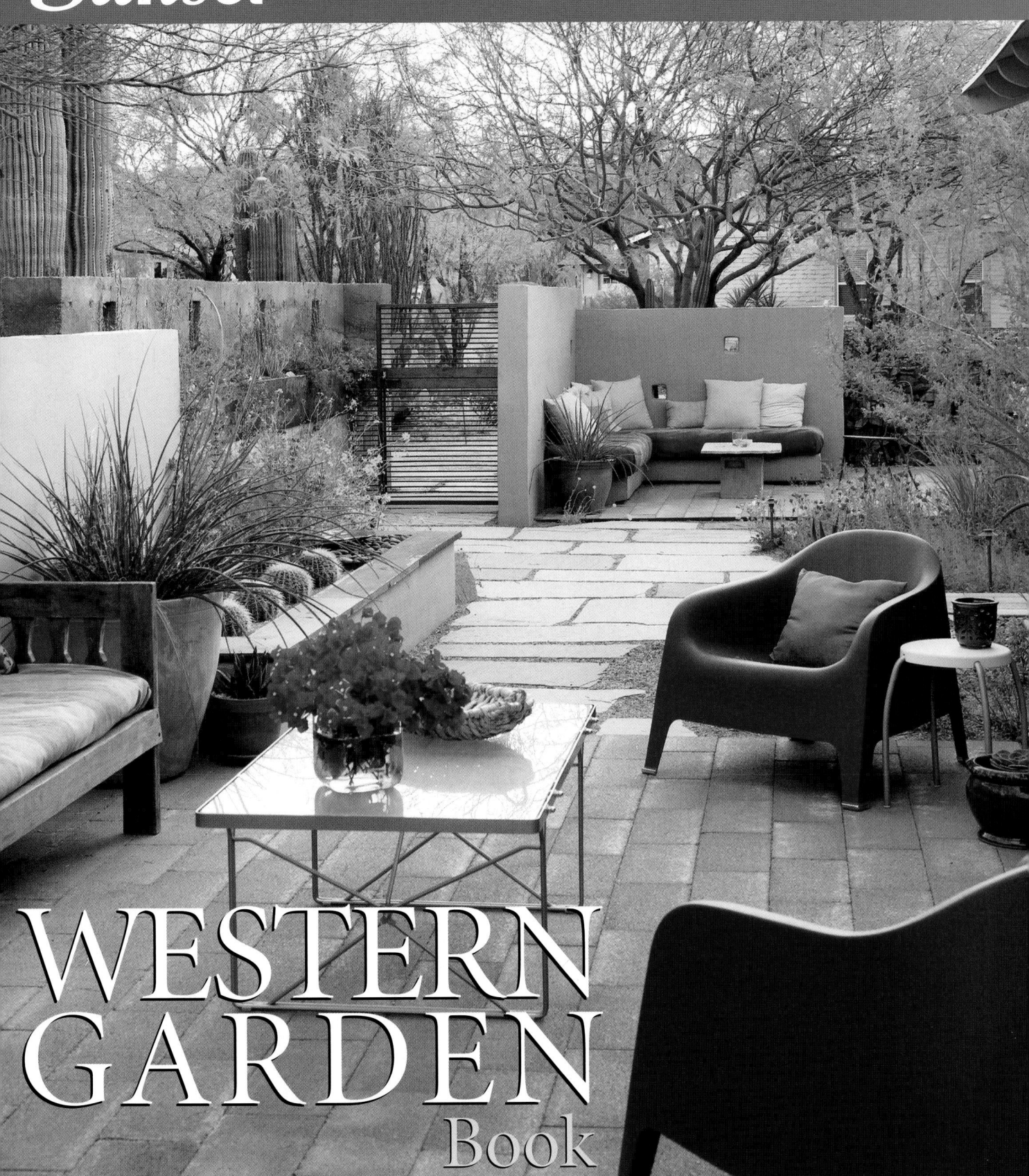

Sunset

WESTERN GARDEN Book

Edited by Kathleen Norris Brenzel

Sunset Western Garden Book

EDITOR
Kathleen Norris Brenzel

MANAGING EDITORS
Fiona Gilsenan, Mike MacCaskey

SENIOR EDITORS
Philip Edinger, Jim McCausland,
Lance Walheim, Tom Wilhite

CONSULTING EDITOR
Marianne Lipanovich

WRITERS AND CONTRIBUTORS
Lisa Albert, Debra Lee Baldwin,
Sharon Cohoon, Sean Hogan,
Mary-Kate Mackey, Lynn Ocone,
Nan Sterman, Vicki Webster,
Hazel White, Marty Wingate

COPY EDITORS
Julie Harris, John Edmonds

PROOFREADERS
David Sweet, Clare Chatfield,
Joan Erickson, Denise Griffiths,
Kathleen Lawrence, Michelle Pollace

INDEXER
Mary Pelletier-Hunyadi

ART DIRECTION
Hespenheide Design: Randy Miyake,
Christine Rocha, Gary Hespenheide,
Bridget Neumayr, Natalie Richmond,
Patti Zeman

PHOTO EDITORS
Carrie Dodson Davis, Danielle Johnson

PRODUCTION SPECIALIST
Linda M. Bouchard

PRINCIPAL PHOTOGRAPHERS
David Cavagnaro, Saxon Holt,
Jerry Pavia

ILLUSTRATION
Tracy LaRue Hohn, Mimi Osborne,
Erin O'Toole, Jenny Speckels

MAP DESIGN AND CARTOGRAPHY
Reineck & Reineck, San Francisco

COVER
Purple coneflower (*Echinacea purpurea*): Photo by Envision/Corbis;
design by Vasken Guiragossian

Sunset Books

VP, GENERAL MANAGER
Richard A. Smeby

VP, EDITORIAL DIRECTOR
Bob Doyle

DIRECTOR OF OPERATIONS
Rosann Sutherland

MARKETING MANAGER
Linda Barker

ART DIRECTOR
Vasken Guiragossian

SPECIAL SALES
Brad Moses

contents

Sunset Publishing Corporation

SENIOR VP
Kevin Lynch

VP, EDITOR-IN-CHIEF, *SUNSET* MAGAZINE
Katie Tamony

VP, PUBLISHER
Tom Marshall

VP, ADMINISTRATION AND MANUFACTURING
Lorinda Reichert

VP, MARKETING DIRECTOR
Beth Whiteley

VP, CONSUMER MARKETING DIRECTOR
Eleanor Hong

VP, GENERAL MANAGER
Mark Okean

10 9 8 7 6 5 4 3
First Printing January 2007.
Copyright ©2007 Sunset Publishing
Corporation, Menlo Park, CA 94025.
Printed in the United States of America.

Eighth edition.
LIBRARY OF CONGRESS CONTROL NUMBER
2006932574
HARDCOVER EDITION
ISBN-13: 978-0-376-03917-0
ISBN-10: 0-376-03917-5
SOFTCOVER EDITION
ISBN-13: 978-0-376-03916-3
ISBN-10: 0-376-03916-7

For additional copies of the *Sunset Western
Garden Book* or any other Sunset book,
visit us at www.sunsetbooks.com or
call 1-800-526-5111.

Special Contributors

Jim Becker owns and operates Goodwin Creek Gardens in southern Oregon, which specializes in herbs, lavenders, scented pelargoniums, everlasting flowers, and fragrant plants.

VJ Billings grows herbs and perennials by the thousands at Mountain Valley Growers in Squaw Valley, California. All her plants are USDA certified organic.

Dr. Paul Bosland is director of the chile breeding and genetics program at New Mexico State University's Chile Pepper Institute. Fondly known as the Chileman on campus, Dr. Bosland is often called upon for commentary by magazine, television, and radio producers.

Scott Calhoun writes, lectures, and designs gardens in Tucson, Arizona. He enjoys exploring the deserts of the Southwest and Mexico looking for interesting plants, gardens, and regional foods. Much of his design inspiration, he says, comes from badlands and taco stands, a style he describes as "Taqueria Chic." His first book, *Yard Full of Sun*, was awarded the 2006 American Horticultural Society Book Award; his second book is *Chasing Wildflowers*.

Tom Carruth, head of the hybridization program for Weeks Roses in Upland, California, has won nine All-American Rose Selection (AARS) awards in the past ten years. He's known for producing roses that stand out in a crowd, including boldly striped 'Scentimental', bicolored 'Betty Boop', and smoky-red 'Hot Cocoa', all AARS winners.

Mike Darcy, one of Portland's foremost gardening authorities and host of the KXL radio program "In the Garden with Mike Darcy," has spent more than two decades teaching and promoting proper gardening techniques through his radio and television programs. An award-winning horticulturist, he has served on the boards of the Hardy Plant Society of Oregon, the Portland Rose Society, and the Pacific Northwest Clematis Society.

Owen Dell, a landscape architect and contractor, shares his expertise as co-host of the Santa Barbara television series "Garden Wise Guys." He is the owner of County Landscape and Design, a fixture on the Santa Barbara gardening scene since 1971, specializing in native plants and sustainable landscaping. He also lectures on such issues as landscaping for fire safety and water conservation.

Dick Dunmire, a former literature professor, first came to Sunset to assist with preparation of the 1967 edition of the *Western Garden Book*. He served as a garden writer and editor for *Sunset* magazine for more than twenty years. His broad horticultural knowledge has been central to the development of this book throughout its last six editions.

Nancy Fiers is one of the West's leading Japanese maple experts and owner of Mountain Maples in Laytonville, California. She was mentored by Oregon State University's J.D. Vertrees, who also supplied much of her nursery's original stock.

David Fross is the founder of Native Sons Wholesale Nursery, specializing in plants from Mediterranean climate regions of the world. He teaches horticulture at California Polytechnic State University and directed the development of the California Collection at the University's Leaning Pine Arboretum. He also co-authored the award-winning *California Native Plants for the Garden*.

Dianna Gibson turned her passion for growing lilies into a business when she founded B&D Lilies in Port Townsend, Washington. The company's bulbs are all American grown in the Pacific Northwest.

Nicholas Gitts and his brother Ted are second-generation owners of the family business, Swan Island Dahlias. Their farm in Canby, Oregon, contains more than 40 acres of dahlias.

John Greenlee, author of *The Encyclopedia of Ornamental Grasses,* is a garden consultant, landscape designer, and meadow specialist. His nursery, in Southern California, carries the largest selection of native grasses on the West Coast.

Jackie Heinricher, who developed a fascination with bamboo at an early age thanks to her father, founded Boo-Shoot Gardens in 1998 to bring beautiful bamboos to the wholesale and retail markets.

Eamonn Hughes has more than thirty years of experience in the design and construction of naturalistic water gardens, both in Europe and in the United States. His company, Hughes Water Gardens in Tualatin, Oregon, offers water garden supplies and plants, as well as design and construction services.

Gary Ibsen has farmed certified organic heirloom tomatoes for more than forty years. He is author of *The Great Tomato Book* and founder of Gary Ibsen's Carmel TomatoFest, the West's largest annual celebration of tomatoes. His website, www.tomatofest.com, keeps more than 500 varieties of heirloom tomatoes in circulation.

Arthur Lee Jacobson is a Seattle-based plant expert, writer, and consultant with a passion for both wild and cultivated plants. His books include *Trees of Seattle*, *Wild Plants of Greater Seattle*, and *North American Landscape Trees*.

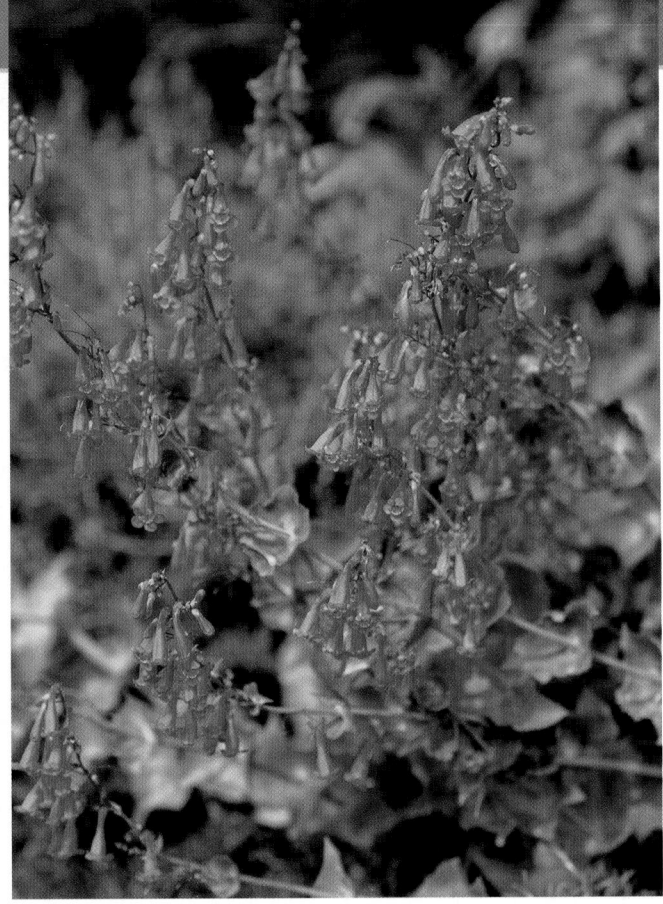

Panayoti Kelaidis, director of outreach for the Denver Botanic Gardens, designed the plantings for the Rock Alpine Garden there—one of the most extensive collections of alpine plants in North America. An internationally known plant authority, he travels extensively to study and collect. He also lectures widely and has published more than 300 articles.

Ted King has been growing chrysanthemums for more than half a century. He is the founder of King's Mums, a family-owned and operated nursery offering a comprehensive collection of chrysanthemums gathered from around the world.

David Leaser is a member of the International Palm Society and a longtime palm tree enthusiast. As founder of Westwood Pacific Publishing, David shares his love for palms in Westwood's first book, *Palm Trees: A Story in Photographs.*

Jeff Lowenfels is a garden writer, columnist, lecturer, lawyer, co-author of *Teaming with Microbes: A Gardener's Guide to the Soil Food Web,* and former host of the public television series "Alaska Gardens with Jeff Lowenfels." He established a program in Anchorage that came to be known as Plant A Row for the Hungry; the idea has been taken up nationwide and now results in the donation of more than a million pounds of produce to food banks each year.

Ciscoe Morris is a horticulturist, master gardener, certified arborist, lecturer, and host of his own gardening programs on radio and television. He writes a weekly garden column for the *Seattle Post Intelligencer* and has co-authored two books, including *Ask Ciscoe.*

Lauren Springer Ogden and Scott Ogden are well-known horticultural consultants and designers whose work emphasizes plants, site sensitivity, and the knowledge of natural processes and relationships. They have designed public and private gardens across the country.

Judith Phillips is a horticulturist, author, landscape designer, and leader in the push for water conservation in garden design. Her books include *Natural by Design, Plants for Natural Gardens,* and *Southwestern Landscaping with Native Plants,* as well as *New Mexico Gardener's Guide.*

Janet Rademacher, marketing director for Mountain States Wholesale Nursery, works to educate the gardening community about native and desert-adapted plants. She holds an M.S. in Ornamental Horticulture from the University of Arizona.

Lon Rombough is a well-known garden writer, nurseryman, and fruit grower. He has more than forty years' experience growing grapes and maintains hundreds of varieties in his small vineyard in Oregon.

Renee Shepherd is an innovator who introduced numerous international vegetables, flowers, and herbs to home gardeners and gourmet restaurants alike. Her company, Renee's Garden, specializes in flower, herb, and vegetable seeds from around the world.

Tom Sjulin has devoted much of his life's work to breeding the perfect strawberry. Formerly associated with Washington State University and Driscoll Strawberry Associates, he now works as a freelance fruit breeder.

Richie Steffen is the horticulture coordinator for the Elisabeth C. Miller Botanical Garden in Seattle, Washington, where he oversees the garden's special collections. He is currently on the selection committee for the Great Plant Picks program, and is also an avid plant photographer.

Bob Tanem, host of the popular radio program "Bob Tanem in the Garden" for KSFO in San Francisco, has been in the nursery business for 40 years, while logging more than 20 years of airtime as a broadcaster. He is author of five gardening books, including four that he co-wrote with Don Williamson: *Annuals for Northern California, Perennials for Northern California, Tree and Shrub Gardening for Northern California,* and *Gardening Month by Month in Northern California.*

Neil and Lore Van Lierop operate the business that Neil's father founded in the 1930s. Visitors and locals alike enjoy spring tours of the growing grounds and gardens of Van Lierop Bulb Farm in Puyallup, Washington.

Lance Walheim, a citrus grower and horticulturist based in California's Central Valley, has authored or contributed to more than 30 gardening books. Walheim, a former garden writer for *Sunset* magazine, is regularly called upon to offer his expertise on radio and television programs.

Paul Wood, once a nurseryman and landscape contractor in California, now lives in Keokea, Maui, where he combines his passions for writing, botany, and native Hawaiian culture. Among his books are *Tropical Trees of Hawai'i, Proteas in Hawai'i, Flowers and Plants of Hawai'i,* and *The Orchid Isles.*

Gardening Among Friends

On a sparkling fall evening after I'd addressed a dinner meeting of the California Association of Nurserymen at Knott's Berry Farm in Buena Park, one of the group's officers gave me a lapel pin with the image of a potted plant enameled in the center, and the words "Friends through Horticulture" printed around the perimeter. I have always cherished that pin for the memories it stirs of that warmhearted gathering, as well as for what it represents: a community of people who share a love for gardening and plants.

Over a supper of fried chicken, mashed potatoes with brown gravy, warm muffins, and tangy-sweet boysenberry preserves, our spirited conversations bounced from the search for a true blue rose, to new shrubs headed our way from Australia, to the hot color bowls flying off nursery shelves on weekends. We learned a lot from each other, and we wrapped up the evening energized.

It was indeed a gathering of friends, but not the first, nor the last, during my tenure as garden editor for *Sunset* magazine. I've had the pleasure of meeting and working with many wonderful gardeners, designers, landscape architects, plant collectors, botanists, backyard tinkerers, and just ordinary folks who have discovered the delights of stopping awhile to sniff the flowers. Plant lovers are some of the most generous people I know. They freely share their tomatoes, their roses, their time, their knowledge. And they are only too happy to share their gardens as well.

Wherever I've traveled in the West—from Aspen to Honolulu and Tucson to Eagle River, Alaska—gardeners and garden experts have welcomed me warmly. Strolling with Dan Dinkel, professor emeritus of horticulture at the University of Alaska, Fairbanks, through his 5-acre garden, we watched his dog, Dawg, shuck corn, while Dan shared his secrets for growing 89-pound cabbages for the state fair competition. On Hawaii's Kona Coast, horticulturist Brian Lievens showed me gardens from dry, lowland lava fields to cloud forests on Mauna Kea's misty slopes, and he introduced me to dwarf plumerias and the frothy pink-and-white 'Thai Delight' bougainvillea. A gardener in Washington's Maple Valley who grows dahlias for Pike Place Market on Seattle's waterfront gave me armloads of beautiful blooms and showed me some plant staking tips that I still use in my own garden.

So perhaps it's not surprising that, as word spread in early 2006 that we planned to revise the *Sunset Western Garden Book,* experts were only too eager to help. The same horticulturists, botanists, growers, and professors who use this book on a daily basis, it turns out, also care passionately about its content. And they understand that it needs to be revised every few years to reflect changing technologies and plants new to the marketplace.

For this reason, we invited many of them to put a bigger stamp on the eighth edition of the book they call "the gardening bible." In the introduction that follows, some share their thoughts on gardening in their regions. Throughout the rest of the book, others generously divulge tips, secrets, and favorite varieties.

To all of you—our readers and "Friends through Horticulture"—who turn to these pages for advice and guidance, this book's for you. We hope you find it as inspiring as it is useful.

Kathleen N Brenzel

*A garden near Malibu
by Nick Williams and
Associates.*

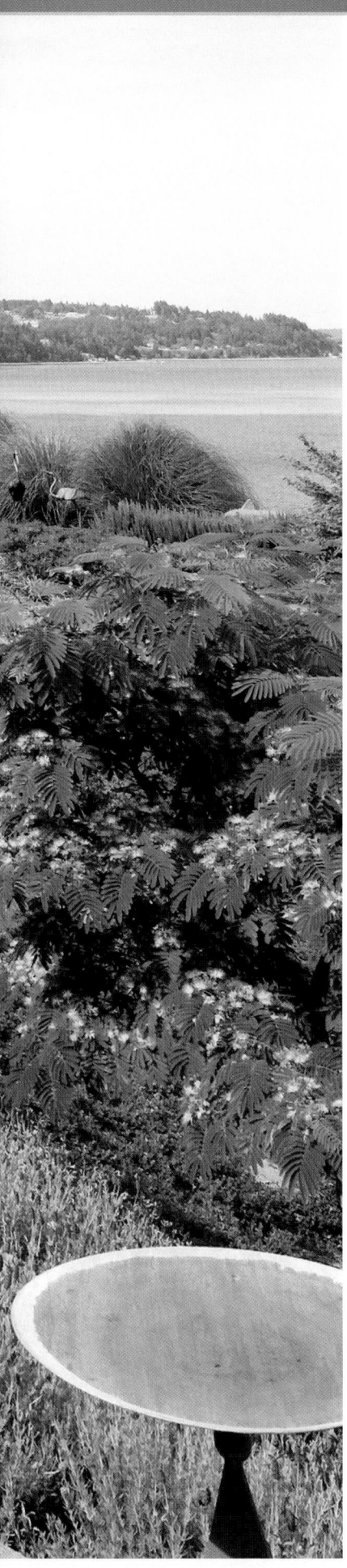

Postcard Washington

CISCOE MORRIS ON PLANT COLLECTING

If you love plants, you'd love gardening in the Pacific Northwest. Our mild climate enables us to grow trees, shrubs, perennials, and more, from practically every corner of the globe. In my Seattle garden, I've planted hardy succulents such as agaves and aloes from the Southwest and Mexico, bromeliads from South America, fire trees from Chile, giant bananas from Japan, palms from Brazil, spooky Jack-in-the-pulpits from China, and winter-blooming grevilleas from Australia. The pièce de résistance is my rice paper plant (*Tetrapanax papyriferus* 'Steroidal Giant'), a 20-foot-tall native of Taiwan whose magnificent 4-foot-wide leaves resemble umbrellas. And that's just in the strip along my driveway.

Still, gardening here presents challenges. For one thing, it's so much fun that everyone is eager to get into the act. That's tough when you have a family of gardeners all wanting to make their mark on a single small plot. My wife, Mary, has become an avid gardener, and we each have our own ideas about what to plant. We've argued so much every time we've gardened together that we finally divided our yard down the middle. She gets her side, and I get mine. Whenever visitors come over, we stand shoulder to shoulder and demand, "Whose side looks the best?" They usually point to hers; I'm positive she's been bribing them.

The other problem is that nurseries sell rare and unusual gems, and are forever introducing new ones that I can't resist buying. At the rate I'm going, I'll have at least one of every type of plant on earth in my garden within the next five years. I don't worry about the garden beds getting too jam-packed, though, as I know I can transplant practically any time of year. Making room for a newcomer is as easy as moving furniture. Of course, that means I have to find a spot for the plant that I just dug up, then something else has to move, and on and on. Eventually even the porches, the balconies, and a roof deck are covered with plants. I end up moving about 473 plants every time I bring home a new purchase.

Yes, it's expensive buying all of those rare treasures. But I know it's worth it when I see my spouse drooling over my latest acquisition. The new find, I hope, will make my side look better than hers.

GIG HARBOR *Spanish lavender, red Japanese maples, mugho pines, ground-covers, and a pink-flowered* Albizia *cloak a slope overlooking Puget Sound. Design: Scott Junge, Rosedale Gardens, Gig Harbor. Above, a bumblebee sips nectar from a* Lithodora diffusa.

Postcard Oregon

MIKE DARCY ON FINDING TRANQUILITY

Let's face it: Life is hectic. So I ease into each day with a stroll through my garden near Lake Oswego, just me and my coffee. On cold mornings, I can see my breath through the steam rising from my cup. Filbert shells crunch beneath my feet; I like them as path coverings because they look natural and keep the mud off my shoes in winter. Here in Oregon, they're as plentiful as—well, filberts.

COTTAGE GROVE *A cascade of small waterfalls spills into a placid pond beside a patio. Ferns, maples, and pines that grow on terraces edged with basalt echo the native landscape beyond the garden's boundaries. Design: Jim Robinson, Daichi Landscape; for Alan Bair and Elizabeth Chandra La Husen.*

Passing a *Melianthus major*, I notice water droplets on its leaves. Winter has been good to this old favorite of mine, as the plant doesn't appear to have suffered any damage from the cold. Farther down the path, *Viburnum × bodnantense* 'Dawn' is blooming, and I bend to sniff the fragrant pink flowers that dangle on bare stems. Hellebores are blooming too, while peonies poke their red stems through the ground. They take me back in time, remind me of my grandmother's garden.

Everywhere in the garden I see beauty, and I see imperfections. My garden is not "designed." It's a horticultural lovefest, a collection of plants that continues to grow and change each year. Do I plant things in the wrong place? Yes, often. Do I move them? Yes, often. I never think of gardening as an exact science, nor do I think a garden is ever complete. There is always a new must-have plant on the market. And no matter how crowded a bed might be, I manage to find room for more.

On this glistening morning, as on most mornings, I find my way to a garden bench, where I sit, finish my coffee, and pause to enjoy the beauty around me. I am constantly in awe of what nature provides, and I savor it. Only then am I ready to begin my day—fully refreshed.

Postcard Northern California

BOB TANEM ON CREATIVE GARDENING

As a longtime nurseryman and an enthusiastic gardener all of my life, I've tilled the soil from the Sierra Nevada foothills to the Northern California coast. In Placerville, where I was born, it was mostly decomposed granite containing lots of micronutrients but little nitrogen. To help it yield decent crops, my father hauled 6 to 7 yards of rotted turkey manure into his vegetable plot every year. My mother considered herself fortunate if she could grab some of this brown gold for her flower beds before it went into Dad's garden. The manure produced phenomenal results; the garden was a winner. And it taught me my first lesson about the land: that growing things successfully takes a can-do attitude.

During my travels throughout this state, I've seen gardens flourish against all odds—in brick-hard clay soil and in sand that can't hold water for long. I've seen bougainvillea bloom where cool fogs blot out the sun in summer, ginger thriving in the Sierra where the snow covers the ground in winter, and barrel cactus surviving rains along the coast. I've even seen quaking aspens at sea level and river birch in the high desert.

None of this surprises me. Because here in Northern California, garden challenges are really opportunities in disguise. Want a tropical feeling in your garden? It's possible. Want an English garden? It's also possible, using quintessential California plants like catmints, lavenders, and penstemons. Want a cutting garden, an organic vegetable garden, a low-water, easy-maintenance garden, a shade garden, a native plant garden? A water garden? Can do. The list goes on. If it grows somewhere in the world, chances are you can grow it here.

This is the excitement of California gardening. We gardeners love to experiment, and to share our green-thumb experiences. Gardening just doesn't get any better than that.

NEAR SANTA ROSA *A garden on Taylor Mountain plays off the region's agricultural roots. Above, echeverias and sedums embrace a wall. Below, a carpet of* Thymus × citriodorus *'Lime'. Opposite: Santolina, blue fescue, lamb's ears, and Spanish lavender grow in steel livestock feeding tanks. Design: Landscape architect Richard William Wogisch for the home he shares with partner Bassam Salameh.*

POINT LOMA *Summers are mild but at times damp near San Diego's bayfront—challenging conditions for roses. Yet Dick and Bonnie Goff have discovered disease-resistant varieties that thrive in beds around their waterfront patio. These include red and gold 'Chihuly'; apricot 'Just Joey'; and yellow miniature 'Sun Sprinkles', which they mix with tough perennials such as lavender-blue pincushion flower.*

Postcard Southern California

OWEN DELL ON CUTTING-EDGE HORTICULTURE

On Thanksgiving Day 1920, the genial English gardener Edward Owen Orpet spontaneously alit from the train in Santa Barbara, impressed by abundant lantana blooms next to the tracks. He stayed to become one of the most beloved horticulturists in a community filled with trailblazing plantsmen and landscape architects. The train station and the lantana still stand, and Santa Barbara is still a mecca of cutting-edge horticulture. For good reason. The air is balmy here between the craggy Santa Ynez Mountains and the placid Pacific coastline. Vibrant bougainvillea blooms shamelessly, and blue-flowered jacaranda trees line some streets. Spanish colonial revival estates with names like Casa del Herrero acknowledge the region's roots, while horticultural fantasies—such as the strangely beautiful gardens at famed opera star Madame Ganna Walska's Lotusland estate—indulge the imagination. The Santa Barbara Botanic Garden, founded not long after Orpet's arrival, teaches about climate-appropriate native plants and responsible landscaping.

Garden design and management continue to change, even in my own garden. I just came down from my roof with a handful of pasilla chiles, grown up there in boxes along with tomatoes, herbs, and other sun-loving edibles. It's the kind of thing that Santa Barbara gardeners do—the oddball innovation, the radical transformation, the inventive response to changing conditions. During the drought of the late 1980s, we painted our lawns green (probably the least admirable event in our long history of progressive gardening). Later we developed the world's first firescape demonstration garden, pioneered the replacement of front lawns with more water-efficient plants, and paved our driveways with permeable concrete to allow rainwater to trickle through to plant roots. These days I'm working with a group of locals on gardening techniques designed to reduce or eliminate materials composed of fossil fuels: PVC pipe, chemical fertilizers, and pesticides, for instance. With oil getting scarcer and more costly, we believe in the need to retrain gardeners for the changing times. We hope to develop a demonstration garden in front of the old train station that so captivated Edward Owen Orpet, where we can display sustainable and permaculture gardening techniques.

I like to think I'm carrying on a tradition of innovation that began long before Orpet. I know that at this moment, in this community, gardeners are more determined than ever to develop hauntingly beautiful gardens that make sense for our climate and terrain. Maybe I'm just proud, but I think Santa Barbara is gardening heaven.

Postcard Arizona

SCOTT CALHOUN ON THE BEAUTY OF DESERT PLANTS

I'm a fourth-generation Arizonan. After I'd lived out of state during college, the desert called me home. I love the scent of creosote bush after rain, the columnar saguaros and lime green palo verde trees, the wide-open spaces. This is my landscape. In Tucson, we don't have Japanese maples or river birches or even much lawn grass. But we can grow some of the planet's most fascinating plants. "Tucson doesn't value lawns," says Mark Dimmitt, director of natural history at the Arizona-Sonora Desert Museum. "But it's the center of the universe for cactus."

I've become accustomed to—even learned to enjoy—handling prickly and thorny plants. Like Frank Lloyd Wright and Georgia O'Keeffe, I've fallen in love with the desert's dramatic and otherworldly geometry: the flaming pink spires of a Parry's penstemon, the zigzag lightning-shaped ocotillo, the twisted trunk of a velvet mesquite tree. The desert offers its own beauty in a palette that is richer than most.

Gardening here is not easy. In my rocky, compacted clay soil, I need a pick or digging bar, and occasionally a 42-pound electric jack-hammer with a spade bit, to prepare the soil for planting one-gallon plants. But the right ones do thrive. For me this is the real lesson of Southwest gardening: plant what grows here naturally.

Each fall I sow seeds of desert wildflowers, including arroyo lupine, desert bluebells, brittlebush, Mexican gold poppies, and penstemons. They sprout and grow over the cool winter months. By spring, my yard is a river of gentian blue, hot pink, and brilliant yellow—an ephemeral crescendo that I relish. In June, I prepare for monsoon rains by sowing the seeds of summer wildflowers. If the rains do come, my Texas ranger is covered with purple flowers that smell like grape Kool-Aid, while my yard is dotted with red, orange, yellow, and lavender flowers from Arizona poppies, desert senna, devil's claws, golden dogbane, firewheel, and Goodding's verbena. Late June is also a good time to grab a pair of taco tongs, pick some prickly pear fruits, and stir their syrup into lemonade, turning it magenta like an Arizona sunset.

Yes, there are times when the misty rain and rich loam of the Pacific Northwest beckon. But mostly I am happily situated in my desert garden, surrounded by all of my pointed plants and neon flowers under a big blue sky.

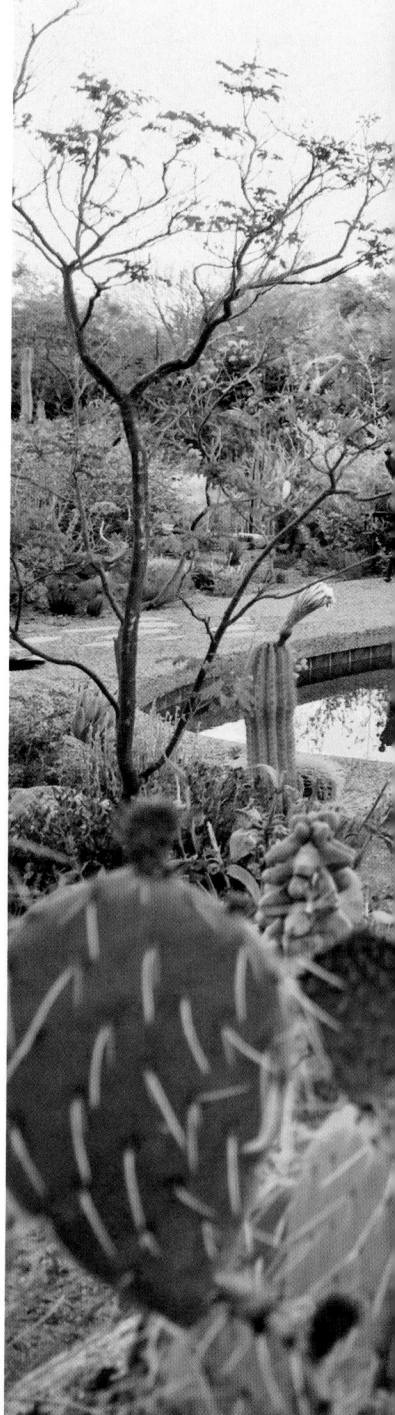

SCOTTSDALE *Mike and Vi Platta's garden makes the most of desert plants. A stone fountain adds accent (left), while Parry's penstemon and cactus add seasonal bloom (right). Near the pool, bougainvillea and sweet acacia create a soft backdrop.*

NEAR SANTA FE *Deciduous trees shade a front-yard courtyard (right), while the property's backyard meadow of blue gramma grass (below) embraces the natural landscape. Design: Richard Wilder of Wilder Landscaping, Santa Fe.*

Postcard New Mexico

JUDITH PHILLIPS ON THE HIGH-DESERT LANDSCAPE

Three things I love most about New Mexico's landscape are the color palette that any painter would envy, a change of seasons, and the plants that grow naturally here. Western New York State, where I grew up, inspired my love for green. But gardening in New Mexico has broadened my tastes to include shades of gray and blue-green, olive, and gold.

The climate of New Mexico, like that of New York, changes dramatically through the year. Spring is windy along the Rio Grande but not wet as in New York. Summer can be scorching, though rarely muggy. Few red oaks or maples grow here to color autumn gardens, but purple asters and dotted gayfeather bloom among chamisa, and golden aspen and cottonwood trees shimmer against a brilliant blue sky. Winter days are mild enough to coax me outdoors for a bit of garden cleanup, but the nights are cold and make me yearn for a bowl of green chile stew and a crackling piñon fire. Though I can't say I miss deep snow, New Mexico's high peaks are usually white by mid-January. Those Magdalena Mountains, filled in summer with the soothing scents of pine and honeyed wildflower meadows, satisfy any nostalgia I may still have for the woodland green of my childhood.

But the real surprise is the rainbow of plants that thrive in the high desert's brilliant sunlight, gritty soils, and dry air in spite of our wide temperature swings. These have become my passion. After heavy winter rains, the countryside is awash in Mexican gold poppies, creamy orange globemallows, and pink and purple verbena. The distant hills turn a soft green. Cacti and succulents are striking for their armor, architecture, and glorious flowers. But it's the subtle, wind-sculpted shapes of desert trees, the fine-textured aromatic foliage of native shrubs, the self-cooling silver sages, and the dance of dryland grasses that lend high-desert gardens their authenticity. These plants, more than any others, have changed me. A former New Yorker, I'm now a Westerner at heart.

Postcard Colorado

PANAYOTI KELAIDIS ON APPROPRIATE PLANTINGS

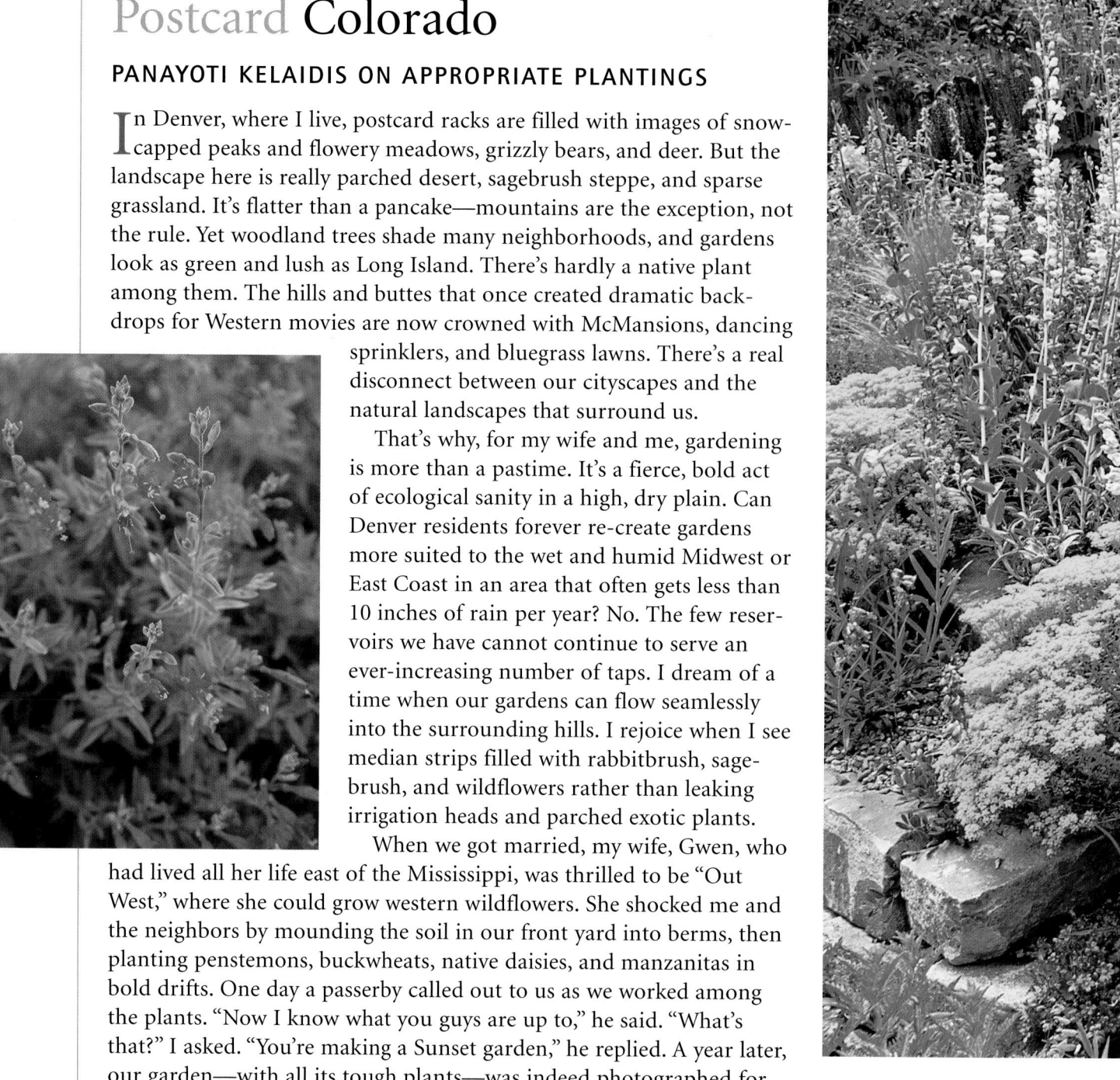

In Denver, where I live, postcard racks are filled with images of snow-capped peaks and flowery meadows, grizzly bears, and deer. But the landscape here is really parched desert, sagebrush steppe, and sparse grassland. It's flatter than a pancake—mountains are the exception, not the rule. Yet woodland trees shade many neighborhoods, and gardens look as green and lush as Long Island. There's hardly a native plant among them. The hills and buttes that once created dramatic backdrops for Western movies are now crowned with McMansions, dancing sprinklers, and bluegrass lawns. There's a real disconnect between our cityscapes and the natural landscapes that surround us.

That's why, for my wife and me, gardening is more than a pastime. It's a fierce, bold act of ecological sanity in a high, dry plain. Can Denver residents forever re-create gardens more suited to the wet and humid Midwest or East Coast in an area that often gets less than 10 inches of rain per year? No. The few reservoirs we have cannot continue to serve an ever-increasing number of taps. I dream of a time when our gardens can flow seamlessly into the surrounding hills. I rejoice when I see median strips filled with rabbitbrush, sagebrush, and wildflowers rather than leaking irrigation heads and parched exotic plants.

When we got married, my wife, Gwen, who had lived all her life east of the Mississippi, was thrilled to be "Out West," where she could grow western wildflowers. She shocked me and the neighbors by mounding the soil in our front yard into berms, then planting penstemons, buckwheats, native daisies, and manzanitas in bold drifts. One day a passerby called out to us as we worked among the plants. "Now I know what you guys are up to," he said. "What's that?" I asked. "You're making a Sunset garden," he replied. A year later, our garden—with all its tough plants—was indeed photographed for and featured in *Sunset* magazine.

The fact is, we love gardens that look like they belong in the West. Casual, easy to maintain. Ones sensibly designed to conserve water. Such gardens honor this vast and visually rich region we are blessed to live in. Let's grow more agastache, delosperma, eriogonum, poppy mallow. More natives and plants adapted to our dry climate. These are the ones that bring the color and spectacle of our native hills back into our daily lives.

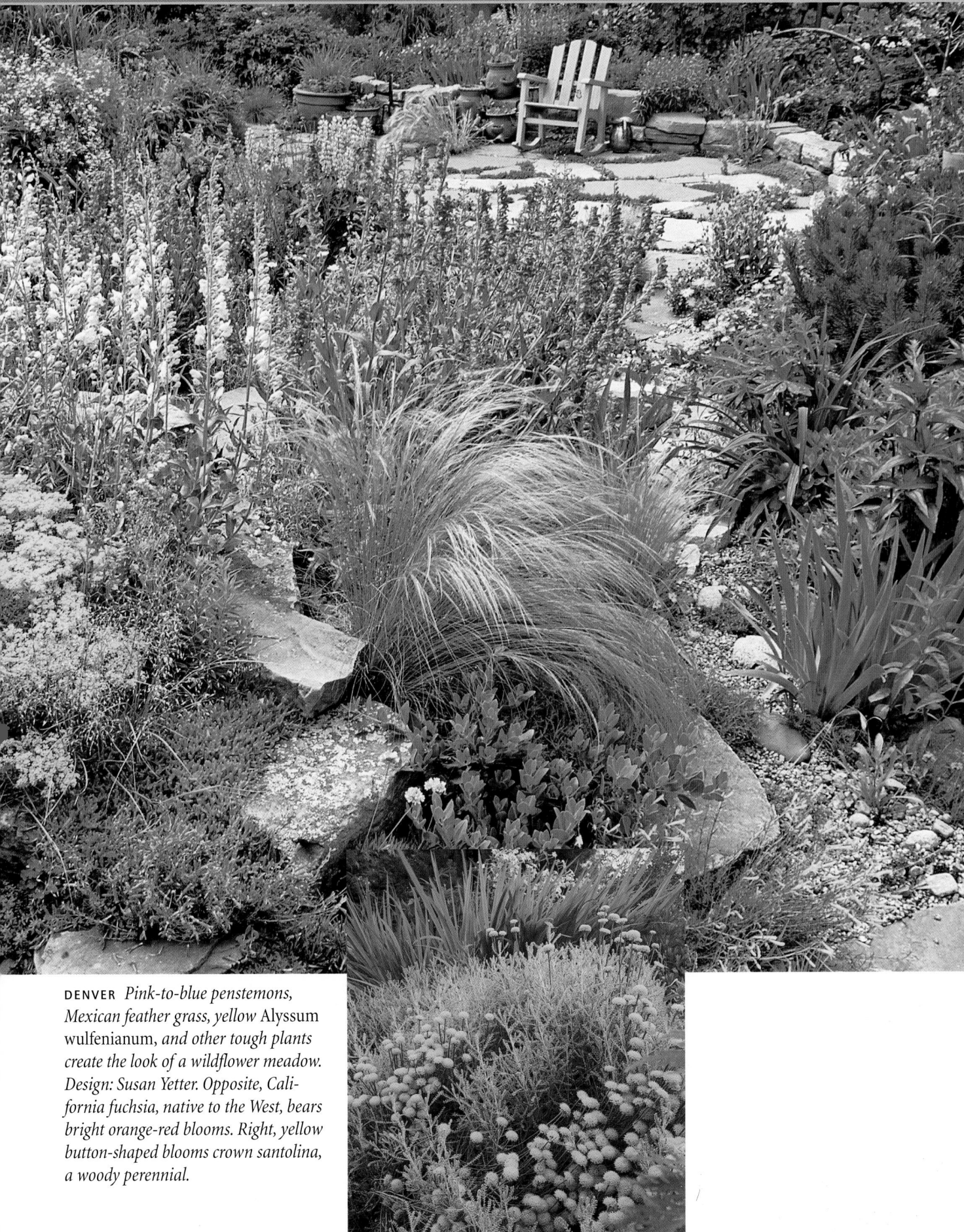

DENVER *Pink-to-blue penstemons, Mexican feather grass, yellow* Alyssum wulfenianum, *and other tough plants create the look of a wildflower meadow. Design: Susan Yetter. Opposite, California fuchsia, native to the West, bears bright orange-red blooms. Right, yellow button-shaped blooms crown santolina, a woody perennial.*

Postcard Alaska

JEFF LOWENFELS ON GARDENING IN THE FAR NORTH

I used to joke that snow peas, iceberg lettuce, snowball cauliflower, and glacier-size cabbages were all you could grow in Alaska. I arrived here some 30 years ago from New York, and I've since discovered that the joke really was on me. Back then, Alaska gardeners grew lots of flowers, mostly in hanging baskets. While the size and color of the blooms would make an English gardener drool, the goods were limited. Nurseries sold quantities of just four plants that could thrive in our cool summer climate: tuberous begonias, fuchsias, lobelia, and pelargoniums. Vegetable gardens featured cole crops, including peas.

Ah, but now it is our turn! Call it global warming or persistence, but we have more plant choices than ever. Cabbages, broccoli, and cauliflower still predominate, but we've discovered we can grow the herbs to flavor our salmon and halibut. Tomatoes developed in Siberia bear fruit outside a greenhouse, and kiwis from northern China also yield tasty crops here. We've experimented, and as a result, we can choose from an expanding number of subarctic apple varieties, even apricots and cherries. We've recently begun to succeed with artichokes as well.

Advances are not limited to fruits and vegetables. The hanging baskets are still here, but tourists also rave about our huge ligularias and the much-coveted blue Himalayan poppy. Annuals and perennials are everywhere. We spend a good part of our dreadfully long, dark winter studying catalogs. Advances in shipping plants have helped our gardeners make more sophisticated choices, and our landscapes are stunning in summer.

HOMER (ON THE KENAI PENINSULA) *In summer, a floral display shimmers with color against a backdrop of glaciers and mountains. Pink cosmos, marigolds, and poppies fill the beds. Above: a Himalayan poppy* (Meconopsis betonicifolia).

Gardening in the far north definitely has advantages. Long, cool summer days urge many plants to great heights and girth. Delphiniums can reach 12 to 14 feet tall, and cabbages can weigh up to 90 pounds apiece. Best of all, we don't have snakes. Bears I don't mind as much as snakes. And I don't mind the sight of a moose in my vegetable patch, even though these animals seem to have a taste for any plant that costs more than 10 dollars. Other than these mighty Alaskans, and slugs, our gardens are pretty pest-free. That's great, because most of us use organic gardening methods. Now if we could only figure out how to deal with mosquitoes.

I've seen a lot of changes during my years in the Last Frontier, but one thing hasn't changed. Everyone gardens here. In fact, you are not a true Alaskan unless you do.

Postcard Hawaii

PAUL WOOD ON SUSTAINABLE ISLAND GARDENING

It is true that I once tossed an avocado pit off my lanai, waited four years, then picked an avocado from the resulting tree. And, yes, some of my weeds are your houseplants. But gardening in the islands is not as easy as you might think. Hawaii is to gardening as Moab, Utah, is to bicycle riding. Radical. The land demands full-contact, high-impact response. Plants seem to sneak around when you're not looking. They swallow paths overnight, make sudden lunges at your garage. You find yourself hacking down head-high flowers just to keep the driveway open.

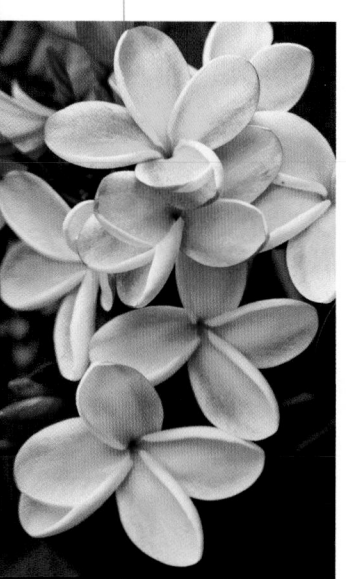

Just about every plant thrives in Hawaii, but oddly enough, not everywhere. Gardening is always peculiar to one's island and to one's position on that island. Hawaii is a place full of places, full of weathers. A five-mile drive can take you from storm to sun, heat to chill. Dig up a plant that's booming in leeward Lahaina and move it around the coast to windward Haiku, and it will sulk. Move it a few miles up the mountain—that's like transplanting it from Cancun to Seattle. The trick is to find out which plants want your place, then make sure your chain saw is sharp.

That's why Hawaii's crops are regional particularities. The ugly but marvelous oranges from Kau, for example. Kula's onions, sweetening across the road from protea farms. The Kona Coast's coffee, of course, because of the dependable afternoon cloud cover that hangs low over the slopes there. Anthuriums in wet, humid Hilo. Orchids on Oahu.

Island soils are lousy—subsurface layers in some areas are raw blue rock honeycombed with lava tubes. Yet they're able to support lush rain forests in places like Hana. Our mild, no-freeze climate is a delight for bugs and mildew. And invasive species are moving to Hawaii faster than California realtors; many of them have their antennae out for my eggplants.

But one force compensates for all the woes: our liquid sunshine. Hawaiians call it the life-giving water of Kane, pure rainwater that seems to fall directly from the sun onto the garden. Just by working with sticks and stones, relatively few plants brought in canoes from the South Pacific, and this life-giving water, the first Hawaiian settlers built a robust population. Experts in engineering waterways from stacked stone, they sculpted Hawaii's streambeds into systems of flowing ponds and farm patches and created an eternally sustainable food supply, with plenty of bananas, breadfruit, coconuts, sugarcane, taro, and yams for everyone. I think they were the most radical gardeners who ever lived.

We can learn from the first Hawaiians. Rely less on jets and barges, more on island resources, and the life-giving waters of Kane.

KAHALU'U, OAHU *As in a tropical rain forest, Leland Miyano's garden uses a diverse mix of foliage plants—artillery plant, bromeliads, cycads, heliconias, philodendron, and ti beneath a canopy of palms and other tropical trees—to create a self-sustaining garden that thrives on rainwater alone. Basalt stones are accents. Paths are laid without mortar to maximize water percolation into the soil. Design: Leland Miyano.*

A beach garden in Carpinteria, California, re-creates a dune grass wilderness. Beach strawberry, thrift, and a grass (Leymus condensatus 'Canyon Prince') native to San Miguel Island across the channel line the sandy path. Design: Susan Van Atta. Opposite: A pond and aspen trees frame a view of distant Elk Mountains near Aspen, Colorado. Design: Richard Shaw for DesignWorkshop.

From the sea to the mountains, our plants

and landscapes create a definite sense of place.

The West's Climate Zones

In this book, we have assigned climate zones to almost every listed plant.

The maps on the following pages show where these numbered climate zones are throughout the West. Take a few minutes to find your zone on the maps (see the locator map right for page numbers) and read the description. It will outline the conditions that combine to make your climate hospitable to some plants, trouble for others.

Several important factors combine with temperature to make each of our climate zones unique. Plants live and die by these elements.

LATITUDE Generally, the farther an area is from the equator, the longer and colder are its winters. Closer to the poles, the number of daylight hours increases in summer and decreases in winter.

ELEVATION Gardens high above sea level get longer and colder winters, often with intense sunlight, and lower night temperatures all year.

OCEAN INFLUENCE Weather that blows in off the Pacific Ocean tends to be mild and laden with moisture in the cool season.

CONTINENTAL AIR INFLUENCE The North American continent generates its own weather, which—compared with coastal climates—is colder in winter, hotter in summer, and more likely to get precipitation any time of year. The farther inland you live, the stronger this continental influence. Incessant wind also becomes a major factor in open interior climates.

MOUNTAINS, HILLS, AND VALLEYS These determine whether areas beyond them will be influenced most by marine air or by continental air. The Coast Ranges take some marine influence out of the air that passes eastward over them. The Sierra-Cascades and Southern California's interior mountains further weaken marine influence. East of the Rocky Mountains, continental and arctic air dominate. In the opposite direction, first the Rockies, then the interior ranges, and finally the Coast Ranges reduce the westward influence of continental air.

MICROCLIMATES Local terrain can sharply modify the climate within any zone. South-facing slopes get more solar heat than flat land and north-facing slopes. Slope also affects airflow: warm air rises, cold air sinks. Because hillsides are never as cold in winter as the hilltops above them or the ground below them, they're called thermal belts. Lowland areas into which cold air flows are called cold-air basins. Microclimates also exist within every garden.

Each zone's growing season—the average number of days between the last frost in spring and the first frost in fall—is shown below each zone title as a green band on a bar. The yellowish green color at each end of the green band indicates shoulder seasons, when light frosts could occur but wouldn't likely bother cool-season crops.

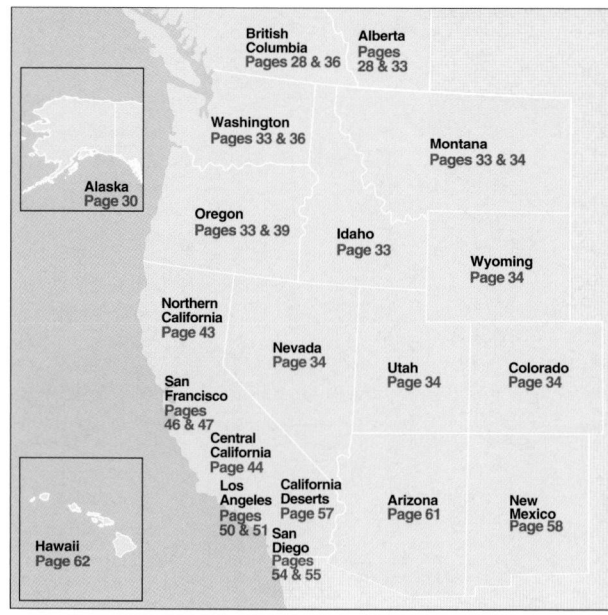

To find your garden's climate zone, start with this locator map and then turn to the page listed for your area. And because climate zones blend into one another, it is important that you learn about adjacent zones as well.

Growing Season

J F M A M J J A S O N D

Growing seasons, however, don't tell the whole story. For example, Zone 5 has a much longer average growing season than Zone 3a, but Zone 3a's extra heat makes it a much more favorable climate for heat-loving summer fruits and vegetables such as melons and peppers.

SOIL Although soil is not a climate condition, it too can influence or limit plant growth. If your soil is heavy and slow to drain, choose plants that can tolerate those conditions. You can amend or replace enough of it to grow a fair number of favored plants. When that isn't practical, you can install raised garden beds. In any case, you will need to learn which plants can handle tough soils.

Canada's Climate Zones

Oceans, mountains, and latitude make all the difference in southwestern Canada. The Pacific Ocean keeps the coastal area (Zones 4 and 5) mild and moist as storms move onshore every month of the year. The mountains (Zone 1a) check the ocean's influence, creating warmer summers in the valleys (Zone 2a), colder winters everywhere, and a shorter growing season. In the Canadian prairies (Zone 1b), continental air ensures more wind all year, very cold winters, mild summers, and shorter growing seasons as it moves north.

ZONING IN ON CLIMATE

In this chapter, climate zones range from the mildest (Hawaii's Zone H2) to the coldest (Alaska's Zone A1).

The Hawaii Difference

The West's southernmost state has the only true tropical zones in the Western U.S. Its two climates include the higher-elevation H1, which is cool enough for many temperate-zone plants, and the lower-elevation H2, which is evenly warm and frost-free. Moderated by the Pacific Ocean and persistent northeasterly trade-winds, Hawaii is mild year-round with two seasons: the cool season (October through April) and the warm season (May through September). But the same sheer cliffs, deep valleys, broad slopes, ridges, high volcanic peaks, and windy points that give the islands their awesome beauty also create an array of microclimates.

Rainfall can vary immensely within a short distance. The upper Manoa Valley on Oahu, for example, can receive 160 inches of rainfall per year, while Waikiki, just 4 miles away, gets 20 inches per year.

Below about 6,000 feet elevation, it's difficult to grow plants that need winter chill to thrive. Such plants grow better at higher elevations on Maui and the Big Island, where air temperatures are cooler. Throughout the islands, the same benign climates that nurture a wide variety of plants to lush growth also help some introduced species spread, crowding out native plants. Some plants that are well-mannered on the mainland have become tenacious wanderers in the islands. Among these are kahili ginger, *Lantana camara*, banana passion vine, princess flower, strawberry guava, and Queensland

Dwarf fireweed (Epilobium latifolium) *and nootka lupine* (Lupinus nootkantensis) *glow in the evening light at Bering Glacier, Alaska.*

umbrella tree. Gardeners should avoid importing any plants (or pieces of plants) without proper permits or inspections.

The Alaska Difference

Though many may try to compare Alaska with cold-winter parts of the Lower 48, this really can't be done. With its unmatched, huge seasonal differences in day length, wild swings in temperature, permafrost, Arctic desert, rain forests, warm-summer interior, and wind-scoured coasts, Alaska is a land apart.

Alaska's Zone A1 encompasses the interior climate centered in Fairbanks; Zone A2, Anchorage and areas along Cook Inlet; and Zone A3, the mild marine climate along the state's southern coast. (The mildest, southernmost part of Alaska tips into Zone 4 of the Lower 48.)

Garden successes here are striking, from the trial grounds for vegetables, annuals, and perennials at Georgeson

Botanical Gardens in Fairbanks to the whopping vegetables in the Matanuska Valley, and intimate flower gardens that border southeastern Alaska's rain forests. But to grow anything in the face of permanently low soil temperatures, gardeners throughout Alaska cover annual vegetable and flower beds with infrared-transmitting (IRT) plastic sheeting at planting time, which raises soil temperatures by 10 to 30 degrees. They also make masterful use of microclimates, press native plants into service, and share ideas and innovation freely, contributing to Alaska's success as a gardening state.

Why Don't We Use Other Climate Zones?

The U.S. Department of Agriculture (USDA) calculates climate zones based on a winter minimum temperature. It provides a useful index for plant hardiness—the ability to withstand frost and low temperatures—but it has some important drawbacks. This focus on cold-tolerance alone, for instance, places the Olympic rain forest and the Sonoran Desert in the same zone.

Similarly, the American Horticultural Society (AHS) has developed a system based on the average number of days above 86°F/30°C (the temperature at which cellular protein is damaged in many plants).

Neither of these systems are relevant to many areas of the West, particularly mild coastal areas which seldom experience extreme temperatures. Our method of zoning considers the broad range of factors based on information from all over the West. It gives Western gardeners a more accurate picture of which plants will thrive in each zone. Our thanks to the many institutions and experts who continue to help us refine the *Sunset* climate zones.

Taro fields spread out across the Hanalei River Valley on the island of Kauai, Hawaii.

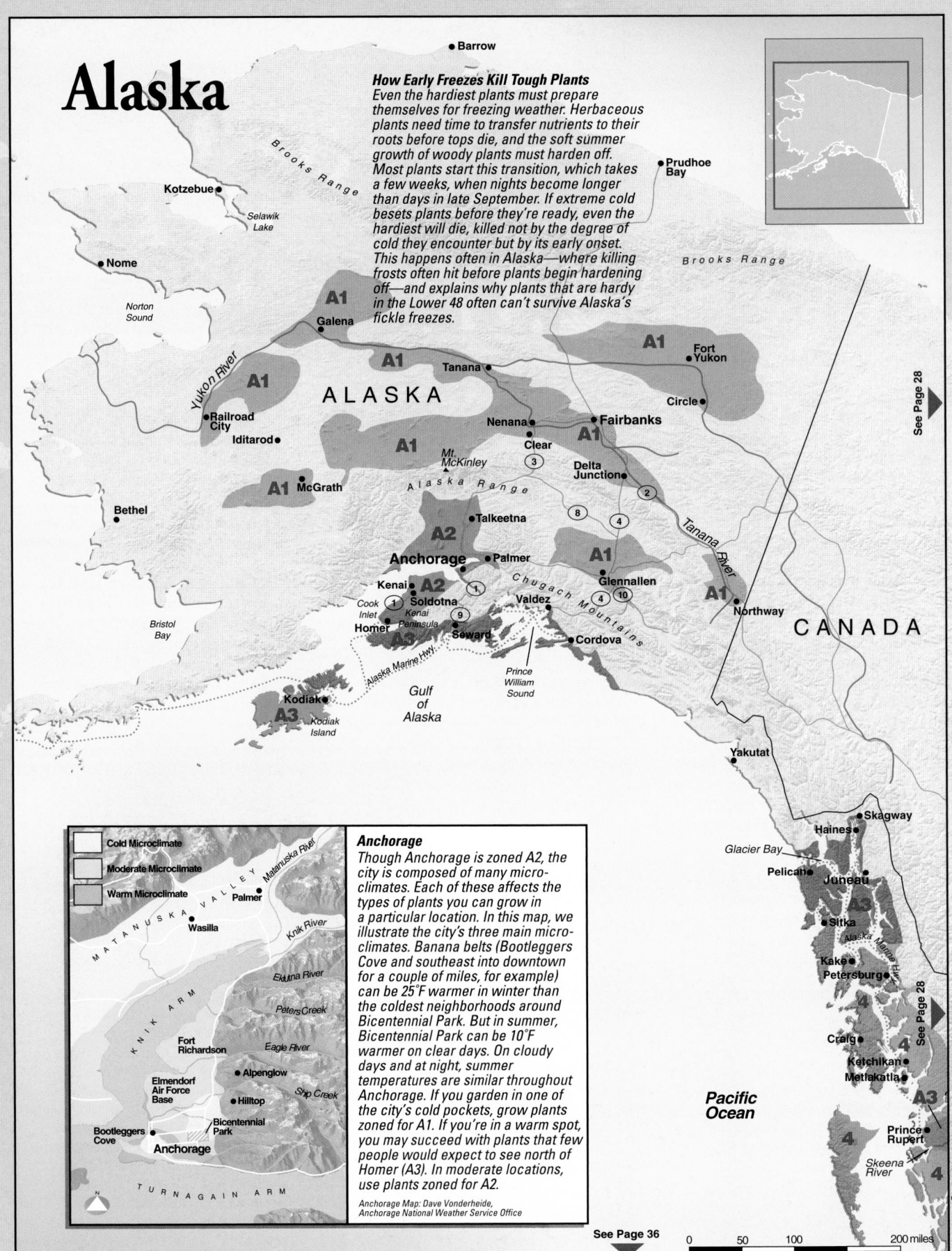

Alaska

How Early Freezes Kill Tough Plants
Even the hardiest plants must prepare themselves for freezing weather. Herbaceous plants need time to transfer nutrients to their roots before tops die, and the soft summer growth of woody plants must harden off. Most plants start this transition, which takes a few weeks, when nights become longer than days in late September. If extreme cold besets plants before they're ready, even the hardiest will die, killed not by the degree of cold they encounter but by its early onset. This happens often in Alaska—where killing frosts often hit before plants begin hardening off—and explains why plants that are hardy in the Lower 48 often can't survive Alaska's fickle freezes.

Barrow

Prudhoe Bay

Kotzebue

Brooks Range

Selawik Lake

Nome

Norton Sound

Brooks Range

A1
Galena

A1
Tanana

A1
Fort Yukon

A1
Yukon River

A L A S K A

Circle

Railroad City

Iditarod

A1

Nenana

Fairbanks A1

Clear
③

Delta Junction

A1
McGrath

Mt. McKinley

Alaska Range

②

Bethel

A2
Talkeetna

⑧ ④

Tanana River

Anchorage Palmer

A1
Glennallen

A1
Northway

Kenai A2

①
Soldotna

Valdez

④ ⑩

Cook Inlet

Kenai Peninsula

Chugach Mountains

C A N A D A

Homer ⑨

Seward

Cordova

Bristol Bay

A3

Prince William Sound

Kodiak
A3 *Kodiak Island*

Alaska Marine Hwy.

Gulf of Alaska

Yakutat

See Page 28

Skagway
Haines

Glacier Bay

Pelican Juneau

A3
Sitka

Kake
Petersburg

Pacific Ocean

④

Craig

④

Ketchikan
Metlakatla

A3

Prince Rupert

Skeena River

④

See Page 28

Anchorage map inset

Cold Microclimate
Moderate Microclimate
Warm Microclimate

MATANUSKA VALLEY

Matanuska River

Palmer

Wasilla

Knik River

Eklutna River

Peters Creek

KNIK ARM

Fort Richardson

Eagle River

Elmendorf Air Force Base

Alpenglow

Hilltop

Ship Creek

Bootleggers Cove

Bicentennial Park

Anchorage

TURNAGAIN ARM

Anchorage
Though Anchorage is zoned A2, the city is composed of many microclimates. Each of these affects the types of plants you can grow in a particular location. In this map, we illustrate the city's three main microclimates. Banana belts (Bootleggers Cove and southeast into downtown for a couple of miles, for example) can be 25°F warmer in winter than the coldest neighborhoods around Bicentennial Park. But in summer, Bicentennial Park can be 10°F warmer on clear days. On cloudy days and at night, summer temperatures are similar throughout Anchorage. If you garden in one of the city's cold pockets, grow plants zoned for A1. If you're in a warm spot, you may succeed with plants that few people would expect to see north of Homer (A3). In moderate locations, use plants zoned for A2.

Anchorage Map: Dave Vonderheide, Anchorage National Weather Service Office

See Page 36

0   50   100   200 miles

Climate Zones   A1 A2 A3   4

ZONE **A1**

Alaska's coldest climate—Fairbanks and the interior

Growing Season

J	F	M	A	M	J	J	A	S	O	N	D

Encompassing most of interior Alaska in a region between the Alaska and Brooks ranges, Zone A1 is Alaska's gardening surprise. During summer, plants benefit from long, warm days, while in winter, gardeners can usually depend on snow to insulate plants. And in permafrost areas, the ground usually thaws to below root level during the warm months.

The keys to beating temperature extremes—with everything from strawberries to snapdragons, beans to sweet corn—include taking advantage of microclimates (especially south and west exposures), boosting soil temperatures with mulches or IRT plastic sheeting, and choosing the right plant varieties. Many birches, for example, reach nearly unparalleled proportions in Fairbanks, as do hardy perennials and a long list of annuals. It also helps to plant in raised beds, whose soil warms up earlier in spring.

Average winter minimums are −10 to −20°F (−23 to −29°C), with occasional dips to −60°F (−51°C). Summer highs are in the 70s, with rare spikes to 90°F (32°C). The average growing season in Fairbanks is 113 days.

Sunflowers and float planes at Fairbanks International Airport.

Famous Matanuska cabbages in the garden of Don and Bonnie Dinkle.

ZONE **A2**

The intermediate climate of Anchorage and Cook Inlet

Growing Season

J	F	M	A	M	J	J	A	S	O	N	D

The Alaska Range protects this area from continental extremes to the north, while the Kenai and Chugach Mountains strip most of the wind and moisture from storms blowing in from the Gulf of Alaska. The salt water of Cook Inlet moderates temperatures as well. However, seasons are well defined and permafrost hides here on north-facing slopes and in sheltered hollows.

Plants like showy mountain ash, late lilac, Siberian larch, Amur chokecherry, Swiss stone pine, and Colorado blue spruce do well in Zone A2. But success depends much on each area's microclimate (see Anchorage map, facing page).

Winter lows average 6°F (−14°C) at Anchorage Airport, 0°F (−18°C) in Palmer and Wasilla, with drops to −20 or −30°F (−29 or −34°C) once in a while. Summer days are usually cloudy and in the mid-60s, with occasional jumps into the high 70s. The growing season ranges from 105 days on the Kenai Peninsula to 138 days in Anchorage. When sowing seeds, take note that plants grow more slowly here than seed packets indicate. You can speed annuals along by starting seed indoors a few weeks before transplant, or outdoors in a cold frame.

ZONE **A3**

The mild maritime climate from Kodiak to Juneau and Prince Rupert

Growing Season

J	F	M	A	M	J	J	A	S	O	N	D

This zone includes southeastern Alaska north of Sitka clear to Skagway, plus Kodiak Island, Homer, Seward, and Prince William Sound. It also touches Prince Rupert, where cold interior air drains down the Skeena River. (Zone 4 covers southeastern Alaska; see page 38.)

Summers are cool and cloudy, while winters are typically windy and rainy. Annual precipitation runs from 80 inches at Kodiak to 200 inches near Sitka. The ground freezes every winter, and repeated freeze-thaw cycles in spring play havoc with cold-hardy plants like hybrid tea roses.

Hardy rhododendrons, azaleas, Japanese maples, and dwarf conifers do well here. The easiest bedding plants to grow include pansies, violas, and snapdragons. Planting in raised beds of light, sandy soil assures good drainage in wet areas and quick warm-up of soil in spring.

Winter minimums average 20 to 30°F (−7 to −1°C), with occasional drops to −5°F (−21°C). Summer highs are in the low 60s, with occasional jumps to 80°F (27°C). The growing season runs from 113 days in Cordova to 162 days in Haines. But cool summer temperatures offset the advantages of summer day length. Plants take longer to grow than seed packets describe.

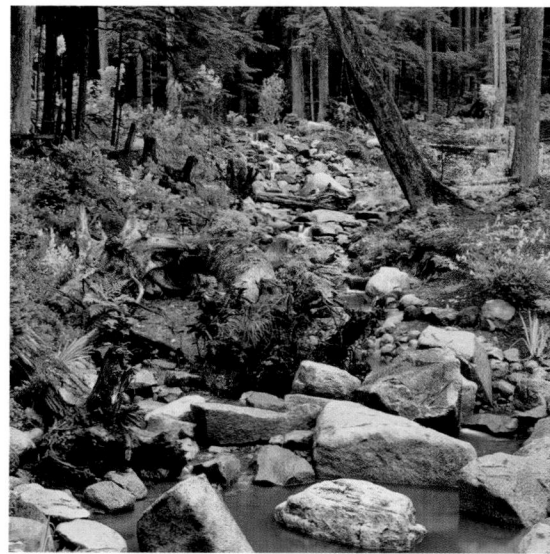

Woodland plants line a rocky creek at Glacier Gardens, Juneau.

ZONE **1A**

Coldest mountain and intermountain areas throughout the contiguous states and southern British Columbia

Growing Season

J F M A M J J A S O N D

Marked by a short growing season and relatively mild summer temperatures, Zone 1a includes the coldest regions west of the Rockies, excluding Alaska, and a few patches of cold country east of the Great Divide. The mild days and chilly nights during the growing season extend the bloom of summer perennials like columbines and Shasta daisies. If your garden gets reliable snow cover (which insulates plants), you'll be able to grow perennials listed for some of the milder zones. In years when snow comes late or leaves early, protect plants with a 5- or 6-inch layer of organic mulch. Along with hardy evergreen conifers, tough deciduous trees and shrubs form the garden's backbone. Gardeners can plant warm-season vegetables as long as they are short-season varieties. To further assure success, grow vegetables from seedlings you start yourself or buy from a nursery or garden center.

Winter lows average in the 0 to 11°F (–18 to –12°C) range; extremes range from –25 to –50°F (–32 to –46°C). The growing season is 50 to 100 days.

Shasta daisies (Chrysanthemum maximum) *carpet a hillside garden in Aspen, Colorado.*

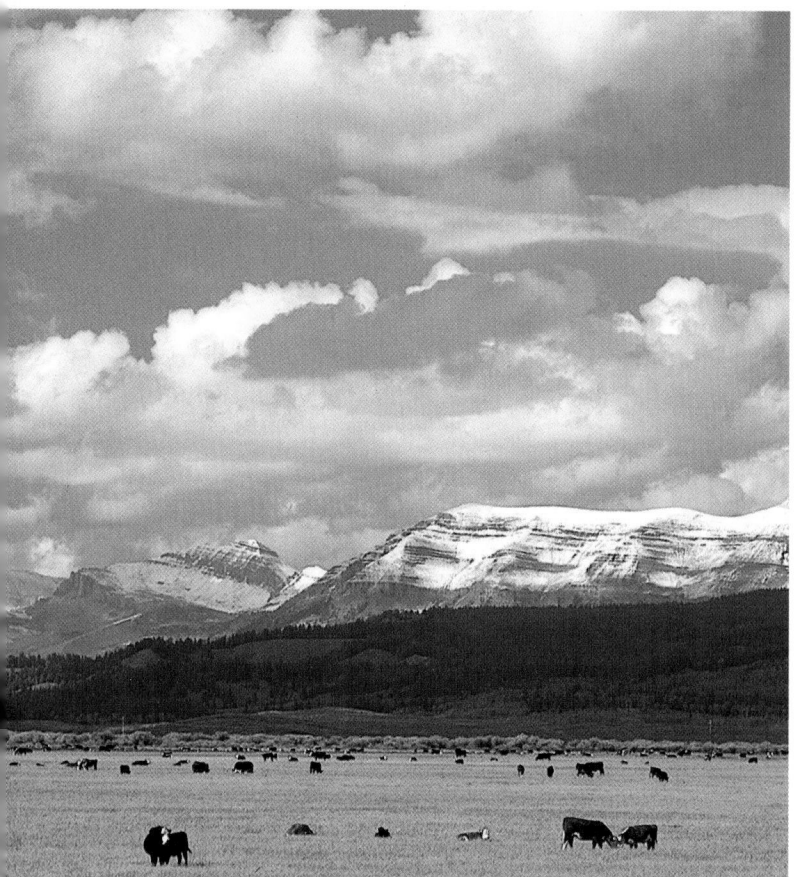

An arctic weather front slides down the east flank of the Rocky Mountains to the open plains in Wyoming.

ZONE **1B**

Coldest Eastern Rockies and plains climate of Colorado, Wyoming, Montana, and Southern Alberta

INTERMOUNTAIN: PAGES 33, 34

Growing Season

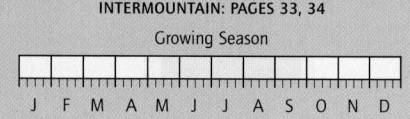

J F M A M J J A S O N D

Centered over the plains of Wyoming and Montana, this zone sees January temperatures from 0 to 12°F (–18 to –11°C), with extremes between –30 and –50°F (–34 to –46°C). Zone 1b lies east of the Great Divide, where the continental climate reigns supreme. Arctic cold fronts sweep through 6 to 12 times a year, sometimes dropping temperatures by 30 or 40°F in 24 hours. The summer growing season tends to be warm and generous at 110 to 140 days long; but constant winds—12 miles per hour average, year-round in many places—call for windbreaks and shade trees, like hackberries and cottonwoods, whose leaves are animated by the wind. Few shrubs are better loved here than lilacs, and few plants are better adapted than native ornamental grasses and prairie flowers. With protection, annual vegetables and flowers thrive, as do wind-tolerant perennials such as buckwheats, grasses, and penstemons. Where hail is a problem, gardeners favor small-leafed plants; where winters are dry and snow cover light, they compensate with mulch and extra water.

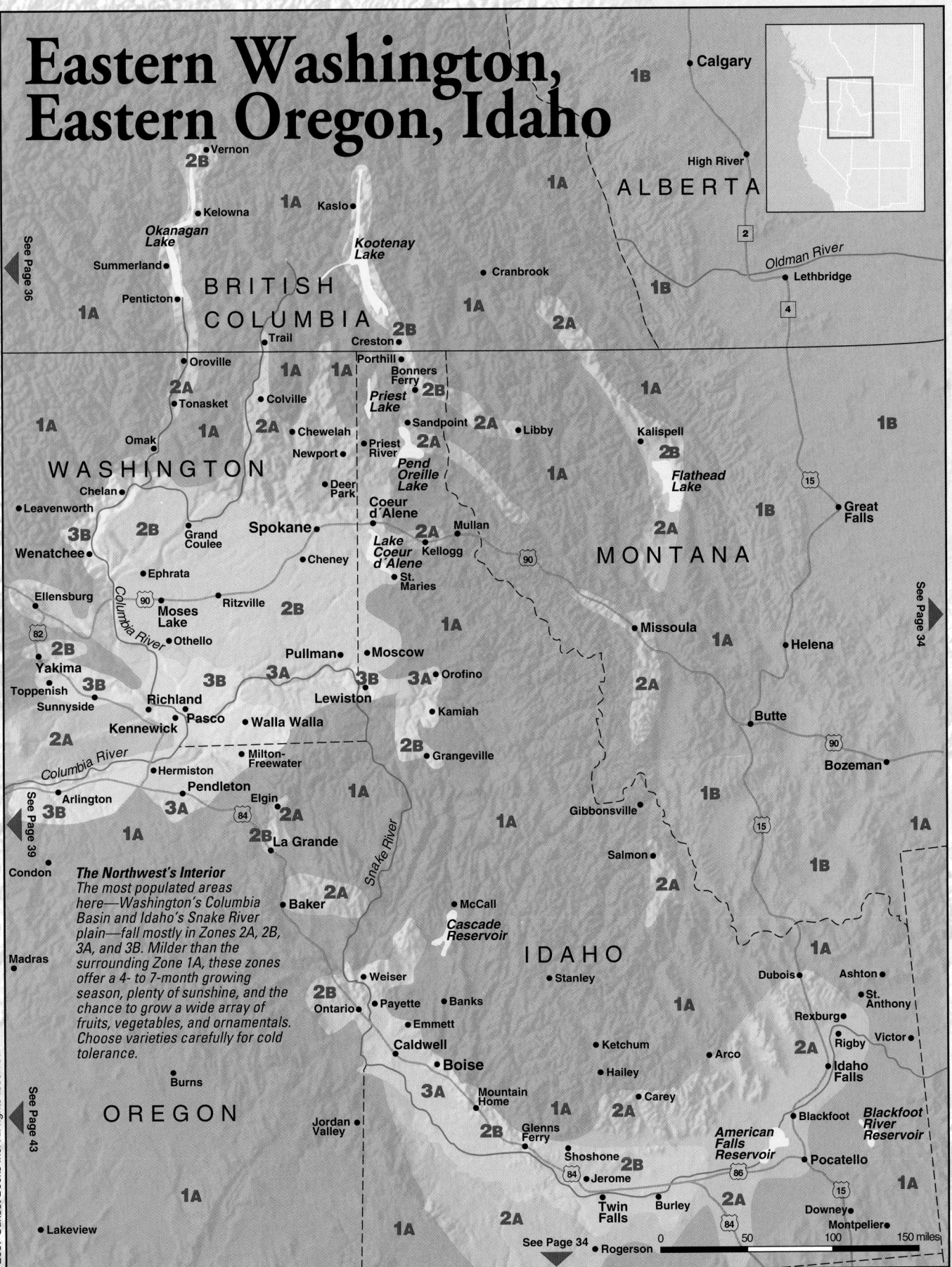

Eastern Washington, Eastern Oregon, Idaho

ALBERTA

BRITISH COLUMBIA

WASHINGTON

MONTANA

IDAHO

OREGON

Okanagan Lake

Kootenay Lake

Priest Lake

Pend Oreille Lake

Flathead Lake

Lake Coeur d'Alene

Cascade Reservoir

American Falls Reservoir

Blackfoot River Reservoir

Columbia River

Snake River

Calgary · 1B
High River ·
Oldman River
Lethbridge ·
Cranbrook ·
Vernon · 2B
Kelowna ·
Kaslo ·
Summerland ·
Penticton ·
Trail ·
Creston · 2B
Oroville ·
Porthill
Bonners Ferry · 2B
Tonasket ·
Colville ·
Chewelah ·
Sandpoint · 2A Libby · Kalispell · 2B
Omak ·
Newport ·
Priest River
Chelan ·
Leavenworth ·
Deer Park ·
Coeur d'Alene
Spokane · Mullan ·
Kellogg
Grand Coulee
Cheney ·
St. Maries
Wenatchee
Ephrata ·
Ellensburg
Ritzville ·
Moses Lake
Othello ·
Yakima
Toppenish ·
Sunnyside ·
Pullman · Moscow · Orofino ·
Richland Lewiston
Pasco · Kamiah ·
Kennewick Walla Walla
Milton-Freewater · Grangeville ·
Hermiston ·
Arlington Pendleton
Condon · Elgin ·
La Grande
Madras · Baker ·
McCall ·
Weiser · Stanley ·
Ontario Payette · Banks ·
Emmett ·
Caldwell
Boise
Burns · Ketchum · Arco ·
Hailey ·
Mountain Home Carey ·
Jordan Valley · Glenns Ferry
Shoshone · Jerome
Twin Falls Burley ·
Lakeview · Rogerson ·
Great Falls ·
Missoula · Helena ·
Butte ·
Bozeman ·
Gibbonsville ·
Salmon ·
Dubois · Ashton ·
St. Anthony
Rexburg · Victor ·
Rigby ·
Idaho Falls
Blackfoot ·
Pocatello ·
Downey ·
Montpelier ·

The Northwest's Interior
The most populated areas here—Washington's Columbia Basin and Idaho's Snake River plain—fall mostly in Zones 2A, 2B, 3A, and 3B. Milder than the surrounding Zone 1A, these zones offer a 4- to 7-month growing season, plenty of sunshine, and the chance to grow a wide array of fruits, vegetables, and ornamentals. Choose varieties carefully for cold tolerance.

See Page 36
See Page 34
See Page 39
See Page 43
See Page 34

0   50   100   150 miles

Climate Zones   1A 1B 2A 2B 3A 3B

Nevada, Montana, Wyoming, Utah, Colorado

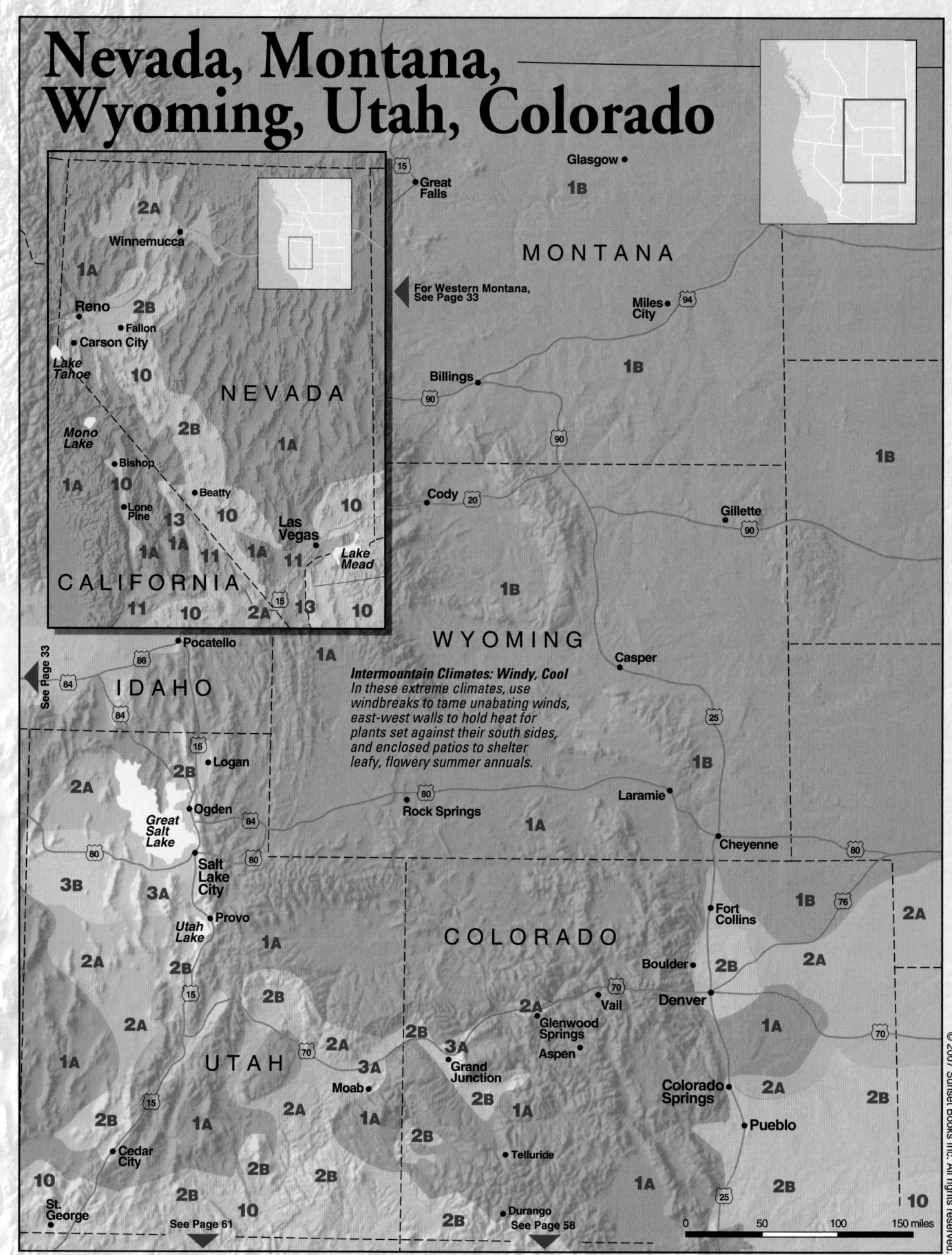

Glasgow •
1B

MONTANA

• Great
Falls

◄ For Western Montana,
See Page 33

Miles
City • 94

Billings •
90

1B

2A
Winnemucca •

1A

Reno • 2B
• Fallon
• Carson City

*Lake
Tahoe*

10

NEVADA

1A

Cody • 20

1B

Gillette •
90

90

*Mono
Lake*

2B

1A   • Bishop
10

13   • Beatty
10

• Lone
Pine

1A   1A   11

Las
Vegas •

1A

11

*Lake
Mead*

10

10

WYOMING

1B

Casper •

25

CALIFORNIA

11   10   2A   15   13   10

• Pocatello
86

1A

Intermountain Climates: Windy, Cool
In these extreme climates, use
windbreaks to tame unabating winds,
east-west walls to hold heat for
plants set against their south sides,
and enclosed patios to shelter
leafy, flowery summer annuals.

See Page 33 ◄
84

IDAHO
84

2B   • Logan

2A

• Ogden
84

80
Rock Springs •

Laramie •
1B

1A

*Great
Salt
Lake*
80

80

• Salt
Lake
City

Cheyenne •
80

1B   76

3B   3A

2A

*Utah
Lake*   • Provo

1A

COLORADO

1B
• Fort
Collins

2A

2A   2B

15

2A

2B

Boulder • 2B
70
Vail •

2A

Denver •

2A

70

*Glenwood
Springs*

1A

70

2A
70
• Aspen

UTAH

2A   3A

Moab •

3A   • Grand
Junction

2B

1A

Colorado
Springs •

2A   2B

1A

• Pueblo

2B

2B

2B

• Telluride

1A   25   2B

10
• Cedar
City

2B

2B   2B

15

1A

• St.
George

2B

10   **See Page 61** ▼

2B   • Durango
See Page 58 ▼

0   50   100   150 miles

10

Climate Zones   ▨ 1A 1B 2A 2B 3A 3B   10 11   13

ZONE **2A**

Cold mountain and intermountain areas

INTERMOUNTAIN: PAGES 33, 34 • CALIFORNIA: PAGES 43, 44, 51
SOUTHWEST DESERTS: PAGES 57, 58, 61

Growing Season

J F M A M J J A S O N D

Another snowy winter climate, Zone 2a covers several regions that are considered mild compared with surrounding climates. You'll find this zone stretched over Colorado's northeastern plains, a bit of it along the Western Slope and Front Range of the Rockies, as well as mild parts of river drainages like those of the Snake, Okanogan, and the Columbia. It also shows up in western Montana and Nevada and in mountain areas of the Southwest. This is the coldest zone in which sweet cherries and many apples grow. Winter temperatures here usually hover between 10 and 20°F (–12 to –7°C) at night, with drops between –20 and –30°F (–29 and –34°C) every few years. When temperatures drop below that, orchardists can lose even their trees. The growing season is 100 to 150 days.

As winter chill gives way, waves of spring tulips and perennials appear.

Prairie flowers meander down a slope into a garden near Denver, Colorado.

ZONE **2B**

Warmer-summer intermountain climate

INTERMOUNTAIN: PAGES 33, 34 • CALIFORNIA: PAGE 43 • SOUTHWEST: PAGES 58, 61

Growing Season

J F M A M J J A S O N D

This is a zone that offers a good balance of long, warm summers and chilly winters, making it an excellent climate zone for commercial fruit growing. That's why you'll find orchards in this zone in almost every state in the West. You'll also find this warm-summer, snowy-winter climate along Colorado's Western Slope and mild parts of the Front Range; in Nevada from Reno to Fallon, then north to Lovelock; in large areas of northern Arizona and New Mexico; and in mild parts of the Columbia and Snake River basins.

Winter temperatures are milder than in neighboring Zone 2a, minimums averaging from 12 to 22°F (–11 to –6°C), with extremes in the –10 to –20°F (–23 to –29°C) range. The growing season here in Zone 2b runs from 115 days in higher elevations and more northerly areas to more than 160 days in southeastern Colorado.

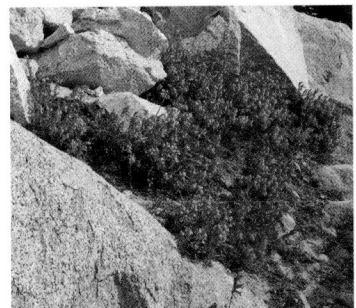

Penstemons look as natural in this rock garden as they do in the wilderness.

Western Washington

BRITISH COLUMBIA

Powell River

Comox

1A

19

BRITISH COLUMBIA

West Vancouver

1A

Port Alberni

Tofino

Bamfield

5

1A

Vancouver Island

Nanaimo

1

Strait of Georgia

4

Duncan

4

Saanich

5

Victoria

Sooke

Vancouver

99

Fraser River

Abbotsford

4

1

4

Pacific Ocean

5

4

La Push

Forks

1A

101

4

Port Angeles

Sequim

4

Port Townsend

Keystone

Anacortes

San Juan Islands

Oak Harbor

20

Mt. Vernon

5

Sedro Woolley

4

20

1A

Maple Falls

Bellingham

Hope

Chilliwack

4

5

Darrington

Arlington

4

▲ *Mt. Olympus*

1A

5

Everett

Sultan

Gold Bar

Skykomish

4

405

Redmond

Lake Washington

Carnation

Bellevue

Lake Sammamish

Snoqualmie

1A

90

Issaquah

Kent

5

Auburn

Puget Sound

Bremerton

Seattle

5

Enumclaw

Puyallup

Tacoma

101

4

Shelton

4

Olympia

5

4

The Northwest's Inland Sea: Windy, Dry, or Wet

Three weather patterns mark western Washington's climate. Northeasters roar down the Fraser River valley, spilling over Bellingham and the San Juan Islands all the way to Sequim and dropping temperatures 20 degrees in a few hours, which can kill otherwise hardy plants. The rain shadow—protected from rainstorms by Olympic and Vancouver Island mountains— covers much of the same area, holding rainfall there to under 30 inches per year. Pacific storms drench the rest of Puget Sound with 40 to 60 inches of annual rainfall.

Queets

Pacific Beach

4

5

Hoquiam

Aberdeen

Elma

101

Raymond

5

Long Beach

4

4

Astoria

5

Seaside

See Page 39

4

6

Chehalis

Centralia

Pe Ell

Toledo

6

4

WASHINGTON

1A

4

1A

▲ *Mt. Rainier*

Ashford

Packwood

Washington's Great Divide

Climates on the west side of the Cascades are generally milder and moister than on the east side, where warmer summers and colder winters are the norm.

▲ Mt. St. Helens

1A

Longview

6

Inset map

Vancouver

Fraser River Valley

Mt. Baker

Bellingham

San Juan Islands

Victoria

Sequim

Rain Shadow

Olympic Peaks

Seattle

Tacoma

Olympia

Mt. Rainier

See Page 33

| 0 | 20 | 40 | 60 miles |

Climate Zones 1A 4 5 6

ZONE **3A**

Mild areas of mountain and intermountain climates

NORTHWEST INTERIOR: PAGES 33, 39
INTERMOUNTAIN: PAGE 34
CALIFORNIA: PAGE 44
SOUTHWEST DESERTS: PAGES 58, 61

Growing Season

| J | F | M | A | M | J | J | A | S | O | N | D |

East of the Sierra and Cascade ranges, you can hardly find a better gardening climate than Zone 3a. Winter minimum temperatures average from 15 to 25°F (–9 to –4°C), with extremes between –8 and –18°F (–22 and –28°C). Its frost-free growing season runs from 150 to 186 days. The zone tends to occur at lower elevations in the northern states (eastern Oregon and Washington as well as Idaho), but at higher elevations as you move south crossing Utah's Great Salt Lake and into northern New Mexico and Arizona. Fruits and vegetables that thrive in long, warm summers, such as melons, gourds, and corn, tend to do well here. This is another great zone for all kinds of deciduous fruit trees and ornamental trees and shrubs. Just keep them well watered.

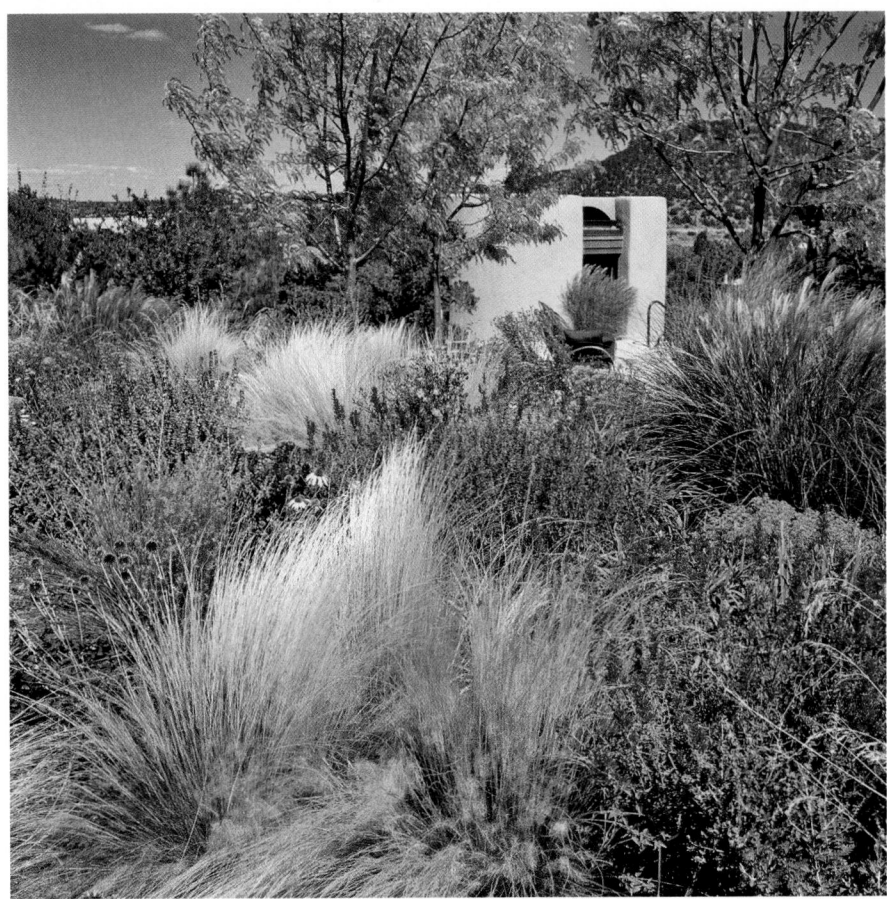

A blend of grasses and drought-tolerant perennials fits seamlessly with classic Santa Fe adobe.

A fire pit cuts the evening chill in this Yakima Valley, Washington, garden.

ZONE **3B**

Mildest areas of intermountain climates

NORTHWEST INTERIOR: PAGES 33, 39
INTERMOUNTAIN: PAGE 34
SOUTHWEST: PAGES 58, 61

Growing Season

| J | F | M | A | M | J | J | A | S | O | N | D |

Zone 3b is much like Zone 3a, but with slightly milder winter averages of 19 to 29°F (–7 to –2°C) and extremes that usually bottom out between –2 and –15°F (–19 to –26°C). Summer temperatures are a bit higher than in Zone 3a—mostly in the high 80s and low- to mid-90s. Zone 3b offers one of the longest growing seasons of the intermountain climates. Gardeners here count on 180 to 210 frost-free days with plenty of heat. However, it's one of the smallest zones. Most of it lies in the warmest parts of eastern Washington's Columbia Basin, with bits in Lewiston, Idaho, and parts of the Southwest. This is fabulous country for annual vegetables and flowers and a long list of perennials, trees, shrubs, and vines.

ZONE 4

Cold-winter areas of the north coast and mild-winter areas of Alaska and British Columbia

ALASKA: PAGE 30 • NORTHWEST: PAGES 36, 39 • CALIFORNIA: PAGE 43

Growing Season

J F M A M J J A S O N D

One of the West's most narrow, linear climates, Zone 4 runs from high in the coastal mountains of Northern California to southeastern Alaska, losing elevation as it moves north. It gets considerable influence from the Pacific Ocean, but also from the continental air mass, higher elevation, or both. As it extends north, the zone first touches salt water in northern Puget Sound and is almost entirely surrounded by salt water in southeastern Alaska.

In the contiguous states, Zone 4 has more cold than neighboring Zone 5, more snow, and a shorter growing season. Compared to neighboring zones in Alaska and Canada, however, it has less winter cold and a longer growing season. No zone grows better perennials and bulbs; people who like woodland plants and rock plants love Zone 4. But beware: though you can grow winter vegetables in the southern part of Zone 4, it doesn't get enough winter sunlight in Alaska to sustain them.

A low-maintenance blend of conifers, shrubs, and perennials adorns the terraces of this Skagit Valley, Washington, weekend house.

Average winter lows in Zone 4 range from 34°F (1°C) down to 28°F (−2°C), with extreme lows averaging 8 to 0°F (−13 to −18°C). The growing season is 150 to 200 days long, but because Zone 4 summers are temperate (highs average from the low 60s to the 70s), plants take more time to develop. If you're growing vegetables, for example, add at least 50 percent to the days-to-harvest figure listed on the seed package, or start your garden from transplants.

This viewing terrace in a Seattle garden, half concealed by shrubbery, also displays garden art.

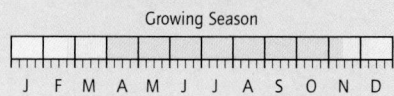

ZONE 5

Marine influence along the Northwest coast, Puget Sound, and South Vancouver Island

NORTHWEST: PAGES 36, 39, 43

Growing Season

J F M A M J J A S O N D

Mild ocean air moderates Zone 5, allowing it to produce some of the finest rhododendrons, Japanese maples, and rock garden plants anywhere. Heaths and heathers thrive in sandy soils along the coast and inland, and katsura trees reach their prime, rarely scorching as they may inland. It's also fine country for native woodland ferns, trilliums, piggyback plants, vine maples, and dogwoods.

Summer highs run between 65 and 70°F (18 and 21°C) along the coast, and between 70 and 75°F (21 and 24°C) inland and around Puget Sound. Such mild temperatures favor leaf vegetables, which are slow to bolt, and flowering ornamentals like begonias. Steady breezes and lower temperatures, especially along the coast, make windbreaks and warm microclimates critical for heat-loving plants.

Average January minimum temperatures range from 33 to 41°F (1 to 5°C), with annual lows averaging a few degrees colder, and 10-year extremes ranging from 20 to 6°F (−7 to −14°C). Some locations (Coupeville, Raymond, Long Beach, Tillamook, Newport) get 10-year lows between 6° and 10°F (-14° and −12°C), but much of the region, especially along the Oregon coast, is mild enough to let gardeners get away with growing plants like *Washingtonia robusta* and hardy forms of *Agave americana*.

Big freezes do considerable damage when they come very early or very late. And while these occasional disasters clear the slate of most borderline plants, they should not serve as a general gauge of plant hardiness here.

Though the growing season averages between 200 and 250 days, heat accumulation is low, and warm-season vegetables develop slowly.

Western Oregon

Portland: Mild to Wild

In winter, when cold air builds east of the Cascades, winds can blast through Columbia Gorge at tree-ripping speed. They hit east Portland hard and usually curve south, sometimes icing up trees clear to Milwaukie. If you live in the Portland area east of Interstate 205, plant trees whose limbs bear up well in ice storms—for example, black walnut, ginkgo, linden, and sweet gum.

Vancouver
Portland
Columbia Gorge
Mt. Hood
Gresham
Mt. Scott
Milwaukie
Lake Oswego

Willamette Valley Is Berry Country

The Willamette Valley is mild but sufficiently cool to make it one of the country's prime regions for growing boysenberries, blueberries, red raspberries, and such wine grapes as Chardonnay, Pinot Noir, and Riesling.

WASHINGTON
OREGON
CALIFORNIA
Pacific Ocean

See Page 36 / See Page 33 / See Page 43

Astoria, Seaside, Garibaldi, Tillamook, Lincoln City, Newport, Waldport, Florence, Reedsport, Coos Bay, Coquille, Bandon, Port Orford, Gold Beach, Brookings, Longview, Vancouver, Portland, Forest Grove, Milwaukie, Newburg, McMinnville, Salem, Dallas, Corvallis, Albany, Eugene, Springfield, Drain, Cottage Grove, Oakridge, Roseburg, Grants Pass, Medford, Ashland, Hood River, The Dalles, Madras, Redmond, Bend, Klamath Falls, Crater Lake, Upper Klamath Lake, Mt. Hood

0 10 20 30 miles

Climate Zones
1A 2B 3A 3B 4 5 6 7 17

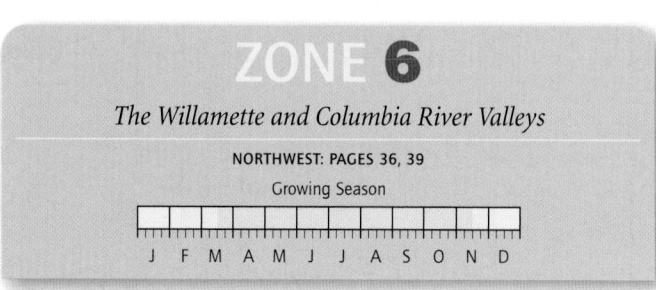

A woodland waterfall welcomes Craig Prunty to the entry of his Beaverton, Oregon, home.

ZONE 6

The Willamette and Columbia River Valleys

NORTHWEST: PAGES 36, 39

Growing Season

J F M A M J J A S O N D

Warmer summers and cooler winters distinguish Zone 6 from coastal Zone 5. Tucked between the Coast Range and the Cascades, Zone 6 includes the Willamette Valley in Oregon, the Columbia River Valley between Vancouver and Longview, and the Cowlitz drainage from Longview to Toledo.

The Coast Range buffers the impact of Pacific storms, but Zone 6 is still a maritime climate, with a long growing season (from 155 days at Cottage Grove to 280 days in Portland neighborhoods) and 40 to 55 inches of annual precipitation most places. The continental influence is felt two to four times each winter when chilly interior air flows west through the Columbia Gorge and produces wind and freezing rain clear to the Portland airport. In spite of this, Portland is among the mildest parts of Zone 6—a great place to experiment with borderline plants like eucalyptus, acacias, and oleanders.

Summer temperatures in Zone 6 average 10 to 15°F (5 to 8°C) higher than those along the coast, while winters are cold enough to trigger good fruit set. Ten-year extremes average 0 to 10°F (−18 to −12°C). Warm summers and chilly winters make the Willamette Valley one of the West's best-known growing areas for berries, hazelnuts, roses, flowering fruit trees, and broadleafed evergreens.

The Willamette Valley's hills and small mountain ranges create many microclimates. South- and west-facing slopes are warm enough to produce world-class Pinot Noir grapes, while north- and east-facing slopes are perfect for shade tolerant plants like rhododendrons, fatsias, and camellias. These hills have perfect air drainage, so winters get less frost than the valley floor.

The Willamette Valley, Oregon, hills give grapes the perfect balance of heat, good soil, and drainage.

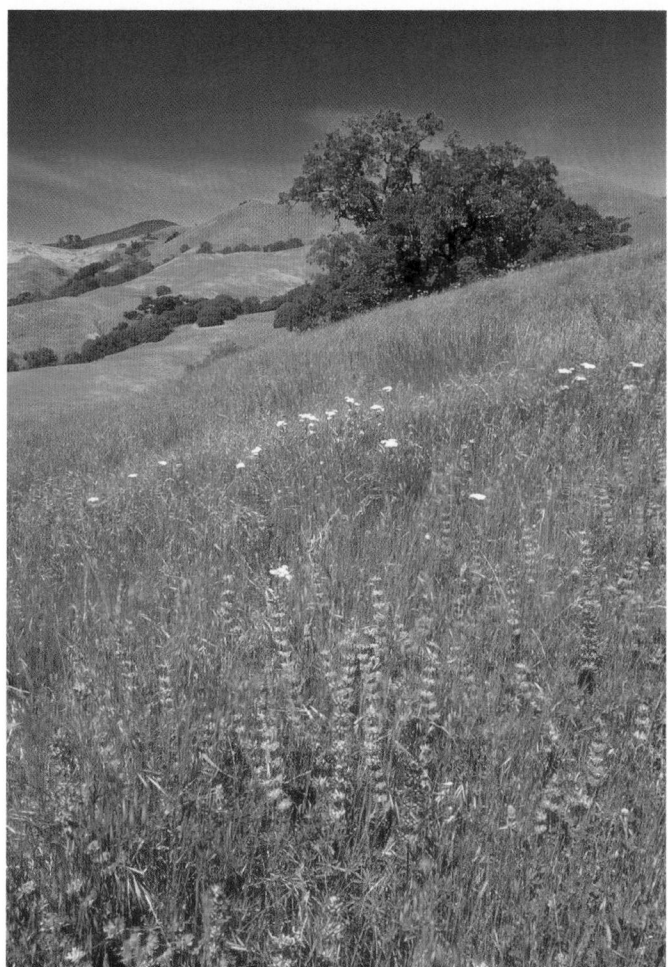

Rolling golden hills traverse much of Zone 7, as shown here at Mount Diablo, California.

ZONE 7

California's Gray Pine Belt, Oregon's Rogue River Valley, and Southern California mountains

OREGON: PAGE 39 • CALIFORNIA: PAGES 43, 44, 46–47

Growing Season

J F M A M J J A S O N D

Zone 7 encompasses several thousand square miles west of the Sierra Nevada and Cascade ranges, and in the mountains that separate the Southern California coast from interior deserts. Because of the influence of latitude, this climate lies mostly at low elevations in Oregon's Rogue Valley, middle elevations around California's Central Valley, and at middle to higher elevations farther south. Gray pines define the heart of Zone 7 around the Central Valley, but more adaptable incense cedars replace them farther north and south.

Hot summers and mild but pronounced winters give Zone 7 sharply defined seasons without severe winter cold or enervating humidity. The climate pleases plants that require a marked seasonal pattern to do well—flower bulbs, peonies, lilacs, and flowering cherries, for example. Deciduous fruit trees do well also; the region is noted for its pears, apples, peaches, and cherries.

Gardeners in a few spots around the San Francisco Bay will be surprised to find their gardens mapped in Zone 7. These areas are too high and cold in winter to be included in milder Zones 15 and 16.

In the mildest parts of Zone 7—in the extreme southern Salinas Valley, for example—you can get away with growing borderline plants such as citrus, oleanders, and almonds if you choose a spot with good air drainage to take the edge off winter chill.

At weather-recording stations in Zone 7, typical winter lows range from 35 to 26°F (2 to –3°C), with record lows averaging from 18 to -0° F (–8 to –18°C).

ZONE 8

Cold-air basins of California's Central Valley

CALIFORNIA: PAGES 43, 44, 46–47

Growing Season

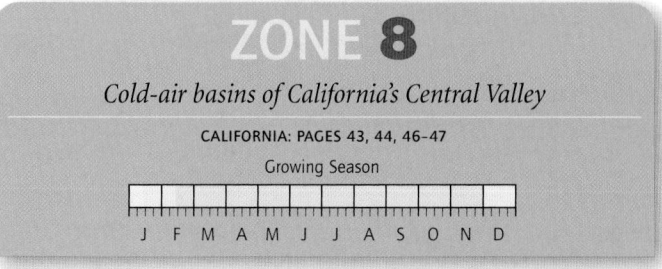

J F M A M J J A S O N D

Zone 8 makes up most of the valley floor in California's Sacramento and San Joaquin Valleys. Only a shade of difference exists between Zone 8 and Zone 9, but it's an important difference—crucial in some cases. Zone 9 is a thermal belt, meaning that cold air can flow from it to lower ground—and that lower ground is found here in Zone 8. Citrus furnish the most meaningful illustration. Lemons, oranges, and grapefruit, which flourish in Zone 9, cannot be grown commercially in Zone 8 because the winter nights are frequently cold enough to injure the fruit or the trees; the trees would need regular heating to deliver decent crops. The same winter cold can damage many garden plants. That cold often shows itself in winter, when cold air rolls off the Sierra Nevada and pools on the valley floor, condensing into thick tule fog.

Zone 8 differs from Zone 14, which it joins near the latitudes of north Sacramento and Modesto, in that Zone 14 occasionally gets some marine influence. Low temperatures in Zone 8 over a 20-year period ranged from 29 to 13°F (–2 to –11°C). Certain features that Zones 8 and 9 share are described under Zone 9.

In winter, tule fog envelops a lone oak in California's Central Valley.

On the eastern slopes of the Central Valley, a vineyard turns autumn gold.

ZONE 9

Thermal belts of California's Central Valley

CALIFORNIA: PAGES 43, 44, 46–47

Growing Season

J F M A M J J A S O N D

As cited in the description of Zone 8, the biggest readily apparent difference between Zones 8 and 9 is that Zone 9, a thermal belt, is a safer climate for citrus than Zone 8, which contains cold-air basins. The same distinction, thermal belt versus cold-air basin, determines which species and varieties—hibiscus, melaleuca, pittosporum, and other plants—are recommended for Zone 9 but not for Zone 8.

Zones 8 and 9 have the following features in common: summer daytime temperatures are high, sunshine is almost constant during the growing season, and growing seasons are long. Deciduous fruits and vegetables of nearly every kind thrive in these long, hot summers; winter cold is just adequate to satisfy the dormancy requirements of the fruit trees. Fiercely cold, piercing north winds blow for several days at a time in winter, but they are more distressing to gardeners than to garden plants. You can minimize them with windbreaks.

In both Zones 8 and 9 tule fogs (dense fogs that rise from the ground on cold, clear nights) appear and stay for hours or days during winter. The fogs usually hug the ground at night and rise to 800 to 1,000 feet by afternoon.

Heat-loving plants such as oleander and crape myrtle perform at their peak in Zones 8 and 9 (and 14). Plants that like summer coolness and humidity demand some fussing; careful gardeners accommodate them by providing filtered shade from tall trees and plenty of moisture. In Zone 9, winter lows over a 20-year period ranged from 28 to 18°F (–2 to –8°C).

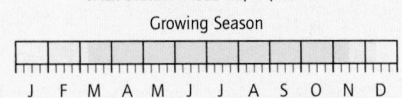

ZONE 14

Northern California's inland areas with some ocean influence

CALIFORNIA: PAGES 43, 44, 46–47

Growing Season

J F M A M J J A S O N D

Marine air moderates parts of Zone 14 that otherwise would be colder in winter and hotter in summer. The opening in Northern California's Coast Ranges created by San Francisco and San Pablo bays allows marine air to spill much farther inland. The same thing happens, but the penetration is not as deep, in the Salinas Valley. Zone 14 includes the cold-winter valley floors, canyons, and land troughs in the Coast Ranges from Santa Barbara County to Humboldt County.

The milder-winter, marine-influenced areas in Zone 14 and the cold-winter inland valleys within Zone 14 differ in humidity. For example, lowland parts of Contra Costa County are more humid than Sacramento.

Fruits that need winter chill do well here, as do shrubs needing summer heat (oleander, gardenia). Over a 20-year period, this area had lows ranging from 26 to 16°F (–3 to –9°C). Weather records show all-time lows from 20 down to 11°F (–7 to –12°C).

A mix of unthirsty perennials, grasses, and shrubs borders a naturalistic path in a Napa Valley garden.

Northern California

OREGON

CALIFORNIA

Pacific Ocean

Pacific Ocean

See Page 39

See Page 34

Dry Foothills of Zone 7
Tens of thousands of foothill gardeners find themselves in Zone 7, which tends to be warm and dry in summer. If you're one of these people, you probably have fast-draining mineral soil. That's great for plants that thrive on minimal water, including many California natives such as flannel bush, oaks, and most manzanitas.

Brookings
Ashland
Dorris
Tulelake
Klamath Lake
Tule Lake
Crescent City
Yreka
Happy Camp
Klamath
Weed
Mt. Shasta
Mt. Shasta
Alturas
Dunsmuir
Willow Creek
Burney
Korbel
Eureka
Trinity Lake
Shasta Lake
Weaverville
Fortuna
Rio Dell
Redding
Anderson
Susanville
Mineral
Garberville
Red Bluff
Chester   Westwood
Greenville
Keddie
Quincy
Corning
Covelo
Rockport
Dos Rios
Laytonville
Paradise
Portola
Chico
Sierraville
Downieville
Willows
Oroville
Lake Oroville
Fort Bragg
Willits
Mendocino
Gridley
Truckee
Upper Lake
Nevada City
Grass Valley
Ukiah
Lakeport
Clear Lake
Colusa
Williams
Marysville
Yuba City
Colfax
Tahoe City
Boonville
Lake Tahoe
Hopland
Point Arena
Lincoln
Auburn
South Lake Tahoe
Cloverdale
Middletown
Roseville
Rio Linda
Folsom Lake
Camino
Placerville
Folsom
Fair Oaks
Lake Berryessa
Woodland
Sacramento
Santa Rosa
Sutter Creek
Jackson
San Andreas
Vallejo
Angels Camp
San Rafael

See San Francisco Bay Area and Inland Map, Pages 46 & 47

0   20   40   60 miles

Climate Zones   1A   2A 2B   4   5   7   8   9   14 15 16 17

© 2007 Sunset Books Inc. All rights reserved.

Central California

Central Valley—Apples to Oranges
Rich soils, a long and warm growing
season, and a pronounced but mild
winter make this a great
food-growing region. From apples to
oranges, nearly everything is
possible.

Pacific
Ocean

Monterey
Bay

Mono Lake

See Page 43

See Page 34

See Page 57

See Los Angeles
and Inland Map,
Pages 50 & 51

See San Francisco
Bay Area and Inland
Map, Pages 46 & 47

Channel
Islands

Pt.
Conception

0   10   20   30 miles

Climate Zones   1A   2A   3A   7   8   9   11   14 15 16 17 18 19 20 21 22 23 24

ZONE 15

Chilly winters along the Coast Range

CALIFORNIA: PAGES 43, 44, 46–47

Growing Season

J F M A M J J A S O N D

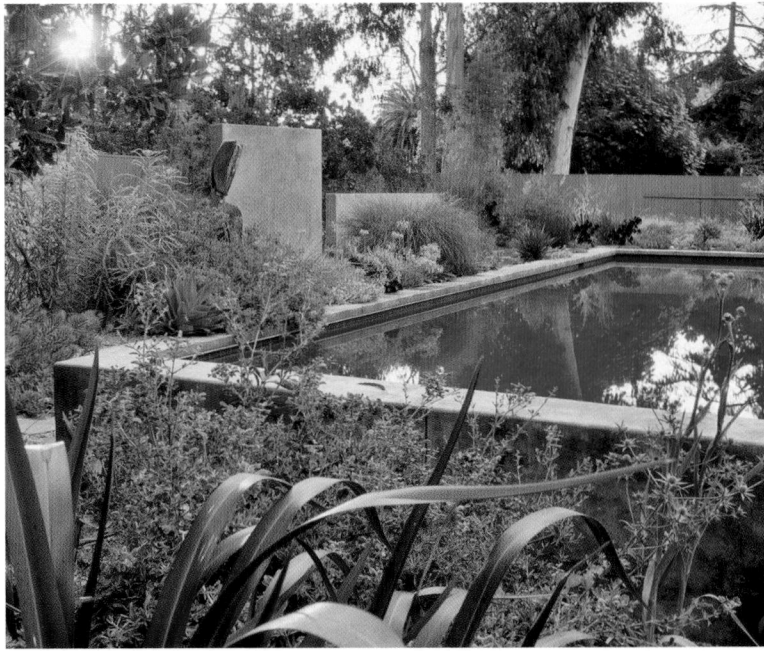

In Palo Alto, graceful eucalyptus trees and tough poolside plantings are reflected in the water.

Zones 15 and 16 are areas of Central and Northern California that are influenced by marine air approximately 85 percent of the time and by inland air 15 percent of the time. Also worthy of note is that although Zone 16 is within the Northern California coastal climate area, its winters are milder because the areas in this zone are in thermal belts (explained on page 28). The cold-winter areas that make up Zone 15 lie in cold-air basins, on hilltops above the thermal belts, or far enough north that plant performance dictates a Zone 15 designation.

Many plants that are recommended for Zone 15 are not suggested for Zone 14 mainly because they must have a moister atmosphere, cooler summers, milder winters, or all three conditions present at the same time. On the other hand, Zone 15 still receives enough winter chilling to favor some of the cold-winter specialties, such as English bluebells, which are not recommended for Zones 16 and 17.

Most of this zone gets a nagging afternoon wind in summer. Trees and dense shrubs planted on the windward side of a garden can disperse it, and a neighborhood full of trees can successfully keep it above the rooftops. Lows over a 20-year period ranged from 28 to 21°F (–2 to –6°C), and record lows from 26 to 16°F (–3 to –9°C).

Zone 15 is found on cooler hilltops and in valleys, including these in San Luis Obispo. Zone 16 lies on the hillside slopes between.

San Francisco Bay Area and Inland

The Coastal Strip

Right along the shore, steady winds and salt spray make windbreaks useful. Just a few miles inland, more heat and less wind greatly improve gardening conditions.

San Pablo Bay

Marine air flowing through the Golden Gate causes steady afternoon winds in summer.

San Francisco's Summer Fog

As warm summer air moves over California's cold coastal waters, it cools and condenses into low clouds and fog. At the same time, Central Valley air heats and rises, creating low pressure at ground level that pulls moist marine air in from the coast. The fog thickens as it moves over San Francisco, the coastal side of Bay Area mountains, and lowlands all the way to the San Joaquin Delta, where the air warms and the fog clears. This process creates San Francisco's cool summers—great for everbearing strawberries like 'Seascape', rhododendrons, camellias, New Zealand Christmas tree, cool-season vegetables and flowers, and stretching out the perennial bloom season, but disastrous for corn, melons, peppers, and other heat-loving plants.

San Francisco Bay

As you move south from San Francisco, summer temperatures increase and fog decreases.

Climate Zones   7 8 9   14 15 16 17

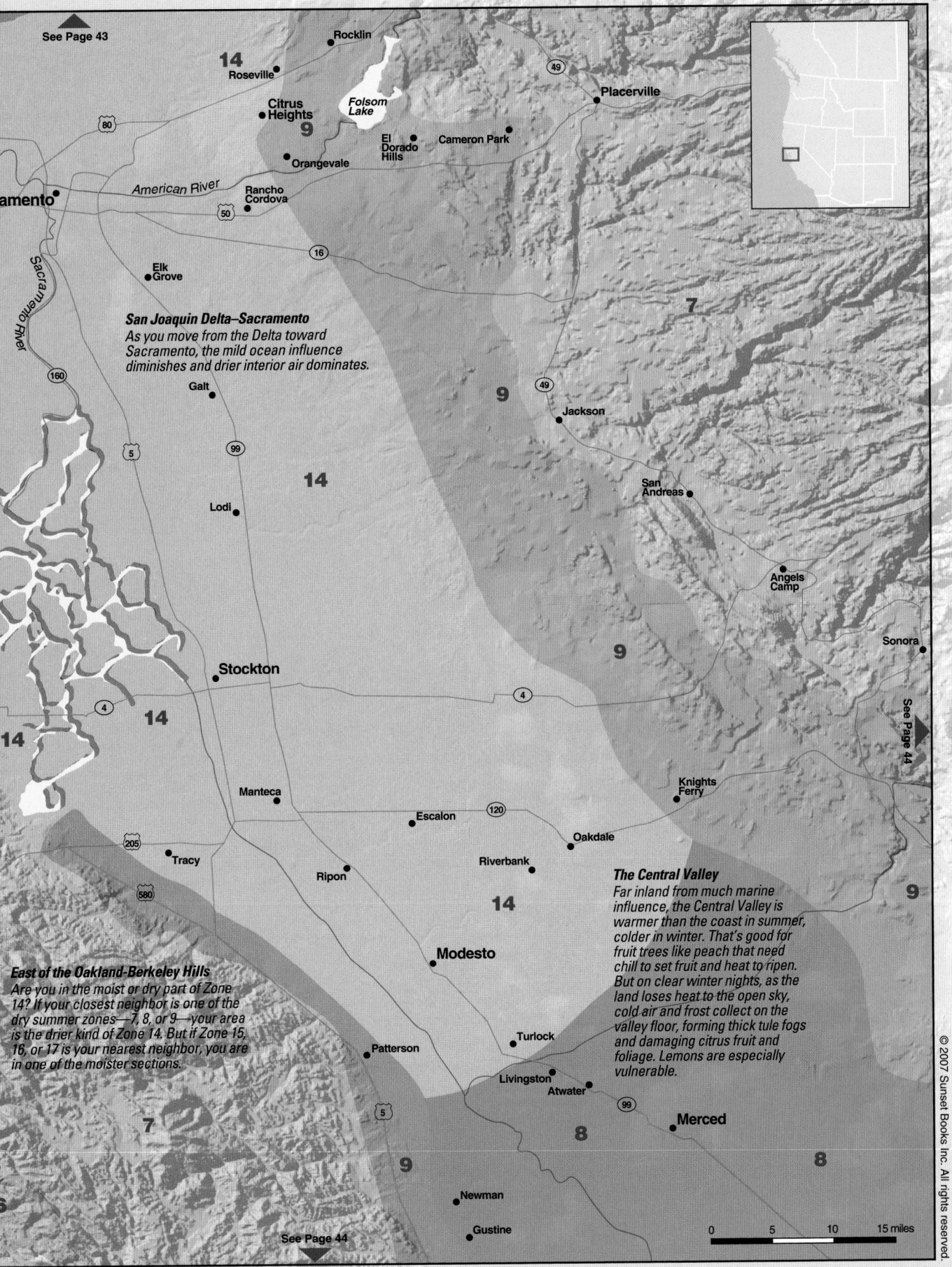

See Page 43

14

Rocklin
Roseville

Citrus
Heights

9

Folsom
Lake

49

Placerville

El
Dorado
Hills
Cameron Park

Orangevale

80

American River

ramento

Rancho
Cordova

50

16

7

Elk
Grove

San Joaquin Delta–Sacramento
As you move from the Delta toward
Sacramento, the mild ocean influence
diminishes and drier interior air dominates.

Galt

9

49

Jackson

160

14

San
Andreas

Lodi

99

5

Stockton

Angels
Camp

9

Sonora

14

4

See Page 44

14

14

Knights
Ferry

Manteca

Escalon

120

Oakdale

9

205

Tracy

Ripon

Riverbank

14

580

The Central Valley
Far inland from much marine
influence, the Central Valley is
warmer than the coast in summer,
colder in winter. That's good for
fruit trees like peach that need
chill to set fruit and heat to ripen.
But on clear winter nights, as the
land loses heat to the open sky,
cold air and frost collect on the
valley floor, forming thick tule fogs
and damaging citrus fruit and
foliage. Lemons are especially
vulnerable.

Modesto

East of the Oakland-Berkeley Hills
Are you in the moist or dry part of Zone
14? If your closest neighbor is one of the
dry summer zones—7, 8, or 9—your area
is the drier kind of Zone 14. But if Zone 15,
16, or 17 is your nearest neighbor, you are
in one of the moister sections.

Turlock

Patterson

Livingston

Atwater

5

99

Merced

7

8

8

9

6

Newman

See Page 44

Gustine

0   5   10   15 miles

ZONE **16**

Central and Northern California coast thermal belts

CALIFORNIA: PAGES 43, 44, 46–47

Growing Season

J F M A M J J A S O N D

This benign climate exists in patches and strips along the Coast Ranges from western Santa Barbara County north to northern Marin County. It's one of Northern California's finest horticultural climates. It consists of thermal belts (slopes from which cold air drains) in the coastal climate area, which is dominated by ocean weather about 85 percent of the time and by inland weather about 15 percent.

Typical lows in Zone 16 over a 20-year period ranged from 32 to 19°F (0 to –7°C). The lowest recorded temperatures range from 25 to 18°F (–4 to –8°C). This zone gets more heat in summer than Zone 17, which is dominated by maritime air, and has warmer winters than Zone 15. That's a happy combination for gardening.

A summer afternoon wind is an integral part of this climate. Plant trees and shrubs on the windward side of your garden to help disperse it.

Chaparral-cloaked slopes surround this poolside patio in Monte Sereno.

The influence of the nearby ocean keeps Zone 17 mild and lush, as seen in this El Cerrito garden.

ZONE **17**

Marine effects in Southern Oregon, Northern and Central California

CALIFORNIA: PAGE 43, 44, 46–47

Growing Season

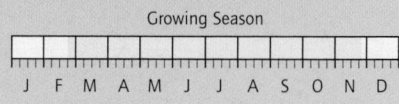

J F M A M J J A S O N D

The climate in this zone features mild, wet, almost frostless winters and cool summers with frequent fog or wind. On most days and in most places, the fog tends to come in high and fast, creating a cooling and humidifying blanket between the sun and the earth, reducing the intensity of the light and sunshine. Some heat-loving plants (citrus, hibiscus, gardenia) don't get enough heat to fruit or flower reliably.

In a 20-year period, the lowest winter temperatures in Zone 17 ranged from 36 to 23°F (2 to –5°C). The lowest temperatures on record range from 30 to 20°F (–1 to –7°C). Of further interest in this heat-starved climate are the highs of summer, normally in the 60 to 75°F (16 to 24°C) range. The average highest temperature in Zone 17 is only 97°F (36°C). In all the other adjacent climate zones, average highest temperatures are in the 104 to 116°F (40 to 47°C) range.

Warm summers in Zone 18 make patio umbrellas and shade structures essential, as in this Riverside backyard.

ZONE **18**

Above and below the thermal belts in Southern California's interior valleys

CENTRAL CALIFORNIA: PAGE 44
SOUTHERN CALIFORNIA: PAGES 50–51, 54–55, 57

Growing Season

J F M A M J J A S O N D

Zones 18 and 19 are classified as interior climates. This means that the major influence on climate is the continental air mass; the ocean determines the climate no more than 15 percent of the time.

Many of the valley floors of Zone 18 were once regions where apricot, peach, apple, and walnut orchards flourished, but the orchards have now given way to homes. Although the climate supplies enough winter chill for some plants that need it, it is not too cold (with a little protection) for many of the hardier subtropicals like amaryllis. It is too hot, too cold, and too dry for fuchsias but cold enough for tree peonies and many apple varieties, and mild enough for a number of avocado varieties. Zone 18 never supplied much commercial citrus, but home gardeners who can tolerate occasional minor fruit loss can grow citrus here.

Over a 20-year period, winter lows averaged from 22 to 17°F (−6 to −8°F). The all-time lows recorded by different weather stations in Zone 18 ranged from 22 to 7°F (−6 to −14°C).

ZONE **19**

Thermal belts around Southern California's interior valleys

CENTRAL CALIFORNIA: PAGE 44
SOUTHERN CALIFORNIA: PAGES 50–51, 54–55, 57

Growing Season

J F M A M J J A S O N D

Like that of neighboring Zone 18, the climate in Zone 19 is little influenced by the ocean. Both zones, then, have very poor climates for such plants as fuchsias, rhododendrons, and tuberous begonias. Many sections of Zone 19 have always been prime citrus-growing country—especially for those kinds that need extra summer heat in order to grow sweet fruit. Likewise, macadamia nuts and most avocados can be grown here.

The Western Plant Encyclopedia cites many ornamental plants that do well in Zone 19 but are not recommended for its neighbor because of the milder winters in Zone 19. Plants that grow well here, but not in much colder zones, include bougainvillea, bouvardia, calocephalus, Cape chestnut *(Calodendrum),* flame pea *(Chorizema),* several kinds of coral tree *(Erythrina),* livistona palms, Mexican blue and San Jose hesper palms *(Brahea armata, B. brandegeei),* giant Burmese honeysuckle *(Lonicera hildebrandiana),* myoporum, several of the more tender pittosporums, and lady palm *(Rhapis excelsa).*

Extreme winter lows over a 20-year period ranged from 28 to 22°F (−2 to −6°C) and the all-time lows at different weather stations range from 23 to 17°F (−5 to −8°C). These are considerably higher than the temperatures in neighboring Zone 18.

This garden in Valley Center displays the colorful aloes and other succulents that thrive in this dry, mild zone.

Los Angeles and Inland

See Page 44

18

24
Santa Barbara

Carpinteria

23

21

20
Ojai

21

Fillmore

Santa Paula

22

126

21

19

Moorpark

18

101

Camarillo

23

Thousand Oaks

21

Ventura

Oxnard

101

Pacific Ocean

1

24

21

20

23

Pacific Coast Highway

Santa Cruz Island

24

The Coast: Great for Variety

Coastal fogs and mild weather make Zone 24 Southern California's best climate for growing colorful flowers like tuberous begonia, pelargonium, and bougainvillea. Scores of plants from Chile, Australia, New Zealand, the Canary Islands, and the moister parts of South Africa also thrive here, making it a prime area for growing exotics such as palms, New Zealand flax, protea, banksia, and grevillea.

The Santa Anas: Nature's Desiccants

Every fall and winter, the Santa Ana wind revs up as the interior's cold, heavy air flows downhill toward the Southern California coast. As this air loses elevation, it compresses, heats up, dries out, and roars ferociously through the passes behind Los Angeles and San Bernardino. Cajon Pass and Soledad Canyon are two main routes, although the wind is named for Santa Ana Canyon. When the Santa Ana winds hit the Los Angeles Basin, they're so hot and dry they can dehydrate plants to a crisp in a few hours. Sprinklers, windbreaks, and row covers help protect them. Santa Anas usually play out near the coast, though sometimes they blow all the way to Santa Catalina Island.

Soledad Canyon

Cajon Pass

San Fernando Valley

Pasadena

San Bernardino

Riverside

San Gorgonio Pass

Los Angeles

Santa Ana Canyon

Anaheim

Santa Ana

Long Beach

Temecula

San Clemente

Pacific Ocean

Santa Catalina Island

Climate Zones

| 1 | 2A | | 7 | 11 | | 18 | 19 | 20 | 21 | 22 | 23 | 24 |

18

18

11

14

Newhall

5

18

2A

7

19

San Fernando

Foothill Freeway

18

Golden State Freeway

7

2A

See Page 57

19

Van Nuys

19

20

18

210

La Cañada

Hollywood Freeway

20

Burbank

2

21

Azusa

19

Claremont

Ventura Freeway

18

Woodland Hills

134

Glendale

Altadena

Foothill Freeway

Upland

19

San Diego Freeway

21

Beverly Hills

Hollywood

Pasadena

Arcadia

21

Covina

210

10

San Bernardino Freeway

10

Ontario

23

Pacific Palisades

101

Pasadena Freeway

Alhambra

20

Pomona

18

24

22

Los Angeles

605

20

60

19

Santa Monica

405

Culver City

10

Santa Monica Freeway

710

23

60

Pomona Freeway

Chino

18

90

22

110

Montebello

20

Long Beach Freeway

Inglewood

5

24

1

Downey

Whittier

21

El Segundo

105

Century Freeway

Hawthorne

22

23

Manhattan Beach

Gardena

Compton

Artesia Freeway

Norwalk

Fullerton

57

Riverside Freeway

91

Hermosa Beach

San Gabriel River Freeway

Lakewood

91

Buena Park

18

Torrance

Harbor Freeway

405

605

5

Anaheim

Redondo Beach

710

55

241

Rolling Hills

110

Orange

23

Palos Verdes Estates

1

22

Garden Grove Freeway

22

261

San Pedro

47

Long Beach

Pacific Coast Highway

San Diego Freeway

Santa Ana

Costa Mesa Freeway

22

241

24

23

Foothill Transit Corridor

24

Pacific Coast Highway

24

405

Santa Ana Freeway

Huntington Beach

55

Irvine

133

San Joaquin Hills Transit Corridor

Newport Beach

1

23

22

22

Mission Viejo

23

Laguna Beach

22

5

24

Santa Catalina Island

San Juan Capistrano

See Page 54

23

5

Avalon

0   5   10   15 miles

ZONE 20

Cool winters in Southern California's areas of occasional ocean influence

CENTRAL CALIFORNIA: PAGE 44
SOUTHERN CALIFORNIA: PAGES 50–51, 54–55, 57

Growing Season

J F M A M J J A S O N D

In Zones 20 and 21, the same relative pattern prevails as in Zones 18 and 19. The even-numbered zone is the climate made up of cold-air basins and hilltops, and the odd-numbered one comprises thermal belts. The difference is that Zones 20 and 21 get weather influenced by both maritime air and interior air. In these transitional areas, climate boundaries often move 20 miles in 24 hours with the movements of these air masses.

Because of the greater ocean influence, this climate supports a wide variety of plants. You can see the range of them at the Los Angeles County Arboretum in Arcadia. Typical winter lows are 37° to 43°F (3 to 6°C); extreme 20-year lows average from 25 to 22°F (−4 to −6°C). All-time record lows range from 21 to 14°F (−6 to −10°C).

A brilliantly colored meadow of mixed wildflowers at the LA County Arboretum in Arcadia.

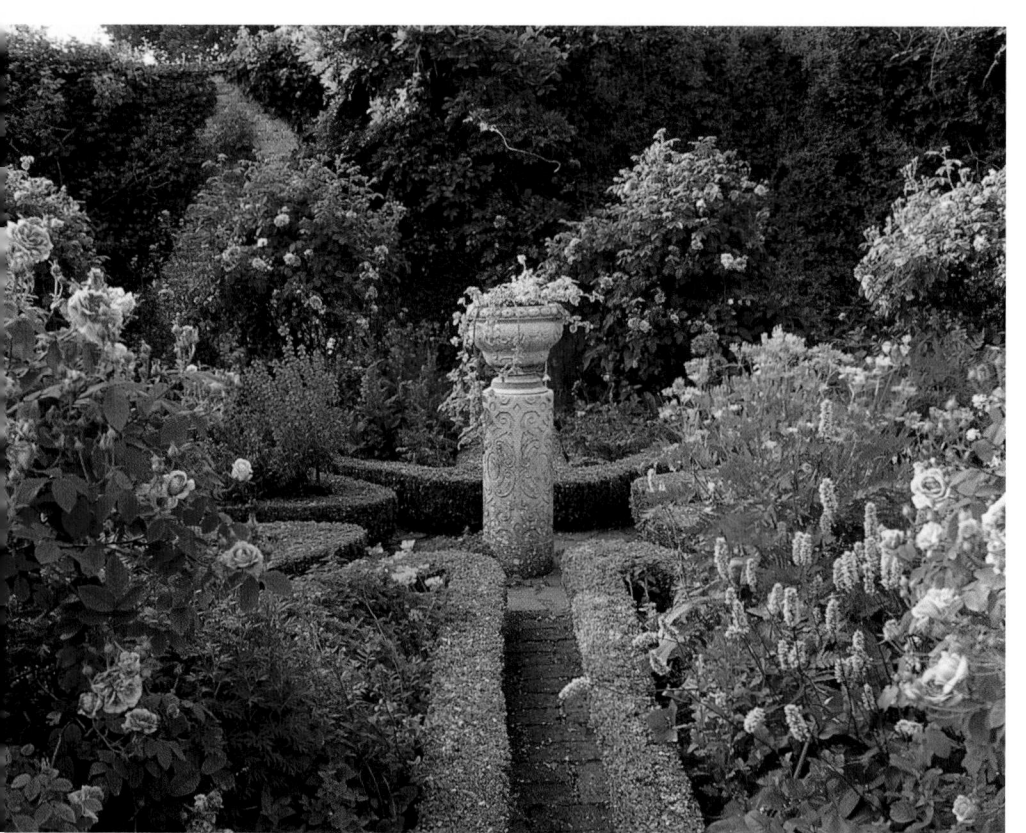

Vigorous and colorful roses thrive in a sunny formal garden in Zone 21.

ZONE 21

Thermal belts in Southern California's areas of occasional ocean influence

CENTRAL CALIFORNIA: PAGE 44
SOUTHERN CALIFORNIA: PAGES 50–51, 54–55, 57

Growing Season

J F M A M J J A S O N D

The combination of weather influences described for Zone 20 applies to Zone 21 as well. Your garden can be in ocean air or a high fog one day and in a mass of interior air (perhaps a drying Santa Ana wind from the desert) the next day.

Because temperatures rarely drop very far below 30°F (−1°C), this is fine citrus-growing country. At the same time, Zone 21 is also the mildest zone that gets sufficient winter chilling for most forms of lilacs and certain other chill-loving plants. Extreme lows—the kind you see once every 10 or 20 years—in Zone 21 average 28 to 25°F (−2 to −4°C). All-time record lows in the zone were 27 to 17°F (−3 to −8°C).

Cacti, grasses, and an orange tree adorn this sunny Los Angeles garden.

ZONE 22

Cold-winter portions of Southern California's coastal climate

CENTRAL CALIFORNIA: PAGE 44 • SOUTHERN CALIFORNIA: PAGES 50–51, 54–55, 57

Growing Season

J F M A M J J A S O N D

Areas falling in Zone 22 have a coastal climate (they are influenced by the ocean approximately 85 percent of the time). When temperatures drop in winter, these cold-air basins or hilltops above the air-drained slopes have lower winter temperatures than those in neighboring Zone 23.

Actually, the winters are so mild here that lows seldom fall below freezing. Extreme winter lows (the coldest temperature you can expect in 20 years) average 28 to 25°F (–2 to –4°C).

Gardeners who plant under overhangs or tree canopies can grow subtropical plants that would otherwise be burned by a rare frost. Such plants include bananas, tree ferns, and the like. The lack of a pronounced chilling period during the winter limits the use of such deciduous woody plants as flowering cherry and lilac. Many herbaceous perennials from colder regions fail here because the winters are too warm for them to go dormant.

ZONE 23

Thermal belts of Southern California's coastal climate

CENTRAL CALIFORNIA: PAGE 44 • SOUTHERN CALIFORNIA: PAGES 50–51, 54–55, 57

Growing Season

J F M A M J J A S O N D

One of the most favored areas in North America for growing subtropical plants, Zone 23 has always been Southern California's best zone for avocados. Frosts don't amount to much here, because 85 percent of the time, Pacific Ocean weather dominates; interior air rules only 15 percent of the time. A notorious portion of this 15 percent consists of those days when hot, dry Santa Ana winds blow. Zone 23 lacks either the summer heat or the winter cold necessary to grow pears, most apples, and most peaches. But it enjoys considerably more heat than Zone 24—enough to put the sweetness in 'Valencia' oranges, for example—but not enough for 'Washington' naval oranges, which are grown farther inland.

Temperatures are mild here, but severe winters descend at times. Average lows range from 43 to 48°F (6 to 9°C), while extreme lows average from 34 to 27°F (1 to –3°C).

Drought-tolerant succulents and ice plants can thrive in Zone 23, as can avocados.

San Diego and Environs

18 18 18 18 See Page 51 11

19 19 19 7

23 19 18 18

22 Perris 19 18

405 18 215 Hemet Idyllwile

Irvine 18 Elsinore 18 18 7

23 22 5 Mission Viejo 23 19 18

Laguna Beach 22 San Juan Capistrano 23 **Coastal San Diego**
The mildest gardens lie on the west-facing coastal slopes not far from salt water (Zone 24). But there's a price to pay for their no-frost feature: Some crops, like apples, don't get enough chill to set fruit. 18

24 San Clemente 22 19 18

Fallbrook 19 7

23 Valley Center 15

Pacific Ocean Oceanside Vista 21 18 7

5 24 San Marcos 20 Escondido

Encinitas Rancho Santa Fe Rancho Bernardo Ramona 20

Why Is San Diego So Mild?
Follow San Diego's latitude around the globe, and you run into Bermuda, Casablanca, and Shanghai—all subtropical climates. That explains the fishtail palms, macadamias, plumerias, and papayas growing outdoors here. But the mild climate is derived as much from San Diego's warm ocean water as from its latitude. Off Ensenada, a branch of the cold southbound California Current hooks east, then north, pulling warmer Mexican waters along with it. This keeps the waters off San Diego mild, usually in the high 50s to low 70s. The temperature of the ocean water affects the air temperature over it, and this in turn moderates temperatures over the coastal strip.

Solana Beach 23 Poway 21 19

Del Mar Lakeside Alpine

La Jolla 24 El Cajon 8 18

805 5 La Mesa 22

24 23 **Inland San Diego**
Don't be too sure about setting out tender plants here. In winter, the large canyons that drain the mountains also drain cold air. When frost comes, it's usually just inland from canyon mouths, where hills meet the coastal plain.

Los Angeles

San Diego

San Diego National City Chula Vista 5 24 805 19

Ensenada

Pacific Ocean Imperial Beach 21

Tijuana

Climate Zones 2B 7 11 13 18 19 20 21 22 23 24

See Page 57

11

13

gs

Palm
Desert

Indio

11

13

7

11

11

10

13

13

11

Salton
Sea

APPLE ALLEY BAKERY
JULIAN→
APPLE PIE

13

See Page 57

Coast to Desert
Drive northeast from the San Diego area and you'll pass through three very different climates. Near the ocean (Zone 24), tender plants such as poinsettias and succulents thrive outdoors. Julian's high elevation (Zone 7) creates enough winter chill to deliver hefty crops of apples and grapes. In Palm Desert (Zone 13), arid conditions favor the growth of such tough, unthirsty heat-lovers as gazanias, cacti, spiky ocotillo, and brittlebush.

7

13

El
Centro

8

7

13

8

7

• Calexico
• Mexicali

Jacumba •

MEXICO

0   5   10   15 miles

ZONE 24

Marine influence along the Southern California coast

CENTRAL CALIFORNIA: PAGE 44
SOUTHERN CALIFORNIA: PAGES 50-51, 54-55, 57

Growing Season

| J | F | M | A | M | J | J | A | S | O | N | D |

Stretched along Southern California's beaches, this climate zone is almost completely dominated by the ocean. Where the beach runs along high cliffs or palisades, Zone 24 extends only to that barrier. But where hills are low or nonexistent, it runs inland several miles.

This zone has a mild marine climate (milder than Northern California's maritime Zone 17) because south of Point Conception, the Pacific is comparatively warm. The winters are mild, the summers cool, and the air seldom really dry. On many days in spring and early summer, the sun doesn't break through the high overcast until afternoon. Tender perennials like geraniums and impatiens rarely go out of bloom here; spathiphyllums and pothos become outdoor plants; and tender palms are safe from killing frosts. In this climate, gardens that include such plants as ornamental figs, rubber trees, and schefﬂeras can become jungles.

Spiky succulents and New Zealand flax spill over the edges of a pathway leading to this classic California-style patio.

In a modern interpretation of Zone 24, this garden in Santa Monica combines bamboo, water plants, and a cozy fire pit.

Zone 24 is coldest at the mouths of canyons that channel cold air down from the mountains on clear winter nights. Several such canyons between Laguna Beach and San Clemente are visible on the map. Numerous others touch the coast between San Clemente and the Mexican border. Partly because of the unusually low temperatures created by this canyon action, there is a broad range of winter lows in Zone 24. Winter lows average from 42°F (5°C) in Santa Barbara to 48°F (9°C) in San Diego. Extreme cold averages from 35° to 28°F (2 to −2°C), with all-time lows in the coldest stations at about 20°F (−6°C).

The all-time high temperatures aren't greatly significant in terms of plant growth. The average all-time high of weather stations in Zone 24 is 105°F (41°C). Record heat usually comes in early October, carried to the coast by Santa Ana winds. The wind's power and dryness usually causes more problems than the heat itself—but you can ameliorate scorching with frequent sprinkling.

Southwest Deserts: Southern California

11

● China
Lake
● Ridgecrest

13

10

11   10

NEVADA

See Page 34

1A

🛣15
● Las
Vegas

11

11

11

2A

See Page 44

10

11

2A

● Searchlight

13

● California
City

11

🛣15

● Baker

Shade Makers for Lancaster, Las Vegas
*More welcome here than anywhere else,
garden trees temper the desert sun and
take the edge off nighttime chill. Choices
include catalpa, desert willow, eucalyptus,
honey locust, locust, loquats, mesquites,
and palo verdes.*

10

See Page 61

● Mojave   🛣58

● Barstow

11

● Ludlow   🛣40

11

11

Needles

🛣40

● Lancaster

🛣15

● Palmdale   ● Victorville   10

13

12

13

CALIFORNIA

7

Big
Bear
City ●

11

11

● San
Bernardino   2B

● Redlands

● Yucca
Valley

● Twentynine
Palms

13

18   7

● Beaumont

● Riverside   ● Banning

19   18

11   🛣10   13

11

11

See Page 50

7   ● Palm
Springs

19

● Hemet   Palm
Desert ●   ● Indio

🛣215   Idyllwild   2B

18   7   🛣10   Desert
Center

13   11

19   7

Blythe   🛣10

23   🛣15   19

11   11   *Salton
Sea*

San
Marcos   Valley
Center

● Warner
Springs   13

11   13

12

ARIZONA

● Escondido   18

● Borrego

20   ● Ramona   7   7   13   13

Poway   20   ● Julian

21   ● Lakeside

● Brawley

22   ● Alpine   7   13   13

23   21   19   13   13

🛣8   ● El Centro   🛣8   13

24   Jacumba ●   ● Calexico   0   10   20   30 miles

● Yuma

MEXICO

Climate Zones   1A   2A 2B   7 10 11 12 13   18 19 20 21 22 23 24

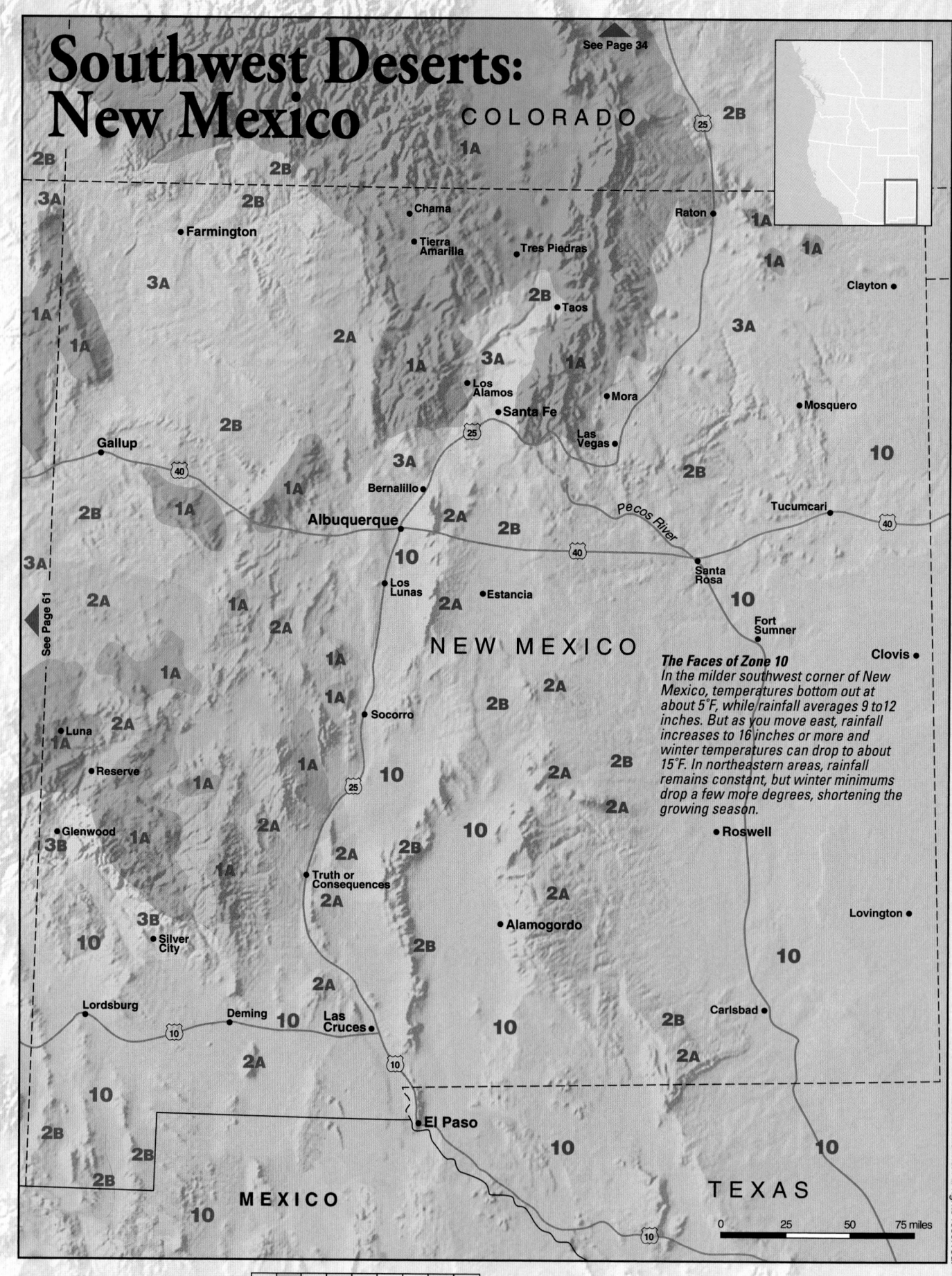

Southwest Deserts: New Mexico

See Page 34

COLORADO

2B

2B

1A

2B

3A

2B

• Chama

Raton •

1A

• Farmington

• Tierra
Amarilla

• Tres Piedras

1A

1A

3A

2B

Clayton •

3A

1A

1A

1A

2A

• Taos

2B

1A

3A

1A

3A

• Mora

• Mosquero

• Los
Alamos

• Santa Fe

2B

Las
Vegas •

10

Gallup •

40

25

3A

2B

Bernalillo •

1A

2B

1A

Albuquerque

2A

2B

Pecos River

Tucumcari •

40

40

3A

10

Santa
Rosa •

See Page 61

2A

10

• Los
Lunas

2A

• Estancia

10

Fort
Sumner •

Clovis •

1A

2A

NEW MEXICO

The Faces of Zone 10
In the milder southwest corner of New Mexico, temperatures bottom out at about 5°F, while rainfall averages 9 to12 inches. But as you move east, rainfall increases to 16 inches or more and winter temperatures can drop to about 15°F. In northeastern areas, rainfall remains constant, but winter minimums drop a few more degrees, shortening the growing season.

• Luna

2A

1A

2A

1A

• Reserve

1A

1A

• Socorro

10

2B

2A

2B

2A

• Glenwood

1A

3B

2A

25

10

2B

10

• Roswell

3B

• Silver
City

2A

• Truth or
Consequences

2A

2B

2A

Lovington •

10

• Alamogordo

2A

Lordsburg

2B

10

Carlsbad •

10

• Deming

10

• Las
Cruces

2A

2A

10

10

2B

2A

• El Paso

10

MEXICO

TEXAS

0   25   50   75 miles

Climate Zones   1A   2A 2B 3A 3B   10

ZONE **10**

High desert areas of Arizona and New Mexico

SOUTHWEST DESERTS: PAGES 57, 58, 61,
NEVADA DESERT: PAGE 34

Growing Season

J F M A M J J A S O N D

This zone consists mostly of the 3,300- to 5,000-foot elevations in parts of Arizona and New Mexico. It also includes parts of southern Utah and Nevada, and adjacent California desert. Zone 10 has a definite winter season—75 to more than 100 nights below 32°F (0°C). That favors deciduous fruits, though late frosts can work against apricot crops. In Albuquerque, New Mexico, and Benson and Kingman, Arizona, average winter minimums range from 32 to 23°F (0 to –5°C). Lows of 25 to 22°F (–4 to –6°C) often come in. The cold winter season calls for spring planting.

Growing seasons are very long—up to 225 days. More rain falls in the east than in the west, and the Pecos River drainage receives more precipitation in summer than in winter.

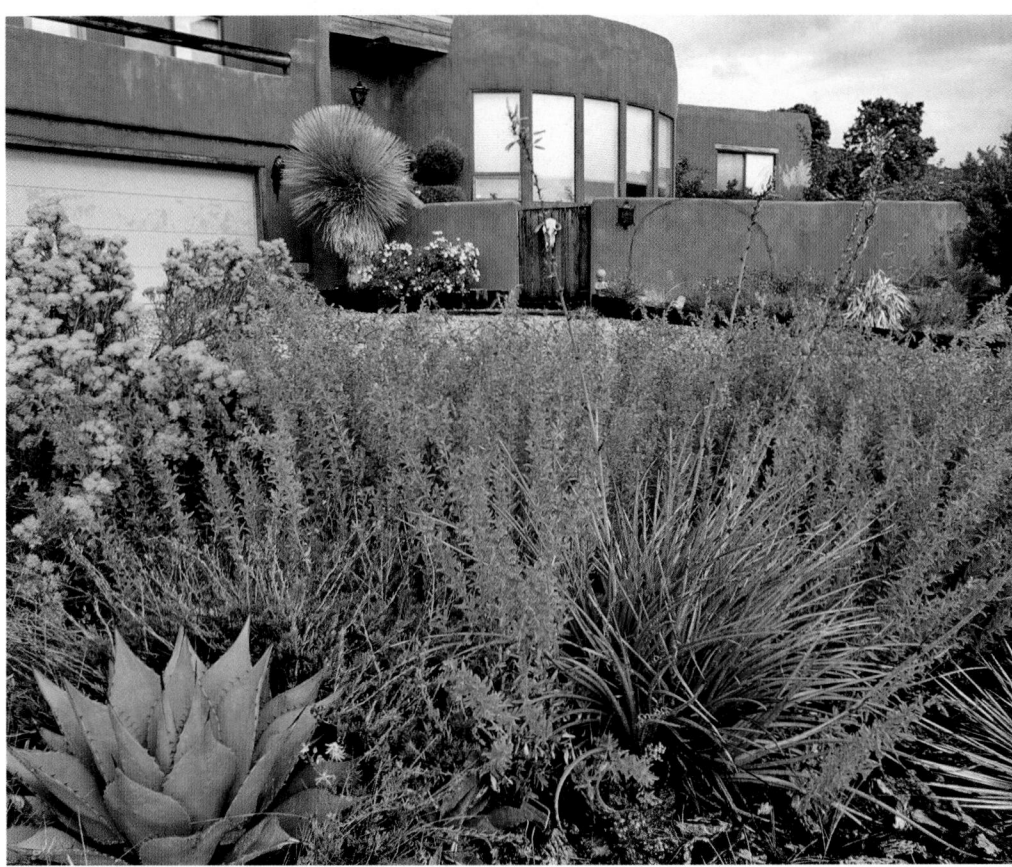

Drought-tolerant perennials like scarlet Zauschneria *thrive in both hot and cold conditions in Albuquerque, New Mexico.*

A Las Vegas, Nevada, garden recreates Mojave style with opuntias, ocotillos, yuccas, and grasses.

ZONE **11**

Medium to high desert of California and southern Nevada

SOUTHWEST DESERTS: PAGES 34, 44, 51, 55, 57, 61
NEVADA DESERT: PAGE 34

Growing Season

J F M A M J J A S O N D

This climate zone shares similarities with its neighbors—the cold-winter Zones 1, 2, and 3, and the subtropical low desert, Zone 13. Like Zones 1 to 3, Zone 11 has cold winters, and like Zone 13, it has hot summers. Hot summer days are followed by mild nights; near-freezing winter nights are followed by daytime temperatures near 60°F (16°C). On average, there are 110 summer days above 90°F (32°C), with the highest temperatures recorded between 111 and 117°F (44 to 47°C). About 85 nights have temperatures below 32°F (0°C), with lows between 11 and 0°F (–12 to –18°C).

If soil moisture is inadequate, the characteristic winds and bright sunlight may combine to dry out normally hardy evergreen plants, killing or badly injuring them.

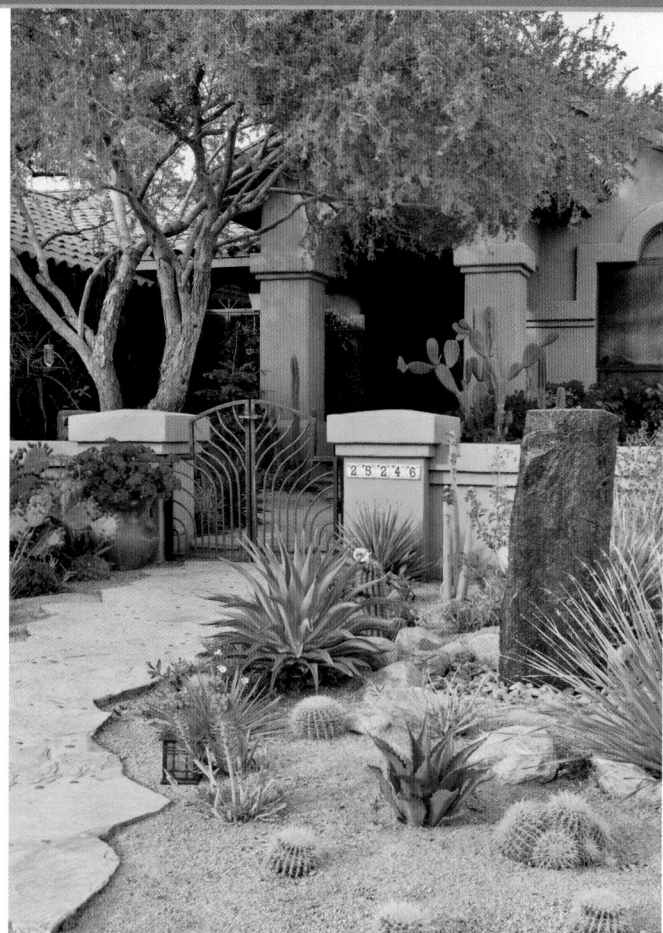

A Sonoran desert garden features barrel cactus in a gravel bed under an olive tree.

ZONE **12**

Arizona's intermediate desert

SOUTHWEST: PAGES 57, 61

Growing Season

J F M A M J J A S O N D

The crucial difference between Arizona's intermediate desert (Zone 12) and the low desert (Zone 13) is winter cold. But though the intermediate desert averages only 5 more freezing nights than the low desert (20 in Tucson compared with 15 in Phoenix and El Centro), it has harder frosts spread over a longer cold season. Zone 12 averages about 8 months between freezes, 9 months between killing frosts of 28°F (−2°C) or lower. Zone 13, on the other hand, averages more than 11 months between killing frosts, when it gets them at all. Extreme low temperatures of 6°F (−14°C) have been recorded in Zone 12. The mean maximums in July and August are 5 or 6°F cooler than the highs of Zone 13.

Many subtropicals that do well in Zone 13 aren't reliably hardy here, but succeed with protection against the extreme winters. Although winter temperatures are lower than in Zone 13, the total hours of cold are not enough to provide sufficient winter chilling for some deciduous fruits.

From March to May, strong winds (to 40 miles per hour) can damage young tender growth. Windbreaks help. Here, as in Zone 13 and the eastern parts of Zone 10, summer rains are to be expected and can be more dependable than winter rains. And as in Zone 13, the best season for cool-season crops (salad greens, root vegetables, cabbage family members) starts in September or October.

ZONE **13**

Low or subtropical desert areas

CALIFORNIA DESERT: PAGES 54, 57 • SOUTHWEST: PAGE 61

Growing Season*

J F M A M J J A S O N D

*heat stops growth in summer

Ranging from below sea level in the Imperial Valley and Death Valley to 1,100 feet around Phoenix, Zone 13 is a subtropical desert. Average summer high is 107°F (42°C); the world's second-highest temperature—a scorching 134°F (56°C)—was recorded in Death Valley on July 10, 1913. Winters are short and mild, with brief frosts occurring up to 15 nights per year. Average winter minimums range from 36 to 42°F (2 to 6°C), with extreme lows from 27 to 15°F (−3 to −9°C).

The gardening year begins in fall for most vegetables and annual flowers, although crops like corn and melons are planted in late winter. Fall-planted crops grow slowly in winter, pick up speed in mid-February, and race through the increasing temperatures of March and April. Spring winds can set back plants, but summer storms cool down gardens, shield plants from the sun, and supply a little extra water.

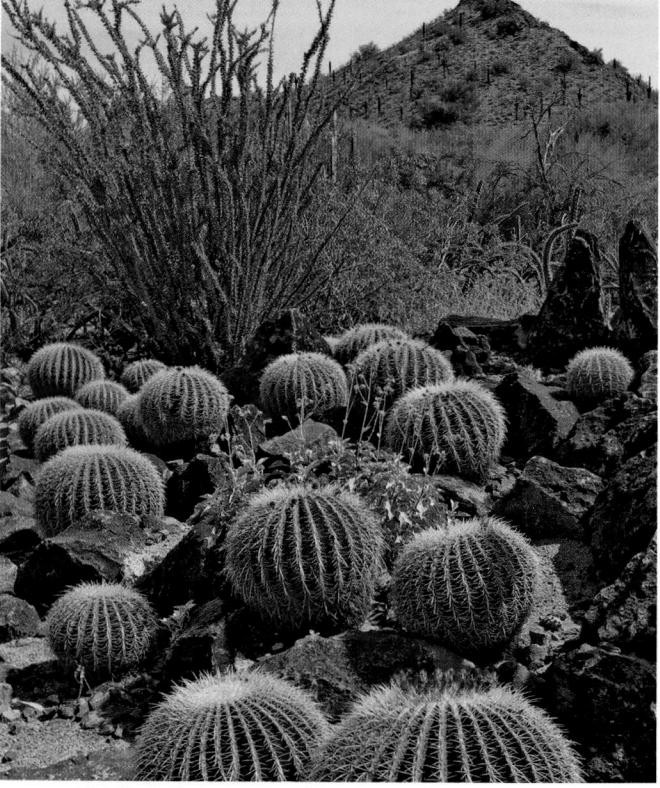

An arrangement of cacti, ocotillo and rocks in a Phoenix, Arizona, garden echoes the native desert beyond.

Southwest Deserts: Arizona

NEVADA

UTAH

ARIZONA

NEVADA

MEXICO

The Low Desert: Opportunities and Limits
Heat-loving subtropicals such as bougainvilleas and date palms thrive in this climate. Though lack of winter chill rules out fruits with high chill requirements, such as most apples and peaches, winter here is perfect for many warm-season flowers and vegetables.

See Page 34

See Page 57

See Page 58

Mesquite

Fredonia

Page

Las Vegas

Lake Mead

Boulder City

Tuba City

Window Rock

Kingman

Williams

Flagstaff

Winslow

Sedona

Holbrook

Needles

Prescott

St. Johns

Parker

Wickenburg

Blythe

Phoenix

Globe

Yuma

Florence

Clifton

Casa Grande

Safford

Ajo

Tucson

Benson

Tombstone

Bisbee

Nogales

Douglas

0   25   50   75 miles

Climate Zones   1A   2A 2B 3A 3B   10 11 12 13

Hawaii

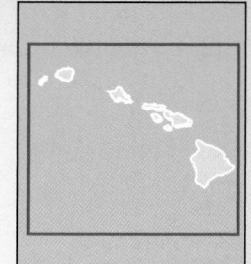

KAUAI

Kilauea

Kapaa

Lihue

Waimea

Poipu

H2

H2　NIIHAU

**Pacific
Ocean**

Laie

Waialua　Haleiwa

Waialua

Wahiawa　H2

Makaha　H2

Nanakuli

Pearl
City

Kaneohe　Kailua

H2

Ewa

Honolulu　Waikiki　Hawaii
Kai

OAHU

MOLOKAI

Hoolehua

H2

Maunaloa

Kaunakakai

MAUI

Kaanapali　Paia

H2　Lahaina　Wailuku　Kahului　Makawao

Lanai
City　Kihei　H2

Kula

LANAI　Wailea　Keokea　Hana

Ulupalakua　H1　Haleakala
National
Park

Kaupo

KAHOOLAWAE

Hawi

Kohala
Forest
Reserve　Honokaa

Kawaihae　Kamuela　HAWAII

H2　H1

Ookala

Kailua-
Kona　Hualalai　Mauna
Kea

Holualoa　H1　Hilo

Captain
Cook　H2

Mauna
Loa　Pahoa

Volcano

H1

Hawaii
Volcanoes
National
Park

Papa　Pahala

H1　Naalehu

H2

Oahu

Ewa

LEEWARD

Honolulu

Waikiki

Diamond
Head

WINDWARD

TRADE WINDS

Wet and Dry
*On all the islands except Hawaii, the north and east
(windward) sides are wet, the south and west (leeward)
sides are dry. From the ocean off the windward sides,
evaporation rises. Carried by trade winds, this warm, moist
air passes over land, increasing clouds and showers, then
over mountains, where it cools. Heavy rains are the result.
Leeward, the air warms as it descends, leaving these south
and west sides mostly sunny and dry.*

　*The Big Island, though, is different. Its high volcanic
peaks (Mauna Loa, Mauna Kea, and Hualalai) block and
deflect the trade winds, leaving local winds to drive Kona
Coast weather. Here, especially in summer, upslope winds
give rise to afternoon clouds and rain at elevations from
1,000 to 4,000 feet (prime for growing coffee).*

Hawaii

TRADE WINDS

LEEWARD

Mauna
Kea

Mauna
Loa　Hilo

Kailua-
Kona

WINDWARD

N

0　20　40　60 miles

Climate Zones　Z　H1　H2

ZONE **H1**

Cooler volcanic slopes: 2,000 to 5,000 feet

Growing Season

J F M A M J J A S O N D

This zone includes Kula and Ulupalakua on Maui and Kamuela and Volcano on Hawaii (the Big Island). Cooler air temperatures make these areas higher up the volcanic slopes better for growing standard cymbidiums, hydrangeas, proteas, and sweet bulbing onions (Maui onions). Low-chill varieties of apples, peaches, and plums grow throughout this zone. The slightly higher elevations are also better for growing plants that can't abide much heat, including Douglas fir and Japanese maples. Lower soil temperatures and cooler nights, too, help some gardeners at the 4,000- to 6,000-foot elevations on the dry sides succeed with plants from Mediterranean climates.

Warm-season highs range from 65 to 80°F (19 to 27°C); cool-season lows can dip to the mid-40s. Frosts can occur above this zone. The growing season is year-round.

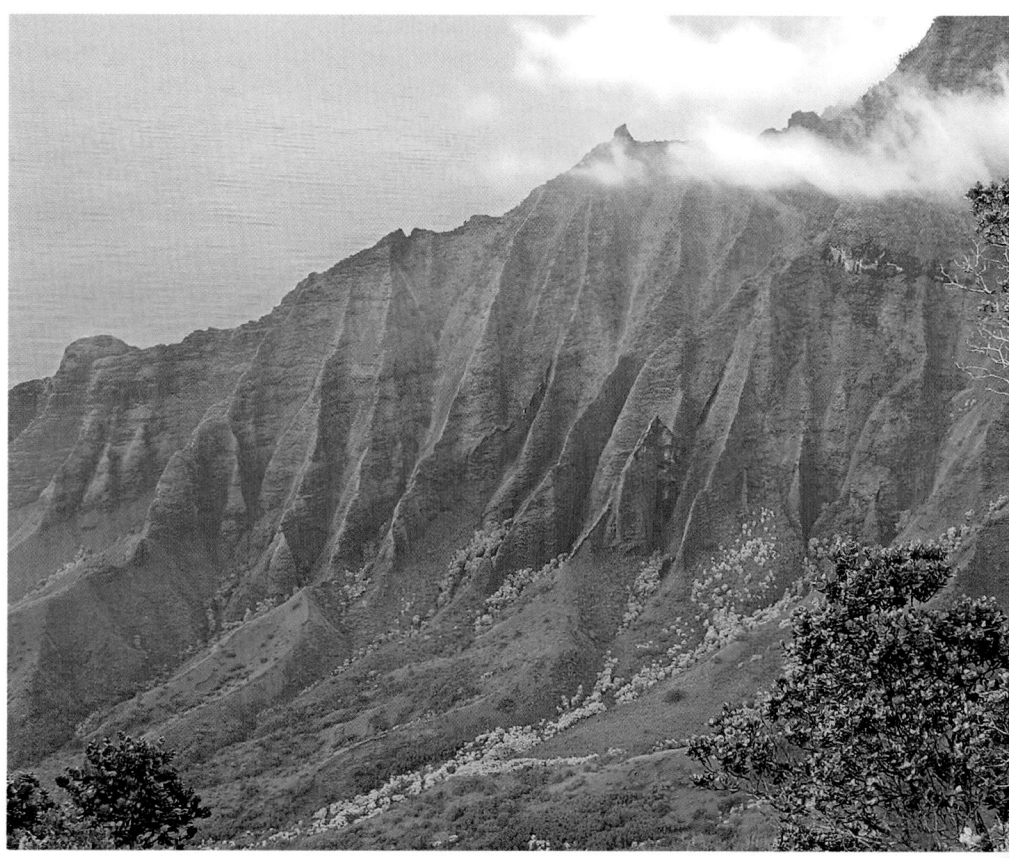

The view over the Kalalau Valley and the distant Na Pali Coast on Kauai.

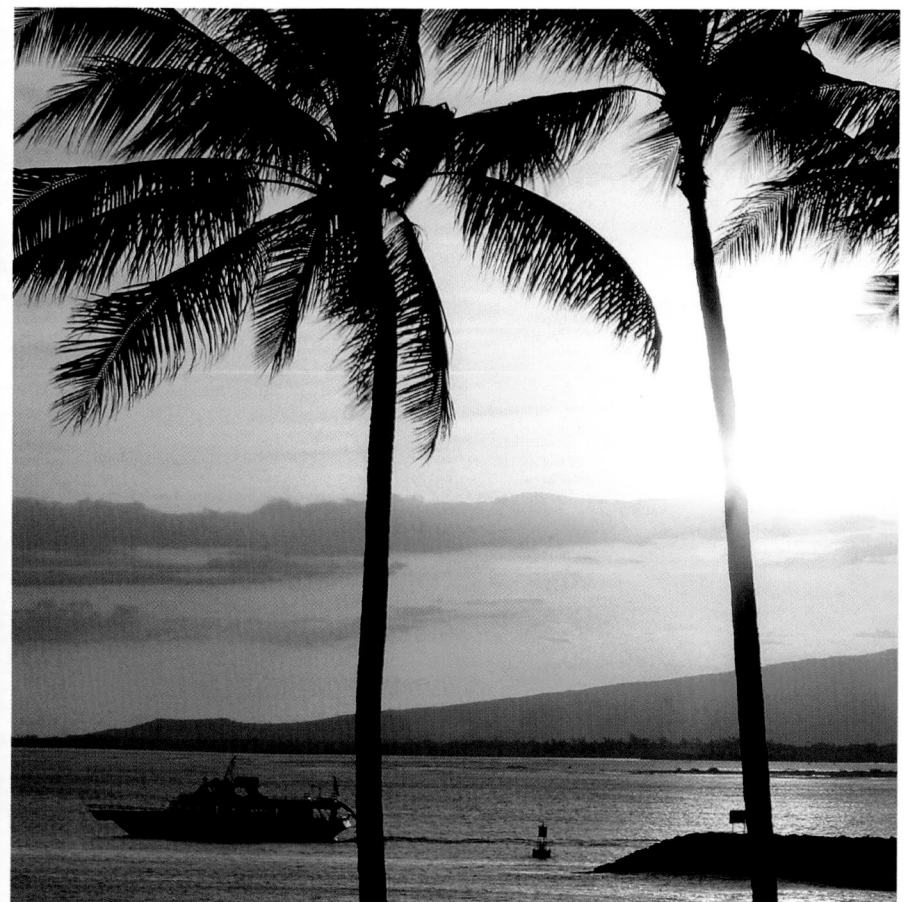

Much of Zone H2 is within view of the ocean, as here in Honolulu, Oahu.

ZONE **H2**

Coconut palm belt: sea level to 2,000 feet

Growing Season

J F M A M J J A S O N D

Zone H2 includes the Ewa plain, Hawaii-Kai, Kailua, Kaneohe, Honolulu, and Waikiki on Oahu; Kahului, Kihei, and Lahaina on Maui; and the Hilo, Kailua-Kona, and Kohala coasts on Hawaii. Most lowland lees in this zone get their heaviest rains between November and March, and May through September is relatively dry. Sunny days urge bougainvilleas, poincianas, plumerias, and shower trees *(Cassia)* into spectacular bloom. On the wet windward sides, where rain comes from passing storms and year-round tradewind showers, bananas, gingers, and heliconias do well.

The Kona Coast, however, gets more rain in the warm season than in the cool season. The same plants grow here as elsewhere in Zone H2 but may have slightly different cultural requirements.

Highs in this zone hover in the 80s; lows can dip to the mid-60s. The growing season is year-round.

Plant Selection Guide

Choosing the right plants for your garden from among the hundreds of thousands available can be a challenge. But with the selection guides in this chapter, you can head to the nursery with confidence. Let these lists guide you in choosing plants to achieve the result you want, whether it's a distinctive effect from flowers or foliage, an attractive planting for a problem spot, a basic garden framework of trees, shrubs, and ground covers, or something special—perhaps a butterfly garden or a tropical "jungle."

Washingtonia filifera

In each list, certain symbols are used to specify every plant's needs (and allow you to determine its suitability for your garden).

☼ Grows best in full sunlight all day long or almost all day—except for an hour or so of shade at the beginning or end of a summer day

◑ Needs partial shade—shade for half the day or for at least 3 hours during the hottest part of the day

● Prefers little or no direct sunlight —for example, it does best on the north side of a house or in shade cast by a broad, dense tree

✎ Refers to the climate zones (explained and mapped in The West's Climate Zones, pages 28–63) where the plant typically grows best

Color

Imperata cylindrica 'Rubra'

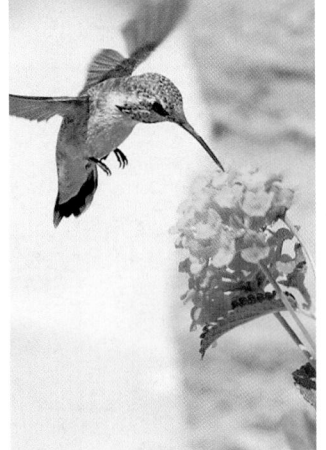

Lantana camara

Basic Landscaping

Special Situations

Ferocactus

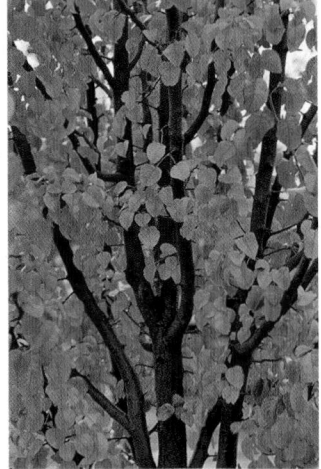

Pyrus calleryana

Problem Solvers

Primula japonica

Perennials

These garden mainstays flower reliably, year after year—one trait that has long endeared them to gardeners. Unlike annuals, which live for only a year, perennials are semipermanent plants that need occasional cutting back and periodic division and replanting to keep up a spectacular display. Some are evergreen; others die to the ground at the end of the growing season, then reappear from their roots the following year.

Tall *Gaura* (top left) and asters create a lacy screen behind lower-growing *Rudbeckia hirta*, dahlia, and purple penstemon.

ACHILLEA p. 170	**AQUILEGIA** p. 195
Yarrow	*Columbine*
☼ ◑ ✿ A1–A3; 1–24	☼ ◑ ✿ ZONES VARY
ACTAEA p. 171	**ARCTOTIS (some)** p. 198
◑ ✿ 1–7, 17	*African daisy*
	☼ ✿ ALL ZONES
ACONITUM p. 171	**ARMERIA** p. 200
Aconite	*Thrift*
☼ ◑ ✿ A1–A3; 1–9, 14–21	☼ ✿ ZONES VARY
ADENOPHORA p.172	**ARUNCUS** p. 202
Lady bells	*Goat's beard*
☼ ◑ ✿ A2, A3; 1–10, 14–24	☼ ◑ ✿ ZONES VARY
AGAPANTHUS p. 174	**ASCLEPIAS tuberosa** p. 204
Lily-of-the-Nile	*Butterfly weed*
☼ ◑ ✿ ZONES VARY	☼ ✿ 1–24
AGASTACHE p. 174	**ASTER** p. 206
☼ ◑ ✿ ZONES VARY	☼ ✿ ZONES VARY
ALSTROEMERIA p. 182	**ASTILBE** p. 207
☼ ◑ ✿ 5–9, 14–24; H1	*False spiraea*
ANEMONE × hybrida p. 185	☼ ◑ ✿ A2, A3; 1–7, 14–17
Japanese anemone	
◑ ✿ 2B–24	

Achillea millefolium

Agastache

Alstroemeria

Aster novae-angliae

Campanula portenschlagiana

ASTRANTIA p. 208
Masterwort
☼ ◑ ✿ 1–9, 14–24
AURINIA saxatilis p. 209
Basket-of-gold
☼ ◑ ✿ 1–24
BAPTISIA p. 217
False indigo
☼ ✿ 1–24
BERGENIA p. 222
☼ ● ✿ A1–A3; 1–9, 12–24
BOLTONIA asteroides p. 227
☼ ◑ ✿ 1–24
CAMPANULA (some) p. 246
Bellflower
☼ ◑ ✿ 1–9, 14–24
CENTAUREA (some) p. 259
☼ ✿ ZONES VARY
CENTRANTHUS ruber p. 260
Jupiter's beard
☼ ◑ ✿ 2–9, 12–24; H1

Coreopsis grandiflora 'Flying Saucers'

CERASTIUM tomentosum p. 261
Snow-in-summer
☼ ◑ ✿ A1, A2; 1–24
CHRYSANTHEMUM p. 271
☼ ✿ ZONES VARY
COREOPSIS (some) p.289
☼ ✿ ZONES VARY
CORYDALIS p. 294
◑ ✿ 2–9, 14–24
DELPHINIUM p. 311
☼ ✿ ZONES VARY
DIANTHUS p. 313
Pink
☼ ◑ ✿ A2, A3; 1–24

Dianthus

Dicentra spectabilis

Felicia amelloides

Gerbera jamesonii

DIASCIA — p. 314
Twinspur
☼ ◐ ✓ ZONES VARY

DICENTRA — p. 315
Bleeding heart
◐ ● ✓ 1-9, 14-24

DICTAMNUS albus — p. 316
Gas plant
☼ ◐ ✓ 1-9

DIGITALIS — p. 317
Foxglove
NEEDS, ZONES VARY

ECHINACEA purpurea — p. 323
Purple coneflower
☼ ✓ A2, A3; 1-24

ECHINOPS — p. 324
Globe thistle
☼ ✓ A2, A3; 1-24

ERIGERON — p. 331
Fleabane
☼ ◐ ✓ ZONES VARY

ERIOGONUM — p. 335
Wild buckwheat
☼ ✓ ZONES VARY.

**ERYNGIUM
amethystinum** — p. 336
Sea holly
☼ ✓ 1-24

**ERYSIMUM
'Bowles Mauve'** — p. 336
☼ ◐ ✓ 4-9, 14-24

EUPATORIUM — p. 345
☼ ◐ ✓ ZONES VARY

EUPHORBIA (some) — p. 345
NEEDS, ZONES VARY

FELICIA amelloides — p. 350
Blue marguerite
☼ ✓ 8, 9, 14-24

FILIPENDULA — p. 354
Meadowsweet
☼ ◐ ● ✓ ZONES VARY

**GAILLARDIA ×
grandiflora** — p. 361
☼ ✓ 1-24; H1, H2

GAURA lindheimeri — p. 364
☼ ✓ 2B-24

GAZANIA — p. 364
NEEDS, ZONES VARY

GERANIUM — p. 366
Cranesbill
☼ ◐ ✓ ZONES VARY

GERBERA jamesonii — p. 368
Transvaal daisy
☼ ◐ ✓ 8, 9, 12-24; H1, H2

Gaillardia × grandiflora 'Summer's Kiss'

GEUM — p. 369
☼ ◐ ✓ 2-24

GYPSOPHILA — p. 382
☼ ✓ ZONES VARY

HELENIUM autumnale — p. 387
Sneezeweed
☼ ✓ 1-24

HELLEBORUS — p. 390
Hellebore
◐ ● ✓ ZONES VARY

HEMEROCALLIS — p. 390
Daylily
☼ ◐ ✓ 1-24; H1, H2

HEUCHERA — p. 393
Coral bells
☼ ◐ ✓ ZONES VARY

**HIBISCUS
moscheutos** — p. 395
Perennial hibiscus
☼ ✓ 2-24; H1

IBERIS sempervirens — p. 404
Evergreen candytuft
☼ ◐ ✓ 1-24

KNIPHOFIA uvaria — p. 428
Red-hot poker
☼ ◐ ✓ 2-9, 14-24

Hemerocallis

LIGULARIA — p. 443
◐ ✓ 1-9, 14-17

LIMONIUM (some) — p. 446
Statice
☼ ✓ ZONES VARY

LINARIA purpurea — p. 447
Toadflax
☼ ◐ ✓ 2-10, 14-24

LINUM perenne — p. 448
Perennial blue flax
☼ ✓ 2-24

LOBELIA cardinalis — p. 450
Cardinal flower
☼ ◐ ✓ 1-7, 14-17

LUPINUS (some) — p. 454
Lupine
☼ ✓ ZONES VARY

LYCHNIS chalcedonica — p. 455
Maltese cross
☼ ◐ ✓ A1-A3; 1-10, 14-24

MACLEAYA cordata — p. 458
Plume poppy
☼ ◐ ✓ A2, A3; 1-24

MALVA alcea — p. 469
Mallow
☼ ✓ 1-9, 14-24

Echinacea purpurea 'Doubledecker'

Erigeron glaucus

Mimulus aurantiacus

Nierembergia caerulea

Perovskia atriplicifolia

Tough but Pretty Perennials

Scott Ogden and Lauren Springer Ogden know something about difficult climate conditions; they garden in rural northern Colorado. In Springer Ogden's book, *The Undaunted Garden,* she describes her techniques for gardening in the face of "extreme temperatures, drought, wind, hail and alkaline soil." What kind of perennials do these tough-minded gardeners like to use in such challenging circumstances?

"What we look for are plants that are long-lived, with great blooms and foliage. They should have a good tolerance of drought and poor soil. And of course they should have overall great looks," says Springer Ogden. Here are their favorite, sure-bet perennials for the Interior West.

Agastache rupestris Licorice mint
Eriogonum umbellatum Sulfur flower
Nepeta racemosa 'Walker's Low' Catmint
Oenothera macrocarpa incana 'Silver Blade' Ozark sundrops
Penstemon pinifolius 'Mersea Yellow' Beard tongue
Perovskia × *hybrida* Russian sage
Sedum sediforme
Veronica pectinata Speedwell

MIMULUS p. 482
Monkey flower
NEEDS, ZONES VARY

NEPETA p. 494
☼ ◐ ✴ 1-24

NIEREMBERGIA p. 496
Cup flower
☼ ◐ ✴ ZONES VARY

OENOTHERA p. 498
Evening primrose
☼ ◐ ✴ ZONES VARY

OSTEOSPERMUM p. 505
African daisy
☼ ✴ 8, 9, 12-24

PAEONIA (herbaceous) p. 508
Peony
☼ ◐ ✴ A1-A3; 1-11, 14-20

PAPAVER orientale p. 510
Oriental poppy
☼ ✴ A1-A3; 1-11, 14-21

PELARGONIUM p. 524
Geranium
☼ ◐ ✴ A2, A3; 1-24

PENSTEMON (many) p. 526
Beard tongue
☼ ◐ ✴ ZONES VARY

PEROVSKIA p. 529
Russian sage
☼ ✴ 2-24

PHLOMIS (some) p. 534
☼ ✴ ZONES VARY

PHLOX subulata p. 535
Moss pink
☼ ◐ ✴ 1-17

PHYGELIUS p. 537
Cape fuchsia
☼ ◐ ✴ 4-9, 14-24; H1, H2

PHYSOSTEGIA virginiana p. 538
False dragonhead
☼ ◐ ✴ A2, A3; 1-9, 14-24

PLATYCODON grandiflorus p. 547
Balloon flower
☼ ◐ ✴ 1-10, 14-24

POLEMONIUM p. 555
◐ ● ✴ 1-11, 14-17

PRIMULA (many) p. 560
Primrose
☼ ◐ ● ✴ ZONES VARY

PRUNELLA p. 564
Self-heal
☼ ◐ ✴ 2-24

Scabiosa columbaria

Fuchsia boliviana

PULMONARIA p. 570
Lungwort
◐ ● ✴ 1-9, 14-17

ROMNEYA coulteri p. 593
Matilija poppy
☼ ✴ 4-12, 14-24; H1

RUDBECKIA p. 604
☼ ✴ 1-24

SALVIA p. 607
Sage
NEEDS, ZONES VARY

SCABIOSA p. 616
Pincushion flower
☼ ✴ ZONES VARY

SEDUM spectabile, S. telephium p. 621
☼ ◐ ✴ 1-24

SIDALCEA malviflora p. 625
Checkerbloom
☼ ✴ 2-9, 14-24

SILENE p. 625
☼ ◐ ✴ ZONES VARY

STOKESIA laevis p. 635
Stokes' aster
☼ ✴ 2-10, 12-24

THALICTRUM p. 646
Meadow rue
◐ ✴ 2-10, 14-17

TROLLIUS p. 656
Globeflower
☼ ◐ ✴ A2, A3; 1-6

VERBENA p. 663
☼ ✴ ZONES VARY

VERONICA p. 663
Speedwell
☼ ✴ ZONES VARY

Veronica spicata 'Red Fox'

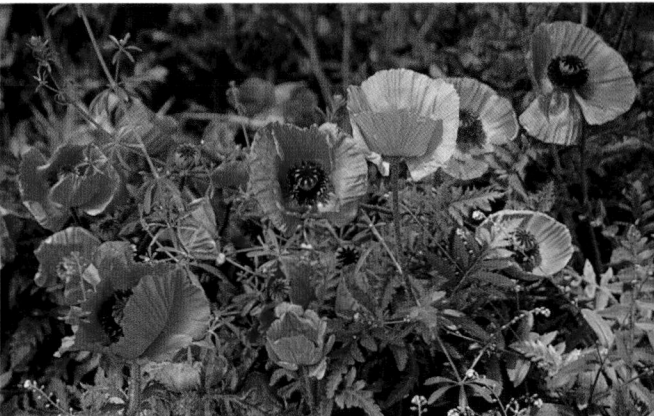

Papaver orientale

Bulbs & Bulblike Plants

Some of the garden's showiest flowers come from plants that grow from true bulbs, corms, tubers, rhizomes, and tuberous roots. Gardeners often call all these underground structures bulbs—and all store food that keeps the plant alive through a dormant period, ready to grow again once dormancy has ended. Some bulbs (daffodil and iris, for example) thrive in most of the West; others, such as caladium, have a more restricted range. You can enjoy many bulbs outside their preferred climate zones by growing them in pots, or by digging and storing them over winter in a frostless location. A few even thrive as houseplants.

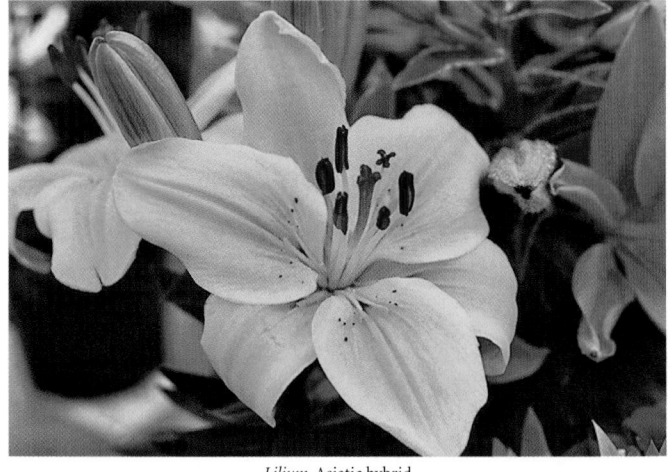
Lilium, Asiatic hybrid

Fall-planted Bulbs

ALLIUM   p. 179
Ornamental allium
☼ ◐ ✎ ZONES VARY

AMARYLLIS belladonna   p. 183
Belladonna lily
☼ ✎ 4–24

ANEMONE   p. 185
Windflower
NEEDS, ZONES VARY

BABIANA   p. 211
Baboon flower
☼ ◐ ✎ 4–24

BRODIAEA   p. 231
☼ ✎ ZONES VARY

CHIONODOXA   p. 269
Glory-of-the-snow
☼ ◐ ✎ A2–A3; 1–7, 14–20

CONVALLARIA majalis   p. 288
Lily-of-the-valley
◐ ✎ 1–A3; 1–7, 14–20

CROCUS   p. 300
☼ ◐ ✎ 1–24

Allium sphaerocephalum

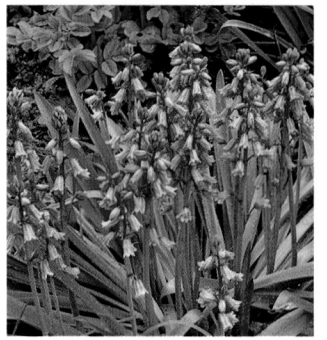
Hyacinthoides hispanica

ERANTHIS hyemalis   p. 330
Winter aconite
☼ ◐ ✎ 1–9, 14–17

FREESIA   p. 358
☼ ◐ ✎ 8, 9, 12–24

FRITILLARIA   p. 359
Fritillary
◐ ✎ ZONES VARY

GALANTHUS   p. 362
Snowdrop
☼ ◐ ✎ 1–9, 14–17

GALTONIA candicans   p. 362
Summer hyacinth
☼ ◐ ✎ 4–24; H1

HIPPEASTRUM   p. 396
Amaryllis
☼ ◐ ✎ ZONES VARY

HYACINTHOIDES   p. 400
Bluebell
◐ ✎ ZONES VARY

Hippeastrum

HYACINTHUS orientalis   p. 400
Common hyacinth
☼ ✎ 8, 9, 11–24

HYMENOCALLIS   p. 402
☼ ◐ ✎ 5, 6, 8, 9, 14–24

IPHEION uniflorum   p. 408
Spring star flower
☼ ◐ ✎ 2B–24

IRIS (some)   p. 409
NEEDS, ZONES VARY

IXIA   p. 415
African corn lily
☼ ✎ 7–9, 12–24

LEUCOJUM   p. 440
Snowflake
☼ ◐ ✎ ZONES VARY

LILIUM   p. 444
Lily
☼ ◐ ✎ ZONES VARY

MUSCARI   p. 487
Grape hyacinth
☼ ◐ ✎ ZONES VARY

Narcissus

Nerine filifolia

NARCISSUS   p. 489
Daffodil
☼ ◐ ✎ A2, A3; 1–24

NERINE   p. 495
☼ ◐ ✎ 5, 6, 8, 9, 13–24

OXALIS (some)   p. 506
NEEDS, ZONES VARY

PUSCHKINIA scilloides   p. 572
☼ ◐ ✎ 1–11, 14

RANUNCULUS asiaticus   p. 579
Persian ranunculus
☼ ✎ ALL ZONES

SCILLA   p. 619
Squill
☼ ◐ ✎ ZONES VARY

SPARAXIS tricolor   p. 630
Harlequin flower
☼ ✎ 9, 12–24

TRITELEIA   p. 655
☼ ✎ 3–9, 14–24

TRITONIA crocata   p. 656
Flame freesia
☼ ✎ 9, 13–24

TULBAGHIA   p. 657
☼ ✎ 13–24; H1, H2

Tulbaghia violacea 'Silver Lace'

Crocosmia × crocosmiiflora

Liatris spicata

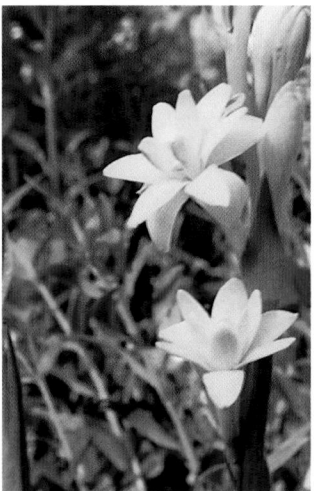

Polianthes tuberosa 'The Pearl'

TULIPA   p. 657
Tulip
:Ò: :Ò: ✂ 1–24

WATSONIA borbonica   p. 670
:Ò: :Ò: ✂ 4–9, 12–24

ZANTEDESCHIA   p. 675
Calla
NEEDS VARY, ✂ 5, 6, 8, 9, 12–24; H1, H2

Winter- & Spring-planted Bulbs

BEGONIA, tuberous   p. 220
:Ò: ✂ 4–9, 14–24; H1

CALADIUM bicolor   p. 236
Fancy-leafed caladium
:Ò: ● ✂ H2

CANNA   p. 248
:Ò: ✂ 6–9, 12–24; H1, H2

COLOCASIA esculenta   p. 287
Taro
:Ò: ✂ 12, 16–24; H1, H2

CROCOSMIA   p. 299
:Ò: :Ò: ✂ ZONES VARY BY SPECIES

CYCLAMEN persicum   p. 304
Florists' cyclamen
:Ò: :Ò: ✂ 15–24

DAHLIA   p. 307
:Ò: :Ò: ✂ 1–24

GLADIOLUS   p. 370
:Ò: ✂ 4–9, 12–24; H1

**GLORIOSA superba
'Rothschildiana'**   p. 371
Glory lily
:Ò: :Ò: ✂ 24; H1, H2

Dahlia

HIPPEASTRUM   p. 396
Amaryllis
:Ò: :Ò: ✂ ZONES VARY

HOMERIA collina   p. 397
:Ò: ✂ 4–24

HYMENOCALLIS   p. 402
:Ò: :Ò: ✂ 5, 6, 8, 9, 14–24

LIATRIS spicata   p. 442
Gayfeather
:Ò: ✂ A2, A3; 1–10, 14–24

LILIUM, Oriental hybrids   p. 444
:Ò: :Ò: ✂ 1–9, 14–24

POLIANTHES tuberosa   p. 555
Tuberose
:Ò: ✂ 7–9, 14–24; H1, H2

SCHIZOSTYLIS coccinea   p. 618
Crimson flag
:Ò: :Ò: ✂ 5–9, 14–24; H1, H2

TIGRIDIA pavonia   p. 649
Tiger flower
:Ò: :Ò: ✂ 4–24; H1

**ZANTEDESCHIA
aethiopica**   p. 675
Common calla
:Ò: :Ò: ✂ 5, 6, 8, 9, 12–24; H1, H2

ZEPHYRANTHES   p. 676
Zephyr flower
:Ò: :Ò: ✂ ZONES VARY

Summer-planted Bulbs

COLCHICUM   p. 286
Meadow saffron
:Ò: ✂ 2–10, 14–24

**CROCUS
(fall-flowering)**   p. 300
:Ò: :Ò: ✂ 1–24

**CYCLAMEN
(except florists' types)**   p. 304
:Ò: :Ò: ✂ ZONES VARY

IRIS (some)   p. 409
NEEDS, ZONES VARY

LYCORIS   p. 457
Spider lily
:Ò: :Ò: ✂ ZONES VARY

STERNBERGIA lutea   p. 634
:Ò: ✂ 3–10, 14–24

Begonia, tuberous

Canna 'Tropicana'

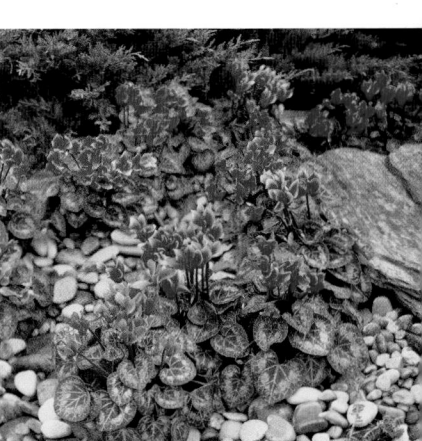

Cyclamen persicum

Annuals

Flowering annuals provide quick color to liven up almost any part of the garden. You can choose from a dazzling array of colors and floral styles; size varies just as widely, from ground-hugging to knee-high to towering. Cool-season annuals (such as calendula and sweet pea) prosper in cool soils and mild temperatures—fall through spring in mild-winter climates, early to late spring elsewhere. Warm-season annuals such as cosmos and zinnia are planted after the year's last frost and usually grow best between late spring and fall—though in the low desert and hot interior climates, some perform better from early to late spring.

Cosmos sulphureus

Calendula officinalis

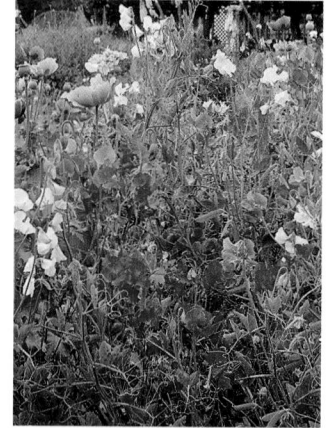

Lathyrus odoratus

Cool-season Annuals

ANTIRRHINUM majus p. 188
Snapdragon
☼ ✿ A1–A3; 1–24

CALENDULA officinalis p. 238
Calendula
☼ ✿ A2, A3; 1–24; H1

CENTAUREA cyanus p. 260
Cornflower
☼ ✿ 1–24; H1, H2

CLARKIA p. 281
☼ ◑ ✿ A1, A2; 1–24

CONSOLIDA ajacis p. 287
Larkspur
☼ ✿ 1–24

CYNOGLOSSUM amabile p. 305
Chinese forget-me-not
☼ ✿ A2, A3; 1–24; H1, H2

DIANTHUS (some) p. 313
Pink
☼ ◑ ✿ A2, A3; 1–24

DIMORPHOTHECA p. 318
African daisy
☼ ✿ 1–24

ESCHSCHOLZIA californica p. 338
California poppy
☼ ✿ 1–24; H1

IBERIS umbellata p. 404
Globe candytuft
☼ ◑ ✿ 1–2

LATHYRUS odoratus p. 433
Sweet pea
☼ ✿ ALL ZONES

LINARIA maroccana p. 447
Baby snapdragon
☼ ◑ ✿ 1–24

MATTHIOLA incana p. 475
☼ ◑ ✿ 1–24

MYOSOTIS sylvatica p. 488
Forget-me-not
◑ ✿ A1–A3; 1–24

NEMESIA strumosa p. 493
☼ ✿ 1–24

PAPAVER (some) p. 510
Poppy
☼ ✿ ZONES VARY

PRIMULA (many) p. 560
Primrose
☼ ◑ ● ✿ ZONES VARY

SCHIZANTHUS pinnatus p. 618
Poor man's orchid
☼ ✿ 1–6, 15–17, 21–24

SENECIO × hybridus p. 622
Florists' cineraria
☼ ◑ ● ✿ 16, 17, 22–24

VIOLA p. 666
Viola
NEEDS, ZONES VARY

Warm-season Annuals

AGERATUM houstonianum p. 176
Floss flower
☼ ◑ ✿ 1–24

BRACHYSCOME iberidifolia p. 230
Swan river daisy
☼ ✿ 1–24

BROWALLIA speciosa p. 232
Amethyst flower
◑ ✿ 17, 23, 24; H1, H2

CALLISTEPHUS chinensis p. 240
China aster
☼ ✿ 1–24

CATHARANTHUS roseus p. 255
Madagascar periwinkle
☼ ◑ ✿ 1–24; H1, H2

CELOSIA p. 259
Cockscomb
☼ ✿ 1–24; H1, H2

CERINTHE major p. 263
Honeywort
☼ ◑ ✿ 1–24

Celosia

Ageratum houstonianum 'Hawaii Blue'

Browallia speciosa

Catharanthus roseus

Brachyscome 'Toucan Tango'

Callistephus chinensis

Cleome hasslerana

Convolvulus tricolor 'Blue Ensign'

Gomphrena globosa

Petunia × *hybrida*

Torenia fournieri

Eustoma grandiflorum

Portulaca grandiflora 'Sundial'

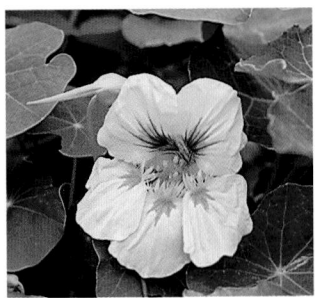
Tropaeolum majus

CLEOME hasslerana p. 283
Spider flower
☼ ✿ 1–24

CONVOLVULUS tricolor p. 288
Dwarf morning glory
☼ ◐ ✿ 1–24

COREOPSIS tinctoria p. 290
Annual coreopsis
☼ ✿ 1–24; H1, H2

COSMOS p. 295
☼ ✿ 1–24

DOLICHOS lablab p. 319
Hyacinth bean
☼ ✿ ALL ZONES

EUSTOMA grandiflorum p. 347
Lisianthus
☼ ◐ ✿ 1–24

GAILLARDIA pulchella p. 361
☼ ✿ 1–24; H1, H2

GOMPHRENA p. 372
Globe amaranth
☼ ◐ ✿ 1–24; H1, H2

GYPSOPHILA elegans p. 382
☼ ✿ 1–24

HELIANTHUS annuus p. 387
Common sunflower
☼ ✿ ALL ZONES

HELICHRYSUM bracteatum p. 388
Strawflower
☼ ✿ ALL ZONES

IMPATIENS p. 406
Balsam
NEEDS, ZONES VARY

IPOMOEA p. 408
Morning glory
☼ ✿ ZONES VARY

LIMONIUM (some) p. 446
Statice
☼ ✿ ZONES VARY

LOBELIA erinus p. 450
☼ ◐ ✿ ALL ZONES

LOBULARIA maritima p. 451
Sweet alyssum
☼ ◐ ✿ ALL ZONES

MIMULUS × hybridus p. 482
◐ ● ✿ 1–24

MOLUCCELLA laevis p. 484
Bells-of-Ireland
☼ ✿ 1–24; H1, H2

NICOTIANA p. 495
Flowering tobacco
☼ ◐ ✿ ALL ZONES

PETUNIA × hybrida p. 531
Petunia
☼ ✿ ALL ZONES

PHLOX drummondii p. 534
Annual phlox
☼ ✿ A2, A3; 1–24; H1

PORTULACA grandiflora p. 558
Rose moss
☼ ✿ ALL ZONES

SALPIGLOSSIS sinuata p. 607
Painted tongue
☼ ✿ 1–24

SALVIA splendens p. 612
Scarlet sage
☼ ✿ ALL ZONES

SANVITALIA procumbens p. 614
Creeping zinnia
☼ ✿ 1–24

SCABIOSA atropurpurea p. 616
Pincushion flower
☼ ✿ 1–24; H1, H2

SILENE coeli-rosa p. 625
Viscaria
☼ ◐ ✿ ALL ZONES

TAGETES p. 642
Marigold
☼ ✿ ZONES VARY

TITHONIA rotundifolia p. 650
Mexican sunflower
☼ ✿ 1–24; H1, H2

TORENIA fournieri p. 653
Wishbone flower
☼ ◐ ✿ 1–24; H1, H2

TROPAEOLUM majus p. 656
Garden nasturtium
☼ ◐ ✿ ALL ZONES

VERBENA p. 663
☼ ✿ ZONES VARY

ZINNIA p. 677
☼ ✿ 1–24; H1, H2

Helichrysum bracteatum

Salpiglossis sinuata

Zinnia elegans

Colored Foliage

Not all color comes from flowers or fruit. The plants listed below offer long-term garden accents in the form of colored leaves: gray or silver, bronze, red or purple, yellow or gold, blue, and variegated. They can be used to enliven the basic green of other garden foliage, to form contrasting combinations (such as gray and red) with one another, to complement flower colors in season, and to provide eye-catching focal points.

Achillea 'Moonshine'

Artemisia 'Powis Castle'

Festuca glauca

Eucalyptus

Gray, Silver Trees & Shrubs

CEDRUS atlantica 'Glauca'   p. 258
Atlas cedar
☀ ✎ 3B–10, 14–24

CHAMAECYPARIS lawsoniana (some)   p. 264
Port Orford cedar
☀ ◐ ✎ A3; 3–6, 15–17

CISTUS (several)   p. 275
Rockrose
☀ ✎ 4–9, 14–24

CONVOLVULUS cneorum   p. 288
Bush morning glory
☀ ◐ ✎ 5–9, 12–24

CUPRESSUS arizonica glabra   p. 303
Smooth Arizona cypress
☀ ✎ 7–24

ELAEAGNUS angustifolia   p. 326
Russian olive
☀ ◐ ✎ A2, A3; 1–3, 7–14, 18, 19

ELAEAGNUS 'Coral Silver'   p. 326
☀ ◐ ✎ 2B–24

EUCALYPTUS (many)   p. 339
☀ ✎ 5, 6, 8–24; H1, H2

FEIJOA, Pineapple guava   p. 350
☀ ✎ 6–9, 12–24; H1, H2

HELIANTHEMUM nummularium (some)   p. 387
Sunrose
☀ ✎ 2B–9, 14–24

HOSTA (several)   p. 398
Plantain lily
◐ ● ✎ ZONES VARY

JUNIPERUS (many)   p. 418
Juniper
☀ ◐ ✎ ZONES VARY

LAVANDULA (most)   p. 434
Lavender
☀ ✎ ZONES VARY

LEUCOPHYLLUM frutescens   p. 440
Texas ranger
☀ ✎ 7–24; H1, H2

PANICUM virgatum (some)   p. 510
Switch grass
☀ ◐ ✎ 1–11, 14–23

PICEA pungens (some)   p. 539
Colorado spruce
☀ ◐ ✎ A2, A3; 1–10, 14–17

ROSA glauca   p. 601
☀ ◐ ✎ A1–A3; 1–24

SALVIA leucophylla   p. 610
Purple sage
☀ ✎ 8, 9, 14–17, 19–24

SANTOLINA chamaecyparissus   p. 614
Lavender cotton
☀ ✎ 2–24; H1, H2

TEUCRIUM fruticans   p. 646
Bush germander
☀ ✎ 4–24

Gray, Silver Perennials

ACHILLEA (many)   p. 170
Yarrow
☀ ✎ A1–A3; 1–24

ARTEMISIA (many)   p. 201
☀ ✎ ZONES VARY

CENTAUREA cineraria   p. 259
Dusty miller
☀ ✎ 8–24; H1, H2

CERASTIUM tomentosum   p. 261
Snow-in-summer
☀ ◐ ✎ A1, A2; 1–24

ECHEVERIA (many)   p. 323
☀ ◐ ✎ ZONES VARY

Picea pungens 'Hoopsii'

Juniperus procumbens 'Nana'

Senecio mandraliscae

ERYSIMUM
'Bowles Mauve' p. 336
Wallflower
☼ ◑ ✎ 4–9, 14–24

FESTUCA (several) p. 351
Fescue
☼ ◑ ✎ ZONES VARY

HELICHRYSUM petiolare p. 388
Licorice plant
☼ ✎ 16, 17, 22–24

LYCHNIS coronaria p. 455
Crown-pink
☼ ◑ ✎ 1–9, 14–24

PEROVSKIA p. 529
Russian sage
☼ ✎ 2–24

ROMNEYA coulteri p. 593
Matilija poppy
☼ ✎ 4–12, 14–24; H1

SALVIA chamaedryoides p. 608
Germander sage
☼ ✎ 8, 9, 12, 14–24

SALVIA officinalis
'Berggarten' p. 611
Garden sage
☼ ✎ 2–24; H1, H2

SENECIO (several) p. 621
NEEDS, ZONES VARY

STACHYS byzantina p. 633
Lamb's ears
☼ ◑ ✎ 1–24

THYMUS (several) p. 648
Thyme
☼ ◑ ✎ ZONES VARY

ZAUSCHNERIA p. 675
California fuchsia
☼ ◑ ✎ ZONES 2–11, 14–24

Bronze, Red, Purple Trees & Shrubs

ACER palmatum (some) P. 168
Japanese maple
☼ ◑ ✎ A3; 2–10, 12, 14–24

Acer palmatum 'Filiferum Purpureum'

Berberis thunbergii 'Atropurpurea'

ACER platanoides (some) p. 169
Norway maple
☼ ◑ ✎ A2, A3; 1–9, 14–17

BERBERIS thunbergii
(several) p. 221
Japanese barberry
☼ ◑ ✎ A3; 2B–24

CERCIS canadensis
'Forest Pansy' p. 262
Eastern redbud
☼ ◑ ✎ 1–24

CORDYLINE australis
'Atropurpurea' p. 289
☼ ✎ 5, 8–11, 14–24; H1, H2

CORYLUS (several) p. 294
Filbert
☼ ◑ ✎ 2–9, 14–20

COTINUS coggygria
(some) p. 296
Smoke tree
☼ ✎ 2–24

DODONAEA
viscosa **'Purpurea'** p. 319
Purple hop bush
☼ ◑ ✎ 7–24; H1, H2

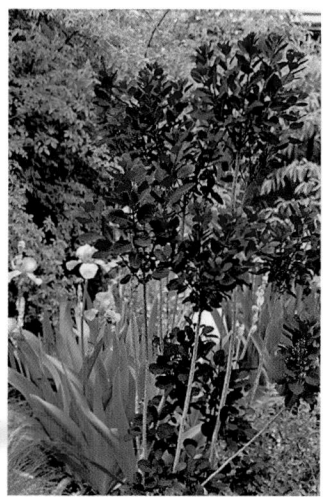

Cotinus coggygria

ERIOBOTRYA deflexa p. 334
Bronze loquat
☼ ◑ ✎ 8–24

FAGUS sylvatica (some) p. 348
European beech
☼ ◑ ✎ A3; 2B–9, 14–21

MALUS (some) p. 469
Flowering crabapple
☼ ✎ 1–11, 14–21

PRUNUS cerasifera (most) p. 568
Cherry plum
☼ ✎ 3–22

PRUNUS × cistena p. 568
Dwarf red-leaf plum
☼ ✎ A3; 1–22

Bronze, Red, Purple Perennials

AEONIUM arboreum
'Atropurpureum' p. 173
☼ ◑ ✎ 15–17, 20–24

Aeonium arboreum 'Atropurpureum'

Canna 'Durban'

AJUGA reptans (several) p. 177
Carpet bugle
☼ ◑ ✎ A2, A3; 1–24

ANTHRISCUS sylvestris
'Ravenswing' p. 188
☼ ◑ ✎ 1–9, 14–24

ASTILBE × arendsii 'Fanal' p. 208
False spiraea
☼ ◑ ✎ A2, A3; 1–9, 14–24

BEGONIA (many) p. 219
◑ ✎ ZONES 14–24; H1, H2

BERGENIA (some) p. 222
☼ ● ◑ ✎ A1, A3; 1–9, 12–24

CANNA (some) p. 248
☼ ✎ 6–9, 12–24; H1, H2

EUPHORBIA amygdaloides
'Purpurea' p. 345
☼ ✎ 2B–24

HEUCHERA (many) p. 393
Coral bells
☼ ◑ ✎ 1–10, 14–24

IMPERATA cylindrica
'Rubra' p. 407
Japanese blood grass
☼ ◑ ✎ 2B–24

Pennisetum setaceum 'Rubrum'

**PENNISETUM setaceum
'Rubrum'** p. 526
☼ ✿ 8–24; H1, H2

**PHORMIUM tenax
(several)** p. 536
New Zealand flax
☼ ◑ ✿ 5–9, 14–24; H1, H2

Yellow, Gold
Trees & Shrubs

**ACER shirasawanum
'Aureum'** p. 170
Golden fullmoon maple
◑ ✿ 3B–6, 14–16

**CALLUNA vulgaris
(several)** p. 240
Scotch heather
☼ ✿ 1A, 2–6, 15–17

**CARYOPTERIS × clandonensis
'Worcester Gold'** p. 253
Blue mist
☼ ✿ 2B–9, 14–24

CEDRUS deodara 'Aurea' p. 258
Deodar cedar
☼ ✿ 3B–10, 14–24

CHAMAECYPARIS (some) p. 264
False cypress
☼ ◑ ✿ ZONES VARY

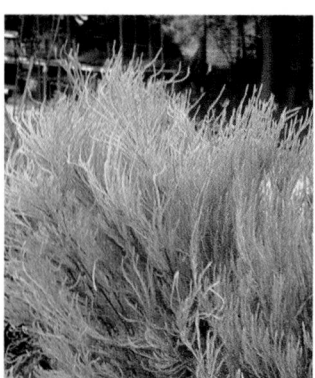

Coleonema pulchellum 'Sunset Gold'

Robinia pseudoacacia 'Frisia'

**CHAMAECYPARIS
lawsoniana (some)** p. 264
Port Orford cedar
☼ ◑ ✿ A3; 3–6, 15–17

**COLEONEMA pulchellum
'Sunset Gold'** p. 287
Pink breath of heaven
☼ ✿ 7–9, 14–24

**GLEDITSIA triacanthos
'Sunburst'** p. 371
Honey locust
☼ ✿ 1–16, 18–20

JUNIPERUS (several) p. 418
Juniper
☼ ◑ ✿ ZONES VARY

LIGUSTRUM 'Vicaryi' p. 443
Vicary golden privet
☼ ◑ ✿ 2–24

**PLATYCLADUS orientalis
(several)** p. 547
Oriental arborvitae
☼ ◑ ✿ 2–24; H1, H2

**ROBINIA pseudoacacia
'Frisia'** p. 592
☼ ✿ 1–24

SAMBUCUS (some) p. 613
Elderberry
☼ ◑ ✿ ZONES VARY

**SPIRAEA japonica
(several)** p. 631
☼ ◑ ✿ A2, A3; 2–10, 14–21

TAXUS baccata (several) p. 644
English yew
☼ ◑ ● ✿ A3; 3–9, 14–24

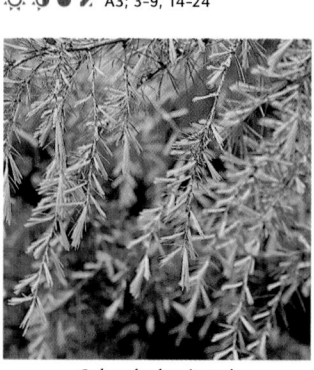

Cedrus deodara 'Aurea'

Aucuba japonica 'Variegata'

THUJA occidentalis (some) p. 646
American arborvitae
☼ ◑ ✿ ZONES VARY

THUJA plicata p. 647
Western red cedar
☼ ◑ ✿ A3; 1–9, 14–24

**VIBURNUM opulus
'Aureum'** p. 665
☼ ◑ ✿ A2, A3; 1–9, 14–24

Yellow, Gold
Perennials

ACORUS gramineus 'Ogon' p. 171
Japanese sweet flag
☼ ◑ ✿ 3B–10, 14–24

**CHRYSANTHEMUM
parthenium 'Aureum'** p. 273
Feverfew
☼ ✿ 2–24

**HELICHRYSUM petiolare
'Limelight'** p. 388
Licorice plant
☼ ✿ 16, 17, 22–24

HOSTA (several) p. 398
Plantain lily
◑ ● ✿ ZONES VARY

**MILIUM effusum
'Aureum'** p. 481
Bowles' golden grass
☼ ✿ 3B–9, 14–17

ORIGANUM (several) p. 502
Oregano
☼ ✿ ZONES VARY

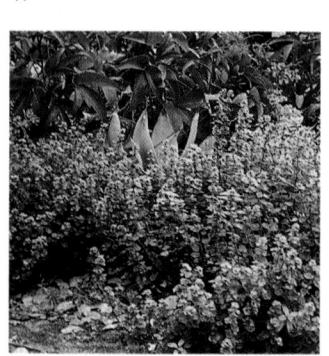

Origanum vulgare 'Aureum'

Hosta 'Great Expectations'

Variegated
Trees & Shrubs

**ACER negundo
'Variegatum'** p. 168
Variegated box elder
☼ ◑ ✿ A2, A3; 1–10, 12–24

AUCUBA japonica (several) p. 209
Japanese aucuba
◑ ● ✿ 4–24

BOUGAINVILLEA (some) p. 227
☼ ✿ 5, 6, 12–17, 19, 21–24; H1, H2

**BUDDLEJA davidii
'Harlequin'** p. 234
Butterfly bush
☼ ◑ ✿ 2–24; H1

COPROSMA p. 288
☼ ◑ ✿ ZONES VARY

CORNUS (several) p. 291
Dogwood
☼ ◑ ✿ ZONES VARY

**COTONEASTER horizontalis
'Variegatus'** p. 296
Rock cotoneaster
☼ ✿ A3; 2B–11, 14–24

**DAPHNE odora
'Marginata'** p. 310
Winter daphne
☼ ✿ 4–10, 12, 14–24

ELAEAGNUS (some) p. 325
☼ ◑ ✿ ZONES VARY

EUONYMUS (some) p. 344
NEEDS, ZONES VARY

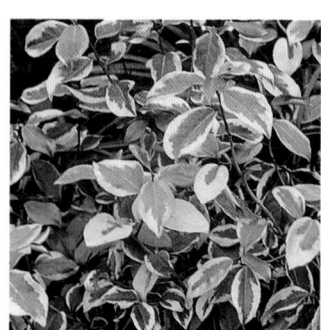

Elaeagnus × ebbingei 'Gilt Edge'

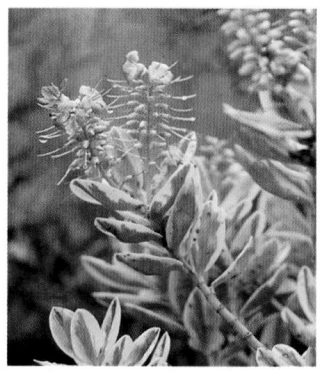

Hebe speciosa × andersonii 'Variegata'

FAGUS sylvatica 'Tricolor' p. 348
Tricolor beech
☼ ◐ ✎ A3; 2B-9, 14-21

HEBE (many) p. 385
☼ ◐ ✎ ZONES 14-24

HYDRANGEA macrophylla (several) p. 401
Big-leaf hydrangea
☼ ◐ ✎ 3B-9, 14-24; H1

ILEX (several) p. 404
Holly
☼ ◐ ✎ ZONES VARY

JUNIPERUS (several) p. 418
Juniper
☼ ◐ ✎ ZONES VARY

LEUCOTHOE fontanesiana 'Rainbow' p. 441
Drooping leucothoe
☼ ◐ ● ✎ 4-7, 15-17

MYRTUS communis (several) p. 488
Myrtle
☼ ◐ ✎ 8-24; H1, H2

OSMANTHUS heterophyllus 'Variegatus' p. 505
☼ ◐ ✎ 4-10, 14-24

PIERIS japonica 'Variegata' p. 540
Lily-of-the-valley shrub
◐ ✎ 2B-9, 14-17

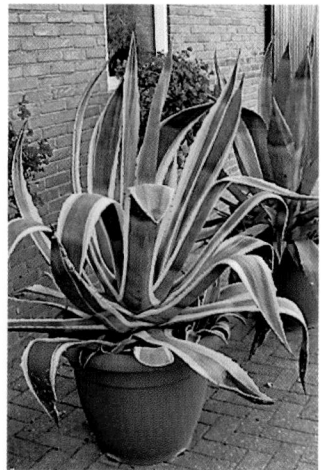

Agave americana

PITTOSPORUM tobira (several) p. 546
Tobira
☼ ◐ ✎ 4-24; H1, H2

VIBURNUM tinus 'Variegatum' p. 666
☼ ◐ ✎ 4-9, 14-24

WEIGELA hybrid 'Variegata' p. 670
☼ ◐ ✎ 1-11, 14-21

Variegated Vines

ACTINIDIA kolomikta p. 171
☼ ◐ ✎ A1-A3; 1-9, 14-17

BOUGAINVILLEA (some) p. 227
☼ ✎ ZONES 5, 6, 12-17, 19, 21-24; H1, H2

HEDERA (some) p. 385
Ivy
☼ ◐ ✎ ZONES VARY

LONICERA japonica 'Aureo-reticulata' p. 452
Goldnet honeysuckle
☼ ◐ ✎ 1-24; H1, H2

Variegated Perennials

AEGOPODIUM podagraria 'Variegatum' p. 173
☼ ◐ ● ✎ A1-A3;1-9, 12, 14-24

AGAVE (some) p. 175
☼ ◐ ✎ ZONES VARY

AJUGA reptans (some) p. 177
Carpet bugle
☼ ◐ ✎ A2, A3; 1-24

ALOE p. 181
☼ ◐ ✎ 8, 9, 12-24

ATHYRIUM niponicum Pictum p. 208
Japanese painted fern
◐ ● ✎ 1-9, 14-24

CALADIUM bicolor p. 236
Fancy-leafed caladium
◐ ● ✎ H2

EUPHORBIA p. 345
☼ ◐ ● ✎ ZONES VARY

GAURA lindheimeri (some) p. 364
☼ ✎ 2B-24

HELICHRYSUM petiolare 'Variegatum' p. 388
Licorice plant
☼ ✎ 16, 17, 22-24

HEUCHERA (some) p. 393
Coral bells
☼ ◐ ✎ ZONES VARY

Bougainvillea 'Hawaii'

HOSTA (many) p. 398
Plantain lily
◐ ● ✎ ZONES VARY

HOUTTUYNIA cordata 'Variegata' p. 399
☼ ◐ ● ✎ 2-9, 14-24

HYPOESTES phyllostachya p. 403
Freckle face
✎ 23, 24, H1, H2

IMPATIENS, New Guinea hybrids p. 406
☼ ◐ ● ✎ 24; H1, H2

LAMIUM (several) p. 431
Dead nettle
◐ ● ✎ ZONES VARY

LIRIOPE muscari (some) p. 449
Big blue lily turf
☼ ◐ ● ✎ 2B-10, 14-24; H1, H2

MISCANTHUS sinensis (several) p. 482
Eulalia
☼ ◐ ✎ 2-24

PACHYSANDRA terminalis 'Variegata' p. 507
Japanese spurge
◐ ● ✎ 2-10, 14-21

PELARGONIUM (several) p. 524
Geranium
☼ ◐ ✎ A2, A3; 1-24

PHLOX paniculata p. 535
Summer phlox
☼ ◐ ✎ 1-14, 18-21

PHORMIUM (some) p. 536
New Zealand flax
☼ ◐ ✎ 7-9, 14-24; H1, H2

Impatiens New Guinea hybrid

Hypoestes phyllostachya

PHYSOSTEGIA virginiana 'Variegata' p. 538
False dragonhead
☼ ◐ ✎ A3; 1-9, 14-24

POLYGONATUM odoratum 'Variegatum' p. 556
Solomon's seal
☼ ◐ ✎ A1-A3; 1-9, 14-17

PULMONARIA (several) p. 570
Lungwort
◐ ● ✎ 1-9, 14-17

SALVIA officinalis (some) p. 611
Garden sage
☼ ◐ ✎ 2-24; H1, H2

THYME (some) p. 648
Thymus
☼ ◐ ✎ ZONES 1-24

TULBAGHIA violacea (some) p. 657
Society garlic
☼ ✎ 13-24; H1, H2

VINCA (some) p. 666
Periwinkle
☼ ◐ ● ✎ ZONES VARY

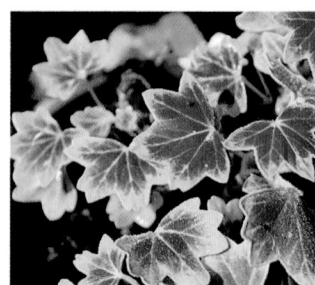

Pelargonium × hortorum 'Golden Ears'

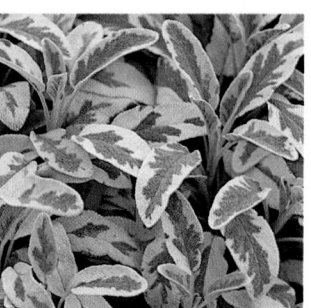

Salvia officinalis 'Tricolor'

Fall Color

Yellow, gold, russet, orange, red, burgundy: in much of the West, foliage in these warm colors means autumn has arrived. To bring these hues to your fall garden, look to the following plants. Because color can vary within a species, it is wise to shop in fall, while colors are changing—or simply to buy selected varieties with known, reliable fall color. Keep in mind that climate can affect color change; in general, it's less of a feature in mild-winter areas.

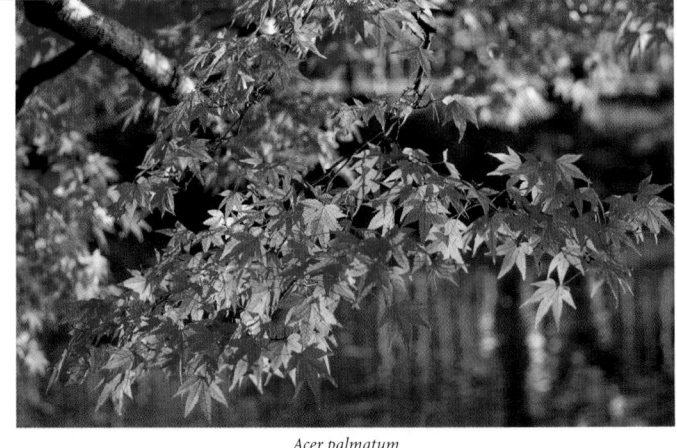
Acer palmatum

Trees

ACER (many)   p. 167
Maple
☼ ◑ ⚡ ZONES VARY

BETULA   p. 223
Birch
☼ ⚡ ZONES VARY

CERCIDIPHYLLUM japonicum   p. 262
Katsura tree
☼ ◑ ⚡ 2B-6, 14-16, 18-20

CERCIS canadensis   p. 262
Eastern redbud
☼ ◑ ⚡ 1-24

CLADRASTIS kentukea   p. 280
Yellow wood
☼ ⚡ 2-9, 14-16

CORNUS (many)   p. 291
Dogwood
☼ ◑ ⚡ ZONES VARY

CRATAEGUS (some)   p. 298
Hawthorn
☼ ⚡ 2-12, 14-17

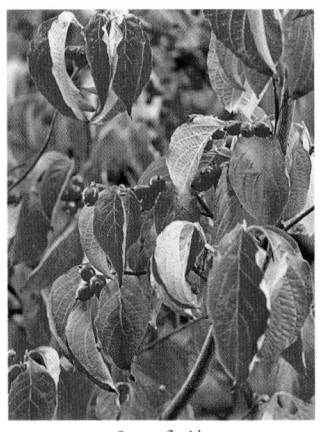
Cornus florida

FRAXINUS (deciduous)   p. 357
Ash
☼ ⚡ ZONES VARY

GINKGO biloba   p. 369
Maidenhair tree
☼ ⚡ A3; 1-10, 12, 14-24

GLEDITSIA triacanthos   p. 371
Honey locust
☼ ⚡ 1-16, 18-20

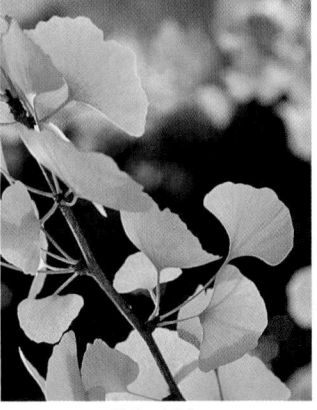
Ginkgo biloba

HALESIA   p. 383
☼ ⚡ 2B-9, 14-21

HAMAMELIS   p. 383
Witch hazel
☼ ◑ ⚡ ZONES VARY

KOELREUTERIA bipinnata   p. 428
Chinese flame tree
☼ ⚡ 8-24; H1

Lagerstroemia indica

LAGERSTROEMIA indica   p. 430
Crape myrtle
☼ ⚡ 7-10, 12-14, 18-21; H1, H2

LARIX   p. 432
Larch
☼ ⚡ ZONES VARY

LIQUIDAMBAR   p. 448
Sweet gum
☼ ⚡ ZONES VARY

LIRIODENDRON tulipifera   p. 448
Tulip tree
☼ ⚡ 2-12, 14-24

Cercidiphyllum japonicum

Liquidambar styraciflua

Populus, Quercus

Metasequoia gylptostroboides

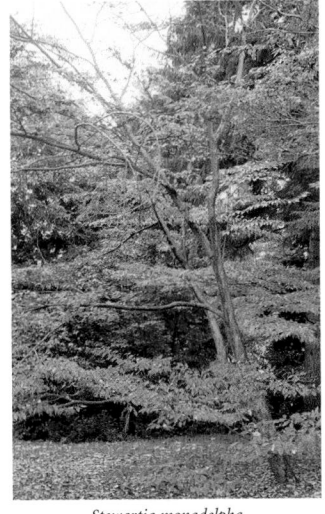

Stewartia monadelpha

LYANOTHAMNUS floribundus   p. 455
Catalina ironwood
☼ ✎ 14-17, 19-24

MALUS   p. 460
Flowering crabapple
☼ ✎ 1–11, 14–21

MELALEUCA quinquenervia   p. 477
Cajeput tree
☼ ✎ 9, 12, 13, 15-17, 20-24; H1, H2

METASEQUOIA glyptostroboides   p. 480
Dawn redwood
☼ ✎ A3; 3–10, 14–24

MORUS ALBA   p. 485
White mulberry
☼ ✎ 2-24; H1, H2

NYSSA sylvatica   p. 497
Sour gum
☼ ◑ ✎ 2-10, 14-21

OXYDENDRUM arboreum p. 506
Sourwood
☼ ✎ 2B-9, 14-17

PARROTIA persica   p. 513
Persian parrotia
☼ ◑ ✎ 2B-7, 14-17

PERSIMMON   p. 530
☼ ✎ ZONES VARY

PISTACIA chinensis   p. 545
Chinese pistache
☼ ✎ 4–16, 18-23

POPULUS (some)   p. 557
Poplar
☼ ✎ ZONES VARY

PRUNUS (deciduous)   p. 564
NEEDS, ZONES VARY

Salix 'Flame'

PYRUS (deciduous)   p. 573
Ornamental pear
☼ ✎ ZONES VARY

QUERCUS (deciduous)   p. 574
Oak
☼ ✎ ZONES VARY

SALIX   p. 606
Willow
☼ ✎ ZONES VARY

SAPIUM sebiferum   p. 614
Chinese tallow tree
☼ ✎ 8, 9, 12–16, 18-21; H1

Quercus

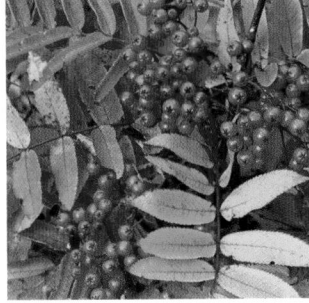

Sorbus americana

SORBUS   p. 629
Mountain ash
☼ ◑ ✎ ZONES VARY

STEWARTIA   p. 634
☼ ◑ ✎ 4-6, 14-17, 20, 21

STYRAX japonicus   p. 637
Japanese snowdrop tree
☼ ◑ ✎ 4-9, 14-21

TILIA   p. 649
Linden
☼ ✎ 1-17

ZELKOVA serrata   p. 676
Sawleaf zelkova
☼ ✎ 3-21

Malus 'David'

Pistacia chinensis

Pyrus calleryana

Berberis thunbergii 'Roseglow'

Cotoneaster horizontalis

Shrubs

AMELANCHIER p. 183
Juneberry
☼ ◐ ✂ ZONES VARY

BERBERIS (deciduous) p. 221
Barberry
☼ ◐ ✂ ZONES VARY

BLUEBERRY (many) p. 226
☼ ✂ ZONES VARY

CERCIS p. 262
Redbud
☼ ◐ ✂ ZONES VARY

CORNUS (deciduous) p. 291
Dogwood
☼ ◐ ✂ ZONES VARY

COTINUS p. 295
Smoke tree
☼ ✂ 2-24

Viburnum prunifolium

Cotinus 'Grace'

COTONEASTER
(most deciduous) p. 296
☼ ✂ ZONES VARY

ENKIANTHUS p. 327
☼ ◐ ✂ 3-9, 14-21

EUONYMUS (deciduous) p. 344
NEEDS, ZONES VARY

HAMAMELIS p. 383
Witch hazel
☼ ◐ ✂ ZONES VARY

HYDRANGEA quercifolia p. 401
Oakleaf hydrangea
☼ ◐ ✂ 2B-23

LAGERSTROEMIA indica p. 430
Crape myrtle
☼ ✂ 7-10, 12-14, 18-21; H1, H2

NANDINA domestica p. 489
Heavenly bamboo
☼ ◐ ● ✂ 3-24; H1, H2

PHOTINIA villosa p. 537
☼ ✂ 3-9, 14-17

PUNICA granatum p. 571
Pomegranate
☼ ✂ 5-24; H1, H2

RHODODENDRON
(deciduous) p. 583
Azalea
☼ ✂ ZONES VARY

RHUS (deciduous) p. 590
Sumac
☼ ✂ ZONES VARY

SPIRAEA (most) p. 631
☼ ◐ ✂ ZONES VARY

VIBURNUM (many) p. 664
NEEDS, ZONES VARY

Euonymus alatus

Euonymus europaeus

Hamamelis × intermedia 'Ruby Glow'

Grape

Vines

GRAPE p. 373
☼ ◐ ✂ ZONES VARY

PARTHENOCISSUS p. 513
☼ ◐ ● ✂ ZONES VARY

WISTERIA p. 671
NEEDS, ZONES VARY

Parthenocissus tricuspidata

Wisteria sinensis

Trees

When you shop for a tree, carefully consider how well it will suit its intended location. Because garden size is a crucial determinant, the trees in this list are grouped in three size categories. Patio trees are generally small, as trees go, and reward close viewing of details: flowers, fruits, fall foliage, decorative bark. All produce minimal litter from flowers, fruits, leaves, and branches, and have root systems not likely to crack or raise pavement. Patio trees are also fine for garden planting, but the list of garden trees includes others that may have litter or root attributes that exclude them from patios but that are not issues in a garden setting. Large landscape trees are generally too massive for small gardens but are choice candidates for planting wherever there's room for them to achieve their full majesty.

Cercis occidentalis

Acer palmatum 'Ever Red'

Corylus avellana 'Contorta'

Cornus florida 'Welchii'

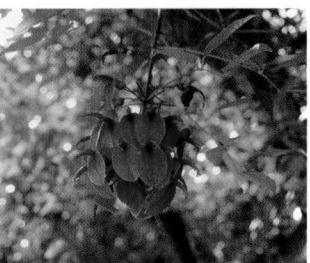

Erythrina crista-galli

Patio Trees, Deciduous

ACER buergeranum p. 167
Trident maple
☼ ◑ ✿ 2–9, 14–17, 20, 21

ACER circinatum p. 167
Vine maple
☼ ◑ ✿ A3; 2B–6, 14–17

ACER davidii p. 167
David's maple
☼ ◑ ✿ 2–6, 15–17, 20, 21

ACER palmatum p. 168
Japanese maple
☼ ◑ ✿ A3; 2–10, 12, 14–24

ACER tataricum ginnala p. 170
Amur maple
☼ ◑ ✿ A1–A3; 1–9, 14–16

AMELANCHIER p. 183
Juneberry
☼ ◑ ✿ ZONES VARY

BAUHINIA p. 218
Orchid tree
☼ ✿ ZONES VARY

CERCIDIUM p. 262
Palo verde
☼ ✿ 8–14, 18–20

CERCIS p. 262
Redbud
☼ ◑ ✿ ZONES VARY

Cercidium floridum

CHILOPSIS linearis p. 268
Desert willow
☼ ✿ 3B, 7–14, 18–23

CHIONANTHUS p. 269
Fringe tree
☼ ✿ ZONES VARY

× CHITALPA tashkentensis p. 270
☼ ✿ 3–24

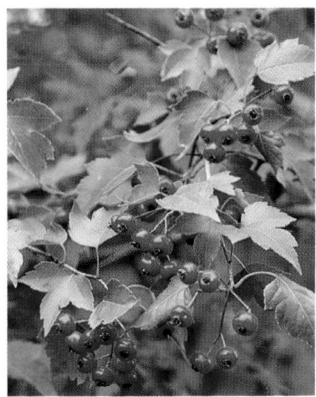

Crataegus phaenopyrum

CHORISIA speciosa p. 271
Floss silk tree
☼ ✿ 12–24; H1, H2

CLADRASTIS kentukea p. 280
Yellow wood
☼ ✿ 2–9, 14–16

CORNUS florida p. 292
Flowering dogwood
☼ ◑ ✿ 2B–9, 14–16

CORNUS kousa p. 292
Kousa dogwood
☼ ◑ ✿ 2–9, 14–17

CORYLUS (most) p. 294
Filbert, hazelnut
☼ ◑ ✿ 2–9, 14–20

COTINUS coggygria p. 296
Smoke tree
☼ ✿ 2–24

CRATAEGUS p. 298
Hawthorn
☼ ✿ 2–12, 14–17

DAVIDIA involucrata p. 311
Dove tree
☼ ◑ ✿ 4–9, 14–21

ERYTHRINA (most) p. 336
Coral tree
☼ ✿ ZONES VARY

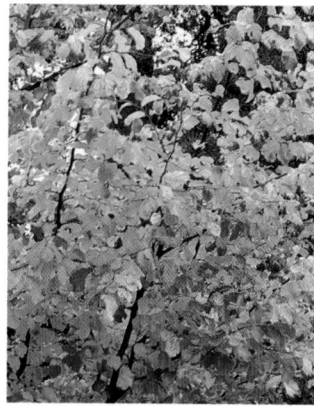

Malus 'Weeping Candied Apple'

Parrotia persica

Koelreuteria paniculata 'September Gold'

FRANKLINIA alatamaha p. 357
☼ ◐ ✄ 3B-6, 14-17

HALESIA carolina p. 383
Snowdrop tree
◐ ✄ 2B-9, 14-21

KOELREUTERIA p. 428
☼ ✄ ZONES VARY

LAGERSTROEMIA (most) p. 430
Crape myrtle
☼ ✄ ZONES VARY

LYSILOMA microphylla thornberi p. 455
Feather bush
☼ ✄ 12-24; H1, H2

MAGNOLIA (small) p. 458
☼ ◐ ✄ ZONES VARY

MALUS p. 469
Flowering crabapple
☼ ✄ 1-11, 14-21

OXYDENDRUM arboreum p. 506
Sourwood
☼ ✄ 2B-9, 14-17

PARROTIA persica p. 513
Persian parrotia
☼ ◐ ✄ 2B-7, 14-17

PRUNUS (flowering cherry) p. 596
☼ ✄ ZONES VARY

PRUNUS cerasifera p. 568
Cherry plum
☼ ✄ 3-22

Prunus × subhirtella

PRUNUS mume p. 567
Japanese flowering apricot
☼ ✄ 3-9, 12-22

SAPIUM sebiferum p. 614
Chinese tallow tree
☼ ✄ 8, 9, 12-16, 18-21; H1

STEWARTIA (small) p. 634
☼ ◐ ✄ 4-6, 14-17, 20, 21

TABEBUIA p. 642
☼ ✄ 15, 16, 20-24; H1, H2

Patio Trees, Evergreen

ACACIA podalyriifolia p. 165
Pearl acacia
☼ ✄ 8, 9, 13-24

BRUGMANSIA p. 232
Angel's trumpet
☼ ◐ ● ✄ 12, 13, 16-24; H1, H2

Cupressus arizonica

Citrus (mandarin)

CASSIA leptophylla p. 253
Gold medallion tree
☼ ✄ 15, 16, 20-24; H1, H2

CITRUS p. 276
☼ ✄ 8, 9, 12-24; H1, H2

CLETHRA arborea p. 284
Lily-of-the-valley tree
☼ ◐ ✄ 15-17, 21-24

COCCULUS laurifolius p. 285
☼ ◐ ● ✄ 8, 9, 12-24

CORDIA boissieri p. 289
Texas olive
☼ ✄ 8-24

CUPRESSUS (some) p. 303
Cypress
☼ ✄ ZONES VARY

DODONAEA viscosa p. 319
Hop bush
☼ ◐ ✄ 7-24; H1, H2

DRIMYS winteri p. 321
Winter's bark
☼ ◐ ✄ 5-9, 14-24

Arthur Lee Jacobson on Fragrant Trees

When a lilac or a crabapple tree is in bloom it can perfume an entire city block. But Seattle-based tree expert Arthur Lee Jacobson cautions against falling for the seductive charms of brief bloomers. "A mock orange is a lovely but transitory pleasure," says Jacobson. He prefers the longer lasting delights to be found in a crushed twig or a handful of fragrant foliage. Here are his suggestions for some garden trees that provide unexpected and durable sources of scent.

Abies grandis Lowland fir ("tangerine smell")

Cinnamomum camphora Camphor tree ("leaves smell like camphor when crushed")

Eucalyptus (many) ("strong odor of menthol")

Juniperus occidentalis Western juniper ("the most fragrant juniper")

Liquidambar styraciflua American sweet gum ("sweetly resinous")

Magnolia wilsonii Wilson magnolia ("rich and fruity floral fragrance lasts for months")

Toona sinensis ("pungent leaves")

Umbellularia californica California laurel ("savory smell")

Zanthoxylum piperitum Japan pepper ("powerful pepper fragrance")

Laurus nobilis

Podocarpus falcatus

Albizia julibrissin

Calodendrum capense

ERIOBOTRYA deflexa p. 334
Bronze loquat
☼ ◑ ✎ 8–24

EUCALYPTUS (some) p. 339
☼ ✎ SEE CHART

GEIJERA parviflora p. 365
Australian willow
☼ ✎ 8, 9, 12–24

HAKEA laurina p. 382
Sea urchin
☼ ✎ 9, 12–17, 19–24

**HETEROMELES
arbutifolia** p. 392
Toyon
☼ ◑ ✎ 5–9, 14–24

**LAURUS nobilis
'Saratoga'** p. 434
Sweet bay
☼ ◑ ✎ 5–9, 12–24; H1, H2

**LEPTOSPERMUM
laevigatum** p. 438
Australian tea tree
☼ ✎ 14–24; H1, H2

LIGUSTRUM p. 443
Privet
☼ ◑ ✎ ZONES VARY

**MELALEUCA
quinquenervia** p. 477
Cajeput tree
☼ ✎ 9, 12, 13, 15–17, 20–24; H1, H2

MICHELIA doltsopa p. 480
☼ ◑ ✎ 14–24; H1, H2

NERIUM oleander p. 495
Oleander
☼ ✎ 8–16, 18–24; H1, H2

**OLEA europaea
(fruitless)** p. 500
Olive
☼ ✎ 8, 9, 11–24; H1, H2

OSMANTHUS fragrans p. 505
Sweet olive
☼ ◑ ✎ 5–9, 12–24; H1

PALMS (some) p. 508
NEEDS, ZONES VARY

PHOTINIA × fraseri p. 537
✎ 3B, 4–24

PODOCARPUS p. 554
☼ ◑ ✎ ZONES VARY

PYRUS kawakamii p. 573
Evergreen pear
☼ ✎ 8, 9, 12–24

**RHAPHIOLEPIS
'Majestic Beauty'** p. 582
☼ ◑ ✎ 4–10, 12–24; H1, H2

RHUS lancea p. 590
African sumac
☼ ✎ 8, 9, 12–24

SCHEFFLERA p. 617
☼ ◑ ✎ ZONES VARY

SCHINUS terebinthefolius p. 617
Brazilian pepper tree
☼ ✎ 13–17, 19–24; H1, H2

SOPHORA secundiflora p. 628
Mescal bean
☼ ◑ ✎ 8–16, 18–24

STENOCARPUS sinuatus p. 634
Firewheel tree
☼ ✎ 16, 17, 20–24

THEVETIA thevetioides p. 647
Giant thevetia
☼ ✎ 12, 13, 22–24; H2

TRISTANIOPSIS laurina p. 655
Water gum
☼ ✎ 15–24

XYLOSMA congestum p. 673
☼ ◑ ✎ 8–24

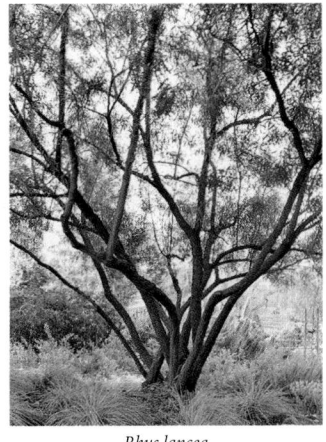

Rhus lancea

Small to Medium Trees, Deciduous

ACER griseum p. 167
Paperbark maple
☼ ◑ ✎ 2–9, 14–21

ALBIZIA julibrissin p. 178
Silk tree
☼ ◑ ✎ 4–23

ALNUS cordata p. 180
Italian alder
☼ ◑ ● ✎ 2B–9, 14–24

BETULA p. 222
Birch
☼ ✎ ZONES VARY

BRACHYCHITON p. 229
☼ ✎ ZONES VARY

CALODENDRUM capense p. 241
Cape chestnut
☼ ✎ 15, 16, 19, 21–24

CARPINUS p. 251
Hornbeam
NEEDS, ZONES VARY

CELTIS p. 259
Hackberry
☼ ◑ ✎ ZONES VARY

**CERCIDIPHYLLUM
japonicum** p. 262
Katsura tree
☼ ◑ ✎ 2B–6, 14–16, 18–20

Betula jacquemontii

Cercidiphyllum japonicum

ELAEAGNUS angustifolia p. 326
Russian olive
☼ ◑ ✎ A2, A3; 1–3, 7–14, 18, 19

ERYTHRINA (some) p. 336
Coral tree
☼ ✎ ZONES VARY

FRAXINUS (several) p. 357
Ash
☼ ✎ ZONES VARY

GLEDITSIA triacanthos p. 371
Honey locust
☼ ✎ 1–16, 18–20

Fraxinus pennsylvanica

Laburnum anagyroides

Morus alba 'Chaparral'

Parkinsonia aculeata

Pistacia chinensis

LABURNUM   p. 429
Goldenchain tree
☼ ◑ ✿ 1–10, 14–17

MAGNOLIA (many)   p. 458
☼ ◑ ✿ ZONES VARY

MALUS   p. 469
Flowering crabapple
☼ ✿ 1–11, 14–21

MORUS alba   p. 485
White mulberry
☼ ✿ 2–24; H1, H2

NYSSA sylvatica   p. 497
Sour gum
☼ ◑ ✿ 2–10, 14–21

PARKINSONIA aculeata   p. 512
Jerusalem thorn
☼ ✿ 8–24; H1, H2

PERSIMMON   p. 530
☼ ✿ ZONES VARY

PISTACIA chinensis   p. 545
Chinese pistache
☼ ✿ 4–16, 18–23

POPULUS tremuloides   p. 558
Quaking aspen
☼ ✿ A1–A3; 1–7, 14–19

PROSOPIS   p. 563
Mesquite
☼ ✿ ZONES VARY

PRUNUS   p. 564
Flowering cherry, peach, plum
☼ ✿ ZONES VARY

PUNICA granatum   p. 571
Pomegranate
☼ ✿ 5–24; H1, H2

PYRUS   p. 573
Ornamental pear
☼ ✿ ZONES VARY

SOPHORA japonica   p. 628
Japanese pagoda tree
☼ ◑ ✿ 2–24

SORBUS aucuparia   p. 629
European mountain ash
☼ ◑ ✿ A1–A3; 1–10, 14–17

STYRAX   p. 637
☼ ◑ ✿ 4–9, 14–21

Punica granatum

TILIA (most)   p. 649
Linden
☼ ✿ ZONES VARY

TIPUANA tipu   p. 650
Tipu tree
☼ ✿ 12–16, 18–24; H1, H2

VITEX agnus-castus   p. 668
Chaste tree
☼ ✿ 4–24; H1, H2

Small to Medium Trees, Evergreen

ACACIA baileyana   p. 164
Bailey acacia
☼ ✿ 8, 9, 13–24

ACACIA cognata   p. 164
Bower wattle
☼ ✿ 16–24

ACACIA pendula   p. 165
Weeping acacia
☼ ✿ 13–24

ACACIA smallii   p. 166
☼ ✿ 8, 9, 12–24

Populus tremuloides

Prunus × yedoensis

Acacia baileyana

Garrya elliptica

Magnolia stellata

Metrosideros excelsus

ACACIA stenophylla p. 166
Shoestring acacia
☼ ⚊ 8, 9, 12–24

AGONIS p. 176
☼ ◐ ⚊ 15–17, 20–24

ARBUTUS 'Marina' p. 197
☼ ⚊ 8, 9, 14–24

ARBUTUS unedo p. 197
Strawberry tree
☼ ◐ ⚊ 4–24

ARCTOSTAPHYLOS manzanita
'Dr. Hurd' p. 198
☼ ◐ ⚊ 4–9, 14–24

CALLISTEMON citrinus p. 239
Lemon bottlebrush
☼ ⚊ 8, 9, 12–24; H1, H2

CALLISTEMON viminalis p. 239
Weeping bottlebrush
☼ ⚊ 6–9, 12–24

CERATONIA siliqua p. 261
Carob
☼ ⚊ 9, 13–16, 18–24; H1

CORNUS capitata p. 291
Evergreen dogwood
☼ ◐ ⚊ 8, 9, 14–20

CRINODENDRON patagua p. 299
Lily-of-the-valley tree
☼ ⚊ 14–24

CUPRESSUS macrocarpa p. 303
Monterey cypress
☼ ⚊ 17

ERIOBOTRYA japonica p. 334
Loquat
☼ ◐ ⚊ 6–24; H1, H2

ERYTHRINA falcata p. 337
Coral tree
☼ ⚊ 19–24; H1, H2

EUCALYPTUS (many) p. 339
☼ ⚊ SEE CHART

FICUS benjamina p. 352
Benjamin tree
☼ ◐ ● ⚊ 13, 23, 24; H1, H2

FICUS microcarpa p. 353
Indian laurel fig
☼ ⚊ 9, 13, 16–24; H1, H2

FICUS rubiginosa p. 353
Rustyleaf fig
☼ ⚊ 18–24; H1, H2

GARRYA elliptica p. 363
Coast silktassel
☼ ◐ ⚊ 4–9, 14–24

HYMENOSPORUM flavum p. 402
Sweetshade
☼ ◐ ⚊ 8, 9, 14–24

ILEX (many) p. 404
Holly
☼ ◐ ⚊ ZONES VARY

LAGUNARIA patersonii p. 431
Primrose tree
☼ ⚊ 13, 15–24; H1, H2

LOPHOSTEMON confertus p. 453
Brisbane box
☼ ⚊ 15–17, 19–24; H1, H2

LUMA apiculata p. 454
☼ ⚊ 14–24

MAGNOLIA (some) p. 458
☼ ◐ ⚊ ZONES VARY

MAYTENUS boaria p. 475
Mayten
☼ ⚊ 8, 9, 14–24

MELALEUCA (several) p. 476
☼ ⚊ ZONES VARY

METROSIDEROS excelsus p. 480
New Zealand Christmas tree
☼ ◐ ⚊ 16, 17, 23, 24; H1, H2

OLNEYA tesota p. 500
Desert ironwood
☼ ⚊ 8–9, 11–14, 18–23

PICEA (some) p. 539
☼ ◐ ⚊ ZONES VARY

PINUS contorta p. 542
Shore pine
☼ ⚊ A3; 4–9, 14–24; H1

PISTACIA lentiscus p. 545
Mastic
☼ ⚊ 8, 9, 12–24

PITTOSPORUM (several) p. 545
☼ ◐ ⚊ ZONES VARY

PRUNUS caroliniana p. 564
Carolina laurel cherry
☼ ⚊ 5–24

SABAL palmetto p. 605
Cabbage palm
☼ ⚊ 12–17, 19–24; H1, H2

UMBELLULARIA californica p. 660
California laurel
☼ ◐ ● ⚊ 4–9, 14–24

Melaleuca quinquenervia

Picea

Umbellularia californica

Acer platanoides

Liriodendron tulipifera

Platanus × acerifolia

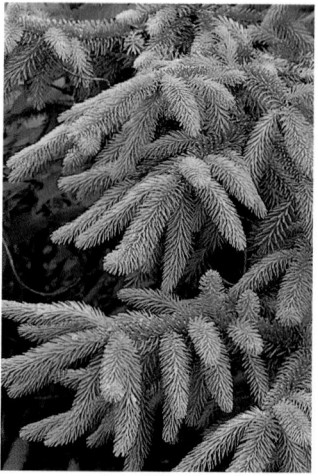
Picea mariana

Large Trees, Deciduous

ACER (several) p. 167
Maple
☼ ◐ ✦ ZONES VARY

CATALPA p. 254
☼ ◐ ✦ 3-10, 14-24

FAGUS sylvatica p. 348
European beech
☼ ◐ ✦ A3; 2B-9, 14-21

GINKGO biloba p. 369
Maidenhair tree
☼ ✦ A3; 1-10, 12, 14-24

JACARANDA mimosifolia p. 415
☼ ✦ 12, 13, 15-24; H1, H2

LARIX p. 432
Larch
☼ ✦ ZONES VARY

LIQUIDAMBAR p. 448
Sweet gum
☼ ✦ ZONES VARY

LIRIODENDRON tulipifera p. 448
Tulip tree
☼ ✦ 2-12, 14-24

METASEQUOIA glyptostroboides p. 480
Dawn redwood
☼ ✦ A3; 3-10, 14-24

NYSSA sylvatica p. 497
Sour gum
☼ ◐ ✦ 2-10, 14-21

PLATANUS p. 546
Plane tree
☼ ✦ ZONES VARY

QUERCUS (many) p. 574
Oak
☼ ✦ ZONES VARY

ROBINIA × ambigua 'Idahoensis' p. 592
Idaho locust
☼ ✦ 2-24

ROBINIA pseudoacacia p. 592
Black locust
☼ ✦ 1-24

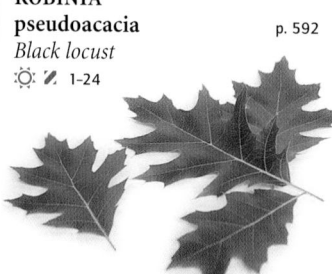
Quercus rubra

ULMUS pumila p. 660
Siberian elm
☼ ✦ A1-A3, 1, 2, 10, 11

ZELKOVA serrata p. 677
Sawleaf zelkova
☼ ✦ 3-21

Large Trees, Evergreen

CASTANOSPERMUM australe p. 254
Moreton Bay chestnut
☼ ✦ 18-22

CASUARINA cunninghamiana p. 254
River she-oak
☼ ✦ 8,9,12-24; H1, H2

CEDRUS p. 258
Cedar
☼ ✦ ZONES VARY

CINNAMOMUM camphora p. 274
Camphor tree
☼ ◐ ✦ 8, 9, 12-24; H1, H2

ELAEOCARPUS decipiens p. 326
Japanese blueberry tree
☼ ◐ ✦ 8, 9, 14-24; H1

PICEA p. 538
Spruce
☼ ◐ ✦ ZONES VARY

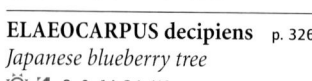

PINUS (many) p. 541
☼ ✦ ZONES VARY

QUERCUS agrifolia p. 575
Coast live oak
☼ ✦ 7-9, 14-24

QUERCUS ilex p. 576
Holly oak
☼ ✦ 4-24

QUERCUS suber p. 577
Cork oak
☼ ✦ 5-7, 8-16, 18-24

QUERCUS virginiana p. 577
Southern live oak
☼ ✦ 4-24

SEQUOIA sempervirens p. 623
Redwood
☼ ◐ ● ✦ 4-9, 14-24

TSUGA canadensis p. 657
Canada hemlock
☼ ◐ ✦ A3; 2-7, 17

Sequoia sempervirens

Jacaranda mimosifolia

Robinia pseudoacacia

Cedrus deodora

Shrubs

Size alone doesn't reliably separate trees from shrubs. Better distinguishing characteristics are aspect and use. Shrubs usually carry their foliage to ground level, revealing little or none of their branch framework. In simplest terms, you walk *under* a tree but *around* a shrub. Shrubs form the framework of a landscape—they're the stable plantings that influence views, direct circulation, and make a smooth transition from tree canopy to ground level. They can be used to punctuate the landscape and, of course, they have a traditional use as a "foundation planting" around a home. Among the shrubs listed here are many that offer seasonal focal points such as showy flowers, fruits, and autumn foliage color.

Alyogyne huegelii 'White Swan'

Anisodontea × hypomandarum

Brunfelsia pauciflora

Echium candicans

Erica ciliaris 'Maweana'

Spring, Evergreen

ABUTILON (most) p. 163
Flowering maple
☀ ◐ ✎ 8, 9, 12-24; H1, H2

ALYOGYNE huegelii p. 183
Blue hibiscus
☀ ✎ 13-17, 20-24; H1, H2

ANISODONTEA × hypomandarum p. 187
Cape mallow
☀ ◐ ✎ 14-24

BERBERIS (some) p. 221
Barberry
☀ ◐ ✎ ZONES VARY

BRUNFELSIA pauciflora p. 233
◐ ✎ 12-17, 20-24; H1, H2

CAMELLIA (many) p. 242
☀ ◐ ✎ 4-9, 12, 14-24

CEANOTHUS p. 255
Wild lilac
☀ ✎ 5-9, 14-24

CHOISYA ternata p. 270
Mexican orange
☀ ◐ ✎ 4-9, 14-24

CISTUS p. 275
Rockrose
☀ ✎ 4-9, 14-24

COLEONEMA p. 286
Breath of heaven
☀ ◐ ✎ 7-9, 14-24

COTONEASTER (some) p. 296
NEEDS, ZONES VARY

CYTISUS p. 306
Broom
☀ ✎ ZONES VARY

DAPHNE × burkwoodii p. 309
☀ ◐ ✎ 2B-6, 14-17

DENDROMECON p. 312
Bush poppy
☀ ✎ ZONES VARY

ECHIUM candicans p. 325
Pride of Madeira
☀ ✎ 14-24

ERICA (most) p. 331
Heath
☀ ◐ ✎ ZONES VARY

EURYOPS p. 347
☀ ✎ ZONES VARY

FREMONTODENDRON p. 359
Flannel bush
☀ ✎ 4-24

GAULTHERIA mucronata p. 364
☀ ◐ ✎ 4-7, 15-17

GREVILLEA (some) p. 378
NEEDS, ZONES VARY

JASMINUM (some) p. 416
Jasmine
☀ ◐ ✎ ZONES VARY

KALMIA latifolia p. 425
Mountain laurel
☀ ✎ 2-7, 16, 17

LANTANA p. 432
☀ ✎ 8-10, 12-24; H1, H2

Ceanothus 'Frosty Blue'

Fremontodendron californicum

Leptospermum scoparium 'Nanum Tui'

Loropetalum chinense 'Sizzlin' Pink'

Deutzia gracilis 'Nikko'

Forsythia

LEPTOSPERMUM   p. 438
Tea tree
☼ ✦ 14–24

LOROPETALUM chinense   p. 453
☼ ◑ ✦ 6–9, 14–24

MAHONIA (some)   p. 467
NEEDS, ZONES VARY

MELALEUCA (some)   p. 476
☼ ✦ ZONES VARY

MICHELIA figo   p. 481
Banana shrub
☼ ◑ ✦ 6, 9, 14–24; H1, H2

NANDINA domestica   p. 489
Heavenly bamboo
☼ ◑ ● ✦ 3, 4–24; H1, H2

PHLOMIS (some)   p. 534
☼ ✦ ZONES VARY

PHOTINIA (most)   p. 537
☼ ✦ ZONES VARY

PIERIS   p. 540
◑ ✦ ZONES VARY

PLUMBAGO auriculata   p. 552
Cape plumbago
☼ ◑ ✦ 8, 9, 12–24; H1, H2

PROSTANTHERA   p. 563
Mint bush
☼ ✦ 14–17, 19–24

Rhododendron 'Happy Days'

RHAPHIOLEPIS indica   p. 582
Indian hawthorn
☼ ◑ ✦ 4–10, 12–24; H1, H2

RHODODENDRON   p. 583
Azalea and rhododendron
◑ ✦ ZONES VARY

ROSMARINUS officinalis   p. 602
Rosemary
☼ ✦ 4–24; H1, H2

SOPHORA secundiflora   p. 628
Mescal bean
☼ ◑ ✦ 8–16, 18–24

VIBURNUM (some)   p. 665
NEEDS, ZONES VARY

Spring, Deciduous

BERBERIS (some)   p. 221
Barberry
☼ ◑ ✦ ZONES VARY

BUDDLEJA alternifolia   p. 234
Fountain butterfly bush
☼ ◑ ✦ 2B–24

CERCIS occidentalis   p. 262
Western redbud
☼ ◑ ✦ 2–24

CHAENOMELES   p. 264
Flowering quince
☼ ✦ 2–23

CORNUS kousa   p. 292
Kousa dogwood
☼ ◑ ✦ 2–9, 14–17

COTONEASTER (some)   p. 296
NEEDS, ZONES VARY

CYTISUS (some)   p. 306
Broom
☼ ✦ ZONES VARY

DEUTZIA   p. 313
☼ ◑ ✦ 2–11, 14–17

ENKIANTHUS   p. 327
☼ ◑ ✦ 3–9, 14–21

EXOCHORDA   p. 348
Pearl bush
☼ ✦ 2–9, 14–23

FORSYTHIA   p. 355
☼ ✦ ZONES VARY

FOTHERGILLA   p. 356
☼ ◑ ✦ 2B–9, 14–17

KERRIA japonica   p. 426
☼ ◑ ✦ 2–23

KOLKWITZIA amabilis   p. 428
Beauty bush
☼ ◑ ✦ 2–11, 14–20

LONICERA (some)   p. 451
Honeysuckle
☼ ◑ ✦ ZONES VARY

MAGNOLIA (several)   p. 458
☼ ◑ ✦ ZONES VARY

PAEONIA (tree)   p. 508
Tree peony
☼ ◑ ✦ 2–12, 14–23

PEDILANTHUS macrocarpus   p. 525
Lady's slipper
☼ ◑ ✦ 12, 13, 19–24

Mahonia aquifolium

Rosmarinus officinalis

Viburnum × burkwoodii

Paeonia
tree

Philadelphus lewisii

Ribes sanguineum

Rosa 'Abraham Darby'

Callistemon citrinus

Abelia × grandiflora

Fuchsia triphylla
'Gartenmeister Bonstedt'

Abutilon hybrid

Acalypha wilkesiana

Hypericum reptans

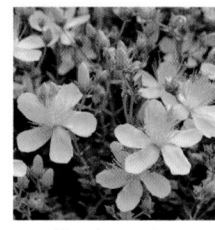

Hakea laurina

PHILADELPHUS (some) p. 533
Mock orange
☼ ◑ ✂ ZONES VARY

PHOTINIA villosa p. 537
☼ ✂ 3–9, 14–17

PHYSOCARPUS p. 538
Ninebark
☼ ◑ ● ✂ ZONES VARY

PSOROTHAMNUS spinosus p. 569
Smoke tree
☼ ✂ 12, 13

RIBES (some) p. 591
Currant
☼ ◑ ✂ ZONES VARY

RHODODENDRON p. 583
Rhododendron and azalea
NEEDS, ZONES VARY

ROSA p. 593
Rose
☼ ✂ ZONES VARY

RUBUS deliciosus p. 603
Rocky Mountain thimbleberry
☼ ◑ ✂ 1–6, 10

RUSH aromatica p. 590
Fragrant sumac
☼ ✂ 1–3, 10

SAMBUCUS (some) p. 613
Elderberry
☼ ◑ ✂ ZONES VARY

SPIRAEA (some) p. 631
☼ ◑ ✂ ZONES VARY

SYRINGA p. 640
Lilac
☼ ◑ ✂ ZONES VARY

VIBURNUM (some) p. 664
NEEDS, ZONES VARY

WEIGELA p. 670
☼ ◑ ✂ 1–11, 14–21

Summer, Evergreen

ABELIA p. 162
☼ ◑ ✂ ZONES VARY

ABUTILON p. 163
Flowering maple
☼ ◑ ✂ 8, 9, 12–24; H1, H2

ACALYPHA wilkesiana p. 166
Copper leaf
◑ ✂ 24; H2

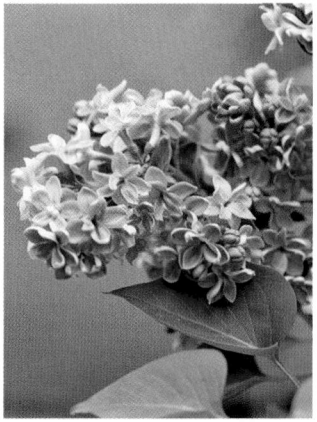

Syringa vulgaris 'Olivier de Serres'

ALLAMANDA schottii p. 179
Bush allamanda
☼ ✂ 23, 24; H1, H2

ALYOGYNE huegelii p. 183
Blue hibiscus
☼ ✂ 13–17, 20–24; H1, H2

ANISODONTEA × hypomandarum p. 187
Cape mallow
☼ ◑ ✂ 14–24

BORONIA molloyae p. 227
Pink boronia
☼ ◑ ✂ 15–17, 20–24

BRUNFELSIA pauciflora p. 233
◑ ✂ 12–17, 20–24; H1, H2

CAESALPINIA (some) p. 236
☼ ✂ ZONES VARY

CALLISTEMON p. 239
Bottlebrush
☼ ✂ ZONES VARY

CALLUNA vulgaris p. 240
Scotch heather
☼ ✂ 1A, 2–6, 15–17

CARPENTERIA californica p. 251
Bush anemone
☼ ◑ ✂ 5–9, 14–24

CERATOSTIGMA (most) p. 261
☼ ◑ ✂ ZONES VARY

DABOECIA p. 307
Irish heath
☼ ◑ ✂ ZONES VARY

ESCALLONIA p. 338
☼ ◑ ✂ 4–9, 14–24

EURYOPS pectinatus p. 347
☼ ✂ 8, 9, 12–24; H1, H2

FUCHSIA p. 360
☼ ◑ ✂ ZONES VARY

GARDENIA augusta p. 362
☼ ◑ ✂ 7–9, 12–16, 18–24; H1, H2

GREVILLEA (some) p. 378
NEEDS, ZONES VARY

GREWIA occidentalis p. 380
Lavender starflower
☼ ✂ 8, 9, 12–24; H1, H2

HEBE p. 385
☼ ◑ ✂ ZONES VARY

HETEROMELES arbutifolia p. 392
Toyon
☼ ◑ ✂ 5–9, 14–24

HIBISCUS p. 394
☼ ✂ ZONES VARY

HYPERICUM (some) p. 402
St. Johnswort
☼ ◑ ✂ ZONES VARY

JASMINUM (some) p. 416
Jasmine
☼ ◑ ✂ ZONES VARY

JUSTICIA (some) p. 423
NEEDS, ZONES VARY

LANTANA p. 432
☼ ✂ 8–10, 12–24; H1, H2

Alyogyne huegelii

Solanum rantonnetii 'Royal Robe'

Clethra alnifolia 'Hummingbird'

Spiraea cantoniensis 'Flore-Pleno'

LAVANDULA p. 434
Lavender
☼ ◼ ZONES VARY

LAVATERA p. 437
Tree mallow
☼ ◼ ZONES VARY

LEONOTIS leonuris p. 438
Lion's tail
☼ ◼ 8-24; H1, H2

LEUCOPHYLLUM p. 440
Texas ranger
☼ ◼ 7-24

MELALEUCA (some) p. 476
☼ ◼ ZONES VARY

NERIUM oleander p. 495
Oleander
☼ ◼ 8-16, 18-24; H1, H2

PLUMBAGO auriculata p. 552
Cape plumbago
☼ ◐ ◼ 8, 9, 12-24; H1, H2

SALVIA (some) p. 607
Sage
NEEDS, ZONES VARY

SOLANUM rantonnetii p. 627
☼ ◐ ◼ 12, 13, 15-24; H1, H2

SOLLYA heterophylla p. 628
Australian bluebell creeper
☼ ◐ ◼ 8, 9, 14-24; H1, H2

TECOMA stans p. 644
Yellow bells
☼ ◼ 12, 13, 21-24; H1, H2

TIBOUCHINA urvilleana p. 649
Princess flower
☼ ◐ ◼ 14-17, 21-24; H1, H2

Summer, Deciduous

ABELIA chinensis p. 162
☼ ◐ ◼ 4-24

BUDDLEJA (some) p. 233
Butterfly bush
☼ ◐ ◼ ZONES VARY

Buddleja davidii

CAESALPINIA pulcherrima p. 236
Red bird of paradise
☼ ◼ 12-16, 18-23; H1, H2

CALLICARPA p. 239
Beautyberry
☼ ◐ ◼ ZONES VARY

CARYOPTERIS p. 252
Bluebeard
☼ ◼ ZONES VARY

CERATOSTIGMA willmottianum p. 262
☼ ◐ ◼ 4-9, 14-24

CLERODENDRUM trichotomum p. 284
Harlequin glorybower
◐ ◼ 15-17, 20-24

CLETHRA p. 284
☼ ◐ ◼ ZONES VARY

Caryopteris × clandonensis

Punica granatum

DEUTZIA (some) p. 313
☼ ◐ ◼ 2-11, 14-17

FUCHSIA (some) p. 360
☼ ◐ ◼ ZONES VARY

HIBISCUS (some) p. 394
☼ ◼ ZONES VARY

HYDRANGEA p. 400
☼ ◐ ◼ ZONES VARY

PHILADELPHUS (some) p. 533
Mock orange
☼ ◐ ◼ ZONES VARY

PLUMERIA rubra p. 553
Nosegay frangipani
☼ ◐ ◼ 12, 13, 19, 21-24; H1, H2

POTENTILLA p. 555
Cinquefoil
☼ ◐ ◼ ZONES VARY

PUNICA granatum p. 571
Pomegranate
☼ ◼ 5-24; H1, H2

ROSA (some) p. 593
Rose
☼ ◐ ◼ ZONES VARY

SPIRAEA (some) p. 631
☼ ◐ ◼ ZONES VARY

Fall, Evergreen

ALYOGYNE huegelii p. 183
Blue hibiscus
☼ ◼ 13-17, 20-24; H1, H2

ANISODONTEA × hypomandarum p. 187
Cape mallow
☼ ◼ 14-24

ARBUTUS unedo p. 197
Strawberry tree
☼ ◐ ◼ 4-24

BRUGMANSIA p. 232
Angel's trumpet
☼ ◐ ● ◼ 12, 13, 16-24; H1, H2

CAMELLIA sasanqua p. 245
☼ ◐ ◼ 4-9, 12, 14-24

Hydrangea macrophylla

Daphne odora 'Marginata'

Escallonia rubra

ESCALLONIA　　　p. 338
☼ ◐ ⚬ 4–9, 14–24

FUCHSIA　　　p. 360
☼ ◐ ⚬ ZONES VARY

HIBISCUS (some)　　　p. 394
☼ ⚬ ZONES VARY

LAVATERA　　　p. 437
Tree mallow
☼ ⚬ ZONES VARY

MELALEUCA (some)　　　p. 476
☼ ⚬ ZONES VARY

NERIUM oleander　　　p. 495
Oleander
☼ ⚬ 8–16, 18–24; H1, H2

PLUMBAGO auriculata　　　p. 552
Cape plumbago
☼ ◐ ⚬ 8, 9, 12–24; H1, H2

SALVIA (some)　　　p. 607
NEEDS, ZONES VARY

TIBOUCHINA urvilleana　　　p. 649
Princess flower
☼ ◐ ⚬ 14–17, 21–24; H1, H2

Rosa 'Heritage'

Fuchsia × *hybrida* 'Lord Beaconsfield'

Salvia greggii 'Alba'

Fall, Deciduous

BUDDLEJA 'Lochinch'　　　p. 234
Butterfly bush
☼ ◐ ⚬ 3B–9, 14–24

HEPTACODIUM miconioides　　　p. 391
Seven sons flower
☼ ◐ ⚬ 2B–6, 14–17

ROSA (some)　　　p. 593
☼ ◐ ⚬ ZONES VARY

Winter, Evergreen

ACACIA (some)　　　p. 164
☼ ⚬ ZONES VARY

CAMELLIA (many)　　　p. 242
☼ ⚬ 4–9, 12, 14–24

CHAMAELAUCIUM uncinatum　　　p. 265
Geraldton waxflower
☼ ⚬ 8, 9, 12–24

COLEONEMA　　　p. 286
Breath of heaven
☼ ◐ ⚬ 7–9, 14–24

Acacia longifolia

Camellia hybrid

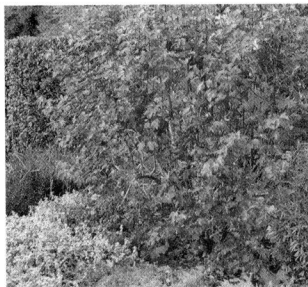

Viburnum opulus

DABOECIA　　　p. 307
Irish heath
☼ ◐ ⚬ 3B–9, 14–24

DAPHNE odora　　　p. 310
Winter daphne
☼ ◐ ⚬ 4–10, 12, 14–24

ERICA (many)　　　p. 331
Heath
☼ ◐ ⚬ ZONES VARY

EUPHORBIA pulcherrima　　　p. 346
Poinsettia
☼ ⚬ 13, 16–24; H1, H2

GREVILLEA (some)　　　p. 378
NEEDS, ZONES VARY

JASMINUM mesnyi　　　p. 416
Primrose jasmine
☼ ◐ ⚬ 4–24; H1, H2

MAHONIA (some)　　　p. 467
NEEDS, ZONES VARY

PROTEA (several)　　　p. 564
☼ ⚬ 16, 17, 21–24; H1

RHODODENRON　　　p. 588
Azalea Kurume hybrids
☼ ⚬ 5–9, 14–24; H1, H2

SENNA　　　p. 622
NEEDS, ZONES VARY

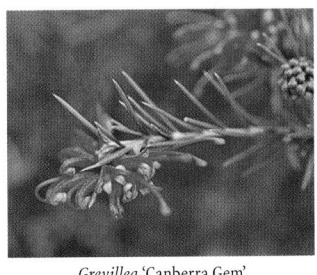

Grevillea 'Canberra Gem'

VIBURNUM (some)　　　p. 664
NEEDS, ZONES VARY

WESTRINGIA fruticosa　　　p. 670
Coast rosemary
☼ ⚬ 8, 9, 14–24

Winter, Deciduous

ABELIOPHYLLUM distichum　　　p. 162
White forsythia
☼ ◐ ⚬ 1–11, 14–19

CHAENOMELES　　　p. 264
Flowering quince
☼ ⚬ 2–23

CHIMONANTHUS praecox　　　p. 268
Wintersweet
☼ ◐ ⚬ 4–9, 14–21

CORNUS mas　　　p. 292
Cornelian cherry
☼ ◐ ⚬ 1–6

CORYLOPSIS　　　p. 294
Winter hazel
☼ ◐ ⚬ ZONES VARY

DAPHNE (some)　　　p. 309
NEEDS, ZONES VARY

FORSYTHIA　　　p. 355
☼ ◐ ⚬ ZONES VARY

HAMAMELIS (most)　　　p. 383
Witch hazel
☼ ◐ ⚬ ZONES VARY

JASMINUM nudiflorum　　　p. 416
Winter jasmine
☼ ◐ ⚬ 2–21

KERRIA japonica　　　p. 426
☼ ◐ ⚬ 2–23

RIBES　　　p. 591
Currant
☼ ◐ ⚬ ZONES VARY

Hamamelis × *intermedia* 'Velena'

Hedges & Screens

Whether you want to block out noise or traffic or to divide areas of the garden, plants with densely packed foliage from top to bottom make ideal living fences. Large shrubs are good candidates for screens; if grouped close together, they can block an objectionable view or direct attention to a garden focal point. Shearing can transform some plants into formal hedges. Low-growing shrubby plants are useful for edging walks or paths.

Symbol ▲▲▲ indicates plants that can be clipped into formal shapes.

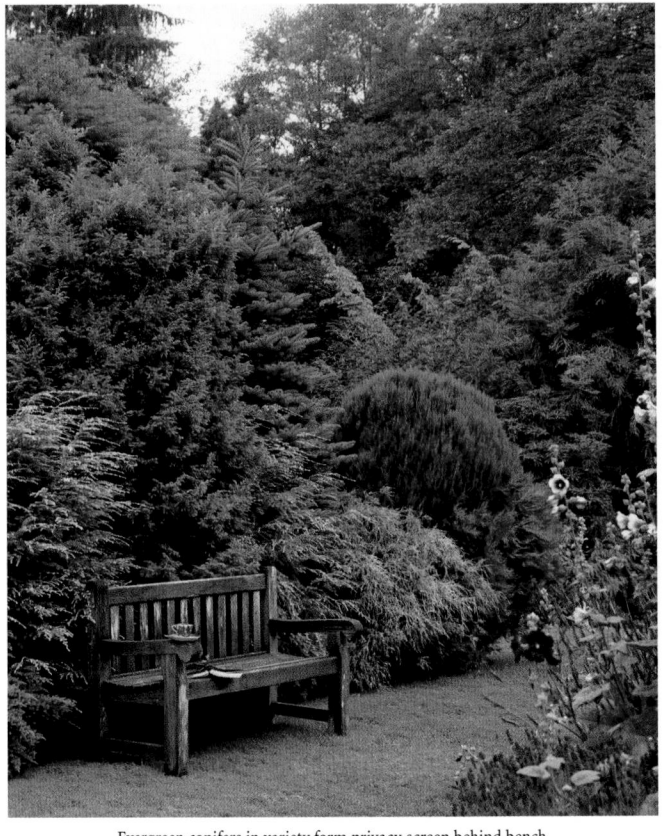

Evergreen conifers in variety form privacy screen behind bench.

Deciduous

ACER campestre — p. 167
Hedge maple
☼ ◑ ▲▲▲ ✂ 2–9, 14–17

BERBERIS (some) — p. 221
Barberry
☼ ◑ ▲▲▲ ✂ ZONES VARY

CARPINUS betulus — p. 251
European hornbeam
☼ ◑ ▲▲▲ ✂ 2–9, 14–17

CHAENOMELES — p. 264
Flowering quince
☼ ✂ 2–23

CRATAEGUS monogyna — p. 299
☼ ▲▲▲ ✂ 1–12, 14–17

ELAEAGNUS angustifolia — p. 326
Russian olive
☼ ◑ ✂ A2, A3; 1–3, 7–14, 18, 19

LIGUSTRUM (some) — p. 443
Privet
☼ ◑ ▲▲▲ ✂ ZONES VARY

MACLURA pomifera — p. 458
Osage orange
☼ ✂ 2, 3, 10–13

**RHAMNUS frangula
'Columnaris'** — p. 581
Tallhedge buckthorn
☼ ◑ ▲▲▲ ✂ 1–7, 10, 11

Berberis thunbergii 'Atropurpurea'

SALIX purpurea 'Gracilis' — p. 607
Dwarf purple osier
☼ ✂ A2, A3; 1–11

**VIBURNUM opulus
'Nanum'** — p. 665
European cranberry bush
☼ ◑ ✂ A2, A3; 1–9, 14–24

Evergreen

ABELIA × grandiflora — p. 162
Glossy abelia
☼ ◑ ✂ 4–24; H1, H2

ARBUTUS unedo — p. 197
Strawberry tree
☼ ◑ ✂ 4–24

BAMBOO (many) — p. 212
☼ ◑ ✂ ZONES VARY

BERBERIS (some) — p. 221
Barberry
☼ ◑ ▲▲▲ ✂ ZONES VARY

BUXUS — p. 235
Boxwood
☼ ◑ ● ▲▲▲ ✂ ZONES VARY

CALLISTEMON (some) — p. 239
Bottlebrush
☼ ▲▲▲ ✂ ZONES VARY

CALOCEDRUS decurrens — p. 241
Incense cedar
☼ ◑ ✂ 2–12, 14–24

CARISSA macrocarpa — p. 251
Natal plum
☼ ◑ ● ▲▲▲ ✂ 22–24; H2

**CHAMAECYPARIS
lawsoniana (several)** — p. 264
Port Orford cedar
☼ ◑ ✂ A3; 3–6, 15–17

CHOISYA TERNATA — p. 270
Mexican orange
☼ ◑ ✂ 4–9, 14–24

CITRUS — p. 276
☼ ✂ 8, 9, 12–24; H1, H2

**× CUPRESSOCYPARIS
leylandii** — p. 302
☼ ▲▲▲ ✂ 3B–24

CUPRESSUS (most) — p. 303
Cypress
☼ ▲▲▲ ✂ ZONES VARY

DODONAEA viscosa — p. 319
Hop bush
☼ ◑ ✂ 7–24; H1, H2

Chaenomeles

Abelia × grandiflora

Arbutus unedo

Callistemon citrinus

Euonymus japonicus 'Aureo-Variegatus'

ELAEAGNUS (some) p. 325
☼ ◐ ✸✸✸ ✂ ZONES VARY

ESCALLONIA p. 338
☼ ◐ ✸✸✸ ✂ 4–9, 14–24

EUONYMUS (most) p. 344
NEEDS, ZONES VARY ✸✸✸

FEIJOA, Pineapple Guava p. 350
☼ ✂ 6–9, 12–24; H1, H2

GARRYA elliptica p. 363
Coast silktassel
☼ ◐ ✂ 4–9, 14–24

GREVILLEA (many) p. 378
NEEDS, ZONES VARY

HETEROMELES arbutifolia
Toyon p. 392
☼ ◐ ✂ 5–9, 14–24

HIBISCUS rosa-sinensis p. 395
Chinese hibiscus
☼ ✂ 9, 12–16, 19–24; H1, H2

ILEX p. 404
Holly
☼ ◐ ✸✸✸ ✂ ZONES VARY

JUNIPERUS
(shrub, columnar) p. 418
Juniper
☼ ◐ ✸✸✸ ✂ ZONES VARY

LEPTOSPERMUM (most) p. 438
Tea tree
☼ ✸✸✸ ✂ 14–24

Hibiscus rosa-sinensis 'Brilliant'

LEUCOPHYLLUM
frutescens p. 440
Texas ranger
☼ ✂ 7–24, H1, H2

LIGUSTRUM (some) p. 443
Privet
☼ ◐ ✸✸✸ ✂ ZONES VARY

MAHONIA (tall) p. 467
NEEDS, ZONES VARY

MYRICA californica p. 488
Pacific wax myrtle
☼ ✸✸✸ ✂ 4–9, 14–24

MYRSINE africana p. 488
African boxwood
☼ ◐ ✸✸✸ ✂ 8, 9, 14–24

MYRTUS communis p. 488
Myrtle
☼ ◐ ✸✸✸ ✂ 8–24; H1, H2

NANDINA domestica p. 489
Heavenly bamboo
☼ ◐ ● ✂ 3–24; H1, H2

NERIUM oleander p. 495
Oleander
☼ ✂ 8–16, 18–24; H1, H2

OSMANTHUS (several) p. 504
☼ ◐ ✂ ZONES VARY

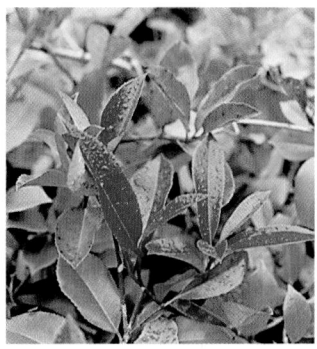

Photinia × fraseri

PHOTINIA p. 537
☼ ✂ ZONES VARY

PITTOSPORUM (several) p. 545
☼ ◐ ✸✸✸ ✂ ZONES VARY

PODOCARPUS p. 554
☼ ◐ ✂ ZONES VARY

PRUNUS (evergreen) p. 564
NEEDS, ZONES VARY ✸✸✸

PYRACANTHA p. 572
Firethorn
☼ ✸✸✸ ✂ ZONES VARY

RHAMNUS (many) p. 581
NEEDS, ZONES VARY ✸✸✸

RHAPHIOLEPIS p. 582
☼ ◐ ✂ 4–10, 12–24; H1, H2

SYZYGIUM paniculatum p. 641
Brush cherry
☼ ◐ ✸✸✸ ✂ 16, 17, 20–24; H1, H2

TAXUS p. 644
Yew
☼ ◐ ● ✸✸✸ ✂ ZONES VARY

TECOMA capensis p. 644
Cape honeysuckle
☼ ◐ ✂ 12, 13, 20–24; H1, H2

TEUCRIUM fruticans p. 646
Bush germander
☼ ✂ 4–24

THUJA p. 646
Arborvitae
☼ ◐ ✸✸✸ ✂ ZONES VARY

Bambusa multiplex (Bamboo)

VACCINIUM ovatum p. 661
Evergreen huckleberry
☼ ◐ ● ✂ 4–7, 14–17, 22–24

VIBURNUM (several) p. 664
NEEDS, ZONES VARY

XYLOSMA congestum p. 673
☼ ◐ ✸✸✸ ✂ 8–24

Pyracantha

Taxus baccata

Garrya elliptica

Nandina domestica

Thuja occidentalis

Xylosma congestum

Vines

Vines are among the most tractable of plants. In contrast to the generally rigid and inflexible branches of trees and shrubs, their stems are fairly limber and can be guided to grow in any direction you want—upward or outward on a wall or fence, up and around a post or tree trunk, up and over an arbor or pergola. Many can also serve as ground covers. Though all vines have long, pliable stems, they climb in different ways. Some are equipped with tendrils; some twine; others cling (see page 740). And some are scrambling plants with no natural means of attachment; they climb only if their stems are securely tied to a support.

Evergreen

ALLAMANDA cathartica p. 179
Allamanda
☼ ✎ 23, 24; H1, H2

BEAUMONTIA grandiflora p. 219
Herald's trumpet
☼ ◑ ✎ 12, 13, 16, 17, 21–24; H1, H2

BIGNONIA capreolata p. 223
Crossvine
☼ ◑ ✎ 4–9, 14–24

BOUGAINVILLEA p. 227
☼ ✎ 5, 6, 12–17, 19, 21–24; H1, H2

CISSUS p. 275
NEEDS, ZONES VARY

CLEMATIS armandii p. 282
Evergreen clematis
☼ ✎ 4–9, 12–24

CLYTOSTOMA callistegioides p. 285
Violet trumpet vine
☼ ◑ ✎ 8, 9, 12–24

DALECHAMPIA dioscoreifolia p. 309
Costa Rican butterfly vine
☼ ◑ ✎ 17–24

DISTICTIS p. 318
☼ ◑ ✎ ZONES VARY

EUONYMUS fortunei (some) p. 344
☼ ◑ ● ✎ 2B–17

FALLOPIA baldschuanica p. 349
Silver lace vine
☼ ✎ A1–A3; 1–24

GELSEMIUM sempervirens p. 365
Carolina jessamine
☼ ◑ ✎ 4–24

HARDENBERGIA p. 384
Lilac vine
☼ ◑ ✎ ZONES VARY

HIBBERTIA scandens p. 394
Guinea gold vine
☼ ◑ ✎ 16, 17, 21–24

JASMINUM (several) p. 416
Jasmine
☼ ◑ ✎ ZONES VARY

LAPAGERIA rosea p. 432
Chilean bellflower
◑ ✎ 5, 6, 15–17, 23, 24

LONICERA (several) p. 451
Honeysuckle
☼ ◑ ✎ ZONES VARY

Jasminum angulare

MACFADYENA unguis-cati p. 457
Cat's claw
☼ ◑ ✎ 8–24; H1, H2

MANDEVILLA p. 473
☼ ◑ ✎ ZONES VARY

MERREMIA p. 479
Yellow morning glory
☼ ✎ ZONES VARY

MILLETTIA reticulata p. 481
Evergreen wisteria
☼ ✎ 6–9, 14–24

MUEHLENBECKIA complexa p. 486
Mattress vine
☼ ◑ ✎ 8, 9, 14–24

PANDOREA p. 510
☼ ◑ ✎ 16–24; H1, H2

PASSIFLORA (some) p. 514
Passion vine
☼ ◑ ✎ ZONES VARY

PETREA volubilis p. 531
Queen's wreath
☼ ✎ 19–24; H1, H2

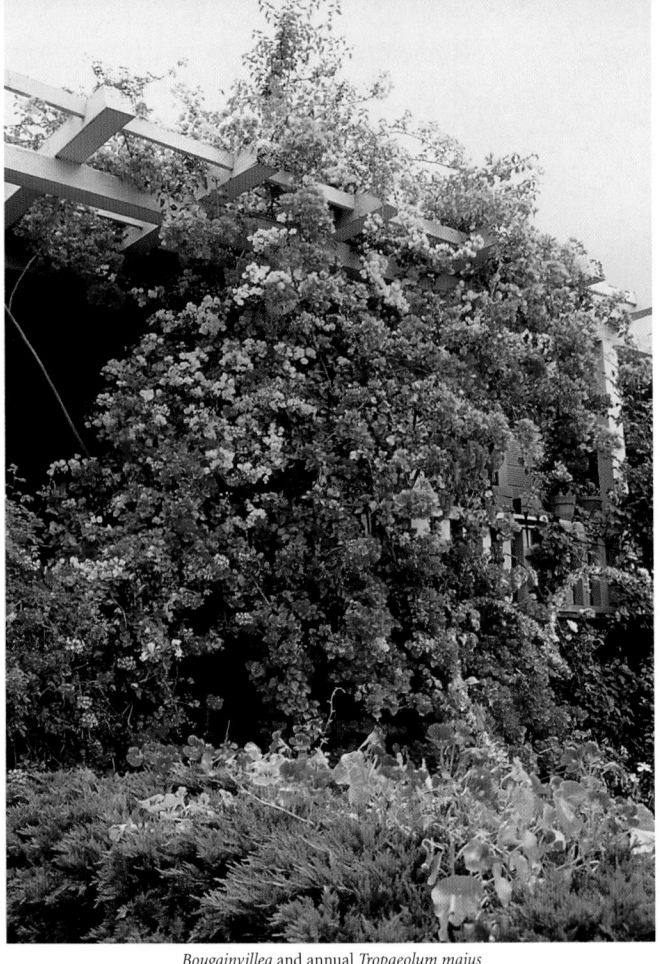
Bougainvillea and annual *Tropaeolum majus*

Mandevilla splendens 'Scarlet Pimpernel'

Passiflora jamesonii 'Coral Glow'

Solanum jasminoides

PODRANEA ricasoliana p. 554
Pink trumpet vine
☼ ◐ ✎ 9, 12, 13, 19–24; H1, H2

PYROSTEGIA venusta p. 573
Flame vine
☼ ✎ 13, 16, 21–24; H1, H2

RHOICISSUS capensis p. 590
Evergreen grape
☼ ✎ 16, 17, 21–24; H2

SOLANDRA maxima p. 626
Cup-of-gold vine
☼ ✎ 15–24; H2

SOLANUM (some) p. 627
☼ ◐ ✎ ZONES VARY

STEPHANOTIS floribunda p. 634
Madagascar jasmine
◐ ✎ 23, 24; H2

STREPTOSOLEN jamesonii p. 637
Marmalade bush
☼ ◐ ✎ 13, 16, 17, 23, 24; H1

TECOMA capensis p. 644
Cape honeysuckle
☼ ◐ ✎ 12, 13, 20–24; H1, H2

THUNBERGIA p. 647
☼ ◐ ✎ ZONES VARY

TRACHELOSPERMUM p. 653
Star jasmine
☼ ◐ ✎ ZONES VARY

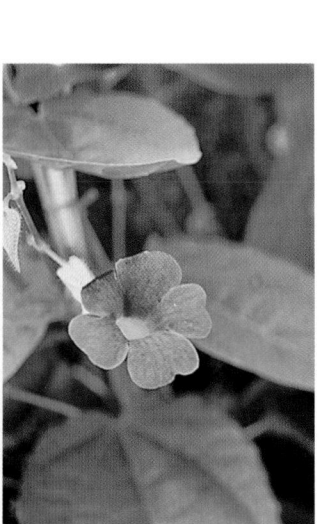

Thunbergia grandiflora

Deciduous

ACTINIDIA kolomikta p. 171
☼ ◐ ✎ A1–A3; 1–9, 14–17

AKEBIA quinata p. 177
Fiveleaf akebia
☼ ◐ ● ✎ 2–24

AMPELOPSIS brevipedunculata p. 184
Porcelain berry
☼ ◐ ● ✎ 2–24

ANTIGONON leptopus p. 188
Coral vine
☼ ✎ 12, 13, 18–24; H1, H2

ARISTOLOCHIA p. 200
NEEDS, ZONES VARY

CAMPSIS p. 246
Trumpet creeper
☼ ◐ ✎ ZONES VARY

CELASTRUS p. 258
Bittersweet
☼ ✎ ZONES VARY

CLEMATIS (most) p. 281
☼ ◐ ✎ ZONES VARY

FALLOPIA baldschuanica p. 349
Silver lace vine
☼ ✎ A1, A3; 1–24

GRAPE p. 373
☼ ◐ ✎ ZONES VARY

Aristolochia

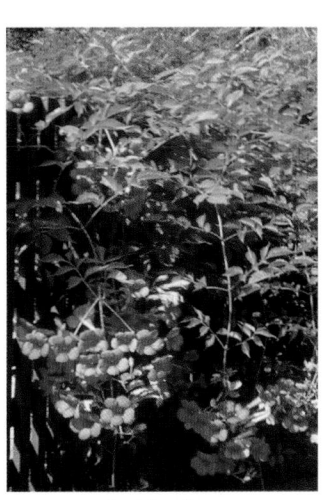

Campsis radicans

HUMULUS lupulus p. 399
Common hop
☼ ✎ A2, A3; 1–10, 14–21

HYDRANGEA anomala petiolaris p. 401
Climbing hydrangea
☼ ◐ ✎ A2, A3; 2–21

IPOMOEA p. 408
Morning glory
☼ ✎ ZONES VARY

JASMINUM nudiflorum p. 416
Winter jasmine
☼ ◐ ✎ 2–21

LONICERA (some) p. 451
Honeysuckle
☼ ◐ ✎ ZONES VARY

MANDEVILLA laxa p. 473
Chilean jasmine
☼ ✎ 4–9, 14–24; H1

MASCAGNIA p. 474
Orchid vine
☼ ✎ 12–24

PARTHENOCISSUS p. 513
NEEDS, ZONES VARY

Clematis 'Etoile Violette'

Vitis (grape)

PASSIFLORA (some) p. 514
Passion vine
☼ ◐ ✎ ZONES VARY

ROSA (climbing types) p. 593
Rose
☼ ✎ ZONES VARY

SCHIZOPHRAGMA hydrangeoides p. 618
Japanese hydrangea vine
◐ ✎ 2–9, 14–17

SOLANUM wendlandii p. 627
Costa Rican nightshade
☼ ◐ ✎ 16, 21–24; H1, H2

VIGNA caracalla p. 666
Snail vine
☼ ✎ 12–24; H1, H2

VITIS p. 668
Grape
☼ ◐ ✎ ZONES VARY

WISTERIA p. 671
NEEDS, ZONES VARY

Wisteria sinensis

Ground Covers

Lawn is the best-known ground cover, unsurpassed as a surface to walk and play on. But where foot traffic is undesirable or infrequent, many other plants offer much of a lawn's neatness with far less maintenance. These plants run the gamut of foliage textures and colors, and many are noted for their flowers; you can combine different plants to form a lovely tapestry. Heights vary from virtually flat to knee-high. Some spread by rooting stems or underground runners; others form clumps and require close spacing to achieve a solid cover. Shrubby types spread from individual root systems; space them according to their expected width at maturity.

Symbol ⚘ indicates ground covers that can take some foot traffic.

Sasa veitchii (Bamboo)

Campanula portenschlagiana

Diascia 'Little Charmer'

Perennials

Armeria maritima

ACHILLEA tomentosa p. 170
Woolly yarrow
☼ ⚡ A1–A3; 1–24

AEGOPODIUM podagraria p. 173
Bishop's weed
☼ ◐ ● ⚡ A1–A3; 1–9, 12, 14–24

AJUGA reptans p. 177
Carpet bugle
☼ ◐ ⚡ A2, A3; 1–24

ALCHEMILLA p. 178
Lady's-mantle
☼ ◐ ⚡ ZONES VARY

ANEMONE blanda p. 185
Windflower
◐ ⚡ 2–9, 14–23

APTENIA cordifolia p. 195
☼ ◐ ● ⚡ 12, 13, 15–17, 21–24; H1, H2

ARABIS p. 196
Rockcress
☼ ⚡ ZONES VARY

ARCTOTHECA calendula p. 198
Cape weed
☼ ⚡ 8, 9, 13–24

ARENARIA p. 199
Sandwort
NEEDS, ZONES VARY

ARMERIA p. 200
Thrift
NEEDS, ZONES VARY

ARTEMISIA (several) p. 201
☼ ⚡ ZONES VARY

Aptenia cordifolia 'Red Apple'

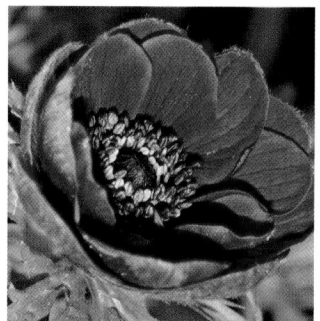
Anemone blanda

ASARUM p. 203
Wild ginger
◐ ● ⚡ ZONES VARY

ASTILBE chinensis 'Pumila' p. 208
False spiraea
☼ ◐ ⚡ ZONES A2, A3, 1–9, 14–24

BAMBOO (several) p. 212
☼ ◐ ⚡ ZONES VARY

BERGENIA p. 222
◐ ● ⚡ A1–A3; 1–9, 12–24

CAMPANULA (some) p. 246
Bellflower
☼ ◐ ⚡ 1–9, 14–24

CAREX comans p. 250
New Zealand hair sedge
☼ ◐ ⚡ 2B–9, 14–24

CAREX flacca p. 250
Blue sedge
☼ ◐ ⚡ 3–9, 14–24

CERASTIUM tomentosum p. 261
Snow-in-summer
☼ ◐ ⚡ A1, A2; 1–24

CERATOSTIGMA plumbaginoides p. 261
Dwarf plumbago
☼ ◐ ⚡ 2B–10, 14–24

CHAMAEMELUM nobile ⚘ p. 265
Chamomile
☼ ◐ ⚡ 2–24

CONVALLARIA majalis p. 288
Lily-of-the-valley
☼ ⚡ A1–A3; 1–7, 14–20

CONVOLVULUS sabatius p. 288
Ground morning glory
☼ ◐ ⚡ 4–9, 12–24

CORONILLA varia p. 293
Crown vetch
☼ ⚡ 1–24

CYMBALARIA muralis p. 304
Kenilworth ivy
◐ ● ⚡ 3B–24

DAMPIERA diversifolia p. 309
☼ ⚡ 15–24

DIASCIA p. 314
Twinspur
☼ ◐ ⚡ ZONES VARY

DICHONDRA micrantha ⚘ p. 315
☼ ◐ ⚡ 8–10, 12–24; H1, H2

DRYAS p. 321
☼ ⚡ A1–A3; 1–6

Convallaria majalis

Dichondra micrantha

Festuca glauca

Origanum vulgare 'Wood's Compact'

Dryas octopetala

Galium odoratum

Gazania hybrid

Osteopermum fruticosum

DUCHESNEA indica   p. 322
Indian mock strawberry
☼ ◑ ● ✓ 1–24; H1, H2

DYMONDIA margaretae   p. 322
☼ ◑ ✓ 15–24

EPIMEDIUM   p. 329
◑ ✓ 2–9, 14–17

ERIGERON karvinskianus   p. 331
Mexican daisy
☼ ◑ ● ✓ 8, 9, 12–24; H1, H2

ERODIUM reichardii   p. 335
Cranesbill
☼ ◑ ✓ 7–9, 14–24

FESTUCA   p. 351
Fescue
☼ ◑ ✓ ZONES VARY

FRAGARIA chiloensis   p. 356
Beach strawberry
☼ ◑ ✓ 4–24; H1

GALIUM odoratum   p. 362
Sweet woodruff
◑ ● ✓ A2, A3; 2–6, 15–17

GAZANIA   p. 364
NEEDS, ZONES VARY

GERANIUM (some)   p. 366
Cranesbill
☼ ◑ ✓ ZONES VARY

GLECHOMA hederacea   p. 371
Ground ivy
☼ ◑ ● ✓ A2, A3; 1–10, 14–24

GYPSOPHILA repens   p. 382
☼ ✓ 1–11, 14–16, 18–21

HERNIARIA glabra ✿   p. 392
Green carpet
☼ ◑ ● ✓ 2B–24

Erigeron karvinskianus

HOUTTUYNIA cordata   p. 398
☼ ◑ ● ✓ 2–9, 14–24

ICE PLANTS   p. 404
NEEDS, ZONES VARY

LAMIUM   p. 431
Dead nettle
◑ ● ✓ ZONES VARY

LIRIOPE spicata   p. 449
Creeping lily turf
☼ ◑ ● ✓ 3–10, 14–24; H1, H2

LOTUS   p. 453
☼ ◑ ✓ ZONES VARY

LYSIMACHIA (some)   p. 456
☼ ◑ ✓ ZONES VARY

MAZUS reptans   p. 475
☼ ◑ ✓ 1–9, 14–24

NEPETA (some)   p. 494
☼ ◑ ✓ 1–24

NIEREMBERGIA   p. 496
Cup flower
☼ ◑ ✓ ZONES VARY

OENOTHERA (many)   p. 498
Evening primrose
☼ ◑ ✓ ZONES VARY

OPHIOPOGON japonicus   p. 501
Mondo grass
☼ ◑ ● ✓ 5–9, 14–24; H1, H2

ORIGANUM (some)   p. 502
Oregano, marjoram
☼ ◑ ✓ ZONES VARY

OSTEOSPERMUM fruticosum   p. 505
Trailing African daisy
☼ ✓ 8, 9, 12–24; H1, H2

OXALIS oregana   p. 506
Redwood sorrel
☼ ◑ ● ✓ 4–9, 14–24

PACHYSANDRA terminalis   p. 507
Japanese spurge
◑ ● ✓ 2–10, 14–21

PELARGONIUM peltatum   p. 525
Ivy geranium
☼ ◑ ✓ A2, A3; 1–24

PERSICARIA (several)   p. 530
Knotweed
☼ ◑ ✓ ZONES VARY

PHLOX subulata   p. 535
Moss pink
☼ ◑ ✓ 1–17

Dymondia margaretae

Herniaria glabra

Persicaria capitata

Pratia pedunculata

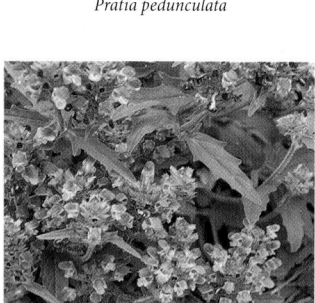

Prunella grandiflora

PHYLA nodiflora ⚘ p. 538
Lippia
☼ ⚡ 8-24; H1, H2

**PLECOSTACHYS
serpyllifolia** p. 547
☼ ⚡ 8, 9, 14-24

POTENTILLA (several) p. 555
Cinquefoil
☼ ◐ ⚡ ZONES VARY

PRATIA ⚘ p. 560
☼ ◐ ⚡ 4-9, 14-24

PRUNELLA p. 564
Self-heal
☼ ◐ ⚡ 2-24

PULMONARIA (several) p. 570
Lungwort
◐ ● ⚡ 1-9, 14-17

**RANUNCULUS
repens pleniflorus** p. 579
Creeping buttercup
☼ ◐ ● ⚡ 1-10, 14-24

SAGINA subulata ⚘ p. 605
Irish moss
☼ ◐ ⚡ 1-11, 14-24

Thymus

Saxifraga stolonifera

Sedum

SAPONARIA ocymoides p. 615
☼ ⚡ 1-11, 14-24

SAXIFRAGA p. 615
Saxifrage
◐ ● ⚡ ZONES VARY

SCAEVOLA p. 616
☼ ⚡ 8, 9, 14-24; H1, H2

SEDUM (many) p. 620
Stonecrop
☼ ◐ ⚡ ZONES VARY

SENECIO mandraliscae p. 622
☼ ◐ ⚡ 12, 13, 16, 17, 21-24; H1, H2

SENECIO serpens p. 622
☼ ◐ ⚡ 16, 17, 21-24

SOLEIROLIA soleirolii p. 627
Baby's tears
☼ ◐ ⚡ 4-24; H1, H2

TEUCRIUM (some) p. 645
Germander
☼ ⚡ ZONES VARY

THYMUS (some) p. 648
Thyme
☼ ◐ ⚡ ZONES VARY

Vinca major

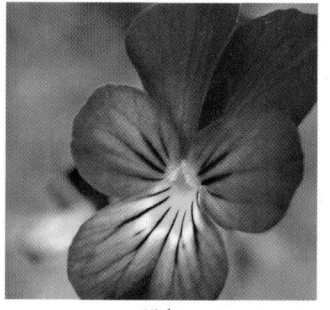

Viola

VANCOUVERIA p. 661
☼ ◐ ⚡ ZONES VARY

VERBENA (many) p. 663
☼ ⚡ ZONES VARY

VERONICA (several) p. 663
Speedwell
☼ ⚡ ZONES VARY

VINCA p. 666
Periwinkle
☼ ◐ ● ⚡ ZONES VARY

VIOLA (several) p. 666
Viola
NEEDS, ZONES VARY

ZAUSCHNERIA p. 675
California fuchsia
NEEDS, ZONES VARY

ZOYSIA tenuifolia ⚘ p. 677
Korean grass
☼ ◐ ⚡ 8, 9, 12-24; H1, H2

Shrubs

**ABELIA× grandiflora
'Prostrata'** p. 162
Glossy abelia
☼ ◐ ⚡ 4-24; H1, H2

ACACIA redolens p. 166
☼ ⚡ 8, 9, 12-24

**ARCTOSTAPHYLOS
(several)** p. 197
Manzanita
☼ ◐ ⚡ ZONES VARY

ARDISIA japonica p. 199
Marlberry
◐ ● ⚡ 6, 15-17

Arctostaphylos 'Emerald Carpet'

Calluna vulgaris 'Carmen'

Carissa macrocarpa

ATRIPLEX semibaccata p. 209
Australian saltbush
☼ ⚡ 8-10, 12-24

BACCHARIS pilularis p. 212
Dwarf coyote brush
☼ ⚡ 5-11, 14-24

CALLUNA vulgaris (some) p. 240
Scotch heather
☼ ⚡ 1A, 2-6, 15-17

**CAMELLIA
sasanqua (some)** p. 245
☼ ◐ ⚡ 4-9, 12, 14-24

**CARISSA macrocarpa
(some)** p. 251
Natal plum
☼ ◐ ⚡ 22-24; H2

CEANOTHUS (some) p. 255
Wild lilac
☼ ⚡ 5-9, 14-24

CISTUS (some) p. 275
Rockrose
☼ ⚡ 4-9, 14-24

COPROSMA (some) p. 288
☼ ◐ ⚡ ZONES VARY

CORNUS canadensis p. 291
Bunchberry
☼ ● ⚡ A1-A3; 1-9, 14-16

Cistus 'Sunset'

CORREA (some) p. 293
Australian fuchsia
☼ ◑ ✎ 14-24

COTONEASTER (some) p. 296
☼ ✎ ZONES VARY

ERICA (some) p. 331
Heath
☼ ✎ ZONES VARY

EUONYMUS fortunei (some) p. 344
☼ ◑ ● ✎ 2B-17

FORSYTHIA (some) p. 355
☼ ✎ ZONES VARY

GAULTHERIA (some) p. 364
☼ ✎ ZONES VARY

GENISTA (some) p. 365
Broom
☼ ✎ ZONES VARY

GREVILLEA (several) p. 378
NEEDS, ZONES VARY

HELIANTHEMUM nummularium p. 387
Sunrose
☼ ✎ 2B-9, 14-24

HYPERICUM (some) p. 402
St. Johnswort
☼ ◑ ✎ ZONES VARY

JUNIPERUS (many) p. 419
Juniper
☼ ◑ ✎ ZONES VARY

LANTANA (some) p. 432
☼ ✎ 8-10, 12-24; H1, H2

MAHONIA (some) p. 467
NEEDS, ZONES VARY

Correa reflexa

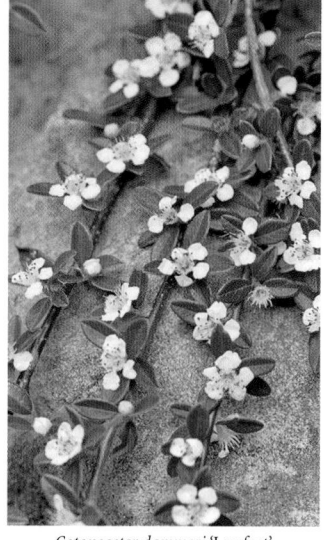

Cotoneaster dammeri 'Lowfast'

MYOPORUM (some) p. 487
☼ ✎ ZONES VARY

NANDINA domestica (some) p. 489
Heavenly bamboo
☼ ◑ ● ✎ 3-24; H1, H2

PAXISTIMA canbyi p. 515
☼ ◑ ✎ 1-10, 14-21

PYRACANTHA (some) p. 572
Firethorn
☼ ✎ ZONES VARY

RHUS aromatica p. 590
Fragrant sumac
☼ ✎ 1-3, 10

RIBES viburnifolium p. 592
Catalina perfume
☼ ◑ ✎ 5, 7-9, 14-17, 19-24

ROSMARINUS officinalis (some) p. 602
Rosemary
☼ ✎ 4-24; H1, H2

RUBUS pentalobus p. 603
☼ ◑ ✎ 4-6, 14-17

SANTOLINA p. 614
☼ ✎ ZONES VARY

SARCOCOCCA hookeriana humilis p. 615
Sweet box
◑ ● ✎ 3-9, 14-24

SOLLYA heterophylla p. 628
Australian bluebell creeper
☼ ◑ ✎ 8, 9, 14-24; H1, H2

TAXUS baccata 'Repandens' p. 644
Spreading English yew
☼ ◑ ● ✎ A3; 3-9, 14-24

VACCINIUM vitis-idaea p. 661
Cowberry
◑ ● ✎ 2-7, 14-17

Erica cinerea 'Purple Beauty'

Parthenocissus quinquefolia

Hedera helix

Helianthemum nummularium 'Buttercup'

Gelsemium sempervirens

Lonicera japonica

Vines

AKEBIA quinata p. 177
Fiveleaf akebia
☼ ◑ ● ✎ 2-24

BOUGAINVILLEA p. 227
☼ ✎ 5, 6, 12-17, 19, 21, 22-24; H1, H2

CISSUS (some) p. 275
NEEDS, ZONES VARY

× FATSHEDERA lizei p. 350
◑ ● ✎ 4-10, 12-24; H1, H2

GELSEMIUM sempervirens p. 365
Carolina jessamine
☼ ◑ ✎ 4-24

HEDERA p. 385
Ivy
☼ ◑ ✎ ZONES VARY

HIBBERTIA scandens p. 394
Guinea gold vine
☼ ◑ ✎ 16, 17, 21-24

JASMINUM (some) p. 416
Jasmine
☼ ◑ ✎ ZONES VARY

LONICERA japonica p. 452
Japanese honeysuckle
☼ ◑ ✎ 1-24; H1, H2

Bougainvillea

MACFADYENA unguis-cati p. 457
Cat's claw
☼ ◑ ✎ 8-24; H1, H2

MUEHLENBECKIA p. 485
Wire vine
☼ ◑ ✎ ZONES VARY

PARTHENOCISSUS p. 513
☼ ◑ ● ✎ ZONES VARY

RHOICISSUS capensis p. 590
Evergreen grape
☼ ◑ ✎ 16, 17, 21-24; H2

ROSA (some) p. 597
Ground cover roses
☼ ◑ ✎ ZONES VARY

TETRASTIGMA voinieranum p. 645
◑ ✎ 13, 17, 20-24; H1, H2

TRACHELOSPERMUM p. 653
Star jasmine
☼ ◑ ✎ ZONES VARY

Rosmarinus officinalis 'Prostratus'

Palms & Cycads

Whether they bring to mind a desert oasis or a tropical beach, it's clear that palms are evocative plants. And not all have the classic silhouette of a single trunk and a topknot. They may have one trunk or many, be fan leafed or feather leafed, soft and graceful or stiff and architectural. Cycads resemble small feather palms but they're very slow growing—making them good choices for smaller gardens.

Washingtonia filifera

Butia capitata

Cocos nucifera

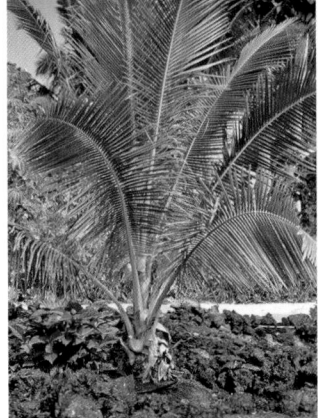
Phoenix canariensis

Palms

ARCHONTOPHOENIX
cunninghamiana   p. 197
King palm
:Ò: :Ò: ✂ 21–24

BRAHEA   p. 230
:Ò: ✂ ZONES VARY

BUTIA capitata   p. 235
Pindo palm
:Ò: :Ò: ✂ 8, 9, 12–24; H1, H2

CARYOTA   p. 253
Fishtail palm
:Ò: :Ò: ● ✂ 23, 24; H2

CHAMAEDOREA   p. 265
:Ò: ● ✂ 16, 17, 22–24; H2

CHAMAEROPS humilis   p. 265
Mediterranean fan palm
:Ò: :Ò: ✂ 4–24; H1, H2

COCOS nucifera   p. 286
Coconut palm
:Ò: ✂ H2

DYPSIS   p. 322
NEEDS, ZONES VARY

HEDYSCEPE
canterburyana   p. 387
:Ò: :Ò: ✂ 17, 23, 24; H1, H2

HOWEA   p. 399
:Ò: ✂ 17, 21–24; H1, H2

JUBAEA chilensis   p. 417
Chilean wine palm
:Ò: ✂ 12–24

LIVISTONA   p. 450
:Ò: ✂ 9, 13–17, 19–24; H1, H2

PHOENIX   p. 535
Date palm
:Ò: ✂ ZONES VARY

PRITCHARDIA   p. 563
Loulu palm
:Ò: ✂ ZONES VARY

PTYCHOSPERMA   p. 570
● ✂ 23, 24; H2

RHAPIDOPHYLLUM
hystrix   p. 582
Needle palm
:Ò: :Ò: ● ✂ 2–24

RHAPIS   p. 582
Lady palm
:Ò: ● ✂ ZONES VARY

RHOPALOSTYLIS   p. 590
:Ò: :Ò: ✂ 17, 23, 24; H1, H2

ROYSTONEA   p. 603
Royal palm
:Ò: ✂ 24; H2

SABAL   p. 605
Palmetto
:Ò: ✂ 12–17, 19–24; H1, H2

SYAGRUS
romanzoffianum   p. 639
Queen palm
:Ò: ✂ 12, 13, 15–17, 19–24; H1, H2

TRACHYCARPUS fortunei p. 653
Windmill palm
:Ò: :Ò: ✂ 4–24

WASHINGTONIA   p. 669
:Ò: ✂ 8–24; H1, H2

Cycads

CYCAS   p. 304
:Ò: ✂ ZONES VARY

DIOON   p. 318
:Ò: ✂ ZONES VARY

ZAMIA   p. 674
:Ò: ● ✂ 21–24; H1, H2

Brahea armata

Rhapis excelsa

Dioon edule

Succulents & Cacti

Although traditionally associated with desert gardens, this diverse group of plants is increasingly making its way into gardens throughout the West. In fact, some of those listed below—notably *Sempervivum* and many *Sedum*—will survive winters in the coldest zones. Used in the right setting, succulents and cacti are unsurpassed for beauty and drama. And they thrive where other plants can't: in rock gardens in nutrient-poor soil, on arid slopes, between paving stones, and in pots that busy owners forgot to water. Their one enemy is excessive moisture, so be sure to give them excellent drainage and just enough water to keep their stems and leaves plump.

Adenium obesum

Aloe arborescens

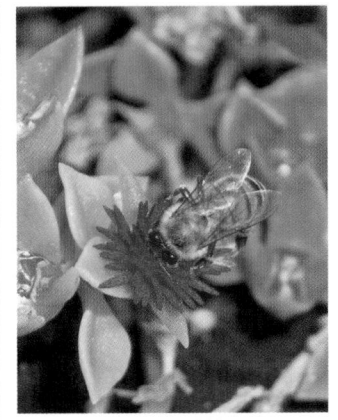

Aptenia cordifolia

Succulents

ADENIUM obesum   p. 172
☼ ✚ 23, 24; H2

AEONIUM   p. 173
☼ ◑ ✚ 15-17, 20-24

AGAVE   p. 175
☼ ✚ ZONES VARY

ALOE   p. 180
☼ ◑ ✚ ZONES VARY

APTENIA cordifolia   p. 195
☼ ◑ ● ✚ 12, 13, 15-17, 21-24; H1, H2

CARPOBROTUS   p. 252
Ice plant
☼ ✚ ZONES VARY

CEPHALOPHYLLUM
'Red Spike'   p. 261
☼ ◑ ✚ 8, 9, 11-24

CEROPEGIA linearis woodii p. 263
Rosary vine
◑ ✚ 21-24

COTYLEDON   p. 297
☼ ◑ ✚ ZONES VARY

CRASSULA   p. 297
☼ ✚ ZONES VARY

DELOSPERMA   p. 311
Ice plant
☼ ◑ ✚ ZONES VARY

DOROTHEANTHUS   p. 320
Livingstone daisy
☼ ✚ A2; 1-24

DROSANTHEMUM   p. 321
☼ ✚ 14-24; H1

DUDLEYA   p. 322
☼ ✚ ZONES VARY

ECHEVERIA   p. 323
☼ ◑ ✚ ZONES VARY

EUPHORBIA (some)   p. 345
☼ ◑ ✚ ZONES VARY

Dudleya hassei

Cotyledon orbiculata

Aloe vera

Carpobrotus chilensis

Delosperma 'Alba'

Echeveria agavoides

Kalanchoe daigremontiana

Cereus peruvianus

A saguaro *(Carnegiea gigantea)* in the Arizona desert

KALANCHOE p. 424
☼ ◑ ✓ ZONES VARY

LAMPRANTHUS p. 431
Ice plant
☼ ✓ ZONES VARY

LITHOPS p. 450
Stoneface
☼ ✓ 12, 13

MALEPHORA p. 469
Ice plant
☼ ✓ ZONES VARY

MESEMBRYANTHEMUM crystallinum p. 479
Ice plant
☼ ✓ 15–17, 23, 24

PACHYPODIUM lamerei p. 507
Madagascar palm
☼ ◑ ✓ 13, 21–24

Sempervivum tectorum

PLUMERIA p. 552
Frangipani
☼ ◑ ✓ ZONES VARY

PORTULACARIA afra p. 558
Elephant's food
☼ ◑ ● ✓ 8, 9, 12–24; H1, H2

SEDUM p. 620
Stonecrop
☼ ◑ ✓ ZONES VARY

SEMPERVIVUM p. 621
Houseleek
☼ ◑ ✓ ZONES 2–24

SENECIO mandraliscae p. 622
☼ ◑ ✓ 12, 13, 16, 17, 21–24; H1, H2

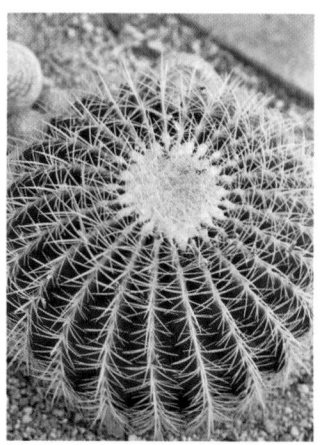

Echinocactus grusonii

Cacti

CARNEGIEA gigantea p. 251
Saguaro
☼ ✓ 12, 13, 18–21

CEPHALOCEREUS senilis p. 260
Old man cactus
☼ ✓ 13, 21–24, H1

CEREUS peruvianus p. 263
☼ ◑ ✓ 13, 16, 17, 21–24; H2

CORYPHANTHA vivipara p. 295
☼ ✓ 1–24

ECHINOCACTUS p. 324
Barrel cactus
☼ ◑ ✓ 12–24

ECHINOCEREUS p. 324
Hedgehog cactus
☼ ✓ ZONES VARY

ECHINOPSIS p. 324
☼ ✓ ZONES VARY

EPIPHYLLUM p. 329
Orchid cactus
◑ ✓ 8, 9, 14–24; H1, H2

ESPOSTOA lanata p. 338
Peruvian old man cactus
☼ ◑ ✓ 12–24

FEROCACTUS p. 351
Barrel cactus
☼ ◑ ✓ 12–24

Ferocactus

MAMMILLARIA p. 473
☼ ◑ ✓ ZONES VARY

OPUNTIA p. 501
☼ ✓ ZONES VARY

RHIPSALIDOPSIS gaertneri p. 583
Easter cactus
◑ ✓ 16, 17, 21–24; H1, H2

SCHLUMBERGERA p. 618
☼ ✓ 16, 17, 21–24; H1, H2

STENOCEREUS thurberi p. 634
Organpipe cactus
☼ ✓ 12–24

Opuntia

Plumeria rubra

Espostoa lanata

Orchids & Bromeliads

Orchids vary so widely that many species and cultivars are unrecognizable as members of this huge family of plants. They come in every color except true black, and range from tiny miniatures to towering giants. At one time, orchids were considered too delicate to be grown outside of a greenhouse. Today many can be grown in indoor gardens and some will thrive outdoors in the West's mildest climate zones. Most bromeliads make ideal houseplants, thriving on neglect. Their cupped leaf bases form a water reservoir, which, in nature, allows them to survive droughts. Indoors, they need only periodic watering.

Cymbidium

Cattleya

Epidendrum

Oncidium

Paphiopedilum

Orchids

BLETILLA striata p. 225
Chinese ground orchid
☾ ✂ 2B–9, 12–24

CATTLEYA p. 255
☾ ✂ H2

CYMBIDIUM p. 305
☾ ✂ ALL ZONES

DENDROBIUM p. 312
☾ ✂ ZONES VARY

EPIDENDRUM p. 328
☀ ☾ ✂ ZONES VARY

LAELIA p. 429
☾ ✂ ZONES VARY

ONCIDIUM p. 500
☾ ✂ 17, 20–24; H1, H2

PAPHIOPEDILUM p. 512
Lady's slipper
☾ ✂ ZONES VARY

Laelia

Pineapple

Dendrobium

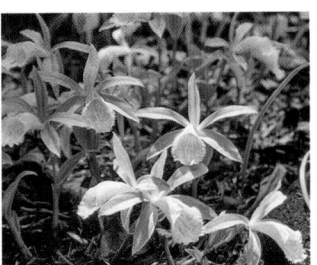
Pleione formosana

PHALAENOPSIS p. 533
Moth orchid
☾ ✂ H2

PLEIONE formosana p. 548
☾ ✂ 5–9, 14–24

VANDA p. 662
☾ ✂ H2

Bromeliads

AECHMEA p. 173
☾ ✂ 22–24; H1, H2

BILLBERGIA p. 224
☾ ✂ 12–24; H1, H2

BROMELIA balansae p. 232
Heart of flame
☀ ✂ 13, 19–24; H1, H2

CRYPTANTHUS zonatus p. 300
☾ ● ✂ 17, 23, 24; H1, H2

Phalaenopsis

NEOREGELIA p. 493
☾ ● ✂ 21–24; H1, H2

PINEAPPLE p. 540
☀ ☾ ✂ 24; H1, H2

PUYA berteroana p. 572
☀ ✂ 9, 13–17, 19–24

TILLANDSIA p. 650
Air plant
☀ ☾ ✂ 22–24

Neoregelia carolinae 'Tricolor'

Puya berteroana

Ornamental Grasses & Grasslike Plants

Unlike lawn grasses, what we call ornamental grasses (including other grasslike plants such as sedges and rushes) rarely need mowing. Denizens of prairie, seashore, forest, meadow, and marsh, they offer fountains, hummocks, and waves of foliage that vary widely in texture, color, and overall character. Some are evergreen; others are deciduous but hold their dried stems and flowers through the cold months, providing year-round interest.

Calamagrostis × *acutiflora*

Alopecurus pratensis 'Aureus'

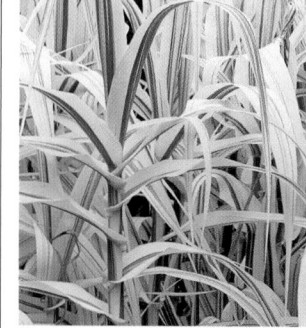

Arundo donax 'Variegata'

Briza media

Hakonechloa macra 'Aureola'

Grasses

ACHNATHERUM speciosum　　p. 170
Indian rice grass
☀ ✔ 1–3, 10–13

AGROPYRON　　p. 176
Wheatgrass
☀ ✔ 1–3, 10

ALOPECURUS pratensis 'Aureus'　　p. 181
Yellow foxtail grass
☀ ◑ ✔ 2–10, 14–17, 21–24

ANDROPOGON gerardii　　p. 185
Big bluestem
☀ ◑ ✔ 1–9, 14–24

ARRHENATHERUM elatius bulbosum 'Variegatum'　　p. 201
Bulbous oat grass
☀ ◑ ✔ 1–7, 15–17, 23, 24

ARUNDO donax　　p. 203
Giant reed
☀ ✔ 3–24

BAMBOO　　p. 212
☀ ◑ ✔ ZONES VARY

BOUTELOUA　　p. 229
Grama grass
☀ ✔ 1–3, 7–11, 14, 18–21

BRIZA maxima　　p. 231
Rattlesnake grass
☀ ✔ 1–24

BRIZA media (perennial)　　p. 231
Rattlesnake grass
☀ ✔ ZONES 1–24

CALAMAGROSTIS　　p. 237
Reed grass
☀ ◑ ✔ 2B–24

CHASMANTHIUM latifolium　　p. 266
Sea oats
☀ ◑ ✔ 2–10, 14–24

COIX lacryma-jobi　　p. 286
Job's tears
☀ ◑ ✔ 12–24; H1

CORTADERIA selloana　　p. 293
Pampas grass
☀ ✔ 3–24; H1

CYMBOPOGON citratus　　p. 305
Lemon grass
☀ ✔ 12, 13, 16, 17, 23, 24; H1, H2

DESCHAMPSIA　　p. 313
Hair grass
☀ ◑ ✔ 2–24

ELYMUS magellanicus　　p. 327
Magellan wheatgrass
☀ ◑ ✔ 3–6, 14–17, 21–24

Andropogon gerardii

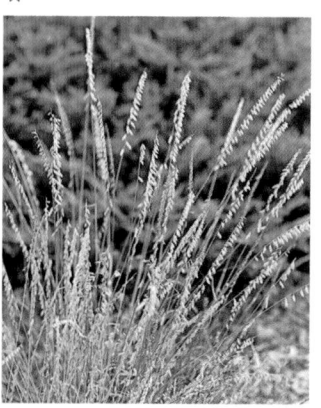

Bouteloua curtipendula

Giant Grasses

Look closely at the stems and nodes of a bamboo plant and you can see that these plants belong to the grass family *Poaceae*. And like their cousins, they can grow in either a clumping or a running fashion. Some running bamboos have a deserved reputation for invasiveness, but there are plenty of well-behaved clumping bamboos for Western gardens. See pages 212–215 for some of the best.

Chusquea coronalis

Bambusa multiplex 'Alphonse Karr'

Phyllostachys nigra

Deschampsia cespitosa

Cortaderia selloana

ERAGROSTIS p. 330
Love grass
☼ ◐ ✀ ZONES 1-24

FESTUCA p. 351
Fescue
☼ ◐ ✀ ZONES VARY

HAKONECHLOA macra p. 383
Japanese forest grass
☼ ◐ ● ✀ 2B-9, 14-24

**HELICTOTRICHON
sempervirens** p. 389
Blue oat grass
☼ ✀ 1-24, 14-24

**IMPERATA cylindrica
'Rubra'** p. 407
Japanese blood grass
☼ ◐ ✀ 2B-24

LEYMUS p. 442
Lyme grass
☼ ◐ ✀ ZONES VARY

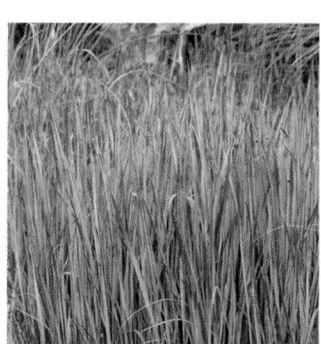

Imperata cylindrical 'Rubra'

**MILIUM effusum
'Aureum'** p. 481
Bowles' golden grass
◐ ✀ 3B-9, 14-17

MISCANTHUS p. 482
Silver grass
☼ ◐ ✀ ZONES VARY

MOLINIA caerulea p. 483
Moor grass
☼ ◐ ✀ 1-9, 14-17

MUHLENBERGIA p. 486
☼ ◐ ✀ ZONES VARY

NASSELLA p. 491
Needle grass
☼ ✀ ZONES VARY

PANICUM virgatum p. 510
Switch grass
☼ ◐ ✀ 1-11, 14-23

PENNISETUM p. 526
Fountain grass
☼ ◐ ✀ ZONES VARY

**PHALARIS arundinacea
picta** p. 532
Ribbon grass
☼ ◐ ✀ A1-A3; 1-10, 14-24

RHYNCHELYTRUM p. 591
Natal ruby grass
☼ ✀ 2B-24; H1, H2

**SCHIZACHYRIUM
scoparium** p. 617
Little bluestem
☼ ✀ 1-24

Festuca glauca

Panicum virgatum 'Cloud Nine'

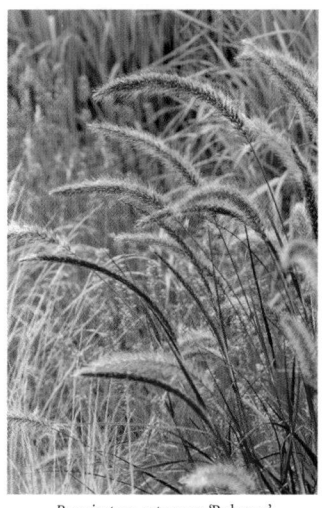

Pennisetum setaceum 'Rubrum'

SESLERIA p. 624
Moor grass
☼ ◐ ✀ ZONES VARY

SPARTINA p. 630
Prairie cord grass
☼ ✀ 1-9, 14-24

SPOROBOLUS airoides p. 632
Alkali sacaton
☼ ✀ 1-24

STIPA p. 635
Feather grass
☼ ✀ ZONES VARY

VETIVERIA zizanioides p. 664
Vetiver
☼ ◐ ✀ 20-24; H1, H2

ZOYSIA p. 677
☼ ◐ ✀ ZONES VARY

Grasslike
Plants

CAREX p. 250
Sedge
☼ ◐ ✀ ZONES VARY

**CHONDROPETALUM
tectorum** p. 270
Cape rush
☼ ◐ ✀ 8, 9, 14-24

Elegia capensis

Carex phyllocephala 'Sparkler'

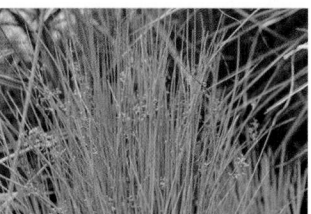

Juncus patens 'Occidental Blue'

CYPERUS p. 306
☼ ◐ ● ✀ ZONES VARY

ELEGIA capensis p. 326
Fountain rush
☼ ◐ ✀ 8, 9, 14-24

EQUISETUM hyemale p. 330
Horsetail
☼ ◐ ✀ 1-24

**ISCHYROLEPIS
subverticillata** p. 414
Broom restio
☼ ◐ ✀ ZONES 14-24

JUNCUS p. 418
Rush
☼ ◐ ✀ ZONES VARY

PHORMIUM p. 536
☼ ◐ ✀ 5-9, 14-24; H1, H2

UNCINIA rubra p. 660
Red hook sedge
☼ ◐ ✀ 4-6, 15-17

XEROPHYLLUM tenax p. 673
Bear grass
☼ ◐ ✀ 1-7, 14-17

Uncinia rubra

Ferns

Think of ferns and you may envision a lush, shady, forest nook—and, in fact, many ferns are woodland natives. In size, they range from forest-floor creepers to the majestic tree ferns that seem to belong to the age of dinosaurs. Foliage may be soft, thin, and silky or firm, thick, and leathery. Fronds are sometimes undivided, reminiscent of lances or spearpoints. More often, though, they're divided—either palmate, resembling a hand with outstretched fingers, or pinnate, looking more like a bird's feather. In the more elaborate types, the fronds are further divided to give the effect of green lace.

Polypodium

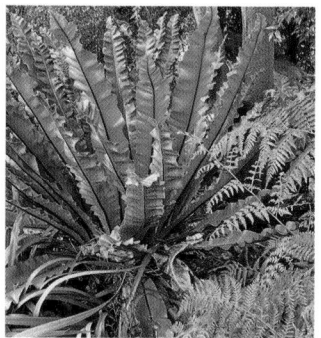

Asplenium scolopendrium

ADIANTUM   p. 172
Maidenhair fern
☼ ● ✎ ZONES VARY

ARACHNIODES simplicior   p. 196
☼ ● ✎ 4–24

ASPLENIUM   p. 206
☼ ● ✎ ZONES VARY

ATHYRIUM   p. 208
☼ ● ✎ ZONES VARY

BLECHNUM   p. 225
☼ ● ✎ ZONES VARY

CYRTOMIUM   p. 306
☼ ● ✎ ZONES VARY

DAVALLIA
trichomanoides   p. 310
Squirrel's foot fern
☼ ✎ 17, 23, 24; H1, H2

Blechnum spicant

Dryopteris

DRYOPTERIS   p. 321
Wood fern
☼ ● ✎ ZONES VARY

HUMATA tyermannii   p. 399
Bear's foot fern
☼ ✎ 17, 23, 24; H1, H2

MATTEUCCIA
struthiopteris   p. 475
Ostrich fern
☼ ☼ ● ✎ A1–A3; 1–10, 14–17

Matteuccia struthiopteris

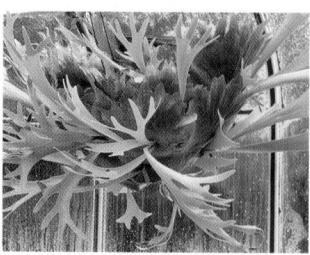

Platycerium

MICROLEPIA   p. 481
☼ ● ✎ 17, 23, 24

NEPHROLEPIS   p. 494
Sword fern
☼ ● ✎ ZONES VARY

OSMUNDA   p. 505
☼ ☼ ✎ ZONES VARY

PELLAEA   p. 525
Cliff-brake
☼ ✎ ZONES VARY

PLATYCERIUM   p. 546
Staghorn fern
☼ ✎ ZONES VARY

POLYPODIUM
glycyrrhiza   p. 556
Licorice fern
☼ ● ✎ A3; 4–6, 14–24

POLYPODIUM scouleri   p. 556
Leather polypody
☼ ● ✎ 4–6, 15–17, 24

POLYSTICHUM   p. 557
☼ ● ✎ ZONES VARY

Pellaea

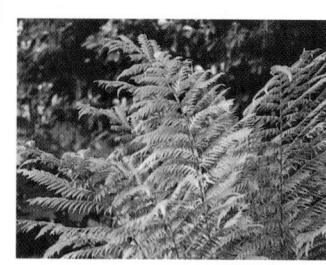

Woodwardia fimbriata

PTERIDIUM
aquilinum   p. 569
Bracken
☼ ☼ ✎ 1–10, 14–24

PTERIS   p. 570
Brake
☼ ● ✎ ZONES VARY

RUMOHRA adiantiformis   p. 604
Leather fern
☼ ☼ ✎ 14–17, 19–24; H1, H2

WOODWARDIA fimbriata   p. 673
Giant chain fern
☼ ● ✎ 2B–9, 14–24

Tree Ferns

CIBOTIUM glaucum   p. 274
Hapu´u
☼ ☼ ✎ 17, 23, 24; H2

CYATHEA cooperi   p. 303
Australian tree fern
☼ ☼ ✎ 15–24; H1, H2

DICKSONIA antarctica   p. 316
Tasmanian tree fern
☼ ☼ ● ✎ 8, 9, 14–17, 19–24; H1

Dicksonia antarctica

Western Natives

Regional native plants are wise additions to the garden. They bring diverse textures and colors to your plantings. Because they are naturally suited to the climate, they typically need less maintenance than many popular non-native plants. Where water is scarce, they're an appropriate (and thrifty) choice, likely to thrive on nothing more than natural rainfall. On these pages, we list natives for six Western regions: Alaska, the Pacific Northwest, the Rocky Mountain area, California, the Southwest, and the Hawaiian Islands. Be aware, though, that these broad areas encompass a good deal of variation. Check the descriptions in the Western Plant Encyclopedia for climate zone adaptation, exposure preference, and moisture needs; then choose the plants best suited to your climate and site. If you start with nursery-raised plants, remember that drought-tolerant natives will need dry-season watering for a year or two until they're established.

View from the Denali highway, Alaska, with *Epilobium augustifolium* (foreground)

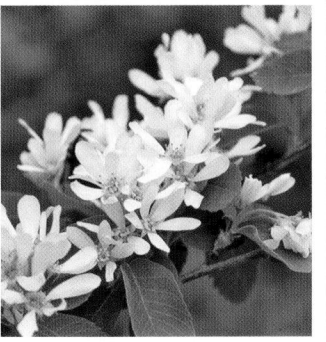
Amelanchier alnifolia

Alaska, Trees & Shrubs

AMELANCHIER alnifolia p. 183
Saskatoon
☼ ◐ ✎ A1–A3; 1–6

CORNUS stolonifera p. 292
Redtwig dogwood
☼ ◐ ✎ A1–A3; 1–9, 14–21

ELAEAGNUS commutata p. 325
Silverberry
☼ ◐ ✎ A1–A3; 1–3

PICEA glauca p. 539
White spruce
☼ ◐ ✎ A1–A3; 1–7, 14–17

POPULUS tremuloides p. 558
Quaking aspen
☼ ✎ A1–A3; 1–7, 14–19

ROSA rugosa p. 602
Ramanas rose
☼ ◐ ✎ A1–A3; 1–24

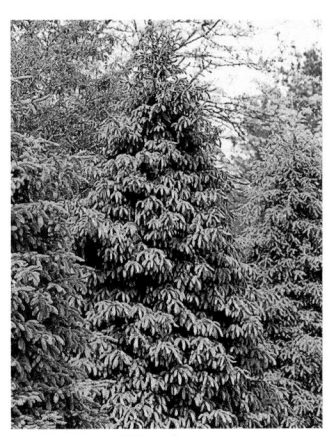
Picea glauca

VIBURNUM edule p. 664
Highbush cranberry
☼ ◐ ✎ A1–A3; 1–11

Alaska, Ground Covers & Perennials

ALLIUM schoenoprasum p. 179
Chives
☼ ✎ A1–A3; 1–24

ARCTOSTAPHYLOS uva-ursi p. 198
Bearberry
☼ ◐ ✎ A1–A3; 1–9, 14–24

CHRYSANTHEMUM arcticum p. 271
Arctic chrysanthemum
☼ ✎ A1–A3; 1–10, 14–21

Populus tremuloides

EPILOBIUM angustifolium p. 328
Fireweed
☼ ✎ A1–A3; 1–7, 14–21

IRIS setosa p. 413
☼ ✎ A1–A3; 1–9, 14–17

JUNIPERUS communis 'Effusa' p. 418
☼ ◐ ✎ A1–A3; 1–24

MATTEUCCIA struthiopteris p. 475
Ostrich fern
☼ ◐ ● ✎ A1–A3; 1–10, 14–17

POLEMONIUM pulcherrimum p. 555
◐ ● ✎ A1–A3; 1–11, 14–17; H1

PULSATILLA patens p. 571
Eastern pasque flower
☼ ✎ A1–A3; 1–6, 15–17

RUBUS arcticus 'Kenai Carpet' p. 603
Nagoonberry
☼ ◐ ✎ A1–A3; 1–3

Cornus stolonifera

Rosa rugosa

Allium schoenoprasum

Arctostaphylos uva-ursi

Matteuccia struthiopteris

Pulsatilla patens

Lupinus and *wyethia* with native oaks in the Colombia River Gorge, Oregon

Pacific North-west, Trees

ABIES concolor   p. 163
White fir
☼ ◐ ⚫ ✦ A2, A3; 1–9, 14–24

ABIES lasiocarpa   p. 163
Alpine fir
☼ ◐ ✦ A2, A3; 1–9, 14–17

ACER circinatum   p. 167
Vine maple
☼ ◐ ✦ A3; 2B–6, 14–17

ARBUTUS menziesii   p. 197
Madrone
☼ ✦ 4–7, 14–19

CHAMAECYPARIS nootkatensis   p. 264
Nootka cypress
☼ ◐ ✦ A2, A3; 2–6, 15–17

CORNUS nuttallii   p. 292
Pacific dogwood
☼ ◐ ✦ 3B–9, 14–20

FRAXINUS latifolia   p. 358
Oregon ash
☼ ✦ 3–9, 14–24

PINUS   p. 542
Shore pine
☼ ✦ A3; 4–9, 14–24; H1

PSEUDOTSUGA menziesii   p. 569
Douglas fir
☼ ◐ ✦ A2, A3; 1–10, 14–17

Cornus nuttallii

Pseudotsuga menziesii

Acer macrophyllum

QUERCUS garryana   p. 576
Oregon white oak
☼ ✦ 2A–11, 14–23

TAXUS brevifolia   p. 644
Western yew
☼ ◐ ⚫ ✦ A3; 3–7, 14–17

THUJA plicata   p. 647
Western red cedar
☼ ◐ ✦ A3; 1–9, 14–24

TSUGA mertensiana   p. 657
Mountain hemlock
☼ ◐ ✦ A1–A3; 1–7, 14–17

Pacific North-west, Shrubs

ACER glabrum   p. 167
Rocky Mountain maple
☼ ◐ ✦ 1–7, 10

ACER macrophyllum   p. 168
Bigleaf maple
☼ ◐ ✦ 2–9, 14–24

AMELANCHIER alnifolia   p. 183
Saskatoon
☼ ◐ ✦ A1–A3; 1–6

ARCTOSTAPHYLOS columbiana   p. 197
Hairy manzanita
☼ ◐ ✦ 4–6, 15–17

CORNUS stolonifera   p. 292
Redtwig dogwood
☼ ◐ ✦ A1–A3; 1–9, 14–21

CORYLUS cornuta californica   p. 295
Western hazelnut
☼ ◐ ✦ 2–9, 14–20

Myrica californica

GAULTHERIA ovatifolia   p. 364
☼ ✦ 3–7, 14–17

GAULTHERIA shallon   p. 364
Salal
☼ ✦ 4–7, 14–17

HOLODISCUS discolor   p. 397
Cream bush
☼ ✦ 1–9, 14–19

MAHONIA aquifolium   p. 467
Oregon grape
☼ ◐ ⚫ ✦ 2–12, 14–24

MAHONIA nervosa   p. 468
Longleaf mahonia
◐ ⚫ ✦ 2B–10, 14–24

MYRICA californica   p. 488
Pacific wax myrtle
☼ ✦ 4–9, 14–24

RIBES aureum   p. 591
Golden currant
☼ ◐ ✦ A2, A3; 1–12, 14–23

Ribes sanguineum

RIBES sanguineum   p. 592
Pink winter currant
☼ ◐ ✦ A3; 4–9, 14–24

VACCINIUM ovatum   p. 661
Evergreen huckleberry
☼ ◐ ⚫ ✦ 4–7, 14–17, 22–24

Pacific North-west, Ground Covers, Vines & Perennials

ADIANTUM aleuticum   p. 172
Five-finger fern
◐ ⚫ ✦ 1–7, 14–21

AQUILEGIA formosa   p. 195
Western columbine
☼ ◐ ✦ A1–A3; 1–11, 14–24

ASARUM caudatum   p. 203
Wild ginger
☼ ⚫ ✦ 4–6, 14–24

Asarum caudatum

Camassia quamash

Dryas octopetala

BLECHNUM spicant p. 225
Deer fern
2B–7, 14–19, 24

CAMASSIA quamash p. 242
Camass
1–10, 14–17

CORNUS canadensis p. 291
Bunchberry
A1–A3; 1–9, 14–16

DRYAS octopetala p. 321
A1–A3; 1–6

DRYOPTERIS filix-mas p. 322
Male fern
2–9, 14–17

**ERYTHRONIUM
revolutum** p. 338
1–7, 14–17

FRAGARIA chiloensis p. 356
Beach strawberry
4–24; H1

**FRITILLARIA
camschatcensis** p. 359
Black lily
A1–A3; 1–7, 15–17

Fragaria chiloensis

Lewisia cotyledon

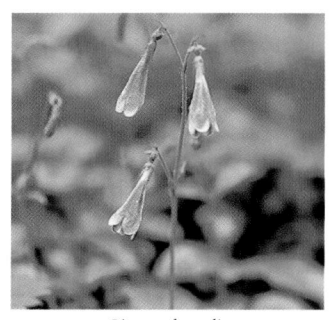

Linnaea borealis

LEWISIA p. 441
1–7, 14–17

LILIUM columbianum p. 445
Columbia lily
2–7, 14–19

LINNAEA borealis p. 447
Twinflower
A1–A3; 1, 2, 4–6, 14–17

MAHONIA repens p. 468
Creeping mahonia
2B–9, 14–24

**MAIANTHEMUM
dilatatum** p. 468
False lily-of-the-valley
A2, A3; 2–9, 14–17

**MAIANTHEMUM
racemosum** p. 468
False Solomon's seal
1–7, 14–17

POLYSTICHUM munitum p. 557
Western sword fern
A3; 2–9, 14–24

SEDUM spathulifolium p. 624
2–9, 14–24

Polystichum munitum

Tolmiea menziesii

TOLMIEA menziesii p. 650
Piggyback plant
A3; 4–9, 14–17, 20–24

TRILLIUM ovatum p. 655
Wake robin
2–7, 14–17

Trillium ovatum

VANCOUVERIA p. 661
ZONES VARY

Rocky Mountains, Trees

ABIES concolor p. 163
White fir
A2, A3; 1–9, 14–24

BETULA occidentalis p. 223
Water birch
A3; 1–7, 10

**JUNIPERUS
monosperma** p. 422
1–3, 10–11

**JUNIPERUS scopulorum
'Tolleson's Blue Weeping'
(tree form)** p. 423
1–24

PICEA pungens p. 539
Colorado spruce
A2, A3; 1–10, 14–17

PINUS (several) p. 541
Pine
ZONES VARY

POPULUS × acuminata p. 558
Lanceleaf cottonwood
1–11, 14–21

POPULUS tremuloides p. 558
Quaking aspen
A1–A3; 1–7, 14–19

PRUNUS americana p. 568
Wild plum
1–3, 10

**PSEUDOTSUGA
menziesii** p. 569
Douglas fir
A2, A3; 1–10, 14–17

An alpine meadow in Colorado's Rocky Mountains

Rocky Mountain, Shrubs

ACER glabrum p. 167
Rocky Mountain maple
☼ ◐ ✎ 1–7, 10

AMELANCHIER alnifolia p. 183
Saskatoon
☼ ◐ ✎ A1–A3; 1–6

ARTEMISIA tridentata p. 202
Big sagebrush
☼ ✎ 1–3, 6–11, 14–24

CEANOTHUS velutinus p. 255
Tobacco brush
☼ ✎ 2–7, 15–17

CERCOCARPUS ledifolius p. 263
Curl-leaf mountain mahogany
☼ ✎ 1–3, 7–10, 14–21

CERCOCARPUS montanus p. 263
Mountain mahogany
☼ ✎ 1–3, 7–10

CHRYSOTHAMNUS nauseosus p. 274
Rabbitbrush
☼ ✎ 1–3, 10, 11

CORNUS stolonifera p. 291
Redtwig dogwood
☼ ◐ ✎ A1–A3; 1–9, 14–21

ELAEAGNUS commutata p. 326
Silverberry
☼ ◐ ✎ A1–A3; 1–3

FALLUGIA paradoxa p. 349
Apache plume
☼ ✎ 2–23

FORESTIERA neomexicana p. 355
New Mexican privet
☼ ✎ 1–3, 7–24

HOLODISCUS dumosus p. 397
Mountain spray
◐ ✎ 1–3, 10

JUNIPERUS communis 'Compressa' p. 422
☼ ◐ ✎ A1–A3; 1–24

PHILADELPHUS lewisii p. 533
Wild mock orange
☼ ◐ ✎ 1–10, 14–24

PRUNUS besseyi p. 567
Western sand cherry
☼ ✎ A1–A3; 1–3, 10

QUERCUS gambellii p. 575
Gambell oak
☼ ✎ 1–3, 10

RHUS glabra p. 590
Smooth sumac
☼ ✎ 1–10, 14–17

RHUS trilobata p. 591
Squawbush
☼ ✎ 1–12, 14–21

RIBES aureum p. 591
Golden currant
☼ ◐ ✎ A2, A3; 1–12, 14–23

ROBINIA neomexicana p. 592
Desert locust
☼ ◐ ✎ 2, 3, 7–11, 14, 18–24

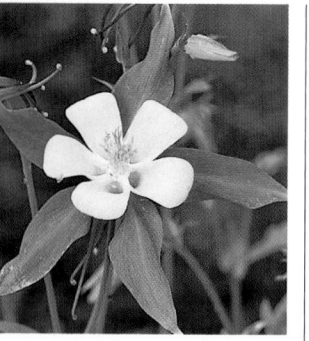

Aquilegia caerulea

RUBUS deliciosus p. 603
Rocky Mountain thimbleberry
☼ ◐ ✎ 1–6, 10

SHEPHERDIA argentea p. 624
Silver buffaloberry
☼ ✎ 1–3, 7, 10

SYMPHORICARPOS albus p. 640
Common snowberry
☼ ◐ ✎ A3; 1–11, 14–21

YUCCA baccata p. 674
Banana yucca
☼ ✎ 1–3, 7, 9–14, 18–24

Rocky Mountain, Ground Covers & Perennials

ANTENNARIA dioica p. 187
Pussy toes
☼ ✎ A1, A2; 1–3, 6, 7, 14–16

AQUILEGIA caerulea p. 195
Rocky Mountain columbine
☼ ◐ ✎ A1–A3; 1–11, 14–24

ARCTOSTAPHYLOS uva-ursi p. 198
Bearberry
☼ ◐ ✎ A1–A3; 1–9, 14–24

CALLIRHOE involucrata p. 239
Poppy mallow
☼ ◐ ✎ 1–3, 7–14, 18–24

CALYLOPHUS hartwegii p. 242
Sundrops
☼ ◐ ✎ 1–3, 6–16, 18–24

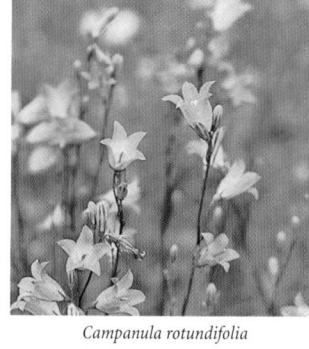

Campanula rotundifolia

CAMPANULA rotundifolia p. 248
Bluebell of Scotland
☼ ◐ ✎ A1–A3; 1–10, 14–24

ERIOGONUM umbellatum p. 335
Sulfur flower
☼ ✎ 1–24

GEUM triflorum p. 369
Prairie smoke
☼ ◐ ✎ 1–3

HUMULUS lupulus neomexicanus p. 399
Common hop
☼ ✎ A2, A3; 1–10, 14–21

MAHONIA repens p. 468
Creeping mahonia
☼ ◐ ✎ 2B–9, 14–24

MELAMPODIUM leucanthum p. 477
Blackfoot daisy
☼ ✎ 2, 3, 10–13

MONARDA fistulosa p. 484
Bee balm
☼ ◐ ✎ A2, A3; 1–10, 14–17

Geum triflorum

Cornus stolonifera

Callirhoe involucrata

Monarda fistulosa

Oenothera speciosa

Penstemon strictus

OENOTHERA caespitosa p. 499
Tufted evening primrose
☼ ☀ ✿ 1-3, 7-14, 18-21

OENOTHERA speciosa p. 499
Mexican evening primrose
☼ ☀ ✿ 2B-24; H1, H2

PENSTEMON (many) p. 526
Beard tongue
☼ ☀ ✿ ZONES VARY

RATIBIDA columnifera p. 580
Mexican hat
☼ ✿ ALL ZONES

ZINNIA grandiflora p. 677
☼ ✿ 2-24

Ratibida columnifera

California, Trees

ABIES (several) p. 162
Fir
☼ ☀ ✿ ZONES VARY

Aesculus californica

AESCULUS californica p. 173
California buckeye
☼ ✿ 3-10, 14-24

ARBUTUS menziesii p. 197
Madrone
☼ ✿ 4-7, 14-19

CALOCEDRUS decurrens p. 241
Incense cedar
☼ ☀ ✿ 2-12, 14-24

CHAMAECYPARIS lawsoniana p. 264
Port Orford cedar
☼ ☀ ✿ A3; 3-6, 15-17

CORNUS nuttallii p. 292
Pacific dogwood
☼ ☀ ✿ 3B-9, 14-20

LITHOCARPUS densiflorus p. 449
Tanbark oak
☼ ☀ ✿ 4-7, 14-24

LYONOTHAMNUS floribundus p. 455
Catalina ironwood
☼ ✿ 14-17, 19-24

PICEA breweriana p. 539
Brewer's weeping spruce
☼ ☀ ✿ 2B, 3-7, 14-17

PINUS (several) p. 541
Pine
☼ ✿ ZONES VARY

PLATANUS racemosa p. 546
California sycamore
☼ ✿ 4-24

POPULUS fremontii p. 558
Western cottonwood
☼ ✿ 1-12, 14-21

POPULUS tremuloides p. 598
Quaking aspen
☼ ✿ A1-A3; 1-7, 14-19

QUERCUS (many) p. 574
Oak
☼ ✿ ZONES VARY

SEQUOIA sempervirens p. 623
Coast redwood
☼ ☀ ✿ 4-9, 14-24

UMBELLULARIA californica p. 662
California laurel
☼ ☀ ● ✿ 4-9, 14-24

Quercus

Calycanthus occidentalis

California, Shrubs

ARCTOSTAPHYLOS (many) p. 197
Manzanita
☼ ☀ ✿ ZONES VARY

BACCHARIS pilularis p. 212
Dwarf coyote brush
☼ ✿ 5-11, 14-24

CALYCANTHUS occidentalis p. 242
Spice bush
☼ ☀ ✿ 4-9, 14-24

CARPENTERIA californica p. 251
Bush anemone
☼ ☀ ✿ 5-9, 14-24

CEANOTHUS (many) p. 255
Wild lilac
☼ ☀ ✿ 5-9, 14-24

CERCIS occidentalis p. 262
Western redbud
☼ ☀ ✿ 2-24

DENDROMECON harfordii p. 312
Island bush poppy
☼ ✿ 7-9, 14-24

Arctostaphylos densiflora

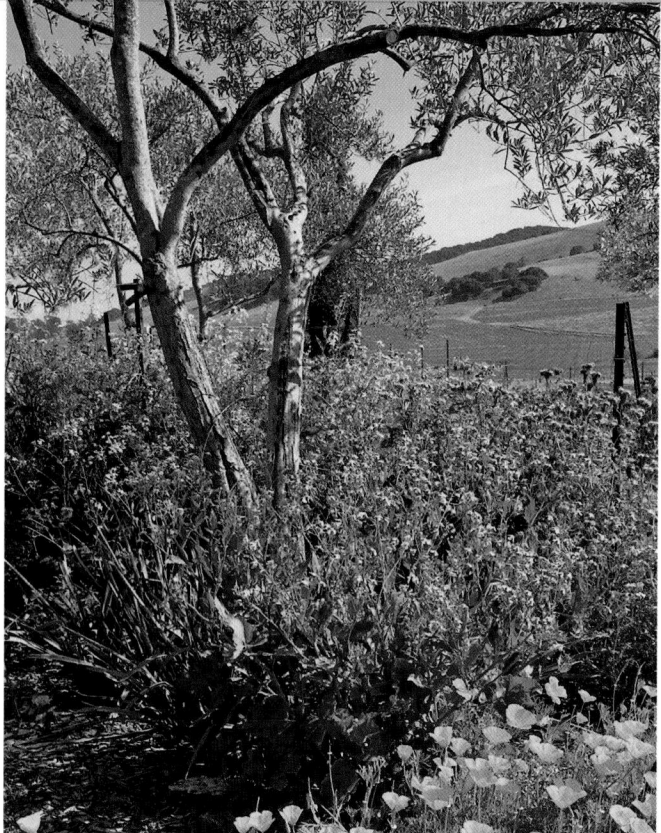

Napa Valley scene with *Eschscholzia californica* (foreground)

Fremontodendron mexicanum

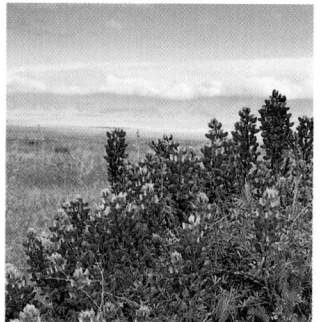

Lupinus arboreus

ERIOGONUM (many)   p. 335
Wild buckwheat
☼ ✂ ZONES VARY

FREMONTODENDRON (several)   p. 359
Flannel bush
☼ ✂ 4-24

GALVEZIA speciosa   p. 362
Island bush snapdragon
☼ ◑ ✂ 14-24

GARRYA (several)   p. 363
Silktassel
☼ ◑ ✂ ZONES VARY

HETEROMELES arbutifolia   p. 392
Toyon
☼ ◑ ✂ 5-9, 14-24

LAVATERA assurgentiflora   p. 437
Tree mallow
☼ ✂ 14-24

LUPINUS arboreus   p. 454
Lupine
☼ ✂ 4, 5, 14-17, 22-24

MAHONIA (several)   p. 467
NEEDS, ZONES VARY

MYRICA californica   p. 488
Pacific wax myrtle
☼ ✂ 4-9, 14-24

PENSTEMON centranthifolius   p. 527
Scarlet bugler
☼ ◑ ✂ 7-23

PHILADELPHUS lewisii   p. 533
Wild mock orange
☼ ◑ ✂ 1-10, 14-24

PRUNUS ilicifolia   p. 564
☼ ◑ ✂ 5-9, 12-24

RHAMNUS californica   p. 581
Coffeeberry
☼ ◑ ✂ 3A-10, 14-24; H1, H2

Rhododendron occidentale

RHODODENDRON occidentale   p. 589
Western azalea
◑ ✂ 4-7, 14-17, 19-24

RHUS integrifolia   p. 590
Lemonade berry
☼ ✂ 8, 9, 14-17, 19-24

RHUS ovata   p. 591
Sugar bush
☼ ✂ 9-12, 14-24

RIBES (several)   p. 591
Currant
☼ ◑ ✂ ZONES VARY

SALVIA clevelandii   p. 608
Cleveland sage
☼ ✂ 8, 9, 12-24

SALVIA leucophylla   p. 610
Purple sage
☼ ✂ 8, 9, 14-17, 19-24

SAMBUCUS (some)   p. 613
Elderberry
☼ ◑ ✂ ZONES VARY

SYMPHORICARPOS albus   p. 640
Common snowberry
☼ ◑ ✂ A3; 1-11, 14-21

TRICHOSTEMA lanatum   p. 654
Woolly blue curls
☼ ✂ 14-24

VACCINIUM parvifolium   p. 661
Red huckleberry
◑ ● ✂ A3; 2-7, 14-17

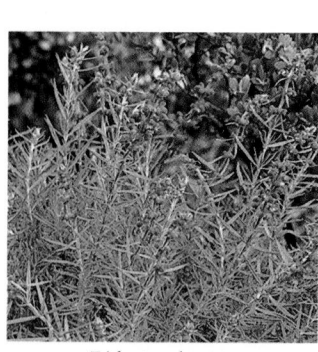

Trichostema lanatum

California, Ground Covers & Perennials

AQUILEGIA formosa   p. 195
Western columbine
☼ ◑ ✂ A1-A3; 1-11, 14-24

ARCTOSTAPHYLOS (many)   p. 197
Manzanita
☼ ◑ ✂ ZONES VARY

ARISTOLOCHIA californica   p. 200
California Dutchman's pipe
◑ ✂ 5-10, 14-24

ARTEMISIA californica   p. 201
California sagebrush
☼ ✂ 7-9, 14-24

ASARUM caudatum   p. 203
Wild ginger
◑ ● ✂ 4-6, 14-24

CEANOTHUS (many)   p. 255
Wild lilac
☼ ✂ 5-9, 14-24

ERIGERON glaucus   p. 331
Beach aster
☼ ◑ ✂ 4-6, 15-17, 22-24

Aquilegia formosa

Erigeron glaucus

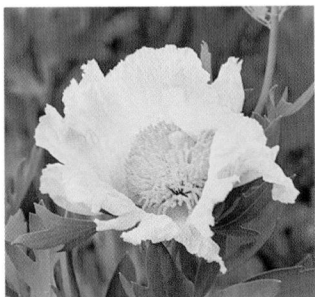

Romneya coulteri

ESCHSCHOLZIA californica   p. 338
California poppy
☼ ◐ ⚡ 1–24; H1

HEUCHERA (some)   p. 393
Coral bells
☼ ◐ ⚡ ZONES VARY

IRIS, Pacific Coast   p. 412
☼ ◐ ⚡ 4–9, 14–24

LEYMUS condensatus   p. 442
Lyme grass
☼ ◐ ⚡ 7–12, 14–24

LILIUM humboldtii   p. 445
Humboldt lily
☼ ◐ ⚡ 3, 7, 14–24

LILIUM pardalinum   p. 445
Leopard lily
☼ ◐ ⚡ 2–7, 14–24

Iris douglasiana

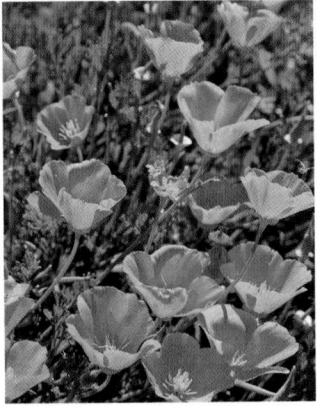

Eschscholzia californica

MIMULUS   p. 482
Monkey flower
NEEDS, ZONES VARY

MUHLENBERGIA rigens   p. 486
Deer grass
☼ ◐ ⚡ 4–24

NASSELLA pulchra   p. 491
Purple needle grass
☼ ⚡ 5–9, 11, 14–24

PENSTEMON heterophyllus   p. 527
Beard tongue
☼ ◐ ⚡ 7–24

PENSTEMON spectabilis   p. 528
Royal beard tongue
☼ ◐ ⚡ 7, 14–23

ROMNEYA coulteri   p. 593
Matilija poppy
☼ ⚡ 4–12, 14–24; H1

SIDALCEA malviflora   p. 625
Checkerbloom
☼ ⚡ 2–9, 14–24

SISYRINCHIUM idahoense bellum   p. 626
Blue-eyed grass
☼ ◐ ⚡ 2–9, 14–24

SISYRINCHIUM californicum   p. 626
Yellow-eyed grass
☼ ◐ ⚡ 4–9, 14–24

Sisyrinchium californicum

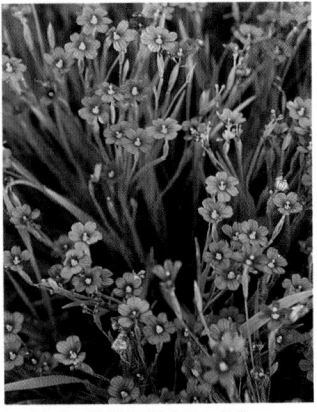

Sisyrinchium idahoense bellum

VANCOUVERIA planipetala   p. 661
Inside-out flower
◐ ⚡ 4–7, 14–17

ZAUSCHNERIA   p. 675
California fuchsia
NEEDS, ZONES VARY

Southwest, Trees

ACACIA constricta   p. 164
White thorn
☼ ⚡ 8, 9, 10–24

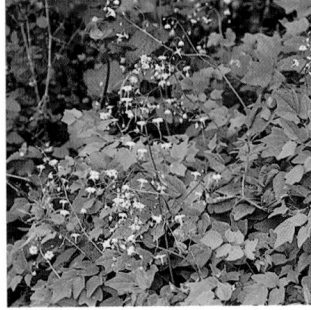

Vancouveria planipetala

ACACIA smallii   p. 166
☼ ⚡ 8, 9, 12–24

CERCIDIUM floridum   p. 262
Blue palo verde
☼ ⚡ 8–14, 18–20

CERCIDIUM microphyllum   p. 262
Littleleaf palo verde
☼ ⚡ 8–14, 18–20

CERCIDIUM praecox   p. 262
Palo brea
☼ ⚡ 12, 13, 18–20

CHILOPSIS linearis   p. 268
Desert willow
☼ ⚡ 3B, 7–14, 18–23

CUPRESSUS arizonica   p. 303
Arizona cypress
☼ ⚡ 7–24

LEUCAENA retusa   p. 440
Golden ball lead tree
☼ ⚡ 10–13

LYSILOMA microphylla thornberi   p. 455
Feather bush
☼ ⚡ 12–24; H1, H2

OLNEYA tesota   p. 500
Desert ironwood
☼ ⚡ 8, 9, 11–14, 18–23

PLATANUS wrightii   p. 546
Arizona sycamore
☼ ⚡ 10–12

PROSOPIS (several)   p. 563
Mesquite
☼ ⚡ 10–13, 18–24

QUERCUS emoryi   p. 575
Emory oak
☼ ⚡ 10–13

WASHINGTONIA filifera   p. 669
California fan palm
☼ ⚡ 8–24; H1, H2

A yucca plant rises from a sea of *Baileya multiradiata*

Larrea tridentata

Tagetes lemmonii

Antigonon leptopus

Echinocactus grusonii

Southwest, Shrubs

ANISACANTHUS thurberi   p. 187
Chuparosa
☼ ✎ 8-13, 18-23; H1, H2

CALLIANDRA californica   p. 238
Baja fairy duster
☼ ✎ 10-24

CALLIANDRA eriophylla   p. 238
Fairy duster
☼ ✎ 10-24

CHRYSOTHAMNUS nauseosus   p. 274
Rabbitbrush
☼ ✎ 1-3, 10, 11

CORDIA boissieri   p. 289
Texas olive
☼ ✎ 8-24

DALEA frutescens   p. 309
Black dalea
☼ ✎ 10-13

DALEA pulchra   p. 309
Indigo bush
☼ ✎ 12, 13

DODONAEA viscosa   p. 319
Hop bush
☼ ◑ ✎ 7-24; H1, H2

ENCELIA farinosa   p. 327
Brittlebush
☼ ✎ 8-16, 18-24; H1

FALLUGIA paradoxa   p. 349
Apache plume
☼ ✎ 2-23

JUSTICIA californica   p. 424
Chuparosa
☼ ✎ 10-14, 18-24

LARREA tridentata   p. 433
Creosote bush
☼ ✎ 7-14, 18-21

LEUCOPHYLLUM   p. 440
Texas ranger
☼ ✎ 7-24

RHUS ovata   p. 591
Sugar bush
☼ ✎ 9-12, 14-24

RHUS trilobata   p. 591
Squawbush
☼ ✎ 1-12, 14-21

SALVIA greggii   p. 609
Autumn sage
☼ ✎ 8-24

SALVIA microphylla   p. 610
☼ ◑ ✎ 7-24

SIMMONDSIA chinensis   p. 625
Jojoba
☼ ✎ 7-24

SOPHORA secundiflora   p. 628
Mescal bean
☼ ◑ ✎ 8-16, 18-24

TAGETES lemmonii   p. 642
Copper canyon daisy
☼ ✎ 8-10, 12-24; H1

TECOMA stans   p. 644
Yellow bells
☼ ✎ 12, 13, 21-24; H1, H2

VAUQUELINIA californica   p. 662
Arizona rosewood
☼ ◑ ✎ 10-13

Tecoma stans

Southwest, Ground Covers & Vines

ANTIGONON leptopus   p. 188
Coral vine
☼ ✎ 12, 13, 18-24; H1, H2

BAILEYA multiradiata   p. 212
Desert marigold
☼ ✎ 1-3; 7-23

BACCHARIS sarothroides   p. 212
Desert broom
☼ ✎ 7-24

CALYLOPHUS hartwegii   p. 242
Sundrops
☼ ◑ ✎ 1-3, 6-16, 18-24

DALEA greggii   p. 309
Trailing indigo bush
☼ ✎ 10-13

MASCAGNIA macroptera   p. 474
Yellow orchid vine
☼ ✎ 12-24

MERREMIA aurea   p. 479
Yellow morning glory
☼ ✎ 12-24

OENOTHERA speciosa   p. 499
Mexican evening primrose
☼ ◑ ✎ 2B-24; H1, H2

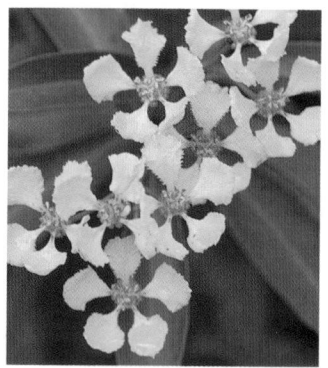

Mascagnia macroptera

OENOTHERA stubbei   p. 499
Saltillo evening primrose
☼ ◑ ✎ 10-14, 18-24

ZINNIA grandiflora   p. 677
☼ ✎ 1-24; H1, H2

Southwest, Accent Plants

AGAVE parryi   p. 175
☼ ◑ ✎ 2B, 3, 6-24

ECHINOCACTUS (many)   p. 324
Barrel cactus
☼ ◑ ✎ 12-24

ECHINOCEREUS (some)   p. 324
Hedgehog cactus
☼ ✎ ZONES VARY

FEROCACTUS (some)   p. 351
Barrel cactus
☼ ✎ 8-24

FOUQUIERIA splendens   p. 356
Ocotillo
☼ ✎ 10-13, 18-20

HESPERALOE parviflora   p. 392
Red yucca
☼ ◑ ✎ 2B, 3, 7-16, 18-24

Hesperaloe parviflora

Fouquieria splendens

Opuntia ficus-indica

Baileya multiradiata

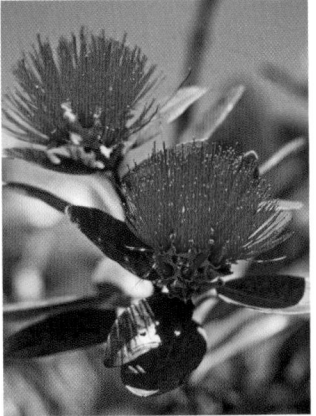

Metrosideros polymorphus

MUHLENBERGIA
dumosa   p. 486
Bamboo muhly
☼ ◑ ✓ 8–24

MUHLENBERGIA rigens   p. 486
Deer grass
☼ ◑ ✓ 4–24

OPUNTIA (many)   p. 501
☼ ✓ ZONES VARY

STENOCEREUS thurberi p. 634
Organpipe cactus
☼ ✓ 12–24

YUCCA (many)   p. 673
☼ ✓ ZONES VARY

Southwest, Annuals & Perennials

BAILEYA multiradiata p. 212
Desert marigold
☼ ✓ 1–3, 7–23

Stenocereus thurberi

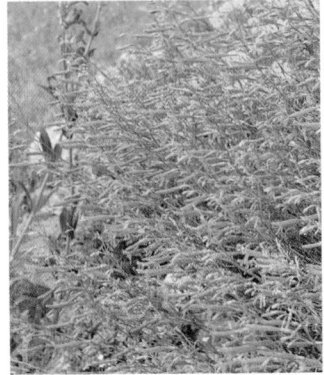

Penstemon pinifolius

MELAMPODIUM
leucanthum   p. 477
Blackfoot daisy
☼ ✓ 2, 3, 10–13

OENOTHERA caespitosa p. 499
Tufted evening primrose
☼ ◑ ✓ 1–3, 7–14, 18–21

PENSTEMON (many)   p. 526
☼ ◑ ✓ ZONES VARY

RATIBIDA columnifera p. 580
Mexican hat
☼ ✓ ALL ZONES

SALVIA farinacea   p. 609
Mealycup sage
☼ ✓ ALL ZONES

VERBENA bipinnatifida p. 663
☼ ✓ 1–24

VERBENA gooddingii   p. 663
☼ ✓ 7–24

Hawaii, Trees & Shrubs

ACACIA koa   p. 165
Koa
☼ ✓ H1, H2

ARTEMISIA australis   p. 201
Ahinahina
☼ ✓ H1, H2

Hibiscus waimeae

CIBOTIUM glaucum   p. 274
Hapu'u
☼ ◑ ✓ 17, 23, 24; H2

DODONAEA viscosa   p. 319
Hop bush
☼ ◑ ✓ 7–24; H1, H2

ERYTHRINA sandwicensis p. 337
Wiliwili
☼ ✓ H2

HIBISCUS waimeae   p. 396
White Kauai hibiscus
☼ ◑ ✓ H1

METROSIDEROS
polymorphus   p. 480
'Ohi'a lehua
☼ ◑ ✓ H1, H2

Sida fallax

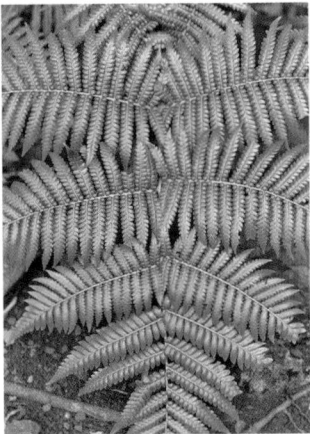

Cibotium glaucum

PRITCHARDIA
hillebrandii   p. 563
Loulu lelo
☼ ✓ 23, 24; H1, H2

SCAEVOLA taccada   p. 616
Beach naupaka
☼ ✓ H2

SIDA fallax   p. 624
'Ilima
☼ ✓ 23, 24; H1, H2

Hawaii, Ground Covers & Perennials

ALYXIA oliviformis   p. 183
Maile
◑ ● ✓ H1, H2

HELIOTROPIUM anomalum
argenteum   p. 389
Hinahina
☼ ✓ H2

PLECTRANTHUS
parviflorus   p. 548
'Ala 'ala wai nui
☼ ✓ 22–24; H2

Plants that Attract Butterflies

Butterflies are welcome visitors to most gardens. Choose the right plants and you can encourage them to stay a while. Butterfly larvae (caterpillars) need food plants; adult butterflies need nectar plants. Sunny areas that are sheltered from the wind and contain amenities such as leaf litter, rock crevices, brush piles, damp places, and even weeds are the most welcoming of gardens for butterflies. When you choose plants, keep in mind that not every plant will attract butterflies in every region. And never use pesticides, unless you can target the specific pest without harming the butterflies.

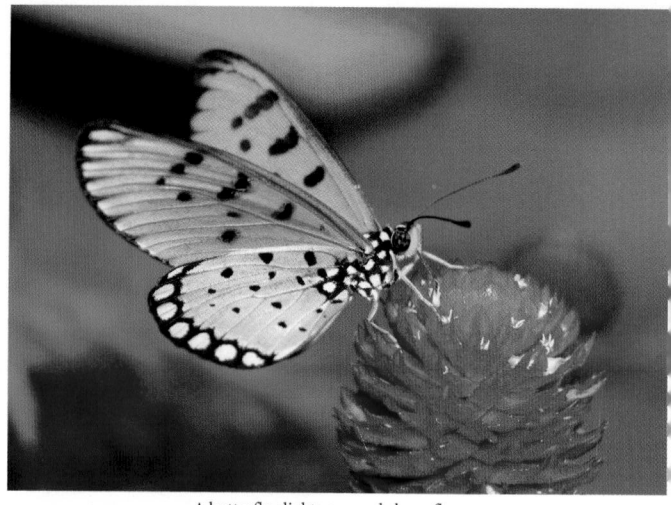

A butterfly alights on a red clover flower.

Aster novi-belgii

Asclepias incarnata

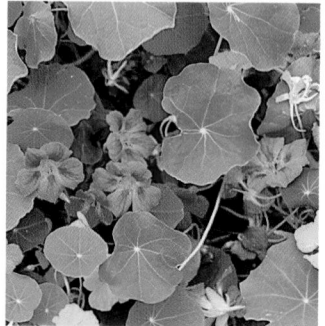

Tropaeolum majus

Butterfly Larvae, Perennials & Annuals

ACHILLEA millefolium   p. 170
Common yarrow
☼ ✀ A1–A3, 1–24

ALCEA rosea   p. 178
Hollyhock
☼ ◑ ✀ 1–24

ANTIRRHINUM majus   p. 188
Snapdragon
☼ ✀ A1–A3; 1–24

ASCLEPIAS   p. 203
☼ ✀ ZONES VARY

ASTER   p. 206
☼ ✀ ZONES VARY

DICENTRA   p. 315
Bleeding heart
◑ ● ✀ 1–9, 14–24

DIGITALIS purpurea   p. 317
Common foxglove
☼ ◑ ● ✀ A2, A3; 1–24

ERIOGONUM   p. 335
Wild buckwheat
☼ ✀ ZONES VARY

FOENICULUM vulgare   p. 355
Common fennel
☼ ✀ ZONES VARY

HELIANTHUS   p. 387
Sunflower
☼ ✀ ZONES VARY

LINARIA purpurea   p. 447
Toadflax
☼ ◑ ✀ 2–10, 14–24

LOBULARIA maritima   p. 451
Sweet alyssum
☼ ◑ ✀ ALL ZONES

LUPINUS   p. 455
Lupine
☼ ✀ ZONES VARY

MALVA   p. 469
Mallow
☼ ✀ 1–9, 14–24

MIMULUS aurantiacus   p. 482
Sticky monkey flower
☼ ◑ ✀ 5–9, 14–24

PENSTEMON   p. 526
Beard tongue
☼ ◑ ✀ ZONES VARY

RUTA graveolens   p. 605
Rue
☼ ✀ 2–24

SIDALCEA malviflora   p. 625
Checkerbloom
☼ ✀ 2–9, 14–24

TROPAEOLUM majus   p. 663
Garden nasturtium
☼ ◑ ✀ ALL ZONES

VERONICA
Speedwell
☼ ✀ ZONES VARY

Butterfly Larvae, Ground Covers & Vines

FRAGARIA   p. 356
Ornamental strawberry
☼ ◑ ✀ ZONES VARY

Alcea rosea

Helianthus annus 'Chianti'

Lupinus hybrid

Passiflora caerulea

HUMULUS lupulus p. 399
Common hop
☼ ☀ A2, A3; 1–10, 14–21

PASSIFLORA p. 514
Passion vine
☼ ◑ ☀ ZONES VARY

WISTERIA p. 671
☼ ◑ ☀ ZONES VARY

Butterfly Larvae, Shrubs

CASSIA p. 253
☼ ☀ ZONES VARY

CEANOTHUS p. 255
Wild lilac
☼ ☀ 5–9, 14–24

HIBISCUS p. 394
☼ ☀ ZONES VARY

HOLODISCUS discolor p. 397
Cream bush
◑ ☀ 1–9, 14–19

LAVATERA p. 437
Tree mallow
☼ ☀ ZONES VARY

PLUMBAGO auriculata p. 552
Cape plumbago
☼ ◑ ☀ 8, 9, 12–24; H1, H2

Rhamnus californica

Ribes sanguineum

RHAMNUS p. 581
NEEDS, ZONES VARY

RIBES p. 591
Currant
☼ ◑ ☀ ZONES VARY

SPIRAEA p. 631
☼ ◑ ☀ ZONES VARY

VIBURNUM p. 664
☼ ◑ ☀ ZONES VARY

Butterfly Larvae, Trees

AESCULUS p. 115
Horsechestnut
☼ ☀ ZONES VARY

BETULA p. 222
Birch
☼ ☀ ZONES VARY

CITRUS p. 276
☼ ☀ 8, 9, 12–24; H1, H2

CORNUS p. 291
Dogwood
NEEDS, ZONES VARY

Aesculus × carnea

Citrus (orange)

CRATAEGUS p. 298
Hawthorn
☼ ☀ 2–12, 14–17

MALUS p. 469
Flowering crabapple
☼ ☀ 1–11, 14–21

PINUS p. 541
Pine
☼ ☀ ZONES VARY

PLATANUS p. 546
Plane tree, sycamore
☼ ☀ ZONES VARY

POPULUS p. 557
Poplar
☼ ☀ ZONES VARY

PROSOPIS p. 563
Mesquite
☼ ☀ 10–13, 18–24

PRUNUS p. 564
NEEDS, ZONES VARY

PSEUDOTSUGA menziesii p. 569
Douglas fir
☼ ◑ ☀ A2, A3; 1–10, 14–17

QUERCUS p. 574
Oak
☼ ☀ ZONES VARY

SALIX p. 606
Willow
☼ ☀ ZONES VARY

Adult Butterflies, Annuals & Perennials

ACHILLEA p. 170
Yarrow
☼ ☀ A1–A3; 1–24

AGAPANTHUS p. 174
Lily-of-the-Nile
☼ ◑ ☀ 4–9, 12–24; H1, H2

ANTIRRHINUM majus p. 188
Snapdragon
☼ ☀ A1–A3; 1–24

AQUILEGIA p. 195
Columbine
☼ ◑ ☀ ZONES VARY

ARMERIA p. 200
Thrift
☼ ☀ ZONES VARY

ASCLEPIAS tuberosa p. 204
Butterfly weed
☼ ☀ 1–24

ASTER p. 206
☼ ☀ ZONES VARY

ASTILBE p. 207
False spiraea
☼ ◑ ☀ A2, A3; 1–9, 14–24

BORAGO officinalis p. 227
Borage
☼ ◑ ☀ A2, A3; 1–24; H1

Achillea

Holodiscus discolor

Aquilegia hybrid

Antirrhinum majus

Armeria maritima

Centranthus ruber

Sedum spectabile

Penstemon heterophyllus

Cosmos sulphurens

Rudbeckia hirta

Monarda didyma

Phlox subulata

CATANANCHE caerulea   p. 255
Cupid's dart
☼ ✿ 1-10, 14-24

CENTRANTHUS ruber   p. 260
Jupiter's beard
☼ ◐ ✿ 2-9, 12-24; H1

CHRYSANTHEMUM maximum   p. 273
Shasta daisy
☼ ◐ ✿ A1-A3; 1-24; H1

COREOPSIS   p. 289
☼ ✿ ZONES VARY

COSMOS   p. 295
☼ ✿ 1-24

CYNOGLOSSUM   p. 305
NEEDS, ZONES VARY

DELPHINIUM   p. 311
☼ ✿ ZONES VARY

DIANTHUS   p. 313
Pink
☼ ◐ ✿ A2, A3; 1-24

ECHINACEA purpurea   p. 323
Purple coneflower
☼ ✿ A2, A3; 1-24

ECHINOPS   p. 324
Globe thistle
☼ ✿ A2, A3; 1-24

ERIGERON   p. 331
Fleabane
☼ ◐ ✿ ZONES VARY

ERIOGONUM   p. 335
Wild buckwheat
☼ ✿ ZONES VARY

ERYNGIUM amethystinum   p. 336
Sea holly
☼ ✿ 1-24

ERYSIMUM cheiri   p. 336
English wallflower
☼ ◐ ✿ 4-6, 14-17, 22, 23

GAILLARDIA × grandiflora   p. 361
☼ ✿ 1-24; H1, H2

HELIOTROPIUM arborescens   p. 389
Common heliotrope
☼ ◐ ✿ ALL ZONES

IBERIS   p. 404
Candytuft
☼ ◐ ✿ ALL ZONES

LATHYRUS odoratus   p. 433
Sweet pea
☼ ✿ ALL ZONES

LIATRIS spicata   p. 442
Gayfeather
☼ ✿ A2, A3; 1-10, 14-24

LOBELIA   p. 450
NEEDS, ZONES VARY

LOBULARIA maritima   p. 451
Sweet alyssum
☼ ◐ ✿ ALL ZONES

MONARDA   p. 484
Bee balm
☼ ◐ ✿ ZONES VARY

ORIGANUM vulgare   p. 502
Oregano, Marjoram
☼ ✿ ZONES VARY

PENSTEMON   p. 526
Beard tongue
☼ ◐ ✿ ZONES VARY

PHLOX   p. 534
☼ ◐ ✿ ZONES VARY

RANUNCULUS   p. 579
NEEDS, ZONES VARY

RUDBECKIA   p. 604
☼ ✿ ZONES VARY

SALVIA   p. 607
Sage
NEEDS, ZONES VARY

SCABIOSA   p. 616
Pincushion flower
☼ ✿ ZONES VARY

Delphinium elatum hybrid

Ranunculus asiaticus

Tagetes erecta

Lantana camara

Lavandula angustifolia

SEDUM (most)   p. 620
Stonecrop
NEEDS, ZONES VARY

SOLIDAGO   p. 628
Goldenrod
☼ ◐ ✎ 1–11, 14–23

TAGETES   p. 642
Marigold
☼ ✎ ZONES VARY

VERBENA   p. 663
☼ ✎ ZONES VARY

ZAUSCHNERIA   p. 675
California fuchsia
NEEDS, ZONES VARY

Adult Butterflies, Shrubs

ABELIA   p. 162
☼ ◐ ✎ ZONES VARY

ABUTILON   p. 163
Flowering maple
☼ ◐ ✎ 8, 9, 12–24; H1, H2

ARCTOSTAPHYLOS   p. 197
Manzanita
☼ ◐ ✎ ZONES VARY

BUDDLEJA   p. 233
Butterfly bush
☼ ◐ ✎ ZONES VARY

CALLUNA vulgaris   p. 240
Scotch heather
☼ ✎ 1A, 2–6, 15–17

CARYOPTERIS   p. 252
Bluebeard
☼ ✎ ZONES VARY

CEANOTHUS   p. 255
Wild lilac
☼ ✎ 5–9, 14–24

CHOISYA ternata   p. 270
Mexican orange
☼ ◐ ✎ 4–9, 14–24

CLETHRA alnifolia   p. 284
Summersweet
☼ ◐ ✎ A2, A3; 1–6

ESCALLONIA   p. 338
☼ ◐ ✎ 4–9, 14–24

HEBE   p. 385
☼ ◐ ✎ 14–24

HETEROMELES arbutifolia   p. 392
Toyon
☼ ◐ ✎ 5–9, 14–24

LANTANA   p. 432
☼ ✎ 8–10, 12–24; H1, H2

LAVANDULA   p. 434
Lavender
☼ ✎ ZONES VARY

LONICERA   p. 451
Honeysuckle
☼ ◐ ✎ ZONES VARY

MAHONIA   p. 467
NEEDS, ZONES VARY

PHILADELPHUS (single-flowered)   p. 533
Mock orange
☼ ◐ ✎ ZONES VARY

POTENTILLA   p. 559
Cinquefoil
☼ ◐ ✎ ZONES VARY

RHAMNUS californica   p. 581
Coffeeberry
☼ ◐ ✎ 3A–10, 14–24; H1, H2

RHODODENDRON   p. 583
◐ ✎ ZONES VARY

RHUS   p. 590
Sumac
☼ ✎ ZONES VARY

RIBES   p. 591
Currant, gooseberry
☼ ◐ ✎ ZONES VARY

ROSMARINUS officinalis   p. 602
Rosemary
☼ ✎ 4–24; H1, H2

SAMBUCUS   p. 613
Elderberry
☼ ◐ ✎ ZONES VARY

SPIRAEA   p. 631
☼ ◐ ✎ ZONES VARY

SYRINGA   p. 640
Lilac
☼ ◐ ✎ ZONES VARY

VACCINIUM   p. 661
NEEDS, ZONES VARY

Adult Butterflies, Trees

ACER   p. 167
Maple
☼ ◐ ✎ ZONES VARY

AESCULUS   p. 173
Horsechestnut
☼ ✎ ZONES VARY

APPLE   p. 189
☼ ✎ ZONES VARY

CITRUS   p. 276
☼ ✎ 8, 9, 12–24; H1, H2

SALIX   p. 606
Willow
☼ ✎ ZONES VARY

VITEX   p. 668
Chaste tree
☼ ✎ ZONES VARY

Buddleja davidii

Lonicera sempervirens

Aesculus hippocastanum

Plants that Attract Birds

To keep birds coming to your garden, you need to create a living smorgasbord that includes plants with berries, foliage, fruit, and nectar. Mix up natives and non-natives, and include plants that bloom at different times of the year. If your garden lacks food during certain months, put up bird feeders. Birds also need leafy or twiggy shrubbery to protect them from predators and to provide nesting places. For more information on attracting birds to your garden, see pages 751–752.

Malus (crabapple)

Aloe arborescens

Aquilegia hybrid

Digitalis purpurea

Leonotis leonurus

Nectar Plants, Annuals & Perennials

AGASTACHE p. 174
☼ ◐ ✎ ZONES VARY

ALCEA rosea p. 178
Hollyhock
☼ ◐ ✎ 1–24

ALOE p. 180
☼ ◐ ✎ 8, 9, 12–24

ALSTROEMERIA p. 182
☼ ◐ ✎ 5–9, 14–24; H1

AQUILEGIA p. 195
Columbine
☼ ◐ ✎ ZONES VARY

ASCLEPIAS tuberosa p. 204
Butterfly weed
☼ ✎ 1–24

CLARKIA p. 281
☼ ◐ ✎ A2, A3; 1–24

CLEOME hasslerana p. 283
Spider flower
☼ ✎ 1–24

CROCOSMIA
×crocosmiiflora p. 300
Montbretia
☼ ◐ ✎ 5–24; H1, H2

DELPHINIUM p. 311
☼ ✎ ZONES VARY

DICENTRA p. 315
Bleeding heart
☼ ◐ ✎ 1–9, 14–24

DIGITALIS p. 317
Foxglove
NEEDS, ZONES VARY

GLADIOLUS p. 370
☼ ✎ 4–9, 12–24; H1

HEUCHERA p. 393
Coral bells
☼ ◐ ✎ ZONES VARY

KNIPHOFIA p. 427
Red-hot poker
☼ ◐ ✎ ZONES VARY

LEONOTIS leonurus p. 438
Lion's tail
☼ ✎ 8–24; H1, H2

LOBELIA (red-flowered) p. 450
☼ ◐ ✎ ZONES VARY

LUPINUS p. 454
Lupine
☼ ✎ ZONES VARY

MIMULUS p. 482
Monkey flower
NEEDS, ZONES VARY

MONARDA p. 484
Bee balm
☼ ◐ ✎ ZONES VARY

PELARGONIUM p. 524
Geranium
☼ ◐ ✎ A2, A3; 1–7, 8–11, 12–24

Alstroemeria hybrid

Dicentra spectabilis

Monarda didyma

Salvia

Penstemon pinifolius

Tecoma capensis

Abutilon pictum 'Thompsonii'

Buddleja davidii

Correa pulchella

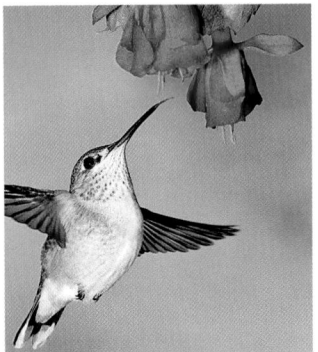

Fuchsia × hybrida

PENSTEMON (many)   p. 526
Beard tongue
☼ ◑ ✿ ZONES VARY

SALVIA (many)   p. 607
Sage
NEEDS, ZONES VARY

VERONICA   p. 663
Speedwell
☼ ✿ ZONES VARY

ZAUSCHNERIA   p. 675
California fuchsia
NEEDS, ZONES VARY

ZINNIA   p. 677
☼ ✿ ZONES VARY

Nectar Plants, Vines

CAMPSIS   p. 246
Trumpet creeper
☼ ◑ ✿ ZONES VARY

IPOMOEA quamoclit   p. 409
Cypress vine
☼ ✿ ALL ZONES

LONICERA   p. 451
Honeysuckle
☼ ◑ ✿ ZONES VARY

PYROSTEGIA venusta   p. 573
Flame vine
☼ ✿ 13, 16, 21–24; H1, H2

TECOMA capensis   p. 644
Cape honeysuckle
☼ ◑ ✿ 12, 13, 20–24; H1, H2

Nectar Plants, Shrubs

ABELIA   p. 162
☼ ◑ ✿ ZONES VARY

ABUTILON   p. 163
Flowering maple
☼ ◑ ✿ 8, 9, 12–24; H1, H2

ACACIA   p. 164
☼ ✿ ZONES VARY

ARBUTUS unedo   p. 197
Strawberry tree
☼ ◑ ✿ 4–24

ARCTOSTAPHYLOS   p. 197
Manzanita
☼ ◑ ✿ ZONES VARY

BOUVARDIA (red-flowered)   p. 229
☼ ✿ 8–10, 12, 14–24

BUDDLEJA   p. 233
Butterfly bush
☼ ◑ ✿ ZONES VARY

CAESALPINIA   p. 236
☼ ✿ ZONES VARY

CALLIANDRA   p. 238
☼ ✿ ZONES VARY

CALLISTEMON   p. 239
Bottlebrush
☼ ✿ ZONES VARY

CEANOTHUS   p. 255
Wild lilac
☼ ✿ 5–9, 14–24

CERCIS occidentalis   p. 262
Western redbud
☼ ◑ ✿ 2–24

CESTRUM   p. 263
◑ ✿ ZONES VARY

CHAENOMELES   p. 264
Flowering quince
☼ ✿ 2–23

CORREA   p. 293
Australian fuchsia
☼ ◑ ✿ 14–24

COTONEASTER   p. 296
☼ ✿ ZONES VARY

FEIJOA, Pineapple Guava   p. 350
☼ ✿ 6–9, 12–24; H1, H2

FUCHSIA   p. 360
☼ ◑ ✿ ZONES VARY

GREVILLEA (red-flowered)   p. 378
NEEDS, ZONES VARY

HETEROMELES arbutifolia   p. 392
Toyon
☼ ◑ ✿ 5–9, 14–24

HIBISCUS   p. 394
☼ ✿ ZONES VARY

JUSTICIA (several)   p. 423
NEEDS, ZONES VARY

KOLKWITZIA amabilis   p. 429
Beauty bush
☼ ◑ ✿ 2–11, 14–20

LANTANA   p. 432
☼ ✿ 8–10, 12–24; H1, H2

Lonicera japonica

Lantana camara

Lantana camara 'Patriot Honeylove'

Lavandula angustifolia 'Hidcote Giant'

LAVANDULA (many)   p. 434
Lavender
☼ ⚡ ZONES VARY

LEUCOPHYLLUM   p. 440
Texas ranger
☼ ⚡ 7–24

LONICERA   p. 451
Honeysuckle
☼ ◐ ⚡ ZONES VARY

MELALEUCA   p. 476
☼ ⚡ ZONES VARY

RIBES   p. 591
Currant
☼ ◐ ⚡ ZONES VARY

ROSMARINUS officinalis   p. 602
Rosemary
☼ ⚡ 4–24; H1, H2

SAMBUCUS   p. 613
Elderberry
☼ ◐ ⚡ ZONES VARY

SYRINGA   p. 640
Lilac
☼ ◐ ⚡ ZONES VARY

Rosmarinus officinalis

TECOMA stans   p. 644
Yellow bells
☼ ◐ ⚡ 12, 13, 21–24; H1, H2

TRICHOSTEMA lanatum   p. 654
Woolly blue curls
☼ ⚡ 14–24

WEIGELA   p. 670
☼ ◐ ⚡ 1–11, 14–21

Nectar Plants, Trees

ALBIZIA julibrissin   p. 178
Silk tree
☼ ◐ ⚡ 4–23

CHILOPSIS linearis   p. 268
Desert willow
☼ ⚡ 3B, 7–14, 18–23

CITRUS   p. 276
☼ ⚡ 8, 9, 12–24; H1, H2

ERYTHRINA   p. 336
Coral tree
☼ ⚡ ZONES VARY

Tecoma stans

Lonicera × brownii

Albizia julibrissin

EUCALYPTUS   p. 339
☼ ⚡ ZONES VARY

Seed & Berry Plants, Evergreen Trees

ABIES   p. 162
Fir
☼ ◐ ⚡ ZONES VARY

ILEX   p. 404
Holly
☼ ◐ ⚡ ZONES VARY

JUNIPERUS   p. 418
Juniper
☼ ◐ ⚡ ZONES VARY

MAGNOLIA grandiflora   p. 460
Southern magnolia
☼ ◐ ⚡ 4–12, 14–24; H1, H2

PICEA   p. 538
Spruce
☼ ◐ ⚡ ZONES VARY

Abies magnifica

Pinus strobus

Thuja occidentalis

PINUS   p. 541
Pine
☼ ⚡ ZONES VARY

QUERCUS   p. 574
Oak
☼ ⚡ ZONES VARY

THUJA   p. 646
Arborvitae
☼ ◐ ⚡ ZONES VARY

TSUGA   p. 657
Hemlock
☼ ◐ ⚡ ZONES VARY

Seed & Berry Plants, Deciduous Trees

ACER   p. 167
Maple
☼ ⚡ ZONES VARY

ALNUS   p. 180
Alder
☼ ◐ ● ⚡ ZONES VARY

BETULA   p. 222
Birch
☼ ⚡ ZONES VARY

CARPINUS   p. 251
Hornbeam
☼ ◐ ● ⚡ ZONES VARY

CELTIS   p. 259
Hackberry
☼ ◐ ⚡ ZONES VARY

Acer palmatum

Betula nigra

Malus (crabapple)

Pyracantha coccinea

Callicarpa japonica

Cornus florida

CORNUS p. 291
Dogwood
☼ ◐ ⚘ ZONES VARY

CRATAEGUS p. 298
Hawthorn
☼ ⚘ 2–12, 14–17 EXCEPT AS NOTED

ELAEAGNUS angustifolia p. 326
Russian olive
☼ ◐ ⚘ A2, A3; 1–3, 7–14, 18, 19

FRAXINUS velutina p. 358
Arizona ash
☼ ⚘ 3B–24

LARIX p. 432
Larch
☼ ⚘ ZONES VARY

LIQUIDAMBAR p. 448
Sweet gum
☼ ⚘ ZONES VARY

MALUS p. 469
Flowering crabapple
☼ ⚘ 1–11, 14–21

MORUS (fruiting kinds) p. 485
Mulberry
☼ ⚘ ZONES VARY

PRUNUS p. 564
☼ ⚘ ZONES VARY

RHUS p. 590
Sumac
☼ ⚘ ZONES VARY

SORBUS p. 629
Mountain ash
☼ ◐ ⚘ ZONES VARY

Seed & Berry Plants, Evergreen Shrubs

ARCTOSTAPHYLOS p. 197
Manzanita
☼ ◐ ⚘ ZONES VARY

ATRIPLEX p. 208
Saltbush
☼ ⚘ ZONES VARY

BERBERIS p. 221
Barberry
☼ ◐ ⚘ ZONES VARY

COTONEASTER p. 296
☼ ⚘ ZONES VARY

GARRYA p. 363
Silktassel
☼ ◐ ⚘ ZONES VARY

HETEROMELES arbutifolia p. 392
Toyon
☼ ◐ ⚘ 5–9, 14–24

HYPTIS emoryi p. 403
Desert lavender
☼ ⚘ 8–14, 18–24

ILEX p. 404
Holly
☼ ◐ ⚘ ZONES VARY

LIGUSTRUM p. 443
Privet
☼ ◐ ⚘ ZONES VARY

MAHONIA p. 467
☼ ◐ ● ⚘ ZONES VARY

PHOTINIA p. 537
☼ ⚘ ZONES VARY

Crataegus

Rubus pentalobus 'Emerald Carpet'

PYRACANTHA p. 572
Firethorn
☼ ⚘ ZONES VARY

RHAMNUS p. 581
☼ ◐ ● ⚘ ZONES VARY

RHUS p. 590
Sumac
☼ ⚘ ZONES VARY

RUBUS p. 603
Bramble
☼ ◐ ⚘ ZONES VARY

VIBURNUM p. 664
☼ ◐ ⚘ ZONES VARY

Seed & Berry Plants, Deciduous Shrubs

AMELANCHIER p. 183
Juneberry
☼ ◐ ⚘ ZONES VARY

Viburnum trilobum

ATRIPLEX p. 208
Saltbush
☼ ⚘ ZONES VARY

BERBERIS p. 221
Barberry
☼ ◐ ⚘ ZONES VARY

CALLICARPA p. 239
Beautyberry
☼ ◐ ⚘ ZONES VARY

CERCIS p. 262
Redbud
☼ ◐ ⚘ ZONES VARY

CORNUS p. 291
Dogwood
☼ ◐ ⚘ ZONES VARY

COTONEASTER p. 296
☼ ⚘ ZONES VARY

ELAEAGNUS p. 325
☼ ◐ ⚘ ZONES VARY

EUONYMUS p. 344
☼ ◐ ● ⚘ ZONES VARY

ILEX p. 404
Holly
☼ ◐ ⚘ ZONES VARY

LIGUSTRUM p. 443
Privet
☼ ◐ ⚘ ZONES VARY

LONICERA p. 451
Honeysuckle
☼ ◐ ⚘ ZONES VARY

MALUS toringo sargentii p. 472
Sargent crabapple
☼ ⚘ 1–11, 14–21

Ilex

RHAMNUS p. 581
☼ ◐ ● ⚡ ZONES VARY

RHUS p. 590
Sumac
☼ ⚡ ZONES VARY

RIBES p. 591
Currant
☼ ◐ ⚡ ZONES VARY

ROSA (small-fruited kinds) p. 593
Rose
☼ ◐ ⚡ ZONES VARY

RUBUS p. 603
Bramble
☼ ◐ ⚡ ZONES VARY

SAMBUCUS p. 613
Elderberry
☼ ◐ ⚡ ZONES VARY

SHEPHERDIA p. 624
Buffaloberry
☼ ⚡ ZONES VARY

SYMPHORICARPOS p. 640
Snowberry, Coralberry
☼ ◐ ● ⚡ ZONES VARY

VACCINIUM parvifolium p. 661
Red huckleberry
☼ ● ⚡ A3; 2-7, 14-17

VIBURNUM p. 664
☼ ◐ ⚡ ZONES VARY

Nigella damascena

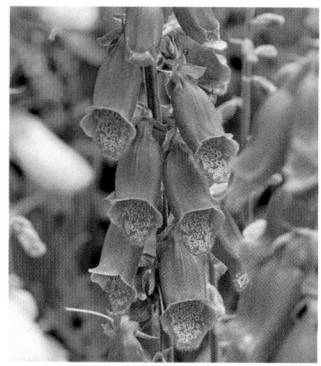
Digitalis purpurea

Seed & Berry Plants, Annuals & Perennials

AQUILEGIA p. 195
Columbine
☼ ◐ ⚡ ZONES VARY

CALENDULA officinalis p. 238
Calendula
☼ ⚡ A2, A3; 1-24; H1

CENTAUREA cyanus p. 260
Cornflower
☼ ⚡ 1-24; H1, H2

Lobularia maritima

COREOPSIS p. 289
☼ ⚡ ZONES VARY

COREOPSIS tinctoria p. 290
Annual coreopsis
☼ ⚡ 1-24; H1, H2

COSMOS p. 295
☼ ⚡ 1-24

DIGITALIS p. 317
Foxglove
☼ ◐ ● ⚡ ZONES VARY

ECHINACEA purpurea p. 323
Purple coneflower
☼ ⚡ A2, A3; 1-24

ERIOGONUM p. 335
Wild buckwheat
☼ ⚡ ZONES VARY

GAILLARDIA pulchella p. 361
☼ ⚡ 1-24; H1, H2

HELIANTHUS annuus p. 387
Common sunflower
☼ ⚡ ALL ZONES

LOBULARIA maritima p. 451
Sweet alyssum
☼ ◐ ⚡ ALL ZONES

NIGELLA damascena p. 496
Love-in-a-mist
☼ ◐ ⚡ ALL ZONES

Zinnia elegans and *Helianthus annuus*

RUDBECKIA p. 604
☼ ⚡ ZONES VARY

SCABIOSA atropurpurea p. 616
Pincushion flower
☼ ⚡ 1-24; H1, H2

SOLIDAGO p. 628
Goldenrod
☼ ◐ ⚡ 1-11, 14-23

TAGETES p. 642
Marigold
☼ ⚡ ZONES VARY

TITHONIA rotundifolia p. 650
Mexican sunflower
☼ ⚡ ALL ZONES

ZINNIA p. 677
☼ ⚡ 1-24; H1, H2

Cercis occidentalis

Rosa

Sambucus nigra 'Marginata'

Helianthus annuus 'Sunbright'

Rudbeckia nitida 'Herbstsonne'

Malus toringo sargentii

Symphoricarpos albus

Vaccinium parvifolium

Solidago hybrid

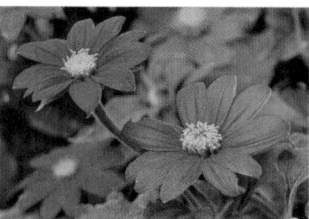
Tithonia rotundifolia 'Fiesta Del Sol'

Trees & Shrubs for Containers

Annuals, perennials, herbs, and even vegetables are standard choices for container gardening. Sometimes, however, only larger, woody plants will suit your needs. Perhaps you want a tall accent for the patio, maybe you long to grow a favorite camellia but have no available ground for planting. Perhaps you have your heart set on a lemon tree, but the climate is too chilly in winter to permit its survival outdoors. The trees and shrubs on these pages adapt well to life in larger containers.

Acer palmatum 'Ever Red'

Abutilon megapotamicum

Citrus (mandarin)

Trees

ACER japonicum   p. 168
Fullmoon maple
☼ ◐ ✂ 2–6, 14–16

ACER palmatum   p. 168
Japanese maple
☼ ◐ ✂ A3; 2–10, 12, 14–24

**ACER shirasawanum
'Aureum'**   p. 170
Golden fullmoon maple
◐ ✂ 3B–6, 14–16

APPLE (dwarf)   p. 189
☼ ✂ ZONES VARY

CITRUS   p. 276
☼ ✂ 8, 9, 12–24; H1, H2

FIG, edible   p. 353
☼ ✂ 4–9, 12–24; H1, H2

PINUS (several)   p. 541
☼ ✂ ZONES VARY

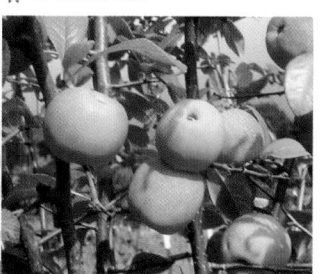

Apple *malus*

**WISTERIA
(trained as tree)**   p. 671
☼ ◐ ✂ ZONES VARY

Shrubs

ABUTILON   p. 163
Flowering maple
☼ ◐ ✂ 8, 9, 12–24; H1, H2

**ANISODONTEA
× hypomandarum**   p. 187
Cape mallow
☼ ◐ ✂ 14–24

**ARBUTUS unedo
(smaller cultivars)**   p. 197
Strawberry tree
☼ ◐ ✂ 4–24

AUCUBA japonica   p. 209
Japanese aucuba
◐ ● ✂ 4–24

Bougainvillea

BERBERIS thunbergii   p. 221
Japanese barberry
☼ ◐ ✂ A3; 2B–24

**BOUGAINVILLEA
(shrubby cultivars)**   p. 227
☼ ✂ 5, 6, 12–17, 19, 21–24; H1, H2

BRUGMANSIA   p. 232
Angel's trumpet
☼ ◐ ● ✂ 12, 13, 16–24; H1, H2

BRUNFELSIA pauciflora   p. 233
◐ ✂ 12–17, 20–24; H1, H2

BUXUS   p. 235
Boxwood
☼ ◐ ● ✂ ZONES VARY

CAMELLIA   p. 242
◐ ✂ 4–9, 12, 14–24

CHOISYA ternata   p. 270
Mexican orange
☼ ◐ ✂ 4–9, 14–24

Brugmansia 'Charles Grimaldi'

Buxus sempervirens

COROKIA cotoneaster   p. 293
☼ ◐ ✂ 4–24

CORREA   p. 293
Australian fuchsia
☼ ◐ ✂ 14–24

**CORYLUS avellana
'Contorta'**   p. 294
Harry Lauder's walking stick
☼ ◐ ✂ 2–9, 14–20

CUPRESSUS (dwarf types) p. 303
Cypress
☼ ✂ ZONES VARY

Fuchsia × hybrida

DAPHNE odora p. 310
Winter daphne
�½ ☽ ✓ 4–10, 12, 14–24

ENKIANTHUS p. 327
☼ ☽ ✓ 3–9, 14–21

ERIOBOTRYA deflexa p. 334
Bronze loquat
☼ ☽ ✓ 8–24

ESCALLONIA (smaller types) p. 338
☼ ☽ ✓ 4–9, 14–24

FATSIA japonica p. 350
Japanese aralia
☽ ● ✓ 4–9, 14–24; H1, H2

FUCHSIA p. 360
☼ ☽ ✓ ZONES VARY

GARDENIA p. 362
☼ ☽ ✓ ZONES VARY

HIBISCUS (several) p. 394
Mountain laurel
☼ ✓ ZONES VARY

HYDRANGEA macrophylla (some) p. 401
Bigleaf hydrangea
☼ ☽ ✓ 3B–9, 14–24; H1

ILEX (many) p. 404
Holly
☼ ☽ ✓ ZONES VARY

JUSTICIA brandegeeana p. 423
Shrimp plant
☼ ☽ ✓ 12, 13, 15–17, 21–24; H1, H2

LAGERSTROEMIA indica (dwarf forms) p. 430
Crape myrtle
☼ ✓ 2–10, 12–24; H1, H2

LANTANA p. 432
☼ ✓ 8–10, 12–24; H1, H2

LAURUS nobilis p. 434
Sweet bay
☼ ☽ ✓ 5–9, 12–24; H1, H2

LAVANDULA p. 434
Lavender
☼ ✓ ZONES VARY

Hibiscus rosa-sinensis

Hydrangea macrophylla

Lantana 'Radiation'

LIGUSTRUM japonicum p. 443
Japanese privet
☼ ☽ ✓ 4–24; H1, H2

MAHONIA (most) p. 467
NEEDS, ZONES VARY

MELIANTHUS major p. 477
Honey bush
☼ ☽ ✓ 8, 9, 12–24; H1, H2

MYRSINE africana p. 488
African boxwood
☼ ☽ ✓ 8, 9, 14–24

NANDINA domestica p. 489
Heavenly bamboo
☼ ☽ ● ✓ 3–24; H1, H2

NERIUM oleander (especially dwarf cultivars) p. 495
Oleander
☼ ✓ 8–16, 18–24; H1, H2

OSMANTHUS fragrans p. 505
Sweet olive
☼ ☽ ✓ 5–9, 12–24; H1

PEACH (genetic dwarfs) p. 516
☼ ✓ ZONES VARY

PICEA glauca (smallest forms) p. 539
White spruce
☼ ☽ ✓ A1–A3; 1–7, 14–17

Yucca

Rosa 'Wanona'

Rhododendron (azalea) 'Phoenicia'

PITTOSPORUM tobira p. 546
Tobira
☼ ☽ ✓ 4–24; H1, H2

PLUMERIA p. 552
Frangipani
☼ ☽ ✓ ZONES VARY

PODOCARPUS macrophyllus p. 554
Yew pine
☼ ☽ ✓ 4–9, 12–24; H1, H2

PODOCARPUS nagi p. 554
☼ ☽ ✓ 8, 9, 14–24; H1, H2

PUNICA granatum (dwarf cultivars) p. 571
Pomegranate
☼ ✓ 5–24; H1, H2

RHODODENDRON p. 583
☽ ✓ ZONES VARY

ROSA p. 593
Rose
☼ ☽ ✓ ZONES VARY

SKIMMIA japonica p. 626
☽ ✓ 4–9, 14–22

SOLANUM rantonnetii p. 627
☼ ☽ ✓ 12, 13, 15–24; H1, H2

SOLLYA heterophylla p. 628
Australian bluebell creeper
☼ ☽ ✓ 8, 9, 14–24; H1, H2

TAXUS p. 644
Yew
☼ ☽ ● ✓ ZONES VARY

YUCCA p. 673
☼ ✓ ZONES VARY

Plants for Tropical Effects

You may be able to create the atmosphere of one of your favorite vacation spots in your own garden. A surprising number of tropical and exotic-looking plants prosper in milder Pacific Coast climates, even in such decidedly non-tropical cities as Seattle or Vancouver, B.C. Listed here is a rich array of trees, vines, shrubs, and perennials with flashy flowers, bold foliage, or an overall lushness that defines tropical destinations worldwide.

Aloes, palm trees, and New Zealand flax make a striking entryway.

Trees

ARALIA p. 196
☼ ◑ ✀ ZONES VARY

BAUHINIA p. 218
Orchid tree
☼ ✀ ZONES VARY

CATALPA p. 254
☼ ◑ ✀ 3–10, 14–24

CHORISIA p. 270
Floss silk tree
☼ ✀ ZONES VARY

ERYTHRINA p. 336
Coral tree
☼ ✀ ZONES VARY

FICUS lyrata p. 353
Fiddleleaf fig
☼ ◑ ✀ 22–24; H1, H2

FIRMIANA simplex p. 355
Chinese parasol tree
☼ ◑ ✀ 5, 6, 8, 9, 12–24

MUSA p. 486
Banana
☼ ◑ ✀ ZONES VARY

PALMS p. 508
NEEDS, ZONES VARY

PAULOWNIA tomentosa p. 515
Empress tree
☼ ✀ 4–9, 11–24

TABEBUIA p. 642
Trumpet tree
☼ ✀ 15, 16, 20–24; H1, H2

Vines

BEAUMONTIA grandiflora p. 219
Herald's trumpet
☼ ◑ ✀ 12, 13, 16, 17, 21–24; H1, H2

BOUGAINVILLEA p. 227
☼ ✀ 5, 6, 12–17, 19, 21–24; H1, H2

CAMPSIS p. 246
Trumpet creeper
☼ ◑ ✀ ZONES VARY

× FATSHEDERA lizei p. 350
☼ ● ✀ 4–10, 12–24; H1, H2

LONICERA hildebrandiana p. 452
Giant burmese honeysuckle
☼ ◑ ✀ 9, 14–17, 19–24; H1, H2

MANDEVILLA p. 473
☼ ◑ ✀ ZONES VARY

MONSTERA deliciosa p. 484
Split-leaf philodendron
☼ ✀ 16, 17, 22–24; H1, H2

PANDOREA p. 510
☼ ◑ ✀ 16–24; H1, H2

PASSIFLORA p. 514
Passion vine
☼ ◑ ✀ ZONES VARY

SOLANDRA maxima p. 626
Cup-of-gold vine
☼ ✀ 15–24; H2

TETRASTIGMA voinieranum p. 645
☼ ✀ 13, 17, 20–24; H1, H2

Shrubs

ABUTILON p. 163
Flowering maple
☼ ◑ ✀ 8, 9, 12–24; H1, H2

BRUGMANSIA p. 232
Angel's trumpet
☼ ◑ ● ✀ 12, 13, 16–24; H1, H2

CROTALARIA agatiflora p. 300
Canary bird bush
☼ ◑ ✀ 13, 15–24; H1, H2

EUPHORBIA cotinifolia p. 345
Caribbean copper plant
☼ ✀ 23, 24; H1, H2

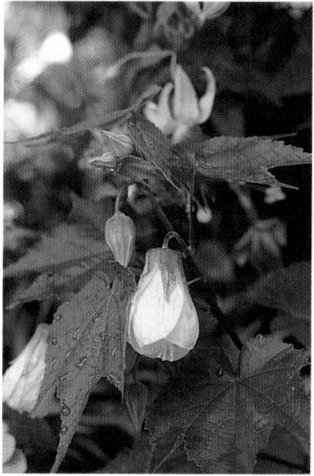
Abutilon hybrid

EUPHORBIA pulcherrima p. 346
Poinsettia
☼ ✀ 13, 16–24; H1, H2

FATSIA japonica p. 350
Japanese aralia
☼ ● ✀ 4–9, 14–24; H1, H2

Erythrina crista-galli

Bougainvillea 'Hawaii'

Brugmansia 'Charles Grimaldi'

Bauhinia × *blakeana*

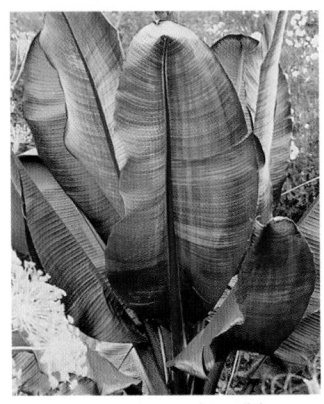

Ensete ventricosum 'Maurellii'

FICUS auriculata   p. 352
☼ ◐ 20–24; H1, H2

HIBISCUS rosa-sinensis   p. 395
Chinese hibiscus
☼ ◐ 9, 12–16, 19–24; H1, H2

IOCHROMA cyaneum   p. 408
☼ ◐ ◑ 15–17, 19–24

MELIANTHUS major   p. 477
Honey bush
☼ ◐ ◑ 8, 9, 12–24; H1, H2

PLUMERIA   p. 552
Frangipani
☼ ◐ ◑ ZONES VARY

SCHEFFLERA   p. 617
☼ ◐ ◑ ZONES VARY

STRELITZIA   p. 637
Bird of paradise
☼ ◐ ◑ ZONES VARY

TECOMA stans   p. 644
Yellow bells
☼ ◐ ◑ 12, 13, 21–24; H1, H2

TETRAPANAX papyrifer   p. 645
Rice paper plant
☼ ◐ ◑ 15–24; H1, H2

TIBOUCHINA urvilleana   p. 649
Princess flower
☼ ◐ ◑ 16, 17, 21–24; H1, H2

Tibouchina urvilleana

Perennials

ALOCASIA   p. 180
Elephant's ear
◐ ◑ 22–24; H1, H2

ALPINIA   p. 182
Ginger lily
◐ ◑ 14–24; H1, H2

ANTHURIUM andraeanum p. 188
Spathe flower
◐ ◑ H2

ASPIDISTRA elatior   p. 205
Cast-iron plant
◐ ● ◑ 4–10, 12–24; H1, H2

BAMBOO   p. 212
☼ ◐ ◑ ZONES VARY

Alocasia × amazonica

Alpinia zerumbet

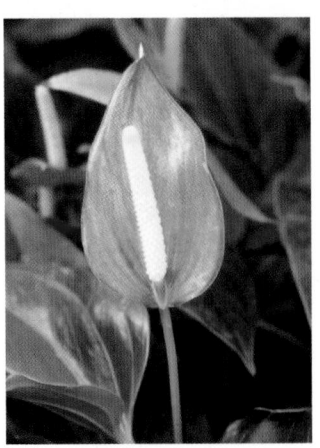

Anthurium andraeanum

BILLBERGIA   p. 224
◐ ◑ 12–24; H1, H2

CALADIUM bicolor   p. 236
Fancy-leafed caladium
◐ ● ◑ H2

CANNA   p. 248
☼ ◐ ◑ 6–9, 12–24; H1, H2

CLIVIA miniata   p. 284
◐ ● ◑ 12–17, 19–24; H1, H2

COLOCASIA esculenta   p. 287
Taro
◐ ◑ 12, 16–24; H1, H2

CRINUM   p. 299
☼ ◐ ◑ 8, 9, 12–24; H1, H2

ENSETE ventricosum   p. 328
Abyssinian banana
☼ ◐ ◑ 13, 15–24; H1, H2

EPIPHYLLUM   p. 329
Orchid cactus
◐ ◑ 8, 9, 14–24; H1, H2

GUNNERA   p. 381
◐ ◑ 4–6, 14–17, 20–24

HEDYCHIUM   p. 386
Ginger lily
◐ ◑ 8, 9, 14–17, 19–24; H1, H2

Canna 'Wyoming'

Caladium bicolor

Schefflera arboricola 'Gold Capella'

KNIPHOFIA   p. 427
Red-hot poker
☼ ◐ ◑ ZONES VARY

PHILODENDRON   p. 533
NEEDS, ZONES VARY

PLATYCERIUM   p. 546
Staghorn fern
◐ ◑ ZONES VARY

XANTHOSOMA   p. 672
◐ ◑ 12, 13, 16, 17, 21–24; H1, H2

ZANTEDESCHIA aethiopica   p. 675
Common calla
☼ ◐ ◑ 5, 6, 8, 9, 21–24; H1, H2

ZINGIBER officinale   p. 676
True ginger
◐ ◑ 9, 14–24; H1, H2

Gunnera tinctoria

Plants for Dry Areas

In most parts of the West, gardeners recognize that they must carefully manage their use of supplemental water for their plants. In places, a short rainy season is followed by many dry months during which there is no rainfall at all. Municipalities often place limits on supplemental watering, especially during drought years. Fortunately, there are many fine plants that, once established, thrive with little or no additional irrigation.

Lagerstroemia indica 'Petite Orchid'

Pinus patula

Cupressus

Grevillea

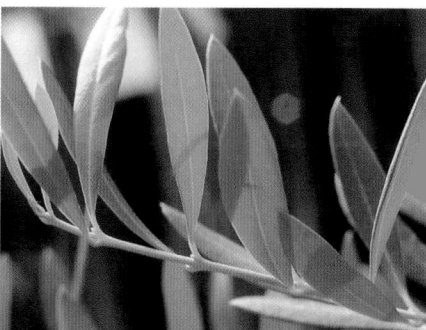

Olea europaea

Trees

ACACIA (many) p. 164
☼ ☀ ZONES VARY

ARBUTUS p. 197
☼ ☀ ZONES VARY

BRACHYCHITON p. 229
☼ ☀ ZONES VARY

CALOCEDRUS decurrens p. 241
Incense cedar
☼ ◑ ☀ 2–12, 14–24

CASUARINA p. 254
Beefwood
☼ ☀ 8, 9, 12–24; H1, H2

CEDRUS p. 258
Cedar
☼ ☀ ZONES VARY

CELTIS p. 259
Hackberry
☼ ◑ ☀ ZONES VARY

CERATONIA siliqua p. 261
Carob
☼ ☀ 9, 13–16, 18–24; H1

CERCIDIUM p. 262
Palo verde
☼ ☀ 8–14, 18–20

CHILOPSIS linearis p. 268
Desert willow
☼ ☀ 3B, 7–14, 18–23

✕ CHITALPA tashkentensis p. 270
☼ ☀ 3–24

CUPRESSUS p. 303
Cypress
☼ ☀ ZONES VARY

ELAEAGNUS angustifolia p. 326
Russian olive
☼ ◑ ◐ ☀ A2, A3; 1–3, 7–14, 18, 19

EUCALYPTUS (most) p. 339
☼ ☀ 5, 6, 8–24; H1, H2

GEIJERA parviflora p. 365
Australian willow
☼ ☀ 8, 9, 12–24

GREVILLEA p. 378
☼ ◑ ☀ ZONES VARY

LAGERSTROEMIA indica p. 430
Crape myrtle
☼ ☀ 2–10, 12–24; H1, H2

LAURUS nobilis p. 434
Sweet bay
☼ ◑ ☀ 5–9, 12–24; H1, H2

LEUCAENA retusa p. 440
Golden ball lead tree
☼ ☀ 10–13

LOPHOSTEMON confertus p. 453
Brisbane box
☼ ☀ 15–17, 19–24; H1, H2

MACLURA pomifera p. 458
Osage orange
☼ ☀ 2, 3, 10–13

OLEA europaea p. 495
Olive
☼ ☀ 8, 9, 11–24; H1, H2

OLNEYA tesota p. 500
Desert ironwood
☼ ☀ 8, 9, 11–14, 18–23

PARKINSONIA aculeata p. 512
Jerusalem thorn
☼ ☀ 8–24; H1, H2

PINUS (most) p. 541
Pine
☼ ☀ ZONES VARY

PISTACIA p. 545
Pistache
☼ ☀ ZONES VARY

PROSOPIS p. 563
Mesquite
☼ ☀ 10–13, 18–24

QUERCUS (many) p. 574
Oak
☼ ☀ ZONES VARY

Calocedrus decurrens

Eucalyptus viminalis

Quercus agrifolia

Robinia × ambigua

Schinus molle

Calliandra californica

Acacia cultriformis

Umbellularia californica

Cistus ladanifer

Coprosma
'Rainbow Surprise'

Cotinus coggygria
'Royal Purple'

Aloysia triphylla

RHUS lancea   p. 590
African sumac
☼ ◐ 8, 9, 12–24

ROBINIA   p. 592
Locust
☼ ◐ ZONES VARY

SCHINUS molle   p. 617
California pepper tree
☼ ◐ 8, 9, 12–24; H1, H2

SOPHORA japonica   p. 628
Japanese pagoda tree
☼ ◐ ◑ 2–24

TAMARIX   p. 642
Tamarisk
☼ ◐ ZONES VARY

**UMBELLULARIA
californica**   p. 660
California laurel
☼ ◐ ● ◑ 4–9, 14–24

Shrubs

ACACIA (many)   p. 164
☼ ◐ ZONES VARY

**ADENOSTOMA
fasciculatum**   p. 172
Chamise
☼ ◐ 6–9, 14–24

ALOYSIA triphylla   p. 182
Lemon verbena
☼ ◐ 4–9, 10, 12–21

ANISACANTHUS thurberi   p. 187
Chuparosa
☼ ◐ 8–13, 18–23; H1, H2

**ANISODONTEA
× hypomandarum**   p. 187
Cape mallow
☼ ◐ ◑ 14–24

ARBUTUS unedo   p. 197
Strawberry tree
☼ ◐ ◑ 4–24

ARCTOSTAPHYLOS   p. 197
Manzanita
☼ ◐ ◑ ZONES VARY

ARTEMISIA (most)   p. 201
☼ ◐ ◑ ZONES VARY

ASTARTEA fascicularis   p. 206
☼ ◐ ◑ 15–24

ATRIPLEX   p. 208
Saltbush
☼ ◐ ZONES VARY

BACCHARIS   p. 212
☼ ◐ ZONES VARY

CAESALPINIA   p. 236
☼ ◐ ZONES VARY

CALLIANDRA (some)   p. 238
☼ ◐ ZONES VARY

**CARPENTERIA
californica**   p. 251
Bush anemone
☼ ◐ ◑ 5–9, 14–24

**CARYOPTERIS
× clandonensis**   p. 253
Blue mist
☼ ◐ 2B–9, 14–24

CEANOTHUS   p. 255
Wild lilac
☼ ◐ 5–9, 14–24

CERCIS occidentalis   p. 262
Western redbud
☼ ◐ ◑ 2–24

CERCOCARPUS   p. 263
Mountain mahogany
☼ ◐ ZONES VARY

**CHAMELAUCIUM
uncinatum**   p. 265
Geraldton waxflower
☼ ◐ 8, 9, 12–24

CISTUS   p. 275
Rockrose
☼ ◐ 4–9, 14–24

**CONVOLVULUS
cneorum**   p. 288
Bush morning glory
☼ ◐ ◑ 5–9, 12–24

COPROSMA (most)   p. 288
☼ ◐ ◑ ZONES VARY

CORDIA (some)   p. 289
☼ ◐ ZONES VARY

CORREA   p. 293
Australian fuchsia
☼ ◐ ◑ 14–24

COTINUS coggygria   p. 296
Smoke tree
☼ ◐ 2–24

COTONEASTER   p. 296
☼ ◐ ZONES VARY

Baccharis pilularis 'Twin Peaks'

Cotoneaster horizontalis

Cytisus scoparius 'Moonlight'

Encelia farinosa

Justicia carnea

Leucophyllum frutescens

Dodonaea viscosa 'Purpurea'

Fouquieria splendens

Lavandula multifida

Leucadendron 'Safari Sunset'

CYTISUS p. 306
Broom
☼ ◑ ✄ ZONES VARY

DALEA p. 309
☼ ✄ ZONES VARY

DENDROMECON p. 312
Bush poppy
☼ ✄ ZONES VARY

DODONAEA viscosa p. 319
Hop bush
☼ ◑ ✄ 7–24; H1, H2

ELAEAGNUS (some) p. 325
☼ ◑ ✄ ZONES VARY

**ELEUTHEROCOCCUS
sieboldianus** p. 326
☼ ◑ ● ✄ 2B–10, 14–17

ENCELIA farinosa p. 327
Brittlebush
☼ ◔ ✄ 8–16, 18–24; H1

EREMOPHILA (most) p. 330
Emu bush
☼ ✄ 8, 9, 13–24

EURYOPS p. 347
☼ ✄ ZONES VARY

FALLUGIA paradoxa p. 349
Apache plume
☼ ✄ 2–23

**FEIJOA,
Pineapple Guava** p. 350
☼ ✄ 6–9, 12–24; H1, H2

FOUQUIERIA splendens p. 356
Ocotillo
☼ ✄ 10–13, 18–20

FREMONTODENDRON p. 359
Flannel bush
☼ ✄ 4–24

GALVEZIA speciosa p. 362
Island bush snapdragon
☼ ◑ ✄ 14–24

GARRYA (some) p. 363
Silktassel
☼ ◑ ✄ ZONES VARY

GENISTA p. 365
Broom
☼ ✄ ZONES VARY

HAKEA p. 382
☼ ✄ 9, 12–17, 19–24

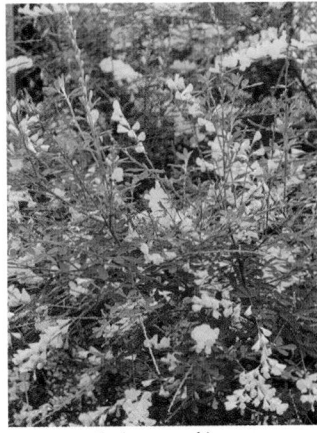

Genista × spachiana

× HALIMIOCISTUS p. 383
☼ ✄ 4–24

HALIMIUM p. 383
☼ ✄ 5–9, 12–24

**HETEROMELES
arbutifolia** p. 392
Toyon
☼ ◑ ✄ 5–9, 14–24

HOLODISCUS p. 397
◑ ✄ ZONES VARY

JUNIPERUS (some) p. 418
Juniper
☼ ◑ ✄ ZONES VARY

JUSTICIA (some) p. 423
NEEDS, ZONES VARY

LANTANA p. 432
☼ ✄ 8–10, 12–24; H1, H2

LAVANDULA p. 434
Lavender
☼ ✄ ZONES VARY

**LAVATERA
assurgentiflora** p. 437
Tree mallow
☼ ✄ 14–24

Lantana 'Radiation'

LEONOTIS leonurus p. 438
Lion's tail
☼ ✄ 8–24; H1, H2

LEPTOSPERMUM p. 438
Tea tree
☼ ✄ 14–24

LEUCADENDRON p. 439
☼ ✄ 16, 17, 20–24; H1

LEUCOPHYLLUM p. 440
Texas ranger
☼ ✄ 7–24

LUMA apiculata p. 454
☼ ✄ 14–24

MAHONIA (many) p. 467
NEEDS, ZONES VARY

Juniperus

Nerium oleander

Salvia spathacea

Teucrium fruticans

Osmanthus × burkwoodii

Plumbago auriculata 'Imperial Blue'

Westringia fruticosa 'Morning Light'

MELALEUCA (most) p. 476
☼ ⚡ ZONES VARY

MYOPORUM p. 487
☼ ⚡ ZONES VARY

MYRTUS communis p. 488
Myrtle
☼ ◐ ⚡ 8-24; H1, H2

NANDINA domestica p. 489
Heavenly bamboo
☼ ◐ ● ⚡ 3-24; H1, H2

NERIUM oleander p. 495
Oleander
☼ ⚡ 8-16, 18-24; H1, H2

OPUNTIA p. 501
☼ ⚡ ZONES VARY

OSMANTHUS p. 504
☼ ◐ ⚡ ZONES VARY

PHLOMIS p. 534
☼ ⚡ ZONES VARY

PLUMBAGO auriculata p. 549
Cape plumbago
☼ ◐ ⚡ 8, 9, 12-24; H1, H2

PORTULACARIA afra p. 558
Elephant's food
☼ ◐ ● ⚡ 8, 9, 12-24; H1, H2

PROSTANTHERA p. 563
Mint bush
☼ ⚡ 14-17, 19-24

PRUNUS ilicifolia p. 564
☼ ⚡ 5-9, 12-24

PYRACANTHA p. 572
Firethorn
☼ ⚡ ZONES VARY

RHAMNUS (most) p. 581
NEEDS, ZONES VARY

RHUS p. 590
Sumac
☼ ⚡ ZONES VARY

RIBES (most) p. 591
Currant
☼ ◐ ⚡ ZONES VARY

ROSA rugosa p. 602
Ramanas rose
☼ ◐ ⚡ A1-A3; 1-24

Rosmarinus officinalis 'Blue Spire'

ROSMARINUS officinalis p. 602
Rosemary
☼ ⚡ 4-24; H1, H2

RUBUS p. 603
Bramble
☼ ◐ ⚡ ZONES VARY

RUSCUS p. 604
Butcher's broom
◐ ● ⚡ 4-24; H1

SALVIA (many) p. 607
Sage
NEEDS, ZONES VARY

SANTOLINA chamaecyparissus p. 614
Lavender cotton
☼ ⚡ 2-24; H1, H2

SIMMONDSIA chinensis p. 625
Jojoba
☼ ⚡ 7-24

SOPHORA (some) p. 628
☼ ◐ ⚡ ZONES VARY

SYMPHORICARPOS p. 640
Snowberry
NEEDS, ZONES VARY

TEUCRIUM p. 645
Germander
☼ ⚡ ZONES VARY

TRICHOSTEMA lanatum p. 654
Woolly blue curls
☼ ⚡ 14-24

VAUQUELINIA californica p. 662
Arizona rosewood
☼ ◐ ⚡ 10-13

WESTRINGIA fruticosa p. 670
☼ ⚡ 8, 9, 14-24

Ground Covers & Vines

ACACIA redolens p. 166
☼ ⚡ 8, 9, 12-24

ARCTOSTAPHYLOS uva-ursi p. 198
Bearberry
☼ ◐ ⚡ A1-A3; 1-9, 14-24

ARCTOTHECA calendula p. 198
Cape weed
☼ ⚡ 8, 9, 13-24

CALYLOPHUS hartwegii p. 242
Sundrops
☼ ⚡ 1-3, 6-16, 18-24

CISSUS (some) p. 275
NEEDS, ZONES VARY

DALEA greggii p. 309
Trailing indigo bush
☼ ⚡ 10-13

FALLOPIA baldschuanica p. 349
Silver lace vine
☼ ⚡ A1-A3; 1-24

Rosa rugosa

Ice plant *(Carpobrotus chilensis)*

Achillea millefolium 'Lavender Beauty'

Armeria maritima

Arctotis hybrid

Centaurea cyanus 'Frosted Mix'

HYPERICUM calycinum p. 403
Aaron's beard
☼ ◐ ✶ 2B–24

ICE PLANTS p. 404
NEEDS, ZONES VARY

JUNIPERUS (some) p. 418
Juniper
☼ ◐ ✶ ZONES VARY

LANTANA p. 432
☼ ✶ 8–10, 12–24; H1, H2

MACFADYENA unguis-cati p. 457
Cat's claw
☼ ◐ ✶ 8–24; H1, H2

MAHONIA (some) p. 467
NEEDS, ZONES VARY

MALVASTRUM lateritium p. 473
Trailing mallow
☼ ✶ 8, 9, 14–24

MASCAGNIA p. 474
Orchid vine
☼ ✶ 12–24

MYOPORUM parvifolium p. 488
☼ ✶ 8, 9, 12–24

RIBES viburnifolium p. 592
Catalina perfume
☼ ◐ ✶ 5, 7–9, 14–17, 19–24

ROSA banksiae p. 601
Lady Banks' rose
☼ ◐ ✶ 4–24; H1, H2

ROSMARINUS officinalis p. 602
Rosemary
☼ ✶ 4–24; H1, H2

TECOMA capensis p. 644
Cape honeysuckle
☼ ◐ ✶ 12, 13, 20–24; H1, H2

THYMUS p. 648
Thyme
☼ ◐ ✶ 1–24

VERBENA (some) p. 663
☼ ✶ ZONES VARY

WISTERIA p. 671
NEEDS, ZONES VARY

Annuals, Bulbs & Perennials

ACHILLEA p. 170
Yarrow
☼ ✶ A1–A3, 1–24

AGAPANTHUS p. 174
Lily-of-the-Nile
☼ ◐ ✶ 4–9, 12–24; H1, H2

AGASTACHE p. 174
☼ ◐ ✶ ZONES VARY

AGAVE (most) p. 175
☼ ◐ ✶ ZONES VARY

ALOE p. 180
☼ ◐ ✶ 8, 9, 12–24

AMARYLLIS belladonna p. 183
Belladonna lily
☼ ✶ 4–24

ARCTOTIS p. 198
African daisy
☼ ✶ ALL ZONES

ARMERIA maritima p. 200
Common thrift
☼ ✶ A2, A3; 1–9, 14–24

ARTEMISIA p. 201
☼ ✶ ZONES VARY

BALLOTA pseudodictamnus p. 212
☼ ✶ 2, 3, 6–9, 14–24

CALAMINTHA p. 237
Calamint
☼ ◐ ✶ 1–9, 14–24

CENTAUREA p. 259
☼ ✶ ZONES VARY

CENTRANTHUS ruber p. 260
Jupiter's beard
☼ ◐ ✶ 2–9, 12–24; H1

COREOPSIS (most) p. 289
☼ ✶ ZONES VARY

DASYLIRION wheeleri p. 310
Desert spoon
☼ ◐ ✶ 10–24

ECHIUM p. 324
☼ ✶ ZONES VARY

ERIGERON karvinskianus p. 331
Mexican daisy
☼ ◐ ✶ 8, 9, 12–24; H1, H2

ERIOGONUM p. 335
Wild buckwheat
☼ ✶ ZONES VARY

Eriogonum grande rubescens

Agapanthus orientalis

Agave americana

Gaura lindheimeri

Nassella tenuissima

Phormium 'Maori Queen'

Sedum acre

EUPHORBIA (most) p. 345
NEEDS, ZONES VARY

GAURA lindheimeri p. 364
2B–24

HESPERALOE parviflora p. 392
Red yucca
2B, 3, 7–16, 18–24

IRIS, bearded p. 410
1–24

IRIS foetidissima p. 412
Gladwin iris
3–24

LIMONIUM perezii p. 446
Statice
13, 15–17, 20–24

LINUM p. 447
Flax
ZONES VARY

LOBELIA laxiflora p. 451
7–9, 12–24

MELAMPODIUM leucanthum p. 477
Blackfoot daisy
2, 3, 10–13

MIMULUS aurantiacus p. 482
Sticky monkey flower
5–9, 14–24

MONARDELLA p. 484
ZONES VARY

MUHLENBERGIA p. 486
ZONES VARY

NARCISSUS p. 489
Daffodil
A2, A3; 1–24

NASSELLA p. 491
Needle grass
ZONES VARY

NOLINA p. 496
ZONES VARY

OENOTHERA p. 498
Evening primrose
ZONES VARY

PENNISETUM setaceum p. 526
Fountain grass
8–24; H1, H2

PENSTEMON (many) p. 526
Beard tongue
ZONES VARY

PEROVSKIA p. 529
Russian sage
2–24

PHLOMIS p. 534
ZONES VARY

PHORMIUM p. 536
5–9, 14–24; H1, H2

ROMNEYA coulteri p. 593
Matilija poppy
4–12, 14–24; H1

SALVIA (some) p. 607
Sage
NEEDS, ZONES VARY

SANTOLINA p. 614
ZONES VARY

SEDUM (many) p. 620
Stonecrop
NEEDS, ZONES VARY

SISYRINCHIUM idahoense bellum p. 626
Blue-eyed grass
2–9, 14–24

STACHYS byzantina p. 633
Lamb's ears
1–24

STIPA gigantea p. 635
Giant feather grass
4–9, 14–24

VERBENA (many) p. 663
ZONES VARY

WATSONIA p. 669
4–9, 12–24

YUCCA (most) p. 673
ZONES VARY

ZAUSCHNERIA p. 675
California fuchsia
NEEDS, ZONES VARY

ZINNIA grandiflora p. 677
ALL ZONES

Watsonia pillansii

Zauschneria californica latifolia

Mimulus aurantiacus

Yucca filamentosa 'Bright Edge'

Verbena bonariensis

Plants for Shade

Shady spots, whether created by leafy canopies, sun-blocking walls, or an overhead structure, are too dark and cool for many garden favorites. Sun-loving plants can dwindle away, fail to bloom, or become leggy and sparse in the absence of direct sunlight. But there are plenty of colorful choices that will thrive with less heat and warmth. Below are trees, shrubs, vines, perennials, bulbs, and annuals for those shady spots.

Acer palmatum

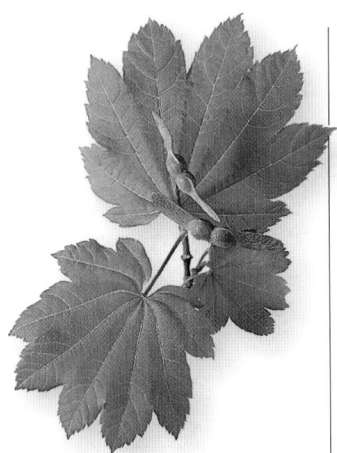

Acer circinatum

CERCIS canadensis	p. 262
Eastern redbud	
☼ ◑ ✂ 1–24	
CORNUS	p. 291
Dogwood	
☼ ◑ ● ✂ ZONES VARY	
DAVIDIA involucrata	p. 311
Dove tree	
☼ ◑ ✂ 4–9, 14–21	
HALESIA	p. 383
☼ ◑ ✂ 2B–9, 14–21	
PARROTIA persica	p. 513
Persian parrotia	
☼ ◑ ✂ 2B–7, 14–17	
PODOCARPUS	p. 554
☼ ◑ ✂ ZONES VARY	
STEWARTIA	p. 634
☼ ◑ ✂ 4–6, 14–17, 20, 21	

Trees

ACER circinatum	p. 167
Vine maple	
☼ ◑ ✂ A3; 2B–6, 14–17	
ACER palmatum	p. 168
Japanese maple	
☼ ◑ ✂ A3; 2–10, 12, 14–24	
ARBUTUS unedo	p. 133
Strawberry tree	
☼ ◑ ✂ 4–24	

Shrubs

ABUTILON	p. 163
Flowering maple	
☼ ◑ ✂ 8, 9, 12–24; H1, H2	
AUCUBA japonica	p. 209
Japanese aucuba	
◑ ● ✂ 4–24	

AZARA	p. 211
◑ ✂ ZONES VARY	
BRUNFELSIA pauciflora	p. 233
◑ ✂ 12–17, 20–24; H1, H2	
BUXUS	p. 235
Boxwood	
☼ ◑ ● ✂ ZONES VARY	
CAMELLIA	p. 242
◑ ✂ 4–9, 12, 14–24	
CARPENTERIA californica	p. 251
Bush anemone	
☼ ◑ ✂ 5–9, 14–24	
CLETHRA alnifolia	p. 284
Summersweet	
☼ ◑ ✂ A2, A3; 1–6	
CLEYERA japonica	p. 284
◑ ✂ 4–6, 8, 9, 14–24; H1	

COPROSMA repens	p. 288
Mirror plant	
☼ ◑ ✂ 14–24; H1	
CORNUS	p. 291
Dogwood	
☼ ◑ ● ✂ ZONES VARY	
CYCAS	p. 304
☼ ◑ ✂ ZONES VARY	

Aucuba japonica 'Variegata'

Cornus kousa

Camellia japonica

Daphne odora

Hydrangea macrophylla 'Tricolor'

Fuchsia × hybrida
'Marinka Golden Treasure'

Rhododendron (azalea) 'Osakazuki'

Skimmia japonica

DAPHNE odora p. 310
Winter daphne
◑ ◿ 4–10, 12, 14–24

ENKIANTHUS p. 327
☼ ◑ ◿ 3–9, 14–21

EUONYMUS fortunei p. 344
☼ ◑ ● ◿ 2B–17

FATSIA japonica p. 350
Japanese aralia
◑ ● ◿ 4–9, 14–24; H1, H2

FUCHSIA p. 360
☼ ◑ ◿ ZONES VARY

GARDENIA augusta p. 362
☼ ◑ ◿ 7–9, 12–16, 18–24; H1, H2

GAULTHERIA p. 364
◑ ◿ ZONES VARY

HAMAMELIS p. 383
Witch hazel
☼ ◑ ◿ ZONES VARY

HYDRANGEA p. 400
☼ ◑ ◿ ZONES VARY

ILEX p. 404
Holly
☼ ◑ ◿ ZONES VARY

KALMIA latifolia p. 425
Mountain laurel
◑ ◿ 2–7, 16, 17

LEUCOTHOE p. 441
☼ ◑ ◿ ZONES VARY

LOROPETALUM chinense p. 453
☼ ◑ ◿ 4–9, 14–24

MAHONIA p. 467
NEEDS, ZONES VARY

NANDINA domestica p. 489
Heavenly bamboo
☼ ◑ ● ◿ 3–24; H1, H2

OSMANTHUS p. 504
☼ ◑ ◿ ZONES VARY

PIERIS p. 540
☼ ◑ ◿ ZONES VARY

PITTOSPORUM p. 545
☼ ◑ ◿ ZONES VARY

RHAMNUS (some) p. 581
NEEDS, ZONES VARY

RHODODENDRON p. 583
Rhododendron, Azalea
◑ ● ◿ ZONES VARY

RIBES sanguineum p. 592
Pink winter currant
☼ ◑ ◿ A3; 4–9, 14–24

SARCOCOCCA p. 615
Sweet box
◑ ● ◿ 4–9, 14–24

SKIMMIA japonica p. 626
◑ ◿ 4–9, 14–22

SYMPHORICARPOS (some) p. 640
Snowberry
NEEDS, ZONES VARY

TERNSTROEMIA gymnanthera p. 645
◑ ● ◿ 4–9, 12–24

VACCINIUM p. 661
NEEDS, ZONES VARY

VIBURNUM (evergreen) p. 664
☼ ◑ ◿ ZONES VARY

Vines

CISSUS (some) p. 275
NEEDS, ZONES VARY

× FATSHEDERA lizei p. 350
◑ ● ◿ 4–10, 12–24; H1, H2

HEDERA p. 385
Ivy
☼ ◑ ◿ ZONES VARY

PARTHENOCISSUS p. 513
☼ ◑ ● ◿ ZONES VARY

TRACHELOSPERMUM jasminoides p. 653
Star jasmine
☼ ◑ ◿ 8–24; H1, H2

Parthenocissus quinquefolia

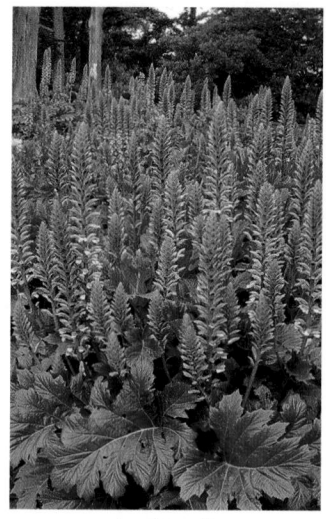

Acanthus mollis

Perennials, Bulbs & Annuals

ACANTHUS mollis p. 167
Bear's breech
☼ ◑ ● ◿ 5–24

ACONITUM p. 171
Aconite
☼ ◑ ◿ A1–A3; 1–9, 14–21

AJUGA p. 177
Carpet bugle
☼ ◑ ◿ A2, A3; 1–24

ALCHEMILLA p. 178
Lady's-mantle
☼ ◑ ◿ ZONES VARY

ANEMONE (some) p. 185
Windflower
NEEDS, ZONES VARY

AQUILEGIA p. 195
Columbine
☼ ◑ ◿ ZONES VARY

ARUM p. 202
◑ ● ◿ ZONES VARY

ARUNCUS p. 202
Goat's beard
☼ ◑ ◿ ZONES VARY

Ajuga reptans

Bergenia cordifolia 'Morning Red'

Brunnera macrophylla

Digitalis purpurea

Epimedium pinnatum

ASARUM   p. 203
Wild ginger
◐ ● ✄ ZONES VARY

ASPIDISTRA elatior   p. 205
Cast-iron plant
◐ ● ✄ 4–10, 12–24; H1, H2

ASTILBE   p. 207
False spiraea
☼ ◐ ✄ A2, A3; 1–9, 14–24

ASTILBOIDES tabularis   p. 208
◐ ✄ 2B–9, 14–17

ASTRANTIA   p. 208
Masterwort
☼ ◐ ✄ 1–9, 14–24

BEGONIA   p. 219
◐ ✄ 14–24; H1, H2

BERGENIA   p. 222
◐ ● ✄ A1–A3; 1–9, 12–24

BLETILLA striata   p. 225
Chinese ground orchid
◐ ✄ 2B–9, 12–24

BROWALLIA   p. 232
Amethyst flower
◐ ✄ ZONES VARY

BRUNNERA macrophylla   p. 233
Brunnera
☼ ◐ ✄ 1–24

CALADIUM bicolor   p. 236
Fancy-leafed caladium
◐ ● ✄ H2

CAMPANULA (some)   p. 246
Bellflower
☼ ◐ ✄ 1–9, 14–24

CLIVIA miniata   p. 284
◐ ● ✄ 12–17, 19–24; H1, H2

COLOCASIA esculenta   p. 287
Taro
◐ ✄ 12, 16–24; H1, H2

CONVALLARIA majalis   p. 288
Lily-of-the-valley
◐ ✄ A1–A3; 1–7, 14–20

CORYDALIS   p. 294
◐ ✄ 2–9, 14–24

CYCLAMEN   p. 304
☼ ◐ ✄ ZONES VARY

DIANELLA tasmanica   p. 313
Flax lily
☼ ◐ ✄ 8, 9, 14–24

DICENTRA (most)   p. 315
Bleeding heart
◐ ● ✄ 1–9, 14–24

DIGITALIS   p. 317
Foxglove
NEEDS, ZONES VARY

DORONICUM   p. 320
Leopard's bane
◐ ✄ A2, A3; 1–7, 14–17

EPIMEDIUM   p. 329
◐ ✄ 2–9, 14–17

ERYTHRONIUM   p. 337
◐ ✄ ZONES VARY

FARFUGIUM japonicum   p. 349
☼ ◐ ● ✄ 4–10, 14–24; H1, H2

FILIPENDULA   p. 354
Meadowsweet
☼ ◐ ● ✄ ZONES VARY

FRANCOA ramosa   p. 357
Maiden's wreath
◐ ✄ 4–9, 14–24

GALIUM odoratum   p. 362
Sweet woodruff
◐ ✄ A2, A3; 2–6, 15–17

GENTIANA   p. 366
Gentian
☼ ◐ ✄ 2–6, 14–17

GERANIUM (some)   p. 366
Cranesbill
☼ ◐ ✄ ZONES VARY

HEDYCHIUM   p. 386
Ginger lily
◐ ✄ 8, 9, 14–17, 19–24; H1, H2

HELLEBORUS   p. 390
Hellebore
◐ ● ✄ ZONES VARY

Begonia, tuberous

Solenostemon scutellarioides

Astilbe × arendsii

Geranium 'Rozanne'

Heuchera 'Amethyst Mist'

Lamium maculatum 'White Nancy'

Mertensia virginica

Trillium ovatum

Impatiens walleriana

Helleborus hybrid

Oxalis

THALICTRUM   p. 646
Meadow rue
☼ ☽ ☇ 2–10, 14–17

TIARELLA   p. 648
Foamflower
☼ ● ☇ ZONES VARY

TOLMIEA menziesii   p. 650
Piggyback plant
☼ ● ☇ A3; 4–9, 14–17, 20–24

TRADESCANTIA virginiana   p. 654
Spiderwort
☼ ☼ ● ☇ 1–24; H1

TRICYRTIS   p. 655
Toad lily
☼ ☇ ZONES VARY

TRILLIUM   p. 655
Wake robin
☼ ● ☇ ZONES VARY

TROLLIUS   p. 656
Globeflower
☼ ☼ ☇ A2, A3; 1–6

VANCOUVERIA   p. 661
☼ ☇ ZONES VARY

VINCA   p. 666
Periwinkle
☼ ☼ ● ☇ ZONES VARY

VIOLA   p. 666
Violet, Pansy
☼ ☼ ● ☇ ZONES VARY

HEUCHERA   p. 393
Coral bells
☼ ☼ ☇ ZONES VARY

× HEUCHERELLA   p. 394
☼ ☇ 1–10, 14–24

HOSTA   p. 398
Plantain lily
☼ ● ☇ ZONES VARY

HYACINTHOIDES   p. 400
Bluebell
☼ ☇ ZONES VARY

IMPATIENS (most)   p. 406
Balsam
NEEDS, ZONES VARY

IRIS foetidissima   p. 412
Gladwin iris
☼ ☼ ● ☇ 3–24

KIRENGESHOMA palmata   p. 426
Yellow waxbells
☼ ☇ 2–9, 14–24

LAMIUM   p. 431
Dead nettle
☼ ● ☇ ZONES VARY

LIGULARIA   p. 443
☼ ☇ 1–9, 14–17

LIRIOPE   p. 448
Lily turf
☼ ☼ ● ☇ ZONES VARY

LOBELIA (most)   p. 450
NEEDS, ZONES VARY

MERTENSIA   p. 479
☼ ● ☇ ZONES VARY

MIMULUS × hybridus   p. 482
☼ ● ☇ 1–24

MYOSOTIS   p. 488
Forget-me-not
☼ ☇ A1–A3; 1–24

OXALIS   p. 506
NEEDS, ZONES VARY

PACHYSANDRA   p. 507
☼ ● ☇ ZONES VARY

POLEMONIUM   p. 555
☼ ● ☇ 1–11, 14–17

POLYGONATUM   p. 556
Solomon's seal
☼ ● ☇ A1–A3; 1–9, 14–17

PRIMULA   p. 560
Primrose
☼ ☼ ● ☇ ZONES VARY

Polemonium

PULMONARIA   p. 570
Lungwort
☼ ● ☇ 1–9, 14–17

REHMANNIA elata   p. 581
Chinese foxglove
☼ ☼ ● ☇ 6–10, 12–24

SAXIFRAGA   p. 615
Saxifrage
☼ ● ☇ ZONES VARY

SENECIO × hybridus   p. 622
Florists' cineraria
☼ ● ☇ 16, 17, 22–24

SOLENOSTEMON scutellarioides   p. 627
Coleus
☼ ● ☇ ALL ZONES

Tricyrtis hirta

Pulmonaria saccharata

Viola × wittrockiana

Saxifraga stolonifera

Moisture-loving Plants

Whether you're planning a pond or stream garden, or just deciding how best to deal with a patch of perpetually boggy ground, you'll find that most standard nursery offerings are not up to the challenge. Constantly saturated soils lack the air that most plants need for good growth—the reason why not just any plant will grow in a swamp. These two pages list the best choices for wet (even underwater) soil: true aquatics, with roots that grow beneath the water's surface; plants that take shallow water or soggy soil; and those that need the constant moisture found in nature beside a pool or brook.

Nymphaea

Aquatic
(submerged only)

APONOGETON distachyus p. 189
Cape pondweed
☼ ◐ ✓ 4–9, 12–24

EICHHORNIA crassipes p. 325
Water hyacinth
☼ ✓ 8, 9, 13–24; H1, H2

NELUMBO p. 492
Lotus
☼ ◐ ✓ 1–24; H1, H2

NYMPHAEA p. 497
Water lily
☼ ✓ 1–24; H1, H2

PETASITES japonicus p. 531
Japanese coltsfoot
☼ ◐ ● ✓ 2B–9, 14–17

PISTIA stratiotes p. 545
Water lettuce
☼ ◐ ✓ 24; H2

PONTEDERIA cordata p. 557
Pickerel weed
☼ ◐ ✓ 1–24; H1, H2

Damp Soil or Shallow Water

ACORUS p. 171
Sweet flag
☼ ◐ ✓ ZONES VARY

BACOPA monnieri p. 212
Water hyssop
☼ ✓ 8–24; H1, H2

CALTHA palustris p. 241
Marsh marigold
☼ ◐ ● ✓ A1–A3; 1–9, 14–24

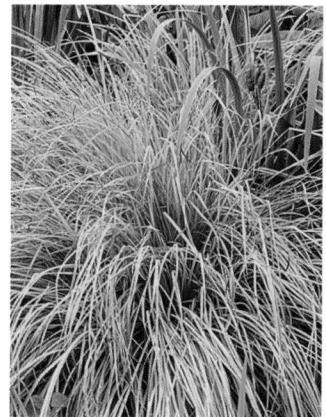

Carex elata 'Aurea'

CAREX elata 'Aurea' p. 250
Sedge
☼ ◐ ✓ 2–9, 14–24

CHONDROPETALUM elephantinum p. 270
Cape rush
☼ ◐ ✓ 8, 9, 14–24

COLOCASIA esculenta p. 287
Taro
◐ ✓ 12, 16–24; H1, H2

Acorus calamus 'Variegatus'

CYPERUS p. 306
☼ ◐ ● ✓ ZONES VARY

EQUISETUM hyemale p. 330
Horsetail
☼ ◐ ✓ 1–24

IRIS, Japanese p. 411
☼ ✓ 1–10, 14–24

IRIS laevigata p. 413
☼ ◐ ✓ 1–10, 14–24

IRIS, Louisiana p. 412
☼ ◐ ✓ 3–24; H1, H2

Cyperus papyrus

Iris pseudacorus

Equisetum hyemale

IRIS pseudacorus p. 413
Yellow flag
☼ ◐ ✓ A2, A3; 1–24

IRIS versicolor p. 413
Blue flag
☼ ◐ ✓ 1–9, 14–17

IRIS virginica p. 413
Southern blue flag
☼ ◐ ✓ 3–9, 14–17

JUNCUS p. 418
Rush
☼ ◐ ✓ ZONES VARY

OENANTHE javanica p. 498
Japanese watercress
☼ ✓ 9, 14–24

PRIMULA florindae p. 561
☼ ◐ ● ✓ A2, A3; 3–6, 15–17

PRIMULA japonica p. 561
☼ ◐ ● ✓ A3; 2–6, 15–17

SCHOENOPLECTUS lacustris tabernaemontani 'Zebrinus' p. 618
☼ ◐ ✓ 5–24

Aconitum napellus

Chelone lyonii

Myosotis sylvatica   *Tradescantia virginiana*

Rodgersia aesculifolia   *Isolepis cernua*   *Matteuccia struthiopteris*

Damp Soil Only

ACONITUM p. 171
Aconite
☼ ◐ ⚘ A1–A3; 1–9, 14–21

ALOCASIA p. 180
Elephant's ear
☼ ⚘ 22–24; H1, H2

ASCLEPIAS incarnata p. 204
Swamp milkweed
☼ ⚘ 1–9, 14–24

ASTER novae-angliae p. 207
New England aster
☼ ⚘ 1–24

ASTILBOIDES tabularis p. 208
◐ ⚘ 2B–9, 14–17

ATHYRIUM p. 208
◐ ● ⚘ ZONES VARY

CHELONE lyonii p. 266
Turtlehead
☼ ◐ ⚘ 1–9, 14–24

DARMERA peltata p. 310
Umbrella plant
◐ ⚘ 2–7, 14–20

EUPATORIUM purpureum p. 345
Joe Pye weed
☼ ◐ ⚘ 1–9, 14–17

FARFUGIUM japonicum p. 349
◐ ● ⚘ 4–10, 14–24; H1, H2

FILIPENDULA (most) p. 354
Meadowsweet
☼ ◐ ● ⚘ ZONES VARY

GUNNERA p. 381
◐ ⚘ 4–6, 14–17, 20–24

HOSTA p. 398
Plantain lily
◐ ● ⚘ ZONES VARY

HOUTTUYNIA cordata p. 398
☼ ◐ ● ⚘ 2–9, 14–24

IRIS setosa p. 413
☼ ⚘ A1–A3; 1–9, 14–17

IRIS, Siberian p. 412
☼ ◐ ⚘ A2, A3; 1–10, 14–23

ISOLEPIS cernua p. 414
Fiber optics plant
◐ ⚘ 7–24

LIGULARIA p. 443
◐ ⚘ 1–9, 14–17

LOBELIA (several) p. 450
NEEDS, ZONES VARY

LYSIMACHIA p. 456
☼ ◐ ● ⚘ ZONES VARY

MATTEUCCIA struthiopteris p. 475
Ostrich fern
◐ ● ⚘ A1–A3; 1–10, 14–17

MILIUM effusum 'Aureum' p. 481
Bowles' golden grass
◐ ⚘ 3B–9, 14–17

MIMULUS cardinalis p. 482
Scarlet monkey flower
☼ ◐ ● ⚘ 2–24

MOLINIA caerulea p. 483
Moor grass
☼ ◐ ⚘ 1–9, 14–17

MYOSOTIS p. 488
Forget-me-not
◐ ⚘ A1–A3; 1–24

OSMUNDA regalis p. 505
Royal fern
☼ ◐ ⚘ 1–9, 14–17

PANICUM virgatum p. 510
Switch grass
☼ ◐ ⚘ 1–11, 14–23

PHALARIS arundinacea picta p. 532
Ribbon grass
☼ ◐ ⚘ A1–A3; 1–10, 14–24

RHEUM p. 582
Ornamental rhubarb
☼ ◐ ⚘ 2B–7, 14–17

RODGERSIA p. 593
☼ ◐ ⚘ 2–9, 14–17

TRADESCANTIA virginiana p. 654
Spiderwort
☼ ◐ ● ⚘ 1–24; H1

TROLLIUS p. 656
Globeflower
☼ ◐ ⚘ A2, A3; 1–6

WOODWARDIA fimbriata p. 672
Giant chain fern
◐ ● ⚘ 2B, 4–9, 14–24

XANTHOSOMA p. 672
◐ ⚘ 12, 13, 16, 17, 21–24; H1, H2

ZANTEDESCHIA aethiopica p. 675
Common calla
☼ ◐ ⚘ 5, 6, 8, 9, 12–24; H1, H2

Aster novae-angliae

Millium effusum 'Aureum'

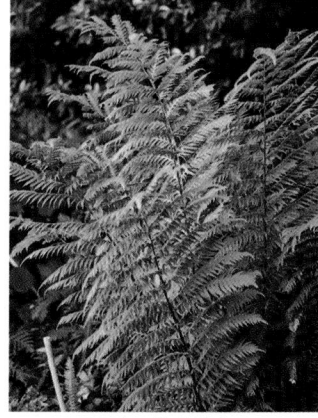

Woodwardia fimbriata

Rock Garden Gems

Dwarf trees, tiny shrubs, miniature bulbous plants, perennials and annuals that form low tufts or creeping mats of foliage are premier rock garden plants. Favorites in all categories are listed below. Classic European alpine gardens can be replicated in cool parts of the Pacific Northwest, but to create the same effect in hotter, drier, or colder regions, you'll need a different assortment of plants. Be sure to heed climate zone adaptations and cultural needs.

Calocephalus brownii

Daboecia cantabrica 'Cinderella'

Pieris japonica

Shrubs

BERBERIS × stenophylla 'Corallina Compacta' p. 221
Rosemary barberry
☼ ◑ ✿ 4–9, 14–24

BERBERIS thunbergii (smaller) p. 221
Japanese barberry
☼ ◑ ✿ A3; 2B–24

BETULA pendula 'Trost's Dwarf' p. 223
European white birch
☼ ✿ A2, A3; 1–12, 14–24

CALLUNA vulgaris (dwarf) p. 240
Scotch heather
☼ ✿ 1A, 2–6, 15–17

CALOCEPHALUS brownii p. 241
Cushion bush
☼ ✿ 16, 17, 19, 21–24

CISTUS (some) p. 275
Rockrose
☼ ✿ 4–9, 14–24

COTONEASTER (dwarf) p. 296
☼ ✿ ZONES VARY

DABOECIA cantabrica p. 307
Irish heath
☼ ◑ ✿ 3B–9, 14–24

DAPHNE cneorum p. 310
Garland daphne
☼ ◑ ✿ 2B–9, 14–17

ERICA (dwarf) p. 331
Heath
☼ ◑ ✿ ZONES VARY

GAULTHERIA (most) p. 364
◑ ✿ ZONES VARY

GENISTA (several dwarf types) p. 365
Dwarf broom
☼ ✿ ZONES VARY

HALIMIUM p. 383
☼ ✿ 5–9, 12–24

HEBE (several dwarf types) p. 385
☼ ◑ ✿ 14–24

HELIANTHEMUM nummularium p. 387
Sunrose
☼ ✿ 2B–9, 14–24

HYPERICUM coris p. 403
St. Johnswort
☼ ◑ ✿ 4–9, 14–24

ILEX crenata (several dwarf types) p. 405
Dwarf Japanese holly
☼ ◑ ✿ 3–9, 14–24

JUNIPERUS (many dwarf types) p. 418
Juniper
☼ ◑ ✿ ZONES VARY

PIERIS japonica (dwarf) p. 540
Lily-of-the-valley shrub
◑ ✿ 2B–9, 14–17

RHODODENDRON (dwarf types) p. 584
☼ ◑ ✿ ZONES VARY

RHODODENDRON (azalea) p. 588
Macrantha hybrids
◑ ✿ 5–9, 14–24

TEUCRIUM (low-growing) p. 645
Germander
☼ ✿ ZONES VARY

Cotoneaster dammeri 'Lowfast'

Hebe

Rhododendron (azaleas) and Ferns

Aeonium

Aster alpinus

Dianthus deltoides

Perennials

ACHILLEA (dwarf)   p. 170
Yarrow
☼ ✎ A1–A3; 1–24

AEONIUM   p. 173
☼ ◐ ✎ 15–17, 20–24

AETHIONEMA   p. 174
Stonecress
☼ ✎ 1–9, 14–21

AJUGA genevensis   p. 177
Carpet bugle
☼ ◐ ✎ A2, A3; 1–24

ANACYCLUS depressus   p. 184
Mount Atlas daisy
☼ ✎ 2–24

ANDROSACE   p. 185
Rock jasmine
☼ ✎ 1–6, 14–17

ANTENNARIA dioica   p. 187
Pussy toes
☼ ✎ A1, A2; 1–3, 6, 7, 14–16

AQUILEGIA (dwarf)   p. 195
Columbine
☼ ◐ ✎ ZONES VARY

ARABIS   p. 196
Rockcress
☼ ✎ ZONES VARY

Arabis procurrens

ARENARIA   p. 199
Sandwort
NEEDS, ZONES VARY

ARMERIA   p. 200
Thrift
☼ ✎ ZONES VARY

ASTER alpinus   p. 206
☼ ✎ 1–4

AUBRIETA deltoidea   p. 209
Common aubrieta
☼ ◐ ✎ 1–9, 14–21

AURINIA saxatilis   p. 209
Basket-of-gold
☼ ◐ ✎ 1–24

CAMPANULA (smallest)   p. 246
Bellflower
☼ ◐ ✎ 1–9, 14–24

CERASTIUM tomentosum   p. 261
Snow-in-summer
☼ ◐ ✎ A1, A2; 1–24

DELOSPERMA   p. 311
Ice plant
☼ ◐ ✎ ZONES VARY

Aurinia saxatilis

Campanula portenschlagiana

Gentiana asclepiadea

DIANTHUS (smallest)   p. 313
Pink
☼ ◐ ✎ A2, A3; 1–24

DRABA   p. 320
☼ ✎ ZONES VARY

DRYAS   p. 321
☼ ✎ A1–A3; 1–6

ECHEVERIA (many)   p. 323
☼ ◐ ✎ ZONES VARY

ERIGERON (dwarf)   p. 331
Fleabane
☼ ◐ ✎ ZONES VARY

ERIOGONUM (dwarf)   p. 335
Wild buckwheat
☼ ✎ ZONES VARY

ERODIUM reichardii   p. 335
Cranesbill
☼ ◐ ✎ 7–9, 14–24

EUPHORBIA myrsinites   p. 346
☼ ✎ 2–24

GENTIANA   p. 366
Gentian
☼ ◐ ✎ 2–6, 14–17

Leontopodium alpinum

GERANIUM (smallest)   p. 366
Cranesbill
☼ ◐ ✎ ZONES VARY

GYPSOPHILA (several dwarf types)   p. 382
☼ ✎ ZONES VARY

HERNIARIA glabra   p. 392
Green carpet
☼ ◐ ● ✎ 2B–24

HEUCHERA   p. 393
Coral bells
☼ ◐ ✎ ZONES VARY

HOSTA (smallest)   p. 398
Plantain lily
◐ ● ✎ ZONES VARY

IBERIS sempervirens   p. 404
Evergreen candytuft
☼ ◐ ✎ 1–24

LEONTOPODIUM alpinum   p. 438
Edelweiss
☼ ✎ 1–9, 14–17

LEWISIA   p. 441
☼ ◐ ✎ 1–7, 14–17

LITHODORA diffusa   p. 450
☼ ◐ ✎ 5–7, 14–17

Origanum vulgare

Portulaca

Cyclamen hederifolium

Galanthus nivalis

Primula japonica

Silene acaulis

Fritillaria meleagris

Muscari

ORIGANUM (low-growing) p. 502
Oregano, Marjoram
☼ ◐ ✿ ZONES VARY

OXALIS p. 506
☼ ◐ ✿ ZONES VARY

PENSTEMON (subshrubs or mat-forming) p. 526
Beard tongue
☼ ◐ ✿ ZONES VARY

PHLOX (trailing or creeping) p. 534
☼ ◐ ✿ ZONES VARY

PLEIONE p. 548
◐ ✿ 5–9, 14–24

POLEMONIUM reptans p. 555
◐ ● ✿ 1–11, 14–17

PORTULACA grandiflora p. 558
Rose moss
☼ ✿ ALL ZONES

POTENTILLA (most) p. 559
Cinquefoil
☼ ◐ ✿ ZONES VARY

PRIMULA (most) p. 560
Primrose
☼ ◐ ● ✿ ZONES VARY

PULSATILLA vulgaris p. 571
Pasque flower
☼ ✿ 2B–6, 15–17

SAPONARIA ocymoides p. 615
☼ ✿ 1–11, 14–24

SAXIFRAGA p. 615
Saxifrage
NEEDS, ZONES VARY

SEDUM (many) p. 620
Stonecrop
NEEDS, ZONES VARY

SEMPERVIVUM p. 621
Houseleek
☼ ◐ ✿ 2–24

SENECIO (some) p. 621
NEEDS, ZONES VARY

SILENE acaulis p. 625
Cushion pink
☼ ◐ ✿ A1–A3; 1–11, 14–16, 18–21

SISYRINCHIUM (smallest) p. 626
☼ ◐ ✿ 4–9, 14–24

THYMUS p. 648
Thyme
☼ ◐ ✿ 1–24

VERONICA (mat-forming) p. 663
Speedwell
☼ ✿ ZONES VARY

Bulbs, Bulb-like Plants

ALLIUM (smallest) p. 179
Ornamental allium
☼ ◐ ✿ ZONES VARY

CHIONODOXA p. 269
Glory-of-the-snow
☼ ◐ ✿ A2, A3; 1–7, 14–20

CROCUS p. 300
☼ ◐ ✿ 1–24

CYCLAMEN (except C. persicum) p. 304
☼ ◐ ✿ ZONES VARY

FREESIA p. 358
☼ ◐ ✿ 8, 9, 12–24

FRITILLARIA (smallest) p. 359
Fritillary
◐ ✿ ZONES VARY

GALANTHUS p. 362
Snowdrop
☼ ◐ ✿ 1–9, 14–17

IPHEION uniflorum p. 408
Spring star flower
☼ ◐ ✿ 2B–24

IRIS (smallest) p. 409
NEEDS, ZONES VARY

MUSCARI p. 487
Grape hyacinth
☼ ◐ ✿ ZONES VARY

NARCISSUS (small) p. 489
Daffodil
☼ ◐ ✿ A2, A3; 1–24

RHODOHYPOXIS baurii p. 589
☼ ✿ 4–7, 14–24

STERNBERGIA lutea p. 634
☼ ✿ 3–10, 14–24

TULIPA (species only) p. 657
Tulip
☼ ◐ ✿ 1–24

ZEPHYRANTHES p. 676
Zephyr flower
☼ ◐ ✿ ZONES VARY

Freesia

Sempervivum tectorum

Pulsatilla vulgaris

Crocus vernus

Zephyranthes grandiflora

Dwarf Conifers

Dwarf conifers are all about foliage, with colors that range from gold to palest cream, lime green to apple green, and deep plum to smoky blue. You can use dwarf conifers to weave a leafy tapestry in a rock garden, to fill in the understory in a woodland garden, or to serve as permanent filler plants in beds and borders. Many also make fine container subjects.

Chamaecyparis lawsoniana 'Lutea Nana'

Cryptomeria japonica 'Globosa Nana'

ABIES balsamea 'Nana'　p. 163
Balsam fir
☼ ◐ ✎ A3; 1–7, 15–17

ABIES koreana 'Horstmann's Silberlocke'　p. 163
Korean fir
☼ ◐ ✎ 3B–9, 14–24

CEDRUS deodara 'White Imp'　p. 258
Deodar cedar
☼ ◐ ✎ 3B–10, 14–24

CHAMAECYPARIS lawsoniana (dwarf kinds)　p. 264
Port Orford cedar
☼ ◐ ✎ A3; 3–6, 15–17

CHAMAECYPARIS obtusa (dwarf kinds)　p. 264
Hinoki false cypress
☼ ◐ ✎ A3; 2B–6, 15–17

CHAMAECYPARIS pisifera (dwarf kinds)　p. 265
Sawara false cypress
☼ ◐ ✎ A3; 2B–6, 15–17

CRYPTOMERIA japonica (dwarf kinds)　p. 301
Japanese cryptomeria
☼ ✎ 4–9, 14–24

PICEA abies (dwarf types)　p. 539
Norway spruce
☼ ◐ ✎ A2, A3; 1–6, 14–17

PICEA glauca albertiana 'Conica'　p. 539
Dwarf Alberta spruce
☼ ◐ ✎ A2, A3; 1–7, 14–17

PICEA glauca densata 'Sander's Blue'　p. 539
Black hills spruce
☼ ◐ ✎ A2, A3; 1–6

PICEA mariana 'Nana'　p. 539
Black spruce
☼ ◐ ✎ A1–A3; 1–7

PICEA pungens glauca　p. 539
Colorado blue spruce
☼ ◐ ✎ A2, A3; 1–10, 14–17

PINUS densiflora 'Pendula'　p. 542
Japanese red pine
☼ ✎ 2–9, 14–17; H1

PINUS flexilis 'Vanderwolf's Pyramid'　p. 543
Limber pine
☼ ✎ A1–A3; 1–11, 14–21

PINUS mugo　p. 543
Mugho pine
☼ ✎ A1–A3; 1–11, 14–24

PINUS strobus Nana group　p. 544
White pine
☼ ✎ 1–6

Pinus mugo

PINUS sylvestris 'Nana'　p. 544
Scotch pine
☼ ✎ A1–A3; 1–9, 14–21

PLATYCLADUS orientalis (dwarf kinds)　p. 547
Oriental arborvitae
☼ ◐ ✎ 2–24; H1, H2

SEQUOIA sempervirens 'Adpressa'　p. 623
Redwood
☼ ◐ ✎ 4–9, 14–24

THUJA occidentalis 'Hetz Midget'　p. 647
American arborvitae
☼ ◐ ✎ A2, A3; 1–9, 15–17, 21–24; H1, H2

THUJA plicata 'Spring Grove'　p. 647
Western red cedar
☼ ◐ ✎ A3; 1–9, 14–24

THUJOPSIS dolabrata 'Nana'　p. 647
False arborvitae
☼ ◐ ✎ 3B–7, 14–17

TSUGA canadensis (dwarf kinds)　p. 657
Canada hemlock
☼ ◐ ✎ A3; 2–7, 17

Chamaecyparis pisifera 'True Blue'

Picea pungens glauca

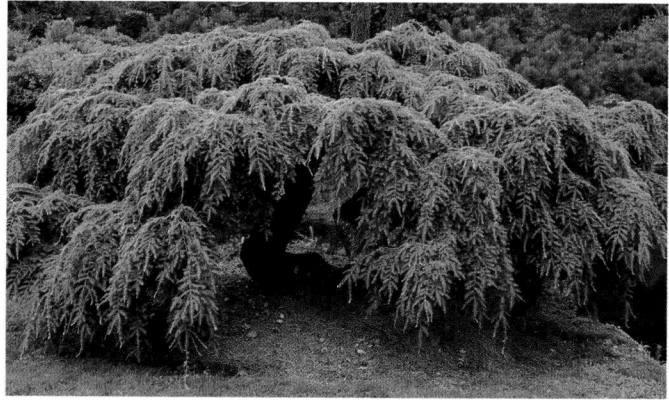

Tsuga canadensis 'Pendula'

Deer-resistant Plants

Browsing deer don't dine indiscriminately. Some plants are particular favorites; others are left more or less alone. If you live in deer country, you'll find it far simpler to build your garden from less-favored plants than to protect the choicer morsels. Deer generally ignore the plants listed below. Few are really deerproof, though: deer in different areas may have different tastes, and tastes may vary from year to year or even from season to season.

Acer palmatum

Trees

ABIES   p. 162
Fir
☼ ◐ ✴ ZONES VARY

ACACIA   p. 164
☼ ✴ ZONES VARY

Crataegus phaenopyrum

Fig, edible

ACER circinatum   p. 167
Vine maple
☼ ◐ ✴ A3; 2B-6, 14-17

ACER palmatum   p. 168
Japanese maple
☼ ◐ ✴ A3; 2-10, 12, 14-24

ALBIZIA   p. 177
☼ ◐ ✴ ZONES VARY

CALLISTEMON   p. 239
Bottlebrush
☼ ✴ ZONES VARY

CEDRUS   p. 258
Cedar
☼ ✴ ZONES VARY

CELTIS   p. 259
Hackberry
☼ ◐ ✴ ZONES VARY

CERATONIA siliqua   p. 261
Carob
☼ ✴ 9, 13-16, 18-24; H1

Cocos nucifera (palm)

Magnolia stellata

CERCIS occidentalis   p. 262
Western redbud
☼ ✴ 2-24

CHAMAECYPARIS   p. 264
False cypress
☼ ◐ ✴ ZONES VARY

CRATAEGUS   p. 298
Hawthorn
☼ ✴ 2-12, 14-17

CUPRESSUS   p. 303
Cypress
☼ ✴ ZONES VARY

EUCALYPTUS (some)   p. 339
☼ ✴ ZONES VARY

FIG   p. 353
☼ ✴ 4-9, 12-24; H1, H2

FRAXINUS   p. 357
Ash
☼ ✴ ZONES VARY

Olea europaea

GINKGO biloba   p. 369
Maidenhair tree
☼ ✴ A3; 1-10, 12, 14-24

MAGNOLIA   p. 458
☼ ◐ ✴ ZONES VARY

MAYTENUS boaria   p. 475
Mayten
☼ ✴ 8, 9, 14-24

MELALEUCA   p. 476
☼ ✴ ZONES VARY

OLEA europaea   p. 499
Olive
☼ ✴ 8, 9, 11-24; H1, H2

PALMS   p. 508
NEEDS, ZONES VARY

PICEA   p. 538
Spruce
☼ ◐ ✴ ZONES VARY

PINUS   p. 541
Pine
☼ ✴ ZONES VARY

PODOCARPUS   p. 554
☼ ◐ ✴ ZONES VARY

PSEUDOTSUGA menziesii   p. 569
Douglas fir
☼ ◐ ✴ A2, A3; 1-10, 14-17

Pseudotsuga menziesii

Aesculus californica

Anisodontea × hypomandarum

Bamboo

Buddleja davidii

Buxus sempervirens

Chaenomeles

Choisya ternata

Cistus

QUERCUS p. 574
Oak
☼ ✿ ZONES VARY

SEQUOIA sempervirens p. 623
Redwood
☼ ◐ ✿ 4-9, 14-24

UMBELLULARIA californica p. 660
California laurel
☼ ◐ ● ✿ 4-9, 14-24

Shrubs

ABELIA × grandiflora p. 162
Glossy abelia
☼ ◐ ✿ 4-24; H1, H2

AESCULUS californica p. 173
California buckeye
☼ ✿ 3-10, 14-24

ALYOGYNE huegelii p. 183
Blue hibiscus
☼ ✿ 13-17, 20-24; H1, H2

ANISODONTEA × hypomandarum p. 187
Cape mallow
☼ ◐ ✿ 14-24

ARCTOSTAPHYLOS p. 197
Manzanita
☼ ◐ ✿ ZONES VARY

BAMBOO p. 212
☼ ◐ ✿ ZONES VARY

BERBERIS p. 221
Barberry
☼ ◐ ✿ ZONES VARY

BUDDLEJA p. 233
Butterfly bush
☼ ◐ ✿ ZONES VARY

BUXUS p. 235
Boxwood
☼ ◐ ● ✿ ZONES VARY

CALLISTEMON p. 239
Bottlebrush
☼ ✿ ZONES VARY

CALLUNA vulgaris p. 240
Scotch heather
☼ ✿ 1A, 2-6, 15-17

CALYCANTHUS occidentalis p. 242
Spice bush
☼ ◐ ● ✿ 4-9, 14-24

CARPENTERIA californica p. 251
Bush anemone
☼ ◐ ✿ 5-9, 14-24

CASSIA p. 253
Senna
☼ ✿ ZONES VARY

CEANOTHUS p. 255
Wild lilac
☼ ✿ 5-9, 14-24

CHAENOMELES p. 264
Flowering quince
☼ ✿ 2-23

CHOISYA ternata p. 270
Mexican orange
☼ ◐ ✿ 4-9, 14-24

CISTUS (most) p. 275
Rockrose
☼ ✿ 4-9, 14-24

COLEONEMA p. 286
Breath of heaven
☼ ◐ ✿ 7-9, 14-24

COPROSMA p. 288
☼ ◐ ✿ ZONES VARY

COROKIA cotoneaster p. 293
☼ ◐ ✿ 4-24

CORREA p. 293
Australian fuchsia
☼ ◐ ✿ 14-24

COTONEASTER p. 298
☼ ✿ ZONES VARY

Dendromecon harfordii

DAPHNE p. 309
NEEDS, ZONES VARY

DENDROMECON p. 312
Bush poppy
☼ ✿ ZONES VARY

DODONAEA viscosa p. 319
Hop bush
☼ ◐ ✿ 7-24; H1, H2

ELAEAGNUS p. 325
☼ ◐ ✿ ZONES VARY

ERICA p. 331
Heath
☼ ◐ ✿ ZONES VARY

ERIOGONUM p. 335
Wild buckwheat
☼ ✿ ZONES VARY

ESCALLONIA p. 338
☼ ◐ ✿ 4-9, 14-24

FEIJOA, Pineapple Guava p. 350
☼ ✿ 6-9, 12-24; H1, H2

Calluna vulgaris 'Corbett Red'

Calycanthus occidentalis

Cotoneaster apiculatus

Erica canaliculata

Heteromeles arbutifolia

Ilex aquifolium

FREMONTODENDRON p. 359
Flannel bush
☼ ✎ 4–24

GAULTHERIA shallon p. 364
Salal
◑ ✎ 4–7, 14–17

GREVILLEA p. 378
NEEDS, ZONES VARY

HAKEA suaveolens p. 382
Sweet hakea
☼ ✎ 9, 12–17, 19–24

HETEROMELES arbutifolia p. 392
Toyon
☼ ◑ ✎ 5–9, 14–24

HYPERICUM p. 402
St. Johnswort
☼ ◑ ✎ ZONES VARY

ILEX p. 404
Holly
☼ ◑ ✎ ZONES VARY

Lavandula

Kerria japonica

Mahonia aquifolium

JUNIPERUS p. 418
Juniper
☼ ◑ ✎ ZONES VARY

KERRIA japonica p. 426
☼ ◑ ✎ 2–23

LANTANA p. 432
☼ ✎ 8–10, 12–24; H1, H2

LAVANDULA p. 434
Lavender
☼ ✎ ZONES VARY

LAVATERA p. 437
Tree mallow
☼ ✎ ZONES VARY

LEONOTIS leonurus p. 438
Lion's tail
☼ ✎ 8–24; H1, H2

LEPTOSPERMUM p. 438
Tea tree
☼ ✎ 14–24

MAHONIA p. 467
NEEDS, ZONES VARY

MYOPORUM p. 487
☼ ✎ ZONES VARY

Myoporum parvifolium

MYRICA californica p. 488
Pacific wax myrtle
☼ ✎ 14–24

MYRTUS communis p. 488
Myrtle
☼ ◑ ✎ 8–24; H1, H2

NANDINA domestica p. 489
Heavenly bamboo
☼ ◑ ● ✎ 3–24; H1, H2

NERIUM oleander p. 495
Oleander
☼ ✎ 8–16, 18–24; H1, H2

PHLOMIS p. 534
☼ ✎ ZONES VARY

PLUMBAGO auriculata p. 552
Cape plumbago
☼ ◑ ✎ 8, 9, 12–24; H1, H2

POTENTILLA p. 559
Cinquefoil
☼ ◑ ✎ ZONES VARY

PYRACANTHA p. 572
Firethorn
☼ ✎ ZONES VARY

RHODODENDRON (not azaleas) p. 583
◑ ✎ ZONES VARY

RHUS p. 590
Sumac
☼ ✎ ZONES VARY

RIBES p. 591
Currant
☼ ◑ ✎ ZONES VARY

ROSMARINUS officinalis p. 602
Rosemary
☼ ✎ 4–24; H1, H2

Nerium oleander

Spiraea cantoniensis 'Flore-Pleno'

SALVIA p. 607
Sage
NEEDS, ZONES VARY

SARCOCOCCA p. 615
Sweet box
◑ ● ✎ ZONES VARY

SENNA p. 622
☼ ◑ ✎ ZONES VARY

SOLLYA heterophylla p. 628
Australian bluebell creeper
☼ ◑ ✎ 8, 9, 14–24; H1, H2

SPIRAEA p. 631
☼ ◑ ✎ ZONES VARY

SYMPHORICARPOS p. 640
Snowberry
NEEDS, ZONES VARY

SYRINGA p. 640
Lilac
☼ ◑ ✎ ZONES VARY

TEUCRIUM p. 645
Germander
☼ ✎ ZONES VARY

TIBOUCHINA urvilleana p. 649
Princess flower
☼ ◑ ✎ 16, 17, 21–24; H1, H2

TRICHOSTEMA lanatum p. 654
Woolly blue curls
☼ ✎ 14–24

VACCINIUM ovatum p. 661
Evergreen huckleberry
☼ ◑ ● ✎ 4–7, 14–17, 22–24

VIBURNUM p. 664
NEEDS, ZONES VARY

WESTRINGIA fruticosa p. 670
Coast rosemary
☼ ✎ 8, 9, 14–24

Rhododendron hybrid

Syringa vulgaris

Ground Covers & Vines

AJUGA p. 177
Carpet bugle
☼ ◑ ✎ A2, A3; 1–24

ARABIS p. 196
Rockcress
☼ ✎ ZONES VARY

BOUGAINVILLEA p. 227
☼ ✎ 5, 6, 12–17, 19, 21–24; H1, H2

CERATOSTIGMA plumbaginoides p. 261
Dwarf plumbago
☼ ◑ ✎ 2B–10, 14–24

FRAGARIA chiloensis p. 356
Beach strawberry
☼ ◑ ✎ 4–24; H1

GALIUM odoratum p. 362
Sweet woodruff
◑ ● ✎ A2, A3; 2–6, 15–17

GAZANIA p. 364
NEEDS, ZONES VARY

GELSEMIUM sempervirens p. 365
Carolina jessamine
☼ ◑ ✎ 4–24

HEDERA helix p. 386
English ivy
☼ ◑ ✎ 3–24; H1

HIBBERTIA scandens p. 394
Guinea gold vine
☼ ◑ ✎ 16, 17, 21–24

JASMINUM p. 416
Jasmine
☼ ◑ ✎ ZONES VARY

Armeria maritima

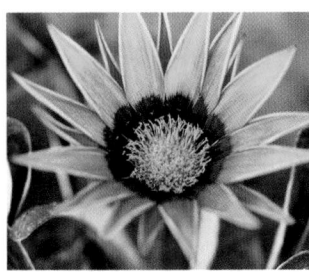

Gazania 'Daybreak Bronze'

OSTEOSPERMUM fruticosum p. 505
Trailing African daisy
☼ ✎ 8, 9, 12–24; H1, H2

PACHYSANDRA terminalis p. 507
Japanese spurge
◑ ● ✎ 2–10, 14–21

SCAEVOLA p. 616
☼ ✎ 8, 9, 14–24; H1, H2

SOLANUM laxum p. 627
Potato vine
☼ ✎ 8, 9, 12–24; H1, H2

TECOMA capensis p. 644
Cape honeysuckle
☼ ◑ ✎ 12, 13, 20–24; H1, H2

VINCA p. 666
Periwinkle
☼ ◑ ● ✎ ZONES VARY

WISTERIA p. 671
NEEDS, ZONES VARY

Perennials & Bulbs

ACANTHUS mollis p. 167
Bear's breech
☼ ◑ ● ✎ 5–24

ACHILLEA p. 170
Yarrow
☼ ✎ A1–A3; 1–24

AGAPANTHUS p. 174
Lily-of-the-Nile
☼ ◑ ✎ 4–9, 12–24; H1, H2

AGAVE p. 175
☼ ◑ ✎ ZONES VARY

Wisteria sinensis

Achillea filipendulina

Agapanthus orientalis

ALOE p. 180
☼ ◑ ✎ 8, 9, 12–24

AQUILEGIA p. 195
Columbine
☼ ◑ ✎ ZONES VARY

ARMERIA p. 200
Thrift
☼ ✎ ZONES VARY

ARTEMISIA p. 201
☼ ✎ ZONES VARY

ASTER p. 206
☼ ✎ ZONES VARY

ASTILBE p. 207
False spiraea
☼ ◑ ✎ A2, A3; 1–9, 14–24

BEGONIA, tuberous p. 220
◑ ✎ 4–9, 14–24; H1

Begonia, tuberous

Aquilegia caerulea

Aster novi-belgii

BRACHYSCOME p. 230
Swan River daisy
☼ ✎ ZONES VARY

CAMPANULA poscharskyana p. 248
Serbian bellflower
☼ ◑ ✎ 1–12, 14–24

CAREX p. 250
Sedge
☼ ◑ ✎ ZONES VARY

CENTAUREA p. 259
☼ ✎ ZONES VARY

CENTRANTHUS ruber p. 260
Jupiter's beard
☼ ◑ ✎ 2–9, 12–24; H1

CERASTIUM tomentosum p. 261
Snow-in-summer
☼ ◑ ✎ A1, A2; 1–24

CHRYSANTHEMUM frutescens p. 272
Marguerite
☼ ✎ 14–24; H1

COREOPSIS p. 289
☼ ✎ ZONES VARY

CROCOSMIA p. 299
☼ ◑ ✎ ZONES VARY

CROCUS p. 300
☼ ◑ ✎ 1–24

DAHLIA p. 307
☼ ◑ ✎ 1–24

DICENTRA p. 315
Bleeding heart
◑ ● ✎ 1–9, 14–24

Dahlia, cactus form

Digitalis grandiflora

Echinacea purpurea

Gaillardia × grandiflora

DIETES p. 317
Fortnight lily
☼ ◐ ✄ 8, 9, 12–24; H1, H2

DIGITALIS p. 317
Foxglove
NEEDS, ZONES VARY

ECHINACEA purpurea p. 323
Purple coneflower
☼ ✄ A2, A3; 1–24

ECHIUM candicans p. 325
Pride of Madeira
☼ ✄ 14–24

ERIGERON p. 331
Fleabane
☼ ◐ ✄ ZONES VARY

ERODIUM reichardii p. 335
Cranesbill
☼ ◐ ✄ 7–9, 14–24

ERYSIMUM p. 336
Wallflower
☼ ◐ ✄ ZONES VARY

ESCHSCHOLZIA californica p. 338
California poppy
☼ ✄ 1–24; H1

EUPHORBIA p. 345
NEEDS, ZONES VARY

EURYOPS p. 347
☼ ✄ ZONES VARY

FELICIA amelloides p. 350
Blue marguerite
☼ ✄ 8, 9, 14–24

FESTUCA glauca p. 351
Common blue fescue
☼ ◐ ✄ 1–24

FREESIA p. 358
☼ ◐ ✄ 8, 9, 12–24

GAILLARDIA × grandiflora p. 361
Blanket flower
☼ ✄ 1–24; H1, H2

GERANIUM p. 366
Cranesbill
☼ ◐ ✄ ZONES VARY

HELICHRYSUM p. 388
☼ ✄ ZONES VARY

HELLEBORUS p. 390
Hellebore
◐ ● ✄ ZONES VARY

HEMEROCALLIS p. 390
Daylily
☼ ◐ ✄ 1–24; H1, H2

IBERIS p. 404
Candytuft
☼ ◐ ✄ 1–24

IRIS p. 409
NEEDS, ZONES VARY

IXIA p. 415
African corn lily
☼ ✄ 7–9, 12–24

KNIPHOFIA p. 427
Red-hot poker
☼ ◐ ✄ ZONES VARY

LAMIUM p. 431
Dead nettle
☼ ● ✄ ZONES VARY

LEUCOJUM p. 440
Snowflake
☼ ◐ ✄ ZONES VARY

LIMONIUM p. 446
Statice
☼ ✄ ZONES VARY

LIRIOPE p. 448
Lily turf
☼ ◐ ● ✄ ZONES VARY

LITHODORA diffusa p. 450
☼ ◐ ✄ 5–7, 14–17

LUPINUS p. 454
Lupine
☼ ✄ ZONES VARY

LYCHNIS coronaria p. 455
Crown-pink
☼ ◐ ✄ 1–9, 14–24

MIMULUS p. 482
Monkey flower
NEEDS, ZONES VARY

MISCANTHUS sinensis p. 482
Eulalia
☼ ◐ ✄ 2–24

MONARDA p. 484
Bee balm
☼ ◐ ✄ ZONES VARY

MYOSOTIS scorpioides p. 488
Forget-me-not
◐ ✄ A1–A3; 1–24

NARCISSUS p. 489
Daffodil
☼ ◐ ✄ A2, A3; 1–24

NEPETA p. 494
☼ ◐ ✄ 1–24

Helleborus hybrid

Hemerocallis 'Huapango'

Limonium tataricum

Mimulus × hybridus

Iris, tall bearded

Narcissus

Erysimum 'Bowles Mauve'

Euphorbia griffithii 'Fireglow'

Nepeta × faassenii

Phormium 'Rainbow Warrior'

Santolina rosmarinifolia

Ageratum houstonianum

ORIGANUM   p. 502
Oregano, Marjoram
☼ ◐ ✎ ZONES VARY

PAPAVER   p. 510
Poppy
☼ ✎ ZONES VARY

PENNISETUM   p. 526
Fountain grass
☼ ◐ ✎ ZONES VARY

PENSTEMON   p. 526
Beard tongue
☼ ◐ ✎ ZONES VARY

PHLOMIS   p. 534
☼ ✎ ZONES VARY

PHLOX subulata   p. 535
Moss pink
☼ ◐ ✎ 1–17

PHORMIUM   p. 536
☼ ◐ ✎ 5–9, 14–24; H1, H2

Pennisetum orientale

ROMNEYA coulteri   p. 593
Matilija poppy
☼ ✎ 4–12, 14–24; H1

RUDBECKIA hirta   p. 604
Gloriosa daisy
☼ ✎ 1–24

SANTOLINA   p. 614
☼ ✎ ZONES VARY

SAXIFRAGA   p. 615
Saxifrage
NEEDS, ZONES VARY

SCABIOSA (some)   p. 616
Pincushion flower
NEEDS, ZONES VARY

SCILLA   p. 619
Squill
☼ ◐ ✎ ZONES VARY

SISYRINCHIUM   p. 626
☼ ◐ ✎ ZONES VARY

Rudbeckia hirta

STACHYS byzantina   p. 633
Lamb's ears
☼ ◐ ✎ 1–24

STIPA   p. 635
Feather grass
☼ ✎ ZONES VARY

TAGETES lemmonii   p. 642
Copper Canyon daisy
☼ ✎ 8–10, 12–24; H1

THYMUS   p. 648
Thyme
☼ ◐ ✎ ZONES VARY

TULBAGHIA violacea   p. 657
Society garlic
☼ ✎ 13–24; H1, H2

VERBENA   p. 663
☼ ✎ ZONES VARY

VERONICA   p. 663
Speedwell
☼ ✎ ZONES VARY

VIOLA odorata   p. 667
Sweet violet
☼ ◐ ● ✎ 1–24

ZANTEDESCHIA   p. 675
Calla
☼ ◐ ✎ 5, 6, 8, 9, 12–24; H1, H2

ZAUSCHNERIA   p. 675
California fuchsia
NEEDS, ZONES VARY

Annuals

AGERATUM houstonianum p. 176
Floss flower
☼ ◐ ✎ 1–24

CALENDULA officinalis   p. 238
Calendula
☼ ✎ A2, A3; 1–24; H1

CAMPANULA   p. 246
Bellflower
☼ ◐ ✎ ZONES VARY

CATHARANTHUS roseus   p. 255
Madagascar periwinkle
☼ ◐ ✎ 1–24; H1, H2

CLARKIA amoena   p. 281
Farewell-to-spring
☼ ◐ ✎ A2–A3; 1–24

IMPATIENS   p. 406
Balsam
NEEDS, ZONES VARY

MYOSOTIS sylvatica   p. 488
◐ ✎ A1–A3; 1–24

PAPAVER rhoeas   p. 511
Flanders field poppy
☼ ✎ A1–A3; 1–24

SCABIOSA (some)   p. 616
Pincushion flower
NEEDS, ZONES VARY

SENECIO × hybridus   p. 622
Florists' cineraria
◐ ● ✎ 16, 17, 22–24

Papaver orientale

Stachys byzantina

Campanula glomerata

Wind-resistant Plants

Regular strong winds can wreak havoc on plants. Water stress is one common problem; constant wind pulls moisture from foliage faster than roots can draw it from the soil. And really powerful winds can virtually destroy many plants—defoliate them, uproot them, wrench off branches with such force that trunks may split. Fortunately, the plants listed below will endure high winds without much damage to health or appearance. For plants unfazed by ocean winds, see "Plants for Seacoast Gardens" (page 152).

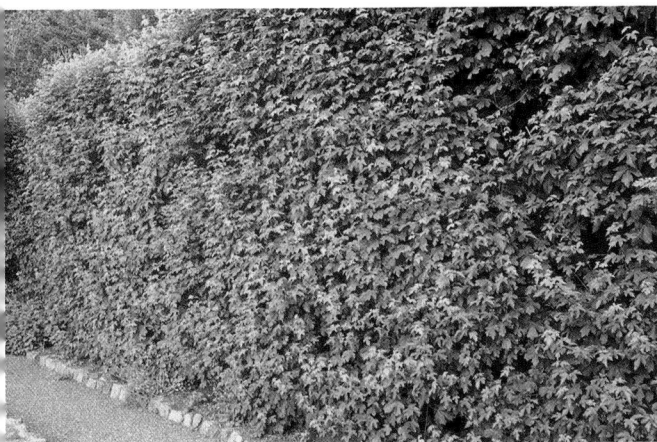

Acer campestre

Trees

ACACIA (some) p. 164
☼ ⚊ ZONES VARY

ACER campestre p. 167
Hedge maple
☼ ◗ ⚊ 2-9, 14-17

BROUSSONETIA papyrifera p. 232
Paper mulberry
☼ ⚊ 3B-24; H1, H2

CALOCEDRUS decurrens p. 241
Incense cedar
☼ ◗ ⚊ 2-12, 14-24

CASUARINA p. 254
Beefwood
☼ ⚊ 8, 9, 12-24; H1, H2

CHAMAECYPARIS lawsoniana p. 264
Port Orford cedar
☼ ◗ ⚊ A3; 3-6, 15-17

CHILOPSIS linearis p. 268
Desert willow
☼ ⚊ 3B, 7-14, 18-23

× CUPRESSOCYPARIS leylandii p. 302
☼ ⚊ 3B-24

CUPRESSUS (most) p. 303
Cypress
☼ ⚊ ZONES VARY

ELAEAGNUS angustifolia p. 326
Russian olive
☼ ◗ ⚊ A2, A3; 1-3, 7-14, 18, 19

EUCALYPTUS (most) p. 339
☼ ⚊ ZONES VARY

Cupressus sempervirens 'Stricta'

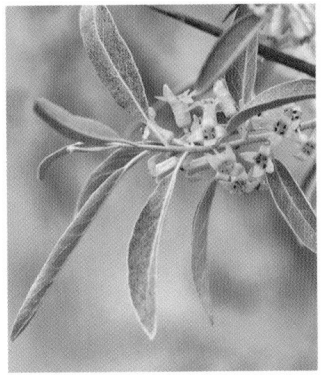

Elaeagnus angustifolia

FRAXINUS 'Fan West' p. 357
Ash
☼ ⚊ 2-14

FRAXINUS velutina 'Rio Grande' p. 358
Fan-tex ash
☼ ⚊ 8-24

LAGUNARIA patersonii p. 431
Primrose tree
☼ ⚊ 13, 15-24; H1, H2

LIGUSTRUM lucidum p. 443
Glossy privet
☼ ◗ ⚊ 5-24; H1, H2

MACLURA pomifera p. 458
Osage orange
☼ ⚊ 2, 3, 10-13

MELALEUCA (most) p. 476
☼ ⚊ ZONES VARY

MELALEUCA quinquenervia p. 477
Cajeput tree
☼ ⚊ 9, 12, 13, 15-17, 20-24; H1, H2

OLEA europaea p. 499
Olive
☼ ⚊ 8, 9, 11-24; H1, H2

PALMS p. 508
NEEDS, ZONES VARY

Eucalyptus deglupta

Populus

PARKINSONIA aculeata p. 512
Jerusalem thorn
☼ ⚊ 8-24; H1, H2

PICEA abies p. 539
Norway spruce
☼ ◗ ⚊ A2, A3; 1-6, 14-17

PINUS (many) p. 541
Pine
☼ ⚊ ZONES VARY

PITTOSPORUM (except P. phillyreoides) p. 545
☼ ◗ ⚊ ZONES VARY

POPULUS (several) p. 557
☼ ⚊ ZONES VARY

PROSOPIS glandulosa p. 563
Honey mesquite
☼ ⚊ 10-13, 18-24

PSEUDOTSUGA menziesii p. 569
Douglas fir
☼ ◗ ⚊ A2, A3; 1-10, 14-17

Prosopis glandulosa

Cocos nucifera (palm)

Schinus molle

QUERCUS ilex   p. 576
Holly oak
☼ ✺ 4–24

QUERCUS virginiana   p. 577
Southern live oak
☼ ✺ 4–24

SCHINUS molle   p. 617
California pepper tree
☼ ✺ 8, 9, 11, 12–24; H1, H2

SEQUOIA sempervirens   p. 623
Redwood
☼ ◑ ✺ 4–9, 14–24

TAMARIX   p. 642
Tamarisk
☼ ✺ ZONES VARY

Tamarix parviflora

THUJA occidentalis   p. 646
American arborvitae
☼ ◑ A2, A3; 1–9, 15–17, 21–24; H1, H2

THUJA plicata   p. 647
Western red cedar
☼ ◑ ✺ A3; 1–9, 14–24

ULMUS pumila   p. 660
Siberian elm
☼ ✺ A1–A3; 1–11, 14–21

Shrubs

ARBUTUS unedo   p. 197
Strawberry tree
☼ ◑ ✺ 4–24

ARCTOSTAPHYLOS   p. 197
Manzanita
☼ ◑ ✺ ZONES VARY

Arbutus unedo

Artemisia tridentata

ARTEMISIA   p. 201
☼ ✺ ZONES VARY

BACCHARIS pilularis   p. 212
Dwarf coyote brush
☼ ✺ 5–11, 14–24

BERBERIS   p. 221
Barberry
☼ ◑ ✺ ZONES VARY

BUXUS   p. 235
Boxwood
☼ ◑ ● ✺ ZONES VARY

CALLISTEMON   p. 239
Bottlebrush
☼ ✺ ZONES VARY

CEANOTHUS   p. 255
Wild lilac
☼ ✺ 5–9, 14–24

Ceanothus

Callistemon citrinus

Cistus × purpureus

Cotoneaster horizontalis

CHAMAECYPARIS   p. 264
False cypress
☼ ◑ ✺ ZONES VARY

CISTUS   p. 275
Rockrose
☼ ✺ 4–9, 14–24

CORREA   p. 293
Australian fuchsia
☼ ◑ ✺ 14–24

COTONEASTER   p. 296
☼ ✺ ZONES VARY

DODONAEA viscosa   p. 319
Hop bush
☼ ◑ ✺ 7–24; H1, H2

ELAEAGNUS   p. 325
☼ ◑ ✺ ZONES VARY

ESCALLONIA   p. 338
☼ ◑ ✺ 4–9, 14–24

EUONYMUS japonicus   p. 344
Evergreen euonymus
☼ ✺ 4–20; H1

GRISELINIA littoralis   p. 380
☼ ◑ ✺ 9, 14–17, 20–24

HAKEA   p. 382
Sweet hakea
☼ ✺ 9, 12–17, 19–24

JUNIPERUS   p. 418
Juniper
☼ ◑ ✺ ZONES VARY

Lantana camara

Lavatera thuringiaca 'Baby Barnsley'

Leptospermum scoparium 'Helene Strybing'

Cerastium tomentosum

LANTANA   p. 432
☼ ✎ 8–10, 12–24; H1, H2

LAURUS nobilis   p. 434
Sweet bay
☼ ◐ ✎ 5–9, 12–24; H1, H2

LAVANDULA   p. 434
Lavender
☼ ✎ ZONES VARY

LAVATERA   p. 437
Tree mallow
☼ ✎ ZONES VARY

LEPTOSPERMUM   p. 438
Tea tree
☼ ✎ 14–24

LEUCOPHYLLUM   p. 440
Texas ranger
☼ ✎ 7–24

LIGUSTRUM japonicum 'Texanum'   p. 443
Japanese privet
☼ ◐ ✎ 3A–24; H1, H2

MYRICA californica   p. 488
Pacific wax myrtle
☼ ✎ 4–9, 14–24

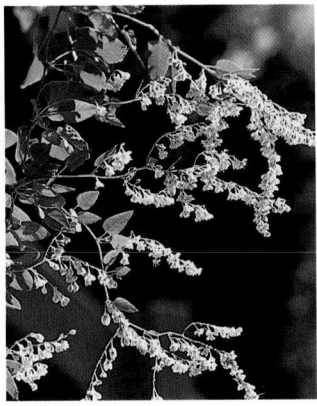

Fallopia baldschuanica

NANDINA domestica   p. 489
Heavenly bamboo
☼ ◐ ● ✎ 3–24; H1, H2

NERIUM oleander   p. 495
Oleander
☼ ✎ 8–16, 18–24; H1, H2

PITTOSPORUM (most)   p. 545
☼ ◐ ✎ ZONES VARY

PRUNUS (evergreen)   p. 564
☼ ✎ ZONES VARY

PYRACANTHA   p. 572
Firethorn
☼ ✎ ZONES VARY

RHAMNUS (some)   p. 581
NEEDS, ZONES VARY

RHAPHIOLEPIS (most)   p. 582
☼ ◐ ✎ 4–10, 12–24; H1, H2

RHUS (some)   p. 590
Sumac
☼ ✎ ZONES VARY

ROSMARINUS officinalis   p. 602
Rosemary
☼ ✎ 4–24; H1, H2

WESTRINGIA fruticosa   p. 670
Coast rosemary
☼ ✎ 8, 9, 14–24

XYLOSMA congestum   p. 673
☼ ◐ ✎ 8–24

Vines

BOUGAINVILLEA   p. 227
☼ ✎ 5, 6, 12–17, 19, 21–24; H1, H2

FALLOPIA baldschuanica   p. 349
Silver lace vine
☼ ✎ A1–A3; 1–24

MUEHLENBECKIA complexa   p. 486
Mattress vine
☼ ◐ ✎ 8, 9, 14–24

TECOMA capensis   p. 644
Cape honeysuckle
☼ ◐ ✎ 12, 13, 20–24; H1, H2

Perennials

AGAPANTHUS   p. 174
Lily-of-the-Nile
☼ ◐ ✎ 4–9, 12–24; H1, H2

AGAVE   p. 175
☼ ◐ ✎ ZONES VARY

ALOE   p. 180
☼ ◐ ✎ 8, 9, 12–24

ASPARAGUS densiflorus 'Sprengeri'   p. 205
Sprenger asparagus
☼ ◐ ✎ 12–24; H1, H2

CAREX   p. 250
Sedge
☼ ◐ ✎ ZONES VARY

CERASTIUM tomentosum   p. 261
Snow-in-summer
☼ ◐ ✎ A1, A2; 1–24

CHRYSANTHEMUM frutescens   p. 272
Marguerite
☼ ✎ 14–24; H1

CRASSULA ovata   p. 298
Jade plant
☼ ◐ ✎ 8, 9, 12–24; H1, H2

ERIOGONUM   p. 335
Wild buckwheat
☼ ✎ ZONES VARY

EUPHORBIA   p. 345
NEEDS, ZONES VARY

EURYOPS   p. 347
☼ ✎ ZONES VARY

FELICIA amelloides   p. 350
Blue marguerite
☼ ✎ 8, 9, 14–24

Agave americana

Halimium lasianthum

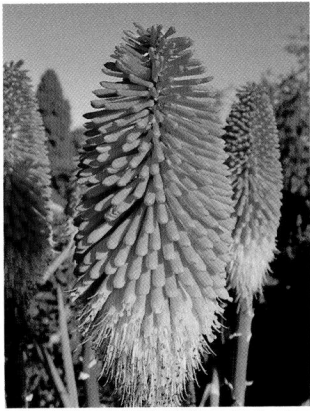

Kniphofia uvaria

HALIMIUM   p. 383
☼ ✎ 5–9, 12–24

HEMEROCALLIS   p. 390
Daylily
☼ ◐ ✎ 1–24; H1, H2

KNIPHOFIA   p. 427
Red-hot poker
☼ ◐ ✎ ZONES VARY

MISCANTHUS   p. 482
Silver grass
☼ ◐ ✎ ZONES VARY

PELARGONIUM   p. 524
Geranium
☼ ◐ ✎ 8, 9, 12–24

PENSTEMON   p. 526
Beard tongue
☼ ◐ ✎ ZONES VARY

PHLOMIS   p. 534
☼ ✎ ZONES VARY

PHORMIUM   p. 536
☼ ◐ ✎ 5–9, 14–24; H1, H2

SALVIA   p. 607
Sage
NEEDS, ZONES VARY

SANTOLINA   p. 614
☼ ✎ ZONES VARY

SIDALCEA   p. 625
Checkerbloom
☼ ✎ ZONES 2–10, 14–24

YUCCA   p. 673
☼ ✎ ZONES VARY

Plants for Seacoast Gardens

A walk on the beach is a pleasure in fine weather, but on less pleasant days, blustery, salt-laden winds can send you scurrying for shelter. Plants, unfortunately, have no escape: they have to tough it out. Even on the breeziest coastlines, though, the plants listed below look fresh and healthy whatever the weather.

Coccoloba uvifera

Metrosideros excelsus

Limonium perezii

Trees

COCCOLOBA uvifera   p. 285
Sea grape
☼ ◐ ✿ 24; H2

✕ CUPRESSOCYPARIS leylandii   p. 302
☼ ✿ 3B–24

EUCALYPTUS (some)   p. 339
☼ ✿ 5, 6, 8–24; H1, H2

FICUS rubiginosa   p. 353
Rustyleaf fig
☼ ✿ 18–24; H1, H2

MELALEUCA quinquenervia   p. 477
Cajeput tree
☼ ✿ 9, 12, 13, 15–17, 20–24; H1, H2

METROSIDEROS   p. 480
☼ ◐ ✿ ZONES VARY

MYOPORUM laetum   p. 487
☼ ✿ 8, 9, 14–17, 19–24

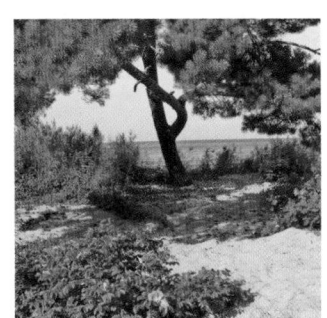

Pinus

PALMS   p. 508
NEEDS, ZONES VARY

PINUS (some)   p. 541
Pine
☼ ✿ ZONES VARY

QUERCUS ilex   p. 576
Holly oak
☼ ✿ 4–24

Umbellularia californica

UMBELLULARIA californica   p. 660
California laurel
☼ ◐ ● ✿ 4–9, 14–24

Shrubs

ARBUTUS unedo   p. 197
Strawberry tree
☼ ◐ ✿ 4–24

CARISSA macrocarpa   p. 251
Natal plum
☼ ◐ ✿ 22–24; H2

CISTUS   p. 275
Rockrose
☼ ✿ 4–9, 14–24

COPROSMA   p. 288
☼ ◐ ✿ ZONES VARY

COROKIA cotoneaster   p. 293
☼ ◐ ✿ 4–24

CORREA   p. 293
Australian fuchsia
☼ ◐ ✿ 14–24

COTONEASTER (many)   p. 296
☼ ✿ ZONES VARY

CYTISUS   p. 306
Broom
☼ ✿ ZONES VARY

DODONAEA viscosa   p. 319
Hop bush
☼ ◐ ✿ 7–24; H1, H2

ELAEAGNUS   p. 325
☼ ◐ ✿ ZONES VARY

ESCALLONIA   p. 338
☼ ◐ ✿ 4–9, 14–24

EUONYMUS japonicus   p. 344
Evergreen euonymus
☼ ✿ 4–20; H1

GENISTA   p. 365
Broom
☼ ✿ ZONES VARY

GRISELINIA   p. 380
☼ ◐ ✿ 9, 14–17, 20–24

Eucalyptus

Washingtonia filifera (palm)

Kalanchoe blossfeldiana

Nerium oleander 'Petite Pink'

Leptospermum scoparium 'Gaiety Girl'

Aloe arborescens

Carpobrotus edulis (ice plant)

Protea compacta

Rosa rugosa

Muhlenbergia capillaris

Echium candicans

HAKEA   p. 382
☼ ✔ 9, 12–17, 19–24

HEBE   p. 385
☼ ◑ ✔ 14–24

JUNIPERUS   p. 418
Juniper
☼ ◑ ✔ ZONES VARY

KALANCHOE   p. 424
☼ ◑ ✔ ZONES VARY

LANTANA   p. 432
☼ ✔ 8–10, 12–24; H1, H2

LAVANDULA   p. 434
Lavender
☼ ✔ ZONES VARY

LEPTOSPERMUM
Tea tree   p. 438
☼ ✔ 14–24

MELALEUCA (most)   p. 476
☼ ✔ ZONES VARY

NERIUM oleander   p. 495
Oleander
☼ ◑ ✔ 8–16, 18–24; H1, H2

PHLOMIS fruticosa   p. 534
Jerusalem sage
☼ ✔ 3B–24

PITTOSPORUM crassifolium   p. 545
☼ ◑ ✔ 9, 14–17, 19–24

PITTOSPORUM tobira   p. 546
Tobira
☼ ◑ ✔ 4–24; H1, H2

PROTEA compacta   p. 564
☼ ✔ 16, 17, 21–24; H1

RHAMNUS alaternus   p. 581
Italian buckthorn
☼ ◑ ✔ 4–24

RHAPHIOLEPIS   p. 582
☼ ◑ ✔ 4–10, 12–24; H1, H2

RHUS integrifolia   p. 590
Lemonade berry
☼ ✔ 8, 9, 14–17, 19–24

ROSA rugosa   p. 602
Ramanas rose
☼ ◑ ✔ A1–A3; 1–24

ROSMARINUS officinalis   p. 602
Rosemary
☼ ✔ 4–24; H1, H2

VIBURNUM (most evergreen species)   p. 664
☼ ◑ ✔ ZONES VARY

WESTRINGIA fruticosa   p. 670
Coast rosemary
☼ ✔ 8, 9, 14–24

Perennials

ACHILLEA   p. 170
Yarrow
☼ ✔ A1–A3; 1–24

AGAPANTHUS   p. 174
Lily-of-the-Nile
☼ ◑ ✔ 4–9, 12–24; H1, H2

ALOE arborescens   p. 181
Tree aloe
☼ ◑ ✔ 8, 9, 12–24; H1, H2

ARMERIA maritima   p. 200
Common thrift
☼ ✔ A2, A3; 1–9, 14–24

Chrysanthemum frutescens

ARTEMISIA   p. 201
☼ ✔ ZONES VARY

CAREX (some)   p. 250
Sedge
☼ ◑ ✔ ZONES VARY

CENTRANTHUS ruber   p. 260
Jupiter's beard
☼ ◑ ✔ 2–9, 12–24; H1

CHONDROPETALUM elephantinum   p. 270
Cape rush
☼ ◑ ✔ 8, 9, 14–24

CHRYSANTHEMUM frutescens   p. 272
Marguerite
☼ ✔ 14–24; H1

CONVOLVULUS sabatius   p. 288
Ground morning glory
☼ ◑ ✔ 4–9, 12–24

DIANTHUS   p. 313
Pink
☼ ◑ ✔ A2, A3; 1–24

ECHIUM candicans   p. 325
Pride of Madeira
☼ ✔ 14–24

ERIGERON   p. 331
Fleabane
☼ ◑ ✔ ZONES VARY

ERIOGONUM   p. 335
Wild buckwheat
☼ ✔ ZONES VARY

EUPHORBIA   p. 345
NEEDS, ZONES VARY

EURYOPS   p. 347
☼ ✔ ZONES VARY

FELICIA amelloides   p. 350
Blue marguerite
☼ ✔ 8, 9, 14–24

GAZANIA hybrids   p. 364
☼ ✔ 8–24; H1, H2

ICE PLANTS   p. 404
Carpobrotus
NEEDS, ZONES VARY

LIMONIUM perezii   p. 446
Sea lavender
☼ ◑ ✔ 13, 15–17, 20–24

MUHLENBERGIA capillaris   p. 486
☼ ◑ ✔ ZONES VARY

NASSELLA tenuissima   p. 491
Mexican feather grass
☼ ✔ 2B–24

PELARGONIUM   p. 524
Geranium
☼ ◑ ✔ 8, 9, 12–24

PHORMIUM   p. 536
☼ ◑ ✔ 5–9, 14–24; H1, H2

SANTOLINA   p. 614
☼ ✔ ZONES VARY

SUCCULENTS (many)   p. 638
NEEDS, ZONES VARY

YUCCA   p. 673
☼ ✔ ZONES VARY

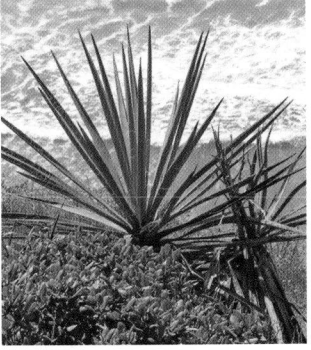
Yucca

Plants for Swimming Pools

When you're selecting plants to enhance a swimming pool or spa area, keep several requirements in mind. First, look for smooth branches, foliage, and flowers; anything bristly, prickly, sharp, or thorny can injure pool users. Second, choose plants that are virtually litter-free; any leaves or spent flowers they do shed should be too large to pass into the pool's filter (which rules out many conifers). Finally, of course, aim for good-looking plants that will enhance this enjoyable part of your landscape.

Camellia japonica

Trees and Shrubs

AUCUBA japonica p. 209
Japanese aucuba
◑ ● ✓ 4–24

BAUHINIA × blakeana p. 218
Hong Kong orchid tree
☼ ✓ 13, 19, 21, 23, 24; H1, H2

BRUGMANSIA p. 232
Angel's trumpet
☼ ◑ ● ✓ 12, 13, 16–24; H1, H2

CAMELLIA p. 242
◑ ✓ 4–9, 12, 14–24

COCCULUS laurifolius p. 285
☼ ◑ ● ✓ 8, 9, 12–24

Cycas revoluta

Cordyline australis

CORDIA boissieri p. 289
Texas olive
☼ ✓ 8–24

CORDYLINE p. 289
NEEDS, ZONES VARY

CYCAS revoluta p. 304
Sago palm
☼ ✓ 8–24; H1, H2

DRACAENA p. 320
☼ ◑ ● ✓ ZONES VARY

ENSETE ventricosum p. 328
Abyssinian banana
☼ ◑ ✓ 13, 15–24; H1, H2

ERIOBOTRYA deflexa p. 334
Bronze loquat
☼ ◑ ✓ 8–24

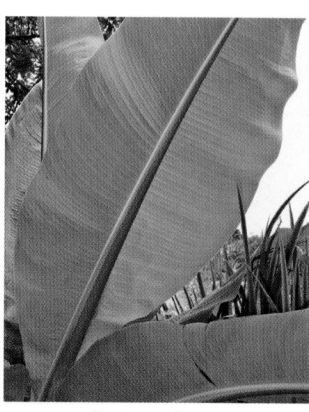

Ensete ventricosum

FATSIA japonica p. 350
Japanese aralia
◑ ● ✓ 4–9, 14–24; H1, H2

FEIJOA, Pineapple Guava p. 350
☼ ✓ 6–9, 12–24; H1, H2

FERNS (tree types) p. 351
NEEDS, ZONES VARY

FICUS auriculata p. 352
☼ ✓ 20–24; H1, H2

FIG, edible p. 353
☼ ✓ 4–9, 12–24; H1, H2

FIRMIANA simplex p. 355
Chinese parasol tree
☼ ◑ ● ✓ 5, 6, 8, 9, 12–24

Fig, edible

Feijoa

Hydrangea macrophylla

GEIJERA parviflora p. 365
Australian willow
☼ ✓ 8, 9, 12–24

HIBISCUS rosa-sinensis p. 395
Chinese hibiscus
☼ ✓ 9, 12–16, 19–24; H1, H2

HYDRANGEA macrophylla p. 401
Bigleaf hydrangea
☼ ◑ ✓ 3B–9, 14–24; H1

LANTANA p. 432
☼ ✓ 8–10, 12–24; H1, H2

Lantana 'Radiation'

Lavandula × intermedia

Persimmon

Bougainvillea

Solandra maxima 'Variegata'

LAVANDULA p. 434
Lavender
ZONES VARY

MELIANTHUS major p. 477
Honey bush
8, 9, 12-24; H1, H2

MUSA p. 486
Banana
ZONES VARY

PALMS (some) p. 508
NEEDS, ZONES VARY

PERSIMMON p. 530
ZONES VARY

PITTOSPORUM tobira
'Wheeler's Dwarf' p. 546
4-24; H1, H2

PLUMERIA p. 552
Frangipani
ZONES VARY

PORTULACARIA afra p. 558
Elephant's food
8, 9, 12-24; H1, H2

RHAPHIOLEPIS
'Majestic Beauty' p. 582
4-10, 12-24; H1, H2

SCHEFFLERA p. 617
ZONES VARY

STENOCARPUS sinuatus p. 634
Firewheel tree
16, 17, 20-24

TABEBUIA chrysotricha p. 642
Golden trumpet tree
13, 15, 16, 20-24; H1, H2

TERNSTROEMIA
gymnanthera p. 645
4-9, 12-24

VIBURNUM davidii p. 665
4-9, 14-24

Vines

BEAUMONTIA
grandiflora p. 219
Herald's trumpet
12, 13, 16, 17, 21-24; H1, H2

BOUGAINVILLEA p. 227
5, 6, 12-17, 19, 21-24; H1, H2

× FATSHEDERA lizei p. 350
4-10, 12-24; H1, H2

LONICERA
hildebrandiana p. 452
Giant Burmese honeysuckle
9, 14-17, 19-24; H1, H2

MANDEVILLA p. 473
ZONES VARY

MONSTERA deliciosa p. 484
Split-leaf philodendron
16, 17, 22-24; H1, H2

SOLANDRA maxima p. 626
Cup-of-gold vine
15-24; H2

TETRASTIGMA
voinieranum p. 645
13, 17, 20-24; H1, H2

Perennials

AEONIUM p. 173
15-17, 20-24

AGAPANTHUS p. 174
Lily-of-the-Nile
4-9, 12-24; H1, H2

AGAVE attenuata p. 175
13, 20-24; H1, H2

ALOCASIA p. 180
Elephant's ear
22-24; H1, H2

Plumeria rubra

Ternstroemia gymnanthera

Lonicera hildebrandiana

Aeonium decorum 'Sunburst'

Palms

Mandevilla 'Moonlight Parfait'

Agapanthus 'Peter Pan'

Aloe

Dietes grandiflora

Erysimum 'Bowles Mauve'

Miscanthus sinensis

Miscanthus sinensis

Philodendron bipinnatifidum

ALOE — p. 180
☼ ◐ ✎ 8, 9, 12–24

ALPINIA — p. 182
☼ ✎ 14–24; H1, H2

ALSTROEMERIA (evergreen types) — p. 182
☼ ◐ ✎ 5–9, 14–24; H1

ANIGOZANTHOS — p. 186
Kangaroo paw
☼ ✎ 15–24

ARTEMISIA 'Powis Castle' — p. 201
☼ ✎ 2–24

Alstroemeria aurea

Anigozanthos hybrid

Strelitzia reginae

ASPIDISTRA elatior — p. 205
Cast-iron plant
◐ ● ✎ 4–10, 12–24; H1, H2

CANNA — p. 248
☼ ◐ ✎ 6–9, 12–24; H1, H2

CAREX (many) — p. 250
Sedge
◐ ● ✎ ZONES VARY

CLIVIA miniata — p. 284
◐ ● ✎ 12–17, 19–24; H1, H2

COLOCASIA esculenta — p. 287
Taro
☼ ◐ ✎ 12, 16–24; H1, H2

COREOPSIS — p. 289
☼ ✎ ZONES VARY

CRASPEDIA globosa — p. 297
Drumsticks
☼ ✎ 8, 9, 14–24

CRASSULA ovata — p. 297
Jade plant
☼ ✎ 8, 9, 12–24; H1, H2

Clivia miniata

Craspedia globosa

Coreopsis grandiflora 'Flying Saucer'

Crassula ovata

CYPERUS — p. 306
☼ ◐ ● ✎ ZONES VARY

DIETES — p. 317
Fortnight lily
☼ ◐ ✎ 8, 9, 12–24; H1, H2

ECHEVERIA — p. 323
◐ ● ✎ ZONES VARY

ERYSIMUM 'Bowles Mauve' — p. 336
☼ ◐ ✎ 4–9, 14–24

GAZANIA — p. 364
NEEDS, ZONES VARY

HEDYCHIUM — p. 386
Ginger lily
☼ ✎ 8, 9, 14–17, 19–24; H1, H2

HEMEROCALLIS — p. 390
Daylily
☼ ◐ ✎ 1–24; H1, H2

HESPERALOE parviflora — p. 392
Red yucca
☼ ✎ 2B, 3, 7–16, 18–24

IRIS pseudacorus — p. 413
Yellow flag
☼ ◐ ✎ A2, A3; 1–24

KNIPHOFIA — p. 427
Red-hot poker
☼ ◐ ✎ ZONES VARY

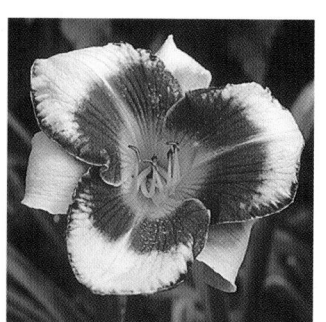

Hemerocallis 'Vintage Bordeaux'

LIMONIUM perezii — p. 446
☼ ✎ 13, 15–17, 20–24

LIRIOPE — p. 448
Lily turf
☼ ◐ ● ✎ ZONES VARY

MISCANTHUS sinensis — p. 482
Eulalia
☼ ◐ ✎ 2–24

PHILODENDRON (treelike types) — p. 533
☼ ◐ ● ✎ ZONES VARY

PHLOMIS — p. 534
☼ ✎ ZONES VARY

PHORMIUM — p. 536
☼ ◐ ✎ 5–9, 14–24; H1, H2

SANTOLINA — p. 614
☼ ✎ ZONES VARY

SCAEVOLA — p. 616
☼ ✎ ZONES VARY

SEDUM dendroideum — p. 620
☼ ◐ ✎ 8, 9, 12, 14–24

SEDUM praealtum — p. 621
☼ ◐ ✎ 8, 9, 12, 14–24

STRELITZIA — p. 637
Bird of paradise
☼ ◐ ✎ ZONES VARY

XANTHOSOMA — p. 672
◐ ✎ 12, 13, 16, 17, 21–24; H1, H2

YUCCA (some) — p. 673
☼ ✎ ZONES VARY

ZINGIBER officinale — p. 676
True ginger
◐ ✎ 9, 14–24; H1, H2

Gazania hybrid

Phormium 'Rainbow Warrior'

Small-space Solutions

Small-space gardens can be low-maintenance and highly functional, but they come with their own design challenges. Chief among them is how to maximize the use of a minimal space. Poor plant choices can quickly lead to an overgrown jumble of plants, making a modest space seem positively cramped. The key is to choose a framework of plants—trees, shrubs, vines, and ground covers—that will become permanent residents of the garden without overstepping their bounds. Then you can fill in empty spots and containers with colorful annuals and perennials.

Cercidium floridum

Acer palmatum 'Sango Kaku'

Bauhinia variegata 'Candida'

Malus (crabapple)

Erythrina crista-galli

Trees, Deciduous

ACER circinatum   p. 167
Vine maple
☀ ◐ ✎ A3; 2B-6, 14-17

ACER palmatum   p. 168
Japanese maple
☀ ◐ ✎ A3; 2-10, 12, 14-24

AMELANCHIER   p. 183
Juneberry
☀ ◐ ✎ ZONES VARY

BAUHINIA variegata   p. 218
Purple orchid tree
☀ ✎ 13, 18-24; H1, H2

CERCIDIUM (most)   p. 262
Palo verde
☀ ZONES VARY

CHILOPSIS linearis   p. 268
Desert willow
☀ ✎ 3B, 7-14, 18-23

CHIONANTHUS   p. 269
Fringe tree
☀ ✎ ZONES VARY

CORNUS kousa   p. 292
Kousa dogwood
☀ ◐ ✎ 2-9, 14-17

ERYTHRINA crista-galli   p. 337
Cockspur coral tree
☀ ✎ 7-9, 12-17, 19-24; H1, H2

LAGERSTROEMIA (many)   p. 430
Crape myrtle
☀ ✎ ZONES VARY

LYSILOMA microphylla thornberi   p. 455
Feather bush
☀ ✎ 12-24; H1, H2

MAGNOLIA × soulangeana (many)   p. 463
Saucer magnolia
☀ ◐ ✎ 2B-10, 12-24

MALUS   p. 469
Flowering crabapple
☀ ☀ ✎ 1-11, 14-21

PRUNUS cerasifera (several)   p. 568
Cherry plum
☀ ✎ 3-22

Trees, Evergreen

ACACIA podalyriifolia   p. 165
Pearl acacia
☀ ✎ 8, 9, 13-24

BRUGMANSIA   p. 232
Angel's trumpet
☀ ◐ ● ✎ 12, 13, 16-24; H1, H2

Chionanthus retusus

Chilopsis linearis

Magnolia × soulangeana

Prunus cerasifera

Potentilla fruticosa 'Klondike'

Spiraea japonica 'Goldflame'

Citrus (lemon)

Rosa 'Baby Eclipse'

Viburnum opulus 'Compactum'

CITRUS   p. 276
☼ ✎ 8, 9, 12–24; H1, H2

CORDIA   p. 289
☼ ✎ ZONES VARY

DODONAEA viscosa   p. 319
Hop bush
☼ ◐ ✎ 7–24; H1, H2

DRIMYS winteri   p. 321
Winter's bark
☼ ✎ 5–9, 14–24

GEIJERA parviflora   p. 365
Australian willow
☼ ✎ 8, 9, 12–24

LEPTOSPERMUM laevigatum   p. 438
Australian tea tree
☼ ✎ 14–24; H1, H2

NERIUM oleander   p. 495
Oleander
☼ ✎ 8–16, 18–24; H1, H2

PODOCARPUS nagi   p. 554
☼ ◐ ✎ 8, 9, 14–24; H1, H2

RHAPHIOLEPIS 'Majestic Beauty'   p. 582
☼ ◐ ✎ 4–10, 12–24; H1, H2

RHUS lancea   p. 590
African sumac
☼ ✎ 8, 9, 12–24

SOPHORA secundiflora   p. 628
Mescal bean
☼ ◐ ✎ 8–16, 18–24

XYLOSMA congestum   p. 673
☼ ◐ ✎ 8–24

Shrubs, Deciduous

BERBERIS thunbergii (small kinds)   p. 221
Japanese barberry
☼ ✎ A3; 2B–24

CARYOPTERIS × clandonensis   p. 253
Blue mist
☼ ✎ 2B–9, 14–24

CLETHRA alnifolia 'Hummingbird'   p. 284
Summersweet
◐ ✎ A2, A3; 1–6

DEUTZIA × rosea   p. 313
☼ ◐ ✎ 2–11, 14–17

GENISTA lydia   p. 366
☼ ✎ 2B–6, 14–17

ILEX verticillata (smaller kinds)   p. 406
Winterberry
☼ ◐ ✎ A2, A3; 1–7

LAGERSTOEMIA indica (dwarf kinds)   p. 430
Crape myrtle
☼ ✎ 7–10, 12–14, 18–21; H1, H2

PEACH, genetic dwarf   p. 516
☼ ✎ ZONES VARY

POTENTILLA (shrubby kinds)   p. 559
Cinquefoil
☼ ◐ ✎ A1–A3; 1–11, 14–21

PUNICA granatum (dwarf selections)   p. 571
Pomegranate
☼ ✎ 5–24; H1, H2

ROSA (especially miniatures)   p. 593
Rose
☼ ◐ ✎ ZONES VARY

SPIRAEA japonica (smaller kinds)   p. 631
☼ ◐ ✎ A2, A3; 2–10, 14–21

VIBURNUM opulus 'compactum', 'Nanum'   p. 665
European cranberry bush
☼ ◐ ✎ A2, A3; 1–9, 14–24

WEIGELA hybrids   p. 670
☼ ◐ ✎ ZONES 1–11, 14–21

Shrubs, Evergreen

BUXUS   p. 235
Boxwood
☼ ◐ ● ✎ ZONES VARY

CALLUNA vulgaris   p. 240
Scotch heather
☼ ✎ 1A, 2–6, 15–17

Buxus sempervirens

Berberis thunbergii

Nerium oleander

Weigela 'Red Prince'

Gardenia augusta

Pieris japonica 'Cavatine'

Rhododendron (deciduous azalea)

Hebe glaucophylla

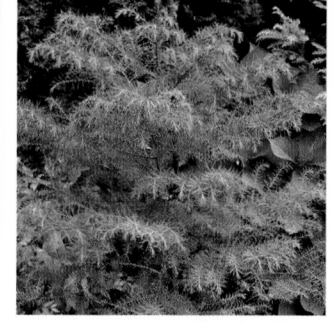

Cryptomeria japonica (dwarf conifer)

CARISSA macrocarpa (some) p. 251
Natal plum
☼ ◑ ✿ 12, 13, 16–24; H2

DABOECIA cantabrica p. 307
Irish heath
☼ ◑ ✿ 3B–9, 14–24

DWARF CONIFERS p. 142
☼ ◑ ✿ ZONES VARY

ERICA (many) p. 331
Heath
☼ ◑ ✿ ZONES VARY

ESCALLONIA (dwarf kinds) p. 338
☼ ◑ ✿ 4–9, 14–24

GARDENIA augusta (several) p. 362
☼ ◑ ✿ 7–9, 12–16, 18–24; H1, H2

HEBE (several) p. 385
☼ ◑ ✿ ZONES VARY

HELIANTHEMUM nummularium p. 387
Sunrose
☼ ✿ 2B–9, 14–24

ILEX cornuta (some) p. 405
Chinese holly
☼ ◑ ✿ 3–24

ILEX crenata (several) p. 405
Japanese holly
☼ ◑ ✿ 3–9, 14–24

ILEX glabra 'Compacta' p. 405
Inkberry
☼ ◑ ✿ 2B–24

ILEX vomitoria (several) p. 406
Yaupon
☼ ◑ ✿ 3–9, 11–24; H1, H2

KALMIA latifolia (dwarf selections) p. 425
Mountain laurel
☼ ◑ ✿ 2–7, 16, 17

LAURUS nobilis p. 434
Sweet bay
☼ ◑ ✿ 5–9, 12–24; H1, H2

LAVANDULA p. 434
Lavender
☼ ✿ ZONES VARY

MYRTUS communis 'Compacta' p. 438
Myrtle
☼ ◑ ✿ 8–24; H1, H2

NANDINA domestica (smaller kinds) p. 489
Heavenly bamboo
☼ ◑ ● ✿ 3–24; H1, H2

NERIUM oleander (several) p. 495
Oleander
☼ ✿ 8–16, 18–24, H1, H2

PIERIS japonica (dwarf selections) p. 540
Lily-of-the-valley shrub
◑ ✿ 2B–9, 14–17

PITTOSPORUM tobira (smaller kinds) p. 546
Tobira
☼ ◑ ✿ 8–24; H1, H2

PRUNUS laurocerasus 'Mount Vernon' p. 566
English laurel
☼ ◑ ✿ 4–9, 14–24

PYRACANTHA (smaller kinds) p. 572
Firethorn
☼ ✿ ZONES VARY

RHAPHIOLEPIS indica (smaller kinds) p. 582
Indian hawthorn
☼ ◑ ✿ 4–10, 12–24; H1, H2

RHODODENDRON (smaller kinds) p. 583
Rhododendron and azalea
◑ ✿ ZONES VARY

ROSMARINUS officinalis (most) p. 602
Rosemary
☼ ✿ 4–24; H1, H2

SALVIA greggii p. 609
Autumn sage
☼ ◑ ✿ 8–24

SANTOLINA p. 614
☼ ✿ ZONES VARY

TEUCRIUM (several) p. 645
Germander
☼ ✿ ZONES VARY

Lavandula stoechas

Salvia greggii 'Alba'

Laurus nobilis

Pittosporum tobira 'Wheeler's Dwarf'

Santolina pinnata

Clematis hybrid

Thunbergia gregorii

Ajuga reptans

Arabis caucasica

Chamaemelum nobile

Thymus

Vines, Deciduous

CLEMATIS alpina p. 282
☼ ✿ A2, A3; 1–11, 14–18

CLEMATIS macropetala p. 282
Downy clematis
☼ ✿ A2, A3; 1–11, 14–18

CLEMATIS texensis p. 282
Scarlet clematis
☼ ✿ 2B–11, 14–24

CLEMATIS, large-flowered hybrids p. 283
☼ ◑ ✿ A2, A3; 2–11, 14–24

LONICERA × brownii p. 451
Scarlet trumpet honeysuckle
☼ ◑ ✿ A3; 1–7

LONICERA × heckrottii p. 452
Goldflame honeysuckle
☼ ◑ ✿ 2–24; H1, H2

ROSA (smaller climbers) p. 593
☼ ◑ ✿ ZONES VARY

THUNBERGIA (some) p. 647
☼ ◑ ✿ ZONES VARY

Lonicera × heckrottii

Vines, Evergreen

BOUGAINVILLEA (some) p. 227
☼ ✿ 5, 6, 12–17, 19, 21–24; H1, H2

HARDENBERGIA p. 384
Lilac vine
☼ ◑ ✿ ZONES VARY

HIBBERTIA scandens p. 394
Guinea gold vine
☼ ◑ ✿ 16, 17, 21–24

LAPAGERIA rosea p. 432
Chilean bellflower
◑ ✿ 5, 6, 15–17, 23, 24

MANDEVILLA (most) p. 473
☼ ◑ ✿ ZONES VARY

SOLANUM crispum p. 627
☼ ◑ ✿ 8, 9, 12–24

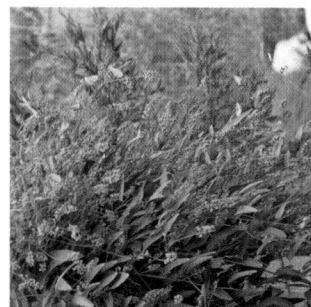

Hardenbergia violacea

Ground Covers

AJUGA reptans p. 177
Carpet bugle
☼ ◑ ✿ A2, A3; 1–24

ARABIS caucasica p. 196
Wall rockcress
☼ ◑ ✿ A1; 1–10, 14–24

ARENARIA p. 199
Sandwort
☼ ◑ ● ✿ ZONES VARY

CEPHALOPHYLLUM 'Red Spike' p. 261
Red spike ice plant
☼ ◑ ✿ 8, 9, 11–24

CHAMAEMELUM nobile p. 265
Chamomile
☼ ◑ ✿ 2–24

DELOSPERMA p. 311
Ice plant
☼ ◑ ✿ ZONES VARY

GAULTHERIA (some) p. 364
◑ ✿ ZONES VARY

LAMPRANTHUS (some) p. 431
Ice plant
☼ ✿ ZONES VARY

MAZUS reptans p. 475
☼ ◑ ✿ 1–9, 14–24

Delosperma cooperi

OPHIOPOGON japonicus (smaller selections) p. 501
Mondo grass
☼ ◑ ● ✿ 5–9, 14–24; H1, H2

PHYLA nodiflora p. 538
Lippia
☼ ✿ 8–24; H1, H2

PRATIA p. 560
☼ ◑ ✿ 4–9, 14–24

SAPONARIA ocymoides p. 615
☼ ✿ 1–11, 14–24

SCAEVOLA 'Mauve Clusters' p. 616
☼ ✿ 8, 9, 14–24; H1, H2

STACHYS byzantina 'Silver Carpet' p. 633
Lamb's ears
☼ ◑ ✿ 1–24

TANACETUM densum amani p. 643
☼ ✿ 3–24

THYMUS p. 648
Thyme
☼ ◑ ✿ ZONES VARY

VANCOUVERIA hexandra p. 661
◑ ✿ 4–7, 14–17, 19–24

Vancouveria hexandra

Western Plant Encyclopedia

Many of the plants sold at nurseries in the West, from tall trees to tiny succulents, are described in the pages that follow. Ornamental plants and herbs are listed alphabetically by their botanical names—*Quercus* (oak) and *Ocimum* (basil), for example. Common names are cross-referenced to help you find the botanical names. Fruits and vegetables, on the other hand, are simply listed by their common names—Apple and Pumpkin, for example.

The sample entry below illustrates the format used throughout the encyclopedia. The plant's botanical name is listed first. Where applicable, alternate botanical names—former names that are still in common parlance or new ones that haven't yet taken hold—are shown in parentheses. Next is the plant's common name or names, followed by the family name. The four lines that follow list the type of plant and cultural information. And a final line is added, wherever needed, to note any problems with toxicity.

Rosa banksiae 'Lutea'

Colchicum
MEADOW SAFFRON,
AUTUMN CROCUS
Liliaceae
PERENNIALS FROM CORMS

🌿 ZONES 2–10, 14–24; OR INDOORS
☼ FULL SUN; BRIGHT INDIRECT LIGHT
💧 REGULAR WATER DURING GROWTH AND BLOOM
◊ ALL PARTS ARE POISONOUS IF INGESTED

Colchicum

Climate

🌿 refers to the Sunset climate zones (see pages 28–63) where the plant grows best. In this example, the plant is recommended for Zones 2–10 or 14–24. If the entry reads "All Zones," the plant will grow anywhere in the West. If the zone line includes the words "or indoors," the plant can be grown outdoors in the designated zones and indoors there or in colder climates.

Exposure

☼ means that the plant grows best with unobstructed sunlight all or almost all day; you can overlook an hour or so of shade at the beginning or end of a summer day. ◑ means the plant needs partial shade—that is some shade for half the day or for at least 3 hours during the hottest part of the day. ● indicates that a plant prefers little or no direct sun—for example, it does best on the north side of a house or beneath a broad, dense-foliaged tree.

Some listings contain qualifications. For example, "☼ ◑ Partial shade in hottest climates" means the plant succeeds in full sun or partial shade except in the hottest areas, where it must have partial shade. If a plant can be grown indoors, outdoor exposure needs are followed by indoor light requirements. In the sample entry, the plant needs full sun outdoors, bright indirect light indoors.

Watering

Moisture needs are given for established plants. Bear in mind that even plants that will survive at maturity on rainfall alone need regular moisture for a time after planting—perhaps a single season for a perennial, up to 2 to 5 years for a tree. ◌ indicates the most drought-tolerant plants; some require no supplemental irrigation once established, while others may need a little. ◔ means the plant needs less than regular moisture; this may mean a soaking every 2 or 3 weeks. ● means the plant requires regular moisture: soil shouldn't be too dry or too wet. ●● is reserved for plants needing ample moisture, such as bog and aquatic plants and streambed natives. Many plants show a range; for example, ●●● means the plant can take regular moisture or wetter conditions.

Toxicity

◊ indicates that the plant or some of its parts are known to have toxic or irritant properties.

A

AARON'S BEARD.
See **HYPERICUM calycinum**

ABELIA
Caprifoliaceae
EVERGREEN, SEMIEVERGREEN,
DECIDUOUS SHRUBS

🌿 ZONES VARY BY SPECIES
☀️ 🌤️ BEST IN SUN, TOLERATE SOME SHADE, EXCEPT AS NOTED
💧 REGULAR WATER

Graceful, arching branches densely
clothed with oval, usually
glossy leaves ½–1½ in. long;
bronzy new growth. Tubu-
lar or bell-shaped
flowers in clusters at
ends of branches or
among leaves. Though
small, blossoms are plentiful enough to be showy,
mostly during summer and
early fall. When
blooms drop, they
usually leave purplish
or copper-colored sepals that provide color into the fall months.
Leaves also may take on bronzy
tints in fall.

Abelia × grandiflora

To keep the shrub's graceful
form, prune selectively; don't
shear. The more stems you cut to
the ground in winter or early
spring, the more open and arching
next year's growth will be. Abelias
are adaptable plants, useful in
shrub borders, as space dividers
and visual barriers, and near
house walls; lower kinds are good
bank or ground covers.

A. chinensis. Deciduous. Zones
4–24. Chinese native to 4–5 ft.
tall and wide, with fragrant, pink-
tinted white flowers.

A. floribunda. MEXICAN
ABELIA. Evergreen. Zones 9, 12–
24; with periodic damage in Zones
7, 8. Severely damaged at 20°F/
–7°C. Native to Mexico. Usually
3–6 ft. tall; sometimes 10 ft. tall
and up to 12 ft. wide. Arching, reddish, downy or hairy stems. Pendulous reddish purple flowers appear
singly or in clusters. Heaviest
bloom is in summer, with sporadic
re-bloom during rest of year. Needs
partial shade in hot climates.

A. × grandiflora. GLOSSY
ABELIA. Evergreen to semiever-

green. Zones 4–24; H1, H2. This
cross between two Chinese species
is the best known and most popular of the abelias. To 8 ft. or taller,
spreading to 5 ft. or wider. Loses
most of its leaves at 15°F/–9°C.
Freezes to the ground at 0°F/
–18°C but usually recovers to
bloom the same year, making a
graceful border plant 10–15 in.
high. The following are among
the varieties grown.

'Confetti'. Dense, 2–3 ft. high,
4–5 ft. wide, with leaves variegated
white, turning maroon in cold
weather. White flowers.

'Edward Goucher'. Zones 5–24.
Less hardy, lacier, and more compact (to 3–5 ft. tall and wide) than
A. × grandiflora. Bears small lilac
pink flowers with orange throats.

'Francis Mason'. Compact (to
3–4 ft. high and wide) and densely
branched, with pink flowers and
yellow-variegated leaves.

'Kaleidoscope'. Compact (2–3 ft.
tall, 3–4 ft. wide) with yellow variegated leaves and white flowers.

'Little Richard'. Dwarf (to 2–3 ft.
high, 4 ft. wide) with shiny, dark
green leaves that hold on for a
long time even in cold winters.
White flowers.

'Panache' ('Silver Anniversary').
Low, to 1½–2 ft. high, spreading
4–5 ft.; silvery cream leaf edges,
red stems. White flowers.

'Prostrata'. Low grower (1½–2 ft.
tall, spreading 4–5 ft. wide) useful
as ground cover, bank planting,
foreground shrub. White flowers.

'Sherwoodii'. Dense, compact,
refined growth to 3–4 ft. tall, 5 ft.
wide. Lavender flowers.

'Sunrise'. Densely branched,
with bronzy green leaves that turn
red and purple in fall. To 3–6 ft.
tall and wide. White flowers.

'White Marvel'. Dense (5 ft.
high and wide), with white, cream,
pink, and yellow new growth.
Mature leaves green with cream to
gold edges. Pink flowers.

ABELIOPHYLLUM
distichum
WHITE FORSYTHIA,
ABELIA-LEAF
Oleaceae
DECIDUOUS SHRUB

🌿 ZONES 1–11, 14–19
☀️ 🌤️ BEST IN SUN, TOLERATES SOME SHADE
💧 REGULAR WATER

Korean native resembling forsythia
in growth habit and abundance
of mid- to late winter blooms. To
3–4 ft. tall and wide, with bluish

*Abeliophyllum
distichum*

green, 1–2-in.-long leaves. Pink
buds along deep brown or black
branches open to very fragrant
white blossoms (sometimes
flushed pink). 'Roseum' is a pink-
flowering form. After bloom,
remove some of oldest branches at
base to keep flowering wood coming. Or cut branches while in bud
or bloom to use for decoration;
budded branches can be forced to
flower indoors.

ABELMOSCHUS
Malvaceae
PERENNIALS OFTEN GROWN AS
ANNUALS

🌿 ZONE H2; ANNUALS IN ZONES 1–24
☀️ 🌤️ AFTERNOON SHADE IN HOTTEST CLIMATES
💧 REGULAR WATER

Hibiscus relatives from tropical
Asia with deeply divided leaves
and large, five-petaled flowers.
Most commonly grown as summer
annuals; will bloom first year from
seed sown early. Thrive in good
garden soil. The annual *A. esculen-
tus* is a vegetable; see Okra.

**A. manihot (Hibiscus mani-
hot).** To 6 ft. or taller, 2–3 ft. wide.
Large, coarse leaves and 3–5-in.,
cream to deep yellow flowers with
maroon central blotch.

**A. moschatus (Hibiscus
moschatus).** SILK FLOWER.
Bushy plant about 1½ ft. high and
wide, with deep green, deeply cut

Abelmoschus moschatus

leaves. Five-petaled, 3–4½-in.,
cherry red or deep pink blooms
resemble those of tropical hibiscus. Can be grown as a houseplant
in 6-in. pot; set on a windowsill in
bright light.

ABIES
FIR
Pinaceae
EVERGREEN TREES

🌿 ZONES VARY BY SPECIES
☀️ 🌤️ FULL SUN OR LIGHT SHADE, EXCEPT AS NOTED
💧 💧 MODERATE TO REGULAR WATER, EXCEPT AS NOTED

In nature, firs are tall, erect, symmetrical trees with uniformly
spaced branch whorls. Though
sometimes confused with spruces
(Picea), they have softer needles
that fall directly from the stems
(spruces leave short pegs behind),
and their large cones grow up
rather than down. Cones shatter
after ripening, leaving a spiky
stalk. Most (but not all) firs are
native to North America and are
high-mountain plants that do best
in or near their natural environments. They grow slowly if at all in
hot, dry, windy areas at low elevations, though firs from some other
parts of the world do well in warm,
dry climates.

Christmas tree farms grow native
firs for cutting, and nurseries in
the Pacific Northwest and Northern
California grow a few species for
the living Christmas tree trade.
Licensed collectors in the Northwest dig picturesque, contorted firs
at high elevations near the timberline and market them through
nurseries as "alpine conifers." Use
these in rock gardens; small specimens are good container or bonsai
subjects. Birds are attracted by fir
seeds. New growth on firs is susceptible to aphid damage.

Allow ample growing room at
planting; if you later try to restrict a
fir tree's size by pruning, you'll only
ruin its natural shape. Pruning is
rarely necessary; plants are more
attractive with branches all the way
to the ground.

A. amabilis. SILVER FIR,
CASCADE FIR. Zones 3–7, 15–17.
Native to southern Alaska south
through Coast Ranges and Cascades of Washington and Oregon.
Imposing tree in the wild, smaller
(20–50 ft. tall and 12–15 ft. wide)
in lowland gardens in the Pacific
Northwest. Dark green needles,
silvery beneath, curve upward
along the branches.

A. balsamea. BALSAM FIR. Zones A3; 1–7, 15–17. Native to eastern North American mountains. Dwarf 'Nana' is the form most commonly sold in the West. It's an interesting rock garden subject, very slowly forming a dense, dark green cushion 2–3 ft. high and wide. Needs partial shade, regular water.

A. bracteata (A. venusta). SANTA LUCIA FIR, BRISTLE-CONE FIR. Zones 6–9, 14–21. From steep, rocky slopes on the seaward side of California's Santa Lucia Mountains. A tall tree (to 70 ft. in 50 years), with spreading lower branches (to 15–20 ft.) and slender steeplelike crown. Stiff, 1½–2½-in.-long needles are dark green above, with white lines beneath; needle points are unusually sharp. Roundish cones are unusual—about 4 in. long, with a long, slender, pointed bract on each cone scale. Exceptionally tolerant of heat and aridity.

A. concolor. WHITE FIR. Zones A2, A3; 1–9, 14–24. Native to mountains of southern Oregon, California, southern Rocky Mountains, Baja California. One of the big five in the timber belt of the Sierra Nevada, along with ponderosa pine, sugar pine, incense cedar, and Douglas fir. A popular Christmas tree and one of the most commonly grown native firs in Western gardens. Needs no irrigation where native; some elsewhere.

Large, symmetrical tree (80–120 ft. tall and 15–20 ft. wide) in its native range and in the Northwest. Slower growing in California gardens; has reached 30 ft. in as many years in lowland California. Best as container plant in Southern California. Bluish green, 1–2-in.-long needles. Some consider 'Candicans', with bluish white foliage, the "bluest" of all conifers.

A. grandis. LOWLAND FIR, GRAND FIR. Zones 1–9, 14–17. From British Columbia inland to Montana, southward to Northern California, where it grows near the ocean. Many Northwest gardeners live and garden successfully under this fir; they prune it high. It's one of the largest firs, reaching 300 ft. in the wild (smaller in cultivation—80–200 ft. tall, 15–25 ft. wide). Handsome, deep green,

1–1½-in.-long needles are glossy above, with white lines beneath; they grow in two rows along branches. 'Johnsonii' is suited to urban gardens, growing 65 ft. tall and 10 ft. wide.

A. koreana. KOREAN FIR. Zones 3b–9, 14–24. Native to Korea. Slow-growing, compact, pyramidal tree seldom over 30 ft. tall and 20 ft. wide. Shiny, short green needles. Sets cones on young, small trees. 'Aurea', with gold-green foliage, is even smaller, slower growing. 'Horstmann's Silberlocke' provides a dwarf silver accent; its needles turn upward, showing silvery white undersides.

A. lasiocarpa. ALPINE FIR, ROCKY MOUNTAIN FIR. Zones A2, A3; 1–9, 14–17. Native to Alaska, south through the high Cascades of Washington and Oregon; nearly throughout the Rocky Mountains. In the wild in good, moist soil, it is a narrow, steeple-shaped tree, 60–90 ft. tall and 10 ft. wide. In gardens, usually grows much shorter and loses its narrow shape; allow for 15–20-ft. spread in Northwest. Extremely slow growing in California gardens. Bluish green, 1–1½-in.-long needles.

A. l. arizonica. Zones 2–9. Native to San Francisco Peaks, Arizona, at 8,500-ft. elevation. Thick, corky, creamy white bark gives the tree its common name, "cork fir." Blue, often silvery, needles. Very handsome as a youngster; good bonsai. Excellent substitute for blue spruce (*Picea pungens*) in smaller spaces, and more disease free.

Abies concolor

A. magnifica. RED FIR. Zones 2–7. Native to the mountains of southern Oregon and parts of California's Sierra Nevada and Coast Ranges. This is the "silver tip" fir of the California cut Christmas tree trade. Stately (80–120 ft. tall and 15–20 ft. wide in the wild), with symmetrical, horizontal, rather short branches. New growth silvery gray. Mature needles blue green, 1 in. long. Hard to grow at low elevations.

A. nordmanniana. NORDMANN FIR. Zones 1–11, 14–24. Native to the Caucasus, Asia Minor, Greece. Vigorous, densely foliaged fir, 30–50 ft. tall and 20 ft. wide in cultivation. Dark green,

shiny, ¾–1½-in.-long needles, with whitish bands beneath. More adaptable to California gardens than native firs, becoming a symmetrical, densely branched, cone-shaped tree. Needs regular water; will submit to long-term container growing.

A. pinsapo. SPANISH FIR. Zones 5–11, 14–24. Native to Spain. Very slow growing, to 25 ft. tall and 10 ft. wide in 40 years. In Southern California, good dwarf effect for years. Dense, symmetrical form; sometimes taken for a spruce. Stiff, deep green, ½–¾-in.-long needles are set uniformly around branches. 'Glauca' needles are blue gray.

A. procera (A. nobilis). NOBLE FIR. Zones 2–6, 15–17. Native to the Siskiyou Mountains in California, northern mountains of Oregon and Washington. Similar to *A. magnifica* in appearance; grown in Northwest nurseries as a living Christmas tree. Grows 90–200 ft. tall and 20–30 ft. wide in the wild, almost as tall in Northwest gardens. Short, stiff branches; blue-green, 1-in.-long needles. Large cones (6–10 in. long, 3 in. wide) with extended bracts as in *A. bracteata.*

A. sibirica. SIBERIAN FIR. Zones A1–A3; 1–3. Native to Siberia, Mongolia. Narrowly conical tree to about 30 ft. tall. Aromatic, bright green needles just over 1 in. long are arranged all around the twigs and point toward twig tips. Short cones (about 3 in. long) are bluish at first, becoming brown. Does best in cool, moist climates; valuable for tolerance to extreme cold.

ABUTILON
FLOWERING MAPLE, CHINESE BELLFLOWER, CHINESE LANTERN
Malvaceae
EVERGREEN SHRUBS

🖋	ZONES 8, 9, 12–24; H1, H2; EXCEPT AS NOTED
☀ ◑	PARTIAL SHADE IN HOTTEST CLIMATES
💧 💧	MODERATE TO REGULAR WATER, EXCEPT AS NOTED

Native to warm regions around the world, especially South America. Planted primarily for its showy flowers. Good drainage is essential. Control whitefly and scale insects. In cold-winter climates, can be grown as potted plants; keep indoors in winter, put out on terrace or patio in summer.

A. hybrids. Grown in zones listed and also as an annual in colder climates. The best-known flowering maples. Upright, arching growth to 8–10 ft. tall, with equal spread. Broad maplelike leaves, sometimes variegated white; drooping bell-like flowers in white, yellow, pink, or red. Main bloom season is spring, but white and yellow forms flower almost continually. Many hybrids are available, including dwarf varieties and ones with more spreading habits.

Abutilon hybrid

A. megapotamicum. Vine-shrub from Brazil. Vigorous growth to 10 ft. and as wide, with arrowlike, 1½–3-in.-long leaves. Flowers resembling red-and-yellow lanterns gaily decorate the long, rangy branches in spring and summer. Pinch branch tips to control size, make bushier. More graceful in detail than in entirety but can be trained to an interesting pattern. Usually best as loose, informal espalier. Good hanging basket plant. 'Marianne' has better, more intense flower color; 'Variegata' has leaves mottled with yellow; 'Victory' is compact and floriferous, with small deep yellow blooms.

A. palmeri. INDIAN MALLOW. Zones 8, 9, 11–13. From low deserts of Arizona, California. To 5 ft. tall and wide. Clustered spring flowers are orange yellow, about 1 in. wide. Grown primarily for its soft, velvety, heart-shaped to roundish leaves, to 6 in. wide and 8 in. long. Little water.

A. pictum 'Thompsonii'. Variety of a Brazilian species. Similar in form to hybrids, but foliage is strikingly variegated with creamy yellow. Blooms almost continually, bearing pale orange bells veined with red.

A. vitifolium (Corynabutilon vitifolium). Zones 5, 6, 15–17. From Chile. To 15 ft. tall, 8 ft. wide. Gray-green, maplelike leaves to 6 in. or longer. In summer, lilac blue to white flowers are borne singly or in clusters on long stalks. Needs high humidity.

A

ABYSSINIAN BANANA.
See **ENSETE ventricosum**

ABYSSINIAN SWORD LILY.
See **GLADIOLUS callianthus**

ACACIA

Fabaceae (Leguminosae)
EVERGREEN AND DECIDUOUS
SHRUBS AND TREES

🗲 ZONES VARY BY SPECIES

☼ FULL SUN

◖ LITTLE OR NO WATER

▶ SEE CHART

Native to tropics or warm regions of world, notably Australia, Mexico, and the southwestern U.S. Of the many species tested over the last 150 years, more than two dozen serve beautifully and functionally in Western landscapes, and new species are continually being tested.

Of species in use today, several offer fountains of clear yellow flowers in early or midwinter. Some are quite fragrant when in bloom. Many decorate and protect hillsides, banks, freeway landscapes. Some serve well in beach plantings. All are attractive to birds. Those listed in chart are evergreen except where noted.

Most nurseries sell only a few of the many acacia species, but you can easily grow acacias from seed you collect yourself or order from a specialist.

The acacias differ widely in foliage and growth habit. Some have feathery, much-divided leaves; others have flattened leafstalks that fulfill the function of leaves. Many start life with feathery leaves and later develop leathery ones.

You can prune acacias or leave them to their own devices. Larger-growing species may end up as shrubs or trees depending on how they are treated in youth. Remove the lead shoot and the plant grows as a shrub; remove the lower branches and it will be treelike. It's best to prune trees to open up their interiors; this will

*Acacia
melanoxylon*

Acacia baileyana

reduce dieback of shaded branches and prevent wind damage. Thin by removing branches all the way to the trunk.

Many acacias are relatively short lived—20 to 30 years. But if a plant reaches 20 ft. high in 3 years, the short life can be accepted.

Acacias seldom suffer pest damage. Where water is bad and salts accumulate, many become chlorotic (as do numerous other plants in such soil).

ACACIA

NAME	ZONES	HEIGHT	SPREAD	LEAVES	FLOWERS	COMMENTS
Acacia aneura MULGA	8, 9, 12–24	15–20 ft.	15–20 ft.	Narrow and pendulous, leathery, gray green to silver	Yellow, rodlike. Winter to spring	Thornless, rounded tree
A. baileyana BAILEY ACACIA (often called "mimosa" as cut flowers)	8, 9, 13–24	20–30 ft.	20–40 ft.	Feathery, finely cut, blue gray	Yellow, in clusters. Fragrant. Profuse in early to midwinter	Most commonly planted and one of hardiest. Wonderful tree on banks when grown as multitrunked shrub-tree
A. b. 'Purpurea' PURPLE-LEAF ACACIA	8, 9, 13–24	20–30 ft.	20–30 ft.	Same as above, except for lavender to purple new growth	Same as above	Cut back to encourage new growth, prolong foliage color
A. berlandieri GUAJILLO	10–24	5–12 ft.	5–20 ft.	Feathery, finely divided, light green	White, fragrant. Early spring	Thornless large shrub forms especially useful for background or screen
A. boormanii SNOWY RIVER WATTLE	8, 9, 12–24	10–15 ft.	6–15 ft.	Narrow, gray green, 2–3 in. long	Bright yellow, fragrant puffs at branch ends. Winter	Shrub that can sucker to form thickets. Tolerates winter wet
A. cognata **(A. subporosa)** BOWER WATTLE, RIVER WATTLE	16–24	20–30 ft.	20–30 ft.	Narrow, drooping, bright green, to 4 in. long	Paired pale yellow puffs. Spring	Graceful weeping tree. Damaged at 20°F/–7°C. Selections include 'Emerald Cascade' and 'Emerald Showers'
A. confusa FORMOSAN KOA	H1, H2	30–50 ft.	To 30 ft.	Dark green, slightly curved	Bright yellow puffs in spring, summer	Open, upright to round headed
A. constricta WHITE THORN, MESCAT ACACIA	8, 9, 10–24	10–18 ft.	To 18 ft.	Tiny, feathery	Yellow, fragrant. Spring, summer	Open, spiny, deciduous shrub native from Texas to Arizona. Valuable in desert for texture, summer flowers
A. covenyi BLUE BUSH	8, 9, 12–24	15–20 ft.	8–10 ft.	Narrow, blue gray	Yellow, globular. Late winter to spring	Fast-growing large shrub or small tree with chocolate brown branches. Excellent windbreak or screen
A. craspedocarpa LEATHERLEAF ACACIA	8, 9, 12–24	8–10 ft.	5–10 ft.	Round, thick, leathery, gray green	Bright yellow, drooping. Spring through summer	Dense, round to upright shrub with attractive flat seedpods. Can be trained as a tree. Very drought tolerant

ACACIA

NAME	ZONES	HEIGHT	SPREAD	LEAVES	FLOWERS	COMMENTS
A. cultriformis KNIFE ACACIA	12–24	10–15 ft.	10–15 ft.	Silvery gray, shaped like 1-in.-long paring knife blades	Yellow, in clusters. Early spring	Naturally a multistemmed tree. Barrier or screen. Useful on banks, slopes
A. cyanophylla (see **A. saligna**)						
A. dealbata (**A. decurrens dealbata**)	8, 9, 14–24; borderline in 6	To 50 ft.	40–50 ft.	Feathery, silvery gray	Similar to *A. baileyana*	Twigs and young branches are silvery gray; attractive. A very fast growing tree
A. farnesiana SWEET ACACIA (see also **A. smallii**)	13–24	To 20 ft.	15–25 ft.	Deciduous, feathery, finely divided leaves on thorny branches	Deep yellow, fragrant balls in winter. May freeze in cold snaps	Shrub or small tree that needs frost-free location in Zone 13. Can freeze to stump at 28°F/–2°C. Better for desert is similar *A. smallii*, often sold as *A. farnesiana*
A. greggii CATCLAW ACACIA	10–24	15–25 ft.	15 ft.	Finely divided, feathery, dark green; carried on spiny branches	Creamy yellow. Spring and intermittently through fall	Native California to Texas. Shrubby in drought, treelike with water
A. iteaphylla WILLOW WATTLE	8, 9, 12–24	8–12 ft.	10–12 ft.	Gray green with reddish pink new growth	Profuse, pale yellow. Winter to spring	Beautiful, slightly weeping, spreading shrub. Good screen or low windbreak, especially near coast
A. koa KOA	H1, H2	To 60 ft.	To 60 ft.	Feathery in young trees; later leathery, curved, 6 in. long, up to ½ in. wide	Yellow, in clusters. Spring	Native Hawaiian tree produces a beautiful hardwood
A. longifolia (often sold as **A. latifolia**) SYDNEY GOLDEN WATTLE	8, 9, 14–24	To 20 ft.	To 20 ft.	Bright green, 3–6 in. long	Golden yellow, loose, 2½-in.-long spikes along branches in late winter, early spring	Usually big, rounded, billowy shrub. Very fast growing; very tolerant. Used as road screening against dust and headlights. Good soil binder near the beach (winds make it prostrate). Resists oak root fungus
A. melanoxylon BLACKWOOD ACACIA, BLACK ACACIA	8, 9, 13–24	To 40 ft.	To 20 ft.	Dark green, 2–4 in. long	Creamy to straw color, in short clusters. Spring	Fast, dense, upright tree. Aggressive roots, litter, brittle branches a problem in confined areas. Thrives in intense heat, coastal winds, poor soil, drought
A. merinthophora ZIGZAG WATTLE	13–17, 19–24	9–12 ft.	9–12 ft.	Long, narrow, gray green	Bright yellow. Winter to spring	Weeping shrub
A. minuta (see **A. smallii**)						
A. pendula WEEPING ACACIA, WEEPING MYALL	13–24	To 25 ft.	To 15 ft.	Blue gray, to 4 in. long, on long, weeping branches	Yellow, in pairs or clusters. Blooms erratically in spring	Beautiful weeping tree. Perfect for cascading from behind wall. Makes graceful espalier. Interesting structure in maturity. Slow grower, seldom looks good in container
A. podalyriifolia PEARL ACACIA	8, 9, 13–24	10–20 ft.	12–15 ft.	Roundish, 1½ in. long, silvery gray, soft and satiny to touch	Light yellow, fluffy, in long clusters. Late fall, winter	Grow as shrub or train as rounded, open-headed tree. Excellent for patio. Good winter color. Won't tolerate summer water. Prune heavily after flowering to keep it compact
A. pravissima OVENS WATTLE	12–24	12–20 ft.	12–20 ft.	Short, triangular, gray green; tightly packed along branches	Profuse, bright yellow, scented. Winter, spring	Shrub or small tree. Endures frost, heat, wind, marine exposure

A

ACACIA

NAME	ZONES	HEIGHT	SPREAD	LEAVES	FLOWERS	COMMENTS
A. redolens	8, 9, 12–24	Variable; 1–6 ft.	Variable; to 15 ft.	Narrow, gray green, leathery	Puffy yellow balls. Spring	Ground cover for banks, large areas of poor soil. Endures drought, heat. 'Desert Carpet' and 'Low Boy' are low-growing forms: 2 ft. high, spreading to 12 ft.
A. rigidula BLACKBRUSH ACACIA	10–13	10–15 ft.	10–15 ft.	Deep green, rounded leaflets	Fragrant, pale yellow, 2–3-in. spikes; almost glow on a bright spring day	Slower growing than other acacias becoming a shrub or small tree. Naturally multitrunked. To train to single trunk, pull off suckers at base
A. salicina WILLOW ACACIA, AUSTRALIAN WILLOW	8, 9, 12–24	20–40 ft.	To 15 ft.	Dark green, narrow, to 3 in. long	Cream-colored balls. Blooms most of year; heaviest in fall, winter	Fast-growing tree, with semiweeping habit. Prune to keep open. Don't overwater
A. saligna (**A. cyanophylla**) BLUE-LEAF WATTLE	8, 9, 12–24	20–30 ft.	15–20 ft.	Narrow, blue green, 6–12 in. long	Nearly orange balls in clusters. Heavy bloom in spring	Screen for privacy or wind control. Multitrunked big shrub or tree
A. schaffneri	8, 9, 12–24	To 18 ft.	To 20 ft.	Deciduous, finely divided, closely set along branches	Yellow balls, fragrant. Spring	Shrub or small tree with curving, nearly black branches. Prune to form trunk and shape branches. Short thorns hidden in leaves
A. smallii (**A. minuta**)	8, 9, 12–24	Variable; 10–35 ft.	15–25 ft.	Deciduous, finely divided leaves on thorny branches	Yellow, fragrant, puffy balls. Spring	Desert Southwest native often sold as *A. farnesiana*, which is cold tender. Plant *A. smallii* where frost occurs
A. stenophylla SHOESTRING ACACIA	8, 9, 12–24	To 30 ft.	To 20 ft.	Long (to 16 in.), narrow, drooping, pale green; maroon new bark	Creamy, ½-in. balls. Late winter, spring	Fast-growing, open, weeping tree; makes good shadows on walls, provides lightest shade for underplantings
A. subporosa (see **A. cognata**)						
A. verticillata	14–24	To 15 ft.	To 15 ft.	Dark green, needlelike, ¾ in. long, in whorls	Pale yellow, in 1-in.-long spikes. Spring	Looks like an airy, shrubby conifer. Good low hedge in wind. Unpruned, it develops open form with many spreading, twisting trunks. Sheared, it grows dense and full. Good at beach. Resists oak root fungus
A. vestita HAIRY WATTLE	13, 15–17, 19–24	12–15 ft.	12–15 ft.	Green, narrow	Beautiful, yellow, ball shaped. Spring	Attractive weeping shrub. Can be used as a low screen or windbreak. Tolerates brief periods of flooding
A. willardiana PALO BLANCO	12–24	To 20 ft.	To 10 ft.	Deciduous fernlike leaves fall early, leaving narrow leaflike stalks 3–12 in. long	Pale yellow. Early spring	Striking feature is white or cream-colored, papery, peeling bark

ACALYPHA

Euphorbiaceae
EVERGREEN SHRUBS

✂ ZONES 24; H2; OR INDOORS

☼ PARTIAL SHADE; BRIGHT INDIRECT LIGHT

💧 REGULAR WATER

All three species described are native to Southeast Asia and the Pacific Islands. Beyond their hardiness range, they can be grown indoors; *A. wilkesiana* and *A. pendula* can be used as annuals in Zones 22 and 23. All bloom intermittently during the warmest months, must have good drainage. Pinch young plants regularly to encourage bushy growth.

A. hispida. CHENILLE PLANT. Can grow to a bulky 10 ft. tall, 6 ft. wide. Heavy, rich green leaves to 8 in. wide. Flowers

Acalypha hispida

come in hanging, 1½-ft.-long clusters that resemble tassels of crimson chenille. Heaviest bloom in early summer; scattered bloom all year. Thrives in tropical climates. Can also be grown in greenhouse or enclosed patio or, with heavy pruning, as a houseplant.

A. pendula (**A. repens**). FIRETAIL. Resembles *A. hispida* in flower form, but plant is much smaller; shorter tassels droop from trailing branches. Good in hanging basket.

A. wilkesiana (**A. tricolor**). COPPER LEAF. Foliage more colorful than many flowers. Often used as an annual, substituting for flowers from late summer to frost. Leaves to 8 in. long, in color combinations including bronzy green mottled with red and purple; red with crimson and bronze; and green edged with crimson and stippled with orange and red. In a warm, sheltered spot it can grow as a shrub to 6 ft. or taller, nearly as wide. Outdoor potted plants should be kept slightly dry through winter.

ACANTHOPANAX sieboldianus.
See **ELEUTHEROCOCCUS
sieboldianus**

ACANTHUS
BEAR'S BREECH
Acanthaceae
PERENNIALS

📈 **ZONES VARY BY SPECIES**

☀ ☼ ● **SUN OR SHADE**

◐ ● **MODERATE TO REGULAR WATER**

Native to southern Europe and
the Mediterranean. Large, deeply
lobed, sometimes spiny leaves
in clumps to
about 3 ft. wide.
Bloom in late
spring or
summer, when
foliage clumps
send up tall
spikes of hooded
whitish, rose,
or purple flow-
ers beneath
spiny green or
purplish bracts.
Lop off the
prickly spikes
after flowers fade.

Acanthus mollis

These tough plants have spreading roots and can become invasive.
Give them plenty of room, or confine them with an 8-in.-deep barrier. In dry-summer regions, they
will lose their leaves if deprived of
moisture in summer, then leaf out
again with winter rains; occasional
soakings will keep leaves green
during hot weather. To propagate,
dig and divide between midfall
and early spring. Control snails,
slugs. Plants are effective in shade
with bamboo and large-leafed
ferns but will survive in dry,
sunny spots.

A. balcanicus (A. hungaricus).
Zones 2–24. Somewhat smaller
than *A. mollis,* with more finely
cut and toothed leaves.

A. mollis. Zones 5–24. Most
commonly grown species. To
4–5 ft. high in bloom. Spineless
leaves to 2 ft. long are deeply lobed
and cut. 'Latifolius' has larger
leaves and is hardier. Foliage of
'Hollard's Gold' is yellow in spring
and throughout summer.

A. spinosus. Zones 4–24. Similar to *A. mollis* in size, but leaves
are more finely cut and armed
with long spines. Foliage is silvery
on the true species. Hybrids have
bright green leaves and are known
as the Spinosissimus Group.

ACCA sellowiana. See **FEIJOA**

ACER
MAPLE
Aceraceae
DECIDUOUS TREES AND SHRUBS

📈 **ZONES VARY BY SPECIES**

☀ ☼ **FULL SUN OR PARTIAL SHADE**

◐ ● **MODERATE TO REGULAR WATER**

When you talk about maples,
you're talking about many trees—
large and midsize shade trees;
smaller trees; and dainty, picturesque shrub-trees. Leaves range
from simple ovals to deeply lobed
and finely dissected shapes. One
element common to all maples
is the fruit (seed capsule), which
resembles a hardware store wingnut. In general, maples are highly
favored in the Pacific Northwest,
in the intermountain areas, and,
to a lesser extent, in Northern
California; with the few exceptions
noted here they are not adapted to
Southern California or the Southwest's desert areas. Practically all
maples in Southern California
show marginal leafburn after mid-
June and lack the fall color of
maples in colder areas. In all
regions, for good fall leaf display,
look for a maple that colors well
in your locale; visit nurseries while
the foliage is changing hue.

The larger maples have extensive fibrous root systems that take
water and nutrients from the topsoil. The great canopy of leaves
calls for a steady, constant supply
of water—not necessarily frequent
watering but constantly available
water throughout the root zone.
Occasional deep watering and
periodic feeding will help keep
roots deep.

Medium to large maple species
need little pruning. On smaller
types, prune to accentuate the natural shape. To minimize sap bleed,
make any cuts in summer or early
fall in mild-winter areas, or from
summer to the end of January
where temperatures remain below
freezing.

A. buergerianum. TRIDENT
MAPLE. Tree. Zones 2–9, 14–17,
20, 21. Native to China, Japan.
Grows 20–25 ft. high and wide.
Roundish crown of 3-in.-wide,
glossy green, three-lobed leaves
that are paler green beneath. Fall
color is usually red, sometimes
orange or yellow. Attractive flaking
bark on older wood. Low, spreading growth; stake and prune to
make it branch high. This is a
decorative, useful patio tree and
favorite bonsai subject.

A. campestre. HEDGE MAPLE.
Tree. Zones 2–9, 14–17. Native to
Europe, western Asia. Slow growing to 70 ft., seldom over 30 ft. tall
and wide in cultivation. Forms a
very dense, compact, rounded
head in the Northwest; thinner in
California. Leaves 2–4 in. wide,
with three to five lobes, dull green
above, downy beneath; turn yellow
in fall. 'Queen Elizabeth' has more
glossy foliage, more erect habit.
'Carnival' grows slowly to about
10 ft. high and wide; new growth
is pink, gradually turning green
with white margins.

A. capillipes. Tree. Zones 2–9,
12, 14–24. Native to Japan. Moderate growth rate to 30 ft. tall and
wide. Young branches red, turning
brown with white stripes with age.
Shallowly three-lobed leaves are
3–5 in. long; red when new,
retain red leafstalks and
midribs at maturity, then
turn scarlet in fall. In
warmer climates, does
best in partial shade.

A. cappadocicum.
COLISEUM MAPLE.
Tree. Zones 3–6. Native to western
Asia. Known in the West by its
variety 'Rubrum', red coliseum
maple. Grows to 35 ft. tall and
wide; forms compact, rounded
crown. Leaves with five to seven
lobes, 5½ in. wide. Foliage is
bright red when new, later turns
rich dark green. Leaves of 'Aureum'
emerge red, turn yellow green,
then green, and finally yellow
in fall.

A. circinatum. VINE MAPLE.
Shrub or tree. Zones A3; 2b–6,
14–17. Native to moist woods,
stream banks in coastal mountains
of British Columbia south to
Northern California. In the forest
shade, it is crooked, sprawling, and
vinelike, with many stems from
the base. In the open, it becomes a
nearly symmetrical small tree
5–35 ft. high, with one or several
trunks. Leaves nearly circular, to
6 in. across, with 5–11 lobes; red
tinted when new, light green as
they mature, then orange, scarlet,
or yellow in fall. Tiny reddish
purple spring flowers are followed
by winged red seeds. 'Monroe' has
deeply cut foliage. 'Sunglow' grows
slowly 6–10 ft. high and wide,
with orange-pink new growth.

Let it go untrimmed to make
natural bowers, ideal settings for
ferns and woodland flowers. Use
under a canopy of tall conifers
where its blazing fall color offers
brilliant contrast. Can be espa-

liered against shady side of a wall.
Its contorted leafless branches
make an intricate pattern in
winter.

A. crataegifolium 'Veitchii'.
VARIEGATED HAWTHORN
MAPLE. Shrub or small tree. Zones
3–6, 14–17. From Japan. Slow
growth to 12–15 ft., with equal
spread, developing into a broad,
round-headed to vase-shaped tree.
Green bark. Small leaves, almost
unlobed, are splashed with white
and pink, turning purple and pink
in fall. Tends to revert to unvarie-
gated form; prune out any new
growth with plain green leaves.
Does best planted in moist,
shady spots.

A. davidii. DAVID'S MAPLE.
Tree. Zones 2–6, 15–17, 20, 21.
Native to central
China. To 20–35 ft.
high and wide.
This maple is
distinctive on
several counts.
Bark is shiny
green striped
with silvery
white, particularly
striking in winter.

*Acer
davidii*

Leaves are glossy green, oval or
lobed, 2–7 in. long, 1½–4 in. wide,
deeply veined. New foliage bronze
tinted; fall color combines bright
yellow, red orange, and purple.
Clustered greenish yellow flowers
are showy in spring. Plant in part
shade in warmer areas.

A. × freemanii. See A. rubrum

A. ginnala. See A. tataricum
ginnala

A. glabrum. ROCKY MOUN-
TAIN MAPLE. Shrub or tree.
Zones 1–7, 10. Multitrunked
clumps may be only 6 ft. tall or up
to 30 ft. under ideal conditions.
Slender, upright branches spread
one-half to two-thirds plant
height. Leaves 2–5 in. wide, three
to five lobed or divided into three
leaflets, borne on dark red twigs.
Fruit tinged red. Fall foliage yellow. Needs well-drained soil and
regular moisture. *A. g. douglasii (A.
douglasii)* grows along shores of
southeastern Alaska, south into
Canada and parts of the Pacific
Northwest and mountain states
(Zones A2, A3; 1–7, 10). It reaches
20–30 ft. tall, 20 ft. wide, has shallowly three-lobed leaves.

A. grandidentatum. See
A. saccharum grandidentatum

A. griseum. PAPERBARK
MAPLE. Tree. Zones 2–9, 14–21.
Native to China. Grows to 25 ft.
or higher; may be half as wide to

A

equally as wide as tall. In winter it makes a striking picture with bare branches angling out and up from main trunk and reddish bark peeling away in paper-thin sheets. Late to leaf out in spring. Leaves are divided into three coarsely toothed leaflets 1½–2½ in. long, dark green above, silvery below. Inconspicuous red flowers in spring develop into showy winged seeds. Foliage turns brilliant red in fall.

A. japonicum. FULLMOON MAPLE. Shrub or tree. Zones 2–6, 14–16. Native to Japan. Grows 20–30 ft. high, with equal or greater spread. Nearly round, 2–5-in.-long leaves cut into 7–11 lobes. Good fall color in red, orange, and golden tones. Give regular moisture, part shade in warm regions. The following varieties are small, slow growing, and best placed as shrubs.

'Aconitifolium'. FERNLEAF FULLMOON MAPLE. Grows about 15 ft. tall and 20 ft. wide. Leaves are deeply cut, almost to leafstalk; each lobe is also cut and toothed.

'Aureum'. GOLDEN FULLMOON MAPLE. See A. shirasawanum 'Aureum'

'Green Cascade'. Weeping form, with finely cut, rich green leaves. Grows only 4–5 ft. high, spreading twice as wide.

'Vitifolium'. Broad and round-topped tree can reach 35–40 ft. tall and wide with age. Bears very large, grapelike leaves.

A. macrophyllum. BIGLEAF MAPLE. Tree. Zones 2–9, 14–24. Native to stream banks, moist canyons, southern Alaska to foothills of California. Dense shade tree grows 30–75 ft. tall, 30–50 ft. wide—too big for a small garden or a street tree. Large three- to five-lobed leaves are 6–15 in. wide, sometimes bigger on young, vigorous sapling growth; leaves turn from medium green to yellow in fall. Small, greenish yellow spring flowers are followed by tawny winged seeds hanging in long, chainlike clusters. Yellow fall color spectacular in cool areas. Resistant to oak root fungus.

A. negundo. BOX ELDER. Tree. Zones A2, A3; 1–10, 12–24. Native to most of U.S. The plain species is a weed tree of many faults—it seeds readily, hosts box elder bugs, suckers badly, and is subject to breakage. Fast growing to 60 ft. (usually less)

Acer macrophyllum

and as wide or wider. Leaves divided into three to nine oval, 2–5-in.-long leaflets with toothed margins; yellow in fall. Several varieties improve on the species.

A. n. californicum. Zones 1–9, 14–24. From central and Northern California. A bit smaller than the species. Can be valuable in a native planting or for stabilizing a stream bank.

'Flamingo'. White and pink leaf markings. Needs some shade in warmer areas.

'Sensation'. Slower growth (to 40 ft. tall, 30 ft. wide) and better branch structure than the species. Doesn't sucker. Good deep pink fall color.

'Variegatum'. VARIEGATED BOX ELDER. Not as large or weedy as the species. Combination of green and creamy white leaves is a standout. Large, pendent clusters of white fruit are spectacular.

A. nigrum. BLACK MAPLE. Zones 1–10, 14–20. Similar to *A. saccharum* but more resistant to heat and drought. Light green leaves turn yellow in fall. 'Greencolumn' can reach 65 ft. tall, 25 ft. wide.

A. palmatum. JAPANESE MAPLE. Shrub or tree. Zones A3; 2–10, 12, 14–24. Native to Japan and Korea. Slow growing to 20 ft. with equal or greater spread; normally many-stemmed. Most airy and delicate of all maples. Leaves 2–4 in. long, deeply cut into five to nine toothed lobes. All-year interest: young spring growth is glowing red; summer leaves are soft green; fall foliage is scarlet, orange, or yellow; slender leafless branches in greens and reds provide winter pattern.

Grafted garden varieties are popular, but common seedlings have uncommon grace and usefulness: they are more rugged, faster growing, more drought tolerant, and they stand more sun and wind than named forms do. Japanese maples thrive everywhere in the Northwest, where they make good small street trees. They can be

Acer palmatum

grown with success in California if given shelter from hot, dry, or constant winds. Filtered shade is best, but full sun can be satisfactory. In California, consider the local soil and water; wherever azaleas are difficult to grow and suffer from salt buildup in the soil, Japanese maples will show burn on leaf edges. Give same watering treatment as azaleas—flood occasionally to leach out salts. Resistant to oak root fungus.

Used effectively on north and east walls, in patios and entryways, as small lawn trees. Attractive in groves (like birches) as woodland planting; for natural effect, set out plants of different sizes with varying spacing. Good under oaks, as background for ferns and azaleas, alongside pools. Invaluable in tubs and for bonsai. Japanese maple is inclined to grow in flat, horizontal planes, so pruning to accentuate this growth habit is easy.

The grafted garden forms are usually smaller than seedlings, more weeping and spreading, brighter in foliage color, and more finely cut in leaf. In California, it seems that the more finely cut the leaf, the more likely leafburn will occur. The following list includes some of the best.

'Atropurpureum'. RED JAPANESE MAPLE. Purplish or bronze to bronzy green leaves, brighter in sun. Holds color all summer.

'Bloodgood'. Vigorous, upright growth to 15 ft. Deep red spring and summer foliage, scarlet in fall. Blackish red bark.

'Bonfire'. Orange-pink spring and fall foliage; twisted trunk, short branches, and drooping branchlets.

'Burgundy Lace'. To 12 ft. high, 15 ft. wide. Leaves more deeply cut than those of 'Atropurpureum'; branchlets bright green.

'Butterfly'. Small (to 7-ft.) shrub with small bluish green leaves edged in white. Cut out growth that reverts to plain green.

'Crimson Queen'. Small, shrubby, 9-ft. mound, with finely

cut leaves that hold color all summer, turn scarlet before dropping off in fall.

'Dissectum' ('Dissectum Viridis'). LACELEAF JAPANESE MAPLE. Small shrub to 6 ft. high, 12 ft. wide, with drooping branches, green bark; pale green leaves turn gold in autumn.

'Ever Red' ('Dissectum Atropurpureum'). A 7-ft. mound with weeping branches. Finely divided, purple-tinged, lacy foliage turns crimson in fall.

'Garnet'. Similar to 'Crimson Queen' and 'Ever Red'; somewhat more vigorous grower.

'Katsura'. Upright and spreading; usually reaches only 6–10 ft. high and wide. Small, compact leaves emerge orange yellow, then turn orange and finally bright green in summer. Yellow-orange fall color.

'Mikawa Yatsubusa'. Upright dwarf grows 3–5 feet high and wide, has densely overlapping green leaves that turn yellow orange in autumn.

'Orangeola'. Compact, weeping form to about 6 ft. high, not quite as wide. Finely dissected leaves are orange as they emerge, then gradually turn green. Fall color is fiery orange red.

'Osakazuki'. Upright grower, becoming wider with age; eventually makes a round-topped tree 20–25 ft. tall. Large leaves (to 5 in. wide) turn from rich green in summer to brilliant crimson in fall. Considered by many to be the Japanese maple with the best fall color. Tolerates sun and heat.

'Oshio Beni'. Like 'Atropurpureum' but more vigorous; has long, arching branches.

'Red Dragon' ('Dissectum Red Dragon'). Resembles 'Ever Red' but with deeper red-purple foliage. Holds color throughout summer; turns crimson in fall.

'Sango Kaku' ('Senkaki'). CORAL BARK MAPLE. Vigorous, upright, treelike. Yellow fall foliage. Twigs, branches striking coral red in winter.

'Seiryu'. THREADLEAF JAPANESE MAPLE. Upright grower to 10–12 ft. high and wide. Lacy, finely divided leaves, reddish in spring, green in summer, then golden yellow touched with crimson in fall.

'Tamukeyama'. Vigorous, cascading growth to 8 ft. high (if central leader is staked upright), spreading wider. Leaves open crimson in spring, then turn to a deeper reddish purple; color holds well through summer. Scarlet fall color. Leaves less lacy than 'Crimson Queen', branches more cascading.

'Waterfall'. Similar to 'Dissectum' but a little smaller, forming a weeping mound 4–6 ft. high and twice as wide. Green leaves finely cut, fernlike, flowing, and elegant. Brilliant yellow and gold fall color.

'Wolff' ('Emperor I'). Vigorous, upright growth to 20–25 ft. high,

eventually wider than tall. Rich red leaves, slightly darker than 'Bloodgood'. Leaves hold color well into summer, turn deep crimson in fall.

A. pentaphyllum. Tree. Zones 4–9, 14–17. Native to China. Rare plant to 20–30 ft. tall and nearly as wide, with leaves divided down to the leafstalk into five narrow, 3-in. leaflets spread out like fingers on a hand. Late to leaf out in spring. Medium green leaves turn pale orange to red in fall.

A. platanoides. NORWAY MAPLE. Tree. Zones A2, A3; 1–9, 14–17. Native to Europe, western Asia. Broad-crowned, densely foliaged tree to 50–60 ft. tall, from two-thirds as wide to equally as wide as high. Leaves five lobed, 3–5 in. wide, deep green above, paler beneath; turn yellow in fall. Showy clusters of small, greenish yellow flowers in early spring. Very adaptable, tolerating many soil and environmental conditions. Once a widely recommended street tree but now strongly objected to because of voracious roots, self-sown seedlings, and aphid-caused honeydew drip and sooty mold. Here are some of the best varieties (purple-leafed forms perform poorly in alkaline soils unless soil is conditioned).

'Cleveland II'. Shapely, compact, well-formed tree about 50 ft. tall, 40 ft. wide.

'Columnare'. Slower grower, narrower form than the species (about 20 ft. wide).

'Conquest'. Columnar sport of 'Crimson King'. Symmetrical; reaches 25–30 ft. high and only 6 ft. wide.

'Crimson King'. Holds purple foliage color until leaves drop. Slower growing than the species. Fine in Northwest and California foothills.

'Crimson Sentry'. Compact growth to 25 ft. tall. Dense foliage, brighter red in spring than 'Crimson King'.

'Deborah'. Like 'Schwedler' but faster growing, straighter.

'Drummondii'. Leaves are edged with silvery white; unusual and striking. Some shade in warm climates.

'Easy Street'. Similar to 'Columnare' but slightly wider, more pyramidal, to 40 ft. high. Dark green foliage turns yellow in fall.

'Emerald Queen'. Fast-growing oval, at least 40–50 ft. high and 25–30 ft. wide. Reddish new growth matures to glossy green, then turns yellow in fall.

'Globosum'. Slow growing with dense, round crown; eventually reaches 20–25 ft. high.

'Jade Glen'. Vigorous, straight-growing form with bright yellow fall color.

'Parkway'. A broader tree than 'Columnare' (about 25 ft. wide), with a dense canopy.

'Princeton Gold'. Oval shape to 35 ft. high. Golden yellow leaves hold their color all season, then turn bright gold in fall.

'Royal Red'. A 40-ft.-tall, red- or purple-leafed form.

'Scarlet Sentinel'. Columnar form, to about 25 ft. wide. Fast growing.

'Schwedler' ('Schwedleri'). Purplish red leaves in spring turn to dark bronzy green by summer, gold in autumn.

'Summershade'. Fast-growing, upright, heat-resistant selection.

'Superform'. Uniform, rounded to oval tree, 40–50 ft. high and wide. Yellow fall color.

A. pseudoplatanus. SYCAMORE MAPLE. Tree. Zones 1–9, 14–20. Native to Europe, western Asia. Moderate growth to 40 ft. high or more, and two-thirds as wide to equally as wide as tall. Leaves 3–5 in. wide, five lobed, thick, prominently veined, dark green above, pale below. No particular fall color. 'Atropurpureum' ('Spaethii') has leaves that are rich purple underneath. 'Brilliantissimum' is smaller, at 15–20 ft. tall, with light pink new growth.

A. pseudosieboldianum. Tree. Zones 2b–10, 14–18. Native to Korea, Manchuria. Rounded tree to 20 ft. tall and wide. Resembles *A. palmatum* in size, form, leaf shape, and fall color and is hardier to cold.

A. rubrum. RED MAPLE, SCARLET MAPLE. Tree. Zones A2, A3; 1–9, 14–17. Native to low, wet areas of eastern North America. Fairly fast growth to 60 ft. tall, 40 ft. wide (or even larger). Faster growing than *A. platanoides* or *A. pseudoplatanus.* Red twigs, branchlets, and buds; quite showy flowers. Dull red fruit. Leaves 2–4 in. long, with three to five lobes, shiny green above, pale beneath; brilliant scarlet fall color in frosty areas. Tolerates most soils. Not at its best in urban pollution. Some of the trees below,

although sold as *A. rubrum,* are actually *A.* × *freemanii*—hybrids between it and *A. saccharinum.*

'Armstrong' and 'Armstrong II' (*A.* × *freemanii*). Very narrow (15-ft.-wide) trees. Fall color (often poor) is orange to red.

'Autumn Blaze' (*A.* × *freemanii*). Dense oval, upright crown, excellent orange-red fall color.

'Autumn Fantasy' (*A.* × *freemanii*). Dense oval, with beautiful red fall color.

'Autumn Radiance'. Dense oval form, orange-red fall color.

'Bowhall'. Narrow (15 ft. wide), cone shaped, with orange-red foliage in fall.

'Columnare'. Narrow (10 ft. wide), with orange-red fall color.

'Karpick'. Narrow grower (20 ft. wide) with red twigs, yellow to red fall color.

'New World'. Narrow (to 15 ft.), upright (to 30 ft.), with bright reddish orange fall color.

'Northwood'. Rounded form. Extremely cold hardy.

'October Glory'. Tall, round-headed tree; last to turn color in fall.

'Red Sunset'. Upright, vigorous branching pattern.

'Schlesingeri'. Tall, broad, fast growing, with regular form; orange-red fall color.

'Somerset'. Narrow oval with brilliant, long-lasting, red fall color. 'Sun Valley' is similar.

A. saccharinum. SILVER MAPLE. Tree. Zones A2, A3; 1–9, 12, 14–24. Native to eastern North America. Grows fast to 40–100 ft. tall and wide. Open form, with semipendulous branches; casts fairly open shade. Silvery gray bark peels in long strips on old trees. Leaves 3–6 in. wide, five lobed, light green above, silvery beneath. In colder part of range, fall color is a mixture of scarlet, orange, and yellow—often in same leaf. Aggressive roots are hard on sidewalks, sewers. You pay a penalty for the advantage of fast growth: weak wood and narrow crotch angles make this tree break easily. Unusually susceptible to aphids and cottony scale. Suffers from chlorosis in alkaline soils. Many rate it the least desirable of maples, but nonetheless it is often planted for fast growth and graceful habit.

Acer rubrum

'Silver Queen'. More upright form than the species, seedless. Bright gold fall color.

'Wieri' ('Laciniatum'). CUT-LEAF SILVER MAPLE, WIER MAPLE. Same as species, but leaves are much more finely cut; provides open shade. 'Skinner's Cutleaf' is similar.

A. saccharum. SUGAR MAPLE. Tree. Zones 1–10, 14–20. Native to eastern North America. The source of maple sugar. Moderate growth to 60 ft. or taller. Stout branches with upward sweep usually form fairly compact canopy to about 40 ft. wide. Leaves 3–6 in. wide, with three to five lobes, green above, pale below. In cold-winter climates, spectacular fall color ranging from yellow and orange to deep red and scarlet. Varieties include the following.

'Bonfire'. Bright red fall foliage.

'Commemoration'. Heavy leaf texture; orange, yellow, and red fall color.

A. s. grandidentatum (A. grandidentatum). WASATCH MAPLE, BIG-TOOTH MAPLE, ROCKY MOUNTAIN SUGAR MAPLE. Deciduous. Zones 1–3. Grows as shrub or tree, 20–30 ft. tall and wide. Leaves have three to five lobes and large, blunt teeth. Brilliant fall color in tones of yellow, orange, and rose red. In nature, grows in canyons and on stream banks. In gardens, requires well-drained soil on the dry side.

'Green Mountain'. Tolerant of heat and drought; autumn leaves vary from yellow to orange to reddish orange.

'Legacy'. Fast growing, drought resistant. Fall color is red, sometimes yellow orange.

'Sweet Shadow'. Leaves are deeply cut, as is each lobe. Orange fall color.

A. shirasawanum 'Aureum'. GOLDEN FULLMOON MAPLE. Shrub or tree. Zones 3b–6, 14–16. Grows to 20 ft. tall and wide. Leaves open pale gold in spring and remain pale chartreuse all summer. Plant in partial shade. *A. s.* 'Autumn Moon' has burnt orange new growth, orange and red fall color.

A. tataricum. TATARIAN MAPLE. Shrub or tree. Zones A2, A3; 1–6, 14–16. Native to southeastern Europe, western Asia. Reaches 20–25 ft. high and wide. Tooth-edged leaves (lobed on young plants) are 2–3½ in. long. Showy red-winged seeds appear in summer. Yellow to reddish brown fall color.

A. t. ginnala. AMUR MAPLE. Zones A1–A3; 1–9, 14–16. Native to Manchuria, northern China, Japan. Toothed leaves are three lobed, even on mature plants. Clusters of small, fragrant yellowish flowers bloom in early spring; these are followed by handsome bright red, winged seeds. Striking red fall color. 'Flame', 15–20 ft. high and wide, has especially fiery foliage in autumn.

A. truncatum. Tree. Zones A2, A3; 1–9, 14–23. Native to China. Grows fairly rapidly to 25 ft., with equal or slightly smaller spread. Like a small *A. platanoides* with more deeply lobed leaves to 4 in. wide. Emerging leaves are purplish red, summer leaves green, autumn leaves yellow to orangish. A good lawn or patio tree.

A. 'White Tigress'. WHITE TIGRESS MAPLE. Shrub or tree. Zones 2b–7, 14–17. Hybrid involving *A. tegmentosum.* Multitrunked growth to 30 ft. high and nearly as wide. Beautiful green bark striped with gray and bright white. Large, lobed leaves turn bright yellow in fall.

ACHILLEA
YARROW
Asteraceae (Compositae)
PERENNIALS

🌱 ZONES A1–A3; 1–24
☀️ FULL SUN
💧 LITTLE TO MODERATE WATER

Yarrows are among the most carefree and generously blooming perennials for summer and early fall, several being equally useful in the garden and as cut flowers (taller kinds may be cut and dried for winter bouquets). Leaves are gray or green, bitter-aromatic, usually finely divided (some with toothed edges). Flower heads are usually in flattish clusters. Yarrows need only routine care: some watering (though they endure drought once established), cutting back after bloom, dividing when clumps get crowded.

Achillea tomentosa

A. ageratifolia (A. serbica). GREEK YARROW. Native to Balkan region. Low, foot-wide mats of silvery leaves, toothed or nearly smooth edged. Topped by white flower clusters ½–1 in. across on stems 4–10 in. tall.

A. clavennae. SILVERY YARROW. Native to Europe. Silvery gray, silky leaves, lobed somewhat like chrysanthemum leaves, form mats about 8 in. wide. Loose, flat-topped clusters of ½–¾-in.-wide, ivory white flower heads on 5–10-in. stems. Often sold as *A. argentea.*

A. filipendulina. FERNLEAF YARROW. From Caucasus. Tall, erect plants 4–5 ft. high and to 3 ft. wide, with deep green, fernlike leaves. Bright yellow flower heads in large, flat-topped clusters. Dried or fresh, they are good for flower arrangements. Several horticultural varieties are available. 'Gold Plate' has flower clusters up to 6 in. wide. Hybrid 'Coronation Gold', to about 3 ft. high, also has large flower clusters.

A. × kellereri. To 6 in. high, 1 ft. wide, with gray-green ferny leaves. Clusters of flower heads look like white daisies with yellow centers.

A. millefolium. COMMON YARROW, MILFOIL. Native to Europe, western Asia. Erect plant with narrow green or grayish green leaves and flat-topped white flower clusters on 3-ft. stems. Spreads by underground runners. A form that grows wild on California's Channel Islands has bright pink blossoms. Many garden varieties have been selected for their flower color, which includes shades of cream to yellow, pink, and red.

A. 'Moonshine'. Resembles *A. × taygetea,* but grows somewhat taller (to 2 ft. high) and bears deeper yellow flowers.

A. ptarmica. From Europe, Asia. Erect plant to 2 ft. high and wide. Narrow leaves with finely toothed edges. White flower heads in rather open, flattish clusters. 'The Pearl' has double flowers.

A. × taygetea. Native to the eastern Mediterranean. Grows to 1½ ft. high and wide. Gray-green, divided leaves 3–4 in. long. Dense clusters of bright yellow flower heads fade to primrose yellow—excellent contrast in yellow until it's time to shear off old stalks. Good cut flowers.

A. tomentosa. WOOLLY YARROW. From Europe, western Asia. Makes a flat, spreading mat (to about 1½ ft. wide) of fernlike, gray-green, hairy leaves. Golden flower heads in flat clusters top 6–10-in. stems. A good edging and

a neat ground cover for small areas; used in rock gardens. Shear off dead flowers to leave attractive gray-green mat.

ACHIMENES
Gesneriaceae
PERENNIALS FROM RHIZOMES

🌱 ALL ZONES
☀️ LIGHT SHADE
💧 REGULAR WATER

Group of hybrids derived from species native to Central America and the Caribbean. Related to African violet and gloxinia. To 1–2 ft. high; slender stems may be upright, spreading, or trailing. Crisp, hairy leaves are bright to dark green. Throughout summer and early fall, offer a lavish display of five-lobed, flat-faced, 1–3-in.-wide trumpets in purple, orchid, lavender, blue, white, pink, red, or orange.

Can be grown in beds as ground cover in mildest climates. Even there, usually kept to containers (protected from direct sun and wind).

Achimenes

In late winter or early spring, plant rhizomes ½–1 in. deep in moist peat moss and sand; maintain at 60°F/16°C to encourage sprouting. When 3 in. high, plant in pots for best show—6 to 12 plants in 6–7-in. pot or hanging basket. Use potting mix of equal parts peat moss, perlite, leaf mold. Pinch back new growth for bushy plants; let trailing stems grow unchecked in hanging baskets. When flowering ends, cut back on water so plants die down. Leave rhizomes in dry soil over winter; or turn out of pots and store in dry perlite or vermiculite in a cool, dry place. Repot in fresh soil before spring growth begins.

ACHNATHERUM hymenoides (Oryzopsis hymenoides)
INDIAN RICE GRASS
Poaceae (Gramineae)
PERENNIAL GRASS

🌱 ZONES 1–3, 10–13
☀️ FULL SUN
💧 LITTLE OR NO WATER

Native to dry regions of the Southwest and northward to Canada. Forms a clump 1–2 ft. tall and

A

wide; tight at the base, spreading and open above. Very narrow, 6–8-in.-long leaves are bright green in cool weather, turning golden brown when summer heat comes. Open, airy flower clusters (attractive for cutting) produce seeds that were harvested by Native Americans for food. Useful plant in desert landscapes.

Achnatherum hymenoides

ACIDANTHERA bicolor. See **GLADIOLUS callianthus**

ACMENA smithii (Eugenia smithii)
LILLY-PILLY TREE
Myrtaceae
EVERGREEN SHRUB OR TREE

🌿 **ZONES 15–17, 19–24**
☀ **FULL SUN**
🔵 **REGULAR WATER**

Australian native's big feature is its dramatic, long-lasting winter show of clustered, ¼–½-in.-wide, edible berries in white, lavender, or lavender pink. If trained, can grow as tree 10–25 ft. high and 8–15 ft. wide. Irregular habit improved by pruning; remove wayward growth at any time. Shiny, pinkish green to green, 3-in.-long leaves. Many small white flowers are clustered at branch tips in summer. Takes ordinary garden care but is at its best with deep, rich, moist soil. Easy to grow from seed.

Acmena smithii

ACONITUM
ACONITE, MONKSHOOD
Ranunculaceae
PERENNIALS

🌿 **ZONES A1–A3; 1–9, 14–21**
☀ ◑ **FULL SUN OR PARTIAL SHADE**
🔵 **REGULAR WATER**
◆ **ALL PARTS ARE POISONOUS IF INGESTED**

Leaves, usually lobed, in basal clusters. Flowers shaped like hoods or helmets, along tall spikes. Monkshood has a definite place under trees, at the back of flower beds, or even at the edge of a shaded bog garden. Substitute for delphinium in shade.

Need some winter chill; hard to establish in warm, dry climates. Sow seeds in spring; or sow in late summer or early fall for bloom the next year. Moist, rich soil for best growth and bloom. Divide in early spring or late fall, or leave undivided for years. Die back in winter; mark site.

A. carmichaelii (A. fischeri). Native to central China. Densely foliaged plant 2–4 ft. high, nearly as wide. Leathery dark green leaves are lobed and coarsely toothed. Blooms from late summer into fall; deep purple-blue flowers form dense, branching clusters 4–8 in. long. 'Wilsonii' grows 6–8 ft. high and 1–2 ft. wide, has more open flower clusters 10–18 in. long.

A. napellus. GARDEN MONKSHOOD. Native to Europe. Upright leafy plants 2–5 ft. high to 1 ft. wide. Leaves 2–5 in. wide, divided into narrow lobes. Late summer flowers usually blue or violet, in spikelike clusters.

Aconitum napellus

ACORUS
SWEET FLAG
Araceae
PERENNIALS

🌿 **ZONES VARY BY SPECIES**
☀ ◑ **LIGHT SHADE IN HOTTEST CLIMATES**
💧 **AMPLE WATER**

Found throughout the Northern Hemisphere, these bog or aquatic plants will succeed in water or in rich, well-irrigated soil. They look like clumps or tufts of iris but are related to calla (*Zantedeschia*). Flowers are inconspicuous. Use plants in damp borders, at pool edges, or in shallow water.

Acorus gramineus 'Variegatus'

A. calamus. SWEET FLAG. Zones 2–10, 14–24. Sword-shaped leaves are 1½ in. wide, 4–5 ft. long, in a clump about 2 ft. wide. Foliage is fragrant when bruised, as are the thick rhizomes. 'Variegatus' has very showy white-bordered leaves. Plants die to the ground in winter.

A. gramineus. JAPANESE SWEET FLAG. Zones 3b–10, 14–24. Fans of 6–12-in., narrow, semievergreen leaves ½ in. wide rise from the ends of slowly creeping rhizomes that eventually form large clumps. Leaves of 'Licorice' are 1½ ft. long, with a licorice flavor; 'Ogon' has narrow (¼-in.), arching, 10-in.-long leaves of golden yellow. 'Variegatus' has 6–12-in.-long leaves striped with white. Dwarf 'Pusillus', 3–5 in. high, spreads very slowly and is useful between stepping-stones or as a companion plant for bonsai.

ACTAEA (including Cimicifuga)
Ranunculaceae
PERENNIALS

🌿 **ZONES 1–7, 17**
◑ **PARTIAL SHADE**
🔵 **REGULAR WATER**
◆ **BERRIES OF SOME TYPES ARE POISONOUS**

Botanists recently combined this genus with *Cimicifuga*, and in doing so, they lumped together plants of markedly different sizes and garden uses. The baneberries (*Actaea*) are small (under 2½ ft. tall), with short clusters of flowers that turn into attractive but poisonous berries. The bugbanes (*Cimicifuga*) are considerably taller (up to 7 ft. in bloom), with long, spikelike flower clusters that ripen into dry seed capsules. Baneberries associate with smaller woodland plants, while bugbanes are stately back-of-the-border plants, looking most at home with a forest background. Both have shiny, much-divided leaves that give an overall airy effect. They grow best in rich, moist, well-drained soil and at

Actaea racemosa

least partial shade (can take more sun in cool-summer zones, provided they don't dry out).

A. alba (A. pachypoda). WHITE BANEBERRY, DOLL'S EYES. From eastern North America. To 2½ ft. tall and not quite as wide. Small white flowers appear in spring on a stalk that swells and reddens after flowers fade; highly toxic 1½-in.-wide berries that follow are white with a dark spot at the tip.

A. japonica (Cimicifuga japonica). Native to Japan. White autumn flowers on purplish black, leafless stalks. In bloom, plant is 3–4 ft. tall, 2 ft. wide.

A. racemosa (Cimicifuga racemosa). BLACK SNAKEROOT. From eastern North America. Forms a leafy clump 3–4 ft. tall, 3 ft. wide. Typically branched stalks carry dense spikes of white flowers in midsummer or early fall, increasing plant height to 7 ft.

A. rubra. RED BANEBERRY. Native to North America. Similar to *A. alba*, but poisonous berries are scarlet, somewhat larger, and borne on slender stems.

A. simplex (Cimicifuga simplex). KAMCHATKA BUGBANE. Native to Siberia and Japan. Foliage clump to 2 ft. tall and wide, with 3–4-ft. flower stalks in fall. 'Atropurpurea' has purplish leaves and pink-tinted flower buds on 5-ft. stems. 'Brunette' and 'Hillside Black Beauty' have even darker foliage and pinkish flowers.

ACTINIDIA kolomikta
Actinidiaceae
DECIDUOUS VINE

🌿 **ZONES A1–A3; 1–9, 14–17**
☀ ◑ **FULL SUN OR PARTIAL SHADE**
💧 **MODERATE TO REGULAR WATER**

Most kiwi vines are grown for delicious fruit, but this eastern Asian species is grown for its flamboyant foliage. Grows rapidly to 15 ft. or more, producing a marvelous foliage mass made up of 3–5-in.-long leaves with elongated heart shape: some in solid green, others white-splashed green, and others green heavily variegated in pink to red. Female varieties

Actinidia kolomikta

produce a bonus crop of small fruits, but male plants (which are nonfruiting) typically have better leaf color. Colors are best in cool weather and—in warmer zones—in partial shade. Clusters of small, fragrant, white flowers appear in early summer. Plants climb by twining; provide sturdy support and train new stems into place as they lengthen. Thin out growth in late dormant season.

For information on growing various types of kiwi vines for their fruit, see Kiwi.

ADAM'S NEEDLE.
See **YUCCA filamentosa**

ADENANTHOS
WOOLLYBUSH
Proteaceae
EVERGREEN SHRUBS

🌡	ZONES 8, 9, 14–24
☀ ◐	PARTIAL SHADE IN HOTTEST CLIMATES
◌ ◍	LITTLE TO MODERATE WATER

Australian natives related to and resembling grevilleas. Valued most for silvery, furry, finely divided foliage. Colorful tubular blossoms are attractive viewed close up but are often borne sporadically. Need excellent drainage.

Adenanthos sericea

A. × cunninghamii (A. drummondii). To 3–4 ft. high and 5–6 ft. wide. Scarlet flowers are mostly concealed by fine-textured, silver-gray foliage, which is useful in fresh and dried arrangements.

A. sericea. To 6–20 ft. tall and wide. Exceptionally silky, silvery foliage. Red, 1½-in. flowers are borne scantily throughout the year. Can be treated as a small tree by removing bottom limbs.

ADENIUM obesum
Apocynaceae
SUCCULENT SHRUB

🌡	ZONES 23, 24; H2; OR INDOORS
☀	FULL SUN; BRIGHT INDIRECT LIGHT
◌	REGULAR WATER
◈	MILKY SAP IS POISONOUS IF INGESTED

Twisted branches grow from a huge, fleshy, half-buried trunk or rootstock. Grown outdoors in the ground, can reach 9 ft. tall and half

Adenium obesum

as wide. Leaves are sparse, and plant is leafless for long periods. Clustered saucer-shaped, deep pink blossoms, each 2 in. or more across, are extremely showy; plant is known as "desert rose" or "desert azalea" in eastern tropical Africa, where it is native.

This plant cannot take frost, winter chill, cold soil. Relocate potted plant to warm area when a freeze threatens. Needs heat, good light, perfect drainage, regular water during growth, dryness during dormancy—in short, this is a plant for careful enthusiasts and collectors. *A. o. swazicum* differs from the species only in technical details.

ADENOPHORA
LADY BELLS
Campanulaceae (Lobeliaceae)
PERENNIALS

🌡	ZONES A2, A3; 1–10, 14–24
☀ ◐	FULL SUN OR PARTIAL SHADE
◌ ◍	MODERATE TO REGULAR WATER

Plants and flowers resemble those of medium-size campanulas. Blue or white, drooping, bell-shaped flowers in branching clusters are fragrant. Sometimes planted at woodland edge or in sunny border. Prefer fertile, well-drained soil. Long lived; resent moving once well established.

Adenophora liliifolia

A. bulleyana. From western China. To 3 ft. tall, 1 ft. wide. Pale blue bells in autumn.

A. confusa. From western China. To 3 ft. tall, 2 ft. wide. Dark blue flowers in summer.

A. liliifolia. Native from central Europe to Siberia. To 1½ ft. high, 1 ft. wide. Pale blue or white flowers in midsummer.

ADENOSTOMA
Rosaceae
EVERGREEN SHRUBS

🌡	ZONES 6–9, 14–24
☀	FULL SUN
◌	NO IRRIGATION NEEDED

These California natives resemble heather (*Calluna*) and tolerate heat, aridity, and poor, rocky soil; need good drainage in moister climates. Both of the species described below are highly flammable, so don't plant them near houses or other structures.

Adenostoma fasciculatum

A. fasciculatum. CHAMISE, GREASEWOOD. Native to coastal hills of California. Tiny, needlelike, clustered leaves; tiny white flowers in dense, 2–5-in. clusters at branch tips. Ordinarily a sparse shrub 5–12 ft. tall and nearly as wide, but a prostrate form is available and makes a good ground cover for rugged slopes.

A. sparsifolium. RED SHANKS. Native to Southern California. To 6–18 ft. tall and about half as wide, with shredding red bark. Needles not clustered; flower clusters somewhat longer and more open than those of *A. fasciculatum*.

ADIANTUM
MAIDENHAIR FERN
Polypodiaceae
FERNS

🌡	ZONES VARY BY SPECIES
◐ ●	PARTIAL OR FULL SHADE
◍◍	AMPLE WATER

Most are of tropical origin; some are western natives. All form spreading clumps over time. Stems are thin, wiry, and dark. Fronds are finely cut; leaflets are mostly fan shaped, bright green, thin textured. Plants need steady moisture and soil rich in organic matter. Protect from snails and slugs.

Most maidenhair ferns die back to some extent in winter. Kinds listed

Adiantum aleuticum

as indoor or greenhouse plants may succeed in sheltered outdoor spots in mild-winter areas.

A. aleuticum (A. pedatum subpumilum). FIVE-FINGER FERN, WESTERN MAIDENHAIR. Zones 1–7, 14–21. Native to North America. Fronds fork to make a fingerlike pattern atop slender stems reaching 1–2½ ft. tall. General effect is airy and fresh. Excellent choice for containers or shaded beds.

A. capillus-veneris. SOUTHERN MAIDENHAIR. Zones 5–9, 14–24; H1, H2. Native to North America. To 1½ ft. tall. Fronds are twice divided but not forked.

A. hispidulum. ROSY MAIDENHAIR. Native to tropics of Asia, Africa. Indoor or greenhouse plant. To 1 ft. tall. Young fronds rosy brown, turning medium green, shaped somewhat like those of *A. aleuticum*.

A. pedatum. AMERICAN MAIDENHAIR FERN, FIVE-FINGER FERN. Zones A3; 1–7, 14–17. Eastern equivalent of *A. aleuticum*, with similar fronds and shiny black stems. Very cold hardy.

A. peruvianum. SILVER DOLLAR MAIDENHAIR. Native to Peru. Indoor or greenhouse plant. To 1½ ft. or taller. Segments of leaves quite large, to 2 in. wide.

A. raddianum (A. cuneatum). Native to Brazil. Indoor or greenhouse plant. Fronds cut three or four times, 15–18 in. long. Many named kinds differing in texture and compactness. Grow in pots; move outdoors to a sheltered, shaded patio for summer. Commonly sold are 'Fritz Luth', 'Gracillimum' (very finely cut), and 'Pacific Maid'.

A. tenerum. Native to tropical America. Indoor or greenhouse plant. Long, broad fronds arch gracefully, are finely divided into many deeply cut segments ½–¾ in. wide. Most commonly sold is 'Farleyense'.

A. venustum. HIMALAYAN MAIDENHAIR. Zones 3–7, 14–17. Chinese native to 8 in. high. Young fronds are bright bronzy pink, maturing to medium green. Spreads slowly to form a 3–5-ft. clump. Shear in late winter to encourage new growth.

A

AECHMEA
Bromeliaceae
PERENNIALS

🌡 ZONES 22-24; H1, H2; OR INDOORS
☼ PARTIAL SHADE; SUNNY WINDOW
💧 KEEP CUP WITHIN LEAF ROSETTE FILLED WITH WATER

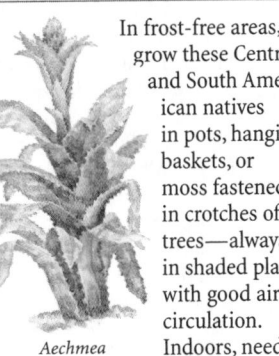

*Aechmea
fasciata*

In frost-free areas, grow these Central and South American natives in pots, hanging baskets, or moss fastened in crotches of trees—always in shaded places with good air circulation. Indoors, need lots of light (such as east or west window) to bloom. Indoors or outdoors, soil should be fast draining but moisture retentive. Keep central tube or cup within leaves filled with water; water soil (or moss) when it's dry. Bromeliad specialists list dozens of species and varieties, and new hybrids appear frequently in nurseries.

A. chantinii. Leaves 1–3 ft. long, green to gray green banded with silver or darker green. Tall flower clusters have orange, pink, or red bracts, yellow-and-red flowers. White or blue fruit.

A. fasciata. Leaves to 2 ft. long, gray green crossbanded with silvery white. From the center grows a cluster of rosy pink bracts in which nestle pale blue flowers that change to deep rose. 'Silver King' has unusually silvery leaves; leaves of 'Marginata' are edged with creamy white bands.

A. fulgens. Leaves 12–16 in. long, green dusted with gray. Flower cluster usually held above the leaves. Blossoms are red, blue, and blue violet; berries are pinkish red. *A. f. discolor* has brownish red or violet red leaves, usually faintly striped.

A. hybrids. The following are among the most commonly grown hybrid bromeliads.

'Foster's Favorite'. Bright wine red, lacquered leaves about 1 ft. long. Drooping, spikelike flower clusters are coral red and blue.

'Royal Wine'. Forms open rosette of somewhat leathery, glossy light green leaves that are burgundy red beneath. Drooping clusters of orange-and-blue flowers.

A. pectinata. Stiff rosette of leaves to 1½ ft. long, strongly

marked pink or red at bloom time. Flowers whitish and green.

A. weilbachii. Shiny leaves to 2 ft. long, green or suffused with red. Dull red, 1½-ft. flower stalk has orange-red berries tipped with lilac.

AEGOPODIUM
podagraria
BISHOP'S WEED, GOUT WEED
Apiaceae (Umbelliferae)
PERENNIAL

🌡 ZONES A1-A3; 1-9, 12, 14-24
☼ ☽ ● SUN OR SHADE
💧 MODERATE WATER

Native Europe to western Asia; naturalized in North America. Rampant ground cover, especially in rich soil. Spreads by creeping underground rootstocks; best contained by underground barrier of wood, concrete, or metal extending 8–12 in. into soil. Many light green, three-leafleted leaves make a dense mass to 6 in. high. Flat-topped clusters of inconsequential flowers rise above the leaves in summer. To neaten, mow two or three times yearly. Shear off flowering stems before they set seed to limit volunteer seedlings. Deciduous even in mild-winter areas.

*Aegopodium
podagraria
'Variegatum'*

'Variegatum' is the most widely planted form; commonly used in intermountain and mountain regions. Leaflets are edged white, look luminous in shade. Set plants 1 ft. apart. Pull any that revert to solid green. In warm climates, give light shade during hottest part of day.

AEONIUM
Crassulaceae
SUCCULENT PERENNIALS

🌡 ZONES 15-17, 20-24
☼ ☽ FULL SUN IN COOLER CLIMATES ONLY
💧 MODERATE WATER

Most are native to the Canary Islands. Among the best succulents for decorative effects, in pots or in the ground. Fleshy leaves are held in rosettes at branch tips. After several years, rosettes produce a single flower stalk in spring or summer; branches that have flowered die. With age, plants become

*Aeonium
arboreum*

leggy; to encourage branching, cut back branches several inches below rosettes. Cuttings are easily rooted: let dry for a few days, then plant in sandy soil kept barely moist until new growth appears.

A. arboreum. To 3 ft. tall and wide. Each branch tip carries a 6–8-in.-wide rosette of bright green, fleshy leaves. Yellow flowers in long clusters. 'Atropurpureum', with magenta-and-green rosettes, is more striking and more widely grown than species. 'Zwartkop' has nearly black rosettes.

A. canariense. Large rosettes (to 10 in. wide) of fuzzy, light green leaves, tinged salmon at tips if grown in full sun. Pale green flowers.

A. 'Cyclops'. Resembles a giant version of *A. arboreum* 'Zwartkop' but with a green center or "eye." It grows 4–5 ft. tall and 2 ft. wide.

A. decorum. Bushy, rounded, many-branched plant to 10 in., each branch ending in a 2-in. rosette. Fleshy, reddish-tinted leaves with red edges. Neat, compact. Pink flowers.

A. haworthii. Free branching, shrubby, to 2 ft. tall and 4 ft. wide, with blue-green, red-edged rosettes 2–3 in. wide. Cream-colored flowers.

A. 'Kiwi'. Low-growing, tight mound of light green rosettes. Leaves have pale yellow variegation and bright red edges. Pale yellow flowers.

A. simsii (A. caespitosum). Low, dense, spreading, cascading, very leafy, 6 in. tall. Bright green leaf rosettes. Pale yellow flowers.

A. 'Sunburst'. Very showy, with 12-in.-wide rosettes of green leaves variegated in white and edged with red. Grows 18 in. high and about 2 ft. wide. Cream-colored flowers.

A. undulatum. Often mislabeled *A. pseudotabuliforme*. Green, 10-in.-wide rosettes atop thick 3-ft. stalks. Makes offsets freely. Yellow flowers.

A. urbicum. "Dinner plate" rosettes to 8–10 in. wide. Long, narrow, gray-green leaves, loosely arranged, have reddish edges. Forms stems several feet tall, unbranched except for offsets at the base. White or pinkish flowers.

AESCULUS
HORSECHESTNUT, BUCKEYE
Hippocastanaceae
DECIDUOUS TREES OR SHRUBS

🌡 ZONES VARY BY SPECIES
☼ FULL SUN
💧 REGULAR WATER, EXCEPT AS NOTED
◆ SEEDS OF ALL ARE SLIGHTLY TOXIC IF INGESTED

Leaves are divided fanwise into large, toothed leaflets. Showy spring flowers, borne at ends of branches in long, dense clusters, attract hummingbirds. In autumn, leathery fruit capsules enclose glossy seeds. Prune established horsechestnuts only to eliminate dead or damaged wood and any awkward-looking branches.

A. × arnoldiana 'Autumn Splendor'. Tree. Zones A2, A3; 1–9, 14–16. Very attractive, cold-hardy hybrid growing 35–40 ft. tall and nearly as wide. Glossy, dark green leaves with five (rarely seven) leaflets turn brilliant maroon in autumn and are resistant to leaf scorch. Yellow flowers, each with an orange-red blotch, are borne in clusters to 8 in. long. Best with some shade.

A. californica. CALIFORNIA BUCKEYE. Shrub or tree. Zones 3–10, 14–24. Native to dry slopes and canyons above 4,000-ft. elevation in Coast Ranges and Sierra Nevada foothills. Often multi-trunked. Grows 10–20 ft. or taller, spreads 30 ft. or wider. New foliage is pale apple green; mature leaves have five to seven rich green, 3–6-in.-long leaflets. Striking sight in spring, when fragrant, cream-colored flower plumes make it a giant candelabra. Big pear-shaped fruits split to reveal shiny brown seeds favored for dried flower arrangements. Seeds sprout freely; seedlings make unusual bonsai subjects.

In the wild, plant drops its leaves by July, but if given moderate water will hold them until autumn. After leaf drop, silvery trunk, branches, and branchlets create an interesting silhouette.

*Aesculus
× carnea*

A. × carnea. RED HORSE-CHESTNUT. Tree. Zones 1–10, 12, 14–17. Hybrid between *A. hippocastanum* and *A. pavia*. To 40 ft. high, 30 ft. wide—smaller than *A. hippocastanum* and a better fit for small gardens. Round headed, with large dark green leaves, each divided into five leaflets; casts dense shade. Bears hundreds of 8-in.-long plumes of soft pink to red flowers; 'Briotii' has rosy crimson blossoms, 'Fort McNair' has pink flowers with a yellow throat, and 'O'Neill Red' has single flowers of bright red.

A. hippocastanum. COMMON HORSECHESTNUT. Tree. Zones 1–10, 12, 14–17. Native to Europe. Reaching 60 ft. high with a 40-ft. spread, this bulky, densely foliaged plant gives heavy shade. Invasive roots can break up paved surfaces. Leaves are divided into five to seven toothed, 4–10-in.-long leaflets. Spectacular flower show: ivory blooms with pink markings are borne in 1-ft.-long plumes. 'Baumannii' has double flowers and sets no seed.

A. pavia. RED BUCKEYE. Shrub or tree. Zones 2–9, 14–24. Native to eastern U.S. Bulky, to 12–20 ft. tall, with irregular rounded crown that is nearly as wide. Glossy deep green leaves with five to seven 3–6-in.-long leaflets. Narrow, erect, 10-in. clusters of bright red or orange-red (rarely yellow) flowers. Best choice for humid climates.

AETHIONEMA
STONECRESS
Brassicaceae (Cruciferae)
PERENNIALS

🗺	ZONES 1–9, 14–21
☀	FULL SUN
💧 💧	LITTLE TO MODERATE WATER

Native to Mediterranean region and Asia Minor. Choice shrublets, attractive in or out of bloom. They are best adapted to colder climates and are favorites among rock gardeners. Grow best in a light, porous soil with considerable lime. Bloom late spring to summer. Deadhead flowers to extend bloom season.

Aethionema × warleyense

A. schistosum. To 5–10 in. high, 1 ft. wide. Erect, unbranched stems densely clothed with narrow, slate blue, ½-in.-long leaves. Fragrant, rose-colored flowers; petals about ¼ in. long.

A. × warleyense (A. 'Warley Rose'). Neat, compact plant to 8 in. high and wide. Pink flowers in dense clusters. Most commonly planted stonecress in warmer climates.

AFRICAN BOXWOOD.
See **MYRSINE africana**

AFRICAN CORN LILY. See **IXIA**

AFRICAN DAISY.
See **ARCTOTIS, DIMORPHO-THECA, OSTEOSPERMUM**

AFRICAN IRIS. See **DIETES**

AFRICAN MASK.
See **ALOCASIA × amazonica**

AFRICAN TULIP TREE.
See **SPATHODEA campanulata**

AFRICAN VIOLET.
See **SAINTPAULIA**

AFROCARPUS.
See **PODOCARPUS**

AGAPANTHUS
LILY-OF-THE-NILE
Amaryllidaceae
PERENNIALS FROM FLESHY RHIZOMES

🗺	ZONES 6–9, 12–24, H1, H2 FOR EVERGREEN KINDS; ZONES 4–9, 12–21 FOR DECIDUOUS KINDS
☀ ◐	FULL SUN OR PARTIAL SHADE
💧 💧	LITTLE TO REGULAR WATER

All of these South African natives form fountainlike clumps of strap-shaped leaves that are evergreen in some species and varieties, deciduous in others. In summer, the clumps give rise to bare stems ending in spherical clusters of funnel-shaped flowers, each cluster like a burst of blue or white fireworks. Some nursery plants are labeled only as "blue" or "white"; if you want a particular shade of blue, choose plants while they're in bloom.

Prosper in full sun or light shade where summers are mild; need some afternoon shade in hottest areas. Evergreen kinds need protective winter mulch in Zone 6. Best in loamy soil but will grow in heavy soils. Thrive with regular water, but established plants in the ground year-round can grow and bloom without irrigation during prolonged dry periods in most areas; need supplemental water in the low desert.

For mass plantings, space plants from 1–1½ ft. apart (use the tighter spacing for smaller varieties). Divide infrequently; every 6 years or so is usually sufficient. These are superb container plants. Good near pools. Protect from snails and slugs.

Names of species have been very much confused over the

Agapanthus praecox orientalis

years, largely because the plants hybridize so easily. It has even been suggested that all agapanthus are merely forms of one species.

A. africanus. Evergreen. Leaves shorter, narrower than those of *A. praecox orientalis;* flower stalks shorter (to 1½ ft. high) with fewer flowers (20–50 per cluster). Blossoms are deep blue. Often sold as *A. umbellatus.* 'Summer Gold' has gray-green leaves edged in yellow.

A. campanulatus. Deciduous. To 3 ft. high, with drooping dark blue flowers. 'Albus' is white flowered.

A. inapertus. Deciduous. As tall as *A. praecox orientalis* and nearly as many-flowered, but its deep blue blossoms droop.

A. praecox orientalis (A. orientalis). Evergreen. Most commonly planted. Broad, arching leaves in big clumps. Stems to 4–5 ft. tall bear up to 100 blue flowers. There are white ('Albus'), double ('Flore Pleno'), and light to fairly dark blue varieties. Other varieties have striped leaves. Often sold as *A. africanus, A. umbellatus.*

A. selections and hybrids. Types sold by variety or hybrid name include the following. All are evergreen, except as noted.

'Bluestorm'. Abundant, deep purple-blue flowers rise on sturdy 2½-ft. stalks above foot-tall foliage clumps.

'Elaine.' Large clusters of nodding bluish purple blossoms borne on 4-ft.-tall stems.

'Ellamae'. Large dark blue flowers on stems to 5 ft. tall.

Headbourne Hybrids. Deciduous. Flowers come in a range of blues and in white on 2½-ft.-tall stems above fairly narrow, rather upright foliage.

'Henryi'. Resembles 'Peter Pan' but has white flowers.

'Midknight Blue'. To 3–4 ft. tall, with deepest blue flowers.

'Mood Indigo'. Deciduous. Hybrid involving *A. inapertus,* with

---

deep violet blooms on stems that grow 3–4 ft. tall.

'Peter Pan'. Outstanding free-blooming dwarf variety. Foot-high foliage mass and blue flowers on 1½-ft. stems.

'Queen Anne'. Foliage clump to 1½ ft. high; blue blossoms on stems to 2 ft.

'Rancho White'. Foliage clump 1–1½ ft. high; broad leaves. Flower stalks 1½–2 ft. tall carry heavy clusters of white flowers. Also known as 'Dwarf White' and 'Rancho'. 'Peter Pan Albus' is similar or identical.

'Snowstorm'. Abundant, snow white blooms on stems 2½ ft. tall. Foliage clump is 1–1½ ft. high.

'Storm Cloud'. Evergreen in warmer part of range. Developed from deciduous 'Mood Indigo' and an evergreen agapanthus. Deep blue-violet blossoms on 4-ft. stems.

'Streamline'. Dwarf form to just 1½ ft. high, with grassy leaves and grayish blue flowers. Blooms over a long period.

'Tinkerbell'. To 2 ft. tall, with light blue flowers and white-striped leaves.

AGASTACHE
Lamiaceae (Labiatae)
PERENNIALS

🗺	ZONES VARY BY SPECIES
☀ ◐	FULL SUN OR PARTIAL SHADE
💧	MODERATE WATER

Summer-blooming perennials with aromatic foliage, whorls of pink, purple, blue, red, or orange flowers in spikelike clusters. All rebloom if deadheaded. Favorites with hummingbirds. Species from Mexico and the Southwest need excellent drainage, especially in wet-winter areas.

A. aurantiaca. ORANGE HUMMINGBIRD MINT. Zones 3–24. Native to northern Mexico. To 2½ ft. tall, 2 ft. wide, with pink flowers that fade to orange. Can be grown as an annual in cold or wet regions. 'Coronado' has yellow-orange blooms.

Agastache foeniculum

A. barberi. Zones 2–24. From Arizona, New Mexico. To 2 ft. tall and wide, with reddish purple flowers.

A. breviflora. Zones 6–24. From Arizona, New Mexico, northern Mexico. To 2 ft. tall, 1½ ft.

A

across, with spikes of purplish red blossoms.

A. cana. TEXAS HUMMING-BIRD MINT. Zones 2–24. Native to Texas, New Mexico. To 2–3 ft. tall, 1½ ft. across. Blooms heavily, bearing reddish pink flowers that smell like bubble gum. A seed-grown selection, 'Heather Queen', blooms the first year from seed sown early in the season.

A. foeniculum. ANISE HYSSOP. Zones A3; 1–24. From north-central North America. Erect, narrow plant to 3 ft. tall and 2 ft. wide, with dense clusters of lilac blue flowers. Its anise- or licorice-scented leaves make a tasty tea. Useful and attractive in perennial borders and herb gardens. More tolerant of winter cold and wet than other species.

'Golden Jubilee' is a bit smaller, with yellow-green new growth that's brightest in full sun.

A. hybrids. Zones 4–24, except as noted. The following are among the many fine hybrids sold.

'Apricot Sunrise'. Zones 2b–24. To 2½ ft. tall, 2 ft. wide. Deep orange flowers fade to apricot on opening.

'Blue Fortune'. To 3 ft. tall, 1½ ft. wide, with powder blue flower spikes.

'Firebird'. To 1½–2 ft. tall, 1½ ft. wide; blooms of coppery orange red.

'Summer Breeze'. Zones 6–24. To 3 ft. tall, 2 ft. wide. Large lavender-pink flowers; dark gray-green leaves.

'Tangerine Dreams'. Zones 6–24. Forms a compact, 1½–2-ft.-wide clump; orange flowers, larger and deeper in color than those of 'Apricot Sunrise', are carried atop many 2–3-ft. stems.

'Tutti Frutti'. Zones 2b–24. To 3–4 ft. tall, 1–2 ft. wide, with purplish red blooms set off nicely by gray-green foliage.

A. mexicana. GIANT MEXICAN LEMON HYSSOP. Zones 3–24. Rangy Mexican native to 2–3 ft. (possibly to 5 ft.) tall and 1 ft. wide. Bears masses of pink flowers, starting in spring and continuing until late fall. Lemon-scented leaves can be used in tea and as a flavoring. Plants in the Acapulco series bear flowers in salmon pink, rose pink, and orange.

A. rugosa. KOREAN HUMMINGBIRD MINT. Zones 4–24. Native to Korea. To 5 ft. tall, 2 ft. wide. Licorice-scented foliage is

glossy green with a purple tinge. Flowers are purplish blue. Like *A. foeniculum*, tolerates wet winters. 'Honey Bee Blue' and 'Honey Bee White' are compact growers 2–2½ ft. high. The species and its varieties will bloom the first year from seed sown early.

A. rupestris. LICORICE MINT, SUNSET HYSSOP. Zones 1–24. From southern Arizona, northern Mexico. To 1½–2½ ft. tall and 1½ ft. wide, with narrow, fragrant gray-green leaves and spikes of orange flowers with lavender calyxes. Outstanding garden performance.

Agastache rupestris

AGATHAEA coelestis. See **FELICIA amelloides**

AGAVE
Agavaceae
SUCCULENT PERENNIALS

✎ ZONES VARY BY SPECIES
☼ ◑ FULL SUN OR PARTIAL SHADE
◌ ◖ LITTLE TO MODERATE WATER, EXCEPT AS NOTED

Sculptural succulents with rosettes of fleshy leaves. Impressive, sometimes colorful, flower stalk emerges from the rosette's center looking something like a giant asparagus; some kinds produce clusters of flowers on side branches, while others have flowers packed along the stalk. After flowering—which may not occur for years—the foliage clump dies, usually leaving behind suckers that make new plants. The plants shrivel from serious drought but plump up again with watering or rainfall. Provide good drainage. Species listed here are native to Mexico, except as noted.

A. americana. CENTURY PLANT. Zones 10, 12–24; H1, H2. Blue-green leaves grow to 6 ft. long, and have hooked spines along margins with a wicked spine at the tip. Be sure you really want one before planting it: its bulk (to 10 ft. wide) and spines make it formidable to remove. After 10 years or more, a branched, 15–40-ft. flower stalk bearing yellowish green flowers appears. There are varieties available with yellow- or white-striped

Agave attenuata

leaves. Among them is 'Mediopicta Alba', to 4 ft. tall and wide, with a broad creamy central stripe.

A. attenuata. Zones 13, 20–24; H1, H2. Leaves 2½ ft. long, soft green or gray green, fleshy, somewhat translucent, without spines. Makes clumps to 5 ft. across; older plants develop a stout trunk to 5 ft. tall. Greenish yellow flowers borne densely on arching spikes to 12–14 ft. long. Will take poor soil but does best in rich soil with regular water. Protect from frost and hot sun. Statuesque container plant. Good near ocean or pool. Variegated forms are sometimes available. 'Nova' ('Boutin Blue') has broader and bluer leaves than the species, with a straight rather than arching flower spike.

A. 'Blue Flame'. Zones 13, 19–24; H1, H2. Elegant hybrid that forms rosettes of blue-green leaves 2½ ft. high and 2 ft. wide. Looks like parent *A. attenuata* but has upward-curving leaf tips that suggest flames, and is hardier (to 25°F/–4°C).

A. bracteosa. SPIDER or SQUID AGAVE. Zones 7–9, 12–24. Small, open grower to 12 in. high and 18–24 in. wide; spreads slowly to form large, mounding colony. Arching, twisting, pale green leaves have neither teeth nor terminal spines. Creamy white flowers appear on a short spike; one of the few agaves that does not die after flowering. Ideal for pots.

A. desmettiana. Zones 13, 20–24. Grows 2–3 ft. high and wide, with gracefully arching blue-green to yellow-green leaves with few if any teeth. Some forms have leaves edged in yellow.

A. filifera. Zones 12–24. Hardy to 17°F/–8°C. Rosettes less than 2 ft. wide; narrow dark green leaves are lined with white and edged with long white threads.

A. geminiflora. TWIN-FLOWERED AGAVE. Zones 13, 20–24; H1. To 2–3 ft. high and wide, with narrow, dark green, pencil-thin leaves. Yellow flowers, touched with red, are held in pairs along a very tall spike. Tolerates considerable shade.

A. parryi. Zones 2b, 3, 6–24. Attractive, compact, cold-hardy species native to Arizona and northern Mexico. Thick, blue-green or gray-green leaves are tipped with sharp black spines. Mature size about 2–3 ft. high and

Janet Rademacher on Agaves in Pots

Agaves look dramatic in pots and thrive with little care. In fact, according to Janet Rademacher of Mountain States Wholesale Nursery in Glendale, AZ, "too much water or fertilizer causes agaves to grow too fast, actually shortening their life span."

Rademacher's favorites for pots are *A. geminiflora*, *A. parryi*, and *A. victoriae-reginae*. Plant them in 1- to 2-foot-deep, bowl-shaped containers filled with fast-draining potting soil. "Let the soil dry before watering, but then soak it," Rademacher advises, adding, "and apply a water-soluble fertilizer only once or twice a year." Don't forget to position spiny plants away from paths.

wide; spreads by offsets to form colonies. Sometimes called "artichoke agave" because the rosettes on some forms resemble giant artichokes. When about 20 years old, plants push up a stout stalk with clusters of yellow flowers. Thrives in part shade. Several popular varieties, often confused, are larger and have a less artichoke-like appearance. *A. p. truncata* has a distinct artichoke look.

A. potatorum. BUTTERFLY AGAVE. Zones 12–24. To 1–2 ft. high and 2–3 ft. wide. Short, broad, toothed, blue-gray leaves flare outward, appear ruffled; tipped with a distinctive, often twisted, reddish spine. Best in full sun.

A. 'Sharkskin'. Zones 8, 9, 13–17, 19–24. Hybrid to 2–3 ft. high and 3–4 ft. wide. Stout habit, with handsome, gray-green leaves that are toothless but tipped with sharp spines. Best in full sun.

A. victoriae-reginae. Zones 10, 12, 13, 15–17, 21–24. Clumps only a foot or so across. The many dark green leaves are 6 in. long, 2 in. wide, stiff, thick, with narrow white lines and sharp black tips. Slow growing; will stand in pot or ground 20 years before flowering.

A. vilmoriniana. OCTOPUS AGAVE. Zones 12–24. Pale green or yellowish green rosettes up to 6 ft. wide. Leaves 3–4 in. wide, fleshy, deeply channeled above, with a single long spine at the end. Arching, twisted leaves give plant look of an octopus or a huge spider. Handsome in pots. ▶

A

A. weberi. WEBER AGAVE. Zones 8, 9, 12–24. Big, dramatic plant, to 5 ft. high and 10 ft. wide. Wide, fleshy, gray-green leaves are finely toothed. Branched stalk produces yellow flowers.

AGERATINA altissima. See **EUPATORIUM rugosum**

AGERATUM houstonianum

FLOSS FLOWER
Asteraceae (Compositae)
ANNUAL

🌱 **ZONES 1–24**

☀️ ◐ **FULL SUN IN COOLER CLIMATES ONLY**

💧 **REGULAR WATER**

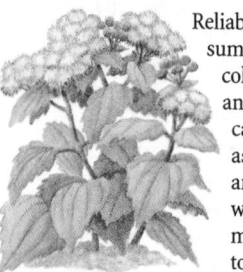

Ageratum houstonianum

Reliable favorite for summer and fall color in borders and containers; can be grown as a winter annual in mild-winter climates. Native to Central America, West Indies. Hairy, soft green leaves are roundish, usually heart shaped at the base. Tiny blue flowers in dense clusters resemble powder puffs. Dwarf kinds (4–6 in. high) include 'Blue Blazer', 'Blue Danube' ('Blue Puffs'), 'Blue Surf', and 'Royal Delft'. 'Neptune', 6–8 in. high, produces its new blooms directly above and concealing older flowers. Somewhat taller (9–12-in.) types include 'Blue Mink' and 'North Sea'. 'Capri' and 'Southern Cross', to 1 ft. high, have clusters of blue flowers with white centers. 'Blue Horizon', to 2½ ft. tall, good as midborder plant and for cutting. Good varieties in other colors are 'Pink Powder-puffs' and white-blooming 'Summer Snow', both 9 in. high. Plants in the Artist series grow 8–18 in. high and bloom in shades of blue, violet, purple, or rose. Most floss flowers form foot-wide clumps.

Best in rich, moist soil. Easy to transplant even when in bloom. Low growers make excellent edgings or pattern plantings with other annuals of similar size. Taller types provide good cut flowers.

AGLAONEMA

Araceae
PERENNIALS

🌱 **ZONE H2; OR INDOORS**

◐ **PARTIAL SHADE; CAN TAKE VERY LOW LIGHT**

💧 **REGULAR WATER**

Tropical Asian plants valued mostly for their ornamental foliage. Flowers resemble small, greenish white callas (*Zantedeschia*). Used in shady borders in Hawaii; elsewhere, they're houseplants. Among the best plants for poorly lighted situations. In fact, few plants can get by on as little light as aglaonema; *A. modestum* is especially tolerant of low light.

Potted plants need a rich, porous potting mix; thrive with lots of water but get by with little. Cut stems will grow for a long time in water. Exudation from leaf tips, especially of *A. modestum*, spots wood finishes.

A. commutatum. Grows to 2 ft. tall and wide. Deep green leaves to 6 in. long, 2 in. across, with pale green markings on veins. Flowers are followed by inch-long clusters of yellow to red berries. *A. c. maculatum*, with many irregular gray-green stripes on leaves, is the most common. 'Pseudobracteatum', 1–2 ft. tall, has white leafstalks and deep green leaves marked pale green and creamy yellow. 'Treubii' has narrow bluish green leaves marked with silvery gray.

A. costatum. Slow growing to 2½ ft. high and wide. Broad deep green leaves have white spots and a broad white stripe along the midrib. 'Foxii' is similar or identical.

A. crispum (A. roebelenii). To 4 ft. tall and broad. Robust plant with leathery leaves to 10 in. long, 5 in. wide, dark green with pale green markings. Sometimes sold as *A.* 'Pewter'.

A. modestum. CHINESE EVERGREEN. Easy to grow, in time forming substantial, several-stemmed clumps 2–3 ft. high and wide. Shiny dark green leaves to 1½ ft. long, 5 in. wide. Often sold as *A. simplex*.

A. 'Silver King' and **'Silver Queen'.** Both are heavy producers of narrow, dark green leaves strongly marked with silver. Both grow to 2 ft. high and wide, but 'Silver King' has larger leaves.

Aglaonema 'Silver King'

AGONIS

Myrtaceae
EVERGREEN TREES OR SHRUBS

🌱 **ZONES 15–17, 20–24**

☀️ ◐ **FULL SUN OR PARTIAL SHADE**

💧💧💧 **LITTLE TO REGULAR WATER**

Native to Australia. Very tolerant of different soil types and watering practices. Related to *Leptospermum* and *Melaleuca*.

A. flexuosa. PEPPERMINT TREE, AUSTRALIAN WILLOW MYRTLE. One of the best small trees for California gardens where temperatures stay above 27°F/ –3°C. Will freeze to the ground at 25°F/–4°C but may come back from a stump if not severely frozen. Spreading, medium-fast grower to 25–35 ft. tall and 15–30 ft. wide. Narrow, willowlike leaves to 6 in. long densely clothe the weeping branches. Leaves smell like peppermint when crushed. Small white flowers bloom profusely in late spring. Use it in a lawn, train it as an espalier, or use it as a tub plant. 'Jervis Bay Afterdark' grows slightly smaller and has beautiful burgundy foliage.

Agonis flexuosa

A. juniperina. JUNIPER MYRTLE. More open and finely textured than *A. flexuosa* but grows to about the same size. Narrow, ¼–½-in.-long, soft green leaves. Bears fluffy white flower clusters, summer into fall.

AGROPYRON

WHEATGRASS
Poaceae (Gramineae)
PERENNIAL GRASSES

🌱 **ZONES 1–3, 10**

☀️ **FULL SUN**

💧 **MODERATE WATER**

Two kinds of wheatgrass, both basically pasture grasses, make reasonably attractive lawns in Rocky Mountains and high plains. They can survive with 8–18 in. of rainfall per year, but when planted close and mowed at 2 in. they should be soaked to 18–20 in. every month. Plant 2 lbs. of seed per 1,000 sq. ft.

A. cristatum. CRESTED WHEATGRASS. Eurasian native; naturalized in U.S. Bunching rather than sod-forming grass. Fairway strain, used for low-maintenance, low-irrigation lawns, is shorter, denser, and finer than common kind.

Agropyron smithii

A. magellanicum. See Elymus magellanicus

A. smithii. WESTERN WHEATGRASS. Native to western U.S. Forms sod, but slowly. Tolerates intense heat and cold; takes moderately alkaline soil.

AGROSTEMMA githago

CORN COCKLE
Caryophyllaceae
ANNUAL

🌱 **ZONES 1–24**

☀️ **FULL SUN**

💧 **MODERATE WATER**

☠️ **ALL PARTS ARE POISONOUS IF INGESTED**

An attractive weed of roadsides and grain fields, this Mediterranean species has naturalized in North America. Several varieties offered are superior plants; they're 2–3 ft. tall and 1 ft. wide, wispy but sturdy. (Like the species, they will self-sow.) Blooms are 2–3 in. wide, on 6–12-in. stems; make good cut flowers. 'Milas' has deep purplish pink blossoms lined and spotted in deep purple and centered with a white eye; 'Purple Queen' bears deeper purple-pink blooms; 'Ocean Pearl' has white flowers with black flecks. Sow seeds in spring or early summer for summer and fall bloom (or in fall for bloom from winter to spring in mild-winter climates). Mass at rear of border, among shrubs, or in front of fence or hedge. Self-sown seedlings of varieties tend to revert to the dark pink–flowered, plain species over time.

Agrostemma githago

A. coeli-rosa. See Silene coeli-rosa

AGROSTIS
BENT, BENT GRASS
Poaceae (Gramineae)
PERENNIAL GRASSES

- ✔ ZONES 1-10, 14-24; BEST WHERE SUMMERS ARE COOL TO MILD
- ☀ FULL SUN
- ◑ ◐ REGULAR TO AMPLE WATER

Agrostis stolonifera

All except *A. gigantea* make beautiful velvety lawns under proper conditions and with constant care. They need frequent close mowing and feeding, occasional topdressing, and much water. In hot weather they succumb to fungal diseases.

In San Francisco Bay Area and western Oregon and Washington, bent grasses (planted intentionally or distributed by birds) tend to dominate bluegrasses and fescues.

A. gigantea. REDTOP. Coarser than other bents; not generally used in lawns. Has been used as quick-sprouting nurse grass in mixtures or for winter overseeding of Bermuda and other winter-dormant grasses.

A. stolonifera (A. palustris). CREEPING BENT. Premium lawn but requires the most care, including frequent mowing to ½ in. tall with special mower. Seed-grown strains include Emerald, Penncross, and Seaside. In some areas you can buy sprigs or sod of the choice strains Congressional, Old Orchard.

A. tenuis. COLONIAL BENT. More erect than *A. stolonifera;* somewhat easier to care for but still fussy. Astoria and Highland are best-known strains; the latter is tougher, hardier, more disease resistant. Mow to ¾ in.

AHINAHINA.
See **ARTEMISIA australis**

AILANTHUS altissima
TREE-OF-HEAVEN
Simaroubaceae
DECIDUOUS TREE

- ✔ ZONES 2B-24
- ☀ FULL SUN
- ◌ ◑ ◐ LITTLE OR NO WATER TO REGULAR WATER

Native to China, but naturalized over much of the U.S. Planted in the 1800s in California's gold country, where it now runs wild. Fast growth to 50 ft. tall and wide. Leaves 1–3 ft. long are divided into 13–25 leaflets 3–5 in. long. Flowers on male trees are smelly. On the female trees, the inconspicuous greenish flowers are usually followed by handsome clusters of red-brown, winged seedpods in late summer and fall; great for dried arrangements. Though often condemned as a weed tree because it suckers profusely and self-seeds, it must be praised for its ability to create beauty and shade under adverse conditions—aridity, hot winds, extreme air pollution, and every type of difficult soil. It is the tree that survived against all odds in *A Tree Grows in Brooklyn.*

Ailanthus altissima

AIR PLANT. See KALANCHOE pinnata, TILLANDSIA

AJANIA pacifica. See CHRYSANTHEMUM pacificum

AJUGA
CARPET BUGLE
Lamiaceae (Labiatae)
PERENNIALS

- ✔ ZONES A2, A3; 1-24
- ☀ ◑ FULL SUN OR PARTIAL SHADE
- ◐ REGULAR WATER

Of the European natives listed below, one is a rock garden plant; the others are ground covers. Of the latter, the highly variable *A. reptans* is better known and more useful, though it will escape into lawns unless contained. All bloom from spring to early summer.

A. genevensis. Rock garden plant 5–14 in. high, 1½ ft. wide; does not spread by runners. Grayish, hairy stems and coarse-toothed leaves to 3 in. long. Flowers in blue spikes; rose and white forms are also sold.

A. pyramidalis. Erect plant 2–10 in. high, 1½–2 ft. wide; does not spread by runners. Stems, with long grayish hairs, have many roundish 1½–4-in.-long leaves. Violet blue flowers are not obvious among the large leaves. 'Metallica Crispa' has reddish brown leaves with a metallic glint.

A. reptans. The popular ground cover carpet bugle spreads quickly by runners, making a mat of dark green leaves in the basic species. Each oval to tongue-shaped leaf is 2–3 in. wide in full sun, to 4 in. wide in part shade; entire foliage mass tops out at around 4 in. high. Blue flowers in 6-in. spikes appear in spring and early summer. Plant 1 ft. apart in spring or early fall. Subject to root rots and fungal diseases where drainage or air circulation is poor. Mow or trim off old flower spikes. Many varieties of this species are available, some sold under several names. The following are among the best choices; all have blue flowers unless otherwise noted. Varieties with bronzy or metallic-looking leaves keep color best in sun.

'Alba'. White-blooming form.
'Black Scallop'. Blackish purple foliage with scalloped edges.
'Burgundy Lace' ('Burgundy Glow'). Reddish purple foliage variegated with white and pink.
'Catlin's Giant'. Large, bronzy green leaves and flower spikes to 8 in. tall.
'Chocolate Chip'. Narrow, chocolate brown leaves. Dwarf plant.
'Giant Bronze'. Deep metallic bronze leaves are larger, more vigorous, and crisper than in basic species. To 6 in. high in sun, 9 in. in part shade.
'Giant Green'. Like 'Giant Bronze' but with bright green leaves.
'Jungle Bronze'. Clumps of large, rounded, wavy-edged, bronze-toned leaves; flower spikes to 8–10 in. high.
'Jungle Green'. Large-leafed variety with green foliage. Less mounded than 'Jungle Bronze'.

Ajuga reptans

'Multicolor'. Leaves are green blended with white and pinkish purple.
'Purpurea' ('Atropurpurea'). Bronze-tinted green leaves.
'Rosea'. Pink blossoms.
'Variegata'. Leaves edged and splotched with creamy yellow.

AKEBIA quinata
FIVELEAF AKEBIA
Lardizabalaceae
DECIDUOUS VINE, SEMIEVERGREEN IN MILD WINTERS

- ✔ ZONES 2-24
- ☀ ◑ ● SUN OR SHADE
- ◐ REGULAR WATER

Native to Japan, China, and Korea. Twines to 15–30 ft. Grows fast in mild regions, more slowly where winters are cold. Valued chiefly for its dainty leaves on 3–5-in. stalks, each divided into five deep green leaflets 2–3 in. long, notched at tips. Dangling clusters of quaint, dull purple, vanilla-scented flowers in spring are more a surprise than a show. The edible fruit, if produced, looks like a thick, 2½–4-in.-long, purplish sausage. 'Shirobana' ('Alba') bears white flowers.

Akebia quinata

Give support for climbing. Keep plant under control to prevent it from becoming rampant. Prune each winter. Recovers quickly when cut to the ground. For a tracery effect on post or column, prune out all but two or three basal stems. Can also be used as ground cover in large spaces; plant 6 ft. apart.

A. trifoliata, threeleaf akebia, is like the above but with three instead of five leaflets per leaf.

ALASKA CEDAR. See CHAMAECYPARIS nootkatensis

ALBIZIA (Albizzia)
Fabaceae (Leguminosae)
DECIDUOUS AND SEMIEVERGREEN TREES

- ✔ ZONES VARY BY SPECIES
- ☀ ◑ FULL SUN OR PARTIAL SHADE
- ◌ ◐ ◐ WATER NEEDS VARY BY SPECIES

These trees have twice-divided, finely textured foliage and powder-puff flowers that are attractive to birds.

A

A. distachya (A. lophantha, Paraserianthes lophantha). PLUME ALBIZIA. Semievergreen. Zones 15–17, 22–24. Native to Australia. Not as hardy as the better-known *A. julibrissin*. In California coastal areas, it often naturalizes. Needs no irrigation; will grow in pure sand at beach. Fast growing to 20 ft. tall, with irregular, sprawling habit. Foliage is dark velvety green and fernlike. Late spring flowers are greenish yellow, in fluffy, 2-in.-long spikes. Best as a temporary screen at beach while slower permanent planting develops. Grown inland, it gets shabby looking.

A. julibrissin. SILK TREE, MIMOSA. Deciduous. Zones 4–23. Native to Asia, ranging from Iran to Japan. Rapid growth to 40 ft., with a canopy spreading to as much as twice the tree's height. Can be cut back to make a 10–20-ft.-tall umbrella. Ferny, pale yellowish green

Albizia julibrissin

leaves are light sensitive and fold at night. Fluffy pink flowers like pincushions bloom in summer. 'Rosea' has richer pink flowers and is considered hardier. 'Boubri' ('Ombrella') bears hot pink blooms. 'Summer Chocolate' has rich burgundy foliage. Silk tree does best with high summer heat; it's one of the best sellers in inland valleys of Southern California. In Zones 4 and 5, choose the warmest locations possible. With regular water grows fast; given skimpy moisture usually survives but grows slowly, looks yellowish.

Unique flat-topped, spreading canopy makes this a good patio tree, despite fallen leaves, flowers, and pods. Because of undulating form and flowers held above the foliage, it's especially beautiful when viewed from above, as from a deck or hilltop. Most attractive if allowed to assume its natural habit, as a multistemmed tree. Somewhat of a problem to get started as a high-headed tree: it must be staked and trained (any buds too low on the trunk should be rubbed out with the thumb). You'll have best success with trees planted from containers established at least 1 year.

ALCEA rosea (Althaea rosea)
HOLLYHOCK
Malvaceae
BIENNIAL OR SHORT-LIVED PERENNIAL

- ZONES 1–24
- PARTIAL SHADE IN HOTTEST CLIMATES
- REGULAR WATER

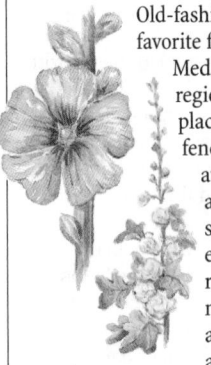

Old-fashioned favorite from the Mediterranean region has its place against a fence or wall or at the back of a border. Old single varieties can reach 9 ft. tall; newer strains and selections are shorter.

Alcea rosea

Big, rough, roundish heart-shaped leaves, more or less lobed, form a clump to about 3 ft. wide. Summer flowers are 3–6 in. wide, carried on spikes; they may be single, semi-double, or double and come in colors including white, pink, rose, red, purple, creamy yellow, apricot. Chater's Double is a fine perennial strain; 6-ft. spires have 5–6-in.-wide flowers. So-called annual strains (biennials treated as annuals) that bloom first year from seed include 5–6-ft.-tall Summer Carnival, with double 4-in. flowers, and 2½-ft.-tall Majorette, with 3–4-in. blossoms.

Sow seeds in ground in late summer for next season's bloom; seed annual strains in early spring for bloom that summer. After flowers fade, cut stalks just above the ground; continue to feed and water plants to encourage late summer or early fall rebloom. Destroy any rust-infected leaves as soon as disease appears. Watch for slugs, snails.

ALCHEMILLA
LADY'S-MANTLE
Rosaceae
PERENNIALS

- ZONES VARY BY SPECIES
- FULL SUN IN COOLER CLIMATES ONLY
- REGULAR WATER

Rounded, pale green, lobed leaves have a silvery look; after rain or overhead watering, they hold beads of water on their surfaces.

Alchemilla mollis

Summer flowers are yellowish green, in large branched clusters, individually inconspicuous but attractive as a mass. Useful for edgings in shady places, as ground cover, and as soothing contrast to brightly colored flowers.

A. alpina. Zones 1–9, 14–17. Native to northern Europe, Greenland. Mat-forming plant creeping by runners, with flowering stems 6–8 in. tall. Leaves 2 in. wide, divided into five to seven leaflets.

A. ellenbeckii. Zones 14–24. Native to mountains of East Africa. Attractive small-scale ground cover to about 2 in. high, with creeping, rooting stems and leaves less than 1 in. wide.

A. erythropoda. Zones 1–9, 14–24. Native to mountains of Balkans, Turkey. Similar to *A. glaucescens* but leaves more deeply lobed and flower stems red-tinted.

A. glaucescens (A. pubescens). Zones 3–9, 14–24. Native to Europe. Dense and wide spreading. Leaves have seven to nine lobes. Flowering stems 8 in. high.

A. mollis. Zones A2, A3; 1–9, 14–24. Native to Asia Minor. Most commonly planted lady's-mantle. Clump-forming plant to 2 ft. or taller, 2½ ft. wide. Nearly circular, scallop-edged leaves to 6 in. across. Self-sows. 'Auslese' bears bright lime green flowers. 'Thriller' has shiny, gray-green leaves and golden yellow blooms.

A. pectinata. Zones 14–24. Native to Mexico. Tiny, creeping ground cover with inch-wide leaves.

ALDER. See ALNUS

ALEURITES moluccana
KUKUI, CANDLENUT TREE
Euphorbiaceae
EVERGREEN TREE

- ZONES 23, 24; H2
- FULL SUN
- REGULAR WATER

Native to Polynesia and southern Asia; has naturalized in Hawaii, where it has been designated the official state tree. Fast growing to 35–60 ft. high and as wide, with upright to spreading habit. Leaves are variable, often lobed, up to 8 in. long, covered with short hairs that give them a distinctive frosted appearance. Tiny white flowers, produced in branched clusters, are followed by green, 2-in. fruits. These are rich in oil used by Polynesians for fuel and cooking; the polished kernels are used

Aleurites moluccana

in leis. Kukui is useful as a specimen or massed in a grove where litter won't present a problem. Needs well-drained soil. Moderate tolerance to wind, salt. Will take some shade.

ALEXANDRA PALM. See ARCHONTOPHOENIX alexandrae, PTYCHOSPERMA elegans

ALGERIAN IVY. See HEDERA canariensis

ALKALI SACATON. See SPOROBOLUS airoides

ALLAMANDA
Apocynaceae
EVERGREEN VINES OR SHRUBS

- ZONES 23, 24; H1, H2; ANYWHERE AS INDOOR/OUTDOOR PLANTS
- FULL SUN
- REGULAR WATER
- ALL PARTS ARE POISONOUS IF INGESTED

These handsome plants from tropical South and Central America tolerate very little frost and require considerable heat for proper growth and bloom; warm nights as well as warm days seem necessary. Trumpet-

Allamanda cathartica

shaped flowers (borne nearly year-round) and foliage are both imposing. Permanent outdoor plants only in the mildest climates. Elsewhere, grow as summer-blooming potted plants; keep indoors during cold weather.

A. blanchetii (A. violacea).
PURPLE ALLAMANDA. Shrubby
or with a few vining stems; usually
grows 6–10 ft. tall and wide.
Somewhat downy leaves up to
5 in. long. Rose purple flowers are
4½ in. across. 'Chocolate Cherry'
and 'Chocolate Swirl' have pinkish
purple flowers with purple-brown
throats. 'Cherries Jubilee'
(A. 'Cherries Jubilee') has brilliant
burgundy red blooms.

A. cathartica. ALLAMANDA,
GOLDEN TRUMPET. Can grow to
great heights (over 50 ft.) as a
vine; it can clamber through trees
but must be tied to other supports.
Often pinched back to grow as a
large freestanding shrub. Leaves
are glossy, leathery, 4–6 in. long.
Yellow trumpets are 5 in. wide,
3 in. long. 'Flore Pleno' has double
yellow flowers. 'Hendersonii' bears
exceptionally attractive orange-
yellow blooms.

A. schottii (A. neriifolia).
BUSH ALLAMANDA. A shrubby
grower to 4–6 ft. high and wide;
occasionally produces climbing
stems. Flowers are 3 in. wide,
tinted orange or red.

ALLIUM
ORNAMENTAL ALLIUM
Liliaceae
PERENNIALS FROM BULBS

🌡 ZONES VARY BY SPECIES; OR DIG
AND STORE

☀ ◑ FULL SUN OR PARTIAL SHADE

💧 REGULAR WATER DURING GROWTH
AND BLOOM

About 500 species, all from the
Northern Hemisphere, many
from mountains of the
West. Relatives of the
edible onion, they are
peerless as cut flowers
(fresh or dried) and use-
ful in borders; smaller kinds
are effective in rock gardens.
Bear small flowers in
roundish, compact or loose
clusters at ends of leafless
stems that range in height
from 6 in. to 5 ft. or taller.
Many are delightfully fragrant; those with onion
odor must be bruised
or cut to give it off.   *Allium*
Bloom in spring or   *giganteum*
summer, with flowers in white and
shades of pink, rose, violet, red,
blue, and yellow.

All prefer well-drained soil
(preferably on the sandy side),
enriched before planting with
organic matter. In fall or spring,
plant bulbs as deep as their height

or width, whichever is greater.
Space smaller species 4–6 in.
apart, larger ones 8–12 in. apart.
Cut back on watering or let soil go
dry when foliage begins to yellow
after flowering. Foliage dies to the
ground, even in mild-winter areas.
Lift and divide only after clumps
become crowded. In areas colder
than stated hardiness, dig and
store; or grow in pots and protect
during winter.

A. aflatunense. Zones 2–24.
Clusters of lilac flowers on stems
2½–5 ft. tall. Resembles *A. giganteum* but with smaller (2–3-in.)
flower clusters; blooms in spring.

A. albopilosum. See
A. cristophii

A. atropurpureum. Zones
1–24. Stems to 2½ ft. tall carry
2-in. clusters of dark purple to
nearly black flowers in summer.

A. caeruleum (A. azureum).
BLUE ALLIUM. Zones 1–24.
Cornflower blue flowers in dense
clusters to 2 in. across on 1-ft.-tall
stems. Late spring bloom.

**A. carinatum pulchellum
(A. pulchellum).** Zones 3–24.
Tight clusters of reddish purple
flowers on 2-ft. stems in summer.

A. cepa. See Onion

A. cristophii (A. albopilosum).
STAR OF PERSIA. Zones 1–24.
Distinctive. Very large clusters
(6–12 in. across) of lavender to
deep lilac, starlike flowers with
metallic sheen, late spring. Stems
12–15 in. tall. Leaves to 1½ ft.
long, white and hairy beneath.
Dried flower cluster looks like an
elegant ornament.

A. giganteum. GIANT
ALLIUM. Zones 2–24.
Summer bloomer bearing
spectacular softball-size
clusters of bright lilac
flowers on stems to 5 ft. or
taller. Leaves 1½ ft. long,
2 in. wide.

A. 'Globemaster'.
Zones 2–24. Bears
6–8-in. clusters of deep
violet flowers in sum-
mer, on stems rising to
2½ ft. or a little taller.

A. karataviense.
TURKESTAN ALLIUM. Zones
1–24. Bears large, dense flower
clusters in midspring, varying
in color from pinkish to beige
to reddish lilac. Broad, recurved
leaves, 2–5 in. across.

A. moly. GOLDEN GARLIC.
Zones 1–24. Bright, shining yellow
flowers in open clusters on 9–
18-in.-tall stems, late spring. Flat
leaves 2 in. wide, almost as long as
flower stems.

A. narcissiflorum. Zones 3–24.
Foot-tall stems with loose clusters
of ½-in., bell-shaped, bright rose
flowers. Summer bloom.

A. neapolitanum. Zones 4–24.
Spreading clusters of large white
flowers on 1-ft. stems bloom in
midspring. Leaves 1 in. wide.
'Grandiflorum' is larger, blooms
earlier. A form of 'Grandiflorum'
listed as 'Cowanii' is considered
superior. Grown commercially as
cut flowers.

**A. oreophilum (A. ostrow-
skianum).** Zones 1–24. Large,
loose clusters of rose-colored
flowers on 8–12-in. stems in late
spring; two to three narrow, gray-
green leaves. 'Zwanenburg' has
deep carmine red flowers, 6-in.
stems. Good for rock gardens,
cutting.

A. porrum. See Leek

A. pulchellum. See A. carinatum pulchellum

A. rosenbachianum. Zones
2–24. Similar to *A. giganteum* but
slightly smaller; blooms in late
spring. 'Album' has greenish white
flowers.

A. sativum. See Garlic

A. schoenoprasum. CHIVES.
Zones A1–A3; 1–24; H1, H2.
Clumps to 2 ft. high (usually
shorter). Leaves look grasslike but
are round and hollow in cross section. Clusters of rose purple spring
flowers (like clover blossoms) atop
thin stems. Use as edging in flower
border or herb garden. Small divisions can be potted in rich soil and
grown on a windowsill. Chop or
snip leaves; use as garnish for delicate onionlike flavor.

A. scorodoprasum. See Garlic

A. siculum. See Nectaroscordum siculum

A. sphaerocephalum. DRUM-
STICKS, ROUND-HEADED
GARLIC. Zones 1–24. Tight, dense,
spherical red-purple flower clusters on 2-ft. stems in
summer. Spreads freely.

A. tuberosum.
CHINESE CHIVES,
GARLIC CHIVES,
ORIENTAL GARLIC.
Zones 1–24; H1, H2.
Clumps of gray-green,
flat leaves ¼ in.
wide, 1 ft. long or
less. Abundance
of 1–1½-ft.-tall
stalks bear clus-
ters of white
flowers in sum-
mer. Flowers
have scent of vio-
lets, are excellent
for fresh or dry

Allium tuberosum

arrangements. Leaves have mild
garlic flavor, are useful in salads
and cooked dishes.

A. unifolium. Zones 3–9,
14–24. California native.
Extremely handsome satiny,
lavender-pink flowers on 1–2-ft.
stems in late spring.

ALLOPLECTUS nummularia. See
NEMATANTHUS gregarius

ALLSPICE, CAROLINA.
See **CALYCANTHUS floridus**

ALMOND
Rosaceae
DECIDUOUS TREES

🌡 ZONES 2B, 3B, 8–10, 12–16, 19–21

☀ FULL SUN

💧 MODERATE WATER

Almond

Botanically known
as *Prunus dulcis*;
native to Asia
Minor and
North Africa.
As a tree, it is
nearly as
hardy as peach
(its close relative),
but as a nut pro-
ducer it is more
exacting in cli-
mate adaptation.
Trees bear best
where summers are
long, hot, and dry;
nuts will not develop
properly in areas with
cool summers or high humidity.
Need some winter chill yet must
be spared from frosts at the wrong
time. Trees bloom early (winter
or early spring), and frost then
will cut the crop; late frosts will
destroy small nuts that are forming. To experiment in areas where
frost is a hazard, choose late-
blooming varieties. Unless you
choose a self-fruitful type, two
varieties that bloom at the same
time are needed for pollination
(they can be planted in the same
hole if space is tight).

Nuts are borne on
spurs that are pro-
ductive for about
5 years; each dor-
mant season, remove
about a fifth of the
oldest fruiting wood to
encourage develop-
ment of new spurs.
Trees reach 20–
30 ft. high, erect
when young, spreading and
dome shaped in age. Leaves
are 3–5 in. long, pale green with

A

gray tinge; flowers are palest pink or white. Fruit looks like leathery, flattened, undersize green peach; in late summer or fall, the hull splits to reveal the pit, which is the almond. Harvest nuts after hulls have cracked open and are partially dry. You can knock or shake them from the tree; waiting for nuts to drop takes too long, carries risk of rotting. Peel off hulls and spread nuts in the sun for a day or two to dry. To test for adequate dryness, shake nuts—kernels should rattle.

Adapt to all soils except heavy, slow-draining ones. Need deep soil (at least 6 ft). Subject to attack by brown rot (causes fruit rot, twig dieback, cankers on trunk and branches) and mites (cause premature yellowing and falling of leaves). The following are the main varieties sold for nuts. For flowering almonds, see *Prunus glandulosa* and *P. triloba*.

'All-in-One'. Semidwarf tree blooms with 'Mission' and 'Nonpareil'. Medium to large sweet, soft-shelled nuts. Self-fruitful. Best variety for home gardens.

'Butte'. Semihard-shelled nut, slightly smaller than 'Mission'. Very productive tree. Late bloomer, flowering just before 'Mission'. Pollinate with 'All-in-One', 'Nonpareil', or 'Mission'.

'Garden Prince'. Genetic dwarf with showy pink blooms and medium-size soft-shelled nuts. Self-fruitful.

'Hall' ('Hall's Hardy'). Hard-shelled, bitter, small nut of low quality. Pink bloom comes late, an advantage in late-frost regions. Tree may actually be a peach-almond hybrid. Partially self-fruitful but better with 'Mission' as pollenizer.

'Mission' ('Texas'). Small, semihard-shelled nut. Regular, heavy producer. Late bloomer, one of the safest for cold-winter, late-frost areas. Pollinate with 'Hall'.

'Ne Plus Ultra'. Large kernels in attractive soft shells. Pollinate with 'Nonpareil'.

'Nonpareil'. Excellent all-around variety. Easily shelled by hand. Midseason bloomer; some bud failure where summers are very hot. Pollinate with 'All-in-One', 'Mission', 'Ne Plus Ultra'.

'Titan'. Sweet, high-quality kernel in thin shell. Late bloomer. Pollinate with 'Hall' or any peach blooming at the same time.

ALMOND, FLOWERING. See **PRUNUS glandulosa, P. triloba**

ALNUS
ALDER
Betulaceae
DECIDUOUS TREES

🌿	ZONES VARY BY SPECIES
☼ ◐ ●	SUN OR SHADE
◐ ◑	REGULAR TO AMPLE WATER

Moisture-loving trees that thrive in moist or wet soils, even tolerate periodic flooding. Good near creeks and other waterways. Very fast growing. In all species, clusters of tassel-like, greenish yellow male flower catkins give interesting display before leaf-out. Female flowers develop into small woody cones that decorate bare branches in winter; these delight flower arrangers. Seeds attract birds. Alders need little pruning except to remove suckers, crossing branches, and dead wood.

A. cordata. ITALIAN ALDER. Zones 2b–9, 14–24. Native to Italy, Corsica. Young growth vertical; older trees to 40 ft. tall, spreading to 25 ft. Heart-shaped, 4-in. leaves, glossy rich green above, paler beneath. Short deciduous period. More restrained than *A. rhombifolia*. Favored in Southwest, except high desert.

A. glutinosa. BLACK ALDER. Zones 1–10, 14–24. Native to Europe, North Africa, Asia. Not as fast growing as *A. rhombifolia*. Probably best as multistemmed tree. Grows to 70 ft. tall, 30 ft. wide. Roundish, 2–4-in., coarsely toothed leaves in lustrous dark green. Makes dense mass from ground up. Good for screen.

A. rhombifolia. WHITE ALDER. Zones 1b–10, 14–21. Native along streams throughout most of California's foothills except along coast; mountains of Oregon, Washington, British Columbia, and Idaho. Very fast growing to 50–90 ft. tall, 40 ft. wide. Branches spread out, then droop at tips. Coarsely toothed, 2½–4½-in. leaves are dark green above, paler green beneath. Very tolerant of heat and wind. Susceptible to tent caterpillars and borers in its native range.

A. rubra (A. oregona). RED ALDER. Zones 3–7, 14–17. Native to stream banks and marshy places from Alaska south to Northern California; usually found in areas with maritime influence. Most

Alnus rhombifolia

common alder of lowlands in Pacific Northwest. Can grow to 90 ft. high but is usually seen at 45–50 ft. tall, 20–30 ft. wide. Attractive smooth, light gray bark. Dark green, 2–4-in. leaves, rust colored and hairy beneath; coarsely toothed margins are rolled under. Can take a surprising amount of brackish water and is useful wherever underground water is somewhat saline. This tree is generally disliked in the Pacific Northwest because it's a favorite of tent caterpillars.

A. tenuifolia. MOUNTAIN ALDER, THIN-LEAF ALDER. Zones A1–A3; 2, 3, 7, 10. Shrub or small tree to 20–25 ft. tall, 15–20 ft. wide. Extremely hardy to cold.

ALOCASIA
ELEPHANT'S EAR
Araceae
PERENNIALS

🌿	ZONES 22–24; H1, H2, EXCEPT AS NOTED; OR INDOORS
◐	PARTIAL SHADE; BRIGHT INDIRECT LIGHT
◐ ◑	REGULAR TO AMPLE WATER
◆	SAP IS POISONOUS IF INGESTED

Native to tropical Asia. Handsome, lush plants for tropical effects. Flowers like those of calla (*Zantedeschia*). Tropical plant specialists sell many kinds with leaves in coppery and purplish tones, often with striking white veins. Provide rich soil, frequent light feedings, and wind protection.

A. × amazonica. AFRICAN MASK. Leathery, deep bronzy green leaves to 16 in. long have wavy edges, heavy white main veins. Plants may grow as tall as 4 ft. and about half as wide. This species is the one most commonly available as a houseplant.

A. cucullata. CHINESE TARO, CHINESE APE. Zones H1, H2. Slow-growing, clumping evergreen

Alocasia macrorrhiza

plant to 2 ft. high. Grown for shiny, deep green, pointed leaves to 15 in. long, 1 ft. wide. Usually massed as a ground cover; plant 1½–2 ft. apart. Requires moist, rich, well-drained soil and protection from wind. Excellent container plant.

A. gageana. DWARF ELEPHANT'S EAR. Looks like a smaller version of *A. macrorrhiza*, reaching only 3–4 ft. high and wide. Bright green leaves, to 2 ft. across, are prominently veined.

A. macrorrhiza. Evergreen at 29°F/–2°C; loses leaves at lower temperatures but comes back in spring if frosts are not too severe. Large, arrow-shaped leaves to 2 ft. or longer, on stalks to 5 ft. tall, form a dome-shaped plant 4 ft. across. Tiny flowers on spike surrounded by greenish white bract. Flowers followed by reddish fruit, giving spike the look of corn on the cob.

A. odora. Similar to *A. macrorrhiza* but not quite as hardy. Fragrant flowers.

A. plumbea. Resembles *A. macrorrhiza*, but leaves are dark olive green or purplish green (or nearly black, in some forms).

A. sanderiana. Grows to 6 ft. tall and wide. Arrow-shaped, deeply lobed leaves about 12–16 in. long, metallic dark purplish green with silver veining on surface.

ALOE
Liliaceae
SUCCULENT TREES, SHRUBS, AND PERENNIALS

🌿	ZONES 8, 9, 12–24, EXCEPT AS NOTED
☼ ◐	FULL SUN OR LIGHT SHADE, EXCEPT AS NOTED
○ ◐	LITTLE TO MODERATE WATER, EXCEPT AS NOTED
◆	SAP BENEATH THE SKIN IS AN IRRITANT

Primarily South African natives, the aloes range from 6-in. miniatures to trees; all form clumps of fleshy, pointed leaves and bear branched or unbranched clusters of orange, yellow, cream, or red flowers. Different species bloom every month; biggest show comes from midwinter through summer. Leaves may be green or gray green, often strikingly banded or streaked with contrasting colors. Showy and easy to grow in well-drained soil in reasonably frost-free areas; need little water but can take more. Except as noted, give full sun in cooler climates, light shade in hotter regions. Where winters are too cold for all-year outdoor culture, grow in pots and shelter from frosts. Most kinds make outstanding container plants. Highly valued as ornamentals, in the ground or in pots. Aloes listed here are only a few of the many kinds.

A. arborescens. Zones 8, 9, 12–24; H1, H2. Forms a large, rounded shrub, to 10 ft. high and wide. Branching stems carry big clumps of gray-green, spiny-edged leaves. Vermillion (occasionally yellow) winter flowers held above foliage in spiky clusters. Withstands salt spray. Tolerates shade. Foliage damaged at 27°F/–3°C, but plants have survived 17°F/–8°C. Not reliably hardy in Zone 12. There is also a variegated form.

A. aristata. Cold-hardy (to around 15°F/–9°C) dwarf for pots, edging, ground cover; just 8–12 in. tall and wide. Rosettes packed with 4-in.-long, ¾-in.-wide leaves ending in whiplike threads. Pink to red summer flowers in 1–1½-ft.-tall clusters.

A. barbadensis. See A. vera

A. barberae (A. bainesii). Slow-growing tree to 20–30 ft. or taller, with heavy, forking trunk and branches. Rosettes of 2–3-ft. leaves, spikes of rose pink flowers on 1½–2-ft. stalks. Used for stately, sculpturesque pattern in landscape. Tender to frost.

A. 'Blue Elf'. Dwarf hybrid with 6-in. rosettes of tooth-edged blue-green foliage. Eventually forms a dense mound 1–2 ft. high and wide. Has never been known to flower. Similar or identical to 'Walmsley's Blue'.

A. brevifolia. Low, spreading clumps of blunt, thick, blue-green, spiny-edged leaves 3 in. long. Clusters of orange flowers on 20-in. stalks, intermittent all year.

A. ciliaris. Zones 8, 9, 12–24; H1, H2. Climbing, sprawling form with pencil-thick stems to 10 ft. long. Small leaves of soft green are edged with white "eyelashes" where the leaf clasps the stem. Long-stalked, 3–6-in. flower clusters with 20–30 green- or yellow-tipped scarlet flowers; intermittent bloom all year. Takes a bit more shade than the other species, but tolerates little frost.

A. dichotoma. KOKERBOOM, QUIVER TREE. Forms a stocky, thick-trunked, compact tree with gray-green, fingerlike leaves; short clusters of bright yellow flowers appear in winter. Very slow grow-

Aloe arborescens

ing, but eventually reaches 12 ft. high or more, with a massive, sculptural trunk. Hardy to about 27°F/–3°C.

A. distans. JEWEL ALOE. Running, rooting, branching stems make clumps of 6-in., fleshy green leaves with yellow teeth along the edges (white in shade). Forked flower stems, 1½–2 ft. tall, carry rounded clusters of red flowers in summer.

A. ferox. Large single trunk rises 6–10 ft. high (after 10 years), topped by a single crown of gray-green, spiny, red-toothed leaves 3–4 ft. long and 6–8 in. wide. Each branched inflorescence holds hundreds of bright scarlet or orange blossoms in winter.

A. 'Johnson's Hybrid'. Compact growth to 1 ft. high and 2 ft. wide. Thin, bright green leaves with faint white spots and small teeth. Bright orange flowers on foot-high stalks bloom nearly year-round. Hardy to 20°F/–7°C.

A. maculata (A. saponaria). SOAP ALOE. Short-stemmed rosettes a foot or more wide feature broad, white-spotted green leaves to 8 in. long. Multibranched, 1½–2½-ft. flower stalks rise in spring, topped with tight heads of nodding blossoms in salmon orange or yellow. Sends out suckers to form dense, expanding colonies. Dig and separate when plants become too crowded. 'Yellow Form' corresponds to A. m. fixburgeana. The old hybrid 'Commutata' is similar, but with pink to red flowers.

A. marlothii. Large, treelike aloe with a stout trunk to 12 ft. tall, topped with a single dense foliage rosette. Leaves are green or grayish, 3–4 ft. long and up to 8 in. wide, often spined on both surfaces and margins. Dried leaves persist on trunk. Winter flower clusters branch horizontally, holding many spikes in yellow, orange, or (rarely) red or bicolors.

A. × nobilis. Dark green leaves edged with small hooked teeth grow in rosettes to 1 ft. wide and high. Clustered orange-red flowers on 2-ft. stalks in early summer. Good in pots—takes limited root space.

A. plicatilis. Slow growing, with thick, forking trunks that are

Aloe maculata

crowned with fans (not rosettes) of smooth, gray-green, foot-long leaves. Scarlet flowers in clusters to 1½ ft. long in late winter to early spring. Statuesque container plant when young; reaches 3–5 ft. in 10 years. Not suited to intense summer heat; tender to frost.

A. polyphylla. Zones 15–17. Hardy to 10°F/–12°C. To 16 in. tall, 2–3 ft. across. Striking rosette, with overlapping rows of leaves that all spiral in the same direction, producing a pinwheel-like or "spinning" effect when plant is viewed from above. Mature plants produce a branching, 3-ft.-tall stalk of nodding, light red to salmon pink blossoms in spring (may fail to bloom some years). Prefers moist, slightly acidic soil. Withhold fertilizer in summer. Partial shade in hot areas.

A. saponaria. See A. maculata

A. × spinosissima. Dense, compact, multibranched shrub, expanding slowly to 4–6 ft. high and wide. Leaf surfaces are not as spiny as name suggests. Unbranched, 1½-ft.-tall flower stalks bear scarlet blossoms from late winter to early spring.

A. striata. CORAL ALOE. Broad leaves to 20 in. long are spineless, gray green, with narrow pinkish red edge. They grow in rosettes 2 ft. wide on short trunk. Brilliant coral pink to orange flowers in branched clusters, midwinter into spring. Handsome, tailored plant. A hybrid between this species and A. maculata is also common; it is similar, with teeth along the leaf margins and some spotting.

A. striatula. Scrambling, hardy shrub with dark green leaves; distinctly striped leaf bases surround the stem. Multiple stems form a dense mound 5–6 ft. tall and to 15 ft. across, but plant may be kept much more compact with occasional hard pruning. Single spikes of yellow flowers, flushed with orange in bud, rise 6–18 in. above the foliage in summer.

A. variegata. PARTRIDGE-BREAST ALOE, TIGER ALOE. Foot-high, tight rosette of fleshy, triangular, dark green, 5-in.-long leaves strikingly banded and edged with white. Loose clusters of pink to dull red flowers appear in late winter to early spring.

A. vera (A. barbadensis). MEDICINAL ALOE, BARBADOS

ALOE. Zones 8, 9, 12–24; H1, H2. Clustering rosettes of narrow, fleshy, stiffly upright leaves 1–2 ft. long. Yellow flowers in dense spike atop 3-ft. stalk, spring and summer. Favorite folk medicine plant used to treat burns, bites, inflammation, and a host of other ills. Among best aloes for Zones 12, 13. Survives without extra water but needs some to look good.

ALOPECURUS
pratensis 'Aureus'
YELLOW FOXTAIL GRASS
Poaceae (Gramineae)
PERENNIAL GRASS

🖊 ZONES 2–10, 14–17, 21–24
☼ ◑ PARTIAL SHADE IN HOTTEST CLIMATES
💧 REGULAR WATER

Golden-variegated selection of a cool-season grass native to Eurasia and naturalized in North America. May be sold as 'Variegatus' or 'Aureovariegatus'. Smaller and less vigorous than plain (green-leafed) species. To 1 ft. high; spreads slowly to form mats 1½ ft.

Alopecurus pratensis 'Aureus'

wide or wider. Translucent foliage ranges from green striped with gold to almost entirely yellow; in part shade, it is chartreuse. When flower spikes form in midspring, shear them off to keep foliage attractive longer (as summer heat pushes it toward dormancy) and to prevent the appearance of volunteer seedlings, which would be green leafed. Fresh new growth resumes in fall and persists until the first hard freeze. Nearly evergreen in climates with cool summers and mild winters. Dislikes drought, excessive moisture, and extremes of heat. Good for border, rock garden, ground cover. Divide every 2 or 3 years in spring or fall.

ALOYSIA
Verbenaceae
DECIDUOUS OR SEMIEVERGREEN SHRUBS

🖊 ZONES VARY BY SPECIES
☼ FULL SUN
💧 REGULAR WATER

These are aromatic shrubs with tiny flowers and a sparse growth habit; they are native to warmer parts of North and South America. Provide good drainage.

A

A. triphylla (Lippia citriodora). LEMON VERBENA. Zones 9, 10, 12–21; marginal in Zones 4–8. Native to Argentina, Chile.

Legginess is its natural state; it's the herb that grew like a gangling shrub in gardens of long ago, reaching 6 ft. or taller and sprawling to 6 ft. wide. Prized for lemon-scented leaves used to flavor teas and iced drinks; when you read of the fragrance of verbena in literature about the antebellum South, this is the plant. Narrow leaves to 3 in. long are arranged in whorls of three or four along branches. Bears open clusters of very small lilac or whitish flowers in summer.

Aloysia triphylla

Grow among lower plants to hide its legginess; or locate it against a wall or fence and pinch-prune to create interesting tracery. Can also be trained into a standard and tolerates clipping into a hedge. Borderline hardy as far north as Seattle if planted against a warm wall. In colder climates, grow it as a houseplant (pinch frequently) and let it spend warm months outdoors.

A. wrightii. OREGANILLO, MEXICAN OREGANO. Zones 8–13, 19–24. Native to desert mountains from California to Texas and northern Mexico. Dense grower to 5 ft. high and wide, with numerous small stems and small (½-in.) leaves. From spring through fall, produces very sweet-scented white flowers that can be used as a flavoring or for tea. Performs best when it gets lots of heat. Good in natural landscape, herb garden, as informal hedge.

Often confused with *A. lycioides*, a larger plant (to 8 ft. tall and 6 ft. wide) bearing blossoms that have a more vanillalike fragrance and are sometimes tinged with purple. Plants sold under either name may be one or the other—but both are outstanding ornamentals. Both make excellent honey. *A. lycioides* is Mexican oregano of spice trade.

ALPINE STRAWBERRY.
See **FRAGARIA vesca**

ALPINIA

GINGER LILY
Zingiberaceae
PERENNIALS

🌿	ZONES 14–24; H1, H2
🔆	LIGHT SHADE
💧	AMPLE WATER

Rhizomes produce leafy clumps that are evergreen in Zones 22–24, H1, and H2. Roots are hardy to about 15°F/–9°C. Tops die back in prolonged cool winter weather, but new shoots appear in spring. Needs good soil, no wind. Must be established for at least 2 years in order to bloom. Each year, remove canes that have flowered.

A. purpurata. RED GINGER. To 9–12 ft. tall, 2–3 ft. wide, with 2½-ft.-long leaves. Blooms in late summer, producing brilliant inflorescence of red bracts and small white flowers. In California, blooms only in a greenhouse.

A. sanderae (A. vittata). VARIEGATED GINGER. Native to Solomon Islands. To 3–4 ft. tall, 2 ft. wide, with 8-in.-long leaves striped with white. Rarely blooms. A good container plant.

A. zerumbet (A. nutans, A. speciosa). SHELL GINGER, SHELL FLOWER. Native to tropical Asia and Polynesia. Grandest of gingers, best all-year appearance. To 8–9 ft. tall, 3–4 ft. wide. Leaves shiny, 2 ft. long, 5 in. wide, with distinct parallel veins; leafstalks are maroon at maturity. Waxy white or pinkish, shell-like, fragrant flowers marked red, purple, or brown in pendent clusters on arching stems in late summer.

Alpinia zerumbet

ALSOPHILA australis, A. cooperi.
See **CYATHEA cooperi**

ALSTROEMERIA

Liliaceae
PERENNIALS FROM TUBEROUS ROOTS

🌿	ZONES 5–9, 14–24; H1
🔆	AFTERNOON SHADE IN HOTTEST CLIMATES
💧	REGULAR WATER DURING GROWTH AND BLOOM
⚠	CAN CAUSE DERMATITIS IN ALLERGIC PEOPLE

These perennials fall into two horticultural classes, which might be called "deciduous" and "evergreen."

Both produce masses of color in borders, bearing clustered flowers at the tops of leafy stems. The flowers, brightly colored and marked with contrasting blotches and flecks, are superb cut flowers and a favorite with florists for their lasting quality. Plants appreciate good drainage. Mulch deeply where winters are severe.

Alstroemeria aurea

Deciduous types. For many years, deciduous alstroemerias were the only ones readily available as garden subjects. The seed-grown Ligtu hybrids and Dr. Salter's hybrids have azalea-like flowers in beautiful, edible-sounding colors—orange, peach, shrimp, salmon—as well as red and near-white; all types are flecked and striped with deeper colors. They produce leafy shoots 2–5 ft. tall in late winter and into spring; as these shoots begin to brown, the flowering shoots appear, with blooms following in early to midsummer. If allowed to set seed, they will self-sow. Plants go dormant after bloom and need no water unless winter rains fail. They naturalize where winters are not severe. Sow seeds in fall, winter, or earliest spring, either where plants are to grow or in pots for later planting out.

Evergreen types. Evergreen alstroemerias include two species and a number of hybrids. The hybrids, available in various colors, were once grown only by commercial florists, who jealously guarded their plants from the home gardening public. American breeders have now produced similar hybrids, which are offered as potted plants. These will produce flowering shoots as long as the soil does not get too warm; repeat bloom can be stimulated by pulling up flowering shoots from the base rather than cutting them.

A. aurea (A. aurantiaca). Grows 3–4 ft. tall, with numerous leafy flowering stems topped by yellow, orange, or orange-red flowers liberally sprinkled with dark stripes and flecks. Sometimes available in winter or spring as dormant roots; these are frail and easily broken. Plant them 8 in. deep and 1 ft. apart. Once established, the plant is vigorous, possibly even invasive.

A. hybrids. These include series such as Meyer, Cordu, Premier, and Inca. They vary in height and come in many colors, mostly in the purple–pink–red range with dark flecks. Usually sold by color; buy in bloom. New hybrids show up constantly, some root-hardy to 0°F/–18°C. Check with local nurseries for availability.

A. psittacina (A. pulchella). Odd looking rather than beautiful. Flowering stems to 2½ ft. tall are crowned by a few dark red flowers marked with green and blotched dark purple. Travels by rhizomes but is not a pest; prefers partial to fairly deep shade. A variegated form has foliage marked in white.

ALTERNANTHERA tenella

JOYWEED
Amaranthaceae
PERENNIAL OFTEN TREATED AS ANNUAL

🌿	ZONES H1, H2; ANYWHERE AS ANNUAL
🔆	FULL SUN
💧	MODERATE WATER

Colorful foliage plant, native from Mexico to Argentina. To 6–12 in. high; plant 4–10 in. apart for best impact. Useful as edging, ground cover, or massed for special landscape effect. Accepts most well-drained soils but is not salt tolerant; will take some shade. Grow from cuttings. Keep planting compact by shearing.

Alternanthera tenella

Among the many varieties are 'Bettzickiana' (known by the common names "Jacob's coat" and "calico plant"), with spoon-shaped leaves blotched yellow and red; 'Magnifica', dwarf form with red-bronze leaves; and 'Parrot Feather' and 'Versicolor', with broad green leaves marked with yellow and pink veins. A form from Thailand that is grown in Hawaii has larger green leaves with irregular white margins.

ALTHAEA rosea.
See **ALCEA rosea**

ALUM ROOT. See **HEUCHERA**

ALYOGYNE huegelii (Hibiscus huegelii)
BLUE HIBISCUS
Malvaceae
EVERGREEN SHRUB

- ☀ ZONES 13–17, 20–24; H1, H2
- ☀ FULL SUN
- ◊ ◊ LITTLE TO MODERATE WATER

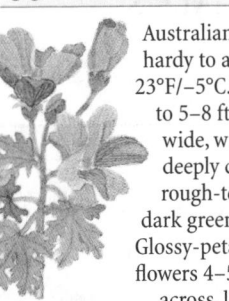

Australian native hardy to about 23°F/–5°C. Upright, to 5–8 ft. tall and wide, with deeply cut, rough-textured dark green foliage. Glossy-petaled flowers 4–5 in. across, lilac blue to deep purple.

Alyogyne huegelii

Blooms off and on all year; individual flowers last 2 or 3 days. Pinch or prune as needed to keep it compact. Variable from seed. 'Santa Cruz' is a good deep blue selection; 'Monterey Bay' and 'Mood Indigo' are deeper blue. 'White Swan' has white blossoms.

ALYSSUM
Brassicaceae (Cruciferae)
PERENNIALS

- ☀ ZONES 1–24
- ☀ ☀ FULL SUN OR LIGHT SHADE
- ◊ MODERATE WATER

Mostly native to Mediterranean region. Mounding plants or shrublets that brighten spring borders and rock gardens with their cheerful bloom. They thrive in poor, rocky soil as long as it is well drained.

A. montanum. To 8 in. high, 1½ ft. wide; leaves gray, hairy (more so on underside). Fragrant yellow flowers in dense, short clusters.

Alyssum montanum

A. saxatile. See Aurinia saxatilis

A. wulfenianum. Prostrate and trailing to about 1½ ft. wide, with fleshy, silvery leaves and sheets of pale yellow flowers.

ALYSSUM, SWEET. See **LOBULARIA maritima**

ALYXIA oliviformis
MAILE
Apocynaceae
EVERGREEN SHRUBBY VINE

- ☀ ZONES H1, H2
- ☀ ● PARTIAL OR FULL SHADE
- ◊ ◊ MODERATE TO REGULAR WATER

A Hawaiian native, this plant is found in various habitats—dry to wet, sea level to high elevation—and is correspondingly quite variable in appearance. In the wild, can be seen straggling along the ground as well as twining in trees. Bears small, tubular greenish yellow flowers followed by shiny purple-black fruits. Main feature, however, is dark green, glossy foliage that is fragrant when bruised, as is bark of stems. Both foliage and stems are widely used in leis. Makes an attractive cover for a shaded trellis. Best in rich, well-drained soil.

Alyxia oliviformis

AMARACUS dictamnus. See **ORIGANUM dictamnus**

AMARANTHUS
AMARANTH
Amaranthaceae
ANNUALS

- ☀ ZONES 1–24; H1, H2
- ☀ ☀ FULL SUN OR PARTIAL SHADE
- ● REGULAR WATER

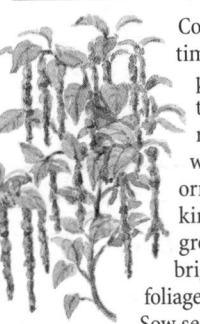

Coarse, sometimes weedy plants native to many regions of the world; a few ornamental kinds are grown for their brightly colored foliage or flowers. Sow seed in place in early summer—soil temperature must be above 70°F/21°C for germination. Or start indoors for planting out after frost danger is past in zones where the growing season is short.

Amaranthus caudatus

Picked when young and tender, leaves and stems of many species (even some of the weedy ones) can be used like spinach, taking its place in hot weather. Some species have seeds that look like sesame seeds, have a high protein content, and can be used as grain.

A. caudatus. LOVE-LIES-BLEEDING, TASSEL FLOWER. Sturdy, branching plant 3–8 ft. high, 1½–3 ft. wide; leaves 2–10 in. long, ½–4 in. wide. Red flowers in drooping, tassel-like clusters. A curiosity, not a pretty plant, but produces grain.

A. hypochondriacus (A. hybridus erythrostachys). PRINCE'S FEATHER. To 5 ft. high, 2 ft. wide, with leaves 1–6 in. long, ½–3 in. wide, usually reddish. Red or brownish red flowers in many-branched clusters. Some strains are grown as a spinach substitute or for grain.

A. tricolor. JOSEPH'S COAT. Branching plant 1–4 ft. high, 1–1½ ft. wide. Leaves 2½–6 in. long, 2–4 in. wide, blotched in shades of red and green. Selections such as 'Early Splendor', 'Flaming Fountain', and 'Molten Fire' bear masses of yellow to scarlet foliage at tops of main stems and principal branches. Green-leafed strains used as spinach substitute are sold under the name "tampala."

× AMARCRINUM memoria-corsii. See **CRINUM**

AMARYLLIS belladonna (Brunsvigia rosea)
BELLADONA LILY, NAKED LADY
Amaryllidaceae
PERENNIAL FROM BULB

- ☀ ZONES 4–24
- ☀ FULL SUN
- ◊ NO IRRIGATION NEEDED
- ◊ ALL PARTS ARE POISONOUS IF INGESTED

Native to South Africa. Performs best in areas with warm, dry summers. Bold, straplike leaves form clump about 1 ft. high, 2 ft. wide in fall and winter; foliage dies back by early summer. About 6 weeks later, 2–3-ft. stalks rise from bare earth, each topped by a cluster of 4–12 fragrant, trumpet-shaped, rosy pink flowers.

Amaryllis belladonna

Grows in almost any well-drained soil. Gets all the moisture it needs from winter rains. Plant bulbs 1 ft. apart right after bloom period ends. Where winter tem-

peratures stay above 15°F/–9°C, keep tops of bulb necks at or slightly above soil level. In colder-winter areas, choose a protected southern exposure and set bulbs slightly below ground level. Lift and divide clumps rarely; they may not bloom for several years if disturbed at the wrong time. Very long lived. For plants with common name "amaryllis," see *Hippeastrum*.

A. hallii. See Lycoris squamigera

AMELANCHIER
JUNEBERRY, SHADBLOW, SERVICEBERRY
Rosaceae
DECIDUOUS SHRUBS OR SMALL TREES

- ☀ ZONES VARY BY SPECIES
- ☀ ☀ FULL SUN OR PARTIAL SHADE
- ◊ ● MODERATE TO REGULAR WATER

Graceful, airy plants grow about twice as high as wide. Bloom in early spring, just before or during leaf-out, bearing drooping clusters of white or pinkish flowers that are showy but short lived. Fruits follow in summer; they are similar to blueberries though with a somewhat musty flavor.

Amelanchier laevis

Use them in pies and preserves—if you can get to them before the birds do (in Alaska, birds have thus far seemed uninterested in fruit). Purplish new spring foliage turns deep green in summer, fiery in fall.

Locate these plants against a dark background to show off flowers, form, fall color. Choose a site where litter from fruit and birds won't be a problem. Prune after bloom to remove crossing, crowded, diseased, or dead branches. The common name "serviceberry" is often pronounced "sarvisberry."

A. alnifolia. SASKATOON. Zones A1–A3; 1–6. Native to western Canada and mountainous parts of western U.S. To about 20 ft. tall, spreading by rhizomes. Selections grown for larger, sweeter berries than the species include 'Smoky', 'Martin', 'Northline', 'Thiessen', and dwarf 'Regent' (only 4–6 ft. tall).

A. canadensis. Zones A2, A3; 1–6. Plants offered under this name may actually belong to other species. Grows to 25 ft. tall, with short, erect clusters of flowers. ▶

A. × grandiflora. Zones 1–6. Hybrids between *A. arborea* (similar to *A. canadensis* but larger) and *A. laevis.* Many named selections are available and may be sold under any of the three names. Most grow to 25 ft. tall, with drooping flower clusters. 'Autumn Brilliance' has blue-green foliage that turns orange red in fall. 'Cole's Selection' and 'Princess Diana' are similar. Strong stems, profuse bloom, and brilliant fall color make them good choices for ornamental use.

A. laevis. ALLEGHENY SERVICEBERRY. Zones 2–6. Native to eastern North America. To 30 ft. tall, with nodding or drooping clusters of flowers. Sweet fruit. 'Spring Flurry' forms an upright oval and turns orange in autumn. Hybrid 'Cumulus' has a narrower habit and yellow-orange to red fall color.

AMETHYST FLOWER. See **BROWALLIA**

AMMI majus

BISHOP'S LACE
Apiaceae (Umbelliferae)
ANNUAL

📋 ALL ZONES	
☀️ ☼ FULL SUN OR PARTIAL SHADE	
⬤ ⬤ MODERATE TO REGULAR WATER	
⬥ SAP CAUSES A RASH	

Ammi majus

From southern Europe, Turkey, north Africa. Well-behaved relative of the roadside weed Queen Anne's lace (*Daucus carota*), offering similar delightful flowers without spreading all over creation. Slender, branched stems grow quickly to 1–3 ft. tall, 1 ft. wide, with attractive light green leaves 6–8 in. long and divided into many lance-shaped leaflets. In summer, each stem tip produces a 4–6-in.-wide, dome-shaped cluster of tiny white flowers. Lacy, delicate blooms are long lasting in a vase; also good in dried arrangements (hang upside down in a cool, dark place for 2 or 3 weeks to dry). Beautiful when massed in the garden. May self-sow, but not rampantly.

Wash hands with soap and water after handling plants, as the sap can cause a rash. Plants are injurious to livestock.

AMPELOPSIS brevipedunculata

PORCELAIN BERRY
Vitaceae
DECIDUOUS VINE

📋 ZONES 2-24	
☀️ ☼ ⬤ SUN OR SHADE	
⬤ ⬤ MODERATE TO REGULAR WATER	

Native to Asia. Rampant woody vine climbs 20–30 ft. by stem tendrils. Large, handsome, three-lobed, 2½–5-in.-wide leaves are dark green. In warm climates, leaves turn red and most drop in fall; more leaves come out, redden, and drop all winter. Many clusters of small, grapelike berries turn from greenish ivory to brilliant metallic blue in late summer and fall; attract birds. Needs strong support: superb on concrete and rock walls or on sturdy arbors. Thin out and shorten stems each winter; dig out suckers. You can cut the vine to the ground and still get berries, since it blooms and fruits on new growth.

Ampelopsis brevipedunculata

'Elegans' has leaves variegated with white and pink and is smaller, less vigorous, and less hardy than the species. Makes a splendid hanging-basket plant.

Boston ivy and Virginia creeper, formerly included in genus *Ampelopsis,* are now placed under *Parthenocissus* because, unlike *Ampelopsis,* both have disks at ends of their tendrils.

AMSONIA

BLUESTAR
Apocynaceae
PERENNIALS

📋 ZONES 2-24	
☀️ ☼ FULL SUN OR LIGHT SHADE	
⬤ ⬤ MODERATE TO REGULAR WATER	

Elegant oleander (*Nerium oleander*) relatives from southeastern U.S. To 2–3 ft. high and wide, with narrow leaves and erect stems topped by clusters of small, star-shaped blue flowers in late spring. Bright yellow fall foliage is a

bonus. Tough plants that succeed in ordinary soil and tolerate occasional lapses in watering.

A. ciliata. Crowded, needlelike (but soft) leaves to 2 in. long; exceptional fall color. Pale blue flowers.

A. hubrichtii. HUBRICHT'S BLUESTAR. Soft, very narrow, almost needlelike leaves; fall foliage is exceptionally bright, clear gold. Sky blue flowers. Considered by many to be the finest of bluestars.

A. illustris. SHINING BLUE-STAR. Leathery, shiny green, willowlike leaves to 3 in. long. Pale blue blossoms.

Amsonia tabernaemontana

A. tabernaemontana. Dull dark green, willowlike leaves to 3 in. long. Slate blue flowers.

AMUR CHOKECHERRY. See **PRUNUS maackii**

ANACYCLUS depressus (A. pyrethrum depressus)

MOUNT ATLAS DAISY
Asteraceae (Compositae)
PERENNIAL

📋 ZONES 2-24	
☀️ FULL SUN	
⬤ ⬤ LITTLE TO MODERATE WATER	

Native to North Africa, Spain. Slowly forms dense, spreading mat somewhat like chamomile (*Chamaemelum*). Grayish, finely

Anacyclus depressus

divided leaves. Single daisylike summer flowers to 2 in. across, with yellow center disks and white rays (red on reverse side). Good in sunny, dry, hot rock gardens. May freeze in severe winters or rot in cold, wet, heavy soil. Dislikes humidity.

ANAGALLIS

PIMPERNEL
Primulaceae
ANNUALS AND PERENNIALS OR BIENNIALS

📋 ZONES VARY BY SPECIES	
☀️ FULL SUN	
◐ ⬤ ⬤ LITTLE TO REGULAR WATER	

Two species sometimes seen, one a weed. Newer hybrids becoming popular. Less aggressive types attractive in rock gardens.

A. arvensis. SCARLET PIMPERNEL. Annual. Zones 1–24. Low-growing weed from Europe, with ½-in., brick red flowers. *A. a. caerulea* has deep blue, larger flowers.

Anagallis monelli linifolia

A. hybrids. Summer annuals. 'Cinnamon' has medium-pink blooms; those of 'Spice' are light pink. Both are low (3 in. high) and spreading, with small, spicily scented leaves. The Wildcat series is taller, to 6–12 in. high, and comes in shades of blue, orange, and pink. All are good in pots and hanging baskets.

A. monelli. Perennial or biennial. Zones 4–9, 12–24. Mediterranean native to 1½ ft. high and wide, with ¾-in. flowers of intense blue. 'Pacific Blue' is a superior selection; 'Phillipsii' is compact, 1 ft. tall; *A. m. linifolia* has narrower leaves than the species. All three bloom from summer to frost.

ANCHUSA

Boraginaceae
ANNUALS, BIENNIALS, AND PERENNIALS

📋 ZONES VARY BY SPECIES	
☀️ FULL SUN	
⬤ ⬤ MODERATE TO REGULAR WATER	

Related to forget-me-not (*Myosotis*) but larger and showier. Worth growing for vibrant blue color; also appreciated for being rela-

Anchusa capensis

tively easy-to-grow plants. Give well-drained soil. High humidity inhibits performance.

A. azurea (A. italica). Perennial. Zones 1–24. Native to the Mediterranean region. Coarse, open, spreading; to 3–5 ft. tall, 2 ft. wide. Leaves 6 in. or longer, covered with bristly hairs. Clusters of bright blue blossoms, ½ to ¾ in. across, in summer and fall. Horticultural forms include gentian blue 'Dropmore', sky blue 'Opal', and rich blue 'Loddon Royalist'.

A. capensis. CAPE FORGET-ME-NOT, SUMMER FORGET-ME-NOT. Biennial in Zones 6–24; annual anywhere. Native to South Africa. To 1½ ft. tall, 8 in. wide. Narrow, 5-in.-long leaves about ½ in. wide. Bright blue, ½-in.-wide flowers with white throats come in clusters about 2 in. long. Use in summer borders.

ANDROMEDA. See PIERIS

ANDROMEDA
polifolia
BOG ROSEMARY
Ericaceae
EVERGREEN SHRUB

🌡	ZONES A1–A3; 1–6
☀ ◑	FULL SUN OR LIGHT SHADE
💧	AMPLE WATER

Andromeda polifolia

Mounding shrub to 1–1½ ft. high and 2–3 ft. wide; native to northern climates in North America, Europe, Asia. Narrow, leathery leaves ½–2 in. long, dark green above, blue gray beneath. Flask-shaped, nodding spring flowers are white to pink, carried in clusters of up to eight at top of stems. Requires strongly acid soil and protection from hottest sun. Connoisseur's plant for rock garden, pot culture, or streamside or bog garden. Varieties include 'Grandiflora', a dwarf with blue-green leaves and large, creamy, pink-shaded flowers; 'Nana', very com-

pact and vigorous, with nearly round pink flowers; and 'Blue Ice', with powder blue foliage and profuse soft pink blooms.

ANDROPOGON
gerardii
BIG BLUESTEM, TURKEYFOOT
Poaceae (Gramineae)
PERENNIAL GRASS

🌡	ZONES 1–9, 14–24
☀ ◑	FULL SUN OR LIGHT SHADE
◌ ◐ ●	LITTLE TO REGULAR WATER

Andropogon gerardii

This is the classic tall prairie grass of the Midwest, where it can reach 8 ft. high. In drier climates, it's more likely to grow 3–5 ft. tall. A clump former (to about 3 ft. wide), it does not ordinarily spread by rhizomes. Thin blades are blue green in summer, turning bronzy red or coppery in fall. Flowers are unshowy but interesting: purplish spikes to 4 in. long, borne at stem ends in sets of three or more (arranged like a turkey's foot). Tolerates a range of soil and moisture conditions. Cut dried stems to base yearly before new spring growth begins. Divide clump when center starts to die. Effective screen when massed if given regular water. A single plant makes a good accent in a mixed border.

ANDROSACE
ROCK JASMINE
Primulaceae
PERENNIALS

🌡	ZONES 1–6, 14–17
☀	FULL SUN
◐	MODERATE WATER

Choice rock garden miniatures grown mostly by alpine plant specialists. Clusters of small flowers in summer. All types require perfect drainage and are best adapted to gravelly banks in rock gardens. Protect from more aggressive rockery plants such as alyssum, aubrieta, rockcress (*Arabis*). Rarely succeed in warm-winter areas.

These species are native to the Himalayas.

A. lanuginosa. Trailing plant forms mats 3 ft. across. Silvery leaves to ¾ in. long, covered with silky white hairs. Pink flowers on 2-in. stems. *A. l. leichtlinii* has white flowers with a crimson eye.

A. primuloides. Spreads by runners. Leaves ½–2 in. long, in rosettes covered with silvery hairs. Pink flowers held on 5-in. stems.

A. sarmentosa. Spreads by runners. Leaves to 1½ in. long, arranged in rosettes, covered with silvery hairs when young. Rose-colored flowers on 5-in.-tall stems. *A. s. chumbyi* forms a dense clump, has woolly leaves.

Androsace lanuginosa

ANEMANTHELE lessoniana. See STIPA arundinacea

ANEMONE
WINDFLOWER, ANEMONE
Ranunculaceae
PERENNIALS

🌡	ZONES VARY BY SPECIES
☀ ◑ ●	EXPOSURE NEEDS VARY BY SPECIES
◐	REGULAR WATER
◈	ALL PARTS ARE POISONOUS IF INGESTED

A rich and varied group of plants ranging in size from alpine rock garden miniatures to tall Japanese anemones grown in borders; bloom extends from very early spring to fall, depending on species.

Most of the anemones described below have fibrous roots or creeping rhizomes or rootstocks, but *A. blanda, A. coronaria,* and *A.* × *fulgens* are grown from tubers requiring special attention. Set out *A. blanda* in fall; where winter temperatures drop below –10°F/ –23°C, apply a thick mulch after first hard frost. Plant *A. coronaria* and *A.* × *fulgens* in fall where they are hardy in the ground; in cooler regions, plant in early spring. In warmer climates, some gardeners soak tubers for a few hours before planting.

Plant tubers scarred side up (look for depressed scar left by base of last year's stem), setting them 1–2 in. deep and 8–12 in. apart in rich, light, well-drained

loam. Or start in flats of damp sand; set out in garden when stems are a few inches tall. Keep soil moist during growth and bloom. Protect from birds until leaves toughen. In high-rainfall areas, excess moisture induces rot. Tuberous types best treated as annuals in rainy-summer or warm-winter climates, where they tend to be short lived; *A. blanda,* in particular, needs distinct winter chill for good performance. Tuberous anemones make good container plants.

A. blanda. Zones 2–9, 14–23. Native to southeastern Europe; sometimes called Greek windflower. Tubers produce spreading mat of finely divided, softly hairy leaves (clumps are wider spreading in colder climates). In spring, each 2–8-in. stem bears one sky blue flower, 1–1½ in. across. Often confused with *A. apennina,* which has more pointed leaf segments. Selections with 2-in. flowers on 10–12-in. plants include 'Blue Star', 'Pink Star', 'White Splendor', and purplish red 'Radar'. All work well as underplantings for tulips, as ground cover drifts under deciduous shrubs and trees, and naturalized in short grass. Partial shade.

Anemone blanda 'White Splendor'

A. canadensis. Zones 1–4. To 1–2 ft. tall, spreading by creeping rhizomes. Inch-wide, yellow-centered white flowers appear in twos and threes from the upper joints of divided leaves. Produces profuse bloom from late spring to early summer. Can be invasive in small gardens. Partial shade.

A. coronaria. POPPY-FLOWERED ANEMONE. Zones 4–24. Native to the Mediterranean; grows from a tuber. Species is rarely seen in gardens; it has been replaced by showy large-flowered hybrids valued for cutting and for spectacular spring color in borders or mass plantings. Blossoms are 1½–2½ in. across, borne singly on 6–18-in. stems above finely divided leaves; colors include red, blue, tones and mixtures of these colors, and white. Among the most popular strains are De Caen (single flowers) and St. Brigid (semidouble to double). Full sun or partial shade.

A. × fulgens. SCARLET WINDFLOWER. Zones 4–9, 14–24. To 1 ft.; grows from a tuber. Basal leaves are divided, stem leaves undivided. Spring flowers 2½ in. across, brilliant scarlet with black stamens. St. Bavo strain comes in unusual color range including pink and rusty coral. Same uses as for *A. coronaria.* Partial shade.

A. × hybrida (A. japonica, A. hupehensis japonica). JAPANESE ANEMONE. Zones 2b–24. Long-lived, fibrous-rooted perennial indispensable for fall flower color. Graceful, branching stems 2–4 ft. high rise from clump of dark green, three- to five-lobed leaves covered with soft hairs. Single or semidouble flowers in white, silvery pink, or rose. Many named varieties. Slow to establish, but once started it spreads readily if roots are not disturbed. Space plants 2 ft. apart. May need staking. Mulch in fall where winters are severe. Increase by divisions in fall or early spring or by root cuttings in spring. Effective in clumps in front of tall shrubbery or under high-branching trees. Partial shade.

A. nemorosa. WOOD ANEMONE. Zones 1–9, 14–24. European native to 1 ft. high, with creeping rhizomes, deeply cut leaves, and inch-wide white (rarely pinkish or blue) spring flowers held above the foliage. Spreads slowly to make an attractive woodland ground cover. Many named varieties exist; 'Allenii' has large blue flowers, and there are double forms. Partial or full shade.

A. pulsatilla. See Pulsatilla vulgaris

A. quinquefolia oregana. Zones 4–7, 15–17. Native to Pacific Northwest and Northern California. Attractive woodland ground cover resembling *A. nemorosa,* with inch-wide white (sometimes blue or pink) spring flowers. Partial shade.

A. sylvestris. SNOWDROP ANEMONE. Zones 1–10, 14. European native growing from creeping rootstock to 1½ ft. tall. Fragrant, 1½–3-in., yellow-centered white flowers in spring, followed by cottony seed heads. Plant spreads readily in damp, wooded locations. 'Grandiflora' has larger blossoms; 'Flore Pleno' is double flowered. Partial or full shade.

A. tomentosa. Zones 2b–9, 14–21. Vigorous, fibrous-rooted Tibetan native often sold as *A. vitifolia* 'Robustissima'. Foliage resembles grape leaves, grows in a spreading clump that gives rise to branching, 3½-ft.-high stems bearing single pink flowers in late summer, early fall. Allow 3 ft. between plants. Partial shade.

ANETHUM
graveolens
DILL
Apiaceae (Umbelliferae)
ANNUAL

🌿 ZONES 1–24
☼ FULL SUN
💧 REGULAR WATER

Anethum graveolens

Native to southwestern Asia and naturalized in northern U.S. To 3–4 ft. tall, with soft, feathery leaves and umbrellalike, 6-in.-wide clusters of small yellow flowers in summer (winter in the desert). Seeds and leaves have pungent aroma. Sow seeds where plants are to grow; for constant supply, sow several times in spring and summer (germinates and grows better in spring). In the desert, sow in later summer or fall. Thin seedlings to 1½ ft. apart. An easy way to grow dill in a casual garden is to let a few plants go to seed. Seedlings can be pulled and chopped for use in cooking. Use seeds in pickling and vinegar; use fresh or dried leaves in cooked dishes, salads, sauces.

ANGELICA
archangelica
ANGELICA
Apiaceae (Umbelliferae)
BIENNIAL

🌿 ZONES A2, A3; 1–10, 14–24
☼ ◑ FULL SUN IN COOLER CLIMATES ONLY
💧 REGULAR WATER

Native to northern Europe and western Asia. Tropical-looking plant with divided and toothed,

Angelica archangelica

yellow-green leaves 2–3 ft. long. When it blooms (in early summer), it sends up a thick, hollow stem to 6 ft. tall topped by a large (4-ft.-wide), umbrellalike cluster of greenish yellow flowers. Grow in moist, rich soil. Propagate from seeds as soon as they ripen in fall. Because angelica is taprooted and doesn't transplant well, sow in place. To prolong plant's life for a few years, cut out flowering stem after it has formed. Angelica leaves are a nice addition to salads; the leafstalks can be cooked and eaten like asparagus. Both leafstalks and hollow flower stems can be candied and used to decorate pastries. Seeds are used commercially to flavor wines, vermouth, and liqueurs.

ANGELICA TREE.
See **ARALIA elata**

ANGELITA DAISY.
See **TETRANEURIS acaulis**

ANGELONIA
angustifolia
Scrophulariaceae
PERENNIAL OFTEN TREATED
AS ANNUAL

🌿 ZONES 1–24; H1, H2
☼ FULL SUN
💧 REGULAR WATER

Native to the tropics of the Americas, angelonia looks a bit like a miniature delphinium. Showy 8-in.-tall spikes of small blue, purple, pink, or white blossoms appear in summer atop plants that grow 1–1½ ft. tall and about 1 ft.

Angelonia angustifolia

wide. Medium green leaves are narrow and pointed, up to 3 in. long. Excellent as a bedding plant and in containers; provides long-lasting cut flowers. Easy to grow in moist, well-drained soil. Very heat tolerant. Not bothered by pests. Many improved hybrids available, some with flowers marked with more than one color.

ANGEL'S HAIR.
See **ARTEMISIA schmidtiana**

ANGEL'S TEARS.
See **NARCISSUS triandrus, SOLEIROLIA soleirolii**

ANGEL'S TRUMPET.
See **BRUGMANSIA**

ANIGOZANTHOS
KANGAROO PAW
Haemodoraceae
PERENNIALS

🌿 ZONES 15–24
☼ FULL SUN
💧 REGULAR WATER

Evergreen native to open eucalyptus forests in western Australia. Thick rootstocks send up clumps of dark green, smooth, swordlike leaves. Spikes of striking, fuzzy, tubular flowers in red, purple, green, or yellow, curved at tips like kangaroo paws (tips split into six segments). Flowers attract hummingbirds. Intriguing in flower, otherwise not outstanding. Bloom from late spring to fall if spent flowering spikes are cut to ground. Good cut flowers. Light sandy soil or heavier soil with good drainage. Control snails and slugs.

A. flavidus (A. flavida). Branching stems to 5 ft. tall bear 1–1½-in.-long, yellow-green flowers tinged with red. Foliage clump is 2–3 ft. wide.

Anigozanthos flavidus

A. hybrids. Kangaroo paws hybridize freely in nature and in cultivation. The following are among the many superior garden plants that have been developed. Foliage clumps range from a foot across (for most dwarf varieties) to about 3 ft. wide; the smaller types make good container subjects.

'Big Red'. Extra-large bright red blossoms top 3–4-ft.-tall stems.

Bush Gems Hybrids. All resist leaf and root diseases that afflict kangaroo paws. Two of the best are 2½–3-ft., easy-to-grow 'Bush Gold', which bears clear lemon yellow flowers above lime green leaves over a long bloom season, and 1½–2½-ft. 'Bush Ranger', a long-lived variety with clear red blooms. Other good varieties include 'Bush Baby', with flowers blending red, orange, and yellow on 1½-ft. stems; 'Bush Emerald', bearing surprising green flowers with contrasting yellow throats and brilliant orange anthers on 2–2½-ft. stems; 'Bush Lantern', a bright yellow dwarf 1–2 ft. tall; and 'Bush Pearl', with bubble-gum pink blossoms on 2-ft. stems.

'Harmony'. Yellow flowers on tall (4–6-ft.) stems clothed with bright red hairs.

'Pink Joey'. Silvery pink flowers on stems 1–3 ft. high.

A. manglesii. Unbranched green stems to 3 ft. high, thickly covered with red hairs; 3-in. flowers in brilliant deep green, red at base. Foliage clump is 1½–2 ft. wide.

ANISACANTHUS
DESERT HONEYSUCKLE
Acanthaceae
EVERGREEN OR DECIDUOUS SHRUBS

| ✿ ZONES 8–13, 18–23; H1, H2 |
| ☀ ◑ EXPOSURE NEEDS VARY BY SPECIES |
| ◔ MODERATE WATER |

Heat-loving shrubs have nectar-filled tubular flowers with two lobes above the mouth, three on the lower lip. Highly favored by hummingbirds and butterflies. Fairly drought tolerant; water deeply every 2 to 3 weeks in summer.

A. quadrifidus wrightii (A. wrightii). Deciduous. Native to southeastern Texas, northeastern Mexico. To 3 ft. tall, 4 ft. wide, with dark green leaves 2 in. long and 1 in. wide. Spikes of 2-in.-long, brilliant red-orange flowers from early summer to fall. Rabbits love new shoots; protect with wire cage until a woody structure is estab-

lished. For compact shape and prolific bloom, cut back by one-half to two-thirds before new spring growth commences. 'Mexican Flame' is a superior selection grown from cuttings. Full sun or light shade.

A. thurberi. CHUPAROSA. Mostly evergreen. Native to northern Mexico and canyons and washes of the Sonoran Desert of southern Arizona and New Mexico. In mild-winter areas, grows to 4 ft. tall (or more) and as wide, with stout branches. Looks best when treated as perennial, cut to ground before spring growth begins. Valued for spikes of 1½-in.-long, yellow-orange flowers held above light green leaves 1½–2 in. long, ½ in. wide. Blooms most prolifically in spring, with occasional blossoms in summer and fall. Full sun. Plants with red or orange-red flowers sold under this name may be *Justicia spicigera*.

Anisacanthus thurberi

ANISE. See **PIMPINELLA anisum**

ANISE TREE. See **ILLICIUM**

ANISODONTEA × hypomandarum
CAPE MALLOW
Malvaceae
EVERGREEN SHRUB

| ✿ ZONES 14–24 |
| ☀ ◑ FULL SUN OR LIGHT SHADE |
| ◔ ◔ LITTLE TO MODERATE WATER |

Fast-growing South African shrub with rounded growth to 4 ft. tall and wide; small (1½-in.), lobed, bright green leaves. Notable for profuse production of inch-wide, dark-veined, dark-eyed pink to purplish blooms resembling miniature individual hollyhocks; flowers come throughout warm weather, year-round in mildest climates. Good for borders, large containers. Often sold as single-trunk standard or "patio tree."

Anisodontea × hypomandarum

'Tara's Wonder' is an open grower to 6 ft. tall and wide, freely branching, with darker, narrowly lobed leaves and very large dark pink flowers. 'Tara's Pink' is bushier, with larger, more widely lobed leaves and lighter pink blossoms.

ANNONA cherimola.
See **CHERIMOYA**

ANTENNARIA dioica
PUSSY TOES
Asteraceae (Compositae)
PERENNIAL

| ✿ ZONES A1, A2; 1–3, 6, 7, 14–16 |
| ☀ FULL SUN |
| ◔ ◔ MODERATE TO REGULAR WATER |

Native to Europe, North America. Forms inch-high mats of woolly foliage that slowly spread among rocks, between paving stones, or at front of border. Furry puffs of flowers are pinkish white in the basic species, deep pink in 'Rubra', and rose pink in 'Rosea'. Extremely hardy to cold; will withstand some light foot traffic.

Antennaria dioica

ANTHEMIS
Asteraceae (Compositae)
PERENNIALS

| ✿ ZONES VARY BY SPECIES |
| ☀ FULL SUN |
| ◔ ◔ MODERATE TO REGULAR WATER |

Some species are weedy, but those listed here (from southern Europe and Turkey) are good garden plants with long-lasting daisylike or buttonlike flowers. Many-segmented leaves are aromatic, especially when bruised. Provide good drainage.

A. carpatica (A. cretica carpatica). Zones 3b–10, 14–24. Forms low, 2-ft.-wide mounds of green to gray-green foliage. Stems about 6 in. high rise from foliage clumps in spring and summer, bearing 1½-in. white daisies with yellow centers.

A. marschalliana (A. biebersteiniana). Zones 1–9, 14–24. Rounded plant 1 ft. tall and wide, with finely cut, fernlike, silvery leaves and 1-in., brilliant yellow daisylike blooms in summer.

Anthemis tinctoria
'E. C. Buxton'

A. nobilis. See Chamaemelum nobile

A. punctata cupaniana. Zones 4–9, 14–24. Mound of silvery foliage 1 ft. tall and at least as wide, topped by 2½-in. long-lasting white daisies in summer.

A. tinctoria. GOLDEN MARGUERITE. Zones 1–11, 14–24. Erect, shrubby plant to 2–3 ft. tall and wide, with angular stems, light green leaves, and gold-yellow, 2-in. daisies in summer and early fall. Excellent cut flower. Cut back lightly after first flush of bloom to keep flowers coming. Plants are short lived; root new ones from stem cuttings in spring or divide clumps in spring or fall. Varieties include 'Beauty of Grallagh', golden orange flowers; 'E. C. Buxton', white with yellow centers; 'Kelwayi', golden yellow; and 'Moonlight', pale yellow.

ANTHRISCUS
Apiaceae (Umbelliferae)
ANNUALS AND PERENNIALS OR
BIENNIALS

| ✿ ZONES VARY BY SPECIES |
| ☀ ◑ EXPOSURE NEEDS VARY BY SPECIES |
| ◔ REGULAR WATER |

Native to Europe, North Africa, and Asia. Though both of these plants produce many umbrella-shaped clusters of tiny flowers, they are valued for their fernlike foliage. In the first species, the leaves are used in cooking; in the second, the foliage brings deep, striking color to the perennial border.

Anthriscus cerefolium

A. cerefolium. CHERVIL. Annual. Zones 1–24. Low foliage mounds about a foot wide. Flower stems, 1–2 ft. topped with white blossoms in summer. The leaves have a parsleylike flavor with overtones of anise; use

A

like parsley, fresh or dried. Sow seeds in place in early spring (in cold-winter areas) or in fall (where winters are mild). In the following years, volunteer seedlings will keep you supplied with new plants. Goes to seed quickly in hot weather; keep flower clusters cut to encourage leafy growth. Grow in partial shade.

A. sylvestris 'Ravenswing'. Perennial or biennial. Zones 1–9, 14–24. Very attractive purple-black foliage in clump 1½ ft. high, 2½ ft. wide. In late spring or early summer, flowering stems to 3 ft. tall bear white blossoms with purplish pink bracts. Deadhead for best appearance and to prevent self-sowing. Grow in full sun or light shade.

ANTHURIUM
SPATHE FLOWER,
FLAMINGO FLOWER
Araceae
PERENNIALS

☀	ZONE H2, EXCEPT AS NOTED; OR INDOORS
☼	PARTIAL SHADE; BRIGHT INDIRECT LIGHT
💧	REGULAR WATER

Native to tropical American rain forests. Exotic plants with handsome dark green leaves and lustrous flower bracts. Bloom best in moderate shade. Among species listed here, all but *A. hookeri* are usually grown as potted plants, even in tropical climates.

Anthurium andraeanum

Anthuriums make unusual houseplants in cooler climates. As such, they are no more difficult to grow than some orchids. The higher the humidity, the better. Leaves lose shiny texture and may die if humidity drops below 50 percent for more than a few days. Keep pots on trays of moist gravel, in bathroom, or under polyethylene cover. Sponge or spray leaves several times daily. For good bloom, locate by window with good light but no direct sun. Generally grow best in 80 to 90°F/27 to 32°C temperature range but will get along at normal house temperature. Growth stops below 65°F/18°C, is damaged below 50°F/10°C. Protect from drafts. Pot in coarse, porous mix of leaf mold, sandy

soil, and shredded osmunda. Give light feeding every 4 weeks.

A. andraeanum. Dark green, oblong leaves to 1 ft. long and 6 in. wide, heart shaped at base. Spreading, heart-shaped flower bracts in shades of red, rose, pink, and white shine as though lacquered. Bracts reach 6 in. long, surround yellow, callalike flower spike. Bloom more or less continuously—plant may have from four to six flowers during the year. Flowers last 6 weeks on plant, 4 weeks after cutting.

A. crystallinum. Leaves to 1½ ft. long, 1 ft. wide, deep green with striking white veining. Flowers unexciting, with small, narrow, greenish bracts. Many similar anthuriums exist in florist trade; plants offered as *A. crystallinum* may be *A. clarinervium, A. magnificum,* or some other species.

A. hookeri. Grown in the tropical landscape for handsome foot-wide "nest" of large (to 8-in.-long) leaves. Excellent accent in a wind-sheltered garden or as a tubbed specimen. Needs high humidity. Grow in well-aerated, rich, moist soil; feed regularly.

A. scandens. Climbing or trailing plant to 2 ft., with 3-in.-long, tapered oval leaves; small, fragrant, greenish flowers; translucent lilac berries.

A. scherzerianum. Zones 23, 24; H2. Slow-growing, compact plant to 2 ft. Dark green leaves 8 in. long, 2 in. wide. Flower bracts broad, 3 in. long, deep red varying to rose, salmon, white. Yellow flower spikes spirally coiled. Easier to handle than *A. andraeanum* and often thrives under good houseplant conditions.

ANTIGONON
leptopus
CORAL VINE, QUEEN'S WREATH,
ROSA DE MONTANA
Polygonaceae
EVERGREEN OR DECIDUOUS VINE

☀	ZONES 12, 13, 18–24; H1, H2
☼	FULL SUN
💧	MODERATE TO REGULAR WATER

Native to Mexico. Where summers are long and hot, this tuberous-rooted perennial vine grows quickly, climbing by tendrils to 40 ft. Makes an open, airy foliage cover; leaves are bright green, 3–5 in. long, heart shaped or arrow shaped. Small rose pink flowers are carried in long, trailing sprays from

midsummer to fall. Evergreen in mild-winter areas; cut back vigorous growth in late winter or early spring. In frosty areas, leaves drop in fall and most of top dies, but recovery is quick when weather warms up. Where winter temperatures dip below 25°F/–4°C, protect roots with mulch. Remove frost-killed stems from their support before new growth emerges in spring. Varieties include rare white 'Album' and hot rose pink (nearly red) 'Baja Red'; the latter's color is variable from seed, but the best are as red as 'Barbara Karst' bougainvillea.

Antigonon leptopus

A wonderful vine in the low deserts of California and Arizona; there, it can grow without irrigation but may die back to ground in summer. Elsewhere give it hottest place in garden; choose a warm, wind-sheltered spot in Southern California coastal gardens. Let it shade a patio or terrace or drape its foliage and blossom sprays along eaves, fence, or garden wall.

ANTIRRHINUM
majus
SNAPDRAGON
Scrophulariaceae
PERENNIAL TREATED AS ANNUAL

☀	ZONES A1–A3; 1–24
☼	FULL SUN
💧	REGULAR WATER

Among best flowers for sunny borders and cutting, at their best in spring and early summer. In regions with mild winters and hot summers, will bloom in winter and spring. Snapdragon flowers have five lobes, which are divided

Antirrhinum majus

into upper and lower "jaws"; by pinching sides of flower lightly, you can make jaws snap open. Later developments include the double flower; the bell-shaped kind, with round, open flowers; and the azalea-shaped bloom, which is a double bellflower. All available in many colors.

Tall "snapping" snapdragons (2½–3-ft.) include Rocket and Topper strains (single flowers) and Double Supreme strain. Intermediate (to 1–2 ft.) are Cinderella, Coronette, Minaret, 'Princess White with Purple Eye', the Ribbon series, Sprite, and Tahiti. Dwarfs (6–8 in. high) include Dwarf Bedding Floral Carpet, Kim, Kolibri, and Royal Carpet. Bell-flowered strains include Bright Butterflies and Wedding Bells (both 2½ ft.), La Bella (1½ ft.), and Little Darling and Liberty Bell (both 15 in.). Azalea-flowered strains include Madame Butterfly (2½ ft.) and Sweetheart (1 ft.). Plants range from about 6 in. across for smallest types to 2 ft. wide for tallest.

In a category of its own is the Chinese Lanterns strain: this bell-flowered snapdragon with trailing, cascading stems is ideal for hanging baskets.

Sow seed in flats from late summer to early spring for later transplanting or buy plants at nursery. Set out plants in early fall in mild-winter areas, spring in colder climates. If snapdragons set out in early fall reach bud stage before night temperatures drop below 50°F/10°C, they will start blooming in winter and continue until weather gets hot.

Valuable cut flowers. Tall and intermediate forms are splendid vertical accents in borders. Dwarf kinds are effective as edgings in rock gardens and raised beds, or in pots.

APACHE PLUME.
See **FALLUGIA paradoxa**

APHELANDRA
squarrosa
ZEBRA PLANT
Acanthaceae
EVERGREEN SHRUB

☀	ZONES 23, 24; H2; OR INDOORS
☼	SOME SHADE; BRIGHT INDIRECT LIGHT
💧	REGULAR WATER

Native to Mexico, South America. Appreciated for striking foliage and flowers. Leaves are 8–12 in. long, dark green veined with

Aphelandra squarrosa

white. Green-tipped yellow blooms and waxy, golden yellow flower bracts make colorful upright spikes at stem tips. In tropical climates, plant reaches 6½ ft. tall and wide, but as houseplant rarely exceeds 1–2 ft. Best-known variety is 'Louisae', but newer 'Apollo White' and 'Diana' are more compact and show more white venation.

Occasionally used as an accent in protected spots in Southern California gardens. If plant freezes, cut it to the ground; new shoots will appear when weather warms up. Indoors, provide bright filtered light or morning sun. When bracts fade, cut back their stalk to a pair of sturdy leaves to keep plants bushy. Repot annually after bloom. Propagate every few years, as older plants decline rapidly; take stem cuttings from late winter to late spring.

APONOGETON distachyus
CAPE PONDWEED, WATER HAWTHORN
Aponogetonaceae
AQUATIC PLANT

☀ ◑ ZONES 4–9, 12–24
☀ ◑ FULL SUN OR PARTIAL SHADE
◔◔ LIVES IN WATER

Native to South Africa. Suitable for small water gardens. Like a miniature water lily, it produces floating leaves from a submerged tuber.

Aponogeton distachyus

The leaves are long and narrow; ⅓-in.-long white, fragrant flowers stand above water in double-branched clusters. In hot-summer climates, blooms in cool weather and is dormant in hottest weather; where winters are cold, blooms in summer and is dormant in winter. Culture is the same as water lily (*Nymphaea*).

APPLE
Rosaceae
DECIDUOUS FRUIT TREES

🖋 ZONES VARY BY VARIETY
☀ FULL SUN
💧 REGULAR WATER DURING FRUIT DEVELOPMENT
▶ SEE CHART NEXT PAGE

Most widely adapted deciduous fruit. Ripens from July to early November, depending on variety. Mild winters of the low desert and the marine and coastal climates of Southern California do not provide enough cold for most standard varieties—in those areas, be sure to choose apples with low winter chill requirement (such low-chill varieties are noted in the chart). In many apple-growing areas, demand for the popular varieties seen on fruit stands often causes nurseries to sell unsuitable selections. For this reason, the chart indicates where some varieties perform best as well as where they are sold. In the coldest climates, including Alaska, rootstock is as important as variety; apples in such areas are best grown on hardy crabapple rootstocks such as *Malus baccata*, *M. antonovka*, or *M. ranetka*. Apple-crabapple hybrids offer another option for coldest-winter areas.

Although many apples are partially self-fruitful to varying degrees ('Golden Delicious', 'Mollie's Delicious', and 'Chehalis' are closest to self-fruitful), it is generally recommended that, unless there are apples growing nearby in your neighborhood, two or more varieties be planted for cross-pollination and good fruit set. Certain varieties (triploids) do not produce fertile pollen and will not fertilize either their own flowers or those of other apples. Don't use 'Gravenstein' or any other pollen-

Apple

What Apples Need

WINTER CHILL Most varieties demand 900 to 1,200 hours of temperatures at or below 45°F/7°C. In mild-winter areas, look for low-chill varieties (100 to 400 hours).

FULL SUN Essential for a good crop—so don't crowd an apple tree into a partially shaded site. To plant more than one variety in a small space, choose dwarf or multiple-variety trees.

WATERING When fruit is developing, make up for any lack of rainfall with periodic deep soakings.

POLLINATION If you have a tree that is not bearing, graft a branch of another variety onto it or place fresh bouquets of blossoms from another variety (in a can of water) at base of tree.

'Spitzenberg'

sterile tree to pollinate an unfruitful tree.

A standard apple tree grows about 20 ft. tall, 20–25 ft. wide. If space is at a premium, consider dwarf trees. For very small yards, multiple-variety trees provide an assortment of different apples as well as cross-pollination—all on a single tree. Available in standard and dwarf sizes, these trees have three to five varieties grafted onto a single trunk and rootstock.

In choosing varieties, remember that good apples are not necessarily red. Skin color is not an indicator of quality or taste. Make sure that name, eye appeal, or taste preference, does not influence you to choose a difficult-to-grow variety. For example, if to your taste 'Golden Delicious' and 'Red Delicious' are nearly equal (and you live in an area where either can be grown), consider differences in growing them. 'Golden Delicious' produces fruit without a pollenizer and comes into bearing at a younger age. It keeps well, while 'Red Deli-

cious' becomes mealy if not stored at temperatures of 35 to 40°F/12 to 4°C or lower. And it can be used for cooking, while 'Red Delicious' is principally a fresh eating apple.

If you want nearly perfect fruit, the apple tree will need much care in most regions. But even with less-than-perfect fruit, an apple tree is ornamental; it has more character, better form, and a longer life than most other deciduous fruit trees. It does best in deep, well-drained soil but gets by in many imperfect situations, including heavy soils.

Codling moth is the universal insect pest of apples. Pheromone traps, trichogramma wasps, or horticultural oil may be enough to thwart this pest in home gardens, but proper timing of controls is critical. Synthetic pesticides such as carbaryl are also effective. Apple maggot is a problem in some areas (particularly western Washington); infested fruit is soft, rotten, and unusable. Various types of sticky traps may be of some help, but frequent insecticide sprays from midsummer to harvest are often needed for complete control. Apple scab causes hard, corky spots on the fruit, with subsequent defoliation and stunting of immature fruit. It is particularly severe in coastal areas of the Pacific Northwest. Planting disease-resistant varieties (see chart) is the best way to avoid the problem. Leaf rollers and aphids are potentially troublesome. Powdery mildew and fireblight can also infect apples in some regions. For timing of sprays and other control measures for any of the above problems, consult your Cooperative Extension Office or a reliable local nursery.

Dwarf and spur apples. Dwarf apples (5–8 ft. tall and wide) are made by grafting wood from standard apple varieties onto dwarfing rootstocks such as M9, EMLA27, and P22. Dwarfs take up little room and bear at a younger age than standard apples, but they have shallow roots and need the support of a post, fence, wall, or sturdy trellis to withstand wind and heavy rain. They are not reliable in the coldest regions. They also need good soil and extra ▶

A

A

APPLE

NAME	ZONES	RIPENING DATE	FRUIT	COMMENTS
'Adina'	18-24; H1	Early to midseason	Large, round, fragrant, dark red. Firm, sweet, creamy white flesh with cinnamon overtones	Low-chill variety
'Akane'	1-7, 14-16	Early to midseason	Small to medium, round to flat. Red skin, crisp white flesh	Scab and mildew resistant
'Anna'	7-24; H1	Early. Sometimes bears light second and third crops later in the season	Large, pale green blushed red. Crisp, sweet with some acid	Begins producing at a young age. Low-chill variety; useful in warmest winter areas. Good annual bearer. Good pollenizer for 'Dorsett Golden' and 'Ein Shemer'
'Arkansas Black'	1-3, 10, 11	Late	Medium size; deep dark red. Hard, crisp	Best after storage for 2 months. 'Arkansas Black Spur' is spurred variation
'Ashmead's Kernel'	4-9, 14-17	Late	Medium size; red-orange blush over rough yellow-green skin	Good disease resistance
'Beverly Hills'	18-24	Early	Small to medium. Yellow skin splashed and striped red. Tender, somewhat tart. Fair quality. Somewhat resembles 'McIntosh'	Definitely for cool areas; will not develop good quality in hot interiors. One of the best for Southern California coast
'Braeburn'	1-3, 6, 14-16 18-23	Late	Medium size; orange-red blush over yellow ground. Crisp, sweet-tart flesh. Stores well	Fruit drops in hot climates. Thin fruit to prevent bearing in alternate years. Very susceptible to mites
'Chehalis'	4-6	Early	Large, yellow green, similar to 'Golden Delicious'. Soft but bakes well. Mild flavor, melting flesh; good in salads. Poor keeper	Self-fruitful. Resists scab
'Cox's Orange Pippin'	7, 14-16	Midseason	Medium size. Dull orange-red skin; yellow, firm, juicy flesh. Superb flavor. English dessert favorite	Susceptible to scab and cracking. Dense growth; thin out branches. Dislikes extreme cold, heat, low humidity. Worth trying for its unique flavor
'Delicious' ('Red Delicious')	Sold wherever apples will grow; best in 2, 3, 7	Midseason	Pointed blossom end with five knobs. Color varies with strain, climate; best with sunny, warm days, cool nights. Mildly sweet. Good finish. Often older, striped kinds taste better than highly colored commercial types	Many strains that vary in ripening season, depth and uniformity of coloring. 'Crimson Spur' and 'Bisbee Spur' are popular home varieties. All types susceptible to scab; difficult for home gardeners to grow in Zones 4-6
'Dorsett Golden'	13, 17-24; H1	Early	Medium to large, yellow or greenish yellow; sweet flavor. Good for eating fresh or cooking. Keeps a few weeks	Seedling of 'Golden Delicious' from Bermuda. Low-chill variety. Good pollenizer for 'Anna' and 'Ein Shemer'
'Ein Shemer'	13, 17-24; H1	Early	Medium size, yellow to greenish yellow. Juicy, crisp, mildly acid	Low-chill variety. Good pollenizer for 'Anna' and 'Dorsett Golden'
'Empire'	2, 3, 6, 7, 14-16	Midseason	Cross between 'McIntosh' and 'Delicious'. Small to medium size, roundish, dark red. Creamy white flesh is juicy, crisp, mildly tart	Semispur growth habit. Good tree structure. Susceptible to spring frost damage. Better adapted to hot-summer areas than 'McIntosh'
'Enterprise'	1-9, 14-16	Late	Medium size, firm; red blush. Sweet; keeps well	Immune to scab; subject to preharvest fruit drop
'Fiesta'	1-9, 14-16	Midseason to late	Firm fruit is larger and even better flavored than 'Cox's Orange Pippin' and doesn't crack. Red-striped skin	Productive; no preharvest fruit drop
'Fuji'	6-9, 14-16, 18-22	Late	Medium to large; yellow-green ground with red stripes. Firm flesh with excellent, very sweet flavor. Stores exceptionally well	Tends to bear heavy crops in alternate years. Needs a long growing season (160 days) to ripen properly. Fairly low chill requirement. 'Red Fuji' is an excellent red-skinned form. 'Beni Shogun Fuji' is good for areas with short, cool growing seasons
'Gala'	6-9, 14-16	Early to midseason	Medium size; beautiful red-on-yellow color. Yellow flesh is highly aromatic, firm, crisp, juicy, sweet. Loses flavor in storage	Vigorous, heavy bearer with long, supple branches that break easily; provide support if necessary. Very susceptible to fireblight. Several color strains are available

APPLE

NAME	ZONES	RIPENING DATE	FRUIT	COMMENTS
'Garden Delicious'	1–3, 6–9, 14–20	Midseason	Medium to large, golden green with red blush	Genetic dwarf 5–8 ft. tall and as wide
'Ginger Gold'	1–9, 14–16	Early midseason	Medium to large, yellow, firm, crisp, mild. Resembles 'Golden Delicious'. Good keeper; one of the best early yellow apples	Ripens over 2 to 3 weeks. Susceptible to mildew. Resistant to sunburn
'Golden Delicious' ('Yellow Delicious')	1–3, 6–11, 14–24	Late midseason	Medium to large. Clear yellow color, though it may develop skin russeting in some climates. Similar in shape to 'Delicious', with less prominent knobs. Highly aromatic, crisp. Excellent for eating fresh and cooking	Not related to 'Red Delicious'; different taste, habit. Long bloom season, heavy pollen production make it a good pollenizer. Self-fruitful. Various strains available. Spur types include 'Goldspur', 'Yellospur'
'Golden Russet'	1–3, 6–9, 14–16, 18, 19	Early to midseason	Medium size; greenish yellow to golden brown with heavy russeting. Creamy yellow, sweet flesh. Good fresh or cooked	Vigorous and productive. Partially self-fruitful but better crop with pollenizer
'Gold Rush'	1–3, 6–9, 14–16	Late	Medium size, yellow, often with some russeting. Best after storage	Immune to scab. Good resistance to mildew; some resistance to fireblight
'Gordon'	18–24; H1	Midseason	Large, greenish yellow blushed red. Sweet-tart flavor	Tree vigorous, upright, semidwarf. Many closely spaced spurs. Long blooming, bearing periods. Low-chill variety
'Granny Smith'	7–11, 14–16	Midseason (later in cool-summer areas)	Large, bright to yellowish green, firm fleshed, tart. Good quality. Stores well; makes good pies, sauce	Australian favorite before it came to U.S. Chancy in cold areas because of late ripening
'Gravenstein'	Widely sold in 4–11, 14–24; best in 15–17	Early to midseason	Large, with brilliant red stripes over deep yellow ground. Crisp, aromatic, juicy. Excellent for fresh eating; makes applesauce with character	Justly famous variety of California's north coast apple district. Pollen-sterile; will not pollinate other varieties. Susceptible to mildew in Zones 4–6. 'Red Gravenstein' is more highly colored
'Haralson'	1–3, 7, 14–16	Early to midseason	Medium size; red ground with deeper red stripes. Crisp, juicy, mildly tart white flesh	Hardy, vigorous, productive tree. Moderate resistance to fireblight
'Honeycrisp'	1–7, 14–16	Midseason	Medium size, red, firm, crisp; excellent sweet-tart flavor	Hardy apple from Minnesota. Resistant to fireblight; somewhat resistant to scab
'Hudson's Golden Gem'	2–6, 7, 14–16	Early to midseason	Elongated, with light brown–russeted skin and crisp, nutty flesh. Good for desserts	Productive; fruit holds well on the tree. Resistant to scab, mildew, and fireblight
'Idared'	4–6, 15–17	Late	Medium to large, bright red apple with firm white flesh, tart at picking time. Stores well, and flavor sweetens in storage	Begins bearing at a young age. Heavy producer
'Jonagold'	2–9, 14–17	Late midseason	Large; heavy red striping over yellow ground. Firm, juicy; fine mildly tart flavor. A frequent taste-test favorite	Productive medium-size tree. Pollen-sterile; won't pollinate other varieties. Not pollinated by 'Golden Delicious'
'Jonathan'	Sold everywhere; best in 2, 3, 7	Midseason	Small to medium, roundish oblong apple with bright red skin. Juicy, moderately tart, crackling crisp, sprightly. All-purpose apple, good keeper	Subject to mildew, somewhat resistant to scab
'Karmijn de Sonnaville'	4–6	Late	Medium size. Deep red over yellow; russeted. Excellent sweet-tart flavor. Great fresh or stored	Intense, complex flavor
'Liberty'	4–9, 14–16	Late midseason	Medium size, heavy red blush. Crisp, with fine sweet-tart flavor, dessert quality	Productive tree. Immune to scab; can get mildew west of Cascades. Resists rust, fireblight
'Lodi'	A2, A3; 1–3, 6–11, 14–16	Early	Medium size, greenish yellow, tart. Good for cooking, keeps well	Large, hardy tree; tends to bear heavily in alternate years
'McIntosh'	2, 3, 14–16	Midseason	Medium to large, bright red, nearly round. Snowy white, tender flesh. Excellent tart flavor	Fine choice for cooler climates if given good care. Very susceptible to scab, preharvest fruit drop

A

APPLE

NAME	ZONES	RIPENING DATE	FRUIT	COMMENTS
'Melrose'	1–7, 15, 16	Late	Medium to large, roundish, red ground striped deeper red. Flesh white, mildly tart, aromatic. Stores exceptionally well; good dessert apple	Cross between 'Jonathan' and 'Delicious'. Somewhat mildew resistant. Considered one of the best in Northwest
'Mollie's Delicious'	8, 9, 14–20	Early	Large, light yellow blushed red. Light yellow, aromatic, juicy, sweet flesh. Stores well	Self-fruitful; bears from an early age. Low-chill variety
'Mutsu' ('Crispin')	7–9, 15, 16	Late	Very large, greenish yellow blushed red. Cream-colored, very crisp flesh, somewhat tarter than 'Golden Delicious'. Excellent dessert and cooking apple with long storage life	Exceptionally large and vigorous tree. Pollen-sterile; won't pollinate other varieties
'Newtown Pippin' ('Yellow Newtown', 'Yellow Pippin')	1–11, 14–22	Late	Large, green. Crisp and tart, fair for eating, excellent for cooking	Large, vigorous tree. Excellent California central coast commercial variety. Susceptible to mildew in Zones 4–6
'Norland'	A1–A3; 1–3	Early	Medium size, oblong, pinkish striped with red. Good fresh or cooked. Stores well	Hardy variety from Canada. Other Canadian introductions such as 'Noran', 'Noret', 'Norson', 'Parkland', and 'Westland' are also good in coldest-winter areas
'Northern Spy'	1–3, 6, 7, 14–16	Late	Large, red skinned. Tender, fine-grained flesh with sprightly flavor. Not attractive but excellent dessert and cooking apple. Keeps well	Slow to reach bearing age
'Oriole'	A2, A3; 1–3, 7, 14–16	Early	Large apple with yellow-orange skin striped or spotted with red. Excellent fresh or cooked	Productive tree with excellent hardiness. Susceptible to mildew
'Paulared'	2, 3, 6, 7, 14–16	Early	Large, round to flattish; solid red blush. Crisp, mildly tart flesh. One of the best early apples	Strong, upright tree. Thrives west of Cascades in Northwest. Somewhat resistant to scab
'Pettingill'	23, 24	Midseason to late	Large, thick skinned, red-blushed green to red. Firm, tasty, moderately acid white flesh	Large, upright, productive tree; regular bearer. Very low chill requirement
'Pink Lady'	6–15	Late	Medium to large. Pink to light red blush over yellow skin; firm, juicy flesh. Sweet-tart flavor. Improves with storage. Good fresh, baked, or as sauce	From Australia; does well in warm-summer areas. Very susceptible to fireblight. Moderately low chilling requirement. Self-fruitful
'Pink Pearl'	1–9, 14–16	Early	Medium size. Pale green skin, sometimes blushed red. Sweet-tart pink flesh. Makes colorful sauce. Good keeper	Very attractive in bloom; blossoms deeper pink than on most other varieties
'Pristine'	3–11, 14–16, 18, 19	Early	Medium; bright yellow skin, mildly tart white flesh. Good for eating, baking, applesauce	Immune to scab; somewhat resistant to mildew, fireblight
'Redfree'	4–9, 14–17	Early	Medium size. Red skin; firm, crisp flesh with good flavor	Heavy bearer. Immune to scab
'Rome Beauty' ('Red Rome')	3, 6, 7, 10, 11	Late	Large, round, smooth red apple with greenish white flesh. Original 'Rome Beauty' has been supplanted by more uniformly red-skinned types like 'Red Rome'. Outstanding baking apple, only fair for eating fresh	Bears at an early age
'Rubinette'	4–6	Midseason	Small to medium. Golden with red stripes, some russeting. Excellent, sweet-tart flavor	Resists scab and mildew
'Sierra Beauty'	2, 3, 6–9, 14–16	Late	Large, exceptionally attractive yellow apple with red stripes. Firm, sweet-tart flesh. Keeps well	Productive tree
'Spartan'	4–7, 15, 16	Midseason	Medium size. Dark red with purplish bloom; crisp flesh. Good flavor, similar to that of 'McIntosh'	Good tree habit. Heavy producer

APPLE

A

NAME	ZONES	RIPENING DATE	FRUIT	COMMENTS
'Spitzenberg' ('Esopus Spitzenberg')	1–7, 14–16; best in 1–3	Late	Medium to large, red-dotted yellow. Crisp, fine grained, tangy, spicy	Old favorite that still rates high. Subject to fireblight, mildew
'Stayman'	1–3, 7, 10, 11	Late	Large red apple with green and russet dots. Fine-grained, firm, juicy flesh with lively flavor	Pollen-sterile; won't pollinate other varieties. Old-timer that still has its devotees. Susceptible to scab
'Summerred'	A2, A3; 1–7, 15, 16	Early	Medium size, bright red; tart and good chiefly for cooking until fully ripe, then good dessert quality too	Hardy. Consistent annual bearer for western Oregon and Washington. Goes overripe too fast in hot-summer climates
'Sundowner'	6–15	Midseason to late	Medium size. Red with crispy, sweet flesh. Stores well	Newer variety from Australia. Tends to bear heavily in alternate years
'Tropical Beauty'	18–24; H1	Early	Medium to large, bright red. Juicy white flesh with mild, sweet flavor	Partially self-fruitful; production enhanced if it grows near 'Adina'
'Wealthy' ('Red Wealthy', 'Double Red Wealthy')	1–7	Early midseason	Medium to large, rough, red. Flesh white with pink veining, firm, tart, juicy. Good cooking variety	Small, cold-hardy tree that tends to bear in alternate years. Not for hot climates
'William's Pride'	1–7	Early	Medium-size, dark red fruit with sweet-spicy flavor. One of the best early red apples	Immune to scab; resistant to fireblight; susceptible to mildew
'Winter Banana'	7–9, 14–24	Late midseason	Large, attractive, pale yellow blushed pink; waxy finish. Tender, tangy, aromatic	Low-chill variety. There is a 'Spur Winter Banana'
'Winter Pearmain' ('White Winter Pearmain')	20–24	Midseason	Medium to large. Pale greenish yellow skin with pink blush. Tender, fine-grained flesh; excellent flavor	Low-chill variety. Performs better than standard cold-winter varieties in Southern California
'Yellow Transparent'	A2, A3; 1–3, 7, 14–16	Early	Medium size. Thin yellow skin with tart white flesh. Good for cooking if harvested when greenish yellow	Tall, vigorous tree with excellent hardiness

'Crimson Spire' Columnar apple tree

TOP: 'Jonathan'
BOTTOM: 'Newtown Pippin'

TOP: 'Gravenstein'
BOTTOM 'Pink Pearl'

'Gala'   'Braeburn'   'William's Pride'   'Pettingill'   'Anna'   'Jonagold'   'Gordon'   'Mutsu'   'Gala'   'Liberty'   'Winter Pearmain'

A

care in feeding and watering. Genetic dwarf apples, such as 'Garden Delicious', are naturally small and stay that way; even grafting them onto a standard (nondwarfing) rootstock would not produce a standard-size tree.

Semidwarf trees are larger than dwarfs but smaller than standard trees. They bear bigger crops than dwarfs and take up less space than standards. Many commercial orchards get high yields by using semidwarf trees and planting them close together. Semidwarfing rootstocks MARK, M26, and M7 reduce normal tree height by about half; the trees may be espaliered or trellised if planted 12–16 ft. apart and allowed to grow 8–12 ft. tall. Semidwarfing rootstocks MM106 and MM111 reduce height by approximately 15 to 25 percent.

Apples bear flowers and fruit on spurs—short branches that grow from wood 2 years old or older. Spurs normally begin to appear only after tree has grown in place 3 to 5 years. On spur-type apples, spurs form earlier (within 2 years after planting) and grow closer together on shorter branches, giving more apples per foot of branch. Spur apples are natural or genetic semidwarfs about two-thirds the size of standard apple trees. They can be further dwarfed by grafting onto dwarfing rootstocks; EMLA27, M9, P22, and MARK give smallest trees.

Columnar apple trees develop a single spirelike trunk to 8 ft. tall, with fruiting spurs directly on the trunk or on very short branchlets. Total width does not exceed 2 ft. Varieties include 'Crimson Spire', red fruit with tart-sweet white flesh; 'Emerald Spire', mellow, sweet green fruit with gold blush; 'Golden Sentinel', sweet, juicy yellow fruit; 'Northpole', crisp, juicy McIntosh-type apple; 'Scarlet Sentinel', large, sweet green-yellow fruit with red blush; 'Scarlet Spire', juicy red-and-green eating apple; and 'Ultra Spire', tart, tangy red apple with yellowish blush. Two varieties are needed for pollination. Columnar trees are easy to maintain and attractive as accent, screen, or container plants. Plant at least 18 in. apart.

Training and pruning apple trees. For most home use, plant dwarf or semidwarf trees for ease in maintenance and harvest. Even commercial growers favor these smaller trees, since closer spacing permits more trees to the acre and a heavier crop. Preferred style is pyramidal or modified leader, in which widely angled branches are encouraged to grow in spiral placement around the trunk. Don't worry about fruit production the first 4 or 5 years—prune to develop strong, evenly spaced scaffold branches. Keep narrow-angled crotches from developing; don't let side branches outgrow the leader or secondary branches outgrow the primary branches.

To prune mature trees (do it late in the dormant season), remove weak, dead, or poorly placed branches and twigs, especially those growing toward the center of the tree (bearing is heaviest when some sun can reach the middle). Removing such growth will encourage development of strong new wood with new fruiting spurs (on apples, spurs may produce for up to 20 years but they tend to weaken after about 3 years) and discourage mildew. If you have inherited an old tree, selective thinning of branches will accomplish the same goal.

Dwarf trees can be grown as espaliers tied to wood or wire frames, fences, or other supports. The technique requires manipulating the branches to the desired pattern and pruning out excess growth. On columnar apples, just remove any wayward growth.

For ornamental relatives, see *Malus*.

APRICOT
Rosaceae
DECIDUOUS FRUIT TREES

- ⚡ **ZONES VARY BY VARIETY**
- ☀ **FULL SUN**
- ♦ **REGULAR WATER DURING FRUIT DEVELOPMENT**

Known botanically as *Prunus armeniaca,* this stone fruit originated in China. It can be grown throughout much of the West, with some limitations. Because apricot trees bloom early in the season, they will not fruit in regions with late frosts. In cool, humid coastal areas, tree and fruit are usually subject to brown rot and blight; in mild-winter areas of Southern California, only varieties with low requirements for winter chill do well.

Standard apricot trees reach 15–20 ft. high and wide and make good, easily maintained dual-purpose fruit and shade trees; they can also be espaliered. Thin, roundish leaves to 3 in. long are reddish when new, maturing to bright green; flowers are pink or white.

Apricot trees bear most of their fruit on short spurs that form on the previous year's growth and remain fruitful for about 4 years. Most varieties ripen from late spring into summer. To get a good crop of large fruit, do this: in midspring, thin excess fruit from branches, leaving 2–4 in. between individual fruits. Prune in summer (rather than in the dormant season, as is usually recommended) to avoid Eutypa dieback, a disease characterized by sudden limb dieback and oozing cankers; it is spread by rain and can infect trees through pruning wounds.

Apricots are subject to various other diseases and insect pests. To avert some problems, consult your Cooperative Extension Office for a local timetable and directions for preventive spraying. Essential treatment dates are during dormancy, before and after flowering, and at red-bud stage.

The following is a good representation of nursery varieties; many are available on dwarf and semidwarf rootstocks. Some varieties need a pollenizer, as indicated. For ornamental relatives, see *Prunus*.

'August Glo'. Zones 8, 9, 12–16, 18–23. Medium-size fruit with exceptional sweet-tart flavor. Late.

Apricot

'Autumn Royal'. Zones 2, 3, 6–9, 12–16, 18–24. Resembles 'Blenheim' but fruit ripens very late; only fall-ripening apricot tree.

'Blenheim' ('Royal'). Zones 2, 3, 6–23. Standard variety in California's apricot regions. Good for canning or drying. Early to midseason.

'Chinese' ('Mormon'). Zones 1–3, 6. Late bloom, hardy tree; good production in late-frost and cold-winter regions. Mid- to late season.

'Floragold'. Zones 2, 3, 6–23. Full-size fruit grows on natural semidwarf tree (about two-thirds the size of standard apricot tree). Reliable producer. Early.

'Goldcot'. Zones 1–3. Developed for cold climates. Sweet flavor. Midseason.

'Golden Amber'. Zones 2, 3, 6–9, 12–16, 18–23. Like 'Blenheim' but blooms over month-long period; fruit ripens late.

'Gold Kist'. Zones 8, 9, 12–16, 18–23. Excellent sweet-tart flavor. Heavy bearing, even in mild-winter areas. Early.

'Harcot'. Zones 1–11, 14–16. Medium to large fruit is sweet, rich, and juicy. Frost hardy, blooms late. Early.

'Harglow'. Zones 1–11, 14–16. Medium-size orange fruit, sometimes blushed red. Firm, sweet, flavorful. Late blooming; disease resistant. Early.

'Katy'. Zones 2, 3, 6–23. Large yellow fruit with red blush. Mild, sweet flavor. Favorite in mild-winter areas. Early.

'King'. Zones 8, 9, 12–16, 18–23. Very large, very highly colored.

What Apricots Need

CLIMATE Ideal climate provides chilly winters, freedom from late frosts, and fairly warm, dry springs.

POLLINATION Most varieties are self-fruitful; some need pollen from another apricot variety.

PRUNING Moderation is the key. The goal is to conserve enough new growth to produce adequate new fruiting spurs and to remove old, exhausted spurs.

'Puget Gold'

DISEASE PREVENTION Several rounds of preventive sprays may keep some problems at bay.

Hard to pollinate; 'Perfection' does best job. Early.

Manchurian apricot (*Prunus armeniaca mandshurica*). Zones A2, A3; 1–3. Hardy shrub to small tree. Small, mild-flavored orange fruit, good for drying. Early.

'Montrose'. Zones 2–3, 6–12, 14–18. Yellow skin with a red blush; sweet and juicy, with excellent flavor. Large fruit and "sweet" edible kernel. A hardy, frost-resistant variety from Montrose, Colorado. Late.

'Moongold'. Zones 1–3. Plum-size, golden, sweet, and sprightly fruit. Developed for cold-winter climates. Late.

'Moorpark'. Zones 2, 3, 6–11, 14–16. Very large fruit, fine flavor. Color develops unevenly. Good home dessert or drying variety, poor canner. Midseason.

'Newcastle'. Zones 10–12, 20–23. Good Southern California variety; needs little winter chill. Midseason.

'Perfection' ('Goldbeck'). Zones 2–9, 12–16, 18–23. Fruit very large but flavor only mediocre. Low chill requirement; hardy tree. Needs pollenizer. Early.

'Puget Gold'. Zones 4–6. Consistent bearer in Puget Sound area; fairly resistant to apricot diseases. Medium-size fruit with good flavor; low in acid. Late.

'Riland'. Zones 2, 3, 6. Highly colored, roundish fruit. Needs pollenizer. Midseason.

'Rival'. Zones 2–6. Large, oval orange fruit blushed red. Needs early-flowering pollenizer, such as 'Perfection'. Early.

'Royalty'. Zones 2, 3, 6–9, 12–23. Extra-large fruit on heavy, wind-resistant spurs. Begins bearing at early age. Ripens early.

'Sun-Glow'. Zones 2–6. Highly colored, early fruit. Hardy tree with extra-hardy fruit buds. Midseason.

'Sungold'. Zones 1–3. Plum-size, slightly flattened, bright orange, sweet, mild fruit. Developed for cold-winter climates. Early.

'Tilton'. Zones 1–8, 10, 11, 18, 20. Higher chill requirement than 'Blenheim' but less subject to brown rot and sunburn. Midseason.

'Tomcot'. Zones 8, 9, 12–16. Large fruit with sweet orange flesh. Needs a pollenizer for best production. Early.

'Wenatchee' ('Wenatchee Moorpark'). Zones 2, 3, 6. Large fruit, excellent flavor. Midseason.

APRIUM.
See **PLUM HYBRIDS**

APTENIA cordifolia (Mesembryanthemum cordifolium)
Aizoaceae
SUCCULENT SHRUBBY PERENNIAL

🌿 ZONES 12, 13, 15–17, 21–24; H1, H2

☀️ ◑ ⬤ SOME SHADE IN HOTTEST CLIMATES

◌ 💧 LITTLE TO MODERATE WATER

Aptenia cordifolia

South African ice plant relative. Trailing stems to 2 ft. long are profusely set with inch-wide, heart-shaped or oval, fleshy bright green leaves. Purplish red, inch-wide flowers bloom in spring and summer. Despite fleshy foliage, it looks less like ice plant than most other related plants do. Use as low trailer in rock garden, on slope or wall; plant 2 ft. apart. Also good in hanging pot. 'Variegata' has white-bordered leaves; hybrid 'Red Apple' has brighter red flowers.

AQUILEGIA
COLUMBINE
Ranunculaceae
PERENNIALS

🌿 ZONES VARY BY SPECIES

☀️ ◑ FULL SUN OR LIGHT SHADE

💧 REGULAR WATER

Lacy foliage and beautifully poised flowers in exquisite pastels, deeper shades, and white give columbines a fairylike, woodland-glen quality. Plants are erect and range from 2 in. to 4 ft. high, depending on species or hybrid. Divided leaves reminiscent of maidenhair fern (*Adiantum*) may be fresh green, blue green, or gray green. Slender, branching stems carry erect or nodding flowers to 3 in. across, often with sepals and petals in contrasting colors; they usually have backward-projecting, nectar-bearing spurs. Some columbines have large flowers and very long spurs; these have an airier look than short-spurred and spurless kinds. Double-flowered types lack the delicacy of the single-flowered

sort, but they make a bolder color mass. Bloom season comes in spring and early summer.

Plants are not fussy about soil as long as it is well drained. On all columbines, cut back old stems for second crop of flowers. All kinds attract hummingbirds. Most are not long-lived and will need to be replaced every 3 or 4 years. Allow spent flowers to form seed capsules to ensure a crop of volunteer seedlings. If you're growing hybrids, the seedlings won't necessarily duplicate the parent plants, but seedlings from species (if grown isolated from other columbines) should closely resemble the originals. Leaf miners are a potential pest, especially on hybrids.

A. alpina. ALPINE COLUMBINE. Zones A1–A3; 1–9, 14–24. Native to the Alps. Grows 1–2 ft. tall, 1 ft. wide. Nodding, bright blue flowers to 2 in. across, with curved spurs to 1 in. long. Good rock garden plant.

A. caerulea. ROCKY MOUNTAIN COLUMBINE. Zones A1–A3; 1–11, 14–24. Native to the Rockies; state flower of Colorado. To 1½–3 ft. high, 2 ft. wide. Blue-and-white flowers erect, 2 in. or more across, with straight or spreading spurs to 2 in. long. An important parent of many long-spurred hybrids.

A. chrysantha. GOLDEN COLUMBINE, GOLDEN-SPURRED COLUMBINE. Zones 1–24. Native to Arizona, New Mexico, and adjacent Mexico. One of the showiest species. Large, many-branched plant to 3–4 ft. tall, 1–2 ft. wide. Undersides of leaflets densely covered with soft hairs. Upright, clear yellow, 1½–3-in. flowers with slender, hooked spurs 2–2½ in. long.

A. desertorum. ARIZONA COLUMBINE. Zones 2b, 3, 6–24. Native to northern Arizona, Utah, New Mexico. To 1½ ft. high, 15 in. wide. Rich bright orange to yellow, 1½-in. flowers. Spurs are held in the same plane as the rest of the blossom and extend beyond it, giving the bloom as a whole a distinct arrowhead shape.

A. flabellata. Zones A2, A3; 1–9, 14–24. Native to Japan. Stocky plant 8 in.–1½ ft. high, 1 ft. wide, with nodding, 1½-in., two-tone flowers of lilac blue and creamy white. Hooked spurs to 1 in. long.

Differs from most other columbines in having thicker, darker leaves with often overlapping segments. The Cameo series is dwarf (4–8 in. high) and comes with two-toned flowers of white and blue, pink, or rose. *A. f. minor* is a very dwarf form (just 4 in. high). Good rock garden plant.

A. formosa. WESTERN COLUMBINE. Zones A1–A3; 1–11, 14–24. Native Alaska to Northern California, Montana, Utah. Grows 1½–3 ft. tall, 1½ ft. wide. Nodding red-and-yellow flowers are 1½–2 in. across, with stout, straight red spurs. Good in woodland garden. Allow it to set seeds, which are relished by song sparrows, juncos, and other small birds. *A. f. truncata* (sometimes sold as *A. californica*) bears yellow-and-orange blossoms that have red spurs.

A. hybrids. Zones A2, A3; 1–10, 14–24. Derived from several species. Preferred tall hybrid strains include graceful, long-spurred McKana Hybrids and double-flowering 'Spring Song' (both to 3 ft. tall, 2 ft. wide). Nora Barlow Mixed, reaching 2–2½ ft. tall and 2 ft. wide, has double flowers in a wide range of colors (the original 'Nora Barlow' has reddish pink blooms with white margins). About the same size is Vervaeneana Woodside Variegated Mixed, with variegated leaves and various flower colors.

Lower-growing strains include Biedermeier and Dragonfly (1 ft. high and wide); long-spurred Music (1½ ft. high and wide); long-blooming Origami (16–18 in. high); and single to double, upward-facing Fairyland (15 in. high and wide).

Aquilegia McKana Hybrid

A. longissima. Zones 1–11, 14–24. Native to southwest Texas, southern Arizona, and northern Mexico. Grows 2½–3 ft. tall, 1½–2 ft. wide. Similar to *A. chrysantha*. Numerous erect, pale yellow blossoms with very narrow, drooping, 4–6-in.-long spurs.

A. saximontana. Zones 1–10, 14–24. Native to the Rocky Mountains. In effect, a miniature *A. caerulea*, just 4–8 in. high and wide.

A. sibirica. Zones A1–A3; 1–6. To 2 ft. tall and wide, with short-spurred, 1½-in., blue to dark purplish red flowers on leafless stalks.

A. vulgaris. EUROPEAN COLUMBINE. Zones A2, A3; 1–10, 14–24. Naturalized in eastern U.S. Grows 1–2½ ft. tall, 1 ft. wide. Nodding blue or violet flowers to 2 in. across; short, knobby spurs about ¾ in. long. Many selections and hybrids offer single to fully double blooms, either short spurred or spurless.

ARABIS
ROCKCRESS
Brassicaceae (Cruciferae)
PERENNIALS

| 🌿 ZONES VARY BY SPECIES |
| ☀️ FULL SUN |
| 💧 MODERATE WATER |

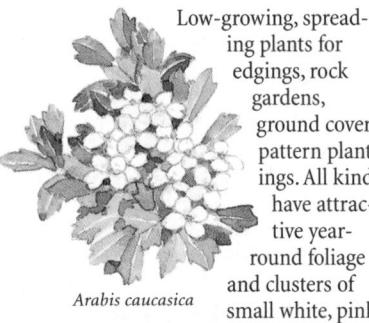
Arabis caucasica

Low-growing, spreading plants for edgings, rock gardens, ground covers, pattern plantings. All kinds have attractive year-round foliage and clusters of small white, pink, or rose purple flowers in spring. Give good drainage.

A. alpina. MOUNTAIN ROCKCRESS. Zones 1–7. Native to high elevations of Europe. Low, tufted, rough-hairy plant 4–10 in. high, 2 ft. wide. White flowers in dense, short clusters. 'Rosea' bears pink flowers; 'Variegata' has yellow-edged green leaves. Plants sold as *A. alpina* are often really *A. caucasica*.

A. blepharophylla. CALIFORNIA ROCKCRESS, ROSE CRESS. Zones 5, 6, 15–17. Native to rocky hillsides and ridges along Northern California coast. Tufted plant to about 8 in. high and wide. Fragrant rose purple flowers in short, dense clusters. Good in rock garden, containers.

A. caucasica (A. albida). WALL ROCKCRESS. Zones A1; 1–10, 14–24. Dependable old favorite; native Mediterranean region to Iran. Forms mat of gray-green leaves to 6 in. high, 1½ ft. wide. White flowers almost cover plant during bloom season. Excellent ground cover and base planting for spring-flowering bulbs such as daffodils and 'Paper White' narcissus. Provide some shade in hot climates. 'Variegata' has gray leaves with creamy white margins; 'Flore Plena' is double flowered; 'Rosabella' and 'Pink Charm' bear pink blossoms.

A. ferdinandi-coburgi. Zones 2b–10, 14–24. Native to Bulgaria. Tight clumps to 4 in. high, 1 ft. wide. White blossoms. Most common form is 'Variegata', with leaves heavily edged and splashed with white.

A. procurrens. Zones 3–10, 14–24. Native to southeastern Europe. Creeping plant with 1½-in. leaves and white flowers clustered on 4–12-in. stems. Over time, spreads widely.

A. × sturii. Zones 1–10, 14–24. Dense, fist-size cushions of small bright green leaves eventually grow into small mats bearing clusters of white flowers on 2–3-in. stems. Some consider it among the finest rock garden plants.

ARACHNIODES
simplicior
Dryopteridaceae
FERN

| 🌿 ZONES 4–24 |
| ◐ PARTIAL OR FULL SHADE |
| 💧💧 REGULAR TO AMPLE WATER |

From Japan and China; sometimes referred to as holly fern. Usually seen in its variety 'Variegata', growing 10–16 in. tall and twice as wide. Fronds are broadly triangular, and once-divided, the divisions deeply cut. Each division is marked by a yellow stripe along its full length. Evergreen where winters are warm; deciduous in frosty regions.

Arachniodes simplicior
'Variegata'

ARALIA
Araliaceae
DECIDUOUS SHRUB-TREES

| 🌿 ZONES VARY BY SPECIES |
| ☀️◐ FULL SUN OR PARTIAL SHADE |
| 💧💧 MODERATE TO REGULAR WATER |

Most are striking bold-leafed plants that may eventually grow to 25–30 ft. tall under ideal conditions. Not for small gardens. Often shrublike and multi-stemmed (because of suckering habit), especially in colder areas where they may grow to 10 ft. tall.

Aralia elata

Clumps may be from one-half to almost as wide as they are tall. Branches are nearly vertical or slightly spreading, usually very spiny. Huge leaves, clustered at ends of branches and divided into many leaflets, have effective pattern value. White flowers, small but in such large, branched clusters that they are showy in midsummer, are followed by purplish berrylike fruit enjoyed by birds.

Grow in well-drained soil. Not good near swimming pools because of spines; even leafstalks are sometimes prickly. Protect plants from wind to avoid burning foliage. Need minimal pruning; dig out suckers to limit spread.

A. elata (A. chinensis). ANGELICA TREE. Zones 1–10, 14–24. Native to Asia. Only moderately spiny. Leaves 2–3 ft. long, divided into toothed, stalkless, 2–6-in.-long leaflets. 'Variegata' has leaflets strikingly bordered with creamy white.

A. elegantissima. See Schefflera elegantissima

A. papyrifera. See Tetrapanax papyrifer

A. sieboldii. JAPANESE ARALIA. See Fatsia japonica

A. spinosa. HERCULES' CLUB, DEVIL'S WALKING STICK. Zones 3–9, 14–24. Native to eastern U.S. Puts up several spiny, usually unbranched stems, each of them crowned by 2–6-ft.-long leaves. This is one of the most tropical-looking genuinely hardy plants. Has a coarse appearance in winter.

ARAUCARIA
Araucariaceae
EVERGREEN TREES

| 🌿 ZONES VARY BY SPECIES |
| ☀️ FULL SUN |
| 💧 REGULAR WATER |

These strange-looking conifers provide a distinctive silhouette with their evenly spread tiers of stiff branches. Most have stiff, closely overlapping, dark to bright green leaves. All do well in a wide range of soils with adequate drainage.

Make impressive skyline trees and are seen in that role in many parks and old estates in California —but they become so towering that they really do need the space they have in a park or large, open property. And they are not trees to sit under—with age they bear large, spiny, 10–15-lb. cones that fall with a crash. They thrive in containers for several years, even in desert areas.

A. araucana (A. imbricata). MONKEY PUZZLE TREE. Zones 4–9, 14–24; H1, H2. Native to Chile. Arboreal oddity with heavy, spreading branches and ropelike branchlets closely set with sharp-pointed dark green leaves. Slow growing in youth, it eventually reaches 70–90 ft. tall, 30 ft. wide. Hardiest of araucarias.

A. bidwillii. BUNYA-BUNYA. Zones 7–9, 12–24; H1, H2. Native to Australia. Probably most widely planted araucaria in both coastal and valley

Araucaria araucana

areas of California. Moderate growth to 80 ft. tall, 60 ft. wide; broadly rounded crown supplies dense shade. Juvenile leaves are glossy, rather narrow, ¾–2 in. long, stiff, more or less spreading in two rows; mature leaves are oval, ½ in. long, rather woody, spirally arranged and overlapping along branches. Unusual houseplant; very tough and tolerant of low light.

A. heterophylla (A. excelsa). NORFOLK ISLAND PINE. Zones 17, 21–24; H1, H2. Native to Norfolk Island near Australia. Moderate growth rate to 100 ft. tall, 60 ft. wide. Pyramidal shape. Juvenile leaves rather narrow, ½ in. long, curved, sharp pointed; mature leaves somewhat triangular, densely overlapping. Can be held

Araucaria heterophylla

in pots for years—outdoors in mild climates, indoors anywhere. Popular Christmas tree in Hawaii.

ARBORVITAE. See THUJA

ARBUTUS
Ericaceae
EVERGREEN TREES OR SHRUBS

⬛ ZONES VARY BY SPECIES

☀ FULL SUN, EXCEPT AS NOTED

◍ LITTLE TO REGULAR WATER, EXCEPT AS NOTED

All have ornamental bark, clusters of little urn-shaped flowers, decorative edible fruit, handsome foliage. Provide good drainage, especially if plant receives regular water. Thin growth of all types as needed.

Arbutus unedo

A. andrachne. Zones 8, 9, 14–24. Native to eastern Mediterranean. To 20–40 ft. tall and wide. Like *A. menziesii* but is not as difficult to grow and has smaller, less shiny leaves. Peeling bark is beautiful.

A. 'Marina'. Zones 8, 9, 14–24. Hybrid of uncertain parentage. To 30 ft. tall (usually less) and equally wide. Resembles *A. unedo* but has larger leaves and rosy pink fall flowers. Good garden substitute for *A. menziesii*.

A. menziesii. MADRONE, MADRONA. Zones 4–7, 14–19. Native from British Columbia to Southern California in Coast Ranges, occasionally in middle elevations of Sierra Nevada. Mature height ranges from 20 to 100 ft. Forms broad, round head almost as wide as tall. In groves, plants are more slender. Main feature is smooth, reddish brown bark that peels in thin flakes. Leathery, 3–6-in.-long leaves are shiny dark green on top, dull gray green beneath. In spring, large clusters of white to pinkish, bell-shaped flowers appear at branch ends. These are followed in early fall by clusters of brilliant orange to red, rough-coated berries that remain on tree most of winter if birds don't get them.

If you live in madrone country and have a tree in your garden, treasure it. Its requirements in gardens outside its native area are exacting: it must have fast drainage and nonalkaline water. Irrigate just enough to keep plants going until they are established, and then give only infrequent and deep watering.

A. unedo. STRAWBERRY TREE. Zones 4–24; damaged in severe winters in Zones 4–7 but worth the risk. Native to southern Europe, Ireland. Remarkably good performance in wide range of climates and soils, from desert to seashore; tolerates wind at the beach. In California, it is one of the best lawn or raised-bed trees. Sun or part shade; needs some shade in the desert.

Slow to moderate growth to 8–35 ft. with equal spread. Normally has basal suckers, stem sprouts. Can thin branches to make open-crowned tree, or plant several and leave unpruned to make screen. Trunk and branches have rich red-brown, shredding bark; tend to become twisted and gnarled in age. Dark green, handsome, red-stemmed leaves are oblong and 2–3 in. long. Clusters of small white or greenish white, urn-shaped flowers and round, ¾-in. fruit, yellow (young) and red (mature), like strawberries in texture, appear at the same time in fall and winter; fruit is edible but usually mealy and bland in flavor. Individual plants may produce tasty fruit.

Varieties include 'Elfin King', a dwarf form (not over 5 ft. tall at 10 years old) that flowers and fruits nearly continuously; 'Compacta', seldom exceeding 10 ft. high; and 'Oktoberfest', a 6–8-ft.-tall plant with deep pink flowers.

ARCHONTO-PHOENIX
Arecaceae (Palmae)
PALMS

⬛ ZONES 21–24; OR INDOORS

☀ SUN OR PART SHADE; BRIGHT INDIRECT LIGHT

◍ MODERATE TO REGULAR WATER

Native to rain forests of eastern Australia; called bangalow or piccabeen palms in that country. They grow to 50 ft. or taller, with 10–15-ft. spread. Mature palms are handsome, stately, difficult to transplant. Where winds are strong, plant in lee of buildings to prevent damage. Young trees can't take frost; mature plants may stand 28°F/–2°C. They tolerate shade and can grow for many years grouped under tall trees. Old leaves shed cleanly, leaving smooth green trunks. Feathery leaves

Archontophoenix cunninghamiana

on mature trees are 8–10 ft. long, green above, gray green beneath. Good potted plants indoors or out.

A. alexandrae. ALEXANDRA PALM. Trunk enlarged toward base.

A. cunninghamiana (Seaforthia elegans). KING PALM. More common than *A. alexandrae*. Trunk not prominently enlarged at base. Clustered amethyst flowers are handsome in summer. Highly recommended for nearly frost-free areas.

ARCTANTHEMUM arcticum. See CHRYSANTHEMUM arcticum

ARCTOSTAPHYLOS
MANZANITA
Ericaceae
EVERGREEN SHRUBS

⬛ ZONES VARY BY SPECIES

☀ FULL SUN OR LIGHT SHADE

◍ LITTLE TO MODERATE WATER

This enormous clan of evergreen woody plants is native to the Far West. Plants vary from creeping ground covers to treelike shrubs, but all have small, urn-shaped white or pink flowers, usually in late winter to early spring, followed by berrylike red or brown fruits that attract birds. (Fruits are noted in descriptions below if they are particularly attractive.) Most are characterized by (and admired for) crooked branches with smooth red to purple bark.

Manzanitas require excellent drainage, but they can tolerate poor soil and in fact

Arctostaphylos densiflora

prefer rocky or sandy, acid soils to rich, heavy ones. To get quick coverage from low ground cover types, plant about 2 ft. apart, then mulch to suppress weeds and encourage rooting along stems. The first summer after planting any manzanita, water every 4 to 7 days, depending on the weather. Once established, plants in warm-summer areas generally thrive on once-a-month watering in well-drained soil; in heavy soil and where summers are cool, they need less frequent irrigation. You may get away with watering just once or twice a summer.

Regular pruning is not required. To make plants denser and more uniformly compact, pinch new spring growth to force branching. On types with interesting branch structure, remove any limbs that detract from effect. Don't cut into bare wood; plants won't send out new growth.

A. 'Austin Hill'. Zones 4–9, 14–24. Smaller (to 8 ft. tall and wide) than *A. manzanita* 'Dr. Hurd', but otherwise similar, with burgundy-colored bark and good tolerance for garden watering.

A. bakeri 'Louis Edmunds'. Zones 4–9, 14–17. Selection of a species native to Sonoma area, California. Upright shrub to 5–6 ft. tall and wide. Gray-green foliage; pink flowers in hanging clusters. Good tolerance for garden watering.

A. × coloradensis. Zones 1–3. Naturally occurring hybrid from cold, high elevation regions of Colorado. Grows 3–4 ft. high and 4–6 ft. wide. Brownish red, peeling bark. Pink spring flowers followed by red fruit. Best in partial shade.

A. columbiana. HAIRY MANZANITA. Zones 4–6, 15–17. Treelike species native to low coastal mountains, central California to British Columbia. Form propagated and sold in northwestern nurseries is called 'Oregon Hybrid'. Low-growing, compact shrub about 3 ft. high and 5–7 ft. wide, with reddish brown bark and 3-in. gray-green leaves. White flowers, red-cheeked brownish fruit. Useful plant, tough enough for highway landscaping in western Oregon and Washington.

A. densiflora. VINE HILL MANZANITA. Zones 7–9, 14–21. Native to Sonoma area, California. Generally low and spreading; outer branches take root when they touch soil. Slender, crooked main stems; smooth, reddish black bark. Small, glossy, light or dark green leaves. White or pink flowers. In bank planting, low types do best on east- or northeast-facing slopes, in loose soil with good drainage.

'Howard McMinn' forms a mound to 5–6 ft. tall (usually much lower), spreading as far as 7 ft. in 5 years. If you prune branch tips (but not those of prostrate branches) after flowering, plant becomes as dense as sheared Kurume azalea. Whitish

A

pink flowers. A similar but somewhat taller and broader variety is 'Harmony'. It's less well known than 'Howard McMinn' but considered the best form by some specialists. 'Sentinel', to 6 ft. or taller and spreading to 8 ft., has light green, downy leaves and more upright growth. Can be trained as small tree by selecting dominant stem or stems and removing others. It is sensitive to salt burn, root rots.

A. edmundsii. LITTLE SUR MANZANITA. Zones 6–9, 14–24. Foot-tall species from coastal Monterey area, California. Several named selections are good ground covers, forming broad mats to about 12 ft. wide. Fast-growing 'Carmel Sur', with neat gray-green foliage and soft pink flowers, has exceptionally good form; very garden-water tolerant. 'Danville' has light green, roundish, inch-long leaves on red stems and bears pink flowers in early to midwinter. Slow-growing 'Little Sur' has dense, flat habit, pointed leaves with reddish margins (bronze when new), and soft pink flowers; good hillside planting. 'Parvifolia' has exceptionally shiny foliage (new growth is rich bronze) and showy pink flowers in early spring.

A. 'Emerald Carpet'. Zones 6–9, 14–24. One of the greenest, most uniform ground cover manzanitas. Forms a dense carpet 8–14 in. tall, mounding slightly higher after many years. Spreads about 5 ft. Roundish oval, ½-in.-long leaves, bright green even in hottest, driest weather. Small pink flowers are not showy. In hot interior valleys, it needs deep irrigation every 2 to 3 weeks.

A. franciscana. Zones 6–9, 14–24. Native to San Francisco but nearly extinct there. Grows to 2½ ft. high, spreads slowly (in 15 years) to 7 ft. White flowers.

A. glauca. Zones 4–9, 14–24. Native California to Baja California. Spreading shrub to 15 ft. tall, 20 ft. wide, with dark reddish brown bark and 3-in., blue-gray leaves. Large, branched clusters of pink to white flowers.

A. hookeri. MONTEREY MANZANITA. Zones 6–9, 14–24. Native to Monterey, California. Slowly forms a dense mound 1½–4 ft. high, spreading 6 ft. or more. Small, glossy green leaves; white to pinkish flowers; shiny, bright red fruit; smooth, red-brown bark. Good on hillsides. 'Monterey Carpet' is a compact grower to 1 ft. high, 12 ft. wide. 'Wayside'

grows 4 ft. tall, 8 ft. or wider; may be slow to fill in but eventually forms dense, attractive mound.

A. 'Indian Hill'. Zones 6–9, 14–24. Ground cover that looks like a small-leafed A. edmundsii. Near-white flowers in winter. Very tolerant of garden watering.

A. insularis. ISLAND MANZANITA. From Channel Islands, California. Zones 16–24. Large, dense shrub to 10–15 ft. tall and wide. Bright green leaves; large, drooping clusters of white flowers in midwinter. 'Canyon Sparkles' is a compact selection (about 4 ft. tall, 6 ft. wide).

A. 'John Dourley'. Zones 6–9, 14–24. One of the best of the newer selections, it grows to 3 ft. tall, 6–10 ft. wide, with gray-green foliage (bronze when new) and pink-tinged white flowers. Good tolerance for garden watering.

A. manzanita. COMMON MANZANITA. Zones 4–9, 14–24. Native to inner Coast Ranges, Sierra Nevada foothills; widely adapted. Tall shrub or shrub-tree 6–20 ft. high, 4–10 ft. wide. Picturesque, crooked branching habit; purplish red bark. Small, shiny, bright to dull green, broadly oval leaves. White to pink flowers in drooping clusters. Fruit starts out white, then turns deep red. 'Dr. Hurd' is a treelike form to 15 ft. tall and as wide or wider, with mahogany bark, large light green leaves, and white winter flowers.

A. × media. Zones 4–9, 14–24. May be a natural hybrid of A. uva-ursi and A. columbiana. Looks like a taller-growing A. uva-ursi (up to 2 ft.), with brighter red branches and leathery dark green leaves; also spreads faster. 'Wood's Red' has leaves that turn reddish in cold weather; it offers a reliable crop of large berries and grows best in the Northwest and in Northern California.

A. nummularia. FORT BRAGG MANZANITA. Zones 14–24. Dense foliage; nearly dome-shaped, low shrub, usually under 2½ ft. high. Small, almost circular bright green leaves; little white flowers. Attractive but considered difficult to grow outside its native north coastal California forests. Needs good drainage, acid soil, and some shade except near coast.

A. 'Pacific Mist'. Zones 7–9, 14–24. To 2½ ft. tall, at least 10 ft. wide. Spreading stems turn upward near ends. Deep reddish brown bark, narrow gray-green leaves, sparse white bloom. Needs

pinching to force branching, but eventually forms a good, dense ground cover.

A. pajaroensis. PAJARO MANZANITA. Zones 14–24. Native to central Monterey Bay area, California. To 3–8 ft. tall, 10–12 ft. wide. New growth bronzy, maturing to bluish green. Pink to white flowers. 'Paradise' is a choice pink-flowered selection with long-lasting bronze foliage color. 'Warren Roberts' is similar, but mature leaves are more bluish color and new growth is darker bronze.

A. pumila. DUNE MANZANITA. Zones 16, 17. Native to dunes around Monterey Bay, California. Spreading, prostrate habit, to 1–2½ ft. high; branches root freely where they touch ground. Plant 6 ft. apart. Narrowish, dull green leaves. Short, dense clusters of small white to pink flowers. Good ground cover in sandy soil near coast.

A. 'Sunset'. Zones 6–9, 14–24. Natural hybrid between A. hookeri and A. pajaroensis. Foliage is coppery red when new, maturing to bright green. Mounding growth to 4–5 ft. tall, 4–6 ft. wide. Pinkish white flowers.

A. uva-ursi. BEARBERRY, KINNIKINNICK. Zones A1–A3; 1–9, 14–24. Native from Northern California north to Alaska; also widespread in other northern latitudes. Long a popular ground or bank cover in Pacific Northwest and intermountain areas. Plant is prostrate, spreading and rooting as it grows; eventually forms a mat 15 ft. wide. Small, glossy, leathery leaves are bright green, turning red or purplish in winter. White or pinkish flowers are followed by red fruits. Plants are slow to become established; mulch heavily between plants to suppress weeds until branches provide cover. The following named, cutting-grown varieties provide uniform appearance in large plantings.

'Alaska'. Flat grower with small, round dark green leaves.

'Massachusetts'. Small leafed, flat growing. Abundant pinkish white flowers and plentiful fruit. Good resistance to leaf spot and leaf gall in Northwest.

'Point Reyes'. Dark green leaves closely set along branches. More tolerant of heat and drought than 'Radiant'.

'Radiant'. Leaves lighter green and more widely spaced than those of 'Point Reyes'. Heavy crop of large fruit in fall, lasting into winter (but sometimes fails to

fruit if pollinating insects are not active at bloom time).

'Vancouver Jade'. Flat growing like 'Alaska' and 'Massachusetts', but not as wide spreading as those two varieties. Jade green leaves turn bronzy red in winter.

'Wood's Compact'. Compact grower with red branches densely clad in dark green leaves. Pink flowers.

ARCTOTHECA
calendula
CAPE WEED
Asteraceae (Compositae)
PERENNIAL

🖋 ZONES 8, 9, 13–24
☼ FULL SUN
◌ LITTLE OR NO WATER

South African native is a tough, easy-to-grow evergreen ground cover. Plants spread by runners to make a thick cover 6–12 in. high; space 1½ ft. apart for fast cover. Elongated gray-green leaves are deeply cleft. Yellow, 2-in. daisies bloom most of

*Arctotheca
calendula*

the year, peaking in spring. Not fussy about soil. Suffers some frost damage when temperature dips just below freezing, but recovers quickly. Not for small areas, since plants can easily spread out of bounds (though they're easy to remove). Good on hillsides. Mow shaggy plantings to tidy them.

ARCTOTIS
AFRICAN DAISY
Asteraceae (Compositae)
ANNUALS AND PERENNIALS

🖋 ALL ZONES, EXCEPT AS NOTED
☼ FULL SUN
◌ MODERATE WATER

The name "African daisy" can refer to any of several plants from southern Africa, and identities are often confused, even by many seed companies and nurseries. *Arctotis* species have lobed leaves that are rough, hairy, or woolly; their flower heads usually have a contrasting ring of color around the central eye. *Dimorphotheca* species (commonly used for mass color in winter) have smooth green foliage, blooms that are white or in the yellow–orange–salmon range. Trailing ground cover African

A

Arctotis acaulis

...daisies and woody, shrubby white, yellow, or purple African daisies are *Osteospermum*.

In cold-winter areas, set out annuals (or perennials that are grown as annuals) in spring for summer bloom. Where winters are mild, plant in fall or winter for bloom from spring into early summer. Plants suffer in extreme heat and humidity.

A. acaulis. Perennial. Zones 5–9, 14–24. Spreading, stemless clumps of leaves to 1 ft. high. Yellow, 3½-in.-wide flower heads with purplish black centers. 'Magenta' has purplish red flowers.

A. breviscapa. Annual. Smaller than *A. acaulis* (to about 6 in. high), with brown-centered orange-yellow flowers.

A. fastuosa alba (Venidium fastuosum). Annual. Bushy growth to 2 ft. tall and 1½ ft. wide, with gray-green, slightly hairy leaves; white, 3-in.-wide daisies with a yellow ring surrounding a deep blue eye. In selection 'Zulu Prince', an inner ring of yellow and purple encircles a black center.

A. hybrids. Most representatives of *Arctotis* sold in nurseries are hybrids that grow 1–1½ ft. tall and wide. The 3-in.-wide flowers come in white, pink, red, purplish, cream, yellow, and orange, usually with a dark ring around a nearly black central eye. Will self-sow but tend to revert to orange; to perpetuate colors you like, take cuttings. Plants survive as perennials in Zones 7–9, 14–24, but even there they bloom best in their first year.

ARDISIA
MARLBERRY
Myrsinaceae
EVERGREEN SHRUBS

📋 ZONES VARY BY SPECIES

◐ ● PARTIAL OR FULL SHADE

💧 REGULAR WATER

This genus comprises 150 shrub species, but only the following two Asian natives are typically grown

in Western gardens. Valued for handsome foliage and ornamental, beadlike, bright red berries that persist during winter. Provide rich, moisture-retentive, well-drained soil. If necessary, prune lightly before bloom period.

A. crenata (A. crenulata, A. crispa). Zones 15–24; H1, H2; or indoors. In warmest frost-free climates, often grown in the ground or in patio planters. Most familiar as a 1½-ft., single-stemmed houseplant; in a large tub, though, it can reach 4 ft. tall and almost that wide. Spirelike clusters of tiny white or pinkish flowers bloom in spring, carried above the shiny, wavy-edged, 3-in.-long leaves. Houseplants require indirect light in summer, several hours of direct sun in winter.

A. japonica. Zones 6, 15–17. Low shrub that spreads by runners to produce a series of upright branches 6–18 in. high. Makes a good-quality ground cover in shade; set plants about 2 ft. apart. Leathery, 4-in.-long, bright green leaves are clustered at tops of branches. White, ½-in. flowers, two to six in a cluster, appear in fall. Forms with white or gold foliage variegation are sometimes sold.

Ardisia japonica

ARECA lutescens. See **DYPSIS lutescens**

ARECASTRUM romanzoffianum. See **SYAGRUS romanzoffianum**

ARENARIA
SANDWORT
Caryophyllaceae
PERENNIALS

📋 ZONES VARY BY SPECIES

☼ ◐ ● EXPOSURE NEEDS VARY BY SPECIES

💧💧 WATER NEEDS VARY BY SPECIES

Low evergreen plants carpet the ground creating a dense mat of mosslike foliage, have small white

Arenaria montana

flowers in late spring and summer. They are often used as lawn substitutes, between stepping-stones, or for velvety green patches in rock gardens. Can be invasive; hard to eradicate in well-watered gardens. Provide good drainage.

A. balearica. CORSICAN SANDWORT. Zones 4–9, 14–24. Mediterranean native forms a mat to 3 in. high, 1½ ft. wide. Leaves oval, thick, glossy, to ⅛ in. long. Grows best in shade with regular water. Adapted to planting in small areas—for example, to cover soil of container-grown tree.

A. montana. Zones 2–9, 14–24. Native to mountains of southwestern Europe. Grows 2–4 in. high; weak stems up to 1 ft. long, usually covered with soft hairs. Leaves grayish green, ½–¾ in. long. Good plant to let trail over rock or tumble over low wall. Full sun. Moderate water.

A. verna (A. v. caespitosa). See Sagina subulata

ARGEMONE
PRICKLY POPPY
Papaveraceae
ANNUALS OR BIENNIALS

📋 ZONES VARY BY SPECIES

☼ FULL SUN

◌ LITTLE OR NO WATER

Argemone mexicana

Prickly-leafed and prickly-stemmed plants to 3 ft. tall, 1½ ft. wide, with large, showy poppies that bloom mainly in summer. Easy to grow from seeds sown in place or in pots (transplant gently). Will reseed and colonize. Provide good drainage. Seed specialists may offer other species.

A. mexicana. MEXICAN POPPY. Annual. Zones 2, 3, 7–24; H1, H2. Native to West Indies and probably Central America and Florida; naturalized in the Southwest and Hawaii. Yellow to orange, 1½–2½-in. flowers. 'Yellow Lustre' grows 1½–2 ft. tall, has lemony orange blooms.

A. polyanthemos (A. intermedia). Annual or biennial. Zones 2, 3, 7–24. Western native with white, 2½–4-in. flowers.

ARGYRANTHEMUM frutescens. See **CHRYSANTHEMUM frutescens**

ARISAEMA
JACK-IN-THE-PULPIT
Araceae
PERENNIALS FROM TUBERS

📋 ZONES VARY BY SPECIES

◐ ● PARTIAL OR FULL SHADE

💧 REGULAR WATER DURING GROWTH AND BLOOM

Curious rather than beautiful relatives of calla (*Zantedeschia*), attractive both to children and to fanciers of the odd. Flowers are tiny, crowded on a club-shaped fleshy spike (spadix) surrounded by an overarching flower bract (spathe) that is usually green or dull purple in color and often striped in a contrasting color. In late spring, tubers send up one to three leaves, each divided into three or more leaflets. Inflorescences appear on a separate stalk in spring or early summer. As flowers fade, spathe withers and spadix forms orange to red seeds.

Arisaema sikokianum

These are woodland plants, appreciative of organic material in the soil. Plant in fall, setting tubers 1 ft. apart, 2 in. deep. Plants die to the ground in winter; don't let dormant tubers dry out completely. Species other than those listed below may appear from time to time in specialists' catalogs.

A. sikokianum. Zones 3–6, 14–17. From Japan. To 20 in. tall, with 6-in. leaflets. A 4–12-in. stalk supports a 6-in. spathe that is erect rather than arching. Spathe is purplish brown on the outside, yellowish white within; spadix is pure white and expanded at the tip.

A. speciosum. Zones 4–6, 14–17. Himalayan native. A single leaf grows to 2 ft., with 8–16-in.-long leaflets on a stalk marbled with dark purple. Spathe is blackish purple outside, whitish within, and up to 8 in. long; spadix has a long, whiplike tip that can reach 2½ ft. long.

A. tortuosum. Zones 4–6, 14–17. Himalayan native. Can reach 4 ft. tall. Leaves have many narrow leaflets. Green or purple spathe to 6 in. long; spadix protrudes from spathe, then curves upward for several inches.

A. triphyllum. Zones 1–6. From eastern North America; the

A

common Jack-in-the-pulpit familiar to easterners. Grows to 2 ft. tall. Both spathe and spadix are green or purple; spathe is striped in white or green.

ARISTEA ecklonii
Iridaceae
PERENNIAL

| 🌿 ZONES 8, 9, 12–24 |
| ☀️ ◐ FULL SUN OR PARTIAL SHADE |
| 💧 MODERATE WATER |

Native to southern Africa. Swordlike evergreen leaves form clump 2 ft. tall and wide, above which rise winged, flattened, 2½-ft. branching flower stalks that bear bright blue six-petaled flowers less than an inch wide. Individual flowers are short lived, but new ones appear over a long season. Remove spent flower stems to prevent aggressive self-sowing. 'Sonja' has larger leaves and flowers than the species.

Aristea ecklonii

ARISTOLOCHIA
Aristolochiaceae
DECIDUOUS AND EVERGREEN VINES

| 🌿 ZONES VARY BY SPECIES |
| ☀️ ◐ ● EXPOSURE NEEDS VARY BY SPECIES |
| 💧 💧 REGULAR TO AMPLE WATER |

Twining vines noted for curiously shaped flowers in rather sober colors; they resemble curved pipes with flared bowls or birds with bent necks. Vigorous growers; thin out unwanted growth in late dormant season or wait until after bloom. If plant is too thick and tangled for selective thinning, cut it to the ground before spring growth begins.

A. californica. CALIFORNIA DUTCHMAN'S PIPE. Deciduous.

Aristolochia littoralis

Zones 5–10, 14–24. Native to Coast Ranges and Sierra Nevada foothills of Northern California. Will cover an 8- by 12-ft. screen with some training or climb by long, thin shoots 10–16 ft. into any nearby tree without harming it. Flower display comes before leaf-out in winter or early spring; pendulous, 1-in.-long blooms are cream colored with red-purple veins. Bright green, heart-shaped leaves to 5 in. long. Interesting and useful where many less hardy vines would freeze. Sometimes used as a ground cover. Grows from seed. Accepts any soil; needs partial shade.

A. gigantea. GIANT DUTCHMAN'S PIPE. Evergreen. Zones H1, H2; 21–24. From Panama and Brazil. To 15–20 ft. Triangular to heart-shaped, dark green leaves can reach 4 in. across. Blooms from summer to early winter, bearing spectacular flowers to 1 ft. long and half as wide; blossoms are burgundy with creamy white netting and a golden throat. They have an unusual fragrance reminiscent of lemony furniture polish. *A. g.* 'Brasiliensis' (*A. brasiliensis*) has flowers to 10 in. long and 7 in. wide with an intricate netting pattern of white and brown. Grows best in frost-free areas. Sun or partial shade.

A. littoralis (A. elegans). CALICO FLOWER. Evergreen. Zones 23, 24; or indoors. Native to Brazil. Grows 15–25 ft. in native habitat. Wiry, slender stems; heart-shaped leaves 3 in. long. Blooms in summer; whitish buds shaped like little pelicans open to 3-in.-wide, heart-shaped flowers of deep purple veined in creamy white. Needs rich soil, partial shade.

A. macrophylla (A. durior). DUTCHMAN'S PIPE. Deciduous. Zones 2–24; short lived in warm-winter areas. Native to eastern U.S. Easily grown from seed. Large (6–14-in.-long), kidney-shaped deep green leaves are carried in shinglelike pattern to form dense cloak on trellis; the vine will cover a 15- by 20-ft. area in a single season and was once a favorite for screening a porch. Blooms in late spring, early summer. Flowers are almost hidden by leaves; each is a yellowish green, 3-in., curved tube flaring into three brownish purple lobes about 1 in. wide. Thrives in full sun to heavy shade. Average to good soil and ample water produce the fastest growth and the largest leaves. Dutchman's pipe will not stand strong winds.

ARMERIA
THRIFT, SEA PINK
Plumbaginaceae
PERENNIALS

| 🌿 ZONES VARY BY SPECIES |
| ☀️ FULL SUN |
| ◔ 💧 LITTLE TO MODERATE WATER |

Narrow, stiff, evergreen leaves grow in compact tufts or basal rosettes; small white, pink, rose, or red flowers are carried in dense, globular heads. Main bloom period is spring to early summer, but shearing off faded flowers may prolong flowering. Sturdy, dependable plants for edging walks or borders and for tidy mounds in rock gardens or raised beds. Attractive in containers.

Good drainage is essential and permits regular watering, but safest tactic is to water moderately in dry climates, sparingly in moister regions. Tolerate seaside conditions, infertile soil. Clumps spread slowly and need dividing only when bare centers show.

A. alliacea. Zones 1–9, 14–24. From southern Europe. Clumps 2–6 in. high and 20 in. wide produce 8–16-in. blossom stalks with bright pink flowers. 'Leucantha' has white blooms.

Armeria maritima

A. caespitosa (A. juniperifolia). Zones 2b–9, 14–24. Stiff, needle-shaped leaves ½ in. long form low, extremely compact rosettes about 6 in. across. Rose pink or white flowers are carried on 2-in. stems. This little mountain native is very touchy about drainage; apply mulch of fine gravel around plants to prevent basal stem rot, especially in summer.

A. girardii (A. juncea, A. setacea). Zones 6–9, 14–24. From southern France. Narrow, needlelike foliage in dense mounds to 10–12 in. high and wide. Lavender-pink flowers.

A. maritima (Statice armeria, A. vulgaris). COMMON THRIFT. Zones A2, A3; 1–9, 14–24. Native to Europe, North America. Tufted

mounds spread to 1 ft.; leaves are 6 in. long. White to rose pink flowers in tight clusters atop 6–10-in. stalks. Bloom is profuse in spring (goes on almost all year in mildest climates). 'Bloodstone' has rose red flowers, 'Cotton Tail' has white blooms, and 'Splendens' has rose pink blossoms. 'Rubrifolia', with purplish red foliage and rosy pink blossoms, brings color to a rock garden for much of the year.

ARONIA
CHOKEBERRY
Rosaceae
DECIDUOUS SHRUBS

| 🌿 ZONES VARY BY SPECIES |
| ☀️ ◐ FULL SUN OR LIGHT SHADE |
| 💧 💧 💧 MODERATE TO AMPLE WATER |

Native to southern Canada and the eastern U.S., chokeberries are tough, undemanding shrubs, useful as fillers or background plantings. Small white or pinkish flowers in

Aronia arbutifolia

1–2-in. clusters are pretty but not showy—but the fruits that follow are highly decorative and last well into winter. Fall foliage is brightly colored. All chokeberries tend to spread by suckering and are somewhat leggy (good for planting beneath). Tolerate many soils. Prune oldest stems to ground in late dormant season; restrict height and increase bushiness by heading back upright stems.

A. arbutifolia. RED CHOKE-BERRY. Zones 1–7. Clumping shrub to 6–8 ft. tall, with many erect stems bearing shiny leaves that are rich green above, paler beneath. Clustered, long-lasting fruits are ½ in. wide, brilliant red. Fall foliage is likewise bright red, and plants tend to color early. 'Brilliant' ('Brilliantissima') is a selected form with especially fine fall color.

A. melanocarpa. BLACK CHOKEBERRY. Zones A2, A3; 1–7. Typically lower than *A. arbutifolia*—usually 3–5 ft. high, rarely to 10 ft. Purple-red fall foliage. Shiny black fruits, ½ in. wide, may be used for juice or preserves. Can handle soils in low, wet areas as well as dry, sandy sites. Suckers profusely; may get out of hand in small gardens. 'Autumn Magic' has fragrant flowers, reliable fall color.

ARRHENATHERUM
elatius bulbosum
'Variegatum'
BULBOUS OAT GRASS
Poaceae (Gramineae)
PERENNIAL GRASS

⚡ ZONES 1–7, 15–17, 23, 24
☀ ◐ FULL SUN OR PARTIAL SHADE
💧 REGULAR WATER

Arrhenatherum elatius bulbosum
'Variegatum'

Attractive variety of a European species, with narrow leaves boldly edged and striped in white. Good looking in a perennial border or large rock garden; useful for brightening dark places under trees or big shrubs. Makes a graceful clump about 1 ft. high and wide. Flowering stems in summer double the plant's height. Goes dormant in summer in hot climates; performs best in cool seasons and cool climates. If it flops over in heat, shear for fresh growth in fall. Bulbous structures at stem bases root on contact with soil to produce new plants; clumps may periodically need curtailing. Divide and replant as needed.

ARROWWOOD.
See VIBURNUM dentatum

ARTEMISIA
Asteraceae (Compositae)
PERENNIALS AND EVERGREEN SHRUBS

⚡ ZONES VARY BY SPECIES
☀ FULL SUN, EXCEPT AS NOTED
◯ 💧 LITTLE TO MODERATE WATER, EXCEPT AS NOTED

Several species are valuable for interesting leaf patterns and silvery gray or white aromatic foliage (flowers are generally insignificant). Most kinds are excellent in mixed borders, where their white or silvery leaves soften harsh reds and oranges and blend beautifully with blues, lavenders, and pinks. Provide good drainage. Cut nonwoody-stemmed perennials to ground in fall to rejuvenate; prune back woody perennials and shrubs (into older wood if necessary) before first flush of spring growth. Divide perennials in spring or fall; propagate shrubs by cuttings.

A. abrotanum. SOUTHERN-WOOD, OLD MAN. Woody perennial. Zones 2b–24. Native to southern Europe. To 3 ft. tall and wide. Beautiful feathery, lemon-scented gray-green foliage; yellowish white flower heads. Use for pleasantly scented leaves in shrub border. Hang dried sprigs in closet to discourage moths. Burn a few leaves on stove to kill cooking odors.

A. absinthium. COMMON WORMWOOD. Woody perennial. Zones 2–24. Native to Europe, temperate Asia. To 2–4 ft. tall, 2 ft. wide. Silvery gray, finely divided leaves with bitter taste, pungent odor. Tiny yellow flowers. Prune to shape. Divide every 3 years. Background shrub; good gray feature in flower border, particularly fine with delphiniums. 'Lambrook Silver' is a 1½-ft.-tall form with silvery white, especially finely cut leaves.

A. arborescens. Evergreen shrub or woody perennial. Zones 7–9, 14–24. Mediterranean native to 3 ft. (sometimes 5–6 ft.) tall and 4–5 ft. wide. Silvery white, very finely cut foliage. Highly attractive but more tender than other artemisias.

A. australis. AHINAHINA, HINAHINA KUAHIWI. Evergreen shrub or woody perennial. Zones H1, H2. Native to Hawaii. To 3–4 ft. tall and wide, with lacy, silvery leaves. Thrives in rock gardens, in coastal gardens, on steep cliffs, in containers. Needs good drainage.

A. californica. CALIFORNIA SAGEBRUSH. Evergreen shrub. Zones 7–9, 14–24. Native to coastal region from Northern California to Baja California. To 1½–5 ft. tall, 4–7 ft. wide, with finely divided grayish white foliage. Drought tolerant but will drop leaves in extreme drought. 'Canyon Gray' and 'Montara' are superior selections.

A. cana (Seriphidium canum). Evergreen shrub. Zones 2, 3, 7, 14–21. Native to region east of the Sierra-

Artemisia abrotanum

Cascade divide. To 3–5 ft. tall and wide. Narrow, silvery green leaves. Very hardy to drought and cold.

A. caucasica. SILVER SPREADER. Evergreen shrublet. Zones 2–11, 14–24. Caucasus native grows 3–6 in. high, spreads to 2 ft. wide. Silky, silvery green foliage; small yellow flowers. Bank or ground cover; plant 1–2 ft. apart. Needs good drainage. Takes extremes of heat and cold.

A. dracunculus. FRENCH TARRAGON, TRUE TARRAGON. Perennial. Zones A1–A3; 2b–10, 14–24. French tarragon (may be labeled 'Sativa') is a sprawling, largely flowerless plant with shiny dark green, aromatic, flavorful leaves. Slowly spreads by creeping rhizomes, the stems becoming slightly woody and the whole plant remaining less than 2 ft. high. Makes an attractive container subject. Russian tarragon (may be labeled 'Inodorus') is a less desirable plant, lacking the characteristic flavor and aroma of true tarragon; it has upright, branching growth to about 3 ft. and small white flowers. Any seeds you find for sale will be for this culinarily inferior Russian tarragon. Cut sprigs in early summer for seasoning vinegar. Use fresh or dried leaves to season salads, cooked dishes. Plants in all zones die to the ground in winter. Divide every 3 or 4 years to keep vigorous. Propagate by divisions or cuttings. Povide moderate to regular water.

Artemisia dracunculus

A. frigida. FRINGED WORMWOOD. Perennial. Zones A1; 1–3, 7–10, 14, 18–21. Native to Southwest, interior Northwest, Alaska. To 1–1½ ft. tall and wide. Finely cut white leaves; small yellow flowers. Plants are compact when young, becoming rangy as they grow; cut back as needed.

A. 'Huntington'. Woody perennial. Zones 4–24. To 3 ft. tall and 4 ft. wide, with spreading stems covered by a thick dome of very silvery foliage. Similar to 'Powis Castle' but with bigger, softer leaves.

A. lactiflora. WHITE MUGWORT. Perennial. Zones 1–9, 14–21. Tall, straight column to 4–5 ft. tall, 2 ft. wide. This native of western China is one of the few artemisias with attractive flowers, bearing large (1½-ft.), branched sprays of creamy white blooms in late summer. Dark green leaves have broad, tooth-edged lobes. Moderate to regular water. Members of the Guizhou Group have purple stems but are otherwise similar to the species.

A. ludoviciana albula (A. albula). SILVER KING ARTEMISIA. Perennial. Zones 1–24. Native to desert Southwest and mountains. To 2–3½ ft. tall, 2 ft. wide, with slender, spreading branches and silvery white, 2-in. leaves. Lower leaves have three to five lobes; upper ones are narrow and unlobed. Cut foliage is useful in arrangements. 'Valerie Finnis' (which may be a variety of the plain species) is a compact grower to 2 ft. tall, with broader, nearly white leaves slightly lobed toward the tip.

A. pontica. ROMAN WORMWOOD. Evergreen shrub or woody perennial. Zones 2–24. Native to southeastern and central Europe; naturalized in eastern North America. Grows 2–4 ft. tall. Spreads invasively by rhizomes—makes a good ground cover if given ample room. Feathery silver gray leaves. Heads of nodding, whitish yellow flowers in long, open, branched clusters. Leaves are used in sachets.

A. 'Powis Castle'. Woody perennial. Zones 2–24. *A. absinthium* is a probable parent of this hybrid. Silvery, lacy mound to 3 ft. tall, 6 ft. wide. Makes a splendid background for bright flowers of other plants and is tough enough to use as a bank or berm cover.

A. pycnocephala. SANDHILL SAGE. Evergreen shrub or woody perennial. Zones 4, 5, 7–9, 14–17, 19–24. Native to beaches of Northern California. Rounded, somewhat spreading plant to 2 ft. tall, 3 ft. wide. Erect-growing stems are crowded with soft, silvery white or gray leaves divided into narrow lobes. Spikes of very small yellow flowers; remove them as they open to keep plant compact. Becomes unkempt after 2 years or so and should be removed and replaced at that time. 'David's Choice' is a foot-tall selection.

A. schmidtiana. ANGEL'S HAIR. Woody perennial. Zones A1–A3; 1–10, 14–24. Japanese native forms a 2-ft.-high, 1-ft.-wide dome of woolly, silvery white, finely cut leaves. 'Silver Mound' grows 1 ft. high.

A. stelleriana. BEACH WORMWOOD, OLD WOMAN, DUSTY MILLER. Perennial. Zones A1–A3; 1–10, 14–24.

Native to northeastern Asia; naturalized in eastern North America. Dense, silvery gray plant to 2½ ft. tall, 3 ft. wide, with lobed, 1–4-in. leaves. Hardier than *Senecio cineraria* (another dusty miller) and often used in its place in colder climates. Yellow flowers in spikelike clusters. 'Silver Brocade' is a superior, dense-growing selection.

A. tridentata (Seriphidium tridentatum). BIG SAGEBRUSH. Evergreen shrub. Zones 1–3, 6–11, 14–24. Native to Great Basin region of the West. Many-branched, silvery-looking plant to 4–15 ft. tall, 3–10 ft. wide. Narrow, very aromatic, hairy gray leaves ¾ in. long, usually with three teeth at tip. Insignificant flowers. Emits the pungent fragrance for which Western deserts are known. Grows easily in any sunny, well-drained spot. Does well with no irrigation.

A. versicolor 'Sea Foam'. ARTEMISIA. Zones A3, 1–24. Perennial. Mounding growth to 6–12 in. high and 1½–3 ft. wide. Lacy, silvery blue foliage; flowers not showy. Useful as a ground cover in full sun or partial shade.

A. vulgaris 'Oriental Limelight'. Zones A2, A3; 1–24. Perennial. Mounding growth to 2–3 ft. high and wide. Finely cut, green leaves are variegated in yellow and gold. Clusters of small white flowers in summer. Spreads underground; can be invasive.

ARTICHOKE

Asteraceae (Compositae)
PERENNIAL

🖋	ZONES VARY; SEE BELOW
☼	FULL SUN
💧	REGULAR WATER

Native to southern Mediterranean region. In Zones 8, 9, 14–24, grow artichoke as dependable perennial crop. In Zones 11–13, usually treated as an annual and planted in fall for spring harvest, but may hang on to be a perennial. In Zones 4–7, plant in spring when offered and hope for the best—you will get foliage, maybe flowers, and a crop if you're lucky. A big, coarse, ferny-looking plant with irregular, somewhat fountainlike form to 4 ft. high, 6–8 ft. wide. Leaves are silvery green. Big flower buds form at

Artichoke

tops of stalks: they are the artichokes you cook and eat. If not cut, buds open into spectacular purple-blue, 6-in., thistlelike flowers that can be cut for arrangements (cut them just before blooms are fully open).

In Zone 17, where it is grown commercially, artichoke can be both a handsome ornamental plant and a producer of fine, tender artichokes from early fall to late spring. In Zones 8, 9, 14–16, 18–24, in partial shade, the plant grows luxuriantly at least from spring through fall; edible buds come as a dividend in early summer only.

Plant dormant roots or plants from containers in winter or early spring. Set root shanks vertically, with buds or shoots just above soil level; space 4–6 ft. apart in a full-sun location. Where roots are not available or in cold-winter areas (even Alaska), you can grow artichokes from seed. 'Imperial Star' produces the first season (150 to 180 days from seed to harvest) and can be grown as an annual; 'Green Globe' is ready to harvest the second summer after seeding. Start seeds indoors 8 to 12 weeks before last frost; set transplants outdoors in a sunny area when the soil has warmed and frost danger is past, spacing them 4–6 ft. apart.

After active growth starts, water plants thoroughly once a week, wetting the entire root system. If grown only for ornamental value, artichokes can tolerate much drought, going dormant in summer heat. Control aphids; after buds start to form, just use strong jets of water to blast off aphids. Also keep snails, slugs, and earwigs away from plants. For gopher control, plant in raised beds lined with hardware cloth at the bottom or in large containers.

Harvest buds while they are still tight and plump. To encourage a second crop, cut off main stalk an inch above ground after harvesting the last bud of the first crop; new sprouts at base will grow faster and produce sooner than an uncut plant would. In all recommended climate zones, cut off old stalks near ground level when leaves begin to yellow. In cold-winter regions, cut tops to 1 ft. in fall, tie

them over root crown, and mulch heavily to protect from frost.

ARTOCARPUS altilis.
See **BREADFRUIT**

ARUGULA

ROCKET, ROQUETTE, RUGOLA
Brassicaceae (Cruciferae)
ANNUAL

🖋	ALL ZONES
☼	FULL SUN
💧	REGULAR WATER

Weedy Mediterranean native. Grown for its 1–4-in.-long leaves, which look like small mustard leaves and lend a nutty zing to green salads. Start from seed in winter or spring; grows best in cool weather. Thin to about 6 in. apart. Harvest tender young leaves; older, larger ones usually taste too sharp. Eventually, plants will shoot up to 3 ft. tall, then bloom; tender buds and flowers taste like the young leaves. Plants reseed.

Arugula

ARUM

Araceae
PERENNIALS FROM TUBERS

🖋	ZONES VARY BY SPECIES
☽ ●	PARTIAL OR FULL SHADE
💧	REGULAR WATER DURING GROWTH AND BLOOM
⬥	SAP IS AN IRRITANT IF INGESTED

Tubers give rise to attractively veined, arrow-shaped leaves in fall or winter. Short stalks bear curious callalike blooms featuring a bract (spathe) that half encloses a thick, fleshy spike (spadix) set with tiny flowers. These blossoms are followed by dense clusters of fruit, typically bright red, that look like little ears of corn and persist after leaves have died to the ground. Use in shady flower borders. Plant tubers in late summer or early fall (toward the end of their dormancy), setting them 8–12 in. apart and about 2 in. deep. Dormant plantings accept summer

Arum italicum 'Pictum'

moisture but don't need it. *A. palaestinum* and *A. pictum* are sometimes used as houseplants in colder climates.

A. italicum. ITALIAN ARUM. Zones 2–24. Native to southern and western Europe. Leaves 1 ft. long on leafstalks of equal length appear in fall or early winter. Very short stems carry white or greenish white (sometimes purple-spotted) flowers in spring and early summer, followed by orange-red fruits. Spathe first stands erect, then folds over and conceals short yellow spadix. Leaves die to ground after bloom. In favorable situations, will naturalize by volunteer seedlings. 'Pictum' has white-veined leaves.

A. palaestinum. BLACK CALLA. Zones 14–24. Native to Israel. Leaves emerge in winter; about 8 in. long, on 1-ft. leafstalks. Spathe is 8 in. long, green outside; opens outward and curls back at tip to reveal purple interior and black spadix. Blooms spring and early summer, then leaves die back.

A. pictum. Zones 7–9, 14–24. Native to western Mediterranean. May be called black calla, like *A. palaestinum*—but unlike that species, it has an 8-in. violet spathe with a white base that encloses a dark purple spadix. Flowers appear in fall—sometimes with emerging foliage, sometimes before. Light green leaves with fine white veins reach 10 in. long and are borne on equally long leafstalks. Foliage dies to ground in hot weather.

ARUNCUS

GOAT'S BEARD
Rosaceae
PERENNIALS

🖋	ZONES VARY BY SPECIES
☼ ☽	FULL SUN ONLY IN COOLER CLIMATES
💧	REGULAR WATER

These perennials resemble astilbe, with slowly spreading clumps of finely divided leaves topped in summer by plumy, branched clusters of tiny white or cream flowers. Good in perennial borders or at edge of woodland against a dark background.

A. aethusifolius. Zones 1–9, 14–17. Native to Korea. Deep green, finely divided leaves make a mound 1 ft. tall and wide. White flower plumes reach 16 in. high. Useful in rock garden, as edging, for small-scale ground cover.

Aruncus dioicus

A. dioicus (A. sylvester). Zones A2, A3; 1–9, 14–17. Native to Eurasia and to southeastern and south-central Alaska. Grows to 6 (sometimes 7) ft. tall, 4 ft. wide, with foamy plumes of white flowers in 20-in., much-branched clusters. 'Kneiffii' is half the size of the species, with more finely divided, near-ferny leaves. 'Child of Two Worlds' ('Zweiweltenkind'), sometimes sold as *A. chinensis,* grows to 5 ft. tall, with gracefully drooping flower clusters.

ARUNDO donax
GIANT REED
Poaceae (Gramineae)
PERENNIAL GRASS

🌿	**ZONES 3–24**
☀	**FULL SUN**
💧💧💧	**MODERATE TO AMPLE WATER**

Giant grass from the Mediterranean. Once valued for its bold effect in garden fringes and near water and for use as a fast-growing windbreak. Now, however, it has run wild in many areas, particularly in mild-winter parts of California, clogging waterways (supplanting the native waterside trees and shrubs) and even damaging bridges. Grows as tall as 30 ft., with 2-ft.-long leaves; spreads by thick rhizomes. Particularly rampant in areas where the flower clusters set fertile seeds,

Arundo donax

such as Southern California. Even where it is less invasive, its size makes it difficult to dig out or divide. In cold climates, it may die back in winter.

'Versicolor' ('Variegata') has leaves with white or yellowish stripes; it grows to about half the height of the species and is less likely to bloom, though it too can get out of bounds in warm climates. Attractive in a large, sturdy container.

ASARINA
CLIMBING SNAPDRAGON, CHICKABIDDY
Scrophulariaceae
PERENNIALS OFTEN GROWN AS ANNUALS

🌿	**ZONES 17–24, EXCEPT AS NOTED; ZONES 1–16 AS ANNUALS**
☀	**ROOTS COOL, TOPS IN SUN**
💧	**REGULAR WATER**

Climbing, sprawling, or trailing tender perennials have twining stems and triangular to ovate leaves. Tubular flowers, borne singly in leaf axils, flare at the mouth like snapdragon (*Antirrhinum,* a close relative). Plants

Asarina antirrhiniflora

from early sowings will bloom in late spring and through the summer. Grow on a trellis, in window boxes or hanging baskets, or as ground cover. Need good drainage.

A. antirrhiniflora (Maurandella antirrhiniflora). Zones 17–24; H1, H2. Native to southwestern U.S., Mexico. Grows 3–6 ft. tall, with 1-in., yellow-throated flowers in lavender, violet, blue, and red. A mixed-color seed strain offers red-and-yellow or blue-and-white flowers.

A. barclaiana (Maurandya barclayana). Native to Mexico. Vigorous, woody-based plant to 12 ft., with 2–3-in. flowers in white, pink, or purple. 'Angel's Trumpet' is a pink bloomer.

A. scandens (Lophospermum scandens). From Mexico. Similar

to *A. barclaiana* but smaller (4–8 ft. tall), bearing somewhat smaller flowers that are in the same color range.

ASARUM
WILD GINGER
Aristolochiaceae
PERENNIALS

🌿	**ZONES VARY BY SPECIES**
☼ ●	**PARTIAL OR FULL SHADE**
💧💧	**REGULAR TO AMPLE WATER**

Asarum caudatum

American and European species are handsome ground covers, forming a lush, lustrous carpet of heart-shaped leaves. The small, three-cornered, typically brownish red, attractive spring flowers are bell shaped, with three tapering "tails." Roots and leaves of wild gingers have a scent somewhat like that of culinary ginger but are not used as seasoning. Grow in average soil, but spread faster, are luxuriant in rich, humusy soil. Start from divisions or container-grown plants; set about a foot apart. Watch for slugs and snails.

A few specialist nurseries offer a number of species from Japan and China. These are true collectors' plants, with ornately mottled leaves, some with flowers in odd shades of near-black and white. Most are expensive and difficult to grow.

A. canadense. Zones 1–6. Native to eastern North America. Deciduous, dark green, kidney-shaped leaves to 6 in. wide. Purplish brown flowers.

A. caudatum. Zones 4–6, 14–24. Native to the West Coast. Evergreen where winters are mild. Heart-shaped leaves are 2–7 in. wide. In fog belt, it makes a choice ground cover for shade and survives with just occasional water.

A. europaeum. Zones 2–6. Native to Europe. Evergreen, kidney-shaped, shiny dark green leaves 2–3 in. wide. Slow spreader.

A. shuttleworthii. Zones 3b–6. Native to the Appalachians. Evergreen, 4-in., shiny green leaves are heart-shaped or roundish and usu-

ally variegated with silvery markings. Slow growing.

A. splendens. Zones 3–6, 15–17. Native to China. Evergreen leaves are dark green, heavily mottled with silver, and heart-shaped with an elongated tip; may reach 7 in. long and 3 in. wide. Large (2-in.-wide), dark purple flowers. Grows vigorously in rich, loose soil, forming large colonies.

ASCLEPIAS
Asclepiadaceae
PERENNIALS

🌿	**ZONES VARY BY SPECIES**
☀	**FULL SUN**
💧 💧💧	**WATER NEEDS VARY BY SPECIES**
◆	**ALL PARTS OF MANY SPECIES ARE POISONOUS IF INGESTED**

Milkweeds (so named for their milky sap) are the best-known representatives of this group of plants. Bloom in summer, typically bearing many small, starlike flowers in broad, flattened clusters at branch tips. All have inflated seedpods with silky seeds. Just a few species are cultivated in gardens.

Asclepias tuberosa

A. curassavica. BLOOD FLOWER. Zones 8, 9, 12–24; H1, H2; all zones as annual. Native to South America. Woody-based plant with stiff stems and narrow 6-in. leaves; grows 3 ft. tall, 2 ft. wide. Clusters of vivid red flowers. 'Silky Gold' is similar but bears bright yellow to yellow-orange blooms. Moderate water.

A. fruticosa (Gomphocarpus fruticosus), A. physocarpa (G. physocarpus). SWAN PLANT, GOOSE PLANT. Zones 14–24. These two very similar woody-based plants from southern Africa sometimes volunteer in gardens. They grow upright to 3–6 ft. tall, 2–3 ft. wide, with many stems clothed in gray-green, willowlike leaves. Sometimes sold by nurseries for puffy, inflated pale green seedpods that are covered with soft, fleshy prickles and have curving stems like swans' necks; the flowers themselves are not showy. Stripped of leaves and dried, seedpod-bearing stems make striking arrangements. Provide good drainage, regular water. ▶

A

A. incarnata. SWAMP MILK-WEED. Zones 1–9, 14–24. Native to eastern U.S. Herbaceous perennial to 2–4 ft. tall, 2 ft. wide. Narrow, pointed leaves to 6 in. long; ball-shaped clusters of pinkish purple flowers. 'Ice Ballet' has pure white blooms. Provide regular to ample water.

A. tuberosa. BUTTERFLY WEED. Zones 1–24. Native to eastern U.S. From a perennial root, many herbaceous stems rise every year to form a clump about 3 ft. tall, 1 ft. wide. Clusters of bright orange flowers attract swarms of butterflies. Gay Butterflies strain features yellow, red, orange, pink, or bicolored blossoms; 'Hello Yellow' has bright yellow blooms. All types make long-lasting cut flowers. Provide good drainage, moderate water.

ASH. See **FRAXINUS**

ASH, MOUNTAIN. See **SORBUS**

ASIAN GREENS
Brassicaceae (Cruciferae)
ANNUALS

| ✎ ALL ZONES |
| ☼ ◑ FULL SUN IN COOLER CLIMATES ONLY |
| ● REGULAR WATER |

The annual vegetables in this large group are mainstays of stir-fry dishes and excellent in salads. They are primarily quick-maturing cool-season crops planted at the same time as other cool-season vegetables: late winter to early spring for spring-to-summer harvest, late summer to early fall for harvest in fall and winter. In areas with short growing seasons and in mild-summer coastal regions, they can be grown all summer.

Many Asian greens, especially the mustards, are attractive foliage plants that make a colorful addition to the vegetable garden and also look good mixed with flowering annuals and spring bulbs.

Chinese mustard greens

Listed here are some of the most common Asian greens (specialty seed catalogs may carry additional kinds). For planting depth and row spacing, follow the instructions on the seed packet.

Broadleaf mustard (dai gai choy). Large green leaves with a pungent, somewhat bitter, mustardlike flavor that gets stronger as the plant matures. Hot weather or inadequate moisture also increases pungency. Best used in soup to tone down the sharp flavor.

Thin or transplant seedlings to 10 in. apart. Harvest plants when they are loose headed and 10–14 in. high, about 65 days after sowing.

Chinese broccoli (gai lohn). Similar in flavor and texture to standard broccoli, but with a slight pungency like that of mustard. Thin or transplant seedlings to 10 in. apart. Harvest central stalk and side shoots when stalk is 8–10 in. tall or when flower buds just begin to form, usually about 70 days after sowing.

Chinese mustard greens (gai choy). Milder member of the mustard family. Thin or transplant seedlings to 10 in. apart. Harvest the first greens when the plants are 2 in. high; continue harvesting

---

Renee Shepherd on Asian Greens

Renee Shepherd knows how to cook up a feast from the garden. Her secret? Asian greens. They grow fast—seemingly overnight—and take only minutes to prepare. "I heat up peanut oil, then throw in some scallions, garlic, and ginger," she explains. "After a few minutes, I add the greens and cook them quickly."

Through her seed company, Renee's Garden, in Felton, CA, Shepherd sells blends of Asian greens, usually including mizuna ("one of the sweetest") and bok choy ("pretty, sturdy, reliable, very juicy, and tender"). She grows these greens cut-and-come-again style. "Plant densely and harvest leaves using kitchen scissors when they are 3 to 5 inches tall, leaving 1-inch crowns so plants regrow," says Shepherd. "You'll be able to harvest these two or three times, depending on time of year and weather."

---

until leaves turn tough or bitter. It usually takes 45 days after sowing for plants to reach mature height of 6–8 in.

Chinese white cabbage (bok choy, pak choi). One of the more familiar Asian greens. Tender-crisp, sweet, very mild; good alone, with meat, in soups and stir-fries. Many varieties are sold. Tatsoi is similar but more compact.

Thin or transplant seedlings to 6–12 inches apart. Harvest approximately 50 days after sowing seed, when plants are loose headed and 10–12 in. tall.

Flowering cabbage (yao choy, choy sum, ching sow sum). Tender, delicate, broccoli-type vegetable. Thin or transplant seedlings to about 6 in. apart. Harvest about 60 days after sowing, when 8–12 in. high.

Mizuna. Mild-flavored, leafy vegetable with finely cut, frilly, white-stemmed leaves. Great in salads. Thin or transplant seedlings to 8–10 in. apart. Start cutting leaves when plants are a few inches tall or wait until mature at 8–10 in. high, about 40 days after sowing.

ASIMINA triloba. See **PAWPAW**

ASPARAGUS
Liliaceae
PERENNIAL

| ✎ ZONES A1–A3; 1–24 |
| ☼ FULL SUN |
| ● REGULAR WATER |

Native to seacoasts of Europe, North Africa, Asia. One of most permanent and dependable of home garden vegetables. Plants take 2 or 3 years to come into full production but then furnish delicious spears every spring for 10 to 15 years. They take up considerable space but do so in the grand manner: plants are tall, feathery, graceful, highly ornamental. Use along sunny fence or as background for flowers or other vegetables.

Seeds grow into strong young plants in one season (sow in spring), but roots are far more widely used. Set out seedlings or roots (not wilted, no smaller than an adult's hand) in fall or winter in mild-winter climates, in early spring in cold-winter areas. Make trenches 1 ft. wide, 8–10 in. deep; space trenches 4–6 ft. apart. Heap loose, manure-enriched soil at bottom of trenches and soak. Space

Asparagus

plants 1 ft. apart, setting them so that tops are 6–8 in. below surface; spread roots out evenly. Cover with 2 in. of soil and water again. (Where drainage is very bad, plant in raised beds.)

As young plants grow, gradually fill in the trench, taking care not to cover growing tips. Soak deeply whenever the soil begins to dry out at root depth. Don't harvest any spears the first year; the object at this time is to build a big root mass. When plants turn brown in late fall or early winter, cut stems to the ground. In cold-winter areas, permit dead stalks to stand until spring; they will help trap and hold snow, which will furnish protection to root crowns.

The following spring you can cut your first spears; cut only for 4 to 6 weeks or until appearance of thin spears indicates that roots are nearing exhaustion. Then permit plants to grow. Cultivate, feed, and irrigate heavily. The third year you should be able to cut spears for 8 to 10 weeks. Spears are ready to cut when they are 5–8 in. long. Thrust knife down at 45° angle to soil; flat cutting may injure adjacent developing spears.

Cleaning up debris from asparagus beds in fall will help get rid of overwintering asparagus beetles. Use row covers over beds in spring. If the beetles appear during cutting season, handpick them, knock them off plants using water jets, or spray them with malathion (carefully noting label precautions).

Asparagus seeds and roots are sold as "traditional" ('Mary Washington' and others) and "all-male" ('UC 157', 'Jersey Giant', and 'Jersey Knight'). The latter kinds are bred to produce more and larger spears because they don't have to put energy into seed production. Such varieties still produce an occasional female plant.

ASPARAGUS, ORNAMENTAL
Liliaceae
PERENNIALS, SHRUBS, OR VINES

⚡ ZONES 12–24, EXCEPT AS NOTED

☀️ ◑ SUN OR PART SHADE

💧 REGULAR WATER

There are about 150 kinds of asparagus besides the edible one—all members of the lily family. Those listed here are native to South Africa. Best known is fern asparagus *(A. setaceus)*, which is not a true fern. Although valued mostly for handsome foliage of unusual textural quality, some of the ornamental species have small but fragrant flowers and colorful berries. Green foliage sprays are made up of what look like leaves. Needlelike or broader, these are actually short branches called cladodes. The true leaves are inconspicuous dry scales.

Most ornamental asparagus look greenest in partial shade but thrive in sun in cool-summer climates. Leaves yellow in dense shade. Plant in well-drained soil amended with peat moss or ground bark. Because of fleshy roots, plants can go for some time without water, but they grow better when watered regularly. Feed in spring with complete fertilizer. Trim out old shoots to make room for new growth. Ornamental asparagus will survive light frosts but may be killed to ground by severe cold. After frost, plants often come back from roots.

A. asparagoides. SMILAX ASPARAGUS. Much-branched vine with spineless stems to 20 ft. or more. Often seen in older gardens. Leaves to 1 in. long, sharp pointed, stiffish, glossy grass green. Small, fragrant white flowers in spring followed by blue berries. Birds feed on berries, drop seeds that sprout at random about the garden. (Plant also self-sows readily.) Roots are nearly immortal, surviving long drought and sprouting when rains come. Cut foliage sprays are prized for table decoration. If it gets little water, plant dies back in summer, revives with fall rains. Becomes tangled mass unless trained. May escape gardens and become a pest.

'Myrtifolius', commonly called baby smilax, is a more graceful form with smaller leaves.

A. crispus. BASKET ASPARAGUS. Airy, graceful plant for hanging baskets. Drooping, zigzag stems have bright green, three-angled leaves held in whorls of three. Often sold as *A. scandens* 'Deflexus'.

A. densiflorus. Zones 12–24; H1, H2; or indoors. The species is less commonly grown than its forms. The following are the two most popular.

'Myers'. MYERS ASPARAGUS. Several to many stiffly upright stems to 2 ft. or more, densely clothed with needlelike deep green leaves that give the plant a fluffy look. Forms a 3–4-ft.-wide clump. Performs well in containers. A little less hardy than 'Sprengeri'. Sometimes sold as *A. meyeri* or *A. myersii.*

'Sprengeri'. SPRENGER ASPARAGUS. Arching or drooping stems 3–6 ft. long. Shiny, bright green, needlelike leaves, 1 in. long, in bundles. Bright red berries. Popular for hanging baskets or containers, indoors and out. Train on trellis; climbs by means of small hooked prickles. Used as billowy ground cover where temperatures stay above 24°F/–4°C. Grows in ordinary or even poor soil. Will tolerate dryness of indoors. Sometimes sold as *A. sprengeri.* Form sold as 'Sprengeri Compacta' or *A. sarmentosus* 'Compacta' is denser, with shorter stems.

A. falcatus. SICKLE-THORN ASPARAGUS. Leaves resemble those of *Podocarpus macrophyllus;* they are 2–3 in. long, in clusters of three to five at ends of branches. Tiny, fragrant white flowers in loose clusters; these are followed by brown berries. Derives its common name from curved thorns along its stems, which it uses to clamber rapidly as high as 40 ft. in its native area (in gardens, it usually reaches about 10 ft.). Makes an excellent foliage mass to cover fence or wall or provide shade for pergola or lathhouse.

A. macowanii. See A. retrofractus

A. meyeri, A. myersii. See A. densiflorus 'Myers'

Asparagus densiflorus 'Sprengeri'

A. officinalis. See Asparagus

A. plumosus. See A. setaceus

A. retrofractus. (A. macowanii) Erect, shrubby, slightly climbing, very tender. Slender, silvery gray stems grow slowly to 8–10 ft. high. Leaves threadlike, 1 in. long, in fluffy, rich green tufts. Clusters of small white flowers. Handsome in containers; useful in flower arrangements. Cut foliage lasts about 10 days out of water, several weeks in water.

A. sarmentosus. See A. densiflorus 'Sprengeri'

A. scandens. BASKET ASPARAGUS. Slender, branching vine climbing to 6 ft. Deep green, needlelike leaves on zigzag, drooping stems. Greenish white flowers ⅛ in. long. Scarlet berries.

A. scandens 'Deflexus'. See A. crispus

A. setaceus (A. plumosus). FERN ASPARAGUS. Zones 12–24; H1, H2; or indoors. Branching woody vine climbs by wiry, spiny stems to 10–20 ft. Tiny threadlike leaves form feathery dark green sprays that resemble fern fronds. Tiny white flowers; purple-black berries. Dense, fine-textured foliage mass useful as screen against walls, fences. Florists use foliage as filler in bouquets; holds up better than delicate ferns. Sometimes called emerald feather. Dwarf 'Nanus' is good in containers. 'Pyramidalis' has upswept, windblown look, is less vigorous than common fern asparagus.

A. sprengeri. See A. densiflorus 'Sprengeri'

ASPEN. See **POPULUS**

ASPEN DAISY. See **ERIGERON speciosus macranthus**

ASPERULA odorata. See **GALIUM odoratum**

ASPHODELINE lutea
YELLOW ASPHODEL, KING'S SPEAR
Liliaceae
PERENNIAL

⚡ ZONES 3B–24

☀️ ◑ FULL SUN OR PARTIAL SHADE

💧 REGULAR WATER

Mediterranean native with a rhizomatous rootstock. Forms a low clump (about 9 in. high, 1 ft. wide) of blue-green to dark green, grassy leaves to 1 ft. long. In spring, stiff, unbranched stems to 3 ft. high rise from clump, topped by narrow clusters of fragrant, 1-in., yellow flowers that peer out from shaggy

Asphodeline lutea

buff or reddish brown bracts. Grow in well-drained soil. Divide in fall.

ASPIDISTRA elatior (A. lurida)
CAST-IRON PLANT
Liliaceae
PERENNIAL

⚡ ZONES 4–10, 12–24; H1, H2; OR INDOORS

◑ ● PARTIAL OR FULL SHADE; BRIGHT TO DIM LIGHT

💧💧 ● MODERATE TO REGULAR WATER

This sturdy, long-lived evergreen foliage plant from China is best known as a houseplant, but it also makes striking accent clumps outdoors. Spreads slowly by rhizomes. Tough, arching, glossy, dark green leaf blades with distinct parallel veins are 1–2½ ft. long, 3–4 in. wide; each is supported by a grooved, 6–8-in.-long leafstalk. Inconspicuous brownish flowers bloom near ground level in spring. 'Variegata' has white-striped leaves but loses its variegation if planted in too-rich soil. Other variegated and spotted forms are available.

Aspidistra elatior

True to its common name, this plant has a cast-iron constitution, thriving in conditions unacceptable to most plants. Although extremely tolerant and requiring only minimal care, it grows best in porous, organically enriched soil and responds to spring and summer feeding. Will grow in dark, shaded areas (under decks or stairs) as well as in filtered sun—except in Zones 12 and 13, where it takes full shade only. Indoors, prefers bright indirect light but also does well in low light. It can live for many years in the same

A

container before repotting is necessary. To keep leaves dust free and glossy, hose them off occasionally or clean with a soft brush or cloth.

ASPIDIUM capense.
See **RUMOHRA adiantiformis**

ASPLENIUM
Polypodiaceae
FERNS

🌡	ZONES VARY BY SPECIES
◐ ●	PARTIAL OR FULL SHADE
💧 💧	REGULAR TO AMPLE WATER

Widespread and variable group of rhizomatous ferns, once called spleenwort for alleged medicinal value. These evergreen species resemble one another only in botanical details and in their need for shade and liberal watering. Unlike many other ferns, they need a rest period from late fall to early spring when grown indoors; during that time, reduce watering and withhold fertilizer.

Asplenium bulbiferum

A. bulbiferum. MOTHER FERN. Zones 14 (protected), 15–17, 20–24; or indoors. From Australia, New Zealand. Graceful, very finely cut light green fronds to 4 ft. tall. Plant grows about 4 ft. wide. Fronds produce plantlets that can be removed and planted. Hardy to 26°F/–3°C. Watch for snails and slugs.
   A. daucifolium (A. viviparum). Indoor plant. Tropical species similar to *A. bulbiferum* but smaller (to 2 ft.), with more finely divided fronds. Also produces plantlets.
   A. nidus (A. nidus-avis). BIRD'S NEST FERN. Zones 23, 24; H2; or indoors. Tender fern native to many tropical regions. Showy, undivided apple green fronds to 4 ft. long, 8 in. wide, growing upright in cluster. Striking foliage plant. Grow potted plant indoors in winter, move to shady patio in summer. One snail or slug can ruin a frond.

Asplenium nidus

A. scolopendrium. HART'S TONGUE FERN. Zones 2b–9, 14–24. Native to Europe, eastern U.S. Odd fern with undivided, strap-shaped leaves 9–18 in. long; forms a clump about 2 ft. wide. Fanciers collect various dwarf, crested, or forked varieties. Needs humus; also add some limestone chips if soil is deficient in calcium. Difficult to grow where water quality is poor. Striking in woodland or rock gardens and with rhododendrons and azaleas. Durable container plant; grows in a tight crown and can remain in the same pot for years.
   A. trichomanes. MAIDEN-HAIR SPLEENWORT. Zones 2–6. Native to much of the Northern Hemisphere, this delicate fern grows in a clump to 6 in. high, 8 in. wide. Narrow bright green fronds are 4–8 in. long; round (or nearly so) leaflets are only ½ in. long. Likes lime. Attractive in wall crevices where it can be seen close up or in a shady rock garden.

ASTARTEA
fascicularis
Myrtaceae
EVERGREEN SHRUB

🌡	ZONES 15–24
☀ ◐	FULL SUN OR PARTIAL SHADE
○	NO IRRIGATION NEEDED

Australian native related to *Leptospermum* but with smaller leaves and flowers. Varieties more commonly grown than species. 'Bremer Bay' grows to 3 ft. or taller and is somewhat wider, with short, narrow, needlelike leaves in bundles thickly arranged along the stems. White or pink, ⅓-in.-wide flowers are borne in incredible profusion over a very long period, with the heaviest bloom in winter. Branches last well when cut.

Astartea fascicularis

'Prostrate Form' is a few inches tall, 3 ft. wide. 'Winter Pink' resembles 'Bremer Bay', but its deeper pink flowers bloom over a shorter season in winter and early spring.

ASTELIA
Liliaceae
PERENNIALS

🌡	ZONES 5, 6, 14–17, 19–24
☀ ◐	FULL SUN OR PARTIAL SHADE
💧	MODERATE WATER

Grown for their silky, silvery, straplike foliage, these increasingly popular evergreen perennials offer a handsome contrast to low, mounding plants or billowing grasses. They make a striking centerpiece in a big container or a perennial border. Small spring flowers are borne in branched clusters on female plants but are not as showy as the berries that follow. Must have excellent drainage. Prefer rich, acidic soil that is high in organic matter. The following are native to New Zealand.
   A. banksii. SHORE ASTELIA. Grows 2–3 ft. high and 3–4 ft. wide, with arching, narrow, silvery green leaves. Greenish flowers are followed by berries that mature to purple black. Best in light shade.

Astelia chathamica

A. chathamica (A. nervosa chathamica). SILVER LEAF. Shiny, silvery swordlike leaves are 3–4 ft. long and 2–4 in. wide, forming a clump 4 ft. tall and 6 ft. wide. Small, cream-colored flowers are borne in clusters 20 in. tall; berries are orange.
   A. nervosa. Variable in size and color, to 2–3 ft. high and wide, with foliage that is silvery green above, green to bronzy beneath, with green midribs. Arching leaves may reach 7 ft. long. Greenish yellow to bronzy purple flowers appear on tall stalks; orange berries follow. 'Westland' is lower growing, with a dusty red wash over silvery green foliage.
   A. nivicola 'Red Gem'. Clumps reach about 1½ ft. tall and 2 ft. wide. Narrow, arching leaves about

a foot long have maroon stripes on a green background with typical silvery sheen. Excellent in containers.

ASTER
Asteraceae (Compositae)
PERENNIALS

🌡	ZONES VARY BY SPECIES
☀	FULL SUN, EXCEPT AS NOTED
💧	REGULAR WATER

There are more than 600 species of true asters, ranging from 6 in. high alpine kinds forming compact mounds to open-branching 6 ft. tall plants. Flowers come in white or shades of blue, red, pink, lavender, or purple, mostly with yellow centers. Bloom time comes in late summer to early fall, except as noted. Taller asters are invaluable for abundant color in large borders or among shrubs. Large sprays effective in arrangements. Compact dwarf or cushion types make tidy edgings, mounds of color in rock gardens, good container plants. For the common annual or China aster sold at nurseries, see *Callistephus chinensis*.
   True asters are adapted to most soils, but growth is most luxuriant in fertile soil. Few problems except for mildew on leaves in late fall. Strong-growing hybrids have invasive roots; they can regrow from small fragments left in soil and spread to become nuisances. Divide yearly in late fall or early spring. Replant vigorous young divisions from outside of clump; discard old center. Divide smaller, tufted, less vigorously growing kinds every 2 years.
   A. alpinus. Zones 1–4. Native to Alps, Pyrenees. Mounding plant to 1 ft. high, 1½ ft. wide. Leaves ½–5 in. long, mostly in basal tuft. Several stems grow from the leafy clump, each carrying one violet blue flower 1½–2 in. across. Late spring to early summer bloom. Best in cold-winter areas. White and pink forms are uncommon.
   A. amellus. ITALIAN ASTER. Zones 2–24. Native to Europe, western Asia. Sturdy, hairy plant to 2 ft. tall, 1½ ft. wide. Branching stems bear yellow-centered violet flowers 2 in. across.
   A. cordifolius. BLUE WOOD ASTER. Zones 1–10, 14–21. To 6 ft. tall, 3 ft. wide, with loose, branching clusters of inch-wide lavender flowers. Native to eastern North America. Sun or light shade.
   A. divaricatus. WHITE WOOD ASTER. Zones 1–10, 14–21. Native

A

to eastern North America. To 3 ft. tall and wide, with a strong horizontal branching pattern and a generous show of white flowers aging to pink. Thrives in shade.

A. ericoides. HEATH ASTER. Zones 1–10, 14–24. Native to eastern North America. To 3 ft. tall and 1 ft. wide, with narrow leaves and strong horizontal branching. Flower heads are small and profusely borne, in white, pink, or blue.

A. × frikartii. Zones 2b–24. One of the finest, most useful and widely adapted perennials. Hybrid between *A. amellus* and *A. thomsonii,* this is a hairy-leafed, lilac-flowered, 3-ft.-tall species native to the Himalayas. Bears abundant clear lavender to violet blue single flowers that are 2½ in. across. Open growth to 2 ft. high and wide. Blooms early summer to fall—almost all year in mild-winter areas if spent flowers are removed regularly. May be short lived. 'Wonder of Staffa' and 'Mönch' are favorites with blossoms in lavender blue.

Aster × frikartii

A. fruticosus. See Felicia fruticosa

A. laevis. Zones 1–10, 14–21. Native to eastern North America.

Aster × frikartii
'Mönch'

Aster novae-angliae
'Alma Potschke'

To 3½ ft. tall, 1½ ft. wide, with smooth, mildew-free foliage and clustered 1-in. flower heads of deep purplish blue.

A. lateriflorus. Zones 1–10, 14–21. North American native. Species grows to 4 ft. tall, 1 ft. wide. Garden selections are shorter (to 2 ft.), with profuse branching, tiny leaves, and a haze of small purplish pink flowers. Foliage turns a coppery purplish red in early fall. 'Prince' has blackish purple stems and leaves; its blooms are white with a red center.

A. novae-angliae. NEW ENGLAND ASTER. Zones 1–24. Native from Vermont to Alabama, west to North Dakota, Wyoming, and New Mexico. Stout-stemmed plant to 3–5 ft. tall and nearly as wide, with hairy leaves to 5 in. long. Flowers are 2 in. wide; they are violet blue in the basic form, with selections in other blue shades, white, pink, nearly red, and deep purple. Very tolerant of wet soils. Reseeds. 'Alma Potschke' bears salmon pink single blooms on 3-ft. stems from late summer to early fall. 'Harrington's Pink' produces clear pink single flowers over a long autumn season on 3–4-ft. stems. 'Purple Dome' is a compact grower to only 1½ ft. tall, with brilliant purple blooms.

A. novi-belgii. NEW YORK ASTER, MICHAELMAS DAISY. Zones 1–24. Native to eastern North America. To 4 ft. tall and 3 ft. wide, with full clusters of bright blue-violet flowers. Similar to *A. novae-angliae* but with smooth leaves. Hundreds of selections are available, varying in height from less than a foot to over 4 ft.; flower colors include white, cream, blue, lavender, purple, rose, and pink. Among the many choices are 'Persian Rose' (rose pink) and

Aster novi-belgii
'Professor Anton Kippenberg'

semidouble 'Professor Anton Kippenberg' (lavender blue), both under 1 ft. high and 1½ ft. wide. Robust 'Climax' bears large sprays of single medium blue blossoms on stems to 6 ft. high. Farmington Michaelmas daisy ('Baldco'), 1 ft. tall and 2 ft. wide, has lilac blooms and resists mildew.

A. pilosus pringlei. Zones 1–9. Eastern U.S. native known in cultivation through its variety 'Monte Cassino', a familiar florists' cut flower. Grows to 5 ft. tall and 1½ ft. wide; tall, narrow stems have many short side branches set with starry white, ¾-in. flowers. This plant is often sold as *A. ericoides* 'Monte Cassino'.

A. sibiricus. Zones A1–A3; 1–5. From northern parts of North America and Eurasia. To 16 in. high and as broad, with 9-in.-long basal leaves, purplish stems, and ¾-in. purple flowers borne singly or a few to the cluster.

A. tataricus. Zones 1–10, 14–21. Native to Siberia, China, Japan. Not for small gardens, this giant grows to 5–7 ft. tall and 3 ft. wide, with 2-ft.-long leaves and sheaves of inch-wide blue flowers in flat clusters in fall. Can be invasive. Takes sun or shade.

A. tongolensis (A. subcaeruleus, A. yunnanensis). Zones 3–24. From China, Himalayas. Dark green leaves in basal tufts; clumps grow to 1½ ft. high, 1 ft. wide. Each stem bears a single lavender blue, orange-centered flower in late spring to early summer. 'Napsbury' has dark blue rays.

ASTERISCUS (Pallenis)
Asteraceae (Compositae)
PERENNIALS

🗡	ZONES VARY BY SPECIES
☼	FULL SUN
◐ ●	LITTLE TO MODERATE WATER

Leafy, evergreen, almost shrubby plants with showy yellow, 1½–2-in. daisies throughout most of the year. Shear spent flowers to neaten appearance and prolong bloom.

A. maritimus (Pallenis maritima, Odontospermum maritimum). Zones 9, 15–24. Native to the Mediterranean region and the Canary Islands. Often sold as 'Gold Coin'. Attractive, silvery green–foliaged ground cover to 1 ft. tall, 4 ft. wide. Tough, tolerant plant for most soils; takes seaside conditions. 'Compact Gold Coin' is less sprawling and more mounding; good in containers.

Asteriscus maritimus

A. sericeus (Nauplius sericeus, Odontospermum sericeus). CANARY ISLAND DAISY. Zones 16, 17, 19–24. To 3 ft. tall and wide, shrubbier than *A. maritimus*. Silky, silvery leaves set off bright yellow flowers for a silver-and-gold effect. The foliage has an odd odor; old leaves tend to blacken and adhere to the stems. If groomed, makes a striking container plant.

ASTILBE
FALSE SPIREA
Saxifragaceae
PERENNIALS

🗡	ZONES A2, A3; 1–7, 14–17; SHORT LIVED IN ZONES 8, 9, 18–24
☼ ◐ ●	FULL SUN IN COOLER CLIMATES ONLY
●	REGULAR WATER

Valued for light, airy quality of plumelike flower clusters and attractive foliage and for ability to provide color from late spring through summer. Leaves are typically divided, with toothed or cut leaflets, though in some species they are simply lobed, with cut margins. Small white, pink, or red flowers are carried in graceful, branching, feathery plumes held on slender, wiry stems ranging from 6 in. to 3 ft. or taller. Most plants grow 2–3 ft. wide.

Astilbes are the mainstay of the shady perennial border, although in cool-summer climates they can withstand full sun if watered adequately. Effective at the edge of pools, along shady

Astilbe × arendsii

paths, in containers. Need moist (but not boggy), rich soil with ample humus. Cut off faded flowering stems and divide clumps every 4 or 5 years. Survival in coldest areas (Zones 1a, 1b, 2a) depends on good snow cover.

A. × arendsii. Most astilbes sold belong to this hybrid group or are sold as such. Parentage is complex, but plants often have *A. japonica, A. chinensis,* and/or *A. thunbergii* in their ancestry. The plants differ chiefly in technical details. The following are some of the best varieties.

'Amethyst'. Late. Lavender, 3–4 ft.

'Bridal Veil'. Midseason to late. Full white plumes, 3 ft.

Color Flash series. Midseason. Pink flowers and colorful foliage; about 2 ft. tall. Leaves of 'Color Flash' gradually turn from green to burgundy. 'Color Flash Lime' has light green foliage that picks up bright yellow tones.

'Deutschland'. Early. White, 1½ ft. Bright green leaves.

'Fanal'. Early. Blood-red flowers, bronzy foliage, 1½–2½ ft.

'Ostrich Plume' ('Straussenfeder'). Midseason to late. Drooping pink clusters, 3–3½ ft. Often sold as a variety of *A. thunbergii.*

'Peach Blossom'. Midseason. Light salmon pink, 2 ft.

'Rheinland'. Early. Deep pink, 2–2½ ft.

A. chinensis. Resembles *A. × arendsii* hybrids, but generally blooms in late summer, grows taller, and tolerates dryness a little better. Varieties include the following:

A. c. davidii. Dense, narrow pink plumes to 3 ft. tall. Pink-flowered 'Finale' blooms latest, grows 18–20 in. tall.

'Pumila'. Low mats of leaves topped with lilac pink flower clusters that rise 12–15 in. high.

A. c. taquetii 'Superba'. Bright pinkish purple flowers in spike-like clusters 4–5 ft. tall. 'Purple Candles' is deeper purple, slightly shorter.

'Visions'. Upright grower to 15 in. tall, with raspberry pink plumes above bronzy green leaves. Blooms a little earlier than other *A. chinensis* selections.

A. simplicifolia. Grows to 16 in. high. Leaves are merely cut or lobed, not divided into leaflets. Known for its garden varieties. 'Sprite' (the best known) is a low-growing, compact plant that

blooms profusely in summer, bearing drooping pink, 1-ft. spires above bronze-tinted foliage. 'Hennie Graafland' is similar but grows a few inches taller and blooms a little earlier.

A. taquetii 'Superba'. See A. chinensis taquetii 'Superba'

ASTILBOIDES tabularis (Rodgersia tabularis)
Saxifragaceae
PERENNIAL

| 🌿 **ZONES 2B–9, 14–17** |
| 🔆 **PARTIAL SHADE** |
| 💧 **AMPLE WATER** |

Large plant from China and Korea, with imposing (2-ft.-wide), nearly round leaves attached at the centers to 3-ft.-long stems. Small white flowers in large clusters appear in summer on stalks to 5 ft. high. Plants spread slowly from thick, creeping rhizomes; count on at least a 3-ft. spread. Needs plenty of water; leaves wilt quickly in hot, dry weather. Striking plant for woodland or pondside garden. Good substitute for hostas where slugs and snails cause problems.

Astilboides tabularis

ASTRANTIA
MASTERWORT
Apiaceae (Umbelliferae)
PERENNIALS

| 🌿 **ZONES 1–9, 14–24** |
| 🔆 🔅 **FULL SUN OR PARTIAL SHADE** |
| 💧 **REGULAR WATER** |

Summer flowers in dense, tight clusters surrounded by papery bracts resemble pincushions or, superficially, daisies. Flowering stems rise from leafy clumps. Blossoms make attractive, long-lasting cut flowers and can also be dried for winter arrangements. Useful plants for woodland or cottage gardens—native to alpine woods and meadows of Europe. Spread by underground runners. Die back in winter, even in mild climates. Need good drainage.

A. carniolica. To 1½ ft. tall and wide, with finely divided leaves. Bracts are shorter than in other species. 'Rubra' has dark

red flowers with silvery accents.

A. major. To 3 ft. high, 1–2 ft. wide, with inch-wide clusters of blossoms that are white-green or white-pink. 'Abbey Road', 'Hadspen Blood', and 'Ruby Wedding' have deep pink to purplish red blooms.

Astrantia major

A. maxima. Similar to *A. major* but grows 2 ft. high and bears pink flowers.

ATHEL TREE. See TAMARIX aphylla

ATHYRIUM
Polypodiaceae
FERNS

| 🌿 **ZONES VARY BY SPECIES** |
| 🔆 ● **PARTIAL OR FULL SHADE** |
| 💧💧 **REGULAR TO AMPLE WATER** |

Fronds of most types turn brown after repeated frosts. Leave dead foliage on plants through winter to provide mulch and to shelter delicate emerging fronds in early spring; cut back after new fronds have appeared. Species described here prefer rich, damp soil and will tolerate considerable sun if grown in constantly moist soil. Propagate by dividing old clumps in early spring.

A. filix-femina. LADY FERN. Zones A1–A3; 1–9, 14–24. Native to much of North America. To 4 ft. or taller, 2–3 ft. wide. Vigorous root system can be invasive. Thin, finely divided fronds. Rootstock rises up on older plants to make short trunk. Vertical effect; narrow at bottom, spreading at top. Specialists stock many varieties with oddly cut and feathered fronds. In 'Frizelliae' (about 8 in. high, 1 ft. wide), the frond divisions are reduced to balls, giving each frond the look of a string of beads. 'Vernoniae Cristatum' (to 2½ ft. tall and wide) has crested and feathered fronds.

Athyrium filix-femina

A. 'Ghost'. Zones 1–9, 14–24. Popular hybrid between *A. niponicum* 'Pictum' and *A. filix femina.* Upright growth to about 2½ tall and 2 ft. wide, with silvery gray fronds and dark purple midribs.

A. niponicum 'Pictum' (A. goeringianum 'Pictum'). JAPANESE PAINTED FERN. Zones 1–9, 14–24. Fronds grow to 1–1½ ft. long, making a tight, slowly spreading, foot-high clump. Leaflets are purplish at the base, then lavender, then silvery greenish gray toward the tip.

A. otophorum. ENGLISH PAINTED FERN. Zones 3–9, 14–24. Actually an Asian native. It resembles Japanese painted fern, but its dark green fronds have a reddish or purple midrib.

ATRIPLEX
SALTBUSH
Chenopodiaceae
EVERGREEN AND DECIDUOUS SHRUBS

| 🌿 **ZONES VARY BY SPECIES** |
| 🔆 **FULL SUN** |
| 🌓 **LITTLE OR NO WATER** |

Unusually tolerant of direct seashore conditions and highly alkaline desert soils, saltbushes are grown for their gray or silvery foliage. Flowers and seeds attract birds. Need good drainage. Often become straggly with age; to keep them compact, cut back previous year's growth by one-third each year before the first flush of spring growth. Plants are fire resistant.

Atriplex hymenelytra

A. barklayana. Evergreen. Zones 16–24. Dwarf saltbush from Baja California forms a dense 1½-ft.-high mound 4 ft. across. Inch-long leaves are covered with white powder.

A. canescens. FOUR-WING SALTBUSH. Evergreen. Zones 1–3, 7–24. Native throughout much of arid part of West. Dense growth 3–6 ft. high, spreading to 4–8 ft. Narrow gray leaves ½–2 in. long. Often sheared into a hedge.

A. confertifolia. SHADSCALE. Deciduous. Zones 1–3, 10. Native to high plains and mesas from eastern Oregon and California to North Dakota, south to northern Arizona, western Texas, and Mexico. Mounded, woody, spiny subshrub, 8 in.–3 ft. tall and wide, with rounded, whitish leaves and pinkish or yellowish flower spikes in early summer.

A. hymenelytra. DESERT HOLLY. Evergreen. Zones 3, 7–14, 18, 19. Native to deserts of Southern California, western Arizona, southern Nevada, southwestern Utah. Compact shrub 1–3 ft. high, 3 ft. wide. Whitish branches and silvery, deeply toothed, roundish leaves to 1½ in. long. Has Christmas holly look—in silvery white; much used for decorations. Outside native range, needs very fast drainage. Can take heavy watering from midwinter into spring.

A. lentiformis. QUAIL BUSH. Deciduous. Zones 3, 7–14, 18, 19. Native to alkali wastes in California valleys and deserts and east to Nevada, Utah, Arizona, and New Mexico. Densely branched, sometimes spiny shrub, 3–10 ft. high, 6–12 ft. wide. Oval, bluish gray leaves ½–2 in. long. Useful as salt-tolerant informal hedge or windbreak.

A. l. breweri. BREWER SALTBUSH. Nearly evergreen. Zones 8, 9, 12–24. Native to California coast south of San Francisco Bay and to Channel Islands. Like *A. lentiformis* but not spiny. To 5–7 ft. high, 6–8 ft. wide. Useful gray plant on ocean front; will grow in reclaimed marine soil. Sometimes sheared into a hedge.

A. nummularia. Evergreen. Zones 15–24. Native to Australia but naturalized in parts of Southern California. Dense, rounded, nearly white shrub to 6 ft. tall, 3 ft. wide. Tolerates summer drought, winter flooding. Will grow in full sun or light shade.

A. polycarpa. DESERT SALTBUSH, CATTLE SPINACH. Evergreen to deciduous. Zones 3, 7–13, 18, 19. A tough desert shrub of alkali flats and dry lakebeds from California's Owens Valley east to Utah and south to Baja California and Sonora, Mexico. Dense covering of grayish white scales gives the densely branched, symmetrical, 3–6-ft. mound a silvery glow. Needs no irrigation but leaves will drop during periods of extreme drought and heat.

A. semibaccata. AUSTRALIAN SALTBUSH. Evergreen. Zones 8–10, 12–24. Native to Australia but naturalized in parts of the West and Southwest. Forms a dense, foothigh mat of ½–1½-in.-long, gray-green leaves. Spreads from 1 ft. to 6 ft. or even wider. Excellent ground cover; plant 3 ft. apart.

AUBRIETA deltoidea
COMMON AUBRIETA
Brassicaceae (Cruciferae)
PERENNIAL

🌿 ZONES 1–9, 14–21

☀️ 🌤️ FULL SUN OR LIGHT SHADE

💧 REGULAR WATER

Native from eastern Mediterranean region to Iran. Mat-forming perennial—popular in Northwest and high-elevation rock gardens, where it blooms in early spring, with basket-of-gold, rockcress, perennial candytuft, and moss pink. Ideal for chinks in dry stone walls or between pavers. Grows 2–6 in. high, 1–1½ ft. across. Small gray-green leaves with a few teeth at tips. Tiny rose to deep red, pale to deep lilac, or purple flowers. 'Novalis Blue' is a fine seed-grown variety with dark blue blossoms. 'Rokey's Purple' is a heavy producer of rich purple flowers. Selections with white- or yellow-variegated leaves are also available.

Aubrieta deltoidea

Provide good drainage. Needs regular moisture before and during bloom; takes some drought later on. After bloom, shear off flowers before they set seed. Don't cut back by more than half—always keep some foliage. After trimming, top-dress with mixture of gritty soil and bonemeal. Sow seeds in late spring for blooms the following spring. Difficult to divide clumps; make cuttings in late summer.

AUCUBA japonica
JAPANESE AUCUBA
Cornaceae
EVERGREEN SHRUB

🌿 ZONES 4–24

🌤️ ⚫ PARTIAL OR FULL SHADE

💧 💧 MODERATE TO REGULAR WATER

Native from Himalayas to Japan. Seedlings vary in leaf form and variegations; many varieties offered. Standard green-leafed aucuba grows at a moderate rate up to 6–10 ft. (sometimes to 15 ft.)

Aucuba japonica 'Variegata'

high and almost as wide. Plant can be kept lower by pruning. Buxom shrub, densely clothed with polished, dark green, toothed leaves 3–8 in. long, 1½–3 in. wide.

Minute dark maroon flowers in earliest spring are followed by clusters of bright red, ¾-in. berries in fall and winter. Both sexes must be planted to ensure fruit crop. Green-leafed 'Rozannie' is self-fruitful, producing a heavy crop of berries without a pollenizer.

Other green-leafed varieties include 'Longifolia' ('Salicifolia'), narrow willowlike leaves (female); 'Nana', dwarf to about 3 ft. tall (female); 'Serratifolia', long leaves with coarsely toothed edges (female).

Variegated varieties (usually slower growing) include 'Crotonifolia', leaves heavily splashed with white and gold (male); 'Fructu Albo', leaves variegated with white, berries pale pinkish buff (female); 'Picturata' ('Aureo-maculata'), leaves centered with golden yellow, edged with dark green dotted yellow (female); 'Sulphur', green leaves with broad yellow edge (female). 'Variegata', often called gold dust plant, is the best-known aucuba. It has dark green leaves spotted with yellow; plants may be male or female. 'Mr. Goldstrike' has heavier gold splashings.

Tolerant of wide range of soils but will grow better and look better if poor or heavy soils are improved. Requires shade from hot sun, accepts deep shade. Grows well in low light under trees, competes successfully with tree roots. Tolerates sea air. Gets mealybug and mites. Prune to control height or form by cutting back to a leaf joint.

All aucubas make choice tub plants for shady patio or in the house. Use variegated forms to lighten up dark corners. Plants combine effectively with ferns, hydrangeas.

AURICULA.
See **PRIMULA auricula**

AURINIA saxatilis
(Alyssum saxatile)
BASKET-OF-GOLD
Brassicaceae (Cruciferae)
PERENNIAL

🌿 ZONES 1–24

☀️ 🌤️ FULL SUN OR LIGHT SHADE

💧 MODERATE WATER

Mustard relative native to mountains of central and southern Europe, Turkey. Gray leaves (sometimes variegated white) form a spreading evergreen mound 8–12 in. high; dwarf forms are half as tall. Dense clusters of single or double, tiny, yellow to apricot flowers cover the plant in spring and early summer. Use as foreground plant

Aurinia saxatilis

in borders, in rock gardens, atop walls; plant about 1½ ft. apart. Poor soils or moderately fertile ones suit the plant perfectly—as long as drainage is good. Shear lightly (don't cut back stems by more than half) right after bloom. Generally hardy but may be killed in extremely cold winters. Self-sows readily.

AUSTRALIAN BLUEBELL CREEPER.
See **SOLLYA heterophylla**

AUSTRALIAN FUCHSIA.
See **CORREA**

AUSTRALIAN PEA VINE.
See **DOLICHOS lignosus**

AUSTRALIAN TEA TREE. See **LEPTOSPERMUM laevigatum**

AUSTRALIAN TREE FERN.
See **CYATHEA cooperi**

AUSTRALIAN WILLOW.
See **ACACIA salicina,**
GEIJERA parviflora

AUSTRIAN BRIER.
See **ROSA foetida**

AUSTROSTIPA ramosissima.
See **STIPA ramosissima**

AUTUMN CROCUS.
See **COLCHICUM**

AUTUMN FERN.
See **DRYOPTERIS erythrosora**

AVENA sempervirens.
See **HELICTOTRICHON sempervirens**

A

AVOCADO

NAME	ZONES	HARVEST PERIOD	FRUIT	COMMENTS
'Bacon'	9, 15–24	Midfall through winter	Medium size, green skinned. Good quality	Mexican. Upright grower. Bears heavier in alternate years. Type A flower. 'Jim Bacon' is a slightly hardier seedling selection
'Don Gillogly'	9, 15–24	Late summer into fall	Large, with black, easy-to-peel skin. Excellent flavor	Mexican. Hardy to 27°F/–3°C. Type A flower
'Fuerte'	9, 15, 19–24	Late fall through spring	Medium size, green skinned. High quality	Hybrid. Hardy to 27°F/–3°C. Well-known variety. Large tree. Early blooming. Tends to bear in alternate years. Type B flower
'Gwen'	19–24	Spring into fall	Medium size, green skinned. Good quality	Guatemalan. Medium tree with narrow habit. Bears in alternate years. Type A flower
'Hass'	16, 17, 19–24	Spring into fall	Medium to large. Dark purple (almost black), pebbly, thick but pliable skin. Excellent flavor	Hybrid. Hardy to 30°F/–1°C. Large, spreading tree. Bears heavier in alternate years. Type A flower. 'Lamb Hass' is more productive, with slightly larger fruit
'Holiday'	19–24	Midfall through winter	Large, green skinned. Very good flavor	Guatemalan. Medium tree with weeping habit. Bears in alternate years. Type A flower
'Jim'	9, 15, 19–24	Late fall into winter	Medium size, with green skin and long neck	Mexican. Type B flower
'Kahaluu'	H2	Fall into winter	Medium to large, green skinned. Superb flavor	Hybrid. Hardy to 30°F/–1°C. Light producer. Type B flower
'Mexicola'	9, 15–24	Late summer into fall	Small, with tender, dark purple skin. Outstanding, nutty flavor. Large seed	Mexican. Very cold-hardy, to 20°F/–7°C. Heavy producer. Type A flower. 'Mexicola Grande' is larger and a bit hardier
'Murashige'	H2	Spring to late summer	Medium to large, with green, pebbly skin. Very good quality. Small seed	Hybrid. Hardy to 30°F/–1°C. Heavy producer. Type B flower
'Nabal'	19–24	Summer into fall	Medium to large, green skinned. Excellent flavor	Guatemalan. Tends to bear in alternate years. Type B flower
'Pinkerton'	9, 15, 19–24	Winter through spring	Medium to large, green skinned. Very good quality	Guatemalan. Large tree. Consistent producer. Type A flower
'Reed'	21–24	Summer into fall	Medium to large, with green, pebbly skin. Fine flavor	Guatemalan. Slender, upright tree. Tends to bear well alone. Type A flower
'Sharwil'	H2	Fall into spring	Medium size, with green, pebbly skin. Excellent flavor	Hybrid. Hardy to 30°F/–1°C. Heavy producer. Type B flower
'Stewart'	9, 15–24	Fall to winter	Small to medium, with dark purple skin. Excellent flavor	Mexican. Compact tree. Type B flower
'Wertz' ('Wurtz')	19–24	Summer	Medium size, with green, pebbly skin. Rich flavor	Guatemalan. Medium tree with weeping branches; good for small gardens. Tends to bear in alternate years. Often sold as 'Dwarf', 'Littlecado', or 'Minicado'. Type A flower
'Whitsell'	19–24	Midwinter into fall	Medium size, green skinned. Very good quality	Guatemalan. Medium tree. Tends to bear in alternate years. Type B flower
'Yamagata'	H2	Late spring through summer	Medium to large, with green, pebbly skin. Rich flavor	Hybrid. Hardy to 30°F/–1°C. Heavy producer. Type B flower
'Zutano'	9, 16–24	Midfall to midwinter	Medium size, green skinned. Average quality	Hybrid. Hardy to 24°F/–4°C. Upright grower. Used to cross-pollinate 'Hass'. Type B flower

AVOCADO
Lauraceae
EVERGREEN TREES

- ⚡ **ZONES VARY BY VARIETY**
- ☀ **FULL SUN**
- 💧 **REGULAR WATER**
- ▶ **SEE CHART AT LEFT**

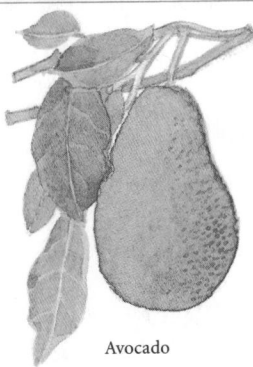

Avocado

In California, two races of avocados are grown: Guatemalan (*Persea americana guatemalensis*) and Mexican (*P. a. drymifolia*). Widely planted varieties 'Hass' and 'Fuerte' are hybrids. Ideal climates for Guatemalan varieties (generally hardy to 30°F/–1°C) are Zones 21, 23, and 24, but good results can be had in Zones 19, 20, and 22, and some success can be expected in Zones 9 and 15. Mexican varieties, which bear smaller, less attractive fruit, are hardier (down to at least 24°F/–4°C) and grow in Zones 9, 15–24, and some warmer locations in Zones 8 and 14. (See chart for cold-hardiness of hybrids.) Avocados bloom in late winter to late spring, so even though older trees will survive these lows, temperatures much below freezing will damage flowers or fruit. In Hawaii, Guatemalan and hybrid varieties are best adapted to (and are grown throughout) Zone H2, but away from exposure to salt spray.

The all-important factor in growing avocados is good drainage. A high water table in the winter rainy season is often fatal, even in well-drained soil. Keep the soil evenly moist by using sprinkler irrigation when the soil near the surface begins to dry. Give plants an occasional deep soaking to wash accumulated salts from the soil around the roots. Let fallen leaves build up under the tree as mulch. Feed young trees lightly; mature trees need 1 lb. of actual nitrogen per year, split into two or more applications and applied in spring and summer. Control chlorosis with iron and zinc chelates.

Pollination is complex. Avocado varieties have flowers categorized as either type A or type B, depending on the time of day they open and when pollen is released. In areas where avocados are common, isolated trees may produce enough fruit for home consumption, but for best production, plant one of each type or graft a limb of one type into a bearing tree of the other type. Flower type for each variety is noted in the chart.

The fruit of many avocado varieties is not ready to harvest until a year or more after fruit set. Time required for maturation varies from approximately 6 months ('Zutano', 'Bacon') to nearly 18 months ('Holiday').

When using avocados in the landscape, remember that most varieties will reach 30–40 ft. tall and spread wider (although size can be controlled to some degree by pruning). They will also produce dense shade and shed leaves consistently throughout the year.

Avocado trees are very susceptible to *Phytophthora* root rot. Added mulch and gypsum can create soil conditions that suppress this fungus. After an avocado is planted, cover the soil around it with a 6–12-in.-deep layer of organic mulch or wood chips, but keep the mulching material at least 6 in. away from the trunk. Scatter a total of 25 lbs. of gypsum per year around the tree a little at a time.

Persea mite is a problem in Southern California; it causes small yellow and black dead spots on the foliage and excessive leaf drop. It can be partially controlled by releasing one of several species of predatory mites. For more information, contact your Cooperative Extension Office.

Unless otherwise noted, fruit of all varieties listed in chart has thin, pliable, smooth skin.

AZALEA.
See **RHODODENDRON**

AZARA
Flacourtiaceae
EVERGREEN SHRUBS OR SMALL TREES

- ⚡ **ZONES VARY BY SPECIES**
- ◑ **PARTIAL SHADE**
- 💧 **REGULAR WATER**

Native to lakesides and woodland edges in Chile, Argentina. Attractive evergreen foliage; fluffy yellow flowers that smell like chocolate to some, vanilla to others. Need fast drainage, regular fertilizer, protection from hot afternoon sun. Prune after bloom to remove crowded or wayward branches.

A. dentata. Zones 5 (with shelter), 6, 15–17. To 15 ft. tall, 12 ft. wide. Toothed, rounded, shiny leaves about 1 in. across. Dense branching and rounded shape make it useful for screen or informal hedge. Tolerates considerable shade. Blooms in spring.

A. lanceolata. LANCELEAF AZARA. Zones 5 (with shelter), 15–17. Large, arching plant to 20 ft. tall, 15 ft. wide. Equal to *A. microphylla* in pattern value, but its bright yellow-green, rather narrow leaves are much larger (to 2½ in. long), producing a lusher effect. Blooms in spring.

A. microphylla. BOXLEAF AZARA. Zones 5–9, 14–24. Best-known species. Slow growing when small, faster when established. Typically reaches 12–18 ft. tall, 8–12 ft. wide, but may attain a treelike 30 ft. tall in great old age. Shiny, roundish dark green leaves are ½–¾ in. long. Flat-branching habit and neatly arranged foliage make it natural for espalier or free-standing wall plant. Blooms in late winter.

Azara microphylla

A. petiolaris (A. gilliesii). Zones 15–17. Shrubby growth to 15–20 ft. tall, 12 ft. wide, but easily trained to form a single-stemmed tree. Oval to roundish, lustrous deep green leaves are 1½–3 in. long, look somewhat like those of holly; they hang from branches like aspen leaves. Blooms in late winter.

AZORELLA trifurcata.
See **BOLAX gummifera**

AZTEC LILY.
See **SPREKELIA formosissima**

BABACO. See **PAPAYA**

BABIANA
BABOON FLOWER
Iridaceae
PERENNIALS FROM CORMS

- ⚡ **ZONES 4–24; OR DIG AND STORE**
- ☀◑ **FULL SUN OR LIGHT SHADE**
- 💧 **REGULAR WATER DURING GROWTH AND BLOOM**

These natives of sub-Saharan Africa are grown for spikes of freesialike flowers in blue, lavender, purple, red, and white. In mid- to late spring, each flowering stem produces six or more blooms, each to 2 in. across. Strongly ribbed, usually hairy leaves typically grow in fans. Corms are reportedly tasty to

Babiana stricta

baboons, hence the plant's common name. Plant them 4 in. deep and 4–6 in. apart—along edge of border or path, in rock garden, in deep pots. In Zones 8–24, plant in fall; in colder areas, plant in early spring, waiting until temperatures will remain above 20°F/–7°C. Cut back on water as leaves yellow. Trim off foliage after it dies back. Where corms can overwinter in ground, leave them in place for several years—they'll increase and bloom more profusely with each year. Beyond hardiness range, dig and store as for gladiolus.

B. rubrocyanea. Ruby-throated royal blue blossoms on 6-in. stems.

B. stricta. Royal blue flowers on 1-ft. stems. Varieties with purple, lavender, white, and blue-and-white blooms are sold.

BABINGTONIA.
See **BAECKEA**

BABY BLUE EYES.
See **NEMOPHILA menziesii**

BABY'S BREATH.
See **GYPSOPHILA paniculata**

BABY SNAPDRAGON.
See **LINARIA maroccana**

BABY'S TEARS.
See **SOLEIROLIA soleirolii**

BACCHARIS
Asteraceae (Compositae)
EVERGREEN SHRUBS

- ⚡ ZONES VARY BY SPECIES
- ☼ FULL SUN
- ◔ ◗ LITTLE TO MODERATE WATER

Main value of these plants is their toughness and ability to grow in difficult conditions: they withstand heat, wind, and poor soil. Most are densely foliaged. Male and female flowers, borne on separate plants, are inconspicuous. Female plants produce cottony seed clusters that can make a mess when blown about by wind; grow male varieties if they're available (or hoe out seedlings if they appear where you don't want them).

B. 'Centennial'. Zones 7–24; best in 10–13. Female hybrid between *B. pilularis* and *B. sarothroides*. Grows 3 ft. tall, 4–5 ft. wide, with narrow leaves and tufted tan seed capsules in spring. Tolerates desert heat; resists root rot caused by water molds.

B. pilularis. DWARF COYOTE BRUSH. Zones 5–11, 14–24. Native to Northern California coast. Remarkable climate and soil adaptation. Near the coast it thrives with no water at all; inland it looks better with monthly watering. In California's high desert, it's the most dependable of all ground covers. Everywhere, it's a very valuable, reliable bank and flatland cover for low-maintenance areas in sun.

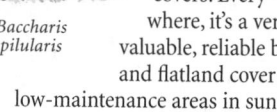

Baccharis pilularis

Makes dense, rather billowy, bright green mat, 8–24 in. high and spreading to 6 ft. or more. Small (½-in.), toothed leaves are closely set on branches. Needs shearing once a year in early spring before new growth starts. Cut out old arching branches and thin to rejuvenate. Feed with a nitrogen fertilizer immediately after cutting back. The plants available in most nurseries are produced by cuttings from male plants. 'Twin Peaks' ('Twin Peaks #2') has small dark green leaves and a moderate growth rate. 'Pigeon Point' has larger leaves in a lighter green and grows faster (9 ft. wide in 4 years); can make a 2–3-ft.-high hedge.

B. sarothroides. DESERT BROOM. Zones 7–24; most useful in 10–13. Native to Southwest. Nearly leafless, but branches are bright green throughout year. Grows 5 ft. tall and wide; can be clipped to 2–3 ft. Extremely drought tolerant. Can take good or poor drainage. Useful for erosion control, replanting disturbed land, or natural landscape in desert regions.

B. 'Starn' (B. 'Thompson'). Zones 7–24; best in 10–13. Has the same size and habit as 'Centennial' but offers an improvement, since it is a male plant and won't produce seed clusters.

BACHELOR'S BUTTON.
See **CENTAUREA cyanus**

BACOPA. See **SUTERA cordata**

BACOPA monnieri
WATER HYSSOP
Scrophulariaceae
AQUATIC PERENNIAL

- ⚡ ZONES 8–24; H1, H2
- ☼ FULL SUN
- 💧 AMPLE WATER

Bacopa monnieri

The true bacopa is a trailing, succulent plant native to the tropics and parts of the southeastern U.S., with ¾-in. leaves and small white or pale blue flowers. It forms mats at the water's edge, often extending its growth into the water. Grow it at a pond edge or in a pot in the water. For the familiar terrestrial bacopa seen as a hanging basket or bedding plant, see *Sutera cordata*.

BAECKEA virgata
(Babingtonia virgata)
Myrtaceae
EVERGREEN SHRUB

- ⚡ ZONES 15–24
- ☼ ◗ FULL SUN OR LIGHT SHADE
- 💧 REGULAR WATER

Australian native with tiny needle-like leaves and profuse small white, honey-scented flowers that resemble miniature blossoms of tea tree (*Leptospermum*). Blooms in spring and summer. Reaches 8 ft. or taller, 4–4½ ft. wide. Pinch

Baeckea virgata

young plants to promote branching; thin out old, weak growth after flowering is over.

BAGAUAK. See **CLERODENDRUM quadriloculare**

BAILEYA multiradiata
DESERT MARIGOLD
Asteraceae (Compositae)
ANNUAL OR PERENNIAL

- ⚡ ZONES 1–3, 7–23
- ☼ FULL SUN
- 💧 MODERATE WATER

Baileya multiradiata

Western desert native grows 1–1½ ft. high, displaying inch-wide, bright yellow flowers above gray-green foliage. Basic bloom period is spring through fall, but year-round bloom is possible in low desert and other mild-winter areas if plants receive periodic moisture. Sow seed in fall or spring, rake in, and water thoroughly. Keep moist until seeds sprout, then reduce watering to once or twice weekly. Thin to 1½ ft. apart. To prolong bloom, water every week or two. Self-sows.

BALD CYPRESS.
See **TAXODIUM distichum**

BALLOON FLOWER.
See **PLATYCODON grandiflorus**

BALLOTA pseudodictamnus
Lamiaceae (Labiatae)
SHRUBBY PERENNIAL

- ⚡ ZONES 2, 3, 6–9, 14–24
- ☼ FULL SUN
- ◔ ◗ LITTLE TO MODERATE WATER

Dense, rounded Mediterranean native to 1½ ft. high, 2 ft. wide, with opposite pairs of roundish, inch-wide, furry gray-green leaves. Bears whorls of unimportant small white flowers. Use in mixed perennial beds or bank plantings. Provide good drainage. Cut back hard in spring before new growth starts.

Ballota pseudodictamnus

BALSAM. See **IMPATIENS**

BALSAM PEAR.
See **BITTER MELON**

BAMBOO
Poaceae (Gramineae)
GIANT GRASSES

- ⚡ SEE CHART FOR HARDINESS
- ☼ ◗ SUN OR PARTIAL SHADE
- ◔ ◑ ◗ LITTLE TO REGULAR WATER
- ▶ SEE CHART NEXT PAGE

Though some grow as tall as trees, all bamboos are actually grasses. Plants consist of woody stems (culms) that are divided into sections (internodes) by obvious joints (nodes). Upper nodes grow buds that develop into branches and leaves. Bamboos spread by underground stems (rhizomes) that, like the aboveground culms, are jointed and carry buds. The manner in which the rhizomes grow is different in running and clumping bamboos, an important distinction for the gardener.

In clumping bamboos (*Bambusa, Borinda, Chusquea, Drepanostachyum, Fargesia, Himalayacalamus, Otatea*), rhizomes grow a few inches from the edge of the clump, then send up stems. Clumps expand continually but slowly. Most clumping bamboos are tropical or subtropical.

In running bamboos (*Chimonobambusa, Indocalamus, Phyllostachys, Pleioblastus, Pseudosasa, Sasa, Semiarundinaria*), rhizomes grow rapidly to various distances from the parent plant before sending up vertical shoots. These bamboos eventually form large patches or

Bambusa multiplex

BAMBOO

For explanation of height and growth habit, see page 216. Hardiness is temperature at which leaf damage occurs.

NAME	ALSO SOLD AS	CONTROLLED (UNCONTROLLED) HEIGHT	GROWTH HABIT	STEM DIAMETER	HARDINESS	COMMENTS (FORM, CHARACTERISTICS, USES)
CLUMPING TYPES						
Bambusa multiplex 'Alphonse Karr' ALPHONSE KARR BAMBOO		8-10 ft. (15-35 ft.)	II	½-1 in.	15°F/-9°C	Branches from base to top. Dense growth. Culms brilliantly striped green on yellow. New culms pinkish and green
B. m. 'Fernleaf' FERNLEAF BAMBOO	*B. nana, B. disticha*	6-10 ft. (10-20 ft.)	II	½ in.	15°F/-9°C	Closely spaced leaves, 10-20 to twig, give ferny look. Loses this look, grows coarser with rich soil, ample water
B. m. 'Golden Goddess' GOLDEN GODDESS BAMBOO		6-8 ft. (6-10 ft.)	II	½ in.	15°F/-9°C	Golden-stemmed variety with graceful, dense, arching growth. Good container or screen plant. Give tops room to spread
B. oldhamii OLDHAM BAMBOO, CLUMPING GIANT TIMBER BAMBOO	*Sinocalamus oldhamii*	15-25 ft. (20-55 ft.)	IV	4 in.	20°F/-7°C	Densely foliaged, erect clumps; good for big, dense screens. Or use single plant as imposing vertical mass. Most common big bamboo in Southern California
B. textilis WEAVER'S BAMBOO		16-20 ft. (30-50 ft.)	IV	5 in.	20°F/-7°C	Stately, upright, forming a very tight column of blue-powdered canes that arch at the top. Grows taller where winters are warmer. Screen or specimen
B. tuldoides ventricosa BUDDHA'S BELLY BAMBOO		3-6 ft. (15-30 ft.)	II or IV	2 in.	20°F/-7°C	Stays small, produces swollen culms that give it its name only when grown in tubs or in poor, dryish soil. Otherwise a giant bamboo with straight culms
B. vulgaris 'Vittata' PAINTED BAMBOO		15-25 ft. (to 50 ft.)	IV	4 in.	32°F/0°C	Yellow culms have vertical green stripes. For Hawaii, mildest coastal climates, and well-lit interiors
Borinda fungosa	*Fargesia fungosa*	10-12 ft. (15-20 ft.)	II	1 in.	10°F/-12°C	Graceful, weeping, fountain shaped. Culms on side facing sun turn rich chocolate brown. Best in half-day sun. Screen or specimen
Chusquea coronalis		8-12 ft. (12-15 ft.)	II	¾ in.	32°F/0°C	Arching culms bear masses of tiny leaves on short, whorled branches. Exceptionally attractive. Sun or light shade. Rare
Drepanostachyum falcatum BLUE BAMBOO	*Himalayacalamus hookerianus*	10-15 ft. (20-30 ft.)	II	2 in.	15°F/-9°C	Culms are sky blue with white powder, sometimes developing a reddish blush. Medium-large blue-green leaves. Spectacular specimen plant
Fargesia murieliae UMBRELLA BAMBOO	*Sinarundinaria murielae*	6-8 ft. (to 15 ft.)	II	¾ in.	-20°F/-29°C	Light, airy, tight clump, arching and drooping at top. Best in shade. Select new-generation plants that will not bloom soon
F. nitida FOUNTAIN BAMBOO	*Sinarundinaria nitida*	6-8 ft. (15-20 ft.)	II	¾ in.	-20°F/-29°C	Graceful, weeping, fountain shaped with wide-spreading foliage. Greenish purple culms mature to deep purplish black. Needs shade to look its best. Rare. New culms of 'Jiuzhaigou' are bright red; grows best with morning sun
F. rufa		6-8 ft. (12-15 ft.)	II	½ in.	-20°F/-29°C	Culm sheaths orange red. Resembles *F. nitida*. Good as specimen, hedge
Himalayacalamus asper PRINCESS BAMBOO	*Neomicrocalamus microphyllus*	8-10 ft. (15-20 ft.)	II	1½ in.	15°F/-9°C	Fountain shaped, forming tight clump. Culms bright green in shade, shiny maroon in sun. Delicate, small leaves. Shade to half-day sun. Good screen or specimen

BAMBOO

For explanation of height and growth habit, see page 216. Hardiness is temperature at which leaf damage occurs.

B

NAME	ALSO SOLD AS	CONTROLLED (UNCONTROLLED) HEIGHT	GROWTH HABIT	STEM DIAMETER	HARDINESS	COMMENTS (FORM, CHARACTERISTICS, USES)
Otatea acuminata aztecorum MEXICAN WEEPING BAMBOO	*Yushania aztecorum, Arthrostylidium longifolium*	8–10 ft. (to 20 ft.)	II	1½ in.	20°F/–7°C	Extremely narrow leaves (6 in. by ⅛ in.) give lacy look. Foliage masses bend nearly to ground. Fairly drought resistant when established. Rare
RUNNING TYPES						
Chimonobambusa quadrangularis SQUARE-STEM BAMBOO	*Bambusa quadrangularis*	10–15 ft. (20–30 ft.)	III	1 in.	10°F/–12°C	Squarish culms have prominent joints, carry heavy whorls of branches. Valued for vertical effect and cascading leaves. Can be grown indoors. Culms grow in winter
Indocalamus tessellatus	*Arundinaria ragamowskii*	2–3 ft. (3–6 ft.)	I	¼ in.	–10°F/–23°C	Broad, handsome leaves are up to 2 ft. long, 3–4 ft. wide and spread like fingers from stem and branch tips. Very shade tolerant. Rapid spreader. Rare
Phyllostachys aurea GOLDEN BAMBOO		6–10 ft. (10–20 ft.)	III	2 in.	0°F/–18°C	Erect, stiff culms, usually with crowded joints at base—good identifying mark. Dense foliage makes it good screen or hedge. Can take much drought but looks better with regular water. Good choice for growing in tubs
P. aureosulcata YELLOW GROOVE BAMBOO		12–15 ft. (15–25 ft.)	III	1½ in.	–10°F/–23°C	Like more slender, more open *P. aurea.* Young culms green with pronounced yellowish groove
P. bambusoides GIANT TIMBER BAMBOO, JAPANESE TIMBER BAMBOO	*P. reticulata*	15–35 ft. (25–45 ft.)	IV	6 in.	–5°F/–21°C	Once the most common of large, hardy timber bamboos. Most perished during blooming period in 1960s–70s. New plants from seed are available. Makes beautiful groves
P. b. 'Castillon'	*P. castillonis*	10–15 ft. (15–20 ft.)	III	2 in.	0°F/–18°C	Yellow culms show green stripe above each branch cluster. Lightly variegated leaves
P. b. 'Holochrysa' ALL GOLD BAMBOO		14–18 ft. (25–35 ft.)	III	2½ in.	0°F/–18°C	Light orange to beige culms with occasional green stripes and variegated leaves. Takes bright light to full sun
P. nigra BLACK BAMBOO		4–8 ft. (10–30 ft.)	III	1½ in.	0°F/–18°C	New culms green, turning black in second year (rarely olive green dotted black). Where summers are hot, does best in afternoon shade
P. n. 'Daikokuchiku' GIANT BLACK BAMBOO		25–30 ft. (45–60 ft.)	IV	3⅓ in.	0°F/–18°C	Identical to *P. nigra* but grows twice as tall and wide. Does well in hot summers
P. n. 'Hale'		15–18 ft. (20–30 ft.)	III	2¾ in.	–5°F/–21°C	Most culms turn jet black within 3–6 months of emerging, so the entire clump is solid black most of the year
P. n. 'Henon'		20 ft. (to 54 ft.)	III	3½ in.	–5°F/–21°C	Much larger than *P. nigra.* Culms whitish green, not changing to black, rough to touch
P. vivax		15–20 ft. (55–70 ft.)	IV	4–6 in.	–5°F/–21°C	Hardiest giant bamboo and the quickest to attain large size. 'Aureocaulis' has golden yellow culms randomly striped with green

BAMBOO

For explanation of height and growth habit, see page 216. Hardiness is temperature at which leaf damage occurs.

NAME	ALSO SOLD AS	CONTROLLED (UNCONTROLLED) HEIGHT	GROWTH HABIT	STEM DIAMETER	HARDINESS	COMMENTS (FORM, CHARACTERISTICS, USES)
Pleioblastus chino 'Murakamianus'		2–5 ft. (6–10 ft.)	I	1/3 in.	10°F/–12°C	Bright green leaves cleanly striped with white. Prune to 2 in. tall in late winter to refresh foliage. Excellent in containers. Looks best with half-day sun
P. distichus DWARF FERNLEAF BAMBOO	Sasa disticha	1–2 ft. (2–3 ft.)	I	1/8 in.	10°F/–12°C	Delicate in appearance. Tiny, two-ranked ferny leaves. Rampant; cut back to ground if rank or stemmy
P. fortunei DWARF WHITE-STRIPE BAMBOO	P. variegatus	1–2 ft. (2–3 ft.)	I	1/4 in.	–10°F/–23°C	Fast spreader; curb rhizomes. Use in tubs or as deep ground cover. Sun or light shade
P. pygmaea	Sasa pygmaea	3 ft. (3 ft.)	I	1/8 in.	0°F/–18°C	Aggressive spreader; good bank holder, good for erosion control. Can be mowed every few years to keep it from growing stemmy and unattractive
P. shibuyanus 'Tsuboi'	P. variegatus 'Tsuboi'	3–4 ft. (6–8 ft.)	I	1/2 in.	0°F/–18°C	Green foliage striped with light yellow variegation; looks good all year. May be pruned into low ground cover or hedge. Good in pots
P. viridistriatus DWARF GREEN-STRIPE BAMBOO	Arundinaria auricoma, A. viridistriatus	1–2 ft. (to 2 1/2 ft.)	I	1/4 in.	0°F/–18°C	Leaves 8 in. long, 1 1/2 in. wide, strikingly variegated green and gold
Pseudosasa japonica ARROW BAMBOO	Arundinaria japonica	6–10 ft. (10–18 ft.)	III	3/4 in.	0°F/–18°C	Stiffly erect culms with one branch at each joint. Large leaves with long, pointed tails. Rampant thick hedge in mild-winter climates; slow spreader where winters are cold, making dense, erect clumps
Sasa palmata nebulosa		6–8 ft. (12–15 ft.)	I	1/2–1 in.	–10°F/–23°C	Tropical appearance, with broad, handsome leaves. Culms green with black spots. Extremely vigorous
S. veitchii		2–3 ft. (2–3 ft.)	I	1/4 in.	–10°F/–23°C	Rampant spreader with large (7- by 1-in.), dark green leaves that turn whitish buff all around the edges in autumn. Looks good in Japanese gardens if curbed
Semiarundinaria fastuosa NARIHIRA BAMBOO		8–10 ft. (25–30 ft.)	II or III	1 1/4 in.	–10°F/–23°C	Rigidly upright growth. Slow spreader easily kept to a clump. Plant close to make narrow, dense hedge or screen

Phyllostachys nigra

TOP: *Sasa veitchii*
BOTTOM: *Pleioblastus pygmaea*

Bambusa multiplex 'Golden Goddess'

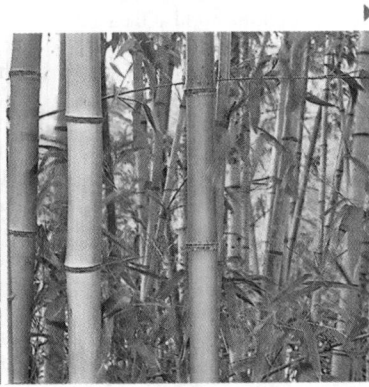

Phyllostachys bambusoides

groves. They are generally fairly hardy plants from temperate regions in China and Japan, and they will grow in a wide variety of soils. Such bamboos require regular maintenance if grown in gardens.

Mature bamboos grow very fast during their brief growth period. The season of shoot growth for runners varies, but is primarily March to July. The more tropical clumpers produce shoots spring, summer, or fall and sometimes twice a year, again depending upon the species. Culms of all bamboos have already attained their maximum diameter when they emerge

*Phyllostachys
aurea*

from the ground. In mature plants, new shoots usually reach their maximum height within 1 to 2 months. Culms of giant types may grow in length several feet a day. Don't expect such growth the first year after transplanting, though. Giant timber bamboo (*Phyllostachys bambusoides*), for instance, needs 3 to 5 years to build up a rhizome system capable of supporting its fast-growing culms; growth in early years will be less impressive.

Flowering of bamboos is one of the great mysteries of this unique plant. Most species flower periodically all over the world at the same time for a period of 2 to 7 years at intervals varying from 10 to 120 years, depending on species. Flowering generally weakens these plants, and although they may slowly recover, they often die. Very heavy feeding and watering may speed their recovery. Bamboo flowers are interesting but not usually decorative, resembling the seed heads of other grains.

Difficult to mass-produce and little known, most bamboos are hard to find in nurseries. Inquire about specialists in your area.

The American Bamboo Society has chapters in the Northwest, Northern California, and Southern California. Society members often propagate rare varieties for sale in connection with their meetings. Arboretum and botanical garden sales are other good sources. Plant names change so frequently that vendors cannot always keep up, so you may need to check for them under the principal names listed in the chart as well as under the synonyms.

The chart also lists hardiness for each type—the temperature at which leaf damage occurs. Stems and rhizomes may be considerably hardier.

Planting and propagating.
Container-grown bamboos may be planted at any time of year. Disregard the rule of never buying root-bound plants: the more crowded a bamboo is in the container, the faster it will grow when planted. Do not cut or spread the root ball, as this may kill some canes. Best time to propagate from existing clumps is just before growth begins; divide hardy kinds in late winter or early spring, tropical ones in mid- to late spring. Transplanting at other times is possible, but risk of losing divisions is high in summer heat or winter chill and wet soil. Cut or saw out large divisions with roots and at least three connected culms. If divisions are tall, cut back tops to balance loss of roots and rhizomes. Foliage may wilt or wither, but culms will send out new leaves. Rhizome cutting is another means of propagating runners; a cutting consists of a foot-long length of rhizome with roots and buds. Plant in rich soil mix with ample organic material added; keep moist.

Care and feeding. For best growth water bamboos frequently and deeply, soaking soil around the plant to at least 12 in. Established plants tolerate considerable drought but look best with regular irrigation. Fertilize in-ground plants once a month, March to October, with a high-nitrogen fertilizer; use a balanced controlled-release fertilizer for plants in containers. To restrict size and spread of an established bamboo, cut back on water and fertilizer. Even though individual culms won't grow taller after their first year, they become increasingly leafy. Plants are evergreen, but

there is considerable dropping of older leaves; old plantings develop a nearly weedproof mulch of dead leaves. Individual canes live for several years but eventually die and should be cut out.

Scale, mealybugs, and aphids are occasionally found on bamboo but seldom do any harm; if they excrete honeydew in bothersome amounts, spray with insecticidal soap or summer oil. Mites can cause yellow streaking or disfigurement of leaves. To control them, use insecticidal soap.

Most bamboos are not recommended for year-round indoor culture, but container-grown plants can spend extended periods indoors in cool, humid, bright rooms. You can revive plants by taking them outdoors, but it is important to avoid sudden changes in temperature and light. Overwatering is the greatest threat to bamboo grown indoors. Provide good drainage and do not allow pots to sit in standing water.

Growth habit and height. The accompanying chart classifies each bamboo by growth habit, which determines its use in the garden. *Group I* includes the dwarf types (5–10 ft. tall) and low-growing ground cover types (1–4 ft. tall) of

running bamboos. These bamboos can be allowed to spread for erosion control or contained in small clumps in borders or rock gardens. Cut back in winter to maintain low stature and enhance new growth. *Group II* consists of clumping bamboos with a fountainlike habit of growth and moderate height (10–30 ft. tall). These noninvasive types are probably the most useful for landscaping: they make excellent hedges or screens, which may be pruned into formal shapes, left to grow naturally as an informal screen, or grown singly to show off their graceful form.

Group III bamboos are running types of moderate size (10–30 ft. tall), with more or less vertical growth; they should generally be contained. They make fast-growing screens and hedges, pruned or unpruned, and may also be grown as specimen plants within containment. *Group IV* consists of the giant bamboos. Use running kinds for groves or for Asian effects on a grand scale. Clumping kinds have a tropical look, especially if they are used with broad-leafed tropical plants. All may be thinned and clipped to show off culms. Thin clumps or groves by cutting out old or dead culms at the base.

The chart lists two heights for each bamboo. *Controlled height* means average height under drier conditions with little feeding, or with rhizome spread controlled by barriers. *Uncontrolled height* refers to plants growing under best conditions without confinement. Keep in mind that, even within these categories, climate and cultural practices will affect eventual heights. Consulting with local bamboo experts about growth habits is always a good idea.

Containment and removal. Even though large expanses of concrete or asphalt will not prevent the spread of running bamboos, it isn't difficult to keep them from taking over the neighborhood—provided you understand how they grow. Rhizomes are shallow and spread sideways, not down. Therefore, you can contain runners by installing a 30–36-in.-deep, 40–60-mil-thick, continuous polypropylene plastic sheet around the perimeter of the planting. Leave a 2-in. lip above ground to block runners. Create any size or shape with this nearly seamless material. Never place plastic under roots since they need excellent drainage. Or contain runners by planting them in raised beds or above-ground containers. Continuously dry soil extending 10–20 ft. beyond the planting bed also stops runners.

Equally effective but the most labor intensive method of stopping runners is to periodically insert a spade down to its full length around the plant, severing the rhizomes and isolating the unwanted parts from the main plant. Break off any new shoots from the isolated rhizomes; they are unlikely to resprout. Another method is to dig a foot-deep, foot-wide trench around plants. Fill the trench with loose mulch or sand, then use a small spading fork several times a year to search the trench for any roving rhizomes, which are easily severed.

Clumping types grow in an enlarging circle and do not gracefully adjust their shape, although a barrier on just one side is sometimes useful. They are not the best choice for narrowly contained spaces and should be planted well away from fences and sidewalks. Once a clump has expanded to the desired size, keep it in check by breaking off new shoots where you don't want them.

There are several ways to eliminate unwanted bamboo. Digging it out with mattock and spade is the surest method, though sometimes difficult. Rhizomes may be widespread, and if you don't remove them all, regrowth will occur. Starve out any remaining root fragments by cutting off all shoots before they exceed 2 ft. in height; repeat as needed—probably many times over the course of a year. Translocated herbicide weed killers, such as glyphosate, have only a temporary effect on bamboo. Contact herbicide sprays can be used but are generally not as effective as rhizome removal.

BAMBURANTA.
See **CTENANTHE compressa**

BAMBUSA. See **BAMBOO**

BANANA
Musaceae
PERENNIAL

	FOR ZONES, SEE TEXT
	FULL SUN
	AMPLE WATER

From Southeast Asia. Fast-growing herbaceous perennial with soft, thickish stems; spreads by suckers and underground roots to form clumps 6–10 ft. wide or wider. Spectacular broad, long

Banana

(5–9-ft.) leaves are easily tattered; protect from wind. Orange-yellow spring flowers on long, drooping stalks are also striking. Bananas are attractive plants near pools or anywhere a tropical landscape is desired. All need ample moisture, rich soil, and heavy feeding. They are easily propagated by division.

Fruiting varieties are often grouped botanically under *Musa acuminata*. They are best adapted to Zone H2 in Hawaii and to Zones 21–24 in California, where planting near a warm, south-facing wall often results in sweet fruit. But even in warm microclimates of Zones 15, 16, 19, and 20, gardeners sometimes harvest edible bananas. In Zones 8, 9, 14, and 18, frost usually kills the tops of the plants each year, but the roots resprout in spring and plants are grown as ornamentals. Elsewhere, bananas can be grown in containers as ornamentals and brought indoors in winter. Plantains are bananas that require cooking before eating; most are tall and vigorous.

Dwarf banana varieties are the best bets for home gardens. They mature at about 7–15 ft. high and usually ripen fruit 70 to 100 days after blooming. Look for 'Dwarf Cavendish' ('Chinese'), 'Dwarf Brazilian', 'Enana Gigante', 'Goldfinger', 'Ice Cream', 'Apple', and 'Williams'.

If you want to harvest quality fruit, let only one or two stalks per clump grow; prune out all others as they emerge. Allow replacement stalks (for next year's fruit) to develop after the fruiting stalks have bloomed. Remove the stalks that have fruited.

Harvest season is usually late summer into fall, or whenever the fruit at the top of the cluster starts to turn yellow. Cut the whole cluster and let it ripen at room temperature. If left on the plant, fruit will split and rot. Banana sap will per-

manently stain fabric, so wear old clothes when harvesting or pruning. Control ants on banana trees to help prevent scale, aphids, and sooty mold.

For ornamental species, see *Ensete* and *Musa*.

BANANA SHRUB.
See **MICHELIA figo**

BANEBERRY. See **ACTAEA**

BANKSIA
Proteaceae
EVERGREEN SHRUBS AND TREES

	ZONES 15–24; H1
	FULL SUN
	MODERATE WATER

Few of the many banksia species (all native to Australia) are in cultivation, although botanical gardens occasionally offer some at sales. Leaves are usually long and narrow, sometimes with strikingly saw-toothed edges. Small flowers appear in dense round or cylindrical clusters (often spectacular) and are followed by long-lasting woody seed cones. Flowers are rich in nectar. Plants are subject to root rot fungi and require perfect drainage. Most can withstand long dry periods. Treat chlorosis with iron chelates. Tree species have no special pruning needs; on shrubs, shorten previous season's growth if needed to limit size. Banksias show varying tolerance to coastal conditions in California; in Hawaii, humidity is too high for them at sea level, and they are grown at higher elevations.

B. ericifolia. HEATH BANKSIA. Shrub. To 10–20 ft. tall, 6–12 ft. wide, with short, needlelike leaves and 6–8-in. clusters of orange to red flowers. Tolerates coastal conditions.

B. integrifolia. Tree. To 30–60 ft. tall, 15–30 ft. wide, with smooth-edged or slightly toothed leaves to

Banksia ericifolia

6 in. long, 2 in. wide. Pale yellow flower clusters can reach 6 in. long. Highly tolerant of coastal conditions.

B. speciosa. SHOWY BANKSIA. Shrub. To 10–18 ft. tall, 10–24 ft. wide. Leaves are 8–16 in. long, 1 in. wide, with strongly toothed edges. Flower cones are 6 in. tall, white opening to yellow. Can stand some coastal exposure.

B. spinulosa. HAIRPIN BANKSIA. Shrub. To 2–4 ft. tall, 4–5 ft. wide. Narrow, medium green leaves are serrated. Cylindrical blossoms, up to 5 in. across, are golden yellow to orange, sometimes with red; blooms fall through winter. One of the easier banksias to grow. 'Schnapper Point' has rich yellow-and-red flowers.

BANYAN, CHINESE and INDIAN. See **FICUS microcarpa, F. benghalensis**

BAPTISIA
FALSE INDIGO, WILD INDIGO
Fabaceae (Leguminosae)
PERENNIALS

	ZONES 1–24
	FULL SUN
	MODERATE WATER

Native to eastern and southern U.S. Tolerate poor, sandy soils and take some drought. Blue-green leaves have three leaflets. Small, sweet pea–shaped blooms in early summer on tall, tapering spikes.

Baptisia australis

Inflated seedpods that follow are attractive in dried arrangements. Clumps gradually increase, but don't need division; also resent transplanting once established.

B. alba. WHITE FALSE INDIGO. To 2–3 ft. tall, 3 ft. wide. White or creamy white flowers.

B. australis. BLUE FALSE INDIGO. To 3–6 ft. tall, 4 ft. wide, with deep blue flowers.

BARBERRY. See **BERBERIS**

BARLERIA obtusa
Acanthaceae
EVERGREEN SHRUB

🌿 ZONES 13, 16–24

☼ ◐ LIGHT SHADE IN HOTTEST CLIMATES

💧 REGULAR WATER

Barleria obtusa

South African native to 3 ft. tall and wide, with dark green, 3-in. leaves and loose clusters of blue, 1½-in. flowers in winter and spring. It likes rich soil and regular moisture when in full growth. Pinch to keep compact. Sometimes grown as indoor/outdoor plant or houseplant in cold-winter areas.

BARREL CACTUS. See **ECHINO-CACTUS, FEROCACTUS**

BASEBALL PLANT. See **EUPHORBIA obesa**

BASIL. See **OCIMUM basilicum**

BASKET FLOWER. See **CENTAUREA americana, HYMENOCALLIS narcissiflora**

BASKET-OF-GOLD. See **AURINIA saxatilis**

BASSIA scoparia. See **KOCHIA scoparia**

BASSWOOD. See **TILIA americana**

BAUHINIA
ORCHID TREE
Fabaceae (Leguminosae)
EVERGREEN, SEMIEVERGREEN, DECIDUOUS TREES AND SHRUBS

🌿 ZONES VARY BY SPECIES

☼ FULL SUN, EXCEPT AS NOTED

💧💧 MODERATE TO REGULAR WATER

These flamboyant flowering plants have a very special place in Hawaii and mild-winter areas of California and Arizona. They vary greatly by species and climate. Common to all garden bauhinias

Bauhinia × blakeana

are twin "leaves," actually twin lobes. Thin crowded growth after bloom.

B. × blakeana. HONG KONG ORCHID TREE. Partly deciduous for short period. Zones 13, 19, 21, 23, 24; H1, H2. Umbrellalike growth habit; reaches 20 ft. high and wide. Flowers bloom from late fall to spring and are shaped like some orchids; they are much larger (5½–6 in. wide) than those of other bauhinias. Colors range from cranberry maroon through purple and rose to orchid pink, often in same blossom. Gray-green leaves tend to drop off around bloom time, but the tree does not lose all of its foliage.

B. forficata (B. candicans, B. corniculata). BRAZILIAN BUTTERFLY TREE. Evergreen to deciduous shrub or tree. Zones 9, 12–23. Native to Brazil. Probably hardiest bauhinia. To 20 ft. tall and broad, often with twisting, leaning trunk and picturesque angled branches; good canopy for patio. Short, sharp thorns at branch joints. Narrow-petaled, creamy white flowers to 3 in. wide, spring into summer. Deep green leaves have more pointed lobes than others. Give some afternoon shade in hot climates.

B. galpinii (B. punctata). RED BAUHINIA. Evergreen to semi-evergreen shrub. Zones 13, 15, 16, 18–24; H1, H2. Native to South Africa. Sprawling, half-climbing plant to about 10 ft. tall, spreading to 15 ft. Blooms from spring to fall, bearing brick red to orange flowers as spectacular as those of bougainvillea. Best as espalier on warm wall. With hard pruning, can make splendid flowering bonsai for large pot or box.

B. lunarioides (B. congesta). ANACACHO ORCHID TREE. Evergreen to semievergreen shrub or tree. Zones 10–13, 18–23. Native from western Texas into northeastern Mexico. To 8–12 ft. high, 4–5 ft. wide, with rounded, very small leaves (½ to ¾ in. long). White- and pink-flowering forms are available. Begins bloom in early spring and repeats many times over spring and summer. Open tree in afternoon shade; bushier in full sun.

B. variegata (B. purpurea). PURPLE ORCHID TREE. Semi-evergreen to deciduous shrub or tree. Zones 13, 18–24; H1, H2. Hardy to 22°F/–6°C. Native to India, China. Most frequently planted bauhinia. Inclined to grow as a many-stemmed shrub, but if staked and pruned, becomes an

attractive tree 20–35 ft. tall and wide. Wonderful show of light pink to orchid purple, broad-petaled, 2–3-in.-wide flowers, usually winter into spring; spectacular street tree where spring is reliably and steadily warm. Light green, broad-lobed leaves generally drop in midwinter. After bloom, it produces huge crop of messy-looking beans; trim them off if you wish (trimming brings new growth earlier). 'Candida' is white blossomed but otherwise identical to the species.

BAY. See **LAURUS, UMBELLULARIA californica**

BAYBERRY. See **MYRICA pensylvanica**

BEACH ASTER. See **ERIGERON glaucus**

BEACH STRAWBERRY. See **FRAGARIA chiloensis**

BEAN
Fabaceae (Leguminosae)
ANNUALS AND PERENNIALS GROWN AS ANNUALS

🌿 ALL ZONES

☼ FULL SUN

💧 REGULAR WATER

Gardeners can choose from many types of beans, the most common of which are described below. Except for the broad or fava bean from the Mediterranean region, these are New World plants belonging to the genus *Phaseolus*. Most beans are frost-sensitive heat lovers, easy to grow from seed. With all, moisten soil thoroughly before planting, then do not water again until seedlings have emerged. Once growth starts, keep soil moist. Fertilize soil after plants are in active growth and again when pods start to form. Control aphids, cucumber beetles, spider mites, and whiteflies if any of these pests are problems in your garden.

Scarlet runner bean

Broad bean (fava bean, horse bean). Cool-season bean (actually a giant vetch, *Vicia faba*), best known in coastal climates. Cook and eat immature pods like edible-pod peas; prepare immature and mature seeds in same way as green or dry limas. Note that a very few people (mainly of Mediterranean

ancestry) have an enzyme deficiency that can cause severe reactions to the beans and even the pollen.

In cold-winter areas, plant as early in spring as soil can be worked; in mild climates, plant in fall for harvest in late winter or early spring. Matures in 120 to 150 days. Space rows 1½–2½ ft. apart. Sow seeds 1 in. deep, 4–5 in. apart; thin to 8–10 in. apart. Plants produce bushy growth to 2–4 ft. high.

Dry bean. Same culture as bush form of snap bean. Let pods remain on bush until they turn dry or begin to shatter; then thresh beans from pods, dry, and store them to soak and cook later as needed. 'Pinto', 'Red Kidney', and 'White Marrowfat' belong to this group.

Some varieties are best when harvested at the green shelling stage and cooked like green limas. These include the flageolet bean (a French favorite) and 'French Horticultural Bean', also known as 'October Bean'. Heirlooms such as 'Aztec Dwarf White', 'Mitla White', and 'New Mexico Appaloosa' were used by Native Americans of the Southwest and are very well adapted to that region.

Lima bean. Like snap beans (which they resemble), lima beans come in either bush or vine (pole) form. They develop more slowly than snap beans—bush types need 65 to 75 days from planting to harvest, pole kinds 78 to 95 days—and do not produce as reliably in very hot weather. Shell before cooking, a tedious chore but worth it if you like fresh limas. Grow like snap beans.

Scarlet runner bean. Perennial twining vine grown as annual. Showy and ornamental, with slender clusters of vivid scarlet flowers and bright green leaves divided into three roundish, 3–5-in.-long leaflets. Use it to cover fences, arbors, outbuildings; it provides quick shade on porches. Pink- and white-flowered varieties exist.

Flowers are followed by flattened, very dark green pods that are edible and tasty when young but toughen as they reach full size. Beans from older pods can be shelled and cooked like green limas. Culture is same as for snap beans (see below).

Snap bean

Snap bean (string bean, green bean). The most widely planted bean type. Tender, fleshy pods, not stringy; may be green, yellow (wax beans), or purple (these turn green when cooked). Plants grow as self-supporting bushes (bush beans) or as climbing vines (pole beans). Bush types bear earlier, but vines are more productive. Plants look like scarlet runner bean, but their white or purple flowers are not showy.

Sow seeds as soon as soil is warm. Heavy seed leaves must push through soil, so be sure that soil is reasonably loose and open. Plant seeds of bush types 1 in. deep and 1–3 in. apart, allowing 2–3 ft. between rows. Pole beans can be managed in a number of ways. Set three or four 8-ft. poles in the ground and tie together at top in tepee fashion; or set single poles 3–4 ft. apart and sow six or eight beans around each, thinning to three or four strongest seedlings; or insert poles 1–2 ft. apart in rows and sow seeds as you would bush beans; or sow along sunny wall, fence, or trellis and train vines on web of light string supported by wire or heavy twine. Pods are ready in 50 to 70 days, depending on variety. Pick every 3 to 5 days; if pods mature, plants will stop bearing.

BEARBERRY. See **ARCTO-STAPHYLOS uva-ursi**

BEARD TONGUE. See **PENSTEMON**

BEAR'S BREECH. See **ACANTHUS**

BEAR'S FOOT FERN. See **HUMATA tyermannii**

BEAUCARNEA recurvata. See **NOLINA recurvata**

BEAUMONTIA grandiflora
HERALD'S TRUMPET, EASTER LILY VINE
Apocynaceae
EVERGREEN VINE

| ☑ ZONES 12, 13, 16, 17, 21–24; H1, H2 |
| ☼ ☽ FULL SUN OR PARTIAL SHADE |
| 💧 REGULAR WATER |

From the Himalayas. Rampant vine that uses arching, twining branches to climb as high as 30 ft. and spread about as wide. Large (6–9-in.), oval to roundish dark green leaves, smooth and shiny above, slightly downy beneath, give lush tropical look. From spring through summer, bears fragrant flowers that look like Easter lilies: trumpet shaped, 5 in. long, green-veined white.

Does best in well-drained soil enriched with organic matter; regular feeding produces most lavish display of foliage and flowers. Prune after bloom to shape or limit size; flowers are produced on wood 2 years or older, so keep a good proportion of old wood. Hardy to 28°F/–2°C. Frost kills it to the ground, but it usually comes back from the roots. Use as big espalier on warm, wind-sheltered wall or train along eaves of house; sturdy supports are essential, since growth is heavy. Good choice for planting near swimming pools.

Beaumontia grandiflora

BEAUTYBERRY. See **CALLICARPA**

BEAUTY BUSH. See **KOLKWITZIA amabilis**

BEAVERTAIL CACTUS. See **OPUNTIA basilaris**

BEE BALM. See **MONARDA**

BEECH. See **FAGUS**

BEECH, FALSE or SOUTHERN. See **NOTHOFAGUS**

BEEFWOOD. See **CASUARINA**

BEET
Chenopodiaceae
BIENNIAL GROWN AS ANNUAL

| ☑ ALL ZONES |
| ☼ FULL SUN |
| 💧 REGULAR WATER |

European native known botanically as *Beta vulgaris*. Raised for their edible roots and tender young leaves, beets grow best in relatively cool weather. In hot-summer climates, sow in early spring or late summer so that plants will mature before extreme heat sets in. In mild-winter areas, you can also plant in late summer for fall and winter harvest. To harvest beets over a long season, sow seed at monthly intervals.

Grow in fertile, well-drained soil without lumps or rocks. Sow seed 1 in. apart and cover with ¼ in. of compost, sand, or vermiculite. Thin plants to 2 in. apart while small—the thinnings (both tops and roots) are edible. To keep roots tender, keep soil evenly moist. Begin harvesting when roots are 1 in. wide and complete it before they exceed 3 in.; they will be woody if allowed to grow bigger. In cold climates, harvest all beets before hard frosts in fall.

Types with round, red roots include 'Detroit Dark Red' and 'Crosby's Egyptian' (old favorites) as well as many newer varieties like 'Kleine Bol' and 'Sangria'. 'Bull's Blood' and 'Lutz Green Leaf' are grown for roots and edible greens. Novelties include 'Cylindra' and 'Forma Nova' (with long, cylindrical roots) and 'Chioggia' (rings of red and white); there are also varieties with golden yellow or white roots.

Beet

BEGONIA
Begoniaceae
PERENNIALS, SHRUBS, TUBERS

| ☑ ZONES 14–24; H1, H2, EXCEPT AS NOTED; OR INDOORS; OR DIG AND STORE; OR TREAT AS ANNUALS |
| ☼ FILTERED SUN; BRIGHT INDIRECT LIGHT |
| 💧 REGULAR WATER |

Grown for textured, multicolored foliage, saucer-size flowers, or lacy clusters of smaller blooms. Native to many tropical and subtropical regions of the world. Outdoors, most grow best in pots in the ground or in hanging baskets in filtered shade, with rich, porous, fast-draining soil, consistent but light feeding, and enough water to keep soil moist but not soggy. Most thrive as indoor plants, in greenhouse,

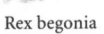

Rex begonia

or under lath. Some prefer terrarium conditions. Almost all require at least moderate humidity. In areas with hot, dry summers or indoors in winter, set pots in pebble-lined saucers or trays kept filled with water to below pot level.

Most are easily propagated from leaf, stem, or rhizome cuttings. They also grow from dust-fine seed. Of the many hundreds of species and varieties, relatively few are sold widely.

Cane-type begonias. They get their name from their stems, which grow tall and woody and have prominent bamboolike joints. The group includes so-called angel-wing begonias. These erect plants have multiple stems, some reaching 5 ft. or more under the right conditions. Most bloom profusely from early spring through autumn, bearing large clusters of white, pink, orange, or red flowers. Some are everblooming. When roots fill 4-in. pots, plants can be placed in large containers or in the ground. Position plants where they will get plenty of light, some sun, and no wind. They may require staking. Protect from heavy frosts. Old canes that have grown barren should be pruned back to two leaf joints in early spring to stimulate new growth.

'Bubbles'. Spotted foliage; pink flowers with apple blossom fragrance. ▶

'Honeysuckle'. Plain green foliage and fragrant pink flowers.

'Irene Nuss'. Dark red-and-green leaves and huge drooping clusters of coral pink flowers.

Hardy begonia. Zones 3–24. Asian species *B. grandis* (*B. evansiana, B. grandis evansiana*) grows from a tuber to 2–3 ft. tall and wide, with branching red stems carrying large, smooth, coppery green leaves with red undersides. Summer flowers are pink or white, carried in drooping clusters. Tops die down after frost. In colder regions, mulch to protect roots.

Hiemalis begonias. Usually sold as Rieger begonias. Bushy, compact; profuse bloomers and outstanding outdoor or indoor plants. Flowers average about 2 in. across and appear over a long season that includes winter. On well-grown plants, green leaves and stems are all but invisible beneath a blanket of bloom. Give indoor plants plenty of light in winter. In summer, keep out of hot noonday sun. Water thoroughly when top inch of soil is dry. Don't sprinkle leaves. Plants may get rangy, an indication of approaching dormancy; if they do, cut stems to 4-in. stubs.

Multiflora begonias. Bushy, compact plants 1–1½ ft. tall and wide. Profuse bloom in carmine, scarlet, orange, yellow, apricot, salmon, pink. Includes Nonstop strain. All are essentially small-flowered, profuse-blooming tuberous begonias; for instructions on care, see Tuberous begonias.

Rex begonias. With their bold, multicolored leaves, these are probably the most striking of all foliage begonias. While many named varieties are grown by collectors, easier-to-find unnamed seedling plants are almost as decorative. The leaves grow from a rhizome; see Rhizomatous begonias for care. In addition, rex begonias should get high humidity (at least 50 percent) to do their best. Provide it by misting with a spray bottle, placing pots on wet pebbles in a tray, or keeping plants in greenhouse. When rhizome grows too far past edge of pot for your taste, either repot into slightly larger container or cut off rhizome end inside pot edge. Old rhizome will branch and grow new leaves. Make rhizome cuttings of the piece you remove and root in mixture of half peat moss, half perlite.

Rhizomatous begonias. Like rex begonias, these grow from a rhizome. Although some have handsome flowers, they are grown primarily for foliage, which varies in color and texture among species and varieties. The group includes so-called star begonias, named for their leaf shape. Rhizomatous begonias perform well as houseplants: give them bright light through a window and water only when the top inch or so of soil is dry. Plant them in wide, shallow pots. They flower from winter through summer, the season varying among specific plants. White to pink flowers appear in clusters on erect stems above the foliage. Rhizomes will grow over edge of pot, eventually forming a ball-shaped plant; if you wish, cut rhizomes back to pot. The old rhizome will branch and grow new leaves. Root the pieces of rhizome in mixture of half peat moss, half perlite.

B. masoniana. IRON CROSS BEGONIA. Large puckered leaves; known for chocolate brown pattern resembling Maltese cross on green background. Flowers are insignificant.

Semperflorens begonias. Fibrous, bedding, or wax begonias. Dwarf (6–8-in.) and taller (10–12-in.) strains grown in garden beds or containers like annuals, producing lots of small flowers in a white-through-red range. Plants bloom from spring through fall (use as a winter annual in hottest-summer climates). Foliage can be green, red, bronze, or variegated. In mild-winter climates, can live for years. Thrive in full sun in cool-summer regions. Prefer broken shade in hotter climates, but dark-foliaged kinds will take sun if well watered.

Shrublike begonias. This large class is marked by multiple stems that are soft and green rather than bamboolike as in the cane-type group. Grown for both foliage and flowers. Leaves are very interesting—some are heavily textured; others grow white or red "hairs"; still others develop a soft, feltlike coating. Most grow upright and bushy, but others are less erect and make suitable subjects for hanging baskets. Flowers in shades of pink, red, white, or peach can come any time, depending on species or variety. Care consists of repotting into larger container as the plant outgrows its pot. Some shrublike begonias can get very large—as tall as 8 ft. Water when soil begins

to dry on surface. Prune to shape; pinch tips to encourage branching.

'Digswelliana'. To 2–3 ft. high, with glossy leaves 2–4 in. long. Red flowers in clusters bloom almost continually from spring to fall.

B. foliosa. Inch-long leaves packed tightly on twiggy plant give fernlike look. Stems arch or droop to 3 ft. Flowers are small, white to red, everblooming in mild weather. 'Miniata' has rose pink to rose red flowers.

'Richmondensis.' To 2 ft. or a little taller. Arching stems carry deep green, shiny, crisp leaves with red undersides. Vivid pink to crimson or white flowers develop from darker buds; nearly year-round bloom. Big and sturdy. Tolerant of sun and wind.

Trailing or climbing begonias. These have stems that trail or climb, depending on how you train them. They are suited to hanging basket culture or planting in the ground where well protected. Growing conditions similar to those for tuberous begonias, though trailing types are not lifted for storage. Sporadic bloom during warm weather.

'Potpourri'. Hybrid developed from *B. solananthera,* with strongly scented deep pink flowers.

B. solananthera. Glossy light green leaves; fragrant white flowers with red centers.

Tuberous begonias. Best in Zones 4–6, 15–17, 21–24, and H1; possible in 7–9, 14, 18–20 with attention to humidity. Among the best-known begonias in the West are these magnificent large-flowered hybrids that grow from tubers. Members of this group range from plants with saucer-size flowers and a few upright stems to multistemmed hanging basket sorts covered in blossoms. With the exception of some rare kinds, they are summer and fall blooming.

Strains are sold as hanging or upright. The former bloom more profusely; the latter have larger flowers. Colors include almost everything but blue; shapes are frilly (carnation), formal double (camellia), and tight-centered (rose). Some have petal edges in contrasting colors (picotee). Popular strains include Double Trumpet

(improved rose form), Prima Donna (improved camellia), and Hanging Sensation.

Most gardeners grow tuberous begonias in containers. Buy dormant tubers (the bigger the better) in midwinter. Set them in pots filled with a rich, humusy soil mix, placing them indented side up and covering them with no more than ¼ in. of mix. If you're planting a number of tubers, it's easiest to start them in a flat or shallow box, spacing them about 4 in. apart. Place pots or flats in a well-lit spot (but not in direct sun) where temperatures will remain above 65°F/18°C; keep soil moist but not saturated during the rooting period. When the tubers have produced two leaves, move them outside, weather permitting (night temperature must remain above 50°F/10°C); or pot up plants started in flats. You can also plant begonias in the ground at this point; amend the existing soil, using 1 part soil to 2 parts potting mix.

Choose a spot in filtered shade, such as under lath; or plant in an open area with eastern exposure. Water enough to keep soil moist but not soggy. For best bloom, mist with water several times a day unless you live in a cool or foggy area. Watch for fuzzy white spots on leaves; these signal powdery mildew. Begin feeding with liquid fertilizer a week or two after plants reach the two-leaf stage. For largest possible blooms, you can use a half-strength solution every other week, but monthly regular-strength feedings yield fine plants.

When leaves begin to yellow and wilt in fall, gradually reduce watering and stop fertilizing. When leaves fall off, lift tubers, shake off soil, and dry in a cool, dry spot for several days. Then store in a cool, dry place such as a shed or garage until spring; when small pink buds appear, plant the tubers once again. (You can also buy small seedling plants each year in early spring and plant them out in pots or in the ground.)

Tuberous begonia

B

BELAMCANDA
chinensis
BLACKBERRY LILY
Iridaceae
PERENNIAL FROM RHIZOME

⚡ ZONES 1-24

☀️ ◑ FULL SUN OR PARTIAL SHADE

💧 REGULAR WATER DURING GROWTH AND BLOOM

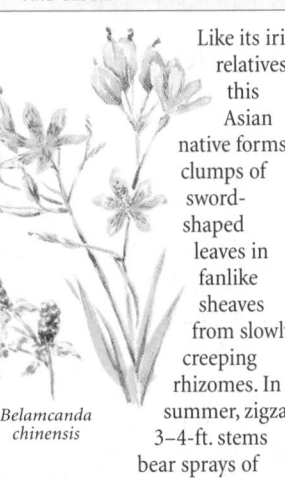
Belamcanda chinensis

Like its iris relatives, this Asian native forms clumps of sword-shaped leaves in fanlike sheaves from slowly creeping rhizomes. In summer, zigzag 3–4-ft. stems bear sprays of 2–3-in., yellowish orange flowers dotted with red. Each flower lasts only a day, but new blossoms keep opening for weeks. As the blooms fade, rounded seed capsules develop; they split open to expose shiny black seeds that look like blackberries (hence the plant's common name). Cut seed-bearing stems for use in dried arrangements.

Effective in groups in border. Set rhizomes 1 ft. apart, with tops just beneath soil surface. Plant in spring in Zones 1–3, in fall elsewhere. Established clumps give best display, so divide infrequently.

BELLADONNA LILY.
See **AMARYLLIS belladonna**

BELLFLOWER.
See **CAMPANULA**

BELLIS perennis
ENGLISH DAISY
Asteraceae (Compositae)
PERENNIAL OFTEN TREATED AS ANNUAL

⚡ ZONES 1-9, 14-24; ANYWHERE EXCEPT HAWAII AS ANNUAL

☀️ ◑ LIGHT SHADE IN HOTTEST CLIMATES

💧 REGULAR WATER

Native to Europe, western Asia. The original English daisies are the kind sometimes seen growing in lawns. Plump, fully double ones sold in nurseries are horticultural varieties that make good edging or bedding plants;

they are also effective with bulbs. Dark green, 1–2-in.-long leaves form rosettes to 8 in. wide. Pink, rose, red, or white flowers are borne on 3–6-in. stems in spring and early summer; deadhead to prolong bloom. Longer lived where summers are cool. Propagate by division.

Bellis perennis

BELLS-OF-IRELAND.
See **MOLUCCELLA laevis**

BELOPERONE guttata.
See **JUSTICIA brandegeeana**

BENJAMIN TREE, BENJAMIN FIG. See **FICUS benjamina**

BENT, BENT GRASS.
See **AGROSTIS**

BERBERIS
BARBERRY
Berberidaceae
EVERGREEN, SEMIEVERGREEN, AND DECIDUOUS SHRUBS

⚡ ZONES VARY BY SPECIES

☀️ ◑ FULL SUN OR LIGHT SHADE

💧💧 MODERATE TO REGULAR WATER

These dense, spiny-stemmed plants, especially the deciduous species, tolerate climate and soil extremes. Require no more than ordinary garden care. Each year, thin out oldest wood and prune as needed to shape—after bloom for evergreen and semievergreen types, late in the dormant season for deciduous kinds. Make attractive hedges. Informal style is best for species grown for spring flowers (yellow, unless otherwise noted) and ensuing berries, which are borne on previous year's growth; species grown for foliage can be sheared. To rejuvenate overgrown or neglected plants, cut them to within a foot of the ground before new spring growth begins.

B. amurensis. Deciduous. Zones A2, A3; 1–6. Hardy to –35°F/–37°C. From northeast Asia. Dense, erect shrub to 10 ft. tall, 7–8 ft. wide, with three-pointed, ¾-in.-long spines and 3-in. leaves divided into three leaflets. Small, fragrant flowers in hanging clusters (up to 25 blooms per cluster) are followed by bright red fruits.

B. buxifolia. MAGELLAN BARBERRY. Evergreen. Zones 4–9, 14–24. Hardy to 0°F/–18°C. Native to Chile, Argentina. Rather rigid and upright, to 6 ft. tall and as wide. Leathery 1-in. leaves. Orange-yellow flowers; dark purple berries, one or two at each leaf cluster. Dwarf 'Nana' ('Pygmaea'), to 1½ ft. high and 2 ft. wide, makes a good hedge or rock garden plant.

B. × chenaultii (B. × hybrido-gagnepainii). Evergreen. Zones 3–9, 14–24. Hardy to 0°F/–18°C. Slow growing to 4 ft. tall, 5 ft. wide, with arching branches. Dark green, spiny-toothed leaves 1–1½ in. long. Bluish black berries. Barrier hedge, foreground planting.

B. darwinii. DARWIN BAR-BERRY. Evergreen. Zones 5–9, 14–24. Hardy to 10°F/–12°C. Very showy barberry from Chile. Fountainlike growth to 5–10 ft. tall, 4–7 ft. wide. Crisp, dark green, hollylike, 1-in. leaves. Orange-yellow flowers are borne so thickly along branches that foliage is hard to see; these are followed by profuse dark blue berries, popular with birds. Spreads by underground runners to form a thicket.

Berberis darwinii

B. × gladwynensis 'William Penn'. Evergreen; drops some leaves at 0 to 10°F/–18 to –12°C. Zones 3b–24. Resembles *B. julianae* in general effect but has broader, glossier leaves and is faster growing, with denser growth, to 4 ft. tall and wide. Good floral display.

B. × irwinii. See B. × stenophylla 'Irwinii'

B. julianae. WINTERGREEN BARBERRY. Evergreen to semi-evergreen. Zones 4–24. Hardy to 0°F/–18°C, but foliage is damaged by winter cold. Chinese native. Dense, upright, to 6 ft. tall and wide; angled branches. Spiny-toothed, dark green, leathery leaves to 3 in. long; reddish fall color. Blue-black berries. One of the spiniest barberries; effective as barrier hedge.

B. koreana. Deciduous. Zones 1–9, 14–17. Hardy to –35°F/–37°C. Korean native grows erect to 4–6 ft. and not quite as wide. Densely foliaged in medium to dark green leaves that turn purple in fall. Fra-grant flowers in drooping, 3–4-in. clusters. Bright red fruit.

B. linearifolia 'Orange King'. Evergreen. Zones 6–9, 14–24. Hardy to 0 to 10°F/–18 to –12°C. This variety of a Chilean species has an open growth habit to 5 ft. tall and wide, with narrow, glossy, 2-in. leaves. Short clusters of deep orange flowers; bluish black fruit.

B. × mentorensis. Evergreen or deciduous. Zones 2–24. Hardy to –20°F/–29°C but loses some or all leaves below about 0°F/–18°C. Compact growth to 7 ft. tall and wide. Dark green, 1-in.-long leaves turn a beautiful red in fall where winters are cold. Berries are dull dark red but are rarely seen. Easy to maintain as a hedge at any height. Tolerates hot, dry weather.

B. × stenophylla. ROSEMARY BARBERRY. Evergreen. Zones 4–9, 14–24. Hardy to 0°F/–18°C. Leaves narrow, ½–1 in. long, with rolled-in edges and spiny tip. Species is 10 ft. tall, 15 ft. wide, but varieties are more commonly grown. 'Corallina Compacta', called coral barberry, reaches 1½ ft. high and wide and bears nodding clusters of bright orange flowers and bluish black fruit; effective in rock garden, as foreground plant. 'Irwinii', to 4–5 ft. tall and wide, resembles a compact-growing *B. darwinii*.

B. thunbergii. JAPANESE BARBERRY. Deciduous. Zones A3; 2b–24. Hardy to –20°F/–29°C. Graceful habit with slender, arch-ing, spiny branches; if not sheared, usually reaches 4–6 ft. tall with equal spread. Densely covered with roundish, ½–1½-in.-long leaves that are deep green above, paler beneath; leaves turn yellow, orange, and red before they fall. Beadlike bright red berries stud branches in fall and through win-ter. Use as hedge, barrier planting, or specimen shrub. The following are among the many attractive varieties grown for vivid foliage.

'Atropurpurea'. RED-LEAF JAPANESE BARBERRY. Plants sold as such vary in plant size and foliage color (from bronzy red to purple red). They must have sun to develop red color (which they will hold all summer).

'Aurea'. Bright golden yellow foliage. Best color in full sun (though it can't take it in hottest climates), but plant will tolerate light shade. Slow growing to 2½–3 ft. tall and wide.

'Bagatelle'. Similar to 'Crimson Pygmy' but with smaller, glossier, deeper red-purple leaves and a more narrow shape, reaching 1½–2 ft. tall and wide. Good slow-growing choice for small spaces.

'Cherry Bomb'. Resembles 'Crimson Pygmy' but is taller (to 4 ft.), with larger leaves and more open growth.

'Crimson Pygmy' ('Atropurpurea Nana'). Selected miniature form, generally less than 1½ ft. high and 2½ ft. wide at 10 years old. Leaves are bright red when new, maturing to bronzy blood red. Must have sun to develop good color.

'Golden Nugget'. Dwarf selection reaching 1–1½ ft. tall and wide, with golden leaves that may be tinged orange. More sun tolerant than other yellow barberries.

'Golden Ring'. Purple leaves with a thin green or golden green border.

'Helmond Pillar'. Purple-leafed form to 4–5 ft. tall, 2 ft. wide.

'Kobold'. Extra-dwarf bright green variety. Like 'Crimson Pygmy' in habit but fuller and rounder.

'Rose Glow'. To 4–6 ft. tall and wide. New foliage marbled bronzy red and pinkish white, deepening to rose and bronze with age. For best color, plant in full sun or lightest shade.

'Royal Cloak'. Compact, mounding to 4 ft. high and at least as wide. Large, dark purple-red leaves.

'Sparkle'. To 5 ft. tall and 6 ft. wide, with rich green foliage that turns vivid yellow, orange, and red in fall.

'Sunsation'. Compact, upright to 3–4 ft. tall and wide. New growth is greenish gold, maturing to bright golden yellow.

B. verruculosa. WARTY BARBERRY. Evergreen. Zones 4–9, 14–24. Hardy to 0°F/–18°C. Native to China. Neat, tailored-looking. Will reach 4–5 ft. tall and wide but can be kept to 1½ ft. Perky, 1-in.-long leaves glossy dark green above, whitish beneath. In fall and winter, the odd red leaf develops as a highlight here and there. Black berries with a purplish bloom. Very choice and effective on banks, in front of leggy rhododendrons or azaleas, in foreground of shrub border.

B. wilsoniae. WILSON BARBERRY. Deciduous to semi-evergreen. Zones 6–9, 14–24. Hardy to 5°F/–15°C. Native to China. To 6 ft. tall and wide, but can be held to 3–4 ft. Light green, roundish, ½–1-in. leaves give the plant a fine-textured look. Beautiful coral to salmon red berries. Makes a handsome barrier hedge.

BERGENIA
Saxifragaceae
PERENNIALS

☀	ZONES A1–A3; 1–9, 12–24; EXCEPT AS NOTED
◐ ●	PARTIAL OR FULL SHADE
💧	REGULAR WATER

Bergenia crassifolia

Native to Himalayas and mountains of China. Thick rootstocks produce rosettes of large, ornamental, glossy green leaves that are evergreen except in coldest areas. In established plantings, foliage clumps may reach 1½ ft. high. Plants bloom in spring, sometimes again in fall, bearing graceful, nodding clusters of small flowers on thick, leafless, 1–1½-ft.-tall stalks; colors include white and shades of pink and red. Plants lend a strong textural quality to borders and plantings under trees, make a bold ground cover. Effective with ferns, hellebores, or hostas and as foreground planting for Japanese aucuba, rhododendrons, Japanese aralia.

Perform best in shade but will tolerate sun in cool-summer climates. Will endure neglect, poor soil, and some drought, but appreciate good soil and regular watering, feeding, and grooming. Plant about 1½ ft. apart. Cut back yearly to prevent legginess. Divide crowded clumps and replant vigorous divisions in late winter or early spring. Control snails and slugs.

B. ciliata (B. ligulata). Zones 5–9, 14–24. Choicest, most elegant species, though more tender than others; foliage damaged in hard frosts. Lustrous light green, nearly round leaves to 1 ft. across, smooth on edges but fringed with soft hairs; bronzy when new. White, rose, or purplish flowers. Plants sold under this name may be garden hybrids.

B. cordifolia. HEARTLEAF BERGENIA. Glossy, roundish leaves are heart shaped at base, with wavy, toothed edges. Bears rose or lilac flowers in pendulous clusters that are partially hidden by leaves. 'Morning Red' ('Morgenrote') has bronzy-toned leaves, dark red flowers. 'Tubby Andrews' has leaves splashed with golden yellow; flowers are pink. 'Winterglut' ('Winter Glow') has bright red flowers and leathery green leaves that turn reddish bronze in fall and winter.

B. crassifolia. WINTER-BLOOMING BERGENIA. Dark green leaves to 8 in. or more across, with wavy, sparsely toothed edges. Rose, lilac, or purple flowers in dense clusters on erect stems that stand well above leaves. Blooms between midwinter and early spring, depending on climate.

B. hybrids. Many hybrids of English or German origin include 'Abendglut' ('Evening Glow'), with dark red flowers and dark reddish leaves with crimped edges; 'Herbstblute' ('Autumn Glory'), with leaves that turn purplish in fall, when it also tends to rebloom; and 'Silberlicht' ('Silver Light'), with large, slightly toothed leaves and white blossoms.

BERLANDIERA
lyrata
CHOCOLATE FLOWER
Asteraceae (Compositae)
PERENNIAL

☀	ZONES 10–13, 18–23; ANYWHERE AS ANNUAL
☀	FULL SUN
💧	MODERATE WATER

Berlandiera lyrata

Native from summer-rainfall areas of Texas west to southeastern Arizona and northern Mexico. Fragrance of chocolate permeates the morning air wherever this daisy blooms. Rounded, somewhat coarse-foliaged plant to 1½–3 ft. high and wide. Blooms in spring and summer, sometimes into fall. Light yellow rays surround a maroon-and-green center. Once seed heads form, shear lightly to encourage more blooms. Native Americans used the flower heads to flavor foods; they dry well for winter bouquets. Sow seeds in place at any time. Thrives in clay soil.

BERMUDA, BERMUDA GRASS.
See CYNODON dactylon

BERMUDA BUTTERCUP.
See OXALIS pes-caprae

BESCHORNERIA
yuccoides
Agavaceae
PERENNIAL

☀	ZONES 13, 16–17, 19–24
☀ ☀	PARTIAL SHADE IN HOTTEST CLIMATES
💧	REGULAR WATER

From Mexico. Rosettes of 2-ft.-long, 2-in.-wide gray-green leaves increase slowly by offsets to make clumps that eventually reach 3–4 ft. wide. Resembles a yucca, but its leaves are soft and spineless. Early summer brings a spectacular flower show: a thick coral pink stalk rises to 3–6 ft. tall, its many pink branches hung with bell-shaped, yellow-tinted green flowers in yellow bracts. A good specimen plant in the ground or in a large container. Must have well-drained soil.

Beschorneria yuccoides

BETA vulgaris.
See BEET, SWISS CHARD

BETHLEHEM SAGE.
See PULMONARIA saccharata

BETULA
BIRCH
Betulaceae
DECIDUOUS TREES

☀	ZONES VARY BY SPECIES
☀	FULL SUN
💧	REGULAR WATER

The white-barked European white birch—the tree that comes to mind when most people think of birches—has relatives that resemble it in graceful habit, thin bark peeling in layers, and smallish, fine-toothed leaves that turn from green to glowing yellow in fall. After leaf drop, the delicate limb structure, handsome bark, and small conelike fruits provide a winter display.

All birches need a regular supply of moisture and nutrients; they are generally too greedy for lawns. Nor should they be planted on a patio or where cars will be parked beneath them, since they are all susceptible to aphids that drip honeydew. Bronze birch borer can be a problem in the northern Rocky Mountain states; leaf miners in the Pacific Northwest. Prune established trees just to remove weak, damaged, or dead growth. To minimize sap bleed, prune in summer or early fall in mild-winter areas; where temperatures remain below freezing, wait until end of January. To avoid providing entry points for pests and diseases, don't make unnecessary or large cuts. If birch borer is present locally, don't prune while it is active (check timing with your Cooperative Extension Office).

B. albo-sinensis. Zones 3–11, 14–24. Native to western China. Large tree (to 100 ft. tall, 30 ft. wide) grown chiefly for beautiful bark: pinkish brown to coppery, covered with a powdery gray bloom. Oval leaves 3 in. long. *B. a. septentrionalis* has flaking, orange to orange-brown bark.

B. jacquemontii (B. utilis jacquemontii). Zones 3–11, 14–17. Native to northern India. Tall, narrow tree with brilliant white bark. Grows about 2 ft. a year to 40 ft., then more slowly to an eventual 60 ft. tall, 30 ft. wide. Seedlings vary in bark color from white to pinkish tan; for guaranteed white bark, look for grafted trees. Some borer resistance.

B. maximowicziana. MONARCH BIRCH. Zones 3–9, 14–24. Native to Japan. Fast growing; open growth when young. More stiffly upright than other birches. Can reach 80–100 ft. tall, 40 ft. wide. Flaking, orange-brown bark eventually turns gray or white. Heart-shaped leaves are the largest among birches—to 6 in. across. Reliable golden fall color even in mild-winter climates. Plants sold under this name are not always the true species.

B. nigra. RIVER BIRCH, RED BIRCH. Zones 1–24. Native to stream banks and lowlands in eastern North America. Very fast

Betula pendula

growth in early years; eventually becomes a pyramidal tree 50–90 ft. tall, 40–60 ft. wide. Trunk often forks near ground, but the tree can be trained to a single stem. Young bark is pinkish, very smooth, and shiny; on older trees, bark flakes and curls in cinnamon brown to blackish sheets. Diamond-shaped leaves are 1–3 in. long, bright glossy green above with silvery undersides. This is the most trouble-free birch. 'Dura-Heat' resists bronze birch borer and is more compact and heat tolerant than the species. 'Heritage' is an excellent selection that has lighter-colored bark and resistance to bronze birch borer.

B. occidentalis (B. fontinalis). WATER BIRCH. Zones A3; 1–7, 10. Native to stream banks from Alaska to Oregon, east to Colorado. Shrubby; usually grows 12–15 ft. tall and wide. Smooth, shiny, cinnamon brown bark. Ovate leaves 2 in. long.

B. papyrifera. CANOE BIRCH, PAPER BIRCH. Zones A1–A3; 1–6. Native to northern part of North America. Similar to *B. pendula* but larger growing (to 50–90 ft. tall, half as wide), with larger leaves (to 4 in. long) that are less densely borne; habit is more open, less weeping. More resistant to borer, leaf miners. Creamy white bark peels off in papery layers.

B. pendula. EUROPEAN WHITE BIRCH. Zones A2, A3; 1–12, 14–24. Native from Europe to Asia Minor. Widely planted in western U.S. Delicate, lacy appearance. Upright main branches, weeping side branches. An average mature tree is 30–40 ft. tall, spreading to half its height. Bark on twigs and young branches is golden brown; as trees mature, bark on trunk and main limbs becomes white, marked with black clefts. Oldest bark (at base of tree) is blackish gray. Glossy, rich green leaves to 2½ in. long are diamond shaped, with a slender, tapered point. Often sold as weeping birch, although trees vary somewhat in habit and young trees show little inclination to weep. Very prone to borer attack. The following are some of the varieties offered.

'Crimson Frost'. Apparently a hybrid between *B. pendula* and

an Asian birch, with burgundy leaf color that persists all summer. Somewhat borer resistant.

'Dalecarlica' ('Laciniata'). CUT-LEAF WEEPING BIRCH. Graceful, open tree with strongly weeping branches, deeply cut leaves. Sunburns in hot, dry weather.

'Fastigiata' (*B. alba* 'Fastigiata'). PYRAMIDAL WHITE BIRCH. Branches upright; habit somewhat like that of Lombardy poplar (*Populus nigra* 'Italica'). Excellent screening tree.

'Purple Rain'. A purple-leafed variety like 'Purpurea', but it holds its color all summer.

'Purpurea' (*B. alba* 'Purpurea'). PURPLE BIRCH. Leaves are maroon purple when new, fading to purplish green in summer. Best in areas with cool summers and winter chill.

'Trost's Dwarf'. To 3 ft. tall and wide. For bonsai, container, rock garden. Needs excellent drainage.

'Youngii'. YOUNG'S WEEPING BIRCH. Decorative, dome-shaped tree with slender branches that hang straight down. Stake to desired height; branches then hang from that point. Sunburns in hot, dry weather.

B. platyphylla japonica (B. mandshurica japonica). JAPANESE WHITE BIRCH. Zones 1–11, 14–24. Native to Japan. Fast growth to 40–50 ft. tall, about half as wide; open habit. White bark. Glossy green, diamond-shaped leaves to 3 in. long. 'Whitespire', to 30–40 ft. tall and only 15 ft. wide, is more borer resistant.

BIDENS ferulifolia
Asteraceae (Compositae)
PERENNIAL

🌿 ZONES 16–24; ANYWHERE AS ANNUAL
☀️ FULL SUN
💧 REGULAR WATER

Native to southern U.S., Mexico, Guatemala. The species grows to 3 ft. tall and wide, but the forms most commonly seen are trailing. Bright green leaves are divided into threadlike segments. Flower

Bidens ferulifolia

heads are bright golden yellow, an inch or so wide, with fewer ray flowers than most daisies and a light honey fragrance. Plants bloom almost continually during mild weather. Extremely heat tolerant. Can be aggressive, clambering into or sprawling over their neighbors; when this happens, cut plants back (they will recover quickly).

Sold under a wide variety of names. Seed-grown kinds include 'Golden Eye', 10–12 in. tall and broad, and 'Golden Goddess', 1½–2 ft. high and wide, with larger (2½-in.) flowers. 'Goldie', 'Goldmarie', and 'Peter's Gold Carpet' are cutting-grown plants similar to 'Golden Eye' in size.

BIG BETONY.
See STACHYS macrantha

BIG BLUESTEM.
See ANDROPOGON gerardii

BIGCONE SPRUCE, BIGCONE DOUGLAS FIR. See PSEUDO-TSUGA macrocarpa

BIGNONIA
capreolata
CROSSVINE
Bignoniaceae
EVERGREEN OR
SEMIEVERGREEN VINE

🌿 ZONES 4–9, 14–24
☀️ ◐ FULL SUN OR LIGHT SHADE
💧 💧 MODERATE TO REGULAR WATER

Bignonia capreolata

Native to southern states. Vigorous, woody vine climbs to a possible 60 ft. by tendrils and holdfast disks, attaching itself to almost any surface. Each shiny dark green leaf consists of two 2–6-in. leaflets and a branching tendril. Leaves turn purplish in cold weather, and some of them drop in the coldest zones. Clustered, 2-in., trumpet-shaped reddish brown to orange or scarlet flowers bloom in mid-spring, with intermittent bloom in summer. 'Dragon Lady' has rich red blooms. 'Jekyll' has slightly smaller flowers that are yellow on the inside, orange on the outside. 'Tangerine Beauty' is a bright orange-red selection. Do any thinning or cutting back before spring growth begins.

The genus *Bignonia* once included many vines with trumpet-shaped, often two-lipped flowers. Although most of these have now been reclassified, they are sometimes still sold as *Bignonia*. Listed below are the older names, followed by the new.

Bignonia australis. See Pandorea pandorana

B. cherere. See Distictis buccinatoria

B. chinensis. See Campsis grandiflora

B. jasminoides. See Pandorea jasminoides

B. radicans. See Campsis radicans

B. speciosa. See Clytostoma callistegioides

B. tweediana. See Macfadyena unguis-cati

B. venusta. See Pyrostegia venusta

B. violacea. See Clytostoma callistegioides

BIG TREE. See SEQUOIA-DENDRON giganteum

BILLBERGIA
Bromeliaceae
PERENNIALS

🌡	ZONES 12, 13; 14 AND 15 WITH PROTECTION; 16–24; H1, H2; OR INDOORS
☼	FILTERED SUN; BRIGHT INDIRECT LIGHT
💧	REGULAR WATER

These pineapple relatives are native to Brazil and other parts of tropical America, where they grow as epiphytes on trees.

Plants grow in basal rosettes of stiff, spiny-toothed evergreen leaves; produce drooping clusters of showy bracts and tubular flowers. Usually grown in containers for display indoors or on patios. In desert zones, Southern California, and Hawaii, however, they are often planted under trees as an easy ground cover, used in borders, or grown on limbs of trees or bark slabs, with roots wrapped in sphagnum moss and leaf mold. Excellent cut flowers.

Billbergia

Need regular moisture during active growth in warm weather;

reduce water as weather cools and growth slows. Plants usually hold water in the funnel-like center of the leaf rosette, which acts as a reservoir. Grow in well-drained soil; or pot in a light, porous mixture of sand, ground bark, and leaf mold. Houseplants need warmth and lots of light. Increase by cutting off suckers from base of plant. Specialists in bromeliads list dozens of varieties.

B. nutans. QUEEN'S TEARS. Most commonly grown. Narrow, spiny green leaves to 1½ ft. long. Long spikes of rosy red bracts; drooping flowers with green petals edged deep blue. Vigorous. Makes offsets freely; easy to grow and propagate.

B. pyramidalis. Leaves to 3 ft. long, 2½ in. wide, with toothed margins. Flowers with red, violet-tipped petals and bright red bracts in dense spikes 4 in. long.

B. sanderana. Leaves are leathery, spiny-toothed, dotted with white, grow to 1 ft. long. Produces loose, nodding, 10-in.-long clusters of flowers with blue petals that are yellowish green at the base; blue-tipped sepals, rose-colored bracts.

BIRCH. See BETULA

BIRD OF PARADISE. See CAESALPINIA, STRELITZIA

BIRD'S-EYE BUSH. See OCHNA serrulata

BIRD'S EYES. See GILIA tricolor

BIRD'S FOOT FERN. See PELLAEA mucronata

BIRD'S FOOT TREFOIL. See LOTUS corniculatus

BIRD'S NEST FERN. See ASPLENIUM nidus

BISHOP'S HAT. See EPIMEDIUM grandiflorum

BISHOP'S LACE. See AMMI majus

BISHOP'S WEED. See AEGOPODIUM podagraria

BITTER MELON
Cucurbitaceae
ANNUAL VINE

🌡	ALL ZONES
☼	FULL SUN
💧	REGULAR WATER

Also called balsam pear or bitter cucumber, bitter melon is classified botanically as *Momordica*

Bitter melon

charantia. Widespread in tropics, naturalized in southeastern U.S. Sprawls or climbs by tendrils to 16 ft. Deeply lobed leaves; yellow to white, 1-in.-wide flowers with fringed petals. Fruit, to 8 in. long, is cylindrical with tapered ends, ridged and warty, bright yellow when ripe, splitting to show scarlet seeds. Immature fruit is cherished in Asian cooking despite its bitter flavor. Ripe fruit is showy, sometimes used in arrangements. Sow seed when soil warms, feed generously, and provide a trellis or other support.

BITTERROOT. See LEWISIA rediviva

BITTERSWEET. See CELASTRUS

BLACKBERRY
Rosaceae
BERRY-PRODUCING VINES

🌡	ZONES VARY BY VARIETY
☼	FULL SUN
💧	REGULAR WATER

Most blackberry varieties are derived from *Rubus* species native to North America; for ornamental relatives, see entries under *Rubus*. The West has its own kinds of blackberries, most of which are trailing vines; these include varieties 'Boysen', 'Logan', 'Marion', and 'Olallie', often simply called boysenberry, loganberry, and so on. Midwestern and eastern blackberries are upright and stiff caned; these erect plants are generally hardier and easier to protect in winter (with a thick mulch) than trailing types. Crosses between trailing and erect blackberries are termed semierect.

Blackberry

Himalayan blackberry, *R. discolor*, better known as *R. procerus*, is an introduced pest that grows anywhere moisture is available. An aggressive spreader, it is hard to control and should be kept out of gardens. Nevertheless, it yields reasonably good fruit and is often tolerated along roadsides.

All kinds of blackberries bear fruit in summer; for good crops, they need deep, well-drained soil and regular moisture throughout the growing season. (But don't locate plants where they will be standing in water during dormancy.) Blackberries can be grown with some success in the desert, though plants may be short lived—for best results, amend soil generously with organic matter, and provide frequent water, heavy mulch, and protection from wind and intense afternoon sun.

In cold-winter regions, planting is usually done after the last hard freeze, when the soil begins to warm. In these areas, blackberries are best located on slight slopes where cold air will "drain" downhill. Set new bare-root plants an inch deeper than they grew at the nursery, covering their crowns with 1 in. of soil. In mild-winter regions, gardeners can plant in spring or gain half a season by transplanting container plants.

Blackberry roots are perennial, but the canes are biennial: they develop and grow one year, bloom and fruit the next. Hence the need to distinguish first- and second-year canes when training and pruning. 'Prime Jan' and 'Prime Jim' are exceptions. They are the first everbearing blackberries, producing two crops per season, like everbearing raspberries. They should be pruned the same way as everbearing raspberries.

Trailing and semierect types should be allowed to grow unrestricted the first year, then trained onto some kind of trellis in their second year. Train year-old canes fanwise onto the trellis; after harvest, cut to the ground all canes that have fruited. Canes of the current season—those growing beneath the trellis—should now be trained onto it. The following pruning must be done by midsummer to avoid reducing next year's crop: with trailing varieties, thin to 12–16 canes, pruning each

B

o 6–8 ft. long; with semierect ypes, thin to 4–8 canes, pruning ach to 5–6 ft. long. These short-ned canes will produce side ranches during remainder of rowing season; cut them back to ft. in early spring. New spring rowth will produce small fruiting ranches from those side branches.

Erect types don't need support, ut tying them to wire helps organize the canes. In the first year, ut canes to 2½ ft. in midsummer o force side growth. Cut resulting side branches to 12–15 in. late in he dormant season. After canes bear fruit in the second year, cut hem to ground. Start the process over again with new canes growing from the ground.

Blackberries are subject to many pests and diseases, includ-ing scale, borers, anthracnose, leaf spot, and powdery mildew, so start with healthy plants from a rep-utable supplier. Also look for resistant varieties. Because they are susceptible to verticillium wilt, do not plant blackberries where potatoes, tomatoes, eggplant, or peppers have grown in prior 3 years. To control red-berry mite (mostly affecting 'Evergreen' and 'Thornless Evergreen'), spider mites, and whitefly, apply a dor-mant spray containing lime sulfur in winter and again as buds are about to break.

Fertilize established plantings in the Pacific Northwest at blos-som time. In California, split the yearly amount into three applica-tions: before new growth starts, in midspring, and in midsummer. Elsewhere, fertilize just before new growth begins. Keep down weeds and pull out suckers; above all, don't let plants get away from you. Some of the varieties available in Western nurseries are listed below. Combine early, midseason, and late varieties to get fresh fruit over the longest possible season.

'Arapaho'. Erect; midseason. Zones 1–24. Thornless, disease resistant. Big crop of medium-size, firm, tasty berries. 'Apache', 'Navaho', and 'Oauchita' are similar thornless varieties; 'Chickasaw', 'Choctaw', 'Kiowa', and 'Shawnee' are also sim-ilar but have thorns. All thrive in hot-summer climates and are easy to grow without a trellis.

'Black Satin'. Erect; midseason. Zones 1–24. Thornless. Very large, juicy, and sweet. Heavy producer; nonsuckering. Good disease resistance.

'Boysen' and 'Thornless Boysen'. Trailing; midseason. Zones 2–24;

not reliably hardy in Zone 1, but will survive winter if canes are left on ground and covered with snow or straw mulch. Popular for high yield and flavor. Very large berries are reddish, soft, sweet-tart, have a delightful aroma, and can be used fresh, cooked, or frozen. Covered with a dusty bloom that slightly dulls color. 'Nectar' is identical variety.

'Brazos'. Erect; early. Zones 4–24. Disease-resistant Texas vari-ety well adapted to hot-summer areas. Large, fairly firm, tart fruit.

'Cherokee'. Erect; early. Zones 1–24. Thorny. Medium-large, firm berries with excellent flavor. Re-sists anthracnose.

'Chester'. Semierect; late. Zones 2–9, 14–24. Thornless. Medium-size, firm berries with good flavor. Late ripening, greatly extending season. Very cold tolerant.

'Dirkson'. Semierect; midseason. Zones 2–9, 14–24. Thornless. High yield of large, semitart berries. Resistant to anthracnose, leaf spot, and powdery mildew.

'Evergreen' and 'Thornless Ever-green'. Trailing; late. Zones 4–6, 8, 9, 12, 13, 20–24. Strong canes bear heavy crop of large, exceptionally firm, black, sweet berries with large seeds.

'Logan' and 'Thornless Logan'. Trailing; early. Same climate adaption as 'Boysen'. Large berries are light red, not darkening when ripe, with fine hairs that dull the fruit's color. Tarter flavor than 'Boysen'; excellent for canning and pies.

'Marion'. Trailing; midseason. Zones 4–9, 14–24. Rich, flavorful fruit sets the standard. 'Marion' types include 'Black Diamond', a thornless variety; late-ripening 'Waldo', with berries that maintain their shape when cooked; and 'Black Butte', 'Silvan', and 'Siskiyou', all early ripeners with excellent flavor.

'Olallie'. Trailing; early. Zones 4–9, 14–24. Berries medium to large, shiny black, firm, with a sweet flavor that has some wild blackberry sprightliness.

'Prime Jan'. Erect; everbearing. Zones 4–6, 16, 17. Like everbear-ing raspberries, bears on new canes in late summer and 2-year-old canes in spring. Can be cut to the ground each winter, resulting in a single late crop the following season. Very productive. Medium-size, sweet-tart berries. 'Prime Jim' is similar.

'Tay' or 'Tayberry'. Trailing; early. Zones 4–9, 14–24. Hybrid

between blackberry and raspberry. Long, thorny canes. Heavy bearer of big, mild-flavored, dark red to purple-black fruit. Bears earlier than most other blackberries.

'Triple Crown'. Semierect; late. Zones 1–9, 14–24. An improved 'Chester' type with large, very flavorful berries. Vigorous canes. Hardy. 'Hull' is similar but not as tasty.

'Young' and 'Thornless Young'. Trailing; midseason. Climate adaption same as for 'Boysen' but not as productive in all climates. Berries are same size and color as 'Boysen' but shiny and somewhat sweeter.

BLACKBERRY LILY.
See **BELAMCANDA chinensis**

BLACK CALLA.
See **ARUM palaestinum**

BLACK-EYED SUSAN.
See **RUDBECKIA hirta**

BLACK-EYED SUSAN VINE.
See **THUNBERGIA alata**

BLACKFOOT DAISY. See
MELAMPODIUM leucanthum

BLACK LILY. See **FRITILLARIA camschatcensis**

BLACK SNAKEROOT.
See **ACTAEA racemosa**

BLANKET FLOWER.
See **GAILLARDIA**

BLAZING STAR.
See **LIATRIS, MENTZELIA**

BLECHNUM
Polypodiaceae
FERNS

🌿	ZONES VARY BY SPECIES
◐ ●	PARTIAL OR FULL SHADE
💧	REGULAR WATER

Evergreen ferns noted for their symmetrical, formal appearance; some form a small trunk. Plants dislike overhead watering when air is humid or still.

B. brasiliense. Zones 19, 21–24. Native to Brazil, Peru. Dwarf tree fern reaching only 4 ft. tall, 5 ft. wide. Nearly erect fronds in compact clusters; reddish when young. 'Crispum' has elegantly ruffled fronds.

B. gibbum. Zones 19, 21–24; H1, H2. Native to Fiji. Dwarf tree fern with 3-ft.-wide crown of fronds atop slender trunk that eventually reaches 3 ft. high. 'Moorei' has wider, more leathery

Blechnum spicant

leaflets and is more attractive in winter.

B. penna-marina. Zones 15–17, 20–24; with protection in Zones 4–6. Native to South Amer-ica. Spreads slowly in cool, moist, sheltered places to make patches of refined-looking, 4–8-in. fronds. Sterile fronds have wider lobes than fertile ones. Can be used as a houseplant.

B. spicant. DEER FERN, DEER TONGUE FERN. Zones 2b–7, 14–19, 24. Native primarily to coastal forests of Northern Califor-nia and Northwest. Glossy deep green fern with two strikingly dif-ferent kinds of fronds: sterile ones are 1¾ in. wide, spreading or angled, 1–3 ft. tall; fertile ones are narrower and stiffly erect, with slender, widely spaced leaflets. Forms a clump to 3 ft. wide.

BLEEDING HEART.
See **DICENTRA**

BLETILLA striata (B. hyacinthina)
CHINESE GROUND ORCHID
Orchidaceae
TERRESTRIAL ORCHID

🌿	ZONES 2B–9, 12–24
◐	FILTERED SUN OR PARTIAL SHADE
💧	REGULAR WATER DURING GROWTH AND BLOOM

Hardy orchid native to China and Japan. Pinkish purple, 2-in.-wide blossoms resembling cattleyas are carried up to 12 on each 1–1½-ft. stem. Bloom lasts for about 6 weeks in late spring or early summer. Pale green leaves, three to six to a plant, remain attractive into early fall. 'Alba' is a white-flowered form. *B. s. albostriata* bears light pink blossoms above leaves striped in green and white.

Grow in pots or ground, under high-branching trees or lath. Plant pseudobulbs any time during dormant period (late fall to early

Bletilla striata

spring), positioning tops 1 in. below soil surface (2 in. in colder regions) and spacing 1 ft. apart. Plant in humus-rich, well-drained soil; mulch if temperatures will drop below 20°F/–7°C. Protect from slugs and snails when leaves emerge. Taper off watering when foliage begins to yellow in fall; discontinue when leaves have died back completely. Forms large clumps over time that can be divided in early spring, before growth starts. (However, blooms best when crowded.)

BLOOD FLOWER.
See **ASCLEPIAS** curassavica

BLOODLEAF. See **IRESINE**

BLOOD LILY. See **SCADOXUS** multiflorus katherinae

BLUEBEARD.
See **CARYOPTERIS**

BLUEBELL. See **CAMPANULA, HYACINTHOIDES, SCILLA**

BLUEBERRY
Ericaceae
DECIDUOUS SHRUBS

✎	ZONES VARY BY TYPE
☀	FULL SUN
💧	AMPLE WATER

Native to eastern North America; for ornamental species in the same genus, see *Vaccinium*. Blueberries thrive under conditions that suit rhododendrons and azaleas, to which they are related. They need cool, moist, well-drained acid soil (pH 4.5–5.5). Where soil isn't acidic enough, either create proper conditions in garden soil or grow in containers filled with acidic potting mix.

Most blueberries grown for fruit are also handsome plants suitable for hedges or shrub borders. Leaves, to 3 in. long, are bronze when new, maturing to

dark green, turning scarlet or yellow in fall. Tiny, urn-shaped spring flowers are white or pinkish. Summer fruit is decorative. Set plants about 3 ft. apart for informal hedge; as individual shrubs, space at least 4–5 ft. apart.

Blueberries are available bareroot or in containers. Plant in early spring in cold-winter regions, autumn in mild climates. Position the crown so that it is no deeper than ½ in. below the ground. Blueberries have fine roots near the soil surface; keep them moist, but don't subject them to standing water. A 3–4-in.-thick mulch of sawdust, ground bark, or the like will protect roots, help conserve soil moisture, and keep weeds down. Don't disturb roots by cultivating around plants. Use acid-forming fertilizers. California growers in particular may need to correct chlorosis with iron sulfate or iron chelate.

Prune to prevent overbearing. Plants shape themselves but often produce so many fruit buds that berries are undersize and plant growth slows down. Keep first-year plants from bearing by stripping off flowers. On older plants, cut back ends of twigs to point where fruit buds are widely spaced. Or simply remove some of oldest branches each year. Also prune out all weak shoots. Plants seldom have serious problems requiring regular control in home gardens. Netting will keep birds at bay.

The following are the major types of blueberries grown. Plant at least two varieties for better pollination, choosing kinds that ripen at different times for a long harvest. For sufficient fruit throughout the season, allow two plants for each household member.

Highbush blueberries. Selections of *Vaccinium corymbosum,* these are the blueberries found in grocery stores. Most varieties grow upright to 6 ft. or more; a few are rather sprawling and under 5 ft. The majority are northern varieties (Zones 2–9, 14–17): they require definite winter cold and ripen fruit from late spring to late summer. The relatively new southern highbush varieties (Zones 8, 9, 14–17, 18–24) are better adapted to mild-winter climates and are

even finding success in Southern California; they ripen their fruit in mid- to late spring, even before rabbiteye types. Except as noted, varieties below are northern types.

'Berkeley'. Midseason. Open, spreading, tall. Large, light blue berries.

'Bluecrop'. Midseason. Erect, tall growth. Large berries. Excellent flavor. Attractive shrub.

'Blueray'. Midseason. Vigorous, tall. Large, highly flavored, crisp berries. Attractive shrub. Tolerates more heat than 'Bluecrop'.

'Chandler'. Midseason to late. Tall, upright. Very large, sweet berries produced over a long season.

'Darrow'. Late. Vigorous, upright. Very large fruit, up to the size of a quarter. Heavy producer.

'Earliblue'. Early. Tall, erect. Large, heavy leaves. Large berries of excellent flavor.

'Elliott'. Late. Tall, upright. Medium to large berries of excellent flavor.

'Ivanhoe'. Early to midseason. Large, dark berries are firm, crisp, tart.

'Jubilee'. Southern highbush. Early. Tall, upright. Medium to large berries with excellent flavor.

'Legacy'. Late. Unusual shrub that doesn't lose its leaves in winter. Will color in cold winters, but stays mostly green in mild areas. Upright, arching. Medium-size berries with fine flavor.

'Misty'. Southern highbush. Very early. Large berries with excellent flavor. Bears heavily.

'Olympia'. Midseason. Medium-size fruit with exceptional, spicy flavor. Large, vigorous, arching bush with great fall color.

'O'Neal'. Southern highbush. Very early. Large, flavorful berries.

'Rubel'. Early to late. Erect, tall growth. Small, firm, tart berries.

'Sharpblue'. Southern highbush. Early to midseason. Large, fast-growing shrub. Large, light blue berries with sweet-tart flavor.

'Southmoon'. Southern highbush. Midseason. Large, bright blue berries with excellent flavor.

'Spartan'. Early. Heavy bearer of large, flavorful fruit.

'Sunshine Blue'. Southern highbush. Midseason. Compact, evergreen, reaching only 3 ft. high; makes an attractive landscape

Blueberry

plant. Large, light blue berries with tangy flavor. Self-fertile. Very low chilling requirement. Tolerates a higher soil pH than most other blueberries.

'Tophat'. Midseason. Dwarf hybrid that stays under 1½ ft.; good for pots. Small fruit with mild flavor.

'Toro'. Midseason. Compact plant with pinkish blooms. Large, firm berries with an excellent, sprightly flavor.

Rabbiteye blueberries. Zones 8, 9, 14–17, 18–24. These selections of *Vaccinium ashei* are native to southeastern U.S. and can be grown in central California, Southern California, and other mild-winter areas if given acid soil conditions. Unlike most blueberries, these tolerate heat. Often taller and rangier than highbush plants, they ripen large, light blue berries from May to July. Quality is not as good as that of highbush blueberries. Varieties include 'Bluebelle', 'Southland', and 'Tifblue'.

Hardy half-high varieties. Zones A2, A3; 1–3. Highbush blueberries have been hybridized with the northeastern U.S. native lowbush blueberry (*Vaccinium angustifolium*) to create very hardy types called half-high blueberries.

'Chippewa'. Midseason. Slightly larger plant than 'Northblue'. Large, light blue fruit with excellent sweet flavor.

'Northblue'. Midseason to late. To 3–4 ft. high. Large, firm, dark blue berries with trace of wild blueberry flavor.

'Northcountry'. Early midseason. Less than 3 ft. tall. Sweet, very light blue berries. Good choice for containers.

'Northsky'. Midseason to late. Densely branched, to 1–1½ ft. high. Light blue berries with hint of wild blueberry flavor. Good in containers.

'Polaris'. Early. To 4 ft. tall; upright, arching. Light blue fruit with delightful flavor.

'St. Cloud'. Early. To 3–4 ft. tall. Large, firm, flavorful berries.

BLUE BLOSSOM.
See **CEANOTHUS** thyrsiflorus

BLUE BUSH.
See **ACACIA** covenyi

BLUE BUTTONS.
See **KNAUTIA** arvensis

BLUE DAWN FLOWER.
See **IPOMOEA** indica

BLUE DAZE. See **EVOLVULUS glomeratus**

BLUE-EYED GRASS. See **SISYRINCHIUM idahoense bellum**

BLUE-EYED MARY. See **OMPHALODES verna**

BLUE GINGER. See **DICHORISANDRA thyrsiflora**

BLUEGRASS. See **POA**

BLUE HIBISCUS. See **ALYOGYNE huegelii**

BLUE LACE FLOWER. See **TRACHYMENE coerulea**

BLUE MARGUERITE. See **FELICIA amelloides**

BLUE MIST. See **CARYOPTERIS × clandonensis**

BLUE OAT GRASS. See **HELICTOTRICHON sempervirens**

BLUE SPIREA. See **CARYOPTERIS incana**

BLUE STAR CREEPER. See **PRATIA pedunculata**

BLUESTAR. See **AMSONIA**

BLUE THIMBLE FLOWER. See **GILIA capitata**

BOCCONIA. See **MACLEAYA cordata**

BOG ROSEMARY. See **ANDROMEDA polifolia**

BOK CHOY. See **ASIAN GREENS**

BOLAX gummifera (B. glebaria, Azorella trifurcata)
Apiaceae (Umbelliferae)
PERENNIAL

- ☒ ZONES 2–6, 14–17
- ☼ ☽ FULL SUN IN COOLER CLIMATES ONLY
- ◑ REGULAR WATER

Native to Chile, Argentina, and the Falkland Islands. The origin of the name is uncertain, but the

Bolax gummifera

plant itself is a low, densely branching perennial with tightly packed rosettes of bright green, glossy, thick, hard leaves ½ in. or so in length. Each leaf is divided into three lobes. Flowers look like tiny, greenish parsley blossoms. The plant forms a firm cushion just 2 in. high and 1½ ft. across. Attractive in rock gardens or as ground cover in light shade, though it can take full sun in cool-summer climates.

BOLTONIA asteroides
Asteraceae (Compositae)
PERENNIAL

- ☒ ZONES 1–24
- ☼ ☽ FULL SUN OR LIGHT SHADE
- ◑ REGULAR WATER

Boltonia asteroides

Native to eastern U.S. In late summer, tall stems bear airy, mounded clusters of small yellow-centered white to blue flowers that resemble Michaelmas daisies (*Aster novi-belgii*). With regular moisture, can reach 6 ft. or taller, 3 ft. wide; may be floppy with overhead watering. 'Pink Beauty' has pink flowers. 'Snowbank' is more compact (to 5 ft. tall) and upright than the species, with larger flowers of a clearer white. 'Nana', with lavender-pink blooms, reaches only 2 ft. high. Plants will survive in poor soil and with reduced water, but have reduced vigor and size and sparser bloom.

BORAGO officinalis
BORAGE
Boraginaceae
ANNUAL

- ☒ ZONES A2, A3; 1–24; H1
- ☼ ☽ FULL SUN OR PARTIAL SHADE
- ◔ MODERATE WATER

Native European herb forms rounded clump to 2–3 ft. high, 1½–2 ft. wide. Bristly gray-green

leaves to 4–6 in. long are edible, with a cucumberlike flavor. Blue, star-shaped summer flowers nod in leafy clusters from branched stems.

Tolerates poor soil. Seeds itself, but doesn't transplant easily because of deep taproot. Best way to start borage is to sow seeds in place in spring after frost danger is past. Good drought-tolerant ground cover and soil binder. Use small, tender leaves in salads; you can also pickle them or cook them as greens. Cut flowers for arrangements or use as a garnish.

Borago officinalis

BORINDA. See **BAMBOO**

BORONIA
Rutaceae
EVERGREEN SHRUBS

- ☒ ZONES VARY BY SPECIES
- ☼ ☽ FULL SUN OR LIGHT SHADE
- ◑ REGULAR WATER

Attractive, relatively short-lived shrubs from Australia. Finely divided leaves produce a wispy look. Bell-shaped blooms are good for cutting. Plants need well-drained, slightly acid, sandy or light loamy soil. Careful watering is important: they should never be completely dry or stay wet at root depth for any length of time. Prune lightly after bloom to promote bushiness and prolong life of plant.

B. clavata. HEATHER WAND. Zones 15–17, 19–24. Compact growth to 4–6 ft. tall and wide, with small, aromatic, light green leaves and lightly scented, greenish yellow flowers in spring. Best in partial shade. Useful, fragrant screen.

Boronia megastigma

B. crenulata. Zones 16–24. To 2–3 ft. tall, 3–4 ft. wide, with tiny dark green leaves and small pink flowers in late winter and spring. 'Rosy Splendor' is more upright (3–4 ft. tall and 2–3 ft. wide), with flowers held on longer stems. 'Shark Bay' is a compact (2-ft.-tall, 3-ft.-wide) selection with pink flowers that appear throughout the

year, most profusely from winter to early summer.

B. denticulata. Zones 15–17, 20–24. To 3–8 ft. tall, 1½–4 ft. wide, with strongly aromatic leaves. Flowers in mauve, pink shades, or more rarely white, in late winter and spring; sporadic bloom otherwise.

B. heterophylla. RED BORONIA. Zones 16–24. Dense grower to 6–8 ft. tall, 4–6 ft. wide, with finely cut foliage and profuse, intensely fragrant, deep pink flowers opening from red buds in late winter and spring.

B. megastigma. BROWN BORONIA. Zones 15–17, 20–24. Only 1–2 ft. tall and wide, with nodding, ½-in., bell-shaped brown to reddish brown flowers with yellow interior; winter bloom. Powerful, pleasant scent combines freesia, orange blossom, and other fragrances. Count on replacing plant every 2 or 3 years from seed or cuttings. Lasts longer grown in light potting mix in containers. 'Jack Maguire's Red' has deep orange-red blooms.

B. molloyae (B. elatior). PINK BORONIA, TALL BORONIA. Zones 15–17, 20–24. Grows 3–12 ft. tall, 3–6 ft. wide. Clouds of ¼-in., bell-shaped pink to rose flowers in spring and summer.

BOSTON FERN. See **NEPHROLEPIS exaltata 'Bostoniensis'**

BOSTON IVY. See **PARTHENOCISSUS tricuspidata**

BO-TREE. See **FICUS religiosa**

BOTTLEBRUSH. See **CALLISTEMON, MELALEUCA**

BOTTLE PALM. See **NOLINA recurvata**

BOTTLE TREE. See **BRACHYCHITON populneus**

BOUGAINVILLEA
Nyctaginaceae
EVERGREEN SHRUBBY VINES

- ☒ ZONES 5, 6, 12–17, 19, 21–24; H1, H2
- ☼ FULL SUN
- ◑◑ MODERATE TO REGULAR WATER

Native to tropical and subtropical South America. Reliably hardy in Zones 22–24, H1, H2, yet widely and satisfyingly grown in areas of minimum frost: Zones 12–17, 19, 21. Use has extended into Zones 5, 6, thanks to low-growing shrubby types that can be purchased in full bloom and grown in containers. ▶

TOP: *Bougainvillea* 'Barbara Karst'
BOTTOM: *Bougainvillea* 'Rosenka'

TOP: *Bougainvillea* 'California Gold'
BOTTOM: *Bougainvillea*
'Mary Palmer's Enchantment'

TOP: *Bougainvillea* 'Raspberry Ice'
BOTTOM: *Bougainvillea* 'San Diego Red'

TOP: *Bougainvillea* 'Orange King'
BOTTOM: *Bougainvillea* 'Texas Dawn'

These are used on patios as summer annuals and moved to a protected area over winter. Where frosts are routine (as in Zones 12, 14, 19, 21), vines need a protected warm wall or warmest spot in garden. If vines get by first winter or two, they will be big enough to take most winter damage and recover. In any case, young plants bloom so readily that replacement is not a real deterrent.

Bougainvillea's vibrant colors come not from the inconspicuous true flowers, but from the large, papery, petal-like bracts that surround them. Bloom reaches its peak in summer, but in mildest-winter regions flowers may appear from spring through fall, and even into winter. Single- and double-flowered types are sold; the double kinds can look messy, because they hold faded blooms for a long time. White- and yellow-flowered varieties need light shade in the hottest climates.

Bougainvillea
'San Diego Red'

Vining bougainvilleas are fast, vigorous growers, reaching 15–30 ft. depending on variety. Long, needlelike thorns arm stiff stems that are moderately to densely clothed in medium green, 2½-in., heart-shaped leaves. Vines are superb on walls and sturdy fences, trellises, arbors. Because they have no means of attachment (though the thorns help them scramble through shrubs and trees), you must tie stems to the support while basic structure is establishing.

In areas that typically have frosts, plant in early spring after danger of frost has passed. Do any major pruning after flowering has ceased (in frost-free regions) or as early as possible in spring after frost danger has passed (in others). During growing season, prune as needed to direct growth.

Heavily pruned vines and shrubby varieties make good self-supporting container plants for terrace or patio. Without support and with occasional corrective pruning, bougainvillea becomes a broad, sprawling shrub, a bank or ground cover, or a hanging-basket plant.

All of the following are tall-growing vines unless otherwise noted.

White: 'Jamaica White' has white bracts veined in light green, is moderately vigorous, and blooms when young. 'Mary Palmer's Enchantment' is a vigorous, large-growing vine with pure white bracts. Thornless 'Singapore White' is shrubby and compact, easily kept to 3–4 ft. high and wide. Bracts of 'White Madonna' are pure white.

Yellow to orange: 'Afterglow' is an open-growing heavy bloomer with yellow-orange bracts and sparse foliage. 'California Gold' ('Sunset') blooms young, with deep golden yellow bracts. 'Orange King' is an open grower with bronzy orange bracts; it needs long summers to bloom well and cannot take frost.

Pink: 'Camarillo Fiesta' has bracts in a blend of hot pink and gold. Double-flowered 'Cherry Blossom' sports rose pink bracts with white to pale green centers. 'Pink Tiara' has abundant pale pink to rose bracts over a long season.

'Rosenka' can be held to shrub proportions if occasional wayward shoots are pruned out; gold bracts age to pink. Thornless 'Singapore Pink' has bright pink bracts; shrubby and compact, it can easily be kept to 3–4 ft. high and wide. 'Southern Rose' has rosy lavender to pink bracts. 'Tahitian Maid' offers extra rows of blush pink bracts that give a double effect.

What Bougainvilleas Need

CAREFUL PLANTING Roots do not knit soil together in a firm root ball, and they are highly sensitive to disturbance. To minimize shock when planting, cut off container bottom and set both plant and container in planting hole. Slide container up over the plant, filling in with soil as you go. Don't worry about damaging the plant as you do so; stems are pliant, with little horizontal growth.

STRONG SUPPORT Tie shoots to a sturdy support so they won't whip in wind. Strong gusts can shred leaves against sharp thorns on stems.

NUTRIENTS Fertilize when growing season begins and again in early summer.

Bougainvillea
'Purple Queen'

MOISTURE Water regularly in spring, moderately during bloom period.

Choice, vigorous 'Texas Dawn' has large sprays of bracts in purplish pink. Unlike other bougainvilleas, 'Torch Glow' ('Bangkok Red') grows erect to form a multistemmed plant to 6 ft. tall that needs no support; its reddish pink flowers are held close to stems and are partially hidden by foliage.

Red: Vigorous 'Barbara Karst' blooms young and for a long period, bearing bracts that are bright red in sun, bluish crimson in shade; it thrives in desert heat and comes back fast after frost. 'Brilliant Variegated' is a spreading, mounding shrub (good for hanging baskets and pots) with leaves variegated with gray-green and silver; bracts are brick red. Vigorous, sprawling 'Crimson Jewel' is good in containers or as a shrubby bank cover, with lower growth and brighter crimson color than 'Temple Fire'; it blooms heavily over a long season. 'La Jolla,' with bright red bracts, has a compact, shrubby habit that makes it a good shrub or container plant. 'Manila Red' has many rows of magenta-red bracts for heavy clusters of double-looking blooms. 'Oo-La-La' is dwarf (1½ ft. tall, 6–8 ft. wide) with magenta-red bracts over a long season; it makes a good ground or bank cover or hanging basket plant. Hardy 'Raspberry Ice' ('Hawaii') is shrubby and mounding (good in hanging baskets), with red bracts and yellow-edged leaves that are tinged red when new. 'Rosea' bears large, rose red bracts on a large vine. 'San Diego Red' ('San Diego', 'Scarlett O'Hara') is one of the best on all counts, with large, deep green leaves that hold on well in cold winters; deep red bracts that appear over a long season; and hardiness equal to old-fashioned purple bougainvilleas. Vigorous and high climbing, it can be trained to tree form by staking and pruning. 'Temple Fire' offers shrublike growth to 4 ft. high, 6 ft. wide on a partially deciduous plant; bracts are bronze red.

Purple: 'Don Mario' is a large, vigorous vine with huge clusters of deep purple-red bracts. Another big vine is 'James Walker', with large, reddish purple bracts. 'Lavender Queen' is an improved form of *B. spectabilis,* with bigger bracts and heavier bloom. Compact 'Purple Queen' sports deep purple bracts on vines that can reach 15 ft. with support; as a trailer, it grows 1½ ft. tall, 6–8 ft. wide. Hardy and vigorous *B. spectabilis (B. brasiliensis)* has purple bracts and blooms well in cool summers (good choice for Zones 16, 17). 'Tahitian Dawn' is a big vine with gold bracts that age to rosy purple.

BOULDER RASPBERRY.
See **RUBUS deliciosus**

BOUNCING BET.
See **SAPONARIA officinalis**

BOUTELOUA
GRAMA GRASS
Poaceae (Gramineae)
PERENNIAL GRASSES

🌿 ZONES 1–3, 7–11, 14, 18–21
☀️ FULL SUN
💧 LITTLE WATER

These natives of dry North American grasslands form clumps of narrow gray-green leaves. Tough, heat- and drought-tolerant plants characterized by oddly attractive flowering stems that carry their summer flowers on one side only.

Bouteloua gracilis

One or a few plants are pretty in a border or large rock garden. Massed, they are useful for creating meadows. Grow from seed or division.

B. curtipendula. SIDE-OATS GRAMA. To 1–2 ft. tall, 2 ft. wide. Flowering stems vary from arching to nearly horizontal, with the purple-tinted green flowers dangling underneath. These, like the leaves, turn yellow in fall, then white in winter.

B. gracilis. BLUE GRAMA, MOSQUITO GRASS. To 1½–2 ft. high, 1 ft. wide. Flowering stems have odd inflorescences springing out at right angles and said to resemble hovering mosquitoes. Reddish in summer, they bleach to white. Tolerates sunny, arid, alkaline conditions in the High Plains and Rocky Mountain areas. Makes a fair low-water-use lawn if mowed to 1½ in. high. Sow seed at 1 lb. per 1,000 sq. ft. in fall to take advantage of winter rain and snow. Irrigate to depth of 1 ft. until established; thereafter, it needs virtually no irrigation.

BOUVARDIA
Rubiaceae
EVERGREEN SHRUBS

🌿 ZONES VARY BY SPECIES
☼ PARTIAL SHADE
💧 WATER NEEDS VARY BY SPECIES

Valued for showy clusters of tubular flowers. Plants have loose, often straggling growth habit. One type has fragrant blossoms, but it is also the most tender and looks poorest after flowers are gone. The nonfragrant red-flowered species are hardier, easier to grow. All appreciate well-drained soil, midday shade. To encourage compact growth, prune hard annually after bloom period ends.

B. glaberrima. Zones 8–10, 12, 14–24. Native to mountain canyons in southern Arizona, New Mexico. To 3 ft. tall and wide. Shrubby, but top growth dies back in cold weather. Smooth green leaves 1–3 in. long. Clustered 1-in., red (rarely pink or white), unscented flowers. Little water.

B. longiflora 'Albatross' (B. humboldtii 'Albatross'). Zones 12, 16, 17, 19–24. Variety of a Mexican species. Jasmine-scented, 3-in. snow white flowers appear at almost any time; excellent in bouquets. Plant is 2–3 ft. high and 2 ft. wide, with paired 2-in. leaves. Pinch out stem tips to make bushier. If soil is poor, grow in

Bouvardia longiflora
'Albatross'

tubs or raised beds in rich, fast-draining soil mix. 'Stephanie' is more compact and floriferous. Regular water.

B. ternifolia (B. jacquinii). Zones 8–10, 12, 14–24. Native to Texas, Mexico. To 3 ft. tall, 2½–3 ft. wide; 2-in. leaves in whorls of three or four. Unscented, inch-long red flowers in loose clusters at branch ends in summer and early fall. Forms have pink, rose, or coral blossoms. Little water.

BOWER VINE.
See **PANDOREA jasminoides**

BOWLES' GOLDEN GRASS.
See **MILIUM effusum 'Aureum'**

BOWSTRING HEMP.
See **SANSEVIERIA trifasciata**

BOX, BOXWOOD. See **BUXUS**

BOX ELDER. See **ACER negundo**

BOYSENBERRY.
See **BLACKBERRY**

BRACHYCHITON
Sterculiaceae
EVERGREEN AND PARTLY OR
WHOLLY DECIDUOUS TREES

🌿 ZONES VARY BY SPECIES
☀️ FULL SUN
💧 LITTLE TO MODERATE WATER

Native to Australia. All have woody, canoe-shaped fruits that delight flower arrangers but are merely litter in the view of some gardeners. Grow in well-drained soil. Tend to form strong central leader; require minimal pruning.

Blooming habit and leaf drop in the two deciduous species listed here can be most erratic. Young trees often bloom only in sections of the tree rather than all over it; those parts will drop their leaves while nonblooming areas retain their foliage. Older trees tend to produce blooms on all branches and drop all their leaves before flowers appear. Bloom is best after a dry winter.

B. acerifolius (Sterculia acerifolia). FLAME TREE, AUSTRALIAN FLAME TREE. Deciduous for brief period. Zones 15–24; H1, H2. Hardy to 25°F/ –4°C. At its best, a spectacular red-flowering tree reaching 60 ft. or taller, 30 ft. wide. Strong, heavy, smooth trunk, usually green. Handsome leaves are glossy bright green, 10-in.-wide fans, deeply lobed. Showiest flowering season usually comes in late spring to early summer, when all or part of tree is covered with clusters of ¾-in., tubular red or orange-red bells.

B. discolor (Sterculia discolor). QUEENSLAND LACEBARK, PINK FLAME TREE. Deciduous for brief period. Zones 15–24. To 40–60 ft. tall; pyramidal in youth but more spreading (to about 30 ft.) in maturity. Ornamental bottle-shaped trunk. Leaves, only 6 in. wide, are narrower than those of *B. acerifolius* and are blue green rather than bright green, with whitish undersides. Leaves on young trees are deeply lobed; lobes become shallower as tree ages. Large, bell-like, deep rose pink flowers in summer; fallen flowers can be messy. Blossoms and subsequent fruit are densely covered with rusty wool on outside.

Brachychiton populneus

B. populneus (Sterculia diversifolia). BOTTLE TREE. Evergreen. Zones 12–24. Moderate growth to 30–50 ft. tall, 30 ft. wide. Common name refers to heavy trunk of mature trees, which is broad at base, tapering toward top. Leaves (2–3 in. long) are fresh green year-round, shimmer in breeze like those of aspens. Clusters of small, bell-shaped white flowers in late spring only noticeable close up. Appreciated

B

in low and intermediate deserts, where it is frequently used as a shade tree and as a screen or high, wide windbreak. Susceptible to Texas root rot.

B. rupestris (Sterculia rupestris). QUEENSLAND BOTTLE TREE. Evergreen. Zones 13, 21, 23, 24. To 25 ft. tall, 15 ft. wide, often much smaller. Leaves on young trees are deeply lobed (like fingers of a hand); on mature trees they are undivided, to 6 in. long. Flowers are small and yellowish. Conspicuous feature is the trunk, which is swollen and bulbous; may measure 5–6 ft. in diameter. Young plants confined to containers often produce grotesquely twisted trunks.

BRACHYGLOTTIS.
See **SENECIO greyi**

BRACHYSCOME
SWAN RIVER DAISY
Asteraceae (Compositae)
ANNUALS AND PERENNIALS

| 🗓 ZONES VARY BY SPECIES |
| ☀ FULL SUN |
| 💧 REGULAR WATER |

Neat, charming Australian daisies make mounds 1 ft. tall, 1½ ft. across, with finely divided leaves and a profusion of inch-wide daisies in spring and summer. Use in rock garden, at front of border, or in containers or raised beds.

B. hybrids. Perennials. Zones 14–24. Choices include 'City Lights', with light lavender-blue flowers; 'New Amethyst', dark purple; and 'Toucan Tango' ('Ultra'), deep lavender blue.

Brachyscome iberidifolia

B. iberidifolia. Annual. Zones 1–24. Flowers are blue, white, or pink. In spring, sow seed where plants are to grow.

B. multifida. Perennial. Zones 14–24. Very similar to *B. iberidifolia*. Blue flowers most common. Propagate by cuttings.

BRACKEN.
See **PTERIDIUM aquilinum**

BRACTEANTHA bracteata (Xerochrysum bracteatum)
BUSH STRAWFLOWER
Asteraceae (Compositae)
SHRUBBY PERENNIAL

| 🗓 ZONES 8, 9, 14–24 |
| ☀ FULL SUN |
| 💧 REGULAR WATER |

Bracteantha bracteata

Australian native formerly considered atypical example of the common annual strawflower (*Helichrysum bracteatum*) has now been given a genus of its own. Flowers, held well above the foliage, resemble those of strawflower in having many rows of papery bracts; narrow leaves are gray green. 'Diamond Head' grows 8 in. high and 1½ ft. wide, with 1½-in., golden yellow flowers. 'Dargan Hill Monarch' is larger overall at 2½ ft. tall and 3–6 ft. wide, with leaves to 6 in. long and golden yellow flower heads to 3½ in. across. 'Cockatoo' resembles the latter but has light yellow blossoms. Newer Sundaze series includes selections with bronzy gold, golden yellow, lemon yellow, pink, or white blossoms on plants 10–14 in. high and wide. Flower heads of all types may be dried for arrangements. Plants need good drainage.

BRAHEA (Erythea)
Arecaceae (Palmae)
PALMS

| 🗓 ZONES VARY BY SPECIES |
| ☀ FULL SUN |
| 💧 LITTLE OR NO WATER TO MODERATE WATER |

These fan palms from Mexico are somewhat like the more familiar washingtonias in appearance. Need some summer water in desert regions.

Brahea armata

B. armata. MEXICAN BLUE PALM. Zones 10, 12–17, 19–24; H1. Hardy to 18°F/–8°C. Grows slowly to 20–40 ft. tall, top spreading 12–25 ft. Silvery blue, almost white leaves. Conspicuous creamy flowers. Takes heat and wind.

B. brandegeei. SAN JOSE HESPER PALM. Zones 13, 19, 21–24; H1, H2. Hardy to 26°F/–3°C. Slow grower to 40 ft. tall and 15 ft. wide, with slender, flexible trunk. Trunk sheds leaves when old. Leaves are 3 ft. long, light gray green.

B. edulis. GUADALUPE PALM. Zones 12–24. Hardy to below 20°F/–7°C. From Guadalupe Island off Baja California. Like *B. armata*, but leaves are light green, flowers less conspicuous. Slow grower, eventually reaching to 30 ft. tall and 15 ft. wide. Old leaves drop, leaving a naked, elephant-hide, stout trunk ringed with scars. Will take beach as well as desert conditions.

B. elegans. FRANCESCHI PALM. Zones 13–17, 19–24. Hardy to 22°F/–6°C. Slowest growing of braheas. Develops a trunk very slowly and reaches only 15 ft. tall; top spreads 15 ft. Gray-green leaves.

BRAKE. See **PTERIS**

BRAMBLE. See **RUBUS**

BRASSAIA actinophylla.
See **SCHEFFLERA actinophylla**

BRAZILIAN BUTTERFLY TREE.
See **BAUHINIA forficata**

BRAZILIAN PLUME FLOWER.
See **JUSTICIA carnea**

BRAZILIAN SKY FLOWER.
See **DURANTA stenostachya**

BREADFRUIT
Moraceae
EVERGREEN TREE

| 🗓 ZONE H2 |
| ☀ FULL SUN |
| 💧 REGULAR WATER |

A distinctly beautiful tropical fruit tree (known botanically as *Artocarpus altilis*) native to the South Pacific region and Malaysia; its Hawaiian name is 'ulu. This impressive evergreen eventually reaches to 40–60 ft. high and just as wide, with huge (to 3-ft.-long), deeply lobed, leathery, shiny dark green leaves. Yellow male catkins and prickly-looking female flowers appear on the same tree but are borne in different clusters.

Bumpy, thin-skinned, round to oblong fruit is 8–12 in. long. Each fruit weighs from 2 to 9 lb. and usually contains large seeds (seeded types are called breadnuts). Fruits in all stages of development are present on the tree throughout the year, as fruiting occurs more or less continually; peak fruiting period in Hawaii is from summer to midwinter. Green fruit can be peeled and the white pulp boiled, roasted, fried, or baked as a vegetable. It can also be used in soups and stews. If left to mature on the tree, the rind of the fruit turns brownish green. The flesh is a sweet, soft pulp that can be baked or steamed as dessert.

Breadfruit

'Ma'afala' and 'Maopo' are good seedless varieties. To fruit abundantly, breadfruit requires heat and moist, fertile soil with excellent drainage. In the greenhouse, plants need high humidity and minimum night temperatures of 60 to 70°F/16 to 21°C.

BREATH OF HEAVEN.
See **COLEONEMA**

BREYNIA nivosa (B. disticha)

SNOW BUSH
Euphorbiaceae
EVERGREEN SHRUB

🌿 **ZONES 22–24; H2; OR INDOORS**

☼ ◐ **FULL SUN OR LIGHT SHADE; BRIGHT INDIRECT LIGHT**

💧 **REGULAR WATER**

Native to Melanesia. Delicate, open growth to 3–4 ft. tall and wide, with gracefully arching branches in zigzag pattern. Thin, roundish leaves nearly opposite each other along the branches are rich green variegated with white. Flowers insignificant. Tends to produce suckers from the roots; can naturalize in humid tropical or subtropical regions. More commonly seen is 'Roseopicta', sweet pea bush or calico plant, with leaves mottled red, pink, white, and green. Colorful houseplant, though prone to mites in dry atmosphere.

Breynia nivosa 'Roseopicta'

BRIMEURA amethystina (Hyacinthus amethystinus)

Liliaceae
PERENNIAL FROM BULB

🌿 **ZONES 1–10, 14–24**

☼ **FULL SUN**

💧 **REGULAR WATER DURING GROWTH AND BLOOM**

European native for rock gardens or naturalizing. In bulb and leaf, resembles small hyacinth, but 10-in. spikes of pendent, bright blue flowers in spring to summer look like bluebells. A pure white

Brimeura amethystina

---

form is available. Plant in mid- to late fall (before ground freezes), 2 in. deep and 3 in. apart. In Zones 1 and 2, mulch soil after first hard frost. Keep soil moist after planting; continue to water regularly until foliage yellows after bloom. Needs no moisture during dormancy.

BRISBANE BOX.
See **LOPHOSTEMON confertus**

BRITTLEBUSH.
See **ENCELIA farinosa**

BRIZA maxima

RATTLESNAKE GRASS, QUAKING GRASS
Poaceae (Gramineae)
ANNUAL GRASS

🌿 **ZONES 1–24**

☼ **FULL SUN**

○ **NO IRRIGATION NEEDED**

Native to Mediterranean region. Ornamental grass of delicate, graceful form, used effectively in dried arrangements and bouquets. Grows 1–2 ft. high. Leaves are ¼ in. wide, to 6 in. long. Clusters

Briza maxima

of nodding, ½-in. or longer, seed-bearing spikelets, papery and straw colored when dry, dangle on threadlike stems. Spikelets resemble rattlesnake rattles. Scatter seed where plants are to grow; thin seedlings to 1 ft. apart. Self-sows; often grows wild along roadsides, in fields. *B. media* is similar but perennial.

BROAD BUCKLER FERN.
See **DRYOPTERIS dilatata**

BROCCOLI

Brassicaceae (Cruciferae)
BIENNIAL GROWN AS ANNUAL

🌿 **ALL ZONES**

☼ **FULL SUN**

💧 **REGULAR WATER**

Among cole crops (cabbage and its other close relatives), broccoli is best all-around choice for the

---

Broccoli

home gardener: bears over long season, is not difficult to raise. Thought to be a Mediterranean native. Grows 2–3 ft. tall, with a branching habit. Sends up a central stalk that bears a cluster (to 6 in. wide) of green or purple flower buds. When central cluster is removed, side branches will lengthen and produce smaller clusters. There are many excellent varieties to choose from. Sprouting broccoli forms many small florets that are harvested when size of buttons. Broccoli raab (broccoli rabe), an Italian relative of broccoli, has slightly stronger flavor. 'Romanesco' broccoli produces light green heads that resemble sea coral and have the flavor and texture of cauliflower. For Chinese broccoli, see Asian Greens.

All types of broccoli are cool-season plants that tend to bolt into flower at high temperatures, so plant them to mature during cool weather. In mild climates, plant in late summer, fall, or winter for crops in winter or early spring. In cold-winter areas, set out young plants 2 to 4 weeks before last frost (young plants resist frost but not hard freezes).

Good guide to planting time is availability of plants in nurseries. Seedlings ready to be planted develop in 4 to 6 weeks from sowing. One pack of seed will produce too many plants for even the largest home garden, so save surplus seed for later plantings. A dozen plants will supply a family. Space plants 1½–2 ft. apart in rows and leave 3 ft. between rows. Keep plants growing vigorously with regular deep irrigation during dry periods and one or two feedings of commercial fertilizer before heads start to form. Harvest 50 to 100 days after setting out plants. Cut heads before clustered buds begin to open. Include 5–6 in. of edible stalk and leaves. Subject to same pests as cabbage.

BRODIAEA

Liliaceae
PERENNIALS FROM CORMS

🌿 **ZONES VARY BY SPECIES**

☼ **FULL SUN**

○ **NO IRRIGATION NEEDED**

Many are natives of the Pacific Coast, where they bloom in sunny fields and meadows in spring and early summer. Plants have a few grasslike leaves; a cluster of funnel-shaped or tubular, ½–2-in.-long flowers tops the stem during bloom. Good cut flowers. After flowering, plants die to the ground.

In nature, these plants are often found in adobe soil, in areas where rainfall is heavy in winter and early spring and corms dry out completely in summer. They appreciate similar conditions in gardens; if you can't keep corms dry in summer, plant in sandy or gritty soil. Set corms 2–3 in. deep and 2–4 in. apart. In cold-winter areas, grow in containers or mulch to protect from freezing and thawing.

Brodiaea includes many plants now listed under different names. Cross-references below will guide you to appropriate entries.

B. coronaria (B. grandiflora). HARVEST BRODIAEA. Zones 4–9, 14–24. Clusters of dark blue, inch-long flowers on 6–10-in. stems.

B. elegans. HARVEST BRODIAEA. Zones 2–9, 14–24. Like *B. coronaria* but to 16 in. tall. Often sold as *B. grandiflora* or *B. coronaria*.

B. grandiflora. See B. coronaria. Another plant known by same name is *Triteleia grandiflora*.

B. hyacinthina. See Triteleia hyacinthina

B. ixioides. See Triteleia ixioides

B. lactea. See Triteleia hyacinthina

B. laxa. See Triteleia laxa

B. lutea. See Triteleia ixioides

B. minor. Zones 7–9, 14–17, 19–24. Dark blue flowers on stems that may be 3–4 in., rarely 1 ft., long.

B. 'Queen Fabiola'. See Triteleia 'Queen Fabiola'

B. tubergenii. See Triteleia tubergenii

B. uniflora. See Ipheion uniflorum

Brodiaea elegans

B

BROMELIA balansae

HEART OF FLAME
Bromeliaceae
PERENNIAL

🌡 ZONES 13, 19–24; H1, H2
☀ FULL SUN
💧 REGULAR WATER

Pineapple relative from South America grows to 4 ft. tall, 4–6 ft. across. Forms impressive cluster of 30–50 arching, saw-toothed leaves, glossy dark green above, whitish beneath. Center leaves turn bright scarlet in spring or early summer. From this center rises a stalk bearing a spike of rose-colored flowers margined with white. Needs warm nights to perform satisfactorily. Takes almost any soil but needs excellent drainage. Grow in light shade in Zone 13. Feed lightly once or twice in summer.

Bromelia balansae

BROOM. See **CYTISUS, GENISTA, SPARTIUM junceum**

BROOM RESTIO. See **ISCHYROLEPIS subverticillata**

BROUSSONETIA papyrifera

PAPER MULBERRY, WAUKE
Moraceae
DECIDUOUS TREE

🌡 ZONES 3B–24; H1, H2
☀ FULL SUN
💧 LITTLE TO REGULAR WATER

Native to China, Japan. Common name comes from inner bark, used for making paper and Polynesian tapa cloth. Has been sold as *Morus papyrifera*. Valuable as shade tree where soil and climate limit choices. Tolerates heat, strong winds, city pollution, and stony, sterile, or alkaline soils. Drought tolerant except in Zones 11–13, where it is considered a high-water-use tree.

Broussonetia papyrifera

Moderate to fast growth to 50 ft. tall, with dense, broad crown to 40 ft. across. Often considerably smaller and more shrublike in gardens. Suckering habit can be problem in rainy climates or highly cultivated gardens. Good in rough bank plantings. Smooth gray bark can become ridged and furrowed

Broussonetia papyrifera

with age. Heart-shaped, 4–8-in. leaves are green and rough on upper surface, gray and velvety beneath; leaf edges are toothed, often lobed when young. Blooms in spring. Flowers on male trees are catkins; on female trees, rounded flower heads are followed by red fruits (in early summer) if a male tree is growing nearby. Needs minimal pruning (done in dormant season).

BROWALLIA

AMETHYST FLOWER
Solanaceae
ANNUALS AND PERENNIALS

🌡 ZONES VARY BY SPECIES
☀ PARTIAL SHADE
💧 REGULAR WATER

Choice plants for connoisseurs of blue flowers. Bear one-sided clusters of lobelia-like blooms in brilliant blue, violet, or white; blue and violet flowers are more striking because of contrasting white eye or throat. Bloom profusely in warm shade or filtered sunlight. Graceful in hanging baskets or pots. Fine cut flowers.

Sow seeds in early spring for summer bloom, in fall for winter color in warmest-winter areas or indoors. You can lift vigorous plants in fall, cut back, and pot; new growth will produce flowers through winter in warm spots. Usually sold as seeds.

B. americana (B. elata). Annual. All zones. Branching, 1–2 ft. high and wide; roundish leaves. Violet or blue flowers ½ in. long, ½ in. across, borne among leaves. 'Sapphire', dwarf compact variety, dark blue with white eye, is very free blooming.

Browallia speciosa
'Marine Bells'

B. speciosa. Perennial in Zones 17, 23, 24; H1, H2; can be grown as annual anywhere. Sprawling, to 1–2 ft. high, nearly a foot wide. Flowers dark purple above, pale lilac beneath, 1½–2 in. across. 'Blue Bells Improved', lavender blue, grows 10 in. tall, needs no pinching to make it branch. 'Marine Bells' has deep indigo flowers, 'Silver Bells' white flowers.

BRUGMANSIA

ANGEL'S TRUMPET
Solanaceae
EVERGREEN TO SEMIEVERGREEN SHRUBS

🌡 ZONES 12, 13, 16–24; H1, H2
☀◐● SUN OR SHADE
💧 REGULAR WATER
☠ ALL PARTS ARE POISONOUS IF INGESTED

South American natives often confused with plants in the genus *Datura* (low-growing, herbaceous plants with upward-pointing flowers and swollen, spiny seedpods). Brugmansias are large, woody shrubs that can be trained into small trees, with typically pendant blooms and bean-shaped seedpods. With their oversize leaves and big, tubular flowers that bloom mainly in summer and fall, they are imposing plants that will astonish your visitors. Blooms of all species except *B. sanguinea* are fragrant, especially in the evening.

Provide a sheltered spot; wind tatters the foliage. In colder part of range, expect frost damage and unattractive winter appearance. In desert zones, they need shade. Before spring growth starts, remove all weak, dead, and crowded stems. Plants growing in containers can overwinter indoors even with low light and very little water.

Brugmansia cubensis
'Charles Grimaldi'

B. arborea. Plants sold under this name are often either *B.* × *candida* or *B.* × *insignis*. The true *B. arborea* has smaller flowers than the plant commonly in cultivation.

B. × candida. Fast growing to 10–12 ft. tall and wide; dull green leaves to 1 ft. long. Sweet-scented, 8–12-in.-long cream to white trumpets hang straight down from the branches. 'Double White' has creamy white double blossoms, distinctly grayish green foliage. 'Variegata' ('Sunset') grows 5 ft. tall and wide, with light golden peach flowers and white-edged leaves.

B. cubensis 'Charles Grimaldi'. Vigorous hybrid between *B.* × *insignis* 'Frosty Pink' and another variety. Fast growing to 10–12 ft. tall and 10 ft. wide. Huge (15-in.), golden yellow to golden orange, powerfully fragrant trumpets cover the plant during bloom season.

B. × insignis. To 10–12 ft. tall and wide. Flowers are large, flaring trumpets that point outward at 45° angle from plant; they have a spicy-sweet fragrance and come in white, pink, yellow, and orange. 'Frosty Pink' has 8–10-in., salmon pink blooms. 'Jamaica Yellow' has light yellow flowers. 'Betty Marshall' bears white blossoms on a compact plant 6–8 ft. high.

B. 'Peaches and Cream'. To 5 ft. tall and wide. Flowers over a long, spring-into-fall season, producing richly perfumed, light peachy pink blossoms to 8 in. long that open from buds that are striped white and green. Blooms profusely, even in small containers. Leaves are dark green, splashed with light green and edged in white and pale yellow.

B. sanguinea. MOUNTAIN ANGEL'S TRUMPET. To 8–12 ft. tall, 6–8 ft. wide. Wavy-edged, narrow green or gray-green leaves to 6–8 in. long; narrow trumpet-shaped blooms to 8 in. long. In the typical form, flowers are orange red with yellow veins; other varieties have orange to yellow or sometimes pink flowers. Doesn't bloom well in hot summers.

B. suaveolens. Plants offered as this species are usually *B.* × *insignis*.

B. versicolor. The most treelike species, to 15 ft. tall and wide. Huge (15-in.) flowers are a peachy apricot color; they hang straight down from the branches, covering the plant during bloom time. Blossoms are sweetly fragrant at night and in the morning. Pink- and white-flowered varieties are also available.

BRUNFELSIA pauciflora (B. calycina)

Solanaceae
EVERGREEN TO SEMIEVERGREEN SHRUB

🌿	ZONES 12–17, 20–24; H1, H2; EXCEPT AS NOTED
🔆	PARTIAL SHADE
💧	REGULAR WATER
◈	ALL PARTS ARE POISONOUS IF INGESTED

Tropical American native grown for showy clusters of white-throated, rich dark purple, tubular flowers opening to flat disks; bloom comes in spring and early summer. In all but warmest locations, loses most of foliage for a short period. These handsome plants deserve extra attention—give them rich, well-drained soil and regular feedings through the growing season. (Where soil tends to be alkaline, as in Zones 12 and 13, add iron to prevent chlorosis.) Prune in spring to remove straggly growth and to shape. Choose a planting location where you can admire the flower show. Performs well in containers. The following forms are available.

'Floribunda'. YESTERDAY-TODAY-AND-TOMORROW. Common name comes from quick color change of blossoms: they turn from purple ("yesterday") to lavender ("today") to white ("tomorrow"). Flowers, several in a cluster and each opening to 2 in. wide, are borne profusely all over plant. Oval leaves, 3–4 in. long and 1½ in. wide, are dark green above, pale green below. Plant will reach 10 ft. or taller with several stems from base, but it can be held to about 3 ft. high by pruning. Has a rather spreading habit, with width nearly equal to height.

'Floribunda Compacta'. About two-thirds the size of the more widely planted 'Floribunda'. Flowers a bit smaller but even more generously produced.

'Macrantha' ('Magnifica'). Zones 12, 13, 16, 17, 20–24; H1, H2. In

Brunfelsia pauciflora 'Floribunda'

addition to being less cold hardy, differs from 'Floribunda' in having fewer but larger flowers, 2–4 in. across. Also has a more slender habit and bigger leaves (to 8 in. long, 2½ in. wide).

BRUNNERA macrophylla

BRUNNERA
Boraginaceae
PERENNIAL

🌿	ZONES 1–24
🔆	FULL SUN IN COOLER CLIMATES ONLY
💧	REGULAR WATER

Eastern European woodland plant to 1½ ft. tall, 2 ft. wide. Leaves heart shaped, dark green, 3–4 in. wide. Airy clusters of tiny, yellow-centered, clear blue flowers reminiscent of forget-me-nots (*Myosotis*). Blooms in spring—often into summer, especially in shade. Several variegated forms are available, including showy 'Jack Frost', with silvery leaves veined in green.

Brunnera is useful as an informal ground cover under high-branching deciduous trees; among spring-flowering shrubs such as forsythia, deciduous magnolias; as filler between newly planted evergreen shrubs. Freely self-sows once established. Seeds you plant may not germinate easily (try freezing them before sowing).

Brunnera macrophylla

Needs well-drained, moisture-retentive soil. Increase by dividing clumps in fall.

BRUNSVIGIA rosea.
See **AMARYLLIS belladonna**

BRUSH CHERRY.
See **SYZYGIUM paniculatum**

BRUSSELS SPROUTS

Brassicaceae (Cruciferae)
BIENNIAL GROWN AS ANNUAL

🌿	ALL ZONES
🔆	FULL SUN
💧	REGULAR WATER

A cabbage relative of unusual appearance. Mature plant has crown of fairly large leaves, and its tall stem is completely covered with small sprouts. Fairly easy to grow where summers are not too hot, long, or dry. 'Jade Cross Hybrid' is most heat tolerant; 'Valiant' has excellent flavor. 'Prince Marvel' is the earliest to harvest in Alaska. You may have to grow your own from seed. In cold-winter climates, set out seedlings you start yourself or nursery transplants in spring for summer-to-fall harvest; in mild-winter areas, plant in late summer and fall for winter-to-spring production.

Brussels sprouts

Treat the same as broccoli. When big leaves start to yellow, begin picking. Snap off little sprouts from bottom first—best when slightly smaller than a golf ball. Leave little sprouts on upper stem to mature. After picking, remove only leaves below harvested sprouts. A single plant will yield from 50 to 100 sprouts. Subject to same pests as cabbage.

BRYOPHYLLUM pinnatum.
See **KALANCHOE pinnata**

BUCHLOE dactyloides

BUFFALO GRASS
Poaceae (Gramineae)
PERENNIAL GRASS

🌿	ZONES 1–3, 10, 11
🔆	FULL SUN
💧	LITTLE WATER

Grass native from central Montana south to Arizona makes a low-maintenance, low-water-need lawn. Slow to sprout and fill in, it spreads rapidly by surface runners once established and makes matted, reasonably dense turf that takes hard wear and looks fairly good with little summer water. Gray green from late spring to hard frost, straw colored through late fall and winter. Runners can invade surrounding garden beds. Given minimal water, it grows to 4 in. tall and requires little or no mowing. More water means higher growth, some mowing.

Buchloe dactyloides

To start from seed, sow 2 lb. per 1,000 sq. ft. Soak occasionally to 1 ft. while grass is getting started. For a faster cover, start from sod, planting 4-in.-wide plugs in prepared soil 3–4 ft. apart in spring; expect coverage in two seasons.

BUCKEYE. See AESCULUS

BUCKTHORN. See RHAMNUS

BUCKWHEAT. See ERIOGONUM

BUDDLEJA

BUTTERFLY BUSH
Buddlejaceae
EVERGREEN, SEMIEVERGREEN, OR DECIDUOUS SHRUBS

🌿	ZONES VARY BY SPECIES
🔆	FULL SUN OR LIGHT SHADE
💧	MODERATE TO REGULAR WATER

Of the many selections—all notable for flower color, fragrance, or both—these are among the most commonly available. Grow in well-drained soil. Blossoms attract butterflies.

B. alternifolia. FOUNTAIN BUTTERFLY BUSH. Deciduous. Zones 2b–24. Native to China. To 12 ft. tall and as wide, with arching, willowlike branches rather thinly clothed with 1–4-in.-long leaves, dull dark green above, gray and hairy beneath. Profuse small clusters of mildly fragrant, lilac purple flowers make sweeping wands of color in spring. Tolerates many soils; thrives in poor, dry gravels. Prune after bloom: remove some of oldest wood to within a few inches of ground. Or train up into single- or multitrunked small tree.

Buddleja globosa

B. asiatica. Evergreen. Zones 8, 9, 14–24; H1, H2. From East Indies. To 10–15 ft. tall and wide. Tiny flowers are carried in narrow, erect spikes to 10 in. long in winter and spring; powerful fragrance suggests that of freesia. Prune after bloom. Freezing weather kills it to the ground, but it recovers to bloom the same year, behaving like a perennial.

B. crispa. Deciduous. Zones 5–7, 14–17. Native to Himalayas. To 6–10 ft. tall and wide, with silvery gray foliage and 4-in. clusters of fragrant lilac flowers with orange or white throats. Peak bloom comes in late summer. For best blooms and to keep plant neat, cut back nearly to ground in late winter. In cold-winter regions, grow in large pots or tubs and protect over winter.

B. davidii. BUTTERFLY BUSH, SUMMER LILAC. Semievergreen to deciduous. Zones 2–24; H1. Native to China, Japan. Fast, rank growth each spring and summer to 3, 4, or even 10 ft. tall and as wide. Tapering leaves are 4–12 in. long, dark green above, white and felted beneath. In midsummer, branch ends are adorned with small, fragrant flowers (lilac with orange eye) in dense, arching, spikelike, slender clusters 6–12 in. long or more. Invasive in disturbed soils in parts of Oregon and Washington. Needs good drainage and

Buddleja davidii

enough water to maintain growth. Cut back heavily before spring growth begins. May die to the ground in freezing weather but will regrow from roots like a perennial and bloom the same year.

The many varieties include 'Harlequin', with deep purple-red flowers and white-edged leaves, and *B. davidii nanhoensis,* which grows only 3–5 ft. tall and wide and comes in forms with white, deep blue, or reddish purple flowers.

B. globosa. ORANGE BUTTERFLY BUSH. Evergreen or semievergreen. Zones 5–9, 14–24. Native to Chile. To 10–15 ft. tall and wide. Dark green leaves are downy beneath. Late-spring or early-summer flowers are tightly clustered into ¾-in. orange balls arranged in spikelike clusters that are 6–8 in. long. Prune as for *B. alternifolia.*

B. 'Lochinch'. Deciduous (retains its leaves in mildest-winter climates). Zones 3b–9, 14–24. Hybrid between *B. davidii* and another Asian species. Grows 5–8 ft. (or taller) and as broad, with gray foliage and light lavender-blue flowers over a long season in late summer and fall. Prune as for *B. davidii.*

B. marrubiifolia. WOOLLY BUTTERFLY BUSH. Zones 10–13, 18–24. Native to southwest Texas and northern Mexico. Densely foliaged shrub to 5 ft. tall and broad, with soft, silvery, woolly foliage and small, ball-shaped, orange flower clusters in spring and summer. Prune after bloom.

B. × weyeriana. Zones 4–24. This hybrid between *B. davidii* and *B. globosa* resembles latter parent but is deciduous (except in mildest-winter climates) and is hardier, with more elongated orange-yellow flower clusters in late spring or early summer. Flowers of 'Sungold' are deeper orange, those of 'Honeycomb' a buttery yellow. Prune as for *B. alternifolia.*

BUFFALO GRASS. See **BUCHLOE dactyloides**

BUGBANE. See **ACTAEA**

BULBINE frutescens (B. caulescens)
Liliaceae
SUCCULENT SHRUBBY PERENNIAL

🗓 ZONES 8, 9, 12–24
☀ ◑ ● PARTIAL OR FULL SHADE IN HOTTEST CLIMATES
◌ ◑ ● LITTLE TO REGULAR WATER

Bulbine frutescens

Native to South Africa. Branching, barely woody stems sprawl to make clump 1 ft. high, 2–3 ft. wide. Leaves are fleshy, bright green, and shaped like slender, pointed pencils. Produces spikelike 6–12-in. clusters of tubular bright yellow flowers resembling those of aloe or red-hot poker (*Kniphofia*) most of the year. 'Hallmark' has gray-green leaves and orange flowers with fuzzy yellow stamens; plant is more compact, less heat tolerant than species. Useful as ground or bank cover in dry, well-drained soil. Don't locate them where they will be stepped on; leaves are slippery when crushed.

BULBINELLA floribunda (B. robusta, B. setosa)
Liliaceae
PERENNIAL

🗓 ZONES 14–24
☀ ◑ ● PARTIAL OR FULL SHADE IN HOTTEST CLIMATES
◑ REGULAR WATER DURING GROWTH AND BLOOM

Native to South Africa. Easy to grow from seed sown in well-drained soil in spring. In fall, forms large clump of narrow, 2-ft.-long, floppy leaves;

Bulbinella floribunda

these are topped in winter with 4-in. spikes of pure yellow flowers, splendid for cutting. Similar to red-hot poker (*Kniphofia*), but flower spikes are shorter and less pointed, and blossoms are bell shaped, not tubular. Foliage dies to the ground after bloom; pull off old, dry leaves. Keep soil on dry side during spring and summer dormancy. Good for low-maintenance borders—makes colonies quickly. Divide crowded clumps in fall.

BULL BAY. See **MAGNOLIA grandiflora**

BULL GRASS. See **MUHLENBERGIA emersleyi**

BUNCHBERRY. See **CORNUS canadensis**

BUNNY EARS. See **OPUNTIA microdasys**

BUNYA-BUNYA. See **ARAUCARIA bidwillii**

BUPLEURUM fruticosum
SHRUBBY HARE'S EAR
Apiaceae (Umbelliferae)
EVERGREEN SHRUB

🗓 ZONES 5–9, 14–24
☀ ◑ SUN OR SHADE
◌ ◑ ● LITTLE TO REGULAR WATER

Tough Mediterranean native and unusual shrub in the parsley family. Grows 5 ft. tall and wide, clothed in thick, smooth, narrowly oval, sea green leaves 4 in. long. In summer, stems are topped by 4–5-in., rounded clusters of chartreuse flowers resembling those of parsley or dill. These last a long time and are followed by brown seeds. Can be trimmed as a hedge. Cut flowering branches make unique arrangements.

Bupleurum fruticosum

BURMESE PLUMBAGO. See **CERATOSTIGMA griffithii**

BURNET. See **SANGUISORBA**

BURNING BUSH. See **KOCHIA scoparia trichophylla**

BURRO TAIL. See **SEDUM morganianum**

BUSH ANEMONE.
See **CARPENTERIA californica**

BUSH MUHLY.
See **MUHLENBERGIA porteri**

BUSH POPPY.
See **DENDROMECON**

BUSH STRAWFLOWER.
See **BRACTEANTHA bracteata**

BUSY LIZZIE.
See **IMPATIENS walleriana**

BUTCHER'S BROOM.
See **RUSCUS**

BUTIA capitata
PINDO PALM
Arecaceae (Palmae)
PALM

🌿 ZONES 8, 9, 12–24; H1, H2

☼ ◐ FULL SUN OR LIGHT SHADE

🌢 REGULAR WATER

Butia capitata

Native to Brazil, Uruguay, Argentina. Very hardy (to 15°F/–9°C), slow-growing palm to 10–20 ft. tall, with a crown of feathery gray-green, arching leaves spreading 10–15 ft. wide. Heavy trunk is patterned with stubs of old leaves; tree is more attractive if stubs are all trimmed same length. Long spikes of small yellow flowers are followed by showy clusters of yellow to red edible fruits in summer.

BUTTERFLY BUSH.
See **BUDDLEJA**

BUTTERFLY FLOWER.
See **SCHIZANTHUS pinnatus**

BUTTERFLY LILY.
See **HEDYCHIUM coronarium**

BUTTERFLY WEED.
See **ASCLEPIAS tuberosa**

BUTTERNUT.
See **JUGLANS cinerea**

BUTTONBUSH.
See **CEPHALANTHUS occidentalis**

BUTTON FERN.
See **PELLAEA rotundifolia**

BUTTONWOOD.
See **PLATANUS occidentalis**

BUXUS
BOXWOOD, BOX
Buxaceae
EVERGREEN SHRUBS

🌿 ZONES VARY BY SPECIES

☼ ◐ ● SUN OR SHADE

🌢 REGULAR WATER

Widely used for edging and hedging. When not clipped, most are soft and billowing. Inconspicuous flowers. All are easy to grow where adapted. Extra care with watering, feeding, and controlling mites and scale will pay off in better color and greater vigor.

Buxus microphylla japonica

B. Green series. Zones 3b–24. Group of Canadian hybrids derived from *B. microphylla koreana* and *B. sempervirens*. Hardy to between –2°F/–19°C and –30°F/–34°C. All feature handsome, rich green foliage and a naturally attractive shape; they need very little pruning. 'Green Gem' slowly forms a mound 3–4 ft. high and wide, with some bronzing of foliage in winter cold. 'Green Mountain' forms a dense cone to 5 ft. high, 3 ft. wide; it was developed as an alternative to dwarf Alberta spruce (*Picea glauca albertiana* 'Conica'). 'Green Velvet' has a rounded habit 3–4 ft. tall and wide, with good green color through winter.

B. microphylla. The species is rarely planted. Its widely used varieties include the following:

'Faulkner'. Zones 3b–24. Hardy to –10°F/–23°C. Glossy, emerald green leaves all year on a dense, slow-growing, rounded plant. May reach 6 ft. high without shaping.

B. m. japonica. JAPANESE BOXWOOD. Zones 3b–24, except as noted. Hardy to –10°F/–23°C but has poor winter appearance in cold-winter areas. Takes dry heat and alkaline soil, but struggles in intense heat, saline soils of desert. Compact; ½–1-in., round-tipped leaves are a lively bright green in summer, brown or bronze in winter in many areas. Grows slowly to 4–6 ft. high and wide if not pruned. Most often clipped as

hedge or shaped into globes, tiers, pyramids in containers. Can keep to 6 in. tall as border edging. The following are commonly grown varieties. 'Green Beauty' holds its deep green color in coldest weather and is considerably greener than *B. m. japonica* in summer heat.

B. m. koreana (B. sinica insularis). KOREAN BOXWOOD. Zones 2b–24. Hardy to –20°F/–29°C. Noted for its hardiness and ability to survive where others freeze. Slower growing and lower (to 2½ ft. high) than *B. m. japonica,* with smaller leaves (¼–½ in.). 'Winter Gem' retains its deep green foliage color through winter.

B. sempervirens. COMMON BOXWOOD, ENGLISH BOXWOOD. Zones 3b–6, 15–17, except as noted. Native to southern Europe, North Africa, western Asia. Dies out in alkaline soils, hot-summer areas. Will grow to height of 15–20 ft. with equal spread. Densely foliaged with medium-size, lustrous dark green, oval leaves.

'Graham Blandy'. Narrow, columnar growth to 7–9 ft. tall, 1 ft. wide.

'Suffruticosa'. TRUE DWARF BOXWOOD. Slower growing than the species; to 4–5 ft. high but generally clipped lower. Small leaves, dense form and texture. A variegated form with silver-edged foliage is available.

'Vardar Valley'. Zones 2b–6, 15–17. To 2–3 ft. tall, 6 ft. wide. Macedonian native; considered hardiest common boxwood.

C

CABBAGE
Brassicaceae (Cruciferae)
BIENNIAL GROWN AS ANNUAL

🌿 ALL ZONES

☼ ◐ TOLERATES LIGHT SHADE IN HOT CLIMATES

🌢 REGULAR WATER

Early varieties mature in 7 to 8 weeks from transplanting into garden; late varieties require 3 to 4 months. Many good types available. In Alaska, 'O.-S. Cross' is standard variety for giant cabbage; use a floating row cover for an early

Cabbage

start. In addition to green cabbage, you can find red and curly-leafed (Savoy) types. For Chinese cabbages, see Asian Greens and Chinese Cabbage.

To avoid overproduction, set out a few plants every week or two, or plant both early and late kinds. Time plantings so heads will form either before or after hot summer months. Sow seeds ½ in. deep about 6 weeks prior to planting-out time. Transplant to rich, moist soil, spacing plants 2–2½ ft. apart. Give frequent light applications of nitrogen fertilizer. Never let plants wilt. Mulch helps keep soil moist and cool. Light frost doesn't hurt cabbage, but harvest and store before heavy freezes occur. In low and intermediate desert, grow as a winter crop in full sun.

To prevent soil-borne pest buildup, plant in different site each year. Row covers will protect plants from some pests such as aphids, cabbage loopers, imported cabbageworms, root maggots. Alternatively, prevent root maggots by ringing base of plant with a tar-paper collar; or cover with a cone fashioned from window screen. Collars made from paper cups or metal cans (with ends removed) also deter cutworms, which chew seedlings off at the base. *Bacillus thuringiensis (Bt)* can be applied to control young larvae of cabbageworms and loopers on plants.

CABBAGE AND KALE, FLOWERING
Brassicaceae (Cruciferae)
BIENNIALS GROWN AS ANNUALS

🌿 ALL ZONES

☼ ◐ BEST IN SUN; TOLERATE SOME SHADE

🌢 REGULAR WATER

Flowering cabbage and flowering kale are grown for their highly ornamental, highly colored leaf rosettes, which look like giant, deep blue-green peonies marbled and edged with white, cream, rose, or purple. Kale differs from cabbage in that its head is slightly looser and its leaf edges are more

C

C

Flowering cabbage

heavily fringed. Both are spectacular in the cool-season garden and appreciate the same soil, care, and timing as conventional cabbage. Plant 15–18 in. apart in open-ground beds, singly in 8-in. pots, or several in a large container. Colors are strongest after first frosts. Single rosette cut and placed on a spike holder in a decorative bowl makes a striking harvest arrangement. Foliage is edible raw or cooked and is quite striking as a salad garnish. For the edible flowering cabbage typically used in Chinese cooking, see Asian Greens.

CABBAGE PALM.
See **SABAL palmetto**

CACTUS

The cactus family contains a huge number of succulent plants (see also Succulents). Generally leafless, they have stems modified into cylinders, pads, or joints that store water in times of drought. Thick skin reduces evaporation, and most species have spines for protection against browsing animals. Flowers are usually large and brightly colored; fruit may also be colorful and is sometimes edible.

Almost all are native to the Americas—from Canada to Argentina, from sea level into high mountains, from deserts to dripping tropical rain forests. Many are native to drier parts of the West.

Cacti range in height from a few inches to 50 ft. tall. Larger species are used to create desert landscapes. Smaller species are grown in pots or, if sufficiently hardy, in rock gardens. Many are easy-care, showy house- or greenhouse plants. Large landscaping types require full sun, well-drained soil. Water newly planted cacti very little; roots are subject to rot before they begin active growth. In 4 to 6 weeks, when new roots are active, water thoroughly; then let soil dry before watering again. Reduce watering in fall to allow plants to

go dormant. Feed monthly in spring and summer. For some larger kinds appropriate for garden use, see *Carnegiea gigantea, Cephalocereus senilis, Cereus peruvianus, Echinocactus, Echinocereus, Espostoa lanata, Ferocactus, Opuntia, Stenocereus thurberi.*

Smaller cacti for pot or rock garden culture usually have interesting forms and brightly colored flowers. Feed and water plants well during warm weather for good display; taper off on fertilizer to encourage winter dormancy. Use fast-draining planting mix. See *Coryphantha vivipara, Echinopsis, Mammillaria.*

Showiest in flower are tropical cacti that grow as epiphytes on trees or rocks. These need rich soil with much humus, frequent feeding and watering, partial shade, and protection from frost. Can be grown outdoors all year in Hawaii; elsewhere, grow in lathhouse or greenhouse, or handle as outdoor/indoor plants. See *Epiphyllum, Rhipsalidopsis, Schlumbergera.*

CAESALPINIA (Poinciana)

Fabaceae (Leguminosae)
EVERGREEN AND DECIDUOUS
SHRUBS AND TREES

✎	ZONES VARY BY SPECIES
☼	FULL SUN
◐ ◑	LITTLE TO MODERATE WATER
✦	PODS AND SEEDS ARE POISONOUS IF INGESTED

Ferny-leafed plants grown for branch-end clusters of colorful blossoms featuring (except in the case of *C. platyloba*) protruding stamens. Blooms attract hummingbirds. Plants grow quickly and easily in hot, sunny locations if given light, well-drained soil and infrequent, deep watering. Prune before first flush of spring growth to remove any dead or damaged wood and wayward branches;

Caesalpinia gilliesii

remove lower limbs for treelike shape in shrubby species.

C. cacalaco. CASCALOTE. Evergreen tree. Zones 12, 13, 21–24. Mexican native grows slowly to 20 ft. tall and wide, with thorny branches and bright green foliage, coarser than that of *C. pulcherrima.* Very showy, large yellow flowers carried well above branches in winter.

C. gilliesii (Poinciana gilliesii). YELLOW BIRD OF PARADISE. Evergreen to deciduous shrub or tree; drops leaves in cold winters. Zones 8–16, 18–24; occasionally seen in Zones 6, 7. From South America. Tough, fast growing to 10 ft. tall, 8 ft. wide, with finely cut foliage and rather open, angular branch structure. Blooms all summer, producing clusters of yellow flowers adorned with bright red stamens.

C. mexicana. MEXICAN BIRD OF PARADISE. Evergreen shrub or tree. Zones 12–16, 18–24. Moderately fast growth to 10–12 ft. tall and wide; can be kept to 6–8 ft. with pruning. Leaves are coarser than those of *C. pulcherrima.* Blooms throughout year except in coldest months, bearing 6-in. clusters of lemon yellow flowers.

C. platyloba. Evergreen tree. Zones 12, 13, 21–24. From Mexico. To 20 ft. tall and wide. Narrow, elongated clusters of tiny yellow flowers in spring lack the long, protruding stamens of other caesalpinias. Best feature is airy appearance due to open branching habit and relatively few leaflets. Leaves turn rust red in fall.

C. pulcherrima (Poinciana pulcherrima). RED BIRD OF PARADISE, DWARF POINCIANA, PRIDE OF BARBADOS. Deciduous shrub; may be evergreen in mild winters. Zones 12–16, 18–23; H1, H2. Native to tropical America. Fast, dense growth to 10 ft. tall and wide. Dark green leaves with many ¾-in. leaflets. Blooms throughout warm weather, bearing clusters of orange or red flowers with red stamens. 'Phoenix Bird' has bright yellow blooms. Various other yellow-flowered forms (including *P. c. flava*) as well as salmon-colored kinds are available in Hawaii. All are useful for quick screening.

Plants freeze to ground in colder part of range but rebound quickly in spring. In milder climates, you can cut them to ground in early spring to make more compact mound.

CAJEPUT TREE. See **MELALEUCA quinquenervia**

CALADIUM bicolor

FANCY-LEAFED CALADIUM
Araceae
PERENNIAL FROM TUBER

✎	ZONE H2; OR DIG AND STORE; OR GROW IN POTS
◐ ●	SOME VARIETIES TOLERATE SOME SUN
● ●	REGULAR TO AMPLE WATER
✦	SAP CAN CAUSE SWELLING IN MOUTH, THROAT

Tropical American natives grown for foliage: large (to 1½-ft.-long), arrow-shaped, long-stalked, almost translucent leaves colored in bands and blotches of red, rose, pink, white, silver, bronze, and green. Most varieties sold in nurseries derive from *C. bicolor*—usually 2 ft. (occasionally to 4 ft.) high and wide. Most require shade. Newer varieties tolerating some sun include 'Fire Chief', 'Rose Bud', 'Red Flash', and 'White Queen'.

Caladiums need rich soil, high humidity, and heat (above 70°F/21°C during days and rarely below 60°F/16°C at nights). In Hawaii, tubers can remain in the ground all year. Elsewhere, dig and store after

Caladium bicolor

leaf dieback, or grow in pots and bring indoors during cold weather.

To grow in ground, plant tubers when days lengthen in spring; place them with knobby side up so tops are level with soil surface. Protect from snails and slugs. Keep well watered and feed lightly throughout growing season. Foliage may be cut back in autumn. Where freezes are likely, dig tubers; remove most of soil; dry tubers for several days in a shaded, dry location; and store in dry peat moss at 50 to 60°F/10 to 16°C.

To grow in pots, start tubers indoors in late winter, outdoors in spring. Use a soil mix made from equal parts coarse sand, leaf mold, and ground bark or peat moss. Use 5-in. pot for a 2½-in. tuber, 7-in. pot for one or two large tubers. Fill halfway with mix; stir in a heaping teaspoon of fish meal. Add 1 in. of potting mix, place tuber on top, cover with 2 in. of mix. Water thoroughly and keep moist until tubers sprout.

CALAMAGROSTIS

REED GRASS
Poaceae (Gramineae)
PERENNIAL GRASSES

- ☑ **ZONES 2B-24**
- ☼ ◑ **FULL SUN OR PARTIAL SHADE**
- ◐ **REGULAR WATER**

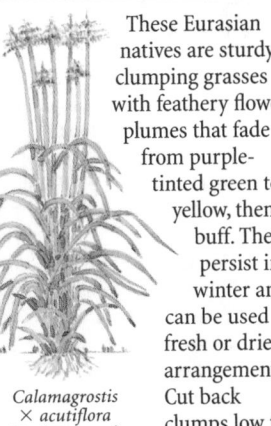

Calamagrostis
× acutiflora
'Karl Foerster'

These Eurasian natives are sturdy, clumping grasses with feathery flower plumes that fade from purple-tinted green to yellow, then buff. These persist into winter and can be used for fresh or dried arrangements. Cut back clumps low to the ground in late winter, before new growth begins.

C. × acutiflora. FEATHER REED GRASS. Known mainly through these evergreen to semi-evergreen selections. 'Karl Foerster' ('Stricta') forms an erect, somewhat arching clump of narrow, bright green leaves 2–3 ft. tall, somewhat broader. Upright flowering stems increase the height to 6 ft. when they first appear in late spring or early summer. 'Overdam' is similar, but its foliage is variegated with white; needs partial shade in hot-summer regions.

C. brachytricha (C. arundinacea brachytricha). FALL-BLOOMING REED GRASS. Deciduous. Upright, arching clump to 1½–2½ ft. tall, 2 ft. wide. In late summer or early fall, broad flower spikes bring plant height to 4 ft. One of the best grasses for partial shade. Great in containers.

CALAMINT. See **CALAMINTHA**

CALAMINTHA

CALAMINT
Lamiaceae (Labiatae)
PERENNIALS

- ☑ **ZONES 1-9, 14-24**
- ☼ ◑ **FULL SUN OR LIGHT SHADE**
- ◐ **MODERATE WATER**

Perennials in the mint family with pleasant-scented foliage and pretty, two-lipped flowers in clusters. Herb fanciers brew tea from the leaves. Plants need well-drained soil. Provide winter protection in coldest zones.

C. grandiflora. Native from Mediterranean region to Iran. Creeping rhizomes produce clump 2 ft. tall and wide, with slender stems and 1½-in. pink summer flowers. Better with some shade.

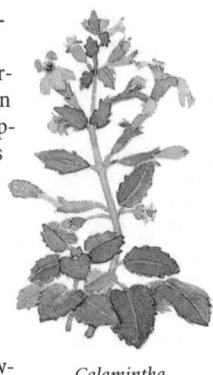

Calamintha grandiflora

C. nepeta (C. nepetoides). Native from Mediterranean region to Great Britain. To 1½ ft. high, 2½ ft. wide. Many tough, slender stems grow outward, then erect. Upper portion of the plant carries a profusion of ½-in. pale lilac to white flowers in late summer and fall.

CALAMONDIN. See CITRUS: Sour-Acid Mandarin

CALANDRINIA

Portulacaceae
PERENNIALS AND ANNUALS

- ☑ **ZONES VARY BY SPECIES**
- ◑ **PARTIAL SHADE IN HOTTEST CLIMATES**
- ◐ ◐ **WATER NEEDS VARY BY SPECIES**

Genus of about 150 species of annuals and evergreen perennials, including some attractive flowering succulents. The three mentioned here come from temperate Pacific coastal regions of North and South America. These plants are related to rose moss (*Portulaca grandiflora*) and, like it, they make good rock garden subjects. Leaves form dense clumps and send up thin stems topped by satiny, cup-shaped flowers. They will tolerate poor soil, provided it is well-drained, but grow and flower best in humus-rich, fast-draining soil. Some members of this genus have recently been reclassified as *Cistanthe*.

Calandrinia grandiflora

C. ciliata (C. ciliata menziesii). RED MAIDS. Annual. All zones. Common wildflower in Northern California, where it populates sunny meadows. Grows about 1 ft. tall and wide, with narrow, fleshy, gray-green leaves to 1½ in. long. From late winter into spring, dainty magenta flowers, about 1 in. wide, are produced on 8-in.-long stems. Moderate water.

C. grandiflora. Perennial. Zones 15–17, 20–24. Native to Chile. Shrubby, clumping growth to 1–3 ft. tall and 2–3 ft. wide. Thick, fleshy gray-green leaves up to 8 in. long are narrowly oval and pointed. From spring into fall, plants produce brilliant magenta blooms along tall (1½–3-ft.) slender stems. Flowers appear to float above the leaves. Lovely addition to perennial beds. Most effective when massed. Easily propagated by cuttings taken in spring. Regular water.

C. umbellata. ROCK PURS-LANE. Perennial often grown as annual. Zones 15–17, 20–24. Native to Chile and Peru. Plants form 6-in.-tall mounds of narrow, bluish to gray-green leaves up to 1½ in. long. Crimson summertime flowers are held just above the foliage on branching stems. Moderate water.

CALATHEA

Marantaceae
PERENNIALS

- ☑ **ZONE H2; OR INDOORS**
- ◑ **PARTIAL SHADE; BRIGHT INDIRECT LIGHT**
- ◐ **REGULAR WATER**

Calathea zebrina

Native to tropical America. Ornamental leaves, beautifully marked in various shades of green, white, and pink, are arranged in basal tufts. Flowers of most are inconspicuous. Need high humidity and warm temperatures (not under 55°F/13°C). Succeed outdoors in Hawaii; elsewhere, they are indoor plants that can be brought outside in summer. Need

porous soil and perfect drainage; if air is dry, also mist plants frequently. Repot as often as necessary to avoid root-bound condition. Calatheas are often mistakenly called marantas.

C. crocata. ETERNAL FLAME. To 1 ft. high, 1½ ft. wide. Leaves 6 in. long, 1–1½ in. wide, dark green above, purple beneath. Spikes, 2 in. long, consist of bright orange flower bracts that look like little torches. Leaf rosette has several shoots; each dies after blooming, but new ones appear to keep up the show. Variable performance as houseplant; subject to mites in low humidity. Does better in greenhouse.

C. lancifolia (C. insignis). To 1½–2½ ft. tall, 2 ft. wide. Long (1–1½-ft.), narrow, wavy-edged leaves are yellow green banded with dark olive green.

C. louisae. To 3 ft. tall, 1½ ft. wide. Foot-long dark green leaves heavily feathered with gray green along midrib.

C. majestica (C. ornata). To 6 ft. tall, 3 ft. wide. Leaves 2–3 ft. long, rich green above, purplish red beneath. Juvenile leaves usually pink striped between veins; intermediate foliage striped white. 'Roseolineata' has pink and white stripes at angle to midrib.

C. makoyana. Showy plant to 2 ft. high, 2½ ft. wide. Foliage colors include pale olive green, cream, and purple in featherlike, blotchy patterns, with a broad darker green border along leaf margins.

C. zebrina. ZEBRA PLANT. Compact plant to 3 ft. high, 2 ft. wide. Ellipse-shaped leaves reach 1–2 ft. long, almost half as wide. Upper surfaces are velvety green with alternating bars of pale yellow green and olive green extending outward from the midrib; undersides are purplish red.

CALCEOLARIA

Scrophulariaceae
PERENNIALS

- ☑ **ZONES VARY BY TYPE**
- ☼ ◑ ◐ **EXPOSURE NEEDS VARY BY TYPE**
- ◐ **REGULAR WATER**

Native from Mexico to Chile. Loose clusters of small pouchlike or slipperlike flowers, usually yellow but sometimes red bronze or spotted with red or orange-brown. Bloom in spring and summer. Plants are many branched, with dark green, crinkly leaves. ▶

C. Herbeohybrida Group.
Zones 14–24; anywhere as annuals or houseplants. This is the florists' calceolaria that produces masses of velvety, inch-long yellow or red flowers, often spotted and marbled. Plants are usually grown from seed sown in spring or summer in light, porous soil; they are ready for final potting or planting out in fall. Calceolaria can reach a height of 2½ ft., but the two most popular strains are lower-growing Multiflora Nana and Multiflora, which reach only 9–15 in. high, 6–12 in. wide. Even where plants winter over, they are usually discarded after flowering. The Anytime strain tolerates high temperatures better than others; start indoors in late winter for summer bloom. Give bedding and outdoor potted plants partial or full shade. Houseplants need a sunny spot.

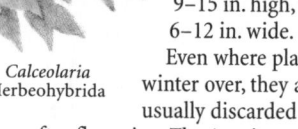

Calceolaria
Herbeohybrida

C. integrifolia. Zones 14–24. Woody-based plant to 3 ft. tall, 1 ft. wide. Leaves about 3 in. long, and about 1 in. wide. Clusters of yellow to red-brown, unspotted flowers ½ in. across. Good cut flower. 'Golden Nugget' has pure golden yellow flowers from spring to fall, 'Russet' and 'Kentish Hero' orange-red to brown blooms. Use in borders, pots, hanging baskets. Best bloom comes when rootbound. Full sun except in hottest climates, where it prefers part shade.

CALENDULA
officinalis

CALENDULA, POT MARIGOLD
Asteraceae (Compositae)
ANNUAL

- ✿ ZONES A2, A3; 1–24; H1
- ☼ FULL SUN
- ◊ MODERATE WATER

Mediterranean native provides sure, easy color from late fall through spring in mild-winter areas, from spring to midsummer in colder climates. Besides familiar daisylike, orange and bright yellow double blooms 2½–4½ in. across, calendulas come in subtler shades of apricot, cream, and soft yellow. Plants somewhat branching, 1–2 ft. high, 1–1½ ft. wide. Leaves are

Calendula officinalis

long, narrow, round on ends, slightly sticky, and aromatic. Plants are effective for masses of color in borders and parking strips, along drives, in containers. Long-lasting cut flowers.

Sow seed in place or in flats in late summer or early fall in mild-winter climates, spring elsewhere. Or buy seedlings at nurseries. Will self-sow to some degree. Adapts to most soils if drainage is fast. Remove spent flowers to prolong bloom. Although it is an excellent pot plant, the common name is actually derived from the plant's earlier use as a "pot herb"—a vegetable to be used in the cooking pot.

Dwarf strains (12–15 in. high) include Bon Bon (earliest), Dwarf Gem, and Fiesta (Fiesta Gitana). Taller (1½–2 ft. high) are Kablouna (pompon centers with looser edges), Pacific Beauty, and Radio (quilled, "cactus"-type blooms).

CALIBRACHOA
MILLION BELLS
Solanaceae
PERENNIAL OFTEN GROWN
AS ANNUAL

- ✿ ZONES 8, 9, 14–24 AS PERENNIAL; ZONES 2–7, 10–13 AS ANNUAL
- ☼ ◐ FULL SUN OR LIGHT SHADE
- ◊ REGULAR WATER

This petunia relative is probably native to Brazil; its garden forms are the result of hybridization. Plants are smaller than petunias, with more wiry, slender stems and tiny, closely set leaves—but not all botanists believe they differ significantly enough from petunias to merit a separate genus. There are two basic types. The trailers, low and flat growing, with leaves ½ in. long and ⅛ in. wide, are called

Liricashower and have white, pink, or purplish blue flowers an inch wide. A more compact and mounding, less trailing series is called Colorburst; it has somewhat larger leaves and cherry, rose, red, or violet flowers. One grower offers both compact and trailing types sold as Million Bells and Superbells that come in a wide range of colors. Superbells are more heat tolerant.

Wiry stems make the plants less subject to breakage than petunias, and tobacco budworms seem uninterested in foliage and flowers. Plants are self-cleaning (spent flowers drop off cleanly). Blooms are produced all season long and plants behave as perennials where frosts are nonexistent or light. Use them in hanging baskets, flower boxes, or as bedding plants (plant 1½ ft. apart).

CALICO FLOWER.
See **ARISTOLOCHIA littoralis**

CALICO PLANT.
See **ALTERNANTHERA tenella 'Bettzickiana', BREYNIA nivosa 'Roseopicta'**

CALIFORNIA BAY.
See **UMBELLULARIA californica**

CALIFORNIA DESERT BLUEBELLS. See **PHACELIA campanularia**

CALIFORNIA DUTCHMAN'S PIPE. See **ARISTOLOCHIA californica**

CALIFORNIA FAN PALM.
See **WASHINGTONIA filifera**

CALIFORNIA FUCHSIA.
See **ZAUSCHNERIA**

CALIFORNIA GERANIUM.
See **SENECIO petasitis**

CALIFORNIA HOLLY.
See **HETEROMELES arbutifolia**

CALIFORNIA HOLLY GRAPE.
See **MAHONIA pinnata**

CALIFORNIA LAUREL. See **UMBELLULARIA californica**

CALIFORNIA NUTMEG.
See **TORREYA californica**

CALIFORNIA POPPY. See **ESCHSCHOLZIA californica**

CALIFORNIA SNOW-DROP. See **STYRAX officinalis rediviva**

Calibrachoa

CALLA. See **ZANTEDESCHIA**

CALLIANDRA
Fabaceae (Leguminosae)
EVERGREEN AND DECIDUOUS
SHRUBS

- ✿ ZONES VARY BY SPECIES
- ☼ FULL SUN, EXCEPT AS NOTED
- ◊ ◐ ● WATER NEEDS VARY BY SPECIES

Group of about 200 species grown mainly for their flowers' long, silky stamens (the blossoms look like feather dusters or powder puffs) and for their ferny foliage. Prune out any dead or damaged wood after bloom.

C. californica. BAJA FAIRY DUSTER. Evergreen. Zones 10–24. Native to Baja California and Sonora, Mexico. To 5 ft. high, 5–6 ft. wide. This species is sometimes likened to *C. eriophylla*, but it's bigger, with more luxuriant foliage and bright deep red stamens.

Both the species and its hybrid 'Maricopa Red' are favorites of hummingbirds. Take little to moderate water. With moderate water, both bloom nearly year-round in Zone 13 (production drops off somewhat in midsummer and earliest winter), and close to that in Zone 12. Blooms throughout the warm parts of the year in other areas.

C. eriophylla. FAIRY DUSTER, FALSE MESQUITE. Deciduous. Zones 10–24. Native from Southern California east to Texas and south into Baja California. Open growth to 3 ft. tall, 4–5 ft. wide. Leaves finely divided into tiny leaflets. Flower clusters show pink to white stamens in fluffy balls to 1½ in. across in late winter or early spring. No irrigation needed, but blooms and leaves (plant is summer-deciduous) will last longer with some summer water.

C. haematocephala. PINK POWDER PUFF. Evergreen. Best in Zones 22–24 and H2; but will grow in Zones 13, 16–21 if protected by overhang or trained to a warm, sunny wall. Native to Bolivia. Big puffs (2–3 in. across) of watermelon red stamens from fall to early spring. There is also a white-flowered form. Leaflets are glossy copper when new, turning dark green; they are longer and broader than those of other species described here. Sprawler, growing quickly to 10 ft. high and wide—or more. Lax growth makes it very well suited to espaliering. Grow in light soil and provide regular water.

Calliandra tweedii

C. tweedii. BRAZILIAN FLAME BUSH, TRINIDAD FLAME BUSH. Evergreen. Best in Zones 22–24; satisfactory in Zones 15–21; freezes back but recovers in Zones 7–9, 12–14. Native to Brazil and Uruguay, though often sold as the true Trinidad native *C. guildingii*. Graceful, picturesque growth to 6–8 ft. tall and wide. In mild-winter climates, can be pruned up to form a handsome small tree, to 15 ft. tall, with a wide, horizontal crown. Lacy, finely divided, fernlike leaves barely hide branching structure. Flower clusters, bright scarlet pompons at branch tips, are highly attractive to hummingbirds. Best flower show comes in early spring and fall, with occasional blossoms in between, but plant will bloom all winter if it gets enough heat. A white-flowered form is rarely offered. Little or no water.

CALLICARPA

BEAUTYBERRY
Verbenaceae
DECIDUOUS SHRUBS

🌿	ZONES VARY BY SPECIES
☀️ 🌤️	FULL SUN OR LIGHT SHADE
💧 💧	MODERATE TO REGULAR WATER

These graceful shrubs with arching branches are cultivated for their pleasing fruit display. Small lilac or pink flowers in summer are followed by tight clusters of little, round, violet to purple fruits that persist well into winter. Effective in woodland gardens or massed in shrub borders. Bloom and fruit occur on current season's growth, so in late winter remove about a third of oldest stems or lop whole plant low to ground. In coldest regions, may freeze to ground but come back from roots.

C. americana. AMERICAN BEAUTYBERRY. Zones 3–9, 14–24. Native to eastern U.S. To 6 ft. tall, 5 ft. wide. Leaves to 6 in. long turn purplish in fall. Biggest, coarsest foliage of the species listed here.

C. bodinieri. BODINIER BEAUTYBERRY. Zones 3–9, 14–24. Native to China. Grows to 6 ft. or more and nearly as wide, with willowlike leaves that turn pink or orange to purple in fall. 'Profusion' is a heavy bearer.

Callicarpa bodinieri

C. dichotoma. PURPLE BEAUTYBERRY. Zones 2b–9, 14–24. Native to China, Korea, Japan. About 4 ft. tall and slightly wider, with slender branches that sweep the ground. Resembles a smaller, finer-textured *C. bodinieri*. 'Issai' bears abundant purple fruits. Those of *C. d. albifructus* are white. 'Early Amethyst' ripens its bright purple fruit earliest.

C. japonica. JAPANESE BEAUTYBERRY. Zones 2b–9, 14–24. Native to China, Taiwan, Japan. To 5 ft. tall and wide, with deep reddish purple fall foliage. 'Leucocarpa' bears white fruit.

CALLIOPSIS. See **COREOPSIS tinctoria**

CALLIRHOE involucrata

POPPY MALLOW, WINE CUPS
Malvaceae
PERENNIAL

🌿	ZONES 1–3, 7–14, 18–24
☀️ 🌤️	PARTIAL SHADE IN HOTTEST CLIMATES
💧 💧	LITTLE TO MODERATE WATER, EXCEPT AS NOTED

Callirhoe involucrata

Native from Missouri to Wyoming, south to Texas. Thick, fleshy root produces a spreading plant 6 in. tall and 2–3 ft. wide, with roundish, deeply cut leaves and a profusion of 2-in., purplish red, mallow-type flowers during hot weather. Needs good drainage but survives in infertile soil and intense heat. Except in desert regions, useful on hot slopes and in areas that get little attention. In hot desert, provide some shade and regular summer water.

CALLISTEMON

BOTTLEBRUSH
Myrtaceae
EVERGREEN SHRUBS OR TREES

🌿	ZONES VARY BY SPECIES
☀️	FULL SUN
💧 💧	MODERATE TO REGULAR WATER

Fast growing, with colorful flowers carried in dense spikes or round clusters consisting mainly of long, bristlelike stamens—hence the common name "bottlebrush." Attractive to hummingbirds. Flowers are followed by woody capsules that can last for years and may resemble rows of beads pressed into bark.

Some bottlebrushes are naturally dense and compact (making good informal hedges); others are sparse and open (can be pruned up to become small trees). Those with pliant branches can be grown as informal espaliers. Very little routine pruning is needed—just remove any weak or dead branches after bloom or before spring growth flush. Don't cut into bare wood beyond leaves—plant may not send out new growth. Generally found in moist ground in their native Australia, they can withstand waterlogged soil. Normally tolerant of saline or alkaline soils but sometimes suffer from chlorosis. Often severely damaged at 20°F/–7°C.

Callistemon citrinus

C. 'Canes Hybrid'. Zones 8, 9, 12–24. Shrub to 10 ft. tall and 15 ft. wide, though easily pruned to keep compact or shape into small tree. Slender, arching branches hold narrow leaves to 3 in. long; foliage is pink tinted when young, maturing to gray green. Soft pink brushes appear in late spring and early summer.

C. citrinus (C. lanceolatus). LEMON BOTTLEBRUSH. Zones 8, 9, 12–24; H1, H2. Most commonly grown bottlebrush; most tolerant of heat, cold, and poor soils. Massive shrub to 10–15 ft. tall and wide, but with staking and pruning in youth easily trained into narrowish, round-headed, 20–25-ft. tree. Nurseries offer it as shrub, espalier, or tree. Narrow, 3-in.-long leaves are coppery when new, maturing to vivid green. Bruised leaves smell lemony. Bright red, 6-in.-long brushes appear in waves throughout the year.

Variable plant when grown from seed. Cutting-grown selections with good flower size and color include 'Improved' and 'Splendens'. 'Compacta' makes a 4-ft. mound with smaller spikes. 'Violaceus' ('Jeffersii'), about 6 ft. tall and 4 ft. wide, has stiffer branching; narrower, shorter leaves; and reddish purple flowers fading to lavender. 'Mauve Mist' is the same but can reach 10 ft. 'Perth Pink', 10 ft. tall, has pink flower clusters.

C. rigidus. STIFF BOTTLEBRUSH. Zones 8, 9, 12–24; H1, H2. Rigid, sparse shrub or small tree to 20 ft. with 10-ft. spread. Leaves sharp pointed, gray green (sometimes purplish). Spring and summer red flower brushes are 2½–4½ in. long. Produces prominent seed capsules. Least graceful of the bottlebrushes.

C. salignus. WHITE BOTTLEBRUSH. Zones 8, 9, 12–24. Shrub or tree to 20–25 ft. tall, 10–15 ft. wide. Dense crown of foliage. New growth bright pink to copper. Willowlike leaves 2–3 in. long. Pale yellow to cream-colored flowers appear in 1½–3-in. clusters in spring, early summer. Train as small shade tree or plant 4–5 ft. apart as hedge.

C. sieberi. ALPINE BOTTLEBRUSH. Zones 5–9, 14–24. Shrub to 3–6 ft. tall and wide, with somewhat upright habit. Small (to 1½-in.-long), dark green leaves densely cover the pendulous branches. Cream to yellow flowers in 1½–6-in.-long brushes appear from late spring to midsummer. Good choice for colder areas.

C. viminalis. WEEPING BOTTLEBRUSH. Zones 6–9, 12–24. Shrub or small tree with pendulous branches. Fast growing to 20–30 ft. tall, with 15-ft. spread. Leaves narrow, light green, 6 in. long. Bright red brushes from late spring into summer, scattered bloom rest of year. Not for windy,

C

Callistemon viminalis

dry areas. As tree, needs staking, thinning to prevent tangled, top-heavy growth. Leaves tend to grow toward ends of long, hanging branches.

'Little John' is a superior dwarf form to 3 ft. tall and wide, with dense growth pattern and blood red flowers in fall, winter, and spring. 'Captain Cook' is a dense, rounded form to 6 ft. tall and wide, suitable for border, low hedge, or screen. 'Red Cascade' grows to a similar height with large, abundant, rosy red blooms. 'McCaskillii' has even denser habit than others, is more vigorous (to 20 ft. tall), and has better flower color and form.

C. viridiflorus. GREEN BOTTLEBRUSH. Zones 4–9, 14–24. Upright and open shrub to 6–8 ft. high and wide. Golden, flaking bark. Dark green leaves are short (to 1¼ in.) and densely held along stems. Three-inch-long green to creamy yellow brushes appear from spring to summer.

CALLISTEPHUS chinensis

CHINA ASTER
Asteraceae (Compositae)
ANNUAL

| ZONES 1–24 |
| FULL SUN |
| REGULAR WATER |

Chinese native is a splendid cut flower and an effective bedding plant when well grown and free of disease. Plants are from 8 in. to 3 ft. high, 10–18 in. wide. Some kinds are branching; others (developed mainly for florists) have strong stems and no side shoots. Leaves are deeply toothed or lobed.

Bloom comes in summer. Many different flower forms: quilled, curled, incurved, ribbonlike, or

with interlaced rays; some have crested centers. Varieties are classified as peony flowered, pompon, anemone flowered, and ostrich feather. Colors range from white to pastel pink, rose pink, lavender, lavender blue, violet, purple, crimson, wine, and scarlet.

Callistephus chinensis

Plant in rich, loamy or sandy soil. After danger of frost is past, sow seed in place or set out plants started in flats. Keep growth steady; sudden checks in growth are harmful. Subject to aster yellows, a viral disease carried by leafhoppers. Discard infected plants; control leafhoppers. All but wilt-resistant types are subject to aster wilt or stem rot, caused by a parasitic fungus that lives in soil and is transmitted through roots into plants. Overwatering produces ideal condition for diseases, especially in heavy or poorly drained soil. Never plant in same location in successive years.

CALLUNA vulgaris

SCOTCH HEATHER
Ericaceae
EVERGREEN SHRUB

| ZONES 1A, 2–6, 15–17 |
| FULL SUN |
| REGULAR WATER |

This, the true and only Scotch heather, which is native from Europe to Asia Minor, has crowded, tiny, scalelike, dark green leaves and spikes of bell-shaped, rosy pink flowers. Garden varieties (far more common than wild species) range from dwarf ground cover and rock garden plants only a couple of inches high to kinds reaching 3 ft. tall. Taller varieties make good backgrounds for lower sorts and are attractive cut flowers. Blossom colors include white, pale to deep pink, lavender, and purple. Foliage—paler and deeper greens, chartreuse, yellow, gray, or russet—often changes color in

winter. Most bloom in mid- to late summer; a few bloom into late fall. But blooming types produce flowers that don't fully open; buds themselves provide long-lasting color. To prune all types, shear off faded flowers and pinch tips immediately after bloom (with types blooming into late fall, delay pruning until late winter).

Heathers thrive in sandy, peaty, fast-draining soil. In the Northwest, they are especially well adapted and require little or no fertilizing. Where watering must be frequent, light feeding with acid plant food—once in late winter, again in early summer—will encourage good growth and bloom.

Here are some of the many varieties available from specialists. All begin blooming in summer, except as noted.

'Allegro'. Vigorous, upright, to 20 in. high, 2 ft. wide. Dark green foliage; ruby flowers.

'Amethyst'. Upright, bushy, to 1 ft. tall, 16 in. wide. Dark green foliage; deep crimson buds last into fall.

'Anette'. Erect, to 1 ft. high, 16 in. wide. Medium green foliage; clear pink buds last well into fall.

'Beoley Gold'. Upright, to 14 in. high, 20 in. wide. One of the best yellow-foliaged varieties. White flowers.

'Blazeaway'. To 14 in. high, 2 ft. wide. Pale foliage with apricot tints, emerging bronzy. Lavender flowers.

'Corbett Red'. Compact grower to 10 in. high, 1½ ft. wide, with dark green foliage. Violet-red flowers.

'County Wicklow'. Mounding, to 10 in. high, 14 in. wide. Medium green foliage; pink double flowers from white buds.

'Cuprea'. Compact, to 1 ft. high, 15 in. wide. Coppery yellow foliage; mauve flowers.

'Dainty Bess'. Tiny gray leaves form a foot-wide, 2–4-in.-tall mat that shapes itself to rocks, crevices. Lavender flowers.

'Dark Beauty'. Compact, to 10 in. high, 14 in. wide. Dark green foliage; deep cherry semi-double flowers.

'Dark Star'. Neat, compact, to 8 in. tall, 14 in. wide. Dark green foliage; crimson semidouble blooms.

'Firefly'. Upright, to 1½ ft. tall, 20 in. wide. Foliage is salmon red in summer, turning bright red in winter. Deep mauve flowers.

'Foxii Nana'. Small mound to 4 in. high, 1 ft. wide. Dark green foliage; purple flowers.

'Gold Haze'. Upright, bushy, to 1 ft. tall, 1½ ft. wide. Yellow foliage; white flowers.

'H. E. Beale'. Loose mound to 2 ft. tall and wide. Dark green foliage; soft pink double flowers. Long spikes are good for cutting.

'Hoyerhagen'. Compact, to 10 in. high, 14 in. wide. Foliage is bright orange gold in summer, turning scarlet red in winter. Pale crimson flowers.

'J. H. Hamilton'. Prostrate, bushy, to 4 in. high, 1 ft. wide. Deep green foliage; profuse double pink blooms.

'Kerstin'. Strong, upright, to 1 ft. high, 1½ ft. wide. Downy, deep green foliage turns lilac gray in winter and sports cream, pink, and red tips in spring. Mauve flowers.

'Kinlochruel'. Compact, to 10 in. tall, 16 in. wide. Bright green foliage; spectacular white double flowers.

'Mair's Variety'. Erect, 2–3 ft. tall and wide. Medium green foliage; white flowers. Easy to grow; good background plant.

'Multicolor'. To 4 in. high, 10 in. wide. Copper-green foliage in summer turns brick red in winter. Scarlet-red new growth in spring. Pale mauve flowers.

'Peter Sparkes'. Mounding, to 15 in. tall, 20 in. wide. Dark green foliage; double deep pink flowers.

'Robert Chapman'. Spreading, to 10 in. high, 2 ft. wide. Greenish to reddish orange foliage; mauve flowers.

Calluna vulgaris

'Ruby Slinger'. Upright, to 10 in. tall, 14 in. wide. Bright green summer foliage; new spring growth cream to yellow. White flowers.

'Silver Knight'. Upright, to 16 in. high, 20 in. wide. Downy gray foliage turns purple gray in winter. Lavender flowers.

'Sister Anne'. Low, spreading, to 4 in. high, 10 in. wide. Downy, gray-green foliage. Mauve flowers.

'Spring Torch'. Spreading, to 1 ft. tall, 20 in. wide. Red-tipped green foliage and pink flowers.

'Tib'. Rounded, bushy, to 1 ft. high, 15 in. wide. Medium green foliage; deepest rosy purple double flowers.

'White Lawn'. Prostrate grower just 2 in. high, 16 in. wide. Bright green foliage. White blooms cover branches.

'Wickwar Flame'. Mounding, to 1½ ft. tall, 2 ft. wide. Yellow to red foliage, lavender flowers.

CALOCEDRUS decurrens (Libocedrus decurrens)

INCENSE CEDAR
Cupressaceae
EVERGREEN TREE

🌿	ZONES 2-12, 14-24
☼ ◐	FULL SUN OR LIGHT SHADE
◌ ◑	NO IRRIGATION TO MODERATE WATER

Native to the mountains of central and southern Oregon, California, western Nevada; also to northern Baja California. Unlike most of its native associates—white fir, Douglas fir, sugar pine—it adapts to many other Western climates. Symmetrical tree to 75–90 ft. tall with dense, narrow, pyramidal crown; give it room for a 10–15-ft. spread at base. Reddish brown bark on trunk. Rich green foliage in flat sprays. Tree gives pungent fragrance to garden in warm weather. Bears small, yellowish brown to reddish brown cones that, when open, resemble ducks' bills.

Although slow growing at first, it may grow 2 ft. per year when established. Takes blazing summer heat and tolerates poor soils. No supplemental water needed in Zones 2, 4–7, 15–17; give moderate water elsewhere. Good tree to make green wall, high screen, windbreak. No pruning required.

Calocedrus decurrens

CALOCEPHALUS brownii (Leucophyta brownii)

CUSHION BUSH
Asteraceae (Compositae)
EVERGREEN SHRUB

🌿	ZONES 16, 17, 19, 21-24
☼	FULL SUN
◑◑	MODERATE TO REGULAR WATER

Native to Australia, Tasmania. Silvery white throughout, this unusual mounding plant to 3 ft. high and wide thrives when buffeted by winds and exposed to salt air and spray. (Grows best in Zones 17, 24.) Tiny threadlike leaves, ⅛ in. long, are pressed tightly against wiry, branching stems. Flower heads are button shaped, ½ in. across, in clusters. Stunning high ground cover or rock garden plant. Effective in large planters with succulents. Fresh or dried foliage is attractive in arrangements. Provide sandy or gravelly soil, fast drainage. Cut out dead wood on older plants.

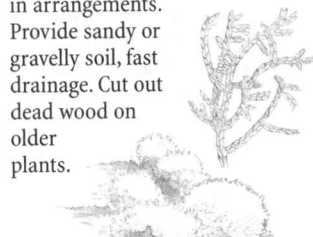
Calocephalus brownii

CALOCHORTUS

Liliaceae
PERENNIALS FROM BULBS

🌿	ZONES VARY BY SPECIES
☼ ◐	FULL SUN OR LIGHT SHADE
◑	REGULAR WATER DURING GROWTH AND BLOOM

Beautiful Western natives, most common in California. One type, sego lily *(C. nuttallii),* is the state flower of Utah. Among the more challenging bulbs for the garden, as they demand the long, warm, dry summers of their native habitats. Sparse, grassy foliage is common to all types, but there are three distinct flower forms. Globe tulips or fairy lanterns have nodding flowers, the petals turning inward to form a globe. Star tulips have upward-facing, cup-shaped flowers, with petal tips often rolled outward; those with long, straight hairs on the inner flower parts are called "cat's ears" or "pussy ears." Mariposa lilies are generally the tallest, with striking cup- or bowl-shaped blossoms. Flower colors include yellow,

Calochortus

purple, lavender, red, pink, and white. Bloom time for most is spring or early summer.

May be difficult to find; check bulb specialists or local plant sales. It's best to plant kinds indigenous to your area; at least one type or another is available in Zones 1–9, 14–24. All can be grown in rock gardens or naturalized on sunny, grassy hillsides if they can be kept dry in summer. Or you can grow them in containers that you bury, then lift after bloom and store. Plant in fall, setting bulbs 3–4 in. deep and about 6 in. apart in well-drained soil.

CALODENDRUM capense

CAPE CHESTNUT
Rutaceae
BRIEFLY DECIDUOUS TREE

🌿	ZONES 19, 21-24; WORTH RISKING IN 15, 16
☼	FULL SUN
◑	REGULAR WATER

Native to South Africa. Slow growing to 25–40 ft. tall and wide, with light to medium green, oval leaves to 6 in. long. Seldom flowers before

Calodendrum capense

the age of about 5 years, but the show is noteworthy when it does come: profuse spikes of rosy lilac, 1½-in.-long flowers. Whole flower cluster measures 10–12 in. high by as much across, and extends well above foliage, giving effect of candelabra. Generally blooms from late spring into summer, but time of flowering and deciduous period varies, depending on where tree is planted. Locate out of prevailing wind. Light, sandy soils are not to its liking.

CALONYCTION aculeatum. See **IPOMOEA alba**

CALTHA palustris

MARSH MARIGOLD
Ranunculaceae
PERENNIAL

🌿	ZONES A1-A3; 1-9, 14-24
☼ ◐ ●	SUN OR SHADE
◑◑	AMPLE WATER
◆	ANY PART CAN CAUSE INFLAMMATION, PAIN IF INGESTED

Native from Alaska to Newfoundland. To 2 ft. tall and wide; well adapted to edges of pools, ponds, streams, other moist situations. With sufficient water it can be grown in borders but must not dry out in summer. Good with bog irises, moisture-loving ferns. Lush, glossy green leaves 2–7 in. across give an almost tropical effect. Clusters of 2-in., vivid yellow flowers in spring; a double-flowered form is available. Marsh marigold is vigorous; increase by divisions or sow seed in boggy soil.

Caltha palustris

CALYCANTHUS

Calycanthaceae
DECIDUOUS SHRUBS

🌿	ZONES VARY BY SPECIES
☼ ◐ ●	SUN OR SHADE
◑	REGULAR WATER
◆	SEEDS CAN PRODUCE CONVULSIONS

Both species described here are bulky, clump-forming shrubs with lush foliage and flowers valued for their fragrance and form. Blooms are produced at ends of current season's growth. Remove twiggy or crowded stems annually, but for best appearance don't prune further.

C

C

C. floridus. CAROLINA
ALLSPICE. Zones 3–9, 14–17.
Native from Virginia to Florida.
Stiffly branched to 6–10 ft. tall and
as wide or wider; suckering, fast
spreading. Oval leaves to 5 in. long
are glossy dark green above, grayish green beneath. Flowers—2 in.
wide, reddish brown, with heady,
strawberrylike fragrance—are carried at ends of leafy branchlets in
late spring or early summer.
Blooms are followed by brownish,
pear-shaped capsules, fragrant
when crushed. Plant in shrub border or around outdoor living space
where flower scent can be appreciated. Aroma varies, so buy plants
in bloom.'Athens'
has yellow flowers.

*Calycanthus
occidentalis*

C. occidentalis.
SPICE BUSH.
Zones 4–9,
14–24. Native
along streams,
moist slopes in Califor-
nia's Coast Ranges and
Sierra Nevada foothills.
To 4–12 ft. high and
wide. Bright green
leaves are 2–6 in. long, 1–2 in.
wide, turn yellow in fall. Brownish
red flowers to 2 in. across, resembling small water lilies, appear in
mid- to late spring or summer,
depending on climate. Both flowers and bruised leaves have fragrance of an old wine barrel. Can
be trained into multistemmed
small tree, but is most useful as
a background shrub or medium
to tall screen. Easily grown
from seed.

CALYLOPHUS

SUNDROPS
Onagraceae
PERENNIALS

| 🗺 ZONES 1–3, 6–16, 18–24 |
| ☀ ◐ FULL SUN OR LIGHT SHADE |
| ◌ ◍ LITTLE TO MODERATE WATER |

Western natives related to and
much resembling evening primrose (*Oenothera),* with bright yellow, four-petaled flowers over a
long summer bloom period. In
Zone 13, flowering declines in
summer heat, and plants flower in
spring and from late summer to
fall. Spread by rhizomes and are
useful for summer color in difficult
climates. Shear just before spring
growth begins. Plant in well-
drained soil. Tolerate regular water
if drainage is superb.

C. drummondianus. To 1½ ft.
high, 2 ft. wide, with narrow,
tooth-edged, somewhat drooping

Calylophus hartwegii

leaves and inch-wide flowers. This
species blooms for a longer period
than *C. hartwegii* in spring, but it
does not rebloom as well in fall.

C. hartwegii. To 1 ft. high,
2 ft. across, with inch-wide flowers; those of 'Sierra Sundrop' are
larger. *C. h. lavandulifolius*
(*C. lavandulifolius)* has narrow,
gray leaves. Excellent in hot, dry
locations and when mixed with
desert perennials.

C. serrulatus. Prairie wildflower found from Saskatchewan
to Texas. To 1½ ft. high and wide,
with ¾-in. flowers.

CALYTRIX tetragona

FRINGE MYRTLE
Myrtaceae
EVERGREEN SHRUB

| 🗺 ZONES 15–24 |
| ☀ ◐ FULL SUN OR LIGHT SHADE |
| ◌ MODERATE WATER |

Australian shrub to 3–6 ft. tall and
wide, with tiny evergreen leaves
and a profusion of small but
showy white or pink star-shaped
flowers from late winter into summer. Calyxes age to deep red or
purple, extending color show even
further. Needs excellent drainage
and should be kept compact by
tip pruning after bloom. Good for
low-maintenance planting or for
screening. Choice cut flower.

Calytrix tetragona

CAMASSIA

CAMASS
Liliaceae
PERENNIALS FROM BULBS

| 🗺 ZONES 1–9, 14–17, EXCEPT AS NOTED |
| ☀ ◐ FULL SUN OR LIGHT SHADE |
| 💧 AMPLE WATER DURING GROWTH AND BLOOM |

Most are native to
moist meadows,
marshes, fields
in Northern
California and
Pacific North-
west. Rosettes
of grasslike
leaves send up
slender spikes
of loosely
spaced, starlike
blossoms in
spring. Plant in

*Camassia
quamash*

fall after weather cools, setting
bulbs 3–4 in. deep, 6 in. apart in
good, moisture-retentive soil.
Locate bulbs where they can
remain undisturbed for many
years. Because plants die down
completely after bloom, set them
where other plants will hide their
yellowing leaves and fill in when
leaves are gone. Bulbs can get by
with less water during summer
dormancy.

C. cusickii. Dense clusters of
pale blue flowers on stems to
3 ft. tall.

C. leichtlinii. Large, handsome
clusters of creamy white flowers
on 4-ft.-tall stems. *C. l. suksdorfii*
(often sold as *C. l.* 'Coerulea') has
blue to deep blue-violet flowers.
This subspecies' variety 'Blue
Danube' is deep blue. Varieties
of the species include 'Alba'
(*C. l. leichtlinii),* white with bluish
tinge, and 'Semiplena', with creamy
white semidouble blooms.

C. quamash (C. esculenta).
Zones 1–10, 14–17. Loose clusters
of blue flowers on 1–2-ft. stems.
Flowers of 'Orion' are deeper
blue, those of 'San Juan Form'
deeper still.

CAMELLIA

Theaceae
EVERGREEN SHRUBS OR TREES

| 🗺 ZONES 4–9, 12, 14–24, EXCEPT AS NOTED |
| ◐ BEST OUT OF STRONG SUN |
| ◍ ◍ MODERATE TO REGULAR WATER |

Native to eastern and southern
Asia. There are over 3,000 named
kinds, and the range in color, size,
and form is remarkable.

The following pages briefly
discuss the cultural requirements
of camellias and describe some
lesser-known species as well as the
widely distributed old favorites
and new varieties. The plant
descriptions include cultural needs
unique to individual species and
varieties, beyond the general
requirements detailed in this
introduction.

Exposure and watering. Though
camellias grow and bloom best
when protected from strong sun,
some kinds are more sun tolerant
than others. Tall old plants prove
that camellias can thrive in full
sun when they are mature enough
for their roots to be shaded by
heavy leaf canopy. Young plants
will grow better and bear more
attractive flowers if grown in partial shade under tall trees, under
lath cover, or on north side of a
building. (Grow in deep shade in
desert.) A few camellias need
shade at any age.

Established plants (over 3 years
old, vigorous, and shading their
own roots) can get by with little
supplemental water. If you give
them regular water, be sure soil is
well drained.

Fertilizing. Fertilize with a commercial acid plant food. Generally,
the time to feed is in weeks and
months following bloom; read fertilizer label for instructions. Don't
use more than recommended; better to cut suggested amounts in
half and feed twice as often. Never
feed sick plants.

Camellia problems. Poor drainage
and water or soil containing excess
salts are the main troublemakers
for camellias. Best cure is to move
plant into aboveground bed of
pure ground bark or peat moss
until it recovers. If you irrigate
your camellias with water high in
salts, leach out accumulated salts
with deep soaking—twice in
summer—to dissolve harmful salts
and carry them deep below the
root zone.

Scorched or yellowed areas in
center of leaves are usually due to
sunburn. Burned leaf edges, excessive leaf drop, or corky spots usually indicate overfertilizing. Yellow
leaves with green veins are signs of
chlorosis; treat with iron or iron
chelates.

One disease may be serious:
camellia petal blight. Flowers rapidly turn an ugly brown. Browning
at edges of petals (especially on
whites and pale pinks) may be

What Camellias Need

SOIL Give them well-drained soil rich in organic material. Never plant so trunk base is below soil line, and never let soil cover base. Keep roots cool with 2-in.-thick mulch (kept away from base).

WATERING Though camellias appreciate regular water (as long as drainage is good), established older plants can survive—even thrive—on fairly little supplemental moisture.

FERTILIZING Feed with a commercial acid plant food, being sure not to overfertilize plants.

SHELTER Protect plants from strong, hot sun and drying winds.

PRUNING Some judicious pruning right after flowering or during summer and fall will improve plant appearance and next year's flower display.

Camellia japonica 'Bob Hope'; irregular semidouble

caused by sun or wind, but if brown rapidly runs into center of flower, suspect petal blight. Sanitation is the best control. Pick up all fallen flowers and petals, pick off all infected flowers from plants, and dispose of them in covered trash bin; encourage neighbors to do the same. Remove any mulch, haul it away, and replace with fresh materials; a deep mulch (4–5 in.) helps keep spores of the fungus from reaching the air.

In the Pacific Northwest, *C. japonica* is very susceptible to cottony camellia scale and soft brown scale; worst symptom is sooty mold on foliage and stems. This damage, along with frequent browning of blossoms in rainy spring weather, has dampened the enthusiasm of gardeners in the Northwest for growing camellias.

Some flower bud dropping in all regions may be natural; many camellias set more buds than they can open. Bud drop can be caused by overwatering, but underwatering is more likely, especially during summer. It can also be caused by spells of very low humidity.

Pruning. Prune away dead or weak wood and thin when growth is so dense that flowers have no room to open properly. Prune at will to get form you want; shorten lower branches to encourage upright growth, or cut back top growth to flatten lanky shrubs. Make cut just above scar that terminates previous year's growth (often a slightly thickened, somewhat rough area where bark texture and color change slightly). A cut just above this point will usually force three or four dormant buds into growth.

Some varieties bear too many flowers. To get nicest display from them, remove buds in midsummer like this: from branch-end clusters remove all but one or two round flower buds (leaf buds are more slender); along stems, remove enough to leave a single flower bud for each 2–4 in. of branch. Removing just the small buds will shorten the bloom season, so remove buds of different sizes.

Camellias in containers. Camellias make outstanding container plants—especially in wooden tubs and half-barrels. As a general rule, plant gallon-size camellias into 12–14-in.-wide containers, 5-gallon ones into 16–18-in. tubs. Fill with a planting mix containing 50 percent or more organic material.

Flower forms. The American Camellia Society defines six basic camellia flower forms; these are illustrated by the photographs on page 244.

Single. One row (a single layer) of up to eight petals surrounding a conspicuous cluster of stamens.

Semidouble. Two or more rows (layers) of regular, irregular, or loose petals surrounding a conspicuous cluster of stamens.

Anemone form. One or more rows (layers) of petals, flat or undulating, surrounding a central mound of intermingled petaloids and stamens.

Peony form. Mounded to nearly ball-shaped flower consisting of petals in no regular arrangement, forming a sort of powder-puff effect. In loose peony form, blossoms contain loose petals (some irregular) intermingled with stamens. In full peony form, flowers are a tighter mass of petals,

petaloids, and stamens, or petals and petaloids with no stamens visible.

Rose-form double. Multiple layers of regularly overlapping (imbricated) petals revealing a central cluster of stamens when flowers are fully open.

Formal double. Flowers consisting of multiple layers of imbricated petals, never showing stamens even when fully open.

C. chrysantha (C. nitidissima nitidissima). GOLDEN CAMELLIA. Tall, vigorous, open grower to 6–16 ft. tall, 10–12 ft. wide, with large (6-in. or longer), glossy, netveined leaves and 2–2½-in., golden yellow flowers. Hybridizers use it to expand the camellia color palette.

C. granthamiana. Becomes a big shrub or small tree of rather open growth to 10 ft. tall, 6 ft. wide, with leathery, glossy, heavily veined, and crinkled leaves 2–6 in. long. Flowers are large, white, single, often with fluted or folded ("rabbit ear") petals and a heavy central tuft of bright yellow stamens. Flowers open in autumn from large, brown, scaly, silkyhaired buds. A cross between this species and *C. reticulata* produced 'China Lady', which looks like a big pink *C. granthamiana*. It has been the parent of several other remarkable seedling camellias. All need excellent drainage; avoid overwatering.

C. hiemalis. Includes a number of varieties formerly listed as sasanquas but differing in their later, longer bloom and heavier-textured flowers. Four good examples follow.

'Chansonette'. Vigorous, spreading growth to 6 ft. high, 8 ft. wide. Large, bright pink, formal double flowers.

'Shishi-Gashira'. One of the most useful and ornamental shrubs. Low growing (3 ft. high and 6 ft. wide), with arching branches that in time pile up tier on tier to make a compact, dark green, glossy-leafed plant. Leaves rather small for camellia, giving medium-fine foliage texture. Flowers rose red, semidouble to double, 2–2½ in. wide, heavily borne over long season—fall through winter in a good year. Full sun or shade.

'Showa-No-Sakae'. To 3 ft. high, 6–8 ft. wide. Faster growing, more open than 'Shishi-Gashira'; wil-

Camellia hiemalis

lowy, arching branches. Semidouble to double flowers of soft pink. Try this as espalier or in hanging basket.

'Showa Supreme'. Very similar to above but with a more compact habit and somewhat larger flowers of peony form.

C. japonica. Zones 4–9, 12, 14–24; H1. This is the plant most gardeners have in mind when they speak of camellias. Naturally a large shrub or small tree but variable in size, growth rate, and habit. Hundred-year-old plants in California reach 20 ft. high and equally wide, and even larger specimens exist. However, most gardeners can consider japonicas to be shrubs 6–12 ft. high and wide. Many are lower growing.

Higo camellias are a category of japonicas that has been bred for more than 200 years in Japan. Generally compact plants, they have dense, heavy foliage and thick-petaled single flowers with a broad, full brush of stamens in the center. In the ideal Higo camellia, mass of stamens should be at least half the diameter of flower. Colors include white, pink, and red—both solid and variegated, as with regular japonicas.

The following list describes japonica varieties that are favorites among Western gardeners. Included here are a number of old standbys whose beauty belies their age. Some of them are among the oldest varieties still in commerce, having been brought to Europe and the U.S. from China and Japan in the 19th century or even earlier (these venerable camellias are noted by date of introduction in the text). The list specifies season of bloom as early, midseason, or late. In California, early means October to January; midseason, January to March; late, March to May. In the Southwest, early means October to December; midseason, January and February; late, March and April. In the Northwest, early means December to February; midseason, March and April; late, May. Flower size is also noted for each variety. Very large blooms are over 5 in. wide; large, 4–5 in.; medium-large, 3½–4 in.; medium, 3–3½ in.; small, 2½–3 in.; and miniature, 2½ in. or less.

'Adolphe Audusson' (1877). Midseason. Very large, dark red

semidouble flowers, heavily borne on a medium-size, symmetrical, vigorous shrub. Hardy. 'Adolphe Audusson Variegated' is identical, but its blossoms are heavily marbled with white on red.

'Alba Plena' (1792). Early. Brought from China over two centuries ago and still a favorite. Large white formal double. Slow, bushy growth. Early bloom is a disadvantage in cold or rainy areas; protect blossoms from rain and wind.

'Betty Sheffield'. Midseason. Large white semidouble to loose peony-form blossoms striped and blotched with red and pink. An upright, medium-size plant, it is the parent of many sports identical save for flower color. 'Betty Sheffield Supreme' has white petals bordered in deep rose red; 'Betty's Beauty' has a narrower pink border. 'Betty Sheffield Blush' is pale pink with a few red marks. 'Betty Sheffield Coral' is coral pink.

'Bob Hope'. Midseason. Large to very large deep red semidouble blooms have prominent golden stamens. Large, vigorous plant.

'Carter's Sunburst'. Early to late. Large to very large flowers, semidouble to peony form to formal double, in pale pink striped with deeper pink. Medium-size, compact plant.

'C. M. Hovey' ('Colonel Fiery') (1853). Midseason to late. Large, formal, dark red blooms. Vigorous and bushy.

'C. M. Wilson'. Early to midseason. Sport of 'Elegans' and identical to it except for its pale pink flower color. 'C. M. Wilson Variegated' has white petal markings; many plants sold as 'C. M. Wilson' are actually the variegated form.

'Covina' (1888). Midseason to late. Medium, rose red semidouble to rose-form double flowers on a compact plant. Highly sun tolerant.

'Daikagura' (1891). Early to late. Large, rose red peony-form blooms on a dense, upright bush.

Very long bloom season. 'Daikagura Variegated' is similar but has rose red blossoms marbled in white; it is often sold as simply 'Daikagura' so you may want to ask which one you are purchasing.

'Debutante'. Early to midseason. Medium-large, light pink peony-form flowers. Profuse bloomer. Vigorous upright growth. Takes some sun.

'Eleanor McCown'. Midseason. Medium, white semidouble to anenome-form flowers streaked with red and pink.

'Elegans' (Chandler); also sold as 'Francine' ('Chandleri Elegans Pink'). 1831. Early to midseason. The founder of a large and growing family of sports. The original plant is slow growing and spreading, bearing large anemone-form blossoms in rose pink; center petaloids are often marked with white. More frequently grown is 'Elegans Variegated', identical except for white variegation on all petals; it is often known simply as Chandleri Elegans. 'Elegans Supreme' is like 'Elegans' with the addition of deep serrations on petal edges. 'Elegans Champagne' is a white sport of 'Elegans Supreme' with creamy central petaloids. 'Elegans Splendor' has white-margined pale pink petals with fringed edges. For other sports in the 'Elegans' family, see 'C. M. Wilson', 'Hawaii', 'Shiro Chan'.

'Glen 40' ('Coquettii'). Midseason to late. Large, deep red formal double. One of the best reds for corsages. Slow, compact, upright growth. Handsome even out of bloom. Hardy; good in containers.

'Grand Slam'. Midseason. Large to very large semidouble to anemone-form deep red flowers. There is a variegated form.

'Guilio Nuccio'. Midseason. Considered by many to be the world's finest camellia. Coral rose, very large semidouble flowers of unusual depth and substance have inner petals fluted in "rabbit ear"

effect. Vigorous upright growth. Forms with variegated, fringed blossoms are available.

'Hawaii'. Early to midseason. A sport of 'C. M. Wilson' with the same plant habit and light pink flower color, but in a full peony form with fringed petals. 'Kona' is a white sport.

'Herme' ('Jordan's Pride'). 1875. Midseason. Medium-large, pink semidouble flowers irregularly bordered in white and streaked with deeper pink. Sometimes bears solid pink blooms on certain branches. Free blooming and dependable.

'Kramer's Supreme'. Midseason. Very large, full peony-form flowers in clear red. Some detect a faint fragrance. Compact, upright, unusually vigorous. Takes some sun.

'Kumasaka' (1896). Midseason to late. Medium-large, rose pink rose-form double to peony-form flowers. Vigorous, compact, upright growth and remarkably heavy flower production make it a choice landscape plant. Hardy. Takes morning sun.

'Magnoliiflora' (1886). Midseason. Medium, pale pink semidouble flowers. Heavy bloomer; good cut flower. Medium-size plant with spreading form. Hardy.

'Mathotiana' (1840s). Midseason to late. Very large rose-form double to formal double blooms in deep crimson, sometimes with purplish cast. Vigorous, upright grower. Takes cold and stands up well in hot-summer areas.

'Mrs. Charles Cobb'. Midseason to late. Flowers are large, deep red semidouble to peony form. Free blooming. Compact plant with dense foliage; best in warmer areas.

'Mrs. D. W. Davis'. Midseason. Spectacular blossoms in palest blush pink: very large, somewhat cup shaped, opening from egg-size buds. Vigorous, upright plant with very handsome, broad leaves.

'Nuccio's Bella Rossa'. Early through midseason. Bears large,

crimson-red formal blossoms over a long period, even on young plants.

'Nuccio's Gem'. Midseason. Medium to large, white, perfectly formed formal double. Full, upright plant.

'Nuccio's Jewel'. Midseason to late. Large flowers in loose to full peony form are white with pink petal edges.

'Nuccio's Pearl'. Midseason. Medium, full formal double blossoms are white with a rim of deep pink outer petals.

'Pearl Maxwell'. Midseason to late. Large, soft shell pink flowers with formal double form.

'Pink Parade'. Midseason. Large, clear pink semidouble to peony-form flowers. Erect and slow growing.

'Prince Eugene Napoleon' ('Pope Pius IX'). 1859. Midseason. Cherry red, medium-large formal double. Compact, upright plant.

'Purity' (1887). Late. Medium white flowers, rose-form double to formal double, usually showing a few stamens. Vigorous, upright plant. Often escapes rain damage.

'Shiro Chan'. Early to midseason. A sport of 'C. M. Wilson' with identical habit and flower form. Blossoms may open palest pink, then fade to white blushed with pink at petal bases. 'Snow Chan' is a pure white sport.

'Silver Waves'. Early to midseason. Large white semidouble blooms with wavy petal edges.

'Swan Lake'. Midseason to late. Very large white flowers with formal double to peony form. Vigorous, upright growth.

'Tiffany'. Midseason to late. Large to very large blossoms in warm pink; rose-form double to loose, irregular semidouble. Vigorous, broad shrub.

'Tom Knudsen'. Early to midseason. Medium to large blooms in dark red with deeper red veining. Formal double to peony form to rose-form double.

Camellia Flower Forms

Camellia sasanqua 'Apple Blossom'; single

Camellia japonica 'C. M. Wilson'; anemone form

Camellia japonica 'Alba Plena'; formal double

Camellia japonica 'Purity'; rose-form double

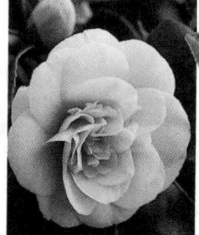

Camellia japonica 'Debutante'; peony form

Camellia hiemalis 'Shishi-Gashira'; semidouble to double

'Tomorrow'. Early to midseason. Very large strawberry red blossoms may be semidouble with petaloids mixed among stamens, or they may have full peony form. Strong, open, slightly pendulous plant. The parent of numerous sports. 'Tomorrow Variegated' is variously marked in white. 'Tomorrow Park Hill' has lightly variegated pale pink petals shading to darker pink at edges. 'Tomorrow's Dawn' reverses the effect, shading from deeper color in petal centers to white at margins. 'Tomorrow's Tropic Dawn' has red-streaked white flowers aging to blush pink.

'Ville de Nantes'. Midseason to late. Large semidouble flowers have white-blotched deep red petals with fringed edges. Bushy, slow-growing plant. 'Lady Kay' is a sport with full peony form.

'Wildfire'. Early to midseason. Medium orange-red semidouble flowers; a vigorous, upright plant.

C. lutchuensis. Shrub to 10 ft. tall, 12 ft. wide, with tiny (1½-in.-long, ½-in.-wide) leaves and profusion of tiny white flowers with strong, pleasant fragrance. Used as parent to introduce fragrance to larger camellias. Long, pliant branches make it an easily trained espalier.

C. oleifera. Shrub or small tree 10–20 ft. tall, 6–12 ft. wide, with open growth habit and somewhat weeping branches. Leaves are 1–3 in. long, glossy green. Flowers are small (1½ in.), white or cream, fragrant. Possibly the hardiest of all camellia species and a parent of hardy hybrids.

C. reticulata. Some of the biggest and most spectacular camellia flowers occur in this species, and likely as not they appear on some of the lankiest and least graceful plants.

Plants differ somewhat according to variety, but generally are rather gaunt and open shrubs that eventually become trees of considerable size—possibly 35–50 ft. tall. In gardens, consider them 10-ft.-tall shrubs, 8 ft. wide. Leaves are also variable but tend to be dull green, leathery, and strongly net veined.

Culture is quite similar to that of other camellias, except that plants seem intolerant of heavy pruning. This, in addition to their natural lankiness and size, makes them difficult to place in garden. They are at their best in light shade of old oaks, where they should stand alone with plenty of room to develop. They are good

container subjects while young but are not handsome out of bloom. They develop better form and heavier foliage in open ground. In Zones 4–6, grow them in containers so you can move them into winter protection, or plant beneath overhang or near wall.

Best-known varieties have very large semidouble flowers with deeply fluted and curled inner petals. These inner petals give great depth to flower. All bloom January to May in California, January to April in Southwest, March to May in Northwest. The following varieties are the best choices for garden use.

'Buddha'. Rose pink flower of very large size; inner petals unusually erect and wavy. Gaunt, open; fast growth.

'Butterfly Wings'. Loose semidouble flower of great size (reported up to 9 in. across), rose pink; petals broad and wavy. Growth open, rather narrow.

'Captain Rawes'. Reddish rose pink semidouble flowers of large size. Vigorous, bushy plant with good foliage. Hardiest of the reticulatas.

'Chang's Temple'. True variety is large, open-centered, deep rose flower, with notched and fluted

Camellia reticulata

center petals. 'Cornelian' (see below) is sometimes sold as 'Chang's Temple'.

'Cornelian'. Large, deep, irregular peony-form flowers with wavy petals, rosy pink to red, heavily variegated with white. Vigorous plant with big leaves that are usually marked with white or yellow. This variety is often sold as 'Chang's Temple' (see description above) or as 'Lion Head'. The true 'Lion Head' is not found in North American gardens.

'Crimson Robe'. Very large, bright red semidouble flowers.

Petals firm textured and wavy. Vigorous plant of better appearance than most reticulatas.

'Purple Gown'. Large, purplish red peony-form to formal double flowers. Compact; best growth habit and foliage in the group.

'Shot Silk'. Large, loose semidouble flowers of brilliant pink with iridescent finish that sparkles in sunlight. Fast, rather open growth.

'Tali Queen'. Very large, deep reddish pink, loose semidouble flowers with heavily crinkled petals. Plant form and foliage very good. Often sold as 'Noble Pearl'; true 'Noble Pearl' is not available in North America.

C. rusticana. SNOW CAMELLIA. To 6–12 ft. tall, 3–10 ft. wide. A class of small-flowered camellias from a cold, extremely snowy part of Japan. Flowers may be white, pink, or red, and single to double in form. Plants tend to be spreading, and branches are remarkably supple. They are no hardier than *C. japonica* and are generally considered to be a subspecies (*C. j. rusticana*).

C. saluenensis. Shrub of dense, leafy growth to 10–15 ft. tall and wide. Leaves elliptic, rather narrow, pointed, thick textured, 1½–2½ in. long and half as wide. Early spring flowers are bell shaped and rather small, varying in color from white to fairly deep pink. Not of great value in itself, it has brought floriferousness, hardiness, and graceful appearance to a large group of its hybrids.

C. sasanqua. Useful broadleafed evergreens for espaliers, ground covers, informal hedges, screening, containers, and bonsai. Plants vary in form from spreading and vinelike to upright and densely bushy; sizes range from 1½ ft. high and 6 ft. wide to 12 ft. tall and wide. Leaves are dark green, shiny, 1½–3½ in. long, a third as wide. Flowers, heavily produced in autumn and early winter, are short lived, rather flimsy, but so numerous that plants make a show for months. Some are lightly fragrant.

Most sasanquas tolerate much sun, and some will thrive in full hot sun with right soil and regular water. The sasanquas are hardy in camellia areas of Pacific Northwest, but flowers are too often damaged by fall and winter rains and frost to call them successful.

'Apple Blossom'. Single white flowers blushed with pink, from pink buds. Upright, somewhat leggy plant.

'Bonanza'. Early. Scarlet-red semidouble flowers. Low-growing, spreading plant.

'Cleopatra'. Rose pink semidouble flowers with narrow, curving petals. Growth is erect, fairly compact. Takes clipping well.

'Hana Jiman'. Large white semidouble flowers with pink edges. Fast, open growth; good espalier.

'Jean May'. Double, shell pink flowers. Compact, upright grower with glossy foliage.

'Kanjiro'. Large semidouble flowers of rose pink shading to rose red at petal edges. Erect growth habit.

'Mine-No-Yuki' ('White Doves'). Large, full peony-form flower. Drops many buds. Spreading, willowy growth; effective espalier.

'Momozono-Nishiki'. Large semidouble flowers are rose, fading to white near the center.

'Setsugekka'. Large, white semidouble flowers with fluted petals. Blossoms have substance; cut sprays hold well in water. Upright and rather bushy shrub.

'Tanya'. Deep rose pink single flowers. Good ground cover.

'Yuletide'. Profusion of small, single, bright red flowers on dense, compact, upright plant.

C. sinensis (Thea sinensis). TEA. In the West, the tea plant grows as a dense round shrub to 15 ft. tall and wide, with leathery, dull dark green leaves to 5 in. long. White, 1½-in.-wide, fragrant fall flowers. Takes well to pruning. Can be trimmed as hedge. Tea can be grown in California but has never been a major crop for economic reasons. 'Blushing Maiden' bears pink flowers, 'Teabreeze' especially fragrant white ones.

C. × vernalis. Certain camellias once classed as sasanquas have been placed here because they bloom later, are often denser in growth, shinier in leaf, and have firmer-textured flowers. They are generally sold as sasanquas. The best-known varieties, both to 9 ft. tall and 6 ft. wide, are the following two.

'Dawn'. Single to semidouble, small white flowers blushed pink. Dense, upright, hardy shrub.

'Hiryu'. Deep red, small, roseform double blooms on a dense, upright plant. 'Hiryu Nishiki' has white markings on flowers.

Hybrid camellias. This term refers to camellias resulting from crosses between two or more species. Several categories of hybrids, described here, have been produced.

C

Medium-flowered hybrids. The first wave of hybridizing involved *C. japonica* and *C. saluenensis.* The resulting hybrids, most of them medium to large shrubs, are of generally good garden form, with foliage like that of *C. japonica* and abundant flowers. See *C. japonica* for explanations of bloom season and flower-size terminology.

'Coral Delight'. Midseason. Coral pink semidouble flowers form garlands along the branches. Slow grower.

'Donation'. Midseason. Large semidouble flowers of orchid pink borne all along stems. Blooms young and heavily on vigorous, somewhat spreading, compact plant with slightly pendulous branches. Quite resistant to cold and sun. Appreciates a little shade in hot, dry areas. There is a form with variegated flowers.

'E. G. Waterhouse'. Midseason to late. Medium formal double of excellent form. Light pink flowers heavily produced on vigorous, upright shrub.

'Fragrant Pink'. Midseason. An exception in that it is a cross between *C. j. rusticana* (*C. rusticana*) and *C. lutchuensis.* Loose peony-form flowers on spreading bush. Flowers are small, deep pink, very fragrant.

'Freedom Bell'. Midseason. Small to medium semidouble, bell-shaped blooms of dark red open beneath branches.

'J. C. Williams'. Early to late. Medium single, cup-shaped flowers of purplish pink over very long season. Vigorous, upright shrub with rather pendulous branches. This and the similar 'Mary Christian' and 'St. Ewe' are good plants for the Pacific Northwest.

'Jury's Yellow'. Early to late. Medium anemone-form blooms with ivory white outer petals, creamy yellow central petaloids. Compact, upright.

'Taylor's Perfection'. Midseason. Profuse light pink semidouble flowers. Fast growing; ideal for trellis or espalier.

Large-flowered hybrids. A second wave of hybridizing, involving *C. japonica* and *C. reticulata,* produced plants that are more spectacular in blossom than the hybrids described above. See *C. japonica* for explanations of bloom season and flower-size terminology.

'Dr. Clifford Parks'. Midseason. Very large blossoms in an orange-toned rich red are semidouble to loose peony form to anemone form. Vigorous, upright plant.

'Flower Girl'. Early to midseason. Large to very large, semidouble to peony-form flowers of bright pink. Vigorous, upright growth. Profuse flowering and small leaves come from its sasanqua parent, big flowers from its reticulata ancestor.

'Francie L.' Midseason to late. Very large semidouble flowers with upright, wavy petals. Deep rose pink.

'Valentine Day'. Midseason to late. Large to very large, salmon pink formal double flowers. Upright grower.

'Valley Knudsen'. Midseason to late. Large to very large, deep orchid pink blooms, semidouble to loose peony form. Compact upright growth.

Hardy hybrids. These camellias, bred from *C. oleifera,* are probably the hardiest of all; they withstand temperatures to –10°F/–23°C given an overhead tree canopy and protection from cold, drying winds. Most produce semidouble flowers; bloom period is fall and winter. Pink varieties include 'Winter's Beauty', 'Winter's Charm', 'Winter's Dream', 'Winter's Fire', 'Winter's Interlude', 'Winter's Peony', and 'Winter's Rose'; white ones include 'Polar Ice', 'Snow Flurry', 'Winter's Hope', and 'Winter's Waterlily'. 'Winter's Star' is purplish red.

CAMPANULA
BELLFLOWER
Campanulaceae (Lobeliaceae)
MOSTLY PERENNIALS;
SOME BIENNIALS OR ANNUALS

🌡	ZONES 1–9, 14–24, EXCEPT AS NOTED
☀ ◐	FULL SUN IN COOLER CLIMATES ONLY
💧 ◐	MODERATE TO REGULAR WATER
▶	SEE CHART NEXT PAGE

Vast and varied group (about 300 species) encompassing trailers, creeping or tufted miniatures, and erect kinds 1–6 ft. or taller. Usually, flower stalks rise above basal leaf rosettes; basal leaves often differ from stem leaves. The perennial species tend to spread indefinitely from the root; width depends mainly on vigor of their rootstocks and time they have been in one spot. Flowers are generally bell shaped, though some are star shaped, cupped, or round and flat. Bloom comes at some time from spring to fall, depending on species. Native throughout the Northern Hemisphere. Kinds featured here come mostly from

Campanula persicifolia
'Telham Beauty'

southern Europe, Turkey, the Caucasus, and northern Asia. *C. lasiocarpa* is a Rocky Mountain and Alaskan native. *C. rotundifolia* is also found in the wild in Alaska.

Uses are as varied as the plants. Gemlike miniatures deserve special settings—close-up situations in rock gardens, niches in dry walls, raised beds, containers. Trailing kinds are ideal for hanging pots or baskets, wall crevices; vigorous, spreading growers serve well as ground covers. Upright growers are valuable in borders, for cutting, occasionally in containers.

Campanulas grow best in good, well-drained soil. Most species are grown fairly easily from seeds sown in spring or early summer. Set out in fall for bloom the following year. Also may be increased by divisions or cuttings. Divide clumps in fall every 3 or 4 years; some may need yearly division. Some species seed freely, and a few have invasive tendencies; may be difficult to remove when entwined with roots of shrubs, trees, or other perennials. For these species, choose sites carefully. Some campanulas are attractive to slugs and snails. Watch for spider mites in hot, dry weather.

CAMPHOR TREE.
See **CINNAMOMUM camphora**

CAMPSIS
TRUMPET CREEPER,
TRUMPET VINE
Bignoniaceae
SEMIEVERGREEN TO DECIDUOUS
VINES

🌡	ZONES VARY BY SPECIES
☀ ◐	FULL SUN OR PARTIAL SHADE
💧 ◐	MODERATE TO REGULAR WATER

Vigorous climbers used for large-scale effects, quick summer screens. All bear radiant, orange-

toned blossoms shaped like flaring trumpets, in clusters at branch tips midsummer to fall. Glossy leaves are divided into 2½-in., ovate leaflets. Stems have aerial rootlets, cling to wood, brick, stucco, and other surfaces. Unless pruned and tied to supporting surface, old plants can become top-heavy and pull away. Each dormant season, shorten some branches and thin others. Pinch back shoot tips in summer to keep plants bushy. Plants spread by suckering roots; pull any that appear. If older plants become unmanageable, cut to ground before spring growth begins and train a few strong new stems.

C. grandiflora (Bignonia chinensis). CHINESE TRUMPET CREEPER. Zones 4–24. Not as vigorous, large, or hardy as the American native *C. radicans,* but flowers are slightly larger and redder. Each leaf has up to nine leaflets. Grows to 30 ft. under ideal conditions. 'Morning Calm' has peach-colored flowers.

Campsis radicans

C. radicans (Bignonia radicans). COMMON TRUMPET CREEPER. Zones 1–21. Native to eastern U.S. Most widely used in cold-winter areas. Deep freeze will kill it to ground, but new stems grow quickly. Each leaf has up to 11 leaflets. Flowers are 3-in.-long orange tubes with scarlet lobes flaring to 2 in. wide. Grows fast to 40 ft. or more, bursting with health and vigor. 'Balboa Sunset' and 'Minnesota Red' have darker red blooms. 'Flava' has yellow blossoms and somewhat lighter green leaves. 'Takarazuka Variegated' ('Summer Snowfall') has leaves marked with white; blooms are orange.

C. × tagliabuana. Zones 3b–24. Hybrid between above two species. 'Mme Galen', best-known variety, has salmon red flowers. 'Crimson Trumpet' bears pure red blooms.

CANARY BIRD BUSH.
See **CROTALARIA agatiflora**

CAMPANULA

NAME, TYPE	GROWTH HABIT, SIZE	FOLIAGE	FLOWERS	USES, COMMENTS
Campanula carpatica (C. turbinata) TUSSOCK BELLFLOWER Perennial	Compact, spreading, leafy tufts, to 6 in. tall. Flower stems upright, branching; usually about 8 in. tall, but may rise 1–1½ ft.	Smooth, bright green, with wavy, toothed edges, 1–1½ in. long. Basal leaves round, often drying up before bloom; stem leaves oval to triangular	Profuse, upward facing, bell or cup shaped, 1–2 in.; light blue, violet, or white. Late spring	Rock gardens, foreground in borders, edging. Variable in flower size and color. 'Blue Chips' and 'White Chips' good dwarf varieties. Easily grown from seed; sometimes sold as 'Blue Clips', 'White Clips'
C. cochleariifolia FAIRY THIMBLES Perennial	Dainty, ground-hugging mat of rosettes from spreading roots. Wiry, erect stems rise 3–6 in. high	Shiny, ¾ in., heart shaped or almost round with 3 large teeth on each side. Stem leaves narrow, lance shaped	Solitary, ½ in., nodding, thimble shaped. 'Bavaria Blue', deep blue; 'Alba', pure white; 'Elizabeth Oliver', multiple powder blue bells, one inside another. All summer in cooler areas	Rock crevices, troughs, between paving stones, edging. Easy to grow, spreads and seeds vigorously
C. collina Perennial	Slow-spreading clump sends up 9–15-in. flowering stems	Basal leaves downy, scallop edged, and heart shaped, on long stems. Stem leaves narrower, smaller	One-sided clusters, each with 1–5 large (1–1½-in.), flaring, deeply cut, nodding bells, usually deep violet blue. Late spring to early summer	Well-behaved garden subject for near front of border, rock garden. Likes moisture, some shade
C. garganica (C. elatines garganica) Perennial Zones 1–9, 14–24	Tight mat, 3–6 in. high, with spreading or trailing flower stems to 6 in.	Small, gray or green, sharply toothed, kidney or heart shaped	Upward-facing, flat, ½-in. stars in violet blue with white centers. One or several atop each stem. 'Baby Blue' is tiny, light blue. Late spring to fall	Rock gardens, troughs, edging. Somewhat like miniature, prostrate C. poscharskyana. 'Dickson's Gold' has golden foliage given enough sun. C. g. fenestrellata is similar to species, but flowering stems incline upward
C. glomerata Perennial Zones A1, A2; 1–10, 14–24	Upright, with erect side branches to 1–2 ft.	Basal leaves broad, wavy edged. Stem leaves broad, toothed. Both somewhat hairy	Narrow, 1-in. bells, flaring at the mouth, in violet, blue, white. Tightly clustered at tops of stems. Spring through summer	Shaded borders or large rock gardens. Plants have proportionately more foliage than flowers. Seed-grown strains include Superba (deepest purple) and Alba (white)
C. isophylla ITALIAN BELLFLOWER, STAR OF BETHLEHEM Perennial Zones 4–9, 14–24	Trailing or hanging soft stems to 2 ft. long, becoming woody at base	Round or heart shaped, light green, toothed, 1–1½ in. long and wide	Loose clusters of upward-facing, light blue, 1-in.-wide stars. 'Alba' has larger, pure white blooms. 'Stella Blue' and 'Stella White' are selections from seed-grown Kristal strain: vigorous, compact, with larger flowers. Late summer, fall (nearly all year in mildest climates)	Hanging baskets, wall pots, tops of walls, rock gardens in filtered shade. Choice ground cover for small areas on slopes in mild-winter climates. In Southern California, best near coast. Indoor/outdoor plant where winters are cold
C. lactiflora Perennial Zones 1–9, 14–24	Erect, branching, leafy, 3½–5 ft. tall	Oblong, pointed, finely toothed, 2–5 in. long	Broadly bell shaped to star shaped, 1 in.; violet to pale blue, white, pink. 'Loddon Anna' is lilac pink. Summer	Rear of border in sun or part shade. Endures even dry shade and is long-lived. 'Pouffe' forms dwarf (10-in.-high) mound covered with lavender blooms
C. lasiocarpa Perennial Zones A1–A3; 1–9, 14–24	Basal tuft to 3 in. high, with flowering stems rising 3–4 in. above foliage	Lower leaves spoon shaped, upper leaves narrow	Usually solitary, 1-in. bells, erect or nearly; violet blue. Summer	Native to Rocky Mountains and Alaska. Rock garden, low carpet plant, in sandy or rocky soil with good drainage
C. medium CANTERBURY BELL, CUP-AND-SAUCER Biennial or annual	Sturdy, hairy, leafy, with erect stems 2½–4 ft. tall. To 1 ft. wide	Lance-shaped, wavy-edged basal leaves 6–10 in. long; stem leaves smaller (3–5 in.)	Bell shaped or urn shaped, 1–2 in.; single or double, held upright in long, loose, open clusters. Purple, violet, blue, lavender, pink, white. Late spring or early summer	Sow seed in late spring for bloom following year, or set out plants from nursery 15–18 in. apart. Good for cutting. 'Calycanthema', commonly called cup-and-saucer, is very popular. Annual variety with bell-shaped (not cup-and-saucer) flowers blooms in 6 months from seed
C. muralis (see C. portenschlagiana)				

C

CAMPANULA

NAME, TYPE	GROWTH HABIT, SIZE	FOLIAGE	FLOWERS	USES, COMMENTS
C. persicifolia PEACH-LEAFED BLUEBELL Perennial	Strong-growing, slender, erect stems 2–3 ft. tall. Plants leafy at base	Basal leaves smooth edged, green, 4–8 in. long. Stem leaves 2–4 in. long, shaped like leaves of peach tree	Open, cup shaped, about 1 in. across, held erect by short side shoots on sturdy stems. Blue, pink, or white. Summer	Choice plant for borders. Easy to grow from seed sown in late spring. 'Telham Beauty', old but still popular, has 3-in. blue flowers. 'Blue Gardenia' and 'White Pearl' have double flowers. 'Powder Puff' has large, white double flowers
C. portenschlagiana (**C. muralis**) DALMATIAN BELLFLOWER Perennial Zones 2–9, 14–24	Low, leafy, mounding or trailing mats 4–6 in. high. Semierect, branching flower stems to 8 in. high	Roundish, heart-shaped, deep green with deeply toothed, slightly wavy edges	Flaring bell shaped, violet blue or grayish white to 1 in. long; several to each stem. Late spring into summer, sometimes blooming again in fall	Fine plant for edging or as small-scale ground cover. Spreads moderately fast; is sturdy, permanent, and not invasive. Easily increased by dividing. 'Resholt' has larger, darker blue flowers
C. poscharskyana SERBIAN BELLFLOWER Perennial Zones 1–12, 14–24	Spreading, mounding, leafy clump to 8 in. high. Branching, semi-upright flower stems to 1 ft. or more	Elongated heart shape, irregularly toothed, slightly hairy, 1–3½ in. long, ¾–3 in. wide	Star-shaped, ½–1-in.-wide blooms in blue lilac, lavender, or grayish white. Spring to early summer	Very vigorous. Shaded border near pools, partially shaded rock gardens, with fuchsias and begonias. Good ground cover for small areas. Needs little water. 'Blue Waterfall' has light blue flowers with white centers
C. punctata Perennial	Flat basal rosette spreads rapidly by underground runners. Wiry 1–1½-ft. flower stems arch over at tip	Dark green, toothed, 4–5 in., heart shaped; leaves narrower on upper stems	Long (2–2½-in.), tubular, waxy, drooping bells; cream through pink to deep maroon, inside paler and spotted with crimson. 'Cherry Bells' is bright, deep rose. Late spring to early summer (scattered bloom until frost)	Forms dense, weed-suppressing mat among shrubs, but too invasive for mixed borders. Some dwarf forms exist
C. pyramidalis CHIMNEY BELLFLOWER Biennial or short-lived perennial Zones 2–9, 14–24	To 2 ft. wide. Sturdy upright stems, unbranched or branched at base, 4–6 ft. or taller	Basal leaves nearly heart shaped, 3–6 in. long with long stalks. Upper leaves lance shaped, stalkless	Dense spikes of 1-in., flat saucers in blue or white. Summer	Back of perennial borders, bays in big shrubbery borders, containers. Stake early to keep stems straight. In cold-winter climates, mulch around plants
C. rotundifolia BLUEBELL OF SCOTLAND, HAREBELL Perennial Zones A1–A3; 1–10, 14–24	Slowly spreading clump, 2–3 in. high. Slender, upright flower stems, some branched, 6–18 in. tall	Green or gray. Basal leaves roundish, long stalked, 1 in.; may dry before bloom. Stem leaves grasslike, 2–3 in.	Broad, bell-shaped bright blue, lavender, or white flowers 1 in. long. One or a few nodding in open clusters	Rock gardens, borders, naturalized under deciduous trees. Self-sows under favorable conditions. 'Olympica' has broader, medium blue bells; dark green, toothed leaves
C. takesimana Perennial Zones A2, A3; 1–9, 14–24	Habit like *C. punctata*, to which it is closely related	Similar to *C. punctata*, but rounder, glossier	Long (2-in.), pendent, pale lilac bells, spotted maroon inside. 'Elizabeth' is deep rosy red with lighter edges. 'Beautiful Trust' has white, deeply split bells, with segments curled back. Early summer	Vigorous, spreading ground cover. Like *C. punctata*, too invasive for mixed borders
C. turbinata (see **C. carpatica**)				

CANNA

Cannaceae
PERENNIALS FROM RHIZOMES

🌿 ZONES 6–9, 12–24; H1, H2; OR DIG AND STORE

☼ FULL SUN

💧 REGULAR WATER DURING GROWTH AND BLOOM

Almost all cannas in nursery trade are hybrids descended from species native to American tropics and subtropics. Large, lance-shaped leaves that may be rich green, bronzy red, or variegated resemble those of banana or ti plants (*Cordyline fruticosa*). Spikes of large, showy, irregularly shaped flowers reminiscent of ginger lilies (*Hedychium*) in red, orange, yellow, pink, cream, white, or bicolors bloom in summer, fall. Old-fashioned garden favorites reach 4–6 ft. tall; lower-growing, more

Canna 'Pretoria'

compact strains include Grand Opera (2 ft.), Pfitzer's Dwarf (2½–3 ft.), Seven Dwarfs (1½ ft.). Once relegated to circular beds on municipal lawns, cannas are undergoing a revival as public taste for tropical effects grows. New varieties too numerous to mention are appearing, many of them flaunting brightly colored leaves as well as showy flowers. Among these are the following 4–6-ft.-tall varieties: 'Minerva' has yellow-striped green leaves and yellow flowers opening from red buds; 'Pretoria' ('Bengal Tiger', 'Striata') has similarly variegated leaves coupled with orange blossoms; 'Tropicanna' ('Phasion') has hot orange blooms over purple foliage that becomes striped with green, yellow, pink, and red. 'Tropicanna Gold' has leaves striped in green and gold; its yellow-orange flowers have dark orange speckles. Two 4-ft. selections with dark foliage are 'Red King Humbert', with reddish bronze leaves and orange-scarlet to red flowers, and 'Wyoming', with bronzy purple foliage and bright orange blooms. 'Black Knight' grows 5–6 ft. high, with blackish bronze foliage and velvety, deep red flowers.

Cannas are most effective in groups of single colors against plain backgrounds. Grow in borders, near poolside, in large pots or tubs on terrace or patio. Leaves useful in arrangements; cut flowers do not keep well. Best adapted to warm- to hot-summer climates; in areas where soil freezes deeply, lift and store over winter. Where hardy in the ground, plant in spring after danger of frost is past. Set rhizomes in rich, loose soil, 2–4 in. deep, 1½–2 ft. apart. For a good head start on bloom in colder regions, start rhizomes indoors 4 to 6 weeks before last frost date; then plant out. Cut each stem to ground after it finishes blooming; new stems will continue

to grow into early fall. Divide clumps every 3 or 4 years.

CANTALOUPE. See **MELON**

CANTERBURY BELL. See **CAMPANULA medium**

CAPE CHESTNUT. See **CALODENDRUM capense**

CAPE COWSLIP. See **LACHENALIA**

CAPE FORGET-ME-NOT. See **ANCHUSA capensis**

CAPE FUCHSIA. See **PHYGELIUS**

CAPE HONEYSUCKLE. See **TECOMA capensis**

CAPE MALLOW. See **ANISODONTEA × hypomandarum**

CAPE MARIGOLD. See **DIMORPHOTHECA**

CAPE PONDWEED. See **APONOGETON distachyus**

CAPE PRIMROSE. See **STREPTOCARPUS**

CAPER. See **CAPPARIS spinosa**

CAPE RUSH. See **CHONDROPETALUM tectorum**

CAPE WEED. See **ARCTOTHECA calendula**

CAPPARIS spinosa
CAPER
Capparidaceae
EVERGREEN OR DECIDUOUS SHRUB

🌿 ZONES 8, 9, 12–24
☼ FULL SUN
○ ● LITTLE TO MODERATE WATER

Native to Mediterranean. Habit varies from sprawling semivine to dense, rounded shrub to 5 ft. tall and wide. Leaves deep green, nearly round, up to 2 in. across (usually less) on vinelike, sometimes spiny branches. In late spring through summer, white, 2–3-in. flowers with showy brushes of lavender stamens rise on

long stalks from every leaf base, open at dawn and close in late afternoon. The pickled unopened buds are commercial capers.

Propagate from cuttings or seed (seeds are slow to sprout and grow). Tolerates poor soil but needs good drainage. Grow as garden curiosity; use sprawling types as ground cover or let spill over a wall.

CARAGANA
PEASHRUB
Fabaceae (Leguminosae)
DECIDUOUS SHRUBS OR SMALL TREES

🌿 ZONES A1–A3; 1–12; EXCEPT AS NOTED
☼ FULL SUN
● MODERATE WATER

Very thorny, spiny plants native to Russia, Manchuria, Siberia. Leaves divided into small leaflets. Spring flowers shaped like bright yellow sweet peas. Useful where choice is limited by cold, heat, wind, bright sun; nearly indestructible in desert, mountain climates. Use as windbreak, cover for wildlife. On the larger species, occasionally prune out old wood to rejuvenate; these can also be clipped as a hedge.

Caragana arborescens

C. arborescens. SIBERIAN PEASHRUB. Fast growing to 20 ft. tall and 15 ft. across; weeping varieties also exist. Leaves to 3 in. long, each with four to six pairs of leaflets.

C. frutex. RUSSIAN PEASHRUB. To 10 ft. tall, 8 ft. wide. Leaves have one or two pairs of 1-in. leaflets.

C. pygmaea. Zones A2, A3; 1–12. May form a 3-ft. mound or grow flat and sprawling to 3–4 ft. wide. Leaves have four ½–¾-in.-long leaflets. No pruning required.

CARAWAY. See **CARUM carvi**

CARDBOARD PALM. See **ZAMIA furfuracea**

CARDINAL CLIMBER. See **IPOMOEA quamoclit**

CARDINAL FLOWER. See **LOBELIA cardinalis**

CARDIOCRINUM giganteum
Liliaceae
PERENNIAL FROM BULB

🌿 ZONES 4–6, 14–17
◐ LIGHT SHADE
● REGULAR WATER

Blossoms of this Himalayan native resemble oversize Easter lilies; glossy dark green leaves are broadly oval to heart-shaped, 1½ ft. long. In summer, foliage rosette gives rise to a leafy stem, 6–12-ft. tall. Stem is flowerless for the first few years, dying back to the ground each fall, but after 3 or

Cardiocrinum giganteum

4 years bears up to 20 fragrant, 6–8-in., white trumpets with dark reddish throats. Flowers set seed, then the whole plant dies—but not before producing many small offset bulbs that grow to flowering size within several years. Set out bulbs (or dig and separate offsets) in early spring or, in mild-winter regions, in fall. Space 2 ft. apart, planting so tops are just beneath soil surface. You can also start new plants from seed, but seedlings may take up to 7 years to reach blooming size. In frost-prone areas, mulch in winter.

CARDOON
Asteraceae (Compositae)
PERENNIAL

🌿 ZONES 4–9, 12–24
☼ FULL SUN
● REGULAR WATER

Mediterranean native classified botanically as *Cynara cardunculus*. Closely related to artichoke but grown for edible leafstalks rather than flower buds. For climate, soil, and other requirements, see Artichoke. To prepare leaves for harvest, blanch them by gathering them together, tying them up,

Capparis spinosa

C

Cardoon

and wrapping with paper to exclude light in late summer to early fall, 4 to 5 weeks before harvesting. To cook, cut heavy leaf midribs into 3–4-in. lengths, parboil until tender, then sauté; or serve boiled with butter or a sauce.

Grown as an ornamental, cardoon is a striking gray-green plant to 5 ft. tall and 4 ft. wide (may reach more than twice that size in the Pacific Northwest), with coarse, spiny, gray-green leaves up to 1½ ft. long. In summer, gray stems produce purple, thistlelike blossoms up to 3 in. across. Blooms can be cut and dried for arrangements. Naturalizes in mild-winter climates; may escape and become a weed.

CAREX

SEDGE
Cyperaceae
PERENNIALS

| ⚡ ZONES VARY BY SPECIES |
| :☀: :◐: FULL SUN OR PARTIAL SHADE, EXCEPT AS NOTED |
| ◌ ◕ ◕ ◕ WATER NEEDS VARY BY SPECIES |

Large group of grasslike, clumping plants found worldwide and grown for foliage effect in borders, rock gardens, containers, water gardens (flowers are generally insignificant); some are used as lawn substitutes, as large-scale ground covers, or erosion control. Long, narrow evergreen leaves are often striped or oddly colored. Specialists offer many varieties. Although characteristically found in damp soils, many sedges will grow under relatively dry conditions in cultivation. Many are short lived in gardens so are used as annuals.

C. barbarae. SANTA BARBARA SEDGE. Zones 4–9, 14–24. A coastal species native from Southern California to Oregon. Rich green leaves 1 ft. long, ½ in. wide

form a slowly spreading clump to 1–3 ft. tall. Good plant for erosion control. Little or no summer water. More aggressive with more water.

C. buchananii. LEATHER LEAF SEDGE. Zones 2b–9, 14–24. From New Zealand. To 3 ft. tall, 2–2½ ft. wide. Curly-tipped, erect blades form clump of striking reddish bronze. Use with gray foliage or with deep greens. Moderate water.

C. comans. NEW ZEALAND HAIR SEDGE. Zones 2b–9, 14–24. Dense, fine-textured clumps reach 1–1½ ft. high. Narrow, silvery green leaves are usually 1 ft. long but may reach 6 ft.; beyond a length of about 2½ ft., they are utterly limp. On flat ground, foliage mounds look about 2½ ft. wide; same is true in areas where foot traffic is common, since leaves often catch on shoes of passersby and snap off. Where leaves are undisturbed on slopes or over ledges, they maintain their length and look like flowing water. 'Bronze' is similar but has coppery brown leaves. Green-leafed selection sold as 'Frosted Curls' or 'Frosty Curls' is usually variety of another sedge, *C. albula*. Moderate water. Occasionally invasive (by self-sowing) in moist areas.

C. conica 'Snowline' ('Marginata'). Zones 3–9, 14–24. Variegated selection of a species native to Japan, Korea. To 2 ft. wide and a little over a foot high, with white-margined dark green leaves. Regular water.

C. divulsa (C. tumulicola). BERKELEY SEDGE. Zones 2b–9, 11–24. Widely sold as the California native *C. tumulicola*, this popular sedge is actually from Europe. Forms arching clumps to 1½ ft. high and 2 ft. wide with spikes of greenish flowers from winter to spring. Shear flowers when they begin to brown with age to keep plants tidy and prevent reseeding. Best in partial shade and with reg-

Carex buchananii

ular water, but grows well under a wide range of conditions. Fine ground cover.

C. elata 'Aurea' ('Bowles Golden'). Zones 2–9, 14–24. Clump to 2½ ft. high, 1½ ft. wide, with narrow leaves that emerge bright yellow in spring and hold some color until late summer. Needs ample moisture; will grow in standing water. Best where it gets some winter chill.

C. flacca (C. glauca). BLUE SEDGE. Zones 3–9, 14–24. From Europe. Many forms of this creeper are in cultivation, ranging from 6 in. to 2 ft. high and wide; foliage may be blue or green. Plant is evergreen only in mildest climates. Not invasive but spreads slowly and can be clipped like a lawn. Endures light foot traffic, moderate shade, competition from tree roots. Tolerates many soils and irrigation schemes; does best with moderate water.

C. flagellifera. Zones 4–9, 14–24. From New Zealand. Closely related to *C. buchananii* and distinguished from it only by small botanical details. It is not quite as erect, and leaves are reddish brown and wider spreading. Moderate water. Often short lived. 'Toffee Twist' grows 10–18 in. high with narrow, iridescent leaves that have a sweeping, almost trailing habit.

C. 'Ice Dance' (C. morrowii 'Ice Dance'). Zones 2b–9, 14–24. Grows 1–2 ft. high and spreads slowly. Dark green leaves edged in creamy white. Good edging or ground cover. Regular water.

C. morrowii. JAPANESE SEDGE. Zones 3–9, 14–24. From Japan. To 1 ft. high, 1½ ft. wide, with shiny, drooping, medium green leaves. Good edging plant; individual plants attractive among stones. Regular water. 'Goldband' ('Fisher's Form') has leaves with creamy yellow margins. Various forms sold as 'Variegata' have leaves edged in white.

C. muskingumensis. PALM SEDGE. Zones 4–9, 14–24. From North America. To 2 ft. tall, spreading widely by rhizomes. Tapering green leaves radiate from lax stems to create the effect of small, feathery palms. Regular water. 'Little Midge', to 10 in. high, is miniature in all its parts. Leaves of 'Oehme' are solid green when new but quickly develop yellow margins.

C. oshimensis 'Evergold' (C. morrowii 'Aurea-variegata'). Zones 3–9, 14–24. Stunning selection of a Japanese native. Clumping growth to 1–2 ft. high, 2–3 ft. wide.

Dark green leaves have a broad central band of creamy white that matures to creamy yellow. Needs shade and regular water.

C. pansa. CALIFORNIA MEADOW SEDGE. Zones 7–9, 11–24. California native. Forms a 6–8-in.-high mat of narrow, dark green leaves that are moderately tolerant of foot traffic; excellent between pavers and stepping-stones. Sometimes used as lawn alternative, with varying success; does best in sandy soil. Needs less care than traditional lawn grasses, but occasional shearing and irrigation will keep it looking its best. Weed control is important during establishment, but it won't tolerate herbicides typically used on lawns.

C. phyllocephala 'Sparkler'. SPARKLER PALM SEDGE. Zones 4–9, 14–24. Selection of a Chinese species. Forms a slowly spreading clump of 1–2-ft.-high, narrow, red-purple stems topped with spirally arranged, dark green leaves edged and striped with creamy white. Candlelike fall blooms, 3–4 in. long, are creamy white, aging to brown. Good-looking ground cover or container plant. Leafy stems are striking in cut-flower arrangements. Best in shady, moist conditions, but will tolerate drier soils.

C. spissa. SAN DIEGO SEDGE. Zones 7–9, 14–17, 19–24. Native to boggy areas in Southern California. Forms slowly spreading clumps. Coarse, upright blue-green leaves to 5 ft. tall. Light golden brown clusters of grass-type flowers appear in spring; cut back after bloom to avoid self-seeding. Needs ample moisture and will grow in standing water.

C. subfusca. RUSTY SEDGE, MOUNTAIN SEDGE. Zones 7–9, 11–24. Low-growing, spreading native of western North America. Dark green leaves to 8–12 in. high form a dense, meadowlike carpet. Native to moist, shady areas but can take sun and some drought. Control spread with edgings or by keeping surrounding areas dry.

C. testacea. Zones 4–9, 14–24. From New Zealand. To 2 ft. tall, 3 ft. wide. Widely arching clumps of light green and reddish brown foliage; leaves develop red and orange highlights in good light. Some tendency to self-seed and spread under moist conditions. Moderate water. Often short lived.

C. texensis (C. retroflexa texensis). CATLIN SEDGE. Zones 7–9, 11–24. Southwestern native.

C

Fine-textured, clumping sedge to 4–6 in. high. Medium green, drooping leaves form a wavy carpet. Excellent small-scale lawn substitute or ground cover. Mow to remove seed heads. Regular water.

CARIBBEAN COPPER PLANT.
See **EUPHORBIA** cotinifolia

CARICA. See **PAPAYA**

CARICATURE PLANT.
See **GRAPTOPHYLLUM pictum**

CARISSA macrocarpa
NATAL PLUM
Apocynaceae
EVERGREEN SHRUB

☀	ZONES 22–24; H2; AND SEE BELOW
☀ ☽	BEST IN SUN; TOLERATES SOME SHADE
○ ◑ ●	LITTLE TO REGULAR WATER

Natal plum's best climates are Zones 22–24 and H2, but so many gardeners find this South African native appealing that it is also grown in Zones 12, 13, 16–21—far beyond safe limits. Fast-growing, strong, upright, rounded shrub of rather loose habit to 5–7 ft. tall and wide (occasionally much larger). Oval, leathery, 3-in. leaves are lustrous rich green. Spines along branches and at end of each twig discourage trespassers.

Carissa macrocarpa

Blooms throughout the year, bearing white flowers almost as fragrant as those of star jasmine (*Trachelospermum jasminoides*) and with the same five-petaled star shape, but larger (to 2 in. across). Blossoms followed by oval, 1–1½-in., fleshy red or purple fruits. Flowers, green fruit, and ripe fruit often appear together. Fruit has cranberrylike flavor and can be eaten fresh or used in jelly, sauce, pie.

Natal plum is easy to grow and accepts a variety of soils. Excellent in ocean wind, salt spray. Prune to

control erratic growth (milky sap oozes from cut stems). Used mainly as screen or hedge in Zones 22–24 and H2; tolerates clipping as formal hedge. In less favorable zones, give it the same protected spot you'd give bougainvillea: warm wall facing south or west, preferably with overhang to keep off frost. Keep it away from walkways—spinniness is a hazard to passersby. Can also be grown as indoor plant in good light.

'Boxwood Beauty'. Exceptionally compact, thornless growth to 2 ft. high and wide. Deep green leaves like those of large-leafed boxwood (*Buxus*). Good for hedging and shaping.

'Fancy'. More upright growth than species, with unusually large fruit.

'Green Carpet'. Low grower to 1–1½ ft. high, spreading to 4 ft. or wider. Smaller leaves than those of species. Excellent ground cover.

'Horizontalis'. To 1½–2 ft. high, spreading, trailing. Dense foliage.

'Prostrata'. Vigorous spreader to 2 ft. high; good ground cover. Prune out any upright growth. Can be trained as espalier.

'Tomlinson'. Thornless. Compact, slow growth to 2–2½ ft. high, 3 ft. wide. Good tub or foundation plant.

'Tuttle' ('Nana Compacta Tuttlei'). Compact, dense growth to 2–3 ft. high, 3–5 ft. wide. Heavy production of flowers and fruit. Effective as a ground cover.

'Variegata'. Grows 2–4 ft. tall, 3–6 ft. wide. Dark green leaves have creamy to yellow variegation.

CARMEL CREEPER.
See **CEANOTHUS griseus horizontalis**

CARNATION.
See **DIANTHUS caryophyllus**

CARNEGIEA gigantea
SAGUARO
Cactaceae
CACTUS

☀	ZONES 12, 13, 18–21
☀	FULL SUN
○	NO IRRIGATION NEEDED

Long-lived desert native grows very slowly to 50 ft. tall; in the wild, may be a column only 3 ft. high after 30 years. Typically produces branches after attaining 12–15 ft. Prominent ribs give fluted appearance. Light brown, ½–3-in.-long spines. Mature

plants bloom in late spring; 3–5-in.-long, single white blossoms (state flower of Arizona) open at night and remain open until next afternoon. Edible oval fruits, sometimes mistaken for flowers, split open to show red pulp.

This is a protected species. When buying a mature specimen, be sure it was collected legally. When choosing a nursery-grown plant, look for one with a good root system. Adapted to dry conditions, but regular water and fertilizer will speed growth. Provide good drainage.

Carnegiea gigantea

CAROB.
See **CERATONIA siliqua**

CAROLINA ALLSPICE.
See **CALYCANTHUS floridus**

CAROLINA JESSAMINE.
See **GELSEMIUM sempervirens**

CAROLINA LAUREL CHERRY.
See **PRUNUS caroliniana**

CARPENTERIA californica
BUSH ANEMONE
Philadelphaceae
EVERGREEN SHRUB

☀	ZONES 5–9, 14–24
☀ ☽	PARTIAL SHADE IN HOTTEST CLIMATES
○ ◑	LITTLE TO MODERATE WATER

Native to a very restricted area in foothills of southern Sierra Nevada in California's Central Valley. Attractive, formal-looking shrub grows slowly to 4–6 ft. tall and wide; many stems rise from base. Older bark light colored and peeling; new shoots, purplish. Thick, narrow, 2–4½-in.-long leaves, dark green above, whitish beneath. In late spring and summer, clusters of

Carpenteria californica

scented, 1½–3-in., yellow-centered white flowers like anemones appear at branch ends. Cutting-grown variety 'Elizabeth' is similar.

Accepts ordinary garden conditions. Inspect occasionally for aphid or mite infestation. Resistant to oak root fungus. If pruning is necessary to shape or restrain growth, do so after flowering.

CARPET BUGLE. See **AJUGA**

CARPINUS
HORNBEAM
Betulaceae
DECIDUOUS TREES

☀	ZONES VARY BY SPECIES
☀ ☽ ●	EXPOSURE NEEDS VARY BY SPECIES
●	REGULAR WATER

Well-behaved, relatively small shade trees. Long life and good habits as street trees. Slow to moderate growth rate. Very hard, tough, heavy wood. Dark green, sawtooth-edged leaves color up in cold-winter climates, hang on late in season. Fruits (small, hard nutlets in leaflike bracts) carried in attractive drooping clusters to 5 in. long. Mature trees need little or no pruning.

C. betulus. EUROPEAN HORNBEAM. Zones 2–9, 14–17. Native Europe to Iran. Dense, pyramidal tree to 40 ft. high and eventually as broad as tall, with drooping outer branches.

Carpinus betulus

▶

C

Carpinus betulus

Handsome, furrowed gray bark somewhat similar to that of *C. caroliniana*. Leaves are 2–5 in. long, turn yellow or dark red in fall. Best in full sun but tolerates light shade. Sometimes clipped into a hedge or screen. Subject to infestation by scale insects. 'Fastigiata' is the variety commonly sold; despite its name (which implies very upright growth), it develops an oval-vase shape with age. 'Frans Fontaine' is the narrowest variety, to 35 ft. high and only 15 ft. wide, with inward-turning branches.

C. caroliniana. AMERICAN HORNBEAM. Zones 1–9, 14–17. Native to eastern North America. Round headed, to 25–30 ft. tall and wide, sometimes larger; can be grown as single- or multi-trunked tree. Smooth blue-gray bark with undulations that look like muscles flexing beneath the surface. Leaves are 1–3 in. long, turn mottled yellow and red (sometimes mostly yellow) in fall; drop before those of *C. betulus*. Does well in exposures from full sun to heavy shade.

CARPOBROTUS
ICE PLANT
Aizoaceae
SUCCULENT WOODY-BASED
PERENNIALS

✂	ZONES VARY BY SPECIES
☼	FULL SUN
◌ ◉	LITTLE TO MODERATE WATER

Trailing plants with coarse, succulent leaves and summer blooms; useful for covering sunny banks (but not steep banks, since their weight could cause the soil to

Carpobrotus chilensis

slide). Plant about 1½ ft. apart. Can rot in very wet conditions; can suffer dieback if severely stressed by lack of water or nitrogen during growth season. Scale insects can cause problems.

C. chilensis (Mesembryanthemum aequilaterale). Zones 12–24. Probably from South Africa; naturalized along coast, Oregon to Baja California. Straight, three-sided, fleshy leaves are 2 in. long; flowers lightly fragrant, rosy purple, about 2 in. across.

C. edulis (Mesembryanthemum edule). HOTTENTOT FIG. Zones 12–24; H1, H2. From South Africa. Curved, 4–5-in.-long leaves; pale yellow to rose, 4-in.-wide flowers. Figlike fruit is edible but not particularly tasty.

CARROT
Apiaceae (Umbelliferae)
BIENNIAL GROWN AS ANNUAL

✂	ALL ZONES
☼	FULL SUN
◉	REGULAR WATER

Carrot

Probably native to Afghanistan. The variety to plant depends on the soil: carrots reach smooth perfection only in light-textured soil that is free of stones and clods. Plant long market kinds only if you can give them a foot of this ideal soil. If you can provide only a few inches, plant half-long varieties such as 'Nantes' and 'Chantenay' or miniature types like 'Lady Finger', 'Short 'n Sweet', or 'Thumbelina' (a short, round carrot). Miniature carrots are also ideal for growing in a container vegetable garden.

Sow lightly in rows at least 1 ft. apart. Soil should be fine enough for root development and loose enough so crusting can't check

sprouting of seeds. If crust should form, keep soil soft by sprinkling. Too much nitrogen or manure will result in excessive top growth and cause forking of roots. Maintain even soil moisture: alternating dry and wet conditions cause split roots. To grow successive plantings, sow seed when previous planting is up and growing; in cold-winter climates, make last sowing 70 days before anticipated killing frost. When tops are 1–2 in. high, thin plants to 1½ in. apart; thin again if roots begin to crowd. Use thinnings steamed in butter or in salads. After first thinning, work in narrow band of commercial fertilizer 2 in. out from the row. Begin harvest when carrots reach finger size, usually 30 to 40 days after sowing; most types reach maturity in 60 to 70 days. In mild-winter climates, carrots store well in the ground; dig as needed.

CARROT WOOD. See **CUPANIOPSIS anacardioides**

CARTHAMUS tinctorius
SAFFLOWER, FALSE SAFFRON
Asteraceae (Compositae)
ANNUAL

✂	ZONES 1–24; H1, H2
☼	FULL SUN
◉	MODERATE WATER

Carthamus tinctorius

This thistle relative (probably an Asian native) is ornamental as well as useful. To 3 ft. tall, 1–1½ ft. wide, with erect, spiny-leafed stems. In summer, bears orange-yellow flower heads above leafy bracts; inner bracts are spiny. Durable cut flower, fresh or dried. Popular in Hawaii for use in leis. Grown commercially for oil extracted from the seeds. The dried flowers have been used for seasoning in place of true saffron, which they somewhat resemble in color and flavor. Sow seeds in

place in spring after frost danger is past. An ornamental spineless form is also available.

CARUM carvi
CARAWAY
Apiaceae (Umbelliferae)
BIENNIAL

✂	ZONES 1–24
☼	FULL SUN
◉	REGULAR WATER

From meadows and grasslands of Asia Minor. Mound of carrotlike leaves grows from taproot to 1–2 ft. high in first year. In second spring, umbrellalike clusters of white flowers rise above foliage; after seeds ripen in midsummer, plant dies. Start seeds in place in fall or early spring; thrives in well-drained soil. Thin seedlings to 1½ ft. apart. Use for flavoring vegetables, pickles, baked goods.

Carum carvi

CARYA illinoinensis. See **PECAN**

CARYOPTERIS
BLUEBEARD
Verbenaceae
DECIDUOUS SHRUBS

✂	ZONES VARY BY SPECIES
☼	FULL SUN
◉	MODERATE WATER

Asian natives valued for contribution of cool blue to flower borders from midsummer to frost. Bear dense stalked clusters of small flowers on current season's growth. Erect form. Generally grown as woody-based perennials —if plants don't freeze back in winter, cut them nearly to ground before spring growth flush to ensure good base for new season's growth. Trim after each wave of bloom to encourage repeat flower-

C

Caryopteris
× clandonensis

...ng. Provide good drainage, since ...lants can rot in wet soil.

C. × clandonensis. BLUE MIST. Zones 2b–9, 14–24. Low-growing mound (to 2 ft. tall and ...vide) of narrow, 3-in.-long leaves. ...lusters of small flowers top ...pper parts of stems. 'Azure', 'Heavenly Blue', and compact 'Petit Bleu' bear deep blue blossoms. 'Dark Knight' and 'Longwood Blue' have deep blue flowers and silvery foliage; 'Worcester Gold' ...as yellow leaves, lavender-blue ...looms. 'Pink Chablis' has pastel pink blooms.

C. incana (C. mastacanthus). COMMON BLUEBEARD, BLUE SPIRAEA. Zones 4–9, 14–24. ...aller than *C. × clandonensis*, ...with looser, more open growth to ...–4 ft. tall, 5 ft. wide. Lavender-blue flowers appear in leaf joints. 'Jason' ('Sunshine Blue') has golden yellow leaves and medium blue ...lowers.

C. odorata. HIMALAYAN BLUEBEARD. Zones 6–9, 14–24. ...o 8 ft. tall, 5 ft. wide, with shiny green foliage and purplish pink ...lower clusters at branch ends.

CARYOTA

FISHTAIL PALM
Arecaceae (Palmae)
PALMS

⚡ ZONES 23, 24; H2; OR INDOORS

☼ ◑ SUN OR PART SHADE; BRIGHT INDIRECT LIGHT

💧 REGULAR WATER

These Southeast Asian natives are feather palms with huge, finely divided leaves made up of leaflets flattened and split at tips like fish tails. Plant in humus-rich soil that provides good drainage. Individual trunks die after flowering, which may not occur for 20 to 25 years.

C. mitis. CLUSTERED FISHTAIL PALM. Slow grower to 10–40 ft. tall, spreading 10–22 ft. Basal offshoots eventually form clustered trunks. Foliage light green. Very tender; thrives only in ideal environment.

C. ochlandra. CANTON FISH-TAIL PALM. Will probably reach 25 ft. and spread half as wide. Medium dark green leaves. Hardiest of the caryotas, it has survived to 26°F/–3°C.

C. urens. FISHTAIL WINE PALM. Handsome single-stemmed palm grows to 50 ft. tall and 15 ft. wide in Southern California. A hardy, high-mountain selection, it is reported to withstand 20°F/7°C once established. Arching, dark green leaves. Avoid handling fruit with bare hands; invisible crystals can cause severe itching.

Caryota ochlandra

CASCADE PALM. See **CHAMAE-DOREA cataractarum**

CASCALOTE.
See **CAESALPINIA cacalaco**

CASCARA.
See **RHAMNUS purshiana**

CASHMERE BOUQUET.
See **CLERODENDRUM bungei**

CASIMIROA edulis.
See **WHITE SAPOTE**

CASSIA

Fabaceae (Leguminosae)
EVERGREEN, SEMIEVERGREEN, AND DECIDUOUS TREES

⚡ ZONES VARY BY SPECIES

☼ FULL SUN

◔◑● WATER NEEDS VARY BY SPECIES

The genus *Cassia* once included many yellow-flowered trees and shrubs now reclassified as *Senna* (see that entry), though some are still sold under their old names. These cassias are showy flowering trees that brighten landscapes in the warmest climates—not just with yellow blooms but also with pink, cerise, and white ones. Flowering dates are approximate, since plants may bloom at any time or bloom intermittently over a long period. Most have long, round seedpods that can present a litter problem. Plant in soil that is well drained. Prune plants when young (to develop a strong framework) and as needed after flowering.

Cassia fistula

C. fistula. GOLDEN SHOWER, YELLOW SHOWER, INDIAN LABURNUM. Semievergreen to deciduous. Zone H2. From India. To 30–40 ft. high and 35 ft. wide. Prized for long, pendent yellow flower clusters borne from spring to fall. Medium green leaves divided into 4–8 pairs of leaflets. A specimen for garden, park, street planting. Good drought tolerance; flowers best in hot, dry locations. Takes little water.

C. grandis. PINK SHOWER, CORAL SHOWER. Deciduous. Zone H2. From tropical America. Fast growing to 20–50 ft. tall and 30 ft. wide. Abundant coral pink flowers in early spring. Leaves divided into 8–20 pairs of small leaflets, pink when young. Use for color accent or as shade, street, or park tree. Somewhat drought tolerant but grows and blooms best with regular water.

C. javanica. PINK AND WHITE SHOWER. Deciduous. Zone H2. From Indonesia. To 30–35 ft. high and 25 ft. wide, with irregular habit. Masses of light pink flowers along branches from spring to fall, peaking in early summer. Leaves divided into 5–15 pairs of oval, 1–2-in.-long leaflets. Useful as color accent or shade, street, or park tree. Good wind tolerance; moderate drought and salt tolerance. Best with moderate water.

C. leptophylla. GOLD MEDAL-LION TREE. Nearly evergreen. Zones 15, 16, 20–24; H1, H2. Native to Brazil. Open-headed, fast-growing tree to 20–25 ft. tall, 30 ft. wide; low spreading with tendency to weep. Very shapely and graceful when pruned to single trunk (otherwise, becomes sprawling). Deep yellow flowers to 3 in. wide come in 6–8-in.-long spikes; main bloom in summer; sporadic bloom later. Little to moderate water.

C. × nealiae. RAINBOW SHOWER. Semievergreen to deciduous. Zone H2. A sterile hybrid between *C. fistula* and *C. javanica*, originating in Hawaii. Moderately fast grower to 30–40 ft. high and 35 ft. wide. Dark green foliage. Thrives in any well-drained soil. Withstands drought well but has only moderate wind tolerance and poor salt tolerance.

Several named varieties are available in a range of flower colors from pale yellow through golden yellow to orange and cerise—the "rainbow" of the common name. Some may produce occasional seedpods.

Cassia × nealiae

'Lunalilo Yellow'. Flowers open to a bright yellow orange, then age to yellow. Late spring to fall bloom.

'Nii Gold'. A sport of 'Wilhelmina Tenney'. Blooms any time from spring to fall; deep gold buds open to blooms that age to strong yellow.

'Queen's Hospital White'. Flowers open pale yellow, fade rapidly to very light yellow to white. Blooms in spring to late summer.

'Wilhelmina Tenney'. Spectacular blossom clusters from spring to fall. Petal exteriors are deep cerise aging to paler shades; interiors are yellow. Adopted as the official tree of Honolulu.

CASTANEA. See **CHESTNUT**

C

CASTANOPSIS
cuspidata

JAPANESE CHINQUAPIN,
COPPER FALSE CHESTNUT
Fagaceae
EVERGREEN TREE

⚡ ZONES 7–9, 14–24

☀ ◑ FULL SUN OR LIGHT SHADE

◐ ◉ MODERATE TO REGULAR WATER

This subtropical relative of oaks
and chestnuts is native to Japan
(where it is widely grown in gardens and parks) and China. Fairly
slow growing to 25–45 ft. tall,
20–25 ft. wide. Drooping branches
bear glossy, leathery, slender-
tipped oval leaves that are deep
green above, bronze below. Bark is
gray and narrowly grooved. Inconspicuous flowers are carried in
erect catkins. Clusters of edible
acornlike nuts, covered with
downy husks, take 2 years to
ripen. Requires well-drained soil.
Resistant to chestnut blight. Handsome tree for garden or parking
strip. 'Shogun' is cutting grown.

Castanopsis cuspidata

CASTANOSPERMUM
australe

MORETON BAY CHESTNUT
Fabaceae (Leguminosae)
EVERGREEN TREE

⚡ ZONES 18–22

☀ FULL SUN

◉ REGULAR WATER

⚠ RAW SEEDS ARE POISONOUS
   IF INGESTED

Native to Australia. Beautiful in
foliage; spectacular in flower. To
50–60 ft. tall, nearly as wide. Large,
shiny, dark green leaves are divided
into 11–15 leaflets about 1½ by 5 in.
Bright red-and-yellow flowers in
stiff spikes about 8 in. long; they
grow from twigs, branches, and
main trunk in summer. Seeds look
like chestnuts but are toxic raw;
they may be eaten safely if roasted
but don't taste very good. Good
lawn or waterside shade tree. Little
pruning required.

*Castanospermum
australe*

CAST-IRON PLANT.
See **ASPIDISTRA elatior**

CASTOR ARALIA.
See **KALOPANAX septemlobus**

CASTOR BEAN.
See **RICINUS communis**

CASUARINA

BEEFWOOD, SHE-OAK
Casuarinaceae
EVERGREEN TREES

⚡ ZONES 8, 9, 12–24; H1, H2

☀ FULL SUN

◐ ◉ ◉ LITTLE TO REGULAR WATER

Native primarily to Australia;
C. equisetifolia is also a Pacific
Island native. Long, thin, jointed,
green branches look like long pine
needles; true leaves are inconspicuous. Tolerate many tough conditions: dry or wet soil, salinity, heat,
wind. Hardy to 15°F/−9°C. Particularly useful in desert areas, where
they are often confused with Athel
tamarisk (*Tamarix aphylla*)
because of similar foliage—but the
casuarinas have conelike fruit.
Cones range from ¼ to 1 in. long in
species described here; those of
C. stricta are largest. Little pruning
required.

C. cunninghamiana. RIVER
SHE-OAK. Tallest and largest
species. To 70 ft. tall, 30 ft. wide.
Finest texture, with dark green
branches.

C. equisetifolia. HORSETAIL
TREE. Fast grower to 40–60 ft. tall,
20 ft. wide. Has pendulous gray-
green branches. Plants sold under
this name may be *C. cunninghamiana* or hybrids between *C. cunninghamiana* and *C. glauca.*

C. stricta (C. verticillata).
MOUNTAIN or DROOPING SHE-
OAK, COAST BEEFWOOD. Fast
grower to 20–35 ft. tall and wide.
Darkest green foliage and largest
cones. Makes beautiful silhouette
against sky. Attractive street tree.
Good at seashore.

Casuarina stricta

CATALINA CHERRY.
See **PRUNUS ilicifolia lyonii**

CATALINA IRONWOOD. See
LYONOTHAMNUS floribundus

CATALINA PERFUME.
See **RIBES viburnifolium**

CATALPA

Bignoniaceae
DECIDUOUS TREES

⚡ ZONES 3–10, 14–24, EXCEPT
   AS NOTED

☀ ◑ FULL SUN OR LIGHT SHADE

◐ ◉ MODERATE TO REGULAR WATER

Catalpas are among the few hardy
deciduous trees that can compete
in flower and leaf with subtropical
species. Large, upright clusters of
trumpet-shaped, 2-in.-wide flowers are pure white, with stripes
and markings in yellow and soft
brown. These are displayed in late
spring and summer above large,
bold, heart-shaped leaves. Flowers
are followed by long, bean-shaped
seed capsules sometimes called
"Indian beans."

Unusually well adapted to
extremes of heat and cold and to
soils throughout the West. Where
winds are strong, plant in lee of
taller trees or buildings to protect
leaves from wind damage. Some
gardeners object to litter of fallen
flowers in summer and seed capsules in autumn. Plants need shaping while young, seldom develop a
well-established dominant shoot.

Shorten side branches as tree
grows. When branching begins at
the desired height, remove lower
branches. On established trees,
head back or thin out any
branches that look out of balance.

For the tree sometimes called
desert catalpa, see *Chilopsis linearis.* Another tree sometimes mistakenly called catalpa is the very
similar *Paulownia tomentosa,* or
empress tree, with lavender flowers. Empress tree shows flower
buds in winter; catalpa does not.

C. bignonioides. COMMON
CATALPA, INDIAN BEAN. Native
to southeastern U.S. Generally
smaller than *C. speciosa.* Grows
to 30–40 ft. tall, with an equal
spread. Leaves are 5–8 in. long,
often arranged in whorls, give off
odd odor when crushed. Becomes
chlorotic in alkaline soil. Resistant
to oak root fungus. Yellow leaves
of 'Aurea' are showier where
summers are cool.

'Nana'. UMBRELLA CATALPA.
A dense globe form usually
grafted high on *C. bignonioides;*
almost always sold as *C. bungei.* It
never blooms. Usually around 6 ft.
high, 5 ft. wide; cut it back to keep
it in scale.

C. × erubescens 'Purpurea'.
Selection of a hybrid between
C. bignonioides and a Chinese
species; resembles *C. bignonioides.*
Young leaves and branchlets are
deep blackish purple, turning purplish green in summer.

Catalpa speciosa

C. speciosa. Zones 2–24. Native
to central U.S. Most widely distributed catalpa in the West. Round-
headed tree to 40–60 ft. tall,
20–40 ft. wide. Leaves 6–12 in.
long, odorless when
crushed. Fewer
flowers per
cluster than for
C. bignonioides.

Catalpa speciosa

CATANANCHE
caerulea
CUPID'S DART
Asteraceae (Compositae)
PERENNIAL

- 🌿 ZONES 1–10, 14–24
- ☀️ FULL SUN
- 💧 MODERATE WATER

Wispy, free-flowering plant from Europe, good for summer borders and fresh or dried arrangements. Gray-green, grassy leaves form a clump to 1 ft. high and wide. Lavender-blue, 2-in. flower heads, reminiscent of cornflowers and surrounded by strawlike, shining bracts, appear atop leafless, 2-ft. stems. Remove faded flowers to prolong bloom. 'Alba' has white blossoms, 'Major' deep blue-violet blooms. Plants will flower first year from seed sown in early spring. Rather short lived, but volunteer seedlings usually provide replacements.

Catananche caerulea

CATHARANTHUS
roseus (Vinca rosea)
MADAGASCAR PERIWINKLE
Apocynaceae
PERENNIAL USUALLY GROWN AS ANNUAL

- 🌿 ZONES 1–24; H1, H2
- ☀️◐ FULL SUN OR PARTIAL SHADE
- 💧 MODERATE WATER

Native to Madagascar. Good for summer-to-fall color in hot climates; thrives in dry or humid heat. Glossy green, 1–3-in.-long leaves cover bushy plant 1–2 ft. high and wide. Phloxlike, 1½-in. flowers in pure white, white with rose or red eye, blush pink, or bright rose. Blooms all summer and keeps flowering after marigolds and zinnias have finished—until Thanksgiving if weather stays mild. Lives over in frost-free areas but may look ragged in winter. In desert regions, may also

Catharanthus roseus

look poor in late summer. Self-sows readily. Provide good drainage and avoid overwatering.

Pacific and Cooler series are compact 15-in. plants with large (2-in.) flowers. The Little series grows 8–10 in. high. Creeping strains, including the Carpet series, grow 4–8 in. tall, 1½ ft. wide. The Mediterranean series, featuring apricot, pink, rose, lilac, or white blooms, grows 5–6 in. high and can spread 2½ ft. wide; it's useful as temporary ground cover or in hanging baskets. All types will bloom first season from seed sown early indoors or in a greenhouse or cold frame. Tropicana series blooms in only 60 days from seed, bears blooms in shades of pink and coral on 1-ft. plants. Nurseries sell plants of the many varieties in late spring.

CATMINT. See **NEPETA faassenii**

CATNIP. See **NEPETA cataria**

CAT'S CLAW. See **MACFADYENA unguis-cati**

CAT'S EARS. See **CALOCHORTUS**

CAT THYME. See **TEUCRIUM marum**

CATTLEYA
Orchidaceae
EPIPHYTIC ORCHIDS

- 🌿 ZONE H2; OR INDOORS
- ◐ LIGHT SHADE; BRIGHT INDIRECT LIGHT
- 💧 REGULAR WATER

Native to tropical America. Among most popular and best known of orchids. Showy flowers are used for corsages.

Species, varieties, and hybrids are too numerous to list here. All have pseudobulbs 1–3 in. thick, bearing leathery leaves and a stem topped with one to four or more flowers. Plants range in size from a few inches tall to 2 ft. or more. Commercial growers offer a wide range of flower colors, including lavender and purple, white, and semialbas (white blossoms with colored lip). Also available are novelties in yellow, orange, red, green, and bronze (many of these are crosses between *Cattleya* and other genera).

Cattleya

Cattleyas are widely grown outdoors year-round in Hawaii, either in containers or naturalized on trees. Elsewhere, they are indoor plants that can be brought outdoors during warm weather. They grow best in a greenhouse where temperature, humidity, and light can be readily controlled. However, they can be grown successfully as houseplants if the following needs are satisfied: (1) warm temperatures (55 to 60°F/13 to 16°C at night, 65 to 80°F/18 to 27°C or higher during the day); (2) relatively high humidity (50 to 60 percent or more); (3) bright indirect light with protection from hot midday sun. Leaves should be light green and held erect; if light intensity is too low, they turn dark green and new growth becomes soft.

CAULIFLOWER
Brassicaceae (Cruciferae)
ANNUAL OR BIENNIAL GROWN AS ANNUAL

- 🌿 ALL ZONES
- ☀️ FULL SUN
- 💧 REGULAR WATER

Related to broccoli and cabbage; all three are members of the genus *Brassica* and are thought to have originated in the Mediterranean region. All share similar cultural requirements, but cauliflower is more difficult to grow. Easiest in cool, humid regions; where summers are hot, grow it to harvest well before or well after midsummer, and select heat-tolerant varieties. Home gardeners usually plant one of the several 'Snowball' varieties or choose hybrids such as 'Early White Hybrid' and 'Snow Crown Hybrid'. An unusual variety is 'Purple Head', a large plant with a deep purple head that turns green when cooked.

Cauliflower

Start with small plants. Space them 1½–2 ft. apart in rows and leave 3 ft. between rows. Water and fertilize as for broccoli. Be sure to keep plants actively growing; any check in growth is likely to cause premature setting of undersize heads. When heads first appear, tie up the large leaves around them to keep them white. (Leaves of self-blanching varieties curl over developing heads without assistance.) Harvest heads as soon as they reach full size. Most varieties are ready to cut 50 to 100 days after transplanting; overwintering types may take 6 months. Cauliflower is subject to same pests as cabbage.

CEANOTHUS
WILD LILAC
Rhamnaceae
EVERGREEN SHRUBS AND GROUND COVERS

- 🌿 ZONES 5–9, 14–24, EXCEPT AS NOTED
- ☀️ FULL SUN
- 🌢 LITTLE OR NO WATER
- ▶ SEE CHART, NEXT PAGE

Some species grow in eastern U.S., Rocky Mountains, the Northwest, and Mexico, but most are native to California. In flower color, they range from white through all shades of blue, from pale powder blue to deep violet blue. Typically flower in spring; bloom time is not indicated in chart unless it is unusual. Plants vary greatly in habit: some are low and spreading, others compact and bushy, still others upright and angular. Generally evergreen; a couple listed

Ceanothus gloriosus

CEANOTHUS

NAME	SIZE	FOLIAGE	FLOWERS	COMMENTS
GROUND COVERS				
Ceanothus 'Centennial'	2 ft. tall, 10 ft. wide	Small, shiny dark green leaves	Very dark blue, in short clusters	More heat resistant than *C. griseus horizontalis*
C. gloriosus POINT REYES CEANOTHUS	1–1½ ft. tall, 12–16 ft. wide	Dark green, oval, 1-in. leaves, tough and spiny	Typically light blue, in 1-in. clusters	Much used in Zones 4–6. Does not do well in summer heat of Zones 7, 14, 18–21
C. g. 'Anchor Bay'	1–1½ ft. tall, 6–8 ft. wide	Very dense	Somewhat deeper blue than above	Dense foliage holds down weeds. 'Heart's Desire' is similar but has smaller, shiny leaves
C. g. exaltatus 'Emily Brown'	2–3 ft. tall, 8–12 ft. wide	Dark green, hollylike, 1-in. leaves	Dark violet-blue 1-in. clusters	Tolerates heavy soil, summer water near coast
C. griseus horizontalis CARMEL CREEPER Zones 5–9, 14–17, 19–24	1½–2½ ft. tall, 5–15 ft. wide	Glossy, oval, 2-in., bright green leaves	Light blue 1-in. clusters	Some sold under this name may be 'Hurricane Point'. Sometimes suffers winter damage in Zones 5–7, 14
C. g. h. 'Hurricane Point'	2–3 ft. tall, to 36 ft. wide	Glossy, oval, 2-in. leaves	Pale blue 1-in. clusters	Very fast, somewhat rank grower. Deer love this and the other forms of *C. griseus*
C. g. h. 'Yankee Point'	2–3 ft. tall, 8–10 ft. wide	Glossy dark green 1½-in. leaves	Medium blue 1-in. clusters	One of best ground-covering kinds. Looks refined
C. hearstiorum	6 in. tall, 6–8 ft. wide	Puckered 1½-in. leaves	Medium blue 1-in. clusters	One of flattest, but lets in weeds. Spreads from center like a star. Variable performance; not dependable
C. 'Joyce Coulter'	2–5 ft. tall, 10–12 ft. wide	Medium green 1-in. leaves	Medium blue, 3–5-in. spikelike clusters	Tolerates heavy soil, some summer water, much pruning
C. maritimus	1–3 ft. tall, 3–8 ft. wide	Blue-green to grayish ½-in. leaves, typically gray or white beneath	White to pale lavender ½-in. clusters	Height and color vary greatly. 'Frosty Dawn' has darker blue flowers. 'Point Sierra' is more tolerant of interior heat
C. prostratus SQUAW CARPET, MAHALA MATS Zones 2–6, 14–16, 18	Prostrate; to 8 ft. wide	Leathery, toothed, light green leaves, ½–1 in. long	Deep to light blue clusters	Useful in native range (higher elevations in northern Sierra Nevada), nearly impossible elsewhere. *C. p. occidentalis*, from northern Coast Ranges, is rare, difficult
C. thyrsiflorus repens CREEPING BLUE BLOSSOM	1–3 ft. tall, 8–9 ft. wide	Shiny green 2-in. leaves	Powdery blue 3-in. clusters	Easy to grow; tolerates heavy soil, summer water
SHRUBS				
C. arboreus 'Cliff Schmidt'	15–20 ft. tall and wide	Glossy dark green leaves, downy white beneath	Powder blue, 5-in. sprays in spring and fall	Excellent near the coast; needs some shade inland
C. 'Blue Jeans'	7–9 ft. tall and wide	Small, dark green leathery leaves	Profuse, pale powder blue clusters	Tolerates heavy soil, drought, summer water. Shear after bloom for low-water-use hedge
C. 'Concha' Zones 6–9, 14–24	6–7 ft. tall, 6–8 ft. wide	Densely clad in dark green 1-in. leaves	Dark blue 1-in. clusters	One of the best for gardens. Tolerates summer water. Hardy to 15°F/−9°C. 'Wheeler Canyon' is similar but has slightly lighter blue flowers
C. 'Cynthia Postan'	6–8 ft. tall and wide	Crinkled, glossy dark green leaves, grayish beneath	Violet-blue flowers, opening from bronzy red buds	Tolerates heavy soils near coast
C. 'Dark Star'	5–6 ft. tall, 8–10 ft. wide	Tiny (¼-in.), dark green leaves	Dark cobalt blue 1½-in. clusters	Similar to *C*. 'Julia Phelps', maybe better
C. × delilianus 'Gloire de Versailles' Zones 3b–9, 14–24	15 ft. tall and wide	Dark green leaves to 3 in. long, evergreen in mild-winter regions, deciduous elsewhere	Fragrant, profuse, light blue	Hybrid of blue-flowered Mexican species with hardy, white-flowered, deciduous eastern U.S. native. Open, rangy; can be espaliered. Only one of this hybrid group to attain popularity
C. fendleri Zones 1–3	From prostrate to 6 ft. tall; to 6 ft. wide	1-in. gray-green leaves, partially evergreen or deciduous	Bluish white	Native to Rocky Mountains. Also useful as large-scale ground cover

CEANOTHUS

C

SPECIES OR VARIETY	SIZE	FOLIAGE	FLOWERS	COMMENTS
SHRUBS (cont'd)				
C. 'Frosty Blue'	6–9 ft. tall, 8–10 ft. wide	Dark green ½-in. leaves. Dense	Deep blue, white-frosted, 2½–3-in. spikelike clusters	White "frosting" makes flowers shimmer. Sturdy stems. Can be shaped as small tree
C. 'Gentian Plume'	10–20 ft. tall, 12–20 ft. wide	Dark green 2½-in. leaves	Dark blue, 10-in. spikelike clusters	Leggy when young; pinching helps. If stems get so long that plants "fall apart," prune them
C. griseus 'Bamico'	4 ft. tall, 6–8 ft. wide	Glossy dark green ¾–1 in. leaves	Rich violet-blue 3-in. clusters	Tolerates heavy soil, summer watering. Can be sheared. Needs partial shade inland
C. g. 'Louis Edmunds'	5–6 ft. tall, 9–20 ft. wide	Bright glossy green 1-in. leaves	Medium sea blue 1-in. clusters	Tolerates heavy soil, summer water. Can also be used as a large-scale ground cover
C. impressus SANTA BARBARA CEANOTHUS	6–9 ft. tall, 10–15 ft. wide	Dense mass of dark green ½-in. leaves	Lovely dark blue 1-in. clusters	Temperamental; does best near coast. Performs quite well in Pacific Northwest
C. 'Julia Phelps'	4½–7 ft. tall, 7–9 ft. wide	Small (½-in.), dark green leaves	Dark indigo 1-in. clusters	One of best colors, best bloomers
C. 'Owlswood Blue'	8–10 ft. tall, 10–12 ft. wide	Dark green, oval, 2½-in. leaves	Dark blue, 4–6-in. spikelike clusters	Reliable, heavy bloom
C. 'Ray Hartman'	12–20 ft. tall, 15–20 ft. wide	Big (2–3-in.), dark green leaves	Medium blue, 3–5-in. spikelike clusters	Can be trained as small tree
C. rigidus 'Snowball'	6 ft. tall, 12–16 ft. wide	Dark green ½-in. leaves	White puffs, ¾ in. wide	Handsome, dense, mounding
C. 'Sierra Blue'	10–12 ft. tall, 8–10 ft. wide	Glossy, medium green 1½-in. leaves	Bright medium blue, 6–8-in. spikelike clusters	Very fast grower; weedy first few years
C. thyrsiflorus BLUE BLOSSOM	6–21 ft. tall, 8–30 ft. wide	Glossy green leaves to 2 in.	Light to dark blue, 3-in. spikelike clusters	One of the tallest and hardiest ceanothus
C. t. 'Skylark'	3–6 ft. tall, 5 ft. wide	Glossy medium green 2-in. leaves	Dark blue clusters; profuse bloom over a long season	Tolerates summer water. C. 'Victoria' is believed to be the same plant
C. t. 'Snow Flurry'	6–10 ft. tall, 8–12 ft. wide	Rich green 2-in. leaves	Profuse pure white clusters	Adaptable, dependable. Good choice for coastal gardens
C. velutinus TOBACCO BRUSH Zones 2–7, 15–17	3–8 ft. tall and wide	Glossy, aromatic leaves 3 in. long	White, late in season	Useful in native plantings in cold climates

here lose leaves in cold weather. Only types with small leaves tend to be deer resistant. New varieties (most of them propagated from selected wild plants) appear frequently in nurseries, while old ones disappear. For the widest choice, deal with a specialist in Western natives. In Zones 1–3, 8, 9, stay with varieties tested and sold locally.

In the wild, these plants grow on rocky slopes; in the garden, they require excellent drainage. Plant in light, well-drained soil. Some demand total dryness during summer, but others (particu-larly coastal ground-cover types) need occasional summer water if grown away from the fog belt.

Ceanothus griseus horizontalis

A few tolerate more frequent summer moisture (see chart). Wait until after blooms have faded to do any pruning, and avoid cutting off any branches more than an inch in diameter. Control plant growth by pinching back shoot tips during the growing season.

Ceanothus sometimes get aphids and whiteflies, but these are easy to control. As a group, plants don't live very long; 5 to 10 years is typical.

CEDAR. See **CEDRUS**

CEDAR, ALASKA. See **CHAMAE-CYPARIS nootkatensis**

CEDAR, ATLANTIC WHITE. See **CHAMAECYPARIS thyoides**

CEDAR, EASTERN RED. See **JUNIPERUS virginiana**

CEDAR, INCENSE. See **CALOCEDRUS decurrens**

CEDAR, LAWSON or PORT ORFORD. See **CHAMAECYPARIS lawsoniana**

CEDAR, WESTERN RED. See **THUJA plicata**

CEDRELA sinensis. See **TOONA sinensis**

CEDRUS
CEDAR
Pinaceae
EVERGREEN TREES

- 🌿 **ZONES VARY BY SPECIES**
- ☀️ **FULL SUN**
- 💧 **MODERATE WATER**

These, the true cedars, are among the most widely grown conifers in Western gardens. Cedars bear needles in tufted clusters. Cone scales, like those of firs *(Abies),* fall from tree, leaving a spiky core behind. Male catkins produce prodigious amounts of pollen that may cover you with yellow dust on a windy day. Plant in deep, well-drained soil. All species are deep rooted and drought tolerant once established. Some botanists contend that the several Mediterranean species are just geographic variants of a single species.

C. atlantica (C. libani atlantica). ATLAS CEDAR. Zones 3b–10, 14–24. Native to North Africa. Slow to moderate growth to 60 ft. or taller. Open, angular growth in youth. Branches usually get too long and heavy on young trees unless tips are pinched out or cut back; branches of any age tend to break in heavy snows. Growth naturally less open with age. Less spreading than other true cedars, but still needs 30-ft. circle.

Needles, less than 1 in. long, are bluish green. Varieties include 'Aurea', needles with yellowish tint; 'Glauca', silvery blue; 'Glauca Pendula', weeping form with blue needles; 'Horstmann', dense, dwarf form (10 ft. tall after 10 years); 'Pendula', vertically drooping branches. Untrained, spreading, informally branching plants are sold as "rustics."

Cedrus atlantica

C. brevifolia. CYPRUS (or CYPRIAN) CEDAR. Zones 5–10, 14–24. Native to Cyprus. Resembles *C. libani* but is smaller (to 50 ft. tall and 40 ft. wide) with shorter needles (¼–½ in.) and smaller cones. Sometimes considered variety of *C. libani.* Very slow growing.

C. deodara. DEODAR CEDAR. Zones 3b–10, 14–24. Native to the Himalayas. Fast growing to 80 ft., with 40-ft. spread at ground level. Lower branches sweep down to ground, then upward. Upper branches openly spaced, graceful. Nodding tip identifies it in skyline. Softer, lighter texture than other cedars. Planted in small lawn, it soon overpowers area. You can control spread of tree by cutting new growth of side branches halfway back in late spring. This kind of pruning also makes tree denser.

Cedrus deodara

Although deodars sold by nurseries are very similar in overall form, many variations occur within a group of seedlings—from scarecrowlike types to low, compact shrubs. Needles, to 2-in. long, may be green or have a blue, gray, or yellow cast. Following variations are propagated by cuttings or grafting.

'Aurea'. New foliage is yellow, gradually turning to golden green in summer.

'Feelin' Blue'. Dwarf, spreading form, to 2 ft. tall and 6 ft. wide. Foliage is blue green.

'Pendula' ('Prostrata'). Grows flat on ground or will drape attractively over rocks or wall.

'Prostrate Beauty'. To 1½–2 ft. tall; may spread 7–8 ft. in 10 years.

'Silver Mist'. Similar to 'Snow Sprite', but tips are white.

'Snow Sprite'. To 12 ft. tall and broad in 10 years. Foliage is silvery green with cream-colored tips.

'White Imp'. Just 3 ft. tall and wide. New growth is white.

C. libani. CEDAR OF LEBANON. Zones 3–10, 14–24. Native Lebanon to Turkey. To 80 ft., but slow growing—to 15 ft. in 15 years. Variable in growth habit. Usually a dense, narrow pyramid in youth. In young trees, needles, less than 1 in. long, are brightest green of the cedars; in old ones, they are dark gray green. Spreads picturesquely as it matures to become majestic sky-line tree with long horizontal limbs and an irregular shape; the tree is ultimately about as broad as high. Rather scarce and expensive because of time to reach salable size. Routine garden care. No pruning needed. 'Sargentii' ('Pendula Sargentii') grows even more slowly, has a short trunk and crowded, weeping branches; choice container or rock garden plant. 'Pendula' is a slow-growing, weeping form.

CEIBA. See CHORISIA

CELASTRUS
BITTERSWEET
Celastraceae
DECIDUOUS VINES

- 🌿 **ZONES VARY BY SPECIES**
- ☀️ **FULL SUN**
- 💧 **REGULAR WATER**

Grown principally for clusters of ornamental summer fruit—yellow-and-orange capsules that split open to display brilliant red-coated seeds. Branches bearing fruit are much prized for indoor arrangements. Since birds seem uninterested in fruit, display extends into winter. To get fruit, you need to plant male and female plants close to each other, but unfortunately, nursery plants are not always labeled. Self-fruitful forms of *C. orbiculatus* are available. Foliage turns yellow in fall.

Vigorous and twining, with ropelike branches; need support.

Celastrus scandens

Don't allow these vines to climb shrubs or small trees—they can kill them by girdling the stems. Prune tangled or intertwined branches before new spring growth begins; prune as needed during summer to manage growth. Growing in poorer soils helps keep vines to more manageable size.

C. orbiculatus. CHINESE BITTERSWEET. Zones 2b–7, 10. Native to Asia. Aggressive grower to 30–40 ft. Leaves roundish, toothed, to 4 in. Fruit on short side shoots is partially obscured until leaves drop.

C. rosthornianus (C. loeseneri). Zones 3b–7, 10. Chinese native. Grows to 20 ft., with oval leaves to 5 in. long. Similar to *C. orbiculatus,* but not as rampant.

C. scandens. AMERICAN BITTERSWEET. Zones A3; 2–7, 10. Native to eastern North America. To 20 ft. or more. Oval, toothed-edged leaves to 4 in. long. Fruit appears in scattered dense clusters; these are held above leaves, making *C. scandens* showier than other two species.

CELERIAC
Apiaceae (Umbelliferae)
BIENNIAL GROWN AS ANNUAL

- 🌿 **ALL ZONES**
- ☀️ **FULL SUN**
- 💧 **REGULAR WATER**

Celeriac

A form of celery grown for its large, rounded, edible roots rather than for leafstalks, this is the "celery root" sold in markets. Roots are peeled, then cooked or used raw in salads.

Growth requirements are same as for celery. Grow plants 6–8 in. apart in rows that are spaced 1½–2 ft. apart. Harvest when roots are 3 in. across or larger—about 100 to 120 days after transplanting. 'Brilliant' and 'Mentor' are among several improved varieties.

CELERY

...piaceae (Umbelliferae)
...IENNIAL GROWN AS ANNUAL

⚡ **ALL ZONES**

☀ **FULL SUN**

💧 **REGULAR WATER**

Celery

Native to Europe and Asia. Needs long period of warmth but not high heat. Plant seeds in flats in early spring; where winters are mild, start in summer for winter crop. (Celery plants started from seed are slow to reach planting size; to save time, you can purchase small nursery plants.) Plant seedlings in rich soil, spacing 6 in. apart in rows 2 ft. apart. Every 2 to 3 weeks, apply liquid fertilizer with irrigation water. To keep plants upright, work some soil up around them as they grow. For whitened stalks, set bottomless milk carton, tar paper cylinder, or similar device over plants to exclude light from stalks (leaves must have sunlight). Or grow self-blanching varieties. Harvest 105 to 130 days after transplanting. Row covers will keep out many pests.

CELERY ROOT. See CELERIAC

CELOSIA

COCKSCOMB, CHINESE
WOOLFLOWER
Amaranthaceae
ANNUALS

⚡ **ZONES 1–24; H1, H2;**
    BEST IN ZONES 8–14, 18, 19; H1, H2

☀ **FULL SUN**

💧 **MODERATE WATER**

Richly colored tropical plants, some with flower clusters in bizarre shapes. Although attractive in cut arrangements with other flowers, in gardens celosias are most effective by themselves. Cut blooms can be dried for winter bouquets. Sow seed in place in late spring or early summer, or set out started plants.

Celosia,   *Celosia,*
crested type   plume type

There are two kinds of cockscombs, both derived from a silvery white–flowered species, *C. argentea,* which has narrow leaves 2 in. long or more. One group, the plume cockscombs (often sold as *C.* 'Plumosa'), has plumy flower clusters. Some of these, like Chinese woolflower (sometimes sold as *C.* 'Childsii'), have plumy flower clusters that look like tangled masses of yarn. Flowers come in brilliant shades of pink, orange red, gold, crimson. You can get forms that grow 2½–3 ft. high and 1½ ft. wide. Dwarf, more compact varieties grow about 1 ft. high and half as wide; they bear heavily branched plumes.

The other group is the crested cockscombs (often sold as *C.* 'Cristata'). These have velvety, fan-shaped flower clusters, often much contorted and fluted. Flower colors include yellow, orange, crimson, purple, and red. Tall kinds grow to 3 ft. tall and 1½ ft. wide; dwarf varieties grow to 10 in. high and 6 in. wide. Good in containers.

CELTIS

HACKBERRY
Ulmaceae
DECIDUOUS TREES

⚡ **ZONES VARY BY SPECIES**

☀ ◐ **FULL SUN OR PARTIAL SHADE**

💧 **MODERATE WATER**

Related to elms (*Ulmus*) and similar to them in most details, but smaller. All have virtue of deep rooting; old trees in narrow planting strips expand in trunk diameter to nearly fill strips without producing surface roots or heaving sidewalk or curb. Good choice for street or lawn tree, even near buildings or paving. Canopy casts moderate shade in spring and summer; leaves turn yellow in fall. Mature trees have picturesque bark with corky warts and ridges. Small berrylike fruits attract birds.

Hackberry is exceptionally tough, tolerating strong winds (stake young trees until well established), desert heat, and dry, alkaline soils. Leaf gall caused by psyllids may disfigure hackberry leaves in some regions (especially in the Rocky Mountain states and Pacific Northwest), but the trees are not harmed. Little pruning required. Bare-root plants, especially in larger sizes, sometimes fail to leaf out. Buy in containers or try for small bare-root trees with big root systems.

C. australis. EUROPEAN HACKBERRY. Zones 8–16, 18–20. Mediterranean native grows at moderate rate to 40 ft. high in 14 or 15 years. Eventually can reach 70–80 ft. tall, 30–35 ft. wide. In youth, branches are more upright than those of other hackberries. Dark green, 2–5-in.-long leaves, more coarsely toothed and sharper tipped than those of *C. occidentalis;* also has shorter deciduous period. Resistant to oak root fungus.

Celtis occidentalis

C. occidentalis. COMMON HACKBERRY. Zones 1–24. Native to eastern North America. To 50 ft. or taller and nearly as wide, with rounded crown and spreading, sometimes pendulous branches. Bright green, oval leaves, 2–5 in. long, with finely toothed edges. Tree does not leaf out until midspring. Resistant to oak root fungus. In Zones 10–13, lives longer than and is superior to commonly planted "Chinese elm" (actually the Siberian elm, *Ulmus pumila*).

C. pallida. DESERT HACKBERRY, GRANJENO. Zones 10–13. Native to southwestern U.S. and northern Mexico. Small tree or shrub with dense, spiny growth to 18 ft. tall; variable in width, sometimes growing wider than tall. Leaves 1 in. or shorter. Small orange berries. Useful in desert as honey source or bird food, for

screen or barrier planting, for erosion control.

C. reticulata (C. douglasii). WESTERN HACKBERRY. Zones 2–24; best in 2, 3, 7–13, 18–21. Native to eastern Washington, northern Oregon, Idaho, through intermountain area to Utah, and in mountains of Arizona and Southern California. To 25–30 ft. tall and wide, with somewhat pendulous branches. Oval, tooth-edged leaves to 2½ in. long, pale beneath, strongly veined.

C. sinensis. CHINESE HACKBERRY, YUNNAN HACKBERRY. Zones 8–16, 18–20. From East Asia. Similar in growth habit to *C. occidentalis,* but smaller (to 40 ft. tall and wide). Leaves to 4 in. long, smoother and glossier than those of other hackberries, with scalloped edges.

CENTAUREA

Asteraceae (Compositae)
ANNUALS, BIENNIALS, AND
PERENNIALS

⚡ **ZONES VARY BY SPECIES**

☀ **FULL SUN**

💧 **MODERATE WATER, EXCEPT AS NOTED**

Out of some 500 species, only a dozen or so are widely cultivated. Of these, annuals are grown mainly for cut flowers; perennial kinds are valued for soft, silvery foliage. All are relatively easy to grow. For best performance, add lime to acid soils. Sow seeds of annuals or set out plants of perennial kinds in spring or fall. (In desert regions, plant all in autumn for winter and spring bloom.)

C. americana. BASKET FLOWER. Annual. Zones 1–24; H1, H2. Native to central and southwestern U.S. To 5–6 ft. tall, 3 ft. wide. Leaves rather rough, oval, to 4 in. long. Summer flowers to 4 in. wide are rose pink, paler toward center. Good in fresh or dried arrangements.

C. cineraria (C. candidissima). DUSTY MILLER. Perennial in Zones 8–24, H1, H2; annual elsewhere. (This common name is

Centaurea cineraria

used for many plants with whitish foliage; see Dusty Miller.) Native to Italy. Compact growth to 1 ft. wide, 1 ft. or taller. Velvety white, strap-shaped leaves with broad, round-ish lobes, mostly in basal clump. Solitary 1-in. flower heads (purple, occasionally yellow) in summer. Trim back after bloom. Blossoms attract bees.

C. cyanus. CORNFLOWER, BACHELOR'S BUTTON. Annual. Zones 1–24; H1, H2. From north-ern temperate regions. A common weed in some areas, such as the Pacific Northwest. To 1–1½ ft. tall, less than a foot wide, branching if given enough space. Narrow gray-green leaves, 2–3 in. long. Spring to midsummer flowers are 1½ in. across, in blue, pink, rose, wine red, or white; blue varieties are traditional favorites for bouton-nieres. 'Jubilee Gem' is a bushy, compact 1-footer with deep blue flowers; Polka Dot strain has all cornflower colors on 16-in. plants.

C. gymnocarpa. DUSTY MILLER. Perennial. Zones 8–24. Italian native considered a form of *C. cineraria.* To 1–3 ft. tall, 1 ft. wide. White, feltlike leaves are more finely divided than those of *C. cineraria.* Usually two or three purple flowers at ends of leafy branches in summer. Trim plants after bloom. Very drought tolerant but can take regular irrigation.

C. hypoleuca 'John Coutts'. Perennial. Zones 2–9, 14–24. Variety of species from Asia Minor. Resembles *C. montana* but has more deeply lobed leaves and deep rose flowers.

C. macrocephala. Perennial. Zones 2–9, 14–24. From the Cau-casus. Attractive, coarse-foliaged, leafy plant 3–4 ft. tall, 2 ft. wide. Blooms in summer, bearing 2-in. clusters of yellow flowers tightly wrapped at the base with overlap-ping, shiny, papery brown bracts. Flower heads resemble thistles. Use in fresh or dried arrangements.

C. montana. Perennial. Zones 2–9, 14–24. Native to mountains of central Europe. It forms a clump 1½–2 ft. tall and wide; grayish green leaves reach 7 in. long. Flowers resembling ragged 3-in. cornflowers top the stems in late spring to midsummer. Pro-tect from snails. Divide every other year. Regular water.

C. moschata (Amberboa moschata). SWEET SULTAN. Annual. Zones 1–24. From Asia Minor. Erect, branching at base, to 10 in. wide, 2 ft. tall (Imperialis strain reaches 3 ft.). Green, deeply

toothed leaves. Fluffy, thistlelike, 1-in. flowers from spring to fall, mostly in shades of lilac through rose, sometimes white or yellow. Musky fragrance. Splendid cut flower. Sow seed directly on soil in spring or set out as transplants. Needs lots of heat; don't give over-head water.

C. rothrockii. Annual or bien-nial. Zones 1–24. Southwest native to 4–6 ft. tall, 2 ft. wide, with 4-in.-long leaves. Flowers like soft thistles bloom from midsummer into fall; these are 5 in. wide, with pink outer rays and a creamy white to yellow center. Frost sensitive; start seeds indoors in cold-winter areas and transplant after last frost. Good for arrangements if cut just before flowers open.

CENTRANTHUS ruber (Valeriana rubra)

JUPITER'S BEARD, RED VALERIAN
Valerianaceae
PERENNIAL

🌱 **ZONES 2–9, 12–24; H1**

☀️ 🌤️ **FULL SUN OR PARTIAL SHADE**

💧 **LITTLE TO MODERATE WATER**

Mediterranean native is a weed in many parts of the West. Self-sows prolifically, thanks to small dandelion-like parachutes on seeds. When used in fringe areas of garden, though, it's hard to beat for long, showy bloom. Forms a bushy clump to 3 ft. high and wide, with bluish green, 4-in.-long leaves. Small (about 1½-in.-wide) flowers, in dense terminal clusters in late spring, early summer. In cool-summer climates, blooms sporadically throughout summer, sometimes into fall. Typical colors

Centranthus ruber

range from deep crimson to pale pink; 'Albus' has white blooms. Plants grow in poor, dry soils and tolerate almost any condition except damp shade. Cut off old flowering stems to shape plants and prevent self-seeding.

CENTURY PLANT. See **AGAVE americana**

CEPHALANTHUS occidentalis

BUTTONBUSH, BUTTON WILLOW
Rubiaceae
DECIDUOUS SHRUB OR TREE

🌱 **ZONES 2–10, 14–21**

☀️ 🌤️ **FULL SUN OR LIGHT SHADE**

💧 💧 **REGULAR TO AMPLE WATER**

Cephalanthus occidentalis

Remarkable for wide distribution —eastern Canada to Florida, Minnesota south through Okla-homa and west to California, with outposts in Cuba, Mexico, and Asia. Grows 3–15 ft. or taller and equally wide, with rounded, rather open habit and bright green, paired or whorled leaves 2–6 in. long. Leafs out late in spring. Creamy white, slender-tubed flowers crowded in rounded, 1–1½-in.-wide heads in late summer. Projecting stigmas give blossom clusters the look of a pincushion. Blossoms attract butterflies. Useful for naturalizing in wet areas. *C. o. californicus* is very similar.

CEPHALARIA gigantea

Dipsacaceae
PERENNIAL

🌱 **ZONES 2–10, 14–24**

☀️ **FULL SUN**

💧 **REGULAR WATER**

Native to the Caucasus. Giant perennial (to 6–8 ft. tall, 2 ft. wide) with coarse, deeply cut leaves to 16 in. long. Pale yellow summer flower heads to 2½ in. wide appear atop long, sparsely branched

Cephalaria gigantea

stems; they resemble those of pin-cushion flower (in fact, plant was once called *Scabiosa gigantea*). Useful in the wild garden or at the back of a border. Despite its height, seldom requires staking.

CEPHALOCEREUS senilis

OLD MAN CACTUS
Cactaceae
CACTUS

🌱 **ZONES 13, 21–24; H1; OR INDOORS**

☀️ **FULL SUN; BRIGHT LIGHT**

💧 **LITTLE OR NO WATER**

Cephalocereus senilis

Native to Mexico. Slender, colum-nar cactus growing slowly to 45 ft. tall in great old age; usually much smaller. Covered with long, grayish white hairs and 1½-in. yellow spines. Only old, quite large (over 15-ft.-tall) plants bloom; they flower in spring, bearing 2-in.-long, rose-colored flowers that open at night. Grow in rocky or loose soil. Supplemental water, fer-tilizer will speed growth of garden plants. Protect from hard frosts. In Zone 13, provide some shade. Indoors, give southern exposure.

CEPHALOPHYLLUM 'Red Spike'

RED SPIKE ICE PLANT
Aizoaceae
SUCCULENT PERENNIAL

🌡 ZONES 8, 9, 11–24

☀☀ FULL SUN OR PARTIAL SHADE

💧💧 MODERATE TO REGULAR WATER

South African native forms a clump 3–5 in. high, slowly spreading to 15–18 in. wide. Spiky green to bronzy red leaves point up. Bright red, 2-in. flowers in winter or early spring, sporadic bloom in other seasons. Blooms attract bees. Grow in well-drained soil. Plant 6–12 in. apart for ground cover. Provide supplemental irrigation during active growth and bloom; cut back watering in summer. In the desert, needs afternoon shade. Sometimes sold as *Cylindrophyllum* 'Red Spike'.

Cephalophyllum
'Red Spike'

CEPHALOTAXUS harringtonii

PLUM YEW
Cephalotaxaceae
EVERGREEN SHRUB OR TREE

🌡 ZONES 4–9, 14–17

☀☀ PARTIAL SHADE IN HOTTEST CLIMATES

💧 MODERATE WATER

Slow-growing conifer from Asia. Related to yew (*Taxus*) but has brighter green needles 1–2½ in. long and (on female plants only)

Cephalotaxus harringtonii

larger fruits that resemble small plums. Species grows at least 10–15 ft. tall and wide, but named varieties are more compact. 'Duke Gardens' grows 3–4 ft. high and at least as wide. 'Fastigiata' ('Stricta') is a broadly columnar form that can reach 10 ft. tall and 6–8 ft. wide. 'Korean Gold' is narrower and has golden new foliage. Plants labeled 'Prostrata' do not form a strong leader and remain 2–3 ft. tall, somewhat wider. Protect all kinds from strong wind. Plants tolerate much pruning and will resprout after being cut back into older wood.

CERASTIUM tomentosum

SNOW-IN-SUMMER
Caryophyllaceae
PERENNIAL

🌡 ZONES A1, A2; 1–24

☀☀ LIGHT SHADE IN HOTTEST CLIMATES

💧💧 MODERATE TO REGULAR WATER

Low-growing European native performs equally well in mild and cold climates, coastal and desert areas. Forms dense, tufty mats of silvery gray, ¾-in. leaves; grows 6–8 in. high, spreads 2–3 ft. in a year. Bears masses of small, snow white flowers in early summer. Use as ground cover on slopes or level ground, as bulb cover, in rock gardens, for edging along paths, between stepping-stones. Plant is not long lived, so avoid extensive planting in prominent situations. Conversely, in the Northwest it grows so enthusiastically it can become a weed.

Cerastium tomentosum

Takes any soil as long as drainage is good. Set divisions or plants 1–1½ ft. apart, or sow seed. To speed growth, water regularly and feed two or three times a year. After bloom ends, shear off faded flower clusters or mow planting. May look a bit shabby in winter but revives rapidly in spring. Repair bare patches in spring or early fall by digging clumps from healthy areas and replanting them in the bare areas.

CERATOIDES lanata (Krascheninnikovia lanata)

WINTER FAT
Chenopodiaceae
EVERGREEN SHRUB

🌡 ZONES 2, 3, 7–14, 18–24

☀ FULL SUN

💧💧 LITTLE TO MODERATE WATER

Ceratoides lanata

Native to much of the arid West. To 1½–3 ft. tall and equally wide, with tiny linear leaves. In autumn, produces spikelike, woolly white seed heads, 1½–7 in. long; these attract birds and can be used in dried arrangements. Tolerates alkaline soil. It has also been known as *Eurotia lanata*. Common name derives from plant's usefulness as winter browse.

CERATONIA siliqua

CAROB, ST. JOHN'S BREAD
Fabaceae (Leguminosae)
EVERGREEN SHRUB OR TREE

🌡 ZONES 9, 13–16, 18–24; H1

☀ FULL SUN

💧💧💧 LITTLE TO REGULAR WATER

Native to eastern Mediterranean region. Often multistemmed, it maintains bushy form with branches to ground when allowed

Ceratonia siliqua

to grow naturally. Use this way as big hedge, informal or trimmed. Trained as tree, with lower branches removed, it grows at a moderate rate to become dense and round headed, to 30–40 ft. tall and wide. Will reach 20 ft. in 10 years. As street tree it needs more than normal space since roots will break sidewalks.

Foliage is glossy dark green, unusually dense. Leaves are divided into four to ten round leaflets averaging about 2 in. long. Small red flowers in spring. Female trees produce (and drop) abundant 1-ft.-long flattened, dark brown, leathery pods. Rich in sugar, the pods are milled to a fine powder and sold in health food stores as chocolate substitute.

Hardy to 18°F/–8°C; give young trees winter protection first year or two. Resistant to oak root fungus. Avoid overwatering in heavy or poorly drained soils, since carob is subject to root-crown rot. Very drought tolerant. If raised for fruit crop, needs regular moisture.

CERATOSTIGMA

PLUMBAGO
Plumbaginaceae
EVERGREEN AND DECIDUOUS SHRUBS AND PERENNIALS

🌡 ZONES VARY BY SPECIES

☀☀ FULL SUN OR PARTIAL SHADE

💧💧 MODERATE TO REGULAR WATER

Valued for clusters of intense blue, phlox-like flowers that bloom in summer to late fall, when cool hues are often especially welcome in the garden. (For pale blue–flowered Cape plumbago, see *Plumbago auriculata*.) Tolerate inconsistent watering. Shrubby species are usually treated like perennials in colder zones; cut them back after bloom and apply a thick mulch.

Ceratostigma plumbaginoides

C. griffithii. BURMESE PLUMBAGO. Evergreen shrub. Zones 4–9, 14–24. Himalayan native similar to *C. willmottianum* in general appearance, but it has rounder leaves and more compact, somewhat lower growth (to 2½–3 ft. high and wide). Also blooms somewhat later. Growth often nipped back by frost.

C. plumbaginoides (Plumbago larpentae). DWARF PLUMBAGO.

C

Perennial. Zones 2b–10, 14–24. Native to China. Wiry-stemmed ground cover to 6–12 in. high. Bronzy to dark green, 3-in.-long leaves turn reddish brown with frosts. Blooms well only in areas with long growing season. Most striking in early or midautumn, when blue blossoms contrast with red fall foliage. In loose soil and where growing season is long, spreads rapidly and (eventually) widely by underground stems. Plant 1–1½ ft. apart for quick cover. Shear or mow annually before spring growth begins. When plants show signs of aging, dig up and replace with rooted stems in spring or summer.

C. willmottianum. CHINESE PLUMBAGO. Deciduous shrub. Zones 4–9, 14–24. Grows as airy mass of wiry stems 2–4 ft. high and wide. Deep green, 2-in.-long leaves are somewhat diamond shaped, with tapering tips; turn yellow or red and drop quickly after frost.

CERCIDIPHYLLUM
japonicum
KATSURA TREE
Cercidiphyllaceae
DECIDUOUS TREE

🌿	ZONES 2B–6, 14–16, 18–20
☀️ ◐	FULL SUN OR LIGHT SHADE
💧	REGULAR WATER

Native to China, Japan. A specimen tree of many virtues if given regular moisture (especially during youth) and sheltered from intense sun and drying wind. Light, dainty branch and leaf pattern. Foliage changes color during growing season: emerges reddish purple, becomes bluish green in summer, then turns yellow to apricot in autumn. To enhance fall color,

Cercidiphyllum japonicum

water less frequently in late summer. Trees grown in acid soil will have best color. Foliage of some katsura trees smells like brown sugar on warm autumn days when leaves are falling.

Rather slow growing, eventually reaching 40 ft. or taller. Pyramidal form when young; tree may remain fairly pyramidal or become more rounded (and as wide as tall) with maturity. Some specimens have single trunk, but multiple trunks are more usual. Brown bark, somewhat shaggy on old trees. Nearly round, 2–4-in. leaves neatly spaced in pairs along arching branches. No serious pest or disease problems. Mature trees need little pruning. Weeping forms include 'Amazing Grace', 'Morioka Weeping', and *C. j. pendulum* (*C. j.* 'Pendulum' or 'Pendula'); all feature fast growth and gracefully weeping branches.

CERCIDIUM
PALO VERDE
Fabaceae (Leguminosae)
DECIDUOUS TREES

🌿	ZONES 8–14, 18–20, EXCEPT AS NOTED
☀️	FULL SUN
💧	LITTLE TO MODERATE WATER

Tough, trouble-free desert trees valued for floral display, shade, colorful bark. Clusters of small, bright yellow flowers nearly hide the spiny branches in spring. Lightly filtered shade is cast by intricate canopy of twigs rather than by tiny leaves, which are shed early. These trees attract birds. Prune only to enhance form, removing crossing, wayward, or too low branches; hold off on pruning when temperatures rise above 100°F/38°C.

C. 'Desert Museum'. This tree carries genes from *Parkinsonia aculeata, Cercidium microphyllum,* and *C. floridum* and combines the best traits of all three. It grows to 20 ft. tall and as wide in 3 to 5 years. Large (1-in.) blossoms appear over a long period; flowering is most profuse in spring, with rebloom possible in summer. Light green stems and leaves. This is a clean, thornless tree that produces few seedpods and scant litter.

C. floridum. BLUE PALO VERDE. Native to deserts of Southern California, Arizona, Baja California. In gardens, grows fast to 35 ft. tall, 30 ft. wide. Bright pure yellow flowers in 2–4½-in. clusters; earliest of these palo

Cercidium floridum

verdes to bloom in spring. Bluish green leaves with one to three pairs of smooth, tiny leaflets; bluish green branches.

C. microphyllum. LITTLE-LEAF PALO VERDE, FOOTHILLS PALO VERDE. From Southern California, Arizona's Sonoran Desert, Baja California. Slow growth to 20 ft. tall and wide. Leaves (with 4–12 pairs of hairy leaflets) and bark are yellowish green. Pale yellow flowers in 1-in. clusters.

C. praecox (C. plurifoliolatum). PALO BREA, SONORAN PALO VERDE. Zones 12 (warmer parts), 13, 18–20. Native Sonoran Desert to South America. Moderate growth to 20 ft. tall and wide. Umbrella form; lime green bark and leaves divided into 12–14 pairs of ¼-in. leaflets.

CERCIS
REDBUD
Fabaceae (Leguminosae)
DECIDUOUS SHRUBS OR TREES

🌿	ZONES VARY BY SPECIES
☀️ ◐	FULL SUN OR LIGHT SHADE
💧	MODERATE TO REGULAR WATER, EXCEPT AS NOTED

Valued for flowers, fruit, foliage. Clusters of small, sweet pea–shaped, rosy to purplish pink blossoms in early spring; where plant is adapted, blooms are borne in great profusion on bare twigs, branches, sometimes even on main trunk. Flowers are followed by clusters of flat, beanlike pods that persist into winter. Attractive broad, rounded leaves are heart shaped at base. All provide fall color with first frost and are attractive in naturalized settings. Do any pruning in dormant season or after bloom.

C. canadensis. EASTERN REDBUD. Zones 1–24. Native to eastern U.S. Largest (to 25–35 ft. tall and wide) and fastest growing of the redbuds, and the most apt to take tree form. Round headed but with horizontally tiered branches in age. Rich green, 3–6-in.-long leaves have pointed tips. Needs

some winter chill for profuse display of rosy pink flowers. Effective as specimen or understory tree. Varieties include 'Alba' (with white flowers), 'Forest Pansy' (a purple-leafed form that needs some shade in hot climates), 'Hearts of Gold' (with lavender flowers followed by leaves that emerge red then mature to yellow and finally green), and 'Silver Cloud' (with leaves marbled with white). 'Lavender Twist' ('Covey') has pinkish purple flowers held on weeping, contorted branches; it does best with afternoon shade.

C. c. mexicana (C. mexicana). Zones 4–24. Includes plants from many sources in Mexico. Most widely distributed is a single-trunked form to 15 ft. tall, with leathery blue-green leaves and pinkish purple flowers.

C. c. texensis 'Oklahoma' (C. reniformis 'Oklahoma'). Wine red flowers and thick, glossy, heat-resistant leaves.

Cercis canadensis

C. chinensis. CHINESE REDBUD. Zones 4–24. Native to China, Japan. Form most often seen is light, open shrub to 10–12 ft. tall, 10 ft. wide. Flower clusters (3–5 in. long) are deep rose, almost rosy purple. Leaves are sometimes glossier and brighter green than those of *C. canadensis*, with transparent line around the edge. Spectacular in high deserts of Arizona. 'Avondale' is a superior form with deep purple flowers.

C. occidentalis. WESTERN REDBUD. Zones 2–24. Native to California, Arizona, Utah, but predominantly found in California foothills below 4,000 ft. Shrub or small tree 10–18 ft. tall and wide; usually produces several trunks from base. Provides all-year interest. Magenta flowers bloom in spring; handsome blue-green, 3-in. leaves, notched or rounded at tip, and newly forming magenta seedpods adorn branches in summer. Foliage turns light yellow or red in fall, and bare branches holding reddish brown seedpods are icturesque in winter. Best floral isplay comes in areas with some vinter chill. Resistant to oak root ungus. Very drought tolerant; xcellent for seldom-watered anks. 'Alba' is a shrub 3–6 ft. tall nd somewhat broader, with white lowers and leaves to 2½ in. wide.

C. reniformis. Zones 3–24. ative to north-central Texas into Oklahoma. Leathery blue-green eaves 2–3 in. wide, with rounded r notched tips. Flowers like those of *C. canadensis;* 'Alba' has white lossoms.

C. siliquastrum. JUDAS TREE. Zones 3b–19. Native to Europe and western Asia. Generally of shrubby habit to 25 ft. tall and wide; occasionally a taller, slender tree with single trunk. Purplish rose flowers. Large (3–5-in.) leaves, deeply heart shaped at base, rounded or notched at tip. Performs best with some winter chill. Occasionally damaged by late frosts in Northwest. Resistant to oak root fungus.

CERCOCARPUS
MOUNTAIN MAHOGANY
Rosaceae
EVERGREEN AND DECIDUOUS
SHRUBS AND TREES

🌿	ZONES VARY BY SPECIES
☀️	FULL SUN
○	LITTLE OR NO WATER

Cercocarpus betuloides

Natives of Western mountains and foothills. Several have a most attractive open structure and branching pattern. Distinguished in fall by long-lasting small fruit topped by a long, twisted, feathery, tail-like plume that sparkles in sunlight. About 20 kinds are native to the West, but the following are most widespread.

C. betuloides. HARDTACK, MOUNTAIN IRONWOOD, SWEET BRUSH. Evergreen shrub or tree. Zones 3, 5, 7–10, 13–24. Native to dry slopes and foothills below 6,000-ft. elevation, south-

western Oregon, California, northern Baja California. Generally a shrub 5–12 ft. high and wide. Can form small tree with wide-spreading crown of arching branches to 20 ft. Wedge-shaped, ½–1-in. leaves cluster on short spurs; leaves are dark green above, pale beneath, with feathery veining and toothed edges.

C. intricatus (C. ledifolius intricatus). Evergreen shrub. Zones 2, 3, 7, 9–11, 14–16, 18–24. Native from eastern California to Utah, Arizona. Slow growth to 3–9 ft. tall and wide, with intricate branching and tiny inrolled leaves, green above, gray underneath.

C. ledifolius. CURL-LEAF MOUNTAIN MAHOGANY. Evergreen shrub or tree. Zones 1–3, 7–10, 14–21. Native to dry mountain slopes throughout the West, from eastern slopes of Sierra Nevada–Cascade divide to Rockies. In warmer western part of its range, it is about the same size as *C. betuloides;* in highest, coldest part of range, it is a very slow growing, excellent hedge or small tree. Leaves leathery, ½–1 in. long, resinous, dark green above, white beneath, with inrolled edges.

C. montanus. Deciduous shrub. Zones 1–3, 7–10. Native to western U.S. mountains. Usually 4–6 ft. tall and as wide, rarely to 8–9 ft. Leaves 1–2 in. long, white beneath. Useful in dry places and coldest climates.

CEREUS peruvianus (C. uruguayanus)
Cactaceae
CACTUS

🌿	ZONES 13, 16, 17, 21–24; H2
☀️ ◐	BEST IN SUN, TOLERATES SOME SHADE
◐ ●	MODERATE TO REGULAR WATER

Native to South America. Tall, tree-like cactus, branching from base, can form bushes to 10 ft. tall with eventual spread of 15 ft. Striking bluish green color, especially when young; ribbed with scattered spines. Large white flowers—6–7 in. long, 5 in. across—open at night in late spring. Big, egg-shaped red fruits split open when fully ripe to reveal white pulp and black seeds. Striking outline; effective in ground or in large containers. Protect from hard frosts. Tolerates much drought, but better appearance with some irrigation and fertilizer during hot, dry months. Propagate by large cuttings (2–6 ft. long) any time of

Cereus peruvianus
'Monstrosus'

year. 'Monstrosus' is smaller and slower growing than species, with ribs irregularly broken up into knobs and crests.

CERINTHE major
HONEYWORT
Boraginaceae
ANNUAL

🌿	ZONES 1–24
☀️ ◐	FULL SUN OR LIGHT SHADE
●	REGULAR WATER

Mediterranean native to 2 ft. tall and approximately as wide. Lower parts of stems bear 2½-in., gray-green leaves; upper parts carry leaflike bracts that partially conceal the flowers, which consist of inch-long purple tubes opening to a yellow interior. Bloom period runs from spring to fall. Though not conspicuous, flowers are rich in nectar and attract honeybees. The species is rarely grown. More often seen is variety 'Purpurascens'; its bracts and upper leaves are purplish blue, making the top of the plant look as if it's been dipped in blue dye. Easy to grow from seed and can self-sow (though not enough to become a pest). In mild-winter climates, seedlings may appear in late summer and

Cerinthe major
'Purpurascens'

bloom the following spring, behaving like biennials or short-lived perennials.

CEROPEGIA linearis woodii
ROSARY VINE
Asclepiadaceae
SUCCULENT VINE

🌿	ZONES 21–24; OR INDOORS
◐	PARTIAL SHADE; BRIGHT LIGHT
●	REGULAR WATER

From South Africa. Little vine with hanging or trailing thin stems growing from tuberous base. Paired heart-shaped leaves—thick and succulent, ⅔ in. long, dark green marbled with white. Little tubers that form on stems can be used to start new plants. Small, dull pink or purplish flowers, not showy but interesting in structure.

Ceropegia linearis woodii

Best grown in pots; stems may trail in thin curtain or be trained on small trellis. Other species are available from specialists. Some are shrubby, some vining, and others stiffly succulent, but all of them have fascinating flower structure.

CESTRUM
Solanaceae
EVERGREEN SHRUBS

🌿	ZONES VARY BY SPECIES
◐	PARTIAL SHADE, EXCEPT AS NOTED
●	REGULAR WATER
◆	FRUIT AND SAP ARE POISONOUS IF INGESTED

All native to the American tropics. Those in cultivation have showy clusters of tubular flowers attractive to hummingbirds. Showy fruit that follows can also attract birds. Fast growing with an arching, lax growth habit that benefits from consistent pruning and pinching back. Best in warm, sheltered spots. May be cut back severely after flowering or fruiting. ▶

Responds well to feeding and organic soil amendments. Frost damage with quick recovery possible in climates specified below.

C. aurantiacum. ORANGE CESTRUM. Zones 16, 17, 21–24; H1, H2. Native to Guatemala. To 8 ft. tall and wide (in frost-free areas may become much larger). Brilliant show of orange flowers in late spring and summer, followed by white berries. Deep green, oval, 4-in. leaves. Good for espalier. May spread by suckers. Loses leaves with cold weather.

C. elegans (C. purpureum). RED CESTRUM. Zones 13, 17, 19–24; H1, H2. Vining shrub from Mexico. To 10 ft. or greater in both height and width, with deep green, 4-in. leaves. Masses of purplish red blossoms in spring and summer are followed by red berries. 'Smithii' has pink flowers.

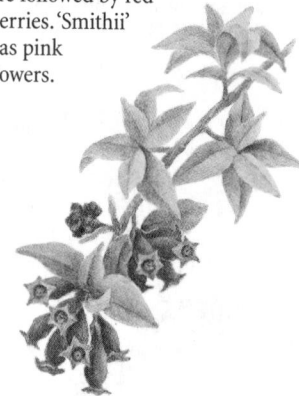

Cestrum elegans

C. fasciculatum. Zones 13, 17, 19–24. Mexican native similar to *C. elegans* but larger in all its parts.

C. 'Newellii'. Zones 13, 17, 19–24. Resembles *C. fasciculatum* but has bright crimson flowers. Some plants listed as *C.* 'Newellii' may in fact be *C. fasciculatum.*

C. nocturnum. NIGHT JESSAMINE. Zones 13, 16–24; H1, H2. Native to West Indies. To 12 ft. tall and wide, with 4–8-in.-long leaves and creamy white summer blossoms. White berries. Powerfully fragrant at night—too much so for some people. Give full sun for best bloom.

CHAENOMELES
FLOWERING QUINCE
Rosaceae
DECIDUOUS SHRUBS

☑ ZONES 2–23
☀ FULL SUN
◐ ◑ MODERATE TO REGULAR WATER

These are among the first shrubs to bloom each year. As early as January, you can take a budded stem

Chaenomeles
'Apple Blossom'

indoors, place it in water in a sunny window, and watch buds break into bloom. Blossoms are 1½–2½ in. across, single to semi-double or double, in white and soft to vibrant shades of pink, orange, and red. Leaves are red tinged when young, maturing to shiny green. Growth habit varies widely among the many available selections: some grow to 10 ft. and spread wider, while others are compact and low growing. Most are thorny, but a few are thornless or nearly so. Some bear small quince-like fruit. All are useful as hedges and barriers.

Flowering quince is easy to grow and virtually indestructible, tolerating extremes of cold and heat, and light to heavy soil. May bloom sparsely or sporadically in warm-winter areas. Prune to shape or to limit growth at any time—but bud and bloom season is a good time for the job, since cut branches can be used for indoor arrangements. New growth that follows bears next year's flowers. Blossoms attract birds.

CHAIN FERN.
See WOODWARDIA

CHAMAEBATIARIA
millefolium
FERNBUSH
Rosaceae
EVERGREEN TO DECIDUOUS SHRUB

☑ ZONES 1–3, 7, 14–21
☀ FULL SUN
◐ ◑ LITTLE TO MODERATE WATER

Native to Rocky Mountains. To 6–8 ft. tall and wide, freely branching from base. Very finely divided, fernlike, aromatic foliage is evergreen in warmer regions, semievergreen or deciduous elsewhere. Midsummer flowers are white, less than ½ in. wide, in many-blossomed upright clusters

Chamaebatiaria millefolium

to 4 in. long. Cut off spent clusters when bloom ends in late summer. Needs good drainage.

CHAMAECEREUS sylvestri.
See **ECHINOPSIS chamaecereus**

CHAMAECYPARIS
FALSE CYPRESS
Cupressaceae
EVERGREEN SHRUBS AND TREES

☑ ZONES VARY BY SPECIES
☀ ◑ FULL SUN OR PARTIAL SHADE
◐ REGULAR WATER

Conifers ranging from rock garden shrublets to timber trees. Sometimes mistaken for arborvitae *(Thuja),* but arborvitae's leaves are entirely green, while false cypresses have white lines on leaf undersides. Most have two distinct types of foliage: juvenile and mature. Juvenile leaves are short, needlelike, soft but often prickly; they appear on young plants and some new growth of larger trees. Mature foliage consists of tiny, scalelike, overlapping leaves. Cones are small and round.

All of the many varieties sold are forms of five species—two from western U.S., two from Japan, one from eastern U.S. New varieties appear each year, while older ones lose market share. Mislabeling is common, since many of these plants closely resemble one another. Numerous dwarf and variegated kinds are available, providing a rich array of choices for bonsai and rock gardens. Pinch out or cut back tips of new growth to control size and shape; don't cut back into old, leafless wood. All types, including trees, can be sheared into hedges. All need good drainage and protection from wind.

C. lawsoniana. PORT ORFORD CEDAR, LAWSON CEDAR. Zones A3; 3–6, 15–17. Pyramidal, 60-ft. Western timber tree with lacy,

drooping foliage. Species is seldom seen in gardens, but its varieties are used there. Blue-green forms include 'Allumii', a slow grower to 30 ft.; 'Ellwoodii', dense, compact to 6–8 ft.; and narrowly conical, 15–18-ft. 'Wisselii', with twisted, irregular growth. Golden-leafed forms include 'Lutea' and 'Stewartii', both conical trees to 30 ft. or more.

Chamaecyparis lawsoniana

C. nootkatensis (Xanthocyparis nootkatensis). NOOTKA CYPRESS, ALASKA CEDAR. Zones A2, A3; 2–6, 15–17. Native from Alaska to California. Pyramidal tree to 80 ft. tall, 25 ft. wide at base. Is coarser than *C. lawsoniana* and stands greater cold, poorer soil. 'Green Arrow' is a narrow selection, reaching 35 ft. tall, only a few feet wide. 'Pendula', to 30 ft., has weeping branches. Twisted branches of 'Torulosa' make a striking silhouette; it grows slowly to 9 ft. tall.

C. obtusa. HINOKI FALSE CYPRESS. Zones A3; 2b–6, 15–17. Native to Japan. There are dozens of golden, dwarf, and fern-leafed forms, but a few varieties are particularly important in landscaping. These include 'Coralliformis', which grows slowly to 6 ft. tall, 4–5 ft. wide, and features contorted branches and fine-textured, blue-green foliage; 'Gracilis', a slender, upright tree to 20 ft. with nodding branch tips; 'Nana Gracilis', a miniature of the former,

Chamaecyparis obtusa
'Nana Gracilis'

reaching 4 ft. in height; 'Nana Lutea', a 4-ft. dwarf with bright yellow foliage; and 'Pygmaea', a slow grower to 3 ft. tall and 5 ft. wide, with red twigs and bright green, fanlike foliage that turns bronze in winter.

C. pisifera. SAWARA FALSE CYPRESS. Zones A3; 2b–6, 15–17. Japanese native to 20–30 ft., rarely seen except in its garden varieties. Silvery blue-green 'Cyano-Viridis' ('Boulevard') is a dense, slow-growing bush to 6–8 ft. high and wide. 'Filifera', a dense mound to 8 ft., has drooping, threadlike branchlets; 'Filifera Aurea' has similar branchlets in yellow. 'Mops' has threadlike branchlets, forms a 1–2-ft. mound; 'Golden Mops' is similar but has yellow foliage.

C. thyoides. ATLANTIC WHITE CEDAR. Zones 1–6, 15–17. Eastern U.S. timber tree is represented in Western gardens by varieties 'Andelyensis', a dense, columnar, gray-green shrub to 10 ft., turning bronze in cold weather; and 'Heather Bun', broader than the former, with leaves that turn intense plum purple in winter.

CHAMAEDOREA
Arecaceae (Palmae)
PALMS

⚡ ZONES 16, 17, 22–24; H2; EXCEPT AS NOTED; OR INDOORS

☼◐ SOME SHADE; BRIGHT INDIRECT LIGHT

💧 REGULAR WATER

Generally small, slow-growing, feather-type palms from Central and South America. Some have single trunks, others clustered trunks. Leaf shape is variable. Good in pots on shaded patio or lanai, in ground on north side of buildings. Some types do well as houseplants. The following are among the most widely grown; other species are also sold.

C. cataractarum. CASCADE PALM, CAT PALM. Native to Mexico. Forms a dense clump to 6 ft. tall, 9 ft. wide. Does best in a moist, partially shaded location with protection from drying winds. Good as hedge, screen, border, or understory plant; fine tubbed specimen, indoors or out.

C. costaricana. If well fed and liberally watered, develops fairly fast into bamboolike clump 8–10 ft. tall and wide. Lacy, feathery leaves 3–4 ft. long. Good potted palm; will eventually need good-size container.

Chamaedorea elegans

C. elegans. Single-stemmed species. Outdoors, grows 6–10 ft. tall, 3–6 ft. wide. Often called parlor palm, this is the best indoor chamaedorea, growing very slowly to an eventual 3–4 ft. as a houseplant. Tolerates crowded roots, poor light. Douse tops with water occasionally, feed regularly, groom by removing old leafstalks. Repot every 2 or 3 years, carefully washing off old soil and replacing it with good potting mix. Plant three or more in one container for effective display. Often sold as *Neanthe bella*.

C. seifrizii. Zones 13, 16, 17, 22–24; H2. Forms clump to 8–10 ft. tall, 6–8 ft. wide. Stems may be somewhat vining on large, established plants. Narrow leaflets.

CHAMAEMELUM
nobile (Anthemis nobilis)
CHAMOMILE
Asteraceae (Compositae)
PERENNIAL

⚡ ZONES 2–24

☼◐ FULL SUN OR PARTIAL SHADE

💧 MODERATE WATER

Chamaemelum nobile

Soft-textured, spreading, 3–12-in.-high mat of bright light green, finely cut, aromatic leaves. Blooms in summer (sometimes continuing into fall in cool climates); blooms winter to spring in hot desert regions. Blossoms of the most commonly grown form look like small yellow buttons, while those of other types resemble little daisies. Makes good lawn substitute if planted 1 ft. apart, mowed or sheared occasionally. Also useful

between stepping-stones or as a low edging along path. 'Treneague' is a nonflowering variety that needs no mowing; 'Flore Pleno' has double daisylike flowers.

The fragrant, sweet, and flavorful chamomile tea comes from the dried flowers of *Matricaria recutita* (*M. chamomilla*).

CHAMAEROPS
humilis
MEDITERRANEAN FAN PALM
Arecaceae (Palmae)
PALM

⚡ ZONES 4–24; H1, H2

☼◐ FULL SUN OR PARTIAL SHADE

💧 MODERATE TO REGULAR WATER

Chamaerops humilis

From western Mediterranean. Probably one of hardiest palms; has survived brief (but not prolonged) temperature drops to 0°F/–18°C or a bit lower. Clumps slowly develop from offshoots, curving to height of 20 ft.; may also reach 20 ft. wide. Growth extremely slow in northern part of range. Green to bluish green leaves on spiny leafstalks. Use plants in containers, mass under trees, grow as impenetrable hedge. Tolerates poor soil, strong winds. *C. h. argentea* (*C. h. cerifera*) has silvery blue foliage.

CHAMELAUCIUM
uncinatum
GERALDTON WAXFLOWER
Myrtaceae
EVERGREEN SHRUB

⚡ ZONES 8, 9, 12–24

☼ FULL SUN

💧 MODERATE WATER

Australian native that is sometimes sold as *C. ciliatum*. Needlelike bright green leaves; showy sprays of pale pink or rosy, ½-in.

Chamelaucium uncinatum

winter flowers cherished for arrangements of long-lasting beauty. Fast growth to 6–8 ft. (perhaps taller when staked) with equal spread. Light and airy, loose and sprawling in appearance; looks somewhat like open-growing heather (*Calluna*). Very old plants have interesting twisted trunks and shaggy bark. Plant on dry, sunny bank or in cutting garden in fast-draining soil. Cut blooming stems freely for arrangements; or cut back after bloom. Seedling plants vary; select in bloom to get color you want. Named varieties include 'Chinchilla' (small, light pink flowers), 'Eric John' (pink), 'Escondido Rose' (reddish purple), 'Purple Pride' (deep rosy purple), 'University' (reddish purple), and 'Vista' (pink). Hybrid 'Lady Stephanie' has light rose blossoms.

CHAMISA. See **CHRYSOTHAMNUS**

CHAMISE. See **ADENOSTOMA fasciculatum**

CHAMOMILE. See **CHAMAEMELUM nobile, MATRICARIA recutita**

CHARD. See **SWISS CHARD**

CHASMANTHE
Iridaceae
PERENNIALS FROM CORMS

⚡ ZONES 13, 15–24; OR DIG AND STORE

☼◐ FULL SUN OR PARTIAL SHADE

💧 NO IRRIGATION NEEDED

South African natives with irislike fans of bright green, 2-ft. leaves that appear shortly after first autumn or winter rains. Narrow, 3–3½-ft.-tall spikes of bright orange-red flowers follow in late winter or early spring, putting on a striking show at a dull time of

C

Chasmanthe aethiopica

year. Plants are fairly hardy, but late frosts may damage flower buds. Cut spent flower spikes to prevent self-sowing. In fall, plant corms in well-drained soil; set them 4 in. deep and 8–12 in. apart. Corms multiply rapidly; dig and divide every 2 or 3 years. During summer dormancy, plants tolerate irrigation (not too much in hot desert regions) but do not need any.

C. aethiopica. Unbranched flower spikes hold blossoms on just one side of spike.

C. floribunda. Once-branched or unbranched spikes bear blossoms along both sides; each spike carries 12–28 flowers. *C. f. duckittii* has yellow flowers.

CHASMANTHIUM latifolium (Uniola latifolia)

SEA OATS, BAMBOO GRASS
Poaceae (Gramineae)
PERENNIAL GRASS

🗺	ZONES 2–10, 14–24
☼ ◐	PARTIAL SHADE IN HOTTEST CLIMATES
💧	REGULAR WATER

Ornamental grass from moist woodlands of eastern U.S. Broad, bamboolike leaves form 2-ft.-wide clump topped in midsummer by arching, 2–5-ft. flowering stems carrying showers of silvery green spikelets that resemble flattened

Chasmanthium latifolium

clusters of oats (or flattened armadillos). These turn copper in fall, look good through winter; they dry to a greenish straw color and are attractive in dried arrangements. Clumps widen slowly and are not aggressive. Leaves turn brown in winter, when plants should be cut back almost to ground. Divide clumps when they become overgrown and bloom diminishes. Stake if flowering stems sprawl.

CHASTE TREE. See **VITEX**

CHAYOTE

Cucurbitaceae
PERENNIAL VINE OFTEN GROWN AS ANNUAL

🗺	ZONES 14–16, 19–24; H1, H2; ANYWHERE AS ANNUAL
☼	FULL SUN
💧	REGULAR WATER

This tropical American native belongs to the same family as squash and resembles a squash vine, though its flowers are inconspicuous. Grown for edible fruit: 3–8 in. long green or yellow green, irregularly oval, grooved, with a large edible seed surrounded by solid, meaty flesh. Flavor similar to that of summer squash. Eat young fruit raw or cooked; boil or bake mature fruit. Large, fleshy tuberous roots can also be eaten—

Chayote

though you cannot, of course, grow the plant as a perennial and consume its roots as well. Chayote is also known as mirliton or christophine.

Needs rich soil. Climbs by tendrils; provide fence or trellis. In areas where fruit is sold in stores, buy in fall and allow to sprout in cupboard; then plant whole fruit edgewise and slanted, with the sprouted end at lowest point, narrow end exposed. If shoot is long, cut it back to 1–2 in. Plant two or more vines to ensure pollination. In mild climates, plant in late winter; in areas where roots may

freeze, pot in 5-gallon container and store in a dark, cool spot until frost danger is past. Plant can produce 20–30-ft. vine in first year, reach 40–50 ft. in second. Tops die down in frost. Bloom starts when day length shortens in fall; fruit is ripe within a month. A well-grown plant can produce 200 or more fruits.

CHECKERBERRY. See **GAULTHERIA procumbens**

CHECKERBLOOM. See **SIDALCEA**

CHECKERED LILY. See **FRITILLARIA meleagris**

CHEIRANTHUS. See **ERYSIMUM**

CHELONE lyonii

TURTLEHEAD
Scrophulariaceae
PERENNIAL

🗺	ZONES 1–9, 14–24
☼ ◐	FULL SUN OR LIGHT SHADE
💧	AMPLE WATER

Chelone lyonii

Leafy, clump-forming perennial native to the eastern U.S. Related to penstemon—but unlike penstemon it is accustomed to life in damp, even boggy, ground. Grows to 4 ft. tall, 2 ft. wide, with 2–6-in. leaves. Short (2-in.) terminal spikes of baggy, inch-long purplish pink flowers with a yellow beard appear in late summer and fall. 'Hot Lips' has bright pink flowers.

CHENILLE PLANT. See **ACALYPHA hispida**

CHENOPODIUM

Chenopodiaceae
ANNUALS AND PERENNIALS

🗺	ZONES VARY BY SPECIES
☼	FULL SUN
💧	REGULAR WATER

Most are weeds; some species are used as food. The plants often have a strong odor. Individual flowers are greenish and insignificant.

C. album. PIGWEED, LAMB'S QUARTERS. Annual. Zones 1–24. Tall weed with leaves to 4 in. long, whitish underneath, smooth pale green above. Leaves can be cooked like spinach.

C. ambrosioides. EPAZOTE, MEXICAN TEA. Perennial. Zones 8, 9, 14–24; H1, H2; Zones 1–7 as annual. Strongly scented leaves to 5 in. long, deeply cut or toothed. Sometimes grown in gardens or collected from the roadside as seasoning for Mexican dishes.

Chenopodium quinoa

C. quinoa. QUINOA. Annual. Zones 1–24, but see below. To 5 ft. tall, with dense flower and seed clusters. A traditional grain of the Andes. Individual seeds look like sesame seeds; they are rinsed to remove surface bitterness, then cooked like rice. Protein content is high. Can't take high heat at blooming or seed setting. Needs short days to bloom; takes light frost. Plant in late spring and harvest in fall. Excellent production in high valleys in the Rocky Mountains. Strains that yield at sea level are available.

CHERIMOYA

Annonaceae
BRIEFLY DECIDUOUS SHRUB OR TREE

🗺	ZONES 21–24; H1, H2
☼	FULL SUN
💧	REGULAR WATER

Native to high elevations in tropics. In Hawaii, grows best above 1,000-ft. elevation. Hardy to about 25°F/−4°C. Grows fast first 3 to 4 years, then slows; eventually forms a tree 15 ft. tall, spreading 15–20 ft. wide. (Unpruned, can reach 30 ft. tall and spread at least as wide.) Leaves are 4–10 in. long, dull green above, velvety-hairy beneath; they drop in late spring, but tree remains leafless only for a brief time. Thick, fleshy, 1-in., hairy brownish or yellow flowers with

Cherimoya

a fruity fragrance begin opening about time of leaf drop and continue forming for 3 to 4 months.

Large fruits weigh ½–1½ lb. Harvest fruit in late fall or winter, when it turns yellowish green. Skin of most varieties resembles short overlapping leaves; some show knobby warts (skin is tender and thin, so handle carefully). Let fruit ripen indoors at room temperature; when ripe, it turns a dull brownish green (some varieties show tan freckles) and yields to gentle pressure like a ripe peach. Refrigerate ripe fruit. Creamy white flesh contains large black seeds and is almost custardlike, with a flavor something like pineapple crossed with banana; eat it with a spoon. Tastes best cold. Specialty nurseries offer several improved varieties, including exceptionally flavorful 'El Bumpo', 'Honeyhart', 'Pierce', and 'Sabor' in California, 'Spain' in Hawaii. 'McPherson' is popular everywhere due to its self-fruitful nature.

Locate tree where you can enjoy fragrance. After it has developed for 4 or 5 years, begin pruning yearly to produce fruiting wood. To ensure fruit set, gather freshly opened flowers and place in a small jar or film canister. Keep in a cool place 12 to 24 hours, by which time the pollen will shed. Use a small paintbrush to pollinate freshly opened flowers.

CHERRY

Rosaceae
DECIDUOUS FRUIT TREES

✎ ZONES VARY BY TYPE

☼ FULL SUN

◆ REGULAR WATER

Both sweet and sour cherries are attractive, productive trees in the home garden. For strictly ornamental relatives, including flowering cherry trees, see *Prunus*.

Sweet cherries. Most common market type and most widely known in the West. Trees 30–35 ft. tall, as broad as high in some varieties; at their best in deep, well-drained soil in Zones 2, 6–9, 14, 15. They have high chilling requirement (need many winter hours below 45°F/7°C) and are therefore not adapted to mild-winter areas of Southern California or low desert. Can't take extreme summer heat or intense winter cold; frosts or rain in spring can damage crop.

Two trees are usually needed to produce fruit, and second tree must be chosen with care. No combination of these will produce fruit: 'Bing', 'Lambert', 'Royal Ann' (they will not pollinate each other). The following varieties will pollinate any other cherry: 'Angela', 'Black Tartarian', 'Republican', 'Sam', 'Stella' (though 'Stella' will not pollinate 'Bing' in mild-winter climates), and 'Van'. However, because 'Lambert' blooms late, it is pollinated best by 'Republican'. 'Craig's Crimson', 'Glacier', 'Lapins', 'Stella', and 'Sweetheart' are self-fruitful (a lone tree will bear).

Cherry trees are easier to grow and harvest when grown on a dwarfing rootstock, such as the Giessen 148 series. Such trees can easily be maintained at less than half the size of those growing on standard rootstocks.

Fruiting spurs are long lived, do not need to be renewed by pruning. Prune trees only to maintain good structure and shape. Fruit appears in late spring to early summer. Use netting to keep birds from eating the crop. For control of brown rot and blossom blight, apply a copper spray just as leaves drop in autumn, then a fungicide when first blooms appear and weekly during bloom. Resume fungicide program about 2 weeks before harvest or if fruit rot begins to appear. Good sanitation will also help limit disease—remove any mummified fruit and prune out and discard diseased twigs as soon as you see them. Spray horticultural oil during the dormant period to control many kinds of pests and diseases, including scale insects and mites.

These are among the best varieties.

'Angela'. Small, glossy black fruit with excellent flavor. Resists cracking. Midseason to late.

'Bing'. Top quality. Large, dark red, meaty fruit of fine flavor. Midseason.

'Black Tartarian'. Fruit smaller than that of 'Bing', purplish black, firm, sweet. Early.

'Craig's Crimson'. Medium to large, deep red to black; superb flavor. Naturally dwarf (about two-thirds normal size). Self-fruitful. Midseason.

'Early Burlat'. Like 'Bing'; ripens 2 weeks earlier.

'Early Ruby'. Dark red, purple-fleshed early cherry that performs well in all sweet cherry areas. 'Black Tartarian', 'Royal Ann', 'Van' are all good pollenizers. Early.

'Emperor Francis'. Medium-size, light red fruit with fine flavor. Favorite in the Northwest. Early.

'Hardy Giant'. Dark red fruit resembles 'Bing'. Good pollenizer, especially for 'Lambert'. Midseason.

'Kristin'. Large black fruit resists cracking. One of the hardiest sweet cherries; worth a try in Zones A2, A3, 1. Midseason.

'Lambert'. Very large, very firm black fruit. Flavor sprightlier than 'Bing'. Late.

Cherry

'Lapins'. Resembles 'Bing' but is self-fruitful. Early to midseason.

'Mona'. Resembles 'Black Tartarian' but is larger. Very early.

'Rainier'. Has yellow skin with pink blush; fruit ripens a few days before 'Bing'.

'Republican' ('Black Republican', 'Black Oregon'). Large, spreading tree. Small, round, purplish black fruit with dark juice, tender yet crisp texture. Good flavor. Late.

'Royal Ann' ('Napoleon'). Large, spreading tree; very productive. Light yellow fruit with pink blush; tender, crisp. Sprightly flavor. Midseason.

'Sam'. Vigorous tree. Large, firm black fruit have excellent flavor. Midseason to late.

'Stella'. Dark fruit like 'Lambert'; ripens a few days later. Self-fruitful

and a good pollenizer for other cherries. 'Compact Stella' is similar, but tree is half the size.

'Sweet Ann'. Medium-size fruit is yellow with a red blush. Excellent flavor. Midseason.

'Sweetheart'. Large, bright red; excellent flavor. Self-fruitful and heavy bearing. Late.

'Utah Giant'. Ripens with 'Bing' but is larger, sweeter; develops sweetness even before fully ripe. Holds color when processed. Pollinate with 'Van' or 'Stella'.

'Van'. Heavy-bearing tree. Shiny black fruit, firmer and slightly smaller than 'Bing'. Good flavor. Ripens earlier than 'Bing' in Northwest, but at the same time in California.

'Vandalay'. Large, black; excellent flavor. Self-fruitful; resists cracking. Midseason.

'White Gold'. Large, yellow with red blush; fine flavor. Self-fruitful and heavy bearing; resists cracking. Midseason.

Sour cherries. Also known as pie cherries. These are spreading trees to 20 ft. tall, best grown in well-drained soil in Zones A2, A3; 1–9, 14–17. They are self-fruitful but poor pollenizers for sweet cherries. There are far fewer types of sour cherries than sweet cherries; these are the most widely grown. The category name notwithstanding, a few varieties listed here are sweet enough to enjoy fresh.

'Early Richmond'. Small, bright red fruit is soft, juicy, and sweet-tart. Early.

'English Morello'. Darker, tarter fruit than that of 'Early Richmond'. Red juice. Late.

'Kansas Sweet' ('Hansen'). Large, semisweet red fruit. Late.

'Meteor'. Fruit similar to that of 'Early Richmond', but tree is smaller. Late.

'Montmorency'. Like 'Early Richmond'. Midseason to late.

'North Star'. Red to dark red skin and sour yellow flesh. Small, very hardy tree. Midseason.

'Surefire'. Bright red skin and flesh; sweet flavor. Late.

CHERRY, FLOWERING.
See PRUNUS

CHERRY OF THE RIO GRANDE.
See EUGENIA aggregata

CHERRY PLUM.
See PRUNUS cerasifera

CHERVIL.
See ANTHRISCUS cerefolium

C

CHESTNUT
Fagaceae
DECIDUOUS TREES

🌿	ZONES 2–9, 14–17, EXCEPT AS NOTED
☀	FULL SUN
💧	MODERATE WATER

The American chestnut (*Castanea dentata*) has become nearly extinct in its native range as a result of chestnut blight, but other species and hybrids are available. They make wonderful, dense shade trees where there is space to accommodate them and where their litter and rank-smelling pollen won't be too obtrusive. All have handsome dark to bright green foliage. Small, creamy white flowers in long (8–10 in.), slim catkins make quite a display in summer. The large edible nuts are enclosed in prickly burs. Nuts fall to the ground when ripe. Gather daily, remove from burs, and let dry in the sun (shade in hot climates). Plant two or more trees to ensure cross-pollination and a substantial crop; single trees bear lightly or not at all. Give occasional deep irrigation.

Chinese chestnut

C. hybrids. Zones 2–9, 14–24. These are mostly offspring of Japanese and European chestnuts (*C. crenata* and *C. sativa*). Trees usually grow 40–60 ft. tall and wide. They do not tolerate alkaline soils. Varieties include 'Colossal', 'Nevada' (small-nutted variety; the proven pollenizer for 'Colossal'), 'Schrader', and 'Skioka'.

C. mollissima. CHINESE CHESTNUT. Native to China, Korea. To 35–40 ft. tall with rounded crown that may spread to 20–25 ft. Leaves 3–7 in. long, with coarsely toothed edges. Most nursery trees are grown from seed, not cuttings; hence, nuts are variable but generally of good quality. Intolerant of alkaline soil.

C. sativa. EUROPEAN CHESTNUT. Native to southern Europe, North Africa, western Asia. Larger, broader than *C. mollissima*: can reach 100 ft. tall with greater spread, but typically grows 40–60 ft. high in gardens. Leaves 4–9 in. long, with sharply toothed edges. Large nuts of excellent quality—the nuts usually sold in markets. Resistant to oak root fungus.

CHICKABIDDY. See **ASARINA**

CHICORY and RADICCHIO
Asteraceae (Compositae)
PERENNIAL

🌿	ALL ZONES
☀	FULL SUN
💧	REGULAR WATER

Native to Mediterranean region; wild form grows as perennial roadside weed 2–4 ft. tall in much of the West and is recognized by its pretty sky blue flowers. Different chicories are grown for three purposes: for salad greens (small-rooted varieties); for roots to make a coffee substitute (large-rooted varieties); and for Belgian or French endive ('Witloof' chicory). To grow 'Witloof', sow seeds in spring or early summer; plants will mature by fall. In winter, trim the greens to an inch of stem; then dig the roots, bury them diagonally in moist sand, and set in dark, cool room until pale, tender new growth has been forced. (For the standard salad green called endive, see Endive.)

Radicchio is the name given to red-leafed chicories grown for salads. 'Rossa de Verona' ('Rouge de Verone'), 'Red Treviso', and 'Rossana' are good varieties. Radicchio makes lettucelike heads that color to a deep rosy red as weather grows cold in fall or winter; its slight bitterness lessens as color deepens.

Chicory

Best sown in mid- to late summer to mature in cool autumn months, though variety 'Giulio' can be sown in spring to harvest in summer.

Sow green-leafed chicory starting in early spring (up to early summer where summers are not too hot); in areas with mild winters, you can also plant in mid- to late summer for fall and winter harvest (or, in the desert, in fall for winter harvest). Sow both green and red types ¼–½ in. deep; thin seedlings to 6–12 in. apart.

CHIHUAHUAN sage. See **LEUCOPHYLLUM laevigatum**

CHILEAN BELLFLOWER. See **LAPAGERIA rosea**

CHILEAN FIRE BUSH. See **EMBOTHRIUM coccineum**

CHILEAN GUAVA. See **UGNI molinae**

CHILEAN JASMINE. See **MANDEVILLA laxa**

CHILEAN WINE PALM. See **JUBAEA chilensis**

CHILOPSIS linearis
DESERT WILLOW,
DESERT CATALPA
Bignoniaceae
DECIDUOUS SHRUB OR TREE

🌿	ZONES 3B, 7–14, 18–23
☀	FULL SUN
💧	LITTLE TO MODERATE WATER

Native to desert washes and streambeds below 5,000 ft. from California to Texas, south into Mexico. To 15–30 ft. tall, 10–20 ft. wide; grows fast at first (as much as 3 ft. in a season), then slows. With age, develops shaggy bark and twisting trunks. Narrow, willow-type leaves 2–5 in. long. Spring to fall, produces fragrant trumpet-shaped blossoms with crimped lobes, similar to those of catalpa; blooms are like small cattleya orchids and attract hummingbirds. Flower color varies among seedlings—may be reddish purple, lavender, rose, pink, or white, often marked with purple and gold. Nurseries select for good color, large size, ruffled form. Gallon-size plants can bloom first year. Drops leaves early; holds a heavy crop of catalpa-like seedpods through winter and can look messy. Thin growth to enhance picturesque shape.

'Burgundy' ('Burgundy Lace'). Deep purplish red flowers.

'Dark Storm'. Lower lip of flower is deep wine red, upper one laven-

Chilopsis linearis

der; lips are usually curved inward. Slow grower to 12–15 ft. high and wide.

'Hope'. White flowers with a pale yellow throat. Wispy, open growth.

'Lois Adams'. Profuse two-tone blooms in pale lavender and magenta; no seedpods. Compact, upright growth.

'Lucretia Hamilton'. Dark purple flowers in large clusters. To 15–18 ft. high and wide.

'Regal'. Combination of lavender and wine red like that of 'Dark Storm', but display is better, since blooms are flat faced and open throated.

'Rio Salado'. Large, ruffled, deep burgundy flowers. Vigorous growth.

'Timeless Beauty'. Long season of two-toned lavender and burgundy blooms; no seedpods. To 15–20 ft. high and wide.

'Warren Jones'. Large, ruffled blossoms in pure, unshaded pink with paler throat. Holds its leaves longer; evergreen in warm-winter climates.

CHIMING BELLS. See **MERTENSIA ciliata**

CHIMONANTHUS praecox (C. fragrans, Meratia praecox)
WINTERSWEET
Calycanthaceae
DECIDUOUS SHRUB

🌿	ZONES 4–9, 14–21
☀◐	AFTERNOON SHADE IN HOTTEST CLIMATES
💧	MODERATE WATER

Native of China, Japan. Needs some winter cold. Winter-blooming shrub with spicy-scented blossoms. Slow, open growth to 10–15 ft. high, 6–8 ft. wide, with many stems from base. Flowers appear on leafless branches in winter or spring and may last for more than a month if not hit by frost. Blossoms are 1 in. wide, translucent pale yellow, with darker centers marked in shades of purple, chocolate, or maroon. Tapered leaves, 3–6 in. long and half as wide, are rough to the touch, medium green; turn yellow green in fall.

In colder part of range, plant in sheltered site to prevent frost damage. In all areas, locate plant where its winter fragrance can be enjoyed. Restrict size by pruning while in flower; shape as a small tree by removing excess basal stems. To rejuvenate a leggy plant, lop it to within a foot of the ground in late winter. Needs good drainage.

Chimonanthus praecox

CHIMONOBAMBUSA.
See **BAMBOO**

CHINA ASTER.
See **CALLISTEPHUS chinensis**

CHINABERRY.
See **MELIA azedarach**

CHINA FIR. See **CUNNINGHAMIA lanceolata**

CHINESE APE.
See **ALOCASIA cucullata**

CHINESE BELLFLOWER.
See **ABUTILON**

CHINESE CABBAGE
Brassicaceae (Cruciferae)
BIENNIAL GROWN AS ANNUAL

🌿	ALL ZONES
☀️	FULL SUN
💧	REGULAR WATER

Makes head somewhat looser than ordinary cabbage, its close relative. Sometimes called celery cabbage. Raw or cooked, it has more delicate flavor than cabbage. There are two kinds: pe-tsai, with tall, narrow heads; and wong bok (Napa cab-

Chinese cabbage

bage), with short, broad heads. Favored pe-tsai variety is 'Michihli'; wong bok varieties include 'Springtime', 'Summertime', and 'Wintertime' (early to late maturing). Definitely cool-season crop; very prone to bolt to seed in hot weather or in the long days of spring and early summer. In Zones 1–6, 10, 11, plant seeds directly in open ground in midsummer; elsewhere, sow in late summer. Sow seeds thinly in rows spaced 2–2½ ft. apart and thin plants to 1½–2 ft. apart. Heads should be ready in 70 to 80 days. Tolerates light shade in hot climates. Subject to same pests as cabbage.

For Chinese white cabbage (bok choy), see Asian Greens.

CHINESE CHIVES.
See **ALLIUM tuberosum**

CHINESE EVERGREEN.
See **AGLAONEMA modestum**

CHINESE FLAME TREE.
See **KOELREUTERIA bipinnata**

CHINESE FORGET-ME-NOT.
See **CYNOGLOSSUM amabile**

CHINESE FOUNTAIN PALM.
See **LIVISTONA chinensis**

CHINESE FOXGLOVE.
See **REHMANNIA elata**

CHINESE GOOSEBERRY VINE.
See **KIWI**

CHINESE GROUND ORCHID.
See **BLETILLA striata**

CHINESE HOUSES.
See **COLLINSIA heterophylla**

CHINESE LANTERN.
See **ABUTILON**

CHINESE LANTERN PLANT.
See **PHYSALIS alkekengi**

CHINESE PARASOL TREE.
See **FIRMIANA simplex**

CHINESE PARSLEY.
See **CORIANDRUM sativum**

CHINESE PLUMBAGO.
See **CERATASTIGMA willmottianum**

CHINESE SCHOLAR TREE.
See **SOPHORA japonica**

CHINESE TALLOW TREE.
See **SAPIUM sebiferum**

CHINESE TARO.
See **ALOCASIA cucullata**

CHINESE WINGNUT.
See **PTEROCARYA stenoptera**

CHINQUAPIN.
See **CHRYSOLEPIS chrysophylla**

CHIONANTHUS
FRINGE TREE
Oleaceae
DECIDUOUS SHRUBS OR TREES

🌿	ZONES VARY BY SPECIES
☀️	FULL SUN
💧💧	MODERATE TO REGULAR WATER

Spectacular flowering plants requiring some winter chill. Common name refers to narrow, fringelike white petals on flowers that are borne in impressive, ample, lacy clusters. Male and female plants are separate; males have larger flowers. If both plants are present, females produce clusters of small, dark olivelike fruit favored by birds. Broad leaves turn bright to deep yellow in fall. Give good drainage. Minimal pruning needed. Resist most pests and diseases, though fungal leaf spot and powdery mildew may occur.

C. retusus. CHINESE FRINGE TREE. Zones 3–9, 14–24. Native to China and Taiwan. Grows about 20 ft. tall, not quite as wide spreading as *C. virginicus*. Usually seen as a big multistemmed shrub but can be trained as a small tree. Leaves

Chionanthus retusus

2–4 in. long. Pure white blossom clusters to 4 in. long appear in late spring or early summer, 2 to 3 weeks before *C. virginicus* comes into flower. A magnificent plant when in bloom, something like a tremendous white lilac. Handsome gray-brown bark (sometimes golden on young stems) provides winter interest.

Chionanthus virginicus

C. virginicus. FRINGE TREE. Zones 2–6, 15–24. Native to southeastern U.S. Leaves and flower clusters often twice as big as those of *C. retusus;* blooms appear a few weeks later. Lightly fragrant, greenish white flowers. Can reach 30 ft. tall, but in gardens usually grows 12–20 ft. high with equal spread. Habit varies from very shrubby and open to more tree-like. In Zones 2–6, where it grows very slowly (the most you can hope for is 12 ft. in 10 years), it is best used as an airy shrub; blooms profusely when just 2–3 ft. tall. In those zones, it is one of the last deciduous plants to leaf out in spring.

CHIONODOXA
GLORY-OF-THE-SNOW
Liliaceae
PERENNIALS FROM BULBS

🌿	ZONES A2, A3; 1–7, 14–20
☀️	FULL SUN DURING BLOOM, LIGHT SHADE AFTER IN HOT CLIMATES
💧	REGULAR WATER DURING GROWTH AND BLOOM

Charming little bulbous plants native to alpine meadows of Crete, Cyprus, and Turkey are among first to bloom in spring. Each bulb produces a stem to 6 in. high, with six-pointed, starlike blossoms in blue, white, or pink spaced along upper part. Straight, narrow leaves are a little shorter than flower stem. In fall, plant bulbs in rich,

C

Chionodoxa luciliae

well-drained soil, setting them 2–3 in. deep and 3 in. apart. In very hot, dry climates, may need some moisture during summer dormancy. When bloom quality declines, dig and divide clumps in early fall. Plantings may also increase from self-seeding.

C. luciliae. Most commonly grown chionodoxa; often confused with other species. Stems typically bear one to four 1½-in., violet-blue blooms. 'Alba' has white flowers larger than those of the species; 'Gigantea' has larger leaves and larger blooms of violet blue; 'Pink Giant' and 'Rosea' bear pink flowers.

C. sardensis. Inch-wide violet-blue flowers with a very small white eye, carried 4–12 to a stem.

× CHITALPA tashkentensis

Bignoniaceae
DECIDUOUS TREE

| 🌿 ZONES 3–24 |
| :☀: FULL SUN |
| ◌ ◑ LITTLE TO MODERATE WATER |

Growing rapidly to 20–30 ft. tall and wide, this tree combines the larger flowers of its *Catalpa bignonioides* parent with the desert toughness and flower color of *Chilopsis linearis,* its other parent. Leaves are 4–5 in. long, 1 in. wide. Erect clusters of frilly, trumpet-shaped flowers in pink, white, or lavender appear from late spring to fall. 'Pink Dawn' has pink blooms, 'Morning Cloud' white ones.

× Chitalpa tashkentensis

Because it constantly drops spent blossoms and leaves in summer, this is not the best tree for planting near patios or walkways. It is susceptible to powdery mildew and anthracnose. Take care not to overwater.

CHIVES.
See **ALLIUM schoenoprasum**

CHLOROPHYTUM

Liliaceae
PERENNIALS

| 🌿 ZONES VARY BY SPECIES; OR INDOORS |
| :◑: PARTIAL SHADE; BRIGHT INDIRECT LIGHT |
| ◑ REGULAR WATER |

Chlorophytum comosum

Frost-tender lily relatives form clumps of attractive evergreen foliage, bear small white flowers in long clusters. In most areas, they are grown as houseplants.

C. bichetii. Indoor plant. West African native grows slowly to 8–10 in. high, 1½ ft. across. Dark green leaves with white stripes, shorter and broader than those of *C. comosum,* gracefully recurved. Flowers carried on 8-in. stalks. Does not produce runners.

C. comosum. SPIDER PLANT. Zones 15–17, 19–24; H1, H2. From South Africa. Forms 1–3-ft.-high clumps of soft, curving leaves like long, broad grass blades. Both 'Variegatum' and 'Vittatum' have white-striped leaves. Flowers about ½ in. long, in loose, leafy-tipped spikes held above foliage. Greatest attraction: miniature duplicates of mother plant, complete with root, at end of curved stems (as with offsets of strawberry plants). These can be cut off and potted individually.

Spider plant is a good choice for hanging baskets. To use as ground cover, set 2 ft. apart in diamond; plants will fill in area in same year. Often sold as *C. capense.*

CHOCOLATE FLOWER.
See **BERLANDIERA lyrata**

CHOCOLATE LILY. See **FRITILLARIA camschatcensis**

CHOISYA ternata

MEXICAN ORANGE
Rutaceae
EVERGREEN SHRUB

| 🌿 ZONES 6–9, 14–24; BORDERLINE IN ZONES 4, 5 |
| :☀: ◑ FULL SUN ONLY IN COOLER CLIMATES |
| ◑ MODERATE WATER |

Mexican native hardy to 15°F/ –9°C. Fast growing to 6–8 ft. high and wide. Lustrous, rich green leaves held toward ends of branches are divided into fans of three leaflets to 3 in. long. Fans give shrub a dense, massive look— but with highlights and shadows. Clusters of fragrant white flowers, somewhat like small orange blossoms, open in late winter or early spring and in bloom continuously for at least two months, then intermittently through summer. Appealing to bees. Sometimes called mock orange. Foliage of 'Sundance' is yellow when young, gradually turning green. 'Aztec Beauty' is a more compact, hybrid

Choisya ternata

form with narrower leaves and fragrant white flowers opening from pink buds in spring and sometimes again in late summer.

Attractive informal hedge or screen. During growing season, thin out older branches in plant's center to force leafy new interior growth. Cut freely for decoration when in bloom. Touchy about soil conditions—difficult to grow in alkaline soils or where water is high in salts. Under such conditions, amend the soil as for azaleas. They are prone to root rot and crown rot if drainage is poor. Subject to damage from sucking insects and mites.

CHOKEBERRY. See ARONIA

CHOKECHERRY.
See **PRUNUS virginiana**

CHOLLA. See OPUNTIA

CHONDROPETALUM elephantinum

CAPE RUSH
Restionaceae
PERENNIAL

| 🌿 ZONES 8, 9, 14–24 |
| :☀: ◑ FULL SUN OR PARTIAL SHADE |
| ◑ ◑ REGULAR TO AMPLE WATER |

Rushlike plant has stems that radiate from the base to form a dense clump 3–5 ft. tall and 4–6 ft. wide. Makes a striking, elegant accent in the ground or in a pot, particularly when a breeze produces a play of light and shadow on its stems. Papery bracts at each stem joint turn from tan to dark brown, then drop off. Narrow clusters of dark brown flower heads (male and female blossoms are on separate plants) top each shoot. Often sold as *C. tectorum,* a closely related but smaller plant (2–3 ft. tall and 3–4 ft. wide).

Chondropetalum elephantinum

Native to South African marshes, it likes to grow with its feet in water, but it is also happy in the ground with regular watering; will even tolerate considerable drought once new growth is complete. Resents high fertility. Cut old growth to the ground just as new sprouts show in spring; or prune out old stems individually if new shoots are already established. Clump expands slowly by rhizomes. Propagate by seed, since roots do not like to be disturbed.

CHORISIA (Ceiba)

FLOSS SILK TREE
Bombacaceae
EVERGREEN TO BRIEFLY DECIDUOUS TREES

| 🌿 ZONES VARY BY SPECIES |
| :☀: FULL SUN |
| ◑ MODERATE WATER |

Native to South America. Heavy trunk is studded with thick spines; it is green in youth, turns gray with age. Leaves divided into

Chorisia speciosa

leaflets like fingers of a hand, drop during autumn flowering or whenever temperatures fall below 27°F/−3°C. Large, showy flowers somewhat resemble narrow-petaled hibiscus blooms. Fast drainage and controlled watering are keys to success. Water established trees about once a month during growing season; ease off in late summer to encourage more flowers. Need little pruning except to remove wayward or dead growth.

C. insignis. WHITE FLOSS SILK TREE. Zones 12, 13, 15–24; H1, H2. To 50 ft. tall and wide. White to pale yellow, 5–6-in. flowers. Blooms from fall into winter; stopped by frost.

C. speciosa. Zones 12–24; H1, H2. Grows 3–5 ft. a year for first few years, then more slowly to an eventual 30–60 ft. tall and wide. Pink, purplish rose, or burgundy flowers are 4 in. or more across. Grafted varieties include 'Los Angeles Beautiful', with wine red flowers, and 'Majestic Beauty', a thornless variety bearing rich pink blooms.

CHORIZEMA
FLAME PEA
Fabaceae (Leguminosae)
EVERGREEN SHRUBS

🌱	ZONES 15–17, 19–24
☀️ ◑	FLOWER COLOR MORE INTENSE IN PARTIAL SHADE
💧	MODERATE WATER

Native to Australia. Hardy to 24°F/−4°C. Both species produce showy clusters of sweet pea–shaped flowers in a blend of orange and purplish red, late winter through spring. A lighter crop often blooms in fall. Fast growing, with slender, graceful branches. Left to go their own way, they are attractive spilling over wall, on banks, in containers or hanging baskets. To keep compact, pinch regularly and cut back after flowering.

C. cordatum. HEART-LEAF FLAME PEA. Grows 3–5 ft. high and wide. Dark green, 1–2-in.-long leaves with small, prickly teeth along the edges. Sometimes erroneously sold as *C. ilicifolium*.

Chorizema cordatum

C. ilicifolium. HOLLY FLAME PEA. To 2–3 ft. high and wide. Oval, ¾–1-in. leaves are similar to those of *C. cordatum*, but edges are wavy and have long, prickly teeth; vaguely resemble leaves of holly (*Ilex*).

CHRISTMAS BERRY. See **HETEROMELES arbutifolia**, **ILEX verticillata**

CHRISTMAS CACTUS. See **SCHLUMBERGERA × buckleyi**

CHRISTMAS CHOLLA. See **OPUNTIA leptocaulis**

CHRISTMAS FERN. See **POLYSTICHUM acrostichoides**

CHRISTMAS ROSE. See **HELLEBORUS niger**

CHRYSACTINIA mexicana
DAMIANITA
Asteraceae (Compositae)
EVERGREEN SHRUB

🌱	ZONES 10–13, 18–24
☀️	FULL SUN
◐ 💧	LITTLE TO MODERATE WATER

Native to Mexico. Heavily branched shrub to 2 ft. tall and wide, with tiny, needlelike, dark green leaves that are strongly aromatic. Golden yellow, 1-in. daisies are borne singly at tips of 2–3-in.-long flowering stems over a long period. Heaviest bloom in spring and fall; eases off in summer in intense heat. A tough plant, endur-

Chrysactinia mexicana

ing extreme heat as well as winter lows to 0°F/−18°C. Tolerant of various soils but does best with reasonably good drainage. Very drought tolerant, but supplemental water in summer encourages more blooms. Valued in folk medicine. Shear annually in early spring; cut back more severely if plant becomes too woody.

CHRYSALIDOCARPUS lutescens. See **DYPSIS lutescens**

CHRYSANTHEMUM
Asteraceae (Compositae)
PERENNIALS AND ANNUALS

🌱	ZONES VARY BY SPECIES
☀️	FULL SUN, EXCEPT AS NOTED
💧	REGULAR WATER, EXCEPT AS NOTED

There are about 160 species of chrysanthemum, mostly native to China, Japan, and Europe. Included are some of the most popular and useful of garden plants—top favorite being *C. × grandiflorum*, whose modern descendants are known as florists' chrysanthemums. Taxonomists have split *Chrysanthemum* into a number of new genera—and, in certain cases, changed their minds and returned some species to the original genus. In the following descriptions, former names are given first, followed by new names in parentheses.

C. arcticum (Arctanthemum arcticum). ARCTIC CHRYSANTHEMUM. Perennial. Zones A1–A3; 1–10, 14–21. Native to Alaska. Very hardy fall bloomer. Forms foot-wide clump of spoon-

Chrysanthemum × grandiflorum

shaped, leathery, usually three-lobed leaves 1–3 in. long. Stems 6–12 in. high bear white or pinkish, 1–2-in. flowers. A group of hybrids known as Northland daisies has been developed from this species; they bear single flowers 3 in. or wider, in shades of pink, rose, rosy purple, and yellow. *C. arcticum* itself is primarily a rock garden plant. Taller-growing hybrids reach 16–20 in. and are best in borders.

C. balsamita (Tanacetum balsamita). COSTMARY. Perennial. Zones 2–24. Native Europe to central Asia. Weedy, rhizomatous plant grown for its sweet-scented foliage (used in salads and sachets) rather than its tiny daisies. Leggy stems reach 3 ft. high; if these are cut

Florists' Chrysanthemum Flower Forms

TOP: 'Firewheel'; spoon
BOTTOM: 'Apricot'; single

TOP: 'Kelvin Mandarin';
pompon
BOTTOM: 'Fireflash';
decorative

TOP: 'Penny Lane'; anemone form
BOTTOM: 'Crimson Tide'; irregular
incurve

TOP: 'Dorridge King'; reflex
BOTTOM: 'Pink Miss Olympia';
laciniated

TOP: 'Super Yellow'; quill
BOTTOM: 'Virginia'; spider

back, the gray-green, finely scallop-margined basal leaves can make a nice edging for an herb garden. Divide clumps and reset divisions in late summer or fall.

C. carinatum (Glebionis carinatum). SUMMER CHRYS-ANTHEMUM, TRICOLOR CHRYSANTHEMUM. Annual. Zones 1–24; H1, H2. Moroccan native grows wild in sand dunes along parts of Southern California coast. To 1–3 ft. high and 3 ft. wide, with deeply cut foliage. Showy bloom in summer and fall: 2-in. single daisies in purple, orange, scarlet, salmon, rose, yellow, or white, with contrasting bands around dark center. Long-lasting cut flowers. Sow seeds in spring, either in pots or open ground. In mild-winter areas, can be sown in fall for winter and spring bloom. Takes light or heavy soil. Court Jesters is an excellent strain.

C. coccineum (Tanacetum coccineum, Pyrethrum roseum). PYRETHRUM, PAINTED DAISY. Perennial. Zones A1; 1–24. Native to Iran, Caucasus. Bushy plant to 2–3 ft. high, 1½ ft. wide, with very finely divided bright green leaves. Bears long-stemmed single daisies in pink, red, or white in spring; if cut back, may bloom again in late summer. Also available in double- and anemone-flowered forms. Excellent for cutting, borders. Needs summer heat to perform well (except in extreme heat of low and intermediate deserts, where it is treated as a winter annual). Sow seeds or divide clumps in spring. Double forms may not come true

from sown seed, may revert to single flowers.

C. coronarium (Glebionis coronarium). CROWN DAISY. Annual. Zones 1–24; H1, H2. Mediterranean native; sometimes seen naturalized on roadsides. To 2½ ft. high and 1½ ft. wide, with coarsely cut light green leaves and yellow daisies in spring, summer. One variety of this species is the vegetable known as shungiku, chop-suey greens, or edible chrysanthemum; it can be cooked like spinach.

C. frutescens (Argyranthemum frutescens). MARGUERITE, PARIS DAISY. Short-lived perennial in Zones 14–24 and H1; summer annual in Zones 3–11; winter annual in Zones 12, 13. Canary Island native has bright green, coarsely divided leaves and woody-based, 3-ft. stems bearing abundant 1½–2½-in. daisies in white, yellow, or pink. Blooms most of the year in mild climates. 'Snow White', double anemone type, has pure white flowers, more restrained growth habit; 'White

Chrysanthemum frutescens

Lady' and 'Pink Lady' produce buttonlike flower heads; 'Silver Leaf' has gray-green leaves and masses of very small white blooms. Dwarf varieties are also available.

All marguerites are splendid in containers and for quick effects in borders, mass displays. A small plant set out in spring can form a 4- by 4-ft. mound by summer. When buying plants, avoid large, vigorous-looking ones with big leaves—they will bloom sparsely. Also avoid plants showing signs of fasciation (flattening or widening of stems) near root crown (at plant's base). Plant in well-drained soil. Grows exceptionally well near coast; also succeeds inland if given sufficient water and good drainage, but may freeze in cold winters. For continued bloom, prune lightly at frequent intervals. In mild-winter areas, do not prune severely, since plants seldom produce new growth from hardened wood; replace every 2 or 3 years. Subject to leaf miner and thrips (which reduce flower quality); old plants are also susceptible to root galls and nematodes.

C. gayanum (Pyrethropsis gayana). Perennial. Zones 14–24. Native to Morocco and Algeria. Woody-based plant to 1½ ft. high, 4 ft. wide, with finely cut gray-green foliage and 1½-in. pink daisies with dark centers. Long bloom season; flowering is heaviest in late winter, early spring. Little water.

C. × grandiflorum. FLORISTS' CHRYSANTHEMUM. Perennial. Zones 2–24; H1. The most useful of all autumn-blooming perennials for borders, containers, and cut-

ting, and the most versatile and varied of all chrysanthemum species, available in many flower forms, colors, plant sizes (from under a foot to 6 ft. tall), flower sizes, and growth habits. Colors include white, yellow, red, pink, orange, bronze, purple, and lavender, as well as multicolors. The following list describes flower forms as designated by chrysanthemum hobbyists.

Anemone form. One or more rows of rays with large raised center disk or cushion. Center disk may be same color as rays or different.

Brush. Narrow, rolled rays give brush or soft cactus dahlia effect.

Decorative. Long, broad rays overlap like shingles to form broad, full flower.

Incurve. Big double flowers with broad rays curving upward and inward.

Irregular incurve. Like above, but with looser, more softly curving rays.

Laciniated is fully double, with rays fringed and cut at tips in carnation effect.

Pompon. Globular, neat, compact, with flat, fluted, or quilled rays. Usually small but can reach 5 in. if buds are thinned to one or two per cluster.

Quill. Long, narrow rolled rays; like spider but less droopy.

Reflex. Big double flowers; rays curl in, out, and sideways, creating shaggy effect.

Semidouble. Somewhat like single or daisy, but with two, three, or four rows of rays around a yellow center.

Single or daisy form. Single row of rays around a yellow center. May be large or small, with broad or narrow rays.

Spider. Long, curling, tubular rays that end with fishhook-curved tips.

Spoon. Tubular rays flattened at tip to make little disks, sometimes in contrasting colors.

Garden culture. It's easy to grow chrysanthemums, not so easy to grow prize-winning chrysanthemums. The latter need more water, feeding, pinching, pruning, grooming, and pest control than most perennials.

Plant in early spring, in an area away from large trees or hedges with invasive roots. In hot climates, choose a spot shaded from afternoon sun. Water deeply at intervals determined by your soil structure—frequently in porous soils, less often in heavy soils. Too

little water causes woody stems and loss of lower leaves; overwatering causes leaves to yellow, then blacken and drop. Stems are attacked by borers in desert areas. Aphids are the only notable pest in all areas. One way to avoid them is to feed plants with systemic insecticide/fertilizer combination. Stake taller plants as needed to keep them upright.

After bloom, cut back plants to within 8 in. of ground. Where soils are heavy and likely to remain wet in winter, dig clumps with soil intact and set on top of ground in inconspicuous place. Cover with sand or sawdust if you wish (a good idea in Zones 2, 3, and 10). Take cuttings from early to late spring (up until May for some varieties) or when shoots are 3–4 in. long. As new shoots develop, you can take additional cuttings from them. In cold-winter areas, store in cold frame or mulch with light, noncompacting material like excelsior.

Pot culture. Pot rooted cuttings midwinter to early spring, using porous, fibrous, moisture-holding planting mix. Move plants to larger pots as growth requires—don't let them become root-bound. Pinch as directed in "What Florists' Mums Need" (at left); stake as required. Plants need water daily in warm weather, every other day in cool conditions. Feed with liquid fertilizer every 7 to 10 days until buds show color.

Off-season, potted chrysanthemums. Florists and even grocery stores sell potted chrysanthemums in bloom every day of the year, though by nature a chrysanthemum blooms in late summer or fall. Growers force these plants to bloom out of season by subjecting them to artificial day lengths, using lights and dark cloths. You can plunge the potted flowering plants right into a garden bed or border for an immediate (but expensive) display, or enjoy them in the house while the flowers remain fresh and then plant them out. Either way, they will not bloom again at the same off-season time the next year. Instead, they will revert to their natural inclination and commence fall bloom once again.

To pot off-season mums after bloom, cut off flowers when they fade, leaving stems 6–8 in. long. Remove soil clump from pot and break apart the several individ-

ual plants that were grown in the pot. Plant these individual plants. When new growth shows from the roots, cut off remainder of old flower stems.

C. hosmariense (Rhodanthemum hosmariense). Perennial. Zones 14–24. Native to Morocco. To 8 in. high, 2 ft. wide, with silvery, finely cut foliage. White daisies bloom over a long season; show is most profuse in winter. Little water.

C. leucanthemum (Leucanthemum vulgare). OX-EYE DAISY, COMMON DAISY. Perennial. Zones A2, A3; 1–24; H1. European native naturalized in many places; spreads by rhizomes and self-seeding. To 2 ft. high, 1 ft. wide, with bright green foliage and yellow-centered daisies from late spring to fall. 'May Queen' begins blooming in early spring.

C. maximum (C. × superbum, Leucanthemum maximum, L. × superbum). SHASTA DAISY. Perennial. Zones A1–A3; 1–24; H1. To 2–4 ft. tall, 2 ft. wide. Original plant with coarse, leathery leaves and gold-centered, 2–4-in.-wide white flowers has been largely superseded by longer-blooming varieties with larger, better-formed flowers. Available in single, double, quilled, and shaggy-flowered forms. All are white, but some show a touch of yellow. All bloom in summer; some start in late spring and continue into fall. All are splendid in borders and as cut flowers. Shasta daisies are easy to grow from seed. Catalogs offer many strains, including dwarf forms that reach only 10–15 in. high.

Set out container-grown plants at any time, divisions in fall or early spring (divide established clumps every 2 or 3 years). Thrive in moist, well-drained, fairly rich soil. Fertilize before and during bloom to encourage large flowers. Prefer sun but do well in partial shade in hot-summer climates; double-flowered kinds hold up better in very light shade. In coldest regions, mulch around plants but do not smother foliage. Shasta daisies are generally easy to grow but have a few problems. One of these is gall, a disease that causes root crown to split into many weak, poorly rooted growing points that soon die. Dig out and discard affected plants and do not replant Shasta daisies in the same spot. When buying plants, avoid those with signs of fasciation (flattening or widening of stems)

near root crown. Control slugs and snails.

C. multicaule (Coleostephus myconis). Annual. Zones A1–A3; 1–24. Native to southern Europe. Blooms in spring, when broad-rayed, buttery yellow daisies ¾ in. across rise above 6–8-in.-wide mats of bright green, fleshy foliage. Blooms best in cool weather; usually sold in fall, winter, or early spring in cell-packs or pots. In Alaska, blooms all summer until frost. In cool-summer/mild-winter climates, plants may live over a second year. 'Moonlight' has lemon yellow flowers.

C. nipponicum (Nipponanthemum nipponicum). Perennial. Zones 3–24. Japanese native resembling a large, rounded, and shrubby Shasta daisy (to 3 ft. tall and 2 ft. wide) with a dense mass of nearly succulent bright green leaves. Long-stemmed white daisies bloom in fall. To maintain compactness, cut back after bloom in mild-winter regions; in colder climates, cut back partway after plants put on strong new growth in spring.

C. pacificum (Ajania pacifica, Pyrethrum marginatum, Dendranthema pacificum). GOLD AND SILVER CHRYSANTHEMUM. Perennial. Zones 3–24. Prohibited in some areas as a host to white rust of chrysanthemum. Semitrailing, woody-based perennial from Japan; to 1 ft. tall, 3 ft. wide. Stems are densely clad in lobed dark green leaves that seem rimmed with white; in fact, woolly white leaf undersides show at edges. Broad clusters of yellow flowers appear in fall; lacking rays, they resemble bunches of brass buttons. Use as bank or ground cover or at the front of perennial border. A tough plant, but lower leaves will die off without regular summer water. Maintain compactness as for *C. nipponicum.* 'Pink Ice' is a pale pink–flowered variety with short rays.

C. paludosum (Leucanthemum paludosum, Melampodium paludosum). Annual. Zones A1–A3; 1–24. Western Mediterranean native forms about 8-in.-wide clumps of dark green, deeply toothed leaves. In summer, bears white flowers resembling miniature Shasta daisies on 8–10-in. stems. Sometimes lives over for a second bloom season. Popularly grown as an annual in Alaska.

C. parthenium (Tanacetum parthenium). FEVERFEW. Perennial. Zones 2–24. Native

C

to southern Europe, Caucasus. Compact, leafy, aggressive, spreading by volunteer seedlings; once favored in Victorian gardens. Leaves have strong peppery scent that some people find offensive. Varieties range from 1 to 3 ft. tall. 'Golden Ball' has bright yellow flower heads and no rays; 'Silver Ball' is fully double, with only the white rays showing. In 'Aureum' (commonly sold in flats as 'Golden Feather'), chartreuse foliage is main attraction. To propagate, divide clumps in spring; or sow seeds in spring for bloom by midsummer.

C. ptarmiciflorum (Tanacetum ptarmiciflorum). DUSTY MILLER, SILVER LACE. Perennial in Zones 16, 17, 19–24; annual in Zones 1–15, 18. Canary Island native grows to 10 in. high and wide. Very finely cut, silvery white leaves. Where winter-hardy, produces white daisies on 1½-ft. stems in summer. Somewhat drought tolerant. (For other plants with the common name "dusty miller," see that entry.)

C. × superbum. See C. maximum

C. weyrichii. Perennial. Zones 2–6. From Japan. Rock garden plant with finely cut leaves; forms a mat to 1–1½ ft. high and 1 ft. wide. Single, 2-in., white to pink daisies with yellow centers appear just above foliage in fall. 'Pink Bomb' has rosy pink rays, and 'White Bomb' has creamy white ones.

C. zawadskii (C. × rubellum). Perennial. Zones 1–24. To 2 ft. high and wide, finely cut leaves, and 2–3-in. daisies over a long season beginning in late summer. 'Clara Curtis' has bright pink flowers; 'Mary Stoker' has blooms of soft yellow touched with apricot.

CHRYSOLEPIS
chrysophylla
CHINQUAPIN
Fagaceae
EVERGREEN TREE OR SHRUB

| ZONES 4–7, 14–17 |
| FULL SUN OR PARTIAL SHADE |
| NO IRRIGATION NEEDED |

Native primarily to Coast and Cascade Ranges from central California to Washington. Habit varies, depending on growing conditions; plant is seen both as a large tree (to 90 ft. tall, 50 ft. wide) and a big shrub. Narrowly oval, 2–6-in. leaves are rich glossy green above, golden beneath from a coating of

Chrysolepis chrysophylla

tiny yellow scales. Fragrant spring flowers in erect or nodding white to creamy white catkins. Fruit a prickly 2-in. bur containing small, sweet-kerneled nuts. Bark is gray and furrowed. Handsome but difficult to grow even in its native range—and extremely difficult elsewhere. Needs excellent drainage, acid soil.

CHRYSOTHAMNUS
RABBITBRUSH, CHAMISA
Asteraceae (Compositae)
DECIDUOUS SHRUBS

| ZONES 1–3, 10, 11 |
| FULL SUN |
| LITTLE OR NO WATER |

High desert, Rocky Mountain natives. Erect, freely branching shrubs to 6 ft. tall, 3 ft. wide; branches are white, with greenish upper surfaces. Gray-green and narrow leaves often drop by bloom time in late summer or fall, when branching, flat-topped or somewhat rounded clusters of fluffy flowers appear at stem ends. Leaves and stems are strongly aromatic. Useful for roadside or naturalistic plantings, revegetation, low-care or no-care borders. Numerous subspecies of both plants described below exist; some are better suited than others to the coldest zones.

Chrysothamnus nauseosus

C. nauseosus. Differs from species below mainly in that its flowers are yellow.

C. viscidiflorus. Flowers are greenish yellow and somewhat sticky.

CHUPAROSA. See **ANISACANTHUS thurberi,** **JUSTICIA californica**

CHUSQUEA. See **BAMBOO**

CIBOTIUM glaucum
HAPU'U, HAWAIIAN TREE FERN
Dicksoniaceae
TREE FERN

| ZONES 17, 23, 24; H2 |
| FULL SUN OR PARTIAL SHADE |
| MODERATE WATER |

Native to Hawaii and the most common tree fern found there; creates a tropical effect in the garden. Very slow grower to 20 ft. tall, with crown spreading 15 ft. wide. Arching, intricately divided, 3–9-ft.-long fronds are medium green above, lighter green beneath. Silky, fawn-colored wool *(pulu)* shrouds the leaf bases and densely covers frond buds at the trunk tip. Needs protection from strong winds. Best with moderate water but tolerates dry or moist conditions. Give some shade in hot, dry areas. Prune to remove old or injured fronds.

Cibotium glaucum

Another tree fern found in lesser numbers in Hawaiian forests is *C. chamissoi.* It has a stout trunk to about 15 ft. tall, covered with blackish, woolly hairs.

CIGAR PLANT. See **CUPHEA ignea**

CILANTRO. See **CORIANDRUM sativum**

CIMICIFUGA. See **ACTAEA**

CINERARIA. See **SENECIO hybridus**

CINNAMOMUM
camphora
CAMPHOR TREE
Lauraceae
EVERGREEN TREE

| ZONES 8, 9, 12–24; H1, H2 |
| FULL SUN OR LIGHT SHADE |
| LITTLE TO REGULAR WATER |

Native to China, Japan. Grows slowly to 50 ft. or taller, 60 ft. wide. Typically a strong-structured tree with heavy trunk and heavy, upright, spreading limbs. Beautiful in rain, when trunk looks black. Aromatic, 2½–5-in.-long leaves smell like camphor when crushed. New foliage in early spring is pink, red, or bronze; matures to shiny yellow green. Inconspicuous but fragrant yellow flowers bloom profusely in late spring, followed by small blackish fruits.

Cinnamomum camphora

Drops leaves quite heavily in early spring; flowers, fruits, and twigs drop later. Plant where litter will not be a problem. Competitive roots also make this tree a poor choice near garden beds and paved areas; roots may invade sewer and drainage lines as well. In desert zones, sometimes affected by salt burn. Subject to verticillium wilt. Symptoms are wilting and dying of twigs, branches, center of tree, or entire tree; wood in twigs or branches shows brownish discoloration. Most susceptible after wet winters or if planted in poorly drained soil. No cure is known, though trees often outgrow the problem. To treat, cut out all damaged branches. Apply nitrogen fertilizer and water it in well.

CINNAMON FERN. See **OSMUNDA cinnamomea**

CINQUEFOIL. See **POTENTILLA**

CISSUS
Vitaceae
EVERGREEN VINES

- ⚡ ZONES VARY BY SPECIES
- ☼ ◐ ● EXPOSURE NEEDS VARY BY SPECIES
- ◔ ◑ ● WATER NEEDS VARY BY SPECIES

These relatives of Virginia creeper, Boston ivy, and grape are valued for their foliage; flowers are inconspicuous. Most climb by tendrils, and most will double as ground covers in mild-winter climates. Easy to grow; not fussy about soil, water, or fertilizer. Prune any time to remove tangled or weak stems or to restrict size. Grown as houseplants, they prefer bright reflected light, moderate water.

C. antarctica. KANGAROO TREEBINE. Zones 16–24; or indoors. Native to Australia. Graceful, densely foliaged vine to 10 ft.; vigorous once established. Glossy, spear-shaped leaves reach 3½ in. long; toothed edges and prominent veins are subtly decorative. In the ground, needs little or no irrigation. Good plant for climbing up or tumbling down—on trellis, wall, or hillside. Sun or shade.

Cissus antarctica

C. capensis. See Rhoicissus capensis

C. discolor. Zone H2; or indoors. Native to Southeast Asia. Can climb to 6–10 ft. but is usually grown in hanging pots. Oval, 4–6-in.-long, toothed leaves resemble those of rex begonia in color and texture; they have showy pink and silver markings, maroon undersurfaces. Needs partial shade, humidity, regular water.

C. hypoglauca. Zones 13–24. Native to Australia. Rapid growth to 15 ft. in one season; eventually reaches 30–50 ft. Climbs by means of flexible stems rather than tendrils. Highly polished, bronze-tinted leaves are divided into five rounded, leathery, 3-in.-long leaflets. New growth is covered with rust-colored fuzz. Use as climber or erosion-controlling bank cover. Sun or light shade. Little or no water.

C. quadrangula (C. quadrangularis). Zones 24; H2; or indoors.

Cissus rhombifolia

Native to tropical Africa, Arabian Peninsula, and eastern India. Odd-looking succulent vine, usually grown in hanging baskets. Generally leafless, with thick, jointed, four-angled or winged stems that climb or trail several feet. Leaves occasionally appear; they are oval or three lobed, 2 in. long. Easy to grow if given regular water, excellent drainage, and full sun.

C. rhombifolia. GRAPE IVY. Zones 13, 15, 16, 21–24; H1, H2; or indoors. Native to South America. Beautiful dark green leaves divided into diamond-shaped, toothed leaflets 1–4 in. long. Veins on leaf undersides have reddish hairs, giving foliage a bronzy overtone. Popular houseplant; tolerates low light. Outdoors, it grows to 20 ft. and can be trained on a support. Full sun to fairly deep shade; moderate water. 'Mandaiana' is more upright and compact than species, with larger, more substantial leaflets. 'Ellen Danica' is smaller than species, with lobed leaflets.

C. striata. Zones 13–24; or indoors. Native to South America. Handsome vine reaching 20 ft. Looks very similar to a miniature Virginia creeper (*Parthenocissus quinquefolia*), with small, leathery leaves divided into three to five 1–3-in.-long leaflets. Foliage contrasts with reddish stems. Train it to make a tracery against a wall surface, let it spill over wall, or use as ground cover. Sun or shade. Moderate water.

C. trifoliata. GRAPE IVY. Zones 10–13; evergreen only in warmest locations. Native to the Southwest and Mexico. Climbs by simple or forked tendrils to 30 ft., or sprawls along the ground. Smooth dark green leaves are typically divided into three 3–4-in. leaflets but are sometimes merely three lobed. Flowering stalks are reddish; inconspicuous flowers are followed in summer by black berries on bright red stalks. Useful for covering chain-link fences or trellises. Contact with plant may cause a skin rash in sensitive people. Full sun. Little to moderate water.

C. voinieriana. See Tetrastigma voinierianum

CISTUS
ROCKROSE
Cistaceae
EVERGREEN SHRUBS

- ⚡ ZONES 6–9, 14–24; BORDERLINE IN ZONES 4, 5
- ☼ FULL SUN
- ◔ LITTLE OR NO WATER

Mediterranean natives; hardy to 15°F/–9°C. In their favored dry-summer climate, they are carefree shrubs bearing a profusion of showy flowers for a month or more from spring into early summer; may also bloom sporadically at other times. In some rockroses, leaves are coated with a perfumed resin; others have foliage covered with gray wool. When plants are out of bloom, their soft green, silver, or grayish foliage and mounded form add subtle color and texture to the landscape.

Sun loving, fast growing, tolerant of aridity. Accept poor soil, cold ocean winds, salt spray, desert heat. Often planted in fire-hazard areas. Good erosion-control cover for dry banks. Useful in big rock gardens, in rough areas along drives, in wild plantings. Taller kinds make attractive informal hedges. Give plants well-drained soil if they will be watered. When locating in an area that won't be irrigated, take particular care not to plant root-bound plants; cut circling roots and spread out the mass so roots can grow down to lower soil levels. Most rockroses resent hard pruning. To keep plants vigorous and neat, periodically cut out a few old stems. Tip-pinch young plants to thicken growth, or give a light overall summer shearing to new growth and stems that have not become woody. If plants become woody and sparse after several years, it is often easiest to replace them.

C. albidus. WHITE-LEAVED ROCKROSE. To 4 ft. tall, 8 ft. wide, with furry gray leaves. Bright purplish pink, 2-in. flowers. Repeat bloom in fall is common.

C. 'Brilliancy'. See C. 'Sunset'

C. × corbariensis. See C. × hybridus

C. crispus. To 3 ft. tall, 5 ft. wide, with furry, wavy-edged gray-green leaves and 2–2½-in. purplish pink flowers. 'Santa Cruz' is a compact, dense selection or hybrid with fuzzy gray foliage and 3-in. blossoms in deeper purplish

Cistus × purpureus

rose. 'Descanso' grows 1 ft. tall and 4 ft. wide, bears a profusion of 1½-in. cerise flowers; often mistakenly labeled 'Warley Rose'.

C. 'Doris Hibberson'. Compact grower to 3 ft. tall and wide. Oval gray-green leaves; clear pink, 3-in. flowers with crinkled, silky petals.

C. × hybridus (C. × corbariensis). WHITE ROCKROSE. Widely grown. To 3–4 ft. tall, 4–8 ft. wide. Gray-green, crinkly, 2-in.-long leaves are fragrant on warm days. White flowers 1½ in. across, yellow centers.

C. incanus (C. villosus). Bushy plant to 3–5 ft. tall and wide. Oval, 1–3-in. leaves are densely covered with down. Purplish pink flowers, 2–2½ in. wide. 'LASCA Select' grows 3 ft. high and 5–8 ft. wide, with deep mauve blooms among soft grayish green leaves with white undersides. *C. i. creticus (C. creticus)* is similar but has wavy-edged leaves.

C. ladanifer (C. ladaniferus maculatus). CRIMSON-SPOT ROCKROSE. Compact growth to 3–5 ft. high with equal spread. Fragrant leaves to 4 in. long are dark green above, lighter beneath; 3-in.-wide flowers are white with a dark crimson spot at each petal base. 'Cordoba' is a choice selection, 'Albiflorus' an unspotted form. *C. l. latifolius (C. palhinhae)* is a lower grower (to 2 ft.) but has larger blooms (3–4 in. across). Hybrids include 'Maculatus', to 6 ft. tall, 4–5 ft. wide; and 'Blanche' (to 8–12 ft. high, 6–8 ft. wide) and 'Frank Birch' (to 6–8 ft. tall and wide), both bearing 4-in. pure white blossoms.

C. laurifolius. Stiff, erect growth to 4–6 ft. high and wide. Dark green, 5-in. leaves with pale undersides. White, 2–2½-in. flowers come in long-stalked clusters of three or more. 'Bennett's White' has 3–4-in. flowers resembling those of Matilija poppy (*Romneya coulteri*), with wavy, crepe paper–textured petals around a large cluster of yellow stamens. Good hedge or background shrub for dry areas.

C. 'Peggy Sammons'. To 3–6 ft. tall and wide, with gray-green leaves and 2½-in. pink flowers.

C. × purpureus. ORCHID ROCKROSE. Compact grower to 4 ft. tall and wide, often shorter and wider when subjected to constant ocean winds. Leaves 1–2 in. long, dark green above, gray and hairy beneath. The 3-in., reddish purple flowers have a red spot at each petal base. Very fine where cool winds and salt spray limit choice of plants.

C. salviifolius. SAGELEAF ROCKROSE. Sometimes sold as *C. villosus* 'Prostratus'. Wide-spreading shrub to 2 ft. high, 6 ft. wide. Light gray-green leaves about 1 in. long, crinkly, veined, crisp looking. Very profuse show of 1½-in.-wide flowers, white with yellow spot at base of each petal. Good bank or ground cover for rough situations.

C. × skanbergii. To 3 ft. tall, 8 ft. wide. Gray-green leaves; great profusion of 1-in., pure pink flowers.

C. 'Sunset' ('Brilliancy'). Dense, spreading growth to 2 ft. tall, 6–8 ft. wide, with resinous gray-green leaves and 2-in.-wide flowers in dark magenta pink.

C. 'Victor Reiter'. Stiffly erect plant to 3–4 ft. high and wide. Gray-green leaves; 2½–3½-in.-wide blossoms in hot pink with paler pink center. Sister seedling of 'Doris Hibberson' but superior to it.

C. villosus. See C. incanus
C. villosus 'Prostratus'. See C. salviifolius

CITRON. See **CITRUS**

CITRUS
Rutaceae
EVERGREEN TREES AND SHRUBS

✎ ZONES 8, 9, 12–24; H1, H2; OR INDOORS

☀ FULL SUN; BRIGHT LIGHT

💧 REGULAR WATER

As landscaping plants, citrus offer year-round attractive form and glossy deep green foliage; also bear fragrant flowers and decorative fruit in season. If you want quality fruit, your choice of varieties will depend on the total amount of heat available through the fruit-developing period (need varies according to type) and on the winter cold in your zone. Citrus flowers attract bees.

Heat requirements. Generally, sweet-fruited varieties need moderate to high heat to form sugars, sour types less heat. Lemons and limes require the least warmth and will produce usable fruit in cool-summer areas (as long as winter temperatures are not too low). 'Valencia' orange has a lower heat requirement and greater frost tolerance; it is adapted to areas

near Southern California coast. Navel oranges demand even more warmth and are better suited to inland regions; their fruit development period is shorter than that of 'Valencia', so trees will produce palatable fruit between winter frosts if summer heat is high. Mandarins (tangerines) require high heat for top flavor and are best adapted to inland areas. Grapefruit develops full flavor only where trees receive prolonged high heat, as in the low desert. (In cooler areas, you're better off growing grapefruit-pummelo hybrids 'Oroblanco' and 'Melogold', which produce sweet fruit in more moderate temperatures.)

Hardiness. Citrus plants of one type or another are grown outdoors all year round in regions with warm to hot summers and mild winters. Lemons, limes, and citrons are most sensitive to freezes. Sweet oranges, 'Improved Meyer' lemon, grapefruit, and most mandarins and their hybrids are intermediate in cold resistance. Kumquats, satsuma mandarins, sour oranges, and calamondin are the most cold resistant, with kumquats—the hardiest of all—withstanding temperatures in the high teens.

Other factors affecting a tree's cold tolerance include preconditioning to cold (it has greater endurance if exposed to cold slowly and if first freeze comes late), type of rootstock, and location in garden. Prolonged exposure to freezing weather is more damaging than a brief plunge in temperature. All citrus fruit is damaged at several degrees below freezing—hence the importance of choosing early-ripening varieties in freeze-prone areas. For information on protecting plants from frost and cold, see "A Practical Guide to Gardening."

Growing citrus in Hawaii. Home gardeners in Hawaii can grow many of the varieties grown on the mainland, plus some specialty types adapted only to the islands (these are included in the variety descriptions). However, citrus grows differently in Hawaii, and the fruit often looks and tastes quite a bit different from the same variety grown in California or Arizona. The trees tend to bloom almost year-round, so harvest is nearly continual. The lack of cool nights results in a rind that's thinner and more greenish than the thicker,

brightly colored skin of fruit grown in California. Lack of cool nights also reduces acid content, which is why Hawaiian citrus tastes sweeter. The fruit is very juicy as well.

Standard or dwarf. Practically all citrus plants sold have been budded or grafted on an understock. Grafted trees begin bearing fruit in just a few years, contrasted to 10 to 15 years for seedling trees. Standard trees (20–30 ft. tall and as wide) are grown on a variety of understocks. Dwarf trees are grown on understocks of trifoliate orange (*Poncirus trifoliata*) or 'Flying Dragon'; the latter is a naturally dwarf, contorted, spiny form of trifoliate orange. Ordinary trifoliate orange understocks produce trees 8–10 ft. tall (some may reach 15–20 ft.). 'Flying Dragon' produces even smaller trees (5–7 ft. at 13 years). Check citrus trees periodically for suckers (branches that arise below the graft line) and remove them before they compete with (or overwhelm) the desired variety. Some tender citrus, such as limes, are grown from cuttings; if such trees are killed to the ground by severe cold, they will resprout from the roots true to type.

Harvest periods. Most citrus varieties ripen their fruit from late fall into winter, but some varieties, such as 'Valencia' orange, ripen into spring and summer. In addition, many types can hold their fruit on the tree for long periods without loss of quality. By growing both 'Washington' navel and 'Valencia' oranges, for example, you can have fresh fruit almost 10 months of the year. Everbearing citrus like lemons and limes can produce throughout the year, but they fruit most heavily in winter and spring.

Citrus fruit ripens only on the tree. The best way to judge its ripeness is to pick a fruit and taste it; rind color is a poor indicator, since many varieties are fully colored before they are edible.

Drainage. Fast drainage is essential. If soil drains slowly, don't attempt to plant citrus in it regardless of how you condition it. Instead, plant above soil level in raised beds or on a soil mound. Drainage in average soil (and

water retention in sandy soil) will be improved by digging in a 4–6-in. layer of organic matter (such as garden compost or ground bark) to a depth of about 1 ft.

Watering. Citrus trees need moist soil, but never standing water. They also need air in the soil. Danger from overwatering is greatest in clay soil where air spaces are minute. In soil with proper drainage, water newly planted trees almost as frequently as trees in containers—twice a week in normal summer weather, more frequently during hot spells. Water established trees every other week during summer. In clay soils, space watering intervals so top 4–6 in. of soil dries between irrigations. Don't let tree reach wilting point. Be sure to water consistently. Fluctuating soil moisture can aggravate fruit splitting—a problem that can affect all citrus, but especially navel oranges (typically in autumn).

If you build basins, make them wider than spread of branches. Citrus roots extend out twice as far as the distance from the trunk to branch ends. Keep trunk dry by starting basin 6 in. or more from trunk. When you water, be sure to wet the entire root zone (that is, soak the soil to a depth of 3–4 ft.).

Orange

Mulching. Since citrus roots grow near the surface as well as deeper, a mulch over the soil is beneficial. Use a 2–3-in. layer of compost or other organic matter to help maintain soil moisture. In mild-summer areas, large pebbles or gravel will increase reflected heat and hasten ripening. Don't allow grass to grow near the trunks of citrus trees. Instead, maintain a grass-free, mulched area under the canopy.

Fertilizing. Nitrogen is the main nutrient that must be supplied in all regions. If you garden in sandy soil, choose a complete fertilizer containing a full range of nutrients. Apply 2 oz. actual nitrogen the first year after a newly planted tree puts on new growth; then increase the amount by 4 oz. each year for the next few years. After the fifth year, apply 1–1½ lb. yearly. (Depending on tree size, give plants growing in raised beds or with restricted root space as well as trees grafted onto 'Flying Dragon' rootstock about a third to half the recommended amount after the fifth year.) To determine weight of actual nitrogen, multiply percentage of total nitrogen (as stated on fertilizer label) by total weight of fertilizer.

Divide total fertilizer into several feedings throughout the growing season. In freeze-prone areas, start feeding in late winter and stop in late summer. Make sure trees are well watered before feeding. Spread the fertilizer beneath and a foot or two outside the branch spread of the tree; then water it in deeply.

Citrus trees that receive too much or too little nitrogen show the evidence in leaf color. Dark green, lush leaves with burned tips or edges indicate too much nitrogen; yellowish leaves are a sign of nitrogen deficiency.

Citrus may suffer from chlorosis due to iron, manganese, or zinc deficiency. In iron chlorosis, leaves turn yellow from edges inward; veins remain dark green. (Same symptom may be caused by overwatering, so check your irrigation practices.) Manganese deficiency shows up as fine mottling, usually on young leaves, and as pale or yellowish areas between dark green veins. Signs of zinc deficiency are yellowish blotching or mottling between leaf veins. Manganese and zinc deficiencies may occur together and be difficult to distinguish from each other. Commercial products containing chelates of all three nutrients are available as foliar sprays.

Pests and diseases. Citrus can get aphids, mites, scale insects, and mealybugs. If these pests' natural enemies fail to handle the infestations, and if jets of water fail to keep the pests in check, spray with appropriate chemicals. If scale remains troublesome, spray with horticultural oil in early spring. Control snails and slugs whenever necessary, especially during warmnight spells in winter and spring.

Copper bands, available in some areas, will keep snails out of trees. Where it is legal to do so (in Southern California), colonize citrus groves with decollate snails, which prey on the garden snail.

The citrus bud mite causes weirdly deformed fruit (especially lemons). Control with horticultural oil spray in spring and in fall; spray only in fall in hot-summer areas. Reduce harmful insect populations by keeping ants out of trees with sticky bands on trunks. (Ants prey on natural insect predators of the mites.)

The few fungal ailments of citrus occur in poorly drained soil. Water molds, causing root rot, show up in yellowing and dropping foliage. Best control is to correct your watering schedule.

Brown rot gummosis usually occurs in older trees at base of trunk. Keep base of trunk dry; trim and clean the oozing wounds, removing decayed bark to a point where discolored wood does not show. Paint areas with Bordeaux paste mixture.

Sunburn. The bark of newly planted citrus trees is subject to sunburn in hot-sun areas. Trunks should be wrapped (paper trunk bands are available commercially). When heavy pruning exposes trunks or limbs, protect bark with whitewash or latex paint diluted by half with water.

Pruning. Commercial trees are allowed to carry branches right to ground. Production is heaviest on lower branches. Growers prune only to remove twiggy growth and weak branches or, in young plants, to nip back wild growth and balance the plant. You can prune garden trees to shape as desired; espaliering is traditional, though espaliered citrus is not very productive. Lemons and sour oranges are often planted close and pruned as hedges. 'Lisbon' and 'Eureka' lemons should be pruned to keep the trees within bounds and the fruit easily reachable. Many citrus are thorny, so wear gloves and a long-sleeved shirt when picking fruit or pruning. In freezeprone areas, don't prune in fall or winter. Wait until late spring or summer to prune frost-damaged trees—new growth will make it clear which wood is dead. If you're growing a multiple-variety citrus tree, you must continually cut back the vigorous growers (lemon, lime, pummelo, grapefruit) so the weaker ones (sweet orange, mandarin) can survive. On all citrus, remove fruit from newly planted trees so that the trees energy will be channeled into new growth rather than fruiting.

Citrus in containers. In general, containers should have a diameter of at least 1½ ft., though calamondin and 'Chinotto' sour orange can stay in 8–10-in. pots for years. Plant in light, well-drained soil mix. Daily watering may be necessary in hot weather. Fertilize monthly from midwinter to midautumn with high-nitrogen liquid fertilizer containing chelated zinc, iron, and manganese.

Potted citrus can stay outdoors all year in mild-winter climates, but plants should be moved to a protected location if a freeze is predicted. In cold-winter regions, shelter plants in winter; a cool greenhouse is best, but a basement area or garage with good bright light is satisfactory. Most container-grown citrus will need to be root-pruned and repotted in fresh soil every 4 or 5 years to remain healthy.

Citrus as houseplants. There's no guarantee of flowering or fruiting indoors, though plants are still appealing. 'Improved Meyer' and 'Ponderosa' lemons, 'Bearss' lime,

Lance Walheim on Mandarins

Lance Walheim is a big fan of mandarins because of their sweet, complex flavor as well as for their attractiveness in the landscape. As a citrus grower and horticulturist based in California's Central Valley, Walheim makes it his business to know the best-tasting varieties. Among his favorite introductions are 'Page' ("juicy, with a rich, unique sweetness"), 'Pixie' ("easy to peel, seedless, and mouthwatering"), 'Gold Nugget' ("delicious fruit produced over a long season"), and 'Seedless Kishu' ("a great snack fruit—just peel and eat in one bite"). And for early ripening and heavy production of luscious fruit, Walheim says, "it's hard to beat the 'Owari' satsuma."

'Pixie' mandarin

kumquats, calamondin, and 'Rangpur' sour-acid mandarin are most likely to produce good fruit. Locate no farther than 6 ft. from a sunny window, away from radiators or other heat sources. Ideal humidity level is 50 percent. Increase moisture by misting tree; also ring tree with pebble-filled trays of water. Water sparingly in winter.

SWEET ORANGE
The commercial oranges of the West are typified by 'Washington' navel and 'Valencia'. In the following list, 'Washington' and the other navel varieties are described first, then 'Valencia' and its counterparts, and finally the other, lesserknown sweet oranges.

'Washington' navel. Widely adapted except in desert regions; best in warm interiors. Standard tree is 20–25-ft. globe. On dwarf stock, it grows 8–12 ft. high. Bears early to midwinter. 'Tabata' is identical (or nearly so) to 'Washington'; it is grown in Hawaii, as is the standard 'Washington'.

'Cara Cara'. First rosy-fleshed navel; bears about the same time as 'Washington'. Rich flavor.

'Lane Late'. Late-ripening navel, extending the season well into summer. 'Summernavel' is also late ripening, but fruit flavor and quality is not as good.

'Robertson'. Variant of 'Washington'. Fruit identical but earlier by 2 to 3 weeks. Tends to carry fruit in clusters. Tree generally smaller than 'Washington'. Has same climate adaptation. Dwarf trees produce amazing amounts of fruit.

'Skaggs Bonanza'. Another variant of 'Washington'. Fruit colors and ripens earlier; tree produces fruit at young age. Very heavy bearing.

'Valencia'. The juice orange of stores. Most widely planted orange in the world. Widely adapted in California but a poor risk in Arizona; if you plant it there, select a warm location or provide some protection to fruit, which must overwinter on tree. One of Arizona Sweets (see next page) would be a safer bet. 'Valencia' oranges mature in summer and store on tree for months, improving in sweetness. Vigorous tree, fuller growing than 'Washington', both as standard and dwarf.

C

C

'Campbell', 'Delta', and 'Mid-knight' are early-ripening, nearly seedless selections of 'Valencia'.

Arizona Sweets is a group of varieties grown in Arizona. They include 'Diller', which bears small to medium-size oranges with few seeds and high-quality juice in late fall (before heavy frost) on a vigorous, large, dense tree with large leaves; 'Hamlin', similar but not as hardy, producing medium-size fruit; 'Marrs', with tasty, low-acid, early-ripening fruit on a naturally semidwarf tree that bears young; and 'Pineapple', tending to bear rich-flavored, seedy fruit in alternate years.

Blood oranges are characterized by red pigmentation in flesh, juice, and (to a lesser degree) rind. Flavor is excellent, with raspberry overtones. Generally, they thrive wherever sweet oranges produce good fruit. Pigmentation varies with local microclimates and weather. 'Moro' bears fruit with deep red flesh and variable amounts of red on the rind from early winter to early spring (no rind pigmentation on the coast); 'Sanguinelli' has red-skinned fruit and flesh streaked with red from late winter to midspring; and 'Tarocco' produces fruit with red or red-suffused pulp and pink to red juice from early to midwinter (color varies from year to year), with good quality in cooler areas. 'Tarocco' is very vigorous and open growing, with long, willowy, vinelike branches; dwarf makes ideal espalier.

'Shamouti' ('Palestine Jaffa'). Originated in Israel and considered there to be finest orange. Large, seedless, no navel. Not a commercial orange in California because not sufficiently superior to 'Washington' navel. Grown on dwarf rootstock for home gardens because of beauty in form and foliage. It is wider than tall. Larger leaves than those of navel oranges. Heavy crop of fruit in early spring. 'Pera' is a 'Shamouti' relative grown in Hawaii.

'Trovita'. Originated from seedling of 'Washington' navel. Thin skinned and about navel size, but without navel. Ripens in early spring. Apparently requires less heat than other sweet oranges and develops good-quality fruit near (though not on) coast. Nevertheless, it tolerates heat well enough to pass as one of the Arizona Sweets. Dwarf tree has 'Washington' navel look, with handsome dark green leaves.

SOUR ORANGE
Very ornamental trees with attractive leaves and big, perfumed, waxy white flowers. Clusters of deep red-orange, tart fruits ripen midfall to winter, hold for a year. For all citrus-growing regions.

'Bouquet de Fleurs' ('Bouquet'). Big shrub or small tree to 8–10 ft. Graceful, dark green foliage. Use as hedge or windbreak. Flowers unusually large, very fragrant. Small, bitter fruit used only in marmalade.

'Chinotto' (myrtle-leaf orange). Dense, bushy, round headed, with closely set, small, almost myrtle-like leaves. Very slow grower to 7–20 ft. tall. Formal appearance; often rounded high on stem and clipped. Makes an ideal tub plant.

Decorative small, round, bright orange fruit is used in Europe for candying.

'Seville'. Thorny, upright to 20–30 ft. high. Used as a street tree in Arizona and Southern California. Good specimen plant or for hedge or tall screen. Seedy fruit makes superior marmalade.

MANDARIN (INCLUDES TANGERINE)
Large and diverse group of citrus that includes many varieties and hybrids. Varieties with orange-red peel are usually called tangerines. Many mandarins tend to bear heavily in alternate years. Some are always seedless, while others produce more seeds; the latter give seedier fruit if pollinated by another mandarin or mandarin hybrid or by 'Valencia' orange.

'Clementine' (Algerian tangerine). Fruit a little larger than 'Dancy', with fewer seeds. Ripens late fall into winter; remains on tree for months, staying juicy and sweet. Seems to develop full flavor in areas that are too cool for a good 'Dancy'. Tree reaches 12 ft., semiopen with vertical, spreading, somewhat willowy branches. Usually bears light crops without another variety for pollination.

'Dancy'. Standard tangerine in markets before Christmas. Smaller and seedier than other mandarins. Best flavor in Zones 12 and 13 but good in Zones 21–23. Ripens late fall into winter; holds well on tree. Upright tree with erect branches. Dwarf tree handsome in container or as espalier.

'Encore'. Light orange, thin-skinned fruit ripens in summer (latest of all mandarin varieties), holds until fall. Good quality. Erect tree with slender branches and narrow leaves.

'Fairchild'. Hybrid between 'Clementine' mandarin and 'Orlando' tangelo. Medium-size, deep orange fruit peels easily, is seedy but juicy and tasty. Ripens late fall into winter. Small, compact tree bears every year. Needs another variety for pollination. Best in desert areas.

'Fremont'. Medium-size, bright orange fruit ripens late fall into winter. Good flavor. Tends to bear in alternate years; thin fruit when crop is unusually heavy.

'Gold Nugget'. Small to medium size, seedless, with rich, sweet flavor. Light yellow orange, often with rough rind (like 'Pixie'); easy to peel. Holds well on the tree and ripens late winter to spring.

'Honey'. Small, seedy fruit with rich, sweet flavor; matures winter into spring. Typically bears heavily in alternate years. Vigorous tree. Not the same as 'Murcott', a tangor often sold in markets as 'Honey'.

'Kara'. Large fruit (2½ in. wide) for mandarin. Tart-sweet, aromatic flavor when ripened in warm interior climates. Ripens winter to spring. From one season to another may be very seedy or nearly seedless. In form, tree resembles 'Owari' satsuma, one of its parents. Spreading, often drooping branches with large leaves. Grows to a rounded 15–20 ft., half that size as dwarf.

'Kinnow'. Medium-size fruit with rich flavor and fragrance. Stores well on tree. Ripens winter to early spring. Handsome tree—

Citrus Types

: 'Minneola' tangelo
: 'Sanguinelli' blood orange

: 'Oroblanco' grapefruit
: 'Chandler' pummelo

: 'Nagami' kumquat
: 'Valencia' orange

: 'Bearss' lime
: 'Dancy' mandarin

: 'Etrog' citron
: 'Improved Meyer' lemon

columnar, dense, very symmetrical to 20 ft. (dwarf will reach 10 ft.). Densely foliaged with slender leaves. Good in any citrus climate.

'Mediterranean' ('Willow Leaf'). The important mandarin of the Mediterranean region. The sweet, aromatic fruit ripens in spring. Spreading tree with thin, willowy branches and narrow leaves.

'Page'. Hybrid between 'Clementine' mandarin and 'Minneola' tangelo. Many small, juicy, sweet fruits autumn into winter. Few seeds, even with another variety for pollination.

'Pixie'. Easy peeling, seedless fruit with excellent flavor, usually with a bumpy rind. Ripens midseason to late. Upright tree.

Satsuma. This group of mandarins is the source of imported canned "mandarin oranges." Sweet, delicate flavor; nearly seedless, medium to large fruit. Loose skin. Earliest mandarin to ripen—early fall to late December. Quickly overripens if left on tree but keeps well in cool storage. Standard trees are spreading, to 10–15 ft. high. Dwarf trees can be used as 6-ft. shrubs. Open, angular growth when young, becoming more compact with age. Not suited to the desert. 'Owari' is the main satsuma grown in the West.

'Seedless Kishu'. Very small, loose skinned, easy to peel; exceptionally rich flavor. Ripens late fall to winter.

'Shasta Gold', 'Tahoe Gold', and 'Yosemite Gold' are three recent introductions from the University of California. All produce large, seedless, deep orange fruit that is easy to peel and has a sweet, rich flavor. Ripen late winter to spring, 'Tahoe Gold' being the earliest of the three.

'W. Murcott' ('Afourer'). Mid- to late-season, medium-size fruit with excellent flavor. Often sold as Delite in supermarkets. Many seeds if cross-pollinated. A seedless form, called 'Tango', has recently been released but may be hard to find in nurseries.

SOUR-ACID MANDARIN

These fairly compact plants produce usable fruit (and are everbearing in mild climates), but their best feature is good looks. They thrive outdoors in the ground or in pots in all citrus-growing areas; indoors, they fruit reliably and are very decorative.

Calamondin. Fruit looks like tiny (¾–1½-in.) orange. Hundreds hang from tall, columnar plant

(8–10 ft. tall and about half as wide, even as dwarf). Also available in a variegated form, with leaves marked with creamy yellow; developing fruit may be striped in yellow and green. Flesh is tender, juicy, sour, with a few small seeds. Skin and flesh good in marmalades.

'Otaheite' (Tahiti orange). Despite the common name, not a true orange. Natural dwarf only a few feet tall. Usually grown indoors as decorative potted plant. Will bear very young. Orange to reddish orange fruit is small, round, and rough skinned; insipid in flavor.

'Rangpur'. Commonly called Rangpur lime, but probably not a lime at all: fruit looks and peels like a mandarin, does not have lime flavor. Less acid than lemon but with flavor overtones that make it a rich, interesting base for punches and mixed drinks. Good landscape tree: vigorous, sturdy, bushy, growing quickly to 15 ft. tall and wide (as dwarf to 8 ft.). Dense when pruned, open otherwise. Fruits are colorful and ornamental, hang on tree throughout year.

PUMMELO

Forerunner of the grapefruit. Bears clusters of enormous round to pear-shaped fruits with thick rind and pith. Once peeled, fruit is just slightly bigger than a grapefruit. Different varieties range in flavor from sweet to fairly acidic. Need a little less heat than grapefruit. Ripen starting in winter in warmest areas. To eat, peel fruit; separate segments and remove membrane surrounding them. Because fruit is so heavy, prune pummelo trees to encourage strong branching.

'Chandler'. Most widely grown variety. Pink fleshed, flavorful, moderately juicy, usually seedless.

'Reinking'. White fleshed, seedy. Not as sweet as 'Chandler'.

'Tahitian' ('Sarawak'). Greenish white flesh; moderately acidic flavor with lime overtones.

GRAPEFRUIT

Trees can reach 25–30 ft. tall (most are shorter), with large, dark green leaves. True grapefruit needs heat for sweet-tart fruit; best in the desert, where fruit ripens in 9 months (can take a year or

Grapefruit

longer where there's less heat). Elsewhere, pummelo-grapefruit hybrids 'Oroblanco' and 'Melogold' are better; they will ripen in 9 to 12 months, depending on climate. At the end of the following list is a variety ('Cocktail') sold as a grapefruit, though it really isn't one.

'Flame'. Seedless red flesh similar to that of 'Rio Red'; slight rind blush.

'Marsh' ('Marsh Seedless'). Main white-fleshed commercial variety. Large, light yellow fruit.

'Melogold'. Grapefruit-pummelo hybrid developed by the University of California. Needs less heat than true grapefruit, but fruit doesn't hold as well on the tree. Fruit is bigger, heavier, and thinner skinned than 'Oroblanco', and its seedless white flesh has more of a sweet-tart flavor.

'Oroblanco'. Sister fruit to 'Melogold', with sweeter seedless white flesh. Has same low heat requirement but is smaller and thicker skinned.

'Redblush' ('Ruby', 'Ruby Red'). Seedless grapefruit with red-tinted flesh. Red internal color fades to pink, then buff by end of season.

'Rio Red'. Seedless grapefruit with good rind blush and flesh nearly as red as that of 'Star Ruby'. More dependable producer than 'Star Ruby'.

'Star Ruby'. Seedless grapefruit with reddest color. Tree is prone to cold damage, erratic bearing, and other growing problems. Doesn't withstand desert heat.

'Cocktail'. Labeled a grapefruit, but actually a mandarin-pummelo hybrid. Large fruit with greenish orange (or mottled orange-and-green) skin and pale orange, very seedy flesh. Sweeter than grapefruit, with distinctive flavor. Best quality in warm-summer areas, but worth growing in cooler regions.

LEMON

Low heat requirement makes lemons widely adapted and especially appreciated in regions where sweet oranges and grapefruit won't

ripen. Do best year-round near the coast, though some varieties are very successful in the desert. Standard varieties like 'Eureka' and 'Lisbon' are best pruned every year or two to maintain size.

'Eureka'. Standard lemon of markets. Bears all year. Not as vigorous as 'Lisbon'. To 20 ft. tall, with somewhat open growth; branches have few thorns. As a dwarf, it is a dense tree with large, dark leaves. New growth on both standard-size and dwarf plants is bronzy purple.

'Improved Meyer'. The word "improved" refers to fact that it is a disease-free form, the only one that can be sold in California (neither original nor improved forms can be sold in Arizona). This is the best lemon for Hawaii. Fruit is quite different from commercial lemon—rounder, thinner skinned, orange yellow in color. Tangy aroma but less acidic flavor than standard lemon; very juicy. Bears fruit year-round and starts bearing at an early age. Tree is not a dwarf on its own roots, though it is sometimes sold as an own-root plant that can reach 12 ft. tall, 15 ft. wide. On a dwarf rootstock, it's half that size.

'Lisbon'. Vigorous, upright, thorny tree to 20–25 ft. tall; denser than 'Eureka'. Can be trimmed up into highly decorative small tree. Fruit practically identical to 'Eureka'. Ripens mostly in fall but has some ripe fruit all year. More resistant to cold than 'Eureka' and better adapted to high heat; best lemon for Arizona. There is also a seedless form.

'Ponderosa'. A novelty. Bears huge, rough lemons with thick, coarse skin; 2 lb. fruits are not unusual. Mild lemon flavor. Bears at early age, frequently at gallon-can size. Main crop in winter, with some fruit through year. Open, angular branching; large, widely spaced leaves. To 8–10 ft. tall; dwarf reaches 4–6 ft.

'Sungold'. Attractive semidwarf lemon (to 14 ft. tall, 8 ft. wide) with green-striped yellow fruit and leaves that are mottled with white and cream. Main crop in fall and winter.

Lemon

'Variegated Pink' ('Pink Lemonade'). Sport of 'Eureka' with green-and-white leaves and green stripes on immature fruit; everbearing like 'Eureka'. Light pink flesh

C

doesn't need heat to develop color. Handsome landscape tree.

'Villa Franca'. Generally similar to 'Eureka', but tree is larger and more vigorous, with denser foliage and thornier branches. Fruit is similar to 'Eureka'; comes mainly from fall through winter. Sold in Arizona to grow in Zones 12, 13; not common in California.

LIME

The various limes range from moderately to extremely cold sensitive; they are most reliable in areas where hard frosts are uncommon. Can succeed in colder areas if grown in pots and protected in winter. Depending on variety, fruit may be intensely sour or nearly devoid of acid.

'Bearss'. Best lime for California and Hawaii gardens. It is a type of the "Persian" or "Tahitian" lime commonly grown in Florida. Tree is quite angular and open when young but forms a dense, round crown when mature; reaches 15–20 ft. (half that size on dwarf rootstock). It is thorny and inclined to drop many leaves in winter. Fruit is green when immature, light yellow when ripe, almost the size of a lemon; it is especially juicy when fully ripe. Seedless. Main crop comes from winter to late spring, though some fruit ripens all year.

'Kieffer'. Leaves are used in Thai and Cambodian cooking, as is bumpy, sour springtime fruit. Available mainly in California.

'Mexican'. Sometimes called key lime in Hawaii. Small, green to yellow-green fruit; standard bartender's lime. Main harvest fall to winter, though you'll get some fruit all year. Very thorny tree to 12–15 ft., with upright, twiggy branches (there is also a thornless form). Very cold sensitive; best suited to Zones 21–23. Can be grown in Hawaii but is subject to viral diseases there.

'Palestine Sweet' (Indian lime). Shrubby plant with acidless fruit resembling that of 'Bearss'. Used in Mideastern, Indian, and Latin American cooking. Ripens fall or winter.

TANGELO

Early citrus-breeding experiments produced the tangelo, a cross between a mandarin and a grapefruit. A cross between a tangelo and a grapefruit ('Wekiwa') is sometimes called a tangelolo. All these hybrids produce their best fruit in warm-summer areas.

'Minneola'. Hybrid of 'Dancy' mandarin and a white-fleshed grapefruit. Large, smooth, bright orange-red fruit tastes much like a mandarin. Few seeds. Ripens mid- to late winter; stores on tree for 2 months. Tree not as large or dense as grapefruit.

'Orlando'. Same parents as 'Minneola'. Medium-large fruit looks like a flattened orange. Both rind and flesh are orange; rind adheres to flesh. Very juicy, mildly sweet; matures early in season. Tree is similar to 'Minneola' but has distinctly cupped leaves, is less vigorous, and is more resistant to cold.

'Wekiwa' (may be sold as pink tangelo or 'Lavender Gem'). A cross between a tangelo and a grapefruit; looks like a small grapefruit but is eaten like a mandarin. Juicy, mild flesh tastes like a mix of sweet orange, grapefruit, and mandarin; color is purplish rose in hot climates. Fruit ripens from late fall into winter.

TANGOR

Hybrid between mandarin and sweet orange; often labeled as an orange—or, in the case of 'Murcott', as a tangerine—when sold in grocery stores. These three tangors are thought to be naturally occurring hybrids rather than breeder-developed varieties. 'Temple' is widely grown in low desert; 'Murcott' and 'Ortanique' are sometimes grown in Hawaii.

'Murcott'. Bears more heavily in alternate years. Vigorous, upright tree bears very sweet, seedy, yellowish orange fruit from late winter into spring. Marketed in stores as 'Honey' tangerine (no relation to 'Honey' mandarin).

'Ortanique'. Sweet, juicy, variably seedy fruit ripening from spring to summer. Sometimes has a small navel. Large, spreading tree.

'Temple'. Flattened, deep bright orange fruit is loose skinned and easy to peel. Tender-textured, juicy pulp is flavorful but not too sweet. Fruit has best quality in Zone 13; it is too acidic in more temperate climates. Ripens in early spring. Bushy, thorny tree to 12 ft. high with greater spread; 6–8 ft. wide on dwarf stock. More cold sensitive than other tangors.

KUMQUAT

Shrubby plants to 6–15 ft. or taller, with yellow to red-orange fruits that look like tiny oranges. Eat whole and unpeeled—spongy rind is sweet, pulp is tangy. Best in areas with warm to hot summers

and chilly nights during fall or winter ripening. Hardy to at least 18°F/–8°C.

'Fukushu'. Large, oval fruit with a prominent neck. Skin and juice are sweet, but not as sweet as 'Meiwa'. Compact, thornless, very attractive tree.

'Marumi'. Slightly thorny plant with round fruit. Sweeter peel than 'Nagami', but the slightly seedy flesh is more acidic.

'Meiwa'. Round fruit is sweeter, juicier, and less seedy than that of other varieties. Performs better than other types in cool-summer areas. Considered the best kumquat for eating fresh. Nearly thornless.

'Nagami'. Main commercial variety. Oval, slightly seedy fruit is more abundant and sweeter in hot-summer climates. Plant is thornless.

KUMQUAT HYBRIDS

These were the results of early experiments by the citrus industry to produce cold-tolerant kinds of citrus. Fruit has never been a commercial success, but it's good for home gardens. Plants tend to be fairly small even as standards; on dwarfing rootstocks, they reach only 3–6 ft.

Limequat. These hybrids of 'Mexican' lime and kumquat are more cold tolerant and need less heat than their lime parent. Good lime substitutes; edible rind like kumquat parent. Some fruit all year, but main crop comes from fall to spring. 'Eustis' bears fruit shaped like a big olive. 'Tavares' has elongated oval fruit on a more compact, better-looking plant than 'Eustis'.

Orangequat. Most commonly grown is 'Nippon', a cross between 'Meiwa' kumquat and satsuma mandarin. It is cold tolerant and has a fairly low heat requirement. Small, round, deep orange fruit with sweet, spongy rind and slightly acidic flesh. Sweeter than kumquat when eaten whole. Ripens winter and spring, but holds on the tree for months.

CITRON

Citron was the first type of citrus to be cultivated. Plant is small, thorny, irregular in shape; grown for big, fragrant, unusual fruit. Very sensitive to cold.

'Buddha's Hand'. Fruit is divided into "fingers" that contain all rind and no pulp. Bears some fruit all year round. This plant has absolutely no tolerance for frost.

'Etrog'. Fruit resembles a big, warty-skinned lemon with dry pulp; the peel is sometimes candied. Used in Jewish Feast of the Tabernacles.

CLADRASTIS
kentukea (C. lutea)
YELLOW WOOD
Fabaceae (Leguminosae)
DECIDUOUS TREE

🌿 ZONES 2–9, 14–16
☀ FULL SUN
💧 REGULAR WATER

Native to Kentucky, Tennessee, and North Carolina. Slow-growing tree to 30–50 ft. tall, with broad, rounded head half as wide as tree is high. Leaves are 8–12 in. long, divided into many (usually 7–11) oval leaflets resembling those of English walnut (See Walnut). Foliage is yellowish green when new, turning bright green in summer and brilliant yellow in fall. Bark is gray in maturity; the common name "yellow wood" refers to the color of the freshly cut heartwood.

Cladrastis kentukea

May not flower until 10 years old and may skip bloom some years, but the late spring display is spectacular when it comes: clusters of fragrant, wisterialike white flowers (those of 'Rosea' are pink) to 14 in. long. Blooms followed by flat, 3–4-in.-long seedpods. Attractive as terrace, patio, or lawn tree even if it never blooms. Deep rooted, so you can grow other plants beneath it. Tolerates alkaline soils; withstands some drought.

Prune when young to shorten side branches or correct narrow, weak branch crotches, which are susceptible to breakage in storms. Usually low branching; you can remove lower branches entirely when tree reaches desired height.

Prune in summer, since cuts made in winter or spring bleed profusely.

CLARET CUP. See **ECHINOCEREUS triglochidiatus**

CLARKIA (includes Godetia)

Onagraceae
ANNUALS

⚡ ZONES A2, A3; 1–24

☼ ☽ LIGHT SHADE IN HOTTEST CLIMATES

🌢 REGULAR WATER

Native to western South and North America; especially numerous in California. Plants grow during cool times of year, bloom in spring and early summer. Attractive in mixed borders or in mass displays. Cut branches keep for several days; cut when top bud opens (others open successively). Sow seed in place in fall (in mild-winter areas) or spring. Seedlings are difficult to transplant, but volunteer seedlings grow well. Best in sandy soil without added fertilizer. Keep soil moist from seeding to flowering.

C. amoena (Godetia amoena, G. grandiflora). FAREWELL-TO-SPRING, GODETIA. Native California to British Columbia. Two wild forms: one has coarse stems and sprawls 4–5 in. high; the other has more slender stems and grows 1½–2½ ft. high. Tapered leaves are ½–2 in. long. On both forms, upright buds open into cup-shaped, 2-in.-wide, slightly flaring pink or lavender flowers, usually blotched or penciled in crimson. Although seeds of named varieties are rarely sold in the U.S. (more available in England), strains of mixed colors are easy to find. Dwarf Gem grows 10 in. tall; Tall Upright reaches 2–3 ft.

C. concinna. RED-RIBBONS. California native. To 1½ ft. tall. Deep pink to lavender flowers

Clarkia amoena

with three-lobed, fan-shaped petals. Rounded leaves are ½–2 in. long. May be found in wildflower seed mixes.

C. pulchella. Native to Pacific Northwest. Slender, upright, mostly unbranched, 1–1½ ft. high. Reddish stems; narrow, 1–2-in.-long, sparse leaves. Flowers are single and four petaled; petals have a three-lobed tip and taper to a clawlike base. There are semidouble and dwarf forms. Some garden clarkias are probably hybrids between *C. pulchella* and *C. unguiculata*.

C. unguiculata (C. elegans). CLARKIA, MOUNTAIN GARLAND. California native. Erect, to 1–4 ft. Reddish stems, 1–1¾-in.-long leaves, 1-in. flowers in rose, purple, white. Some varieties have double flowers in white, orange, salmon, crimson, purple, rose, pink, or creamy yellow. Double-flowered kinds are the ones usually sold in seed packets.

CLARY. See **SALVIA**

CLEMATIS

Ranunculaceae
DECIDUOUS AND EVERGREEN VINES AND PERENNIALS

⚡ ZONES VARY BY SPECIES

☼ ☽ FULL SUN OR PARTIAL SHADE, EXCEPT AS NOTED

🌢 REGULAR WATER, EXCEPT AS NOTED

Of the more than 200 clematis species, most are deciduous vines; exceptions include useful evergreen vines *C. armandii* and *C. cirrhosa,* as well as some interesting upright herbaceous types. Attractive blooms come in a wide variety of shapes; they may resemble bells, stars, tulips, saucers, urns—even miniature lanterns. Each flower consists of a central brush of stamens surrounded by petal-like segments called sepals. Range of flower colors is wide, from pastel pinks to crimson red; periwinkle blue through soft lavender shades, rich magenta, and dark purple; and pure white through creamy tones and even golden yellow. Unless otherwise specified, blooms are 4–6 in. across. Float cut flowers in a bowl of water to make a choice indoor display. Burn cut ends of stems with a match to make flowers last longer. The blossoms of the large-flowered hybrids and a few species are followed by fluffy clusters of seed heads, also useful for flower arrangements. Leaves vary from pale to dark green, usually divided

Clematis armandii

into leaflets. Leafstalks twist and curl to hold plant to its support.

Choosing a site. When deciding where to plant your clematis, remember that most types need 5 to 6 hours of sunlight to produce the greatest number of blooms. Site vining types next to an obelisk, trellis, fence, or arbor to give stems support for twining; or plant near the base of a shallow-rooted shrub or tree and let the vine scramble up into it. You can disregard the advice to plant clematis "with their feet in the shade and their head in the sun"— provided your plants are kept properly mulched and watered. To reduce competition for nutrients and moisture, make sure any closely neighboring plants are not too vigorous; shallow-rooted annuals and delicate ground covers are good choices.

Planting. Dig a large hole, up to 2 ft. wide and deep, and plant in rich, loose, fast-draining soil; add generous quantities of organic matter. Add lime only if soil tests indicate a calcium deficiency. For large-flowered hybrids, as well as species such as *C. crispa, C. integrifolia, C. pitcheri, C. terniflora, C. texensis,* and *C. viticella,* plant with the crown (the point where the stems emerge from the soil in the nursery container) 3–5 in. below ground level. Deep planting ensures disease- or cold-damaged plants will resprout. Others can be planted with their crowns at ground level. Stems are easily broken, so plant carefully and protect with wire netting if near a path or where pets or children might brush by and snap them off at the base. Apply a 2–3-in.-thick layer of mulch around (but not touching) the stems to keep the roots cool. In desert areas plant where there is protection from afternoon sun and strong winds.

If you're planting a deciduous clematis, cut stems back to 6–12 in. from the ground or to two or three pairs of growth buds, whichever is lower. Late in the following dormant season, cut the plant back to two or three pairs of buds; train shoots emerging that second spring. Don't prune evergreen vines at first; just start training shoots onto their support.

Plant care. Clematis need regular watering and a steady supply of nutrients. Don't let them dry out, and apply a complete liquid fertilizer monthly during the growing season.

Pruning. The basic objective of pruning mature clematis vines is to get the greatest display of flowers on the shapeliest plant. Pruning is not complicated, and these are forgiving plants that will soon recover from any mistakes. The type of pruning you do depends on when your plants flower. If you don't know which kind you have, watch them for a year to see when they bloom, then proceed accordingly. Do keep in mind that dormant stems of clematis can look dead.

Spring-blooming clematis (which may actually bloom in late fall or winter in mild-winter areas) bloom on stems produced the previous year. After bloom has finished, thin out weak or tangled stems, remove any dead or damaged growth, and cut stems back to the first (topmost) pair of healthy leaf buds.

Summer- and fall-blooming clematis bloom at the ends of new stems that were produced in spring of the same year. These vines should be pruned when their leaf buds emerge—this can be any time from late fall to early spring depending whether you live in a mild- or cold-winter climate. Cut all the stems back to 12–18 in. above ground level, making each cut just above a pair of healthy leaf buds.

Twice-flowering clematis bloom on the previous year's stems in spring, then again on the current year's shoots in summer and fall. In late fall or early spring, prune lightly to thin out excess shoots or untangle stems. After the early blooms fade, prune more heavily so that new shoots will develop for the second round of flowers.

Pests and diseases. Aphids, mealybugs, scale, and whiteflies occasionally affect clematis. ▶

Snails, slugs, and earwigs may require control. Powdery mildew can be a problem on some types. Stem rot is a potentially serious disease of clematis. This fungal infection causes browning and wilting of leaves along an entire stem (it is sometimes referred to as "wilt"). Infection begins at the base of the stem, near the soil line. Small stems are more likely to become infected, so buy the biggest plant possible, and try not to break new shoots when planting. To treat infected plants, cut off all diseased parts, then disinfect your shears with diluted household bleach or another broad-range disinfectant. Dispose of diseased stems in a sealed plastic bag to avoid spreading fungal spores. Infected plants will produce healthy new shoots.

C. alpina. Deciduous vine. Zones A2, A3; 1–11, 14–18. Native to Europe and Asia. To 6–8 ft., with lacy, soft green foliage. Early-spring blooms are nodding and bell shaped, with four pointed sepals in white, pink, periwinkle blue, or purple, depending on the variety. An inner "skirt" of stamens is creamy white in most varieties. Blooms are followed by decorative seed heads. Plants are extremely cold hardy. Varieties include 'Burford White' (white), 'Constance' (reddish pink), 'Frances Rivis' (sky blue), 'Frankie' (soft blue), 'Ruby' (rosy pink), and 'Willy' (pale pink).

C. armandii. EVERGREEN CLEMATIS. Zones 4–9, 12–24. From China. Fast-growing vine to 15–20 ft. Leathery leaves are divided into three glossy, dark green leaflets to 6 in. long; they droop downward, creating a strongly textured look. Creamy white, vanilla-scented, saucer-shaped flowers, 1½–2 in. across, are borne in clusters in early to midspring. Leaves burn badly at the tips in areas where the soil or water contains excess salts. Best planted in a sunny, sheltered spot (out of harsh winds) with adequate support, such as a sturdy fence. Slow to start but races once established. Makes a great privacy screen if not allowed to become bare at the base. Do some pruning each year after bloom to avoid buildup of dead thatch and tangling on the inner part of the vine. Choice varieties include 'Apple Blossom' (pinkish white blooms), 'Snowdrift' (pure white flowers), 'Hendersonii Rubra' (soft pink flowers, reddish bronze new growth).

C. cirrhosa. Evergreen vine. Zones 4–9, 14–24. Native to southern Europe and the Mediterranean. Grows to 15 ft. under ideal conditions. Small, glossy, dark green leaves have three lobes. Flowers are 1½–2 in. wide and look like cream-colored bells; these appear in fall, later in the season than the blooms of most other clematis. Requires excellent drainage and a sunny, sheltered position, such as a south- or southwest-facing wall that is protected from wind. Varieties include 'Freckles' (creamy flowers speckled with dark red) and 'Wisley Cream' (greenish cream; blooms mid- to late fall).

C. crispa. Deciduous vine. Zones A2, A3; 2–11, 14–24. From the southeastern U.S. To 5–8 ft. or more. Delicate leaves are divided into two to five leaflets. Fragrant flowers are dainty bells of pale lavender blue, 1–1½ in. across; sepal tips flare and curl back. Long bloom season in mild-winter climates, beginning in late spring and continuing into fall; blooms from summer to fall where winters are cold. Flowers are followed by interesting feathery seed heads. Train into a shrub to help protect delicate stems.

C. discoreifolia. See C. terniflora.

C. × durandii (C. integrifolia 'Durandii'). Herbaceous perennial. Zones A2, A3; 2–11, 14–24. Nonclimbing hybrid reaches 3–5 ft. tall and 3 ft. wide, with dark green, undivided leaves. Long-lasting blooms appear summer to fall; these are 4 in. wide and saucer shaped, with deeply ribbed, indigo blue sepals. Provide support such as a small pillar or allow it to grow among small shrubs or flowering perennials. Attractive in containers.

C. integrifolia. Herbaceous perennial. Zones A1–A3; 1–11, 14–24. Native to Europe and Asia. Nonclimbing growth to 2–3 ft. or taller and about 2 ft. wide, with dark green, undivided 2–4-in.-long leaves. Nodding, sometimes fragrant, bell-shaped blue flowers, 1½–2 in. wide, appear in summer. Useful as a border plant because

of its diminutive size. Varieties include white 'Alba' and bright pink 'Rosea', both 2–3 ft. tall. 'Rooguchi' grows to 3–4½ ft. tall, with stunning deep purple blooms; plant it in a sunny location to prevent powdery mildew.

C. macropetala. DOWNY CLEMATIS. Deciduous vine. Zones A2, A3; 1–11, 14–18. Native to northern China and Siberia. To 6–10 ft., with feathery leaves. Nodding, bell-shaped, double-looking flowers are 2½–3½ in. across and appear in early spring. Outer sepals come in light to periwinkle blue, purple, pink, mauve, or white. An inner skirt of cream-colored sepals looks like a ballerina's tutu. Handsome, long-lasting, silvery seed heads. Varieties include 'Blue Bird' (mauve blue), 'Jan Lindmark' (purplish violet), 'Markham's Pink' (pink), 'Rosy O'Grady' (pinkish mauve), and 'White Swan' (creamy white).

C. montana. ANEMONE CLEMATIS. Deciduous vine. Zones 3b–9, 14–18. Native to the Himalayas. Vigorous grower to 20 ft. or more, with massive display of 2–2½-in.-wide, anemone-like flowers from late spring to early summer; blooms in shades of pink. Give it plenty of room to roam; prune as for spring-blooming types. Varieties include 'Elizabeth' (to 20 ft., with soft pink flowers and bronzy foliage that matures to green) and 'Mayleen' (20–30 ft., with deep pink flowers and medium green to bronzy foliage); both have vanilla-scented blossoms. *C. m. rubens* grows to 25 ft., with pale pink flowers and new foliage that is rich bronze, maturing to bronzy green. Its selection 'Tetrarose' reaches 20 ft., with bronze foliage; its mauve-pink blooms have a spicy scent.

C. pitcheri. Deciduous vine. Zones A2, A3; 2–11, 14–24. Native to south central U.S. Grows fast to 10 ft. or more, with medium green leaves composed of three to five leaflets. Prolific production of delicate, urn-shaped flowers up to 1 in. across that are rich purple outside,

Clematis montana rubens

white near the tips of the curving sepals. Long bloom period in summer—up to three months. Despite its small blossoms, this is a real showstopper.

C. tangutica. GOLDEN CLEMATIS. Deciduous vine. Zones A1–A3; 1–11, 14–24. Native to Mongolia, northern China. Varieties range in height from 6 to 20 ft.; gray-green leaves have five to seven leaflets. Nodding, bell- or lantern-shaped, bright yellow flowers, 1½–2 in. across, appear in profusion from midsummer to midfall. Blossoms are followed by handsome, silvery, mop-headed seed clusters. Tolerant of poor soil. On a trellis, the vine will cascade so that the flowers dance in the wind. Top varieties include 'Bill MacKenzie' (10 ft. or more), 'Golden Harvest' (10 ft. or more), and 'Helios' (6–8 ft.).

C. terniflora (C. discoreifolia, C. maximowicziana). SWEET AUTUMN CLEMATIS. Deciduous vine (semievergreen in milder areas). Zones 2–11, 14–24. Native to Japan. Very fast growing to 20 ft., with dark green leaves consisting of three to five oval leaflets. Produces masses of fragrant, creamy white flowers in late summer to fall. Can reseed. Plant in a warm, sunny location. Makes good privacy screen, arbor cover. Often sold as *C. paniculata*, a similar species from New Zealand.

C. texensis. SCARLET CLEMATIS. Deciduous vine. Zones 2b–11, 14–24. Native to Texas. Fast growth to 6–10 ft., with blue-green leaves divided into three to five heart-shaped leaflets. Tulip-shaped scarlet flowers, 2–3 in. across, are produced in abundance from early summer until late fall. Use on posts or tall trellis in a location with full sun and good air circulation to prevent powdery mildew. Crosses with large-flowered hybrids have produced eye-catching varieties such as the vivid pink 'Duchess of Albany', crimson 'Gravetye Beauty', and rich pink 'Princess Diana'.

C. viticella. Deciduous vine. Zones A2, A3; 2–11, 14–24. From southern Europe and western Asia. To 8–10 ft., with medium green leaves comprising five to seven small leaflets. Open, bell-shaped flowers are 1½–4 in. wide and come in a range of colors, depending on variety. Provides an outstanding display of blooms in summer and fall. Very versatile; good in combination with largelowered hybrid types. One of the easiest clematis to grow; very tolerant of heat and poor soil. Varieties include 'Abundance' (rosy pink), 'Alba Luxurians' (white with green tips), 'Etoile Violette' (purple), 'Little Nell' (creamy white sepals edged with soft violet), 'Pagoda' (mauve pink), 'Purpurea Plena Elegans' (double blooms in rosy purple), 'Royal Velours' (reddish purple), and 'Venosa Violacea' (white sepals edged with a wide band of deep purple).

Large-flowered hybrids. Deciduous vines. Zones A2, A3; 2–11, 14–24. Grow 6–10 ft. Flowers of most are saucer shaped and 6–8 in. across. Although there are hundreds of large-flowered hybrids in commerce, local nurseries usually offer only a limited selection of the old favorites and perhaps some of the newer, branded varieties sold as Signature, Patio, and Garland clematis. Mail-order catalogs are the best source for collectors seeking the new and different. Following is a list of time-honored hybrids along with some noteworthy newer varieties.

White: 'Henryi' is the standard. 'Huldine', 'Hyde Hall', 'Jackmanii Alba', 'Marie Boisselot', and 'Snow Queen' are also excellent choices, as is longtime favorite *C. lanuginosa* 'Candida'.

Pink: Look for 'Caroline' (pale pink sepals marked with dark pink), 'Comtesse de Bouchaud' (bright mauve pink), 'Hagley Hybrid' (mauve pink), 'Kakio' (also known as 'Pink Champagne', with vivid pink sepals and a pale central band), and 'Proteus' (double flowers of mauve pink). Where summers are hot, plant in bright shade to prevent these soft colors from fading.

Red: Great choices include vivid magenta 'Ernest Markham', deep red 'Niobe', velvety crimson 'Rouge Cardinal', carmine red 'Ville de Lyon', and deep maroon 'Warsaw Nike' ('Warszawska Nike').

Purple: The classic 'Jackmanii', with velvety, dark purple sepals, remains the most popular. Other fine choices include rich dark purple 'Aotearoa'; deep blue-violet 'Daniel Deronda'; velvety, dark violet 'Gipsy Queen'; rosy purple 'Richard Pennell'; purple-blue 'The President'; and rosy mauve 'Viola'.

Blue: Sky blue 'Ramona' is deservedly popular. Other varieties include 'H. F. Young' (periwinkle blue, tinged with mauve), 'Ken

Donson' (deep lavender blue), and 'William Kennett' (lilac blue).

Bicolor: Choices include 'Asao' (deep rosy pink sepals with a pale pink central bar), 'Barbara Jackman' (lavender with vivid magenta bar), 'Charissima' (cerise pink with deep pink bar), the ever-popular 'Nelly Moser' (purplish pink with reddish bar), and 'Piilu' (pastel pink with raspberry bar). In hot-summer areas, plant these varieties in bright shade to prevent fading.

Double: Fully double, roselike blooms in early summer on old wood are usually followed later by single or semidouble flowers on new wood. Choice varieties include silvery blue 'Belle of Woking', lavender-blue 'Blue Light', white 'Duchess of Edinburgh', and lavender-blue 'Multi Blue'. 'Josephine' has unusual flowers of mauve pink with a dark blue central stripe.

CLEOME hasslerana (C. spinosa)
SPIDER FLOWER
Capparidaceae
ANNUAL

- ZONES 1–24
- FULL SUN
- MODERATE TO REGULAR WATER

Cleome hasslerana

Shrubby, branching South American native topped in summer and fall with many open, fluffy clusters of pink or white flowers with extremely long, protruding stamens. Slender seed capsules follow the blossoms. Stems have short, strong spines; lower leaves are divided, upper ones undivided. Leaves and stems are clammy to the touch, and have a strong but not unpleasant smell.

Plant grows 4–6 ft. tall, 4–5 ft. wide; especially vigorous in warm, dry inland areas. Grow in background, as summer hedge, against walls or fences, in large containers; or—since plants self-sow to a fault—naturalize in fringe areas of

garden. Flowers and dry seed capsules useful in arrangements.

Sow seeds in place in spring; they sprout rapidly in warm soil. A number of varieties can be grown from seed.

CLERODENDRUM
Verbenaceae
EVERGREEN AND DECIDUOUS SHRUBS AND VINES

- ZONES VARY BY SPECIES
- EXPOSURE NEEDS VARY BY SPECIES
- REGULAR WATER

Diverse group of plants grown for big clusters of showy, brightly colored flowers that are fragrant in some species. Bloom comes on current season's growth. Provide support for climbing species. Grow in well-drained soil. Good greenhouse plants in areas beyond their hardiness limits.

C. buchananii fallax (C. speciosissimum). PAGODA FLOWER. Evergreen to deciduous shrub. Zones 24; H2. From Indonesia. Erect growth to 12 ft. tall, 6 ft. wide. Plant produces brilliant scarlet flowers much of the year. Densely pubescent, large heart-shaped leaves to 1 ft. long. Suitable shrub for mass plantings, hedges, or colorful screens; also makes a good container plant. Prune to improve appearance and shape as needed. Full sun or partial shade.

C. bungei (C. foetidum). CASHMERE BOUQUET. Evergreen shrub. Zones 5–9, 12–24. Native to China. Plant grows rapidly to 6 ft. tall and wide; spreads rapidly by suckers, eventually forming a thicket if not restrained. Big (to 1-ft.), coarse, broadly oval leaves with toothed edges are dark green above and have a rust-colored fuzz beneath. Leaves smell unpleasant when bruised or crushed. Loose clusters of delightfully fragrant rosy red flowers in summer, sometimes into fall. Plant where its appearance (except during bloom time) is not important. Prune severely in spring and pinch back throughout the growing sea-

Clerodendrum bungei

son to make a compact, 2–3-ft. shrub. Resistant to oak root fungus. Deer resistant. Deep shade in desert regions, partial shade elsewhere.

C. chinense pleniflorum (C. fragrans pleniflorum). Evergreen to semievergreen shrub. Zones 8, 9, 12–24. Native to southern China. Coarse plant to 5–8 ft. tall, spreads freely by root suckers unless controlled or confined. Its 10-in. leaves resemble those of *C. bungei* but are not malodorous when bruised or crushed. (This species may also be called cashmere bouquet, a name more often applied to *C. bungei*.) Pale pink double flowers with a sweet, clean fragrance are carried in broad clusters resembling hydrangea. Partial shade.

C. myricoides 'Ugandense' (C. ugandense). Evergreen shrub. Zones 9, 14–24; H1, H2. Native to tropical Africa. Grows to 10 ft. tall and about half as wide, though often much smaller in California. Glossy dark green leaves to 4 in. long. Each five-petaled blossom has one violet-blue petal and four pale blue ones; pistil and stamens arch outward and upward. Partial shade; can take full sun in Hawaii.

Clerodendrum myricoides 'Ugandense'

C. quadriloculare. BAGAUAK. Evergreen shrub. Zone H2. From the Philippines. To 15 ft. tall, spreading by root suckers. Has an upright habit; can be trained to tree form. Clusters of fragrant pink flowers in fall and spring enhance the deep purple of the leaf undersides. Use as color accent, hedge, screen, or tubbed specimen for the lanai. Protect from harsh winds. Prune to shape. Full sun.

C. × speciosum. CLERODENDRUM VINE. Evergreen shrubby vine. Zones 22–24; H2. Hybrid between *C. splendens* and *C. thomsoniae*. Moderate to rapid growth to 30 ft. Produces clusters of flowers at branch tips in winter and spring. Bicolored blooms have a dull pink or red calyx surrounding a short tube in deep crimson with violet shades; calyxes hang on. Full sun.

C. splendens. RED CLERODENDRUM. Evergreen vine. Zones 23, 24; H2. From tropical

C

Africa. Climbs rapidly to 30 ft. Large clusters of bright red flowers bloom profusely during winter. Protect from strong winds. Best in sun on vertical supports such as a fence or trellis, and can be trained along eaves.

C. thomsoniae (C. balfouri). BLEEDING HEART GLORY-BOWER. Evergreen vine. Protected spots in Zones 22–24; H2; or indoor/outdoor potted plant. Native to West Africa. Restrained and mannerly growth to no more than 12 ft. Distinctly ribbed, oval, shiny dark green leaves, 4–7 in. long. Blooms from summer to fall, bearing flattish, 5-in. clusters of up to 20 flowers. White calyxes reminiscent of paper lanterns surround scarlet flowers, giving a striking two-tone contrast. Use it on sheltered patio walls or arbor posts. Grows well in large containers; move it to a frost-free shelter in winter. Partial shade.

C. trichotomum. HARLEQUIN GLORYBOWER. Deciduous shrub. Zones 15–17, 20–24. Plant can be grown in Zones 5 and 6 but may periodically freeze to the ground and come back from roots. Native to Japan. Shrub reaches 10–15 ft. tall and as wide, with many stems growing from base. Can be trained as a small tree. Soft, hairy, oval dark green leaves to 5 in. long. Fragrant blossoms—each a white tube almost twice as long as the prominent, fleshy, scarlet calyxes surrounding it—come in late summer. Calyxes hang on and contrast pleasingly with metallic-looking turquoise or blue-green fruit. Give this shrub plenty of room to spread at top; add plants underneath it to hide its legginess. *C. t. fargesii,* from China, is somewhat hardier and smaller; it has smooth leaves and green calyxes that turn pink. Partial shade.

CLETHRA
Clethraceae
DECIDUOUS SHRUBS AND EVERGREEN TREES

🌡	ZONES VARY BY SPECIES
☼ ◑	BEST IN PARTIAL SHADE BUT ADAPTABLE
💧	REGULAR WATER

These attractive plants are grown for the small, five-lobed, sweet-scented white or pink flowers that cluster at branch tips in mid- to late summer. Fairly soil tolerant but do best in moist, organic, slightly acidic, well-drained soil. Plants prefer partial shade but can

adapt successfully to less light as well as to full sun, though they need some shade where summers are very hot. On deciduous shrubs, remove some old wood from base annually before spring growth begins. Evergreen tree described below (*C. arborea*) doesn't need routine pruning.

C. alnifolia. SUMMERSWEET, SWEET PEPPERBUSH. Deciduous shrub. Zones A2, A3; 1–6. Eastern U.S. native grows 4–10 ft. tall and wide; spreads slowly by suckers. Thin, strong branches form vertical pattern. Dark green, toothed-edged, 2–4-in.-long leaves appear late in spring, turn golden yellow to brownish in fall. During bloom season, each branch tip carries several 4–6-in.-long spires of tiny, gleaming white flowers with a spicy perfume.

Selections include the following; most grow a bit wider than tall and hold their flowers loosely upright.

'Hummingbird' is a white-flowered dwarf form that grows to about 2½–3 ft. tall.

'Pink Spires' (to 4 ft.) has deep pink blooms.

'Rosea' (6–10 ft.) has pale pink flowers.

'Ruby Lace' (to 5 ft.) bears deep pink blooms.

'Ruby Spice' (to 6–8 ft.) has dark rosy pink flowers.

'Sixteen Candles' is similar to 'Hummingbird', but flower spikes are held straight up like candles on a birthday cake.

Clethra alnifolia 'Pink Spires'

C. arborea. LILY-OF-THE-VALLEY TREE. Evergreen tree. Zones 15–17, 21–24. Native to Madeira. Rather stiff upright growth to 20 ft. tall and about half as wide. Plant is densely clothed with 4-in. leaves in glossy, bronzy green. White flowers in upright, branched clusters resemble lily-of-the-valley (*Convallaria majalis*) in looks and even in fragrance. Leaf

tips burn with frost, but plant comes back from old wood or from roots when damaged. You may need to control spider mites in summer. For another lily-of-the-valley tree, see *Crinodendron patagua*. For lily-of-the-valley shrub, see *Pieris japonica*.

C. barbinervis. JAPANESE SWEET SHRUB. Deciduous shrub. Zones 5–9, 14–24. Slow-growing plant reaches 15–18 ft. tall and about one-half to two-thirds as wide. Shrub has attractive, peeling, glossy gray to brown bark when plant matures. Produces drooping, 4–6-in. clusters of fragrant, bell-shaped white flowers. Heavily veined, sharply toothed leaves turn bright yellow in fall.

CLEYERA japonica (Eurya ochnacea)
Theaceae
EVERGREEN SHRUB

🌡	ZONES 4–6, 8, 9, 14–24; H1
◑	PARTIAL SHADE
💧💧	MODERATE TO REGULAR WATER

Native to Japan, southeast Asia. Handsome but not widely known bushy shrub related to camellia. Similar in character to *Ternstroemia gymnanthera.* Grows at moderate rate to 15 ft. tall and as wide, with graceful, spreading, arching branches. New leaves are beautiful deep brownish red. Mature leaves are 3–6 in. long, glossy dark green with reddish midrib. Plant produces small clusters of fragrant creamy white flowers in early fall that are followed by small, dark red, puffy berries; fruit lasts through winter. Flowers and berries are attractive but not showy; they don't form on young plants. No routine pruning needed. 'Tricolor' (*C. fortunei*) has yellow-and-rose variegation on its young leaves.

Cleyera japonica

CLIANTHUS puniceus
PARROT BEAK
Fabaceae (Leguminosae)
EVERGREEN SHRUBBY VINE

🌡	ZONES 8, 9, 14–24; H1
☼ ◑	FULL SUN ONLY IN COOLER CLIMATES
💧	REGULAR WATER

New Zealand native grows to 12 ft. high and nearly as wide. Sprays of 3–6-in., glistening dark green leaves divided into many narrow leaflets hang gracefully, forming an open foliage pattern. In late spring or early summer, bright red, sweet pea–shaped flowers with 3-in. keels resembling parrot beaks swing downward between the leaves. Pods that follow are 3 in. long. Forms with pink or white flowers are also available. To display beauty of leaves and flowers, train as espalier or on a support. Mix an organic soil amendment into heavy soil. Watch for slugs, snails, spider mites.

Clianthus puniceus

CLIFF-BRAKE. See PELLAEA

CLIMBING LILY. See GLORIOSA superba 'Rothschildiana'

CLIMBING SNAPDRAGON. See ASARINA

CLIVIA miniata
Amaryllidaceae
PERENNIAL FROM TUBEROUS RHIZOMES

🌡	ZONES 12–17, 19–24 (SEE BELOW); H1, H2; OR INDOORS
◑ ●	SOME SHADE; BRIGHT INDIRECT LIGHT
💧	REGULAR WATER

Native to South Africa. Showy and striking member of the amaryllis family for garden borders, beds, or containers. Plant produces brilliant, large clusters of funnel-shaped orange flowers on 2-ft.

talks that appear above dense lumps of dark green, strap-shaped, 1½-ft.-long evergreen eaves; flowering period ranges from early winter to midspring, but most are spring bloomers. Ornamental red berries follow flowers.

French and Belgian hybrids have very wide leaves and yellow to deep red-orange blooms on thick, rigid stalks. 'Flame' is an exceptionally hot orange red. Solomone hybrids have pale to deep yellow flowers.

Clivias are damaged by freezing temperatures (32°F/0°C) and will survive only to about 25°F/−4°C.

Clivia miniata

In frostless areas or well-protected parts of garden, they are handsome in borders with azaleas, ferns, other shade plants. Set them 1½–2 ft. apart; let clumps grow undisturbed for years. In areas too cold for year-round outdoor culture, grow in pots; move to shelter or bring indoors (and water sparingly) in winter. Container plants bloom best with regular fertilizing, crowded roots.

CLOVER. See **TRIFOLIUM**

CLUSTERED GOLDFLOWER. See **TETRANEURIS scaposa**

CLYTOSTOMA callistegioides
VIOLET TRUMPET VINE
Bignoniaceae
EVERGREEN VINE

| % ZONES 8, 9, 12–24 |
| ☼ ◑ FULL SUN OR PARTIAL SHADE |
| ◑ ◑ MODERATE TO REGULAR WATER |

Formerly classified as *Bignonia violacea, B. speciosa*. Strong-growing vine from Brazil and Argentina will clamber over anything by tendrils; needs support on walls. Each leaf divided into two glossy dark green leaflets with wavy margins. Extended terminal

Clytostoma callistegioides

shoots hang down to give a curtainlike effect. Blooms from late spring to fall, when sprays of trumpet-shaped violet, lavender, or pale purple flowers, 3 in. long and nearly as wide at the flare, appear at ends of shoots. Top is hardy to 20°F/−7°C, roots to 10°F/−12°C. Prune in late winter to discipline growth and prevent tangling. At other times of year, remove unwanted long runners and spent flower sprays.

CNEORUM tricoccon
SPURGE OLIVE
Cneoraceae
EVERGREEN SHRUB

| % ZONES 14–24 |
| ☼ FULL SUN |
| ◐ LITTLE WATER |

Western Mediterranean native. Twiggy growth to 2 ft. tall and broad, with 1–2 in., shiny green or gray-green leaves set closely on stems. Looks something like boxwood *(Buxus)*. In early summer, small bright yellow flowers open at

Cneorum tricoccon

branch ends; these are followed by small, dry red fruits that resemble three little berries pressed together. Fruits eventually turn black. Tough, undemanding plant for hot, dry places. Can be used in rock garden or as edging. Thin out older wood before spring growth begins.

COAST ROSEMARY.
See **WESTRINGIA fruticosa**

COBAEA scandens
CUP-AND-SAUCER VINE
Polemoniaceae
PERENNIAL VINE USUALLY GROWN AS ANNUAL

| % ZONES 24, H1, H2 AS PERENNIAL; ZONES 3–23 AS ANNUAL |
| ☼ FULL SUN |
| ● REGULAR WATER |

Cobaea scandens

Native to Mexico. Extremely vigorous growth to 25 ft. in only one season. Bell-shaped flowers are first greenish, then violet or rose purple; there is a white-flowered form. Called cup-and-saucer vine because 2-in.-long cup of petals sits in large, green, saucerlike calyx. Leaves divided into two or three pairs of oval, 4-in. leaflets. At ends of leaves are curling tendrils that enable vine to climb rough surfaces without support.

The hard-coated seeds may rot if sown outdoors in cool weather. Start indoors in 4-in. pots; notch seeds with knife and press edgewise into moistened potting mix, barely covering seeds. Keep moist but not wet; transplant seedlings to warm, sunny location when weather warms. Protect from strong winds. Blooms first year from seed. May not bloom until very late summer in coolest climates. In mildest-winter areas, lives from year to year, eventually reaching over 40 ft. long and blooming heavily in midsummer the first year, from spring to fall in subsequent years.

COCCOLOBA uvifera
SEA GRAPE
Polygonaceae
EVERGREEN SHRUB OR TREE

| % ZONES 24; H2 |
| ☼ ◑ FULL SUN OR LIGHT SHADE |
| ◐ ◑ LITTLE TO MODERATE WATER |

From tropical America; hardy to 30°F/−1°C. To 20–40 ft. high and spreading to 20 ft. wide. Excellent for seaside planting; tolerant of wind, sand, salt, and drought. Can be grown as large, bushy shrub or trained to form a single-trunked

Coccoloba uvifera

tree. Withstands severe pruning and can be espaliered. Its rounded glossy green leaves have reddish veins and grow up to 8 in. wide; coppery when young. Small white blossoms in winter and spring are followed by clustered fruits, green maturing to purple, that can be made into jelly.

COCCULUS laurifolius
Menispermaceae
EVERGREEN SHRUB OR TREE

| % ZONES 8, 9, 12–24 |
| ☼ ◑ ● SUN OR SHADE |
| ● REGULAR WATER |

Himalayan native useful as screen, background plant. Grows slowly at first, then moderately fast to 25 ft. or more. Usually multistemmed shrub with arching, spreading growth as wide as high, though it can be kept smaller with pruning. Staked and trained as a tree, it takes on an umbrella shape. Long, willowy branches are as easy to train as vines; fastened to a trellis, they make an effective screen. Can also be espaliered. Shiny, leathery, oblong leaves to 6 in. long have three strongly marked veins running from base to tip.

Cocculus laurifolius

COCKSCOMB. See **CELOSIA**

COCKSPUR THORN.
See **CRATAEGUS crus-galli**

C

C

COCOS nucifera
COCONUT PALM, NIU
Arecaceae (Palmae)
PALM

| 🖊 ZONE H2 |
| ☼ FULL SUN |
| 💧 MODERATE WATER |

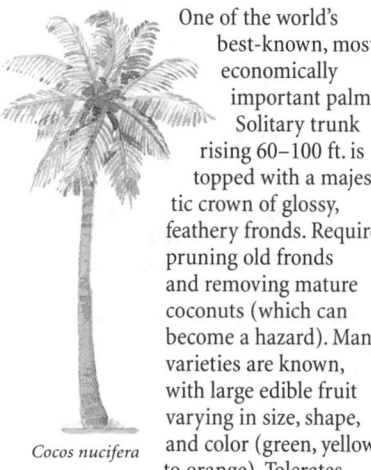
Cocos nucifera

One of the world's best-known, most economically important palms. Solitary trunk rising 60–100 ft. is topped with a majestic crown of glossy, feathery fronds. Requires pruning old fronds and removing mature coconuts (which can become a hazard). Many varieties are known, with large edible fruit varying in size, shape, and color (green, yellow to orange). Tolerates many different soil conditions; has excellent salt and drought tolerance and can also be found growing in brackish water. Superb for large gardens, parks, or avenues. Dwarf forms are available and more suitable for the medium-size garden; some of these reach 10–15 ft. tall, with a feathery crown about equally wide. For queen palm, formerly called *C. plumosa*, see *Syagrus romanzoffianum*.

CODIAEUM variegatum 'Pictum'
CROTON
Euphorbiaceae
EVERGREEN SHRUB

| 🖊 ZONES 24; H2; OR INDOORS |
| ☼ ◐ ● SOME FORMS TAKE SUN, OTHERS SHADE |
| 💧💧 REGULAR TO AMPLE WATER |

Native to the tropics. Grown outdoors in a frost-free climate, it can reach 6 ft. or taller, with equal spread; elsewhere, it's usually seen

Codiaeum variegatum 'Pictum'

as single-stemmed houseplant to about 2 ft. high. Grown principally for its large, leathery, glossy leaves, which may be green, yellow, red, purple, bronze, pink, or almost any combination of these colors. Leaves vary in shape; they may be oval, lance shaped, or very narrow, with smooth or lobed margins. Dozens of named forms are available.

Outdoor exposure depends on the variety. Give bright light, regular misting indoors; does well in a warm, humid greenhouse. Can be brought outdoors during warm times of year. Contact with croton leaves can cause a skin rash in some people.

COFFEA arabica
COFFEE
Rubiaceae
EVERGREEN SHRUB

| 🖊 ZONES 21–24; H1, H2; OR INDOORS |
| ◐ ● SOME SHADE; BRIGHT INDIRECT LIGHT |
| 💧 REGULAR WATER |

Coffea arabica

Native to east Africa. The coffee tree of commerce can be grown as a specimen or in shrub borders in the mildest-winter regions; it's also a handsome container plant for patios, lanais, and large well-lit rooms in any climate. Upright shrub to 15–20 ft. tall and about half as wide outdoors; rarely more than 4–6 ft. high indoors. Evenly spaced tiers of branches are clothed with shiny, dark green, oval leaves to 6 in. long. Small (¾-in.), fragrant white flowers are clustered near leaf bases. Blooms are followed by 1½-in. fruits that turn from green (when they first appear) to purple or red. Each contains two seeds—coffee beans. Grow in rich, well-drained soil. Protect from frosts.

COFFEEBERRY.
See **RHAMNUS californica**

COFFEE FERN.
See **PELLAEA andromedifolia**

COIX lacryma-jobi
JOB'S TEARS
Poaceae (Gramineae)
ANNUAL GRASS

| 🖊 ZONES 12–24; H1; COLDER ZONES AS NOTED BELOW |
| ☼ ◐ FULL SUN OR PARTIAL SHADE |
| 💧 REGULAR WATER |

A curiosity from Southeast Asia, grown for its ornamental beadlike seeds. Leaves are 1½ in. wide, to 2 ft. long, growing in loose, sprawling clumps to 1½ ft. across. Smooth, prominently jointed stems to 6 ft. long bear separate male and female flower spikelets in autumn. Outside coverings of female flowers harden as seeds ripen, turning to shiny, ¼–½-in. "beads" in pearly white, gray, or violet; these can be strung like actual beads. For use in dried arrangements, cut stems before seeds dry and shatter.

Coix lacryma-jobi

Sow seeds in place in early to midspring. Plants need heat and a long growing season to flower. In zones colder than those listed, start seeds indoors and set out plants after danger of frost is past. Where summers are short and cool, give plants the warmest spot in the garden—even reflected heat next to wall.

COLCHICUM
MEADOW SAFFRON, AUTUMN CROCUS
Liliaceae
PERENNIALS FROM CORMS

| 🖊 ZONES 2–10, 14–24; OR INDOORS |
| ☼ FULL SUN; BRIGHT INDIRECT LIGHT |
| 💧 REGULAR WATER DURING GROWTH AND BLOOM |
| ☠ ALL PARTS ARE POISONOUS IF INGESTED |

Native to Mediterranean region. Many species; sometimes called autumn crocus, but not true

Colchicum

crocuses. Shining, brown-skinned, thick-scaled corms send up clusters of long-tubed, flaring lavender-pink, rose purple, or white flowers to 4 in. across in late summer or early autumn, whether corms are sitting in dish on windowsill or planted in soil. When corms are planted out, broad leaves 6–12 in. long emerge in spring, last for a few months, and then die long before flower cluster rises from ground. Best planted where they need not be disturbed more often than every 3 years or so.

Corms are available during a brief dormant period in the summer. Hybrids include 'The Giant', single lavender, and 'Waterlily', double violet. Plant corms 3 in. deep and 6–8 in. apart. Cut back on watering during dormancy, but don't let the soil dry out. To plant in bowls, set upright on 1–2 in. of pebbles or in special fiber sold for this purpose, and fill with water to the base of the corms.

COLEONEMA
BREATH OF HEAVEN
Rutaceae
EVERGREEN SHRUBS

| 🖊 ZONES 7–9, 14–24 |
| ☼ ◐ FULL SUN OR LIGHT SHADE |
| 💧 REGULAR WATER |

Native to South Africa. Plants of filmy appearance and delicate character, with slender branches and narrow, heathlike leaves that are fragrant when brushed or bruised. Tiny flowers are borne freely over long season in winter and spring. Plants can continue with scattered bloom at any other time.

You may find plants in nurseries under either *Coleonema* or their former name, *Diosma*. Actually, your choice amounts to a white- or a pink-flowering breath of heaven.

Good on banks or hillsides, along paths where you can break off and bruise a twig to enjoy the foliage's fragrance. Frequently used next to buildings, though a little wispy for such use. Plant in light soil; fast drainage is a must. To control size and promote compactness, shear lightly after main bloom is over. For even more filmy look, thin out some interior stems.

C. album (Diosma alba). WHITE BREATH OF HEAVEN. To 5 ft. or taller and as wide, with white flowers. Often sold as *Diosma reevesii;* once known as *D. ericoides.*

C. pulchellum (C. pulchrum). PINK BREATH OF HEAVEN, PINK DIOSMA. Grows to 5 ft. tall and as wide, occasionally to 10 ft. Bears tiny pink flowers. Species often sold as *Diosma pulchra.* 'Sunset Gold' has yellow foliage, grows 1½ ft. tall, 4 ft. wide.

Coleonema pulchellum

COLEOSTEPHUS myconis. See **CHRYSANTHEMUM multicaule**

COLEUS × hybridus. See **SOLENOSTEMON scutellarioides**

COLLARDS. See **KALE AND COLLARDS**

COLLINSIA
heterophylla
(C. bicolor)
CHINESE HOUSES
Scrophulariaceae
ANNUAL

- **ZONES 1–24**
- **PART SHADE IN HOTTEST CLIMATES**
- **REGULAR WATER**

Native to California. This is a rather uncommon plant in nature; blooms from spring to early summer, with 1-in.-long blossoms that resemble snapdragons (*Antirrhinum*). Flowers are held in tiers at top of 1–2-ft.-tall, somewhat hairy stems. The upper lip of the flower is white, the lower one rose

Collinsia heterophylla

or violet. Plant produces oblong leaves to 2 in. long. Gives light, dainty effect in front of borders, scattered under deciduous trees, or as bulb cover. Sow seed in place in fall or early spring in rich, moist soil. Can also be sown in late spring for early fall bloom. Self-sows under favorable conditions.

COLOCASIA
esculenta
TARO, ELEPHANT'S EAR
Araceae
PERENNIAL FROM TUBER

- **ZONES 12, 16–24; H1, H2; OR DIG AND STORE**
- **BEST IN WARM, FILTERED SHADE**
- **AMPLE WATER**
- **ALL PARTS MAY CAUSE INDIGESTION IF INGESTED RAW; CONTACT WITH SAP MAY IRRITATE SKIN**

Colocasia esculenta

Native to tropical Asia and Polynesia. Fast growing to 6 ft. tall. Leathery green to gray-green, heart-shaped leaves are mammoth in size (to 2½ by 3 ft.), carried at ends of succulent stalks from spring through fall. Sometimes available are varieties with foliage marked in various purple shades; two of the most striking are 'Black Magic', with solid purple leaves, and 'Illustris' with green-veined, charcoal black foliage. All create a

lush effect in the course of a single season. Flowers resembling greenish callas (*Zantedeschia*) appear only in the warmest climates. The starchy tubers were once a staple food of Polynesians, who ate other parts of the plant as well. In Hawaii, where nearly 300 forms of wetland and upland (dry) taro are recorded, the plant is still grown commercially for the edible roots.

Enrich soil with organic matter before planting. Set tubers 1–1½ ft. apart and about 2 in. deep. Tops die down at 30°F/–1°C. In listed zones, tubers can be left in ground all year; in Zones 14 and 15, a thick mulch will allow in-ground survival over the average winter. Elsewhere, lift and store tubers after foliage is killed by frost; or grow in containers (good in any zone) and shelter over winter. Effective with tree ferns and other large-leafed tropical plants. Handsome in large tubs, in raised beds, near swimming pools. Protect plants from wind, which tears leaves. Feed lightly once a month during growing season. When clumps become overcrowded, divide them in early spring.

COLUMBINE. See **AQUILEGIA**

COMAROSTAPHYLIS
diversifolia
SUMMER HOLLY
Ericaceae
EVERGREEN SHRUB OR TREE

- **ZONES 7–9, 14–24**
- **FULL SUN IN COOLER CLIMATES ONLY**
- **MODERATE WATER**

Native to coastal Southern California, Baja California. Rather formal growth to 6–18 ft. high, 4–8 ft. wide. Gray bark. Leathery, 1–3-in.-

Comarostaphylis diversifolia

long leaves are shiny dark green above, white and hairy beneath, with inrolled margins. (Variety *C. d. planifolia* has flat leaves.) Small, white, bell-shaped flowers in spring, followed by clusters of red, warty berries similar to those of madrone (*Arbutus menziesii*). Needs little pruning, but some thinning improves appearance.

COMFREY. See **SYMPHYTUM officinale**

CONEFLOWER, PRAIRIE or YELLOW. See **RATIBIDA pinnata**

CONEFLOWER, PURPLE. See **ECHINACEA purpurea**

CONEFLOWER, ROSE. See **ISOPOGON formosus**

CONFEDERATE JASMINE. See **TRACHELOSPERMUM jasminoides**

CONFEDERATE ROSE. See **HIBISCUS mutabilis**

CONSOLIDA ajacis
(Delphinium
ambiguum)
LARKSPUR, ANNUAL
DELPHINIUM
Ranunculaceae
ANNUAL

- **ZONES 1–24**
- **FULL SUN**
- **REGULAR WATER**
- **ALL PARTS, ESPECIALLY SEEDS, ARE POISONOUS IF INGESTED**

Native to southern Europe. Upright plants grow 1–4 ft. tall, 1 ft. wide, with deeply cut, almost ferny leaves. Blossom spikes densely set with 1–1½-in.-wide flowers (most are double) in white or shades of blue, lilac, pink, rose, salmon, carmine; there are also blue-and-white bicolors. Best bloom in cooler spring and early summer months. Giant Imperial strain has many 4-ft., compactly placed vertical stalks. Regal strain has 4-ft. base-branching stems, thick spikes of large flowers similar to perennial delphiniums. Super Imperial strain is base branching, has large flowers in 1½-ft. cone-shaped spikes.

Consolida ajacis

C

Steeplechase is base branching, has biggest double flowers on 4-ft. spikes; it is heat tolerant. Sow seed where plants are to grow; fall planting is best except in heavy, slow-draining soils. Thin plants to avoid crowding, get biggest flowers. Nursery transplants are also available for early-spring planting.

CONVALLARIA
majalis

LILY-OF-THE-VALLEY
Liliaceae
PERENNIAL FROM RHIZOME

🌿	ZONES A1–A3; 1–7, 14–20
☼	PARTIAL SHADE
💧	REGULAR WATER
⬥	ALL PARTS ARE POISONOUS IF INGESTED

Native to many northern regions of the Old World; naturalized in U.S., Canada. Lush, spreading, 6–8-in.-high ground cover. Blooms for a short period in early spring, sending up arching stems that bear small, nodding, sweet-scented, waxy white bells along one side. Broad, glossy green,

Convallaria majalis

deciduous leaves are attractive throughout growing season. Bright red berries (poisonous, like the rest of the plant) may appear in fall. Double- and pink-flowered forms are sold, as are types with variegated leaves. All are charming as carpet between camellias, rhododendrons, or pieris, under deciduous or high-branching evergreen trees. Can become invasive where well adapted.

Plant single rhizomes (called pips) or clumps in rich soil in fall before ground freezes. Set 1½ in. deep; space clumps 1–2 ft. apart, single pips 4–5 in. apart. Mulch planting each year before new growth emerges. Large, prechilled pips for forcing are available in winter (even in mild climates) and can be potted for bloom indoors. After bloom, plunge pots in ground in a cool, shaded area.

Once plants are dormant, remove them from pots and set out in garden; or wash soil off pips, enclose them in plastic bags, and refrigerate them (in vegetable bin) until time to repot in December or January.

CONVOLVULUS

Convolvulaceae
ANNUALS, PERENNIALS, AND EVERGREEN SHRUBS

🌿	ZONES VARY BY SPECIES
☼ ☽	BEST IN SUN, TOLERATE SOME SHADE
💧	MODERATE WATER

Mediterranean natives with funnel-shaped morning glory flowers. Common vining morning glories (*Ipomoea*) are sometimes sold as *Convolvulus.*

C. althaeoides tenuissimus. Perennial. Zones 7–9, 14–24. To 6 in. high, 2–3 ft. wide. Two kinds of foliage. Basal leaves are less than 1 in. long, oval to arrow shaped, sometimes lobed; leaves on trailing or creeping flowering stems are divided into narrow segments. Summer flowers are pink, 1–1½ in. wide. Spreads by rhizomes and can be invasive. Good in rock gardens, hanging baskets.

C. cneorum. BUSH MORNING GLORY. Evergreen shrub. Best in Zones 7–9, 12–24; marginal in Zones 5, 6. Grows fast to 2–4 ft. tall and as wide. Silky-smooth, silvery gray, lance-shaped leaves 1–2½ in. long. White or pink-tinted morning glories with yellow throats open from pink buds in late spring and summer. Give light soil and fast drainage. Prune severely to renew plant; can get leggy if left alone.

C. sabatius (C. mauritanicus). GROUND MORNING GLORY. Perennial. Zones 4–9, 12–24. Grows 1–2 ft. high with branches trailing to spread 3 ft. or more. Soft, hairy, gray-green, roundish, evergreen leaves ½–1½ in. long. Lavender-blue, 1–2-in.-wide flowers bloom from early summer into fall. Grows well in light, gravelly soil with good drainage but will take clay soil if not overwatered. Tends to become woody; prevent by trimming in late winter.

C. tricolor. DWARF MORNING GLORY. Annual. Zones 1–24. Bushy, branching, somewhat trailing plant to 1 ft. high and 2 ft. wide. Small, narrow leaves. Summer flowers, 1½ in. across, variable in color but usually blue with yellow throat. Nick tough seed coats

Convolvulus tricolor

with knife and plant in place when soil has warmed up. In mild-winter climates, can be planted in fall for spring bloom. Use as edging or at top of wall. 'Blue Flash' and Ensign series (red, blue, rose, white) grow 6 in. tall.

COOLIBAH.
See **EUCALYPTUS microtheca**

COONTIE. See **ZAMIA pumila**

COPPER CANYON DAISY.
See **TAGETES lemmonii**

COPPER LEAF.
See **ACALYPHA wilkesiana**

COPROSMA

Rubiaceae
EVERGREEN SHRUBS

🌿	ZONES VARY BY SPECIES
☼ ☽	FULL SUN OR PARTIAL SHADE
◐ ◑ ●	LITTLE TO REGULAR WATER

Native to New Zealand. Where hardy, all are valued for ease of maintenance in difficult situations and for handsome, glossy foliage. Male and female flowers are borne on separate plants; female plants bear attractive small fruits when a male is nearby for pollination.

C. 'Coppershine'. Zones 8, 9, 14–24. Male hybrid. Rounded form to 6 ft. high and wide; fast growing while young. Leathery leaves are 1–1¾ in. long, less than half as wide, polished bright green heavily shaded with coppery brown. New growth is even more heavily tinted; entire plant is bright copper in winter. Good hedge, screen.

C. 'Evening Glow'. Zones 8, 9, 14–24. Upright, rounded growth to 4–5 ft. tall and nearly as wide. Glossy green leaves are variegated gold during growing season and turn orange red in fall and winter. Colorful accent for borders or in pots. Avoid pruning in hot summer months. 'Rainbow Surprise' is similar in size and habit, with leaves variegated with cream and

pink, washed with red in fall and winter.

C. × kirkii. Zones 14–24; H1, H2. To 1–3 ft. high or nearly prostrate; spreading 4–6 ft. wide. Long, straight stems slant outward from base. Small (½–2-in.), narrow yellow-green leaves are closely set on stems. White fruits speckled red. Tough ground cover or bank cover; prune regularly to keep dense. Grows in wide range of soils; tolerates coastal winds, salt spray. Slightly drought tolerant near coast. Give part shade inland. 'Variegata', 6–24 in. high and up to 5 ft. wide, has white-edged gray-green leaves and translucent white berries; good trailing plant for wall pot, hanging basket.

C. petriei (C. pumila). Zones 8, 9, 14–24. Spreading, mounding plant to 2–2½ ft. high, eventually 6–8 ft. wide. Small, roundish oval leaves are bright shiny green. Set 2–2½ ft. apart for ground cover in 3 years. Cut out upward-growing branches. Tolerates more cold, heat than *C. × kirkii*. Egg-shaped fruits are translucent purplish red or blue. 'Verde Vista' (*C.* 'Prostrata'), a natural hybrid, is an improvement on the parent.

C. repens (C. baueri). MIRROR PLANT. Zones 14–24; H1. Rapid growth to 10 ft. tall, 6 ft. wide; much lower and more compact when subjected to seacoast conditions. Inland, an open, straggly shrub if neglected—but beautiful, dense form if pruned twice yearly (at any height desired). Oval or oblong leaves are 3 in. long, 1½ in. wide, dark to light green, almost unbelievably shiny and glossy. Yellow or orange fruits. Use as hedge, screen, informal espalier.

Coprosma repens

Variegated forms include 'Argentea', with green leaves flecked silvery white; 'Marble Queen', to 2–3 ft. tall, with creamy white leaves irregularly splashed and dotted with green; 'Marble King', slow grower with cream-colored leaves heavily speckled in

me green; 'Picturata', green leaves
[bl]otched creamy yellow in the
[m]iddle; 'Exotica', female version
[o]f 'Picturata' with orange-yellow
[fr]uits; 'Marginata', with green
[le]aves irregularly edged in creamy
[w]hite; 'Pink Splendor', green leaves
[w]ith yellow margin that takes on a
[p]ink edging with maturity.

[C]ORAL BELLS.
[S]ee **HEUCHERA sanguinea**

[C]ORALBERRY.
[S]ee **SYMPHORICARPOS**

[C]ORAL FOUNTAIN.
[S]ee **RUSSELIA equisetiformis**

[C]ORAL TREE. See **ERYTHRINA**

[C]ORAL VINE.
[S]ee **ANTIGONON leptopus**

[C]ORDIA
[B]oraginaceae
[E]VERGREEN SHRUBS AND TREES

✔ ZONES VARY BY SPECIES
☼ FULL SUN
◐ ◑ ● WATER NEEDS VARY BY SPECIES

[Th]ese members of the forget-me-
[n]ot family are grown for their
[s]howy flowers. Some species are at
[h]ome in the desert Southwest,
[o]thers in more tropical climates.

Cordia boissieri

C. boissieri.
TEXAS OLIVE.
Shrub or tree.
Zones 8–24.
Native to New
Mexico, Texas, Mexico;
[a]dapted to low and intermediate
[d]eserts. To 12 ft. tall, 8–10 ft. wide.
[O]val, rough-surfaced, grayish
[g]reen leaves to 5 in. long. Clus-
[t]ered, 2½-in. white flowers with
[y]ellow throats begin bloom in
[m]idspring and continue over a
[l]ong season; repeat bloom is possi-
[b]le in autumn. Can be kept pruned
[a]s a low (3–5-ft.) shrub or trained
[i]nto a small tree. Moderate water.

C. parvifolia. LITTLE-LEAF
CORDIA. Shrub. Zones 8–14,
18–24. Native to Baja California.
Similar to *C. boissieri* but somewhat smaller, with smaller leaves
(most are ½ in. or less); flowers
(to 1½ in. wide). Plant 8–9 ft. apart
for informal hedge or barrier. Little
to moderate water.

C. sebestena. GEIGER TREE,
KOU HAOLE. Shrub or tree.
Zones 24; H1, H2. Native to the
Caribbean Islands and tropical
America. A popular street tree in
Hawaii's dry lowlands. To 10–25 ft.
high and 15 ft. wide, with dense,
round head. Dark green leaves are
9–12 in. long and half as wide, so
rough surfaced they are almost
sandpapery. Clusters of brilliant
orange-red flowers are produced
much of the year at branch tips.
Good wind and salt tolerance;
takes drought but does best with
regular water.

C. subcordata. KOU. Tree.
Zones H1, H2. From seashores of
East Africa to Polynesia. A good
shade tree in Hawaii's hot coastal
areas. Dense growth to 25–35 ft.
high, 25 ft. wide. Smooth, thin, oval
leaves, 4–8 in. long. Clusters of
crepey light orange flowers much
of year. Regular water.

CORDYLINE
Agavaceae
EVERGREEN PALMLIKE SHRUBS
OR TREES

✔ ZONES VARY BY SPECIES; OR INDOORS
☼ ◐ EXPOSURE NEEDS VARY BY SPECIES
◐ ● WATER NEEDS VARY BY SPECIES

Woody plants with swordlike
leaves, related to yuccas and agaves
but usually ranked with palms in
nurseries and landscapes. Good
next to swimming pools. As houseplants, prefer bright indirect light
but tolerate low light; rarely bloom
indoors. To keep indoor plants
from getting too big, grow them in
undersize pots and repot annually
in fresh potting soil. Cordyline is
often sold as *Dracaena;* for true
Dracaena, see that entry.

**C. australis (Dracaena aus-
tralis).** Zones 5, 8–11, 14–24; H1,
H2. From New Zealand. Hardiest
of cordylines, surviving to at least
15°F/–9°C. In youth, forms a fountain of narrow (2–5-in.-wide),
3-ft.-long leaves. Upper leaves are
erect; lower ones arch and droop.
In maturity, a tree to 20–30 ft. tall,
6–12 ft. wide, branching high on
trunk; rather stiff looking (like

Cordyline australis 'Red Star'

Joshua tree, *Yucca brevifolia*).
Fragrant, ¼-in. flowers in long,
branching clusters in late spring.
For more graceful plant, cut back
when young to force multiple
trunks. Grows fastest in soil deep
enough for big, carrotlike root.
Used for tropical effects, with
boulders and gravel for desert
look, near seashore. Full sun.
Moderate to regular water.

Colorful varieties include 'Atropurpurea', known as bronze dracaena, with bronzy red leaves; 'Pink
Stripe', bronze with pink margins;
'Red Star', purplish red; and 'Sundance', green with a pink midrib.

C. baueri. Zones 8, 9, 14–24.
From New Zealand. To 8–10 ft.
high, 3 ft. wide, with 2-ft.-long
leaves in deep purple red. Fragrant
white flowers in summer. Full sun,
moderate water.

C. 'Festival Grass'. Zones 8, 9,
14–24. Unusual hybrid forms a
fountainlike clump 2–3 ft. high
and wide. Glossy, brilliant burgundy leaves are ¾ in. wide and
2–3 ft. long. Great in pots or as
an accent.

C. fruticosa (C. terminalis).
TI PLANT. Zones 21–24; H1, H2.
Frequently used as houseplant.
From tropical Southeast Asia.
Many named forms with red, yellow, or variegated leaves. White or
red, foot-long flower clusters in
summer or sporadically throughout year. Plants are usually started
from "logs"—small sections of
mature stems imported from
Hawaii. Lay logs flat in mixture of
peat moss and sand, covering them
to about one-half their diameter.
Keep moist. When shoots grow out
and root, cut them off and plant
them. In frost-free locations where
it receives regular water and soil
stays warm, reaches 6–15 ft. high,
3–8 ft. wide. Full sun or partial
shade (types with colorful leaves
show more intense hues in sun).

C. indivisa. BLUE DRACAENA.
Zones 16, 17, 20–24. Hardy to

26°F/–3°C. From New Zealand.
Trunk grows to 25 ft. tall and is
topped with 8–10-ft.-wide crown
of huge (6-ft.-long, 6-in.-wide),
rather stiff leaves. White summer
flowers in 4-ft.-long clusters. Tolerates seaside conditions. Give full
sun, moderate water.

C. stricta. Zones 13, 16, 17,
20–24; H1, H2. Hardy to 26°F/
–3°C. From Australia. Slender,
erect stems clustered at base or
branching low. Leaves are 2 ft.
long, dark green, and with hints
of purple. Very decorative during
spring bloom, bearing fragrant
lavender flowers in large, branched
clusters. Reaches 15 ft. high and
6 ft. wide but can be kept lower by
cutting tall canes to ground; new
canes replace them. Long cuttings
stuck in ground will root quickly.
Fine container plant indoors or
out; good for tropical-looking
background in narrow areas,
lanais, side gardens. Needs some
shade except in cool-summer climates. Regular water.

C. terminalis. See *C. fruticosa*

COREOPSIS
Asteraceae (Compositae)
PERENNIALS AND ANNUALS

✔ ZONES VARY BY SPECIES
☼ FULL SUN
◐ ● LITTLE TO MODERATE WATER, EXCEPT AS NOTED

Easy-to-grow members of the
sunflower family yielding a profusion of yellow, orange, maroon,
or reddish flowers. Deadhead for
longer bloom; use hedge shears
to remove large numbers of spent
blooms. Both annual and perennial kinds are easy to propagate—
annuals from seed sown in place
or in pots, perennials from seed or
division. Plants tend to self-sow;
seeds attract birds. The following
species are from the eastern and
southern U.S. unless otherwise
noted.

C. auriculata 'Nana'. Perennial.
Zones 1–24. Makes 5–6-in.-high
mat of 2–5-in.-long leaves. Under
ideal conditions, it will spread by
underground runners to form a
2-ft.-wide clump in a year. Bright
orange-yellow, 1–2½-in. flowers
rise well above foliage; blooms
profusely over a long season
(from spring to fall) if you deadhead faithfully. Best used in
front of taller plants, in borders,
as edging.

C. gigantea. Perennial.
Zones 14–17, 19–24. Native to
coastal Southern California,

C

Baja California. Grows to 3 ft. (occasionally 10 ft.) tall, with asymmetric form. Succulent trunks to 4 in. across hold a few branches of varying lengths tipped with clusters of fernlike leaves. Clusters of 3-in. yellow daisies in spring. Showy in seaside plant collection; rarely sold in nurseries.

C. grandiflora. Perennial. Zones 2–24; H1, H2. To 1–2 ft. high, spreading to 3 ft. Narrow dark green leaves with three to five lobes. Bright yellow, 2½–3-in. single flowers bloom all summer, carried high above foliage on long, slender stems. 'Flying Saucers' is a nearly sterile selection with single, flat, 2-in.-wide yellow flowers over a long period. 'Sunburst' has semidouble flowers; it will bloom the first year from seed sown early in spring, then spread by self-sowing. 'Early Sunrise' is similar and blooms even earlier. 'Sunray' is a dense, compact selection with double and semidouble flowers. All are tough enough for use in roadside beautification.

Coreopsis grandiflora

C. lanceolata. Perennial. Zones 1–24; H1, H2. Grows to 1–2 ft. high, 1–1½ ft. wide. Narrow, somewhat hairy foliage, mostly in tuft near plant's base; some leaves on lower part of flower stems have a few lobes. Yellow, 1½–2-in. blossoms on pale green stems bloom in late spring and summer, make excellent cut flowers. When well established, persists year after year. Has naturalized in Hawaii. 'Sterntaler' has yellow flowers with a reddish brown circle in the center.

C. 'Limerock Ruby'. Perennial. Zones 1–24. Hybrid to about 1½ ft. tall and 2½ ft. wide; forms a clump

of fine-textured foliage similar to that of *C. verticillata*. Ruby red flowers to 1 in. across appear in late spring through summer. Moderate water. 'Limerock Passion' is similar, but with yellow-centered, lavender-pink flowers.

C. maritima. Perennial. Zones 14–24. Native to coast of Southern California. Sometimes called sea dahlia. Grows from a tuberous taproot to reach 1–3 ft. high, 1–2 ft. wide. Stems are hollow; leaves are somewhat succulent, divided into very narrow lobes. True yellow, 2½–4-in. blossoms on 9–12-in. stems in spring; make striking cut flowers. Use in borders, for naturalizing.

C. rosea. Perennial. Zones 2b–24. Fine-textured plant 1½–2 ft. tall, 1 ft. wide, with pink, yellow-centered daisylike flowers from summer to fall. Unlike other species, prefers moist soil. 'American Dream' has rosy pink flowers with a yellow center. 'Heaven's Gate' is pink with a dark crimson ring around the center. 'Sweet Dreams' has threadlike leaves and masses of big white flowers with a raspberry ring surrounding a yellow eye.

C. 'Tequila Sunrise'. Perennial. Zones 2a–24. To 1½ ft. high, 1 ft. wide. Narrow, olive green leaves are irregularly variegated with cream and yellow, with touches of pinkish red in spring and deeper red in fall. Golden yellow, 1½-in. flowers with deep orange-red centers appear continually in summer. Moderate water.

C. tinctoria. ANNUAL COREOPSIS, CALLIOPSIS. Annual. Zones 1–24; H1, H2. Native to much of North America. Slender, upright, 1½–3 ft. tall, 1–1½ ft. wide, with wiry stems; much like cosmos in growth habit. Smooth leaves and stems. Summer-to-fall flowers in yellow, orange, maroon, bronze, and reddish, banded with contrasting colors; purple-brown centers. Dwarf and double varieties are available. Sow seed in place in dryish soil.

C. verticillata. Perennial. Zones 1–24. To 2½–3 ft. tall, half as broad. Many erect or slightly leaning stems carry many whorls of finely divided, very narrow leaves. Bright yellow, 2-in. daisies are freely borne at stem tips over a long bloom season—from summer through autumn. One of the most tolerant of drought, neglect. 'Moonbeam', 1½–2 ft. tall, has pale yellow flowers; 'Zagreb', 1 ft. tall, has golden yellow flowers.

CORIANDRUM sativum
CORIANDER, CHINESE PARSLEY, CILANTRO
Apiaceae (Umbelliferae)
ANNUAL

| ✎ ALL ZONES |
| ☼ ◑ LIGHT SHADE IN HOTTEST CLIMATES |
| ● REGULAR WATER |

Mediterranean native grows 1–1½ ft. high, 9 in. wide. Delicate fernlike foliage; flat clusters of pinkish white flowers in summer. Both fresh leaves (cilantro) and seeds (coriander) are widely used as seasoning. Leaves are popular in salads and many cooked dishes;

Coriandrum sativum

crush the aromatic seeds for use in sausage, beans, stews, baked goods. Grow in good, well-drained soil. Start from seed (including coriander seed sold in grocery stores) in early spring after all danger of frost is past. In low-desert areas, plant in autumn; goes to seed and dies in late spring heat. Sow in place; plant is taprooted and transplants poorly. Grows quickly, self-sows.

CORN
Poaceae (Gramineae)
ANNUAL

| ✎ ALL ZONES |
| ☼ FULL SUN |
| ● REGULAR WATER |

Sweet corn is the one cereal crop that home gardeners are likely to grow; it requires considerable space but is still well worth planting. Once standard sweet corn is picked, its sugar changes to starch very quickly; by rushing ears from garden directly to boiling water, you can capture full sweetness. Sugar-enhanced and supersweet

varieties of corn are actually sweeter than standard kinds, and they maintain their sweetness longer after harvest because of a gene that increases the quantity of sugar and slows its conversion to starch. A very few people consider these varieties overly sweet.

Corn needs heat, but suitable early hybrid varieties will grow even in cool-summer areas. In Alaska, grow short-season varieties; plant seeds you have pre-germinated and grow with black plastic mulch and a cover. In Hawaii, try varieties developed especially for Island gardens, such as supersweet kinds 'Waimanolo SS' and 'UH-10'.

Corn grows in various soils but does best in deep, rich ones; good drainage is important. Sow seed 2 weeks after average last-frost date, then make three or four more plantings at 2-week intervals; or plant early, midseason, and late varieties. In Hawaii, you can plant corn year-round. Plant in blocks of four or more short rows rather than in single long row; pollination is by wind, and unless a good supply of pollen falls on silks, ears will be poorly filled. Don't plant popcorn near sweet corn; pollen of one kind can affect characteristics of other. For the same reason, some supersweet varieties must be grown at a distance from standard sweet kinds.

Sweet corn

Plant in rows 3 ft. apart and thin seedlings to 1 ft. apart. Or plant in "hills" (actually clumps) spaced 3 ft. apart on all sides. Plant six or seven seeds in each hill and thin to three strongest plants.

Give plants plenty of water. Feed with high-nitrogen fertilizer when stalks are 12–15 in. tall, again when they are 2–2½ ft. high. Just as tassel emerges from stalk, give good deep watering that thoroughly wets entire root zone; repeat when silks form. Don't remove suckers that appear. Check your crop when ears are plump and silks have withered; corn is usually ready to eat 3 weeks after silks first appear. To check, pull back husks and try popping a kernel with your thumbnail. It should squirt milky juice; watery juice means that corn is immature, while doughy consistency indicates overmaturity.

Corn earworm is the principal insect pest. There is no simple control. Most gardeners expect some harvested ears to show worm damage at the silk ends, and they just cut off those ends. The prevention (it's tedious) goes like this: 3 to 7 days after silks appear, use a medicine dropper to put two drops of mineral oil just inside the tip of each ear.

Baby corn. Special varieties that are harvested very early, when the ears are only a few inches long. The tender ears are eaten whole, often pickled or used in salads or Asian cuisine. Plant seeds 1–2 in. apart; thin seedlings to 4 in. apart. Harvest shortly after the first silks appear, which may be only a few weeks after sowing.

Ornamental corn. Some kinds of corn are grown for the beauty of their shelled ears rather than for eating. Calico, Indian, Squaw, and Rainbow are some names given to strains with bright-colored kernels —red, brown, blue, gray, black, yellow, or mixed colors. 'Indian Summer' has brightly colored, edible kernels. Grow ornamental corn well away from sweet corn; mix of pollen can affect the latter's flavor. For ornamental display, grow like sweet corn, but let ears ripen fully; silks will be withered, husks will turn the color of straw, and kernels will be firm. Cut ear from plant,

Ornamental corn

including 1½ in. of stalk below ear; pull back husks (leave attached to ears) and dry thoroughly.

Zea mays japonica includes several kinds of corn grown for ornamental foliage. One occasionally sold is 'Gracilis', a dwarf corn with bright green leaves striped white.

Popcorn. Grow and harvest just like ornamental corn. When ears are thoroughly dry, rub kernels off cobs and store in dry place. White, red, and yellow kinds of popcorn look like other types of corn.

Popcorn

Strawberry popcorn, grown either for its ornamental value or for popping, has stubby, fat, strawberry-like ears packed with red kernels.

CORN COCKLE.
See **AGROSTEMMA githago**

CORNELIAN CHERRY.
See **CORNUS mas**

CORNFLOWER.
See **CENTAUREA cyanus**

CORN PLANT.
See **DRACAENA fragrans**

CORN SALAD. See **MACHE**

CORNUS
DOGWOOD
Cornaceae
DECIDUOUS AND EVERGREEN
SHRUBS AND TREES AND A
PERENNIAL

🔲 ZONES VARY BY SPECIES

☼ ☽ ● FULL SUN OR LIGHT SHADE, EXCEPT AS NOTED

💧 REGULAR WATER, EXCEPT AS NOTED

All dogwoods offer attractive foliage and blossoms; some have spectacular fruit or winter bark. Leaves of many types turn brilliant colors in fall. What appear to be flower petals in many dogwoods are actually bracts—petal-like modified leaves. These surround the inconspicuous true flowers.

C. alba. TATARIAN DOGWOOD. Deciduous shrub. Zones A2, A3; 1–9, 14–24. Native to Siberia, northern China, Korea. In cold-winter areas, its bare, blood red twigs are colorful against snow. Wide spreading, eventually producing thicket of many upright stems to about 10 ft. tall. Branches densely foliaged with leaves to 2½–5 in. long, 2½ in. wide; leaves are deep rich green above and paler beneath, turn red in fall. Spring bloom; small, fragrant, creamy white flowers in 1–2-in., flattish clusters. Small bluish white to white fruits. In species and following varieties, new wood is brightest; cut back in late dormant season to force new growth.

'Argenteomarginata' (C. 'Elegantissima'). Showy green-and-white leaves on red stems.

'Gouchaultii'. Leaves have yellow borders suffused with pink.

'Ivory Halo' is compact, to 3–6 ft. tall and wide; red stems hold white-edged green leaves.

'Sibirica'. SIBERIAN DOGWOOD. Smaller and not as wide spreading as species; grows to about 7 ft. high, 5 ft. wide. Gleaming coral red branches.

C. alternifolia. PAGODA DOGWOOD. Deciduous shrub or tree. Zones 2–6. Native to eastern North America. Multitrunked plant to 20 ft. high and wide. Strong horizontal branching pattern provides attractive winter silhouette. Light green leaves turn red in fall. Creamy spring flowers come in small clusters, are not showy. Blue-black fruit follows. Foliage of 'Argentea' has white markings.

C. canadensis. BUNCHBERRY. Perennial. Zones A1–A3; 1–7; difficult but possible in Zones 8, 9, 14–16. Native from Northern California to Alaska and eastward. Ground cover 6–9 in. high, found in the wild under trees by lakes and streams. Creeping rootstocks send up stems topped by whorls of oval or roundish, 1–2-in.-long, deep green leaves that turn yellow in fall, die down in winter. In late spring or early summer, plants bear small, compact clusters of tiny flowers surrounded by (usually) four oval, ½–¾-in., pure white bracts. Clusters of small, shiny red fruits follow in late summer.

Best performance in part or full shade in cool, moist climates, in acid soil with generous amounts of organic matter. Set out small plants from pots about 1 ft. apart. Small rooted pieces gathered from the woods may not establish easily. Excellent with rhododendrons, ferns, trilliums, lilies.

C. capitata. EVERGREEN DOGWOOD. Shrub or tree. Zones 8, 9, 14–20. Himalayan native hardy to 15°F/–9°C. Not reliably evergreen; may drop all its leaves in cold weather, and often loses half of them in mild winters. To 20–30 ft. tall and wide, with 2–4-in.-long, gray-green leaves; some turn red or purplish in fall. Unless grown from cuttings, trees don't flower until 8 to 10 years old— but when they do bloom, they are delightful. Small springtime clusters of flowers are surrounded by four to six 1½–2-in., creamy to pale yellow bracts. Large (1-in.), showy, strawberrylike crimson fruit in fall can be a litter problem, though birds may do some of the cleanup for you.

C. c. emeiensis. Zones 4–9, 14–17. From China; hardier than the species. To 35 ft. tall and wide. Foliage in upper portion of tree turns purple, while lower leaves remain green. New leaves replace the old ones in spring. Usually sold as *C. omeiense* 'Summer Passion'.

C. controversa. GIANT DOGWOOD. Deciduous tree. Zones 4–9, 14, 18, 19. From Asia. Resembles typical big shrubby dogwoods in leaves, flowers, and fruit, but grows rapidly into a magnificent tree 40–60 ft. tall and wide, with picturesque horizontal branches. Luxuriantly foliaged with oval, 3–6-in.-long leaves that are dark green above, silvery green beneath, glowing red in fall. Creamy white spring flowers in fluffy, flattish, 3–7-in. clusters are not spectacular, but so abundant they give a good show. Blossoms are followed in late summer by ½-in., shiny blue-black fruit enjoyed by birds. Full sun for best bloom, brightest fall color. 'June Snow' bears abundant large flower clusters and has mottled orange-yellow, red, and purplish red fall leaf color. Foliage of 'Variegata' is edged white.

C. 'Eddie's White Wonder'. Deciduous tree. Zones 3–9, 14–20. Hybrid between *C. florida*

Cornus florida 'Rubra'

C

and *C. nuttallii*. A little taller and more erect than *C. florida*, twiggier and easier to transplant than *C. nuttallii*. Midspring bloom. Clusters of tiny true flowers are surrounded by four to six white bracts.

C. florida. FLOWERING DOGWOOD, EASTERN DOGWOOD. Deciduous tree. Zones 2b–9, 14–16. Native to eastern U.S. May reach 40 ft. high and wide, but more commonly seen at 20–30 ft. Trees tend to branch low, the branches building up in horizontal layers (with gray twigs pointing upward at branch ends). Mature trees—often wider than tall—have a gently rounded to flat crown. Small flower clusters are surrounded by four roundish, 2–4-in. bracts with notched tips. The species has white bracts, but selections offer bracts in pink shades to nearly red (as well as white). Bracts form in fall; tips may dry out in harsh, dry winters, preventing inflorescence from opening fully. Flowers almost cover the tree in midspring before the leaves expand. Oval, 2–4-in.-long leaves are bright green above, lighter green beneath; turn glowing red in fall. Clusters of small, oval scarlet fruit last into winter or until birds eat them. Subject to anthracnose, a fungus that can cause leaf damage, stem cankers, and decline or death of the tree. Avoid injury to bark from mowers and string trimmers; try to keep the tree healthy with adequate feeding, watering, and air circulation.

The following are among the varieties offered. (*C. florida* has been bred with *C. kousa* to produce more disease resistant hybrids; for those, see *C. × rutgersensis*.)

'Cherokee Brave'. Red bracts with white centers. Resists mildew.

'Cherokee Chief'. Deep rosy red bracts, paler at base.

'Cherokee Daybreak' ('Daybreak'). Green leaves with white variegation turn pink and red in fall. White bracts.

'Cherokee Princess'. Unusually heavy display of white blooms.

'Cherokee Sunset' ('Sunset'). Yellow-variegated leaves turn red purple in fall. Reddish bracts. Resistant to anthracnose.

'Cloud Nine'. White-bracted selection blooms young and very heavily. Gives better bloom in cold climates than other *C. florida* varieties; also tolerates heat and lack of winter chill better than other varieties.

'Rubra'. Longtime favorite for its pink or rose bracts.

'Welchii'. TRICOLOR DOGWOOD. Leaves about 4 in. long, variegated in creamy white, pink, deep rose, and green throughout spring and summer; turn solid deep rose to almost red in fall. Rather inconspicuous pinkish to white bracts are not profuse. Best with some shade.

C. kousa. KOUSA DOGWOOD. Deciduous shrub or tree. Zones 2–9, 14–17. Native to Japan and Korea. Can be a big multistemmed shrub or—with training—a small tree to 20 ft. tall and wide (or even larger). Dense, spreading, horizontal growth habit and delicate limb structure. Lustrous medium green leaves, 4 in. long, have rusty brown hairs at base of veins on undersurface. Flowers along tops of branches show above leaves in late spring or early summer (later than other flowering dogwoods). Creamy white, rather narrow, 2–3-in.-long bracts with slender, sharp-pointed tips turn pink along edges. In late summer and fall, inch-wide red fruits appear, resembling large raspberries hanging below branches. Yellow or scarlet autumn leaf color. Less susceptible to anthracnose than *C. florida* and *C. nuttallii*. Except as noted, the following selections bear white bracts.

Cornus kousa

'Autumn Rose'. To 20 ft. tall, 25 ft. wide. Leaves are light green when new, pink to red in fall.

C. k. chinensis. Larger leaves and bracts than species.

'Gold Star'. To 12 ft. tall and wide, with yellow-centered green leaves.

'Heart Throb'. Large, deep red to rose pink flowers over a long period.

'Milky Way'. More floriferous than species.

'National'. To 25–30 ft. tall, 12–15 ft. wide, with earlier bloom than species and bright red fall color.

'Satomi' ('Satomi Red', 'Rosabella'). Reaches 20 ft. tall and wide. Rose red bracts.

'Wolf Eyes'. Gray-green leaves edged with white. Pinkish red fall color.

C. mas. CORNELIAN CHERRY. Deciduous shrub or tree. Zones 1–6. Native to southern Europe, Asia. Usually an airy, twiggy shrub but can be trained as small tree (15–20 ft. high and wide). One of earliest dogwoods to bloom, bearing clustered masses of small, soft yellow blossoms on bare twigs in mid- to late winter. Oval, 2–4-in.-long leaves turn from shiny green to yellow (or red, in some forms) in autumn. Fall color is enhanced by clusters of cherry-size, bright scarlet fruits that hang on until birds get them. Fruit can be used for preserves. In winter, flaking, mottled gray-and-tan bark provides interest. Tolerates alkaline soils. Leaves of 'Variegata' are marbled creamy white.

C. nuttallii. PACIFIC DOGWOOD, WESTERN DOGWOOD. Deciduous tree. Zones 3b–9, 14–20. Native to Pacific Northwest and Northern California. To 50 ft. tall, 20 ft. wide, with one trunk or several. Gray branches in pleasing horizontal pattern. Spectacular when it shows off its gleaming white bracts on bare branches in spring; there is often a second flowering in late summer, when tree is in full leaf. Flowers ringed by four to eight large (to 3-in.-long), rounded or pointed bracts; they may be white or pink-tinged white. Oval, 3–5-in. green leaves turn yellow, red, and pink in autumn. Decorative red fruit in knoblike clusters in fall.

Dislikes routine garden watering, fertilizing, pruning; injury to tender bark provides entrance for insects and diseases. For better chance of success, give exceptionally good drainage and infrequent summer water, and plant under high-branching trees so bark will not sunburn. In Northwest, however, planting under larger trees is not advisable. *C. nuttallii* is very susceptible to anthracnose in this region, and a location under larger trees creates conditions that favor the disease—reduced air circulation and shadiness that extend time for wet foliage to dry.

Named varieties better tolerate garden conditions. 'Colrigo Giant' is vigorous and heavy trunked, with low-branching but erect habit; bears profusion of 6-in. flower heads. 'Goldspot' has leaves splashed with creamy yellow; because it is grafted, it blooms from an early age (when only 2 ft. high).

'Starlight' is a hybrid between *C. nuttalli* and *C. kousa*, with an upright habit to 30 ft. tall and 20 ft. wide. Blooms are white; fall leaf color is red. Resists anthracnose and powdery mildew. 'Venus', another cross between these two species, grows 25 ft. tall and 20 ft. wide, with very large (6-in.) white blooms and few fruits.

C. omeiense 'Summer Passion'. See *C. capitata emeiensis*

C. × rutgersensis. STELLAR DOGWOOD. Deciduous trees. Zones 3–9, 14–17. These disease-resistant single-trunked hybrids between *C. florida* and *C. kousa* grow to about 20 ft. tall, 25–30 ft. wide. Bloom comes between midspring bloom of *C. florida* and late-spring or early-summer bloom of *C. kousa*. Blossoms appear along with the leaves. 'Aurora', 'Celestial', and 'Ruth Ellen' have broad white bracts; 'Constellation' and 'Stardust' have narrow white ones, giving a starlike effect. 'Stellar Pink' produces pink bracts. All have brilliant fall color.

C. sanguinea. BLOODTWIG DOGWOOD. Deciduous shrub. Zones 1–7. From Europe. Grows as large multistemmed shrub to 12 ft. high, about 8 ft. wide. Big show comes in fall, thanks to dark blood red foliage, and in winter, when bare, purplish to dark red twigs and branches are on display. Prune severely in late dormant season to produce new branches and twigs for winter color. Dark green, 1½–3-in.-long leaves; greenish white late-spring flowers in 2-in. clusters. Black fruit. 'Midwinter Fire' has brilliant orange-red fall color and red berries.

C. stolonifera (C. sericea). REDTWIG DOGWOOD, RED-OSIER DOGWOOD. Deciduous shrub. Zones A1–A3; 1–9, 14–21. Like *C. sanguinea*, this one is grown for brilliant red fall foliage and winter twigs, and it too should be cut back severely in late dormant season. Native to moist places, Northern California to Alaska and eastward. Thrives not only in the coldest mountain areas of West but also throughout California—even in intermediate valleys of Southern California if given frequent water. Grows rapidly to form a multistemmed shrub 7–9 ft. high; spreads to 12 ft. or wider by creeping underground stems and rooting branches. Oval, 1½–2½-in.-long,

C

Cornus stolonifera

fresh deep green leaves. Small, creamy white flowers in 2-in. clusters appear among leaves throughout summer; white or bluish fruits follow.

Use as a space filler on moist ground (good for holding banks) or plant along property line as a screen. Shade tolerant. To control spread, use a spade to cut off roots; also trim branches that touch ground.

C. s. baileyi. To 6–8 ft. tall; exceptionally bright red twigs.

C. s. coloradensis. COLORADO REDTWIG. Native from Yukon to New Mexico and California. To 5–6 ft. high, with brownish red stems. Its selection 'Cheyenne' is redder.

'Flaviramea'. YELLOWTWIG DOGWOOD. Yellow twigs and branches.

'Isanti'. Compact grower to 5 ft. tall, with bright red stems.

'Kelseyi' ('Nana'). Dwarf form seldom exceeding 1½ ft. tall. Stems not as red as those of species.

'Silver and Gold'. Yellow branches and cream-edged green leaves.

COROKIA
Cornaceae
EVERGREEN SHRUBS

🌿 ZONES 4–24

☀️ ◐ FULL SUN OR PARTIAL SHADE

💧 MODERATE WATER

New Zealand natives grown for zigzag branching habit; small, starlike yellow flowers; and red, orange, or yellow fruits. Night lighting from below emphasizes bizarre branch pattern and casts interesting shadows. Sculptural form is enhanced by selective removal of a third or more of the branches and by heading back strong new shoots to maintain a compact outline. If intertwining branches are left intact, plants make dense hedges. Need good drainage. Thrive in containers.

C. cotoneaster. Slow growing to 8–10 ft. high and wide, but usually seen as a 2–4-ft. container plant. Slim, contorted, reddish to nearly black branches. Sparse, oval leaves to ¾ in. long, dark glossy green above, white beneath. Yellow, ½-in. flowers are followed on older plants by small orange or red fruit. 'Little Prince' grows 4 ft. high, has bright red fruit.

Corokia cotoneaster

C. × virgata. A series of hybrids with more erect growth habit than *C. cotoneaster;* eventually reach 10 ft. tall, 6 ft. wide. Most have spoon-shaped leaves up to 1½ in. long. Use in pots, as accent plants in garden, as hedge or screen. 'Red Wonder' and 'Yellow Wonder' are named for the color of their showy fruits. 'Bronze King' has tiny, bronze-tinged leaves; 'Bronze Lady' has darker bronze foliage (of the usual size) and bright red fruit. 'Sunsplash' has bronzy stems and bright green leaves margined with creamy yellow.

CORONILLA varia
CROWN VETCH
Fabaceae (Leguminosae)
PERENNIAL

🌿 ZONES 1–24

☀️ FULL SUN

💧 MODERATE WATER

Weedy European native related to peas, beans, and clovers. Creeping roots and rhizomes make it a tenacious ground cover. Sprawling stems to 2 ft. long are set with leaves divided into 11–25 oval, ½–¾-in.-long leaflets. Lavender-pink flowers in 1-in. clusters bloom from summer into fall; these are followed by bundles of brown, fingerlike seedpods. Dies to the ground in winter, even in mild climates. Too invasive and rank for flower beds; use it for covering erosion-prone banks and at garden

Coronilla varia

fringes. Mow, feed, and—if rains are absent—irrigate in early spring for best appearance. Difficult to eliminate once established. 'Penngift' takes sun or shade.

CORREA
AUSTRALIAN FUCHSIA
Rutaceae
EVERGREEN SHRUBS

🌿 ZONES 14–24

☀️ ◐ PARTIAL SHADE IN HOTTEST CLIMATES

💧 MODERATE WATER

These Australian natives may resemble fuchsia in their flower form, but in all other ways they are far from fuchsialike. Plants range from low growing to tall, are usually dense and spreading. Roundish, 1-in. leaves, densely felted underneath; gray or gray-green color contrasts subtly with other grays, distinctly with dark greens. All are valued for their long flowering season, usually late fall into spring (*C. alba* is a summer bloomer). Small (½–¾-in.) flowers hang from branches like little bells; they are individually handsome but not showy.

Need fast drainage; do well in poor, rocky soil. Easy to kill with kindness (overwatering, overfertilizing). Should not get reflected heat from wall or pavement. Use as ground cover on banks or slopes. Attractive in large pots placed where flowers can be enjoyed close up.

C. alba. To 8 ft. high and wide, with rusty-haired stems and dark green leaves. Flowers are white, more open and star-shaped than those of other correas. Withstands seashore conditions. Apparently not relished by deer. *C. a. pannosa* 'Western Pink Star' grows 3–4 ft. tall and 4–6 ft. wide, with pale pink flowers.

C. backhouseana. Upright and rather sprawling growth to 4–5 ft. tall and wide. Chartreuse flowers. More successful in Southern California than *C. pulchella.* Often sold as *C. magnifica.*

C. 'Dusky Bells' ('Carmine Bells'). Low growing (2–2½ ft.), spreading as wide as 8 ft. Deep red flowers.

C. 'Ivory Bells'. Resembles 'Dusky Bells' but has creamy white flowers.

C. pulchella. To 2–2½ ft. high, spreading as wide as 8 ft. Leaves green above, gray green below; flower color ranges from light pink to reddish orange. Most widely grown correa in Northern California. 'Mission Bells' has deep

Correa pulchella

pink to red flowers; 'Orange Flame' has somewhat smaller orange blossoms. 'Pink Eyre' is compact, 2–3 ft. high and wide, with showy rose pink blooms nearly year-round. 'Pink Flamingo' is similar, with salmon pink blooms.

C. reflexa. Variable species, with many forms ranging from 1 to 9 ft. tall, 3 to 9 ft. wide. Flowers are 1–1½ in. long, tubular, with color that varies from yellow green to red, with yellow to green tips. 'Cape Carpet' reaches 1 ft. high and 8–10 ft. wide; flowers are bright red with chartreuse tips. 'Carpenter Rocks' flowers are similar but grow just 3–4 ft. high and wide. 'Yanakie' is 4 ft. tall and wide, with large red flowers tipped in cream or green.

CORTADERIA
selloana
PAMPAS GRASS
Poaceae (Gramineae)
PERENNIAL GRASS

🌿 ZONES 3–24; H1

☀️ FULL SUN

💧 ANY AMOUNT OF WATER

Native to Argentina. Grows very fast in rich soil in mild climates—from gallon-can size to 8 ft. in one season. Established plants may reach 20 ft. tall, up to about

C

13 ft. wide. Each plant is a fountain of saw-toothed, grassy leaves; long stalks bearing 1–3-ft., white to chamois or pink flower plumes rise above the foliage in late summer. 'Pumila' ('Ivory Feathers') is smaller (to 3 ft. tall, 4 ft. wide), with white plumes rising to 6 ft. 'Sun Stripe' has yellow-striped foliage in clumps to 4 ft. tall, 5 ft. wide, with white flower plumes to 6 ft. high.

Cortaderia selloana

This well-known landscaping form of *Cortaderia*—like its truly weedy and noxious cousin *C. jubata*—may send its seeds into the wind under certain circumstances to germinate and grow wherever they land. For that reason, nurseries in some areas no longer sell *Cortaderia* at all. Many horticulturists recommend against further landscaping with *C. selloana* and suggest removing it from gardens that border wild lands. Be sure to grub out volunteer *Cortaderia* seedlings whenever they appear.

CORYDALIS

Fumariaceae
PERENNIALS

| ☀ ZONES 2–9, 14–24 |
| :◐ PARTIAL SHADE |
| ● REGULAR WATER |

Handsome clumps of dainty divided leaves like those of bleeding heart (*Dicentra,* to which it is closely related) or maidenhair fern (*Adiantum*). Clusters of small, spurred flowers. Plant in rich, moist soil. Effective in rock crevices, in open woodland, near pool or streamside. Divide clumps or sow seed in spring or fall. Plants self-sow. Tend to be short lived in mild-winter Southern California zones.

C. cheilanthifolia. Chinese native, 8–10 in. high and wide, with fernlike green foliage. Clusters of yellow, ½-in.-long flowers in spring.

C. curviflora rosthornii 'Blue Heron'. Clumping growth to 10 in. high, 8 in. wide. Finely cut gray-green foliage. Large, very fragrant, sapphire blue flowers from spring into summer. Doesn't reseed.

C. flexuosa. From western China. Typically to 1 ft. high, 8 in. wide, but under favorable conditions it rapidly spreads wider from bulblets on the roots. Finely divided foliage and spikelike clusters of blue flowers in early spring, often continuing into summer. May go dormant in summer, especially in hot climates, but will reappear the following spring. Selections include 'Blue Panda', with gentian blue flowers; 'China Blue', pure sky blue flowers; 'Nightshade', blue-and-lavender flowers; 'Père David', lavender to light blue flowers. 'Purple Leaf', the earliest bloomer, has purplish blue flowers and green leaves blotched purple.

C. lutea. Native to southern Europe. To 15 in. tall, 1 ft. wide. Masses of delicate foliage on many stems. Golden yellow, ¾-in.-long, short-spurred flowers throughout summer. Self-sows and can become somewhat weedy.

Corydalis lutea

C. solida. From northern Europe, Asia. To 10 in. high, 8 in. wide. Blooms in spring, producing spikes containing up to 20 purplish red flowers. Grow from fall-planted tubers.

CORYLOPSIS

WINTER HAZEL
Hamamelidaceae
DECIDUOUS SHRUBS

| ☀ ZONES VARY BY SPECIES |
| :☼: :◐ FULL SUN OR PARTIAL SHADE |
| ● REGULAR WATER |

Asian natives valued for sweet-scented, bell-shaped, soft yellow flowers that hang in short, chain-like clusters on bare branches in early spring. New foliage that follows is often tinged pink; it later turns bright green. Toothed, nearly round leaves somewhat resemble those of hazelnut (*Corylus*); fall color varies from none to poor to a good clear yellow. Rather open structure with attractive, delicate branching pattern. Give same soil conditions as you would rhododendrons. Grow in wind-sheltered location in shrub border or at edge of woodland.

C. glabrescens. FRAGRANT WINTER HAZEL. Zones 2–7, 14–17. Hardiest species. To 8–15 ft. high and wide. Can be trained as a small tree. Flower clusters are 1–1½ in. long.

C. pauciflora. BUTTERCUP WINTER HAZEL. Zones 4–7, 14–17. Dainty habit to 4–6 ft. high and wide. Blossom clusters are 1¾ in. long, each containing two or three blooms.

C. sinensis. Zones 4–7, 14–17. A variable species. The typical form is a spreading shrub to 15 ft. tall and wide, bearing crowded flower spikes to 2 in. long. *C. s. sinensis* (*C. willmottiae*) has velvety blue-green leaves, hairy leafstalks, and flower clusters to 3 in. long. Its selection 'Spring Purple' has purplish young stems that mature to green. *C. sinensis calvescens* (*C. platypetala*) has smooth leaf surfaces and largely hairless leafstalks.

Corylopsis spicata

C. spicata. SPIKE WINTER HAZEL. Zones 3b–7, 14–17. To 8 ft. high, 10 ft. wide. New growth is purple, maturing to bluish green; 6–12 blossoms in each 1½-in.-long flower cluster.

Corylopsis spicata

CORYLUS

FILBERT, HAZELNUT
Betulaceae
DECIDUOUS SHRUBS AND TREES

| ☀ ZONES 2–9, 14–20, EXCEPT AS NOTED |
| :☼: :◐ FULL SUN OR PARTIAL SHADE |
| ● REGULAR WATER, EXCEPT AS NOTED |

Although usually grown for their edible nuts (see Filbert, Hazelnut), the following make very attractive ornamental shrubs or small trees. The plants have separate female and male flowers. Female blossoms are inconspicuous; male ones are showy, appearing in pendent catkins on bare branches in winter or early spring. Leaves are roundish to oval, with toothed margins. Thin branches as needed in late winter; remove suckers when you see them.

Corylus avellana
'Fusco-rubra'

Oregon currently prohibits the planting of all *Corylus* species in home gardens, in an effort to stop the spread of eastern filbert blight. Though Western native *C. cornuta californica* is blight resistant, it too is banned because of difficulty in distinguishing it from blight-prone *C. avellana.* Before planting any of these trees, check to see if the ban is still in effect.

C. avellana. EUROPEAN FILBERT. Shrub. To 10–15 ft. high and wide. One of the species grown commercially for nuts. The following are widely grown ornamental varieties.

'Contorta'. HARRY LAUDER'S WALKING STICK. Rounded to 8–10 ft. tall and wide. Grown for fantastically gnarled and twisted branches and twigs, revealed after its 2–2½-in. leaves turn yellow and drop in autumn. Branches are used in flower arrangements. Plants are almost always grafted, so suckers arising from the base below the

raft should be removed; they
on't have contorted form.

'Fusco-rubra' ('Atropurpurea').
rows to 10–15 ft. high and
ide, with 3–4-in., reddish purple
aves.

C. colurna. TURKISH HAZEL.
ree. Zones 2b–9, 14–20. From
outheast Europe into western
sia. Pyramidal in form; usually
0–50 ft. (possibly to 75 ft.) tall
nd about half as wide, with
eaves to 6 in. long. Can be grown
s a single- or multitrunked tree.
laking, mottled bark provides
vinter interest. Produces small
lusters of edible nuts. Flourishes
n areas with hot summers and
old winters. Attractive tree in
ts own right, and a parent (with
C. avellana) of hybrids called
azels. Quite drought tolerant
nce established.

C. cornuta californica.
WESTERN HAZELNUT. Shrub.
Native to damp slopes below
7,000-ft. elevation, northern Coast
Ranges and Sierra Nevada of Cali-
ornia, north to British Columbia. Open, multistemmed, to 5–12 ft.
igh and wide. Roundish, somewhat hairy, coarsely toothed,
½–3-in. leaves turn bright yellow
n fall. Small nuts with flavorful
kernels are enveloped in a leafy
husk with a long, attenuated beak.

C. maxima. Shrub or tree.
Zones 2b–9, 14–17. Native to
southeastern Europe. One of the
species grown commercially for
nuts. Suckering shrub to 12–15 ft.
high and wide; can be trained as
a small tree. Most widely grown
ornamental form is 'Purpurea',
with rich dark purple leaves to 6 in.
long and heavily purple-tinted
male catkins. Leaf color fades to
green in hot climates.

CORYMBIA. See **EUCALYPTUS**

CORYNABUTILON vitifolium.
See **ABUTILON vitifolium**

CORYNOCARPUS
laevigatus
NEW ZEALAND LAUREL
Corynocarpaceae
EVERGREEN SHRUB OR TREE

📏	ZONES 16, 17, 20–24; H1, H2; BEST IN ZONES 17, 24; H1, H2
☀️ ◐	FULL SUN OR PARTIAL SHADE
💧	REGULAR WATER
🍎	FRUIT IS EXTREMELY POISONOUS IF INGESTED

Handsome, upright, 20–40 ft. high,
5–15 ft. wide. Beautiful, dark
green, very glossy, leathery leaves,

Corynocarpus laevigatus

to 7 in. long by 2 in. wide. (Leaves
of 'Variegata' have a showy yellow
border.) Flowers noticeable but
of no importance—tiny, whitish,
in 3–8-in.-long upright clusters.
Orange, oblong fruit to 1 in. long.
Good in containers. Slow growing;
keeps attractive form for years.
Needs only minimal pruning. Use
as screen or large hedge, background. Good in sheltered areas,
entryways, beneath overhangs.
Has naturalized in Hawaii.

CORYPHANTHA
vivipara
Cactaceae
CACTUS

📏	ZONES 1–24; OR INDOORS
☀️	FULL SUN; BRIGHT SUNNY WINDOW
💧💧	LITTLE TO REGULAR WATER

Native from Alberta to north
Texas, west to Arizona, Utah,
Nevada, and deserts of California.
Has single or clustered globular,
2-in. bodies covered with little
knobs bearing white spines. Showy
pink to purple flowers to 2 in. long.
Wide spreading. One of the hardiest cacti; subspecies from the cold-

Coryphantha vivipara

est zones will take temperatures
far below zero. Also thrives as a
houseplant; cut back on moisture
during winter. Usually sold as
Mammillaria vivipara.

COSMOS
Asteraceae (Compositae)
PERENNIALS AND ANNUALS

📏	ZONES 1–24, EXCEPT AS NOTED
☀️	FULL SUN
💧	MODERATE WATER

Native to tropical America, mostly
Mexico. Showy summer- and
fall-blooming plants, open and
branching in habit, with bright
green divided leaves and daisylike flowers in many colors and
forms (single, double, crested, and
frilled). Heights vary from 2½ to
8 ft. Use for mass color in borders
or background, or as filler among
shrubs. Useful in arrangements
if flowers are cut just after they
open and placed immediately in
deep, cool water. Sow seed in open
ground where plants are to grow
or set out transplants from spring
to summer. Plant in not-too-rich
soil. Plants self-sow freely, are
attractive to birds.

Cosmos bipinnatus

C. atrosanguineus. CHOCO-
LATE COSMOS. Perennial from
tuberous roots. Zones 4–9, 14–24.
Where winters are colder, dig and
store as for dahlias. Grows 2–2½ ft.
tall, 1½ ft. wide, with coarsely cut
foliage. Blooms in late summer
and fall, with deep brownish red,
nearly 2-in.-wide flowers with a
strong perfume of chocolate (or
vanilla). Attractive companion for
silvery-foliaged plants. Provide
well-drained soil. Winter mulch is
prudent in all but mildest regions
(where plant tends to be rather
short lived).

C. bipinnatus. Annual. Heights
up to 8 ft., widths to 1½–2½ ft.
Blossoms are 3–4 in. wide, with
tufted yellow centers and rays in
white and shades of pink, rose,

lavender, purple, or crimson.
Among the many types are 3–4-ft.-
tall 'Candystripe', with white-and-
rose flowers; 'Picotee', to 2½ ft.
high, white flowers edged red;
Sensation strain, 3–6 ft. tall,
including 'Dazzler' (crimson) and
'Radiance' (rose with red center);
and 'Sea Shells', to 3 ft. tall, grown
for quilled ray flowers that look
like long, slender cones. Sonata is a
dwarf strain 1½–2 ft. high; 'Sweet
Dreams' reaches 3 ft. tall and has
pale pink to white blossoms with
rose centers; Versailles strain, bred
for cut flowers, reaches 3½ ft.
and bears its blossoms on long,
strong stems.

C. sulphureus. YELLOW
COSMOS. Annual. To 7 ft. tall,
1½–2½ ft. wide, with yellow-
centered, yellow or orange-yellow
single flowers. Tends to become
weedy looking at end of season.
Two 3–4-ft.-tall, semidouble-
flowering strains are Bright Lights,
with 3½-in. flowers in yellow,
gold, orange, and orange red; and
Klondike strain, with 2-in. flowers
ranging from scarlet orange to
yellow. Dwarf Klondike or Sunny
strain is 1½ ft. tall, bears 1½-in.
flowers. Foot-tall semidouble
bloomers include Ladybird mix,
with 2½-in. scarlet, yellow, and
orange flowers; and 'Sunny Red',
with orange-red blooms.

**COSTA RICAN BUTTERFLY
VINE.** See **DALECHAMPIA
dioscoreifolia**

COSTMARY. See **CHRYSAN-
THEMUM balsamita**

COTINUS
SMOKE TREE
Anacardiaceae
DECIDUOUS SHRUBS OR TREES

📏	ZONES 2–24
☀️	FULL SUN
💧	MODERATE WATER

Unusual and colorful shrub-trees
creating broad, urn-shaped mass
usually as wide as high. Naturally
multistemmed, but can be trained
to a single trunk. Common name
derived from dramatic puffs of
"smoke" from fading flowers: as
the tiny greenish blooms wither,
they send out elongated stalks
clothed in a profusion of fuzzy
lavender-pink hairs.

Plants are at their best under
stress in poor or rocky soil. In
cultivated gardens, give them fast
drainage and avoid overly wet
conditions. Resistant to oak root

C

Cotinus coggygria
'Royal Purple'

fungus. For another plant with the common name "smoke tree," see *Psorothamnus spinosa.*

C. coggygria. Native from southern Europe to central China. Typically 12–15 ft. high and wide, though it may eventually reach 25 ft. The roundish, 1½–3-in. leaves are bluish green in the species, but purple-leafed types are more commonly grown. Leaves of 'Nordine' ('Nordine Red') and 'Purpureus' emerge purple, then gradually turn green; 'Notcutt's Variety', 'Royal Purple', and 'Velvet Cloak' hold their purple color through most of the summer. Those with purple foliage have richer purple "smoke puffs" than the species. 'Golden Spirit' reaches about 7 ft. high and 6 ft. wide, with leaves that are lime green in spring and turn golden yellow in summer. 'Pink Champagne' is a green-leafed selection with pinkish tan puffs. Leaves of all types change in fall, taking on colors ranging from yellow to orange red.

C. 'Grace'. Hybrid between *C. coggygria* and *C. obovatus.* To 15 ft. tall and wide, with blue-green foliage shaded purple, large deep pink puffs. Orange and purple-red fall foliage.

C. obovatus. From eastern U.S. Grows 20–30 ft. tall and wide. Bluish to dark green leaves turn yellow, orange, and reddish purple in fall.

COTONEASTER
Rosaceae
EVERGREEN, SEMIEVERGREEN,
AND DECIDUOUS SHRUBS

| 🌡 ZONES VARY BY SPECIES |
| ☼ FULL SUN, EXCEPT AS NOTED |
| ◐ ◑ LITTLE TO MODERATE WATER |

Native to China, Himalayas, northern India. Plants range from low types used as ground covers to small, stiffly upright shrubs to tall (25-ft.) shrubs of fountainlike

growth with graceful, arching branches. White or pinkish spring-time flowers resembling tiny single roses are pretty because of their abundance, though not especially showy. Berries (typically red or orange red) follow the blossoms in fall and winter. All cotoneasters grow vigorously and thrive with little or no maintenance. In fact, they look better and produce better crops of berries if planted on dry slopes (where they can reduce erosion) or in poor soil rather than in rich, moist garden soil.

While some medium and tall growers can be sheared, they look best when allowed to maintain natural fountain shapes. Prune only to enhance graceful arch of branches. Keep medium growers looking young by pruning out portion of oldest wood each year. Prune ground covers to remove dead or awkward branches. Give flat growers room to spread. Don't plant near walk or drive where branch ends will need stubbing.

Cotoneasters are useful, if not striking, shrubs and can be good looking in the proper setting. Some are especially attractive in form and branching pattern *(C. congestus, C. horizontalis),* while some others *(C. lacteus, C. microphyllus)* are notable for colorful fruit that is long lasting if birds don't get it. Trailing varieties make excellent ground covers. Low horizontal kinds die out in desert heat.

C. acutifolius. PEKING COTONEASTER. Deciduous. Zones A1–A3; 1–3. To 10 ft. tall and as wide, with glossy green foliage turning red in fall. Fruit is black. Useful as hedge or screen.

C. adpressus praecox. Deciduous. Zones 2–24. To 1½ ft. tall, 6 ft. wide, with shiny leaves turning maroon red in fall and a profusion of bright red, ½-in. fruit. Bank or ground cover. Takes some shade. *C. adpressus* is similar, somewhat smaller.

C. apiculatus. CRANBERRY COTONEASTER. Deciduous. Zones A3; 2–24. Best in cold-winter climates. Dense grower to 3 ft. tall, 6 ft. wide, with small, round leaves turning deep red in autumn. Clustered fruits about the size of large cranberries. Can take some shade. Use as bank cover, hedge, background planting. 'Tom Thumb' is a miniature mound 4–6 in. high, 10 in. wide.

C. congestus (C. microphyllus glacialis). PYRENEES COTONEASTER. Evergreen. Zones 3b–24.

Slow grower reaches to 3 ft. tall and as wide, with dense, downward-curving branches and tiny dark green leaves. Plant produces small, bright red fruit. Use in containers, in rock gardens, and above walls.

C. dammeri (C. humifusus). BEARBERRY COTONEASTER. Evergreen. Zones 2–24. Fast, prostrate growth to 8 in. high, 10 ft. wide. Branches root along ground. Leaves are bright glossy green, fruit bright red. 'Coral Beauty' (*C.* × *suecicus* 'Coral Beauty') is 6 in. tall; 'Eichholz' grows 10–12 in. high, shows a scattering of red-orange leaves in fall; 'Lowfast' is 1 ft. high; 'Skogsholmen' grows 1½ ft. tall. 'Streib's Findling' (which may be a hybrid with *C. procum-bens* or a selection of that species) grows 4–6 in. high, has dark bluish green foliage. All are good ground covers in sun or partial shade and can drape over walls, cascade down slopes.

C. divaricatus. SPREADING COTONEASTER. Deciduous. Zones 1–24. Stiff growth to 6 ft. tall and wide. Dark green leaves closely set on branches turn orange red in fall. Egg-shaped, bright red fruits are ½ in. long. Informal hedge, screen, bank planting.

C. franchetii. Evergreen. Zones 3b–9, 14–24. Arching growth to 10 ft. tall, 6–9 ft. wide. Leaves are grayish green when new, maturing to bright green; undersides are fuzzy. Pink-tinged white flowers in clusters of up to 20 are followed by orange-red berries.

C. glaucophyllus. Evergreen. Zones 11–14, 18–20. To 6–8 ft. tall and broad, with gracefully arching branches clothed in gray-green foliage. Dense clusters of white

Cotoneaster glaucophyllus

flowers are followed by dark red berries. Attractive in shrub beds or as informal hedge.

C. horizontalis. ROCK COTONEASTER. Deciduous. Zones A3; 2b–11, 14–24. Can be 2–3 ft. tall, 15 ft. wide, with stiff

Cotoneaster horizontalis

horizontal branches and many branchlets set in herringbone pattern. Small, roundish, bright green leaves turn orange and red before falling. Leafless period may be brief. Showy red fruit. Effective when given enough room to spread; disfigured by cutting branches short to accommodate traffic. Fine bank cover or low traffic barrier. 'Variegatus' has leaves edged in white. *C. h. perpusillus* is smaller, more compact.

C. lacteus (C. parneyi). Evergreen. Zones 4–24. Graceful, arching habit to 8 ft. or taller, 10 ft. or wider, with 2-in. leaves that are dark green above, whitish green

Cotoneaster lacteus

underneath. White flowers in 2–3-in. clusters followed by a heavy crop of long-lasting red fruit. Best as informal hedge, screen, or espalier. Can be clipped as formal hedge, but form suffers.

C. microphyllus. ROCKSPRAY COTONEASTER. Evergreen. Zones A3; 2–9, 14–24. Its horizontal branches trail and root, forming a mass 6 ft. across; secondary branches grow erect to 2–3 ft. Leaves are very small (⅓ in.), dark green, gray beneath. Fruit is rosy red. *C. m. thymifolius,* 2–3 ft. high and wide, has even tinier leaves, with edges rolled under. Both are effective in rock gardens or on banks. 'Cooperi', a miniature mound-forming selection to 1 ft. across, is a good rock garden plant.

C. multiflorus. Deciduous. Zones 1–12, 14–21. Vigorous grower to 6–10 ft. tall, 12–15 ft. wide, with graceful arching and trailing branches. Let grow as spreading shrub or train as small tree. Dark green leaves are 2½ in. long. Showy clusters of white flowers, pinkish red fruits.

C. salicifolius. WILLOWLEAF COTONEASTER. Evergreen or semievergreen. Zones 3b–24. Shrub to 15–18 ft. tall and wide, with narrow, dark green leaves 1–3½ in. long and bright red fruits. Graceful screening or background plant but can be invasive. Some shade in low desert.

Better known are the trailing forms used as ground cover. 'Emerald Carpet' is 12–15 in. tall, to 8 ft. wide, with compact habit and small leaves. 'Herbstfeuer' ('Autumn Fire') grows 2–3 ft. high and up to 8 ft. wide. 'Repens' is similar in appearance; it is sometimes grafted to a tall stem of some other cotoneaster species and used as a weeping tree.

C. × watereri. Evergreen. Zones 4–9, 14–24. A group of large hybrids (to 25 ft. tall and wide) that resemble haystacks. Leaves to about 4 in. long; large clusters of long-lasting fruit. Examples are 'Cornubia' (*C. frigidus* 'Cornubia') and 'John Waterer', both with red fruit, and 'Rothschildianus', with bright yellow fruit.

COTTONWOOD. See POPULUS

COTYLEDON
Crassulaceae
SUCCULENT SHRUBS

✎	ZONES VARY BY SPECIES; OR INDOORS
☼ ◐	BEST IN LIGHT SHADE; SUNNY SPOT
◌ ◑	LITTLE TO MODERATE WATER

South African natives vary in size and appearance. Easily grown from cuttings and handsome in containers, raised beds, or open

Cotyledon orbiculata

ground beds. Aphids may attack during bloom season.

C. orbiculata. Zones 12, 13, 16, 17, 21–24. Grows quickly to 3 ft. tall, 2 ft. wide. Opposing pairs of fleshy leaves are 2–3 in. long, rounded, gray green to nearly white, narrowly edged red. Green-leafed forms are available. Flower stems rise above plant and carry clusters of orange, bell-shaped, drooping flowers in summer. Good landscaping shrub in mild climates and well-drained soils. Splendid container plant.

C. undulata. Zones 17, 23, 24. Striking 1½-ft. plant with broad, thick leaves dusted with white powder. Wavy leaf edges. Orange, clustered flowers in spring and early summer. Overhead watering washes off powder.

COWBERRY.
See **VACCINIUM vitis-idaea**

COYOTE BRUSH, DWARF.
See **BACCHARIS pilularis**

COYOTE MINT.
See **MONARDELLA villosa**

CRABAPPLE
Rosaceae
DECIDUOUS FRUIT TREES

✎	ZONES A1–A3; 1–9, 11–21
☼	FULL SUN
◉	REGULAR WATER DURING FRUIT DEVELOPMENT

Crabapple

Crabapple is a small, usually tart apple, typically used for jelly and pickling. For the many kinds grown for their springtime flowers and small, typically inedible, colorful fruit, see flowering crabapple, described under *Malus*.

Of the crabapple varieties grown for fruit, one of the most popular is 'Transcendent', with

2-in., red-cheeked yellow crabapples that ripen in summer. Others include 'Centennial' and 'Dolgo', both with 1½-in. fruit; that of 'Centennial' is sweet. The red-fruited 'Maypole' is a newer columnar dwarf crabapple variety. 'Rescue' and 'Trailman' are very hardy apple-crabapple hybrids that can be eaten fresh or cooked. To fruit well, crabapple trees need about 600 hours of temperatures at 45°F/7°C or lower. In coldest areas, crabapples should be grafted onto hardy rootstocks (for more information, see Apple).

CRAB CACTUS.
See **SCHLUMBERGERA truncata**

CRAMBE
Brassicaceae (Cruciferae)
PERENNIALS

✎	ZONES A2, A3; 2–9, 14–17
☼ ◐	FULL SUN OR LIGHT SHADE
◉	REGULAR WATER

Cabbage relatives; both are ornamental, one edible. They produce large, smooth blue-green leaves like those of cabbage and large, loose heads of small, honey-scented, white flowers in summer. Leaves turn yellow and fade after bloom, leaving an empty space to plant with annuals. Watch out for cabbage worms on foliage.

Crambe cordifolia

C. cordifolia. From the Caucasus. Forms a 2–3-ft. mound of long-stalked, 1–3-ft.-long leaves. Intricately branched flowering stems bear huge, billowing cloud of blossoms. When in bloom, it may occupy a space 6 ft. high, 4–6 ft. wide.

C. maritima. SEA KALE. From coastal northern Europe; naturalized on the Oregon coast. To 2 ft. tall and wide, with blue-green leaves a foot wide. In Europe (but apparently not in the U.S.), plants are blanched in late winter or early spring by covering with pots or a deep mulch; the pale sprouts are harvested like asparagus. Grow from seed.

CRANBERRY.
See **VACCINIUM macrocarpon**

CRANBERRY BUSH.
See **VIBURNUM trilobum**

CRANESBILL. See ERODIUM reichardii, GERANIUM

CRAPE MYRTLE.
See **LAGERSTROEMIA**

CRASPEDIA globosa
DRUMSTICKS
Asteraceae (Compositae)
PERENNIAL

✎	ZONES 8, 9, 14–24; ANNUAL IN OTHER ZONES
☼	FULL SUN
◉	REGULAR WATER

Odd, attractive, offbeat Australian daisy. Silvery leaves form 8–12-in.-wide clumps, send up 2-ft. stalks, each topped by a 1-in. globe of tiny yellow flowers. Bloom may occur at any time of year. Flowers are useful, fresh or dry, in arrangements.

Craspedia globosa

CRASSULA
Crassulaceae
SUCCULENT PERENNIALS

✎	ZONES 8, 9, 12–24, EXCEPT AS NOTED; OR INDOORS
☼	FULL SUN, EXCEPT AS NOTED; BRIGHT LIGHT
◌	LITTLE TO NO WATER

Most are from South Africa. All have succulent foliage; many have strange geometric forms. Need good drainage. May not survive winter without overhead protection in Zones 8, 9, 12–15, 18–21. To cope with extreme summer heat in Zones 12 and 13, grow in pots or coolest sites (such as a northern exposure).

C. arborescens (C. atropurpurea arborescens). SILVER JADE PLANT, SILVER DOLLAR. A shrubby, heavy-branched plant much like jade plant (*C. ovata*),

C

but with gray-green, red-edged, red-dotted leaves. Produces summer flowers (usually seen only on old plants) that are star shaped, white aging to pink. Good change of pace from jade plant; smaller and slower growing.

C. argentea. See C. ovata

C. capitella thyrsiflora (C. corymbulosa). To 6–30 in. high and a little wider than tall. Slightly branched, with rosettes of long, triangular, fleshy leaves; leaves are dark red when plant is grown in intense sunlight and poor soil. Tiny white flowers in summer.

C. falcata. Zones 8, 9, 12–24; H1, H2. Grows to 4 ft. high, 2½ ft. wide. Thick, fleshy, gray-green, sickle-shaped leaves are vertically arranged in two overlapping columns on erect stems. Dense clusters of scarlet flowers are held well above the leaves in late summer.

Crassula falcata

C. lactea. Spreading, semishrubby plant grows 1–2 ft. tall and 3 ft. wide, with fleshy dark green leaves. Bears white flowers in 4–6-in. clusters during fall. Grows in shade, even dense shade. Fine rock garden plant.

C. lycopodioides. WATCH CHAIN. Leafy, branching, erect stems to 1 ft. high and wide, closely packed with tiny green leaves in four rows; effect is that of braided chain or of some strange green coral. Very small, inconspicuous greenish flowers. Easy to grow and useful in miniature and dish gardens.

C. 'Morgan's Pink' ('Morgan's Pride'). Fine miniature hybrid. Densely packed, fleshy leaves in tight cluster to 4 in. high and wide. Big, brushlike clusters of pink flowers are nearly as big as the plant; spring bloom.

C. multicava. Zones 8, 9, 12–24; H1, H2. To 1–1½ ft. high, 3 ft. wide. Dark green, spreading ground cover or hanging plant. Loose clusters of light pink flowers that resemble mosquitoes bloom in late winter and spring. Rampant grower in sun or shade, in any soil.

C. ovata (C. argentea). JADE PLANT. Zones 8, 9, 12–24; H1, H2. Sometimes sold as *C. portulacea*. Top-notch houseplant, large container plant, landscaping shrub in mildest climates. Use only as potted plant in hottest desert regions.

Crassula ovata

Plant has a stout trunk and sturdy limbs, even when small; and plants stay small in container. In time, can reach 9 ft. high, half as wide, but is usually smaller. Leaves are thick, oblong, fleshy pads 1–2 in. long, glossy bright green, sometimes with red-tinged edges. 'Crosby's Dwarf' is a low, compact grower; variegated kinds are 'Sunset' (yellow tinged red) and 'Tricolor' (green, white, and pinkish). 'Gollum' and 'Hobbit' have reddish, concave leaf tips. Clusters of pink, star-shaped flowers bloom in profusion, from fall into spring. Good near swimming pools.

C. pyramidalis. Interesting oddity grows to 3–4 in. high and wide; flat, triangular leaves closely packed in four rows give plant a squarish cross section.

C. schmidtii. Mat-forming, spreading plant to 4 in. tall, 1 ft. wide, with long, slender, rich green leaves. Clusters of small dark rose or purplish flowers put on a show in winter and spring. Good choice for pots or rock gardens.

C. tetragona. Upright plants with treelike habit, 1–2 ft. high and a little narrower. Leaves are narrow, 1 in. long; cream-colored flowers are borne in clusters. Widely used in dish gardens to suggest miniature pine trees.

CRATAEGUS
HAWTHORN
Rosaceae
DECIDUOUS TREES

✎	ZONES 2–12, 14–17, EXCEPT AS NOTED
☼	FULL SUN
◐	MODERATE WATER

These members of the rose family are known for clusters of pretty, usually white flowers after leaf-out in spring and for showy fruit resembling tiny apples in summer and fall (and often into winter). Typically multitrunked, with thorny branches that need some pruning to thin out excess twiggy growth. Many hawthorns produce water sprouts, which should be pruned out. Attract bees, birds.

Hawthorns will grow in any soil as long as it is well drained. It's best to grow them under somewhat austere conditions, since good soil, regular moisture, and fertilizer promote succulent new growth that is particularly susceptible to fireblight. The disease makes entire branches die back quickly. Aphids and scale are potential pests.

C. ambigua. RUSSIAN HAWTHORN. Zones 1–10, 14. Native to southeastern Russia, Turkey, Iran. Extremely cold hardy. To 15–25 ft. tall and as wide or wider. Vase-shaped form and twisting branches give attractive silhouette. Leaves to 2½ in. long, deeply cut. Profuse small red fruit.

C. 'Autumn Glory'. Dense, twiggy hybrid grows vigorously to 25 ft. with 15-ft. spread. Dark green leaves similar to those of *C. laevigata* but more leathery. Very large, glossy, bright red fruit, autumn into winter. Highly susceptible to fireblight.

C. crus-galli. COCKSPUR THORN. Native to eastern U.S. and Canada. Zones 1–12, 14–17. To 20–30 ft. high, 20–35 ft. wide. Stiff thorns to 3 in. long. Smooth-textured, tooth-edged leaves are glossy dark green, turning orange to red in fall. Dull orange-red fruit. *C. c. inermis* is a thornless variety.

C. laevigata (C. oxyacantha). ENGLISH HAWTHORN. Zones A2, A3; 2–12, 14–17. Native to Europe and North Africa. To 18–25 ft. high, 15–20 ft. wide. Leaves are similar to those of *C. monogyna* but have toothed lobes. Best

Crataegus laevigata

known through its varieties, among them 'Paul's Scarlet', with clusters of double rose to red flowers; 'Double White' and 'Double Pink', double-flowered forms that set little fruit; and 'Crimson Cloud' ('Superba'), with white-centered, bright red single flowers and vivid red fruit. All have toothed, lobed,

2-in. leaves that lack good fall color. In Northwest, susceptible to a leaf spot fungus that can defoliate trees in late spring to early summer.

C. × lavallei (C. carrierei). CARRIERE HAWTHORN. Zones 3–12, 14–21. To 25 ft. with 15–20-ft. spread. More erect and open branching than other hawthorns, with less twiggy growth. Dark green, leathery, toothed leaves are 2–4 in. long, turn bronze red after first sharp frost and hang on well into winter. Loose clusters of ¾-in., orange to red fruit last all winter. Fruit makes a mess on walks.

C. mollis. DOWNY HAWTHORN. Zones 1–12, 14–17. Native to central North America. Big, broad tree to 30 ft. tall, 35 ft. wide; looks like mature maple tree. Lobed, toothed leaves to 4 in. long, covered with down. Red, 1-in.-wide fruit is also downy; it doesn't last very long on tree but has value in jelly making.

C. monogyna. Zones 1–12, 14–17. Native to Europe, North Africa, western Asia. Classic hawthorn of English countryside for hedges and boundary plantings. Represented in Western nurseries mainly by upright variety 'Stricta', 30 ft. tall and 8 ft. wide. Plant 5 ft. apart for dense, narrow screen. Leaves 2 in. long, with three to seven deep, smooth-edged lobes. Clusters of small red fruit are rather difficult to see.

C. oxyacantha. See C. laevigata

C. phaenopyrum (C. cordata). WASHINGTON THORN. Native to southeastern U.S. Moderate growth to 25 ft. with 20-ft. spread. Graceful, open limb structure. Glossy, 2–3-in.-long leaves with three to five sharp-pointed lobes (like some maples); foliage turns beautiful orange, scarlet, or purplish in fall. Shiny red fruit hangs on well into winter. More graceful and delicate than other hawthorns, preferred street or lawn tree. One of the least prone to fireblight.

C. pinnatifida. Native to northeastern Asia. To 20 ft. high, 10–12 ft. wide. Leaves lobed like those of *C. laevigata* but bigger and thicker; turn red in fall. Slightly smaller fruit than that of *C. × lavallei*.

C. 'Toba'. Zones A3; 1–10. Canadian hybrid with great cold tolerance. To 20 ft. tall and a bit wider. Leaves similar to those of *C. × lavallei*. White flowers age to pink. Sparse crop of large fruit.

C. viridis. GREEN HAWTHORN. Native to eastern U.S. To 25–30 ft. high and wide, with broad, spreading crown. Leaves turn yellowish in fall; they aren't showy. Clustered white flowers are followed by red fruit. 'Winter King' is vase shaped, with silvery stems and larger red fruit that lasts all winter; it's an attractive and trouble-free hawthorn.

CREAM BUSH.
See **HOLODISCUS discolor**

CREEPING BUTTERCUP.
See **RANUNCULUS repens** '**Pleniflorus**'

CREEPING CHARLIE. See **PLECTRANTHUS verticillatus**

CREEPING JENNY.
See **LYSIMACHIA nummularia**

CREEPING ZINNIA.
See **SANVITALIA procumbens**

CREOSOTE BUSH.
See **LARREA tridentata**

CRESS, GARDEN
Brassicaceae (Cruciferae)
ANNUAL

🗓	ALL ZONES
🔆 🌓	FULL SUN OR PARTIAL SHADE
💧💧	REGULAR TO AMPLE WATER

Sometimes called pepper grass; tastes like watercress. Easy to grow as long as weather is cool. Sow seed as early in spring as possible. Plant in rich, moist soil. Make rows 1 ft. apart; thin plants to 3 in. apart (eat thinnings). Cress matures fast; make successive sowings every 2 weeks up to middle of

Garden cress

May. Where frosts are mild, sow through fall and winter. Try growing garden cress in shallow pots of soil or planting mix in sunny kitchen window. It sprouts in a few days, can be harvested (with scissors) in 2 to 3 weeks. Or grow it by sprinkling seeds on pads of wet cheesecloth; keep damp until harvest in 2 weeks.

CRIMSON FLAG.
See **SCHIZOSTYLIS coccinea**

CRIMSON GLORY VINE.
See **VITIS coignetiae**

CRINODENDRON
Elaeocarpaceae
EVERGREEN SHRUBS OR TREES

🗓	ZONES VARY BY SPECIES
🔆	FULL SUN
💧	AMPLE WATER

Little-known evergreen shrub-trees from Chile with leathery leaves, somewhat stiff growth habit, and attractive flowers. Thrive in wet spots; take regular lawn watering but should be watered deeply once a month to encourage deep rooting. Need good drainage.

C. hookerianum. Zones 5, 6, 16, 17. To 12–15 ft. tall and about as wide. Stiff branches clothed with narrow, sharply toothed leaves; in late spring or early summer, drooping, 1-in.-long red flowers open from buds resembling cherries. Easy to root from cuttings but hard to raise to maturity. Needs cool summers, high humidity. Spider mites are a constant problem.

Crinodendron patagua

C. patagua (C. dependens, Tricuspidaria dependens). LILY-OF-THE-VALLEY TREE. Zones 14–24. Somewhat like evergreen oak in general appearance; sometimes called flowering oak. To 25 ft. tall and almost as wide, with upright branching and a rounded crown. Leaves 2½ in. long, dark green above, gray green beneath, with irregular toothed edges. Bears hundreds of ¾-in.-long, bell-shaped white flowers in summer, sometimes into fall. Blossoms are followed by attractive cream-and-red seed capsules that drop and

can be messy on paving. Tends to be shrubby; or some branches may turn down while others stick up. Early staking and pruning are important in training as tree. Prune any time to thin out brushy growth in center and remove branches that hang down. For another lily-of-the-valley tree, see *Clethra arborea.*

CRINUM and × AMARCRINUM
Liliaceae
PERENNIALS FROM BULBS

🗓	ZONES 8, 9, 12–24; H1, H2; EXCEPT AS NOTED; OR INDOORS
🔆 🌓	SOME SHADE IN HOTTEST CLIMATES; BRIGHT FILTERED LIGHT
💧 💧💧	REGULAR TO AMPLE WATER
☠	ALL PARTS ARE POISONOUS IF INGESTED

Native to many warm and tropical parts of the world. Lush foliage and lilylike flowers of impressive size. Each bulb tapers to an elongated, stemlike neck, from which radiate long, broad, strap-shaped leaves. Evergreen in mild-winter climates if given year-round moisture. Thick stems to 4 ft. or taller rise from the foliage, each bearing a cluster of long-stalked flowers. Blossoms resemble those of belladonna lily *(Amaryllis belladonna),* but they're twice as big and open out a bit wider. Many are highly fragrant; colors include white and many shades of pink, from light to dark. Most bloom in spring or summer; flowering goes on all year in Hawaii.

Bulbs generally are available year-round, but spring and fall are best times to plant. Amend soil with plenty of humus. Set bulbs 2–4 ft. apart, with tops of necks even with soil surface. Divide infrequently. Protect from snails and slugs. In colder part of range, mulch heavily in winter; move plants in containers to a frostproof location. These plants (especially *C. × powellii* and × *Amarcrinum)* are grown as houseplants in most areas; don't let soil dry out.

C. asiaticum. SPIDER LILY, GRAND CRINUM, ST. JOHN'S LILY. Zones 20–24. From Southeast Asia. Can form a mass 4–6 ft. high, 7 ft. wide. Clusters of large, spidery-looking, fragrant white flowers, 6–8 in. across. Tolerant of poor soils, salt, drought, light shade. *C. a. procerum* is an even larger plant. Its variety 'Splendens', with purple leaves and pink flowers,

is called Queen Emma lily, as is the following species.

C. augustum. QUEEN EMMA LILY. Zones 20–24. From Mauritius and the Seychelles. Similar to *C. asiaticum* but slightly larger, with wider white flower segments and dark red markings.

C. bulbispermum (C. longifolium). From South Africa. Long, narrow, twisting gray-green leaves tend to lie on the ground. Fragrant flowers are deep pink.

C. 'Ellen Bosanquet'. Broad bright green leaves. Flowers are deep rose, nearly red; fragrant.

C. moorei. From South Africa. Large (6–8-in.-wide) bulbs with stemlike necks to 1 ft. or longer. Long, thin, wavy-edged bright green leaves. Fragrant, bell-shaped flowers typically are soft pink, though colors run from white to pinkish red.

C. × powellii. Resembles *C. moorei* (one of its parents) but has fragrant flowers on shorter (2-ft.) stems. Range of flower colors is similar to that of *C. moorei.* 'Album' is a pure white form, vigorous enough to serve as a tall ground cover in shade.

Crinum × powellii

× Amarcrinum memoria-corsii (Crinodonna corsii). Hybrid between *Amaryllis belladonna* and *C. moorei.* Resembles *Crinum* in growth habit and foliage, but its soft pink, very fragrant flowers look more like those of *Amaryllis belladonna,* with narrower funnel shape than blooms of most crinums.

CROCOSMIA
Iridaceae
PERENNIALS FROM CORMS

🗓	ZONES VARY BY SPECIES; OR DIG AND STORE
🔆 🌓	SOME SHADE IN HOTTEST CLIMATES
💧	REGULAR WATER DURING GROWTH AND BLOOM

Native to tropical and southern Africa. Formerly called tritonia; related to freesia, ixia, sparaxis. Sword-shaped leaves in basal clumps. Small orange, red, or yellow flowers bloom in summer (spring in hottest areas) on branched stems. Useful for splashes of garden color and for cutting. ▸

Plant in well-drained, enriched soil; set corms 2 in. deep, 3 in. apart. Where winter temperatures remain above 10°F/–12°C, needs no winter protection. Where lows range from 10 to –5°F/12 to –21°C, provide winter mulch. In colder areas, dig and store over winter. Divide clumps only when vigor, flower quality begin to decline.

C. × crocosmiiflora (Tritonia crocosmiiflora). MONTBRETIA. Zones 5–24; H1, H2. A favorite for generations, mont-bretias can still be seen in older gardens where they have spread freely, as though native to those sites, producing orange-crimson flowers 1½–2 in. across on 3–4-ft. stems. Sword-shaped leaves grow to 3 ft. tall, ½–1 in. wide.

Crocosmia × crocosmiiflora

Many once-common named forms in yellow, orange, cream, and near-scarlet are making a comeback. Good for naturalizing on slopes or in fringe areas. Montbretia has established itself in wild lands throughout the Hawaiian Islands.

C. hybrids. Zones 4–24. Among 2-ft.-high choices are 'Citronella', light yellow flowers with dark eye; 'Emily McKenzie', orange with red eye; and 'Solfatare', bronze foliage and yellow flowers. In the 2–3-ft. range are 'Babylon' (orange flowers with scarlet throats), 'Emberglow' (scarlet), and 'Jenny Bloom' (golden yellow). 'Lucifer' grows 4 ft. tall, with bright red blossoms.

C. masoniorum. Zones 5–24. Leaves 2½ ft. long, 2 in. wide. Bright orange to orange-scarlet flowers, 1½ in. across, borne in dense, one-sided clusters on 2½–3-ft. stems

Crocosmia masoniorum

that arch over at the top. Buds open slowly from base to tip of clusters, and old flowers drop cleanly from stems. Flowers last about 2 weeks when cut.

CROCUS
Iridaceae
PERENNIALS FROM CORMS

⚡	ZONES 1–24; BEST IN COLD-WINTER AREAS
☼ ◖	FULL SUN DURING BLOOM, LIGHT SHADE AFTER IN HOT CLIMATES
💧	REGULAR WATER DURING GROWTH AND BLOOM

Low growers, mainly from Mediterranean region, Caucasus. All have grasslike leaves, often with silvery midrib; foliage comes before, with, or after flowers, depending on species. Flowers in a wide range of colors are 1½–3 in. long, with long, stemlike tubes and flaring or cup-shaped petals; the short (true) stems are hidden underground.

Most crocuses bloom in winter or earliest spring, but some bloom in fall, the flowers rising from bare earth weeks or days after planting. Mass them for best effect. Attractive in rock gardens, between stepping-stones, in containers. Set corms 2–3 in. deep, 3–4 in. apart, in light, porous soil. Protect from gophers. Divide every 3 or 4 years. Won't naturalize where winters are warm.

C. ancyrensis. Small golden yellow flowers in early winter.

C. angustifolius. CLOTH OF GOLD CROCUS. Formerly *C. susianus.* Orange-gold, starlike flowers with dark brown center stripe. Early winter blooming.

C. biflorus. SCOTTISH CROCUS. White flowers with yellow throat, striped purple on the outside. Late winter bloom. Highly variable in the wild; some forms are fall blooming.

C. chrysanthus. Orange-yellow, sweet-scented blooms. Hybrids and selections of species range from white and cream through yellows and blues, often marked with deeper colors. Usually even more free-flowering than *C. vernus,* but with smaller flowers. Blooms in spring. Popular varieties include

Crocus vernus

'Blue Pearl', palest blue; 'Cream Beauty', pale yellow; 'E. P. Bowles', yellow with purple featherings; 'Ladykiller', outside purple edged white, inside white feathered purple; 'Princess Beatrix', blue with yellow center; and 'Snow Bunting', pure white.

C. goulimyi. Plant produces deep lavender-blue flowers during fall. Needs warmth, excellent drainage; tolerates warm winters of Southern California.

C. imperati. Bright lilac inside, buff veined purple outside, saucer shaped. Early spring.

C. korolkowii. Bright yellow to bronze-yellow flowers in late winter. Very cold tolerant.

C. kotschyanus (C. zonatus). Pinkish lavender or lilac flowers in early fall.

C. sativus. SAFFRON CROCUS. Lilac flowers in fall. Interesting rather than showy. Orange-red stigma is true saffron of commerce. To harvest saffron, pluck the stigmas as soon as flowers open, dry them, and store them in glass or plastic vials. Stigmas from a dozen flowers will season a good-size paella or similar dish. To get continued good yield of saffron, divide corms as soon as leaves turn brown; replant in fresh or improved soil. Mark planting site with low-growing ground cover so you won't accidentally dig up dormant bulbs.

C. sieberi. Delicate lavender blue with golden throat. One of the earliest to bloom in winter.

C. speciosus. Showy blue-violet flowers in early fall. Lavender and mauve varieties available. Fast increase by seed and division. Showiest autumn-flowering crocus.

C. tommasinianus. Slender buds; star-shaped, silvery lavender-blue flowers, sometimes with dark blotch at tips of segments. Blooms very early in the year.

C. vernus. DUTCH CROCUS. Familiar crocus in shades of white, yellow, lavender, and purple, often penciled and streaked. Late winter or early spring bloom. This is the most vigorous crocus (and the only one widely sold in all areas).

CROSSVINE. See **BIGNONIA capreolata**

CROTALARIA agatiflora
CANARY BIRD BUSH
Fabaceae (Leguminosae)
EVERGREEN SHRUB

⚡	ZONES 13, 15–24; H1, H2
☼ ◖	FULL SUN OR PARTIAL SHADE
💧	REGULAR WATER
◈	ALL PLANT PARTS ARE POISONOUS IF INGESTED

Native to East Africa. Fast, rank growth to 12 ft. tall and wide unless pruned frequently (should be pruned two or three times a year). Common name is well earned: unique 1½-in. flowers are strung along flower spike (to 14 in. long) like so many chartreuse birds. Blossoms harmonize with most colors. Heaviest bloom in summer or fall, but in frost-free areas it blooms intermittently for 10 months. Foliage is a pleasing gray green, with leaves divided into 3-in.-long leaflets. Recovers quickly after frost damage.

Crotalaria agatiflora

CROTON. See **CODIAEUM variegatum 'Pictum'**

CROWN DAISY. See **CHRYSAN-THEMUM coronarium**

CROWN IMPERIAL. See **FRITILLARIA imperialis**

CROWN OF THORNS. See **EUPHORBIA milii**

CROWN-PINK. See **LYCHNIS coronaria**

CROWN VETCH. See **CORONILLA varia**

CRYPTANTHUS zonatus
Bromeliaceae
PERENNIAL

⚡	ZONES 17, 23, 24; H1, H2; OR INDOORS
◖ ●	SOME SHADE; BRIGHT INDIRECT LIGHT
💧	MODERATE WATER

Native to Brazil. Bromeliad grown for showy leaves in spreading, low-growing clusters to 1½ ft. wide, usually less. Individual leaves wavy, dark brownish red, banded crosswise with green, brown, or white. Unimportant little white

Cryptanthus zonatus

flowers grow among leaves. Pot in equal parts coarse sand, shredded osmunda, and ground bark or peat moss. Most effective in mass or mixed plantings, terrariums.

C. bivittatus is similar to *C. zonatus* in cultural needs and general appearance but has green leaves with lengthwise stripes of creamy white. Many other striped and banded species and hybrids are available from specialists.

CRYPTOMERIA japonica

JAPANESE CRYPTOMERIA
Taxodiaceae
EVERGREEN TREE

🌿	ZONES 4–9, 14–24
☼	FULL SUN
💧	REGULAR WATER

Graceful conifer, fast growing (3–4 ft. a year) in youth. Eventually skyline tree to 100 ft. tall, 30 ft. wide at base. Straight columnar trunk; thin red-brown bark peels off in strips. Foliage soft bright green to bluish green in growing season, brownish purple in cold weather. Slightly pendulous branches are clothed in ½–1-in.-long, needlelike leaves. Roundish, red-brown cones ¾–1 in. wide. These trees are sometimes used in closely planted groves for a Japanese garden effect. Resistant to oak root fungus.

Cryptomeria japonica

'Cristata'. Unusual, twisted, cockscomblike growth at branch ends. Grows into an upright cone 12–15 ft. tall, 6–7 ft. wide after 10 years, eventually twice as large.

'Elegans'. PLUME CEDAR, PLUME CRYPTOMERIA. Quite unlike species. Feathery, grayish green foliage turns rich coppery red or purplish in winter. Grows slowly into a dense pyramid 20–60 ft. tall, about 20 ft. wide. Trunks may lean or curve. For effective display, give it room. 'Elegans Aurea' is similar but turns yellow in winter.

'Nana' ('Lobbii'). Upright dwarf grows very slowly to 4 ft. high and wide. Dark green foliage.

'Pygmaea' ('Nana'). DWARF CRYPTOMERIA. Bushy dwarf 1½–2 ft. high, 2½ ft. wide. Dark green, needlelike leaves; twisted branches.

'Sekkan-sugi' ('Sekkan'). Slow-growing, cone-shaped tree to 18–25 ft. high and 12–20 ft. wide. New growth is creamy yellow.

'Tansu'. An extreme dwarf, seldom exceeding 15 in. high and wide.

'Vilmoriniana'. Slow-growing dwarf to 1–2 ft. high and wide. Fluffy gray-green foliage turns bronze during late fall and winter. Rock garden or container plant.

'Yoshino'. Resembles the species but is smaller (to 30–40 ft. tall and 20 ft. wide), with bluish green foliage that takes on reddish tones in winter.

CTENANTHE

Marantaceae
PERENNIALS

🌿	ZONES 23, 24; H1, H2; OR INDOORS
◑	PARTIAL SHADE; BRIGHT INDIRECT LIGHT
💧💧	AMPLE WATER

Native to Brazil. Leaves are the big feature; they may be short stalked and set along stems, or long stalked and rising from plant's base only. Insignificant white flowers form under bracts in spikes at ends of branches. Use with other tropical foliage plants such as philodendron, alocasia, tree ferns. Plant in rich, moist soil; feed regularly.

C. 'Burle Marx'. Grows to 2 ft. tall, 1½ ft. wide. Leaves are gray green feathered with dark green on their upper surfaces, maroon undersides; leafstalks are also maroon. Tender and best grown as a houseplant, except in Hawaii.

C. compressa. BAMBURANTA. To 2–3 ft. high, 1½ ft. wide. Leaves

Ctenanthe oppenheimiana

leathery, oblong, lopsided, to about 15 in. long, waxy green on top, gray green beneath, held at angle on top of wiry stems. This plant is often sold as *Bamburanta arnoldiana*.

C. lubbersiana (Maranta lubbersiana). To 2½ ft. tall and wide. Yellow, 8-in. leaves with green markings.

C. oppenheimiana. GIANT BAMBURANTA. Compact, branching plant, 3–5 ft. high, 3 ft. wide. Narrow, leathery leaves, dark green banded with silver above, purple beneath, set at angle on downy stalks. 'Tricolor' has showy cream patches with its other colors.

CUBAN OREGANO. See **PLECTRANTHUS amboinicus**

CUCUMBER

Cucurbitaceae
ANNUAL VINE

🌿	ALL ZONES
☼	FULL SUN
💧	REGULAR WATER

Each vine needs at least 25 sq. ft., but you can use a fence or trellis to conserve space. Seeds require warm soil to sprout, and flowers need heat for pollination.

There are long, smooth, green, slicing cucumbers; numerous small pickling cucumbers; and roundish, yellow, mild-flavored lemon cucumbers. Novelties include Asian varieties (long, slim, very mild), Armenian cucumber (actually a long, curving, pale green, ribbed melon with cucumber look and mild cucumber flavor), and English greenhouse cucumber. The last type must be grown in greenhouse to avoid pollination by bees, with subsequent loss of form and flavor; when well grown, it's the mildest of all cucumbers. 'Sweet Success' is a mild, seedless cucumber with the flavor and character of a greenhouse cucumber; plant is

female, but flowers do not require pollination.

Bush cucumbers—varieties with compact vines—take up little garden space. Burpless varieties resemble hothouse cucumbers in shape and mild flavor but can be grown out-of-doors. Pickling cucumbers should be harvested as soon as they have reached the proper size—tiny for sweet pickles (gherkins), larger for dills or pickle slices. They grow too large very quickly.

Plant seeds in a sunny spot 1 to 2 weeks after the average date of last frost. To grow cucumbers on trellis (the best way to keep them straight), plant seeds 1 in. deep and 1–3 ft. apart and permit main stem to reach top of support. Pick while young to ensure continued production.

Cucumber

Row covers will protect seedlings from slugs, snails, and various insect pests, including cucumber beetles and flea beetles; remove covers when flowering begins so that pollination can occur. Whiteflies are a potential pest late in season; hose off plants regularly or hang yellow sticky traps. Misshapen fruit is usually due to uneven watering or poor pollination; bitter fruit is usually a result of uneven irrigation.

CUCUMBER TREE. See **MAGNOLIA acuminata**

CULANTRO. See **ERYNGIUM foetidum**

CUNNINGHAMIA lanceolata

CHINA FIR
Taxodiaceae
EVERGREEN TREE

🌿	ZONES 4–6, 14–21
☼	FULL SUN
💧	MODERATE WATER

Native to China. Picturesque conifer with heavy trunk; stout, whorled branches; and drooping

C

C

*Cunninghamia
lanceolata*

branchlets. Grows at moderate rate to 30 ft. tall with 20-ft. spread. Stiff, needlelike, sharp-pointed leaves are 1½–2½ in. long, green above, whitish beneath. Brown, 1–2-in. cones are interesting but not profuse. Among palest of needled evergreens in spring and summer; turns red bronze in cold winters. Needs protection from hot, dry wind in summer and cold wind in winter. Becomes less attractive as it ages. Prune out dead branchlets. 'Glauca', with striking gray-blue foliage, is more widely grown and hardier than the species.

CUP-AND-SAUCER.
See **CAMPANULA medium**

CUP-AND-SAUCER VINE.
See **COBAEA scandens**

CUPANIOPSIS
anacardioides
CARROT WOOD
Sapindaceae
EVERGREEN TREE

| 🌿 ZONES 16–24; H1, H2 |
| ☀ FULL SUN |
| 🌢🌢🌢🌢 ANY AMOUNT OF WATER |

Native to Australia. Slow to moderate growth to 40 ft. tall, 30 ft. wide; glossy dark green leaves divided into six to ten leathery, 4-in.-long leaflets. Tolerates seacoast conditions, heat, drought, poor soil. Generally neat in appearance. As trees approach maturity, they may produce marble-size, leathery, yellow to orange fruit that splits but does not squash or stain.

Some trees fruit heavily enough to be an annoyance, while others never fruit, for reasons not understood. One theory is young trees selected for unusual vigor and broader-than-usual leaflets will produce less fruit than others. Another is trees under stress tend to develop more female flowers, hence more fruit. It is also believed that thinning out the tree every 2 years or so will result in production of young, nonfruiting wood. In its younger years, it makes an

*Cupaniopsis
anacardioides*

attractive, well-behaved tree. Consider underplanting with a ground cover deep enough to swallow the fruit drop. If you do so, be prepared to pull volunteer seedlings when they appear. Many landscape architects feel that the tree's virtues outweigh its faults.

CUP FLOWER.
See **NIEREMBERGIA**

CUPHEA
Lythraceae
EVERGREEN SHRUBS OR WOODY PERENNIALS

| 🌿 ZONES 16–24; H1, H2; EXCEPT AS NOTED; ANNUALS ANYWHERE |
| ☀ ◑ FULL SUN OR PARTIAL SHADE |
| 🌢 REGULAR WATER |

Native to Mexico, Central America. Provide color throughout warm months; use in small beds, as formal edging for borders, along paths, in containers. Flowers attract hummingbirds. Pinch tips of shoots for compact growth; severely cut back older plants in late fall or early spring. Reliably perennial only in frost-free areas, though they may survive light frosts in Zones 16, 17, 21–23. Easy to grow from

cuttings. *C. hyssopifolia* and *C. ignea* have both naturalized on Hawaii (Big Island).

C. hyssopifolia. FALSE HEATHER, HAWAIIAN HEATHER, MEXICAN HEATHER. Grows 1–2 ft. tall, to about 2½ ft. wide. Flexible, leafy branchlets clothed in very narrow, ½–¾-in.-long leaves. Tiny flowers (scarcely half as long as leaves) in pink, purple, or white. Plants in the Itsy Bitsy series grow 8 in. tall, 18 in. wide; they're excellent in rock gardens. 'Riverdene Gold', 1 ft. tall and 2 ft. wide, has golden foliage and deep pink blooms. 'Caribbean Sunset', to 2 ft. tall, has orange blooms.

C. ignea. CIGAR PLANT. Zones 11–13, 16–24; H1, H2. Leafy, compact plant to 1 ft. or taller, as wide as tall. Narrow dark green leaves, 1–1½ in. long. The flowers explain the "cigar" of the common name: they're tubular, ¾ in. long, bright orange red with white tip and dark ring at end. 'David Verity' has orange-red blooms.

Cuphea ignea

C. llavea. BAT-FACED CUPHEA. Zones 11–13, 21–24; H1, H2. To 2–3 ft. tall, 3 ft. wide. Leaves to 3 in. long. Red-and-purple, 1½-in.-long flowers are said to look like a bat's face. Occasionally spreads by seed in gardens. Though cultivated in the desert, it is not drought tolerant—in nature, it grows along stream banks in Mexico. Compact varieties (12–16 in. high, 18 in. wide) include 'Flamenco Rumba', with coral red flowers; and 'Flamenco Tango', with vibrant pink blooms.

C. micropetala. To 4 ft. tall, 3–4 ft. wide. Arching stems closely set with narrow, 5-in. leaves and topped by a slender, spikelike cluster of 1½-in., bright red flowers tipped with yellow. Deciduous in cold weather.

C. × purpurea. Zones 11–13, 21–24; H1, H2. Hybrid to 1–1½ ft.

high and wide; excellent as a ground cover or spilling from a hanging basket. Red flowers to 1¼ in. long; dark green leaves to 3 in. long. 'Firecracker' has dark purple flowers with two earlike bright red petals.

CUPID'S DART.
See **CATANANCHE caerulea**

CUP-OF-GOLD VINE.
See **SOLANDRA maxima**

× CUPRESSO-
CYPARIS leylandii
Cupressaceae
EVERGREEN TREE

| 🌿 ZONES 3B–24 |
| ☀ FULL SUN |
| 🌢🌢 MODERATE TO REGULAR WATER |

Hybrid between *Chamaecyparis nootkatensis* and *Cupressus macrocarpa*. Grows very fast—from cuttings to 15–20 ft. high in 5 years. Most often planted as quick screening. In gardens, usually reaches 60–70 ft. tall, 8–15 ft. wide; can be pruned into tall (10–15-ft.) hedge but will quickly get away from you without regular maintenance. Long, slender, upright branches with flattened gray-green foliage sprays give youthful trees a narrow, pyramidal form, though they can become open and floppy. Produces small cones composed of scales. Will accept a wide variety of soils and climate conditions; takes strong wind. In warm-summer regions, loses stiff, upright habit and is subject to coryneum canker fungus; may reach only 30–40 ft. tall before dying from the disease (see *Cupressus macrocarpa* for information on this fungus). 'Naylor's Blue' has grayish blue foliage; 'Castlewellan' has golden new growth and narrow, erect habit; 'Emerald Isle' has bright green foliage on a plant 20–25 ft. tall, 6–8 ft. wide.

*× Cupressocyparis
leylandii*

CUPRESSUS
CYPRESS
Cupressaceae
EVERGREEN TREES

- 🌿 ZONES VARY BY SPECIES
- ☀ FULL SUN
- ◑ 💧 LITTLE TO MODERATE WATER, EXCEPT AS NOTED

These conifers have tiny scalelike leaves that are closely set on cordlike branches and bear interesting globular, golf ball–size cones made up of shield-shaped scales. Need little pruning.

Cupressus arizonica

C. arizonica. ARIZONA CYPRESS. Zones 7–24. Native to central Arizona. To 40 ft. tall, 20 ft. wide. Seedlings variable, with foliage from green to blue gray or silvery. Rough, furrowed bark. *C. a. glabra* (often sold as *C. glabra*) is virtually identical to the species but has smooth cherry red bark. Other forms include 'Blue Pyramid', a dense blue-gray pyramid to 20–25 ft. high; 'Carolina Sapphire', to 30 ft. with steely blue-green foliage and a broad, symmetrical form; 'Gareei', with silvery blue-green foliage; and compact, symmetrical 'Pyramidalis'. Mass for windbreak or screen.

C. cashmeriana. KASHMIR CYPRESS. Zones 8, 9, 14–24. Native to Kashmir and Tibet. Striking, narrowly pyramidal tree, 40–60 ft. tall and 15–20 ft. wide. Main branches are upright but produce beautiful long, pendulous, flattened branchlets of aromatic blue-green foliage. Best with regular water. Not tolerant of strong winds or extreme heat.

C. forbesii. TECATE CYPRESS. Zones 8–14, 18–20. Native to

coastal mountains of Southern California. Low-branching tree to 10–25 ft. tall and 20 ft. wide, with cherry red bark and green foliage. Very fast growing. In fact, it may get too top heavy for size of root system; keep on the dry side to slow growth, thus lessening likelihood that tree will topple in strong winds. Useful as hedge or screen.

C. macrocarpa. MONTEREY CYPRESS. Best in Zone 17. Native to California's Monterey peninsula. Beautiful tree to 40 ft. or taller, with rich bright green foliage. Narrow and pyramidal in youth, spreading as wide as high as it grows older; picturesque in age, especially in windy coastal conditions. Away from cool coastal winds, it is very subject to coryneum canker fungus, for which there is no cure. Look for foliage that first turns yellow, then deep reddish brown, and falls off slowly. Destroy infected trees. A fast-growing windbreak tree in coastal conditions.

Cupressus sempervirens

C. sempervirens. ITALIAN CYPRESS. Zones 4–24; H1, H2; best in Zones 8–15, 18–21. Native to southern Europe, western Asia. Species has horizontal branches and dark green foliage, but variants such as 'Stricta' ('Fastigiata'), columnar Italian cypress, and 'Glauca', blue Italian cypress (blue green in color), are more common and are classic Mediterranean landscaping plants; both are dense, narrow trees to 60 ft. high, 5–10 ft. wide at maturity. 'Swane's Golden' is a narrowly columnar form with golden yellow new growth. 'Tiny Tower' is a slow, dense grower that reaches only 8 ft. tall and 2 ft. wide after 10 years; foliage is deep blue green.

CURCUMA
alismatifolia
SIAM TULIP
Zingiberaceae
PERENNIAL FROM RHIZOMES

- 🌿 ZONES 14–24; H1, H2; OR DIG AND STORE
- ☀◑ FULL SUN OR LIGHT SHADE
- 💧 AMPLE WATER DURING GROWTH AND BLOOM

From Thailand. Not unlike a tulip in appearance (hence the common name), but it's actually a ginger rather than a tulip. Grows 2 ft. tall, with foliage like small canna leaves. Flowering stem is topped by a cluster of pink, rose, or white bracts that hide tiny flowers. The inflorescence is shaped a bit like a flaring pinecone. Plant in spring, setting rhizomes 1 in. deep, 6 in. apart. Blooms from early summer to early fall. Each blossom lasts for several weeks and is replaced by others as new plants arise from the rhizome. Plant goes dormant in winter. Beyond its hardiness range, dig and store over winter, being careful not to damage the bulbous storage organs on the roots.

Curcuma alismatifolia

CURRANT
Grossulariaceae (Saxifragaceae)
DECIDUOUS SHRUB

- 🌿 ZONES A1–A3; 1–6, 15–17
- ☀◑● SOME SHADE IN HOTTEST CLIMATES
- 💧 REGULAR WATER

Many-stemmed, thornless shrub to 3–5 ft. high and wide, depending on vigor and variety. Attractive lobed, toothed leaves to 3 in. wide drop early in fall, sometimes turning bright red, orange, or yellow first. Drooping clusters of white or yellowish flowers bloom in early spring, followed in summer by fruit used for jellies, jams, preserves. For ornamental relatives, see *Ribes*.

Currant worm can defoliate plants; control with *Bt*. Like other members of *Ribes*, currant may be host to white pine blister rust and is still banned in some areas where white pines grow; check with your Cooperative Extension Office or a local nursery for regulations in your area. Black currant, derived from *R. nigrum* or *R. odoratum* (see descriptions under *Ribes*), is favored host. Rust-immune black currant hybrids include 'Consort', 'Crusader', 'Mina Smyriou', and 'Titania'; all have rich, pungent

Currant

flavor and are good in jams and preserves. 'Ben Sarek' has good-quality fruit on compact, mildew- and rust-resistant plants. Red and white currants, derived from *R. sativum*, are less likely to be hosts to the rust; they are tart flavored and used mainly for jelly. Red-fruited varieties include 'Cherry', 'Jonkheer Van Tets', 'Perfection', 'Red Lake', and 'Wilder'; white types include 'Primus' and 'White Imperial'.

Generally self-fruitful. Do not grow where water or soil is high in sodium. Mulch well. Prune during dormant season. On red and white currants, cut stems older than 3 years to the ground; on black currants, remove stems older than 2 years. Older canes are often darker and peeling.

CURRY PLANT.
See **HELICHRYSUM italicum**

CUSHION BUSH.
See **CALOCEPHALUS brownii**

CUSHION PINK.
See **SILENE acaulis**

CYATHEA cooperi
AUSTRALIAN TREE FERN
Cyatheaceae
TREE FERN

- 🌿 ZONES 15–24; H1, H2
- ☀◑ PARTIAL SHADE IN HOTTEST CLIMATES
- 💧 REGULAR WATER

Fastest growing of the fairly hardy tree ferns (to 20°F/−7°C, but with damage to fronds). To an eventual 20 ft. tall, 12 ft. wide. Starts

C

Cyathea cooperi

out as a low, wide clump (can spread from 1 ft. to as much as 6 ft. in a year) before growing upward. Broad, bright green, finely cut fronds. Brownish hairs on leafstalks and leaf undersurfaces can irritate skin; wear long sleeves, hat, and neckcloth when grooming plants. Reasonably certain to survive in sheltered places along coast and in warm coastal valleys of California. Becoming a pest in Hawaiian rain forests. 'Brentwood' is a more robust form. Often sold as *Alsophila australis, A. cooperi,* or *Sphaeropteris cooperi.*

CYCAS
Cycadaceae
CYCADS

🌿 ZONES VARY BY SPECIES	
☼ PARTIAL SHADE	
💧 REGULAR WATER	

Neither ferns nor palms, these evergreen plants are primitive, cone-bearing relatives of conifers, excellent for tropical effects. A rosette of dark green, feathery leaves grows from a central point at the top of a single trunk (sometimes several trunks). Eventually as wide as tall. Female plants bear conspicuous, egg-shaped red to orange seeds.

C. circinalis. QUEEN SAGO. Zones 23, 24; H1, H2. Native to Old World tropics. Beautiful specimen plant to 20 ft. tall. Graceful,

Cycas revoluta

drooping leaves to 8 ft. long atop unbranched trunk. Protect from frost.

C. revoluta. SAGO PALM. Zones 8–24; H1, H2; hardy to 15°F/–9°C. Native to Japan. As a 2–3-ft.-tall youngster, has an airy, fernlike appearance; with age (grows very slowly to as high as 10 ft.), looks more like a palm. Leaves are 2–3 ft. long (larger on very old plants), divided into many narrow, leathery segments. Tough, tolerant house- or patio plant; also good subject for bonsai.

CYCLAMEN
Primulaceae
PERENNIALS FROM TUBERS

🌿 ZONES VARY BY SPECIES	
☼ ◐ FULL SUN OR PARTIAL SHADE	
💧 REGULAR WATER	

Native to Europe, Mediterranean region, Asia. Grown for pretty flowers carried atop attractive clump of basal leaves; blossoms resemble shooting stars or butterflies, typically come in white and shades of pink, rose, red. Most go through near-leafless or leafless dormant period at some time during summer.

Large-flowered florists' cyclamen *(C. persicum)* is most often seen as a container-grown gift plant, though it can be used as a bedding plant in favorable climates. The other species described here are smaller-flowered, hardier plants better adapted to outdoor culture. Use them in rock gardens, in naturalized clumps under trees, or as carpets under camellias, rhododendrons, and large noninvasive ferns; hardy types also grow well under native oaks. All are good container plants if grown out of direct sun.

All cyclamens grow best in fairly rich, porous soil with lots of humus. Plant tubers 6–10 in. apart, ½ in. deep. (Florists' cyclamen is an exception: upper half of tuber should protrude above soil level.) Best planting time for tubers is dormant period in summer— except for florists' cyclamen, which is always sold as a potted plant and can be planted out anytime. Topdress annually with light application of potting soil with complete fertilizer added (being careful not to cover top of florists' cyclamen tubers). Do not cultivate around roots.

Plants grow readily from seed. Small-flowered hardy species take several years to bloom; older

strains of florists' cyclamen need 15 to 18 months from seed, while newer strains can bloom 7 months after planting. Grown outdoors in open ground, plants often self-sow.

C. × atkinsii. Zones 4–9, 14–24. Crimson flowers on 4–6-in. stems in winter. Deep green, silver-mottled leaves. There are also varieties with pink or white blooms.

C. cilicium. Zones 3–9, 14–24. Fragrant pale pink flowers with purple blotches on 2–6-in. stems, fall into winter. Leaves are mottled. 'Album' has white blossoms.

C. coum. Zones 2–9, 14–24. Deep crimson rose flowers on 4–6-in. stems in winter and early spring. Round deep green leaves. Varieties with pink or white flowers are available.

C. europaeum. See C. purpurascens

C. hederifolium (C. neapolitanum). Zones 2–9, 14–24. Large light green leaves marbled silver and white. Rose pink flowers bloom on 3–4-in. stems in late summer, early fall. One of the most vigorous and easiest to grow; very reliable in cold-winter climates. Set tubers a foot apart. There is a white-flowered variety.

Cyclamen persicum

C. persicum. FLORISTS' CYCLAMEN. Zones 15–24. Original species has 2-in., fragrant, deep to pale pink or white blooms borne on 6-in. stems. Selective breeding has resulted in large-flowered florists' cyclamen (the old favorites) and newer, smaller strains; with rare exceptions, fragrance has disappeared. Plants typically have heart- or kidney-shaped dark green leaves, often with silvery mottling. They bear crimson, red, salmon, purple, pink, or white flowers on 6–8-in. stems from late fall to spring. Good choice for color in place to be occupied in

summer by tuberous begonias. Shade is required where summers are hot. Plants lose leaves and go dormant in hot weather, but usually survive if drainage is good and soil not waterlogged. Protect from slugs and snails; plants are especially vulnerable because tops of tubers and growing points are exposed.

Dwarf or miniature florists' cyclamens are replicas of standards with half- or three-quarter–size leaves and blossoms. Can bloom in 7 to 8 months from seed. Miniature strains (profuse show of 1½-in. flowers on 6–8-in. plants) include Miracle and Laser, both with fragrant blossoms.

C. purpurascens (C. europaeum). Zones 4–9, 14–24. Distinctly fragrant crimson flowers on 5–6-in. stems, late summer or early fall. Bright green leaves mottled silvery white; almost evergreen.

C. repandum. Zones 4–9, 14–24. Bright crimson flowers with long, narrow petals on 5–6-in. stems in spring. Rich green, ivy-shaped leaves are marbled silver, toothed on edges.

CYDONIA. See CHAENOMELES

CYDONIA oblonga. See QUINCE, FRUITING

CYLINDROPHYLLUM 'Red Spike'. See CEPHALOPHYLLUM 'Red Spike'

CYMBALARIA
Scrophulariaceae
PERENNIALS

🌿 ZONES 3B–24	
☼ ● PARTIAL OR FULL SHADE	
💧 REGULAR WATER	

European natives related to snapdragons *(Antirrhinum)*. Not showy, but they have their uses as

Cymbalaria muralis

small-scale ground covers in cool, shady places or as decorations for terrarium or hanging basket. In ground, can be invasive.

C. aequitriloba. Inch-deep mat that looks like small-scale dichondra. Leaves have three to five shallow lobes. Purple, snapdragon-shaped flowers are pretty but too tiny to make a show. Use as moss substitute.

C. muralis (Linaria cymbalaria). KENILWORTH IVY. Usually grown as annual. Dainty creeper that may appear uninvited in shadier parts of garden, sometimes even sprouting in chinks of stone or brick wall. Trailing stems root at joints. Smooth leaves 1 in. wide or less, with three to seven toothlike lobes. Blooms mainly in spring, with small lilac blue flowers carried singly on stalks a little longer than leaves.

CYMBIDIUM
Orchidaceae
TERRESTRIAL ORCHIDS

✿	ALL ZONES—SUBJECT TO CONDITIONS BELOW
☼	PARTIAL SHADE
●	REGULAR WATER

Native to high altitudes in Southeast Asia. Very popular because of their relatively easy culture. In areas subject to frost, grow in containers in lathhouse, greenhouse, or beneath overhang or high-branching tree. You can bring indoors when in flower. Excellent cut flower. Long, narrow, grasslike foliage forms sheath around short, stout, oval pseudobulbs. Long-lasting flowers grow on erect or arching spikes. Standard types usually bloom from midwinter to midspring. Bloom season for miniatures starts in earliest fall, is heaviest late fall into winter.

Miniature cymbidium

For best bloom, give as much light as possible without burning foliage. Plants do well under shade cloth or lath. Plants with yellow-green leaves generally flower best; dark green foliage means too much shade. During flowering period, give plants shade.

To set buds, plants need 50 to 55°F/10 to 13°C night temperatures. Daytime temperatures of 60 to 75°F/16 to 24°C (or even as high as 80 to 90°F/27 to 32°C) suit them. They will stand temperatures as low as 28°F/−2°C for short time only; where there's danger of harder frosts, cover plants with polyethylene film. Flower spikes are more tender than other plant tissues.

Potting mix for cymbidiums should drain fast yet retain moisture. Many commercial orchid mixes are available. Keep potting medium moist when new growth is developing and maturing—usually spring through summer. In winter, water plants just enough to keep bulbs from shriveling. On hot summer days, mist foliage early in day. Watch for slugs and snails at all times.

Feed with complete liquid fertilizer every 10 days to 2 weeks. Use a high-nitrogen formula winter to early summer, a low-nitrogen product from late summer through fall. Transplant potted plants when bulbs fill pots. When dividing plants, keep minimum of three healthy bulbs (with foliage) in each division. Dust cuts with sulfur or charcoal to discourage rot.

Most cymbidium growers list only hybrids—large-flowered varieties with white, pink, yellow, green, or bronze blooms. Most have yellow throat, dark red markings on lip. Large-flowered forms produce 12 or more 4½–5-in. flowers per stem. Miniature varieties, about a quarter the size of large-flowered forms, are popular for their size, free-blooming qualities, and flower colors. A growing class of intermediate-climate cymbidiums (the only types suited to Zone H2) will thrive alongside cattleyas in a greenhouse or in climates where night temperatures are too warm for standard cymbidiums. Many cymbidiums bloom in summer and fall, and some are fragrant.

CYMBOPOGON
citratus
LEMON GRASS
Poaceae (Gramineae)
PERENNIAL

✿	ZONES 12, 13, 16, 17, 23, 24; H1, H2
☼	FULL SUN
●	REGULAR WATER

From India. All plant parts are strongly lemon scented and widely used as an ingredient in Southeast Asian cooking. Clumps of inch-

Cymbopogon citratus

wide leaves grow 3–4 ft. tall (or more) and 3 ft. wide. Base of clump, composed of overlapping leaf bases, is nearly bulbous in appearance. Occasionally grown in gardens. It can live over in the mildest-winter regions, but it's safer to pot up a division and keep it indoors or in a greenhouse over winter.

CYNODON dactylon
BERMUDA GRASS, BERMUDA
Poaceae (Gramineae)
PERENNIAL GRASS

✿	ZONES 5–10, 12–24; H1, H2
☼	FULL SUN
●●	MODERATE TO REGULAR WATER

Subtropical fine-textured grass that spreads rapidly by surface and underground runners. Tolerates heat and looks good if well maintained. It turns brown in winter; some varieties stay green longer than others, and most stay green longer if well fed. Can be overseeded with cool-season grasses for winter color. Needs sun and should be cut low; 1 in. is desirable for common Bermuda, ½–¾ in. for hybrid Bermuda. Needs dethatching—removal of matted layer of old stems and stolons beneath the leaves—to look its best.

Cynodon dactylon

Common Bermuda is a good minimum-maintenance lawn for large area. Needs feeding, careful and frequent mowing to remove seed spikes. Roots invade shrubbery and flower beds if not carefully confined. Can become extremely difficult to eradicate. Plant from hulled seed or sprigs.

Hybrid Bermudas are finer in texture and better in color than the common kind. They will crowd out common Bermuda in time but are harder to overseed with rye, bluegrass, or red fescue. Help them stay green in winter by feeding in early fall and by removing thatch. Useful in areas with short dormant season. Grow from sprigs (stolons), plugs, or sod.

'Santa Ana'. Deep green, coarse, smog resistant. Takes hard wear; holds color late.

'Tifdwarf'. Extremely low and dense; takes very close mowing. Slower to establish than others, but slower to spread where it's not wanted. Useful as small-scale ground cover on banks, among rocks.

'Tifgreen'. Fine textured, deep blue green, dense. Few seed spikes, sterile seeds. Takes close mowing; preferred for putting greens.

'Tifway'. Low growth; dense, fine texture. Stiff dark green blades. Wear resistant. Slow to start. Sterile (no seeds).

'U-3'. Finer in texture than common Bermuda but with obvious and unattractive seed spikes. Very tough. Grow from sprigs; not dependable from seed, tending to revert to mixture of many types. Not up to other hybrids in quality.

CYNOGLOSSUM
Boraginaceae
PERENNIALS AND BIENNIALS
GROWN AS ANNUALS

✿	ZONES VARY BY SPECIES
☼ ☼ ●	EXPOSURE NEEDS VARY BY SPECIES
◯ ●	WATER NEEDS VARY BY SPECIES

Bedding, border, or wild garden plants with little blue, white, or pink flowers like forget-me-nots (*Myosotis*), to which they are related.

C. amabile. CHINESE FORGET-ME-NOT. Biennial grown as annual. Zones A2, A3; 1–24; H1, H2. East Asian native reaching 1½–2 ft. tall, 1 ft. wide. Lance-shaped leaves are soft, hairy, grayish green. Loose sprays of rich blue, pink, or white flowers (larger than forget-me-nots)

C

Cynoglossum amabile

appear in spring, continue into summer where weather is cool. Widely available 'Firmament', the most popular variety, has rich blue blooms on compact plants about 1½ ft. high. All varieties bloom from seed sown in fall or early spring, preferably in location where plants are to grow. Hardy except in most severe winters. Give full sun, regular water.

C. grande. WESTERN HOUND'S TONGUE. Perennial. Zones 4–9, 14–24. Native to Oregon and California Coast Ranges and to Sierra Nevada slopes below 4,000 ft. Hairy, mostly basal leaves 6–12 in. long. Blue spring flowers with white centers. Plants reach 1–2½ ft. tall and 1 ft. wide; die back in summer to a heavy underground root. Choose a shaded, woodsy site with cool soil; provide little or no summer water.

CYPERUS
Cyperaceae
PERENNIALS

	ZONES VARY BY SPECIES
☼ ◐ ●	SUN OR SHADE
💧💧	AMPLE WATER

These African natives are sedges—grasslike plants distinguished from true grasses by three-angled, solid stems and very different flowering parts. Valued for striking form, silhouette, shadow pattern.

Most cyperus grow in rich, moist soil or with roots submerged in water. Keep plants groomed by removing dead or broken stems; divide and replant vigorous plants when the clump becomes too large, saving smaller, outside divisions and discarding the overgrown centers. Beyond their hardiness range, pot up divisions and keep them over the winter as houseplants.

C. albostriatus (C. diffusus). Zones 14–24. Resembles *C. alternifolius,* but tends to be less hardy, shorter (to 20 in.), with broader

leaves and lusher, softer appearance. Vigorous, invasive plant; best used in contained space.

C. alternifolius. UMBRELLA PLANT. Zones 8, 9, 12–24; H1, H2. Narrow, firm, spreading leaves arranged like ribs of umbrella at tops of 2–4-ft. stems. Flowers are held in dry greenish brown clusters. Grows in water or moist soil. Effective near pools, in pots or planters, or in dry stream beds or small rock gardens. Self-sows. Can become weedy and take over a small pool. Naturalized in parts of Hawaii. 'Gracilis' ('Nanus') is a dwarf form to 1½ ft. high.

C. papyrus. PAPYRUS. Zones 16, 17, 23, 24; H1, H2. Tall, graceful, dark green stems 6–10 ft. high, topped with clusters of green threadlike parts to 1½ ft. long (longer than small leaves at base of cluster). Will grow quickly in 2 in. of water in shallow pool, or can be potted and placed on bricks or inverted pot in deeper water. Protect from strong wind. Also grows well in rich, moist soil out of water. Naturalized on Kauai. Used by flower arrangers.

Cyperus papyrus

C. prolifer (C. isocladus). DWARF PAPYRUS. Zones 16, 17, 23, 24; H1, H2. Flowers and long, thin leaves combine to make filmy brown and green clusters on slender stems about 1½ ft. high. Use in Asian-style gardens; sink in pots in water gardens where delicate design of slender, leafless stems will not be lost among larger and coarser plants.

CYPHOMANDRA betacea. See **TREE TOMATO**

CYPRESS. See *Cupressus.* True cypresses are all *Cupressus;* many plants erroneously called cypress are under *Chamaecyparis* and *Taxodium.*

CYPRESS SPURGE. See **EUPHORBIA cyparissias**

CYPRESS VINE. See **IPOMOEA quamoclit**

CYPRIPEDIUM. For tropical and subtropical orchids sold under this name, see *Paphiopedilum.* True cypripediums, the hardy lady's slipper orchids, are rare or endangered in the wild and extremely difficult to maintain in gardens. Nursery-grown plants are scarce, expensive, and hard to establish.

CYRTANTHUS
Amaryllidaceae
PERENNIALS FROM BULBS

	ZONES 16–24
◐	LIGHT SHADE
●	REGULAR WATER

South African natives with glossy, strap-shaped, evergreen leaves that remain attractive all year. Flowers appear in clusters at ends of stems that rise just above the leaves. Plants are frost sensitive; give sheltered spot in Zones 18–22. Plant in spring, in well-drained, enriched soil; set bulbs 1–1½ ft. apart, with tips just beneath soil surface. Give less water during semidormant period (winter and spring for *C. elatus,* summer for *C. mackenii*), but don't let plants dry out. To increase plantings, remove bulblets that form around larger bulb and plant separately. Good potted plants.

Cyrtanthus elatus

C. elatus (C. purpureus, Vallota speciosa). SCARBOROUGH LILY. Looks like a more delicate version of Dutch hybrid amaryllis (*Hippeastrum*). Leaves 1–2 ft. long. In summer and early fall, each thick flower stalk is topped with up to ten 3–4-in., funnel-shaped orange-red blooms. (White- and pink-flowered forms are less common.) Succeeds in competition with tree roots. Excellent houseplant.

C. mackenii. Foot-long, narrow leaves, somewhat wavy edges.

Each stem holds up to five tubular curved, 2-in.-long, fragrant white blooms in spring. There are also cream- and yellow-flowered forms and hybrids in coral, orange, and red shades. If in pots, will need annual repotting.

CYRTOMIUM
Polypodiaceae
FERNS

	ZONES VARY BY SPECIES
☼ ●	PARTIAL OR FULL SHADE
●	REGULAR WATER

Coarse-textured but handsome ferns with firm-textured, glossy fronds 2–3 ft. long. Provide soil with high organic content; do not plant too deeply.

C. falcatum. JAPANESE HOLLY FERN. Zones 5–9, 14–24; H1, H2; or indoors. Native to Asia, South Africa, Polynesia; naturalized in Hawaii. Fronds to 10 in. wide, with 3–11 pairs of divisions. Takes houseplant conditions well.

Cyrtomium falcatum

C. fortunei. Zones 4–9, 14–24. From China, Japan, Korea. Fronds to 6 in. wide; more finely cut and with more divisions (12–26 pairs) than those of other species.

C. macrophyllum. Zones 7–9, 13–24. From China, Himalayas. Fronds (to 10 in. wide) are the coarsest among the species listed here, with three to eight pairs of divisions.

CYTISUS
BROOM
Fabaceae (Leguminosae)
EVERGREEN, SEMIEVERGREEN, AND DECIDUOUS SHRUBS

	ZONES VARY BY SPECIES
☼	FULL SUN
○	LITTLE OR NO WATER

Most widely planted brooms belong to this genus, but look for other choice shrubs under *Genista.*

weet pea–shaped flowers, often ragrant. Plants tolerate wind, eashore conditions, and rocky, nfertile soil. Where soil is highly lkaline, give them iron sulfate. rune after bloom to keep to rea onable size, lessen production of nsightly seedpods.

C. battandieri. ATLAS BROOM. emievergreen or deciduous. ones 4–6, 14–17. Moroccan ative puts on fast growth to 2–15 ft. high and as wide. Can be rained as small tree. Leaves di ided into three roundish leaflets o 3½ in. long, 1½ in. wide, covered vith silvery, silky hairs. Fragrant, ure yellow flowers in spikelike -in. clusters at branch ends in ummer.

Cytisus battandieri

C. canariensis (Genista canariensis). CANARY ISLAND BROOM. Evergreen. Zones 8, 9, 12–24. Damaged at 15°F/–9°C but recovers quickly. Many-branched, upright shrub to 6–8 ft. high, 5– 6 ft. wide. Bright green leaves divided into ½-in. leaflets. Bright yellow, fragrant flowers bloom in short clusters at branch tips in spring, summer. Aggressive; has escaped from gardens.

C. × kewensis. KEW BROOM. Evergreen. Best in Zones 2–6; less vigorous but satisfactory in Zones 16, 17. Low (less than 1 ft. high) and spreading, with trailing, cas cading branches to 4 ft. or more. Creamy white, ½-in. flowers in spring. Tiny leaves.

C. lydia. See Genista lydia

C. × praecox. WARMINSTER BROOM. Deciduous. Zones 2–9, 14–22. Compact growth to 3–5 ft. high and 4–6 ft. wide, with many slender stems. Mounding mass of pale yellow to creamy white flow ers in spring. Small leaves fall early. Effective as informal screen or hedge, along drives, paths, garden steps. 'Allgold', slightly taller, has bright yellow flowers; 'Hollandia' has pink ones. 'Moon light', formerly considered to be

C. × praecox variety, is now thought to be form of *C. scoparius*.

C. purgans. PROVENCE BROOM. Deciduous. Zones 1–7. From Europe, North Africa. Dense, mounding growth to 3 ft. high and wide. Roundish, silky, hairy leaves are ¼–½ in. long. Fragrant chrome yellow flowers in late spring, early summer. 'Spanish Gold' grows 4 ft. tall, 6 ft. wide; it is hardy in the Colorado Rockies to an elevation of 8,000 ft.

C. racemosus. See C. × spachianus

C. scoparius. SCOTCH BROOM. Evergreen. Zones 2–9, 14–22; H1. This aggressive Euro pean species has given all brooms a bad name. Upright-growing mass of wandlike green stems (often leafless or nearly so) may reach 10 ft. Golden yellow, ¾-in. flowers, spring and early summer. A tenacious weed from Seattle to San Diego and in Hawaii, espe cially on the Big Island.

Cytisus scoparius 'Burkwoodii'

Much less aggressive are lower- growing, more colorful forms. Most of these grow 5–8 ft. tall and wide. 'Burkwoodii' has red blooms touched with yellow; 'Carla', pink- and-crimson flowers lined in white; 'Dorothy Walpole', rose pink and crimson; 'Lena', red and lemon yellow; 'Lilac Time', lilac pink blooms on a compact plant; 'Lord Lambourne', scarlet and cream; 'Minstead', white flushed lilac and deep purple; 'Moonlight', pale yel low blossoms, compact grower; 'Pomona', orange and apricot; 'St. Mary's', white; 'San Francisco' and 'Stanford', red.

C. × spachianus (C. racemo sus, Genista racemosa). Ever green. Zones 7–9, 11–24. Similar in growth habit to *C. canariensis* but with larger leaflets and longer, looser spikes of fragrant yellow flowers in late spring. Naturalizes where adapted. Often sold as *Genista fragrans*.

D

DABOECIA cantabrica
IRISH HEATH
Ericaceae
EVERGREEN SHRUB

🌿 ZONES 3B–9, 14–24

☀️ 🌤️ FULL SUN ONLY IN COOLER CLIMATES

💧 REGULAR WATER

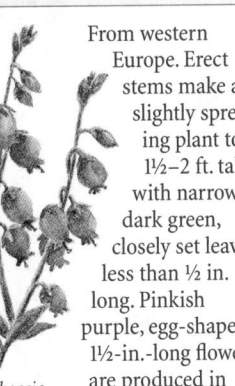

From western Europe. Erect stems make a slightly spread ing plant to 1½–2 ft. tall, with narrow, dark green, closely set leaves less than ½ in. long. Pinkish purple, egg-shaped, 1½-in.-long flowers are produced in narrow clusters 3– 5 in. long from late spring to early autumn; in warmer part of range, bloom may begin in early spring. Needs fast-draining, acidic soil. Most useful on hill sides and in rock gardens or natural landscapes.

Daboecia cantabrica

Daboecia cantabrica

Varieties include white-flowered 'Alba' and magenta-blooming 'Waley's Red' and 'Arielle'. 'Cin derella' has bicolored white-and- pink flowers and gray-green leaves. *D. c. scotica* 'William Buchanan' (*D. × scotica* 'William Buchanan') is a low grower (just 10 in. tall) with reddish purple blossoms; 'William Buchanan Gold' is similar but shows some yellow variegation in the foliage.

DAFFODIL. See **NARCISSUS**

DAHLBERG DAISY. See **THYMOPHYLLA tenuiloba**

DAHLIA
Asteraceae (Compositae)
PERENNIALS FROM TUBEROUS ROOTS

🌿 ZONES 1–24, EXCEPT AS NOTED

☀️ 🌤️ LIGHT SHADE IN HOTTEST AREAS

💧 REGULAR WATER

Native to Mexico, Guatemala. Through centuries of hybridizing and selection, dahlias have become tremendously diversified, available in numerous flower types and flower sizes (from 2 to 12 in. across) and all colors but true blue.

Bush and bedding dahlias range from 1 ft. to over 7 ft. tall. The tall bush forms are useful as summer hedges, screens, and fillers among shrubs; lower kinds give mass color in borders and containers. Modern dahlias, with their strong stems, long-lasting blooms that face outward or upward, and sub stantial, attractive foliage, make striking cut flowers. Leaves are generally divided into many large, deep green leaflets. Some forms have brownish purple leaves; a well-known example is 'Bishop of Llandaff'.

Dahlia flower forms. The dahlia flower has composite (daisylike) blooms containing many individual flowers called florets. One type of dahlia flower is composed of ray florets (which look like petals) surrounding a central cluster of petal-less disk flo rets. A second type has ray florets only. The American Dahlia Society has classified dahlias according to the flower forms described below. Blooms range in size from giant (over 10 in.), large (8–10 in.), and medium (6–8 in.) to small (4–6 in.), miniature (2–4 in.), and mignon (under 2 in.).

Dahlia hybrid

Anemone form. Single or multi ple layers of rays surround tubular disk florets that form a "pincush ion" center.

Collarette. One layer of long rays and a second, inner layer of shorter ones that form a "collar" around the center of the flower.

Orchid form. A single layer of rays with inrolled margins for two-thirds or more of their length, giving the flower a pinwheel appearance.

Peony form. Central disk flo rets are surrounded by two or

Dahlia Flower Forms

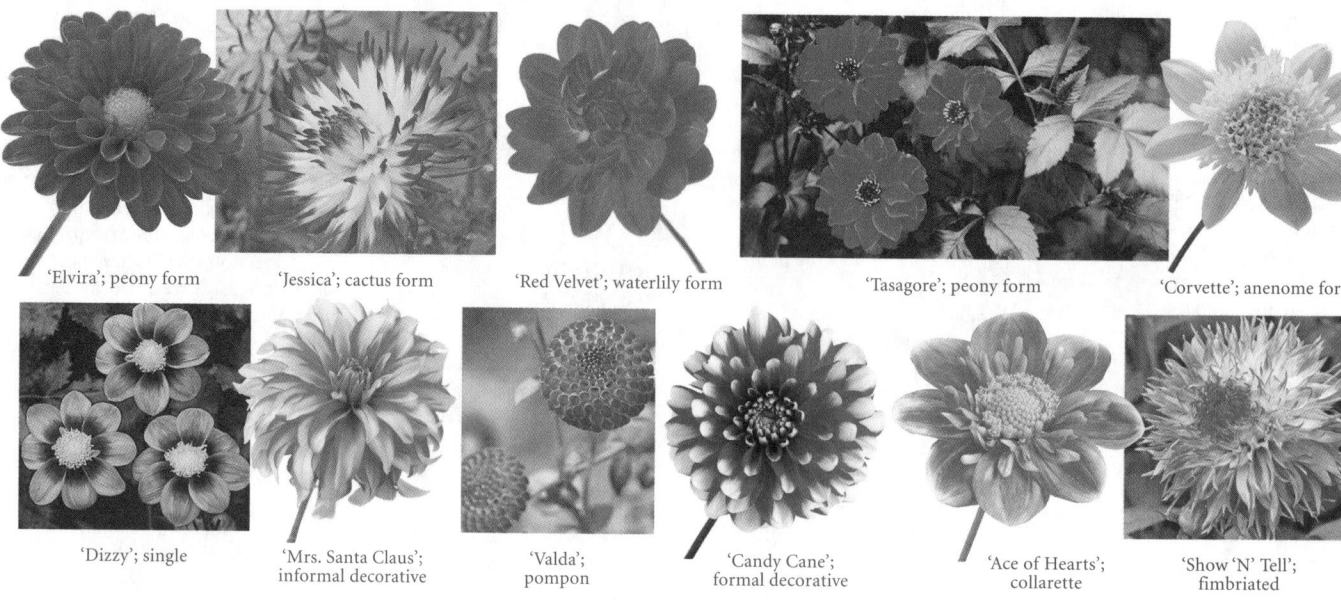

'Elvira'; peony form   'Jessica'; cactus form   'Red Velvet'; waterlily form   'Tasagore'; peony form   'Corvette'; anenome form

'Dizzy'; single   'Mrs. Santa Claus'; informal decorative   'Valda'; pompon   'Candy Cane'; formal decorative   'Ace of Hearts'; collarette   'Show 'N' Tell'; fimbriated

more rows of rays; innermost rays may be curled or twisted.

Single. One layer of rays arranged in a plane around a central cluster of disk florets.

The following forms are composed of ray florets only.

Ball. Flower looks spherical, though it's flattish in profile. Rays have inrolled margins for at least half their length. *Pompon* form is similar, but rays are inrolled, giving them a tubular look.

Cactus form. Ray margins roll downward; tips are pointed.

Straight cactus rays radiate in all directions from center; may be straight or curved downward, margins rolled for over half their length. *Incurved cactus* rays are similar, but they curve upward. *Semicactus* flowers have broad-based rays with margins rolled along outer half (portion farthest from center); the rays may be straight or curve upward or downward.

Decorative. Full flowers of two types. *Formal decorative* has many overlapping layers of symmetrically arranged, fairly flat rays that tend to curve downward. *Informal decorative* is just as full, but rays are curved, curled, or twisted and often arranged in a more irregular pattern.

Fimbriated. All rays split at tips with split portions twisted, giving the flower a fringed appearance.

Waterlily form. Rays broad, curving slightly upward; flower profile is flat to saucer shaped, resembling a waterlily bloom.

Novelty. Any flower form not covered in previous categories.

Planting. Most dahlias are started from tuberous roots planted in spring after frost is past and soil is warm. Several weeks before planting, dig the soil in the planting area to 1 ft. deep and work in plenty of organic matter, such as garden compost or ground bark. At planting time, dig a foot-deep hole for each root; make holes 1½ ft. wide for dahlias that grow over 4 ft. tall, and 9–12 in. wide for smaller types. Space holes for larger vari-

eties 4–5 ft. apart, smaller ones 1–2 ft. apart. Incorporate about ¼ cup of granular low-nitrogen fertilizer into the soil at the bottom of each planting hole, then add 4 in. of soil before placing the root in the center of the hole, with its growth bud pointing up. Before planting a tall variety, drive a 5–6-ft. stake into the hole just off center, then place the root horizontally in the bottom of the hole, 2 in. from the stake and with the growth bud pointing toward it. Cover roots with 3 in. of soil, and water thoroughly. As shoots grow, gradually fill hole with soil.

Dahlias can be started from seed. For tall types, start seeds early indoors; transplant seedlings into garden beds after frost danger is past. For dwarf dahlias, sow seed in place after soil is warm, or buy and plant started seedlings from the nursery. Dwarf dahlias are usually replaced each year, though they can be lifted and stored.

Thinning, pinching. On tall-growing dahlias, thin out shoots when they're about 6 in. high, leaving only the strongest one or two. When remaining shoots have three sets of leaves, pinch off tops just above upper set; dahlias with smaller flowers, such as pompons, singles, and dwarfs, need only this first pinching. For best show of larger-flowered types, pinch again by removing all but terminal flower buds on side shoots.

Plant care. After shoots are above-ground, start watering regularly to

a foot deep; continue throughout active growth. Dahlias planted in enriched soil shouldn't need additional food, but if your soil is light or if roots stayed in the ground the previous year, apply a granular low-nitrogen fertilizer when the first flower buds show. Mulch to discourage weeds and to eliminate cultivating, which may injure feeder roots.

Cutting flowers. Pick nearly mature flowers in early morning or evening. Immediately place cut stems in 2–3 in. of hot water; let stand in gradually cooling water for several hours or overnight.

Lifting, storing. In climates where ground freezes in winter, dig and store tuberous roots in fall. In other regions, roots may remain in place as long as drainage is excellent and winter temperatures remain above 20°F/−7°C. In borderline climates, mulch with 4-in. layer of straw or similar material. Gardeners in most areas, however, prefer to dig the roots annually.

To lift the roots, cut stalks to 4 in. above-ground after the tops turn yellow or are frosted. Dig a 2-ft.-wide circle around each plant; carefully pry up clump with spading fork, shake off loose soil, and let the clump dry in sun for several hours. From that point, follow either of the following methods.

Method 1: Divide clumps immediately. Freshly dug roots are easy to cut, and eyes (growth buds) are easy to recognize at this time. To divide, cut the stalks with a sharp knife, leaving 1 in. of stalk attached to each section; make sure each division has an eye, so it will produce a new plant. Dust cut surfaces with sulfur to prevent rot; bury in dry sand, sawdust, peat moss, or perlite and store over winter in a cool (40 to 45°F/ 4 to 7°C), dark, dry place.

Method 2: Leave clumps intact. Cover them with dry sand, sawdust, peat moss, or perlite and store in cool, dark, dry place as directed in method above. With Method 2, roots are less likely to shrivel.

About 2 to 4 weeks before planting in spring, separate intact clumps, cutting them apart as described under Method 1. Then place all roots—whether fall- or spring-divided—in moist sand to plump them up and encourage sprouting.

D. imperialis. TREE DAHLIA. Zones 4–6, 8, 9, 14–24. Multistemmed tree grows each year from permanent roots to a possible 10–20 ft. tall, 4–6 ft. wide. Daisylike, 4–8-in.-wide lavender flowers with yellow centers bloom at branch ends in late fall. Leaves divided into many leaflets. Frost kills tops completely; cut back to ground afterward. If tree dahlia were longer blooming or evergreen, it would be a valued landscape plant, but annual dieback relegates it to tall novelty class. Available from specialists; seldom sold in nurseries. Grow from cuttings taken near stem tops (or from side shoots) in fall; root in pots of moist sand kept in a protected place over winter. Or dig root clump and divide in fall. Give full sun or partial shade. *D. excelsa, D. maxonii* are similar.

DALBERGIA sissoo

ROSEWOOD
Fabaceae (Leguminosae)
SEMIEVERGREEN TREE

| 🌿 ZONES 13, 19, 21–24; H1, H2 |
| ☀️ 🌤️ FULL SUN OR PARTIAL SHADE |
| 💧 REGULAR WATER |

Soft, green, thornless growth makes rosewood look more like a tropical tree than a desert native. Rapid growth to 25–50 ft. tall, 35–50 ft. wide.

Dalbergia sissoo

Handsome leaves divided into three to five 3-in., oval or roundish leaflets with narrow, elongated tips. Short clusters of pendulous, cream-colored, very fragrant flowers in spring. From India, where it is an important timber tree.

DALEA

Fabaceae (Leguminosae)
EVERGREEN AND DECIDUOUS SHRUBS

| 🌿 ZONES VARY BY SPECIES |
| ☀️ FULL SUN |
| 💧 LITTLE TO MODERATE WATER |

Extremely useful and attractive desert shrubs from the southwestern states and northern Mexico. All have finely divided foliage and clusters of small sweet pea–shaped flowers. The taller shrub types should be cut back by half during their first 3 or 4 years to encourage dense growth. Overwatering or summer drought can result in partial leaf drop.

Dalea greggii

D. bicolor. INDIGO BUSH. Deciduous. Zones 10–13. To 6–8 ft. tall, 5–6 ft. wide. Silvery leaves; deep blue autumn flowers. Rapid regrowth from hard winter pruning brings a quick crop of fresh foliage. 'Monterrey Blue' is a cutting-grown selection with especially good flower color.

D. capitata. Evergreen. Zones 10–13. Ground cover to 8 in. high and 3 ft. wide. Finely divided light green foliage has a lemon scent. Bears yellow flowers during spring and autumn. Control whiteflies. Requires some water in summer and survives regular irrigation. 'Sierra Gold' is a cutting-grown variety.

D. frutescens. BLACK DALEA. Evergreen. Zones 10–13. Mounded growth to 3 ft. tall, 4 ft. across, with silvery green, lacy foliage. Purple flower clusters appear from fall to spring. A cutting-grown form is called 'Sierra Negra'.

D. gattingeri. See Petalostemon purpureum

D. greggii. TRAILING INDIGO BUSH. Evergreen. Zones 10–13. Has mounding habit to 1½ ft. high and spreading 6 ft. wide. Pearl gray foliage and clusters of lavender to purple flowers in spring and early summer. Good desert ground cover.

D. lutea. Evergreen. Zones 12, 13. To 6 ft. tall and wide, with deep green leaves and clustered yellow flowers in late fall. 'Sierra Moonrise' is a selected form.

D. pulchra. INDIGO BUSH. Evergreen. Zones 12, 13. To 8 ft. high and 5 ft. wide. Silvery foliage; purple flowers in spring.

D. spinosa. See Psorothamnus spinosus

DALECHAMPIA dioscoreifolia

COSTA RICAN BUTTERFLY VINE
Euphorbiaceae
EVERGREEN VINE

| 🌿 ZONES 17–24 |
| ☀️ 🌤️ FULL SUN OR LIGHT SHADE |
| 💧 REGULAR WATER |

From Central and South America. Twining vine to 16–25 ft., with oval, pointed leaves to 3 in. long and 1 in. wide; leaves are dull dark green above, paler green and fuzzy beneath. Blossoms measure up to 6 in. across and are thought by some to resemble purple butterflies, with tiny yellow flowers appearing between two violet bracts. With adequate warmth and moisture, growth is rapid and blooms abundant. Heaviest bloom comes from early summer to late fall, but vine can flower nearly year-round.

Dalechampia dioscoreifolia

DAME'S ROCKET. See **HESPERIS matronalis**

DAMIANITA. See **CHRYSACTINIA mexicana**

DAMPIERA diversifolia

Goodeniaceae
PERENNIAL

| 🌿 ZONES 15–24 |
| ☀️ FULL SUN |
| 💧 REGULAR WATER |

Australian ground cover to 3 ft. high, 6 ft. wide. It spreads steadily in loose, well-drained soil by suckering and by roots that sprout from trailing stems, but it is not invasive or weedy. Evergreen, narrowly oval leaves to 1 in. long. In spring and summer, many small dark blue flowers appear at ends of new growth.

Dampiera diversifolia

DAPHNE

Thymelaeaceae
EVERGREEN, SEMIEVERGREEN, AND DECIDUOUS SHRUBS

| 🌿 ZONES VARY BY SPECIES |
| ☀️ 🌤️ EXPOSURE NEEDS VARY BY SPECIES |
| 💧 MODERATE WATER, EXCEPT AS NOTED |
| ⚠️ ALL PARTS, ESPECIALLY FRUITS, ARE POISONOUS IF INGESTED |

Although some daphnes are easier to grow than others, all require fast-draining soil and careful summer watering. They are generally more temperamental in California than in the Northwest. Plants respond to heavy pruning but rarely need more than the occasional snip to correct their shape. Cut back to lateral branches or to just above obvious growth buds. You can cut budded branches of deciduous types for forced bloom indoors.

D. bholua. Semievergreen to deciduous. ZONES 4–9, 14–17. Native to Himalayas. Upright growth to 6–12 ft. tall and 5–6 ft. wide, with leathery, dark green leaves to 4 in. long. Clusters of fragrant white flowers with a purplish pink blush appear in late winter. Small blackish purple fruit. Plant in part shade and provide regular water.

D. × burkwoodii. Evergreen or semievergreen to deciduous. Zones 2b–6, 14–17. Erect, compact growth to 3–4 ft. tall and wide, densely foliaged with narrow leaves. Abundant small clusters of fragrant flowers (white fading to pink) appear at branch ends in late spring and again in late summer. 'Briggs Moonlight' has pale yellow leaves with a narrow green border; 'Carol Mackie' has gold-edged green leaves. 'Somerset' is larger (to 4 ft. tall and 6 ft. wide) and bears pink flowers. Use all in shrub borders, at woodland edges, as foundation plantings. Full sun or light shade.

D. cneorum. GARLAND DAPHNE. Evergreen. Zones 2b–9, 14–17. From mountains of central and southern Europe. Forms mat less than 1 ft. high and 3 ft. wide. Good container plant. Trailing branches covered with narrow, 1-in.-long, dark green leaves. Clusters of fragrant rosy pink flowers appear in spring. Choice rock garden plant; give it light shade in warm areas, full sun in cool-summer areas. After bloom is through, top-dress with mix of peat moss and sand to keep roots cool and induce additional rooting of trailing stems.

Varieties include 'Eximia', lower than the species (to 8 in. high) and with larger flowers; 'Pygmaea Alba', 3 in. tall, 1 ft. wide, with white flowers; 'Ruby Glow', with larger, more deeply colored flowers than the species and with late-summer rebloom; and 'Variegata', with gold-edged leaves.

D. genkwa. LILAC DAPHNE. Deciduous. Zones 4–6, 16, 17. From China. Erect, open growth to 3–4 ft. high and wide. Before leaves expand, clusters of lilac blue, scentless flowers wreathe the branches, making foot-long wands of blossoms. White fruit follows flowers. Leaves oval, 2 in. long. Use in rock garden, shrub border. Full sun or light shade.

D. mezereum. FEBRUARY DAPHNE. Deciduous. Zones 2–7, 14–17. From Europe, Caucasus, Siberia. Rather gawky, stiff-twigged, erect growth to 4 ft. tall and 3 ft. wide, with thin, roundish, 2–3-in.-long leaves; should be planted in groups for best appearance. Fragrant reddish purple flowers in short, stalkless clusters are carried along branches in mid- or late winter before leaf-out and continue into spring. May go dormant in summer. Clustered red fruit follows flowers. Full sun or

light shade. 'Alba' has white flowers and yellow fruit and is not as rangy as the species.

D. odora. WINTER DAPHNE. Evergreen. Zones 4–10, 12, 14–24. From China, Japan. So prized for its pervasive floral perfume that it continues to be widely planted despite its unpredictable behavior—it can die despite the most attentive care, or flourish with little attention until you invite all your gardening friends over to admire it, at which point it promptly succumbs without warning just to show you who's in charge. Very neat, handsome plant, usually to about 4 ft. high (occasionally 8–10 ft. high) and 6 ft. wide. Rather narrow, 3-in.-long leaves are thick and glossy. Nosegay clusters of charming, intensely fragrant flowers—pink to deep red on outside, with creamy pink throats—appear at branch ends in winter. 'Alba' has white flowers; terminal growth sometimes distorted by fasciation (growths resembling cockscombs). 'Leucanthe' is relatively disease resistant, with white-throated pale pink blooms; 'Aureo-marginata' ('Marginata'), more widely grown than species, has yellow-edged leaves.

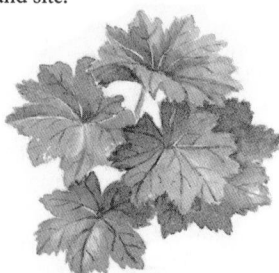

Daphne odora 'Aureo-marginata'

This species needs much air around its roots, so plant in porous soil (as you would rhododendrons). Always set plant a bit high, so the juncture of roots and stems is 1–2 in. above soil grade. Where soil is heavy and poorly drained, grow in porous, organic soil mixture in raised bed or container.

In Zones 18–24, transplanting an existing *D. odora* often fails—digging cuts roots, the plant suffers, and water molds get at it. Transplanting has a somewhat better chance of success in Zones 4–9, 14–17.

Plant this daphne where it can get at least 3 hours of shade each day around midday. If possible, shade soil around roots with living ground cover. A soil pH of 7.0 is right for it (important in Zones 4–6). Feed right after bloom with complete fertilizer but not acid plant food.

During dry season, water as infrequently as plant will allow. Little or no water in summer increases flowering next spring

and helps prevent death from water molds.

D. × transatlantica 'Jim's Pride'. Semievergreen to deciduous. Zones 2b–9, 14–17. Hybrid often sold as *D. caucasica*. Mounded growth to 3–4 ft. tall and 5–6 ft. wide after 10 years. Small gray-green leaves. Very fragrant, pink-flushed white flowers bloom over long season, from spring to fall. Produces the most blooms in full sun but can take part shade. 'Summer Ice' is similar but leaves are edged with creamy white.

DARMERA peltata (Peltiphyllum peltatum)

UMBRELLA PLANT, INDIAN RHUBARB
Saxifragaceae
PERENNIAL

🌿	ZONES 2–7, 14–20
◐	PARTIAL SHADE
💧	AMPLE WATER

Native to mountains of Northern California and Oregon. Large, round clusters of pink flowers appear on bare stalks to 6 ft. tall in spring. Shield-shaped, 1–2-ft.-wide leaves appear later on 2–6-ft. stalks. Each plant spreads 4–8 ft. wide. Stout rhizomes to 2 in. thick grow in damp ground or even into streams. A spectacular plant for pond, stream, or damp, cool woodland site.

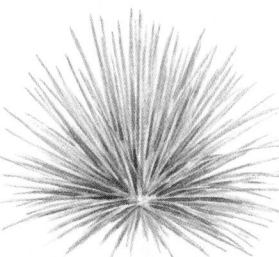

Darmera peltata

DASYLIRION

Agavaceae
EVERGREEN SHRUBS

🌿	ZONES VARY BY SPECIES
☀◐	FULL SUN OR LIGHT SHADE
◐💧	LITTLE OR NO WATER TO MODERATE WATER

Native to deserts and mountains of the Southwest and Mexico. Clumps of narrow, grassy leaves spring from a woody base that can, with age, grow into a treelike trunk. Tiny flowers are tightly clustered on a tall, narrow spike. Provide good drainage. Very

drought tolerant, but some irrigation will speed growth. Definitely need summer water in Zone 13.

D. longissimum (D. quadrangulatum). MEXICAN GRASS TREE. Zones 12–24. Smooth-edged green leaves in fountainlike clump to about 5 ft. high and wide. Trunk is slow to form, but may reach 10 ft. tall. Eventually bears white to cream-colored flowers in early summer.

D. texanum. GREEN DESERT SPOON. Zones 10–24. Forms neat clump about 5 ft. high and wide. Narrow, leathery, dark green leaves have small teeth along the edges. In summer, plant produces an 8-ft.-tall spike of creamy white flowers.

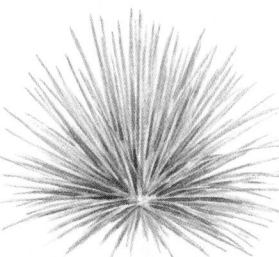

Dasylirion wheeleri

D. wheeleri. DESERT SPOON, SOTOL. Zones 10–24; most widely used in 10–13. Forms a near-spherical clump 3–5 ft. high, 4–5 ft. wide. Spiky bluish gray leaves to 3 ft. long have teeth along the edges and are stiffer than those of *D. longissimum*. Leaves slowly form a trunk to 3 ft. tall, covered with dried, drooping shag of old leaves. Base of each leaf broadens where it joins the trunk to form a long-handled "spoon" prized in dried arrangements. Eventually produces white flowers on 9–15-ft.-tall spike in early summer.

DATE PALM. See PHOENIX

DATIL. See YUCCA baccata

DATURA. See BRUGMANSIA

DAVALLIA trichomanoides

SQUIRREL'S FOOT FERN
Polypodiaceae
FERN

🌿	ZONES 17, 23, 24; H1, H2; OR INDOORS
◐	PARTIAL SHADE; BRIGHT INDIRECT LIGHT
💧	MODERATE TO REGULAR WATER

Asian native. Very finely divided evergreen fronds to about 1 ft. long, 6 in. wide, rise from light reddish brown, furry rhizomes (resembling

Davallia trichomanoides

quirrel's feet) that creep over soil urface. Hardy to 30°F/–1°C; can e used in mild-winter areas as mall-scale ground cover in partly haded areas. Best use in any cliate is as hanging basket plant. Jse light, fast-draining soil mix. eed occasionally. For a similar ern, see *Humata tyermannii*.

DAVIDIA involucrata

OVE TREE
Nyssaceae
ECIDUOUS TREE

🌿 ZONES 4–9, 14–21

☼ ◑ PARTIAL SHADE IN HOTTEST CLIMATES

⬤ REGULAR WATER

Native to China. Grows to 35–65 ft. all, with strong branching pattern and a rounded crown 15–40 ft. wide. Has a clean look both in and out of leaf. Roundish to heartshaped, 3–6 in.-long leaves are vivid green. Comes into bloom in spring; general effect is that of white doves resting among green

Davidia involucrata

leaves—or, as some say, like handkerchiefs drying on branches. Small, clustered, red-anthered flowers are carried between two large white or creamy white bracts that are unequal in size—one is 6 in. long, the other about 4 in. Because leaves are already present at bloom time, the large blossoms aren't as showy as smaller flowers of many deciduous fruit trees.

Trees often take 10 years to come into flower, and then may bloom more heavily in alternate years. The variety 'Sonoma' blooms as young as 2 years old. Brown fruits about the size of golf balls persist on tree well into winter, sometimes until spring. Plant this tree by itself; it should not compete with other flowering trees. Looks pleasing in front of dark conifers, where its vivid green and white stand out.

DAWN REDWOOD.
See **METASEQUOIA glyptostroboides**

DAYLILY. See **HEMEROCALLIS**

DEAD NETTLE.
See **LAMIUM maculatum**

DEER FERN, DEER TONGUE FERN. See **BLECHNUM spicant**

DEER GRASS.
See **MUHLENBERGIA rigens**

DEERHORN CEDAR.
See **THUJOPSIS dolabrata**

DELONIX regia

ROYAL POINCIANA,
FLAMBOYANT TREE
Fabaceae (Leguminosae)
PARTIALLY OR WHOLLY
DECIDUOUS TREE

🌿 ZONES 22, 23; H2

☼ FULL SUN

◌ LITTLE WATER

This native of Madagascar, which Hawaiians call *ohai'ula*, is as flamboyant as it is shapely. Its large trusses of 4-in., orange to scarlet flowers with white or yellow markings put on a spectacular display in late spring or early summer. The blooms are followed by 2-ft.-long black seedpods that hang on the bare winter branches. Rapidly attains 30–40 ft. tall and as wide, with umbrella-shaped

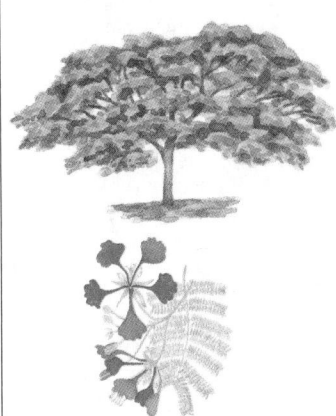

Delonix regia

silhouette. Fernlike leaves, finely cut into many tiny leaflets, give filtered shade. Good drought tolerance; moderate tolerance to wind and salt. A form with pure yellow flowers, called yellow royal poinciana, is also grown in Hawaii.

DELOSPERMA

ICE PLANT
Aizoaceae
SUCCULENT PERENNIALS

🌿 ZONES 2–24, EXCEPT AS NOTED

☼ ◑ LIGHT AFTERNOON SHADE IN HOTTEST CLIMATES

⬤◌ MODERATE TO REGULAR WATER

This group of ice plants includes a useful ground cover (*D.* 'Alba') and several unusually hardy South African rock garden plants. With the latter, withhold water in fall to harden off plants for winter; they also appreciate a gravel mulch to keep crowns dry. All species do best with regular water in summer, but they will get by with just enough water to keep them looking bright and fresh. Except as noted, fleshy leaves are rich green.

Delosperma cooperi

D. 'Alba'. WHITE TRAILING ICE PLANT. Zones 12–24. Spreading dwarf plant, rooting freely from stems. Roundish leaves; small white summer flowers that attract bees. Good ground and bank cover; plant 1 ft. apart for quick cover.

D. basuticum. Zones 1–24. Grows ½ in. high, 9 in. wide, with roundish leaves and inch-wide, daisylike bright yellow flowers with white central zones. Spring to early-summer bloom.

D. cooperi. Reaches 3 in. tall, 1½ ft. wide, with cylindrical leaves and a summer-long display of rich purple flowers.

D. floribundum 'Starburst'. Clumping to 4 in. tall and 10–18 in. wide. Roundish leaves and 1-in., pink to magenta, daisylike flowers; blooms late spring to fall.

D. 'Kelaidis' (D. 'Mesa Verde'). Vigorous, cold-tolerant hybrid grows 2 in. tall and 1–2 ft. wide, with pale salmon pink flowers (1½ in. across) from spring until fall.

D. nubigenum 'Lesotho'. Only 1 in. tall, spreading to 3 ft. The cylindrical leaves turn red in fall and winter, green up again in spring. Bright golden yellow, 1–1½-in. flowers cover the plant in late spring.

D. sphalmanthoides. Only ½ in. high and 8 in. wide, with tiny, plump gray-green leaves and an early spring show of pinkish purple flowers.

DELPHINIUM

Ranunculaceae
PERENNIALS, SOME TREATED AS
BIENNIALS OR ANNUALS

🌿 ZONES VARY BY SPECIES

☼ FULL SUN, EXCEPT AS NOTED

⬤ REGULAR WATER

Most people associate delphiniums with blue flowers, but colors also include white and shades of red, pink, lavender, and purple. Leaves are lobed or fanlike, variously cut and divided. Taller hybrids offer rich colors in elegant spires. All kinds are effective in borders and make good cut flowers; lowergrowing kinds serve well as container plants. Blossoms attract birds. For an annual delphinium (larkspur), see *Consolida ajacis*.

All kinds of delphiniums are easy to grow from seed. In mildwinter areas, sow fresh seed in flats or pots of light soil mix in summer; set out transplants in early fall for bloom in late spring and early summer. (In mild-winter climates, most perennial forms are short lived, often treated as annuals.) In cold climates, refrigerate summer-harvested seed in airtight containers until time to sow. Sow seed in spring and set out transplants in early summer for first bloom by late summer; plants will live over and bloom again earlier in the following summer.

Delphiniums need rich, porous soil and regular fertilizing. Improve poor or heavy soils by blending in soil conditioners. Add lime to strongly acid soils. Work small amount of superphosphate into soil around the root ball. Be careful not to cover root crown with soil. Protect from snails, slugs. In Alaska, the delphinium defoliator eats the plants' leaves in its green caterpillar stage;

handpick caterpillars or spray with *Bt*.

D. ambiguum. See Consolida ajacis

D. × belladonna. Zones 1–9, 14–24. Sturdy and bushy, to 3–4 ft. tall, 2 ft. wide. Deeply cut leaves and short-stemmed, airy flower clusters. Varieties include light blue 'Belladonnna', dark blue 'Bellamosum', white 'Casablanca', and deep turquoise blue 'Cliveden Beauty'. All have flowers 1½–2 in. wide; longer lived than tall hybrids listed under *D. elatum*.

D. cardinale. SCARLET LARKSPUR. Zones 7, 14–23. Native to California coastal mountains. To 3–6 ft. tall and 2 ft. wide, with erect stems growing from deep, thick, woody roots. Leaves 3–9 in. wide, with deep, narrow lobes. Flowers 1 in. across, with scarlet calyx and spur and scarlet-tipped yellow petals. Sow seed early for first-year bloom.

D. elatum. CANDLE DELPHINIUM, CANDLE LARKSPUR. Zones A1–A3; 1–10, 14–24. Siberian native to 3–6 ft. tall, 2 ft. wide, with small flowers in dark or dull purple. This species is among the parents of modern delphinium strains, with flower colors including shades of lilac pink to deep raspberry rose, clear lilac, lavender, royal purple, and darkest violet.

Delphinium elatum

Pacific strain (also called Pacific Giants, Pacific Coast hybrids, and Pacific hybrids) grows 5–8 ft. tall. Available as seed-raised mixed-color plants and in named series that produce specific colors, including light blue 'Summer Skies'; medium blue 'Blue Bird'; medium to dark blue 'Blue Jay'; 'Galahad', clear white with white center; 'Percival', white with black

center. Additional purple, lavender, and pink selections are sold.

Blue Fountains, Blue Springs, and Magic Fountains strains are like Pacific strain but shorter (2–2½ ft. tall). Stand Up strain is even shorter (15–20 in. high). These lower-growing types seldom require staking.

Centurion is a long-stalked (4–5-ft.-tall), large-flowered hybrid strain similar to the Pacific strain. It too will bloom the first year from seed, but it's more reliably perennial.

English Delphinium Mix grows 6–8 ft. tall, produces double flowers of blue, purple, mauve, pink, and white. The spikes are much denser looking than those of Pacific strain. English types may be sold under other names such as 'English Seedlings'.

D. grandiflorum (D. chinense). CHINESE or BOUQUET DELPHINIUM. Short-lived perennial treated as biennial or annual. Zones A1–A3; 1–10, 14–24. Bushy, branching, to 1 ft. tall or less and about as wide as high. Varieties include 'Dwarf Blue Mirror', 1 ft. tall, upward-facing flowers of deep blue; and 'Tom Thumb', 8 in. tall, pure gentian blue flowers. Blue Butterfly strain grows 14 in. high, has deep blue blooms.

D. nudicaule. SCARLET LARKSPUR. Zones 5–7, 14–17. Native of Northern California, southwestern Oregon. Slender plant to 1–3 ft. tall and less than a foot wide. Long-stalked, mostly basal leaves are broadly divided. Sparse show of long-spurred red flowers. Sun or part shade; best in woodland situations.

DENDRANTHEMA pacificum. See **CHRYSANTHEMUM pacificum**

DENDROBIUM

Orchidaceae
EPIPHYTIC ORCHIDS

🌡	ZONES VARY BY TYPE; OR INDOORS
☀	LIGHT SHADE; BRIGHT INDIRECT LIGHT
💧	REGULAR WATER

This huge genus (it may include as many as 1,400 species and even more hybrids) ranges from Japan and the Himalayas to Australia and the Pacific islands. Many are grown by orchid fanciers in greenhouses (outdoors in the tropics or mildest subtropical and Mediterranean climates); many are also commercially grown for the cut flower

Dendrobium nobile

trade. Some have thin, canelike pseudobulbs (see Orchids), others short, fat ones. Only a few of the more widely grown are mentioned here. Culturally they fall into two classes. Intermediate-climate types are evergreen; they need water throughout the year (somewhat less in winter) and temperatures similar to those required by cattleyas. Cool growers drop some or all of their leaves during a period of winter dormancy, at which time they need very little water (only enough to keep pseudobulbs from shrinking) and temperatures suitable for green-leafed paphiopedilums.

D. bigibbum phalaenopsis (D. phalaenopsis). Intermediate grower. Zone H2. Native to Australia, New Guinea. Blooms throughout the year, with canes up to 3 ft. tall producing arching spikes that carry as many as ten 3-inch purple flowers. The parent of many hybrids.

D. hybrids. Zone H2. A bewildering number of hybrids have been produced in Hawaii and elsewhere, both for ornamental potted plants and for cut flowers and leis. Most are intermediate growers. Buy plants in bloom to get desired flower color and bloom season.

D. kingianum. Cool grower. Zones 16, 17, 22–24; H1. Native to Australia. Makes large clumps of 2–20-in. pseudobulbs topped by 4-in. leaves. In late winter or early spring, erect spikes to 8 in. long carry a few or up to as many as 20 fragrant, inch-wide flowers in pink, white, or red. Thrives outdoors along California coast if protected from frost.

D. nobile. Cool grower. Zone H1. Himalayan native. Canes 12–20 in. tall carry two ranks of 2–3½-in. leaves; leaves last for about 2 years. Short inflorescences borne on leafy and leafless canes carry two to four fragrant, 1½-in., white to purplish pink flowers with a yellow or white zone surrounding a dark purple eye.

Blooms almost any time of year. The parent of many colorful hybrids.

D. speciosum. Cool grower. Zones 16, 17, 22–24; H1. From Australia. Large masses of 4-in. to 3-ft. pseudobulbs topped with 1½–10-in.-long leaves. Blooms in late winter or early spring. Inflorescences are crowded spikes of fragrant, creamy to yellow flowers; they resemble bushy foxtails, can reach 2–2½ ft. long.

DENDROMECON

BUSH POPPY
Papaveraceae
EVERGREEN SHRUBS

🌡	ZONES VARY BY SPECIES
☀	FULL SUN
💧	NO IRRIGATION NEEDED

Both species described below give showy display of bright yellow, 2-in.-wide, poppylike flowers. Use on banks and roadsides, with other native shrubs.

D. harfordii (D. rigida harfordii). ISLAND BUSH POPPY. Zones 7–9, 14–24. Native to Santa Cruz and Santa Rosa islands off coast of Southern California. Rounded or spreading large shrub or small tree 8–20 ft. tall and as wide. Deep green leaves to 3 in. long, half as wide. Free flowering from spring into early summer, with scattered bloom throughout year. Prune to thin or shape after bloom.

Dendromecon harfordii

D. rigida. BUSH POPPY. Zones 4–12, 14–24. In Zones 4 and 5, grows best as a south-wall shrub. Native to dry chaparral in lower elevations in California. Untidy growing wild. Freely branched shrub 4–8 ft. tall and 4–6 ft. wide, with shredding yellowish gray or white bark. Thick, veiny, gray-green leaves 1–4 in. long. Flowers in spring. Prune back to about 2 ft. after bloom.

DESCHAMPSIA

HAIR GRASS
Poaceae (Gramineae)
PERENNIAL GRASSES

| ✓ ZONES 2-24, EXCEPT AS NOTED |
| :☀: :☀: FULL SUN OR PARTIAL SHADE |
| ◐◐ WATER NEEDS VARY BY SPECIES |

Hair grasses are grown for their graceful clumps of arching foliage and airy clouds of flowers. Although they grow over much of North America, most garden selections are imports from Europe. Use in mass plantings.

D. cespitosa. TUFTED HAIR GRASS. Clumps of narrow dark green leaves to 1–2 ft. tall and 2 ft. wide, evergreen except in colder climates. Airy inflorescences in late spring or early summer can increase plant height to 4 ft. or taller; they are green to greenish gold, turning straw color in winter. Good subject for planting under native oaks. 'Bronzeschleier' ('Bronze Veil') has bronzy yellow inflorescences; those of 'Goldgehänge' and 'Goldstaub' are golden yellow. *D. c. vivipara*, also known as 'Fairy's Joke', produces plantlets instead of seeds; these droop to the ground and may take root. All of the above forms of *D. cespitosa* take regular water.

Deschampsia cespitosa vivipara

D. c. holciformis, Pacific hair grass, grows in Zones 4–9, 14–24. It has darker green foliage than the species and dense, narrow, relatively coarse inflorescences. Takes marshy, even brackish conditions.

D. flexuosa. CRINKLED HAIR GRASS. Smaller than *D. cespitosa* (usually less than 2 ft. tall and about a foot wide in bloom), with more open, bronze to pale greenish yellow inflorescences in midsummer. Succeeds in dry woodland shade as well as in sunnier or moister situations.

DESERT BROOM.
See **BACCHARIS sarothroides**

DESERT CHRISTMAS CACTUS.
See **OPUNTIA leptocaulis**

DESERT HOLLY.
See **ATRIPLEX hymenelytra**

DESERT HONEYSUCKLE.
See **ANISACANTHUS**

DESERT IRONWOOD.
See **OLNEYA tesota**

DESERT LAVENDER.
See **HYPTIS emoryi**

DESERT MARIGOLD.
See **BAILEYA multiradiata**

DESERT OLIVE.
See **FORESTIERA neomexicana**

DESERT SPOON.
See **DASYLIRION wheeleri**

DESERT WILLOW.
See **CHILOPSIS linearis**

DEUTZIA

Saxifragaceae
DECIDUOUS SHRUBS

| ✓ ZONES 2-11, 14-17, EXCEPT AS NOTED |
| :☀: :☀: FULL SUN OR LIGHT SHADE |
| ● REGULAR WATER |

These shrubs are best used among evergreens, where they can make a show when in flower, then blend back in with other greenery later on. Bloom season coincides with that of late-spring bulbs such as tulips and Dutch iris. Prune shrubs after bloom. With low- or medium-growing kinds, cut some of oldest stems to ground every other year. Prune tall-growing kinds severely by cutting back wood that has flowered. Cut to outward-facing side branches.

D. crenata. Native to Japan. Similar to *D. scabra,* but with white flowers. Deep purple-red fall foliage. *D. c. nakaiana,* dwarf and spreading, has double flowers.

D. × elegantissima. Grows to 6 ft. tall and wide, with pink flowers. 'Rosealind', 4–5 ft. tall and wide, has deep rose flowers.

D. gracilis. SLENDER DEUTZIA. Native to Japan. To 2–4 ft. (possibly 6 ft.) tall, 3–4 ft. wide. Many slender stems arch gracefully, carry bright green, 2½-in., sharply toothed leaves and clusters of snowy white flowers. 'Nikko' grows only 1–2 ft. by 5 ft. and can be used as a ground cover.

D. hybrids. Zones 2b–9, 14–23. These include 'Pink-a-Boo', an erect grower to 6–8 ft. tall and 6 ft. wide, with large clusters of pink

flowers; and 'Magicien', similar but with dark red flowers.

Deutzia 'Pink-a-Boo'

D. × rosea. To 3–4 ft. tall and wide, with finely toothed, 1–3-in.-long leaves. Short clusters of pinkish flowers with white interiors.

D. scabra. Native to Japan, China. To 7–10 ft. by 6 ft. Oval, scallop-toothed, 3-in.-long, dull green leaves are roughish to touch. White or pale pink flowers in narrow, upright clusters. 'Pride of Rochester' has large clusters of small, frilly, double white flowers tinged pink. 'Codsall' ('Codsall Pink') bears double pink blooms. Leaves of 'Variegata' are marked with white.

DEVIL'S BACKBONE.
See **PEDILANTHUS tithymaloides smallii**

DEVIL'S TOBACCO.
See **LOBELIA tupa**

DEVIL'S WALKING STICK.
See **ARALIA spinosa**

DIANELLA

FLAX LILY
Liliaceae
PERENNIALS

| ✓ ZONES 8, 9, 14-24 |
| :☀: :☀: FULL SUN IN COOLER CLIMATES ONLY |
| ● REGULAR WATER |

These interesting plants are grown for their grassy, straplike foliage and small, star-shaped blue flow-

Dianella tasmanica

ers followed by shiny berries. Provide rich, porous soil and routine fertilizing. Attractive near swimming pools.

D. caerulea. BLUE FLAX LILY. Native to eastern Australia. Tufted or mat-forming plants 1–2 ft. tall and 2–3 ft. wide. Shiny, medium green leaves are lightly toothed, to 2½ ft. long. Light or dark blue flowers about ¾ in. across have prominent yellow stamens and are followed by translucent blue to purple berries.

D. tasmanica. From southeastern Australia, including Tasmania. Grows 3–4 ft. tall; narrowly upright when young but spreading slowly by rhizomes with age. Sturdy, medium green leaves (striped white in 'Variegata' and yellow in 'Yellow Stripe'). Loose clusters of small blue summer flowers on straight, slender stalks are followed by large (¾-in.) glistening blue berries that last 2 months or longer on the plant.

DIANTHUS

PINK
Caryophyllaceae
PERENNIALS, BIENNIALS, AND ANNUALS

| ✓ ZONES A2, A3; 1-24, EXCEPT AS NOTED |
| :☀: :☀: LIGHT SHADE IN HOTTEST CLIMATES |
| ● REGULAR WATER |

Over 300 species and extremely large number of hybrids. Most kinds form attractive evergreen mats or tufts of grasslike green, gray-green, blue-green, or gray-blue leaves. Single, semidouble, or double flowers in white and shades of pink, rose, red, yellow, and orange; many have rich, spicy fragrance. Main bloom period for most is spring into early summer; some kinds rebloom later in season or keep going into fall if faded flowers are removed.

Among dianthus are favorites such as cottage pink and sweet William, highly prized cut flowers such as carnation (clove pink), and rock garden miniatures. Many named varieties not mentioned here are available locally.

All kinds of dianthus thrive in light, fast-draining soil. Carnations, sweet William, and cottage pinks need fairly rich soil; rock garden or alpine types require a gritty growing medium, with added lime if soil is acid. Avoid overwatering. Sow seed of annual kinds in flats or directly in garden. ▶

D

Propagate perennial kinds by cuttings made from tips of growing shoots, by division or layering, or from seed. Carnation and sweet William are subject to rust and fusarium wilt.

D. 'Allwoodii'. Perennial. Group of pinks derived from crossing carnation (*D. caryophyllus*) and cottage pink (*D. plumarius*). Plants vary in size, but most are 12–15 in. high and 2 ft. wide, with gray-green foliage and two blossoms per stem. Pink, white, or red flowers are strongly clove-scented. Long bloom period if deadheaded regularly. More compact and floriferous than their *D. plumarius* parent.

D. arenarius. Perennial. From Europe. Tufted plant to 1½ ft. tall and wide, with narrow, grass green leaves and 1½-in.-wide, fringed white flowers sometimes marked with green or purple. Highly fragrant; can tolerate some shade.

D. barbatus. SWEET WILLIAM. Vigorous biennial often grown as annual. From southern Europe. To 20 in. tall and 1 ft. wide, with sturdy stems. Leaves are flat, light to dark green, 1½–3 in. long. Dense clusters of white, pink, rose, red, purplish, or bicolored flowers, about ½ in. across, set among leafy bracts; not very fragrant. Sow seed in late spring for bloom the following year. Double-flowered and dwarf strains are obtainable from seed. Indian Carpet is only 6 in. tall. Roundabout and Summer Beauty strains (1 ft.) bloom the first year from seed.

D. caryophyllus. CARNATION, CLOVE PINK. Perennial. Zones A2, A3; 1–24; H1. Highly bred Mediterranean species. Two distinct categories exist: florists' and border types. Both have double flowers, bluish green leaves, and branching, leafy stems that often become woody at base.

Border carnations are bushier and more compact (12–14 in. high and wide) than florists' type. Fragrant, 2–2½-in.-wide flowers are borne in profusion. Effective as shrub border edgings, in borders of mixed flowers, and also in containers. Hybrid carnations grown from seed are usually treated as annuals but often live

Dianthus caryophyllus

over. 'Juliet' makes compact, foottall clumps and bears 2½-in. scarlet flowers over a long season; 'Luminette', 2 ft. tall, is similar. Pixie Delight strain is also similar but includes full range of carnation colors. Knight series has strong stems, blooms in 5 months from seed; Bambino strain is a little slower to bloom. There is also a strain called simply Hanging Mixed, with pink- or red-flowered plants that sprawl or hang from pot or window box. Newer varieties include bright red 'Cinnamon Red Hots', to 1 ft. tall; rose pink 'Pinkie', reaching 6 in. high; and foot-tall 'Velvet 'n Lace', with frilly dark red flowers edged in white.

Florists' carnations are grown commercially in greenhouses, outdoors in gardens in mild-winter areas, including higher-elevation gardens in Hawaii. Greenhouse-grown plants reach 4 ft., have fragrant flowers 3 in. wide in many colors—white, shades of pink and red, orange, purple, yellow; some are variegated. For large flowers, leave only terminal bloom on each stem, pinching out all other buds down to fifth joint, below which new flowering stems will develop. Stake to prevent sprawling. Start with strong cuttings taken from the most vigorous plants of selected named varieties. Sturdy plants conceal supports, look quite tidy.

D. chinensis. CHINESE PINK, RAINBOW PINK. Biennial or short-lived perennial; most varieties grown as annuals. Erect plant to 6–30 in. high and 6–10 in. wide; stems branch only at top. Stem leaves narrow, 1–3 in. long, ½ in. wide, hairy on margins. Basal leaves are usually gone by flowering time. Flowers about 1 in. across, rose lilac with deeper-colored eye; lack fragrance.

Modern strains are compact domes (1 ft. tall or less) covered with bright flowers in white, pink, red, and all variations and combinations of those colors. 'Fire Carpet' is a brilliant solid red, 'Snowfire' white with a red eye. Telstar is a bushy, extra dwarf (6–8-in.) strain with dark green leaves. Petals are deeply fringed on some, smooth edged on others. Some flowers have intricately marked eyes. Sow directly in ground in spring, in full sun, for summer bloom. Pick off faded flowers with their bases to prolong bloom.

Dianthus caryophyllus

D. deltoides. MAIDEN PINK. Perennial (even though it blooms in just a few weeks from seed). From Europe and Asia. To 8–12 in. high, forming a loose mat to 1 ft. wide. Blossoms about ¾ in. wide, with sharp-toothed petals, are borne at ends of forked flowering stems with short leaves. Colors include white and light or dark rose to purple, spotted with lighter colors. Blooms in summer, sometimes again in fall. Useful, showy ground or bank cover. Can tolerate half-day shade.

Varieties include white 'Albus', deep red 'Vampire', bright scarlet 'Zing', and rose red 'Zing Rose'. Microchip is a mixture including pinks, reds, and white, often with a contrasting eye.

D. gratianopolitanus (D. caesius). CHEDDAR PINK. Perennial. From Europe. Neat, ground-hugging, foot-wide mat of blue-gray foliage. Stems 6–10 in. high bear small, typically pink to rose, single blossoms (less than an inch across) that are very fragrant. Bloom season lasts from spring to fall if plants are deadheaded regularly. Effective as ground cover or edging or in rock garden.

'Bath's Pink'. Fringed, soft pink blooms on 12–15-in. stems.

Dianthus gratianopolitanus
'Bath's Pink'

'Little Boy Blue'. Foot-high stems bearing white flowers dotted with pink; foliage is intense blue gray.

'Little Joe'. Crimson flowers on 6-in. stems.

'Rose Bowl'. Cerise rose blossoms on 6-in. stems.

'Spotty'. Looks much like 'Rose Bowl', but flowers are heavily spotted with white.

'Tiny Rubies'. Dwarf selection with double ruby red flowers on 4-in. stems; clump spreads 4 in. wide.

D. plumarius. COTTAGE PINK. Perennial. Zones A1; 1–24. Charming, almost legendary European species, cultivated for hundreds of years and used in developing many hybrids. Typically has loosely matted gray-

green foliage in clump to 2 ft. wide. Flowering stems 10–18 in. tall; spicily fragrant, dark-centered flowers in rose, pink, or white, with more-or-less fringed petals. Highly prized are old laced pinks, with white flowers in which each petal is outlined in red or pink. Cottage pinks bloom from summer to fall if deadheaded. Indispensable edging for borders or for peony or rose beds. Perfect addition to small arrangements and old-fashioned bouquets.

Choice selections include 'Dad's Favorite', which bears red-edged double white flowers on 10-in. stems; 'Essex Witch', with semidouble rose pink flowers on 5-in. stems; and 'Musgrave's Pink', a foot-tall classic that is at least 200 years old and bears intensely fragrant, single white blooms with a green eye.

DIASCIA
TWINSPUR
Scrophulariaceae
PERENNIALS AND ANNUALS

🌿	ZONES VARY BY SPECIES
☀ ☼	PARTIAL SHADE IN HOTTEST CLIMATES
◐ ●	MODERATE TO REGULAR WATER

South African natives related to snapdragon (*Antirrhinum*). The coral to purplish pink flowers each have two prominent spurs on the back; these bear oils attractive to pollinating bees. Blooms are carried in spikelike clusters at stem ends from spring through early summer and often into fall. At their best used in rock gardens, borders, or containers. With the exception of *D. barberae*, all of the species listed here are perennial, though these perennials may die in winter if planted in heavy, wet soil. Shear back after bloom period.

D. barberae. Perennial often grown as an annual. Zones 1–10, 14–24. Mat-forming plant to 10 in. tall, 20 in. wide, with rose pink

Diascia barberae

blossoms. 'Blackthorn Apricot' bears apricot-colored flowers.

D. cordata (D. barberae 'Fisher's Flora'). Zones 7–9, 14–24. Low green mat to 6 in. high and 20 in. wide, with 10-in. sprays of salmon pink blossoms.

D. fetcaniensis. Zones 4–9, 14–24. To 10 in. high and 20 in. wide, with rose pink blooms.

D. hybrids. Zones 4–9, 14–24. These include 'Emma', an especially cold-hardy selection to 2 ft. tall and 4 ft. wide, with raspberry-colored blossoms; 'Ice Pole', to 10–14 in. high and 18 in. wide, with pure white flowers; 'Langthorn's Lavender', to 1 ft. tall, with lavender blooms; and 'Red Start', to 8 in. high and 1 ft. wide, with watermelon red flowers. 'Ruby Field', to 10 in. high and 2 ft. wide, bears salmon pink blossoms; it is similar to *D. cordata*, one of its parents, but has a longer bloom season. A group of new hybrids from England (all 7–10 in. high and 1½ ft. wide) includes coral pink 'Coral Belle'; 'Little Charmer', pink with a dark red eye; rosy red 'Red Ace'; and deep pink 'Strawberry Sundae'. Plants in the Flying Colors series have large flowers in shades of red, pink, apricot, and coral; most grow 6–12 in. high (some grow upright, others are more trailing).

D. integerrima. Zones 2–9, 14–24. To 1½ ft. tall, creeping to 3–4 ft. wide. Small, linear leaves are 1 in. long. Loose spikes of rich purplish pink flowers. 'Coral Canyon' grows 12–15 in. high and 1½ ft. wide, bears salmon pink flowers.

D. rigescens. Zones 7–9, 14–24. To 1 ft. high. Sprawling stems form clumps to 1 ft. tall, 2 ft. wide, turn up at ends to display 6–8-in. spikes of rich pink flowers. Cut out old stems.

D. vigilis. Zones 4–9, 14–24. To 20 in. high and slightly wider, with fleshy green leaves and light pink flowers. 'Jack Elliott' has large blooms that are pink with yellow and maroon markings.

DICENTRA
BLEEDING HEART
Fumariaceae
PERENNIALS

Delicate-looking plants. Graceful, divided, fernlike foliage. Dainty pendent flowers, usually heart shaped, in pink, rose, yellow, or

white on leafless, horizontal to arching stems. In general, dicentras need rich, light, moist, porous soil. Never let water stand around roots. Foliage dies down even in mild-winter climates; mark clumps to avoid digging into roots in dormant season. Short lived in mild-winter areas.

D. chrysantha. GOLDEN EARDROPS. Native to inner Coast Ranges and Sierra Nevada foothills of California. Erect plant with sparse, blue-gray, divided leaves on stout, hollow, 4–5-ft. stems. Golden yellow, short-spurred flowers, held upright in large clusters. Plant grows 1½ ft. wide. Requires warmth. Unlike many dicentras, this species needs soil that is not too rich; make sure drainage is good. Plant has deep taproot and does not need irrigation during its flowering in spring and summer. Seed available from wildflower specialists.

D. eximia. FRINGED BLEEDING HEART. Native to northeastern U.S. Forms tidy clump 1–1½ ft. high and wide. Blue-gray basal leaves are more finely divided than those of *D. formosa*. Deep rose pink flowers with short, rounded spurs bloom from midspring into summer. Cut back for second growth and occasional repeat bloom. Does not spread by rhizomes but may extend itself by self-sowing.

D. formosa. WESTERN BLEEDING HEART. Native to moist woods along Pacific Coast. To 1½ ft. tall, 3 ft. or wider. Blue-green foliage. In spring, leafless flower stalks hold clusters of pendulous pale or deep rose flowers on reddish stems. Spreads freely by rhizomes and seeding, forming large colonies. 'Zestful' is everblooming, with deep rose flowers. *D. f. oregana* grows to 1 ft. tall, has silvery green leaves and cream-colored flowers that are tipped with purple.

D. hybrids. *D. eximia* and *D. formosa* cross freely to yield hybrids, many of which have been named. The following are among the most commonly cultivated; they grow 1–1½ ft. high and 1½–2 ft. across (eventually spreading more widely) and bloom from spring into summer.

'Bacchanal'. Finely cut, gray-green leaves and dark red flowers.

'Bountiful'. Dark blue-green foliage and purplish pink to dusky red flowers.

'King of Hearts'. Finely cut blue-green leaves with rosy pink flowers produced over a long period.

'Langtrees'. Silvery green foliage and white flowers shaded pink.

'Luxuriant'. Zones A1–A3; 1–9, 14–24. Medium to dark green leaves and red flowers.

D. spectabilis. COMMON BLEEDING HEART. Zones A1–A3; 1–9, 14–24. Native to Japan. Old garden favorite; showiest and largest leafed of all bleeding hearts. To 2–3 ft. high, 3 ft. wide; stems are set with soft green leaves. Blooms in late spring, bearing flowers on one side of arching stems—rose pink, pendulous, heart shaped, with protruding white inner petals. 'Alba' ('Pantaloons') is a pure white form. 'Gold Heart' has bright yellow foliage.

Plants generally die down and become dormant by midsummer, but they'll keep going longer in cool-summer climates if given adequate moisture. Plant summer-maturing perennials nearby to fill the gap. Dormant roots—fleshy and sometimes even woody—are available at nurseries from late fall to earliest spring; plant as soon as they become available in your area. In the Southwest, you can sometimes establish plants permanently in a cool, moist spot in foothill canyons, but the usual practice there is to plant new roots in ground or container each year and discard plants in early summer after blooming. In Southern California, plants usually last for only one season. Best in partial shade.

Dicentra spectabilis

DICHONDRA
Convolvulaceae
PERENNIALS

Low-growing plants that spread by rooting surface runners. One species is an often-seen small-scale ground cover; the other is an interesting new foliage plant.

D. argentea 'Silver Falls'. Grows 2–3 in. tall and spreads 4–6 ft. wide. Heart-shaped leaves up to 1 in. wide are covered with silvery down, as are the stems. Eye-catching, shimmering container plant; cascades over the edge of pots or window boxes. Can also be used as a small-scale ground cover. Easy to grow from seed. Use as an annual in cold-winter areas.

D. micranthra. Small (up to 1½ in.) round leaves look like miniature water lily pads. In shade and with regular moisture and nutrients it can grow to 6 in. high and require frequent mowing. Spreads widely. Once favored and commonly used as a lawn, but large

Dichondra micrantha

plantings were so often devastated by flea beetles that it is now used mainly in limited spaces. Good in small areas that are subject to foot traffic—as between stepping-stones—where it stays low and seldom (if ever) needs trimming or mowing. Often sold as *D. carolinensis* or *D. repens*.

DICHORISANDRA
thyrsiflora
BLUE GINGER
Commelinaceae
PERENNIAL

This Brazilian native is not a true ginger but rather a robust and upright-growing relative of wandering Jew (*Tradescantia*). Fleshy, unbranched or sparsely branched stems to 6–8 ft. rise from a fleshy rhizome. Deep green, oval, 6–12-in.-long, evergreen leaves are spirally arranged around the stem, forming a 3-ft.-wide foliage clump. Flowers are deep violet blue, and come in 6-in. spikes at tops of stems throughout the year. Best in moist soil enriched with

D

Dichorisandra thyrsiflora

organic matter. Easy to propagate by cuttings. As a houseplant or in greenhouse, grows 3 ft. tall in an 8-in. pot, taller in a larger one.

DICKSONIA
Dicksoniaceae
TREE FERNS

✎	ZONES VARY BY SPECIES
☼ ◐ ●	FULL SUN IN COOLER CLIMATES ONLY
●	REGULAR WATER

Hardy, slow growing, from Southern Hemisphere. Easy to transplant and establish. See Ferns for culture.

D. antarctica. TASMANIAN TREE FERN. Zones 8, 9, 14–17, 19–24; H1. Native to southeastern Australia, Tasmania. Hardiest of tree ferns; well-established plants tolerate 20°F/–7°C. Thick, red-brown, fuzzy trunk grows slowly to 15 ft. Many arching, 3–6-ft. fronds grow from top of trunk; mature fronds are more finely cut than those of Australian tree fern (*Cyathea*).

Dicksonia antarctica

D. squarrosa. Zones 17, 23, 24; H1. Native to New Zealand. Slender, dark trunk grows slowly to 20 ft. tall. Flat crown of 8-ft.-long, stiff, leathery fronds with whitish undersides. Much less frequently grown than *D. antarctica*.

DICLIPTERA
Acanthaceae
PERENNIALS

✎	ZONES VARY BY SPECIES
☼ ◐	FULL SUN OR PARTIAL SHADE
◌ ◔ ●	WATER NEEDS VARIES BY SPECIES

Tender perennials with narrow, tubular, two-lipped blossoms. Where stems are not killed to ground by frost, shear to about 6 in. high in late winter.

D. resupinata. Zones 13, 18–23; root hardy to about 22°F/–6°C. Native to washes and rocky slopes from southeastern Arizona and southwestern New Mexico into Mexico. Open, sparse growth to 2 ft. tall, 2–3 ft. wide. Elongated heart-shaped, 1-in.-long leaves are dark green, with an attractive purplish cast in cool weather. Slender, rosy purple, ¾-in.-long flowers from late spring to fall. Sometimes reseeds but is not invasive. Little or no water.

Dicliptera suberecta

D. suberecta (Jacobinia suberecta, Justicia suberecta). Zones 12, 13, 15–17, 19, 21–24. Native to Uruguay. Woody-based perennial 2 ft. tall, 1½ ft. wide, with grayish green, softly downy leaves 1½–3 in. long and half as wide. Summertime clusters of bright orange-red, 1½-in.-long flowers attract hummingbirds. Moderate to regular water.

DICTAMNUS albus
GAS PLANT, FRAXINELLA
Rutaceae
PERENNIAL

✎	ZONES 1–9
☼ ◐	FULL SUN OR LIGHT SHADE
● ●	MODERATE TO REGULAR WATER
⬨	OIL FROM IMMATURE SEED CAPSULES MAY CAUSE AN ALLERGIC SKIN REACTION

Native Europe to northern China. Sturdy, long lived, extremely permanent in colder climates, need-

ing little care once established. Forms clumps 2½–4 ft. high, 3 ft. wide. In early summer, produces loose spires of blossoms at branch tips; each flower resembles a wild azalea, with narrow petals and prominent greenish stamens. Pink is the basic color, but nurseries offer lilac purple 'Purpureus' and white 'Albiflorus'. Seedpods that follow can be left in place for fall interest. Glossy olive green leaves with 9 to 11 leaflets, each 1–3 in. long, are handsome throughout the growing season.

Dictamnus albus
'Purpureus'

Plant emits strong lemony scent when rubbed or brushed against. In warm, humid weather, oils from immature seed capsules may briefly ignite if you hold a lighted match immediately beneath a flower cluster—hence the common name "gas plant" (this "ignition test" does not harm plant).

Effective in borders; good cut flower. Divide infrequently, since divisions are difficult to establish and often take 2 or 3 years to bloom well. Propagate from seed sown in fall or spring; or take root cuttings in spring.

DIDISCUS coeruleus.
See **TRACHYMENE coerulea**

DIEFFENBACHIA
DUMB CANE
Araceae
PERENNIALS

✎	ZONES 24; H1, H2; OR INDOORS
☼ ◐ ●	SUN OR SHADE; BRIGHT INDIRECT LIGHT
●	MODERATE WATER
⬨	SAP BURNS MOUTH, MAY PARALYZE VOCAL CORDS

From forests of tropical America. Grown for their strikingly variegated evergreen foliage—in colors varying from dark green to yellow

green and chartreuse, with variegations in white or pale cream. In warmest climates, will grow year-round outdoors, either potted or in the ground as accent plants. Elsewhere, use them indoors. Small plants generally have single stems, while older ones may develop multiple stems. Taller than wide; those listed here are 1½–2 ft. wide. Mature plants bear flowers resembling odd, narrow callas (*Zantedeschia*).

Give container plants fast-draining potting mix and feed with half-strength liquid fertilizer bimonthly in spring and summer. Underfed, underwatered plants show amazing endurance, recovering from severe wilting when better conditions come. Repotting is necessary when roots begin pushing plant up out of pot. Once repotted, plants usually send out new basal shoots. Sudden change from low to high light level will burn leaves, but you can move houseplants to a sheltered patio or lanai in summer. If plants get leggy, you can cut them back to 6 in. above the soil line; gangly specimens cut back in this way will usually resprout with multiple stems. Or start new plants by air layering or taking stem cuttings; discard the original, overly leggy looking plant.

Some of the types described below may be sold as varieties of *D. seguine*.

Dieffenbachia amoena

D. amoena. To 6 ft. or taller. Broad, dark green, 1½-ft.-long leaves with narrow, slanting white stripes on either side of midrib.

D. × bausei. To 3 ft. or taller. Greenish yellow, 1-ft.-long leaves have deep green blotches and white flecks.

D. 'Exotica'. To 3–4 ft. tall, with small leaves featuring dull green edges and extensive creamy white variegation. Midrib is creamy white.

D. maculata (D. picta). Grows to 6 ft. or taller. Broad, oval, green leaves reach 10 in. or longer, have greenish white dots and patches. Variety 'Rudolph Roehrs' has pale chartreuse foliage blotched with ivory and edged with green. Foliage of 'Superba' is thicker and slightly more durable than that of species and is more generously marked with creamy dots and patches.

DIERAMA

FAIRY WAND
Iridaceae
PERENNIALS FROM CORMS

☀	ZONES 4–24
☼	FULL SUN
●	REGULAR WATER

Native to South Africa. Evergreen; will die to the ground in extreme cold. Swordlike leaves to 2 ft. long; slender, tough, arching stems 4–7 ft. tall, topped in late spring or early summer with pendulous flowers that range in color from purplish pink to other pink shades to white. Blooms of *D. pendulum* are bell shaped, those of *D. pulcherrimum* more funnel shaped.

Dierama pulcherrimum

Effective against background of dark green shrubs or at end of pool where graceful form can be displayed. Plant in spring, setting corms 3–5 in. deep and about 2 ft. apart. When dividing clumps, include several corms in each division.

DIETES

FORTNIGHT LILY, AFRICAN IRIS
Iridaceae
PERENNIALS FROM RHIZOMES

☀	ZONES 8, 9, 12–24; H1, H2
☼ ☼	FULL SUN OR PARTIAL SHADE
● ●	MODERATE TO REGULAR WATER

Irislike plants with fans of stiff, narrow evergreen leaves; form dense, long-lasting clumps. Flow-ers resembling small Japanese irises consist of three outer and three inner segments; they appear on branched stalks throughout spring, summer, and fall, some-times well into winter in mild climates. Bloom bursts seem to occur at 2-week intervals, hence the common name "fortnight lily." Flowers come in solid colors— white, cream, yellow; each of the three outer segments features a small blotch of contrasting orange, yellow, or brown. Each flower lasts only a day (with one exception), but supply of flowers on a stem is seemingly endless. Excellent in permanent landscape plantings with pebbles and rocks, shrubs and other long-lived perennials.

Plant from containers (bare rhi-zomes are not sold) at any time of year, setting plants about 2 ft. apart. All types look best with good soil and regular watering, but once established will perform sat-isfactorily even in poor soil or with infrequent or erratic water-ing. Clumps can remain undis-turbed for years; when you need to divide, do so in fall or winter.

D. bicolor. From South Africa. Stems 2–3 ft. tall. Flowers about 2 in. wide and circular in outline, light yellow with dark brown to maroon blotches. Flower stems last only one year.

D. grandiflora (D. iridioides 'Johnsonii'). From South Africa. In general aspect, this is a some-what taller (up to 3-ft.), larger ver-sion of *D. iridioides* and is usually sold as a variety of that species. Other differences include brown markings at the bases of inner segments and, on outer segments, yellow blotches that are actually bearded. Unlike all others, this species has flowers that last for 3 days before folding; flower stems are perennial (see *D. iridioides*).

D. hybrids. 'Lemon Drops' and 'Orange Drops' are hybrids of *D. bicolor* and resemble it save for flower color. 'Lemon Drops' is ivory with yellow blotches, 'Orange Drops' ivory with orange blotches. As is true for their other parent, *D. iridioides,* these hybrids' flower stems last more than a year; see below for care.

D. iridioides (D. vegeta, Moraea iridioides). From East Africa. Stems to 3 ft. tall. Waxy white flowers to 3 in. across have yellow-orange blotches, a few orange marks at bases of inner three segments; three style arms— appendages radiating from flower's center—are usually pale violet. To

Dietes iridioides

prevent self-sowing and prolong bloom, break off blossoms individ-ually. Don't cut flower stems (they last for more than a year) until they clearly have stopped produc-ing blooms; then cut back to lower leaf joint near base of stem. For the plant sold as *D. iridioides* 'Johnsonii', see *D. grandiflora*.

DIGITALIS

FOXGLOVE
Scrophulariaceae
PERENNIALS AND BIENNIALS

☀	ZONES VARY BY SPECIES
☼ ☼ ●	EXPOSURE NEEDS VARY BY SPECIES
●	REGULAR WATER, EXCEPT AS NOTED
☣	ALL PARTS ARE POISONOUS IF INGESTED

Mainly from Europe, Mediter-ranean region. Erect plants 2–8 ft. high form low clumps of hairy gray-green leaves topped by spikes of tubular flowers shaped like fin-gertips of a glove; colors include purple, yellow, white, pastels. Blos-soms attract hummingbirds. Com-mon foxglove (*D. pupurea*) is widely grown for height and color display in shaded gardens, though it will thrive in full sun in cool-summer regions. In parts of Cali-fornia and the Pacific Northwest, it has escaped from gardens to deco-rate roadsides. Other, less well known species are deserving sub-jects for borders, woodland edges, and larger rock gardens. Most tend to be biennials, but some can be coaxed into a second year of bloom if spent flowers are removed before they set seed.

Foxgloves need moist, well-drained soil, appreciate enrich-ment. Set out plants in fall for bloom the following spring and summer. Sow seed in spring. Con-trol snails and slugs. After first flowering, cut off main spike; side shoots will develop and bloom late in the season. In hottest climates, plants will usually die out in sum-mer heat. Plants self-sow freely; blooms of volunteers are often white or light colored.

D. ferruginea. RUSTY FOXGLOVE. Biennial or short-lived perennial. Zones 1–10, 14–24. To 4 ft. tall, 1½ ft. wide, with stems densely clothed in deeply veined leaves. Long, dense spikes of ¾–1¼-in.-long, yellowish flowers netted with rusty red. Full sun or light shade.

D. grandiflora (D. ambigua). YELLOW FOXGLOVE. Biennial or short-lived perennial. Zones 1–10, 14–24. To 3 ft. tall, 1½ ft. wide. Toothed leaves wrap around stem. Flowers are 2–3 in. long, yellowish marked with brown. 'John Innes Tetra' is a choice selection to 20 in. tall, with gray-green leaves and pale yellow flowers richly netted with gold and brown. Full sun or light shade.

D. laevigata. Perennial. Zones 3b–10, 14–24. To 3 ft. high, 1½ ft. wide, with smooth, narrow dark green leaves and inch-long, creamy yellow flowers speckled with purplish brown. Full sun; tolerates light shade.

D. lanata. GRECIAN FOX-GLOVE. Biennial or short-lived perennial. Zones 2b–10, 14–24. To 2 ft. high and 1 ft. wide, with cream to light tan flowers netted with brown. Full sun or light shade.

D. lutea. Perennial. Zones 1–10, 14–24. Mediterranean native. To 2–2½ ft. tall, 15 in. wide, with nar-row, tightly packed spires of pale yellow flowers dotted with brown. Partial or full shade; can take full sun in cool-summer climates.

D. × mertonensis. Perennial. Zones 1–10, 14–24. Spikes to 2–3 ft. high, bearing attractive coppery rose blooms above a foot-wide clump of furry leaves. Though a hybrid, it comes true from seed. Partial or full shade; can take full sun in cool-summer climates.

D. obscura. NARROW-LEAF FOXGLOVE. Woody-based peren-nial. Zones 2–10, 14–24. To 1½ ft. tall, 1 ft. wide, with lance-shaped leaves and spikes of drooping brown-and-yellow bells. Takes full sun or light shade, well-drained but not rich soil, and occasional deep watering.

D. purpurea. COMMON FOXGLOVE. Biennial or short-lived perennial. Zones A2, A3; 1–24. Variable, appearing in

D

many garden forms. Bold, erect growth to 4 ft. or taller, with stems rising from clumps of large, rough, woolly light green leaves. Short-stalked stem leaves become smaller toward top of plant; these are the source of digitalis, a valued but highly poisonous medicinal drug. Pendulous flowers 2–3 in. long, borne in one-sided, 1–2-ft.-long spikes, purple with darker spots on lower, paler side. Partial or full shade; can take full sun in cool-summer climates.

Garden strains include Camelot, which reaches 3½–4 ft. tall in sun or shade and blooms consistently the first and second year in shades of rose, white, lavender, or cream with a speckled throat; 5-ft.-tall Excelsior, with fuller spikes than species and flowers held more horizontally to show off interior spotting; 3-ft. Foxy, which performs as an annual and blooms in 5 months from seed; 4-ft. Gloxiniiflora, bearing flowers that are larger and open wider than those of species; 3-ft.-high Peloric Mixed, with topmost flower of each spike open or bowl shaped and 3 in. wide; and Shirley, a tall (6-ft.), robust strain with a full range of colors.

D. thapsi. Perennial. Zones 2–10, 14–24. From Spain. To 1 ft. tall and wide, with furry foliage and short spires of drooping purplish pink flowers. Thrives under the same conditions as *D. obscura.* 'Spanish Peaks' is a selection chosen as outstanding by the Denver Botanic Garden.

Digitalis purpurea

DILL. See ANETHUM graveolens

DIMORPHOTHECA

AFRICAN DAISY, CAPE MARIGOLD
Asteraceae (Compositae)
ANNUALS

🌿	ZONES 1–24; BETTER IN WARM-SUMMER CLIMATES
☼	FULL SUN
💧	MODERATE WATER

Gay, free-blooming South African natives with daisy flowers, unsurpassed for winter and spring color in dry-summer, warm-winter areas. In those regions, broadcast seeds in late summer or early fall

where plants are to grow (preferably in light soil). In colder climates, sow in spring for summer bloom. Flowers close when shaded, on heavily overcast days, and at night. Use in broad masses as ground cover, in borders and parking strips, along rural roadsides, as filler among low shrubs. For other plants known as African daisy, see *Arctotis* and *Osteospermum fruticosum.*

D. barberae. See Osteospermum jucundum

D. ecklonis. See Osteospermum ecklonis

D. fruticosa. See Osteospermum fruticosum

D. pluvialis (D. annua). Branched stems 4–16 in. high. Leaves to 3½ in. long, 1 in. wide, coarsely toothed. Yellow-centered, 1–2-in.-wide flower heads, with rays that are white above, violet or purple beneath. Variety 'Glistening White', dwarf form with flower heads 4 in. across, is especially desirable.

D. sinuata (D. aurantiaca). Best known of annual African daisies. To 4–12 in. high. Narrow, 2–3-in.-long leaves with a few teeth or shallow cuts. Flowers 1½ in. wide with yellow centers or dark centers with flecks of yellow, and orange-yellow rays sometimes deep violet at base. Hybrids between this species and *D. pluvialis* come in white and shades of yellow and light orange, often with contrasting dark centers.

Dimorphotheca sinuata

Widely used for winter-to-spring color in Zones 10–13, where plantings reseed yearly. Provide some supplemental water if winter rains don't come; leave dry over summer. Highly invasive in hot desert regions; should not be used near parks, preserves, natural areas.

DIOON

Zamiaceae
CYCADS

🌿	ZONES VARY BY SPECIES
◐	PARTIAL SHADE
💧	REGULAR WATER

In general, resemble *Cycas revoluta* and take same culture. Dioons are more tender, even slower growing, and less frequently sold.

D. edule. Zones 12, 13, 17, 19–24; H1, H2. Very slow growing. Eventually forms cylindrical trunk 6–10 in. wide, 3 ft. high. Leaves spreading, slightly arching, 3–5 ft. long, made of many smooth-edged leaflets (sometimes toothed at tips on young plants). Leaves on young plants are dusty blue green, soft, feathery; those of mature plants are shiny, darker green, more rigid.

Dioon edule

D. spinulosum. Zones 21–24; H1, H2. Slow growth to 12 ft. high. Leaves to 5 ft. long, with up to 100 narrow, spine-toothed, dark green, 6–8-in.-long leaflets. Protect from frosts.

DIOSMA. See COLEONEMA

DIOSPYROS. See PERSIMMON

DIPLACUS aurantiacus. See **MIMULUS aurantiacus**

DIPLADENIA splendens. See **MANDEVILLA splendens**

DIPOGON lignosus. See **DOLICHOS lignosus**

DISANTHUS cercidifolius

Hamamelidaceae
DECIDUOUS SHRUB

🌿	ZONES 4–7, 14–17
☼ ◐	LIGHT SHADE IN HOTTEST CLIMATES
💧	REGULAR WATER

Native to Japan. Slender-branched shrub to 10–12 ft. tall and wide, grown for magnificent fall color.

Disanthus cercidifolius

Nearly round, smooth, 2–4-in.-wide leaves turn from bluish green to shades of deep red with orange tints with the onset of colder weather. Tiny, purplish fall flowers are mildly scented. Provide rich soil and protection from wind. No special pruning needed.

DISTICTIS

Bignoniaceae
EVERGREEN VINES

🌿	ZONES VARY BY SPECIES
☼ ◐	FULL SUN OR PARTIAL SHADE
💧	REGULAR WATER

These Mexican natives are spectacular vines for milder climates, reaching heights of 20–30 ft. Glossy leaves consist of two leaflets with a central, three-part tendril that plants use for climbing. All bear long-lasting, trumpet shaped flowers. Plant in good, well-drained soil; provide sturdy support, since growth is dense and heavy. Prune in winter to thin stems, control size.

D. buccinatoria (Bignonia cherere, Phaedranthus buccinatorius). BLOOD-RED TRUMPET VINE. Zones 8, 9, 14–24; H1. Oblong to oval leaflets 2–4 in. long. Clusters of 4-in.-long, yellow-throated flowers in orange red fading to bluish red; blossoms stand out well from vine. Blooms in bursts throughout year when weather warms. Give protected site in interior valleys of California.

Distictis buccinatoria

D. laxiflora (D. lactiflora, D. cinerea). VANILLA TRUMPET VINE. Zones 16, 22–24; H1, H2. More restrained than most trumpet vines and requires less pruning. Oblong, 2½-in.-long leaflets. Vanilla-scented, 3½-in.-long trumpets appear in generous clusters throughout warmer months, sometimes giving 8 months of bloom; they are violet at first, fading to lavender and white.

D. 'Rivers'. ROYAL TRUMPET VINE. Zones 16, 22–24; H1, H2. Plants sold under this name are nearly a match for *D. buccinatoria* in vigor and foliage and have flowers of about the same size that are mauve to purple with a yellow to orange throat. Sometimes labeled *D. riversii.*

Distictis 'Rivers'

DITTANY OF CRETE.
See **ORIGANUM dictamnus**

DIZYGOTHECA elegantissima.
See **SCHEFFLERA elegantissima**

DODECATHEON
SHOOTING STAR
Primulaceae
PERENNIALS

🖊	ZONES VARY BY SPECIES
☼ ◐	FULL SUN OR PARTIAL SHADE
●	REGULAR WATER DURING GROWTH AND BLOOM

Mostly native to the West. Form basal rosette of pale green leaves (which later dry up in summer heat). Spring flowers somewhat like small cyclamen blooms, few to many in a cluster on leafless stems ranging from a few inches to 2 ft. tall. Rarely available in nurseries; buy seed for types native to your area (not all are hardy everywhere) from specialists in native plant seeds. Give porous, rich, well-drained soil. Let soil dry out after bloom.

Many species with flower colors ranging from white to pink, laven-

Dodecatheon hendersonii

der to magenta. Western *D. hendersonii* (Zones 7–9, 14–24), for example, bears blossoms in white, pink shades, or magenta, carried 3–15 to each 1½-ft. stalk. Plant has 6-in. leaves, forms a clump just under a foot wide.

DODONAEA
HOP BUSH, HOPSEED BUSH
Sapindaceae
EVERGREEN SHRUBS

🖊	ZONES VARY BY SPECIES
☼ ◐	FULL SUN OR LIGHT SHADE
○ ◑ ●	LITTLE TO REGULAR WATER

Tough shrubs mostly from Australia, although the most common species, *D. viscosa,* is native to the American Southwest and Hawaii as well as to many other parts of the world. All tolerate wind, poor soil, heat. Foliage is finely divided and fernlike in some, undivided in others. Flowers are insignificant, but seedpods are often showy and long lasting.

D. adenophora, D. microzyga. Zones 8, 9, 12–24. Plants sold under these names are probably forms of *D. tenuifolia.* Spreading shrub 3–10 ft. tall and somewhat wider, with finely cut leaves and very showy red fruits.

D. boroniifolia. Zones 8, 9, 14–24. Grows 1½–6 ft. tall, 3–9 ft. wide, with spreading branches and shiny, dark green, finely cut leaves 1½ in. long. Fruiting capsules are pink to purplish red, ¾ in. wide.

D. viscosa. Zones 7–24; H1, H2. Native to many warmer regions, such as Arizona and Hawaii (where it is called 'a'ali'i). Fast-growing shrub with many upright stems; reaches 10–15 ft. high and spreads almost as wide (can be trained to tree form by cutting out all but single stem). Willowlike green leaves to 4 in.

long. Inconspicuous flowers followed in late spring or summer by ornamental, papery seed capsules that may be red, pink, tan, yellow, or green. In Hawaii, the capsules are used in leis.

'Purpurea', purple hop bush, is a selected form with strongly bronze-tinted foliage that darkens in winter; seedlings can vary greatly in color. Cutting-grown 'Saratoga' is uniformly deep purple. Seed capsules cream to pinkish in color. Plant purple-leafed kinds in full sun to retain rich foliage color; they will turn green in shade.

Dodonaea viscosa 'Purpurea'

You can prune all members of this species into an espalier or hedge or plant 6–8 ft. apart and leave unpruned for a big informal screen. Plants take any kind of soil, ocean winds, and dry desert heat. Quite tolerant of aridity when established but will also take regular water (grows well in flower beds).

DOG-TOOTH VIOLET.
See **ERYTHRONIUM dens-canis**

DOGWEED.
See **THYMOPHYLLA**

DOGWOOD. See **CORNUS**

DOLICHOS
Fabaceae (Leguminosae)
PERENNIAL VINES

🖊	ZONES VARY BY SPECIES
☼	FULL SUN
●	REGULAR WATER

These twining vines produce dense cover of light green leaves divided like fans into three leaflets.

D. lablab (Lablab purpureus). HYACINTH BEAN. Perennial vine

usually grown as annual. All zones. Fast growing to 10 ft. Broad, oval, medium green leaflets to 3–6 in. long. Sweet pea–shaped purple or white flowers in loose clusters on long stems stand out from foliage. Flowers followed by velvety, beanlike magenta purple pods to 2½ in. long. Grow like string beans for quick screening. Needs good drainage. Naturalized in Hawaii. 'Ruby Moon' has dark green leaves with purple undersides.

Dolichos lablab

D. lignosus (Dipogon lignosus). AUSTRALIAN PEA VINE. Zones 16, 17, 21–24; H2. Somewhat woody vine to 10 ft. or more, with small, triangular, 1½-in.-long leaflets and small rose purple flowers clustered at ends of long stalks. Evergreen in mild winters. Grow from seed and train on trellis or frame for summer screen.

DOLL'S EYES. See **ACTAEA alba**

DOMBEYA
Sterculiaceae
EVERGREEN SHRUBS AND TREES

🖊	ZONES 21–24; H2
☼ ◐	FULL SUN OR PARTIAL SHADE
◑ ●	WATER NEEDS VARY BY SPECIES

Around 225 species of trees and shrubs native to Africa, Madagascar, and nearby islands in the Indian Ocean. Grown primarily for their big, dense flower clusters, which dangle from branches on long stems. Many also have attractive large leaves.

D. cacuminum. STRAWBERRY SNOWBALL TREE. Native to Madagascar. Tree to 40–50 ft. tall and 15–25 ft. wide. Very large, maplelike leaves are glossy green. In spring, coral red flowers in

D

D

clusters to 1 ft. across hang from branches; these fall to the ground before drying to create a colorful carpet. Best in full sun with occasional deep irrigation.

Dombeya wallichii

D. wallichii. PINK BALL TREE. Zones 19–24. Native to East Africa and Madagascar. Shrub or small tree to 15–25 ft. tall and 15–30 ft. wide. Large (6–8-in.), heart-shaped, bright green leaves pick up brownish cast with first frost. Fragrant pink flowers appear in 4–6-in.-wide clusters in fall to winter; these fade to light pink then brown as they dry on the plant. Best with regular water.

DONKEY TAIL.
See **SEDUM morganianum**

DORONICUM
LEOPARD'S BANE
Asteraceae (Compositae)
PERENNIALS

🌱	ZONES A2, A3; 1–7, 14–17
☼	PARTIAL SHADE
💧	REGULAR WATER

Summer is the season for most yellow daisies, but these European natives bear a profusion of showy daisylike flowers in early to mid-spring. Blossoms are carried on long, slender, branching stems that rise from low, spreading, dense clumps of tooth-edged dark green leaves that are rounded to heart-shaped at base. Good cut flowers.

Doronicum cordatum

Mark location of plants before they die back, and provide some moisture during dormancy. Young plants bloom best; divide clumps every 2 or 3 years in early autumn. Tolerate full sun in cool-summer climates; light, dappled, or partial shade otherwise.

D. cordatum (D. caucasicum, D. columnae, D. orientale). Flower heads to 2 in. wide, borne singly on 1–1½-ft. stems above a foot-wide foliage clump. Usually dies back in summer. 'Magnificum' and 'Finesse' are a little taller, with bigger blossoms. 'Little Leo' is compact, growing just 12–15 in. tall and wide.

D. plantagineum. PLANTAIN LEOPARD'S BANE. Larger, coarser-leafed plant than *D. cordatum*, suitable for a wild garden. Stout stems 2½–4 ft. tall rise above a 2-ft.-wide clump, each producing a few 2–4-in. flowers. Goes dormant in summer.

DOROTHEANTHUS
bellidiformis
LIVINGSTONE DAISY
Aizoaceae
SUCCULENT ANNUAL

🌱	ZONES A2; 1–24
☼	FULL SUN
💧	MODERATE WATER

From South Africa. Unlike most others, this ice plant is an annual. Pretty and useful temporary carpet. Trailing, basally branching plant a few inches high, with fleshy, bright green leaves and daisylike, 2-in. flowers in white, pink, orange, red. Sow seed in warm weather. Comes into bloom quickly. Attracts bees. Tolerates poor, dry soil.

Dorotheanthus bellidiformis

DOUBLE BRIDAL WREATH.
See **SPIRAEA cantoniensis**

DOUGLAS FIR.
See **PSEUDOTSUGA menziesii**

DOVE TREE.
See **DAVIDIA involucrata**

DOXANTHA unguis-cati.
See **MACFADYENA unguis-cati**

DRABA
Brassicaceae (Cruciferae)
PERENNIALS

🌱	ZONES VARY BY SPECIES
☼	FULL SUN
💧	REGULAR WATER

Some 300 species native to mountainous and subarctic regions of the world. All are low mat- or cushion-forming plants with tightly clustered, tiny leaves in rosettes and four-petaled yellow (rarely white) flowers in short, spikelike clusters. Rock garden plants that require perfect drainage, dislike soggy soil. Can endure great cold. The following are two of the most commonly planted species.

Draba aizoides

D. aizoides. Zones 2–7. Tufts of tiny rosettes form clumps 2–4 in. across. Flowering stems up to 4 in. tall hold four to ten or more bright yellow flowers.

D. oligosperma. Zones 1–7. One of more than a dozen species native to the Rocky Mountain area. Makes silvery mats that spread up to 1 ft. wide topped with loose clusters of yellow flowers carried on 4-in. stems.

DRACAENA
Agavaceae
EVERGREEN PALMLIKE TREES

🌱	ZONES VARY BY SPECIES; OR INDOORS
☼	SUN OR PART SHADE; BRIGHT INDIRECT LIGHT
💧	MODERATE WATER

Foliage plants most widely grown indoors or on patio or lanai. Some show graceful, fountainlike form with broad, curved, ribbonlike leaves, occasionally striped with chartreuse or white. Others have very stiff, sword-shaped leaves. Outdoors, give all but *D. draco* a wind-protected site. In containers, water only when top ½–1 in. of soil is dry. Almost never bloom as

houseplants. For other plants often called dracaena, see *Cordyline*.

D. australis. See Cordyline australis

D. deremensis. Zones 24; H2. Native to tropical Africa. Most commonly sold is variety 'Warneckii': erect, slow growing to an eventual 15 ft. tall, 3 ft. wide, with 2-ft.-long, 2-in.-wide leaves in rich green striped white and gray. 'Bausei' is green with white center stripe; 'Longii' has broader white center stripe; 'Janet Craig' has broad, dark green leaves. Compact versions of 'Janet Craig' and 'Warneckii' exist.

D. draco. DRAGON TREE. Zones 16, 17, 21–24; H1, H2. Native to Canary Islands. Stout trunk with upward-reaching or spreading branches topped by clusters of heavy, 2-ft.-long, sword-shaped leaves. Grows slowly to 20 ft. high and as wide. Makes odd but interesting silhouette. Clusters of greenish white flowers form at branch ends. After blossoms drop, stemmy clusters remain. Trim them off to keep plants neat.

Dracaena draco

D. fragrans. CORN PLANT. Zones 21, 23, 24; H2. Native to West Africa. Upright, eventually reaching 20 ft. high and 5 ft. wide, but slow growing. Heavy, ribbon-like, blue-green leaves to 3 ft. long, 4 in. wide. (Typical plant in 8-in. pot will bear leaves about 1½ ft. long.) 'Massangeana' has broad yellow band in center of leaf. Other striped varieties are 'Lindenii' and 'Victoriae'.

D. marginata. Zones 21, 23, 24; H2. Very easy to grow, very popular. To 12 ft. tall, 5–6 ft. wide. Slender, erect, smooth gray stems carry chevron markings where old leaves have fallen. Stems topped by crowns of narrow, leathery leaves to 2 ft. long, ½ in. wide. Leaves are

Dracaena marginata

eep glossy green with narrow
argin of purplish red. If plant
rows too tall, cut off crown and
eroot it. New crowns will appear
n old stem. 'Tricolor' ('Candy
ane') adds narrow gold stripe to
reen and red.

D. sanderana. Zones 21, 23, 24;
12. Native to West Africa. Neat
nd upright, to 6–10 ft. tall, 2 ft.
ide, somewhat resembling young
orn plant. Strap-shaped, 9-in.-
ng leaves striped with white.

RAGON TREE.
ee **DRACAENA draco**

REPANOSTACHYUM.
ee **BAMBOO**

RIMYS winteri
INTER'S BARK
Winteraceae
VERGREEN TREE

🗓 ZONES 5–9, 14–24

☀ ◑ FULL SUN IN COOLER CLIMATES
ONLY

💧 REGULAR WATER

Native to southern Chile and
Argentina. Slender tree to 25 ft. tall,
20 ft. wide; distinguished chiefly by

Drimys winteri

---

its attractive foliage and dignified
presence. Stems and branches,
which tend to droop gracefully,
have aromatic, mahogany red bark.
Leathery, fragrant, bright green
leaves are elliptical, 5–10 in. long.
Small clusters of jasmine-scented,
inch-wide, creamy white flowers
appear in winter and spring. Tree
is usually multistemmed but easily
trained to a single trunk. It may
require pruning from time to
time to maintain a pleasingly
symmetrical outline. Provide a
frost-sheltered location in Zones
5–7. Requires good drainage.

DROPSEED. See **SPOROBOLUS**

DROPWORT.
See **FILIPENDULA vulgaris**

DROSANTHEMUM
Aizoaceae
SUCCULENT PERENNIALS

🗓 ZONES 14–24; H1

☀ FULL SUN

💧 LITTLE TO MODERATE WATER

These two South African ice plants
are often confused with each other.
Leaves of both are covered by
glistening dots that look like ice
crystals; both also have flowers
with many narrow petals, bloom
in late spring and early summer,
and endure poor soil. Beyond that,
however, they are quite different.

Drosanthemum floribundum

D. floribundum. ROSEA ICE
PLANT. Grows to 6 in. tall, but
stems trail to considerable length
or drape over rocks, walls. Best
ice plant for reducing erosion on
steep slopes (plant 1½ ft. apart).
Pale pink, ¾-in.-wide flowers
form shimmering sheets of
bloom, attract bees. Often sold
as *D. hispidum*.

D. hispidum. To 2 ft. tall, 3 ft.
wide, less inclined to stem-root
than *D. floribundum*. Showy, 1-in.
purple flowers.

DRUMSTICKS.
See **ALLIUM sphaerocephalum**,
CRASPEDIA globosa

DRYAS
Rosaceae
PERENNIALS

🗓 ZONES A1–A3; 1–6

☀ FULL SUN

💧 MODERATE WATER

Choice plants for rock gardens.
Evergreen or partially so; somewhat shrubby at base, forming a
carpet of leafy, creeping stems.
Oblong leaves look like little oak
leaves. Bloom from late spring into
summer, bearing shiny white or
yellow flowers that resemble
strawberry blossoms. Ornamental
seed capsules with silvery white
tails follow the blooms.

D. drummondii. To 4 in. high,
spreading 3 ft. or wider. Leaves
1½ in. long, white and woolly
beneath. Nodding, ¾-in. yellow
flowers.

D. octopetala. To 2–3 in. high
and 3 ft. wide, with inch-long
leaves and erect, 1½-in. white
flowers.

Dryas octopetala

D. × suendermannii. Hybrid
between the two species above.
To 4 in. high, 3 ft. wide. Leaves
1–1½ in. long. Nodding, 1¼-in.
flowers are yellowish in bud, white
in full bloom.

DRYLAND TEA TREE.
See **MELALEUCA lanceolata**

DRYOPTERIS
WOOD FERN
Polypodiaceae
FERNS

🗓 ZONES VARY BY SPECIES

☀ ◑ PARTIAL OR FULL SHADE

💧 REGULAR WATER

One of the largest genera of ferns,
with well over 100 species from
many parts of the world. Use in
shade or woodland gardens, where
their fronds contrast nicely with
the foliage of other plants, especially large-leafed sorts such as
hostas and hydrangeas. Wood
ferns grow best in rich soil with
plenty of organic matter and regular moisture. They tolerate dry
shade. As a rule they are rather
forgiving; a good choice for begin-

---

ning gardeners. These plants
are seldom bothered by deer or
other pests.

D. affinis. GOLDEN MALE
FERN. Semievergreen. Zones
3b–9, 14–24. Native to Europe and
southwestern Asia. To 3–5 ft. high
and wide. Finely cut, arching
fronds are chartreuse green when
they unfold, dark green later. 'Cristata' ('Cristata The King') is more
compact, with 3-ft. arching fronds
with crested tips. 'Crispa Gracilis' is
an evergreen dwarf form to only
6–12 in. tall and wide.

D. carthusiana. (D. spinulosa).
NARROW BUCKLER FERN,
SHIELD FERN. Deciduous. Zones
A2; 1–9, 14–17. A native of
Europe, Asia, and North America.
Clumps reach 2 ft. tall, 1 ft. across.
Coarsely cut, yellowish green
fronds to 6–18 in. tall, half as
wide, have shaggy black scales on
frond stem and lower part of
midrib. Tolerates bog conditions.

D. × complexa 'Robust'.
Semievergreen. Zones 3b–9,
14–17. Sometimes sold as *D. filix-
mas* 'Undulata Robusta', this
hybrid is similar to parent *D. affinis*, with 3–4-ft.-long, dark green
fronds that are deeply divided,
with undulating edges. Vigorous
and easy to grow.

D. dilatata (D. austriaca).
BROAD BUCKLER FERN. Usually
deciduous. Zones 2–7, 14–17.
From western and central Europe.
Vigorous grower to 3–4 ft. high
and wide, with rich green fronds
that are broadly triangular. Stalks
and midribs are covered in dark
brown scales. Adaptable and easy
to grow. 'Lepidota Cristata' is a
2-ft.-tall form with narrower
fronds.

D. erythrosora. AUTUMN
FERN. Semievergreen. Zones 2–9,
14–24. Native to China and Japan.
Erect growth to 2 ft. tall, 1½ ft.
wide. One of the few ferns with
seasonal color variation. Expanding fronds in spring are a blend of

Dryopteris erythrosora

copper, pink, and yellow; they turn green in summer, then rusty brown in fall. Bright red spores, produced on leaf undersides, are an attractive winter feature. 'Brilliance' has especially bright coppery-red new growth.

D. filix-mas. MALE FERN. Usually evergreen, sometimes deciduous. Zones 2–9, 14–17. Native to much of the Northern Hemisphere. Grows 2–5 ft. tall and wide, with finely cut, medium green fronds to 1 ft. wide. 'Linearis Polydactyla', to 2½ ft. tall, is easy to grow and has very narrow leaf divisions with spreading, fingerlike tips; fronds are favorites for cut arrangements. All male ferns tolerate considerable drought when grown in full shade.

D. wallichiana. WALLICH'S WOOD FERN. Semievergreen. Zones 4–6, 14–17. Native to India, China. Stately fern 3–5 ft. high, not quite as wide. Bright golden green fronds turn dark green as they mature; brown stems have shiny black scales. Slow growing.

DUCHESNEA indica
INDIAN MOCK STRAWBERRY
Rosaceae
PERENNIAL

| 🌿 ZONES 1–24; H1, H2 |
| ☀️ ☁️ ● SUN OR SHADE |
| 💧 MODERATE WATER |

Native to Japan, eastern Asia, India. Grows like strawberry, with trailing stems that root firmly along ground. Bright green, long-stalked leaves with three leaflets. Yellow, ½-in. blossoms are followed by red, ½-in., nearly tasteless fruit that stands above foliage rather than under leaves as in true strawberry. Grows readily without much care. Best used as ground cover among open shrubs or small

Duchesnea indica

trees. Plant 1–1½ ft. apart. In a well-watered garden, it can become a rampant invader. Fruit attracts birds.

DUDLEYA
Crassulaceae
SUCCULENT PERENNIALS

| 🌿 ZONES VARY BY SPECIES |
| ☀️ FULL SUN |
| 💧 MODERATE WATER |

Native to California, Arizona, coastal Oregon, Baja California. About 40 species are known, some common on California's coastal cliffs or inland hills.

Best known species in cultivation is Baja California native *D. brittonii* (Zones 16, 17, 21–24), with 1½-ft.-wide leaf rosettes on stems that gradually lengthen into 1–2-ft. trunks; these lean or become prostrate as the plant ages. Fleshy leaves are covered with a heavy coat of chalky powder that can be rubbed off. When plants flourish, they produce reddish stalks with little yellow flowers in spring. Striking plant when

Dudleya brittonii

well grown; needs bright light and shelter from rain, hail, and frost. Best under glass or plastic roof to keep powder from being washed off.

Others are valued for use in containers, rock gardens, low borders. *D. caespitosa* (from Southern California; grows in Zones 9, 14–17, 19–24) and *D. farinosa* (Northern California and southern Oregon coast; succeeds in Zones 5, 7, 14–17, 19–24) are familiar sea-cliff plants; both are sometimes called cliff lettuce.

DUMB CANE.
See **DIEFFENBACHIA**

DURANTA
Verbenaceae
EVERGREEN SHRUBS

| 🌿 ZONES VARY BY SPECIES |
| ☀️ FULL SUN |
| 💧 REGULAR WATER |
| ☠️ D. ERECTA BERRIES ARE POISONOUS IF INGESTED |

Glossy green leaves arranged in pairs or whorls along the stems. Attractive blue flowers in clusters draw butterflies in summer, are followed by bunches of berrylike yellow fruit. Plants sold as *D. stenostachya* are often actually *D. erecta*; distinguishing characteristics are described below. Use as quick, tall screen. Thrive in hot-summer areas. Need continual thinning and pruning to stay under control.

Duranta erecta

D. erecta (D. repens, D. plumieri). SKY FLOWER, GOLDEN DEWDROP, PIGEON BERRY. Zones 13, 16, 17–24; H1, H2. Native to southern Florida, West Indies, Mexico to Brazil. Fast growing to 10–25 ft. tall, 6–10 ft. wide. Tends to form multistemmed clumps; branches often drooping and vinelike. Stems may or may not have sharp spines. Oval to roundish leaves are 1–2 in. long, rounded or pointed at tip. Tubular violet-blue flowers flare to less than ½ in. wide. Waxy yellow berries in clusters 1–6 in. long. 'Alba' has white flowers. 'Sweet Memory' is thornless, with flower petals edged in white. 'Gold Mound', only 1½ ft. high and wide, has brilliant gold leaves; it rarely flowers but is excellent for adding color to container plantings.

D. stenostachya. BRAZILIAN SKY FLOWER. Zones 13, 16, 21–23; H2. Not as hardy as *D. erecta;* seems to require more heat. Makes neater, more compact shrub than *D. erecta,* growing to about 4–6 ft. tall, 3–5 ft. wide (under ideal conditions, 15 ft. high). Stems are spineless. Leaves

are larger (3–8 in. long) than those of *D. erecta* and taper to long, slender point. Lavender-blue flowers are also somewhat larger; fruit clusters grow to 1 ft. long.

DUSTY MILLER. This name is given to a number of plants with gray foliage. The dusty miller of one region may be unknown in another. Among many dusty millers are *Artemisia stellerana, Centaurea cineraria, C. gymnocarpa, Chrysanthemum ptarmiciflorum, Lychnis coronaria, Senecio cineraria,* and *S. viravira.*

DUTCHMAN'S PIPE.
See **ARISTOLOCHIA**

DYMONDIA
margaretae
Asteraceae (Compositae)
PERENNIAL

| 🌿 ZONES 15–24 |
| ☀️ ☁️ FULL SUN OR LIGHT SHADE |
| 💧💧 MODERATE TO REGULAR WATER |

Ground cover native to South Africa. Forms a tight mat 2–3 in. high, spreading slowly by offsets to 20 in. wide. Narrow (⅛-in.), evergreen leaves are 2–3 in. long, deep grayish green above, rolled in at the edges to show cottony white undersides. Summer flowers are yellow, 1–1½-in.-wide daisies half-buried in the foliage. Deep roots give established plants considerable drought tolerance, but they'll spread faster if watered. Use between paving blocks and stepping-stones, in rock gardens; can take light foot traffic.

Dymondia margaretae

DYPSIS (Neodypsis, Chrysalidocarpus)
Arecaceae (Palmae)
EVERGREEN TREES

| 🌿 ZONES VARY BY SPECIES; OR INDOORS |
| ☀️ ☁️ EXPOSURE NEEDS VARY BY SPECIES |
| 💧💧 WATER NEEDS VARY BY SPECIES |

Madagascar natives better known by the alternative botanical names shown above. Both of these tropical species are rather tender, small

Dypsis lutescens

…medium-size feather palms
…ith graceful foliage and attractive
…unks. Good container plants for
…atio, lanai. Give indoor plants
…right filtered light.

**D. decaryi (Neodypsis
…ecaryi). TRIANGLE PALM.**
…ones 20–24; H2. Slow growing,
…ngle-trunked palm reaches
…8–20 ft. tall, 12–15 ft. wide.
…runk is triangular in cross sec-
…on because heavily keeled leaf-
…talks grow in three ranks about
…e stem. Gray-green fronds to
…5 ft. long are strongly upright but
…rching at tips. Native to arid parts
…f Madagascar and requires little
…ater. Full sun or light shade.

**D. lutescens (Chrysalido-
…arpus lutescens, Areca lute-
…cens). CANE PALM.** Zones 23
…light shade), 24; H1, H2 (full sun).
…lumping palm with slender yel-
…owish trunks, yellow-green leaves,
…nd clusters of golden yellow fruit.
…low growth to 28 ft. tall, 20 ft.
…vide; unlikely to reach that size in
…alifornia. Protect from hot, dry
…vind. Drought tolerant but does
…est with regular water. Moderate
…alt tolerance.

…DYSSODIA.
…See **THYMOPHYLLA**

E

…ASTER CACTUS.
…See **RHIPSALIDOPSIS gaertneri**

…ASTER EGG BUSH. See
…REMOPHILA racemosa

…ASTER LILY VINE.
…See **BEAUMONTIA grandiflora**

ECHEVERIA
Crassulaceae
SUCCULENT PERENNIALS

- ZONES VARY BY SPECIES
- ☼ ◑ FULL SUN OR PARTIAL SHADE, EXCEPT AS NOTED
- ◐ MODERATE WATER, EXCEPT AS NOTED

Mexican natives that form rosettes
of fleshy green or gray-green
leaves, often marked with deeper
colors. Long, slender, sometimes
branched clusters of bell-shaped,
nodding flowers, usually pink, red,
or yellow. Good in rock gardens.
Those that grow in Zone 12 need
cool spot, partial shade there. Those
suitable for Zone 13 need extra
attention to grow outdoors in that
area. Some types make good
houseplants.

**E. agavoides (Urbinia
agavoides).** Zones 8, 9, 12–24.
Rosettes 6–8 in. across. Stiff, fleshy,
sharp-pointed leaves are smooth
and bright green, marked deep
reddish brown at tips and edges.
Flower stalks to 1½ ft. bear small
red-and-yellow blooms.

Echeveria agavoides

E. crenulata. Zones 17, 21–24;
or indoors. Loose rosettes, 1½ ft.
across, on short, thick stems. Pale
green or white-powdered leaves
grow to 1 ft. long and 6 in. wide,
with wavy, crimped, purplish red
edges. Flower clusters to 3 ft. high,
with a few yellow-and-red flowers.
Striking plant. Shelter from
hottest sun; water frequently
during warm weather.

E. elegans. HEN AND CHICKS.
Zones 8, 9, 12–24. Tight grayish
white rosettes to 4 in. across,
spreading freely by offsets. Pink
flowers lined in yellow, in clusters
to 8 in. long. Useful for pattern
planting, edging, containers. Can
burn in hot summer sun.

E. hybrids. Zones 8, 9, 12–24;
or indoors. Generally have large,
loose rosettes of big leaves on
single or branched stems; plant
size varies by hybrid. Leaves are
crimped, waved, wattled, or heavily
shaded with red, bronze, or purple.

All are splendid potted plants;
they do well in open ground in
mild-summer areas. Among them
are 'Arlie Wright', with large, open
rosettes of wavy-edged, pinkish
leaves; 'Cameo', with large blue-
gray leaves, each centered with a
large raised bump of the same
color; and 'Perle von Nürnberg',
with pearly lavender-blue foliage.
'Doris Taylor' is smaller, with
short, close-set leaves densely covered with short hairs. Showy, nodding flowers are red and yellow.

**E. × imbricata. HEN AND
CHICKS.** Zones 8, 9, 12–24.
Rosettes 4–6 in. across, saucer
shaped, gray green. Loose clusters
of small, bell-shaped, orange-red
flowers. Makes offsets very freely.
Probably most common hen and
chicks in California gardens.

Echeveria × imbricata

**E. secunda. HEN AND
CHICKS.** Zones 8, 9, 14–24. Gray-
green or blue-green rosettes to
4 in. across. Makes offsets freely.
E. s. glauca (E. glauca) leaves are
faintly edged purple red, and the
blue-green rosettes have a
purplish tinge.

E. setosa. Zones 17, 23, 24.
Dense rosettes to 4 in. across are
dark green, and densely covered
with stiff white hairs. Red flowers
are tipped with yellow. Good
choice for rock gardens, shallow
containers. Very tender.

ECHINACEA
CONEFLOWER
Asteraceae (Compositae)
PERENNIALS

- ZONES A2, A3; 1–24
- ☼ FULL SUN
- ◐◐ MODERATE TO REGULAR WATER

These are tough, colorful perennials from central and eastern
North America. Daisylike flowers,
usually with narrow, arching rays,
have brownish orange, dome-
shaped centers and are held on
straight stems above clumps of
bristly foliage. Flowers are often
lightly fragrant. Generally bloom
over a long period in summer
(may start in spring in mild-
winter climates). Flowering may
continue until frost.

Use on the outskirts of gardens
or in wide borders with other
robust perennials. Also excellent in
containers. Generally do not need
staking. Perform well in summer
heat (though not in the hottest
desert areas, where they are
mainly spring blooming). Good
cut flowers. Clumps spread slowly,
become crowded after 3 or 4 years.
Fleshy rootstocks can be difficult
to separate; divide carefully, making sure each division has a shoot
and roots. Plantings can also be
increased by taking root cuttings,
seeding, or transplanting self-
sown seedlings.

E. hybrids. Complex crosses
have produced hybrid coneflowers
that are popular for their vigor
and extended color range. 'Mango
Meadowbrite' grows 2–3 ft. high
and wide; orange-yellow petals
surround orange-brown centers.
'Orange Meadowbrite' ('Art's
Pride') grows about the same size,
bears reddish orange flowers.
'Pixie Meadowbrite' grows only
about 1½ ft. tall and a bit wider,
with pink, nondrooping petals
surrounding a yellow-brown center. Plants in the Big Sky series
grow 2–3 ft. high and 2 ft. wide;
choices include butter yellow
'Sunrise', bright orange 'Sunset',
and reddish orange 'Sundown'
('Evan Saul').

**E. purpurea. PURPLE
CONEFLOWER.** Bristly, oblong,
3–4-in.-long leaves form a 2-ft.-
wide, dense foliage clump from
which rise sparsely leafed flowering stems 3–4 ft. high. Showy, 4-in.
flowers have drooping, rosy purple
rays and a central orange-brown
cone that resembles a beehive. If
faded flowers are left in place,
bristly seed heads hang on into
winter; seeds are favored by
finches.

Echinacea purpurea ▶

Many fine varieties are available. 'Bravado' is a 2-ft.-high selection with rosy purple blooms. 'Doubledecker' ('Doppelganger'), another 2-footer, has something extra: a second set of pink petals emerging from the top of the cone. 'Fragrant Angel' grows 2–2½ ft. tall with sweetly scented white flowers. 'Kim's Knee High' grows 1½–2 ft. tall and has clear pink flowers. 'Magnus' grows 3–4 ft. tall and has deep purplish pink, orange-centered flowers to 7 in. wide. 'Rubinstern' ('Ruby Star') grows 2–3 ft. high with carmine red, nondrooping rays. Both 'White Lustre' (2½ ft. tall) and 'White Swan' (1½–2 ft. high) have white rays and orange-yellow cones.

E. tennesseensis 'Rocky Top'. Narrow, medium green leaves form a mound 1½–2 ft. high and nearly as wide. Flowers 2–3 in. across consist of narrow, rich pink rays that bend distinctively upward around a large, greenish black cone.

ECHINOCACTUS
BARREL CACTUS
Cactaceae
CACTI

🌿	ZONES 12–24
☼ ◐	PARTIAL SHADE IN HOTTEST CLIMATES
💧	MODERATE WATER

Numerous kinds of large, cylindrical cacti with prominent ribs and stout thorns. Many are native to Southwest. Best known in gardens is *E. grusonii*, golden barrel, a Mexican cactus of slow growth to 4 ft. high, 2½ ft. in diameter. With age, often produces offsets to form clumps 6 ft. across. Showy, stiff, yellow 3-in. spines; yellow, 1½–2-in. flowers at top of plant in summer. Protect from hard frosts. Water every couple of weeks in summer.

Echinocactus grusonii

ECHINOCEREUS
HEDGEHOG CACTUS
Cactaceae
CACTI

🌿	ZONES VARY BY SPECIES
☼	FULL SUN
💧	MODERATE WATER

Nearly 50 species of hedgehog cactus grow in the southwestern U.S. and northern Mexico, with some growing at fairly high elevations in Utah and Colorado, where they are subject to freezing temperatures. All have cylindrical, ribbed bodies in clumps; showy red, yellow, purple, or white flowers with many rows of petals; and fleshy fruit, edible in some species. Although cold hardy in most zones, and often seen in collections, they are used in landscaping chiefly in desert or interior mountain gardens.

E. engelmannii. Zones 2, 3, 7, 10–24. Clumps 1–2 ft. tall, 3 ft. wide, with 3–4-in.-thick stems. Lavender to deep purplish red flowers 2–3 in. wide. Inch-long red fruits are edible.

Echinocereus engelmannii

E. triglochidiatus. CLARET CUP. Zones 2, 3, 10–14, 18–23. Dense clump, up to 3 ft. wide, sometimes with hundreds of 2–3-in.-diameter stems to a foot tall. Flowers are 3½ in. wide, orange to red; inch-long fruits (not edible) are pink to red.

ECHINOPS
GLOBE THISTLE
Asteraceae (Compositae)
PERENNIALS

🌿	ZONES A2, A3; 1–24
☼	FULL SUN
💧	MODERATE WATER

Well-behaved, decorative thistle relative for the perennial border. Rugged-looking, erect, rigidly branched plant 2–4 ft. tall and 2 ft. wide, with coarse, prickly, deeply cut gray-green leaves to 1 ft. long. Distinctive flower heads are spherical, about the size of golf balls;

Echinops exaltatus

they look like pincushions stuck full of tubular metallic blue pins. Bloom midsummer to late fall.

Plants may be offered as *E. exaltatus, E. humilis, E. ritro,* or possibly *E. sphaerocephalus.* Whatever name you encounter, you're likely to get a plant closely resembling the general description above. 'Taplow Blue' has bright blue blossoms on 3–4 ft. stems. 'Veitch's Blue' has darker blue flowers on a plant 2½–3 ft. high.

Grow from divisions in spring or fall, or sow seed in flats or open ground in spring. Provide average, well-drained soil and moderate water. (With enriched soil and regular moisture, may grow too robustly and require staking.) Clump can be left in place, undivided, for many years. Flowers are excellent for dried arrangements; cut them before they open and dry them upside down.

ECHINOPSIS
Cactaceae
CACTI

🌿	ZONES 8–10, 12–24, EXCEPT AS NOTED; OR INDOORS
☼	FULL SUN; BRIGHT SUNNY WINDOW
💧	REGULAR WATER

Small, spiny cacti from South America, generally grown in pots. Enormous number of species, hybrids, and selections; genus now includes plants formerly named *Lobivia* and *Lobivopsis* and still often sold under those names. All are showy and easy to grow, with many-petaled flowers in white and shades of yellow, pink, red, and orange. Free blooming during warm months if given good light, regular moisture from spring to fall, and fast-draining soil. Give little or no water in winter.

E. bruchii (Lobivia bruchii). SOUTH AMERICAN GOLDEN BARREL. Single, nearly round stem is 1 ft. tall and thick, with

yellow spines and red, 3-in. flowers.

E. caespitosa (Lobivia caespitosa). Clustered and cylindrical bodies, each 6 in. high and 2 in. thick, have dark, inch-long spines and orange, 3-in. flowers.

E. chamaecereus (Chamaecereus sylvestri). PEANUT CACTUS. To 4 in. high, 1–2 ft. wide. The cylindrical, ribbed, 2–3-in. joints fall off easily and root just as easily; even tiny ones produce flowers. Blooms are bright scarlet, nearly 3 in. long. Great favorite with children.

Echinopsis chamaecereus

E. chrysantha (Lobivia chrysantha). Single stem is 2½ in. high, 3 in. wide. Orange-yellow, 2-in.-wide flowers with purple center.

E. eyriesii. Zones 16, 17, 21–24. Cylindrical, dark-spined cactus to 6–12 in. high and 2–4 in. wide. Very large white flowers 8–10 in. long, 2–4 in. wide. Eventually forms clumps.

E. haageana (Lobivia haageana). Single stem grows 1 ft. tall, 3 in. thick. Flowers are 3 in. long, yellow with red throat.

E. hamatacantha. Zones 16, 17, 21–24. Rounded, to 4 in. high and 2 in. thick, with red to yellow, 3-in. flowers.

E. pentlandii (Lobivia boliviensis). Clustered round stems to 4 in. high and wide. Red, 2½-in.-long flowers.

ECHIUM
Boraginaceae
BIENNIALS, PERENNIALS, AND SHRUBS

🌿	ZONES VARY BY SPECIES
☼	FULL SUN
💧	LITTLE TO MODERATE WATER
⬧	E. VULGARE IS POISONOUS IF INGESTED

Grown for striking form and flower clusters. All do well in dry, poor soil but need good drainage. All are excellent for seacoast gardens. Flowers attract bees. Give

Echium candicans

...ttle or no water in mild-summer climates, weekly irrigation during summer in hotter areas.

E. candicans (E. fastuosum). PRIDE OF MADEIRA. Shrub. Zones 14–24. From Madeira, as its common name indicates. Large, picturesque plant to 5–6 ft. tall, 8–10 ft. wide, with many coarse, heavy branches. Narrow, hairy, gray-green leaves form roundish, irregular mounds at ends of stems. Great spikelike clusters of ½-in., bluish purple flowers stand out dramatically, well above foliage, in spring. Branch tips and developing flower spikes may be killed by late frosts. Use for bold effects against walls, at back of wide flower borders, on slopes. Prune lightly to keep bushy. Cut off faded flower spikes.

E. pininana. Woody-based perennial. Zones 16, 17, 22–24. From the Canary Islands. Sparsely branched, to 18 ft. tall, 2–3 ft. wide. Stems packed with long, narrow, bristly gray-green leaves and topped with long, spikelike clusters of blue flowers. Typically short lived and rarely sold but occasionally seen in old gardens near California coast.

E. vulgare. Biennial grown as annual. Zones 4–9, 14–24. European native blooms first year if sown between early fall and earliest spring. To 1–3 ft. tall, 1 ft. wide. Leaves covered with stiff white bristles; blue, white, or pink flowers in spikelike clusters. Endures aridity, poor soil. Seeds freely and can become a pest if seedlings are not hoed out.

E. wildpretii. TOWER OF JEWELS. Biennial. Zones 15–17, 21–24. Striking oddity from the Canary Islands spends its first year as an attractive, roundish mass of long, narrow leaves covered with silvery gray hairs. In its second

year, it starts to grow. By mid- or late spring, it forms a column of countless little rose to rose red flowers 6–10 ft. high and a foot or more in diameter. When all flowers have faded, the plant dies, leaving behind a vast amount of seed. The resulting seedlings may grow and bloom the next year if they are not hoed out.

EDELWEISS.
See **LEONTOPODIUM alpinum**

EDGEWORTHIA
chrysantha
(E. papyrifera)
PAPER BUSH
Thymelaeaceae
DECIDUOUS SHRUB

| ZONES 5–9, 14–24 |
| FULL SUN OR LIGHT SHADE |
| REGULAR WATER |

Native to China. Daphne relative grown in Asia for its bark, used in the manufacture of fancy paper. To 6 ft. tall and wide, with pliable stems produced freely from the base and 4-in. leaves that cluster toward branch tips. In winter or earliest spring, many small, fragrant pale yellow flowers in tight clusters to 2 in. across open from interesting-looking silky whitish buds formed the previous fall. Protect blossoms from late spring frosts. Little pruning required.

Edgeworthia chrysantha

EGGPLANT
Solanaceae
ANNUAL

| ZONES 1–24; H1, H2 |
| FULL SUN |
| REGULAR WATER |

Few vegetable plants are handsomer than eggplant, a Southeast Asian native. Resembles a little tree, 2–3 ft. high and equally wide. Big leaves (usually lobed) are purple tinged; drooping violet flowers are 1½ in. across. And, of course, big purple fruits are spectacular.

Effective in large containers or raised beds; a well-spaced row of eggplant makes a distinguished border between vegetable and flower garden.

Most gardeners plant large roundish or oval varieties such as 'Black Beauty', 'Burpee Hybrid', 'Dusky', or 'Early Beauty'. The Japanese, who prefer their eggplant small and very tender, prefer long, slender varieties sold under a number of names, such as 'Ichiban'. Specialists in imported vegetable seeds offer numerous colored varieties, including the full-size 'White Beauty' and a host of smaller varieties in a range of sizes (down to ½ in.) and colors—white, yellow, red, green. Some of the smaller ones genuinely resemble eggs. All are edible as well as attractive.

Eggplant 'Black Beauty'

Can be grown from seed (sow indoors 8 to 10 weeks before date of last expected frost), but starting from nursery-grown plants is much easier. To produce a crop, eggplant needs 2 to 3 months of warm days and nights (night temperatures no lower than 65°F/18°C). Set plants out in spring when frost danger is past and soil is warm. Space 3 ft. apart in loose, fertile soil. Feed once every 6 weeks; control weeds.

If you enjoy tiny whole eggplants, allow plants to produce freely. If you prefer larger fruits, keep too much fruit from setting by pinching out some terminal growth and some blossoms; three to six large fruits per plant will result. Harvest fruits after they develop some color, but don't wait until they lose their glossy shine. A second crop for late summer and fall harvest can be grown in warmest climates.

Flea beetles can be a problem on young plants; grow under row covers until big enough to tolerate leaf damage. Control aphids and whiteflies.

EGLANTINE.
See **ROSA eglanteria**

EICHHORNIA
crassipes
WATER HYACINTH
Pontederiaceae
AQUATIC PLANT

| ZONES 8, 9, 13–24; H1, H2; ANNUAL IN COLDER CLIMATES |
| FULL SUN |
| LOCATE IN PONDS OR POOLS |

Native to tropical America. Feathery roots; floating leaves ½–5 in. wide, nearly circular, on inflated stems. Showy 2-in. flowers, carried many to a spike, are lilac blue; upper petals have a yellow spot in center. Needs warmth to flower profusely. Where it is perennial, it can become an extremely serious, ineradicable pest; do not turn it loose in natural or large bodies of water.

Eichhornia crassipes

ELAEAGNUS
Elaeagnaceae
DECIDUOUS AND EVERGREEN SHRUBS AND TREES

| ZONES VARY BY SPECIES |
| FULL SUN OR PARTIAL SHADE |
| LITTLE TO REGULAR WATER |

All are splendid screen plants. All grow fast when young, becoming dense, full, firm, and tough—and they do it with little upkeep. All tolerate seashore conditions, heat, and wind.

Foliage is distinguished in evergreen forms by silvery (sometimes brown) dots that cover leaves, reflecting sunlight to give plants a special sparkle. Deciduous kinds have silvery gray leaves. Small, insignificant, but usually fragrant

E

E

flowers are followed by decorative fruit, usually red with silvery flecks. Evergreen kinds bloom in fall; in addition to their prime role as screen plants, they are useful as natural espaliers, clipped hedges, or high bank covers.

E. angustifolia. RUSSIAN OLIVE. Deciduous tree. Zones A2, A3; 1–3, 7–14, 18, 19. Native from Europe to Asia. To 20 ft. high and wide, but can be clipped to make a medium-height hedge. Angular trunk and branches (sometimes thorny) are covered with shredding dark brown bark that is picturesque in winter. Bark contrasts with narrow, willowlike, 2-in.-long silvery gray leaves. Small, very fragrant, greenish yellow flowers in early summer are followed by fruit that resembles miniature olives. Can take almost any kind of punishment, including hot summers, bitterly cold winters, drought, poor soil. Has naturalized in many areas east of the Cascades in the Pacific Northwest. Doesn't do as well in mild-winter, cool-summer climates. Good background or barrier plant. Resistant to oak root fungus. 'Red King' ('King Red') has fruit in a bright rust red shade.

E. commutata. SILVERBERRY. Deciduous shrub. Zones A1–A3; 1–3. Native to Alaska, Rocky Mountains, northern plains of U.S. and Canada. Grows upright to 12 ft. tall, 6 ft. wide, with open form and slender, spineless, red-brown branches that become coated with silvery scales. Oval leaves are silvery gray on both surfaces. Tiny, fragrant spring flowers followed in early fall by dry, mealy, ⅓-in.-long, oval fruits, also silver coated and a favorite of birds. Plant spreads by suckers to form colonies.

E. 'Coral Silver'. Shrub. Zones 2b–24. Evergreen in Zones 19–24, deciduous or partially deciduous elsewhere. Has unusually bright gray foliage, coral red berries in autumn.

E. × ebbingei. Evergreen shrub. Zones 4–24. More upright (to 10–12 ft. high and wide) than *E. pungens,* with thornless branches. Leaves 2–4 in. long, silvery on both sides when young, later dark green above and silvery beneath. Tiny, fragrant silvery flowers. Red fruit

makes good jelly. 'Gilt Edge' has striking yellow margins on its leaves.

E. multiflora. Deciduous shrub. Zones 2b–24. From China, Japan. To 6–10 ft. high and wide. Leaves silvery green above, silvery brown below. Small, fragrant spring flowers followed by attractive, ½-in.-long, bright orange-red berries on 1-in. stalks. Fruit is edible but tart, loved by birds.

E. pungens. SILVERBERRY. Evergreen shrub. Zones 4–24. Has rather rigid, sprawling, angular habit of growth to 10–15 ft. high and wide; can be kept lower and denser by pruning. Even tolerates shearing into a hedge. Grayish green, 1–3-in.-long leaves have wavy edges and brown tinting from rusty dots. Branches are spiny, also covered with rusty dots. Overall color of shrub is olive drab. Oval fruit, ½ in. long, red with silver dust. Tough container plant in reflected heat, wind. Forms listed below are more commonly planted than the plain olive drab variety and have a brighter, lighter look in the landscape, but they are less hardy (grow in Zones 5–24). All make effective barriers, thanks to dense, twiggy, spiny growth.

Elaeagnus pungens

'Fruitlandii'. Large silvery leaves.

'Maculata'. GOLDEN ELAEAGNUS. Leaves have large gold blotch in center.

'Marginata'. SILVER-EDGE ELAEAGNUS. Silvery white leaf margins.

'Variegata'. YELLOW-EDGE ELAEAGNUS. Yellowish white leaf margins.

ELAEOCARPUS decipiens (E. sylvestris ellipticus)

JAPANESE BLUEBERRY TREE
Elaeocarpaceae
EVERGREEN TREE

🌿 ZONES 8, 9, 14-24; H1
☀️ FULL SUN
💧 REGULAR WATER

From Japan, China. To 30–60 ft. tall, 20–30 ft. wide, with densely branched upright habit. New leaves are rusty and hairy, turning

Elaeocarpus decipiens

smooth and bright green. Oldest leaves eventually drop, turning red before they fall. Blooms in summer, producing tiny, scented white flowers in 1½–3-in.-long clusters; these are followed by blue-black fruits that look like small olives. Attractive street or lawn tree. Grow in rich, well-drained soil. Needs little pruning. 'Little Emperor' is a slow, dense grower to 6–10 ft. tall and wide, with interesting twisted leaves; a good choice for hedge or screen.

ELDERBERRY. See **SAMBUCUS**

ELEGIA capensis

FOUNTAIN RUSH
Restionaceae
EVERGREEN PERENNIAL

🌿 ZONES 8, 9, 14-24
☀️🔆 FULL SUN OR LIGHT SHADE
💧💧 REGULAR TO AMPLE WATER

Native to streamsides and other moist areas in South Africa. Stately, reedlike stems 6–8 ft. tall are decorated at evenly spaced nodes with dense whorls of long, feathery branches and golden, papery leaf bracts. Plants spread by rhizomes to form dense clumps

Elegia capensis

up to 7 ft. wide. Small, coppery brown flowers are borne in attractive clusters atop stems from fall into winter. Needs constant moisture and well-drained soil that is not too rich; avoid fertilizers high in phosphorus. Arching stems sway and rustle gently in the wind. Beautiful near swimming pools or ponds. Can also be grown in very large pots.

ELEPHANT'S EAR. See **ALOCASIA, COLOCASIA esculenta**

ELEPHANT'S FOOD. See **PORTULACARIA afra**

ELEUTHEROCOCCUS sieboldianus (Acanthopanax sieboldianus)

Araliaceae
DECIDUOUS SHRUB

🌿 ZONES 2B-10, 14-17
☀️🔆● SUN OR SHADE
💧💧● ANY AMOUNT OF WATER

Native to China, Japan. Grows 8–10 ft. tall and wide; erect, eventually arching stems have short thorns below each leaf. Bright green leaves have five to seven

Eleutherococcus sieboldianus 'Variegatus'

1–2½-in.-long leaflets arranged like fingers on a hand. Small, inconspicuous white flowers are borne in clusters; these are rarely followed by clusters of small black berries. This plant's virtues are its somewhat tropical appearance, adaptability (takes rich or poor soil, any exposure, any amount of irrigation), and high tolerance for difficult conditions, including air pollution. 'Variegatus', a 6–8-ft. shrub with white-bordered leaflets, is more widely grown than the species.

ELM. See **ULMUS**

ELYMUS arenarius. See **LEYMUS arenarius**

ELYMUS
magellanicus
(Agropyron magellanicus)

MAGELLAN WHEATGRASS
Poaceae (Graminea)
PERENNIAL GRASS

- 🌱 ZONES 3–6, 14–17, 21–24
- ☼ PARTIAL SHADE IN HOTTEST CLIMATES
- 💧 REGULAR WATER

Botanists have moved some species formerly in this genus to *Leymus* (see that entry for other blue-leafed grasses). Of the species remaining in *Elymus*, this clump-forming

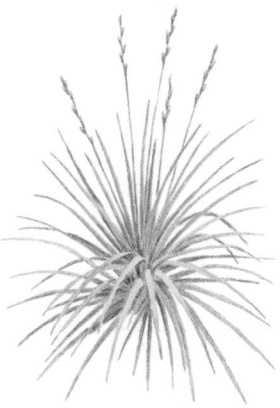

Elymus magellanicus

native of South American mountains is the most ornamental. Grows 1½ ft. high and wide, with metallic blue leaves (probably the bluest of all grasses). Cool-season grass, nearly evergreen in mild climates; grown for its foliage rather than the flower spikelets produced in summer. Likes humidity along the California coast and well-drained soil. To increase your planting, divide in spring. Good container plant.

EMBOTHRIUM
coccineum

CHILEAN FIRE BUSH
Proteaceae
EVERGREEN OR DECIDUOUS SHRUB OR TREE

- 🌱 ZONES 5, 6, 14–17, 21–24
- ☼ FULL SUN OR LIGHT SHADE
- 💧 REGULAR TO AMPLE WATER

From many altitudes and latitudes in Chile. Sometimes a large, suckering shrub of variable habit, sometimes a tree to 50 ft. tall and half as wide. It may be evergreen or deciduous; the latter forms are hardier. All have shiny green leaves that are oblong to narrow, up to

Embothrium coccineum

4½ in. long; all put on a showy floral spectacle in late spring or early summer, bearing clusters of long, narrow, brilliant red flowers. *E. c. lanceolatum* is a narrow-leafed semievergreen form.

Needs good drainage, acid soil, nonalkaline water, cold-wind protection.

EMPRESS TREE.
See **PAULOWNIA tomentosa**

EMU BUSH. See **EREMOPHILA**

ENA'ENA. See **GNAPHALIUM sandwicensium sandwicensium**

ENCELIA
Asteraceae (Compositae)
DECIDUOUS SHRUBS

- 🌱 ZONES VARY BY SPECIES
- ☼ FULL SUN
- 💧 LITTLE OR NO WATER

Much-branched shrubs to 3 ft. high and 4 ft. wide, with typically sparse foliage that tends to drop in times of drought. Loose clusters of yellow daisies bloom in spring; after bloom, cut back by at least a third to encourage repeat flowering. Useful for out-of-the-way places out of reach of irrigation. Be especially careful not to overwater in summer in hot desert regions.

Encelia farinosa

E. californica. Zones 7–16, 18–24. Native to Southern California. Bright green leaves to 2½ in. long; brown-centered flowers to nearly 3 in. across.

E. farinosa. BRITTLEBUSH, INCIENSO. Zones 8–16, 18–24; H1. Native to the Southwest. Rounded, aromatic, stiff-branched shrub (sap is fragrant) with silvery, woolly leaves to 3 in. long in dense clusters. Shrub bears a profusion of yellow- or brown-centered daisies that are somewhat smaller than those of *E. californica.*

ENDIVE
Asteraceae (Compositae)
BIENNIAL OR ANNUAL

- 🌱 ALL ZONES
- ☼ FULL SUN
- 💧 REGULAR WATER

Mediterranean native. Includes curly as well as broad-leafed endive (escarole), both of which form a rosette of leaves. Tolerates more heat than lettuce, grows faster in cold weather. Matures in 90 to 95 days from seed. In cold-winter areas, sow from spring into summer; in mild-winter climates, sow so that plants mature after summer heat is past.

Endive

Plant in rows 15–18 in. apart. Be sure to thin plants to 10–12 in. apart. When plants have reached full size (a foot across), pull outer leaves over center and tie them up at top (but not when they're wet, as that may cause decay). Covered center leaves will blanch to yellow or white. Endive can be used unblanched by cutting outer leaves, as for Swiss chard. 'Green Curled' is standard curly endive; 'Broad-leaved Batavian' is a good full-leafed variety.

Belgian or French endives are the blanched sprouts of a kind of chicory; see Chicory.

ENDYMION.
See **HYACINTHOIDES**

ENGLISH DAISY.
See **BELLIS perennis**

ENGLISH LAUREL.
See **PRUNUS laurocerasus**

ENGLISH PAINTED FERN.
See **ATHYRIUM otophorum**

ENKIANTHUS
Ericaceae
DECIDUOUS SHRUBS

- 🌱 ZONES 3–9, 14–21, EXCEPT AS NOTED
- ☼ FULL SUN ONLY IN COOLER CLIMATES
- 💧 REGULAR TO AMPLE WATER

Native to Japan. Upright stems with tiers of nearly horizontal branches; plants are narrow in youth, broader in age, but always attractive. Leaves are clustered or crowded near branch ends, turn orange or red in autumn. Clusters of nodding, bell-shaped flowers bloom in spring. Like rhododendrons, require moist, well-drained acid soil enriched with plenty of organic matter such as peat moss or ground bark. Prune only to remove dead or broken branches. Plant in location where silhouette, flowers, and fall color can be enjoyed close up.

E. campanulatus. Zones 2–9, 14–21. Slow-growing shrub to 10–20 ft. tall and half as wide. Bluish green, 1½–3-in.-long leaves turn brilliant red in fall. In late spring, pendulous clusters of yellow-green, red-veined, ½-in.-long bells hang below leaves. 'Albiflorus' bears white blooms; 'Red Bells' has red flowers and notably deep red fall color. *E. c. palibinii* bears deep red blossoms. *E. c. sikokianus* has deep red flowers streaked with pink and yellow; autumn leaves are orange and red.

Enkianthus campanulatus

E. cernuus. Seldom over 10 ft. tall and wide, with 1–2-in.-long leaves. White flowers. Not as well known as *E. c. rubens,* which has translucent deep red flowers in late spring. Leaves turn yellow and red in autumn.

E. perulatus. To 6–8 ft. high and wide. Roundish, 1–2-in.-long leaves; exceptionally good scarlet fall color. Small white flowers open in early spring before leaves emerge.

ENSETE ventricosum (Musa ensete)
ABYSSINIAN BANANA
Musaceae
PERENNIAL

- ZONES 13, 15–24; H1, H2
- FULL SUN OR PART SHADE
- REGULAR WATER

African native is grown for its lush, attractive tropical-looking foliage. For fruit-bearing banana trees, see Banana. Fast growing to 15–20 ft. high, 10–15 ft. wide. Dark green leaves with stout midribs grow out in arching form from a single vertical stem; each leaf is 10–20 ft. long, 2–4 ft. wide.

Ensete ventricosum

'Maurelii' has dark red leafstalks and leaves tinged with red on upper surface, especially along edges. Bloom typically occurs 2 to 5 years after planting, when inconspicuous flowers form within a cylinder of bronzy red bracts at end of stem. Plant dies to roots after flowering; it's possible then to grow new plants from shoots that sprout from the crown, but easier to simply discard the old plant and replace it with a new one from the nursery.

Leaves are easily shredded by wind, so plant in a wind-sheltered location. Evergreen in mildest climates. In Zones 13, 15, 16, 18, will die back in a cold winter, regrow in spring. Attractive near swimming pools. Good container subject to grow outdoors in summer, move indoors or into a greenhouse over winter.

EPAULETTE TREE.
See **PTEROSTYRAX hispida**

EPAZOTE. See **CHENOPODIUM ambrosioides**

EPHEDRA
MORMON TEA, JOINT FIR
Ephedraceae
EVERGREEN SHRUBS

- ZONES VARY BY SPECIES
- FULL SUN
- LITTLE OR NO WATER TO MODERATE WATER

Shrubby plants from arid parts of the West. Leaves are insignificant and soon drop; interest lies in slender, jointed, much-branched stems that come in various shades of green and turn yellow with age. Male and female flowers are borne on separate plants. The many species include upright-growing as well as clambering types, but those listed here are erect and densely branched. Some have papery cones, others fleshy and colorful ones. Tough plants that will tolerate dry, exposed conditions and poor soils. Must have good drainage.

E. equisetina. BLUESTEM JOINT FIR. Zones 2, 3, 7–16, 18–23. To 4–6 ft. tall, 3–8 ft. wide. Fine-textured, powdery blue-green stems. Conspicuous yellow flowers are followed by red cones.

E. nevadensis. Zones 3, 7, 9–14, 18–23. To 3 ft. high and wide, with pale green stems. Round yellow-green cones, sometimes tinged with pink, in late winter to midspring.

E. trifurca. Zones 3, 7–16, 18–23. To 15 ft. tall (though 6 ft. or so is common) and 8–10 ft. wide. Blue-green stems have thorny tips.

Ephedra nevadensis

Papery, translucent reddish brown cones appear in late winter to early spring.

E. viridis. Zones 1–3, 7–24. To 3–4 ft. high and wide, with bright green to yellow-green stems. Membranous or papery yellowish cones produced in spring.

EPIDENDRUM
Orchidaceae
EPIPHYTIC OR TERRESTRIAL ORCHIDS

- ZONES VARY BY SPECIES
- FULL SUN OR PARTIAL SHADE
- REGULAR WATER

All are easy to grow and bear large clusters of blooms. The genus formerly included a number of plants with hard, round pseudobulbs and thick, leathery leaves, but most of those species have been reassigned to *Encyclia*. Described below are reed-stemmed epidendrums with thin, stemlike pseudobulbs.

The first two species listed below are cool growers. They need plenty of sun to flower but also coolness and shade at roots. Mulch plants growing in the ground. If sun is too hot, foliage turns bright red and burns. Tip growth damaged at 28°F/−2°C; killed at about 22°F/−6°C. In cold-winter areas, grow plants in pots and move them indoors in winter.

All three species listed grow well in ground bark or other orchid media. Feed with diluted high-nitrogen liquid fertilizer during the growing season. Feed plants grown in ground bark at every other watering; plants in other media monthly. When blooms fade, cut flower stems back to within one or two joints above soil. For more information, see Orchids.

E. ibaguense (E. radicans). Zones 17, 21–24; H1, H2; or indoors. Native to Colombia. Erect, leafy stems are 2–4 ft. high. Globular clusters of 1–1½-in., orange-yellow flowers with fringed lips held at tips of slender stems well above foliage. Blooms almost continually in warm weather. Hybrids available in shades of yellow, orange, pink, lavender, and white.

E. × obrienianum. Zones 17, 21–24; H1, H2; or indoors. Best-known of these hybrids. Stems rise 1–2 ft. above foliage; clusters of vivid red flowers look like tiny cattleyas. Nearly continuous bloom in warm weather.

E. pseudepidendrum. Zone H2; or greenhouse plant. Native to

Epidendrum × obrienianum

Costa Rica, Panama. Intermediate grower. Erect stems to 3 ft. tall, with narrow, 8-in.-long, dark green leaves on upper half. Clusters of shiny apple green blooms (to 3 in. wide) with intense orange lip, in winter and spring.

EPILOBIUM angustifolium
FIREWEED
Onagraceae
PERENNIAL

- ZONES A1–A3; 1–7, 14–21
- FULL SUN
- MODERATE WATER

Native to northern parts of North America (including Alaska and the Northwest) and Eurasia. To 2–5 ft. tall, 1½–3 ft. wide; narrow leaves to 10 in. long. Loose clusters of pink to rosy purple, four-petaled flowers in early summer. ('Album' has white flowers.) Seeds itself freely in open spaces, especially after forest fires. Attractive but generally considered weedy. For low-growing, red-flowering forms, see *Zauschneria*.

Epilobium angustifolium

EPIMEDIUM

Berberidaceae
PERENNIALS

✓ ZONES 2–9, 14–17, EXCEPT AS NOTED

☼ PARTIAL SHADE

◊ MODERATE WATER

Low growers with creeping underground stems. Thin, wiry leafstalks hold leathery leaves divided into heart-shaped leaflets 3–4 in. long. Foliage is bronzy pink in spring, green in summer, bronze in fall; even in deciduous species, leaves last late into the year. In spring, plants bear loose spikes of small, waxy flowers in pink, red, creamy yellow, or white. The flowers have four petals, which may be spurred or hooded, and eight sepals—four inner ones resembling petals and four (usually small) outer ones.

Use as ground cover under trees or among rhododendrons, azaleas, camellias; set out plants 1 ft. apart. Good in large rock gardens, containers. Tolerate heavy shade. Foliage and flowers are long lasting in arrangements. Cut back in late winter before new growth resumes. Divide large clumps in spring or fall by cutting through tough roots with a sharp spade. Keep your eyes open for interesting new species coming in from China and Japan.

Epimedium grandiflorum

E. alpinum. Zones 1–9, 14–17. From southern Europe. Evergreen, 6–9 in. high. Small flowers have red inner sepals and yellow petals. Spreads faster than other epimediums.

E. × cantabrigiense. To 8–12 in. tall, with olive-tinted semievergreen foliage and small red-and-yellow flowers.

E. grandiflorum. BISHOP'S HAT, LONGSPUR EPIMEDIUM. From China, Korea, Japan. Deciduous epimedium to about 1 ft. high. Relatively large blooms (to 2 in. across) are shaped like a bishop's mitre, with red outer sepals, pale violet inner sepals, and white petals with long spurs. There are varieties with white, pinkish, or violet flowers. 'Rose Queen' bears crimson flowers with white-tipped spurs; 'White Queen' has silvery white blooms.

E. × perralchicum. Evergreen hybrid between *E. perralderianum* and *E. pinnatum colchicum.* Grows 16 in. high; bears ¾-in. yellow flowers. Yellow blooms of 'Frohnleiten' and yellow-and-bronze ones of 'Wisley' are 1 in. across.

E. perralderianum. From North Africa. To 1 ft. tall, with shiny evergreen leaves and ¾-in., bright yellow flowers.

E. pinnatum. Zones A2; 2–9, 14–17. From northern Iran. To 8–12 in. high, with nearly evergreen foliage. Flowers have yellow sepals and very short reddish brown spurs. *E. p. colchicum* is taller (to 16 in.), with larger flowers; its selection 'Black Sea' (*E.* 'Black Sea') has foliage that turns inky purple-black in winter.

E. × rubrum. This semievergreen hybrid between *E. alpinum* and *E. grandiflorum* grows to 1 ft. high. Flowers, borne in showy clusters, have crimson inner sepals, pale yellow or white petals, and upward-curving spurs. Selections include rosy pink 'Pink Queen' and white 'Snow Queen'.

E. × versicolor. Best known of several selections is 'Sulphureum', 12–20 in. tall, with light yellow flowers and semievergreen leaves marked with brownish red.

E. × warleyense. Evergreen hybrid to 1½ ft. tall, with light green foliage and clusters of small, coppery orange-red flowers. 'Orangekönigin' has paler orange-red flowers.

E. × youngianum 'Niveum'. Deciduous; to 8–12 in. high. Bears pure white flowers.

EPIPHYLLUM

ORCHID CACTUS
Cactaceae
CACTI

✓ ZONES 8, 9, 14–24; H1, H2; OR INDOORS

☼ PARTIAL SHADE; BRIGHT INDIRECT LIGHT

◊ REGULAR WATER

Growers use the name "epiphyllum" to refer to a wide range of plants—both the genus *Epiphyllum* itself and a number of crosses with related plants. All are tropical (not desert) cacti, and most grow on tree branches as epiphytes, like some orchids. In California zones above, protect by growing under lath or trees. Plants need rich, quick-draining soil with plenty of

Epiphyllum hybrid

sand and leaf mold, peat moss, or ground bark. Cuttings are easy to root in spring or summer. Let the base of the cutting dry for a day or two before potting it up. Overwatering and poor drainage cause bud drop.

In winter, epiphyllums need frost protection. Most have arching (to 2 ft. high), trailing stems and look best in hanging pots, tubs, or baskets. Stems are long, flat, smooth, quite spineless, and usually notched or scalloped along edges. Spring flowers vary in size from medium to very large (up to 10 in. across); color range includes white, cream, yellow, pink, rose, lavender, scarlet, and orange. Many varieties have blends of two or more colors. Feed with low-nitrogen fertilizer before and after bloom.

EPIPREMNUM
pinnatum 'Aureum' (Pothos aureus)

POTHOS
Araceae
EVERGREEN VINE

✓ ZONES 24; H2; OR INDOORS

☼☼● SUN OR SHADE; BRIGHT INDIRECT LIGHT

◊ REGULAR WATER

Philodendron relative from the Solomon Islands. Oval, pointed, 2–4-in.-long, leathery dark green

Epipremnum pinnatum 'Aureum'

leaves splashed or marbled with yellow. Best known as a houseplant. Commonly used as an attractive trailer in pots, window boxes, larger terrariums; requires same care as vining philodendrons. Outdoors and in greenhouses where it is given ample room, the plant becomes a big, tropical-looking vine with deeply cut leaves 2–2½ ft. long. It's capable of climbing the tallest trees and is sometimes used as a ground cover at the base of trees. Grows well in shade but has better foliage color in sun.

EPISCIA

FLAME VIOLET
Gesneriaceae
PERENNIALS

✓ ZONE H2; OR INDOORS

● FULL SHADE; BRIGHT INDIRECT LIGHT

◊◊ AMPLE WATER

Low-growing tropical American natives spread by runners that form new plants at their tips; excellent display in hanging pots. Leaves are 2–5 in. long, 1–3 in. wide; typically oval, velvety, and beautifully colored. Flowers that look something like African violets (*Saintpaulia ionantha*) come in red, pink, orange, yellow, lavender, or white, appear at scattered intervals throughout the year. Plants bloom well in high humidity of greenhouse but will also succeed as houseplants. Can grow outdoors year-round in Hawaii. In mild-winter areas on the mainland, potted plants can stay outside most of the year if given a warm, shady, wind-protected location.

E. cupreata has red flowers. *E. c. viridifolia* has green leaves with creamy veins; 'Metallica', olive green leaves with pale stripes, red edges; 'Chocolate Soldier', chocolate brown, silver-veined leaves; and 'Silver Sheen', silver leaves with darker margins.

Episcia cupreata viridifolia

E

EQUISETUM hyemale

HORSETAIL
Equisetaceae
PERENNIAL

| 🌿 ZONES 1–24 |
| :☼: :◐: FULL SUN OR PARTIAL SHADE |
| 💧 LOCATE IN MARSHY AREA OR POOL |

Rushlike survivor of Carboniferous Age in Europe, North America. There are several species, but *E. hyemale* is most common. Slender, hollow, 4-ft. stems are bright green, with a ring of black and ash gray at each joint. Spores are borne in conelike spikes at stem ends. Miniature *E. scirpoides* is similar, but only 6–8 in. high. The common name "horsetail" refers to the bushy look produced by the many whorls of slender, jointed green stems that radiate out from joints of main stems on some of the other species.

Equisetum hyemale

Although horsetail is effective in some garden situations, especially near water, use it with caution: it is extremely invasive and difficult to get rid of. Best confined to containers. In open ground, root-prune or dig out unwanted shoots rigorously and constantly.

ERAGROSTIS

LOVE GRASS
Poaceae (Gramineae)
PERENNIAL GRASSES

| 🌿 ZONES VARY BY SPECIES |
| :☼: :◐: FULL SUN TO PARTIAL SHADE |
| 💧 LITTLE TO MODERATE WATER |

Of about 250 species native to many temperate and tropical regions of the world, only a few love grasses are cultivated in gardens. These form graceful clumps of fine-textured foliage; airy floral plumes float like clouds above the leaves. Useful as textural accents or as bank or ground covers. All are drought tolerant and need excellent drainage; they grow best in sandy soils. Reseed readily. Plants are tough and carefree; cut back to a few inches tall in late fall or winter to make way for new spring growth.

E. curvula. WEEPING LOVE GRASS. Zones 4–24. From southern Africa and India. Billowing mass of slender, dark green, hairlike leaves reaches 3 ft. tall and wide. In summer, lavender-gray flower plumes increase plant height to 4 ft. Foliage picks up yellow and bronzy hues in cold weather. Evergreen in mild-winter zones. Excellent for massing. Tolerates almost any soil and may be used to control erosion.

E. elliottii. ELLIOT'S LOVE GRASS. Zones 8, 9, 14–24. From Puerto Rico, Virgin Islands, and southeastern U.S. Narrow leaves form a blue-gray clump 3 ft. high and wide; foliage turns plum purple in fall. Airy tan flower plumes are held above the leaves in spring and keep their good looks well into fall. Dramatic as a specimen plant.

E. spectabilis. PURPLE LOVE GRASS. Zones 1–24. Native from Maine to Minnesota, south to Florida, Arizona, and Mexico. Light green leaves form a compact clump to about 1½ ft. tall and wide. In late summer, plants are covered with wispy clouds of rosy purple plumes that increase the overall height to 2 ft. Leaves turn reddish purple in fall, when flowers have faded to soft cream. Good color combination with gray-leafed plants.

Eragrostis curvula

E. trichodes. SAND LOVE GRASS. Zones 1–24. Native from Illinois to Colorado and Texas. Narrow, bright green leaves grow in an upright clump to 1½–2 ft. tall and wide; foliage turns bronze red in fall. Delicate bronze to purplish blooms appear on stout stems to 4 ft. tall in late summer and last well into winter.

ERANTHIS hyemalis

WINTER ACONITE
Ranunculaceae
PERENNIAL FROM TUBER

| 🌿 ZONES 1–9, 14–17 |
| :☼: :◐: FULL SUN DURING BLOOM, PART SHADE DURING REST OF YEAR |
| 💧 REGULAR WATER DURING GROWTH AND BLOOM |

Native to Europe, Asia. Charming plant that reaches 2–8 in. high, blooming in late winter or early spring. Single yellow flowers

Eranthis hyemalis

resembling buttercups are about 1½ in. wide, with five to nine petal-like sepals; each bloom sits on a single, deeply lobed, bright green leaf that looks like a ruff. Round basal leaves divided into narrow lobes emerge immediately after the flowers bloom. All traces of the plant disappear by the time summer arrives. The species *E. cilicica* is similar but blooms later, bears slightly larger flowers, and has bronze-tinted new leaves.

Plant tubers in late summer; if they look dry or shriveled, plump them up in wet sand before planting. Plant 3 in. deep and 4 in. apart, in moist, porous soil. Reduce water in summer but don't let soil dry out completely. Divide clumps infrequently; when doing so, separate into small clumps rather than single tubers.

EREMOPHILA

EMU BUSH
Myoporaceae
EVERGREEN SHRUBS

| 🌿 ZONES 8, 9, 13–24 |
| :☼: FULL SUN |
| 💧💧 LITTLE TO MODERATE WATER, EXCEPT AS NOTED |

Of the more than 200 species of these Australian shrubs, just a few are grown in warmer parts of California and the Southwest. All tolerate aridity, heat, wind, and poor soil but like good drainage. All have slender stems that change direction abruptly and interlace to form dense growth. Some may become leggy, but all respond well to pruning. Common name comes from the flightless bird that eats the small fruits of some species. In North America, fruits are food for many birds and animals. Hummingbirds visit the flowers.

E. decipiens. Compact, spreading mound 3 ft. high and wide. Leaves are about 1 in. long and seem to clasp the stems. Brilliant scarlet, slender-tubed blossoms to 1 in. long provide winter color for 2 to 3 months. Thrives without irrigation.

E. glabra. COMMON EMU BUSH. Variable species with creeping or upright growth to 5 ft. tall, 3–10 ft. wide. Narrow leaves to 2 in. long; tubular, 1¼-in.-long flowers in red, orange, yellow, or green from early spring to autumn. 'Murchison River' grows 3 ft. high and wide, has silvery foliage and bright red flowers.

E. laanii. Spreading shrub 3–6 ft. tall and 4–10 ft. wide, with narrow, 2-in. gray-green leaves. White, pink, or light red flowers to 1 in. long. White-flowered form reputedly is more vigorous and may sucker. Very adaptable species. Tolerates dappled shade.

E. maculata. SPOTTED EMU BUSH. Most widely grown type occurs naturally on flood plains; more tolerant of moisture and humidity than other species. Variable in habit. Most forms grow 3 ft. tall and twice as wide, but some are much larger. Narrow leaves are often hairy when young. Heavy winter and spring crop of flowers, with a scattering at other times of year. Blossoms are 1–2 in. long and come in dark red, yellow, orange, or pink, often with dark spotting inside. 'Aurea' has lighter green leaves and bears 1-in.-long, unspotted yellow flowers; it grows 3–6 ft. tall and to 10 ft. wide with

E

Eremophila laanii

irrigation. 'Pink Beauty' grows 10–12 ft. tall (to 6 ft. tall even without irrigation) and 4–6 ft. wide, bears profuse bluish pink, 1½-in. blossoms in late winter.

E. racemosa. EASTER EGG BUSH. Upright grower to 4–5 ft. tall and 3–4 ft. wide, with narrow, pale green leaves. Tubular flowers start as yellow buds that turn orange, then shades of pink and purple as they mature, looking like a collection of brightly colored Easter eggs. Blooms heavily in spring then intermittently in summer. Blooms are followed by grapelike berries. Prune to encourage bushy growth. Good in containers.

E. 'Valentine'. Upright growth 6–8 ft. tall and 5 ft. wide. Brilliant rose red, 1-in.-long blossoms in late winter almost hide the foliage. Leaves have a purplish cast that makes this shrub particularly handsome even when out of bloom. 'Rosea' is similar, if not identical.

EREMURUS
FOXTAIL LILY, DESERT CANDLE
Liliaceae
PERENNIALS FROM TUBEROUS
ROOTS

⚡ ZONES 2–10, 14–16, 18–21

☀ FULL SUN

💧 REGULAR WATER DURING GROWTH AND BLOOM

Imposing lily relatives from western and central Asia, grown for 3–9-ft.-tall spires of blooms. Bell-shaped, ¼–1-in.-wide white, pink, or yellow flowers are massed closely in graceful, pointed spikes on upper one-third to one-half of stem. Plants bloom in late spring, early summer; need winter cold to bloom well. Rosettes of strap-shaped basal leaves appear in early spring, fade away after bloom in summer. Magnificent in large borders against background of dark green foliage, wall, or solid fence. Dramatic in arrangements; cut when lowest flowers on spike open.

Handle the thick, brittle roots carefully; they tend to rot when bruised or broken. Plant them in rich, fast-draining soil, setting crown just below surface in mild-winter climates, 4–6 in. deep in colder ones. Space roots 2–4 ft. apart. When leaves die down, mark spot; don't disturb roots. Don't let soil dry out completely during dormancy. Provide winter mulch in coldest areas.

E. himalaicus. To 4–8 ft. tall, with white flowers. Leaves to 1½ ft. long.

Eremurus himalaicus

E. × isabellinus. Probably best known in this group are the Shelford Hybrids, 4–5 ft. tall, with blossoms in mixed colors (white, yellow, pink, orange). 'Cleopatra' is a 3–6-ft.-tall, orange-and-red selection of the Ruiter Hybrids, a Dutch strain featuring bright, clear flower colors.

E. robustus. To 6–9 ft. tall, with pink flowers that are lightly veined with brown. Dense basal rosettes of leaves to 2 ft. long.

E. stenophyllus (E. bungei). To 3–5 ft. tall, with bright yellow flowers aging to orange brown. Leaves to 1 ft. long.

ERICA
HEATH
Ericaceae
EVERGREEN SHRUBS

⚡ ZONES VARY BY SPECIES

☀ ◐ PARTIAL SHADE IN HOTTEST CLIMATES

💧 REGULAR WATER

▶ SEE CHART NEXT PAGE

Grown for small, needlelike leaves and abundant, usually small flowers that may be bell shaped, urn shaped, or tubular. By choosing

Erica carnea
'Springwood'

varieties of both heaths and their close relative heather *(Calluna)* carefully, you can have color year-round.

The hardiest heaths, native to northern and western Europe, are widely used as shrubs or ground cover plants in cool-summer, humid regions of California and the Pacific Northwest. Fanciers sometimes plant the shortest types in masses for a multicolored Persian-carpet effect. Good on slopes. South African species are tender to frost and about as hardy as fuchsias; where temperatures dip below 28°F/–2°C, it is safest to grow them in containers and provide shelter. A third group of heaths, native to the Mediterranean and southern Europe, is intermediate in hardiness. Taller heaths can be used as screens. All attract bees.

Heaths demand excellent drainage, and most need acid soil. Sandy soil amended with organic matter such as peat moss and compost is ideal; heavy clay is usually fatal. Feeding with an annual sifting of compost is usually sufficient, but if plants lose color, feed lightly with acid plant food in early spring. When it comes to watering, be careful and consistent. Heaths will not tolerate standing water or absolute dryness. To keep plants looking neat, shear or cut off faded flower spikes. Don't cut back into leafless wood; new growth may not resprout.

ERIGERON
FLEABANE
Asteraceae (Compositae)
PERENNIALS

⚡ ZONES VARY BY SPECIES

☀ ◐ FULL SUN OR LIGHT SHADE

💧 MODERATE WATER

Free-blooming plants with daisy-like flowers. Similar to closely related Michaelmas daisy *(Aster*

novi-belgii), except that erigeron's flower heads have threadlike rays in two or more rows rather than broader rays in a single row. White, pink, lavender, or violet flowers, usually with yellow centers. Cut back after flowering to prolong bloom. Grow best in sandy soil. Rock garden species need especially fast drainage.

E. glaucus. BEACH ASTER, SEASIDE DAISY. Zones 4–6, 15–17, 22–24. Native to California, Oregon coast. Burns in hot sun inland. Forms a clump to 1 ft. high and 1½ ft. wide, with blue-green foliage and stems. Stout, hairy stems are topped by lavender, 1½–2-in.-wide flower heads in spring, summer. 'Sea Breeze' has large pink flowers. 'Arthur Menzies' is a compact selection to 8 in. high with lavender-pink blooms. 'Wayne Roderick' ('W. R.'), also grows to 8 in. high, bears large lavender blooms in summer; possibly a hybrid, it's similar to *E. glaucus* but has larger leaves and does better in warmer areas.

E. karvinskianus. MEXICAN DAISY, SANTA BARBARA DAISY. Zones 8, 9, 12–24; H1, H2. Native to Mexico. Graceful, trailing plant 10–20 in. high, 3 ft. wide. Leaves 1 in. long, often toothed at tips. Dainty flower heads ¾ in. across with numerous white or pinkish rays. Rarely out of bloom. Use as ground cover in garden beds or large containers, in rock gardens, in hanging baskets, on dry walls. Drought tolerant. Naturalizes easily (a pest in Hawaii); invasive unless controlled. 'Moerheimii' is more compact, with slightly larger leaves and lavender-tinted flower heads.

E. speciosus. Zones 1–9, 14–24. Native to Pacific Northwest. Erect, leafy stemmed, 2 ft. high and wide. Summer flowers are 1–1½ in. across, with dark

Erigeron speciosus

ERICA

NAME, ZONES, ORIGIN	GROWTH HABIT, SIZE	LEAVES	FLOWER COLOR, SEASON	COMMENTS
Erica arborea TREE HEATH Zones 15–17, 21–24 Southern Europe, North Africa	Dense shrub or tree to 10–20 ft. tall, 8–10 ft. wide. One or many trunks, often heavy burl at base	Bright green; new growth lighter green	White, fragrant. Spring	Slow growing. Performs well enough in Zones 4–6 in years between big freezes. Burls are the "briar" used for making pipes
E. a. alpina	Dense, upright shrub to 6 ft. tall, 3–4 ft. wide	As above	White. Spring	Slow to reach blooming age, then free blooming. Slightly hardier than *E. arborea;* a surer bet in Zones 4–6
E. australis SOUTHERN HEATH Zones 5–9, 14–24 Spain, Portugal	Upright, spirelike, 6–10 ft. tall, 3–5 ft. wide	Dark green	Rosy or red. Clustered at ends of shoots. Spring	'Mr. Robert' is a white form
E. canaliculata (usually sold as **E. melanthera** and often called Scotch heather) Zones 15–17, 20–24 South Africa	Bushy, spreading, but with general spired effect. To 6 ft. tall, 4 ft. wide	Dark green above, white beneath	Pink to rosy purple. Fall, winter	Sometimes called Christmas heather because of winter bloom. Pink-flowered form is sold as 'Rosea', reddish purple form as 'Rubra'. One of the best for Southern California. Cut flowers last for weeks, whether stems are immersed in water or not
E. c. 'Boscaweniana' (sometimes sold as **E. melanthera 'Rosea'**)	Upright bush or small tree to 18 ft. tall, 10–12 ft. wide	Same as above	Pale lilac pink to nearly white. Winter, spring	Like *E. canaliculata,* good source of cut flowers
E. carnea (**E. herbacea**) Zones A3; 2–10, 14–24 European Alps	Dwarf to 6–16 in. high, 2 ft. wide. Upright branchlets rise from prostrate main branches	Medium green	Rosy red. Winter, spring	Unsightly unless pruned every year. This species and its varieties tolerate neutral or slightly alkaline soil
E. c. 'December Red'	To 6 in. high, 1½ ft. wide	Medium green	Pink to reddish purple. Winter	Early blooming
E. c. 'Myretoun Ruby'	To 6 in. high, 1½ ft. wide	Dark green	Magenta to crimson. Winter, spring	Very striking red
E. c. 'Pink Spangles'	To 6 in. high, 1½ ft. wide. Vigorous, spreading	Medium green	Shell pink to deep pink. Winter, spring	Reliable old standard
E. c. 'Ruby Glow'	To 8 in. high, 1½ ft. wide	Dark green	Deep ruby red. Winter, spring	One of richest in color
E. c. 'Springwood' (**'Springwood White'**)	To 8 in. high, 14 in. wide	Light green	White; open from creamy buds. Winter, spring	Toughest, fastest-growing heath; one of neatest looking
E. c. 'Vivellii'	To 6 in. high, 1½ ft. wide	Dark green; bronzy red in winter	Carmine red. Winter, spring	Relatively tidy. Interesting for seasonal change in foliage color as well as for bloom

Erica arborea

Erica arborea alpina

Erica canaliculata

Erica canaliculata 'Rosea'

Erica carnea 'Myretoun Ruby'

Erica carnea 'Vivellii'

ERICA

NAME, ZONES, ORIGIN	GROWTH HABIT, SIZE	LEAVES	FLOWER COLOR, SEASON	COMMENTS
E. ciliaris DORSET HEATH Zones 4–6, 15–17 England, Ireland	Trailing, 6–12 in. high, 20 in. wide	Pale green	Rosy red. Summer	Good for massing
E. c. 'Mrs. C. H. Gill'	To 1 ft. high, 20 in. wide	Dark green	Deep red. Summer, early fall	Showy, bell-like flowers
E. c. 'Stoborough'	Same as above, but taller, to 1½ ft.	Medium green	White. Summer, early fall	Free blooming, showy
E. cinerea TWISTED HEATH Zones 4–6, 15–17 British Isles, northern Europe	To 1 ft. high, 2½ ft. wide. Forms low mat	Dark green, dainty	Purple. Summer	Good ground cover
E. c. 'Atrosanguinea'	To 9 in. high, 2½ ft. wide	Dark green, dainty	Scarlet. Summer, early fall	Dwarf, slow growing
E. c. 'C. D. Eason'	To 10 in. high, 20 in. wide	Dark green	Red. Late spring, summer	Outstanding; good summer flower display
E. c. 'P. S. Patrick'	To 15 in. high, 20 in. wide	Dark green	Purple. Summer	Long, sturdy spikes of large flowers
E. × darleyensis 'Darley Dale' (E. mediterranea hybrida) Zones 2–10, 14–24	Bushy grower to 1 ft. tall, 2 ft. wide	Medium green	Shell pink to light rosy purple; darken with age. Fall to midspring	Tough, hardy plant that takes both heat and cold surprisingly well. Tolerates neutral soils. In Northern California, most foolproof heath
E. × d. 'Furzey'	Bushy, 14–18 in. high, 2 ft. wide	Dark green	Deep rose pink. Winter, early spring	Spreading, vigorous plant
E. × d. 'Kramer's Rote'	Bushy, to 14 in. high, 2 ft. wide	Dark bronze green	Magenta. Winter, early spring	One of the best all around
E. × d. 'Silberschmelze' ('Molten Silver', E. × d. 'Alba', 'Mediterranea Hybrid White')	To 1½–2 ft. high, 2½ ft. wide	Medium green	White, fragrant. Winter, spring	Easy to maintain. Vigorous
E. herbacea (see E. carnea)				
E. lusitanica (E. codonodes) SPANISH HEATH Zones 5–9, 14–24 Spain, Portugal	Upright feathery shrub, to 6–12 ft. high, 2–4 ft. wide	Light green	Pinkish white, slightly fragrant. Winter	Remarkably profuse bloom. Needs frost-sheltered spot in Northwest. One of best in Zones 20–24

Erica cinerea 'C. D. Eason'

Erica × darleyensis 'Darley Dale'

Erica quadrangularis

Erica tetralix

Erica vagans

ERICA

NAME, ZONES, ORIGIN	GROWTH HABIT, SIZE	LEAVES	FLOWER COLOR, SEASON	COMMENTS
E. mediterranea hybrida (see E. × darleyensis 'Darley Dale')				
E. melanthera (see E. canaliculata)				
E. quadrangularis Zones 15–17, 20–24 South Africa	Stiff, upright shrub to 2 ft. tall, 1½ ft. wide	Bright green	Tiny, rose or white. Late winter, early spring	Offered as potted plants or sold as cut branches. Often sold as *E. persoluta*
E. tetralix CROSS-LEAFED HEATH Zones 4–6, 15–17 England, northern Europe	Upright, to 1 ft. tall, 2 ft. wide	Dark green, silvery beneath	Rosy pink. Summer, early fall	Best if given moist, acid, well-drained soil, afternoon shade
E. t. 'Alba Mollis'	Upright, slightly spreading, to 1 ft. high and wide	Silvery gray	Pure white. Summer, early fall	Foliage sheen pronounced in spring, summer
E. t. 'Darleyensis'	Spreading, open growth to 8 in. high, 1 ft. wide	Gray green	Rosy pink. Summer	Good color. Do not confuse with *E. × darleyensis*, which blooms at some point from fall to midspring, depending on variety
E. vagans CORNISH HEATH Zones 3b–6, 15–17, 20–24 Cornwall, Ireland	Bushy, open, to 2–3 ft. high and wide	Bright green	White to shell pink or rose. Summer	Robust and hardy
E. v. 'Lyonesse'	Bushy, rounded, to 1½ ft. high and wide	Bright, glossy green	White. Summer, early fall	Best white Cornish heath
E. v. 'Mrs. D. F. Maxwell'	Same as above	Dark green	Cherry pink or red. Summer, early fall	Outstanding for color and heavy bloom; widely grown
E. v. 'St. Keverne'	Same as above	Light green	Rose pink. Summer, early fall	Heavy bloom. Compact if pruned annually
E. ventricosa Zones 15–17, 20–24 South Africa	To 3 ft. tall and wide	Medium green, needlelike	Pale to medium pink, shiny. Late spring, early summer	Heavy flower spikes at tips of branches. Occasionally sold as small pot plant in spring
E. × watsonii 'Dawn' Zones 4–9, 14–24	Spreading mound, 1 ft. tall, 2–3 ft. wide	Green; new growth golden	Deep pink. Summer, early fall	Excellent ground cover. Easy to grow. Hybrid between *E. ciliaris* and *E. tetralix*

violet or lavender rays. Widespread through Rocky Mountain area is *E. s. macranthus,* aspen daisy, which bears three to five flowers on each stalk; stalks nod near top. Hybrids between *E. speciosus* and other species are available; they have larger flowers and come in white and pink as well as blue shades. Some of the best are azure blue 'Blue Beauty', violet-blue 'Darkest of All', light violet 'Strahlenmeer', 'Pink Jewel' (with blooms in various pink shades), carmine pink 'Förster's Liebling' (Förster's Darling'), and white 'Schneewittchen' ('Snow White').

ERIOBOTRYA
LOQUAT
Rosaceae
EVERGREEN TREES OR SHRUBS

✂ ZONES VARY BY SPECIES

☀ ◐ FULL SUN OR PARTIAL SHADE

⚫ 💧 MODERATE TO REGULAR WATER

Both species described here (one of which bears edible fruit) are Chinese natives with large, prominently veined, sharply toothed leaves that can be cut and used for indoor decoration. Both can be espaliered on fence or trellis (but not in reflected heat) and make

good container plants. Attractive to birds. Plant in well-drained soil. Subject to fireblight. Moderate water for ornamental plants; regular moisture for a good fruit crop.

E. deflexa. BRONZE LOQUAT. Zones 8–24. Fast-growing, shrubby plant. Though easily trained into small tree similar in size to *E. japonica*, it is often espaliered. New leaves emerge bright copper and hold that color for a long time before turning green. The leaves are shinier, more pointed, less leathery, and less deeply veined than those of *E. japonica*. Garlands of creamy

white flowers in spring. No edible fruit.

E. japonica. Zones 6–24; H1, H2. Though this loquat produces edible fruit, it's most often used as an ornamental. Grows 15–30 ft. tall; spreads as wide as it is high in sun, grows narrower in shade. Leathery, crisp, stoutly veined and netted leaves are 6–12 in. long, 2–4 in. wide, deep glossy green above, woolly and rust colored beneath. New branches are woolly. Small dull white flowers, fragrant but not showy, appear in woolly 3–6-in. clusters in fall. Orange to yellow, 1–2-in.-long fruit with large

Eriobotrya japonica

seeds in the center ripens in winter or spring. Flesh may be sweet, sweet-tart, or tart, depending on tree and variety. Eat fresh or use in preserves, pies.

Most trees are sold as seedlings, good ornamental plants with unpredictable fruit quality. If you want to harvest a crop, look for a grafted variety such as 'Champagne' (best in warm areas), 'Gold Nugget' (best in cooler regions), or 'MacBeth' (exceptionally large fruit). For good fruit, thin the branches somewhat to let light into tree's interior. If the tree sets fruit heavily, remove some while it's small to increase size of the remaining fruit and to prevent limb breakage.

ERIOGONUM
WILD BUCKWHEAT
Polygonaceae
SHRUBBY PERENNIALS

🌿 ZONES VARY BY SPECIES
☼ FULL SUN
○ ◐ LITTLE TO MODERATE WATER

Native to most areas of the West (the few sold at nurseries are mostly native to California coast). Individual blossoms are tiny but grow in long-stemmed or branched clusters —usually domed, flattish, or ball-like. Flowers age to an attractive tan or reddish brown and persist for a long time; good in dried arrangements. Flowers attract butterflies; birds enjoy the seeds.

Grow best in well-drained, loose, gravelly soil. Useful for covering dry banks, massing among rocks; smaller forms make good specimens in rock gardens. May self-sow; transplant when they're small to extend planting or replace overgrown plants. Shrubby kinds

get leggy after several years. You can do some pruning to shape if you start when plants are young, but if they have had no attention, it's better to replace them. Most buckwheats withstand wind and heat. In hottest climates, plants look best with deep watering twice monthly in summer.

E. arborescens. SANTA CRUZ ISLAND BUCKWHEAT. Zones 5, 7–9, 14–24. Native to Santa Cruz, Santa Rosa, and Anacapa islands, Southern California. Grows 3–4 ft. (sometimes 8 ft.) high, spreading to 4–5 ft. or more. Trunk and branches with shredding gray to reddish bark make attractive open pattern. Rather narrow, ½–1½-in.-long, gray-green leaves

Eriogonum arborescens

cluster at ends of branches. Long-stalked, flat clusters of pale pink to rose flowers, late spring through summer.

E. cinereum. ASHYLEAF BUCKWHEAT. Zones 5, 14–17, 19–24. Native to coastal bluffs and canyons of Southern California. Grows 2–5 ft. tall and 3 ft. wide, with ash-colored, 1-in. leaves and pale pink flowers in ball-shaped clusters in summer. Best planted in groups.

E. crocatum. SAFFRON BUCKWHEAT. Zones 14–24. Native to Southern California. Low, compact plant to 1½ ft. high, 2 ft. wide. Stems and roundish, 1-in.-long leaves are covered with white wool. Sulfur yellow flowers in broad, flattish clusters, early spring to late summer.

E. fasciculatum. CALIFORNIA BUCKWHEAT. Zones 7–9, 12–24. Native to foothills of California (from Santa Clara to San Diego) and to desert mountain slopes of Southern California. Forms a clump 1–3 ft. high, spreading to 4 ft. Leaves narrow, ½–¾ in. long; may be dark green above, white and woolly beneath, or gray and

hairy. White or pinkish flowers in headlike clusters, late spring to early fall. Good for erosion control. 'Theodore Payne' is lower growing, makes an attractive green ground cover.

E. f. polifolium. ARIZONA BUCKWHEAT. Native to inland mountains and deserts of California into western Utah, Arizona, and northwest Mexico. Differs from the species only in minor botanical details.

E. giganteum. ST. CATHERINE'S LACE. Zones 5, 7–9, 14–24. Native to Santa Catalina and San Clemente islands, Southern California. Differs from *E. arborescens* in its more freely branching habit; grayish white, broadly oval, 1–2½-in.-long leaves; and longer period of bloom.

E. grande rubescens (E. rubescens, E. latifolium rubescens). RED BUCKWHEAT. Zones 5, 14–24. Native to San Miguel, Santa Rosa, and Santa Cruz islands, Southern California. Woody stems at the base; branches tend to lie on ground, spreading to 1–1½ ft., with upright tips about 10–12 in. high. Gray-green, oval leaves 1–3½ in. long. Branch tips and sturdy upright branchlets are topped by headlike clusters of rosy red flowers in summer.

E. umbellatum. SULFUR FLOWER. Zones 1–24. Plants grow to timberline and above. Low, broad mats of woody stems set with 1-in. leaves that are green above, white and felted beneath. In late spring or early summer, 4–12-in. stalks carry clusters of tiny yellow flowers that age to rust. 'Shasta Sulfur' makes a silvery green mound 1½ ft. high and 3 ft. wide, adorned in spring with sulfur yellow flowers. 'Sierra' (grown from seed and somewhat variable) forms a dome 1–2 ft. high and 3–4 ft. wide, above which rise golf ball–size clusters of bright yellow flowers.

E. wrightii. WRIGHT'S BUCKWHEAT. Zones 7–11, 14–24. Widely distributed species native from eastern and southern California to western Texas and northern Mexico. Selections from higher elevations and northern part of range take more cold. Wandlike stems form a mound 1½ ft. high by 2 ft. wide. Silvery green, felted leaves, ½ in. long and ¼ in. wide, narrow to a point. Tiny white or pinkish flowers appear in clusters along stalks from midsummer through fall.

ERODIUM reichardii (E. chamaedryoides)
CRANESBILL
Geraniaceae
PERENNIAL

🌿 ZONES 7–9, 14–24
☼ ◐ FULL SUN OR PARTIAL SHADE
● REGULAR WATER

Native to Balearic Islands and Corsica. Dainty-looking but tough plant, forming dense foliage tuft 3–6 in. high, 1 ft. across. Long-stalked, dark green, roundish, ⅓-in.-long leaves with scalloped edges. Profuse, cup-shaped, ½-in.-wide flowers with white or rose pink, rosy-veined petals notched at tips, early spring into fall. Good small-scale ground cover, rock garden plant. A double-flowered pink and a single-flowered white form exist. Plant in porous soil.

Erodium reichardii

E. chrysanthum has silvery foliage and pale yellow flowers. *E. petraeum crispum* (*E. foetidum*) has white flowers with lavender veins and a conspicuous purple spot on one petal.

ERYNGIUM
SEA HOLLY, AMETHYST ERYNGIUM
Apiaceae (Umbelliferae)
ANNUALS, BIENNIALS, AND PERENNIALS

🌿 ZONES 2–24, EXCEPT AS NOTED
☼ FULL SUN
◐ ● WATER NEEDS VARY BY SPECIES

Mostly spiny-leafed, rosette-forming plants that produce erect, thistlelike, leafy stalks bearing tight, silvery or blue-tinted flower heads surrounded by showy bracts. Bloom in summer (sometimes into fall). Upper leaves, leafstalks, bracts, and flowers may all be frosted with silver or tinted in shades of blue or amethyst.

Sea hollies from dry, rocky areas in Europe, North Africa, Turkey, central Asia, China, and Korea tend to be taprooted; prefer dry,

E (margin tab)

well-drained, poor to moderately rich soils; need protection from excessive winter water. Those from wet grasslands in Mexico, Brazil, and Argentina have fibrous root systems, prefer moist, well-drained soils. Taprooted forms are difficult to divide but may be propagated by root cuttings. If seeding, sow in place. Some species reseed vigorously. Watch out for snails and slugs. Useful in rock gardens and for long displays in borders. Good choice for dried arrangements.

E. alpinum. ALPINE SEA HOLLY. Perennial. From southeastern Europe. To 2½ ft. high, 1½ ft. wide, with taproot. Spiny, heart-shaped basal leaves 3–6 in. long. Upper leaves and stems are tinged with soft blue to steel blue near top. The conical, 1½-in. flower heads are surrounded by purplish blue, intricately cut bracts. Tolerates very light shade. Moderate water.

E. amethystinum. Perennial. Zones 1–24. From Italy and the Balkans. To 2½ ft. high and 1½ ft. wide, with taproot. Spiny, medium green leaves to 6 in. long. Silvery blue stems and conical, 1-in. amethyst flower heads surrounded by 2-in., silvery blue bracts. Moderate water.

Eryngium amethystinum

E. foetidum. CULANTRO. Biennial grown as an annual where temperatures drop below 0°F/–18°C. Zones 4–9, 12–24; H1, H2. Native to American tropics. To 2 ft. tall and wide. Rosettes of green, spiny, lance-shaped leaves to 5 in. long; foliage has aroma similar to coriander or cilantro. Succulent new leaves can substitute for true coriander and are produced long after the latter has gone to seed. Flowering stems bear dark green, ¾-in., egg-shaped flower heads. Fertile soil, regular water.

E. giganteum. MISS WILL-MOTT'S GHOST. Biennial to short-lived perennial. From the Caucasus and Iran. To 3–4 ft. or taller, 2½ ft. wide. Oval or heart-shaped, medium green leaves to 6 in. long. Three-lobed stem leaves. In late summer, bears blue or pale green, conical flower heads surrounded by silvery, 2½–4-in. bracts; the plant dies after flowering ends. Reseeds well. Provide fertile soil, regular water.

E. planum. FALSE SEA HOLLY. Perennial. From southeast Europe to central Asia. To 3 ft. tall, 1½ ft. wide, with taproot. Oblong to heart-shaped, deep green leaves to 4 in. long. Stem leaves are blue tinted, with three to five lobes or sections. Rounded, ½–¾-in.-wide, light blue flower heads are surrounded by narrow blue-green bracts. Moderate water.

E. variifolium. MOROCCAN SEA HOLLY. Perennial. Zones 4–9, 14–24. From Morocco. To 1½ ft. high, 10 in. wide, with taproot. Oval, tooth-edged, spiny, somewhat fleshy leaves are 2 in. long, heart shaped at base, dark green marbled with white veins. Stiff, silvery blue, branching stems bear 1-in. blue-gray flower heads surrounded by silvery blue bracts to ½ in. Moderate to regular water.

E. yuccifolium. RATTLE-SNAKE MASTER, BUTTON SNAKEROOT. Perennial. From central and eastern U.S. To 4 ft. tall, 2 ft. wide. Sword-shaped, spiny-edged, blue-gray leaves to a little over 3 ft. long. Strong, branched stems. Cylindrical, whitish green to pale blue flower heads are 1½ in. across, lack showy bracts. Fertile soil, regular water.

ERYSIMUM
WALLFLOWER
Brassicaceae (Cruciferae)
PERENNIALS, SOME GROWN AS BIENNIALS OR ANNUALS

✎	ZONES VARY BY SPECIES
☼ ◐	FULL SUN OR LIGHT SHADE
◌ ◑ ●	WATER NEEDS VARY BY SPECIES

This genus swallowed up *Cheiranthus*, which included the old-fashioned biennial bedding-plant wallflowers and several choice perennials. All have the typical clustered four-petaled flowers that give the crucifers their name, but their habits and uses differ widely.

E. × allionii. SIBERIAN WALLFLOWER. Perennial, often grown as biennial or annual. Zones A3; 1–9, 14–24. Branching plants 1–1½ ft. tall and somewhat

Erysimum × allionii

wider are covered in spring with fragrant flowers in rich orange or yellow. In mild-winter climates, sow seed in fall; elsewhere, sow in spring for well-established plants by fall. Full sun, moderate water. Sometimes sold as *E. asperum* or *E. hieraciifolium.*

E. cheiri (Cheiranthus cheiri). ENGLISH WALLFLOWER. Perennial in Zones 4–6, 14–17, 22, 23, but usually grown as a biennial or annual. From southern Europe. Best in cool, moist regions. Branching, woody-based plants 1–2½ ft. tall, 1–1½ ft. wide, with narrow bright green leaves and broad clusters of showy, sweet-scented flowers in spring. Blossoms are yellow, cream, orange, red, brown, or burgundy, sometimes shaded or veined with contrasting color. Main bloom period falls between that of primroses and summer bedding plants. Under ideal conditions in coastal Pacific Northwest may bloom year-round. Sow seeds in spring for bloom the following year (some strains flower the first year if seeded early); or set out plants in fall or earliest spring. May self-sow. Regular water.

E. hybrids. Perennials. Zones 4–9, 14–24. Many excellent choices available. Most popular is 'Bowles Mauve', 3 ft. tall and 4–6 ft. wide, with narrow gray-green leaves held on erect stems, each topped by a 1½-ft.-long, narrow, spikelike cluster of mauve flowers. Best in areas with cool summers and mild winters, where bloom is practically continual; elsewhere plants bloom from winter through spring. Often short lived. 'Compact Bowles Mauve' is about half the size. 'Lemon Zest' grows 8–12 in. high and wide, with pale to lemon

yellow blooms in early spring. 'Wenlock Beauty' grows 2 ft. high and wide, with springtime flowers varying from buff to purple in a single spike. All these hybrids take moderate water.

E. insulare suffrutescens (E. suffrutescens). Perennial. Zones 14–17, 22–24. Native to central and southern California coasts. Woody-based growth 6–24 in. high, 4–12 in. wide, with narrow leaves and fragrant orange-yellow flowers in spring. Little water.

E. kotschyanum. Perennial in Zones 3b–11, 14–21; often treated as a winter annual in hot-summer climates. Light green leaves form a mat 6 in. high and a foot wide; in spring, fragrant deep yellow flowers appear on 2-in. stems. Use in rock garden or with other small perennials between paving stones. If plants hump up, cut out central portion, transplant it, and press original plant flat again. Divide clumps in fall. Provide moderate water.

E. linifolium 'Variegatum'. Zones 4–6, 14–24. Shrubby growth to 2 ft. tall, 2–3 ft. wide. Prized for its narrow, 3½-in.-long leaves, which are gray-green and edged in creamy white. Mauve flowers about ½ in. across appear from spring to fall. Moderate water.

ERYTHEA. See **BRAHEA**

ERYTHRINA
CORAL TREE
Fabaceae (Leguminosae)
DECIDUOUS OR NEARLY EVERGREEN TREES AND SHRUBS

✎	ZONES VARY BY SPECIES
☼	FULL SUN
◐	MODERATE WATER
◆	SEEDS ARE POISONOUS IF INGESTED

Many species; known and used chiefly in Southern California. Some are also cultivated in Hawaii, and a few are grown in Arizona. Valued for brilliant flowers in colors ranging from greenish white through yellow to light or vivid shades of orange and red. The flat, beanlike pods following bloom contain poisonous seeds. Leaves are divided into three leaflets. These are typically thorny plants with strong structural value, both in and out of leaf. To eliminate too rapid, succulent growth and limb breakage in larger species, give little or no irrigation during dry weather and prune after flowering.

E. × bidwillii. Deciduous shrub. Zones 8, 9, 12–24. To 8 ft.

all and as wide; sometimes tree-like to 20 ft. or taller. Spectacular spring-to-winter display of 2-ft.-long clusters of pure red flowers on long, willowy stalks; main show in summer. Cut back flowering wood after blossoms fade. Very thorny; plant away from paths and use long-handled pruners when trimming.

E. caffra (E. constantiana). CORAL TREE. Briefly deciduous tree. Zones 21–24; H2. Native to South Africa. To 24–40 ft. tall, 40–60 ft. wide. Drops leaves in early winter; then angular bare branches produce big clusters of deep red-orange, tubular flowers that drip nectar. In late winter or earlier, flowers give way to fresh, light green foliage.

Erythrina caffra

E. coralloides. NAKED CORAL TREE. Deciduous tree. Zones 12, 13, 19–24. Native to Mexico. To 30 ft. high and as wide or wider, but easily contained by pruning. Fiery red blossoms like fat candles or pinecones bloom at tips of naked, twisted, black-thorned branches in spring. At end of flowering season, 8–10-in. leaves develop; they give shade in summer, turn yellow in late fall, then drop—revealing a bizarre branching structure that's almost as valuable as spring flower display. Sometimes sold as *E. poianthes.*

E. crista-galli. COCKSPUR CORAL TREE, COMMON CORAL TREE. Nearly evergreen (in Hawaii) to deciduous tree. Zones 7–9, 12–17, 19–24; H1, H2. Shrub or tree to 15–20 ft. tall and as wide in nearly frostless areas; perennial to half that size in colder part of range. Native to South America.

Erythrina crista-galli

Many-stemmed, rough-barked plant, with 6-in. leaves divided into 2–3-in.-long leaflets. First flowers form after leaves unfurl in spring, when each branch tip flaunts a big, loose, spikelike cluster of velvety, birdlike blossoms in warm pink to wine red (color varies with the plant). Depending on environment, there may be as many as three distinct flowering periods, spring through fall. Cut back old flower stems after each wave of bloom.

E. falcata. Nearly evergreen tree. Zones 19–24; H1, H2. Native to Brazil and Peru. Upright habit reaching 30–40 ft. high. Must be in ground several years before it flowers (may take 10 to 12 years). Dark red (occasionally orange-red), sickle-shaped flowers in hanging, spikelike clusters at branch ends in winter, early spring. Some leaves drop at bloom time.

Erythrina humeana

E. humeana. NATAL CORAL TREE. Normally deciduous tree (sometimes almost evergreen). Zones 12, 13, 20–24; H1, H2. Native to South Africa. May grow to 30 ft. tall, but begins blooming when only 3 ft. high. Flowers continually from late summer to late autumn, carrying bright orange-red blossoms in long-stalked clusters at branch ends well above the leaves (unlike many other types). Dark green foliage. 'Raja' is shrubbier and has leaflets with long, pointed "tails."

E. lysistemon. Deciduous tree. Zones 13, 21–24; H2. Native to South Africa. Similar to *E. caffra* in size but slower growing. Light orange (sometimes shrimp pink) flowers. Time of bloom varies greatly; may bloom intermittently from early fall to late spring, occasionally in summer. Many handsome black thorns. A magnificent tree of great landscape value. Very sensitive to wet soil. Sometimes erroneously sold as *E. princeps.*

E. sandwicensis. WILIWILI, HAWAIIAN CORAL TREE. Deciduous tree. Zone H2. Hawaiian native to 20–45 ft. high and as wide. Masses of white to chartreuse, coral, orange, red, or bicolored flowers bloom in late summer to winter, preceding the flush of new foliage. Extremely drought tolerant; good selection for xeriscape gardens.

E. × sykesii. Deciduous tree. Zones 19–24. Hybrid from Australia. To 24–30 ft., with spreading habit. Showy red flowers appear in winter before leaves emerge. Unlike the other species, does not form pods.

E. variegata. INDIAN CORAL TREE, TIGER'S CLAW. Deciduous tree. Zone H2. Native from India to southern Polynesia. To 60 ft. tall, 25–35 ft. wide, with a prickly trunk and branches and leaves comprising three broad, triangular leaflets to 6 in. long. Large clusters of brilliant coral red flowers are produced in winter before new leaves appear. Forms are available with white flowers and variegated leaves. All types are adapted to wide range of soil conditions.

'Tropic Coral'. TROPIC CORAL TALL ERYTHRINA. Columnar, evergreen to semievergreen form of *E. variegata* to 50 ft. high, 10–15 ft. wide. Bright orange flowers appear at the top of the tree in spring. Used as a windbreak or screen and near tall buildings when space is limited.

ERYTHRONIUM
Liliaceae
PERENNIALS FROM BULBS

🌿 ZONES VARY BY SPECIES

☼ LIGHT SHADE

💧 REGULAR WATER DURING GROWTH AND BLOOM

Spring-flowering plants with dainty, nodding, lily-shaped blooms 1–1½ in. across, on stems usually 1 ft. high or less. All have two (rarely three) broad, tongue-shaped basal leaves; these are mottled in many species. Set out in groups under deciduous trees, in rock gardens, beside pools or streams; give rich, porous soil. Plant bulbs in fall, as soon as you receive them; don't let them dry out. Set 2–3 in. deep, 4–5 in. apart. Western species need no water during dormancy, but give *E. dens-canis* moisture year-round. Divide clumps infrequently—only when vigor and bloom quality decline.

Erythronium tuolumnense

E. californicum. FAWN LILY. Zones 4–7, 14–17. Native to Northern California. Leaves mottled with brown. Creamy white or yellow flowers with deeper yellow band at base, on 6–10-in. stems.

E. dens-canis. DOG-TOOTH VIOLET. Zones 1–7, 15–17. From Europe. Leaves mottled brown and white. Deep pink to purple flowers on 6–12-in. stems. Specialists can supply named varieties with white, pink, rose, or violet blossoms. Needs some shade during hot afternoon hours.

E. hendersonii. Zones 4–7, 15–17. Native to Northern California and southern Oregon. Foot-tall stems carry light to deep lavender flowers that are dark maroon at base, deeply curled back at tips. Dark green leaves are attractively mottled with brown.

▶

E. revolutum. Zones 1–7, 14–17. Western native quite similar to *E. californicum*, but foliage and flowers are larger; stems up to 16 in. Blossoms are usually pink marked yellow in the center, but varieties 'Pink Beauty' (pure pink without yellow center) and 'White Beauty' are available.

E. tuolumnense. Zones 2–7, 14–17. Native to California. Robust plant with solid green leaves and 12–15-in.-tall stems. Golden yellow flowers, greenish yellow at base. 'Kondo' and 'Pagoda' are extra-vigorous selections.

ESCALLONIA
Escalloniaceae
EVERGREEN SHRUBS

| 🌿 ZONES 4–9, 14–24 |
| ☼ ◐ PARTIAL SHADE IN HOTTEST CLIMATES |
| ● REGULAR WATER |

Native to South America, principally Chile. Wind tolerant, clean looking, with glossy leaves. Clusters of flowers in summer and fall (nearly year-round in mild climates). May freeze badly at 10 to 15°F/–12 to –9°C, but will recover quickly. Will take direct coastal conditions and coastal winds. Tolerant of most soils but damaged by high alkalinity. Drought tolerant, but look better with regular water. Prune taller ones by removing one-third of old wood each year after bloom, cutting to the base; or shape into multitrunked trees. Tip-pinch smaller kinds to keep them compact. Can be sheared as hedges, but this may sacrifice some bloom. Fast growing; good screen plants. Attractive to bees. Foliage of some exudes resinous fragrance.

E. 'Apple Blossom'. Dense grower to 5 ft. high and wide, sprawling unless pinched back. Pinkish white flowers open from pink buds.

E. 'Balfouri'. Graceful plant up to 10 ft. tall and wide, with drooping branchlets and narrow clusters of pink-tinted white flowers. Good as espalier.

E. bifida (E. montevidensis). WHITE ESCALLONIA. As shrub, can be kept to 8–10 ft. high and wide, useful as big screening plant; can also grow as multitrunked small tree to 25 ft. tall. Glossy dark green leaves are 3–4 in. long. White flowers in large, rounded clusters at branch ends. Many plants sold under this name are *E. illinita*, a plant to 10 ft. tall with smaller flower clusters and a pronounced resinous odor.

E. 'C. F. Ball'. See E. rubra

E. 'Compakta'. To 3 ft. high and wide, with rose red flowers.

E. 'Frades' (E. 'Fradesii'). Compact growth to 5–6 ft. high (lower with pinching) and wide. Resembles *E. laevis,* but has smaller, glossy green leaves and prolific show of pure pink to rose flowers. Good as espalier.

E. 'Ingramii'. See E. rubra macrantha

E. 'Jubilee'. Compact-growing, 6-ft. shrub that is densely leafy right to the ground. Clustered pinkish to rose flowers. Set 4 ft. apart for informal hedge or screen.

E. laevis (E. organensis). PINK ESCALLONIA. Leafy, dense-growing shrub to 12–15 ft. tall and wide. Bronzy green leaves. Pink to red buds open into white to pink flowers in short, broad clusters. Use as a large screen or train as a small tree. Leaves burn in seacoast wind and salt as well as in high heat.

E. montevidensis. See E. bifida

E. 'Newport Dwarf'. Grows 2½ ft. tall, 4 ft. wide, with deep pink to red flowers.

E. organensis. See E. laevis

E. 'Pride of Donard'. Dense, mounding shrub to 5 ft. high and 8 ft. wide, with glossy dark green leaves and pink flowers.

E. 'Red Elf'. Dense, spreading shrub to 8 ft. tall, 12 ft. wide, with inch-long, dark glossy green leaves and short clusters of deep red flowers.

E. rubra. Upright, compact shrub 6–15 ft. tall and wide. Leaves smooth, very glossy dark green. Red or crimson flowers in 1–3-in. clusters. Much used as screen or hedge, especially near coast. Compact varieties are 'C. F. Ball', 5–6 ft. high and wide (to 3 ft.

Escallonia rubra

with some pinching), and 'William Watson', to 4 ft. tall and wide, with ruddy cerise flowers, spindly habit unless pruned. *E. r. macrantha* ('Ingramii') resembles the species but has larger flowers.

E. virgata. Partially deciduous shrub grows to 6 ft. tall and 8 ft. wide, with ¾-in. leaves. Plant produces short clusters of pale rose or white flowers. The hardiest escallonia; does well in frostiest parts of these plants' hardiness range.

ESCHSCHOLZIA
Papaveraceae
PERENNIALS AND ANNUALS

| 🌿 ZONES 1–24; H1 |
| ☼ FULL SUN |
| ◐ ◑ ● LITTLE TO REGULAR WATER |

Poppy relatives with upward-facing, four-petaled yellow or orange blooms above finely cut foliage. Individual plants grow about 1½ ft. wide. Of the several species native to western North America and Mexico, *E. californica* is the most outstanding and the most widely used; it is the state flower of California. All are drought tolerant, but giving them summer water will extend their flowering season.

E. caespitosa. Annual. Native to California and southwestern Oregon. Smaller plant than *E. californica;* garden variety 'Sundew', for example, has densely tufted growth to 6 in. high. Plants bear bright yellow, 1-in. flowers. Use for edging, in containers.

E. californica. CALIFORNIA POPPY. Perennial often grown as annual. Native to California, Oregon. Free branching from base, with slender, 8–24-in.-long stems and blue-green, finely divided leaves. Single, satiny-petaled flowers about 2 in. wide; color varies from pale yellow to deep orange. Flowers close at night and on overcast days. In mild climates, it blooms from spring to summer and reseeds freely. Naturalized not just in California but also in parts of Hawaii. In cold-winter areas, generally used as a summer annual.

California poppy is not the best choice for important beds viewed close up—unless you trim off dead flowers regularly, plants go to seed and all parts turn straw color. It can't be surpassed, however, for naturalizing on sunny hillsides, along drives, or in dry fields, vacant lots, parking strips, or country gardens.

Eschscholzia californica

Sow seeds where plants are to grow; seedlings don't transplant well. Sow in fall in mild-winter areas, in spring in colder regions. Broadcast on cultivated, well-drained soil; if rain is absent, water to keep ground moist until seeds germinate. For large-scale sowing, use 3–4 lb. of seeds per acre. Birds are attracted to the seeds.

There are also garden forms with blooms of yellow, pink, rose, flame orange, red, cream, and white. Sunset strain has single flowers, Mission Bells has semidouble ones, and Ballerina blooms are semidouble with frilled and fluted petals. Thai Silk strain has bronze-tinted foliage, semidouble flowers in full color range. Among the many California poppy selections are 'Apricot Flambeau', yellow with orange-pink borders; 'Carmine King', a blend of deep pink and white; 'Dalli', orange-red blooms with yellow eye; and 'Inferno', orange scarlet. Names of 'Cherry Ripe', 'Milky White', and 'Purple Cap' describe flower color. 'Champagne and Roses' has heavily frilled flowers in rose or light pink. 'Golden Tears' bears single golden yellow blooms on trailing stems to 2 ft. long. Garden forms usually revert to orange or yellow when they reseed.

ESPOSTOA lanata
PERUVIAN OLD MAN CACTUS
Cactaceae
CACTUS

| 🌿 ZONES 12–24; OR INDOORS |
| ☼ ◐ SUN OR LIGHT AFTERNOON SHADE; BRIGHT LIGHT |
| ◐ ● LITTLE TO MODERATE WATER |

Columnar cactus, branching with age. Slow growing in pots, fairly fast (to 8 ft. tall and 2 ft. wide) in open ground. Light brown, bristly, ½–2-in.-long thorns are usually concealed in long white hair that covers plant. Hair is especially long and dense near summit. Tubular, pink, 2-in.-long flowers in spring. Protect from hard frosts.

Espostoa lanata

ETERNAL FLAME. See **CALATHEA crocata**

ETLINGERA elatior (Phaeomeria magnifica)

TORCH GINGER
Zingiberaceae
PERENNIAL

✿ ZONE H2

☼ ◑ FULL SUN OR PARTIAL SHADE

● REGULAR WATER

Malaysian and Indonesian jungles are home to this herbaceous, clump-forming plant to 20 ft. high and as wide (spreading wider over time). One of Hawaii's best-loved gingers. Canelike stems are clothed with dark green, pointed leaves, each 12–28 in. long and 4–6 in. wide. Plant blooms most of the year, producing striking bright red or pink, conelike inflorescences on 2–5-ft.-long stalks that rise directly from the ground. Best in rich, organic soil with protection from wind.

Etlingera elatior

EUCALYPTUS
Myrtaceae
EVERGREEN TREES AND SHRUBS

✎ ZONES 5, 6, 8–24; H1, H2 (SEE HARDINESS IN CHART)

☼ FULL SUN

◌ LITTLE OR NO WATER, EXCEPT AS NOTED

▶ SEE CHART NEXT PAGE

With few exceptions, these plants are native to Australia. More than 600 different species grow there, ranging from sprawling shrubs (many of them bearing the common name "mallee") to skyline trees. About 150 species have been grown in areas of California and Arizona that have climates similar to the plants' native Australian habitats; many have been grown as solitary representatives in arboretums. Eucalypts are the most widely planted non-native trees in these two Western states—for several hundred miles in parts of California, you never lose sight of one.

The first eucalypts were planted in this country in 1856, and from 1870 on they were widely grown for windbreaks, firewood, and shade. From 1904 to 1912, thousands of acres were planted in an ill-advised hardwood timber scheme. Although they were popular landscape trees through much of the latter twentieth century, serious pest problems and smaller lot sizes have lessened their popularity, especially in California.

Eucalyptus nicholii

California and Arizona do not have a monopoly on eucalypts, however. Many can be grown in western Washington and Oregon, and gardeners in the mildest parts of Vancouver Island have also experimented with them. Safest for beginners in these milder-winter areas of the Pacific Northwest are *E. gunnii,* cider gum, and *E. pauciflora,* the ghost gum.

The two species most commonly planted in Hawaii are

E. citriodora, lemon-scented gum, and *E. deglupta,* Mindanao gum. *E. robusta,* swamp mahogany, is a less common landscape choice; it is used mainly in reforestation.

Eucalyptus ficifolia

Eucalypts are appealing on several levels: Depending on the species, they may show attractive form, striking bark, good-looking foliage, or some combination of these features. Some even have showy blossoms, though flowers of many are unimportant. Juvenile and adult leaves differ; when juvenile foliage is significantly different, it is noted in the chart. Also pay attention to plant size; many species are best suited to larger properties.

Some botanists now divide *Eucalyptus* into several genera, with most of the plants listed here assigned to *Symphyomyrtus.* Exceptions are listed with their new names in parentheses in the chart that follows.

Hardiness. The chart gives approximate hardiness for each species, but these temperatures are not absolute. In addition to air

Eucalyptus polyanthemos

temperature, take into account the plant's age (older plants are generally hardier) and its condition, as well as the date of frost (a freeze is more damaging in November than it would be in January, after the plant has experienced weeks of low temperatures) and its duration. If temperatures in your area are likely to fall within the frost-damage range for a certain species, plant it as a risk. If they regularly drop below the given range, don't plant it.

Planting. A few species grow as much as 10 ft. annually in their early years. Such a growth rate is typically associated with short-lived trees, but not in this case—fast-growing tree eucalypts can live for at least a century if given proper care from the start.

Generally, the best way to grow eucalypts is from seed—it's as easy as starting many annuals and perennials. Sow seeds in a flat in spring or summer; keep shaded and water sparingly. When seedlings are 2–3 in. tall, lift gently, separate, and transplant to another flat of prepared soil, spacing 3 in. apart. Or transplant into gallon cans or other large pots. Plant in ground in 2 to 3 months, when seedlings are 6–12 in. high.

When buying plants, select the most vigorous looking ones, not the biggest. Avoid those with many leafless twigs or evidence of hard pruning. If possible, do not buy root-bound plants. If such plants are all you can get, do this: wash soil off roots and cut off any kinked roots that cannot be straightened; then spread remaining roots out as straight as possible (in a fan shape) in premoistened planting hole, with stem's old soil line ½–1 in. below grade. Immediately fill in around roots with moistened soil and irrigate heavily. If plants are top-heavy, cut back and stake (chart prescribes staking for certain species).

Eucalyptus sideroxylon

Fertilizing and watering. Complete fertilizer is seldom needed, although iron often is required for eucalypts whose leaves chronically turn yellow between veins (chlorosis). In the desert, plants are especially subject to chlorosis in

E

E

dense or shallow soils. Iron chelate applied in spring and fall is helpful for young trees. Overwatering can cause chlorosis. Newly planted trees may need water every day for their first week if weather is hot and dry, once or twice a week for rest of first growing season. Once established, most eucalypts need no watering at all, except in low desert.

Foliage. Most eucalypts have two conspicuously different kinds of foliage: soft, variously shaped juvenile leaves, found on seedlings, saplings, and new branches that grow from stumps; and (typically) tougher adult or mature leaves. Where a species' juvenile foliage is significant, it is mentioned in chart. Almost all eucalyptus leaves, juvenile and adult, have a distinctive pungent aroma, though foliage must sometimes be crushed to release its scent. Beyond the fragrance common to all types, some are accented with lemon or other perfumes. For the types grown for their decorative foliage, trim frequently to encourage a steady supply of handsome leaves.

Pruning. Many eucalypts need pruning to improve shape or to remove dead or dying growth. The ideal time for the job is between March and August. (Where eucalyptus beetles are a problem—see "Pests"—avoid pruning from May to October.) Some descriptions in the chart recommend that you cut back plants to make them bushier or stouter. Wait until plant has been in the ground at least a year, then cut back to just above a side branch or bud. If there are no side branches or visible buds, cut back trunk to desired height—if plant is established, new growth will break out beneath cut. Later, remove all excess new branches that form; keep only those that are well placed.

Occasional deep or prolonged freezes may kill even large eucalyptus trees. Don't be too quick to remove them; they can sprout new growth from trunk or large branches, though heavy freeze damage may alter their appearance. Delay removal or heavy pruning until summer (late fall or earliest spring in areas where beetles are present).

Pests. Eucalyptus was pest-free until 1984, when the eucalyptus long-horned beetle—one of the tree's native attackers in

EUCALYPTUS

NAME, HARDINESS	HEIGHT	SPREAD	LEAVES, BARK	FLOWERS, FRUIT	COMMENTS
Eucalyptus camaldulensis (E. rostrata) RED GUM 12 to 23°F/ −11 to −5°C	45–150 ft.	45–105 ft.	Long, slender, lance-shaped, pendulous green leaves. Tan, mottled, curved trunk	Unimportant white to pale yellow flowers, small capsules	Large tree with spreading crown, weeping branches. For highways, broad streets, parks, skylines. Gets chlorosis in desert
E. cinerea SILVER DOLLAR TREE 14 to 17°F/ −10 to −8°C	20–55 ft.	20–45 ft.	Roundish gray-green juvenile leaves, 1–2 in. long. Long, narrow green mature leaves	Unimportant small white flowers, small capsules	Cut back often for a supply of decorative foliage. Withstands wind. Best in dry site or with fast drainage. Can be used as perennial in borderline climates
E. citriodora (Corymbia citriodora) LEMON-SCENTED GUM 24 to 28°F/ −4 to −2°C	45–90 ft.	15–45 ft.	Leaves long (3–7 in.), golden green, lemon scented. Trunk white to pinkish	Small white flowers, little urn-shaped capsules	Attractive, narrow tree; can grow close to walls, walks. Lower half to two-thirds of tree is bare trunk. Trunk is weak when young; stake stoutly. Cut back and thin often to strengthen. Can take much or little water
E. cladocalyx (E. corynocalyx) SUGAR GUM 23 to 28°F/ −5 to −2°C	45–90 ft.	45–75 ft.	Shiny, reddish, 3–5-in. leaves, oval or variably shaped. Tan bark peels to show creamy patches	Unimportant creamy white flowers, small capsules	Planted for structure. Skyline tree on Southern California coast with characteristic puffy clouds of foliage separated by open spaces. Tough. 'Nana' is a small grower to 20–25 ft.
E. conferruminata (usually sold as **E. lehmannii**) BUSHY YATE 25 to 28°F/ −4 to −2°C	12–27 ft.	15–30 ft.	Elongated oval, light green, 2-in. leaves; some turn red in fall	Green flowers in 4-in. clusters open from horn-shaped buds. Large woody capsules remain on branches	Fast-growing, flat-topped, dense tree for windbreak or seashore. Left unpruned, branches touch ground
E. deglupta MINDANAO GUM 24 to 26°F/ −4 to −3°C	75–200 ft.	30–75 ft.	Dark green leaves. Flaking bark strikingly colored in blue, green, yellow, red, purple	Flowers, fruit inconspicuous	Fast-growing, erect tree from jungles of Indonesia, Philippines, New Guinea. Trunk is the spectacular feature. Regular water
E. erythrocorys (Eudesmia erythrocoryos) RED-CAP GUM 23 to 26°F/ −5 to −3°C	12–30 ft.	9–25 ft.	Thick, shiny, deep green, lance-shaped leaves, 4–7 in. long. White trunk	Bright red caps tilt up and fall off to reveal yellow flowers in clusters like brushes. Blooms any time of year, heaviest from fall to early spring	Best with multiple trunks; sprawling but attractive. To make dense, head back main shoots several times. Can take much water if drainage is good. Can be grown in lawn. Attractive in desert

EUCALYPTUS

NAME, HARDINESS	HEIGHT	SPREAD	LEAVES, BARK	FLOWERS, FRUIT	COMMENTS
E. ficifolia (Corymbia ficifolia) RED-FLOWERING GUM 25 to 30°F/ −4 to −1°C	18–45 ft.	15–60 ft.	Deep green, leathery, 3-7-in.-long leaves; look like rubber plant foliage	Showy foot-long clusters of red flowers (sometimes white, cream, pink, or orange) all year, peaking in summer. Heavy 1-in. seed capsules like dice cups	Usually single trunked, round headed. Unpredictable flower color from seed. Prune seed capsules from young trees to avoid weighing down branches, spoiling form. Seldom thrives in lawns or hottest climates
E. globulus BLUE GUM 17 to 22°F/ −8 to −6°C	45–165 ft.	30–75 ft.	Oval, silvery juvenile leaves; mature leaves are sickle shaped, dark green, 6-10 in. long	Flowers white to yellowish. Warty seed capsules	Good as a windbreak, but not the best choice for gardens due to greedy roots, brittle wood, messiness— produces considerable litter from falling leaves, bark, capsules. Smaller form 'Compacta' is just as greedy, almost as messy
E. gunnii CIDER GUM 5 to 10°F/ −15 to −12°C	30–75 ft.	18–45 ft.	Silvery blue-green young foliage. Dark green, 3-5-in.-long mature leaves. Green-and-tan bark	Small creamy white flowers. Clusters of tiny capsules	One of the fastest-growing, hardiest eucalypts. Dense form good for shade, windbreak, or screen. May take temperatures a few degrees colder than indicated, if not for an extended period
E. lehmannii (see **E. conferruminata**)					
E. leucoxylon WHITE IRONBARK 14 to 18°F/ −10 to −8°C	30–90 ft.	18–60 ft.	Gray-green, sickle-shaped leaves, 3-6 in. long. Trunk brownish or bluish gray, shedding to reveal white new bark	Flowers variable—white to cream, pink, or reddish. Little goblet-shaped capsules	Habit somewhat variable; usually slender, upright, open, with pendulous branches. Tolerates adverse conditions, including heat, wind, and heavy soils or light, rocky ones
E. macrocarpa 8 to 12°F/ −13 to −11°C	6-12 ft.	9–36 ft.	Light gray-blue leaves, 2-5 in. long, in pairs close to stem. Greenish white bark	Golf ball–size gray buds open to round, fluffy, flat-topped pink, red, or white flowers 4-7-in. across; blossoms are stalkless, "sit" on branches. Followed by 3-in. capsules	Sprawling and awkward, but showy. For dry places. Can be espaliered on sunny fence or wall
E. microtheca COOLIBAH 5 to 10°F/ −15 to −12°C	30–60 ft.	24–54 ft.	Blue-green, ribbonlike leaves to 8 in. long	Insignificant creamy white flowers. Tiny capsules create no litter	Bushy, round-headed, single- or multitrunked tree. Wind resistant. One of the best eucalypts for Arizona
E. nicholii NICHOL'S WILLOW-LEAFED PEPPERMINT 12 to 15°F/ −11 to −9°C	36–48 ft.	15–36 ft.	Narrow, 3-5-in.-long, light green leaves. Furrowed, rich reddish brown bark	Inconspicuous whitish flowers, tiny capsules	Graceful, weeping garden or street tree. Crushed leaves said to smell like peppermint. Too much water can cause chlorosis
E. papuana (Blakella papuana) GHOST GUM 22°F/−6°C	30–54 ft.	20–45 ft.	Lance-shaped, 2-5-in., light green leaves, tinted purplish by frost. Smooth white bark	Small white flowers. Fruit inconspicuous	Semiweeping growth. White bark is most striking feature. Produces only sparse litter. Does well in desert soils
E. pauciflora GHOST GUM 10 to 15°F/ −12 to −9°C	24–60 ft.	18–45 ft.	Narrow gray-green leaves, 3-6 in. long. White trunk	Insignificant flowers, fruit	White trunk and branches and open crown make it a good specimen tree. Good in lawns. Takes wet or dry soil. Very little litter. In youth, remove erratic branches

EUCALYPTUS

NAME, HARDINESS	HEIGHT	SPREAD	LEAVES, BARK	FLOWERS, FRUIT	COMMENTS
E. polyanthemos SILVER DOLLAR GUM 14 to 18°F/ −10 to −8°C	30–75 ft.	15–45 ft.	Gray-green, nearly round, 2–3-in. juvenile leaves; dark green, lance-shaped mature leaves	Unimportant whitish flowers	Young leaves used in fresh and dried arrangements. Select young trees carefully; some have leaves less round and gray than others. Specimen, street tree. Can be used as perennial in borderline climates
E. pulverulenta SILVER MOUNTAIN GUM 15 to 21°F/ −9 to −6°C	18–30 ft.	6–15 ft.	Silver-gray, shish kebab–style juvenile foliage (stems appear to pierce leaves). Mature leaves usually long and pointed. Ribbony bark	Small, fuzzy, creamy white flowers sandwiched between round leaves along stems, fall to spring. Cup-shaped capsules	Garden curiosity. Source of branches for arrangements. Cut back often to encourage juvenile foliage
E. robusta SWAMP MAHOGANY 11 to 15°F/ −12 to −9°C	60–75 ft.	30–75 ft.	Dark green, leathery, shiny leaves 4–7 in. long. Stringy, dark red-brown bark	Pink-tinted, creamy white flowers anytime, mainly winter	Densely leafed, ultimately round headed. Strong tree; good windbreak. Performs well in moist or saline soil. Darkest green eucalypt in desert
E. rostrata (see **E. camaldulensis**)					
E. rudis FLOODED GUM 12 to 18°F/ −11 to −8°C	30–60 ft.	24–40 ft.	Gray-green to green, 4–6-in., lance-shaped leaves. Rough bark	White flower clusters (not showy). Small fruit	Often weeping. Use as shade or street tree. Takes coastal conditions, wind, much or little water, sandy or saline soil. Not good in desert unless in deep, gravelly, well-drained soil
E. salmonophloia SALMON GUM 20 to 25°F/ −7 to −4°C	To 40 ft.	To 40 ft.	Narrow, glittering bright green leaves. Salmon-colored bark	Flowers white to cream, capsules inconspicuous	Slow growing; eventually flat-topped. Bark is main feature. Tolerates drought, some salt in soil. Good choice for home landscape in desert
E. salubris GIMLET 20 to 25°F/ −7 to −4°C	20–25 ft.	20–25 ft.	Glossy deep green leaves to 4 in. long. Smooth, shiny, ridged red-brown bark	Flowers rather large, creamy white, conspicuous. Fruits inconspicuous	Can be single- or multitrunked. Like a smaller *E. salmonophloia*. Withstands heavy soils. Good in desert
E. sargentii SALT RIVER MALLET 22°F/−6°C	30–40 ft.	30–40 ft.	Narrow green leaves to 4 in. long. Dark gray, peeling bark	Cream-colored flowers open from slender buds with long horns	Stout single or multiple trunks. Exceptionally tough, very salt tolerant. Good in desert
E. sideroxylon RED or PINK IRONBARK 20 to 25°F/ −7 to −4°C	30–90 ft.	30–60 ft.	Slim blue-green leaves turn bronze in winter. Furrowed, nearly black trunk	Fluffy light pink to crimson flowers in pendulous clusters, mainly fall to late spring. Small capsules	Variable: open or dense, slender or squat, weeping or upright. Use as specimen, screen, street tree. Gets chlorotic in wet, heavy soils
E. torquata CORAL GUM 17 to 22°F/ −8 to −6°C	18–36 ft.	15–30 ft.	Light green to yellow-green leaves, long and narrow or blunt and round	Flower buds like tiny Japanese lanterns, opening to flowers of coral red and yellow, on and off all year	Grown for bloom (good cut flowers) and small tree size. Stake and prune or head back to make graceful. Branches often droop from weight of flowers, seed capsules. Good in desert
E. viminalis MANNA GUM 12 to 15°F/ −11 to −9°C	30–150 ft.	24–45 ft.	Light green, narrow, 4–6-in. leaves. Whitish trunk with shedding bark	Small white flowers, fruit usually too high to be seen	Needs plenty of room—good for parks, highways. Best in good soil but can take poor soil. Creates debris

E

Australia—was observed in Southern California. It has now been successfully controlled by natural predators introduced from Australia. But since then, several other beetles (including an additional species of long-horned beetle and three leaf-eating beetle species), at least one gall wasp species, and as many as eight psyllid species have been introduced. Without natural predators to keep them in check, many have become serious pests, especially on stressed trees. Signs of long-horned beetle infestation include oval holes in the plant's wood, and individual branches or the whole plant dying with leaves still attached. Freshly cut wood attracts the pest, so avoid pruning during its active period (May to October). If you see tunnels under bark of firewood, immediately burn or bury the wood. Remove dead or dying trees; bury logs or cover tightly with tarpaulins for at least 6 months. Tightly cover eucalyptus firewood and do not transport it. Species that have proved at least partially resistant to long-horned borers include *E. camaldulensis*, *E. citriodora*, *E. cladocalyx*, *E. robusta*, and *E. sideroxylon*.

Eucalyptus citriodora

Psyllids were first discovered in Southern California in 1998; the tiny insects have spread throughout the state, attacking many eucalyptus species. The red gum lerp psyllid was identified in Arizona in 2005; it, too, attacks several species. Psyllids suck sap from leaves, excreting honeydew in the process; foliage may look black due to sooty mold growing on the honeydew. If present in high numbers, the pest can cause severe leaf drop. Infested plants are more susceptible to attack by other pests, including borers. Minimize stress by irrigating deeply (but not near the trunk) during long dry spells; don't fertilize. Don't spray leaves with any kind of insecticide—

parasitoid wasps have been released to control the psyllid. Soil drenches and trunk injections of the systemic insecticide imidacloprid protect healthy trees from psyllids.

For the most current information on pests of eucalyptus, including resistant species, contact your county's Cooperative Extension Office.

EUCOMIS
PINEAPPLE FLOWER
Liliaceae
PERENNIALS FROM BULBS

| 🌿 ZONES 4–9, 14–24; H1, H2 |
| 🔆 🌓 FULL SUN OR LIGHT SHADE |
| 💧 REGULAR WATER DURING GROWTH AND BLOOM |

Unusual-looking plants from tropical southern Africa. Thick spikes closely set with ½-in.-long flowers are topped with clusters of leaflike bracts that resemble pineapple tops. Make good cut flowers. Bloom in summer; persistent purplish seed capsules carry on the show even longer. Need rich soil with plenty of humus. Plant in ground in fall, setting bulbs 4–6 in. deep, 1 ft. apart. Also fairly easy to grow from seed sown in spring. In areas where ground freezes, mulch to protect plantings. Divide every 5 or 6 years. Interesting potted plants; set bulbs with tips just beneath soil surface and repot yearly in fresh soil mix.

E. bicolor. Spikes to 2 ft. tall; green flowers with purple-edged petals. Attractive, wavy-edged leaves to 1 ft. long, 3–4 in. wide.

Eucomis comosa

E. comosa (E. punctata). Thick spikes 2–3 ft. tall are set with greenish white flowers tinged pink or purple. Stems are spotted purple at the base. Leaves grow to 2 ft. long and are less wavy than those of *E. bicolor*. 'Sparkling Burgundy' has dark purple leaves.

EUCOMMIA
ulmoides
HARDY RUBBER TREE
Eucommiaceae
DECIDUOUS TREE

| 🌿 ZONES 3–10, 14–21 |
| 🔆 FULL SUN |
| 💧💧 MODERATE TO REGULAR WATER |

From central China. Rubber can be made from this tree's sap, but the process isn't economically feasible—instead, the plant is grown for its ornamental qualities.

Eucommia ulmoides

Attractive rounded habit; can reach 40–60 ft. tall, with equal or greater spread. Leaves resemble those of elm *(Ulmus)* but are glossier and more leathery. When a leaf is slowly torn in two, sap from the veins congeals into threads of rubber, holding the two halves together. Fall color is negligible; flowers and fruit are not conspicuous. Tolerates a wide variety of soils but requires good drainage. Not troubled by pests.

EUCRYPHIA
Eucryphiaceae
EVERGREEN OR SEMIEVERGREEN
SHRUBS OR TREES

| 🌿 ZONES 5, 6, 15–17 |
| 🔆 🌓 BEST IN SUN, TOLERATE SOME SHADE |
| 💧 REGULAR WATER |

Many attractive species and varieties. The kinds most frequently sold in the West have shiny evergreen leaves and 2½-in.-wide, pure white flowers with big tufts of yellow stamens in center. Give them neutral or slightly acid soil and shelter from strong winds. In

Zones 5 and 6, protect young plants from temperatures below 15°F/–9°C.

E. glutinosa. Native to central Chile. Upright growth to 10–25 ft. high and 5–15 ft. wide. Shiny dark green leaves are 2½ in. long and divided into three to five leaflets with serrated edges; they turn yellow, orange, or red in fall. Fragrant flowers to 2½ in. across appear in late summer.

E. lucida. Native to Tasmania. To 20–30 ft. tall, half as wide. Smooth-edged, glossy leaves 1½–3 in. long. Fragrant blooms in early summer. 'Pink Cloud' has red-centered rosy pink blossoms. In Zones 5 and 6, plants may be damaged in coldest winters; those that are sheltered (growing at woodland edges, for example) fare better.

E. × nymansensis. Group of hybrids between two species from Chile. Best known is 'Mount Usher', to about 20 ft. tall and 8 ft. wide, with toothed leaves—some simple, some divided into three to five 2–4-in.-long leaflets. Often bears double flowers. 'Nymansay', to 15 ft. tall and 10 ft. wide, is somewhat faster growing. Both bloom in late summer.

Eucryphia × nymansensis

EUGENIA
Myrtaceae
EVERGREEN SHRUBS OR TREES

| 🌿 ZONES VARY BY SPECIES |
| 🔆 🌓 FULL SUN OR PARTIAL SHADE |
| 💧 REGULAR WATER |

Grown for attractive foliage, white flowers, edible "cherries." Perform best with rich, well-drained soil, moist atmosphere, sheltered planting location. Some species have been reclassified. For *E. myrtifolia* and *E. paniculata,* see *Syzygium paniculatum;* for *E. smithii,* see *Acmena smithii.*

E. aggregata. CHERRY OF THE RIO GRANDE. Zones 23, 24. Native to Brazil. To 15 ft. tall and

E

10 ft. wide, with bark peeling in thin layers. Narrow, elliptical, glossy dark green leaves to 3 in. long. Fruit to 1 in. long ripens from orange red to deep purplish red, is said to taste like cherries. Eat fresh or use for jams, jellies.

Eugenia uniflora

E. uniflora. SURINAM CHERRY, PITANGA. Zones 21–24; H1, H2. From tropical America. Very slow, open growth to 15–25 ft. tall and 10–15 ft. wide, though it's commonly seen at 6–8 ft. tall with equal spread. Glossy coppery green leaves reach 2 in. long, deepen in color to purplish or red in cold weather. Fragrant, showy, ½-in.-wide white flowers with prominent stamens. Fruit is about 1 in. in diameter, ripens from yellow to orange to deep red; edible when fully ripe. Fruit of seedlings ranges from quite sweet and cherrylike to very sour. 'Lolita' has sweet black fruit and is far superior in flavor to seedlings. Good for jams, jellies. Grafted varieties are sometimes available. Good screen. Can be sheared into a hedge, but by doing so you'll sacrifice fruit.

EULALIA.
See **MISCANTHUS** sinensis

EUONYMUS
Celastraceae
EVERGREEN AND DECIDUOUS
SHRUBS AND VINES

✎	ZONES VARY BY SPECIES
☼ ◑ ●	EXPOSURE VARIES BY SPECIES
◖ ◗	MODERATE TO REGULAR WATER

Deciduous and evergreen euonymus species are distinct: the characteristic squarish "hatbox" fruit common to both offers the only hint that they're related. Deciduous types are valued for fall leaf color or showy fruit. Evergreen sorts, used mainly for landscape structure (background and foundation plants, hedges, dividers),

include some of the most cold-tolerant broad-leafed plants. Most species take a range of exposures, from full sun to fairly deep shade; deciduous kinds with fall color give best display in a sunny location. Some species are very susceptible to mildew. Scale can be a problem on any euonymus.

E. alatus. WINGED EUONYMUS. Deciduous shrub. Zones A3; 2–10, 14–16. From China, Japan. Though nursery tags may indicate a much smaller plant, the species can reach 15–20 ft. high and wide. Dense, twiggy, flat-topped shrub with horizontal branching. Twigs have flat, corky wings that disappear on older growth. Though fruit is smaller and less profuse than that of *E. europaeus,* fall color is impressive: the dark green leaves turn flaming red. (On plants grown in shade, fall color is pink.)

'Compacta', a smaller plant (to 6–10 ft. high and a little narrower) with smaller corky wings, isn't quite as hardy as the species (Zones A3; 2b–10, 14–16). 'Timber Creek' ('Chicago Fire'), to 8 ft. high and wide, is an extra-hardy selection that succeeds in Zones A3, 1–10, 14–16. 'Rudy Haag' is a dense grower to just 4–5 ft. high and wide, with rose to red fall color. 'Little Moses' ('Odom') is smaller still, just 2½–3 ft. high and slightly wider, with particularly long lasting fall color. Larger types make good screens. All make wonderful specimen plants; set them off against dark evergreens for greatest color impact. 'Compacta' is also excellent as an unclipped hedge.

Euonymus alatus

E. americanus. STRAWBERRY BUSH. Deciduous shrub. Zones 3b–9, 14–17. From eastern U.S. To 4–6 ft. tall and wide, with tough, leathery dark green leaves that turn yellow in autumn. Plentiful fall crop of scarlet fruits that open to show orange seeds. Tolerates much shade; good in woodland plantings.

E. europaeus. SPINDLE TREE. Deciduous shrub or tree. Zones 1–9, 14–16. From Europe, western Asia. Can reach 20 ft. tall and 15 ft. wide but is usually smaller. Green branches bear shiny green leaves to 3 in. long; fall color varies from yellowish green to yellow to red. Inconspicuous flowers mature into showy pink to red fruits that split to reveal white seeds with a fleshy bright orange appendage. 'Aldenham' ('Aldenhamensis') is a vigorous selection with bright pink-and-orange fruits and red fall foliage. Full sun or partial shade.

E. fortunei. Evergreen vine or shrub. Zones 2b–17. From China. One of the best broad-leafed evergreens where temperatures drop below 0°F/–18°C. Trails or climbs by rootlets. If plant is used as a shrub, its branches will trail and sometimes root; if allowed to climb, it will form a spreading mass to 20 ft. or more. Prostrate forms can be used to control erosion. Rich deep green leaves are 1–2½ in. long, with scallop-toothed edges; flowers are inconspicuous. Mature growth (like that of ivy) is shrubby and bears fruit; cuttings taken from this shrubby wood produce upright plants. Grows in sun or shade. In desert, takes full sun better than ivy.

The varieties of *E. fortunei,* some of which are listed here, are better known than the species itself. Many nurseries still sell them as forms of *E. radicans,* once thought to be the species but now considered another variety (see *E. f. radicans*).

'Canadale Gold'. Compact growth to 4 ft. high, 3–3½ ft. wide, with light green leaves edged in yellow.

'Colorata'. PURPLE-LEAF WINTER CREEPER. To 2 ft. high, 6–8 ft. wide. Same sprawling growth habit as *E. f. radicans,* though it makes a more even ground cover. Leaves turn dark purple in fall and winter.

'Emerald Gaiety'. To 4–5 ft. high, 3 ft. wide. Dense-growing, erect shrub with deep green leaves edged in white.

'Emerald 'n Gold'. Similar to above but with gold-edged leaves.

'Golden Prince'. To 4 ft. high and wide. New growth tipped gold; older leaves turn solid green. Extremely hardy; good hedge plant.

'Greenlane'. To 3–4 ft. high, 4–5 ft. wide, with erect branches, deep green foliage, orange fall fruits.

'Harlequin' grows 6–12 in. high and 12–18 in. wide. New growth is

Euonymus fortunei
'Emerald 'n Gold'

almost all white, becoming mottled green and white. Makes a nice edging.

'Ivory Jade'. To 3 ft. high, 6 ft. wide. Resembles 'Greenlane' but has creamy white leaf margins that show pink tints in cold weather.

'Moonshadow'. To 3 ft. high, 4 ft wide. Bright yellow leaves with dark green margins.

E. f. radicans. COMMON WINTER CREEPER. Zones 4–9, 14–17. Tough, hardy, trailing or vining shrub from Korea, Japan. Dark green, thick-textured, 1-in. leaves. Given no support, it's a sprawling, foot-high ground cover. Given a wall to cover, it does the job completely.

'Sunspot'. To 3–6 ft. high and wide. Dark green leaves have a central bright yellow spot.

E. japonicus. EVERGREEN EUONYMUS. Evergreen shrub. Zones 4–20; H1. From China, Korea, Japan. Upright grower to 8–10 ft. high, 6 ft. wide; usually kept lower. Inconspicuous flowers. Older shrubs are attractive trained as trees, pruned and shaped to show their curving trunks and umbrella-shaped tops. Can be grouped to form a hedge or screen. Very glossy, leathery deep green leaves are 1–2½ in. long, oval to roundish.

Though the species and its varieties are very tolerant of heat, unfavorable soil, and seacoast conditions, they tend to suffer from various problems. They are prone to scale, thrips, and spider mites. They are notorious for susceptibility to powdery mildew; to lessen likelihood of mildew infection, give a full-sun location with good air circulation.

Variegated forms are the most popular and are among the few shrubs to maintain their variegaon in full sun in hot-summer climates. (There may be some confusion in nursery labeling of these varieties.)

'Aureo-Variegatus'. To 10 ft. tall, ft. wide. Green leaves with a brilliant yellow central blotch.

'Chollipo'. Narrow, erect plant o 12 ft. tall, 2–3 ft. wide. Green eaves bordered with white.

'Grandifolius'. To 6–8 ft. high, –6 ft. wide, with shiny dark green eaves larger than those of species. ompact, well branched, good for hearing into pyramids, globes.

'Green Spire' is columnar, to ft. high and only 1–2 ft. wide. xcellent as a narrow hedge.

'Microphyllus' (E. j. pulchellus). OX-LEAF EUONYMUS. Comact, small-leafed shrub to 1–2 ft. igh and half as wide. Formal ooking; usually trimmed as ow hedge. Similar in form are Microphyllus Butterscotch' (with ellow-variegated leaves) and Microphyllus Variegatus' (with eaves splashed in white).

'Silver King'. To 6 ft. tall and bout half as wide, with green eaves edged silvery white.

'Silver Princess'. Like 'Microphyllus Variegatus' but larger (to 3 ft. all, 2 ft. wide), with larger leaves.

E. kiautschovicus (E. patens). ones 3–10, 14–19. From China. o 8 ft. tall and as wide or wider. ully evergreen in mild-winter limates and nearly so in harsh winters where there's no snow over. May lose leaves or suffer eaf damage at around 0°F/–18°C. lossy dark green, rather thin-extured leaves. Inconspicuous ruit is pink with orange seeds. Manhattan' is the selection from Manhattan, Kansas—testimony o its toughness. Full sun or artial shade.

EUPATORIUM
steraceae (Compositae)
ERENNIALS

ZONES VARY BY SPECIES

LIGHT SHADE IN HOTTEST CLIMATES

WATER NEEDS VARY BY SPECIES

hese are generally large plants with big domes of small flower eads that are rich in nectar and ollen. Blossoms attract butter-es. Most of the species (includng two of the four described ere) are wild plants of eastern .S. meadows, little noted until ecently but now popular in erennial borders and naturalistic eadow plantings.

E. dubium 'Little Joe'. DWARF JOE PYE WEED. Zones 1–9, 14–17. From eastern U.S. To 4 ft. high and about as wide. Large domes (to 10 in. across) of small lavender flowers are held above whorls of deep green foliage in late summer and fall. Moderate water.

E. greggii. Zones 3, 10–13. Native to Arizona, Texas. Weak-stemmed plant to 1½–2½ ft. tall, 2–3 ft. wide, with clusters of fluffy lavender flowers that are similar in form to those of floss flower (*Ageratum*). Spring to fall bloom. Lacy, divided leaves are somewhat hairy and usually sparse. Excellent for attracting butterflies. Native to dry, hot, rocky places but prefers some shade in low desert. Drought tolerant but looks best with occasional water. 'Boothill', first found near Tombstone, Arizona, is a choice form.

E. maculatum. See E. purpureum maculatum

Eupatorium purpureum maculatum 'Gateway'

E. purpureum. JOE PYE WEED. Zones 1–9, 14–17. From eastern U.S. To 3–9 ft. tall, 1–3 ft. wide, with clump of hollow stems set with tiered whorls of strongly toothed leaves to a foot long. Leaves have a vanilla scent when bruised. Big domes of pale purple flowers in late summer or fall. *E. p. maculatum* is similar but somewhat smaller (to 6 ft.), with purple-spotted stems. Most common in gardens is 5-ft.-tall 'Gateway', with reddish purple stems topped by mauve to dusky purple flowers. All put on best show with rich soil, ample water.

E. rugosum (Ageratina altissima). WHITE SNAKEROOT. Zones 1–10, 14–17. From eastern U.S. To 4 ft. tall, 2 ft. wide. Stems and lance-shaped leaves to 5 in. long are heavily marked with deep brownish red; 'Chocolate' has especially deep color. Fluffy white flowers in late summer and early fall. Give rich soil, ample water.

EUPHORBIA
Euphorbiaceae
ANNUALS, BIENNIALS, PERENNIALS, AND EVERGREEN AND DECIDUOUS SHRUBS OR TREES

ZONES VARY BY SPECIES

EXPOSURE NEEDS VARY BY SPECIES

MODERATE TO REGULAR WATER, EXCEPT AS NOTED

SAP IS IRRITATING OR POISONOUS IN MANY SPECIES

Large genus of about 2,000 species. What is called a "flower" is technically a cyathium, consisting of fused bracts that form a cup around the much-reduced true flowers. Cyathia may appear singly or in clusters. In some cases, as with poinsettia (*E. pulcherrima*), additional bracts below provide most of the color. Fruit is usually a dry capsule that releases seeds explosively, shooting them up to several feet away. Many euphorbias are succulents; these often mimic cacti in appearance and are as diverse in form and size. Only a few succulent types are listed here, but specialists in cacti and succulents can supply scores of species and varieties. All euphorbias have milky white sap that is irritating on contact or toxic if ingested (degree of irritation or toxicity varies, depending on species). Before using cut flowers in arrangements, dip stems in boiling water or hold in a flame for a few seconds to prevent sap bleed. Plant all in well-drained soil.

E. amygdaloides. Perennial. Zones 2b–24. From Europe and Turkey. To 3 ft. tall, 1 ft. wide, with reddish green stems. Evergreen, 1–3-in.-long, dark green leaves have red undersides that turn darker red in winter. Greenish yellow flowers in clusters to 8 in. long at stem ends in midspring to early summer. Best in sun but tolerates some shade. 'Purpurea' has foliage heavily tinted purple, bright green inflorescences.

E. a. robbiae. MRS. ROBB'S BONNET. Shorter (to 1 ft. tall) and more shade tolerant than the species; also more spreading, expanding its territory by rhizomes and sometimes becoming invasive. It has interbred with the plain species, and intermediates are often sold as this variety.

E. antisyphilitica. CANDELILLA. Succulent shrub. Zones 12, 13, 18–21. Native to southwestern U.S., Mexico. Erect plant to 3 ft. high, spreading by underground stems. Cylindrical pale green stems

are covered with wax used commercially in making candles. Inflorescence consists of red bracts and white petal-like appendages in a star shape. Good for rock gardens, containers. Withstands light frosts. Full sun, little water.

E. biglandulosa. See E. rigida

E. 'Blue Haze'. Zones 7–9, 14–17. Hybrid between *E. seguieriana niciciana* and a species from central and eastern Europe. Compact, bushy growth to 1½ ft. tall and 2 ft. wide, with narrow, powder blue leaves held on reddish stems. Practically covered in chartreuse inflorescences from late spring well into summer. Full sun to partial shade. Tolerates aridity.

E. characias. Perennial. Zones 4–24. Mediterranean native. Upright stems crowded with narrow blue-green leaves form a dome-shaped bush 4 ft. high and wide. Chartreuse or lime green flowers in dense, round to cylindrical clusters appear in late winter, early spring. Color holds with only slight fading until seeds ripen; then stalks turn yellow and should be cut out at base, since new shoots have already made growth for next year's flowers. 'Humpty Dumpty' is a shorter (to 2½-ft.-high), vigorous selection. 'Tasmanian Tiger' grows 3 ft. tall and wide, with leaves and flower bracts edged in white. *E. c. wulfenii* (*E. veneta*), the most commonly grown form, has broader clusters of yellow flowers. All are fairly drought resistant and perform best in full sun.

Euphorbia characias wulfenii

E. cotinifolia. CARIBBEAN COPPER PLANT. Shrub or tree. Deciduous in Zone 23; evergreen in Zones 24, H1, H2. From tropical America. Usually a multistemmed shrub 9–10 ft. high and wide, though it can become a small tree to 18 ft. tall if grown in a warm, frost-free spot. Long-stalked leaves to 4 in. long, 3 in. wide, usually borne in threes, are similar to those of smoke tree (*Cotinus*); 'Atropurpurea', the form most commonly grown, has wine red leaves. Loose flower clusters have small white bracts, are not showy. Likes full sun, heat, good drainage; can't take frost. Older plants may fall over under their own weight unless staked.

E. cyathophora. See E. heterophylla

E

E. cyparissias. CYPRESS SPURGE. Perennial. Zones 2–24. European native forms feathery clump to 8 in. (possibly to 16 in.) high; spreads vigorously by rhizomes, often becoming invasive. Slender, erect stems branch toward tips. Crowded blue-green, needle-like leaves. Terminal clusters of yellow-green flowers appear in late spring to early summer; these may turn orange in poor soils. Plant may go dormant in winter. Full sun or light shade. Little to moderate water.

E. 'Diamond Frost'. Perennial. Zones 13, 21–24; H1, H2. Annual elsewhere. Delicate, airy mounds to 12–18 in. high and twice as wide. Small white flowers look like snowflakes interspersed with the sparse, olive green foliage. Plant resembles baby's breath (Gypsophila paniculata). Blooms year-round in mild winter areas, spring to fall elsewhere. Excellent in pots and hanging baskets. Full sun to partial shade.

E. dulcis 'Chameleon'. Perennial. Zones 2b–24. Forms a mound to 2 ft. high and wide. New spring growth is burgundy, maturing to dark bronzy green. Greenish yellow flower heads with a purplish tint appear at stem ends in early summer. Leaves and bracts turn rich purple in fall. Spreads by self-sowing; comes true from seed. Full sun. Tolerates dry soil.

E. epithymoides. See E. polychroma.

E. griffithii. Perennial. Zones 2–10, 14–24. Erect-stemmed Himalayan native to 3 ft. tall and wide; spreads by creeping roots but is not aggressive. Narrow, medium green leaves are red tinged when new. Reddish orange to red bracts in early summer; those of 'Fireglow' are vivid orange red. Dies back in winter. Full sun or light shade.

E. heterophylla. FALSE POINSETTIA, MEXICAN FIRE PLANT, PAINTED SPURGE. Annual. Zones 1–24; H1, H2. Plants labeled as this species are almost always E. cyathophora, a native of eastern U.S. and Mexico. To 3 ft. tall, 1 ft. wide. Bright green leaves of varying shapes, larger ones resembling those of poinsettia (E. pulcherrima); flowers unimportant. In summer, upper leaves are blotched bright red and white, giving the appearance of a second-rate poinsettia. Useful in hot, dry borders in poor soil. Sow seed in place after danger of frost is past. Heavy reseeder in desert gardens. Full sun.

E. lambii. Deciduous shrub. Zones 14–24. From Canary Islands. Reaches 3–7½ ft. tall and almost as wide; spreads slowly by self-seeding. Single trunk branches slowly, first in two, later in threes, creating an inverted cone shape. Each branch is topped with a rosette of bluish to yellow-green leaves. Terminal clusters of chartreuse flowers in early spring. Tolerates various soil types. Full sun. Give regular water during growth and bloom; doesn't need any during summer dormancy.

E. lathyris. GOPHER PLANT, MOLE PLANT. Biennial. Zones 2–10, 14–24. From Europe, northwest Africa. Legend claims that it repels gophers and moles. Stems have poisonous, caustic milky juice; keep away from skin and especially eyes, as painful burns can result. Juice could conceivably bother a gopher or mole enough to make it beat a hasty retreat. Single-stemmed plant to 5 ft. tall and 1 ft. wide. Stem is densely set with large leaves growing at right angles to the stem and to each other (forming four longitudinal rows along stem). In second summer, produces short-lived cluster of unspectacular yellow flowers at top of stem. Flowers soon go to seed, after which the plant dies. Start from seed; plant will keep going by self-sowing. Sun or shade. Little to regular water.

E. marginata. SNOW-ON-THE-MOUNTAIN. Annual. Zones 1–24. From central North America. To 2 ft. high, 1 ft. wide. Oval light green leaves; upper ones striped and margined white, sometimes even solid white. Summer flowers are variegated in green and white. Good for contrast with bright-colored bedding plants. 'Summer Icicle' has particularly bright white markings. Sow seeds in place in spring, in sun or partial shade. Thin to only a few inches apart, since plants are somewhat rangy.

E. × martinii. Perennial. Zones 3–24. Hybrid between E. amygdaloides and E. characias. To 2–3 ft. tall and wide. Resembles a compact E. characias, with dense clusters of brown-centered chartreuse flowers in late winter, spring. Evergreen leaves often tinged purple when young. Stems are red in winter. Full sun or partial shade. Fairly drought resistant. 'Red Martin' has leaves held nearly upright, showing off red color of stems and new foliage.

E. milii (E. splendens). CROWN OF THORNS. Woody shrub; evergreen but sparsely leafed. Zones 13, 21–24; H1, H2; or indoors. Some frost damage below 28°F/–2°C. From Madagascar. To 1–4 ft. high, 1½ ft. wide. Stems armed with long, sharp thorns. Roundish, thin, light green leaves usually appear only near branch ends. Clustered pairs of red bracts put on a show nearly all year. Many varieties and hybrids varying in form, size, and bract color (yellow, orange, pink). Plants in the Supergrandiflora series are hybrids (often sold as varieties of E. × lomi) with large flowers in shades of yellow, pink, orange, and red; some are attractively speckled.

In windy or frost-prone areas, grow against a sheltered wall; or grow in container. Salt tolerance makes it an ideal choice for seaside plantings. Grow in porous but not rocky soil, in full sun or light shade (needs afternoon shade in Zone 13). Indoors, give bright light.

Euphorbia myrsinites

E. myrsinites. Perennial. Zones 2–24. Native from southern Europe to central Asia. To 6 in. high, 1 ft. wide. Evergreen plant with stems that trail outward from central crown, then rise toward tips. Stiff, roundish blue-gray leaves set closely in spirals around stems. Flattish clusters of chartreuse to yellow flowers top stem ends in late winter, early spring. Cut out old stems as they turn yellow. Withstands cold, heat, and aridity but is short lived in warm-winter areas. Use in sunny rock garden with succulents and gray-leafed plants.

E. obesa. BASEBALL PLANT. Succulent perennial. Zone 24; or indoor/outdoor plant. South African native forms a solid, fleshy, gray-green sphere (or short cylinder) to 8 in., with brownish horizontal stripes and brown dots that outline vertical ridges. Flowers unimportant. Give bright light, warmth, no sudden temperature changes. Little to moderate water; keep dryish in winter.

E. palustris. Perennial. Zones 2b–9, 14–17. From Europe, western Asia. Forms robust clump to 3 ft. high and wide, with many medium green, 2–3-in. leaves that turn yellow and orange in fall. Wide-branching clusters of yellow flowers in spring, early summer. Dies back in winter. Self-sows. Full sun or partial shade. One of the few euphorbias that will grow in damp or boggy conditions; also does well in ordinary garden soil, whether dry or moist.

E. polychroma (E. epithymoides). Perennial. Zones A2; 1–24. From Europe. Neatly rounded hemisphere to 1½ ft. high, 2 ft. wide, with deep green leaves symmetrically arranged on closely set, hairy stems. From midspring to midsummer, plant is covered with rounded clusters of bright yellow flowers surrounded by whorls of yellow-green bracts. Effect is of a gold mound suffused with green. Displays good fall color (yellow to orange or red) before going dormant. 'Bonfire' has leaves that emerge green but then mature to red and hold their color all summer. Use in rock gardens, perennial borders. Needs some shade in hottest climates. Short lived but reseeds.

E. pulcherrima. POINSETTIA. Evergreen, semievergreen, or deciduous shrub. Zones 13, 16–24; H1, H2; or indoors. From Mexico. Leggy plant to 10 ft. or taller, 6 ft. wide. Coarse leaves grow on stiffly upright canes. Showy part of plant consists of petal-like bracts; true flowers in center are yellowish, inconspicuous. Red single form is the most familiar; less well known are double-bracted red sorts and forms with white, yellowish, pink, or marbled bracts. Plants bloom only when they experience long nights—in winter and into spring. Milky sap is not poisonous; most people find it either completely harmless or at

Euphorbia pulcherrima

most mildly irritating to skin or stomach.

Useful garden plant in well-drained soil and full sun (light shade in Zone 13). Where adapted outdoors, needs no special care. Grow as informal hedge in frost-free areas; where winter weather is frosty (but not severely cold), plant against sunny wall, in sheltered corner, under south-facing eaves (east-facing ones in Zone 13). Thin branches in summer to produce larger bracts; or prune them back at 2-month intervals for bushy growth (but often smaller bracts). To improve red color, feed every 2 weeks with high-nitrogen fertilizer, starting when color begins to show.

To care for holiday gift plant, keep in a sunny window and avoid sudden temperature changes. Keep soil moist but don't let water stand in pot saucer. When leaves drop in late winter or early spring, cut stems back to two buds and reduce watering to minimum. Store in a cool place until danger of frost is past; then set plant out in garden or keep in pot in a sunny spot on the patio. Potted plant will probably grow too tall for indoor use the next winter, but may survive winter if well sheltered. Start new plants by making late-summer cuttings of stems with four or five eyes (joints).

To get potted plant to bloom at Christmas time (earlier than in nature), do this: starting in early October, move it to a completely darkened closet each night for 14 hours; then, in the morning, move it into light for a maximum of 10 hours. Continue the process for 10 weeks.

E. rigida (E. biglandulosa). Perennial. Zones 4–24. Mediterranean native forms a 3–5-ft.-wide clump of stems that angle outward, then rise up to 2 ft. high. Fleshy gray-green leaves to 1½ in. long are narrow and pointed, their bases set tightly against stems. Broad, domed flower clusters in late winter or early spring are chartreuse yellow fading to pinkish. After seeds ripen, stems die back and should be removed; new stems take their place. Reseeds in mildest-winter areas, but not enough to become a pest. Showy display plant in borders, rock gardens, containers. Full sun. Tolerates drought.

E. robbiae. See E. amygdaloides robbiae

E. seguieriana niciciana. Perennial. Zones 4–24. From Balkans to Pakistan. Resembles a delicate, fine-textured E. characias. To 1½ ft. high and wide, with narrow, inch-long blue-gray leaves and chartreuse inflorescences. Full sun. Tolerates aridity.

E. tirucalli. MILKBUSH, PENCILBUSH, PENCIL TREE. Succulent tree or shrub. Zones 13, 23, 24; H1, H2; or indoors. From tropical eastern Africa. Grown for striking pattern of silhouette or shadow. Fast growing to possible 30 ft. tall and 6 ft. wide, usually much smaller. Single or multiple trunks support tangle of light green, pencil-thick, succulent branches with tiny leaves present only on actively growing tips. Flowers are unimportant. 'Sticks on Fire' has pale pink to fiery salmon pink stems; new growth has the most intense color in bright light. Both species and variety very tolerant of seacoast conditions. Full sun. Be sure to keep milky sap away from eyes, as it can cause severe damage. As houseplant, thrives in driest atmosphere; needs all the light you can give it, well-drained potting mix, routine watering and fertilizing.

E. veneta, E. wulfenii. See E. characias

EUROPEAN BIRD CHERRY. See **PRUNUS padus**

EURYA emarginata
Theaceae
EVERGREEN SHRUB

| ✒ ZONES 4–6, 15–17, 21–24 |
| :☼: LIGHT SHADE |
| 💧 REGULAR WATER |

Native to Japan. Slow growing to 6 ft. tall and wide, with branches rising at a 45° angle from base of plant. Easily kept to 3–4 ft. by pruning to side buds or branches. Grown for refined foliage—teardrop-shaped, dark green, leathery, ½-in.-long leaves closely

Eurya emarginata

set on branches. (*E. e. microphylla* has even tinier leaves—just ¼ in. long.) Young plants don't bloom, but old ones bear small greenish yellow flowers in late spring; most people consider the blossoms malodorous. Grow in organically enriched, acid, moist, well-drained soil. For the plant sometimes called *E. ochnacea,* see *Cleyera japonica.*

EURYOPS
Asteraceae (Compositae)
EVERGREEN SHRUBS

| ✒ ZONES VARY BY SPECIES |
| :☼: FULL SUN |
| 💧 💧 💧 LITTLE TO REGULAR WATER |

Native to South Africa. Leaves are finely divided; flower heads are daisylike. Long bloom season; keep old flowers picked off. Plants need excellent drainage. They thrive on buffeting ocean winds but are damaged by sharp frosts. Take well to container culture.

E. acraeus. Zones 5–9, 12–24. Mounded growth to 2 ft. high and wide. Silvery gray leaves to ¾ in. long. Inch-wide, bright yellow daisies cover plant in spring. Mountain native and thus hardier to frost than *E. pectinatus* and its varieties. Has been used as a rock garden plant in western Washington and Oregon. May not survive winters in colder zones unless protected from excess moisture.

Euryops pectinatus

E. pectinatus. Zones 8, 9, 12–24; H1, H2. To 3–6 ft. high and wide. Easy care and extremely long flowering season make it a good filler, background plant, or low screen. Gray-green, deeply divided, 2-in.-long leaves. Bright yellow, 1½–2-in.-wide daisies on 6-in. stems bloom most of the year. Cut back in late spring or early summer to maintain compactness and limit size. 'Viridis' is like species in all but leaf color; its

foliage is deep green. 'Munchkin', with gray-green foliage, grows to 3 ft. tall, 4 ft. wide.

EUSTOMA grandiflorum (Lisianthus russellianus)
LISIANTHUS, TULIP GENTIAN, TEXAS BLUEBELL
Gentianaceae
BIENNIAL OR SHORT-LIVED PERENNIAL GROWN AS ANNUAL

| ✒ ZONES 1–24 |
| :☼: :☼: FULL SUN OR LIGHT SHADE |
| 💧 REGULAR WATER |

Native to high plains of the West, but garden forms introduced from Japan. Plants grow better and have longer stems where nights are warm; best cut flowers are produced in greenhouses. In summer,

Eustoma grandiflorum

a foot-wide clump of gray-green foliage sends up 1–3-ft. stems topped by tulip-shaped, 2–3-in. flowers in purplish blue, pink, or white; bloom lasts all summer if old blossoms are cut off. Fully double flowers of Double Eagle and Echo strains resemble roses. Color range of single-flowered Heidi strain includes a so-called yellow (actually ivory). 'Forever White' and 'Forever Blue' are bushy and compact, to about 1 ft. tall, with large single blooms. 'Red Glass' has rose red single flowers. Mermaid and Lizzy are dwarf (8-in.) strains.

Start with nursery plants or, with much care, from dust-fine seeds. Sprinkle seeds on surface of potting soil; don't cover with soil. Soak well, then cover the pot with glass or plastic until seedlings emerge. At four-leaf stage (about 2 months), transplant three or four plants into each 6-in. pot; plant out in beds after plants put on some growth. Needs good garden soil, good drainage. Use in pots, borders, cutting gardens.

E

E

EVENING PRIMROSE.
See **OENOTHERA**

EVERGREEN GRAPE.
See **RHOICISSUS capensis**

EVERGREEN PEAR.
See **PYRUS kawakamii**

EVERGREEN WISTERIA.
See **MILLETTIA**

EVERLASTING.
See **HELIPTERUM**

EVOLVULUS
glomeratus
Convolvulaceae
PERENNIAL USUALLY GROWN
AS ANNUAL

🌿	ZONES 24; H2; ANYWHERE AS ANNUAL
☀️ ◐	FULL SUN OR LIGHT SHADE
💧	REGULAR WATER

Evolvulus glomeratus 'Blue Daze'

Native to Brazil. Small trailing morning glory with stems to 20 in. long and oval leaves ⅓–1¼ in. long. Half-inch-wide blue flowers in summer; they close in the evening and on dark, cloudy days. Plants most widely offered are labeled 'Blue Daze', 'Hawaiian Blue Eyes', or *E. g. grandiflorus;* or they may simply bear the common name "blue daze." These plants vary somewhat: foliage may be green or gray, blossoms bright blue or powder blue. Stems of all root where they touch the ground, and cuttings root very easily in water or moist soil. Use in hanging baskets, beds, borders.

EXACUM affine
PERSIAN VIOLET
Gentianaceae
ANNUAL OR SHORT-LIVED
PERENNIAL GROWN AS ANNUAL

🌿	ALL ZONES; OR INDOORS
◑ ●	SOME SHADE; BRIGHT INDIRECT LIGHT
💧 💧	REGULAR TO AMPLE WATER

Native to Socotra, an island off the Horn of Africa. Small, rounded plant with egg-shaped, inch-long leaves and blue, sweet-scented, star-shaped flowers centered with

Exacum affine

tufts of bright yellow stamens. (A white variety is also available.) Five plants in a 5-in. pot make attractive showing. Needs rich soil, high humidity. Deadhead to prolong bloom. Good plant for house or cool greenhouse.

EXOCHORDA
PEARL BUSH
Rosaceae
DECIDUOUS SHRUBS

🌿	ZONES 2–9, 14–23
☀️	FULL SUN
💧	REGULAR WATER

From China. Loose, spikelike clusters of 1½–2-in. white flowers open from a profusion of buds resembling pearls. Flowers bloom in spring, at about the same time the roundish, 1½–2-in.-long leaves expand. Foliage and arching growth suggest the related spirea, but pearl bush has larger individual blossoms. Prefers well-drained, acid soil; will take considerable neglect. Prune after bloom to control form, size. To make larger kinds fit small gardens, you can remove the lower branches to create upright, airy, multistemmed small trees.

Exochorda racemosa

E. giraldii. To 9 ft. tall and somewhat wider. Red tints in leaf veins and flower stalks.

E. × macrantha. 'The Bride', the only generally available form of this hybrid group, is a compact shrub 6 ft. tall and wide.

E. racemosa (E. grandiflora). COMMON PEARL BUSH. Loose, open, slender shrub to 10–15 ft. tall and wide. Resistant to oak root fungus.

F

FAGUS
BEECH
Fagaceae
DECIDUOUS TREES

🌿	ZONES VARY BY SPECIES
☀️ ◐	FULL SUN OR LIGHT SHADE
💧💧 💧	MODERATE TO REGULAR WATER

Fagus sylvatica 'Purpurea Pendula'

Of the beeches described here, European beech (*F. sylvatica*) is by far the most widely grown. The species differ very little except in leaf details. Capable of growing 90 ft. tall and 60 ft. wide, but usually much smaller. Typically have a broad cone shape, with wide, sweeping lower branches that can reach the ground unless pruned off. Smooth gray bark contrasts well with the glossy dark green foliage. In fall, leaves first take on a bronze to red-brown color, then turn brown; many hang on the tree well into winter. Lacy branching pattern and pointed leaf buds provide an attractive winter silhouette. New foliage has a silky sheen. Little three-cornered nuts enclosed in spiny husks are edible but too small to be of value; they often fail to fill, especially on solitary trees.

All beeches cast heavy shade and have a dense network of fibrous roots near soil surface, inhibiting growth of lawn or other plants beneath. Transplant from containers or, if moving an in-ground tree, dig with a substantial ball of earth. Give any good garden soil. Salts in soil or water stunt growth, turn leaves brown. Woolly

beech aphids cause little trouble except for dripping honeydew. Trees withstand heavy pruning; they can be planted close together and trimmed to form a dense, impassable hedge as low as 4 ft.

F. crenata. JAPANESE BEECH. Zones 2b–6. From Japan. Scalloped-edged leaves are somewhat smaller than those of other beeches. Reddish brown fall color.

F. grandifolia. AMERICAN BEECH. Zones 1–6. From eastern North America. Toothed leaves 3–6 in. long turn golden bronze in fall.

F. sylvatica. EUROPEAN BEECH. Zones A3; 2b–9, 14–21. Native from central Europe to Caucasus. Glossy green leaves to 4 in. long, turning russet and bronzy in autumn. Many varieties, including the following.

'Asplenifolia'. FERNLEAF BEECH. Large, robust, spreading tree with delicate foliage: narrow leaves are deeply lobed or cut nearly to midrib.

'Atropunicea'. COPPER BEECH, PURPLE BEECH. To 50–60 ft. high, 35–45 ft. wide. Deep reddish or purple leaves. Good in containers. Often sold as 'Riversii' or 'Purpurea'. Seedlings of copper beech are usually bronzy purple, turning bronzy green in summer.

Fagus sylvatica

'Dawyck Gold'. Columnar tree to 60 ft. tall, 22 ft. wide. New leaves emerge yellow, mature to light green, turn yellow again in fall.

'Dawyck Purple'. Columnar, to 70 ft. tall, 15 ft. wide, with purple foliage.

'Fastigiata'. DAWYCK BEECH. Narrow, upright tree, like Lombardy poplar (*Populus nigra* 'Italica') in form; 8 ft. wide when 35 ft. tall. Broader in great age, but still narrower than the species.

'Laciniata'. CUTLEAF BEECH. Narrow, deeply cut green leaves.

'Pendula'. WEEPING BEECH. regular, spreading form. Long, weeping branches reach to ground. Green leaves. Without staking to establish vertical trunk, will grow wide rather than high.

'Purple Fountain'. To 25 ft. tall and 12 ft. wide, with weeping branches from an upright trunk that needs staking only in youth. Purple to purple-red foliage.

'Purpurea Pendula'. WEEPING COPPER BEECH. Purple-leafed weeping form. Usually no larger than 10 ft. high and wide; may need staking to maintain upright growth. Splendid container plant.

'Red Obelisk'. Columnar tree with dark purple-red foliage. Some leaves are deeply cut, others smooth edged.

'Rohan Gold'. Leaves with wavy scalloped edges open yellow and gradually fade to green, then turn gold again in fall.

'Rohanii'. Similar to the above but with brownish purple leaves maturing to dark green; unimpressive fall color (reddish or purplish brown).

'Tricolor'. TRICOLOR BEECH. Green leaves marked white and edged pink. Slow to 24–40 ft. tall, usually much less. Foliage burns in hot sun or dry winds. Choice container plant.

'Zlatia'. GOLDEN BEECH. Young leaves yellow, aging to yellow green. Subject to sunburn. Slow grower; good container plant.

FAIRY DUSTER.
See **CALLIANDRA eriophylla**

FAIRY LANTERN.
See **CALOCHORTUS**

FAIRY LILY.
See **ZEPHYRANTHES**

FAIRY THIMBLES.
See **CAMPANULA cochleariifolia**

FAIRY WAND. See **DIERAMA**

FALLOPIA
Polygonaceae
EVERGREEN OR DECIDUOUS VINES

| 🌡 ZONES A1–A3; 1–24 |
| ☀ ◑ EXPOSURE NEEDS VARY BY SPECIES |
| 💧 LITTLE TO REGULAR WATER |

The two plants described here were formerly listed as *Polygonum*. Both offer showy flowers, but they also require vigilance, as they spread by rhizomes and can be highly invasive and difficult to eradicate.

Fallopia baldschuanica

F. baldschuanica (F. aubertii, Polygonum aubertii). SILVER LACE VINE. Zones A1–A3; 1–24. Deciduous in Zones A1–A3, 1–7, 10–12; evergreen elsewhere. This extremely vigorous vine from Asia can cover a large space (40 ft.) in a short time. Heart-shaped, waxy-edged, glossy green leaves are 1½–2½ in. long. From spring to fall, the vine is covered in a frothy mass of creamy white flowers that are sometimes tinged with pink; these develop into papery, pinkish white fruits. Use to cover a fence or arbor or as a rough bank cover. Tolerates coastal conditions; succeeds in the desert only if given deep, rich soil and regular watering. Prune severely to keep in bounds; can be cut back to the ground in winter, but blooms will be delayed until late summer. Full sun.

F. japonica (Polygonum cuspidatum, Reynoutria japonica). JAPANESE KNOTWEED. Zones A1–A3; 1–24. Deciduous perennial from eastern Asia. Tough, vigorous plant with wiry, reddish stems that form large clumps to 4–8 ft. tall. Pale green leaves are nearly heart shaped, to 5 in. long. Showy clusters of greenish white flowers in late summer and fall. Rampant. Spreads by underground runners and is particularly hard to control; shoots have been known to push up through asphalt. Good choice for bank cover or erosion control where little else will grow. Full sun or partial shade.

'Crimson Beauty' bears fiery red flowers on 7–8-ft. stems from late summer through fall. It's better behaved than the species, forming clumps that are not invasive. 'Variegata' has creamy white leaves splashed with dark green; spring new growth is coral pink. Foliage a favorite for flower arrangements.

FALLUGIA paradoxa
APACHE PLUME
Rosaceae
SEMIEVERGREEN SHRUB

| 🌡 ZONES 2–23 |
| ☀ FULL SUN |
| 💧 NO IRRIGATION NEEDED |

Native to mountains of medium and high deserts of California, southwestern U.S., northern Mexico. Grows 4–6 ft. tall, 5 ft. wide, with straw-colored branches and flaky bark. Small, lobed leaves are deep green on top, rusty beneath; carried in clusters. Flowers resembling single white roses just 1½ in. wide bloom in spring, summer. Large, showy clusters of feathery seedheads follow; greenish at first, later turning pink or taking on reddish tinges, they create a soft-colored, changing haze through which you can see the shrub's rigid branch pattern. Needs gritty, well-drained soil. Pruning usually not needed.

Fallugia paradoxa

FALSE ARBORVITAE.
See **THUJOPSIS dolabrata**

FALSE BABY'S BREATH.
See **GALIUM mollugo**

FALSE BIRD-OF-PARADISE.
See **HELICONIA**

FALSE CYPRESS.
See **CHAMAECYPARIS**

FALSE DRAGONHEAD.
See **PHYSOSTEGIA virginiana**

FALSE HEATHER.
See **CUPHEA hyssopifolia**

FALSE INDIGO. See **BAPTISIA**

FALSE LILY-OF-THE-VALLEY.
See **MAIANTHEMUM dilatatum**

FALSE MESQUITE.
See **CALLIANDRA eriophylla**

FALSE POINSETTIA.
See **EUPHORBIA heterophylla**

FALSE SANDALWOOD.
See **MYOPORUM sandwicense**

FALSE SOLOMON'S SEAL. See **MAIANTHEMUM racemosum**

FALSE SPIREA.
See **ASTILBE, SORBARIA**

FALSE SUNFLOWER.
See **HELIOPSIS helianthoides**

FANCY-LEAFED CALADIUM.
See **CALADIUM bicolor**

FAN PALM. See **CHAMAEROPS, PRITCHARDIA, WASHINGTONIA**

FAREWELL-TO-SPRING.
See **CLARKIA amoena**

FARFUGIUM
japonicum (Ligularia tussilaginea)
Asteraceae (Compositae)
PERENNIAL

| 🌡 ZONES 4–10, 14–24; H1, H2; OR INDOORS |
| ☀ ◑ SOME SHADE; BRIGHT INDIRECT LIGHT |
| 💧 AMPLE WATER |

From China, Japan. Forms a clump to about 2 ft. tall and wide. Glossy bright green, kidney-shaped, scalloped, or shallowly lobed leaves are 7 in. long, 15 in. wide, carried on long (1–2-ft.) leafstalks. Flower stems are 1½–2 ft. tall, each carrying several 1½–2-in. yellow daisy flowers. The species is not as popular or widely grown as its selections.

Farfugium japonicum
'Aureo-maculatum'

'Argenteum' has somewhat smaller deep green leaves marbled with gray green and white. 'Aureo-maculatum', also known as leopard plant, has thick, leathery leaves that are heavily, evenly speckled with yellow. 'Crispatum', sometimes called pie crust ligularia, has thick, ruffle-edged gray-green leaves.

All are choice container plants for shady beds or entryways. Tops hardy to 20°F/–7°C. Plants

F

die back to roots at 0°F/–18°C, put on new growth in spring. Control snails and slugs.

FARGESIA. See **BAMBOO**

× **FATSHEDERA lizei**
Araliaceae
EVERGREEN SHRUB OR VINE

| 🌡 ZONES 4–10, 12–24; H1, H2 |
| ◑ ● PARTIAL OR FULL SHADE |
| 💧 REGULAR WATER |

Hybrid between Japanese aralia (*Fatsia japonica*) and English ivy (*Hedera helix*), with characteristics of both parents. Highly polished, 4–10-in.-wide leaves with three to five pointed lobes look like giant ivy leaves; plant also sends out long, trailing or climbing stems like ivy, though without aerial holdfasts. This hybrid inherited shrubbiness from its Japanese aralia parent, though its habit is more irregular and sprawling.

× *Fatshedera lizei*

Leaves of 'Variegata' are bordered in white; those of 'Media-Picta' have a central yellow blotch.

Leaves are injured at 15°F/–9°C, tender new growth at 20 to 25°F/–7 to –4°C. Seems to suffer more from late frosts than from winter cold. Give it protection from hot, drying winds. Watch out for slugs and snails. Good near swimming pools.

This plant tends to grow in a straight line, but it can be shaped if you work at it. Pinch tip growth to force branching. Two or three times a year, guide and tie stems before they become brittle. If plant gets away from you, cut it back to ground; it will regrow quickly. If you use it as ground cover, cut back vertical growth every 2 or 3 weeks during growing season. Grown as vine or espalier, plants are heavy, so give them strong supports. Even a well-grown vine is leafless at base.

FATSIA japonica (Aralia sieboldii, A. japonica)
JAPANESE ARALIA
Araliaceae
EVERGREEN SHRUB

| 🌡 ZONES 4–9, 14–24; H1, H2 |
| ◑ ● PARTIAL OR FULL SHADE |
| 💧 REGULAR WATER |

From Korea, Japan. Tropical-looking shrub with long-stalked, big, glossy dark green, deeply lobed, fanlike leaves to 16 in. wide. Moderate growth to 5–8 ft. high and wide (rarely more); sparsely branched. Many roundish clusters of small, creamy white flowers in fall and winter, followed by clusters of small, shiny black fruit.

Grows in nearly all soils except soggy ones. Adapted to containers. If leaves are chronically yellow, add iron to soil. During prolonged dry spells, wash occasionally with hose to clean leaves and to lessen insect attack. Control slugs and snails. Established plants sucker freely; keep suckers or remove them with spade. Rejuvenate spindly plants by cutting back hard in early spring. Plants that set fruit often self-sow.

Fatsia japonica

A natural landscaping choice where bold pattern is wanted. Most effective when thinned to show some branch structure. Provides year-round good looks for shaded entryway or patio. Useful near swimming pools. 'Moseri' has compact habit. 'Variegata' has leaves edged golden yellow to creamy white.

FAWN LILY. See **ERYTHRONIUM californicum**

FEATHER BUSH.
See **LYSILOMA microphylla thornberi**

FEATHERED HYACINTH.
See **MUSCARI comosum 'Monstrosum'**

FEATHERFLOWER.
See **VERTICORDIA plumosa**

FEATHER GRASS. See **STIPA**

FEATHER GRASS, MEXICAN.
See **NASSELLA tenuissima**

FEATHER REED GRASS.
See **CALAMAGROSTIS acutiflora**

FEATHERTOP.
See **PENNISETUM villosum**

FEIJOA, PINEAPPLE GUAVA
Myrtaceae
EVERGREEN SHRUB OR TREE

| 🌡 ZONES 6 (MARGINAL), 7–9, 12–24; H1, H2 |
| ☀ FULL SUN |
| 💧 REGULAR WATER |

South American native known botanically as *Feijoa sellowiana* (*Acca sellowiana*). Hardiest of so-called subtropical fruits. Normally a large multistemmed plant; reaches 18–25 ft. with equal spread if not pruned or killed back by frosts. Can take almost any amount of training or pruning (late spring is the best time) to shape as espalier, screen, hedge, or small tree. Oval, 2–3-in.-long leaves are glossy green above, silvery white beneath. Blooms in spring, bearing unusual inch-wide flowers with big central tufts of red stamens and four fleshy white petals tinged purplish on inside; blossoms attract bees and birds. Flowers are edible and can be added to fruit salads or used for jams and jellies. Plant is drought tolerant, but give it regular water for best fruiting.

Fruit ripens 4 to 5½ months after flowering in warmest regions, 5 to 7 months after bloom in cooler areas. Oval, grayish green, 1–4-in.-long fruit has soft, sweet to bland pulp with flavor somewhat like pineapple. The best way

Feijoa

to harvest is to wait until first fruit drops, then spread a tarp underneath and give the tree a shake. Repeat every few days. Fruit is sometimes sold in markets; it may be labeled "feijoa" or "pineapple guava."

Improved varieties 'Beechwood', 'Coolidge', 'Mammoth', 'Nazemetz', and 'Trask' are self-fruitful, although cross-pollination will produce a better crop. Single plants of seedlings or other named varieties may require cross-pollination.

FELICIA
Asteraceae (Compositae)
SHRUBS, PERENNIALS, AND ANNUAL

| 🌡 ZONES VARY BY SPECIES |
| ☀ FULL SUN |
| ◐ 💧 WATER NEEDS VARY BY SPECIES |

Daisy relatives, typically with blue flowers; native to South Africa. Though more than 80 species are known, only a few are commonly cultivated in Western gardens.

F. amelloides (F. aethiopica, Agathaea coelestis). BLUE MARGUERITE. Woody perennial in Zones 8, 9, 14–24; treated as winter annual in Zone 13 and summer annual elsewhere. Despite the common name, not the true

Felicia amelloides

marguerite (*Chrysanthemum frutescens*). About 1½ ft. tall and spreading 4–5 ft. wide, with roughish, oval, rather aromatic green leaves about 1 in. long. Produces an abundance of 1¼-in., yellow-centered sky blue daisies. As a perennial, blooms almost continually if dead flowers are picked off; prune back hard in late summer to encourage new blooming wood. Grow in pots or containers, let spill over wall or edge of raised bed, or plant in any sunny spot. Regular water.

F. bergeriana. KINGFISHER DAISY. Annual. Zones 1–24. Freely branching plant with grayish, 1½-in. leaves makes mat 4–6 in. high, up to a foot across. Bright blue, inch-wide flowers appear all summer long. Sow in early spring (in fall where winters are warm). Good in pots, window boxes, borders, edgings. Regular water.

F. fruticosa (Aster fruticosus). SHRUB ASTER. Evergreen shrub. Zones 8, 9, 14–24. Bushy, densely branched growth to 2–4 ft. tall, 3 ft. wide. Narrow, ½–¾-in.-long, dark green leaves. Profuse, inch-wide lavender flowers in spring. Prune after bloom. Needs no irrigation.

FELT PLANT.
See **KALANCHOE beharensis**

FENNEL, COMMON.
See **FOENICULUM vulgare**

FERNBUSH. See **CHAMAEBATIARIA millefolium**

FERN-OF-THE-DESERT. See **LYSILOMA microphylla thornberi**

FERN PINE. See **PODOCARPUS gracilior**

FERNS

Large group of perennial plants grown for their attractive leaves (fronds). Ferns vary in height from a few inches to more than 50 ft. and are found in all parts of the world. Most are forest plants, but some grow in deserts, in open fields, or near the timberline. Frond shapes vary from feathery plumes to undivided blades, and colors include lime to emerald green, soft bluish gray, burgundy, and even reddish orange; some are variegated with white or creamy tones. New fronds grow from the base in uncoiling structures called crosiers or fiddleheads. Ferns do not flower but reproduce by spores that form directly on the fronds. Fertile fronds may have a have a different shape and color than sterile ones.

Uses. For ground cover, choose spreading, colonizing ferns such as Adiantum, Blechnum, Matteuccia, Nephrolepis, and Polypodium. Types with horizontally arching fronds are also good ground cover candidates; see Davallia, Polypodium, and Polystichum.

As accent plants, evergreen ferns with shiny, waxy foliage are especially fine; see Cyrtomium,

Dryopteris, Polystichum, and Rumohra adiantiformis. For colorful accents, use ferns with burgundy, silver, or creamy foliage, such as named varieties of Athyrium and Pteris; newly emerging orange fronds of Dryopteris erythrosora are outstanding.

For large focal points in frost-free areas, tree ferns are the obvious choice. See Blechnum, Cibotium, Cyathea, and Dicksonia. Frost-tolerant ferns of impressive size include larger types of Dryopteris, Osmunda, and Woodwardia.

Choices for a woodland garden are many. See Adiantum, Asplenium, Athyrium, Blechnum, Dryopteris, Microlepia, Nephrolepis, Osmunda, Pellaea, Polypodium, Polystichum, Rumohra, and Woodwardia.

Almost any fern can thrive in a container outdoors. For mixed plantings, choose a fern with an upright habit or single crown, such as Blechnum, Dryopteris, Polystichum, or Osmunda. For hanging baskets, plant Davallia, Platycerium, and Pyrrosia.

Care. Most ferns tolerate a variety of soil types, but all grow best in well-drained soil enriched with organic matter. They also benefit from a generous layer of mulch to keep soil moist and roots cool. Established ferns growing in reasonably fertile soil rarely need more than a yearly application of well-rotted manure or organic compost. If foliage yellows, apply a half-strength organic fertilizer such as blood meal or fish emulsion; concentrated fertilizers can burn surface roots. Fertilize potted ferns annually with a long-term (9 months or more) controlled-release fertilizer.

Regular watering suits most ferns, but some grow in wet soil (see Athyrium, Matteuccia, Osmunda, and Woodwardia). Others do well in dry shade, such as under trees or next to house foundations (see Dryopteris, Microlepia, Pellaea, and Polystichum). Some ferns grow in considerable sun, provided they are regularly watered (see Blechnum, Osmunda, and Pellaea rotundifolia).

Cut off broken or misshapen fronds any time of year. In cold climates, leave spent foliage in place through the winter months to protect the plant's crown; remove old fronds when spring bulbs emerge. Prune fronds of evergreen ferns when stems become limp.

Ferocactus cylindraceus

FEROCACTUS
BARREL CACTUS
Cactaceae
CACTI

🪴 ZONES 8–24
☀ FULL SUN
💧 NO IRRIGATION NEEDED

Medium to large cacti. Ribbed and formidably spiny; globular when young, cylindrical with increasing age.

F. cylindraceus (F. acanthodes). COMPASS BARREL CACTUS. Native to Southern California, Nevada, Arizona, Baja California. Grows slowly to 8–9 ft. tall, 3 ft. wide. Yellow to orange, bell-shaped flowers, 3 in. across, bloom midspring into summer. Plant grows faster on its shady side than on sunny side, producing curve toward the south.

F. wislizenii. FISHHOOK BARREL CACTUS. Native to Arizona, Texas, Mexico. Similar to above, with yellow or yellow-edged red flowers in summer.

FESTUCA
FESCUE
Poaceae (Gramineae)
PERENNIAL GRASSES

🪴 ZONES VARY BY SPECIES
☀ ◑ BEST IN SUN; TOLERATE SOME SHADE
💧💧 MODERATE TO REGULAR WATER

Some of these grasses are ornamental; others are used for lawns, erosion control, or pasture. All need good drainage, can withstand dry conditions and severe frosts. Clumps can be divided in fall.

F. amethystina. Zones 2–10, 14–24. From the Alps and southern Europe. To 1½ ft. high, 10 in. wide. Extremely fine-textured, threadlike leaves are blue green to intensely blue gray. Drooping, violet-tinged flower spikes held above foliage in late spring, early summer. Use like *F. glauca*.

F. arundinacea. TALL FESCUE. Zones A1–A3; 1–10, 14–24. From

Europe, northern Asia; naturalized in cooler parts of North America. Clumping, tall-growing pasture grass (to 4 ft.) also used for moderately low-water-use lawns. Tough blades, tolerance of compacted soils make it a good turf for playing or sports; finer-textured strains are used alone or mixed with bluegrass. Check locally for best-adapted varieties. Forms no runners, so plants must be close together to make dense turf; sow 8–10 lb. of seed per 1,000 sq. ft. Sow in fall in mild-winter areas, in spring in colder part of range. After grass is 2–3 in. high, soak deeply if rains fail; soak again to 1 ft. when blades begin to fold or curl. Feed lightly—monthly in summer, three times during fall, winter. Mow to 2–3 in. Left unmowed, it makes an excellent, deep-rooted erosion control cover on slopes, banks.

F. californica. CALIFORNIA FESCUE. Zones 4–9, 14–24. Native to the Coast Ranges from Northern California to Oregon. Grows as loose clump of blue-green or blue-gray leaves to 2–3 ft. high, 1–2 ft. wide; topped by airy flowers in late spring, early summer. Flower spikes are green at first, later turning purple and finally maturing to deep yellow. Long lived and does well in various soil types. Tolerates summer drought in its cooler climate zones. Use as specimen plant or massed as ground cover. 'Serpentine Blue' has intensely blue-gray foliage.

F. glauca (F. cinerea). COMMON BLUE FESCUE. Zones 1–24. From Europe. To 1 ft. high, 10 in. wide. Dense tuft of very narrow, fine leaves; color varies from blue gray to silvery white. Summer flowers in spikes. Use as edging or ground cover. Center of clump commonly dies out after several years. Sometimes sold as *F. ovina glauca*. 'Blausilber' ('Blue Silver') is one of the best silver-leafed selections. 'Elijah Blue' forms an 8-in.-high clump of intensely silver-blue leaves and is one of the tougher, longer-lived

Festuca glauca

F

selections. 'Siskiyou Blue', to 1–2 ft. high, has luminous blue leaves.

F. idahoensis. Zones 1–10, 14–24. Native from British Columbia to Alberta, south to central California and Colorado. Blue-green to silvery blue foliage in dense clump to 14 in. high, 10 in. wide. Longer lived than *F. glauca,* and clumps are less likely to die out in center. May also be more tolerant of wet winter soils. Good slope stabilizer.

F. mairei. MAIRE'S FESCUE, ATLAS FESCUE. Zones 2–11, 14–24. Native to mountainous areas of Morocco. Grows 2–3 ft. tall and wide, forming a neat, dense mound of fine-textured, golden green leaves. Very slender, gray-green flower spikes are held above foliage mass in early summer. Evergreen in mild-winter areas. Drought and heat tolerant. Good for erosion control or as a large-scale ground cover; also makes an attractive specimen.

F. rubra. RED FESCUE, CREEPING RED FESCUE. Zones A2, A3; 1–10, 14–24. From Europe, North America. Spreads by rhizomes. Principal use is in blends with bluegrass or other lawn grasses; also used to overseed Bermuda lawns in winter. Narrow dark green blades. Not fussy about soil. Can be used alone (many varieties available); mow to 1½–2 in. high. One of most shade tolerant of good lawn grasses. Unmowed, all types of red fescue make attractive meadow on slopes too steep to mow. Need regular water for good growth. For drought-tolerant red fescues, look for blue-leafed California selections.

F. trachyphylla. SHEEP'S FESCUE. Zones 1–24. From many temperate-climate areas of the world. Forage and meadow grass producing dense, foot-high tufts of fine-textured, green to gray-green leaves and small purple-tinged flowers in mid- to late summer.

F. valesiaca. WALLIS FESCUE. Zones 2b–10, 14–24. European native to 1½ ft. high and wide. Similar to *F. glauca.* Winter dormant. Known largely in its selection 'Glaucantha', which has fine-textured blue-green leaves in a clump under 6 in. high.

FEVERFEW. See **CHRYSANTHEMUM parthenium**

FIBER OPTICS PLANT. See **ISOLEPIS cernua**

FICUS
Moraceae
EVERGREEN AND DECIDUOUS TREES, SHRUBS, AND VINES

✎	ZONES VARY BY SPECIES
☀ ◐ ●	EXPOSURE NEEDS VARY BY SPECIES
💧	REGULAR WATER

The average gardener would never expect to find the commercial edible fig, small-leafed climbing

Ficus auriculata

fig, banyan tree, and potted rubber tree under one heading—but they are classed together because they bear small or large figs (inedible in most species). Ornamental types are discussed here; for sorts grown for tasty fruit, see Fig.

Many ornamental species make good houseplants. Generally, they thrive on rich, steadily moist (not wet) soil, frequent light feedings, and bright, indirect light.

F. auriculata (F. roxburghii). Briefly deciduous shrub or small tree. Zones 20–24; H1, H2. Native to India. To 25 ft. high and wide. Leaves have sandpapery texture, are unusually large—broadly oval to round, about 15 in. across. New growth is mahogany red, turning to rich green. Large figs are borne in clusters on trunk and framework branches. Can be shaped as small tree or espaliered. Beautiful in large container; good near swimming pools. Grow in wind-protected, sunny location.

F. benghalensis. INDIAN BANYAN. Evergreen tree. Zones 23, 24; H2. Native to India and Pakistan. On the mainland, it grows very slowly. In Hawaii, it is a very large, fast-growing tree to 80 ft. tall and initially as wide, spreading (potentially up to several acres) by accessory trunks developing from aerial roots. This is the most spectacular of the many banyans grown in Hawaii, but it should be used with extreme caution and only in large spaces. Full sun.

Ficus benjamina

F. benjamina. BENJAMIN TREE, BENJAMIN FIG, WEEPING FIG. Zones 13, 23, 24; H1, H2; or indoors. From India and Malaysia. In Hawaii, fast growing to 60 ft. tall with an even greater spread. Good shade or specimen tree for larger gardens or parks, since it requires space for its invasive surface root system. In Southern California and Arizona, plant reaches about half the size it does in Hawaii and is often used as entryway or patio tree; also good as screen, espalier, or clipped hedge. Leathery, 5-in.-long, shiny green leaves densely clothe drooping branches. 'Exotica' has wavy-edged leaves with long, twisted tips; often sold simply as *F. benjamina.* New plants are easy to start from cuttings taken between late spring and early summer. Give a frost-free, wind-protected location in sun or shade.

One of the most popular houseplants. Sudden leaf shedding is a common problem, often resulting from plant being moved to a new location. If shedding begins shortly after a move, be patient; leaves usually grow back. If leaves that fall are green, insufficient water is another possible cause; try to keep soil evenly moist. If fallen leaves are yellow, overwatering may be to blame. If shedding is accompanied by sweet smell and sticky leaves, look for and control scale insects. For an indoor tree that is similar in size and habit to *F. benjamina* but doesn't drop its foliage (leaves are long, resembling those of many eucalyptus), try *F. binnendijkii* 'Alii'.

Ficus deltoidea diversifolia

F. carica. See Fig

F. deltoidea diversifolia. MISTLETOE FIG. Evergreen shrub. Zones 19–24; H1, H2; or indoors. Native to Southeast Asia. Grows very slowly to 8–10 ft. high, about half as wide. Interesting open, twisted branch pattern. Thick, dark green, roundish, 2-in. leaves are sparsely stippled with tan specks on upper surface and a few black dots below. Attractive, small greenish to yellow fruit borne continuously. As outdoor plant, most often grown in container on patio. Part shade.

F. elastica. RUBBER TREE. Evergreen shrub or tree. Zones 13, 16, 17, 19–24; H1, H2; or indoors. Native to India and Malaysia. In Hawaii, it is a wide-spreading tree 60–80 ft. high (up to 100 ft. in damp, tropical forests). On the mainland, it can become a 40-ft. tree in frost-free zones; often seen as a small tree or shrub in shaded "tunnel" garden entrances in cooler part of range. Comes back quickly if killed to ground by frost. Narrow, leathery dark green leaves are 8–12 in. long. New

Ficus elastica 'Decora'

leaves unfold from rosy pink sheaths that soon wither and drop. Partial or full shade.

One of most foolproof indoor pot subjects; can take less light than most big houseplants. If potted plant becomes too tall and leggy, you can cut off the top and select a side branch to form a new main shoot. Or get a new plant by air layering the top section; when roots form, cut branch section with attached roots and pot it up. The best varieties include:

'Abidjan' ('Burgundy'). West African selection made from 'Decora'. New growth, leaf sheaths, and leaf midribs are red. On plants grown in bright light, older leaves are dark maroon.

'Decora' ('Belgica'). The common rubber plant sold for indoor use is usually this variety. Superior to the species because of its broader, glossier leaves. Foliage is bronzy when young.

'Doescheri'. Leaves are marbled in green and gray green, with green margins, creamy yellow midribs, and pink leafstalks.

'Rubra'. New leaves are reddish and retain a red edge as rest of leaf turns green. Sometimes grown as shrub or small tree in Zones 22–24.

'Variegata'. Long, narrow leaves marked in yellow and green. Variegation is interesting when leaves are viewed close up in container—but as an outdoor tree, plant has a sickly look.

F. lyrata (F. pandurata). FIDDLELEAF FIG. Evergreen tree or shrub. Zones 22–24; H1, H2; or indoors. Native to tropical Africa. Dramatic structural form with prominently veined, fiddle-shaped, huge leaves (to 15 in. long, 10 in. wide) in glossy dark green. In Hawaii, forms a dense, round-headed tree 35–50 ft. tall and about 35 ft. wide. In California, can grow to 20 ft. high and as wide, with trunks 6 in. thick. Good near swimming pools. To increase branching, pinch back when plant is young. Full sun or light shade. Highly effective as a houseplant.

F. macrophylla. MORETON BAY FIG. Evergreen tree. Zones 17, 19–24; H1, H2. Native to Australia. Grows to enormous dimensions. A tree in Santa Barbara, California, planted in 1877 is about 75 ft. tall and 150 ft. wide, with massive buttressed trunk and surface roots. Blunt, oval, leathery leaves, 10 in. long and 4 in. wide, glossy green above, brownish beneath. Rose-colored leaf sheaths appear like candles at branch ends. Inch-long figs are purple spotted with white. Although plant is tender when young, it acquires hardiness with size. Shows damage at 24 to 26°F/–4 to –3°C. Be sure to give it plenty of room. Full sun.

F. microcarpa (F. retusa). INDIAN LAUREL FIG, CHINESE BANYAN. Evergreen tree. Zones 9, 13, 16–24; H1, H2. Native from Malay peninsula to Borneo. One of the more common banyans in Hawaiian landscapes, where it grows quickly to 60 ft. high, with a dense canopy spreading to about 75 ft. wide; produces multiple aerial roots in wet areas. In California and Arizona, it grows at a more moderate rate to 25–30 ft. high, 35–40 ft. wide. Beautiful weeping form, with long, drooping branches thickly clothed with blunt-tipped,

Ficus lyrata

2–4-in.-long leaves. Light rose to chartreuse new leaves, produced almost continuously, give pleasing two-tone effect. Plants sold as *F. m. nitida* (a name with no botanical standing) may have the same weeping form as the species or may have upright-growing branches.

Prune at any time of year to shape as desired. Remove lower branches to reveal slim, light gray trunk. Responds well to shearing into formal hedge as low as 5 ft. Where pest free, makes a highly satisfactory tree or tub plant. Unfortunately, subject to thrips damage in California; hard to control, since the pest quickly curls new leaves (thus protecting itself from sprays). Afflicted leaves show stippling, then drop. 'Green Gem' has thicker, darker green leaves and is apparently unaffected by thrips. Full sun.

F. m. crassifolia. WAX FIG, TAIWAN FIG. To 10–12 ft. high and sprawling as wide. Tolerates salt, wind, drought, various soil types. In Hawaii, more likely to be used for hedges or containers than the species. Easily pruned to maintain size and shape. Full sun or partial shade.

F. pandurata. See F. lyrata

F. pumila (F. repens). CREEPING FIG. Evergreen vine. Zones 8–24; H1, H2; or indoors. Native to China, Japan, Australia. Has a most unfiglike habit; it is one of few plants that attaches itself securely to wood, masonry, or even metal in barnacle fashion. Because it is grown on walls and thus protected, it is found in colder climates more often than any other evergreen fig. Grows in sun or shade; not for hot south or west wall.

Looks innocent enough in youth, making a delicate tracery of tiny, heart-shaped leaves. Neat little juvenile foliage ultimately develops into big (2–4-in.-long), leathery leaves borne on stubby branches that bear large oblong fruits. In time, stems will envelop a three- or four-story building so completely that it becomes necessary to keep them trimmed away from windows. It's safe to use on house walls if you cut it to the ground every few years; also control by removing fruiting stems from time to time as they form.

Roots are invasive. 'Minima' has shorter, narrower leaves than species. Small, lobed leaves of 'Quercifolia' look like miniature oak leaves. 'Variegata' has standard-size leaves with creamy white markings.

F. religiosa. PEEPUL, BO-TREE. Briefly deciduous tree. Zones 13, 19, 21, 23, 24; H1, H2. Native India to Southeast Asia. In Hawaii, to 80–100 ft. tall with almost equal spread. On mainland, may reach 40 ft. high and wide after 25 years or more. Foliage is quite open and delicate, revealing structure of tree at all times. Bark is warm, rich brown. Pale green, 4–7-in.-long leaves are thin textured and rather crisp, roundish in shape but with a long, tail-like point. They move easily even in the slightest breeze, giving the foliage mass a fluttering look. Leaves drop completely in late spring or early summer—a frightening experience for the gardener who has bought an "evergreen" fig. Full sun.

F. repens. See F. pumila

F. retusa. See F. microcarpa

F. roxburghii. See F. auriculata

F. rubiginosa. RUSTYLEAF FIG. Evergreen tree. Zones 18–24; H1, H2. Native to Australia. Single- or multitrunked, densely foliaged tree to 20–50 ft. tall, with broad crown 30–50 ft. wide. Leaves about 5 in. long, deep green above, generally rust colored and woolly beneath. May develop hanging aerial roots characteristic of many of the evergreen figs that grow in tropical environments. A small-leafed form has been sold as *F. microphylla.* Full sun.

F. r. australis is virtually identical to the species but may vary in having leaf undersides with a less pronounced rust color. Its selections 'El Toro' and 'Irvine' have exceptionally dark green leaves; 'Florida' has lighter green foliage. 'Variegata', with leaves mottled green and cream, is sometimes sold as a houseplant.

FIG
Moraceae
DECIDUOUS FRUIT TREES

🖊 ZONES 4–9, 12–24; H1, H2; OR IN POTS
☀️ FULL SUN
💧 REGULAR WATER

Native to western Asia, eastern Mediterranean, *Ficus carica* is grown for edible fruit; for ornamental relatives, see *Ficus*. Grows

fairly fast to 15–30 ft. tall; generally low branched, spreading at least as wide as high. Where hard freezes (below 10 to 15°F/–12 to –9°C) are common, fig wood freezes back severely and plants act like big shrubs. Can be held to 10 ft. in a large container; can also be trained as espalier along fence or wall.

Fig

Heavy, smooth, gray trunks are gnarled in really old trees, picturesque in silhouette. Rough bright green leaves with three to five lobes are 4–9 in. long and nearly as wide. Casts dense shade. Winter framework, tropical-looking foliage, strong trunk and branch pattern make fig a top-notch ornamental tree, especially near patio where it can be illuminated from beneath. Fruit drop is problem immediately above deck or paving. Protect container plants in winter.

Not particular about soil. In colder part of range, trees planted near south walls or trained against them benefit from reflected heat. Cut back tops hard at planting. As tree grows, prune lightly each winter, cutting out dead wood, crossing branches, and low-hanging branches that interfere with traffic. Pinch back runaway shoots in any season. Avoid deep cultivation (which may damage surface roots) and high-nitrogen fertilizers (which stimulate leafy growth at the expense of fruit). Gophers love fig roots; if they or other burrowing animals are a problem in your garden, plant fig trees in ample wire baskets. Ripe fruit may need protection from birds.

Home-garden figs do not need pollinating, and most varieties bear two crops a year. The first comes in early summer on last year's wood; the second, more important one comes in late summer or early fall from the current year's growth. When figs are ripe, they detach easily when lifted and bent back toward the branch. Keep fruit picked as it ripens; protect from birds if you can. In late fall, pick

F

off any remaining ripe figs and clean up fallen fruit.

Varieties differ in climate adaptability. Most need prolonged high temperatures to bear good fruit, while some thrive in cooler conditions. Familiar dried figs from the market are usually 'Calimyrna' or imported Smyrna figs. These require special pollenizers (male trees called caprifigs) and a special pollinating insect and are not recommended for home gardens.

'Black Jack'. Purple skin with sweet pink flesh. Similar to 'Mission'. Widely adapted to California climates. Easily kept small by pruning.

'Brown Turkey' ('Black Spanish', 'San Pedro'). Brownish purple fruit. Adaptable to most fig-growing climates. Good, small garden tree.

'Celeste' ('Blue Celeste', 'Celestial'). Violet-tinged bronzy skin, rosy amber flesh. Good fresh; resists spoilage. Dries well on tree in California.

'Conadria'. Choice thin-skinned white fig blushed violet; white to red flesh with fine flavor. Best in hot areas; takes intense heat without splitting.

'Desert King'. One late-summer crop of green-skinned, red-fleshed fruit. Adapted to all fig climates but better in cooler areas like Northwest.

'Genoa' ('White Genoa'). Greenish yellow skin, strawberry-colored to yellow flesh. Good quality; good in coastal valleys, California coast.

'Italian Everbearing'. Resembles 'Brown Turkey' but has somewhat larger fruit with reddish brown skin. Good fresh or dried.

'Kadota' ('White Kadota'). Tough-skinned fruit is greenish yellow. One of the best figs for Hawaii; in California, grows best in hot interior valleys.

'Lattarula'. Also known as Italian honey fig. Green skin, amber flesh. Grown in Northwest, where it can ripen in summer and produce fall crops in good seasons.

'Mission' ('Black Mission'). Large tree; purple-black figs with pink flesh; good fresh or dried. Widely adapted; popular in California.

'Osborn Prolific' ('Neveralla'). Dark reddish brown skin; amber flesh, often tinged pink. Very sweet; best eaten fresh. Best in Northern California coastal areas and Pacific Northwest. Light bearing in warm climates.

'Panachée' ('Striped Tiger', 'Tiger'). Greenish yellow skin with dark green stripes. Strawberry-colored flesh is sweet but dry. Best eaten fresh. Requires long, warm growing season. One crop late in summer.

'Peter's Honey' ('Rutara'). Greenish yellow skin, amber flesh. Needs hot exposure in Northwest and coastal areas.

'Texas Everbearing'. Mahogany to purple skin, strawberry-colored flesh. Bears at a young age. Produces well in short-season areas of Southwest.

FILBERT, HAZELNUT
Betulaceae
DECIDUOUS NUT TREES

🌡 ZONES 2–7
☀ ◐ AFTERNOON SHADE IN HOTTEST CLIMATES
💧 REGULAR WATER

These plants are selections of European species *Corylus avellana* and *C. maxima* that are grown for nut production (their nuts are the commercial ones sold in stores). To 10–18 ft. high and wide; look more like trees than the ornamental species (see *Corylus*). Handsome and nicely structured, good choice for garden or terrace. From spring to fall, the roundish, ruffle-edged leaves cast a pleasant spot of shade. Showy catkins (male flowers) hang long and full on bare branches in winter.

Plant in late winter or early spring in deep, well-drained soil. Trees tend to sucker; clear these out three or four times a year if you wish to maintain a clean trunk. For a boundary hedgerow, plant mixed varieties 4 ft. apart and let suckers grow.

Filbert

Eastern filbert blight, a destructive bark disease, has devastated old standby varieties 'Butler', 'Du Chilly', 'Daviana', and 'Ennis'; they are no longer recommended in the prime filbert-growing areas of Oregon and Washington. To protect commercial orchards, filberts and hazelnuts (including ornamentals) are quarantined in Oregon and can no longer be planted in home gardens there.

The blight is evident as raised, oval black bumps in vertical lines on infected branches and twigs. Individual branches die out, and the entire plant can succumb. To protect existing plants, spray with copper and horticultural oil together at bud break (usually late March), again in mid-April, and a third time in early May. Remove dead branches, cutting 2 ft. back into healthy growth. Burn or bury prunings. Severely infected trees should be removed entirely.

Filberts ripen in late summer and drop in early fall; the roundish or oblong nuts form inside frilled husks. A 10-year-old tree may yield up to 20 lb. of nuts per year. Harvest by picking up nuts from the ground, then dry them in the sun for a few days. Squirrels and jays are a nuisance, often picking the nuts before they fall. Handpicking when the nuts are tree-ripe (when they separate easily from the hulls) will thwart animal thieves.

Since cross-pollination is necessary, plant at least two varieties. Best crops in cold-winter areas. 'Santiam' is a new blight-resistant variety that produces abundant, high-quality nuts on a smallish tree. Its pollenizer, 'Zeta', is also immune but is not productive. The following are blight resistant to varying degrees; none is totally immune.

'Barcelona'. Fine flavor. Some resistance to blight.

'Casina'. Thin-shelled nuts with excellent flavor. Intermediate blight resistance.

'Hall's Giant'. Flavorful. Good resistance to blight.

'Lewis'. Good-quality nut. Highly resistant to blight.

'Tonda di Giffoni'. Excellent flavor. Highly resistant to blight.

Two types of hybrids called filazels and trazels can be grown into Zone 1. They vary in blight resistance and cannot be planted in Oregon. Filazels—hardy, 10–15-ft. producers of good-quality nuts—are hybrids between *C. avellana* and the native beaked hazelnut (*C. cornuta*). Trazels—upright, 20–30-ft. trees producing

sweet, fine-flavored nuts—are crosses between *C. avellana* and Turkish hazel (*C. colurna*). Plant two of the same type for cross-pollination.

FILIPENDULA
MEADOWSWEET
Rosaceae
PERENNIALS

🌡 ZONES VARY BY SPECIES
☀ ◐ ● FULL SUN IN COOLER CLIMATES ONLY
💧 💧💧 REGULAR TO AMPLE WATER

Like *Astilbe*, these bear plumes of tiny flowers above large, coarsely divided leaves. Bloom in summer. Dormant in winter, even in mild-winter areas. Most species prefer moist to constantly damp soil. Good in borders, naturalistic landscapes, beside ponds.

F. purpurea. Zones 3b–9, 14–17. Pink, 3–4-ft. plumes rise above a 2-ft.-wide foliage clump. Leaves are 5–7 in. long, look like maple leaves.

Filipendula rubra
'Venusta'

F. rubra. QUEEN OF THE PRAIRIE. Zones A1–A3; 1–9, 14–17. Given plenty of moisture and rich soil, can reach 8 ft. high in bloom; bears pink plumes above 4-ft.-wide clump of jagged-edged leaves with big, lobed leaflet at tip. 'Venusta' has purplish pink flowers and is a little shorter (4–6 ft. high).

F. vulgaris (F. hexapetala). DROPWORT. Zones A1–A3; 1–9, 14–17. White plumes on 3-ft. stems rise above a 1½-ft.-wide mound of ferny leaves divided into inch-long leaflets. Double-flowered 'Flore Pleno' has heavier-looking plumes. Needs less water than other species; also prefers full sun in all but the warmest regions.

FINOCCHIO. See **FOENICULUM vulgare azoricum**

FIR. See **ABIES**

FIRETAIL.
See **ACALYPHA pendula**

FIRETHORN.
See **PYRACANTHA**

FIREWEED.
See **EPILOBIUM angustifolium**

FIREWHEEL TREE.
See **STENOCARPUS sinuatus**

FIRMIANA simplex
(F. platanifolia)
CHINESE PARASOL TREE
Sterculiaceae
DECIDUOUS TREE

- ZONES 5, 6, 8, 9, 12–24
- FULL SUN OR PARTIAL SHADE
- REGULAR WATER

Native to China, Japan. Slow growing to about 15–30 ft. tall and half as wide, with smooth, light gray-green bark. Trunk often unbranched for 4–5 ft. before dividing into three or more slender, upright, slightly spreading branches that carry lobed, tropical-looking, 1-ft. leaves. Each stem

Firmiana simplex

looks as if it could be cut off and carried away as a parasol. Tree bears large, loose, upright clusters of greenish white flowers at branch ends in summer. Fruit looks like a green pea pod opened out flat, with seeds on pod margins. Leafless for long period in winter (unusual for tropical-looking tree). Tolerates all soil types. Does well in patios and courtyards protected from wind. Good near swimming pools.

FISHTAIL PALM. See **CARYOTA**

FIVE-FINGER FERN.
See **ADIANTUM**

FLAG. See **IRIS**

FLAMBOYANT TREE.
See **DELONIX regia**

FLAME BUSH.
See **CALLIANDRA tweedii**

FLAMEGOLD.
See **KOELREUTERIA elegans**

FLAME OF THE WOODS.
See **IXORA coccinea**

FLAME PEA. See **CHORIZEMA**

FLAME TREE.
See **BRACHYCHITON acerifolius**

FLAME VINE.
See **PYROSTEGIA venusta**

FLAME VIOLET. See **EPISCIA**

FLAMINGO FLOWER.
See **ANTHURIUM**

FLANNEL BUSH.
See **FREMONTODENDRON**

FLAX. See **LINUM**

FLAX, NEW ZEALAND.
See **PHORMIUM**

FLAXLEAF PAPERBARK.
See **MELALEUCA linariifolia**

FLAX LILY. See **DIANELLA**

FLEABANE. See **ERIGERON**

FLOSS FLOWER.
See **AGERATUM houstonianum**

FLOSS SILK TREE.
See **CHORISIA**

FLOWERING ALMOND, CHERRY.
See **PRUNUS**

FLOWERING CRABAPPLE.
See **MALUS**

FLOWERING CURRANT.
See **RIBES**

FLOWERING MAPLE.
See **ABUTILON**

FLOWERING NECTARINE, PEACH, PLUM. See **PRUNUS**

FLOWERING QUINCE.
See **CHAENOMELES**

FLOWERING TOBACCO.
See **NICOTIANA**

FOAMFLOWER. See **TIARELLA**

FOENICULUM
vulgare
COMMON FENNEL
Apiaceae (Umbelliferae)
PERENNIAL SOMETIMES TREATED
AS ANNUAL

- ZONES VARY BY FENNEL TYPE
- FULL SUN
- MODERATE WATER

Two forms of this Mediterranean native are commonly grown—one as a perennial for its flavorful seeds and young leaves, the other as an annual for its edible leaf bases.

Foeniculum vulgare

The plain species, which is cultivated for licorice-flavored seeds and young leaves, is a perennial in Zones 2b–11, 14–24, H1, H2, a winter annual in Zones 12, 13. Grows 3–5 ft. tall. Similar in appearance to dill (*Anethum graveolens*), but its yellow-green foliage, though finely cut, is coarser. Plant produces flat clusters of yellow flowers in summer. Bronze fennel ('Purpurascens', 'Smokey') reaches 6 ft. tall, has bronzy purple foliage. Start from seed where plants are to be grown. Sow in light, well-drained soil; thin seedlings to 1 ft. apart. Use seeds to season baked goods; use young leaves as garnish for salads, fish, and other dishes. Common fennel often escapes as a roadside or garden weed (in Hawaii and parts of California, it can be invasive); it's attractive until tops turn brown, and even then birds like the seeds. New stems grow in spring from perennial root.

F. v. azoricum, Florence fennel or finocchio, is a summer annual in all zones except 12 and 13, where it is a winter annual. It is lower growing than the species (to 2 ft. high), with larger, thicker leafstalk bases that are used as a vegetable, cooked or raw. Its feathery leaves are used as a garnish and seasoning.

FORESTIERA
neomexicana
NEW MEXICAN PRIVET, DESERT
OLIVE
Oleaceae
DECIDUOUS SHRUB

- ZONES 1–3, 7–24
- FULL SUN
- LITTLE TO MODERATE WATER

Native to New Mexico, Colorado, Arizona west to California. Little used outside arid regions. Grows 12–18 ft. tall, 12 ft. wide. Smooth, medium green leaves to 1½ in. long turn yellow in fall. Inconspicuous flowers. Small (¼-in.-long), egg-shaped fruits, blue-black when mature, are not always produced (some plants do not have both male and female flowers); when they do appear, they attract birds. Fairly fast growth makes it a good screen plant; can be trained as a small multitrunked tree.

Forestiera neomexicana

FORGET-ME-NOT.
See **MYOSOTIS**

FORSYTHIA
Oleaceae
DECIDUOUS SHRUBS

- ZONES A2, A3; 2B–11, 14–16, 18, 19; EXCEPT AS NOTED
- FULL SUN
- MODERATE TO REGULAR WATER

Native to China, Korea. From late winter to early spring, these fountain-shaped shrubs' bare branches are covered with ¾–1½-in. yellow flowers; budded branches can be forced for indoor bloom. During rest of growing season, foliage—medium green, rounded leaves with pointed tips—blends well with other background shrubs. Use as screen, espalier, or bank cover; or plant in shrub border. Tolerate most soils. Prune after bloom by cutting to ground a third of the branches that have flowered; also remove oldest branches and weak or dead wood. In coldest-winter climates, flower buds may be destroyed by temperatures of –15 to –20°F/–26 to –29°C. The hardiest varieties are noted below. For white forsythia, see *Abeliophyllum distichum*.

F. 'Arnold Dwarf'. Grows to about 1½–3 ft. tall, 6 ft. wide. Flowers are sparse and not especially attractive, but plant is a useful, fast-growing ground cover for cold climates.

F. hardy hybrids. Zones A2, A3; 1a, 2–11, 14–16, 18, 19. Recent introductions have extended the range of forsythia into regions formerly too cold for successful flowering—or even for the plant's survival.

'Meadowlark'. To 6–9 ft. tall and 10 ft. wide, with semiarching habit. Bright yellow flowers open from buds hardy to –35°F/–37°C.

'New Hampshire Gold'. Mounding habit to 5 ft. tall and broad, with drooping yellow flowers. Buds are hardy to –35°F/–37°C.

'Northern Sun'. Erect grower to 8–10 ft. tall and slightly narrower; reliably bud-hardy to –30°F/–34°C.

F. × intermedia. This group of hybrids between parents *F. suspensa* and *F. viridissima* includes the following selections.

'Beatrix Farrand'. Upright to 10 ft. tall, 7 ft. wide. Branches thickly set with deep yellow flowers marked with orange.

'Fiesta'. To 3–4 ft. tall and somewhat broader, with deep yellow flowers and yellow-variegated leaves.

'Goldtide'. To 20 in. high and 4 ft. wide, with profuse yellow blooms.

'Goldzauber'. Erect growth to 6–8 ft. tall and slightly narrower. Deep yellow blooms.

'Karl Sax'. Resembles 'Beatrix Farrand' but is lower growing (to about 8 ft.), neater, and more graceful.

'Lynwood' ('Lynwood Gold'). Stiffly upright to 7 ft., with 4–6-ft. spread. Profuse tawny yellow blooms survive spring storms.

'Spectabilis'. Dense, upright, vigorous shrub to 10 ft. high, 6 ft. wide. Deep yellow flowers.

'Spring Glory'. To about 6 ft. tall and wide, with heavy crop of pale yellow flowers.

F. mandshurica 'Vermont Sun'. Zones A2, A3; 1–11, 14–16. Erect, extremely bud-hardy shrub to 8 ft. tall, 6 ft. wide; lemon yellow flowers appear before those of other forsythias.

F. ovata. KOREAN FORSYTHIA. To 4–6 ft. high, 10 ft. wide. Early bloomer (about a week after *F. mandshurica* 'Vermont Sun') bearing a profusion of bright yellow flowers. 'Tetragold' is lower growing (about 3 ft. high), has deep yellow blooms.

F. suspensa. WEEPING FORSYTHIA. Dense, upright shrub reaches to 8–10 ft. tall, 6–8 ft. wide; bears golden yellow blossoms. Drooping, vinelike branches root where they touch damp soil. Useful as a large-scale bank cover. Plant can also be trained as a vine; if you support main branches, branchlets will cascade.

F. viridissima. GREENSTEM FORSYTHIA. Zones A2, A3; 2b–11, 14–16, 18, 19. Stiff-looking shrub 6–10 ft. tall and wide, with deep green foliage, olive green stems, and greenish yellow flowers. 'Bronxensis' is a slow-growing dwarf to 1 ft. high, 2–3 ft. wide; use as ground cover or in borders.

FORSYTHIA, WHITE. See **ABELIOPHYLLUM distichum**

FORTNIGHT LILY. See **DIETES**

FOTHERGILLA
Hamamelidaceae
DECIDUOUS SHRUBS

🌿 ZONES 2B–9, 14–17
☀️ 🌤️ PARTIAL SHADE IN HOTTEST CLIMATES
💧 REGULAR WATER

Native to southeastern U.S. Grown mainly for fall foliage color, but spring bloom is pretty: small, honey-scented white flowers in 1–2-in., brushlike clusters on zigzagging stems. Blossoms may

Forsythia × intermedia

appear before or with leaves. Performs best in moist, well-drained, acid soil.

F. gardenii. DWARF FOTHERGILLA. Typically 2–3 ft. high (though it can grow considerably taller) and as wide or wider, with 1–2½-in.-long, dark green leaves. Foliage turns intense yellow to orange to scarlet in autumn, often with all three colors in same leaf. 'Blue Mist' is a blue-foliaged variety that doesn't color up as well in fall.

Fothergilla major

F. major (F. monticola). Erect shrub to 9 ft. tall and 6 ft. wide, with roundish, 2–4-in.-long leaves turning yellow to orange to purplish red in autumn. 'Mount Airy' is smaller (3–5 ft. high and wide), with abundant bloom, good dark green leaf color, and consistently superb fall color in yellow, orange, and scarlet.

FOUNTAIN GRASS. See **PENNISETUM**

FOUQUIERIA
Fouquieriaceae
DECIDUOUS SHRUBS OR TREES

🌿 ZONES VARY BY SPECIES
☀️ FULL SUN
💧💧 LITTLE TO MODERATE WATER

Desert natives with grooved, spiny branches. Drop leaves during hot, dry periods, then resprout and bloom quickly after rains, bearing tubular flowers to 1 in. long. They can survive on rainfall but grow and bloom best if soaked deeply once a month. Need excellent drainage, intense summer heat. Easily propagated from softwood cuttings in warm weather; cut branches stuck in ground will root and grow.

F. macdougalii. MEXICAN TREE OCOTILLO. Zones 11–13. Native to Mexico. Brown branches covered with gray spines rise from a short, smooth, yellowish green trunk. In frost-free climates, plant

can reach 20 ft. tall (with trunk making up 3 ft. of height) but is more typically seen around 6–8 ft. tall, 4 ft. wide (trunk about a foot high, often less). Lance-shaped light gray leaves to 1½ in. long. Deep red flowers come in open sprays reminiscent of exploding skyrockets. In frost-prone areas, grow in container and move indoors in winter.

F. splendens. OCOTILLO. Zones 10–13, 18–20. Native to Colorado and Sonoran deserts east to Texas and south into Mexico. Forms a 5–10-ft.-wide clump of stiff, whip-thin, gray stems 8–25 ft. high, heavily furrowed and covered with stout thorns. Fleshy, roundish, ½–1-in.-long leaves. Attractive foot-long clusters of flowers; color ranges from bright to deep red orange (occasionally yellow). Use as screen, impenetrable hedge, living fence for animal enclosures; or grow for silhouette against bare walls.

Fouquieria splendens

FOUR O'CLOCK. See **MIRABILIS**

FOXGLOVE. See **DIGITALIS**

FOXTAIL LILY. See **EREMURUS**

FRAGARIA
ORNAMENTAL STRAWBERRY
Rosaceae
PERENNIALS

🌿 ZONES VARY BY SPECIES
☀️ 🌤️ AFTERNOON SHADE IN HOTTEST CLIMATES
💧 REGULAR WATER

For strawberries grown strictly for their edible fruit, see Strawberry; the plants described here are grown for their ornamental qualities, though *F. vesca* also produces delectable fruit. Grow in sandy or other well-drained soil.

F. chiloensis. BEACH STRAWBERRY, SAND STRAWBERRY. Zones 4–24; H1. Native to Pacific Coast beaches and bluffs of North

Fragaria chiloensis

and South America. A parent of the commercial strawberry; forms lush, compact mat 4–8 in. high. Glossy dark green leaves have three tooth-edged leaflets, take on red tones in winter. White, 1-in. flowers in spring, occasionally followed by a few bright red, seedy, ¾-in. fruits in fall. For ground cover, set out nursery-grown plants 1–1½ ft. apart. Mow or cut back annually in early spring to force new growth and prevent stem buildup.

F. 'Lipstick'. Zones 2b–24. Results from a cross between *Fragaria* and *Potentilla*. Similar to *F. chiloensis* in general appearance but bears rich rosy red flowers in spring and intermittently through summer. Use in borders, edgings, rock gardens. Produces very few fruits.

F. 'Pink Panda'. Zones 4–24. Resembles *F.* 'Lipstick' and is used in the same way, but it bears pink flowers from spring to fall.

F. vesca. ALPINE STRAWBERRY, FRAISE DU BOIS, WOOD STRAWBERRY. Zones 2b–9, 14–24; H2. This one bears a small crop of tiny but fragrant, delicious berries over a long summer season, but it's usually grown as an edging for flower or herb beds (space plants 8–12 in. apart). Does not produce runners but may be grown from seed; bears the first year from seed sown early. Varieties include red-fruiting 'Alexandria', 'Baron Solemacher', 'Improved Rügen', 'Mignonette', and 'Semperflorens'; there are also yellow- and white-fruiting selections.

FRAISE DU BOIS.
See **FRAGARIA** vesca

FRANCESCHI PALM.
See **BRAHEA** elegans

FRANCOA ramosa
MAIDEN'S WREATH
Saxifragaceae
PERENNIAL

🌿	ZONES 4–9, 14–24
◑	PARTIAL SHADE
◌◌●	MODERATE TO REGULAR WATER

Native to Chile. Large, wavy-edged leaves to 6 in. long in a basal clump 1–2 ft. high, 3 ft. wide (and spreading wider by rhizomes). Graceful, almost leafless flowering stems 2–3 ft. long appear in midsummer, with upper portions carrying spikes of many tiny pure white (occasionally pinkish) blossoms. Good cut flowers. Plants are distributed mainly by neighborliness—more of them pass over back fences than

Francoa ramosa

through nurseries. Grows in rich soil. In just a few years, one plant increases sufficiently in size to let you divide and replant fresh new segments from clump's outside edges. Best in dappled shade all day or with sun for half the day. *F. sonchifolia* is similar but bears pink flowers.

FRANGIPANI. See PLUMERIA

FRANKLINIA alatamaha (Gordonia alatamaha)
Theaceae
DECIDUOUS TREE

🌿	ZONES 3B–6, 14–17
☼◑	PARTIAL SHADE IN HOTTEST CLIMATES
●	REGULAR WATER

Though once native to Georgia, this tree has apparently been extinct in the wild since before 1800. Open, airy form; may grow 30 ft. tall but more typically

Franklinia alatamaha

reaches 10–20 ft. high. When grown with single trunk, tends to be fairly slender; grown with multiple trunks, spreads wider than high. Attractive gray bark has faint white vertical striping. Glossy green 4–6-in.-long leaves turn orange and red in fall. In late summer, round white buds open to fragrant white blossoms resembling single camellias: 3 in. wide, five petaled, with central clusters of yellow stamens. Bloom may coincide with fall foliage color. Small, woody capsules follow the flowers. Tree blooms shyly during wet autumns in Northwest. Provide well-drained, rich, light, acid soil. Easy to grow from seed, flowering in 6 or 7 years. Makes an unusual lawn or patio tree; good for contrast in azalea and rhododendron plantings.

FRAXINELLA.
See **DICTAMNUS albus**

FRAXINUS
ASH
Oleaceae
DECIDUOUS AND EVERGREEN TREES

🌿	ZONES VARY BY SPECIES
☼	FULL SUN
◌◌●●	WATER NEEDS VARY BY SPECIES

Fairly fast-growing trees, most of which tolerate hot summers, cold winters, and many kinds of soil, including alkaline sorts. Chiefly used as street, shade, lawn, and patio shelter trees. In most cases, leaves are divided into leaflets. Male and female flowers (generally inconspicuous, in clusters) grow on separate trees in some species, on the same tree in others. In the latter case, flowers are often followed by clusters of single-seeded, winged fruit, often in such abundance that they can be a litter

problem. When flowers are on separate trees, you'll get fruit on female tree only if a male tree grows nearby.

Ashes are prone to borers. In some parts of California, ash whitefly is a problem; the chalky white, ⅛-in.-long insects colonize in patches on leaf undersides. Outbreaks are usually controlled by natural enemies; avoid spraying with broad-spectrum insecticides, which are likely to wipe out these beneficial predators.

F. americana. WHITE ASH. Deciduous. Zones 1–11, 14–17. Native to eastern U.S. Grows to 80 ft. or taller, with straight trunk and oval-shaped crown to 50 ft. wide. Leaves 8–15 in. long with five to nine dark green, oval leaflets, paler beneath; turn purplish in fall. Leaf edges burn in hot, windy areas. Regular water.

Male and female flowers are on separate trees, but plants sold are generally seedlings, so you don't know what you're getting. If you end up with both male and female trees, you will get a heavy crop of seed; both litter and seedlings can be a problem. Seedless selections include 'Autumn Applause', 'Autumn Purple', and 'Royal Purple', all with exceptionally good, long-lasting purple fall color; 'Champaign County', a dense grower; 'Rosehill', with bronzy red fall color; 'Skyline', an upright, somewhat narrow oval with brown and purple fall color; and 'Greenspire', another upright and narrowish oval with orange-red fall color.

F. angustifolia oxycarpa. Deciduous. Zones 2b–9, 12–24. Mediterranean native. Fairly compact, small-leafed, fine-textured ash with delicate, lacy look. Apparently not grown in the West, except in its variety 'Raywood' (Raywood ash or claret ash), a round-headed, compact, fastgrowing tree 25–35 ft. tall, 25 ft. wide, with purple-red fall color, no seeds. Prone to dieback in parts of California. Moderate water.

F. 'Fan West'. Deciduous. Zones 2–14. Seedless hybrid between *F. pennsylvanica* and *F. velutina coriacea* 'Modesto'. Resembles the latter in size and habit. Light olive green leaves, good branch structure; tolerates cold, desert heat, and wind. Best with regular water but tolerates some aridity.

F. greggii. LITTLE LEAF ASH. Evergreen. Zones 10–13. Native Arizona to Texas. To 25 ft. tall and 20 ft. wide, with leaves divided into three to seven ¾-in., leathery

F

F

leaflets. Useful desert tree. Little water.

F. latifolia (F. oregona). OREGON ASH. Deciduous. Zones 3–9, 14–24. Native to Sierra Nevada and west of the Cascades from Northern California to British Columbia. To 40–80 ft. tall, 30–50 ft. wide. Leaves 6–12 in. long, divided into five to seven oblong to oval, light green, hairy or smooth leaflets; end leaflet to 4 in. long, larger than side leaflets. Male and female flowers on separate trees. Will grow in standing water during winter months. Needs no dry-season irrigation. Subject to many pests and diseases; not a first-rate tree.

F. mandshurica 'Mancana'. MANCHURIAN ASH. Deciduous. Zones A1–A3; 1–3. Very cold-hardy, seedless, cutting-grown variety to 35 ft. tall and 25 ft. wide, with a dense, oval crown. Original tree was grown from a seed collected in Manchuria. Foot-long, yellowish green leaves have up to 11 coarsely toothed leaflets to 5 in. long; take on good yellow color in fall. Thrives on regular water but tolerates drought.

Fraxinus ornus

F. ornus. FLOWERING ASH. Deciduous. Zones 3–9, 14–17. Native to southern Europe and Asia Minor. Grows rapidly to 40–50 ft., with broad, rounded crown 20–30 ft. wide. Supplies luxuriant mass of foliage. Leaves 8–10 in. long, divided into 7–11 oval, medium green, 2-in.-long leaflets with toothed edges. Foliage turns to soft shades of lavender and yellow in fall. In spring, displays quantities of fluffy, branching, 3–5-in.-long clusters of fragrant white to greenish white blossoms followed by unsightly seed clusters

that hang on until late winter unless removed. Moderate water.

F. pennsylvanica (F. lanceolata). GREEN ASH, RED ASH. Deciduous. Zones A2, A3; 1–6. Native to eastern U.S. To 30–40 ft. tall and wide, with compact, oval crown. Gray-brown bark; dense, twiggy structure. Leaves 10–12 in. long, divided into five to nine bright green, rather narrow, 4–6-in.-long leaflets. Male and female flowers on separate trees. Takes wet soil and severe cold, but foliage burns in hot, dry winds. Regular water. Seedless varieties include fast-growing, cold-tolerant 'Bergeson'; round-headed 'Emerald', not as cold hardy as other selections; 'Marshall', fast-growing tree with tapered crown; 'Patmore', tolerant of extreme cold; 'Summit', with upright habit and good golden yellow fall color; and 'Urbanite', with pyramidal form and bronze fall color.

F. quadrangulata. BLUE ASH. Deciduous. Zones 2–6. Native to central U.S. Grows rapidly to 60–80 ft. tall with crown to about 40 ft. wide. Branches distinctly square in cross section, usually with flanges along edges. Oval dark green leaflets (7–11 per leaf) are 2–5 in. long and have toothed edges. Foliage turns purplish in fall. Fruit may become a litter problem if you have both female and male trees. Regular water.

F. uhdei. EVERGREEN ASH, SHAMEL ASH. Evergreen to semievergreen. Zones 9, 12–24. Native to Mexico and a favorite in Southern California and low-elevation deserts. Grows fast to 25–30 ft. tall in 10 years; reaches 40 ft. in 20 years and may eventually attain 70–80 ft. or taller. Upright, narrow tree about 15 ft. wide when young; eventually takes on a spreading form as it grows older (may reach 60 ft. wide at maturity). Leaves divided into five to nine glossy dark green, finely tooth-edged leaflets about 4 in. long. Foliage may burn if subjected to hot winds. In mildest climates, leaves hold on through winter; in colder areas, tree loses most or all of its foliage, but leafless period often lasts only for a short time. Sharp frosts may kill branch tips; tree will suffer serious damage at 15°F/ –9°C or lower.

Cut back any long, unsightly branches when tree is young. Eliminate deep crotches by pruning out weaker branches. Texas root rot sometimes causes dieback and will kill young trees, but

established ones usually survive. Resistant to oak root fungus. Tolerates aridity but does best with regular water and an occasional deep soaking.

'Majestic Beauty'. Has exceptionally large leaves and is more reliably evergreen than species.

'Sexton'. Very compact, rounded crown. Larger, deeper green leaflets than those of species.

'Tomlinson'. Grows more slowly than species (to 18 ft. in 10 years) and is more upright and dense when young. Leaflets are more leathery, with wavy-toothed margins.

F. velutina. ARIZONA ASH. Deciduous. Zones 3b–24. Native to southwestern U.S. and Mexico. Withstands hot, dry conditions; cold hardy to about –10°F/–23°C. Grows about 30 ft. (possibly to 50 ft.) tall. Pyramidal when young; spreading to 30–40 ft. wide when mature, with more open form. Leaves divided into three to five narrow to oval, 3-in.-long leaflets; turn bright yellow in fall. Male and female flowers on separate trees. Regular water.

'Berrinda'. Zones 3–24. Very tough, cold-hardy selection from New Mexico, with a strongly upright form to 35 ft. high and about as wide.

'Bonita'. Zones 8–24. Good substitute for 'Modesto', especially in the Southwest. Broadly oval to 30–35 ft. high and slightly wider. Bright yellow fall color lasts longer than that of 'Modesto'.

F. v. coriacea. MONTEBELLO ASH. Zones 8, 9, 12–24. Native mostly to Southern California. Broader, more leathery leaves than the species.

'Modesto'. MODESTO ASH. Zones 3–24. Originated in Modesto, California. Vigorous form growing to about 50 ft. tall, with 30-ft. spread. Leaflets are medium green, glossier than those of species; bright yellow fall color. Resistant to oak root fungus but subject to numerous other problems that have caused many communities to remove it from their lists of recommended trees. In many areas, leaves get a scorched look due to anthracnose fungus if springtime weather is wet. In agricultural regions, verticillium wilt is prevalent (there is no control for it; young trees may die once infected, but established trees often survive). In some areas, mistletoe—an evergreen parasitic plant—can infest Modesto ash so heavily that the trees seem to be in

Fraxinus velutina coriacea 'Modesto'

leaf in winter. Control is difficult; the best defense is to prune out mistletoe as soon as you notice it. In desert, tree is subject to ash decline syndrome, an ailment of unknown origin. Keep tree vigorous; if it succumbs, replace with 'Bonita', 'Rio Grande', *F. angustifolia oxycarpa* 'Raywood', or *F. uhdei*.

'Rio Grande'. FAN-TEX ASH. Zones 8–24. Thrives in hot, dry climates and alkaline soils. Has larger, darker green, more succulent leaflets than 'Modesto'; they turn golden yellow in late fall. Foliage resistant to wind burn.

FRECKLE FACE. See **HYPOESTES phyllostachya**

FREESIA
Iridaceae
PERENNIALS FROM CORMS

🗡 **ZONES 8, 9, 12–24**

☀ ◑ **FULL SUN OR PARTIAL SHADE**

💧 **REGULAR WATER DURING GROWTH AND BLOOM**

South African natives prized for the rich perfume of their flowers. In spring, wiry, 1–1½-ft. stems bear spikes of tubular flowers that reach 2 in. long, flare to 2 in. wide.

Freesia hybrids

Each stem bends at nearly a right angle just beneath the lowest bud. Narrow, sword-shaped leaves to 1 ft. tall grow in irislike fans. In the past, the most widely available freesia was creamy white, powerfully sweet-scented *F. leichtlinii*, which naturalized in its preferred climates. Today, though, the most popular freesias are hybrids (Dutch and Tecolote hybrids represent the majority of those sold) with larger, single or double blossoms in yellow, orange, red, pink, lavender, purple, blue, and white—mixed or in single-color varieties. Volunteers tend to revert to cream marked with purple and yellow. These newer hybrid freesias are generally not as fragrant as the old-fashioned type.

Hardy to 20°F/–7°C. Plant in fall, setting corms 2 in. deep and 2 in. apart in well-drained soil. Cut back on watering when leaves start to yellow in late spring; withhold moisture during summer dormancy. In dry-summer regions, corms can be left in ground; in rainy-summer climates, it's best to dig them when foliage yellows and store the corms until it's time to replant them in early fall. Plantings will increase rapidly; dig and divide when vigor and quality of bloom decline.

In cold-winter areas, freesias can be grown in pots in sunny window; keep room temperature as cool as possible at night. Flowering potted freesias (grown from chilled and stored corms) are available all year. In subsequent years, they will bloom at the normal time in spring.

FREEWAY DAISY. See **OSTEOSPERMUM fruticosum**

FREMONTO-DENDRON (Fremontia)

FLANNEL BUSH
Sterculiaceae
EVERGREEN SHRUBS OR TREES

🌿 ZONES 4–24

☀ FULL SUN

◌ NO IRRIGATION NEEDED

Native to California; *F. californicum* is also native to parts of central Arizona. Fast-growing plants with a typically irregular shape, reaching 20 ft. tall and 12 ft. wide except as noted. Leathery leaves are dark green above, felted beneath. Very showy, typically saucer-shaped yellow blossoms in spring. Flowers are followed by persistent conical

seed capsules covered with bristly, rust-colored hairs; some people consider them unsightly, and they can irritate skin. Plants are completely drought tolerant and will accept occasional moisture during their normally dry period in summer only if drainage is excellent (hillside planting is recommended). Roots are shallow, so stake plants while young to prevent them from being blown over in windy areas. Pinch young growth to encourage branching; prune off overly long shoots. Remove lower branches to shape into small trees. Locate in front of a sunny wall in marginal climates. Plants are usually short lived.

Fremontodendron
'California Glory'

F. 'California Glory'. Hybrid between *F. californicum* and *F. mexicanum*. Rich yellow flowers to 3 in. across have red-tinged backs. Prolific bloom over long period.

F. californicum. COMMON FLANNEL BUSH. Eye-catching show of lemon yellow, 1–1½-in. flowers; tend to bloom all at once. Roundish, 1-in.-long, unlobed or three-lobed leaves.

F. 'Dara's Gold'. Compact hybrid resulting from a cross between *F. mexicanum* and a low-growing form of *F. californicum*. Grows just 3–4 ft. high and 6–8 ft. wide. Leaves are glossy green. Sunny yellow flowers to 2 in. wide appear over a long period from late winter to late spring. Excellent in large containers.

F. 'Ken Taylor'. Cross between *F.* 'California Glory' and a lower-growing species. To 4–6 ft. tall and 12 ft. wide, bearing somewhat cup-shaped golden flowers with orange backs.

F. mexicanum. SOUTHERN FLANNEL BUSH. Brilliant display of orange-tinted yellow blossoms

to 2½ in. across. Blooms less profusely than *F. californicum*, but flowers appear over a longer period. Leaves reach 3 in. long, have three to five distinct lobes.

F. 'Pacific Sunset'. Hybrid between *F. californicum* and *F. mexicanum*. To 12–15 ft. tall and wide. Deep orange-yellow, 3½–4-in.-wide flowers. Bloom peaks in spring, is sporadic later.

F. 'San Gabriel'. Looks much like 'California Glory' and has the same parentage, but its leaves are more deeply cut, resembling maple leaves.

FRINGE CUPS.
See **TELLIMA grandiflora**

FRINGE HYACINTH.
See **MUSCARI comosum**

FRINGE MYRTLE.
See **CALYTRIX tetragona**

FRINGE TREE.
See **CHIONANTHUS**

FRITILLARIA

FRITILLARY
Liliaceae
PERENNIALS FROM BULBS

🌿 ZONES VARY BY SPECIES

☼ LIGHT SHADE, EXCEPT AS NOTED

● REGULAR WATER DURING GROWTH AND BLOOM

In spring, unbranched stems ranging from 6 in. to 3 ft. high are topped by bell-shaped, nodding flowers, often unusually colored and mottled. Use in woodland gardens, rock gardens, or borders. In fall, plant bulbs in porous soil with ample humus. Set smaller bulbs 3–4 in. deep and 6 in. apart; set largest ones (*F. imperialis*) 4–5 in. deep, 8–12 in. apart. Bulbs sometimes rest for a year after planting or after blooming, so put in enough for yearly display. All appreciate some winter chill and tend to perform poorly where summers are hot and dry. Reduce watering as foliage dies back in summer. Once it is gone, withhold water from *F. biflora* until fall. *F. meleagris* needs moderate to regular water during dormancy; the others require some summer moisture. Clumps seldom need dividing.

F. biflora. MISSION BELLS. Zones 7, 14–21. California native to 6–16 in. high, with one to six brownish, 1½-in. bells on each blossom stalk. 'Martha Roderick' has rusty orange flowers with a white center.

F. camschatcensis. BLACK LILY, CHOCOLATE LILY. Zones A1–A3; 1–7, 15–17. Native near Pacific coast, Japan to northwestern U.S. Grows 9–18 in. high, with whorls of leaves around the stem. Flowering stem carries one to eight 1¼-in.-long, deep purple to nearly black bells.

Fritillaria imperialis

F. imperialis. CROWN IMPERIAL. Zones 1–7, 14–17. Native to Europe. Stout stalk to 3 ft. tall, clothed with broad, glossy leaves and crowned by circle of large (2–3-in.-long) bells in red, orange, or yellow; a tuft of leaves tops the flowers. Bulb and plant have musky odor that some people find offensive. Can take full sun in cooler climates.

F. meleagris. CHECKERED LILY, SNAKESHEAD. Zones 1–7, 15–17. Native to damp meadows in Europe, Asia; tolerates occasional flooding. One to three showy, 2-in. bells top each 1–1½-ft. stem; blossoms are checkered and veined with reddish brown and purple. Lance-shaped, 3–6-in.-long leaves. There is a white-blossomed form.

F. michailovskyi. Zones 2–7, 14–17. From Turkey. To 6 in. high. Each stem bears one to six 1–1½-in. bells that are purplish brown at base, bright yellow toward tip.

F. pallidiflora. Zones A1–A3; 1–7. From northern China, Siberia. Each 2–3-ft. stem carries one to six 1¼-in. bells in pale yellow tinted with green.

F. persica 'Adiyaman'. Zones 2–7, 14–17. Variety of a species from western Asia. Stems 2–3 ft. tall carry up to 30 deep plum purple, inch-long flowers on upper half. Foliage is grayish. Plant is hardy and easy to grow, but emerging stems need protection from late frosts in colder regions. Can take full sun in cooler climates.

F

FUCHSIA

Onagraceae
EVERGREEN AND DECIDUOUS
SHRUBS

🗹 ZONES VARY BY SPECIES

☼ ◐ FULL SUN OR PARTIAL SHADE

💧 REGULAR WATER

From wet, mountainous areas, mainly in tropical America. Most fuchsias bloom from late spring to first frost (and some bloom even longer), bearing unscented flowers frequented by hummingbirds. Popular showy-blossomed fuchsias are forms of *F. × hybrida* and are discussed under that heading. Some species fuchsias have blooms that are smaller overall than those of hybrids; others bear large, tubular flowers in unusual colors.

Fuchsias grow best in cool-summer areas with much moisture in atmosphere and soil. Plant in-ground fuchsias in full sun in the Northwest; give potted ones there and all fuchsias farther south either morning sun or all-day dappled shade. If you live where fog rolls in on summer afternoons, any place in your garden will supply ideal conditions. Where summers are warm, windy, or dry, seek or create favorable exposure protected from wind and hot afternoon sun. A heavy mulch (1½–3 in. thick) helps keep soil moist in hot climates. Frequent overhead sprinkling is beneficial in several ways: it keeps leaves clean, discourages some pests, and counteracts low humidity.

Fuchsia × hybrida,
double type

Blooms appear on new wood, so do any pruning before spring growth begins. In addition to removing broken or crossing branches, you can prune as little or as much as desired to maintain size or to shape the plant. In colder areas, wait to cut out frost-damaged stems until all danger of frost is past.

Fuchsia gall mite has caused serious problems for fuchsia growers primarily in California. Most hybrid fuchsias sold today have susceptible parentage and are prone to infestation, but many species fuchsias are resistant. The tiny mites, visible only under magnification, cause large, unsightly masses of distorted leaves, usually covered with reddish hairs. Cut off and destroy all distorted tissue. The pest can live on some resistant species and hybrids without producing any symptoms, allowing reinfection of susceptible fuchsias nearby. In the Northwest, aphids are the main pest. Spider mites and whiteflies are other common pests of fuchsias, though in the Northwest they tend to cause trouble primarily on potted plants.

F. boliviana. Evergreen. Zones 17, 22–24. From South America. Woody, erect growth to 12 ft. or taller and 8 ft. wide, with softly hairy pale green leaves to 7 in. long. Blooms throughout the year, producing large, pendent clusters of red flowers with slender tubes to 3 in. long. Pinkish red fruit. May spread by seed in moist gardens. Resistant to fuchsia gall mite. 'Alba' has two-tone flowers in white and pinkish red; fruit is white.

F. campos-portoi. Deciduous. Zones 3b–9, 14–24. From Brazil. Similar to *F. magellanica* and bears very similar blossoms, but has a denser habit and smaller leaves. Inflated buds with rounded teardrop shape; profuse bloomer. Can be grown as a dense shrub or allowed to clamber up into trees. Resistant to fuchsia gall mite.

F. denticulata. Evergreen. Zones 17, 22–24. From Peru, Bolivia. Parent of many new mite-resistant hybrids. Best known of these is 'Fanfare', which produces strong canes to 10 ft. or longer if given support of a tree or garden structure; excellent trained on trellis or as espalier. Dark green, 2–7-in.-long leaves. Blooms in summer and fall. Flowers are up to 3 in. long; petals orange red, sepals and slender floral tubes red. Resistant to fuchsia gall mite.

F. fulgens. Evergreen. Zones 15–17, 22–24. From Mexico. To 5 ft. tall and wide, with heart-shaped, light green leaves 5–8 in. long (or longer). Blooms from winter into spring, bearing pendent clusters of orange-red flowers to 3 in. long. Resistant to fuchsia gall mite.

F. glazioviana. Evergreen. Zones 16, 17, 22–24. From Brazil. Vigorous, fast-growing plant to 6–12 ft. tall and wide. Grow it as a dense shrub or let it scramble into trees. Small, shiny leaves and single pink-and-purple flowers just under an inch long. Resistant to fuchsia gall mite.

F. × hybrida. HYBRID FUCHSIA. Zones 4–6 (with protection), 15–17, 22–24, H1; can also be grown with some difficulty in Zones 7–9, 14, 20, 21. Where frosts are light, plants lose their leaves, and tender growth may die. Where freezes are hard, most plants die back to hard wood, sometimes to the ground.

Fuchsia × hybrida,
single type

The vast majority of fuchsias with showy flowers fall into this hybrid group. Many hundreds of selections are sold in the West, offering a wide variety of combinations of all colors in the range. Sepals (top parts that flare back) are always white, red, or pink. Corolla (inside part of flower) may be almost any color in range of white, blue violet, purple, pink, red, and shades approaching orange. Flowers range from shelled-peanut size to giants as big as a child's fist. Some flowers are single, with just one layer of closely set petals in corolla; some are very double, with many sets of ruffled petals in corolla. Small-flowered types often have small leaves, while big-flowered sorts have large leaves.

Plant form varies widely; choices range from erect-growing shrubs 3–6 ft. high and wide to trailing types grown in hanging baskets. You can also train (or buy) fuchsias as espaliers and standards (miniature tree forms).

Gardeners in California should note that, due to susceptible parentage, many if not most hybrids are susceptible to mite damage. Mite-resistant selections include 'Carnival', 'Mrs. Victor Reiter', and 'Trumpeter'.

Main concern in Northwest is winter protection. Most hybrid fuchsias there are grown in containers and brought into a garage or basement in winter; if container-grown plants are left outdoors, roots will freeze and the plants will die. In-ground fuchsias will have a better chance of survival if planted deeper than normal. Dig hole deep enough so you can place juncture of roots and stems 4–5 in. below soil level; gradually fill in soil as plant grows. Most hybrids need the insulation of a thick mulch in winter; mounding a 5–6-in. layer of sawdust over roots is effective. Hardier selections, however, will survive winters unmulched. These include 'Cardinal', 'Jingle Bells', 'June Bride', 'Mrs. Popple', 'Phyllis', 'Rufus', 'Santa Cruz', 'Speciosa', 'Surprise', 'Tessie', 'Voltaire', 'Whiteknights Amethyst', and 'Whiteknights Pearl'.

Fuchsias in all regions—whether in containers or beds—need porous, water-retentive soil rich in organic matter. Remember that those in hanging baskets need more watering than any other form. To keep blooms coming, apply light doses of complete fertilizer frequently.

Prune potted fuchsias severely before spring growth begins, cutting back each stem of last year's growth to one or two pairs of buds. Let about three pairs of leaves develop, then pinch off stem tips to stimulate branching. Continue pinching new growth for several weeks. Pick off old flowers as they start to fade. Prune in-ground fuchsias mainly to remove dead growth and to shape as desired; pinching is unnecessary.

You can take cuttings of favorite hybrids and grow them into flowering plants in a few months to a year. Cut 2–3-in. pieces of stem (preferably tips) and stick lower halves into damp sand to root.

F. magellanica. Zones 3b–9, 14–24; H1. Deciduous where frosts are light. Top dies back with first hard frost; protection of a mulch is needed in coldest-winter areas. Native to Chile, Argentina. In virtually frost-free areas, attains 10 ft. or taller and as wide or wider. In the Northwest, will reach 5–6½ ft. tall and wide if not frozen back; can grow 4–5 ft. in a season after being frozen back. Profuse production of drooping, 1½-in.-long, red-and-violet flowers. Oval, ½–1-in.-long leaves in groups of two or three. Very vulnerable to fuchsia gall mite. Parent of most hybrid fuchsias, which have inherited its mite susceptibility.

F. paniculata. Evergreen. Zones 16, 17, 22–24. From Mexico and Central America. Woody, erect growth to 12–14 ft. tall and 8 ft. wide (or larger), with small-toothed, somewhat shiny leaves to 8 in. long. Each lavender-pink flower is tiny, but blooms are massed in clusters to 10 in. across. Resistant to fuchsia gall mite. Often confused with and difficult to distinguish from *F. arborescens*, which is not reliably mite resistant.

F. procumbens. Semievergreen or deciduous. Zones 4–6, 15–17, 21–24. From New Zealand. Prostrate, spreading growth to about 6 in. high and 3–4 ft. wide. Heart-shaped, half-inch-long leaves. Small, petal-less flowers in summer have pale orange sepals with green markings and purple tips; anthers and pollen are blue. Showy, ¾-in. red berries. Good in shady rock gardens and containers. Resistant to fuchsia gall mite.

F. thymifolia. Evergreen. Zones 14–17, 20–24. From Mexico. Erect grower 3–9 ft. tall and wide, with ½–1-in.-long leaves and profuse, dangling white to pink flowers that age to deeper pink. Attractive close up; good for bonsai. Pollinated by bees rather than by hummingbirds. Resistant to fuchsia gall mite.

F. triphylla. Evergreen. Zones 16–17, 23, 24. From the West Indies. The species is seldom seen, but hybrid 'Gartenmeister Bonstedt' is well known. Somewhat more tender than most fuchsia hybrids but said to be more tolerant of heat. To 1½–2 ft. tall and wide. (Many plants sold are actually 'Thalia', nearly identical to

Fuchsia triphylla 'Gartenmeister Bonstedt'

'Gartenmeister Bonstedt' but reaching about 3 ft.) Leaves are reddish bronze above, purplish beneath. Drooping clusters of intense orange-red, long-tubed flowers. Blooms all year in mildest climates. Protect from frost. Susceptible to fuchsia gall mite.

FURCRAEA
Agavaceae
SUCCULENT PERENNIALS

| 🌡 ZONES 13, 16–17, 19–24; H1, H2 |
| ☀ ◑ LIGHT SHADE IN HOTTEST CLIMATES |
| 💧 MODERATE WATER |

These *Agave* relatives are native to Mexico and South America; many hail from the deciduous tropical forests of Venezuela and Colombia. Plants are grown for their dramatic form—they're bold specimen plants that bring an exotic look to the garden. Large, fleshy, sword-shaped leaves are held in huge rosettes (up to 8 ft. across) that grow into attractive fountain shapes in some species and are held like a pinwheel atop a trunk in others. Mature plants (at least 10 years old) send up spectacular bloom spikes, to 25 ft. tall, lined with pendent, greenish white, bell-shaped flowers that are powerfully fragrant in some species. Plants die after bloom, but the small plantlets (bulbils) that develop from the flowers can be easily pulled off and planted to reproduce the parent.

Provide rich, well-drained soil and allow it to dry between waterings. Plants need little water in winter but thrive with moderate summer irrigation. Protect from frost.

F. foetida. MAURITIUS HEMP. Forms a practically stemless clump of slightly glossy, deep green leaves 5–8 in. wide and up to 8 ft. long. Leaf margins have few teeth and are slightly wavy, suggesting undulating ribbons. Excellent for tropical gardens; grows well in a large container. The species was once grown commercially for the strong, hemplike fibers in its leaves. Considered invasive in Hawaii. Popular 'Mediopicta' (*F. f. mediopicta*) bears foliage with broad cream stripes edged in green striations.

F. macdougalii. Slender, rigid, gray-green leaves, to 7 ft. long and less than 3 in. wide, are held stiffly upright, resembling a group of javelins. Leaf margins are lined with small, widely spaced teeth.

Furcraea foetida 'Mediopicta'

With age, plants form a thick trunk that can grow to 20 ft. or taller.

F. roezlii. Trunk-forming species, eventually reaching 20 ft. tall and 8–10 ft. wide. Slender, leathery, blue-green leaves to 4 ft. long and 3 in. wide have tiny teeth along the margins. Dry leaves persist on the trunk, forming an interesting shaggy skirt. Tolerates much drought in all but the hottest areas.

F. selloa. Clumps grow to 6 ft. wide, eventually forming a 5-ft.-tall trunk. Attractive, dark green leaves, to 4 ft. long and 3 in. wide, are narrow at the base, wide in the middle, and sharply pointed at the tip. Wavy leaf margins are lined with brown, hooked teeth. *F. s. marginata* is a popular variegated form with a thin strip of creamy yellow along the leaf edges.

GAILLARDIA
BLANKET FLOWER
Asteraceae (Compositae)
PERENNIALS AND ANNUALS

| 🌡 ZONES 1–24; H1, H2 |
| ☀ FULL SUN |
| 💧 MODERATE WATER |

Native to central and western U.S. Low-growing summer bloomers with daisylike flowers in warm colors—yellow, bronze, scarlet. Plants thrive in heat, need good drainage. Easy to grow from seed and fine for cutting and borders; often reseed.

G. aristata. Perennial. Parent of popular hybrid *G. × grandiflora*. Has been largely replaced in garden culture by its many offspring, but the wild form is still much used in revegetation and wild-

flower mixes. Grows to 2–2½ ft. tall and 2 ft. across. Flower heads to 4 in. wide are yellow to red; the most common form has red rays with a jagged yellow border. 'Indian Yellow' has pure golden yellow flowers.

G. × grandiflora. Perennial. Hybrid of *G. aristata* and *G. pulchella*. Grows to 2–4 ft. high, 1½ ft. wide, with roughish gray-green foliage and single or double flowers 3–4 in. across. Much variation in flower color; range includes various warm shades of red and yellow, with orange or maroon bands. Exceptionally long bloom period for perennial—early summer until frost. Plants flower first year from seed.

Gaillardia × grandiflora

Many strains and varieties are available, including dwarf kinds and types with extra-large flowers. 'Goblin' is a good compact variety (1 ft. tall) with large deep red flowers bordered in bright yellow. 'Goblin Yellow' is similar but has yellow blooms. 'Baby Cole', another red-and-yellow type, grows 7–8 in. high. 'Mandarin' grows 2 ft. tall, with mahogany centers and flame orange petals tipped in yellow. Among 2½-ft.-tall varieties are deep red 'Burgundy'; pure orange 'Tokajer'; and 'Torchlight', bearing yellow blooms bordered with red. 'Yellow Queen', with pure yellow flowers and yellow centers, may reach 3 ft. tall.

G. pulchella. Annual. To 1½–2 ft. high, 1 ft. wide, with soft, hairy leaves and long, whiplike stems carrying 2-in. flowers in warm shades of red, yellow, gold. Easy to grow; sow seeds in warm soil after danger of frost is past (in Zones 12 and 13, sow in fall). 'Red Plume' and 'Yellow Plume' are double flowered, with 2-in. blossoms on uniform 12–14-in. plants.

G

G

GALANTHUS
SNOWDROP
Amaryllidaceae
PERENNIALS FROM BULBS

🌢	ZONES 1–9, 14–17, EXCEPT AS NOTED
☼ ◐	FULL SUN DURING BLOOM, LIGHT SHADE AFTER
●	REGULAR WATER
✦	BULBS ARE POISONOUS IF INGESTED

These natives of Europe and Asia Minor perform best in cold-winter climates. Closely related to and often confused with *Leucojum* (snowflake). Among the first bulbs to bloom as winter ends. Nodding, bell-shaped white flowers are borne one per stalk; inner flower segments are infused or marked with green, while larger outer segments are pure white. Plants have two or three strap-shaped basal leaves. Use in rock gardens or under flowering shrubs, naturalize in woodland, or grow in pots. Plant in fall, setting bulbs 3–4 in. deep and 3 in. apart in moist soil with ample humus. Prefer year-round moisture. Do not divide often; when division is necessary, do the job right after bloom.

G. elwesii. GIANT SNOWDROP. Foot-high stems carry 1½-in. flowers; inner segments are heavily infused with green. Better adapted to mild-winter zones than *G. nivalis*.

G. ikariae. Zones 4–9, 14–24. Vigorous grower to 4–6 in. high. Glossy, rich green leaves are curved and slightly broader than those of other species listed here. Large green spot marks inner petals of flowers, which appear a little later than blooms of other snowdrops.

G. nivalis. COMMON SNOWDROP. More delicate version of *G. elwesii*. Stems 6–9 in. high bear inch-long flowers, their inner segments marked at tips with a green crescent. 'Flore Pleno' has double blooms.

Galanthus nivalis

GALIUM
Rubiaceae
PERENNIALS

🌢	ZONES 1–6, 15–17, EXCEPT AS NOTED
◐ ●	PARTIAL OR FULL SHADE
● ●●	REGULAR TO AMPLE WATER

All have whorls of narrow leaves at intervals along thin, usually sprawling stems. Flowers are tiny, often profuse. Plants are not showy, but one (*G. odoratum*) is a useful ground cover for a shady site, while others have been grown for medicine, food, or dye. Can become invasive.

G. boreale. NORTHERN BEDSTRAW. Zones A1–A3; 1–6, 15–17. From Alaska, Canada, northern Europe, Asia. To 2½ ft. tall and wide, with 2-in. leaves. Clusters of tiny white flowers appear in profusion in summer. Nice wildflower for shade.

G. mollugo. FALSE BABY'S BREATH. From North America, Europe. Sprawling, weak-stemmed plant to 5 ft. tall and wide. Tiny leaves; loose, open clusters of tiny white flowers in summer and fall. Roots were once used to make red dye, and leaves in curdling milk for cheese.

Galium odoratum

G. odoratum (Asperula odorata). SWEET WOODRUFF. Zones A2, A3; 2–6, 15–17. Native to Europe, North Africa, Siberia. Attractive low spreader that brings to mind deep, shady woods. Slender, square stems encircled every inch or so by six to eight aromatic, bristle-tipped leaves. Clusters of tiny white flowers appear above foliage in late spring and summer. When dried, leaves and stems give off a fragrance like hay; they are used to make May wine. In shade gardens, best used as a ground cover or pathway edging. Spreads rapidly in rich soil with abundant moisture and can become a pest if allowed to grow unchecked. Self-

sows freely; can also be increased by division in fall or spring.

G. verum. LADY'S BEDSTRAW. From Europe, Asia. Much like *G. mollugo* and also blooms in summer and fall, but is somewhat smaller (to 3½ ft. high and wide) and bears yellow rather than white flowers.

GALTONIA
candicans
SUMMER HYACINTH
Liliaceae
PERENNIAL FROM BULB

🌢	ZONES 4–24; H1; OR DIG AND STORE
☼ ◐	LIGHT SHADE IN HOTTEST CLIMATES
●	REGULAR WATER DURING GROWTH AND BLOOM

Native to South Africa. Strap-shaped leaves, 2–3 ft. long. In summer, the stout, 2–4-ft. stems are topped with loose, spikelike clusters of 1–1½-in.-long, sweet-scented white flowers—drooping, funnel shaped, the three outer segments often tipped green. Plant in fall where winter lows won't fall below 10°F/–12°C, in spring in colder regions; set bulbs 6 in. deep and 1 ft. apart, in organically enriched soil. Floral display is best if clump is not disturbed from one year to the next. Where winter lows range from 10 to –20°F/ –12 to –29°C, mulch planting after foliage dies down. In colder regions, dig annually and store as for gladiolus. Control slugs and snails.

Galtonia candicans

GALVEZIA speciosa
ISLAND BUSH SNAPDRAGON
Scrophulariaceae
EVERGREEN SHRUB

🌢	ZONES 14–24
☼ ◐	LIGHT SHADE IN HOTTEST CLIMATES
◊	NO IRRIGATION NEEDED

Native to Catalina, San Clemente, and Guadalupe islands (off the coast of Southern California). Usually grows 3 ft. high and 5 ft. wide, but can climb or lean on

Galvezia speciosa

other shrubs and reach 8 ft. Leaves are about 1 in. long, half as wide. Scarlet, tubular, 1-in.-long flowers cluster toward tips of branches. Bloom is heaviest in midspring but intermittent throughout year. Endures light or heavy soils if drainage is adequate. 'Firecracker' is a compact form (2–3 ft. high and 3 ft. wide) with bright red flowers.

GARDENER'S GARTERS. See **PHALARIS arundinacea picta**

GARDENIA
Rubiaceae
EVERGREEN SHRUBS

🌢	ZONES VARY BY SPECIES
☼ ◐	FULL SUN OR PARTIAL SHADE
● ●●	REGULAR TO AMPLE WATER

White or yellowish, intensely fragrant blossoms contrast sharply with shiny, leathery dark green leaves. Double forms are classic flowers for corsages.

G. augusta (G. jasminoides). Zones 7–9, 12–16, 18–24, H1, H2, except as noted. Native to China, Taiwan, Japan. Glossy bright green, lance-shaped leaves

Gardenia augusta

nd intensely fragrant, single or double white flowers. Hardy to 0°F/–7°C or even lower but must ave summer heat to thrive and loom well. Hard to grow in adobe r alkaline desert soils. Give orthern or eastern exposure n desert.

Provide fast-draining but moisture-retentive soil conditioned with plenty of organic matter such as peat moss or ground ark. Plant gardenias high (like zaleas and rhododendrons) and void crowding from other plants nd competing roots. To help suppress weeds, mulch plants instead of cultivating around them. Unless water is high in salts (residue from alt in water may burn leaves), mist lants in early morning except during bloom time. Where water ontains dissolved salts, irrigate deeply once a month to leach salts rom soil. Feed every 3 to 4 weeks during growing season with acid plant food, fish emulsion, or blood meal. Magnesium deficiency can esult in yellow leaves with green veins; treat by dissolving one tablespoon of Epsom salts in a gallon of water and soaking the root zone (best done in early spring). Prune to remove dead wood, straggling branches, faded flowers. To control aphids and brown scale, wash plants frequently with jet spray from hose or spray plants with light horticultural oil. (In hot weather, spray in the evening—though not if temperatures exceed 90°F/32°C—then wash off foliage next morning.)

Plants are useful in containers or raised beds, as hedges, espaliers, low screens, or specimens. Named varieties include the following.

'Aimée' ('First Love', 'Amy Yoshida'). Upright grower to 4–6 ft. tall and wide. Very large, very double, 4-in.-plus, roselike blossoms with elegantly spiraled form. Starts blooming in spring and continues well into summer.

'August Beauty'. Erect growth to 4–6 ft. high, 3–4 ft. wide. Loosely double, 2–3-in.-wide flowers produced primarily in early summer.

'Belmont' ('Hadley'). Vintage estate variety to 5 ft. high (or taller) and 5 ft. wide, with 4-in., roselike blossoms. Bulk of bloom comes from late spring to early summer. Leaves are large (up to 6 in. long).

'Chuck Hayes'. Zones 6–9, 12–16, 18–24; H1, H2. Extra-hardy variety; possibly as cold tolerant as 'Kleim's Hardy'. To 4 ft. high and wide. Double, 3-in. flowers in sum-

mer, with heavy rebloom in autumn. Very heat tolerant.

'Kimura Shikazaki' ('Four Seasons'). Compact growth to 2–3 ft. tall and wide. Flowers similar to those of 'Veitchii' but slightly less fragrant. Extremely long bloom season, from spring to fall.

'Kleim's Hardy'. Zones 6–9, 12–16, 18–24; H1, H2. Slow growing, forming a mound 2–3 ft. high and wide. Intensely fragrant single, star-shaped flowers are 1–3 in. wide. Blooms profusely in early summer, sporadically through rest of growing season. Reportedly has survived to 0°F/–18°C, suffering only damage to foliage.

'Miami Supreme'. To 6 ft. tall and wide, with large (4-in. or wider), very double flowers in spring; periodic rebloom through summer.

'Mystery'. Grows 6–8 ft. high and wide, even larger in time. Pure white, formal, 4–5-in. blossoms are the standard variety for florists' corsages. Blooms from midsummer through early fall—longer if warm weather continues. Intense fragrance carries through the air, even in dry climates. Rangy growth needs pruning to keep it neat and within bounds.

'Radicans' ('Prostrata'). True miniature gardenia. Grows 6–12 in. high and 2–3 ft. wide, with inch-long dark green leaves and many inch-wide double flowers, mainly in early summer. Good small-scale edging, ground cover, container plant. 'Radicans Variegata' ('Prostrata Variegata') has medium green leaves irregularly edged or splashed with creamy yellow and white; same habit as 'Radicans' but somewhat less vigorous.

'Veitchii'. Sometimes sold as "everblooming gardenia." Compact form 3–4½ ft. high, to 6 ft. wide; leaves to 2½ in. long. Oldest variety, but still most reliable bloomer. Roselike, 1½–2-in.-wide, pure white blossoms from late spring to fall; bloom may continue during a warm winter.

'White Gem'. Dense, compact dwarf to 1–2 ft. high and wide. Rounded, five- or six-petaled, 1½–2-in. single flowers bloom continuously from spring through summer. Sweet, carrying fragrance. Good in containers, foreground of borders.

G. taitensis. TIARE TAHITI, TAHITIAN GARDENIA, KIELE. Zone H2. Native to Polynesia. Dense-crowned large shrub or small tree to 18 ft. tall and wide.

Shiny dark green leaves to 8 in. long, 4 in. wide. White, 4-in.-wide, pinwheel-shaped flowers are produced throughout the year; they are powerfully fragrant and a favorite for leis. Plants can be pruned into small trees or planted as an informal hedge. Best in full sun; will tolerate shade. Withstands beach conditions if protected from salt, winds.

G. thunbergia. Zones 16, 17, 21–24; H1, H2. Native to South Africa. Winter-blooming shrub to 10 ft. tall, 20 ft. wide. Angular branches; dark green leaves to 6 in. long. Single, 3–4-in. flowers have a long tube and typically eight overlapping, petal-like lobes. Somewhat more tolerant than *G. augusta* of cool conditions and less-than-perfect soil, but tender to frost. With age, becomes more vigorous and blooms more profusely. Rough, brownish gray, elliptical fruits to 5 in. long remain on plant for 2 or 3 years.

GARLAND FLOWER.
See **HEDYCHIUM coronarium**

GARLIC
Liliaceae
PERENNIAL

| 🗡 ALL ZONES EXCEPT A1 |
| ☀ FULL SUN |
| 💧 REGULAR WATER |

These onion relatives are not known in the wild. Seed stores and some mail-order seed houses sell disease-free mother bulbs ("sets") for planting—and some gardeners have had good luck planting bulbs from grocery stores. In mild-winter areas, plant in fall for early summer harvest; where winters are cold, plant in early spring. Break up bulbs into individual segments ("cloves") and select

Garlic

largest ones. Plant in rich, well-drained soil, setting cloves pointed end up, 1 in. deep, 3–6 in. apart, in rows 15 in. apart. Harvest when leafy tops fall over; lift out with garden fork rather than pulling. Air-dry bulbs, cut off most of tops and roots, and store in cool, well-ventilated place out of sunlight. Giant or elephant garlic has unusually large (fist-size) bulbs and mild garlic flavor. Grow as for regular garlic, but space 8–12 in. apart. For ornamental relatives, see *Allium*.

GARLIC CHIVES.
See **ALLIUM tuberosum**

GARRYA
SILKTASSEL
Garryaceae
EVERGREEN SHRUBS

| 🗡 ZONES VARY BY SPECIES |
| ☀ ◐ FULL SUN OR PARTIAL SHADE |
| ◐ 💧 WATER NEEDS VARY BY SPECIES |

Grown mainly for their pendulous male and female catkins, which appear on separate plants; male catkins are longer, more slender, and more decorative than female ones. Both sexes must be present for female plants to produce their grapelike clusters of fruit.

Garrya elliptica

G. elliptica. COAST SILKTASSEL. Zones 4–9, 14–24. Native to Coast Ranges from southern Oregon to Southern California. Densely foliaged plant reaches 10–20 ft. high and as wide. Plant can be trained as a small tree. Elliptical, wavy-edged leaves to 2½ in. long are dark green above with gray and woolly undersides. Clustered flower tassels appear in winter. Male catkins are yellowish to greenish yellow, 3–8 in. long; female ones are pale green, rather

G

stubby, 2–3½ in. long. Clustered purplish fruits on female plants hang on all summer—even longer if not eaten by birds. Excellent foliage plant; use as screen, informal hedge, or specimen. For unusually long catkins, plant male varieties 'Evie' (10 in.) or 'James Roof' (1 ft.). Moderate water.

G. fremontii. FREMONT SILKTASSEL. Zones 3–10, 12, 14–17. Native to mountains of Washington, Oregon, California, Arizona. To 9 ft. tall and wide. Differs from *G. elliptica* in its leaves, which are glossy, smooth edged, and lively yellow green on both upper and lower surfaces. Yellowish or purple catkins; purple or black fruit. Takes heat and cold better than *G. elliptica.* No irrigation needed.

GAS PLANT.
See **DICTAMNUS albus**

GAULTHERIA
Ericaceae
EVERGREEN SHRUBS

🌿	ZONES VARY BY SPECIES
◐	PARTIAL SHADE, EXCEPT AS NOTED
💧	REGULAR WATER

These shrubs bear urn-shaped flowers and fleshy, berrylike fruit. They all need moist, acid soil rich in organic matter. Smaller kinds are favored for rock gardens and woodland plantings. Larger kinds are good companions for other acid-loving shrubs such as rhododendrons and azaleas.

G. mucronata (Pernettya mucronata). Zones 4–7, 15–17. From Chile, Argentina. Grows 2–3 ft. tall, spreading by underground runners to form a 4-ft.-wide clump. Small leaves are glossy dark green; some turn red or bronzy in winter. Tiny, bell-shaped, white to pink flowers appear in late spring, followed by colorful, long-lasting berries in white, pink, red, rose, purple, or near black, all with a notable metallic sheen. To get more fruit, grow several plants together to ensure cross-pollination. Can be invasive; control by trimming roots with a spade. Thin regularly and shear lightly to keep plant compact and attractive. Interesting as an informal low hedge or border plant; also good in tubs or large window boxes. Grows well in partial shade; takes full sun in all but hottest climates.

G. ovatifolia. Zones 3–7, 14–17. Native to the mountains in Northern California to British

Columbia, east to northern Idaho. Plant is spreading and trailing, with upright branches to about 8 in. high. Oval, leathery, dark green leaves about ¾–1½ in. long and nearly as wide. Bears tiny white to pinkish flowers in summer and bright red, ¼-in.-wide berries in fall and winter that are edible, have a wintergreen flavor. Small-scale ground cover in woodland.

G. procumbens. WINTERGREEN, CHECKERBERRY, TEABERRY. Zones 1–7, 14–17. Native to eastern North America. Creeping stems send up erect branches to 6 in. high, with oval, 2-in., glossy dark green leaves clustered toward tips. Foliage

Gaultheria procumbens

emits a strong wintergreen odor when bruised, turns reddish with winter cold. Small pinkish white summer flowers are followed by scarlet berries. Both berries and foliage have flavor of wintergreen (or teaberry). Use as ground cover; plant 1 ft. apart. 'Macrocarpa' is a compact variety bearing a heavy crop of fruit. 'Red Baron' has notably large fruits.

G. shallon. SALAL. Zones 4–7, 14–17. Native from central California coast north to British Columbia. In good growing conditions, can reach 4–10 ft. tall and slightly wider; in poor, dry soil and full sun, it's a tufted plant only

Gaultheria shallon

1–2 ft. high (makes a good low bank cover in these circumstances). Glossy bright green leaves are nearly round, 1¾–4 in. long. Loose, 6-in.-long clusters of white or pinkish flowers on reddish stalks bloom in spring. Edible black fruits resembling large huckleberries follow the blossoms; they're bland flavored, but birds like them. Only neglected plantings need pruning; cut back in spring, remove dead wood, and mulch with organic material such as leaf mold or peat moss. Cut branches are sold by florists as "lemon leaves."

GAURA lindheimeri
Onagraceae
PERENNIAL

🌿	ZONES 2B–24
☀	FULL SUN
💧	MODERATE WATER

Native to Texas and Louisiana. Airy growth to 2½–4 ft. high, 2–3 ft. wide. Leaves are 1½–3½ in. long and stalkless, growing directly from stems. Branching

Gaura lindheimeri

flower spikes bear many closely set, 1-in.-long white blossoms that open from pink buds. Long bloom period (often from late spring into fall), with only a few flowers opening at a time. Blossoms age to a rosy shade, then drop off cleanly, but seed-bearing spikes should be removed to improve overall appearance, prolong bloom period, and prevent overly enthusiastic self-sowing. Long-lived plant. Division not necessary—and difficult in any case, since gaura grows from a deep taproot

(which makes it very drought tolerant). For additional plants, let a few seedlings grow.

Selected forms include 2–2½-ft 'Corrie's Gold', featuring gold-edge foliage; 'Passionate Blush', upright and compact, to 1½ ft. tall and slightly wider, with red stems and pink flowers; 'Pink Cloud', an upright grower to 2½–3 ft. tall, with plentiful deep pink flowers; 'Pink Fountain', 2–3 ft. high, with lateral branching that makes for an especially dense mass of soft pink flowers; 2-ft. 'Siskiyou Pink', with maroon-mottled leaves and deep maroon buds opening to ros pink flowers; 'Whirling Butterflies with slightly larger white flowers on a 3-ft. plant; and the similar bu slightly smaller and denser 'White Fountain'.

GAYFEATHER. See **LIATRIS**

GAZANIA
Asteraceae (Compositae)
PERENNIALS, SOME GROWN
AS ANNUALS

🌿	ZONES VARY BY SPECIES
☀◐	EXPOSURE NEEDS VARY BY SPECIES
💧	MODERATE TO REGULAR WATER

Native to South Africa. Low, clumping or spreading plants grown for colorful daisies over long bloom season. Tolerate seacoast conditions. Grow well in enriched or unamended soil, and with regular or only occasional irrigation.

G. hybrids. Zones 8–24, H1, H2 as perennials; in colder climates, carry plants through winter by taking cuttings in fall as you would for pelargoniums. Dazzling color display during peak bloom in late spring, early summer. In mild-winter climates, they continue to bloom intermittently through the rest of year. Grow in full sun. There are basically two types: clumping and trailing.

Clumping gazanias (complex hybrids between a number of species) form a mound of evergreen, typically lobed leaves that are dark green above with gray and woolly undersides. Flowering stems are 6–10 in. tall, bearing 3–4-in.-wide blossoms in colors including yellow, orange, white, and rosy pink; undersides of rays are reddish purple. Blossoms often have dark centers. You can also get a mixture of hybrids (as plants or seeds) in different colors. Flowers open on sunny days and close at night and in cloudy weather.

Among seed-grown kinds is the Daybreak series—low-growing, spreading plants that bloom in 12 weeks from seed (good choice for areas with short growing season) and feature blossoms in orange, bronze, yellow, yellow striped with red, and mixed colors. Harlequin Hybrids are 12–15 in. tall and offer a full range of colors; blossoms have striking zones in contrasting colors. Other seed-grown sorts are Sundance Mixed, with 4–5-in. flowers on 10–12-in. plants; Sunshine Mix, which grows to 10–12 in. tall, displaying several zones of color on each 4-in. flower; and 8-in.-tall Talent Mix, showing off 2½-in. blossoms against silvery foliage.

Gazania hybrid

Named hybrids of special merit include 'Aztec Queen' (multicolored), 'Burgundy', 'Copper King', and 'Fiesta Red'; these are best used in small-scale plantings, though the last is sturdy enough for large expanses. 'Moonglow' is double-flowered bright yellow of unusual vigor; unlike most gazanias, it has blooms that stay open even on dull days.

Use clumping gazanias in parking strips, as edging along sunny paths, in rock gardens. Good temporary fillers between young shrubs or as replaceable ground cover for relatively level areas not subject to severe erosion.

Trailing gazanias are derived from *G. rigens leucolaena*, formerly sold as *G. uniflora* or *G. leucolaena*. They grow about as tall as clumping types but spread rapidly by long, trailing stems. Foliage is a clean silvery gray; flowers are yellow, white, orange, or bronze. *G. rigens* 'Variegata' bears orange flowers over leaves variegated in creamy white. Newer, larger-flowered hybrids include 'Sunburst' (orange with black eye) and 'Sunglow' (yellow). 'Sunrise Yellow' has large, black-centered yellow flowers; leaves are green instead of gray. These newer hybrids are superior to older kinds in length of bloom, resistance to dieback.

Trailing gazanias are useful on banks as well as level ground. Or grow them at the top of a wall and let them drape over the edge. Attractive in hanging baskets.

G. krebsiana. Zones 3, 7–24. Grows about 6 in. high and 1 ft. wide, with deeply divided leaves that are dark green on top and silvery white beneath; foliage takes on purple hues in cold weather. Rich reddish orange flowers 2½–3 in. across have a central disk of orange or dark yellow; base of each petal is green and black, with a single white spot. Long bloom season, from spring to fall. May reseed a bit. Full sun.

G. linearis 'Colorado Gold'. Zones 2–9, 14–19. Unlike other gazanias, this is a hardy perennial in much of the cold-winter West. One of the many surprisingly hardy plants brought back from the high mountains of South Africa, it has succeeded in Denver and northern New Mexico. Grows 4 in. high, 15 in. wide. Strap-shaped leaves are dark green above, woolly white beneath. Bright yellow flowers to 3 in. wide bloom all summer. Self-sows. Full sun or partial shade.

GEIGER TREE.
See **CORDIA sebestena**

GEIJERA parviflora
AUSTRALIAN WILLOW, WILGA
Rutaceae
EVERGREEN TREE

	ZONES 8, 9, 12–24
☼	FULL SUN
◐ ◑	LITTLE TO MODERATE WATER

Graceful, fine-textured tree from Australia. To 25–30 ft. tall and 20 ft. wide, with main branches sweeping up and out, little

Geijera parviflora

branches hanging down. Distant citrus relative; called a willow because its narrow, drooping, 3–6-in.-long leaves give a weeping willow effect. Casts light shade. With age, produces loose clusters of unimportant small, creamy white flowers in early spring and early fall. Has much of willow's grace and eucalyptus's toughness. Trouble-free patio, street, or grove tree. Deep, noninvasive roots. Grow in well-drained soil. Needs pruning only to correct form (much less pruning than true willow).

GELSEMIUM
Loganiaceae
EVERGREEN VINES

	ZONES 4–24
☼ ◐	FULL SUN OR PARTIAL SHADE
◐ ◑ ◖◗	WATER NEEDS VARY BY SPECIES
◑	ALL PARTS ARE POISONOUS IF INGESTED

Native to southeastern U.S. Shrubby, twining vines grow to about 20 ft., with pairs of shiny, light green, 1–4-in.-long leaves borne on long branches that look almost like streamers. Flowers are bright yellow trumpets. Often trained onto fences and mailboxes.

Gelsemium sempervirens

On a trellis, these vines will cascade and swing in the wind; trained against a house wall, they make a delicate green curtain of branches. Thin stems will not damage their support. Can get top-heavy; if this happens, cut back to stimulate fresh new growth. Also used as ground covers, especially nice tumbling down banks. Keep trimmed to 3 ft. high. In full sun, the plants are more shrubby and floriferous; in partial shade, they grow longer and bloom a bit less.

G. rankinii. SWAMP JESSAMINE. Scentless, inch-wide flowers bloom in spring and fall. Needs

regular to ample water; tolerates boggy soil.

G. sempervirens. CAROLINA JESSAMINE. Fragrant, 1½-in.-long flowers appear in late winter, early spring, with occasional sporadic bloom in fall. Needs regular water in youth but is fairly drought tolerant once established. 'Pride of Augusta' ('Plena') is a double-flowered form.

GENISTA
BROOM
Fabaceae (Leguminosae)
DECIDUOUS AND EVERGREEN SHRUBS

	ZONES VARY BY SPECIES
☼	FULL SUN
◐ ◑	LITTLE TO MODERATE WATER

Leaves are often small and short lived. Green branches give these deciduous plants an evergreen look. Flowers are yellow (rarely white or pink) and sweet pea shaped. Less aggressive than other brooms *(see Cytisus)*; the species listed here are not invasive. Smaller kinds are attractive in rock gardens and bank plantings. These shrubs tolerate rocky or infertile soil. Need good drainage. The various species are native to central, southern, and eastern Europe.

G. aetnensis. MT. ETNA BROOM. Leafless or nearly so. Zones 5–9, 14–24. Large shrub or small tree to 18 ft. or more, with graceful arching, weeping green branchlets, bare or with a very few tiny leaves during growing season. Branches are covered with blooms in summer. Not likely to survive temperatures below 5°F/–15°C.

Genista lydia

G. canariensis (Cytisus canariensis). CANARY ISLAND BROOM. Evergreen. Zones 8, 9, 14–24. Damaged at 15°F/–9°C but recovers quickly. Many-branched, upright shrub 6–8 ft. tall, 5–6 ft. wide. Bright green leaves divided into ½-in. leaflets. Fragrant flowers at ends of branches in spring and summer. The genista of florists. Grows like a weed and spreads by self-sown seedlings.

G. fragrans. This white-flowered species is not in the nursery trade. Plants sold under this name are *G.* × *spachiana.*

G. hispanica. SPANISH BROOM. Deciduous. Zones 4–22. Mass of spiny stems to 1–2 ft. high, up to 5 ft. wide; stems set with ½-in.-long leaves. Clusters of flowers at stem tips in spring.

G. lydia. Nearly leafless. Zones 2b–6, 14–17. Often erroneously sold as *Cytisus lydia.* Shrub grows to 2 ft. tall and 3 ft. wide; makes a good ground cover. Bears profuse show of blossoms at tips of shoots in late spring. Sets few seeds.

G. monosperma (Retama monosperma). BRIDAL VEIL BROOM. Nearly leafless. Zones 16, 17, 22–24. Upright growth to 20 ft. high, 10 ft. wide, with slender, graceful gray-green branches. Fragrant white flowers in winter, spring.

G. pilosa. Deciduous. Zones 2b–22. Fairly fast growing prostrate shrub, ultimately to 1–1½ ft. tall with 7-ft. spread. Intricately branched gray-green twigs bear roundish, ¼–½-in.-long leaves. Blooms in spring. 'Vancouver Gold' is a good selection. 'Gold Flash' is compact, reaching just 6–12 in. tall and 2–3 ft. wide.

G. racemosa. See G. × spachiana

G. sagittalis. Leafless. Zones 2–22. Rather rapid grower to 1 ft. high and 3 ft. wide. Upright, flattened bright green branchlets appear jointed. Makes a sheet of bloom in late spring and early summer.

G. × **spachiana (G. racemosa).** Evergreen. Zones 7–9, 14–24. Similar to *G. canariensis,* but with larger leaflets and longer, looser spikes of fragrant flowers in late spring. Naturalizes where adapted. Often sold as *G. fragrans.*

G. tinctoria. DYER'S GREEN-WEED, WOADWAXEN. Deciduous. Zones 2–24. To 6 ft. tall and wide, with undivided leaves to 2 in. long. Upright flower spikes in late spring or early summer. 'Royal Gold' is a compact selection 2 ft. tall and wide.

GENTIANA
GENTIAN
Gentianaceae
PERENNIALS

- ⚬ ZONES 2–6, 14–17, EXCEPT AS NOTED
- ☼ ◑ FULL SUN OR LIGHT SHADE, EXCEPT AS NOTED
- ● REGULAR WATER

Low, spreading, or upright plants, generally with tubular flowers in intense blue shades. Many are difficult to grow, but even they are prized by rock garden enthusiasts. Need perfect drainage. Most require lime-free soil. If they thrive, they are worth the care because they produce some of the richest blues in the garden.

G. acaulis. From Europe. Leafy-stemmed rosette to 4 in. high, 1 ft. wide, with inch-long, glossy dark green leaves. Rich blue flowers to 2 in. long in summer. Grows well but often fails to bloom.

G. asclepiadea. WILLOW GENTIAN. Native to Europe and western Asia. Forms a clump of arching stems to 2 ft. tall, 1½ ft. wide. Dark green, 2–3-in.-long leaves. Blooms in late summer and early fall, when deep blue, 1½-in. flowers that open into stars appear singly or in twos or threes in joints of upper leaves. Not difficult to grow. Partial shade.

G. clusii (G. acaulis clusii). This European native is similar to *G. acaulis* but bears larger flowers.

G. cruciata. CROSS GENTIAN. From Europe, Turkey, Siberia. Foot-wide basal rosette of thick, glossy, medium green, 4–8-in.-long leaves sends up leafy, 12–16-in. stalks bearing clustered 1-in., dark blue flowers. Blooms in summer and early fall. Easy to grow.

G. septemfida. Zones A1–A3; 1–6, 14–17. From Turkey, Iran to central Asia. Arching or sprawling stems 9–18 in. long form a spreading mass about 8 in. high, 1 ft. wide. Medium green, oval leaves to 1½ in. long. Clusters of 2-in., dark blue flowers in late summer. Easy to grow. *G. s. lagodechiana,* the

form commonly sold, is similar but has more widely spaced flowers.

G. sino-ornata. From China, Tibet. Bright green foliage rosette to 7 in. high and somewhat wider sends out trailing stems that end in 2-in. flowers of brightest blue in early fall. Fairly easy to grow in half shade.

G. verna. SPRING GENTIAN. From mountains of Europe. Dark green leaves to 1 in. long form a rosette to 2 in. high, 4 in. wide. Bright blue, 1-in. flowers in spring. Not a good competitor against sturdier plants; grow in pots or troughs. Needs some lime.

Gentiana acaulis

GERANIUM
CRANESBILL
Geraniaceae
PERENNIALS

- ⚬ ZONES VARY BY SPECIES
- ☼ ◑ AFTERNOON SHADE IN HOTTEST CLIMATES
- ● REGULAR WATER, EXCEPT AS NOTED

The common indoor/outdoor plant most people know as geranium is, botanically, *Pelargonium.* Considered here are true geraniums, which are mostly hardy plants. Many types bloom over a long period, bearing flowers that are attractive though not always as showy as those of pelargoniums. Carried singly or in few-flowered clusters, blossoms have five overlapping petals that look alike. (Pelargonium flowers also have five petals, but two point in one direction, while the other three point in the opposite direction.) Colors include blue, purple, magenta, and bluish rose; some are pure pink or white. Beaklike fruit that follows the flowers accounts for the common name "cranesbill." Leaves are roundish or kidney shaped, lobed or deeply cut; plants may be upright or trailing. Good in rock gardens, perennial borders; some are useful as small- or large-scale ground covers. A few shrubby species are good for holding slopes.

Best climates for most geraniums are cool- and mild-summer regions, where plants can grow in full sun or light shade. In hot-summer areas, give afternoon shade. South African species are less cold hardy but more tolerant of heat, afternoon sun. All species appreciate moist, well-drained soil. Some geraniums benefit from being cut back after flowering or in the fall; these are noted in text. Clumps of most types can be left in place for many years before they decline due to crowding; at that point, divide in early spring. Increase by transplanting rooted portions from a clump's edge; or take cuttings. Many produce lots of seedlings, and some can become naturalized pests.

G. 'Ann Folkard'. Zones 2b–9, 14–24. Mounding, billowing plant (1½ ft. high, to 5 ft. wide) with chartreuse leaves that age to light green. Saucer-shaped, 1½-in.-wide blossoms are rich magenta purple suffused with pink and blue, centered and veined in black. Blooms from spring into fall. Effective planted at edge of patio and sprawling onto it.

G. anemonifolium. See G. palmatum

G. armenum. See G. psilostemon

G. 'Brookside'. Zones 2b–9, 14–24. Hybrid developed by crossing *G. pratense* and a purple form of *G. clarkei.* To 2½ ft. tall and as wide, with deeply serrated, 3-in.-wide leaves. Plant is covered from late spring into summer with bowl-shaped flowers to 2 in. across. Long-lasting blooms are rich, deep blue with pale centers and pink veins. Its seedling 'Orion' is similar, but with larger flowers (2½ in. across) of an even richer blue. Both can be cut back after flowering for repeat bloom.

G. × **cantabrigiense.** Zones 1–24. Excellent ground cover, 6–8 in. high, spreading slowly but widely. Pleasantly scented, dark green leaves are 1½–2½ in. wide and deeply cut with multiple lobes. Long-lasting flowers are about 1 in. across. Plants may be sheared in late fall for fresh spring growth. 'Biokovo' has white blooms with a pale pink blush. Blossoms of 'Karmina' and 'Cambridge' are bright bluish pink, and those of 'Westray' are dark pinkish red. All bloom from late spring to early summer.

G. cinereum. Zones 1–24, but very short lived where summers are hot. From the Pyrenees. Forms wide, 8–12-in.-tall mats

Geranium cinereum
'Ballerina'

composed of 1–1½-in., soft gray-green leaves—rounded, bluntly lobed, and deeply cut. In early to midsummer, slender, trailing stems bear many cupped, 1–1½-in.-wide flowers in pale pink with dark veins. 'Ballerina' is pinkish lilac with dark veins radiating from a wine-colored center; continues blooming into fall. The slightly larger 'Laurence Flatman' has light lavender blossoms with reddish center blotches in between red veins. For the plant sometimes listed as *G. c. subcaulescens*, see *G. subcaulescens*.

G. clarkei 'Kashmir White'. Zones 2b–9, 14–24. From Kashmir. To 2 ft. tall when in bloom; spreads widely by rhizomes. Medium green, deeply cut, 2–6-in.-wide leaves with seven narrow lobes are carried on 1½-ft. leafstalks. White, 1½-in.-wide flowers with pale pink veins from late spring to early summer. Cut back after bloom for a repeat flower show.

G. dalmaticum. Zones 1–24. From the Balkans. Low (4–5-in.) carpeting plant, creeping slowly by rhizomes to 2 ft. or wider. Glossy, 1½-in., deeply cut dark green leaves. Soft pink, 1-in. flowers in late spring. Red fall leaf color. Good in rock gardens.

G. endressii. Zones 1–9, 14–24. From southern Europe to southwest Asia. Bushy, 1–1½-ft.-high mound, spreading by rhizomes to 2 ft or wider. Light green, 2–3-in.-wide leaves are deeply cut in fine lobes; evergreen in mild climates. Funnel-shaped blossoms with notched petals are rose pink with a silvery sheen, about 1 in. across. Blooms late spring into fall in mild-summer areas; peters out in early summer where summers are hot.

G. 'Frances Grate' ('Silver Sugar Plum'). Zones 14–24. Billowy, woody, scrambling plant 1½ ft. tall by 5 ft. or wider. Finely cut 2-in.-wide leaves are gray green above, silvery beneath.

Saucer-shaped, wide-petaled lilac mauve flowers to 1 in. across, early spring through fall. Takes hot afternoon sun. Seeds profusely and can be invasive; seedlings vary widely.

G. grandiflorum. See *G. himalayense*

G. harveyi. Zones 5–9, 14–24. From South Africa. Woody-based mound to 8 in. high by 2 ft. or wider. Deeply five-lobed, silky, 1-in. leaves are gray green above, silvery underneath. Magenta, 1¼-in.-wide flowers from late spring through fall. Tolerates hot sun. Good on slopes or trailing among rocks.

G. himalayense (G. grandiflorum). Zones 1–24. Himalayan native to 1½ ft. high, spreading by rhizomes. Long-stalked, medium green, 2½-in.-wide leaves are roundish, with prominent veins and five broad, deeply divided lobes. Blooms from late spring into summer; 1-ft. stems bear clusters of 1½–2-in.-wide blue flowers with reddish veins and purple eye. Excellent deciduous small-scale bulb cover; plant 1–1½ ft. apart. 'Gravetye' is a dependable selection typical of the species. 'Baby Blue' has larger light blue flowers. 'Plenum' ('Birch Double') is less vigorous, with double light lavender blossoms.

G. ibericum. Zones 2–9, 11–24. From Turkey and the Caucasus. To 2 ft. tall and 3 ft. wide, with medium green, hairy, 4-in.-wide, deeply divided leaves with 9–11 lobes. Bowl-shaped, 2-in. lavender-blue flowers with purple veins in late spring.

G. incanum. Zones 14–24. From South Africa. To 6–10 in. high, spreading fast to form a 2-ft.-wide cushion of finely cut leaves. Inch-wide light magenta flowers appear from spring to fall. Cut to ground every 2 or 3 years to keep neat. Endures heat and drought better than most geraniums, but needs some summer water. Self-seeds profusely and can be invasive.

G. 'Johnson's Blue'. Zones A2, A3; 2–9, 14–24. Hybrid resembling its *G. himalayense* parent, but leaf divisions are narrower. Mounds 1½–2 ft. wide and spreads by rhizomes; excellent summer ground cover. Abundant 2-in., blue-violet flowers in loose clusters from spring to fall. Blossoms are sterile. Much of material sold under this name is 'Gravetye' or another *G. himalayense* form, with a shorter bloom season and fertile flowers.

G. macrorrhizum. Zones 1–24. From southern Europe. To 8–10 in. high, spreading fast by underground rootstocks and fleshy rhizomes that root on soil surface. Thick, hairy, sticky, five- to seven-lobed leaves 3–4 in. across; foliage has a strong, musky fragrance and attractive autumn coloring ranging from dull yellow to orange and scarlet. Inch-wide flowers in white, pink, or magenta. Blooms late spring through early summer; some repeat in fall. Good ground cover for small areas, though it can overwhelm smaller plants. 'Bevan's Variety' has vibrant combination of deep magenta petals and red sepals. 'Ingwersen's Variety' has soft bluish pink flowers, longer blooming season. 'Album' is white-flushed pale pink, with pink sepals and stamens.

G. maculatum. WILD CRANESBILL, SPOTTED CRANESBILL. Zones 1–24. Native to moist woodlands and meadows of eastern North America; the only commonly cultivated U.S. native cranesbill. To 1½ ft. tall, 2 ft. wide, with deeply divided, five- to seven-lobed leaves. Profuse lilac pink, 1–1½-in. flowers in spring to early summer. 'Album' has white blossoms. Leaves of 'Elizabeth Ann' and 'Espresso' are dark chocolate brown. All may be cut back after bloom to encourage fresh foliage and flowers.

G. maderense. Zones 14–24. Dramatic native of Madeira likes moist conditions, shade. Largest of all geranium leaves (1½–2 ft. long)—overlapping, glossy, deeply divided, shaped like giant snowflakes. Reddish brown leafstalks help buttress the 3–4-ft. "trunk" supporting hundreds of densely packed, fuzzy buds and magenta-eyed deep pink blossoms. Blooms early spring through midsummer. Biennial or short-lived perennial; dies after blooming but spawns many seedlings.

G. × magnificum. Zones 1–9, 14–24. Vigorous sterile hybrid has been cultivated for more than a century. Spreads steadily, forming broad clumps 2–2½ ft. high and wide. Rounded, quilted, 3-in. leaves are divided into broad segments. Profuse 2-in. violet blossoms heavily veined in deep purple; blooms in late spring and early summer.

G. magniflorum. Zones 2b–7. From South Africa. This diminutive alpine gem forms compact mounds of evergreen foliage 6–

10 in. high and 15–20 in. wide. Bright green, finely cut leaves look something like parsley; take on purple and scarlet hues in winter. Vivid pinkish purple flowers are produced in spring and summer. Needs very well drained soil, such as gravelly loam. Pretty in a rock garden or spilling from a large container. Plants can be neatened with a light shearing after bloom. Moderate water.

G. × oxonianum. Zones 2–9, 14–24. Among best selections is 'Claridge Druce', which forms a vigorous clump 2–3 ft. tall, 3 ft. wide. Rounded, 3–4-in. leaves are deeply cut between broad, toothed lobes. Funnel-shaped, broad-petaled, 1½–1¾-in., cool pink flowers with purplish veins bloom late spring to summer. Good large-scale ground cover but can overwhelm adjacent plants. Self-sows profusely; seedlings resemble parent, but blossoms often have narrower petals. Can be cut back hard after flowering to encourage fresh foliage and discourage reseeding. 'Wargrave Pink' is similar in habit but a little less vigorous, with glossy warm pink blossoms that resemble those of *G. endressii* (one of the parents). 'Winscombe' has flowers that open pale pink and turn deep pink with age, giving an overall multicolored effect.

G. palmatum (G. anemonifolium). Zones 4–9, 14–24. From Madeira; similar to *G. maderense*, another giant geranium from that island. Plants reach 4 ft. tall and wide, with huge, ferny leaves (to 14. in. across) that are dark green, turning reddish in sun. Purplish pink 1½-in.-wide flowers with deep crimson centers appear in great numbers in late spring to summer. Grows best in a sunny, sheltered spot. Will reseed.

G. 'Patricia'. Zones 2–9, 14–24. This hybrid between *G. endressii* and *G. psilostemon* is durable and easy to grow. Plants reach 2½ ft. tall and 3 ft. wide, with medium green leaves up to 6 in. across that are deeply lobed and veined. Eye-catching flowers, to 1½ in. wide, are a warm reddish magenta with deep burgundy veins and centers. Long bloom period, from spring to late summer. Cut back after first flush of bloom for fresh growth and flowers.

G. phaeum. MOURNING WIDOW, DUSKY CRANESBILL. Zones 2b–9, 14–24. Shade-loving native of southern and central European mountains. To 2 ft. high, 1½ ft. wide. Leaves are

G

Geranium phaeum
'Samobor'

basal, 3–4 in. across, shallowly cut into seven to nine tooth-edged lobes, often with brown markings. Clusters of dusky purple or maroon blossoms bloom from spring to fall. Cut back flowering stems after bloom to neaten appearance and encourage rebloom. 'Lily Lovell' has purplish maroon blooms with a white eye. 'Samobor' has light maroon flowers and leaves heavily marked with maroon.

G. 'Philippe Vapelle'. Zones 3–9, 14–24. Tight clump 1 ft. tall and 1½ ft. wide. Medium green, 3-in., rounded leaves are quilted, shallowly cut into scalloped lobes. Violet-blue flowers with darker veins have deeply notched petals. Blooms spring through midsummer.

G. 'Pink Spice'. Zones 3b–9, 14–24. Compact mound 8–10 in. tall, to 1 ft. wide. Reddish bronze, 1½-in. leaves form a dark background for 1-in.-wide pink blossoms on long, trailing stems. Blooms from late spring through fall. Foliage color is best with at least half-day direct sun.

G. platypetalum. Zones 3b–9, 14–24. From Turkey and the Caucasus. Clump 1½ ft. high and wide with rounded, quilted leaves, shallowly cut into seven to nine scalloped lobes. Saucer-shaped, 1½–1¾-in. summer flowers with notched petals are deep violet blue with paler center and dark veins.

G. pratense. MEADOW CRANESBILL. Zones 2–7, 14–24. Native from Ireland to Siberia and Japan. Forms a clump 1½–2 ft. tall, 2–3 ft. wide. Hairy, 3–6-in. leaves on

Geranium
pratense

upright stalks are deeply cut into seven narrow, pointed, divided lobes. Flowers about 1 in. wide, typically blue with reddish veins; bloom from spring through summer. Self-seeds profusely; cut to ground when flowers fade to prevent seedlings and encourage rebloom. 'Midnight Reiter' is dramatic, with dark purple leaves and rich blue blooms. 'Mrs. Kendall Clark' has pale blue flowers with lighter veins. 'Plenum Caeruleum' has double flowers of lavender blue. 'Striatum' has white blossoms irregularly splashed, streaked, or spotted with violet blue.

G. psilostemon (G. armenum). Zones 2b–9, 14–24. Native to Armenia, Turkey. Large clump—to 4 ft. tall and wide—with big, deeply cut leaves and an early summer show of 1–1½-in. magenta flowers with black centers and veins. Leaves turn brilliant flame color in fall.

G. renardii. Zones 2b–9, 14–24. From the Caucasus. Compact grower to 1 ft. high and wide. Velvety gray-green leaves have deeply etched veins and scalloped lobes. Early to midsummer flowers are white with violet veining; overall effect is pearly gray. May be cut back hard in fall. Blooms of 'Tcschelda' are pale violet with dark purple veins.

G. × riversleaianum. Zones 2b–9, 14–24. Forms foot-high, wide-spreading mat of silky, silvery green leaves. Continuous show of rounded, ¾-in. blossoms on long, trailing stems from late spring through fall. 'Mavis Simpson' has soft shell pink blossoms with dark veins. 'Russell Prichard' is brilliant magenta rose.

G. robustum. Zones 14–24. Shrubby species from South Africa grows 3 ft. high, 4 ft. wide. Finely divided leaves to 3 in. across are silky gray green above, silvery below. Summer flowers 1 in. across, light purple with a white eye. Survives with little water. Use on slopes with other drought-tolerant plants like lavender (Lavandula), rockrose (Cistus). Self-sows profusely.

G. 'Rozanne'. Zones 2–11, 14–24. This naturally occurring hybrid between G. himalayense

and G. wallichianum 'Buxton's Variety' is very popular and easy to grow. Plants reach 1½–2 ft. tall and spread a little wider, forming a lush mound of deeply lobed, 2-in.-wide dark green leaves; foliage takes on attractive red tones in the fall. Stunning flowers, to 2½ in. wide, are rich violet blue with a large white eye. A vigorous grower that blooms all summer and into autumn, doing especially well in warm, sunny spots. For freshest spring growth, cut back plants in late fall.

G. 'Salome'. Zones 4–6, 14–17. A cross between two Himalayan species. This low, trailing plant grows about 1 ft. tall and 3–4 ft. wide. Leaves to 5 in. wide emerge golden green and age to a fresh light green. Foliage is a lovely foil

Geranium renardii

for the 1¼-in. blossoms of pale violet pink, centered and veined with deepest violet. Blooms midsummer to late fall; cut back after bloom period to freshen plants. Good choice for cooler parts of Pacific Northwest; struggles in heat.

G. sanguineum. BLOODY CRANESBILL. Zones A2, A3; 1–9, 14–24. Native from western Europe to the Caucasus and Turkey. Forms dense clump 8–18 in. high, spreading by rhizomes to 2½ ft. or wider. Dark green, 1–2-in.-wide leaves are deeply divided into five to seven lobes, each with three narrow segments; turn blood red in fall. Typical forms have deep purple to almost crimson flowers 1½ in. wide; bloom late spring well into summer and will rebloom if cut to ground. Good 1–1½-ft.-tall selections include white 'Album'; 'John Elsley', pink with deeper pink veins; reddish purple 'Max Frei'; and 'New Hampshire', reddish magenta petals with magenta veins. 'Vision', a variable seed-grown strain, has magenta

flowers with dark purple veins. *G. s. striatum (G. s. lancastriense)* is a compact form only 5–6 in. high. It bears light pink flowers heavily veined with red (its seedlings may vary somewhat) and makes an excellent rock garden or foreground plant.

G. 'Silver Sugar Plum'. See G. 'Frances Grate'

G. subcaulescens (G. cinereum subcaulescens). Zones 3–24, but short lived where summers are hot. Native to the Balkans, Turkey. Like *G. cinereum,* but with darker green leaves and brilliant crimson-magenta flowers with black centers and veins.

G. sylvaticum. WOOD CRANESBILL. Zones 2–9, 14–24. Native from Ireland to Siberia, south to Turkey. Shade- and moisture-loving plant to 2½ ft. tall and wide. Late spring to early summer flowers an in. across, range in color from white through pink to reddish purple.

G. wallichianum. Zones 2–9, 14–24. Himalayan native of low, sprawling or trailing but not rooting habit, 1 ft. tall and 3 ft. wide. Blooms from early summer until fall, bearing 1–1½-in.-wide flowers in lilac or purplish blue with a white eye. 'Buxton's Variety' has pure blue flowers with large white eye. Stout taproot is not easy to divide; propagate from seed.

G. wlassovianum. Zones A2, A3; 1–7. Native to Siberia, Mongolia, northeastern China. Clump-forming plant to 1½ ft. high, 2 ft. wide. Velvety, 2-in., divided leaves emerge pinkish bronze, mature to dusky green tinged with brown, and then turn cinnamon brown in fall. Reddish purple, 1¼-in.-wide flowers with small white eye and deep violet veins. Blooms midsummer to early fall.

GERBERA jamesonii
TRANSVAAL DAISY
Asteraceae (Compositae)
PERENNIAL OFTEN GROWN AS ANNUAL

🌡 ZONES 8, 9, 12–24; H1, H2; ANYWHERE AS ANNUAL
☼ ◑ PARTIAL SHADE IN HOTTEST CLIMATES
💧 REGULAR WATER

This South African native is among the most elegant and sophisticated of daisies. Clump of tongue-shaped, lobed, 10-in.-long leaves sends up slim yet sturdy stems to 1½ ft. high, each bearing one slender-petaled, 4–5 in. daisy. Colors are pure, unshaded, and glowing;

Gerbera jamesonii

include cream through yellow to coral, orange, flame, and red. Basic flower has single ring of rays surrounding prominent central disk. Hybrid forms may have two rows of long rays, or an outer ring of long rays and a central ring of short, tufted ones; or they may be fully double, with a fluffy look. Many strains are sold, including dwarf types only 7 in. tall. As perennial, can bloom any time of year, with peaks in early summer and late fall. Beyond hardiness range, treat as summer annual. In Zones 12 and 13, best as winter annual (may last longer during a cool spring).

Needs organically enriched soil with excellent drainage (if soil drains poorly, grow in raised bed). Plant 2 ft. apart; to avoid rot, keep root crown slightly above soil level. Protect from snails and slugs. Water deeply and let soil become nearly dry before watering again. For best flowering, fertilize monthly. Divide (in late winter) only when clump is crowded and flowering declines. When cutting blooms for arrangements, slit the bottom inch of the stem before placing in water.

GERMANDER. See **TEUCRIUM**

GERMAN IVY.
See **SENECIO mikanioides**

GERMAN STATICE.
See **GONIOLIMON tataricum**

GEUM
Rosaceae
PERENNIALS

🌿	ZONES 2–24, EXCEPT AS NOTED
☀️ ◐	PARTIAL SHADE IN HOTTEST CLIMATES
💧	REGULAR WATER

Double, semidouble, or single roselike flowers in bright orange, yellow, or red over long season (spring to late summer) if dead

blooms are removed. Handsome foliage, with leaves divided into many leaflets; evergreen except in coldest winters. Good in borders and for cut flowers. Ordinary garden soil; need good drainage. Grow from seed sown in early spring, or divide plants in autumn or early spring.

G. chiloense. Native to Chile. Foliage mounds to 15 in. high, 2 ft. wide. Leafy flowering stems to 2 ft. high carry flowers about 1½ in. across. Varieties include 'Fire Opal', with semidouble orange-scarlet

Geum chiloense

blooms; double yellow 'Lady Stratheden'; double scarlet 'Mrs. Bradshaw'; and double copper 'Princess Juliana'. Hybrid 'Georgenberg', to 12–15 in. high and wide, has light yellow-orange blooms. Petals of semidouble-flowered 'Fireball' are yellow orange with red margins.

G. coccineum. From the Balkans, Asia Minor. To 12–20 in. tall and wide, with coarsely divided foliage and brick red, 1½-in. flowers. 'Borisii' is a compact (1- by 1-ft.) variety with bright orangered flowers. Use in rock garden or front of border. 'Red Wings', to 28 in. tall and broad, has semidouble scarlet flowers.

G. 'Starker's Magnificum'. To 1½ ft. high and wide, with double flowers in tangerine orange over a long season.

G. triflorum. PRAIRIE SMOKE, OLD MAN'S WHISKERS. Zones 1–3. From North America. Footwide leafy mound produces stems to 20 in. tall, each bearing clusters of nodding maroon flowers. Entire plant is often furry. Seeds have long, feathery gray "tails."

GHOST GUM. See **EUCALYPTUS papuana, E. pauciflora**

GHOST PLANT. See **GRAPTO-PETALUM paraguayense**

GIANT REED.
See **ARUNDO donax**

GIANT SACATON.
See **SPOROBOLUS wrightii**

GIANT SEQUOIA. See **SEQUOIADENDRON giganteum**

GILIA
Polemoniaceae
ANNUALS

🌿	ZONES 1–24
☀️	FULL SUN
💧	LITTLE TO MODERATE WATER

Western natives related to phlox. Slender plants with finely cut leaves and colorful flowers from late spring to early fall. Useful in wild garden or borders. In fall or early spring, sow seeds in well-drained soil where plants are to grow. Thin seedlings to avoid crowding.

G. aggregata. See Ipomopsis aggregata

Gilia capitata

G. capitata. BLUE THIMBLE FLOWER. Native from British Columbia to California. Grows 8–30 in. tall, to 8 in. wide. Pale violet-blue to blue flowers with blue pollen are carried in dense, ½–1½-in.-wide clusters that look like pincushions.

G. rubra. See Ipomopsis rubra
G. tricolor. BIRD'S EYES. Native to California. To 10–20 in. high, 8 in. wide. Flowers, carried singly or in clusters of two to five, are ½ in. wide or wider; pale to deep violet with yellow throat spotted purple; blue pollen.

GIMLET.
See **EUCALYPTUS salubris**

GINGER. See **ALPINIA, ZINGIBER officinale**

GINGER, WILD. See **ASARUM**

GINGER LILY.
See **ALPINIA, HEDYCHIUM**

GINKGO biloba
MAIDENHAIR TREE
Ginkgoaceae
DECIDUOUS TREE

🌿	ZONES A3; 1–10, 12, 14–24
☀️	FULL SUN
💧💧	MODERATE TO REGULAR WATER

Ancient survivor from prehistoric times (200 million years ago), when it grew worldwide; now native only to two small areas in China. Graceful tree, attractive in any season, especially in fall when leathery light green leaves of spring and summer suddenly turn gold (they practically glow when backlit by the sun). Leaves hang on for a time, then drop quickly and cleanly to make golden carpet where they fall. Related to conifers but differs in having broad (1–4-in.-wide), fan-shaped leaves rather than needlelike foliage. In shape and veining, leaves resemble leaflets of maidenhair fern, hence tree's common name. Can grow to 70–80 ft. tall, but most mature trees are 35–50 ft. May be gawky in youth, but becomes well proportioned with age—narrow to spreading or even umbrella shaped. Typical width is no more than one-half to two-thirds of height. Usually grows slowly, about 1 ft. a year, but under ideal conditions can grow up to 3 ft. a year.

Ginkgo biloba

G

G

Plant male trees (grafted or grown from cuttings of male plants); female trees produce messy, fleshy, ill-smelling fruit in quantity. Named varieties listed below are male. Use as street tree, lawn tree. Plant in deep, loose, well-drained soil. Be sure nursery plants are not root-bound. Young growth may be brittle, but wood becomes strong with age. Ginkgos are not usually bothered by insects or diseases, and they're very tolerant of air pollution, heat, and acid or alkaline conditions. Resistant to oak root fungus. Water young trees regularly until they reach about 20 ft. tall, then cut back to occasional irrigation. On young trees, cut back any awkward branches and vertical shoots growing parallel to central leader. Older trees need minimal pruning; just remove weak, broken, or dead branches.

'Autumn Gold'. Upright to 40 ft., eventually rather broad and spreading to about 30 ft.

'Fairmount'. Fast-growing, pyramidal form similar to 'Princeton Sentry'.

'Princeton Sentry'. Erect to 50 ft. high; 20-ft. spread at base, tapering toward top.

'Saratoga'. Similar to 'Autumn Gold', with a distinct central leader.

GLADIOLUS
Iridaceae
PERENNIALS FROM CORMS

🗡	ZONES 4–9, 12–24; H1; EXCEPT AS NOTED; OR DIG AND STORE
☀	FULL SUN
💧	REGULAR WATER DURING GROWTH AND BLOOM

All have sword-shaped leaves and tubular, often flaring or ruffled flowers in unbranched or branching, usually one-sided spikes. Extremely wide color range. Flowers come from spring to fall, depending on kind of gladiolus and planting time. Superb cut flowers. Good in borders or beds behind mounding plants that cover lower parts of stems, or in large containers with low annuals at base.

Plant corms of baby gladiolus in fall or early spring for flowers in late spring. Plant all others from midwinter (in mildest regions) into spring, after soil has warmed. Grandiflora hybrids will flower about 100 days after planting; the smaller hybrids and species will bloom in about 80 days. For an extended flowering season, plant

Gladiolus callianthus

at 1- to 2-week intervals over a period of 4 to 6 weeks. Where growing season is long enough, gardeners often time plantings so that bloom will be over before onset of hottest weather, when thrips can seriously disfigure the flowers. That means planting from January through March in Zones 7–9, 14–24, H1; April through June in Zones 4–6; and November through January in Zones 12, 13.

Start off with corms that are high crowned for their width; broad, flat ones are older and less vigorous. Best planted in rich, sandy loam. Set corms about four times deeper than their height; plant somewhat more shallowly in heavier soils. Space big corms 6 in. apart, smaller ones 4 in. apart. You can cut flower spikes when lowest buds begin to open, but keep at least four leaves on plants to build up corms.

Corms can be left in the ground from year to year where plants are perennial (dig, divide, and replant when performance declines). After blossoms fade, trim off stems beneath lowest flower—uncut stems will set seeds, diverting energy from food storage. In colder areas, dig after foliage yellows completely (in rainy areas, dig while leaves are still green to avoid botrytis infection). Dry corms on a flat surface in a dark, dry area for 2 to 3 weeks; then store over winter in a single layer in flats or ventilated trays in a cool place (40 to 50°F/4 to 10°C).

Baby gladiolus. Zones 4–9, 12–24, H1 for most; also Zones 2b, 3 for winter-hardy types. Hybrid race resulting from breeding red-flowered *G. colvillei* with other species. Flaring, 2½–3¼-in. flowers in short, loose spikes on 1½-ft.

stems in late spring. Blooms may be white, pink, red, or lilac, either solid or blotched with contrasting color. When left in the ground in borders or among shrubs, these glads will form large clumps.

Butterfly gladiolus. See Primulinus and butterfly hybrids

G. callianthus (Acidanthera bicolor). ABYSSINIAN SWORD LILY. Native to Africa. In late summer and fall, each 2–3-ft. stem bears two to ten fragrant, creamy white flowers with chocolate brown markings on lower segments. Blossoms are 2–3 in. wide, 4–5 in. long. 'Murielae' is taller, with purple-crimson blotches.

G. communis byzantinus (G. byzantinus). BYZANTINE GLADIOLUS. From southern Europe. Summer bloom of mainly maroon, sometimes reddish or coppery, 1–3-in. flowers in groups of 6–12 on 2–3-ft. stems. Narrower leaves than grandiflora hybrids.

Grandiflora hybrids. GARDEN GLADIOLUS. These are the best-known gladiolus, producing spikes that reach from 3 to 6 ft. high, depending on variety and growing conditions. Late spring and summer flowers (up to 30 per spike) are widely flaring, up to 8 in. across; colors include white, cream, yellow, orange, apricot, salmon, red, rose, lavender, purple, smoky shades, buff, and even green. More diminutive selections from grandiflora breeding are grouped as small and miniature gladiolus; these grow 3–4 ft. high, stand upright without staking, and bear up to eighteen 2½–3-in.-wide flowers per spike. Though perennial, grandiflora hybrids are usually dug and stored yearly even in mild-winter regions.

Grandiflora hybrid gladiolus

Primulinus and butterfly hybrids. These summer bloomers derive in part from *G. dalenii* (formerly *G. primulinus*), an African species with hooded (rather than funnel-shaped), primrose yellow flowers. Named varieties grow 3–4 ft. tall, each spike carrying up to 18 widely spaced, somewhat hooded blossoms in a wide range of colors. Group known as butterfly gladiolus has 2–3-ft. stems bearing more closely spaced blossoms; distinct throat markings or blotches of contrasting color give butterfly appearance.

Butterfly hybrid gladiolus

G. tristis. Native to South Africa. Dainty species with 2½–3-in. flowers on slender, 1½-ft. stems in summer. Creamy to yellowish white blossoms are veined with purple, fragrant at night. *G. t. concolor* has soft yellow to nearly white flowers.

GLAUCIUM
HORNED POPPY, SEA POPPY
Papaveraceae
BIENNIALS AND PERENNIALS OFTEN GROWN AS ANNUALS

🗡	ZONES VARY BY SPECIES
☀	FULL SUN
💧	MODERATE WATER
❂	ROOTS ARE POISONOUS IF INGESTED

Gray-green leaves are lobed or finely cut. Cup-shaped, four-petaled, 2-in. flowers are individually short lived, but they keep coming during summer bloom season. Flowers are followed by unusually long (to 1 ft.), slender seed capsules. Sow seeds in place in fall or early spring.

G. corniculatum. Biennial grown as annual. Zones 2–24. From Europe, southwest Asia. Grows 1–1½ ft. high and as wide.

Glaucium flavum

Orange-red flowers with dark spot at base.

G. flavum. Perennial or biennial. Zones 8–24; grows anywhere as annual. From Europe, Canary Islands, North Africa, Turkey. Grows 1–3 ft. tall, 1½ ft. wide. Orange to brilliant yellow flowers look varnished. Cut back to new basal leaves yearly.

GLEBIONIS.
See **CHRYSANTHEMUM carinatum, C. coronarium**

GLECHOMA hederacea (Nepeta hederacea)
GROUND IVY
Lamiaceae (Labiatae)
PERENNIAL

| 🌿 ZONES A2, A3; 1–10, 14–24 |
| ☼ ◐ ● SUN OR SHADE |
| 💧 REGULAR WATER |

From Europe; naturalized in North America. Trailing plant with neat pairs of round, scallop-edged bright green or white-bordered leaves to 1½ in. across, spaced along stems. 'Variegata' leaves are splashed irregularly with creamy yellow. Small, trumpet-shaped blue flowers in spring and summer are not especially showy. Can be planted as small-scale ground cover or used in hanging baskets. To 3 in. high, with stems trailing to 1½ ft., rooting at joints. Can become a pest in lawns.

Glechoma hederacea

GLEDITSIA triacanthos
HONEY LOCUST
Fabaceae (Leguminosae)
DECIDUOUS TREE

| 🌿 ZONES 1–16, 18–20 |
| ☼ FULL SUN |
| 💧 💧 MODERATE TO REGULAR WATER |

Native to central and eastern North America. Fast growing to 35–70 ft. tall and 25–35 ft. wide, with upright trunk and spreading, arching branches. Bright green, fernlike leaves to 10 in. long are divided into many oval, ¾–1½-in.-long leaflets. Late to leaf out; leaves turn yellow before dropping early in autumn. Inconspicuous flowers followed by broad, 1–1½-ft.-long pods filled with sweetish pulp (edible but insipid) and hard, roundish seeds.

Foliage casts filtered shade, allowing growth of lawn or other plants beneath tree's canopy. Small leaflets dry up and filter into grass,

Gleditsia triacanthos

decreasing raking chores. Not good in narrow area between curb and sidewalk, since roots on old plants will heave pavement. Tolerant of acid or alkaline conditions, salt, drought, cold, heat, wind. Does best in areas with sharply defined winters, hot summers. Prune out any wayward or crossing branches. Mimosa webworm (chews leaves) and pod gall midge (deforms foliage) are main pests. Additionally, honey locust borer (tunnels into limbs and trunks) may attack stressed tree.

Trunks and branches of the species are formidably thorny, and its pods make a mess. These selections of its thornless form *G. t. inermis* are better choices for gardens, normally having few or no pods.

'Halka'. Fast growing. Forms sturdy trunk early, has strong hori-

Gleditsia triacanthos

zontal branching pattern. Can bear a heavy crop of seedpods.

'Imperial'. Tall, spreading, symmetrical tree to about 35 ft. More densely foliaged than other forms; gives heavier shade.

'Moraine'. MORAINE LOCUST. Best-known garden selection. Graceful, spreading, and fast-growing tree with branches angled upward, then outward. Subject to wind breakage.

'Rubylace'. Deep red new growth. Subject to wind breakage.

'Shademaster'. More upright and faster growing than 'Moraine'—to 24 ft. tall, 16 ft. wide in 6 years.

'Skyline'. Pyramidal and symmetrical.

'Sunburst'. Golden yellow new foliage; showy against background of deep green. Defoliates easily in response to temperature changes, drought. Subject to wind breakage.

'Trueshade'. Rounded head of light green foliage.

GLOBE AMARANTH.
See **GOMPHRENA**

GLOBE DAISY.
See **GLOBULARIA**

GLOBEFLOWER. See **TROLLIUS**

GLOBE MALLOW.
See **SPHAERALCEA**

GLOBE THISTLE.
See **ECHINOPS**

GLOBE TULIP.
See **CALOCHORTUS**

GLOBULARIA
GLOBE DAISY
Globulariaceae
EVERGREEN SHRUBS

| 🌿 ZONES VARY BY SPECIES |
| ☼ FULL SUN |
| 💧 MODERATE WATER |

Globe daisies are mat-forming or mounding plants with leathery dark green leaves. Their small (½–¾-in.) lavender-blue flowers

are gathered into tight, round heads on stalks standing above the foliage mound. They are not true daisies, although the flower heads resemble rayless daisies or small powder puffs.

G. 'Blue Eyes'. Zones 3–9, 14–24. Probable hybrid grows about 2 ft. tall, spreading at least twice as wide. Attractive foliage. Produces lots of dark-centered blooms in late summer.

G. cordifolia. Zones 3–9, 14–24. From mountains of central and southern Europe. To 5 in. tall, 1 ft. wide, with creeping, rooting stems. Summer bloom. Good in rock gardens.

Globularia × indubia

G. × indubia. Zones 8, 9, 14–24. To 1–2 ft. tall, 5 ft. wide. Blooms in summer and fall. Tough plant; good for hot, dry banks.

GLORIOSA DAISY.
See **RUDBECKIA hirta**

GLORIOSA superba 'Rothschildiana' (G. rothschildiana)
GLORY LILY, CLIMBING LILY
Liliaceae
PERENNIAL FROM TUBER

| 🌿 ZONES 24; H1, H2; OR GROW IN POTS |
| ☼ ◐ LIGHT SHADE IN HOTTEST CLIMATES |
| 💧 REGULAR WATER DURING GROWTH AND BLOOM |
| ☠ ALL PARTS ARE POISONOUS IF INGESTED |

Lily relative native to tropical Africa and Asia. A tendril at the tip of each tapering, lance-shaped, 5–7-in. leaf wraps around any handy support, helping plant climb to 6 ft. In summer, top part of plant bears flashy 4-in. blossoms, each with six recurved, wavy-edged segments in brilliant red banded with yellow.

Can survive outdoors all year in completely frost-free areas, but even there is best grown in pots. ▶

Gloriosa superba 'Rothschildiana'

For appearance of permanent planting, sink containers into garden bed. Set tubers horizontally, one to a container (pot should be at least 8 in. in diameter), about 4 in. deep in rich, loose soil mix. Start indoors or in greenhouse in winter; set out after frosts. Give climbing stems support from trellis, wires, string, or even loose-growing shrubs. Feed with liquid fertilizer every 3 weeks. Withhold water and fertilizer when leaves begin to yellow and die back in fall. Sever dead stems and move pots to dry, cool spot for winter. In late winter, knock tubers out of containers; repot in fresh soil mix. Or dig tubers from pots in fall and store.

GLORYBOWER.
See **CLERODENDRUM**

GLORY LILY. See **GLORIOSA superba** 'Rothschildiana'

GLORY-OF-THE-SNOW.
See **CHIONODOXA**

GLOXINIA.
See **SINNINGIA speciosa**

GNAPHALIUM
sandwicensium sandwicensium
'ENA 'ENA
Asteraceae (Compositae)
PERENNIAL

🌿 ZONES H1, H2

☼ FULL SUN

💧 MODERATE WATER

Native to nearly every island of Hawaii, this herbaceous, clumping perennial grows from sea level to high elevations. Valued for silvery green, hairy leaves to about 4 in. long and for small size of foliage clumps (4–5 in. high and wide). Foliage has a strong balsamlike fragrance. Clusters of brownish

flowers with yellow bracts are unremarkable; some gardeners pinch off stalks (which can reach 1½ ft. tall) as they appear to keep plant looking neat. Needs well-drained soil. Good in borders and rock gardens.

Gnaphalium sandwicensium sandwicensium

GOAT'S BEARD. See **ARUNCUS**

GODETIA. See **CLARKIA**

GOLD COIN.
See **ASTERISCUS maritimus**

GOLD DUST PLANT. See **AUCUBA japonica** 'Variegata'

GOLDEN BALL LEAD TREE. See **LEUCAENA retusa**

GOLDENCHAIN TREE. See **LABURNUM**

GOLDEN CUP. See **HUNNEMANNIA fumariifolia**

GOLDEN DEWDROP. See **DURANTA erecta**

GOLDEN EARDROPS. See **DICENTRA chrysantha**

GOLDENEYE. See **VIGUIERA**

GOLDEN FLEECE. See **THYMOPHYLLA tenuiloba**

GOLDEN GARLIC. See **ALLIUM moly**

GOLDEN GLOBES. See **LYSIMACHIA congestiflora**

GOLDEN LARCH. See **PSEUDOLARIX amabilis**

GOLDEN MARGUERITE. See **ANTHEMIS tinctoria**

GOLDENRAIN TREE. See **KOELREUTERIA paniculata**

GOLDENROD. See **SOLIDAGO**

GOLDEN SHOWER. See **CASSIA fistula**

GOLDEN TRUMPET. See **ALLAMANDA cathartica**

GOLDEN WONDER SENNA. See **SENNA splendida**

GOLDFISH PLANT. See **NEMATANTHUS gregarius**

GOLD FLOWER. See **HYPERICUM × moserianum**

GOLD MEDALLION TREE. See **CASSIA leptophylla**

GOLD TREE. See **TABEBUIA donnell-smithii**

GOMPHOCARPUS. See **ASCLEPIAS fruticosa**

GOMPHRENA
GLOBE AMARANTH
Amaranthaceae
ANNUALS AND PERENNIALS
GROWN AS ANNUALS

🌿 ZONES 1–24; H1, H2

☼ ◑ FULL SUN OR PARTIAL SHADE

💧 MODERATE WATER

Stiffly branching plants to 2 ft. tall, 1 ft. wide, covered in summer and fall with rounded, papery, clover-like heads ¾–1 in. wide. These may be dried quickly and easily, retaining color and shape for winter arrangements. Narrow oval leaves are 2–4 in. long.

Gomphrena globosa

G. globosa. Annual. From Central America. White, pink, lavender, or purple flower heads on 1–2-ft. stems. 'Strawberry Fields' has hot red, ½-in. blossoms on 2-ft. stems. Dwarf varieties for use as edging or bedding plants include 9-in. 'Buddy' (purple) and 'Cissy' (white). All types can be planted closely in large containers —six to a shallow 10-in. pot—for a long-lasting living bouquet.

G. haageana. Perennial treated as annual. From southern U.S., Mexico. Heads of tightly clustered bright orange bracts resembling inch-wide pinecones are borne on 2-ft. stems. Tiny yellow flowers peep from the bracts. Often sold as 'Haageana Aurea' or orange gomphrena.

GONIOLIMON
tataricum (Limonium tataricum)
GERMAN STATICE
Plumbaginaceae
PERENNIAL

🌿 ZONES 2–21

☼ FULL SUN, EXCEPT AS NOTED

💧 MODERATE WATER

From southern Russia, Caucasus. Dense clumps of dark green, narrowly oval leaves grow from a woody rootstock. In summer, leafless flower stalks rise to 1½ ft., forking repeatedly to form a broad, domed cluster to 1½ ft.

Goniolimon tataricum

wide. Tiny flowers are light purplish to white. Entire inflorescence can be dried for winter arrangements. Plant withstands both cold and heat. Best where summers are hot and dry. Needs partial shade in Zone 13.

GOOSEBERRY
Grossulariaceae (Saxifragaceae)
DECIDUOUS SHRUB

🌿 ZONES A1–A3; 1–6, 15–17; EXCEPT AS NOTED

☼ ◑ ● SOME SHADE IN HOTTEST CLIMATES

💧 REGULAR WATER

Multistemmed plants to 3–5 ft. high and wide; varieties range from thorny to nearly spineless. Lobed, somewhat maplelike leaves usually turn bright colors in fall. Fruit is often decorative, marked with longitudinal stripes; ripens from late spring to summer and is used for pies, canning. Needs same grow-

Gooseberry

ing conditions as currant; prune as for red and white currants. Like currant, prohibited in some areas where white pines grow; also subject to currant worm. Generally self-fruitful. Derived from several *Ribes* species; for strictly ornamental relatives, see *Ribes*.

Selection 'Captivator' has large, teardrop-shaped, sweet pink fruit on an extra-hardy, mildew-resistant, nearly thornless plant. 'Fredonia' is a fairly open grower producing large dark red fruit. 'Invicta' has large green fruit and is resistant to mildew. 'Oregon Champion' bears a heavy crop of green fruit. Pink-fruited 'Pixwell' is an extremely hardy, nearly thornless variety. 'Poorman' has red fruit sweet enough to eat fresh off bush, though skin is tart. 'Welcome' bears medium-large, dull red, tart fruit on a productive plant with hardly any spines.

Jostaberries are disease-resistant black currant–gooseberry hybrids. Their black fruit tastes like currants but isn't as astringent; it makes great jams and jellies. Plants are less hardy than currants or gooseberries; they grow in Zones A3, 1–6, 15–17.

GOOSE PLANT.
See **ASCLEPIAS fruticosa**

GOOSE PLUM.
See **PRUNUS americana**

GOPHER PLANT.
See **EUPHORBIA lathyris**

GORDONIA alatamaha.
See **FRANKLINIA alatamaha**

GOSSYPIUM
tomentosum
HAWAIIAN COTTON, MA'O
Malvaceae
EVERGREEN SHRUB

| 🌿 ZONE H2 |
| ☀ FULL SUN |
| ◌ LITTLE WATER |

Native to Hawaii and adapted to hot, dry areas. Spreading shrub grows to 3–6 ft. high and equally

as wide. Pure yellow, 2–3-in.-wide flowers are produced much of the year and show off nicely against the attractive silvery green, maple-like leaves. Seed capsules have brown fuzzy seeds with short cottony hairs. This plant is not grown

Gossypium tomentosum

commercially for cotton fiber but used in breeding of disease- and insect-resistant commercial cotton plants. Good as specimen shrub, informal hedge, or high ground cover. Performs best in well-drained soil.

GOURD
Cucurbitaceae
ANNUAL VINES

| 🌿 ALL ZONES |
| ☀ FULL SUN |
| ◌ REGULAR WATER |

Many plants bear gourds. One of the most commonly planted is *Cucurbita pepo ovifera*, a yellow-flowered vine that produces small ornamental gourds in various shapes and sizes, solid colored or striped; many of the little gourds you see in stores likely come from this plant. *Luffa cylindrica (L. aegyptiaca)*, called dishcloth

Gourd

gourd or vegetable sponge gourd, is another yellow-flowered plant; it bears cylindrical, 1–2-ft.-long fruits with a fibrous interior that, when dried, may be used in place of a sponge or cloth for scrubbing or bathing. *Lagenaria siceraria (L. vulgaris),* white-flowered gourd, produces fruits from 3 in. to 3 ft. long, in round, crook-necked, coiled, bottle, dumbbell, or spoon shapes.

All gourd vines grow fast and will reach 10–15 ft. Sow seeds when ground is warm; start indoors if growing season is short. Gourds need all the summer heat they can get to develop fruit by frost. If planting for ornamental gourd harvest, give vines wire or trellis support to hold ripening fruits off ground. Set out transplants or thin seedlings to 2 ft. apart. You can harvest gourds when tendrils next to their stems are dead, but it's best to leave them on the vine as long as possible—until the gourds turn yellow or brown. They can even stay on the vine through frosts, but a heavy frost can discolor them. Cut each gourd with some stem attached, so you can hang it up to dry slowly in a cool, airy spot. When thoroughly dry, preserve with coating of paste wax, lacquer, or shellac.

GOUT WEED.
See **AEGOPODIUM podagraria**

GRAMA GRASS.
See **BOUTELOUA**

GRANJENO. See **CELTIS pallida**

GRAPE
Vitaceae
DECIDUOUS VINES

| 🌿 ZONES VARY BY VARIETY |
| ☀ FULL SUN |
| ◌ MODERATE WATER |
| ▶ SEE CHART PAGE 375 |

Grown for fresh fruit, wine, shade, and fall color. (For strictly ornamental types, see *Vitis*.) A single grapevine can produce enough new growth every year to arch over a walk, roof an arbor, form a leafy wall, or provide an umbrella of shade over a deck or terrace. Grape is one of the few fruiting vines that offer bold textured foliage, colorful edible fruit, and a dominant trunk and branch pattern for winter interest. To produce good-quality fruit, you must choose a variety that suits your climate well, train it carefully, and prune it regularly.

There are several basic grape types. European grapes (*Vitis vinifera*) have tight skin, a generally high heat requirement, and cold tolerance to around 5°F/–15°C. These are the table grapes of the market, including 'Thompson Seedless'. The classic wine grapes, such as 'Cabernet', 'Chardonnay', and 'Pinot Noir', are also European in origin. Production of European wine grapes has greatly increased in the Northwest, but the bulk of the commercial crop is grown in California. For more information about growing wine grapes in your region, consult your local Cooperative Extension Office.

American grapes stem from *V. labrusca,* with some influence from other American native species. These are slipskin grapes of the 'Concord' type, which have a moderate summer heat requirement (as opposed to high heat needs of European table grapes) and tolerate temperatures well below 0°F/–18°C. American grapes are used in jelly, in unfermented grape juice, and as a flavoring for

G

Lon Rombough on Cool Table Grapes

Many of the nation's table grapes come from hot, sunny California vineyards—but there are varieties that thrive where summers are cool. Just ask Lon Rombough, who has harvested plenty of sweet, fresh fruit from the 200 grape varieties he grows in Aurora, Oregon. "A mature vine of the right variety can produce more than 30 pounds of fruit per year here, usually plenty for a family of four," he says.

For successful production in cool areas, Rombough advises choosing a variety that ripens early, is cold-hardy, and can take fall rains without the fruit cracking. American and American hybrid varieties make his list of tastiest table grapes for the cool Northwest. His favorite seeded grapes are 'New York Muscat', 'Price', and 'Swenson Red'. Among seedless varieties, he recommends 'Canadice', 'Interlaken' (it ripens well in the cool Puget Sound area), 'Reliance', and 'Vanessa' (which has exceptional rain resistance).

soft drinks; some wine, usually sweet, is also made from these grapes.

Hybrid grape varieties have characteristics intermediate between those of their parents. In general, these vines are almost as disease resistant and hardy as American species (most will need protection below −15°F/ −26°C), but the fruit is more like that of European grapes. Varieties called French hybrids—examples include 'Aurore', 'Seyval Blanc', 'Foch', and 'Baco Noir'—can be used for making wine in cold-winter climates. Consult your Cooperative Extension Office for varieties that will grow best locally.

Almost all grapes are self-fruitful and do not require pollination from another variety to bear fruit—but since they differ greatly in hardiness and heat requirements, choosing the right type and variety is important. Varieties listed in the chart, beginning on the following page, are widely available and of high quality where adapted, but they represent only a small portion of what can be grown.

The Pacific Northwest is primarily American grape country, but there are many opportunities to grow European grapes as well; the warmest parts of the Columbia River basin and the lower Williamette Valley are the best European grape–growing areas there. Regions of California and Arizona with a long warm season favor European varieties; California's coastal and inland valleys offer an ideal climate for most types. In short-season, high-elevation areas, choose either American or hardy European varieties, and plant in warm microclimates. If your climate is cooler or growing season shorter than is desirable for grape growing, look for early-ripening varieties.

The popularity of European grapes, especially wine varieties, has led to their being tried beyond their normal range. In cold-winter climates, the crop may be ruined by spring frosts and summer rains in some years, but vines that are protected or planted in warm microclimates can produce harvestable fruit in other years. Even in Hawaii, European wine grapes are being successfully grown in some high-elevation areas. At lower elevations, where grapes are ravaged by the hard-to-control Chinese rose beetle, crops are rarely successful.

What Grapes Need

SOIL Deep, fertile, well-drained sandy loam is ideal.

AIR CIRCULATION Free air movement is important. If you garden on hilly terrain, it's better to plant grapes on a slope than in a low-lying basin, where trapped air increases danger from frost or mildew.

PRUNING High-quality crop depends on initial training and regular dormant-season pruning (see text).

HARVESTING Cut bunches from vines in late summer or fall, when grapes are sweet and fully colored.

'Black Monukka', European

Support. Once they are established, grapevines are rampant. Provide a sturdy trellis, arbor, chain-link or rail fence, or wall strung with wire to support these big vines and their heavy bunches of fruit. To build a custom wire trellis large enough to accommodate two grapevines, set stout posts in the ground 15–20 ft. apart; posts should rise 5 ft. above the soil. Set two smaller posts (support stakes for the vines) 4–5 ft. from the end posts. String sturdy galvanized wire (10- or 11-gauge) across the four post tops. For a double-wire trellis, string a lower wire at the 2½-ft. level. Space multiple trellises 10–12 ft. apart.

Planting and care. Purchase year-old bare-root vines, and plant during the dormant season (winter in mild-winter regions, about 3 weeks before the last expected frost date in cold-winter areas). Trim roots to 6 in. just before planting in holes spaced 8–10 ft. apart. If planting at an arbor or fence, position each hole about 1½ ft. away from the structure, and set the plant at a 45° angle so it leans toward the support. Cut back top growth to two or three buds. Place vines as deep in the soil as they grew in the nursery, spreading roots in all directions. In some areas, planting deeper, with all but the top bud buried, is

recommended; check with a local nursery or Cooperative Extension Office.

Water and weed regularly. Grapes are prone to fungal diseases, so avoid splashing water on leaves; drip irrigation is ideal. Fertilize each spring with a balanced fertilizer; for newly planted vines apply one-fourth the amount recommended on the bag, then gradually increase the amount each year until the fourth year, when you can start applying the full recommended dose each spring.

Initial training. If all you want is a leafy cover for an arbor or patio, you need only train a strong vine up and over its support and thin out entangling growth each year. But most people plant grapes for the delicious fruit. To prepare grapevines for good production, train them into a basic framework on an arbor or wire trellis.

The first summer after planting, let each vine grow unchecked from the base of its support structure. During the first winter, select the sturdiest shoot for the trunk and tie it to the support; shorten it to the three or four lowest buds and remove all other shoots at their base. In the second spring, once the buds have grown out to 6–8-in.-long shoots, choose the strongest upright shoot for the continuation of the trunk and tie it to the post. (If you're training plants on a two-wire trellis or against a fence, also select two strong lower shoots for "arms" and tie them to the lower horizontal support.) Cut off all other shoots.

If you're growing your grapevine on a wire trellis, the second summer is the time to stop its vertical ascent. When the trunk reaches the top wire of the trellis, pinch it back to force branching. Train the two strongest resulting shoots along the top wire and remove any others. (For a two-wire trellis, also tie the lower arms' new growth along the lower wire; pinch back any lateral shoots developing from those arms to about 10 in. long.) In the

Grape

second winter, cut back all growth on the trunk and arms and make sure that both sets of arms are loosely tied to the wire. During the third summer, allow the vine to grow but remove any shoots sprouting on the trunk. At this point, you've established a permanent framework for your trellis-grown vine, and you can choose between cane pruning and spur pruning from the third winter on (see "Yearly pruning," below).

If you're training your vine onto an arbor, the second summer is the time to direct its growth onto the roof of the structure. When the vine has grown just beyond the top of the vertical support, gently bend it over and secure it to the roof as it grows. Remove side shoots to encourage the tip to grow. During the second winter, cut back the main stem to a point just beyond where you want the last set of branches. Cut off all the side shoots. During the third spring, thin new shoots to 1 ft. apart. In the third winter, you're ready to create the final framework; its form depends on how you plan to prune your vines in subsequent years. If you're planning to do spur pruning, cut back each of the shoots you selected in the spring to two buds. If you will be cane pruning your vines, cut branches alternately to long canes (12 buds) and spurs (two buds).

Yearly pruning. Grapes are produced on stems that develop from year-old wood—stems that formed in the previous season. These year-old stems have smooth bark, whereas older stems have rough, shaggy bark. The purpose of yearly pruning is to limit the amount of potential fruiting wood to ensure that the plant doesn't produce too much fruit and that the fruit it does bear is of good quality. Pruning should be done in the dormant season—that is, in winter or earliest spring before the buds swell.

The two most widely used methods for pruning grapevines are spur pruning and cane pruning; see accompanying chart for recommended method for each variety. Begin using either method in the third winter, and repeat yearly thereafter.

GRAPE

VARIETY	ZONES	SEASON	PRUNING	COMMENTS
AMERICAN and AMERICAN HYBRID VARIETIES				
'Alden'	6–22	Early midseason	Spur	Large, firm, seeded reddish blue grape with light muscat flavor. Good for fresh eating, juice, wine. Very productive. Good fall leaf color
'America'	7–22	Midseason	Cane or spur	Seeded blue grape with intense flavor. Good for juice, fresh eating, wine. Resistant to Pierce's disease
'Black Spanish' ('Lenoir')	7–9, 11–24	Late midseason	Spur	Very old black grape. Small seeded fruit is fine for eating but best for wine and juice. Resistant to Pierce's disease
'Bluebell'	2–7	Early	Cane or spur	Seeded blue grape with a flavor like that of 'Concord'. Excellent for juice, good for eating fresh. Very hardy (to –35°F/–37°C). Grows in warm-summer areas but may taste flat there
'Buffalo'	2–7	Early	Cane or spur	Seeded black fruit with spicy flavor. Good for fresh eating or juice. Can produce secondary crop if frosted in spring
'Campbell Early'	5–22	Early midseason	Spur	Large, seeded black grape of 'Concord' type for fresh eating, juice. Colors before achieving full flavor
'Canadice'	2b–9, 11–21	Early	Spur	Seedless red fruit. Excellent for fresh eating or juice. Ripens in very cool areas, such as around Puget Sound. Overcrops easily; must be pruned hard or have crop thinned. Hardy to –20°F/–29°C if well pruned
'Champanel'	7 (warmer parts), 8, 9, 11–16, 18–24	Midseason	Cane	Seeded black grape. Good for juice, fresh eating. Tolerant of alkaline soil; resistant to Pierce's disease
'Concord'	2b, 3, 6–9, 14–23	Midseason	Cane or spur	Seeded blue fruit. Standard American slipskin for cooking, juice, jelly
'Edelweiss'	2–9, 14–21	Early	Cane or spur	Seeded white grape. Fresh eating or juice. Milder flavor than 'Niagara', but vine is more manageable. Flavor goes flat in hot-summer areas
'Golden Muscat' AMERICAN HYBRID	3b, 6–24	Late	Spur	Very large, juicy, seeded green-yellow fruit. Flavor is citruslike, not true muscat; good for eating fresh. Ripens 2 weeks after 'Concord'. Cracks in wet weather
'Himrod' AMERICAN HYBRID	3–9, 11–21	Very early	Cane	Seedless white fruit with spicy flavor. For fresh eating. Very vigorous, suited to arbors. Hardy to –15°F/–26°C

'Buffalo'

'Canadice'

'Concord'

'Golden Muscat'

GRAPE

VARIETY	ZONES	SEASON	PRUNING	COMMENTS
AMERICAN and AMERICAN HYBRID VARIETIES (continued)				
'Interlaken' AMERICAN HYBRID	2–9, 14–21	Very early	Cane or spur	Firm, seedless green or yellow grape with fruity flavor. Ripens a week earlier than 'Himrod'. One of few that matures in the coolest areas of Pacific Northwest. Excellent for fresh eating; only one for raisins in cool-summer areas
'Lakemont'	3, 6–22	Early	Cane or spur	Seedless white fruit with mild flavor; very productive. Fine table grape; keeps well in cold storage
'Mars'	4–9, 14–21	Early midseason	Cane or spur	Blue fruit; large for a seedless grape. Fine for fresh eating, juice, wine, raisins. Flavor improves after harvest
'New York Muscat'	2b–9, 14–21	Early	Cane or spur	Seeded blue grape with sweet muscat flavor. Excellent for fresh eating, juice, wine. Less vigorous than other varieties. Can be tried in hotter areas, but quality may suffer
'Niabell'	7–9, 14–16, 18–22	Early	Cane or spur	Large, seeded black grape similar to 'Concord' at its best. Excellent for arbors. Vigorous and productive in wide range of climates. Succeeds in hot interiors where 'Concord' fails
'Niagara'	2, 3, 6–10, 14–21	Midseason	Cane	Seedless green to pale yellow fruit. Good for fresh eating, juice, wine
'Price'	2–9, 14–21	Very early	Spur	Seeded blue grape. Sweet and juicy, with refined 'Concord'-type flavor. Very good for eating fresh and fine for juice. Ripens in coolest areas of range, even around Puget Sound. May even succeed in Zone 1 with cold protection
'Reliance' AMERICAN HYBRID	2b–9, 14–21	Early midseason	Spur	Seedless red grape with mild, sweet flavor. Good for fresh eating or juice. Dependably productive
'Swenson Red'	2–9, 14–21	Early	Spur	Firm, meaty, seeded red or red-blue grape with unique fruity flavor. Excellent for fresh eating, juice, wine
'Valiant'	A2, A3; 1–9	Early	Spur	Seeded blue fruit with 'Concord'-like flavor. Makes very good juice and jelly. Hardy to –50°F/–46°C
'Vanessa'	2–9, 14–21	Early	Cane	Firm, seedless red grape with fruity flavor. Resists cracking. Good replacement for European variety 'Flame' in cool-summer areas. Use for fresh eating or raisins
'Venus'	3–9, 14–21	Early midseason	Cane or spur	Seedless blue grape. Fruity, muscatlike flavor; fine choice for fresh eating or juice. Excellent fall color

'Himrod'

'Lakemont'

'Niagara'

'Reliance'

GRAPE

VARIETY	ZONES	SEASON	PRUNING	COMMENTS
EUROPEAN VARIETIES				
'Autumn Royal'	6–9, 11–16, 18–21	Midseason to late	Cane or spur	Large, seedless purplish black grape. Good for fresh eating or raisins
'Autumn Seedless'	6–9, 11–16, 18–21	Midseason	Cane or spur	Seedless pale green to golden grape. Good for fresh eating or raisins
'Black Monukka'	3, 6–16, 17 (warmer parts), 18–24	Early midseason	Cane or spur	Seedless purplish black fruit in large, loose clusters. Popular home variety. One of hardiest European grapes
'Crimson Seedless'	6–9, 12–16, 18–22	Late	Cane	Large, seedless red grape with excellent flavor. For fresh eating, raisins
'Delight'	6–9, 12–16, 17 (warmer parts), 18–24	Early	Spur	Large, seedless, dark greenish yellow. Good for fresh eating, raisins. Succeeds in mild-winter areas
'Early Muscat'	6–9, 11–16, 18–24	Early midseason	Spur	Seeded green fruit in large clusters. Excellent muscat flavor. Used for muscat wine in Northwest
'Fantasy'	6–9, 11–14, 18–21	Midseason	Cane	Large, seedless bluish black fruit with sweet, rich flavor. Good fresh or for wine. Vigorous; leave six to eight canes when pruning
'Flame'	6–9, 11–16, 17 (warmer parts), 18–24	Early midseason	Cane or spur	Seedless red grape. For fresh eating, raisins. Very vigorous. Keep on dry side to reduce vigor, encourage ripening
'Muscat' ('Muscat of Alexandria')	6–9, 11–16, 18–21	Late midseason	Spur	Large, rounded, seeded green to amber fruit. Renowned for sweet, musky, aged-in-the-vat flavor. Fine for fresh eating, juice, wine, raisins
'Muscat Hamburg'	6–9, 11–16, 18–21	Late midseason	Spur	Seeded black grape. Intense, almost orangelike muscat flavor. Good fresh or for wine
'Perlette'	6–9, 11–16, 17 (warmer parts), 18–24	Early	Spur	Pale yellow, seedless fruit. Earlier, larger, less sweet than 'Thompson Seedless'. Excellent fresh. Needs less heat than most European varieties
'Ribier'	7–9, 11–16, 18–21	Early midseason	Spur	Very large, seeded black grape with mild flavor. Good for fresh eating
'Ruby Seedless' ('King's Ruby')	7–9, 12–16, 18–24	Late midseason	Cane or spur	Large clusters of seedless red to reddish black fruit. Sweet dessert grapes. Very susceptible to powdery mildew
'Thompson Seedless'	7–14, 18, 19	Midseason	Cane	Big clusters of small, sweet, seedless greenish amber fruit. For fresh eating, raisins. Widely planted but does best in hot, dry areas

'Crimson Seedless'

'Flame'

'Perlette'

'Ribier'

'Ruby Seedless'

G

Spur pruning. Start by removing weak side shoots from the arms. Leave the strongest shoots (spurs) spaced 6–10 in. apart; cut each to two buds. Each spur will produce two fruit-bearing shoots during the next growing season. The next winter and every winter thereafter, remove the lower shoot on each spur and cut the upper stem to two buds. Those buds will develop into stems that bear fruit the following summer.

Cane pruning. Select one strong lateral shoot near the trunk on each arm, cut it back to 12 buds, and tie it to the support; these will produce fruiting shoots in the coming summer. Select another strong lateral shoot near the trunk on each arm, and cut it back to two buds; these will be the renewal spurs. Remove all other shoots. Each winter, remove the arms that have fruited, and choose as their replacements the two longest and strongest shoots that grew from the renewal spurs. Cut each to 12 buds and tie the two shoots to the support; select the two next-best shoots as renewal spurs, and cut each to two buds. Remove all other shoots.

Pests and diseases. Pierce's disease, caused by a bacterium spread by the sharpshooter insect, is a serious threat to grapes in California. It causes afflicted vines to lose productivity, wilt, and die in a matter of only a season or two. For more information, contact your Cooperative Extension Office.

The grape leafhopper may cause leaf drop on grapevines in California. Get rid of nearby weeds, which may harbor the pest. Spraying with insecticidal soap is somewhat effective; grape leafhopper infestations are rarely serious enough to warrant a stronger pesticide. Grape mealybug may infest vines in the Northwest and parts of California; control with horticultural oil spray in late winter.

Powdery mildew is a serious disease of European grapes (most American varieties are immune). To control, dust vines with sulfur when shoots are 6 in. long, again at 12–15 in. long, then every 2 weeks until harvest.

GRAPEFRUIT. See CITRUS

GRAPE HYACINTH.
See **MUSCARI**

GRAPE IVY. See CISSUS rhombifolia, C. trifoliata

GRAPTOPETALUM paraguayense
GHOST PLANT
Crassulaceae
SUCCULENT PERENNIAL

- ☀ ZONES 13, 16–17, 19–24; OR INDOORS
- ☼ ☽ FULL SUN OR PARTIAL SHADE
- ○ LITTLE WATER

Thick-leafed succulent native to Mexico. Stems branch as they creep along the ground, cascade over walls, or spill from containers. Plants form mounds 7 in. high and at least 1 ft. wide. Suitable as a

Graptopetalum paraguayense

ground cover in areas where there is no foot traffic or as filler for hanging baskets and rock gardens. Fleshy, pointed leaves grow along stems and form rosettes that range in color from pale blue gray (when grown in bright shade) to yellow pink (in full, hot sun). Star-shaped flowers are white or yellow, on branching stems. Grow in coarse, well-drained soil that goes dry between waterings. Does not do well in desert heat, but will tolerate temperatures down to about 25°F/–4°C. Plants grow readily from cuttings; handle carefully, as leaves break off easily.

GRAPTOPHYLLUM pictum
CARICATURE PLANT
Acanthaceae
EVERGREEN SHRUB

- ☀ ZONES H2; 24; OR INDOORS
- ☼ LIGHT SHADE; BRIGHT FILTERED LIGHT
- ● REGULAR WATER

This frost-tender native of New Guinea is prized for its beautiful foliage. Grows 6–8 ft. tall and wide, with glossy deep green leaves to 6 in. long and half as wide. Irregular cream-colored marbling decorates each leaf along the midrib. In summer, reddish

Graptophyllum pictum
'Chocolate'

purple tubular flowers to 1½ in. long are borne in short clusters. 'Chocolate' has leaves mottled burgundy green and bronze, with pinkish cream marbling and deep pink midribs. 'Tricolor' has bright green leaves with white marbling and pink midribs.

In frost-free zones, may be used as a landscape plant in light shade and well-drained soil; excellent contrast to ferns. Elsewhere, grow in pots that can be moved indoors to a bright location in winter; reduce water. Pinch out growing tips to make plants bushy.

GRASSES

The grasses in this book are either lawn or ornamental plants—except for corn, the only cereal commonly grown in home gardens. All are described under entries headed by their botanical names; to find these, check lists below.

Bamboos, which are grasses, are charted under Bamboo. Although not true grasses, sedges in the genus *Carex* are often grouped with ornamental grasses for their similar appearance and uses.

The most common lawn grasses in the West are *Agrostis*, bent grass, redtop; *Buchloe*, buffalo grass; *Cynodon*, Bermuda grass; *Festuca*, fescue; *Lolium*, ryegrass; *Poa*, bluegrass; *Stenotaphrum*, St. Augustine grass; and *Zoysia*, zoysia grass. Specialty lawn grasses include *Agropyron*, wheatgrass; *Bouteloua*, grama grass; and *Paspalum*, seashore paspalum.

Ornamental grasses continue to increase in popularity, with new types reaching nurseries each year. They bring texture, color, and motion to the garden; combine well with a variety of other plants; and often change dramatically from season to season. See *Achnatherum*, Indian rice grass; *Alopecurus*, yellow foxtail grass; *Andropogon*, big bluestem, turkey-

foot; *Arrhenatherum*, bulbous oat grass; *Arundo*, giant reed; *Briza*, rattlesnake grass; *Calamagrostis*, reed grass; *Chasmanthium*, sea oats; *Coix*, Job's tears; *Cortaderia*, pampas grass; *Deschampsia*, hair grass; *Elymus*, wheatgrass; *Eragrostis*, love grass; *Festuca*, fescue; *Hakonechloa*, Japanese forest grass; *Helictotrichon*, blue oat grass; *Imperata*, Japanese blood grass; *Leymus*, lyme grass; *Milium*, Bowles golden grass; *Miscanthus*, eulalia, silver grass; *Molinia*, moor grass; *Muhlenbergia*, including bamboo muhly and deer grass; *Nassella*, needle grass; *Panicum*, switch grass; *Pennisetum*, fountain grass; *Phalaris*, ribbon grass; *Rhynchelytrum*, natal ruby grass; *Schizachyrium*, little bluestem; *Sesleria*, moor grass; *Spartina*, prairie cord grass; *Sporobolus*, dropseed; and *Stipa*, feather grass.

GRASS NUT.
See **TRITELEIA laxa**

GRASS TREE.
See **NOLINA, XANTHORRHOEA**

GREASEWOOD.
See **ADENOSTOMA fasciculatum**

GRECIAN LAUREL.
See **LAURUS nobilis**

GREEN CARPET.
See **HERNIARIA glabra**

GREENWEED, DYER'S.
See **GENISTA tinctoria**

GREVILLEA
Proteaceae
EVERGREEN SHRUBS AND TREES

- ☀ ZONES VARY BY SPECIES
- ☼ ☽ EXPOSURE NEEDS VARY BY SPECIES
- ○ LITTLE OR NO WATER, EXCEPT AS NOTED

Australia is home to a multitude of grevillea species (over 250) and hybrids; many of these have great garden merit, including plants not described here. Also watch for new introductions that often show up in nurseries. Though grevilleas vary in size and appearance, they generally have fine-textured foliage and long, slender, curved flowers, usually borne in dense clusters. Many cannot tolerate salt-laden soils, poor water quality, heavy summer irrigation, or heavy frost, but all are attractive enough to warrant some risk taking. Like other members of the protea family, they are sensitive to high levels of phosphorus in the soil. Fertilize lightly and avoid high-phosphorus fertilizers.

G. alpina. MOUNTAIN GREVILLEA. Shrub. Zones 15–24. Highly variable in size and form. Among most widely distributed is 'East Grampians', a low spreader (to 2½ ft. high and 5 ft. wide) with inch-long bright green leaves and masses of red-and-yellow flowers from fall through spring. Full sun or light shade.

G. asplenifolia. Shrub. Zones 15–24. To 9–15 ft. tall, 9–20 ft. wide, with foot-long leaves less than ½ in. wide. Deep red, 2½-in.-long flower clusters appear in late winter and spring. Showy in bloom and useful for screening. Takes sun but prefers partial shade.

G. 'Austraflora Fanfare'. See G. 'Fanfare'.

G. australis. ALPINE GREVILLEA. Shrub. Zones 15, 16, 23, 24. Spreading or erect habit; reaches 1–7 ft. tall, 4–9 ft. wide. Narrow dark green to olive green leaves are ½–1 in. long. Cream-colored flowers—not showy, but powerfully fragrant—bloom in winter and spring. Full sun or partial shade.

G. banksii. Shrub or tree. Zones 16–24; H1. Often sold as G. b. 'Bushy Form' or 'Forsters'. To 9 ft. tall and 12 ft. wide, with 4–10-in.-long leaves deeply cut into narrow lobes. Erect, 3–6-in.-long clusters of dark red flowers appear sporadically all year but are most profuse in late spring. Showy used singly against high wall, near entryway, or grouped with other large-scale shrubs. Freezes at 24°F/–4°C; takes wind. Full sun. Little to regular water.

G. 'Boongalla Spinebill'. Shrub. Zones 15–24. Sprawling growth to 3–5 ft. high, 15 ft. wide. Deeply cut, 6-in.-long leaves are coppery when new, later turn deep green. Toothbrushlike clusters of red flowers bloom nearly all year, most heavily in late winter. Full sun or partial shade.

G. 'Canberra Gem' ('Canberra'). Shrub. Zones 8, 9, 12–24. Open, graceful growth to 8 ft. tall, 12 ft. wide. Needlelike, bright green, 1-in. leaves. Clusters of red flowers in winter and spring (and intermittently at other times). Has been sold as 'Pink Pearl'. Full sun or partial shade.

G. 'Constance'. See G. 'Poorinda Constance'.

G. curviloba. Shrub. Zones 14–24. Often sold as G. tridentifera or G. biternata. Variable habit; may

reach 6 ft. high and 10–15 ft. across or grow as a low (2-ft.) spreader, also to 10–15 ft. wide. Finely divided bright green leaves; cream-colored, honey-scented blossoms in winter and spring. To use as ground or bank cover, prune out any stems that grow upright. Full sun or partial shade.

G. 'Fanfare' ('Austraflora Fanfare'). Shrub. Zones 15–24. Thought to be a hybrid involving G. × gaudichaudii. Like that parent, it is low and spreading, to 1 ft. tall and 10–15 ft. wide. Narrow, sawtoothed leaves up to 7 in. long are coppery red and covered with silky hairs when young, maturing to dark green. Toothbrushlike flowers in deep red appear winter to spring. Excellent tough, fast-growing ground cover; tip prune after flowering to keep dense. Full sun or partial shade.

G. × gaudichaudii. Shrub. Zones 15–24; H1. Prostrate plant spreading 10–15 ft. wide. Lobed leaves resembling oak leaves are bronzy when they emerge, then mature to dark green. Toothbrushlike clusters of dark red flowers in winter and spring. Provide good drainage, moderate water. Takes sun but prefers partial shade. Tolerates extended wet periods.

G. 'Ivanhoe'. Shrub. Zones 14–24. Dense grower to 6–15 ft. tall, 9–15 ft. wide. Finely divided leaves to 6 in. long. Pinkish red flowers in toothbrushlike clusters form at branch tips in late winter, spring. Full sun or light shade.

G. lanigera. WOOLLY GREVILLEA. Shrub. Zones 15–24. Spreading, mounding growth to 3–6 ft. tall, 6–10 ft. across. Closely set, narrow, ½-in.-long leaves are covered with hairs that give foliage a grayish cast. Clusters of narrow, curved, crimson-and-cream flowers profuse in winter and spring; attractive to hummingbirds. Good bank cover in hot, sunny area; good transition beween garden and wild area.

Compact varieties are attractive in rock gardens or as ground covers. These include 'Coastal Gem' (about 1½ ft. high, 4–5 ft. wide), which starts blooming in fall; 'Low Form' (2 ft. tall, 4 ft. wide), which is very dense and looks good in containers; and 'Mt. Tamboritha' (2 ft. tall, 4–6 ft. wide), which blooms practically year-round. Full sun or partial shade. Plants tolerate extended wet periods.

G. lavandulacea. LAVENDER GREVILLEA. Shrub. Zones 15–24.

Variable, but all forms are dense growers with half-inch-long gray leaves. 'Billywing', to 2½ ft. high and 6 ft. wide, has red-and-cream flowers in winter and spring. 'Penola', to 5 ft. tall and 8 ft. wide (or larger), bears deep rose red blossoms fall through spring. 'Tanunda' is 1½–3 ft. high, 3–6 ft. wide, with profuse coral pink flowers; main show comes in winter, with occasional repeat bloom in midsummer. Tolerates light shade.

G. 'Long John'. Shrub. Zones 15–24. To 10 ft. tall and 15 ft. wide, with 8-in. leaves divided into many narrow lobes. Early spring brings a heavy display of pink-and-red flowers. Useful for screening. Full sun or partial shade.

G. 'Moonlight'. Shrub. Zones 15–17, 21–24. Big, soft-looking plant grows quickly to 8–12 ft. tall and 6–8 ft. wide. Ferny, dark gray-green leaves make a pretty backdrop for the many creamy to pale yellow, cylindrical blossoms produced in winter and spring, nearly year-round in ideal conditions. Good cut flowers. To keep plants compact and encourage fresh new growth and bloom, shear or cut back by about one-third after flowering. Full sun or partial shade.

G. 'Noellii' (G. 'Noell'). Shrub. Zones 8, 9, 12–24. To 4 ft. tall, 4–5 ft. wide. Densely clad with narrow, 1-in.-long, glossy medium green leaves. Clusters of pink-and-white flowers bloom in spring. Full sun. Moderate water.

Grevillea 'Noellii'

G. 'Poorinda Constance' ('Constance'). Shrub. Zones 8, 9, 12–24. Resembles 'Canberra Gem'

in size and habit, but has broader leaves that are deep green above, almost white beneath. Bears large clusters of orange-red flowers in spring, often again in fall. Full sun.

G. 'Red Hooks'. Shrub. Zones 16–24. Grows to 12 ft. tall and up to 18 ft. across, with finely cut 5-in. leaves. Coral red, toothbrushlike flower clusters from late winter to late spring, with a scattering at other times of year. Full sun or light shade.

G. robusta. SILK OAK. Tree. Zones 8, 9, 12–24; H1, H2. Weedy in parts of Hawaii. Fast growing to 50–60 ft. (rarely 100 ft.) tall. Young trees are symmetrical and pyramidal. Old ones are broad topped (30–35 ft. wide), usually with a few heavy, horizontal limbs; picturesque against skyline. Ferny leaves are golden green to deep green above, silvery beneath. Heavy leaf fall in spring, sporadic leaf drop throughout year. Large clusters of bright golden orange flowers in early spring. Wood is brittle and easily damaged in high winds. For sturdier branches, cut central leader back hard at planting time and shorten branches to well-balanced framework. Thrives in heat; one of lushest greens for low desert. Useful as quick, tall screen; can be clipped as tall hedge. Full sun. Grows in poor, dense soils if not overwatered; can take regular water in fast-draining soils. Young trees damaged at 24°F/–4°C; older ones hardy to 16°F/–9°C. Beyond hardiness range, sometimes grown as potted plant or houseplant and discarded when it gets too big.

G. 'Robyn Gordon'. Shrub. Zones 16–24. To 6–7 ft. tall and wide. Large (6–8-in.) light green leaves divided into many narrow segments. Pendent 6-in. clusters of bright red flowers are showy most of year. Full sun.

G. rosmarinifolia. ROSEMARY GREVILLEA. Shrub. Zones 8, 9, 12–24. To 6 ft. tall, nearly as broad. Narrow, 1½-in.-long leaves are dark green on top, silvery beneath; look somewhat like those of rosemary. Red-and-cream flower clusters (rarely pink or white) in

Grevillea robusta

fall and winter; scattered bloom in other seasons. Use as clipped or informal hedge in dryish places. Impervious to heat and aridity. A dwarf form, just 3 ft. high and 6 ft. wide, bears pink-and-cream flowers in waves throughout the year, most heavily in spring and fall. 'Scarlet Sprite', another dwarf, is similar but bears blooms in bright red and cream. Full sun or partial shade.

G. 'Ruby Clusters'. Shrub. Zones 14–24. Dense growth to 6 ft. tall and broad, with narrow, 3-in.-long dark green leaves. Deep red flowers appear nearly nonstop throughout the year, with the heaviest show in early spring. Responds well to pruning. Full sun or partial shade.

G. 'Sylvia'. Shrub. Zones 16–24. Similar to 'Robyn Gordon' but slightly larger, with leaves a bit darker and glossier; its raspberry pink flowers are held a bit more upright. Strong stems make blooms good for cutting. Shear or cut back plant by one-third after bloom to keep compact. Full sun.

G. thelemanniana. HUMMINGBIRD BUSH, SPIDER-NET GREVILLEA. Shrub. Zones 9, 14–17, 19–24. Graceful, rounded habit 5–8 ft. high and wide. Dark green, 1–2-in.-long leaves divided into narrow segments. Clusters of bright red flowers tipped yellow can appear in any season. Airier, more open, less adapted to hedge and screen use than *G. rosmarinifolia.* Among the many forms is a dwarf gray-leafed selection 6 in. high and 6 ft. wide, useful for trailing over a wall or down a bank. 'Magic Lantern' ('Gilded Dragon') also has gray leaves but grows 2–3 ft. tall and 4–6 ft. wide. All forms can be temperamental in Northern California; prefer dry, warm winters of Southern California. Full sun or partial shade.

G. victoriae. Shrub. Zones 8, 9, 14–24. Variable in size; the form most commonly seen is 6 ft. or taller and as wide, with gray-green, narrowly oval, 4-in. leaves and orange-red flowers in drooping clusters during late winter and spring. 'Murray Valley Queen' is an outstanding selection with profuse flowers; new growth is covered with attractive rust-colored hairs. Occasional summer water will prevent bud drop. Takes sun but prefers partial shade.

G. 'White Wings'. Shrub. Zones 15–24. To 6 ft. tall and spreading 10–15 ft. wide, with finely divided, 2-in.-long bright green leaves. Masses of fragrant white flowers

appear in spring, with a scattering at other times. Good for bank or slope planting. Full sun or partial shade.

GREWIA occidentalis
LAVENDER STARFLOWER
Tiliaceae
EVERGREEN SHRUB

🌿 ZONES 8, 9, 12–24; H1, H2
☼ FULL SUN
💧 REGULAR WATER

Fast-growing, sprawling South African native can be used in various ways. Tends to branch freely in flat pattern, making a natural espalier if given the support of a warm, sunny wall or fence. Becomes dense with pinching and pruning. Unstaked, it grows 6–10 ft. tall (sometimes higher) with equal spread. Can be planted 4 ft. apart and used as tall clipped hedge or screen. If plant is allowed to sprawl and upright stems are removed, it can serve as a bank cover. Can be trained as a single-trunked tree or tied in place to cover arbor or trellis.

Grewia occidentalis

Dark green, oblong, finely toothed leaves 3 in. long. Star-shaped, inch-wide flowers are lavender pink with yellow centers. Blooms in late spring and sporadically into fall, especially if cut back lightly after first heavy bloom. Do any major pruning in fall after flowering is over. Tolerates wind.

GRISELINIA
Cornaceae
EVERGREEN SHRUBS

🌿 ZONES 9, 14–17, 20–24
☼ ◐ FULL SUN OR PARTIAL SHADE
💧💧 MODERATE TO REGULAR WATER

Native to New Zealand. Upright form and thick, leathery, lustrous green leaves. Flowers and fruit

are insignificant. Always look well groomed. Good near swimming pools.

G. littoralis. A 50-ft. tree in New Zealand, but usually seen in the West as 10-ft.-high shrub of equal spread. Leaves roundish, to 4 in. long. With regular moisture, it can reach 8 ft. in 3 years. Dense, compact screen or windbreak. Fine beach plant, good espalier. 'Variegata' has leaves marked with cream.

Griselinia littoralis

G. lucida. Slower growing, a little smaller, more open and slender than *G. littoralis,* with larger (to 7-in.-long) leaves. Excellent foliage plant for partial shade. Thrives in containers. 'Variegata' has white markings on leaves.

GROUND CHERRY. See **POHA**

GROUND IVY.
See **GLECHOMA hederacea**

GUADALUPE PALM.
See **BRAHEA edulis**

GUAIACUM
Zygophyllaceae
EVERGREEN TREES OR SHRUBS

🌿 ZONES VARY BY SPECIES
☼ ◐ FULL SUN OR LIGHT SHADE
💧 MODERATE WATER

Related to creosote bush (*Larrea tridentata)* and puncture vine (the weed *Tribulus terrestris*), the guaiacums belong to a small genus noted for hard, heavy wood and for producing resin.

G. coulteri. Zones 13, 23, 24. This Mexican native has light gray bark and dark green leaves divided into six to ten narrow, ½–1-in. leaflets. Clusters of deep blue-violet, ¾-in. flowers appear sporadically from spring through summer. Tolerates drought, but irrigation during dry periods will promote heavier bloom. Needs good drainage. Where subject to

Guaiacum coulteri

light frosts, plant tends to be shrubby, around 5–12 ft. high and wide. In a frost-free site, it can become a multitrunked tree to 20 ft. high and nearly as wide. Leaves and branch tips may be damaged by temperatures just below freezing point; prune out only after new growth appears in spring.

G. officinale. LIGNUM-VITAE. Zones H1, H2. From dry coastal areas of Central America and the West Indies. A very slow growing, bushy tree that can be trained to single or multiple trunks. With time, it may reach 25–35 ft. high and 20–25 ft. wide, but it is often seen at half that size or smaller. Attractive medium green leaves to 3½ in. long are composed of two or three pairs of leathery, oval leaflets. Masses of lavender-blue flowers are produced in late spring; these are followed by heart-shaped, yellow-orange capsules, about ¾-in. long, that may split, revealing bright red fruit. Adapted to wide range of soils; has good wind and drought tolerance. Only light pruning required to shape. Useful in entry court or as accent or screen in the landscape; does well in a container.

GUAJILLO.
See **ACACIA berlandieri**

GUAVA
Myrtaceae
EVERGREEN SHRUBS OR TREES

🌿 ZONES VARY BY SPECIES
☼ ◐ FULL SUN OR PART SHADE
💧 REGULAR WATER

Native to tropical America; known botanically as *Psidium*. Plants bear white flowers composed mainly of a brush of stamens. The blossoms develop into round to pear-shaped, berrylike fruits that mature from late summer into fall, though some may be produced year-round. Though guavas are self-fruitful, trees may yield a heavier crop with another variety of the same species to pollinate them. Grow best in rich soil. Drought tolerant ut need regular moisture for ood fruit quality. Fruit is best icked when skin is fully colored, hough it can be harvested when till greenish and ripened at room emperature (placing green fruit in ag with an apple or a banana will asten ripening). Good eaten fresh r used in jellies, purées, juice rinks. Plants take pruning well; hey can be sheared into a hedge but at expense of fruit).

Common or tropical guava P. guajava) grows in Zones 23, 24, 1, H2 (it is weedy in Hawaii, here it is choking out native pecies). To 25 ft. tall and nearly as ide, with strongly veined leaves o 6 in. long. May lose some of its eaves briefly in spring; new

Guava

rowth is an attractive salmon olor. Yellow-skinned, 1–3-in.-ide fruit has white, pink, or yel-ow flesh and a musky, mildly acid lavor. 'Holmberg', 'Indonesian eedless', and 'Ruby × Supreme' re sweeter dessert varieties rown mostly in Hawaii. Beaumont', 'Ka Hua Kula', and Waiakea', tarter and used mainly or juice, are also grown primarily n Hawaii.

Strawberry guava or purple trawberry guava (P. cattleianum r P. littorale longipes) is hardier o cold than common guava, rowing in Zones 9 and 14 (shel-ered locations), 15–24, H1, H2 it has naturalized throughout Hawaii but is less invasive than ommon guava). In Hawaii, it is usually grown as single-trunked ree to 20 ft. tall and wide; in alifornia, it is more often seen as shrub to 8–10 ft. high and wide, hough it is sometimes trained as multitrunked tree 10–15 ft. tall.

Especially beautiful reddish to golden brown bark. Leaves to 3 in. long are bronze when new, matur-ing to glossy green. Fruit is dark red (nearly black when fully ripe), 1½ in. wide, with white flesh and a sweet-tart, slightly resinous flavor. Yellow strawberry guava or lemon guava (P. cattleianum lucidum) differs in its more open, taller growth habit (to 30 ft. tall by 15 ft. wide in Hawaii), greenish gray to golden bark, and larger, yellow-skinned fruit.

For the plant known as pine-apple guava, see Feijoa.

GUERNSEY LILY.
See **NERINE sarniensis**

GUINEA GOLD VINE.
See **HIBBERTIA scandens**

GUM. See **EUCALYPTUS**

GUNNERA
Gunneraceae
PERENNIALS

| 🌿 ZONES 4–6, 14–17, 20–24 |
| 🔆 PARTIAL SHADE |
| 💧 AMPLE WATER |

Big, bold, awe-inspiring South American plants to 8 ft. high and as wide or wider, with giant leaves (4–8 ft. across) on 4–6-ft.-long stalks covered in stiff hairs. Leaves are conspicuously veined, with

Gunnera tinctoria

lobed and cut edges. Given space (they need plenty) and the neces-sary care, these plants can be the ultimate summertime conversation pieces. New sets of leaves grow each spring. In mild-winter areas, old leaves remain green for more than a year. Elsewhere, leaves die back completely in winter. Flower clusters to 1½ ft. long resemble corncobs, form close to roots. Tiny fruits are red.

Soil must be rich in nutrients and organic material. Feed three

times a year, beginning when new growth starts, to keep leaves maxi-mum size. Give overhead sprin-kling when humidity is low or drying winds occur. Use plants where they can be focal point in summer—beside a pool or domi-nating a bed of low, fine-textured ground cover.

G. manicata. Native to Brazil, Colombia. Leaves carried fairly horizontally. Spinelike hairs on leafstalks and leaf ribs are red. Leaf lobes are flatter than those of *G. tinctoria* and do not have frilled margins.

G. tinctoria (G. chilensis). From Chile. Most common species. Leaf margins are lobed, toothed, somewhat frilled. Leaves are cupped and flaring, held more vertically than those of *G. manicata*.

GYMNOCLADUS dioica
KENTUCKY COFFEE TREE
Fabaceae (Leguminosae)
DECIDUOUS TREE

| 🌿 ZONES 1–3, 7–10, 12–16, 18–21 |
| ☀️ FULL SUN |
| 💧 REGULAR WATER |

Native to eastern U.S. Grows very fast as a sapling but slows once it hits 8–10 ft. Give it plenty of room, since it will ultimately reach 60–100 ft. tall and 45–50 ft. wide. Provides year-round interest. Attractive leaves 1½–3 ft. long, divided into many 1–3-in. leaflets; pinkish when emerging late in spring, deep bluish green by summer. In leaf, the tree casts light shade. Fall color usually not effec-tive, but foliage sometimes turns bright yellow. The relatively few, heavy, contorted branches and stout twigs make bare tree pictur-esque in winter.

Gymnocladus dioica

Gymnocladus dioica

Male and female plants are sep-arate. Narrow, creamy to greenish white flower panicles at ends of branches in spring are up to 1 ft. long (and fragrant) on female trees, to 4 in. long on males. Blos-soms on female trees are followed by flat, 6–10-in.-long, reddish brown pods containing hard black seeds. Pods persist through winter. Early settlers roasted the seeds to make a coffee substitute, hence the tree's common name. Grows best in moist, rich, deep soil but adapts to poor soil, drought, city condi-tions. Can take much heat and cold. Needs minimal pruning.

GYNURA aurantiaca
PURPLE VELVET PLANT
Asteraceae (Compositae)
PERENNIAL

| 🌿 ZONE H2; OR INDOORS |
| 🔆 LIGHT SHADE; BRIGHT INDIRECT LIGHT |
| 💧 REGULAR WATER |

From East Indies. Grows 2–3 ft. tall and somewhat wider; upright and shrubby in youth, clambering when mature. Grown for its strik-ing foliage and stems, which are covered in velvety purple hairs.

Gynura aurantiaca
'Purple Passion'

Oval, pointed leaves are 6–8 in. long and 2½–4 in. wide, with deeply toothed margins. Yellow to orange, ½-in. flowers have an unpleasant odor; pinch out flower buds as they form. 'Purple

Passion' ('Sarmentosa'), often sold as *G. sarmentosa,* has smaller leaves and a strong climbing or trailing habit; excellent for use in hanging baskets.

Grow in rich, loose, well-drained soil. Needs strong indirect light for best color. Cut back old, woody plants to produce fresh, colorful foliage.

GYPSOPHILA
Caryophyllaceae
ANNUALS AND PERENNIALS

🌿	ZONES VARY BY SPECIES
☼	FULL SUN
💧	MODERATE WATER

Slender-stemmed, much-branched plants are upright or spreading, ranging from 3 in. to 4 ft. tall. Bloom is profuse in summer, covering plants in clusters of tiny single or double flowers in white, pink, or rose. Leaves (sparse when plants are in bloom) are typically blue green. Use for airy look in borders and bouquets, for contrast with large-flowered, coarse-textured plants. Dwarf kinds are ideal for rock gardens, for trailing from pockets in walls or over tops of dry rock walls.

Gypsophila repens

Add lime to strongly acid soils before planting. Perennial kinds are not always easy to transplant (especially *G. paniculata,* which has deep, carrotlike roots). If possible, do not disturb them often. Protect roots from gophers; protect tender new growth from snails and slugs. To encourage repeat bloom on perennial sorts, cut back flowering stems before seed clusters form.

G. cerastioides. Perennial. Zones 2–10, 14–21. Native to the Himalayas. Gray foliage forms a mat to 3 in. high and twice as broad; clustered flowers vary from pink-veined white to pure pink. Use in rock garden, between stepping-stones.

G. elegans. Annual. Zones 1–24. Native to Asia Minor, Caucasus, southern Ukraine. Upright grower to 1½ ft. high and wide. Lance-shaped, rather fleshy leaves to 3 in. long. Profuse single white flowers to ½ in. wide or wider; pink and rose forms are also avail-

able. Plants live only 5 to 6 weeks; for continuous bloom, sow seed in open ground every 3 to 4 weeks from late spring into summer. Excellent cut flower.

G. paniculata. BABY'S BREATH. Perennial. Zones A2, A3; 1–10, 14–16, 18–21; H1. Native to central Asia, central and eastern Europe. This is the classic filler in bouquets. To 3 ft. or taller and as broad. Slender, sharp-pointed leaves 2½–4 in. long. Single white flowers about $\frac{1}{16}$ in. across, hundreds in a spray. 'Bristol Fairy' is an improved, more billowy form to 4 ft. high, covered with double blossoms ¼ in. wide. Florists' favorite is 'Perfecta', which bears even larger flowers (to about ½ in. wide). These dwarf varieties have double flowers: 'Compacta Plena' (1½ ft. high, with white flowers), 'Pink Fairy' (1½ ft. high, with pink blooms), and 'Viette's Dwarf' (12–15 in. high, with pink flowers).

G. repens. Perennial. Zones 1–11, 14–16, 18–21. Alpine native 6–9 in. high, with trailing stems 1½ ft. long. Leaves narrow, less than 1 in. long. Clusters of small white or pink flowers. To propagate, take cuttings in midsummer. Varieties include 'Alba' (white) and 'Rosea' (pink).

H

HABRANTHUS
Amaryllidaceae
PERENNIALS FROM BULBS

🌿	ZONES 8, 9, 12–24
☼ ☼	FULL SUN OR LIGHT SHADE
💧	REGULAR WATER DURING GROWTH AND BLOOM

Native from Texas to Argentina, where they sprout and flower almost immediately after ground has been moistened by summer rainfall. Grassy foliage and trumpet-shaped to funnel-shaped blossoms similar to those of fairy lily (*Zephyranthes*), a close relative. Usually one blossom per stem.

Plant in spring, in well-drained soil; set bulbs with tops at soil level and space 3 in. apart. If you live in a frost-free climate and can withhold moisture for about a month after flowering is over, you may get another bloom cycle in fall. Use in rock gardens or naturalize. Plantings don't need dividing for many years. Where soil freezes, grow in pots.

H. robustus. Flowers—sometimes two to a stem—usually bloom before leaves emerge. Light pink, 3-in. blossoms with green throats and deeper pink veining are carried on 9-in. stems.

Habranthus robustus

H. tubispathus (H. andersonii). Flowers 1½ in. long, yellow veined in red on exterior of petals. Stems and leaves about 6 in. high. 'Cupreus' is coppery orange. A bright yellow form on slightly taller stems, known in Texas as copper lily, is probably a naturally occurring variety.

HACKBERRY. See **CELTIS**

HAEMANTHUS katherinae. See **SCADOXUS multiflorus katherinae**

HAIR GRASS. See **DESCHAMPSIA**

HAKEA
Proteaceae
EVERGREEN SHRUBS

🌿	ZONES 9, 12–17, 19–24
☼	FULL SUN
💧	NO IRRIGATION NEEDED

Native to Australia. Especially good for seacoast. Tougher than many other Proteaceae family

members; adapt to a wide variety of soil types (including poor soils). Fertilizer is usually not needed; if you do apply it, make sure it is low in phosphorus.

In addition to the species described below, other hakeas are offered from time to time by experimentally minded nurseries. Remarkably diverse in foliage and flower, all are high-quality shrubs for difficult sites.

H. laurina. SEA URCHIN, PINCUSHION TREE. Dense, rounded habit to 10–25 ft. high and 9–30 ft. wide; often trained as single-trunked tree. Narrow, gray-green, 6-in.-long leaves are often red margined. Showy flower clusters look like round crimson pincushions stuck with golden pins. Blooms in winter, sometimes in late fall. Good small patio tree.

Hakea laurina

H. suaveolens. SWEET HAKEA. Dense, broad, upright plant to 10–20 ft. tall and wide. Stiff, dark green, 4-in. leaves, branched into stiff, needlelike, stickery segments. Small, fragrant white flowers in dense, fluffy clusters, fall and winter. Useful, fast-growing barrier plant, background, or screen. Good with conifers. Can be pruned into tree form.

H. victoria. ROYAL HAKEA. Erect, narrow plant to 6–15 ft. high and 5–9 ft. wide. Leathery leaves to 8 in. long and 5 in. wide, flat or slightly cupped, stemless, toothed, deep green beautifully netted with yellow and variegated with cream and orange. Flowers insignificant. Cut foliage dries well, lasts well in arrangements.

HAKONECHLOA
macra
JAPANESE FOREST GRASS
Poaceae (Gramineae)
PERENNIAL GRASS

🌡 ZONES 2B–9, 14–24

☼ ◐ ● FULL SUN IN COOLER
CLIMATES ONLY

💧 REGULAR WATER

Clumps of gracefully arching leaves characterize this choice grass from Japan. To 1–3 ft. tall, somewhat wider. Spreads slowly by underground runners; never invasive. Tolerates full sun in fog belt or cool northwestern gardens. Prefers rich, moist, well-drained soil. Choice for shade garden, cool rock garden, containers. All-green leaves of species turn coppery orange in fall. Colored-leaf selections are more widely grown.

Hakonechloa macra
'Aureola'

'Albostriata' ('Albovariegata'). To 3 ft. high. Green leaves with longitudinal white stripes.

'All Gold'. As the name implies, leaves of this vigorous selection are entirely golden yellow. Similar in size to 'Aureola' but more upright.

'Aureola'. Most widely grown variety. To 14 in. high. Green leaves have longitudinal yellow stripes. In dense shade, the color turns to chartreuse; in full sun in cool climates, it may become paler, turning to creamy yellow. Foliage is sometimes suffused with pink in cool fall weather.

HALESIA
Styracaceae
DECIDUOUS TREES

🌡 ZONES 2B–9, 14–21

◐ PARTIAL SHADE

💧 REGULAR WATER

Elegant flowering trees native to southeastern U.S.; put on best floral show in cold-winter areas. Bell-shaped white flowers bloom in spring, usually just as leaves begin to appear. Because blossoms are pendent, they show off best when you can look up into tree. Leaves turn yellow in fall. Brown, winged

fruits hang on almost all winter—or even into spring or summer. Plants grow best in cool, deep, humus-rich soil. Attractive in woodland gardens, with rhododendrons and azaleas planted beneath.

H. carolina (H. tetraptera). SNOWDROP TREE, SILVER BELL. To 30–40 ft. tall, with 20–35-ft. spread. Clusters of ½–¾-in. bells. Oval, finely toothed, 2–5-in.-long leaves. Fruit has four wings. Train plant to single trunk when young or it will grow as large shrub. 'Wedding Bells', to about 15 ft. tall and wide, has larger flowers.

Halesia carolina

H. diptera. To 20–30 ft. tall and as wide, often with multiple trunks. Deeply lobed bells are ½–¾ in. long; appear 2 to 3 weeks later than those of other species. Leaves and fruits are similar in size to those of *H. carolina*, though fruits have two rather than four wings. Larger and more profuse blooms appear on *H. d. magniflora.*

H. monticola. MOUNTAIN SILVER BELL. Similar to *H. carolina* but taller (eventually to 60–80 ft.), with bigger leaves (3–6 in. long) and flowers (1 in.). Four-winged fruits are also somewhat larger. 'Arnold Pink' has rosy pink blooms; those of 'Rosea' are pale pink.

× HALIMIOCISTUS
Cistaceae
EVERGREEN SHRUBS

🌡 ZONES 4–24

☼ FULL SUN

💧💧 LITTLE OR NO WATER TO
MODERATE WATER

These mound-forming, densely foliaged hybrids between *Halimium* and *Cistus salviifolius* combine the good qualities of both

× Halimiocistus sahucii

parents, offering abundant bloom and high tolerance for sun and heat. They need excellent drainage and cannot live in wet soil; water from lawn sprinklers can kill them. Use in rock gardens, on dry banks, spilling over a wall. Or plant on sunny side of the house under eaves where rains seldom reach.

× H. sahucii. To 1–2 ft. high, 3–4 ft. wide, with narrow dark green leaves to 1½ in. long. Profuse, 1½-in. white flowers with central puff of yellow stamens in spring.

× H. wintonensis. To 2 ft. high, 4–5 ft. wide, with furry gray-green leaves to 2 in. long. Sheets of 2-in. white flowers with pronounced dark reddish purple central blotch in spring and early summer.

HALIMIUM
Cistaceae
EVERGREEN SHRUBS

🌡 ZONES 5–9, 12–24

☼ FULL SUN

💧 LITTLE WATER

From southwestern Europe. Closely related to sunrose (*Helianthemum*) and sometimes sold under that name; cultural requirements and uses are the same. Halimiums have gray-green, ½–1½-in.-long leaves, bear loose clusters of flowers in spring.

Halimium lasianthum

H. lasianthum. To 3 ft. tall and 5 ft. wide, with ¼-in.-wide leaves. Flowers are 1½ in. across, bright yellow with brownish purple blotch near petal bases.

H. ocymoides. To 2 ft. tall, 3 ft. wide. Leaves slightly narrower than those of *H. lasianthum.* Inch-wide flowers are bright yellow with black-and-purple blotch at base of petals.

H. umbellatum. To 1½ ft. high and 2 ft. wide, with very slender leaves resembling those of rosemary. White, ¾-in.-wide flowers with yellow blotch at petal bases.

HAMAMELIS
WITCH HAZEL
Hamamelidaceae
DECIDUOUS SHRUBS OR TREES

🌡 ZONES VARY BY SPECIES

☼ ◐ FULL SUN OR PARTIAL SHADE

💧 REGULAR WATER

Medium-size to large shrubs, sometimes treelike, usually with spreading habit and angular or zigzag branches. Valued for bright fall foliage and nodding clusters of interesting yellow to red blooms that typically appear in winter. Flowers consist of many narrow, crumpled petals and are said to resemble shredded coconut, mop heads, or spiders. Most witch hazels are fragrant and bloom over a long period. They appreciate rich, organic soil. Prune only to guide growth, remove poorly placed branches and suckers, or obtain flowering stems for scented winter bouquets.

H. × intermedia. Zones 3–7, 15–17. Group of winter-blooming hybrids between *H. mollis* and *H. japonica*. Big shrubs (12–15 ft. high and wide). Often grafted; remove any growth originating from below graft. The following varieties are among the best.

'Allgold'. Deep yellow flowers with red sepals; yellow fall foliage.

'Arnold Promise'. Bright yellow flowers. Yellow, orange, and red fall foliage.

'Carmine Red'. Light red flowers; red-orange fall foliage.

'Diane'. Dark red flowers aging to orange red. Red-purple fall foliage.

'Hiltingbury'. Coppery red flowers; orange-yellow fall color.

'Jelena' ('Copper Beauty', 'Orange Beauty'). Coppery orange flowers. Fall foliage in orange, red, and scarlet.

'Magic Fire' ('Fire Charm', 'Feuerzauber'). Flowers in

H

Hamamelis mollis

coppery orange blended with red. Fiery red fall foliage.

'Moonlight'. Pale yellow blooms marked red at base; yellow fall foliage.

'Pallida'. Luminous light yellow blossoms; yellow fall foliage.

'Primavera'. Broad-petaled light yellow flowers. Yellow-orange autumn foliage.

'Ruby Glow'. Coppery red flowers; bright red fall foliage.

'Sunburst'. Heavy clusters of radiant yellow, unscented flowers. Yellow fall foliage.

'Westerstede'. Unshaded yellow-orange flowers. Orange-red fall foliage.

H. japonica. JAPANESE WITCH HAZEL. Zones 2b–7, 15–17. From Japan. Much like *H.× intermedia,* though perhaps somewhat more erect and treelike (to 12–20 ft. tall and broad). Small, lightly scented yellow flowers in late winter or earliest spring. Chief draw is fall foliage in shades of red, purple, and yellow. *H. j. flavopurpurascens* has yellow-orange flowers that are purple at the base, and reddish yellow fall foliage. *H. j.* 'Arborea' grows 20–25 ft. tall, has yellow blossoms and yellow autumn leaves.

H. mollis. CHINESE WITCH HAZEL. Zones 2b–7, 15–17. From China. Moderately slow-growing shrub to 8–10 ft. tall and wide, or small tree that may reach 30 ft. Roundish, 3½–6-in.-long leaves are dark green and rough above, gray and felted beneath, turning good pure yellow in fall. Sweetly fragrant, 1½-in.-wide, rich golden yellow flowers with red-brown sepals bloom on bare stems in

winter. Flowering branches are excellent for cutting. Selections include 'Coombe Wood', a very heavy bloomer with especially fine fragrance; 'Early Bright', earliest to bloom; and 'Goldcrest', with larger flowers that appear later than those of the others.

H. vernalis. OZARK WITCH HAZEL. Zones 2–7, 15–17. From central and southern U.S. Multistemmed, suckering shrub to 6–10 ft. tall, spreading even wider. Rather small, fragrant yellow to orange flowers from winter to spring. Medium to dark green, 2–5-in.-long leaves turn bright yellow in fall and hold for several weeks in favorable weather. 'Lombart's Weeping' is a 5–6-ft. tree with somewhat drooping branches. 'Sandra' bears yellow spring flowers of no great distinction, but it has reddish purple new growth and brilliant red fall foliage.

H. virginiana. COMMON WITCH HAZEL. Zones 1–9, 14–16, 18–21. Native to eastern North America. Sometimes reaches 25 ft. tall but usually grows 10–15 ft. high and wide. Open, spreading, rather straggling habit. Moderately slow growing. Bark is the source of the liniment witch hazel. Roundish leaves similar to those of *H. mollis* but not gray and felted beneath; turn yellow to orange in fall. Small, fragrant golden yellow blossoms appear in fall but tend to be lost in colored foliage.

HAMELIA patens

SCARLET BUSH
Rubiaceae
EVERGREEN OR DECIDUOUS
SHRUB OR TREE

⚹ ZONES 13, 23, 24; H1, H2
☼ FULL SUN
●●● REGULAR TO AMPLE WATER

Relative of gardenia and coffee; native from southern Florida to South America. Grows 6–10 ft. tall (possibly much taller) and 5–6 ft. wide. Whorls of 6-in., oval gray-green leaves; red leafstalks and flower stems. Clusters of ¾-in., tubular, orange to bright red flowers form at branch tips all summer long. Thanks to flower shape and color, the plant is also known by the names "firecracker shrub" and "fire bush." Flowers are followed by small dark red, purple, or black fruits that are much relished by birds. Give lots of water while in active growth, regular

Hamelia patens

water at other times. Needs good drainage. Tolerant of salt and heat. Evergreen in Zones 24 and H1; loses its leaves in colder areas. In Zone 13, it will die to the ground without overhead shelter or other cold protection.

HAPU'U.
See **CIBOTIUM glaucum**

HARDENBERGIA

LILAC VINE
Fabaceae (Leguminosae)
EVERGREEN SHRUBBY VINES

⚹ ZONES VARY BY SPECIES
☼ ◑ PARTIAL SHADE IN HOTTEST CLIMATES
● MODERATE WATER

Native to Australia. Grow at moderate rate to 10 ft., climbing by twining stems. Attractive flowers shaped like sweet peas bloom from late winter to early spring, carried in clusters of several to many. Need light, well-drained soil. Provide support for climbing and cut back after bloom to prevent tangling. Good against trellises in large containers (use soil mix rich in organic matter). Subject to spider mites, nematodes; otherwise fairly free of pests and diseases.

Hardenbergia comptoniana

H. comptoniana. Zones 15–24. Light, delicate foliage pattern; leaves divided into three to five dark green, narrow, 2–3-in.-long leaflets. Flowers are violet-blue, ½-in.-long, and held in long, narrow clusters. Where temperatures drop below 24°F/–4°C, plant beneath overhang.

H. violacea (H. monophylla). Zones 8–24. Coarser textured than *H. comptoniana;* leaves usually undivided, 2–4 in. long. Flowers are lilac or violet to rose or white. 'Happy Wanderer' is a tough, vigorous selection with pinkish purple blooms; 'Icicle' has pure white blossoms, 'Rosea' pink ones. 'Mini-Ha-Ha' is a shrubby dwarf form growing 3 ft. tall and wide.

HARDTACK.
See **CERCOCARPUS betuloides**

HARDY RUBBER TREE.
See **EUCOMMIA ulmoides**

HAREBELL.
See **CAMPANULA rotundifolia**

HARE'S FOOT FERN.
See **POLYPODIUM aureum**

HARLEQUIN FLOWER.
See **SPARAXIS tricolor**

HARRY LAUDER'S WALKING STICK. See **CORYLUS avellana 'Contorta'**

HART'S TONGUE FERN.
See **ASPLENIUM scolopendrium**

HAU. See **HIBISCUS tiliaceus**

HAWAIIAN COTTON. See **GOSSYPIUM tomentosum**

HAWAIIAN TREE FERN.
See **CIBOTIUM glaucum**

HAWORTHIA

Liliaceae
SUCCULENT PERENNIALS

⚹ ZONES 15–17, 20–24; OR INDOORS
◑ PARTIAL SHADE; BRIGHT INDIRECT LIGHT
◊ ● LITTLE TO MODERATE WATER

Diminutive, rosette-forming succulents from South Africa. Many types produce offsets to form dense, spreading colonies. Fleshy leaves may be slender and rough textured or pillowlike and smooth; some have small white bumps or ridges. Tiny flowers are held on long, whiplike stems from spring to fall; these may be clipped off as they fade to keep plants tidy.

Haworthias are well suited to containers, and their small size

Haworthia attenuata

and tolerance of low humidity make them good houseplants. In pots or in the ground, provide sandy, fast-draining soil that is allowed to dry between waterings. Protect from frost and hot sun. Acclimate nursery plants to the garden gradually or leaves may sunburn. Numerous species and hybrids make these variable plants popular with collectors.

H. attenuata. ZEBRA PLANT. To 6 in. tall. Rigid, dark green leaves up to 3 in. long are slender and triangular; each leaf is dotted with white bumps on the inner surface and banded with raised white horizontal ridges on the outside. Give just enough sun to make outer leaves blush red orange.

H. coarctata. Tightly stacked rosettes of bronzy green leaves form upright or leaning columns to 6 in. or taller. Tolerates more sun than other species, turning shades of burgundy in brighter conditions.

H. cymbiformis. To 3 in. tall, looking something like a small, chubby artichoke. Wedge-shaped leaves up to 2 in. long have light and dark green markings.

H. fasciata. Similar to *H. attenuata*, but inner leaf surface is smooth.

HAWTHORN. See **CRATAEGUS**

HAZELNUT. See **CORYLUS; FILBERT, HAZELNUT**

HEAL-ALL. See **PRUNELLA**

HEART OF FLAME. See **BROMELIA balansae**

HEATH. See **DABOECIA, ERICA**

HEATHER, SCOTCH. See **CALLUNA vulgaris**

HEATHER WAND. See **BORONIA clavata**

HEAVENLY BAMBOO. See **NANDINA domestica**

HEBE
Scrophulariaceae
EVERGREEN SHRUBS

⚟ ZONES 14–24, EXCEPT AS NOTED

☼ ◑ PARTIAL SHADE IN HOTTEST CLIMATES

💧 REGULAR WATER

New Zealand natives closely related to *Veronica* and occasionally still sold under that name. Most types are grown mainly for attractive form and foliage (neat pairs of opposite leaves); some give good flower display in summer, and a few produce a scattering of bloom throughout the year. Most are fast growing. All do best in cool-summer, mild-winter climates—in the San Francisco area, for example. Dry summer heat and winter frosts shorten their lives. Larger-leafed types are more susceptible to winter damage. Very prone to root rot if drainage is anything less than excellent. Take seacoast conditions. Prune after bloom, shortening stems that have flowered by about half to keep plants compact and bushy. Rejuvenate ragged plants by cutting back severely; they'll resprout easily from old, leafless wood.

H. 'Amy'. Zones 5, 6, 14–24. To 5 ft. high and wide, with 2–3-in.-long, dark green leaves tinged purple on top, purplish red beneath. Foliage is dark bronzy purple when new and takes on that color in winter as well. Short, dense spikes of reddish purple flowers. Summer is the main bloom season.

H. × andersonii. Mounding, compact plant to 5–6 ft. tall and wide. Fleshy deep green leaves to 4 in. long. Flowers are white at base, violet at tip, carried in 2–4 in. spikes. 'Variegata' has white-bordered leaves.

H. 'Autumn Glory'. Zones 5, 6, 14–24. Compact grower to 2 ft. high and wide. Dark green leaves are 1½ in. long. Many 2-in., deep lavender-blue flower spikes in late summer, fall.

H. buxifolia (H. odora). BOXLEAF HEBE. Rounded and symmetrical, to an eventual 5 ft. high and wide; easily shaped into 3-ft. hedge. Deep green, ⅓-in.-long

Hebe 'Autumn Glory'

leaves densely cover branches. Small white flowers in dense clusters.

H. carnosula. To 1 ft. high and 2–3 ft. wide, thickly foliaged in ½-in., rounded grayish green leaves. Small white flowers in dense spikes.

H. 'Coed'. Compact shrub to 3 ft. high and wide. Reddish stems densely clothed with 1½-in. dark green leaves. Profuse spikes of small pinkish purple flowers.

H. elliptica. Much-branched shrub 5–6 ft. high. Medium green leaves 1½ in. long. Clusters of fragrant bluish flowers.

H. glaucophylla. Zones 5–7, 14–24. Compact, rounded, about 2 ft. high and wide. Half-inch-long, roundish blue-green leaves. White flowers in short, dense clusters. Good low foundation plant or tidy divider between lawn and walkway.

H. 'Great Orme'. Zones 5–7, 14–24. Rounded form to 4 ft. high and wide, with narrow, 2-in.-long, medium green leaves. Deep pink, 3-in.-long flower spikes fade to white at base.

H. imperialis. See H. speciosa 'Imperialis'

H. 'Lake' ('Veronica Lake'). Dense growth to 3 ft. high and wide, with 1½-in. dark green leaves and abundant short spikes of lilac flowers.

H. 'Patty's Purple'. Dense, to 3 ft. high and wide. Wine red stems; tiny dark green leaves. Purple flowers on slender spikes. Use in masses, flower borders. Can be sheared.

Hebe 'Autumn Glory'

H. pinguifolia. Zones 5–7, 14–17, 22–24. To 3 ft. tall and wide. Blue-gray leaves (sometimes with a pinkish edge) are 1½-in.-long ovals, very closely set or even overlapping. White flowers are tiny

but profuse. 'Pagei' is a prostrate form that can grow 9 in. high and 4 ft. across in 5 years; it is easily increased by cutting off and planting branches that have rooted. 'Sutherlandii' grows 1½ ft. tall and 3 ft. wide, with beautiful gray foliage.

Hebe glaucophylla

H. 'Red Edge' (H. albicans 'Red Edge'). Zones 5–7, 14–24. Low and rounded, to 1½–2 ft. high and 2–3 ft. wide. Blue-gray leaves to 1 in. long have a distinctive red edge, especially on new growth or in cold weather. Pale lilac flowers are held in 2-in. spikes.

H. speciosa. SHOWY HEBE. Zones 14–24; H1. Dense shrub to 5 ft. high, 4 ft. wide. Stout stems bear glossy dark green, 2–4-in.-long leaves. Reddish purple flowers held in 3–4-in. spikes. 'Imperialis' has reddish foliage, magenta flowers.

H. 'Wiri Blush'. Zones 5–7, 14–24. Rounded form to 3 ft. high and 4 ft. wide, with narrow, 2-in.-long, shiny dark green leaves. Bright pink, 3-in.-long spikes of flowers.

H. 'Wiri Dawn'. Zones 5–7, 14–24. Compact growth to about 1 ft. high and 1½–2 ft. wide, with narrow, 1½-in.-long, olive green leaves and short spikes of pale pink flowers that open from rosy pink buds.

HEDERA
IVY
Araliaceae
EVERGREEN VINES

⚟ ZONES VARY BY SPECIES

☼ ◑ SOME SHADE IN HOTTEST CLIMATES

💧💧 MODERATE TO REGULAR WATER

Ivy is appreciated by some gardeners for its ability to cover quickly, reviled by others—particularly in the Pacific Northwest—for its invasive tendencies. Often used as a ground cover because of its horizontal growth habit, it also

H

H

climbs to cover walls, fences, and trellises, attaching itself firmly by aerial rootlets (a factor to consider when planting against surfaces that must be painted). This type of growth occurs during the plant's juvenile stage, which can last up to 10 years; during this stage, the thick, leathery leaves are usually lobed. At maturity, ivies become shrubby, with stiff branches clothed in unlobed leaves, and they begin blooming: domelike clusters of greenish white flowers appear in late summer and are followed by black berries in fall.

English ivy (*H. helix*) and several of its varieties have been placed on noxious-weed lists in some parts of the West because of their ability to crowd out native plants and endanger trees upon which they grow. Whether they creep out of gardens over ground or spread into natural areas by birds that eat the berries, invasive ivies are destructive when left to grow unchecked. They can grow to 90 ft., with stems to 1 ft. in diameter, and can completely cover the trunks of large trees, promoting rot. Once they grow up into the canopy, these ivies can shade out the foliage of deciduous trees and make any type of tree top-heavy and thus more prone to breakage. In areas where ivy is invasive, it is recommended to grow only named varieties and, if possible, to confine the ivy to containers or well-defined garden areas, where its growth can be monitored. Ivy has been widely planted on hillsides in the belief that it will decrease erosion, but studies have shown that slopes covered in single species are actually more prone to slides.

Plant ivy in spring; where winters are not excessively cold, you can also plant in fall. Ivy can be grown from cuttings, but planting from pots is more dependable and gives faster growth. Standard spacing is 1½–2 ft. apart. Amend soil (to depth of 8–12 in. if possible) with organic matter such as ground bark or peat moss. Before planting, thoroughly moisten soil; also make sure transplants' roots are moist and their leaves and stems full of moisture (not wilted). Feed with high-nitrogen fertilizer after planting (for spring-planted ivy) or, for fall-planted ivy, in first spring after planting. Feed again in midsummer. For best growth, continue to feed every year in early spring and midsummer.

Most ivy ground covers should be trimmed around edges two or three times a year (use hedge shears or a sharp spade). Fence and wall plantings also need trimming two or three times a year. When ground cover builds up higher than you want, mow it with rugged rotary power mower or cut it back with hedge shears. Do this in spring so ensuing growth will quickly cover bald look.

Many trees and shrubs can grow compatibly in ivy ground cover, but small, soft, or fragile plants will be smothered. Ivy ground covers can be a haven for slugs and snails and can also harbor rodents, especially if the ivy is never cut back.

H. canariensis (H. algeriensis). ALGERIAN IVY. Zones 5–9, 12–24. Native to Canary Islands, Mediterranean coast of North Africa. Shiny, rich green leaves 5–8 in. wide with three to five shallow lobes. Leaves are more widely spaced along stems than those of *H. helix*. Coarse-looking plant; aggressive grower. 'Variegata' ('Gloire de Marengo') has dark leaves marbled with gray green and irregularly margined in creamy white; it does not take extreme heat.

H. colchica. PERSIAN IVY. Zones 3b–24. Native to Turkey, Caucasus mountains. Oval to heart-shaped leaves are largest among all ivies: 3–7 in. wide, to 10 in. long. 'Dentata' has slightly toothed leaves; 'Dentata Variegata' is marbled with deep green, gray green, and creamy white. 'Sulphur Heart' ('Paddy's Pride') has central gold variegation.

H. helix. ENGLISH IVY. Zones 3–24, H1, except as noted. From Europe. Dull dark green, three- to five-lobed leaves with paler veins are 2–4 in. wide at base and as long.

Many small- and miniature-leafed forms of English ivy are good choices for pots and hanging

Hedera helix 'Gold Heart'

baskets, for training into intricate patterns on walls, and for small-scale ground covers. These varieties are also used to create topiary shapes on wire frames. In general, their leaves are about half as large as those of the species, and some are even smaller. Leaf shapes vary widely: they may be deeply lobed and cleft, ruffle edged, arrow shaped and narrow, or divided into distinct leaflets. 'Baltica', with whitish-veined leaves, is often considered the hardiest variety of English ivy (Zones 2b–24); its leaves take on purplish tones in winter. 'Hahn's Self Branching' is a dense-branching form with light green leaves that does best in partial shade. 'Conglomerata' is a slow-growing dwarf; 'Minima' has especially small leaves (½ to 1 in. wide). Other varieties include 'Buttercup', 'California', 'Fluffy Ruffles', 'Glacier', 'Gold Dust', 'Gold Heart', 'Heart', 'Needlepoint', 'Ripple', 'Shamrock', 'Silverdust', and 'Star'.

HEDGEHOG CACTUS. See **ECHINOCEREUS**

HEDYCHIUM

GINGER LILY
Zingiberaceae
PERENNIALS

| ZONES 8, 9, 14–17, 19–24; H1, H2 |
| LIGHT SHADE |
| AMPLE WATER |

Native to tropical Asia, India, Himalayas. Leaves grow in a single plane along stems rising from stout rhizomes. Foliage is especially handsome in tropical conditions, as in Hawaii. Dense spikes of richly fragrant flowers are produced in late summer or early autumn.

Does best in rich soil high in organic matter. To encourage fresh new growth, remove old stems after flowers fade. Plants spread indefinitely from rhizomes and in time can outgrow even generous garden spaces. Frost can kill them to ground, but new stalks appear in early spring. Good near swimming pools, at the beach, in shade gardens, in big borders. Useful in large containers but will not grow as tall there as in open ground. Potted plants can be moved out of sight when unattractive.

H. coccineum. RED GINGER LILY, SCARLET GINGER LILY. To 6–9 ft. tall, with leaves to 20 in. long and 2 in. wide. Particularly showy, bearing orange-scarlet flowers with prominent red stamens on blossom spikes to 10 in. long. Flowers of cold-hardy 'Tara' are tangerine.

H. coronarium. WHITE GINGER, BUTTERFLY LILY, GARLAND FLOWER. To 3–7 ft. high, with leaves 8–24 in. long and 2–5 in. wide. White flowers in 6–12-in.-long clusters are especially fragrant; good cut flowers. Naturalized in Hawaii, where the flowers are used in leis. In California, it looks best where humidity is moderate to high (in coastal areas, for example).

H. densiflorum. To 9 ft. or taller, with leaves to 14 in. long and 4 in. wide. Orange-yellow flowers are produced in dense spikes to 8 in. long.

H. flavescens. YELLOW GINGER. To 6 ft. or taller, with oblong leaves 4–22 in. long and 1–4 in. wide. Heavily perfumed yellow flowers to 3 in. across are produced in oval heads with many broad, overlapping green bracts. Naturalized in Hawaii.

H. flavum. Like *H. flavescens* but a little shorter (to about 5 ft.) and with yellow or orange flowers in slightly smaller heads.

Hedychium gardnerianum

H. gardnerianum. KAHILI GINGER. Plant grows to 8 ft. high, with leaves 8–18 in. long, 4–6 in. wide. Pure yellow flowers with red stamens are borne in 1½-ft.-long

Hedera helix

pikes. Naturalized in Hawaii and onsidered a pest on the Big sland.

H. greenei. To 5 ft. tall. Leaves 8–10 in. long, 2 in. wide; orange-ed flowers in 5-in. spikes.

H. spicatum acuminatum. Grows to 3 ft. high. Leaves reach 6 in. long and 4 in. wide, have downy undersides. Bears creamy white flowers in loose spikes to 8 in. long.

HEDYSCEPE canterburyana

Arecaceae (Palmae)
PALM

☑	ZONES 17, 23, 24; H1, H2
☼ ◐	FULL SUN OR LIGHT SHADE
💧	REGULAR WATER

Hedyscepe canterburyana

From Lord Howe Island in the South Pacific. Related to *Archon-tophoenix* but smaller, broader, and lower growing, with wider leaf segments and more arching, lighter green feather-type leaves. To 30 ft. tall, with fronds spreading 15 ft. wide. Hardy to 30°F/−1°C.

HELENIUM

SNEEZEWEED
Asteraceae (Compositae)
PERENNIALS

☑	ZONES VARY BY SPECIES
☼	FULL SUN
💧	REGULAR WATER, EXCEPT AS NOTED

Rather coarse looking, but valuable for profuse late summer and autumn bloom. Numerous leafy stems yield great sheaves of daisy-like, typically brown-centered blossoms with yellow, orange, red, or coppery rays. In many sneeze-weeds, the ray flowers are reflexed. Trim off faded blossoms to encourage long bloom. Perform best in hot-summer areas. Can survive an occasional missed irrigation but look better with regular moisture. Give good drainage. Need little fertilizer. Taller kinds require staking and are best in the back of borders. All need division and replanting every few years.

Helenium autumnale

H. autumnale. Zones 1–24. Native to much of North America. To 5 ft. tall and 1½ ft. wide. Yellow, 2-in.-wide flowers with reflexed rays. Most plants sold under this name are really hybrids; see *H.* hybrids.

H. bigelovii. Zones 1–10, 14–24. From California, Oregon. To 2–3 ft. tall, 1 ft. wide. Yellow blossoms to 2½ in. across have reflexed rays. 'Tip Top' is compact and free flowering.

H. hybrids. Zones 1–24. Most types of sneezeweeds sold are hybrids—even if often sold as *H. autumnale.* Flowers are 2–3 in. across, come in shades of yellow, orange, red, rust, copper, and blends of these colors. Tall types (4–5 ft. high, 2 ft. wide) include 'Baudirektor Linne', brownish red with a brown center; 'Butterpat', light yellow with a deeper yellow center; 'Mardi Gras', yellow splashed with red and orange, and a brown center; and 'Waldtraut', with coppery brown rays around a dark central disk. Compact varieties (about 3 ft. high, 1½ ft. wide) include 'Coppelia', copper orange with a brown disk; 'Crimson Beauty', dusky deep red with a brown disk; 'Moerheim Beauty', coppery red with a brown center; 'Rubinzwerg', rusty red with a yellow-and-brown center; and 'Wyndley', butter yellow with a yellow-brown central disk.

HELIANTHEMUM nummularium

SUNROSE
Cistaceae
EVERGREEN SHRUB

☑	ZONES 2B–9, 14–24
☼	FULL SUN
💧	MODERATE WATER

Commonly sold under this name are a number of forms of this species, as well as hybrids between it and other species; all are native to Europe and Asia Minor. All grow 6–8 in. high and spread to 3 ft. Leaves are ½–1 in. long; they may be gray on both surfaces, or glossy green above and fuzzy gray beneath. Midspring to early summer display of 1-in.-wide, single or double flowers in bright or pastel colors—flame red, apricot, orange, yellow, pink, rose, peach, salmon, or white. Each blossom lasts only a day, but new buds continue to open. Shear plants back after flowering to neaten appearance and encourage repeat bloom.

Specialists offer many named varieties; especially noteworthy are: 'Annabel', with double pink blooms; 'Cheviot', with peachy flowers above gray foliage; 'Raspberry Ripple', with deep pink flowers streaked and tipped with white; 'Wisley Pink' ('Rhodanthe Carneum'), with large pink flowers; and 'Wisley Primrose' with gray foliage and light lemon yellow flowers.

Helianthemum nummularium

Let sunroses tumble over rocks, set them in niches in dry rock walls, or grow them in planters on a sunny patio. Use them at seashore or in rock gardens; let them ramble over gentle slopes. If used as ground cover, set out 2–3 ft. apart. In cold-winter areas, lightly cover plants with evergreen boughs to keep foliage from dehydrating. Plants will be hardier if soil is not too rich and is kept on the dry side (good drainage is essential). The object is to encourage hard, nonsucculent growth.

HELIANTHUS

SUNFLOWER
Asteraceae (Compositae)
ANNUALS AND PERENNIALS

☑	ZONES VARY BY SPECIES
☼	FULL SUN
💧💧	REGULAR TO AMPLE WATER, EXCEPT AS NOTED

Coarse, sturdy plants with bold blooms. Most are prime subjects for cut flowers. Plants are tough and widely adapted. Perennial kinds spread rapidly, may become invasive. Tall kinds are not for tidy gardens; may need staking. All bloom in summer and fall.

Helianthus annuus

H. annuus. COMMON SUNFLOWER. Annual. All zones. The wild ancestor of today's familiar sunflowers is a coarse, hairy plant with 2–3-in.-wide flowers, native to much of the central U.S. and southward to Central America. It is the state flower of Kansas and the only plant native to the lower 48 states to have become an important agricultural commodity. It has been bred to produce giant plants as well as a host of smaller (but still significant) varieties for garden decoration and cut flowers.

Best known among the giant forms are 'Mammoth Russian' and 'Russian Giant'. They grow 10 ft. (possibly 15 ft.) tall and 2 ft. wide and typically produce a single huge head (sometimes more than a foot across) consisting of a circle of short yellow rays with a brown central cushion of seeds. Newer variety 'Kong' is as large as the older varieties. 'Sunspot' carries flower heads 10 in. wide on 2-ft.-high plants. For children, annual

H

sunflowers are easy to grow and bring a sense of great accomplishment. Sow seeds in spring where plants are to grow. Large-flowered kinds need rich, moist soil. People eat the roasted seeds; birds enjoy the raw ones in fall and winter.

Sunflowers for cutting come on compact, branching plants and bear 4–8-in.-wide blooms in a rich variety of colors. They fall into two basic categories: pollen-bearing types and pollenless ones. Kinds with pollen include 'Del Sol', early-blooming yellow, 5 ft. tall; 'Indian Blanket', red with yellow tips, 4–5 ft.; 'Italian White', creamy yellow to near white, 5 ft.; 'Lemon Eclair', light yellow, 4–6 ft.; 'Moonshadow', pale yellow to cream, 4 ft.; Parasol Mix, lemon, orange, red, and bicolor, to 4–5 ft.; and 'Soraya', orange, with sturdy stem, to 6 ft. 'Teddy Bear', only 1½ ft. high, has fully double, 6-in.-wide flowers that look like pompons.

Kinds without pollen, classified as *H. × hybridus*, have the advantage of not shedding on tabletops. They include Large Flowered Mix, yellow, red, and bronze, 6–10 ft. tall; 'Bright Bandolier', yellow-and-mahogany bicolor, 5–7 ft.; 'Cinnamon Sun', cinnamon bronze, 4–7 ft.; 'Prado Red', deep garnet, 3½–4 ft.; 'Valentine', light yellow, 4–5 ft.; and 'Velvet Queen', combination of bronze, burgundy, chestnut red, and mahogany, 6–8 ft.

H. 'Lemon Queen'. Perennial. Zones 2–24. Selected from a hybrid of two species native to the U.S. Fast growth to 6–8 ft. tall and 3–4 ft. wide, with narrow, 5-in.-long leaves. Produces many 2-in.-wide, semidouble, pale yellow flowers with a dark brown center. Use at back of casual border or in combination with large ornamental grasses. Takes moist or dry soil. Does not require staking, provided soil is not too rich and plants are not overfertilized.

H. maximilianii. Perennial. Zones 1–24. From central and southwestern U.S. Forms a clump 3 ft. wide, with 10-ft.-tall stems clothed in narrow, 8–10-in.-long leaves and topped by a narrow spire of 3-in. yellow flowers. Often seen peering over adobe walls in the Southwest.

H. × multiflorus. Perennial. Zones 1–24. To 5 ft. tall and 3 ft. wide, with thin, tooth-edged, 3–8-in.-long leaves and many yellow, 3-in., yellow-centered blossoms. Excellent for cutting. 'Loddon Gold' ('Flore Pleno') is double flowered. 'Capenoch Star' single, but disk flowers are quilled (rolled into long, slender tubes), giving a pincushion effect.

H. salicifolius (H. orgyalis). Perennial. Zones 1–24. Native to central U.S. To 6–8 ft. tall, 3 ft. wide, with narrow, gracefully drooping leaves to 8 in. long. Stems are topped by sheaves of 2-in. yellow flowers with purplish brown centers.

H. tuberosus. JERUSALEM ARTICHOKE. Perennial. Zones 2–24. From eastern and central North America. To 6–7 ft. tall, 3 ft. wide; oval leaves to 8 in. long. Bright yellow flowers to 4 in. across. Grown as commercial crop; tubers are edible, sold in markets as "sunchokes." Harvest tubers every year; save two or three for replanting. Plant can become a pest. If controlled, makes a good, quick temporary screen or hedge.

Helianthus tuberosus

HELICHRYSUM
Asteraceae (Compositae)
ANNUALS AND PERENNIALS

🖉 ZONES VARY BY SPECIES
☀ FULL SUN
💧 MODERATE WATER

Best known is *H. bracteatum*, the annual strawflower used in fresh and dried arrangements. Others, though less familiar, are choice plants for landscape use.

H. bracteatum. STRAWFLOWER. Annual. All zones. From Australia. To 2–3 ft. tall, 1 ft. wide, with straplike, 2–5-in.-long, medium green leaves. Blooms from summer until frost, bearing many papery, 2½-in. flowers that look like prickly pompons. Colors include yellow, orange, red, pink, and white. Known as "everlasting" because its blossoms last indefinitely when dried. Sow in place in late spring or earliest summer (at same time as zinnias). Dwarf forms are also available.

For shrubby perennial forms (such as 'Cockatoo', 'Dargan Hill Monarch', and 'Diamond Head') previously included with annual

Helichrysum petiolare
'Limelight'

strawflower, see *Bracteantha bracteata.*

H. italicum (H. angustifolium). CURRY PLANT. Perennial. Zones 13–24. From southern Europe. To 2 ft. high and wide, with woody base and crowded, narrow, nearly white leaves to 1½ in. long. Leaves emit a strong fragrance of curry powder when bruised or pinched. Not used in curry, but a few can add a pleasant aroma to a salad or meat dish. Bright yellow, ½-in. flowers in clusters 2 in. across appear from midsummer to autumn.

H. petiolare. LICORICE PLANT. Perennial in Zones 16, 17, 22–24; annual elsewhere. From South Africa. To 1½–3 ft. high, with trailing stems to 4 ft. White, woolly, inch-long leaves; insignificant flowers. A licorice aroma is sometimes noticeable—in hot, still weather, for example, or when leaves are dry. 'Limelight' has luminous light chartreuse leaves; 'Licorice Splash' has variegated yellow-green foliage; 'Variegatum' has leaves with white markings. All are useful for their trailing branches, which thread through mixed plantings or mingle with other plants in large pots, hanging baskets. In parts of coastal Northern California, licorice plant has escaped cultivation to become an invasive pest; to reduce seed production, shear off blooms when they begin to fade. For the so-called dwarf form, see *Plecostachys serpyllifolia.*

HELICONIA
LOBSTER-CLAW,
FALSE BIRD-OF-PARADISE
Heliconiaceae
PERENNIALS

🖉 ZONES 24; H1, H2; EXCEPT AS NOTED; OR GROW IN POTS
☀ ◑ FULL SUN OR LIGHT SHADE
💧 AMPLE WATER

More than 100 species of tropical American plants grown for big, showy, waxy flower clusters that

consist of brightly colored bracts; small true flowers peep out from the bracts. Clusters may be erect or drooping, from a few inches to several feet in length; used in spectacular tropical flower arrangements. In growth habit, plants resemble banana or canna. Oblong to spoon-shaped evergreen leaves are large (sometimes very large), and plants form sizable clumps that keep increasing with age. Best with rich soil, heavy feeding, and plenty of water—all of which will keep clump expanding. Cut away stems that have flowered to make room for new growth. In areas with frosts, grow plants in tubs and shelter from winter cold. Potted plants can bloom anytime; those in the ground flower in spring and summer.

H. angusta. To 4–10 ft. tall, with leaves to 3 ft. long. Erect flower clusters to 2½ ft. long. Yellow or orange to vermilion or scarlet bracts; white or yellow-tipped green flowers.

Heliconia angusta

H. bihai (H. humilis). To 6–15 ft. tall, with 2–6-ft.-long leaves. Erect blossom clusters 1½–3½ ft. long. Reddish orange bracts with green margins; white to pale green flowers.

H. brasiliensis (H. farinosa). To 3–5 ft. tall, with 2½-ft. leaves. Erect clusters of red bracts enfold white or red flowers.

H. caribaea. WILD PLANTAIN. To 6–15 ft. tall, with 5-ft.-long leaves and erect flower clusters to 1½ ft. Bracts are red or yellow, often marked with contrasting colors; flowers are white with green tips.

H. latispatha. Can reach 10 ft. tall, with leaves to 5 ft. long. Erect flower clusters to 1½ ft. tall, with pirally set orange, red, or yellow bracts and green-tipped yellow flowers.

H. pendula (H. collinsiana). To 6 ft. tall; 2–3-ft.-long leaves. Pendulous 2-ft. inflorescence with spirally arranged red bracts, yellow flowers.

H. psittacorum. PARROT HELICONIA. Highly variable species; more vigorous than other heliconias. Grows 4–8 ft. tall, with leaves to 20 in. long, blossom clusters to 7 in. long. Bracts spread upward at a 45° angle. They vary in color; may be red, sometimes shading to cream or orange, and are often multicolored. Flowers are yellow, orange, or red, usually tipped in dark green or white. Many named selections are available.

H. rostrata. To 4–6 ft. tall, with 2–4-ft.-long leaves. Hanging inflorescences to 1–2 ft. long contain red bracts shading to yellow at the tip; flowers are greenish yellow.

H. schiedeana. Zones 21–24; H1, H2. To 6–10 ft. tall, with leaves to 5 ft. long. Upright, 1½-ft.-long blossom clusters feature red or orange-red, spiraling bracts that enclose yellow-green flowers. 'Fire and Ice' has bright yellow flowers with deep red bracts.

H. wagneriana. To 6–12 ft. tall, with 4–6-ft.-long leaves. Erect flower clusters 6 in.–1½ ft. long. Heavy, overlapping, green-edged bracts are deep pink to pale crimson, shading to cream at base; flowers are white.

HELICTOTRICHON sempervirens (Avena sempervirens)

BLUE OAT GRASS
Poaceae (Gramineae)
PERENNIAL GRASS

| 🌱 ZONES 1–12, 14–24 |
| 🔆 FULL SUN |
| 💧 REGULAR WATER |

Native to western Mediterranean region. Bright blue-gray, narrow leaves in fountainlike clump 2–3 ft. high and wide; resembles giant clump of blue fescue (*Festuca glauca*) but is more graceful. In spring, stems to 2 ft. or taller rise above foliage, bearing wispy, straw-colored flower clusters. Grows best in rich, well-drained soil. Attractive in borders or with boulders in rock garden. Pull out occasional withered leaves. Evergreen in mild-winter climates; semievergreen in colder areas.

Helictotrichon sempervirens

'Saphirsprudel' ('Sapphire') has leaves that are slightly wider and brighter blue than the species.

HELIOPSIS helianthoides

OX-EYE SUNFLOWER, FALSE SUNFLOWER
Asteraceae (Compositae)
PERENNIAL

| 🌱 ZONES 1–11, 14–24 |
| 🔆 FULL SUN |
| 💧 MODERATE WATER |

Native to the eastern half of North America, extending southwest to Arizona. Species is rarely offered, but several varieties are available. Most grow 3–4 ft. tall and 3 ft. wide, with rough-textured 6-in.-long oval leaves with pointed tips. Yellow blooms resembling 2–3-in.-wide sunflowers top the plants from late summer into fall. Plants may be staked or allowed to arch gracefully.

Outstanding 4-ft.-tall selections include 'Bressingham Doubloon',

Heliopsis helianthoides
'Summer Sun'

with semidouble golden yellow flowers, and 'Prairie Sunset', with dark green leaves, deep purple stems, and golden yellow flowers sporting a dark red spot at the base of each petal. 'Summer Sun' ('Sommersonne'), to 2½ ft. tall and 1½ ft. wide, has dark green foliage and bright yellow flowers that may be single or semidouble. 'Loraine Sunshine' is about the same size, but its leaves are white with green veins, and its single yellow flowers begin blooming in midsummer.

HELIOTROPE. See **HELIOTROPIUM arborescens, VALERIANA officinalis**

HELIOTROPIUM

Boraginaceae
PERENNIALS, ONE USUALLY TREATED AS ANNUAL

| 🌱 ZONES VARY BY SPECIES |
| 🔆 🔅 EXPOSURE NEEDS VARY BY SPECIES |
| 💧 REGULAR WATER |
| ⚠ ALL PARTS OF H. ARBORESCENS ARE POISONOUS IF INGESTED |

Both species produce clusters of tiny flowers with a sweet, delicate fragrance. Foliage is handsome. Provide well-drained soil.

H. anomalum argenteum. HINAHINA. Zone H2. Native Hawaiian coastal ground cover. Rosettes of succulent gray-green to silvery leaves form a mat 3 in.–1 ft. high; in winter and spring, clusters of white flowers are held well above the foliage. Set out plants 6–8 in. apart. Both blossoms and leaf rosettes are used in leis. Thrives in coastal gardens with wind and saturating salt spray. Tolerates drought but does better with regular moisture. Full sun.

H. arborescens. COMMON HELIOTROPE. From Peru. This old-fashioned favorite grows to 4 ft. tall, 2 ft. wide as a perennial (Zones 15–17, 23, 24; H1, H2), but it's typically treated in all regions

Heliotropium arborescens

as a summer bedding annual to 1½–2 ft. high, 1–1½ ft. wide. Dark violet, purple, blue, or white blossoms are densely set in curved, one-sided spikes that form rounded, 3–4-in. clusters. Veined leaves have a darkish purple cast. 'Black Beauty' and 'Iowa' are varieties with deep purple flowers; there are also dwarf forms under 1 ft. high. All are good in pots (in cold climates, overwinter them in a frost-free spot). They can take full sun in cooler climates but need partial shade in warmer ones.

HELIPTERUM

EVERLASTING, SUNRAY
Asteraceae (Compositae)
ANNUALS AND PERENNIALS

| 🌱 ZONES VARY BY SPECIES |
| 🔆 🔅 EXPOSURE NEEDS VARY BY SPECIES |
| 💧 REGULAR WATER |

This large Australian genus contains primarily annuals but also includes some perennials. All have daisylike flower heads with papery rays that retain their color and form when dried. Plants are useful for winter arrangements and for garden color.

H. anthemoides. CHAMOMILE SUNRAY. Perennial. Zones 8, 9, 14–24. Forms a compact gray-green mound 1 ft. tall, 2 ft. wide. Foliage has a chamomile scent when bruised. Blooms in late winter and early spring, with scattered bloom later; bright red buds open to white, ½–1-in.-wide daisies. Give full sun in cool-summer climates, partial shade in hotter regions.

Helipterum roseum

H. roseum (Acroclinium roseum). PINK AND WHITE EVERLASTING, PINK PAPER DAISY. Annual. Zones 1–24. Topnotch flower for cutting, drying. Grows 2 ft. tall, with scanty, narrow leaves and 1–2-in., pink or

H

white daisy flowers. Grow in full sun in warm soil, sowing seeds where plants are to grow after danger of frost is past. Thin to 6–12 in. apart.

HELLEBORUS

HELLEBORE
Ranunculaceae
PERENNIALS

- 🟦 ZONES VARY BY SPECIES
- 🟡⚫ PARTIAL OR FULL SHADE
- 💧💧 WATER NEEDS VARY BY SPECIES
- ☣ ALL PARTS ARE POISONOUS IF INGESTED

Distinctive, long-lived plants that add color to the garden for several months in winter and spring, hellebores are also appreciated for their attractive foliage. Each leaf consists of a long leafstalk ending in large, leathery leaflets grouped together like fingers on an outstretched hand.

All hellebores form tight clumps of many growing points, but species differ in their manner of growth. Some have stems that rise from the ground, bearing leaves all along their length; stems produce flowers at their tip in their second year, then die to the ground as new stems emerge to replace them. In other species, leaves are not carried on tall stems but arise directly from growing points at ground level; separate (typically leafless) flower stems spring from the same points.

Flowers are usually shaped like cups or bells (those of *H. niger* are saucer shaped), either outward facing or drooping; they consist of a ring of petal-like sepals ranging in color from white and green through pink and red to deep purple (rarely yellow). Flowers of all hellebores persist beyond the bloom periods listed below, gradually turning green. Blossoms are attractive in arrangements: after you cut them, slice the stems lengthwise or seal cut ends by searing over a flame or immersing in boiling water for a few seconds. Then place in cold water. Or simply float flowers in a bowl of water.

Plant in good, well-drained soil amended with plenty of organic matter. Plants prefer soil that is somewhat alkaline but will also grow well in neutral to slightly acid conditions (*H. niger* is an exception; it must have alkaline soil). Feed once or twice a year. Don't disturb once planted; they resent moving and may take 2 or more years to re-establish (if they

survive at all). If well sited, however, they may self-sow, and young seedlings can be transplanted in early spring. Offspring may not exactly resemble the parent, but all are attractive. Mass under high-branching trees, on north or east side of walls, or in beds. Not damaged by deer or rodents.

Intensive breeding here and abroad has widened the range of colors and forms. Check specialists' catalogs for choice new plants.

H. argutifolius (H. corsicus). CORSICAN HELLEBORE. Zones 3b–9, 14–24. From Corsica, Sardinia. Erect or sprawling, to 2–3 ft. tall and wide. Substantial enough to use as a small shrub. Blue-green, 6–9-in. leaves divided into three sharply toothed leaflets. Leafy stems carry clusters of 2-in., pale green flowers from winter into spring. Best hellebore for Southern California; more sun tolerant than others. Moderate water. Two varieties with white-marbled leaves are 'Janet Starnes' (which has a touch of pink in the foliage) and 'Pacific Frost'. Seedlings of these plants, sold as Janet Starnes strain and Pacific Frost strain, closely resemble the parents. 'Silver Lace' has blue-gray foliage overlaid with a silver lace pattern that fades slightly in summer.

H. foetidus. BEAR'S-FOOT HELLEBORE. Zones 2b–9, 14–24. From western and central Europe. To 2½ ft. high and wide, the stems clothed with dark green leaves divided into seven to ten narrow, leathery leaflets to 8 in. long. Clusters of inch-wide flowers are light green with purplish red edges, bloom winter to spring. Plant parts are malodorous if crushed or bruised (don't smell bad otherwise). Tolerates sun in cool, humid areas. Self-sows freely where adapted. Moderate water. 'Red Silver' has red stems, narrow leaflets with a silver sheen, and green flowers with a red edge. Wester Flisk strain has stems, flower stems, and leafstalks infused with purplish red, with the color extending into leaf bases.

H. hybrids. Zones 2b–10, 14–24. Leaves have no obvious stems. These hybrid plants gener-

ally resemble principal parent, *H. orientalis,* but flower color range has been extended and superior parents selected for seed production. Some are sold under the breeder's name, such as Ballard's Group, which has flowers in several colors. Others are sold as color strains, such as Sunshine Selections (white, pink, yellow, or red flowers), Royal Heritage strain (pink, purple, maroon, or white blooms), and Winter Queen mix (white, pink, maroon, or spotted flowers). Others are grouped according to form, such as Party Dress Group, which has double flowers. Moderate to regular water.

H. 'Ivory Prince' (H. × nigersmithii 'Walhelivor'). Zones 2–9, 14–17. Hybrid of complex parentage, with foliage like that of *H. niger.* Grows 1 ft. tall, 1½–2 ft. wide, with red buds opening into ivory white flowers that take on rose and chartreuse tones as they age. Regular water.

H. lividus. Zones 5 (with protection), 6–9, 14–24. From Majorca. To 1½ ft. high and twice as wide. Leaves resemble those of *H. argutifolius* but lack noticeable teeth and have purplish undersides and a network of pale veins above. Winter-to-spring flowers in clusters of up to ten are pale green washed with pinkish purple. Moderate water.

H. niger. CHRISTMAS ROSE. Zones 1–7, 14–17. From Europe. Leaves have no obvious stems. Elegant plant to 1 ft. tall, 1½ ft. wide, blooming Christmas time into spring. Often planted in warm-winter climates but seldom thrives there. Plants of *H. orientalis* are often mislabeled Christmas rose. Lustrous dark green leaves are divided into seven to nine lobes with a few large teeth; they seem to rise directly from the soil. White, 2-in. flowers appear singly or in groups of two or three on a stout stem about the same height as the foliage clump. Blooms turn pinkish with age. Less tolerant of light than other hellebores; needs more definite shade. Needs alkaline soil; if your soil is acidic, mulch plants with ½-in.-deep layer of lime or granite chips available at stone

Helleborus orientalis

yards. Regular water. 'White Magic' is a large-flowered variety.

H. orientalis. LENTEN ROSE. Zones 2b–10, 14–24. Greece, Turkey, Caucasus. Leaves have no obvious stems. Much like *H. niger* in growth but more tolerant of warm-winter climates. Basal leaves with 5–11 sharply toothed leaflets; branched flowering stems to 1 ft. tall, with leaflike bracts at branching points. Blooms in late winter and spring; flowers are 2–4 in. wide, in colors including white, pink, purplish, cream, and greenish, often spotted with deep purple. Easier to transplant than other hellebores. A widely variable plant, but all forms are attractive. Encourage self-sowing and keep the colors you like. Hybridizes quite freely with many other species; many nursery plants may actually be hybrids. Moderate to regular water.

H. × sternii. Zones 4–9, 14–24. Hybrid between *H. argutifolius* and *H. lividus,* with bluish green foliage netted with white or cream. Greenish flowers suffused with pink bloom from winter to spring. Variable from seed. Moderate water. 'Boughton Beauty' has silver-gray leaves with pink stems.

HELXINE soleirolii.
See **SOLEIROLIA soleirolii**

HEMEROCALLIS

DAYLILY
Liliaceae
PERENNIALS FROM TUBEROUS ROOTS

- 🟦 ZONES 1–24; H1, H2; EXCEPT AS NOTED
- ☀🟡 PARTIAL SHADE IN HOTTEST CLIMATES
- 💧 REGULAR WATER

Tuberous, somewhat fleshy roots give rise to large clumps of arching, sword-shaped leaves— evergreen, semievergreen, or

Helleborus argutifolius

Hemerocallis hybrid

deciduous, depending on daylily type. Deciduous types go completely dormant in winter and are the hardiest, surviving without protection to about –35°F/–37°C; where winters are very mild, however, they may not get enough chill to perform well. Evergreen kinds succeed in mild-winter regions as well as in colder areas, but they need a protective mulch (such as a 4–6-in. layer of hay) where temperatures dip below –20°F/–29°C. Semievergreen sorts may or may not retain their leaves, depending on where they are grown.

Clusters of flowers like lilies appear at the ends of generally leafless stems that stand well above foliage. Older yellow, orange, and rust red daylilies have in most part been replaced by newer kinds in an expanded range of colors and patterns; both tall and dwarf varieties are available. Many species daylilies exist, but only a few are offered by nurseries; most of those available are hybrids.

Use in borders, mass on banks under high-branching deciduous trees or along driveways and roadsides in country gardens, or group among evergreen shrubs near pools, along streams. Plant dwarf daylilies in rock gardens or as edgings or low ground covers. All are good cut flowers. Cut stems with well-developed buds; these open on successive days, though each flower is slightly smaller than the preceding one. Arrange individual blooms in low bowls. One caution: plants are reportedly toxic to cats.

Few plants are tougher, more persistent, or more trouble free. Daylilies adapt to almost any kind of soil. You can set out bare-root plants at any time during the growing season; spring and summer are better in cold-winter zones, while fall and winter are preferred where winters are warm. Plant from containers at any time from early spring through midautumn (year-round in mild-

winter areas). For best results, provide well-drained soil amended with organic matter; give regular moisture from spring through fall. When clumps become crowded (usually after 3 to 6 years), divide them in fall or early spring in hot-summer areas, during summer in cool-summer regions or where growing season is short.

H. fulva. TAWNY DAYLILY, COMMON ORANGE DAYLILY. Deciduous. From China or Japan. To 3–5 ft. high and 4 ft. wide; may spread into colonies. Leaves are 2 ft. or longer. Tawny orange-red, 3–5-in., unscented flowers in summer. A tough, persistent perennial suitable for holding banks; not often sold but commonly seen in old gardens and along roadsides. Double-flowered 'Kwanso' ('Kwanso Flore Pleno') is sometimes seen in the same locales.

Hemerocallis hybrid

H. hybrids. Deciduous, evergreen, and semievergreen. Standard-size hybrids generally grow 2½–4 ft. tall, 2–3 ft. wide; some selections reach 6 ft. high. Dwarf types grow just 1–2 ft. tall and wide. Flowers of standard kinds are 4–8 in. across, those of dwarfs 1½–3½ in. wide. Some have broad petals, others narrow, spidery ones; many have ruffled petal edges. Colors range far beyond the basic yellow, orange, and rusty red to pink, vermilion, buff, apricot, plum or lilac purple, cream, and near-white, often with contrasting eyes or midrib stripes that yield a bicolor effect. Many varieties are sprinkled with tiny iridescent dots known as diamond dust. Selections with semidouble and double flowers exist. Tetraploid varieties have unusually heavily textured petals.

Bloom usually begins in mid-spring, but early and late bloomers are also sold. By planting all three types, you can extend bloom period. Scattered bloom may occur during summer, and reblooming types put on second display in late summer to mid-autumn. Some varieties bloom throughout warm weather. These include 3-ft.-tall Starburst series, which comes in a variety of colors, as well as 2-ft.-high dwarf varieties 'Black-eyed Stella' (yellow with red eye), bright yellow 'Happy Returns' and 'Stella de Oro', and red 'Pardon Me'.

New hybrids appear in such numbers that no book can keep up. To get the ones you want, visit daylily specialists, buy plants in bloom at your local nursery, or study catalogs. Look for varieties that have won awards from the American Hemerocallis Society. AM stands for Award of Merit, given to ten varieties each year. HM means Honorable Mention, awarded to any plant receiving ten votes from the selection committee. SM stands for Stout Medal, the highest award a daylily can receive. Past SM winners include the long-blooming 'Stella de Oro' and the free-blooming yellow tetraploid 'Mary Todd'. An old variety that has maintained its popularity is 'Hyperion', a 4-footer with exceptionally fragrant yellow blooms.

H. lilioasphodelus (H. flava). LEMON DAYLILY. Deciduous. From China. Reaches 3 ft. high and wide, with 2-ft.-long leaves; 4-in., fragrant, pure yellow flowers bloom in mid- to late spring. Newer hybrids may be showier, but this species is still cherished for its delightful perfume and early bloom time.

H. minor. GRASS-LEAF DAYLILY. Deciduous. Zones A1–A3; 1–9, 14–17. From eastern Asia. To 2 ft. high and wide, with narrow (¼-in.-wide) leaves. Blooms for a relatively short time in late spring or early summer, when fragrant, bright golden yellow flowers are held just above the foliage. This is among the few daylilies hardy enough to succeed in Alaska's interior.

HEMLOCK. See **TSUGA**

HEN AND CHICKENS. See **SEMPERVIVUM tectorum**

HEN AND CHICKS. See **ECHEVERIA**

HEPATICA
LIVERLEAF
Ranunculaceae
PERENNIALS

🌿 ZONES 1–6, 14–17

☼ ◐ PARTIAL OR FULL SHADE

💧 REGULAR WATER

These low-growing woodland plants (reaching 6–9 in. high and 6 in. wide) with evergreen or nearly evergreen leaves resemble the smaller anemones (and were formerly considered anemones). Leaves were once thought to resemble the liver in shape, hence the common name. Flowers appear in early spring, each rising on its own stalk above the clump of last year's leaves. A new crop of leaves follows bloom. Flowers have numerous narrow, petal-like sepals arranged around a central mass of yellow stamens. These are choice plants for woodland gardens and shaded rock gardens. Though little known in North America except among wildflower fanciers, they are popular with plant collectors in Japan, where many varieties are cultivated.

Hepatica americana

H. acutiloba. Native to eastern and central North America. Leathery, 4-in. leaves are divided into three sharp-pointed lobes. Flowers are lilac and white, ½–1 in. across, on stems to 9 in. high.

H. americana. Native to eastern and central North America. Leathery, 4-in. leaves with three rounded lobes. Flowering stems are usually just 6 in. high. Flowers are typically light blue, but sometimes pink or white, ½–1 in. wide.

H. nobilis (H. triloba). Native to Europe. Very similar to species *H. americana*. Bears flowers that are usually bluish purple but are sometimes white or pink.

HEPTACODIUM
miconioides
SEVEN SONS FLOWER
Caprifoliaceae
DECIDUOUS SHRUB OR TREE

🌿 ZONES 2B–6, 14–17

☼ ◐ FULL SUN OR LIGHT SHADE

💧 REGULAR WATER

From China. Fountain-shaped shrub to 15–20 ft. tall, 8–10 ft. wide. Large, narrowly

H

H

heart-shaped leaves are shiny green, deeply veined. Fragrant, creamy white flowers in large clusters at branch ends open over a long bloom season in late summer and fall. Blooms are succeeded by even showier masses of small fruits with bright purplish red calyxes. Common name derives from the number of flowers in each of the clusters forming part of the larger inflorescence. Picturesque even in winter, when bark is on show: thin, pale tan strips peel away to reveal dark brown bark beneath. Not fussy about soil; not bothered by pests or diseases. Some consider it a worthy substitute for crape myrtle (*Lagerstroemia*) where that plant does not succeed. Can be trained as a single- or multitrunked tree.

Heptacodium miconioides

HEPTAPLEURUM arboricolum. See **SCHEFFLERA arboricola**

HERALD'S TRUMPET. See **BEAUMONTIA grandiflora**

HERB-OF-GRACE. See **RUTA graveolens**

HERCULES' CLUB. See **ARALIA spinosa**

HERNIARIA glabra
GREEN CARPET,
RUPTURE WORT
Caryophyllaceae
PERENNIAL SOMETIMES
TREATED AS ANNUAL

| 🌿 ZONES 2B–24; ANNUAL ELSEWHERE |
| ☀️ ◐ ● SUN OR SHADE |
| 💧 REGULAR WATER |

From Eurasia and North Africa, especially the Mediterranean area. Trailing plant 1–3 in. high, with crowded, tiny (less than ¼-in.-long) bright green leaves. Bloom negligible. Where temperatures remain above –20°F/–29°C, grown as an evergreen perennial; foliage turns bronzy red in winter. In colder areas, treated as an annual. Spreads well by rooting stems but

Herniaria glabra

won't grow out of control. Use it between stepping-stones, on mounds, among rocks, or in parking strips. Plant 1 ft. apart. Endures the occasional footstep but not constant traffic. Provide well-drained soil.

HESPERALOE
Agavaceae
PERENNIALS

| 🌿 ZONES VARY BY SPECIES |
| ☀️ ◐ FULL SUN OR LIGHT SHADE |
| 💧 ● LITTLE TO MODERATE WATER |

Clumps of narrow evergreen leaves with threadlike fringe along edges give rise to tall, branching inflorescences set with many tubular flowers. Foliage clumps resemble yucca or coarse grass. Plants require little maintenance aside from removal of spent flower clusters. Established plants can get by with little summer water, but they look and bloom better with a soaking every 2 weeks or so during warm weather.

Hesperaloe parviflora

H. funifera. Zones 12, 13. From northern Mexico. Clumps grow to 6 ft. tall and 6–8 ft. wide. Stems up to 15 ft. high bear inch-wide, greenish white flowers in late spring or early summer.

H. nocturna. Zones 12, 13. From northern Mexico. Foliage clump 5 ft. tall, 6 ft. wide. Flowers in late spring and early summer, producing blossom spikes up to 12 ft. high that bear many 1-in., night-blooming, slightly fragrant greenish lavender flowers.

H. parviflora. RED YUCCA. Zones 2b, 3, 7–16, 18–24. From Texas and New Mexico. Leaf clumps 3–4 ft. tall and wide produce 5-ft. stalks carrying many rose red to bright red flowers from late spring through midsummer, sometimes into early fall. Especially heat tolerant; can take full sun, even reflected heat. Excellent container plant. There is a yellow-flowered form.

HESPERIS matronalis
DAME'S ROCKET
Brassicaceae (Cruciferae)
PERENNIAL OR BIENNIAL

| 🌿 ZONES A2, A3; 1–24 |
| ☀️ ◐ FULL SUN OR LIGHT SHADE |
| 💧 REGULAR WATER |

Old-fashioned cottage garden plant from central and southern Europe; naturalized in North America. Free-branching, to 3 ft. tall and wide, with 4-in., tooth-edged leaves. From late spring into

Hesperis matronalis

summer, bears rounded clusters of ½-in., four-petaled lilac to purple flowers similar to those of stock (*Matthiola*); blossoms are fragrant at night. Grows readily from seed and often self-sows. When plants get old and woody, replace them with young seedlings. White- and double-flowered forms exist.

HETEROCENTRON elegans (Schizocentron elegans)
SPANISH SHAWL
Melastomataceae
PERENNIAL

| 🌿 ZONES 15–24 |
| ☀️ PARTIAL SHADE |
| 💧 ● MODERATE TO REGULAR WATER |

Native from Mexico to Guatemala. To 2–4 in. high, 1½ ft. wide, with creeping, vinelike habit. Glossy, oval evergreen leaves to ½ in. wide, each with three well-marked veins. Leaves and stems often take on reddish tones as the season

Heterocentron elegans

advances. In summer, inch-wide magenta flowers appear among the leaves; calyxes remain after blossoms have withered. When used as a ground cover, blooming plants look like a carpet of bright bougainvillea. Good subject for hanging baskets. Needs frost protection in Zones 15, 16, 18–20. Best in partial shade but tolerates full sun (in cooler climates) as well as full shade. Protect from snails and slugs.

HETEROMELES arbutifolia
TOYON, CHRISTMAS BERRY, CALIFORNIA HOLLY
Rosaceae
EVERGREEN SHRUB OR TREE

| 🌿 ZONES 5–9, 14–24 |
| ☀️ ◐ FULL SUN OR PARTIAL SHADE |
| 💧 MODERATE WATER |

Native to California Coast Ranges, Sierra Nevada foothills, Baja California. Grows as a dense shrub to 6–10 ft. tall and broad or a multitrunked small tree 15–25 ft. tall and spreading almost as wide (can be pruned to form a single-trunked tree). Thick, leathery, glossy dark green leaves are 2–4 in.

Heteromeles arbutifolia

long, edged with bristly, pointed teeth. Small white flowers in flattish clusters appear in summer; these are followed in fall to winter by pea-size bright red (rarely yellow) berries, much relished by birds. Flowers attract bees. *H. a. macrocarpa,* from Southern California's Channel Islands, has larger berries.

Toyon improves under cultivation. If trimmed to give abundance of year-old wood, it produces even more berries than in the wild. Valuable as screen or bank planting. Subject to fireblight. Tolerates drought but looks better with moderate irrigation.

HEUCHERA

CORAL BELLS, ALUM ROOT
Saxifragaceae
PERENNIALS

🌱 **ZONES VARY BY SPECIES**

☼ **FULL SUN IN COOLER CLIMATES ONLY**

💧💧 **MODERATE TO REGULAR WATER**

Compact evergreen clumps of roundish leaves with lobed or scalloped edges. A vast array are grown for their colorful foliage. Slender, wiry 1–3-ft. stems bear loose clusters of nodding, bell-shaped flowers, typically ⅛ in. across or smaller. Dainty blossoms consist of colorful fused sepals and often lack petals; they are long lasting in cut arrangements. Color range includes shades of red to pink (attractive to hummingbirds) and less showy white or green. Bloom time varies by type from early spring to late summer; some kinds continue into fall.

Use in rock gardens or as ground cover, mass in borders or in front of shrubs, or use as edging for beds of taller perennials. They make good container plants, especially when combined with other perennials and even small shrubs.

Grow in well-drained, humus-rich soil. Will take full sun in cool climates, but in warmer regions they do best with afternoon shade or a northern exposure with open sky above. Divide clumps every 3 or 4 years in spring (or in fall in mild-winter climates). Use young, vigorous rooted divisions, or cut old woody stems to within an inch of the ground and let them regrow. Easy to propagate from cuttings started in sand in spring or from seed sown in spring. Strawberry root weevils chew on foliage, but these can be shaken off lifted plants. Mealybugs can damage base of plants; treat with insecticidal soap.

H. × brizoides. Zones 1–10, 14–24. Diverse group of hybrids between *H. sanguinea* and other species. To 1–2½ ft. tall, 1–1½ ft. wide, with spring or summer bloom. Seed-grown strain called Bressingham Hybrids offers flowers in white and shades of pink and red. Selected cutting-grown varieties include 'Firefly' ('Leuchtkäfer'), with fragrant, fiery scarlet bells; 'Freedom', profuse rosy pink flowers; 'Bressingham White', long-blooming white; 'June Bride', large pure white blossoms; 'Snowstorm', deep reddish pink flowers above white-variegated foliage.

H. Canyon series. Zones 2–11, 14–24. Spring-blooming group of mat-forming hybrids. Foliage mounds are 3–6 in. high, 1–2 ft. or more wide, with rounded, medium green, ¾–1½-in. leaves. Three choices with sprays of ½-in. flowers on 16–20-in. stems are rose red 'Canyon Delight', medium pink 'Canyon Pink', and rich red 'Canyon Belle'. The following are smaller, with more diminutive blossoms on stems topping out at 8–12 in.: 'Canyon Chimes', dark pink calyx with slightly protruding white petals; 'Canyon Duet', strongly bicolored pink and white; and 'Canyon Melody', medium pink calyx with protruding white petals.

H. hybrids. Zones 1–9, 14–24; often short lived in warm-summer areas. Most of these have as a parent *H. americana*, a species from the central U.S. that forms a mound 8 in. to 2 ft. high and wide, with leaves 1½–4½ in. across, marbled and veined. These varieties have been selected for their marvelously colored and sometimes ruffled foliage. Tiny summer flowers are held on thin stalks to 3 ft. high and are white to cream unless otherwise noted.

'Amethyst Mist.' Deep purple leaves that age to silver with green or purple veins.

'Chocolate Ruffles'. Leaves dark chocolate above, burgundy below; burgundy color also shows in ruffles on leaf edges. Purple blossom spikes and flowers.

'Chocolate Veil'. Chocolate-colored leaves with maroon undersides; top surfaces of leaves marbled with light purple and silver between veins. Purple flowers tinged lime green.

'Crème Brûlée'. Peachy orange foliage and creamy yellow flowers.

'Crimson Curls'. Deep red, ruffled leaves, fading to gray green in summer.

'Garnet'. Deep red winter foliage; brighter new foliage in spring.

'Green Spice'. Silver-gray leaves with purple veins.

'Lace Ruffles'. Ruffled, scalloped green leaves mottled silvery white.

'Lime Rickey'. Chartreuse leaves with ruffled edges.

'Marmalade'. Bright red new growth that ages to shades of orange and rich reddish brown; deep red flowers.

'Obsidian'. Foliage deepest burgundy, nearly black, with glossy sheen.

'Peach Flambé'. Bright leaves of apricot to peach, taking on purple tones in winter.

'Persian Carpet'. Silver leaves with dark purple veins and leaf edges.

'Pewter Moon'. Silvery leaves with maroon undersides; pink blooms.

'Pewter Veil'. Shining silvery leaves; small purple flowers.

'Plum Pudding'. Plum purple leaves with a silver coating.

'Ring of Fire'. Silvery, purple-veined leaves that develop a red rim in fall.

'Ruby Veil'. Large (8-in.) silvery leaves; veins red near leaf base.

'Shenandoah Mountain'. Purple and bronze leaves with a silver sheen.

'Silver Scrolls'. Silvery leaves with dark purple veins.

'Snow Angel'. Light green leaves splashed with cream; pinkish red flowers.

'Stormy Seas'. Leaves with tones of silver, lavender, and pewter, with red undersides that show on curly edges.

'Velvet Night'. Deep bluish purple leaves.

'Vesuvius'. Burgundy-purple foliage topped by bright red flowers.

H. maxima. ISLAND ALUM ROOT. Zones 15–24. Native to Channel Islands off coast of Southern California. Foliage clumps 1–2 ft. tall, spreading 3–4 ft. or more in time. Lobed dark green leaves have a roundish heart shape. Hundreds of small whitish or pinkish blossoms appear on each narrowly branched, wiry 1½–2½-ft. stem in early spring. Good casual ground cover.

H. micrantha. Zones 1–10, 14–24. Native to California, Washington, Oregon, Idaho. Adapts easily to garden conditions. Plant in protected spot in coldest part of range; in desert, give full shade but good light. Long-stalked, roundish, gray-green, 1–3-in.-wide leaves are toothed and lobed, hairy on both sides. Late spring to early summer flowers are whitish or greenish, about ⅛ in. long, carried in loose clusters on leafy, 2–3-ft. stems. Hybrid forms developed from *H. micrantha* are more adaptable than the species itself. Seed-grown varieties include 'Martha Roderick', with bright green leaves and profuse rose pink flowers; 'Painted Lady', with purple leaves marked with silvery gray; 'Palace Purple', with maplelike, rich brownish or purplish leaves that retain their color all year if given adequate sunlight; and 'Ruffles', with leaves that are deeply lobed and ruffled around the edges.

Heuchera micrantha
'Palace Purple'

H. Rancho Santa Ana hybrids. Zones 14–24. These hybrids between *H. sanguinea* and *H. maxima* are vigorous and free flowering. Foliage clumps grow 1–2 ft. tall and 2–4 ft. wide, with leaves 2–4 in. across. Stems 2–3 ft. tall carry a profusion of small flowers. Long bloom season, from late spring through summer, nearly all year in mild-winter areas. 'Genevieve' has green leaves marbled with gray; deep pink, white-centered flowers. 'Opal' has medium green leaves and white flowers that open from pink buds. 'Santa Ana Cardinal' sports

H

shiny dark green leaves and rose pink flowers. Leaves of 'Wendy' are light green, pretty in combination with its medium pink flowers.

H. sanguinea. Zones A1–A3; 1–11, 14–24. Native to New Mexico and Arizona. Round, 1–2-in. leaves with scalloped edges form neat foliage tufts. From spring into summer, slender, wiry, 1–2-ft. stems bear open clusters of nodding, bell-shaped flowers. 'Cherry

Heuchera sanguinea

Splash' has red flowers and white-and-gold variegation on the leaves. 'Frosty' has red flowers and silver-variegated foliage. Pink-flowered 'Geisha's Fan' has silver leaves with purple veins. 'Snow Storm' has green leaves heavily splashed with white and flowers that are cerise red. 'White Cloud' has light green, silver-flecked foliage and profuse white blossoms. Seed-grown Bressingham hybrids bear loads of flowers in white and shades of pink, red, and coral.

× HEUCHERELLA

Saxifragaceae
PERENNIALS

🗺	ZONES 1–10, 14–24
☼	LIGHT SHADE
💧	REGULAR WATER

These hybrids combine the flowering habit of coral bells (*Heuchera*) with the heart-shaped leaves of foamflower (*Tiarella cordifolia*). Most produce foliage clumps 4–5 in. high and about 1 ft. wide; leaves are lobed and 1½–4 in. across. Late spring or summer blooms of pink or white are held on thin stalks 1–2 ft. tall, creating a candlelike effect. Excellent choice for shaded rock gardens or as woodland ground cover. Require well-drained, humus-rich soil.

× H. alba 'Bridget Bloom'. Bright green leaves marked with

× *Heucherella alba* 'Bridget Bloom'

reddish brown; pink flowers from spring to midsummer.

× H. 'Burnished Bronze'. Large, bronze-red leaves; pink flowers.

× H. 'Chocolate Lace'. Chocolate-red, deeply lobed foliage and soft pink blooms.

× H. 'Heart of Darkness'. Silver-coated green leaves centered and veined in maroon; white flowers.

× H. 'Kimono'. Deeply lobed leaves patterned green and silver with purple veins; flowers are tawny white and not showy. Mounding clumps to 1 ft. high and wide.

× H. 'Pink Frost'. Silvery green foliage; pink blooms from spring to fall.

× H. 'Stoplight'. Large chartreuse leaves that are veined and centered with bright red; white blossoms. Clumps reach 6 in. high and 1½ ft. wide.

× H. 'Sunspot'. Bright yellow leaves with red central veins; pink flowers.

× H. tiarelloides. Light green leaves and sprays of pink flowers spring to midsummer, often with repeat bloom in autumn.

× H. 'Viking Ship'. Green foliage shaped like maple leaves, with a profusion of showy coral-pink flowers.

HIBA CEDAR.
See **THUJOPSIS dolabrata**

HIBBERTIA

Dilleniaceae
EVERGREEN SHRUBS AND VINES

🗺	ZONES VARY BY SPECIES
☼ ☼	FULL SUN OR PARTIAL SHADE
💧	REGULAR WATER

Most are native to Australia, including those described below. All types have bright yellow flowers resembling wild roses. Low-growing species for rock gardens

are worth seeking out; these include *H. vestita*, to 6 in. high and 2–3 ft. wide, with tiny dark green leaves and comparatively large (1½-in.) blossoms. The following species are more widely grown.

H. cuneiformis (Candollea cuneiformis). Shrub. Zones 12, 13, 15–24. Grows to 4 ft. tall and 6 ft. wide. Polished green, 1-in.-

Hibbertia cuneiformis

long leaves are tapered at base, toothed at tip. Flowers carried all along new growth in spring. Prune after flowering to control outline. Requires exceptionally fast drainage. Tolerates wind.

H. scandens (H. volubilis). GUINEA GOLD VINE. Zones 16, 17, 21–24. Fast-growing vine climbs by twining stems to 8–10 ft. In ideal climate, foliage is handsome all year—narrow, waxy dark green leaves to 3 in. long. Blooms from spring into early fall. Good for small garden areas if trained on trellis or against low fence; can be grown as ground cover. Do any significant thinning in late fall or winter; remove errant stems as needed during bloom time. Recovers quickly from light frosts.

Hibbertia scandens

HIBISCUS

Malvaceae
PERENNIALS, ANNUALS, AND EVERGREEN AND DECIDUOUS SHRUBS OR TREES

🗺	ZONES VARY BY SPECIES
☼	FULL SUN
💧	REGULAR WATER

Among the showiest flowering plants in Western gardens; some are very tender tropical species grown in Hawaii. Plants typically bear funnel-shaped blossoms, often with prominent stamens. The many species offer a wide range of flower colors. The giant whitefly is a relatively new pest of hibiscus in coastal Southern California, but a parasitoid wasp has been released to control it.

Hibiscus rosa-sinensis 'The Path'

H. arnottianus. HAWAIIAN WHITE HIBISCUS. Shrub or tree. Zones 23, 24; H1, H2. Native to Hawaii, island of Oahu. To 30 ft. high, 25 ft. wide. Blooms almost year-round, producing slightly fragrant white flowers with central column of magenta stamens. Beautiful for small entryway tree or as landscape accent.

H. brackenridgei. Shrub or tree. Zones 23, 24; H1, H2. Native to Hawaii—and the official state flower there. Plant grows to 8–15 ft. high and about half as wide, with a profusion of large, pure yellow flowers borne in spring and early summer. Somewhat short lived (4 to 6 years in the wild).

H. calyphyllus (H. rockii). Woody-based perennial or shrub. Zones 23, 24; H1, H2. Native to tropical Africa. Sprawling growth to 3–9 ft. high and as wide. Flowers are 3–4 in. wide, sulfur yellow marked brownish red to maroon at the base.

H. huegelii. See Alyogyne huegelii

H. manihot. See Abelmoschus manihot

H. moschatus. See Abelmoschus moschatus

H. moscheutos. PERENNIAL HIBISCUS, ROSE-MALLOW. Perennial. Zones 2–24; H1. Native to eastern U.S. Largest flowers of all hibiscus, some reaching 1 ft. across, on a plant 6–8 ft. high and 3 ft. wide. Bloom starts in late spring or early summer and continues until frost. Oval, toothed leaves are deep green above, whitish beneath. Plants die to the ground in winter, even in mild climates. For most spectacular bloom, feed at 6- to 8-week intervals during growing season. Protect from wind.

Seed-grown strains often flower the first year if sown indoors and planted outdoors early. Southern Belle grows 4 ft. tall; Disco Belle, Frisbee, and Rio Carnival reach 2–2½ ft. tall. All have 8–12-in.-wide flowers in red, pink, rose, or white, often with red eye. The many cutting-grown selections and hybrids include these 4-footers: 'Blue River II', 10-in. pure white flowers; 'George Riegel', 10-in. ruffled pink blooms with red eye; 'Lady Baltimore', with 6–8-in. glowing pink flowers with a large red center; 'Lord Baltimore', 10-in. deep red; 'The Clown', 6–8-in. light pink with red eye; and 'Turn of the Century', 5–10-in. blooms with red eye and bicolor petals of pink and white. 'Crimson Wonder' can reach 5 ft. tall and wide, with slightly ruffled rose red flowers 9–11 in. across.

H. mutabilis. CONFEDERATE ROSE. Deciduous shrub. Zones 4–24; H1, H2. From China. In warmest climates, shrubby or tree-like to 15 ft. tall, 8 ft. wide. Behaves more like perennial in colder part of range, growing flowering branches from woody base or short trunk. Broad, oval leaves with three to five lobes. Summer flowers are 4–6 in. wide, opening white or pink and changing to deep red by evening. 'Rubrus' has red flowers. Double-flowered forms exist.

H. rockii. See H. calyphyllus

H. rosa-sinensis. CHINESE HIBISCUS, TROPICAL HIBISCUS. Evergreen shrub. Zones 9, 12–16, 19–24; H1, H2. Probably from tropical Asia; has been in cultivation for centuries. Provide overhead protection where winter lows frequently drop below 30°F/ –1°C. Where temperatures go much lower, grow in containers and shel-

ter indoors over winter; or treat as annual, setting out fresh plants each spring. Also makes a good houseplant.

One of most flamboyant flowering shrubs. Reaches 30 ft. tall and 15–20 ft. wide in Hawaii, but more typical size on mainland is 8–15 ft. tall, 5–8 ft. wide. Glossy leaves vary somewhat in size and texture depending on variety. Growth habit may be dense and dwarfish or loose and open. Summer flowers are single or double, 4–8 in. wide. Colors range from white through pink to red, from yellow and apricot to orange. Individual flowers last only a day, but the plant blooms continuously.

This shrub requires excellent drainage; if necessary, improve soil for best drainage or set plants in raised beds or containers. Can be used as screen, espalier, or specimen. To develop good branch structure, prune poorly shaped young plants when you set them out in spring. To keep a mature plant growing vigorously, prune out about a third of old wood in early spring. Pinching out tips of stems in spring and summer increases flower production. All varieties susceptible to aphids. There are thousands of selections; the following are some of those sold in the West. Varieties are listed below by flower color.

White. 'Bridal Veil' has large, pure white, single flowers that last 3–4 days on the bush. 'Bride' has very large, single, palest blush pink to white flowers; slow, open-branched growth to 4–5 ft. 'Powder Puff' has creamy white double flowers in a puffball shape; plants reach 8–10 ft. tall. 'White Wings' bears profuse, narrow-petaled, single white flowers with a small red eye; this vigorous, open, upright grower is best pruned to control legginess (a compact form with smaller flowers is available).

Yellow and orange. 'All Aglow' has large single blooms with broad, gold-blotched orange petals

and a pink halo around a white throat. 'Butterfly' has small, single, bright yellow flowers; slow, upright growth to 7 ft. 'California Gold' produces a heavy yield of single flowers in yellow with a red center; grows slowly to moderately to a compact 7 ft. 'Cherie' offers a profuse show of single, bright orange flowers with deep maroon throat; grows 6–8 ft. tall. 'Crown of Bohemia' has double gold flowers with petals that shade to carmine orange toward base; plant is bushy and upright, with moderate or fast growth to 5 ft. 'Empire' has single, warm orange flowers in profusion; grows 6–8 ft. high. 'Fiesta' has large, frilly, single, bright orange flowers with white central eye edged in red; strong, erect growth to 6–7 ft. 'Fullmoon' has pure yellow double flowers; moderately vigorous growth to a compact 6 ft. 'Golden Dust' bears single flowers of bright orange with yellow-orange centers on a compact, thick-foliaged plant to 4 ft. 'Hula Girl' has large, single, canary yellow flowers with a deep red eye; flowers last for several days on this compact 6-footer. 'Itsy Bitsy Peach' has small leaves and small (2–3-in.), single, peach-colored flowers. 'The Path' has ruffled, single, buttercup yellow flowers with a bright pink center; bushy, upright shrub grows 6–8 ft. tall.

Pink. 'Agnes Galt' bears large single flowers on a vigorous plant; prune to prevent legginess. 'Amour' has big, single, soft pink flowers; grows 6–8 ft. tall. 'Erin Rachel' produces large, neon pink flowers with orange edges; grows slowly to 5–6 ft. 'Itsy Bitsy Pink' has small leaves and small (2–3-in.) single flowers. 'Kona' flowers are ruffled and double on a vigorous, upright, bushy plant that benefits from regular pruning. 'Kona Improved' has fuller flowers of a richer pink. 'Kona Princess' produces small double flowers on a 6–7-ft. shrub. 'Morning Glory' has blush pink, single blooms that age to warmer pink with white petal tips; grows

Hibiscus rosa-sinensis 'Empire'

8–10 ft. tall. 'Ross Estey' grows to 8 ft. and has large ruffled leaves that are polished dark green; its single blooms are very large and long lasting (2 or 3 days on the plant), with broad, overlapping petals shading to coral orange toward tips. 'Seminole Pink' bears bright pink single flowers almost year-round; grows 8–10 ft. tall.

Red. 'Brilliant' ('San Diego Red') is a vigorous grower with bright red single flowers in profusion. 'Cooperi' bears small, single, deep red flowers, but principal attraction is the foliage—narrow leaves variegated with white. 'Diamond Head' has large double flowers in deepest red (nearly black); compact growth to 5 ft. 'Ecstasy' produces large, single, bright red flowers with striking white variegation; upright growth to 4 ft. 'Flamenco Flame' has double red flowers and grows to 6–7 ft. 'Itsy Bitsy Red' has small leaves; its single flowers are 2–3 in. across. 'Jason Okumoto' bears semidouble, scarlet-throated flowers with a cup-and-saucer look (thick central group of shorter orange petals surrounded by collar of large pink petals). 'Kate Sessions' has large, broad-petaled, single flowers in red with a gold tinge on the petal undersides; upright, open growth to 10 ft. 'President' bears large single blooms of intense red, shading to deep pink in the throat; grows upright and compact to 6–7 ft. tall. 'Red Dragon' ('Celia') has small to medium, double, dark red flowers; upright, compact plant reaches 6–8 ft. tall. 'Vulcan' has yellow buds that open into large, single red flowers with yellow on back of petals; compact growth to 4–6 ft.

All of the above varieties are what might be called landscape hibiscus. They are plants sturdy enough to survive reliably in open ground wherever hibiscus are hardy, and they bloom reliably with routine good care. Plants of another group—one that might be called show or connoisseur's hibiscus—are becoming available. These have large (8–10-in.), single or double flowers in striking colors, including novel shades such as gray, tan, mauve, brown, and blue. Most show blends of two or three colors. Plants are grafted onto sturdy rootstocks. They grow to 4–8 ft. tall and wide in the ground, 3–4 ft. in containers. To bloom, they need night temperatures in the 60s or higher, warmer temperatures by day, and at least 1 hour of direct sun daily. The following selections, all with single

H

H

flowers, are a few of the many varieties that are available.

'Fifth Dimension'. Gunmetal gray edged with orange and yellow; white lines radiate from the center toward the edges.

'Georgia's Pearl'. Pure light yellow blossoms have a dark red eye surrounded by a narrow zone of pink.

'Rainbow Christie'. Pink with a dark red eye and a wide white, cream, or yellow border.

'Silver Memories'. Unusual combination of silvery white with yellow or orange border.

H. sabdariffa. ROSELLE, JAMAICA SORREL, JAMAICA FLOWER. Annual. Zones 1–24; H1, H2. Native from India to Malaysia. Narrowish plant reaches 4–7 ft. high. Oval, 3-in.-long leaves with three to five lobes. Grown for fleshy red calyxes that surround bases of yellow flowers. These calyxes are used for making sauce, jelly, cool drinks, or teas; dried, they are known as Jamaica flowers. Their flavor is reminiscent of cranberry or currant. Plants need long, hot summer to ripen flowers. Bloom begins as days shorten; early frosts prevent harvest. Grow like tomatoes; space plants 1½–2 ft. apart in rows. Can be used as narrow temporary hedge.

Hibiscus schizopetalus

H. schizopetalus. FRINGED HIBISCUS, CORAL HIBISCUS. Evergreen shrub. Zones 23, 24; H1, H2. From tropical East Africa. To 9–15 ft. high, 6–12 ft. wide, with a weeping habit. Throughout most of the year, produces unusual pink flowers with fringed petals. There are a number of hybrids with pure white, pink, red, or yellow blossoms. Plants are sometimes kept small and grown in hanging baskets.

H. syriacus. ROSE OF SHARON, SHRUB ALTHAEA. Deciduous shrub. Zones 2–24; H1.

Hibiscus syriacus 'Diana'

From eastern Asia. To 10–12 ft. tall and 6 ft. wide. Upright and compact when young, spreading and open with age. Easily trained to a single trunk with a treelike top or as an espalier. Sometimes kept trimmed as a hedge. Leaves to 4 in. long, often three lobed, coarsely toothed. Leafs out later in spring than most other deciduous shrubs; foliage drops in fall without coloring. Blooms from mid- or late summer until frost, resembling a bush covered with hollyhocks. Blossoms are single, semidouble, or double, 2½–3 in. across; some have a conspicuously contrasting red to purple throat. Single flowers are slightly more effective, opening somewhat wider, but they tend to produce many unattractive capsule-type fruits—which in turn produce many unwanted seedlings.

Easy to grow. Prefers heat, tolerates some drought. Prune to shape; for bigger flowers, cut back previous season's growth in winter, cutting down to two buds. Where winter temperatures drop to −10°F/−23°C or lower, protect young plants with a winter mulch for first few years. The following, some of them hard to find, are among the best varieties.

'Albus'. Single pure white blooms to 4 in. across.

'Anemoniflora' ('Paeoniflora'). Semidouble red blossoms with a deeper crimson eye.

'Ardens'. Double purple.

'Blue Bird'. Single blue with deep red eye.

'Blushing Bride'. Double bright pink.

'Boule de Feu'. Double deep violet pink.

'Coelestis'. Single violet blue with reddish purple throat.

'Collie Mullens'. Double purplish lavender.

'Lavender Chiffon'. Single lavender with center tuft of petals.

'Lucy'. Double deep rose with red eye.

'Meehanii'. Small, pale purple with dark centers; variegated foliage with creamy white margins.

'Purpurea'. Semidouble purple with red eye.

'Red Heart'. Single white with red eye.

'White Chiffon'. Single white with center tuft of petals.

'Woodbridge'. Single deep rose with red eye.

Newer selections are sterile triploids, which have a long blooming season and set few or no seedpods. They include 'Aphrodite', rose pink with deep red eye; 'Diana', pure white; 'Helene', white with deep red eye; and 'Minerva', ruffled flowers of lavender pink with reddish purple eye.

H. tiliaceus. TREE HIBISCUS, HAU, MAHOE. Evergreen tree. Zones 23, 24; H1, H2. Native to tropical Asia and Polynesia. Reaches 30 ft. tall and wide, with broad, leathery, unlobed green leaves to 6 in. long. The 4-in. flowers, each lasting a day, open yellow and deepen to orange by day's end. Excellent tolerance of salt, wind, drought, and heat. Tangled mess in the wild; requires heavy pruning to shape into suitable tree form and regular pruning to maintain form.

H. waimeae. WHITE KAUAI HIBISCUS, KOKIO KEOKEO. Evergreen shrub or tree. Zone H1. Native to Kauai. To 18–25 ft. tall and about half as wide. Blooms much of the year. Each fragrant, 5–8-in. flower lasts just one day; blossoms open white in the morning, turn light pinkish by afternoon. Rounded, downy light green leaves to 7 in. long. Use singly as a specimen or mass as a screen. Protect from wind. Full sun or light shade.

HIDALGO.
See **STACHYS albotomentosa**

HIMALAYACALAMUS.
See **BAMBOO**

HIMALAYAN HONEYSUCKLE or PHEASANTBERRY.
See **LEYCESTERIA formosa**

HIMALAYAN POPPY.
See **MECONOPSIS betonicifolia**

HINAHINA. See **HELIOTROPIUM anomalum argenteum**

HIPPEASTRUM
AMARYLLIS
Amaryllidaceae
PERENNIALS FROM BULBS

🖋	ZONES VARY BY TYPE; OR INDOORS
☀ ◐	LIGHT SHADE IN HOTTEST CLIMATES; BRIGHT LIGHT
💧	REGULAR WATER DURING GROWTH AND BLOOM
☣	BULB IS TOXIC IF INGESTED

Almost all amaryllis sold are hybrids; they can be grown outdoors year-round in Zones 13, 15–17, 21–24, H1, H2, and (with some shelter) in Zones 8, 9, 14, 18, 20. Usually marketed as giant amaryllis or Royal Dutch amaryllis (though developed by hybridizers around the world from species native to Central and South America). Named varieties or color selections are available in reds, pinks, salmon, near-orange, and white, some striped and variously

Hippeastrum hybrid

marked. Two to several flowers, often 8–9 in. across, form on a stout, 2-ft. stem. Newer forms include double-flowered varieties in white (some with picotee edges), creamy yellow, and pink; miniatures with 3–5-in. flowers topping 12–15-in. stems; and an unusual evergreen Brazilian species, *H. papilio* (Zones 8, 9, 13–24), with 5-in. greenish white flowers heavily patterned in dark red.

Where amaryllis are grown outdoors, flowers bloom in spring, appearing either before or with the broad, strap-shaped leaves. Indoors, they bloom just a few weeks after planting.

Where hardy in the ground, they can be planted in large clumps or drifts. In fall, set bulbs 1 ft. apart in organically enriched, well-drained soil; keep tops of bulb necks even with soil surface. Protect from slugs and snails. Water thoroughly, then keep soil barely moist until leaves emerge. Once plants have sprouted, increase watering, giving enough to keep soil moist but not soggy. Leaves will grow through summer and disappear in fall if plants are dried off; otherwise, some foliage will remain. Divide infrequently.

Even where they are hardy, amaryllis are usually grown in containers. Plant them from midautumn through winter in a rich, sandy potting mix amended with bonemeal or superphosphate. Allow a 2-in. space between the bulb and the edge of the pot; set upper half of bulb above soil surface. Firm soil, water well, and then keep soil barely moist until plant growth begins. When flowers fade, cut off stem; keep up regular watering and feeding until late summer. At this point, cut back on watering. When leaves are completely yellow, withhold water and let plants dry out. Repot in late fall or early winter.

HIPPOPHAE rhamnoides

SEA BUCKTHORN
Elaeagnaceae
DECIDUOUS SHRUB OR TREE

🌡	ZONES A2, A3; 1–6
☼	FULL SUN
💧	MODERATE TO REGULAR WATER

Native from Europe to Mongolia. Usually seen as an open, mounding shrub 8–10 ft. tall and wide, but it can grow much taller and spread by suckering from the roots. Thorny branches carry nar-

Hippophae rhamnoides

row (¼-in.-wide), 3-in.-long, silvery green to grayish green leaves. Flowers are inconspicuous, but fruits on female plants are showy —bright orange, round or oval, to ⅓ in. long. Fruit persists on the plant into winter—apparently it is too acidic to appeal to birds. High in vitamin C, it can be made into sauces or jam. You need both male and female plants to get fruit.

Sea buckthorn tolerates cold, wind, poor soil (as long as it is well drained), and salt spray. Good screen plant for difficult situations.

HOARY MINT.
See **POLIOMINTHA incana**

HOGAN CEDAR.
See **THUJA plicata 'Fastigiata'**

HOLLY. See **ILEX**

HOLLY FERN, BRAUN'S.
See **POLYSTICHUM braunii**

HOLLY FERN, JAPANESE.
See **CYRTOMIUM falcatum**

HOLLY FERN, LONG-EARED.
See **POLYSTICHUM neolobatum**

HOLLYHOCK. See **ALCEA rosea**

HOLLYLEAF CHERRY.
See **PRUNUS ilicifolia**

HOLODISCUS

Rosaceae
DECIDUOUS SHRUBS

🌡	ZONES VARY BY SPECIES
☼	PARTIAL SHADE
💧	LITTLE TO REGULAR WATER

Both species described here are Western natives, similar in appearance to the related *Spiraea*. Nodding, branched clusters of many small, creamy white flowers at branch tips in late spring or early summer make quite a show and attract birds. Flowers age to tannish gold, remain attractive for a long time. Prune by thinning after flowers have turned brown and clusters have withered. Use these shrubs in native plantings or rural low-maintenance gardens where they can fend for themselves.

H. discolor. CREAM BUSH, OCEAN SPRAY. Zones 1–9, 14–19. Native to Coast Ranges, Sierra Nevada; north to British Columbia, east to Rocky Mountains. May reach 20 ft. tall and 15 ft. wide in moist, rich soil. In dry, sunny situations, such as east of Cascades in Oregon and Washington, may grow just 3 ft. tall and

4 ft. wide. Triangular leaves to 3 in. long are deep green above, white and hairy beneath; edges are coarsely toothed. Flower clusters to 1 ft. long.

Holodiscus discolor

H. dumosus. MOUNTAIN SPRAY, ROCK SPIRAEA. Zones 1–3, 10. Native to eastern slopes of the Cascades of Oregon and to shady canyons in the Rockies from Wyoming southward. Generally smaller than *H. discolor* (may reach 15 ft. tall in good conditions), with narrower, shorter flower clusters (to 7 in. long). Coarsely toothed leaves less than 1 in. long.

HOMERIA collina (Moraea collina)

Iridaceae
PERENNIAL FROM CORM

🌡	ZONES 4–24; OR DIG AND STORE
☼	FULL SUN
💧	REGULAR WATER DURING GROWTH AND BLOOM

Native to South Africa, where it is often found growing on slopes from low to high altitudes. Recently reclassified as *Moraea*. First comes one floppy, grasslike leaf. It is followed by branching or unbranched, 1½-ft. stems bearing 2½–3-in.-wide flowers in soft yellow or muted orange. Soon after bloom, the foliage yellows and dies down. Where adapted, plant anytime from fall through winter, setting corms 2 in. deep, 3 in. apart; in such regions, corms can be left in the ground and allowed to multiply freely. If they will receive moisture during their long dormancy, however, soil must be very well drained. If drainage is less than excellent and you can't keep planting area dry, dig after leaves have died down and store over

Homeria collina

summer; or grow in pots. In areas beyond hardiness range, plant in spring (as soon as soil can be worked) for summer flowers; lift corms in late summer or early fall and store over winter. In areas where the species has escaped gardens and naturalized, it has been found toxic to livestock.

HONEY BUSH.
See **MELIANTHUS major**

HONEY LOCUST.
See **GLEDITSIA triacanthos**

HONEY MYRTLE.
See **MELALEUCA**

HONEYSUCKLE.
See **LONICERA**

HONEYWORT.
See **CERINTHE major**

HOP. See **HUMULUS**

HOP BUSH, HOPSEED BUSH.
See **DODONAEA**

HOREHOUND.
See **MARRUBIUM vulgare**

HORNBEAM. See **CARPINUS**

HORNED POPPY.
See **GLAUCIUM**

HORSECHESTNUT.
See **AESCULUS**

HORSEMINT. See **MONARDA**

HORSERADISH

Brassicaceae (Cruciferae)
PERENNIAL

🌡	ALL ZONES
☼	FULL SUN
💧	REGULAR WATER

Native to southeastern Europe. Large (to about 3-ft.), coarse, weedy-looking plant grown for

Horseradish

its large white roots, which are peeled, grated, and mixed with vinegar or cream to make a condiment. Does best in rich, moist soils in cool regions. Grow it in some sunny, out-of-the-way corner. In late winter or early spring, set root horizontally in a 3–4-in.-deep trench and cover with 2 in. of soil. One plant should provide enough horseradish for a family of four. For multiple plants, space 2½–3 ft. apart. Through fall, winter, and spring, harvest pieces of horseradish roots from the outside of the root clump as you need them—that way you'll have your horseradish fresh and tangy.

HORSETAIL.
See **EQUISETUM hyemale**

HORSETAIL TREE.
See **CASUARINA equisetifolia**

HOSTA
PLANTAIN LILY
Liliaceae
PERENNIALS

| 🌿 ZONES VARY BY SPECIES |
| 🌤 ⬤ PARTIAL OR FULL SHADE |
| 💧 REGULAR WATER |

These plants' real glory is in their foliage—the thin spikes of blue or white trumpet-shaped flowers that last for several weeks in summer are a dividend. Leaves may be heart shaped, lance shaped, oval, or nearly round, carried at the ends of leafstalks that rise from the ground and radiate from the center of a clump. They overlap to form symmetrical, almost shingled-looking foliage mounds ranging in size from dwarf (as small as 3–4 in. across) to giant (as broad as 5 ft.). Leaves may be glossy or dull, with smooth, quilted, or puckery texture and smooth or wavy edges. Foliage colors range from light to dark green to chartreuse (sometimes almost yellow), gray, and blue. There are also color combinations, including variegations in

white, cream, or yellow. (Color of variegation may differ with climate and soil type.)

New varieties enter the scene in ever-increasing numbers. To be sure you are getting the one you want, buy the plant in full leaf or deal with an expert. Many hostas are available only from mail-order specialists. All are native to eastern Asia.

Generally, hostas are shade lovers, though some will tolerate sun (those with considerable white or yellow in leaves are least sun tolerant), and most will take considerable sun in cool-summer zones. Plants grown in sun will be more compact and will produce more flowers. Good in containers. Hostas grow most luxuriantly in good, organically enriched soil, with regular feeding during the growing season. All go dormant in winter (even in mild climates), collapsing to almost nothing. Clumps expand in size over the years and shade out weeds; remain vigorous without division— clumps become more beautiful as they grow larger. To increase a planting, carefully remove plantlets from a clump's perimeter. Or cut a wedge-shaped piece from a clump and transplant it; the clump will fill in quickly. Protect from slugs and snails with a nontoxic control, such as iron phosphate pellets. Hostas with heavily textured or waxy leaves are less attractive to these pests.

H. fortunei. Zones A1–A3; 1–10, 14–21. Variable plant known mainly for its many varieties, which offer a wide range of foliage colors. Two choices, both to 2 ft. tall and 3 ft. wide, are *H. f. aureomarginata*, with distinctly veined, deep olive green leaves irregularly rimmed in yellow, and *H. f. hyacinthina*, which has slightly puckered gray-green leaves edged with a fine white line. Both bear lavender blooms in late spring.

H. hybrids. Zones 1–10, 14–21; some succeed in Zones A2, A3, and 22–24. The following list represents just a few of the many hundreds of possibilities. Size given at the start of each listing is for foliage clump. Performance in

Zones 22–24 will vary, but all are worth a try in these areas.

'Blue Angel'. To 2½ ft. tall, 6 ft. wide. Blue leaves; near-white flowers on 4-ft. stalks.

'Blue Cadet'. To 15 in. tall and wide. Dense, neat clumps of blue-green leaves good for edging. Lavender blooms.

'Francee'. To 15 in. tall, 3 ft. wide. Dark green leaves with a sharply defined white border; light lavender flowers on 2½-ft. stalks.

'Frances Williams'. To 20 in. tall, 3 ft. wide. Heavily corrugated blue leaves are bordered with yellow. White flowers on 2-ft. stalks.

'Gold Standard'. To 2 ft. tall, 3 ft. wide. Bright golden leaves with a blue-green margin. Lavender flowers.

'Great Expectations'. To 2 ft. tall, 2½ ft. wide. Leaves are creamy yellow in center, surrounded by a wide blue-green edge. White flowers on 3-ft. stalks.

'Honeybells'. To 2½ ft. high, 4 ft. wide. Wavy-edged yellow-green leaves; lightly scented pale lilac flowers on stalks 3 ft. tall.

Hosta
'Great Expectations'

'June'. To 14–16 in. tall, 2½ ft. wide. Heart shaped leaves are blue gray at margins, irregularly variegated with greenish yellow and bright yellow. Lavender blooms on 1½-ft.-tall stems.

'Krossa Regal'. To 2½ ft. high and wide, with big, leathery, frosty blue leaves that arch upward and outward to form a vase-shaped plant. Lavender flower spikes can reach 5–6 ft. tall.

'Patriot'. To 15 in. tall, 3 ft. wide. Resembles 'Francee', but leaves have a wider white border. Lavender flowers on 2½-ft. stems.

'Royal Standard'. To 2 ft. high, 3–4 ft. wide. Glossy, light green leaves are oval to heart shaped and ribbed, with undulating margins. Fragrant white flowers on 3-ft.-tall stalks.

'Sagae'. To 2 ft. tall, 3 ft. wide, with upswept foliage forming a vase shape. Blue-gray leaves with a wide creamy white border. Lavender flowers on 4½-ft. stalks.

'Sum and Substance'. To 3 ft. high, 6 ft. wide, with textured chartreuse leaves that turn golden with age. Pale lavender flowers.

H. plantaginea. FRAGRANT PLANTAIN LILY. Zones 1–10, 14–24. To 2 ft. high, 3 ft. wide.

Glossy bright green leaves to 10 in. long, broadly oval with parallel veins and quilted surface. Large, noticeably fragrant white flowers on 2½-ft. stalks. 'Venus' forms a slightly shorter clump and has double flowers.

H. sieboldiana. Zones 1–10, 14–21. To 3 ft. high, 4 ft. wide. Blue-green, broadly heart-shaped leaves, 10–15 in. long, heavily veined and puckered. Many slender pale lilac flowers nestle close to leaves. Foliage of 'Elegans' is covered in a blue-gray bloom.

H. ventricosa (H. caerulea). BLUE PLANTAIN LILY. Zones 1–10, 14–24. To 2 ft. high, 3 ft. wide. Common name refers to violet-blue blossoms on 3-ft. stalks, not to foliage color: leaves are glossy deep green, broadly heart shaped, prominently veined, to 8 in. long. Leaves of 'Aureo-maculata' are yellowish green with a green border. 'Aureo-marginata' ('Variegata') has green leaves edged with creamy white.

HOTTENTOT FIG.
See **CARPOBROTUS edulis**

HOUSELEEK.
See **SEMPERVIVUM**

HOUTTUYNIA
cordata
Saururaceae
PERENNIAL

| 🌿 ZONES 2–9, 14–24 |
| 🌤 🌤 ⬤ SUN OR SHADE |
| 💧 💧 REGULAR TO AMPLE WATER |

From China, Japan. Spreading underground stems send up 9-in.-high blanket of foliage—heart-shaped green leaves to 3 in. long that look very much like those of English ivy (*Hedera helix*). Foliage emits an odd scent when crushed, reminiscent of orange peel. Inconspicuous clusters of white-bracted flowers like tiny dogwood

Houttuynia cordata
'Chameleon'

(Cornus) blossoms. Unusual ground cover that disappears completely in winter, even in mild climates. Most commonly grown form of species is 'Chameleon' ('Tricolor', 'Variegata'), with showy splashes of cream, pink, yellow, and red on foliage; colors are most intense in sun.

Can spread aggressively in wet ground. For ground cover, plant 1½–2 ft. apart; curb growth with wood, concrete, or metal barrier extending 8–12 in. into the soil. Attractive in containers.

HOWEA

Arecaceae (Palmae)
PALMS

- ZONES 17, 21–24; H1, H2; OR INDOORS
- PARTIAL SHADE; BRIGHT INDIRECT LIGHT
- REGULAR WATER

Feather palms native to Lord Howe Island in the South Pacific. Slow growing; reach full height in tropics but only perhaps half as tall in California, where they are typically planted under other trees for frost protection. With age, finely divided leaves drop to show clean, green trunk ringed with leaf scars. These are the kentia palms of florists' shops (usually sold there under the name "kentia") and make ideal potted plants—the classic parlor palms. To minimize spider mite problems, keep fronds clean and dust free. Indoor plants withstand drafts, some watering neglect.

H. belmoreana. SENTRY PALM. Less common than *H. forsteriana*. Tends to be smaller than the latter (grows to 25 ft. tall and 15 ft. wide), with 6–7-ft.-long leaves.

H. forsteriana. PARADISE PALM. To 60 ft. tall, 20 ft. wide, with leaves to 9 ft. long; leaflets are long and drooping.

Howea forsteriana

HOYA

WAX FLOWER, WAX PLANT
Asclepiadaceae
PERENNIALS

- ZONES VARY BY SPECIES; OR INDOORS
- PARTIAL OR FULL SHADE; BRIGHT LIGHT
- REGULAR WATER

Tropical plants with thick, waxy, evergreen leaves and tight clusters of small, waxy flowers that appear in leaf joints during summer. These plants prefer rich, loose, well-drained soil. When grown as container plants, they bloom best when pot-bound. Do not prune out the short stalks that bear flowers, because new flower clusters will develop on them. Specialists list dozens of available species and hybrids, with growth habit varying from vining to shrubby.

H. carnosa. WAX FLOWER, WAX PLANT. Zones H1, H2; with overhead protection, also in Zones 15–24 (but even there it is quickly damaged by temperatures much below freezing). From India, Burma, southern China. Vining plant grows to 10–20 ft., with green, oval, 2–4-in.-long rigid

Hoya carnosa

leaves. Fragrant (more pronounced at night) flowers in big, round, convex clusters; each ½-in. blossom is creamy white, centered with a five-pointed pink star. Red young leaves give extra color. Attractive trained on a pillar or trellis. Indoors, traditionally trained on wire in a sunny window. In cool climates, allow plant to go dormant in winter, giving only enough water to keep it from shriveling.

'Variegata' has leaves edged in white suffused with pink; it is not as vigorous or hardy as the plain species. 'Exotica' shows yellow-and-pink variegation. 'Krinkle Kurl' has crinkly leaves closely spaced on short stems; it is often sold as 'Compacta' or as Hindurope plant.

H. lanceolata bella. Zones H1, H2; indoor/outdoor plant elsewhere. Native from Himalayas to Burma. Shrubby growth to 1½–3 ft. high and wide, with fleshy green leaves to 1½ in. long and sweetly aromatic clusters of ½-in., purple-centered white flowers. Slender, upright branches droop as they grow older. Best used in hanging basket.

HUCKLEBERRY. See **VACCINIUM ovatum, V. parvifolium**

HUMATA tyermannii

BEAR'S FOOT FERN
Polypodiaceae
FERN

- ZONES 17, 23, 24; H1, H2; OR INDOORS
- PARTIAL SHADE
- REGULAR WATER

Native to China. This small fern has furry, creeping rhizomes that look something like bear's feet. Fronds 8–10 in. long, very finely cut, rising at intervals from the rhizome. Like squirrel's foot fern *(Davallia trichomanoides)* in appearance, culture, and uses, but slower growing. Sometimes listed as *Davallia tyermannii*.

Humata tyermannii

HUMBOLDT COUNTY FUCHSIA. See **ZAUSCHNERIA septentrionalis**

HUMMINGBIRD BUSH. See **GREVILLEA thelemanniana**

HUMMINGBIRD FLOWER. See **ZAUSCHNERIA**

HUMMINGBIRD MINT. See **AGASTACHE**

HUMMINGBIRD TRUMPET. See **ZAUSCHNERIA californica**

HUMULUS

HOP
Cannabaceae
PERENNIAL VINES

- ZONES A2, A3; 1–10, 14–21
- FULL SUN
- REGULAR WATER

Extremely fast-growing perennial vines with large, deeply lobed, toothed leaves to 6 in. long are attractive for summer screening on trellises or arbors—and one species yields the hops used in beer. Bloom in late summer. Male plants produce flower panicles; females bear blossoms in greenish spikes resembling pinecones. Squarish, hairy stems twine vertically; to get horizontal growth, twine stem tips by hand. Cut stems to ground after frost turns them brown; regrowth comes the following spring.

H. japonicus. JAPANESE HOP. From eastern Asia. Grows to 20–30 ft. Bears ¾-in. female flower spikes. Dark green leaves have five to seven lobes; 'Variegatus' marked with white. Sow seeds in place in spring.

H. lupulus. COMMON HOP. From many northern temperate regions of the world. This species produces the traditional flavoring for beer. The hops, or female flowers, are soft, flaky, 1–2-in., light green cones of bracts and blossoms that emit a fresh, piny fragrance. Bright green leaves have three to five lobes. Tender top shoots can be cooked as a vegetable. Plants sold in nurseries are typically female; no pollenizer needed. May be offered as potted plants or as dormant roots. The roots should be planted in rich soil in early spring; set just below surface of soil with thick end up. Many varieties are available, including 'Aureus', which has attractive chartreuse foliage. *H. l. neomexicanus (H. americanus)*, native to central and southern Rockies, differs from the plain species only in botanical details.

Humulus lupulus

H

H

HUNNEMANNIA fumariifolia

MEXICAN TULIP POPPY, GOLDEN CUP
Papaveraceae
PERENNIAL USUALLY TREATED AS ANNUAL

🌿	ZONES 1–24; H1, H2
☀️	FULL SUN
💧💧	LITTLE OR NO WATER TO MODERATE WATER

Mexican native related to California poppy (*Eschscholzia*). Bushy, open grower to 2–3 ft. high; finely divided blue-green leaves. Cup-shaped, pure yellow blooms, 3 in. across with crinkled petals, in

Hunnemannia fumariifolia

summer, early fall. If cut in bud, blooms last for a week in water. Plant from containers or start from seed, sowing seed in place in warm, sunny location and thinning seedlings to 1 ft. apart. Showy when massed. Reseeds. Needs excellent drainage.

HYACINTH BEAN.
See **DOLICHOS lablab**

HYACINTHOIDES

BLUEBELL, WOOD HYACINTH
Liliaceae
PERENNIALS FROM BULBS

🌿	ZONES VARY BY SPECIES
🌤️	FILTERED SUN OR LIGHT SHADE
💧	REGULAR WATER DURING GROWTH AND BLOOM
🌸	BULBS MAY CAUSE AN ALLERGIC SKIN REACTION

These spring-blooming bulbs were once classed in the genus *Scilla* and are still popularly known by that name; some bulb dealers continue to list them as such. They were later reclassified as *Endymion* and now have been renamed *Hyacinthoides*. They resemble hyacinths but are taller, with looser flower clusters and fewer, narrower leaves.

Climate will determine which species is better for your area.

Spanish bluebell (*H. hispanica*) is the better choice for warmer regions. The English species (*H. non-scripta*) definitely prefers colder winters and moderate to cool summers. When grown near each other, the two species sometimes hybridize, producing intermediate forms. Plant bulbs in fall, setting them 3 in. deep in mild climates, as deep as 6 in. where winters are severe. Space about 6 in. apart. Propensity for reseeding makes these good subjects for naturalizing; lovely in informal drifts among tall shrubs, under deciduous trees, among low-growing perennials. Need regular moisture from planting time until foliage dies and at least some moisture in summer. Divide infrequently; when division is needed, do it in fall. Plants thrive in pots, and flowers are good for cutting.

H. hispanica (Scilla campanulata, S. hispanica). SPANISH BLUEBELL. Zones 1–11, 14–24. From Spain, North Africa. Prolific and vigorous, with inch-wide, strap-shaped leaves and sturdy, 20-in. stems bearing 12 or more nodding, unscented bells about ¾ in. long. Blue is the most popular color, 'Excelsior' (deep blue) the most popular variety. There are also white, pink, and rose forms. Leaves can look a trifle ratty before dying back.

Hyacinthoides non-scripta

H. non-scripta (Scilla non-scripta). ENGLISH BLUEBELL, WOOD HYACINTH. Best in Zones 2b–6, 15. From western Europe. Fragrant blue flowers are narrower and smaller than those of *H. hispanica,* on 1-ft. stems that nod at the tip. Leaves are also narrower—only about ½ in. wide. 'Alba' is white flowered; 'Rosea' has pink blossoms.

HYACINTHUS

HYACINTH
Liliaceae
PERENNIALS FROM BULBS

🌿	ZONES VARY BY TYPE
☀️	FULL SUN
💧	REGULAR WATER DURING GROWTH AND BLOOM
🌸	BULBS MAY CAUSE AN ALLERGIC SKIN REACTION

Springtime bloomers grown for spikes of bell-shaped, fragrant flowers that rise from basal bundle of narrow bright green leaves. Two species formerly sold as *Hyacinthus* have been reclassified; the species that remains is the common hyacinth.

H. amethystinus. See Brimeura amethystina

H. azureus. See Muscari azureum

Hyacinthus orientalis

H. orientalis. COMMON HYACINTH. To most gardeners, hyacinths are the highly fragrant, fat-spiked Dutch hybrids derived from this species. They grow to 1 ft. tall, with straplike leaves that may be erect or arching. Large flower spikes are tightly packed with waxy blooms in white, cream, buff, yellow, pink, salmon, red, blue, or purple. Largest bulbs (called exhibition size) produce largest spikes and are the best choice for containers and forced flowers. Next largest size is good for massing in beds and borders. Smallest bulbs produce smaller, looser flower spikes—same results you'll get from larger bulbs left in the ground year to year. Dutch hybrids can be grown in all zones outside Hawaii, but bulbs left in the ground will persist only in regions with distinct winter cold. Best treated as annuals in Zones 8, 9, 11–24.

Roman or French Roman hyacinth (*H. o. albulus*), native to south of France, is smaller than the Dutch hybrids and blooms earlier. Each bulb usually produces several slender, foot-tall stems, each with loose spikes of white, pale blue, or pink flowers. Good for naturalizing and informal drifts. Thrives in regions with little or no winter chill; will persist year after year in Zones 4–24.

Both Dutch hybrids and Roman hyacinth must be planted early enough to establish roots before ground freezes. Where winter temperatures drop below 20°F/−7°C, set out bulbs in earliest fall; in warmer regions, delay until mid- to late fall (keep bulbs cool until then). Plant in organically enriched, sandy, well-drained soil. Set largest Dutch hybrid bulbs 4–5 in. deep, 5 in. apart; set smaller hybrid bulbs and Roman hyacinth bulbs 3 in. deep, 4–5 in. apart. (Hyacinth bulbs have invisible barbs on their surfaces that can cause some people's skin to itch; after handling, wash hands before touching face or eyes.) If bulbs will remain in the ground, fertilize just as blossoms fade, remove spent spikes, and keep watering regularly until foliage yellows.

Choice container plants. Pot in porous mix with tip of bulb near surface. Cover potting mix with thick mulch of sawdust, wood shavings, or peat moss to keep bulbs cool, moist, and shaded until top growth shows; remove mulch and place in full light.

To grow hyacinths in water in a special hyacinth glass, keep in a dark, cool place until rooted, then give light when top growth appears; place hyacinths in sunny window when leaves have turned uniformly green.

HYDRANGEA

Hydrangeaceae (Saxifragaceae)
DECIDUOUS SHRUBS AND VINES, EXCEPT AS NOTED

🌿	ZONES VARY BY SPECIES
☀️🌤️	PARTIAL SHADE IN HOTTEST CLIMATES
💧	REGULAR WATER

Big, bold leaves and large clusters of long-lasting flowers in white, pink, red, or blue. Summer and fall bloom. Flower clusters may contain sterile flowers (conspicuous, with large, petal-like sepals) or fertile flowers (small, starry petaled); or they may feature a cluster of small fertile flowers surrounded by ring of big sterile ones (these are called lacecap hydrangeas). Sterile flowers last for a long time (often holding up for months), gradually fading in color.

In some hydrangea varieties, blue or pink flower color is affected by soil pH—bluest color is produced in strongly acid soils (below pH 5.5), pink or red in neutral to alkaline soils (pH 7.0 and higher). Florists control flower color of potted hydrangeas by controlling soil mix; blue-flowered florists' plants may show pink blossoms when planted out in less acid soil, and pink-flowered types will turn blue in less alkaline soil. In either case, the plants may go through a year or two of transition, showing murky purple flower colors. Flowers can be made (or kept) blue by applying aluminum sulfate to the soil, kept red (or pink) or made redder by liming the soil or applying superphosphate in quantity. Flower-color treatment is not effective unless started well ahead of bloom. Varieties with white flowers stay white.

Hydrangeas are good looking as single plants, massed, or in tubs on the patio. Easy to grow in rich, porous soil. Fast growing. Prune as needed to control form—in late dormant season for those producing blooms on new growth, after bloom for those flowering on previous year's growth. To get biggest flower clusters, reduce number of stems; for numerous medium-size clusters, keep more stems.

H. anomala petiolaris (H. petiolaris). CLIMBING HYDRANGEA. Vine. Zones A2, A3; 2–21. From Russia, Korea, Japan. Climbs high (as far as 60 ft.) with its clinging aerial rootlets; shrubby and sprawling without support. Green, 2–4-in.-long leaves have a rounded heart shape. Mature plants develop short, flowering branches with flat, white, 6–10-in.-wide lacecap flower clusters. Becomes woody with age. Prune out overly vigorous growth only after vine is well established and climbing. Can be rejuvenated by cutting back to framework in late dormant season. 'Mirranda' has leaves with irregular yellow margins; it is slower growing than the species.

H. arborescens. SMOOTH HYDRANGEA. Shrub. Zones A3; 1–21. Native from New York to Iowa, south to Florida, Louisiana. Upright, dense growth to 10 ft. tall and wide. Oval, grayish green,

4–8-in. leaves; white flowers. In basic species, most flowers in a cluster are fertile; the few sterile ones are not plentiful enough for full lacecap effect. Much showier is 'Annabelle', which produces enormous (to 1-ft.) globular clusters of sterile flowers on a plant about 4 ft. tall and wide. 'Grandiflora' is another 4-footer; its flower clusters are 6 in. across. 'White Dome' grows about 5 ft. tall and wide, with sturdy stems holding white, dome-shaped flower clusters to 10 in. across; a few sterile flowers surround the tightly packed fertile ones. *H. a. radiata*, sometimes called silverleaf hydrangea, has leaves with a coating of minute white hairs on the underside. Prune all of these in late dormant season.

H. aspera. Shrub. Zones 4–9, 14–24. From eastern Asia. Imposing shrub to 10–12 ft. tall, spreading nearly as wide. Dark green, somewhat hairy leaves to 10 in. long, 4 in. wide. Rather flat, 10-in. flower clusters contain purplish white to pink fertile flowers surrounded by 1-in. white, pink, or purple sterile blooms. 'Macrophylla' has leaves larger than those of the species; its wide domes of purple-blue fertile flowers are surrounded by white sterile blooms. Prune in late dormant season. To make a broad, many-stemmed plant, cut back hard for first 3 years; flowering will be delayed, but the plant's form will be improved.

H. a. sargentiana (H. sargentiana) has broader, more heavily furred leaves. Fertile flowers are light purple; sterile ones are pinkish white, about 1½ in. across.

Villosa Group *(H. villosa)* has blue or purple fertile flowers and 1-in.-wide, pale pinkish purple sterile flowers.

H. macrophylla (H. hortensia, H. opuloides, H. otaksa). BIGLEAF HYDRANGEA, GARDEN HYDRANGEA. Shrub. Zones 3b–9, 14–24; H1. From Japan. Symmetrical, rounded habit; grows to 4–8 ft. high (or more) and as wide. Thick, shiny, coarsely toothed leaves to 8 in. long; flow-

Hydrangea macrophylla

ers of white, pink, red, or blue (often depending on soil pH) are held in big clusters. Great performer in areas where winters are fairly mild; disappointing where plants freeze to ground every year (they may never bloom under these conditions, since flower buds are produced on old wood). Protect in colder zones by mounding soil or leaves over base of plants. Prune after bloom.

Varieties with rounded flower clusters (sometimes called mophead or hortensia types) include 'All Summer Beauty', which produces its dark blue or pinkish blooms on new wood and should be pruned in late dormant season; 'Ayesha', with light purplish pink cupped flowers (like little buttons); 'Buttons 'n Bows', only 3–4 ft. tall and wide, with deep pink flowers featuring white-edged petals; 'Domotoi', an old favorite with clusters of pink or blue double sterile flowers; 'Endless Summer', which produces pink or blue blooms on both old and new wood; 'Merritt's Beauty', with deep carmine-red flowers; 'Nigra', with dark purple-black stems bearing light green leaves and flowers that vary from soft pink to blue; 'Nikko Blue', with large blue blossom clusters; 'Pia' ('Pink Elf'), a dwarf at just 1½ ft. tall and 2 ft. wide, with deep pink flowers; 'Pink 'n Pretty', with bright pink blooms on a compact plant 4–6 ft. high and 3–4 ft. wide; and 'Red 'n Pretty', which is similar but has flowers of deep rosy pink.

Varieties with lacecap flowers include 'Blue Wave', with light blue to pink sterile flowers and darker fertile flowers; 'Lady in Red', featuring red stems and leaf veins, light pink flowers that age to burgundy, and lovely red fall color; 'Lanarth White', just 3–4 ft. tall and wide, with white sterile flowers and fertile flowers of blue or pink; 'Lemon Wave', with leaves irregularly variegated with yellow and cream and flowers in mauve tones; 'Lilacina' ('Mariesii Lilacina'), with dark blue fertile flowers and mauve sterile ones held out on long stems; 'Shooting Star,' with double white flowers is sold in

pots during winter holidays. 'Teller Red' ('Teller Rot'), with a double row of rose red sterile flowers surrounding pink-and-blue fertile ones; and old favorite 'Tricolor' ('Mariesii Variegata', 'Variegata'), with dark green leaves strongly marked with cream and light green; flower color depends on soil pH.

H. paniculata. Shrub. Zones A2, A3; 1–21. Native to Japan and China. Upright, spreading growth to 10–20 ft. tall and wide or larger. Medium to dark green leaves are oval and pointed, 3–6 in. long. Flowers begin as elongated clusters of greenish white buds in early summer, opening to 4–8-in.-long cones of white sterile flowers hiding tiny fertile flowers within. Blooms age to tawny pink, giving a show that lasts for months; flower spikes can be removed in late fall to neaten plant's appearance. Prune to shape in late dormant season.

Best known is the old variety 'Grandiflora'; its flower clusters can reach 1½ ft. long. Newer varieties include 'Burgundy Lace', with 10-in.-long pink flower clusters; 'Ruby' with blooms that deepen to carmine by late summer; 'Tardiva', which is similar to 'Grandiflora' but blooms later, in early and midautumn; 'Unique', with big flower clusters, to 16 in. long and 10 in. wide; and 'White Moth', with rounded flower clusters up to 14–16 in. across.

H. petiolaris. See H. anomala petiolaris

H. 'Preziosa' (H. serrata 'Preziosa'). Shrub. Zones 3b–9, 14–24. From Japan and Korea. Grows 4–5 ft. tall and wide, with medium green leaves that are oval, pointed, and about 6 in. long. Round, 3–5-in.-wide clusters of white sterile flowers age to red, blue, or mauve, depending on soil acidity. Prune after bloom.

H. quercifolia. OAKLEAF HYDRANGEA. Shrub. Zones 2b–23. From southeastern U.S. Broad, rounded shrub to 6 ft. tall and 8 ft. wide, with handsome, deeply lobed, 8-in.-long leaves that resemble those of oaks, turn bronze or crimson in fall. Elongated clusters of white flowers (to 8 in. long) in late spring and early summer turn pinkish purple as they age; fertile flowers are usually concealed by larger sterile flowers. 'Alice' has foliage that turns rich red in fall; 'Pee Wee' grows 4 ft. tall and wide and has 5-in.-long flower clusters; 'Sike's Dwarf' is

Hydrangea quercifolia

H

a little shorter, to 3 ft. tall and 4 ft. wide; 'Snow Queen' has larger flower clusters than the species; 'Snowflake' bears double flowers; 'Vaughn's Lillie' has flower heads up to 1 ft. long, so full they look almost round. Prune after bloom. Stems and flower buds may be damaged where temperatures go much below –10°F/–23°C; in these areas, oakleaf hydrangea is best grown for its handsome foliage.

H. sargentiana. See H. aspera sargentiana

H. seemannii. Evergreen vine. Zones 5–9, 14–24. From Mexico. Grows 15–30 ft. tall, with long stems clinging to support with aerial rootlets; also puts out bushy growth from base. Glossy dark green leaves are oval and pointed, to 6 in. long. In summer, 6-in. white lacecap flowers emerge from huge round buds. Grow this elegant vine in morning sun or bright shade, with protection from wind. Pruning is seldom necessary but may be done after flowers fade.

H. serrata. Shrub. Zones 3b–9, 14–24. From Korea, Japan. Resembles *H. macrophylla*. To 4–6 ft. tall and wide. The following selections have lacecap flowers. 'Beni Gaku' has pale blue fertile blooms surrounded by white, red-edged sterile flowers that age to rosy purple. 'Bluebird' has deep blue fertile flowers surrounded by pale blue sterile ones. 'Fuji Waterfall' is compact, just 3–4 ft. tall and a little wider, with double white sterile flowers on long stems that appear to dance above the flower heads. 'Grayswood' has sterile white flowers that droop outward, showing red reverse; the fertile blooms are mauve blue. 'Miyama-yae-Murasaki' ('Purple Tiers') sports pink sterile flowers that are double and look like fireworks shooting from the flower heads.

'Woodlander' is compact, to 4 ft. tall and wide, with leaves that age to a dusky purple; nice contrast to the dainty white to shell pink sterile flowers. Prune all after bloom.

H. villosa. See H. aspera Villosa Group

HYMENOCALLIS
Amaryllidaceae
PERENNIALS FROM BULBS

🌿	ZONES 5, 6, 8, 9, 14–24; OR DIG AND STORE
🔆 🌓	FULL SUN OR PARTIAL SHADE
💧	REGULAR WATER DURING GROWTH AND BLOOM
⬥	BULBS ARE POISONOUS IF INGESTED

Native to southern U.S. and South America. To picture this summer bloomer, imagine a cross between a belladonna lily (*Amaryllis belladonna*) and a daffodil. Like belladonna lily, it has strap-shaped, 2-ft.-long leaves and thick flower stems carrying several large, fragrant flowers—though leaves and flowers appear together in hymenocallis. Like daffodils, the flowers have two sets of segments: inner ones form a funnel, while outer ones are longer, spidery, and recurved.

Plant in rich, well-drained soil—in late fall or early winter in frostless areas, after frost danger is past in colder climates. Set bulbs with tips 1 in. below surface; space 1 ft. apart. Foliage keeps all summer if watered, dies in fall. Dig bulbs after leaves have yellowed (do not cut off fleshy roots), dry with roots facing up, and store in open trays in cool, dry, dark place.

H. × festalis. Each stem bears about four horizontally held flowers 3–5 in. across. Outer segments are very spidery, resembling curled white ribbons; these surround a

Hymenocallis narcissiflora

broadly chalice-shaped cup with fringed lobes. 'Zwanenburg' has larger flowers.

H. narcissiflora (Ismene calathina). BASKET FLOWER, PERUVIAN DAFFODIL. From Peruvian Andes. Most commonly grown hymenocallis, with green-striped white flowers about 4 in. wide and held in clusters of two to five. 'Advance' has pure white flowers faintly lined with green in throat.

H. 'Sulphur Queen'. Soft primrose yellow blossoms with green stripes in the throat; they reach 6 in. wide and have a more circular cup surrounded by broader, less spidery segments than other hymenocallis described here.

HYMENOCYCLUS. See **MALEPHORA**

HYMENOSPORUM flavum
SWEETSHADE
Pittosporaceae
EVERGREEN SHRUB OR TREE

🌿	ZONES 8, 9, 14–24
🔆 🌓	FULL SUN OR LIGHT SHADE
💧	MODERATE WATER

Native to Australia. Slow to moderate growth to 12–40 ft., with 9–20-ft. spread. Graceful, upright, slender, open habit. Narrow, glossy dark green leaves, 2–6 in. long. In early summer, bears yellow flowers with pronounced fragrance of orange-blossom honey. Early training is necessary to correct two problems. First, branches spread out in almost equal threes,

Hymenosporum flavum

creating weak crotches that are likely to split. Second, leaves tend to cluster near ends of branches and twigs. Frequent pinching and shortening of growth in early years will result in stronger, denser plant. Best located away from strong winds. Grow in well-drained soil.

Hymenosporum flavum

HYMENOXYS. See **TETRANEURIS**

HYPERICUM
ST. JOHNSWORT
Hypericaceae
EVERGREEN, SEMIEVERGREEN, AND DECIDUOUS SHRUBS OR PERENNIALS

🌿	ZONES VARY BY SPECIES
🔆 🌓	PARTIAL SHADE IN HOTTEST CLIMATES
⬥💧	MODERATE TO REGULAR WATER

All bear yellow flowers resembling single roses with prominent sunburst of stamens in center. Shallowly cup-shaped, five-petaled blooms range in color from creamy yellow to gold; flowers may be solitary or in clusters. Neat, fresh green foliage. Various species used for mass plantings, ground covers, informal hedges, borders. Grow especially well in mild, moist regions.

A difficult-to-control rust is extensively infecting plantings (especially those of the species *H. calycinum*) in the Pacific Northwest. Remove and destroy blighted leaves and any leaf litter; avoid overhead watering of plants in the evening.

H. androsaemum. Semievergreen shrub. Zones 3b–24. Shade-tolerant native of Europe, western Asia. To 3 ft. tall and wide, with stems arching toward the top. Leaves are medium green above, paler beneath, to 4 in. long and 2 in. wide. Clusters of ¾-in., golden yellow flowers in summer. Blossoms are followed by inedible berrylike fruits that turn from red to purple to black as they age. Useful as tall ground cover at edge of woods, on shaded slopes, in a wild garden. 'Albury Purple', to 2 ft. tall and wide, has new growth flushed dusky purple. Leaves of 'Glacier' are pink when new, then heavily splashed with white. 'Gladis Brabazon' has foliage variegated with cream and pink.

H. calycinum. AARON'S BEARD, CREEPING ST. JOHNSWORT. Evergreen to semievergreen shrub; tops often killed in cold winters but come back in spring. Zones 2b–24. From Bulgaria, Turkey. Grows to 1 ft. high and spreads by vigorous underground stems. Short-stalked leaves to 4 in. long are medium green in sun, yellow green in shade. Bright yellow blossoms about 3 in. across throughout summer. Tough, dense ground cover that competes successfully with tree roots, takes poor soil. Fast growing; will control erosion on hillsides. May invade other plantings unless confined. Plant from flats or as rooted stems; set 1½ ft. apart. Clip or mow yearly during dormant season.

Hypericum calycinum

H. coris. Evergreen shrub. Zones 4–9, 14–24. From Europe. To about 6–12 in. or taller and about 1 ft. wide. Narrow, medium green, ½–1-in.-long leaves in whorls of four to six. Bears loose clusters of yellow, ¾-in.-wide flowers in spring or early summer. Good choice as ground cover or rock garden plant.

H. frondosum. Deciduous shrub; evergreen in mildest climates. Zones 2b–24. From southeastern U.S. Grows 1–3 ft. tall, with mounding form. Blue-green leaves set off clusters of 1½-in., bright yellow flowers that bloom from midsummer to early fall. 'Sunburst' forms a tight mound to 3 ft. tall and wide.

H. 'Hidcote' (**H. patulum 'Hidcote'**). Evergreen to semievergreen shrub; perennial that dies to the ground in coldest part of range. Zones 3–9, 14–24. To 4 ft. tall and 5 ft. wide in mildest climates; in cold areas, freezes keep plant to about half that size. Dark green leaves 2–3 in. long. Yellow, 3-in. flowers all summer.

H. × moserianum. GOLD FLOWER. Evergreen shrub; peren-nial that dies to the ground in coldest part of range. Zones 3–9, 14–24; H1. Mounding habit to 3 ft. tall and wide, with arching, reddish stems. Leaves 2 in. long, medium green above, blue green beneath. Golden yellow, 2½-in.-wide blossoms are borne singly or in clusters of up to five. Blooms in summer, possibly into fall. Cut back in early spring. 'Tricolor' has gray-green leaves edged in white and tinged with pink.

Hypericum × moserianum 'Tricolor'

H. patulum 'Hidcote'. See H. 'Hidcote'

H. reptans. Evergreen shrub. Zones 3b–6, 15–17. Himalayan native only about 2 in. high, 1½ ft. or wider; roots along ground. Medium green, ¼–½-in.-long leaves crowded along stems; golden summer blooms to 1¾ in. wide. Good in rock gardens. Protect from frosts in colder regions.

H. 'Rowallane'. Evergreen to semievergreen shrub; perennial that dies to the ground in coldest part of range. Zones 4–9, 14–24. Upright, rather straggly growth to 6 ft. tall and 3 ft. wide. Profuse show of bright yellow flowers, 2½–3 in. wide, in late summer and fall. Dark green leaves 2½–3½ in. long. Remove older branches annually.

HYPOESTES phyllostachya (H. sanguinolenta)
FRECKLE FACE, PINK POLKA-DOT PLANT
Acanthaceae
PERENNIAL OFTEN GROWN AS ANNUAL

🌡 ZONES 23, 24; H1, H2; ANNUAL ANYWHERE; OR INDOORS
☀ ◑ FULL SUN OR LIGHT SHADE; BRIGHT LIGHT
● REGULAR WATER

This South African native is actually a perennial, but outside of Hawaii it is almost always used as

Hypoestes phyllostachya

a summer bedding annual or houseplant. Grows 1–2 ft. tall, about 1 ft. wide. Slender stems bear oval, 2–3-in.-long leaves spotted irregularly with pink or white. Selected form 'Splash' has larger spots. Plants bloom very rarely. Tip-pinch to make bushy. For indoor use, plant in loose, peaty mixture in pots or planters. Growth can be cut to within an inch or so of the soil in early spring to renew; plants tend to become woody and need replacing every few years.

HYPTIS emoryi
DESERT LAVENDER
Lamiaceae (Labiatae)
EVERGREEN SHRUB

🌡 ZONES 8–14, 18–24
☀ FULL SUN
◐ ● LITTLE TO MODERATE WATER

Native to desert Southwest. Erect or spreading shrub 3–10 ft. tall, 3–8 ft. wide. Woolly gray, roundish leaves to 1 in. long, with scalloped and toothed edges. Numerous tiny blue-violet flowers crowded into short spikes near branch ends can appear at any time throughout year, but bloom is heaviest in spring. Plant gives off pleasant lavender fragrance following rains or when brushed against. May die

Hyptis emoryi

back to roots at about 25°F/–4°C. Needs excellent drainage. Drought tolerant but looks better with irrigation. 'Silver Lining' is slightly more narrow and upright, with silvery white leaves and purple-flushed stems.

HYSSOP. See AGASTACHE, HYSSOPUS officinalis

HYSSOP, WATER. See BACOPA monnieri

HYSSOPUS officinalis
HYSSOP
Lamiaceae (Labiatae)
PERENNIAL

🌡 ZONES 1–24
☀ ◑ FULL SUN OR LIGHT SHADE
● ● MODERATE TO REGULAR WATER

From southern Europe. Compact growth to 1½–2 ft. tall, 3 ft. wide. Narrow, glossy dark green leaves on woody-based stems; foliage has pungent scent. Profusion of dark blue flower spikes throughout summer and into autumn; not a dramatic show but pleasant looking. Selections with white, pink, or lavender blooms exist.

Hyssopus officinalis

Start from seed sown in early spring or from stem cuttings in late spring or early summer. Once established, it may self-sow. Tolerates some drought but will thrive with regular moisture if drainage is good. Tolerates trimming as a low hedge or as border for a knot garden. Peppery-tasting leaves are sometimes used in cooking.

Hyssopus officinalis

H

I

IBERIS

CANDYTUFT
Brassicaceae (Cruciferae)
PERENNIALS AND ANNUALS

🌣 ZONES 1–24, EXCEPT AS NOTED
☼ ◑ FULL SUN OR PARTIAL SHADE
◐ REGULAR WATER

Free-blooming plants from southern and western Europe with clusters of white, lavender, lilac, pink, rose, purple, carmine, or crimson blossoms. Perennial candytufts flower from early spring to summer. Annual species bloom in spring and summer; they are most floriferous where summer nights are cool. Use all kinds in borders, containers, for cutting. Perennials are also good as edgings, in rock gardens, as small-scale ground covers.

All types need well-drained soil. In spring or (in mild climates) fall, sow seeds of annuals in place or in flats for later transplanting. Set out perennial plants in spring or fall. Shear lightly after bloom to stimulate new growth.

I. amara. HYACINTH-FLOWERED CANDYTUFT, ROCKET CANDYTUFT. Annual. To 12–15 in. high, 6 in. wide. Fragrant white flowers in tight, round clusters that elongate into spikes resembling those of hyacinth. Narrow, slightly fuzzy leaves.

I. gibraltarica. Perennial. Zones 4–9, 14–24. Resembles *I. sempervirens* but bears flatter clusters of light pinkish or purplish flowers, which may be white near the center.

I. sempervirens. EVERGREEN CANDYTUFT. Perennial. To 8–12 in. (or even 1½ ft.) high, spreading about as wide. Narrow, shiny dark green leaves are attractive all year. Pure white flower clusters carried on stems long enough to cut for bouquets. Lower, more compact varieties include 'Alexander's White', a 6-in.-high plant with

Iberis sempervirens

fine-textured foliage; 'Kingwood Compact', also 6 in. high; 'Little Gem', 4–6 in. tall; 'Purity', 6–12 in. tall and wide spreading; and 'Snow Cushion', 5 in. tall and 1 ft. wide. 'Snowflake', 4–12 in. high and 1½–3 ft. wide, has broader, more leathery leaves than the species; also has larger flowers in larger clusters on shorter stems. It is extremely showy in spring, with sporadic bloom through summer and fall. 'Autumnale' and 'Autumn Snow' bloom in spring and again in fall.

I. umbellata. GLOBE CANDYTUFT. Annual. Bushy plants 12–15 in. high, 9 in. wide. Lance-shaped leaves to 3½ in. long; flowers in pink, rose, carmine, crimson, salmon, lilac, and white. Lower-growing strains Dwarf Fairy and Magic Carpet, available in the same colors, reach 6 in. high.

ICE PLANTS

These low-growing, succulent perennials (and a few annuals) were once conveniently lumped together as *Mesembryanthemum*, but they are now classified under several genus names. Where hardy, they are among the most useful and colorful of flowering ground covers. In colder climates, grow them as summer bloomers in window boxes or hanging baskets; or treat as houseplants. All grow best in well-drained soils; none will tolerate foot traffic. Feed lightly in fall, again after bloom. The various perennial genera included in this book are *Aptenia, Carpobrotus, Cephalophyllum, Delosperma, Drosanthemum, Lampranthus,* and *Malephora. Dorotheanthus* is an annual genus. *Mesembryanthemum*—the original, all-encompassing genus—now contains annuals that have naturalized along the California coast but are seldom seen elsewhere.

ILEX

HOLLY
Aquifoliaceae
EVERGREEN AND DECIDUOUS SHRUBS AND TREES

🌣 ZONES VARY BY SPECIES
☼ ◑ FULL SUN OR PARTIAL SHADE
◐ REGULAR WATER

English holly (*I. aquifolium*) is the most familiar in song and legend (and in Christmas wreaths), but

this species thrives only in the Pacific Northwest and in coastal Northern California; in fact, it has become invasive there, spreading into native habitats. Other hollies are better adapted to other parts of the West. In size, they range from foot-high dwarfs to trees 40–50 ft. tall. Many hundreds of species and hybrids exist. Smaller kinds are attractive as foundation plantings or low hedges; larger evergreen sorts make attractive and impenetrable tall hedges or screens.

Nearly all holly plants are either male or female, and as a rule both sexes must be present in order for female plants to set fruit. Best bet is to plant a male of the same species as fruiting females; if you use a different species, berries will form only if both plants flower at the same time. Varieties described below are female unless otherwise noted. A few are self-fruitful; these also are noted.

Most hollies prefer rich, slightly acid garden soil with good water drainage. (A few exceptions are noted.) All appreciate a mulch to deter weeds and keep soil cool and moist. Though plants will grow in sun or part shade, choose a sunny spot for best berry production and most compact growth. Scale can cause problems in all holly-growing areas. Holly bud moth and leaf miner need attention on English holly in the Northwest; for control, employ only products currently registered for use against those pests. Diseases are rarely a problem for home gardeners.

Most hollies tend to be dense and symmetrical. Prune mainly to remove poorly placed, broken, or dead branches. Winter holiday season is good time to prune, because clipped branches can be used for indoor decoration. You can restore a holly that has become too open or ragged by severely shortening its branches and allowing new growth to fill in. Small-leafed hollies can be sheared into formal hedges or topiary figures.

I. × altaclerensis 'Wilsonii' (**I. wilsonii**). WILSON HOLLY. Evergreen shrub or tree. Zones 3b–24. Hybrid between *I. aquifolium* and a species from the Canary Islands. One of the best hollies, especially in warmer regions. Takes wind, almost any soil. Usually a shrub 6–8 ft. high and wide, but easily trained as single-stemmed tree 15–20 ft. high, 10–12 ft. wide. Evenly spine-toothed, rich green leaves are thick, leathery, 5 in. long,

3 in. wide. Heavy producer of bright red berries. Makes a good espalier, screen, or informal or clipped hedge.

I. aquifolium. ENGLISH HOLLY. Evergreen shrub or tree. Zones 4–9, 14–17; H1 (above 4,000 ft.). Native to southern and central Europe, Great Britain. Slow growth to 40 ft. tall and 25 ft. wide, usually much less. Highly variable in leaf shape, color, and degree of spininess. Some varieties produce seedless berries without a pollenizer, but these berries are usually small, slow to develop, and quick to drop. Needs protection from sun in hot, dry areas and soil conditioning where soils are alkaline. Resistant to oak root fungus. The following are among the best-known varieties.

Ilex aquifolium

'Angustifolia'. Male selection with narrow form, narrow leaves, and purple stems.

'Balkans'. Hardiest of English hollies, this variety was originally grown from seed collected in the mountains of the Balkan region. Upright plants with smooth dark green leaves. Male and female (fruiting) forms are available.

'Big Bull'. Very ornamental male with large, nearly smooth-edged leaves.

'Boulder Creek'. Typical English holly with large leaves. Brilliant red berries.

'Ciliata Major'. Vigorous, erect plant with purple bark on young shoots. Large, olive-tinged dark green leaves are flat, long spined, very glossy. Good berry producer.

'Ferox'. HEDGEHOG, PORCUPINE HOLLY. Male with sterile pollen. Twisted, fiercely spined leaves are what give it its common names.

'Fertilis'. Sets light crop of seedless berries without pollination.

'J. C. Van Tol' ('Van Tol'). Glossy green leaves. Produces large dark red berries at young age. Sometimes sold as a variety of I. × altaclerensis.

'San Gabriel'. Bears seedless berries without pollination.

'Sparkler'. Strong, upright grower to about 12 ft. tall, 8 ft. wide. Heavy crop of glistening red berries at an early age.

'Teufel's Deluxe'. Exceptionally dark green leaves. Large, early-ripening red berries.

'Teufel's Zero'. Upright with long slender branches, weeping. Dark red berries ripen early. Unusually hardy.

Varieties with variegated leaves are also sold. Types that have silver-edged leaves are 'Argenteo-marginata', 'Silvery', 'Silver Queen' (male). Types with silver-centered leaves are 'Argentea-mediopicta', 'Silver Star', 'Silver Milkmaid'. Gold-edged leaves: 'Aureo-marginata', 'Gold Coast' (6–8-ft.-tall male), 'Golden Queen' (male), 'Lily Gold'. Gold-centered leaves: 'Golden Milkmaid', 'Pinto'.

I. × aquipernyi. Evergreen shrub or tree. Zones 4–9, 14–24. Hybrid between I. aquifolium and I. pernyi. To 20 ft. tall (or more), 12 ft. wide, with cone-shaped habit and dense foliage. Spiny-edged, 2–4-in.-long leaves are closely set on branches. 'San Jose' and 'Brilliant' produce small red berries without a pollenizer. Resistant to oak root fungus.

I. cornuta. CHINESE HOLLY. Evergreen shrub or tree. Zones 8–24, but needs long warm season to set fruit. In desert climates, give protection from hot sun; grow in eastern or northern exposure. From China, Korea. Dense or open growth to 10 ft. or taller, often wider in maturity. Leaves are typically glossy, leathery, nearly rectangular, with spines at the four corners and at tip. Exceptionally large, long-lasting bright red berries. Selections show great variation in fruit set, leaf form, spininess. In the following list, those setting fruit do so without a male variety.

'Berries Jubilee'. Dwarf, dome-shaped plant to 4–6 ft. high and wide, with large leaves and heavy crop of large bright red berries. This variety has larger, spinier leaves than those of 'Burfordii', on a much smaller plant.

'Burfordii'. BURFORD HOLLY. To 15 ft. tall, 10 ft. wide. Widely planted in low-elevation California. Leaves nearly spineless, cupped downward. Useful as espalier.

'Carissa'. Dwarf, dense grower to 3–4 ft. high and 4–6 ft. wide, with small leaves. Use for small containers, low hedge. Female, but no berries.

'Dazzler'. Compact, upright growth to 8–10 ft. high and wide. Glossy leaves have a few stout spines along wavy margins. Loaded with berries.

'Dwarf Burford' ('Burfordii Nana'). Resembles 'Burfordii' but is much smaller—to just 6 ft. high and wide. Branches densely set with small (1½-in.), light green, spineless leaves.

'Rotunda'. DWARF CHINESE HOLLY. Compact low grower to 3–4 ft. high, 6–8 ft. wide. Female, but does not produce berries. A few stout spines and rolled leaf margins between spines make the medium-size light green leaves nearly rectangular.

'Willow-leaf'. Large shrub or small tree to 15 ft. tall and wide, with dense growth. Long, narrow, dark green leaves. Good crop of dark red berries.

Ilex cornuta 'Burfordii'

I. crenata. JAPANESE HOLLY. Evergreen shrub. Zones 3–9, 14–24. From Russia, Japan, Korea. Looks more like boxwood (Buxus) than holly. Dense, erect, usually to 4–10 ft. high and wide, sometimes much larger. Narrow, finely toothed, ½–¾-in.-long leaves. Black berries. Extremely useful where winter cold limits choice of polished evergreens for hedges, edgings. Varieties include the following.

'Compacta'. Rounded shrub to 6 ft. high and wide, with dense habit. Many different plants sold under this name.

'Convexa'. Compact, rounded shrub to 4–6 ft. high and somewhat wider. Leaves are roundish, cupped downward at the edges. Use as clipped or unclipped hedge. Many different plants sold under this name.

'Glory'. Small, dense, round grower to 5 ft. tall, 8 ft. wide. Male. Extremely hardy.

'Golden Gem'. Slow growth to 3½ ft. tall and 4–5 ft. wide, with yellow-green leaves that turn a brighter yellow in winter.

'Green Island'. Open, spreading; to 3 ft. tall and twice as wide.

'Helleri'. Remains very small (about 1 ft. high, 2 ft. wide) for many years. May reach twice that size in 30 years.

'Hetzii'. Like 'Convexa' but with larger leaves and more vigorous growth.

'Mariesii'. Very slow-growing columnar holly with dense, tiny, round leaves. To 2 ft. high, 4–6 in. wide in about 10 years; eventually to 6 ft. tall, 16 in. wide. Good plant for rock garden, bonsai, containers.

'Northern Beauty'. To 4 ft. high, 4–5 ft. wide, with lustrous leaves.

'Sky Pencil'. Columnar plant to 6 ft. tall and only 10 in. wide.

I. dimorphophylla. OKINAWAN HOLLY. Evergreen shrub. Zones 15–17, 19–24. From Japan. To 5 ft. tall, 3 ft. wide. Leaves less than 1 in. long, closely set with short spines. Small red berries. Tender to frost.

I. 'Ebony Magic'. Evergreen shrub. Zones 3–9, 12–24. Pyramidal form. Typically grows 8–12 ft. tall and 6–8 ft. wide, though may reach 20 ft. tall and half as wide. Blackish purple bark; shiny dark green, spiny-edged leaves. Large orange-red berries last through spring. 'Ebony Male' is often used for pollination.

I. glabra. INKBERRY. Evergreen shrub. Zones 2b–24. Native to eastern North America. To 10 ft. tall and wide, with thick, spineless dark green leaves and black berries. More widely available are the dwarf forms 'Compacta' (female) and 'Nordic' (male), which grow to 4 ft. tall and wide but can be sheared to make a 2-ft. hedge.

I. latifolia. Evergreen tree. Zones 4–7, 15–17, 20–24. Native to China, Japan. Slow-growing, stout-branched plant to 25 ft. tall, 15 ft. wide. Dull dark green leaves are 6–8 in. long (largest of all hollies), thick and leathery, fine toothed. Big clusters of large, dull orange-red berries. 'Purple Power' has dark, glossy 5-in. leaves that are purple when new.

I. 'Little Rascal'. Evergreen shrub. Zones 3b, 14–17. Dense, rounded, compact growth to just 2 ft. tall and 3 ft. wide. Medium green leaves turn deep purple in winter. Male.

I. × meserveae. Evergreen shrub. Zones 3–9, 14–17. Most plants in this category are hybrids between I. aquifolium and a cold-tolerant species from northern Japan. Dense, bushy plants; apparently the hardiest of hollies with the true holly look. To 10 ft. high and wide, though more commonly seen 3–5 ft. tall and broad. Purple stems and spiny, glossy blue-green leaves. Red-fruiting female varieties include 'Blue Angel', 'Blue Girl', and 'Blue Princess'; male pollenizers include 'Blue Boy' and 'Blue Prince'. 'Golden Girl' has yellow berries. 'China Boy' and red-fruited 'China Girl' are crosses between I. cornuta and the northern Japanese species; slightly hardier and more tolerant of summer heat than the other hybrids.

I. 'Nellie R. Stevens'. Evergreen shrub or tree. Zones 4–9, 14–24. Hybrid between I. cornuta and I. aquifolium. Fast growing, densely conical to 15–20 ft. tall, 10 ft. wide. Glossy, leathery, sparsely toothed leaves to 3 in. long. Self-fruitful but forms a heavier crop if pollinated by male variety of I. cornuta.

I. opaca. AMERICAN HOLLY. Evergreen tree. Zones 2–9, 14–17, 19–23. Native to eastern U.S. Slow growing to 40–50 ft. tall, 20–40 ft. wide; pyramidal or round-headed. Dull or glossy green, 2–4-in.-long leaves with spiny margins. Red berries; not quite as numerous as on I. aquifolium. Resistant to oak root fungus. Some of the many varieties are occasionally available in the West. They include 'Cardinal', 'Old Heavy Berry', and 'Torchbearer'.

I. pedunculosa. Evergreen shrub or tree. Zones 2b–9, 14–17. From China, Japan. To 15–20 ft. tall, 12–15 ft. wide; has awkward shape when young. Narrow and smooth-edged leaves 1–3 in. long. The ¼-in., bright red berries dangle like cherries on 1–1½-in. stalks in autumn.

I. pernyi. Evergreen tree. Zones 4–9, 14–24. Native to China. Slow growth to 20–30 ft. tall, 10 ft. wide. Glossy, 1–2-in.-long, triangular leaves with one to three spines on each side; closely packed against branchlets. Red berries set tightly against stems.

I. 'San Jose Hybrid'. Evergreen shrub or tree. Zones 4–9, 14–24. Resembles I. × altaclerensis 'Wilsonii' but has somewhat longer, narrower leaves. Upright growth; heavy berry production.

I. 'September Gem'. Evergreen shrub. Zones 4–9, 14–24. Dense, conical dark green plant to 6 ft. tall, 3 ft. wide, with sparsely spined, 2-in.-long leaves. Early crop of bright orange-red fruit.

I. 'Sparkleberry'. Deciduous shrub or tree. Zones 1–7. Hybrid between *I. serrata* and *I. verticillata.* Upright growth to 12–15 ft. high and wide. Tooth-edged dark green leaves to 4 in. long persist until early winter before dropping. Masses of bright red berries from fall into spring. 'Apollo' is a male pollenizer.

I. verticillata. WINTERBERRY, CHRISTMAS BERRY. Deciduous shrub. Zones A2, A3; 1–7. Native to eastern North America. Unlike most hollies, will thrive in boggy soils, although it also succeeds in any moist, organic soil. Grows 6–10 ft. tall and spreads wider by suckering. Oval leaves to 3 in. long. Enormous crop of bright red berries ripens in early fall and lasts all winter (unless eaten by birds). 'Afterglow' has orange-red berries on a globe-shaped plant. 'Winter Gold' has apricot-colored berries. 'Cacapon', 'Fairfax', 'Sunset', and 'Winter Red' have dark red berries. 'Red Sprite' is a dwarf (to 3 ft. high and wide) with larger red fruit. Plant a male variety for pollination —good choices include 'Dwarf Male' (to 2 ft. tall); 'Jim Dandy' and 'Late Male' (both to 4 ft.); and 'Southern Gentleman' (to 6 ft.).

I. vomitoria. YAUPON. Evergreen shrub or tree. Zones 3–9, 11–24; H1, H2. Native to southeastern U.S. Takes extremely alkaline soils better than other hollies. To 15–20 ft. tall and 10–15 ft. wide, with narrow, inch-long, shallowly toothed dark green leaves. Often trained as standard or sheared into columnar form; good topiary plant. Pea-size scarlet berries borne in profusion. Varieties include the following.

'Nana'. DWARF YAUPON. To 3–5 ft. high and slightly wider. Refined, attractive; formal appearance when sheared. Fruit often hidden among leaves.

'Pendula'. Weeping branches show to best effect when plant is trained as standard. Male and female forms available.

'Pride of Houston'. Upright, freely branching plant to 15 ft. tall, 5–10 ft. wide. Profuse berry production. Good screen or hedge.

'Stokes' ('Stokes Dwarf', 'Schillings'). To 3–4 ft. high and wide, with closely set dark green leaves. Male.

'Will Fleming' ('William Fleming'). Columnar; 10 ft. tall, 2 ft. wide. Male.

I. wilsonii. See I. × altaclerensis 'Wilsonii'

'ILIMA. See **SIDA fallax**

ILLICIUM

ANISE TREE
Illiciaceae
EVERGREEN SHRUBS OR TREES

🌡	ZONES 4–9, 14–24
◑ ●	PARTIAL OR FULL SHADE
💧	AMPLE WATER
◈	ALL PARTS OF I. ANISATUM ARE POISONOUS IF INGESTED

Little-used but attractive clan of shrubs or small trees noted for thick, leathery, glossy leaves (anise-scented when crushed) and spring flowers with many petal-like segments reminiscent of small magnolia blossoms. Fruits that follow are small, one-sided pods arranged in a ring. The star anise of Chinese cookery is the fruit of the tropical tree *I. verum,* apparently not grown in North America. All like rich soil with abundant organic material. Big, bold foliage gives the impression of rhododendrons. Seldom need pruning.

Illicium anisatum

I. anisatum (I. religiosum, I. japonicum). ANISE SHRUB, JAPANESE ANISE. Native to Japan, South Korea, Taiwan. To 6–10 ft. (possibly 15 ft.) tall, 6–8 ft. wide; conical growth habit. Oval to lance-shaped, blunt-tipped, glossy leaves to 5 in. long, 2 in. wide. Inch-wide, scentless flowers on short, nodding stalks cluster in leaf axils; they open yellowish green, then fade to creamy white. Much planted in Buddhist cemeteries; cut branches are used to decorate graves. Highly fragrant wood used for incense. Seeds, foliage, and wood are toxic if ingested.

I. floridanum. FLORIDA ANISE TREE. Native from Florida to Louisiana. Reaches 6–10 ft. or taller, equally wide. Pointed oval leaves 6 in. long and 2 in. wide, with prominent midribs. Waxy, nodding maroon flowers 1–2 in. across on 1½–2-in.-long stalks; most people find scent unpleasant. 'Halley's Comet' is more compact, with larger, redder flowers than the species; often blooms into fall. 'Album' is white flowered; 'Variegatum' has maroon purple flowers with subtle green-on-green leaf variegation. 'Woodland Ruby' is a hybrid with ruby pink, 2-in. flowers shaped like starfish; flowering period extends through summer.

I. mexicanum. MEXICAN ANISE. Shrub. Native to northern Mexico. To 4 ft. tall and wide. Narrowly oval, pointed leaves to 2 in. long are medium green with red stems. Reddish pink flowers, to 2 in. across, are produced mainly in spring, with some repeat bloom through summer. 'Aztec Fire' is larger growing, to about 8 ft. tall and 6 ft. wide, with darker red flowers.

IMMORTELLE. See **XERANTHEMUM annuum**

IMPATIENS

BALSAM, TOUCH-ME-NOT, SNAPWEED
Balsaminaceae
PERENNIALS AND ANNUALS

🌡	ZONES VARY BY SPECIES
☀ ◑ ●	EXPOSURE NEEDS VARY BY SPECIES
💧	REGULAR WATER

Of the hundreds of species, only the following are usually seen in gardens. Most of these are annuals or tender perennials treated as annuals; all are valuable for long summer bloom. When lightly touched, ripe seed capsules burst open and scatter seeds.

I. auricoma 'Jungle Gold'. Perennial. Zones 24; H1, H2; grow as annual elsewhere. Selection from an African species. Dense, bushy plant to 1½ ft. tall and wide, with glossy, bright green leaves that are oval, pointed, and up to 6 in. long; leaf margins are serrated and toothed. Intricate orchidlike blooms to 1 in. long are rich golden, with throats marked in red. Give shade and regular applications of balanced fertilizer for profuse bloom over a long period in summer. Superb in containers.

I. balfourii. Annual. All zones. From the Himalayas. To 20 in.

Impatiens auricoma 'Jungle Gold'

high and broad, with 4–5-in. leaves and loose clusters of inch-wide, pink-tinted white flowers. Seldom planted but often pops up unannounced. It can become a pest by reseeding, but it is attractive in shady, informal plantings.

I. balsamina. BALSAM. Annual. All zones. From Southeast Asia. Erect, branching plant reaches 8–30 in. high and 6–8 in. wide. Sharp-pointed, 1½–6-in.-long leaves with deeply toothed edges. Large, spurred flowers borne among leaves along main stem, branches. Solid colored or variegated, in white or shades of pink, rose, lilac, or red. Compact, double camellia–flowered forms are most frequently grown. Sow seeds in flats or pots in early spring; after frost danger is past, set out young plants (or purchased transplants) in full sun (light shade in hottest climates).

I. glandulifera (I. roylei). Annual. All zones. From the Himalayas. To 3–6 ft. tall, with thick, juicy stems and leaves to 8 in. long. Abundance of yellow-spotted purple to white flowers. Like a larger *I. balfourii* and just as likely to self-sow all over the place. Light to full shade.

I. holstii. See I. walleriana

I. New Guinea hybrids. Perennials in Zones 24, H1, H2; can be grown as annuals in all zones. A varied group of striking plants developed from a number of species native to New Guinea, especially *I. hawkeri (I. schlechteri).* Plants can be upright to

Impatiens New Guinea hybrid 'Tango'

spreading; most are 1–2 ft. tall and as wide or wider (though some are smaller, such as 8-in.-high Baby Bonita series). Leaves are typically large, often variegated with cream or red. Flowers usually large (3 in. wide) though not profuse, held well above foliage; colors include lavender, purple, pink, red, orange, and white. Once considered primarily pot plants, they may also be grown in the open ground; provide ample fertilizer and give somewhat more sun than you would common impatiens (*I. walleriana*).

Popular strains include Celebration (with 3-in. flowers), Infinity, Paradise, and Pure Beauty. Most New Guinea hybrids are cutting-grown plants, but Spectra (Firelake) and Java strains can be grown from seed. Spectra offers a mix of flower colors and has leaves variegated with cream or white; bronze-leafed Java is available in single or mixed colors. 'Tango', also seed-grown, has bright orange blooms and bronze-green foliage.

I. sodenii (I. oliveri). POOR MAN'S RHODODENDRON. Perennial in Zones 15–17, 21–24; indoor/outdoor plant elsewhere. From eastern tropical Africa. To 4–8 ft. tall, 10 ft. wide, with woody-based stems clothed in whorls of 8-in.-long, glossy dark green leaves. Produces many 2½-in., slender-spurred flowers in lilac, pale lavender, or pinkish shades, and white; 'Madonna' ('Full Moon', 'Alba') has white flowers to 3 in. across. Tolerates seacoast conditions. Frosts kill it to ground, but it regrows in spring. Blooms in partial or deep shade; takes sun in cool-summer areas.

I. sultani. See I. walleriana
I. walleriana. BUSY LIZZIE. Perennial in Zones 17, 24, H1, H2; can be grown as an annual in all zones. Native to eastern Africa. Includes plants formerly known as *I. holstii* and *I. sultani*. Rapid, vigorous growth; tall types to about 2 ft. high, dwarf kinds 6–12 in. high. Narrow, glossy dark green, 1–3-in.-long leaves on juicy pale green stems. Flowers 1–2 in. wide, in all colors but yellow and true blue. All types are useful for many

months of bright color in partial or full shade. Grow plants from seed or cuttings; or buy them in cell-packs or pots. Space taller types 1 ft. apart, dwarfs 6 in. apart. If plants overgrow, cut them back as low as 6 in. above ground—it's a tonic. New growth emerges in a few days, and flowers cover it in 2 weeks. Plants in moist ground often reseed.

Among the many strains and varieties are the following, all bearing the typical five-petaled blooms.

Accent. To 10 in. high. Popular, in numerous individual colors or a mix.

Accent Star. Variation of Accent strain, with white central star extending across the petals.

Blitz. To 16 in. tall, with 2-in. flowers in mixed or single colors.

Bruno. To 10–12 in. Tetraploid strain (double the usual number of chromosomes), with large (2½-in.) flowers on extremely sturdy plants. Available in single or mixed colors.

Butterfly. To 10 in. high. Blossoms show contrasting central patch in butterfly form.

Mosaic. To 12–14 in. Irregular splashes of white against base color of several lilac or rosy shades.

Pride. To 10–16 in. Flowers are larger than usual (to 2½ in. across), in single or mixed colors.

Stardust. To 12–14 in. Central white star tapers off into a dusting of white.

Super Elfin. To 8–10 in. Comes in an exceptionally wide range of individual colors and blends of harmonizing hues. One example is 'Blue Pearl', with flowers in an unusual bluish lilac shade.

Swirl. To 10–12 in. Pastel shades with picotee edges of deeper color.

Many novelty strains and selections are available. They include Firefly, dwarf series to 6–8 in. high, with ½-in. flowers in the full range of impatiens colors; Confection, 10–12 in., producing high percentage of double and semidouble flowers from seed; and 'Victorian Rose', 10–12 in., with frilly rose pink and semidouble flowers. Other double impatiens with flowers resembling rosebuds include cutting-grown Fiesta and

Impatiens walleriana

Tioga strains. The double-flowered types are best used in containers, located where flower detail can be observed close up.

IMPERATA cylindrica 'Rubra' ('Red Baron')

JAPANESE BLOOD GRASS
Poaceae (Gramineae)
PERENNIAL GRASS

🌱 ZONES 2B–24
☼ ◑ FULL SUN OR PARTIAL SHADE
💧 REGULAR WATER

From Japan. Forms upright clump 1–2 ft. tall, 1 ft. wide. In spring, leaves emerge medium green at base, red at tip; red color extends along leaf and intensifies in summer and fall. Top half or more of each leaf may be brilliant red. Striking in borders, especially where sun can shine through blades. Rarely (if ever) flowers. Turns straw colored in winter; best cut to the ground yearly. Spreads slowly by underground runners.

Imperata cylindrica 'Rubra'

INCARVILLEA

Bignoniaceae
PERENNIALS

🌱 ZONES VARY BY SPECIES
☼ ◑ LIGHT SHADE IN HOTTEST CLIMATES
💧 REGULAR WATER

These plants from the Himalayas and China have showy trumpet-shaped flowers like their trumpet vine relatives (*Bignonia, Campsis,* and the like). Flowers are large for the size of the plant. Many species are coming into cultivation, but only the following two have reached North American gardens in any numbers. Leaves are 2–8 in. long, divided featherwise into leaflets. Plants are deep rooted and need reasonably deep soil and excellent drainage. In cold-winter regions, mulch plants after ground

has frozen (to prevent ground from heaving). Protect from slugs and snails.

I. arguta. Zones 4–6, 15–24; can be treated as annual elsewhere, since it will bloom first year from seed if started in earliest spring. Erect plant to 5 ft. tall and 3 ft. wide, or sprawling to 3 ft. tall and 5 ft. wide; somewhat shrubby at base. Leaves divided into 4–12 leaflets, each up to 2 in. long. Blooms in spring and summer; inflorescences have 5–20 pink or white, 1½-in.-long flowers. Effective leaning over walls or spilling down slopes. Self-sows but does not become a pest.

Incarvillea delavayi

I. delavayi. Zones 2–24. Grows 2 ft. high, 1 ft. wide. Like *I. arguta,* has divided leaves and trumpet-shaped flowers—but in other respects, it is entirely different. Grows from a carrot-shaped perennial root and forms a rosette of foot-long leaves, each divided into many leaflets. The foot-long flower stalk is topped by 2–12 blossoms that are 3 in. long and wide, rosy purple outside, yellow and purple within. Blooms in late spring, early summer. Division is difficult. 'Snowtop' has white flowers.

INCENSE CEDAR.
See **CALOCEDRUS decurrens**

INDIAN HAWTHORN.
See **RHAPHIOLEPIS indica**

INDIAN LABURNUM.
See **CASSIA fistula**

INDIAN MALLOW.
See **ABUTILON palmeri**

INDIAN MOCK STRAWBERRY.
See **DUCHESNEA indica**

INDIAN RHUBARB.
See **DARMERA peltata**

INDIAN RICE GRASS. See **ACHNATHERUM hymenoides**

INDIGO BUSH.
See **DALEA, INDIGOFERA**

INDIGOFERA
INDIGO BUSH
Fabaceae (Leguminosae)
DECIDUOUS SHRUBS

| 🌾 ZONES 2B–9, 14–21 |
| ☀️ ◐ EXPOSURE NEEDS VARY BY SPECIES |
| 💧 REGULAR WATER |

Woody-stemmed plants with finely divided, almost ferny foliage; dense clusters of tiny sweet pea–shaped flowers in summer. Plants can be killed to the ground in a hard winter, but they recover quickly from the roots and bloom on new wood in spring and summer. Even in mild-winter areas, plants are more compact and attractive when cut back hard in late dormant season. Provide good drainage.

I. australis. AUSTRAL INDIGO. Zones 14–24. Native to temperate Australia. To 5 ft. high and wide, with erect and arching shoots. Magenta flowers are clustered close to the stems. Partial shade.

I. decora. From China, Japan. To 1–2½ ft. tall and 3 ft. wide, with arching branches. Narrow, somewhat drooping blossom clusters to 8 in. long hold as many as 40 small white blooms suffused with pink. Full sun.

Indigofera kirilowii

I. kirilowii. Native to Northern China, Korea, Japan. To 2½–3 ft. tall, 3 ft. wide, with upright shoots and erect, 5-in. clusters of rose pink flowers. Full sun.

INDOCALAMUS. See **BAMBOO**

INKBERRY. See **ILEX glabra**

INSIDE-OUT FLOWER.
See **VANCOUVERIA planipetala**

IOCHROMA
Solanaceae
EVERGREEN VINING SHRUBS

| 🌾 ZONES 15–17, 19–24 |
| ☀️ ◐ FULL SUN OR PARTIAL SHADE |
| 💧 REGULAR WATER |

Genus of about 20 species from forests of Central and South America. Fast-growing, softwooded, vining shrubs with drooping tubular or trumpet-shaped flowers in clusters of up to 20 near ends of branches. Blooms from early spring through fall—or year-round in frost-free areas. Leaves 5–8 in. long, 1½–3 in. wide. Fruits are pulpy berries

Lax growth is best staked up, espaliered, or draped over a fence or wall. For continuity of bloom, prune selectively to maintain size and shape. Avoid pruning in late fall or when cold weather approaches. Hard pruning is all right otherwise, though it will

Iochroma cyaneum

delay bloom. Protect from hard frosts. Cucumber beetles love to eat the leaves. Flowers attract hummingbirds.

I. cyaneum. Grows to 8 ft. or more, with dull dark green leaves. Stems and new shoots covered with soft, grayish down. Narrow trumpets are 2–3 in. long. Blossom color of seedlings varies from blues through violets and deep reds to purplish rose and pink. All have a metallic sheen. Buy plants in bloom to get the color you want; or select named varieties. 'Burgundy' is wine red to crimson. 'Indigo' is glossy violet blue, 'Royal Blue' a lighter, more brilliant blue; 'Sky King' is a pure light blue.

I. fuchsioides. To 10 ft. or more, with glossy bright green leaves. Brilliant orange-scarlet, tubular flowers with yellow throats; look like fuchsia flowers.

IPHEION uniflorum (Brodiaea uniflora, Triteleia uniflora)
SPRING STAR FLOWER
Liliaceae
PERENNIAL FROM BULB

| 🌾 ZONES 2B–24 |
| ☀️ ◐ FULL SUN OR PARTIAL SHADE |
| 💧 REGULAR WATER DURING GROWTH AND BLOOM |

Spring-blooming Argentine native with wildflower charm. Each bulb produces several slender stems, each bearing a single half-inch blossom with six overlapping

Ipheion uniflorum
'Rolf Fiedler'

petals. Usual color is white tinged with blue, but variants include white 'Album', bright blue 'Rolf Fiedler', and dark blue 'Wisley Blue'. All have narrow, nearly flat leaves that smell like onions when bruised.

Use in borders or under deciduous shrubs; or naturalize in woodland areas or among low grasses. In fall, set bulbs 2 in. deep and 2 in. apart. Prefers dry conditions during summer dormancy but will accept water if drainage is good. Divide infrequently—plantings become more attractive over the years as bulbs multiply.

IPOMOEA
MORNING GLORY
Convolvulaceae
PERENNIAL AND ANNUAL VINES

| 🌾 ZONES VARY BY SPECIES |
| ☀️ FULL SUN |
| 💧💧 MODERATE TO REGULAR WATER |

Native to tropical and subtropical regions of the world. This genus includes many ornamental twining vines as well as the edible sweet potato (see Sweet Potato); it does not include the weedy plant known as wild morning glory or bindweed (*Convolvulus arvensis*). The plants described here may self-sow, but they do not spread by nearly ineradicable underground runners as does wild morning

glory. Plants tend to have hard seeds; to encourage faster sprouting, nick the coating or soak overnight in water before planting. For annual display, sow seeds in place after frost danger is past; or for an earlier start, sow seeds indoors, then set out plants 6–8 in. apart. Use morning glory vines on fence or trellis or as ground cover. Or grow in containers; provide stakes or a wire cylinder for support, or let plant cascade. For cut flowers, pick stems with buds in various stages of development and place in deep vase; buds open on consecutive days.

I. alba (Calonyction aculeatum). MOONFLOWER. Perennial in Zones 15–17, 23, 24, H1, H2; annual elsewhere. Fast growing (20–30 ft. in a season), providing quick shade for arbor, trellis, or fence. Luxuriantly clothed in heart-shaped leaves to 8 in. long, closely spaced on stems. Blooms in the evening, showing off fragrant, 6 in. funnel-shaped white blossoms after sundown and into the night (flowers also open on cloudy or dark days). Needs heat to bloom.

I. batatas. SWEET POTATO. Perennial from tuberous roots. Zones 13, 21–24; H1, H2; indoor/outdoor plant. For the edible sort, see Sweet Potato; following are fancy-leafed forms grown for ornament. Trailing in habit, they have leaves that vary in size from 2 to 4 in. long and in shape from heart shaped to deeply lobed.

'Ace of Spades' has heart-shaped deep purple leaves. 'Blackie' is a fast grower with purple-black leaves. 'Ladyfingers' has medium green leaves divided into long, fingerlike lobes; leafstalks are burgundy. 'Marguerite' (alternate spellings include 'Margurite' and 'Margarita') has golden green foliage. A variety variously called 'Tricolor' and 'Pink Frost' has green leaves with white and pink variegation. All are attractive in hanging baskets.

I. indica (I. acuminata, I. learii). BLUE DAWN FLOWER. Perennial. Zones 8, 9, 12–24; H1, H2. Vigorous, rapid growth to 15–30 ft. Dark green, heart-shaped or three-lobed leaves. Clusters of 3–4-in., funnel-shaped flowers from spring into fall; blooms open bright blue, then fade to pinkish purple by day's end. Use to cover large bank, wall, or unsightly fence or other structure. Blooms in 1 year from seed; can also be grown from cuttings, divisions, and layering of established plants.

I. nil. MORNING GLORY. Annual. All zones. Summer bloomer resembling *I. tricolor*. The large-flowered (to 6-in.-wide) Imperial Japanese strain belongs to this species. Other available selections include rosy red 'Scarlett O'Hara', odd pinkish tan 'Chocolate', and the mixed-color Early Call strain which is useful where summers are short.

I. quamoclit (Quamoclit pennata). CYPRESS VINE, CARDINAL CLIMBER. Annual. All zones. To 20 ft., with 2½–4-in.-long leaves finely divided into slender threads. Summer flowers are 1½-in.-long tubes that flare at mouth into a five-pointed star; they are usually scarlet, rarely white.

I. tricolor. MORNING GLORY. Annual. All zones. Vigorous growth to 10–15 ft., with large, heart-shaped leaves. Showy, funnel-shaped to bell-like flowers are single or double, in solid colors of blue, lavender, pink, red, or white, often with throats in contrasting colors; some are bicolored or striped. Most types open only in morning, fade in afternoon. Bloom from summer until frost. Among the most popular selections is 'Heavenly Blue', to 15 ft., bearing 4–5-in., pure sky blue flowers with yellow throat. 'Tie Dye', to 6–8 ft., bears 6-in.-wide lavender blooms marked with deep purple swirls, stripes, and flecks; its foliage is splashed silvery white. Dwarf strain with white markings on the leaves (known as Spice Islands or simply as Variegated) grows only 4 in. high and spills to 1 ft. across; flower colors include red, pink, blue, and bicolors.

I. tuberosa. See Merremia tuberosa

Ipomoea tricolor
'Heavenly Blue'

IPOMOPSIS
Polemoniaceae
BIENNIALS OR PERENNIALS

- 🌿 ZONES VARY BY SPECIES
- ☼ FULL SUN
- ○ NO IRRIGATION NEEDED

Erect single stems, finely divided leaves, and tubular red (or yellow-and-red) flowers. Individual plants are narrow and somewhat startling in appearance; best massed.

Ipomopsis aggregata

Good in wild garden, where they survive on rainfall—but can take irrigation if grown in watered border. Sow seeds in spring or early summer for bloom the following summer.

I. aggregata (Gilia aggregata). Biennial. Zones 1–3, 6–14, 18–21. Native from California to British Columbia, east to Rocky Mountains. To 2½ ft. tall and 1 ft. wide. Flowers are red marked yellow (sometimes pure yellow), an inch or so long; borne in long, narrow clusters.

I. rubra (Gilia rubra). Biennial or perennial. Zones 2, 3, 7–9, 14–24. Native to southern U.S. To 6 ft. tall and 1 ft. wide. Flowers red outside, yellow marked red inside.

IRESINE
BLOODLEAF
Amaranthaceae
PERENNIALS

- 🌿 ZONES VARY BY SPECIES; OR INDOORS
- ☼ FULL SUN; BRIGHT LIGHT
- ● REGULAR WATER

Tender, upright plants grown for their vibrant leaf colors; flowers are inconspicuous and may be

Iresine herbstii

pinched out. Grow best in rich, well-drained soil. Pinch tips of young plants to encourage bushiness. Good in containers. Beyond hardiness range, bring indoors for winter, treat as annuals, or grow as houseplants. Easy to propagate from cuttings taken in fall and grown for spring and summer display.

I. herbstii. Zones 22–24; H1, H2. From Brazil. To 1–3 ft. high and wide, or larger under ideal conditions. Leaves are 1–3 in. long, oval to round, usually notched at the tip. Leaf color may be purplish red with light midrib and veins, or green or bronze with yellowish veins. Stems may be green, purple, or red.

I. lindenii. Zones 21–24; 15–17 with protection. From Ecuador. To 3 ft. tall and wide, with glossy, deep red leaves with prominent dark or light red veins. Leaves are egg shaped to lance shaped, to 4 in. long.

IRIS
Iridaceae
PERENNIALS FROM BULBS
AND RHIZOMES

- 🌿 ZONES VARY ACCORDING TO SPECIES OR TYPE
- ☼◑● EXPOSURE NEEDS VARY BY SPECIES
- ●●●● WATER NEEDS VARY BY SPECIES

A large and remarkably diverse group of 200 to 300 species, varying in flower color and form, cultural needs, and blooming periods (although the majority flower in spring or early summer). Leaves are swordlike or grasslike. Flowers (fragrant, in many kinds) are showy and complex in structure. The three inner segments (the standards) are petals; they are usually erect or arching but, in some

kinds, may flare to horizontal. The three outer segments (the falls) are petal-like sepals; they are held at various angles, from nearly horizontal to drooping.

Irises grow from bulbs or rhizomes. In floral detail, there are three categories: bearded (each fall bears an adornment resembling a fuzzy caterpillar); beardless (each fall is smooth); and crested (each fall bears a comblike ridge instead of a full beard).

Described here are the irises most available in the West. Tall bearded irises (and other bearded classes) are the most widely sold; many new hybrids are cataloged every year. Specialty growers abound. A smaller number offer various beardless classes and some species. Retail nurseries carry bulbous irises for fall planting; more and more nurseries are also selling Pacific Coast irises.

BULBOUS IRISES

Irises that grow from bulbs have beardless flowers. Bulbs become dormant in summer and can be lifted and stored until planting time in fall.

Dutch iris

Dutch and Spanish irises. Zones 2b–24. The species that parented this group come from Spain, Portugal, Sicily, and northern Africa. (Dutch irises acquired their name because the hybrid group was developed by Dutch bulb growers.) Flowers are borne atop slender stems that rise up from rushlike foliage. Standards are narrow and upright; oval to circular falls project downward. Colors include white, mauve, blue, purple, brown, orange, yellow, and bicolor combinations—usually with a yellow blotch on falls. Dutch iris flowers reach 3–4 in. across, on stems 1½–2 ft. tall; these are the irises sold by florists. Bloom period is early spring in warm-winter climates, late spring in colder areas. Spanish irises are similar but have smaller flowers that bloom about 2 weeks after Dutch irises.

Plant bulbs in autumn, setting them 4 in. deep, 3–4 in. apart; give full sun. Bulbs are hardy to about –10°F/–23°C, but in coldest adapted zones, apply a mulch in winter. Give regular water during growth. Bulbs can be left in the ground for several years where summers are dry; elsewhere, they should be lifted. After bloom, let foliage ripen before digging; store bulbs in a cool, dry place for no more than 2 months before replanting. Dutch and Spanish irises are good in containers; plant five bulbs in a 5–6-in. pot.

The widely sold 'Wedgwood' is a Dutch hybrid hardy only in Zones 4–24. Large flowers are lavender blue with yellow markings, blooming earlier than others (generally coinciding with 'King Alfred' daffodils). Bulbs are larger than those of average Dutch hybrid. Vigorous foliage dies down after bloom and is best masked by bushy annuals or perennials that will mature later in the season.

English irises. Zones 3–6, 15–17, 21–24. The species (*I. latifolia*) from which named selections were made is native to the Pyrenees, where it grows in moist meadows. Early botanists first noticed the iris growing in southern England, where it had been taken by traders. Flowers are similar in structure to Dutch and Spanish irises, but falls are broader and decorated with a hairline stripe of yellow. Colors include bluish purple, wine red, maroon, blue, mauve, white. Bloom comes in early summer. Plant bulbs in fall, 3–4 in. deep, 4 in. apart, in cool, moist, acid soil. Choose a partly shaded location in warm-summer areas, full sun where summers are cool. Because English irises don't need complete dryness after flowering, they can be left in the ground in suitable climates (bulbs are hardy to about –10°F/–23°C). Or the bulbs can be lifted and replanted.

Reticulata irises. Zones 3–24; safer in pots in colder zones. The netted outer covering on the bulbs gives the group its name. These are classic rock garden and container plants, the flowers (like small Dutch irises) appearing on 6–8-in. stems in early spring (midwinter in mild areas). Narrow blue-green leaves appear after bloom. Available species include *I. reticulata,* with 2–3-in. violet-scented flowers (purple, in the usual forms), and bright yellow–flowered *I. danfordiae.* Pale blue–flowered *I. histrio* and large-flowered, blue-and-yellow *I. histrioides* may be carried by some specialists. Far more common are named hybrids such as 'Cantab' (pale blue with orange markings), 'Harmony' (blue marked in yellow), 'J. S. Dijt' (reddish purple).

Bulbs are hardy to about –10°F/–23°C and need some subfreezing winter temperatures to thrive. Plant in autumn, in well-drained soil in a sunny location; set bulbs 3–4 in. deep and 3–4 in. apart. Need regular moisture from fall through spring. Soil should be kept dry during summer dormant period; in rainy climates, lift bulbs in summer or grow in pots so you can control moisture. Divide only when vigor and flower quality deteriorate. Watch for slugs and snails.

RHIZOMATOUS IRISES

Irises that grow from rhizomes (thickened, modified stems with fleshy roots) may have bearded, beardless, or crested flowers; among this group are the most widely grown types. Leaves are swordlike, overlapping each other to form flat fans of foliage.

Bearded irises. Zones 1–24. The most widely grown irises fall into the bearded group. More than a century of breeding has produced a vast array of beautiful hybrids. All have upright standards and flaring to pendent falls that have characteristic epaulette-like beards. Tall bearded irises are the most familiar of these, but they represent just one subdivision of the entire group.

July to October is best planting period; in regions with mild winters and cool to moderate summers, you can plant throughout this time. In cold-winter zones, plant during July or August; where summer temperatures are high, plant in September or October.

Bearded irises need good drainage. They'll grow in soils from sandy to claylike, but in clay soils plant in raised beds or on ridges to assure drainage, avoid rhizome rot. Plant in full sun in cool climates; in hottest regions, they'll accept light shade during the afternoon. Space rhizomes 1–2 ft. apart; set with tops barely beneath soil surface, spreading roots well. Growth proceeds from the leafy end of rhizome, so point that end in direction you want growth initially to occur. For quick show, plant three rhizomes 1 ft. apart—two with growing ends pointed outward, the third aimed to grow into the space between them. On slopes, set rhizomes with growing end facing uphill. Water to settle soil and start growth. Thereafter, water judiciously until new growth shows plants have rooted; then water regularly until fall rains or frosts arrive. If weather turns hot, shade newly planted rhizomes to prevent sunscald, possible rot. Where winters are severe, mulch new plantings to prevent heaving from alternate freezing, thawing.

From the time growth starts in late winter or early spring, water regularly until about 6 weeks after flowers fade; increases and buds for next year's flowers form during postbloom period. During summer, plants need less water. In heavy soil, it may be sufficient to water every other week in hot climates, monthly in cool ones. In lighter soils, try watering weekly in hot areas, every other week in cool ones. For best performance, feed plants with moderate-nitrogen commercial fertilizer as growth begins in spring, then after bloom has finished. In cool, moist spring, leaf spot may disfigure foliage; use an appropriate fungicide at first sign of infection. Remove old and dry leaves in fall.

Clumps become overcrowded after 3 or 4 years; quantity and quality of bloom decrease. Lift and divide crowded clumps at best planting time for your area. Save large rhizomes with healthy leaves; discard old and leafless ones from clump's center. Break rhizomes apart or use a sharp knife to separate. Trim leaves, roots to about 6 in.; let cut ends heal for several

Tall bearded iris 'Beverly Sills'

Dutch iris
'White Wedgwood'

Reticulata iris
'Harmony'

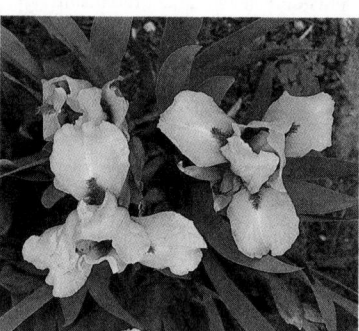

Standard dwarf bearded iris
'Sarah Taylor'

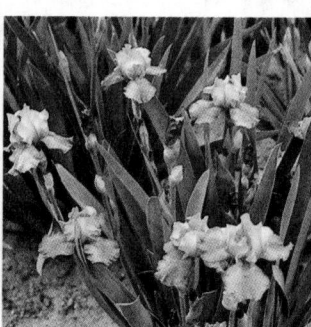

Bearded iris
'Brown Lasso'

hours to a day before replanting. If replanting in the same soil, amend it with organic matter.

Dwarf and median irises. These irises generally have flowers shaped like the familiar tall beardeds, but flower size, plant size, and stature are smaller. Median iris is a collective term for the categories standard dwarf, intermediate and border bearded, and miniature tall bearded.

Miniature dwarf bearded irises. Grow to 8 in. tall; flowers large for size of plant. Earliest to bloom of bearded irises (about 6 weeks before main show of tall beardeds). Hardy, need winter chill. Plants multiply quickly. Shallow root systems need regular moisture and periodic feeding.

Standard dwarf bearded irises. Grow 8–15 in. tall. Flowers and plants are larger than miniature dwarfs. Profuse bloom. Easier to grow than miniature dwarfs in Western gardens but perform best with some winter chill.

Intermediate bearded irises. Grow 15–28 in. tall, bear flowers 3–5 in. across. Flower later than dwarfs but 1 to 3 weeks before tall bearded irises. Most are hybrids of standard dwarfs and tall bearded varieties and resemble larger standard dwarfs rather than border beardeds. Some give second bloom in fall.

Border bearded irises. Grow 15–28 in. tall—proportionately smaller versions of tall beardeds in the same wide range of colors and patterns. Bloom period is same as for tall bearded.

Miniature tall bearded irises. Grow 15–28 in. high and flower with tall beardeds. Their small flowers (2–3 in. wide), narrower foliage, and pencil-thin stems give them

appearance of tall bearded irises reduced in every proportion. Good for cutting and arrangements—hence their original name, "table irises."

Tall bearded irises. Among choicest perennials for borders, massing, cutting. Easy to grow. Midspring flowers, on branching stems 2½–4 ft. high. All colors but pure red and green; patterns of two colors or more, blends produce infinite variety. Countless named selections are available. Modern hybrids often have elaborately ruffled, fringed flowers. Available variegated-foliage selections include 'Pallida Variegata' (often cataloged as 'Zebra'), with green leaves striped with cream; and 'Argentea', producing green leaves with white stripes. Both bear smallish blue-lavender flowers on stems to 2 ft. high.

Remontant (or reblooming) tall bearded irises flower in spring, again in mid- to late summer, fall, or winter, depending on variety and climate. In mild climates, some are nearly everblooming. Plants need fertilizer, regular moisture for best performance. Specialists' catalogs offer increasing numbers of remontant tall beardeds.

Aril and arilbred irises. The aril species and interspecies hybrids (characterized by an aril, or collar,

Japanese iris

on their seeds) offer strange and often remarkably beautiful flowers on unattractive plants. Exacting cultural requirements. Most species come from semidesert areas of the Near East and central Asia; they need limy soil, perfect drainage, full sun, and no summer water (and thus do best in areas with scant or no summer rain). There are two main groups: *Oncocyclus* and *Regelia. Oncocyclus* group includes a number of species with huge, nearly globular flowers in lavender, gray, silver, maroon, and gold, often intricately veined and stippled with deeper hues. *Regelia* group has smaller, narrower-petaled flowers, veined or unmarked; they come in brighter shades than *Oncocyclus*, often with a lustrous sheen. *Oncocyclus* are more difficult to grow; somewhat easier are *Regelia* group and hybrids between the two *(Oncogelia)*.

Arilbreds—hybrids between the arils and bearded irises—offer some of the arils' exotic beauty on plants nearly as easy to grow as tall beardeds, given well-drained, neutral to alkaline soil. Amount of aril ancestry can determine ease of culture: hybrids containing half aril ancestry or more usually are more demanding than those of one-quarter or three-eighths aril ancestry. Specialists' catalogs often state hybrid ancestries for this reason.

Beardless irises. Flowers in this group all have smooth, "beardless"

falls but otherwise differ considerably in appearance from one type or species to another. Rhizomes have fibrous roots (unlike fleshy roots of bearded types); most prefer or demand more moisture than bearded irises. Many can perform well from crowded clumps but will eventually need division. Timing varies; dig and replant quickly, keeping roots moist until planted.

The following five hybrid groups contain the most widely sold beardless irises. Also described are individual species (and their named selections) available from growers of specialty irises and perennials.

Japanese irises. Zones 1–10, 14–24. Derived solely from *I. ensata* (formerly *I. kaempferi)*, these irises feature sumptuous blossoms 4–12 in. across on slender stems to 4 ft. high. Flower shape is essentially flat. "Single" types have three broad falls and much-reduced standards, giving triangular flower outline; "double" blossoms have standards marked like the falls and about the same size and shape, resulting in circular flower outline. Colors are purple, violet, pink, rose, red, white—often veined or edged in contrasting shade. Plants have graceful narrow, upright leaves with distinct raised midribs. Purple-flowered 'Variegata' has white-margined leaves.

Plants need much moisture during growing, flowering period. Acid to neutral soil and water are required. If soil or water is alkaline, apply aluminum sulfate or iron sulfate (1 oz. to 2 gallons water) several times during growing season. Plant rhizomes in fall or spring, 2 in. deep and 1½ ft. apart; or plant up to three per 12-in. container. Use in moist borders, at edge of pools or streams, or even in boxes or pots plunged halfway to rim in pond or pool

Miniature tall bearded iris
'Rosemary's Dream'

Bearded iris
'Edith Wolford'

Arilbred iris
'Jeweled Veil'

Japanese iris

during growing season. Full sun except in hottest areas.

Louisiana irises. Zones 3–24; H1, H2. Approximately four species from the lower Mississippi region and Gulf Coast compose this group of so-called swamp irises. Graceful, flattish blossoms on stems 2–5 ft. tall, carried above and among leaves that are long, narrow, and unribbed. The range of flower colors and patterns is extensive—nearly the equal of tall beardeds.

Specialists offer a vast array of named hybrids; some may carry the basic species as well. *I. brevicaulis (I. foliosa)* has blue flowers with flaring segments carried on zigzag stems among the foliage. *I. fulva* has coppery to rusty red (rarely yellow) blossoms with narrow, drooping segments. *I. giganticaerulea* is indeed a "giant blue" (sometimes white) with upright standards and flaring falls; stems may reach 4 ft. or more, with proportionally large leaves. *I. hexagona* also comes in blue shades with upright standards, flaring falls. *I. × nelsonii*, a natural hybrid population derived from *I. fulva* and *I. giganticaerulea*, resembles the *I. fulva* parent in flower shape and color (but also including purple and brown tones) and approaches the *I. giganticaerulea* parent in size.

Plants thrive in well-watered, rich garden soil as well as at pond margins; soil and water should be neutral to acid. Locate in full sun where summer is cool to mild; choose light afternoon shade where summer heat is intense. Plant in late summer; set rhizomes 1 in. deep, 1½–2 ft. apart. Mulch for winter where ground freezes.

Pacific Coast irises. Best in Zones 4–9, 14–24; grown with mixed success in Zone 3. Eleven species native to Pacific Coast states constitute a homogeneous group

within the genus *Iris*, from which breeders have developed hybrids in a broad range of colors and patterns; flowers may be white, blue shades, pink, copper, brown, maroon, violet—many with elaborate veining or patterning. Foliage is narrow; clumps are like coarse grass. Slender flower stems reach 8–24 in., depending on variety.

Best conditions are sun to light shade, well-drained soil, moderate to scant water in summer. Intense heat coupled with water and poor drainage can be fatal; in clay soil, grow in raised beds in organically amended soil. Plant from containers anytime, though spring and fall are best. Timing is critical in digging, dividing, and replanting. Best moment is when new roots are starting to form (scrape away soil at plant base to check); this ranges from early fall in colder regions to midwinter in mild-winter areas.

Specialists sell several species prominent in the ancestry of hybrids. *I. douglasiana* is native to California coast from Santa Barbara into Oregon. Evergreen leaves 1½–2 ft. long; stems 1–2 ft., sometimes branched, with flowers in purple and blue shades to white, cream. Tolerates less-than-perfect conditions. *I. innominata* comes from northwestern California and southwestern Oregon. Evergreen leaves; 8–12-in. stems bear flowers in yellow, orange, lavender, purple, brown, many attractively veined. Best in mild-summer regions, in woodland or rock garden. *I. tenax*, from Washington and Oregon, makes grassy clumps of foot-tall deciduous leaves. Flowers may be white, blue, purple, pink, cream, often veined in purple or brown. Best with mild summers, some winter chill.

Siberian irises. Zones A2, A3; 1–10, 14–23. The most widely sold members of this group are named

hybrids derived from *I. sibirica* and *I. sanguinea* (formerly *I. orientalis*) —species native to Europe, Asia. Clumps of narrow, almost grasslike leaves (deciduous in winter) produce slender stems to 4 ft. high (depending on variety), each bearing two to five blossoms with upright standards and flaring to drooping falls. Colors include white and shades of blue, lavender, purple, wine, pink, and light yellow.

Siberian iris

Give plants full sun (partial or dappled shade where summer is hot), neutral to acid soil. Set rhizomes 1–2 in. deep, 1–2 ft. apart. In cold-winter regions, plant in early spring or late summer; plant in autumn in milder regions. Water liberally from onset of growth until several weeks after bloom. Divide infrequently—when clumps show hollow centers—at best planting time for your region.

Specialists may offer various Sino-Siberian species. Most feature drooping falls and erect to flaring standards. Predominantly yellow colors are found in *I. forrestii* and *I. wilsonii;* predominantly purple to violet flowers occur in *I. chrysographes, I. clarkei, I. delavayi,* and *I. dykesii.* These species and their hybrids perform best in Zones 4–6, 15–17, where climate is moist and relatively mild. Give plants good, acid soil, regular moisture. Interesting hybrids between these species and Pacific Coast irises are

called Cal-Sibes; flowers resemble the Siberian parents but have expanded color range. Garden needs are the same as for Sino-Siberian types.

Spuria irises. Zones 2–24. In flower form, the spurias resemble Dutch irises. Older members of this group had primarily yellow or white-and-yellow blossoms; *I. orientalis* (universally known as *I. ochroleuca*) has naturalized in many parts of the West, its 3–5-ft. stems bearing white flowers with yellow blotches on the falls. Dwarf *I. graminea* bears narrow-petaled, fragrant blue-and-maroon blossoms on foot-high stems. Modern hybrids show a great color range: blue, lavender, gray, orchid, tan, bronze, brown, purple, earthy red, and near black—often with a prominent yellow spot on the falls. Flowers are held closely against 3–6-ft. stems, rising above handsome clumps of narrow dark green leaves. Flowering starts during latter part of tall bearded bloom and continues for several weeks beyond.

Plant rhizomes in late summer or early fall, in rich, neutral to slightly alkaline soil; set them 1 in. deep, 1½–2 ft. apart. Plants grow well in full sun but will also take light shade for part of the day. They need ample moisture from onset of growth through bloom period but little moisture during summer. Divide clumps (not an easy task) infrequently; mulch clumps for winter where temperatures drop to –20°F/–29°C or lower.

SPECIES IRISES

I. foetidissima. GLADWIN IRIS. Zones 3–24. Native to Europe. Glossy evergreen leaves to 2 ft. make handsome foliage clumps. Stems 1½–2 ft. tall bear subtly attractive flowers in blue gray and dull tan; specialists may offer color variants in soft yellow and lavender blue, as well as a form

Louisiana iris

Pacific Coast iris 'Dorothea's Ruby'

Siberian iris 'Caesar's Brother'

Spuria iris 'Barbara's Kiss'

Iris laevigata

ith white-variegated leaves
Variegata'). Real attraction is
rge seed capsules that open in
ll to show numerous round,
ange-scarlet seeds; the cut stems
ith seed capsules are attractive in
rangements. Grow in sun to
ade in cool-summer regions,
ght or partial shade to full shade
sewhere. Extremely tolerant
aridity.

I. laevigata. Zones 1–10,
–24. Native to China, Korea,
pan. Smooth, glossy leaves reach
–2½ ft. high, to 1 in. wide.
ower stems grow to about the
me height, bearing violet-blue
ossoms with upright standards
d drooping falls enlivened with
llow central stripes. Bloom
riod comes after that of tall
arded irises. Named color vari-
ts include kinds with white,
agenta, and patterned purple-
d-white blooms, as well as a
rple-flowered selection with
aves striped in ivory white. There
so are varieties whose standards
imic falls in shape, pattern, and
rriage, producing the effect of a
uble blossom. This is a true bog
ant, growing best in constantly
oist, acid soil—even in shallow
ater. Full sun.

I. missouriensis. WESTERN
LUE FLAG, ROCKY MOUNTAIN
IS. Zones 1–10, 14–24. Native
extensive Western area—from
estern Nebraska and Dakotas
to Sierra Nevada/Cascade moun-
in ranges and mountains of
uthern California, from the
kon southward into northern
exico. Elevation range is also
tensive—from 2,000 to about
,000 ft. In zones where plant is
apted, local forms are more
kely to succeed. Narrow, flat,
uish green, winter-deciduous
aves range from 12 to 22 in.
gh. Blooms in late spring and
mmer, bearing blossoms with
arrow, upright standards and
miflaring to drooping falls, on

stems a bit higher than the foliage.
Colors range from lavender to
white, with veins in darker lavender to purple; the darker colors are
found in the more southerly and
westerly forms. Give a sunny location and neutral to alkaline, water-
retentive soil that is kept moist
throughout growth and bloom,
dry thereafter. Best time to plant
or transplant is from early spring
into the flowering period.

A similar species, *I. longipetala*,
is considered by some botanists
to be a form of *I. missouriensis*. It
differs from *I. missouriensis* in its
nativity (northern and central California Coast Ranges, up to about
1,200 ft.) and in having evergreen
foliage and an early spring bloom
period. Cultural preferences are the
same as for *I. missouriensis*.

I. prismatica. Zones 2–6.
Native to eastern North America.
Foliage and flowers suggest a small
Siberian iris. Typical form grows
about 1 ft. high, bearing dainty
purple-and-white blossoms on
branching, sinuous stems. A pure
white form exists. *I. p. austrina*,
native to the southern Appalachians, is a bit taller and coarser, with
lilac-blue blossoms. Give plants full
sun and moist (but not boggy),
acid soil. Rhizomes spread widely,
forming loose colonies rather than
tight clumps.

I. pseudacorus. YELLOW
FLAG. Zones A2, A3; 1–24. Native
to Europe but now found worldwide in temperate regions; seeds
float, aiding plant's dispersal.
Impressive foliage plant; under
best conditions, upright leaves
may reach 5 ft. tall. Flower stems
grow 4–7 ft. (depending on culture), bear bright yellow flowers
3–4 in. across. Selected forms offer
ivory and lighter yellow flowers,
double flowers, variegated foliage,
and plants with shorter and taller
leaves. Plant in sun to light shade.
Needs acid soil and more than
average moisture; thrives in shal-

low water and can become invasive where running water spreads
its seeds.

Several hybrids are excellent
foliage plants with distinctive blossoms. All prefer ample water (but
not pond conditions), sun to light
shade. 'Holden Clough' perhaps has
I. foetidissima as its other parent.
Flowers, 3–4 in. across, are soft tan
heavily netted with maroon veins;
stems grow to 4 ft.; leaves reach
4–5 ft. but tips arch over. Two of
its seedlings are similar but larger.
'Phil Edinger' grows to 4½ ft. with
arching foliage; 4–5-in. flowers are
brass colored, heavily veined in
brown. 'Roy Davidson' is similar,
but flowers are dark yellow with
fine brown veining and maroon
thumbprint on falls.

I. setosa. Zones A1–A3; 1–6.
Native to Siberia (extending to
Kamchatka), Alaska, eastern
Canada, and New England. Leaves
are a slightly grayed green, ½–1 in.
wide; plants vary from less than
1 ft. to about 2 ft. high, with flower
stems taller than leaves. Blooms in
late spring and summer, bearing
typically blue-purple to red-purple
flowers with broadly rounded falls,
standards reduced to mere bristles.
Form sold as 'Nasuensis' is larger
in all parts than species, reaches
about 3 ft. high; will also grow in
Zones 7–9, 14–17. Garden culture
as for Siberian irises: moist, well-
drained, neutral to acid soil, and
full sun except in hottest areas.
Will grow where buffeted by salt-
laden ocean spray. Plant in late
summer, early fall.

I. unguicularis (I. stylosa).
WINTER IRIS. Zones 4–9, 14–24.
Native to Greece, the Near East,
northern Africa. Dense clump of
narrow dark green leaves. Depending on variety and mildness of
winter, flowers appear from
November to March. Typical form
has violet-tinted blue blossoms
elevated on 6–9-in. tubes that
serve as stems. Named selections

vary in flower color (lighter and
darker lavender, orchid pink,
white) and coarseness and length
of foliage. Plants need neutral to
acid soil, heat, and scant water
during summer (but will take
moderate water if soil is very well
drained). In Zones 4 and 5, grow
against sunny wall or house foundation to increase summer heat
and to lessen winter cold. Divide
overcrowded clumps in early fall
(mild regions) or in late winter
after flowering (colder regions).
Slugs and snails are attracted to
the flowers.

I. versicolor. BLUE FLAG.
Zones 1–9, 14–17. Widely distributed North American species,
found in bogs and swamps from
Mississippi Valley to eastern
Canada. Grows 1½–4 ft. tall; narrow leaves are thicker in the center
but not ribbed. Shorter-growing
forms have upright leaves, but
foliage of taller types may recurve
gracefully. The typical wild flowers
are a light violet blue, but lighter
and darker forms exist; a wine
red variant has been sold as 'Ker-
mesina'. Named selections include
pink 'Rosea' and 'Vernal', as well as
others with flowers in violet red.
Like *I. pseudacorus*, this species
thrives in sun to light shade, in
moist, acid soil or shallow water.

Specialty growers offer hybrids
between *I. versicolor* and other
species such as *I. ensata, I. laevigata*, and *I. virginica*. Violet-
flowered 'Gerald Darby', a hybrid
with *I. virginica*, has striking wine
red stems.

I. virginica. SOUTHERN BLUE
FLAG. Zones 3–9, 14–17. Native to
Eastern seaboard, from Virginia
south and west to Mississippi
River and Gulf Coast. Similar to
I. versicolor in form and flower;
distinguishing floral feature is
longer standards. Flower colors
include light to dark blue, wine
red, pink, lavender, and white.
A plant sold as 'Giant Blue' is

Iris pseudacorus

Iris unguicularis 'Walter Butt'

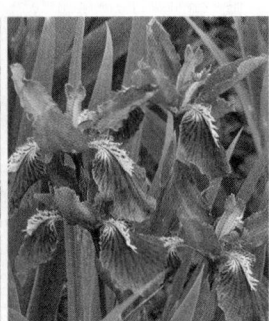
Iris cristata

Iris tectorum

distinctly larger in all parts, approaching *I. pseudacorus* in size. Plant in moist, acid soil or grow in shallow water. In deep ponds, plant in large pots barely submerged beneath the surface. Sun to light shade.

Crested irises. Though these are botanically placed with beardless irises, they represent a transition between beardless and bearded: each fall bears a narrow, comblike crest where a beard would be in bearded sorts. Slugs and snails are especially attracted to foliage and flowers.

I. cristata. Zones 2b–6. Leaves 4–6 in. long, ½ in. wide; slender greenish rhizomes spread freely. Flowers white, lavender, or light blue with golden crests. Give light shade, organically enriched soil, regular water. Divide just after bloom or in fall after leaves die down.

I. tectorum. ROOF IRIS. Zones 3–9, 14–24; H1, H2. Native to Japan, where it is planted on cottage roofs. Foliage fans to 1 ft. tall look like those of bearded irises, but leaves are ribbed and glossy. Flowers suggest an informal bearded iris with fringed petals and crests in place of beards. Colors are violet blue with white crests or white with yellow crests; standards are upright at first, opening to horizontal as flower matures. Provide organically enriched soil, light shade, regular water. Short lived in regions where summers are hot and dry. 'Paltec', a hybrid of *I. tectorum* with a bearded iris, will grow with bearded irises; it reaches about 1 ft. high, with lavender flowers suggesting a bearded iris with beards superimposed on crests.

Tender crested irises. Several tender species and hybrids form bamboo-type stems carrying foliage fans aloft; flower stems to 2 ft. are widely branched, bearing orchidlike sprays of fringed flowers in lavender to white with orange crests. These include *I. confusa, I. japonica, I. wattii,* and hybrids such as 'Nada' and 'Darjeeling'. Grow in sun where summer is cool, light shade elsewhere; plant in organically enriched soil. Regular water during growth. Reliable outdoors in Zones 17, 23, 24, and H1; in other zones, grow in containers and move to shelter over winter.

IRISH LACE.
See **TAGETES filifolia**

IRISH MOSS.
See **SAGINA subulata**

IRONBARK. See **EUCALYPTUS**

ISCHYROLEPIS subverticillata
BROOM RESTIO
Restionaceae
PERENNIAL

🌿 ZONES 14–24
☀️ 🌤 FULL SUN OR PARTIAL SHADE
💧 MODERATE WATER

Native to South Africa. Reedlike plant to 6 ft. tall and 4 ft. wide; looks something like a big, feathery, clumping horsetail (*Equisetum hyemale*). Erect or slightly arching, canelike stems hold whorls of long, thin leaves at evenly spaced nodes. Insignificant flowers appear

Ischyrolepis subverticillata

at branch tips in late summer; small, silvery seed heads that follow are showy. Remove outer stems every 2 or 3 years to rejuvenate plant. Good in large pots. Stems are excellent in cut-flower arrangements.

ISLAND BUSH SNAPDRAGON.
See **GALVEZIA speciosa**

ISMENE calathina. See
HYMENOCALLIS narcissiflora

ISOLEPIS cernua (Scirpus cernuus)
FIBER OPTICS PLANT
Cyperaceae
PERENNIAL

🌿 ZONES 7–24
🌤 PARTIAL SHADE
💧 AMPLE WATER

Grasslike sedge from British Isles, Europe, and North Africa. To 6–10 in. high (but usually lower), flopping over to become about

Isolepis cernua

twice as wide. Blooms all year; small brown flower spikelets appear at ends of the drooping, threadlike green stems. Occasional division and resetting will keep it small. An ideal plant for edge of shallow pond. Good container plant, especially when displayed on a pedestal or plant stand so its flowing habit is easier to appreciate.

ISOPOGON formosus
ROSE CONEFLOWER
Proteaceae
EVERGREEN SHRUB

🌿 ZONES 15–24
☀️ 🌤 FULL SUN OR LIGHT SHADE
☀️ MODERATE WATER

From Australia. Slender, erect habit to 4–9 ft. high, 3–6 ft. wide. Stems are densely clothed with finely divided leaves and topped by dense, 2½-in., conelike clusters of long, slender rosy purple florets in late winter or spring. Excellent cut flower—and cutting in bloom stimulates denser growth. Tip-pinching also makes plants bushier. Easily propagated from cuttings.

Isopogon formosus

Like most proteas, this species cannot tolerate high phosphorus levels and should be fertilized lightly with nitrogen. Avoid watering in hot weather (above 90°F/32°C).

ISOTOMA fluviatilis.
See **PRATIA pedunculata**

ITEA
SWEETSPIRE
Escalloniaceae
EVERGREEN, SEMIEVERGREEN, AND DECIDUOUS SHRUBS

🌿 ZONES VARY BY SPECIES
☀️ FULL SUN, EXCEPT AS NOTED
💧 REGULAR WATER

Only a few of the ten or so species are seen in gardens. One feature they have in common is small, scented flowers in long, narrow, tightly packed clusters. Little pruning required.

I. ilicifolia. HOLLYLEAF SWEETSPIRE. Evergreen. Zones 4–9, 14–24. Native to China. Shrub has graceful, arching, open habit to 10–15 ft. tall and 10 ft. wide. Leaves are oval, spiny-toothed, to 4 in. long; new foliage is bronzy red, matures to glossy dark green.

Itea ilicifolia

Lightly fragrant greenish white flowers in nodding or drooping clusters to 1 ft. long in autumn; blooms sparsely where winters are mild. Not striking, but a graceful plant of distinction. Attractive near water or espaliered against a wall. Needs partial shade in hottest climates.

I. japonica 'Beppu'. Semievergreen. Zones 4–6. Native to Japan. Dwarf shrub to 2½ ft. tall and suckering widely. Leaves and flowers resemble those of *I. virginica,* under which name this shrub is often mistakenly sold. Foliage turns reddish purple in fall.

I. virginica. Deciduous. Zones 2b–6, 15–17. Native to eastern U.S. To 3–15 ft. tall, spreading by suckers to form large patches where well adapted. Narrow, oval, 4-in.-long, dark green leaves turn purplish or bright red in fall, hang on the plant for a long time—

possibly all winter. Fragrant, creamy white summer flowers in erect clusters to 6 in. long. Compact varieties include 'Sarah Eve', to 5 ft., with red new growth, flowers that open blushed pink, and good red fall color; 'Henry's Garnet' (3–4 ft.), a superior selection with brilliant purplish red fall foliage; 'Saturnalia', about the same height but less prone to suckering than the others listed here; 'Merlot' (3 ft.), with rich red fall foliage; and the charming 2-ft.-tall 'Little Henry'. All are good in woodland gardens.

ITHURIEL'S SPEAR.
See **TRITELEIA laxa**

IVY. See **HEDERA**

IXIA
AFRICAN CORN LILY
Iridaceae
PERENNIALS FROM CORMS

- 🗷 **ZONES 7–9, 12–24; OR DIG AND STORE**
- ☼ **FULL SUN**
- 💧 **REGULAR WATER DURING GROWTH AND BLOOM**

Clump of narrow, almost grasslike leaves sends up wiry, 18–20-in. stems topped by short spikes of 2-in. flowers in late spring. Each six-petaled blossom opens out nearly flat in full sun but remains cup shaped or closed on overcast days. Colors include cream, yellow, red, orange, and pink, typically with dark centers. Most ixias sold are hybrids of the South African species *I. maculata*.

Grow in well-drained soil. Where winter lows usually stay above 20°F/–7°C, plant corms in early fall, setting them 2 in. deep and about 3 in. apart. In climate zones where temperatures may drop down to 10°F/–12°C, plant them in late fall, setting the corms 4 in. deep; cover planting with

Ixia maculata hybrid

mulch. In colder areas, plant in spring for flowers in early summer. Let soil go dry when foliage yellows after bloom. Where corms won't be subject to rainfall or irrigation during dormant period, they can be left undisturbed until the planting becomes crowded or flowering declines. When this occurs, dig corms in summer and store as for gladiolus until recommended planting time in your area. Where corms will receive summer moisture, dig and store them after foliage dies back; or treat as annuals. Potted corms (planted close together and about 1 in. deep) can be stored in pots of dry soil.

IXIOLIRION
tataricum
(I. montanum)
Amaryllidaceae
PERENNIAL FROM BULB

- 🗷 **ZONES 2 AND 3 WITH SHELTER, 4–11, 14–21; OR DIG AND STORE**
- ☼ **FULL SUN**
- 💧 **MODERATE WATER DURING GROWTH AND BLOOM**

Native to central Asia. Wiry, 12–16-in. stems rise from a clump of narrow gray-green leaves, bearing loose clusters of 1½-in. flowers in late spring. Each blue-violet blossom has six narrow petals marked with a darker central line.

Ixiolirion tataricum

Foliage dies down in summer, not to reappear until following spring. Bulbs accept moderate summer moisture but don't need any.

Plant in fall, setting bulbs 3 in. deep, 3 in. apart. Beyond hardiness range, however, plant in early spring; dig in fall and store until planting time the next year. Where bulbs are hardy in the ground, they can remain in place for many years. Dig and divide clumps in fall when they become crowded.

IXORA
Rubiaceae
EVERGREEN SHRUBS

- 🗷 **ZONE H2, EXCEPT AS NOTED**
- ☼ **FULL SUN OR LIGHT SHADE**
- 💧 **REGULAR WATER**

Large group of tropical plants with handsome, leathery, medium to dark green leaves and showy clusters of flowers that bloom throughout much of the year. These shrubs thrive in well-drained, fertile, acid soil. Require little pruning but will tolerate heavy pruning. Use as specimen shrub, hedge or screen, or tubbed plant for lanai or patio. Beyond the hardiness range, can be grown only in greenhouse.

Ixora coccinea

I. casei 'Super King'. SUPER KING IXORA. Native to the Caroline Islands of the western Pacific. To 12 ft. tall, 8–10 ft. wide, with bright red flower clusters to 6 in. across.

I. chinensis 'Nora Grant'. NORA GRANT IXORA. Native from south China into the Malay peninsula. Grows 6 ft. high and about 4 ft. wide, with large clusters of coral flowers.

I. coccinea. FLAME OF THE WOODS, JUNGLE FLAME. Zones 24; H2. Native to Sri Lanka and southern India. Long in cultivation in southern Florida and Hawaii; many selections are available, featuring blossoms in shades of red, orange, pink, or yellow. Grows 7–10 ft. high and about 6 ft. wide but is often kept lower by tip pinching.

I. 'Thai Dwarf'. THAI DWARF IXORA. A group of compact dwarf ixoras introduced into Hawaii from Thailand. Growing 4 ft. high and wide, they provide abundant, dense clusters of small flowers in a range of brilliant colors—red, orange, gold, pink, yellow.

JACARANDA
mimosifolia
Bignoniaceae
DECIDUOUS OR SEMIEVERGREEN TREE

- 🗷 **ZONES 12, 13, 15–24; H1, H2**
- ☼ **FULL SUN**
- 💧 **MODERATE WATER**

Often sold as *J. acutifolia*. Brazilian native to 25–40 ft. high, 15–30 ft. wide, with open, irregular, oval-headed habit; sometimes multi-trunked or even shrubby. Finely cut, ferny leaves usually drop in late winter. New leaves may emerge quickly, or branches may remain bare until tree comes into bloom—typically in mid- to late spring, though blossoms may appear earlier or open at any time throughout summer. Flowers are lavender blue, tubular, 2 in. long, carried in profuse 8-in.-long clusters. White-flowered 'Alba' is sometimes sold; it has lusher foliage and sparser bloom over a longer season. All forms have flat, roundish seed capsules, quite decorative in arrangements.

Tree is fairly hardy after it gains some mature, hard wood. Young trees are tender below 25°F/–4°C but often rebound from freezes to make multistemmed, shrubby plants. Takes wide variety of soils

Jacaranda mimosifolia

but does best in sandy soil. Often fails to flower in path of ocean winds or where heat is inadequate. Resistant to oak root fungus. Established trees need little pruning; cut any awkward limbs back to strong laterals.

JACK-IN-THE-PULPIT.
See **ARISAEMA**

JACOBEAN LILY.
See **SPREKELIA formosissima**

JACOBINIA carnea, J. ovata. See **JUSTICIA carnea, J. candicans**

JACOBINIA suberecta.
See **DICLIPTERA suberecta**

JACOB'S COAT. See **ALTERNANTHERA tenella 'Bettzickiana'**

JACOB'S LADDER.
See **PEDILANTHUS tithymaloides smallii, POLEMONIUM caeruleum**

JADE PLANT.
See **CRASSULA ovata**

JAMAICA FLOWER or SORREL.
See **HIBISCUS sabdariffa**

JAPANESE ARALIA.
See **FATSIA japonica**

JAPANESE BLOOD GRASS. See **IMPERATA cylindrica 'Rubra'**

JAPANESE BLUEBERRY TREE.
See **ELAEOCARPUS decipiens**

JAPANESE CHINQUAPIN.
See **CASTANOPSIS cuspidata**

JAPANESE COLTSFOOT.
See **PETASITES japonicus**

JAPANESE FALSE OAK.
See **LITHOCARPUS edulis**

JAPANESE FELT FERN.
See **PYRROSIA lingua**

JAPANESE FLOWERING APRICOT, JAPANESE FLOWERING PLUM. See **PRUNUS mume**

JAPANESE FOREST GRASS.
See **HAKONECHLOA macra**

JAPANESE HYDRANGEA VINE.
See **SCHIZOPHRAGMA hydrangeoides**

JAPANESE KNOTWEED.
See **FALLOPIA japonica**

JAPANESE PAGODA TREE.
See **SOPHORA japonica**

JAPANESE PAINTED FERN.
See **ATHYRIUM niponicum**

JAPANESE SILVER TREE.
See **NEOLITSEA sericea**

JAPANESE SNOWBALL.
See **VIBURNUM plicatum**

JAPANESE SNOWBELL, JAPANESE SNOWDROP TREE.
See **STYRAX japonicus**

JAPANESE SWEET SHRUB.
See **CLETHRA barbinervis**

JAPANESE TASSEL FERN. See **POLYSTICHUM polyblepharum**

JAPANESE WATERCRESS.
See **OENANTHE javanica**

JAPAN PEPPER.
See **ZANTHOXYLUM piperitum**

JASMINUM
JASMINE
Oleaceae
EVERGREEN, SEMIEVERGREEN, AND DECIDUOUS SHRUBS AND VINES

| ☑ ZONES VARY BY SPECIES |
| ☀ ◐ FULL SUN OR LIGHT SHADE |
| ◓ ◖ MODERATE TO REGULAR WATER |

When one thinks of fragrance, jasmine is one of the first plants that comes to mind. Yet not all jasmines are fragrant; and despite its common name, the intensely sweet star jasmine is not a true jasmine at all, but a member of the genus *Trachelospermum*. Growth habits of jasmines range from vining to vining-shrubby to decidedly shrubby. True vining types climb by twining stems. Vining shrubs do not twine, but rather put out long, slender, lax stems that must be tied into place if the plants are to function as vines. Otherwise, they'll flop over to make green haystacks of foliage. To grow these plants as shrubs, shorten any shoots that become too long. Only one of the species listed below, *J. parkeri*, is a true shrub; its dwarf size suits it to rock gardens.

Jasmines grow more rapidly in good soil and bloom more profusely in sunny sites, but all adapt well to less-than-perfect conditions. When plants become tangled or untidy, cut them back heavily just before spring growth begins. Pinch and prune as needed throughout the year to control growth.

J. angulare. SOUTH AFRICAN JASMINE. Evergreen vining shrub. Zones 16–24; H1. From South Africa. Vigorous grower with stems 10–20 ft. long. Rich green leaves are divided into three leaflets. Summer-blooming white flowers over 1 in. wide are borne in groups of three; some gardeners detect a subtly sweet scent, others no fragrance at all.

J. azoricum. Evergreen vining shrub. Zones 17–24; H1, H2. From the Azores. To 10–15 ft. high, with dark green leaves divided into three leaflets and clusters of fragrant white flowers in summer.

J. floridum. Evergreen or semievergreen vining shrub. Zones 4–9, 12–24; H1. From China. To 5 ft. high. Dark green leaves divided into three (rarely five) small (½–1½-in.-long) leaflets. Clusters of golden yellow, ½–¾-in., scentless flowers bloom primarily from spring into fall.

J. humile. ITALIAN JASMINE. Evergreen vining shrub. Zones 5–10, 12–24; H1, H2. From the Mideast, Myanmar, and China. Erect, willowy shoots reach 20 ft., arch to make 10-ft. mound. Light green leaves with three to seven 2-in.-long leaflets. Clusters of ½-in., fragrant bright yellow flowers all summer. Can be trained as a shrub or clipped into a hedge. 'Revolutum' has larger flowers (to 1 in. wide) and larger, darker green leaves than the species.

Jasminum laurifolium nitidum

J. laurifolium nitidum (J. nitidum). SHINING JASMINE, ANGELWING JASMINE. Evergreen or semievergreen vine. Zones 12, 16, 19–24; H1, H2. From Admiralty Islands in the southwest Pacific. Requires long, warm growing season to bloom satisfactorily. Hardy to about 25°F/−4°C. Moderate growth to 10–20 ft. Undivided glossy green leaves to 2 in. long. Very fragrant flowers shaped like 1-in. pinwheels open from purplish buds in late spring and summer. Flowers are white above, purplish beneath, borne in clusters of three. Can be used as ground cover or container plant. Often sold as *J. magnificum*.

J. leratii. PRIVET-LEAFED JASMINE. Evergreen vine. Zones 22–24; H1, H2. Native to New Caledonia. To 15 ft., with glossy dark green leaves to 2 in. long that resemble those of privet (*Ligustrum*). Slightly fragrant white flowers in spring.

J. magnificum. See J. laurifolium nitidum

Jasminum mesnyi

J. mesnyi (J. primulinum). PRIMROSE JASMINE. Evergreen vining shrub. Zones 4–24; H1, H2. From China. Long, arching branches 6–10 ft. long. Dark green leaves with three lance-shaped, 2–3-in. leaflets. Bright lemon yellow, unscented flowers to 2 in. across are semidouble or double, produced singly rather than in clusters. Main bloom in winter or spring; may flower sporadically at other times. Needs space. Best tied up at desired height and permitted to spill down in waterfall fashion. Use to cover pergola, bank, large wall, or clip as a 3-ft.-high hedge. In any form, may need occasional severe pruning to avoid brush pile look.

J. multiflorum. DOWNY JASMINE, PIKAKE-HOKU. Evergreen vining shrub. Zones 21–24; H1, H2. From India. Leaves (to 2 in. long) and stems have a downy coating, producing an overall gray-green effect. Clustered white flowers in early spring; not strongly scented. Often called star jasmine in Hawaii, where it is commonly used as a hedge.

J. nudiflorum. WINTER JASMINE. Deciduous vining shrub. Zones 2–21; best adapted to cooler climates. From China. If unsupported, reaches 4 ft. or higher and 7 ft. wide; if trained on a trellis or wall, can grow to 15 ft.

lender, willowy green stems
tand out in winter landscape.
Unscented, bright yellow, 1-in.
flowers appear in winter or early
spring, before handsome, glossy
green, three-leafleted leaves
unfurl. Good bank cover; spreads
by rooting where stems touch soil.
Attractive planted at the top of
retaining walls, with branches
cascading over side. Can also be
trained like *J. mesnyi* (tie plant at
desired height and let branches
spill down like a waterfall). A variegated form is available.

J. officinale. COMMON
WHITE JASMINE, POET'S
JASMINE. Semievergreen or
deciduous vine. Zones 5–9, 12–24;
H1. From Himalayas, Caucasus. To
30 ft. Very fragrant white flowers
to 1 in. across; blooms throughout
summer and into fall. Rich green
leaves have five to nine leaflets,
each to 2½ in. long. 'Argenteo-
variegatum' has leaves edged in
creamy white. 'Aureum' has striking golden yellow foliage.

J. o. affine (J. grandiflorum).
SPANISH JASMINE. Main difference from basic species is size—
this form climbs only to 15 ft. but
bears larger (1½-in.) blooms.

J. parkeri. DWARF JASMINE.
Evergreen shrub. Zones 5–9,
12–24. From India. Dwarf, twiggy,
tufted shrub to 1 ft. high and
1½–2 ft. wide. Bright green, ½–
1-in.-long leaves with three to five
tiny leaflets. Small, scentless yellow
flowers borne profusely in spring.
Good choice in rock garden or as
container plant.

J. polyanthum. Evergreen
vine. Zones 5–9, 12–24; H1. From
China. Fast-climbing, strong-
growing vine to 20 ft. Bright to
dark green leaves are slightly
paler on undersides, have five to
seven leaflets with the terminal
leaflet slightly longer than the
rest. Highly fragrant blossoms are
white inside, rose colored outside,
borne in dense clusters. Blooms in
late winter and spring; sporadic
flowers rest of year. Can be used
as ground cover; sometimes grown
in large containers or hanging baskets. 'Variegatum' has leaves with
pale yellow margins.

J. primulinum. See J. mesnyi
J. sambac. ARABIAN
JASMINE, PIKAKE. Evergreen
vining shrub. Zones 13–21, 23,
24; H1, H2. Thought to be native
to tropical Asia. To 6–10 ft.
Undivided glossy green leaves
to 3 in. long. Blooms in summer,
bearing clusters of powerfully
fragrant, ¾–1-in. white flowers.

'Grand Duke' has double flowers.
In Hawaii, blossoms of this species
are a favorite for leis and are used
in making perfume. In Asia, they're
used in jasmine tea.

J. × stephanense. Evergreen or
deciduous vine. Zones 5–9, 14–24.
To 15–20 ft., with dull green
foliage that persists year-round in
Southern California. Leaves may
be undivided and about 2 in. long
or divided into five 2-in.-long
leaflets. Pale pink, ½-in., fragrant
flowers in clusters of five or more
appear in late spring and summer.

JERUSALEM ARTICHOKE.
See **HELIANTHUS tuberosus**

JERUSALEM CHERRY.
See **SOLANUM pseudocapsicum**

JERUSALEM SAGE.
See **PHLOMIS fruticosa**

JERUSALEM THORN.
See **PARKINSONIA aculeata**

JEWEL MINT OF CORSICA.
See **MENTHA requienii**

JICAMA
Fabaceae (Leguminosae)
ANNUAL VINE

🌱	BEST IN ZONES H1, H2; MAINLY ORNAMENTAL IN ZONES 8, 9, 12–14, 18–24
☀️	FULL SUN
💧	AMPLE WATER
◆	SEEDS ARE POISONOUS IF INGESTED

The edible part of this tropical
American plant is actually an
enlarged taproot; it develops
underground like a beet and tastes
something like a sweet water
chestnut. Very attractive vine,
twining to 14 ft. high or more; has
luxuriant deep green foliage and
upright spikes of pretty, sweet
pea–shaped purple or violet
flowers in summer. Leaves have
three leaflets.

Jicama

Cultivate jicama for edible root
in Hawaii and as an ornamental
elsewhere. Plants produce poor-
quality roots in Southern California, and you'll usually get only
foliage and flowers in Northern
California. Grow on trellis or on
the ground as a trailing mound.
Plant in spring, after danger of
frost is past. Sow seeds 2 in. deep
and 4 in. apart; thin seedlings to
8–12 in. apart. Needs long, warm
growing season and rich soil.
Apply high-nitrogen fertilizer
monthly. Flowers should be
pinched off for maximum root
production (each vine yields one
edible root weighing from 1 to
6 lbs.), but you can allow seed for
next year's crop to form on one
or two plants. Roots enlarge in fall
as days begin to grow shorter, but
weather must stay warm to produce a good crop; harvest them
before first frost in regions where
frosts are likely (if you're fortunate
enough to get a crop). In frost-free
areas, you can leave them in the
ground until they're needed. Peel
off the rough brown skin and eat
the white flesh raw or cooked.

JOB'S TEARS.
See **COIX lacryma-jobi**

JOE PYE WEED.
See **EUPATORIUM purpureum**

JOHNNY-JUMP-UP.
See **VIOLA tricolor**

JOINT FIR. See **EPHEDRA**

JOJOBA.
See **SIMMONDSIA chinensis**

JONQUIL.
See **NARCISSUS jonquilla**

JOSEPH'S COAT.
See **AMARANTHUS tricolor**

JOSHUA TREE.
See **YUCCA brevifolia**

JOYWEED.
See **ALTERNANTHERA tenella**

JUBAEA chilensis
CHILEAN WINE PALM
Arecaceae (Palmae)
PALM

🌱	ZONES 12–24
☀️	FULL SUN
◐	LITTLE OR NO WATER

From Chile. Slow-growing single-
stemmed palm to 50–60 ft. tall,
25 ft. wide. Massive trunk may
grow to 3 ft. thick; patterned with

Jubaea chilensis

scars of leaf bases. Feather-type
leaves; insignificant flowers. Hardy
for a palm (to 20°F/–7°C).

JUDAS TREE.
See **CERCIS siliquastrum**

JUGLANS
WALNUT
Juglandaceae
DECIDUOUS TREES

🌱	ZONES VARY BY SPECIES
☀️	FULL SUN
◐ ◐◐	WATER NEEDS VARY BY SPECIES

Usually large and spreading; leaves
are divided into many leaflets and
have a featherlike appearance.
Bear oval or round nuts enclosed
in a fleshy husk. English walnut is
a well-known orchard tree (see
Walnut). American native species
are sometimes planted as shade
trees (with a bonus of edible nuts)
or used as an understock for grafting English walnut. Nuts of these
species typically contain little
meat, and the shells are very thick
and hard to crack.

J. californica. CALIFORNIA
BLACK WALNUT. Known chiefly
through the following two geographic variants. Both produce
roundish nuts with rich flavor;
they are resistant to oak root fungus and require no irrigation.

J. c. californica. Zones 18–24.
Native to Southern California.
Grows 15–30 ft. high and wide,
usually with several stems from
ground level. Leaves are 6–12 in.
long, with 9–19 leaflets (each
2½ in. long). Tree is not grown
commercially but is worth saving
if it grows as a native.

J. c. hindsii. Zones 5–9, 14–20.
Native to scattered localities in
Northern California. To 30–60 ft.
high and wide, with a single
trunk. Leaves have 15–19 leaflets,

J

each 3–5 in. long. Widely used as a rootstock for English walnut in California.

J. cinerea. BUTTERNUT. Zones 1–9, 14–17. Native to eastern North America. To 50–60 ft. tall and 40–50 ft. wide. Butternut resembles black walnut (*J. nigra*), but tree is smaller, leaves have fewer leaflets, and the flavorful nuts are elongated or oval instead of round. Regular water.

J. major (J. rupestris major). NOGAL, ARIZONA WALNUT. Zones 10–13. Native to Arizona, New Mexico, northern Mexico. Broad-headed tree to 50 ft. tall and wide. Leaves have 9–13 leaflets. Small, round nuts are enclosed in husks that dry on the tree; nuts drop still in the husk. Rich flavor like that of *J. nigra*. Takes desert heat and wind. Needs deep soil, moderate water.

Juglans nigra

J. nigra. BLACK WALNUT. Zones 1–9, 14–21. Native to eastern North America. High-branched tree to about 100 ft. tall, 70 ft. wide, with round crown and furrowed blackish brown bark. Leaves have 11–23 leaflets, each 2½–5 in. long. Round, 1½-in.-diameter nuts have rich flavor. Big, hardy shade tree for large sites. Don't plant near flower or vegetable gardens, rhododendrons, or azaleas; black walnut curbs these plants either by secreting a

growth-inhibiting substance or by root competition. Long dormant season. Moderate water.

J. regia. See Walnut

JUJUBE

Rhamnaceae
DECIDUOUS TREE

🌿	ZONES 6–16, 18–24; H1
☀ ◐	BEST IN SUN; TOLERATES SOME SHADE
◌ ◖	MODERATE TO REGULAR WATER

Native to temperate regions of Asia and known botanically as *Ziziphus jujuba*. Slow to moderate growth to 15–20 ft. tall (possibly 30 ft.) and 10–15 ft. wide. Spiny, gnarled, somewhat pendulous branches. Glossy bright green, 1–2-in.- long leaves with three prominent veins; good yellow fall color. Clusters of small yellowish flowers in late spring or summer. Round to oval fruit with a central pit matures in fall; it can be eaten fresh from the tree or dried. Harvest fruit for fresh eating when it begins to turn from yellow green to reddish brown; it has a crisp texture and tastes like a sweet apple. If allowed to turn completely brown and become mushy, fruit is better for drying. The dried fruits look and taste like dates—for that reason, the plant is sometimes called Chinese date. Fruit may not ripen fully on tree in cool-summer areas; pick at half-brown stage and ripen indoors. Fruit of seedling trees is ½–1 in. long. The two most common cultivated varieties are 'Lang', with 1½–2-in., elongated fruit, and 'Li', bearing 2-in., round fruit with a very small pit. 'Lang' needs 'Li' as pollenizer; 'Li' is more productive

Jujube

with 'Lang' planted nearby, though it will produce some fruit if planted alone.

Jujube is deep rooted and takes well to desert conditions. The tree is very cold hardy but not productive in short-summer areas. Tolerates drought. Takes saline and alkaline soils but grows better in good garden soil and thrives in lawns if there is adequate drainage (though suckering from roots can be a problem, particularly in moist soil). Has no serious pests but is subject to Texas root rot in deserts. Prune in winter to shape, encourage weeping habit, or reduce size. Attractive silhouette, foliage, fruit, and toughness make it a good decorative tree, especially for high desert.

JUNCUS

RUSH
Juncaceae
PERENNIALS

🌿	ZONES VARY BY SPECIES
☀ ◐	FULL SUN OR LIGHT SHADE
◖	AMPLE WATER

Rushes somewhat resemble grasses, with leaflike, cylindrical stems and tiny, inconspicuous flowers clustered near stem tips. Specialists usually suggest planting them with grasses or aquatic plants at the edge of a pond or stream, in shallow water, or among stones and pebbles. These rushes die back in winter in colder zones; in warmer areas, plants that have grown shabby may be cut to the ground in late winter for fresh spring growth.

Juncus effusus
'Spiralis'

J. effusus. SOFT RUSH. Zones 1–24; H1. Native to many temperate regions of the world. To 2½ ft. high and wide. Medium green stems are ⅛–¼ in. thick; erect at first, they arch somewhat toward tips. Stems turn brown with frost. 'Carman's Japanese' grows 1½–2 ft. tall, with an overall finer texture.

'Spiralis' has stems that coil in spirals.

J. patens. CALIFORNIA GRAY RUSH. Zones 4–9, 14–24. Native to California and Oregon. To 2 ft. high and wide, with stiffly upright green or gray-green stems. Tolerates more heat and drought than *J. effusus* but thrives best in moist soil or even shallow water. 'Carman's Gray' and 'Elk Blue' are good gray-stemmed selections.

J. polyanthemos. AUSTRALIAN SILVER RUSH. Zones 14–24; H1, H2. Native to mainly coastal areas of Australia. Grows to 4 ft. tall, 3 ft. wide. Erect gray-green stems are easily moved about by breezes, lending motion to the garden.

JUNEBERRY.
See **AMELANCHIER**

JUNGLE FLAME.
See **IXORA coccinea**

JUNIPER MYRTLE.
See **AGONIS juniperina**

JUNIPERUS

JUNIPER
Cupressaceae
EVERGREEN SHRUBS AND TREES

🌿	ZONES VARY BY SPECIES
☀ ◐	FULL SUN OR PARTIAL SHADE; SEE CARE BOX, PAGE 423
◌ ◖ ◖	LITTLE OR NO WATER TO REGULAR WATER; SEE CARE BOX, PAGE 423
▶	SEE CHART FACING PAGE

Ranging from low ground covers to large trees, these widely grown plants are conifers, though they produce fleshy, berrylike fruits instead of woody cones. Foliage may consist of small, prickly needles (juvenile foliage) or tiny overlapping scales (mature foliage); or the same plant may show both types. Leaf colors include green shades as well as silvery blue, gray, and creamy yellow.

In the accompanying chart, junipers are grouped by form: ground covers, shrubs, columnar types, and trees. Look for the general size and shape that will serve your purpose in the landscape, so that you won't later be forced to lop off branches to make the juniper fit the spot. Be aware, however, that many of the shrub junipers can eventually grow to the size of small trees.

The ground cover group includes plants from a few inches to a few feet high; the lower sorts are particularly useful in rock

JUNIPERUS

NAME	ZONES	HEIGHT	WIDTH	COMMENTS
GROUND COVERS				
Juniperus chinensis 'Parsonsii'	1–24	To 1½ ft.	8 ft. or more	Slow growing. Dense, short twigs on flat, rather heavy branches. Blue-green new leaves mature to dark green
J. c. 'San Jose'	1–24	To 2 ft.	6 ft. or more	Slow growing and heavy trunked. Dark sage green, with both needle and scale foliage
J. c. sargentii SARGENT JUNIPER, SHIMPAKU	A2, A3; 1–24	To 2½ ft.	6–10 ft.	Feathery gray-green or green foliage. Classic bonsai plant
J. c. s. 'Glauca'	1–24	1½–2 ft.	6–10 ft.	Blue-green version of *J. c. sargentii*
J. c. s. 'Saybrook Gold'	1–24	2–3 ft.	To 6 ft.	Like *J. c. sargentii* but with rich yellow foliage
J. c. s. 'Viridis'	1–24	1½–2 ft.	6–10 ft.	Bright green version of *J. c. sargentii*
J. communis 'Alpine Carpet'	A2–A3; 1–24	8 in.	3–4 ft.	Slow growing. Deep blue-green, soft-looking foliage
J. c. communis (J. c. saxatilis)	1–24	To 1 ft.	6–8 ft.	Prostrate and trailing, with upturned branches like tiny candles. Color varies from gray to gray green
J. c. 'Effusa'	A1–A3; 1–24	To 1 ft.	6–10 ft.	Sparsely foliaged, showing off reddish brown stems
J. horizontalis 'Bar Harbor' BAR HARBOR JUNIPER	A1–A3; 1–24	To 1 ft.	8–10 ft.	Fast growing. Feathery blue-gray foliage turns plum color in winter. As plant ages, foliage dies back in center to expose limbs, especially in hot climates
J. h. 'Blue Chip'	A1–A3; 1–24	To 1 ft.	6–8 ft.	Silvery blue foliage
J. h. 'Blue Rug' (see **J. h. 'Wiltonii'**)				
J. h. 'Douglasii' WAUKEGAN JUNIPER	A1–A3; 1–24	To 1 ft.	To 10 ft.	Steel blue foliage turns purplish in fall. Rich green new growth
J. h. 'Glomerata'	1–24	To 6 in.	To 10 ft.	Deep green, turning plum color in winter. Scale foliage gives it a soft look
J. h. 'Hughes'	A1–A3; 1–24	To 1 ft.	6–8 ft.	Showy silvery blue foliage
J. h. 'Huntington Blue'	1–24	9–12 in.	6–7 ft.	Dense foliage in bright blue gray
J. h. 'Icee Blue'	1–24	4 in.	8 ft.	Maintains dense crown of silvery blue foliage
J. h. 'Mother Lode'	1–24	To 4 in.	8–10 ft.	Similar to *J. h.* 'Wiltonii' but with yellow foliage that turns bronze in winter
J. h. 'Plumosa' ANDORRA JUNIPER	1–24	To 1½ ft.	To 10 ft.	Feathery foliage is gray green in summer, turns plum color in winter. Flat branches with upright branchlets
J. h. 'Prince of Wales'	A1–A3; 1–24	To 8 in.	8–10 ft.	Medium green foliage turns purplish in fall
J. h. 'Wiltonii' ('Blue Rug') BLUE CARPET JUNIPER	A1–A3; 1–24	4–6 in.	6–8 ft.	Very flat juniper. Dense, short branchlets on long, trailing branches. Foliage is an intense silver blue. Similar to *J. h.* 'Bar Harbor' but denser; it rarely exposes limbs with age
J. h. 'Youngstown'	1–24	To 1 ft.	To 6 ft.	Resembles *J. h.* 'Plumosa' but is flatter, more compact
J. h. 'Yukon Belle'	A1–A3; 1–24	To 6 in.	6–8 ft.	Silvery blue foliage

J

JUNIPERUS

NAME	ZONES	HEIGHT	WIDTH	COMMENTS
J. procumbens JAPANESE GARDEN JUNIPER	1–24	1–2½ ft.	To 12 ft.	Feathery yet substantial blue-green foliage on strong, spreading branches
J. p. 'Green Mound'	1–24	To 8 in.	To 6 ft.	Mounding habit; will trail over walls. Light green foliage
J. p. 'Nana'	1–24	To 1 ft.	To 6 ft.	Curved branches radiating in all directions. Shorter needles and slower growth than *J. procumbens*. Can be staked into upright, picturesque shrub. Give it some protection from sun in hot climates
J. rigida conferta SHORE JUNIPER	3–9, 14–24; H1, H2	To 1 ft.	6–8 ft.	Native to Japan. Prostrate and trailing, with soft bluish green needles. Excellent for seashore but will stand warmer climates if given moist, well-drained soil
J. r. c. 'Blue Pacific'	3–9, 14–24	To 1ft.	6–8 ft.	Denser, bluer, more heat tolerant than *J. r. conferta*
J. r. c. 'Emerald Sea'	3–9, 14–24	To 1 ft.	6–8 ft.	Bright green-leafed form of *J. r. conferta*
J. sabina 'Arcadia'	1–24	To 1 ft.	6–8 ft.	Lacy bright green foliage
J. s. 'Blue Danube'	1–24	To 1½ ft.	To 5 ft.	Blue-green foliage
J. s. 'Broadmoor'	A2, A3; 1–24	2–3 ft.	To 10 ft.	Dense, mounding habit. Soft bright green leaves
J. s. 'Buffalo'	A2, A3; 1–24	8–12 in.	To 8 ft.	Soft, feathery bright green foliage
J. s. 'Calgary Carpet'	A2, A3; 1–24	6–9 in.	10 ft.	Soft green foliage
J. s. 'Moor-Dense'	1–24	To 1 ft.	To 8 ft.	Resembles *J. s.* 'Broadmoor' but is denser. Has layered look
J. s. 'Scandia'	A2, A3; 1–24	To 1 ft.	6–8 ft.	Dense bright green foliage
J. s. 'Tamariscifolia' **(J. tamariscifolia)** TAMARIX JUNIPER, TAM	A2, A3; 1–24	1½–2½ ft.	10 ft. or more	Symmetrically spreading, with dense blue-green foliage. Widely used, probably overused. More pest problems than other junipers. *J. s.* 'Tamariscifolia New Blue' foliage is bluer
J. scopulorum 'Blue Creeper'	A2, A3; 1–24	To 2 ft.	6–8 ft.	Spreading, mounding habit. Bright blue-green foliage
SHRUBS				
J. chinensis 'Aurea' **('Gold Coast')**	1–24	To 4 ft.	To 4 ft.	Compact shrub with rich golden yellow foliage. More upright than *J. × pfitzeriana*; more arching than *J. × p.* 'Armstrongii'
J. c. 'Blaauw' BLAAUW'S JUNIPER, BLUE SHIMPAKU	1–24	To 4 ft.	To 3 ft.	Vase shaped, dense, compact. Blue foliage

Juniperus chinensis 'Parsonsii'

Juniperus chinensis 'San Jose'

Juniperus horizontalis 'Blue Chip'

Juniperus rigida conferta 'Blue Pacific'

Juniperus sabina 'Buffalo'

JUNIPERUS

NAME	ZONES	HEIGHT	WIDTH	COMMENTS
J. c. 'Kaizuka' ('Torulosa') HOLLYWOOD JUNIPER	1–24; H1, H2	To 15 ft.	To 10 ft.	Irregular and upright, with twisted appearance. Rich green foliage
J. c. 'Kaizuka Variegata' VARIEGATED HOLLYWOOD JUNIPER	1–24; H1, H2	8–10 ft.	To 6 ft.	Irregular cone, though growth is more regular than that of J. c. 'Kaizuka'. Green foliage variegated with creamy white
J. c. 'Maneyi'	1–24	To 10 ft.	To 10 ft.	Semierect, with steeply angled, spreading branches. Blue-gray foliage
J. c. 'Mint Julep'	1–24	4–6 ft.	6–8 ft.	Vase shaped, with arching branches. Mint green foliage
J. c. 'Sea Green'	1–24	4–5 ft.	4–5 ft.	Compact dark green selection with fountainlike, arching branches
J. c. 'Torulosa' (see J. c. 'Kaizuka')				
J. × pfitzeriana PFITZER JUNIPER	A2, A3; 1–24; H1, H2	5–6 ft.	10–12 ft.	Arching, with sharp-needled, feathery gray-green foliage
J. × p. 'Armstrongii' ARMSTRONG JUNIPER	1–24	4–5 ft.	4–5 ft.	Upright, with medium green foliage. More compact than J. × pfitzeriana
J. × p. 'Aurea' GOLDEN PFITZER JUNIPER	1–24; H1, H2	4–5 ft.	8–10 ft.	Blue-gray foliage; current season's growth is golden yellow. J. × p. 'Old Gold' is similar or identical
J. × p. 'Compacta' NICK'S COMPACT PFITZER JUNIPER	A2, A3; 1–24; H1, H2	To 2 ft.	4–6 ft.	Compact, densely branched gray-green variety
J. × p. 'Daub's Frosted'	1–24	2–3 ft.	6 ft.	Yellow new growth matures to blue green. Mounding habit
J. × p. 'Glauca'	1–24; H1, H2	5–6 ft.	6–8 ft.	Arching branches; silvery blue foliage
J. sabina SAVIN JUNIPER	A2, A3; 1–24	4–6 ft.	5–10 ft.	Creeping or shrubby dark green plant. Exceedingly tough
J. scopulorum 'Table Top Blue'	1–24	To 5 ft.	7–12 ft.	Flat-topped gray plant
J. squamata 'Blue Star'	1–24	2–3 ft.	3–4 ft.	Uniform branching; silver blue foliage
J. s. 'Holger'	1–24	To 6 ft.	To 6 ft.	Dense, broad, flat topped. Yellow-tipped new growth
J. s. 'Meyeri' MEYER OR FISHBACK JUNIPER	A3; 1–24	6–8 ft.	2–3 ft.	Upright, with stiff, oddly angled branches. Broad needles in blend of colors: green, gray, and reddish
J. virginiana 'Hetzii' HETZ BLUE JUNIPER	1–24	To 15 ft.	To 15 ft.	Inverted pyramid, with branches spreading outward and upward at 45° angle. Blue-gray foliage

J

Juniperus ×
pfitzeriana

Juniperus squamata
'Blue Star'

Juniperus virginiana
'Hetzii'

Juniperus chinensis
'Robusta Green'

Juniperus occidentalis

JUNIPERUS

NAME	ZONES	HEIGHT	WIDTH	COMMENTS
COLUMNAR TYPES				
J. chinensis 'Blue Point'	1–24	To 12 ft.	To 8 ft.	Densely branched blue-green cone
J. c. 'Columnaris' CHINESE BLUE COLUMN JUNIPER	1–24	12–15 ft.	To 6 ft.	Narrow blue-green cone
J. c. 'Hetz's Columnaris'	1–24	To 15 ft.	To 5 ft.	Dense rich green column. Largely mature (scalelike) leaves; little juvenile foliage. Threadlike branchlets
J. c. 'Robusta Green'	1–24	12–16 ft.	3–5 ft.	Brilliant green, dense column
J. c. 'Spartan'	1–24	To 15 ft.	3–5 ft.	Dense rich green column
J. communis 'Compressa'	A1–A3; 1–24	To 2 ft.	To 6 in.	Dwarf column; for rock gardens
J. c. 'Stricta' (J. c. hibernica) IRISH JUNIPER	A1–A3; 1–24	12–20 ft.	3–4 ft.	Very narrow dark green pillar with closely compact branch tips
J. scopulorum 'Cologreen'	1–24	To 15 ft.	5–7 ft.	Narrow bright green column
J. s. 'Gray Gleam'	1–24	To 15 ft.	5–7 ft.	Slow growing, attaining full height in 30–40 years. Symmetrical blue-gray column
J. s. 'Green Ice'	1–24	To 15 ft.	7–10 ft.	Dense habit makes it a good windbreak. Gray-green foliage is paler when new
J. s. 'Medora'	1–24	To 10 ft.	To 2½ ft.	Slow growing, narrow, dense, bluish green
J. s. 'Moonglow'	1–24	9 ft.	4–5 ft.	Broadly pyramidal, dense growth
J. s. 'Pathfinder'	1–24	To 25 ft.	To 12 ft.	Gray-blue cone
J. s. 'Skyrocket'	A2, A3; 1–24	15–20 ft.	2–3 ft.	Very narrow blue-gray spire. Sometimes sold as *J. virginiana* 'Skyrocket'
J. s. 'Wichita Blue'	A2, A3; 1–24	10–15 ft.	4–6 ft.	Broad silver blue cone
J. virginiana 'Blue Arrow'	A2, A3; 1–24	15 ft.	2 ft.	Blue-green foliage, pencil-like form
J. v. 'Cupressifolia' HILLSPIRE JUNIPER	A3; 1–24	10–15 ft.	6–8 ft.	Compact dark green cone
J. v. 'Idyllwild'	A2, A3; 1–24	15 ft.	5 ft.	Dark green foliage, upright form. Good for hedges
J. v. 'Prairie Pillar'	A2, A3; 1–24	15–20 ft.	2–3 ft.	Blue-green foliage, columnar form. Short branches hold up under heavy snow
TREES				
J. californica CALIFORNIA JUNIPER	3, 6–12, 14–24	10–40 ft.	10–40 ft.	Native to desert regions of California and Southwest. Yellowish to rich green foliage
J. deppeana pachyphlaea ALLIGATOR JUNIPER	1–3, 10–12	10–60 ft.	10–60 ft.	Native to Southwest and Mexico. Blue-gray foliage; striking checked bark (like alligator hide)
J. monosperma (J. erythrocarpa)	1–3, 10–11	10–40 ft.	10–40 ft.	Native to southwestern U.S. Similar to *J. osteosperma;* bluish green foliage

JUNIPERUS

NAME	ZONES	HEIGHT	WIDTH	COMMENTS
J. occidentalis WESTERN JUNIPER	1–10, 14, 18–21	50–60 ft.	30–50 ft.	Massive, long-lived native of Sierra Nevada and intermountain regions from central Washington to Southern California. Fragrant green foliage
J. osteosperma UTAH JUNIPER	1–3, 10, 11	10–30 ft.	10–30 ft.	Native to arid West, mainly Great Basin Mountains. Adapted to high desert landscapes. Yellowish green foliage
J. recurva (J. recurva coxii)	4–6, 15–17	20–50 ft.	12–25 ft.	Native to Himalayas. Erect, with strongly weeping branches. Less hardy than other junipers
J. scopulorum 'Tolleson's Blue Weeping' ('Repandens')	1–24	To 20 ft.	To 10 ft.	Drooping branchlets clothed in blue-green foliage make a graceful, weeping tree
J. s. 'Tolleson's Green Weeping'	1–24	To 20 ft.	To 10 ft.	Like J. s. 'Tolleson's Blue Weeping' but with dark green foliage
J. virginiana EASTERN RED CEDAR	A3; 1–24	40–50 ft. or more	15–30 ft.	Native to eastern North America. Conical dark green tree; turns reddish in cold weather

J

Juniperus chinensis
'Kaizuka'

gardens. In the first few years after planting, a mulch will help keep soil cool and suppress weeds as the junipers fill in.

Shrub types range from low to quite tall. Shapes include mounding, gracefully spreading, irregularly twisted, and spirelike. In the chart, the latter type of shrubs—the columnar sort—is listed separately, since these narrow, upright plants perform a distinct function in the landscape. They're excellent accents and perfect for tight spots where you want some height, offering you a wider vari-

What Junipers Need

EXPOSURE In cool-summer areas, junipers grow best in full sun (but do tolerate light shade). In warmer climates, they prefer partial shade.

SOIL They will grow in virtually any soil—light to heavy, acid to alkaline—as long as drainage is good.

WATERING In cool-summer areas, junipers may get by with no supplemental irrigation if they're growing in loam or clay soils; in lighter soils, give them little to moderate water. Where summers are warm to hot, plants in lighter soils should have moderate to regular water, while those in heavier soils will do well on little to moderate water. Wherever drainage is slow, be careful to avoid overwatering—when junipers fail, the cause is usually too much moisture.

PRUNING Very little trimming is needed if you choose a plant of the right size and shape to fill the allotted space.

Juniper

ety of choices than other plants do. Tree junipers (grown more rarely than shrubs) are valued for picturesque habit. Their height and form vary greatly, depending on growing conditions; plants are lower and shrubbier in poor soil and arid climates, much larger if given good soil and more moisture. Many of the larger junipers serve well as screens or windbreaks in cold-winter areas.

Though junipers are extremely tolerant of various soil types, you can expect root rot if the soil is waterlogged (plants will turn yellow and collapse). Avoid planting junipers so close to sprinklers that their roots stay wet. Deer don't usually browse junipers, but the plants are subject to a number of pests and diseases. Pests to watch for include spider mites (symptoms are gray or yellow, dry-looking plants with fine webbing on twigs); aphids (look for sticky deposits, falling needles, sooty mold); twig borers (browning and dying branch tips). Juniper blight causes twigs and branches to die back; control with copper sprays in summer. To confirm a problem or decide on control measures, consult your Cooperative Extension Office or local garden center.

JUPITER'S BEARD.
See **CENTRANTHUS ruber**

JUSTICIA
Acanthaceae
EVERGREEN, SEMIEVERGREEN, AND DECIDUOUS SHRUBS

🖊 ZONES VARY BY SPECIES
☀ ◐ ● EXPOSURE NEEDS VARY BY SPECIES
○ ◐ ● ◗ WATER NEEDS VARY BY SPECIES

Group of plants grown chiefly for their tubular, tightly clustered flowers—or, in the case of *J. brandegeeana*, for showy spikes of bracts. Blossoms of all species attract hummingbirds. Leaves are paired, opposite each other on the stems.

J. brandegeeana (Beloperone guttata). SHRIMP PLANT. Evergreen. Zones 12, 13, 15–17, 21–24; H1, H2; elsewhere as annual or indoor/outdoor plant. Native to Mexico. To 3–4 ft. high and wide. Apple green, oval to elliptic leaves to 2½ in. long. Tubular white flowers spotted with purple are enclosed in overlapping coppery bronze bracts to form compact, drooping, jointed-looking spikes

Justicia brandegeeana

3 in. long (eventually lengthening to 6–7 in.). Spike formation somewhat resembles a large shrimp. Blooms produced mainly from spring to fall, sporadically rest of year. 'Chartreuse' has chartreuse yellow bracts that sunburn more easily than the coppery kind.

Good in pots or tubs and for close-up planting near terraces, patios, entryways. To shape, pinch young plants continuously until compact mound of foliage is obtained, then let bloom. To encourage bushiness, cut back stems when bracts turn black. Leaves often drop in cold weather or if soil is too wet or dry. Give moderate water. Takes full sun, but bracts and foliage fade unless plant is grown in partial shade. Give at least half-day shade in hottest climates.

J. californica. CHUPAROSA, CALIFORNIA BELOPERONE. Semievergreen or deciduous. Zones 10–14, 18–24. Native from edges of southeastern California's Colorado Desert to Arizona and northern Mexico. To 6 ft. high and wide, with arching, grayish branches and sparse, ¼-in., roundish light green leaves. Clusters of tubular, bright red, 1½-in.-long flowers give a good show from fall through spring. ('Yellow' has yellow blossoms.) Often freezes to ground in winter but comes back quickly in spring. Full sun or light shade. Little to moderate water. Summer-deciduous but will maintain much of its foliage if irrigated during long dry periods.

J. candicans (J. ovata, Jacobinia ovata). Evergreen. Zones 12, 13, 21–24. Native to southern Arizona, Mexico. Erect growth to 3 ft. high and wide, with gray branchlets and dark green, heart-shaped leaves to 3 in. long. Clusters of 1-in., tubular, vivid red flowers from fall to early summer, with intermittent bloom later in summer. Full sun or light shade. Regular water.

J. carnea (Jacobinia carnea). BRAZILIAN PLUME FLOWER. Evergreen. Zones 8, 9, 13–24, H1, H2; elsewhere as annual or indoor/outdoor plant. From South America. Soft-wooded, erect shrub to 4–6 ft. high, 2½–3 ft. wide. Medium green, prominently veined leaves to 10 in. long. Dense clusters of pink to crimson, tubular flowers from midsummer to fall. 'Huntington Form' is a more compact plant (3–4 ft. high) with deeper pink flowers and leaves that are bronze

colored on lower surfaces. Cut back plants in early spring to encourage strong new growth. Upper portions of branches freeze at 29°F/–2°C. Give partial or full shade, rich soil, regular to ample water.

Justicia carnea

J. ghiesbreghtiana. See J. spicigera

J. spicigera. MEXICAN HONEYSUCKLE. Evergreen. Zones 12–24. From Mexico and Central America. To 3 ft. tall, 4 ft. wide, with light green, smooth or velvety leaves. Few-flowered clusters of 1½-in. orange or orange-red flowers appear nearly year-round, peaking in spring and fall. Full sun or partial shade. Little to regular water. Often sold as *J. ghiesbreghtiana* or, in Arizona, as *Anisacanthus thurberi*.

J. suberecta. See Dicliptera suberecta

K

KAHILI GINGER.
See **HEDYCHIUM gardnerianum**

KALANCHOE
Crassulaceae
SUCCULENT PERENNIALS

🖊	ZONES VARY BY SPECIES; OR INDOORS
☀ ◐	FULL SUN OR PARTIAL SHADE; BRIGHT LIGHT
💧 💧	MODERATE TO REGULAR WATER

From Old World tropics. Kalanchoes have fleshy, typically green leaves and bell-shaped flowers; they are used principally as houseplants but can be grown outdoors year-round where winters are mild or warm. In Zone 13, grow in a

shady spot. In borderline climates, give protection of lath, eaves, or other overhead structure.

K. beharensis. FELT PLANT. Zones 13, 21–24; H1, H2. Stems usually unbranched, to 4–5 ft. (sometimes 10 ft.) tall. Very narrow plant—just 1–2 ft. wide. Thick, triangular to lance-shaped leaves (usually six to eight pairs) at stem tips. Leaves are 4–8 in. or longer, half as wide as long, strikingly waved and crimped at edges, covered with dense, feltlike coating of white to brown hairs. Flowers not showy. Hybrids between this and other species differ in leaf size, color, and degree of felting and scalloping. Striking in big rock garden, raised bed.

K. blossfeldiana. Zones 17, 21–24; H1, H2. To 1½ ft. high and wide. Shiny, red-edged dark green leaves to 2½ in. long, 1–1½ in. wide; may be smooth edged or slightly lobed. Small bright red flowers in big clusters held above

Kalanchoe blossfeldiana

leaves. Hybrids and named varieties come in various sizes and flower colors, including yellow, orange, and salmon. 'Pumila' and 'Tetra Vulcan' are choice dwarf (6-in.) seed-grown selections. Species and all selections bloom in winter, early spring. Popular houseplant at Christmas. Often summered outdoors and brought in before the first frost.

K. daigremontiana. MATERNITY PLANT. Zones 13, 23, 24; H2. Upright, single-stemmed plant 1½–3 ft. tall, 1 ft. wide. Gray-green leaves spotted in red, 6–8 in. long, 1¼ in. or more wide. Leaf edges are notched; young plants sprout in notches and may root on the plant. Clusters of small, drooping, grayish purple flowers in winter.

K. luciae. PADDLE PLANT. Zones 13, 17, 21–24; H1, H2. From southeastern Africa. Colorful, sculptural plant grows 1–1½ ft.

high and wide, spreading by offsets. Short, thick trunk holds fleshy, broadly oval leaves to 8 in. long and 6–8 in. wide. Leaves are gray green, with margins that turn bright red in full sun. In winter or early spring, a single stem rises 2–3 ft. high and bears clusters of ½–¾-in.-long, tubular, dark yellow flowers with a pleasing fragrance. Provide protection from slugs and snails, which can permanently disfigure leaves. Often sold as *K. thyrsiflora*.

K. manginii. Zones 23, 24; H2. Hanging basket plant. Stems spreading or trailing, to 1 ft. long. Thick, 1-in.-long leaves. Drooping, inch-long, bright red flowers in spring.

K. pinnata (Bryophyllum pinnatum). AIR PLANT. Zones 23, 24; H2. Naturalized throughout Hawaiian Islands. To 2–3 ft. tall and about as wide. First leaves to form are undivided and scallop edged; later ones are divided into three to five leaflets, these also scalloped. Produces many plantlets in indented parts of leaf edges. Indoors, leaves are sometimes removed and pinned to a curtain, where they will produce plantlets until they dry up. Greenish white to reddish flowers in clusters to 3 in. long; not particularly attractive. Likes moisture.

K. pumila. Zones 13, 17, 21–24; H1, H2; or indoors. Native to Madagascar. Mounded, trailing plant to about 1 ft. high and 2 ft. wide. Gray-green leaves, to 1½ in. long, are covered with fine white powder, giving an overall frosted look; toothed leaf edges are lightly tinged with pink. Blooms in winter, with each leafy stem producing a cluster of ½-in. pink flowers with yellow anthers. Tolerates considerable shade and drought. If growing indoors, site in a sunny window; in winter, reduce watering and provide temperatures below 60°F/16°C to promote flowering. Lovely in hanging baskets.

K. tomentosa. PANDA PLANT. Zones 13, 23, 24; H2. Branching plant eventually reaches 3 ft. high, 8 in. wide. Leaves 2 in. long, with dense, feltlike coating of white hairs. Leaf tips and shallow notches in leaves are strongly marked dark brown. Yellowish green flowers in spring.

K. uniflora. Zones 23, 24; H2. Trailing plant 6 in. high, 2 ft. wide; good in hanging pots. Thick, 1-in.-long leaves have a few scallops near rounded tips. Inch-long summer flowers; color ranges from red to purple.

KALE and COLLARDS
Brassicaceae (Cruciferae)
BIENNIAL GROWN AS ANNUAL

⚡ **ALL ZONES**

☼ ☼ **FULL SUN OR LIGHT SHADE**

💧 **REGULAR WATER**

These cool-season cabbage relatives (members of the genus *Brassica*) are grown for their leaves, which can be steamed, stir-fried, sautéed, or added to soups. Curly-leafed kales (such as 'Dwarf Blue Curled' and 'Dwarf Siberian') form compact clusters of leaves that are tightly curled. 'Toscano' is a noncurly green kale, 'Red Russian' a noncurly red kale (its leaves are actually gray green with purple veins). So-called flowering kale is similar to flowering cabbage, with brightly colored, decorative foliage; it too is edible and is sometimes sold in markets under the name "salad savoy." The type of kale known as collards is a large, smooth-leafed plant that does not form a head. Collard varieties include 'Champion', 'Georgia', and 'Vates'.

Kale

Sow seeds in place and thin to 1½–3 ft. apart; or set out transplants at the same spacing. Plant kale in late summer for a fall crop; in cool-summer areas, it can also be planted in early spring for a summer crop (intense sun in hotter climates makes leaves turn bitter). Plant collards in summer for fall and winter harvest; or plant in early spring for a spring-into-summer crop (collards are heat tolerant). Vigorous plants will grow 2–3 ft. high.

For all types of kale and collards, harvest leaves by removing them from the outside of clusters; or harvest entire plant. Light frost sweetens flavor. Both kale and collards are high in vitamins A and C, and in calcium. Plants suffer far fewer pest and disease problems than most other crops in the cabbage family.

KALMIA
Ericaceae
EVERGREEN SHRUBS

⚡ **ZONES VARY BY SPECIES**

☼ ☼ **EXPOSURE NEEDS VARY BY SPECIES**

💧 **REGULAR WATER**

⚠ **LEAVES AND FLOWER NECTAR ARE POISONOUS IF INGESTED**

Elegant flowering shrubs related to rhododendron, with somewhat similar showy flower clusters. Notable difference is that each long flower stalk bears a small bud resembling a fluted turban; the buds open to chalice-shaped blooms with ten starlike points. Plants share rhododendron's need for moist atmosphere and moist, acid, humus-rich soil.

Kalmia latifolia

K. latifolia. MOUNTAIN LAUREL, CALICO BUSH. Zones 2–7, 16, 17. Native to eastern North America. Slow growing to 6–8 ft. or taller, with equal spread. Glossy, leathery, oval leaves are 3–5 in. long, dark green on upper surface, yellowish green beneath. Blooms in late spring, bearing clusters to 5 in. across. Flowers are typically 1 in. wide, light pink or white opening from darker pink buds—but blossoms often have subtly different color in their throats and may have contrasting stamens. Hardy well below 0°F/–18°C. Partial shade. Has proved difficult to grow in the ground in Zones 16, 17; seems to do better in containers there. In Zones 2 and 3, give plants protection from winter sun and winds, which could cause dehydration.

Many named varieties are available. Those with flowers marked in contrasting colors include 'Carousel', light pink blooms with intricate pattern of white and purplish red inside; 'Freckles', white with spots and splashes of purplish red; 'Kaleidoscope', red with a white center and white rim; 'Keep-sake', burgundy red with a white edge; 'Peppermint', white with red banding from center to edge; and 'Pinwheel', red with scalloped white border. 'Bullseye' has cream-colored blossoms with white and purple-red markings in throat, white edge, and broad, purple-red band around the inside; new foliage is reddish.

Red-budded selections include 'Nathan Hale', 'Nipmuck', and 'Olympic Fire', which all have pink flowers; 'Ostbo Red', with blossoms that open pink and deepen in color with age; 'Raspberry Glow' and 'Richard Jaynes', deep pink blooms; and 'Sarah', reddish pink flowers.

'Pristine' is a white-flowered selection. Dwarf varieties (to 3 ft. in 10 years) include 'Elf', with pink buds opening to white flowers; 'Little Linda', red buds opening to pink flowers; 'Minuet', light pink buds opening to white flowers with a maroon ring inside; and 'Tiddlywinks', pink buds opening to pink flowers.

K. polifolia microphylla (K. microphylla). WESTERN LAUREL, ALPINE LAUREL. Zones A2, A3; 1–7, 16, 17. Native from Alaska to Northern California. To 1 ft. high and 8 in. wide, with spreading branches and erect branchlets. Small (to ¾-in.) leaves are dark green above, whitish beneath. Rounded clusters of ½-in., rose to purple flowers bloom in summer. Provide partial shade; where summers are cool, can also be grown in full sun.

KALMIOPSIS leachiana
Ericaceae
EVERGREEN SHRUB

⚡ **ZONES 4–6, 14–17**

☼ **PARTIAL SHADE**

💧 **REGULAR WATER**

Rhododendron relative native to mountains of southwest Oregon. Slow growing to 1 ft. tall, with 2-ft.

Kalmiopsis leachiana

spread. Many branches densely clothed with thick, dark green leaves. Blooms early spring, with clusters of profuse, ½-in., rose pink flowers. May rebloom. Same culture as rhododendron, but fussier: roots need perfect drainage, higher organic content in soil. Good rock garden plant.

KALOPANAX septemlobus (K. pictus)
CASTOR ARALIA, TREE ARALIA
Araliaceae
DECIDUOUS TREE

⚡ **ZONES 2–6, 14–17**

☼ **FULL SUN**

💧 **REGULAR WATER**

Native to eastern Asia. Unusual in being the only cold-hardy large tree in its family. Also notable for the tropical look conferred by big (7–10-in.) leaves with five to seven lobes. On young trees, leaves may exceed 1 ft. in width.

Kalopanax septemlobus

In maturity, tree is 40–60 ft. tall and equally wide, with a spiny trunk and relatively few coarse, spiny branches. With age, spines eventually disappear from trunk and larger branches. Open and gaunt in youth but eventually develops an attractive, rounded habit. Tiny white flowers appear in flattish, 1–2-ft. clusters at branch ends in summer. Tiny black fruits follow the blossoms; they are quickly consumed by birds.

KANGAROO PAW. See **ANIGOZANTHOS**

K

KANGAROO TREEBINE.
See **CISSUS antarctica**

KATSURA TREE. See
CERCIDIPHYLLUM japonicum

KECKIELLA
Scrophulariaceae
EVERGREEN OR DECIDUOUS SHRUBS

	ZONES 7–9, 12–24
☼ ☽	EXPOSURE NEEDS VARY BY SPECIES
◐ ◕ ●	LITTLE TO REGULAR WATER

These woody-stemmed Southern California natives with tubular, lipped flowers were once listed as shrubby penstemons. They are extremely drought tolerant but will drop their leaves in summer unless watered. Need excellent drainage.

K. antirrhinoides. Erect to spreading habit to 4 ft. tall, 3 ft. or wider; leaves less than 1 in. long. Abundant show of fragrant yellow flowers in late spring and summer. Full sun.

Keckiella cordifolia

K. cordifolia. Previously sold as *Penstemon cordifolius.* To about 5 ft. tall and wide, sprawling. Behaves almost like a vine when growing among taller shrubs. Dark green leaves are 1–2½ in. long. Red, 1–2-in.-long, unscented flowers from late spring into early summer; attract hummingbirds. A yellow-flowered variety is available. Full sun or partial shade.

KENILWORTH IVY.
See **CYMBALARIA muralis**

KENTIA PALM. See **HOWEA**

KENTUCKY COFFEE TREE.
See **GYMNOCLADUS dioica**

KENYA IVY.
See **SENECIO macroglossus**

KERRIA japonica
Rosaceae
DECIDUOUS SHRUB

	ZONES 2–23
☼ ☽	FULL SUN IN COOLER CLIMATES ONLY
◐ ◕	MODERATE TO REGULAR WATER

Native to China and Japan. Open, graceful, rounded shrub to 6 ft. high, with 8-ft. spread. Slender stems are yellowish green to bright green in winter, providing welcome color in cold climates. Toothed, heavily veined bright green leaves somewhat triangular, 2–4 in. long. They unfold early in spring, turn yellow in fall. Flowers

Kerria japonica
'Pleniflora'

are similar to small (1¼–2-in.), single, yellow roses and appear in spring. Plant continues to bloom off and on into early summer. 'Golden Guinea' has larger (2–2½-in.) flowers. 'Picta' has white-edged leaves. 'Pleniflora', the most commonly grown kerria, is a vigorous grower to 8–10 ft. tall and wide; it has double yellow, 1¼-in. blossoms that appear throughout the summer and sometimes into early fall. Flower color of all forms fades in strong sunlight.

Allow room for plant to display its arching form. Plants produce clumps of stems from roots; 'Pleniflora' in particular is likely to spread freely. Cut out any unwanted shoots to keep clumps more compact. Prune heavily after bloom, cutting out branches that have flowered and all dead or weak wood. The green branches are a favorite subject in Japanese wintertime flower arrangements.

KEY LIME.
See **CITRUS: Limes,** '**Mexican**'

KIELE. See **GARDENIA taitensis**

KINGFISHER DAISY.
See **FELICIA bergeriana**

KING PALM. See **ARCHONTO-PHOENIX cunninghamiana**

KING'S MANTLE.
See **THUNBERGIA erecta**

KING'S SPEAR.
See **ASPHODELINE lutea**

KINNIKINNICK.
See **ARCTOSTAPHYLOS uva-ursi**

KIRENGESHOMA palmata
YELLOW WAXBELLS
Hydrangeaceae (Saxifragaceae)
PERENNIAL

	ZONES 2–9, 14–24
☽	PARTIAL SHADE
●	REGULAR WATER

Native to Japan, Korea. A perennial of great elegance. Reaches 2–4 ft. high, 1 ft. wide, with dark purplish stems carrying deeply lobed and toothed leaves to 8 in. across. Pale yellow flowers, borne in clusters of three, appear in joints of upper leaves and at tops of stalks in late summer and early autumn. Blossoms are drooping and narrowly bell shaped, 1½ in. long. Lovely in partially shaded border or woodland garden. Needs ample organic matter in soil.

Kirengeshoma palmata

KIWI
Actinidiaceae
DECIDUOUS VINES

	ZONES VARY BY SPECIES
☼ ☽	FULL SUN OR PARTIAL SHADE
●	REGULAR WATER

From eastern Asia. Fast-growing, twining vines grown for fruit with flavor that is a combination of melon, strawberry, and banana. Fuzzy-skinned kiwifruit (the type sold in markets) has a delicious

piquancy; the other kinds are sweeter. Unless you have a self-fruitful variety, you will need to grow a male plant nearby to pollinate the female (fruit-bearing) plant. Supply sturdy supports, such as a trellis, an arbor, or a patio overhead. You can also train kiwi vines to cover walls and fences; guide and tie vines to the support as necessary. These vines prefer good, well-drained soil and regular applications of nitrogen fertilizer. Plants are sensitive to salt burn in alkaline soils. In fall, harvest fruit while it is firm and let it ripen off the tree; fruit left on the vine too long will spoil or be eaten by birds. Start harvesting when the first fruits just start to soften or when fuzzy kiwis turn from greenish brown to fully brown.

Kiwi

During dormant season, prune for form and fruit production. Cut back to one or two main trunks and remove closely parallel or crossing branches. Fruit is borne on shoots from year-old or older wood; cut out shoots that have fruited for 3 years and shorten younger shoots, leaving three to seven buds beyond previous summer's fruit. In summer, shorten overlong shoots and unwind any shoots twining around main branches. Because male pollenizer's sole purpose is flower production, you can prune it back drastically after bloom.

Fuzzy-skinned kiwi (*Actinidia deliciosa* or *A. chinensis*) grows and fruits best in Zones 4–9, 12–24 (note, however, that a vine can take up to 5 years from planting to flower or set fruit). Sometimes called Chinese gooseberry vine, it twines to 30 ft. if not curbed. Roundish, 5–8-in.-long leaves are rich dark green above, velvety white below. New growth often has rich red fuzz. Spring flowers are 1–1½ in. wide, opening cream colored and fading to buff.

Fuzzy, brown-skinned, green-fleshed fruit is the size and roughly the shape of an egg. 'Hayward' is the most common fruiting variety. 'Saanichton', a female type from Vancouver Island, Canada, is a good choice for cooler areas. Use 'Chico Male' or plants sold simply as "male" to pollinate 'Hayward' and 'Saanichton'. 'Vincent' needs little winter chill and is a good variety for warmest-winter climates; use 'Chico Male' as a pollenizer for it. Male hardy kiwi varieties can also supply pollen for female fuzzy-skinned kiwis.

Hardy kiwi (*A. arguta*) grows and produces well in Zones A1–A3; 1–10, 12, 14–24. It is much like fuzzy-skinned kiwi vine in appearance but has smaller leaves (which are smooth and fuzzless), flowers, and fruit. The 1–1½-in.-long, fuzzless fruit can be eaten skin and all. Green-fruited female varieties 'Ananasnaja', 'Jumbo', and 'Hood River' need a male variety (may be sold simply as "male") for pollen. 'Issai', also with green fruit, is a self-fruitful variety. *A. purpurea* and its hybrid 'Ken's Red' produce small red fruit with red flesh; each needs a pollenizer.

Arctic beauty kiwi (*A. kolomikta*) is best suited to Zones A2, A3; 1–9, 14–17. Male plants are ornamental vines grown for their splashy, heart-shaped foliage (see description under *A. kolomikta*). Female plants typically have somewhat less colorful leaves than males, but they produce small green fruit about the size of hardy kiwi fruit; a male vine must be growing nearby to supply pollen. Plants typically grow to 15 ft. or more. Prefers partial shade, especially in hotter climates. 'September Sun' has sweet fruit and the best foliage variegation among female varieties.

KIWI, ORNAMENTAL.
See **ACTINIDIA kolomikta**

KLEINIA. See **SENECIO**

KNAUTIA
Dipsacaceae
PERENNIALS

✿	ZONES 2–10, 14–24
☼	FULL SUN
●	REGULAR WATER

Related to pincushion flower (*Scabiosa*), with blossoms that are similar in structure—clustered in tight heads above ruffs of leafy bracts on bare stems. Basal leaves are barely lobed, but those on upper stems are deeply divided. These are meadow plants that make few demands on the gardener; they are at home in cottage gardens, wild gardens, perennial borders, roadside plantings. Cut flowers are good for fresh or dried arrangements.

K. arvensis. BLUE BUTTONS. From Europe, Caucasus, Mediterranean region. To 1–5 ft. tall, 1½ ft. wide. Blue, 1½-in. flower heads in summer.

Knautia macedonica

K. macedonica. From central Europe. To 1½–3 ft. tall and as wide. Deep purplish red flower heads bloom from early summer to fall. Reseeds manageably. 'Mars Midget', to 16 in. high, is more upright and has crimson flowers.

K. Melton Pastels. To 1½–3 ft. or taller, 1½ ft. wide. Flower heads in tones of blue, mauve, pink, rose, salmon pink, and crimson from late spring to fall.

KNIPHOFIA
RED-HOT POKER, TORCH LILY
Liliaceae
PERENNIALS

✿	ZONES VARY BY SPECIES
☼ ◐	FULL SUN OR PARTIAL SHADE
◑ ●	MODERATE TO REGULAR WATER

Dense clumps of grasslike, finely toothed foliage produce bare stems topped by nodding, tubular flowers in tight, overlapping clusters. Flowering stems look like glowing pokers or torches, hence the common names. Blossoms open from bottom to top over the course of several days, changing color as they mature. Increasing numbers of species—mostly from South Africa—are now grown in gardens and hybridized. The old 3-ft.-high forms of *K. uvaria* in shades of coral orange and yellow have given way to kinds with blooms ranging from coral red through every conceivable shade of orange, peach, and yellow to near-white and light green, on plants varying in size from 1½-ft. dwarfs to 6-ft. giants. The flowers attract hummingbirds.

Red-hot pokers require adequate moisture when blooms are forming and will fail to flower if conditions are too dry then. In summer, they'll tolerate even marshy conditions—but for winter survival, well-drained soil is essential. Most of these plants flower in summer, but some start in late spring and repeat throughout the growing season; others bloom all winter in mild climates. Where winter temperatures drop to 0°F/–18°C or below, tie foliage over clumps in fall to protect growing points (or at least leave all foliage in place over winter). In milder climates, cut or pull out any ratty-looking leaves in fall; new leaves will replace them by spring. Crowns increase slowly, forming clumps 2–3 ft. or wider at base; you will get the best show if clumps are left in place for several years. Increase plantings by division in spring except for types still blooming then; for these, wait until summer to divide. New strains are available as seed (be aware that seedlings will vary in color and quality). Protect from slugs and snails.

K. caulescens. Zones 4–9, 14–24. Blue-green leaves (purple at base) are 3–4 ft. long, 2–3 in. wide; they are produced in rosettes on short, branching, woody stems like trunks. Stalks 2 ft. tall bear heads of coral red to terra-cotta buds that open to pale yellow flowers. Blooms from midsummer into fall.

K. citrina. Zones 2–9, 14–24. Smallish species with narrow, dark bluish green leaves and globular flower heads in various yellow shades on 2–2½-ft.-tall stems. Summer to fall bloom. 'Lime Select' has bright lime green buds that open chartreuse and fade to cream.

K. hybrids. Zones 2–9, 14–24, except as noted. Although they involve several species, these hybrids generally share the narrow leaves and summer bloom season of *K. uvaria*. A distinct departure is 'Christmas Cheer', a hybrid of vigorous species *K. rooperi*.

'Alcazar'. Dark, bronzy stems to 3½ ft., with brick red flowers that age to pinkish orange.

'Bee's Sunset'. Stems to 3 ft. high, with glowing yellow-orange buds opening light yellow.

'Border Ballet'. Buds are a soft, dusty coral pink opening to cream blooms. Stems reach 4–4½ ft.

'Bressingham Comet'. Stems to 2 ft. tall; flower clusters are orange with a yellow base.

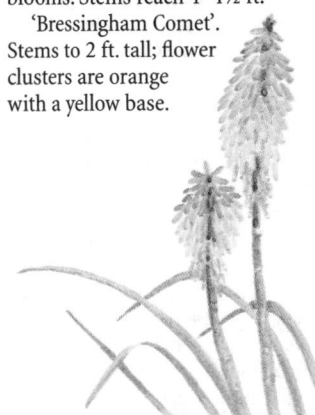

Kniphofia
'Bressingham Comet'

'Christmas Cheer'. Zones 19–24. Brilliant orange buds open to deep gold flowers on 4–5-ft. stems. Blooms fall through late spring in mild-winter areas, fall until frost elsewhere. Give it room; leaves (to 5 ft. long and 2 in. wide) become lax and collapse on the ground, smothering any plants in their way. Clump increases rapidly to 6–8 ft. or more across. Divide in early summer after flowering stops.

'Cobra'. Stems 3–4 ft. tall. Flower clusters are orange at the top, fading through peach to creamy white at the base.

'Flamenco'. Seed-grown strain that blooms first year in early fall, in subsequent years in summer. Flower colors range from coral through orange and yellow to creamy white. Stems to 2½ ft. tall.

'Gold Mine'. Glowing orange-yellow buds opening golden amber on 3–3½-ft. stems.

'Little Maid'. Thin, grassy leaves and narrow flower stems to 2 ft. tall. Creamy white blossoms open from buds in buff-tinted pale yellow.

'Malibu Yellow'. Stems 5–6 ft. tall bear 8–10-in.-long heads of lime green buds that open primrose yellow.

'Peaches and Cream'. Stems about 4 ft. high bear peach-colored buds opening to cream blossoms.

'Percy's Pride'. To 4 ft. tall, with green-tinted yellow buds opening cream.

'Primrose Beauty'. To 3 ft. tall, with blossoms in clear light yellow. ▶

K

'Shining Scepter'. Plant sold in North America under this name is 3 ft. tall, with tangerine orange flowers; the English original is 4 ft. tall, with pale yellow buds opening ivory.

'Sunningdale Yellow'. Broad blue-green leaves. Spikes to 4 ft. tall hold 9-in.-long flowers that open yellow green and change to bright yellow before fading to apricot.

'Toffee Nosed'. Stems to 2 ft., with flower spikes that are creamy white at the base and tawny orange at the top.

'Vanilla'. Stems 2–2½ ft. tall; buds are light yellow, opening cream.

K. northiae. Zones 4–9, 14–24. Very large, dramatic-looking species with solitary rosette of broad bluish green leaves (up to 6 in. wide at base, 5 ft. long) on a woody, trunklike stem 1–3 ft. tall. Does not form clumps. Thick blossom stalks rise 1–2 ft. above foliage in summer, bearing large, oblong heads of orange buds opening light yellow.

K. thomsonii. Zones 6–9, 14–24. Alpine species from East Africa. Clumps grow 3–5 ft. high and 2–4 ft. wide. Narrow blue-green leaves grow to about 3 ft. long. Individual blooms are orange, not as tightly packed onto the spike as those of other *Kniphofia* species and hybrids.

K. uvaria. Zones 2–9, 14–24. Leaves to 1 in. wide, 2 ft. long. Oblong flower heads on stems 3–3½ ft. tall. Coral red buds open to orange or deep yellow blossoms in summer (in fall, in cold-winter climates). Most varieties sold under this name are hybrids (see *K.* hybrids).

Kniphofia uvaria

KNOTWEED. See **PERSICARIA**

KOA. See **ACACIA koa**

KOCHIA scoparia (Bassia scoparia)
SUMMER CYPRESS
Chenopodiaceae
ANNUAL

⊘ ALL ZONES
☀ FULL SUN
💧 REGULAR WATER

Native to Eurasia. To 3 ft. high and 2 ft. wide. Branches are so thickly clothed in soft, narrow light green leaves that plant is too dense to see through. Grow individually for its gently rounded form; or group plants for low, temporary hedge or edging. Can be sheared into any shape. Grow from seed sown in early spring or (in mild-winter climates) in fall. Tolerates high heat, performs well in short-summer areas.

Kochia scoparia

K. s. trichophylla (Bassia scoparia trichophylla). MEXICAN FIRE BUSH, BURNING BUSH. Same as above, but foliage turns red in fall. Can reseed profusely enough to become a pest; hoe out unwanted seedlings when they're small.

KOELREUTERIA
Sapindaceae
DECIDUOUS TREES

⊘ ZONES VARY BY SPECIES
☀ FULL SUN
💧 MODERATE TO REGULAR WATER

Small trees native to eastern Asia noted for large, loose clusters of yellow flowers followed by fat, papery fruit capsules resembling little Japanese lanterns. Capsules are used in both fresh and dried arrangements. Good patio, lawn, or street trees. Very adaptable to different soils as long as drainage is fairly good. Control self-sown seedlings.

K. bipinnata (K. integrifoliola). CHINESE FLAME TREE. Zones 8–24; H1. To 20–40 ft. tall and wide, eventually flat topped. Leaves 1–2 ft. long, divided into 7–12 oval leaflets; turn yellow for short time before dropping. Late-summer flower clusters are like those of *K. paniculata*, but 2-in. capsules are more colorful, in shades of orange, red, or salmon. Capsules come quickly after flowers and persist into fall. Prune tree to develop high branching. Wood is brittle and may break under a heavy load of snow. Roots are deep but not invasive; good tree to plant under.

K. elegans (K. formosana). FLAMEGOLD. Zones 14–24; H1, H2. Round-headed tree 20–30 ft. tall and equally broad. Leaves about 1½ ft. long, with 9–16 leaflets. Bright yellow fall flowers in tall, erect clusters are followed by especially showy clusters of long-lasting, puffy orange-red to salmon fruits. Fall foliage is yellow but not consistent; show is often poor.

K. paniculata. GOLDENRAIN TREE. Zones A2; 2–24. To 20–35 ft. tall, 25–40 ft. wide. Open branching, giving slight shade. Leaves to

Koelreuteria paniculata

15 in. long with 7–15 oval, toothed or lobed leaflets, each 1–3 in. long. New leaves are purplish, maturing to bright green in summer; may turn yellow to gold in fall, but fall foliage color is unreliable. Very showy, 8–14-in.-long flower clusters in early to midsummer. Fruit capsules are red when young, maturing to buff and brown shades; last well into autumn. Tree takes cold, heat,

drought, wind. Prune to shape; can be gawky without pruning. 'Fastigiata' is 25 ft. tall, only 3 ft. wide. 'Rose Lantern' has seed pods flushed with pink. 'September' blooms about a month later than the species.

KOHLRABI
Brassicaceae (Cruciferae)
BIENNIAL GROWN AS ANNUAL

⊘ ALL ZONES
☀ FULL SUN
💧 REGULAR WATER

Cool-season cabbage relative. Leaves and leafstalks are edible, but edible part most commonly associated with kohlrabi is its enlarged, bulblike portion of the

Kohlrabi

stem formed just above the soil surface. Standard varieties are 'Early White Vienna' and 'Early Purple Vienna'—similar in size and flavor, differing only in skin color. Other white varieties include 'Triumph' and early-maturing 'Grand Duke'. 'Kolibri' is a popular purple-skinned variety. Plants are very fast growing, ready to harvest in 50 to 60 days from seed. Quality declines if harvest is delayed. Sow seed ½ in. deep in rich soil about 2 weeks after average date of last frost. Follow first planting with successive sowings 2 weeks apart. In areas with warm winters, plant again in late fall and early winter. Space rows 1½ ft. apart; thin seedlings to 4–6 in. apart. Plants are not usually bothered by pests or diseases. Harvest bulbous part when 2–3 in. wide. Peel, slice, and serve raw; or steam or sauté slices or chunks. Steam young leaves and leafstalks.

KOKERBOOM.
See **ALOE dichotoma**

KOLKWITZIA amabilis
BEAUTY BUSH
Caprifoliaceae
DECIDUOUS SHRUB

- ZONES 2–11, 14–20
- FULL SUN OR PARTIAL SHADE
- REGULAR WATER

Native to central China. Graceful, upright growth to 10–12 ft. tall and about as wide. If grown in partial shade, it has an arching form; in full sun, it's denser and shorter. Gray-green leaves to 3 in. long sometimes turn reddish in fall. Blooms heavily in mid- to late spring, bearing clusters of 1-in.-long, yellow-throated pink flowers. Blossoms are followed by conspicuous pinkish brown, bristly fruits that prolong color display. Brown, flaky bark gradually peels from stems during winter. 'Pink Cloud' is a particularly floriferous selection with light pink blooms that are slightly larger than those of the species.

Kolkwitzia amabilis

Adapts to many soils and climates. Blooms on wood formed the previous year. Thin out oldest stems after blossoms have faded; or, to enjoy the fruit, wait until early spring to prune, then do so lightly. Plant can be renewed by cutting to ground after bloom.

KOREAN GRASS.
See **ZOYSIA tenuifolia**

KOREAN ROCK FERN.
See **POLYSTICHUM tsus-simense**

KOU, KOU HAOLE. See **CORDIA subcordata, C. sebestena**

KOWHAI.
See **SOPHORA tetraptera**

KRASCHENINNIKOVIA lanata.
See **CERATOIDES lanata**

KUKUI.
See **ALEURITES moluccana**

KUMQUAT. See **CITRUS**

LABLAB purpureus.
See **DOLICHOS lablab**

LABURNUM
GOLDENCHAIN TREE
Fabaceae (Leguminosae)
DECIDUOUS TREES OR SHRUBS

- ZONES 1–10, 14–17
- AFTERNOON SHADE IN HOTTEST CLIMATES
- MODERATE TO REGULAR WATER
- ALL PARTS, ESPECIALLY SEEDPODS, ARE HIGHLY POISONOUS IF INGESTED

These upright growers are usually pruned into single-trunked trees, but can be shrubby if permitted to keep basal suckers and low branches. Green bark; bright green leaves divided into three leaflets (like clover leaves). Handsome during bloom in mid- to late spring, when yellow, sweet pea–shaped flowers appear in hanging clusters similar to those of wisteria. Use as specimen in lawn or border, plant in groups in front of neutral background, or space regularly in long border of perennials, rhododendrons, or lilacs. Flexible branches make plants easy to espalier. Both species are native to central and southern Europe.

Provide well-drained soil. Prune regularly after bloom to keep tidy; remove dead or crowding branches in tree's center (avoid large cuts, because cut areas callus over slowly). Remove seedpods if possible—not only are they toxic, but a heavy crop drains the plant's strength.

L. alpinum. SCOTCH LABURNUM. To 30–35 ft. tall, 20–25 ft. wide. Flower clusters 10–15 in. long. 'Pendulum' has weeping branches.

L. anagyroides. COMMON GOLDENCHAIN. To 20–30 ft. tall, 15–20 ft. wide. Flower clusters 6–10 in. long. Like *L. alpinum*, it has a weeping variety, 'Pendulum'.

L. × watereri. Hybrid between above two species. To 15–30 ft. tall,

Laburnum × watereri

10–20 ft. wide, with 10–20-in.-long flower clusters. 'Vossii' is the most widely grown, most graceful variety, with flower clusters near 20 in. long.

LACE FERN.
See **MICROLEPIA strigosa**

LACE VINE.
See **FALLOPIA baldschuanica**

LACHENALIA
CAPE COWSLIP
Liliaceae
PERENNIALS FROM BULBS

- ZONES 16, 17, 23, 24; OR INDOORS
- LIGHT SHADE IN HOTTEST CLIMATES; BRIGHT LIGHT
- REGULAR WATER DURING GROWTH AND BLOOM

South African natives resembling hyacinths. Each bulb usually produces just two broad, succulent, strap-shaped leaves, often spotted with brown. Spikes of pendent, typically tubular blossoms appear at tops of thick flowering stems in late winter or early spring.

Planted in the ground, cape cowslip does best in mild-winter, dry-summer regions. In other areas, grow in pots in house or greenhouse. Plant in late summer or early fall. Set bulbs in well-drained soil, 1–1½ in. deep, 3 in. apart. Water sparingly until growth starts, then give regular moisture until foliage yellows after bloom. Gradually let soil dry out and keep as dry as possible until next fall. Protect plants from slugs and snails.

After planting for indoor bloom, water thoroughly and keep in a cool, dark place until leaves appear; then bring into light, provide cool night temperatures (50°F/10°C), and feed when flower spikes show. Store bulbs dry in pots over summer.

L. aloides (L. tricolor). Stems 10–12 in. high, with yellow flowers tipped in red and green. Inch-wide leaves. 'Aurea' has bright orange-yellow blossoms; 'Nelsonii' bears bright yellow blooms tinged with green. 'Pearsonii' has yellow-orange flowers with red-orange bases; stems are slightly taller than those of species.

L. bulbifera (L. pendula). Stems to 15 in. high, with coral red and yellow flowers tipped in purple. Leaves are 2 in. wide. 'Superba' has orange-red blooms.

Lachenalia bulbifera

L. contaminata. Stems and narrow (less than ⅛-in.-wide), upright leaves both reach 9 in. high. Tight spikes of nearly spherical bells are red to brown with white tips. Reminiscent of grape hyacinth (*Muscari*).

LADY BELLS.
See **ADENOPHORA**

LADY FERN.
See **ATHYRIUM filix-femina**

LADY PALM. See **RHAPIS**

LADY'S BEDSTRAW.
See **GALIUM verum**

LADY'S-MANTLE.
See **ALCHEMILLA mollis**

LADY'S SLIPPER.
See **PAPHIOPEDILUM, PEDILANTHUS macrocarpus**

LAELIA
Orchidaceae
EPIPHYTIC ORCHIDS

- ZONES VARY BY SPECIES; OR INDOORS
- LIGHT SHADE; BRIGHT LIGHT
- REGULAR WATER

More than 60 species belong to this genus, which is closely related to and resembles *Cattleya*. Pseudobulbs may be plump (like those of cattleya), with plants bearing large flowers; or they may be slender and canelike, with plants bearing clusters of smaller flowers. All have fleshy leaves. Laelias cross freely with cattleyas. A few are hardy enough to grow outdoors along the California coast as far north as San Francisco. Outdoor plants are usually grown on tree trunks or in pots on the patio; indoor plants can be brought outdoors at warm times of year. For cultural needs, see *Cattleya.*

L. anceps. Zones 16, 17, 21–24; H1, H2. From Mexico. Plump pseudobulbs carry thick 6-in. leaves. Flower spikes range from 6 in. to 3 ft. long, carry three to six fragrant, 4-in. pinkish lilac flowers in winter. Some varieties have pink, white, purple, or lavender-blue blossoms.

Laelia anceps

L. autumnalis. Zones 16, 17, 21–24; H1, H2. From Mexico. This species is similar to *L. anceps,* but its scented flowers bloom in autumn. Rosy purple flowers have a pinkish white lip with purple and yellow markings.

L. cinnabarina. Zone H2. From Brazil. Narrow, canelike pseudobulbs to 20 in. tall bear narrow, foot-long leaves and spikes of up to 12 bright red-orange, 3–4-in. flowers in spring.

L. purpurata. Zone H2. From Brazil. Plump pseudobulbs produce 12–16-in.-long leaves. Flower spikes to 1 ft. high carry three to eight 8-in. flowers, typically white with a purple lip. Forms with pink or blue lips exist. Blooms in late spring or early summer.

LAGENARIA. See GOURD

LAGERSTROEMIA
CRAPE MYRTLE
Lythraceae
DECIDUOUS SHRUBS AND TREES

| 🖉 ZONES VARY BY SPECIES |
| ☼ FULL SUN |
| ◐ MODERATE WATER |

The crape myrtles are among the most satisfactory of plants for hot-summer regions; showy summer flowers, good-looking bark, and (in many cases) brilliant fall color make them attractive all year round. Long, cool autumns yield the best leaf display; the first hard frost ends the show. (In cool-summer regions, these plants flower less, and mildew is a more serious problem among susceptible varieties.)

Most crape myrtles seen in gardens are varieties of *L. indica* or hybrids of that species with *L. fauriei.* The latter species has attracted some attention for its hardiness and exceptionally showy bark, although it is scarcely grown in the West.

Crape myrtles bloom on new wood and should be pruned in winter or early spring. On large plants, remove basal suckers, twiggy growth, crossing branches, and branches growing toward the center of the plant. Also gradually remove side branches up to a height of 4–5 ft.; this exposes the handsome bark of the trunks. If you need to reduce a large crape myrtle's height, shorten the topmost branches by 1–3 ft. in late winter, cutting back to a side branch or bud. For branches more than 2 in. thick, cut back to the crotch or trunk. Also prune dwarf forms periodically throughout the growing season, thinning out small, twiggy growth. Snip off spent flower clusters of all types to neaten appearance and promote a second, lighter bloom. Heavy watering and any fertilizing in summer can significantly decrease hardiness in marginal climates. Where adapted, plants perform best with infrequent but deep watering.

L. fauriei. JAPANESE CRAPE MYRTLE. Tree. Zones 7–10, 12–14, 18–21. Native to Japan. To 20–30 ft. tall and as wide, with upright habit and outward-arching branches. Leaves are light green, 4 in. long, 2 in. wide, turning yellow in fall. Smooth gray bark flakes away to reveal shiny cinnamon bark beneath. White flowers are carried in 4-in. clusters. Highly mildew resistant; the parent of many resistant hybrids.

L. hybrids. Zones 7–10, 12–14, 18–21; H1, H2. Introductions of the U.S. National Arboretum, these hybrids between *L. indica* and *L. fauriei* have been selected for hardiness and mildew resistance. Grow as shrubs or train into small trees.

'Acoma'. To 10 ft. tall, 11 ft. wide, with pendulous branches. White flowers, dark red fall color.

'Arapaho'. To 20 ft. tall, 10 ft. wide. Cranberry red flowers. New growth is deep red, fades to green; red-purple fall color.

'Biloxi'. To 20 ft. tall and 12 ft. wide. Pale pink flowers, dark red fall color.

'Comanche'. To 12 ft. tall, 13 ft. wide. Deep coral pink flowers and orange-red to purple-red fall color.

'Hopi'. To 8 ft. tall and 10 ft. wide. Medium pink flowers, orange-red autumn color.

'Lipan'. Grows to 13 ft. high and as wide. Lavender flowers, orange to red fall color.

'Miami'. To 16–20 ft. tall, 8–12 ft. wide. Dark pink flowers, orange fall color.

'Muskogee'. To 25 ft. tall and 12 ft. wide. Lavender flowers, red fall color.

'Natchez'. Reaches 25 ft. tall and 12 ft. wide. White flowers, orange-red autumn color.

'Pecos'. To 8 ft. tall, 6 ft. wide. Pink flowers, maroon fall color.

'Tonto'. To 15–20 ft. tall and wide. Large clusters of red flowers; red autumn color.

'Tuscarora'. To 22 ft. tall, 12 ft. wide. Pinkish red flowers. Orange-red autumn color.

'Tuskegee'. To 15 ft. tall and 18 ft. wide. Deep pink blooms, orange-red fall color.

Lagerstroemia indica

'Yuma'. To 13 ft. tall, 12 ft. wide. Lavender flowers; fall color from yellow to russet.

'Zuni'. To 9 ft. tall, 8 ft. wide. Lavender flowers, orange-red fall color.

L. indica. CRAPE MYRTLE. Tree or shrub. Excellent performance in Zones 7–10, 12–14, 18–21; H1, H2. Mildew is a serious problem in Zones 15–17, 22–24. Hardy in Zones 4 and 5 but seldom flowers well there except in hottest summers. Thrives in Zone 6 but flowers very late. Sometimes treated as perennial in Zones 2

Lagerstroemia indica

and 3; will come back from roots if frozen to the ground.

Native to China. To 25 ft. tall and wide. Dark green leaves are 1–2½ in. long and somewhat narrower, often tinged red on opening and frequently turning brilliant orange or red in the fall. Crinkly-petaled, crepelike, 1–1½-in. flowers in dense clusters range from white through pink to red and purple. Trained as a tree, develops an attractive trunk and branch structure. Smooth gray or light brown bark peels off to reveal smooth, pinkish inner bark. Winter trunk and branches look polished.

The following list contains many of the best selections, including trees, large shrubs, and dwarfs. Mildew can be a problem; the best solution is to plant mildew-resistant hybrids (see *L. hybrids*).

'Catawba'. Roundish, dense growth to 6–10 ft. high and equally wide (can be trained as a 15-ft. tree). Dark purple flowers, orange-red fall color.

'Centennial'. Dwarf, rounded plant to 3–5 ft. tall and wide. Lavender flowers, orange fall color.

'Centennial Spirit'. Multistemmed large shrub or small tree to 20 ft. tall and as wide or nearly so. Dark red flowers, orange-red fall color.

'Chica Pink' and 'Chica Red'. Compact, dense, 3–4 ft. tall and wide. Pink or rosy red flowers; both have yellow fall color.

Dixie series. Dwarf, weeping shrubs for border, ground cover, or hanging basket. Varieties include deep red 'Beverly' ('Baton Rouge') and lavender 'Louisa' ('Cordon Bleu'), both to 3 ft. high and wide; purple-flowered 'Passion', to 3 ft. high, 5 ft. wide; and pink-blossomed 'Pink Blush' ('Delta Blush'), to 2 ft. high and 4 ft. wide.

Dwarf series. These grow 3–6 ft. tall and wide. Colors are indicated by variety names: 'Dwarf Pink', 'Dwarf Purple', 'Dwarf Red', 'Dwarf White'.

'Glendora White'. As a shrub, grows erect to 9 ft. tall and 6–7 ft. wide. With training, makes a tree to 25 ft. tall and 20 ft. wide. Bears white flowers. Red fall foliage.

'Near East' ('Shell Pink'). Rounded growth to 15–20 ft. tall and wide, with soft pink flowers. Orange-red fall color.

'Peppermint Lace'. Erect shrub 6–7 ft. tall and wide, or tree to 15–20 ft. tall and wide. Deep pink flowers with a white picotee edge. Red fall color.

Petite series. To 5 ft. tall and 4 ft. wide, with names that describe their flower color: 'Petite Embers', 'Petite Orchid', 'Petite Pinkie', 'Petite Plum', 'Petite Red Imp', 'Petite Snow'. All have yellow fall foliage.

'Pink Velour'. Vase-shaped shrub or small tree to 10 ft. tall and wide. Neon pink flowers and yellow-orange fall color.

'Seminole'. To 6–12 ft. tall and as wide. Bright pink flowers, red fall color.

'Watermelon Red'. Rounded habit to 20–25 ft. tall and as wide. Bright red flowers, yellow fall color.

'White Chocolate'. To 8–10 ft. tall and wide. Foliage emerges burgundy in spring, then matures to chocolate-tinged green. Pure white flowers. Bright orange-yellow fall color.

L. speciosa. GIANT CRAPE MYRTLE. Tree. Zones H1, H2. Native from India to Australia. To 80 ft. tall, 30 ft. wide, with leaves 8–12 in. long, 4 in. wide. White to purple flowers are borne in clusters to 16 in. long. Sometimes planted as street tree in Hawaii.

LAGUNARIA
patersonii
PRIMROSE TREE,
COW ITCH TREE
Malvaceae
EVERGREEN TREE

| 🌿 ZONES 13, 15–24; H1, H2 |
| ☀️ FULL SUN |
| 💧 MODERATE WATER |

Native to South Pacific and Australia. Rather fast growth to 20–50 ft. Young trees narrow and erect; old ones sometimes spreading to as wide as 40 ft., with flat-topped look. Densely foliaged in thick, oval, 2–4-in.-long leaves that are

Lagunaria patersonii

olive green above, gray beneath. Pink to rose, 2-in.-wide summer blossoms look similar to hibiscus flowers, fade almost to white with age. 'Royal Purple' has purple blossoms. Brown seed capsules, popular with flower arrangers, hang on for a long time; they split into five sections, revealing bright brown seeds. Handle pods carefully, since they contain short, stiff fibers that can irritate skin and eyes.

Lagunaria patersonii

Tolerates wide variety of soils and growing conditions. Resists ocean wind, salt spray; tolerates intense heat. Foliage is damaged at 25°F/–4°C but recovers quickly. Blooms best in coastal conditions. Use as specimen tree; or plant in groups as a showy windbreak or screen.

LAMB'S EARS.
See **STACHYS byzantina**

LAMB'S LETTUCE. See MACHE

LAMB'S QUARTERS.
See **CHENOPODIUM album**

LAMIASTRUM galeobdolon.
See **LAMIUM galeobdolon**

LAMIUM
DEAD NETTLE
Lamiaceae (Labiatae)
PERENNIALS SOMETIMES
GROWN AS ANNUALS

| 🌿 ZONES VARY BY SPECIES |
| ◐ ● PARTIAL OR FULL SHADE |
| 💧 REGULAR WATER |

Native from Europe to western Asia. Vigorous growers with opposite pairs of tooth-edged, typically heart-shaped leaves, often marked with silver or white. Clustered flowers come in pink, white, or yellow. Evergreen in mild-winter climates.

L. galeobdolon (Lamiastrum galeobdolon). DEAD NETTLE, YELLOW ARCHANGEL. Perennial in Zones 2–11, 14–24; winter annual in Zones 12, 13. Trailing or clump-forming plant with roundish or heart-shaped leaves to 2½ in. long. Blooms in late spring, bearing yellow flowers (not showy). One popular variety is 'Hermann's Pride', a clump former

to 2 ft. tall and wide, with 1¼-in.-long, sharply tapered leaves that are evenly and symmetrically marked with white spots and streaks. Also commonly sold is *L. g. montanum* 'Florentinum' (*L .g.* 'Variegatum'), a trailing plant with stems that root as they spread. Dull medium to dark green leaves are edged in green and marbled with silvery gray in the center. Attractive plant in hanging baskets, where it will trail to 2–3 ft., or as an informal ground cover (it can be invasive but is easily curbed).

L. maculatum. DEAD NETTLE, SPOTTED NETTLE. Perennial in Zones A2, A3; 1–11, 14–24; winter annual in Zones 12, 13. To 8 in. high; spreads by rhizomes and stolons to 3 ft. wide but

Lamium maculatum

is not a rampant grower. Leaves are 1–3 in. long, green with a central white stripe or zone. Pink or white flowers in late spring and early summer. Choice selections include the following. 'Anne Greenaway' has pink flowers and green leaves edged in yellow and striped with silver down the center. 'Beacon Silver' has pink flowers and green-edged, silvery gray leaves; similar in leaf color are 'Orchid Frost' (orchid pink flowers), 'Purple Dragon' (purple blooms), 'Red Nancy' (deep rosy pink flowers), and 'White Nancy' (white blooms). 'Chequers' has pink flowers and green leaves with a white center stripe. 'Pink Pewter' has pink blooms and silvery leaves edged in greenish gray. All bloom from spring to midsummer and make excellent ground covers for shady spots, nicely lighting up darker garden areas. They are also useful in hanging baskets. They need some grooming to remove old, shabby growth.

LAMPRANTHUS
ICE PLANT
Aizoaceae
SUCCULENT PERENNIALS

| 🌿 ZONES 14–24, EXCEPT AS NOTED |
| ☀️ FULL SUN |
| 💧 LITTLE OR NO WATER |

From South Africa. Most of the ice plants with large, brilliant flowers belong to this genus, which includes plants formerly called *Oscularia*. Plants are fleshy, erect or trailing, woody at base. Select in bloom for the color you want. Cut back lightly after bloom to eliminate fruit capsules, encourage new leafy growth. Good at seashore. Flowers attract bees.

L. aurantiacus. To 10–15 in. tall. Gray-green, inch-long, three-sided leaves. Flowers 1½–2 in. across, bright orange; midwinter to spring bloom. 'Glaucus' has bright yellow flowers; those of 'Sunman' are golden yellow. Plant 15–18 in. apart for bedding, borders, low bank cover.

L. deltoides (Oscularia deltoides). Stems to 2 ft. long; they grow erect to 1 ft., then begin to lean and trail. Triangular blue-green leaves with a pink flush are short (less than 1 in. long), very thick and fleshy, closely set on stems. Fragrant, purplish rose, ½-in.-wide flowers in late spring, summer. Attractive trailing over walls or in hanging baskets.

Lampranthus deltoides

L. filicaulis. REDONDO CREEPER. Thin, creeping stems; fine-textured, glistening green foliage. Spreads slowly to form mats about 3 in. high. Small pink flowers bloom in early spring. Use for small-scale ground cover, mound, or low bank cover. Plant 3 ft. apart.

L. pedunculatus (Oscularia pedunculata). Like *L. deltoides* but with fragrant flowers in pale pinkish mauve.

L. productus. To 15 in. high, spreading 1½–2 ft. wide. Gray-green leaves tipped bronze. Profuse show of inch-wide purple

L

Lampranthus spectabilis

flowers from early winter into spring; scattered bloom at other times.

L. spectabilis. TRAILING ICE PLANT. Zones 12–24. Sprawling or trailing to 1 ft. high, 1½–2 ft. wide. Three-sided gray-green leaves. Planting becomes a carpet of gleaming color from late winter to spring, when the 2–2½-in.-wide, pink, rose pink, red, or purple flowers are in bloom.

LANCEWOOD.
See **PSEUDOPANAX crassifolius**

LANTANA
Verbenaceae
EVERGREEN SHRUBS

🌿	ZONES 8–10, 12–24; H1, H2; ANNUALS ELSEWHERE
☀	FULL SUN
◐ ⬤	LITTLE TO MODERATE WATER
✤	FRUITS ARE POISONOUS IF INGESTED

Fast-growing tropical American natives with tiny flowers in tight clusters that look like miniature nosegays. Valued for profuse show of color over long season—every month of the year in frost-free areas. Light frosts merely keep plants in check. Heavier freezes (possible in Zones 8–10, 14) may seriously damage or kill plants in some but not all winters. In colder zones, lantana is grown as a summer annual, typically used in containers, hanging baskets, and window boxes.

Prone to mildew in shade or during prolonged overcast weather. Prune hard in spring to remove dead wood and prevent woodiness. Too much water and fertilizer cuts down on bloom. Shrubby kinds are used as low hedges or foundation plants or as substitutes for annuals in beds or containers. Spreading kinds are excellent bank covers and will control erosion. Effective spilling from raised beds, planter boxes, or hanging baskets. Crushed foliage has a pungent odor that some people find objectionable.

Blackberry-like fruits are attractive but highly toxic, especially before ripening. Remove spent flowers before berries form.

L. camara. One of the two species used in hybridizing. Coarse, upright grower to 6 ft. tall and wide. Rough dark green leaves; yellow, orange, or red flowers in 1–2-in. clusters. In lowland areas of Hawaii, this species long ago escaped from cultivation and is considered a noxious weed; various insects that attack it have been imported in attempts to control it.

L. montevidensis (L. sellowiana). The other species used in cross breeding. This one is sold at nurseries. A little hardier than *L. camara*, it's a ground cover to about 2 ft. high, with branches trailing to 3 or even 6 ft. Dark green, 1-in.-long, coarsely toothed leaves are sometimes tinged red or purplish, especially in cold weather. Rosy lilac flowers in 1–1½-in.-wide clusters. 'White Lightnin' has white flowers. 'Lavender Swirl' has flower clusters in pure white, solid purple, and white-and-purple.

Lantana montevidensis

L. selections and hybrids. In the following list, some of the selections are forms of *L. camara* or hybrids between those forms; others, hybrids between *L. camara* and *L. montevidensis*.

'American Red'. To 4–6 ft. tall and wide. Bright red flower clusters with yellow florets in center.

Bandana series. Compact growth to 2–2½ ft. tall and wide. Large flowers open yellow and turn orange, pink, or cherry red.

'Christine'. To 6 ft. by 5 ft. Cerise pink. Can be trained into small patio tree.

'Confetti'. To 2–3 ft. by 6–8 ft. Blossoms mix yellow, pink, purple.

'Cream Carpet'. To 2–3 ft. by 6–8 ft. Cream with bright yellow throat.

'Dwarf Pink'. To 2–4 ft. by 3–4 ft. Light pink. Rather tender.

'Dwarf White'. To 2–4 ft. by 3–4 ft.

'Dwarf Yellow'. To 2–4 ft. high and wide.

'Gold Rush'. To 1½–2 ft. by 4–6 ft. Rich golden yellow.

'Irene'. To 3 ft. by 4 ft. Compact. Magenta and lemon yellow clusters.

'Lemon Swirl'. Slow growing to 2 ft. tall, 3 ft. wide. Bright yellow band around each leaf; yellow flowers.

'Miss Huff'. To 3–5 ft. by 10 ft. Orange and pink. Hardier than other lantanas, surviving sharp frosts.

'New Gold'. To 2–3 ft. by 6–8 ft. Golden yellow.

Patriot series. Plants range from 12–15 in. tall and wide to 4–5 ft. tall and wide, depending on variety. Multicolored flowers in different combinations of yellow, pink, purple, orange, and red.

'Radiation'. To 3–5 ft. high and wide. Rich orange red.

'Rainbow' ('Patriot Rainbow'). Compact plant to 1 ft. by 15 in. Flowers combine yellow, orange, and fuchsia pink.

'Spreading Sunset'. To 2–3 ft. tall by 6–8 ft. wide. Vivid orange red.

'Spreading Sunshine'. To 2–3 ft. tall by 6–8 ft. wide. Bright yellow.

'Sunburst'. To 2–3 ft. tall by 6–8 ft. wide. Bright golden yellow.

'Tangerine'. To 2–3 ft. tall by 6–8 ft. wide. Burnt orange.

LAPAGERIA rosea
CHILEAN BELLFLOWER
Liliaceae
EVERGREEN VINE

🌿	ZONES 5, 6, 15–17, 23, 24
◐	PARTIAL SHADE
⬤	REGULAR WATER

The national flower of Chile. Likes high humidity, moderate summer temperatures. Slender stems twine to 10–20 ft. Glossy, leathery, oval leaves to 4 in. long. Blooms off and on through late spring, summer,

Lapageria rosea

and fall. Beautiful, 3-in.-long, rosy red, pendent, bell-shaped flowers (frequently spotted with white) have unusually heavy, waxy texture; hold up as long as 2 weeks after cutting. Good vine for post, trellis, or tree trunk. Give it wind protection and loose, well-drained, organically enriched soil. Protect from snails and slugs.

LARIX
LARCH
Pinaceae
DECIDUOUS TREES

🌿	ZONES VARY BY SPECIES
☀	FULL SUN
⬤	REGULAR WATER

These conifers form slender pyramids with horizontal branches and drooping branchlets. Needles are ½–1½ in. long, in fluffy tufts; except as noted, those of the following species are soft to the touch. Woody, roundish, ½–1½-in.-long cones are scattered all along branchlets. Notable for color in spring and fall and for winter silhouette. In spring, shows off pale green tufts of new needles,

Larix decidua

bright purple-red new cones. In fall, needles turn brilliant yellow and orange before dropping. Winter interest is enhanced by the many cones, which turn brown with age and hang on to create a polka-dot pattern against the sky. Best in regions with relatively cool summers and cool to cold winters. Not particular about soils. Plant with dark evergreen conifers as background or near water for reflection. Larches attract birds.

L. decidua (L. europaea). EUROPEAN LARCH. Zones A1–A3; 1–9, 14–17. From mountains of Europe. Moderate to fast growth to 30–60 ft. tall, 10–25 ft. wide. Grass green summer foliage. In 'Pendula', branches arch out and down and branchlets hang nearly straight down. Plants sold under this variety name may actually be *L. kaempferi* 'Pendula'.

L. gmelinii. DAHURIAN LARCH. Zones A1–A3. Native to eastern Siberia. Tall tree to 100 ft. high and 30 ft. wide; shrubby in extremely cold or very windy regions. Summer leaves are light green. Cones are brown, oval, 1 in. long.

L. kaempferi. JAPANESE LARCH. Zones 1–9, 14–19. Native to Japan. Most frequently planted larch in the West. Fast growing to 60 ft. or taller, 20–30 ft. wide, but can be dwarfed in containers. Summer foliage is bluish green. A weeping form, 'Pendula', is often sold as a variety of *L. decidua*.

L. occidentalis. WESTERN LARCH, TAMARACK. Zones A3; 1–7. Native to Cascades of Washington and Oregon, eastern Oregon, northern Rocky Mountains. Grows 150–200 ft. tall as timber tree, but usually just 30–50 ft. tall, 10–15 ft. wide in gardens. Sharp, stiff needles are blue green to gray green in summer.

L. sibirica (L. russica). Zones A1–A3; 1, 2. Native from northeastern Europe to Siberia. Narrowly conical tree to 30–90 ft. tall and 15 ft. wide, with horizontal or upward-angled branches and yellow twigs. Needles are bright green in summer. Tolerates extreme cold but can be damaged by spells of early warming followed by hard freezes. 'Pendula' has weeping branches.

LARKSPUR.
See **CONSOLIDA ajacis**

LARKSPUR, CANDLE.
See **DELPHINIUM elatum**

LARKSPUR, SCARLET.
See **DELPHINIUM cardinale, D. nudicaule**

LARREA tridentata
CREOSOTE BUSH
Zygophyllaceae
EVERGREEN SHRUB

🌿 ZONES 7–14, 18–21

☀ FULL SUN

◐◔ LITTLE OR NO WATER TO
       MODERATE WATER

One of the most common native shrubs in deserts of southeastern California, Arizona, southern

Larrea tridentata

Utah, Texas, northern Mexico. Grows 4–8 ft. tall and wide, with many upright branches. Straggly and open in shallow, dry soil; attractive, dense, rounded but spreading where water accumulates. Leathery yellow-green to dark green leaves divided into two tiny, ⅜-in.-long crescents; gummy secretion makes them look varnished and yields distinctive creosote odor, especially after rain. Small yellow flowers off and on all year, followed by small roundish fruit covered with shiny white or rusty hairs. With water and fertilizer, grows taller and denser with larger, shiny dark green leaves. Use as wind or privacy screen, or trim into formal hedge. Sometimes sold as *L. divaricata*.

LATHYRUS
SWEET PEA
Fabaceae (Leguminosae)
ANNUALS AND PERENNIALS

🌿 ZONES VARY BY SPECIES

☀ FULL SUN

◐◔◕ WATER NEEDS VARY
         BY SPECIES

✦ SEEDS CONTAIN TOXIC AMINO ACIDS

In this group is one of the best-known garden flowers—the delightfully fragrant and colorful sweet pea. Throughout this book you will find flowers described as "sweet pea shaped." The flower of the sweet pea is typical of the many members of the pea family (Fabaceae). Each flower has one large, upright, roundish petal (banner or standard), two narrow side petals (wings), and two lower petals that are somewhat united, forming a boat-shaped structure (keel).

L. latifolius. PERENNIAL SWEET PEA. Zones 1–24. Native

to Europe. Strong-growing vine to 9 ft., with blue-green foliage. Flowers are usually mixes of reddish purple, white, and pink; single colors may be sold. Blooms all summer if not allowed to go to seed. Grows with little care, tolerates aridity (give moderate water). May escape and become naturalized, even weedy. Use as bank cover, as trailer over rocks, on trellis or fence.

L. odoratus. Annual. All zones. Native to the Mediterranean region. Blooms in winter, spring, or summer, bearing many spikelike clusters of crisp-looking flowers with a clean, sweet perfume. Blossoms come in single and mixed colors. Mixes include deep rose, blue, purple, scarlet, white, cream, salmon, bicolors. Vining types grow to 5 ft. or more; bush kinds grow 8 in. to 3 ft. tall. Sweet peas make magnificent cut flowers in quantity.

Lathyrus odoratus

To hasten germination, soak seeds for a few hours before planting. In less-than-perfect soil, prepare ground by digging a 1–1½-ft.-deep trench. Mix 1 part peat moss or other organic soil amendment to 2 parts soil, also adding a complete fertilizer according to label directions; backfill trench with mix. Sow seeds 1 in. deep and 1–2 in. apart. When seedlings are 4–5 in. high, thin to at least 6 in. apart. Pinch out tops to encourage strong side branches. Where climate prevents early planting or soil is too wet to work, start three or four seeds in each small peat pot, indoors or in a protected place, and set out when weather has settled. Plant peat pots 1 ft. apart, thinning each to one strong plant. This method is ideal for bush types. Protect young seedlings from birds and control slugs and snails. Never let

vines lack for water; soak heavily. To prolong bloom, cut flowers at least every other day and remove all seedpods. Regular monthly feeding will keep vines vigorous and productive.

For vining sweet peas, provide trellis, strings, or wire before planting. Seedlings need support as soon as tendrils form. Free-standing trellis running north and south is best. When planting against fence or wall, keep supports away from wall to ensure good air circulation.

The following entries describe vine-type sweet peas (heirloom types first, then in groups by time of bloom) and bush types.

Heirloom varieties. Not as large and showy as modern hybrids, these old spring-blooming varieties (some dating back hundreds of years) are notable for powerful fragrance.

'America'. Crimson to scarlet with white stripes.

'Blanche Ferry'. Carmine rose standard, pink wings. Similar to 'Painted Lady' but with more intense color.

'Cupani'. Deep blue standard, purple wings. More vigorous than 'Matucana'.

'Matucana'. Same coloring as 'Cupani'. This and 'Cupani' are very close to the original wild *L. odoratus*.

Old Spice Mix. A mixture of eight old-fashioned varieties with flowers in white and in shades of pink, red, and purple.

'Painted Lady'. Dates from the 18th century; bears small rose-and-white flowers.

Early flowering (Early Flowering Multiflora, Early Multiflora, formerly called Early Spencers). The name "Spencer" once described a type of frilled flower (with wavy petals) that is now characteristic of almost all varieties. "Multiflora" indicates that the plants carry more flowers per stem than the old Spencers did.

The value of early-flowering varieties is that they will bloom in midwinter when days are short. (Spring- and summer-flowering types will not bloom until days have lengthened to 15 hours or more.) Where winter temperatures are mild (Zones 12, 13, 17, 21–24; H1, H2), sow seeds in late summer for winter bloom. Use these varieties for forcing in greenhouse. They are not heat resistant. Generally sold in mixed colors.

L

Spring flowering (Spring-Flowering Heat-Resistant Cuthbertson Type, Cuthbertson's Floribunda, Floribunda-Zvolanek strain). Both mixtures and single-color named varieties are available in seed packets. Flowers have a wide color range: pink, lavender, purple, white, cream, rose, salmon, cerise, carmine, red, blue. Royal or Royal Family are somewhat larger flowered, more heat resistant than the others. In Zones 7–9, 12–24, plant between early fall and earliest winter. Elsewhere, plant just as soon as soil can be worked.

Summer flowering (Galaxy, Plenti-flora). Available in named varieties and mixtures in wide color range. Bloom from early summer on. Large flowers, five to seven on each long stem. Heat resistant, but not enough so for Zones 7–15, 18–21.

Bush type. The so-called bush-type sweet peas are strong vines with predetermined growth, heights. Unlike vining kinds, these stop their upward growth at 8 in. to 3 ft. high. Some kinds are completely self-supporting; others need support of a few sticks or pieces of brush (similar to what you would provide for many perennials). Suitable for all regions. Flowers come in full range of colors. Most are early or spring blooming; follow planting dates given for early- or spring-flowering vining types.

Bijou. To 1 ft. Available in single or mixed colors. Each 5–7 in. stem produces four or five flowers. Self-supporting plants are spectacular in borders, beds, window boxes, containers. Not as heat resistant or as long stemmed as Knee-Hi; performs better in containers.

Cupid. To 4–6 in. by 1 ft. Trails on ground or hangs from containers.

Jet Set. Bushy plants grow 2–3 ft. tall; need some support.

Knee-Hi. To 2½ ft.; need some support. Large, long-stemmed blooms are carried five or six to the stem. Has all the virtues and color range of Cuthbertson's Floribunda, but on bush-type plants. Good for mass display in beds, borders. Growth will exceed 2½ ft. where planting bed joins a fence or wall; keep in the open for uniform height.

Little Sweethearts are rounded bushes to about 8 in. tall; they need no support, bloom over a long season. Snoopea (12–15 in.)

and Supersnoop (2 ft.) need no support.

L. splendens. PRIDE OF CALIFORNIA. Perennial. Zones 14–24. Native to chaparral in San Diego County and adjacent Baja California. To 8–10 ft. Each stem bears clusters of three to ten deep red blooms in early spring. Start from seed in pots in fall or spring; plant out in fall or winter. Long lived in dry, well-drained soil.

LAUREL. See **LAURUS nobilis, PRUNUS, UMBELLULARIA californica**

LAUREL, SIERRA. See **LEUCOTHOE davisiae**

LAUREL, WESTERN or ALPINE. See **KALMIA polifolia microphylla**

LAURENTIA fluviatilis. See **PRATIA pedunculata**

LAURUS nobilis
SWEET BAY, GRECIAN LAUREL
Lauraceae
EVERGREEN SHRUB OR TREE

> 🌿 ZONES 5–9, 12–24; H1, H2; OR INDOOR/OUTDOOR PLANT

> ☼ ◑ FULL SUN OR PARTIAL SHADE

> 💧 MODERATE WATER

This Mediterranean native grows slowly to 12–40 ft. tall and wide. Natural habit is compact and multistemmed, with broad base; plant often resembles a gradually tapering cone. Leathery, aromatic leaves are the traditional bay leaves of cookery—oval, 2–4 in. long, dark green. Clusters of small yellow spring flowers are followed by black or dark purple, ½–1-in. fruit. 'Saratoga' has broader leaves and a more treelike habit.

Not fussy about soil but needs good drainage. Subject to black

scale and laurel psyllid ('Saratoga' is resistant to psyllid). Tends to sucker heavily. Dense habit makes it a good large background shrub, screen, or small tree (though trees eventually will be large). Takes well to clipping into standards, hedges, or topiary shapes such as globes and cones. A classic formal container plant. In areas too cold for growing sweet bay in the ground, grow it in a container and move to a greenhouse or cool, well-lighted room when temperatures drop to about 20°F/–7°C.

LAURUSTINUS. See **VIBURNUM tinus**

LAVANDIN. See **LAVANDULA × intermedia**

LAVANDULA
LAVENDER
Lamiaceae (Labiatae)
EVERGREEN SHRUBS

> 🌿 ZONES VARY BY SPECIES

> ☼ FULL SUN

> 💧 MODERATE WATER

Native to Mediterranean region, Canary Islands, and Madeira. Prized for fragrant lavender or purple flowers, often set off by colorful bracts. Blossom spikes of some species are used for perfume, aromatic oil, soap, medicine, sachets. Aromatic gray, gray-green, or yellowish green foliage. Use as informal hedge or edging, in herb gardens, or in borders with plants needing similar cultural conditions—sunrose (*Helianthemum*), catmint (*Nepeta*), rosemary, santolina, verbena. Where winters are too cold for year-round growth outdoors, lavenders are good container plants for sunny windows. When they are grown outside in marginal climates, self-sown seedlings often show up in summer after parent plants die from winter cold. Most lavenders attract bees and butterflies.

Lavenders need well-drained soil and little or no fertilizer. They will succeed in cool coastal or mountain climates or inland valleys and deserts but succumb to root rot in areas where heat is accompanied by humidity. Fern-leaf sorts (*L. canariensis, L. minutolii, L. multifida*) as well as *L. × allardii, L.* 'Goodwin Creek Grey', and *L. × heterophylla* are tender, but they're more resistant to heat and humidity than English lavenders and lavandins (*L. angustifolia, L. × intermedia*). Give good air

circulation. If mulching around lavenders, use pea gravel, decomposed granite, or sand rather than organic materials. To keep plants neat and compact, shear back by one-third to one-half (even by two-thirds) every year immediately after bloom. If plants become woody and open in center, remove a few of the oldest branches; take out more when new growth comes. If this doesn't work, dig and replace.

For sachets and potpourri, cut flower spikes or strip flowers from stems just as blossoms show color; dry in a cool, shady place. Dried spikes make fragrant wreaths, swags, wands. Dried flowers can be used to scent water or soap. To flavor ice cream, pastries, salads, you can use fresh flowers of *L. angustifolia* and *L. × intermedia* varieties; other species contain harmful chemicals that should not be ingested.

Laurus nobilis

Since lavenders have been in cultivation for centuries and some species cross easily, many varieties and hybrids have arisen. Names are often confused, so some of the variety names that follow may not agree with those you see on nursery labels. Be aware that only cutting-grown stock is truly uniform. Several varieties originally propagated by cuttings are now grown from seed (for example, plants labeled Hidcote Strain and Munstead Strain); seedlings vary in color and growth habit.

L. × allardii. Zones 8, 9, 12–24. A natural hybrid of *L. dentata* and *L. latifolia*—and the real identity of most lavenders sold in the U.S. as *L. × heterophylla*. Fairly open growth to 3–3½ ft. tall, 3 ft. wide. Dull gray-green leaves vary from entirely smooth edged to toothed near the tip, all on the same plant. Bright violet-blue flower spikes are slender, interrupted (that is, with blossom clusters separated on the stem rather than massed together), carried on long, wiry, sometimes branched stems. Blooms from mid- to late summer. Scent is more medicinal than sweet. More tolerant of heat and humidity than English lavenders and lavandins.

L. angustifolia (L. officinalis, L. vera). ENGLISH LAVENDER. Zones 2–24. This is the sweetly fragrant lavender used for perfume and sachets. Common name notwithstanding, it is native not to England but to mountains of southern Europe. It's the hardiest, most widely planted species. In Zones 2 and 3, it is shorter lived, lasting only 3 to 5 years. Most varieties are fairly low growing, forming mounds of foliage from 8 in. to 2 ft. high and wide. Narrow, smooth-edged, gray-green or silvery gray leaves to 2 in. long. Unbranched flower stems rise 4–12 in. above foliage, and are topped with 1–4-in.-long spikes of flowers in white, pink, lavender blue, or various shades of purple. Blooms mainly from early to midsummer, but some varieties repeat in late summer or fall. Named selections include the following.

'Alba'. To 1½–2 ft. high and wide. Pure white flowers, gray-green foliage.

'Blue Cushion'. To 1½ ft. tall, 2 ft. wide. Profuse bright violet-blue flowers above medium green foliage.

'Buena Vista'. Repeat bloomer to 1½–2 ft. high and wide. Deep

violet-blue flowers with superb fragrance.

'Compacta'. To 1½ ft. high and wide; good dwarf hedge plant. Light violet flowers; gray-green leaves.

'England'. To 1 ft. high, 15 in. wide. Light violet-blue flowers; downy, silvery foliage.

'Gray Lady'. To 1½–2 ft. tall and wide. Lavender-blue flowers; silvery gray foliage.

'Hidcote'. The original had deep violet flowers and medium green foliage on a plant 1½–2 ft. tall. The plants sold under this name today are frequently grown from seed; they may bear gray foliage and/or vary in size from the original. 'Hidcote Blue' (with deep blue flowers) and 'Hidcote Superior' (compact, uniform, 16 in. tall and 18 in. wide) are popular selections.

'Irene Doyle' ('Two Seasons Lavender'). To 1½–2 ft. high and wide, with gray-green leaves. Light violet flowers bloom in early summer and give a repeat performance in late summer.

'Jean Davis'. To 1½–2 ft. high and wide. Flowers in pale lilac pink; gray-green foliage.

'Lady' ('Lavender Lady', 'Cambridge Lady'). Seed-grown strain that blooms in 3 months from spring-sown seed. Gray-green foliage. Very short spikes of lavender-blue flowers on a plant 1–1½ ft. high and wide; some variation in flower color and growth habit.

'Martha Roderick'. Compact growth to 1½–2 ft. high and wide. Dense gray foliage. Bright violet-blue blossoms in great abundance from late spring to early summer.

'Melissa'. Dense, compact grower to 1½ ft. high and wide. Good pink flower color, fading to white in hottest sun. Gray-green leaves.

'Mitcham' ('Mitcham Grey'). Named for the former center of English perfume production. Semi-open habit to 2 ft. high and wide. Bright violet-blue flowers; gray foliage.

'Munstead'. The original is 1½ ft. tall, 2 ft. wide, with bright lavender-

blue flowers and medium green foliage. Long bloomer; makes a good low hedge. Quite variable when grown from seed.

'Nana' ('Dwarf Blue'). Slow growing to 1 ft. high, 16 in. wide. Stiff lavender-blue flower spikes in midsummer; gray foliage. Ideal for rock garden or edging. Somewhat hardier than most other English lavenders.

'Nana Alba'. White-flowered version of 'Nana'.

'Rosea'. To 1½–2 ft. high and wide. Light mauve pink flowers; light green foliage.

'Sharon Roberts'. Semi-open growth a little over 2 ft. high and to 2 ft. wide. Profuse show of bright violet-blue flowers begins in late spring, often repeats in fall. Medium green to gray-green foliage.

'Skylark'. To 20 in. high and wide. Deep violet-blue spikes in profusion; gray-green foliage.

'Thumbelina Leigh'. Very compact mound of medium green leaves to just 6 in. high and 12 in. wide. Bright violet-blue flowers rise 6 in. above foliage.

'Twickel Purple'. Grows to 2–2½ ft. high, 3 ft. wide. Heavy, dense spikes of light violet flowers on long, wiry stems, fanning out around an open mound of gray-green foliage.

L. canariensis. CANARY ISLAND LAVENDER. Zones 16–24. Bushy, rounded habit to 3–4 ft. high and wide. Divided, ferny-looking light green leaves 3 in. long, 2 in wide. Spikes of bright lavender-blue flowers are held on branched stems well above foliage. Blooms from early spring to late fall (all year in warm-winter areas). Resents hard pruning; remove faded bloom stems to keep tidy.

L. dentata. FRENCH LAVENDER, TOOTHED LAVENDER. Zones 8, 9, 12–24. To 3–4 ft. tall, 4–6 ft. wide. Narrow green or gray-green leaves are 1½ in. long, ½ in. wide, with square-toothed edges. Purple flowers in short, rounded spikes, each topped with a pair of flaglike bracts that look like rabbit ears. Long spring-into-summer

flowering period; almost year-round in mild-winter areas. 'Linda Ligon' has smaller leaves with irregular creamy white variegation. *L. d. candicans* ('French Gray') has grayer, somewhat larger leaves than the species, with dense grayish white down on young foliage.

L. 'Goodwin Creek Grey'. Zones 8, 9, 12–24. Most likely a hybrid between *L. lanata* and *L. dentata*. This densely foliaged plant grows to 2½–3 ft. high and 3–4 ft. wide, with silvery leaves that are toothed at tips. Deep violet-blue flowers from spring to late fall; virtually year-round in mild-winter climates. Similar to *L. × allardii* in scent and tolerance for heat and humidity.

L. × heterophylla. SWEET LAVENDER. Zones 8, 9, 12–24. The original is probably a cross between *L. dentata* and *L. angustifolia,* occurring wild in southern France. Most plants labeled as this lavender are actually *L. × allardii*. Both *L. × heterophylla* and *L. × allardii* hybrids have dull gray-green leaves, but the true *L. × heterophylla* has upper leaves that are mostly smooth edged, while those near the plant's base are usually toothed in the middle and near the tip. *L. × heterophylla* is also a shorter plant (grows to about 1½–2 ft. tall) with shorter, unbranched spikes of bright violet flowers—and the spikes are less interrupted, having one whorl of blossoms below the main flower spike. Bloom starts in midsummer. Similar to *L. × allardii* in fragrance and tolerance for heat and humidity, but slightly hardier to cold.

L. × intermedia. LAVANDIN, HEDGE LAVENDER. Zones 4–24. This group of sterile hybrids between parents *L. angustifolia*

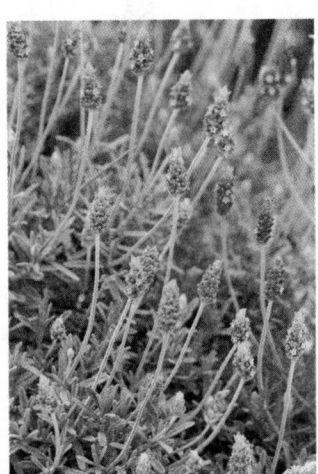

Lavandula dentata

Lavandula angustifolia

and *L. latifolia* is distinguished from the English lavenders by larger growth and by branching stems topped with interrupted flower spikes; blooms from mid- to late summer. Long used in the perfume and soap industries, lavandins are vigorous, fragrant plants. Almost as hardy as English lavender parent and more tolerant of warm, humid summers. They include the following selections.

'Abrialii'. Once the mainstay of the French lavender oil industry. To 2½ ft. high, 3 ft. wide, with gray-green foliage. Dark violet-blue blossoms in narrow, conical, 3½–5-in.-long spikes are excellent for drying.

'Dutch' ('Hortensis'). To 3 ft. tall and 2–2½ ft. wide, with gray foliage. Few-branched stems topped with narrow, conical, 2–3-in. spikes of flowers in deep blue violet.

'Fred Boutin'. To 3–4 ft. tall and wide. Dense, silvery gray foliage topped in early to midsummer with 1½–3-in.-long spikes of violet-blue blossoms on unbranched stems.

'Grappenhall'. To 3 ft. tall and wide (or larger). Profuse, slightly fragrant, blue-violet flower spikes; medium green foliage.

'Grey Hedge'. To 3 ft. or more in height and width. Dense foliage in a very silvery gray; profuse lavender-blue flowers on few-branched stems. Excellent rounded or square-sheared hedge; set plants 2 ft. apart.

'Grosso' ('Fat Spike'). Widely planted commercial variety in France and Italy; possibly the most fragrant lavandin of all. Compact growth to 2½ ft. high and wide. Silvery foliage; large (2–3½-in.-

Lavandula × intermedia
'Grosso'

thick), conical spikes of violet-blue flowers with darker calyxes. Often gives repeat bloom in late summer. Excellent flower for drying.

'Hidcote Giant'. To 2½ ft. high and 3 ft. wide, with gray-green foliage. Stout stems topped by fat spikes of vivid violet-blue flowers.

'Provence'. Though it is often described as a traditional perfume lavandin, this selection does not produce the kind of oil that is used in perfumery. Grows to 2 ft. high, 3 ft. wide, with fragrant light violet flower spikes that dry well. Good hedge plant.

'Silver Edge' ('Walberton's Silver Edge'). To 2½ ft. tall and wide, with lavender-blue flowers held above broad, gray-green leaves uniformly edged in creamy white. Remove stems with foliage that reverts to green.

'Super'. Superb, sweet perfume, close to that of the English lavender parent; yields high-quality essential oil. To 3 ft. high and wide, with gray-green foliage. Lavender-blue flower spikes on long, graceful, laterally branched stems.

'White Spikes' ('Alba'). To 2½ ft. high and wide, with silvery leaves. Spikes of white blossoms and sage green calyxes are 1½–2 in. long, bloom from early summer through fall. Becomes woody with age.

L. lanata. WOOLLY LAVENDER. Zones 8, 9, 12–24. To 1½–2½ ft. high, 2–3 ft. wide. Thickly woolly, near-white leaves are broad (¼–⅜ in. wide), 1½–2 in. long. Widely branching stems that are 10–18 in. long support 1–4-in.-long, interrupted spikes of deep violet blossoms in late summer. Very slow growing; do not cut back hard. This shrub needs perfect drainage; more subject to root rot than English lavenders and lavandins. Difficult to propagate. Many plants sold under this name are varieties of *L. × intermedia.*

L. lanata hybrids. Zones 4–24. The following crosses of *L. lanata* with forms of *L. angustifolia* bloom in mid- to late summer.

'Lisa Marie'. Compact growth to 12–15 in. high and 1½–2 ft. wide, with silvery leaves that have the color but not the woolly texture of *L. lanata.* Short spikes of deep violet blossoms with distinct white base, giving bicolor effect. Has cold hardiness and resistance to root disease of *L. angustifolia.*

'Richard Gray'. Dense growth to 15 in. high and wide. Silvery gray foliage. Flower stems 4–8 in. long carry short (1–1¼-in.) spikes of

vivid violet blossoms; both buds and calyxes are deep violet blue, with a woolly coating.

'Silver Frost'. Semi-open plant 1½ ft. high and wide, with bright silvery foliage. Flower stems radiate in all directions, bear 2-in. spikes of deep violet blossoms with silvery blue calyxes.

L. latifolia (L. spica). SPIKE or BROADLEAF LAVENDER. Zones 4–24. Compact growth to 3 ft. tall and 1½–2 ft. wide, with gray-green leaves 3 in. long, ¼ in. wide; resembles *L. angustifolia.* Slender, widely branching flower stems support interrupted spikes 1½–4 in. long; blossoms range from soft mauve to bright violet blue, with woolly gray calyxes tipped in violet. Blooms in late summer.

L. minutolii. GREEN FERN-LEAF LAVENDER. Zones 8, 9, 14–24. Native to Canary Islands. To 2 ft. tall and 3 ft. wide, with deeply divided green foliage similar to that of *L. canariensis.* Tiny, bright blue flowers are held on stems up to 3 ft. tall summer through fall. Very tolerant of heat and humidity. Responds well to pruning.

L. multifida. FERNLEAF LAVENDER. Zones 16–24. Sprawling growth to 1½ ft. tall and 2–3 ft. across. Gray-green to silvery foliage is finely divided into branched segments that are heavily felted with fine hairs. Wiry, branching flower stems rise 10–14 in. above the leaves, with deep blue-violet flowers arranged spirally around a 3–4-in. spike. Blooms spring to fall (all year in mild-winter areas). Remove faded bloom stalks and oldest stems to keep it neat. Has a strong, earthy, medicinal scent. Plants offered as *L. pinnata* are likely to be *L. multifida.*

L. officinalis. See *L. angustifolia*

L. pinnata. See *L. multifida.*

L. stoechas. SPANISH LAVENDER. Zones 4–24. Includes several subspecies, all stocky plants 1½–3 ft. tall and wide, with narrow gray or gray-green, ½–1-in.-long leaves. Small flowers are typically blackish maroon, borne on short, fat, 2-in. spikes topped by two to four flaglike bracts resembling rabbit ears; the bracts come in shades of pink and purple. Blossoms open first in four vertical rows around the spike; then rest of spike fills in with flowers. Blooms spring into summer; often repeats if sheared.

Lavandula stoechas
'Otto Quast'

Flower stem length varies from 1½ in. to 8 in. or more. Very drought resistant. Seeds profusely; can be invasive. Named forms include the following.

'Hazel'. To 2½ ft. tall, 2 ft. wide. Dense, sturdy mound of gray-green foliage is topped by darkest purple flowers and bright violet bracts. Heavy bloom in spring, modest autumn rebloom.

'Lemon Leigh'. Forms a dense mound of gray-green foliage about 2 ft. tall, with equal or greater width. Flowers are palest yellow; bracts are soft yellow to chartreuse. Lovely in combination with lavenders in the more usual hues. Unusually heavy fragrance.

'Leucantha' ('Spanish White', 'Snowman'). To 1½–2 ft. high and wide, with pale gray-green foliage and stems. White flowers and creamy white bracts with green veining.

Madrid series. To 1½ ft. tall and wide. 'Madrid Blue' has sky blue flowers, white bracts. 'Madrid Pink' has deep rose pink flowers, lavender-pink bracts. 'Madrid White' has white flowers and bracts.

'Otto Quast' ('Quasti'). To 2 ft. high or a bit more, 2½–3½ ft. wide. Flower stems 2–3 in. long, with maroon blossoms and red-purple bracts. Medium green to gray-green leaves. Plants sold under this name are usually grown from seed and often are shorter than the plant just described, with shorter flower stalks.

L. s. pedunculata. Taller than other forms, with longer flower stems. Green or gray-green foliage. Its selection 'Atlas' grows 2½–3 ft. tall, about as wide, with 7–14-in. flower stalks and vibrant red-violet bracts.

'Willow Vale'. Vigorous, upright, o 1½ ft. tall and wide. Wispy gray-reen leaves; deep blue-violet flow-rs and bluish purple bracts. Short 1–2-in.) flower stems.

'Wings of Night'. Heavy bloomer hat resembles 'Otto Quast' but has broader habit.

'Winter Bee'. About 2 ft. tall, vith equal or greater spread. Gray-reen foliage. Dark purple flowers nd lavender bracts appear in arly spring, about 3 weeks earlier han those of other Spanish laven-ers. Blooms are long lasting.

L. vera. See L. angustifolia

L. viridis. GREEN LAVENDER, YELLOW LAVENDER. Zones 8, 9, 2–24. To 2–3 ft. high and wide, vith bright green, pine-scented oliage. Short, densely packed, ylindrical flower heads are car-ied on 1–2-in.-long stems in pring. White or creamy flowers; racts vary in color from cream hrough light yellow to bright hartreuse or pale green. Closely elated to L. stoechas, with which t crosses readily, producing ybrids with foliage in gray, gray reen, or yellow green; flowers nd bracts come in white, cream, ellow, shrimp pink, salmon, nagenta, rose pink, shades of ed violet and blue violet, and various greens.

LAVATERA
TREE MALLOW
Malvaceae
ANNUALS AND EVERGREEN SHRUBS

- 🌡 ZONES VARY BY SPECIES
- ☀ FULL SUN, EXCEPT AS NOTED
- 💧 REGULAR WATER, EXCEPT AS NOTED

These easy-to-grow plants bear blossoms resembling single holly-hocks (Alcea).

L. assurgentiflora. Evergreen shrub. Zones 14–24. Native to Southern California's Channel Islands but naturalized on the coastal mainland. Erect growth to

Lavatera assurgentiflora

12 ft. tall and wide. Maplelike leaves 3–5 in. long, lobed and toothed. Rosy lavender, white-striped, 2–3-in.-wide flowers bloom almost throughout the year, heaviest from midspring to late summer. Resists wind, salt spray. Use as fast-growing wind-break hedge. Will reach 5–10 ft. and bloom first year from seed. Shear to keep dense. Little to moderate water.

L. maritima (L. bicolor). Ever-green shrub. Zones 6–9, 12–24. Native to western Mediterranean. Grows quickly to 6–8 ft. tall and about as wide, with gray-green, 2½-in. maplelike leaves and a summer-long show of light pink, 2–3-in. flowers with dark rose veining and a deep purple center. Open grower; cut back hard to keep it compact. Needs partial to full shade in Zones 12 and 13.

L. thuringiaca. Evergreen shrub. Zones 2–9, 14–24. Native to central and southeastern Europe. Resembles L. maritima but has denser growth, greener leaves. Flowers are purplish pink, 3 in. across, nearly everblooming (except in colder-winter zones). 'Barnsley' grows 6–8 ft. tall and 6 ft. wide, and has lighter pink flowers with deep pink centers. 'Bredon Springs' is a strong grower to 6 ft. tall and wide, with rose pink flow-ers and soft gray-green foliage. 'Burgundy Wine', to 4–5 ft. tall and wide, has reddish pink flowers. 'Kew Rose' sports large, mauve-pink flowers on an open-growing plant to 12 ft. tall. 'Red Rum' grows about 4–5 ft. tall and 3–4 ft. wide, with deep pink flowers held on burgundy stems. 'Rosea', to 6 ft. tall and 6 ft. wide, has pink blossoms. Plants need winter protection in Zones 2 and 3.

L. trimestris. ANNUAL MALLOW. All zones. Mediter-ranean native reaches 3–6 ft. tall and wide from spring-sown seed. Satiny flowers up to 4 in. across. Species is seldom seen in gardens; more commonly grown are named varieties with blossoms in white, pink, rosy carmine. Bloom extends from midsummer to frost if spent flowers are removed to halt seed production. Thin seedlings to allow each plant ample room to spread. Makes a colorful, fast-growing summer hedge or back-ground planting. In mild-winter regions, can also be sown in fall for winter-to-spring bloom. Com-pact (2–3-ft.) varieties include 'Mont Rose', rose pink; 'Mont Blanc', white; and 'Silver Cup',

bright pink. 'Ruby Regis', to 2 ft. high and wide, has 3½-in. flowers of deep rose veined in a deeper shade. 'Loveliness' has similar blos-soms but grows up to 3–4 ft. tall and wide.

LAVENDER. See **LAVANDULA**

LAVENDER COTTON. See **SANTOLINA chamaecyparissus**

LAVENDER STARFLOWER. See **GREWIA occidentalis**

LAYIA platyglossa
TIDYTIPS
Asteraceae (Compositae)
ANNUAL

- 🌡 ZONES 1–10, 14–24
- ☀ FULL SUN
- 💧 LITTLE OR NO WATER

California native usually obtained in mixed wildflower seed packets or from specialists dealing in native plant seeds. Rapid growth to 5–16 in. high and wide. Narrow, softly hairy, gray-green leaves to 1¼ in. long; lower leaves toothed or lobed, upper ones smooth edged. Flowers are about 2 in. across, with light yellow rays neatly marked white at the tips.

Layia platyglossa

Blooms in spring; in cool-summer climates, flowering continues into early summer.

Takes poor and rather heavy soils (though it won't tolerate standing water). To give seedlings a good start, however, prepare soil as for any garden bed. Seeds are usually sown in fall but can also be planted in early spring. Self-sows and will naturalize on banks or in other well-drained sites as long as competition from grasses is minimal. Very drought tolerant; give occasional water if winter rains fail.

LEATHER FERN. See **RUMOHRA adiantiformis**

LEEK
Liliaceae
BIENNIAL GROWN AS ANNUAL

- 🌡 ZONES A3; 1–24; H1, H2
- ☀ ◐ PARTIAL SHADE IN HOTTEST CLIMATES
- 💧 REGULAR WATER

Leeks are related to onions but don't form distinct bulbs. To 2–3 ft. tall, with an edible, mild-flavored stem that resembles a long, fat green onion. Give very rich soil. Performs best in cool-summer climates, but also does well in hotter areas if given some shade.

Leek

In cold-winter regions, set out transplants in early spring, or direct sow seeds in late summer for harvest the following year. In mild-winter areas, set out transplnts in fall. Sow seeds indoors, ½ in. deep, 1 in. apart, 8 weeks prior to plant-ing date. Space seedlings 2–4 in. apart in a 5-in.-deep furrow. As plants grow, mound soil around stalks to blanch them (this makes the stem bottoms white and mild), keeping mounded soil just below leaf joints.

Harvest when stems are ½–2 in. thick, usually about 4 to 7 months after setting out plants. In cold-winter climates, harvest before ground freezes. (Where ground doesn't freeze, you can leave leeks in place and harvest as needed.) Lift out with spading fork. Any offsets may be detached and replanted. If leeks bloom, small bulbils may appear in flower clus-ters; plant these for later harvest. To prepare leeks for cooking, slice off the roots and all but 2–3 in. of the green leaves; rinse thoroughly, separating layers. Leeks are not bothered by many of the pests and diseases that attack onions.

L

LEMAIREOCEREUS thurberi.
See **STENOCEREUS thurberi**

LEMON. See **CITRUS**

LEMONADE BERRY.
See **RHUS integrifolia**

LEMON BALM.
See **MELISSA officinalis**

LEMON GRASS.
See **CYMBOPOGON citratus**

LEMON VERBENA.
See **ALOYSIA triphylla**

LENTEN ROSE.
See **HELLEBORUS orientalis**

LEONOTIS leonurus
LION'S TAIL
Lamiaceae (Labiatae)
EVERGREEN SHRUB

- ☘ ZONES 8–24; H1, H2
- ☀ FULL SUN
- ◐ LITTLE OR NO WATER

Mint-family member from South
Africa. Branching to 4–6 ft. tall
and wide. Hairy, square stems
carry opposite pairs of narrow,
toothed,
2–5-in.-
long leaves.
Blooms in
summer and
into autumn,
with showy,
dense whorls
of tubular,
deep orange,
2-in. flowers
covered with
furlike coat
of fine hairs.
Striking
if kept well
groomed. If
frost hits, cut
plant back to
live growth in spring. Naturalized
in Hawaii. There is also a white-
flowered form, *L. l. albiflora*.

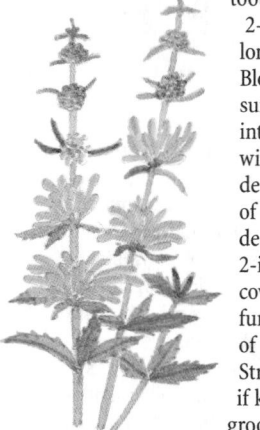
Leonotis leonurus

LEONTOPODIUM alpinum
EDELWEISS
Asteraceae (Compositae)
PERENNIAL

- ☘ ZONES 1–9, 14–17
- ☀ FULL SUN
- ● REGULAR WATER

Short-lived perennial from mountains of Europe. Rock garden plant
growing 6–12 in. high and 1 ft.
wide, with woolly white stems,
leaves, and bracts. Small white

Leontopodium alpinum

flower heads are crowded at stem
tips; a collar of slender leaves radiates out from below each flower
head like the arms of a starfish.
Tiny bracts of flower heads are
tipped with black. Blooms in early
summer. Needs excellent drainage.

LEOPARD PLANT.
See **FARFUGIUM japonicum**
'Aureo-maculatum'

LEOPARD'S BANE.
See **DORONICUM**

LEPECHINIA
PITCHER SAGE
Lamiaceae (Labiatae)
EVERGREEN SHRUBS

- ☘ ZONES 7–9, 14–24, EXCEPT AS NOTED
- ☀◐ PARTIAL SHADE IN HOTTEST CLIMATES
- ◐◒ LITTLE OR NO WATER TO MODERATE WATER

These aromatic members of the
mint family are attractive in wild
gardens. They reach 6 ft. tall and
nearly as wide; once established,
they can do without irrigation
except in the hottest regions. All
have opposite pairs of 1½–5-in.-
long leaves and short, spikelike

Lepechinia calycina

clusters of tubular, 1¼-in. flowers
with a gaping mouth and prominent calyx. Except as noted,
species listed here are from California's Coast Ranges and bear
white to pale pink or lavender
blooms.

L. calycina. Lance-shaped to
narrowly egg-shaped leaves.
Blooms in late spring.

L. fragrans. Furry gray-green
leaves, somewhat squared off at
base. Blooms in spring and
summer.

L. hastata. Zones 7–9, 14–24;
H1. From Mexico; possibly native
to Hawaii, where it is called
pakaha. Spreads by rhizomes.
Arrow-shaped leaves; reddish purple flowers. Main bloom comes in
summer, with sporadic flowering
during the rest of the year.

LEPTOSPERMUM
TEA TREE
Myrtaceae
EVERGREEN SHRUBS OR TREES

- ☘ ZONES 14–24, EXCEPT AS NOTED
- ☀ FULL SUN
- ◐◒ LITTLE OR NO WATER TO MODERATE WATER

Native to Australia, New Zealand.
Called tea tree because Captain
Cook brewed a tea from the leaves
and gave it to his crew as a scurvy
preventive. Substantial and useful
plants year round; soft and casual
looking (never rigid or formal).
Most make a display of five-
petaled single flowers (somewhat
like tiny wild roses) along stems
among the small leaves. Petals surround a hard central cone or cup
that matures to a woody seed capsule that hangs on for a long time
after the petals drop. Flowers typically white, pink, or red.

If planted in well-drained,
slightly acid soil, tea trees are
long-lived plants requiring little
care. Where drainage is poor, they
sometimes succumb quickly to
root rot. Need minimal pruning,
though you may want to thin
growth to emphasize a picturesque habit. When clipping or
shearing into hedges, don't cut
into bare wood—new growth is
unlikely to sprout. Old shrubs that
become overgrown or bare at the
base can be limbed up into small
trees. Plants thrive in seacoast
conditions.

L. horizontalis. See L. scoparium 'Horizontalis'

L. laevigatum. AUSTRALIAN
TEA TREE. Zones 14–24; H1, H2.
Large shrub or small tree 10–30 ft.

high and wide, with oval or
teardrop-shaped, dull green to
gray-green leaves to 1 in. long.
Blooms in spring, bearing white
flowers to ½ in. across. Solitary
plants allowed to grow to full size
develop picturesque character, with
shaggy, gray-brown, muscular-
looking trunks that twist and
curve gracefully, reach 2 ft. across
at base. Handsome branches range
out from trunk and carry canopies
of finely textured foliage; some
weeping branches hang down
from the foliage canopies. To make
a windbreak, screen, or clipped
hedge, set the plants 3–6 ft. apart,
depending on ultimate size of
selection. Used in these roles,
plants do not develop any visible
branching character, but they
do form a solid bank of fine-
textured foliage.

'Compactum', to 5–8 ft. high
and 6 ft. wide, is somewhat more
open and sparser blooming than
species; 'Reevesii' grows only 4–5 ft.
high and wide, has rounder,
slightly larger, more densely set
leaves. Neither of these varieties
develops the picturesque form of
the species.

**L. macrocarpum (L. nitidum
'Macrocarpum').** To 3–8 ft. high
and wide. Tiny, narrow leaves
(½ in. long, ⅛ in. wide) are reddish when new, then mature to
purplish bronze. Spring flowers
nearly 1 in. wide, chartreuse yellow
with dark green central disk.

L. petersonii. LEMON-
SCENTED TEA TREE. To 9–20 ft.
tall, 6–15 ft. wide. Erect, somewhat
open growth with arching or
weeping branchlets. Medium
green leaves are 1–2 in. long, ⅛ in.
wide, give off strong lemon scent
when bruised; Australians occasionally use the dried leaves to
make tea. Flowers are small, white,
inconspicuous.

L. polygalifolium. Variable size
and habit; ranges from 3 to 18 ft.
tall, 1½ to 9 ft. wide, and can be
upright or spreading. Narrow deep
green leaves are less than 1 in.
long. Showy, very profuse bloom
from late spring into summer,
when stems are densely set with
white, honey-scented, ¾-in.-wide
flowers. Attractive cut flowers and
foliage. 'Yarra River' has red leaves.

L. rotundifolium. Variable in
size and habit, but usually reaches
about 6 ft. high and 9 ft. wide, with
spreading, arching branches. Tiny
roundish leaves. Spring flowers to
1 in. across vary in color from
white to deep purplish pink.
Extremely showy in bloom but has

shorter flowering period than *. scoparium*. 'Manning's Choice' has deep lavender pink blossoms.

L. scoparium. NEW ZEALAND TEA TREE, MANUKA. Zones 14–24; H1, H2. Basic species is rarely seen, but its many varieties are valuable garden plants. Not as bold in form or as serviceable in hedges and screens as *L. laevigatum*, but its half-inch flowers are showier: single or double, in white, pink, or red, profuse in spring and summer. Branches densely set with needlelike green leaves, ¼–½ in. long. Good in containers.

Leptospermum scoparium
'Ruby Glow'

'Apple Blossom'. Upright growth to 8 ft. tall and wide. Pale pink double flowers age to white. Leaves tinge pink in cold weather.

'Burgundy Queen'. Upright, dense grower to 12 ft. tall, 10 ft. wide. Double flowers are deep burgundy. Cold weather flushes foliage with burgundy tones.

'Crimson Glory'. Grows 6–7 ft. tall and wide. Crimson double flowers; bronzy foliage.

'Gaiety Girl'. Slow growing to 5 ft. tall, 4 ft. wide. Double flowers are pink with lilac tint. Reddish foliage.

'Helene Strybing'. To 6–10 ft. tall and wide with an open, picturesque habit. Rich, deep pink, single flowers are a bit larger than those of other varieties.

'Horizontalis'. Fast growing to 3–4 ft. tall, 12 ft. wide, with horizontal branches and drooping branchlets. Single white flowers. Good bank cover.

'Nanum Ruru'. Dense grower to just 2 ft. tall and wide. Dark pink single flowers; tiny dark green leaves. Especially good in containers or as a ground cover.

'Nanum Tui'. Low, rounded growth to 2 ft. high, 3 ft. wide. Light pink single flowers, darker at center.

'Pink Cascade'. To 1 ft. tall, 3–4 ft. wide. Single pink flowers on sprawling, weeping branches. Attractive trailing over walls, among rocks.

'Pink Damask'. Dense habit to 6–8 ft. tall, 4–5 ft. wide. Double ruby red flowers; red-tinged leaves.

'Pink Pearl'. To 6–10 ft. tall, 5–8 ft. wide. Pale pink buds open into double blush pink to white flowers.

'Red Ensign'. Upright, dense habit to 6–8 ft. tall and not quite as wide. Heavy bloomer, with single flowers of deep crimson.

'Ruby Glow'. Compact, upright growth to 6–8 ft. tall, 4–5 ft. wide. Dark foliage and ¾-in. double blooms in oxblood red; entire shrub looks red.

'Silver and Rose'. Dense growth to 4–5 ft. tall and wide. Abundant rose pink, green-centered flowers; bright gray-green foliage.

'Snow White'. Spreading, compact growth 2–4 ft. high, 4–5 ft. wide. Double white flowers with green centers.

LETTUCE
Asteraceae (Compositae)
ANNUAL

A short browse through a seed catalog, seed display rack, or selection of nursery seedlings will reveal enough variety to keep your salad bowl crisp and colorful throughout the growing season. There are four principal types of lettuce: crisphead, butterhead or Boston, loose-leaf, and romaine.

Crisphead is the most exasperating for home gardeners to produce. Heads form best when monthly average temperatures are 55 to 60°F/13 to 16°C. In mild climates, this type of lettuce does well over a long season, but in hot-summer areas, timing of planting becomes critical. Best varieties include 'Great Lakes', 'Summertime', and 'Nevada'.

Butterhead or Boston type has a loose head with green, smooth outer leaves and yellow inner leaves. Good varieties include 'Bibb' ('Limestone'), 'Buttercrunch', and 'Tom Thumb'. 'Mignonette' ('Manoa') stands heat without bolting to seed.

Loose-leaf lettuce makes a rosette rather than a head. Stands heat better than other types. Choice selections include 'Black-seeded Simpson', 'Green Ice', and 'Oak Leaf' (all with green leaves); 'Salad Bowl' (with deeply cut green leaves); and 'Prizehead' and 'Ruby' (red-tinged leaves).

Romaine lettuce has an erect, cylindrical head of smooth leaves; outer leaves are green, inner ones whitish. Stands heat moderately well. Try 'Medallion', 'Olga', or 'Parris Island'.

Lettuces with bronzy to pinkish red leaves add color to a salad. 'Freckles', 'Marveille des Quatre Saisons', and 'Perella Red' are butterheads; 'Lollo Rosso', 'Red Oak Leaf', 'Red Sails', and 'Ruby' are loose-leaf varieties; 'Rouge d'Hiver' and 'Sierra' are romaines.

Lettuce

Various loose-leaf and romaine lettuce varieties are typically included in mesclun mixes— mixtures of fast-growing, tender salad greens (usually some mild and some tangy) that may include mustards, arugula, cress, chicory, radicchio, and/or mizuna.

All lettuces need loose, well-drained soil. Sow in open ground; barely cover seeds. Loose-leaf lettuce can be grown as close as 4 in. apart; thin all other types to 1 ft. apart. Grow mesclun in blocks 4 in. wide and don't thin.

For prolonged harvest, sow at 2-week intervals. In cold-winter regions, begin sowing seed for all types after frost, as soon as soil is workable; where summers are very short, sow indoors, then transplant seedlings outdoors after last frost. In mild-winter, cool-summer regions, sow in early spring for spring and summer harvest, then make further sowings in late summer or early fall for winter harvest. In mild-winter, hot-summer areas, grow only as a winter and early spring crop.

Feed plants lightly and frequently. Control snails, slugs, and earwigs. Harvest when heads or leaves are of good size; once lettuce reaches maturity, it rapidly goes to seed, becoming quite bitter. With loose-leaf lettuce, you can clip off just the outer leaves as you need them. Likewise, snip off young leaves of mesclun mix for salads.

LEUCADENDRON
Proteaceae
EVERGREEN TREES AND SHRUBS

South African native related to *Protea;* see that entry for culture. Male and female flowers are borne on separate plants. Inflorescences form at stem tips. In some shrubby species, conelike male flower clusters sit above showy colored bracts and have the look of giant daisies. Those of *L. discolor* and *L. tinctum* make striking cut flowers that dry well. Female flower clusters are less showy and develop into conelike seed clusters.

Leucadendron argenteum

L. argenteum. SILVER TREE. Tree. Young plants are narrow, stiffly upright, and, thanks to their more symmetrical form, more spectacular in effect than older ones. Mature trees have twisted gray trunks and a spreading, irregular silhouette; can reach 40 ft. by 25–30 ft., though they are more typically seen at about half that size. Silky, silvery white, 3–6-in.-long leaves densely cover the branches. This is a foliage plant; flowers and fruit are inconsequential. Leaves are good for arrangements.

Needs fast-draining soil; will not thrive in clay or alkaline soil or in soil amended with animal manure. Needs humid air; takes ocean winds but not dry winds. Hard to use, due to cultural problems and striking appearance— it doesn't blend well with most plants. Small plants are picturesque container subjects for 3 or 4 years; larger ones are effective on slopes (good way to provide them with the excellent drainage they need) when combined with boulders, succulents, and pines in sheltered seaside gardens. Use singly or in groups.

L. discolor. Shrub. Upright, slightly spreading growth to 4–8 ft. tall and wide. Stems are densely set with gray-green leaves. Red-centered gold inflorescences in early fall or winter. 'Pom Pom' is a showy male selection with white to pale yellow bracts surrounding orange-red cones.

L. galpinii. Shrub. Erect growth to 6–8 ft. tall and 4–6 ft. wide. Narrow, gray-green foliage. Male plants sport yellow pompon flowers; female plants produce soft gray, pink-tinged cones that are great in arrangements.

L. hybrids. Shrubs. The following are among the best of the many available hybrids. 'Pisa' is a fast, dense grower to 6 ft. tall, 3–5 ft. wide, with willowy, gray-green leaves; silver cones are surrounded by yellow-green bracts in spring. 'Safari Sunset' is vigorous and upright, to 8–10 ft. tall and 6–8 ft. wide, with intensely red bracts in summer that fade to light yellow in the center by late winter; tolerant of frost and clay soils. 'Safari Sunshine' is smaller (4–5 ft. tall and wide) and less vigorous, with rich red bracts in late winter and spring; eye-catching leaves are heavily variegated in pink and creamy white.

L. tinctum. Shrub. Upright, slender habit to 8 ft. tall and 3–4 ft.

wide. Dark green foliage. Spring inflorescences are rose to red, sometimes yellow.

LEUCAENA retusa
GOLDEN BALL LEAD TREE
Fabaceae (Leguminosae)
EVERGREEN OR DECIDUOUS
SHRUB OR TREE

🌿 ZONES 10–13
☀️ FULL SUN
💧 LITTLE TO MODERATE WATER

Native to Texas, northern Mexico. Grows 12–20 ft. tall and wide, with light green leaves twice divided into many tiny leaflets. Showy spring flowers are fluffy yellow balls 1 in. across; they are followed by flattened, beanlike pods 6–10 in. long. Useful tree for mini-oasis or transition between cultivated garden and native desert. Good choice for small patio tree. Evergreen in milder winters; deciduous otherwise.

Leucaena retusa

LEUCANTHEMUM.
See **CHRYSANTHEMUM**

LEUCOJUM
SNOWFLAKE
Amaryllidaceae
PERENNIALS FROM BULBS

🌿 ZONES VARY BY SPECIES
☀️ ◐ FULL SUN DURING BLOOM, LIGHT SHADE AFTER IN HOT CLIMATES
💧 REGULAR WATER DURING GROWTH AND BLOOM

Native to Europe. Easy-to-grow, permanent plants with strap-shaped leaves and nodding, bell-shaped white flowers with six green-tipped segments. Good naturalized under deciduous trees, in

Leucojum aestivum

shrub borders or orchards, or on cool slopes. Plant in fall, setting bulbs 3–4 in. deep, 4 in. apart. Give some water during summer dormancy; *L. aestivum* can get by without any if soil is shaded. Do not disturb clumps until they are really crowded. When this occurs, dig clumps after foliage dies down, then divide and replant immediately.

L. aestivum. SUMMER SNOWFLAKE. Zones 1–10, 14–24. Leaves 1–1½ ft. long. Stems are 1½ ft. tall, each carrying three to five inch-long flowers. 'Gravetye Giant' is a bit taller and larger flowered than the species and bears as many as nine flowers per stem. Common name "summer snowflake" is misleading—in mild-winter areas, plants can bloom during the period from late fall through winter; in colder regions, blossoms appear in midspring.

L. vernum. SPRING SNOWFLAKE. Zones 1–6. Flourishes in areas with definite winter cold; generally unsuccessful where temperatures remain above 20°F/–7°C. Leaves 9 in. long. In earliest spring, each foot-long stem bears a single large white flower (occasionally two).

LEUCOPHYLLUM
TEXAS RANGER, SILVERLEAF
Scrophulariaceae
EVERGREEN SHRUBS

🌿 ZONES 7–24, EXCEPT AS NOTED
☀️ FULL SUN
💧 LITTLE TO MODERATE WATER

Native to the Southwest and northern Mexico, these compact, slow-growing shrubs are highly useful and attractive in desert gardens. Most have silvery foliage and a good show of ½–1-in.- wide flowers with an open bell shape. Flowering may occur at varying

times of the year, often after summer showers. Need very good drainage. Tolerate heat, wind, and alkaline soil. Use as informal or clipped hedges, massed as tall ground cover, or in mixed dry-country gardens. Unless formally hedged, plants require little pruning. Old, straggling plants can be rejuvenated by cutting close to the ground.

L. candidum. VIOLET SILVERLEAF. To 5 ft. high and wide, with small (½-in.), silvery leaves and deep purple flowers. 'Silver Cloud' is a heavy bloomer with very white foliage. 'Thunder Cloud' is smaller than the species (to 3–4 ft. high and wide) and has deeper purple, more closely spaced blossoms.

L. frutescens. TEXAS RANGER, TEXAS SAGE, CENIZO. Zones 7–24; H1, H2. To 6–8 ft. tall and wide, with gray foliage and light purple flowers. 'Green Cloud' has bright green foliage and dark rose or magenta flowers; it may be deciduous in coldest winters. 'White Cloud' has gray foliage and white flowers. 'Compacta', with gray foliage and pink flowers, grows 5 ft. high and wide.

Leucophyllum frutescens

L. laevigatum. CHIHUAHUAN SAGE. Open, angular growth to 4 ft. tall, 5 ft. wide. Tiny dark green leaves; profuse lavender flowers.

L. langmaniae. Dense grower to 5 ft. high and wide, with bright green leaves and lavender flowers. 'Lynn's Legacy' ('Lynn's Everblooming') flowers profusely over a long period in summer. 'Rio Bravo' has rich green foliage and requires little pruning to maintain a tight, rounded form.

L. pruinosum. Open growth habit to 6 ft. tall and wide, with silvery foliage. Purple flowers have a strong fragrance of grape bubble gum.

L

L. 'Rain Cloud'. Hybrid derived from *L. frutescens.* Erect growth to [?] ft. tall, 3–4 ft. wide. Small, silvery leaves; violet-blue flowers.

L. revolutum. Slow growth to about 4 ft. tall, 4–5 ft. wide, with light green, somewhat succulent foliage. Bears purple flowers that appear in fall, later than for other leucophyllums. 'Houdini' has larger, showier blossoms than the species.

L. zygophyllum. To 3 ft. tall and wide, with gray-green, slightly cupped leaves and light blue flowers. 'Cimarron' is a dense grower with bluish purple flowers tightly packed along stems; leaves have a distinctly cupped shape.

LEUCOPHYTA brownii. See **CALOCEPHALUS brownii**

LEUCOSPERMUM

PINCUSHION
Proteaceae
EVERGREEN SHRUBS

🌱	**ZONES 15–17, 21–24; H1**
☼	**FULL SUN**
💧	**MODERATE WATER**

South African shrubs related to *Protea;* see that entry for culture. Like proteas, these shrubs are difficult to grow, but extra effort is rewarded with spectacular clusters of many long, slender tubular flowers in a large, thistlelike head. These make stunning cut flowers that last for a month in water. Leaves are narrow, stalkless ovals, crowded along stems. Bloom peaks in late winter and early spring, but can start earlier and last up to 6 months in mild winters. Well-established plants can take several degrees of frost; side buds will produce flowers even if main flower buds freeze. Prune only to shape or remove dead flowers.

Leucospermum reflexum

L. cordifolium (L. nutans). NODDING PINCUSHION. Compact habit to 4 ft. tall and wide. Medium green leaves. Best species for cut flowers: blossom clusters are 4 in. across, with individual tube-shaped, yellow-tipped coral flowers that curve gracefully outward, then inward again. Selections in varying colors include 'Flame Spike' (salmon red), 'Red' (orange red), and 'Yellow Bird' (light yellow).

L. reflexum. ROCKET PINCUSHION. Sprawling growth to 12 ft. tall and wide, with attractive gray foliage. Orange-rose, 4-in. flower heads. As the flowers age, the "pins" curl downward, giving blossom a shaggy look.

LEUCOTHOE

Ericaceae
EVERGREEN SHRUBS

🌱	**ZONES VARY BY SPECIES**
☼ ◐	**FULL SUN IN COOLER CLIMATES ONLY**
💧	**WATER NEEDS VARY BY SPECIES**
☠	**LEAVES AND NECTAR ARE POISONOUS IF INGESTED**

Relatives of *Pieris,* with leathery leaves and clusters of small, urn-shaped creamy white flowers. Need deep, acid, humus-rich soil; well-suited to woodland gardens. Keep out of drying winds. Best used in masses; not especially attractive individually. Good planted in front of taller, leggy broad-leafed evergreens. All have suckering growth; for shape and neatness, prune oldest stems to the ground occasionally.

L. axillaris. COAST LEUCO-THOE. Zones 4–7, 15–17. Native to southeastern U.S. Spreading, arching plant 2–4 ft. tall, 3–6 ft. wide. Leaves to 4 in. long are bronze when they emerge; they mature to dark green, then turn red in winter. Drooping, 1-3-in.-long flower clusters held along stems in midspring. Regular water.

L. davisiae. SIERRA LAUREL. Zones 2, 4–7, 15–17. Native to bogs and wet places in Siskiyou and Sierra Nevada mountains. Upright shrub to 3 ft. high and 5 ft. wide. Glossy rich green leaves to 3 in. long are bronze-tinted in winter. Flowers in erect, 2–4-in.-long clusters bloom in early summer. Ample water.

L. fontanesiana (L. catesbaei, L. walteri). DROOPING LEUCO-THOE. Zones 4–7, 15–17. Native to eastern U.S. Grows slowly to 3–6 ft. high and wide, spreading by underground stems. Branches arch gracefully. Leaves are 3–6 in. long, turn bronzy purple in fall (remain greener in deep shade). Drooping, 1½–2½-in.-long clusters of flowers bloom in midspring. Moderate water.

Leucothoe fontanesiana

'Lovita'. To 2 ft. high and 4 ft. wide. Leaves are smaller and darker green than those of species; turn mahogany in winter.

'Nana'. To 2 ft. high, spreading to 6 ft. wide. Leaves turn bronzy red in winter.

'Rainbow'. To 5 ft. high and 6 ft. wide, with green leaves marbled cream and pink.

'Rollissoni'. Grows 3 ft. high and 6 ft. wide, with shorter, narrower leaves that turn beet red in fall.

'Scarletta'. To 2 ft. high and 4 ft. wide. Leaves are bright red when new; they turn green by summer, then deep red in fall and winter.

LEVISTICUM officinale

LOVAGE
Apiaceae (Umbelliferae)
PERENNIAL

🌱	**ZONES 4–9, 12–24**
☼ ◐	**LIGHT AFTERNOON SHADE IN HOTTEST CLIMATES**
💧	**REGULAR WATER**

From the eastern Mediterranean region. Ornamental herb with divided, glossy deep green leaves to 2½ ft. long. Hollow stems rise from the foliage clumps in summer, crowned by sprays of flat-topped greenish yellow flower clusters. Flowering plants may reach 6 ft. tall under ideal conditions, but more usual size is 3 ft. high and wide. Plant has a history of culinary uses; seeds are valued

Levisticum officinale

for their celery flavor, leaves are added to salads and soups. Grow from seeds sown in place in fall; or start seeds in containers and transplant into garden in spring. You can also divide an established clump in early spring. Volunteer seedlings are another source of extra plants.

LEWISIA

Portulacaceae
PERENNIALS

🌱	**ZONES 1–7, 14–17, EXCEPT AS NOTED**
☼ ◐	**FULL SUN OR LIGHT SHADE**
💧	**LITTLE TO MODERATE WATER**

Beautiful plants for rock gardens, collections of alpine plants. Often difficult to grow. All need excellent drainage; plant with fine gravel around crowns. Of the many offered by specialists, the following are outstanding.

L. cotyledon. From Northern California and southern Oregon. To about 1 ft. high, 10 in. wide. Rosettes of narrow, fleshy, evergreen leaves bear 10-in. stems topped by large, extremely showy clusters of 1-in., white or pink flowers often striped with rose or red. Blooms from spring to early summer. *L. c. howellii* is similar but has wavy-edged leaves and somewhat larger flowers. Prune out side growth to maintain air circulation around root crown. Can be grown in pots of fast-draining sterilized soil or growing mixes.

Several floriferous hybrids are available. 'Dark Cloud' produces 6–10-in. stems bearing large purplish red flowers; similar 'Pink Cloud' has bright pink blooms. 'Sunset Strain' has flowers ranging from apricot to rose and bright cherry red. 'Little Plum', a cross between *L. cotyledon* and a species native to the Sierra Nevada, sports abundant rose-purple flowers with a hint of orange over a long period.

L. rediviva. BITTERROOT. Native to mountains of the West. To 2 in. high, 4 in. wide. State flower of Montana. Fleshy roots; short stems with short, succulent, strap-shaped leaves to 2 in. long that typically die back before flowers appear (seemingly from bare earth) in spring. Flowers, borne singly on short stems, look like 2-in.-wide water lilies in rosy pink or white. Not difficult if drainage is excellent; risky otherwise.

Lewisia tweedyi

L. tweedyi. Zones A2, A3; 1–7, 14–17. Native to mountains of south central Washington. To 8 in. high, 1 ft. wide. Stunning big, satiny, salmon pink flowers, one to three to a stem, bloom above fleshy, evergreen, 4-in. leaves. Prune out side growth to keep root crown open to air. Winter moisture is a problem; grow plants in pots and turn them on their sides in wet weather.

LEYCESTERIA formosa
HIMALAYAN HONEYSUCKLE, HIMALAYAN PHEASANTBERRY
Caprifoliaceae
DECIDUOUS SHRUB

| 🌡 ZONES 4–6, 14–17, 20–24 |
| ☼ ◐ FULL SUN OR LIGHT SHADE |
| 💧 REGULAR WATER |

Native to Himalayas and western China. Fast-growing shrub to 6 ft. high and wide; the branches do not become woody until their second year. Stems are a handsome gray green when young, later turning bright green. Paired bright green leaves to 6 in. long.

From summer to early fall, inflorescences form at branch tips and in upper leaf joints; the small white flowers are less conspicuous

Leycesteria formosa

than the purplish bracts that partially conceal them. Inflorescences are 1–2 in. long at first, then gradually lengthen to 6 in. Blossoms are followed by berries much appreciated by birds; fruit starts out green but rapidly turns deep red, then purplish black (all three colors are present simultaneously). In cold-winter areas, shoots may freeze back; cut them to the ground in late winter or early spring (regrowth is rapid).

LEYMUS
LYME GRASS, WILD RYE
Poaceae (Gramineae)
PERENNIAL GRASSES

| 🌡 ZONES VARY BY SPECIES |
| ☼ ◐ FULL SUN OR LIGHT SHADE |
| 💧 💧 LITTLE TO MODERATE WATER |

These wild ryes or lyme grasses were formerly assigned to *Elymus* but are now known as *Leymus* (simply an anagram of the former generic name). They are grown principally for their blue-gray or silvery blue foliage. Very drought tolerant; will remain evergreen with some summer water. For other types of blue-leafed grasses, see *Elymus magellanicus, Festuca,* and *Helictotrichon sempervirens.*

L. arenarius (Elymus arenarius). BLUE LYME GRASS. Zones A2, A3; 1–9, 14–24. From coastal northern and western Europe.

Leymus arenarius

Low, vigorous clump of gray-blue leaves topped by clusters of inconspicuous flowers. To 3–4 ft. in bloom, spreading widely by thick rhizomes. Good soil binder; may need curbing. Flowers are not especially attractive, and plant looks best when cut back after bloom to stimulate fresh foliage. Does best in cool weather but withstands considerable heat. Grows in sandy soils in the wild; tolerates clay soils. Often sold as 'Glaucus', which is identical to the species. 'Findhorn' is a compact variety.

L. condensatus. Zones 7–12, 14–24. Native to coastal Southern California and Channel Islands. Basic species is usually green leafed, reaching 9 ft. tall and 6 ft. wide in bloom. More commonly grown is 'Canyon Prince', to 4 ft. tall and 3 ft. wide; its foliage is greenish when new, maturing to brilliant silvery blue. Spreads slowly by rhizomes.

LIATRIS spicata
GAYFEATHER, BLAZING STAR
Asteraceae (Compositae)
PERENNIAL

| 🌡 ZONES A2, A3; 1–10, 14–24 |
| ☼ FULL SUN |
| 💧 REGULAR WATER |

From eastern and central North America. Showy bloomer to 4 ft. tall, 1½ ft. wide. Basal tufts of grassy leaves grow from thick, often tuberous rootstocks. In summer, tufts lengthen into tall stems densely set with leaves and topped by "foxtails" of small light purple

Liatris spicata

flowers with prominent stamens. Blossom spikes open from the top downward. Best-known selection is 'Kobold' (2 ft. tall), with bright rosy lilac flowers. 'Floristan White' (3 ft. tall) is a white-flowered selection. 'Silvertips' (to 2½–3 ft. tall) has lavender flowers with white tips.

Endures heat, cold, aridity, poor soil. Needs moderately fertile,

well-drained soil; sensitive to soggy soil during winter dormancy. Plant in spring, in clumps or drifts; you can start from nursery transplants or set out rootstocks 2 in. deep, 6–8 in. apart. When performance declines, divide clumps in early spring. Often sold as *L. callilepis* by Dutch bulb growers.

LIBERTIA
Iridaceae
PERENNIALS

| 🌡 ZONES 8, 9, 14–24 |
| ☼ ◐ LIGHT SHADE IN HOTTEST CLIMATES |
| 💧 REGULAR WATER |

Iris relatives with swordlike leaves in fans and clusters of white flowers from late spring to midsummer. Blooms consist of three large petals and three much smaller ones, giving them a triangular look.

L. formosa. From Chile. Leathery bright green leaves form a clump 6–18 in. high, 2 ft. wide. Flowering stems to 3 ft. tall carry dense, spikelike clusters of 1¼-in. flowers.

L. grandiflora. From New Zealand. Bright green leaves in a clump 2 ft. high, 1½ ft. wide. Branching clusters of ¾-in. flowers on 2½-ft. stems.

Libertia peregrinans

L. peregrinans. From New Zealand. To 2 ft. high, 1 ft. wide; forms colonies by rhizomes. Narrow, stiffly erect olive green leaves have an orange to brownish orange center stripe; especially attractive when backlit. Branching clusters of inch-wide flowers on stems shorter than leaves. Good in containers. 'Bronze Sword' is more compact at 1–1½ ft. tall.

LIBOCEDRUS. See **CALOCEDRUS**

LIGULARIA

Asteraceae (Compositae)
PERENNIALS

✔ ZONES 1–9, 14–17, EXCEPT AS NOTED
☽ PARTIAL SHADE, EXCEPT AS NOTED
♦ AMPLE MOISTURE

Stately perennials from China and Japan. Form 3-ft.-wide clumps of large leaves topped by daisy-type flowers in yellow to orange. All need rich soil and plenty of moisture; they do not tolerate heat or low humidity. Best with morning or afternoon sun and midday shade; or with dappled shade all day. The more sun they get, the more water they need. Good around pools, along stream beds, in bog gardens. Control slugs and snails. Clumps can remain undisturbed for years; if more plants are needed, divide clumps in early spring.

L. dentata. Grown primarily for big, attractive leaves (to more than a foot across), roundish with heart-shaped base. In midsummer to early fall, sends up 3–5-ft. stems topped by large, branching heads of 4-in.-wide, orange-yellow daisies. 'Othello' (grows in Zones A2, A3; 1–9, 14–17) and 'Desdemona' have deep purple leafstalks, veins, and leaf undersides; upper surfaces of leaves are green.

L. 'Gregynog Gold'. Clump of 4-in.-wide, heart-shaped, toothedged leaves sends up stems to 6 ft. tall. In late summer and fall, stems bear conical clusters of 4-in. yellow flowers.

L. przewalskii. Deeply lobed and cut leaves grow to 1 ft. wide. Dark purplish flowering stalks rise to about 6 ft., topped with dense, narrow spires of ¾-in. yellow daisy flowers in summer. In the Pacific Northwest, can take full sun.

L. stenocephala. Zones A2, A3; 1–9, 14–17. Especially stunning flower spikes. Usually represented by variety 'The Rocket', which forms a large clump of foot-wide, irregularly toothed leaves topped by tall (up to 5-ft.), narrow, darkstemmed spires bearing many ½-in. yellow daisies in summer.

Ligularia stenocephala 'The Rocket'

L. tussilaginea. See Farfugium japonicum

L. wilsoniana. Zones 2–9, 14–17. Bears kidney-shaped leaves that reach 20 in. wide. Stems grow to 6 ft. tall, carry spikes of inchwide yellow daisies in summer.

LIGUSTRUM

PRIVET
Oleaceae
EVERGREEN, SEMIEVERGREEN, AND
DECIDUOUS SHRUBS AND TREES

✔ ZONES VARY BY SPECIES
☀☽ FULL SUN OR PARTIAL SHADE
♦ REGULAR WATER
♦ LEAVES AND FRUITS CAUSE GASTRIC
   DISTRESS IF INGESTED

Most widely used as hedges, though one type is a street tree; can also be clipped into formal shapes and featured in tubs or large pots. All bear abundant, showy clusters of white to creamy white flowers in late spring or early summer (some people find the scent unpleasant). Flowers attract bees. Clipped hedges bloom less heavily, since shearing removes most of the flower-bearing branches. Blossoms are followed by small blue-black berries; birds eat them, thus distributing seeds. Most privets grow well in any soil.

Nurseries sometimes misidentify certain privets. The plant sold as *L. japonicum* very often turns out to be the tree species *L. lucidum*. The true *L. japonicum* is available in two or more forms. The tall, shrubby kind is the true species; the lower-growing and more densely foliaged form is often sold as *L. texanum* but probably should be called *L. japonicum* 'Texanum'.

Smaller-leafed hardy privets used for hedging are also often confused. *L. amurense, L. ovalifolium,* and *L. vulgare* look much alike, and any of these is likely to be sold as "common privet"— a name that rightly belongs only to *L. vulgare*.

L. amurense. AMUR PRIVET. Shrub. Zones A2, A3; 1–24. Deciduous in coldest areas, where it is widely used for hedge and screen planting. Partially evergreen in milder climates but seldom planted there. Native to northern China. Much like *L. ovalifolium* in appearance, but foliage is not as glossy.

L. japonicum. JAPANESE PRIVET, WAX-LEAF PRIVET. Evergreen shrub. Zones 4–24; H1, H2; except as noted. From northern China, Korea, Japan. To 10–12 ft. tall, 8 ft. wide, with dense, compact habit. Roundish oval leaves are 2–4 in. long, with a thick, slightly spongy feel; they are glossy medium to dark green above, distinctly paler to almost whitish beneath. Excellent plant for hedges or screens and for shaping into globes, pyramids, and other shapes. With lower limbs pruned off, also makes an attractive small standard tree. Sunburns in hot spells. In areas where there is hardpan or where Texas root rot prevails, grow it in containers. Often confused with its variety 'Texanum'.

'Recurvifolium'. Leaves are wavy edged, twisted at the tip, and slightly smaller than those of the species. Somewhat open grower.

'Rotundifolium' ('Coriaceum'). To 5 ft. tall and 3 ft. wide, with nearly round leaves to 2½ in. long. Give partial shade in hottest climates.

Ligustrum lucidum

'Silver Star'. To 6–8 ft. tall, 4–6 ft. wide. Deep green leaves with graygreen mottling and startling creamy white edges. Provides a good contrast to deep green foliage.

'Texanum'. Zones 3a–24; H1, H2. Very similar to species but lower growing (to 8–10 ft. tall, 4–6 ft. wide), with somewhat denser, lusher foliage. Useful as a windbreak. This plant is often sold as the species.

'Variegatum'. Leaves have creamy white margins and blotches.

L. lucidum. GLOSSY PRIVET. Evergreen tree. Zones 5–24; H1, H2. Native to China, Korea, Japan. Round-headed tree to 20–40 ft. high and wide, with one or several trunks. Glossy, 4–6-in.-long leaves are tapered and pointed, medium to dark green on both sides. They feel leathery but lack the slightly spongy feel of *L. japonicum* leaves. Flowers bloom in especially large, feathery clusters in late spring and early summer; they are followed by a profuse crop of fruit. Can be used as lawn tree or planted 10 ft. apart for tall privacy screen or windbreak. Performs well in large containers.

Before planting this tree, carefully consider its disadvantages. Eventual fruit crop is immense; never plant where fruit will fall on cars, walks, or other paved areas (it stains). Fallen seeds (and those dropped by birds) sprout profusely in ground covers and will need pulling. Many people dislike the flowers' odor, and fruiting clusters are bare and unattractive after fruit drop.

L. ovalifolium. CALIFORNIA PRIVET. Semievergreen shrub; evergreen only in warmest winter climates. Zones 3b–24; H1, H2. Native to Japan. Dark green, oval, 2½-in. leaves. Grows rapidly to 8–15 ft. tall, 6–10 ft. wide, but can be kept sheared as a 4-ft. hedge. For use as a hedge, set plants 9–12 in. apart. Clip early and frequently to encourage low, dense branching. Greedy roots. Well-fed, wellwatered plants hold their foliage longest. Tolerates heat. 'Aureum', golden privet, has yellow-edged leaves; it is often sold as 'Variegatum'.

L. 'Suwannee River'. Evergreen shrub. Zones 4–24. Reported to be a hybrid between *L. japonicum* 'Rotundifolium' and *L. lucidum*. Slow-growing, compact plant reaches 1½ ft. tall in 3 years, eventually grows 3–4 ft. high and wide. Leathery, somewhat twisted dark green leaves; no fruit. Use as low hedge, as foundation planting, in containers.

L. 'Vicaryi'. VICARY GOLDEN PRIVET. Deciduous shrub. Zones 2–24. To 8–10 ft. high and wide. Yellow leaves; color is most pronounced on plants in full sun. Best planted alone; color does not develop well under hedge shearing.

L

L. vulgare. COMMON PRIVET. Deciduous shrub. Zones 2–24; H1. From northern Europe, Mediterranean, Asia Minor. To 15 ft. tall, 12 ft. wide. Dark green leaves are less glossy than those of *L. ovalifolium,* and root system is not as greedy. Clusters of black fruit are conspicuous on unpruned or lightly pruned plants. 'Lodense' ('Nanum') is a dense dwarf that reaches only 4 ft. high and wide.

LILAC. See **SYRINGA**

LILAC VINE. See **HARDENBERGIA**

LILIUM

LILY
Liliaceae
PERENNIALS FROM BULBS

| 🖊 ZONES VARY BY SPECIES OR TYPE |
| ☀ ☽ ROOTS COOL, TOPS IN SUN OR FILTERED LIGHT |
| 💧 REGULAR WATER, EXCEPT AS NOTED |

Most stately and varied of bulbous plants, ranging in height from 1 to 9 ft. For many years, only the species—the same plants growing wild in parts of Asia, Europe, and North America—were available, and many of these were difficult to grow.

Around 1925, lily growers began a significant breeding program. They bred new hybrids from species with desirable qualities and also developed strains and varieties that were healthier, hardier, and easier to grow than the original species. They produced new forms and new colors; what is more important, they developed methods for growing healthy lilies in large quantities. Today, hybrids and strains typically provide the best garden lilies, but it is still possible to get some easily grown species.

Plant bulbs in fall or spring as soon as possible after you get them. If you must wait, keep them in a cool place briefly until you plant. Don't buy bulbs with dry, withered scales; they won't rehydrate, and their appearance may indicate that the growing tip inside is dead.

Before planting bulbs, remove any injured portions, then let the bulbs callus in a cool place for a few hours before planting. For each bulb, dig a generous planting hole (1 ft. deeper than height of bulb). Place enough soil at bottom of hole to bring it up to proper level for bulb (see next paragraph).

Set bulb with its roots spread; fill in hole with soil, firming it in around bulb to eliminate air pockets. If your area is infested with gophers, you may have to plant each bulb in a 6-in.-square wire basket made of ½-in. hardware cloth. (The depth of the basket will depend on the planting depth.)

Planting depth varies according to size and rooting habits of bulbs. General rule is to bury each bulb 2½ times as deep as its diameter. Planting depth can be quite flexible. It is better to err by planting too shallowly rather than too deeply; lily bulbs have contractile roots that draw them down to proper depth if the soil has been deeply loosened before planting. Ideal spacing for lily bulbs is 1 ft. apart, but you can plant as close as 6 in. for densely massed effect.

Since most lilies never really enter a dormant period, they need moisture year-round; water when the top 2 in. of soil has dried out. Cut back on watering somewhat after tops turn yellow in fall, but never let roots go completely dry. Exceptions to this rule are species native to dry-summer areas with gravelly soils (*L. columbianum, L. humboldtii, L. pardalinum*). These are adapted to dry periods after bloom and will rot if they get too much water.

Flooding is preferable to overhead watering, which can help to spread disease spores and also topple tall lilies when they're in flower. If you use drip irrigation, keep the emitter 8 in. from the stem. Irrigate in the morning, so leaves have time to dry before disease sets in. Pull weeds by hand if possible; hoeing may injure roots. Avoid pre-emergent weed suppressants; they can also suppress lily root growth.

Remove faded flowers to prevent seed formation. Wait until stems and leaves turn yellow before you cut plants back. If clumps become too large and crowded, dig, divide, and transplant them in fall. If you're careful, you can lift lily clumps at any time, even when they are in bloom.

Lilies are fine container plants. Place one bulb in a deep 8-in. pot or five in a 16-in. pot. A half oak barrel can easily handle a dozen bulbs. Plant at the same depth required for planting in the ground (as described previously). Place bulbs with roots spread and pointing downward, fill the container with soil, and gently hand-pack it until the soil surface is firm. Leave

an inch of space between surface of soil and rim of pot for watering. Water thoroughly and place in a cool room, a garage, or a greenhouse that is heated (in colder climates) just enough to keep out frost. During root-forming period, water whenever the top 2 in. of soil dries out. Move pots to a partially shaded area during blooming period if temperatures rise above 90°F/32°C. Later, if you wish to repot bulbs, do so in late fall.

Incurable viral infection troubles lilies. To avoid the problem, buy healthy bulbs from reliable sources. Dig and destroy any lilies that display mottled leaves or seriously stunted growth (unless those problems are linked to hail or other severe weather). Control aphids, which spread the infection. Reduce risk of botrytis blight (a fungal disease) by maintaining good air circulation around plants; don't let dense foliage surround lilies. Botrytis can be controlled with a fungicide and by keeping lily foliage dry; if you've struggled with botrytis in the past, spray the ground with fungicide as new lilies emerge in spring.

Although the official classification of lilies lists eight divisions of hybrids and a ninth division of

Lilium columbianum

species, the following describes just the lilies ordinarily available to Western gardeners. Advances in breeding continue to produce new lilies faster than books can list them. Consult specialists' catalogs to learn about these wonders.

ASIATIC HYBRIDS
Zones A1–A3; 1–9, 14–24. Derived primarily from Chinese species. These are easy to grow and the most reliable for the average garden; they are also the earliest to bloom (early summer). Flowers are usually unscented. Some of the hybrids have upward-facing flowers, while others have horizontally held or drooping blooms. Stems are strong, erect, and range in height from short (1½ ft.) to moderate (4½ ft.). Flowers come in virtually every color but blue. Many have dark spots or contrasting bands of color.

AURELIAN HYBRIDS (TRUMPET LILIES)
Zones 3–9, 14–24. Derived from Asiatic species such as *L. henryi* and *L. regale* (but not *L. auratum* or *L. speciosum*). Midsummer bloomers with trumpet- or bowl-shaped flowers, usually scented. Blossoms range in color from white and cream through yellow and pink, many with green, brown, or purple shading on their outer surfaces. Plants are typically 3–6 ft. tall; each stem carries 6–15 flowers. Examples include 'Copper King', with rich melon blooms; 'Golden Splendor', deep gold with maroon striping on petal backs; the Pink Perfection strain; and 'Ortega', an ivory white flower with a cinnamon lined, buttery yellow throat.

ORIENTAL HYBRIDS
Zones 1–9, 14–22. The most exotic of the hybrids, bred primarily from Japanese species. Bloom midsummer to early fall, with big (to 9-in.), fragrant flowers of white or pink, often banded with gold or red on the center of each petal, and spotted with red. Most are 3–5 ft. tall, with flowers that face upward or outward (a few have nodding blooms). If you live where summer temperatures routinely rise above 90°F/32°C, plant these in dappled afternoon shade. Examples are 'Casablanca' (pure white), 'Acapulco' (hot pink), and 'Stargazer' (rose red with white margins).

NTERDIVISIONAL HYBRIDS
During the past few years,
reeders have accomplished con-
iderable hybridization between
divisions, resulting in the two
main groups described below.
One of the best lilies ever, 'Black
Beauty' (with deep maroon, white-
dged petals that are strongly
ecurved), is an interdivisional
ybrid, but its exact parentage is
unknown. In addition to the fol-
owing two categories, work is
eing done on Oriental-Asiatic
ybrids, which have an Easter lily
hape, light fragrance, and gener-
lly softer colors than LA hybrids.

OT hybrids (also called
Orienpets). Zones 1–9, 14–23.
Descended from Oriental and
rumpet lilies. These heavy-
temmed lilies grow 3–5 ft. tall.
They tolerate a little more heat
nd demand less winter chill than
heir Oriental parents, and most
ave a light, sweet fragrance with
emony overtones. The color range
s mostly in shades of yellow but
lso includes reds and pinks;
whites should be available soon.
Examples include 'Conca d'Or'
heady perfume), lemon yellow
etals with pale edges; 'Sweet-
eart', a mango yellow flower with
bright red splotch covering most
f the middle of each petal; and
Vice Versa', a solid coral red.

LA hybrids. Zones A2, A3; 1–9,
4–24. Hybrids between Easter
ilies (L. longiflorum) and Asiatic
ybrid lilies. These plants grow
quickly to 3–4 ft., bloom early, and
ake great cut flowers. Blooms
ace up and are available in yellow,
ink, red, white, and orange.

Examples include 'Royal Sunset'
(pink with soft yellow center),
'Red Alert' (deep, shiny red), and
'Auckland' (white). 'Dipo Lolo' (soft
pink flowers) is a 1½-ft. dwarf
that's perfect for pots. LA hybrids
are among the best-performing
lilies for Southern California.

SPECIES AND VARIANTS
A number of excellent species
lilies are listed below. Those
described as having Turk's cap
flowers bear blooms with strongly
recurved petals.

L. amabile. Zones 2b–9, 14–17.
Native to Korea. To 3 ft. tall, with
one to five flowers per stem in
early summer. Orange-red Turk's
cap blossoms with dark purple
spots. Scent is slightly unpleasant.
Tolerates alkaline soils.

L. auratum. GOLD-BAND
LILY. Zones 1–7, 14–17. Native to
Japan. To 4–6 ft. tall. Very fragrant
white flowers with crimson spots
and gold band are carried 6–30
per stem. Blooms in late summer.

Lilium auratum

L. cernuum. Zones 1–9, 14–24.
Native to Korea, Manchuria,
Siberia. Summer bloomer only
12–20 in. high, with fragrant lilac-
colored flowers often dotted in
darker purple. Usually bears up
to six blossoms per stem. Needs
sandy soil.

L. columbianum. COLUMBIA
LILY, TIGER LILY. Zones 2–7,
14–19. Native from British Columbia to Northern California. To 5–
6 ft. tall, with one to six small,
golden orange, unscented lilies
per stem in midsummer.

L. henryi. Zones 1–10, 14–21;
H1. Native to China. Slender stems
to 8–9 ft., each topped by 10–20
barely scented, bright orange
Turk's cap flowers. Summer bloom.
Does best in light shade in all
regions.

L. humboldtii. HUMBOLDT
LILY. Zones 3, 7, 14–24. Native to
open woodlands of the Sierra
Nevada. To 3–6 ft. tall. Unscented,
nodding Turk's cap blooms are
bright orange with large maroon
dots; early summer bloom.
L. h. ocellatum is similar, but its
maroon dots are margined in red.

L. lankongense. Zones 2b–24.
Alpine native of China. To 3–5 ft.
tall, spreading by stoloniferous
stems. Powerfully fragrant Turk's
cap flowers in rose red with purple
spots, carried up to 15 per stem.
Midsummer bloom. Tolerates
alkaline soils. Many consider this
the most beautiful lily.

L. leucanthum centifolium.
Zones 2–9, 14–24. Native to China.
To 7–8 ft. tall. Up to 18 fragrant,
white, midsummer flowers with
external purple-red streaks.

Funnel-shaped blooms, slightly
pendulous. The most common
selection is 'Black Dragon', which
has white petals shaded pale
yellow inside, brownish maroon
outside.

L. longiflorum. EASTER LILY.
Zones 2–9, 14–24; H1. Native to
Japan, Taiwan. Up to six trumpet-
shaped, very fragrant white
flowers on each short stem.
Usually purchased in bloom at
Easter. Stems will die down. Plant
may rebloom in fall; in 1 or 2
years, will likely begin flowering
in midsummer, its normal bloom
season. Recent hybridization has
yielded pink, red, and yellow
types.

L. martagon. TURK'S CAP
LILY. Zones 1–10, 14–17. Native
from Europe to Mongolia. To 3–5 ft.
tall. In midsummer, each stem
bears up to 50 pendent flowers
1–2 in. across with sharply
recurved petals. Blossoms are typically purplish pink with darker
spots, but darker colored and pure
white variants exist. Easy to grow
but slow to establish; eventually
forms big clumps.

L. pardalinum. LEOPARD
LILY. Zones 2–7, 14–17. Native
from southwestern Oregon to
Southern California. To 4–8 ft. tall,
with unscented Turk's cap flowers
in orange or red orange shading
to yellow, with brown spotting in
center. Up to 10 flowers per stem.
Blooms in late spring or early
summer.

L. pumilum. CORAL LILY.
Zones 1–10, 14–24. Native to
northern China, Mongolia, Siberia.
To 1–1½ ft. high, with up to

L

TOP: Asiatic hybrid lily 'Orange Mountain' BOTTOM: OT hybrid lily 'Conca d'Or'

TOP: Aurelian hybrid lily 'Golden Splendor' BOTTOM: *Lilium longiflorum*

TOP: Oriental hybrid lily 'Casablanca' BOTTOM: *Lilium martagon*

TOP: Interdivisional hybrid 'Black Beauty' BOTTOM: *Lilium pardalinum*

TOP: *Lilium henryi* BOTTOM: *Lilium regale*

Dianna Gibson on Fragrant Lilies

Erstwhile perfume merchant and founder of B & D Lilies in Port Townsend, Washington, Dianna Gibson has definite opinions about lily fragrance.

"The Oriental hybrid lilies smell spicy, like carnations," she says. "The trumpets (Aurelian hybrids) have an intense floral scent, like Grandma's perfume." That makes both lily types effective along walkways or beside patios, where breezes waft the scent through the garden.

But indoors, the scent of either kind can be overpowering. That's where Oriental-trumpet (OT) hybrids come in. Gibson thinks they have the most pleasing fragrance for the vase: the scent is "lighter than either parent, with a hint of lemon."

Gibson's fragrance favorites? Of the Orientals, two stand out: 'Casablanca' and 'Acapulco'. Among the trumpets, she likes 'Ortega' and the Pink Perfection strain. And of the OT hybrids, 'Conca d'Or' and 'Sweetheart' have the fragrances she likes the best.

Lilium pumilum

20 fragrant red Turk's cap flowers per stem. Blooms in early summer.

L. regale. REGAL LILY. Zones 1–9, 14–24. Native to western China. Popular and easy to grow. Stems to 6 ft. tall; in midsummer, each bears up to 25 fragrant, funnel-shaped white blossoms flushed purple outside; carried horizontally.

L. speciosum. Zones 1–7, 14–17. Native to China, Japan, Taiwan. To 3–5 ft. tall. Large, wide, fragrant Turk's cap flowers are white, heavily suffused with rose pink and sprinkled with raised crimson dots. Usually up to 12 flowers per stem. Blooms in late summer. *L. s. album* has pure white blooms, *L. s. rubrum* red ones. 'Uchida' is the most popular selection; it has white-edged pink blooms with deep pink speckles and red anthers.

LILLY-PILLY TREE. See **ACMENA smithii**

LILY. See **LILIUM**

LILY-OF-THE-NILE. See **AGAPANTHUS**

LILY-OF-THE-VALLEY. See **CONVALLARIA majalis**

LILY-OF-THE-VALLEY SHRUB. See **PIERIS japonica**

LILY-OF-THE-VALLEY TREE. See **CLETHRA arborea, CRINODENDRON patagua**

LILY TURF. See **LIRIOPE, OPHIOPOGON**

LIME. See **CITRUS**

LIMEQUAT. See **CITRUS: Kumquat hybrids**

LIMNANTHES douglasii
MEADOWFOAM, POACHED EGGS
Limnanthaceae
ANNUAL

| 🌿 ZONES 1–9, 14–24 |
| ☀ FULL SUN |
| 💧 REGULAR WATER |

Native to wet meadows and other damp, sunny locales in California and southwestern Oregon. Pro-

Limnanthes douglasii

duces a blanket of flowers in spring; can be coaxed into a longer bloom period if given some supplemental water as the ground starts drying out later in spring. Grows 6–12 in. tall and broad, with yellowish green, finely divided leaves and clusters of inch-wide flowers. Blossoms may be white or yellow but are most commonly yellow with white petal tips. Sow seeds in fall or earliest spring. Plants self-sow where adapted.

LIMONIUM
STATICE, SEA LAVENDER
Plumbaginaceae
PERENNIALS AND ANNUALS

| 🌿 ZONES VARY BY SPECIES |
| ☀ FULL SUN |
| 💧 MODERATE WATER |

Large, leathery, green basal leaves contrast with airy clusters of tiny, delicate flowers on nearly leafless, many-branched stems. The flowers consist of two parts: an outer, papery envelope (the calyx) and an inner part (the corolla). Calyx and corolla are often of different colors. Flowers are good for cutting and keep their color when dried. Plants tolerate heat and many kinds of soil but need good drainage. They often self-sow. For spring and summer bloom of annual kinds, sow indoors and move to garden when weather warms up. Or sow outdoors in early spring for later bloom.

L. gmelinii. Perennial. Zones 1–10, 14–24. From eastern Europe, Siberia. Much like a slightly smaller *L. platyphyllum*, with 5-in. basal leaves and widely branching clusters of blue flowers in mid- to late summer.

L. perezii. Perennial. Zones 13, 15–17, 20–24. Native to the Canary Islands. Often freezes in Zones 14, 18, 19. To 3 ft. tall, with flower clusters spreading nearly as wide. Calyx is rich purple, corolla white. Long spring and summer bloom. Leaves up to 1 ft. long, including stalks. First-rate beach plant. Often naturalizes in coastal Southern California. Damaged at 25°F/–4°C but useful even where it freezes out occasionally; nursery-grown seedlings develop quickly. Needs afternoon shade in Zone 13.

L. platyphyllum (L. latifolium). Perennial. Zones 1–10, 14–24; H1. Native to central and southeastern Europe. Vigorous plant to 2½ ft. tall, covered in a haze of flowers up to 3 ft. wide in

Limonium perezii

summer. Calyx is white, corolla bluish; pure white and pink kinds exist. Smooth-edged leaves to 10 in. long.

L. sinuatum. Annual. All zones. Mediterranean native widely grown for use as a cut flower in both fresh and dried arrangements. To 1½ ft. tall and 1 ft. wide, with basal leaves lobed nearly to midrib and flower stems distinctly winged. Calyx is blue, lavender, or rose; corolla is white. Improved garden strains come in many colors, including yellow, apricot, orange, peach, rose, light blue, deep blue, purple, and white.

L. suworowii. See Psylliostachys suworowii

L. tataricum. See Goniolimon tataricum

L. vulgare. Perennial. Zones 4–9, 14–24. Native to British Isles and coastal regions of Western Europe, Mediterranean, and North Africa. Grows 1–2 ft. tall and wide. Dainty lavender blooms appear in summer on branched stems held above foliage. Leaves are narrowly oval, with pointed tips, reaching 6–8 in. long. Division is difficult; best to grow from seed or root cuttings.

LINANTHUS grandiflorus
MOUNTAIN PHLOX
Polemoniaceae
ANNUAL

| 🌿 ZONES 1–9, 14–24 |
| ☀ FULL SUN |
| 💧 LITTLE OR NO WATER TO MODERATE WATER |

Native to Northern California, this phlox relative somewhat resembles annual phlox (*Phlox drummondii*), bearing heads of inch-wide, pink-tinged white or lavender-pink blossoms with yellow throats. Good cut flower. Plant grows to 2 ft. tall, 1 ft. wide. Sow seeds in fall or earliest spring. In cooler areas, needs little

Linanthus grandiflorus

or no water for spring bloom; in warmer regions, give occasional irrigation.

LINARIA
TOADFLAX
Scrophulariaceae
ANNUALS AND PERENNIALS

- ZONES 1-24, EXCEPT AS NOTED
- FULL SUN OR LIGHT SHADE
- REGULAR WATER

Brightly colored blooms like small, spurred snapdragons (*Antirrhinum*). Medium green, very narrow leaves. Easy to grow. Best in masses; individual plants are rather wispy.

L. cymbalaria. See Cymbalaria muralis

L. Fantasy Hybrids. Annuals. Compact plants 1 ft. tall or less and 6–8 in. wide, with very narrow bluish green leaves. Clusters of small (½–1-in.) flowers in spring and summer. 'Fantasy Blue' has bright blue flowers with a touch of yellow in the throat. Other selections are available in magenta, pink, yellow, and white.

L. maroccana. BABY SNAP-DRAGON, TOADFLAX. Annual. From Morocco. Grows to 1½–2 ft.

Linaria maroccana

high, 6 in. wide. Summer flowers in red-and-gold, rose, pink, mauve, chamois, blue, violet, or purple, blotched with a different shade on the lip. Spur is longer than flower. Northern Lights strain offers shades of red, orange, and yellow as well as bicolors. Fairy Bouquet strain is only 9 in. tall and has larger flowers in pastel shades. For a showy display, sow seeds in quantity in early spring, after danger of frost is past. In Zones 10–13, sow in fall for winter bloom.

L. purpurea. Perennial. Zones 2–10, 14–24. From southern Europe. Narrow, bushy, erect growth to 2½–3 ft. high, 1 ft. wide. Blue-green foliage; violet-blue flowers from spring to late fall. 'Canon Went' is a pink form.

L. reticulata. Annual. From Portugal, North Africa. To 2–4 ft. tall, 10 in. wide, with very narrow bluish green leaves and showers of small purple-and-orange flowers in late spring and summer. 'Flamenco' (1–1½ ft. high) has yellow flowers with a conspicuous maroon blotch.

LINDEN. See TILIA

LINDERA
SPICEBUSH
Lauraceae
DECIDUOUS SHRUBS OR TREES

- ZONES VARY BY SPECIES
- FULL SUN OR PARTIAL SHADE
- REGULAR WATER

Spicebushes are grown principally for the beauty of their fall foliage; early spring clusters of small, greenish yellow flowers on leafless shoots are attractive but not conspicuous. On female plants, fruits will follow the blossoms if a male plant is nearby. Best used at woodland edge or as space fillers. Need good drainage; tolerate some drought. The common name refers to the spicy odor of the crushed leaves.

L. benzoin. Zones 2–6. Native to woodlands in eastern U.S. Reaches 6–12 ft. tall and broad. Light green leaves are 3–5 in. long, half as wide. Yellow fall color and plant form are best in full sun; if grown in shade, foliage color isn't as pronounced and habit is loose and open. Fruits (noticeable after leaf fall) are bright red, to ½ in. long.

L. obtusiloba. JAPANESE SPICEBUSH. Zones 3b–6, 14–17. Native to Japan, China, Korea. To 10–20 ft. tall and a little narrower.

Leaves are 5 in. long, 4 in. wide, occasionally lobed near the tip to give leaf a mitten shape. Fall color is an exceptionally brilliant yellow that develops even in shade and holds for 2 weeks or more. Small (¼-in.-wide) red fruits eventually turn black.

Lindera obtusiloba

LINGONBERRY. See VACCINIUM vitis-idaea minus

LINNAEA borealis
TWINFLOWER
Caprifoliaceae
PERENNIAL

- ZONES A1–A3; 1, 2, 4–6, 14–17
- PARTIAL OR FULL SHADE
- REGULAR WATER

Native to much of North America; in the West, found from Northern California to Alaska and Idaho.

Linnaea borealis

Delicate, flat mats of evergreen, 1-in., glossy green leaves spread to about 3 ft. by runners. Blooms in summer, carrying pairs of pale pink or rosy pink, fragrant, trumpet-shaped, ⅓-in.-long flowers on 3–4-in. stems. Collector's item or

small-scale ground cover for woodland garden. Keep area around plants mulched with leaf mold to induce spreading. Tolerates sun in cool-summer climates.

LINUM
FLAX
Linaceae
PERENNIALS AND ANNUALS

- ZONES VARY BY SPECIES
- FULL SUN
- MODERATE WATER

Plants with erect, branching stems and narrow leaves produce an abundance of shallow-cupped, five-petaled flowers over a long bloom period. Each bloom lasts only a day, but others keep coming. The flax of commerce—*L. usitatissimum*—is grown for its fiber and seeds, which yield linseed oil.

Use in borders; some naturalize freely in uncultivated areas. Light, well-drained soil. Most perennial kinds live only 3 or 4 years and should be replaced regularly. Easy to grow from seed; perennials also can be propagated from cuttings. Difficult to divide.

L. flavum. GOLDEN FLAX. Perennial. Zones 2–24. From central and southern Europe. To 12–15 in. high, 1 ft. wide, with somewhat woody base. Grooved branches, green leaves. Spring and summer flowers are golden yellow, about 1 in. wide, carried in many-branched clusters. Often called yellow flax—a name correctly applied to the closely related *Reinwardtia indica*. 'Compactum' is just 6 in. high and wide.

L. grandiflorum. FLOWERING FLAX. Annual. Zones 1–24. From North Africa. To 1½–2½ ft. tall and 6–12 in. wide, with narrow gray-green leaves. Summer flowers are rose pink, 1–1½ in. wide. Sow seed thickly in place in early spring or (in mild-winter climates) in fall. Self-sows without becoming a pest and is often included in wildflower mixes. Two selections far more common than the species are: 'Rubrum', scarlet flax, with bright red flowers; and 'Bright Eyes', bearing white flowers with a brownish red eye.

L. narbonense. Perennial. Zones 3–24. Wiry-stemmed Mediterranean native to 2 ft. tall, 1½ ft. wide. Narrow blue-green leaves. Open clusters of 1¾-in., azure blue flowers with white eye; blooms in late spring and early summer. 'Six Hills' has rich sky blue blossoms.

L

L. perenne. PERENNIAL BLUE FLAX. Perennial. Zones 2–24. Native Europe to central Asia. Most vigorous blue-flowered flax, to 2 ft. tall, 1½ ft. wide. Stems are usually leafless on lower part. Profuse bloomer, producing branching clusters of light blue flowers that close in shade or late in the day. Blooms in late spring and summer. Self-sows freely.

Linum perenne

LION'S TAIL.
See **LEONOTIS leonurus**

LIPPIA citriodora.
See **ALOYSIA triphylla**

LIPPIA repens.
See **PHYLA nodiflora**

LIQUIDAMBAR

SWEET GUM
Hamamelidaceae
DECIDUOUS TREES

🌡 ZONES VARY BY SPECIES
☀ FULL SUN
💧 MODERATE TO REGULAR WATER

Valuable for form, foliage, fall color, easy culture. Moderate growth rate. Young and middle-aged trees are generally upright, somewhat cone shaped; older ones have a more spreading habit. Lobed, maplelike leaves. Flowers are inconspicuous; fruits are spiny balls that ornament trees in winter, must be raked up throughout the year.

Give neutral or slightly acid, well-amended garden soil; chlorosis in strongly alkaline soil is hard to correct (the reason why none of these trees is recommended for desert zones). Trees branch from the ground up and look most natural that way, but lower limbs can be removed to expose a definite trunk. To develop a strong central leader on young trees, pinch back side branches. Without proper training in youth, trees can develop weak branching pattern.

Mature trees need little or no pruning.

Good street trees only if given a wide parking strip in which to grow: their surface roots can crack sidewalks, create a nuisance in lawns. Round, spiny seedpods are hard enough to damage bicycle tires. Effective planted 6–10 ft. apart to form tall screens or groves. Brilliant fall foliage (color is less effective in mildest climates or in mild, late autumns).

L. formosana. CHINESE SWEET GUM. Zones 4–9, 14–24. Native to China. To 40–60 ft. tall, 25 ft. wide. Free-form outline; sometimes pyramidal, especially when young. Three- to five-lobed leaves are 3–4½ in. across, violet red when expanding, maturing to deep green. Fall color ranges from red in northern part of range to yellow beige in Southern California. Leaves drop late, usually in early winter. 'Afterglow' has lavender-purple new growth, rosy red fall color.

L. orientalis. ORIENTAL SWEET GUM. Zones 5–9, 14–24. Native to Turkey. To 20–30 ft. tall and wide. Leaves 2–3 in. wide, deeply five lobed, each lobe again lobed to give a lacy effect. Leafs out early after short dormant period. Fall color varies from deep gold and bright red in cooler areas to dull brownish purple in coastal Southern California. Resistant to oak root fungus.

L. styraciflua. AMERICAN SWEET GUM. Zones 3–9, 14–24. Native to eastern U.S. About 60 ft. tall in gardens; much taller in the wild. Narrow and erect in youth, with lower limbs eventually spreading to 20–25 ft. Tolerates damp soil; resists oak root fungus. Good looking all year. Branching pattern, furrowed bark, and corky wings on twigs all provide winter interest, as do hanging seedpods— 1½-in., spiky spheres reminiscent of tiny medieval maces. On mature trees, seedpods are profuse enough to cause a litter problem (especially on lawns, where they interfere with mowing), and they're painful to walk on in bare feet.

Five- to seven-lobed, 3–7-in.-wide leaves are deep green in

Liquidambar styraciflua

spring and summer, turning to purple, yellow, or red in fall. Even seedling trees usually give good fall color, though color may vary somewhat from year to year. To get desired and uniform color, purchase budded trees of a named variety, preferably while they are in fall leaf. Good selections include the following. (Note that 'Burgundy', 'Festival', and 'Palo Alto' were developed in California and color better there than in the Northwest.)

'Aurora'. Compact, pyramidal grower to 30 ft. tall and 10–15 ft. wide. Outstanding fall colors of yellow, orange, red, and purple, even in warm-winter regions.

'Burgundy'. Deep purple-red fall color. Foliage hangs on late into winter—or even into early spring if storms are not heavy.

'Cherokee'. Produces very few or no seedpods. Fall color is burgundy red (yellow on trees grown in shade).

'Festival'. Narrow, columnar. Light green foliage turns a combination of yellow, peach, pink, orange, and red in fall.

'Golden Treasure'. Deep green leaves bordered in gold. In fall, gold rim lightens to pale yellow, then white; green center turns burgundy.

'Palo Alto'. Orange-red to bright red fall color.

'Rotundiloba'. Leaves have rounded rather than sharp-pointed lobes. Sets no seedpods. Fall colors are yellow, red, burgundy, and purple.

'Variegata'. Green leaves with yellow streaks and splotches. In fall, the yellow variegation turns pink; green part of leaf becomes red.

'Worplesdon'. Narrow-lobed leaves turn orange red in fall.

LIRIODENDRON tulipifera

TULIP TREE
Magnoliaceae
DECIDUOUS TREE

🌡 ZONES 2–12, 14–24
☀ FULL SUN
💧 REGULAR WATER

Eastern U.S. native. Fast growth to 60–80 ft., eventually spreading to 40 ft. wide; considerably larger in

the wild. Straight, columnar trunk with spreading, rising branches that form a tall, pyramidal crown. The 5–6-in. leaves are unique; variously described as lyre shaped, saddle shaped, or truncated, they're like blunt-tipped maple leaves missing the end lobe. Foliage turns from bright yellow green to bright yellow in fall. (This is one of the best deciduous trees for Southern California, where it turns yellow most autumns.) Tulip-shaped, 2-in.-wide flowers in late spring are greenish yellow, orange at base; they are handsome at close range but not showy on the tree, since they are carried high up and well concealed by leaves. Trees usually do not bloom until they are 12 to 15 years old.

Liriodendron tulipifera

Thrives in deep, rich, well-drained, neutral to slightly acid soil. Give this tree plenty of room to grow; it makes a good large shade or lawn tree. Wide-spreading network of shallow, fleshy roots, however, makes it difficult to garden under. Control scale insects and aphids as necessary. Immune to oak root fungus.

Nurseries may carry two selections that are slower growing and somewhat smaller than the species. Columnar 'Arnold' ('Fastigiata') reaches about 10–15 ft. wide; it will bloom just 2 to 3 years after planting. 'Aureomarginatum' ('Majestic Beauty') has yellow-edged leaves.

LIRIOPE

LILY TURF
Liliaceae
PERENNIALS

🌡 ZONES VARY BY SPECIES
☀ ◑ ● SOME SHADE IN HOTTEST CLIMATES
💧 REGULAR WATER

These popular and durable plants from Asia form tufts of evergreen grasslike leaves and bear summer flowers in spikelike or branched clusters. Blossoms come in white and various shades of purple; some are quite showy. Last well in flower arrangements. Use as casual ground cover in small areas. Also attractive as borders along paths, between flower bed and lawn, among rock groupings, or in rock gardens. Grow well along streams and around garden pools. They compete well with roots of other plants; try them under bamboo or to cover bare soil at bases of trees or shrubs (either in the ground or in large containers). None is satisfactory as mowed lawn. Tolerate indoor conditions. For a closely related plant that is not quite as cold-hardy, see *Ophiopogon*.

Provide filtered sun to full shade; can take full sun in cool-summer regions. Plant in well-drained soil. Become ragged and brown with neglect. Cut back shaggy old foliage after new leaves appear. Plants don't need heavy feeding. To increase, divide in early spring before new growth starts. These plants aren't usually attractive to deer, but they do need protection from snails and slugs.

Plants look best from spring until cold winter weather arrives. Extended freezes may cause them to turn yellow; they take quite a while to recover. Can show tip burn on leaves if soil contains excess salts or if plants are kept too wet where drainage is poor.

L. muscari. BIG BLUE LILY TURF. Zones 2b–10, 14–24; H1, H2. Forms large clumps 1–1½ ft. tall and eventually a bit wider—but does not spread by underground stems. Loose growth habit, with arching, typically dark green leaves to 2 ft. or longer, ½–¾ in. wide. Dense, spikelike, 6–8-in. flower clusters reminiscent of grape hyacinth (*Muscari*) blooms appear on 5–12-in. stems. Flowers are held above the foliage on young plants, partly hidden by leaves on older ones. Round, shiny

Liriope muscari

black fruits follow flowers. The following are among the best varieties; all grow 12–15 in. tall unless otherwise noted.

'Big Blue'. To 18 in. tall. Stiffly arching, narrow leaves; dark violet flowers. Does well even in dry shade.

'Gold Band'. Broad green leaves are edged with bright gold. Lavender flower spikes are held well above foliage.

'John Burch'. Broad yellow-green leaves with creamy yellow margins. Large flower spikes like lavender cockscombs stand well above the foliage. Performs best in full sun.

'Lilac Beauty'. Dark green leaves; pale violet flowers.

'Majestic'. To 1½ ft. high. Somewhat open growing clumps. Blooms heavily, bearing large (up to 10-in.-long) clusters of dark violet blossoms resembling cockscombs; flowers are held well above the leaves on young plants.

'Monroe's White'. Broad leaves. Large white flower spikes stand well above foliage. Fruit is purple. Prefers more shade than most types.

'Pee Dee Ingot' ('Pee Dee Gold Ingot'). To 10–12 in. tall. New growth emerges bright gold in spring, ages to chartreuse. Purple flowers show up well against foliage.

'Royal Purple'. Similar to 'Majestic' but with deeper purple flowers.

'Silvery Sunproof'. Strong, open, vertical growth. Medium green leaves have gold stripes that age to white; whole leaf is whiter in sun, more yellow or green in shade. Lilac flowers are held well above foliage. One of the best for full sun and for flowers.

'Variegata'. Forms loose, soft clumps. Leaves are green with yellow edges when new, then turn solid dark green in second season. Violet flowers are held well above the leaves. May be sold as *Ophiopogon jaburan* 'Variegatus'.

L. spicata. CREEPING LILY TURF. Zones 3–10, 14–24; H1, H2. Dense ground cover that grows 8–9 in. high and spreads widely by underground stems; can be invasive. Deep green, grasslike leaves are just ¼ in. wide. Foliage is not as upright as that of *L. muscari*. Pale lilac to white flowers appear in spikelike clusters barely taller than the leaves. Set plants 1 ft. apart for quick cover. For best effect, mow yearly in early spring, before new growth emerges. In Northwest, suffers less winter

damage than *L. muscari*. 'Silver Dragon' is slower growing and has a somewhat sparser habit, its leaves are striped in silvery white, and its pale purple flowers are held on short spikes; it makes a fine ground cover for shade.

LISIANTHUS.
See **EUSTOMA grandiflorum**

LITCHI
LITCHI NUT, LYCHEE
Sapindaceae
EVERGREEN TREE

- ⚘ ZONES 21–24; H1, H2
- ☼ FULL SUN
- ⬤ REGULAR WATER

From China and known botanically as *Litchi chinensis*. Slow-growing, round-topped tree to 20–40 ft. tall and wide. Leathery leaves are coppery red when new, maturing to dark green; each has three to nine 3–6-in.-long leaflets. Tiny cream-colored flowers bloom in late spring. Usually self-fruitful, though an individual tree may set more male flowers than female ones, reducing fruit production.

Litchi

Allow fruit to ripen on the tree; when warty, brittle, easy-to-peel rind turns from green to red, fruit is ready to harvest. The smooth, white, edible portion inside looks somewhat like a grape but has a pit in the middle. The most desirable varieties have a small or shriveled seed known as a chicken tongue. Fruit of all types is sweet—juicy when fresh, raisin-like when dried. Varieties include small-pitted 'Groff', 'Kaimana' (the best variety for Hawaii), and 'Kwai Mi' ('Mauritius'). 'Sweet Cliff' has a small to medium-size seed; the slightly more acidic 'Brewster' has a large one.

Litchi needs a frost-free site, acid soil, moist atmosphere, light

nitrogen fertilizer. Has fruited in a few coastal areas of Southern California; reliable in Hawaii.

LITHOCARPUS
Fagaceae
EVERGREEN TREES

- ⚘ ZONES VARY BY SPECIES
- ☼ ☼ FULL SUN OR LIGHT SHADE
- ⬤ MODERATE WATER

Genus of oaklike trees and shrubs, mostly from East and Southeast Asia but with one species from the western U.S. Grown primarily for their attractive foliage. They provide a stately presence in garden or open woodland settings. Provide well-drained soil.

Lithocarpus densiflorus

L. densiflorus. TANBARK OAK. Zones 4–7, 14–24. Native to Coast Ranges from southern Oregon to Santa Barbara, California. To 40–80 ft. tall, 30–50 ft. wide. Tree reaches taller end of height range under forest conditions; in the open, it is lower growing and broader, with the lower branches sometimes touching the ground. Leathery, 1½–4-in.-long, sharply toothed leaves are covered with whitish or yellowish wool when they expand, then mature to smooth green above, gray green beneath. Tiny, whitish male flowers in large, branched clusters bloom in summer, giving off an odd odor that some people find offensive. Acorns in burlike cups. As street or lawn tree, it resembles holly oak (*Quercus ilex*) but has lusher foliage. *L. d. echinoides* is a shrub 3–10 ft. tall and wide; its bluish leaves are smaller than those of the species and bear few or no teeth.

Sudden oak death, caused by a fungus called *Phytophthora ramorum*, is decimating tanbark oak trees throughout their native range; many oak species are also susceptible. To learn more about this disease, see *Quercus*. See also page 574.

L. edulis (Pasania edulis). JAPANESE FALSE OAK. Zones 7, 9, 14–24. From Japan. To 25–45 ft. tall and wide, with smooth grayish bark and leathery, glossy green leaves 3–6 in. long. Differs from oak *(Quercus)* in having male catkins that are erect (instead of drooping) and acorns that are tightly clustered in groups (instead of solitary or paired). The inch-long acorns have edible kernels. Susceptibility to sudden oak death is unknown.

LITHODORA diffusa
Boraginaceae
PERENNIAL

| 🌿 ZONES 5–7, 14–17 |
| ☼ ☽ LIGHT SHADE IN HOTTEST CLIMATES |
| 💧 MODERATE WATER |

Native to southern and western Europe. Forms a prostrate, somewhat woody, slightly mounded mass 6–12 in. high, 3–4 ft. wide. Narrow evergreen leaves are ¾–1 in. long; both foliage and stems are hairy. In late spring (and often later), plant is sprinkled with brilliant blue, tubular, ½-in.-long flowers. Give loose, well-drained, lime-free soil. Use in rock gardens, spilling over walls, as small-scale ground cover.

Lithodora diffusa

Best suited to mild-summer climates. 'Heavenly Blue' and 'Grace Ward' are the forms most commonly seen. 'Star' ('Blue Star') has white-edged blue blossoms. The plant was formerly called *Lithospermum diffusum* or *L. prostratum*.

LITHOPS
STONEFACE
Aizoaceae
SUCCULENT PERENNIALS

| 🌿 ZONES 12, 13; OR INDOORS |
| ☼ FULL SUN; BRIGHT SUNNY WINDOW |
| 💧 LITTLE WATER |

Of the so-called living rocks or pebble plants of South Africa, these are among the best known. Shaped like inverted cones 2–4 in. high; tops resemble stones with a fissure across the middle. Colors

Lithops

include gray and gray green, often mottled with tan or brown. During bloom season, a single stemless flower emerges from the fissure; blossom resembles an ice plant flower and is typically yellow or white. New leaves also emerge from fissure. Many species are available, all of them interesting. Grow in pots of fast-draining soil mix. Can be grown outdoors year-round in the warmest desert regions. There, they bloom in winter and go dormant in summer. Indoors, they bloom in midsummer to midautumn and are dormant in winter. Give thorough but infrequent drenchings during the growing season; withhold water during dormancy.

LITHOSPERMUM. See **LITHODORA diffusa**

LITTLE BLUESTEM. See **SCHIZACHYRIUM scoparium**

LIVERLEAF. See **HEPATICA**

LIVINGSTONE DAISY. See **DOROTHEANTHUS bellidiformis**

LIVISTONA
Arecaceae (Palmae)
PALMS

| 🌿 ZONES 9, 13–17, 19–24; H1, H2 |
| ☼ FULL SUN |
| 💧 REGULAR WATER, EXCEPT AS NOTED |

These slow-growing fan palms somewhat resemble *Washingtonia* but generally have shorter, darker,

Livistona australis

shinier leaves. They are hardy to about 22°F/–6°C. All make good potted plants.

L. australis. From coastal forest of eastern Australia. To 40–50 ft. tall, 15 ft. wide. Has clean, slender trunk with interesting-looking leaf scars. Dark green leaves are 3–5 ft. wide.

L. chinensis. CHINESE FOUNTAIN PALM. From Japan, Taiwan. Very slow growing; eventually to 40 ft. tall, 15 ft. wide. Roundish, bright green, 3–6-ft.-wide leaves droop strongly at outer edges.

L. decipiens. RIBBON FAN PALM. From northeastern Australia. To 30–40 ft. tall and 15 ft. wide in 20 years. Stiff, open head of deeply divided leaves that are green on top, bluish beneath, 2–5 ft. across. Leaves are carried on long, spiny stems, and have wispy terminal leaflets that hang downward.

L. mariae. From hot, dry interior Australia. To 10–15 ft. tall after many years (ultimately to as high as 80 or even 100 ft.), 15 ft. wide. Leaves 3–4 ft. wide. Young plants and those grown in containers have attractive reddish leaves and leaf stems. Little to moderate water.

LOBELIA
Campanulaceae (Lobeliaceae)
PERENNIALS AND ANNUALS

| 🌿 ZONES VARY BY SPECIES |
| ☼ ☽ EXPOSURE NEEDS VARY BY SPECIES |
| 💧💧💧💧 WATER NEEDS VARY BY SPECIES |
| ☠ MOST CONTAIN POISONOUS ALKALOIDS |

All are grown for their tubular, lipped flowers, which resemble those of honeysuckle *(Lonicera)* or salvia. Annual kinds are low plants for edgings or hanging baskets; perennial sorts are larger, vertical-growing plants with flowering stalks that rise above the foliage.

L. cardinalis. CARDINAL FLOWER. Perennial. Zones 1–7, 14–17. Native to eastern U.S. and to a few sites in mountains of the Southwest. Erect, single-stemmed plant to 2–4 ft. high, 1 ft. wide. Sawtooth-edged leaves are set directly on the stems. Spikes of flame red, inch-long flowers in summer. A bog plant in nature, it needs rich soil and ample moisture throughout the growing season. Full sun or partial shade.

L. erinus. Annual. All zones. From South Africa. Popular, depen-

dable edging plant to 3–6 in. high. Compact forms reach 5–9 in. wide; trailing types spread to 1½ ft. Leafy, branching stems with green or bronzy green foliage. Blooms from early summer to frost, bearing ¾-in.-wide flowers in light blue to violet (sometimes pink, reddish purple, or white) with white or yellowish throats. Lives over winter in mild climates. In mild-winter, hot-summer regions, grow it as a winter-to-spring annual. If started from seed sown in pots, takes about 2 months to reach planting size. Give rich soil, regular water. Self-sows where adapted. Can take full sun in cooler climates; needs some shade in warmer regions.

Lobelia erinus

Compact types include 'Cambridge Blue', with pure, soft blue flowers and green leaves; and 'Crystal Palace', with rich deep blue blossoms and bronzy green leaves. Trailing kinds include the Cascade series, with carmine red, violet-blue, blue, pink, or white blooms, and 'Sapphire', with bright blue flowers; both are green leafed. Trailers are well suited to hanging baskets. They also make a graceful underplanting in containers, where the stems, loaded with flowers, can spill over the edges.

L. fulgens (L. splendens). Perennial. Zones 4–9, 14–24. Native to Mexico. Similar to *L. cardinalis* but with narrower leaves; both stems and leaves have deep red undertones. Give same growing conditions as *L. cardinalis*.

L. × gerardii. Perennial. Zones 2–9, 14–17. Group of summer-blooming hybrids between *L. cardinalis* and *L. siphilitica*. Most

ommon is 4-ft. 'Vedrariensis', with
oppery green foliage and bright
urple flowers. 'Grape Knee-Hi',
ft. high, is a sturdy plant with
ich purple blooms. 'Rosea', 2½ ft.
all, has rose pink flowers. 'Ruby
Queen', to 3 ft. tall, has ruby red
looms. All form clumps about
ft. wide. Provide rich soil, regular
ater, partial shade.

L. laxiflora. Perennial. Zones
7–9, 12–24. Native to Arizona,
Mexico. To 3 ft. tall, 3–6 ft. wide.
Erect stems set with narrow leaves
grow from creeping underground
rootstock, bear open clusters of
tubular orange-red flowers over a
ong summer season. Withstands
considerable aridity and neglect;
often persists in abandoned gardens. Can be invasive. Little water.
Full sun or partial shade.

L. siphilitica. Perennial. Zones
1–9, 14–17. Native to eastern U.S.
Leafy plant to 2–3 ft. tall and 1 ft.
wide. Blue flowers in summer.
Ample water, partial shade.

L. × speciosa. Perennial.
Zones 2–9, 14–17. Group of
hybrids of uncertain ancestry. Can
reach 5 ft. tall, 1 ft. wide; many
combine red leaves and red flowers. Two 4–5-footers are 'Queen
Victoria', with purple-red foliage
and scarlet flowers; and 'Dark Crusader', with dark purple leaves and
deep magenta flowers. 'Monet
Moment' reaches 3 ft. tall, with big
clusters of rich violet-pink blossoms. Compliment series, to 2½ ft.
high, has dark green leaves; blossoms may be scarlet, deep red, or
blue purple. Ample water. Full sun
or partial shade.

L. tupa. DEVIL'S TOBACCO.
Perennial. Zones 4–9, 14–24. This
impressive Chilean native has a distinctly tropical look. Plants form a
3–4-ft.-wide clump of upright, red
stems holding felted, light green,
lance-shaped leaves to 1 ft. long.
Each stem is topped in mid- to late
summer by a bloom spike that
brings the overall height to 6 ft.
Clusters of tubular, 2-in.-long flowers in a rich, warm red are held
on reddish stems; blooms attract
hummingbirds. Grow in a sunny,
wind-sheltered position in fertile,
well-drained soil. In cold-winter
zones, mulch plants until well established. Does not require division, but
if more plants are desired, divide
clumps in spring. Regular water.

LOBIVIA, LOBIVOPSIS.
See **ECHINOPSIS**

LOBSTER-CLAW.
See **HELICONIA**

LOBULARIA
maritima
SWEET ALYSSUM
Brassicaceae (Cruciferae)
ANNUAL

| 🖊 ALL ZONES |
| ☼ ☼ BEST IN SUN; TOLERATES LIGHT SHADE |
| 💧 REGULAR WATER |

Mediterranean native. Low,
branching, trailing plant to 1 ft.
high and wide, with narrow or
lance-shaped leaves ½–2 in. long.
Crowded clusters of tiny, four-
petaled white flowers with a sweet
honey fragrance. In cold-winter
regions, blooms from spring until
frost; in mild climates, blooms all
year from self-sown seedlings.
Seeds are sometimes included in
wildflower mixes or erosion-
control mixes for bare or disturbed earth.

Lobularia maritima
'Rosie O'Day'

Easy, quick, dependable. Blooms
from seed in 6 weeks; grows in
almost any soil. Useful for carpeting, edging, bulb cover; temporary
filler in rock garden or perennial
border; between flagstones; in
window boxes or containers.
Flowers attract bees. If you shear
plants halfway back 4 weeks after
they come into bloom, new growth
will make another crop of flowers,
and plants won't become rangy.

Garden varieties are better
known than the species. These
varieties self-sow too, but
seedlings tend to revert to taller,
looser growth and bear smaller,
paler blossoms than the parent.
'Carpet of Snow' (2–4 in. tall), 'Little Gem' (4–6 in.), and 'Tiny Tim'
(3 in.) are good compact whites.
'Tetra Snowdrift' (1 ft.) has long
stems, large white flowers. 'Rosie
O'Day' (2–4 in.) and 'Pink Heather'
(6 in.) have lavender pink blooms.
'Oriental Night' (4 in.) and 'Violet
Queen' (5 in.) bear rich violet purple flowers.

LOCUST. See **ROBINIA**

LOGANBERRY.
See **BLACKBERRY**

LOLIUM
RYEGRASS
Poaceae (Gramineae)
ANNUAL AND PERENNIAL GRASSES

| 🖊 ZONES VARY BY SPECIES |
| ☼ FULL SUN |
| 💧 REGULAR WATER |

These European natives are
clumping, not running, grasses.
Not considered the choicest lawn
grasses, but useful in special conditions and situations (lawns, pasture, soil reclamation). To make
tight turf, sow heavily. Ryegrass is
often mixed with other lawn grass
species for low-cost, large-area
coverage in cool-summer climates.
In Bermuda grass country, it is
often sown in fall on recondi-
tioned Bermuda lawns to give
winter green.

L. multiflorum. ANNUAL
RYEGRASS, ITALIAN RYEGRASS.
Annual. Zones 1–24. Larger,
coarser than perennial ryegrass.
Some plants live for several seasons in mild climates. Fast growing, deep rooted. Hybrid between
L. multiflorum and *L. perenne* is
common or domestic ryegrass,
often used as winter cover on soil
or winter-dormant lawns.

Lolium perenne

L. perenne. PERENNIAL
RYEGRASS. Perennial. Zones A2,
A3; 1–6, 15–17. Finer in texture
than *L. multiflorum;* deep green
with high gloss. Sprouts quickly and
grows fast. Best in cool-summer
climates. Has become the most
popular lawn grass in the Northwest, west of the Cascades. 'Manhattan' is finer, more uniform.

Other recommended varieties
include 'Pennfine', 'Derby', 'York-
town', and 'Loretta'. Mow all at
2 in. high.

LONDON PRIDE.
See **SAXIFRAGA umbrosa**

LONICERA
HONEYSUCKLE
Caprifoliaceae
EVERGREEN, SEMIEVERGREEN, AND
DECIDUOUS SHRUBS AND VINES

| 🖊 ZONES VARY BY SPECIES |
| ☼ ☼ FULL SUN OR PARTIAL SHADE, EXCEPT AS NOTED |
| 💧💧 MODERATE TO REGULAR WATER, EXCEPT AS NOTED |

Most honeysuckles are valued for
their clustered or paired, often fragrant flowers. Blossoms are tubular
in form. Some have two flaring,
unequal lips; others are trumpets
or straight tubes, sometimes flaring at the mouth into five equal
lobes. Flowers attract hummingbirds, and the red or purple
berries that follow provide food
for many other kinds of birds.
Blossoms typically deepen in color
after opening, so clusters contain
both pale and darker blooms.
Vining species climb by twining
and need staking until they are tall
enough to reach a trellis or other
support. As they grow, they may
need to be tied to the support
here and there to distribute the
branches well.

Provide good drainage. Honeysuckles typically need some thinning; ideal time for the job is after
bloom. Cut old, straggling honeysuckles to the ground before spring
growth begins; they will regrow
rapidly. Generally free of serious
pests, though aphids sometimes
infest them.

L. × brownii. SCARLET
TRUMPET HONEYSUCKLE.
Deciduous vine. Zones A3; 1–7.
Represented in nurseries by its
superior selection 'Dropmore
Scarlet', which climbs to 9–10 ft.
Unscented, bright red flowers that
look like trumpets bloom from
late spring or early summer until
frost. Pairs of triangular blue-
green leaves to about 3 in. long
appear to be joined at the bases.

L. caerulea edulis. SWEET-
BERRY HONEYSUCKLE. Deci-
duous shrub. Zones A1–A3; 1–3.
Native to northern Europe and Asia.
To 4–6 ft tall and 4–5 ft. wide, with
pointed bright green leaves to 3 in.
long. Small, unscented, pale yellow
flowers are straight tubes ending
in five equal lobes. Blooms in early

L

spring. Edible, teardrop-shaped blue berries ripen in mid- to late spring; they resemble highbush blueberries but are not as sweet, though experimentation in Russia is producing improved varieties. Produce crops even north of the Arctic Circle. Early warm spells sometimes induce flowers to open before the last frost; they then suffer cold damage. For best fruiting, set at least two plants in a sunny location and keep soil moist. Watch to see if you need to protect berries from birds. For an ornamental hedge, space plants 3–4 ft. apart; for living snow fence, space 1½–2 ft. apart.

L. fragrantissima. WINTER HONEYSUCKLE. Deciduous shrub, semievergreen in mild-winter areas. Zones 1–9, 14–24. Native to China. Arching, rather stiff growth to about 8 ft. high and wide. Oval, 1–3-in.-long leaves are dull dark green above, blue green beneath. Creamy white, half-inch-long, two-lipped flowers from late winter to early spring; blossoms are richly fragrant (like *Daphne odora*) but not showy. Red berries. Can be used as a clipped hedge or background plant. Bring budded branches indoors for bloom.

Lonicera fragrantissima

L. × heckrottii. GOLDFLAME HONEYSUCKLE, CORAL HONEYSUCKLE. Deciduous or semievergreen vining shrub. Zones 2–24; H1, H2. Vigorous. To 12–15 ft. tall, with 2½-in., oval, blue-green leaves. Free blooming spring to frost. Clusters of coral pink buds open to 1½-in., slightly fragrant, two-lipped flowers that are bright coral pink outside and rich yellow within. Train as espalier or on wire along eaves.

L. henryi. HENRY'S HONEYSUCKLE. Vine. Evergreen in mild-winter climates, semievergreen in cold-winter regions. Zones 2b–9, 14–21. From western China. Strong, twining climber to 10–30 ft. Glossy, deep green leaves are oblong and pointed, 2–4 in. long,

and held in pairs along branches. Downy shoots emerge from leaf bases in early to midsummer to produce clusters of ¾-in.-long, yellow-throated flowers in shades of pink, sometimes with hints of orange or maroon. Bluish black fruit follows. May be used as a ground cover. Best with regular water and in partial shade.

Lonicera hildebrandiana

L. hildebrandiana. GIANT BURMESE HONEYSUCKLE. Evergreen vine. Zones 9, 14–17, 19–24; H1, H2. Native to China. Fast-growing to 30 ft., with 4–6 in., oval, glossy dark green leaves on ropelike stems. Bears fragrant, 6–7-in., two-lipped, summer flowers that open white, then turn yellow to dull orange; blossoms slow to drop. May bear dark green berries. Thin out older stems occasionally and remove some of the growth that has bloomed. Striking along eaves, on arbor or wall. Needs sturdy support.

L. japonica. JAPANESE HONEYSUCKLE. Vine. Evergreen in mild-winter climates, semievergreen or deciduous in colder areas. Zones 1–24; H1, H2. Native to eastern Asia. Can reach 30 ft. Rampant (even invasive) plant that can become a weed, since birds spread the seeds; consider planting the similar but less aggressive *L. periclymenum.* Basic species has oval deep green leaves to 3 in. long and sweet-scented, two-lipped, purple-tinged white flowers from spring to fall.

Several varieties are grown, all better known than the species. 'Aureo-reticulata', goldnet honeysuckle, with leaves veined in yellow, is better behaved than *L. japonica*; variegation is especially strong in full sun. 'Halliana', Hall's honeysuckle, is the most vigorous and widely grown variety; it bears pure white flowers that age to yellow and attract bees. 'Purpurea' (proba-

bly same as *L. j. chinensis*) has leaves with purple-tinged undersides and flowers that are purplish red outside, white inside.

Of the above, 'Halliana' is the most commonly used as bank and ground cover and for erosion control in large areas; as ground cover, set plants 2–3 ft. apart. Unless curbed, it can become a weed, smothering less vigorous plants. Needs severe pruning once a year to prevent undergrowth from building up and becoming a fire hazard. Cut back almost to framework with hedge shears. Train as privacy or wind screen on chain link or wire fence. Takes dryness pretty well when established; tolerates poor drainage.

L. korolkowii floribunda 'Blue Velvet'. Deciduous shrub. Zones 1–9, 14–21. Native to central Asia. To 12 ft. tall and 8 ft. wide. Tidy-looking, rounded, 2-in. leaves are light blue when young, maturing to gray green. Showy, fragrant, two-lipped light pink flowers open in mid- to late spring and are followed by bright red berries. Does best in full sun but tolerates part shade. Little to moderate water. A choice plant for the high plains and intermountain zones of the West.

L. 'Mandarin'. Deciduous vine. Zones 2b–9, 14–21. Hybrid between a Chinese species and *L. × brownii* 'Dropmore Scarlet'. Fast growing, as much as 6 ft. per year, to 15–20 ft. at maturity. Foliage emerges coppery in spring, deepens to glossy green; accented by young stems of deep purplish brown. Appearing in late spring to midsummer (and sometimes again in fall) are deep red buds that open into 2–3-in.-long flowers that are orange red outside, golden yellow within. Flowers are not particularly fragrant, and they are not followed by fruit.

L. nitida. BOX HONEYSUCKLE. Evergreen shrub. Zones 4–9, 14–24; H1, H2. Native to southwestern China. To 11 ft. tall, 10 ft. wide. Branches densely clothed in tiny (½-in.), egg-shaped, shiny dark green leaves that may turn an attractive bronze to plum color in winter. Late spring or early summer flowers are straight tubes—fragrant, creamy white, ½ in. long. Translucent blue-purple berries. Grows fast and tends toward untidiness but is easily pruned as specimen plant or hedge. Tolerates salt spray. 'Baggesen's Gold', to 4–6 ft. high and wide, has foliage that is golden in

sun (though very strong sun may burn leaves), chartreuse in shade. 'Lemon Beauty', to 4–6 ft. high and wide, has dark green leaves edged in shades of lemon and chartreuse. 'Maigrün', to 3 ft. high and 8 ft. wide, has leaves that are pale green when young, dark green when mature; it can be used as a tall ground cover. 'Red Tips', to 4–6 ft. high and wide, has deep raspberry red new growth that ages to dark green with red-tinted tips and edges. 'Silver Beauty', 3–4 ft. high and wide (possibly up to 6 ft.), has bright silver leaf margins.

L. periclymenum. WOODBINE. Evergreen or deciduous vine. Zones 1–24. Native to Europe and the Mediterranean region. Grows 10–20 ft. tall. Resembles *L. japonica* but is less rampant. Whorls of 2-in.-long, fragrant, two-lipped flowers in summer and fall. Blooms of 'Serotina' (also known as late Dutch honeysuckle) are purple outside, yellow inside. 'Berries Jubilee' has yellow flowers followed by a profusion of red berries. 'Belgica' (also called early Dutch honeysuckle) is less vining and more bushy than most, with abundant purple-flushed white flowers that fade to yellow and are followed by large red fruit. 'Graham Thomas' has white flowers aging to copper-tinted yellow. 'Winchester' has leaves that are purple tinged when young, pinkish red flowers with creamy throats, and bright reddish purple berries.

L. pileata. PRIVET HONEYSUCKLE. Semievergreen shrub. Zones 3b–9, 14–24; H1. Native to China. To 2–3 ft. tall and 8 ft. wide. Low and spreading, with stiff, horizontal branches. Dark green, 1½-in. leaves like those of privet (*Ligustrum*). Small, fragrant white flowers are shaped like straight tubes; they bloom in midspring and are followed by translucent violet berries. Good bank cover. Does well at the seashore. Give partial or full shade in hot climates.

L. sempervirens. TRUMPET HONEYSUCKLE. Evergreen in mild-winter climates, semievergreen or deciduous in colder areas. Zones 2–24. Native to eastern and southern U.S. Can climb 10–20 ft. tall but shrubby if not given support. Showy, unscented, trumpet-shaped flowers are 1½–2 in. long, orange-yellow to scarlet, carried in whorls at branch ends from late spring into summer. Scarlet fruit. Oval, ½–3-in.-long leaves are medium green above, bluish green

Lonicera sempervirens

beneath. 'Cedar Lane' is a vigorous selection with deep red flowers; 'Leo' produces vivid coral red blooms with orange throats over a long period; *L. s. sulphurea* has yellow blooms. Forms with larger flowers may be sold as 'Magnifica' or 'Superba'. For hybrid 'Dropmore Scarlet', see *L.* × *brownii* (the latter is a hybrid between *L. sempervirens* and *L. hirsuta*).

L. × **tellmanniana.** REDGOLD HONEYSUCKLE. Deciduous vine. Zones 3–9, 14–21. Hybrid involving a large-flowered form of *L. sempervirens*. Vigorous grower to 15 ft., with attractive, deep green leaves to 4 in. long. Rich amber to coppery orange flowers, up to 2 in. long, appear from late spring to midsummer. A choice honeysuckle for partial shade.

LOOSESTRIFE. See **LYSIMACHIA, LYTHRUM virgatum**

LOPHOMYRTUS
× ralphii
Myrtaceae
EVERGREEN SHRUB

🌿 ZONES 8–9, 14–24

☼ ☼ FULL SUN OR PARTIAL SHADE

◐ ◑ MODERATE TO REGULAR WATER

The genus *Lophomyrtus* contains just two species, both native to New Zealand. This hybrid between the two grows 6–15 ft. tall and 5–8 ft. wide, with attractive, dark green leaves that are broadly oval, up to 1 in. long, and held in pairs along the stems. Small white summer flowers resemble those of closely related myrtle (*Myrtus communis*) and are followed by reddish black berries. Can be pruned into a hedge or trained as a small tree. Stems of many forms are popular in the cut-flower trade. Colored-leaf forms show more pronounced color in full sun. Grow in moderately fertile, well-drained soil.

Forms selected for their dense growth habit include 'Kathryn', to 6–8 ft. tall and wide, with glossy,

puckered maroon leaves; 'Lilliput', just 2–3 ft. high and wide, with bronzy leaves; and 'Sundae', to 8–12 ft. tall and 4–8 ft. wide, with glossy, puckered, burgundy-flushed green leaves edged in creamy yellow.

Lophomyrtus × *ralphii* 'Kathryn'

LOPHOSPERMUM scandens. See **ASARINA scandens**

LOPHOSTEMON
confertus
(Tristania conferta)
BRISBANE BOX
Myrtaceae
EVERGREEN TREE

🌿 ZONES 15–17, 19–24; H1, H2

☼ FULL SUN

◐ ◐ ◑ LITTLE TO REGULAR WATER

Australian native somewhat resembling eucalyptus. Erect, moderate to fast growth to 30–45 ft. tall and 25 ft. wide. Trunk and limbs

Lophostemon confertus

resemble those of madrone (*Arbutus menziesii*), with reddish brown bark flaking off to reveal smooth, light-colored bark beneath. Oval, leathery bright green leaves are 4–6 in. long, tend to cluster at tips of branchlets; those of 'Variegata' are edged in a strikingly brilliant yellow. White to cream-colored, ¾-in. flowers in clusters of three to seven appear in summer, followed by woody capsules like those of eucalyptus. Takes almost any soil, but young plants get a better start with good soil; chlorosis can be a problem in poor soils. Pinch and prune to get more twiggy growth. Good street or lawn tree.

LOQUAT. See **ERIOBOTRYA**

LOROPETALUM
chinense
Hamamelidaceae
EVERGREEN SHRUB

🌿 ZONES 6–9, 14–24; BORDERLINE IN ZONES 4, 5

☼ ☼ PARTIAL SHADE IN HOTTEST CLIMATES

◑ REGULAR WATER

Native to China, Japan. To 6–10 ft. high and wide. Neat, compact habit, with tiers of arching or drooping branches. Roundish,

Loropetalum chinense 'Razzleberri'

light green, soft-textured leaves 1–2 in. long; throughout the year, the occasional leaf turns yellow or red, providing a nice touch of color. White to greenish flowers, each with four narrow, twisted, inch-long petals, appear in clusters of four to eight at branch tips. Flowering is heaviest in spring, but some bloom is likely at any time.

Subtly beautiful plant; good in foreground, raised beds, woodland garden. Young plants can be grown in hanging baskets. Provide rich, well-drained soil. Can take any amount of pruning. In Pacific Northwest, needs protection against hard freezes.

The following varieties all have purple foliage and pink to purple flowers and look much alike: 'Blush', 'Burgundy', 'Fire Dance', 'Pippa's Red', 'Razzleberri', 'Ruby', 'Sizzlin' Pink', 'Suzanne'. All are attractive, but the species makes a more striking show—its white flowers contrast better with green foliage than pink blooms with purple leaves.

LOTUS
Fabaceae (Leguminosae)
PERENNIALS

🌿 ZONES VARY BY SPECIES

☼ ☼ FULL SUN OR PARTIAL SHADE

◑ REGULAR WATER

Produces trailing stems that are often completely prostrate. Leaves are divided into leaflets. Flowers are sweet pea shaped, in shades of red to yellow. (For plants with the common name "lotus," see *Nelumbo*.)

L. berthelotii. PARROT'S BEAK. Zones 9, 15–24; H1. Woody-based perennial native to the Canary Islands and Cape Verde Islands. To 8–12 in. high, with trailing, 2–3 ft.-long stems thickly covered with silvery gray leaves with three to five leaflets. Very narrow, 1-in., scarlet blossoms in summer. Space plants 2 ft. apart as ground cover; cut back occasionally to induce bushiness. Also very effective in hanging baskets or as cascader over wall or rocks. Dies back in cold weather; suffers root rot where drainage is poor. Not a long-lived plant in Southern California.

L. corniculatus. BIRD'S FOOT TREFOIL. Zones 2–24. From Europe, Asia. Herbaceous plant 6–12 in. high, with prostrate stems; forms a mat of dark green, cloverlike, three-leafleted leaves. Clusters of small yellow flowers in summer and fall. Seedpods at tops of flower stems spread into segments like a bird's foot, hence the common name. Use as ground cover or coarse lawn substitute; sow seeds or set out plants (if they are available). Mow occasionally. Goes dormant where winters are cold. Has become invasive in parts of the Northwest.

L

L. maculatus. Zones 9, 15–24. Canary Island native resembling *L. berthelotii.* To 8–12 in. high, 2–3 ft. wide. Known mainly through its selections. 'Gold Flash' has bright yellow flowers with striking orange-red markings; needs cool nights to set flower buds. 'New Gold Flash' (blossom color similar to that of 'Gold Flash') and 'Amazon Sunset' (bright orange red) are similar in plant and flower form to 'Gold Flash', but they bloom better where nights remain warm.

Lotus maculatus 'Gold Flash'

L

LOULOU PALM. See **PRITCHARDIA**

LOVAGE. See **LEVISTICUM officinale**

LOVE GRASS. See **ERAGROSTIS**

LOVE-IN-A-MIST. See **NIGELLA damascena**

LOVE-LIES-BLEEDING. See **AMARANTHUS caudatus**

LUCKY CLOVER. See **OXALIS tetraphylla**

LUFFA. See **GOURD**

LUMA apiculata (Myrtus luma)
Myrtaceae
EVERGREEN SHRUB OR TREE

🌱 ZONES 14–24
☀️ FULL SUN
💧💧💧 LITTLE TO REGULAR WATER

Native to Chile, Argentina. Fast grower to 6–8 ft. (possibly 20 ft.) tall and wide, densely foliaged in closely set, oval to roundish, dark green leaves ½–1 in. long. Like common myrtle (*Myrtus*) but is denser, deeper green. Old plants develop beautiful smooth bark the

Luma apiculata

color of cinnamon. Blooms in late summer and early fall, with white to pinkish, four-petaled, about ½-in.-wide flowers with a central brush of stamens. Blue-black, ½-in. fruits are edible but not especially tasty.

LUNARIA annua
MONEY PLANT
Brassicaceae (Cruciferae)
BIENNIAL

🌱 ZONES 2–10, 14–24
☀️ ☽ AFTERNOON SHADE IN HOTTEST CLIMATES
💧💧💧 LITTLE TO REGULAR WATER

Native to Europe. Old-fashioned garden plant grown for the translucent, 1¼-in.-wide circles that hang onto flower stalks; these "coins" are all that remains of the ripened seedpods after the outer coverings have dropped with seeds. Reaches 1½–3 ft. high, 1 ft. wide, with coarse, heart-shaped, tooth-edged leaves. Spring flowers resemble wild mustard blooms but are purple or white. Plant in an out-of-the-way spot in poor soil or in mixed flower bed where shining pods can be admired before they are picked for dried arrangements. Tough and persistent; can reseed and become weedy.

Lunaria annua

LUNGWORT. See **PULMONARIA**

LUPINUS
LUPINE
Fabaceae (Leguminosae)
ANNUALS, PERENNIALS, AND EVERGREEN SHRUBS

🌱 ZONES VARY BY SPECIES
☀️ FULL SUN
💧💧💧💧 WATER NEEDS VARY BY SPECIES

Leaves are divided into many leaflets that spread out like fingers of a hand. Sweet pea–like flowers are borne in dense spikes at ends of stems. There are hundreds of species, many of them native to the western U.S. and found in a wide range of habitats. The most commonly grown lupines are the Russell hybrids. Most lupines are not fussy about soil, though hybrids prefer rich, slightly acidic soil. All need good drainage. Except as noted, start plants from seed sown in fall, winter, or early spring. To hasten germination, soak seeds for a few hours before planting.

L. arboreus. Evergreen shrub. Zones 4, 5, 14–17, 22–24. Native to California coastal areas. To 5–8 ft. tall and wide. Spring flowers, in clusters 4–16 in. long, are usually yellow but may be lilac, bluish, white, or some mixture of those colors. Striking beach plant. Little or no water.

L. argenteus. SILVERSTEM LUPINE. Perennial. Zones 1–7. Native to Southwest, Sierra Nevada, Rocky Mountains. To 2 ft. high, 1 ft. wide, with silvery-haired stems and (usually) smooth leaves. Flowers variable in color—usually blue, sometimes lilac or white. Moderate to regular water.

L. hartwegii. Annual. Zones 1–24. Native to Mexico. To 1½–3 ft. tall, 1 ft. wide. Flowers in shades of blue, white, and pink. Sow seeds in place in spring for summer bloom. Moderate water.

L. hybrids. Perennials. Zones A1–A3; 1–7, 14–17. To 4–5 ft. tall, 2 ft. wide. These English-bred hybrid groups are descended from plants native to western America. Self-sown seedlings won't resemble parents. Regular water.

Russell hybrids—the classic lupines—bloom during late spring or early summer, bearing tall flower spikes in white, cream, yellow, pink, red, orange, blue, purple, or bicolors. Little Lulu and Minarette are small strains—to 1½ ft. high and wide. All Russell hybrids tend to be short lived. They are prone to powdery

mildew; provide good air circulation. Grow from seed or buy nursery plants.

New Generation hybrids have all the merits of the Russell hybrids (from which they were developed) but are sturdier, needing no staking; longer lived, requiring replacement only after 7 or 8 years; and mildew resistant. They also come in a wider range of brighter, more intense colors, including interesting bicolors such as yellow-and-orange combinations. Bloom period is longer, too—from late spring to the end of summer, with possible autumn rebloom if plants are deadheaded regularly. Sold as seedling plants.

Lupinus Russell hybrids

L. microcarpus densiflorus (L. densiflorus). Annual. Zones 3–24. California native to 1½–2 ft. high and wide, with white, yellow, pink, or lavender-tinged flowers in spikes to 1 ft. long. 'Ed Gedling', a selection of *L. densiflorus aureus,* is a choice form with bright yellow flowers. Sow in fall for spring bloom. Good roadside decoration. Little or no water to moderate water.

L. nanus. SKY LUPINE. Annual. Zones 3–24. Native from California to British Columbia. To 8–24 in. high, 9–12 in. wide. Spring flowers are rich blue marked with white. Sow seeds in fall or winter; combine California poppies (*Eschscholzia*) with the lupines for contrast. Self-sows readily where it gets little competition. Excellent for barren banks. No irrigation needed except in desert zones.

L. polyphyllus. Perennial. Zones 3–7, 14–21. Native to moist places from California to British Columbia. Grows 1½–4 ft. tall, 2–2½ ft. wide. Blooms in summer, bearing blue, purple, or reddish flowers in clusters 6–24 in. long.

One important ancestor of the Russell hybrids. Regular water.

L. succulentus. Annual. Zones 7–24. California native. To 3 ft. tall, 2½ ft. wide; lush and leafy, with 6-in. spikes of blue flowers in spring. Normally found in damp places but adapts elsewhere; sometimes used for erosion control. Moderate to ample water.

LYCHEE. See **LITCHI**

LYCHNIS
Caryophyllaceae
PERENNIALS, SOME TREATED AS ANNUALS

🌡	ZONES VARY BY SPECIES
☼ ◐	FULL SUN OR LIGHT SHADE
💧💧💧	WATER NEEDS VARY BY SPECIES

Old-fashioned garden flowers. All plants tolerate poor soils. The different kinds vary in appearance, but all come in eye-catching colors.

L. × arkwrightii. Short-lived perennial best treated as annual. Zones 3–9, 14–24. To 1½ ft. tall, 1 ft. wide, with brown-tinted dark green leaves. Clusters of 1½-in. orange-scarlet flowers. 'Vesuvius' has brownish purple leaves. Regular water.

L. chalcedonica. MALTESE CROSS. Perennial. Zones A1–A3; 1–10, 14–24. Native to Russia. Loose, open form. Grows to 2–3 ft. high, 1 ft. wide. Leaves and stems are hairy; scarlet, ½-in. flowers with deeply cut petals are borne in dense terminal clusters. Particularly effective in large borders alongside white-flowered or gray-foliaged plants. 'Alba' has white blossoms. Regular water.

L. coeli-rosa. See Silene coeli-rosa

L. coronaria. CROWN-PINK, DUSTY MILLER, MULLEIN PINK, ROSE CAMPION. Perennial. Zones 1–9, 14–24. From southeastern Europe. To 1½–2½ ft. tall, 1½ ft. wide, with attractive, silky white foliage and magenta to crimson flowers a little less than an inch across. Effective massed. 'Alba' produces white flowers; 'Angel's Blush' bears white blooms with a cherry red eye. All self-sow freely if faded blossoms are not removed. Moderate water.

L. flos-cuculi. RAGGED ROBIN. Perennial. Zones 1–7, 14–17. Alpine native to 2½ ft. tall and wide. Bluish green leaves; loose clusters of inch-wide, pale to deep pink or white flowers with fringed petals. Ample water.

Lychnis coronaria

L. viscaria 'Splendens'. Perennial. Zones 1–10, 14–24. Selection of a Eurasian native to 1 ft. high and wide. Forms a low, compact, evergreen clump of grasslike leaves to 5 in. long; stalks with clusters of ½-in.-wide, pink to rose blooms rise above the foliage clump. 'Splendens Flore Pleno' is a double-flowered selection. Good rock garden plant; flowers last well when cut. Regular water.

LYCIANTHES rantonnetii.
See **SOLANUM rantonnetii**

LYCORIS
SPIDER LILY
Amaryllidaceae
PERENNIALS FROM BULBS

🌡	ZONES VARY BY SPECIES; OR GROW IN POTS
☼	FULL SUN
💧	REGULAR WATER DURING GROWTH AND BLOOM

Native to China, Japan. Narrow, strap-shaped leaves appear in fall (in mild-winter regions) or in spring; they remain green until some point in summer, then die down completely. Leafless flower stalks emerge after the foliage disappears. In late summer or early fall, each stalk bears a cluster of blooms with narrow, pointed petal-like segments and—in some species—projecting, spidery-looking stamens. Blossoms may be funnel shaped or have segments splayed outward or reflexed.

Grow in a sunny site that stays dry during summer dormancy. (In areas with summer rainfall, grow in pots that can be protected from moisture.) Plant in late summer, setting bulbs in well-drained soil about 1 ft. apart. Keep tops of bulb necks at or just above soil surface—except in coldest part of range, where tops of necks should

be just under surface. Water regularly while plants are growing and again when flower stalks emerge. It's best to withhold water and let soil go dry in summer when foliage begins to wither, though plants can take some summer water if drainage is excellent. Disturb clumps (after bloom) only when you want to move them or divide them to increase a planting. Beyond hardiness range, grow spider lilies in containers and overwinter them indoors.

L. aurea. GOLDEN SPIDER LILY. Zones 16, 17, 19–24; H1. Bright yellow, 3-in. flowers on 2-ft. stems. Slightly protruding stamens.

L. radiata. Zones 4–9, 12–24; H1. Best known and easiest to grow. Stems 1½ ft. tall bear 1½–2-in., coral red flowers with a golden sheen; stamens are very prominent. 'Alba' has white flowers.

Lycoris radiata

L. sanguinea. Zones 4–24. To 2 ft. tall, with 2½-in., bright red to orange-red blooms. Stamens do not protrude.

L. sprengeri. Zones 4–24. Similar to *L. squamigera*, but with slightly smaller flowers in a more purplish pink.

L. squamigera (Amaryllis hallii). Zones 2–24. Fragrant, lilac pink, 3-in. blossoms on 2-ft. stems resemble those of belladonna lily (*Amaryllis belladonna*). Stamens do not protrude.

LYME GRASS. See **LEYMUS**

LYONOTHAMNUS floribundus
CATALINA IRONWOOD
Rosaceae
EVERGREEN TREE

🌡	ZONES 14–17, 19–24
☼	FULL SUN
💧	MODERATE WATER

Native to Channel Islands off coast of Southern California. The species has lobed or scallop-

Lyonothamnus floribundus asplenifolius

edged leaves that are not divided into leaflets; it is seldom seen in cultivation. Much better known is *L. f. asplenifolius*, fernleaf Catalina ironwood. It grows at a moderate rate to 20–35 ft. high, 15 ft. wide. Red-brown bark peels off in long, thin strips; young twigs are often reddish. Leaves are 4–6 in. long, deep green above, gray and hairy beneath, divided into three to seven deeply notched or lobed leaflets. Blooms in late spring or early summer, bearing small white blossoms in flat, 8–18-in.-wide clusters that contrast well with the dark foliage. Old clusters turn brown; if it is practical to do so, cut them off.

Needs excellent drainage and should be pruned in winter to shape and control growth. Sometimes suffers from chlorosis in heavy soils. Easiest to grow near coast. Handsome in groves.

LYSILOMA microphylla thornberi (L. thornberi)
FEATHER BUSH, FERN-OF-THE-DESERT
Fabaceae (Leguminosae)
EVERGREEN OR DECIDUOUS SHRUB OR TREE

🌡	ZONES 12–24; H1, H2
☼	FULL SUN
💧	NO IRRIGATION NEEDED

Native to foothills of Arizona's Rincon Mountains. To 12–15 ft. tall and as wide, with multiple stems and a broad canopy of finely cut bright green leaves somewhat like those of acacia. Blooms in late spring or early summer, bearing masses of ½–1-in.-wide, creamy white, clustered flowers like little puffballs emerging from round buds. These are followed by flat, ridged brown seedpods 4–8 in. long. Good informal background shrub, patio tree (can be trained

*Lysiloma microphylla
thornberi*

to a single stem), or transition plant between garden and desert. To accentuate plant's filmy look, thin out crowded and weak branches in center. Evergreen in frost-free areas; deciduous elsewhere. May be killed to the ground by heavy frosts but usually comes back from the roots.

LYSIMACHIA
Primulaceae
PERENNIALS

| 🌱 ZONES VARY BY SPECIES |
| 🔆 🌤 FULL SUN OR PARTIAL SHADE |
| 💧💧 MODERATE TO REGULAR WATER |

Most are vigorous perennials capable of spreading beyond their allotted space, especially if they receive plenty of water. Police them to be sure they don't invade choicer plantings. Useful for naturalizing at woodland edges or in barely maintained areas. Blossoms are yellow or white; except as noted, they appear in summer.

L. barystachys. Zones 3b–9, 14–21. Native to eastern Russia and Asia. To 2 ft. high, 1½ ft. wide, with narrow green leaves 3-in. long. Small white flowers held in foot-long spikes that start out horizontal and then turn upright.

L. ciliata. Zones 1–9, 14–21. Native to northeastern U.S. Erect clump to 4 ft. tall, 2 ft. wide, with narrow green leaves to 6 in. long. Nodding, 1-in., yellow flowers with red-brown centers appear singly or in loose clusters in upper leaf joints. 'Atropurpurea' ('Firecracker') is similar but has reddish leaves.

L. clethroides. GOOSENECK LOOSESTRIFE. Zones A2, A3; 1–9, 14–24. Native to China, Korea, Japan. To 3 ft. tall, quickly spreading as wide or wider. Erect stems are clothed with pointed olive green leaves to 5 in. long. Flower spikes densely packed with tiny white blooms are 6–8 in. long, arched like a goose's neck. Long lasting as a cut flower.

L. congestiflora. GOLDEN GLOBES. Zones 8, 9, 14–24; H1, H2. Native to China. Mat-forming plant grows to 4 in. high and 1 ft. or wider. Oval green leaves to 2 in. long. Upturned yellow flowers, ½ in. across, grow in leafy terminal clusters. Plant blooms from spring to summer. 'Outback Sunset' produces red-tinged leaves with yellow variegation and bears yellow flowers with red centers.

L. ephemerum. Zones 2b–10, 14–24. Native to southwestern Europe. Leathery gray-green leaves to 6 in. long form a neat clump to 3 ft. tall and 1 ft. wide. Slender clusters of white, ½-in.-wide, longlasting flowers. Not invasive.

L. nummularia. CREEPING JENNY, MONEYWORT. Zones 1–9, 14–24. Native to Europe; naturalized in eastern North America. To 4–8 in. high, spreading 2 ft. or more, rooting as it goes. Forms attractive mat of roundish, light green, 1-in. leaves. Yellow flowers about 1 in. across appear singly in leaf joints. Best use is in corners or containers where it need not be restrained. Will spill from wall, hanging basket. 'Aurea' has bright yellow leaves; needs shade.

*Lysimachia
nummularia*

L. punctata. LOOSESTRIFE. Zones 1–9, 14–24. Native to central Europe, Asia Minor. To 3 ft. tall, spreading to 2 ft. or more by underground stems. Narrow green leaves to 3 in. long are borne in whorls on erect stems; inch-wide yellow flowers, also in whorls, appear on top third of stems. 'Alexander', to 2–3 ft. tall and wide, has leaves edged with creamy white; 'Golden Alexander', to 2 ft. tall and wide, has yellow-edged leaves. Both selections are fast growing but somewhat less vigorous than the species. Divide clumps every 2 or 3 years in early spring.

LYTHRUM virgatum
PURPLE LOOSESTRIFE
Lythraceae
PERENNIAL

| 🌱 ZONES 1–9, 14–24 |
| 🔆 FULL SUN |
| 💧 REGULAR WATER |

Native to Europe, Asia. Showy plant for pond margins, but often escapes its boundaries by freely self-sowing. Has naturalized in many areas, displacing native vegetation; wild populations have

Lythrum virgatum

clogged waterways in parts of the Northwest and the mountain states. Foliage clumps to 2 ft. wide send up 2½–5-ft.-high stems—the lower portions clothed with narrow leaves, the upper parts densely set with ¾-in., magenta flowers in late summer and fall. Hybrids (often sold as varieties of *L. salicaria,* a similar plant) include 'Morden Gleam', 'Morden Pink', 'Pink Spires', 'Roseum Superbum', and 'Rosy Spires'. They are not self-fertile, but they cross-pollinate with other lythrums and become a nuisance. Planting purple loosestrife and its variants is forbidden in some places and unwise wherever the plants will have reliable moisture through much of the year.

M

MAACKIA
Fabaceae (Leguminosae)
DECIDUOUS TREES

| 🌱 ZONES 1–10, 14–17 |
| 🔆 FULL SUN |
| 💧 REGULAR WATER |

Related to locust (*Robinia*) and yellow wood (*Cladrastis*), these are small to medium-size trees with leaves divided like feathers into many small, narrow leaflets. They grow at a slow to moderate rate. Summer flowers resemble small sweet peas; creamy to yellowish white, crowded into erect, 4–6-in.-long, spikelike clusters. Flat, 2–3-in.-long seedpods follow the blossoms. Plants are not fussy about soil. Need minimal pruning.

M. amurensis. AMUR MAACKIA. Native to Manchuria, Siberia. Possibly to 60 ft. tall and wide but unlikely to exceed 30 ft. in gardens. Broad, rounded head; dark green leaves. Bark on trunk is an attractive bronze color and peels in curling flakes. *M. a. buergeri* differs only in that its leaves have fuzzy undersides.

Maackia amurensis

M. chinensis. CHINESE MAACKIA. Chinese native reaches 20–30 ft. high and wide. Shrubbier than *M. amurensis,* with leaves divided into more and smaller leaflets. Foliage unfolds silvery grayish green, matures to dark green.

MACADAMIA

Proteaceae
EVERGREEN TREES

⚡ ZONES 9, 16, 17, 19–24; H1, H2

☀ FULL SUN

💧 REGULAR WATER

Native to Australia. Clean, handsome ornamental trees where frosts are light. Where best adapted (Zones 23, 24, H1, H2), produce clusters of delicious hard-shelled nuts, usually within 3 to 5 years after planting.

Set out macadamias from containers any time of year, but they'll suffer less stress from moisture loss and heat if planted in fall. Avoid windy sites. Perform best in deep, rich soil, with light applications of fertilizer at least twice a year. Trees are weak wooded, so prune young plants to encourage strong structure. New growth that emerges during winter is usually yellow; this is caused by cold, not health problems. Later growth will be green. Macadamias are resistant to oak root fungus.

Though most macadamias are sold under the name *M. ternifolia*, any tree you buy will nearly always be one of the two species (or their hybrids) described below. Trees grow 30–40 ft. tall and almost as wide, with whorls of glossy, leathery, 5–12-in.-long leaves; mature foliage is durable and attractive in arrangements. Look for grafted, named varieties of proven nut-bearing ability. Seedlings take longer to bear nuts, and their quality is unpredictable. Macadamias are self-fruitful, but planting two different varieties often produces bigger harvests. Trees bloom in winter and spring, bearing small, sometimes fragrant white to pink flowers in dense, pendent, 1-ft. clusters. Roundish fruit to 1½ in. wide consists of a leathery husk containing a hard-shelled nut. To harvest nuts, pick them up as they fall from tree (husks of ripe nuts split, making the nuts easy to remove).

M. hybrids. Crosses between *M. integrifolia* and *M. tetraphylla*. 'Beaumont' is one of the best varieties for Southern California, bearing over a very long period. It produces medium to large nuts with moderately thick shells; new leaves are reddish. 'Cooper' has small nuts, also with moderately thick shells. 'Vista' produces small to medium-size, very thin-shelled nuts.

M. integrifolia. SMOOTH-SHELL MACADAMIA. Commercial species best adapted to Hawaii. Can be grown near the coast in Southern California. Leaves are smooth edged. Nuts ripen from late fall to late spring. Popular varieties include 'Kakea', 'Kau', 'Keaau', 'Mauka', and 'Purvis'.

Macadamia tetraphylla

M. tetraphylla. ROUGH-SHELL MACADAMIA. More widely grown than *M. integrifolia* in California, where it performs best slightly inland. Differs from *M. integrifolia* in having a more open growth habit, spiny leaves, and thinner-shelled nuts that ripen from fall to midwinter. Varieties include 'Burdick', 'Cate', and 'Fenton'.

MACARTHUR PALM. See **PTYCHOSPERMA macarthuri**

MACFADYENA
unguis-cati
CAT'S CLAW, YELLOW TRUMPET VINE
Bignoniaceae
EVERGREEN OR DECIDUOUS VINE

⚡ ZONES 8–24; H1, H2

☀ ☽ FULL SUN OR PARTIAL SHADE

💧 MODERATE WATER

Native from Mexico and West Indies to Uruguay. Vigorous vine formerly known as *Doxantha unguis-cati* and *Bignonia tweediana*. Climbs high (to 25–40 ft.) and fast by hooked, clawlike, forked tendrils. Each leaf consists of two oval, glossy light green leaflets to 2 in. long; a tendril is centered between them. Blooms in early spring, bearing lobed yellow trumpets to 2 in. long, 4 in. across.

Macfadyena unguis-cati

Succeeds in cool-summer areas but is faster growing and stronger where summers are hot—even on south walls in Zones 12, 13. Can climb any surface that isn't slick, including stone, wood, chain link fences, tree trunks; vines are even seen clinging to undersides of freeway overpasses. Tends to produce leaves and flowers at stem ends; after bloom, cut back some stems nearly to the ground to stimulate new growth lower down. During growing season, pinch back vigorous shoots as needed. Can be used as a ground cover; it puts down roots where stems touch the ground, making it a good choice for erosion control on slopes. Evergreen where frosts are light or absent; partially to almost completely deciduous in colder areas.

MACHAERANTHERA
tanacetifolia
TAHOKA DAISY, PRAIRIE ASTER
Asteraceae (Compositae)
ANNUAL OR BIENNIAL

⚡ ZONES 1–24

☀ FULL SUN

💧💧💧 LITTLE TO REGULAR WATER

Native to much of central and western North America—from Alberta south to Texas and Mexico, west to California. Much-branched plant to 1–1½ ft. high and wide, with finely divided bright green leaves. Blooms in late

Machaeranthera tanacetifolia

spring and summer, bearing 2-in., yellow-eyed, lavender-blue daisies; each blossom is carried on its own inch-long stalk just above the foliage clump. Sow seeds in fall or early spring in well-drained soil. Tolerates drought but performs better with some moisture.

MACHE

Valerianaceae
ANNUAL

⚡ ZONES A1–A3; 1–24; H1

☀ FULL SUN

💧 REGULAR WATER

This cool-season crop, sometimes called corn salad or lamb's lettuce, is among the most cold-hardy of traditional salad and cooking greens. Plants form rather loose rosettes of spoon-shaped leaves to 6 in. long with a mild, nutty flavor. Grow in well-drained soil. In warmer climates, sow seeds from

Mache

fall through early spring for harvest in about 90 days. In cooler climates, sow seeds directly in the ground in summer (for fall harvest), or in late winter as soon as soil is workable (for spring harvest). Space rows 8 in. apart; sow seeds ½ in. deep and 1 in. apart. Thin to 6 in. apart. Start extra plants so a few can reseed. Plants overwinter in areas where the ground does not freeze. Harvest entire rosette at once.

MACHILUS thunbergii. See **PERSEA thunbergii**

MACKAYA bella

Acanthaceae
EVERGREEN SHRUB

⚡ ZONES 15–24

☽ ● PARTIAL OR FULL SHADE

💧💧 MODERATE TO REGULAR WATER

From South Africa. Grows 4–5 ft. high and wide, sometimes much taller, with glossy dark green leaves to 5 in. long. From spring into early summer, produces

M

Mackaya bella

loose, 9–10-in.-long clusters of trumpet-shaped, 2-in.-long flowers with flaring lobes; blossoms are lavender with deep purple lines in the throat. Give well-drained soil. Minimal pruning needed.

MACLEAYA
PLUME POPPY
Papaveraceae
PERENNIALS

| 🌱 ZONES VARY BY SPECIES |
| :☀: :☀: LIGHT SHADE IN HOTTEST CLIMATES |
| 💧 REGULAR WATER |

These tall perennials from China and Japan are often still listed under *Bocconia*, a name properly belonging to their shrubby tropical relatives. Tall, branching stems carry clouds of tiny flowers. Leaves are large and deeply lobed. Plants look tropical, and their garden value lies in size and structure rather than floral impact. Spread by creeping rhizomes and can be invasive if not controlled; plant them among sturdy shrubs rather than among delicate perennials.

M. cordata. Zones A2, A3; 1–24. To 7–8 ft. tall and 3 ft. wide, with grayish green, 10-in. leaves. White to beige flowers. Considered less invasive than *M. microcarpa*.

M. microcarpa. Zones 2b–24. Similar to *M. cordata* but has

Macleaya microcarpa

pinkish beige flowers. Blossoms of 'Coral Plume' are more decidedly pink.

MACLURA pomifera
OSAGE ORANGE
Moraceae
DECIDUOUS TREE

| 🌱 ZONES 2, 3, 10–13 |
| :☀: FULL SUN |
| 🌑🌣🌑 LITTLE OR NO WATER TO REGULAR WATER |

Native from Arkansas to Oklahoma and Texas. Fast growth to 60 ft. tall and 40 ft. wide (though often less), with spreading, open habit. Young branches are thornier than mature ones. Wood is orange in color and very hard. Glossy medium green leaves to 5 in. long. If a male plant is present, female plants may bear 4-in.-wide, inedible fruits (so-called hedge-apples) that look like bumpy yellow-green oranges. 'Whiteshield' and 'Wichita' are thornless male selections.

Maclura pomifera

Withstands heat, cold, wind, poor soil, moderate alkalinity, and wet or dry conditions. Immune to oak root fungus. Easily propagated from seed, stem cuttings, or root cuttings; easy to transplant. Useful as big, tough, rough-looking tall hedge or background plant. Prune to any size from 6 ft. up; pruned high, becomes a shade tree.

MADAGASCAR JASMINE.
See **STEPHANOTIS floribunda**

MADAGASCAR PALM.
See **PACHYPODIUM lamerei**

MADAGASCAR PERIWINKLE.
See **CATHARANTHUS roseus**

MADRONE, MADRONA.
See **ARBUTUS menziesii**

MAGELLAN wheatgrass.
See **ELYMUS magellanicus**

MAGNOLIA
Magnoliaceae
DECIDUOUS AND EVERGREEN TREES AND SHRUBS

| 🌱 ZONES VARY BY SPECIES |
| :☀: :☀: FULL SUN OR PARTIAL SHADE |
| 💧 REGULAR WATER |
| ▶ SEE CHART NEXT PAGE |

Magnificent flowering plants featuring blossoms in white, pink, red, purple, or—a more recent development—rich yellow. These plants show a remarkable variety of leaf shapes and plant forms. The following text classifies magnolias by general type; the chart lists them alphabetically. New varieties and hybrids appear every year, but distribution is spotty in local nurseries. Many more kinds are available from mail-order specialists.

MAGNOLIA TYPES
Magnolias include both evergreen and deciduous types. Most have large, striking blossoms composed of petal-like segments, but a few are grown for use as foliage plants.

Evergreen magnolias. In California and Arizona, "magnolia" usually means *M. grandiflora*, the classic Southern magnolia with glossy leaves and big, fragrant white blossoms. Loved for its foliage and flowers, it also offers the advantages of heat resistance and tolerance for damp soil. On the other hand, it requires a fair amount of maintenance and has limited uses. It's messy, shedding its big, hard leaves (they look almost like plastic) and other litter constantly from late spring into earliest autumn. And though it's generally considered a street or lawn tree, it tends to lift paved walks with its surface roots, and it

Magnolia grandiflora

casts dense, year-round shade that prevents the growth of a healthy lawn beneath. Furthermore, it is slow growing in heavy soil or where root area is restricted. Before planting this tree, carefully consider whether its advantages outweigh its drawbacks. Other evergreen options are *M. delavayi* and *M. virginiana*.

Deciduous magnolias with saucer flowers. This group includes saucer magnolia (*M.* × *soulangeana*) and its many varieties, often called tulip trees because of the shape and bright colors of their flowers. Also included here are yulan magnolia (*M. denudata*) and lily magnolia

Magnolia × soulangeana

(*M. liliiflora*). All are hardy to cold, thriving in various climates throughout the West—but early flowers of all forms are subject to frost damage, and all do poorly in hot, dry, windy areas. Related to these, but more tender to cold (and heat), are the big, spectacular Oriental magnolias from western China and the Himalayas— *M. campbellii, M. dawsoniana, M. sargentiana robusta*, and *M. sprengeri* 'Diva'. Their early flowers are also subject to frost and storm damage.

Deciduous magnolias with star flowers. Included in this group are *M. kobus, M. stellata* and its varieties (the star magnolias), and *M. salicifolia*. All are hardy, slow-growing, early-blooming plants with wide climatic adaptability.

Other magnolias. Less widely planted is a group of magnolias generally considered foliage plants or shade trees; they bloom as leaves appear or after they unfurl.

▶ page 467

MAGNOLIA

NAME	ZONES	TYPE	HEIGHT	SPREAD	AGE AT BLOOM	FLOWERS	USES, CHARACTERISTICS, COMMENTS
Magnolia acuminata CUCUMBER TREE	2–9, 14–21	Deciduous	60–80 ft.	30 ft.	12 yrs.	Greenish yellow, to 3½ in. wide; glossy, not conspicuous. Appear after leaves in late spring, summer. Handsome reddish seed capsules with red seeds	Shade or lawn tree. Canopy of 5–9-in. leaves provides dense shade. Hardy to cold; dislikes hot, dry winds. 'Koban Dori' is a smaller selection, to 15–20 ft. tall, with canary yellow flowers
M. a. subcordata (**M. cordata**) YELLOW CUCUMBER TREE, YELLOW MAGNOLIA	4–9, 14–21	Deciduous	25–35 ft.	20–35 ft.	12 yrs.	Yellow to yellow-green flowers larger than those of species (to 4 in.); appear as leaves start to expand. Mild lemon scent	Slow-growing lawn or border tree. Showier, lower, and shrubbier than *M. acuminata*. Not ordinarily a tree you can walk or sit under. 'Miss Honeybee' is a selection with larger, pale yellow flowers
M. 'Apollo'	4–9, 14–24	Deciduous	To 35 ft.	18–20 ft.	2 yrs. from grafts	Abundant, fragrant, star-shaped flowers to 10 in. across. Blooms in early to midspring, before leaf-out. First blossoms to open are deep violet outside, paler inside; later ones are deep rose pink	Smallish, round-headed tree
M. 'Athene'	3b–9, 14–24	Deciduous	18–25 ft.	18–25 ft.	3–4 yrs.	Large (8–10 in.) cup-and-saucer-shaped blooms. Rosy purple at base shading to pale pink, with ivory white interior. Richly fragrant	Similar to *M.* 'Iolanthe' but more upright. Moderate to fast growth. Flowers well when young
M. auriculata (see **M. fraseri**)							
M. 'Butterflies'	2b–9, 14–24	Deciduous	To 20 ft.	To 15 ft.	2 yrs. from grafts	Produces many 4–5-in., light yellow flowers with red stamens. Blooms in midspring, before leaves emerge	Hybrid of *M. acuminata* and *M. denudata*. Upright and pyramidal when young; later spreading. Leaves 8 in. long, medium to dark green, sparsely hairy. Hardy to –29°F/–34°C without injury
M. campbellii	4–9, 14–21 (best in 15–17)	Deciduous	60–80 ft.	To 40 ft.	20 yrs.; grafts bloom younger, at 4–5 yrs.	Magnificent 6–10-in., bowl-shaped blooms in crimson to rose pink, with central segments cupped over rose-colored stamens. Late winter to spring, before leaves emerge	Plant in lee of evergreens to protect flowers from strong winds. Make it focus of garden and give it room. 'Alba', 'Strybing White' are white forms; 'Hendricks Park', 'Late Pink' are good pinks. 'Charles Raffill' has very large bright pink flowers with white interior. 'Kew's Surprise' is similar, but outside of bloom is deep pink
M. conspicua (see **M. denudata**)							
M. cordata (see **M. acuminata subcordata**)							
M. dawsoniana DAWSON MAGNOLIA	4–9, 14–21	Deciduous	40–50 ft.	25–30 ft.	10 yrs. from grafts	Large (8–10-in.), faintly scented white blossoms with rose shading. Narrow, slightly pendulous segments. Profuse early bloom	Good choice for big gardens. Puts on a magnificent show; a little untidy close up. Very dark green leaves. Quite cold hardy when established; needs hardening off in fall. Blooms of 'Chyverton' are deep pink, lighter at tips and within

M

MAGNOLIA

NAME	ZONES	TYPE	HEIGHT	SPREAD	AGE AT BLOOM	FLOWERS	USES, CHARACTERISTICS, COMMENTS
M. 'Daybreak'	4–9, 14–24	Decid-uous	To 30 ft.	To 10–15 ft.	3 yrs.	Large (8–10 in.), very fragrant, bright rose pink flowers. Blooms in late spring, escaping frost damage	Narrow form; useful in small lots, side yards
M. delavayi	7–9, 14–21	Ever-green	20–30 ft.	To 20 ft.	4–5 yrs.	Dull creamy white, 6–8 in. wide. Fragrant, short lived; shatter day they open. Long summer bloom	Foliage is the feature: leaves are 8–14 in. long, 5–8 in. wide, stiff, leathery, gray green, tropical looking. Use as single tree or giant shrub in lawn or large corner. Hard to train as single-stemmed tree
M. denudata (M. conspicua, M. heptapeta) YULAN MAGNOLIA	3b–9, 14–24	Decid-uous	To 35 ft.	To 30 ft.	6–7 yrs.	Fragrant white flowers, some-times tinged purple at base. Blossoms are erect; somewhat tulip shaped, 3–4 in. long, spreading to 6–7 in. Early bloom on base branches; often a few flowers appear in summer	Tends toward irregular form; good in informal garden or at woodland edge. Choose a site where it can be shown off against dark background or sky. Leaves 4–7 in. long. Does well in Southern California
M. 'Elizabeth'	3b–9, 14–24	Decid-uous	To 40 ft. or more	To 20 ft.	2–6 yrs. from grafts	Fragrant soft yellow flowers, 6–7 in. wide. Color is paler in mild-winter areas. Blossoms appear before or with the leaves	Hybrid between M. acuminata and M. denudata. Grow as single-trunked tree or multitrunked shrub-tree. Hardy to at least –20°F/–29°C
M. fraseri (M. auriculata)	4–9, 14–21	Decid-uous	To 30 ft.	To 20 ft.	10–12 yrs.	Creamy to yellowish white, fragrant, 8–10 in. wide. Blooms in late spring, when leaves are full grown. Rose red, 5-in. seed capsules are showy in summer	Single lawn or woodland tree. Thin, stiff, brittle leaves 16–18 in. long, with two earlike lobes at base; borne in whorls at branch ends. Effect is that of parasols. Handsome dark brown fall color
M. 'Galaxy'	3b–9, 14–24	Decid-uous	To 40 ft.	To 25 ft.	5 yrs. from grafts	Abundant bright red-purple, slightly fragrant, goblet-shaped blossoms to 5 in. across. Blooms in midspring, before leaves emerge but usually after last frost	Fast-growing, broadly conical tree. Medium green leaves to 8 in. long. Cross between M. liliiflora and M. sprengeri 'Diva'
M. glauca (see M. virginiana)							
M. grandiflora SOUTHERN MAGNOLIA, BULL BAY	4–12, 14–24; H1, H2	Ever-green	To 80 ft.	To 60 ft.	15 yrs., some-times much less; 2–3 years from grafts or cuttings	Pure white, aging buff; large (8–10 in. across), powerfully fragrant. Usually have six seg-ments. Species and its varieties bloom throughout summer, fall	Street or lawn tree, big container plant, wall or espalier plant. Unpredictable in form and age of bloom. Grafted plants more predict-able but need pruning to become single-trunked trees. Can grow as multitrunked tree. Glossy, leathery leaves, 4–8 in. long. Needs warmest location (or warm wall) in Zones 4, 5. Expect breakage, some yearly pruning (see page 467) in Zones 6, 7. Give wind-sheltered spot in desert. In Hawaii, does best in Zone H1 and in inland valleys of H2
M. g. 'D. D. Blanchard'	4–12, 14–24; H1, H2	Ever-green	To 50 ft. or more	25–35 ft.	2 yrs.	Like those of M. grandiflora	Handsome pyramidal tree. Lustrous dark green leaves are orange-toned brown on undersides
M. g. 'Edith Bogue'	4–12, 14–24; H1, H2	Ever-green	To 35 ft.	To 20 ft.	2–3 yrs. from grafts	Like those of M. grandiflora. Young plants slower to come into heavy bloom than some other varieties	Shapely, vigorous tree. One of hardiest selections of M. grandiflora; has withstood –24°F/–31°C. The one to try in coldest regions. Keep out of strong winds

M

MAGNOLIA

NAME	ZONES	TYPE	HEIGHT	SPREAD	AGE AT BLOOM	FLOWERS	USES, CHARACTERISTICS, COMMENTS
M. g. 'Little Gem'	4–12, 14–24; H1, H2	Evergreen	Slow to 20–25 ft.	10–15 ft.	2 yrs. from grafts	Small (5–6-in.-wide) flowers from spring through late summer (fewer blooms form during midsummer heat)	Narrow form makes it good in container, as espalier, in confined area. Branches to ground. Half-size leaves are dark green above, rusty beneath
M. g. 'Majestic Beauty'	7–12, 14–24; H1, H2	Evergreen	35–50 ft.	To 20 ft.	2 yrs. from grafts	Very large (to 1 ft. across)	Vigorous, dense-branching street or shade tree of broadly pyramidal form. Leaves are exceptionally long, broad, and heavy
M. g. 'Russet'	4–12, 14–24; H1, H2	Evergreen	Fast to 80 ft.	To 20 ft.	2 yrs. from grafts	Flattish, 10-in.-wide blooms	Useful where fast-growing, narrow evergreen tree is needed. Densely foliaged. Narrow, glossy leaves with russet wool on undersides
M. g. 'Samuel Sommer'	4–12, 14–24; H1, H2	Evergreen	Fairly fast to 30–40 ft.	To 30 ft.	Same as M. grandiflora	Full and very large, ranging from 10 to 14 in. wide	Large, leathery, glossy leaves are very dark green above, with heavy rusty red felting on underside
M. g. 'San Marino'	4–12, 14–24; H1, H2	Evergreen	Slow to 25 ft.	To 20 ft.	Same as M. grandiflora	Profuse show of 4-in. flowers	Grow this plant as a large shrub, small round-headed tree, or espalier. Densely foliaged to the ground unless shaped
M. g. 'St. Mary'	4–12, 14–24; H1, H2	Evergreen	Usually 20 ft.; much larger in old age	To 20 ft.	Same as M. grandiflora	Heavy production of 8–10-in. flowers on small tree	Fine where standard-size magnolia would grow too large and too fast. Left alone, it will form a big, dense bush. Can be trained as a small tree. Good plant for containers and espalier
M. g. 'Victoria'	4–12, 14–24; H1, H2	Evergreen	To 20 ft.	To 15 ft.	2–3 yrs. from grafts	Like those of M. grandiflora	Parent plant came from Victoria, British Columbia. Withstands –10°F/–23°C with little damage, but should be located out of wind. Leaves dark green, exceptionally broad and heavy
M. heptapeta (see M. denudata)							
M. hypoleuca	4–9, 14–21	Deciduous	To 50 ft.	To 30 ft.	15 yrs.	Strongly perfumed flowers to 8 in. across; creamy white with purplish red stamens. Blooms in early summer, after leaves expand (blossoms are partly concealed by foliage). Red, 5–8-in.-long fruits	For large lawn or garden. Coarse-textured plant with attractive gray bark; leaves to 16 in. long
M. 'Iolanthe'	3b–9, 14–24	Deciduous	To 25 ft.	To 25 ft.	3–5 yrs.	Abundant, bowl-shaped blossoms 10–12 in. across, in soft pink with paler pink interior; open from large, hairy, outward-facing buds. Blooms in late winter and early spring, before leafout	Small, wide-spreading tree has survived brief periods down to –12°F/–24°C. Outward-facing blooms are more desirable than the more common upturned or downturned magnolia flowers
M. kobus KOBUS MAGNOLIA	2b–9, 14–24	Deciduous	To 30 ft.	To 20 ft.	15 yrs.	White, slightly fragrant blossoms to 4 in. wide. Blooms in early to midspring, before leaves emerge	Cold-hardy, sturdy tree for planting singly in a lawn or in informal shrub and tree groupings. M. k. borealis is much larger (to 75 ft.), with larger leaves

M

MAGNOLIA

NAME	ZONES	TYPE	HEIGHT	SPREAD	AGE AT BLOOM	FLOWERS	USES, CHARACTERISTICS, COMMENTS
M. k. stellata (see **M. stellata**)							
M. Kosar-De Vos hybrids (the so-called "Little Girl" series)	2b–9, 14–24	Deciduous	To 12 ft.	To 15 ft.	4–5 yrs.	Flower color ranges from deep to pale purple (sometimes with pink or white interior), depending on variety. Trees bloom in spring before leafout; sporadic rebloom in summer	Hybrids between *M. liliiflora* 'Nigra' and *M. stellata* 'Rosea'; bred to bloom later than *M. stellata*, thus avoiding frost damage. Erect, shrubby growers bearing girls' names: 'Ann', 'Betty', 'Jane', 'Judy', 'Pinkie', 'Randy', 'Ricki', 'Susan'. Use in shrub border or singly in lawn
M. lennei (see **M. × soulangeana 'Lennei'**)							
M. liliiflora (**M. quinquepeta**) LILY MAGNOLIA	2b–9, 14–24	Deciduous	To 12 ft.	To 15 ft.	4–5 yrs.	White inside, purplish outside. Blooms over long spring, summer season. Tends to have two distinct bloom periods in Northwest	Good for shrub border; strong vertical effect in big flower border. Spreads slowly by suckering. Leaves 4–6 in. long. Blooms of 'Gracilis', 'Nigra', and 'O'Neill' are dark purplish red outside, pink inside
M. × loebneri	2b–9, 14–24	Deciduous	Slow to 12–15 ft.; can reach 50 ft.	12–15 ft.	3 yrs.	Narrow, strap-shaped flower segments similar to those of *M. stellata*, but generally fewer and somewhat longer and wider. Blooms appear before leaves in midspring. Some selections are fragrant	Hybrids between *M. kobus* and *M. stellata*. 'Ballerina', white with faint pink blush, and taller, pure white 'Spring Snow' are both fragrant. Very lightly scented are 'Leonard Messel', with pink blooms from darker buds, and 'Merrill' ('Dr. Merrill'), a vigorous, free-flowering white-blossomed form. Use in lawn, shrub border, at woodland edge
M. macrophylla BIGLEAF MAGNOLIA	4–9, 14–21	Deciduous	Slow to 30 ft.	To 20 ft.	12–15 yrs.	Fragrant white flowers to 16 in. across in late spring and early summer, after leafout	Showy tree with leaves 1–3 ft. long and 9–12 in. wide. Needs to stand alone. Be sure to give it some shade in warm climates
M. officinalis	4–9, 14–21	Deciduous	To 50 ft.	To 25 ft.	15 yrs.	Fragrant, creamy white flowers to 8 in. wide. Blooms in midspring, after leafout	Much like *M. hypoleuca*. Big and exotic-looking tree for big garden or large lawn
M. quinquepeta (see **M. liliiflora**)							
M. 'Royal Crown'	2b–9, 14–24	Deciduous	20–25 ft.	20–25 ft.	3–5 yrs.	Candle-shaped pink buds open to upright, 10–12-in. blooms with narrow segments; blossoms dark red to violet outside, white inside. Blooms in early spring, before leafout	Vigorous, densely branched hybrid of *M. liliiflora* and *M. × veitchii*
M. salicifolia ANISE MAGNOLIA	2b–9, 14–21	Deciduous	Slow to 18–30 ft.	To 12 ft.	2–10 yrs.	White, fragrant, to 4 in. across; narrow segments. Blooms in midspring, before leaves emerge	Usually upright, with slender branches, graceful appearance. Can be used for shrub border. Leaves are 3–6 in. long, have anise scent when crushed; turn bronzy red in fall. 'Kochanakee' and 'W. B. Clarke' are large flowered, bloom young and heavily. Another heavy bloomer is 'Miss Jack'

MAGNOLIA

NAME	ZONES	TYPE	HEIGHT	SPREAD	AGE AT BLOOM	FLOWERS	USES, CHARACTERISTICS, COMMENTS
M. sargentiana robusta	5–9, 14–24	Decid-uous	To 35 ft.	To 35 ft.	10–12 yrs.; 8–10 yrs. from grafts	Huge (8–12-in.), fragrant mauve pink bowls open erect, then nod. Blooms in mid- to late spring, before leaves open	Among most spectacular of flowering plants. Leaves 6–8 in. long. Not for hot, dry areas. Must have ample room
M. sieboldii OYAMA MAGNOLIA	4–9, 14–24	Decid-uous	6–15 ft.	6–15 ft.	5 yrs.	Cup-shaped, fragrant, white flowers centered with crimson stamens. Blooms from late spring through late summer. Bright pink seedpods	Good for small gardens. Buds look like white Japanese lanterns. Nice planted upslope or at top of wall so people can look up into somewhat nodding flowers. Leaves 3–6 in. long. Best in part shade
M. × soulangeana SAUCER MAGNOLIA (often called TULIP TREE)	2b–10, 12–24	Decid-uous	To 25 ft.	To 25 ft. or more	3–5 yrs.	White to pink or purplish red, fragrant, variable in form and size (from 3 to 6 in. wide). Blooms from late winter into spring, both before leaves emerge and as they open	Hybrid of *M. denudata* and *M. liliiflora*. Good lawn plant; good anchor plant in big container plantings. Seedlings highly variable; look for named selections (especially later-blooming ones for frost-prone regions). Medium green, rather coarse-looking leaves 4–6 in. long or longer
M. × s. 'Alba' ('Amabilis', 'Alba Superba')	2b–10, 12–24	Decid-uous	To 30 ft.	To 25 ft. or more	3–5 yrs.	Purple-suffused buds open to large, nearly pure white flowers. Early	Same uses as for *M. × soulangeana*. Rather more upright in growth than most varieties
M. × s. 'Black Tulip'	2b–10, 14–24	Decid-uous	To 30 ft.	To 15 ft.	3–5 yrs. from grafts	Large, goblet-shaped blooms of deep wine red. Blooms in early spring, before foliage emerges	Slender, upright grower. Excellent specimen for small gardens. In mild climates, can be grown in containers when young. Can be pruned as a hedge. Protect from strong winds
M. × s. 'Brozzonii'	2b–10, 12–24	Decid-uous	To 25 ft.	To 25 ft. or more	3–5 yrs.	White blossoms very slightly flushed purplish rose at base; 8 in. across. Late	One of the most handsome white-flowered magnolias. Vigorous tree
M. × s. 'Burgundy'	2b–10, 12–24	Decid-uous	To 25 ft.	To 25 ft. or more	3–5 yrs.	Large, cup- or bowl-shaped flowers are deep purple halfway up from base; then color pales to pink. Early	Earlier bloom than most makes it more susceptible to frost damage. San Francisco's Japanese Tea Garden has many of these, pruned into picturesque shapes
M. × s. 'Coates'	2b–10, 12–24	Decid-uous	To 25 ft.	To 25 ft. or more	3–5 yrs.	Large, attractive blooms resemble those of *M.* 'Royal Crown'. Midseason	Large, shrubby. Quick grower
M. × s. 'Lennei' (M. lennei)	2b–10, 12–24	Decid-uous	To 25 ft.	To 25 ft. or more	3–5 yrs.	Very large, globe-shaped blossoms are deep purple outside, white inside. Late	Spreading, vigorous plant. Late bloom helps it escape frosts in cold areas
M. × s. 'Lennei Alba' (M. lennei 'Alba')	2b–10, 12–24	Decid-uous	To 25 ft.	To 25 ft. or more	3–5 yrs.	Like those of 'Lennei', but white in color, slightly smaller, and earlier (midseason)	Spreading, vigorous plant

M

Magnolia campbellii

Magnolia 'Elizabeth'

Magnolia 'Galaxy'

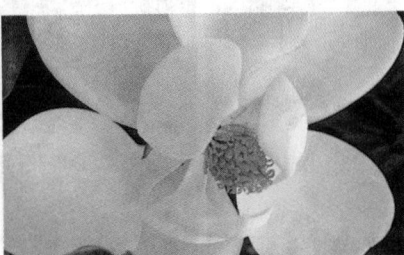
Magnolia grandiflora

MAGNOLIA

NAME	ZONES	TYPE	HEIGHT	SPREAD	AGE AT BLOOM	FLOWERS	USES, CHARACTERISTICS, COMMENTS
M. × s. 'Lilliputian'	2b–10, 12–24	Deciduous	To 18 ft.	10–15 ft.	3–5 yrs.	Flowers are pink outside, white inside, somewhat smaller than those of other M. × *soulangeana* selections. Late	Good where a smaller magnolia is called for
M. × s. 'Norbertii'	2b–10, 12–24	Deciduous	To 18 ft.	10–15 ft.	3–5 yrs.	White, suffused with purple on outside. Late	Upright, dense habit
M. × s. 'Pink Superba'	2b–10, 12–24	Deciduous	To 25 ft.	To 25 ft. or more	3–5 yrs.	Large deep pink blooms are white inside. Early	Best where late frosts are not a problem. Identical to M. × s. 'Alba' except for flower color
M. × s. 'Rustica Rubra'	2b–10, 12–24	Deciduous	To 25 ft.	To 25 ft. or more	3–5 yrs.	Large, cup-shaped, deep reddish purple flowers. Blooms somewhat past midseason. Big (6-in.) dark rose seedpods	Vigorous grower for large areas. More treelike than many M. × *soulangeana* varieties
M. × s. 'San Jose'	2b–10, 12–24	Deciduous	To 25 ft.	To 25 ft. or more	3–5 yrs.	Large white flowers flushed with pink. Very early	Exceptionally early bloom puts it at risk for frost damage in cold areas
M. sprengeri 'Burncoose'	5–9, 14–24	Deciduous	To 40 ft.	To 20 ft.	5–8 yrs.	Stunning, upright, 10–12-in. flowers are rich rose to violet and sweetly fragrant. Blooms early to midspring before leafout	More upright, stronger growing than M. s. 'Diva'
M. s. 'Diva'	5–9, 14–24	Deciduous	To 40 ft.	To 30 ft.	3 yrs.	Spectacular, erect, sweet-scented blooms to 8 in. wide are bright rose pink outside, pink-suffused white with deeper pink lines inside. Blooms late winter to early spring, before leaves open	Buds more frost resistant than those of M. sargentiana robusta. Big shrub that can be trained as tree. Young plants are broad, twiggy
M. s. 'Eric Savill'	5–9, 14–24	Deciduous	To 30 ft.	To 20 ft.	5–8 yrs.	Full, fragrant, deep red purple flowers. Blooms in early spring	Outstanding seedling of M. s. 'Diva'
M. 'Star Wars'	3b–9, 14–24	Deciduous	30–35 ft.	To 20 ft.	4 yrs.	Rich bright pink blossoms (paler inside), 11 in. across. Blooms for 1–2 months, beginning in early spring (before leafout)	Cross between M. campbellii and M. liliiflora. Especially good magnolia for Southern California and inland areas
M. stellata (M. kobus stellata) STAR MAGNOLIA	2b–9, 14–24	Deciduous	To 10 ft.	To 20 ft.	3 yrs.	White flowers to 3 in. across, with 12–18 narrow, strap-shaped segments. Profuse bloom comes very early—late winter to early spring, before leafout. Some varieties are fragrant	Slow growing, shrubby; use for borders, entryway gardens, edge of woods. Good idea to plant this early bloomer where you can see flowers from indoors. Quite hardy, but flowers often nipped by frost in colder part of range. Fine texture in twig, leaf. Fair yellow-and-brown fall leaf color

Magnolia kobus

Magnolia kobus

Magnolia 'Randy' (Kosar-De Vos hybrid)

Magnolia liliiflora

Magnolia × *loebneri*

MAGNOLIA

NAME	ZONES	TYPE	HEIGHT	SPREAD	AGE AT BLOOM	FLOWERS	USES, CHARACTERISTICS, COMMENTS
M. s. 'Centennial'	2b–9, 14–24	Deciduous	To 10 ft.	To 20 ft.	3 yrs.	White blossoms faintly marked pink, 5 in. across, with 40–50 segments. Midspring	Same uses as *M. stellata*. Like an improved *M. s. 'Waterlily'*
M. s. 'Dawn'	2b–9, 14–24	Deciduous	To 10 ft.	To 20 ft.	3 yrs.	White flowers have 25 or more segments, each with a longitudinal pink stripe	Same uses as *M. stellata*
M. s. 'Jane Platt'	2b–9, 14–24	Deciduous	12–15 ft.	10–12 ft.	3–5 yrs.	Rich pink, 4–5-in. blossoms with 40–50 segments. Blooms in early spring	Typical shrubby *M. stellata* plant form
M. s. 'Rosea' PINK STAR MAGNOLIA	2b–9, 14–24	Deciduous	To 10 ft.	To 20 ft.	3 yrs.	Pink buds; flowers open pink-flushed white, age to plain white. Late winter	Same uses as *M. stellata*. Various plants are sold under this name
M. s. 'Royal Star'	2b–9, 14–24	Deciduous	18–20 ft.	To 15 ft.	3 yrs.	Fragrant white blooms with 25–30 segments. Blooms 2 weeks later than species	Same uses as *M. stellata*. Faster growing
M. s. 'Rubra'	2b–9, 14–24	Deciduous	To 10 ft.	To 20 ft.	3 yrs.	Rosy pink blooms to 5 in. across	More treelike in form than other *M. stellata* varieties
M. s. 'Waterlily'	2b–9, 14–24	Deciduous	To 10 ft.	To 20 ft.	3 yrs.	Pink buds open to very fragrant white blossoms to 5 in. across, with 40–50 segments. Blooms late, after most other *M. stellata* varieties	Faster growing than most star magnolias. Various plants are sold under this name
M. 'Sundance'	3b–9, 14–24	Deciduous	25–30 ft.	To 20 ft.	4–5 yrs. from grafts	Fragrant, pale golden yellow, saucer-shaped flowers to 8 in. across. Blooms in spring, before leafout	Hybrid between *M. acuminata* and *M. denudata*. Fast-growing, pyramidal tree
M. 'Timeless Beauty'	4–9, 14–24	Evergreen	15–20 ft.	20–25 ft.	2 yrs.	Creamy white, fragrant flowers to 10 in. wide. Blooms in spring and summer	Extremely dense crown with spreading branches. A natural hybrid between *M. grandiflora* and *M. virginiana*
M. × veitchii VEITCH MAGNOLIA	4–9, 14–24	Deciduous	30–40 ft.	To 30 ft.	4–5 yrs.	Profuse show of goblet-shaped, 8–10-in.-wide blooms in soft white flushed with pink. Blooms in midspring, before leafout	Spectacular tree. Hybrid between *M. campbellii* and *M. denudata*. Fast growing and vigorous. Needs plenty of room. Protect from wind; branches are brittle. Good magnolia for Southern California. Give it afternoon shade in hottest areas

M

Magnolia salicifolia 'W. B. Clarke'

Magnolia salicifolia

Magnolia × soulangeana

Magnolia stellata 'Rubra'

MAGNOLIA

NAME	ZONES	TYPE	HEIGHT	SPREAD	AGE AT BLOOM	FLOWERS	USES, CHARACTERISTICS, COMMENTS
M. × veitchii 'Columbus'	4–9, 14–24	Deciduous	30–35 ft.	15–20 ft.	2 yrs.	Cup-shaped, 4–5-in.-wide, white with purple highlight at base of each segment. Late winter or early spring, before leafout	Has a thicker trunk and stronger branching structure than other magnolias, making it a sturdy choice for urban plantings
M. virginiana (M. glauca) SWEET BAY	4–9, 14–24	Evergreen to deciduous	To 50 ft., usually less	To 20 ft.	8–10 yrs.	Creamy white, fragrant, nearly globular blossoms are 2–3 in. wide. Late spring to late summer	Prefers moist, acid soil. Grows in swamps in eastern U.S. Big evergreen or semievergreen tree in milder climates; deciduous shrub in colder areas. Leaves bright green above, nearly white beneath, 2–5 in. long. Twigs and branches are bright green, adding winter interest if leaves fall
M. v. 'Moonglow' ('Jim Wilson')	3–9, 14–24	Evergreen to deciduous	35–40 ft.	15–18 ft.	4 yrs.	Like those of M. virginiana	A bit hardier and more upright than M. virginiana, with glossy, dark green leaves. Grows fast and starts blooming young
M. 'Vulcan'	4–9, 14–24	Deciduous	To 25 ft.	To 25 ft.	1 yr. from grafts	Showy, ruby red blossoms to 10–12 in. across. Flowers borne in tree's younger years may be smaller and paler than those on older trees. With good care, trees will produce mature flowers in 3 or 4 years. Blooms in spring, before leafout	Open form when young, becoming more rounded with age
M. 'Wada's Memory'	2b–9, 14–24	Deciduous	To 30 ft.	To 20 ft.	3–5 yrs. from grafts	White, slightly fragrant blossoms over 4 in. across. Blooms in early to midspring, before leaves emerge	Also sold as M. × kewensis 'Wada's Memory' or as M. × proctoriana 'Wada's Memory'. Same uses as M. kobus; grows faster than M. kobus. Coppery red new leaves
M. wilsonii WILSON MAGNOLIA	4–9, 14–24	Deciduous	To 25 ft.	To 25 ft.	10 yrs.	Fragrant, pendulous, 3–4-in.-wide, white blossoms with red stamens. Late spring	Spreading shrub or tree with rich purple-brown twigs. Leaves 3–6 in. long; may be narrow or somewhat broad. Plant high on bank where you can look up into flowers. Best in light shade. Effect similar to that of M. sieboldii
M. 'Yellow Bird'	3b–9, 14–24	Deciduous	To 40 ft.	To 20 ft.	2 yrs. from grafts	Deepest yellow color of the yellow hybrids. Slight green tinge at base of erect, 3-in.-long flower segments. Blooms for 2–3 weeks in early to midspring, as leaves emerge	Hybrid of M. acuminata and M. × bronxensis 'Evamaria'. Upright and pyramidal when young, broadly oval when mature. Furrowed bark. Sometimes available as a multi-trunked form
M. 'Yellow Fever'	3b–9, 14–24	Deciduous	To 40 ft.	15–20 ft.	4–5 yrs.	Fragrant, 6–8-in. yellow flowers fade to cream. Blooms in spring, before foliage appears	Vigorous, upright hybrid between M. acuminata and M. denudata
M. 'Yellow Lantern'	3b–9, 14–24	Deciduous	To 50 ft.	20–25 ft.	2–3 yrs. from grafts	Clear yellow blossoms (darker than those of M. 'Elizabeth', paler than those of M. 'Yellow Bird') with upright or slightly spreading segments to 6 in. long. Open from large, furry buds. Midspring, before leafout	Hybrid of M. acuminata and M. × soulangeana 'Alexandrina'. Upright, single-trunked tree

M

What Magnolias Need

CAREFUL SITING Pick a location where the shallow, fleshy roots won't be damaged by digging or by soil compaction from constant foot traffic.

SOIL Magnolias appreciate fairly rich, well-drained, neutral to slightly acid soil amended with plenty of organic matter at planting time. They will grow in somewhat alkaline soil but may develop chlorosis.

MULCHING At least in the early years, keep a cooling mulch over the root area.

WATERING Irrigate deeply and thoroughly, but don't waterlog the soil or the tree will drown. Only *M. virginiana* can take constantly wet soil.

FERTILIZING Treat chlorosis with iron chelates. Feed trees if new growth is scanty or weak, or if you see significant dieback despite adequate watering and drainage; use a controlled-release product. For more on fertilizing, see text.

PRUNING For deciduous magnolias, best time is after bloom; for evergreen kinds, do the job before the spring growth flush. Best method is to remove the entire twig or limb right to the base. Cuts on deciduous kinds are often slow to callus over, so prune these only when necessary to correct shape, eliminate or cut back wayward branches, or remove lower branches from trunk as tree gains height.

Magnolia × soulangeana

Among them are *M. hypoleuca*, a big tree with large leaves and large (but not especially noticeable) flowers; and *M. fraseri* and *M. macrophylla*, medium-size trees with huge leaves and blooms. *M. acuminata* is a big shade tree with inconspicuous greenish yellow flowers; the similar *M. a. subcordata* is a smaller tree with slightly showier blossoms. Hybrids of the latter are grown for their flowers, which show better yellow color than their parent. Blossoms of some of these hybrids appear on bare branches; others bloom as leaves emerge. *M. sieboldii* and *M. wilsonii* constitute another flowering category; they bear drooping, cup-shaped, fragrant white blossoms after leafout.

Magnolia culture

For any magnolia, choose planting site carefully—virtually all these trees are hard to move once established. Magnolias never look their best when crowded. Larger deciduous types are most effective standing alone against a background that will display their flowers and, in winter, their strongly patterned, typically gray limbs and big, fuzzy flower buds. Smaller deciduous magnolias show up well in large flower or shrub borders and make choice ornaments in Japanese gardens. All magnolias may be used as lawn trees; try to provide a good-size grass-free area around the trunk, and don't plant under the tree. In frost-prone areas, plant early-flowering magnolias in a northern exposure to delay bloom as long as possible and lessen frost damage.

Balled-and-burlapped plants are available in late winter and early spring; container plants are sold any time. Do not set plants lower than their original soil level. In windy locations, stake single-trunked or very heavy plants to keep them from rocking to and fro—the movement would tear the thick, fleshy, sensitive roots.

Soggy soil can topple newly planted large magnolias, so stake big specimens if planting them just before the rainy season; to avoid damaging roots, set stakes in planting hole before placing tree. Remove stakes as soon as the tree is firmly rooted.

Magnolias are generally not bothered by pests or diseases. Watch for scale and aphids at any time and for spider mites in hot weather. Protect lower leaves of shrubby types from snails and slugs. Magnolias are not immune to oak root fungus, but they seem somewhat resistant.

More troublesome are problems caused by nutrient deficiencies. (Also see "What Magnolias Need," above.) Chlorosis from lack of iron in alkaline soils shows up as yellowing between leaf veins; iron chelates will correct this condition. Fertilizer will remedy nitrogen deficiency. Feed trees if new growth is sparse and weak, or if the tree shows a fair amount of dieback despite adequate watering and drainage. Use a slow-release product, since magnolias are very susceptible to salt damage from overfertilizing, resulting in burned leaf edges. The same leaf damage can result from excess mineral salts in the soil or salts in irrigation water. The latter is a problem in Southern California and, typically, the factor limiting success of magnolias in desert regions. Frequent heavy waterings will help leach out salts and carry them to lower soil levels—as long as drainage is good. In the Northwest, late frosts may burn edges of new leaves.

MAHONIA
Berberidaceae
EVERGREEN SHRUBS

🌿 ZONES VARY BY SPECIES
☼ ☼ ● EXPOSURE NEEDS VARY BY SPECIES
◔ ◑ ● WATER NEEDS VARY BY SPECIES

Related to barberry (*Berberis*) and described under that name by some botanists. Easy to grow; good looking all year. Typically spiny-edged leaves are divided into leaflets; foliage can be quite prickly, so avoid setting mahonias too close to walkways or in other areas where they might snag passersby. Yellow flowers are borne in dense, rounded to spikelike clusters and followed by berrylike, typically blue or blue-black (sometimes red or brown) fruit with a powdery bloom. Generally disease resistant, though foliage is sometimes disfigured by a small looper caterpillar. Fruit of all mahonias attracts birds. In general, pruning is needed only to remove old, damaged stems or to correct rank growth; cut those stems all the way to the ground.

M. aquifolium. OREGON GRAPE. Zones 2–12, 14–24. Native from British Columbia to Northern California, mostly west of the Cascades. State flower of Oregon. Dense, bushy plant grows erect to 6 ft. high, spreading by underground stems to 5 ft. wide. Leaves are typically glossy green, 6–12 in. long, with five to nine leaflets that resemble holly leaves. Ruddy or bronze new growth; scattered mature red leaves throughout the year (more pronounced in fall and

Mahonia aquifolium

winter). Leaves turn purplish or bronze in winter, especially in cold-winter areas or where plants are grown in full sun. Early spring flowers appear in 2–3-in. clusters along stems. Edible blue-black fruit with gray bloom (makes good jelly).

'Compacta' grows 2–3 ft. high and spreads to 5 ft. or more. New foliage is a glossy light to coppery green; mature leaves are matte medium green. 'John Muir' is about the same size, with somewhat finer foliage and denser growth. 'Orange Flame', 2 ft. tall and 3 ft. wide, has bronzy new growth, glossy green mature leaves that turn wine red in winter.

Mass as foundation planting or as low screen or garden barrier; plant in woodland or in tubs. Control height and form by pruning; if any woody stems jut out too far, cut them down to ground (new growth fills in quickly). Can be sheared as a formal hedge. Resistant to oak root fungus. Give wind protection in cold-winter areas. Can take any exposure but performs best with shade in hottest climates (northern exposure recommended in desert). Little to regular water.

M. fortunei. Zones 5–9, 14–24. Native to China. To 6 ft. high and 3 ft. wide, with an unusual stiff charm. Erect stems bear 10-in.-long leaves with 7–13 leaflets; matte green above, yellowish green with heavily netted veins on undersides. Short clusters of flowers in late fall. Full sun or light shade. Regular water.

M. fremontii. DESERT MAHONIA. Zones 2b–24. Native to deserts of Southwest. Upright, many-stemmed plant to 3–12 ft. tall, 6 ft. wide. Gray-green to yellowish green leaves, each with

M

three to five thick, inch-long leaflets that are edged with very sharp, tough spines. Flowers in 1–1½-in.-long clusters in late spring; dark blue to brown fruit. Full sun or light shade. Little or no water.

M. 'Golden Abundance'. Zones 2b–12, 14–24. Vigorous, densely foliaged plant reaches 6 ft. high, spreading by underground stems to 5 ft. wide. Glossy green leaves with red midribs. Profuse bloom in early spring with clusters of yellow flowers; later produces an abundant crop of purplish blue berries with gray bloom. Full sun in cooler climates, some shade in hotter ones. Little to regular water.

M. gracilipes. Zones 4 (borderline), 5–9, 14–24. Native to China. Grows 5–6 ft. tall and wide, spreading slowly by underground stems. Plant sprawls gracefully rather than growing upright. Dark green leaves have light green veins and chalky white undersides. Pendent sprays of purplish red and creamy yellow flowers are held on long racemes in late summer or early fall; powdery blue fruit follows. Not particular about soils, but grows best in humus-rich, well-drained soil. Full sun or light shade. Regular water.

M. japonica Bealei Group. LEATHERLEAF MAHONIA. Zones 3b–12, 14–24. Native to China. To 10–12 ft. high and 10 ft. wide, with strong pattern of vertical stems and horizontal leaves. The leaves reach over a foot long, divided into 7–15 broad, thick, leathery leaflets to 5 in. long. Foliage is yellowish green above, gray green below, with a small yellow patch at the base of each leaflet. Blooms in late winter, producing erect, 3–6-in.-long blossom spikes at ends of branches. Powdery blue berries. Truly distinguished plant against background of stone, brick, wood, glass. Plant in rich soil amended with ample organic matter. Takes sun in cool-summer areas; does best in partial shade elsewhere. Regular water.

M. lomariifolia. Zones 6 (borderline), 7–9, 14–24. Native to China. To 6–12 ft. high and 6 ft. wide, with erect stems that branch only slightly. Young plants often have a single, vertical unbranched stem; older ones produce more branches (almost vertical-growing) from near base. Clustered deep green leaves are held horizontally near ends of branches. Each leaf reaches 2 ft. long, has 19–41 barbed leaflets arranged symmet-

Mahonia lomariifolia

rically along both sides of central leafstalk (with a single leaflet at the tip). Midwinter flowers grow in long, erect clusters at branch tips, just above topmost cluster of leaves. Blue berries. Strong-structured plant for dramatic effect. Partial shade, especially in afternoon. Regular water.

M. × media. Zones 6–9, 14–24. Hybrids between *M. lomariifolia* and a Japanese species. Plants bear upright clusters of fragrant flowers in late fall and winter; generally resemble *M. lomariifolia* and require the same conditions. 'Arthur Menzies' grows 10–12 ft. tall, 8–10 ft. wide; 'Buckland' and 'Charity' grow to 15 ft. high, 12 ft. wide; 'Faith' reaches 6–10 ft. high and 6 ft. wide; 'Hope' and 'Lionel Fortescue' both grow to 6 ft. high and wide; and 'Winter Sun' reaches 4–5 ft. high and as wide.

M. nervosa. LONGLEAF MAHONIA. Zones 2b–10, 14–24. Native from British Columbia to Northern California, mostly west of the Cascades. To 2 ft. (occasionally 3–4 ft.) high and 3 ft. wide, spreading by underground stems. Clustered at stem tips are 10–18-in.-long leaves divided into 9–19 leaflets, each 1–3 in. long; plant creates the impression of a stiff, leathery fern. Early spring flowers are borne in upright, 3–6-in.-long clusters. Blue berries. Use as woodland ground cover, facing for taller mahonias, low barrier plant. Partial or full shade; little to moderate water. This plant is an excellent choice for dry shade.

M. nevinii. NEVIN MAHONIA. Zones 7–24. Native to scattered areas in Southern California. Many-branched shrub to 6 ft. high and wide. Gray leaves with three to five 1-in.-long leaflets. Loose, 1–2-in. clusters of spring flowers are followed by red berries. Resistant to oak root fungus. Use individually or as screen, hedge, barrier. Full sun or partial shade. Little or no water to regular water.

M. pinnata. CALIFORNIA HOLLY GRAPE. Zones 4–9, 14–24. Native from southern Oregon to Southern California. To 4–5 ft. high (often taller along the coast) and as wide. Similar to *M. aquifolium* but with spinier, more crinkly leaves; new growth often shows lots of red and orange. Spikelike springtime flower clusters; dark blue berries. 'Ken Hartman' has dense, uniform growth. Full sun in cooler areas, light shade in hottest climates. No irrigation needed (takes aridity better than *M. aquifolium*).

M. repens. CREEPING MAHONIA. Zones 2b–9, 14–24. Native from British Columbia to Northern California, eastward to Rocky Mountains. To 1 ft. high and 3 ft. wide, spreading by underground stems. One of the best mahonias for winter color: dull blue-green leaves turn bronzy or pinkish when cold weather arrives. Short clusters of flowers in mid- to late spring are followed by blue berries. Good ground cover. Full sun or partial shade. Little or no water.

M. 'Skylark'. Zones 4–9, 14–24. Grows to 5 ft. high or higher, 5 ft. wide. Shiny leaves to 6 in. long are reddish when new; they mature to deep green, then take on purple tints in winter. Spring flowers in dense, 4–6-in. spikes. Dark blue berries. Full sun in cooler areas, partial shade in hotter ones. No irrigation needed.

M. trifoliolata. Zones 3, 10–13. Native to Arizona, southern New Mexico, Texas. To 8 ft. high and about half as wide. Blue-green leaves with three wavy-edged leaflets. Short flower clusters in spring are followed by orange-red berries sometimes used for jelly. Full sun. Moderate water.

MAIANTHEMUM
Liliaceae
PERENNIALS

🌿	ZONES VARY BY SPECIES
◐	PARTIAL SHADE
💧	REGULAR WATER

Botanists have recently brought two familiar Western natives together under this single genus name. Both are woodland plants that need loose, rich, slightly acidic soil to look their best.

M. dilatatum. FALSE LILY-OF-THE-VALLEY. Zones A2, A3; 2–9, 14–17. Native from Northern California to Alaska, Idaho. Also known as *M. bifolium* or as

M. d. kamtschaticum. To 6–8 in. high; in good growing conditions, spreads rapidly by creeping rootstocks to form broad mats. Stems 2–6 in. high bear neat, roundish to heart-shaped, heavily veined leaves to 8 in. long and half as wide. Bears foamy clusters of white flowers in spring that are followed by red berries in summer. Makes an attractive woodland-type ground cover but is capable of overwhelming more delicate plants growing nearby. Disappears in winter.

Maianthemum dilatatum

M. racemosum (Smilacina racemosa). FALSE SOLOMON'S SEAL. Zones 1–7, 14–17. Commonly seen in shaded woods from California to British Columbia, east to the Rockies. Grows 1–3 ft. tall, spreading by creeping rhizomes to form dense colonies. Each single, arching stalk has several medium green, oval to lance-shaped, 3–10-in.-long leaves with hairy undersides; foliage turns golden yellow in fall. In spring, stalks are topped by fluffy, conical clusters of small, fragrant, creamy white flowers. Red berries with purple spots ripen in autumn; they are favored by wildlife. Good for naturalizing in wild gardens. Tolerates more sun in cool-summer climates. Resembles true Solomon's seal (*Polygonatum*).

MAIDEN GRASS.
See **MISCANTHUS sinensis 'Gracillimus'**

MAIDENHAIR FERN.
See **ADIANTUM**

MAIDENHAIR SPLEENWORT.
See **ASPLENIUM trichomanes**

MAIDENHAIR TREE.
See **GINKGO biloba**

MAIDEN'S WREATH.
See **FRANCOA ramosa**

MAILE. See **ALYXIA oliviformis**

MAJORANA hortensis.
See **ORIGANUM majorana**

MALCOLMIA
maritima
VIRGINIAN STOCK
Brassicaceae (Cruciferae)
ANNUAL

🌿 **ZONES 1–24**

☀ **FULL SUN**

💧 **REGULAR WATER**

Low-growing Mediterranean native reaches only 8–15 in. high. Single stemmed or branching from base, with oblong gray-green leaves to 2 in. long. From spring to fall, plant is covered with nearly scentless, four-petaled flowers in

Malcolmia maritima

white, yellow, pink, lilac, or magenta. Will bloom from seed in 6 weeks; sow seed in place (in moderately rich soil) at any time except during hot or very cold weather. Thin seedlings to about 8 in. apart. Does not reseed readily. Good choice as bulb cover. May not flower well in hot, humid conditions.

MALE FERN. See **DRYOPTERIS**

MALEPHORA
(Hymenocyclus)
ICE PLANT
Aizoaceae
SUCCULENT PERENNIALS

🌿 **ZONES VARY BY SPECIES**

☀ **FULL SUN**

💧 **LITTLE OR NO WATER**

Ground cover plants from South Africa. Dense, smooth, 1–1¾-in.-long fleshy leaves are highly resistant to heat, wind, exhaust fumes, and fire. Widely used for both streetside and freeway plantings.

Plants bloom over a long season, but their daisylike flowers are scattered rather than in sheets. Attractive to bees.

Malephora lutea

M. crocea. Zones 11–24. To 6 in.–1 ft. high and 6 ft. wide, with blue-green foliage. Sparse production of reddish yellow flowers nearly year-round, with heaviest bloom in spring. Good choice for moderately steep slopes. *M. c. purpureo-crocea* has bluish green foliage, salmon-colored flowers.

M. lutea. ROCKY POINT ICE PLANT. Zones 12–24. To 1 ft. high and 6 ft. wide, with bright green foliage. Inch-wide yellow flowers bloom during most of year. More vigorous than *M. crocea*.

MALLEE. See **EUCALYPTUS**

MALLOW.
See **MALVA, SPHAERALCEA**

MALLOW, ANNUAL.
See **LAVATERA trimestris**

MALLOW, TRAILING.
See **MALVASTRUM lateritium**

MALLOW, TREE.
See **LAVATERA**

MALOSMA laurina.
See **RHUS laurina**

MALTESE CROSS.
See **LYCHNIS chalcedonica**

MALUS
FLOWERING CRABAPPLE
Rosaceae
DECIDUOUS TREES

🌿 **ZONES 1–11, 14–21, EXCEPT AS NOTED IN CHART**

☀ **FULL SUN**

💧 **MODERATE TO REGULAR WATER**

▶ **SEE CHART NEXT PAGE**

From North America, Europe, Asia. Valued for brief, lavish show of white, pink, or red flowers and for fruit that is showy, edible, or both. (Most of the trees listed in the chart bear fruit that is enjoyed primarily by birds. For crabapples used chiefly in cooking, see Crabapple.) Hundreds of different kinds are cultivated, and new varieties appear every year. Most grow about 20 ft. high, though size ranges from as low as 4 ft. to as tall as 35 ft. Leaves are pointed

ovals, often fuzzy, varying in color from medium green to nearly purple. Fall foliage is rarely noteworthy. Bloom in spring (usually before leaves unfurl), bearing masses of single, semidouble, or double flowers that sometimes have a musky, sweet scent. Small red, orange, or yellow apples, ranging from under ¾ in. to almost 2 in. wide, ripen from midsummer into autumn; in some varieties, the fruit hangs on well after leaves drop and even into winter. Some varieties bear flowers and fruit more heavily in alternate years.

Malus floribunda

Plant bare-root trees in winter or early spring; set out container plants anytime. Best in fertile, well-drained, deep soils but will grow in rocky or gravelly ones. They take acidic to slightly alkaline soil. Flowering crabapples are hardier, more tolerant of wet soil, and longer lived than flowering cherries and other flowering stone fruits. Take heat but are not at their best in low desert. For optimal growth and productivity, plants need winter chill—about 600 hours at 45°F/7°C or lower.

Flowering crabapple varieties differ widely in disease resistance. Many of the most popular varieties of years past are highly prone to one or more of the diseases that can plague these trees: apple scab, cedar-apple rust, fireblight, powdery mildew. Today, the nursery trade places great emphasis on promoting disease-resistant varieties—thus displacing many of the old favorites. The chart beginning on the following page notes degree of resistance or susceptibility for each variety. In the Pacific Northwest, it's imperative to choose trees that resist cedar-apple rust, scab, and powdery mildew. Fireblight may afflict susceptible trees anywhere when conditions are favorable for its development.

Flowering crabapples are subject to attack from the same pests that affect apple. Scale, aphids, spider mites, and tent caterpillars may require control; codling moths and apple maggots should be controlled if you intend to harvest the fruit.

Malus toringo sargentii

These are fine lawn trees, but their bark can easily be nicked by mowers, creating an entry point for diseases. Protect them by creating a sod-free, mulched area around the trunk. Or underplant with primroses, spring-blooming bulbs, or shade-loving bedding plants. Plant them near fences to heighten the screening effect.

Prune only to build a good framework, remove any suckers, and correct the shape. Crabapple trees can be trained as espaliers.

MALVA
MALLOW
Malvaceae
PERENNIALS OR BIENNIALS

🌿 **ZONES 1–9, 14–24, EXCEPT AS NOTED**

☀ **FULL SUN**

💧 **REGULAR WATER**

From Europe; naturalized in U.S. These plants are related to and somewhat resemble hollyhock (*Alcea*), but they are bushier, with smaller, roundish to heart-shaped leaves. Bloom from summer to fall. Easy to grow; need good drainage, average soil. Grow from seed; usually bloom first year. Use in perennial borders or for a quick tall edging. Not long lived.

M. alcea. Perennial. To 4 ft. tall, 2 ft. wide; upper leaves deeply divided. Saucer-shaped pink flowers to 2 in. wide. Most common form is 'Fastigiata'; it is narrower than the species and looks much like hollyhock.

M. moschata. MUSK MALLOW. Perennial. Zones A2, A3; 1–9, 14–24. Erect, branching plant to 3 ft. tall, 2 ft. wide. Finely cut leaves; pink or white flowers

▶ page 473

M

MALUS

NAME	HABIT, SIZE	FLOWERS	FRUIT	COMMENTS
Malus 'Adams' Zones A2, A3; 1–21	Dense, round headed, to 20 ft. tall and wide	Red buds open to single pink flowers	Dull red, small, long lasting	Orange fall foliage. Good disease resistance
M. 'Adirondack'	Columnar, to 12 ft. by 6 ft.	Red buds; large, red-tinged, single, waxy white flowers	Red to orange red	Formal in appearance. High disease resistance
M. 'Ames White'	Dense, upright, to 25 ft. tall and wide	Pink buds open to single white flowers	Yellow	High disease resistance
M. × arnoldiana ARNOLD CRABAPPLE	Broad, to 25 ft. by 35 ft.	Red buds open to single pink flowers that fade to white. Fragrant	Red-blushed yellow	Susceptible to scab and fireblight. Bears more heavily in alternate years
M. × atrosanguinea CARMINE CRABAPPLE	Erect, dense, irregular, to 18 ft. by 25 ft.	Single deep pink to red flowers. Fragrant	Reddish or greenish yellow, turning brown; hangs on all winter	Foliage has a purplish sheen. Moderate disease resistance
M. 'Brandywine'	Vigorous, shapely, to 15–20 ft. tall and wide	Double rose pink. Fragrant	Yellowish green	Leaves have a reddish cast. Fair disease resistance
M. 'Callaway'	Attractive, round headed, to 18 ft. by 16 ft.	Pink buds open to single white flowers	Deep red, large, long lasting	Low chill requirement for bloom; good in warmer-winter areas. High disease resistance
M. 'Centurion'	Oval crowned, to 25 ft. by 15–20 ft.	Red buds open to single red flowers	Shiny deep red, long lasting	Blooms young. High disease resistance
M. 'Coralburst'	Small, dense, to 10–15 ft. by 8–10 ft.	Coral pink buds open to small, double rose pink flowers	Reddish orange, small; scant crop	Usually grafted on a standard; sometimes grown as a shrub. Fair disease resistance
M. coronaria 'Charlottae'	Broadly spreading, to 30 ft. by 35 ft.	Large, double pale pink flowers	Yellowish green, large	Orange-red autumn foliage color. Like the species, blooms late and is susceptible to rust and scab
M. 'Donald Wyman'	Broad, to 20 ft. by 25 ft.	Pink to red buds open to single white flowers	Shiny, bright red, small, long lasting	Lustrous foliage. Good disease resistance
M. 'Dorothea'	Dense, round headed, to 25 ft. tall and wide	Red buds open to large, semidouble pink flowers	Bright yellow, small	Susceptible to scab and fireblight
M. floribunda JAPANESE FLOWERING CRABAPPLE	Broad, dense grower to 12 ft. by 18 ft.	Deep pink buds open to single white flowers. Fragrant, incredibly profuse blooms	Red-blushed yellow, small; does not last long	Moderate disease resistance
M. 'Harvest Gold'	Vigorous, narrow, to 30 ft. by 15 ft.	Pink buds open to single white flowers. Late blooming	Yellow, showy; hangs on until spring	High disease resistance
M. 'Hopa' Zones A2, A3; 1–11, 14–21	Fast growth to 25 ft. by 20 ft.	Single rose red flowers; fragrant	Orange red, large; drops early. Good for jelly	Suckers freely. Old-fashioned variety; very prone to disease except where humidity is very low. Newer, more disease-resistant crabapples are a better choice
M. hupehensis (M. theifera) TEA CRABAPPLE	Broad form; moderate growth to 15 ft. by 25 ft.	Deep pink buds open to single white flowers. Fragrant	Greenish yellow to red, small, not showy	Picturesque form, with branches strongly angled from short trunk. Moderate disease resistance
M. 'Indian Magic'	Round headed, to 15–20 ft. tall and wide	Red buds open to single deep pink flowers	Shiny red to orange, small, long lasting	Moderate susceptibility to disease
M. 'Indian Summer'	Rounded, to 18 ft. tall and wide	Single rose red	Bright red, long lasting	Good orange-red fall leaf color. High disease resistance

MALUS

NAME	HABIT, SIZE	FLOWERS	FRUIT	COMMENTS
M. ioensis 'Plena' BECHTEL CRABAPPLE	Round headed, open, to 30 ft. tall and wide	Double pink flowers. Fragrant	Dull yellow green, large	Highly susceptible to disease. 'Klehm's' is a similar variety that offers better disease resistance
M. 'Jewelberry'	Dwarfish, dense, to 8 ft. by 12 ft.	Pink buds open to single white flowers	Shiny, red, small, long lasting	Bears young. Moderate disease resistance
M. kaido (see **M. × micromalus**)				
M. 'Katherine'	Slow growing to 20 ft. tall and wide	Deep pink buds open to large, double pink flowers that quickly fade to white	Red-blushed yellow, very small	Fair disease resistance. Bears more heavily in alternate years
M. 'Liset'	Roundish, dense growth to 15–20 ft. tall and wide	Crimson buds open to single flowers in deep red to crimson	Dark red to maroon; hangs on well	Deep purplish green leaves. Fair disease resistance
M. 'Louisa'	Broad, weeping, to 15 ft. tall and wide	Single rose pink. Profuse bloomer	Golden orange, small	Excellent, graceful weeper. Glossy, dark green foliage. Good disease resistance
M. 'Madonna'	Narrow, erect tree grows to 15–20 ft. by 10–15 ft.	Pink buds open to double white flowers. Long bloom season	Red-blushed yellow, small	Bronzy new growth. Good disease resistance
M. × micromalus **(M. kaido)** MIDGET CRABAPPLE Zones A2, A3; 1–11, 14–21	Slow growth to 15 ft. by 8–10 ft.	Red buds open to single pink flowers that hold their color. Profuse bloomer	Red or greenish, not showy	Some susceptibility to scab
M. 'Molten Lava'	Spreading, weeping tree to 12 ft. by 15 ft.	Deep red buds open to single white flowers	Red orange, small; lasts well on tree	Attractive yellow winter bark. Good disease resistance
M. 'Narragansett'	Broad, round headed, to 15 ft. tall and wide	Red buds open to single white flowers with faint touch of pink	Bright red, small, showy	High disease resistance
M. 'Oekonomierat Echtermeyer' **('Pink Weeper')** WEEPING CRABAPPLE	Grows at moderate rate to 15 ft. by 20 ft., with weeping branches	Red buds open to single purplish red flowers	Purplish to reddish to greenish brown	Foliage is purple when new, turning purplish green by summer. Prune out any erect-growing branches. Disease prone
M. 'Pink Princess'	Low, broad, to 15 ft. by 12 ft.	Single rose pink	Deep red, small; lasts well on tree	Reddish green foliage. Good disease resistance
M. 'Pink Spires' Zones A2, A3; 1–21	Narrow, upright, to 25 ft. by 12–15 ft.	Deep rose pink buds open to single flowers in a lighter rose pink	Reddish purple; hangs on well	Foliage is red when new, maturing to bronzy green. Moderate disease resistance
M. 'Prairifire'	Round headed, to 20 ft. tall and wide	Red buds open to single flowers in deep pinkish red	Dark red, small; hangs on well	Leaves emerge reddish maroon, turn dark green. High disease resistance
M. 'Profusion'	Upright, spreading, to 20 ft. tall and wide	Deep red buds, single deep purplish pink flowers	Dark red, long lasting	Foliage is purple when young, matures to bronzy green. Moderate disease resistance
M. 'Purple Wave'	Broad, spreading, to 10–15 ft. tall and wide	Large, single to semidouble rose red flowers fade to purplish pink with age	Dark purple red	Purplish foliage. Susceptible to rust, scab
M. 'Radiant' Zones A2, A3; 1–21	Broad, round headed, to 20 ft. tall and wide	Deep red buds open to single deep pink flowers	Bright red; colors early and lasts into winter	Leaves are reddish when they open, later turn green. Susceptible to scab

M

MALUS

NAME	HABIT, SIZE	FLOWERS	FRUIT	COMMENTS
M. 'Red Barron'	Narrow (to 20 ft. by 12 ft.), growing broader with age	Very deep red buds open to single reddish pink flowers	Shiny dark red	New leaves are purple, mature ones bronzy green. Susceptible to scab
M. 'Red Jade' Zones A2, A3; 1–21	Irregular, weeping form; to 15 ft. tall and wide	Small, single white flowers	Bright red, heavy crop; holds well into fall	Moderate disease resistance
M. 'Red Jewel'	Small, round headed, to 15 ft. by 12 ft.	Large, single white flowers	Bright red, small, long lasting	Fair disease resistance
M. 'Red Silver'	Angular, irregular, to 30 ft. tall and wide	Single deep wine red flowers	Dark purplish red. Good for jelly	Reddish foliage covered with silky hairs that give it a silvery look. Very prone to scab
M. 'Robinson'	Dense, upright, vase-shaped tree to 25 ft. by 15 ft.	Deep red buds open to single deep pink flowers	Dark red	Copper-tinged foliage. High disease resistance
M. 'Royal Fountain'	Weeping form; to 15 ft. tall and wide	Single rose red	Deep red	Leaves start out purple, turn bronze in summer. Moderate disease resistance
M. 'Royalty' Zones A1–A3; 1–21	Upright, to 20 ft. by 18 ft.	Single purplish crimson	Dark red	Foliage is dark purple in spring, purplish green in summer, dark purple again in fall. Susceptible to scab, fireblight
M. sieboldii 'Calocarpa' (see M.× zumi calocarpa)				
M. 'Snowdrift' Zones A1–A3; 1–21	Rounded, dense, to 20–25 ft. tall and wide	Red buds open to single white flowers. Long bloom season	Orange red, small, long lasting	Good disease resistance
M. 'Strawberry Parfait'	Open, vase shaped, to 20 ft. by 25 ft.	Red buds open to single pink flowers edged in red; profuse bloomer	Red-blushed yellow	High disease resistance
M. 'Sugar Tyme'	Upright, oval, to 18 ft. by 15 ft.	Delicate light pink buds open to single white flowers. Fragrant	Red, abundant, long lasting	High disease resistance
M. theifera (see M. hupehensis)				
M. 'Thunderchild' Zones A2, A3; 1–21	Erect, oval, to 20 ft. by 18 ft.	Single rose pink	Dark red	Purple foliage. Good disease resistance
M. toringo sargentii SARGENT CRABAPPLE	Broad, densely branched, to 10 ft. by 20 ft.	Single white flowers. Blooms are small, fragrant, profuse	Red, tiny, long lasting	Good disease resistance. 'Candymint' has pink flowers with petals outlined in red. 'Rosea', a pink-flowered form, may be more disease prone than the species. 'Firebird' (5–8 ft. tall and wide) and 'Tina' (4–6 ft. tall and 8–10 ft. wide) are excellent dwarf forms
M. transitoria 'Golden Raindrops' ('Schmidtcutleaf') Zones 3–11, 14–21	Upright, vase-shaped, to 20 ft. tall by 15 ft. wide	Small, star-shaped white flowers from pink buds. Profuse blooms	Golden yellow, abundant, long lasting	Unique crabapple with deeply cut, dark green foliage. Excellent resistance to scab, cedar-apple rust, mildew; fair resistance to fireblight
M. 'Weeping Candied Apple'	Weeping form; to 10–15 ft. by 20 ft.	Outer petals deep pink, inner petals whitish edged in pink, opening from reddish buds	Bright red, small; persists all winter	Good disease resistance
M.× zumi calocarpa (M. sieboldii 'Calocarpa')	Densely branched, rounded, to 15 ft. tall and wide	Single flowers open pale pink, then fade to white. Fragrant	Glossy, bright red, small; lasts well on tree	Moderate susceptibility to fireblight

M

Malva alcea

o 1 in. wide or somewhat wider. Entire plant emits a mild, musky odor if brushed against or bruised. Named selections are more frequently grown than the species. 'Rosea' has pink blossoms; 'Alba' is 2 ft. tall, bears white flowers.

M. sylvestris. Perennial or biennial. Erect, bushy growth to 2–4 ft. tall, 2 ft. wide. Can become invasive. Flowers 2 in. wide; often bloom until frost. Common variety 'Zebrina' (often sold as *M. zebrina*) has blossoms in pale lavender pink with pronounced deep purple veining. 'Mauritiana' has darker, often semidouble flowers.

MALVASTRUM
lateritium
(Modiolastrum
lateritium)
TRAILING MALLOW
Malvaceae
PERENNIAL

- ZONES 8, 9, 14–24
- FULL SUN
- LITTLE OR NO WATER

From South America. Grows 8 in. high, 5 ft. wide, with trailing stems that root as they spread. Roundish, 2–3-in.-wide leaves. Blossoms throughout warm weather, bearing saucer-shaped, 1½–2-in.-wide flowers that are salmon pink with pinkish orange center. Useful for holding soil on a bank or for ground cover (but does not toler-

Malvastrum lateritium

ate foot traffic). Withstands poor soil, heat, much aridity. Its only drawback is invasiveness; keep it away from more delicate plants.

MAMMILLARIA
Cactaceae
CACTI

- ZONES 8–24, EXCEPT AS NOTED
- PARTIAL SHADE IN HOTTEST CLIMATES
- REGULAR WATER

Specialists offer as many as 100 species of these cacti, which are chiefly grown in pots. Plants are small (usually 2–6 in. high), cylindrical or globe shaped, with single or clustered stems. Purple, red, pink, or white flowers (generally small) are arranged in a circle near top of plant. Southwestern natives *M. meiacantha* and *M. wrightii* are hardy to Zone 2. Both are 4 in. high and bear spring flowers; those of *M. meiacantha* are pink or white, those of *M. wrightii* purple or pink.

Mammillaria

All mammillarias are easy to grow. Provide some shade in hot desert regions. Give regular moisture during growing season; keep dry in winter to induce bloom. For the plant sold as *M. vivipara*, see *Coryphantha vivipara*.

MANDARIN. See CITRUS

MANDEVILLA
Apocynaceae
EVERGREEN AND DECIDUOUS
VINES OR VINING SHRUBS

- ZONES VARY BY SPECIES
- FULL SUN OR PARTIAL SHADE
- REGULAR WATER

Grown for showy flowers, the genus *Mandevilla* includes plants formerly called *Dipladenia*. Blossoms feature five broad lobes that flare out from a tubular throat; except as noted, they are unscented. Plants climb by twining. They survive outdoors only in mildest

regions. In colder areas, treat as annuals, or grow them in containers and move them indoors or to a greenhouse for the winter. Need heat to bloom; in coastal areas, train against a protected south- or west-facing wall, preferably with additional reflected heat from paving. Watch for spider mites. Growth may need thinning from time to time.

M. boliviensis. Evergreen. Zones 23, 24; H1, H2. Native to Ecuador and Bolivia. Grows 12 ft. long as a vine; reaches 3 ft. tall and 5 ft. wide as a sprawling shrub. Glossy, pointed leaves to 4 in. long, 1½ in. wide. Blooms throughout the year, producing white, 2½-in.-wide flowers with golden yellow throats.

M. hybrids. Evergreen. Zones 21–24; H1, H2. The hybrid mandevillas described here are sometimes sold as selections of *M.* × *amabilis* or *M.* × *amoena*. Plants grow to 15–20 ft., with glossy dark green, oval leaves 3–8 in. long. Most widely grown is 'Alice du Pont', with clusters of glowing pink, 2–4-in. flowers appearing among the leaves from spring to fall; even very small plants in 4-in. pots will bloom. 'Magic Dream' ('Crimson Jewel') has crimson red flowers. 'Moonlight Parfait' has pink buds that open to large white blossoms with a pink, double-petaled center. 'Pink Parfait' ('Rita Marie Green') has long-lasting, hot pink, double flowers. 'Ruby Star' is a slightly more compact plant with narrower-lobed, 3-in.-wide flowers; blossoms open deep pink, then mature to magenta with a touch of yellow deep in the throat. 'Summer Snow' bears blush pink blossoms that eventually fade to white. 'Tango Twirl' offers upright clusters of light pink double blooms. 'White Delight' has pale pink buds opening to white blooms with a light yellow throat.

Plant all hybrids in rich soil and provide a frame, trellis, or stake for support. Pinch tips of young plants to induce bushiness.

M. laxa (M. suaveolens). CHILEAN JASMINE. Deciduous; evergreen in frost-free areas. Zones 4–9, 14–24; H1. From Chile and Argentina. Grows to 15 ft. or

*Mandevilla
'Alice du Pont'*

more, with heart-shaped, 2–6-in.-long leaves. Blooms in summer. Clustered flowers are white, 1½–2 in. across, with a powerful perfume like that of gardenia. Requires less heat to bloom than other mandevillas. Provide rich soil. If plant becomes badly tangled, cut to ground in winter; it will resprout and bloom on new growth. Roots hardy to about 5°F/–15°C.

M. splendens (M. sanderi, Dipladenia splendens). Evergreen. Zones 21–24; H1, H2. Native to southeastern Brazil. Compact, shrubby plant to 2 ft. tall, 3 ft. wide; eventually starts to twine (to 15–20 ft. tall with support), but you can keep it bushy by pinching climbing shoots. Deep green leaves are 4–8 in. long, tinged with bronze when new. Flowers are 3–4 in. wide, rose pink with yellow throats; color grows paler as blossoms age. Varieties that are lower growing and shrubbier than the species (to 6–8 ft.) are superb in hanging baskets; these include 'My Fair Lady' (white blooms), 'Red Riding Hood' (deep cherry red flowers), and 'Scarlet Pimpernel' (scarlet flowers). Similar in form is 'Strawberry Lemonade', with deep pink, yellow-throated flowers; its leaves are beautifully variegated in mint green, cream, and white, with pink flushes when young.

MANFREDA
maculosa
TEXAS TUBEROSE
Agavaceae
SUCCULENT PERENNIAL

- ZONES 4–24
- SUN OR SHADE
- LITTLE TO REGULAR WATER

Native to southern Texas, northern Mexico. Fleshy, 6–12-in.-wide leaves grow from a bulblike rootstock to form a 1-ft.-tall, 2-ft.-wide plant that resembles a small, virtually spineless century plant (*Agave americana*). Deep green leaves are strikingly blotched with purple; markings are more pronounced in sun than in shade. In summer, 3–4½-ft. stalks bear fragrant, 2-in.-long, tubular flowers in creamy white aging to purple; long stamens give them a spidery look.

M

Manfreda maculosa

Flowers attract hummingbirds. Good in containers or in the ground. Leaves die back in winter but reappear quickly when warm weather arrives. Plants form new clumps by offsets. Some botanists consider this plant to be an agave.

MANGIFERA indica.
See **MANGO**

MANGLE DULCE.
See **MAYTENUS phyllanthoides**

MANGO

Anacardiaceae
EVERGREEN TREE

✂	ZONES 23, 24; H1, H2
☼	FULL SUN
💧	REGULAR WATER
◆	SAP AND JUICE FROM FRUIT CAUSE SKIN RASH IN SOME PEOPLE

Tropical Asian native, known botanically as *Mangifera indica.* In Hawaii, mango trees reach upwards of 50 ft. tall and spread to 30 ft. or more. These trees are very long lived and produce heavy crops of fruit. In mildest parts of Southern California, however, plants often remain shrubby and are likely to fruit only in the most favorable frost-free locations. Large (8–16-in.-long), handsome leaves are often coppery red or purple when new; they later turn dark green.

Trees are self-fruitful. Long clusters of yellow to reddish flowers appear at branch ends from spring into summer; these are followed by oval fruits up to 9 in. long, weighing up to 2 lbs. in good growing conditions. Fruit has green to reddish or yellowish skin, a large seed, and very juicy pale yellow to deep orange flesh that tastes somewhat like a peach with flowery overtones. Poorer-quality fruit may be stringy and/or have a flavor reminiscent of varnish or turpentine. In Southern California, skin

may not color well, but fruit quality can still be excellent.

Mangoes are most flavorful if allowed to ripen on the tree; they are usually ready to harvest 4 to 5 months after bloom. Many reliable varieties are sold, among them 'Ah Ping', 'Julie', 'Keitt', 'Pope', and 'Rapoza'. Trees tend to bear more heavily in alternate years.

Trees tolerate fairly poor, shallow soil as long as it is well drained. Fertilize as recommended for citrus. Anthracnose, scale, and powdery mildew can be serious problems. Little pruning is needed.

Mango

MANZANITA.
See **ARCTOSTAPHYLOS**

MAPLE. See **ACER**

MARANTA lubbersiana.
See **CTENANTHE lubbersiana**

MARGUERITE. See
CHRYSANTHEMUM frutescens

MARIGOLD. See **TAGETES**

MARIPOSA LILY.
See **CALOCHORTUS**

MARJORAM. See **ORIGANUM**

MARLBERRY. See **ARDISIA**

MARMALADE BUSH.
See **STREPTOSOLEN jamesonii**

MARRUBIUM
vulgare

HOREHOUND
Lamiaceae (Labiatae)
PERENNIAL

✂	ZONES 1–24
☼	FULL SUN
💧	LITTLE TO MODERATE WATER

Native to Mediterranean region and western Asia; naturalized throughout Europe and the Americas. Coarse, upright plant to 1–3 ft.

Marrubium vulgare

tall, 1–1½ ft. wide, with wrinkled, woolly, aromatic gray-green leaves to 2 in. long. Rounded whorls of white flowers (similar to those of mint) bloom on foot-long, branching stems in summer. Flowers in second year from seed. As a garden plant, it is invasive and rather weedy looking, but it makes a serviceable edging in a garden of gray-leafed plants. Used for medicinal purposes and in candy. Foliage lasts well in bouquets. Requires little water but will take more if drainage is good; otherwise not fussy about soil. Give protection from cold, wind.

MARSH MARIGOLD.
See **CALTHA palustris**

MASCAGNIA

ORCHID VINE
Malpighiaceae
DECIDUOUS VINES

✂	ZONES 12–24
☼	FULL SUN
💧	MODERATE WATER

Twining vines native to Mexico; useful in desert gardens, where they bloom at the hottest time of year. Bright green leaves in opposite pairs resemble those of honeysuckle (*Lonicera*). Bear clusters of five-petaled blossoms (the petals are shaped like Ping-Pong paddles);

Mascagnia lilacina

each bloom is centered with ten stamens. Oddly winged seedpods that look something like butterflies follow the flowers; these are sometimes used in dried arrangements.

M. lilacina. LAVENDER ORCHID VINE. To 15–20 ft., with 1½-in. leaves and lilac flowers that are followed by inch-wide seedpods. Plant is hardy to 15 to 18°F/ –9 to –8°C.

M. macroptera. YELLOW ORCHID VINE. To 15 ft., with 3-in. leaves. Abundant bright yellow flowers are followed by conspicuous 2-in., yellow-green seedpods. Hardy to 22 to 24°F/–6 to –4°C.

MASTERWORT.
See **ASTRANTIA**

MASTIC. See **PISTACIA lentiscus**

MATERNITY PLANT. See
KALANCHOE daigremontiana

MATILIJA POPPY.
See **ROMNEYA coulteri**

MATRICARIA
recutita
(M. chamomilla)

CHAMOMILE
Asteraceae (Compositae)
ANNUAL

✂	ZONES 1–24
☼	FULL SUN
💧	MODERATE WATER

Native to Europe, western Asia; naturalized in North America. Aromatic plant grows to 2 ft. tall and 1½ ft. wide, with finely cut, almost fernlike foliage. White-and-yellow daisy-type flowers to 1 in. wide bloom in summer. Grows easily in ordinary soil; sow seed in late winter or spring. Valued for its herbal use: dried flowers are used in making the familiar, fragrant chamomile tea.

Plants or seeds sold as *Matricaria* 'White Stars', 'Golden Ball', and 'Snowball' are varieties

Matricaria recutita

f *Chrysanthemum parthenium.* hamomile sold as a walk-on round cover is *Chamaemelum obile (Anthemis nobilis).*

MATTEUCCIA struthiopteris

STRICH FERN
olypodiaceae
ERN

- ZONES A1–A3; 1–10, 14–17
- FULL SUN IN COOLER CLIMATES ONLY
- REGULAR TO AMPLE WATER

Native to northern regions of North America, Europe, Asia. Is nardy to extreme cold and does not grow with full vigor in mild-winter areas. Clump is narrow at nase, then spreads out at top like a shuttlecock. Plant can grow 6 ft. tall and 3 ft. wide in moist, moderate climates, but it may reach only a quarter or a third of that size in mountain regions with short growing season, low humidity. Jumbo' is a hefty-looking variety that can reach 7 ft. tall under ideal conditions; mature plants form a short trunk.

Matteuccia struthiopteris

Plant spreads by underground rhizomes. Attractive in woodland or beside pond or stream. Needs rich soil. Unfolding young fronds (fiddleheads) are edible; cook them in boiling water for 10 minutes or steam them for 20 minutes, until tender but still slightly crisp. Also sold as *Matteuccia pensylvanica.*

MATTHIOLA

STOCK
Brassicaceae (Cruciferae)
BIENNIALS OR PERENNIALS GROWN AS ANNUALS

- ZONES 1–24
- FULL SUN OR LIGHT SHADE
- REGULAR WATER

From the Mediterranean region. Old-fashioned favorites, with narrow gray-green leaves and profuse,

erect spikes of fragrant flowers. Best in cool weather.

M. incana. Valued for spicy-sweet perfume, cut flowers. Oblong leaves to 4 in. long. Flowers are single or double, 1 in. wide, in colors including white, pink, red, purple, lavender, blue, yellow, and cream.

Matthiola incana

Many strains are available, ranging from under 1 ft. to as tall as 3 ft., from 10 to 16 in. wide. Earliest bloomer is Trysomic Seven Weeks (flowers in 7 weeks), with branching plants about 12–15 in. tall. Ten Weeks, also branching, reaches 15–18 in. tall. Column and Double Giant Flowering are unbranched plants 2–3 ft. tall; they can be planted 6–8 in. apart in rows and are ideal for cutting. Giant Imperial strain is branching, 2–2½ ft. tall; it comes in solid or mixed colors.

Stock needs light, fertile soil, and good drainage. In cold-winter areas, plant in earliest spring to get flowers before hot weather (choose early bloomers). In mild-winter regions, plants set out in early fall will bloom in winter or early spring. Take moderate frost but will not set flower buds if nights are too chilly; late planting means no flowers until spring. Where winter rainfall is heavy, plant in raised beds for good drainage.

M. longipetala (M. bicornis). EVENING SCENTED STOCK. To 1 ft. or a little taller, 9 in. wide, with lance-shaped leaves to 3½ in. long. Small purplish flowers are not showy, but they give off a powerful fragrance at night. In hot-summer, mild-winter climates, grow as a winter annual.

MATTRESS VINE.
See **MUEHLENBECKIA complexa**

MAURANDELLA antirrhiniflora.
See **ASARINA antirrhiniflora**

MAURANDYA barclayana.
See **ASARINA barclaiana**

MAURITIUS HEMP.
See **FURCRAEA foetida**

MAY APPLE.
See **PODOPHYLLUM peltatum**

MAYBUSH, MAYDAY TREE.
See **PRUNUS padus**

MAYPOP.
See **PASSIFLORA incarnata**

MAYTENUS

Celastraceae
EVERGREEN TREES AND SHRUBS

- ZONES VARY BY SPECIES
- FULL SUN
- WATER NEEDS VARY BY SPECIES

Two species of this genus of primarily South American natives are grown in the West. Both have inconspicuous flowers and fruit, but they are otherwise remarkably dissimilar in appearance.

M. boaria. MAYTEN. Zones 8, 9, 14–24. From Chile. Graceful tree with narrow, 1–2-in.-long, light to medium green leaves. Resembles a small-scale weeping willow *(Salix),* with long, pendulous branchlets hanging down from branches. Slow to moderate growth to an eventual 30–50 ft. high and wide; 20 ft. tall by 15 ft. wide is typical at 12 years of age. For uniformity, plant cutting-grown trees of 'Green Showers'; its weeping branchlets are densely clad with deep green leaves that are a little broader than those of the species.

Give well-drained soil. Disturbing the roots by cultivating may cause suckers to appear. Tree produces much side growth; remove unwanted branches along trunk, or keep some of them for multiple-

Maytenus boaria

trunk effect. May show partial defoliation after a cold snap, but recovery is rapid. Resistant to oak root fungus. Moderate to regular water; irrigate deeply to keep tree from rooting near soil surface and invading planting beds.

M. phyllanthoides. MANGLE DULCE. Zones 12, 13, 23, 24. From Baja California, Mexico, the Caribbean. Like mangroves *(mangle* is Spanish for "mangrove"), this plant grows in or near salt water and in brackish, swampy soils inland. Usually grows as a 6–12 ft. shrub but occasionally a small tree up to 24 ft.; usually as wide as it is tall. Smooth light gray bark; fleshy dark green to gray-green leaves to 1½ in. long. Little to moderate water.

MAZUS reptans

Scrophulariaceae
PERENNIAL

- ZONES 1–9, 14–24
- PARTIAL SHADE IN HOTTEST CLIMATES
- REGULAR WATER

Himalayan native to 2 in. high; spreads 1 ft. or wider by slender stems that creep and root along the ground. Sparsely toothed, rather narrow leaves are bright green, about 1 in. long. Spring and early

Mazus reptans

summer flowers are ¾ in. across, purplish blue with white and yellow markings; they appear in clusters of two to five. In shape, the blossoms resemble those of monkey flower *(Mimulus).* Use in rock garden, as small-scale ground cover, as filler between pavers (takes heavy foot traffic in this last role). Needs rich soil. Evergreen in mild-winter climates; in colder areas, freezes to ground but usually recovers quickly in spring if protected over winter by snow cover or light mulch.

MEADOWFOAM.
See **LIMNANTHES douglasii**

M

MEADOW RUE.
See **THALICTRUM**

MEADOW SAFFRON.
See **COLCHICUM**

MEADOWSWEET.
See **FILIPENDULA**

MECONOPSIS
Papaveraceae
PERENNIALS

| 🌡 ZONES VARY BY SPECIES |
| ◑ ● PARTIAL OR FULL SHADE |
| ● REGULAR WATER |

Ardent collectors and shade garden enthusiasts sometimes attempt the many species offered by specialist seed firms. Most of these are difficult to grow, but the choices listed here are not too trying if given loose, acid soil and cool, humid, shady conditions. Protect seaside plantings from wind.

Plants consist of foliage rosettes with elongated leaves that vary in shape from undivided to lobed or cut; these foliage clumps send up flowering stems at bloom time. Blossoms are large and brilliantly colored. Plants self-sow without becoming invasive. Except as noted, these plants are native to the Himalayas.

M. betonicifolia (M. baileyi). HIMALAYAN POPPY. Zones A1–A3; 1–6, 17. In the right climate, can reach 6 ft. tall and 2 ft. wide. Abundant hairy leaves with serrated edges; silky, 3–4-in., sky blue poppies with yellow stamens. In less favorable locales, it is a much squatter, shorter-lived plant with smaller flowers verging on mauve. Blooms in late spring or early summer.

Meconopsis betonicifolia

M. cambrica. WELSH POPPY. Zones 1–9, 14–17. Native to western Europe. To 1–2 ft. tall, 1 ft. wide, with divided leaves. Easier to grow than *M. betonicifolia*. Produces orange or yellow, 3-in.

poppies from late spring to fall. In the coolest-summer areas, it tolerates full sun, some drought. *M. c. aurantiaca* 'Flore Pleno' has semidouble flowers.

M. grandis. Zones A2, A3; 1–6, 17. To 4 ft. tall, 2 ft. wide. Tooth-edged basal leaves are up to 10 in. long; leaf size is reduced farther up the stems. Leaves and stems have rusty hairs. In late spring, 4–6-in.-wide flowers in pure blue to purplish red are borne on long (to 16-in.) stalks that rise from the uppermost leaves. May be biennial if moisture is not adequate.

M. × sheldonii. Zones A2, A3; 1–6, 17. Hybrid of *M. betonicifolia* and *M. grandis*. Plant grows to 4–5 ft. tall, 2 ft. wide, with toothed leaves and 4-in., pure blue poppies on 8–20-in. stalks. Blooms in late spring or early summer.

MEDITERRANEAN FAN PALM.
See **CHAMAEROPS humilis**

MELALEUCA
Myrtaceae
EVERGREEN SHRUBS OR TREES

| 🌡 ZONES VARY BY SPECIES |
| ☀ FULL SUN |
| ◌ LITTLE WATER, EXCEPT AS NOTED |

Australia is home to 140 or more species of melaleucas, and many of these show up in Western gardens. All have narrow, sometimes needlelike leaves and bear clustered flowers with prominent stamens; the blossoms attract birds. Since each flower cluster resembles a bottlebrush, some melalecas are called bottlebrushes, though that name is more generally applied to members of the genus *Callistemon*. Tight clusters of woody seed capsules are attached directly to branches; these hang on for several years, forming odd, decorative cylinders around twigs and branches. Many melaleucas have interestingly contorted branches and bark that peels off in thick, papery layers.

All melaleucas are easy to grow. Most withstand heat, wind, seacoast conditions, poor soil, limited moisture. Most are vigorous and fast growing; for a natural appearance, control by cutting back selected branches to a well-placed side branch. Almost all melaleucas make good screens; some of the larger ones are useful as flowering or shade trees.

M. armillaris. DROOPING MELALEUCA. Shrub or tree.

Zones 8, 9, 12–24; H1, H2. As sprawling shrub, grows 12–15 ft. high, 15–30 ft. wide; trained as a tree, reaches 15–30 ft. tall and wide. Branches are drooping. Furrowed gray bark peels off in strips near base of trunk. Light green, needlelike leaves to 1 in. long; fluffy white flowers in 1–3½-in.-long spikes from spring to fall. Tough and adaptable; especially useful in sea winds. Use as clipped hedge or unclipped informal screen; prickly leaves make it a good barrier plant.

M. decussata. LILAC MELALEUCA. Shrub or tree. Zones 9, 12–24; H1. To 8–20 ft. tall and wide. Brown, shredding bark. Tiny (½-in.) bluish leaves closely set on arching, pendulous branches. Lilac to purple flowers in 1-in. spikes from late spring to summer. Withstands some neglect. Use it for big masses of fine-textured foliage in the landscape. Thin to improve appearance, show off trunk and branch character.

M. elliptica. GRANITE BOTTLEBRUSH. Shrub or tree. Zones 9, 12–24. To 8–16 ft. high, 10–15 ft. wide. Brown, shredding bark. Branches are fanlike, with each one producing a number of branchlets that spread outward and upward in a single plane; roundish, ½-in., bluish or grayish green leaves are set mostly at branchlet ends. Blooms from early spring to fall, bearing bright pink to crimson, 2–3½-in.-long bottlebrushes on side branches.

M. ericifolia. HEATH MELALEUCA. Shrub or tree. Zones 9, 12–24; H1. To 18–36 ft. tall, 12–24 ft. wide. Soft, fibrous tan or gray bark. Dark green, needlelike, 1-in. leaves like those of heather (*Calluna*). Yellowish white flowers in 1-in. spikes bloom in early spring. Grows fast and tolerates alkaline soil, poor drainage; good near beach. Makes an attractive multitrunked tree.

M. fulgens. SCARLET HONEY MYRTLE. Shrub. Zones 13, 15–24. To 3–9 ft. tall, 5–9 ft. wide, with flat, narrow green to gray-green leaves ¼–1 in. long. Blooms from late winter to early summer, with sporadic rebloom likely; flower clusters are 2 in. long and wide, in pale orange, salmon, or bright scarlet (all with golden anthers). Blossoms appear at ends of branches, and new leafy growth proceeds from center of flower cluster. Showy plant.

M. huegelii. CHENILLE HONEY MYRTLE. Shrub or tree.

Zones 9, 12–24. Highly variable species to 3–25 ft. tall, 6–20 ft. wide. Nearly triangular leaves are less than ½ in. long, set close together on branches, usually overlapping. Profuse spring to summer show of 2–4-in.-long flowers that are pink or red in bud, opening to white or cream (rarely pink). Blossoms are good for cutting. Plant can take hard pruning and serve as hedge or windbreak.

M. hypericifolia. DOTTED MELALEUCA. Shrub. Zones 9, 12–24; H1. To 6–12 ft. tall, 3–12 ft. wide, with thin, peeling pale gray bark and drooping branches. Coppery green to dull green, 1¼-in. leaves. Blooms from late spring through winter, producing bright orange-red flowers in dense 2-in. clusters (often hidden by foliage). Can be clipped into a hedge but blooms more profusely as an informal, unclipped screen. Not suitable for planting right at beach though it takes ocean wind.

M. incana. GRAY HONEY MYRTLE. Shrub or tree. Zones 8, 9, 12–24. Spreading, arching plant with semiweeping branchlets. Gray, furry foliage gives the plant an overall pale, smoky look. Small clusters of yellowish white flowers in spring. Naturally grows as a broad shrub to 9 ft. tall and wide but can be shaped into a handsome small tree.

M. lanceolata. DRYLAND TEA TREE. Shrub or tree. Zones 8, 9, 12–24 . To 18–30 ft. tall, 12–25 ft. wide. Narrow dark green leaves to ½ in. long. White or cream, 2-in. bottlebrush flower clusters bloom from summer into fall, with sporadic bloom the rest of the year. Tolerates most soil types and takes hard frosts. Tends to retain its foliage down to ground level.

M. linariifolia. FLAXLEAF PAPERBARK. Tree. Zones 9, 13–

Melaleuca linariifolia

24; H1. To 20–30 ft. tall, 20–25 ft. wide, with dense, umbrellalike crown. White bark sheds in papery flakes. Slender branchlets covered with stiff, bright green or bluish green, needlelike leaves about 1¼ in. long. In summer, numerous fluffy spikes of small white flowers give effect of snow on branches. Young plants are willowy and need staking until trunk firms up.

M. nesophila. PINK MELALEUCA. Tree or shrub. Zones 13, 16–24; H1. Fast growth to 15–20 ft. high (possibly to 30 ft.) and about as wide. Grows naturally as a small tree. Develops gnarled, heavy branches that sprawl or ascend in picturesque patterns. Grayish cream to pale brown bark is thick and spongy; gray-green leaves are thick, roundish, to 1 in. long. Roundish bottlebrush flower clusters to 1 in. wide are produced at branch ends most of the year; they open mauve pink, fade to white with yellow tips. Use as tree or big, informal screen; or shear as hedge. Takes ocean winds and spray; poor, rocky soil; desert heat. Little to regular water.

M. quinquenervia. CAJEPUT TREE, PAPERBARK TREE. Zones 9, 12, 13, 15–17, 20–24; H1, H2. Upright, open growth to 20–40 ft. tall, 15–25 ft. wide; can become twice as large in the tropics. Pendulous young branches. Thick, spongy, light brown to whitish bark peels off in sheets (you can use these sheets to line wire hanging baskets). Stiff, narrowly oval, 2–4-in.-long leaves are shiny pale green, covered with silky hairs when young. The foliage turns purple with light frosts. Yellowish white (sometimes pink or purple) flowers bloom in 2–3-in. spikes in summer and fall. Good street tree. Trees planted 8–10 ft. apart and thinned occasionally make a pleasant grove. Little to regular water. Has been sold as *M. leucadendra*. In Hawaii, cajeput tree has

Melaleuca quinquenervia

escaped cultivation to become an invasive pest.

M. rhaphiophylla. SWAMP PAPERBARK. Zones 8, 9, 12–24. Shrub or tree to 12–45 ft. tall and 9–24 ft. wide, with papery gray or tan bark and green or gray-green, needlelike leaves ½–2 in. long. Profuse, showy bloom from spring into summer, with fragrant white or cream, 1½-in.-long flower clusters. Can endure some shade. Regular to ample water.

M. styphelioides. PRICKLY PAPERBARK. Tree. Zones 9, 13–24; H1. To 20–40 ft. tall, 10–20 ft. wide, with lacy, open growth and pendulous branchlets. Thick, spongy bark turns from pale tan to charcoal colored with age, peels off in papery layers. Light green, prickly leaves to ¾ in. long are sometimes twisted. Creamy white flowers in 1–2-in. brushes from summer through fall. Thrives in any soil. Resistant to oak root fungus. Good lawn tree. Best trained with multiple trunks.

M. thymifolia. THYMELEAF MELALEUCA. Shrub. Zones 8, 9, 12–24. Low, spreading bush 2–4 ft. high, 4–8 ft. wide. Bark is corky, flaking, grayish brown. Narrow blue-green leaves to ¾ in. long are fragrant when crushed. Blooms spring through early summer, with 2–3-in.-wide flower clusters resembling bundles of tiny ostrich feathers in white, pink, deep mauve, or dusky purple. Many different color forms, including 'Pink Lace' and 'White Lace'. Prefers acid soil but tolerates soils that lack fertility, are somewhat alkaline, or have sluggish drainage. Prune after flowering to keep compact. Takes occasional drought; best with regular water.

M. viridiflora. BROADLEAFED PAPERBARK. Shrub or tree. Zones 13, 19–24. To 12–25 ft. tall, 6–18 ft. wide, with papery gray or light tan bark. Thick, leathery dark green or gray-green leaves less than 1 in. long. Flowering comes sporadically throughout the year; blossoms are narrow brushes to 6 in. long in white, cream, or green. *M. v. rubriflora* has pink to red flowers.

M. wilsonii. VIOLET HONEY MYRTLE. Shrub. Zones 8, 9, 12–24. To 3–10 ft. tall, 5–12 ft. wide, with spreading or arching habit. Leaves very narrow, ½ in. long, dark green. Clusters of two to five pink or purplish pink, ½-in.-wide flowers line the branches to make spikes that may or may not be interrupted by leaves. Can be

pruned as a hedge. A prostrate form just 2 ft. high and 8 ft. wide is available; it makes a good small-scale ground cover. Will tolerate hard frost and occasional flooding. Takes extended dry spells but looks best with regular water.

MELAMPODIUM leucanthum
BLACKFOOT DAISY
Asteraceae (Compositae)
PERENNIAL

🌱 ZONES 2, 3, 10–13
☀ FULL SUN
💧 MODERATE WATER

Short-lived perennial from Arizona, New Mexico, Texas, Mexico. Narrow gray leaves in clumps to 1 ft. tall and wide are topped by clouds of inch-wide, honey-scented white daisies with yellow centers. Showy when in bloom. In mild climates, it flowers off and on during

Melampodium leucanthum

the winter months and more heavily from midspring into early fall—if given some water. Where freezing temperatures are routine, expect bloom in spring and summer only. Grow in fast-draining soil; in nature, blackfoot daisy grows principally in decomposed granite. If plant becomes straggly, cut it back in fall.

For the annual butter daisy, sometimes sold as *M. paludosum*, see *Chrysanthemum paludosum*.

MELIA azedarach
CHINABERRY
Meliaceae
DECIDUOUS TREE

🌱 ZONES 6–24; H1, H2
☀ FULL SUN
💧 MODERATE WATER
◆ FRUIT IS POISONOUS IF INGESTED

Native to China, northern India. To 30–50 ft. high and wide, with irregular habit. Rich green, 1–3 ft.-

Melia azedarach 'Umbraculiformis'

long leaves are cut into many toothed, narrow or oval leaflets 1–2 in. long. In spring or early summer, bears loose clusters of lilac flowers that are fragrant in the evening. Blossoms are followed by hard, berrylike yellow fruits about ½ in. wide. Tough plant; tolerates heat, wind, poor alkaline soil, drought. In areas with year-round moisture, tends to self-sow and become a pest.

'Umbraculiformis', Texas umbrella tree, is less picturesque but far more common than the species. Grows to 20–25 ft. high, with dense, dome-shaped crown and drooping leaves. Grows true from seed.

MELIANTHUS major
HONEY BUSH
Melianthaceae
EVERGREEN SHRUB

🌱 ZONES 8, 9, 12–24; H1, H2
☀◐ PARTIAL SHADE IN HOTTEST CLIMATES
💧💧💧 LITTLE TO REGULAR WATER

Native to South Africa. This soft-wooded plant grows rapidly to 6–12 ft. tall and 8–10 ft. wide but is easily kept much shorter. Irregular habit, with stems that may be semierect or sprawling and spreading. Bold-looking foliage: grayish green, foot-long leaves divided into strongly toothed leaflets. Foliage is malodorous when brushed against or bruised. Foot-tall spikes of reddish brown, 1-in. flowers bloom in late winter, early spring. Adapts to most soils. Use for tropical effects; good as accent plant. To get a tall shrub,

Melianthus major

M

stake a few stems; for a sprawling, bulkier plant, shorten some stems in early spring before new growth begins.

M. minor has greener and shorter leaves than those of *M. major* (6–7 in. long), on a shorter (3-ft.-tall) plant. Its flowers are hidden among the leaves.

MELINIS.
See **RHYNCHELYTRUM**

MELISSA officinalis
LEMON BALM, SWEET BALM
Lamiaceae (Labiatae)
PERENNIAL

| 🗡 ZONES 1–24 |
| ☀ ☽ FULL SUN OR PARTIAL SHADE |
| 💧 REGULAR WATER |

From southern Europe. A single plant grows to about 2 ft. tall, 1½ ft. wide—but plants self-sow and spread rapidly, sometimes becoming pests. Lemon-scented,

Melissa officinalis

heavily veined foliage is light green in the species. Check catalogs to find 'Aurea' and 'All Gold', with solid yellow leaves, and 'Variegata', with green foliage variegated in yellow. Leaves are used fresh in cold drinks, fruit cups, salads, fish dishes; dried leaves give lemon perfume to sachets, potpourris. Likes rich soil. Shear occasionally to keep compact.

MELON
Cucurbitaceae
ANNUALS

| 🗡 ZONES 2–24 |
| ☀ FULL SUN |
| 💧 REGULAR WATER |

Thought to have originated in Africa. The principal types cultivated in the West are muskmelons ("cantaloupes") and late melons. True cantaloupes are a type of hard-shelled melon rarely grown in North America. Also see Watermelon.

Muskmelons are ribbed, with netted skin and typically salmon-colored flesh; they are more widely adapted than late melons. Varieties include 'Ambrosia', 'Burpee Hybrid', 'Earligold', and 'Sweet 'n Early'. Hybrids are superior to others in disease resistance and uniformity of size and quality. (Growing melons resistant to mildew and other diseases is particularly important in humid, coastal regions.) Seed packets and catalogs will usually tell you if the variety you buy is a hybrid. Other muskmelons include small, tasty, highly perfumed types from the Mediterranean, such as white-fleshed 'Ha-Ogen' and orange-fleshed 'Charmel' and 'Charentais'.

Melon

Late melons are a varied group including honeydew, casaba, 'Crenshaw', 'Honey Pearl', 'Persian', and 'Sweet Delight'. Because they need a longer growing season than muskmelons, they are less widely cultivated. They dislike high humidity and grow best in areas with hot, relatively dry summers (Zones 8, 9, 12–14, 18, 19).

To ripen to full sweetness, melons need steady heat for 2½ to 4 months. Sow seeds in light, well-drained soil 2 weeks after average last-frost date; don't rush it, since melons are truly tropical plants and will perish in even a light frost. In regions where summers are cool or relatively short, start plants indoors in pots a few weeks before last-frost date, then plant outdoors in warmest southern exposure. Row covers allow for earlier planting outdoors. Clear plastic mulch (in areas where summers are very short) or black plastic mulch under melons warms soil, speeds harvest, and helps keep fruit from rotting.

Though you can grow melons on sun-bathed trellises, the heavy fruit must be supported in individual cloth slings. These plants are best grown in hills or mounded rows a few inches high at center; you will need to provide considerable space. Make hills about 3 ft. in diameter and space them 3–4 ft. apart; encircle each with a furrow for irrigation. Make rows 3 ft. wide and as long as desired, spacing them 3–4 ft. apart; make furrows for irrigation along both sides. Plant seeds 1 in. deep—four or five seeds per hill, two or three seeds every 1 ft. in rows. When plants are well established, thin each hill to the best two plants; thin rows to one strong plant per foot. Fill furrows with water from time to time (furrows let you water plants without wetting foliage), but do not keep soil soaked. Feed (again in furrows) every 6 weeks.

To determine if a cantaloupe is ready for harvest, lift the fruit and twist; it will easily slip off the stem if ripe. A pleasant, perfumy fragrance also indicates ripeness.

Late melons do not slip from stems when ripe. Honeydews are ready to pick when the area where the melon rests on the ground turns from yellow to white. Harvest 'Crenshaw', casaba, and other late melons when the fruit begins to turn yellow and starts to soften at the blossom end. As 'Crenshaw' approaches maturity, protect fruits from sunburn by shading them on the southwest side with a wooden shingle.

MENTHA
MINT
Lamiaceae (Labiatae)
PERENNIALS

| 🗡 ZONES VARY BY SPECIES |
| ☀ ☽ FULL SUN OR PARTIAL SHADE |
| 💧 REGULAR WATER |

These Mediterranean natives spread rapidly by underground stems and can be quite invasive; to keep them in bounds, grow them in pots or boxes. Tough and unfussy, they grow almost anywhere but perform best with light, moist, medium-rich soil; regular water; and full sun or partial shade. Plants disappear in winter in colder part of range. Replant about every 3 years; propagate from runners.

M. × gracilis (M. × gentilis). GOLDEN APPLE MINT. Zones 3–24. To 2 ft. tall. Smooth deep green leaves with yellow variegation have a spicy apple fragrance and flavor. Inconspicuous flowers. Use in flavoring foods. Foliage is excellent in mixed bouquets.

M. × piperita. PEPPERMINT. Zones A2, A3; 1–24. To 3 ft. tall. Strongly scented, tooth-edged leaves to 3 in. long, dark green often tinged with purple. Small purplish flowers in 1–3-in. spikes. Leaves are good for flavoring tea. *M. × p. citrata*, known as orange mint (crushed leaves have slight orange flavor) or bergamot mint, grows to 2 ft. high and has broad, 2-in.-long leaves and small lavender flowers. It is used in potpourris and in flavoring foods.

M. pulegium. PENNYROYAL. Zones 4–24. Creeping plant 4–16 in. high, with inch-wide, bright green, nearly round leaves. Small lavender flowers in tight, short whorls. Strong mint fragrance and flavor. Poisonous if consumed in large quantities but safe as a flavoring. Needs a cool, moist site.

M. requienii. JEWEL MINT OF CORSICA. Zones 5–9, 12–24.

Creeping, mat-forming mint reaches only ½ in. high. Tiny, round bright green leaves give this plant a mossy appearance; leaves release a delightful minty or sage-like fragrance when bruised. Can be used as an aromatic filler between stepping-stones (won't take heavy foot traffic). Bears tiny, tubular light purple flowers in summer.

M. spicata. SPEARMINT. Zones A2, A3; 1–24. To 1–3 ft. high. Dark green, toothed leaves are slightly smaller than those of *M.* × *piperita*. Leafy spikes of pale blue flowers. Use leaves fresh from the garden or dried, as flavoring for foods, cold drinks, jelly. Leaves of *M. s. crispa* have curly margins. 'Kentucky Colonel' has large, flavorful leaves.

Mentha spicata

M. suaveolens (M. rotundifolia). APPLE MINT. Zones 3–24. Stiff stems grow 1½–3 ft. tall, bearing rounded, slightly hairy gray-green leaves 1–4 in. long. Purplish white flowers in 2–3-in. spikes. Foliage has scent combining fragrances of apple and mint. 'Variegata', pineapple mint, has leaves with white markings, faint scent of pineapple.

MENTHOLATO. See **PLECTRANTHUS cylindraceus**

MENTZELIA
BLAZING STAR
Loasaceae
PERENNIALS, BIENNIALS, AND ANNUALS

🌿 ZONES VARY BY SPECIES
☼ FULL SUN
◐ ◑ ◓ WATER NEEDS VARY BY SPECIES

Native to desert and semidesert areas of western U.S. Tolerate heat, wind, and poor soil, but require good drainage. Star-shaped yellow

blossoms are large and showy. Good in naturalistic plantings.

M. laevicaulis. Biennial or short-lived perennial. Zones 1–3, 7–9, 14–24. Rough, ungainly plant to 3–3½ ft. tall and wide, with narrow, 3–7-in.-long leaves. During spring and summer, spectacular pale yellow, 4-in. stars open in the evening; plant is often given the name "evening star" for that reason. Best used on bare banks. Little or no water.

Mentzelia lindleyi

M. lindleyi. Annual. Zones 4–9, 14–24. To 1–4 ft. tall; usually narrow but sometimes spreading to 1½ ft. Rough-textured light green to gray-green leaves. In spring or early summer, produces flowers that are bright yellow with orange or reddish central ring and a big brush of yellow stamens. Use alone or in wildflower mixtures. Sow seed in place in fall, winter, or earliest part of spring. Provide regular water until plants come into bloom, then reduce or stop watering.

MERREMIA
YELLOW MORNING GLORY, WOOD ROSE
Convolvulaceae
EVERGREEN VINES

🌿 ZONES VARY BY SPECIES
☼ FULL SUN
● REGULAR WATER

Twining vines with leaves divided into leaflets and golden, 3-in. flowers like those of morning glory (*Ipomoea*). Flowers are followed by woody, roundish seed capsules surrounded by woody sepals—the "wood roses" admired by flower arrangers. Tolerate some drought.

M. aurea. Zones 12–24. Native to Baja California. Climbs to 25 ft., with a woody base and leaves divided into five 1½-in. leaflets. Blooms during warm months. Drops leaves in summer drought. May be felled by frost but will resprout from the roots.

Merremia aurea

M. tuberosa (Ipomoea tuberosa). PILIKAI. Zones 23 (borderline), 24; H1, H2. Native to tropical America but naturalized throughout the tropics. Climbs to 50–100 ft., with 6-in. leaves divided into seven lobes. Flowers in late winter and spring.

MERTENSIA
Boraginaceae
PERENNIALS

🌿 ZONES VARY BY SPECIES
◐ ● PARTIAL OR FULL SHADE
● REGULAR WATER

Resemble giant-size forget-me-nots (*Myosotis*) and belong to the same family. Plants emerge and flower early, then go dormant soon after going to seed (usually before midsummer). Typically smooth, gray-green or blue-green leaves. Nodding, bell-shaped flowers are carried in gradually uncoiling clusters. Blooms are pink or lavender in bud, opening to blue flowers that sometimes have a pinkish cast. Good in woodland gardens.

Provide moist, rich soil. Use summer annuals to fill void after plants die back. Clumps can be left in place indefinitely; they will slowly spread. To increase a planting, transplant volunteer seedlings or dig and divide the clump in early fall.

M. ciliata. CHIMING BELLS, MOUNTAIN BLUEBELL. Zones 1–7, 14–17. Native to damp places

Mertensia pulmonarioides

in the Rocky Mountains and the Blue Mountains of Oregon. To 3 ft. tall and 1 ft. wide, with ½–¾-in. flowers. Several other species, most of them lower growing than *M. ciliata*, also are native to mountainous areas of the West.

M. pulmonarioides (M. virginica). VIRGINIA BLUEBELLS. Zones 1–9, 14–21. From eastern U.S. Most widely planted species. To 1–2 ft. tall and 1½ ft. wide, with 1-in. flowers.

MESCAL BEAN. See **SOPHORA secundiflora**

MESEMBRYANTHE-MUM crystallinum
ICE PLANT
Aizoaceae
SUCCULENT ANNUAL OR BIENNIAL

🌿 ZONES 15–17, 23, 24
☼ FULL SUN
◐ ◑ LITTLE OR NO WATER TO MODERATE WATER

Of the many plants commonly called *Mesembryanthemum* or ice plant, this native of South Africa is now considered the only true *Mesembryanthemum*. For other, showier types, see Ice Plants.

Mesembryanthemum crystallinum

M. crystallinum is a sprawling plant a few inches tall and several feet wide. Oval, flat, stalked, fleshy leaves grow to 4 in. long, turn red at dry times of year. Leaves are covered with tiny, transparent blisters that glisten like flecks of ice. Foliage is edible and resembles New Zealand spinach in flavor. White to pinkish, 1-in. flowers bloom in summer. Easy to grow from seed. Has naturalized in parts of California. Very drought tolerant plant when grown in the ground. Best use in gardens, though, is in hanging baskets and window boxes—in which locations this plant will need at least moderate watering.

MESQUITE. See **PROSOPIS**

M

METASEQUOIA glyptostroboides

DAWN REDWOOD
Taxodiaceae
DECIDUOUS TREE

✔	ZONES A3; 3–10, 14–24
☼	FULL SUN
💧	REGULAR WATER

Thought to have been extinct for millions of years, this plant was found growing in a few isolated sites in its native China during the 1940s. It is a pyramidal tree with small cones and soft, pale green needles that turn light bronze in autumn, then drop to reveal attractive winter silhouette. Branchlets tend to turn upward.

Metasequoia glyptostroboides

Young trees have reddish bark; older ones have darker, fissured bark and rugged, fluted trunk bases. Grows very fast when young—sometimes as much as 4–6 ft. a year in California (less in colder areas). Reaches about 90 ft. tall and about 20 ft. wide at the age of 40 or so (trees haven't been in cultivation long enough to determine the maximum garden size). Looks somewhat like bald cypress (*Taxodium distichum*), another deciduous conifer. While in leaf, it also bears superficial resemblance to coast redwood (*Sequoia sempervirens*).

Grows best in good, well-drained soil with regular moisture. Good lawn tree, though in time surface roots may interrupt smooth flow of turf. Not suited to arid regions or seacoast, since dry heat and salty ocean winds will burn foliage. Resistant to oak root fungus.

METROSIDEROS

Myrtaceae
EVERGREEN TREES OR SHRUBS

✔	ZONES VARY BY SPECIES
☼ ◑	BEST IN SUN; TOLERATE SOME SHADE
💧	MODERATE WATER

Grown for attractive, leathery foliage and showy flowers with prominent stamens. Best near coast; tolerate wind, salt spray. Grow in well-drained soil. Sensitive to frost.

M. collina. Zones 16, 17, 23, 24. From Hawaii. Shrubby, upright species with a profusion of powder-puff blossoms in late spring and early summer; attracts butterflies and nectar-feeding birds. Useful as flowering hedge, specimen, container plant. 'Spring Fire' is the best-known variety; it grows 8–12 ft. high and 4–6 ft wide, with orange-red blooms and gray-green leaves. 'Fiji', just 2 ft. tall and wide, has red flowers and coppery new growth.

M. excelsa. NEW ZEALAND CHRISTMAS TREE, POHUTU-KAWA. Zones 16, 17, 23, 24; H1, H2. Native to New Zealand. To 30 ft. tall or more, spreading as wide as tall; prune lower branches to get tree form. On young plants, leaves are glossy green; on older ones, they are dark green above, white and woolly beneath. Big clusters of dark red flowers cover branch ends in late spring and early summer. (Bloom occurs in December in New Zealand, hence common name "New Zealand Christmas tree.") Useful lawn or street tree (if given ample root space) in coastal gardens. 'Aurea' has yellow flowers. Leaves of 'Gala' are centered with bright yellow; its dark red flowers have stamens tipped with gold.

Metrosideros excelsa

M. polymorpha (M. collina polymorpha). 'OHI'A LEHUA, LEHUA. Zones H1, H2. Native to Hawaii. Slow-growing, highly variable plant; may form a small, erect to prostrate shrub or grow as tree up to 100 ft. tall. The foliage is also variable—as are the flowers, which are produced throughout the year. Blossoms are commonly red but are also seen in white and shades of orange, pink, and yellow; they are used in leis.

M. villosa 'Tahiti' (M. kermadecensis 'Tahiti'). DWARF POHUTUKAWA. Zones 16, 17, 23, 24; H1, H2. Native to New Zealand. Compact shrub to 3 ft. tall and wide with thick, round, gray-green leaves. Clusters of orange-red flowers appear in early to late spring; sporadic rebloom. Good plant for containers, small gardens, around pools and foundations. Prolific seed set; remove seed heads to encourage new growth and rebloom.

MEXICAN BLUE PALM. See **BRAHEA armata**

MEXICAN DAISY. See **ERIGERON karvinskianus**

MEXICAN DEER GRASS. See **MUHLENBERGIA dubia**

MEXICAN FEATHER GRASS. See **NASSELLA tenuissima**

MEXICAN FIRE BUSH. See **KOCHIA scoparia trichophylla**

MEXICAN FIRE PLANT. See **EUPHORBIA heterophylla**

MEXICAN FLAME VINE. See **SENECIO confusus**

MEXICAN GRASS TREE. See **DASYLIRION quadrangulatum, NOLINA longifolia**

MEXICAN HAT. See **RATIBIDA columnifera**

MEXICAN HEATHER. See **CUPHEA hyssopifolia**

MEXICAN HONEYSUCKLE. See **JUSTICIA spicigera**

MEXICAN ORANGE. See **CHOISYA ternata**

MEXICAN OREGANO. See **ALOYSIA wrightii, POLIOMINTHA maderense**

MEXICAN PALO VERDE. See **PARKINSONIA aculeata**

MEXICAN POPPY. See **ARGEMONE mexicana**

MEXICAN SHELL FLOWER. See **TIGRIDIA pavonia**

MEXICAN SUNFLOWER. See **TITHONIA rotundifolia**

MEXICAN TARRAGON. See **TAGETES lucida**

MEXICAN TULIP POPPY. See **HUNNEMANNIA fumariifolia**

MICHAELMAS DAISY. See **ASTER novi-belgii**

MICHELIA

Magnoliaceae
EVERGREEN SHRUBS OR TREES

✔	ZONES VARY BY SPECIES
☼ ◑	PARTIAL SHADE IN HOTTEST CLIMATES
💧	REGULAR WATER

Magnolia relatives native to China and the Himalayas. When in flower, they might be mistaken for some kind of magnolia—but unlike magnolias, they bear their blossoms among the leaves rather than singly at branch ends.

M. figo has been in gardens for some 200 years, and *M. doltsopa* has been in cultivation in North America for perhaps half a century. The other species and hybrids listed here, however, are newcomers about which we have much to learn; they have not yet had time to grow to maturity in North American gardens. All are attractive, with lush foliage and profuse, fragrant blossoms divided into petal-like segments.

M. champaca. CHAMPACA. Shrub or tree. Zones 16–24; H1, H2. To 10–20 ft. tall and broad. Glossy bright green, 10-in. leaves. Orange-yellow, 3-in. flowers with up to 20 segments are borne intermittently throughout the year, most often in winter and summer; their perfume is legendary. 'Alba' (*M.* × *alba*) has white flowers.

M. crassipes (M. figo crassipes). Shrub or tree. Zones 5–9, 14–24. Recently introduced and with no long track record in the West. Rich green foliage. Plants have bloomed at a very young age, bearing a profusion of white flowers. Has succeeded in the Puget Sound area.

M. doltsopa. Tree. Zones 14–24; H1, H2. To 90 ft. tall in its native Himalayas; in San Francisco, it has grown to 25 ft. in as many years. Varies from bushy (nearly as wide as high) to narrow and upright (about half as broad as tall); choose plants for desired form,

Michelia doltsopa

then prune to shape. Thin-textured, leathery dark green leaves 3–8 in. long, 1–3 in. wide. In winter and spring, furry brown buds open to blossoms ranging from cream colored to white, with a slight green tinge at the base; they are 5–7 in. across, with 12–16 segments, each 1 in. wide. 'Silver Cloud' presents an abundance of large, cream-colored blossoms in spring.

M. figo (M. fuscata). BANANA SHRUB. Zones 6 (borderline), 9, 14–24; H1, H2. Slow growing to 6–8 ft. high (possibly to 15 ft. tall) and about two-thirds as wide. Densely clothed with glossy, leathery, 3-in. leaves. Plant blooms most heavily in spring but produces scattered flowers throughout summer. Blossoms are 1–1½ in. wide, creamy yellow with a thin brownish purple border on each segment. Notable feature is the powerful, fruity fragrance, like that of ripe bananas; the perfume is strongest in a warm, wind-free spot. Choice plant for entry or patio. 'Port Wine' has rose to maroon flowers.

M. × foggii. Shrub. Zones 9, 14–24. Group of hybrids between *M. figo* and *M. doltsopa*. 'Allspice' grows 15–18 ft. tall, 6–8 ft. wide, with glossy dark green foliage; from spring to summer, bears fruity-scented, 1½-in., light yellow flowers bordered in maroon. 'Jack Fogg', about 18 ft. tall and 6–8 ft. wide, has fragrant spring flowers of white, with each segment bordered in purplish pink.

M. maudiae. Shrub or tree. Zones 5–9, 14–24. This newcomer is a large shrub or small tree, possibly to 25 ft. tall, with 6-in. leaves that are glossy medium green above, gray green beneath. White, 3–4-in. flowers bloom from late spring to midsummer.

M. sinensis (M. wilsonii). Tree. Zones 5–9, 14–24. To 20 ft. tall, possibly much taller in time, with

6-in., glossy green leaves. Blooms in early summer, bearing white flowers with 9–11 segments.

M. yunnanensis. Shrub or tree. Zones 5–9, 14–24. Another newcomer. To 15 ft. tall. Blooms in early spring, when white flowers burst from dark, velvety buds.

MICKEY MOUSE PLANT.
See **OCHNA serrulata**

MICROBIOTA
decussata
SIBERIAN CARPET CYPRESS
Cupressaceae
EVERGREEN SHRUB

| 🌿 ZONES A3; 1–10, 14–17 |
| ☀ ◑ PARTIAL SHADE IN HOTTEST CLIMATES |
| 💧 MODERATE WATER |

Native to Siberian mountains and hardy to any amount of cold. Neat, sprawling shrub that resembles a trailing arborvitae *(Thuja)*. Grows 1½ ft. tall, 7–8 ft. wide, with many

Microbiota decussata

plumy, horizontal or trailing branches closely set with scalelike leaves. Foliage is green in summer, turning purplish or reddish brown in winter. More shade tolerant than junipers. Needs excellent drainage. Use as a bank cover.

MICROLEPIA
Polypodiaceae
FERNS

| 🌿 ZONES 17, 23, 24 |
| ◐ ● PARTIAL OR FULL SHADE |
| 💧 MODERATE WATER |

Sturdy plants useful for landscaping in mild climates. Both species described below can take fairly dry soil—drier than is usual for ferns. Both are hardy to 28°F/–2°C.

M. firma. Native to India. Grows to 2½ ft. high and 2 ft. wide. Dull green, delicately cut, triangular fronds to 3 ft. long. Frond surfaces are densely hairy.

M. strigosa. LACE FERN. Native to tropical Asia. Robust fern with delicate dark green fronds. Grows 2–3 ft. tall and wide. Sometimes sold as *M. speluncae*.

Microlepia strigosa

MICROMERIA chamissonis.
See **SATUREJA douglasii**

MIGNONETTE.
See **RESEDA odorata**

MILFOIL.
See **ACHILLEA millefolium**

MILIUM effusum
'Aureum'
BOWLES' GOLDEN GRASS
Poaceae (Gramineae)
PERENNIAL GRASS

| 🌿 ZONES 3B–9, 14–17 |
| ◑ LIGHT SHADE |
| 💧💧 REGULAR TO AMPLE WATER |

Species is native to eastern North America, Eurasia. Its colorful selection 'Aureum' forms a clump to 2 ft. high and wide. Bright greenish gold leaves first grow erect, then take on arching, weeping form. Foliage is brightest in spring, turns light green by summer. Effective for a spot of color in a woodland garden or shaded rock garden. Does best where summers are cool or mild; in hotter regions, goes partially dormant in summer. Seedlings usually have yellow foliage, though color may vary.

Milium effusum 'Aureum'

MILKBUSH.
See **EUPHORBIA tirucalli**

MILKWEED, SWAMP.
See **ASCLEPIAS incarnata**

MILLETTIA
Fabaceae (Leguminosae)
EVERGREEN OR DECIDUOUS VINES

| 🌿 ZONES 8, 9, 14–24; MARGINAL IN ZONES 6, 7 |
| ☀ FULL SUN |
| 💧 REGULAR WATER |

Genus contains deciduous and evergreen trees and shrubs as well as woody-based, twining climbers. Pealike flowers and leaves divided into many lance-shaped leaflets are similar to those of wisteria. Evergreen in frost-free areas, deciduous elsewhere. Grow in well-drained soils.

M. reticulata. EVERGREEN WISTERIA. From China. Vigorous twining vine usually described as reaching 15 ft. but—like wisteria—can attain great size. Shiny, leathery, bright green leaves. In late summer or early fall, bears tight clusters of dark purple-red flowers with odor of cedar and camphor. Use as cover for arbor, pergola, or chain-link fence. Grows extremely fast and, once established, can overwhelm trees if permitted to climb into them.

Millettia reticulata

M. taiwanensis. CHINESE EVERGREEN WISTERIA. Native to India, Southeast Asia, China, and Taiwan. Vinelike shrub with moderate growth to 4–6 ft. tall and 8–10 ft. wide, with shiny, light green leaves. Produces large clusters of reddish purple blooms in late summer. Good for draping over fences or walls or to cover narrow arched gateways. Can be pruned into a hedge (shear after blooms fade). On slopes and banks, may behave like ground cover.

MILLION BELLS.
See **CALIBRACHOA**

MIMOSA. See ACACIA baileyana, ALBIZIA julibrissin

M

MIMULUS
MONKEY FLOWER
Scrophulariaceae
PERENNIALS, ONE GROWN
AS ANNUAL

🌱	ZONES VARY BY SPECIES
☀ ◐ ●	EXPOSURE NEEDS VARY BY SPECIES
◌ ◑ ◕ ●	WATER NEEDS VARY BY SPECIES

Wide-ranging group of plants with different needs. All have funnel-shaped, two-lipped flowers said to resemble a grinning monkey face—hence the common name.

M. aurantiacus (Diplacus aurantiacus). STICKY or SHRUBBY MONKEY FLOWER. Woody-based perennial. Zones 5 and 6 (with protection), 7–9, 14–24. Native to southern Oregon, California, Baja California. To 4½ ft. tall and wide, with narrow, 1½-in.-long, sticky dark green leaves. Buff-toned orange, 1¾-in. flowers bloom over a long spring-and-summer season. Several subspecies were formerly considered separate species. These include *M. a. bifidus,* with large pale yellow to peach flowers; *M. a. longiflorus,* with cream to orange-yellow blooms; and *M. a. rutilus,* with deep red blossoms. All thrive in full sun or partial shade, with little water.

More important than the subspecies themselves are the showy hybrids derived from them (often called Verity hybrids, after their originator). These plants grow 1–4 ft. tall and wide, with narrow, glossy dark green leaves that are sometimes sticky. Flowers are 1–3 in. long, in colors ranging from white and cream to yellow, orange, copper, salmon, red, and maroon. Plant in full sun or light shade; give good drainage. Prune in spring before growth starts. Pruned again after first flowering, they often rebloom in fall—and, if given moderate water with good drainage, they may flower repeatedly throughout the year. Because plants are not long lived, take cuttings of your favorites; they root easily in moist sand.

M. cardinalis. SCARLET MONKEY FLOWER. Perennial. Zones 2–24. Native to damp or wet locales throughout much of the West. To 2½ ft. high and wide, with upright or sprawling stems and bright green, sticky, 1–3-in. leaves. Tubular, scarlet, 1½–2-in.-long flowers bloom throughout summer. Give full shade in Zones 12 and 13, sun or shade elsewhere. Ample water.

M. × hybridus. Short-lived perennial grown as annual. Zones 1–24. To 1 ft. high and wide, with smooth, succulent leaves. Flowers are 2–2½ in. across, in colors including cream, rose, orange, yellow, scarlet, and brown, usually with heavy brownish maroon spotting or mottling. Mystic Mix series has virtually unspotted flowers. Sow in spring for summer bloom, or set out plants for early spring show. Provide rich soil with high organic content, regular water, partial or full shade.

Mimulus aurantiacus longiflorus

Mimulus × hybridus

MING ARALIA.
See **POLYSCIAS fruticosa**

MINT. See **MENTHA**

MINT BUSH.
See **PROSTANTHERA**

MINTLEAF. See **PLECTRANTHUS madagascariensis**

MIRABILIS
FOUR O'CLOCK
Nyctaginaceae
PERENNIALS, ONE OFTEN
GROWN AS ANNUAL

🌱	ZONES VARY BY SPECIES
☀	FULL SUN
◌	LITTLE WATER
☠	SEEDS AND ROOTS ARE POISONOUS IF INGESTED

Strong-looking, mounding plants with the substance and character of shrubs—albeit only seasonal or temporary ones. In summer, branch ends bear clusters of trumpet-shaped, 2-in.-long flowers that open late in the afternoon. Plants are killed to the ground by frost but resprout from their large tuberous roots. Sow seeds in fall or spring. Plants self-sow freely.

M. jalapa. FOUR O'CLOCK, MARVEL OF PERU. Zones 4–24, H1, H2 as perennial. In colder climates, treat as annual; or dig and store like dahlia. Native to Peru. To 3–4 ft. tall and wide, with green leaves 2–6 in. long. Flowers in white and shades of red, pink, or yellow; several colors may appear on the same plant or even the same flower. Blossoms are fragrant at night. Jingles strain is lower growing than old-fashioned kinds, has flowers splashed and stained in two or three colors at once.

Mirabilis jalapa

M. multiflora. DESERT FOUR O'CLOCK. Zones 1–3, 7–16, 18–24. Native to much of the Southwest. To 1–2 ft. high, 3–5 ft. wide, with magenta flowers and gray-green leaves to 3 in. long.

MIRROR PLANT.
See **COPROSMA repens**

MISCANTHUS
SILVER GRASS
Poaceae (Gramineae)
PERENNIAL GRASSES

🌱	ZONES VARY BY SPECIES
☀ ◐	FULL SUN OR PARTIAL SHADE
◑ ●	MODERATE TO REGULAR WATER

Among the showiest and liveliest looking of ornamental grasses, these are clump-forming plants that range from very large kinds to dwarf types good for small gardens and containers. Attractive flower panicles appear atop tall stalks; they open as tassels and gradually expand into silvery to pinkish or bronze plumes that usually last well into winter. Leaves are broad or narrow, always graceful; they may be solid colored, striped lengthwise, or banded crosswise. In fall and winter, foliage of most species turns shades of yellow, orange, or reddish brown; it looks especially showy against snow or a background of dark evergreens.

Need little care. Cut old foliage back to the ground before new leaves sprout in early spring; in climates with a long growing season, cut back again in midsummer to keep compact and to freshen foliage. Some varieties collapse at bloom time unless given support of four or five narrow stakes inserted inconspicuously at edge of clump, concealed by foliage; wind twine or wire around stakes and clump at two levels. Divide every 2 or 3 years to limit clump size and prevent decline in vigor. Stunning accent plants in large pots or tubs.

M. 'Giganteus'. GIANT SILVER GRASS. Zones 1–24. Impressive upright grass to 10–14 ft. tall, 8–10 ft. wide; self-supporting on stems to 2 in. thick. Arching, drooping leaves to 3 ft. long, 1½ in. wide, dark green with white midrib. In cold-winter areas, plant does not bloom. In other regions, however, flower plumes to 1 ft. long rise 1–2 ft. above foliage in very late summer to fall; they emerge tan, open silver. Leaves turn purplish green in fall, then drop to leave tall, bare stalks over winter. Good summer screen or hedge; provides tropical effect. Takes seacoast conditions. Give partial shade in hottest climates. Often mislabeled as *M. floridulus.*

M. sinensis. EULALIA, JAPANESE SILVER GRASS. Zones 2–24. Native to Japan, Korea, China. Variable in size and foliage. Blooms in late summer or fall. Flowers are usually held well above foliage clumps; they may be cut for fresh or dried arrangements. Many varieties are obtainable, and new ones arrive on the market every year. Here are some of the choicest.

'Adagio'. Very narrow green leaves form a clump 2–3 ft. high and wide. Pink plumes rise to 4–5 ft. Better flower production than similar 'Yaku Jima'. Yellow fall foliage. Good container plant.

M. s. condensatus 'Cabaret'. Boldest variegated miscanthus. Big, upright clump 6–7 ft. tall, 4–5 ft. across; wide (to 1¼-in.), ribbonlike leaves with a broad white center stripe and green edges. Pink-suffused stems to 8–9 ft. bear coppery pink plumes that age to cream. Seed-sterile.

M

M. s. condensatus 'Cosmopol-tan'. Similar in growth and bloom to 'Cabaret', but foliage has the reverse pattern: leaves have a green center (with a white midrib) and white margins.

'Goldfeder' ('Gold Feather'). Clump grows 4–5 ft. high and wide, with ¾-in.-wide leaves edged light golden yellow. Silvery pink flower plumes on lax stems to 7 ft. tall. Stems tend to flop, but do so gracefully; can be staked to keep upright.

'Gracillimus'. MAIDEN GRASS. Narrow dark green leaves with silver midrib; graceful clump to 4–5 ft. high, 6–8 ft. wide. Stems 5–6 ft. tall bear coppery plumes that mature to cream. Tends to flop; divide in spring every year or two to keep compact. Bright orange fall foliage. Seeds profusely and can become a pest.

'Graziella'. Narrow leaves form a clump 4–5 ft. tall, 5–8 ft. wide. Silvery "ostrich" plumes rise to 6–7 ft. Coppery red and orange fall foliage. More refined and upright than 'Gracillimus'.

'Kirk Alexander'. Clump to 3–4 ft. tall and wide, with green leaves horizontally banded in greenish yellow. Pinkish copper plumes on stems to 5 ft. tall.

'Little Kitten'. Seedling of 'Yaku Jima', with narrow, slightly pendulous, silvery green leaves that form a clump just 1½ ft. tall and wide. Sparsely produced beige flower spikes bring overall height to 2½ ft. Foliage turns gold in fall.

'Malepartus'. Dark green leaves are broader than those of species, in a clump 3 ft. high and wide. Flower plumes on 6–7 ft. stalks open rose pink, fade to silvery white, finish tan. Orange fall foliage.

'Morning Light'. Sport of 'Gracillimus', with narrow band of white on leaf margins; less vigorous and more compact than 'Gracillimus'. Grows to 3–4 ft. high and as wide; coppery flower plumes reach 5–6 ft. tall. Where the growing season is long, dig and divide clumps yearly to keep plants compact. Seedlings have leaves like those of 'Gracillimus'—deep green with silvery midrib.

Miscanthus sinensis 'Gracillimus'

'Purpurascens'. FLAME GRASS. Best where summers are not too hot. Upright clump 3–4 ft. high and wide, with green leaves to ½ in. wide. Silvery flower plumes rise 5–6 ft. tall. Foliage turns orange red in fall, fades to reddish brown.

'Sarabande'. Clump grows 5 ft. tall and 3–4 ft. wide. Resembles 'Gracillimus' but with narrower leaves; flowers appear a bit earlier and are held more erect. Fine textured and graceful.

'Strictus'. PORCUPINE GRASS. Narrow, erect clump 4–6 ft. tall, 3–4 ft. wide. Spiky, ½-in.-wide leaves are banded horizontally with creamy yellow, suggesting porcupine quills. Coppery plumes on 5–7-ft.-tall stems. Tends to flop with weight of blooms; should be staked.

'Variegatus'. A fountain of silver. Graceful, weeping clump 3–4 ft. high and as wide, with ¾-in. green leaves edged and striped in white. Spikes 5–6 ft. tall, tend to flop, especially on older plants; need staking. Divide every year or two. Give partial shade in hottest climates.

'Yaku Jima'. Compact, fine-leafed selection similar in form to 'Adagio'. Tan flower plumes; reddish brown fall foliage.

'Zebrinus'. ZEBRA GRASS. Like 'Strictus', but broadly arching and lax; certain to flop in bloom unless staked. Most plants sold under this name are 'Strictus'.

M. transmorrisonensis. EVERGREEN MISCANTHUS. Zones 4–24. Native to Taiwan. Forms a compact clump 2½–3½ ft. high and 3–4 ft. wide, with narrow leaves 2–3 ft. long, ½ in. wide. Foliage remains green into early winter (and is evergreen in mildest-winter areas). Slender, silvery flower plumes on stems 5–7 ft. tall.

Plant begins blooming in spring in mild-winter climates; cutting stems back to ground when plumes begin to fade will produce a second bloom flush—sometimes even a third one. Cutting back stems also keeps clump looking fresh. Where winters are cold, bloom time comes in mid- to late summer. Plumes age to tan and drop seed before winter, leaving bare stems. Makes a good large-scale ground cover if given regular moisture and yearly mowing.

MISSION BELLS.
See **FRITILLARIA biflora**

MISS WILLMOTT'S GHOST.
See **ERYNGIUM giganteum**

MITCHELLA repens
PARTRIDGEBERRY, TWINBERRY
Rubiaceae
PERENNIAL

⚡ ZONES 1-6

◑ ● PARTIAL OR FULL SHADE

💧 💧💧 REGULAR TO AMPLE WATER

Attractive small, creeping evergreen plant native to much of eastern North America. Roundish leaves are less than 1 in. long, borne in pairs along trailing, somewhat woody stems that root where they touch the ground. Paired small white flowers appear

Mitchella repens

in late spring or early summer; these are followed by bright red berries less than ¼ in. across. Use as small-scale ground cover, preferably where it can be seen near eye level—on a shady bank or above a wall. Provide moist, acid soil containing plenty of leaf mold or other organic material.

MIZUNA. See **ASIAN GREENS**

MOCK ORANGE. See **CHOISYA ternata, PHILADELPHUS**

MODIOLASTRUM lateritium. See **MALVASTRUM lateritium**

MOLE PLANT. See **EUPHORBIA lathyris**

MOLINIA caerulea
MOOR GRASS
Poaceae (Gramineae)
PERENNIAL GRASS

⚡ ZONES 1-9, 14-17

☀ ◐ FULL SUN OR PARTIAL SHADE

💧 💧💧 REGULAR TO AMPLE WATER

Native to moist places from the British Isles to Siberia, south to the Caucasus and Turkey; resents dry, alkaline conditions. Long lived but slow growing, taking several years to reach full size. Erect, narrow light green leaves form a neat, dense clump. In summer, spikelike clusters of yellowish to purplish flowers rise above clump; they turn to tan and last well into fall. Inflorescences are profuse but narrow, giving clump a see-through quality. Good cut flowers. In late fall, both leaves and flower clusters detach from bulbous crown, leaving nothing visible above ground. There are two forms of moor grass, each with numerous varieties.

Molinia caerulea

The typical form, often called purple moor grass, produces a leafy clump 1–2 ft. high and wide; flower stalks are 2–3 ft. tall. 'Moorflamme' ('Moor Flame') has airy flower heads held 2 ft. above the foliage, good red-orange autumn foliage color. 'Variegata' has leaves broadly edged in creamy white; yellowish flower stems arch out in all directions, giving perfect fountain effect. 'Heidebraut' ('Heather Bride') produces stems to 5 ft. high; leaves become distinctly yellowish in fall.

M. c. arundinacea, known as tall moor grass, has broader gray-green leaves that form a clump 2–3 ft. high and wide. Flowering stems are 5–8 ft. tall; they arch to the ground when wet, then straighten up as they dry. Give this one space so you can enjoy its form and motion in the wind. Among its forms are old favorite 'Karl Foerster', still one of the best; it has arching, 2½-ft.-long leaves and semierect flower stalks to 7 ft. tall. 'Skyracer' has erect, 3-ft.-tall leaves and 7–8-ft. stems bearing yellow flowers that sparkle with morning dew. Arching, 6-ft. stems of 'Transparent' have a translucent section between highest leaf and beginning of flower spike; plant bears tiny, airy blossoms and has bright orange-yellow fall foliage. 'Windspiel' ('Windplay') has wiry vertical stems 7–8 ft. tall that sway with the slightest breeze.

M

MOLUCCELLA laevis
BELLS-OF-IRELAND,
SHELL FLOWER
Lamiaceae (Labiatae)
ANNUAL

☘	ZONES 1–24; H1, H2
☀	FULL SUN
◐	REGULAR WATER

Though its common name implies Irish origin, this plant is in fact native to the Mideast. To 2–3 ft. high, 10 in. wide. Flowers are carried almost from base in whorls of six. Showy part of flower is large, apple green, shell- or bell-shaped calyx, very veiny and crisp textured; small white tube of united petals in center is inconspicuous. Calyx-blossom spikes are quite attractive and long lasting in either fresh or dried arrangements; be sure to remove the unattractive leaves.

Moluccella laevis

Needs loose, well-drained soil. Doesn't perform well in hot, humid climates. Sow seed in ground in early spring for summer bloom; in mildest climates, can be sown in fall for winter bloom. Usually grown as winter annual in the desert. If weather is warm, refrigerate seed for a week before planting. For long blossom spikes, fertilize regularly.

MONARDA
BEE BALM, OSWEGO TEA, HORSEMINT
Lamiaceae (Labiatae)
PERENNIALS

☘	ZONES VARY BY SPECIES
☀◐	LIGHT SHADE IN HOTTEST CLIMATES
◐◐	REGULAR TO AMPLE WATER

Native to eastern North America. Bushy, leafy clumps to 2–4 ft. high, initially about 1½ ft. wide; spread rapidly at edges but are not really invasive. Dark green, 4–6-in.-long leaves have a strong, pleasant odor like a blend of mint and basil. In summer, upright stems are topped by tight clusters of long-tubed flowers much visited by hummingbirds. Divide every 3 or 4 years. Not long lived in areas with warm winters and long, hot summers.

M. didyma. Zones A2, A3; 1–11, 14–17. Basic species has scarlet flowers surrounded by reddish bracts. Garden selections include scarlet 'Adam'; pink 'Croftway Pink' and 'Granite Pink'; dark rose red 'Jacob Kline'; dark red 'Mahogany'; and bright pinkish red 'Raspberry Wine'. 'Cambridge Scarlet' is a very old variety that is still widely sold. Mildew-resistant varieties include lavender 'Violet Queen', pink 'Marshall's Delight', and rosy lavender 'Petite Delight' (just 1–1½ ft. tall, 2 ft. wide). 'Claire Grace' (*M. fistulosa* 'Claire Grace') is an upright grower to 4–5 ft. tall, with lavenderrose flowers and good resistance to mildew; it performs well in California gardens. All bloom over long period of 2 months or more when spent flowers are removed. Don't let soil dry out.

Monarda didyma
'Marshall's Delight'

M. fistulosa. Zones A2, A3; 1–10, 14–17. Bears lavender to light pink flowers encircled by whitish bracts; they are less showy than blossoms of *M. didyma*. Best suited to wild garden.

MONARDELLA
Lamiaceae (Labiatae)
PERENNIALS

☘	ZONES VARY BY SPECIES
☀	FULL SUN
○	LITTLE WATER

Aromatic mint-family perennials native to California and adjacent states. Typically sprawling, with two-lipped flowers in clusters at stem ends. All require excellent drainage. Use in wild gardens or rock gardens.

M. macrantha. Zones 7–9, 14–24. To 6 in. high, 1 ft. wide. Stems of shiny dark green leaves sprawl, turn up at ends to show tight, 1–1½-in. clusters of bright red, 1½-in.-long flowers in late spring and summer. 'Marian Sampson' is a vigorous and disease-resistant selection.

Monardella macrantha

M. odoratissima. Zones 1–3, 7–10, 14–24. Bushy plant with a sprawling, woody base. Grows from 4 in. to 2 ft. tall, spreading as wide as high. Hairy gray-green leaves; 1-in.-wide heads of small purplish flowers in summer and early fall. Has been used to make a fragrant tea.

M. villosa. COYOTE MINT. Zones 7–9, 14–24. Bushy grower 1–2 ft. tall, 1–1½ ft. wide, with furry gray-green leaves and 1½-in. heads of small purplish, pink, or white flowers in late spring and summer.

MONDO GRASS.
See **OPHIOPOGON**

MONEY PLANT.
See **LUNARIA annua**

MONEYWORT.
See **LYSIMACHIA nummularia**

MONKEY FLOWER.
See **MIMULUS**

MONKEY PUZZLE TREE.
See **ARAUCARIA araucana**

MONKSHOOD. See **ACONITUM**

MONSTERA
Araceae
EVERGREEN VINES

☘	ZONES VARY BY SPECIES; OR INDOORS
◐	FILTERED SUNLIGHT; BRIGHT LIGHT
◐	REGULAR WATER

Tropical American natives related to philodendrons and resembling them in the glossiness and texture of their foliage. Need rich soil. They can be grown outdoors only in the warmest climates. Indoors, direct sun in winter and bright reflected light the rest of the year are ideal; in dim light, leaves will be small and widely spaced on long, droopy stalks. If a tall potted plant gets bare at the base, replant it in a larger container along with a younger, lower plant to fill in; or cut it back and let it regrow from new shoots.

M. deliciosa. SPLIT-LEAF PHILODENDRON. Zones 16, 17, 22–24; H1, H2. To 30–60 ft. if planted in open bed outdoors or in greenhouse. Protect from frost (recovers fairly quickly from frost damage, though). Long, cordlike roots hang from stems and root when they reach soil; also help support plant on trees or on moss logs. Young foliage is uncut; mature leaves are heavy, leathery, dark green, deeply cut and perforated.

Monstera deliciosa

Big plants may bear flowers like those of calla (*Zantedeschia*), with a thick, 10-in.-long spike surrounded by a boatlike white bract. If heat, light, and humidity are high, spike may ripen into edible fruit said to combine flavors of banana and pineapple. Eat only when fully ripe (green, caplike rind will knock off easily, exposing sticky fruit kernels); fruit can be painfully caustic before that stage. Allow plenty of room when growing this species as a houseplant; it may reach 15 ft. Often sold as *Philodendron pertusum*.

M. friedrichsthalii. SWISS CHEESE PLANT. Zones 24; H1, H2. Plant sold under this name is probably *M. obliqua*. Can reach 25 ft. outdoors but is more commonly used as indoor plant. Smaller, thinner-textured leaves than those of *M. deliciosa*, with wavy rather than deeply cut edges. Common name comes from oval holes on either side of leaf midrib.

MONTBRETIA. See
CROCOSMIA × crocosmiiflora

MONTEZUMA CYPRESS.
See **TAXODIUM mucronatum**

MOONFLOWER.
See **IPOMOEA alba**

MOOR GRASS. See **MOLINIA
caerulea, SESLERIA**

MORAEA iridioides.
See **DIETES iridioides**

MORAINE LOCUST.
See **GLEDITSIA triacanthos
inermis 'Moraine'**

MORETON BAY CHESTNUT. See
CASTANOSPERMUM australe

MORINA longifolia
WHORLFLOWER
Morinaceae
PERENNIAL

🌡 **ZONES 2–9, 14–24**

☀ ◐ **FULL SUN OR LIGHT SHADE**

💧 **REGULAR WATER**

This little-known but attractive
Himalayan native looks something
like a thistle. Forms a foot-wide
rosette of glossy dark green, spine-
toothed, deeply cut basal leaves to

Morina longifolia

10 in. long. In midsummer, foliage
clump sends up a 2–3-ft. flower
spike bearing closely spaced
whorls of 1½-in. flowers; blossoms
open white and age to pink, then
red. Easy to grow in average soil.

MORMON TEA. See **EPHEDRA**

MORNING FLAG or IRIS.
See **ORTHROSANTHUS**

MORNING GLORY.
See **CONVOLVULUS, IPOMOEA,
MERREMIA**

MORUS
MULBERRY
Moraceae
DECIDUOUS TREES

🌡 **ZONES VARY BY SPECIES**

☀ **FULL SUN**

💧 **REGULAR WATER**

Deciduous trees with leaves of
variable size and shape, often on
the same plant. Yellow autumn
color ranges from subdued to
bright. Fruits somewhat resemble
miniature blackberries and are
favored by birds. For providing
shade in home gardens, the most
important kinds are fruitless forms
of *M. alba*.

Morus alba

M. alba. WHITE MULBERRY,
SILKWORM MULBERRY. Zones
2–24; H1, H2. Native to China.
Fast-growing tree can reach 30–
50 ft. high and wide, though it's
often smaller. Leaves to 6 in. long
and nearly as wide, often lobed.
Fruit-bearing (female) trees have
inconspicuous flowers followed by
white, pink, or purple fruit that is
sweet but rather insipid; it stains
paved surfaces (as well as clothing). 'Pendula' ('Teas' Weeping') is
a low-growing, strongly weeping
form—but a fruit producer.
Fruitless (male) forms are better
for home gardens, though they
do produce pollen in prodigious
amounts. Varieties include 'Chaparral' (weeping), 'Fan-San', 'Fruitless', 'Kingan', and 'Stribling'
('Mapleleaf').

Tolerates desert heat, alkaline
soil, seacoast conditions. Resistant
to Texas root rot. Subject to sooty
canker disease. Stake new plants;
they quickly develop large crowns,
which may snap from slender
young trunks in high winds. For
first few years, branches may grow
so long that they droop from their
own weight; shorten such branches
to a well-placed upward-growing

bud. Difficult to garden under
because of heavy surface roots.
Takes some aridity but performs
better with regular moisture.

M. australis 'Unryu' (*M. bom-
bycis* 'Unryu', *M. alba* 'Unryu').
CONTORTED MULBERRY. Zones
3–24. Selection of an eastern Asian
native. To 25 ft. tall and wide, with
twisted, contorted branches useful
in dried floral arrangements or for
winter silhouette. Fast growth
means that branches may be cut
freely with no harm to the tree.
Dark green, broadly oval leaves
6–7 in. long.

M. nigra. BLACK MULBERRY,
PERSIAN MULBERRY. Zones
4–24; H1, H2. Likely a native of
western Asia. To 30 ft. tall, 35 ft.
wide, with short trunk and dense,
spreading head. Heart-shaped
leaves to 8 in. long. Large, juicy
dark red to black fruit. 'Oscar'
and 'Wellington' are heavy bearers.
'Black Beauty' is smaller (15 ft.
tall). All do best with regular
water.

M. papyrifera. See Broussonetia papyrifera

M. rubra. RED MULBERRY.
Zones 2–7. Native to eastern and
central U.S. Resembles *M. alba* but
bears fruit that is somewhat larger
and has a better flavor. Fruit is red
when immature; it ripens to black.
Does best in rich soil. 'Illinois
Everbearing' is a hybrid between
this species and *M. alba;* its fruit
ripens throughout summer.

**MOSES-IN-THE-BOAT,
MOSES-IN-THE-CRADLE.**
See **TRADESCANTIA spathacea**

MOSQUITO GRASS.
See **BOUTELOUA gracilis**

MOSS, IRISH and SCOTCH.
See **SAGINA subulata**

MOSS CAMPION.
See **SILENE acaulis, S. schafta**

MOSS PINK.
See **PHLOX subulata**

MOSS ROSE.
See **PORTULACA grandiflora**

MOTHER FERN.
See **ASPLENIUM bulbiferum**

MOTHER-IN-LAW'S TONGUE.
See **SANSEVIERIA trifasciata**

MOTH ORCHID.
See **PHALAENOPSIS**

MOUNTAIN ASH. See **SORBUS**

MOUNTAIN BLUEBELL.
See **MERTENSIA ciliata**

MOUNTAIN FLAX.
See **PHORMIUM cookianum**

MOUNTAIN GARLAND.
See **CLARKIA unguiculata**

MOUNTAIN IRONWOOD.
See **CERCOCARPUS betuloides**

MOUNTAIN LAUREL.
See **KALMIA latifolia**

MOUNTAIN MAHOGANY.
See **CERCOCARPUS**

MOUNTAIN PHLOX.
See **LINANTHUS grandiflorus**

MOUNTAIN PRIDE.
See **PENSTEMON newberryi**

MOUNTAIN SPRAY.
See **HOLODISCUS dumosus**

MOUNT ATLAS DAISY.
See **ANACYCLUS depressus**

MOURNING BRIDE.
See **SCABIOSA atropurpurea**

MOURNING WIDOW.
See **GERANIUM phaeum**

MRS. ROBB'S BONNET.
See **EUPHORBIA amygdaloides
robbiae**

M

MUEHLENBECKIA
WIRE VINE
Polygonaceae
EVERGREEN SHRUBS AND VINES

🌡 **ZONES VARY BY SPECIES**

☀ ◐ **FULL SUN OR PARTIAL SHADE**

💧 **REGULAR WATER**

Unusual New Zealand natives with
thin, wiry stems, small leaves, and
insignificant flowers. Both of the
species below spread by rhizomes,
but one is a noninvasive creeper,
the other a vigorous climber or
sprawler that can overrun other
plants.

M. axillaris (*M. nana*). CREEP-
ING WIRE VINE. Shrub. Zones
3–9, 14–24; H1. Small, dense,
creeping plant; can grow just a few
inches tall or mound to 1 ft. high.
Closely spaced leaves are oblong to

Muehlenbeckia axillaris

nearly round, up to ⅜ in. long, glossy dark green. Bears very small (⅛-in.), translucent white fruits with black seeds. Use in rock garden or plant 1½–2 ft. apart for a small-scale ground cover. Can be mowed yearly to keep flat. Deciduous where winter chill is pronounced.

M. complexa. MATTRESS VINE, WIRE VINE. Vine. Zones 8, 9, 14–24. Twining vine can climb to 20–30 ft. or more; sprawls in the absence of support. Used as a ground cover, spreads over a 30-ft.-wide area. Forms a dense tangle of thin black or brown stems. Light green leaves are ½–¾ in. long, variable in shape—may be oval, rounded, fiddle shaped. Good for beach planting, screen. Curb growth by shearing or cutting back as much as desired; plant will regrow vigorously.

MUGWORT, WHITE. See **ARTEMISIA lactiflora**

MUHLENBERGIA
Poaceae (Gramineae)
PERENNIAL GRASSES

🌿 ZONES VARY BY SPECIES
☀️ 🌤️ FULL SUN OR LIGHT SHADE
💧💧 LITTLE OR NO WATER TO MODERATE WATER

Narrow-leafed grasses large and showy enough to stand out in the garden. Except as noted, evergreen in mild winters but turn tan or brown with hard freezes. They are very drought tolerant plants but look better and grow larger if given some supplemental water.

M. capillaris. PINK MUHLY. Zones 4–24. From eastern U.S. Dark green foliage forms a mound to 3 ft. tall, 6 ft. wide; airy plumes of feathery reddish flowers rise an additional 2½ ft. in fall. Evergreen in low desert. Cut plants back in late winter for fresh new growth in spring. 'Regal Mist' ('Lenca') has deep rosy pink flowers.

M. dubia. PINE MUHLY, MEXICAN DEER GRASS. Zones 3b, 7–24. Native to Arizona, western Texas, New Mexico, and northern Mexico. Densely tufted plant, similar to *M. rigens* but smaller (2–3 ft. tall and wide). Fine-textured leaves and upright, creamy flower spikes in summer and fall. Plant in well-drained soil.

M. dumosa. BAMBOO MUHLY. Zones 8–24. Native to Arizona, Mexico. To 3–6 ft. high and wide. Resembles bamboo, with slender, woody stems set with narrow

bright green leaves to about 3 in. long. Branching flower clusters appear in spring; blossoms are barely distinguishable from foliage.

M. emersleyi. BULL GRASS. Zones 2–24. Native to Arizona, New Mexico, Texas. Glossy green leaves form a mound 1½ ft. tall, 3–4 ft. wide, with flower spikes rising 2–3 ft. above the foliage from summer into fall. Spikes are purplish or reddish, fading to cream with age.

M. lindheimeri. Zones 6–24. From Texas, Mexico. Clump of soft, arching blue-green leaves grows to 5 ft. tall and wide, with amber flower spikes arching 2 ft. above foliage in autumn. Blooms of the species fade to gray; flowers of 'Autumn Glow' are yellow in fall. Attractive in dried arrangements. Semievergreen in mild-winter areas; dies to the ground in colder climates.

M. porteri. BUSH MUHLY. Zones 3, 7–14, 18–24. Native to southwestern U.S., northern Mexico. To 3 ft. tall and wide. Fine, short, blue-green stems and blades. Profuse small, pinkish purple seed heads form a gauzy mass from late summer through fall. Best in well-drained soils but will tolerate heavy soils.

M. pubescens. SOFT BLUE MEXICAN MUHLY. Zones 8–24. From central Mexico. Downy blue-green foliage forms a clump 1 ft. tall, 2 ft. wide. In spring or early summer, soft flower spikes rise 1–1½ ft. above the clump; they are light blue, aging to amber. Light frosts turn foliage purplish red; harder freezes kill it to the ground.

Muhlenbergia rigens

M. rigens. DEER GRASS. Zones 4–24. Native from California to Texas and south into Mexico. Bright green leaves form a dense, tight clump to 4 ft. high and wide. Slender yellow or purplish flower spikes in autumn are erect at first, then leaning; rise 2 ft. above the leaves.

M. rigida. PURPLE MUHLY. Zones 6–24. From Texas, New Mexico. Green clump to 2 ft. high and wide, producing 3-ft. spikes of brownish purple to deep purple flowers in late summer and fall. 'Nashville' flowers are an attractive true purple.

MULBERRY. See **MORUS**

MULGA. See **ACACIA aneura**

MULLEIN. See **VERBASCUM**

MULLEIN PINK. See **LYCHNIS coronaria**

MURRAYA paniculata (M. exotica)
ORANGE JESSAMINE
Rutaceae
EVERGREEN SHRUB

🌿 ZONES 21–24; H1, H2
🌤️ FILTERED SUNLIGHT
💧 REGULAR WATER

Native to Southeast Asia. Open habit; fast grower to 6–15 ft. tall and wide. Good as hedge, filler, foundation plant. Sometimes grown as small single- or multi-trunked tree. Has graceful, pendulous branches with glossy dark green leaves divided into three to

Murraya paniculata

nine oval, 1–2-in. leaflets. Blooms in late summer and fall (sometimes in spring), with white, ¾-in., bell-shaped blossoms with jasmine fragrance. On mature plants, small red fruits follow flowers. Needs rich soil, frequent feeding. Slowly recovers beauty after cold winters. Blooms attract bees.

A dwarf variety is usually sold as *M. exotica*. It is slower growing, more upright, and more compact than the species, reaching 6 ft. tall, 4 ft. wide. Its leaves are a lighter shade of green and have smaller, stiffer leaflets; bloom is usually less profuse.

MUSA
BANANA
Musaceae
PERENNIALS

🌿 ZONES VARY BY SPECIES
☀️ 🌤️ FULL SUN OR PARTIAL SHADE
💧 AMPLE WATER

For information on fruiting types, see Banana. The ornamental bananas described here include tall, medium-size, and dwarf plants; some of the tall sorts are the size of trees. All are fast growing; all have soft, thickish stems and spread by suckers or underground roots to form clumps that are often as wide as or wider than the plant is tall. Spectacular-looking long, typically broad leaves are easily tattered by strong winds, so choose protected planting sites. Will usually regrow from roots if cut down by frost; in frost-prone areas, locate plants where their absence won't be conspicuous. Attractive near swimming pools. Can be grown in tubs and wintered indoors (cut tops off tall plants). Give rich soil; feed heavily.

M. acuminata. Zones 8, 9, 14–24; H1, H2. From Southeast Asia. Many varieties available. Plants are grown for fruit in warmest gardens, but they also make handsome ornamentals there as well as in cooler areas. Some have especially attractive foliage. 'Enano Gigante' grows 6–8 ft. tall and wide, with large, dark green leaves that are marked with red when young; produces rich, creamy fruit. Leaves of 6–10-ft.-tall 'Zebrina' ('Roja', 'Rojo', 'Sumatra', 'Sumatrana') are green with maroon stripes; the plant produces tiny, inedible dark maroon fruit.

M. basjoo. JAPANESE BANANA. Zones 2 and 3 (with protection), 4–9, 14–24; H1, H2. From Japan. The hardiest of the banana clan. To 15 ft. tall, with narrow green leaves about 8 ft. long. Terminal spikes of yellow flowers may be followed by small, unpalatable fruit. Where plants freeze to the ground, spring regrowth will be quicker if trunks are heavily mulched in winter.

M. ensete. See Ensete ventricosum

M. lasiocarpa (Musella lasiocarpa). CHINESE YELLOW BANANA. Zones 5–9, 11–24; H1, H2. From mountains of China. To 5–6 ft. tall, with dark green, 3–4-ft.-long leaves. Grown for unusual inflorescence that looks like a giant (8-in.-wide) yellow

M

artichoke and can last all summer. Plant dies after flowering, but new growth sprouts from base. Not at its best in hot-summer regions.

M. × paradisiaca (M. sapientum). Zones 9, 12–16, 19–24; H1, H2. This is the most common form of the ornamental bananas. Makes a clump to 20 ft. tall and half as wide. Leaves to 9 ft. long. Flower stalks are pendent, bearing large, showy, powdery purple bracts; fruit (usually seedy and inedible) sometimes follows.

Musa × paradisiaca

M. velutina. Zones 23, 24; H2. From India. To 5–7 ft. tall, with 3-ft.-long leaves that are green above, bronzy beneath. Upright pink bracts, orange flowers, and small, velvety pink bananas that are inedible but highly decorative.

MUSCARI
GRAPE HYACINTH
Liliaceae
PERENNIALS FROM BULBS

- 🌿 ZONES VARY BY SPECIES
- ☼ ◐ FULL SUN OR LIGHT SHADE
- 💧 REGULAR WATER DURING GROWTH AND BLOOM

Native to the Mediterranean and southwestern Asia. Clumps of grassy, fleshy leaves appear in fall and live through cold and snow. Spikes of small, typically urn-shaped blue or white flowers (fragrant, in some species) bloom in early spring. Plant in early fall, setting bulbs about 2 in. deep and 3 in. apart in well-drained soil. Plant in masses or drifts under flowering trees or shrubs; use in edgings and rock gardens; grow in containers. Very long lived. Dig and divide when clumps become crowded. Plants self-sow under favorable conditions.

M. armeniacum. Zones A1–A3; 1–24. Bright blue flowers on 8-in.

Muscari armeniacum

stems rise above a clump of floppy foliage. 'Blue Spike' has double blue flowers in a tight cluster at top of spike. 'Early Giant' blooms somewhat earlier than the species, has darker blue flowers edged in white. 'Cantab', with light blue blossoms, grows lower than the species and has neater foliage and a later bloom time.

M. aucheri (M. tubergenianum). Zones A1–A3; 1–24. Stems to 8 in. tall. Flowers on lower part of spike are bright blue; those on upper part are paler blue.

M. azureum (Hyacinthella azurea, Hyacinthus azureus). Zones 2–24. Blossom spires are between those of hyacinth and grape hyacinth in appearance. Stalks to 8 in. high bear tight clusters of fragrant sky blue flowers that have a bell shape (rather than the usual urn shape).

M. botryoides. Zones A1–A3; 1–24. Medium blue flowers on stems to 1 ft. tall. 'Album' has white flowers.

M. comosum. FRINGE HYACINTH, TASSEL HYACINTH. Zones 1–24. Bears rather loose clusters of unusual, tattered-looking flowers on 1–1½-ft. stems. In the species, blossoms are greenish brown on lower part of spike, bluish purple on upper part. 'Monstrosum' ('Plumosum'), feathered or plume hyacinth, bears violet-blue to reddish purple flowers that look like shredded coconut.

M. latifolium. Zones 1–24. Possibly the showiest of the grape hyacinths. Each bulb produces just one leaf and a flowering stem to 1 ft. tall. Flowers on lower part of spike are deepest violet, those on upper part vivid indigo blue.

M. macrocarpum. Zones 5–9, 14–24. Curving, straplike, gray-green leaves to 1 ft. long. Stems to

6–8 in. tall bear tubular flowers that are soft yellow on lower part of spike, brownish purple at its top, with a lovely, sweet perfume. 'Golden Fragrance' has golden yellow flowers below, rich purple ones above.

M. neglectum. STARCH HYACINTH. Zones 1–24. Stems about 6 in. tall. Lower part of bloom spike holds tightly crowded, dark blue blossoms edged in white, while upper part is set with pale blue blooms. Flowers are said to smell like laundry starch.

MUSELLA lasiocarpa. See **MUSA lasiocarpa**

MUSTARD
Brassicaceae (Cruciferae)
ANNUAL

- 🌿 ALL ZONES
- ☼ FULL SUN
- 💧 REGULAR WATER

Two kinds of mustard are popular in Western gardens, both derived from plants native to the Mediterranean eastward into Asia. Curly-leafed mustard looks similar to curly-leafed kale in appearance. It is usually cooked like spinach or cabbage; young leaves are sometimes eaten raw in salads or used as garnishes.

Mustard

Mustard spinach (also called tendergreen mustard) has smooth dark green leaves. It matures earlier than curly-leafed mustard and is more tolerant of hot, dry weather. 'Red Giant' ('Chinese Red') has large, crinkled leaves with strong red shading and is handsome enough for a border. Use young mustard spinach as a salad green; older leaves can be cooked.

Mustard is easy to grow, and it grows fast—it's ready for the table 35 to 60 days after planting. Sow in rows in early spring; make successive sowings when young plants

from each previous planting are established. Thrives in cool weather but quickly goes to seed in summer heat. For fall harvest, sow in late summer; in mild-winter areas, plant again in fall and winter. Thin seedlings to 6 in. apart. Harvest outer leaves as needed. To learn about broadleaf mustard and Chinese mustard greens, see Asian Greens.

MYOPORUM
Myoporaceae
EVERGREEN SHRUBS OR TREES

- 🌿 ZONES VARY BY SPECIES
- ☼ FULL SUN, EXCEPT AS NOTED
- 💧 ◐ LITTLE TO MODERATE WATER, EXCEPT AS NOTED

Bell-shaped flowers attractive at close range but not showy; fruit small but colorful. Shiny dark green leaves with translucent dots. Tough and fast growing.

M. floribundum. Shrub. Zones 15–17, 19–24. Native to Australia. Interesting sculptural form; graceful, open growth to 5–9 ft. tall, 6–12 ft. wide. Sticky, very narrow, 3½-in.-long leaves droop from horizontally held branches. White to cream flowers are borne profusely along branches in spring; they are followed by tiny purplish fruits. Full sun or partial shade. Does best with regular water but takes wetter and drier conditions.

M. insulare. Shrub or tree. Zones 8, 9, 14–17, 19–24. Native to Australia. Varies in height and width, growing 3–20 ft. tall and 6–25 ft. wide. Tends to be shrubby in cooler or coastal areas, more treelike in hot climates. Leaves and flowers are very similar to those of *M. laetum* but somewhat smaller. Bluish purple fruits.

M. laetum. Shrub or tree. Zones 8, 9, 14–17, 19–24. Temperatures below 24°F/–4°C can cause severe

Myoporum laetum

M

damage. Native to New Zealand. Exceptionally fast growth to 30 ft. tall, 20 ft. wide. Densely clothed in rather narrow, 3–4-in.-long leaves. If allowed to grow naturally, it forms a billowing mass, but it can be trained as an attractive multi-trunked tree. To use it as a ground cover, peg down branches so they'll root and spread. Clusters of small white summer flowers with purple markings are followed by reddish purple fruits. Good seaside plant. 'Carsonii' is even faster growing than the species, with larger, broader, darker green leaves; branches are leafy all the way to ground. 'Compactum' is a dense grower to just 16 ft.; good choice for a tall hedge.

M. 'Pacificum'. Shrub. Zones 16–24. Extremely fast growing to 2 ft. tall and 30 ft. wide. As ground cover, can cover 100 sq. ft. in a year. Medium green, 1-in.-long leaves have an elongated oval shape. Bears small white flowers in summer. Performs best in cooler regions. Prune as needed; regrowth is rapid.

M. parvifolium (M. p. 'Prostratum'). Shrub. Zones 8, 9, 12–24. Native to Australia. Ground cover to 3–6 in. high, 9 ft. wide, with dense covering of light green leaves ¼–1½ in. long, ¼ in. or less wide. Tiny white summer flowers are followed by purple fruits. Plant 6–8 ft. apart; plants will fill in within 6 months, rooting where stems touch moist soil. Good on banks, slopes. Will not tolerate foot traffic. 'Burgundy Carpet' has red stems, purple new growth; 'Pink' bears pink flowers. 'Putah Creek' is taller than the species and not quite as wide spreading; it grows 1 ft. high, 8 ft. wide. 'Tucson' is more densely branched than the species and has smaller leaves.

M. sandwicense. FALSE SANDALWOOD, NAIO. Shrub or tree. Zones H1, H2. Moderately slow-growing Hawaiian native to 30 ft. high and wide; extremely variable in the wild, where it is seen both at tree size and as low as 3 ft. Fragrance of wood is similar to that of sandalwood. Pointed, glossy green leaves 2–6 in. long. Blooms come in both spring and summer, bearing small white or pink flowers clustered close to the stems; these are followed by small white fruits that shrivel and turn brown with age. Excellent windbreak, hedge, screen, or specimen plant. Good tolerance for wind, salt, and drought. Needs well-drained soil. Normally does not require pruning but can be shaped during growth.

MYOSOTIS
FORGET-ME-NOT
Boraginaceae
PERENNIALS, BIENNIALS, AND ANNUALS

- 🌿 ZONES A1–A3; 1–24
- ◐ PARTIAL SHADE
- 💧 REGULAR WATER

Both of the forget-me-not species described feature profuse, typically blue springtime flowers, tiny but exquisite. Grow easily and densely as ground covers. Do best in cool, moist areas, as in woodland gardens, at pond edges, along stream banks. They have invaded damp woodlands in some areas. Not usually browsed by deer.

Myosotis sylvatica

M. scorpioides. Perennial. Native to Europe, Asia, North America. Also known as water forget-me-not because roots need nearly constant moisture, such as alongside a stream or pond. This species is similar in most respects to *M. sylvatica*, but it grows a little lower, blooms even longer, and has roots that live over from year to year. Flowers are about ¼ in. wide; they come in blue with a yellow eye, white, or pink. Leaves are shiny, oblong, and bright green. Plant spreads by creeping roots.

M. sylvatica. Annual or biennial. Native to Europe. State flower of Alaska. To 6–12 in. high, 2 ft. wide. Soft, hairy foliage; basal leaves reach 4 in. long, while those set higher on stems are ½–2 in. long. Pure blue flowers with a white eye are ⅓ in. wide, set loosely along top portions of stems. Blooms and seeds profusely for a long season, beginning in late winter or early spring. Self-sows and will persist for years unless weeded out. Often sold as *M. alpestris*. Improved varieties include 'Blue Ball' and 'Royal Blue Improved'. Forget-me-nots are attractive beneath pink, rose, and salmon-colored tulips.

MYRICA
Myricaceae
EVERGREEN AND SEMIEVERGREEN OR DECIDUOUS SHRUBS OR TREES

- 🌿 ZONES VARY BY SPECIES
- ☀ FULL SUN
- 💧 WATER NEEDS VARY BY SPECIES

The two species described here are coastal natives: one comes from the Pacific coast; the other comes from the Atlantic. Both are cultivated for their attractive, pleasantly aromatic foliage. Flowers are inconspicuous, but the fruits that follow are effective in autumn and winter. Plants are useful as screens and as informal or clipped hedges.

M. californica. PACIFIC WAX MYRTLE. Evergreen shrub or tree. Zones 4–9, 14–24. Native to coast and coastal valleys from Southern California to Washington. In windy oceanfront conditions, it can be a low, flattened mass. Grown out of wind, it's a big shrub or tree to 10–30 ft. tall and wide, usually with many upright trunks. One of the best-looking native plants for gardens. Branches are densely clad with tooth-edged, narrow, 2–4½-in.-long leaves that are glossy dark green above, paler beneath, and clean looking throughout the year. Purplish, wax-coated nutlets are attractive to birds. Moderate water. A selection sold as 'Buxifolia' is more densely branched than the species, with smaller leaves.

Myrica californica

M. pensylvanica (M. caroliniensis). BAYBERRY. Deciduous to semievergreen shrub. Zones 1–7. Native to coastal eastern North America. Dense, compact growth to 9 ft. tall, 5–12 ft. wide. Narrowish glossy green leaves to 4 in. long are dotted with resin glands. Roundish fruit is covered with white wax—the bayberry wax used for candles. Tolerates poor, sandy soil. Resistant to oak root fungus. Regular water.

MYROBALAN.
See **PRUNUS cerasifera**

MYRSINE africana
AFRICAN BOXWOOD
Myrsinaceae
EVERGREEN SHRUB

- 🌿 ZONES 8, 9, 14–24
- ☀◐ FULL SUN OR PARTIAL SHADE
- 💧 MODERATE WATER

Native to the Azores, Africa, Himalayas, and China. Shrub grows to 3–8 ft. tall and 2½–6 ft. wide. Form is slightly floppy when young, but plant stiffens as it matures into a dense, rounded bush that is easily kept to 3–4 ft. with pinching and pruning. Erect-growing dark red stems are closely

Myrsine africana

set with very dark green, glossy, rounded, aromatic ½-in. leaves. Insignificant flowers. Good choice for low hedges, topiary, foundation plantings, narrow beds, and containers. Cut foliage is attractive in arrangements. Withstands air pollution.

MYRTLE.
See **MYRTUS communis**

MYRTUS communis
MYRTLE
Myrtaceae
EVERGREEN SHRUB

- 🌿 ZONES 8–24; H1, H2
- ☀◐ FULL SUN OR PARTIAL SHADE
- 💧 LITTLE TO MODERATE WATER

From the Mediterranean. Rounded plant is bulky and dense but has fine-textured foliage. Reaches 5–6 ft. high and 4–5 ft. wide (as much as 15 ft. by 20 ft. in old age). Glossy bright green leaves are pointed, 2 in. long, pleasantly aromatic when bruised or brushed against. White, sweet-scented, ¾-in. flowers with many stamens bloom in summer followed by bluish black, ½-in. berries. Takes any soil, but good drainage is essential. Makes a good informal hedge or screen, requiring little or

M

no pruning; as a specimen shrub, it can be selectively pruned to reveal limb structure. Withstands shearing into formal hedges and topiary.

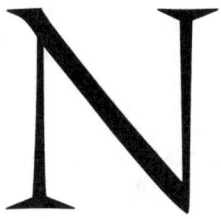

Myrtus communis

Named selections vary in foliage character and overall size. 'Variegata' fits the basic description but has white-edged leaves. 'Boetica' is especially upright, with thick, twisted branches and larger, darker leaves. 'Buxifolia' has small leaves like those of boxwood (*Buxus*). Dwarf forms include 'Compacta', a small-leafed variety popular for edgings and low formal hedges; 'Compacta Variegata', similar but with white-margined foliage; and 'Microphylla', with tiny, closely set leaves.

M. luma. See Luma apiculata
M. ugni. See Ugni molinae

N

NAGEIA falcatus.
See **PODOCARPUS gracilior**

NAGEIA nagi.
See **PODOCARPUS nagi**

NAGOONBERRY. See **RUBUS arcticus 'Kenai Carpet'**

NAIO.
See **MYOPORUM sandwicense**

NAKED LADY.
See **AMARYLLIS belladonna**

NANDINA domestica
HEAVENLY BAMBOO,
SACRED BAMBOO
Berberidaceae
EVERGREEN OR
SEMIEVERGREEN SHRUB

⚡ ZONES 3 (WITH SOME PROTECTION), 4–24; H1, H2

☼ ◐ ● SOME SHADE IN HOTTEST CLIMATES

◇ ◔ ● LITTLE TO REGULAR WATER

From China and Japan. Belongs to the barberry family but is reminiscent of bamboo in its lightly branched, canelike stems and deli-cate, fine-textured, lacy-looking foliage. Slow to moderate growth to 6–8 ft. tall, 3–4 ft. wide. Old clumps may be wider than tall because of slow, steady spread by suckers. Leaves are divided into many 1–2-in. leaflets shaped like pointed ovals. Foliage emerges pinkish and bronzy red, then turns to soft light green; takes on purple and bronze tints in fall and often turns fiery crimson in winter, especially in a sunny location and with some frost. A good filler in bouquets. Pinkish white or creamy white blossoms in loose, erect, 6–12-in. clusters bloom at branch ends in late spring or early summer. If plants are grouped, shiny red berries follow the flowers; isolated plants seldom fruit heavily.

Nandina domestica

In climates where summers are very hot, requires some shade; in milder climates, can take sun or shade. Does best in rich soil with regular water but can even compete with tree roots in dry shade. Subject to chlorosis in alkaline soil. Resistant to oak root fungus. In time, unpruned clumps become top-heavy and bare at base; to encourage denser foliage lower down, cut oldest canes to the ground each year before new growth begins in spring. Loses leaves at 10°F/−12°C; stems are damaged at 5°F/−15°C, but plant usually recovers quickly. Has with-stood −12°F/−24°C with some snow cover and little wind; severely damaged at 0°F/−18°C if exposed to strong winds.

Makes a light, airy-looking hedge, screen, or tub plant. Good for bonsai and in narrow, restricted spaces. Dramatic with night lighting. Varieties include the following.

'Alba' (*N. d. leucocarpa*). To 4–6 ft. tall, 2–3 ft. wide, with creamy white berries and foliage that is lighter green than that of species and lacks red tints. More subject to cold damage than the species.

'Compacta'. To 4–5 ft. tall, 3 ft. wide. Very lacy looking, with more canes and narrower, more numer-ous leaflets than the species.

'Filamentosa' ('San Gabriel'). THREADLEAF NANDINA. Mounding plant to 1–3 ft. tall and wide. Very finely dissected leaves have red tints; turn orange, bronze, or purplish red in fall. Overall effect is lacy and elegant.

'Fire Power'. To 2 ft. tall and wide. Red-tinged summer foliage turns bright red in winter.

'Gulf Stream'. To 3–3½ ft. tall, 1½ ft. wide, with blue-green summer foliage and good red winter color.

'Harbor Dwarf'. To 2–3 ft. tall. Rather than forming a discrete clump, it spreads by rhizomes to make a good ground cover. Foliage has orange-red to bronzy red winter color.

'Moon Bay'. To 2½ ft. high and wide. Leaves are lighter green than those of the species, and they turn bright red in winter. Not known to flower or fruit.

'Moyers Red'. Standard-size plant with broad leaflets. Brilliant red winter color in regions that get frost. Flowers are pinker than those of the species, and berries ripen a month or two earlier.

'Nana' ('Nana Purpurea', 'Atro-purpurea Nana'). To 2 ft. tall, 2–3 ft. wide. Coarse foliage is purplish green in summer, purplish red to bright red in winter. Leaves typi-cally show cupping, curling, and color streaks, though plants sold under the names listed here vary in the degree to which these char-acteristics are present. A very slow grower, best used as an individual plant in a container or against a background of rock or gravel to emphasize its domed habit. Not known to flower or fruit.

'Plum Passion'. To 4–6 ft. tall and 3 ft. wide. Narrow leaves are deep purplish red when young; turn deep green by summer, then reddish purple in winter.

'Royal Princess'. Stiffly upright, fast grower, to 6–8 ft. tall, 2–4 ft. wide. Narrow, lacy foliage turns burgundy in spring, orange red in fall. Especially heavy production of red berries.

'Sienna Sunrise'. Grows 3–4 ft. tall, 2–3 ft. wide. Foliage emerges vivid fiery red, softens to medium green in summer; red highlights return in fall and winter.

'Umpqua Chief'. Slow growing to 3 ft. high and 2 ft. wide in 3 years; matures at 5–6 ft. Tallest stems tend to flop. Leaflets are large, give good winter color.

'Umpqua Princess'. To 3–4 ft. high, 2 ft. wide. Narrow leaflets give it an open appearance.

'Woods Dwarf'. Slow, dense grower to 1½ ft. high and wide. Foliage turns crimson-orange to scarlet in winter.

NANKING CHERRY.
See **PRUNUS tomentosa**

NARCISSUS
DAFFODIL, NARCISSUS, JONQUIL
Amaryllidaceae
PERENNIALS FROM BULBS

⚡ ZONES A2, A3, 1–24, EXCEPT AS NOTED

☼ ◐ FULL SUN DURING BLOOM, PARTIAL SHADE AFTER IN HOT CLIMATES

● REGULAR WATER DURING GROWTH AND BLOOM

Beyond their fascinating variety in flower form and color, these natives of Europe and North Africa offer numerous appealing traits. They are permanent, increasing from year to year; they stand up to cold (most are hardy to −30°F/ −34°C) and heat; and they are use-ful in many garden situations. Given minimum care at planting, they thrive with virtually no fur-ther attention. These plants do not require summer watering (but will take it), need only infrequent divi-sion (and will even survive without it), and are totally unappetizing to gophers and deer. They bloom in late winter or spring.

All plants known by the names "daffodil," "narcissus," and "jon-quil" are properly *Narcissus*. In gardener's terms, however, "daf-fodil" refers to large-flowered kinds, "narcissus" denotes small-flowered (usually early-blooming) types bearing blossoms in clusters, while "jonquil" refers to *N. jonquilla* and its hybrids.

Trumpet daffodil

N

All have the same basic flower structure. Each bloom has a perianth (six outer petal-like segments) held at right angles to the corona (also called trumpet or cup, depending on its length) in the blossom's center. Flowers may be borne singly or in clusters. Colors are basically yellow and white, but there are many variations—shades of orange, red, apricot, pink, cream. Some are fragrant. Leaves may be straight and flat (strap shaped) or narrow and rushlike.

Use among trees and flowering shrubs, in ground-cover plantings, near water, in rock gardens, or in borders. Naturalize in sweeping drifts where space is available. Choose a planting area that will be in full sun while bulbs are blooming; after bloom, partial shade is beneficial, especially in hot-summer regions. One traditional location is beneath high-branching deciduous trees, where spring leafout provides the ideal dappled shade. Flowers usually face the sun—another factor to keep in mind when selecting planting locations. Daffodils perform well in containers. They also make fine cut flowers, though they should have a vase of their own; freshly cut stems release a substance that causes other cut flowers to wilt.

When buying bulbs, look for those that are solid and heavy, with no injury to the basal plate. So-called double-nose bulbs will give you the most and largest flowers the first season after planting. In most climate zones, it's best to plant bulbs in late summer or early fall, as soon as they are available. In regions with long, warm autumns and fairly mild winters, however, put off planting until soil has cooled in midautumn.

Daffodils are not fussy about soil as long as it is well drained. To improve drainage in heavy soils, dig in plenty of organic matter prior to planting. Set bulbs approximately twice as deep as they are tall—typically 5–6 in. deep for large bulbs, 3–5 in. deep for smaller ones. Space bulbs at least 6–8 in. apart. Water newly planted bulbs thoroughly. In many regions, fall and winter are wet or snowy enough to provide all the moisture daffodils require. If precipitation fails before bloom period ends and leaves begin to yellow, keep plantings well watered. Faded blooms can be removed to neaten plants' appearance, but the foliage should be left in place to mature naturally; as long as the leaves are green, they

Neil and Lore Van Lierop on Stretching the Daffodil Season

After decades as daffodil growers, Neil and Lore Van Lierop have learned how to keep bulbs flowering from February to May. They manage this feat yearly at Van Lierop Bulb Farm in Puyallup, WA, but you can duplicate their show nearly anywhere in the West. Just plant each of the following five daffodil varieties.

'February Gold', a yellow Triandrus hybrid, opens the season. "Yellows are first to bloom," Neil says, "and it's still the most popular color."

'Unsurpassable' is a good yellow trumpet daffodil that follows hard on the heels of 'February Gold'.

The popular and dependable trumpet 'Mount Hood' blooms midseason with a yellow blush and matures to snowy white.

'Geranium', a Tazetta with white segments and an intensely orange cup, appears a little later, producing several fragrant flowers per cluster.

Closing the season is the fragrant Poeticus daffodil 'Pheasant's Eye', with white segments and a green-centered yellow cup edged in orange.

All will naturalize, returning more plentifully each year. "Most important," says Neil, "never cut back the leaves before they die back naturally."

Tazetta hybrid 'Geranium'

are using sunlight to rebuild the bulbs' energy for next year's growth. After leaves have turned brown, they should be removed and the soil lightly cultivated so that insects will not have an easy way in. Summer moisture is not needed.

Established clumps need dividing only when flower production and bloom quality decline. It's easiest to dig clumps just after foliage dies down, when you can still see where plants are. After digging bulbs, store them as you

would gladiolus corms until planting time.

To grow daffodils in containers, set bulbs close together, tips level with soil surface. Place pots in a well-drained trench or cold frame and cover with 6–8 in. of moist peat moss, wood shavings, sawdust, or sand. Look for roots in 8 to 10 weeks (tip from pot carefully). Remove pots with well-started bulbs to a greenhouse, a cool room, or a sheltered garden spot to bloom. Keep well watered until foliage yellows; then plant out in the garden. You can sink containers of bulbs in borders when plants are almost ready to bloom, then lift them when flowers fade.

The most serious pest is the narcissus bulb fly. An adult fly resembles a small bumblebee. The female lays eggs on leaves and on necks of bulbs; when eggs hatch, young grubs eat their way into the bulbs. Check bulbs before planting and discard any that are damaged, soft, or infested. Cultivate and mulch around bulbs after leaves die down.

Following are the 12 generally recognized divisions of daffodils and representative varieties in each division.

Trumpet daffodils. Trumpet is as long as or longer than surrounding perianth segments; one flower to each stem. Best known is yellow 'King Alfred', but newer yellow-flowered 'Arctic Gold' and 'Unsurpassable' are superior. Pure white varieties include 'Mount Hood', 'Empress of Ireland'. Bicolors with white segments and yellow trumpet include 'Bravoure', 'Las Vegas', 'Peace Pipe'; among those with yellow segments and white trumpet are 'Honeybird', 'Spellbinder'.

Large-cupped daffodils. Cup is shorter than perianth segments but always more than one-third their length; one flower per stem. Varieties include 'Stainless' (white); 'Carlton' and 'Saint Keverne' (both yellow). Varieties with white perianth segments and

Tazetta hybrid 'Cragford'

colored cup include 'Ice Follies' (yellow cup); 'Romance', 'Salome' (pink cup); 'Johann Strauss', 'Professor Einstein' (orange cup). 'Ambergate', 'Ceylon', and 'Fortissimo' all have yellow perianth segments and pink, orange, or red cup. Those with yellow segments and white cup include 'Daydream', and 'June Jungrund'.

Small-cupped daffodils. Cup no more than one-third the length of perianth segments; one flower per stem. Varieties include 'Audubon' (white segments, pale yellow cup banded pink) and 'Barrett Browning' (white segments, orange-red cup).

Double daffodils. Cup has segments that are separate rather than joined together. Flower looks like a peony rather than a typical daffodil. One flower per stem. Examples are 'Christmas Valley' and 'Replete' (white perianth segments, pink cup segments), 'Tahiti' (yellow segments, red cup), and 'White Lion' (white segments, yellow cup).

Triandrus hybrids. Cup at least two-thirds the length of perianth segments; several flowers to each stem. White 'Thalia' is an old favorite. Others include 'Hawera' (yellow) and 'Silver Chimes' (white segments, yellow cup).

Cyclamineus hybrids. Early bloomers with one flower per stem. Perianth segments are strongly recurved. Yellow 'February Gold' is best known. Yellow 'Peeping Tom' has an especially long trumpet. 'Jack Snipe' and 'Phalarope' have white segments, yellow trumpets.

Jonquilla hybrids. Each stem bears two to four small, very fragrant flowers; foliage is often rushlike. Choices include 'Bell Song' (white perianth segments, pink cup); 'Pipit' (yellow segments, white cup); 'Quail', 'Sun Disc', and 'Trevithian' (solid yellow).

Tazetta daffodils and Tazetta hybrids. Zones 5–24. Hardy to about 10°F/–12°C. Early-blooming, cluster-flowering types popularly known by the name "narcissus." Each stem bears four to eight or more very fragrant flowers with short cup. Many have white perianth segments and yellow cup, but there are

Daffodil Divisions

TOP: Trumpet daffodil 'Bravoure'
BOTTOM: Cyclamineus hybrid

TOP: Small-cupped daffodil 'Barrett Browning'
BOTTOM: Jonquilla hybrid 'Trevithian'

TOP: Large-cupped daffodil 'Fortissimo'
BOTTOM: Tazetta hybrid 'Early Splendor'

TOP: Double daffodil 'Tahiti'
BOTTOM: Poeticus daffodil 'Actaea'

TOP: Triandrus hybrid 'Hawera'
BOTTOM: Split-corona hybrid 'Colblanc'

other color combinations. *N. tazetta* 'Orientalis', Chinese sacred lily, has light yellow segments and darker yellow cup. 'Paper White' is pure white; 'Early Splendor' has white segments, orange cup; 'Grand Soleil d'Or' has yellow segments, orange cup. Newer varieties include 'Cragford' and 'Geranium' (white segments, orange cup); and 'Falconet' and 'Scarlet Gem' (yellow segments, orange cup). Tazettas are often grown indoors in bowls of pebbles and water (keep dark and cool until growth is well along, then gradually bring into light).

Poeticus daffodils. Perianth segments are white; very short, broad cup is in a contrasting color, usually with red edges. 'Actaea' and 'Pheasant's Eye' are old favorites.

Species, varieties, and hybrids. This category includes species, their naturally occurring forms, and wild hybrids. Included here are many miniature types popular with collectors and rock garden enthusiasts. Prominent among these are the following.

N. asturiensis. Often sold as *N.* 'Miniature'. Very early miniature trumpet daffodil. Pale yellow flowers, only 1 in. long, on 3-in.-tall stems.

N. bulbocodium. HOOP PETTICOAT DAFFODIL. Zones 3–24. Plant is hardy to about –10°F/–23°C. Stems to 6 in. tall bear small yellow flowers that are mostly trumpet, with almost threadlike perianth segments. Foliage is grassy.

N. cyclamineus. Zones 3–24. Hardy to about –10°F/–23°C. Small

Narcissus bulbocodium

flowers, one to each 6–12-in. stem, have strongly recurved, lemon yellow perianth segments and narrow, tubular golden cup.

N. jonquilla. JONQUIL. Very fragrant golden yellow flowers with short cups in clusters of two to six on 1-ft. stems. Rushlike foliage.

N. triandrus. ANGEL'S-TEARS. One to six small flowers per stem; blossom colors run from white through cream to pale yellow. Cup is at least half as long as perianth segments. Tallest forms reach 10 in. high.

Split-corona hybrids. Cup is split for at least one-third its length into two or more segments. 'Cassata' (white perianth segments, yellow cup), 'Colblanc' (all-white flowers), and 'Palmares' (white segments, pink cup) are three of the more readily available varieties in this small but growing class.

Miscellaneous. This category contains all types that don't fit the other divisions. 'Tête-à-tête' and 'Jumblie' (both yellow) have flowers like those of Cyclamineus hybrids but are rock garden dwarfs to about 6 in. high.

NARROW BUCKLER FERN. See **DRYOPTERIS carthusiana**

NASSELLA

NEEDLE GRASS
Poaceae (Gramineae)
PERENNIAL GRASSES

🌿	ZONES VARY BY SPECIES
☀	FULL SUN
○	LITTLE OR NO WATER, EXCEPT AS NOTED

These needle grasses were once included in *Stipa*. All are clump formers characterized by long awns—needlelike or threadlike appendages that give a feathery look to the inflorescence. The first three species described are California natives that look much alike; all are useful for revegetation of wild areas, for stabilizing soil, and for restoring natural meadows. They can be started from seed. Clear area of weeds and other grasses first; *Nassella* species can self-sow once established, but initially they cannot compete with other vegetation.

All these needle grasses are cool-season growers that go dormant during hot, dry summers, reviving with cooler autumn weather and rains.

N. cernua. NODDING NEEDLE GRASS. Zones 7–9, 11, 14–24. To 3 ft. tall, 2 ft. wide, with deep green leaves. Purple-toned awns reach 4½ in. long, age to a silvery color. Blooms in late winter, early spring.

N. lepida. FOOTHILL NEEDLE GRASS. Zones 7–9, 11, 14–24. Similar to *N. cernua* in appearance

and bloom season, but awns are shorter (to 2 in. long).

N. pulchra. PURPLE NEEDLE GRASS. Zones 5–9, 11, 14–24. The classic native California bunch grass. Much like the two species listed above, but with 4-in. awns. Same early bloom period.

N. tenuissima. MEXICAN FEATHER GRASS. Zones 2b–24. Native to Texas, New Mexico, Mexico. Among finest textured and most billowy looking of all ornamental grasses. To 2 ft. tall, 2–3 ft. wide, with threadlike bright green

Nassella tenuissima

leaves. In summer, produces very thin flowering stems that arch outward and downward, ending in a cloud of silvery green, 3-in. awns that age to a light straw color and remain attractive into winter. Stays green where summers are cooler. Thrives with little to regular water. Can self-sow in well-irrigated gardens; to prevent, cut plants back before seeds ripen.

NASTURTIUM. See **TROPAEOLUM**

NATAL IVY.
See **SENECIO macroglossus**

NATAL PLUM.
See **CARISSA macrocarpa**

NATAL RUBY GRASS.
See **RHYNCHELYTRUM**

NAUPAKA.
See **SCAEVOLA taccada**

NAUPLIUS sericeus.
See **ASTERISCUS sericeus**

NEANTHE bella.
See **CHAMAEDOREA elegans**

NECTARINE.
See **PEACH and NECTARINE**

NECTAROSCORDUM siculum (Allium siculum)
Liliaceae
PERENNIAL FROM BULB

🌡	ZONES 2B–9, 14–24
☀☽	FULL SUN OR LIGHT SHADE
💧	REGULAR WATER DURING GROWTH AND BLOOM

Onion relative from the Mediterranean region and western Asia. Creates an attractive silhouette. Strap-shaped, 12–16-in.-long

Nectaroscordum siculum

leaves emerge in spring, give off garlic scent if crushed or bruised. Thick, fleshy stems to 4 ft. tall appear in summer, each carrying a cluster of up to 30 nodding, 1-in., bell-shaped flowers. Blooms are white, suffused with pink or purple and tinged green at the base. Leaves die back at or just after bloom. Flowers are followed by upright seed capsules that can be dried for winter arrangements. In fall, plant bulbs 1½ ft. apart and 2 in. deep in well-drained soil, or start from seed in early spring.

NEEDLE GRASS.
See **NASSELLA**

NEEDLE PALM.
See **RHAPIDOPHYLLUM hystrix**

NEILLIA
Rosaceae
DECIDUOUS SHRUBS

🌡	ZONES 2B–9, 14–24
☀☽	FULL SUN OR LIGHT SHADE
💧	REGULAR WATER

From China. Graceful, arching shrubs related to spirea and, like it, useful in shrub borders or as space fillers. Attractive green, glossy foliage. Both species described below bear short, nodding clusters of pink blossoms in spring and early summer. To keep shrubs open and graceful, prune them after bloom, cutting branches that have flowered to the base.

Neillia affinis

N. affinis. To 6 ft. tall and wide, with reddish purple stems; 3½-in., oval to lance-shaped leaves; and 3-in.-long flower clusters.

N. sinensis. Grows about 6 ft. tall and wide (possibly larger), with peeling brown bark; 3-in., lance-shaped leaves; and 2½-in.-long flower clusters.

NELUMBO (Nelumbium)
LOTUS
Nelumbonaceae
AQUATIC PLANTS

🌡	ZONES 1–24; H1, H2
☀☽	FULL SUN OR PARTIAL SHADE
💧	LOCATE IN PONDS, WATER GARDENS

Huge, waxy round leaves attached at their centers to leafstalks rise above the water. Large, fragrant summer flowers form above or below leaves. Ornamental woody

fruit is perforated like a salt shaker, looks attractive in dried arrangements.

If you buy started plants in containers, put them in a pond, positioned so soil in pots is 8–10 in. below surface of water. If you acquire roots, plant them in spring, setting them horizontally and about 4 in. deep in a 1–1½-ft.-deep container of fairly rich soil; then place container at recommended depth in pond, as described above for started plants. Do not let roots freeze; where freezes are possible, cover the pond or fill it deeper with water. Beware of introducing lotus plants or roots to earth-bottom ponds 3–4 ft. or shallower; plants will eventually fill in pond, and rhizomes are difficult to remove.

N. lutea (Nelumbium luteum). AMERICAN LOTUS. Native to much of North America. Similar to *N. nucifera* but somewhat smaller in leaf and flower. Flowers are pale yellow.

N. nucifera (Nelumbium nelumbo). INDIAN or CHINESE LOTUS. Native to Asia, Australia. Round leaves, 2 ft. or wider, carried 3–6 ft. above water surface. Pink, 4–10-in.-wide flowers borne singly on stems. Both tubers and seeds are esteemed in Chinese cookery, and the plant holds great religious significance for Buddhists: it represents the human soul rising from mud and aspiring to light and purity.

Nelumbo nucifera

White, rose-colored, and double varieties exist. 'Speciosum' is the classic, single light pink lotus of Asian art. 'Alba Grandiflora' bears large, very fragrant white flowers. 'Empress' has single white blooms with deep pink edges. Dwarf forms (12–24 in. tall) suitable for tubs or small ponds include 'Tulip' ('Shirokunshi'), single white; and 'Momo Botan', double, deep rose fading to white on 1½–2-ft. stems.

NEMATANTHUS gregarius
GOLDFISH PLANT
Gesneriaceae
PERENNIAL

🌡	ZONES H1, H2; OR INDOORS
☀	PARTIAL SHADE; BRIGHT INDIRECT LIGHT
💧	REGULAR WATER

From tropical South America. Related to African violet (*Saintpaulia*) and has similar cultural needs. Grows to 2½ ft. high, 3 ft. wide, with foot-long, arching branches that are closely set with rich green, oval leaves ¾–1½ in. long. Orange, puffy, roundish flowers are about 1 in. long,

Nematanthus gregarius

pinched at tip into pursed "mouth" like that of a goldfish. Given enough warmth and humidity, this plant will bloom year-round. Easy to root from tip cuttings; stems may also root where they contact damp soil mix. Arching, trailing growth makes it best suited to hanging pots or baskets.

NEMESIA
Scrophulariaceae
ANNUALS AND PERENNIALS

🌡	ZONES VARY BY SPECIES
☀	FULL SUN
💧	REGULAR WATER

Colorful South African natives, some with fragrant flowers. None is at its best in hot weather, though new *N. caerulea* hybrids are more heat tolerant than other types. All need well-drained soil. Remove faded flowers to prolong bloom. Use as bedding or rock garden plants, in hanging baskets, as bulb covers.

N. caerulea (N. foetens, N. fruticans). Perennial in Zones 14–24; annual anywhere. To 2 ft. tall, 1 ft. wide, with small bright green leaves and upright stems carrying many intensely fragrant blossoms in blue, pink, or lavender. Flowers are narrower than those of *N. strumosa*. Often blooms for months without special attention (almost all year in cool-summer, mild-winter climates), but if flowers decline, cut plant back to stimulate new growth and more bloom. Tolerates light afternoon shade.

While the species prefers cool weather, the following hybrids withstand temperatures as high as 95°F/35°C. Growing about 1 ft. tall and wide are 'Compact Innocence', with yellow-centered white flowers, and particularly heat-tolerant 'Blue Bird', with blue-violet blossoms centered with yellow. Even more compact (to about 9 in. tall) are 'New Blue', with flowers slightly redder than those of 'Blue Bird' and with less yellow in their centers, and 'Opalescent' with scentless pearly blue and light pink flowers over a long period. Well-established plantings of the species and hybrids are hardy to 15°F/−9° C.

Nemesia strumosa

N. strumosa. Annual. Zones 1–24. The true species grows 1½ ft. high and 1 ft. wide, but plants sold under this name are usually more compact hybrids between *N. strumosa* and *N. versicolor*; they remain under a foot high, reach about 6 in. wide, and produce small, unscented flowers in clusters to about 4 in. across. Blossoms are chalice shaped, flaring at the mouth into two unequal lips, the lower one larger than the upper. They come in every color but green. Several mixtures offer a wide range of bright solid colors; bicolors include 'Mello Red and White' and blue-and-white 'KLM'.

Buy started plants or sow seeds in place. Time plantings of this rapid grower to avoid frost but come into bloom during cool weather. In cold-winter climates, sow in early spring for late spring, early summer bloom; in mild-winter areas, sow in fall for bloom in winter and spring. Give rich soil and regular moisture. Pinch to induce bushiness. Good bulb cover or hanging basket plant.

N. versicolor. Annual. Zones 1–24. Grows to 8–10 in. high and as wide. Unscented flowers are similar to those of *N. strumosa*, but color range of *N. versicolor* contains more blue, yellow, and white. Flowers of 'Blue Gem' are a rich pure blue with a white center. Time plantings as for *N. strumosa*.

NEMOPHILA
Hydrophyllaceae
ANNUALS

☑	ZONES VARY BY SPECIES
☀ ◑	FULL SUN OR PARTIAL SHADE
💧	REGULAR WATER

To 6–12 in. high and trailing to 1 ft. wide, with bell-shaped flowers to 1 in. across in spring. Pale green, hairy, ferny leaves give plants a delicate appearance. Often used as bulb cover. Broadcast seed in place. In cold-winter areas, sow as soon as the ground is workable in spring; in mild-winter regions, plant in fall. Plant is quickly killed by heat and humidity. Reseeds when grown under cool, moist conditions.

N. maculata. FIVE-SPOT NEMOPHILA. Zones 1–9, 12–24. Native to California. Flowers are white, marked with fine purple lines and dots; a large purple dot appears at the tip of each of the five lobes.

Nemophila menziesii

N. menziesii (N. insignis). BABY BLUE EYES. Zones 1–24. Native to California, southern Oregon. Blooms as freely in gardens as it does in the wild, bearing sky blue blossoms with a white or near-white center. 'Snow Storm' (*N. m. atomaria*), the baby blue eyes variety most commonly grown in Oregon, has white flowers dotted with black. 'Pennie Black' (*N. m. discoidalis*) produces blooms that are blackish purple rimmed in white.

NEODYPSIS decaryi. See **DYPSIS decaryi**

NEOLITSEA sericea
JAPANESE SILVER TREE
Lauraceae
EVERGREEN TREE

☑	ZONES 4–9, 14–24
☀ ◑	FULL SUN TO LIGHT SHADE
💧💧	MODERATE TO REGULAR WATER

Fast-growing tree native to Japan, Korea, China. Related to camphor tree (*Cinnamomum*). Broadly cone shaped, growing 30–45 ft. tall, 25–40 ft. wide. Foliage is aromatic when bruised. New leaves are bronze, drooping, covered with silky white hairs; mature ones are dark green with velvety white undersides, 3–7 in. long. Tiny, inconspicuous flowers are followed by red, ½–¾-in. fruits.

Neolitsea sericea

NEOMARICA
Iridaceae
PERENNIALS

☑	ZONES 16, 17, 21–24; H2; OR INDOORS
☀ ◑	FULL SUN OR LIGHT SHADE; BRIGHT INDIRECT LIGHT
💧	REGULAR WATER

Like iris, these perennials produce fans of lance-shaped leaves. Foliage arises from short rhizomes; leaves and flowering stems grow to about the same height. Flowers are intricate, with three large, rounded outer segments surrounding three smaller, curled segments that are banded in contrasting colors. Individual flowers last only a day, but others follow over an extended period.

N. caerulea. From Brazil. To 5–5½ ft. tall, 2–3 ft. wide, with stiffly erect leaves. As plant grows, lower leaves fan out to the side. Branching flower stems carry a succession of 3–4-in. blue blossoms, their centers intricately banded in yellow, white, and brown. Blooms in early summer. Offsets are produced at flowering points on the stems; they detach easily for additional plants.

Neomarica caerulea

N. gracilis. WALKING IRIS. From Mexico to Brazil. To 2–2½ ft. tall, 1–1½ ft. wide. Blooms in late spring and summer; flower stems resemble the leaves so closely that blossoms appear to emerge directly from the foliage. Flowers are 2½ in. wide. Outer segments are white; inner ones show a combination of blue, brown, and yellow. As flowers fade, the blossom stalk bends downward and produces plantlets that take root— hence the common name.

NEOREGELIA
Bromeliaceae
PERENNIALS

☑	ZONES 21–24; H1, H2; OR INDOORS
☀ ◑	SOME SHADE; BRIGHT INDIRECT LIGHT
💧	KEEP CUP WITHIN ROSETTE FILLED WITH WATER

From South America. Bromeliads with rosettes of leathery leaves, often strikingly colored or marked; short spikes of typically inconspicuous flowers are buried in hearts of rosettes. Keep central tube or cup within leaf rosette filled with water. Need light, open, fast-draining soil mix that holds moisture but does not exclude air; water the mix when it dries out. Feed lightly. Use outdoors year-round only in frost-free locations; can be grown on tree branches with sphagnum moss packed around roots.

N. carolinae. To 1 ft. tall, 2½ ft. wide. Many shiny, medium green

Neoregelia carolinae
'Tricolor'

N

leaves about 1 ft. long, 1½ in. wide. As plant approaches bloom, leaves turn rich red at base. 'Tricolor' has green leaves with lengthwise white stripes; as is true for the species, center of rosette turns red before blooms appear.

N. spectabilis. PAINTED FINGERNAIL PLANT. To 1½ ft. tall, 3 ft. wide. Leaves are about 1 ft. long, 2 in. wide, olive green with bright red tips. Foliage takes on a bronzy color in strong light.

NEPETA
Lamiaceae (Labiatae)
PERENNIALS

☀	ZONES 1–24, EXCEPT AS NOTED
☼ ☽	FULL SUN OR PARTIAL SHADE
⬥	MODERATE WATER

Vigorous, spreading members of the mint family with aromatic foliage. With the exception of catnip *(N. cataria),* these plants are valuable for their spikes of two-lipped blue or blue-violet (or sometimes pink, white, or yellow) flowers. As soon as blossoms fade, shear plants back by half or cut faded flower stems to the ground to encourage rebloom. (Most species seed freely and can become invasive if spent flowers are not removed.) Plants make attractive, informal low hedges or edgings.

In winter or early spring, cut out last year's growth to make way for new stems. At that time, you can also divide clumps for increase, though it's easy to start new plants from cuttings (take them before flower buds form). When buying named varieties, be sure to obtain cutting-grown plants; seedlings vary in flower color and habit. In cold-winter climates, nepetas are occasionally used as a substitute for lavender *(Lavandula)* in borders and edgings. Most species resent heat combined with high humidity. In Zones 12 and 13, most are best treated as winter annuals. Tolerate regular moisture if soil is well drained.

N. cataria. CATNIP. From the Mediterranean and western Asia. To 2–3 ft. high and wide, with downy, heart-shaped, tooth-edged

Nepeta cataria

gray-green leaves. Spikes of small (¼–½-in.) whitish or pinkish flowers in late spring, early summer. Not very ornamental but worthy of a place in the herb garden. Grows easily in light soil and self-sows readily. Common name refers to stimulant effect on cats, but their susceptibility to the herb varies: some felines fall into a rapturous frenzy, rolling wildly on the plant, but others ignore it. If necessary, protect crown of plant with an inverted wire basket; stems will grow through. The same tactic also helps preserve potted plants grown outdoors and brought indoors occasionally for cats to enjoy. You can also sprinkle dried leaves over your cat's food or use them to stuff cloth toys. Some people use catnip to flavor tea. 'Citriodora' has lemon-scented foliage.

N. clarkei. Zones 2b–9, 14–24. Himalayan native to 2½–4 ft. tall, 1½–3 ft. wide. Truest blue flowers of all nepetas, with white patch on lower lip. Blooms in summer and early fall. Lance-shaped green leaves are 1–2½ in. long.

N.× faassenii. CATMINT. Sterile hybrid of *N. racemosa* and a European species; often sold as *N. mussinii.* Soft, silvery gray-green, spreading mound grows to 1 ft. high, 1½–2 ft. wide. Scallop-edged, heart-shaped gray-green leaves to 1 in. long. Attractive to some cats, who enjoy nibbling on and rolling in plantings; insert short sticks in the ground among the foliage to discourage cats and prevent destruction. Loose, lax spikes of ½-in. lavender-blue flowers in late spring, early summer. Set plants 1–1½ ft. apart for ground cover. 'Select Blue' has darker flowers than the species; 'Snowflake' has pure white blooms. 'Dropmore' grows to 1½ ft. high and 3 ft. wide; it may be a hybrid involving another species.

N. grandiflora. Native to Europe, Caucasus. Open clump to 2½ ft. tall, 1½ ft. wide. Gray-green, hairless or sparsely hairy, scallop-edged, egg-shaped leaves to 4 in. long. Violet-blue, ¾-in. flowers in late spring, early summer. 'Bramdean' has lavender-blue blossoms with purple calyxes; 'Dawn to Dusk' has lilac-pink flowers, smoky

violet calyxes. Calyxes of both these varieties persist after flowers have faded.

N. hederacea. See Glechoma hederacea

N. nervosa. Zones 3–10, 14–24. Native to Kashmir. Bushy habit to 1–2 ft. tall, 1 ft. wide. Bright green, conspicuously veined, tooth-edged leaves are lance shaped, 2–4 in. long. Brilliant violet-blue (rarely yellow), ½-in. flowers bloom from midsummer to early fall.

N. racemosa (N. mussinii). Native to the Caucasus, Turkey, Iran. Sprawling plant grows from 6 in. to 1 ft. tall and about 2 ft. or more wide. Roundish, scallop-edged, ½–1¼-in.-long leaves can range in shades from medium green to gray green; they are covered with fine hairs. The typical form produces ⅓-in.-long lavender flowers for a short period in midsummer; may rebloom if sheared. Reseeds prodigiously. Inferior to its hybrid *N.× faassenii,* but there are several worthwhile selections that are more compact than the species and bloom over a longer period. 'Blue Ice' has dense gray-green foliage and pale blue flowers that fade to near-white. 'Superba' has a dense, matlike habit and gray-green leaves that are smaller than those of the species; it bears lavender-blue blossoms from spring through fall. Violet-blue flowers of 'Walker's Low' appear over an equally long season.

N. reichenbachiana. Native to Armenia and the Caucasus. May be a form of *N. racemosa.* Makes a thick, low mound to 1 ft. high, 2–4 ft. wide. Woolly, heart-shaped, deeply veined leaves have pointed tips and scalloped edges; they are pale green above, gray or white beneath, ¾–1¼ in. long. Blooms from late spring through fall, producing 6–8-in.-tall spikes of deep blue flowers with just a hint of violet. Good ground cover; space plants 3 ft. apart.

N. sibirica (N. macrantha, Dracocephalum sibiricum). SIBERIAN CATNIP. Native to Siberia. Sturdy, upright habit to 2–3 ft. tall, 1½–2 ft. wide. Dark green, oblong to lance-shaped, 3-in.-long leaves are softly hairy beneath. Spikes of large (1½-in.) violet-blue blossoms appear for about a month, beginning in early summer.

N. 'Six Hills Giant'. Possibly a hybrid of *N.× faassenii* and similar to it—but grows taller (reaches 2½–3 ft. high and as wide), has greener foliage, and bears deeper

blue flowers. More tolerant of damp climates than other nepetas.

N. 'Souvenir d'André Chaudron' ('Blue Beauty'). Probably a hybrid of *N. sibirica.* Similar to parent but grows only 1½ ft. high and blooms for a longer period, with season extending into late summer.

NEPHROLEPIS
SWORD FERN
Polypodiaceae
FERNS

☀	ZONES VARY BY SPECIES; OR INDOORS
☼ ●	SOME SHADE; BRIGHT INDIRECT LIGHT
⬥	REGULAR WATER

Tough and easy to grow, these are the most widely used of all ferns. For native Western sword fern, see *Polystichum munitum.*

N. cordifolia. SOUTHERN SWORD FERN. Zones 8, 9, 12–24; H1, H2. Native to many tropical regions of the world. To 2–3 ft. tall, 5 ft. wide. Tufts of bright green, narrow (2-in.-wide), upright fronds with closely spaced, finely toothed leaflets. Roots often have small, roundish tubers. Plant spreads by thin, fuzzy runners and can be invasive. Will not take hard frosts but is otherwise adaptable, tolerating poor soil and erratic watering. Good in narrow, shaded beds; can thrive in full sun with adequate water. Effective ground cover; also good in pots and hanging baskets. Often sold as *N. exaltata.*

N. exaltata. Zones 23, 24; H2. Like *N. cordifolia,* this is a tropical species, but it grows larger than *N. cordifolia* (to 7 ft. high and wide) and has broader fronds (to 6 in. wide). Most common are named selections grown as houseplants. Best known is 'Bostoniensis', Boston fern. Growing about 3 ft. high, it is the classic parlor fern, with spreading, arching habit and graceful, eventually drooping fronds broader than those of the species. Among the many forms

Nephrolepis exaltata 'Bostoniensis'

with more finely cut and feathery fronds are 'Fluffy Ruffles', 'Rooseveltii', and 'Whitmanii'.

N. obliterata. Zones H1, H2. From northwestern Australia. Grows to 3–4½ ft. high and wide. Similar to *N. cordifolia* but has darker green, somewhat narrower fronds. Used mainly as a houseplant. Habit is stiffer and more erect than that of *N. exaltata* 'Bostoniensis', and plant is more tolerant of low humidity and both high and low light conditions. Selections include 'Kimberley Queen' and 'Western Queen'.

NERINE
Amaryllidaceae
PERENNIALS FROM BULBS

☀	ZONES 5, 6, 8, 9, 13–24
☼ ◐	PARTIAL SHADE IN HOTTEST CLIMATES
◉	REGULAR WATER DURING GROWTH AND BLOOM

South African relatives of spider lily (*Lycoris*), which they closely resemble. Most have strap-shaped leaves to about 1 ft. long; these die back well before bloom time in late summer or early fall, then reappear later in the year (typically around bloom time or shortly afterward). Some types are essentially evergreen. All have broad, funnelshaped flowers carried in clusters atop leafless stems; each blossom has six spreading segments that are recurved at their tips.

Same planting instructions, cultural conditions as for *Lycoris*. Withhold summer water for species that experience summer dormancy, but keep watering the essentially evergreen kinds. As is true for *Lycoris*, these plants can be grown in pots in areas beyond their hardiness range or where soil cannot be kept dry for summerdormant types.

N. bowdenii. Flowers to 3 in. long, soft pink marked with deeper pink, in clusters of 8–12 on 2-ft. stems. Forms with taller stems and larger flower clusters are available in deeper pink, crimson, and red. 'Crispa' is 1 ft. tall, with pale pink, wavy-edged segments; 'Pink Triumph' is a larger plant that blooms later.

N. filifolia. Essentially evergreen, since new leaves—narrow, grassy, 6–8 in. long—are produced as old ones fade. Inch-wide, rose red flowers with narrow, crinkled segments are carried in clusters of 8–12 on 1-ft. stems. Spreads rapidly.

N. masoniorum. Virtually evergreen species like *N. filifolia*, but it bears its flowers in clusters of 4–12 on 9-in. stems.

Nerine sarniensis curvifolia fothergillii

N. sarniensis. GUERNSEY LILY. Large clusters of 1½-in., iridescent crimson flowers with prominent stamens, borne on stalks to 2 ft. tall. Pink, orange, scarlet, and pure white varieties. *N. s. curvifolia fothergillii* has scarlet flowers overlaid with shimmering gold.

NERIUM oleander
OLEANDER
Apocynaceae
EVERGREEN SHRUB

☀	ZONES 8–16, 18–24; H1, H2
☼	FULL SUN
◐ ◉	LITTLE TO MODERATE WATER
◉	ALL PARTS ARE POISONOUS IF INGESTED. DON'T BURN PRUNINGS; SMOKE CAN CAUSE SEVERE IRRITATION

Mediterranean native. Moderate to fast growth to 3–20 ft. tall and 4–12 ft. wide, depending on variety. Larger types can be easily trained into single or multitrunked trees. Narrow, 4–12-in.-long leaves are dark green, leathery, and semiglossy; attractive in all seasons. Blooms from late spring to fall, bearing 2–3-in.-wide, often fragrant flowers clustered at twig or branch ends. Forms with double and single flowers are sold, in colors ranging from white to shades of yellow, pink, salmon, and red. 'Sister Agnes', single white, is the most vigorous oleander, often reaching 20 ft. tall; 'Mrs. Roeding', double salmon pink, grows 6 ft. tall and has smaller leaves, finer-textured foliage than big oleanders. Flowers of

double types hang on after bloom and turn brown. Single-flowered 'Hawaii' offers the same rich color as 'Mrs. Roeding', but its flowers drop cleanly.

'Petite Pink' and 'Petite Salmon' grow 3–6 ft. high and nearly as wide; keep at lower end of range with moderate pruning. They make excellent informal flowering hedges, though they are not as cold hardy as standard-size oleanders. Bright red 'Little Red', to 3–4 ft. tall and wide, is completely hardy—as are the following, intermediate in size between dwarfs and full-size plants: deep red 'Algiers', white 'Casablanca', bright red 'Ruby Lace' (with 3-in., wavy-edged flowers), and white 'Morocco'.

Oleanders need little water once established, but they can take moderate amounts. They tolerate poorly drained and relatively salty soils. In shade or ocean fog, they produce weak or leggy growth and few flowers. Routine pruning isn't necessary, but you may need to prune to guide growth. To control size and form, cut oldest stems to the ground before spring growth begins; shorten remaining stems to restrict height. To prevent bushiness at base, pull (don't cut) any unwanted suckers. To renew an old, unattractive, leggy plant, lop it to the ground before new growth begins in spring.

Oleander was once the basic landscaping shrub for regions with hot, dry summers and mild winters, but it is now facing a severe threat from leaf scorch, a bacterial disease spread by the glassywinged sharpshooter (an insect pest). Leaves of infected plants turn brown and drop, and the plant quickly declines and dies. No cure is known, although the disease's progress may be slowed by pruning out affected parts of the plant (sterilize pruning tools after each cut). The disease is already serious in Southern California and in parts of Arizona and Texas. Efforts are being made to curb its spread by controlling the insect carrier. Previously, chief problems were scale, yellow oleander aphid, and bacterial gall disease (causing deformed flowers and warty growths).

All parts of this plant are highly toxic. Caution children

Nerium oleander

against eating leaves or flowers; keep prunings and dead leaves away from hay or other animal feed; don't use wood for barbecue fires or skewers. Smoke from burning prunings can cause severe irritation to mucous membranes. Wash hands thoroughly after handling plants.

For a plant called yellow oleander, see *Thevetia*.

NEW MEXICAN PRIVET. See **FORESTIERA neomexicana**

NEW ZEALAND CHRISTMAS TREE. See **METROSIDEROS excelsus**

NEW ZEALAND FLAX. See **PHORMIUM tenax**

NEW ZEALAND LAUREL. See **CORYNOCARPUS laevigatus**

NEW ZEALAND TEA TREE. See **LEPTOSPERMUM scoparium**

NICOTIANA
FLOWERING TOBACCO
Solanaceae
PERENNIALS, MOST GROWN AS ANNUALS

☀	ALL ZONES, EXCEPT AS NOTED
☼ ◐	FULL SUN OR PARTIAL SHADE
◉	REGULAR WATER
◉	ALL PARTS ARE EXTREMELY POISONOUS IF INGESTED

Tender perennials from South America. All but *N. glauca* are grown as annuals, but they may live over in mild-winter areas. Upright-growing plants with large, soft, oval leaves; both foliage and stems are slightly sticky. Flowers— very fragrant, in some species— are tubular, typically flaring at the mouth into five pointed lobes; they appear near tops of branching stems in summer. They usually open at night or on cloudy days, though some kinds open during the day. Some nicotianas reseed readily.

N. alata (N. affinis). Wild species (for which seed is available) grows 2–4 ft. tall (possibly to 6 ft. under ideal conditions), 1 ft. wide. Bears large, intensely fragrant white flowers that open toward evening. Selection and hybridization with other species have produced many garden strains that stay open day and night and come in colors including white, pink shades, red, and lime green, but their perfume is not as strong as that of the "unimproved" common species.

Nicotiana alata

Domino strain grows 12–15 in. high and has upward-facing flowers that take heat and sun better than taller kinds. Nicki strain is taller, to 15–18 in. The older Sensation strain is taller still (to 4 ft.) and looks more at home in informal mixed borders than as a bedding plant. Fragrance in these strains is erratic. If scent (especially during evening) is important to you, plant 3-ft.-tall 'Grandiflora'.

N. glauca. TREE TOBACCO. Zones 7–24. Naturalized in Hawaii and from California to Texas and Mexico. Shrubby or treelike habit to 10–25 ft. tall, 10 ft. wide. Bluish green leaves to 6 in. long; small, unscented yellow-green flowers. Be especially careful with the leaves—they can be deadly if eaten.

N. langsdorffii. To 5 ft. tall, 1½ ft. wide. Branching stems are hung with drooping sprays of bell-shaped bright green flowers. Unusual blossom color blends well with blues, yellows in flower border. No noticeable scent.

N. sylvestris. To 5 ft. tall, 2 ft. wide. Intensely fragrant, long, tubular white flowers are borne in tiers atop a statuesque plant. Striking in a night garden.

NIEREMBERGIA
CUP FLOWER
Solanaceae
PERENNIALS

	ZONES VARY BY SPECIES
	LIGHT SHADE IN HOTTEST CLIMATES
	REGULAR WATER

The first species listed here grows as a spreading mound; the second is a ground-covering mat. Both are blanketed with broadly cup-shaped blooms in summer. Beyond hardiness range, treat as annuals.

N. linariifolia (N. caerulea, N. hippomanica). DWARF CUP FLOWER. Zones 8–24; H1, H2. To 6–12 in. high and wide. Much-branched, mounding plant, with very small, stiff leaves. Flowers are blue to violet. Trimming back plant after bloom to induce new growth seems to lengthen its life. 'Purple Robe', and the white 'Mont Blanc', usually sold as *N. hippomanica*, may be varieties of the similar *N. scoparia*.

Nierembergia repens

N. repens (N. rivularis). WHITE CUP. Zones 5–9, 14–24; H1. Mat to 4–6 in. high, 2 ft. wide, with bright green foliage and white blossoms. For best performance, don't crowd it with more aggressive plants. Not as heat tolerant as *N. linariifolia*.

NIGELLA damascena
LOVE-IN-A-MIST
Ranunculaceae
ANNUAL

	ALL ZONES
	FULL SUN OR PARTIAL SHADE
	REGULAR WATER

Mediterranean native. Old-fashioned favorite to 1–1½ ft. high, 10 in. wide. All leaves, even those that form under collar beneath each flower, are finely cut into threadlike divisions. Blue, white, or rose-colored blooms, 1–1½ in. across, are borne singly at branch ends in spring. Curious papery-textured, horned seed capsules lend an airy effect to

Nigella damascena

bouquets and mixed borders, look very decorative in dried arrangements. 'Miss Jekyll', to 1½ ft. tall, has semidouble cornflower blue blossoms. Persian Jewels, to 15 in. high, is a superior strain in a mix of colors.

Love-in-a-mist comes into bloom quickly in spring, dries up in summer heat. Start from seed in spring, as soon as ground is workable and frost danger is past; can be sown in fall in mild-winter areas. Sow seed where plants are to grow, since long taproot makes transplanting unsatisfactory. Self-sows freely.

NIGHT JESSAMINE. See **CESTRUM nocturnum**

NIGHTSHADE. See **SOLANUM**

NIKAU PALM. See **RHOPALOSTYLIS sapida**

NINEBARK. See **PHYSOCARPUS**

NIPPONANTHEMUM nipponicum. See **CHRYSANTHEMUM nipponicum**

NIU. See **COCOS nucifera**

NOGAL. See **JUGLANS major**

NOLANA paradoxa
Nolanaceae
PERENNIAL GROWN AS ANNUAL

	ALL ZONES
	FULL SUN OR LIGHT SHADE
	MODERATE WATER

Unusual plant from Chile that looks like a trailing, sky blue petunia. To 6–8 in. high and 2 ft. wide, with trailing stems bearing ovate, 2-in.-long leaves. In summer, plant is covered with 2-in., funnel-shaped flowers in bright blue with

Nolana paradoxa

a white or yellow throat. 'Blue Bird' has deep sky blue blossoms with a white throat. Use as edging or in hanging basket. Withstands wide range of temperatures. Needs good drainage.

NOLINA
Agavaceae
PERENNIALS

	ZONES VARY BY SPECIES
	FULL SUN
	LITTLE OR NO WATER TO MODERATE WATER

Accent plants with tough, grassy leaves usually about 3 ft. long, typically on a thick trunk. In spring or summer, 3–4-ft. stalks rise from the center of the foliage rosette, carrying tiny greenish or creamy white flowers. Plants are valued for their strong vertical silhouette rather than their blossoms. Good for desert or other dry landscapes.

N. bigelovii. Zones 7–16, 18–24. Native to California, Arizona. Stout stem to 3 ft. tall is topped by a rosette of gray-green, 3–4-ft. leaves. Plant eventually reaches about 6 ft. wide.

N. longifolia. MEXICAN GRASS TREE. Zones 12–24. Native to central Mexico. In youth, forms a fountain of bright green, grasslike leaves. In time, leafy whorls top trunks 6–10 ft. tall, sometimes with a few branches. Plant can eventually spread to 9 ft. wide.

Nolina longifolia

N. matapensis. TREE BEAR GRASS. Zones 10–13. From Mexico. To 10–25 ft. tall, 10 ft. wide, with a branching trunk that is slow to develop. Each branch ends in a shower of bright green, broad-based leaves with sharp edges; leaves may reach 9 ft. long.

N. microcarpa. Zones 3, 10–13. Native from Arizona to Texas and Mexico. Unlike others, doesn't form a noticeable trunk; instead, branching and slowly spreading underground stems give rise here and there to rosettes of narrow (less than ½-in.-wide) olive green leaves with tips split into tufts. Each foliage clump can reach 3 ft. tall, 6 ft. wide.

N. parryi. Zones 2, 3, 7–24. Native to deserts of Southern California. Resembles *N. bigelovii*, but eaf bases are expanded into a spoonlike shape. Some authorities consider this a subspecies of *N. bigelovii.*

N. recurvata (Beaucarnea recurvata). BOTTLE PALM, PONYTAIL PALM. Zones 13, 16–24, H1, H2; or indoors. Native to Mexico. To 12–15 ft. tall (possibly to 30 ft. in great age), 9–12 ft. wide. One or more trunks rise from greatly swollen base. On young plants, trunk base looks like a big onion sitting on the soil; on old plants, it can measure several feet across. Clusters of bright green leaves arch and droop at ends of branches. Mature outdoor plants may bloom. Does exceptionally well indoors if given bright light and not overwatered.

NORFOLK ISLAND PINE.
See **ARAUCARIA heterophylla**

NORTHERN BEDSTRAW.
See **GALIUM boreale**

NOTHOFAGUS

SOUTHERN BEECH,
FALSE BEECH
Fagaceae
EVERGREEN AND DECIDUOUS TREES

🌿	ZONES 5, 6, 14–17
☀️	FULL SUN
💧	REGULAR WATER

Relatives of beech (*Fagus*); native to Southern Hemisphere. Small dark green leaves and open branch structure give these trees a graceful look. Nuts are so tiny as to go unnoticed. Need high humidity, neutral to acid soil, and good drainage. The three species described below, all from Chile, are sold in Western specialty nurseries; evergreen species from Australia and New Zealand are rarely available so are not covered here.

Nothofagus antarctica

N. antarctica. Deciduous. To 50 ft. tall, 30 ft. wide. Closely set, oval, ½–1½-in. leaves line long, graceful shoots on young trees. Grows fast in youth; fills out with age, but branches maintain their graceful, fern-frond appearance. Yellow fall foliage. Open growth makes for handsome silhouette against wall or sky.

N. dombeyi. Evergreen. To 50–70 ft. tall, 30 ft. wide. Leaves to 1½ in. long, ½ in. wide. Good tree for shading rhododendrons, azaleas; open structure admits filtered light.

N. obliqua. Deciduous. Fast growing to 70–100 ft. tall, 50 ft. wide. Oblong, 3-in. leaves turn yellow, orange, or red in autumn; several colors may be present on a single tree.

NYMPHAEA

WATER LILY
Nymphaeaceae
AQUATIC PLANTS

🌿	ZONES 1–24; H1, H2
☀️	FULL SUN
💧	LOCATE IN PONDS, WATER GARDENS

Floating leaves are rounded, with deep notch at one side where leaf-stalk is attached. Showy flowers either float on surface or stand above it on stiff stalks. There are hardy and tropical kinds. Hardy types come in white, yellow, copper, pink, and red. Tropical types add blue and purple to the color range; recent introductions include an unusual greenish blue. Some tropicals in the white-pink-red color range are night bloomers; all others close at night. Many are fragrant.

Hardy kinds are easiest for beginners. Plant them from February to October in mild-winter areas, from April to July in cold-winter regions. Set 6-in.-long pieces of rhizome on soil at pool bottom or in boxes (not redwood ones, since these can discolor the water), placing rhizome in a nearly horizontal position with its bud end up. In either case, top of soil should be 8–12 in. below surface of water. Feed at planting time and monthly thereafter, using a controlled-release product. Groom plants by removing spent leaves and blossoms. They usually bloom throughout warm weather and go dormant in fall, reappearing in spring. In very cold areas, protect plants by covering pond or by adding more water to it.

Nymphaea

Tropical kinds begin to grow and bloom later in summer but last longer, often until the first frost. Buy started tropical plants and set them at the same depth as hardy rhizomes. Tropical types go dormant but do not survive really low winter temperatures. Their best chance of long-term survival is in regions where orange trees grow. Where winters are colder, store dormant tubers in damp sand over winter or buy new plants each year.

NYSSA sylvatica

SOUR GUM, TUPELO,
PEPPERIDGE
Nyssaceae
DECIDUOUS TREE

🌿	ZONES 2–10, 14–21
☀️ 🌤️	FULL SUN OR PARTIAL SHADE
💧 💧	MODERATE TO REGULAR WATER

Native to eastern U.S. Slow to moderate growth to 30–50 ft. or taller, 15–25 ft. wide. Pyramidal when young; spreading, irregular, and rugged in age. Crooked branches and dark, red-tinged bark make dramatic picture against winter sky. Glossy dark green, 2–5-in.-long leaves emerge rather late in spring. Male and female flowers borne on separate plants. Both sexes bear inconspicuous flowers; females will bear fruit if a male is growing nearby (males may set some fruit as well). Fruits are bluish black, shaped like small olives; birds like them, but the fruits can make a mess on decks and driveways. In fall, even in mild-winter regions, leaves turn yellow

Nyssa sylvatica

and orange, then bright red before dropping. 'Autumn Cascades' has a strongly weeping form.

Sour gum prefers moist, deep, acid, well-drained soil containing lots of organic matter, but tolerates poor drainage and some drought. Does not thrive in polluted air. Excellent specimen or shade tree; very attractive in naturalized landscapes. Select a permanent location, since this tree's taproot makes it difficult to move later on.

N

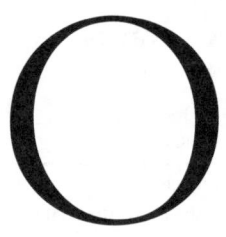

OAK. See **QUERCUS**

OAT GRASS, BLUE.
See **HELICTOTRICHON**
sempervirens

OAT GRASS, BULBOUS.
See **ARRHENATHERUM elatius**
bulbosum 'Variegatum'

OBEDIENT PLANT.
See **PHYSOSTEGIA virginiana**

OCEAN SPRAY.
See **HOLODISCUS discolor**

OCHNA serrulata
(O. multiflora)

BIRD'S-EYE BUSH, MICKEY
MOUSE PLANT
Ochnaceae
EVERGREEN SHRUB

| 🌿 ZONES 14-24 |
| 🌓 PARTIAL SHADE |
| 💧 MODERATE WATER |

From South Africa. Slow, spreading growth to 4–8 ft. high and
wide. Oblong leaves, 2–5 in. long,
are leathery, fine toothed, bronzy
in spring, deep green later. Early
summer flowers are the size of
buttercups *(Ranunculus)*. After

Ochna serrulata

the yellow petals fall, sepals turn
vivid red; then five or more green,
seedlike fruits protrude from red
center. Fruits later turn glossy jet
black, in strong contrast to red
sepals; at this stage the configura-
tion can be said to resemble eyes,
ears, and nose of a mouse. Prefers
slightly acid soil. Good in tub or
box or as small espalier. Makes
an interesting accent in a shrub
border.

OCIMUM basilicum

BASIL
Lamiaceae (Labiatae)
ANNUAL

| 🌿 ALL ZONES |
| ☀️ FULL SUN |
| 💧 REGULAR WATER |

From tropical and subtropical
Asia. Somewhat bushy plant to
2 ft. tall and 1 ft. wide, with green,
shiny, 1–2-in.-long leaves and
spikes of white flowers. Forms
with purple or variegated leaves
have purple flowers. Very popular
culinary herb. Used fresh or dry,
its leaves lend a pleasant, mildly
sweet flavor to sauces and cooked
dishes of all sorts. The best leaves
are from younger stems that have
not yet borne flowers. There is a
dwarf, small-leafed kind that
thrives in containers.

Ocimum basilicum

'Dark Opal' has large leaves in
a deep bronzy purple and small
lavender-pink flowers; it grows
1–1½ ft. high and is attractive
enough for borders and mass
plantings. Other good purple-
leafed varieties include 'Red
Rubin', with uniform dark color,
and 'Purple Ruffles', with deeply
fringed and ruffled leaf edges.
Sow seeds of any basil in early
spring; or set out nursery plants
after all danger of frost is past.
Space plants about 10–12 in.
apart or thin to this distance.
Fertilize once during the growing
season with a complete fertilizer.
To prolong leaf production—
which will cease when plants
come into bloom—pinch out
flower spikes as they form.
Where the growing season is
long, though, flowering always
wins out and plants will mature
and stop producing new growth.
In these regions, make successive

sowings about every 2 weeks to
ensure a steady supply of leaves
throughout the season.

OCOTILLO. See **FOUQUIERIA**

OCTOPUS TREE.
See **SCHEFFLERA actinophylla**

ODONTOSPERMUM maritimum.
See **ASTERISCUS maritimus**

OEMLERIA
cerasiformis
(Osmaronia
cerasiformis)

OSO BERRY, INDIAN PLUM
Rosaceae
DECIDUOUS SHRUB OR TREE

| 🌿 ZONES 4-9, 14-24 |
| 🌓 🌓 ● FULL SUN IN COOLER CLIMATES ONLY |
| 💧 AMPLE WATER |

In damp woodlands and meadows
in the Northwest and in parts of
California, oso berry's tiny, almond-
scented white flowers are among
the first signs of spring. A suckering shrub that grows to 3–15 ft.
tall, eventually spreading into
thickets that become 12 ft. wide or
more. Lance-shaped leaves to 3½
in. long are dark green on top, gray
green and slightly fuzzy beneath.
Crushed leaves have a fresh scent
like that of cucumbers. Bell-
shaped, fragrant blooms in drooping clusters up to 4 in. long appear

Oemleria cerasiformis

with the foliage, which emerges
very early in the year. Male and
female plants are separate; if a
male is nearby, females will bear
small (less than ½-in.-long) blue-
black fruits that are relished by
birds and other wildlife. To keep
the plant looking its best, remove
some of the oldest stems after
bloom. Or revive an old, overgrown
shrub by cutting it back almost to
the ground.

OENANTHE javanica

JAPANESE WATERCRESS,
FLAMINGO CELERY
Apiaceae (Umbelliferae)
PERENNIAL

| 🌿 ZONES 9, 14-24 |
| ☀️ FULL SUN |
| 💧 AMPLE WATER |

Native to eastern Asia. Stems 8–
16 in. long, prostrate or semierect,
set with 4-in., bright green leaves
divided like celery foliage. Flat,
round clusters of whitish flowers
bloom in summer. Stems root
where they touch damp soil, and
plant spreads indefinitely; it will
grow even in water. Can be eaten
as a vegetable; use leaves raw or
shred them into soups.

Oenanthe javanica
'Flamingo'

In North America, the species
is rarely grown. More commonly
seen is 'Flamingo', with grayish
green leaves edged in white; the
white border becomes suffused
with pink during cool weather, the
pink eventually spreading to the
whole leaf. Dormant in winter
except in the mildest climates. Use
as an ornamental around pools
and in wet places.

OENOTHERA

EVENING PRIMROSE,
SUNDROPS
Onagraceae
PERENNIALS OR BIENNIALS

| 🌿 ZONES VARY BY SPECIES |
| ☀️🌓 FULL SUN OR PARTIAL SHADE |
| 💧💧 LITTLE TO MODERATE WATER, EXCEPT AS NOTED |

Valued for showy, four-petaled,
silky flowers in bright yellow, pink,
or white. Some types display their
blossoms during the day, others
open in late afternoon and close
the following morning. Flowers of
some are fragrant. Plants succeed
in tough, rough places.
O. berlandieri. See O. speciosa
'Rosea'

O. caespitosa. TUFTED, FRAGRANT, or WHITE EVENING PRIMROSE. Perennial or biennial. Zones 1–3, 7–14, 18–21. Native to western U.S. Clump to 8–12 in. high, 2 ft. wide, with many rosettes of narrow, fuzzy gray-green leaves to 4 in. long. Fragrant, 3–4-in. flowers fade from white to pink; they open in the evening. Blooms heavily in late spring, early summer.

O. drummondii. See O. stubbei

O. elata hookeri (O. hookeri). Perennial or biennial. Zones 5–7, 14–24. Native to moist places in many parts of western U.S. To 3 ft. high and wide. Basal rosette of medium green, lance-shaped, 2–5-in.-long leaves; branching flower stems are hairy, carry smaller leaves. Evening-blooming plant that produces flowers all summer. The 2–3-in. blossoms are carried in terminal spikes; they open pale yellow, later turn orange red. Reseeds heavily; not recommended for orderly, irrigated gardens. Grow in moist area where it can run wild. Tolerates both drought and flooding.

O. fruticosa. SUNDROPS. Perennial or biennial. Zones 1–21. Native to eastern U.S. Erect growth to 2 ft. high and wide. Branching reddish stems are set with medium green, lance-shaped leaves to 4½ in. long; leaves turn dull red with frost. Clusters of 1–2-in.-wide, deep yellow flowers from late spring through summer; open in daytime. 'Fireworks' ('Fyrverkeri') has red flower buds and leaves tinted purplish brown. Foliage of 'Summer Solstice' ('Sonnenwende') turns bright red in summer, darkens to burgundy in fall. *O. f. glauca (O. tetragona)* has light yellow flowers and red stems; its leaves are broader than those of species and red tinted when young.

O. macrocarpa (O. missouriensis). OZARK SUNDROPS. Perennial. Zones 1–24. Native to south-central U.S. To 6 in. tall and 2 ft. wide, with narrow, lance-shaped leaves to 3 in. long. Late spring to early fall, bears pure yellow, 4-in. flowers that remain open all day. Large winged seedpods follow the flowers. Good in rock gardens. Give partial shade in hottest climates. *O. m. incana* 'Silver Blade' has silvery blue leaves.

O. speciosa. MEXICAN EVENING PRIMROSE. Perennial. Zones 2b–24; H1, H2. Native to southwestern U.S. and Mexico. To 1 ft. high and 3 ft. or more wide, spreading by rhizomes. Forms rosettes of medium green, oblong to lance-shaped, 1–3-in.-long leaves. Fragrant, 2-in. flowers are white to pinkish, aging to pink; despite plant's common name, they open during the day. Blooms spring or early summer into fall, then stems die back. Good ground cover for dry slopes or parking strips, but can be aggressive and is potentially invasive. Varieties include pure white 'Alba', light pink 'Rosea' *(O. berlandieri, O. speciosa childsii),* pink 'Siskiyou', and 'Woodside White' (white blossoms with a chartreuse eye).

Oenothera speciosa 'Rosea'

O. stubbei. SALTILLO EVENING PRIMROSE. Perennial. Zones 10–14, 18–24. Native to Mexico. Evening-blooming plant that forms a dark green mat 5 in. high and 4 ft. wide; prostrate stems root along the ground, forming offset plants. Narrow leaves to 2½ in. long. Yellow, 2½-in. flowers rise on individual stems 6–8 in. above foliage. Blooms most heavily in spring, sporadically throughout the rest of the year. Endures heat and drought but does better with occasional water. Often sold as *O. drummondii.*

O. tetragona. See O. fruticosa glauca

OKRA
Malvaceae
ANNUAL

🗡	ALL ZONES
☼	FULL SUN
💧	REGULAR WATER

Warm-season vegetable from tropical Asia. Large, erect, bushy plant to 6 ft. tall, with big, bold, deeply lobed leaves; the edible pods are produced in leaf joints. Grows well under same conditions as sweet corn. Plant when danger of frost is past and ground has warmed to 70°F/21°C. To speed germination, soak seeds for 24 hours before planting; use only seeds that are swollen. Leave 2½–4 ft. between rows; thin plants to 1–1½ ft. apart. Apply a complete fertilizer when the first pods set, again when plants are shoulder high. Begin picking when pods are 2–4 in. long (wear gloves, since pods are prickly). Pick every 2 days or so; plants stop producing if pods are not harvested. Okra takes 55 to 60 days from planting to harvest.

Okra

'Annie Oakley' and 'Cajun Delight' are early varieties that mature in areas with a short growing season. 'Burgundy' has red leaves and pods, looks attractive in containers. Grown in a large tub in a warm spot, a single okra plant can yield a crop large enough to make it worth growing. Okra is used to flavor and thicken soups and gumbos; it can also be sautéed, steamed, or batter-fried.

OLD MAN.
See ARTEMISIA abrotanum

OLD MAN CACTUS.
See CEPHALOCEREUS senilis

OLD MAN'S WHISKERS.
See GEUM triflorum

OLD WOMAN.
See ARTEMISIA stelleriana

OLEA europaea
OLIVE
Oleaceae
EVERGREEN TREE

🗡	ZONES 8, 9, 11–24; H1, H2
☼	FULL SUN
💧	LITTLE TO MODERATE WATER

From the Mediterranean. Along with palms, citrus, and eucalyptus, olives are regional trademarks along avenues and in gardens of California and southern Arizona. The trees' beauty has been appreciated in those areas since they were introduced to mission gardens for the oil their fruit produces.

Willowlike foliage is a soft gray green that goes well with most colors. Smooth gray trunks and branches become gnarled and picturesque in age. Trees grow slowly, typically to 25–30 ft. high and as wide; however, young ones put on height (if not substance) fairly fast. Begin training early. For single trunk, prune out or shorten side branches below point where you want branching to begin; cut off basal suckers. For multiple trunks, stake lower branches or basal suckers to continue growth at desired angles. Large old trees can (with reasonable care) be boxed and transplanted with near certainty of survival.

Olive trees look best when grown in deep, rich soil, but they will also grow in shallow, alkaline, or stony soil and with little fertilizer. They thrive in areas with hot, dry summers but also perform adequately in coastal areas. They take temperatures down to 15°F/–9°C.

Olea europaea

Olives withstand heavy pruning. Thinning each year shows off branch pattern and eliminates some flowering/fruiting wood, reducing the fruit crop—which can be a nuisance in ornamental plantings.

On fruiting varieties, olives ripen and drop late in the year. Without processing, the olives are inedible, and they can stain paving and harm lawns if not removed. In addition to pruning, reduce crop by spraying with fruit-control hormones when tiny white flowers appear. Or spread tarpaulin at dropping time, knock off all fruit, and dispose of it. So-called fruitless varieties are not always reliably barren.

'Ascolana'. A variety grown commercially for fruit; available as a specimen tree from landscaping firms. Large fruit, small pit. ▶

O

'Bonita'. Sold as fruitless; actually, has tiny fruit resembling that of privet (*Ligustrum*).

'Little Ollie'. Big, dense shrub (to 6–8 ft. high and wide), very dark green; excellent as hedge or screen. Bears almost no fruit.

'Majestic Beauty'. Airy and fluffy looking; suitable as specimen or as hedge or screen. Bears almost no fruit.

'Manzanillo'. Commercial-grove kind most often sold as specimen tree by landscaping firms. More spreading habit than most. Apple-shaped fruit.

'Mission.' Commercial-grove kind sold as specimen tree by landscaping firms. Taller than 'Manzanillo', 'Sevillano'.

'Sevillano'. Commercial-grove kind sold as specimen tree by landscaping firms. Oaklike form.

'Skylark Dwarf'. Typically a large, compact, multitrunked shrub to 16 ft. high and wide. Sets very small fruit crop in some years.

'Swan Hill'. Leaves are deep green. Bears no fruit. Little or no pollen—a boon to allergy sufferers.

'Wilsoni' ('Wilson's Fruitless', 'Fruitless'). Occasionally bears small fruit crop.

OLEANDER.
See **NERIUM oleander**

OLIVE. See **OLEA europaea**

OLNEYA tesota
DESERT IRONWOOD
Fabaceae (Leguminosae)
EVERGREEN TREE

🌿	ZONES 8, 9, 11–14, 18–23
☀️	FULL SUN
💧	LITTLE OR NO WATER TO MODERATE WATER

Thorny native of the Southwest's Sonoran Desert; found in warm-winter areas of California. Grows slowly to 15–30 ft. tall, with equal

Olneya tesota

spread; common name "ironwood" refers to its extremely hard, heavy heartwood. May be single- or multitrunked; prune to maintain desired form. Branches are erect in youth, later spreading. Gray-green leaves, each with two spines at base, are divided into many ¾-in. leaflets. In late spring, clusters of pinkish lavender, ½-in., sweet pea–shaped flowers put on a good show. These are followed by dark brown, fuzzy, 2-in.-long pods. Tree drops leaves heavily around bloom time, but new foliage emerges quickly.

In the wild, this plant grows near washes, where some deep water is usually available. In the garden, it is extremely drought tolerant but will grow faster with occasional summer water. Drops its leaves in hard frosts and cannot endure prolonged freezes.

OMPHALODES
Boraginaceae
PERENNIALS

🌿	ZONES VARY BY SPECIES
◐	PARTIAL SHADE
💧	REGULAR WATER

These resemble forget-me-nots (*Myosotis*) but typically have deeper blue, somewhat larger (½-in.) flowers and more restrained behavior—these plants don't have the irritating habit of reseeding themselves all over the place.

Omphalodes verna

Omphalodes thrive in woodland gardens or shaded rock gardens and look especially attractive on a wall or bank, where their flowers may be viewed at eye level.

O. cappadocica. Zones 2b–9, 14–21. Native to Turkey. Slowly spreading clump of bright green foliage to 1½ ft. wide. Sends up 1–1½-ft.-high sprays of bright blue, white-eyed flowers in spring. 'Lilac Mist' is shorter (to 10 in.), with grayish lavender flowers. 'Starry Eyes', also to 10 in. high, has pale lilac flowers with dark blue spots at the base of each

petal. There also is a form with pure white flowers.

O. verna. BLUE-EYED MARY. Zones 2–9, 14–21. Native to mountains of Europe. Forms a foliage mat 3 in. high, 3 ft. or more wide, with dark green, 4-in. leaves. In spring, leafy stalks to 8 in. tall bear clustered deep blue flowers with a white eye.

ONCIDIUM
Orchidaceae
EPIPHYTIC ORCHIDS

🌿	ZONES 17, 20–24; H1, H2; OR INDOORS
◐	PARTIAL SHADE; BRIGHT INDIRECT LIGHT
💧	REGULAR WATER

Orchids native from Florida and Mexico through central and South America. The several hundred species and countless hybrids range from tiny plants just 1 in. tall to giants with branching flower spikes to 6 ft. or more bearing dozens of blooms. Most produce long spikes of yellow or brown-and-yellow flowers; a few come in white or rose. Some (including the plants described here) have compressed pseudobulbs with one or two large leaves; others are almost without pseudobulbs; still others have cylindrical, pencil-like leaves. Plants typically produce a few large blossoms or many small ones, but some have numerous large flowers and a few bear their blooms singly. In many, flowers have a large, flaring lip reminiscent of a flamenco dancer's skirt; these are sometimes called dancing ladies. Blossoms of some are scented. As outdoor plants, oncidiums are usually grown on tree trunks or in pots on the patio; indoor plants can be brought outdoors during warm weather. Take same houseplant culture as cattleyas. Also see Orchids.

O. crispum. Pseudobulbs are 4 in. high and are topped by 8-in. leaves. In fall, produces a branch-

Oncidium crispum

ing, 3-ft.-tall spike carrying many 4-in. flowers in chestnut brown spotted with yellow. Each bloom has a brown lip with a large bright yellow spot.

O. ornithorhynchum. Pseudobulbs 2½ in. tall are topped by leaves to 1 ft. long. In summer, many branching, 8–12-in.-tall spikes carry a cloud of ½–1-in. pink or purplish pink flowers with yellow markings.

O. Sharry Baby 'Sweet Fragrance'. Powerfully fragrant hybrid selection with 4-in.-high pseudobulbs topped with 8-in. leaves. Bears 2–3-ft. spikes of reddish or purplish brown, inch-wide blossoms in summer and fall. Some liken the flowers' perfume to chocolate, others to vanilla.

ONION
Liliaceae
BIENNIAL GROWN AS ANNUAL

🌿	ALL ZONES
☀️	FULL SUN
💧	REGULAR WATER

Botanically, the onion is *Allium cepa*, a species not known in the wild. More so than for other vegetables, growing onions successfully requires proper variety selection, appropriate planting methods, and good timing. Consult a local nursery or your Cooperative Extension Office for advice on varieties that grow well in your area.

Onion varieties differ in size, shape, color, flavor, and storage life. More important, different types form bulbs in response to varying day lengths. If you choose a type inappropriate for your area, it may bolt, form small premature bulbs, or not bulb up at all.

Long-day varieties need 14 to 16 hours of daylight to form bulbs and are best adapted to northern latitudes, such as Alaska and the Pacific Northwest. They tend to be pungent, and they store well; examples include 'Early Yellow Globe', 'Ebenezer', 'Ruby', 'Southport White Globe', 'Sweet Spanish'. Generally, long-day onions are planted in early spring and form bulbs as the days get longer in summer.

Short-day varieties need 10 to 12 hours of daylight and are best adapted to southern latitudes, such as Southern California, the Southwest, and Hawaii. They are typically planted in fall to early winter, grow vegetatively through winter, then begin to bulb up in spring.

O

These onions tend to be sweet and are poor keepers; examples are 'Bermuda', 'California Red', 'Granex', 'Grano', and 'Super Sweet'.

Intermediate-day onions, requiring 12 to 14 hours of daylight, are best suited to interior valleys of central California. They store moderately well. Examples are 'Autumn Spice', 'Red Torpedo', 'Ringmaker'. They are usually planted in early spring.

(True bunching onions, also sold as scallions, are varieties that do not form bulbs and are harvested like scallions or green onions; they can be grown anywhere.)

Onions can be grown from seed, sets (small bulbs), or transplants. Sets and transplants are easiest for beginners, though starting from seed gives a larger crop for a smaller investment and offers a wider choice of varieties.

Onion

In mild-winter climates, onions grow well from seed planted in fall to early winter. Sets and transplants can be planted all winter long and through early spring, although sets are generally longday varieties that will not bulb up well in southern regions. They can, however, be grown for scallions or green onions—standard onions harvested before they form bulbs. In Hawaii, short-day varieties are usually started from seed from earliest part of cool season; intermediate types are planted later in cool season for warmseason harvest. Types called Maui onions are actually any sweet, bulbing onion grown in Hawaii. In cold-winter climates, planting can begin in early spring as soon as the soil is workable; or start seed indoors in late winter and transplant later.

Soil should be loose, rich, and well drained. If planting sets, push them just under the soil surface so the point of the bulb is visible. Space sets and transplants 4–5 in.

apart (closer if you want to harvest some as green onions). Sow seed ¼ in. deep, in rows 15–18 in. apart. Thin seedlings to separate them by 4–5 in.; they can be eaten or transplanted to extend planting. Trim back tops of transplants about halfway.

Onions are shallow rooted and need moisture fairly near the surface. Feed plants regularly, especially early in the season: the larger and stronger the plant, the bigger the bulb it forms. Carefully eliminate weeds. When most of the tops have begun to yellow and fall over, dig bulbs and let them cure and dry on top of the ground for several days. Cover bulbs with tops to prevent sunburn. When the tops and necks are completely dry, pull off the tops and brush dirt from bulbs; then store bulbs in dark, cool, airy place.

OPHIOPOGON
Liliaceae
PERENNIALS

🌡	ZONES 5–9, 14–24; H1, H2
☀☀◐●	SOME SHADE IN HOTTEST CLIMATES
◔◔	MODERATE TO REGULAR WATER

These grasslike Asian natives are slightly less cold-hardy than their close cousins *Liriope*. They are easy to grow, requiring little more than well-drained soil and protection from snails and slugs. Good as informal ground cover in small areas, along paths, or in rock gardens. Attractive when planted in large sweeps in areas where lawns don't succeed, such as under trees. They also do well in containers. Grow them for their lush, evergreen foliage; the summer flowers, borne on short spikes, are largely hidden by the leaves.

It's easy to obtain more plants by division. Use a sharp spade to divide clumps in early spring; or use a knife to divide clumps sold in flats or cell-packs at garden centers.

O. jaburan. GIANT LILY TURF. Sometimes sold as *Liriope gigantea*. Grows 2–3 ft. tall, 1–1½ ft. wide, with dark green, slightly curved, ½-in.-wide leaves. Forms clumps; does not spread by underground stems. Nodding clusters of small white flowers are followed by showy, ½-in.-long oval fruits in a metallic violet blue (attractive in arrangements). 'Vittatus' (sometimes sold as *Liriope muscari* 'Variegata') has leaves edged in creamy white. Grows best in partial or full shade.

O. japonicus. MONDO GRASS. Forms a dense clump to 6–8 in. high; spreads wider by underground stems, many of which are tuberlike. Slow to establish as ground cover. Light lilac flowers in short spikes, usually hidden by dark green leaves 8–12 in. long and just ⅛ in. wide. Blue fruits are round, about ¼ in. across. If plants look shabby, mow or shear before spring growth begins. Set divisions 6–8 in. apart. 'Kyoto Dwarf' and 'Nana' are half the size of species, spread more slowly. 'Kigimafukiduma' ('Silver Mist') is a whitevariegated form.

Ophiopogon planiscapus 'Nigrescens'

O. planiscapus 'Nigrescens' ('Arabicus', 'Ebony Knight'). BLACK MONDO GRASS. Tufts to 8 in. high, 1 ft. wide. Spreads slowly and does not make a solid cover. Leaves grow to 14 in. long, ⅛–¼ in. wide, emerging green but soon darkening to nearly black. Bell-shaped white or purpleflushed flowers are ¼ in. long. Dramatic in containers, especially when combined with yellow or chartreuse foliage, such as that of yellow creeping Jenny (*Lysimachia nummularia* 'Aurea').

OPUNTIA
Cactaceae
CACTI

🌡	ZONES VARY BY SPECIES
☀	FULL SUN
◔	LITTLE OR NO WATER, EXCEPT AS NOTED

The species described here originate in the desert Southwest and Mexico; other species are native to those areas and/or to other parts of the western U.S., the Great Plains, Canada, and Florida. Many kinds, with varied appearance. Most species fall into one of two sorts: those having flat, broad joints (pads) or those having cylindrical joints. Though the use of common names is somewhat inconsistent, members of the first group are often called prickly

pear; those in the second group are frequently known as cholla. Hardiness is variable. Flowers are generally large and showy. The fruit is a berry, often edible.

O. basilaris. BEAVERTAIL CACTUS. Zones 2, 3, 7–24. Lowbranching plant to 1 ft. high, 4 ft. wide. Oval to roundish gray-green to purplish pads are 2–12 in. wide and ½ in. thick, set with spines up to 2 in. long. Rich rose purple, 2–3-in. spring flowers.

O. bigelovii. TEDDYBEAR CACTUS. Zones 10–24. Slow growing to 3–6 ft. tall, 3 ft. wide, with treelike form. Woody trunk is covered with black spines, which are less conspicuous than their prominent yellow-gold sheaths. Cylindrical, easily detached joints are covered with vicious silvery yellow spines. Most plants never bloom, though may bear 1–1½-in. pale green, yellow, or white flowers (all with lavender markings) in early spring. Grows freely in the hottest, driest deserts.

O. ficus-indica. Zones 8, 9, 12–24; H1, H2. Big, shrubby or treelike cactus to 15 ft. tall, 10 ft. wide, with woody trunks and smooth, flat green pads. Few or no spines; has clusters of bristles. Bears 3–5-in.-wide, yellow to orange flowers in late spring and early summer. Blossoms are followed by roundish, 2–3½-in.-long fruits that ripen from yellow to

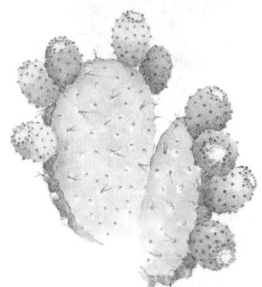

Opuntia ficus-indica

red; these are the prickly pears you may see sold in grocery stores. Handle fruit carefully—bristles break off easily and irritate the skin. Use rubber gloves when peeling fruit, or impale it on a fork and strip skin carefully, avoiding bristly areas. This plant is very drought tolerant, but in hottest regions it needs regular moisture for best fruit. 'Burbank Spineless' is a nearly spineless selection. 'Gray Form' has gray pads.

O. leptocaulis. DESERT CHRISTMAS CACTUS, CHRISTMAS CHOLLA, PENCIL CACTUS. Zones 3, 7–24. To 2–3 ft. (rarely to

O

6 ft.) tall and equally wide. Joints are 1–12 in. long, ¾ in. thick, and have 1–2-in.-long spines. Spring flowers, to ¾ in. across, are green to yellow. Fleshy fruits about the size and shape of olives mature from green to red, usually around Christmastime; hang on all winter. Very striking cold-hardy species.

O. macrocentra (O. violacea). Zones 2, 3, 7–24. To 4 ft. tall and 6 ft. wide, with round, 8-in., purplish green pads that turn rich purple in cool weather. Yellow-and-red flowers in spring are 3–3½ in. wide. 'Tubac' is said to hold its purple pad color more consistently throughout the year.

O. microdasys. BUNNY EARS. Zones 12–24; or indoors. Fast growth to 2–3 ft. high, 4–5 ft. wide (much smaller in pots). Flat, thin, nearly round pads to 6 in. across, in a soft, velvety green; neatly spaced tufts of short golden bristles give a polka-dot effect. 'Albispina' has white bristles. New pads atop larger old ones give plant the shape of an animal's head.

Opuntia microdasys

ORANGE. See **CITRUS**

ORANGE BELLS.
See **TECOMA × alata**

ORANGE CLOCK VINE.
See **THUNBERGIA gregorii**

ORANGE JESSAMINE.
See **MURRAYA paniculata**

ORANGEQUAT.
See **CITRUS: Kumquat hybrids**

ORCHIDS

The orchid family is probably the largest in the plant kingdom, with nearly 800 genera and over 17,000 species. Best known in the West are *Bletilla, Cattleya, Cymbidium, Dendrobium, Epidendrum, Laelia, Oncidium, Paphiopedilum, Phalaenopsis, Pleione,* and *Vanda.*

Orchid growers' terms. Here are definitions of the orchid growers' terms you will encounter in this book.

Epiphytic. In nature, epiphytic orchids cling to high branches of trees in tropical or subtropical jungles, deriving their nourishment from air, rain, and whatever decaying vegetable matter they can trap in their root systems.

Pseudobulb. Epiphytic orchids have thickened stems called pseudobulbs that store food and water and allow the plants to survive drought. These may be short and fat or erect and slender. They vary in color from green to brown. Leaves may grow along pseudobulbs or from their tips.

Terrestrial. Some orchids (including most native North American orchids) are terrestrial and must grow in loose, moist, humus-rich soil. They often occur in wooded areas but sometimes grow in open meadows as well. These orchids require constant moisture and food.

Sepals, petals, and other flower parts. Segments of an orchid flower include three sepals and three petals; stamens, style, and stigma are united into a single organ, the column. One of the petals, usually the lowest one, is called the lip. The lip is usually larger and more brightly colored than the other segments and may be marked with stripes, spots, or streaks. In some orchids, it is unusually shaped (having various appendages) or folded into a slipperlike "pouch."

Rafts, bark. Nearly all orchids, terrestrial or epiphytic, are grown in pots. A few are grown on "rafts" (slabs of bark or wood) or in baskets of wood slats; a few natives are grown in open ground.

Potting and growing orchids. For most epiphytic orchids, the potting materials used for cattleyas (the most commonly grown orchids) work well: osmunda fiber, hapu'u (tree fern stem), or ground bark. Other potting materials suitable for orchids may be available locally. It is sensible to use the ready-made mixes sold by orchid growers; these are blended for proper texture and acidity.

Watering and fertilizing needs vary somewhat depending on the particular orchid. In general, though, water plants when the potting mix dries out and becomes lightweight (usually about once a week), and apply a water-soluble

orchid fertilizer every 2 weeks during the growing season. To provide humidity for plants growing in the house, fill a metal or plastic tray with gravel to within an inch of the top (the space is necessary for air circulation), then add just enough water to reach almost to top of gravel. Stretch hardware cloth over the tray. Set pots on top of hardware cloth; check water level periodically, and add more water to tray as needed.

Temperature requirements. The various orchids of the world's tropical regions can be grown outdoors year-round in one or another part of Hawaii; some thrive outdoors in coastal Southern California. Elsewhere, you may be able to grow certain types outdoors all year or just during warm weather; others must be kept indoors.

The following list divides tropical orchids into three classes according to their temperature needs; lowland natives need the warmest conditions, higher-altitude natives the coolest ones. The terms "cool-growing," "intermediate," and "warm-growing" refer to the greenhouse temperatures that approximate ideal conditions for good growth and regular flowering in the plants' native environments. (Most of these orchids will get along fine in somewhat less than ideal situations, though.)

Cool-growing orchids do best with temperatures of 50 to 55°F/10 to 13°C at night, 60 to 75°F/16 to 24°C during the day. This group includes *Cymbidium* (some), *Dendrobium* (some), *Epidendrum* (some), *Laelia* (some), *Paphiopedilum* (green-leafed forms), *Pleione.* Some cool growers are thoroughly hardy to many cold-winter zones of the West, and others can withstand winters in mildest parts of California.

Intermediate orchids thrive at temperatures of 55 to 60°F/13 to 16°C at night, 65 to 80°F/18 to 27°C during the day. Members of this group include *Cattleya, Cymbidium* (some), *Dendrobium* (some), *Epidendrum* (some), *Laelia* (some), *Oncidium, Paphiopedilum* (the mottled-leafed forms). These can be grown in pots or on a windowsill with other houseplants but will peform best with additional humidity. An excellent method of supplying humidity is described in "Potting and growing orchids" (above). Most can be moved outdoors in

summer; place them in the shade of high-branching trees, on the patio, or in a lathhouse.

Warm-growing orchids do best with temperatures of 60 to 65°F/16 to 18°C at night, 70 to 85°F/21 to 29°C during the day. Warm growers described in this book include *Phalaenopsis* and *Vanda.* These orchids can grow outdoors in warmest parts of Hawaii but need greenhouse conditions (uniform warm temperatures and high humidity) in colder climates.

ORCHID CACTUS.
See **EPIPHYLLUM**

ORCHID TREE.
See **BAUHINIA**

ORCHID VINE.
See **MASCAGNIA**

OREGANILLO.
See **ALOYSIA wrightii**

OREGANO. See **ORIGANUM**

OREGON BOXWOOD.
See **PAXISTIMA myrtifolia**

OREGON GRAPE.
See **MAHONIA aquifolium**

OREGON MYRTLE.
See **UMBELLULARIA californica**

ORGANPIPE CACTUS.
See **STENOCEREUS thurberi**

ORIENTAL ARBORVITAE.
See **PLATYCLADUS orientalis**

ORIENTAL POPPY.
See **PAPAVER orientale**

ORIGANUM
OREGANO, MARJORAM
Lamiaceae (Labiatae)
PERENNIALS

	ZONES VARY BY SPECIES
	FULL SUN, EXCEPT AS NOTED
	LITTLE TO MODERATE WATER

Mint relatives with tight clusters of small flowers. Each blossom has a collar of bracts—large, colorful, and quite decorative in some species—that can overlap to give the inflorescence the look of a small pinecone. Blossoms are especially attractive to bees, butterflies. Many species have aromatic foliage, and the leaves of several have culinary use. Some are good as ground covers, as trailers to cascade over rocks or retaining walls, or in hanging baskets. Those with conspicuous bracts are attractive dried and used in wreaths and arrangements; cut and hang just as first flowers open.

Origanum majorana

Not fussy about soil type but need good drainage. In milder climates, many species can become woody with age, but wood of previous seasons is seldom as productive as new growth from the base. For best results, cut previous year's stems to ground in winter or early spring. Propagate by division or from cuttings taken before flower buds form. The various species hybridize freely, and seedlings may not resemble the parents. Colored-leaf varieties need a half day of direct sun for best color but can burn in afternoon sun in hot-summer areas.

O. amanum. Zones 2b–24. Native to Turkey and the eastern Mediterranean. Low, evergreen mound to 8 in. high, 1 ft. wide, with bright green, hairy, heart-shaped leaves ¾ in. long. Blooms in summer and fall, when arching stems are weighed down by clusters of light green bracts and slender, tubular, five-lobed pink blossoms about 1½ in. long that radiate in all directions. Bracts age to soft purple, making plants decorative even after the flowers fade. Dislikes wet conditions.

O. 'Betty Rollins'. Zones 6–9, 12–24. Hybrid forms a dense, neat mat 3–6 in. tall, 1–1½ ft. wide. Small, oval, dark green leaves are topped in summer by clusters of light pink flowers.

O. calcaratum (O. tournefortii). Zones 8, 9, 12–24. Native to Crete and the Aegean islands. Bushy, many-stemmed plant to 1 ft. tall, 2 ft. wide, with pairs of gray-green, densely furry, ¼–1¼-in.-long leaves evenly spaced along radiating stems. Bright pink flowers emerge from pendent, 2-in.-long clusters of gray-green bracts tinged rose; several clusters to each stem. Blooms from spring through fall.

O. dictamnus (Amaracus dictamnus). DITTANY OF CRETE, HOP MARJORAM. Zones 8, 9, 12–24. Native to Crete. Aromatic herb to 8 in. high, 1½–2 ft. wide, with slender, arching stems to 1 ft. long. Thick, roundish, woolly white leaves to ¾ in. long. Pink to purplish flowers emerge from rose-tinted light green bracts; blooms summer to fall. Shows up best when planted individually in rock garden or in hanging basket.

O. × hybridum. Zones 4–9, 12–24. Resembles parent *O. dictamnus,* but its leaves are gray green and downy rather than woolly.

O. laevigatum. Zones 2–24. Native to Turkey, Cyprus. Sprawling plant with grayish green leaves about 1¼ in. long; reaches 2 ft. tall in bloom. It spreads by rhizomes and arching stems that root at the joints to form a dense clump 2–3 ft. wide. Branching, airy clusters of ½-in., tubular pink or purple flowers and small purplish bracts appear from late spring to fall. Useful as bank or ground cover. 'Herrenhausen' has larger bracts and more compact heads of lilac-pink flowers. 'Hopley's', probably a hybrid with *O. vulgare,* blooms from mid- to late summer, bearing denser heads of purplish pink flowers and purplish bracts; it self-sows freely, producing seedlings with variable foliage and flower color. Both 'Herrenhausen' and 'Hopley's' have purple leaves in cool weather.

O. libanoticum. Zones 2b–24. Native to Lebanon. Attractive trailing plant to 2 ft. high and wide, with small, roundish, smooth green leaves. From midsummer to fall, produces cascades of pale green to pinkish bracts (similar to those of hop, *Humulus*) and small rose pink flowers; heads elongate as the season progresses, ending up several inches long. For best effect, plant at top of wall or in hanging basket.

O. majorana (Majorana hortensis). SWEET MARJORAM, KNOTTED MARJORAM. Zones 8–24; summer annual anywhere. Native to the Mediterranean and Turkey. To 1–2 ft. tall and wide. Oval gray-green leaves to ¾ in. long. Inconspicuous white flowers emerge from clusters of knotlike heads at top of plant. Keep blossoms cut off and plant trimmed to encourage fresh growth. Fresh or dried leaves are used for seasoning meats, scrambled eggs, salads, vinegars, casseroles, tomato dishes. Often grown in pots indoors on sunny windowsill in cold-winter areas. Leaves of 'White Anniversary' have a distinct cream margin.

O. × majoricum. ITALIAN MARJORAM, SICILIAN MARJORAM. Zones 4–24. Similar to *O. majorana* but with wider, greener leaves. Some gourmet cooks consider this the best marjoram for seasoning.

O. 'Marshall's Memory'. Zones 6–9, 12–24. Hybrid to 1–1½ ft. tall, 2 ft. wide. Forms a dense mat of small, rounded leaves that are bright green when new, aging to a darker shade. Profuse bright lavender-pink flowers with rosy bracts in summer. Best with moderate water.

O. microphyllum. Zones 7–9, 11–24. Native to Crete. Grows into a dome 10 in. high, 1 ft. wide. Reddish branches bear tiny gray-green leaves to ¼ in. long. Clusters of small flowers that are pale pink to purple appear in summer. Thrives in dry rock crevices.

O. 'Norton Gold'. Zones 2b–24. Hybrid of *O. laevigatum* and *O. vulgare* 'Aureum'. To 1 ft. tall, 1½–2 ft. or more wide, with open habit like that of *O. laevigatum.* Rounded leaves are brilliant gold with a bluish sheen. Foliage is aromatic, with a good flavor; for mealtime color, use sprays of leaves as garnish. Pink flowers bloom in midsummer. Protect from hottest sun.

O. onites. POT MARJORAM, RHIGANI. Zones 8–24. Eastern Mediterranean native. To 2 ft. tall and wide, with bright green, aromatic, inch-long leaves and 2-in.-wide, flattish heads of white or purplish flowers in late summer. Sometimes called Cretan oregano.

O. rotundifolium. Zones 2b–24. Native to Turkey, Armenia, Georgia. Dense, suckering plant grows 8 in. high, 1 ft. wide, bearing numerous wiry stems set with pairs of virtually stemless, blue-green, 1-in. leaves that have a rounded heart shape. Blooms throughout summer, bearing spikes of small pale pink blossoms and green, 2–3-in.-

Origanum rotundifolium 'Kent Beauty'

long bracts like those of hop (*Humulus*) at stem ends (bracts almost obscure the flowers). 'Kent Beauty' is a hybrid with *O. scabrum;* has a more compact habit (4 in. high, 8 in. wide) and bears conspicuous mauve-toned pink blossoms and deep rose bracts in the summer. 'Rose Beauty' has even darker reddish bracts. 'Barbara Tingey' is a hybrid with *O. calcaratum* and similar to 'Kent Beauty'; its rose pink flowers peep out from under light green bracts that age to deep purplish pink.

O. sipyleum. SHOWY PINK OREGANO. Zones 4–9, 12–24. Native to Turkey. To 1–2 ft. tall. Small, blue-green, oval to lance-shaped leaves. In summer, thin stems hold sprays of pale green bracts and pinkish violet flowers well above the foliage. Good cut flowers for dried arrangements.

O. syriacum (O. maru). BIBLICAL HYSSOP, SYRIAN MARJORAM. Zones 7–24. Native to Syria, Turkey, and Cyprus. With its strong, sweet, pungent flavor, this plant is a favorite herb for flavoring Mideastern dishes. Grows to 1½ ft. tall and wide. Soft gray-green leaves to 1½ in. long. Blooms in late spring and early summer, with pale pink, ¼-in. flowers in branching, 2–3-in. clusters.

O. vulgare. OREGANO, WILD MARJORAM. Zones 1–24, except as noted. Native to most of Europe and temperate Asia. Upright growth to 2½ ft. tall, 2–3 ft. wide. Oval dark green leaves to 1½ in. long and ¾ in. wide; white or purplish pink blossoms from midsummer to early fall. Fresh or dried leaves are used in many dishes, especially Spanish and Italian ones.

Most wild forms have scentless leaves; be sure to choose a selected form with a good aroma and a flavor that you like. For best flavor, keep this plant trimmed to prevent flowering—but let some clumps bloom for bees and butterflies to enjoy.

'Aureum' has white flowers, pink bracts, and bright golden foliage in spring (with morning sun), turning to green by late summer and fall; 'Thumble's Variety' is similar. 'Aureum Crispum' has curly golden leaves. 'Compactum' ('Humile') is a wide-spreading plant just a few inches tall, suitable for a ground cover or between paving stones; it seldom flowers, but leaves turn purple in winter. 'Country Cream' (with white flowers) and lilac-pink-flowered

O

'Polyphant' ('White Anniversary') are compact growers to 4–6 in. and have leaves with a distinct creamy white edge; they are often confused in commerce (and both are sometimes sold as 'Variegatum'). 'Roseum' has bright rose pink flowers, green leaves.

O. v. hirtum (*O. heracleoticum*). GREEK OREGANO. Zones 8, 9, 12–24. Native to Greece, Turkey, the Aegean islands. Like the species, but with broader, slightly fuzzy gray-green leaves. Spicy, pungent flavor.

ORNAMENTAL PEAR.
See **PYRUS**

ORNITHOGALUM
Liliaceae
PERENNIALS FROM BULBS

✔	ZONES VARY BY SPECIES
☼ ☽	FULL SUN OR PARTIAL SHADE
◊ ◒ ●	WATER NEEDS VARY BY SPECIES
♦	ALL PARTS, ESPECIALLY BULBS, ARE POISONOUS IF INGESTED

Clusters of typically star-shaped flowers appear in the spring; *O. dubium* may start blooming in late winter. Leaves vary from narrow to broad and tend to droop. In mild-winter areas, ornithogalums can fill many different roles. Set them in open woodlands, wild gardens, or rock gardens, where many kinds will naturalize; plant them in containers or mass them in borders. Where cold winters prevent growing ornithogalums outdoors, plant the bulbs in pots and force them to early flowering indoors or in a greenhouse.

Plant bulbs in early fall in well-drained soil amended with plenty of organic matter, setting them 3 in. deep and 3–4 in. apart. Provide regular moisture during growth and bloom (*O. longibracteatum*, however, is drought tolerant and needs only moderate water). *O. arabicum* and *O. dubium* both need a dry dormant period: after flowering has finished and leaves have died down, withhold water until new foliage begins to emerge. In areas with summer rainfall, grow them in pots to keep them dry. *O. nutans* and *O. umbellatum* can take moisture during dormancy. *O. longibracteatum* will remain evergreen with some water. Dig and divide plantings of all species only when plant vigor and bloom quality decline.

O. arabicum. STAR OF BETHLEHEM. Zones 5–24. From the eastern Mediterranean. Stems to

2 ft. tall carry clusters of 2-in., waxy-looking white flowers, each centered with a shiny, beadlike black eye. Bluish green, strap-shaped, inch-wide leaves may reach same length as stems, but they're usually floppy. Best where summers are warm and dry.

Ornithogalum dubium

O. dubium. Zones 8, 9, 14–24. From South Africa. Stems 8–12 in. high bear blooms resembling those of *O. arabicum*, but petals surrounding the beady black eye come in shades of yellow orange. Dark green to yellowish green, lance-shaped leaves are about 4 in. long, nearly prostrate.

O. longibracteatum (**O. caudatum**). PREGNANT ONION, FALSE SEA ONION. Zones 21–24; or indoors. From South Africa. Grown for bulb and foliage rather than its tall wands of small green-and-white flowers. To 3 ft. tall in leaf; flowers increase height to 5 ft. Long, strap-shaped light green

Ornithogalum longibracteatum

leaves droop downward. Gray-green, smooth-skinned bulb is 3–4 in. wide and grows on top of, not in, the soil. Bulblets form under skin and grow quite large before they drop out and root. Hardy to 25°F/–4°C; will lose leaves if not given moderate water.

O. nutans. Zones 3–24. From the eastern Mediterranean. To 1½–2 ft. tall. Starlike to nearly bell-shaped flowers are white striped

with green on the outside; they have pronounced central clusters of stamens. Up to 15 blooms are spaced along upper part of each stalk. Narrow, floppy bright green leaves. Spreads rapidly and may become weedy. Sometimes called silver bells.

O. umbellatum. STAR OF BETHLEHEM. Zones 1–24; H1. From the eastern Mediterranean. Stems to 1 ft. tall bear clusters of inch-wide white flowers striped green on the outside. Semierect, grassy-looking leaves about as long as flower stems. Cut flowers last well but close at night. Once established, may naturalize and become weedy.

ORTHROSANTHUS
MORNING FLAG, MORNING IRIS
Iridaceae
EVERGREEN PERENNIALS FROM RHIZOMES

✔	ZONES 14–17, 19–24
☼ ☽	PARTIAL SHADE IN HOTTEST CLIMATES
◒	MODERATE WATER

These *Sisyrinchium* relatives have dark green, grasslike leaves arising from short, woody rhizomes. Showy blooms of blue, lavender, or white open in succession on slim, erect stems in summer. Individual flowers look their best in the morning, then fade as the day progresses. Wonderful plants for sunny slopes, rock gardens, and containers. Tolerate poor, sandy soils but bloom better in fertile, well-drained soil.

O. chimboracensis. Forms clumps 1–1½ ft. tall and wide, with rough-edged leaves up to 16 in. long. Pale to medium blue, 1½–1¾-in. flowers are held on stems to 2 ft. tall.

O. multiflorus. Clumps reach 1–2 ft. tall, 1 ft. wide. Smooth-edged leaves grow to 1½ ft. long. Pale to bright blue flowers are about 1½ in. across. Grassier

Orthrosanthus multiflorus

appearance than *O. chimboracensis;* also tolerates more drought. Effective foliage plant for commercial plantings or home gardens; pretty flowers are a bonus.

ORYZOPSIS hymenoides. See **ACHNATHERUM hymenoides**

OSAGE ORANGE.
See **MACLURA pomifera**

OSCULARIA.
See **LAMPRANTHUS**

OSMANTHUS
Oleaceae
EVERGREEN SHRUBS

✔	ZONES VARY BY SPECIES
☼ ☽	FULL SUN OR PARTIAL SHADE
◊ ◒ ●	LITTLE TO REGULAR WATER

All have clean, leathery, attractive foliage and, typically, white flowers that are inconspicuous but fragrant. Fruits (on female plants) are rarely seen. Plants tolerate broad range of soils, including heavy clay. Most are dense shrubs that can eventually reach tree size. To grow them as background shrubs, pinch tips of new growth on young plants to encourage bushiness; on older, established plants, occasionally cut back any wayward branches. These shrubs also make good informal or lightly clipped tall hedges.

O. × burkwoodii (**× Osmarea burkwoodii**). Zones 4–9, 14–17. Slow growing to 6–10 ft. tall, 8–12 ft. wide. Densely clothed in glossy bright green, tooth-edged leaves 1–2-in. long. Spring bloom. Useful as hedge.

O. decorus (**Phillyrea decora**). Zones 4–9, 14–21. From Georgia, northeastern Turkey. Handsome, densely foliaged shrub to 6–10 ft. tall and somewhat wider. Shiny, leathery leaves are dark green above and yellow green below; these are narrowly oval, pointed, 3–5 in. long and ½–1¾ in. wide. In spring, fragrant, small white flowers appear in clusters at the leaf bases, followed by ½-in.-long oval fruits that mature from reddish to nearly black.

O. delavayi. DELAVAY OSMANTHUS. Zones 4–9, 14–21. From China. Slow-growing, graceful plant with arching branches; reaches 4–6 ft. tall, 6–8 ft. wide. Dark green, oval, tooth-edged leaves to 1 in. long. Blooms profusely in spring, bearing clusters of four to eight blossoms (largest flowers of any osmanthus).

Attractive all year. Good choice for foundation plantings, massing. Handsome on retaining walls where branches can hang down. Needs partial shade in hot-summer areas.

O. × fortunei. Zones 4–10, 14–24. Hybrid between *O. heterophyllus* and *O. fragrans.* Slow, dense growth to an eventual 15–20 ft. tall, 6–8 ft. wide; usually seen at about 6 ft. tall. Oval, 4-in.-long leaves resemble those of holly (*Ilex*). Spring and summer bloom. 'San Jose' blooms in fall, bears flowers ranging in color from cream to orange.

O. fragrans. SWEET OLIVE. Zones 5–7 (with shelter), 8, 9, 12–24; H1. Native to China, Japan, Himalayas. Broad, dense, compact. Grows at a moderate rate to 10 ft. tall, 6–8 ft. wide (though older plants may reach 30 ft. tall, 10–12 ft. wide). Oval, glossy medium green leaves to 4 in. long, toothed

Osmanthus fragrans

or smooth edged. Flowers are powerfully fragrant, with a sweet scent like that of ripe apricots. Bloom is heaviest in spring and early summer, but plants flower sporadically throughout year. Sometimes trained as an espalier. Give afternoon shade in hottest climates. *O. f. aurantiacus* has narrower, less glossy leaves than the species; its crop of wonderfully fragrant, soft apricot orange flowers is concentrated in early autumn. *O. f. thunbergii* has golden blooms, red new growth; an extract from its flowers is used in some of the world's most expensive perfumes.

O. heterophyllus (O. ilicifolius). HOLLY-LEAF OSMANTHUS. Zones 4–10, 14–24. From Japan. Grows to 10–20 ft. tall and slightly wider, with 2½-in., spiny-edged, glossy green leaves. Resembles English holly (*Ilex aquifolium*), but leaves are opposite one another on stems rather than alternate. Late fall and winter bloom. Useful as hedge.

'Goshiki'. Erect growth to 3½ ft. tall, 5 ft. wide. New leaves have pinkish orange markings; in mature foliage, the variegations are creamy yellow (on a deep green background).

'Gulftide'. Dense grower to 8 ft. tall, 10 ft. wide. May actually be a selection of *O. × fortunei.*

'Purpureus' ('Purpurascens'). Same growth habit as species. Leaves are dark purple when new, maturing to purple-toned deep green.

'Rotundifolius'. Slow growing to 5 ft. tall and wide. Small, roundish leaves are lightly spined.

'Variegatus'. Slow growing to about 8–10 ft. tall and wide, with densely set leaves edged in creamy white. Useful for lighting up shady areas. Foliage is somewhat more prone to freeze damage than that of other species.

OSMARONIA cerasiformis.
See **OEMLERIA cerasiformis**

OSMUNDA
Osmundaceae
FERNS

🌱	ZONES VARY BY SPECIES
☼ ◑	FULL SUN OR LIGHT SHADE
💧	AMPLE WATER

Large deciduous ferns for damp (even wet) soils in regions with cold (or at least chilly) winters. Rather coarse looking but handsome nonetheless. They produce large masses of matted roots; root masses of *O. regalis* provide the osmunda fiber used in potting mixes for orchids. Fronds are twice divided; they turn orange, brown, and yellow as they approach dormancy. Use at woodland edges or in cool, moist or wet areas. Both species described here are native to much of the Northern Hemisphere. *O. cinnamomea* has separate sterile and fertile fronds; in *O. regalis,* each frond has a fertile segment near the tip.

O. cinnamomea. CINNAMON FERN, FIDDLEHEADS. Zones 1–6. To 2–5 ft. tall and 2 ft. wide. This fern has two types of fronds.

Sterile fronds are erect, up to 5 ft. tall, and divided in typical fern fashion. Fertile ones are shorter and consist of stalks topped by short, tightly clustered, brown spore-bearing bodies.

O. regalis. ROYAL FERN, FLOWERING FERN. Zones 1–9, 14–17. To 6 ft. tall, 3 ft. wide; each frond segment is quite large. Fertile segments are smaller, clustered near frond tips; they look something like flower buds. 'Cristata' has crested fronds; 'Purpurascens' has purplish red new growth and stems that remain purple throughout the season; and 'Undulata' has wavy or ruffled segment margins. The species and its varieties love moisture and can even grow in shallow water.

Osmunda regalis

OSO BERRY.
See **OEMLERIA cerasiformis**

OSTEOSPERMUM
AFRICAN DAISY
Asteraceae (Compositae)
PERENNIALS

🌱	ZONES 8, 9, 12–24, EXCEPT AS NOTED; ANYWHERE AS ANNUALS
☼	FULL SUN
💧	MODERATE TO REGULAR WATER

Woody-based perennials native to South Africa; closely related to *Dimorphotheca* and often sold as such. Mounded or trailing in habit, bearing a profusion of daisylike flowers over a long season; blossoms are more profuse during cooler parts of bloom period. Grow them as summer annuals in areas beyond hardiness range, as winter annuals in hot desert regions. Narrowish oval leaves are 2–4 in. long, smooth-edged or with a few large teeth. Flowers of most kinds open only in sunlight, but many

have a second color on the backs of rays that shows on half-open flowers during overcast weather.

Tolerate drought and neglect but look better with good garden soil and irrigation. Tip-pinch young plants to induce bushiness. Deadheading produces more blooms. Cut back old, sprawling branches to young side growth in late summer to midautumn. Mass along driveways or paths or use in borders, rock gardens, containers. Types that spread by rooting stems are good on slopes.

O. barberae. See O. jucundum

O. ecklonis (Dimorphotheca ecklonis). To 2–5 ft. tall, 2–4 ft. wide. Long stems bear 3-in. flowers with dark blue centers and rays that are white above, lavender blue on backs. Blooms in spring.

'Lavender Mist'. Zones 2b–24. To 1 ft. tall, 15 in. wide; 3-in. flowers open white, age to soft pale purple. Blooms from midspring until fall.

Passion Mix. Compact growth to 1–1½ ft. high and about as wide, with 2–2½-in. flowers in a variety of colors (pink, rose, purple, white), all with sky blue centers. Blooms throughout the year, more heavily in spring and fall. Blossoms stay open in low light better than those of many nonhybrid varieties.

O. fruticosum (Dimorphotheca fruticosa). TRAILING AFRICAN DAISY, FREEWAY DAISY. Zones 8, 9, 12–24; H1, H2. To 6–12 in. tall, spreading rapidly by trailing, rooting stems; will cover a 2–4-ft.-wide circle in a year. Deep lilac buds open to 2-in.-wide flowers with a dark purple center; rays are lilac above (fading nearly to white by second day), deeper lilac beneath. Blooms intermittently all year, more heavily in

Osteospermum fruticosum

fall and winter. Needs well-drained soil. Does well near the ocean. Use as ground cover or bank cover; if it gets too tall or weedy, mow or cut back in midsummer. Also good planted at top of a wall or in a hanging basket.

The following hybrids reach 18–20 in. high. 'African Queen' and 'Burgundy' have purple blooms. 'Whirlygig' ('Pinwheel') bears unusual white-and-blue flowers with rays that are white on upper surface, blue on back; each ray is pinched in the middle to reveal its blue underside, giving it the look of a spoon with a blue handle and a white bowl. Blossoms of Side Series stay open on overcast days and at night; selections include 'Brightside' (white with a blue eye), 'Highside' (bicolor blooms in white and dark pink), 'Riverside' (butter yellow), 'Seaside' (bicolor in white and light pink), and 'Wildside' (dark purple).

O. jucundum (O. barberae, Dimorphotheca barberae). Grows to 4–20 in. high; spreads by rooting stems to 2–3 ft. across. Bears long-stalked, 2-in.-wide flowers with purple centers; rays vary in color from mauve pink to magenta, with bronzy purple to purplish pink undersides. Blooms more heavily in spring and fall, generally less profusely in summer.

O. j. compactum 'Purple Mountain'. Zones 2b–24. Choice plant for colder climates. To 10 in. high, 1 ft. wide, with a profusion of bright purple, 2–3-in. flowers from spring to midsummer. If deadheaded, continues to bloom (albeit sparingly) until fall.

O. Symphony series. Mounding habit to 8–12 in. high, 3 ft. wide (1 ft. as annual). Among the most heat tolerant of osteospermums, flowering throughout moderately hot summers as well as during cool weather. Flowers are 2–2½ in. wide, with dark blue centers. Choices include 'Cream Symphony' (pale yellow rays), 'Lemon Symphony' (medium yellow), 'Orange Symphony' (light orange). Particularly attractive in window boxes and hanging baskets.

OSTRICH FERN.
See **MATTEUCCIA struthiopteris**

OSWEGO TEA. See MONARDA

OTATEA. See BAMBOO

OUR LORD'S CANDLE.
See **YUCCA whipplei**

OXALIS
Oxalidaceae
PERENNIALS

🖊	ZONES VARY BY SPECIES
☀ ☼	PARTIAL SHADE IN HOTTEST CLIMATES, EXCEPT AS NOTED
💧	REGULAR WATER

Leaves typically divided into three leaflets, giving them the look of clover leaves. Flowers may be pink, white, rose, or yellow. Most can be slightly to highly invasive in the open ground; see individual entries for specific cautions.

O. acetosella. WOOD SORREL, SHAMROCK. Zones 1–10, 14–24. From many northern temperate regions of the world. To 5 in. high, spreading widely by rhizomes. Typical clover-type leaves with three heart-shaped leaflets. Blooms in late spring, bearing ¾-in.-wide white flowers with purple to pink veins; blossoms rise just above the foliage. Can be somewhat invasive in its favored woodland conditions (moist, rich soil and partial shade). See also Shamrock.

Oxalis oregana

O. adenophylla. Zones 4–9, 12–24. Native to South America. Dense, compact, leafy tuft 4 in. high, 6 in. wide. Each leaf has 9–22 crinkly gray-green leaflets. In late spring, 4–6-in.-high stalks bear 1-in., bell-shaped flowers in lilac pink with deeper veins. Good rock garden plant or companion to bulbs such as species tulips or smaller kinds of narcissus, either in pots or in the ground. Needs good drainage. Plant tubers in fall, setting 1 in. deep, 3–5 in. apart.

O. hirta. Zones 8, 9, 14–24. Native to South Africa. To 1 ft. high, 1½ ft. wide, with many upright, branching stems that gradually fall over with weight of leaves and flowers. Small pale green leaves are set directly on the stems or on very short stalks. General effect is feathery. Bright rose pink, 1-in. flowers in late fall or winter. Plant is dormant in summer. Grow from bulbs planted in fall; set them 1 in. deep, 3–5 in. apart. Good for rock gardens, hanging baskets.

O. lasiandra. Zones 8, 9, 12–24; H1, H2. Native to Mexico. Taprooted plant forms a clump to 1 ft. high and wide, with reddish leafstalks and medium green, wheel-shaped

leaves, each with as many as ten narrow leaflets. Dark red, 1-in.-wide flowers through summer and fall.

O. oregana. REDWOOD SORREL, OREGON OXALIS. Zones 4–9, 14–24. Native to coastal forests from Washington to California. Grows to 10 in. high, spreading indefinitely by creeping rhizomes. Medium green, velvety leaves 1½–4 in. wide. Blooms in spring, sometimes again in fall, bearing white (sometimes pink), 1-in.-wide flowers with lavender veining. Makes an attractive ground cover for partial to deep shade in areas with mild winters and cool summers. Plant may outcompete other ground covers. Dies down in winter in colder part of climate range; elsewhere, mow to renovate. Tolerates wet conditions.

O. pes-caprae (O. cernua). BERMUDA BUTTERCUP. Zones 8, 9, 12–24. Native to South Africa. Reaches 1 ft. high, spreading indefinitely by bulbs. Produces clusters of bright green leaves, often spotted with dark brown, that spring directly from soil in fall. Flowering stems rise above the foliage in winter and spring, topped with clusters of 1-in., bright yellow flowers. Will become an invasive pest in an open garden; best grown in pots or baskets.

O. purpurea (O. variabilis). Zones 8, 9, 12–24. Native to South Africa. Grows to 4 in. tall and 6 in. wide; dark green leaves have large (up to 1½-in.-wide) leaflets. Bears 1–2-in., rose red flowers over a long period in fall and winter. Spreads by bulbs and rhizomelike roots but is not aggressive or weedy. Plant bulbs in fall, setting them 1 in. deep, 3–5 in. apart. Improved kinds, sold under the name "Grand Duchess," have larger flowers in rose pink, white, or lavender.

O. tetraphylla (O. deppei). LUCKY CLOVER. Zones 7–9, 12–24. Native to Mexico. Forms a clump 6–10 in. high and wide, spreading slowly by tubers. Medium green leaves to 3 in. across have four leaflets, each one banded purple or maroon toward the base. Each leaf is held like a little umbrella atop a fleshy stem. Bright pink, 1-in. flowers rise above the leaves from late spring through summer. Needs well-drained soil. Good in containers or as a companion plant for larger bulbs and perennials. 'Iron Cross'

Oxalis tetraphylla 'Iron Cross'

has more defined, darker leaf markings that form a cross shape. Its flowers are a deep, rich pink.

O. versicolor. CANDY CANE SORREL. Zones 6–9, 14–24. Native to South Africa. To 3–6 in. high and 8 in. wide. Medium green leaves have deeply notched leaflets less than ½ in. wide. Funnel-shaped flowers are white, over 1 in. wide, with a crimson margin on the petal backs; buds also show striping. Plant bulbs in fall for spring flowers (set them 1 in. deep, 3–5 in. apart); bloom lasts for months.

OX-EYE SUNFLOWER.
See **HELIOPSIS helianthoides**

OXYDENDRUM arboreum
SOURWOOD, SORREL TREE
Ericaceae
DECIDUOUS TREE

🖊	ZONES 2B–9, 14–17
☀	FULL SUN
💧	REGULAR WATER

Native to eastern U.S. Beautiful flowering tree offering year-round interest. Slow to 15–30 ft. (eventually to 50 ft.) high, 20 ft. wide. Pyramidal shape with slender trunk, somewhat rounded crown, and slightly pendulous branches;

Oxydendrum arboreum

reates a handsome winter silhou-
tte. Narrow, 5–8-in.-long leaves
ook a bit like peach leaves; they are
ronze tinted in early spring, rich
reen in summer. In fall, leaves
urn orange, scarlet, or blackish
urple; all colors may be present
n the same tree. Vividly colored
utumn leaves remain on the tree
or a long time, dropping over an
xtended period much like the
eaves of liquidambar. Tree blooms
n the summer, bearing fragrant,
ell-shaped creamy white flowers
n 10-in.-long, drooping clusters at
ranch tips. In autumn, branching
lusters of seed capsules extend
utward and downward from
ranches like fingers; capsules
ipen from greenish to light silvery
ray and hang on late into winter.

Best known in areas with cool
ummers, well-defined winters.
Needs acid, well-drained soil. Not
ompetitive; doesn't do well in
awns without careful attention
you must remove grass from
eneath canopy, mulch well, and
rrigate deeply). Avoid underplant-
ng with anything that may need
ultivation.

Use as specimen in a woodland
arden or as patio shade tree.
Young plants make good container
ubjects.

OZOTHAMNUS
rosmarinifolius
Asteraceae (Compositae)
EVERGREEN SHRUB

- ZONES 14–24
- FULL SUN
- REGULAR WATER

Native to Australia. Dense, erect
habit to 6–10 ft. tall, 3–5 ft. wide.
Close-set, upright branches are
hickly clothed with straight, nar-
ow, 1½-in.-long, dark green leaves
hat resemble those of rosemary. In
early summer, closely packed red
uds appear at branch tips; these
pen into 1½-in. clusters of tiny
white daisies. The entire plant has
a pleasant aroma, especially in
warm weather.

Ozothamnus rosmarinifolius

P

PACHISTIMA, PACHYSTIMA.
See **PAXISTIMA**

PACHYPODIUM
lamerei
MADAGASCAR PALM
Apocynaceae
SUCCULENT SHRUB

- ZONES 13, 21–24; OR INDOORS
- FULL SUN OR PARTIAL SHADE; BRIGHT LIGHT
- REGULAR WATER

From Madagascar. Not a palm,
though it looks something like one.
Easy-to-grow shrub with impressive silhouette: spiny, succulent,
branched or unbranched trunk
topped with a circle of strap-
shaped leaves to 1 ft. long and 1–
4 in. wide. May reach 18 ft. tall
and 5 ft. wide in frostless climates.
Large, old plants may bloom in
summer, bearing lightly fragrant,
trumpet-shaped white flowers to
2 in. across; smaller, younger
plants seldom bloom. Some people
think of older, blooming plants as
spiny plumerias.

Pachypodium lamerei

Madagascar palm can survive
outdoors year-round in areas that
get light frosts, but it will drop its
leaves and go dormant there and
may never grow higher than 8 ft.
If you grow it outdoors in these
regions, give it very little moisture
during dormancy. Beyond hardiness range, grow it in a pot indoors
and summer it outside, or keep it
indoors all year as a houseplant.
Plants can stay in the same pots
for years; they grow better when
their roots are crowded.

PACHYSANDRA
Buxaceae
PERENNIALS

- ZONES VARY BY SPECIES
- PARTIAL OR FULL SHADE
- MODERATE TO REGULAR WATER

Spreading slowly but surely by
underground runners, these are
invaluable ground covers for shady
places. Compact growth and
clean-looking, attractive foliage
are their chief virtues. Spring
flowers are not showy when viewed
casually but are attractive at close
range. Plants have somewhat
woody growth, *P. terminalis* more
so than *P. procumbens*. Compete
successfully with tree roots. Give
them moist, somewhat acid soil,
well amended with organic material; for good coverage, plant both
species 1 ft. apart. Too much sun
yellows the foliage and causes
poor growth. Hardy to cold.

P. procumbens. ALLEGHENY
SPURGE. Zones 2–6, 15–17. From
southeastern U.S. To 6–12 in. high.
Grayish green, broadly oval to
roundish leaves are 2–4 in. long,
clustered near stem tips; they are
often mottled with gray or brown.
Small, fragrant white or pinkish
flowers in 2–4-in. spikes. Spreads
more slowly than species *P. terminalis*. Deciduous in northern part
of range, semievergreen to evergreen farther south.

P. terminalis. JAPANESE
SPURGE. Zones 2–10, 14–21; performs better in northern part of
range. From Japan and northern
China. To 8–12 in. high. Evergreen
leaves are shiny dark green, about
same length as those of *P. procumbens* but somewhat narrower;
upper half of each leaf is shallowly
toothed. Small white flowers are
borne in 1–2-in. spikes. Withstands heavy shade and is widely
used under trees. 'Green Carpet' is
shorter (to 4 in.) and denser than
the species, with deeper green
leaves. Leaves of 'Green Sheen' are
especially glossy; those of 'Silver

Pachysandra terminalis

Edge' ('Variegata') have a creamy
border. 'Cut Leaf' has deeply dissected foliage.

PACIFIC WAX MYRTLE.
See **MYRICA californica**

PADDLE PLANT.
See **KALANCHOE luciae**

PAEONIA
PEONY
Paeoniaceae
PERENNIALS AND DECIDUOUS
SHRUBS

- ZONES VARY BY TYPE
- AFTERNOON SHADE IN HOTTEST CLIMATES
- REGULAR WATER

Though a few species peonies may
be found through specialists' catalogs and seed exchanges, most garden peonies are hybrids. The basic
types are herbaceous and tree
peonies, both descended from
Chinese species. A new third category, the intersectional hybrids,
combines the best traits of herbaceous and tree types. All peonies

Herbaceous peony,
single

are extremely long-lived plants of
significant size; they provide
choice cut flowers and are a mainstay of big perennial borders. They
demand more than ordinary care
in site preparation—but in return
for the effort, they can produce
flowers of outstanding beauty for
a lifetime.

Herbaceous peonies, largely
descendants of the perennial *P. lactiflora*, die to the ground in late fall.
Intersectional hybrids leave woody
stems standing when they die back
after first frost, but since these
stems rarely resprout, they're best
cut to the ground. Both types are
usually grown on their own roots
(compact rhizomes with thick,
tuberous roots and several growth
buds called eyes).

Tree (actually shrub) peonies
produce flowers on permanent
woody branches and are chiefly
descendants of *P. suffruticosa*, a

P

6-ft. shrub. Tree peonies usually start out as grafts on herbaceous peony roots, but in the long run they do best on their own roots. When shopping for tree peonies, look for plants that have already started to form their own substantial root systems.

All peonies are best set out in fall, either as bare-root plants or from nursery containers. Ideally, the planting site for peonies should be deeply dug at least several days before planting. Work in plenty of compost, especially in heavy soil, and incorporate a high-phosphorus fertilizer; then allow the soil to settle before planting. Plant herbaceous peony roots with eyes 2 in. deep in cold climates, 1 in. deep in warmer regions (planting too deeply prevents flowering). Intersectional hybrids should be planted 3 in. deep in cold climates, 2 in. deep in warmer areas. Set tree peonies with the graft line 6–8 in. below soil surface (the aim is to get the shrubby top graft to root on its own). In cold-winter areas, plant at least 6 weeks before the ground usually freezes; mulch only after the ground has frozen. Plants are unlikely to bloom the first spring after planting, but they should bloom every year after that.

Peonies of all types can be grown in large (18–24-in.) containers. Herbaceous and intersectional hybrid peonies do best in pots that are wider than they are deep, while tree peonies prefer containers that are as deep as they are wide. Replant every third autumn in the same or a slightly larger pot, replacing most of the soil when you do.

Feed with low-nitrogen fertilizer (such as 5-10-10) as first leaves unfurl in spring, then again after the last flower fades. When leaves drop in autumn, apply 1 cup of a 50-50 mix of bonemeal and triple superphosphate to the soil around each plant.

To gather peonies for bouquets, cut them just as flower buds begin to open. Leave at least three leaves on every cut stem, and do not remove more than half the blooms from any clump. The object is to preserve leaf growth so that it nourishes the plant for the following year.

During cool, humid periods, the fungal disease botrytis is sometimes a problem, especially on herbaceous peonies. Young buds on infected plants blacken and wither, fuzzy brown spots develop on flowers and leaves, and stems wilt and collapse. To help prevent the problem, provide good air circulation around the plants, and keep the planting area free of fallen leaves. In autumn, cut herbaceous and intersectional peonies to the ground; as new growth emerges in spring, spray with copper fungicide.

Herbaceous peonies. Perennials. Zones A1–A3; 1–11, 14–20. Well-grown clumps reach 2–4 ft. tall and wide. Large, glossy, deep green, attractively divided leaves are an effective background for the plants' spectacular spring or early-summer flowers and look good throughout summer. Flower colors range from pure white through cream to pink and red; some of the reds are very deep, with chocolate brown overtones. Depending on variety, blossoms range from 2 in. to as much as 10 in. across; many have a perfume similar to that of old-fashioned roses, though in some varieties the scent is either unimpressive or absent. In form, they fall into three basic categories: single or semidouble, with one or two rows of petals; Japanese, with a single row of petals and a large central mass of narrow petal-like segments called staminodes; and double, with full flowers composed of many petals.

Herbaceous peonies bloom well only where they experience an extended period of pronounced winter chill. Summer heat is not a problem for the plants, but their flowers do not last as well where spring days are hot and dry. In such areas, choose singles, semidoubles, and Japanese varieties, as they bloom before the season heats up; also give plants some afternoon shade and be sure they have adequate water. (Japanese types in particular do well in the warmest zones.) In the mildest-summer parts of Zones 1–7, where these plants grow best, they thrive in full sun. Provide support for very large or double varieties, which can become so heavy with water during spring rains that they fall over.

Varieties are too numerous to list. Four fragrant doubles—all

Tree peony, double

introduced more than a century ago and still popular—deserve mention because they are most likely to be found in local garden centers and nurseries. These are 'Edulis Superba', bright pink with an outer ring of somewhat lighter petals; 'Felix Crousse', deep red; 'Festiva Maxima', white with a few crimson flecks near the center; and 'Sarah Bernhardt', deep rose pink edged with paler pink.

Divide herbaceous peonies only to increase your stock. Dig clumps in early fall, hose off soil, and divide into sections, making sure that each has at least three eyes; these appear at the tops of root clusters, at or near the bases of the past season's stems. Plant immediately to allow plants time to put down roots before the onset of freezing weather. Transplants may take a year or two to establish before blooming.

Intersectional hybrids. Woody perennials. Zones A1–A3; 1–11, 14–20. Moderate growth rate to about 3 ft. tall and wide. Attractive leaves resemble those of tree peonies. Compared with herbaceous and tree peonies, intersectional hybrids produce more flowers and bloom over a longer period, sport better-looking foliage throughout the growing season, and have superior resistance to botrytis. Flowers may be single or semidouble, in shades of lavender, pink, red, copper, yellow, or cream.

Good examples include 'Cora Louise', a vigorous grower with semidouble blooms of understated beauty: flowers open yellow pink, then fade to cream with lavender-purple markings at the petal bases. 'First Arrival' has semidouble blooms of lavender pink. 'Garden Treasure' has yellow semidouble flowers with pinkish red petal bases and pink-tipped staminodes. 'Pastel Splendor' is a gorgeous single that opens in a warm rose color, then fades through shades of pink, yellow, and ivory, with raspberry-colored petal bases.

Intersectional hybrids require less winter chill than herbaceous peonies. Because this category is still relatively new, prices are high, but they are dropping steadily.

Tree peonies. Deciduous shrubs. Zones 2–12, 14–23. Slow growth to 2–6 ft. tall and eventually as wide, with handsomely divided blue-green to bronzy green leaves. Single to double flowers, typically very large (to 10–12 in. across), appear in spring. These peonies seldom show their full potential until they have spent several years in the garden, but the spectacular results are worth the wait.

Catalogs offer named varieties of Japanese origin in white and shades of pink, red, and purple. These are generally semidouble and display their flowers well. Some of the older European hybrids in pink and yellow are fully double, with flowers so heavy they hang their heads. More recent and more expensive hybrids come in yellow, copper, and a coral that approaches orange; all result from crosses of *P. suffruticosa* with *P. delavayi* and *P. d. lutea*. These bear semidouble blooms that face outward and upward.

Tree peonies require much less winter chill than herbaceous peonies. The large flowers are fragile and should be sheltered from strong winds. Snip off blooms when they fade. After leaf drop in fall, prune to remove dead wood and to control the height of mature plants; do this by removing about half the current season's growth on the tallest branches that have bloomed, always making your cuts just above an outward-facing side branch. In coldest climates, protect from winter sun and wind with a burlap curtain.

PAGODA FLOWER. See **CLERODENDRUM buchananii fallax**

PAINTED DAISY. See **CHRYSANTHEMUM coccineum**

PAINTED FINGERNAIL PLANT. See **NEOREGELIA spectabilis**

PAINTED SPURGE. See **EUPHORBIA heterophylla**

PAINTED TONGUE. See **SALPIGLOSSIS sinuata**

PALLENIS maritima. See **ASTERISCUS maritimus**

PALMETTO. See **SABAL**

PALMS

Most palms are tropical or subtropical; a few are surprisingly hardy (specimens are seen in Edinburgh, London, and southern

Russia, as well as Portland, Seattle, and Denver). These trees offer great opportunity for imaginative planting. In nature, they grow not only in solid stands but also with other plants, notably broad-leafed evergreen trees and shrubs. They are effective near swimming pools.

Most young palms prefer shade, and all tolerate it; this fact makes them good house or patio plants when they are small. As they grow, they can be moved into full sun or partial shade, depending on the species. Growth rates vary, but keeping plants in pots usually slows growth of faster-growing kinds. If temperatures are 60°F/16°C or higher, fertilize potted palms often; also wash them off frequently to provide some humidity and clean the foliage. Washing also dislodges insects, which (indoors, at any rate) are protected from their natural enemies and can increase extremely rapidly.

Some shade-tolerant palms such as *Rhapis, Chamaedorea,* and *Howea* may spend decades in pots indoors. Others that later may reach great size—*Phoenix, Washingtonia, Chamaerops*—make charming temporary indoor plants but must eventually be moved outdoors.

Planting holes for palms should generally be the same depth as the root ball and 1–2 ft. wider; you can use unamended native soil for backfill. If you are planting in very poor, alkaline, or clay soil, however, some experts suggest a different procedure. For a 5-gal.-size palm, dig a 3-ft.-wide hole that is 8 in. deeper than root ball. Place 1–2 cu. ft. of well-rotted manure, nitrogen-fortified sawdust, or other organic amendment in the hole, then mix in a handful or two of blood meal and top with a 6-in. layer of soil. Set in the palm and fill in around it with a mixture of half native soil and half nitrogen-fortified sawdust, ground bark, or peat moss. Water newly planted palms faithfully until established.

Most palms, even big ones, transplant easily in late spring or early summer. Since new roots form from the base of the trunk, the root ball need not be big; a new root system will form and produce lush new growth. When transplanting large palms, contractors usually tie leaves together over the center "bud" or heart to protect it.

Established palms need little maintenance; they thrive in rea-

David Leaser on Potted Palms

A single potted palm with big, luxuriant leaves and a strong silhouette can add a tropical look to any landscape. "There's no easier way to turn a porch into a lanai," says palm enthusiast David Leaser.

Almost any palm will make a good container plant, but the following are Leaser's top choices for both loveliness and the slow growth that will allow them to live for years in a pot: paradise palm (*Howea forsteriana*), *Chamaedorea elegans*, lady palm (*Rhapis excelsa*), Mediterranean fan palm (*Chamaerops humilis*), and pygmy date palm (*Phoenix roebelenii*).

Choose a pot that is taller than it is wide and slightly larger than the nursery container, and be sure it has one or more holes for drainage. "A 5-gallon plant should fit comfortably in a pot that is 14 inches wide and 16 inches deep," says Leaser. "Terra-cotta is a good choice because it absorbs some moisture from the soil and reduces the risk of overwatering."

Leaser suggests using a potting mix that is porous enough to provide good drainage but heavy enough so the palm doesn't tip over. Cactus mix is a good choice—or a mix of equal parts sand, coarse peat moss, and perlite. Water carefully, and never allow your palm to stand in water. Tap on the terra-cotta container to see if water is needed. "If the pot 'rings,' the soil is dry and needs water," says Leaser; "if you hear a dull thud, the soil is sufficiently damp."

Apply a controlled-release fertilizer during the summer months; Leaser recommends an 18-6-18 formula with magnesium. Once you see roots growing out of the drainage hole, repot the palm into a slightly larger container.

sonably fertile soil, with the appropriate amount of moisture (see individual entries for recommendations). All tropical palms do their growing during warm times of year. Winter rains wash the foliage down (and, in areas with salty soil, leach out accumu-

lated salts). Palms growing in dry or dusty areas or beyond the reach of rain or dew should be hosed off periodically; this helps control populations of spider mites and sucking insects that find refuge in the long leaf stems. Beach plantings should also be washed off occasionally to keep salt from accumulating on the leaves.

Feather palms and many fan palms look neater when old leaves are removed after they have turned brown. Make neat cuts close to the trunk, leaving the leaf bases. Some palms shed the old leaf bases on their own. Others, including *Syagrus* and *Chamaedorea*, may hold old bases. You can remove them by slicing them off at the very bottom of base (be careful not to cut into trunk).

Many palm admirers say that dead leaves of *Washingtonia* should remain on the tree, the thatch being part of the palm's character. If you agree but prefer a neater look, you can cut lower fronds uniformly close to trunk, but leave leaf bases, which present a rather attractive lattice surface.

Most species are frost sensitive. Frost becomes more damaging to palms as it extends its stay and is repeated. A light frost that lasts for half an hour may not harm plants at all, but if the same degree of frost persists for 4 hours, it may injure some palms, kill others. Hardiness is also a matter of plant size; larger palms may survive severe frosts without harm, while smaller ones perish. At its least serious, frost damage consists simply of burned leaf edges —but frost may affect whole leaves, parts of trunks, or crown. Damage to the crown is usually fatal (though some trees have recovered from it).

Following are nine roles that the right kinds of palms can fill. Palms in each listing are described under their own entries elsewhere in this book.

Sturdy palms for street trees and vertical effects in large gardens. *Archontophoenix, Brahea, Cocos, Jubaea, Livistona, Phoenix canariensis, P. dactylifera, P. loureiri, P. rupicola, Pritchardia* (some), *Rhopalostylis, Roystonea, Sabal* (tall species), *Syagrus, Washingtonia.*

Small to medium-size palms for frost-free gardens. *Archontophoenix, Caryota, Chamaedorea, Dypsis lutescens, Hedyscepe, Howea, Ptychosperma.*

Small to medium-size palms that tolerate a light, brief frost. *Brahea, Butia, Chamaedorea cataractarum, C. elegans, Dypsis decaryi, Livistona, Phoenix roebelenii, Trachycarpus.*

Hardiest palms. *Brahea armata, B. edulis, Butia capitata, Chamaerops, Jubaea, Phoenix canariensis, P. dactylifera, P. loureiri, Rhapidophyllum, Rhapis, Sabal, Syagrus romanzoffianum, Trachycarpus, Washingtonia.*

Salt-tolerant palms for seaside plantings. *Brahea edulis, Butia, Chamaerops, Cocos, Phoenix canariensis, P. dactylifera, P. reclinata, Sabal blackburniana, S. palmetto, Washingtonia robusta.*

Palms for hot, dry climates. *Brahea armata, Butia, Chamaerops, Livistona chinensis, L. mariae, Phoenix canariensis, P. dactylifera, P. loureiri, P. sylvestris, Sabal mexicana, S. minor, Washingtonia.*

Palms to grow under lath, beneath overhangs, or indoors. *Archontophoenix, Caryota mitis, C. ochlandra, C. urens, Chamaedorea, Hedyscepe, Howea, Livistona* (young), *Phoenix reclinata* (young), *P. roebelenii, Rhapidophyllum, Rhapis, Rhopalostylis, Trachycarpus* (when young). Indoor palms should occasionally be brought outdoors into soft light.

Palms as underplantings. Young palms, especially slow growers such as *Livistona chinensis* and *Chamaerops,* stay low for 5 to 10 years and can be used effectively as plantings under tall trees. Keep in mind that they may have to be moved if they get too tall, a project you may not want to undertake. Two shrubby palms that remain small are *Rhapidophyllum* (6–8 ft. high) and *Sabal minor* (rarely exceeds 6 ft.).

Palms for night lighting. Thanks to their stateliness and spectacular leaves, all palms are good subjects for this. Light them from behind or below; or direct floodlights to silhouette them against light-colored walls.

PALO BLANCO.
See **ACACIA willardiana**

PALO BREA.
See **CERCIDIUM praecox**

PALO VERDE.
See **CERCIDIUM**

PAMPAS GRASS.
See **CORTADERIA selloana**

PANDANUS tectorius

SCREWPINE, HALA
Pandanaceae
EVERGREEN TREE

🌡	ZONE H2
☀	FULL SUN
💧	REGULAR WATER

Native to many Pacific islands, including Hawaii. Palmlike, round-headed tree grows to 20–30 ft. high and 20–40 ft. wide. Striking appearance; sends down aerial roots and bears spirals of stiff, spiny, 3-ft.-long leaves at the ends of stubby branches. Female plants develop large fruits resembling pineapples. Has good wind and salt tolerance; thrives in any well-drained soil, even beach sand. Excellent shade or windbreak tree for the beach garden. Produces litter; needs maintenance to remove old leaves. Young plants can be grown in pots on the patio or indoors.

Pandanus tectorius

PANDA PLANT.
See **KALANCHOE tomentosa**

PANDOREA

Bignoniaceae
EVERGREEN VINES

🌡	ZONES 16–24; H1, H2
☀ ◑	PARTIAL SHADE IN HOTTEST CLIMATES
💧💧	WATER NEEDS VARY BY SPECIES

Twining vines noted for clusters of trumpet-shaped flowers and for rich green, glossy, divided leaves; the foliage is so attractive that the plants look lovely even when out of bloom. Perform best in good, organically enriched soil. Blooms are borne on previous year's growth; prune to shape or thin vines after flowering.

P. jasminoides (Bignonia jasminoides, Tecoma jasminoides). BOWER VINE. Native to Australia. Fast growth to 20–30 ft. Each leaf has five to seven oval, 1–2-in.-long leaflets with pointed tips. Typically unscented flowers are white with pink throats, 1½–2 in. long; bloom from late spring to early fall. 'Alba' and the stronger-growing 'Lady Di' have pure white flowers; 'Rosea' produces soft pink blooms with nearly red throats. 'Rosea Superba' and a variety known simply as 'Deep Pink Form' are fragrant. There is a form with variegated leaves. Plant in lee of prevailing wind. Prolonged freezes will kill this species and its varieties. Regular water.

Pandorea jasminoides

P. pandorana (Bignonia australis, Tecoma australis). WONGA-WONGA VINE. Native to Australia, Pacific islands. More vigorous than *P. jasminoides,* covering twice the space; give it plenty of room. Leaves divided into 8–17 leaflets that are narrower than those of *P. jasminoides* and 1–3 in. long. Small (to ¾-in.-long), unscented spring flowers are typically creamy white, often spotted brownish purple in the throat. 'Golden Showers' has golden yellow blossoms. Tougher, more wind resistant, and less susceptible to freeze damage than *P. jasminoides.* Moderate water.

PANICUM virgatum

SWITCH GRASS
Poaceae (Gramineae)
PERENNIAL GRASS

🌡	ZONES 1–11, 14–23
☀ ◑	FULL SUN OR LIGHT SHADE
💧💧💧	ANY AMOUNT OF WATER

Native to much of the U.S. except the Far West. Upright, 2–4-ft.-wide clump of narrow deep green or gray-green leaves. Bloom begins in midsummer, when slender flower clusters rise above the foliage, increasing height of clump to 4–7 ft.; clusters open into loose, airy clouds of pinkish blossoms that fade to white, then brown. Foliage turns yellow in fall, gradually fades to beige. Both foliage and flowers persist all winter, providing interest in cold-weather gardens. Tolerates coastal winds. The following varieties reach 5 ft. tall in bloom unless otherwise noted.

Panicum virgatum

'Cloud Nine' has metallic blue foliage that turns gold in autumn; billowing clouds of reddish brown flowers bring height to 6 ft. tall.

'Dallas Blues' has powder blue leaves and reddish purple flowers.

'Haense Herms' has an open, fountainlike shape, with delicate, light green leaves that turn bright red in fall, then deepen to burgundy; reaches 4 ft. tall in bloom.

'Heavy Metal' has silvery blue, sturdy leaves that turn bright yellow in fall.

'Northwind' has a strongly vertical form, with olive green foliage that turns yellow in autumn.

'Rotstrahlbusch' is an upright grower, to about 4 ft. tall in flower, with green, red-tinged leaves that turn rich, deep red in fall and burgundy flowers.

'Shenandoah' has a cascading form, with red-tipped blue-green leaves that turn maroon in early fall and airy red flower clusters.

PANSY. See VIOLA

PAPAVER

POPPY
Papaveraceae
PERENNIALS AND ANNUALS

🌡	ZONES VARY BY SPECIES
☀	FULL SUN
💧💧	MODERATE TO REGULAR WATER

Poppies provide gay spring and summer color for borders, containers, and bouquets. Give ordinary, well-drained soil (note exception for *P. alpinum*); feed lightly until established. Perennial species tend to be short lived. When using poppies as cut flowers, sear cut stem ends in a flame before placing them in water.

P. alpinum (P. burseri). ALPINE POPPY. Perennial. Zones 1–9, 14–17. In keeping with its origin in the Pyrenees, Alps, and Carpathians, this species is best adapted to colder climates and requires the exceptionally fast-draining soil of a rock garden. Produces 4-in.-wide basal rosette of divided, 2–6-in.-long leaves; foliage is blue green, nearly hairless. In spring or summer, leafless flower stems to 5–8 in. tall bear 1½–2-in. blossoms in white, orange, yellow, or salmon. Blooms first year from seed sown in fall or early spring. Where adapted, self-sows freely.

P. atlanticum. Perennial. Zones 2b–9, 14–24. Native to Morocco. To 2 ft. tall, with downy gray-green leaves in basal rosette 6 in. across. Flowers are soft orange to red, 2–4 in. across, opening in late spring and early summer. Sow seed in fall. To prolong bloom period, remove spent flowers.

P. commutatum 'Lady Bird'. Annual. Zones 1–24. Selection of a species native to Greece, Turkey, the Caucasus, Iran. To 1½ ft. tall and nearly as wide. Blooms profusely for several weeks in midsummer, producing 3-in., bright red flowers with a black blotch in the middle of each petal. Flower stems are softly hairy. Sow in late winter or early spring; or set out plants in midspring.

P. nudicaule. ICELAND POPPY. Short-lived perennial in Zones A2, A3, 1–6, 10; grown as annual in Zones 7–9, 12–24. Native to subarctic regions. Coarsely hairy, blue-green, divided leaves make basal rosettes 6 in. wide. Hairy, 1–2-ft. stalks bear cup-shaped, slightly fragrant flowers to 3 in. across, in yellow, orange, salmon, rose, pink, cream, white. In cold-winter areas, sow seed in earliest spring for summer bloom; or set out plants in fall for bloom the following year. In mild-winter climates, set out plants in fall for winter and early spring bloom. To prolong flowering, pick flowers freely.

P. orientale. ORIENTAL POPPY. Perennial. Zones A1–A3; 1–11, 14–21. Native to the Caucasus, northeastern Turkey, northern Iran. Needs winter chill for best performance. In mild-winter areas,

Papaver orientale

lowers tend to form without stalks, so they are partly or completely hidden among the leaves. Height is variable; some types are ust 16 in. tall, others reach 4 ft. Plants spread by offsets to 2 ft. or nore. These are among the leafiest poppies, forming bushy clumps of hairy, medium green, coarsely cut leaves to 1 ft. long. Blooms are 4–5 in. across; deeply crinkled petals often have a black blotch at the base. Many named varieties are sold, offering single or double flowers in orange ('Pizzicato', semi-dwarf 'Allegro'), scarlet, red, pink ('Queen Alexandra'), salmon, or white ('Royal Wedding'). Seed-grown mixes such as 'Fruit Punch' are also worth growing.

Plants bloom from late spring to early summer, then die back (sometimes not completely) later in summer. In all types, new leafy growth appears in fall, lasts over winter, and develops rapidly in spring. Set sprawling plants such as baby's breath (*Gypsophila*) nearby to cover the bare areas left after poppies die down. Plant dormant crowns in fall with tops 3 in. deep; or set out container-grown plants. Provide good drainage and room for air circulation. Divide every 3 to 5 years in mid- to late summer, after foliage has died back.

P. rhoeas. FLANDERS FIELD POPPY, SHIRLEY POPPY. Annual. Zones A1–A3; 1–24. Best in cool-summer areas. Native to Eurasia, North Africa. Slender, branching, hairy-stemmed plant to 3 ft. tall,

Papaver rhoeas

1 ft. wide, with short, irregularly divided leaves. Single or double flowers are 2 in. or more wide, in white, pink, red, orange, salmon, scarlet, lilac, soft blue, bicolors. Mix seed with an equal amount of fine sand, then broadcast it where plants are to grow. For bloom from spring through summer, make successive sowings starting in early spring. In low and intermediate desert, plant in fall for outstanding early spring show. For cut flowers, pick when buds first show color. Remove seed capsules (old flower bases) weekly to prolong the bloom season. Notorious self-sower.

Selections bearing single scarlet flowers with a black base are sold as 'American Legion' or 'Flanders Field'. Angels' Choir strain offers double flowers in a wide range of colors, including some with creamy picotee edges. Mother of Pearl strain has single flowers, primarily soft pastels and white, with an occasional red; also includes some bicolors and picotees, as well as speckled blooms.

P. somniferum. OPIUM POPPY, BREADSEED POPPY. Annual; may self-sow or overwinter in mild-winter areas. All zones. Believed to have originated in southeastern Europe and western Asia. To 4 ft. tall. Hairless gray-green leaves have jagged edges. Late spring flowers are 4–5 in. across, in white, pink, red, purple, deep plum, and are sometimes single, usually double; some of the double forms have fringed petals. Blooms are followed by large seed capsules used in dried arrangements. Ripe pods include large quantities of the poppy seed used in baking. Shake pods over a tray to collect the seeds.

Opium is derived from the sap of the green capsules; derivatives include morphine, codeine, and heroin. American federal law permits the sale, possession, and use of opium poppy seed, but it is illegal—a felony, in fact—to grow opium poppy plants. This law is commonly ignored by growers and gardeners alike who appreciate the beauty of the flowers. In a half-hearted effort to circumvent the letter of the law, growers and nurseries usually sell opium poppy seedlings under names such as annual poppy, breadseed poppy, peony-flowered poppy, Turkish poppy, Asian poppy, *Papaver laciniatum, P. paeoniflorum,* or *P. setigerum.* Under any name, you can always identify opium poppy

by its blue-green, hairless leaves. When you rub the tops of them with the backs of your fingers, they burnish nicely.

PAPAYA
Caricaceae
PERENNIALS

☀ ZONES VARY BY SPECIES

☼ FULL SUN, EXCEPT AS NOTED

● REGULAR WATER

They may look like trees or large shrubs, but these members of the genus *Carica* are actually big perennials with hollow stems. All are tall, upright, narrow plants, 3–6 ft. wide at the top. Cream-colored flowers are inconspicuous. Fruit takes 6 to 10 months to ripen, depending on climate; in Hawaii, it is borne throughout the year. Plants produce crops when young. To get most fruit, don't grow papaya as a permanent plant; keep a few plants coming along each year, and destroy old ones. Give regular moisture and fertilizer in warm weather. Grow from seeds saved from fruit or start with purchased plants. Babaco (see following text) is seedless and must be started from transplants. Transplant carefully, disturbing the root ball as little as possible. All types need excellent drainage. Papayas grow quite well in large containers.

C. papaya—the papaya found in markets—is the species grown most frequently. This native of tropical America can be cultivated outdoors in Zones 21–24 and H2, and anywhere in a greenhouse. Needs year-round warmth. Thrives in Hawaii. In California, the key to success is choosing the right location; root rot in cold, wet soil is the principal cause of failure, so locate on south slope or south side of house where winter sun can heat soil. Plant will also benefit from reflected heat in winter.

C. papaya grows 20–25 ft. tall in Hawaii, perhaps half that in California, with a straight stem topped by a crown of broad, fan-like, deeply lobed leaves on 2-ft.-long stalks. Grow three to five "trees" in a group; you ordinarily need both male and female plants for fruit production. Some types are self-fruitful, producing either bisexual flowers or both male and female flowers on the same plant. Varieties with yellow-orange flesh grown primarily in Hawaii include 'Kapoho', 'Solo', and dwarf 'Waimanalo'. Types with pinkish

flesh grown in Hawaii and California include 'Sunrise', 'Sunset', and 'Thai Dwarf'. Varieties grown in Hawaii have pear-shaped fruit as large as 1–2 lbs. Mexican varieties bear much bigger fruit (up to 10 lbs., to more than 1 ft. long) with yellow, orange, or pink flesh and a less intense flavor. Harvest papayas of both types when skin begins to turn yellow; let ripen fully at room temperature. Papaya seeds are edible, with a somewhat peppery flavor.

Papaya

Two other papayas, both from highland areas of South America, are less widely grown. Mountain papaya (*C. pubescens*), native to the Andes, can be grown in Zones 21–24, H1, H2. It reaches 10–12 ft. tall; foliage is borne in dense clusters at tops of its multiple trunks. Elaborately lobed, foot-wide leaves are fan shaped, deeply veined, and sandpapery in texture; they are dark green above, lighter beneath. Small fruit is edible when cooked (it's unpalatable raw). Male and female plants are needed for fruit set.

Babaco is the common name of Ecuadorean native *C. × heilbornii pentagona,* a self-fruitful, naturally occurring hybrid between *C. pubescens* and another Andean species. It can be grown in Zones 17, 19–24, H1. Plant resembles a dwarf (5–8-ft.-tall) *C. papaya.* Foot-long, seedless fruit has juicy flesh similar to that of 'Crenshaw' melon in color and texture; the unique sweet-tart flavor combines papaya, pineapple, and strawberry. Needs partial shade in hottest climates. Can be grown as a houseplant in a sunny window.

PAPERBARK. See **MELALEUCA**

PAPER BUSH.
See **EDGEWORTHIA chrysantha**

PAPER MULBERRY.
See **BROUSSONETIA papyrifera**

P

PAPHIOPEDILUM
LADY'S SLIPPER
Orchidaceae
TERRESTRIAL ORCHIDS

🌿 ZONES VARY BY TYPE; OR INDOORS

◐ PARTIAL SHADE; BRIGHT INDIRECT LIGHT

💧 REGULAR WATER

Sometimes sold as *Cypripedium,* these terrestrial orchids are native to tropical and subtropical regions of Asia. Usually grown in greenhouse or as houseplants; can be brought outdoors in warm weather. Some green-leafed forms can stay outdoors all year in mildest parts of the West Coast (Zones 17, 20–24); more tender, mottled-leafed forms can be grown outdoors year-round in Zone H2.

Leaves are graceful and arching. Plants have no pseudobulbs. Green-leafed types usually flower in winter, mottled-leafed kinds in summer. Most plants obtained from orchid dealers are hybrids rather than species. Blooms are perky, usually one to a stem, occasionally two or more. Many of them shine as if lacquered. Flowers may be white, yellow, green with white stripes, or pure green; or they may show a combination of background colors and markings in tan, mahogany, brown, maroon, green, and white.

Paphiopedilum insigne

A noteworthy species is *P. insigne.* Among the cold-hardiest of the green-leafed types, it can withstand brief exposure to 28°F/–2°C. It blooms at any time from early fall through winter, bearing polished-looking flowers on stiff, hairy brown stems. Sepals and petals show a combination of green and white, with brown spots and stripes; pouch is reddish brown.

For indoor culture, green-leafed forms generally require tempera-tures of 50 to 55°F/10 to 13°C at night, 60 to 75°F/16 to 24°C during the day. Mottled-leafed forms do best with temperatures of about 55 to 60°F/13 to 16°C at night, 65 to 80°F/18 to 27°C during the day. Heat requirements are best met in a greenhouse. The least fussy types can be grown in pots in the house. Lady's slippers have no rest period. Use same potting mix as for cymbidiums. Don't plant in oversize pot; plants thrive when crowded. Flourish with less light than most orchids require.

PAPYRUS.
See **CYPERUS papyrus, C. prolifer**

PARADISE PALM.
See **HOWEA forsteriana**

PARAGUAY NIGHTSHADE.
See **SOLANUM rantonnetii**

PARAHEBE
Scrophulariaceae
SHRUBBY PERENNIALS

🌿 ZONES 5, 6, 15–17, 20–24

☀ ◐ FULL SUN OR LIGHT SHADE

💧 REGULAR WATER

These woody-based, evergreen perennials were formerly classified as *Hebe,* before that as *Veronica.* Sprawling or drooping in habit, they form loose mounds. Leaves are arranged in opposite pairs along stems. Bloom profusely in summer, bearing small (½-in.), saucer-shaped flowers. Attractive in rock gardens, at the front of perennial borders, trailing over walls. Cut back any frost-damaged stems to near base of plant.

P. catarractae. From New Zealand. To 1 ft. high, twice as wide as tall. Narrow dark green leaves to 1¼ in. long. Flowers are white with blue or pink veining and a red eye, carried in narrow clusters to 4 in. long. Stems root where they touch moist soil. If plants begin looking leggy, you can cut them back

Parahebe catarractae

somewhat, but not as severely as *P. perfoliata.*

P. perfoliata (Derwentia perfoliata). From Australia. To 1½–4 ft. tall, 6 ft. wide. The pairs of 2-in.-long, gray-green leaves clasp the stem completely, so that stem seems to be piercing the foliage. Clusters of deep blue flowers appear at branch ends and in upper leaf joints. To restore an old plant to beauty, cut it back nearly to the ground. Thrives beneath blue gum trees (*Eucalyptus globulus*).

PARASERIANTHES lophantha.
See **ALBIZIA distachya**

× PARDANCANDA norrisii
CANDY LILY
Iridaceae
PERENNIAL FROM RHIZOME

🌿 ZONES 2–24

☀ ◐ FULL SUN OR LIGHT SHADE

💧 REGULAR WATER

Group of garden hybrids resulting from a cross between *Belamcanda* (blackberry lily) and *Pardanthopsis,* an iris relative. To 3 ft. tall, 2 ft. wide. Foliage fans are like those of iris. From midsummer to fall, plants produce six-segmented,

× Pardancanda norrisii

3–4-in.-wide flowers in a great range of colors, including yellow, blue, red, purple, pink, white, orange, and bicolors. Each bloom lasts only a day, but new flowers keep the show going. Good cut flowers. Plants are short lived, often blooming themselves to death; they self-sow in areas with warm summers. Grow from seed; in areas where the growing season is long, early sowing results in flowers the first year. Provide good drainage. Drought tolerant.

PARIS
Trilliaceae (Liliaceae)
PERENNIALS

🌿 ZONES 4–7, 14–17

◐ ● PARTIAL OR FULL SHADE

💧 REGULAR WATER

◈ FRUIT IS POISONOUS IF INGESTED

To picture these plants, visualize trilliums that suddenly sprouted four or more leaves instead of the traditional three, then abandoned their traditional flowers for an assemblage of green sepals and narrow yellow petals. These plants bear one blossom per stem; fruit consists of a black or red, berrylike mass of mildly poisonous seeds. Plants spread slowly by rhizomes. Curiosities for woodland or shaded rock garden.

Paris polyphylla

P. polyphylla. Himalayan native 2–3 ft. tall, 1 ft. wide, with four to ten oblong to lance-shaped, medium green leaves to 7 in. long. Summer flowers are 4 in. wide, with broad, triangular sepals and threadlike petals as long as or longer than sepals. Fruit (rarely seen) is scarlet.

P. quadrifolia. HERB PARIS. Native to Europe, eastern Asia. To 6–15 in. high, 1 ft. wide, with four (sometimes more) oval, 3–5-in.-long, dark green leaves. Late-spring flowers have four or more leaflike sepals and eight very narrow, almost threadlike petals. Fruit is black.

PARIS DAISY. See **CHRYS-ANTHEMUM frutescens**

PARKINSONIA aculeata
JERUSALEM THORN, MEXICAN PALO VERDE
Fabaceae (Leguminosae)
DECIDUOUS TREE

🌿 ZONES 8–24; H1, H2

☀ FULL SUN

◐ 💧 LITTLE TO MODERATE WATER

Native to southwestern U.S., Mexico. Rapid growth at first, then slowing; eventually reaches

5–30 ft. high and wide. Yellow-green bark, spiny twigs, picturesque form. Sparse foliage; leaves 5–9 in. long, with many tiny leaflets that quickly fall in drought or cold. Numerous yellow flowers in loose, 3–7-in.-long clusters. Long bloom season in spring; intermittent bloom throughout year. Flowers are followed by 2–6-in.-long seedpods that mature in summer.

Parkinsonia aculeata

Tolerates alkaline soil. Requires minimal attention once established. As shade tree, it filters sun rather than blocking it. Litter drop is a problem. Thorns, sparse foliage rule it out of tailored gardens. Reseeds freely in the desert. Flowering branches are attractive in arrangements.

For information on an excellent hybrid involving this plant, see *Cercidium* 'Desert Museum'.

PARROT BEAK.
See **CLIANTHUS puniceus**

PARROTIA persica
PERSIAN PARROTIA
Hamamelidaceae
DECIDUOUS TREE OR SHRUB

🌡	ZONES 2B–7, 14–17
☼ ☼	FULL SUN OR LIGHT SHADE
💧💧	MODERATE TO REGULAR WATER

Native to Iran. Slow growing to 15–35 ft. tall and wide; naturally multistemmed but can be trained to a single trunk. Oval, 3–6-in.-long leaves have wavy margins; upper half is shallowly toothed. Choice, colorful tree, attractive in all seasons. Most dramatic display comes in autumn: leaves usually turn golden yellow, then orange or rosy pink, and finally scarlet. Smooth gray bark flakes off to reveal white patches; showy when on display in winter. Dense clusters of tiny flowers with red stamens and woolly brown bracts appear in late winter or early spring before

Parrotia persica

leaves open; they give the plant an overall reddish haze. New foliage unfurls reddish purple, matures to lustrous dark green. Prefers slightly acid soil but tolerates alkaline soil.

PARROT'S BEAK.
See **LOTUS berthelotii**

PARSLEY PANAX.
See **POLYSCIAS fruticosa**

PARSNIP
Apiaceae (Umbelliferae)
BIENNIAL GROWN AS ANNUAL

🌡	ALL ZONES
☼	FULL SUN
💧	REGULAR WATER

Carrot relative from Siberia and Europe. Among the most cold hardy of vegetables; grown for its delicately sweet, creamy white to yellowish roots, most often used in stews. For long roots, it needs well-prepared, loose, deep soil (roots of some varieties grow to 15 in.). In cold-winter areas, sow seeds in late spring, harvest in fall; leave surplus in ground to be dug as needed in winter. Cold makes the

Parsnip

roots sweeter. In mild-winter climates, sow in fall and harvest in spring; in these areas, mature roots will continue to grow if left in ground, becoming tough and woody. Soak seeds in water for a day before planting to improve germination. Sow ¼–½ in. deep, in rows spaced 2 ft. apart; thin seedlings to 3 in. apart.

PARTHENOCISSUS
Vitaceae
DECIDUOUS VINES

🌡	ZONES VARY BY SPECIES
☼ ☼ ●	SUN OR SHADE
💧	MODERATE WATER

Valued for handsome foliage—green in summer, reliably turning to superb orange or red shades in fall. Blossoms are insignificant; more noticeable are clusters of small blue-black fruits that form in late summer or fall and hang on into winter if not consumed by birds. Vines typically cling to walls by suction disks at ends of tendrils. All but the fairly restrained *P. henryana* are said to grow to 50–60 ft., but they are really limited only by the size of the support.

Thrive in organically enriched soil. Think twice before letting them attach to shingles, clapboard, or mortared brick or stone. At repainting time their clinging tendrils are hard to remove, and vines can creep under siding. They also hasten deterioration of wood and mortar. When vines reach desired size, prune each dormant season to restrain spread and—for those trained on buildings—to keep them away from doors, windows, and eaves. Cut out any wayward branches; likewise cut out any that have pulled away from their support, since disks will not reattach. Trim as needed during the growing season.

P. henryana. SILVERVEIN CREEPER. Zones 4–9, 14–17. Native to China. Grows to 20 ft.; less aggressive growth than the other species listed. Leaves have five leaflets to 2 in. long; they open purplish, then turn dark bronzy green with pronounced silver veining and purple undersides. Color is best in partial or full shade; in strong light, leaves fade to plain green. Foliage turns rich red in autumn. This vine clings to walls, but it needs some support to get started. Also a good choice for spilling over walls or as a small-scale ground cover.

P. inserta. VIRGINIA CREEPER, WOODBINE. Zones 1–24. Native to Rocky Mountains and eastward; the Western form of *P. quinquefolia*. Scrambles rather than clings; tendrils have few or no suction disks.

P. quinquefolia. VIRGINIA CREEPER. Zones A2, A3; 1–24. Native to eastern U.S. Big, vigorous vine that clings or runs over ground, fences, trellises, arbors, trees. Looser growth than *P. tricuspidata;* has a see-through quality. Leaves divided into five 6-in. leaflets with saw-toothed edges. Foliage is bronze tinted when new, matures to semiglossy dark green, turns crimson and burgundy in early fall. Good ground cover on slopes; can control erosion. *P. q. engelmannii* is a denser grower with smaller leaves; leaves of 'Star Showers' splashed with white, take on pink tones in fall, then turn red.

Parthenocissus quinquefolia

P. tricuspidata. BOSTON IVY. Zones 1–24. Native to China, Japan. Semievergreen in mild-winter areas. This species is even more vigorous than *P. quinquefolia*. Foliage color is similar to that of *P. quinquefolia* in spring and summer but covers a broader spectrum in fall. Leaves are glossy, to 8 in. wide, variable in shape; usually three lobed or divided into three leaflets. Autumn color varies from orange to wine red. Clings tightly, grows fast to make a dense, uniform wall cover. This is the "ivy" of the Ivy League; covers brick or stone in areas where

Parthenocissus tricuspidata

P

English ivy *(Hedera helix)* freezes. In intensely hot regions, plant only on walls with northern or eastern exposure. 'Green Showers' has large (10-in.) leaves that turn burgundy in fall. 'Lowii' and 'Veitchii' produce half-size leaves on less rampant vines.

PARTRIDGEBERRY.
See **MITCHELLA repens**

PASANIA edulis.
See **LITHOCARPUS edulis**

PASPALUM
vaginatum
SEASHORE PASPALUM
Poaceae (Gramineae)
PERENNIAL GRASS

	ZONES 17, 24; H2
	FULL SUN
	MODERATE TO REGULAR WATER

Native to southeastern U.S. Makes an attractive lawn near coast; tolerates salty soil, heat, wear. Color is close to that of bluegrass, and lawns are pest free. In interior climates, it develops tough stems that turn brown after cutting. Mow to ¾ in. with a reel mower and feed only between midautumn and late spring. Usually sold as sod under names like Adalayd and Excalibre.

Paspalum vaginatum

PASQUE FLOWER.
See **PULSATILLA**

PASSIFLORA
PASSION VINE
Passifloraceae
EVERGREEN, SEMIEVERGREEN, AND
DECIDUOUS VINES

	ZONES VARY BY SPECIES
	FULL SUN OR PARTIAL SHADE
	MODERATE TO REGULAR WATER

All but one of the passion vines listed here are South American natives. All climb by tendrils to 20–30 ft. Foliage is typically rich green. Plants bloom during warm weather. Flower parts can be seen to symbolize elements of the passion of Christ, hence plant's common name: the crown represents a halo or crown of thorns; the five stamens, the five wounds; the ten petal-like segments, the ten faithful apostles. Many species produce edible fruit as a bonus; for the species cultivated specifically for its edible crop, see Passion Fruit.

Train passion vines on trellises or walls for their vigor and bright, showy flowers; or use as a soil-holding bank cover. Vigorous, likely to overgrow and tangle; require rigorous thinning and untangling. Winter and early spring are best times for major pruning, but you can thin excess new growth at any time in the growing season. Tolerate many soil types. These vines are the favorite food of caterpillars of the gulf fritillary butterfly.

Passiflora × belotii

P. × belotii (P. × alatocaerulea, P. pfordtii). Evergreen or semievergreen. Zones 5–9, 12–24; H1, H2. Dies to ground in colder part of range. Hybrid between *P. caerulea* and *P. alata,* a species not described here. Among the best-known, most widely planted passion vines, and probably least subject to damage from caterpillars. Three-lobed leaves are 3 in. long; fragrant, 4-in. flowers are white shaded pink and lavender, with deep blue or purple crown. Forms no fruit. In colder areas, give it a warm place out of wind, such as against a wall or beneath an overhang; mulch roots in winter.

P. caerulea. BLUE CROWN PASSION FLOWER. Evergreen or semievergreen. Zones 5–9, 12–24; H1, H2. Dies to the ground in colder part of range. Five-lobed leaves are smaller than those of *P. × belotii;* faintly fragrant flowers in greenish white with white-and-purple crown are also smaller. Egg-shaped, yellow to orange, 2½-in. fruit isn't very tasty. Can be invasive. Has naturalized in Hawaii.

P. edulis. See Passion Fruit

P. × exoniensis. Evergreen. Zones 16, 17, 23, 24; H2. Hybrid descended from *P. mollissima.* Five-lobed, 5-in.-long leaves. Drooping, 5-in., unscented flowers are dark green and brownish red outside, brilliant pink inside, with a touch of purple in the throat and an inconspicuous white crown. Banana-shaped, yellow, 3-in.-long fruit.

P. incarnata. WILD PASSION VINE, MAYPOP. Deciduous. Zones 4–10, 12–24; H1, H2. Native to eastern U.S. Hardiest of the passion flowers, surviving to at least −10°F/−23°C and possibly even lower. Dies to the ground in colder part of range. Three-lobed leaves are 4–6 in. wide. Freely produced fragrant, 3-in. flowers are white or pale lavender, with a showy crown of filaments banded in purple and pink. Egg-shaped, yellow, 2-in. fruit. Spreads vigorously from underground roots and can become an attractive pest. Seldom offered as plants; easy to grow from seed.

P. 'Incense'. Deciduous. Zones 5–24; H1, H2. Hardy to 0°F/−18°C; holds its leaves through short cold spells, dies to the ground when the weather turns colder. Hybrid between *P. incarnata* and an Argentinian species. Flowers are 5 in. wide, violet with lighter crown, with fragrance similar to that of sweet peas *(Lathyrus).* Egg-shaped, 2-in., olive green to yellow-green fruit with fragrant, tasty pulp.

P. jamesonii. Evergreen. Zones 14–24; H1, H2. The true species is probably not in cultivation; plants sold under this name are hybrids of *P. mixta* and other species. Glossy, three-lobed leaves. Profuse, unscented salmon pink flowers lack a conspicuous corona; the floral segments are carried at the end of a long (4-in.) tube. Quick cover for bank or fence. Rampant growth in mild-winter regions has earned these plants an unflattering comparison to kudzu, the vining scourge of the South. 'Coral Glow' and 'Coral Seas' are available selections.

P. 'Lavender Lady'. Evergreen. Zones 16–24; H2. Profuse show of unscented, 4-in., lavender flowers with deep violet crown.

P. mollissima. BANANA PASSION VINE. Evergreen. Zones 13, 15–24; H2. Soft green leaves are three lobed, deeply toothed. Pendulous, unscented rose pink blossoms are similar in shape to those of *P. jamesonii;* they are long tubed, about 3 in. long. Flavorful yellow fruit is oblong, 4–6 in. long. Extremely aggressive grower; useful for covering banks in some areas but a problem if planted among trees or shrubs. In Hawaii, it is a serious pest, smothering trees with its rapid growth.

P. vitifolia. Evergreen. Zones 16, 17, 23, 24; H2. Deep green, 6-in. leaves shaped like grape leaves set off bright red, 3½-in., unscented flowers with red to yellow coronas. Egg-shaped, greenish yellow, 2-in. fruit. Does not attract caterpillars. Has naturalized in Hawaii.

PASSION FRUIT
Passifloraceae
EVERGREEN OR
SEMIEVERGREEN VINE

	ZONES 15–17, 21–24; H1, H2
	FULL SUN
	REGULAR WATER

Known botanically as *Passiflora edulis,* this vigorous South American native climbs by tendrils to 20–30 ft. Light yellow-green, toothed leaves are three lobed. Blooms during warm weather, bearing white, 2–3-in.-wide flowers with white-and-purple crown (for more on flower form,

Passion fruit

see *Passiflora).* Doesn't need cross-pollination to bear fruit. Fragrant, roundish fruit 1½–3 in. wide ripens mainly in summer and fall; at maturity, waxy rind turns from green to deep purple, and fruit falls from the tree. Either pick the fruit when it turns color or gather it from the ground every few days. Pulp is orange in color, with an exotic, citruslike flavor; use for juice or cut fruit in half and eat pulp, seeds and all, with a spoon. There is a form with larger, more acidic, yellow-skinned fruit. Sweet-fruited hybrids that have good-size fruit include red-skinned 'Red Rover' and 'Frederick', and purple-skinned 'Edgehill' (particularly good in Southern California) and 'Kahuna'.

Grow in well-drained soil; give wind protection. Train on trellis or wall to show off flowers. Withhold water during cold months. Prune yearly after harvest: thin out excess stems by cutting them to the ground and cut back vigorous growth by a third. Semievergreen in colder part of range. Plants are often short lived. Has naturalized in Hawaii and become a serious pest there.

PASSION VINE.
See **PASSIFLORA**.

PATRINIA
Valerianaceae
PERENNIALS

🌡	ZONES 2B–6, 15–17
☀	FULL SUN
💧	REGULAR WATER

Native to eastern Asia. Deeply cut or lobed leaves to 6 in. long form mounds of foliage. In summer, plants produce flowering stems bearing few or no leaves and flat-topped clusters of tiny yellow or white blossoms. Good in perennial borders. Long-lasting cut flowers. Appreciate rich, well-drained soil.

Patrinia scabiosifolia

P. scabiosifolia. To 4–6 ft. tall, 2 ft. wide. Flowering stems produce sprays of tiny yellow blossoms. Because stems have a see-through quality, plant can be grown either at front or at rear of border. May need staking.

P. villosa. To 2–3 ft. tall, 2 ft. wide, with leaves that may be divided or uncut. Showers of white blossoms.

PAULOWNIA
tomentosa
EMPRESS TREE
Bignoniaceae
DECIDUOUS TREE

🌡	ZONES 4–9, 11–24
☀	FULL SUN
💧	REGULAR WATER

Native to China. Somewhat similar to catalpa in growth habit, leaves. Grows quickly to 40–50 ft., with nearly equal spread. Heavy trunk and heavy, nearly horizontal branches. Foliage gives tropical effect: light green, roughly heart-shaped, sometimes lobed leaves are 5–12 in. long, 4–7 in. wide. Fall color insignificant. Brown flower

Paulownia tomentosa

buds the size of small olives form in autumn and persist over winter, then open in early spring, before leafout. Fragrant, 2-in., trumpet-shaped flowers are lilac blue, marked on the inside with darker spotting and yellow stripes; they appear in 6–12-in.-long, upright clusters. Flowers are followed by 1½–2-in. seed capsules shaped like tops; these are persistent, remaining on the tree along with next season's flower buds. This tree does not bloom well where winters are very cold (buds freeze) or very mild (buds may drop off).

Grows in many soils but does best in deep, moist, well-drained soil. Tolerates air pollution. Protect from strong winds. Plant where falling flowers and leaves are not a problem. Not a tree to garden under due to dense shade, surface roots. If cut back yearly or every other year from an early age, it will produce a mass of giant-size leaves to 2 ft. long but at the expense of flower production. A tree called "sapphire dragon tree" is *P. kawakamii,* similar to *P. tomentosa* but smaller at maturity.

PAWPAW
Annonaceae
DECIDUOUS TREE

🌡	ZONES 2–9, 14, 18–21
☀	FULL SUN, EXCEPT AS NOTED
💧	REGULAR WATER

From eastern North America. The pawpaw (*Asimina triloba*) is the only hardy member of a tropical family that also includes cherimoya. To 30 ft. tall; spreads as wide

Pawpaw

as high when grown alone but is often seen in thickets of narrow, erect plants that arise from suckering. In hot-summer climates, give it some shade in its first years. Medium green leaves are oval, somewhat drooping, 4–10 in. long; turn bright yellow in fall. Foliage smells unpleasant when crushed. Purplish or brownish (sometimes green) flowers with three prominent petals are large but not showy. Fruits are roughly oval, 3–5 in. long, yellowish green ripening to brown. Soft custardlike flesh has a number of large brown seeds and a flavor somewhat like banana. If possible, get grafted plants of named varieties such as 'Prolific', 'Rebecca's Gold', 'Sunflower', 'Taylor', and 'Wells'; seedlings are highly variable. Plant two varieties for cross-pollination.

PAXISTIMA
(Pachistima,
Pachystima)
Celastraceae
EVERGREEN SHRUBS

🌡	ZONES VARY BY SPECIES
☀ ◑	PARTIAL SHADE IN HOTTEST CLIMATES
💧 💧	MODERATE TO REGULAR WATER

Low-growing shrubs with small, shiny, leathery leaves and insignificant flowers. Hardiness and compact habit make them useful as low hedges, edgings, ground cover in cold-winter areas. Best in well-drained soil.

P. canbyi. Zones 1–10, 14–21. Native to mountains of eastern U.S. Slowly makes a mat to 1 ft.

Paxistima canbyi

high, 3–5 ft. wide. Narrow dark green leaves to ¾ in. long.

P. myrtifolia (P. myrsinites). OREGON BOXWOOD. Zones 2–7, 15, 16. Native to mountains of the West. Dense plant of variable habit; may be nearly prostrate or as tall as 4 ft. Spreads about 4 ft. Growth is more compact in sun. Leaves to 1¼ in. long are dark green above, paler beneath.

PEA
Fabaceae (Leguminosae)
ANNUAL

🌡	ALL ZONES
☀	FULL SUN
💧	REGULAR WATER

Native to southern Europe. Some peas are for shelling, some have edible pods, and others can be eaten either way. If you have space and don't mind the bother, grow tall (vining) peas on trellises, strings, or chicken wire; they climb by tendrils to 6 ft. or more and bear heavily. Bush types are more commonly grown in home gardens; no support is required, though they can be grown on short trellises for easy picking.

Among shelling peas, superior bush varieties include 'Mr. Big', 'Green Arrow', and 'Maestro'. In France, tiny peas called petits pois are considered a delicacy because of their tenderness and sweet flavor. These aren't just immature versions of shelling peas; they're genetically smaller (2–3 in. long at maturity), with six to nine small peas per pod. Two common varieties are 'Waverex' and 'Precovelle'.

An unusually good vegetable (and one popular in Asian cooking) is the edible-pod pea, usually called snow or sugar pea. 'Mammoth Melting Sugar' is a tall variety; 'Manoa Sugar' is a tall type developed for Hawaii gardens. 'Oregon Sugar Pod II' and 'Oregon Giant' are bush varieties. 'Snow Wind' has few leaves on its upper stems, putting all its energy into producing peas.

P

'Super Sugar Snap' (tall), 'Sugar Ann' (bush), and semileafless 'Sugar Lace' (bush) combine the qualities of shelling peas and edible-pod peas. You can eat the immature pods, eat pods and peas together as you would string beans (the most popular way), or wait for the peas to mature and harvest them for shelling.

All peas are easy to grow when conditions are right. They need coolness and humidity and must be planted at just the right time. Where winters are cold, sow as early in spring as the ground can be worked; for a fall crop, sow about 12 weeks before the first frost date. Where winters are mild, plant at any time from fall to early spring—but don't sow after midwinter in areas where spring days quickly become too warm for peas. Successive plantings several days apart will lengthen the bearing season; most varieties are ready to pick 60 to 70 days from planting.

Pea

Grow peas in slightly acid to slightly alkaline soil that is water retentive but fast draining. Soak seeds overnight in water before planting them. If planting in winter, sow ½–1 in. deep. At other times of year, sow 2 in. deep in light soil, ½–1 in. deep in heavy soil. Leave 2 ft. between rows for bush types, 5 ft. for tall vines; thin seedlings to 2–4 in. apart. (Thinnings can be steamed or stir-fried.) Moisten ground thoroughly before planting; then hold off on watering until seedlings are up. Plants need little fertilizer, but if soil is very light give one application of complete fertilizer about 6 weeks after planting. If weather turns warm and dry, supply water in furrows; overhead watering encourages mildew. Provide support for vining peas as soon as tendrils form.

When peas reach harvesting size, pick all pods that are ready; if seeds are allowed to ripen, plant will stop producing. Begin harvesting peas for shelling when the pods have swelled to almost a cylindrical shape but before they lose their bright green color. Harvest edible-pod peas when they're 2–3 in. long, before the seeds begin to swell. Vines are brittle; steady them with one hand while picking with the other. Refrigerate peas unwashed, and use as soon as possible.

PEACH and NECTARINE

Rosaceae
DECIDUOUS FRUIT TREES

🌿 **ZONES VARY BY VARIETY**

☀️ **FULL SUN**

💧 **REGULAR WATER DURING FRUIT DEVELOPMENT**

▶ **SEE CHART NEXT PAGE**

Native to China. Peach *(Prunus persica)* and nectarine *(P. p. nucipersica)* trees look alike and have the same cultural needs. Where fruit is concerned, both peaches and nectarines may be clingstone (flesh adheres to the pit), freestone (flesh easily separates from pit), or semifreestone (between the two); but other than this, nectarines differ from peaches in several respects. They have smooth rather than fuzzy skin; in some varieties, flavor is slightly different; and many are more susceptible to brown rot of stone fruit (controls described at right). Here we consider fruiting peaches and nectarines. For strictly flowering types, see *Prunus*.

In most regions, crops ripen between June and September, depending on variety. Early varieties grown in mild-winter climates may mature as early as April. For good harvests, trees must be exposed to winter chill (see care box); insufficient chilling results in delayed leafout, a scanty crop, and eventual death of the tree. In extremely mild-winter areas, only low-chill varieties do well (and very few of those are satisfactory in the low desert). A few low-chill peach varieties have been tried successfully at higher elevations in Hawaii; nectarines tend to split in Hawaii and so are not commonly grown there. In areas subject to late frosts, early-blooming varieties are risky. Where spring is particularly cold and rainy, plants set few flowers, pollinate poorly, and get peach leaf curl. They need

clear, hot weather during the growing season.

The peach and nectarine varieties listed in the chart are the most widely available and recommended. However, many more are sold, some with local adaptation. For information on the varieties that perform best in your area, consult your local Cooperative Extension Office or an area nursery.

Peach

A standard-size peach or nectarine tree grows rapidly to 25 ft. tall and wide, but properly pruned trees are usually kept to 10–12 ft. high and a little wider. They start bearing large crops when 3 or 4 years old and reach peak production at 8 to 12 years. Genetic or natural dwarf trees, most of which grow to 5–6 ft. tall and produce medium-size fruit, are useful in tubs and small planting areas. You can also save space by planting three or four full-size varieties in one hole: prune the new bare-root trees so that each retains just one primary branch, and point those branches outward as you plant the trees in the hole. With a few exceptions (see comments in chart), peaches and nectarines are self-fruitful.

Peach and nectarine trees require good drainage, regular fertilizing, and heavier pruning than other fruit trees. Genetic dwarf trees need less pruning than standard ones. When planting a bare-root tree that is an unbranched "whip," cut it back to 2–3½ ft. above ground (the thicker the trunk, the less severe the cutting back). New branches will form below cut. After first year's growth, select three well-placed branches for scaffold limbs. On mature trees, in each dormant season cut off two-thirds of previous

year's growth by removing two of every three branches formed that year; or head back each branch to one-third its length; or head back some and cut out others. Trees can be trained as espaliers.

Among the most serious diseases of peaches and nectarines are brown rot of stone fruit and peach leaf curl. The fungus responsible for peach leaf curl causes emerging new leaves to thicken and pucker. Infected foliage may be tinged red, pink, yellow, or white; it usually falls in midsummer. Severely infected trees are weakened and may stop producing. Brown rot fungus causes flowers to wilt and decay, twigs to crack and ooze sap. To control both diseases, practice good sanitation—get rid of diseased plant parts to keep fungus from reinfecting the tree the next year. Also apply fixed copper or lime sulfur dormant sprays once after autumn leaf drop and again just as buds begin to swell but before they open. In coastal areas of the Northwest, where winter and spring are almost always rainy, spray three times, starting in late December and repeating at 2- to 4-week intervals. Some gardeners reduce peach leaf curl by planting the trees under eaves and training them in a fan shape against a south-facing wall. Move potted

▶ page 521

What Peaches and Nectarines Need

WINTER CHILL Most varieties need 600 to 900 hours of winter temperatures at or below 45°F/7°C. Low-chill selections are the best bet for mild-winter regions.

PRUNING They need more pruning than other fruit trees because they produce fruit on 1-year-old branches. Severe annual pruning (see text) not only renews fruiting wood—it also encourages production of fruit throughout the tree rather than at ends of sagging branches that can easily break.

FRUIT THINNING Even with good pruning, peaches and nectarines form too much fruit. When fruits are 1 in. wide, thin out (remove some) to 8–10 in. apart.

DISEASE CONTROL Where peach leaf curl and brown rot of stone fruit are troublesome, apply dormant sprays annually (see text).

P

PEACH AND NECTARINE

NAME	ZONES	FRUIT	COMMENTS
PEACHES			
'Arctic Supreme'	7–9, 14, 15, 18	Large. Clingstone. Red-over-cream skin; white flesh. Superb flavor. Midseason	Among the finest flavored of all peaches
'August Pride'	7–9, 14, 15, 18–24	Large. Freestone. Yellow skin with red blush; yellow flesh. Aromatic fruit with rich flavor. Midseason	Low chill requirement
'Babcock'	12, 13, 15, 16, 19–24; H1	Small to medium. Freestone. Light pink skin with red blush; little fuzz. White flesh reddens near pit. Sweet flavor with some tang. Early	Low chill requirement. Old-timer
'Baby Crawford'	7–9, 14, 15, 18	Small. Freestone. Golden orange, very fuzzy skin with slight blush; yellow flesh. Intense flavor. Midseason	An exceptionally flavorful variety
'Bonanza II'	2, 3, 7–12, 14–16, 18–23	Large. Freestone. Attractive red-and-yellow skin; deep yellow to orange flesh. Good flavor. Midseason	Genetic dwarf. Showy flowers. Fruit more flavorful than that of 'Bonanza', the original dwarf variety for home gardens
'Bonita'	15–24	Large. Freestone. Yellow skin with medium red blush; firm yellow flesh. Fine flavor. Midseason	Low chill requirement
'Champagne'	6–11, 14, 15, 18	Medium to large. Freestone. Yellow skin with light red blush; white flesh with red near the pit. Fine, sweet flavor. Midseason	Vigorous and productive
'Desertgold'	8, 9, 12, 13, 18–24	Medium-size. Semifreestone. Yellow skin and flesh. Good quality. Very early	Very early bloom rules it out wherever spring frosts are likely
'Donut' ('Stark Saturn')	7–9, 13–15, 18–23	Medium-size. Freestone. Shaped like a doughnut, with a sunken middle. White skin with red blush; white flesh. Mildly sweet flavor with a hint of almond. Early	Low chill requirement. Almost evergreen in mild-winter areas
'Earligrande'	8–24	Medium to large. Semifreestone. Yellow with red blush. Excellent flavor. Early	Fine quality. Low-chill variety for mild-winter climates
'Elberta'	1–3, 6–11, 14	Medium to large. Freestone. Yellow skin with red blush; yellow flesh. High quality. Midseason	Needs good amount of winter chill, high summer heat to ripen to full flavor
'El Dorado'	2, 3, 7–12, 14, 15, 18	Medium-size. Freestone. Yellow skin with red blush; yellow flesh. Rich flavor. Early	Genetic dwarf
'Eva's Pride'	12, 13, 18–24	Medium to large. Freestone. Yellow skin and flesh. Fine flavor. Early to midseason	Low chill requirement
'Fay Elberta' ('Gold Medal')	2, 3, 6–11, 14, 15, 18, 19	Medium to large. Freestone. Yellow flesh. Has more red blush on skin and keeps better than 'Elberta'. Midseason; ripens with 'Elberta'	Large, handsome single flowers. 'Fantastic Elberta' is a double-flowered sport; its fruit has excellent flavor
'Flordaprince'	12, 13, 18–24; H1	Medium to large. Semifreestone, becoming freestone when fully ripe. Red-blushed yellow skin; yellow flesh. Very good quality. Very early	Low chill requirement
'Fortyniner'	5–9, 14–16, 18	Large. Freestone. Yellow skin with bright red blush; yellow flesh. Fine flavor. Early midseason	Looks like its parent, 'J. H. Hale'; blooms about 1 week earlier
'Frost'	3–9, 14, 15, 18	Medium-size. Freestone. Yellow skin with slight red blush; yellow flesh. Tangy flavor. Midseason to late	Resistant to peach leaf curl
'Gleason's Early Elberta' ('Lemon Elberta', 'Improved Elberta')	2–11, 14, 15	Like 'Elberta' but has better color and even better flavor; ripens about 10 days later	Late blooming and cold hardy. Needs somewhat less heat than 'Elberta'
'Halehaven'	1–3, 6–11, 14–16	Medium to large. Freestone. Red skin; firm yellow flesh. Juicy and flavorful. Midseason	Flower and leaf buds are very winter hardy. Good fresh or canned

P

PEACH AND NECTARINE

NAME	ZONES	FRUIT	COMMENTS
'Harken'	1–7	Large. Freestone. Yellow skin with red blush; yellow flesh. Very sweet. Midseason	Good performer in cold climates and coastal Northwest
'Honey Babe'	3–12, 14–16, 18–20	Small to medium. Freestone. Yellow skin with red blush; yellow flesh. Fine flavor. Midseason	Genetic dwarf. Needs another genetic dwarf peach or nectarine for pollination in the Northwest
'Indian Blood Cling' ('Indian Cling')	1–3, 6–11, 14–16	Medium-size. Clingstone. Red skin; firm yellow flesh streaked with red. Rich flavor. Late	Old-fashioned variety with small but devoted band of enthusiasts. Good for preserves
'Indian Free'	7–11, 14–16	Large. Freestone. Greenish white skin with red blush; red-tinged yellow flesh, deep red at pit. Rich and aromatic when fully ripe. Late midseason	Needs pollinating by any other peach except 'J. H. Hale'. An old favorite with a unique flavor
'J. H. Hale'	1–3, 7–11, 14–16	Very large. Freestone. Yellow skin overlaid with deep red; little fuzz. Yellow flesh. High quality; fine keeper. Midseason	Needs pollinating by any other peach except 'Indian Blood Cling' or 'Indian Free'
'July Elberta' ('Kim Elberta')	2, 3, 6–12, 14–16, 18, 19	Medium to large. Freestone. Yellow skin blushed red; yellow flesh. High quality. Early, 3 weeks before 'Elberta'	Prolific bearer
'Loring'	7–9, 14, 15, 18	Large. Freestone. Attractive yellow skin blushed red; little fuzz. Moderately juicy yellow flesh. Good quality. Midseason	Vigorous. Showy flowers
'Midpride'	7–9, 12–16, 18–24	Medium-size. Freestone. Red-blushed yellow skin; yellow flesh. Exceptional flavor. Midseason	Excellent variety with low chill requirement
'Nectar'	7–11, 14–16	Medium to large. Freestone. Creamy white skin with red blush; white flesh. Excellent flavor. Early midseason	Among the best white peaches
'New Haven'	1–7	Large. Freestone. Red-blushed yellow skin; yellow flesh. Good quality. Midseason to late	Good performer in cold climates and coastal Northwest
'O'Henry'	7–10, 14–16, 18	Large. Freestone. Yellow skin with red blush; yellow flesh streaked red. Fine flavor. Midseason	Good commercial and home-garden variety
'Pix Zee'	2, 3, 7–9, 14, 15, 18	Large. Freestone. Yellow skin with red blush; yellow flesh. Good flavor. Early to midseason	Genetic dwarf
'Polly'	1–3, 10	Medium-size. Freestone. White skin blushed red; juicy white flesh. Excellent flavor. Late midseason	Tree and buds very hardy to cold
'Q 1-8'	3–9, 14, 15, 18	Medium-size. Semifreestone. Yellow skin with red blush; white flesh. Sweet, flavorful. Early	Resistant to peach leaf curl
'Ranger'	2, 3, 6–12, 14, 15	Large. Freestone. Red-blushed skin; firm, yellow, good-tasting flesh. Early	Vigorous, productive tree. Good for areas with late spring frosts. Good fresh, canned, or frozen
'Red Baron'	7–9, 14–16, 18–23	Large. Freestone. Yellow skin and flesh. Sweet, rich flavor. Midseason to late	Ornamental tree with double red blossoms
'Redhaven'	3, 5, 12, 14–16	Medium-size. Freestone. Yellow skin with bright red blush; firm yellow flesh. Good flavor. Long ripening season permits numerous harvests. Early	Colors up early, so test for ripeness. One of the best varieties. Good fresh or frozen. 'Early Redhaven' ripens 2 weeks earlier
'Redskin'	1–3, 6–12, 14–16	Medium to large. Freestone. Yellow skin heavily blushed red; yellow flesh. Excellent quality. Midseason	Productive tree. Good fresh, canned, or frozen
'Reliance'	1–11	Medium to large. Freestone. Yellow skin blushed dull red; soft yellow flesh. Good flavor. Early	Outstanding cold hardiness
'Rio Grande'	8–10, 15, 18–20	Medium to large. Freestone. Yellow skin with red blush; firm yellow flesh. Good flavor. Early	Productive tree with showy flowers

P

PEACH AND NECTARINE

NAME	ZONES	FRUIT	COMMENTS
'Rio Oso Gem'	3, 7–11, 14, 15	Medium to large. Freestone. Yellow skin with red blush; firm yellow flesh. Excellent flavor. Late midseason	Small tree; not vigorous. Fruit is excellent fresh or frozen
'Santa Barbara'	18–24; H1	Large. Freestone. Red-blushed yellow skin; yellow flesh. Excellent flavor; best used fresh. Midseason	Low chill requirement. Sport of 'Ventura'
'Snow Beauty'	7–9, 14, 15, 18	Large. Freestone. Red skin, white flesh. Midseason	Among the best flavored of white peaches
'Southern Rose'	2, 3, 7–12, 14–16, 18–23	Medium-size. Freestone. Yellow skin with red blush; yellow flesh. Fair flavor. Midseason	Genetic dwarf with low chill requirement. 'Southern Flame' and 'Southern Sweet' are others in the series
'Strawberry Free'	7–9, 14–16, 18–20	Medium-size. Freestone. Medium red blush on yellow skin; firm white flesh. Excellent flavor. Early midseason	An old favorite among white peaches
'Suncrest'	7–9, 14, 15, 18	Large. Freestone. Yellow skin with bright red blush. Excellent flavor. Midseason	Variety made famous in *Epitaph for a Peach: Four Seasons on My Family Farm*, by David Mas Masumoto
'Tra-Zee'	6–9, 14, 15, 18	Medium size. Freestone. Dark red skin; firm yellow flesh. Excellent flavor. Late	Vigorous and productive
'Tropi-berta'	8, 9, 14–16, 18–22; H1	Large. Freestone. Yellow skin blushed red; juicy yellow flesh. Good flavor. Late midseason	Moderately low chill requirement
'Tropic Snow'	12, 13, 18–23; H1	Medium-size. Freestone. Red skin, white flesh. Superb flavor. Early	Best low-chill white peach
'Ventura'	18–23; H1	Medium-size. Freestone. Very smooth yellow skin; yellow flesh. Attractive fruit with fair flavor. Midseason	Low chill requirement. Developed especially for Southern California
NECTARINES			
'Arctic Jay'	7–9, 14–16, 18	Large. Freestone. Deep red skin; white flesh. Excellent, rich flavor. Early to midseason	Among the many excellent white nectarines in the Arctic series; harvest season depends on variety. "Arctic" refers to white color of flesh, not to cold hardiness
'Arctic Rose'	7–9, 14–16, 18	Medium-size. Freestone. White to pale yellow skin with red blush; white flesh. Delicious sweet flavor. Midseason	One of the best-tasting nectarines
'Arctic Star'	7–9, 14, 15, 18–24	Large. Semifreestone. Bright red skin; white flesh. Very sweet, rich flavor. Early	Low chill requirement. One of the best white nectarines for mild-winter areas
'Double Delight'	7–9, 14–16, 18–20	Medium-size. Freestone. Dark red skin; yellow flesh. Rich flavor. Midseason	Ornamental double pink flowers. Low chill requirement
'Fantasia'	3, 7–9, 14–16, 18–22	Large. Freestone. Bright yellow-and-red skin; firm yellow flesh. Sweet, rich flavor. Midseason	Vigorous. Relatively low chill requirement. Good in colder areas
'Flavortop'	2, 3, 6–12, 14, 15, 18	Large. Freestone. Yellow skin, heavily blushed red; yellow flesh. Good flavor. Midseason	Vigorous, productive. Showy flowers

'Frost' peach

'Indian Free' peach

'July Elberta' peach

'Midpride' peach

P

PEACH AND NECTARINE

NAME	ZONES	FRUIT	COMMENTS
NECTARINES (continued)			
'Goldmine'	7–12, 14–16, 18–22	Large. Freestone. Creamy yellow, tough skin with red blush; firm white flesh. Excellent, distinctive flavor. Late midseason	Low chill requirement. Excellent fresh or frozen. 'Arctic Fantasy' is an improved form with even better flavor
'Heavenly White'	7–9, 14–16, 18	Very large. Freestone. Creamy white skin that is heavily blushed with red; white flesh. Especially fine flavor. Midseason	Has been called a connoisseur's delight
'Independence'	7–9, 14–16, 18, 19	Large. Freestone. Red skin, yellow flesh. Good flavor. Early	Moderately vigorous, moderately productive tree
'Juneglo'	3–9, 14–16, 18	Medium-size. Freestone. Red skin, yellow flesh. Fine flavor. Early	One of the most reliable varieties in coastal Northwest
'Le Grand'	7–9, 14–16, 18	Large. Clingstone. Bright yellow-and-red skin; yellow flesh. Delicate, sweet-tart flavor. Late	Fruit holds well on the tree
'Liz's Late'	7–9, 14–16, 18	Medium-size. Freestone. Red-over-yellow skin; yellow flesh. Sprightly, sweet-spicy flavor. Good keeper. Late	Unusual flavor makes this nectarine a favorite
'Mericrest'	1–3, 10, 11, 14–16, 18	Medium-size. Freestone. Bright red skin; yellow flesh. Flavorful. Midseason	May be as cold hardy as 'Reliance' peach. Good resistance to brown rot
'Nectar Babe'	2–12, 14–16, 18–20	Small to medium-size. Freestone. Dark red skin; yellow flesh. Good flavor. Midseason	Genetic dwarf. Good pollinator for 'Honey Babe' peach
'Necta Zee'	2–12, 14–16, 18–20	Medium-size. Freestone. Red skin, yellow flesh. Sweet and flavorful. Early to midseason	Genetic dwarf
'Panamint'	7–9, 14–16, 18–24	Medium to large. Freestone. Bright red skin; yellow flesh. Very good flavor. Midseason	Low chill requirement
'Ruby Grand'	2, 3, 6–12, 14, 15, 18	Large. Freestone. Firm yellow flesh of exceptional flavor and quality. Early to midseason	Good all-purpose nectarine
'Silver Lode'	7–9, 14–16, 18–20	Medium-size. Freestone. Scarlet-and-white skin; white flesh. Good flavor. Early	Low chill requirement
'Snow Queen'	7–9, 14–16, 18–23	Medium-size. Freestone. Red skin; white flesh. Sweet and juicy. Early	Low chill requirement
'Southern Belle'	7–12, 14–16, 18–23	Large. Freestone. Yellow skin with red blush; yellow flesh. Good flavor. Early	Genetic dwarf. Low chill requirement
'Sunred'	18–23	Medium-size. Semifreestone. Bright red skin; yellow flesh. Good flavor. Very early	Low chill requirement

'Redhaven' peach   'Rio Oso Gem' peach   Genetic dwarf peach tree   'Fantasia' nectarine   'Independence' nectarine genetic dwarf peaches and nectarines to a covered location in rainy weather. To control the diseases as well as scale insects, use sprays combining horticultural oil with either lime sulfur or fixed copper.

Peach tree borer, which tends to attack trees stressed by poor growing conditions or wounds, causes defoliation, branch dieback, and possibly death. Jellylike matter exuding from the base of the tree is the first indication of the pest's presence. The insect holes will be evident at or just below ground level. Prevention through good growing conditions is the best control; if a tree is attacked, consult your Cooperative Extension Office for best treatment.

PEACH-LEAFED BLUEBELL.
See **CAMPANULA persicifolia**

PEANUT
Fabaceae (Leguminosae)
ANNUAL

🗺️ **ZONES 2–24**

☀️ **FULL SUN**

💧 **REGULAR WATER**

The peanut originated in South America and bears best where summers are long and warm. It is tender to frost but worth growing even in cool regions. Plants resemble bush sweet peas *(Lathyrus)* 10–20 in. tall. After the bright yellow flowers fade, a "peg" (shootlike structure) develops at each flower's base and grows down into soil; peanuts develop underground. For best performance, give fertile, well-drained soil; sandy or other light-textured soil is ideal for penetration by pegs.

The four basic classes of peanuts are Virginia and Runner types, with two large seeds per pod; Spanish, with two or three small seeds per pod; and Valencia, with three to six small seeds per pod. Buy seeds (unroasted peanuts)

Peanut

from mail-order suppliers. Plant just as soon as soil has warmed in spring, setting seeds (with shells removed but skins intact) 1½–2 in. deep. Sow seeds of Virginia and Runner peanuts 6–8 in. apart; sow Spanish and Valencia peanuts 4–6 in. apart. Fertilize at planting time. In cool-summer areas, grow under floating row covers to hasten growth. In 110 to 120 days after planting, foliage yellows and plants are ready to dig; loosen soil, then pull up plants. Let peanuts dry on vines in a warm, airy, shaded place for 2 to 3 weeks; then strip them from plants.

PEARL MILLET.
See **PENNISETUM glaucum**

PEANUT CACTUS.
See **ECHINOPSIS chamaecereus**

PEAR, ASIAN
Rosaceae
DECIDUOUS FRUIT TREES

🗺️ **ZONES 2–12, 14–21, EXCEPT AS NOTED**

☀️ **FULL SUN**

💧 **REGULAR WATER**

These pears are descendants of two Asian species: *Pyrus pyrifolia (P. serotina)* and *P. ussuriensis.* Trees grow to 25–30 ft. tall and about half as wide, but they're easily kept to half that size with pruning. Unlike European pears, Asian pears are generally round in shape, with a crisp, gritty, firm to hard texture. Asian pears are often called apple pears because of their

Asian pear

roundness and crispness, but they are not hybrids of those two fruits. All pears benefit from pollination by a second variety that flowers at the same time (consult your local nursery). European pears, however, are not reliable pollenizers for Asian types because they generally bloom later. Asian pears should be thinned to one pear per fruiting spur and should be picked ripe.

Fresh Asian pears are excellent combined with other fruits and vegetables in salads. They need the same general culture as European

pears but have a lower chilling requirement (take as few as 400 hours) and a greater resistance to fireblight. Asian pear varieties include 'Chojuro', 'Hosui', 'Ichiban', 'Kikusui', 'Kosui', 'Mishirasu', 'Seuri', 'Shinko', 'Tsu Li', 'Ya Li', 'Yoinashi', and 'Yongi'. 'Shinseiki' grows in Zones 2–13, 14–21. 'Nijisseki' ('Twentieth Century') is a particularly cold-hardy variety.

PEAR, EUROPEAN
Rosaceae
DECIDUOUS FRUIT TREES

🗺️ **ZONES VARY BY VARIETY**

☀️ **FULL SUN**

💧 **REGULAR WATER**

▶️ **SEE CHART NEXT PAGE**

Most pears sold in markets and grown in gardens are varieties of *Pyrus communis,* a European species. The long-lived trees are pyramidal in form, with strongly vertical branching; they grow 30–40 ft. tall (sometimes taller), 15–25 ft. wide. Pears on dwarfing understocks make good small garden trees; they range from one-half to three-fourths the size of standard-size trees. Pears also make excellent espaliers. All types have leathery, glossy bright green leaves and bear handsome clusters of white flowers in early spring. For ornamental relatives, see *Pyrus.*

European pear

To produce good crops, pears need winter chill (see care box). In cold climates, their early bloom makes them prone to damage from spring frosts; in such areas, they are often planted in protected locations, such as on slopes. Hybrids between European pears and the hardy *P. ussuriensis,* such as 'Ure', are worth trying in the coldest regions. Where winters are very mild, choose varieties needing little winter chill. Some low-chill types are Asian hybrids, crosses between European and Asian pears with fruit similar to that of European varieties.

Pears do best in well-drained loam, but they tolerate damp, heavy soil better than other fruit trees. They produce fruit on knobby

European pear

spurs that remain productive for up to 5 years. Thinning the fruit is not usually necessary. Harvest season is July to late October, depending on variety. Fruit does not ripen properly on the tree; pick it when full size but not yet ripe. Fruit of most kinds should be put in a cool, dark place to ripen; exceptions are 'Anjou', 'Bosc', and 'Comice', which should be put in cold storage (32 to 40°F/0 to 4°C) for about a month after picking, then brought into a warm room to ripen.

What European Pears Need

WINTER CHILL Pears need at least 600 hours of winter chill (45°F/7°C or lower), and most do better still with 900 hours. In warmest-winter climates, choose low-chill varieties.

POLLINATION They normally need cross-pollination for good fruit set; plant two or more varieties. Some types, notably 'Bartlett' and 'Comice', are self-fruitful in many parts of California but not usually elsewhere.

PRUNING AND TRAINING Best done when trees are young to establish a good framework of main branches. Prune lightly each year during the dormant season to keep good form, eliminate crowding branches.

HARVESTING Don't wait for pears to ripen on the tree—they will be ruined. Pick unripe, when they're green and firm. If a pear is ready to harvest, the stem will snap free from the branch when you lift the fruit so that it is horizontal. If the stem remains connected, check again in a few days.

'Bartlett'

P

PEAR, EUROPEAN

NAME	ZONES	FRUIT	COMMENTS
'Anjou' ('d'Anjou', 'Beurre d'Anjou')	2, 3, 6–9	Medium to large fruit may be round or have a short neck. Yellow to russeted yellow. Fine flavor. Ripens after cold storage. Late	Upright, vigorous tree. Tie down limbs for more consistent bearing. Moderately susceptible to fireblight. 'Red d'Anjou' is a red-skinned form
'Bartlett'	2–11, 14–18	Medium to large, with short but definite neck. Thin skinned, yellow or slightly blushed, very sweet and tender. Midseason	Standard summer pear of fruit markets. Generally self-fruitful but may need a pollenizer in cool California coastal areas and Northwest; use any variety except 'Seckel'. Tree does not have the best form, is susceptible to fireblight; nevertheless a good home variety
'Blake's Pride'	2–9, 14–18	Medium-size, bell-shaped fruit. Yellow to gold skin with light russeting. Fine, melting flavor. Midseason	Recent introduction with excellent resistance to fireblight
'Bosc' ('Beurre Bosc', 'Golden Russet')	2–9, 14–18; best in Northwest and higher elevations farther south	Medium to large, quite long necked, interesting and attractive in form. Heavy russeting on green or yellow skin. Fine flavor; firm, juicy flesh. Holds shape when cooked. Ripens after cold storage. Late	Large, upright, vigorous tree. Needs pruning in youth. Highly susceptible to fireblight
'Clapp Favorite'	2–9, 14–18; best in Northwest, inter-mountain areas	Resembles 'Bartlett'. Soft, sweet flesh. Early	Productive, shapely tree; attractive foliage. Highly prone to fireblight. 'Bennett', popular in Northwest, is a red-blushed strain
'Comice' ('Doyenne du Comice', 'Royal Riviera')	2–9, 14–18	Large to very large, roundish to pear shaped. Thick, greenish yellow skin is russeted, sometimes blushed. Superb flavor and texture. Ripens after cold storage. Late	Big, vigorous tree; slow to reach bearing age. Bears good crops when soil, climate, and exposure are right. Generally self-fruitful but does better in Northwest with a pollenizer. Moderately susceptible to fireblight. 'Red Comice' is a red-skinned sport
'Conference'	2–9, 14–18	Large, yellow, elongated fruit borne in clusters. Very juicy, sweet flesh with buttery texture. Late	Very productive. Good resistance to fireblight
'Fan Stil'	2, 3, 7–12, 14–23	Medium-size, bell-shaped yellow fruit with slight red blush. Crisp, juicy; good fresh and cooked. Midseason	Asian pear hybrid. Vigorous, upright growth. Consistently large crops. Needs little winter chill; tolerates heat. Highly resistant to fireblight
'Flordahome'	2, 3, 7–23	Small to medium, light green fruit with short pear shape. Juicy flesh. Early	Resistant to fireblight. Needs little winter chill. Pollinate with 'Hood'
'Harrow Delight'	1b, 2–7	Resembles 'Bartlett' but is smaller. Smooth texture, very good flavor. Early	Cold-hardy variety developed in Canada. Excellent resistance to fireblight
'Hood'	2, 3, 7–24; H1	Large yellow-green fruit with typical pear shape. Ripens a little later than 'Flordahome'	Vigorous tree. Resistant to fireblight. Needs very little winter chill. Pollinate with 'Flordahome'

'Anjou'

'Bartlett'

'Bosc'

'Comice'

'Red Comice'　　　　'Sensation Red Bartlett'

P

PEAR, EUROPEAN

NAME	ZONES	FRUIT	COMMENTS
'Kieffer'	2, 3, 7–23	Medium to large, oval; greenish yellow skin blushed red. Gritty texture; fair flavor. Good for canning, baking. Late	Asian pear hybrid. Low-chill variety. Good for hot or cold climates. Quite resistant to fireblight
'Max-Red Bartlett'	2–11, 14–18	Resembles 'Bartlett' but has bright red skin and a somewhat sweeter flavor. Midseason	Red color extends to twigs and tints leaves. Susceptible to fireblight. Bears better in Northwest with a pollenizer; use any except 'Seckel'
'Monterrey'	2, 3, 7–12, 14–23	Large, apple shaped; yellow skin. Good flavor; texture not too gritty. Midseason	Probably an Asian pear hybrid. Needs little winter chill. Very resistant to fireblight
'Moonglow'	2, 3, 7–12, 14–23	Somewhat like 'Bartlett' in looks. Juicy, soft fruit with good flavor. Early	Upright, vigorous tree; very heavy bearer. Highly resistant to fireblight
'Orcas'	2–7, 14–17	Large. Pear shaped but has a pointier stem end than a typical pear. Yellow skin with red blush. Flavorful, melt-in-the-mouth flesh. Midseason	Vigorous, spreading tree
'Orient'	2–21	Large, bell-shaped fruit with russeting on yellow skin. Firm, juicy, and somewhat sweet; good for canning, baking. Late	Asian pear hybrid. Heavy producer. Highly resistant to fireblight
'Rescue'	2–7, 14–17	Large, traditional shape; yellow skin with red-orange blush. Sweet, juicy, and smooth textured. Good keeper. Midseason	Vigorous, productive, upright tree. Northwest favorite
'Seckel' ('Sugar')	2–11, 14–21	Very small, very sweet, aromatic. Roundish to pear shaped; yellow-brown skin, granular flesh. A favorite for home gardens, preserving. Early midseason	Highly productive. Fairly resistant to fireblight. Self-fruitful but bears more heavily with pollenizer (any except 'Bartlett' and its strains will do)
'Sensation Red Bartlett'	2–9, 14–18	Looks much like 'Bartlett', but skin is bright red over most of fruit. Midseason	Medium-size tree, less vigorous than 'Bartlett'. Susceptible to fireblight
'Summer Crisp'	A2, A3; 1–3	Small, roundish. Red-blushed green skin. Crisp, mildly sweet flesh. Late	Cold-hardy variety from Minnesota. Quite resistant to fireblight
'Sure Crop'	2–9, 14–18	Resembles 'Bartlett' in looks and flavor. Late midseason	Consistent annual bearer. Prolonged bloom makes it safe where spring frosts come late. Fairly resistant to fireblight
'Ure'	A2, A3; 1–3	Small, roundish fruit with greenish yellow skin. Sweet and juicy. Good fresh or canned. Midseason	Cold-hardy Asian hybrid developed in Canada. Small tree. Resistant to fireblight
'Warren'	1b–9, 14–18	Medium to large fruit with teardrop shape; pale green skin, often with a red blush. Buttery, juicy flesh with excellent flavor. Good keeper. Late	Cold-hardy tree. Extremely resistant to fireblight
'Winter Nelis'	2, 3, 7–9, 14–18	Small to medium, roundish fruit with rough, dull green or yellowish skin. Not attractive but has a very fine flavor. Very good keeper, fine for baking. Late	Moderately susceptible to fireblight

P

The most trouble-free pear-growing regions are warm, dry areas of California and Oregon, where commercial orchards are located. Fireblight can be a serious problem; in problem-prone areas, fireblight-resistant varieties offer the best chance of success. The disease can cause entire branches to die back quickly; as soon as you see blackened growth, cut it back to a growth bud or stem with green, healthy tissue, disinfecting pruning tools after each cut. To avoid profuse new growth, with resultant risk of fireblight, do not prune heavily in any one dormant season; also fertilize sparingly. Dormant oil sprays will control pear psylla and various other pests that may bother pear trees. Codling moth can ruin fruit; pheromone traps may be an effective control for a few trees in a home garden. For more information on codling moth, see Apple, page 189. Pear trees are resistant to oak root fungus.

PEARL BUSH. See **EXOCHORDA**

PEARL MILLET. See **PENNISETUM glaucum**

PEASHRUB. See **CARAGANA**

PECAN
Juglandaceae
DECIDUOUS TREE

✿	ZONES 2 AND 3 (WARMER PARTS), 6–10, 12–14, 18–20
☼	FULL SUN
●	REGULAR WATER

Native to the south-central U.S.; scientific name is *Carya illinoinensis*. Graceful, shapely tree to 70 ft.

▶

tall and wide; large for small gardens but attractive where space is available. Foliage resembles that of English walnut but is prettier, with a finer texture that casts lighter shade; leaves have more (11–17), narrower, longer (4–7 in.) leaflets. Inconspicuous flowers are followed by nuts enclosed in husks. Best nut production is in areas with long, hot summers (Zones 8–10, 12–14, 18–20); crops in other recommended zones are less certain but possible. Harvest when nuts fall in autumn; remove husks right away, then dry and store.

Most pecans set light crops

Pecan

without cross-pollination. For a good-size crop, plant a type 1 variety near a type 2 variety. (Note that pecans tend to be alternate bearers, with a heavy crop one year followed by a light crop the next.) The best selections include 'Burkett' (type 2), 'Mohawk' (type 2), 'Western Schley' (type 1), and 'Wichita' (type 2). Early-ripening 'Pawnee' (type 1) is the best choice for areas that normally don't have warm summer temperatures over a long enough time for pecans to ripen (Zones 6 and 7 and the warmer parts of Zones 2 and 3). Other early-ripening varieties that may succeed in these short-season areas include 'Shoshoni' and 'Kanza' (both type 2).

Pecan trees need well-drained soil loosened to a depth of 6–10 ft.; they will not grow well in saline soil. Set out bare-root trees in winter. Dig a planting hole deep enough to accommodate the long taproot; position the bud union above soil level. Firm soil around roots, then water thoroughly. If you're counting on a quality nut crop, don't let soil dry out. Prevent pecan rosette (abnormal clumps of twigs caused by zinc deficiency) by spraying zinc sulfate spray on expanding leaves in spring. Because pecan trees are prone to aphid infestations (and resulting sticky honeydew droppings), don't plant a tree where it will overarch a parking area or patio. For severe aphid infestations, consider applying the systemic insecticide imidacloprid to the soil. Pecan trees resist oak root fungus. Pruning is needed only to remove suckers from below the graft union and to clear out dead, broken, or poorly placed limbs.

PEDILANTHUS
Euphorbiaceae
DECIDUOUS AND EVERGREEN SHRUBS

✎	ZONES VARY BY SPECIES
☼ ☼	EXPOSURE NEEDS VARY BY SPECIES
◓	LITTLE WATER
◈	MILKY SAP CAN CAUSE STOMACH UPSET

Both species have decorative stems, but those of the first are bare most of the year. Both have inconspicuous red flowers concealed in tubular or slipper-shaped red bracts.

P. macrocarpus. LADY'S SLIP-PER. Deciduous. Zones 12, 13, 19–24. Native to Mexico. Grows to 5 ft. tall, and 2–3 ft. wide, with small, scanty leaves that drop soon after they emerge. The fleshy, waxy, whitish, forking, half-inch-thick stems are the main feature. Bears 1-in. bracts in late spring; may

Pedilanthus
tithymaloides smallii

repeat in summer after rainfall. Tolerates light shade, but has best form in full sun.

P. tithymaloides smallii 'Variegatus'. DEVIL'S BACK-BONE, JACOB'S LADDER. Evergreen. Zone H2; or indoors. Caribbean native to 1–2 ft. tall, with somewhat fleshy, zigzagging stems and 2–3-in., oval mid-green leaves. 'Variegatus' is a selection with grayish stems and leaves marked with white and pink; fairly common as a houseplant. Under good growing conditions, may produce ½-in. bracts in summer. Partial shade in Zone H2. Give houseplants bright indirect light; fertilize every couple of months during warm months, and keep soil barely moist.

PEEPUL. See FICUS religiosa

PELARGONIUM
GERANIUM
Geraniaceae
SHRUBBY PERENNIALS

✎	ZONES 8, 9, 12–24; A2, A3, 1–7, 10, 11 AS ANNUALS; OR INDOORS
☼ ☼	SOME SHADE IN HOTTEST CLIMATES; BRIGHT SUNNY WINDOW
◓ ◓	MODERATE TO REGULAR WATER

The common name "geranium" is widely used for *Pelargonium*—but botanically speaking, it is not really accurate. To the botanist, pelargoniums are woody-based

perennials (most of them native to South Africa) that endure light frosts but not hard freezes and have slightly asymmetrical flowers in clusters. True geraniums, on the other hand, are annuals and perennials (some woody-based) native mainly to the Northern Hemisphere, bearing symmetrical flowers either singly or in clusters. Some are weeds, while others are valued border or rock garden plants.

In the past, the commonly grown pelargoniums were *P.* × *domesticum*, Lady Washington pelargonium; *P.* × *hortorum*, common geranium (this group also includes variegated forms usually referred to as fancy-leafed or color-leafed geraniums); and *P. peltatum*, ivy geranium. Today, other kinds are increasingly available, including many with scented leaves.

Plants perform best in areas with warm, dry days and cool nights. They can be grown outdoors year-round where winters are very mild; in these areas, they bloom throughout warm weather. Zones 17 and 24 are ideal climates; next best are Zones 15, 16, 22, 23; possible but not as easy are Zones 8, 9, 12–14, 18–21. Elsewhere, they are summer annuals or houseplants. In cold-winter climates, move plants indoors before the first frost or take cuttings for next year.

Plant in any good, fast-draining soil. Amend poor alkaline soil with plenty of organic matter. Geraniums growing in good garden soil need little fertilizer; those in light sandy soil should receive two or three feedings during active growth. Remove faded flowers regularly to encourage new bloom. Pinch growing tips of young, small plants to force side branches. All geraniums do well in pots; they bloom best when somewhat potbound. Common pests include aphids, whiteflies, and spider mites. Geranium (tobacco) budworm may be a problem in some

Pelargonium × *domesticum*

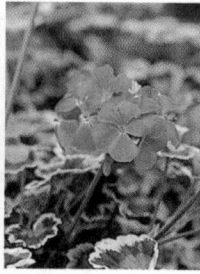

Pelargonium × *hortorum* 'Mrs. Pollock'

Pelargonium peltatum

Scented geranium *Pelargonium graveolens*

Scented geranium *Pelargonium* 'Charity'

P

areas; affected flowers look tattered or fail to open at all. Prevent or limit infestation by spraying plants with *Bacillus thuringiensis (Bt)*.

P. cordifolium (P. cordatum). Rounded plant to 4 ft. tall and wide, with 2½-in., dull green, toothed and lobed leaves. Loose clusters of reddish purple, 1-in. flowers. Good for borders.

P. × domesticum. LADY WASHINGTON PELARGONIUM, MARTHA WASHINGTON PELARGONIUM, REGAL GERANIUM. Erect or somewhat spreading, to 3 ft. tall and wide. Rangier than *P. × hortorum*. Heart-shaped to kidney-shaped leaves are dark green, 2–4 in. wide, with crinkled margins and unequal sharp teeth. Loose, rounded clusters of large (2-in. or wider), showy flowers; colors include white and many shades of pink, red, lavender, purple, with brilliant blotches and markings of darker colors. Can be planted in beds but tends to get rangy. First-class potted plant. Some varieties are used in hanging baskets.

Pelargonium × domesticum

P. × hortorum. COMMON GERANIUM, GARDEN GERANIUM. Succulent stemmed; reaches 1–2 ft. high and wide as an annual. In mild climates where geraniums grow as perennials, older plants become woody and can top 3 ft. Round or kidney-shaped leaves are velvety, hairy, and aromatic, with edges indistinctly lobed and scalloped. Most varieties show a zone of deeper color that looks like a thick halo around the center of the leaf, though some have plain green foliage. Single or double flowers are flatter and smaller than those of *P. × domesticum*, but clusters bear many more blossoms. Varieties are sold in white and shades of pink, rose, red, orange, lavender blue, and violet. Flowers may be solid colored, bicolored, speckled, or splashed with contrasting colors.

Common geraniums may be propagated from seed. Seed of open-pollinated varieties is inexpensive and routinely used to grow large numbers of plants for bedding. Hybrid strains, available from rather expensive seed, produce well-branched, uniform, colorful plants. The Maverick strain, which has an open habit, with many flowering stems and evenly green leaves, is a good example. There are also cactus-flowered, dwarf, and other novelty varieties.

Common geraniums propagated from cuttings are called zonal geraniums, whether or not they have dark-colored zones in the leaves. These plants are uniform, well branched, heat resistant, and available in many colors. Because they cost more than seed-grown geraniums, they're more often purchased for containers than for bedding out. Look for vigorous series such as Americana, Eclipse, and Rocky Mountain; each comes in a wide range of colors. There are also numerous zonal novelties on the market, including ones with speckled petals (such as the Avenida Mosaic series), and ones with single or double, star-shaped flowers (such as the Graffiti series).

Fancy-leaf varieties have zones, borders, or splashes of brown, deep purple, gold, red, white, and green in various combinations. Some also have highly attractive flowers. The Black Velvet series, which can be grown from seed, sports purplish black leaves edged in bright green, with large single- or multicolored blooms. 'Golden Ears', 1 ft. high and wide, has small, deeply cut, almost star-shaped leaves of deep bronzy red with a wide border of chartreuse; flowers are bright coral. 'Vancouver Centennial' is very similar if not identical. 'Mrs. Pollock' has green leaves with a red zone and a creamy yellow margin; it bears vermilion blooms.

P. peltatum. IVY GERANIUM. To 1–1½ ft. tall, trailing to 3–5 ft. wide. Rather succulent, glossy, bright green, 2–3-in.-wide leaves have pointed lobes and look something like those of ivy (*Hedera*). Inch-wide single or double flowers in rounded clusters of five to ten;

Pelargonium × hortorum

colors include white, pink, rose, red, and lavender. Upper petals may be blotched or striped. Many named varieties. The Freestyle series has a semitrailing habit and comes in a wide range of colors, including bicolors. 'L'Elegante' has white-edged foliage; other varieties are available with white or yellow veins in leaves. Summer Showers strain can be grown from seed, features blossoms in mixed colors (white, pink, red, lavender, magenta).

Crosses with zonal geraniums represent a relatively new direction for ivy geraniums. These hybrids combine the heat resistance, better branching, and heavier flowering of zonal geraniums with the glossy leaves and mounding, trailing habit of ivy geraniums. The Galleria series led the way, and the new Caliente series has developed it further; flowers of both series come primarily in the red, coral, and pink color range.

Use ivy geranium in hanging containers, window boxes, or raised beds; it also makes a good bank or ground cover (but not for erosion control). Because it does especially well with cool nights and bright days, ivy geranium is favored along the coast and in mountain gardens.

P. sidoides. Slow-growing; dense mound 1 ft. tall and wide. Silvery gray, heart-shaped leaves to 1½ in. across. Clusters of dark purple, ¾-in. flowers bloom on slender, branching, trailing stems.

P. 'Splendide'. Grows 1–1½ ft. high and wide, with spreading or stiffly trailing stems. Silvery gray, 1–1½-in.-long, oval leaves have slightly toothed edges. Distinctive blossoms, carried a few to a cluster, are 1–1¼ in. wide, have unusual coloring: the two upper petals are dark red, nearly black at the base, while the three lower ones are nearly white. Use in pots, hanging baskets. Often sold as *P. tricolor* or *P. violareum*.

Scented geraniums. Many aromatic species, hybrids, and selections are available. Most grow 1–3 ft. tall, spreading as wide as high. Foliage scent is the main draw; clusters of small, typically white or rosy flowers are secondary in appeal. Leaves vary in shape from nearly round to finely cut and almost ferny; they range in size from minute to 4 in. across. Common names usually refer to the fragrance of their leaves: almond geranium (*P. quercifolium*), apple geranium (*P. odoratissimum*), lime geranium (*P. nervosum*), nutmeg geranium (*P. × fragrans* 'Nutmeg'), peppermint geranium (*P. tomentosum*). There are several rose geraniums, including *P. capitatum*, *P.* 'Charity', *P. graveolens*, and *P.* 'Lady Plymouth'. Various types offer lemon fragrance, including *P. crispum* and *P.* 'Prince Rupert'. All scented geraniums are good for herb gardens, edgings, front of borders, window boxes, hanging baskets; peppermint geranium makes a good ground cover in frost-free gardens. Use fresh leaves of all types for flavoring jelly and iced drinks; use dried leaves in potpourri and sachets.

Scented geranium
Pelargonium tomentosum

Scented geranium
Pelargonium graveolens

PELLAEA

CLIFF-BRAKE
Polypodiaceae
FERNS

☑	ZONES VARY BY SPECIES
☼	FILTERED SUNLIGHT
◐◖◆	WATER NEEDS VARY BY SPECIES

Though these small to medium-size ferns are not striking in overall appearance, they have charmingly detailed foliage, with leaves divided into little narrow to roundish leaflets. Once established, they tolerate drier conditions than most other ferns do. All need well-drained soil.

P. andromedifolia. COFFEE FERN. Zones 7–9, 14–24. Native

P

to dry, stony places in California, southern Oregon, and Baja California. Grows slowly to 1–2 ft. high and wide. Thin, wiry stalks hold finely cut gray-green to bluish green fronds. Common name refers to the small leaflets, shaped somewhat like coffee beans. Grow in bright filtered light. Use in native landscapes, rock gardens. Little water.

P. atropurpurea. PURPLE STEM CLIFF-BRAKE. Zones 2–7, 14–17. Very cold-tolerant fern native from northeastern U.S. south to Guatemala. Grows 1–2 ft. high and wide, with arching fronds. Oblong to lance-shaped, bluish gray leaflets are held on purplish black midribs. Best in bright shade and alkaline soil. Use in rock gardens. Little water.

P. rotundifolia. BUTTON FERN. Zones 14–17, 19–24. From Australia, New Zealand. Grows 1–2 ft. high, 2 ft. wide. Spreading stalks hold small, evenly spaced, rounded leaflets that are dark green and leathery. Use for contrast with finer-textured ferns or in mixed container plantings, where fronds will spill attractively over the sides. Regular water. Pretty houseplant in bright indirect light; tolerates dry indoor air.

Pellaea rotundifolia

P. viridis. GREEN CLIFF-BRAKE. Zones 14–17, 19–24; H2. Native from Africa to India. Grows about 1 ft. high and wide, with shiny, bright green fronds. Oval to lance-shaped leaflets are held on glossy black stems. Thrives with regular water but will tolerate short periods of drought. Use as ground cover, in rock gardens, in containers.

PELTIPHYLLUM peltatum. See **DARMERA peltata**

PENCILBUSH, PENCIL TREE. See **EUPHORBIA tirucalli**

PENCIL CACTUS. See **OPUNTIA leptocaulis**

PENNISETUM
FOUNTAIN GRASS
Poaceae (Gramineae)
ANNUAL AND PERENNIAL GRASSES

- 🌿 ZONES VARY BY SPECIES
- ☀️ ◐ FULL SUN OR PARTIAL SHADE, EXCEPT AS NOTED
- 💧 💧 MODERATE TO REGULAR WATER, EXCEPT AS NOTED

Growing in fountainlike mounds, these are among the most graceful of ornamental grasses. They have long, narrow leaves and arching stems that bear furry, foxtail-like flower plumes in summer, with bloom often extending into fall. Use them in containers, in perennial or shrub borders, as bank covers.

P. alopecuroides. Perennial. Zones 2b–24. From eastern Asia. To 5 ft. high and wide. Clump of bright green foliage is topped by pinkish plumes. Leaves turn yellow in fall, brown in winter. The following reach about 3 ft. high and wide: 'Hameln' (white plumes), 'Moudry' (black plumes), 'Cassian' (light brown plumes, gold fall foliage with red tints). 'Little Bunny' is a dwarf form growing just 1½ ft. high and wide. The species and its varieties all can self-sow; 'Moudry' is an especially heavy self-seeder.

P. 'Burgundy Giant'. Perennial in frost-free zones 23, 24; H1, H2; grow as annual elsewhere. Believed to be a variant of a species from the East Indies. Bold, tropical-looking, very tender grass resembles a reddish purple corn plant. Grows 4–5 ft. tall and 2 ft. across, with foot-long leaves that are broader than those of most other fountain grasses (nearly 1½ in. wide). Foliage is held on strong, upright burgundy stems. Red-purple, 8–12-in.-long flower plumes appear on nodding stems above the foliage in midsummer; fade to cream in fall. Needs full sun and regular water.

P. 'Fairy Tails'. Perennial in Zones 8, 9, 14–24; annual elsewhere. Hybrid of uncertain parentage. Evergreen in mild-winter climates (where temperatures remain above 28°F/−2°C). Grows 3–5 ft. high and wide, with arching, narrow, blue-green leaves. Distinctly vertical, dark wheat–colored plumes appear above them from spring to summer. Plant in full sun. Reaches full size with regular water; grows smaller (but still attractive) under drier conditions.

P. glaucum 'Purple Majesty'. PURPLE MAJESTY ORNAMENTAL MILLET. Annual. Developed from a millet species from Asia and Africa that has long been cultivated for its edible seeds. Grows 3–5 ft. tall and 2–3 ft. wide, with huge, spear-shaped leaves up to 3 ft. long and 2 in. wide. Foliage is rich purple, darkest in full sun. Stiff, cylindrical, purple flower spikes up to 20 in. long appear atop foliage in midsummer. Cut bloom spikes before they mature and use them in dried arrangements, or leave them to reach maturity on the plant, where they'll attract birds. Easy to start from seed. Best in full sun with regular water.

P. orientale. Perennial. Zones 3–10, 14–24. From central and western Asia. To 2 ft. high, 2½ ft. wide, with pinkish plumes standing above a mound of green to gray-green foliage. Plumes mature to light brown; foliage turns straw colored in winter. Seldom self-sows. Two recommended selections grow taller: 'Karley Rose', to 3 ft., has an upright form with dark green foliage and deep pink plumes. 'Tall Tails', to 6 ft. tall, 4 ft. wide, has a more open form with light tan plumes; extremely heat tolerant.

P. setaceum. Perennial in Zones 8–24; H1, H2; often grown as an annual in colder climates. From tropical Africa, southwestern Asia, Arabian Peninsula. To 5 ft. high and wide. Forms a dense clump of medium green foliage; long plumes of coppery pink or purplish flowers are held within the clump or just above it. Dies back in winter, even in mild climates. Full sun. Can take supplemental irrigation but doesn't need any. In arid climates, thrives in gravel beds and other dry sites. Thanks to its heavy self-sowing, this species will threaten to crowd out native vegetation when planted near open country; it has become a rampant pest in the Hawaiian Islands. To prevent seeding, cut off flower plumes before seeds mature. 'Rubrum'

Pennisetum setaceum 'Rubrum'

('Cupreum') has purplish red leaves and rose-colored plumes that fade to beige. 'Eaton Canyon' ('Red Riding Hood') is similar in color but grows just 1½–2 ft. tall and wide; it is evergreen in frost-free areas. Neither usually sets seed. Some believe that these red-leafed plants belong to another species.

P. thunbergii 'Red Buttons' (P. massaicum 'Red Buttons'). RED BUNNY TAILS FOUNTAIN GRASS. Perennial in Zones 4–12, 14–24; annual elsewhere. Selection of a species from Africa. Sometimes offered as *P. messiacum*. Upright growth to about 2 ft. tall and wide, with very narrow, glossy green leaves with burgundy highlights. In spring and summer, foliage is topped by delicate, fuzzy, iridescent red flower plumes that fade to tan. Bloom spikes are 2–3 in. long, held on erect stems that bring plant height to 3 ft. Takes heat and drought but looks best with regular water.

P. villosum. FEATHERTOP. Perennial usually used as an annual. From Africa. Thin, cascading, medium green leaves form a mound about 3 ft. tall and wide. Foliage is topped in summer by soft, feathery, creamy white plumes that look great in fresh or dried arrangements. Easy to start from seed. Will self-sow. Best in full sun with regular water.

PENNYROYAL. See **MENTHA pulegium**

PENSTEMON
BEARD TONGUE
Scrophulariaceae
PERENNIALS

- 🌿 ZONES VARY BY SPECIES
- ☀️ ◐ PARTIAL SHADE IN HOTTEST CLIMATES
- 💧 💧 LITTLE TO MODERATE WATER, EXCEPT AS NOTED

There are some 250 species of penstemon. Most are native to the West, ranging from Canada into Mexico; some grow on highest mountains, some in the desert, others in forest glades, in foothills, on plains. A few are widely available, but most are sold only by specialists. Some of the perennials described here have woody-based stems, while others are herbaceous. Most species have narrowish, pointed leaves; those in basal foliage clump are larger, those on flower stems smaller. Narrowly bell-shaped, lipped flowers (usually ¾–1½ in. long) are most commonly seen in bright reds and blues, but they also come in shades from soft pink through salmon and peach to deep rose, lilac, dark purple, white, and, rarely, yellow. Blossoms of some species attract hummingbirds.

Need fast drainage. Species in particular benefit from rock garden conditions. Usually short lived (3 or 4 years). Hybrids and selections tend to be easier to grow than wild species alongside regular garden plants; wild kinds may die quickly if given too-rich soil and too much water. In dry years or with restricted water, however, plants of wild species may thrive.

P. alamosensis. Zones 3, 7–13, 18, 19. Native to southern New Mexico. Herbaceous growth to 2 ft. high and 1 ft. wide. Beautiful silver-gray, wavy-edged basal foliage. Coral flowers bloom in late spring for an extended period, often visited by hummingbirds.

P. ambiguus. PRAIRIE PENSTEMON, SAND PENSTEMON. Zones 2, 3, 7–15, 18–21. Native to south-central and southwestern U.S. Woody-based growth to 2 ft. high and wide. Grayish green, very narrow leaves. White to pink flowers come in broad (rather than tall) clusters that resemble those of phlox. Blooms from early summer to early fall. Needs heat and sandy soil to perform well. Spreads by underground stems where well adapted.

P. amphorellae. MEXICAN BLUE PENSTEMON. Zones 3b, 7–24. Native to high elevations in Mexico. Woody-based growth forms an airy shrublet to 1½ ft. high and wide, with pale green, very narrow leaves. Puffy light blue flowers bloom all summer.

P. baccharifolius. ROCK PENSTEMON. Zones 10–13. Native to southwestern Texas. Woody-based growth to 1½ ft. high and wide. Small, broad, glossy dark green leaves have a thick, leathery feel. Coral pink flowers bloom all summer and are very attractive to hummingbirds.

P. barbatus. SCARLET BUGLER. Zones 1–20; needs some winter chill for best performance. Native to mountain regions, from Colorado and Utah south to Mexico. Open, somewhat sprawling habit to 3 ft. or more tall, 1½ ft. wide. Bright green foliage. Long, loose spikes of red flowers over a long period, starting at some point from late spring to midsummer. One of the best penstemons for

humid-summer areas. Selections include foot-tall 'Elfin Pink', with clear pink flowers; 2½-ft. 'Rose Elf', with deep rose blooms; and 2-ft. 'Schooley's Yellow', with soft lemon yellow flowers.

P. cardinalis. Zones 2, 3, 7–24. Native to southern New Mexico and Texas. Leafy habit to 2½ ft. tall, 2 ft. wide. Large, leathery, dark green foliage. Dark red flowers bloom all summer; very popular with hummingbirds. Long-lived plant thrives even in areas with humid summers.

P. centranthifolius. SCARLET BUGLER. Zones 7–23. Native to Coast Ranges of California. To 2–3 ft. tall, 1½–2 ft. wide, with waxy gray leaves that vary from lance shaped to oval. Long spikes of narrow bright red flowers in spring or early summer.

P. clutei. SUNSET PENSTEMON. Zones 2, 3, 7–14, 18–21. Native to Sunset Crater in northern Arizona. Grows 2–3½ ft. tall and 2 ft. wide. Toothed, luminescent blue-gray foliage makes a nice contrast with pink flowers that bloom from late spring through much of the summer, frequented by hummingbirds. Excellent performer in the interior West. May self-sow.

P. cobaea. WILD FOXGLOVE, WILD SNAPDRAGON. Zones 2–11, 14–24. Native from Nebraska through the southern Great Plains to Texas. Herbaceous stems rise 1–2 ft. tall; plant spreads to 1 ft. wide. Foliage is bold, profuse, and dark green. Flowers to 2 in. long, the largest of the penstemon clan, appear in late spring or summer in shades of white, pink, lavender, or purple. Long-lived plant. Regular water. Prairie Splendor is a hybrid seed strain with *P. triflorus* that includes rose and burgundy flower colors.

P. cordifolius. See Keckiella cordifolia

P. davidsonii (P. menziesii davidsonii). Zones 1–7, 14, 15. Native to high mountains of Sierra Nevada and western Nevada, north to British Columbia. Forms a mat 4–8 in. high, 1½ ft. wide. Small dark green leaves; violet-blue flowers in midsummer. Prefers snow cover in winter;

without it, hardy only to about −10°F/−23°C. Regular water.

P. digitalis. Zones 1–9, 14–24. Native to eastern and central U.S. To 3–5 ft. tall, 2–3 ft. wide, with long, medium green leaves and clusters of white or pale pink flowers in summer. Tolerates heat and humidity. Regular water. 'Husker Red' grows to 2½–3 ft. tall and has maroon foliage and pinkish white flowers.

P. eatonii. FIRECRACKER PENSTEMON. Zones 1–3, 7–13, 18–21. Native to mountains of desert Southwest. This scarlet-flowered species is similar to *P. centranthifolius*. Grows 1–3 ft. tall and wide and has lance-shaped, leathery green leaves, sometimes with a whitish bloom (but without a waxy coating). Flowers appear on tall spikes in spring to early summer. Tolerates heat.

P. grandiflorus. SHELL-LEAF PENSTEMON, WILD SNAPDRAGON. Zones 1–3, 10. Native to the Great Plains. To 3½ ft. tall, 10 in. wide, with waxy, rounded, pale gray-green leaves. Large (to 1¾-in.) pink to lavender-blue flowers in summer. 'Prairie Snow' has pure white blooms. Prairie Jewel is a silvery-leafed seed strain 1½–3 ft. high, bearing flowers in colors ranging from white through rosy pink to lavender and deep purple. War Axe is a deeper-colored seed strain hybridized with a species from the south-central U.S. The species and its various forms are excellent plants for Rocky Mountain and Great Plains states.

P. heterophyllus. Zones 7–24. California native of variable appearance, with glossy bluish green foliage and crowded spikes of narrow blossoms ranging from reddish purple to deep blue. Blooms in spring and early summer. The following grow 1½–2 ft. high and 2–3 ft. wide: 'Margarita', with sky blue fowers that fade to purple; 'Blue Bedder', with bright blue blossoms; and *P. h. purdyi*, with darker green foliage than the species and rosy lavender to intense blue flowers.

P. hybrids. BORDER PENSTEMON, GARDEN PENSTEMON. Perennials in Zones 6–9, 14–24; treated as annuals elsewhere

Penstemon digitalis

(grow as winter annual in Zones 12, 13). All are compact, bushy, upright plants to 2–4 ft. tall and 3 ft. wide, with narrow green leaves. Large (to 2-in.) summer flowers in loose spikes at stem ends, in almost all colors but blue and yellow. Mass these plants in borders or group with other summer-flowering plants. Where grown as perennials, set out nursery transplants in fall for bloom in late spring and early summer. After the flowers fade, cut back to side growth for another round of bloom in late summer, early fall. This group of penstemons prefers regular water but is subject to root rot in wet, heavy soils.

Among the many hybrids are pale lilac 'Alice Hindley' ('Lady Hindley'); pale pink 'Apple Blossom'; dark maroon 'Blackbird'; 'Evelyn', with rosy pink blooms marked inside with dark pink; scarlet 'Firebird'; wine red 'Garnet'; 'Holly's White', white with pink tinge; and dark purple 'Midnight'. True 'Sour Grapes' has flowers in a combination of violet and metallic blue, but some plants sold under this name may have bright red-violet blooms. The Kissed series features white-throated blooms with lips in bright colors: 'Cerise Kissed', 'Coral Kissed', 'Violet Kissed', 'Wine Kissed'.

P. linarioides coloradoensis. Zones 2, 3, 7–11. Native to Colorado, the Southwest, and Mexico. A small shrublet or semiprostrate mat, growing 8–12 in. high and wide, with needlelike silvery foliage that makes the plant attractive even out of bloom. Lavender or pale blue flowers with white throats appear in profusion in late spring and early summer. Quite long lived. *P.* 'Silverton' is a commercial selection of this species.

P. mensarum. GRAND MESA PENSTEMON. Zones 2, 3, 10. Native to western Colorado. Herbaceous stems 2–3 ft. high and

Penstemon heterophyllus purdyi

1–1½ ft. wide. Dark green basal foliage. In spring, bears the most fiercely brilliant dark blue flowers of the cultivated penstemons. Excellent performer in mountain regions. Tolerates considerable shade and thrives with moderate watering.

P. Mexicali hybrids. Zones 1–3, 10. Bushy growth to 1½ ft. high and wide, with profuse, narrow, shiny green leaves. Blossoms of 'Pike's Peak Purple' are violet, those of 'Red Rocks' bright rose. Burgundy and pink forms are also available. Highly recommended for Rocky Mountain and Great Plains states; rival the border penstemons for showiness of leaf and flower, yet are much hardier to cold. Bloom all summer. Do well with moderate water but tolerate regular moisture.

P. newberryi. MOUNTAIN PRIDE. Zones 1–9, 14–19. Native to higher elevations of the Sierra Nevada. To 1½ ft. high, 3 ft. wide; woody at base. Gray leaves are thick, roundish, tooth edged, ½–1½ in. long. Rose red, ½-in. flowers in summer. Regular water.

P. palmeri. SCENTED PENSTE-MON. Zones 2, 3, 10–13. Native to mountains of desert Southwest. To 4–6 ft. tall and 2–3 ft. wide, with thick grayish blue leaves. This is among the few scented penste-mons, with flower stalks bearing fragrant light pink blossoms in early summer. Will bloom first year from seed. Thrives in hot, dry con-ditions. Sandy or gravelly soil is essential.

P. parryi. PARRY'S PENSTE-MON. Zones 3, 10, 12, 13. Native from Arizona into Mexico. To 2–4 ft. tall and 1–3 ft. wide, with leathery gray-green leaves. Many flower stalks bear reddish pink blossoms in spring. Self-sows.

P. pinifolius. Zones 2–24. Native to southern New Mexico and Arizona. Woody-based growth to 1½ ft. high, 2 ft. wide, with short, needlelike bright green leaves crowded along stems. Red-orange summer flowers. For rock garden, border, small-scale ground cover. Good in dry gardens or regularly watered ones. 'Mersea Yellow', to 1 ft. by 1½ ft., has soft yellow flowers. 'Shades of Mango', about 15 in. tall and wide, has orange and yellow flowers on the same plant.

P. procumbens. MAT PENSTE-MON. Zones 2, 3, 7–10, 14–17. Colorado native. Creeping woody stems form mats 1–2 in. high and eventually 2–3 ft. wide. Tiny, rounded foliage resembles that of thyme (*Thymus*). Dark violet-blue

flowers cover the plant in spring. Often erroneously labeled *P. caespi-tosus* 'Claude Barr'. Tolerates some shade, is long lived, and has proved adaptable to many diverse cli-mates. Other ground-hugging pen-stemons of note, also with blue or purple flowers, are *P. caespitosus*, *P. crandallii*, and *P. teucrioides*.

P. pseudospectabilis. DESERT BEARD TONGUE. Zones 2, 3, 10, 12–21. Native to mountains of Southern California and Arizona. Shrubby, upright plant 2–4 ft. tall, 2 ft. wide. Large bluish green leaves with bases that clasp the stems. Rosy pink to purple flowers from spring into summer.

Penstemon hybrid

P. richardsonii. Zones 2–10, 14–21. Native to the Pacific Northwest. Woody grower 1–1½ ft. high and wide, with toothed, blue-green foliage. Rose, pink, lavender, or white flowers bloom in late summer for an extended period. Grows well in many climates. Tolerates some shade and may self-sow.

P. rostriflorus. Zones 3, 7, 10–13, 18–24. Southwestern native. Woody-based plant 1½ ft. high and wide, with narrow, olive green foliage. Orange-red flowers bloom midsummer into autumn, attracting hummingbirds. Long lived in loose soils. Formerly known as *P. bridgesii*.

P. rupicola. ROCK PENSTE-MON. Zones 2–7, 14–17. Native to Cascades and Siskiyou Mountains. Woody-based growth to 4 in. high, 1½ ft. wide, with trailing, much-branched stems. Small, roundish blue-green leaves have finely toothed edges. Bright rose flowers bloom from late spring into sum-mer. Beautiful in rock gardens or chinks in dry stone walls. White-flowered 'Albus' needs partial shade for best bloom.

P. rydbergii. Zones 1–7, 14–16. Native to many of the northern mountainous areas of the West.

Leafy stems rise 1–2 ft. high and 1½ ft. wide over bright green basal foliage mats. Many small blue flowers in dense whorls bloom in early summer. Excellent, long lived performer in cool mountain regions. Regular to ample water.

P. spectabilis. ROYAL BEARD TONGUE. Zones 7, 14–23. Native to Southern California. To 3–4½ ft. tall and wide, with smooth green or grayish leaves that clasp the stems. Rose-colored to purplish flowers in spring, early summer.

P. strictus. ROCKY MOUNTAIN PENSTEMON. Zones 1–3, 10–13. Native from southern Wyoming to Arizona and New Mexico. To 2–3 ft. tall, 2 ft. wide. Dark green leaves turn purplish in winter. Blooms in early summer, producing large blossoms in near-violet to brilliant bluish purple. Long lived and adaptable.

P. superbus. Zones 12, 13. Native to northern Mexico. To 3–4 ft. tall and wide, with gray-green leaves that blacken when they dry out. Deep rose to red flowers in spring or early summer.

P. triflorus. HILL COUNTRY PENSTEMON. Zones 3, 7–9, 10–14. Native to central Texas. Herbaceous plant 1½–2 ft. high and 1–1½ ft. wide, with rich green foliage. Pink, rose, or white flowers bloom in spring. Long lived and adaptable, performing well in the Southwest as well as in more humid areas.

PENTAS lanceolata

STAR CLUSTERS
Rubiaceae
PERENNIAL OFTEN GROWN
AS ANNUAL

☘ ZONES 23, 24; H1, H2; ANYWHERE AS ANNUAL
☼ FULL SUN
◐ REGULAR WATER

Woody-based perennial from trop-ical Africa. In Hawaii, it grows as large as 6 ft. tall, 3 ft. wide; else-where, it reaches 2–3 ft. high and

Pentas lanceolata

wide. Stems are topped by tight, 4-in.-wide clusters of small, star-shaped flowers in white, pink, lilac, or red. As a perennial, it provides nearly year-round color; as an annual, it blooms in summer. Good cut flowers. Green, somewhat hairy leaves are pointed ovals to 6 in. long. Prune plant heavily each year before spring growth begins to keep it compact and encourage flowering. Deadhead regularly for more blooms. Can be used as a houseplant; set in a bright west- or south-facing window.

PEONY. See **PAEONIA**

PEPINO.
See **SOLANUM muricatum**

PEPPER

Solanaceae
ANNUAL

☘ ALL ZONES
☼ FULL SUN
◐ REGULAR WATER

Vegetable native to tropical South America. All peppers grow on attractive bushy plants ranging from less than a foot high to 4 ft. tall. Peppers are classified as sweet or hot, but breeders have blurred the distinction by developing hot bell peppers and sweet jalapeños.

Bell pepper

Sweet peppers remain mild even after they ripen and change color. This group includes the big stuff-ing and salad peppers commonly called bell peppers. The best known is 'California Wonder', which starts green and ripens red. Others start green or purple, then ripen yellow, orange, or even brown. Hybrids have been bred for early ripening, high yield, and/or disease resistance. Other sweet types include sweet cherry pep-pers, used for pickling; long, slender Italian frying peppers and Hungarian sweet yellow peppers, both used for cooking; and thick-walled, very sweet pimientos (sometimes called pimentos), used in salads, cooking, and canning. (Allspice, also called pimento, is not a pepper but a spicy seasoning made from the fruits of a tree native to Jamaica.)

Hot pepper
'Cayenne'

Hot peppers (chiles) vary from pea-size types to narrow, 6–7-in.-long forms, but all are pungent, ranging from mildly hot Italian peperoncini to nearly incandescent habanero strains like 'Red Savina'. Among the most popular hot peppers are jalapeños, used fresh, dried, or pickled. Others include 'Anaheim', a mildly spicy pepper from New Mexico used for making canned green chiles and the attractively strung bunches called ristras; 'Cayenne', usually dried, powdered, and used as a spice; and 'Hungarian Yellow Wax (Hot)' and 'Fresno Chile Grande', mostly used for pickling and cooking. Mexican cooking calls for a wide variety of hot peppers, among them 'Ancho', 'Mulato', and 'Pasilla'.

Peppers need a long, warm growing season, so in most areas they must be planted outdoors as seedlings in order to produce fruit. In regions with cool or short summers, extend the season by using floating row covers and clear plastic mulches. Sow seed indoors 8 to 10 weeks before the average last-frost date. When the soil is thoroughly warm and night temperatures remain consistently above 55°F/13°C, set seedlings outdoors, spacing them 1½–2 ft. apart. After plants are established (but before blossoms set), give them one or two applications of a balanced liquid fertilizer.

Allow 60 to 95 days from planting to harvest. Most peppers can be picked green or purple after they have reached good size, but flavor typically becomes fuller and sweeter as fruit ripens into its mature color. Pick pimientos only when red-ripe. To harvest any kind

---

Paul Bosland on Pepper Flavor

Horticulture professor Dr. Paul Bosland, director of the Chile Pepper Institute at New Mexico State University at Las Cruces, is internationally recognized as a chile breeder. On campus, he's fondly referred to as Chile Man, and when he talks about peppers, you know you're in the presence of a connoisseur.

The complex flavor of tabascos, he explains, has 23 components, while bell peppers and jalapeños are dominated by only one taste—but it ranks as the single most potent flavor in the world.

From mild to wild, here are some of Bosland's favorites.

For heat-free sweetness, try a salad laced with 'Red Heart' pimientos.

Sample moderate heat by making salsa with multicolored 'NuMex Piñata' jalapeños. They're beautiful and full flavored.

Test your tongue's fire tolerance by cooking up a batch of buffalo wings with 'Red Savina' habaneros. The world's hottest pepper, they are more than 100 times as hot as 'NuMex Piñata'.

For the curious but cautious, 'NuMex Suave Red' offers full habanero flavor at very low heat levels.

---

of pepper, snip the stem with hand pruners or scissors. Possible pests include aphids, whiteflies, and cutworms. To control pepper weevils (both the larvae and adults attack fruit), destroy infested plants after harvest.

PEPPER GRASS.
See **CRESS, GARDEN**

PEPPERIDGE.
See **NYSSA sylvatica**

PEPPERMINT.
See **MENTHA × piperita**

PEPPERMINT TREE.
See **AGONIS flexuosa**

PEPPER TREE. See **SCHINUS**

PEPPERWOOD.
See **UMBELLULARIA californica**

PERICALLIS × hybrida.
See **SENECIO × hybridus**

PERILLA frutescens
SHISO
Lamiaceae (Labiatae)
ANNUAL

☀	ALL ZONES
☀ ☀	FULL SUN OR LIGHT SHADE
●	REGULAR WATER

Native from the Himalayas to eastern Asia. Sturdy, leafy warm-weather plant grows very quickly to 2–3 ft. tall, 1 ft. wide. Broadly ovate, deeply toothed leaves reach 5 in. long. The kind most commonly seen has bronzy or purple leaves that look much like those of coleus. Fancy Fringe strain has deeply cut and fringed leaves in dark bronzy purple.

Perilla frutescens

Shiso makes an attractive addition to summer borders, but various parts of the plant are also edible. Use leaves as a vegetable or flavoring (they taste something like mint, something like cinnamon); fry the long, thin clusters of flower buds in tempura batter and serve as a vegetable. In Asia, the seeds are pressed for edible oil. Extremely easy to grow; self-sows freely.

PERIWINKLE. See **CATHARANTHUS roseus, VINCA**

PERNETTYA mucronata.
See **GAULTHERIA mucronata**

PEROVSKIA
RUSSIAN SAGE
Lamiaceae (Labiatae)
SHRUBBY PERENNIALS

☀	ZONES 2–24
☀	FULL SUN
○ ●	LITTLE TO MODERATE WATER

Native to western and central Asia. Woody-based clump with many grayish white, upright-growing stems clothed in gray-green foliage. Leaves on lower part of stem are 2–3 in. long and deeply

---

cut; those toward stem tip are smaller and merely toothed. In late spring and summer, stems are topped with widely branched sprays of small lavender-blue flowers that seem to form a soft haze above the foliage. To extend the bloom season, trim off spent blossoms. Mature clumps may reach 3–4 ft. tall and wide; they often colonize, spreading by underground stems to send up new clumps. Can be invasive where well adapted.

Perovskia 'Blue Spire'

Russian sage is typically marketed as *P. atriplicifolia*, but most plants sold are probably hybrids between *P. atriplicifolia* and *P. abrotanoides*. Widely grown 'Blue Spire', with deep violet blooms, is sometimes sold as *P. atriplicifolia* 'Superba' or *P.* 'Longin'. For lighter blue flowers, grow 'Blue Mist' or 'Blue Haze'. 'Filagran' has silvery, very finely cut leaves. Mass plants or use them individually in borders. Takes any soil as long as drainage is good. Extremely resistant to heat and drought. Performs best in warm summers. Cut nearly to the ground each spring before new growth starts.

PERSEA americana.
See **AVOCADO**

PERSEA thunbergii
(Machilus thunbergii)
Lauraceae
EVERGREEN TREE

☀	ZONES 8, 9, 14–24
☀	FULL SUN
●	REGULAR WATER

From Japan, China, and Korea. Related to camphor tree (*Cinnamomum*) and avocado, this large tree grows fairly fast to 60–80 ft. tall, 40–60 ft.

Persea thunbergii ▶

P

wide. Thick, glossy leaves are deep green above, paler beneath, to 6 in. long, 2½ in. wide. Tiny yellowish flowers bloom in spring; these are followed in summer by round, blackish purple fruits less than ½ in. wide. A promising tree for parks, streets, or large gardens.

PERSIAN SHIELD.
See **STROBILANTHES dyeranus**

PERSIAN VIOLET.
See **EXACUM affine**

PERSICARIA
KNOTWEED
Polygonaceae
PERENNIALS

🗲 **ZONES VARY BY SPECIES**

☼ ◐ **FULL SUN OR PARTIAL SHADE**

◉ **REGULAR WATER, EXCEPT AS NOTED**

Sturdy plants with jointed stems and small white or pink flowers. Some kinds tend to get out of hand and need to be controlled.

P. affinis (Polygonum affine). Zones 1–9, 14–17. Himalayan native. Spreading plant to 1 ft. high, 2 ft. or more wide. Deep green, lance-shaped, finely tooth-edged leaves are mostly basal; they grow 2–4½ in. long, turn bronze in winter. Dense, erect, 2–3-in. spikes of bright rosy red flowers bloom in summer, early fall. Informal border or ground cover. 'Darjeeling Red' forms 3-in.-high foliage mats, has 10-in. spikes of deep pink flowers that age to red; its foliage turns red in fall. 'Superba' ('Dimity') has pale pink flowers and larger leaves than the species.

P. amplexicaulis (Polygonum amplexicaule). Zones 2b–9, 14–24. Himalayan native. Forms a big clump—to 4 ft. tall and wide when plants are in flower. Medium green leaves are pointed ovals up to 10 in. long. Blooms profusely from midsummer to fall, bearing narrow, 4-in. blossom spikes simi-lar to those of lavender but in a wider range of colors—pink, pur-ple, red, white.

P. bistorta (Polygonum bis-torta). Zones 2–9, 14–24. Native to Eurasia. Makes a clump to 2½ ft. tall, 3 ft. wide, with broadly oval, medium green, 4–12-in.-long leaves. Tight, 2–3-in. spikes of pale pink or white flowers bloom from late spring until well into summer. 'Superba' is a good pink selection.

P. capitata (Polygonum capi-tatum). Perennial in Zones 8, 9,

12–24; annual in colder climates. Himalayan native. Tough, trailing ground cover 3–6 in. high; spreads indefinitely both by rooting stems and by self-seeding. Oval, 1½-in.-long leaves are dark green when new, take on pinkish overtones when mature. Leaves of all ages have a bronzy cast that deepens in cooler weather; they discolor and die below 28°F/−2°C. Stems and small, round flower heads are pink. Blooms almost all year in mild climates. Best in confined spots (where it won't be able to spread) or in uncultivated areas. No irriga-tion needed.

P. vacciniifolia (Polygonum vacciniifolium). Zones 4–7, 15–17. Himalayan native. Prostrate plant forms a foliage mat to 3 in. high, trailing to 2 ft. or wider. Slender, branching, red-dish stems are clothed in oval, ½-in.-long, shiny green leaves that turn red in fall. In late sum-mer, 6–9-in. flower stalks bear dense, upright, foxtail-like, 2–3-in. spikes of rose pink blos-soms. Excellent as a bank cover or for draping over a boulder in a large rock garden.

P. virginiana (Polygonum vir-ginianum, Tovara virginiana). Zones 2–9, 14–17. Native to eastern North America, eastern Asia. To 2–4 ft. tall, spreading indefinitely

Persicaria virginiana
'Painter's Palette'

by creeping rhizomes. Oval green leaves 3–10 in. long; insignificant flowers. The species is rarely found in gardens. More commonly seen is 'Painter's Palette', valued for its flashy foliage: leaves are marbled in green, pale gray green, and ivory, with a ragged chocolate maroon V in the center. On new growth, the ivory patches are closer to yellow, and the central V-shaped mark has a pink cast.

PERSIMMON
Ebenaceae
DECIDUOUS FRUIT TREES

🗲 **ZONES VARY BY SPECIES**

☼ **FULL SUN**

◉◐ **WATER NEEDS VARY BY SPECIES**

Two kinds of persimmons are grown in the West. The native American species is a bigger, more cold-tolerant tree than the Japanese species, but the latter type bears larger fruit and is the sort sold in markets. Both species have inconspicuous flowers, and both are tolerant of many soils (as long as drainage is good) and resistant to oak root fungus.

Japanese or Oriental persimmon *(Diospyros kaki)* grows and fruits best in Zones 6–9, 14–16, 18–24, H1 (fruit-ing may be inconsistent in Hawaii—does best in dry highlands). It reaches 30 ft. tall (or more) and at least as wide. Has a handsome branch pattern and is one of the best fruit trees for ornamental use; makes a good small shade tree or espalier. Leaves are light green when new, matur-ing to dark green, leathery ovals 6–7 in. long. Foliage turns vivid yellow, orange, or red in fall (even in mild climates). After leaves drop, brilliant orange-scarlet, 3–4-in. fruits brighten the tree for weeks and persist until winter unless harvested. Sets fruit without pollination, though pollinated trees often produce tastier, more abun-dant crops.

Persimmon

Prune trees when they are young to establish a good frame-work; thereafter, prune only to remove dead wood, shape the tree, or open up a too dense interior. Remove any suckers that shoot up from below the graft line.

Fruit drop is a common prob-lem in young trees. To avoid it, water regularly and feed once in late winter or early spring; too little or inconsistent mois-ture causes fruit drop, as does overfertilizing.

Some Japanese persimmon varieties are astringent until soft-ripe—at which stage they become very sweet. To save the crop from birds, pick fruit when fully colored but still hard, then let it ripen off the tree. Eat when the flesh is

mushy and puddinglike. Non-astringent varieties are hard (like apples) when ripe, with a mildly sweet flavor; they can be eaten hard, but their flavor improves when they are allowed to soften slightly off the tree.

'Chocolate'. Nonastringent. Medium-size, acorn-shaped fruit. When pollinated, has seeded flesh with dark streaks; when unpolli-nated, has seedless yellow-orange flesh. Fruit from pollinated trees has best flavor.

'Early Fuyu'. Nonastringent. Ripens several weeks earlier than 'Fuyu' and is a good choice where growing seasons are too short or cool to ripen later varieties.

'Fuyu'. Nonastrin-gent. Firm fleshed; about the size of a baseball but flattened like a tomato. Favorite variety in Hawaii. 'Jiro' is very similiar and often mis-labled as 'Fuyu'. Similar but larger is 'Gosho', widely sold as 'Giant Fuyu'.

'Hachiya'. Astringent. Big, slightly pointed fruit. Very shapely tree for ornamental use.

'Izu'. Nonastringent. Medium-size, round fruit borne on a tree about half the standard size. Ripens early.

'Maru'. Like 'Chocolate', non-astringent and seeded if pollinized by another variety. Medium-size, round fruit with shiny, orange-red skin. Flesh is dark cinnamon colored and has best flavor when seeded.

'Nishimura Wase' ('Coffee Cake'). Nonastringent when pollenized by another variety. Large, round fruit with spicy-sweet, chocolate-colored flesh when pollenized. Early. Good choice in climates too cool to ripen 'Fuyu'. Use 'Chocolate' as a pollenizer.

'Saijo'. Astringent. Hardy, pro-ductive, early-ripening variety with sweet, elongated, dull yellow fruit. One of the most reliable for the Pacific Northwest. Hardy.

'Tamopan'. Astringent. Large, acorn-shaped fruit.

American persimmon *(Dio-spyros virginiana)*, native to the eastern U.S., grows best in Zones 3–9, 14–16, 18–23. Can grow to 15–30 ft. high and about as wide, with attractive gray-brown bark that is fissured in a checkered pat-tern. Glossy green, broadly oval leaves to 6 in. long turn yellow, pink, or reddish purple in fall.

Round, 1½–2-in.-wide fruit is yellow to orange (often blushed red); very astringent until soft-ripe, then very sweet. On wild species, fruit ripens in early fall after frost; some varieties do not require winter chill. Both male and female trees are usually needed to get fruit. 'Meader' is self-fruitful; its fruit is seedless if not pollinated. 'Early Golden' has more flavorful fruit; it needs cross-pollination for best crop. Trees usually need pruning only to remove broken or dead branches. Does best with regular moisture but will also perform well with moderate water.

'Russian Beauty' and 'Nikita's Gift', developed in Russia, are hybrids between American and Japanese persimmons. They are as hardy as American persimmon, with larger fruit (2–2½ in. across) that is sweet and flavorful when allowed to fully soften.

PERUVIAN LILY.
See **ALSTROEMERIA**

PERUVIAN OLD MAN CACTUS.
See **ESPOSTOA lanata**

PETALOSTEMON purpureum

PURPLE PRAIRIE CLOVER
Fabaceae (Leguminosae)
PERENNIAL

🌿	ZONES 1–3, 10–12
☀	FULL SUN
◐ ●	LITTLE TO MODERATE WATER

Native from Saskatchewan to Texas. Attractive perennial for the wild garden. To 1½ ft. high and wide, with many rigid, outward-leaning stems covered with dark green leaves. In summer, stems are tipped with tight heads of small reddish purple flowers. Deep roots supply fertility to the soil through nitrogen-fixing bacteria. This is a tough plant, well suited to the extremes of its native prairies and

Petalostemon purpureum

plains. Tolerates any soil. Botanists are divided as to its exact classification; many include it in the genus *Dalea* and identify it as *D. gattingeri*.

PETASITES japonicus

JAPANESE COLTSFOOT, FUKI
Asteraceae (Compositae)
PERENNIAL

🌿	ZONES 2B–9, 14–17
☀ ◐ ●	FULL SUN IN COOLER CLIMATES ONLY
💧	AMPLE WATER

Giant perennial for perpetually moist locales near ponds, streams. Creeping rhizomes give rise to big (2½-ft.-wide), round leaves on edible, 3-ft.-long stalks that are used by the Japanese as a vegetable (called fuki). Short, thick spikes of fragrant white daisies appear in early spring before the leaves

Petasites japonicus

emerge. Locate this plant with care; its thick rhizomes are invasive, and the plant can be difficult to eradicate. *P. j. giganteus* has leaves to 4 ft. wide on 5-ft. stalks. Its selection 'Variegatus', with 3–4-ft. stalks, has 2–3-ft.-wide leaves with bold white markings.

PETREA volubilis

QUEEN'S WREATH, SANDPAPER VINE
Verbenaceae
EVERGREEN VINE

🌿	ZONES 19–24; H1, H2
☀	FULL SUN
●	REGULAR WATER

Woody vine native to Mexico, Central America, and the West Indies. Twines to 20–40 ft. but can easily be kept smaller. Elliptical deep green leaves 8 in. long have a sandpapery surface. Stunning floral display: pendent, foot-long clusters of star-shaped, blue-purple, 1½-in.-wide blossoms. Blue calyxes hang on after the petals drop. Main bloom period comes in winter and spring in Hawaii, late spring and summer in California; lesser displays occur at other times during warm weather.

Petrea volubilis

Beautiful plant trained on arbor or pergola, along eaves, on a high wall. Flowers are sometimes used in leis. Grow this vine in organically enriched, moist but well-drained soil. Provide support for climbing stems. Prune and thin growth as needed in winter. Wind resistant. Frost sensitive; may need some protection in Zones 19–22.

PETROSELINUM crispum

PARSLEY
Apiaceae (Umbelliferae)
BIENNIAL GROWN AS ANNUAL

🌿	ZONES A3; 1–24
☀ ◐	AFTERNOON SHADE IN HOTTEST CLIMATES
●	REGULAR WATER

From southern Europe. Two kinds of parsley are grown, both with finely cut dark green foliage: flat-leafed Italian parsley and curly-leafed French parsley. Leaves are used as a seasoning (both fresh and dried); fresh sprigs and minced leaves are classic garnishes. Flat-leafed parsley grows to 2–3 ft. tall and 2 ft. wide; it is considered more flavorful than curly parsley, which grows to 6–12 in. high and wide and makes a more attractive garnish.

Parsley is best started fresh each year, either from nursery transplants or seed. Set out small plants or sow seed in place—in spring after average last-frost date

Petroselinum crispum

in cold-winter climates; in fall or early spring where winters are mild; in early fall in low desert. Soak seeds in warm water for 24 hours before planting. (Even after soaking, they may not come up for several weeks; according to an old story, parsley seeds must go to the devil and back before sprouting.) Thin seedlings to 1–1½ ft. apart for flat-leafed parsley, 6–8 in. apart for curly parsley; or space plants at these distances. Attractive edging for herb, flower, or vegetable garden; good in window boxes and pots.

PETUNIA

Solanaceae
PERENNIALS GROWN AS ANNUALS

🌿	ALL ZONES
☀	FULL SUN
●	REGULAR WATER

Low-growing, bushy to spreading plants with thick, broad leaves that are slightly sticky to the touch. Flowers vary from funnel-shaped single blooms to densely double, heavily ruffled ones (like carnations). The many colors available include pure white, cream, yellow, and the whole range of reds and blues: from soft pink to deepest red, light blue to deepest purple. Bicolors and picotees are also available, as are types that have contrasting veins on the petals and kinds with fluted or fringed edges. In most climate zones, plants bloom throughout summer until frost. In Zones 12 and 13, summer heat kills them; in these areas, grow them for winter and spring color.

Plants thrive in good garden soil. Single-flowered kinds are not particular about soil quality and will tolerate alkalinity, but they must have good drainage. Space 8–18 in. apart, depending on plant size. After plants are established, pinch back halfway to encourage compact growth. Feed most kinds monthly with a complete liquid fertilizer; hungry trailing petunias—referred to by growers as the teenage boys of the plant world—do best when given controlled-release fertilizer at planting time in addition to weekly applications of liquid fertilizer. Near the end of the main bloom period, cut back rangy plants by half to force new growth. In humid weather, botrytis disease can damage blossoms and foliage of most petunias; Multifloras are somewhat resistant to this disease. Smog damage

P

(spotting on seedling leaves) and geranium (tobacco) budworm (flowers look tattered or fail to open) may cause problems in some areas.

The following petunia categories are still relevant, but as new hybrids and forms are being developed, some growers are starting to reclassify petunias—especially cutting-grown varieties—by flower size alone, designating them as having large, medium-, or mini-size flowers (instead of Hybrid Grandiflora, Hybrid Multiflora, and Hybrid Milliflora).

For the petunia relative called million bells, see *Calibrachoa*.

Hybrid Grandiflora. These hybrid plants bear the largest flowers of all petunia classes but bloom the least profusely. Sturdy plants grow 15–27 in. high and 2–3 ft. across. Flowers are usually single, to 4½ in. across, with ruffled or fringed edges; colors include pink, rose, salmon, red, scarlet, blue, white, pale yellow, and striped combinations.

Petunia

Fluffy Ruffles strain has the largest blossoms, growing to 6 in. across. Cascade, Countdown, and Supercascade series plants have a trailing habit that makes them good selections for hanging baskets. Magic and Supermagic are compact, heavy-blooming plants bearing large (4–5-in.) single flowers in white, pink, red, or blue. Other popular strains are weather-tolerant Storm, compact and ruffled Ultra, cascading Cloud, and Hula Hoop and Frost (both with white-rimmed blossoms). 'Prism Sunshine' is a much-improved yellow. Double Hybrid Grandifloras have heavily ruffled flowers that come in all petunia colors except yellow.

Hybrid Multiflora. This hybrid group is sometimes called Floribunda. Plants are about the same size as Grandifloras, but flowers are single or double, generally smooth edged, and smaller (to 2 in. across). Neat, compact growth makes them ideal for bedding and massing. Many named varieties in pink, rose, salmon, yellow, white, or blue. Joy and Plum strains have single, satiny-textured flowers in

white, cream, pink, coral, red, or blue. 'Summer Sun' has bright yellow single blooms. Prime Time and the rain-tolerant Celebrity strains have single flowers somewhat larger than those of the typical Hybrid Multiflora, and flowers in the Whispers series come in more than a dozen colors.

Hybrid Milliflora. These dwarf petunias form mounds 6–8 in. high and wide; they need no pinching or pruning. Plants cover themselves with small (1–1½-in.) flowers that come in all petunia colors except yellow. Effective planted in groups of a single color; very attractive in containers, hanging baskets, and window boxes. Fantasy is a single-flowered seed-grown strain, while Tiny Tunia is a cutting-grown series. Both come in a wide range of colors, and Tiny Tunia even has double forms.

Trailing and mounding petunias. These low, spreading plants (one can cover a 2–5-ft. circle) are used as ground covers and in tubs, in window boxes, and in hanging baskets. There are seed-grown and cutting-grown types. Plants in the seed-grown Wave series grow 6 in. tall, to 5 ft. wide, and cover themselves with 2½–3-in. flowers of pink, lilac, rose, or purple. The Ramblin' series blooms earlier than Wave, is more upright, grows 3 ft. wide, and comes in the red, pink, burgundy, and lavender range. The Tidal Wave series mounds up to 2 ft. tall if planted 1 ft. apart or against a fence, but mounds just 1 ft. tall if planted 2 ft. apart and given room to spread.

The following cutting-grown types grow slightly lower than the Wave series and spread to 2–4 ft. wide. Surfinias have 1½-in. flowers in pink, violet, purple, blue, yellow, or white. Cascadias are very similar, with heavy bloom and good tolerance of wind and rain. Jamborees are good choices for winter planting in mild parts of southwestern deserts. Supertunias have 2½-in. flowers in shades of pink, violet, or purple; they tend to flower nonstop all summer long. Petunias bear profuse ¾-in. blos-

soms in colors including pink, purple, and white, with darker veins.

Cutting-grown double types such as the Marco Polo series (many colors) and Priscilla (soft lavender with dark purple veins) mound about 6 in. high and spread 2 ft. For a smaller double series, try Sweet Sunshine.

PHACELIA
campanularia
CALIFORNIA DESERT BLUEBELLS
Hydrophyllaceae
ANNUAL

| 🌡 ZONES 1–3, 7–24 |
| ☀ FULL SUN |
| 💧 LITTLE TO MODERATE WATER |

Native to California deserts. To 6–18 in. high and wide, with coarsely toothed gray-green leaves. Clusters of 1-in., bell-shaped deep blue flowers in spring. Takes most well-drained soils. Sow in ground in fall or earliest spring; or sow in pots and transplant while seedlings are very small. Give some water to extend bloom season.

Phacelia campanularia

PHAEDRANTHUS buccinatorius. See **DISTICTIS buccinatoria**

PHAEOMERIA magnifica. See **ETLINGERA elatior**

PHALAENOPSIS
MOTH ORCHID
Orchidaceae
EPIPHYTIC ORCHIDS

| 🌡 ZONE H2; OR INDOORS |
| ☼ FILTERED SUN; BRIGHT INDIRECT LIGHT |
| 💧 REGULAR WATER |

These are tropical orchids with thick, broad, leathery leaves and no pseudobulbs. Leaves are rather flat, to 1 ft. long. From fall to spring, plants bear long (to 3-ft.) sprays of 3–6-in.-wide flowers in white, cream, pale yellow, or light lavender pink; some are spotted or barred or have lips in a contrasting color. Many lovely hybrids are sold. Very popular orchid commercially.

Phalaenopsis

Considered beginner orchids, these are among the easiest to grow indoors. They can be grown in a greenhouse with fairly high humidity and temperatures that average 60 to 65°F/16 to 18°C at night, 70 to 85°F/21 to 29°C during the day. Or grow them in the house; a good location is near a bathroom or kitchen window with light coming through a gauze or other sheer curtain (foliage burns easily in direct sun). Some smaller-flowered new hybrids give promise of being even easier to grow, tolerating somewhat lower night temperatures. Give moth orchids same potting medium as cattleya (see Orchids). During the growing and flowering season, feed weekly with a balanced liquid fertilizer diluted to half-strength. When cutting flowers, cut back to just above one of the tiny bracts on the stem; secondary sprays may form. To promote stronger new growth, many growers prefer to cut out the entire stem after blossoms fade.

PHALARIS
arundinacea picta
RIBBON GRASS, GARDENER'S GARTERS
Poaceae (Gramineae)
PERENNIAL GRASS

| 🌡 ZONES A1–A3; 1–10, 14–24 |
| ☀ ☼ FULL SUN OR PARTIAL SHADE |
| 💧 REGULAR WATER |

Native to North America, Eurasia. Tough, tenacious grass; forms a 2–3-ft.-high clump that spreads aggressively—and indefinitely—by underground runners. Leaves

Phalaris arundinacea picta

are deep green with longitudinal white stripes, turn buff colored in autumn. Airy flower clusters are white, aging to pale brown. To keep this plant in-bounds, grow it in large containers or use same control methods as for running kinds of bamboo (see Bamboo). Less invasive selections are 'Woods Dwarf' ('Dwarf Garters'), about half as tall as the species and with brighter white striping; and 'Feesey' ('Strawberries and Cream'), to 1½–2 ft. tall, with white stripes that usually take on pink tints during cool weather.

PHASEOLUS caracalla.
See **VIGNA caracalla**

PHEASANT'S-TAIL GRASS.
See **STIPA arundinacea**

PHILADELPHUS
MOCK ORANGE
Hydrangeaceae (Philadelphaceae)
DECIDUOUS AND EVERGREEN SHRUBS

☀	ZONES VARY BY SPECIES
☀ ☽	PARTIAL SHADE IN HOTTEST CLIMATES
◖ ◖	MODERATE TO REGULAR WATER

Grown for white or cream-colored, usually fragrant flowers that bloom in late spring or early summer. Blossoms are four petaled, typically 1–2 in. wide; they range from single to fully double. Plants are generally large and vigorous, with fountainlike form. Oval, 2–4-in.-long leaves (typically medium green in color) are arranged in pairs along the stems.

Prune every year just after bloom, cutting out oldest wood and surplus shoots at base. To rejuvenate, cut to the ground. Taller types are striking planted in lawns and as background and corner plantings; smaller kinds can be used near foundations or planted as low screens or informal hedges. Buy this plant in bloom to check for best fragrance. Not fussy about soil type but must have good drainage.

P. 'Belle Etoile'. Deciduous. Zones 2–17. This popular shrub grows 5 ft. tall and 8 ft. wide. Fringed, maroon-centered, single flowers to 2½ in. across are wonderfully fragrant. May be offered as a selection of *P. × purpureomaculatus* or *P. × lemoinei.*

P. 'Buckley's Quill'. Deciduous. Zones 3–17. Dense, compact grower to 4–5 ft. tall and wide, with clusters of 1-in. double flowers. Petals are narrow and pointed.

P. coronarius. SWEET MOCK ORANGE. Deciduous. Zones A1–A3; 1a, 2–24. From southern Europe, Caucasus. Strong-growing old favorite to 10–12 ft. tall and wide. Clusters of especially fragrant, 1½-in. flowers. 'Aureus', to 8 ft. high, has bright golden foliage that turns yellow green in summer.

P. 'Enchantment'. Deciduous. Zones 2b–17. Grows about 5–7 ft. high and wide, with very fragrant double flowers about 1 in. across. May be labeled as *P. × lemoinei* 'Enchantment.'

P. 'Glacier'. Deciduous. Zones A3; 1a, 2–17. Grows 5 ft. high and wide, with fragrant double blossoms to 1¼ in. wide.

P. gordonianus. See P. lewisii
P. lewisii. WILD MOCK ORANGE. Deciduous. Zones 1–10, 14–24. Native to western North America; the state flower of Idaho. Fountain-shaped, loosely branched shrub 4–10 ft. tall, typically broader than high (tall race from west of the Cascades is often called *P. gordonianus*). Satiny single flowers to 2 in. across. Tolerates some aridity. 'Goose Creek' is a double-flowered selection.

Philadelphus lewisii

P. mexicanus. EVERGREEN MOCK ORANGE. Zones 8, 9, 14–24. From Mexico. Vining shrub has long, supple stems clothed with evergreen leaves. Creamy white, 1½-in. flowers in small clusters may bloom sporadically throughout year. Can be kept to 6 ft. high and wide as a free-standing shrub. It is best used, however, as a vine or bank cover; can climb 15–20 ft. if given support.

P. microphyllus. Deciduous. Zones 1–3, 7, 10, 14–16, 18. From southwestern U.S., Mexico. To 4–5 ft. tall and wide (often smaller), with small (¾–1½-in.-long) leaves. Extremely fragrant, inch-wide flowers are borne singly or in pairs. Endures some drought.

P. 'Minnesota Snowflake'. Deciduous. Zones A3; 1a, 2–17. To

6–8 ft. high and wide, with double flowers to 2 in. across. Reputedly hardy to −30°F/−34°C. 'Dwarf Minnesota Snowflake' ('Dwarf Snowflake', 'Miniature Snowflake') grows 3–4 ft. high and wide, with 1–1½-in. double flowers.

P. 'Natchez'. Deciduous. Zones A3; 1a, 2–17. Grows 8–10 ft. high and wide. Very showy in bloom, when branches are covered in 2-in.-wide double flowers.

P. 'Virginal'. Deciduous. Zones A3; 1a, 2–17. To 6–8 ft. high and wide. Fragrant double flowers are 2 in. across.

PHILLYREA decora.
See **OSMANTHUS decorus**

PHILODENDRON
Araceae
EVERGREEN VINES AND SHRUBS

☀	ZONES VARY BY TYPE; OR INDOORS
☀ ☽ ●	EXPOSURE NEEDS VARY BY TYPE; BRIGHT INDIRECT LIGHT
◖	REGULAR WATER

From tropical America. Tough, fast-growing plants favored for attractive, leathery, usually glossy leaves. In good conditions, old plants may bloom; the blossoms resemble those of calla (*Zantedeschia*), with a boatlike bract surrounding a club-shaped structure. Bracts are usually greenish, white, or reddish.

Whether grown in containers or open ground, all philodendrons need rich, loose, well-drained soil. Feed lightly and frequently for good growth and color. Clean dust from leaves of indoor plants. Most philodendrons—especially those grown in containers—tend to drop their lower leaves, leaving a bare stem. Once a plant gets gangly and overgrown, the best course is often simply to discard it and replace it with a new plant. However, you can also cut the plant back to short stub, then let it regrow; or you can air-layer the leafy top, then plant the layer once it roots (and discard parent). Some philodendrons send down aerial roots. Push these into soil or cut them off (removing them won't hurt the plant).

Philodendrons fall into two main classes.

Arborescent; relatively hardy. These are large, shrub-size plants with big leaves and sturdy, self-supporting trunks. They can be grown indoors but need much more space than most houseplants. They grow outdoors in Zones 8, 9,

12–24, H1, H2. As landscape plants, they do best in sun (some shade at midday where light is intense) but can take considerable shade. Use them for tropical effects or as massive silhouettes against walls or glass. Excellent in large containers; effective near swimming pools.

Vining and self-heading; tender. This class includes tender plants of two different habits. They can grow outdoors in Zone H2, where they require partial or full shade; elsewhere, they are houseplants. Many kinds are sold, with many different leaf shapes and sizes. Vining types do not really climb and must be tied to or leaned against a support until they eventually shape themselves to it. The support can be almost anything, but certain water-absorbent columns (sections of tree fern stem, wire and sphagnum "totem poles," slabs of bark) serve especially well, since they can be kept moist. Self-heading types form short, broad plants with leaves radiating out from a central point.

The following list indicates the class of each species and variety. Note that one popular "philodendron"—the so-called split-leaf philodendron—belongs to another genus, *Monstera*.

P. cordatum. See P. scandens oxycardium

Philodendron erubescens

P. erubescens. Vining. Often sold as *P.* 'Hastatum'. To 10–20 ft. high, with foot-long, arrow-shaped deep green leaves. Subject to leaf spot in overly warm, moist conditions. A number of selections and hybrids are available; they are more resistant to leaf spot and tend to be more compact. Some have much red in new foliage and in leafstalks. 'Royal Queen' has bright red new growth; mature leaves are dark green heavily tinged with red. 'Emerald Queen' is a choice deep green form.

P. 'Lynette'. Self-heading. To 1 ft. high, 2 ft. wide. Makes tight

P

cluster of foot-long, broadish, bright green leaves that are strongly patterned by deeply sunken veins. Good tabletop plant.

P. oxycardium. See P. scandens oxycardium

P. pertusum. See Monstera deliciosa

P. scandens. Vining. Among the most common philodendrons. Can reach 50 ft. Deep green, heart-shaped leaves; juvenile leaves are 4–6 in. long, while mature ones reach 1 ft. long. *P. s. micans* has velvety young leaves; mature leaves

Philodendron scandens oxycardium

are smooth. *P. s. oxycardium* (often sold as *P. oxycardium* or *P. cordatum*) has glossy leaves throughout its life. Juvenile forms of both are most popular; they are grown on tree trunks, in hanging baskets and window boxes, as houseplants. Indoors, train them on string or wire for a variety of decorative effects; or grow on moisture-retentive columns.

P. selloum (P. bipinnatifidum). Arborescent. Treelike shrub to 6–15 ft. high and wide, typically with a single, upright trunk that leans with age. Deeply cut leaves to 3 ft. long are held on 3-ft.-long stalks.

P. wendlandii. Self-heading. To 1 ft. high, 2 ft. wide. Compact clusters of 12 or more deep green, foot-long, broadly lance-shaped leaves on short, broad stalks. Indoors, this species is useful where a tough, compact foliage plant is needed. *P.* 'Lynette' is similar.

PHLEBODIUM aureum. See **POLYPODIUM aureum**

PHLOMIS
Lamiaceae (Labiatae)
PERENNIALS AND
EVERGREEN SHRUBS

⚡ **ZONES VARY BY SPECIES**

☀ **FULL SUN**

◐◑ **LITTLE TO MODERATE WATER**

Mediterranean natives. Erect stems are set with widely spaced whorls of hooded, two-lipped flowers in

yellow, purple, or lilac. Moisture-conserving thick, typically furry or hairy leaves are lance shaped to oval, set opposite each other on stems. Not particular about soil but must have good drainage. Need little water where summers are cool; in hot-summer regions, give them more moisture. Cut flowers are striking in mixed arrangements; blooming stems dry well for winter bouquets.

P. 'Edward Bowles' ('Grande Verde', 'Lemon Swirl'). Shrub. Zones 3b–24. To 3–4 ft. tall, 5–6 ft. wide. Hybrid between *P. fruticosa* and *P. russeliana*. Resembles a bulkier *P. fruticosa* and has broader leaves (to 6 in. long, 3 in. wide) and larger, pure yellow flowers. Often sold as *P. fruticosa* and takes the same care.

P. fruticosa. JERUSALEM SAGE. Shrub. Zones 3b–24. To 4 ft. tall and wide, with woolly gray-green leaves to 6–8 in. long, 1¼ in. wide. Deep golden yellow, 1-in. flowers in ball-shaped whorls along upper half of stems. Cut plants back by half in fall to keep them compact. With watering, will produce several waves of bloom in spring and summer if cut back lightly after each flowering. Can tolerate light shade for part of day. Resistant to oak root fungus.

P. italica. Shrub. Zones 5–24. Arching, suckering habit to 3–4 ft. tall, 5–6 ft. or more wide. Gray-green, 2–3-in.-long leaves are covered with silvery wool. Lilac-pink flowers in 1-in. whorls from early to midsummer. To keep plant neat, remove faded flowering stems; cut out basal branches that are more than 3 years old.

P. lanata. Shrub. Zones 7–24. Dense, compact plant to 2½ ft. tall, 4–6 ft. wide. Woolly, wrinkled, 1-in., sage green leaves. Stems and leaf undersides have brownish scales. Whorls of 1-in., deep yellow flowers bloom from spring to fall if faded stems are cut out.

P. purpurea. Shrub. Zones 7–24. Rather lax habit to 4–6 ft. high and wide. Lance-shaped leaves to 4 in. long are gray green, sparsely hairy above, white and woolly beneath; new shoots are also white and woolly. Purplish pink flowers bloom mainly in late spring, but scattered blossoms

appear all year long where winters are mild. After each flowering, cut plant back by one-third to keep it neat and compact.

P. russeliana. Perennial. Zones 2–24. Spreads by rhizomes to make a low clump of furry olive green foliage. Leaves are large (to 8 in. long, 6 in. wide) and heart shaped. Creates an effective weed-suppressing ground cover. Sends up 2–3-ft.-tall stems bearing flowers in soft yellow fading to cream. The main bloom period comes in early summer, but some flowers are produced later as well. Flower spikes are attractive even after blossoms fade; they dry out and remain upright throughout the winter. Tolerates partial shade.

P. samia. Perennial. Zones 2–24. Similar in habit to *P. russeliana*, forming a low mat of oval, scallop-edged, 4–8-in.-long leaves that are medium green above, white and woolly below. Blooms throughout summer, sending up 2–3-ft.-tall stems of flowers in purple or purplish pink (greenish or white in some forms).

P. tuberosa. Perennial from tuberous roots. Zones A1–A3; 1–24. Basal rosette of deep green foliage covered with fine hairs; leaves deeply toothed, arrow shaped, to 10 in. long. Late spring into summer, sends up 3–6-ft. stems with purple or pinkish mauve blossoms

Phlomis fruticosa

along upper third; upper lip of each flower is straight rather than hooded. Blooming plants resemble foxgloves (*Digitalis*). Disappears in winter.

PHLOX
Polemoniaceae
PERENNIALS AND ANNUALS

⚡ **ZONES VARY BY SPECIES**

☀◐ **FULL SUN OR LIGHT SHADE, EXCEPT AS NOTED**

💧 **REGULAR WATER, EXCEPT AS NOTED**

Most are natives of North America. With the exception of *P. drummondii* (annual phlox), the species described here are perennial. The many types show wide variation in form, but all have showy flower clusters. Tall kinds are excellent border plants; dwarf ones are mainstays of the rock garden. Unless otherwise noted, grow in ordinary garden soil and provide

regular moisture. Two major problems affect phlox: red spider mites (attack almost all species) and powdery mildew (*P. paniculata* is especially susceptible).

P. bifida. SAND PHLOX. Zones 2–17. From central U.S. Forms clumps 8–10 in. tall and 1½–2 ft. wide, with narrow, light green leaves. Blooms spring through early summer, bearing profuse, ½-in. lavender to white flowers with deeply notched petals. 'Snowmass' grows only 4–8 in. high and bears white flowers. Thrives with full sun and excellent drainage; best with moderate moisture but tolerates drought well.

P. divaricata. SWEET WILLIAM PHLOX. Zones 1–17. Native to eastern North America. To 1 ft. high, 2 ft. wide, with creeping underground shoots. Slender stems are clothed in oblong, 1½–2-in.-long leaves. Blooms in spring, bearing open clusters of ¾–1½-in.-wide, somewhat fragrant blossoms; color varies from pale blue (sometimes with pinkish tones) to white. Flowers of 'Dirigo Ice' are palest blue, while those of *P. d. laphamii* are bright blue. 'Montrose Tricolor' has lavender-blue blossoms; its leaves emerge pink, then age to green with white margins. Use in rock garden or as bulb cover. Grow in good, deep soil. Light shade.

Phlox divaricata

P. drummondii. ANNUAL PHLOX. Zones A2, A3; 1–24; H1. Native to Texas. To 6–18 in. high, 10–12 in. wide, with erect, leafy stems more or less covered with rather sticky hairs. Lance-shaped to oval, nearly stalkless leaves are 1–3 in. long. Profuse blossoms in tight clusters at tops of stems. Comes in bright and pastel colors (no blue or orange), some with contrasting eye. Tall strains (about 1½ ft. high) in mixed colors include Finest and Fordhook Finest. The Astoria and Intensia strains are intermediate in size (8–12 in. tall) and so freely branching that they take on a rounded shape; both are available in a wide range of colors and are

P

just right for large containers. Dwarf (6–8-in.) strains include Beauty and Globe, both with roundish flowers; and starry-blossomed Petticoat and Twinkle. Bloom period lasts from early summer until frost if faded flowers are removed. Plant in spring in cold-winter regions, in fall in mild climates. Grow in light, rich soil well amended with organic matter. Full sun.

P. maculata. THICK-LEAF PHLOX. Zones 1–14, 18–23. Native to eastern North America. To 3–4 ft. tall, 1½ ft. wide, with thick, narrow, pointed leaves 2–4 in. long. Early summer flowers about ¾ in. wide in 15-in.-long clusters; colors range from white (often with a colored eye) through pink shades to magenta. Shiny, mildew-resistant foliage. Varieties include 'Alpha', rose pink; 'Delta', white with pink eye; 'Omega', white with purplish pink eye; and 'Rosalinde', deep rose pink. Pure white 'Miss Lingard' may be a hybrid between *P. maculata* and another eastern species, *P. carolina*.

P. mesoleuca. See *P. nana ensifolia*

P. nana. SANTA FE PHLOX. Zones 4–24, except as noted. Native to southwestern U.S., Mexico. To 8 in. high, 1½ ft. wide. Sprawling stems are clothed in grayish green, narrow leaves to 1½ in. long. Blooms from spring into fall, bearing 1½-in. blossoms in bright pink, purple, or white. *P. n. ensifolia* (*P. mesoleuca*), Chihuahuan phlox, is more cold hardy (Zones 2–24); it grows to 6 in. high, bears blooms in colors ranging from cream to yellow, orange, and red. *P. nana* and *P. n. ensifolia* both like heat; both do well with little water but will take more moisture if soil is well drained. Tip-pinch plants to keep them from getting straggly.

P. nivalis. TRAILING PHLOX. Zones 4–7. Native to central U.S. Trailing plant to 4–6 in. high, 1 ft. wide. Forms loose mat of narrow, inch-long leaves. Pink or white, 1-in. flowers in fairly large clusters, late spring or early summer. Excellent in rock gardens; needs good drainage.

P. paniculata. SUMMER PHLOX. Zones 1–14, 18–21. From eastern North America. To 3–5 ft. tall, 2 ft. wide, with narrow, 2–5-in.-long leaves tapering to a slender point. Fragrant, 1-in. flowers in large, dome-shaped clusters throughout summer. Colors include white and shades of lavender, pink, rose, and red; blooms of some varieties have a contrasting eye. Plants do not come true from seed—most seedlings tend toward an uncertain purplish pink, though some may be attractive.

Summer phlox thrives in full sun, but flower color may bleach in hottest areas; performance is better in northern than in southern climates. After setting out young plants, pinch stem tips to induce branching. Mulch to keep roots cool. Divide every few years, replanting young shoots from outside of clump.

Very susceptible to mildew at end of bloom season. To minimize the problem, provide good air circulation: don't crowd plants, and thin mature plants to leave only six to eight stems. Mildew-resistant varieties include 'Bright Eyes', rose pink with darker eye; 'David' and 'Mount Fuji' ('Fujiyama'), pure white; 'Eva Cullum' and 'Miss Pepper', pink with red eye; 'Franz Schubert', lilac pink; 'Miss Candy', hot pink; 'Miss Marple', white with reddish pink eye; 'Miss Violet', purple; 'Red Eyes', deep pink with red eye; and the Volcano series (white, purple, lavender, red, pink with white eye, and pink with red eye).

P. stolonifera. CREEPING PHLOX. Zones A2, A3; 1–17. From eastern North America. Creeping, mounding plant to 6–8 in. high, 1 ft. wide, with narrow evergreen leaves to 1½ in. long. Profuse springtime show of 1-in., lavender flowers. Varieties include 'Bruce's White', lavender-blue 'Blue Ridge', and deep lavender 'Sherwood Purple'. Light shade.

P. subulata. MOSS PINK. Zones 1–17. From eastern U.S. Forms a mat to 6 in. high, 1½ ft. or wider, with creeping stems clothed in stiffish, ½-in., needlelike evergreen to semievergreen leaves. Blooms in late spring or early summer, bearing ¾-in. flowers in white and colors including pale to deep shades of pink, and lavender blue. Makes sheets of brilliant color in rock gardens. Plant in loose, not-too-rich soil; give moderate water. After flowering, cut back halfway.

Phlox paniculata

Specialists offer two dozen or more varieties; many are actually selections of other low-growing species, or hybrids between those species and *P. subulata*. 'Tamanonagalei' ('Candy Stripe') has rose pink blossoms edged in white; it is more drought tolerant than the average moss pink and has good fall rebloom.

PHOENIX
DATE PALM
Arecaceae (Palmae)
PALMS

✎ **ZONES VARY BY SPECIES**

☼ **FULL SUN, EXCEPT AS NOTED**

🌢 **REGULAR WATER**

These feather palms are mostly large trees, though the following list includes one dwarf. Trunks are patterned with bases of old leaf-stalks. Small yellowish flowers in large, hanging sprays. On female trees, blossoms are followed by clusters of dates—but only if the tree has been in the ground for at least several years and if a male tree is nearby. Dates of *P. dactylifera* and *P. sylvestris* are used commercially; those of other species don't have as much edible flesh. Date palms hybridize freely, so buy these trees from a reliable nursery that knows the seed or plant source.

Phoenix canariensis

P. canariensis. CANARY ISLAND DATE PALM. Zones 8, 9, 12–24; H1, H2. Canary Island native. Hardy to 20°F/–7°C; slow to develop new head of foliage after damage from hard frosts. Big, heavy-trunked plant to 60 ft. tall, with a great many bright green to deep green, gracefully arching fronds that form a crown to 50 ft. wide. Grows slowly until it forms a trunk, then speeds up a little. Young plants do well in pots for many years, looking something like pineapples. Best planted in parks, along wide streets, or in other large spaces; not for

small city lots. Takes seacoast conditions.

P. dactylifera. DATE PALM. Zones 8, 9, 11–24; H1, H2. Leaves killed at 20°F/–7°C, but plants have survived 4°F/–16°C. Native to the Mideast. Classic palm of desert oases. Slender-trunked tree to 80 ft., with a crown 20–40 ft. wide; gray-green, waxy leaves have stiff, sharp-pointed leaflets. Sends up suckers from base; natural habit is a clump of several trunks. Bears dates of commerce; principal variety is 'Deglet Noor'. Too large and stiff for most home gardens. Does well at seaside, in desert.

Phoenix dactylifera

P. loureirii (P. humilis). Zones 8, 9, 12–24; H1, H2. Hardy to 20°F/–7°C. Native from India to China. Resembles smaller, slimmer, more refined *P. canariensis*. Slow grower to 10–18 ft. tall and wide, with dark green leaves. Does well in containers.

P. reclinata. SENEGAL DATE PALM. Zones 9, 13–17, 21–24; H2. Damaged below 25°F/–4°C. Native to Africa. To 20–30 ft. high and wide. Produces offshoots, forming picturesque clumps with several curving trunks; if you want a single-trunked tree, remove offshoots. Fertilize for fast growth. Good seaside plant.

P. roebelenii. PYGMY DATE PALM. Zones 13, 16, 17, 22–24; H2; or indoors. Foliage browns at around 26°F/–3°C but recovers rapidly in spring. From Laos. Small, slow-growing, single-trunked palm to 6–10 ft. high. Fine-textured, curving leaves form

Phoenix roebelenii

a dense crown 6–8 ft. across. Good in groves or as a potted plant. Full sun or partial shade. Indoors, provide bright indirect light.

P. rupicola. CLIFF DATE PALM. Zones 13, 16, 17, 19–24; H1, H2. Hardy to 26°F/–3°C. Native to India. As stately as *P. canariensis* but slender trunked and much smaller, reaching only 25 ft. high, 15–20 ft. wide. Lime green foliage is soft and lush-looking; lower leaves droop gracefully. Best with some shade when young.

P. sylvestris. SILVER DATE PALM. Zones 8, 9, 12–24; H1, H2. Hardy to 22°F/–6°C. Native to India. Beautiful single-trunked palm to 30 ft. tall, 20–25 ft. wide. Tapering trunk is wide at base, narrow at top. Dense, rounded crown of gray-green leaves. Sap is used commercially for making date sugar.

PHORMIUM

Agavaceae
PERENNIALS

⚡ ZONES 7–9, 14–24; H1, H2; REGROW AFTER FREEZES IN ZONES 5, 6

☀ ☽ FULL SUN OR PARTIAL SHADE

◐ ◑ ● LITTLE TO REGULAR WATER

From New Zealand. Dramatic plants with many swordlike evergreen leaves that grow in a fan pattern; make good garden focal points. The many variegated selections provide year-round color in perennial and shrub borders, on hillsides, in seaside plantings, near swimming pools. Cool weather intensifies foliage colors. On established plants, branched clusters of tubular flowers appear in late spring or early summer, rising to twice the height of the foliage clump in some kinds.

Rugged *P. tenax* varieties are sturdy and fast growing. They take almost any soil, little to regular watering, hot or chilly conditions; do well at seacoast. They will take poor drainage to a point; crown rot can be a problem if they are planted too low in poorly drained soil. Rigid, upright leaves seldom sunburn, even on variegated kinds with light-colored variegation. Subject to summer rot in low desert, but replacement plants set out in fall will grow quickly. Use as windbreak along coast; grow in containers wherever soil doesn't freeze in winter. More finicky than *P. tenax* are forms of *P. cookianium* and the spectacular hybrids between *P. cookianum* and *P. tenax*. To thrive, they require a bit more water; in hot areas, their arching leaves need afternoon shade to prevent burning.

P. tenax, P. cookianum, and their forms and hybrids are all harmed by temperatures below 20°F/–7°C. In cold-winter areas, you can grow smaller sorts indoors or move larger containers to shelter when deep cold threatens.

Nursery plants in containers are deceptively small; when you plant, allow enough room to accommodate a mature specimen. Cut out flower stalks when blossoms wither. As leaves age, colors fade; cut out older ones as close to base as possible to maintain best appearance. On variegated sorts, watch for reversions to solid green or bronze; remove reverted crowns down to root level before they take over the clump. Clumps can remain in place indefinitely. To increase plantings, take individual crowns from clump edges; or divide large clumps (not an easy job).

P. cookianum (P. colensoi). MOUNTAIN FLAX. Medium green leaves (usually pinkish at base) are less rigid than those of *P. tenax;* they arch gracefully, droop at the tips. Leaves are 4–5 ft. long, 2½–3 in. wide; mature clumps are 4–5 ft. high, spreading to 8–10 ft. or more. Yellow flowers on branching, 3–5-ft. stalks; drooping, twisted seedpods. 'Dwarf' is a compact selection only 3 ft. high, 5–6 ft. wide. *P. c. hookeri* 'Tricolor' has green leaves margined in cream and red; foliage is flushed with rose in cool weather. 'Cream Delight' is a sport of 'Tricolor'; its leaves have a broad, creamy yellow central stripe and narrow green margins edged in dark red.

P. hybrids. These are all bird-pollinated, naturally occurring crosses between *P. cookianum* and *P. tenax,* selected for distinctive leaf color.

'Apricot Queen'. To 2½–3 ft. tall, 4–5 ft. wide. Leaves are 2–3 in. wide, light yellow with green margins; blushed with apricot in cool weather.

'Dark Delight'. Arching habit to 3–4 ft. high, 6–8 ft. wide. Leaves are 1–2 in. wide; very dark but vivid reddish brown with a thin orange midrib.

Phormium 'Jester'

'Dazzler'. To 3 ft. tall, 5–6 ft. wide, with twisting, arching, 1½-in.-wide leaves in scarlet striped with maroon.

'Duet'. To 2½–3½ ft. tall and wide. Stiff leaves to 1¾ in. wide are lime green with creamy yellow stripes at margins.

'Ed Carman'. Upright growth to 2–3 ft. tall and wide; 2-in.-wide bronze leaves are edged with narrow bands of light pink to white.

'Firebird'. Stiffly upright, to 5–6 ft. tall, 2–3 ft. wide. Rose red leaves have bronze-green margins.

'Flamingo'. See 'Maori Sunrise'

'Gold Sword'. Fairly stiff, upright plant to 2½–3 ft. tall, 3–5 ft. wide. Bright yellow, 2-in.-wide leaves have green edges and (sometimes) a faint rosy flush in center.

'Guardsman'. To 5–6 ft. tall, 7–8 ft. wide, with rigid, upright leaves to 3 in. wide. Bronzy olive green with red border.

'Jester'. To 1½–2½ ft. tall and wide, with arching, 2-in.-wide leaves that are rich pink with hints of orange, edged in lime green.

'Maori Chief'. Robust, upright to 6 ft. tall, 6–8 ft. wide. Leaves 2½ in. wide, green with rosy edges. Similar to 'Sundowner' but more refined.

'Maori Maiden'. To 3–4 ft. tall, 4–6 ft. wide. Leaves to 1¾ in. wide are salmon pink (fading to cream) with narrow olive green stripes at edges.

'Maori Queen'. To 3 ft. high, 4–5 ft. wide. Shorter, more upright, narrower-leafed version of 'Sundowner'. Stiff leaves to 2¼ in. wide are bronzy green, with broad marginal streaks of coral fading to cream.

'Maori Sunrise'. To 3 ft. high, 5–6 ft. wide, with stiff leaves up to 2½ in. across. Foliage is margined and striped in bronzy green; base color is pinkish orange in younger leaves, aging to cream in older ones. 'Flamingo' is similar or identical.

'Platt's Black'. Somewhat arching growth to 2–3 ft. tall and wide; leaves up to 1 in. wide. One of the darkest varieties, with dark burgundy to black leaves. Grows best in cooler climates.

'Rainbow Warrior'. Similar to 'Maori Maiden' but with leaves in a somewhat darker salmon, fading to cream with age. Foliage turns nearly blood red in winter.

'Red Heart'. Relaxed, arching habit to 3 ft. tall, 4–6 ft. wide. Light red, 1½–2-in.-wide leaves are light green on edges and undersides.

'Sea Jade'. To 4–5 ft. tall, 5–6 ft. wide, with rather stiff leaves to 2½ in. wide. Maroon to bronze in center, with lime green margins and undersides.

'Sundowner'. Erect growth to 5–6 ft. tall, 6–8 ft. wide, with leaves to 3½ in. wide. Olive or bronzy green foliage has stripes of pinkish red (aging to cream) at or near edges and a fine red edge; leaf undersides are grayish green.

'Sunset'. To 4–5 ft. tall and wide. Stiffly upright leaves are 1½ in. wide, with slightly arching tips; color is apricot to pink, striped with green.

'Surfer'. To 3 ft. tall, 5–6 ft. wide. Maroon-bronze, 1½-in.-wide leaves have grayish green undersides and a narrow, gray-green central stripe. Foliage is stiff but arching and twisting.

'Yellow Wave'. To 4–5 ft. high, 5–7 ft. wide, with 2¼-in.-wide leaves in chartreuse with lime green margins. Leaves can burn in hot sun.

P. tenax. NEW ZEALAND FLAX. Large, bold plant with bronzy green leaves to 9 ft. long, 5 in. wide; rigid and mainly upright, curving mainly (if at all) near tips. Mature clumps are about as wide as or a little wider than high. Vertical inflorescences—often to twice the height of foliage clump—contain many dull red or reddish orange flowers; seedpods are twisted but held erect. Many choices, offering great variety in plant size and leaf color. Note that bronze-leafed varieties take on a deeper color in full sun.

'Atropurpureum', 'Bronze', 'Purpureum', 'Rubrum'. These names are used interchangeably in the trade for plants with purplish or brownish red foliage that grow 6–8 ft. tall and wide. Usually grown from seed and somewhat variable; if you want a particular color, make sure you see the actual plant before buying.

'Atropurpureum Compactum' ('Monrovia Red'). To 5 ft. tall and wide, with burgundy-bronze foliage. Uniform; propagated by tissue culture.

'Bronze Baby'. To 3 ft. tall and wide, with 1½-in.-wide leaves. Foliage is deep reddish brown aging to deep bronze; narrow orange leaf edges and midrib (on underside) glow in sunlight.

'Chocolate'. To 4–5 ft. high and wide, with rich brown leaves.

'Dusky Chief'. Dense clump to 6 ft. high and wide. Wine red leaves are 2–3 in. wide and have coral edges that glow when backlit.

'Jack Spratt'. To 1½ ft. high and wide, with ½-in.-wide, twisting, reddish brown leaves.

'Morticia'. To 3–4 ft. high and wide, with stiff, 1½-in.-wide, purple-black leaves.

'Pink Stripe' ('Pink Edge'). To 4–5 ft. high and wide. Gray-green foliage has a purplish tinge. Each leaf has a bright pink margin that is broader at base, gradually narrowing to almost nothing at tip.

'Thumbelina'. Similar to 'Jack Spratt' but more upright growing and a little darker.

'Tiny Tiger' ('Aurea Nana'). Miniature of 'Variegatum', reaching barely 1 ft. high and wide. Leaves are flushed pink in cool weather. 'Tony Tiger' is a 2-ft. version.

'Tom Thumb'. Upright clump to 2–3 ft. high and wide. Green, wavy-edged, ½-in.-wide leaves have red-bronze margins.

Phormium tenax
'Variegatum'

'Variegatum'. To 6–8 ft. tall and wide, with ¾-in.-wide, grayish green leaves that have creamy yellow stripes along edges.

'Veitchianum' ('Radiance', 'Williamsii Variegatum'). To 5–6 ft. tall, 7 ft. wide. Green leaves have a central yellow stripe, lime green margins with a thin orange edge.

PHOTINIA
Rosaceae
EVERGREEN AND DECIDUOUS
SHRUBS OR TREES

🌡 ZONES VARY BY SPECIES

☀ FULL SUN

💧💧 MODERATE TO REGULAR WATER

Related to hawthorn (*Crataegus*) and pyracantha. Densely foliaged plants with elliptical to oval leaves

and bright-colored new growth that matures to dark green. In early spring, all bear flattish clusters of small white flowers. In most types, blossoms are followed in fall by red or black berries that may last into winter. Evergreen species may suffer considerable damage if temperatures remain below 10°F/−12°C for prolonged periods. Good for screen and background plantings. Tip-pinch plants to encourage colorful new growth. Prune to shape before spring growth begins or after bloom; don't allow new growth to get away from you and make long, bare switches. Many photinias can be converted to small trees by limbing up; or they can be trained as trees from the beginning. Berries are attractive to birds. All photinias are susceptible to fireblight; all but *P. × fraseri* are subject to powdery mildew.

P. davidiana (Stranvaesia davidiana). Evergreen shrub or small tree native to China and Vietnam. Zones 4–11, 14–17. Informal, wide-spreading plant grows at a moderate rate to 6–20 ft. high and wide. Oval, pointed, smooth-edged leaves to 4 in. long; new foliage is reddish. Some leaves turn bronze or purple in late fall and winter, a good foil for clusters of showy red berries that form at the same time. White flowers in 4-in. clusters appear late spring to early summer. For best growth give plants plenty of room and soil that is not too rich. In hot interior climates, protect from hot winds and supply adequate water. Looks good with strong-growing Western native plants, or as a screen or background. Berried branches are handsome as holiday cut foliage.

P. d. undulata is lower growing, forming an irregularly shaped 5-ft. shrub with wavy-edged leaves; branch tips and new foliage are bronzy red.

P. × fraseri. Evergreen shrub or tree. Zones 3b (with protection), 4–24. 'Birmingham' is the usual selection sold; for many years, it was the only one available and was simply labeled *P. × fraseri.* Moderate to fast growth to 10–15 ft. high and wide. Leaves to 5 in. long; bright bronzy red when new. Flower clusters resemble those of *P. glabra* but are not followed by berries. Good espalier or small single-stemmed tree. Cut branches are excellent in arrangements. Resists mildew and heat, but leaf spot can be serious in the Pacific Northwest. Sometimes suffers from chlorosis

Photinia × fraseri
'Birmingham'

in Zones 12, 13. Aphids may be a problem. Often used as a formal hedge, but the large leaves look ragged when sheared. For a more attractive appearance, clip plants more lightly or prune selectively to grow as an informal hedge.

Two newer selections about half the size of 'Birmingham' are useful in smaller spaces: 'Indian Princess', with orange-red new growth, and 'Red Robin', with bright red new leaves and good resistance to leaf spot.

P. glabra. JAPANESE PHOTINIA. Evergreen shrub. Zones 4–9, 14–24. From Japan. Broad, dense growth to 6–10 ft. high and wide. Leaves to 3 in. long, coppery when new; scattered leaves turn bright red through fall and winter, adding touches of color. Flowers in 4-in. clusters. Berries are red, aging to black.

P. serratifolia (P. serrulata). CHINESE PHOTINIA. Evergreen shrub or tree. Zones 4–16, 18–22; can be grown in Zones 17, 23, 24, but is especially prone to mildew there. From China. Broad, dense grower; can reach 30 ft. high and wide but is easily held to one-third that size. Stiff leaves to 8 in. long are prickly along edges. Bright copper new growth; scattered crimson leaves in fall, winter. Flower clusters to 6 in. across. Bright red berries often last until winter. 'Aculeata' (frequently sold as 'Nova' or 'Nova Lineata') is more compact; its leaf midribs and main veins are ivory yellow.

P. villosa. Deciduous shrub or tree. Zones 3–9, 14–17. From China, Korea, Japan. To 15 ft. tall, 10 ft. wide. Leaves are 1½–3 in. long; they are pale gold with rosy tints when new, green when mature, bright red or yellow in fall. Flower clusters 1–2 in. across; bright red berries.

PHYGELIUS
CAPE FUCHSIA
Scrophulariaceae
PERENNIALS

🌡 ZONES 4–9, 14–24; H1, H2

☀ ◐ FULL SUN OR LIGHT SHADE

💧 REGULAR WATER

From South Africa. Woody-based perennials that die to the ground in cold climates, remain shrubby in milder areas. Related to snapdragon (*Antirrhinum*) and penstemon, but drooping flowers also suggest fuchsia. Plants grow 3–4 ft. high, spreading about as wide by underground stems or rooting prostrate branches. Dark green leaves are 3½–4½ in. long, oval and pointed, with finely toothed margins. Bloom from summer into fall, bearing tubular, curved flowers in loosely branched clusters at stem ends. To keep plants neat, cut out old flower stalks after bloom. Mulch roots in cold-winter regions. Species can be started from seed; named varieties should be grown from cuttings or by ground layering.

P. aequalis. Pyramidal clusters of dusty rose flowers. 'Sensation' ('Sani Pass') has rich purplish pink flowers that are creamy yellow inside. 'Trewidden Pink' bears dusty pink, yellow-throated blossoms tipped in red. 'Yellow Trumpet' has pale yellow blooms.

P. capensis. More open and sprawling than *P. aequalis,* with loose clusters of orange to red flowers.

Phygelius capensis

P. × rectus. Hybrids between the previous two species. 'African Queen' has orange flowers with a yellow throat; 'Devil's Tears', scarlet with yellow throat; 'Moonraker', solid pale yellow; 'Tommy Knockers', peach with yellow throat. 'Pink Elf' bears pink flowers on a smaller plant than the usual (2 ft. high, 3 ft. wide).

P

PHYLA nodiflora (Lippia repens)

LIPPIA
Verbenaceae
PERENNIAL

⚡	ZONES 8–24; H1, H2
☼	FULL SUN
◠◑●	LITTLE TO REGULAR WATER

From many tropical and subtropical regions of the world. Ground-hugging growth and ability to endure foot traffic have established its use as a lawn substitute in some areas where a traditional lawn is impractical. Creeping stems

Phyla nodiflora

clothed in oval, ¾-in., grayish green leaves form a mat no higher than 2 in. Rounded, ½-in. heads of tiny lavender-pink flowers appear from spring to fall. Blossoms are a magnet for bees; if this bothers you, mow plantings periodically to remove flowers. Set out plants from containers 2 ft. apart; plant rooted sprigs at 1-ft. intervals. Looks shabby in winter, but an early-spring feeding will promote fast new growth. Takes many soils, though performance suffers where nematodes are a problem (in the desert, for example).

PHYLLITIS scolopendrium.
See **ASPLENIUM scolopendrium**

PHYLLOSTACHYS.
See **BAMBOO**

PHYSALIS alkekengi

CHINESE LANTERN PLANT
Solanaceae
PERENNIAL OFTEN GROWN AS ANNUAL

⚡	ZONES 1–24
☼◑	FULL SUN OR LIGHT SHADE
●	REGULAR WATER

From Europe, Asia. Grown not for flowers but for the blossoms' decorative, papery, 2-in. calyxes, which look like lanterns and mature to a striking orange red in late summer and fall. Grows 1½–3 ft. high and wide, with angular branches set with long-stalked, light green, oval,

Physalis alkekengi

2–3-in.-long leaves. Small, star-shaped white flowers appear in leaf joints during summer; these are followed by inedible berries, each enclosed in a colorful inflated husk—the enlarged calyx of the flower. Dry, leafless stalks hung with these gay "lanterns" make choice winter arrangements.

Sow seeds in light soil in spring. Plant is clump forming, spreading widely by long, creeping, whitish underground stems; can become invasive. Increase established plantings by digging and dividing the roots. 'Pygmy' is a dwarf variety just 8 in. high; it makes a good potted plant.

Two other *Physalis* species produce edible fruit within papery husks. See Tomatillo (*P. ixocarpa*) and Poha, Ground Cherry (*P. peruviana*).

PHYSOCARPUS

NINEBARK
Rosaceae
DECIDUOUS SHRUBS

⚡	ZONES VARY BY SPECIES
☼◑●	SUN OR SHADE
◑●	MODERATE TO REGULAR WATER

Ninebarks are so named because of their peeling bark, which strips off to reveal several layers. The plants resemble spirea and are closely related to it, bearing round clusters of tiny white or pinkish flowers in spring or early summer. All have medium green leaves with lobed edges. Among the species described here, only *P. monogynus* has good fall color. Prune plants as needed after bloom; rejuvenate by cutting old stems to the ground.

P. capitatus. Zones 2b, 3–9, 14–19. Native to mountains of western North America. To 8 ft. tall and wide, with 2-in. leaves and dense clusters of white flowers. Clustered buds are as attractive as the opened blossoms.

P. monogynus. MOUNTAIN NINEBARK. Zones A1–A3; 1–3, 10. Rocky Mountain and High Plains native. To 3–5 ft. high and wide, with 1½-in. leaves and pinkish to white flowers carried just a few to a cluster. Leaves turn brilliant orange and red in fall.

P. opulifolius. COMMON NINEBARK. Zones A1–A3; 1–10, 14–17. Native to eastern and central North America. To 9 ft. tall and 10 ft. wide, with leaves to 3 in. long. Many white or pinkish blossoms in each cluster. Varieties are more attractive than the species. 'Diabolo', to 9–12 ft. high and wide, has intense reddish purple leaves (foliage color can tend

Physocarpus opulifolius 'Diabolo'

toward dark green in very hot summers or when plant is grown in partial shade). Leaves of 'Luteus' are yellow when plant is grown in sunlight, yellow green in shade. Compact varieties to 4–6 ft. tall and broad include 'Dart's Gold', similar to 'Luteus' but brighter; 'Nanus', with small, shallowly lobed dark green leaves; and 'Nugget', with leaves that unfold golden yellow, gradually mature to lime green, and then turn gold again in fall.

PHYSOSTEGIA virginiana

FALSE DRAGONHEAD, OBEDIENT PLANT
Lamiaceae (Labiatae)
PERENNIAL

⚡	ZONES A2, A3; 1–9, 14–24
☼◑	FULL SUN OR PARTIAL SHADE
●	REGULAR WATER

From eastern and central North America. To 4 ft. tall, 3 ft. wide—or much wider, if rhizomes are allowed to spread unchecked. Slender, upright stems carry oblong, toothed, 3–5-in.-long leaves with pointed tips. In sum-

Physostegia virginiana 'Vivid'

mer or early fall, each stem is topped by a 10-in.-long spike densely set with funnel-shaped, 1-in. flowers, typically in bright bluish pink. Blossoms resemble snapdragons (hence the name "false dragonhead") and will remain in place if twisted or pushed out of position (hence the name "obedient plant"). 'Bouquet Rose' reaches 3 ft. high, has rose pink flowers. Varieties growing 2 ft. tall include rose pink 'Vivid', white 'Summer Snow', and 'Variegata', with bluish pink flowers and white-edged leaves.

Attractive in borders; good cut flowers. Bloom stalks may need staking to remain upright. Cut to ground after bloom. Vigorous and notoriously invasive; to keep clumps in-bounds, divide them every 2 years in early spring.

PICEA

SPRUCE
Pinaceae
EVERGREEN TREES

⚡	ZONES VARY BY SPECIES
☼◑	FULL SUN OR LIGHT SHADE
◠◑	LITTLE TO MODERATE WATER, EXCEPT AS NOTED

Like firs (*Abies*), spruces are pyramidal, with branches arranged in neat tiers. Unlike firs, however, they have pendent cones, and their needles are stiffer and attached to branches by small pegs that remain behind after the needles drop. Most spruces are tall timber trees that lose their lower branches fairly early in life as they head upward; their canopies thin out noticeably as they age. Many species have dwarf varieties useful for foundation plantings, in rock gardens, in containers; these plants have shallow root systems and so need a reasonably cool location. Spruces generally grow best where summers are cool or mild; they will not thrive in heat and humidity. *P. pungens* tolerates dry conditions better than the other species. Spruces have no special soil requirements. Birds are attracted to these trees—both for seeds and for shelter.

Check spruces for small, dull green aphids in winter; if they're present, take control measures at that time to prevent defoliation in spring. Pine needle scale (look for flat, white scale insects on needles) may encourage sooty mold. In Rocky Mountain states, spruces may be bothered by spider mites and tussock moths. Cooley spruce gall adelgid is an aphidlike insect that attacks many spruce trees, especially in the Pacific Northwest and mountain areas. Its feeding causes green, conelike galls to form at ends of new growth. These galls gradually turn light purplish tan then brown by autumn. Douglas fir is an alternate host for these pests, but it doesn't develop galls. Contact your local Cooperative Extension Office for control measures.

Prune only to shape. If a branch grows too long, cut it back to a well-placed side branch. To slow growth and make it denser, remove part of each year's growth to force side branching. When planting larger spruces, don't place them too close to buildings, fences, or walks; they need space. Can be grown in containers for years as living Christmas trees; in coldest climates, move to a protected location in winter.

P. abies (P. excelsa). NORWAY SPRUCE. Zones A2, A3; 1–6, 14–17. Native to northern Europe. Fast growth to 100–150 ft. tall, 20 ft. wide. Doesn't do as well as North American native spruces in Rocky Mountain states. Stiff, deep green, attractive pyramid in youth; in age, branchlets droop strongly, and oldest branchlets (those nearest trunk) die back. Tolerates heat and humidity better than most spruces. Extremely hardy and wind resistant; valued for windbreaks in cold-winter zones. The following slow growers are among the many dwarf varieties available.

'Little Gem'. Dense grower to 1 ft. high and wide, with short needles and flat top.

'Nidiformis'. BIRD'S NEST SPRUCE. Dense growth to 3–5 ft. tall, 4–6 ft. wide. Individual plants vary in form. Some are flat topped; in others, the semierect main branches curve outward, leaving a shallow depression at the plant's top that gives it the look of a bird's nest.

'Pendula'. Grows naturally as a ground cover about 1½ ft. high, 10 ft. wide. Looks attractive cascading downward from rocks or walls. Can be staked to desired height and grown as a short, weeping tree.

'Sherwoodii'. Picturesque shrub with compact but irregular habit. Parent tree was only 5 ft. tall, 10 ft. wide at 60 years of age.

P. breweriana. BREWER'S WEEPING SPRUCE. Zones 2b, 3–7, 14–17. Native to Siskiyou Mountains in California and Oregon. To 30–50 ft. tall and 10–12 ft. wide in cultivation (to 80–120 ft. tall in native habitat). Stiff, upright pyramid in youth; branchlets become pendulous as the tree ages. Very striking form in maturity, with 7-8-ft.-long branchlets hanging vertically from the main branches. Needles are shiny deep green above, gray green beneath. More tender than most spruces. Requires regular water, cool temperatures.

P. engelmanii. ENGELMANN SPRUCE. Zones A2, A3; 1–7, 10, 14–17. Native from British Columbia south to Oregon and northern California, east to the Rockies. To 60–130 ft. tall, 20–25 ft. wide, with densely pyramidal form. Resembles blue-green forms of *P. pungens,* but needles are softer and tree is not as wide at base. Even 25-ft. specimens will be densely branched to ground. Popular lawn tree in Rocky Mountain region.

P. glauca. WHITE SPRUCE. Zones A1–A3, 1–7, 14–17, except as noted. Native to Canada and northern U.S. Cone-shaped, densely foliaged tree to 60–70 ft. tall and 10–12 ft. wide. Broad when young, narrower in age. Pendulous twigs; silver-green needles. Growth is best where winters are very cold. Many varieties, including the following.

P. g. albertiana 'Conica'. DWARF ALBERTA SPRUCE, DWARF WHITE SPRUCE. Zones A2, A3; 1–7, 14–17. Compact, cone-shaped, bushy shrub grows slowly, reaching 6–8 ft. tall, 4–5 ft. wide in 35 years. Short, soft needles are bright grass green when new, gray green when mature. Needs shelter from drying winds (hot or cold) and from strong, reflected sunlight. Popular tub plant.

P. g. densata. BLACK HILLS SPRUCE. Zones A2, A3; 1–6. Slow-growing, dense pyramid can reach 20–25 ft. tall, 10–12 ft. wide in 35 years. Use in containers; plant

in groves for screening or for alpine meadow effect.

'Jean's Dilly'. Pyramidal tree to 8–10 ft. tall and 12–14 ft. wide, with twisted needles.

'Sander's Blue'. To 6 ft. tall and 4 ft. wide. New growth and mature growth differ in color, giving plant a variegated look: young needles are slate blue, mature ones gray green.

P. mariana. BLACK SPRUCE. Zones A1–A3; 1–7. Native to Alaska and other parts of northern North America. Forms an irregular column to 30–50 ft. tall, 6–10 ft. wide. Bluish green needles. Tolerates cold, wet soils. 'Nana' is a compact variety (to 3 ft. high, 4–6 ft. wide) with blue-gray foliage; it is attractive in rock gardens, borders.

Picea pungens glauca

P. omorika. SERBIAN SPRUCE. Zones 2b–7, 14–17. Native to southeastern Europe. Narrow, conical, slow-growing tree to 50–60 ft. tall and just 6–10 ft. wide. Shiny, dark green needles have whitish undersides. Retains branches to the ground for many years. Considered by some to be the most attractive of all spruces. It is the one least likely to be seriously damaged by Cooley spruce gall adelgid. 'Nana' is a dwarf to 3–4 ft. tall and wide (possibly to 10 ft. high), with short, closely spaced needles.

P. orientalis. ORIENTAL SPRUCE. Zones 2b–7, 14–17. Native to Caucasus, Asia Minor. Dense, compact, cone-shaped tree with very short needles; grows slowly to 50–60 ft. high, 20 ft. wide. Tolerates poor soils as long as they are well drained, but may suffer leaf burn in very cold, dry winds.

Among the many available varieties is 'Aureospicata', with chartreuse new growth that matures to deep green.

P. pungens. COLORADO SPRUCE. Zones A2, A3; 1–10, 14–17. Native to Rocky Mountain region. In gardens, reaches 30–60 ft. tall, 10–20 ft. wide; in the wild, grows to a possible 100 ft. tall, 25–35 ft. wide. Very stiff, regular, horizontal branches form a broad pyramid. Foliage of seedlings varies in color from dark green through all shades of blue green to steely blue. Poor choice for Puget Sound region, where lack of winter cold leads to severe aphid infestations. Throughout its range, subject to an aphid that forms galls. Prefers dry soil.

P. p. glauca. COLORADO BLUE SPRUCE. Like the species but with bluish foliage. Many selections offer good blue color, including the following.

'Fat Albert'. Broad, formal looking tree to 10–15 ft. tall and 10–12 ft. wide.

'Hoopsii'. Dense, conical form with spreading branches and blue-white foliage.

'Koster'. Forms a blue-gray cone, though growth habit may be irregular.

'Moerheimii'. Same blue-gray color as 'Koster', but shape is more compact and symmetrical. Needles are longer than in other selections.

'Montgomery'. Slow-growing dwarf that forms a broad, silver-blue cone to 5 ft. high and wide.

'Pendula'. WEEPING BLUE SPRUCE. Gray-blue plant with weeping branchlets. Can be grown as ground cover; can also be trained to a small, weeping tree by staking at desired height when young.

'Thompsen'. Similar to 'Hoopsii' in color, but needles are twice as thick. Vigorous, symmetrical habit.

P. sitchensis. SITKA SPRUCE. Zones A2, A3; 4–6, 14–17. Native to cool, foggy areas from Alaska to California. The largest of all spruces, this is a pyramidal tree 80–160 ft. tall and 20–40 ft. wide in cultivation; plants in the wild may grow much taller. Horizontal branches hold short, flat, prickly needles that are glossy dark green above, powder blue beneath. Needs moisture both in atmosphere and soil to look its best. Subject to Cooley spruce gall. 'Papoose' ('Tensa') is a dwarf variety to 4 ft. high and wide.

PICKEREL WEED. See **PONTEDERIA cordata**

PIERIS

Ericaceae
EVERGREEN SHRUBS

- ⚡ **ZONES VARY BY SPECIES**
- ☼ **FILTERED SUNLIGHT OR PARTIAL SHADE**
- 💧 **REGULAR WATER**
- ◆ **LEAVES AND NECTAR ARE POISONOUS IF INGESTED**

Elegant in foliage and form the year around, these plants make good companions for rhododendron and azalea, to which they are related. They have whorls of leathery, narrowly oval, glossy, medium to dark green leaves and bear clusters of small, urn-shaped, typically white flowers. Most plants form flower buds by autumn; these resemble strings of tiny beads in greenish pink, red, or white and provide a subtle decorative feature in winter. Flowers open from midwinter to midspring. New spring growth is often brightly colored (pink to red or bronze).

Same cultural requirements as rhododendron and azalea. Need acid, well-drained but moisture-retentive soil and summers that are cool to merely warm; do not thrive in hot, dry conditions. Fairly easy to grow in the Pacific Northwest west of the Cascades, but as you move south and inland, they become increasingly fussy and are often less satisfactory. Where water is high in salts, soil needs careful leaching. Choose a planting location sheltered from wind, where plants will get high shade or dappled sunlight at least during the warmest afternoon hours. Where summers are cool or foggy, plants can take more sun. Prune by removing spent flowers. Thin older specimens by taking out whole branches; or limb them up to reveal attractive peeling bark. Splendid in containers, in woodland and Japanese gardens, in entryways where year-round quality is essential.

P. floribunda (Andromeda floribunda). MOUNTAIN PIERIS. Zones 2–9, 14–17. Native to southeastern U.S. Compact, rounded shrub to 6 ft. tall, 10 ft. wide. Differs from the other species—new growth is pale green, mature leaves dull dark green, 1½–3 in. long. Blossoms in upright clusters. Cold hardy; tolerates sun, heat, and low humidity better than the others.

P. 'Forest Flame'. Zones 3b–9, 14–17. Hybrid between *P. japonica* and a form of *P. formosa forrestii*. To 6–10 ft. tall, 3–5 ft. wide. Leaves are about 3½ in. long—brilliant red when new, fading to creamy pink before maturing to dark green. Blooms profusely, bearing broader, heavier flower clusters than those of *P. japonica*.

P. formosa forrestii (P. forrestii). CHINESE PIERIS. Zones 4–9, 14–17. From China. Dense, broad, to 10 ft. tall, 12 ft. wide. Polished-looking leaves to 6 in. long. New growth ranges from brilliant scarlet (in the best forms) to pale salmon pink. To get good color, buy plants when they are producing new growth; the best selections are sometimes offered as 'Bright Red'. Large, drooping flower clusters. Good espalier in shade.

P. japonica (Andromeda japonica). LILY-OF-THE-VALLEY SHRUB. Zones 2b–9, 14–17. Upright, dense, tiered growth to 9–10 ft. high and wide. New leaves are bronzy pink to red; mature ones are glossy green, 3 in. long. Drooping clusters of white, pink, or nearly red flowers; flower buds are often dark red. Many varieties, some rare.

Pieris japonica

The following are grown for smaller-than-usual size or unusual foliage:

'Bert Chandler'. Salmon pink new foliage ages to cream, then white; then matures to pale green.

'Bisbee Dwarf'. To 1 ft. high and wide, with half-size leaves that are red when young.

'Cavatine'. To 2–3 ft. high and wide, with red new growth.

'Compacta'. Grows to 6 ft. high and wide.

'Crispa'. To 6–7 ft. high and wide, with handsome wavy-edged leaves.

'Flaming Silver'. To 4 ft. high and wide. Young leaves are red with pink margins, mature ones green with white edges.

'Karenoma'. Compact grower to 3–6 ft. high and wide, with upright flower clusters.

'Mountain Fire'. Fiery red new growth.

'Prelude'. To 2–3 ft. high and wide; pink new growth.

'Pygmaea'. Tiny dwarf to 1 ft. high and wide, with very few flowers and narrow leaves to 1 in. long.

'Spring Snow'. Similar to 'Karenoma'.

'Valley Fire'. Brilliant red new growth.

'Variegata'. Slow growing to 6 ft. high and wide. Creamy white leaf variegation; the white markings are tinged pink in spring.

The following varieties are grown principally for their flowers:

'Christmas Cheer'. Early bloomer with bicolored flowers in white and deep rose red; flower stalks are rose red.

'Coleman'. Pink flowers open from red buds.

'Daisen'. Flowers like 'Christmas Cheer', but broader leaves.

'Dorothy Wyckoff'. White flowers open from deep red buds.

'Pink'. Shell pink flowers age to white.

'Purity'. To 3–4 ft. high and wide. Late bloomer with unusually large white flowers.

'Temple Bells'. Slow grower to 3–5 ft. high and wide. Ivory flowers.

'Valley Rose'. Light pink flowers.

'Valley Valentine'. To 5–7 ft. tall and wide. Deep red buds and flowers.

'White Cascade'. Extremely heavy show of pure white blooms.

PIGEON BERRY.
See **DURANTA erecta**

PIGGY-BACK PLANT.
See **TOLMIEA menziesii**

PIKAKE, PIKAKE-HOKU.
See **JASMINUM sambac,**
J. multiflorum

PILIKAI.
See **MERREMIA tuberosa**

PIMPERNEL. See **ANAGALLIS**

PIMPINELLA anisum

ANISE
Apiaceae (Umbelliferae)
ANNUAL

- ⚡ **ZONES 1–24; H1, H2**
- ☼ **FULL SUN**
- 💧 **REGULAR WATER**

Mediterranean native to 2 ft. tall, 1½ ft. wide. First growth produces a clump of bright green, roundish to heart-shaped, tooth-edged leaves. Foliage clumps send up stems set with feathery leaves; in summer, bear umbrellalike clusters

Pimpinella anisum

of tiny white flowers at stem tips. Use fresh leaves in salads; use seeds for flavoring baked goods, confections.

Plant grows quickly in warm weather, but you'll need to allow about 4 months for a crop of seeds to grow and mature. In coldest regions, sow seeds indoors, then set out young plants when frost danger is past. In mild-winter climates, sow directly in the ground in spring for harvest in summer or early fall. Where summers are very hot, sow in fall for spring harvest. Grow in light, well-drained soil. Plants are fairly wispy and look best in groups. They are taprooted and do not transplant easily once they begin to put on size.

PINCUSHION.
See **LEUCOSPERMUM**

PINCUSHION FLOWER.
See **SCABIOSA**

PINCUSHION TREE.
See **HAKEA laurina**

PINDO PALM.
See **BUTIA capitata**

PINE. See **PINUS**

PINEAPPLE

Bromeliaceae
PERENNIAL

- ⚡ **ZONES 24; H1, H2; OR INDOORS**
- ☼ **FULL SUN FOR FRUIT; BRIGHT LIGHT**
- 💧 **REGULAR WATER**

Native to South America. Well adapted to Hawaii, where it is a commercial crop. Has been cultivated outdoors in Southern California in warm, protected sites; black plastic mulch over soil increases chances of success.

To 2½–5 ft. tall, 3–4 ft. wide, with a short, thick stem topped by a rosette of long (1½–6-ft.), narrow dark green leaves with sawtoothed edges. At bloom time, the stem lengthens and produces a head composed of small red or purple flowers. The blossoms develop into the pineapple fruit. Fruits are typically borne one per stem; in ideal outdoor growing conditions, they reach size and heft of pineapples sold in markets. 'Sugarloaf' ('White Sugarloaf') is a low-acid variety with very sweet white flesh and a soft core.

Whether grown outdoors or as a houseplant, pineapple takes up to 2 years to begin bearing. Fruit should be ready to harvest when it reaches a good size and starts to take on a yellow cast, with bottom turning golden; individual leaves can be pulled out easily. After picking, let ripen fully at room temperature. After the fruit is harvested, the plant will continue to produce for several more years.

Pineapple

Outdoors, plants can be grown in the ground or in pots. Plant in well-drained soil. Start from divisions sold in nurseries; or slice off the leafy top of a market pineapple (cut about an inch below the leaf rosette) and let it dry for a couple of days. Plant 1 ft. apart. Set divisions 3–4 in. deep; set pineapple tops 2 in. deep (base of leaf rosette should be buried). Fertilize frequently.

Pineapple can also be grown indoors in a greenhouse or sunny room where temperature stays above 68°F/20°C. Root the base of a leafy pineapple top in water or in fast-draining but moisture-retentive potting mix. When roots have formed, move pineapple to 7–8-in. pot of rich soil. If you're lucky, a pineapple will form, but it will be much smaller than commercial fruit. A variety with pink, white, and olive green leaves is sometimes sold as a houseplant; it can take reduced light, since it is grown for foliage rather than fruit.

PINEAPPLE FLOWER.
See **EUCOMIS**

PINEAPPLE GUAVA.
See **FEIJOA**

PINE MUHLY.
See **MUHLENBERGIA dubia**

PINK. See **DIANTHUS**

PINK BALL TREE.
See **DOMBEYA wallichii**

PINK POLKA-DOT PLANT.
See **HYPOESTES phyllostachya**

PINK SHOWER.
See **CASSIA grandis**

PINK TECOMA.
See **TABEBUIA heterophylla**

PINK TRUMPET VINE.
See **PODRANEA ricasoliana**

PIÑON. See **PINUS edulis**

PINUS
PINE
Pinaceae
EVERGREEN TREES, RARELY SHRUBS

| ⚡ ZONES VARY BY SPECIES |
| ☼ FULL SUN |
| ◐ LITTLE WATER, EXCEPT AS NOTED |

Pines are the great individualists of the garden, each species differing not only in its characteristics but also in the ways it responds to wind, heat, and other growing conditions. Cone appearance (size and shape) is one identifying feature of these trees. Another is the number of needles in a bundle; most pines carry their long, slender needles in groups of two, three, or five. Young trees tend to be pyramidal, while older ones are more open or round topped. The text gives typical dimensions for pines in cultivation, but trees often grow much larger in the wild. Seeds of all species attract birds.

All pines can be shaped, and often improved, by some pruning. The best time to prune is in spring, when new growth emerges. Cut the candles (see "What Pines Need") to promote bushiness or limit the plant's size. You can remove unwanted limbs to accent a pine's branching pattern—but remember that a new one won't sprout to take its place. In time, lower limbs of most pines will die naturally; when this happens, cut them off.

Shaping a pine artistically— in the manner of trees in Japanese gardens—requires some skill, but it isn't difficult. Cut out any branches that interfere with the

desired effect, shorten others, and create an upswept look by removing all twigs that grow downward. Cut the vertical main trunk back to a well-placed side branch to induce side growth; wire or weight branches to produce a cascade effect.

Pines are vulnerable to air pollution, which causes abnormal needle drop and poor growth and may even kill trees. They are also subject to a number of diseases and pests, but healthy, well-grown plants will usually maintain their vigor with comparatively little attention. Many five-needle pines are subject to a blister rust (a bark disease that can be fatal) when grown in the vicinity of currants or gooseberries. In the Pacific Northwest, distorted or dead new shoots on two- and three-needle pines indicate an infestation of European pine shoot moth larvae. In California, engraver beetles sometimes bore into bark of Aleppo, shore, Bishop, Coulter, Monterey, ponderosa, and Torrey pines. Sticky secretions, sooty mold, and yellowing needles indicate aphid infestation. Your Cooperative Extension Office can also offer advice concerning each tree's adaptability to your area and any local environmental or pest problems. The number of available color variants, odd forms, and dwarf pines runs easily into the hundreds: seek them out at specialty nurseries.

P. albicaulis. WHITEBARK PINE. Zones A2, A3; 1–7, 15–17. From high mountains of Northern California and Nevada north to Canada. Grows very slowly to 20–40 ft. tall (usually much less), about half as wide. In youth, slender and symmetrical, with whitish bark; often multitrunked as it ages. Dark green, 1½–3-in.-long needles are held in groups of five. Cones to 3 in. long, roundish, and purple. Licensed collectors dig plants from the wild and sell them under the name "alpine conifer." Densely foliaged pine is good for rock gardens, bonsai.

P. aristata. BRISTLECONE PINE. Zones A2, A3; 1–11, 14–19. Localized populations scattered across high mountains of the West. Grows very slowly to 20 ft. tall (possibly to 45 ft.), 15 ft. wide. Dense, bushy, heavy-trunked tree with ground-sweeping branches. In youth, symmetrical and narrow crowned. Needles are held in groups of five and grow 1–1½ in. long;

Pinus muricata

P

dark green flecked with dots of white resin. Cones to 3½ in. long are narrowly oval, dark purplish brown, bristly. Excellent container, rock garden, and bonsai plant. Protect from wind in cold climates.

P. attenuata. KNOBCONE PINE. Zones 2–10, 14–21. Native to Oregon's northern and central Cascades, Siskiyous and Sierra foothills in California, south to Baja California. Grows rapidly

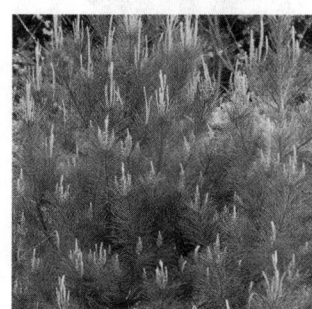

Pinus attenuata

to 20–80 ft. tall, 20–25 ft. wide. Usually rounded and regular in youth, open and irregular in age, though some populations are more regular in form and densely foliaged than others. Yellow-green needles 3–5 in. long are held in groups of three. Light brown cones are 4–6 in. long, narrowly oval, lopsided, and knobby; they stay attached to branches for many years (fire releases them). Grows well in poor soil.

P. austriaca. See P. nigra

P. banksiana. JACK PINE. Zones A1–A3; 1, 2. Native from the Arctic Circle to Minnesota. Slow to moderate growth to 30–50 ft. tall (often less) and 10–15 ft. wide. In youth, a symmetrical pyramid; in age, irregular and more spreading, often picturesque. Sometimes remains shrubby. Olive-green needles to 2 in. long are held in groups of two and are often curved or twisted. Cones are yellowish brown, 1–3 in. long, and slender, with a pointed tip. Tolerates poor soil, even sand. Good windbreak.

P. brutia (P. halepensis brutia). CALABRIAN PINE. Zones 6–9, 12–24. From eastern Mediterranea, southern Russia, southern Italy. Grows fast to 30–80 ft. tall, 15–25 ft. wide. Classic pine shape in youth; top spreads with age. Dark green needles in groups of two reach 5–6½ in. long. Cones are oval to oblong, 3 in. long, reddish brown. Very much like *P. halepensis,* though its form is less interesting at maturity. Thrives in heat, wind, and poor soil.

P. bungeana. LACEBARK PINE. Zones 2–10, 14–21. From northern and central China. Grows 50–75 ft. tall and 20–35 ft. wide. Starts out pyramidal to rounded, then becomes more open, spreading, and picturesque. Often multi-trunked, sometimes shrubby. Smooth, dull gray bark flakes off like that of sycamore *(Platanus)* to reveal creamy white patches. Bright

Pinus bungeana

Pinus canariensis

green needles in groups of three are 2–4 in. long. Oval cones are 2–2½ in. long and yellowish brown. Limbs are brittle, can break under heavy ice or snow load.

P. canariensis. CANARY ISLAND PINE. Zones 8, 9, 12–24. Native to Canary Islands. Grows fast to 50–80 ft. tall, 20–35 ft. tall. Gawky when young, but soon develops into a slender, graceful pyramid, after which it takes on a tiered look, then finally develops a round head. Bark is fissured, reddish brown. Needles 9–12 in. long held in groups of three; bluish green when new, then aging to dark green. Glossy brown cones are oval, reaching 4–9 in. long. Resists oak root fungus.

P. cembra. SWISS STONE PINE. Zones A1–A3; 1–7, 10. Native to the mountains of central Europe.

Pinus cembra

Grows extremely slowly to 50–70 ft. or taller, 20–25 ft. wide. Handsome narrow, dense pyramid in youth; becomes broad, open, and round topped in maturity. Dark green needles are 3–5 in. long, held in groups of five. Broad, oval, purplish blue cones are 3½ in. long. 'Klein' has violet-blue cones; grows 12 ft. tall, 6 ft. wide. Does best with regular water.

P. cembroides. MEXICAN PIÑON PINE. Zones 2–24. Native from Arizona to Baja California, Northern Mexico. Slow grower to 10–25 ft. tall, nearly as wide. Rangy in youth, but older trees develop stout, spreading branches

that form a round head. Dark green needles 1–2 in. long are grouped in twos or threes. Cones are 1–2 in. long, rounded, and yellowish or reddish brown. Good choice in desert. Cones contain edible seeds (pine nuts).

P. contorta. SHORE PINE, BEACH PINE. Zones A3; 4–9, 14–24, H1. Native along the Pacific Coast from Alaska to Northern California. Grows fairly quickly to 20–35 ft. tall and wide. Nursery trees are compact, pyramidal, and somewhat irregular; trees growing along the coast may be dwarfed and shaped by winds. Dark green needles are held in groups of two, reaching 1¼–2 in. long. Narrow, lopsided cones 1–2 in. long are light yellow brown. Good-looking tree in youth; densely foliaged. Responds well to pruning. Good in containers. Among the best pines for small gardens. Tree needs regular water.

P. c. murrayana (P. c. latifolia). LODGEPOLE PINE, TAMARACK. Zones A1–A3; 1–7, 14–17. Native to the mountains of the western U.S. Can grow 50–80 ft. tall, 20–25 ft. wide, but often much smaller. Planted among other trees, lodgepole pine grows tall and slender, but in the open, the trunk can be quite thick, even though the tree remains narrow and dense. Yellow-green needles are grouped in twos, reaching 1½–3 in. long. Cones to 1½ in. long are shiny brown and oval; tend to hang onto branches for a long time. Tree needs regular water.

P. coulteri. COULTER PINE. Zones 3–10, 14–23; H1. Native to dry, rocky mountain California slopes from Mt. Diablo and Mt. Hamilton through the Santa Lucia Range and Southern California to Baja California. Grows moderately fast to 30–80 ft. tall, 20–40 ft. wide, with shapely, open growth and wide-spreading, persistent lower branches. Can develop multiple leaders. Needles are deep green, stiff, 5–10 in. (even 14 in.) long and held in groups of three. Heavy cones are 10–14 in. long, oval, and buff colored; they remain on the tree for a long time.

P. densiflora. JAPANESE RED PINE. Zones 2–9, 14–17; H1. Native to Japan. Grows rapidly when young, ultimately to 40–60 ft. tall (to 100 ft. tall in perfect conditions) and 40 ft. wide. Develops a broad, irregular head, even in youth; often has two trunks. Young branches have flaking, red-orange bark. Bright green needles are grouped

Pinus densiflora 'Oculus-draconis'

in twos and reach 2½–5 in. long. Tawny brown cones are 2 in. long, oval or oblong in shape. Won't take hot, dry, or cold winds. Needs regular water.

'Compacta' is similar in size to 'Umbraculifera' but more dense.

'Oculus-draconis' (dragon eye pine) is about half the size of the species. Each needle has two yellow bands, so branches appear to have concentric green and yellow bands when viewed from the tips.

'Pendula' is a dwarf form with a sprawling, weeping habit—perfect for rock gardens. Can be staked to form a weeping specimen tree.

'Umbraculifera,' Tanyosho pine, grows in Zones 2–10, 14–17. It is a moderate grower to 12–20 ft. tall and 18 ft. wide. Broad, flat-topped tree with many trunks that emerge from the base; often grafted onto a short single trunk. Good for containers, rock gardens, and Asian gardens.

P. edulis (P. cembroides edulis). PIÑON, NUT PINE. Zones 1–11, 14–21. Native from California's desert mountains east to New Mexico and Texas, north to Wyoming. Grows slowly to 10–20 ft. tall, 8–16 ft. wide. Horizontally branching tree, bushy and symmetrical in youth, spreading as it matures and developing a rounded, flat crown. Stiff, dark green needles are usually grouped in twos, reaching ¾–1½ in. long. Roundish, light brown cones to 2 in. long produce the edible pine nuts sold in markets. This is a

Pinus edulis

beautiful, dense small pine for containers and rock gardens, lending a look of age to new gardens. In the Southwest, trees stressed by drought are damaged or killed by bark beetles.

P. eldarica. (P. brutia eldarica) AFGHAN PINE. Zones 6–9, 11–24. From southern Russia, Afghanistan, Pakistan. Growth size, rate, habit, and both needle and cone descriptions match *P. brutia*. Among best pines for much of the desert; also thrives near Pacific Coast. Avoid planting in Southwest areas with elevations of 4,000–8,000 ft. where oaks are prevalent; fatal Comandra blister rust often kills these pines here. Christmas Blue is a blue-green strain.

P. flexilis. LIMBER PINE. Zones A1–A3; 1–11, 14–21. Native to 5,000–11,000-ft. elevations in northern Arizona, Utah, Nevada, Southern California; eastern slopes of Rockies from Alberta to Texas. Grows at a slow to moderate rate to 30–55 ft. tall, 15–25 ft. wide. In youth, forms a rather straggly pyramid; in maturity, develops a thick trunk and an open, round top. Many of its limber branches may droop. At highest elevations it is dwarfed and irregular. Dark green needles are slightly curved or twisted, to 3 in. long, and held in groups of five. Buff to buff orange cones are elongated and oval, growing 3–5 in. long. Takes well to shearing; good bonsai subject. Tolerates wind and grows well on rocky slopes. 'Vanderwolf's Pyramid' has regular form, blue-green needles.

P. griffithii. See P. wallichiana

P. halepensis. ALEPPO PINE. Zones 7–9, 11–24. Native to Medi-

Pinus halepensis

terranean region. Grows at a moderate to fast rate to 30–60 ft. tall and 20–40 ft. wide. Already shows rugged character at 5 years; in age, has open, irregular crown of many short, ascending branches. Light green needles 2½–4 in. long are usually grouped in twos. Reddish

brown cones are 3 in. long, oval to oblong, stalked and bent backward. Takes poor soils, desert heat, seashore conditions, but better trees can be found for milder climates. In the Southwest, Aleppo blight causes temporary dieback in winter. For the plant sometimes sold as *P. h. brutia*, see *P. brutia*.

P. heldreichii (P. h. leucodermis). BOSNIAN PINE. Zones 2–11, 14–24. Native to the Balkans, Greece, Italy. Slow grower to 50–75 ft. tall, 15–20 ft. wide, forming a dense, erect oval or cone shape. Stiff, dark green needles are 2½–3½ in. long and held in groups of two; they persist for 5–6 years, so tree is densely foliaged. Narrowly oval, blue to bright brown cones 2–3 in. long are carried singly or in clusters of three. Young trees have pale grayish bark. Great landscape tree, especially near the ocean where its salt tolerance pays off. Regular water.

P. jeffreyi. JEFFREY PINE. Zones 2–9, 14–19; H1. Native to mountains of California, southern Oregon, western Nevada, Baja California. Moderate growth rate, reaching 60–120 ft. tall, 20–25 ft. wide. Pyramidal form, with straight trunk and pendulous branches; symmetrical in youth, more open with age. Blue-green needles grouped in threes are 5–8 in. long. Cones are 6–12 in. long, oval, and reddish brown, with scales whose spiny tips curve inward. Attractive in youth, with silvery gray bark and bluish foliage. Furrows in the bark of older trees have the fragrance of vanilla, butterscotch, or oranges, depending on the tree and the sniffer. Does best at high altitudes.

P. lambertiana. SUGAR PINE. Zones 2–9, 15–17. Native to Sierra Nevada and California's higher Coast Ranges, high mountains of Southern California and Baja California, north to southwestern Oregon. Grows slowly in youth, then speeds up, ultimately reaching 200 ft. tall (or taller) and 50 ft. wide. In youth, a narrow, open pyramid with spreading, rather pendulous branches; in age, usually flat topped, with a wide-spreading, open head. Dark bluish green needles 3–4 in. long are held in groups of five. Cones are light brown, 10–20 in. long, and almost cylindrical. This is the world's tallest pine. Huge cones are a hazard around play areas, patios, parked cars—but best-ever holiday decorations. Thrives around Puget Sound.

P. monticola. WESTERN WHITE PINE. Zones 1–7. Native from Northern California north to British Columbia, east to Montana. Grows fast at first, then moderately to slowly, to 60 ft. tall, 20 ft. wide. Attractive, narrow, and open crowned in youth; in age, a pyramidal tree with spreading and somewhat drooping branches. Thin, soft needles 1½–4 in. long are blue green, striped with white beneath; held in groups of five. Cones 5–11 in. long are slender and light brown. Bark is purplish, weathering to a silvery color; forms plates rather than furrows.

P. mugo (P. mugo mugo). MUGHO PINE. Zones A1–A3; 1–11, 14–24. From the eastern Alps and Balkan states. Slow growth to 4–8 ft. high, 8–15 ft. wide. From the start, a shrubby, symmetrical little pine. Often spreads in old age. Dark green needles to 2 in. long are held in groups of two and are crowded on branches. Cones to 1½ in. long are oval and tawny to dark brown. Widely used in rock gardens and containers. Pick plants with dense, pleasing form. Pumilio group includes a number of compact selections.

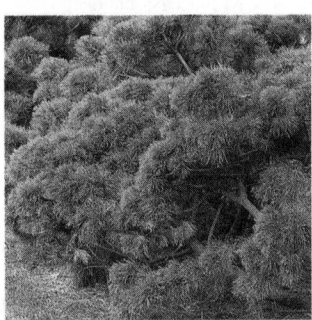

Pinus mugo

P. m. uncinata, Swiss mountain pine, from the mountains of Spain and central Europe to the Balkans, is slow growing and highly variable in size. May be a prostrate shrub, low shrub, or pyramidal tree of moderate size (30–80 ft. high and wide). Nursery plants are generally bushy, twisted, and somewhat open.

P. muricata. BISHOP PINE. Zones 5, 14–17, 22–44. From northern coastal California, Santa Cruz Island, and northwestern Baja California. Rapid grower to 40–75 ft. tall, 20–40 ft. wide. Open and pyramidal form in youth, dense and rounded in middle life, and irregular in old age. Needles are dark green, 4–6 in. long, and held in groups of two. Brown, broadly oval cones are 2–3 in. long, lopsided,

and held in whorls of three to five. Slower growing, denser in youth, and better mannered than *P. radiata*, another pine native to California. Tolerates salt air. First-rate windbreak tree.

P. nigra (P. austriaca). AUSTRIAN BLACK PINE. Zones A3; 2–10, 14–21. From Europe, western Asia. Slow to moderate growth to 40–60 ft. tall and half as wide. Dense, stout, pyramidal tree with uniform crown. Branches grow in regular whorls. In old age, broad and flat topped. Stiff, very dark green needles, 3–6½ in. long, are held in groups of two. Oval, brown cones are 2–3½ in. long. Tree of strong character for landscape decoration or as windbreak in cold regions. Tolerant of urban environment and seacoast conditions. Resistant to oak root fungus. Regular water.

P. parviflora. JAPANESE WHITE PINE. Zones 2–9, 14–24. From Japan and Taiwan. Slow to moderate grower to 20–50 ft. tall and wide or larger. In youth, a dense pyramid; in age, wide spreading and flat topped. Needles are 1½–2½ in. long, bluish green, and held in groups of five. Oval to oblong, reddish brown cones are 2–3 in. long. Widely used and popular as bonsai subject, container tree. Grows well in the Seattle area and in Northern California. Blue-gray and dwarf forms are available. Regular water.

P. patula. JELECOTE PINE. Zones 6–9, 12–24; H1. Native to Mexico. Very fast growth to 60–80 ft. tall and half as wide, forming a symmetrical pyramid with widely spaced tiers of branches. Pendent, grass green needles to 1 ft. long are held in groups of three. Lustrous brown cones are sickle shaped, to 4½ in. long. Graceful tree that casts light shade and provides a handsome silhouette. One of the fastest-growing

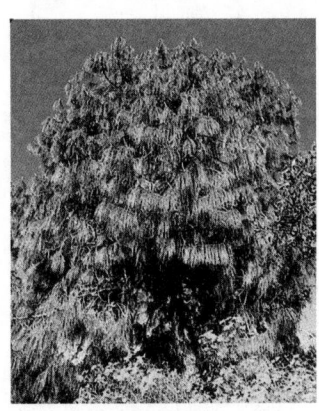

Pinus patula

P

pines in the world. Best near coast. Resistant to oak root fungus. Regular water.

P. pinaster. CLUSTER PINE, FRENCH TURPENTINE PINE, MARITIME PINE. Zones 6–9, 12–24. Native to the Atlantic coast of France, western Mediterranean, and northern Africa. Very fast growth to 80–90 ft. tall, 30–35 ft. wide. Pyramidal tree with spreading or sometimes pendulous branches. Glossy green needles are 5–9 in. long and held in groups of two. Cones are 4–7 in. long, oblong, glossy light brown, and held singly or in clusters. Best near coast and in coastal valleys. Used in San Francisco's Golden Gate Park to help bind sand dunes. May be weak rooted when young.

P. pinea. ITALIAN STONE PINE. Zones 8, 9, 11–24; H1. From southern Europe and Turkey. Moderate growth to 40–80 ft. tall and 40–60 ft. wide. In youth, grows as a stout, bushy globe; in middle life, develops a thick trunk topped with an "umbrella" of many branches. In maturity, tree is broad and flat topped. Stiff needles are bright green to gray green, 5–8 in. long, and held in groups of two. Cones are broadly oval, 4–6 in. long, and glossy chestnut brown. Excellent pine for beach gardens; also tolerates heat. Eventually too large for small gardens. This is the pine depicted in Renaissance paintings; also a source of edible seeds (pine nuts).

P. ponderosa. PONDEROSA PINE, WESTERN YELLOW PINE. Zones 1–10, 14–21; H1. Native from British Columbia to Mexico and east to Nebraska, Texas, northeast Oklahoma. Moderate to fast grower, reaching 50–100 ft. tall, 25–30 ft. wide. May exceed 200 ft. high in the wild. In youth, straight trunked and well branched. Stately in age, with open branches in spirelike crown. Yellow green to dark green, firm needles 4–11 in. long are held in groups of three in clusters at branch ends. Cones are oval, 3–5 in. long, light brown to red brown. Important lumber tree. Handsome orange-brown bark. Useful for groves, shelter belt; also good for bonsai or containers.

Doesn't take desert heat and wind. *P. p. arizonica* has needles in groups of three to five. *P. p. scopulorum*, from the Rockies, has shorter needles and drooping branches.

P. radiata. MONTEREY PINE. Zones 14–24; H1. From central coast of California. Very fast growth to 80–100 ft. tall, 25–35 ft. wide. Puts on 6 ft. a year when young; reaches 50 ft. in 12 years. Shapely, broad cone in youth, then drops its lower branches to develop rounded or flattish crown. Bright green needles 3–7 in. long are held in groups of two or three. Oval, lopsided cones are 3–6 in. long, light brown, and held in clusters that persist on the branches. Often shallow rooted, subject to blowing over in wind. Even in ideal climate, suffers many pests and diseases (including pitch canker) that make it a poor risk. Try to keep established plants healthy with occasional deep watering and feeding.

Pinus pinea

P. sabiniana. GRAY PINE, FOOTHILL PINE. Zones 3–10, 14–21. Fast grower to 40–80 ft. tall, 30–50 ft. wide, with an irregular to rounded head; trunks are usually forked. Gray-green needles are 8–12 in. long and held in groups of three. Cones are 6–10 in. long, oval, and chocolate brown; tips of scales are clawlike. Unusual, lovely tree for large gardens. Crown is bulky yet lacy, almost transparent; offers little shade. Though native to dry foothills, it thrives in Seattle area. Cones contain edible seeds (pine nuts).

P. strobus. WHITE PINE, EASTERN WHITE PINE. Zones 1–6. Slow in seedling stage, then fast to 50–80 ft. tall (or taller), 20–40 ft. wide. Forms a symmetrical pyramid, with horizontal branches in regular whorls. Becomes broad, open, and irregular with age. Fine textured, handsome tree. Blue-green needles are

soft, 3–5½ in. long, held in groups of five. Slender, often curved, light brown cones reach 3–8 in. long. Intolerant of strong winds. Popular varieties include 'Contorta', with twisted branches and needles; 'Pendula', with weeping, trailing branches; and 'Prostrata', very low and trailing.

Plants in the Nana group are broad shrubs, growing slowly to 3–7 ft. tall, 6–12 ft. wide. Useful in rock gardens or containers, though plants sold under this name have been known to grow into small trees. 'Blue Shag' is a blue-needled form. These need regular water.

P. sylvestris. SCOTCH PINE. Zones A1–A3; 1–9, 14–21. From northern Europe, western Asia, northeastern Siberia. Grows fast at first, then moderately to 30–70 ft. (possibly to 100 ft.) tall and 25–30 ft. wide. Forms a narrow, well-branched pyramid when young. In age, becomes irregular, open, and picturesque, with drooping branches. Stiff, 1½–3 in. long, blue-green needles often turn yellow green in winter. Egg-shaped cones to 2 in. long are gray to reddish brown. Popular as a Christmas tree and in gardens. Showy red bark, sparse foliage in maturity. Wind resistant. 'French Blue' keeps its blue color in winter. Handsome and dense 'Fastigiata' grows slowly to 20–30 ft. tall and just 4–6 ft. wide. Dwarf forms 'Nana' and 'Watereri' grow slowly to just 12 ft. high. All need regular water in hottest areas.

P. thunbergii. JAPANESE BLACK PINE. Zones 3–12, 14–21. From Japan. In the Northwest, grows fast to 100 ft. tall and 40 ft. wide; in Southern California and desert, grows slowly to moderately to 20 ft. tall, 10 ft. wide. Spreading branches form a broad, conical tree; irregular and spreading in age, often with a leaning trunk. Bright green needles are stiff, 3–4½ in. long, held in groups of two; new growth (candles) nearly white. Oval, brown cones grow to about 3 in. long. Handsome tree that can be sheared as a Christmas tree or pruned as a cascade or giant bonsai. Regular water in hottest areas. 'Majestic Beauty' tolerates smog and salt. Dwarf 'Thunderhead' (6 ft. tall, 5 ft. wide in 10 years) has dark foliage.

Pinus thunbergii

P. torreyana. TORREY PINE. Zones 8, 9, 14–24. Native to California's coastal San Diego area and Santa Rosa Island. Fast growth to at least 40–60 ft. tall, 30–50 ft. wide. Broad, open, irregular, picturesque habit when exposed to ocean winds; tall, upright, and symmetrical inland. Needles are light gray green to dark green, 8–13 in. long, and held in groups of five. Roundish, chocolate brown cones are 4–6 in. long. Native to coast but accepts hotter, drier conditions. Less open form if grown in heavy soil. Don't prune large branches; they will die back to trunk. Resistant to oak root fungus.

P. wallichiana (P. griffithii). HIMALAYAN WHITE PINE. Zones A2, A3; 4–6, 15–17. From the Himalayas. Slow to moderate growth to 30–50 ft. tall, 15–30 ft. wide. May reach 150 ft. high in the wild. Broad and conical, it often retains branches to ground even in age. Drooping, blue-green needles 6–8 in. long are held in groups of five. Slender, elongated cones are 6–10 in. long and light brown. Good form and color make this a fine choice for featured pine in a big lawn or garden.

PISTACHE. See **PISTACIA**

PISTACHIO NUT
Anacardiaceae
DECIDUOUS TREE

✎	ZONES 7–12, 14, 15, 18–21 (SEE TEXT)
☼	FULL SUN
💧	MODERATE WATER

Botanically known as *Pistacia vera*, this native of southwestern and central Asia produces the pistachio nuts sold in markets; for strictly ornamental members of the genus, see *Pistacia*. Tree grows to 25–30 ft. tall and as wide, with one or several trunks. Its gray-green leaves are divided into three to five roundish, 2–4 in.-long leaflets.

Male and female plants are separate; to get fruit, be sure to include a male tree in your planting. 'Peters' is the most commonly grown male; 'Kerman' is the principal female (fruiting) variety. On female trees, small brownish green spring flowers are followed by heavy clusters of soft, wrinkled, reddish husks that contain the hard-shelled pistachio nuts.

Harvest nuts in early autumn: spread a tarp beneath tree, then shake tree until nuts fall. Strip off and discard husks; dip nuts in water and dry them in the sun

Pistachio nut

until shells split (dipping in water helps the shells split). Some people like to add flavor by boiling the husked nuts in salted water for a few minutes before drying them.

Nut production is best in Zones 8–11, where trees get just the right amount of summer heat and winter chill. Trees grow well in Zones 7, 12, 14, 15, 18–21, but crops are unpredictable—and when they do appear, nut meats often do not properly fill shells.

When planting, avoid rough handling; budded tops are easily broken away from understock. Susceptible to verticillium wilt and oak root fungus; to lessen disease risk, grow in well-drained soil and water deeply and infrequently.

Trees are inclined to spread and droop; stake them and train to a good framework of four or five limbs beginning 4 ft. or so above ground. Take 5 to 8 years to begin bearing and many years to reach full yield. Tend to bear more heavily in alternate years. Established trees will survive with little water, but nut quality is best if trees receive periodic deep soakings.

PISTACIA

PISTACHE
Anacardiaceae
EVERGREEN, SEMIEVERGREEN, AND DECIDUOUS TREES AND SHRUBS

| 🌱 ZONES VARY BY SPECIES |
| ☀️ FULL SUN |
| 🌑🌑 WATER NEEDS VARY BY SPECIES |

These are ornamental species; for the plant grown for edible nuts, see Pistachio Nut. Glossy deep green leaves are divided into leaflets; insignificant flowers. If male trees are nearby, female trees will bear clusters of tiny fruits. Verticillium wilt may strike established trees. Minimize susceptibility by planting in well-drained soil, watering deeply but infrequently. Young trees tend to be irregular in form

and benefit from early training and pruning.

P. atlantica. MOUNT ATLAS PISTACHE. Semievergreen or deciduous tree. Zones 8–24. From the Mediterranean region. Slow to moderate growth to 45–60 ft. tall and wide. More regular and pyramidal than other pistaches, especially in youth. Leaves have 7–11 narrow leaflets to 2 in. long, rounded at tip. Nearly evergreen in mildest-winter areas of range; holds foliage into late autumn where winters are cold. Dark blue or purple fruit. Needs good drainage. Tolerates desert heat and winds. No irrigation needed. Not widely grown as an ornamental but is much used as understock for pistachio nut.

P. chinensis. CHINESE PISTACHE. Deciduous tree. Zones 4–16, 17 (warmer parts), 18–23; little grown in Zones 4–7. From China. Slow to moderate growth to 30–60 ft. tall, with nearly equal spread. Foot-long leaves consist of 10–16 narrow, 2–4-in.-long leaflets. Good fall color, even in mild climates: foliage turns luminous orange to red (sometimes shades of yellow). This is the only tree to color scarlet in the desert. Fruit is red at first,

Pistacia chinensis

then ripens to blue black. Tolerates a wide range of conditions. Accepts various watering regimes, from no water at all (this only in deep soils) to regular lawn watering (though verticillium wilt is a danger with the latter). Takes moderately alkaline soil. Resistant to oak root fungus. Reliable tree for streetside planting, lawn, patio, or garden.

P. lentiscus. MASTIC. Evergreen shrub or tree. Zones 8, 9, 12–24. From the Mediterranean region. Slow growth to 15–25 ft. high, 20–30 ft. wide. Three to five pairs of leaflets to 1 in. long. Fruit ripens from red to black. Useful as a screen plant for hot, dry locations and poor soil. Sap is the source of

mastic, an aromatic resin. Little or no water (monthly soaking is best in Zones 12, 13).

P. vera. See Pistachio Nut

PISTIA stratiotes

WATER LETTUCE
Araceae
AQUATIC PERENNIAL

| 🌱 ZONES 24; H2 |
| ☀️ 🌓 FULL SUN OR LIGHT SHADE |
| 🌑 LOCATE IN PONDS, WATER GARDENS |

Native to many parts of the tropics. Attractive plant that resembles a floating, grayish green loose-head lettuce; each foliage rosette grows to about 4 in. high and wide. The trailing roots provide a refuge for small fish. Inconspicuous flowers. Increases by offsets and can become a pest in open tropical waters.

Pistia stratiotes

PITANGA. See **EUGENIA uniflora**

PITCHER SAGE. See **LEPECHINIA**

PITTOSPORUM

Pittosporaceae
EVERGREEN SHRUBS OR TREES

| 🌱 ZONES VARY BY SPECIES |
| ☀️ 🌓 FULL SUN OR PARTIAL SHADE |
| 🌑🌑 MODERATE TO REGULAR WATER, EXCEPT AS NOTED |

These plants are valued primarily for their foliage and form, though they also bear clusters of small, bell-shaped, often sweetly fragrant flowers followed by fairly conspicuous fruits the size of large peas. All are basic, dependable plants with pleasing outlines when allowed to branch naturally. Prune periodically to enhance form, thinning out weak branches and wayward shoots. Some make good clipped hedges. Excellent for screens, windbreaks. Susceptible to aphids and scale insects; sooty mold on leaves is a sign of infestation. Ripe fruits (usually orange) split open to reveal sticky seeds; fallen fruit can be a nuisance on lawns, paving.

P. brevicalyx. Zones 8, 9, 14–24. Native to China. To 18–20 ft. tall, 16–18 ft. wide. Leathery, glossy dark green leaves have somewhat

silvery undersides, reach 4–5 in. long, 1½–2 in. wide. Large clusters of fragrant bright yellow flowers in spring. Produces very little fruit.

P. crassifolium. Zones 9, 14–17, 19–24. From New Zealand. Can reach 25 ft. tall and 20 ft. wide in 8 to 10 years, but yearly pruning easily keeps it to 6–10 ft. tall, 6–8 ft. wide. Branches are densely clothed in gray-green, 1–2-in.-long leaves with rounded ends. Maroon flowers in late spring. Tolerates seaside conditions. 'Compactum' grows to 3 ft. or a bit taller, with equal spread.

P. eugenioides. Zones 9, 14–17, 19–22; H1, H2. From New Zealand. To 20–40 ft. tall, 15–30 ft. wide. Often seen as a high hedge or screen plant; unpruned, becomes a tree with a curving gray trunk. Yellow-green to medium green, wavy-edged, lance-shaped, 2–4-in.-long leaves. Fragrant yellow flowers in spring. Set 1½ ft. apart for a hedge; force bushiness by shearing 2–6 in. from tops of plants several times each year between midwinter and early fall. A form with foliage edged in creamy white grows just 10 ft. tall; it needs partial shade in hottest climates.

P. phillyreoides. WILLOW PITTOSPORUM. Zones 8, 9, 12–24. Native to Australia. Slow grower to 12–20 ft. tall, 10–15 ft. wide. This species differs from other pittosporums in both habit and leaf shape; it is a weeping plant with trailing branches and dark green, very narrow leaves to 3 in. long. Blooms in late winter and early spring, bearing very fragrant yellow flowers. Deep yellow fruit follows the blossoms. Always looks best standing alone; its strong structure should not be diminished by competing foliage. Good by pool or patio. If drainage is poor, water infrequently but very deeply. Tolerates heat and aridity better than other pittosporums and has even naturalized in some desert areas.

P. rhombifolium. QUEENSLAND PITTOSPORUM. Zones 12–24; H1, H2. From Australia. Grows slowly to 15–35 ft. tall, 12–25 ft. wide. Rich green, glossy, nearly diamond-shaped leaves to 4 in. long. White flowers in late spring. Growth is open enough to let you see the showy clusters of round, 1½-in., yellow to orange fruits that decorate the plant from fall through winter. As a small tree, well suited for lawn or patio (as long as sticky fruit won't pose a problem). Or plant several as a not-too-dense screen that needs

P

little pruning. Resistant to oak root fungus.

P. tenuifolium (P. nigricans). Zones 9, 14–17, 19–24. From New Zealand. To 15–25 ft. tall, 10–15 ft. wide. Similar in form to *P. eugenioides* but has darker twigs and leafstalks; purple flowers; shorter, more oval, deeper green leaves with less wavy edges; and greater tolerance for seacoast conditions. 'Silver Sheen' has a somewhat more open habit than the species and smaller, silvery green leaves. 'Marjorie Channon', to about 8 ft. high and wide, has green leaves bordered in creamy white.

P. tobira. TOBIRA. Zones 8–24; H1, H2. Worth trying in Zones 4–7. From Japan. Dense, rounded growth 6–15 ft. (rarely to 30 ft.) tall and wide. You can remove lower limbs from an older plant to make a small tree, or you can hold plant to 6 ft. by careful heading back and thinning (doesn't look good sheared). Whorls of leathery, narrowly elliptical, shiny dark green leaves to 5 in. long. In early spring, creamy white flowers with fragrance of orange blossoms are borne at branch tips. Seldom flowers in Hawaii. Good for screen, tall hedge, multistemmed specimen of interesting, irregular form. Very tolerant of seacoast conditions. 'Variegata' grows 5–10 ft. high and wide, has leaves in gray green and gray with an irregular creamy white margin. It makes a good hedge or foundation plant; sometimes loses many leaves in winter.

Pittosporum tobira

Several compact selections are available. The most common is 'Wheeler's Dwarf', to 2–3 ft. high and 4–5 ft. wide, with the same handsome leaves as *P. tobira*. It is a choice plant for foreground, low boundary, even small-scale ground cover; good near swimming pools. 'Turner's Variegated Dwarf' is the size of 'Wheeler's Dwarf' but has foliage like that of 'Variegata'. 'Cream de Mint' is smaller—just 2–2½ ft. high and wide—and has mint green leaves with a creamy white border.

P. undulatum. VICTORIAN BOX. Zones 14 and 15 (with protection), 16, 17, 21–24; H1, H2. From Australia. Fairly fast to 15 ft., then slow to 30–40 ft. high and wide. Glossy green, lance-shaped, wavy-edged leaves up to 6 in. long. Creamy white, very fragrant flowers in early spring. Makes dense, single- or multitrunked, dome-shaped tree of great beauty. Plants set 5–8 ft. apart can make a thick, 10–15-ft.-tall screen with selective pruning (not shearing). Roots are strong, becoming invasive with age.

Pittosporum undulatum

P. viridiflorum. CAPE PITTOSPORUM. Zones 15–17, 20–24; H1, H2. From South Africa. Grows 25 ft. tall and wide. Leaves to 3 in. long are glossy deep green above, paler beneath, often with inrolled edges; tips may be sharp or blunt. Dense clusters of fragrant yellowish green flowers in late spring. Resembles a large *P. tobira*. Use as screen, garden tree, street tree.

PLANE TREE.
See **PLATANUS**

PLANTAIN LILY.
See **HOSTA**

PLATANUS
PLANE TREE, SYCAMORE
Platanaceae
DECIDUOUS TREES

✎	ZONES VARY BY SPECIES
☼	FULL SUN
◐	MODERATE TO REGULAR WATER

All are large, with heavy trunk (or trunks) and sculptural branch pattern. Older bark sheds in patches to reveal pale, smooth new bark beneath. Big, rough-surfaced leaves (to 10 in. across) have three to five lobes, resemble maple (*Acer*) leaves. Fall foliage color is yellowish to brown, not striking. Ball-

shaped brown seed clusters, usually on threadlike stalks, hang on the bare branches through winter; these are prized for winter arrangements. Best in rich, deep, moist, well-drained soil. All are subject to anthracnose, which causes early leaf drop and twig dieback. Rake up and dispose of dead leaves, since fungus spores can overwinter on them. Chlorosis may be a problem in the desert.

P. × acerifolia (P. × hispanica). LONDON PLANE TREE. Zones 2–24. Hybrid between *P. occidentalis* and *P. orientalis;* often sold under the latter name. Grows fast to 40–80 ft. tall, with 30–40-ft. spread. Creamy new bark weathers to gray. Looks very handsome in winter. Tolerates many soil types and stands up beautifully to smog, soot, dust, and reflected heat. Susceptible to mildew. Good tree for avenue, street, park, large lawn. When pollarded to create a low, dense canopy, it can fit smaller spaces. 'Bloodgood' is resistant to anthracnose; 'Yarwood' is mildew resistant; 'Columbia' is resistant to both diseases.

Platanus × acerifolia

P. occidentalis. AMERICAN SYCAMORE, BUTTONWOOD. Zones 1–24. Native to eastern U.S. Similar to *P. × acerifolia* but has whiter new bark and a longer leafless period. Irregular habit, contorted branches. Occasionally grows with multiple or leaning trunks. Old trees near streams sometimes reach huge size. Best in a large wild garden.

P. racemosa. CALIFORNIA SYCAMORE. Zones 4–24. Robust native of California foothills and Coast Ranges; grows near streams in the wild. Fast rate of growth to 30–80 ft. tall and 20–50 ft. wide, frequently with multiple or leaning trunks. Smooth branches are often gracefully twisted and contorted. Attractive, patchy bark in brown, gray, white. Deeply lobed leaves

turn dusty brown early in autumn; in mild coastal climates, they hang on until new growth starts. In winter, virtually stemless seed balls are carried three to seven along a single stalk. Tolerates much heat and wind. With careful pruning, can be trained into picturesque multitrunked clump. For large informal or wild garden.

P. wrightii (P. racemosa wrightii). ARIZONA SYCAMORE. Zones 10–12. To 80 ft. tall, 55 ft. wide. Native along streams and canyons in mountains of southern and eastern Arizona. Resembles *P. racemosa*, but leaves are more deeply lobed and seed clusters have individual stems branching from common stalk.

PLATYCERIUM
STAGHORN FERN
Polypodiaceae
EPIPHYTIC FERNS

✎	ZONES VARY BY SPECIES; OR INDOORS
◐	PARTIAL SHADE; INDIRECT LIGHT
●	REGULAR WATER

Native to tropical regions, where they grow on trees. In gardens, they grow best mounted on slabs of bark or tree fern stem, in hanging baskets, or attached to trees. To thrive, they need regular water, very well drained soil, and strong indirect light. Plants have two kinds of fronds. Sterile fronds are flat, pale green, aging to tan and brown; they support the plant and accumulate organic matter to provide nutrients. Fertile fronds are forked, resembling deer antlers (hence the common name). Difficult to grow under normal houseplant conditions, but good in a garden room, sun porch, or attached greenhouse where direct sun can be filtered by a sheer window covering. Water thoroughly but not often. Check moisture levels

Platycerium bifurcatum

by pressing on the sterile brown frond base; water only when dry. Apply balanced liquid fertilizer monthly during growing season.

P. bifurcatum. COMMON STAGHORN FERN. Zones 15–17, 19–24; H2. From Australia and New Zealand. Arching or pendent gray-green fertile fronds, 3 ft. high and wide. Produces numerous offsets, which may be detached for use in propagation. This species shows much variability in form, and several varieties are grouped together as the *P. bifurcatum* complex. Look for named cultivars like 'Netherlands' with distinctive grayish, upward-arching fronds.

P. superbum. GIANT STAGHORN FERN. Zones 23, 24; H2. From Australia. To 6 ft. tall, with 5 ft. spread. Broad, gray-green fertile fronds are spreading or pendent; often forked several times, resembling moose antlers. Sterile fronds are deeply lobed. Protect from frosts.

PLATYCLADUS orientalis (Thuja orientalis)
ORIENTAL ARBORVITAE
Cupressaceae
EVERGREEN TREE

🌡	ZONES 2–24; H1, H2
☀ ◑	PARTIAL SHADE IN HOTTEST CLIMATES
💧💧	MODERATE TO REGULAR WATER

Native to northern China, Manchuria, and Korea. The species grows 25 ft. tall and 15 ft. wide but is rarely grown; nurseries offer more attractive, shrubbier selections. Juvenile leaves are feathery and needlelike; mature leaves are flat and scalelike, carried in irregularly arranged sprays. Foliage is green or yellowish green, may take on bronze tones in winter. Upright cones to ¾ in. long start off gray blue and age to brown; pleasant-smelling when crushed. Widely used around foundations, by doorways or gates, in formal rows. Protect plants from reflected heat of light-colored walls or pavement. In Rocky Mountains, grows best in partial shade; shade during winter is especially helpful. Needs well-drained soil. Blight of leaves and twigs in Northwest is easily controlled by copper sprays applied in early fall and by pruning out and destroying diseased growth. Has survived well in nematode-infested soils. Watch for spider mites.

The following selections are among the best.

Platycladus orientalis 'Aurea Nana'

'Aurea Nana' ('Berckmanii'). DWARF GOLDEN ARBORVITAE, BERCKMAN DWARF ARBORVITAE. Golden-foliaged, compact globe. Usually 3 ft. tall and 2 ft. wide but can grow as high as 5 ft.

'Bakeri'. Compact, cone shaped, bright green. To 5–8 ft. high, 4 ft. wide in 10 years.

'Beverlyensis'. BEVERLY HILLS ARBORVITAE, GOLDEN PYRAMID ARBORVITAE. Upright, globe shaped to conical; somewhat open habit. Golden yellow branchlet tips. In time, can reach 10 ft. tall and wide; give it room.

'Blue Cone'. Dense, upright, conical; good blue-green color. To 8 ft. tall, 4 ft. wide.

'Bonita' ('Bonita Upright', 'Bonita Erecta'). Rounded, full, dense cone to 3 ft. tall, 2 ft. wide. Dark green with slight golden tinting at branch tips.

'Fruitlandii'. FRUITLAND ARBORVITAE. Compact, upright, cone shaped, with deep green foliage.

'Minima Glauca'. DWARF BLUE ARBORVITAE. To 3–4 ft. tall and wide. Blue-green foliage.

'Raffles'. Resembles 'Aurea Nana' but is smaller, denser in growth, brighter in color.

'Westmount'. To 3 ft. tall, 2 ft. wide. Green foliage has yellow tips throughout the growing season.

PLATYCODON grandiflorus
BALLOON FLOWER
Campanulaceae (Lobeliaceae)
PERENNIAL

🌡	ZONES 1–10, 14–24
☀ ◑	LIGHT SHADE IN HOTTEST CLIMATES
💧	REGULAR WATER

From Siberia, northern China, Japan. To 3 ft. tall and 2 ft. wide. Inflated, balloonlike buds are carried on slender stalks at the ends of upright stems clad in broadly oval, 1–3-in.-long, light olive green leaves. Buds open to 2-in.-wide, star-shaped, blue-violet flowers with purple veins. Bloom begins in early summer and continues for 2 months or more if spent blossoms (not entire stems) are removed. Pink, white, and double-flowered varieties are available. Blossoms of 1½–2-ft. 'Komachi' keep their balloon shape, never opening fully. *P. g. mariesii* grows only 1–1½ ft. high and wide; 'Apoyama' reaches 10–12 in. high, 8 in. wide.

Platycodon grandiflorus

Balloon flower is easy to grow from seed, but it is deep rooted and takes 2 or 3 years to get well established. Dies back completely in fall, and new growth appears quite late in spring; mark position to avoid digging up fleshy roots. If you do unearth a root, replace it (or the pieces) right away. Protect roots from gophers. Grow as winter annual in Zones 12, 13.

PLECOSTACHYS serpyllifolia
Asteraceae (Compositae)
PERENNIAL

🌡	ZONES 8, 9, 14–24
☀	FULL SUN
💧	MODERATE WATER

South African native to 1½ ft. tall, spreading to twice as wide or more. Tiny, furry, whitish leaves are closely packed along sprawling,

Plecostachys serpyllifolia

woody-based stems. Grown for its foliage rather than its clusters of small pinkish flowers. This plant has been sold as a dwarf form of *Helichrysum petiolare*, which it resembles in miniature. Attractive gray plant for ground or bank cover, large rock garden, or border.

PLECTRANTHUS
Lamiaceae (Labiatae)
PERENNIALS AND EVERGREEN SHRUBS

🌡	ZONES 22–24; H2; OR INDOORS
◑	PARTIAL SHADE, EXCEPT AS NOTED; BRIGHT INDIRECT LIGHT
💧	REGULAR WATER

Close relatives of coleus; native to many tropical regions of the world. They have square stems, opposite pairs of fleshy, tooth-edged or scalloped leaves, and whorls of tubular, two-lipped blossoms. Some are highly aromatic, used as seasonings or home remedies. Others are grown for their attractive foliage, yet others for their striking floral displays. Some are good bedding plants for summer color; some make dense, weed-suppressing ground covers for frost-protected areas. Several are trailing plants that drape gracefully from hanging baskets or wall pots. All are superb in containers, either alone or in combination with other plants.

Easy to grow. Stems take root wherever they touch the ground. Cuttings root quickly in soil or water. Remove flower spikes after they fade. *P. argentatus* and *P. fruticosus* are the shrubbiest of the species listed here, but the others get somewhat woody at the base after a year or more. Pinch all types to induce branching; discard old plants when they become leggy or too woody and start new ones.

Confusion reigns in *Plectranthus* nomenclature, with different nurseries selling the same plant under different names. Here are some of the most interesting species.

P. amboinicus (Coleus amboinicus). CUBAN OREGANO, SPANISH THYME, INDIAN MINT. From Africa. Summer-blooming trailer to 1 ft. high, 3 ft. wide, with white, lilac-pink, or light purple flowers in 6-in. spikes. Velvety, ovate gray-green leaves are 3 in. long, with broadly toothed edges. Popular in Cuban cooking, they have a fragrance that falls midway between oregano and thyme but has a sweet note not present in either. Leaves of 'Variegatus' are bordered in cream, with the very

P

edge often tinged bright pink; excellent flavor. 'Well-Sweep' ('Wedgwood'), with extra-sweet flavor, has leaves in chartreuse and gray green with a dark green margin; Wedgwood blue flowers.

P. argentatus. From Australia. Erect to spreading plant to 3 ft. tall, 6 ft. or wider. Densely hairy, scallop-edged, oval leaves to 7 in. long are silvery gray green, with a light purplish flush on growing tips and stems. Pink-tinged white flowers in foot-long spikes in late summer, fall. Best in at least half-day direct sun; will take hot afternoon sun if adequately watered.

P. australis. See *P. verticillatus*

P. ciliatus. From southern Africa. Handsome, burgundy-stemmed trailer to 6–12 in. high, 3–5 ft. wide. Excellent dense ground cover. Late summer and fall white or purplish flowers in 8–12-in. spikes. Oval leaves to 3½ in. long, with finely toothed edges and pointed tips; leaves have deep green upper surfaces, burgundy undersides and veins. 'Old Gold' leaves are yellow or chartreuse above, burgundy beneath; new leaves are flushed with burgundy. 'Tricolor' is similar, but tops of leaves also have dark green splotches. Both varieties have white blooms.

P. coleoides 'Marginata'. See *P. forsteri* 'Marginatus'

P. cylindraceus (P. marrubioides). VICK'S PLANT, MENTHOLATO. From Africa. Mounding growth to 1½– 3 ft. high, 2–4 ft. wide. Sometimes blooms, bearing blue or lavender flowers in dense, narrow, pointed spikes 12–15 in. long (there may be a pair of shorter spikes near base). Velvety, triangular gray-green leaves 1½– 3 in. long, with three to five broad teeth on each side of leaf. Foliage smells like a combination of camphor and menthol and is used medicinally in Mexico.

P. forsteri. From Australia, Fiji, New Caledonia. To 10 in. high, 3 ft. wide; stems actually grow 3 ft. tall, but they arch over from weight of foliage. Tip-pinch early to induce branching; repeat to keep compact. Medium green, ovate, irregularly toothed leaves to 4 in. long. White or pale mauve flowers in 6–8-in. spikes are produced intermittently throughout the year. Leaves of

'Marginatus' (*P. coleoides* 'Marginata') are irregularly edged in creamy white. 'Green and Gold' has lime green leaves with a neat gold margin.

P. fruticosus. From South Africa. Upright growth to 3–5 ft. tall, 2–4 ft. wide. Lance-shaped, coarsely toothed leaves to 4 in. long are olive green above, purplish beneath. Blooms in autumn, bearing mauve pink or bluish blossoms in very showy clusters to 1 ft. long, half as wide.

P. madagascariensis. MINT-LEAF. From southern Africa. Vigorous trailer reaches 1 ft. high; spreads 3–4 ft. wide initially, eventually much wider by rooting at leaf joints. Medium green leaves to 2 in. long are hairy, roundish, scallop edged; they smell like mint when crushed. Lavender-blue or white flower spikes in late spring, early summer. 'Variegated Mint-leaf', the most commonly grown form, has irregular white leaf margins. Good ground cover to brighten shady areas. Often mistakenly sold as *Iboza*, another genus in the same family.

P. nummularis. See *P. verticillatus*

P. oertendahlii. MOSAIC SWEDISH IVY, ROYAL CHARLIE, CANDLE PLANT. From South Africa. Easy-care specimen for hanging basket or pot; most often grown as houseplant. To 8–12 in. high, with branches trailing to 1½–2 ft. long. Roundish, irregularly toothed, velvety dark green leaves up to 2½ in. long, with purple undersides and intricate network of silver veins. In fall, whitish flowers bloom in loose, 8–12-in.-long spikes. Foliage of 'Uvongo' is more heavily netted with silver than that of the species; leaves of 'Variegatus' are irregularly edged in creamy white.

Plectranthus oertendahlii

P. parviflorus. 'ALA 'ALA WAI NUI. From Hawaii, Australia. Occurs naturally in dry, exposed locations. Spreading, trailing plant grows to 6–8 in. or possibly higher; spreads to 3 ft. but can be easily restrained. Light green, toothed leaves are covered with short, silvery fuzz. Short spikes of pale blue flowers bloom all year. Use in hanging baskets, rock garden, or as small-scale ground cover.

P. verticillatus. SWEDISH IVY, CREEPING CHARLIE. From southern Africa. Typically grown in hanging basket or pot in the house or outdoors; also makes a good ground cover in a warm, protected spot. To 4–8 in. high, 4–6 ft. wide, with trailing branches. Waxy, shiny dark green, scallop-edged leaves are roundish, to 1½ in. across. White or pale purplish blossoms in 8-in. spikes bloom intermittently all year. To grow as a ground cover, plant cuttings 1–2 ft. apart for quick coverage. Often incorrectly sold as *P. australis* or *P. nummularis*. 'Marmoratus' produces leaves irregularly marked with ivory.

PLEIOBLASTUS. See **BAMBOO**

PLEIONE
Orchidaceae
TERRESTRIAL ORCHIDS

🗺	ZONES 5–9, 14–24; OR INDOORS
☼	PARTIAL SHADE; BRIGHT INDIRECT LIGHT
💧	REGULAR WATER DURING GROWTH AND BLOOM

Dwarf orchids native to high mountains of India and China. Many species, all deciduous. Each pseudobulb produces one or two narrowly oval, pleated-looking leaves; leaves reach 8 in. long in the biggest species. Flowers are large (3–4 in. wide) for the size of the plant and resemble small cattleyas; they usually appear just as the leaves begin to show in early spring. Blossoms of *P. bulbocodioides* are purple with a white lip marked with reddish spots. Those of *P. formosana* are purple, pink, or white; fringed lip has yellow center with brownish red markings.

Where frosts are rare and summer temperatures moderate, these orchids can be grown outdoors all year—provided they have perfect drainage, rich soil that is moist and well aerated, and some winter protection (shelter from excessive rain). Usually grown in rock gardens or in pots. For a good show, plant pseudobulbs close together.

Pleione bulbocodioides

If planting in the ground, bury pseudobulbs, leaving just the tips exposed; or plant in a shallow pot and bury only the bottom quarter of each pseudobulb. Repot yearly before growth begins.

PLUM
(including Prune)
Rosaceae
DECIDUOUS FRUIT TREES

🗺	ZONES VARY BY VARIETY
☼	FULL SUN
💧	MODERATE WATER
▶	SEE CHART OPPOSITE PAGE

Like their cherry, peach, and apricot relatives, these are stone fruits of the genus *Prunus*. For flowering plums, see page 567. For crosses involving plums, apricots, and peaches, see Plum Hybrids. Three categories of edible plums and prunes are grown in the West: European, Japanese, and hardy. All bloom in late winter or early spring; fruit ripens at some point from May into September, depending on variety and climate.

The two most widely grown groups are European (*Prunus* × *domestica*) and Japanese (*P. salicina*). 'Damson' plum, which is sometimes considered a separate species (*P. insititia*), is probably a type of European plum (*P.* × *domestica insititia*); 'Damson' interbreeds freely with other European plums. Prunes are European plum varieties with a high sugar content that makes it possible to sun-dry the fruit without it fermenting.

European plums and prunes bloom later than Japanese plums and are better adapted to areas with late frosts or cool, rainy spring weather. Most European varieties have a moderately high chill need that excludes them from extremely mild-winter areas. Many European and Japanese varieties are self-fruitful, but others need cross-pollination to produce good crops. The chart lists proven pollenizers, but other choices also exist; consult a

PLUM

NAME	ZONES	POLLINATION	FRUIT	COMMENTS
EUROPEAN VARIETIES				
'Brooks'	2–12, 14–22	Self-fruitful	Large. Yellowish red to blue skin; yellow flesh. Sweet with a little tartness. Midseason	Good canning variety or dried prune. Produces reliably in Pacific Northwest
'Coe's Golden Drop'	2–12, 14–22	Any other European plum	Medium to large; oblong. Straw yellow skin, often blushed red; golden flesh. Sweet, juicy, apricot-like flavor. Late	Intense flavor. Highly regarded in Europe
'Damson' ('Blue Damson')	2–23	Self-fruitful	Small. Purple or blue-black skin; green flesh. Very tart. Late	Variety has low chill requirement. Makes fine jam and jelly. Strains of this variety are sold as 'French Damson', 'Shropshire'
'Early Laxton'	2–12, 14–20	Any other European plum	Medium-size. Pinkish orange skin; yellow flesh. Deliciously sweet flavor. Early	Excellent for cooking. Upright, very productive tree
'French Prune' ('Agen', 'Petite')	2, 3, 7–12, 14–22	Self-fruitful	Small. Red to purplish black skin; greenish yellow flesh. Very sweet and mild. Late	Standard drying prune of California. Also suitable for canning
'Green Gage' ('Reine Claude')	2–22; H1	Self-fruitful	Small to medium. Greenish yellow skin; amber flesh. Very rich, sweet flavor. Midseason	Very old variety; still a favorite for eating fresh, cooking, canning, jam. Selected strains are sold as 'Jefferson'
'Imperial' ('Imperial Epineuse')	3–12, 14–18	Any other European plum	Large. Red-purple to black-purple skin; greenish yellow flesh. Fine-quality fruit with sweet, intense flavor. Late midseason	Excellent fresh. Makes a premium dried prune or canned product
'Italian Prune' ('Fellenburg')	2–12, 14–18	Self-fruitful	Medium-size. Purplish black skin; yellow-green flesh. Sweet flavor. Late midseason	Standard variety for prunes in the Pacific Northwest. Excellent fresh as well as for canning; dries well. 'Early Italian' ripens 2 weeks earlier
'Mirabelle'	2–12, 14–22	Any midseason non-'Mirabelle' European plum	Small. Yellow fruit with orange to red dots on the skin. Mild, sweet yellow flesh. Ripening time varies	A type favored in Europe for making brandy. Also good in preserves. Look for 'Geneva Mirabelle' and 'Reine de Mirabelle'
'Opal'	A1, A2; 1–3	Self-fruitful	Small. Reddish purple skin; yellow flesh. Good, sweet flavor. Early	Vigorous and hardy
'Reine Claude de Bavay' ('Bavay Green Gage')	2–12, 14–20	Self-fruitful	Large. Yellow skin with white dots; sweet, juicy yellow flesh. Similar to 'Green Gage' in flavor. Late	Compact tree; good choice for smaller gardens. Form of 'Green Gage' with superior flavor
'Seneca'	2–12, 14–20	Any other European plum	Very large. Red skin; yellow flesh. Deliciously sweet. Late	Productive. One of the best for the Pacific Northwest
'Stanley'	2–12, 14–22	Self-fruitful	Large. Purplish black skin; yellow flesh. Sweet and juicy. Midseason	Good canning variety or dried prune. Fruit resembles a larger 'Italian Prune'
'Sugar'	2–12, 14–22	Self-fruitful	Medium-size. Dark blue skin; yellow flesh. Intensely flavored; very sweet. Early midseason	Good fresh as well as canned; good home-drying prune. This variety tends to bear heavily in alternate years

P

     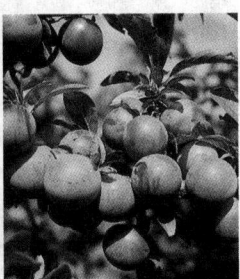

'Brooks' 'Damson' 'Green Gage' 'Stanley' 'Beauty' 'Burbank'

PLUM

NAME	ZONES	POLLINATION	FRUIT	COMMENTS
JAPANESE VARIETIES				
'Autumn Rosa'	7–12, 14–23	Self-fruitful	Medium to large. Purplish red skin; yellow flesh with red streaks. Good, sweet flavor. Very late	Low chill requirement. Ripens over a long period; holds well on tree
'Beauty'	2–24	Self-fruitful; yield improved with 'Santa Rosa'	Medium-size. Bright red skin; amber flesh with scarlet streaks. Good, sweet flavor. Very early	Low chill requirement. Consistent, heavy bearer. Fruit softens quickly and must be harvested promptly
'Burbank'	2–12, 14–20	'Beauty', 'Santa Rosa'	Large. Red skin; amber flesh. Aromatic fruit with excellent, sweet flavor. Midseason	Hardier to cold than most Japanese plums
'Burgundy'	7–12, 14–24	Self-fruitful	Small. Dark red skin and flesh. Excellent, rich flavor. Early to midseason	Low chill requirement. Great fresh or canned. Fruit holds well on the tree
'Casselman'	2, 3, 7–12, 14–22	Self-fruitful	Sport of 'Late Santa Rosa'; skin color is lighter and fruit ripens a few days later	Not subject to cracking of skin
'Catalina'	7–12, 14–24	Self-fruitful	Large. Deep purple skin and flesh. Juicy and sweet. Late	Low chill requirement. Very productive
'Elephant Heart'	2, 3, 7–12, 14–22	'Santa Rosa'	Very large. Dark red skin; rich red flesh. Highly flavored. Midseason to late	Skin is tart until fruit is fully ripe. Long harvest season
'Emerald Beaut'	7–12, 14–20	'Beauty', 'Burgundy', 'Late Santa Rosa'	Medium-size. Light green skin; greenish yellow to orange flesh. Exceptional, sweet, rich flavor. Midseason to late	Fruit holds well on tree without losing quality
'Friar'	2, 3, 7–12, 14–20	'Santa Rosa', 'Late Santa Rosa'	Large. Purplish black skin; amber flesh. Good, sweet flavor. Late midseason	Fruit resists cracking; softens slowly after picking. Very vigorous, productive tree
'Golden Nectar'	2, 3, 7–12, 14–20	Self-fruitful	Very large. Yellow skin and flesh; small pit. Excellent, sweet flavor. Midseason	Fruit keeps well after harvest
'Howard Miracle'	7–10, 14–20	'Santa Rosa', 'Wickson'	Medium-size. Yellow skin with red blush; yellow flesh. Spicy flavor reminiscent of pineapple. Midseason	Very vigorous. Fruit more acid than that of most Japanese plums, but truly distinctive in flavor
'Kelsey'	2, 3, 7–12, 14–18; H1	Self-fruitful	Large. Green to greenish yellow skin splashed red; firm yellow flesh. Sweet but not juicy. Late midseason	Fruit keeps well after harvest
'Laroda'	7–12, 14–22	'Burgundy', 'Santa Rosa', 'Late Santa Rosa'	Large. Red skin; amber flesh (red near skin). Rich and juicy. Midseason	Fruit holds well on the tree
'Late Santa Rosa'	7–12, 14–22	Self-fruitful	Medium to large. Purplish crimson skin; amber flesh (red near skin). Tart-sweet, sprightly flavor. Late	Follows 'Santa Rosa' by a month

'Casselman'

'Friar'

'Howard Miracle'

'Santa Rosa'

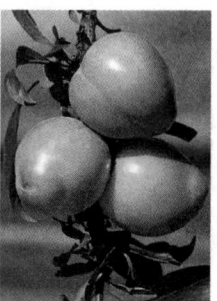
'Satsuma'

'Wickson'

PLUM

NAME	ZONES	POLLINATION	FRUIT	COMMENTS
'Mariposa' ('Improved Satsuma')	2, 3, 7–12, 14–22; H1	'Autumn Rosa', 'Beauty', 'Santa Rosa', 'Late Santa Rosa', 'Wickson'	Large. Purple-red skin; deep red flesh. Sweet. Midseason	Good for cooking and eating
'Methley'	2–9, 12–24; H1	Self-fruitful	Medium-size. Reddish purple skin; dark red flesh. Sweet and mild. Early	Low chill requirement. Good bloom hardiness
'Nubiana'	2, 3, 7–12, 14–20	Self-fruitful	Large. Deep purple-black skin; amber flesh. Sweet and firm. Midseason	Good for eating fresh and for cooking (flesh turns red when cooked). Good keeper
'Santa Rosa'	2, 3, 7–23	Self-fruitful	Medium to large. Purplish red skin with heavy blue bloom; yellow flesh (dark red near skin). Rich, pleasing, tart flavor. Early	Low chill requirement. Important commercial variety for fresh eating. Good canned if skin is removed. 'Weeping Santa Rosa' has unique drooping habit, grows only 6–8 ft. high
'Satsuma'	2–22	'Beauty', 'Santa Rosa', 'Wickson'	Small to medium. Dull deep red skin; dark red, solid, meaty flesh. Mild, sweet flavor. Small pit. Early midseason	Preferred for jams and jellies. Sometimes called blood plum because of red juice
'Shiro'	2, 3, 7–12, 14–22	Self-fruitful	Medium to large. Yellow skin and flesh. Mild but good flavor. Early midseason	Heavy producer. Fruit good for eating fresh or cooking. Pretty in flower and fruit
'Wickson'	2–12, 14–22	'Beauty', 'Santa Rosa'	Large. Greenish yellow to yellow skin, blushed with red when fruit is ripe. Firm yellow flesh. Mild but fine flavor. Early midseason	Showy fruit that keeps well after harvest. Good for jams and jellies
HARDY HYBRIDS				
'Opata'	A2, A3; 1–3	Check locally	Small. Purple skin; green flesh. Sweet. Late	Cherry-plum hybrid from South Dakota. Bush form. Upper branches often freeze in coldest areas, but lower branches usually fruit well. Fruit is good fresh and for preserves
'Pipestone'	A2, A3; 1–3	Check locally	Large. Tough red skin; yellow flesh. A little stringy but juicy and sweet. Midseason	Vigorous Japanese-American hybrid developed in Minnesota. Tree form. Needs little heat to ripen. Very good for fresh eating and jam; good for jelly
'Sapalta'	A2, A3; 1–3	Check locally	Small. Red-purple skin; almost black flesh. Mildly sweet. Late	Cherry-plum hybrid developed in Canada. Bush form. Good for fresh eating, juice, canning, preserves
'Superior'	A2, A3; 1–3	Check locally	Very large. Golden, with, red-blushed, lightly russeted skin. Firm yellow flesh, slightly tart near skin. Dessert quality. Late midseason	Japanese-American hybrid developed in Minnesota. Tree form. Bears at an early age and heavily. Good fresh or for jam, jelly
'Underwood'	A2, A3; 1–3	Check locally	Medium to large. Dark red skin; amber flesh. Tender, juicy, sweet. Early	Vigorous Japanese-American hybrid developed in Minnesota. Tree form. Good for fresh eating and jam; fair for jelly

P

knowledgeable local nursery for more information.

Where winters are severe, a third plum category dominates. This is a complex group of hardy hybrids involving Japanese plum, several species of native American wild plums, and the native Western sand cherry (*P. besseyi*). Those with fruit near the size and quality of Japanese plums are sometimes called Japanese-American hybrids; those with smaller fruit closer in flavor to wild species are often called cherry-plum hybrids. The hardy hybrids originated in Canada, the Dakotas, and Minnesota and are exceptionally tolerant of cold and wind. Pollination of hardy hybrids is difficult; ask local nurseries about effective pollenizers.

Plums come in many colors—both inside and out. Skin may be yellow, red, purple, green, blue, or almost black; flesh may be yellow, red, or green. Japanese plums are the largest and juiciest of the lot, with a pleasant blend of acid and sugar; they are mainly eaten fresh. European plums have flesh that is firmer and can be cooked or eaten fresh; prune varieties are largely used for drying or canning, but they can also be eaten fresh if you like the very sweet flavor. Many hardy plums are tasty fresh, while others are better cooked or used in preserves.

As orchard trees, both Japanese and European plums reach 15–20 ft. tall with somewhat wider spread, but with pruning they are easily kept to 10–15 ft. high and wide. Differences in growth habit are discussed below. There are no truly dwarfing rootstocks for plums, and semidwarf trees are only slightly smaller than stan-

What Plums Need

WINTER CHILL Most Japanese plums require 500 to 900 hours at 45°F/7°C or lower; European plums demand 700 to 1,000 hours of chill.

SOIL Plants tolerate many soil types but do best in fertile, well-drained soil.

FERTILIZING For larger fruit and vigorous growth, feed heavily. Orchardists give Japanese plums 1–3 lbs. of actual nitrogen a year; they give European plums 1–2 lbs. Home gardeners, however, can usually get by with much less. Hardy hybrids need only light applications of nitrogen.

FRUIT THINNING Japanese varieties bear very heavily, producing much small fruit. If the entire crop were allowed to ripen, its weight might damage the tree—so thin fruits to 4–6 in. apart as soon as they are large enough to be seen. Other plums usually don't need thinning unless the tree sets a particularly large amount of fruit.

PRUNING Japanese varieties require heavy annual pruning to ensure fruit set and healthy growth throughout the tree. European plums and hardy hybrids need much less attention.

'Green Gage'

dards. Some of the hardy hybrids are trees; others grow as bushes to about 6 ft. high and at least as broad.

Most Japanese plum trees are trained to a vase shape, with five or six main scaffold branches; fruiting laterals grow from these scaffolds. Where space is limited, trees can be trained in a more

Plum

linear fashion (against a wall or fence, for example). Japanese varieties tend to make tremendous shoot growth, and rather severe pruning is necessary at all ages, regardless of training method. Many varieties produce excessive vertical growth; shorten these shoots to outside branchlets.

European plums do not branch as freely as Japanese types, so selection of framework branches is limited; these plums are usually trained to a central leader. Mature European plums require pruning mainly to thin out annual shoot growth; otherwise, little is needed. If you grow hardy hybrids, prune them to renew unfruitful branches (on shrubby types, remove older shoots to the ground every few years) and to keep the plant's center open.

In the dry-summer West, plums are subject to far fewer problems than peaches or apples. Dormant-season sprays combining horticultural oil with lime sulfur or fixed copper will control the fungal disease brown rot and various insect pests, including scale. Peach tree borer is another potential pest; see Peach and Nectarine.

PLUMBAGO

Plumbaginaceae
EVERGREEN OR SEMIEVERGREEN SHRUBS

| ✔ ZONES VARY BY SPECIES |
| ☼ ☼ FULL SUN OR LIGHT SHADE |
| ◌ ◖ ● LITTLE TO REGULAR WATER |

Sprawling plants that bloom over a long season, bearing phloxlike clusters of blue or white flowers at branch ends. Prune these shrubs back hard in late winter to control their growth and keep them compact. For other plants called plumbago, see *Ceratostigma*.

P. auriculata (P. capensis). CAPE PLUMBAGO. Evergreen or semievergreen. Zones 8, 9, 12–24; H1, H2. Native to South Africa. Makes a mounding shrub to 6 ft. tall, 8–10 ft. wide; or, if tied to a support, grows as a vine to 12 ft. or more. Oblong, 1–2-in, light to medium green leaves. Inch-wide flowers. In seedling plants, blossom color varies from white through pure light blue to sky blue; best way to get good blue color is to buy cutting-grown selections

Plumbago auriculata

such as 'Royal Cape' or 'Imperial Blue'. 'Alba' is a white selection. Blooms from spring through summer—or nearly all year in warm, frost-free locations. Flowers are used in leis.

Evergreen where frosts are absent or light; heavy frost can burn new growth and blacken leaves, but recovery is fast. Prune out any damaged parts when frost danger is past. In colder part of range, plant in spring to give plants time to become established before cold weather arrives. Not fussy about soil type but must have good drainage. Good cover for bank, fence, wall; good background and filler plant.

P. scandens. Evergreen. Zones 12, 13, 21–24; H1, H2. Native from Florida to Arizona, south to Central America. To 4 ft. or more high and wide. Oblong leaves to 4 in. long are deep red when new, maturing to medium green; nearly all foliage turns red in late fall and winter. Blooms year-round (with a short break during hottest part of summer), bearing typically white (sometimes blue-tinged) flowers nearly 1 in. wide. Particularly striking when white blooms appear in combination with red leaves. With this species, hard pruning both controls size and encourages the growth of colorful new foliage. Accepts most soils. Can get powdery mildew in late summer but doesn't seem to be greatly harmed by it. Attractive ground cover. 'Summer Snow' has pure white blooms.

PLUMBAGO larpentae. See **CERATOSTIGMA plumbaginoides**

PLUME CEDAR, PLUME CRYPTOMERIA. See **CRYPTOMERIA japonica 'Elegans'**

PLUME HYACINTH. See **MUSCARI comosum 'Monstrosum'**

PLUME POPPY. See **MACLEAYA**

PLUMERIA

FRANGIPANI, PUA MELIA
Apocynaceae
NEARLY EVERGREEN AND DECIDUOUS SHRUBS OR TREES

| ✔ ZONES VARY BY SPECIES |
| ☼ ☼ PARTIAL SHADE IN HOTTEST CLIMATES |
| ● MODERATE WATER |

Handsome additions to the landscape in the warmest climates, these are natives of tropical America with a spreading to round-headed form. Leathery leaves are clustered near the tips of thick, succulent branches (branches exude caustic sap when injured). Large clusters of showy, waxy, typically fragrant, five-petaled flowers are produced at branch tips much of the year. Widely used in leis.

In Hawaii, plumerias are easy to grow from cuttings. On the mainland, safest method is to begin with container plants (usually sold in leaf and flower in summer). If you want to try cuttings, start with long (15–24-in.) tip sections of stem taken in early spring and allow them to callus over for a week before planting; short cuttings often succumb to rot.

Do best in hot, dry locations in full sun but will grow in light shade. Not fussy about soil type but cannot take cold, wet soils. Some tolerance of salt and wind. Can be pruned at any time of year to maintain desired size and shape; withstands severe pruning (best done in warm season on mainland). Tender to frost. Beyond hardiness range, may be grown in a container and moved indoors in winter to a bright window (for continued bloom) or to a frost-free garage or shed.

: *Plumeria rubra* 'Aztec Gold'
: *Plumeria rubra* 'Daisy Wilcox'

Plumeria rubra

P. obtusa. SINGAPORE PLUME-RIA, BLUNT-NOSE FRANGIPANI. Nearly evergreen. Zones 24; H2. From Cuba, Hispaniola, Yucatán Peninsula. Fast growing to 30–35 ft. high, 15 ft. wide. Dark green leaves are retained most of the year; they grow to 6 in. or longer, have blunt or rounded tips. Sweet-scented, 3-in.-wide, yellow-centered white flowers spring through fall. On mainland, more difficult to grow than *P. rubra.*

P. rubra. PLUMERIA, TEMPLE TREE, NOSEGAY FRANGIPANI. Deciduous. Zones 12, 13, 19, 21–24; H1, H2. Native from Mexico to Panama. Grows at a moderate rate to 25–35 ft. tall, 15–20 ft. wide. Medium green leaves are 8–16 in. long, with narrow, pointed tips. Bloom begins in spring, often before foliage emerges, and contin-ues for more than 6 months. Well over 100 varieties have been devel-oped; flowers are typically 2–4½ in. wide, in colors from white through

: *Plumeria rubra* 'Candystripe'
: *Plumeria rubra* 'Hawaiian Yellow'

yellow, gold, and orange to shades of pink and red; fragrance varies. Dwarf and semidouble-flowered forms (rare on the mainland) are available. The following are full-size varieties with large, very fra-grant single flowers.

'Aztec Gold'. Buttercup yellow shading to white at petal edges.

'Daisy Wilcox'. Extra-large blos-soms in pale pink shading to white at edges.

'Dean Conklin'. Salmon with orange center.

'Guillot's Sunset'. Pink-and-white bicolor with orange center.

'Hawaiian Yellow'. Yellow with white margins. Especially sturdy plant.

'Intense Rainbow'. Yellow blos-soms blending to pink.

'Kauka Wilder'. Combination of reds and yellows gives blossoms an overall rich orange color. Very sweet fragrance.

'Pink Parfait'. Large, reddish pink blooms.

'Smith's Candystripe'. Vibrant pink and white blooms have bright yellow markings on upper surfaces of petals, alternating red and white stripes on undersides. More fragrant than the similar 'Candystripe'.

'Tangerine'. Coral-orange flowers.

PLUM, FLOWERING.
See **PRUNUS**

PLUM HYBRIDS
Rosaceae
DECIDUOUS FRUIT TREES

| 🖋 ZONES VARY BY TYPE |
| ☀ FULL SUN |
| 💧 MODERATE WATER |

These hybrids between plum and apricot and between plum and peach combine characteristics of their parent fruits in varying degrees. The differences among them are somewhat blurred. Like their parents, they need winter chill for good fruit production. Not yet widely tested, so zone listings are preliminary.

Plumcot. Zones 2, 3, 7–12, 14–23. This was the original plum-apricot cross made by Luther Burbank. One modern variety, 'Plum Parfait', is widely sold. It has pinkish orange skin, flesh marbled in crimson and amber, and a wonderfully sweet-tart, plumlike flavor; ripens in mid- to late sum-mer. Tree resembles both plum and apricot but is slightly smaller and more compact than either. Treat as

for Japanese plum. Self-fruitful but takes 5 years or more to begin bearing.

Pluot. Zones 2, 3, 7–12, 14–23. Enjoys similar conditions and is most likely to succeed where 'Santa Rosa' plum does. Fruit is very sweet, close in flavor to a plum. Mid- to late summer ripeners include 'Dapple Dandy' (often sold in markets under the name "dinosaur egg"), with mottled maroon-and-yellow skin and creamy white flesh streaked with red; 'Flavor Grenade', with elon-gated green fruit flushed with red; 'Flavor King', with purplish red skin and flesh; and 'Flavor Queen', with greenish yellow skin and golden flesh. 'Flavor Supreme' has deep red flesh and skin mottled green and maroon; it ripens in late spring or early summer. Both 'Dapple Dandy' and 'Flavor Supreme' will pollinate any other pluot; you can also use a Japanese plum that blooms at the same time. Same culture as for Japanese plum.

'Flavor Delight' aprium

Aprium. Zones 3–22. Will grow where popular apricot varieties suc-ceed. 'Flavor Delight' has sweet, yel-low fruit similar to an apricot, but it's a little juicier and has a touch of plum flavor. Partially self-fruitful, but for best crop pollinate with any apricot that blooms at the same time or with 'Flavor Supreme' pluot. Fruit ripens in late spring or early summer. Tree is similar to apricot and should be maintained as such.

Peach-plum hybrids. Zones 3–9, 14–16, 18. The newest of the plum hybrids resemble peach trees in tree form and climate adapta-tion, and should be maintained in similar fashion. Self-fertile 'Tri-Lite' has red skin with white flesh; its mild, classic peach flavor has a plum aftertaste.

PLUM YEW.
See **CEPHALOTAXUS harringtonia**

PLUOT.
See **PLUM HYBRIDS**

POA
BLUEGRASS
Poaceae (Gramineae)
PERENNIAL AND ANNUAL GRASSES

| 🖋 ZONES VARY BY SPECIES |
| ☀ FULL SUN, EXCEPT AS NOTED |
| 💧 REGULAR WATER |

Native to Europe but naturalized in North America. Of the three species described here, *P. pratensis* is the best-known cool-season lawn grass. Leaves of all have distinctive boat-prow tip.

P. annua. ANNUAL BLUE-GRASS. Annual. All zones. Cool-season weed of lawns that often furnishes much of the green in winter lawns. Bright green, soft-textured grass; it would be attrac-tive were it not for its seed heads and propensity to die off in dry-summer regions just when it is needed most—when rain lessens in late spring. To discourage annual bluegrass in lawns, maintain a thick turf of good grasses.

P. pratensis. KENTUCKY BLUEGRASS. Perennial. Best in Zones A1–A3, 1–3; satisfactory with extra care in Zones 4–11, 14–17. Blue-green lawn grass. Many selections—such as 'A-34', 'America', 'Blacksburg', 'Glade', and 'Midnight'—are available as seed or sod. Mow at 2–2½ in. (dwarf forms can be mowed lower). Use alone or in a mixture with other grasses.

Poa pratensis

P. trivialis. ROUGH-STALKED BLUEGRASS. Perennial. Zones A1–A3; 1–11, 14–17. Fine-textured bright green grass used in meadow and pasture grass mixes. Can become weedy. Also used in lawn mixtures for shady spots—takes shade and damp soil.

POACHED EGGS.
See **LIMNANTHES douglasii**

P

PODOCARPUS
Podocarpaceae
EVERGREEN SHRUBS OR TREES

✔	ZONES VARY BY SPECIES
☀ ◐	FULL SUN OR PARTIAL SHADE
♦	REGULAR WATER

Versatile plants grown for their good-looking foliage and interesting form. They are adaptable to many climates and have many garden uses. Make good screens and background plants. Foliage generally resembles that of related yews *(Taxus)*, but leaves of the better-known species are longer, broader, and lighter in color. If a male plant is growing nearby, female plants bear fruit after many years, producing small, fleshy fruits rather than cones. Grow well (if slowly) in most soils, but may develop chlorosis where soil is alkaline or heavy and damp. Some botanists divide the plants into three genera *(Afrocarpus, Nageia, Podocarpus)*; where they apply, new names are given in parentheses.

P. elongatus. For plants sold under this name, see P. gracilior

P. falcatus (Afrocarpus falcatus). Tree. Zones 8, 9, 14–24; H2. Slow-growing native of South Africa. Differs from *P. gracilior* in nativity, small botanical details. For uses, see *P. gracilior.*

P. gracilior (Afrocarpus elongatus, Nageia falcatus). FERN PINE. Tree, often grown as espaliered vine or even in hanging baskets. Zones 8, 9, 13–24; H1, H2. From eastern Africa. To 20–60 ft. tall, 10–20 ft. wide. Among the cleanest, most pest-free trees for street, lawn, patio, garden; good as big shrub, as hedge, in container.

Method of propagation determines growth habit. If grown from seed, plants are upright even when young (and stay that way); these plants are usually sold as *P. gracilior.* In youth, they have branches set somewhat sparsely with glossy dark green leaves 2–4 in. long, ½ in. wide. With age, they produce 1–2-in., soft grayish green to bluish green leaves that are more closely spaced on branches. Stake seedling plants until a strong trunk develops.

If grown from cuttings or grafts of a mature tree, plants have the smaller, more closely set leaves just described, but they have very limber branches and are often reluctant to make strong vertical growth. These more willowy plants, suitable for espalier, hanging pots, or growing as vines along fences, are often sold as *P. elongatus.* Given staking and tying, *P. elongatus* types eventually become upright trees, though their foliage mass persists in drooping for some time.

P. henkelii. LONG-LEAFED YELLOWWOOD. Tree. Zones 8, 9, 14–24; H1, H2. From eastern and southern Africa. Handsome, erect tree grows slowly to 30–50 ft. tall, 15–20 ft. wide. Bears masses of drooping, shiny green leaves, pointed at both ends. Young plants have leaves 5–7 in. long, ⅓ in. wide; on older plants, leaves are much smaller, to 1–2 in. long, a little over ⅛ in. wide.

P. latifolius. YELLOWWOOD. Tree. Zones 8, 9, 12 (warmest parts), 13–24; H1, H2. From eastern and southern Africa. This is the true yellowwood, an important timber tree in Africa. Resembles *P. henkelii* in most details. Leaves taper only toward tip.

P. macrophyllus. YEW PINE. Shrub or tree. Zones 4–9, 12–24; H1, H2. Native to eastern China, Japan. Generally narrow and upright; to 15–50 ft. tall, 6–15 ft. wide. Bright green leaves 4 in. long, ½ in. wide. Good as a street or lawn tree, screen, large shrub; limber enough to espalier. Easily pruned as clipped hedge, topiary. Does well in tubs. Very heat tolerant.

P. m. maki. SHRUBBY YEW PINE. Slower growing and smaller than species—to 8–15 ft. tall, 2–4 ft. wide. Dense and upright, with leaves to 3 in. long, ¼ in. wide. A choice shrub; one of the best container plants for outdoor or indoor use.

P. nagi (Nageia nagi). Tree. Zones 8, 9, 14–24; H1, H2. From Japan, where it reaches 80–90 ft. tall. In California, more commonly seen at 15–20 ft. tall, 6–8 ft. wide. Pendulous branchlets; leathery, smooth, dark green, sharp-pointed leaves 1–3 in. long, ½–1½ in. wide. Grows upright in youth without staking; plant in groves for slender sapling effect. Makes a decorative foliage pattern against wood or masonry background. Excellent container plant.

P. nivalis. ALPINE TOTARA. Shrub. Zones 4–9, 14–17. From New Zealand. Broad, low-growing, spreading plant that eventually reaches 2–3 ft. high, 6–10 ft. wide. Branches are densely clothed with dark olive green, ¼–¾-in.-long needles like those of yew. Attractive as ground cover or in large rock garden.

P. totara. TOTARA. Tree. Zones 8, 9, 14–24. From New Zealand. In its native environment, this tree reaches 100 ft. tall. In California, more common size is 25–30 ft. tall and 18–25 ft. wide. Dense and rather narrow. Stiff, leathery gray-green leaves to 1 in. long, pointed at tips. General appearance like that of yew.

PODOPHYLLUM
Berberidaceae
PERENNIALS

✔	ZONES VARY BY SPECIES
◑ ●	PARTIAL OR FULL SHADE
♦ ♦	REGULAR TO AMPLE WATER
✦	ALL PARTS (EXCEPT RIPE FRUIT) ARE POISONOUS IF INGESTED

Odd-looking yet striking plants, these herbaceous barberry relatives grow from thick underground rhizomes that send up stalks crowned with large, umbrella-shaped, deeply lobed leaves. Shoots with a single leaf are flowerless; those with two leaves bear a single 2-in.-wide flower (set between the leaves) in mid- to late spring. Blooms are followed by juicy, 2-in. berries; these are edible when fully ripe (poisonous until that stage) but can have a powerful laxative effect. Make attractive, slowly spreading deciduous ground covers for shady areas with moist, organically enriched soil.

P. hexandrum. Zones 4–7, 14–17. From Himalayas, western China. To 2–2½ ft. high, 1½–2 ft. wide. Dark green, brown-mottled leaves to 10 in. wide are divided into three or five lobes; each lobe is further divided. White or pink flowers are followed by bright red berries.

P. peltatum. MAY APPLE. Zones 1–7. From eastern North

Podophyllum hexandrum

America. To 1–1½ ft. high, 1 ft. wide. Foliage is bronze when new; mature leaves are shiny dark green, to 1 ft. wide, divided into five to nine lobes. White flowers followed by bright yellow berries. Spreads fairly fast in its preferred rich, moist soil. Dies back completely in late summer.

PODRANEA
ricasoliana
PINK TRUMPET VINE
Bignoniaceae
EVERGREEN VINE

✔	ZONES 9, 12, 13, 19–24; H1, H2
☀ ◐	FULL SUN OR PARTIAL SHADE
♦ ♦	MODERATE TO REGULAR WATER

Native to South Africa. Sprawling growth to 20 ft.; must be fastened to its support. Glossy dark green leaves consist of two to five opposite pairs of 2-in. leaflets plus one terminal leaflet. Blooms in spring or summer, when tips of new growth produce loose clusters of 2–3-in.-wide, red-veined pink flowers shaped like open trumpets.

Podranea ricasoliana

Grows slowly when young, then speeds up as it matures. Likes heat, good drainage. Use on posts, arbors, trellises, walls, trunks of high-branching trees. Thin out any tangling growth in winter. Light frosts may cause leaves to drop; heavier frosts may kill vine to the ground, but regrowth is almost certain as long as soil doesn't freeze.

Podocarpus gracilior

P

POHA, GROUND CHERRY
Solanaceae
PERENNIAL

- ☑ ZONES H1, H2; ANYWHERE AS ANNUAL
- ☀ FULL SUN
- 💧 REGULAR WATER

From Brazil, but naturalized at higher elevations throughout Hawaiian Islands. Known botanically as *Physalis peruviana* and closely related to tomatillo (*P. ixocarpa*) and Chinese lantern plant (*P. alkekengi*). Bushy plant with heart-shaped, irregularly toothed, somewhat velvety green leaves to 2½–6 in. long. As a perennial, it can reach 6 ft. tall and 4 ft. wide (needs support); as an annual, it is more likely to grow 1½–3 ft. high and wide. Plant produces small, bell-shaped spring flowers that are whitish yellow with brown spots in the throat. After blossoms fade, the enlarged calyx forms a loose, papery, straw-colored husk around the fruit. The seedy, inch-wide yellow fruit ripens from late summer into autumn; it is smaller and sweeter than tomatillo and can be eaten fresh or used in pies and preserves.

Poha

Grow in well-drained soil in a frost-free, wind-protected site. Plant is self-fruitful, but you can help ensure pollination by gently shaking flower stems or spraying them lightly with water. No fertilizer needed. Cut back on watering when fruit is maturing. Harvest fruit when it drops to ground; remove papery husks before using. Plant often self-sows.

POHINAHINA.
See **VITEX rotundifolia**

POHUTUKAWA.
See **METROSIDEROS excelsus**

POINCIANA. See CAESALPINIA, DELONIX regia

POINSETTIA.
See **EUPHORBIA pulcherrima**

POLEMONIUM
Polemoniaceae
PERENNIALS

- ☑ ZONES 1–11, 14–17, EXCEPT AS NOTED
- ◐ PARTIAL OR FULL SHADE
- 💧 REGULAR WATER

Lush rosettes of finely divided, ferny, light to medium green foliage. Blossom stalks are typically leafy and bear clusters of bell-shaped flowers in spring or early summer. Good under trees. Grow from seed or from divisions made after bloom or in spring; give well-drained soil. Many species are choice wildflowers from Western mountains. The following are among those most commonly available in nurseries.

Polemonium caeruleum

P. caeruleum. JACOB'S LADDER. Native to Europe, Asia. Fairly upright-growing plant to 1–3 ft. high, 1–1½ ft. wide. Lavender-blue, pendulous, 1-in. flowers. 'Brise d'Anjou', with each leaflet neatly outlined in white, is one of the most striking of variegated-foliage plants.

P. carneum. Native from Washington west of the Cascades to California. Sprawls to 1–1½ ft. high, 1 ft. wide. Yellowish buds open to ½–1 in., peachy pink blossoms that age to purplish blue. Use in borders.

P. 'Firmament'. Hybrid between *P. caeruleum* and *P. reptans*. To 20 in. high, 1 ft. wide, with bright blue flowers. Use in borders.

P. pulcherrimum. Zones A1–A3; 1–11, 14–17; H1. Native from Alaska to California. Sprawling or erect, to 1 ft. high and wide. Crowded clusters of ¼-in. flowers in blue shades or white, often with yellow throat. Good in shaded rock gardens.

P. reptans. Native to eastern U.S. Weak-stemmed plant to 1–1½ ft. high, 1 ft. wide; light blue,

---

¾-in. flowers. Better known than the species is heavy-blooming 'Blue Pearl'; it grows 10 in. high, 1½ ft. wide and bears bright blue blossoms. Good choice for a shaded rock garden.

POLIANTHES tuberosa
TUBEROSE
Agavaceae
PERENNIAL FROM RHIZOME

- ☑ ZONES 7–9, 14–24; H1, H2
- ☀ FULL SUN
- 💧 REGULAR WATER DURING GROWTH AND BLOOM

Native to Mexico. Noted for heady, powerfully sweet fragrance. Each rhizome (actually a modified rhizome with bulblike top and tuberous roots) produces a fountain of narrow, grassy leaves about 1½ ft. tall. Flower spikes rise above the leaves, bearing loose whorls of tubular, glistening white flowers in summer or early fall. Tallest tuberose (to 3½ ft.) is the form sometimes sold as 'Mexican Single'. More widely sold is double-flowered 'The Pearl', to 2½ ft. tall; it is a good garden variety, but single types provide longer-lasting cut flowers.

To bloom year after year, tuberoses need a long warm season (at least 4 months) before flowering. Where this can be provided outdoors, you can plant rhizomes directly in the ground; elsewhere, start them indoors in pots and plant outside after soil warms in spring. Set rhizomes 2 in. deep, 4–6 in. apart. If soil or water is alkaline, apply acid fertilizer when growth begins. When foliage starts to yellow in fall, stop watering. Where winter temperatures remain above 20°F/–7°C, rhizomes can be left in the ground all year (if you do this, divide clumps about every 4 years). However, many gardeners in these areas (and all gardeners living in colder regions) dig rhizomes and store them over the winter. Dig plants in fall after leaves have yellowed; cut off dead

Polianthes tuberosa

---

foliage, let rhizomes dry for 2 weeks, and store in a cool, dry place until planting time. Tuberoses can also be grown in containers and moved to protection during cold weather.

POLIOMINTHA
Lamiaceae (Labiatae)
EVERGREEN SHRUBS

- ☑ ZONES VARY BY SPECIES
- ☀◐ EXPOSURE NEEDS VARY BY SPECIES
- 💧 REGULAR WATER

These are mint relatives with the family's typical square stems; paired opposite leaves; tubular, two-lipped flowers; and strong, often pleasant aroma. Well-grown plants reach about 3 ft. high and wide. Very tolerant of many soils.

P. incana. HOARY MINT. Zones 10–13. Native to southwestern U.S. Branching gray stems are set with narrow white leaves to ¾ in. long. Blooms profusely in summer, bearing lavender-blue or white flowers less than ½ in. long in spikelike, 2–6-in.-long clusters. Full sun. Can survive with little or no water but looks better with regular moisture.

P. maderensis (P. longiflora). MEXICAN OREGANO. Zones 8–24. Native to eastern Mexico. Habit varies from somewhat cascading to upright. Leaves are shiny deep green, less than ½ in. long, with odor and flavor of true oregano (*Origanum*). Long-tubed (1–1½-in.) flowers open lavender, deepen to purple, and finally fade to white; all three colors are present on the plant at once. Long bloom season, from late spring into fall. Blossoms attract hummingbirds. Give light shade in hottest desert regions, full sun elsewhere.

Poliomintha maderensis

POLYGALA
Polygalaceae
EVERGREEN SHRUBS

- ☑ ZONES VARY BY SPECIES
- ☀◐ FULL SUN OR LIGHT SHADE
- 💧 REGULAR WATER

These plants are grown for colorful, asymmetrical flowers that look somewhat like sweet peas (*Lathyrus*). Grow in well-drained soil.

P. chamaebuxus. Zones 4–6. Native to Europe. To 4 in. high, 1 ft. wide; spreads slowly by underground stems. Leathery dark green, 1–1½-in.-long leaves resemble those of boxwood (Buxus). Flowers combine bright yellow with creamy yellow or white, sometimes with red; spring or early summer bloom. *P. c. grandiflora* bears flowers in a combination of rosy purple and yellow. Good choice for rock gardens.

P. × dalmaisiana. SWEET-PEA SHRUB. Zones 8, 9, 12–24. To 3–5 ft. high and wide; usually bare at base. Grayish green, oval to lance-shaped leaves to 1 in. long. Blooms nonstop from midsummer to fall, producing flowers in a bright, vivid purplish pink that combines well with blue shades and white. To conceal this plant's legginess, set low, bushy plants in front of it. Cut back hard in late winter to promote more compact, bushy growth. Replace plant if it becomes too lanky. Good filler.

Polygala × dalmaisiana

P. fruticosa 'Petite Butterflies'. Zones 8–9, 14–24. Native to South Africa. Dense growth to 2–3 ft. high and wide. Inch-long, rounded leaves are gray green. Purplish pink, sweet pea–shaped blooms are about 1 in. across, with a pale pink central crest. Blooms almost year-round in mildest areas, spring to fall elsewhere. Excellent near coast. Good cut flower.

P. virgata. PURPLE BROOM. Zones 8–9, 14–24. From South Africa. Fast, upright growth to 4–6 ft. high, 3–5 ft. wide. Narrow, bright green leaves up to 2 in. long and ¼ in. wide make a nice backdrop for spikes of purple, sweet pea–shaped, ½-in. flowers in summer and fall. Plants tend to be leafless near the base. Can take short periods of drought.

POLYGONATUM
SOLOMON'S SEAL
Liliaceae
PERENNIALS

🌿	ZONES A1–A3; 1–9, 14–17
◐ ●	PARTIAL OR FULL SHADE
💧	REGULAR WATER

Slowly spreading rhizomes send up arching stems clothed in bright green, broadly oval leaves arranged in nearly horizontal planes. Where leaves join stems, pairs or clusters of small, bell-shaped greenish white flowers appear in spring or early summer, hanging beneath the stems on threadlike stalks. Small blue-black berries may follow flowers. Leaves and stems turn bright yellow in autumn before plant dies to the ground. Attractive in woodland gardens. Grow in loose, woodsy soil. Can remain in place for years; to increase your plantings, dig rhizomes from clump edges in early spring and replant. Good in containers. For the Western native called false Solomon's seal, see *Maianthemum racemosum*.

P. biflorum. Native to eastern North America. To 1–3 ft. tall, 2 ft. wide, with leaves to 4 in. long and flowers usually in pairs or threes. A form sometimes sold as *P. commutatum* or *P. canaliculatum* is much more vigorous, growing 3–7 ft. tall, 3–4 ft. wide. It has leaves to 7 in. long and flowers in groups of two to ten.

Polygonatum biflorum

P. odoratum (P. japonicum, P. officinale). Native to Europe, Asia. To 1½–3½ ft. tall, 2 ft. wide, with 4–6-in. leaves. Flowers are fragrant, usually borne in pairs but sometimes singly. 'Variegatum' has white-edged leaves; its stems are dark red until fully mature.

POLYGONUM.
See **FALLOPIA, PERSICARIA**

POLYPODIUM
Polypodiaceae
FERNS

🌿	ZONES VARY BY SPECIES
◐ ●	PARTIAL OR FULL SHADE
◊ ◊◊	WATER NEEDS VARY BY SPECIES

Widespread, variable group, mostly evergreen. Some are Western natives suitable for wild gardens, among rocks, in woodland, or hanging over walls. Others are tropical plants most commonly used in hanging baskets indoors or in a greenhouse. All have creeping rhizomes and shed spent fronds cleanly as new growth appears.

P. aureum (Phlebodium aureum) HARE'S FOOT FERN. Zones 15–17, 19–24; H1, H2; or indoors. From tropical America. Grows 2½ ft. high, 5 ft. wide, with showy, gracefully arching, blue-green fronds. 'Mandaianum', sometimes called lettuce fern, has fronds with frilled and wavy edges. Regular water.

P. glycyrrhiza. LICORICE FERN. Zones A3; 4–6, 14–24. Mat-forming native of coastal regions from Alaska to California. Grows 1 ft. tall and spreads indefinitely. Use as ground cover in woodland or rock garden. Dark green fronds resemble those of a small sword fern (*Polystichum*). Grow in well-drained soil; mulch with leaf mold or other organic matter. Can take full sun when grown on the coast. Little to regular water.

P. scouleri. LEATHERY POLYPODY. Zones 4–6, 15–17, 24. Native along coast from British Columbia to Southern California. Slow-growing fern to 6 in. high, with indefinite spread. Thick, glossy, deep green fronds. Often found growing on trees and rocks; when grown in the ground, it tends to form a clump. Tolerates salt spray. Same culture as for *P. glycyrrhiza*.

P. subauriculatum 'Knightiae' (Goniophlebium subauriculatum 'Knightiae'). KNIGHT'S POLYPODY. Zones 24; H2; or indoors. Native to tropical Asia. Hanging basket plant with graceful, pendulous, fringed fronds to 3 ft. or longer. Grow in bright indirect light, in moist, well-drained potting mix; feed with controlled-release fertilizer. Spectacular plant when well grown. Regular water.

P. vulgare. COMMON POLYPODY. Zones A2, A3; 2–9, 14–17. Native to Europe and Asia. Found in woodlands, among rocks, or on trees in areas with high rainfall. Grows 1 ft. tall, with indefinite spread. Medium green fronds are held erect. Highly variable; many named forms with crested or dis-

Polypodium aureum 'Mandaianum'

sected leaves are available. Thrives in acidic or alkaline soil with moderate water.

POLYSCIAS
Araliaceae
EVERGREEN SHRUBS OR TREES

🌿	ZONES 24; H1, H2; OR INDOORS
☀ ◐	FULL SUN OR PARTIAL SHADE; BRIGHT INDIRECT LIGHT
💧💧	MODERATE TO REGULAR WATER

Like many other aralia relatives, these Polynesian natives are grown for their handsomely divided leaves; flowers are unimportant and seldom produced. Foliage is typically olive green with a red tinge. Appreciate warmth, humidity, good drainage.

These plants are grown outdoors in Hawaii, where they often serve as hedges, screens, specimens, tub plants. Elsewhere, they are usually treated as houseplants. As indoor plants, they are considered fussy, demanding fresh, fairly still air (they cannot tolerate drafts) and exactly the right amount of water (enough, but not too much). Overwatering and mite damage are the two main causes of failure. Misting is helpful in maintaining their health, as is light feeding.

P. fruticosa. MING ARALIA, PARSLEY PANAX. To 10 ft. tall, 4–6 ft. wide. Leaves to 2½ ft. long are finely divided and redivided into a multitude of narrow, toothed-edged segments.

Polyscias fruticosa

P. guilfoylei. Narrowly upright to 12–20 ft. tall, 4–8 ft. wide. Medium green leaves are usually marked with white; they reach 1½ ft. long, have five to nine leaflets. 'Victoriae', to 15 ft. tall, has white-edged leaflets that are deeply slashed and cut.

P. scutellaria 'Balfourii' (P. balfouriana). To 15 ft. tall, 4–8 ft. wide. Leaves usually have up to three roundish, 4-in.-long leaflets in green irregularly edged with white. *P.* 'Marginata' is similar.

POLYSTICHUM

Polypodiaceae
FERNS

🌡	ZONES VARY BY SPECIES
🌓 ●	PARTIAL OR FULL SHADE
💧	REGULAR WATER

Hardy, symmetrical, easy-to-grow plants with evergreen fronds, except in the case of *P. braunii*. Among the most useful and widely planted ferns; combine well with other plants. Do best in rich, well-drained soil. Use in shady beds, along house walls, and in mixed woodland plantings.

P. acrostichoides. CHRISTMAS FERN. Zones 1–9, 14–24. Native to eastern North America. To 1–1½ ft. tall, about 3 ft. wide. Most useful for shaded sites in cold climates, where the dark green foliage makes a fine contrast to snow or to brown dead leaves during the winter holiday season. Stiff fronds remain upright until pushed over by heavy snow or hard frost.

P. braunii. BRAUN'S HOLLY FERN. Zones 3–6, 14–17. Native to northern latitudes of America and Asia. To 1–3 ft. high and wide. New growth is silvery green, maturing to dark green. Deciduous in colder areas. Once established, can tolerate some dryness.

P. munitum. WESTERN SWORD FERN. Zones A3; 2–9, 14–24. Native from California to Alaska and Montana, Idaho, and South Dakota. Most common fern of Western forests. To 2–4 ft. high and wide. Leathery, lustrous dark green fronds are erect, then spreading. Each leaflet is dagger shaped, with toothed edges and a base that looks rather like a sword hilt. Old plants may have 75–100 fronds. Long lasting when cut for arrangements. Established plants get by with reduced moisture.

Polystichum munitum

P. neolobatum. LONG-EARED HOLLY FERN. Zones 5–7, 14–17. Native to Asia. Upright, arching growth to 2 ft. tall and a bit wider, with shiny, dark green fronds with pale green undersides. Upper

leaflets closest to midrib on each frond are enlarged and somewhat rounded, like little "ears." On some varieties, mature fronds take on a silvery sheen.

P. polyblepharum. JAPANESE TASSEL FERN. Zones 4–9, 14–24. Native to Asia. Handsome, dense, lacy-looking plant to 2–3 ft. tall, 3 ft. wide. Glossy dark green fronds. Golden, bristled unfurling fronds in spring. Sometimes sold as *P. setosum*.

P. setiferum. SOFT SHIELD FERN. Zones 4–9, 14–24. Native to southern Europe. Many forms, varying from 2 to 4½ ft. high and wide. Finely cut fronds give effect of green lace. 'Congestum Cristatum' is a 6–12-in.-tall dwarf with upright gray-green fronds. Divisilobum group features named varieties with particularly lacy appearance. Plantlets form on midribs of older fronds on several types of soft shield fern; these can be detached and planted. The species and its varieties are easy to grow and are splendid in shaded beds or rock gardens.

P. setosum. See P. polyblepharum

P. tsus-simense. KOREAN ROCK FERN. Zones 4–7, 14–17. From Asia. Forms a neat, dainty clump 12–15 in. tall and wide. Erect, leathery, dark green fronds are held on dark stems. Use at front of shaded borders, among rocks, in pots. Established plants can take short periods of dryness.

POMEGRANATE

Punicaceae
DECIDUOUS SHRUB OR TREE

🌡	ZONES 5–24 (BUT SEE TEXT); H1, H2
☀	FULL SUN
💧	REGULAR WATER

Native from Iran to the Himalayan region of northern India; naturalized throughout the Mediterranean. Naturally grows as a rounded plant to 15–20 ft. tall and broad, though it is often kept pruned to about 10 ft. high and wide. Showy red flowers at branch tips in spring; thick calyx persists as a projection at base of fruit. Roundish fruit to 5 in. wide is yellow overlaid with pink or red; it contains sacs of seedy, sweet-tart, juicy pulp. Self-fruitful.

Best-known variety is 'Wonderful', with orange red flowers and burnished red fruit with red pulp. Other varieties are increasingly available, including the following. All have red or orange red flowers.

'Ambrosia' bears huge fruits (up to three times larger than those of 'Wonderful'), pale pink skin, and purple pulp. 'Fleishman', 'Granada', and 'King' have pink flowers and pink pulp. 'Eversweet' ripens very early and bears virtually seedless fruit with transparent red pulp and clear, nonstaining juice. 'Red Silk' bears medium to large red fruit with excellent sweet-tart, red pulp on a small 6–8-ft. tree, ideal for containers. 'Sweet' has yellow flowers and pink pulp. 'White' bears pink fruit with sweet, transparent pulp.

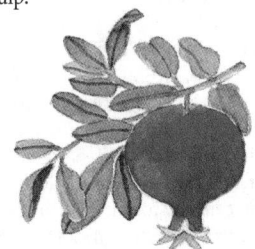

Pomegranate

Pomegranates ripen in fall; harvest them when they reach full color. Fruit left on the tree is likely to split and rot, especially if weather is rainy. Can be stored for up to 7 months in the refrigerator. To eat fresh, cut into quarters or eighths and pull rind back (starting from the ends) to expose the juicy sacs; eat them, seeds and all. To remove juice for drinking fresh or for use in jams, jellies, or sauces, cut fruit in half and ream with a juicer. Or roll fruit firmly on hard surface; then cut a hole in stem end and squeeze juice into a container.

In Zones 5, 6, and 17, where pomegranate grows and blooms but may not fruit, locate against south or west wall. Tolerates a wide variety of soils, growing well even in alkaline soil. Resistant to oak root fungus. Can take considerable drought but produces better fruit with regular moisture. For ornamental pomegranate varieties, see *Punica granatum*.

PONTEDERIA
cordata

PICKEREL WEED
Pontederiaceae
AQUATIC PERENNIAL

🌡	ZONES 1–24; H1, H2
☀ 🌓	FULL SUN OR LIGHT SHADE
💧	LOCATE IN PONDS, WATER GARDENS

Native to eastern North America. To 3–4 ft. high, 2–2½ ft. wide. Long-stalked, glossy green leaves

Pontederia cordata

stand well above surface of water; these are heart shaped, to 10 in. long and 6 in. wide. Blooms from late spring to fall, bearing short spikes of blue flowers at stem ends. Often grown as a companion to water lilies (*Nymphaea*); plant in pots of rich soil placed in 1 ft. of water. Gives an informal garden pool the look of a wild pond. To use in natural ponds, set plants at shoreline—underwater, directly in the soil. Goes dormant in winter.

PONYTAIL PALM.
See **NOLINA recurvata**

POOR MAN'S ORCHID.
See **SCHIZANTHUS pinnatus**

POOR MAN'S RHODODENDRON.
See **IMPATIENS sodenii**

POPCORN. See **CORN**

POPLAR. See **POPULUS**

POPPY. See **PAPAVER**

POPPY, HIMALAYAN.
See **MECONOPSIS betonicifolia**

POPPY, HORNED.
See **GLAUCIUM**

POPPY MALLOW.
See **CALLIRHOE involucrata**

POPPY, MEXICAN.
See **ARGEMONE mexicana**

POPPY, SEA. See **GLAUCIUM**

POPULUS

POPLAR, COTTONWOOD, ASPEN
Salicaceae
DECIDUOUS TREES

🌡	ZONES VARY BY SPECIES
☀	FULL SUN
💧	REGULAR WATER

Fast-growing, tough trees. Grown primarily—and especially appreciated—in interior regions with hot summers and cold winters. Don't do as well in mild-winter areas and in coastal climates where temperature fluctuation is minimal. Trees have aggressive surface roots that crowd out other plants, heave pavement, and clog sewer and drainage lines; best suited to rural areas and fringes of large properties. Most poplars will sucker if their roots are cut or disturbed. They are subject to many pests and diseases.

Despite their liabilities, some of these trees are beautiful or distinctive enough to be widely sold. Many have good fall color. Leaves of most are roughly triangular, sometimes toothed or lobed. Pendulous catkins (denser on male trees) appear in spring before leafout. Female trees later bear masses of cottony seeds that blow about and become a nuisance; for that reason, male (seedless) varieties are the best choice and are usually offered in nurseries.

P. × acuminata. LANCELEAF COTTONWOOD. Zones 1–11, 14–21. Hybrid of *P. angustifolia* and another species; like *P. angustifolia*, thrives at high elevations. To 40–60 ft. tall, 35–45 ft. wide. Narrow, triangular leaves to 4 in. long are glossy dark green above, paler dull green beneath. Yellow fall color. Seedless.

P. alba. WHITE POPLAR. Zones A3; 1–11, 14–21. Native to Europe, Asia. To 40–70 ft. high and wide. Common name refers to woolly white leaf undersides and to light-colored young bark. Leaves are 2–5 in. long, usually with three to five lobes.

A "lively" tree with leaves that move even in light breezes, showing flickering white and green highlights. Poor fall color. Tolerates wide range of soils. Suckers profusely—an advantage if it is planted as a windbreak, otherwise a problem. Seedless variety 'Pyramidalis', called Bolleana poplar (often sold as *P. bolleana*), forms a narrow (15-ft.-wide) column and has a white or light gray trunk like that of birch (*Betula*).

P. angustifolia. NARROWLEAF POPLAR. Zones 1–11, 14–21. Native from Alberta to Mexico, primarily in Rocky Mountains; grows at elevations to 8,000 ft. To 50–60 ft. tall, 35–45 ft. wide, with finely toothed, narrow, willowlike green

leaves to 5 in. long. Young bark is green.

P. × canadensis 'Eugenei'. CAROLINA POPLAR. Zones 1–11, 14–21. Male hybrid to 100 ft. tall, 40 ft. wide. Glossy bright green, tooth-edged leaves to 4 in. long; good yellow fall color.

P. × canescens 'Macrophylla'. Zones A2, A3; 1–11, 14–21. To 100 ft. tall, 50 ft. wide, with exceptionally large leaves (to 9 in. long on vigorous young shoots) that are glossy dark green above, white beneath. Fine yellow or red fall color. Older trees have creamy gray bark.

P. fremontii. WESTERN COTTONWOOD, FREMONT COTTONWOOD. Zones 1–12, 14–21. Native to California and central Rockies south to Mexico. To 40–60 ft. or taller, 30 ft. wide. Glossy yellow-green, coarsely toothed, virtually triangular leaves are thick textured, 2–4 in. wide; turn bright lemon yellow in fall. Leaves persist almost all winter in Zone 12. 'Nevada' is a male variety.

P. nigra 'Italica'. LOMBARDY POPLAR. Zones A3; 1–11, 14–24. Male selection of a European native. Beautiful columnar tree to 40–100 ft. tall, 15–30 ft. wide, with upward-reaching branches. Bright green, 4-in. leaves turn golden yellow in fall. Excellent along country driveways; valuable both as windbreak and skyline decoration. Healthy and attractive in cold, dry interior climates. Suckers profusely. *P. n. thevestina* has white bark.

P. tremula. EUROPEAN ASPEN. Zones A1–A3; 1–7. From Europe, North Africa, Asia. Similar to *P. tremuloides*, but its bark is somewhat darker and its leaves more coarsely toothed. Seedless 'Erecta', sometimes called Swedish columnar aspen, is a narrow grower with red fall color—a good substitute for Lombardy poplar (*P. nigra* 'Italica').

P. tremuloides. QUAKING ASPEN. Zones A1–A3; 1–7, 14–19. Native throughout mountains of the West, at elevations to 9,000 ft. Generally performs poorly or grows slowly in lowlands; usually short lived in warmer climates. To 20–60 ft. tall, 15–30 ft. wide; often grows as a multitrunked tree or in a clump. Smooth, pale gray-green

Populus nigra 'Italica'

to whitish bark. Dainty, roundish, 2–4-in., glossy green leaves flutter with the slightest movement of air. Brilliant golden yellow fall color. Good background tree for native shrubs and wildflowers. Apt to suffer from sudden dieback or borers.

P. trichocarpa. BLACK COTTONWOOD. Zones A2, A3; 1–9, 14–24. Native from Alaska to Southern California. To 30–100 ft. tall, 25–30 ft. wide. Heavy-limbed tree with furrowed dark gray bark, very brittle wood. Leaves are 3–5 in. across, deep green above and distinctly silver beneath; attractive when ruffled by breezes. Good golden yellow fall color.

PORCELAIN BERRY. See **AMPELOPSIS brevipedunculata**

PORCUPINE GRASS. See **MISCANTHUS sinensis 'Strictus'**

PORK AND BEANS. See **SEDUM rubrotinctum**

PORT ORFORD CEDAR. See **CHAMAECYPARIS lawsoniana**

PORTUGAL LAUREL. See **PRUNUS lusitanica**

PORTULACA
ROSE MOSS, PURSLANE
Portulacaceae
ANNUALS

✐ **ALL ZONES**
☼ **FULL SUN**
◐◑ **MODERATE TO REGULAR WATER**

Low-growing, fleshy plants. One is called a weed but can be used in cooking and salads. The others are grown for their brilliant flowers, on display from late spring until frost; generally, the blossoms open fully in bright light and close by midafternoon in hot weather. The various plants described here thrive in high temperatures, intense sunlight. Not fussy about soil. Bright-flowered types are attractive in rock gardens, parking strips, hanging baskets, or as edgings and bank covers; they don't require deadheading to prolong bloom.

P. grandiflora. ROSE MOSS. From South America. To 6 in. high, 1½ ft. across. Trailing, branching reddish stems are set with narrow, cylindrical, pointed leaves to 1 in. long. Inch-wide, lustrous-petaled flowers shaped like tiny roses, in white and many bright and pastel shades of red, cerise, rose pink, orange, and yellow. Available as single colors or mixes, in single-

Portulaca grandiflora

or double-flowered strains: Prize, Magic Carpet, Sunglo, Sunkiss are popular. Afternoon Delight and Sundance strains stay open longer in the afternoon. The newer Sundial strain also resists closing and has larger (2-in.), double blossoms; 'Sundial Peach' is especially attractive. All self-sow, but they often fail to come true from seed.

P. oleracea. PURSLANE. Unimproved form is thought to have originated in India; it's an edible weed with tiny yellow flowers and plump, oval leaves to 1¼ in. long. Warm weather and moisture encourage its growth. Control by hoeing or pulling before it goes to seed; don't let pulled plants lie about, since they can reroot or ripen seed. Stems and leaves can be added to salads, soups, sauces; improved garden strains are sold for the vegetable garden. Called *verdolaga* in Mexico, *pourpier* in France.

P. Wildfire hybrids. Sometimes offered as *P. oleracea*, or *P. grandiflora*, but is actually a strain of *P. umbraticola*. Best in hot-summer areas; popular in the Southwest. Plants grow a few inches tall and spread to 2 ft.; they have the broad leaves of *P. oleracea* but bear brightly colored, 1½-in. single flowers in red, pink, lavender, yellow, orange, peach, white, or bicolors. Each flower lasts only a day, but new ones keep the show going. Plants live over in the absence of frost.

PORTULACARIA
afra
ELEPHANT'S FOOD
Portulacaceae
SUCCULENT SHRUB

✐ **ZONES 8, 9, 12–24; H1, H2**
☼◐● **SUN OR SHADE**
◌◑ **LITTLE TO MODERATE WATER**

Native to South Africa. Can be grown outdoors but needs frost protection in Zones 8, 9, 12, 14, 15, 18–21. To 12 ft. tall and nearly as wide, with thick, juicy stems and glossy green leaves. Looks a bit like jade plant (*Crassula ovata*) and is sometimes sold under the name "miniature jade plant," but it's faster growing and more loosely branched, with tapering, more limber branches and smaller (½-in.-long) leaves. In its native land, it bears clusters of tiny pink flowers, but it seldom blooms in North America.

Portulacaria afra

In frost-free or nearly frostless areas, can be used as a fast-growing informal screen or unclipped hedge. Small specimens are good, easy-care potted plants and can be trained as bonsai. Forms with variegated leaves ('Tricolor', 'Variegata') are slower growing and smaller than the species.

POTATO
Solanaceae
PERENNIAL TREATED AS ANNUAL

✎	ALL ZONES
☀	FULL SUN
●	REGULAR WATER
◆	GREEN SKIN AND RAW SHOOTS ARE POISONOUS IF INGESTED

Andean native, botanically known as *Solanum tuberosum*. For ornamental relatives, see *Solanum*. Though other vegetables are more common in home gardens, growing potatoes can be very satisfying: 2 lbs. of seed potatoes can yield 50 lbs. of potatoes for eating. The many pests and diseases that beleaguer commercial growers are not likely to plague home gardeners. To avoid disease problems, plant certified disease-free starter potatoes or disease-resistant varieties.

Grow from seed potatoes that you cut into 1½-in. cubes (each with at least two eyes) or from small tubers, which are planted whole and are less likely to rot in the ground. Home gardeners have access to a number of varieties, including types with red, white,

yellow, russet brown, or bluish purple skins; depending on variety, flesh may be white or match the skin color of red, yellow, or blue varieties. Shapes vary from round or cylindrical to fingerlike (the latter are called fingerlings). Some varieties mature faster than others, but most reach harvesting size 2½ to 4 months after planting.

Culinary use depends greatly on whether a potato is moist or dry, and whether the starch it contains is branched (holds its shape in salads and stews) or relatively straight (allows the potato to fall apart in cooking). For baking and mashing, most people prefer a light, dry, fluffy potato like 'Butte' or 'Russet Burbank'. For velvety textured soups, try 'Carola', which falls apart nicely when cooked. For stews, boiling, and potato salads, choose a waxy, moist potato like 'Reddale'. For fun, make colorful fries or mashed potatoes with 'All Blue'; 'Elba' is another good choice for these dishes, but with traditional buff-colored skin and white flesh.

There are also potatoes for special situations. If you garden in a short-season climate, try an early all-purpose variety like 'Yukon' or 'Yukon Gold'. In wet climates or soil that tends to be damp, grow 'Nooksack'. If diseases are a problem in your area, try 'Island Sunshine' for resistance to late blight, or 'Reddale' for resistance to verticillium wilt.

Potatoes need fertile, sandy, fast-draining soil; tubers become deformed in heavy, poorly drained soil. In cold-winter climates, plant as soon as the soil is workable in spring. In mild-winter regions, plant in early spring for a summer crop, in early fall for a winter-into-spring crop. Where frosts are not severe, potatoes can be planted in midwinter—as long as the soil isn't too wet from winter rains. Let seed potato pieces dry for a day or two before planting. Then set minitubers or potato pieces 2 in. deep, 1–1½ ft. apart. Add loose soil as plant grows, taking care not to cover stems completely; developing tubers should always be covered with soil to keep skin from turning green.

The above-ground potato plant is sprawling and bushy, with

much-divided dark green leaves somewhat like those of a tomato plant. Clustered inch-wide flowers may be white, pink, light red, or pale blue, depending on variety; blossoms often reflect the color of the tubers, but not always.

Dig early potatoes (so-called new potatoes) when the plants begin to bloom; dig mature potatoes when plants die down. Dig carefully to avoid bruising or cutting the tubers. Well-matured potatoes free of defects are the best keepers; store them in a cool (40°F/4°C), dark, dry place. Where ground doesn't freeze, late potatoes can remain in ground until needed. Dig before warmer temperatures start them growing again.

Another method of growing potatoes is to prepare soil so surface is loose, plant potato pieces or minitubers ½–2 in. deep, and water well. Mound loose soil over plants as directed above; then cover soil with a 1–1½-ft.-thick layer of straw, hay, or dead leaves. Surround the planting with chicken wire to keep loose material from blowing away. Potatoes will form on the soil surface or just beneath it, requiring little digging; you can probe through the mulch with your fingers to harvest them.

Potato

POTATO VINE.
See **SOLANUM laxum**

POTENTILLA
CINQUEFOIL
Rosaceae
PERENNIALS AND
DECIDUOUS SHRUBS

✎	ZONES VARY BY SPECIES
☀ ◐	PARTIAL SHADE IN HOTTEST CLIMATES
● ●	WATER NEEDS VARY BY TYPE

Tough, unfussy perennials and small shrubs with flowers in white, cream, and soft to bright shades of pink, red, yellow, orange. Leaves are divided into leaflets; may be green, gray green, or silvery gray.

Perennials
These include sturdy, clumping plants for use in rock gardens or perennial borders and creeping kinds used as ground covers. Leaves are divided fanwise into leaflets and are reminiscent of strawberry foliage. Moderate to regular water.

P. atrosanguinea. Zones 2b–9, 14–24. Sprawling, clump-forming Himalayan native to 1½ ft. high, 2 ft. wide. Leaves divided into three furry, silvery gray leaflets; deep red, 1-in. flowers in summer. A parent of several superior hybrids, including 'Gibson's Scarlet', with scarlet blossoms.

P. nepalensis 'Miss Willmott'. Zones 2b–9, 14–24. Variety of a Himalayan native. Forms a clump to 1 ft. high, 1½ ft. wide. Each leaf consists of five roundish, bright green leaflets. Summer bloomer, bearing branching clusters of ½–1-in.-wide, salmon pink blossoms. For borders, cut flowers. Performs well near coast.

P. neumanniana (P. verna 'Nana'). Zones A1–A3; 1–24. European native. May also be sold as *P. tabernaemontani*. Dainty-looking yet tough and persistent ground cover to 3–6 in. high; spreads quickly by creeping, rooting stems. Bright green leaves are divided into five leaflets. Butter yellow, ¼-in. flowers bloom in spring and summer. Foliage blankets the ground completely yet is permeable enough to be a good bulb cover; established plantings endure limited foot traffic. Set plants 1 ft. apart in well-drained soil. Plantings look more uniform if mowed annually before spring growth begins; in colder areas, mowing also serves to remove browned winter leaves.

P. recta 'Warrenii'. Zones A2, A3; 1–10, 14–24. Selection of a species from Europe, Siberia. Erect clump to 2 ft. high, 1½ ft. wide, with medium green to gray-green leaves divided into five to seven leaflets. Profuse show of bright yellow, 1-in. flowers in late spring. Tolerates a wide range of soils. Sometimes sold as *P. warrenii*. 'Macrantha' (which may be listed as *P. warrenii* 'Macrantha') is the same or a very similar plant.

P. × tonguei. Zones 2–24. Clumping, to 4 in. high, 1–2 ft. wide; nearly prostrate stems. Dark green leaves are divided into three to five leaflets. Late spring or summer blooms, ½-in.-wide, apricot with a red center.

P. warrenii. See P. recta 'Warrenii'

Shrubs
The shrubby potentillas, most often sold as named forms of *P. fruticosa,* are native to northern latitudes everywhere, including the Cascades and Olympic and Rocky mountains. They perform well in

P

Potentilla fruticosa
'Tangerine' (shrub)

Zones A1–A3, 1–11, 14–21. All have typically bright green to dark green leaves divided into three to seven leaflets; all bloom cheerfully from late spring to early fall, producing 1½–2-in.-wide blossoms.

These are fairly trouble-free plants that do best in well-drained soil with moderate water but tolerate poor soil, drought, and heat. Varieties with red- or orange-tinted blossoms should be grown in light shade; they tend to fade quickly in hot sun. After the bloom period ends, cut out some of the oldest stems from time to time to make room for new growth. Here are some of the many varieties to be found in nurseries.

'Abbotswood'. To 3 ft. high and wide. White flowers.

'Floppy Disc'. To 2–3 ft. tall, 3–4 ft. wide. Deep pink double flowers bleach to pinkish white in high heat.

'Frosty'. To 1 ft. high and 3 ft. wide. Large white flowers.

'Goldfinger'. To 3 ft. tall, 4 ft. wide. Golden yellow flowers.

'Gold Star'. To 2 ft. tall, 2–2½ ft. wide. Bright yellow blooms.

'Jackman's Variety'. To 3–4 ft. tall, 5 ft. wide. Bright yellow blossoms.

'Katherine Dykes'. To 3 ft. tall and wide. Pale yellow flowers.

'Klondike'. Dense grower to 2 ft. high and wide. Deep yellow flowers.

'Mount Everest'. Bushy, upright plant to 4½ ft. high and wide. Pure white blossoms.

'Primrose Beauty'. To 2–3 ft. high and wide, with silvery green foliage and pale yellow flowers.

'Red Ace'. To 2 ft. high, 3–4 ft. wide. Flowers are bright red, with yellow center and yellow petal backs; they fade to solid yellow with age (fading is very rapid in hot-summer climates or under poor growing conditions).

'Sunset'. To 1½ ft. tall, 3 ft. wide. Flowers are red in light shade; in hot sun, they may be reddish orange, orange, or yellow.

'Sutter's Gold'. Grows to 1 ft. high, 3 ft. wide, with soft yellow blooms.

'Tangerine'. To 2½ ft. high and wide, with bright orange-yellow flowers.

POTERIUM.
See **SANGUISORBA**

POTHOS. See **EPIPREMNUM pinnatum 'Aureum'**

POT MARIGOLD.
See **CALENDULA officinalis**

POWDER PUFF.
See **CALLIANDRA**

PRAIRIE ASTER.
See **MACHAERANTHERA tanacetifolia**

PRAIRIE CORD GRASS.
See **SPARTINA pectinata**

PRAIRIE DROPSEED.
See **SPOROBOLUS heterolepis**

PRAIRIE SMOKE.
See **GEUM triflorum**

PRATIA
Campanulaceae (Lobeliaceae)
PERENNIALS

⚡	ZONES 4–9, 14–24
☼ ◑	PARTIAL SHADE IN HOTTEST CLIMATES
💧	REGULAR WATER

Small, ground-hugging plants that reach just 2–3 in. high in bloom, with creeping, branching stems that root at the joints. All are useful low ground covers where soil is reasonably rich and well drained. Set plants 8–12 in. apart; fertilize periodically. Small, closely set leaves and tolerance for an occasional footstep make them choice selections for use between stepping-stones. They resemble baby's tears

Pratia pedunculata

(Soleirolia) but offer appealing flowers as well as attractive foliage. Can be invasive where well adapted.

P. angulata. Native to New Zealand. Dark green, ½-in. leaves set off small white to ice blue summer flowers like those of lobelia, with a two-lobed upper lip and a three-lobed lower lip. Small, round fruit is purplish red.

P. pedunculata (Isotoma fluviatilis, Laurentia fluviatilis). BLUE STAR CREEPER. Native to Australia. Bright green, nearly stemless, ¼-in. leaves; in late spring and summer, these form a backdrop for equally tiny, star-shaped pale blue flowers. 'County Park' has deeper blue flowers.

PREGNANT ONION.
See **ORNITHOGALUM longibracteatum**

PRETTY FACE.
See **TRITELEIA ixioides**

PRICKLY PAPERBARK.
See **MELALEUCA styphelioides**

PRICKLY PEAR. See **OPUNTIA**

PRICKLY POPPY.
See **ARGEMONE**

PRIDE OF CALIFORNIA.
See **LATHYRUS splendens**

PRIDE OF MADEIRA.
See **ECHIUM candicans**

PRIMROSE. See **PRIMULA**

PRIMROSE TREE.
See **LAGUNARIA patersonii**

PRIMULA
PRIMROSE
Primulaceae
PERENNIALS SOMETIMES
GROWN AS ANNUALS

⚡	ZONES VARY BY SPECIES OR TYPE
☼ ◑ ●	FULL SUN IN COOLER CLIMATES ONLY
💧 💧	WATER NEEDS VARY BY TYPE
▶	SEE CHART NEXT PAGE

Most primroses are native to the Himalayas and cool regions of Southeast Asia and Europe. Plants form a foliage rosette; at bloom time, typically circular, sometimes fragrant flowers with five petals rise above the leaves. The petals usually overlap and are often indented at the apex, sometimes so deeply that each flower appears to have ten parts.

Blossoms may be borne on individual stems, in clusters at stem ends, or in tiered, candelabra-like clusters along the stem. Most primroses are spring blooming, but some start flowering in mid- to late winter in mild climates, and a few bloom in early summer. Some go dormant in late fall or winter; mark their location before they disappear (see chart next page).

Nearly all are good plants for the woodland garden. Many thrive in shallow streams or perennially boggy spots; others make excellent bedding or edging plants; and several early varieties are delightful late-winter potted plants for porch or windowsill.

Specialists have organized the hundreds of primrose species, selections, named hybrids, and hybrid strains into dozens of groupings called sections. Get seeds or plants from specialty nurseries and primrose societies. Retail nurseries and garden centers sell most of the primroses listed in the chart.

What Primroses Need

CLIMATE Primroses fare best in areas with chilly winters (*P. malacoides* and *P. obconica* are notable exceptions) and cool summers.

EXPOSURE In cool-summer regions, especially where foggy or overcast weather is common, primroses can take full sun. In hotter, sunnier areas, they prefer filtered or dappled sunlight or bright shade.

SOIL Plant all (except water-loving species) in organically enriched, well-drained soil, with roots mulched to keep them cool.

WATERING Most types thrive with regular water; others need damp or even boggy soil.

DIVIDING Primrose plants form tight clumps that will need dividing when performance declines. When clumps become over-crowded, dig and divide them right after bloom or (in mild-winter areas) in autumn.

Primula vialii

PRIMULA

NAME, ZONES	SIZE	LEAVES	FLOWERS	COMMENTS
Primula acaulis (see **P. vulgaris**)				
P. alpicola MOONLIGHT PRIMROSE 3–6, 17	To 20 in. high, 1 ft. wide	Elliptical, to 4 in. long, wrinkled, medium green	Clusters of sulfur yellow (sometimes white or purple), bell-shaped blossoms. Powerfully fragrant. Summer	Somewhat tender in coldest zones. Regular water
P. auricula AURICULA A2, A3; 1–6, 15–17, 22–24	To 6–8 in. high, 1 ft. wide	Evergreen. Broad, leathery gray-green leaves are toothed or smooth edged, sometimes with mealy, powdery coating that spots and runs in rain	Clustered blooms in white, cream, yellow, orange, pink, rose, red, purple, blue, or brownish, with white or yellow eye. Fragrant. Early spring	Usually grown in pots for display. Some choice named varieties have green or near- black flowers rimmed in mealy powder or in a contrasting color. Regular water
P. beesiana 3–6, 15–17	To 2 ft. high and wide	Oval to lance shaped, toothed, medium green, tapering into leafstalk; to 14 in. long (including stalk)	Tiered blossoms; 2–8 dense whorls per stem. Color is variable but usually reddish purple with yellow eye. Mid- to late spring	Very deep rooted. Regular water in the form of deep soakings
P. bulleyana 3–6, 15–17	To 2 ft. high and wide	Like those of *P. beesiana*, but with reddish midribs Mid- to late spring	Tiered blossoms; 5–7 whorls per stem. Bright yellow, opening from orange buds	Looks showy at woodland edge. Regular water
P. denticulata DRUMSTICK PRIMROSE A2, A3; 1–6	To 1 ft. high and wide	Spoon shaped, medium green, 6–12 in. long. Only half grown at bloom time	Dense, ball-shaped clusters on stout stems. Color ranges from blue violet to purple. Early spring	Pinkish, lavender, and white varieties available. Regular water
P. florindae A2, A3; 3–6, 15–17	To 3 ft. tall, 2 ft. wide	Long-stemmed, toothed, medium green leaves are broadly oval with heart- shaped base, to 9 in. long	Yellow, bell shaped, nodding; carried in clusters of up to 60. Most fragrant primrose and the latest to bloom. Late spring or summer	Ample water; will grow in a few inches of running water or in damp, low spot. Plants are late to appear in spring. Hybrids have red, orange, or yellow flowers
P. helodoxa (see **P. prolifera**)				
P. japonica A3; 2–6, 15–17	To 2½ ft. high, 1½ ft. wide	Spoon shaped, light green, to 9 in. long	Tiered blossoms in purple with yellow eye; up to 5 whorls on each stout stem. Late spring, early summer	'Miller's Crimson' is an excellent red variety, and 'Alba' is a fine white. Pink forms also available. Ample water; will grow at edge of pond, even in very shallow water
P. × juliae (Pruhonicensis hybrids) JULIANA PRIMROSE 2–6, 14–17, 20–23	To 3–4 in. high, 10 in. wide	Rounded, scallop edged, bright green, to 2½ in. long	White, blue, yellow, orange red, pink, or purple, borne singly or in clusters. Early spring	Excellent for edging, woodland, rock garden. Regular water
P. littoniana (see **P. vialii**)				
P. malacoides FAIRY PRIMROSE, BABY PRIMROSE 8, 9, 12–24	To 8–15 in. high, 1 ft. wide	Evergreen. Soft, pale green, oval, 1½–3 in. long, with lobed and cut edges; carried on long stalks	Tiered blossoms in loose, lacy whorls along many upright stems. White, pink, rose, red, lavender. Midwinter to late spring	Perennial in mild-winter areas of California and Arizona, though often grown as annual there. Good under high-branching trees, with spring bulbs. Stands light frost. Treated only as annual, potted plant, or houseplant elsewhere. Regular water
P. obconica 4–9, 14–24	To 1 ft. high and wide	Evergreen. Soft, hairy, medium green, roundish, to 6 in. long; hairy leafstalks. Hairs (except on Freedom and Libre strains) may irritate skin	Large, broad clusters of 1½–2-in.-wide blooms in white, pink, salmon, lavender, reddish purple. Winter, spring; nearly everblooming in cool-summer areas	Perennial, but best treated as annual. Use for bedding where winters are mild, as houseplant in colder regions. Regular water

P

▶

PRIMULA

NAME, ZONES	SIZE	LEAVES	FLOWERS	COMMENTS
P. Polyanthus Group POLYANTHUS PRIMROSE, ENGLISH PRIMROSE 1–24	To 8–12 in. high, 9 in. wide	Fresh green, tongue shaped, to 8 in. long; resemble romaine lettuce leaves. Evergreen in milder climates	Large, full clusters of 1–2-in.-wide blossoms (miniature types are smaller). Almost any color; many very brilliant. Winter to early or midspring	Choose from many large-flowered strains, like Pacific Giant, or look for choice novelties such as 'Gold Lace' (gold-edged, yellow-centered, mahogany petals) and 'Penumbra' (similar, with silver-edged petals). All are excellent for massing, with bulbs, or in pots. Grow as annuals in hot-summer areas. Regular water
P. prolifera (P. helodoxa) 4–6, 15–17	To 2–3 ft. high, 2 ft. wide	Evergreen. Spoon shaped to triangular, deep green, to 14 in. long	Tiered blossoms; up to 7 whorls per stem, each with 3–12 fragrant, light to bright yellow, inch-wide flowers. Late spring, summer	Good beside brooks, in bog gardens. Ample water
P. pulverulenta 3–6, 17	To 3 ft. tall, 2 ft. wide	Elliptical, deep green, wrinkled, to 1 ft. or longer	Tiered blossoms; several to many whorls per stem. Red to red-purple, with purple eye. Flowering stems thickly dusted with white meal. Late spring, summer	Bartley strain has flowers in pink and salmon range. Ample water
P. sieboldii A2, A3; 2–7, 14–17	To 1 ft. high and wide	Oval, light green, deeply lobed and toothed, 2–4 in. long, carried on long leafstalks	White, pink, or purple, all with white eye; 1–1½ in. wide, in clusters of 2–15. Early spring	Many named selections in deep or light colors; flowers of some have fringed petals. Leaves of all types usually die back shortly after flowering. Regular water
P. sinensis CHINESE PRIMROSE Indoors	To 6–8 in. high and wide	Evergreen. Soft, hairy, bright green, roundish, 2–4 in. long, with toothed, lobed edges. Hairs may irritate skin	One or more whorls per stem, each with many 1½-in.-wide blossoms in white, pink, lavender, reddish, or coral. Stellatas have star-shaped flowers. Winter	Tender. Favorite European potted plant; imported seed available from specialists. Regular water
P. × tommasinii A3; 2a–9, 14–24	To 6–12 in. tall, 1½ ft. wide over time	Green, 9 in. long, tongue shaped	Hose-in-hose is most common type sold; looks like one single flower emerging from the center of another. Fragrant	The YOU and ME series includes hose-in-hose flowers in yellow, cream, maroon, red, rose, white, purple, apricot, blue. Regular water
P. veris COWSLIP A3; 2–6, 15–17	To 4–10 in. high, 8 in. wide	Similar to those of polyanthus primrose. Evergreen in milder climates	Clustered flowers are bright yellow, fragrant, ½–1 in. wide. Early spring	Lovely naturalized in wild garden or rock garden. Charming but not as sturdy as polyanthus primrose. Regular water
P. vialii (P. littoniana) 4–6, 15–17	To 1–2 ft. high, 1 ft. wide	Oblong, irregularly toothed, hairy, to 8 in. long	Dense, narrow, 3–5-in.-long spikes of fragrant flowers to ½ in. wide on erect stems. Violet blue, opening from red buds. Late spring or early summer	Not long lived but quite easy to grow from seed. Use in rock garden. Regular to ample water
P. vulgaris (P. acaulis) PRIMROSE, ENGLISH PRIMROSE A3; 2–6, 14–17, 21–24	To 8 in. high, 1 ft. wide	Much like those of polyanthus primrose. Evergreen in milder climates	Borne singly; vigorous garden strains often bear 2 or 3 per stem. White, yellow, red, blue, brown, bronze, or wine colored. Early spring	Single series like Danova, sweet-scented Primera, and large-flowered Supreme are ubiquitous, but doubles and rose-flowered series like Belarina and Rosanna are gaining popularity. Good in woodland gardens, as edging, in containers. Regular water

For bedding out, try *P. malacoides* and *P. obconica* (California favorites); *P. × juliae* and *P. vulgaris* (favored in all areas except the coldest and hottest parts of the West); and *P.* Polyanthus Group (the most weather-resistant primrose in all areas). For growing on boggy sites or in shallow water, nothing is more lovely than a colony of *P. florindae, P. japonica,* or *P. prolifera*. For similar tall, tiered blooms in ordinary woodland garden soil, try *P. beesiana, P. bulleyana,* or *P. pulverulenta*. For head-turning flowers, try individual plants of *P. vialii* or a bed of *P. denticulata*.

The key to success with primroses is the right climate. Almost any primrose flourishes in the cool, humid Pacific Northwest; if given the right amount of moisture and sun protection, these plants can be grown successfully in somewhat warmer, drier regions. Most are quite hardy; many thrive east of the Cascades and in intermountain regions. Where the climate is less than favorable, they are sometimes treated as annuals. Some will grow indoors. All are subject to slug and snail damage.

Primula malacoides

Primula Polyanthus Group

PRINCE'S FEATHER. See **AMAR-ANTHUS hypochondriacus**

PRINCESS FLOWER.
See **TIBOUCHINA urvilleana**

PRITCHARDIA
LOULU PALM
Arecaceae (Palmae)
PALM

🌡	ZONES VARY BY SPECIES
☼	FULL SUN
💧	MODERATE WATER

Complex genus; includes 19 native Hawaiian species and about 25 species restricted to various other tropical Pacific islands. Erect, medium-size fan palms with straight trunk and regular form. Best in well-drained soil with moderate moisture. Plant in groups or use as specimens. Young plants tolerate shade and are good containers, indoors or out.

P. hillebrandii. LOULU LELO. Zones 23, 24; H1, H2. Native to Hawaii. Slow growing to 20 ft. tall, 8 ft. wide. Leaves to 4 ft. long. Full sun brings out the bluish silver color of the foliage. Striking accent in the landscape during the day or under night lighting.

P. minor. Zones 17, 23, 24; H1, H2. From high-elevation Hawaii. Slow growth to 20–30 ft. tall, with attractive, deep green, rounded leaves with a silvery underside. Protect from hot sun when young.

P. pacifica. FIJI FAN PALM. Zone H2. Native to Fiji. Moderately fast growth to 30 ft. tall, 8 ft. wide. Green leaves to about 4 ft. long. Needs protection from drying winds. Moderate salt tolerance.

P. thurstonii. THURSTON FAN PALM. Zone H2. Native to Fiji. Slow-growing, slender-trunked tree to 15–30 ft. tall, 8 ft. wide. Bright green, 5–6-ft.-long leaves. Good salt tolerance.

Pritchardia pacifica

PRIVET. See **LIGUSTRUM**

PROSOPIS
MESQUITE
Fabaceae (Leguminosae)
EVERGREEN AND DECIDUOUS TREES OR SHRUBS

🌡	ZONES 10–13, 18–24, EXCEPT AS NOTED
☼	FULL SUN
💧	LITTLE TO MODERATE WATER

Native to deserts in the Southwest, Mexico, and South America. Though hardy in other environments, they are most commonly grown in deserts, where they are among the toughest and most useful of trees. Much of their success in these harsh conditions is due to their far-reaching roots that will travel great distances to find water (a trait that will cause problems if plants tap into drainage or sewer lines). Once established, these plants are highly drought tolerant, but quickly adapt to regular lawn watering. In poor, rocky soil and without additional water, mesquites are shrubby; in deep soil where roots can reach groundwater, or where irrigation is generous, they grow rapidly to about 30 ft. tall, with a picturesque, spreading canopy approximately as wide.

Because these plants hybridize freely, exact identification is sometimes difficult. They may have one or many trunks; all have dark bark, a thicket of branches, and little leaflets that filter sunlight to cast airy, light shade. Small spikes of tiny greenish yellow flowers in spring and summer are followed by flat, beanlike, 2–6-in.-long pods. Flowers are a source of honey, and the pod contents are edible. Thorniness is variable; thornless varieties are available. Little pruning is needed; do the job only to cut out broken or dead limbs.

P. alba. ARGENTINE MESQUITE. Nearly evergreen. Native to South America. Plants sold under this name are vigorous and fast growing, with an erect single trunk and a rather dense canopy of blue-green leaves and spines. They drop some leaves throughout cold weather. Cutting-grown 'Colorado' is an erect, thornless tree with foliage slightly lighter in color than that of seedling plants. A cutting-grown, thornless form is available, often sold under the name "Chilean mesquite" (even though it is a form of *P. alba*, not of *P. chilensis*).

P. chilensis. CHILEAN MESQUITE. Evergreen in mild-winter climates; deciduous in colder areas. Zones 10–13; H1, H2. Native to South America. Produces a fairly open canopy of deep green leaves. Another tree sold under this name (probably a hybrid) is deciduous, with a denser canopy. In Hawaii, a species first thought to be *P. pallida* has now been classified as *P. chilensis;* it has naturalized in the Hawaiian Islands, where it reaches 50 ft. tall and nearly as wide.

P. glandulosa. HONEY MESQUITE, TEXAS MESQUITE. Deciduous. Native to southwestern U.S., Texas, Mexico. Often multitrunked. Bright green leaves and drooping branchlets give this tree something of the look of California pepper tree (*Schinus molle*). Cutting-grown 'Maverick' is a superior, thornless form. The subspecies *P. g. torreyana* grows naturally westward as far as California.

Prosopis glandulosa torreyana

P. 'Phoenix'. Semievergreen. From South America. Thornless, fast-growing hybrid grows 30–35 ft. high and wide. Large, lush green leaves cast nice shade. Light yellow flowers in spring and summer are followed by a scattering of brown seedpods.

P. pubescens. SCREW BEAN. Deciduous. Native to Arizona, Texas, Mexico. Common name refers to the spirally twisted seedpods, which make an unusual and attractive addition to dried arrangements. Open canopy of bluish green foliage. This is a naturally shrubby plant that is often used as a barrier planting, but it can be trained as a tree.

P. velutina (P. glandulosa velutina). ARIZONA MESQUITE. Deciduous. Native from southeastern Arizona into Mexico and West Texas. Resembles *P. glandulosa* but may be smaller and shrubbier when grown in poor, dry conditions. Common in Arizona.

PROSTANTHERA
MINT BUSH
Lamiaceae (Labiatae)
EVERGREEN SHRUBS

🌡	ZONES 14–17, 19–24
☼	FULL SUN
💧	MODERATE WATER

Australian natives with minty-smelling foliage and an enormous profusion of small flowers, usually in shades of purplish blue or white. These plants require excellent drainage. Although they tend to be short lived, they grow quickly and put on a good show. Prune them carefully; avoid cutting into bare wood or doing any other hard pruning. There are many species available; look for them at specialists' nurseries or at plant sales held by botanical gardens.

P. nivea induta. Upright, compact form. Grows to 6 ft. tall, 3 ft. wide. Narrow, silvery leaves somewhat longer than 1 in. Produces blue flowers in the spring. *P. nivea* is a larger and more open-growing shrub bearing white flowers.

P. 'Poorinda Bride'. Upright growth to 4–6 ft. high and wide. Narrow, 2-in.-long leaves are deep olive green. White flowers have hints of violet and are marked yellowish orange in the throat; appear late spring to summer. Best with partial shade inland. Cut back by up to one-third after bloom to maintain bushiness.

P. rotundifolia. To 6 ft. tall, 5 ft. wide, with small roundish leaves and purple-blue flowers. Selections include 'Ghost Cave', with grayish green leaves and purple flowers; 'Glen Davis', with an especially profuse showing of dark purple flowers; and 'Rosea', to only 3–4 ft., with dark green leaves and deep rose pink flowers.

Prostanthera rotundifolia

PROTEA
Proteaceae
EVERGREEN SHRUBS

〲	ZONES 16, 17, 21–24; H1
☼	FULL SUN
◓	MODERATE WATER

Some 150 species of beautiful flowering plants native to South Africa. Borne at branch ends, the flower heads consist of tight clusters of tubular true flowers surrounded by brightly colored bracts; effect is that of a large, very colorful artichoke or thistle. Superb cut flowers: they hold their color for weeks and retain their shape even after fading. Leaves are leathery, often edged in red.

Widely grown in Hawaii and Southern California for the cutflower trade. In home gardens, these plants are not for beginners: they need perfect drainage (preferably on slopes), protection from dry winds, good air circulation. Give regular moisture until plants are established; thereafter, water only every 2 to 4 weeks. Most need acid soil, though some accept alkaline soil. Smaller species can be grown in containers. Under any conditions, plants are not long lived.

Young proteas are tender to cold; older ones of most species are hardy to 25 to 27°F/–4 to –3°C. Raised from seed, plants bloom in 3 or 4 years. Fertilize lightly with nitrogen; avoid fertilizers containing phosphorus (plants will glut themselves, then die of the overdose). Small applications of iron can remedy chlorosis. The following species are among the easiest to grow.

P. compacta. PINK PROTEA. Erect grower to 6–10 ft. tall, 4–8 ft. wide. Light green, oval leaves to 4 in. long, with downy, wavy edges. Pure rose pink to carmine, 4-in. flower heads appear from spring to summer.

P. cynaroides. KING PROTEA. To 3–5 ft. high and wide, with open, spreading habit. Dark green,

Protea cynaroides

oval leaves to 5½ in. long. Blooms midsummer to winter or early spring; flower heads reach 1 ft. across, with pale pink to crimson bracts surrounding white true flowers. Regular water.

P. eximia. ROSE-SPOON PROTEA. Dense and upright, to 6–8 ft. tall and 3–4 ft. wide. Silvery green, broadly oval leaves to 2½–4 in. long. Profuse bloom in winter; flower heads are rich red, to 5 in. across, with spoon-shaped bracts protruding outward and upward.

P. neriifolia. MINK PROTEA. To 10 ft. tall, 6–8 ft. wide. Leaves are narrow, medium green, to 7 in. long; resemble oleander (*Nerium*) leaves. Blooms in fall and winter; pink to salmon bracts with furry black tips form heads to 5 in. long and 3 in. wide. Withstands temperatures as low as 17°F/ –8°C; will grow in alkaline soil.

P. susannae. SUSANNA PROTEA. To 6–10 ft. high, 9–12 ft. wide. Grayish, elongated oval leaves to 5 in. long. Brownish pink flower heads to 4 in. across in fall and winter. Leaves smell unpleasant; strip them from the stems when cutting flowers for arrangements.

PRUNE. See PLUM

PRUNELLA
SELF-HEAL, HEAL-ALL
Lamiaceae (Labiatae)
PERENNIALS

〲	ZONES 2–24
☼ ◐	FULL SUN OR LIGHT SHADE
◓	REGULAR WATER

Native to Europe. Creeping perennials that spread by surface and underground runners to form low, dense foliage mats. Upright spikes of hooded flowers rise above the leaves in summer. Though names are much confused, all species are tough, tolerant, and deep rooted. They are useful for small-scale ground covers and can endure the occasional footstep; set 1 ft. apart. Choose location carefully, though: these plants are too invasive to risk near choice, delicate rock garden plants. After bloom, shear off spent flower spikes to keep the planting neat and prevent seed formation.

P. grandiflora. Leaves to 4 in. long; stems to 1½ ft. tall, bearing spikes of 1–1½-in. purple blossoms. Varieties include 'Pink Loveliness', 'Purple Loveliness' (lilac purple touched with white), and 'White Loveliness'.

P. vulgaris. This is the common species. Smaller in all its parts

Prunella vulgaris

than *P. grandiflora*, with leaves to 2 in. long, 1-ft. stems, and purple or pink flowers just ⅓ in. long. *P. v. incisa* has deeply cut leaves.

PRUNUS
Rosaceae
EVERGREEN AND DECIDUOUS SHRUBS AND TREES

〲	ZONES VARY BY SPECIES
☼	FULL SUN, EXCEPT AS NOTED
◓◓	MODERATE TO REGULAR WATER, EXCEPT AS NOTED
▶	SEE CHARTS ON FOLLOWING PAGES

Discussed here are ornamental members of the genus *Prunus*. Fruit trees belonging to this genus—collectively known as stone fruits—are described under their common names. See Almond; Apricot; Cherry; Peach and Nectarine; Plum; and Plum Hybrids.

Ornamental species and forms can be divided into two categories: evergreen and deciduous. Evergreen types are used chiefly as hedges, screens, shade trees, street trees. Deciduous flowering trees and shrubs, closely related to the fruit trees mentioned above, are valued for their winter or spring floral display as well as for attractive shape and for foliage form, texture, and sometimes even fall color. Many of these deciduous kinds offer a bonus of edible fruit.

EVERGREEN FORMS

These attractive evergreen species are all large shrubs or small trees.

P. caroliniana. CAROLINA LAUREL CHERRY. Zones 5–24. Native from North Carolina to Texas. As an upright shrub, it branches densely from the base and can serve as a clipped hedge or tall screen to 20 ft. high; can be sheared into formal shapes. Trained as a tree, it typically grows 20–30 ft. high and 15–25 ft. wide but can reach 40 ft. tall with a 30–40 ft. spread; it also looks attractive grown with multiple trunks. Plant is thickly clothed in

2–4-in.-long, smooth-edged, glossy green leaves. Small, fragrant creamy white flowers bloom in 1-in. spikes from late winter to midspring; blossoms are followed by black fruit to ½ in. wide that is inconspicuous among the leaves. Flower and fruit litter can be a problem in paved areas.

Carolina laurel cherry looks best in coastal areas. Often shows salt burn and chlorosis in alkaline soils. Withstands desert heat and wind but appreciates a location protected from hottest sun in the low desert. May need moderate water in hottest climates; succeeds with little or no water elsewhere. 'Bright 'n Tight' and 'Compacta' are more densely branched than the species and reach only 8–10 ft. tall, 6–8 ft. wide.

P. ilicifolia. Zones 5–9, 12–24. The two similar forms described below are both useful as small trees, screens, or medium-size to tall clipped hedges. They often hybridize when growing near each other, producing plants with intermediate characteristics. Avoid planting near paved surfaces or parking areas, since fallen fruit causes stains. Unusually high resistance to oak root fungus. Both need good drainage. Can take extreme drought, but look best with occasional deep soakings.

P. i. ilicifolia. HOLLYLEAF CHERRY. Native to California Coast Ranges. To 10–25 ft. high and wide. Glossy, oval to elliptical leaves to 2 in. long are light green when new, maturing to a rich deep green; they are spiny edged like holly (*Ilex*) leaves but not as prickly. Blooms at leafout, bearing fragrant, ½-in., creamy white flowers in narrow, 3–6-in.-long spikes. Round, ¾-in.-wide, dark red or reddish purple fruit is edible but has a large pit and not much flesh.

P. i. lyonii. CATALINA CHERRY. Native to California's Channel Islands. In the wild, plants can grow as trees to 45 ft. tall and over 30 ft. wide, but in gardens they're more often seen as giant shrubs to 15–20 ft. high and wide. Leaves are similar in color and shape to those of *P. i. ilicifolia*, but they are smooth edged or very faintly toothed. Flowers identical to those of *P. i. ilicifolia*; fruit is darker red to almost black.

P. laurocerasus. ENGLISH LAUREL. Zones 4–9, 14–24, except as noted; best performance in Zones 4–6, 15–17. Native from southeastern Europe to Iran. Fast growing to 15–30 ft. tall and wide. Leathery, oblong, glossy dark green leaves are

PRUNUS–FLOWERING CHERRY

NAME	ZONES	GROWTH HABIT, FOLIAGE	HEIGHT, SPREAD	FLOWERS, SEASON, COMMENTS
Prunus 'Accolade'	2–9, 14–17	Small tree with spreading branches, twiggy growth pattern. Very vigorous	To 25 ft. high and wide	Semidouble blush pink, 1½ in. wide, in large, drooping clusters; open from rose pink buds. Early. Hybrid between *P. sargentii* and *P.* × *subhirtella*
P. campanulata TAIWAN FLOWERING CHERRY	6–9, 14–24	Graceful, slender, upright-growing small tree; densely branched	To 20–25 ft. high and wide	Single, bell shaped, drooping, in clusters of 2–5. Striking shade of bright purplish pink. Early. Red fruit about ½ in. long. Good choice for warm-winter areas
P. 'Hally Jolivette'	3–7, 14–20	Dense, shrubby	Slow to 6–8 ft. high and wide; eventually reaches twice that size	Double white blooms open from pink buds. Early; relatively long bloom, lasting several weeks. Can be used in shrub borders. Hybrid between *P.* × *subhirtella* and *P.* × *yedoensis*
P. 'Okame'	4–9, 14–23	Upright, oval habit. Dark green, fine-textured foliage. Good yellow-orange to orange-red fall color	To 25 ft. by 20 ft.	Single carmine pink. Very early. Hybrid between *P. campanulata* and another species
P. sargentii	2–7, 14–17	Upright, spreading branches form rounded crown. Good orange-red fall color	To 40–60 ft. tall and wide	Single blush pink flowers in clusters of 2–4. Midseason. 'Columnaris' is narrower and more erect than species, though more vase shaped than truly columnar
P. s. 'Pink Flair'	2–7, 14–24	Compact; upright with narrow vase shape	To 25 ft. tall, 15 ft. wide. Good orange-red fall color	Single pink flowers. Midseason
P. serrula	2–7, 14–16	Round-headed tree with narrow, willowlike leaves. Valued for its beautiful, glossy, mahogany red bark	To 30 ft. tall and wide	Bark more notable than small white flowers, which are almost hidden by new leaves. Midseason
P. serrulata		Known through its many varieties. Some are listed here (may be sold by variety name only)		
P. s. 'Amanogawa'	3–7, 14–20	Columnar in youth, becoming vase shaped with age	To 20–25 ft. tall, 4–8 ft. wide	Semidouble light pink with deep pink petal margins. Early midseason
P. s. 'Kwanzan' ('Kanzan', 'Sekiyama')	3–7, 14–20	Branches stiffly upright, forming narrow, inverted cone that spreads with age	To 30 ft. by 20 ft.	Large, double, deep rosy pink, in pendent clusters. Blossoms appear before or with red young leaves. Midseason
P. s. 'Royal Burgundy'	3–7, 14–20	Habit similar to that of 'Kwanzan'. Leaves are reddish purple	Same as 'Kwanzan'	Like those of 'Kwanzan', but deeper pink and with red stems
P. s. 'Shirotae' ('Mt. Fuji')	2–7, 14–20	Strong horizontal branching. Striking yellow-orange fall foliage. Buy a tree that has not been top-pruned; that forces horizontal branching to start much too low	To 20 ft. by 25 ft.	Semidouble. Pink in bud; white when fully open, aging to purplish pink. Early
P. s. 'Shogetsu' ('Shimidsu Sakura')	3–7, 14–20	Spreading growth, arching branches	To 15 ft. by 25 ft.	Semidouble and fully double pale pink, often with white center. Late
P. s. 'Snow Fountains' ('White Fountain')	3–7, 14–20	Slightly curving trunk; weeping branches reach to ground. Sold as small tree or trunkless ground cover	To 12–15 ft. high and wide as tree; to 1 ft. by 10–15 ft. as ground cover	Single white. Early
P. s. 'Snow Goose'	3–7, 14–20	Erect; narrow at first, eventually becoming broader	To 20 ft. high and wide	Single white. Early
P. × subhirtella 'Autumnalis'	2–7, 14–20	Loose-branching, bushy tree with flattened crown	To 25–30 ft. high and wide	Double white or pinkish white. Blooms in fall as well as early spring; may also bloom during warm spells in winter

P

PRUNUS–FLOWERING CHERRY

NAME	ZONES	GROWTH HABIT, FOLIAGE	HEIGHT, SPREAD	FLOWERS, SEASON, COMMENTS
P. × s. 'Pendula' SINGLE WEEPING CHERRY, WEEPING HIGAN CHEERY	2–7, 14–20	Usually sold grafted at 5–6 ft. high on upright-growing understock. Graceful branches hang down, often to ground	To 10–12 ft. high and wide	Profuse show of small, pale pink single flowers. Early
P. × s. 'Rosea'	2–7, 14–20	Wide spreading, horizontally branching	To 20–25 ft. by 30 ft.	Single pink blossoms open from nearly red buds. Profuse, very early bloom. Pacific Northwest favorite
P. × s. 'Whitcomb'	2–7, 14–20	Same as *P.* × *s.* 'Rosea'	To 30 ft. by 35 ft.	Single; pink fading to white. Early
P. × s. 'Yae-shidare-higan' DOUBLE WEEPING CHERRY	2–7, 14–20	Same as *P.* × *s.* 'Pendula'	Same as *P.* × *s.* 'Pendula'	Double rose pink. Midseason
P. 'Tai Haku' GREAT WHITE CHERRY	2–7, 14–20	Vigorous, with rounded crown. Good orange fall color	To 20–25 ft. high and wide	Extra-large (2½-in.), pure white single blooms. Flowers appear with bronzy new leaves. Late midseason
P. × yedoensis YOSHINO FLOWERING CHERRY	3–7, 14–20	Horizontal branches; graceful, open pattern	To 40 ft. by 30 ft.	Single light pink to nearly white. Early. This is the cherry planted around the Tidal Basin in Washington, D.C. Fast growing
P. × y. 'Akebono' (sometimes called **'Daybreak'**)	3–7, 14–20	Same as *P.* × *yedoensis*	To 25 ft. high and wide	Flowers pinker than those of *P.* × *yedoensis*. One of the best, most disease-free flowering cherries in the Pacific Northwest. Early

Prunus laurocerasus 'Zabeliana'

3–7 in. long. Blooms in spring or early summer, bearing 3–5-in. spikes of fragrant, creamy white flowers that are often hidden by the leaves. Flowers are followed by small black fruit.

Needs reasonably good drainage. Can thrive with little to regular water (regular applications of moisture and nutrients will speed growth and keep top dense). Needs some shade in hottest climates; can take sun or shade elsewhere. Tolerates salt spray. Few pests, though it may be troubled occasionally by scale insects. English laurel is often sheared, but doing so mutilates its large leaves;

for a better-looking result, make selective cuts back within the plant. Maintaining this plant as a formal hedge is a problem: its fast growth means frequent trimming. It's best used as a tall unclipped screen or trained as a tree. Smaller-growing varieties make lower, easier-to-maintain hedges.

'Etna'. Grows 5–7 ft. tall and about two-thirds as wide. Compact growth; takes well to shearing. Coppery new leaves contrast nicely with deep green color of mature foliage. Violet berries.

'Marbled White' ('Castlewellan'). To 15 ft. tall and wide; leaves are densely speckled with white. Showiest in cool climates.

'Mount Vernon'. Very slow growing. Forms a dense mound to perhaps 1 ft. high in 5 years; eventually attains 3 ft. high and wide. Though very dwarf, it has full-size leaves like those of the species. Can be used as ground cover.

'Nana'. Slow grower to 4–6 ft. tall and wide. Leaves to about 5 in. long.

'Otto Luyken'. Zones 3a–9, 14–24. To 3–4 ft. high, 5–6 ft. wide (has reportedly reached 6 ft. tall, 10 ft. wide). Leaves to 4½ in. long, exceptionally dark green.

'Schipkaensis'. SCHIPKA LAUREL. Zones 3–9, 14–17. Typically 4–5 ft. tall (possibly to 10 ft.), 7 ft.

wide. Narrow, 2–4½-in.-long leaves. There is some variation in plants sold under this name.

'Zabeliana'. Zones 3–9, 14–21. To 4–6 ft. tall, 6–8 ft. wide (wider with age). Branches angle upward and outward from base. Narrow, willowlike leaves 3–5 in. long. Versatile plant; good for low screen, foundation plant, bank cover (with branches pegged down), espalier.

P. lusitanica. PORTUGAL LAUREL. Zones 4–9, 14–24. From Spain and Portugal. Densely branched shrub 10–20 ft. high and wide; or multitrunked tree to 30 ft. tall and wide. Trained to a single trunk, it is used as a formal street tree. Narrowly oval, glossy dark green leaves to 5 in. long. Small, creamy white flowers in 5–10-in. spikes bloom in spring and early summer; these are followed by clusters of very small, bright red to dark purple fruit. Attractive background plant, screen. Slower grower than *P. laurocerasus* and more tolerant of heat, strong sunlight, wind. Little or no water. 'Variegata' has leaves with narrow, irregular white margins and fruit that ripens from red to black.

P. l. azorica. Native to Azores and Canary Islands, where it grows 60–70 ft. tall. In the West, it is a

large, columnar shrub about 20 ft. tall, 10 ft. wide. Glossy, exceptionally deep green foliage.

DECIDUOUS FLOWERING FRUIT TREES

Grown for beautiful floral displays in winter, spring. Branches of all types can be cut for indoor decoration; follow proper pruning procedures when you cut, and make your selections with an eye to thinning or shaping the canopy. For longest-lasting bloom, cut branches when buds first begin to show color or when they have just opened. Place branches in a deep container of water; strip off any buds or flowers that will be below water level.

Flowering cherry. For zones, see chart. Early to midspring bloom, depending on variety. Usually blossom before leafout, but some bloom with new leaves. Some flowering cherries have especially good fall color; all are good trees to garden under. Large, sprawling kinds make good shade trees; smaller ones are indispensable in Japanese gardens. Cultural needs of all are identical. They require fast-draining, well-aerated soil; those grown in heavy, poorly drained soil are sometimes subject to root rot, for which there is no cure (an affected tree will

P

usually bloom, then send out new leaves that suddenly collapse). If your soil is substandard, plant in raised beds. Even in good growing conditions, foliage may sustain damage from insect pests. *P.* × *subhirtella* varieties are subject to bacterial blight. Best with moderate water. Prune to remove awkward or crossing branches; pinch back the occasional overly ambitious shoot to force branching.

Flowering peach. Zones 3–24 (note, however, that blossoms may suffer frost damage in cold climates and that leafout may be delayed in warm-winter areas). Produces blossoms about 1½ in. wide in late winter and early spring, before leafout. More widely adapted than fruiting peach but identical to it in other respects— plant size, growth habit, cultural needs, pruning requirements, potential problems. Place trees where they will be striking when in bloom yet fairly unobtrusive out of bloom.

Some peach varieties produce both showy blossoms and good fruit; these are described under Peach and Nectarine. The following varieties are strictly "flowering"; that is, they have showy blooms, but fruit is either absent or worthless. In areas with late frosts, choose late bloomers; early bloomers are best in regions with hot, early springs.

'Early Double Pink'. Very early.

'Early Double Red'. Deep purplish red or rose red. Very early. Brilliant color is beautiful but likely to clash with other pinks and reds.

'Early Double White'. Blooms with 'Early Double Pink'.

'Helen Borchers'. Semidouble, pure pink, large (2½-in.) flowers. Blooms late.

'Icicle'. Double white flowers. Blooms late.

'Late Double Red'. Later than 'Early Double Red' by 3 to 4 weeks.

'Peppermint Stick'. Double flowers striped red and white; may also bear all-white and all-red flowers on the same branch. Midseason.

'Weeping Double Pink'. Smaller than other flowering peaches, with weeping branches. Requires staking to develop main stem of suitable height. Midseason.

'Weeping Double Red'. Like above; has deep rose red flowers. Midseason.

'Weeping Double White'. White version of other weeping forms listed above.

Flowering plum. For zones, see chart on next page. Flowers appear between midwinter and mid-spring, usually before leafout. Many flowering plums feature purple foliage. If you are choosing a plum to be planted in a patio or paved area, check its fruiting habit. These trees are less particular about soil than flowering cherry or flowering peach, but they will fail if soil is waterlogged for prolonged periods. Where conditions are boggy, plant in raised beds. Little pruning is needed. Aphids and spider mites are possible pests. Leaf-damaging insects and leaf spot disease are problems in the Pacific Northwest.

ADDITIONAL DECIDUOUS SPECIES

The following shrubs or trees bloom early in the season. In some cases, blossoms are followed by edible fruit.

P. besseyi. WESTERN SAND CHERRY. Shrub. Zones A1–A3; 1–3, 10. Native to the Great Plains. To 3–6 ft. high and wide. Good show of white, ½-in.-wide flowers in mid- to late spring, before leafout, followed by sweet black cherries a little more than ½ in. across. Fruit is used for pies, jams, jellies. Gray-green, 1–2-in.-long leaves. Withstands heat, cold, wind, and drought. A parent of hardy hybrid plums (see Plum).

P. glandulosa. DWARF FLOWERING ALMOND. Shrub. Zones 2–12, 14–19. Native to China, Japan. To 4–6 ft. high and wide; upright, spreading. Light green, willowlike leaves to 4 in. long. In early spring, the many slender, leafless stems are covered with blossoms. Typically sold are white 'Alboplena' and pink 'Sinensis' ('Rosea Plena'), both with 1–1¼-in. double blooms that look like fluffy pompon chrysanthemums. Prune heavily during or after flowering to promote strong new growth for next year's bloom. Can be used as a flowering hedge. Suckers freely. Fireblight can be a problem. Brown rot causes trouble in the Pacific Northwest.

Prunus 'Okame' (Flowering cherry)

P. maackii. AMUR CHOKECHERRY. Tree. Zones A1–A3; 1–7, 10. Native to Manchuria and Siberia; extremely hardy to cold and wind. To 25–30 ft. tall, 25 ft. wide. Main feature is handsome bark on trunk; it is yellowish to cinnamon brown and peels off like birch (*Betula*) bark. Strongly veined, rather narrow, pointed leaves to 4 in. long. Blooms after leafout in midspring, bearing small, fragrant white flowers in narrow, 2–3-in.- long clusters. Black, ¼-in.-wide fruit.

P. mume. JAPANESE FLOWERING APRICOT, JAPANESE FLOWERING PLUM. Tree. Zones 3–9, 12–22. Blooms may be damaged by frost in coldest areas. From China and Korea. Longer lived, tougher, more trouble-free than other flowering fruit trees; common names notwithstanding, it is neither a true apricot nor a true plum. Leaves to 4½ in. long, are broadly oval, pointed. White to dark red, 1–1¼-in. blossoms with a clean, spicy fragrance form on leafless branches in midwinter to early spring. Yellow to green, 1-in. fruit is edible only if pickled.

For profuse bloom on year-old wood, let newly planted trees grow unpruned for their first year. Then prune heavily, as follows. After bloom, prune back all shoots to 6-in. stubs; these stubs will produce long whips that will form next year's flower buds. The next year, cut back half of the young growth to 6-in. stubs; then cut back the other half the following year. Continue this routine in succeeding years. If allowed to develop naturally, Japanese flowering plum grows into a gnarled, picturesque tree 20 ft. tall and wide. Varieties include the following.

'Bonita'. Semidouble rose red.

'Dawn'. Large, ruffled double pink flowers.

'Matsubara Red'. Double, deep red flowers.

'Peggy Clarke'. Double flowers in deep rose, with extremely long stamens and red calyxes.

'Rosemary Clarke'. Double white flowers with red calyxes. Very early; often in bloom on New Year's Day in California.

'W. B. Clarke'. Double pale pink flowers; weeping form. Effective large bonsai or container plant. Bloom and form make it the center of attention in a winter garden.

P. padus. EUROPEAN BIRD CHERRY, MAYDAY TREE, MAYBUSH. Tree. Zones A1–A3; 1–7, 10. Native to Europe, northern Asia. Moderate growth to 15–20 ft. tall and wide, occasionally taller. Rather thin and open in habit when young. Among the first plants to leaf out in spring; leaves are dull dark green, oval, 3–5 in. long. Profuse mid- to late spring show of small, very fragrant white flowers in slender, drooping, 3–6-in. clusters that nearly hide foliage. Small, dark purple fruit follows the flowers; it is bitter but much loved by birds. Fruit is often used for making jelly and wine. Branches are stiff, subject to breakage under heavy snow loads. Older trees tend to sucker. Leaves of 'Merlot' emerge green, but then turn purple in summer.

P. tomentosa. NANKING CHERRY. Shrub. Zones A1–A3; 1–3, 10. From Tibet, China. Like *P. besseyi*, this species is very tough and cold hardy. To 6–8 ft. tall, 10 ft. wide, with shiny reddish brown, peeling bark. Elliptical leaves to 1½ in. long, dull dark green above, woolly beneath. Small, fragrant white flowers open from pinkish buds before leafout in spring; edible, ½-in.-wide, scarlet fruit follows.

P. triloba. FLOWERING ALMOND. Tree or treelike shrub. Zones A1–A3; 1–11, 14–20. Native to China. Slow growth to 8–10 ft. (possibly 15 ft.) tall, with equal spread. May be sold as a single- or multistemmed plant. Rather broad, often three-lobed leaves are 1–2½ in. long, dark green above, lighter green beneath. Pink flowers to 1½ in. wide appear on bare branches in early spring. 'Multiplex' has double pink flowers. A double white form is sometimes available.

P. virginiana. CHOKECHERRY. Shrub or tree. Zones A1–A3, 1–3, 10, except as noted. Native to eastern North America. To 20–30 ft. tall, 18–25 ft. wide, with suckering habit. Broadly elliptical, 2–4-in. leaves. In late spring, very fragrant white flowers appear in slender, 3–6-in. clusters among the leaves; these are followed by astringent, ½-in.-wide, dark red to black

PRUNUS–FLOWERING PLUM

NAME	ZONES	GROWTH HABIT, FOLIAGE	HEIGHT, SPREAD	FLOWERS, FRUIT, COMMENTS
Prunus americana WILD PLUM, GOOSE PLUM	1–3, 10	Thicket-forming shrub or small tree. Dark green foliage	To 15–25 ft. by 10–15 ft.	Clusters of 1-in., single white flowers. Fruit yellow to red, to 1 in., sour but good for jelly. Native to Rockies. Very tough
P. × blireiana	3–22	Graceful form. New leaves reddish purple; turn greenish bronze by summer	To 25 ft. by 20 ft.	Double, fragrant pink to rose flowers. Hybrid of *P. cerasifera* 'Atropurpurea' and *P. mume*
P. cerasifera CHERRY PLUM, MYROBALAN	3–22	Most often used as rootstock for various stone fruits. Dark green leaves	To 30 ft. high and wide	Pure white flowers. Red, 1–1¼-in.-wide fruit is sweet but bland. Self-sows freely; some seedlings bear yellow fruit. Purple- and red-leafed varieties are popular
P. c. 'Allred'	3–22	Upright, slightly spreading. Red leaves	To 20 ft. by 12–15 ft.	Single white flowers. Red, 1½-in., tart fruit good for preserves, jelly
P. c. 'Atropurpurea' (P. 'Pissardii') PURPLE-LEAF PLUM	3–22	Rounded habit. Leaves are coppery red when new, later deepen to dark purple; turn red in autumn	Fast to 25–35 ft. high and wide	Single white flowers. Heavy crop of red, 1–1½-in. fruit
P. c. 'Hollywood'	3–22	Upright habit. Leaves dark green above, red beneath	To 30–40 ft. by 25 ft.	Single light pink to white flowers. Good-quality red plums, 2–2½ in. wide. Hybrid of *P. c.* 'Atropurpurea' and a Japanese plum
P. c. 'Krauter Vesuvius'	3–22	Upright, oval form. Darkest foliage (blackish purple) of any flowering plum	To 18 ft. by 12 ft.	Single light pink flowers. Little or no fruit
P. c. 'Mt. St. Helens'	3–22	Upright, spreading, with rounded crown. A sport of *P. c.* 'Newport' but more robust, with larger leaves of a richer purple color	Faster than 'Newport', to 20 ft. high and wide	Same as 'Newport'
P. c. 'Newport'	2–22	Upright and spreading, with rounded crown. Foliage is dark purple all summer, attractively reddish in autumn	To 15–20 ft. by 20 ft.	Fragrant, single white to pale pink flowers. Will bear a little fruit
P. c. 'Purple Pony'	3–22	Naturally semidwarf; available budded low or high. Deep purple foliage holds color throughout season	Usually not taller than 10–12 ft. by 12 ft.	Single pale pink flowers appear with the leaves. No fruit
P. c. 'Thundercloud'	3–22	Rounded in habit (more so than *P. c.* 'Atropurpurea'). Dark coppery leaves	To 20 ft. high and wide	Fragrant, single light pink to white flowers. Sometimes sets good crop of 1-in. red fruit
P. × cistena DWARF RED-LEAF PLUM	A3; 1–22	Dainty multistemmed shrub. Can be trained as single-trunked tree; good for small patios. Intensely red-purple new leaves mature to coppery purple	To 6–10 ft. by 6–8 ft.	Fragrant, single white flowers appear after leafout (unlike flowering plums above); offer striking contrast to foliage. May produce small (½-in.) blackish purple fruit
P. × c. 'Big Cis'	A3; 1–22	Sport of *P. × cistena*. Dense, globular, and more vigorous than *P. × cistena*, with larger purple leaves	Fast to 14 ft. by 12 ft.	Same as *P. × cistena*

fruit. Good fall foliage display; color varies from bright red to pale yellow. 'Canada Red' has leaves that open green, then turn red as they mature; it is a sport of 'Schubert', which has mature leaves in a more purplish shade. *P. v. demissa*, Western chokecherry (Zones 2–10, 14–24), is native to the Pacific Coast, Sierra Nevada, Great Basin area, and northern Rockies. It tolerates heat and drought.

PSEUDOLARIX amabilis (P. kaempferi)
GOLDEN LARCH
Pinaceae
DECIDUOUS TREE

🌿 ZONES 2–7, 14–17

☀ FULL SUN

💧 REGULAR WATER

Native to China. Slow growing to 40–70 ft. high, often nearly as broad at base; symmetrical, pyramidal form. Wide-spreading branches with pendulous tips grow in whorls. Foliage has a feathery look; 1½–2-in.-long, ⅛-in.-wide needles are clustered in tufts except near branch ends, where they are single. Needles are bluish green during growing season, then turn a magnificent golden yellow very briefly in autumn before dropping. Cones, bare branches present an interesting pattern in winter. Choose a planting spot that

Pseudolarix amabilis

is open, but sheltered from cold winds. Best in deep, rich, well-drained, acid soil; performance is better in colder part of range. Fine for spacious lawns.

PSEUDOPANAX
Araliaceae
EVERGREEN SHRUBS OR TREES

📏	ZONES VARY BY SPECIES
☼ ◑ ●	SUN OR SHADE
●	REGULAR WATER

From New Zealand. Typically slow-growing aralia relatives cultivated for their evergreen foliage. In youth, *P. crassifolius* and *P. ferox* are odd looking and very decorative, with long, narrow, spiny-toothed, colorful leaves. Mature plants of all have dark green, divided or undivided leaves of unremarkable shape. Flowers are inconspicuous. No special pruning needs. All make good container plants.

P. crassifolius. LANCEWOOD. Zones 16, 17, 21–24. In time, a tree to 50 ft. tall, 15 ft. wide. Usually seen as single-stemmed plant 3–5 ft. tall, 8–10 in. wide, with rigid, drooping, strongly toothed leaves to 3 ft. long, ½–¾ in. wide. Young leaves are dark green above and dark purple beneath, with an orange or yellow midrib on upper surface. Upright growth habit makes this plant a good choice for narrow areas.

P. ferox. Zones 16, 17, 21–24. To 10–12 ft. tall, 3–4 ft. wide. Young plants produce strongly toothed leaves to 1–1½ ft. long and ½–1 in. wide. Young leaves are dark green to blackish green above and bronzy beneath, with brown, orange, or red midrib on upper surface.

P. lessonii. Zones 17, 22–24. Moderate growth to 12–20 ft. tall, 6–12 ft. wide. Effective multi-stemmed tree in open ground. Leathery and dark green leaves are divided into three to five leaflets 2–4 in. long.

Pseudopanax lessonii

PSEUDOSASA. See **BAMBOO**

PSEUDOTSUGA
Pinaceae
EVERGREEN TREES

📏	ZONES VARY BY SPECIES
☼ ◑	TOLERATE PARTIAL SHADE IN YOUTH
◐ ● ●	LITTLE OR NO WATER TO REGULAR WATER

The two species described here are quite similar, but they differ greatly in status—the first is little known, while the second is the most prominent tree in the Pacific Northwest.

P. macrocarpa. BIGCONE SPRUCE, BIGCONE DOUGLAS FIR. Zones 3–11, 14–23. Native to Southern California. Stout-trunked tree to about 60 ft. tall and 30 ft. wide. Needles are similar to those of *P. menziesii.* Cones are much larger, reaching 4–7½ in. long, 2–3 in. wide; three-pronged bracts on cones barely protrude from each side.

Pseudotsuga menziesii

P. menziesii (P. taxifolia). DOUGLAS FIR. Zones A2, A3; 1–10, 14–17. Since pioneer days, Northwesterners have gardened under and near this magnificent native tree. In cultivation, it grows 80–160 ft. tall, 20–30 ft. wide; in forests, it reaches 250 ft. tall. Young trees are sharply pyramidal and foliaged to the ground; they are popular as Christmas trees. As trees age, they lose lower limbs. Branches are densely clothed in soft, 1½-in.-long, deep green or blue-green needles that radiate in all directions. Needles are sweetly fragrant when crushed. Ends of branches turn up. Pointed wine red buds form at branch tips in winter, open to apple green new growth in spring. Reddish brown, oval cones are about 3 in. long, with obvious three-pronged bracts; they are pendent, unlike the upright cones of true firs (*Abies*).

The tree's entire range includes Oregon, Washington, and parts of the Rocky Mountains and extends to Alaska and California (as far south as Monterey and Fresno Counties). In coastal climates, it is fast growing, feathery, dark green, with slightly drooping branchlets. The Rocky Mountain form is *P. m. glauca*, a blue-green tree that is slower growing, more cold tolerant, more compact, and stiffer than the species. Compact, weeping, and other forms exist, but they are grown mostly in arboretums and botanical gardens. All tolerate wind, will grow in all soils except boggy ones. For best success, especially in coldest zones, buy plants raised from seed of trees native to your region. Resistant to oak root fungus.

PSIDIUM. See **GUAVA**

PSOROTHAMNUS spinosus (Dalea spinosa)
SMOKE TREE
Fabaceae (Leguminosae)
DECIDUOUS TREE OR SHRUB

📏	ZONES 12, 13
☼	FULL SUN
◐	LITTLE OR NO WATER

Native to deserts of Arizona, Southern California, Baja California. To 10–20 ft. tall, 10–15 ft. wide. Sparsely foliaged in small, hairy white leaves that drop in early spring, revealing an intricate network of silvery gray, spiny branches; the leafless plant is said to resemble a cloud of smoke. In late spring, puts on a good show of fragrant, violet-purple, sweet pea–shaped flowers in 1½–2-in. clusters. Cut branches (in or out of bloom) are good in arrangements. Not always available in nurseries but easily started from seed in warm weather. Provide good drainage. Needs little care.

Psorothamnus spinosus

PSYLLIOSTACHYS suworowii (Limonium suworowii)
Plumbaginaceae
ANNUAL

📏	ZONES 1–24
☼	FULL SUN
●	REGULAR WATER

Native to Iran, Afghanistan, central Asia. Forms a low, 1-ft.-wide rosette of narrow leaves to 8 in. long. In summer, spikes of tiny lavender-pink blossoms increase the plant's height to 1½ ft. Spikes are branched

Psylliostachys suworowii

or unbranched, very slender, and cylindrical; unbranched ones are reminiscent of furry rats' tails. They are excellent in fresh or dried flower arrangements. Sow seeds in ground when danger of frost is past; or start seeds earlier indoors. This plant may be offered as *Statice suworowii.*

PTERIDIUM aquilinum
BRACKEN
Polypodiaceae
FERN

📏	ZONES 1–10, 14–24
☼ ◑	FULL SUN OR PARTIAL SHADE
◐ ● ●	LITTLE TO REGULAR WATER
✦	FRONDS ARE POISONOUS IF INGESTED

Found all over the world, bracken is represented by various subspecies that differ in minor details.

Pteridium aquilinum pubescens

P. a. pubescens is native to the West. It has coarse, much-divided fronds that rise directly from deep, running rootstocks; grows from as low as 2 ft. high to as tall as 7 ft. under good conditions. Occurs naturally in many places; often among the first colonizing plants in disturbed soil. Fine in untamed locations, but do not allow it into the garden. Deep rootstocks make it a tough, invasive weed. Do not gather fiddleheads to cook; they contain a slow carcinogenic poison.

PTERIS
BRAKE
Polypodiaceae
FERNS

🌿	ZONES VARY BY SPECIES
🌓 ●	PARTIAL OR FULL SHADE
🌢 🌢	MODERATE TO REGULAR WATER

Small evergreen ferns of subtropical or tropical origin. Mostly used in dish gardens or small containers, but some are large enough for landscape use.

P. cretica. CRETAN BRAKE, RIBBON FERN. Zones 17, 23, 24; H1, H2. Easy to grow. Reaches 2½ ft. high and 2 ft. wide, with thin fronds and long, narrow leaflets. Can naturalize in Southern California. Numerous varieties available, some with forked or crested fronds, others variegated. 'Albolineata' (*P. c. albolineata, P. nipponica*) has a broad white band down the center of each leaflet. 'Ouvrardii' (*P.* 'Ouvrardii') is vigorous, with dark green fronds. 'Parkeri' is also dark green and grows a bit larger. 'Roweri' is boldly crested. 'Wimsettii' is compact, with dense frilled fronds and forked or crested tips.

Pteris cretica

P. ensiformis 'Victoriae'. Zones 17, 23, 24; H1, H2. Upright to 1–1½ ft. high and wide. Fronds are divided into very narrow leaflets intricately variegated in white.

P. quadriaurita. Zone 24. Reaches 2–4 ft. tall and wide. Rather coarsely divided fronds. Not as easy to grow as other species, but worth the effort for unusual coloring of varieties 'Argyraea' (*P. argyraea),* with green fronds heavily marked white, and 'Tricolor', with fronds marked white, green, and red. Protect from frost; watch for slugs and snails.

P. tremula. AUSTRALIAN BRAKE. Zones 16, 17, 22–24. Upright to 5 ft. tall and 3 ft. wide. Graceful fronds on slender, upright stalks. Good landscape fern, with excellent silhouette. Very fast growing.

PTEROCARYA
stenoptera
CHINESE WINGNUT
Juglandaceae
DECIDUOUS TREE

🌿	ZONES 4–24
☀	FULL SUN
🌢 🌢	MODERATE TO REGULAR WATER

From China. Fast to 40–90 ft. tall, 30–50 ft. wide, with heavy, wide-spreading limbs. Clearly shows its kinship to walnuts in its leaves: 8–16 in. long and divided into many finely toothed, oval leaflets.

Pterocarya stenoptera

Foot-long clusters of small, single-seeded, winged nuts hang from branches. Good looking but has only one real virtue: it succeeds well in compacted, poorly aerated soil in play yards and other high-traffic areas. Aggressive roots make it unsuitable in garden or lawn. *P. fraxinifolia,* Caucasian wingnut, is similar but has slightly larger leaflets, longer nut clusters.

PTEROSTYRAX
hispida
EPAULETTE TREE
Styracaceae
DECIDUOUS TREE

🌿	ZONES 3–10, 14–21
☀	FULL SUN
🌢	REGULAR WATER

Native to Japan. Single- or multi-trunked tree to 20–30 ft. (possibly 40 ft.) tall and equally wide.

Pterostyrax hispida

Rather coarse, oval to oblong, 3–8-in.-long leaves are light green above, gray green beneath. Blooms in late spring or early summer, bearing creamy white, lightly fragrant flowers with fringed petal edges in drooping clusters 4–9 in. long, 2–3 in. wide. Pendent clusters of small, furry gray fruits hang on well into winter, are attractive on bare branches. Best planted where you can look up into it—on bank beside path, above a bench, in a raised bed. Choice selection for woodland edge or as focal point in large shrub border. Established trees need little pruning.

PTYCHOSPERMA
Arecaceae (Palmae)
PALMS

🌿	ZONES 23, 24; H2
🌓	LIGHT SHADE
🌢	REGULAR WATER

Native to Australia and the South Pacific. Small feather palms with slender, ringed trunks and well-defined crown shafts (the smooth, usually green upper portion of the trunk, formed by overlapping bases of newer leaves). Leaflets are toothed at the tip. Often produce red fruit in warmest frost-free climates. Grow in well-drained soil.

P. elegans. ALEXANDER PALM, SOLITAIRE PALM. From Australia. Erect, single-trunked palm to 25 ft. tall, 15 ft. wide. Leaves to 8 ft. long.

Ptychosperma macarthuri

P. macarthuri. MACARTHUR PALM. Native to New Guinea. To 10–25 ft. tall, 12–15 ft. wide, with several clustered trunks. Leaves to 6½ ft. long. Good large understory plant. Often grown in tubs.

PUA MELIA. See **PLUMERIA**

PULMONARIA
LUNGWORT
Boraginaceae
PERENNIALS

🌿	ZONES 1–9, 14–17
🌓 ●	PARTIAL OR FULL SHADE
🌢	REGULAR WATER

Low-growing shade lovers with quiet charm. In many kinds, foliage is attractively dappled with gray or silver. The long-stalked leaves are mostly in basal clumps, though there are a few on the flower stalks. Plants bloom in late winter or early spring (just before leaves appear or as they emerge), bearing drooping clusters of funnel-shaped, typically blue or purplish flowers. After flowering finishes, more leaves arise from the base of the clump. If plants are well watered, foliage will remain ornamental through the growing season. All have creeping roots and can be used as small-scale ground covers or edgings for beds or woodland paths. Need moist, well-drained, organically enriched soil. Clumps may become crowded after a few years; divide them in early fall.

P. angustifolia. COWSLIP LUNGWORT. Native to Europe. To 8–12 in. high, 1½ ft. wide, with narrowish dark green leaves and bright blue flowers that open from pink buds. *P. a. azurea* has sky blue blossoms.

P. longifolia. Native to the British Isles, western Europe. To 8–12 in. high, 1½ ft. wide. Slender leaves to 20 in. long are deep green spotted with silver. Blooms a little later than other species; flowers are purplish blue. 'Bertram Anderson' has deep blue blossoms.

P. 'Roy Davidson'. Hybrid between *P. saccharata* and *P. longifolia.* Resembles *P. longifolia* 'Bertram Anderson' but has slightly wider leaves and flowers that open pink before deepening to blue.

P. saccharata. BETHLEHEM SAGE. To 1–1½ ft. high, 2 ft. wide, with elliptical, medium green, silver-spotted leaves and blue flowers opening from pink buds. Specialists usually offer named selections, including early-blooming

Pulmonaria saccharata 'Mrs. Moon'

'Highdown', with deep blue blossoms; 'Janet Fisk', with blooms that age from pink to blue and leaves that are heavily spotted and marbled with silver; old favorite 'Mrs. Moon', with large leaves and pink flowers aging from pink to blue; 'Sissinghurst White', with large white blooms; and 'Smoky Blue', with blue flowers atop deep green, white-spotted leaves.

PULSATILLA
PASQUE FLOWER
Ranunculaceae
PERENNIALS

- 🌿 **ZONES VARY BY SPECIES**
- ☼ **FULL SUN**
- 💧 **REGULAR WATER**

Low-growing, clumping plants. Woody rootstock produces foot-wide rosette of finely cut leaves covered with silky hairs; smaller leaves clothe the short flowering stems. In early spring, each stem is topped by a single large, cup-shaped, erect or nodding blossom with silky hairs on the outside and a mass of yellow stamens within. The fluffy seed clusters are almost as showy as the flowers; each seed is topped by a long, twisting, feathery appendage. Plants reach 5–6 in. high in bloom, rise to about 1½ ft. tall by the time seeds appear. Best in cool conditions. Need well-drained soil. Good rock garden plants. May go dormant in summer.

Pulsatilla vulgaris

P. patens. EASTERN PASQUE FLOWER. Zones A1–A3; 1–6, 15–17. From Russia, Siberia, North America. Erect, 2–3½-in. flowers in rich purple, occasionally yellow or white.

P. vulgaris (Anemone pulsatilla). PASQUE FLOWER. Zones 2b–6, 15–17. From central Europe. Blooms are 1½–3½ in. wide; erect, then nodding. Colors range from white through pink shades to purple or red.

PUMMELO. See **CITRUS**

PUMPKIN
Cucurbitaceae
ANNUAL

- 🌿 **ALL ZONES**
- ☼ **FULL SUN**
- 💧 **REGULAR WATER**

Thought to have originated in South America; related to squash, gourd, melon. Fruit varies greatly in size, depending on variety. One of the best for a jumbo Halloween pumpkin is 'Atlantic Giant'. 'Orange Smoothie' is smooth skinned, making it easy to decorate with paint. 'Small Sugar', a smaller pumpkin with finer-grained, sweeter flesh, is great for pies. 'Jack Be Little' and 'Wee-B-Little' are miniature (3–4-in.) types used for decoration. Novelties with white skin and orange flesh include miniature 'Baby Boo' and 8–10-in. 'Lumina'. Seeds of all are edible, but the easiest to eat are those of hull-less varieties like 'Trick or Treat'.

Pumpkin

Giant pumpkins aren't special varieties; they are ordinary full-size pumpkins grown in a special way (though gardeners aiming for colossal fruits do have favorites, such as 'Atlantic Giant'). As plant develops, cut off all but two main stems. After blossom set, remove all but one fruit on each stem. Along each stem's length, mound a 4-in.-wide hill of soil every 2 ft.; roots will form there.

Pumpkins are available in vining and bush types. Both need lots of room: a single vine can cover 500 sq. ft., and even bush sorts can spread over 20 sq. ft. Where the growing season is short, start plants indoors and use floating row covers early in the season. In most areas, sow seeds outdoors in late spring after soil has warmed; plant in rich soil. For vining pumpkins, sow five or six seeds 1 in. deep in hills 6–8 ft. apart; thin seedlings to two per hill. Plant bush pumpkins in rows spaced 3 ft. apart; plant seeds 1 in. deep in clusters of three or four, spacing clusters 2 ft. apart along the row. Thin seedlings to one or two plants per cluster.

Give periodic fertilizer. Water regularly during rainless periods, but keep foliage dry to prevent leaf diseases. Plants do not perform well in high heat and humidity. In late summer, slide wooden shingles or other protection under fruit to protect it from wet soil and rot (not necessary if soil is sandy). Depending on variety, pumpkins are ready to harvest 90 to 120 days after sowing, when the shell has hardened. Pick after first frost kills the plant. Use a sharp knife or hand pruners to harvest fruit, leaving 1–2 in. of stem. Subject to same pests and diseases as squash.

PUNICA granatum
POMEGRANATE
Punicaceae
DECIDUOUS SHRUB OR TREE

- 🌿 **ZONES 5–24; H1, H2**
- ☼ **FULL SUN**
- 💧💧 **MODERATE TO REGULAR WATER**

Native from Iran to the Himalayas. For fruiting types, see Pomegranate. The varieties described here either fail to fruit at all or bear fruit that is more decorative than tasty. They make good landscape plants. Taller types can be used as foundation plants, in shrub borders, as tall hedges or small trees; lower-growing varieties are excellent for edgings, in containers. All bear showy single or double summer flowers with ruffled petals surrounding a central cluster of stamens. Narrow leaves are bronzy when new, maturing to glossy bright green or golden green; they turn brilliant yellow in fall except where winters are very mild. Take many soil types, including alkaline soil. In late dormant season, prune as needed to shape. On shrubby

Punica granatum

types, remove oldest stems occasionally to encourage strong new growth.

'Chico'. DWARF CARNATION-FLOWERED POMEGRANATE. Compact shrub to 3 ft. high and wide. Easily kept to 1½ ft. high with occasional pruning. Double orange-red flowers.

'Legrellei' ('Madame Legrelle', 'California Sunset'). To 8–10 ft. high and wide. Creamy white double flowers heavily striped coral red.

'Nana'. DWARF POMEGRANATE. Dense grower to 3 ft. high, 6 ft. wide. Blooms when a foot tall or less. Orange-red single flowers followed by small, dry red fruit. Nearly evergreen in mild winters.

'Nochi Shibori'. To 8–10 ft. high and wide. Double dark red flowers.

'Tanyosho'. To 8–10 ft. high and wide. Double light apricot flowers.

PURPLE BROOM.
See **POLYGALA virgata**

PURPLE CONEFLOWER.
See **ECHINACEA purpurea**

PURPLE HEART. See **TRADESCANTIA pallida 'Purpurea'**

PURPLE-LEAF PLUM.
See **PRUNUS cerasifera 'Atropurpurea'**

PURPLE MAJESTY ORNAMENTAL MILLET. See **PENNISETUM glaucum 'Purple Majesty'**

PURPLE OSIER.
See **SALIX purpurea**

PURPLE PRAIRIE CLOVER. See **PETALOSTEMON purpureum**

PURPLE QUEEN. See **TRADESCANTIA pallida 'Purpurea'**

PURPLE VELVET PLANT.
See **GYNURA aurantiaca**

PURSLANE.
See **PORTULACA oleracea**

PUSCHKINIA
scilloides
Liliaceae
PERENNIAL FROM BULB

> ✂ ZONES 1–11, 14

> ☼ ◑ FULL SUN OR LIGHT SHADE

> ◐ REGULAR WATER DURING GROWTH AND BLOOM

Native to Asia Minor. Late winter or early spring bloomer closely related to squill (*Scilla*) and glory-of-the-snow (*Chionodoxa*). Performs best where ground freezes in winter. Each bulb produces two broad, upright, strap-shaped bright green leaves that are a bit shorter than the 6-in. flower stem. Each stem bears up to 15 star-shaped, inch-wide blossoms in pale blue with a greenish blue stripe down center of each petal. Most widely sold variety is *P. s. libanotica,* which is virtually identical to the species. A white-flowered variant may be offered as *P. s.* 'Alba' or *P. s. libanotica alba.*

Puschkinia scilloides

Most effective in masses; good choice for naturalizing. Plant from late summer into fall, setting the bulbs 3 in. deep, 3 in. apart in well-drained soil. Keep soil slightly moist until foliage appears, then water regularly until leaves start to yellow in early summer. Needs very little water during summer dormant period. Seldom needs dividing.

PUSSY EARS.
See **CALOCHORTUS**

PUSSY TOES.
See **ANTENNARIA dioica**

PUYA berteroana
Bromeliaceae
PERENNIAL

> ✂ ZONES 9, 13–17, 19–24

> ☼ FULL SUN

> ◐ ◑ LITTLE TO MODERATE WATER

Native to Chile. Big, spectacular bromeliad, usually sold as *P. alpestris.* Produces an evergreen foliage clump up to 10 ft. across, crowded with narrow, swordlike gray-green leaves to 2 ft. long; leaves have

Puya berteroana

sharp tips and sharply spined edges. Flower stalks rise from the clump, resembling giant asparagus spears as they develop; they reach 4–6 ft. tall during spring bloom, when they bear massive clusters of 2-in.-wide, bell-shaped blossoms in metallic blue green and steely turquoise, accented with vivid orange anthers. Stiff, spiky branchlet ends protrude from flower clusters. Use in large rock gardens, on banks, in big containers. Good with cacti, succulents. Tolerates poor soil.

PYRACANTHA
FIRETHORN
Rosaceae
EVERGREEN SHRUBS

> ✂ ZONES VARY BY SPECIES

> ☼ FULL SUN

> ◐ MODERATE WATER

Grown for bright fruit, evergreen foliage (may be semievergreen in cold climates), versatility in the landscape, ease of culture. All grow fast and vigorously, varying in habit from upright to sprawling. All have glossy green, 1–4-in.-long, ½–1-in.-wide leaves that are generally oval or rounded at ends; all bear flowers and fruit on spurs along wood of last year's growth. Small, spring flowers are dull creamy white, carried in flattish clusters; they're effective thanks to their profusion. Some people find the scent unpleasant. Nearly all species have needlelike thorns.

The real glory of firethorns is in their thick clusters of pea-size, orange-red berries, which light up the garden for months. Depending on variety, berries color up from late summer to midautumn; some types hang on until late winter,

when they're cleared out by birds, storms, or decay. Dislodge old, withered or rotted berries with a water jet or an old broom. Selections with red, orange, or yellow berries are available; if color is important to you, buy plants when they are in fruit.

As shrubs and ground covers, firethorns look better and produce more heavily if allowed to grow naturally. Prune to check wayward branches. Plants can be espaliered, or be sheared as hedges (though at the expense of much fruit). To grow low-growing, wide-spreading types as ground covers, set plants 4–5 ft. apart. Firethorns tolerate most soils but should not be overwatered. Subject to fireblight, scale insects, woolly aphids, red spider mites. In coastal areas of the Pacific Northwest, apple scab is sometimes a problem in early spring; it can nearly defoliate plants.

P. angustifolia 'Yukon Belle'. Zones 3–24. Variety of a Chinese native. To 8–10 ft. tall, 6–8 ft. wide. Bright orange berries.

P. coccinea. Zones 3–24. From the eastern Mediterranean. Rounded growth to 8–10 ft. tall and wide (potentially larger trained against a wall). Red-orange fruit. Best known for its varieties.

Pyracantha coccinea

'Gnome'. Densely branched plant to 6 ft. tall, 8 ft. wide. Orange berries.

'Kasan'. To 8–10 ft. tall and 6–8 ft. wide. Long-lasting orange-red fruit.

'Lalandei' and 'Lalandei Monrovia'. Similar varieties to 10–15 ft. tall and wide. Orange-red berries. Among the hardiest.

'Lowboy'. To 2–3 ft. tall, 6–8 ft. wide. Bright orange berries.

'Wyattii'. To 9–12 ft. high and wide. Orange-red berries.

P. crenatoserrata (P. fortuneana, P. yunnanensis). Zones 4–24. From China. Vase-shaped plant to 15 ft. tall, 10 ft. wide.

Limber branches make it a good espalier subject. Pale orange to coral berries persist through winter.

'Cherri Berri'. To 10 ft. tall, 8 ft. wide. Deep red berries.

'Graberi'. More erect than the species; to 10–12 ft. tall, 8–10 ft. wide. Huge clusters of dark red berries.

P. hybrids. These are plants of mixed or uncertain heritage. The group includes many of the most desirable firethorns.

'Apache'. Zones 4–24. To 4–5 ft. high and 6 ft. wide. Large, bright red berries last well into winter. Good resistance to fireblight and scab disease.

'Fiery Cascade'. Zones 4–24. To 8 ft. tall, 9 ft. wide. Berries age from orange to red. Good disease resistance.

'Harlequin'. Zones 4–24. To 6 ft. tall and wide. New leaves emerge pinkish white, turn green-and-white by summer, take on pink tones again in winter. Orange-red berries.

'Mohave'. Zones 4–24. To 12 ft. tall and wide. Heavy producer of big orange-red berries that color late and hang on for a long time.

'Orange Glow'. Zones 4–24. To 10 ft. tall and wide; erect at first, then spreading. Orange to orange-red berries.

'Red Elf'. Zones 4–9, 12–24. Low-growing, compact plant to 2 ft. high and wide; good in containers. Bright red berries.

'Ruby Mound'. Zones 4–9, 12–24. Among the most graceful of ground cover firethorns. Long, arching, drooping branches make a 2½-ft.-high mound that spreads to about 10 ft. Bright red berries.

'Teton'. Zones 2b–24. Fairly upright growth to 12 ft. tall, 4–6 ft. wide. Yellow-orange berries.

'Tiny Tim'. Zones 4–24. Compact growth to 3 ft. tall and wide. Small leaves, few or no thorns, red berries. Shorten any runaway vertical shoots.

'Watereri'. Zones 4–24. To 8 ft. tall and wide, with long-lasting bright red berries.

P. koidzumii. Zones 4–24. From Taiwan. Loose, unruly grower to 8–12 ft. tall and wide. Best known for its varieties. Among these are 'Santa Cruz' and 'Walderi', both good bank and ground covers.

'Santa Cruz' ('Santa Cruz Prostrata'). Reaches 6 ft. tall but is easily maintained at 3 ft. or lower by pruning out erect-growing branches. Can spread as wide as 10 ft. Red berries.

P

'Victory'. To 8–10 ft. tall, 6–8 ft. wide. Dark red berries color late but hang on late as well.

'Walderi' ('Walderi Prostrata'). To 3 ft. tall but easily kept to 1½ ft. by pruning out upright branches. Spreads to about 6 ft. wide. Red berries.

PYRETHROPSIS gayana.
See **CHRYSANTHEMUM gayanum**

PYRETHRUM.
See **CHRYSANTHEMUM coccineum, C. pacificum**

PYROSTEGIA venusta (P. ignea, Bignonia venusta)

FLAME VINE
Bignoniaceae
EVERGREEN VINE

- ☀ **ZONES 13, 16, 21–24; H1, H2**
- ☀ **FULL SUN**
- 💧 **MODERATE WATER**

Native to South America. Climbs rapidly by tendrils and twining to reach 20–40 ft.; where well adapted, grows rampantly. Leaves consist of two or three oval, 2-in. leaflets; two-leafleted leaves have a tendril between the leaflets rather than a third leaflet. Impressive in bloom, when tubular, 3-in., orange flowers appear in clusters of 15–20 at branch ends. The main flower display comes in winter; in warmest gardens, bloom starts in fall and continues into spring. In the

Pyrostegia venusta

mildest climates, a scattering of foot-long seed capsules will usually form after flowers fade. This vine is especially striking along fences and eaves, on pergolas and arbors, spilling over the tops of retaining walls, as a bank cover. Tolerates many soils. Revels in heat; in cooler climates, plant in a hot spot such as along a west-facing wall. Do any major pruning in spring or summer, after bloom has finished.

PYRUS

ORNAMENTAL PEAR
Rosaceae
EVERGREEN AND DECIDUOUS
SHRUBS OR TREES

- ☀ **ZONES VARY BY SPECIES**
- ☀ **FULL SUN**
- 💧 **MODERATE WATER**

Fruiting pears are described under Pear, Asian and Pear, European. The following are ornamental species, grown for their profuse late-winter or early-spring show of white flowers and their glossy, attractive leaves. Not at their best in shallow soils but otherwise unfussy about soil, even growing well in heavy clay. Most are subject to fireblight.

Pyrus calleryana 'Chanticleer'

P. calleryana. CALLERY PEAR. Deciduous tree. Zones 2b–9, 14–21. Chinese native. Needs some winter chill. To 50 ft. tall and wide, with strong horizontal branching pattern; young growth is thorny. Broadly oval, scallop-edged, leathery, 1½–3-in.-long leaves are glossy dark green, turning rich purplish red in fall. Blooms very early; late freezes may destroy flower crop. Very small, round, inedible fruit. Less susceptible to fireblight than most pears.

'Aristocrat'. Essentially pyramidal in form, though somewhat open and rounded; to 35–40 ft. tall, 20 ft. wide. Branches curve upward to form a strong structure. Fall color ranges from yellow to red.

'Autumn Blaze'. Rounded form to 30 ft. high, 25 ft. wide. Hardiest of the callery pears. Crimson fall color develops early.

'Bradford'. First variety of *P. calleryana* to be introduced.

Pyramidal tree to 50 ft. tall, 30 ft. wide. Strongly vertical limbs (with no central leader); branching pattern spreads with age. Branch crotches in mature trees have a tendency to split.

'Capital'. Columnar. To 40 ft. tall, 15 ft. wide. Coppery fall color.

'Chanticleer' ('Cleveland Select', 'Stone Hill'). Most plants sold under this name are narrowly pyramidal in form; some are more columnar. To 40 ft. tall, 15 ft. wide. Fall color varies from orange to reddish purple.

'Redspire'. Pyramidal; to 30–35 ft. tall, 20 ft. wide. Especially large blossom clusters; yellow to red fall color.

'Trinity'. Round-headed form to 30 ft. tall and wide. Orange-red fall color.

P. communis. See Pear, European

P. fauriei 'Korean Sun' ('Westwood'). Zones 2b–9, 14–21. This selection of a Korean species is compact and rounded, growing 12 ft. tall and 15 wide; can be pruned into a small tree or grown as a large shrub. Fine textured, cold hardy, and fruitless. Leaves turn orangish red to purple in autumn.

P. kawakamii. EVERGREEN PEAR. Evergreen shrub or tree; partially deciduous in coldest winters. Zones 8, 9, 12–24. From Taiwan. To 15–30 ft. high and wide, with drooping branchlets and glossy green, oval, 2–4-in. leaves with pointed tips. Masses of flowers in winter and early spring. Small, inedible fruit. Left to its own devices, becomes a broad, sprawling shrub. Can be espaliered but is most often grown as a single- or multitrunked tree. To train as a tree, stake one or several stems and shorten side growth; keep tree staked until it is self-supporting. To build up framework limbs, shorten any overlong, pendent branches to upward-facing growth buds or branchlets. An established, well-shaped tree needs little pruning—and heavily pruned plants seldom bloom. Tolerates many soils. Very prone to fireblight.

P. pyrifolia (P. serotina). SAND PEAR, JAPANESE SAND PEAR. Deciduous tree. Zones 2–9, 14–21. Native to China. To 40 ft. tall, 25 ft. wide. Like European fruiting pear in appearance, but leaves are glossier and more leathery. Fall color ranges from brilliant orange red to reddish purple. Profuse early spring blossoms; small, woody, gritty-textured fruit. This species is involved in the parentage of Asian pear varieties.

P. salicifolia 'Pendula'. WEEPING WILLOW-LEAFED PEAR. Deciduous tree. Zones 2–9, 14–21; performs better in cold climates. Native to southeastern Europe, western Asia. Elegant specimen plant to 12–15 ft. tall, 10–12 ft. wide. Grown for silvery, willowlike foliage and beautiful weeping habit; form is showcased in winter, when branches are bare. Flowers appear as leaves emerge in early spring. Leaves to 3½ in. long; silvery white when new, slowly turning silvery green in summer. Fruit is insignificant. Very susceptible to fireblight. Sometimes sold as 'Silver Frost'.

P. ussuriensis. USSURIAN PEAR. Deciduous tree. Zones A1–A3; 1–3, 10. Native to Manchuria, Siberia. Another parent of Asian pear varieties. Dense, rounded tree to 15–40 ft. tall, 15–25 ft. wide. Roundish, 2–4-in., glossy bright green leaves turn red or purple in fall. Large spring flowers are followed by tiny, hard, inedible fruit. Similar to *P. calleryana* and a good substitute for it in colder climates.

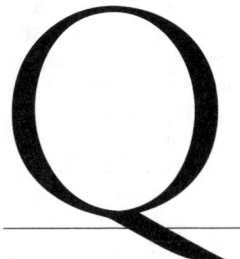

QUAIL BUSH.
See **ATRIPLEX lentiformis**

QUAKING GRASS.
See **BRIZA maxima**

QUAMOCLIT pennata.
See **IPOMOEA quamoclit**

QUEEN EMMA LILY.
See **CRINUM augustum**

QUEEN OF THE PRAIRIE.
See **FILIPENDULA rubra**

QUEEN PALM.
See **SYAGRUS romanzoffianum**

QUEEN SAGO.
See **CYCAS circinalis**

QUEENSLAND LACEBARK.
See **BRACHYCHITON discolor**

QUEEN'S TEARS.
See **BILLBERGIA nutans**

QUEEN'S WREATH.
See **ANTIGONON leptopus,
PETREA volubilis**

Q

QUERCUS

OAK

Fagaceae

DECIDUOUS AND EVERGREEN
TREES AND SHRUBS

✏ **ZONES VARY BY SPECIES**

☼ **FULL SUN**

◐ ◖ ● **WATER NEEDS VARY; SEE TEXT**

The oaks comprise 600 or so species, all native to the Northern Hemisphere. Their appearance and hardiness vary widely, but all produce acorns preceded by inconspicuous flowers. Single nuts are more or less enclosed in a cuplike cap covered with many closely set scales. In some species, the acorns are edible, with a sweet flavor. Some oaks are widely planted over large areas, while others have a limited range. Many wild-growing species may occur naturally in rural or suburban areas but seldom, if ever, find their way into the nursery trade; these are not described here.

Homeowners acquire oaks either by planting them or by inheriting trees that were present before their land was developed. Oaks that have been planted often thrive with no special care. Those from summer-rainfall areas appreciate moderate to regular summer irrigation during dry spells. Mediterranean natives can take irrigation or leave it, and U.S. natives of the Far West—after being watered through the first two dry seasons after planting—are better off without watering. Old, wild oaks from areas without much summer rain must be kept dry during the warm season, since they often succumb to fungal root diseases if given routine summer watering. But don't hesitate to give planted or inherited native oaks monthly soakings in winter if rains fail (and do this every winter in low-rainfall areas like San Diego), applying water at the drip line.

Special treatment for existing native oaks. If possible, do not raise or lower grade level between trunk and drip line. If you must alter grade, put a well around base of trunk so that grade level there is not changed. Never water within 10–15 ft. of trunk, and never let water stand within that area. Protect trunk from earth-moving machinery with cribs of 2-by-4s or heavier timbers. Avoid piling excavated soil around trunk or above root system (which extends

somewhat beyond branch spread); or provide drains for aeration and removal of excess water. Do not excavate or pave above the root zone without consulting an arborist. Avoid regular traffic or other ground-compacting activity in root area; when grading and other landscaping have been completed, be sure the tree has access to adequate water and air in the soil.

In much of the West, native oaks have adapted their root systems to long, dry summers; heavy summer watering can damage roots by activating oak root fungus (see "Pests and diseases," below). To safeguard such native trees, do not locate plantings (especially those needing regular moisture) too close to the trunk, and use only underplantings that require little or no summer water.

Old native oaks benefit from periodic grooming to remove dead wood, but thick branches should not be cut unless there is a good reason to do so. To avoid stimulating out-of-season new growth that will be susceptible to mildew and other problems, prune trees only when they are dormant. With evergreen oaks in the Far West, this means pruning during the dry season—in mid- to late summer.

Pests and diseases. Oaks and their acorns provide sustenance for a complex network of insects, birds, and other wildlife. Any of a number of sucking and chewing insects and mites feed on these trees, but most of the time such creatures are kept in check by other insects and mites, by birds, or by factors we have not even identified. Many kinds of oaks host several kinds of caterpillars that seldom do enough damage to be considered pests. Occasionally, though, an outbreak of some organism gets bad enough to require artificial control. Oak moth caterpillars can be a serious potential pest: heavy infestations can cause defoliation, and severe attacks for 2 or more years in a row can weaken or even kill a tree. However, oak moths tend to be cyclical, striking perhaps every 7 to 10 years; they may run their course and diminish on their own. If control becomes necessary, consult a professional arborist or tree ser-

vice. Oak trees are too large for the limited spray equipment available to the home gardener.

Most oaks produce galls of various colors, shapes, and sizes on twigs or leaf surfaces. The galls are swellings that form after insects (mostly wasps) lay eggs in the plant tissue; the larvae develop inside. Depending on the oak species and the type of insect involved, the galls may resemble apples, potatoes, mushrooms, dunce caps, or other objects. They do little harm and normally do not warrant treatment.

Many fungi are associated with the life cycle of oaks. Some are beneficial, but others are harmful. Oak root fungus (*Armillaria*) often is present in neighborhoods that once contained oak forests or walnut groves. This fungus is normally held in check in summer by drought and in winter by cool temperatures. Summer watering, especially close to the trunk, activates it; it grows rapidly in warm, moist conditions. Consult an arborist about infected trees.

*Quercus
agrifolia*

Over the past decade, a newly identified species of *Phytophthora* fungus, *P. ramorum*, has killed tens of thousands of coast live oaks (*Quercus agrifolia*), California black oaks (*Q. kelloggii*), and the closely related tanbark oaks (*Lithocarpus densiflorus*) in coastal California and Oregon. The fungus affects (but does not kill) several other oak species, as well as California bay laurel (*Umbellularia californica*). The infected condition has been dubbed "sudden oak death." The responsible fungus flourishes in cool, moist conditions and apparently spreads mainly by way of splashing, wind-driven raindrops. It may also be distributed by contact with infected roots, or transfer of infected wood or soil on tools, automobile or bicycle tires, or shoes.

Symptoms of sudden oak death often begin with oozing of reddish or brownish sap from the afflicted tree's trunk and main limbs. Leaves wilt suddenly, turn dull or yellowish, curl up, and dry. The fungus has been accompanied by an epidemic of oak bark beetles and heartwood-boring ambrosia beetles attracted by the fermenting sap of

dying trees. These small, black native insects, each about the size of a grain of rice, previously were not considered serious pests, since they attack only wounded or stressed trees. But with the sudden oak death epidemic, the beetles are multiplying by the millions, hastening the demise of sick trees. New generations of beetles emerge in spring and early fall. Avoid pruning in spring, when beetles are most active.

You can cut down ailing oaks after they wilt if they're unsightly or hazardous, but once the leaves die, the tree will not revive, and the disease will not spread. Do not transport infected wood. You can use it for firewood, but store it in a dry place, since fungal spores can be washed off cut wood and return to the environment to infect other trees. Do not use the wood for mulch.

For more information about sudden oak death, including strategies for prevention, see page 688. In the following entries, oaks that are known to die from sudden oak death are indicated, as are species that can serve as hosts to the fungus and those that are apparently immune to it.

How to grow an oak from an acorn. Select a fallen acorn that is shiny, plump, and free of worm holes; remove cap. To protect the buried acorn from birds, squirrels, and other creatures, dig the planting hole 6 in. deep, 6 in. wide; then roll a 1½-ft.-wide length of aluminum screening into a 6-in.-diameter cylinder and insert one end of it into the hole. Refill the screen-lined hole with unamended soil. Plant the acorn sideways and cover it with 1 in. of soil (if a white root has already sprouted, point it downward). Tie screen closed at top. Or plant several acorns in one area and thin to the best seedling. The first summer, give moderate water—just enough to keep soil moist for good root growth. After first summer, remove the screen to allow roots to grow freely.

How to transplant an oak. If its root ball is otherwise big and firm enough, an oak seedling up to 5–8 ft. tall seems not to suffer from having its vertical root cut. The tree may wilt or lose leaves after root is cut, but if kept watered it should show new growth within 4 to 6 weeks. Best time to transplant is fall or winter (or early spring, in some cold-winter areas).

Oak seedlings in nursery containers should not have a spiraling taproot at the container bottom; better growers cut a seedling's taproot when moving it to a nursery container, so that the young tree will develop a branching root system.

When you dig the tree's planting hole in its new location, mix some oak leaf mold or soil obtained from under an established, healthy oak into the hole to inoculate it with beneficial fungi.

How to train a young oak. Many young oaks are twiggy by nature, with growth divided among so many twigs that none elongates quickly. To promote faster vertical growth, pinch off tips of small side branches, but retain as much leaf surface as possible to sustain maximum growth. Western native shrub oaks are adapted to browsing by deer and lend themselves readily to close planting and eventual shearing into handsome formal hedges. They should be used more widely for this purpose in preference to plants with higher water requirements.

BEST OAKS FOR THE WEST
From among the many hundreds of oak species, here are the choices best suited to Western gardens.

Q. acutissima (Q. serrata). SAWTOOTH OAK. Deciduous tree. Zones 2–7, 14–17. From the Himalayas, China, Korea, Japan. Moderate to fast growth to 35–45 ft. (ultimately 50–70 ft.) tall and wide, usually with open, spreading habit. Dark gray bark with red-brown furrows. Shiny dark green, pointed, oblong leaves are 3½–7 in. long, with bristle-toothed, slightly wavy edges; they look like chestnut (*Castanea*) leaves. Foliage is yellowish when new, turns yellow to yellowish brown in fall; may hang on late into winter. Acorns are blunt cylinders to 1 in. long, enclosed for two-thirds of their length in a burlike cap. Prefers well-drained, slightly acid soil but is fairly tolerant of other soils. Good shade or lawn tree.

Q. agrifolia. COAST LIVE OAK. Evergreen tree. Zones 7–9, 14–24. Native to coastal central and Southern California. Round headed and densely foliaged; to 20–70 ft. tall, often with even greater spread. Smooth dark gray bark, deeply fissured in very old trees. Oval, convex, stiff, leathery dark green leaves, tooth edged and hollylike, 1–3 in. long. Foliage is attractive all

year (unless devoured by oak moth caterpillars). Conical, ¾–1½-in. acorns are enclosed for one-fourth of their length by a cap with thin, overlapping scales. Has greedy roots; drops almost all its old leaves in early spring. Despite flaws, a handsome and worthwhile shade or street tree. Can be sheared to make a 10–12-ft. hedge. Susceptible to sudden oak death.

Q. bicolor. SWAMP WHITE OAK. Deciduous tree. Zones A3; 1–3, 10. Native to eastern North America. Slow to moderate growth to 50–60 ft., rarely taller, with equal or greater spread. Bark of trunk and branches flakes off in scales. Shallowly lobed or scalloped leaves are 3–7 in. long, a little more than half as wide, shiny dark green above, silvery white beneath. Fall color is usually yellow but sometimes orange, fiery red, or purple. Oblong to egg-shaped, 1-in. acorns, enclosed by one-third in rounded cap with hairy scales. Tolerates wet soil; also thrives where soil is well drained.

Q. borealis. See Q. rubra
Q. buckleyi. See Q. texana
Q. chrysolepis. CANYON LIVE OAK, MAUL OAK, GOLDEN-CUP OAK. Evergreen tree. Zones 3–11, 14–24. Native to foothills and desert mountains from southwestern Oregon to Baja California and east into Arizona. Handsome, round-headed or somewhat spreading tree to 20–60 ft. tall and wide. Bark is smooth and whitish when young, checked and gray with age. Oval, 1–2-in.-long leaves may be smooth edged or spiny; shiny medium green above, pale blue or grayish beneath, with thin felting of silvery or golden hairs on undersides when new. Oblong, sharp-tipped acorns among largest (to 2 in. long) found on American oaks; they are enclosed by one- to two-thirds in a turbanlike cap covered with golden fuzz. Most widely distributed and variable of all California oaks, and most adaptable to varying conditions. Susceptible to sudden oak death.

Q. coccinea. SCARLET OAK. Deciduous tree. Zones 2–10, 14–24. Native to eastern U.S. Grows at moderate rate in deep, rich soil. Can reach 60–80 ft. tall, 40–60 ft. wide. Pyramidal when young, round topped in maturity. Gray-brown bark cracked into irregular plates. Bright green leaves are 3–6 in. long, with pointed, deeply cut lobes; turn scarlet where fall nights are cold. Rounded, ¾–1-in. acorns half-covered in a bowl-like cap.

Quercus coccinea

Good street or lawn tree. Deep rooted.

Q. douglasii. BLUE OAK. Deciduous tree. Zones 3–11, 14–24. Native to dry foothills around California's Central Valley and interior valleys of Southern California. Low branching, wide spreading; to 30–50 ft. high, 40–70 ft. wide. Light gray bark is shallowly checked in small squares. Shallowly lobed, oval, decidedly bluish green leaves are 1½–4 in. long, ¾–2 in. wide. Attractive fall colors: pastel pink, orange, yellow. Egg-shaped, ¾–1¼-in. acorns with sharply pointed tip and thin, flat cap. Good in dry, hot situations. Immune to sudden oak death.

Q. durata. LEATHER OAK, NUTTALL'S SCRUB OAK. Evergreen shrub. Zones 5, 7–10, 14–24. Native to northern Coast Ranges to San Luis Obispo area and to Sierra Nevada foothills, south to San Gabriel Mountains. In the wild, mostly confined to serpentine soil (a kind of nutrient-poor soil). Dense, rounded growth to 10 ft. tall and 8–12 ft. wide. Bare and somewhat leggy to 3–5 ft. above ground; then forms open-branched tiers of foliage. Tough, oval, convex, ¾–1-in.-long leaves have smooth or prickly edges; dark green above, pale gray beneath, with a dense coating of fine, soft hairs. Acorns variable: ½–1 in. long, often almost cylindrical, half-enclosed in a warty, bowl-shaped cap.

Q. emoryi. EMORY OAK. Evergreen tree. Zones 10–13. Native

Quercus coccinea

from Arizona to Texas and adjacent Mexico. Handsome and rounded, to 50 ft. tall, 40 ft. wide. Leathery dark green, oval, sharply toothed leaves to 2–3 in. long are hollylike but flat; turn golden and drop just before new growth begins in late spring. Round-tipped, oblong, edible acorns enclosed by up to one-half in bowl-like cap. Grows well in low desert; tolerates a variety of soils. Tree needs periodic soakings in summer.

Q. engelmannii. ENGELMANN OAK, MESA OAK, PASADENA OAK. Evergreen tree. Zones 7–9, 14–24. Native to Southern California. Spreading habit to 40–50 ft. high, often twice as wide. Thick, leathery, dull bluish green, oval or oblong leaves to 2 in. long; wavy surfaced or flat, usually smooth edged. Oval to cylindrical, round-tipped acorns to 1¼ in. long are half-enclosed in a warty cap. Tree grows best with monthly deep soakings in warm season, but don't keep it constantly moist. In its native area, it has the same cherished native status as the more widespread Q. agrifolia.

Q. fusiformis (Q. virginiana fusiformis). ESCARPMENT LIVE OAK, PLATEAU OAK. Briefly deciduous tree or shrub. Zones 3, 10–13. Native to plains of central Texas, southern Oklahoma, far eastern New Mexico. To 30–40 ft. tall and about as wide, with dense crown. Rough dark brown bark with scaly ridges. Shiny, leathery, 1½–4-in.-long leaves are oblong to elliptical; margins smooth or with a few sharp teeth, often rolled under. Foliage remains green through winter but turns yellow and drops for 2 to 4 weeks in spring. Acorns are ½–1 in. long, may have an egg shape or look like an elongated spindle; enclosed by one-third to one-half in goblet-shaped cap. Prefers well-drained alkaline soil. Easily endures heat, winter cold from Phoenix to Albuquerque; needs monthly soakings.

Q. gambellii (Q. utahensis). GAMBELL OAK, ROCKY MOUNTAIN WHITE OAK. Deciduous tree or shrub. Zones 1–3, 10. Native to Nevada, Arizona, east to Colorado, New Mexico. Slow to 15–30 ft. (rarely 50 ft.) tall, half as wide. Often forms colonies from root system. Thick, ridged trunk bark is light gray to whitish. Leaves 3–7 in. long, half as wide, with seven to nine deep lobes; dark green above, pale and densely hairy below. Foliage turns yellow,

Quercus douglasii

orange, or red in fall. Woolly, egg-shaped or globular, sharp-tipped acorns nearly 1 in. long, half-covered by a knobby cap. Characteristic oak of Arizona's Oak Creek Canyon and Colorado foothills south of Denver. Adaptable to wide range of soils and moisture levels; grows rapidly into a substantial tree in deep, rich soil.

Q. garryana. OREGON WHITE OAK, GARRY OAK. Deciduous tree. Zones 2a–11, 14–23. Native from British Columbia to California's Transverse Ranges. Slow to moderate growth to 40–90 ft. tall, 30–60 ft. wide, with rounded crown. Branches are often twisted; bark is gray, scaly, checked. Leathery, 3–6-in.-long, broadly oval leaves with rounded lobes. Foliage is glossy dark green above, rusty or downy beneath; turns reddish brown in fall. Globular, edible acorns to 1¼ in. long, bulging from a small, scale-covered cap. Tree casts moderate shade and has a deep, nonaggressive root system. Immune to sudden oak death.

Q. ilex. HOLLY OAK, HOLM OAK. Evergreen tree. Zones 4–24. Native to Mediterranean region. To 30–60 ft. tall and wide, with dense, rounded head and smooth dark gray bark. Leaves vary in shape and size but are usually oval to lance shaped, 1–3 in. long, with

smooth or prickly edges; rich dark green on top, covered with gray or yellow hairs beneath. Egg-shaped to nearly round, 1–1½-in. acorns are gray brown with darker lines, half-enclosed in deep cap that tapers to stem. Tolerates salt air; will grow in constant sea wind but tends to be shrubby there. Inland, growth rate can be fairly fast but varies with soil and water conditions. Good evergreen street or lawn tree where coast live oak (*Q. agrifolia*) is difficult to maintain, though it lacks that tree's open grace. Can take hard clipping into formal shapes or hedges. Susceptible to sudden oak death.

Q. kelloggii. CALIFORNIA BLACK OAK. Deciduous tree. Zones 5 (inland areas), 6, 7, 9, 14–21. Grows in company with conifers in upland locations from southern Oregon to Southern California. To 30–80 ft. tall and wide, with short trunk, ascending branches, and rounded crown. Dark gray, furrowed, checked bark. Handsome foliage: leaves unfold soft pink or dusty rose, mature to dark glossy green, turn yellow or yellow orange in fall. Leaves 4–10 in. long, 2½–6 in. wide, with deep, sharply tapered lobes ending in bristly points. Oblong or almost conical, 1–1½-in. acorns enclosed by about half in bowl-shaped cap. Good moderate-size tree for spring and fall color; attractive winter trunk and branch pattern. Susceptible to sudden oak death.

Q. lobata. VALLEY OAK, CALIFORNIA WHITE OAK. Deciduous tree. Zones 3b–9, 11–24. Native to interior valleys, Sierra foothills, and Coast Ranges away from direct coastal influence. California's mightiest oak, often reaching 70 ft. or taller, with equal or greater spread. Massive trunk and limbs with thick, distinctly checked gray bark. Straight and erect during its first several decades of growth; more spreading with age. Limbs

Quercus lobata

often picturesquely twisted; long, drooping outer branches sometimes sweep ground. Deeply cut, round-lobed leaves are 3–4 in. long, 2–3 in. wide; dark green above, paler beneath. Shiny, 1½–2½-in. acorns are conical, enclosed by one-third in warty, bowl-shaped cap.

Possibly the largest North American oak, this species tolerates high heat and moderate alkalinity in its native range. Best in deep soils where it can tap groundwater; in such situations, it can grow fast (2½–3 ft. a year). Magnificent tree for shading a big outdoor living area, though constant rain of debris will create a nuisance on any nearby planting areas or paved surfaces. This is the tree that gives much of California's Central Valley the look of a giant park. Fortunately, it is apparently immune to sudden oak death.

Q. macrocarpa. BURR OAK, MOSSYCUP OAK. Deciduous tree. Zones A2, A3; 1–11, 14–23. Native to eastern North America. Rugged-looking tree to 60–75 ft. tall and about half that wide in youth, equally wide in maturity. Flaky grayish brown bark with flattened, narrow ridges. Leaves are 8–10 in.

Quercus macrocarpa

long, broad at tip, tapered at base, with five to seven deeply cut, rounded lobes; glossy green above, whitish beneath, turning yellow and brown in autumn. Round or egg-shaped, 1–1½-in. acorns are almost completely covered by fringed, mossy-looking cap. Similar to *Q. bicolor* but faster growing and more tolerant of adverse conditions.

Q. muehlenbergii. CHINQUAPIN OAK, YELLOW CHESTNUT OAK. Deciduous tree. Zones 2–12, 14–17. Native to central and eastern U.S. To 40–50 ft. tall, 50–60 ft. wide, with wide-spreading, rounded crown. Flaking whitish or gray bark. Deeply toothed, lance-shaped, 4–6-in.-long leaves are shiny green above, whitish and furry below. Foliage turns golden late in fall but hangs on late. Egg-shaped, edible, ½–1-in. acorns are enclosed by one-fourth to one-half in warty cap. Desirable street or shade tree for large area. Long lived but difficult to transplant and establish. Fairly tolerant of alkaline soils.

Q. myrsinifolia. JAPANESE LIVE OAK. Evergreen tree or shrub. Zones 4–7, 14–24. Native to southern China, Japan, Laos; almost extinct in the wild. Reaches 30–50-ft. tall in its native range, but in cultivation it usually grows as a large, round-headed shrub to 20–30 ft. high and as wide (or nearly so). Lance-shaped, glossy dark green leaves 2½–4 in. long, toothed toward tip. Purplish red new foliage. Acorns ¾ in. long, cylindrical with abrupt point, half enclosed in unusual, shallow cap marked with seven to nine concentric rings. Not easily recognized as an oak unless seen with its acorns—unlike most of its relatives, it is wispy and graceful rather than sturdy.

Q. palustris. PIN OAK, SWAMP OAK. Deciduous tree. Zones 2–10, 14–24. Native to eastern U.S. Moderate to fairly rapid growth to 50–80 ft. tall, 30–40 ft. wide. Brownish gray bark with shallow ridges and furrows. Pyramidal in youth, with lower branches sweeping downward. If you remove those branches to gain walking space, the limbs above will simply bend into the same position—so wait to remove lower limbs until tree is mature and has formed an open, rounded top. Glossy dark green leaves are 3–6 in. long, deeply cut into bristle-pointed lobes; in brisk fall weather, leaves turn yellow, red, and finally russet brown. Much of

Quercus garryana

Quercus kelloggii

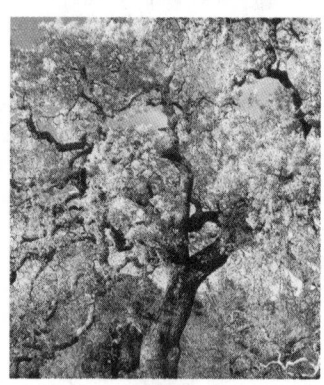

Quercus lobata

the dead foliage hangs on in winter. Nearly round acorns to ¾ in. across, enclosed by about a third in saucer-shaped, fuzzy cap. Less tolerant of dry conditions than most oaks. Develops chlorosis in alkaline soils. Unlike most native Western oaks, it is a fine tree for growing in lawns.

Q. phellos. WILLOW OAK. Deciduous tree. Zones 2–4, 6–16, 18–21. Native to southeastern U.S. To 50–90 ft. tall, 30–50 ft. wide. Pyramidal in youth, spreading wider with age. Smooth gray bark. Leaves look more like those of willow (*Salix*) than those of typical oak—2½–5 in. long, ⅓–1 in. wide, smooth edged. Foliage turns yellowish before falling; in warmer regions, dead leaves may hang on through winter. Has the most delicate foliage pattern of all the oaks.

Quercus phellos

Spherical, ½-in.-wide acorns with a shallow cap enclosing only the end of the nut.

Q. robur. ENGLISH OAK. Deciduous tree. Zones A2, A3; 1–12, 14–21. Native to Europe. Fairly fast grower to 50–60 ft. tall, 30 ft. wide, with rather short trunk and very wide, open head. Dark green, 3–4½-in.-long, 2–3-in.-wide leaves with three to seven pairs of rounded lobes. Leaves hold until late fall without much color change. Acorns are 1–1½ in. long, varying in shape from oval to oblong, coming to an abrupt point at tip; covered by up to one-third in velvety, bowl-shaped cap. 'Sky-

rocket' grows about 45 ft. tall and 15 ft. wide and holds its shape well. 'Skymaster' becomes a broad pyramid 50 ft. tall and half as wide. 'Crimson Spire', a hybrid with white oak (*Q. alba*, a large, handsome oak from eastern North America), is another narrowly upright grower (45 ft. tall, 15 ft. wide); it has reddish fall color and good mildew resistance.

Q. r. fastigiata, upright English oak, is columnar like Lombardy poplar (*Populus nigra* 'Italica') when young (to 50 ft. tall and 15 ft. wide), then matures to a broad, pyramidal shape. 'Regal Prince', similar in height but slightly wider, is a cross between *Q. r. fastigiata* and an oak from the southeastern U.S.; it's adaptable and resistant to mildew.

Q. rubra (Q. r. maxima, Q. borealis). RED OAK, NORTHERN RED OAK. Deciduous tree. Zones 1–10, 14–21. Native to eastern North America. Fast growth to 60–75 ft. tall, 50 ft. wide, with spreading branches and rounded canopy. Bark becomes quite dark and fissured with age. Leaves 5–8 in. long, 4–6 in. wide, with three to seven pairs of sharp-pointed lobes. New leaves and leafstalks are red or bright yellow in spring, dark green in summer, turning dark red, ruddy brown, or orange in fall. Acorns are ¾–1 in. long, shaped like a toy top, enclosed by one-third in shallow cap; often profuse, creating litter on pavement. Needs fertile soil and regular moisture. High-branching habit and reasonably open shade make it a good tree for big lawns, parks, broad avenues. Deep roots make it good to garden under. Known host of the fungus that causes sudden oak death.

Q. serrata. See Q. acutissima

Q. shumardii. SHUMARD RED OAK. Deciduous tree. Zones 2–10, 14–17. Native to eastern U.S. Similar to *Q. coccinea* but slightly

less hardy. Leaves are bright yellow in spring, dark green in summer, yellow to red in autumn. Acorns to 1¼ in. long are egg shaped, coming to an abrupt point; very shallow cap. Tolerates wide range of soils.

Q. suber. CORK OAK. Evergreen. Zones 5–7 (with occasional winter damage), 8–16, 18–24. Native to western Mediterranean, North Africa. To 30–60 ft. high and wide. Trunk and main limbs covered with handsome, thick, corky bark (the cork of commerce). Toothed, 3-in., oval leaves are shiny dark green above, gray beneath. Egg-shaped acorns with a short point are ¾–1½ in. long, covered by one-third to one-half in bowl-shaped cap.

Good garden shade tree; light-textured foliage contrasts interestingly with massive, fissured trunk. Needs good drainage. Fairly tolerant of various soils, but foliage may turn yellow in highly alkaline conditions. One of best oaks for desert. Value as street or park tree diminishes when children find out how easy it is to carve its bark.

Q. texana (Q. buckleyi). TEXAS OAK, SPANISH OAK. Deciduous tree or shrub. Zones 11–13. Native to central and western Texas, southern Oklahoma. To 35 ft. tall and as wide or wider, with trunk branching almost from the base. Bark is light brown and scaly when young, becoming dark gray with platelike scales and deep fissures at maturity. Leaves are 2½–5½ in. long, with three to seven sharply pointed, bristle-tipped lobes. Foliage is densely hairy and reddish when new, matures to yellow green, turns bright scarlet in fall. Egg-shaped, ¾-in. acorns with a sharp tip, one-third enclosed in reddish, densely felted cap. Similar to *Q. shumardii*. Takes alkaline soil.

Q. tomentella. ISLAND OAK. Evergreen tree. Zones 7–9, 14–17, 19–24. Native to California's Channel Islands. To 25–40 ft. tall and wide (occasionally to 60 ft. tall in

cultivation). Slightly toothed leaves to 2–4 in. long, 1–1½ in. wide, dark green above, matted with fine grayish or tan hairs beneath. Egg-shaped, 1–1½-in. acorns bulge from shallow, woolly cap. Endures seacoast conditions. Needs deep soaking every 2 to 3 weeks outside fog belt. Symmetrical tree when well grown; some consider it the handsomest of California's evergreen oaks.

Q. turbinella. DESERT SCRUB OAK, SHRUB LIVE OAK. Evergreen shrub. Zones 2, 3, 7–24. Native to piñon-juniper belt in desert mountains from Southern California and Baja California east to Colorado, western Texas, adjacent Mexico. To 10 ft. high and as wide, with bushy, stiffly branched form; can be trained as a small tree. Gray, smooth mature bark. Hollylike, oval, dull yellowish green, 1–1½-in.-long leaves with sharp, spine-tipped teeth. Foliage hangs on through winter, drops in spring when replaced by new leaves. Acorns to 1¼ in. long vary in shape but often look like a toy top; they are enclosed by one-fourth to one-half in a bowl-shaped cap with short, papery scales. Tough background plant or hedge for dry, cold-winter inland areas; also does well in the temperate maritime climate of the Pacific Northwest.

Q. utahensis. See Q. gambellii

Q. vacciniifolia. HUCKLEBERRY OAK. Evergreen shrub. Zones 1–7, 14–23. Native to mountains of Northern California and southern Oregon. Grows to 2–5 ft. high and at least twice as wide, with sprawling branches. Oblong to egg-shaped, smooth-margined, ¾–1¼-in.-long leaves, pointed or round at the tip; shiny gray green above, gray with sparse golden hairs below. Round to oval acorns to ½ in. long, with shallow cap covered in thin, hairy scales. This tree is sometimes planted in wild gardens, large rock gardens, or mountain gardens; it can also be used as an interesting informal hedge.

Q. virginiana. SOUTHERN LIVE OAK. Evergreen tree; partly or wholly deciduous in cold-winter regions. Zones 4–24. Native to coastal plains of southeastern U.S. Grows at a moderate to fast rate, eventually reaching 40–80 ft. tall, with a heavy-limbed crown spreading twice as wide. Long lived; with age, bark becomes very dark and checked. Smooth-edged, narrowly oval, 1½–5-in.-long leaves are shiny dark green above and whitish beneath. Oval acorns

Quercus palustris

Quercus suber

Quercus virginiana

Q

to 1 in. long, with sharp spine at tip; enclosed by one-fourth in bowl-shaped cap with hairy scales. Best in deep, rich, moist soil. In hot interior climates, it's the most attractive of all evergreen oaks. Best oak for lawn planting i n low desert; fast-growing variety 'Heritage' is recommended for that region. For the tree sometimes called *Q. v. fusiformis,* see *Q. fusiformis.*

Q. wislizenii. INTERIOR LIVE OAK. Evergreen tree. Zones 7–9, 14–16, 18–21. Native to Sierra foothills, eastern side of Coast Ranges, interior valleys from southern Oregon to Southern California. To 30–75 ft. tall, often broader than high, with dense, rounded canopy. Elliptical glossy green leaves 1–4 in. long, with smooth or spiny edges and abruptly pointed tip. Slender, conical, sharp-pointed, ¾–1½-in. acorns are enclosed by one-fourth to one-half in a flat-scaled cap. Handsome tree for parks and big lawns. Young plants are sparse and angular, offering little hint of their ultimate beauty.

QUILLAJA saponaria

SOAPBARK TREE
Rosaceae
EVERGREEN TREE

🌿	ZONES 8, 9, 14–24
☼	FULL SUN
💧💧	MODERATE TO REGULAR WATER

Native to Chile. To 30–45 ft. (occasionally to 60 ft.) tall, half as wide. Young trees are dense columns foliaged right down to ground, with pendulous branches; they give the general effect of a narrow, bushy, weeping coast live oak (*Quercus agrifolia*). Older trees develop a broader, flatter-looking crown; their branchlets are less pendulous than those of young plants. Shiny green, leathery, 2-in.

Quillaja saponaria

leaves are oval and pointed to nearly round. White, ½-in.-wide spring flowers are followed by handsome, inch-wide, brown fruit that opens into a star shape. Tends toward multiple trunks and excessive bushiness but responds quickly to pruning. Fairly tolerant of various soils. Drought tolerant but does better with periodic soakings; accepts lawn watering. Good narrow screening tree, tall hedge. The bark contains saponin, a lather-producing chemical; it is used in parts of Chile for washing and cleaning.

QUINCE, FLOWERING.
See **CHAENOMELES**

QUINCE, FRUITING

Rosaceae
DECIDUOUS OR SEMIEVERGREEN
SHRUBS OR TREES

🌿	ZONES VARY BY SPECIES
☼	FULL SUN
💧💧	MODERATE TO REGULAR WATER

Two spring-blooming species produce early-fall crops of fragrant yellow fruit; it is typically tart and used for jams and jellies. The fruit can also be made into candy or combined with other fruits in pies.

Fruiting quince

These pear relatives need little winter chill to be productive, and they make good landscape plants. Need good drainage. Do not use high-nitrogen fertilizer, which promotes succulent growth susceptible to fireblight. Fruit is borne on new growth; little pruning is required beyond initial shaping and periodic thinning to keep plant's center open to sunlight. For the thorny shrubs grown mainly for flowers, see *Chaenomeles.*

The deciduous common quince (*Cydonia oblonga*), from western Asia, succeeds in Zones 2–24. Slow grower to 10–25 ft. high and wide, with gnarled, twisted branches that look attractive when leafless in

winter. Oval, 2–4-in. leaves are dark green above, whitish beneath; turn yellow in autumn. White or pale pink, 2-in. flowers are followed by 3–4-in., round to pear-shaped fruits. Avoid deep cultivation near trunk; this damages shallow roots and causes suckers. Remove any suckers that sprout around base of tree; they rarely bear fruit and tend to weaken the tree.

'Apple' ('Orange'). This variety is an old favorite. Round fruit with tender orange-yellow flesh.

'Aromatnaya'. Round; sweet yellow flesh that tastes like pineapple. This variety can be thinly sliced and eaten fresh.

'Cooke's Jumbo'. Pear-shaped fruit with white flesh. Can be nearly twice the size of other quinces.

'Havran'. Large and pear shaped variety, with very sweet white flesh.

'Pineapple'. Roundish, with tender white flesh that tastes like pineapple.

'Smyrna'. Round to oblong fruit with white flesh; strongly aromatic.

'Van Deman'. Large, oblong fruit; yellow flesh with spicy flavor.

QUINOA.
See **CHENOPODIUM quinoa**

QUIVER TREE.
See **ALOE dichotoma**

R

RABBITBRUSH.
See **CHRYSOTHAMNUS**

RADICCHIO.
See **CHICORY and Radicchio**

RADISH

Brassicaceae (Cruciferae)
ANNUAL

🌿	ALL ZONES
☼ ◐	LIGHT SHADE IN HOTTEST CLIMATES
💧	REGULAR WATER

Probably native to eastern Mediterranean region. To grow well, radishes need evenly moist soil and some added nutrients. Supply nutrients by blending well-aged manure into soil at least a month before planting. Or feed about 10

Radish

days after planting, applying fertilizer beside rows (as for carrots) or using a liquid fertilizer.

Sow seeds as soon as ground can be worked in spring, then at weekly intervals until warm weather approaches (plants go to seed when temperatures rise, with roots becoming bitter in the process). In mild-winter climates, you can also sow at intervals in fall and winter for harvest during those seasons. Sow seeds ½ in. deep and 1 in. apart; space rows 1–1½ ft. apart. When the tops are up, pull out every other plant; you can eat the thinnings if they are large enough. Radishes are best harvested and eaten as soon as they reach full size; they can become pithy and overly pungent in flavor if left in the ground too long. You can pull them for the table as early as 3 weeks after sowing seeds (the slowest kinds take 2 months to reach table-ready size).

The most familar radishes are short, round, red or red-and-white types like 'Cherry Belle', 'Cherriette', and 'Scarlet White-tipped'. You can also get round radishes in white or pink; 'Easter Egg II' produces a mixture of white, pink, red, and purple. 'French Dressing' and 'Red Flame' are long, narrow, white-tipped types with a sweet flavor; they're known as breakfast radishes. Other long radishes have a more typical radish flavor; white 'Icicle' is the best known of these, but there are also novelties like 'Misato Rose Flesh', which is green outside and pink inside. Some types of long, white radishes with a mildly nippy to hot flavor can be found in markets under the name "daikon."

RAGGED ROBIN.
See **LYCHNIS flos-cuculi**

RAINBOW SHOWER.
See **CASSIA × nealiae**

RANGPUR LIME.
See **CITRUS: Sour-acid mandarin**

RANUNCULUS

Ranunculaceae
PERENNIALS

✿ ZONES VARY BY SPECIES

☼ ◑ ● EXPOSURE NEEDS VARY BY
     SPECIES

💧 REGULAR WATER

This very large genus comprises about 250 species of widely different habit and appearance, but the two listed here are the species most commonly grown in gardens.

R. asiaticus. PERSIAN RANUN-CULUS, TURBAN RANUNCULUS. All zones; see below. Native to Asia Minor. Tuberous-rooted plant to 1½–2 ft. tall and wide, with fresh green, almost fernlike leaves. Blooms profusely in spring, when each flowering stalk bears one to four 3–5-in.-wide, semidouble to fully double blossoms that some say resemble small peony blooms. Flowers come in white, cream, and many shades of yellow, orange, red, pink. Popular Tecolote Giant strain is available in single colors, mixed colors, and picotees. Bloomingdale strain offers the same variety on dwarf plants 8–10 in. high. All types are good in the ground or in pots.

Ranunculus asiaticus

Tuberous roots are hardy to 10°F/−12°C; in Zones 4–9, 12–24, plant in fall for bloom in winter, early spring. Beyond hardiness range, plant in spring as soon as ground is workable; or start roots indoors 4 to 6 weeks before the usual last-frost date. Nurseries sell tuberous roots of various sizes; all produce equally large blossoms, but bigger roots yield a greater number of flowers.

Grow in full sun, in organically enriched, very well-drained soil (if necessary, plant in raised beds). Set roots with prongs down, 2 in. deep (1 in. deep in heavier soils) and 6–8 in. apart. Water thoroughly, then withhold water until leaves emerge. Birds are fond of

ranunculus shoots; protect sprouting plants with netting or wire. Or start plants in pots or flats, then set them in the garden when they're 4–6 in. tall—too mature to appeal to birds. (You can also start with nursery-grown seedlings.) Remove faded flowers to encourage more bloom.

When flowering tapers off and leaves start to yellow, stop watering the plants and allow the foliage to die back. Where tuberous roots are hardy in the ground, they can be left undisturbed—as long as soil can be kept dry during summer. However, most gardeners throughout the West dig plants when foliage turns yellow, cut off the tops, let roots dry for a week or two, and store them in a cool, dry place until planting time.

R. repens pleniflorus. CREEP-ING BUTTERCUP. Zones 1–10, 14–24. From Eurasia; naturalized in North America. Vigorous plant with thick, fibrous roots and runners that root at the joints. Forms lush, glossy green mat to 1 ft. high, 6 ft. wide; leaves are roundish, deeply cut into three tooth-edged, 2-in.-long leaflets. Fully double, 1-in., button-shaped bright yellow flowers are held above foliage on 1–2-ft. stems in spring. Can be invasive in constantly moist soil. Attractive deciduous ground cover for full sun to deep shade. Basic species is single flowered, as aggressive as *R. r. pleniflorus*.

RAOULIA australis

Asteraceae (Compositae)
PERENNIAL

✿ ZONES 2B–9, 14–24

☼ FULL SUN

💧 MODERATE WATER

Ground cover plant from New Zealand. Tiny gray leaves form a very tight carpet to ½ in. high, 1 ft. wide; stems are hidden by the leaves. Inconspicuous pale yellow flowers in spring. Needs sandy soil, perfect drainage. Good in rock gardens.

Raoulia australis

RAPHIOLEPIS.
See **RHAPHIOLEPIS**

RASPBERRY

Rosaceae
DECIDUOUS SHRUBS

✿ ZONES A1–A3; 1–24; BEST IN
     3–6, 15–17

☼ FULL SUN

💧 REGULAR WATER

For ornamental species, see *Rubus;* the plants described here are grown for their luscious fruit. Red and yellow raspberries are derived from *R. idaeus,* native to North America, Europe, Asia. Black raspberries (or blackcaps) are varieties of North American species *R. occidentalis.* Purple raspberries are hybrids between black and red types. All bear clusters of white flowers in spring.

Raspberries grow from perennial roots that produce thorny biennial stems called canes. Generally, raspberry canes grow to full size in the first year, then bear fruit in their second summer. Red and yellow varieties known as everbearing (or fall-bearing) produce two crops on the same canes—one in fall of the first year, the second in summer of the next year. In all instances, the canes die after fruiting in the second year.

For raspberry fruit to reach perfection, plants need winter chill and a lingering springtime with slowly warming temperatures. In warmer zones outside best raspberry climates, satisfactory production may come from plants grown in light shade, mulched heavily to keep soil cool. Good drainage is essential; if you garden in heavy clay, consider planting in raised beds. Rich, slightly acid soil (pH 6 to 6.5) is ideal. Avoid planting where you have previously grown tomatoes, potatoes, peppers, or eggplants, which may have tainted the soil with verticillium wilt.

Plant bare-root stock during the dormant season. Set red and yellow raspberries 2½–3 ft. apart, in rows spaced 6–10 ft. apart. Plant black and purple raspberries in slightly raised mounds 2–3 ft. apart, in rows 6–8 ft. apart; they will develop into clumps of canes. Cut back the cane that rises from the root, leaving only enough (about 6 in.) to serve as a marker. Mulch plantings to discourage

Red raspberry

weeds and keep soil moist. Water need is greatest during flowering and fruiting. Feed at bloom time.

Red and yellow raspberries are produced on erect plants with long, straight canes; they can be grown as freestanding shrubs and staked, but they are tidier and easier to manage if trained on a trellis or confined to a hedgerow (pairs of parallel wires strung at 3 ft. and 5 ft. above ground along either side of a row of plants).

Summer-bearing varieties should produce three to five canes in first year. Tie these to a trellis or confine to a hedgerow. Dig or pull out any canes that grow more than 1 ft. away from trellis or outside hedgerow. In late dormant season, cut canes on trellis to 5–5½ ft. high, those in hedgerow to 4 ft. When growth recommences, new canes will appear all around parent plant and between rows. After the original canes bear fruit, cut them to ground. Then select the best 5–12 new canes and train these (they will bear next summer); cut remaining new canes to ground. Everbearing red and yellow varieties fruit in first autumn on top third of cane, then again in second summer on lower two-thirds of cane. Cut off upper portion of cane after first harvest; cut out cane entirely after second harvest. As an alternative, you can follow the example of growers who cut everbearing canes to the ground yearly in fall after fruiting has finished (wait until late dormant season in cold-winter regions). You'll sacrifice one of the annual crops but get an extended harvest from late summer into fall. Use a power mower in a large berry patch.

Black and purple raspberries are produced on clump-forming plants with arching canes. No support is needed. In the first summer, force branching by heading back new canes of black varieties to 2 ft., of purple varieties to 2½ ft. If you prefer trellising, cut black varieties to 2–2½ ft., purple ones to 2½–3 ft. In late dormant season, remove all weak or broken canes. Leave six to eight canes in a hill or spaced 6–8 in. apart in a row. Shorten the side branches to 8–10 in. for black raspberries, 12–14 in. for purple types. The

R

side branches will bear fruit in summer. After harvest, cut to the ground all canes that have fruited and cut back all new canes as described for first summer's growth.

To control anthracnose and other fungal diseases on all raspberries, spray with lime sulfur during dormancy and again as leaf buds begin to open; this also helps control many insect pests, including spider mites and cane borer. If borers attack, prune out and destroy damaged canes below entry points (pinhead-size holes at or near ground level).

A caution to gardeners in Hawaii: the very vigorous *R. niveus,* called Mysore raspberry (ripe fruit is black, but plant is grown like red raspberry), is sometimes grown in Island gardens; however, it can become a troublesome weed, choking out native vegetation.

Red and yellow varieties. Red varieties are the most common; yellow types are mutations of red raspberries.

'Anne'. Everbearing. Large, apricot gold berries with excellent, sweet flavor.

'Autumn Bliss'. Everbearing. Very large red berries with fine flavor. Resists root rot.

'Bababerry'. Everbearing. Large, firm red berries. Needs little winter chill; stands heat well. Best in hot-summer climates.

'Boyne'. Summer-bearing. Very hardy red raspberry bred in Manitoba. Medium-size fruit. Early ripening. Subject to anthracnose.

'Canby'. Summer-bearing. Large bright red berries. Thornless.

'Caroline'. Everbearing. Large, red berries with excellent flavor and high levels of nutrients and antioxidants.

'Cascade Delight'. Summer-bearing. Long season of large red berries with great flavor. Heavy bearing and resistant to root rot.

'Chilcotin'. Summer-bearing. Very large, firm red berries with excellent flavor. Long harvest season.

'Chilliwack'. Summer-bearing. Very large red berries with fine flavor. Somewhat resistant to root rot.

'Dinkum'. Everbearing. Medium-size, firm red fruit with good flavor.

'Fallgold'. Everbearing. Large yellow fruit with good flavor.

'Fallred'. Everbearing. Large, firm red fruit with outstanding flavor.

'Heritage'. Everbearing. Small red berries are tasty but a bit dry.

'Indian Summer'. Everbearing. Small crops of large, tasty red berries. Fall crop is often larger.

'Kiska'. Summer-bearing. Small red berries with good flavor. Hardy; developed for Alaska.

'Latham'. Summer-bearing. Older, very hardy; for coldest regions. Mildews in humid summers. Late. Large red berries are often crumbly.

'Meeker'. Summer-bearing. Large, firm bright red berries on long, willowy branches.

'Newburgh'. Summer-bearing. Large light red berries. Late-ripening variety. Takes heavy soil fairly well.

'September'. Everbearing. Small to medium-size red berries of good flavor. Fall crop is heavier.

'Summit'. Everbearing. Large red berries with good flavor. Very productive. Resistant to root rot.

'Sumner'. Summer-bearing. Early-ripening variety with some resistance to root rot in heavy soils. Fine-flavored, large red berries.

'Tulameen'. Summer-bearing. Very large, firm red berries with excellent flavor. Long harvest season. Must have well-drained soil.

'Willamette'. Summer-bearing. Large, firm dark red berries that hold color and shape well.

Black and purple varieties. Black raspberries have blue-black fruit that is firmer and seedier than that of red and yellow types, and they have a more pronounced flavor. Purple raspberries are crosses between black and red kind and share characteristics of both.

'Brandywine'. Large purple berries. Tart; good for jams, jellies. Ripens late.

'Cumberland'. Large black berries. Old, heavy-bearing variety.

'Jewel'. Large black berries. Vigorous, disease-resistant plant.

'Morrison'. Large black berries. Productive, late-ripening variety.

'Munger'. Medium-size black berries. Most popular commercial black-fruited variety.

'Sodus'. Large purple berries with a white bloom; rich flavored, excellent in pies. Vigorous plant.

Black raspberry

RATIBIDA
Asteraceae (Compositae)
PERENNIALS

✎	ALL ZONES
☀	FULL SUN
●	REGULAR WATER

Stiffly erect, branched, roughly hairy plants with deeply cut leaves. Flower heads resemble those of black-eyed Susans (*Rudbeckia*) but have fewer ray flowers and a spherical or cylindrical central cone (rather than a flat disk). Use in casual, natural-looking borders with grasses and other minimum-care perennials.

Ratibida columnifera

R. columnifera. MEXICAN HAT. From Great Plains. To 2½ ft. tall, 1 ft. wide. Flowers have drooping yellow or brownish purple rays and a tall, columnar brown cone. Effect is that of a sombrero with a drooping brim.

R. pinnata. PRAIRIE or YELLOW CONEFLOWER. Native to central North America. To 4 ft. tall, 1½ ft. wide, with yellow rays and a nearly globular brown cone.

RATTAN PALM.
See **RHAPIS humilis**

RATTLESNAKE GRASS.
See **BRIZA maxima**

RATTLESNAKE MASTER.
See **ERYNGIUM yuccifolium**

RAVENALA
madagascariensis
TRAVELER'S TREE, TRAVELER'S PALM
Strelitziaceae
EVERGREEN TREE

✎	ZONES 24; H2
☀	FULL SUN
●	REGULAR WATER

Native to Madagascar. Upright clump to 30–40 ft. tall, 25–30 ft. wide, with numerous large, banana-like leaves held in the shape of a gigantic fan atop an

Ravenala madagascariensis

unbranched trunk. Spectacular accent in the garden or displayed against a large building. Protect from strong winds, which will shred the leaves. Small plants have some shade tolerance, can be used as potted specimens.

RED BANEBERRY.
See **ACTAEA rubra**

REDBERRY.
See **RHAMNUS crocea**

REDBIRDS IN A TREE.
See **SCROPHULARIA macrantha**

REDBUD. See **CERCIS**

RED HOOK SEDGE.
See **UNCINIA rubra**

RED-HOT POKER.
See **KNIPHOFIA**

RED MAIDS.
See **CALANDRINIA ciliata**

REDONDO CREEPER.
See **LAMPRANTHUS filicaulis**

RED-RIBBONS.
See **CLARKIA concinna**

RED SHANKS.
See **ADENOSTOMA sparsifolium**

RED SPIKE ICE PLANT. See **CEPHALOPHYLLUM 'Red Spike'**

REDTOP.
See **AGROSTIS gigantea**

RED VALERIAN.
See **CENTRANTHUS ruber**

REDWOOD.
See **SEQUOIA sempervirens**

REDWOOD SORREL.
See **OXALIS oregana**

RED YUCCA.
See **HESPERALOE parviflora**

REED GRASS.
See **CALAMAGROSTIS**

R

REHMANNIA elata
CHINESE FOXGLOVE
Gesneriaceae
PERENNIAL

✓ ZONES 6 (BORDERLINE), 7-10, 12-24

☼ ☽ ● FULL SUN IN COOLER CLIMATES ONLY

◗ REGULAR WATER

Native to China. Grows 3 ft. tall, 1½–2 ft. wide. Clump of coarse, deeply toothed leaves (evergreen in mild-winter climates) sends up stalks loosely set with tubular, 3-in.-long flowers that look something like big, gaping foxgloves

Rehmannia elata

(Digitalis). Common form bears rosy purple blossoms with a yellow throat dotted in red; there is also a fine white form with cream throat that must be grown from cuttings or divisions. Where winters are mild, blooms from midspring well into fall; in colder climates, bloom comes in summer. Long lasting as a cut flower. Provide rich soil. Easy to grow from seed, root cuttings, divisions.

REINWARDTIA indica (R. trigyna)
YELLOW FLAX
Linaceae
SHRUBBY PERENNIAL

✓ ZONES 8-10, 12-24; H1, H2

☼ ☽ FULL SUN OR PARTIAL SHADE

◗ ◗ MODERATE TO REGULAR WATER

Native to mountains from Pakistan to China. To 3–4 ft. high and wide, with deep green or grayish green,

Reinwardtia indica

elliptical evergreen leaves 1–3 in. long. Blooms profusely, bearing brilliant yellow, 2-in. flowers like those of flax (*Linum,* to which it is related). Individual blossoms do not last long, but for weeks new ones open daily. In mild-winter regions, blooms in late fall and early winter; in colder areas, bloom comes in summer. Grow in fertile, well-drained soil. Pinch young plants to encourage branching. Cut back hard after bloom to keep compact.

RESEDA odorata
MIGNONETTE
Resedaceae
ANNUAL

✓ ALL ZONES

☼ ☽ PARTIAL SHADE IN HOTTEST CLIMATES

◗ REGULAR WATER

Native to North Africa. To 1–1½ ft. tall and wide; rather sprawling. Light green leaves. Not a particularly beautiful plant, but the remarkable spicy-sweet fragrance of its flowers makes it well worth growing. The small blossoms are greenish with a coppery or yellow tinge, carried in dense spikes that become loose and open with age. Flowers dry up quickly in hot weather.

Reseda odorata

Sow seed in early spring (or in late fall or winter, in mildest climates). Make successive sowings for the longest bloom period. Does best in rich soil. Plant in masses to get full effect of perfume; or locate a few plants in scentless plantings to provide fragrance. Deadhead to keep blooms coming. Suitable for containers. Strains with longer flower spikes and brighter colors are sold, but they are less fragrant.

RETAMA monosperma.
See **GENISTA monosperma**

RHAMNUS
Rhamnaceae
EVERGREEN AND DECIDUOUS SHRUBS OR TREES

✓ ZONES VARY BY SPECIES

☼ ☽ ● EXPOSURE NEEDS VARY BY SPECIES

◗ ◗ ◗ WATER NEEDS VARY BY SPECIES

Grown for form and foliage; clusters of small flowers are rather inconspicuous. Used chiefly as background plantings, hedges. Berries (typically pea size) are enjoyed by birds; volunteer seedlings may be a nuisance.

R. alaternus. ITALIAN BUCKTHORN. Evergreen shrub. Zones 4–24. Native to Mediterranean region. Fast, dense growth to 10–20 ft. high and wide. Oval, shiny bright green leaves to 2 in. long; small black berries. Easily trained as single- or multitrunked tree. Takes well to shearing and shaping. Tolerates heat; does well with little or no water but also accepts regular watering. Full sun or partial shade. 'John Edwards' is a vigorous, fast-growing, long-lived cutting-grown variety to 15–18 ft. tall, 6–10 ft. wide. Compact 'Variegata' ('Argenteovariegata') grows 6–8 ft. high and equally wide, has cream-edged foliage that looks striking against a dark background (if branches with plain green leaves appear, cut them out or they'll quickly take over).

R. californica. COFFEEBERRY. Evergreen shrub. Zones 3a–10, 14–24; H1, H2. Native to California, southwest Oregon, and Arizona. To 3–15 ft. tall, 8 ft. wide. Grown near the ocean, plant may have a low, spreading habit; in woodlands, it grows upright. Leaves are 1–3 in. long, variable—shiny or dull, dark green to yellowish green, usually paler on undersides (some forms have gray, hairy leaf undersides). Berries turn from green to red to black as they ripen. Among the many named selections are 'Eve Case', a dense grower to 4–8 ft. high and as wide, with large berries; and 'Seaview', a ground cover variety growing 1½–2 ft. high, 6–8 ft. wide. Both have leaves that are distinctly broader, flatter, and brighter green than those of species. 'Mound San Bruno', to 4–6 ft. tall and wide, has narrower leaves than species. All are tolerant of pruning and shaping. Not fussy about soil. Full sun or partial shade. Established plants need no irrigation, but the broader-leafed types look better with moderate water. 'Mound San Bruno' is espe-

Rhamnus californica

cially tolerant where moisture is concerned: it can take regular garden watering or none at all.

R. cathartica. COMMON BUCKTHORN. Deciduous shrub or tree. Zones 1–3. Native to Europe, western and northern Asia. Grows 15–25 ft. tall and wide. Glossy green, elliptical or oval, 1–2½-in.-long leaves. Foliage turns an unremarkable yellow in fall, drops late in the season. Short twigs near branch ends are often tipped with spines. Small black berries. Takes poor soil, wind. Useful hedge or small tree in coldest, driest regions. Little or no water. Full sun.

R. crocea. REDBERRY. Evergreen shrub. Zones 7, 14–24. Native to Coast Ranges from Northern California into Baja California. To 2–3 ft. high, 3–6 ft. wide, with many stiff branches, often spiny at tips. Roundish, ½-in.-long leaves, frequently with finely toothed edges; glossy dark to pale green above, golden or brownish beneath. Small bright red fruit. Takes full sun or partial shade in its native territory; does best with some shade in hotter inland areas. Little water.

R. frangula. ALDER BUCKTHORN. Deciduous shrub or tree. Zones 1–7, 10, 11. Native to Europe, western Asia, North Africa. Grows 10–12 ft. (possibly 18 ft.) tall and wide. Oval to roundish, glossy dark green leaves to 3 in. long; turn yellow in autumn. Berries ripen from red to black. 'Asplenifolia' grows 10–12 ft. high, 6–10 ft. wide, with fernlike, medium to dark green, wavy-edged leaves. 'Columnaris', tallhedge buckthorn, grows 12–15 ft. tall, 4 ft. wide; set plants 2½ ft. apart for a tight, narrow hedge that can be kept as low as 4 ft. Full sun or partial shade. Moderate water.

R. ilicifolia (R. crocea ilicifolia). HOLLYLEAF REDBERRY. Evergreen shrub. Zones 7–10, 14–23. Native to Coast Ranges and

R

Sierra Nevada foothills, mountains of Southern California, Arizona, Baja California. Bulky shrub or shrubby tree to a possible 15 ft. high, nearly as wide. Roundish, spiny-toothed, ½–1¼-in.-long leaves. Takes heat, drought; makes a good informal screen. Full sun or partial shade. No irrigation needed.

R. purshiana. CASCARA, CHITTAM BARK. Deciduous shrub or tree. Zones 1–9, 14–17. Native from Northern California to British Columbia and Montana. To 20–40 ft. tall, 10–30 ft. wide, with smooth gray or brownish bark that has medicinal value. Picturesque branching pattern. Dark green, prominently veined leaves are elliptical, 1½–8 in. long, usually borne somewhat more heavily (in tufts) at branch ends. Good yellow foliage color in fall. Black berries. Takes full sun to dense shade. Regular water.

RHAPHIOLEPIS
Rosaceae
EVERGREEN SHRUBS

✿	ZONES 8–10, 12–24; H1, H2; WORTH THE RISK IN ZONES 4–7
☼ ◐	FULL SUN OR LIGHT SHADE
◌ ◔ ●	LITTLE TO REGULAR WATER

In regions where temperatures never (or very rarely) fall to 0°F/–18°C, these are among the most widely planted shrubs. And for good reason: their glossy, leathery leaves and dense, compact growth habit make them especially attractive background plants and informal hedges. They bloom profusely from late fall or midwinter to late spring, with flowers ranging in color from white to nearly red. Berrylike dark blue fruit follows the flowers (it is not especially showy). New leaves in tones of bronze and red often add more touches of color.

Most are low growers. The taller kinds rarely reach more than 5–6 ft., and pruning can keep them at 3 ft. almost indefinitely. For bushy, compact plants, pinch back branch tips at least once yearly, after flowering. For a more open structure, let plants grow naturally and thin out branches occasionally. Plants in partial shade are less compact and produce fewer flowers than those in full sun. Good seacoast plants; tolerate salt drift. Little bothered by pests, though aphids occasionally attack them. Fireblight and a fungal leaf spot (in cool, wet weather) are possible disease problems. In hot-summer regions, plants will burn in reflected heat; they need some sheltering shade in low desert.

R. × delacourii. Pink-flowered hybrid of *R. indica* and *R. umbellata*. To 6 ft. tall, 8 ft. wide. Small pink flowers in upright clusters. Leaves are 1¼–2¾ in. long.

R. indica. INDIAN HAWTHORN. Native to China. To 4–5 ft. high, 5–6 ft. wide, with 1½–3-in.-long, pointed leaves and ½-in. flowers in white tinged with pink. Species is seldom seen in gardens, but its varieties are widely grown and sold. They differ mainly in flower color and in plant size and form; there is variation even within a variety. Flower color is especially inconsistent: in warmer climates and exposures, blossoms are usually lighter, and in general blooms are paler in fall than in spring. In the Northwest, subject to a leaf spot fungus, which defoliates the plants. Varieties include the following.

'Ballerina'. To 2 ft. tall, 4 ft. wide. Deep rosy pink flowers. Leaves take on a reddish tinge in winter.

'Clara'. To 3–5 ft. tall and wide. White flowers. Red new growth.

'Dancer'. Reaches 4 ft. tall, 5 ft. wide. Pure pink flowers.

Rhaphiolepis indica 'Dancer'

'Enchantress'. To 3 ft. tall, 5 ft. wide, with rose pink blooms. 'White Enchantress' has white blossoms.

'Indian Princess'. Up to 3 ft. high, 5 ft. wide. Light pink flowers.

'Jack Evans'. To 4–5 ft. high, 4 ft. wide. Bright pink flowers. Leaves sometimes have a purplish tinge.

'Pink Lady'. To 5–6 ft. high and wide. Dark pink flowers.

'Spring Rapture'. To 3–4 ft. high and wide. Rose red blossoms.

'Springtime'. Vigorous, upright growth to 4–6 ft. tall and wide. Deep pink flowers.

R. 'Majestic Beauty'. Larger in every detail than the others. Can be trained as a single- or multi-trunked tree to 20–25 ft. tall, 8–10 ft. wide; as a shrub, easily kept at 10–12 ft. tall, 6–8 ft. wide. Fragrant light pink flowers in clusters to 10 in. wide. Leaves are 4 in. long. Thought by some to be a hybrid between *Rhaphiolepis* and loquat (*Eriobotrya*).

R. umbellata (R. u. ovata, R. ovata). Native to Japan, Korea. Vigorous to 4–6 ft. (sometimes to 10 ft.) high and wide. Distinguished from *R. indica* by its leathery dark green, 1–3-in.-long, roundish leaves. White, about ¾-in.-wide flowers. Thick and bushy in full sun. In Northwest, less subject to leaf spot than *R. indica*. Sometimes called Yeddo hawthorn. 'Minor' ('Gulf Green') is a compact, slow-growing form to 3–4 ft. high and wide.

RHAPIDOPHYLLUM hystrix
NEEDLE PALM
Arecaceae (Palmae)
PALM

✿	ZONES 2–24
☼ ◐ ●	SUN OR SHADE
◔ ◑ ●	MODERATE TO AMPLE WATER

Perhaps the hardiest palm in the world, taking temperatures well below 0°F/–18°C. Native to the coastal plains of the southeastern U.S. Shrubby and slow growing, to an eventual 6–8 ft. high and wide; does not have a distinct trunk. Smooth stems bear dramatic fans of lustrous dark green, 3-ft.-wide leaves, each deeply cut into 6–12 segments. Common name refers to the sharp, 4-in.-long black spines on sheaths at bases of leafstalks

Rhapidophyllum hystrix

and on seeds. Tolerates a wide range of soils. Good accent or understory plant. Hard to find in garden centers; available by mail order.

RHAPIS
LADY PALM
Arecaceae (Palmae)
PALMS

✿	ZONES VARY BY SPECIES; OR INDOORS
◐ ●	SOME SHADE; BRIGHT INDIRECT LIGHT
●	REGULAR WATER

These choice, slow-growing fan palms form bamboolike clumps. Foliage is deep green; trunks are covered with a net of dark, fibrous leaf sheaths. Several variegated forms exist, and fanciers are willing to pay very high prices for good examples. Good indoor plants.

R. excelsa. LADY PALM. Zones 12–17, 19–24; H1, H2. Hardy to 20°F/–7°C. From China. To 5–12 ft. tall and wide. One of the finest houseplants. Withstands neglect and poor light but responds quickly to better light, regular watering and fertilizing.

Rhapis excelsa

R. humilis. RATTAN PALM, SLENDER LADY PALM. Zones 16, 17, 20–24; H1, H2. Hardy to 22°F/–6°C. To 18 ft. tall, 3 ft. wide, with tall, slender stems. Larger, longer-leafed palm than *R. excelsa*.

RHEUM
ORNAMENTAL RHUBARB
Polygonaceae
PERENNIALS

✿	ZONES 2B–7, 14–17
☼ ◐	FULL SUN OR LIGHT SHADE
●	AMPLE WATER
✦	LEAVES ARE POISONOUS IF INGESTED

The ornamental rhubarbs are stately plants, good focal points in well-watered perennial borders or at woodland edges. The large leaves arise directly from stout rhizomes; flowering stalks produce smaller leaves and prominent bracts. Blossoms are individually inconspicuous but are massed in tall, branching, plumy clusters, making a great show in late spring or early summer. Grows best in deep, organically enriched soil. For the edible plant, see Rhubarb.

R. australe (R. emodi). From the Himalayas. To 4–10 ft. tall, 6–8 ft. wide. Rounded leaves to 2½ ft. across, with wavy edges and red veins. White flower plumes reach 8–12 in. long.

R. palmatum. From China, Tibet. To 6–8 ft. tall, 6 ft. wide. Nearly round, 2–3-ft.-wide leaves are deeply cut into tooth-edged

Rheum palmatum

lobes. Red flower plumes to 2 ft. long. In variety 'Atrosanguineum', the entire plant is suffused with red. Leaves of *R. p. tanguticum* are less deeply cut than those of the species and often tinted purple; flowers may be white, pink, or red.

RHIPSALIDOPSIS gaertneri (Schlumbergera gaertneri)
EASTER CACTUS
Cactaceae
CACTUS

- ☀ ZONES 16, 17, 21–24; H1, H2; OR INDOORS
- ◐ PARTIAL SHADE; BRIGHT LIGHT
- ● REGULAR WATER

Native to Brazil. For culture and description, see *Schlumbergera*. Much like *S.* × *buckleyi* but initially more upright, then semipendent to 6 in. high, 1 ft. wide (*S.* × *buckleyi* is completely drooping). Blooms in spring, often again in late summer or early fall. Many varieties with blossoms in various shades of pink and red. In marginal climates, give protection of lathhouse or covered terrace. Good houseplant; bring outdoors during warm times of year, if desired. Plant has been renamed *Hatiora gaertneri* but is not generally offered as such.

Rhipsalidopsis gaertneri

RHODANTHEMUM hosmariense.
See **CHRYSANTHEMUM hosmariense**

RHODODENDRON (includes Azalea)
Ericaceae
EVERGREEN AND DECIDUOUS SHRUBS, RARELY TREES

- ✎ FOR ZONES, SEE TEXT
- ◑ FILTERED SUNLIGHT
- ●● REGULAR TO AMPLE WATER
- ✿ LEAVES ARE POISONOUS IF INGESTED

Approximately 800 species belong to this huge group. The International Register lists more than 10,000 named varieties, of which perhaps several thousand are currently available. Botanists have arranged species into series and subseries; one of these series includes the plants called azaleas.

Rhododendron 'Trude Webster'

With careful selection, gardeners in all climates—even the coldest, hottest, and driest ones—can find ways to grow certain members of this genus (in containers or as houseplants, if need be). Rhododendrons generally do best in Zones 4–6, 15–17, though there are many exceptions. The climate adaptation of azaleas, however, differs greatly from that of rhododendrons. For example, evergreen azaleas are grown extensively in Southern California and Hawaii, while rhododendrons require special attention there. Overall, zones for azaleas vary widely, depending on the hybrid group or species; see the azalea listings on pages 587–589 for specifics.

Rhododendrons and azaleas need more air in the root zone than almost all other garden plants, but they also require a constant supply of moisture. Without excellent drainage, they can succumb to root rot (see "What Rhododendrons and Azaleas Need"). Soils rich in organic matter have the desired qualities; if your soil is deficient, amend it liberally with organic material.

In clay or alkaline soil, planting in a raised bed is the simplest way to give these plants the conditions

What Rhododendrons and Azaleas Need

EXPOSURE Generally, they fare best in filtered sunlight. Where summers are mild or foggy, they can take more sun. In general, however, the sunnier or hotter the climate, the more protection plants will need. Some individual varieties and hybrid groups have been bred for sun tolerance.

SOIL Plants need rich, acid soil that is both moisture retentive and fast draining. If plants turn yellow, wilt, or collapse, they are probably suffering from root rot caused by poor drainage.

FERTILIZING Some experts dig fertilizer into the soil to get new plantings off to a good start. Feed established plants with commercial acid fertilizer well before bloom, as buds swell (in early spring, except for the earliest bloomers). Feed again when new leaves begin to grow, just as blooms are fading. Topdress with compost in early fall.

PINCHING This is essential for shaping plants and encouraging thick, bushy growth. For other pruning information, see text.

WINTER PROTECTION In very cold weather, sun and wind can severely damage plants. Protect larger ones in exposed locations with a windbreak of burlap fastened to stakes. Protect roots from damage caused by alternate freezing and thawing by mulching root area after soil has frozen.

Rhododendron 'Anna Rose Whitney'

they need. The finished bed should be 1–2 ft. above original soil level. Mix a generous amount of organic material into the top foot of native soil; then fill bed above it with a mixture of 50 percent organic matter, 30 percent native soil, 20 percent sand. This soil mix will be well aerated but moisture retentive and will permit alkaline salts to leach through. Plant azaleas and rhododendrons with top of root ball slightly above soil level. Never

allow soil to wash in and bury stems. Plants are surface rooters and benefit from a mulch such as pine needles, oak leaves, or wood by-products (for example, redwood or fir bark or chips). Never cultivate around these plants.

Sun tolerance of azaleas and rhododendrons differs by species and variety. Too much sun causes leaf centers to bleach or burn, though most of these plants can take full sun in cool-summer areas. Ideal location is in filtered shade beneath tall trees; east and north sides of house or fence are next best. Too dense shade results in lanky plants that bloom sparsely.

In areas where dissolved salts accumulate, periodically leach the planting by watering heavily—enough to drain through the soil two or three times. If leaves turn yellow while veins remain green, plants have iron chlorosis; apply iron chelates to soil or spray foliage with iron solution.

Insects and diseases seldom cause well-grown plants much harm. Root weevils are the main problem, especially in the Pacific Northwest. Damage by root weevil adults, which notch leaves, is usually minor, but their larvae can girdle roots. A number of pesticides that range from acephate to pyrethrins can help in serious infestations.

During recent years, leaf mildew has become a problem on some varieties of rhododendron. If you want to grow a variety that is susceptible, plant it in a sunny spot that gets plenty of air circulation. The best prevention, however, is to plant resistant varieties.

Both wind and soil salts burn leaf edges; windburn shows up most often on new foliage, salt burn on older leaves. Late frosts often cause deformed leaves.

Pruning rhododendrons is simple; follow these general guidelines. Tip-pinch young plants to make them bushy; prune older, leggy plants to restore shape by cutting back to a side branch, leaf whorl, or cluster of latent buds. Do any extensive pruning in late winter or early spring (wait until danger of frost is past in colder areas). Pruning at this time will sacrifice some flower buds, but the plant's

R

energies will be diverted to latent growth buds, which will then be ready to push out their new growth early in the growing season. (Several varieties will not produce new growth from latent buds.) You can do some shaping while plants are in bloom, using cut branches in arrangements. To prevent seed formation, which can reduce next year's bloom, clip or break off spent flower trusses, taking care not to damage growth buds at base of each truss.

Evergreen azaleas are dense, usually shapely plants; heading back the occasional wayward branch restores symmetry. To keep bushes compact, tip-pinch frequently, starting after flowering ends and continuing until July. Prune deciduous azaleas while they are dormant and leafless (in cold climates, wait until frost danger is past). You don't have to prune azaleas as carefully as you do rhododendrons—the leaves are fairly evenly spaced along the branches, with a bud at base of each leaf, so new growth will sprout from almost anywhere you cut (in either bare or leafy wood). Azaleas can even be sheared into formal hedges.

KINDS OF RHODODENDRONS

Most people know rhododendrons as big, leathery-leafed shrubs with rounded clusters ("trusses") of stunning white, pink, red, or purple blossoms. But there are also dwarfs a few inches high, giants that reach 40 or even 80 ft. tall in their native Southeast Asia, and a host of species and hybrids in every intermediate size, in a color range including scarlet, yellow, near blue, and a constellation of orange, apricot, salmon, and pink shades. Blossoms of some types are spotted in other colors. In other types, flowers have a blotch or flare in a different color on just the upper petal.

The following sections list named varieties by categories, to give you some idea of their adaptability to different climates and garden roles. These varieties are described later. Listed are the generally available kinds, representing only a portion of the many rhododendrons grown in the West.

Ironclad hybrids for coldest winters.
These can take temperatures down to −25°F/−32°C: 'Catawbiense Album', 'Crete', 'English Roseum', 'Henry's Red', 'Northern Starburst', 'Nova Zembla', 'PJM', 'Purple Gem', 'Purple Passion', 'Roseum Elegans', and *R. yakushimanum* and its named selections.

Northern California specials.
Zones 15–17. The following four rhododendrons, called Maddenii hybrids, are too tender for Northwest gardens: 'Else Frye', 'Forsterianum', 'Fragrantissimum', 'Mi Amor'. Good performers in Northern California: 'Anah Kruschke', 'Noyo Chief', 'Percy Wiseman', 'Rubicon', 'Sappho', 'Taurus'.

Vireyas for indoors and frost-free areas.
The Vireya rhododendrons, from the tropics of Southeast Asia, manage nicely in frost-free and nearly frostless zones (17, 23, 24; H2). They are also fine container plants (even indoors), so they can be grown in colder zones if brought inside for the winter. They need an especially fast-draining potting mix (many species are epiphytes in the wild); a combination of equal parts peat moss, ground bark, and perlite works well. Typically, plants flower on and off throughout the year rather than in one blooming season. They bear waxy-textured flowers in exciting shades of yellow, gold, orange, vermilion, salmon, and pink, plus cream, white, and bicolors. Species, named hybrids, and unnamed seedlings are offered by some specialty growers.

Among the best ones you are likely to find are *R. aurigeranum* (a hybrid of *R. brookeanum* commonly listed as 'Gracile'), *R. javanicum*, *R. konori*, *R. laetum*, *R. lochae*, *R. macgregorae*, and the hybrids 'George Budgen' (orange yellow), 'Ne Plus Ultra' (a red-flowering hybrid between *R. laetum* and *R. zoelleri*), and 'Taylori' (pink).

Widely adapted varieties.
All of these are highly regarded, dependable, popular, and easy to grow just about anywhere: 'Anna Rose Whitney', 'Blue Ensign', 'Cotton Candy', 'Crest', 'Hallelujah', 'Jean Marie de Montague', 'Loder's White', 'Mrs. G. W. Leak', 'Purple Splendour', 'Ramapo', 'Trude Webster'.

Low-growing species and hybrids.
Although they are rhododendrons, these have the charm and general appearance of azaleas: 'Blue Diamond', 'Sapphire', *R. impeditum*, *R. keiskei*, *R. moupinense*, *R. pemakoense*, *R. rupicola chryseum*.

Dwarfs and low growers.
Distinctive foliage and bell-shaped or funnel-shaped flowers, not in typical trusses, mark these varieties: 'Cilpinense', 'Ginny Gee', 'Patty Bee', 'Ramapo', 'Snow Lady'.

Rhododendron hybrids and species.
This section identifies some of the best rhododendrons for Western gardens; hybrids are listed first, followed by species. For more information on a given rhododendron, refer to the regional lists of recommended varieties compiled by the American Rhododendron Society (ARS); these may be found on the Web at *www.rhododendron.org*. The ARS lists are updated frequently as new rhododendrons are introduced and old ones drop out of production.

In the following list, we include cold-tolerance data and mature height, following the ARS's practice of using average height at 10 years as basis for plant size. Older plants may be taller; crowded or heavily shaded plants may reach the typical 10-year height at a younger age. Low plants (to 3 ft. or less) are usually slow growing and unlikely to exceed the 10-year height by much. Most rhododendrons tend to grow about as wide as high.

Bloom time given is approximate and varies with weather and location. The bloom season starts as early as December or January (in mildest climates) and extends through August; most types are spring bloomers. In the list below, "very early" corresponds to winter; "early" to early spring; "midseason" to midspring; "late" to late spring; and "very late" to summer. All of the following plants are evergreen, unless noted.

'A. Bedford'. −5°F/−21°C. To 6 ft. Large trusses of lavender-blue blooms with darker flare. Late.

'Alena'. −15°F/−26°C. To 5 ft., with rounded form. Dark green leaves. Fragrant, white, bell-shaped flowers with speckled yellow interior. Midseason.

'America'. −20°F/−29°C. To 5 ft. Dark red. Late.

'Anah Kruschke'. −15°F/−26°C. To 6 ft. Lavender blue to reddish purple. Flower color not the best, but plant has good foliage, is very tolerant of heat and sun. Can be sensitive to root rot in warm, wet soils. Midseason to late.

'Anna Rose Whitney'. −5°F/−21°C. To 6 ft., with excellent foliage. Big trusses of blossoms in rich, deep pink. Late midseason.

'Autumn Gold'. −5°F/−21°C. To 5 ft. Well-branched plant with rather upright growth. Salmon flowers in flat-topped trusses; blooms from an early age. Very late.

'Baden Baden'. −15°F/−26°C. To 2 ft. high, 4 ft. wide. Bright red. Midseason.

'Bambino'. −5°F/−21°C. To 3 ft. Peach pink suffused with yellow and dotted with red. Large calyx gives effect of a double flower. Midseason.

'Besse Howells'. −15°F/−26°C. To 3 ft. Large trusses of rosy red blooms. Early midseason.

'Blaney's Blue'. −5°F/−21°C. To 4–6 ft., with compact, dense, rounded habit. Profuse pale blue flowers from early age. Midseason.

'Blue Diamond'. −5°F/−21°C. To 3 ft.; compact, erect. Small leaves. Small lavender-blue flowers cover plant in early midseason. Takes considerable sun in Northwest.

'Blue Ensign'. −15°F/−26°C. To 4 ft.; compact, well branched, rounded growth. Leaves tend to spot. Lilac-blue flowers with a striking dark blotch. Midseason. Tolerates sun.

'Blue Peter'. −10°F/−23°C. To 4–5 ft. Broad, sprawling growth; needs regular pruning. Large trusses of lavender-blue flowers with purple blotch. Midseason. Tolerates heat and sun.

Rhododendron 'Blue Peter'

'Bow Bells'. −5°F/−21°C. Forms a 3-ft. mound. Rounded leaves; bronzy new growth. Loose clusters of bright pink, cup-shaped flowers open from deeper pink buds. Early midseason.

'Capistrano'. −15°F/−26°C. To 3 ft. tall, 6 ft. wide. Bell-shaped yellow flowers. Midseason to late.

'Carmen'. 0°F/−18°C. To 2 ft., spreading and dense. Deep red, bell-shaped flowers; small, rounded, glossy green leaves. Early midseason.

'Catawbiense Album'. −25°F/−32°C. To 6 ft. Pink buds; white flowers with greenish blotch. Mid-

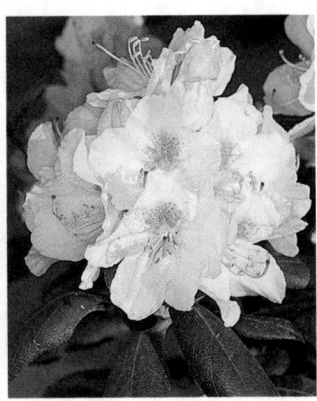

Rhododendron 'Catawbiense Album'

season to late. Takes cold and heat.

'Catawbiense Boursault'. –20°F/ –29°C. Like 'Catawbiense Album' but has pinkish lavender flowers. Takes cold and heat.

'Chionoides'. –15°F/–26°C. To 4 ft.; dense, compact, rounded form. White flowers with light yellow spotting. Late midseason. Takes sun.

'Christmas Cheer'. –10°F/–23°C. Shapely plant to 4 ft. Tight trusses of pink to white flowers; very early. Blooms at Christmas (or earlier) where winters are mild, in March in colder regions. Tolerates sun.

'Cilpinense'. 5°F/–15°C. To 3 ft., with low, spreading habit. Small leaves. Funnel-shaped flowers in apple blossom pink fading to white; loose clusters nearly cover plant. Easy to grow. Effective massed. Early; protect blossoms from late frosts.

'Cinnamon Bear'. –15°F/–26°C. Dense growth to 3 ft. Rosy pink buds open to pink-tinged white flowers. Midseason. New growth is furry, white; older leaves have furry brown undersides.

'Cornubia'. 15°F/–9°C. Strong, upright growth to 7 ft. Blood red flowers in large clusters. Very early.

'Cotton Candy'. 0°F/–18°C. To 6 ft. Tall trusses of large flowers in soft pink. Midseason.

'Crest'. –5°F/–21°C. To 6 ft. Tall, open habit; plant tends to be bare toward base. Large trusses of bright yellow flowers. Early midseason. Outstanding blooms.

'Crete'. –25°F/–32°C. To 4 ft. Pinkish purple buds open to light purple flowers that age to white. Early midseason.

'Cunningham's Blush'. –15°F/ –26°C. Dependable old variety to 4 ft. Blush pink with white blotch. Late midseason.

'Cunningham's White'. –15°F/ –26°C. May actually be hardier than rated; a plant in Finland has survived –45°F/–43°C. To 4 ft. An old-timer bearing white blooms with greenish yellow blotch. Late midseason.

'Cynthia'. –15°F/–26°C. To 6 ft., eventually much taller. Large trusses of rose-colored flowers with dark spots; blooms held above large leaves. This vigorous beauty has been a favorite since Ulysses S. Grant was president. Late midseason.

'Daphnoides'. –10°F/–23°C. To 3 ft. Prolific trusses of lavender-blue flowers. Well-branched, densely foliaged plant. Glossy deep green, oval leaves are convex, unusual among rhododendrons. Late.

'Dora Amateis'. –15°F/–26°C. To 3 ft. Compact, rather small-foliaged plant; good for foreground. Profuse bloomer with green-spotted white flowers. Spicy fragrance. Early midseason.

'Elizabeth'. 0°F/–18°C. To 3 ft. One of the most popular low-growing red rhododendrons, very widely planted. Attractive foliage sets off large, bright red, waxy, trumpet-shaped flowers that are carried in clusters of three to six at branch ends and in upper leaf joints. Blooms very young. Early midseason; often reblooms in early fall. Very susceptible to fertilizer burn, salts in water or soil.

'Else Frye'. 15°F/–9°C. To 4 ft. Long, limber growth makes this a natural for informal espalier. Considerable pinching is needed to achieve compact form. Intensely fragrant flowers are pink-flushed white with a gold throat. Early midseason.

'English Roseum' ('Roseum Pink'). –25°F/–32°C. Erect habit to 6 ft. Lavender-pink blooms. Midseason. Tough and undemanding.

'Fabia Tangerine'. 5°F/–15°C. To 3 ft. Compact plant. Leaves covered with reddish brown fuzz. Open trusses of brilliant orange, bell-shaped flowers. Midseason.

'Fantastica'. –5°F/–21°C. To 3 ft. Compact. Long, elliptical leaves have woolly undersides. Rose pink flowers with white throat, green spotting on petals. Late midseason.

'Fastuosum Flore Pleno'. –15°F/ –26°C. Open, rounded habit to 6 ft. Lavender-blue double blooms marked with gold blotch. Flower center is filled with small, lavender petal-like structures. Midseason. Dependable old-timer. Tolerates heat and sun.

'Fire Rim'. 3°F/–16°C. To 3 ft. Red buds open to a profusion of magenta flowers with red-freckled yellow throats. Midseason.

'Forsterianum'. 15°F/–9°C. To 5 ft. Open, rangy growth. Attractive glossy leaves and red-brown, glossy, peeling bark. Tubular, frilled, fragrant white flowers tinted pink. Very early; buds often damaged by frost in colder areas if plant is not given overhead protection.

'Fragrantissimum'. 15°F/–9°C. Loose, open, rangy growth; bright green, bristly leaves. With hard pinching in youth, a 5-ft. shrub. Easily trained as espalier or vine, reaching 10 ft. or more. Can spill over wall. Large, powerfully fragrant, funnel-shaped white flowers touched with pink. Early midseason. Grow as container plant in Northwest; overwinter indoors in a room that is bright but cool.

Rhododendron 'Fragrantissimum'

'Furnivall's Daughter'. –10°F/ –23°C. To 5 ft. Tall trusses of bright pink flowers with cherry red blotch. Midseason.

'Ginny Gee'. –10°F/–23°C. Striking 2-ft. dwarf with small leaves, dense growth. Small pink bells are dotted inside and out with white. Profuse bloom in early midseason.

'Glowing Gold'. 10°F/–12°C. To 3 ft. Large, funnel-shaped flowers are yellow with pink midribs and orange-yellow throats spotted with orange. Stunning in bloom, bearing 15 blossoms per truss. Early midseason.

'Golfer'. –15°F/–26°C. Low, broad, to 1½ ft. Leaves densely furred with soft, silvery hairs. Bright pink flowers in tight clusters. Early midseason.

'Gomer Waterer'. –15°F/–26°C. To 5 ft. Pink buds open to white flowers with yellowish green blotch. Late midseason. Old-timer. Tolerates sun; endures heat and drought better than most.

'Hachmann's Charmant'. –15°F/ –26°C. To 4 ft. Rounded, rose-edged white flowers have pink throats and red marking on upper lobes. Takes several years to develop abundant annual bloom. Midseason.

'Halfdan Lem'. –5°F/–21°C; may be hardier. To 5 ft. Well shaped and vigorous, with heavy stems and large leaves. Big, tight trusses of luminous red flowers. Midseason.

'Hallelujah'. –15°F/–26°C. To 4 ft. Rose red flowers stand above thick, beautiful forest green foliage. Very strong grower; fine-looking plant with or without flowers. Midseason. Takes full sun.

'Heavenly Scent'. 0°F/–18°C. To 4 ft. Large, medium pink blooms are fragrant. Early midseason.

'Henry's Red'. –25°F/–32°C. To 5 ft.; broader than tall. Dark red flowers. Midseason.

'Holden'. –15°F/–26°C. To 4 ft. Compact plant. Rose red flowers are marked with deeper red. Midseason.

'Honsu's Baby'. 5°F/–15°C. To 1 ft. Dense and well branched. Pink buds open to bell-shaped white flowers with lavender-pink edges. Early midseason.

'Hotei'. 0°F/–18°C. To 3 ft. Compact plant. Canary yellow flowers backed by a prominent calyx come only when plant is 6 to 8 years old. Closest of all varieties to a deep pure yellow. Midseason. Roots can rot easily; needs excellent drainage.

'Janet Blair'. –15°F/–26°C. To 5 ft.; vigorous and spreading. Large, ruffled flowers blend pastel pink, cream, white, and gold; rounded trusses. Midseason to late.

'Jean Marie de Montague'. –5°F/–21°C. To 5 ft., with attractive foliage. Brilliant scarlet flowers. Midseason.

'Johnny Bender'. –5°F/–21°C. To 4–5 ft. Glossy dark green leaves set off blood red flowers. Midseason.

'Kiwi Magic'. –5°F/–21°C. To 3 ft. Lax trusses of peach pink flowers shade to creamy yellow inside. Large calyx. Midseason.

'Lemon Dream'. 0°F/–18°C. To 1 ft. Dense and spreading. Yellow flowers rise above oval, glossy green leaves. Midseason.

Rhododendron 'Fastuosum Flore Pleno'

R

Rhododendron 'Lem's Monarch'

'Lem's Cameo'. –5°F/–21°C. To 4–5 ft. Flowers in a blend of apricot, cream, and pink. Midseason.

'Lem's Monarch' ('Pink Walloper'). –5°F/–21°C. To 6 ft. Big, heavy-branched plant with large leaves. Pink flowers, darker at the edges, bloom in huge, round trusses. Midseason.

'Leo'. –5°F/–21°C. To 5 ft., well clothed in large dark green leaves. Rounded to dome-shaped trusses packed with rich cranberry red blooms. Midseason to late.

Loderi hybrids. 5°F/–15°C. Spectacular group with tall trusses of 6–7-in.-wide, extremely fragrant flowers in shades of pink or white. Midseason. Informal, open growth to 6 ft., eventually becoming much larger and nearly treelike; too large for small garden. Slow to reach blooming age, not easy to grow; maintaining good foliage color is difficult. Best known are 'King George', pink quickly fading to white; 'Pink Diamond', blush pink; and 'Venus', deepest pink of the group.

'Loder's White'. 0°F/–18°C. Shapely growth to 5 ft. Tall trusses of white flowers with faint yellow throat and light pink picotee edge; blooms turn pure white as they mature. Midseason. Blooms freely even when young. Best white for most regions.

'Madame Masson'. –15°F/–26°C. Grows to 5 ft. White with light yellow flare on upper petal. Late midseason. Needs pruning to maintain compact form.

'Mi Amor'. 15°F/–9°C. Striking plant for mild-winter climates. Open, lanky; to 6 ft. Huge (6-in.), powerfully fragrant, bell-shaped white flowers with yellow throat, borne in clusters of three to five. Midseason.

'Moonstone'. –5°F/–21°C. To 3 ft. Low, compact mound with neat, small, rounded leaves. Flaring bells age from pale pink to creamy yel-

low. Early midseason. Fine facing taller rhododendrons, as low foundation planting with 'Bow Bells'.

'Mrs. G. W. Leak' ('Cottage Gardens Pride'). 0°F/–18°C. Strong-growing plant to 6 ft. Light pink flowers with showy reddish purple flare. Early midseason.

'Nancy Evans'. 5°F/–15°C. Compact growth to 3 ft., with bronzy new foliage. Orange-tinged buds open to yellow flowers; each bloom is backed by a calyx that makes it look almost double. Midseason.

'Naselle'. 5°F/–15°C. To 4 ft. Salmon flowers have apricot centers, rose-tinged edges. Early midseason.

'Northern Starburst'. –30°F/–34°C. To 4 ft. Improved form of 'PJM' with larger flowers and bigger, thicker leaves that turn blackish purple in winter. Early to early midseason.

'Nova Zembla'. –25°F/–32°C. To 5 ft. Profuse red flowers in midseason. Takes heat.

'Noyo Chief'. 10°F/–12°C. To 5 ft. Outstanding glossy green, heavily ribbed leaves. Bright red flowers. Midseason.

'Old Copper'. –5°F/–21°C. Well-shaped plant to 5 ft. Coppery orange flowers. Late. Can take more heat than most rhododendrons.

'Olive'. –5°F/–21°C. To 4 ft. Orchid pink flowers on a upright, open plant. Very early. Frost protection ensures better bloom.

'Pacific Sunset'. 0°F/–18°C. To 4 ft. Each coral pink flower has a golden eye and red freckles. Midseason.

'Paprika Spiced'. 0°F/–18°C. To 3 ft. Flowers in a blend of yellow, pink, and orange, dotted with red. Large yellow calyx. Midseason.

'Patty Bee'. –10°F/–23°C. To 1½ ft. Small plant, well clothed with small (1-in.-wide) leaves that turn dark red in winter. Loose trusses of lemon yellow flowers cover even young plants. Early midseason.

'Percy Wiseman'. –10°F/–23°C. To 3 ft. Compact growth. Peachy yellow flowers fade to white. Midseason. Notably heat resistant.

'Pink Pearl'. –5°F/–21°C. To 6 ft.; open and rangy if not pruned. Tall trusses of rose pink flowers. Midseason. Grows and blooms dependably in all except coldest climates.

'PJM'. –25°F/–32°C. Dense, bushy plant to 4 ft. Exceptional purplish pink flowers; profuse bloom. Flowers early, when foliage still has its mahogany winter color. Takes heat as well as cold.

Rhododendron 'Pink Pearl'

'Point Defiance'. –5°F/–21°C. To 6 ft. Rose-edged, pale pink flowers appear on a vigorous, upright plant. Takes 4–5 years to begin blooming. Midseason.

'President Roosevelt'. 0°F/–18°C. To 4 ft. Dark green leaves marked with golden yellow. Tall trusses of red flowers with white centers. Early midseason. Named for Theodore Roosevelt.

'Purple Gem'. –25°F/–32°C. To 2 ft. Dwarf with tiny leaves that emerge bluish, take on rust tones. Blue-purple flowers in early midseason.

'Purple Passion'. –25°F/–32°C. To 6 ft. tall, 5 ft. wide. Dark green leaves and large, deep purple flowers. Midseason.

'Purple Splendour'. –5°F/–21°C. To 5 ft. Informal habit. Ruffled-looking deep purple blossoms with black-purple blotch. Late midseason. Tolerates sun.

'Ramapo'. –20°F/–29°C. Dense, spreading growth to 2 ft. in sun, taller in shade. New growth is dusty blue green, maturing to dark green. Pinkish violet flowers cover plant in early midseason. Useful rock garden or low border plant. Good choice in California.

'Rosamundi'. –5°F/–21°C. To 4 ft. Slow growing and compact. Ball-like trusses of pink flowers. Very early to early.

'Roseum Elegans'. –25°F/–32°C. To 6 ft. Olive green foliage. Lilac-pink flowers. Midseason to late. Tolerates both heat and cold.

'Rubicon'. 5°F/–15°C. To 4 ft. Well-proportioned plant. Red flowers have black freckles. Early midseason.

'Sapphire'. –5°F/–21°C. To 2½ ft. Twiggy, rounded, and dense, with tiny, narrow gray-green leaves. Small, azalea-like light blue flowers. Early midseason.

'Sappho'. –15°F/–26°C. To 6 ft. Easy to grow; gangly without

pruning. Use at back of border. White blossoms, dark purple eye. Midseason.

'Scarlet Wonder'. –15°F/–26°C. May be hardier than its rating; has survived –45°F/–43°C in Finland (perhaps protected by snow cover). Outstanding, compact dwarf to 2 ft. Shiny, quilted-looking foliage forms backdrop for many bright scarlet blossoms. Midseason.

'Scintillation'. –15°F/–26°C. To 5 ft. Compact plant covered in lustrous dark green leaves. Rounded trusses of pastel pink flowers with deep pink markings in throat; blooms age to brownish pink. Midseason.

'Seaview Sunset'. –5°F/–21°C. To 3 ft. Compact growth. Red-orange buds open light yellow with red-orange band, mature to yellow. Early.

'September Song'. 0°F/–18°C. To 4 ft.; broader than tall. Flowers shade from salmon at edges to golden orange in throat, giving trusses an overall orange look. Blooms young. Midseason.

'Skookum'. –20°F/–29°C. To 4 ft. Globe-shaped red flowers on a rounded, well-proportioned plant. Midseason.

'Snow Lady'. 0°F/–18°C. To 2½ ft. Fuzzy light green leaves. Big show of pure white flowers. Early.

'Susan'. –5°F/–21°C. To 6 ft. Handsome foliage; violet-blue flowers are held in large trusses. Midseason.

'Taurus'. –5°F/–21°C. To 6 ft. Vigorous and upright; well clothed in forest green leaves. Deep red buds open to large bright red bells with black spotting. Early midseason. Plants bloom only after reaching 4 to 6 years old.

'Teddy Bear'. 0°F/–18°C. To 3 ft., compact, rounded. Light purplish pink flowers age to white. Early midseason.

'Top Banana'. 0°F/–18°C. Upright plant to 3 ft. high, wider than tall. Brick red buds open to clear bright yellow flowers. Blooms young. Early midseason.

'Trude Webster'. –10°F/–23°C. To 5 ft. Strong-growing plant with large leaves. Huge trusses of pure pink flowers in midseason. One of the best pinks.

'Unique'. –5°F/–21°C. To 4 ft.; outstanding neat, rounded, compact habit. Bright pink buds open to tight, rounded trusses of creamy pale yellow blossoms. Grow in full sun to avoid mildew. Early midseason.

'Vibrant Violet'. 0°F/–18°C. To 3 ft. Violet flowers cover small,

R

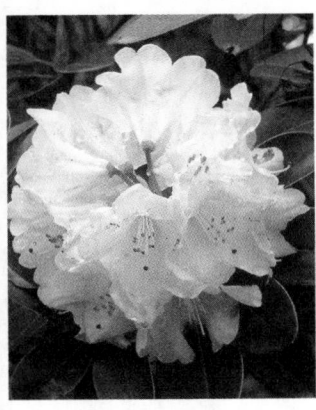

Rhododendron 'Unique'

dark green leaves on a well-branched, mounding plant. Early.

'Vulcan'. –15°F/–26°C. To 5 ft. Bright brick red flowers. Late midseason. New leaves often grow past flower buds, partially hiding them.

'Wanna Bee'. –10°F/–23°C. To 3 ft. Dark yellowish green leaves have bronzy felted undersides. Fuchsia buds open to blush pink blooms that fade to white. Early midseason.

R. augustinii. –5°F/–21°C. Native to western China, Tibet. Open, moderate growth to 6 ft. Bell-shaped flowers in clusters of up to six. Colors range from white to lavender pink to blue. Early midseason. 'Barto Blue', 'Electra', 'Lackamas Blue', and 'Towercourt' are choice blue forms.

R. calophytum. –15°F/–26°C. Native to southwestern China, Tibet. Becomes a small tree in time; to 6 ft. after 10 years. Noted for big leaves (10–14 in. long, 4 in. wide). Trusses of fragrant pale pink flowers with deep red blotch. Early. Protect from wind.

R. calostrotum keleticum. –15°F/–26°C. Native to Burma, Tibet, China. Compact, spreading plant to 1 ft. tall, 3 ft. wide. Leaves are tiny, just ½ in. long, smooth and dark green above, scaly brown beneath. Inch-wide, crimson-purple, saucer-shaped flowers come in upright trusses of three. Fine in rock garden or as bonsai subject. Late midseason.

R. chryseum. See R. rupicola chryseum

R. falconeri. 10°F/–12°C. Native to the Himalayas. Tree to 25 ft. tall. Leathery, 6–12-in.-long leaves with reddish, felted undersides. Clusters of creamy white to pale yellow flowers. Early midseason. Blooms when 15 to 20 years old.

R. forrestii forrestii Repens Group. 5°F/–15°C. Several pros-trate to very low growing plants fall within this group, derived from a species native to China, Myanmar. Bear small clusters of tubular bright red flowers in early midseason. All are useful rock garden plants; require perfect drainage. A plant called simply *R. forrestii forrestii* is actually, according to recent findings, *R. chamaethomsonii chamaethomsonii*.

R. fortunei. –15°F/–26°C. From eastern China. Treelike growth to 6–10 ft. tall, about half as wide; may reach 20 ft. tall after many years. Leaves are oval and pointed, to 7 in. long, matte dark green above and lighter green below. Fragrant pink flowers 2–3 in. across are held in trusses of 6 to 12; they completely cover the plant in midseason. *R. f. discolor* (–5°F/–21°C) is a bit smaller, with a more open habit. Its late-season flowers, up to 4 in. across, are white to pink and come in trusses of eight to ten.

R. impeditum. –15°F/–26°C. From China. Twiggy, dense dwarf to 1 ft., with tiny, closely packed leaves in light grayish green. Small lavender-blue to purple-blue flowers cover the plant in early midseason. Set 15 in. apart for dense ground cover. Takes full sun in cooler areas. Needs excellent drainage to avoid root rot.

R. keiskei. –5°F/–21°C. Native to Japan. Compact growth to 2 ft. Bears light to bright yellow flowers in clusters of three to five. Early midseason. 'Yaku Fairy' is a selected creeping form reaching just 6 in. high.

R. macrophyllum (R. californicum). –5°F/–21°C. COAST RHODODENDRON, WESTERN RHODODENDRON. Native near coast from Northern California to British Columbia. Rangy plant growing 4–10 ft. tall, as high as 20 ft. in some locations. Leathery dark green leaves are 2½–6 in. long. Trusses may hold 20 flowers

Rhododendron augustinii 'Electra'

in pinkish purple to white, spotted with reddish brown. Midseason to late.

R. moupinense. 0°F/–18°C. From China. To 1½ ft., with open, spreading habit. Small, oval leaves are deep red when new, maturing to green. White or pink flowers with red spots. Very early.

R. mucronulatum. –15°F/–26°C. From China, Mongolia, Korea, Japan. Deciduous rhododendron with open, rather thin growth to 5 ft.; makes up for bare, leggy branches with very early bloom. Small clusters of flowers, usually in bright purple. There is also a pink form, 'Cornell Pink'.

R. pemakoense. 0°F/–18°C. From the Himalayas, China. To 1½ ft. Compact, spreading plant with small leaves. Very profuse show of pinkish purple blooms. Early. Useful in rock gardens.

R. racemosum. –5°F/–21°C. Native to China. Several forms are available, including a 6-in. dwarf; a compact, upright shrub to 2½ ft.; and a 7-footer. Small pink flowers in clusters of three to six all along stems. Early to early midseason. Easy to grow; sun tolerant in cooler areas.

R. rupicola chryseum (R. chryseum). –10°F/–23°C. From China, Myanmar. Grows to 1 ft. Dense branching habit; small-leafed dwarf. Bears small, bell-shaped bright yellow blossoms, four or five to a cluster. Early midseason.

R. williamsianum. –5°F/–21°C. Native to Szechuan, China. Compact, mounding growth to 3 ft. tall, 3–4 ft. wide. Attractive, bronzy juvenile foliage matures to rounded, smooth green leaves about 1¾ in. across with blue-green underside. Pink, bell-shaped flowers are 2 in. wide and held on nodding stalks in trusses of two to three. Midseason.

R. yakushimanum. –25°F/–32°C. From Japan. Forms a tight mound to 1–4 ft. high. New growth is covered with a feltlike coat of white hairs; older leaves are glossy dark green above, brown and felted beneath. Clear pink bells age to white. Late midseason. Selections include 'Ken Janeck', a large (to 4-ft.) form with intense pink flowers, and smaller-growing 'Yaku Angel', with pink-tinged buds opening to pure white flowers. There are also a number of hybrids that perform as well in cold climates as they do in milder ones. Among them are 'Mardi Gras', 'Yaku Sunrise', and 'Yaku Princess' (this last selection is part of a good series of hybrids, all with names

including royal titles). The three hybrids just mentioned all have blooms that are white or pink-tinged white.

KINDS OF AZALEAS
Azaleas are divided into two broad categories: evergreen and deciduous. Each category includes both hybrid groups and species.

Evergreen azaleas
Evergreen azaleas fall into more than a dozen groups and species, though an increasing number of hybrids have such mixed parentage that they don't fit into any category. The following list includes some of the most popular groups. Except as noted, bloom season is early (see "Rhododendron hybrids and species," page 584, for bloom-season terms). Plants grown in greenhouses can be forced for winter bloom. Plant size tends to vary within a group, but most individual plants are about as wide as high.

Belgian Indica hybrids. Zones 14–24; H1, H2. These hybrids were originally developed for greenhouse forcing. Where winter lows don't dip below 20°F/–7°C, many of them serve well as landscape plants. They are profuse bloomers with lush, thick foliage and typically semidouble or double, 2–3-in. blossoms. Among the most widely sold are 'Albert and Elizabeth', white with pink edges; 'California Sunset', salmon pink with white border; 'Chimes', dark red; 'Mardi Gras', salmon with white border; 'Mission Bells', red semidouble; 'Mme Alfred Sanders', cherry red; 'Orange Sanders', salmon orange; 'Orchidiflora', orchid pink; 'Paul Schame', salmon. Three choices with pendent growth are 'Red Poppy', deep purple 'Violetta', and orange-red 'William Van Orange'; all are suitable for hanging baskets.

Brooks hybrids. Zones 8, 9, 14–24. Hardy to 20°F/–7°C. Bred in

Rhododendron yakushimanum 'Yaku Angel'

Modesto, California, for heat and drought tolerance, compact form, large flowers. Best known are white 'Madonna'; rose-colored 'My Valentine'; 'Pinkie'; and 'Red Wing'.

Gable hybrids. Zones 4–9, 14–24. Bred to produce azaleas of Kurume type that take 0°F/–18°C temperatures. In Zones 4–6, they may lose some leaves during winter. Bloom heavily in midseason. Frequently sold are bright pink 'Caroline Gable'; purple 'Herbert'; pink 'Louise Gable', 'Pioneer', and 'Rosebud'; 'Purple Splendor'; 'Purple Splendor Compacta' (less rangy growth than 'Purple Splendor'); and white 'Rose Greeley'.

Girard hybrids. Zones 4–9, 14–24. Hardy to –5°F/–21°C or somewhat lower. Originated from Gable crosses. 'Girard's Fuchsia' has reddish purple blossoms; 'Girard's Hot Shot', orange-red flowers and orange-red fall and winter foliage; 'Girard's Roberta', 3-in., double pink flowers.

Glenn Dale hybrids. Zones 4–9, 14–24. Hardy to 0°F/–18°C. Developed primarily for hardiness, though they do drop some leaves in cold winters. Some are tall and rangy, others low and compact. Growth rate varies from slow to rapid. Some have small leaves like Kurume hybrids; others have large leaves. Familiar varieties are orange 'Anchorite'; pale pink 'Aphrodite'; orange-red 'Buccaneer'; white 'Everest' and 'Glacier'; and 'Geisha', white with red stripes.

Gold Cup hybrids. Zones 14–24. Members of this group were originally called Mossholder-Bristow hybrids. Plants combine large flowers of Belgian Indica hybrids with vigor of Rutherfordiana hybrids. Good landscape plants where temperatures don't fall below 20°F/–7°C. Some popular varieties are 'Easter Parade', pink blooms mottled in white; 'Sun Valley', white; and 'White Orchid', white with red throat.

Greenwood hybrids. Zones 4–7, 14–17. Bred in Canby, Oregon. Most of these are compact, hardy plants bearing large double flowers. They were developed to take lows of about 0°F/–18°C but will succeed in colder climates if you keep them from drying out: it's desiccation, not freezing, that does them in.

Kaempferi hybrids. Zones 2–7. Based on *R. kaempferi*, the torch

azalea, a cold-hardy plant with orange-red flowers. These are somewhat hardier than Kurume hybrids (to –15°F/–26°C), with a taller, more open habit. Nearly leafless below 0°F/–18°C. Profuse bloom. Available choices are salmon rose 'Fedora'; 'Holland', a late-season bloomer with large red flowers; orange-red 'John Cairns'; and white 'Palestrina'.

Kurume hybrids. Zones 5–9, 14–24; H1, H2. Hardy to 5°F/–15°C. Compact, twiggy plants, densely clothed in small, glossy leaves. Small flowers are borne in incredible profusion. Plants have mounded or tiered form, look handsome even out of bloom. Widely used as houseplants. Grow well outdoors but cannot endure hot, dry summer winds. Of the many available varieties, these are most widely sold: pink 'Coral Bells', crimson 'Hexe', bright red 'Hino-crimson', cerise red 'Hinodegiri', red-violet 'Sherwood Orchid', orange-red 'Sherwood Red', 'Snow', and dark red 'Ward's Ruby'.

Kurume hybrid azalea 'Ward's Ruby'

Kurume hybrid azalea 'Sherwood Orchid'

Macrantha hybrids. Zones 5–9, 14–24. Includes plants sometimes referred to as Gumpo and Satsuki azaleas. Hardy to 5°F/–15°C. Low-growing plants, some of them true dwarfs; many are pendent enough for hanging baskets. Large flowers come late. Popular varieties include blush pink 'Bunkwa'; orange-red 'Flame Creeper'; white 'Gumpo'; rose pink 'Gumpo Pink'; bright pink 'Hi Gasa'; rose pink

'Rosaeflora'; and 'Shinnyo-No-Tsuki', bearing violet-red blossoms with white center.

Monrovia hybrids. Zones 8, 9, 14–24. Hardy to 10°F/–12°C. Developed by Monrovia Nursery in Southern California, using Belgian Indica and Southern Indica azaleas as parents. They resemble Southern Indicas, form 4–6-ft. mounds, and thrive in warm, dry areas. Sun tolerant. 'Imperial Princess' has single pink flowers; 'Imperial Queen' bears double pink blooms. Midseason.

Pericat hybrids. Zones 5–9, 14–24. These were originally developed for greenhouse forcing but are as hardy as Kurume hybrids (5 to 10°F/–15 to –12°C) and look much the same, though flowers tend to be somewhat larger. Varieties include light pink 'Mme Pericat', blush pink 'Sweetheart Supreme', and rose pink 'Twenty Grand'.

Robin Hill hybrids. Zones 4–9, 14–24. Hardy to 0°F/–18°, probably lower. A large group with typically large flowers. Most are 2–4-ft. plants; some are more dwarf. Late bloom. There are so many good ones—several with "Robin Hill" in their name—that it's difficult to single out only a few. Try pink 'Betty Ann Voss'; 'Conversation Piece', pink with light center; 'Nancy of Robin Hill', pink with red blotch; red-orange 'Robin Hill Gillie'; and 'Hilda Niblett', with blossoms in a combination of light pink, deep pink, and white.

Rutherfordiana hybrids. Zones 14–24. Greenhouse plants; also good in garden where temperatures don't go below 20°F/–7°C. Bushy, 2–4-ft. plants with handsome foliage. Medium-size blossoms may be single, semidouble, or double. Available varieties include 'Alaska', white with chartreuse blotch; light orchid pink 'Constance'; brick red 'Dorothy Gish'; rosy red 'Firelight'; orchid pink 'L. J. Bobbink'; white 'Purity'; deep pink 'Rose Queen'; and 'White Gish', very pale pink fading to white.

Southern Indica hybrids. Zones 8, 9, 14–24. Varieties selected from

Southern Indica hybrid azalea 'Formosa'

Belgian Indica hybrids for vigor and sun tolerance. Most take temperatures of 10 to 20°F/–12 to –7°C, but some are damaged even at the upper end of that range. They generally grow faster, more vigorously, and taller than other kinds of evergreen azaleas. Often sold in California under the name "sun azaleas." Used for massing and as specimens—as shrubs, standards, espaliers. Popular choices include carmine red 'Brilliant'; salmon pink 'Duc de Rohan'; 'Fielder's White'; brilliant rose purple 'Formosa' (also sold as 'Coccinea', 'Phoenicia', 'Vanessa'); light pink 'George Lindley Taber'; 'Iveryana', white with orchid streaks; 'Little John', a dense, rounded bush up to 6 ft. tall (despite the name) bearing burgundy foliage and a few deep red flowers; bright orange 'Orange Pride'; brilliant red 'Pride of Dorking'; watermelon pink 'Southern Charm' (sometimes sold as 'Judge Solomon'); and 'White April'.

Vuykiana hybrids. Zones 2–7. See description of Kaempferi hybrids. Varieties sold include violet-blue 'Blue Danube', 'Vuyk's Rosy Red', and 'Vuyk's Scarlet'.

R. mucronatum. Zones 4–9, 14–24. Hardy to 5°F/–15°C. Typically listed as a species (*R. mucronatum* or *R. indica alba*), this plant is in fact an old Japanese garden hybrid now properly known as *R.* 'Mucronatum'. It has also been sold as 'Indica Alba' and 'Ledifolia Alba'. Grows 6–10 ft. high, with hairy leaves and large (to 3-in.) white flowers. Two of its sports are 'Sekidera' and 'Indica Rosea'; the former has blossoms flushed or blotched with purplish pink, while the latter bears pink-flushed blooms.

Deciduous azaleas
Very few deciduous shrubs can equal deciduous azaleas for show-

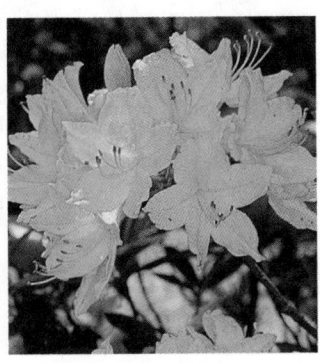

Rhododendron luteum
(deciduous azalea)

iness and color range. Evergreen azaleas can't match them for blooms in the yellow, orange, and flame red range, nor for flowers with bicolor contrasts. Foliage often turns brilliant orange red to maroon in autumn. In the list below, hybrid groups are followed by species. Plant size tends to vary within a group, but most individual plants are roughly equal in height and width. For definition of bloom-season terminology, see "Rhododendron hybrids and species," page 584.

Ghent hybrids. Zones 2b–9, 14–17. Many are hardy to –25°F/ –32°C. Upright growth. Flowers are generally 1½–2¼ in. wide. Colors include shades of yellow, orange, umber, red, and pink. Midseason.

Knap Hill–Exbury hybrids. Zones 3–9, 14–17. Hardy to –20°F/ –29°C. These make up perhaps half of all the deciduous azaleas sold in the Pacific Northwest. Plants vary from upright to spreading, from 4 to 6 ft. tall. Produce the largest flowers found on deciduous azaleas (up to 5 in. across), borne in clusters of 7–18. Blossoms are sometimes ruffled or fragrant, in colors ranging from white through pink and yellow to orange and red, often with contrasting blotches.

Both Knap Hill and Exbury azaleas come from the same original crosses. The first crosses were made at Knap Hill (in England); subsequent improvements were made at both Exbury (also in England) and Knap Hill. The so-called Rothschild azaleas are Exbury plants. Ilam and Arneson hybrids are improvements on the original stock.

Knap Hill–
Exbury hybrid
azalea 'Old Gold'

Midseason to late bloom. If you want to be sure of flower color and size, choose named varieties (this does not mean you should dismiss all seedling plants as inferior—but do select them in bloom). Some of the best named forms are pink 'Cannon's Double'; orange 'Gibraltar'; double deep pink 'Homebush'; golden tangerine 'Klondyke'; 'Old Gold', bearing light orange-yellow blossoms flushed pink and blotched deep orange; and 'Oxydol', white flowers with yellow markings.

Mollis hybrids. Zones A3; 2–9, 14–17. Hardy to –25°F/–32°C. Hybrids of *R. molle* and *R. japonicum*. Upright growth to 4–5 ft. Flowers 2½–4 in. wide, in clusters of 7–13. Colors range from chrome yellow through bright red. Very heavy bloom in midseason. Leaves have a light skunky fragrance when new, but they turn a lovely yellow to orange in autumn.

Northern Lights hybrids. Zones A2, A3; 1–7. The hardiest of all deciduous azaleas, withstanding –45°F/–43°C. Developed by the University of Minnesota. To 2–4 ft., with ball-shaped trusses of fragrant sterile flowers (no need to deadhead after bloom). Late. Most widely available are 'Apricot Surprise', 'Orchid Lights', 'Rosy Lights', and 'White Lights'. Foliage can have the skunky odor of the Mollis ancestors.

Occidentale hybrids. Zones 4–7, 14–17. Hardy to –5°F/–21°C. Hybrids between *R. occidentale* and Mollis azaleas. To 8 ft. Flowers 2½–4 in. wide; wide color range— from white blossoms flushed with rose and marked with yellow blotches, to red blooms with orange blotch. Midseason to late. An outstanding example is 'Washington State Centennial' ('Centennial'), with big, fragrant, frilly flowers in light orange-yellow marked with a large yellow flare; blossoms quickly age to white.

Viscosum hybrids. Zones 3–7. Hardy to –15°F/–26°C. Hybrids between Mollis azaleas and *R. viscosum,* an eastern U.S. native with a powerful clove perfume. Flowers have the colors of Mollis azaleas but the fragrance of *R. viscosum.* Late.

R. japonicum. JAPANESE AZALEA. Zones 3b–7, 14–17. Hardy to –10°F/ –23°C. Native to Japan. Upright, fast growth to 6 ft. Salmon red, 2–3-in.-wide flowers are carried in clusters of 6–12 before leafout. Midseason. *R. j. aureum* has rich yellow flowers.

R. luteum (R. flavum). PONTIC AZALEA. Zones 3–7, 14–17. Hardy to –15°F/–26°C. Native to eastern Europe, Asia Minor. To 8 ft. or more. Blooms before leafout, bearing fragrant, single yellow flowers with darker blotch. Midseason.

R. occidentale. WESTERN AZALEA. Zones 4–7, 14–17, 19–24. Hardy to –5°F/–21°C. Native to mountains and foothills of California and Oregon. Erect growth to 6–10 ft. Clusters of fragrant, funnel-shaped flowers bloom after leafout. Midseason to late. Color varies from white to pinkish white with yellow blotch; some are heavily marked in carmine rose. Superior named cutting-grown plants are scarce but available and worth looking for. 'Leonard Frisbie' is a choice, heavily marked variety.

R. schlippenbachii. ROYAL AZALEA. Zones 3–7, 14–17. Hardy to –20°F/–29°C. Native to Korea and Manchuria. Densely branched shrub to 6–8 ft. Leaves in whorls of five at tips of branches. Blooms in early midseason as leaves are expanding, producing large (2– 4-in.), highly fragrant, pure light pink flowers in clusters of three to six. A white form is also available. Good fall color: yellow, orange, scarlet, crimson. Protect from full sun.

R. vaseyi. PINKSHELL AZALEA. Zones 3–7, 14–17. Hardy to –20°F/ –29°C. Native to mountains of North Carolina. Upright plant with irregular, spreading form. To 10–15 ft. Blooms before leafout, bearing light pink flowers in clusters of five to eight. Midseason.

RHODOHYPOXIS
baurii
Hypoxidaceae
PERENNIAL FROM
RHIZOMELIKE STRUCTURE

ZONES 4–7, 14–24
FULL SUN
REGULAR WATER DURING GROWTH AND BLOOM

From mountains of South Africa. Tufts of narrow, 2–3-in. leaves are nearly obscured by masses of inch-wide, six-petaled flowers over a

Rhodohypoxis baurii

long spring-and-summer bloom period. Typical blossom colors range from pink shades to rosy red, but white varieties are available. Grows from a bulblike structure that is closest to a rhizome but also has characteristics of corm, tuber, and tuberous roots.

Plant roots in early spring, setting them 1 in. deep and 3–5 in. apart in nonalkaline, well-drained soil; choose a location where winter moisture can be kept to minimum. Stop watering when foliage yellows in fall. Divide crowded plantings in early spring, just as growth begins. Good in rock gardens. Often grown in containers to accommodate need for dry winters.

RHODOPHIALA
bifida
Amaryllidaceae
PERENNIAL FROM BULB

ZONES 8, 9, 12–24
FULL SUN
REGULAR WATER DURING GROWTH AND BLOOM

South American native resembling a small amaryllis (*Hippeastrum*) and considered by some to be *H. advenum.* Puts up a few foot-long leaves and a foot-tall flower stalk that bears two to six bright red, 2-in.-long, narrow-petaled blooms in late summer, early autumn. Plants spread willingly and put on a fine show. Grow as for *Hippeastrum.*

Rhodophiala bifida

RHOEO spathacea.
See **TRADESCANTIA spathacea**

R

RHOICISSUS
capensis
(Cissus capensis)
EVERGREEN GRAPE
Vitaceae
EVERGREEN VINE

🌿	ZONES 16, 17, 21–24; H2; OR INDOORS
☀ ◑	ROOTS COOL, TOP IN SUN; BRIGHT OR INDIRECT LIGHT
💧	REGULAR WATER

Native to Africa. Tuberous-rooted vine, growing slowly to 15 ft. or more. Scallop-toothed leaves are roundish to kidney shaped, something like those of true grape in size and appearance. New stems and leaves are covered with red hairs that give them a rosy rust color. Mature leaves are a bold, coppery-tinged light green on upper surface, hairy and rust colored beneath. Flowers are insignificant.

Rhoicissus capensis

Makes a good overhead screen or ground cover in frost-free regions. Fine houseplant; tolerates low light.

RHOPALOSTYLIS
Arecaceae (Palmae)
PALMS

🌿	ZONES 17, 23, 24; H1, H2
☀ ◑	FULL SUN OR PARTIAL SHADE
💧	REGULAR WATER

Feather palms with long, clean trunks marked with closely spaced rings. Moderate growth rate. Best in frost-free gardens.

Rhopalostylis sapida

R. baueri. From Norfolk Island. To 50 ft. tall, 20 ft. wide. The beautiful curving, arching leaves grow to 6–9 ft. long.

R. sapida. NIKAU PALM, SHAVING BRUSH PALM. From New Zealand. To 30 ft. high, 15 ft. wide. Feathery leaves 4–8 ft. long stand upright from prominent bulge at top of trunk. Good container plant where small space dictates an upright palm.

RHUBARB
Polygonaceae
PERENNIAL

🌿	BEST IN ZONES A1–A3; 1–11; ALSO SUCCEEDS IN ZONES 14–24
☀ ◑	PARTIAL SHADE IN HOTTEST CLIMATES
💧	REGULAR WATER
☠	LEAVES ARE POISONOUS IF INGESTED; USE LEAF STEMS ONLY

Foliage is showy enough to qualify this plant for a display spot in the garden. Bears big, crinkled leaves with an elongated heart shape that are carried on thick, typically red-tinted stalks. Leafstalks have a delicious, tart flavor and are typically used like fruit in sauces and pies. Produces insignificant flowers in spikelike clusters. Preferred varieties include 'Cherry' ('Crimson Cherry'), 'MacDonald', and 'Strawberry', all with red stalks; and 'Victoria', which produces greenish stalks. For strictly ornamental species of rhubarb, see *Rheum*.

Rhubarb

Needs some winter chill for thick stems, good red color. Plant divisions (containing at least one bud) in late winter or early spring. In Zones 10 and 11, treat as cool-season annual and plant in fall for winter-into-spring harvest (plants tend to rot in heat of late spring, summer). Set tops of divisions at soil line; space 3–4 ft. apart. Let plants grow for two full seasons before harvesting. In third season, you can pull off leafstalks for 4 or 5 weeks in spring; older, huskier plants can take up to 8 weeks of pulling. To harvest leafstalks, grasp them near base and pull sideways and outward; do not cut with a

knife, since cutting leaves a stub that will decay. Never remove all the leaves from a single plant; stop harvesting when slender leafstalks appear. After harvest, feed and water freely; cut out any blossom stalks that appear. In the mildest areas, plants won't die back completely in winter.

RHUS
SUMAC
Anacardiaceae
EVERGREEN AND DECIDUOUS
SHRUBS AND TREES

🌿	ZONES VARY BY SPECIES
☀	FULL SUN
◌ ◐	LITTLE TO MODERATE WATER

Of the ornamental sumacs, deciduous kinds are extremely hardy to cold; they are noted for brilliant fall leaf color and, on female plants, showy clusters of (usually) red fruits that attract birds. They tend to produce suckers, especially if their roots are disturbed by cultivation. Evergreen species are less hardy. All sumac species thrive in almost any soil, as long as drainage is good (soggy soils can kill them).

Poison oak and poison ivy were once members of the genus *Rhus*, but they have been reclassified as *Toxicodendron*. For more information on these weedy, rash-causing sumac relatives and recommended controls, see "Poison oak, poison ivy" (page 750).

R. aromatica. FRAGRANT SUMAC. Deciduous shrub. Zones 1–3, 10. Native to eastern North America. Fast-growing plant to 3–5 ft. tall, sprawling 5 ft. or wider. Three-leafleted leaves to 3 in. long are fragrant when brushed against or crushed. Foliage turns red in fall. Tiny yellowish flowers in spring; small red fruit. Coarse bank cover, ground cover for poor or dry soils. 'Gro-Low' grows 2–3 ft. high and 6–8 ft. wide.

R. copallina. SHINING SUMAC. Deciduous shrub or tree. Zones 2–9, 14–18. From eastern U.S. To 10–30 ft. tall, spreading indefinitely by suckers. Foot-long leaves are divided featherwise into 9–12 leaflets, each to 4 in. long; turn brilliant red in fall. Greenish, 6-in. flower spikes in summer are followed by clusters of dark red, fuzzy fruits.

R. glabra. SMOOTH SUMAC. Deciduous shrub or tree. Zones 1–10, 14–17. Native to much of North America. Upright grower to 10 ft., sometimes treelike to 20 ft. Spreads widely by suckers; in the

wild, forms large patches. Looks much like *R. typhina* and has the same garden uses, but usually grows lower and does not have velvety branches. Leaves divided into 11–23 tooth-edged, rather narrow, 2–5-in.-long leaflets that are deep green above, whitish beneath; foliage turns scarlet in fall. Inconspicuous flowers in early summer are followed by showy clusters of scarlet fruits that remain on bare branches well into winter. Leaves of 'Laciniata' are deeply cut and slashed, giving the plant a fernlike appearance.

R. integrifolia. LEMONADE BERRY. Evergreen shrub. Zones 8, 9, 14–17, 19–24. Native to coastal Southern California, Channel Islands, Baja California. Generally 3–10 ft. high and wide; rarely treelike to 30 ft. Leathery dark green leaves are oval to nearly round, 1–2½ in. long. White or pinkish flowers in dense clusters from midwinter to spring (sometimes from early winter into summer). Clustered small, flattish fruits are reddish and gummy, with tart pulp that can be used to flavor drinks— hence the common name.

Rhus integrifolia

Grows best near coast, where established plants need no irrigation. Makes a wonderful ground cover on rocky slopes exposed to salt-laden winds; one plant eventually sprawls over a wide area, even down cliffs. In less windy places, use as a tall screen or background plant. Excellent for espalier against fences and walls. Can be trimmed to make a dense formal hedge and maintained just under a foot wide. Useful in erosion control. Highly susceptible to verticillium wilt.

R. lancea. AFRICAN SUMAC. Evergreen tree. Zones 8, 9, 12–24. Slow grower to 20–30 ft. tall, 20–35 ft. wide. Open, spreading habit; graceful, weeping outer branchlets. Dark green leaves are divided into three willowlike, 4–5-in.-long leaflets. Inconspicuous early spring flowers are followed by clusters of pea-size yellow or red fruit that can make a mess on pavement. This species can be trained to a single trunk or allowed to grow as a multitrunked tree somewhat resembling olive (*Olea*). Makes a good specimen, background plant, screen; can also be clipped into a hedge. Takes desert heat; susceptible to Texas root rot.

R. laurina (Malosma laurina). LAUREL SUMAC. Evergreen shrub. Zones 14–17, 19–24. Native mostly to coastal foothills of Southern California and Baja California. Grows rapidly to 6–15 ft. tall and wide; sometimes almost treelike in form, with a rounded crown. Attractive reddish branches. Pleasantly aromatic light green leaves often have pink margins and pink leafstalks; they are 2–4 in. long, shaped like those of laurel (*Laurus*). Small whitish flowers in dense, branched, 2–6-in.-long clusters in late spring and early summer, sometimes continuing through autumn. Berrylike white fruit. Gets rangy unless pruned; useful as espalier or clipped hedge. Good bank cover where frosts are rare. More tender to frost than *R. ovata* or *R. integrifolia;* sometimes freezes in its native range but comes back quickly from a stump.

R. microphylla. DESERT SUMAC. Deciduous shrub. Zones 10–13. Native to southwestern U.S. and Mexico. Grows to 8 ft. (possibly 15 ft.) tall, 12 ft. wide. Leaves are divided featherwise into five to nine small (less than ½-in.-long) leaflets. Clusters of little white flowers appear in spring before leafout; these are followed in early summer by tiny, hairy orange or red fruit.

R. ovata. SUGAR BUSH. Evergreen shrub. Zones 9–12, 14–24. Native to dry slopes away from coast in Southern California, Baja California; dry slopes in Arizona. Upright or spreading habit. Typically grows 4–10 ft. high and wide, though it can be shorter or taller. Takes well to pruning. Glossy, leathery leaves are 1½–3 in. long, somewhat trough shaped, pointed at tips. Dense clusters of white or pinkish spring flowers are followed by small, reddish, hairy fruit coated with a sugary secretion. Same landscape uses as species *R. integrifolia* but for inland areas rather than seacoast. Rarely bothered by pests or diseases.

R. trilobata. SQUAWBUSH, SKUNKBUSH. Deciduous shrub. Zones 1–12, 14–21. Native from Illinois westward to Texas and California, north to Washington. Similar in most details to *R. aromatica,* but most people find the scent of the bruised leaves unpleasant. Clumping habit makes it a natural low hedge; also good for erosion control. Brilliant yellow to red fall color.

R. typhina. STAGHORN SUMAC. Deciduous shrub or tree. Zones A1–A3; 1–10, 14–17. From eastern North America. Upright to 15 ft. (sometimes 30 ft.) tall, spreading much wider by suckers. Very similar to species *R. glabra,* but the branches have a velvety coat of short brown hairs—much like antlers of a deer "in velvet."

Rhus typhina

Leaves are divided into 11–31 toothed, 5-in.-long leaflets; foliage is deep green above, grayish beneath, turns yellow orange to rich red in fall. Blooms in early summer, bearing 4–8-in.-long clusters of tiny greenish blossoms followed by clusters of fuzzy crimson fruits that hang on all winter, gradually turning brown. 'Laciniata' is a female selection with deeply cut leaflets; it grows 10–12 ft. tall. 'Dissecta' is similar.

Both *R. typhina* and *R. glabra* take extreme heat and cold. Big, divided leaves give tropical effect; fall show is brilliant (for best effect, plant among evergreens). Bare branches make a fine silhouette in winter; fruit is decorative. Both species colonize aggressively by root suckers—a potential problem, especially in small gardens. They grow well when confined to large containers.

R. virens. EVERGREEN SUMAC. Evergreen shrub. Zones 10–13. Native to southeastern Arizona, New Mexico, Texas, Mexico. To 12 ft. tall and wide, with dark green leaves divided featherwise into five to nine 1½-in. leaflets. White spring and summer flowers (not showy) are followed by small, berrylike red fruit. Tolerates open shade, making it a good choice for an understory plant beneath tall trees.

RHYNCHELYTRUM (Melinis)

NATAL RUBY GRASS
Poaceae (Gramineae)
PERENNIAL GRASSES

> ⚡ ZONES 2B–24; H1, H2; ALL ZONES AS ANNUALS
>
> ☀ FULL SUN
>
> 💧 REGULAR WATER

These short-lived African natives are harmless weeds in the tropics. In mild-winter climates of the West, they can reseed themselves, and plants may live over from year to year. In cold regions, treat as annuals; or pot up divisions and protect them during winter. Narrow blue-green leaves are erect, then arching; form clumps 1 ft. high and slightly wider. From these rise 2-ft. flower spikes that open deep pink to purplish red and gradually fade to light pinkish tan.

R. nerviglume. A strain of this species introduced by the Denver Botanic Garden is sold as 'Pink Crystals'. It blooms in late summer and has survived winters in Pueblo, Colorado.

Rhynchelytrum nerviglume 'Pink Crystals'

R. repens. Like the above. Blooms in summer or early autumn; flowering may continue throughout mild winters in Southern California.

RHYNCHOSPERMUM. See **TRACHELOSPERMUM**

RIBBON FERN. See **PTERIS cretica**

RIBBON GRASS. See **PHALARIS arundinacea picta**

RIBES

CURRANT, GOOSEBERRY
Grossulariaceae (Saxifragaceae)
EVERGREEN AND DECIDUOUS SHRUBS

> ⚡ ZONES VARY BY SPECIES
>
> ☀ ◐ FULL SUN OR PARTIAL SHADE
>
> 💧 💧 WATER NEEDS VARY BY SPECIES

Those without spines are called currants; those with spines are known as gooseberries. The following species are grown ornamentally; see Currant and Gooseberry for strictly fruiting types. Members of this genus are alternate hosts to white pine blister rust and are still banned in a few areas where white pines grow.

R. alpinum. ALPINE CURRANT. Deciduous shrub. Zones A2, A3; 1–6, 10. Native to Europe. Dense, twiggy growth to 4–5 ft. (rarely taller) and equally wide. Roundish, ½–1½-in.-wide, deep bright green leaves with toothed, lobed edges appear very early in spring. Flowers and fruit are not showy. Good hedge. 'Green Mound' and yellow-leafed 'Aureum' are dwarf forms about half the size of the species. Regular water.

R. aureum. GOLDEN CURRANT. Deciduous shrub. Zones A2, A3, 1–12, 14–23, except as noted. Native to inland regions of the West. Erect growth to 3–6 ft. tall and wide. Light green leaves with lobed, toothed edges. Small, bright yellow spring flowers, usually with a spicy fragrance, in 1–2½-in.-long clusters. Summer berries turn from yellow to red to black. Moderate to regular water.

R. a. gracillimum, the more tender California form (Zones 6–10, 14–24), has unscented blooms that age to reddish orange.

R. indecorum. WHITE FLOWERING CURRANT. Deciduous shrub. Zones 7–9, 11, 14–24. Native to Coast Ranges in Southern California. To 6–9 ft. tall, 4–6 ft. wide. Thickish, scallop-edged leaves to 1½ in. long; dark green and roughly hairy above, white and fuzzy beneath. Clusters of small white flowers enclosed in pink bracts put on a good show in winter. Needs no irrigation but will tolerate garden watering.

R. malvaceum. CHAPARRAL CURRANT. Deciduous shrub. Zones 6–9, 14–24. Native to slopes in California's Coast Ranges. To 5 ft. tall and wide, with hairy, roundish, dull green, 2-in. leaves and short clusters of fragrant pink flowers throughout fall, winter. Red fruit. Needs no irrigation, but give it moderate water if you don't want it to go dormant in summer.

R. nigrum. BLACK CURRANT. Deciduous shrub. Zones A1–A3; 1–7. Native to Europe, Asia. To 3–5 ft. high and wide. Deep green, three-lobed, 2–4-in. leaves have an odd scent. Drooping clusters of whitish spring flowers develop into juicy, shiny black fruit with a sweet-tart flavor like that of blackberry. Regular water.

R

R. odoratum. Deciduous shrub. Zones A2, A3; 1–10, 14–17. Similar to *R. aureum* but native to Midwest and High Plains. Spring flowers have fragrance of carnations (*Dianthus*). Rust-resistant 'Crandall' has large, shiny black fruit with the rich, sweet-tart flavor of *R. nigrum*. Regular water.

R. sanguineum. PINK WINTER CURRANT, RED FLOWERING CURRANT. Deciduous shrub. Zones A3; 4–9, 14–24. Native to Coast Ranges from California to British Columbia. To 5–12 ft. tall and wide, with maplelike, dark green, 2½-in.-wide leaves. In spring, produces drooping, 2–4-in.-long clusters of 10–30 small deep pink to red flowers. Blue-black fruit has a whitish bloom. Most commonly sold is *R. s. glutinosum* (more southerly in origin than the species); its blossoms are typically deep or pale pink, carried in clusters of 15–40. 'Barrie Coate', 'Elk River Red', 'King Edward VII', and 'Pulborough Scarlet' are red-flowering selections. Pink varieties include 'Claremont', with two-tone blossoms aging to red, and 'Spring Showers', with 8-in. flower clusters. 'Album', 'Inverness White', and 'White Icicle' are good white varieties. Little to moderate water.

Ribes sanguineum

R. speciosum. FUCHSIA-FLOWERING GOOSEBERRY. Nearly evergreen shrub. Zones 7–9, 14–24. Native near coast, from central coast of California south to Baja California. Erect to 4–8 ft. tall, 6–10 ft. wide, with spiny, often bristly stems. Thick-textured, maplelike, 1-in. leaves are glossy dark green above, lighter beneath. Deep crimson to cherry red flowers, borne winter to spring, are drooping and fuchsialike, with long, protruding stamens. Gummy, bristly red berries. Excellent barrier. Needs no irrigation, but moderate water keeps it nearly evergreen in summer (it can also take regular moisture). Partial shade in hottest climates.

Ribes speciosum

R. viburnifolium. CATALINA PERFUME, EVERGREEN CURRANT. Evergreen shrub. Zones 5, 7–9, 14–17, 19–24. Native to Catalina Island, Baja California. To 3–6 ft. tall, spreading to 12 ft. wide. Wine red stems are arching or half trailing; they may root in moist soil. Roundish, 1-in., leathery dark green leaves are fragrant after rain or when crushed (some liken the scent to pine, others to apples). Light pink to purplish flowers from midwinter into spring. Red berries. To keep plant low, cut out upright-growing stems. Needs partial shade in hottest climates. Needs no irrigation but can take moderate water. Good on banks or under native oaks where watering is undesirable.

RICE PAPER PLANT.
See **TETRAPANAX papyriferus**

RICINUS communis

CASTOR BEAN
Euphorbiaceae
EVERGREEN SHRUB USUALLY
GROWN AS ANNUAL

🗡	ZONES 23, 24; H1, H2; ALL ZONES AS ANNUAL
☼	FULL SUN
💧	REGULAR WATER
◆	SEEDS (OR BEANS) ARE POISONOUS IF INGESTED

Bold, striking plant from Africa, Asia. Can provide tall screen or leafy background in a hurry; grows 6–15 ft. tall and half as wide in a single season. Where winters are mild, will live over and become quite woody and treelike. Has naturalized in small areas in many climates. Should not be planted in areas where small children play—the poisonous seeds are attractive. Foliage and seeds occasionally cause severe contact allergies as well. To prevent seed formation, pinch off the burlike seed capsules while they are small.

Large-lobed leaves are 1–3 ft. across on vigorous young plants, smaller on older plants. Unimpressive, small white flowers are borne in clusters on foot-high stalks in summer, followed by attractive prickly husks that contain seeds. Grown commercially for castor oil extracted from seeds. Many horticultural varieties. 'Zanzibarensis' has very large green leaves; 'Dwarf Red Spire' is lower growing (to 6 ft.), with red leaves and seedpods.

Ricinus communis 'Dwarf Red Spire'

ROBINIA

LOCUST
Fabaceae (Leguminosae)
DECIDUOUS TREES AND SHRUBS

🗡	ZONES VARY BY SPECIES
☼	FULL SUN
💧	LITTLE OR NO WATER TO MODERATE WATER
◆	BARK, LEAVES, AND SEEDS ARE POISONOUS IF INGESTED

Fairly fast growing plants, well adapted to hot, dry regions. Leaves are divided like feathers into many roundish leaflets. Clusters of white or pink, sweet pea–shaped flowers bloom from midspring to early summer, followed by beanlike pods about 4 in. long. Locust trees tolerate poor soil and can get by on little or no water, but they do have some drawbacks: wood is brittle, roots are aggressive, and plants often spread by suckers.

R. × ambigua. Tree. Zones 2–24. Hybrid between *R. pseudoacacia* and *R. viscosa*, a seldom-grown pink-flowering locust. The following are the best-known varieties.

'Decaisneana'. To 40–50 ft. tall, 20 ft. wide. Flowers like those of *R. pseudoacacia*, but color is pale pink.

'Idahoensis'. IDAHO LOCUST. Tree of moderately fast growth to a shapely 40 ft. tall, 30 ft. wide. Bright magenta rose flowers in 8-in. clusters; one of showiest of locusts in bloom. Good flowering tree for Rocky Mountain gardens.

'Purple Robe'. Resembles 'Idahoensis' but has darker, purple-pink flowers, reddish bronze new growth; blooms 2 weeks earlier and over a longer period.

R. neomexicana. DESERT LOCUST. Shrub or tree. Zones 2, 3, 7–11, 14, 18–24. Native from California's desert mountains to Arizona, New Mexico. Thorny plant; usually seen as a shrub about 6 ft. high and wide but can become a 30-ft. tree. Drooping, 6-in. clusters of inch-wide pink flowers.

R. pseudoacacia. BLACK LOCUST. Tree. Zones 1–24. Native to eastern and central U.S. Fast growth to 40–75 ft. tall, 30–60 ft. wide, with rather sparse, open branching habit. Deeply furrowed brown bark. Thorny branches. Leaves divided into 7–19 leaflets, each 1–2 in. long. White, fragrant, ½–¾-in.-long flowers are held in dense, pendent clusters that reach 4–8 in. long.

Robinia pseudoacacia

Little valued in its native territory except as a source of honey and fence posts, it has been widely planted (and has subsequently escaped) in much of the western U.S. In California's Gold Country, it has gone native. It manufactures its own fertilizer through nitrogen-fixing root nodule bacteria and can colonize the poorest soil. With some pruning and training in its early years, it can be a truly handsome flowering tree. Has been used as a street tree but is not a good choice for narrow parking strips or under power lines. Wood is extremely hard and tough; suckers are difficult to prune out where soil is not watered. Varieties include the following.

'Frisia'. To 50 ft. tall, 25 ft. wide. New growth is nearly orange; mature leaves are yellow, turning greener in summer heat. Thorns and young wood are red.

'Pyramidalis' ('Fastigiata'). Narrow, columnar, to 50 ft. tall, 10 ft. wide.

'Tortuosa'. Slow grower to 50 ft. tall, 30 ft. wide, with twisted branches. Few flowers.

'Twisty Baby' ('Lace Lady'). Dwarf to 8–10 ft. tall, 12–15 ft. wide. Picturesquely twisted branches; few flowers.

'Umbraculifera'. Dense and round-headed tree, to 20 ft. tall and wide. Usually grafted 6–8 ft. high on another locust to create a living green lollipop. Few flowers.

Robinia pseudoacacia

ROCKCRESS. See **ARABIS**

ROCKET. See **ARUGULA**

ROCK JASMINE. See **ANDROSACE**

ROCK PURSLANE. See **CALANDRINIA umbellata**

ROCKROSE. See **CISTUS**

ROCK SPIREA. See **HOLODISCUS dumosus**

RODGERSIA

Saxifragaceae
PERENNIALS

🌱 ZONES 2–9, 14–17

☼ ☼ PARTIAL SHADE IN HOTTEST CLIMATES

💧 AMPLE WATER

Native to China, Japan. Large plants with imposing leaves and clustered tiny flowers in plumes somewhat like those of astilbe; bloom in early to midsummer. Primary feature is handsome foliage, which often takes on bronze tones in late summer. Plants spread by thick rhizomes, need rich soil. The various species hybridize freely. Dormant in winter; provide winter mulch in cold climates. Showy in moist woodland or bog gardens.

Rodgersia aesculifolia

R. aesculifolia. To 6 ft. tall, 3 ft. wide. Leaves are divided like fingers of hand into five to seven tooth-edged, 10-in. leaflets; they are similar to those of horsechestnut *(Aesculus).* Shaggy brown hairs on flower stalks, leaf stems, major leaf veins. White flowers.

R. pinnata. To 4 ft. tall, 2½ ft. wide. Leaves have five to nine 8-in. leaflets. Red flowers.

R. podophylla. To 5 ft. tall, 6 ft. wide. Coppery green leaves divided into five 10-in.-long leaflets. Creamy flowers.

R. sambucifolia. To 3 ft. high and wide. Leaves have up to 11 leaflets. Flat-topped clusters of white or pink flowers.

R. tabularis. See Astilboides tabularis

ROMNEYA coulteri

MATILIJA POPPY
Papaveraceae
SHRUBBY PERENNIAL

🌱 ZONES 4–12, 14–24; H1

☼ FULL SUN

◌ 💧 LITTLE OR NO WATER TO MODERATE WATER

Native from Coast Ranges to coastal valleys of Southern California, Baja California. Spectacular plant to 6–8 ft. or taller, spreading indefinitely by rhizomes. Sends up thick stems clothed in irregularly lobed leaves; stems and foliage are

Romneya coulteri

grayish green. Along their upper part, stems bear huge (to 9-in.), slightly scented flowers often likened to giant-size fried eggs: each blossom has five or six crepe-papery petals centered with a cluster of golden stamens. Blooms from late spring into summer, into fall with some watering. Flowers are handsome in arrangements. 'Butterfly' is a profusely branching plant with smaller flowers of rounded, overlapping petals. 'White Cloud' is exceptionally vigorous, with profuse, very large blossoms.

Use on hillsides as soil binder, along roadsides, in marginal areas, in wide borders. Invasive; don't plant near less vigorous plants. Tolerates many soils. Withhold summer irrigation to keep growth in check. Cut nearly to ground in late fall. New shoots emerge after first rains in winter. Although easy to grow once established, the plant is very difficult to propagate. Easiest way to get more plants is to dig up rooted suckers from spreading roots, but you can try taking cuttings from the thickest roots. To make seeds germinate, mix them with potting soil in a foil-lined flat; burn pine needles on top of flat for 30 minutes, then water and hope for sprouting.

ROSA

ROSE
Rosaceae
DECIDUOUS AND EVERGREEN SHRUBS AND VINES

🌱 ALL ZONES, EXCEPT AS NOTED

☼ ☼ FULL SUN OR LIGHT SHADE

💧 REGULAR WATER, EXCEPT AS NOTED

The rose is the queen of flowers, the most loved and widely planted shrub in all temperate parts of the world. More than 14,000 varieties are grown. Although mostly deciduous, roses can be evergreen in mild climates. Their stems, sometimes quite prickly, may be erect, arching, trailing, or scrambling. Leaves are divided into three, five, or seven leaflets, usually with toothed margins.

Roses are prized for their lovely, often scented flowers. Many types carry their blossoms in clusters, but some (notably hybrid teas) tend to bear their flowers singly, one bud per stem. Some blooms are flattish rosettes; others are cupped; hybrid tea roses have a conical shape, with high, pointed centers. The blossoms range from single (4–8 petals) to semidouble (9–16 petals), double (17–25 petals), full (26–40 petals), and very full (to 150 petals or more). Thanks to the hybridizing efforts of breeders and enthusiastic gardeners over many centuries, roses are now available in all colors except blue and black. Many are blends—different shades of a single color or more than one color.

Rose bushes are natural choices for flower beds and shrub borders; some also make fine hedges or container plants. The largest are the old garden roses, grandifloras, and shrub roses. Hybrid teas and floribundas generally grow with more restraint. Miniature roses are the smallest; some reach only 1 ft.

tall. For a little formality, consider a standard rose, a bush rose grown on a tall, bare stem; a patio rose is a small standard.

Ground cover roses make a low, mounding carpet of color up to 8 ft. wide. They are most often massed on a slope or an area of the garden where other knee-high shrubs might be used. They also make good container plants.

Climbing roses grow on vertical surfaces or freestanding supports. The most vigorous ones will cover a house roof or grow to the top of a large tree. More moderate climbers clothe arbors and tall walls. Small climbers, sometimes called pillar roses, are suitable for a pyramid or trellis. In addition to the roses that are classified as climbers, there are old garden roses and shrub roses that climb, as well as climbing miniature roses.

CONSIDERING CLIMATE

The most reliable way to find roses that grow well in your climate is to visit municipal or private rose gardens in your region. Varieties that are performing well there are obviously good choices—and you'll see how big they grow. Climate affects the size of many roses; for example, 'Sally Holmes' in Seattle might be a 5-ft.-tall bush, but in Southern California it can be a huge rambler, with canes to 35 ft. long. David Austin roses grow with admirable reserve in England and similarly cool climates in the West, but in the warmest zones, they can grow much taller.

In mild-winter regions, some roses adapted to very cold climates produce few flowers. In areas with cool summers, roses with a large number of petals tend to "ball," opening poorly or not at all. In the absence of heat, dark-colored flowers may appear muddy rather than vibrant. Also, because the overcast skies and fog common in cool-summer zones encourage foliar diseases such as mildew, rust, and black spot, varieties noted for their disease resistance grow and bloom better there.

In hot-summer areas, flowers open rapidly. Varieties with few petals (under 30) may go from bud to fully open blossom in just a few hours on a hot day. Those with more petals take longer to open and stay attractive longer. Some colors (the golden yellow in 'Peace', for example) may fade almost to white in very hot weather, and dark reds may sunburn. During intensely hot weather, plants may

R

almost go dormant, causing flower production to drop markedly. (To avoid these problems, plant roses where they will receive afternoon shade, and away from reflected heat from light-colored surfaces.) Best flowering in hot-summer areas is in spring and fall.

If you live in a cold-winter area, choose roses that are sufficiently cold hardy for your region, or check out how to protect less hardy varieties in winter (see "Providing Winter Protection," page 596). In Zones 1–3, hybrid teas, grandifloras, and floribundas need protection. However, the hardy hybrids (bred primarily in Canada and Iowa) can go through winter with little or no special protection. Many old roses (chiefly those that flower only in spring), as well as a number of species roses and their hybrids, also survive in Zones 1–3 with scant or no winter protection. In Alaska, the native Nootka rose is hardy enough to need no protection, as are some of the other extra-hardy species roses and their hybrids, such as the wonderfully fragrant rugosas *(R. rugosa).*

As you research your selections, you can check the American Rose Society (ARS) rose ratings, available in the ARS's *Handbook for Selecting Roses,* sent free to members. (See *www.ars.org* for more information.) The ratings are numeric assessments of each rose from 1 to 10 based on a national average of scores for that plant. The higher the number, the better the rose. But a rating does not tell the entire story: a rose with a low rating may fail in some regions but flourish in others.

BUYING PLANTS
Mail-order catalogs and/or Web sites offer the widest choice of roses; they are practically the only way to shop if you are looking for lesser-known varieties. You'll also find roses for sale in local nurseries and garden centers, home improvement and hardware stores, and even some supermarkets.

Container-grown roses. Plants in plastic or pressed-peat pots are available from retail stores from early spring through fall, year-round in mild-climate regions. The best time to shop is in mid- to late spring, when the plants are in bloom, the largest selection is available, and you have a chance to plant out your purchases before summer heat arrives. You can,

---

What Roses Need

LOCATION Choose a spot in full sun (light afternoon shade in hottest regions). An open area with good air circulation helps discourage foliage diseases. Don't plant where the roots of trees or other shrubs will compete with rose roots.

DRAINAGE Roses need reasonably well drained soil.

WATERING Regular water is essential for strong plants and lots of flowers. Mulch beneath plants to help conserve moisture.

FERTILIZING Repeat-flowering roses need repeated applications of fertilizer throughout the growing season. Roses that bloom only in spring need an application as growth begins and a second one after they have bloomed.

PRUNING Pruning makes all roses more productive and attractive. Thin out dead, weak, and old growth. Then reduce the size of the plant according to the type of the rose.

PEST AND DISEASE CONTROL Check roses regularly; it may be necessary to thwart various troublemakers at some point, but early attention and preventive care are particularly effective.

Hybrid tea rose 'Double Delight'

---

however, plant container-grown roses at any time during the growing season (see "Planting").

Choose plants with strong new growth and healthy-looking leaves. A large (preferably 5-gal.) container is better than a small one; it's less likely that the roots had to be cut back severely to fit in the container when the plant was potted. Avoid plants with roots protruding from the bottom of the container, as well as those showing weak growth or blackened areas of dieback on the canes. These are all signs that the plant has been in the container too long and may not establish well in your garden.

Bare-root roses. During late winter and early spring, nurseries and stores may also offer bare-root

---

roses; these are dormant plants with no soil on the roots. If you shop from mail-order nurseries, typically you'll receive bare-root plants, and the shipping may begin in fall. It doesn't harm the roses to be dug up and transported bare root, and although you can't see your roses in flower, bare-root plants have advantages over plants sold in containers: they are generally less expensive, and they may establish vigorous roots faster.

Bare-root plants are graded 1, 1½, or 2, number 1 being the best. Suppliers usually offer only grade 1 plants, and they will often replace plants that fail to grow. A healthy bare-root rose has thick, green canes and a big cluster of sturdy, fibrous roots. Reject any with dried-out or squishy roots or with canes that are weak, shriveled, or beginning to leaf out.

Be cautious about buying packaged bare-root roses that are displayed indoors on retail store shelves; the roots are wrapped in a moist material, but the indoor heating may cause the material to dry out. Buy these roses as soon as they appear for sale, rather than when they are marked down as bargains.

In milder-winter zones, you can plant bare-root roses throughout winter. In areas where the ground freezes, plant either in fall before the soil freezes (then protect plants over winter) or in early spring after the soil has thawed.

Budded or own-root roses. Many old roses, species roses and their hybrids, and virtually all miniature roses are propagated by cuttings and grown on their own roots. Most modern roses are budded onto a standard understock, a completely different rose variety whose root system thrives in a wide range of soils and climates. There is a current trend, however, to try new varieties on their own roots and grow them that way when successful.

Both budded and own-root roses grow well and produce fine flowers. Budded plants are often larger at the time of purchase than own-root plants, but both kinds will be equally husky within a year or two. Own-root roses do have

---

one advantage: if the plant is killed to the ground by cold (or mowed down by accident), it will regrow from the roots as the rose you want. Regrowth from roots of a budded plant, in contrast, will be from the understock rose.

CHOOSING A PLANTING SITE
Choose a planting place where your rose will receive at least 6 hours of sunshine daily. If your weather is consistently cool or overcast, choose a location that's open all day to any sun that might appear. If summer heat is intense, find a spot that receives filtered sunlight during the hottest afternoon hours.

Soil for roses should drain reasonably well; if the soil in your chosen spot does not, the best alternative is to plant in raised beds. Don't locate roses too close to trees or large shrubs; their roots will steal the water and nutrients intended for your roses. Choose a spot where there is good air circulation, but avoid windy locations. High winds can wreck the flowers and increase transpiration from the leaves, making frequent watering necessary.

PLANTING
In preparation for planting, the first step is to decide on the spacing between plants. Generous spacing between plants aids air circulation, which reduces the incidence of mildew, black spot, and other foliage diseases. Exactly how far apart to plant depends on the growth habit of the roses and on your climate. The colder the winter and the shorter the growing season, the smaller the bushes will be; where the growing season is long and winters are mild, bushes can attain greater size. But some varieties are naturally small, others tall and massive—and those relative size differences will hold in any climate. In the coldest zones, you might plant the most vigorous roses 3 ft. apart; in milder climates, space vigorous sorts 6 or even 8 ft. apart.

The next step is to prepare the soil. Dig it deeply, incorporating organic matter such as ground bark, peat moss, or compost to help aerate dense clay soils and improve moisture retention in sandy soils. Add a complete fertilizer to the soil and dig supplemental phosphorus and potassium into the planting holes. If you are planting new roses in a spot where existing bushes have been growing for 5 or more years, be sure to add plenty of rich organic material, as the soil is most likely quite spent.

Plant roses from containers according to the directions found on page 715 under "Planting from a Container." If your rose is in a pressed-peat pot, see the information on "Removing Plants from Containers," page 713; you can plant your rose in its peat pot if you follow the directions found there, although some gardeners prefer to remove the pot.

Healthy, ready-to-plant bare-root roses should have plump, fresh-looking canes and roots. Before planting, immerse the entire plant in water for up to 2 days to be certain all canes and roots are plumped up. Plant bare-root roses according to the directions on page 714. After planting, some gardeners mound mulch over the bud union (the knob from which the canes grow) and around the canes to conserve moisture, then gradually (and carefully) remove the mulch when the leaves begin to expand.

If you are planting a budded plant (whether container grown or bare root), set the plant in the hole so that the bud union is just above soil level. In Zones A1–A3 and 1–3, some gardeners set the bud union 1–2 in. beneath the soil surface for increased protection from cold, but since this usually results in the production of fewer canes, many gardeners in these cold-winter zones keep to the standard guideline (bud union just above soil level) and give their roses plenty of winter protection.

WATERING AND MULCHING
With the exception of some old garden roses and species roses that thrive on little water once they are established, roses need watering at all times during the growing season. Inadequate water slows or halts growth and bloom.

Water deeply enough to moisten the entire root system (16–18 in. deep). How often you need to water depends on soil type and weather. Big, well-established plants need more water than newly set plants, but you will need to water new plants more frequently until they are established.

Various irrigation options are available. Basin flooding is a simple way to water individual rose plants. If you have a drip irrigation system, you will be able to water many plants at one time. Overhead sprinkling freshens foliage and helps remove dust; it can also

wash away aphids, spider mites, and the spores of powdery mildew and other fungal leaf diseases. On the other hand, overhead sprinkling washes off sprays that were applied to control pests and diseases, and it may leave mineral deposits on foliage if water is hard. If you use an overhead sprinkler, do it early in the day to allow foliage time to dry off during daylight hours; leaves that stay wet for several hours are more likely to develop powdery mildew and other foliage diseases. Even if you irrigate in basins, give plants an occasional morning shower to clean dust off the foliage (if rains don't do it for you).

Each spring, spread a 2–3-in.-thick layer of fresh mulch around your roses. Mulching conserves moisture and deters weed growth. It also helps keep soil cool—a benefit in all but the coolest-summer climates.

FEEDING
Though roses have a reputation for being heavy feeders, their nutrient needs vary depending on rose type and your soil's natural fertility. Many old roses, shrub roses, and species roses do not need regular fertilizer if growth is satisfactory. But for many repeat-flowering modern roses, regular fertilizing is needed to produce the most gratifying results.

In the mildest-winter climates (Zones 8, 9, 12–24; H1, H2), give established roses their initial feeding with a complete fertilizer in February; elsewhere, give the first feeding just as growth begins. Thereafter, time fertilizer applications to bloom periods. For roses that flower repeatedly throughout the growing season, fertilize after each blooming cycle has ended, when new growth is just beginning. For roses that bloom only in spring, one additional feeding just after flowering ends will encourage vigorous new growth and plenty of blooms next year.

Where winters are cold, stop feeding in late summer or fall, at least 6 weeks before the first expected hard frost. In mild-winter zones experiencing virtually no subfreezing weather, you may continue fertilizing until mid-October for a crop of late-fall flowers.

Dry fertilizer, applied to the soil, is most frequently used. A variation on this type is controlled-release fertilizer; follow directions on the package for the amount and frequency of applications. Liquid

fertilizers are useful in smaller gardens using basin watering. Most liquid types can also be sprayed on rose leaves, which absorb some nutrients immediately. If you are looking for an organic fertilizer for roses, try dehydrated alfalfa; it smells better than fish emulsion.

CONTROLLING PESTS AND DISEASES
Although some roses are especially susceptible to pests and diseases, most of these plants thrive with just a little preventive care. Well-tended, healthy roses are less likely to fall prey to pest infestations or diseases. To reduce the risk of trouble, choose roses that are suitable for your climate and are notably disease resistant (breeders have come a long way in producing roses that resist black spot, powdery mildew, and rust); prepare the soil well; feed and water diligently (being careful about the timing of overhead watering); and prune to ensure good air circulation around the leaves.

Start each year with a garden cleanup, removing prunings, leaves, and old mulch, which may harbor overwintering insect eggs and disease spores. Then, if you have reason to think you need it,

Tom Carruth on Fragrant Roses

Ever wondered why so many modern roses, though gorgeous and highly resistant to disease, are completely scentless? The answer, in a word, is heredity.

Tom Carruth, famed rose hybridizer with Weeks Roses in Upland, CA, explains: "Fragrance in roses is a recessive trait, and often comes with a susceptibility to diseases such as powdery mildew and black spot."

It hasn't been easy, but hybridizers have developed several lovely varieties that combine the practical virtues of modern roses with the perfume associated with old roses. Carruth's favorites include 'Memorial Day', a hybrid tea with a strong classic damask rose scent; 'Scentimental', a floribunda with a strong sweet and spicy scent; 'Secret', a hybrid tea with a spicy-sweet fragrance; and 'Yves Piaget', a hybrid tea with an alluring old-fashioned damask scent.

spray the plants and the soil to kill any remaining insect eggs and disease spores. Do this before the plants leaf out, and use a natural product such as dormant-season horticultural oil or lime sulfur.

Allies in the battle against rose pests include ladybugs, lacewings, beetles, flies, spiders, birds, and wasps. You can buy predators such as ladybugs at nurseries and release them in your garden; encourage them to stay awhile by setting out plants that attract them, such as dill, fennel, and yarrow. Avoid using broad-spectrum pesticides, which kill beneficial insects along with pests.

Watchfulness is an excellent strategy for maintaining healthy roses. A very effective way to keep pests from building up large, damaging populations is to pick off the early visitors and drop them in a bucket of soapy water. Or blast the tiny ones from your roses with a jet of water. For more information about pest management and advice on controlling aphids, spider mites, and thrips, see pages 704–710.

Rose midges are a problem in coastal Northern California and the coastal Northwest. The almost microscopic adults lay eggs in the growing tips of rose stems; when the larvae hatch, they bore into the developing rose buds, deforming the buds and leaving blackened, withered tips. The larvae then fall to the ground and pupate, perpetuating the cycle. Snip off and bag any affected shoots as soon as you notice them, and clear and dispose of all leaf litter, weeds, and debris. Try laying black plastic under the plants so the larvae cannot pupate. Lose no time contacting a good local nursery for advice on the best treatments if the damage continues; repeated soil drenches or foliar applications of systemic insecticides may be the only viable options.

Rose slugs—insect larvae that chomp and tatter rose leaves—have been a huge problem in recent years in coastal California. The most effective treatment is Spinosad, a pesticide derived from a soil bacterium. It does not harm most beneficial insects.

Powdery mildew, rust, and black spot are the most likely diseases to appear on your roses at some point. At the first sign of disease, remove affected leaves and debris. Don't wait until the damage is substantial before you spray. For more information on disease

R

management strategies and advice on controlling powdery mildew and rust, see pages 686–688.

Black spot is most troublesome in warm summer weather when there is humidity or rainfall to sustain and spread it. For a nontoxic control, apply a spray made from 2 tsp. of baking soda and 2 tsp. of fine-grade horticultural oil dissolved in 1 gal. of water. In years with wet springs, anticipate downy mildew; some gardeners spray a fungicide preventively in a wet spring to prevent defoliation.

For local help with pests and diseases, consider joining the American Rose Society. Its consulting rosarians advise member gardeners on rose problems at no cost.

PRUNING

Annual pruning contributes to the health, productivity, and longevity of roses. The basic objective is to promote strong growth that will bear good flowers. If left unpruned, a rose can expend its energy making spindly, twiggy growth that produces only substandard flowers.

Because nutrients are stored in the canes, prune conservatively: never chop down a vigorous 6-ft. bush to 1½-ft. stubs unless you want only a few huge blooms for exhibition. (However, in Zones A1–A3 and 1–3, where roses freeze back to their winter protection, you will remove dead wood in spring and may be left with the equivalent of a severely pruned plant.)

The best pruning time for most roses is at the end of the dormant season, when growth buds begin to swell. The exact time varies according to locality but is usually sometime between January (in mild climates) and April (in colder ones). Where late frosts are common, be sure not to prune too early—the resulting new growth will be vulnerable to freezes.

General pruning guidelines. The following pruning recommendations apply to roses in general; the sections that follow offer more specific advice on pruning the various types of roses.

Use sharp pruning shears; make all cuts as described in "Making Pruning Cuts," page 723. Remove wood that is obviously dead, wood that has no healthy growth coming from it, branches that cross through the plant's center or rub against larger canes, branches that make a bush appear lopsided, as well as any unproductive old canes that strong new ones have replaced

during the past season. Removing any foliage that remains on the plant will reduce the incidence of disease later.

Cut back the previous season's growth by one-third to one-half, making cuts above outward-facing buds (except for very spreading varieties, in which some cuts to inside buds will promote more height without producing many crossing branches). The ideal result is a V-shaped bush with a relatively open center.

If any suckers (growth produced from the understock of a budded plant) are present, completely remove them. Dig down to where the suckers grow from the understock and pull them off with a downward motion; this removes growth buds that would otherwise produce additional suckers in subsequent years. Let the wound air-dry before you replace soil around it.

Be certain you are removing a sucker rather than a new cane growing from the bud union. Suckers usually are easy to distinguish from desired canes; differences can be seen in foliage size, shape, and color, as well as in size of thorns. If in doubt, let the presumed sucker grow until you can establish its difference from a cane; its flowers will be noticeably different. A flowerless, climbing cane from a bush rose is almost certainly a sucker.

Consider cutting flowers as a form of pruning. Cut off enough stem to support the flower in a vase, but don't deprive the plant of too much foliage. Always leave a stem with at least two sets of five-leaflet leaves. Make your cut just above an outward-growing bud or a five-leaflet leaf.

Pruning hybrid teas and grandifloras. The most widely planted modern roses—hybrid teas and grandifloras—can be pruned successfully according to the guidelines above.

Pruning floribunda, polyantha, and many shrub roses. These

Shrub rose 'Bonica'

types are grown for the amount of bloom they produce rather than the quality of individual flowers. Follow the general pruning guidelines, but cut back the previous season's growth by only one-fourth, and leave as many strong new canes and stems as the plant produced. On polyanthas and floribundas, remove only one-quarter to one-half of the previous year's foliage. If you have a hedge of one variety, cut back all the plants to uniform height.

Pruning old garden roses and species roses. Most of these need only a light annual pruning—provided you've allowed these typically vigorous roses sufficient space. Remove any dead or weak canes, then prune just the tip of each remaining cane. If the center of the plant is dense and overcrowded, completely remove a few old, woody canes. The roses in this group that produce long, arching canes (many of the hybrid perpetuals, for example) can be pruned the same way as climbers.

Prune old garden and species roses that bloom only once, in spring, after they have flowered. Prune the repeat-blooming types at the end of the dormant season.

Pruning climbing roses. All climbers should be left unpruned for the first 2 or 3 years after planting, but do train the canes, even in the first season. Spread them so they are as horizontal as possible, which will stimulate the production of flowering branches.

Prune climbing roses that bloom only in spring just after they finish flowering, removing old canes that show no signs of strong new growth. For climbers that bloom off and on in other seasons as well as in spring, prune at the same time you'd prune bush roses in your locality. Remove the oldest unproductive canes and any weak, twiggy growth; cut back the lateral branches on the remaining canes to two or three buds.

Pillar roses are not quite bush roses or climbers. They produce tall, somewhat flexible canes that

bloom profusely without having to be trained horizontally. Prune them according to the general pruning guidelines given at the beginning of the "Pruning" section.

Pruning ground-cover roses. Cut back the stems of low-growers such as the Flower Carpet series by about a third. To develop a more prostrate form, cut vertical stems back to the plant's main stem.

Pruning standard roses. Standards, often called tree roses, are an artificial creation: a rose budded onto a tall, bare understock stem. Follow the pruning guidelines for the rose type that forms the head; pay particular attention to maintaining a symmetrical plant, pruning harder on its weak side. Several heights are available. Climbers are often used for 5-ft. standards and allowed to cascade; prune these very lightly (removing only dead wood and spindly stems) for the first couple of years to allow them to develop their form. The 3-ft. standards are generally grandifloras, hybrid teas, or floribundas. Shrub roses, ground cover roses, and large miniatures are usually used for 2-ft. standards. Miniatures are used for 1½ -ft. standards.

Pruning miniature roses. Follow the general pruning guidelines, but cut back the height attained during the previous year by at least half; remove all weak and twiggy stems.

PROVIDING WINTER PROTECTION

Where winter temperatures regularly drop to 10°F/–12°C or lower, roses that are somewhat tender, such as many hybrid teas, floribundas, and grandifloras, need protection against cold. Low temperatures can kill exposed canes; repeated freezing and thawing will kill canes by rupturing their cells; and winter winds can desiccate exposed canes.

A healthy plant that is hardened off before the first hard frost withstands harsh winters better than a weak or actively growing one. Prepare plants for winter by timing your last fertilizer application of the growing season so that bushes will have stopped putting on new growth by the expected date of the first sharp frost. Leave the last crop of blooms on your plants to form hips (fruits), which will aid the ripening process by stopping growth. Keep plants well watered until the soil freezes.

After a couple of hard freezes have occurred and nighttime temperatures remain consistently below freezing, mound soil over the base of each bush to a height of 1 ft. Collect the soil from another part of garden; do not scoop soil from around the roses, exposing their surface roots. Cut excessively long canes back to 2–4 ft. (the lower figure applies in Zones A1–A3 and 1, 2, and 3a). Then use soft twine to tie the canes together and keep them from whipping around in wind.

When the mound has frozen, cover it with evergreen boughs, straw, or other fairly lightweight material that will act as insulation and keep the mound frozen. A 3–4-ft.-high wire-mesh cylinder filled with noncompacting insulating material (such as straw, hay, oak leaves, or pine needles) may preserve much of the cane growth it encloses.

Remove the protection in spring after frost danger is past. Gradually remove the soil mounds as they thaw, working carefully to avoid breaking new growth that may have begun sprouting under the soil.

Protecting climbers. Mound climbing roses in the same manner, but be sure to protect all of their canes. Where winter lows range from –10 to 5°F/–23 to –15°C, insulate the canes by wrapping them in burlap stuffed with straw or a similar material. Where temperatures normally go below –10°F/–23°C, remove canes from their support, gently bend them to ground, and cover them with soil. (A wiser plan, however, is to plant only climbers known to be hardy in such climates.)

Protecting standards. Standards (tree roses) may be insulated in the same manner as climbers, but they still may not survive,

Modern climbing rose 'Blaze'

since the head of the tree is the most exposed. Some gardeners dig up their standards each year, pack the roots loosely in soil or another medium, and store the plants in a cool garage, basement, or shed until replanting time in spring. A simpler technique is to grow standards in large containers and move them in fall to a cool shed or garage where temperatures won't drop below 10°F/–12°C.

Protection in Alaska. If you are growing roses in Alaska, you'll probably agree with the rosarian in Anchorage who told us, "Roses aren't hard to grow in Alaska, just tough to keep." To overwinter tender hybrid roses, dig a trench 2 ft. deep beside the house and bury your roses in it, removing any remaining foliage first. Dig them up for replanting in mid-May. Simply mounding soil over cut-back bushes isn't enough protection.

If the roses are in pots, you can move them to a basement wall under a deck for winter and toss wood shavings over them; or take the pots into a sunroom. Some gardeners inter their roses—they dig a trench in the garden, slip in a bottomless wood box made to fit the trench, put the roses in the box, and cover them with builder's sand.

MODERN ROSES

Most of the thousands of roses for sale are modern roses—ones introduced after 1867, the year the first hybrid tea rose was developed. For more than 100 years after that, breeders raced to produce the most perfect hybrid teas, grandifloras, and floribundas, the flowering "modern" rose bushes that were, and largely still are, the mainstay of public and residential rose gardens. However, in the past few years, landscape roses, particularly the lax and leafy shrub roses, have become almost as popular.

The chart on page 598 presents a list of excellent modern roses grouped by type and color. Refer to the information below to learn about the ancestry and growing characteristics of the different types of modern roses.

Shrub roses. Planting roses for general landscape use is not a new idea; some fine shrub roses date to the early 20th century. Today, however, rose breeders are developing new roses for use purely as flowering shrubs. The emphasis is on plants that bloom prolifically over a long season and have abundant

disease-resistant foliage; some breeders are also developing plants that can survive cold winters with no special attention. Modern shrub roses need little or no pruning to remain shapely. Because they bloom almost continuously, they make excellent partners for perennials and other shrubs in borders.

These shrub roses vary widely in growth habit and flower color; loose categories are listed below. Some shrub roses make tidy small climbers. For more shrub rose choices, check the section on species roses on page 601.

Hybrid musk shrub roses. These were developed in the first 30 years of the 20th century from a descendant of the musk rose (*R. moschata*). Hybrid musks are large (6–8-ft.-tall) shrubs or small climbers that perform well in dappled or partial shade as well as in sun. Most are nearly everblooming, with fragrant, clustered flowers. Like the hardy shrub roses, hybrid musks tend not to flower prolifically in mild climates.

Modern climbing rose 'Golden Showers'

Hardy shrub roses. Canadian and Midwestern breeding programs have produced rose bushes that survive northern and Rocky Mountain winters with virtually no special protection against cold. Some resemble floribundas and grandifloras; their ancestries include hardy species roses as well as floribundas and hybrid tea roses. These have "country" names like 'Country Dancer' and 'Prairie Princess'. Others are mostly large shrubs to small climbers, bred in part from *R. rugosa*. Many of these are named for explorers: 'John Cabot' and 'William Baffin' among them.

Miscellaneous shrub roses. Many modern shrub roses are of complex or unknown ancestry and fall outside the categories listed above. Among these miscellaneous shrub roses are several very well known

ones, such as 'All That Jazz', 'Knock Out', and 'Sally Holmes'.

Trademarked roses. Recognizing public loyalty to brand-name products, some rose breeders have created trademarked "families" to which new varieties can be added over time.

The David Austin English roses were the first in this category to attract significant interest. Developed from crosses of various old roses (albas, centifolias, gallicas) with modern roses, they capture the lovely old rose forms and fragrances, but they are repeat flowering and come in a range of colors found only in today's hybrid tea roses. These roses range from low shrubs to plants determined to be climbers regardless of pruning. Many have Chaucerian or Shakespearean names, though the three most popular—'Abraham Darby', 'Graham Thomas', and 'Mary Rose'—commemorate, respectively, an English industrialist, a noted English horticulturist, and the flagship of Henry VIII's fleet.

In France, the house of Meilland has produced the Romantica roses, most of which are named for well-known figures in European arts and letters (such as 'Yves Piaget'); the color range is contemporary, but the full-petaled flowers recall the early hybrid teas and hybrid perpetuals. The trademarked Meidiland family of roses (including 'Pink Meidiland' and 'White Meidiland') from Meilland are mostly somewhat billowy shrubs.

Another French firm, Guillot (famous for originating the first hybrid tea rose), offers Generosa roses; these are more nearly equivalent to the English roses in variability and old rose style. 'Martine Guillot', with cupped, creamy white blooms blushed with peach, is an example.

The Renaissance roses, developed by the Danish house of Poulsen, are akin to floribundas, with an emphasis on vigor, disease resistance, abundance of bloom, and modern flower form.

Flower Carpet is a family of ground cover roses bred by noted German rosarian Werner Noack for easy care and a long season of prolific bloom.

Ground cover roses. These are low-growing plants, around 2 or 2½ ft. tall, that spread to at least 3½ ft. wide (some reach 6 ft. or wider). Vigor, disease resistance, and a profusion of bloom from

R

MODERN ROSES

The following roses are among the best choices for Western gardens. The designation *WRHF* indicates membership in the World Rose Hall of Fame, *AARS* identifies winners of the All-America Rose Selections award, and *f* indicates roses with dependably powerful fragrance.

SHRUBS

The designation *DA* indicates David Austin roses, *h* hardy shrub roses, and *m* hybrid musk roses.

Red: Alexander Mackenzie *(h)*, Henry Kelsey *(h)*, Home Run, Knock Out *(AARS)*, Red Meidiland, Will Scarlet *(m)*, William Shakespeare 2000 *(DA)*

Pink: All That Jazz *(AARS)*, Aunt Honey *(h)*, Ballerina *(h)*, Bonica *(WRHF) (AARS)*, Carefree Delight *(AARS)*, Carefree Wonder *(AARS)*, Cornelia *(m)*, Country Dancer *(h)*, Erfurt *(f)*, Felicia *(m) (f)*, First Light *(AARS)*, Gertrude Jekyll *(DA) (f)*, Heritage *(DA) (f)*, John Cabot *(h)*, Kathleen *(m)*, Mary Rose *(DA)*, Maytime *(h)*, Penelope *(m)*, Pink Meidiland, William Baffin *(h)*

Orange/warm blend: Abraham Darby *(DA)*, Alchymist *(f)*, Buff Beauty *(m)*, Kaleidoscope, Paul Bocuse, Prairie Princess *(h)*, Westerland

Yellow: Autumn Sunset *(f)*, Baby Love, Golden Celebration *(f)*, Graham Thomas *(DA)*, Molineux *(DA) (f)*, Yellow Jacket

White: Hawkeye Belle *(h)*, Pearl Drift, Sally Holmes, Sea Foam, Starry Night *(AARS)*, White Meidiland (Super Swany)

Lavender/mauve: Outta the Blue

GROUND COVERS

Red: Fire Meidiland, Red Flower Carpet, Ruby Meidiland, Scarlet Flower Carpet

Pink: Appleblossom Flower Carpet, Coral Flower Carpet, Pink Flower Carpet

Yellow: Yellow Flower Carpet

White: White Flower Carpet, White Meidiland (Super Swany)

CLIMBERS

Red: Altissimo, Blaze, Cl. Étoile de Hollande *(f)*, Don Juan *(f)*, Dortmund, Dublin Bay, Fourth of July *(AARS)*

Pink: Cl. Cécile Brünner, Cl. First Prize, Cl. Queen Elizabeth, Eden (Pierre de Ronsard) *(WRHF)*, Jeanne Lajoie (miniature), New Dawn *(WRHF)*, Nozomi, Pearly Gates

Orange/warm blend: America *(AARS) (f)*, Cl. Earthquake (miniature), Cl. Peace, Cl. Rainbow's End (miniature), Handel, Joseph's Coat, Polka *(f)*, Royal Sunset *(f)*

Yellow: Garden Sun, Golden Showers *(AARS)*, Royal Gold

White: Cl. Iceberg, Lace Cascade, White Dawn *(f)*

HYBRID TEAS

Red: Firefighter *(f)*, Ingrid Bergman *(WRHF)*, Mister Lincoln *(AARS) (f)*, Olympiad *(AARS)*, Opening Night *(AARS)*, Veterans' Honor

Pink: Bewitched *(AARS)*, Bride's Dream, Brigadoon *(AARS)*, Color Magic *(AARS)*, Dainty Bess, First Prize *(AARS)*, Gemini *(AARS)*, Memorial Day *(AARS) (f)*, Miss All-American Beauty *(AARS)*, New Zealand *(f)*, Royal Highness *(AARS)*, Secret *(AARS) (f)*, Sheer Bliss *(AARS)*, Tiffany *(AARS) (f)*, Timeless *(AARS)*, Touch of Class *(AARS)*, Yves Piaget *(f)*

Orange/warm blend: Abbaye de Cluny, Artistry *(AARS)*, Brandy *(AARS)*, Cary Grant, Chicago Peace, Double Delight *(WRHF) (AARS) (f)*, Folklore *(f)*, Fragrant Cloud *(WRHF) (f)*, Just Joey *(WRHF) (f)*, Medallion *(AARS)*, Perfect Moment *(AARS)*, Remember Me, Rio Samba *(AARS)*, Sunset Celebration *(AARS)*, Tropicana *(AARS)*, Voodoo *(AARS)*

Yellow: Elina, Mellow Yellow, Midas Touch *(AARS)*, Peace *(WRHF) (AARS)*, St. Patrick *(AARS)*

White: Full Sail, Garden Party *(AARS)*, Honor *(AARS)*, Moonstone, Pascali *(WRHF) (AARS)*, Pristine, Whisper *(AARS)*

Lavender/mauve: Barbra Streisand *(f)*, Fragrant Plum *(f)*, Neptune *(f)*, Paradise *(AARS)*, Stainless Steel *(f)*

GRANDIFLORAS

Red: Crimson Bouquet *(AARS)*, Love *(AARS)*

Pink: Earth Song, Fame! *(AARS)*, Pink Parfait *(AARS)*, Queen Elizabeth *(WRHF) (AARS)*, Tournament of Roses *(AARS)*

Orange/warm blend: Candelabra *(AARS)*, Caribbean *(AARS)*, Glowing Peace *(AARS)*, Octoberfest

Yellow: Gold Medal

White: White Lightnin' *(AARS) (f)*

Lavender/mauve: Lagerfeld *(f)*, Melodie Parfumée

FLORIBUNDAS

Red: Europeana *(AARS)*, Scentimental *(AARS) (f)*, Showbiz *(AARS)*

Pink: Betty Prior, Brilliant Pink Iceberg, Sexy Rexy, Simplicity

Orange/warm blend: Amber Queen *(AARS)*, Betty Boop *(AARS)*, Brass Band *(AARS)*, Day Breaker *(AARS)*, Gingersnap, Livin' Easy *(AARS)*, Marmalade Skies *(AARS)*, Playboy, Singin' in the Rain *(AARS)*

Yellow: Easy Going, Julia Child *(AARS)*, Sun Flare *(AARS)*, Sunsprite *(f)*

White: French Lace *(AARS)*, Iceberg *(WRHF)*, Margaret Merrill *(f)*

Lavender/mauve: Angel Face *(AARS) (f)*, Blueberry Hill, Ebb Tide *(f)*, Intrigue *(AARS) (f)*

POLYANTHAS

Pink: Cécile Brünner *(WRHF)*, China Doll, The Fairy

Orange/warm blend: Margo Koster, Perle d'Or (Yellow Cécile Brünner)

MINIATURES

Red: Little Artist, Robin Red Breast, Starina

Pink: Baby Grand, Giggles, Minnie Pearl, Pierrine

Orange/warm blend: Jean Kenneally, Magic Carrousel, Millie Walters, Party Girl, Rainbow's End

Yellow: Minilights, My Sunshine, Rise 'n' Shine (Golden Sunblaze), Sun Sprinkles *(AARS)*

White: Gourmet Popcorn, Irresistible, Simplex, Snow Bride

Lavender/mauve: Ruby Pendant, Winsome

R

late spring until frost are the hallmarks of this category. Ground cover roses are perfect for covering slopes, creating low barriers to foot traffic on level ground, and growing in containers.

The most commonly available ground cover roses are those in the Flower Carpet series, available in red, scarlet, pink, apple blossom, coral, yellow, and white. Several of the trademarked Meidiland roses, such as 'White Meidiland', are sufficiently low growing to be used as ground covers. 'Sea Foam', a shrub rose, makes a fine ground cover about 3 ft. tall and 6 ft. wide, and some miniature roses have a pretty, sprawling habit. Several of the species roses and some of the climbing roses make good ground covers as well.

Climbing roses. These are simply rose bushes that produce long, strong canes that will grow upright against a wall or arbor. They do not climb by twining or attachment but must be trained through or tied to their support. There are two types of modern climbing roses: large-flowered climbers (LCLs) and climbing sports of bush roses, such as 'Cl. Iceberg' and 'Cl. Cécile Brünner'. The large-flowered climbers generally produce the most blooms, but the climbing sports have the exquisite flowers of their famous parents.

Left to their own devices, many climbers make attractive arching shrubs or even ground covers. For more climbers, including some very large ones, see the species roses section on page 601.

Hybrid tea roses. These are the classic, aristocratic roses, with long, stylish pointed buds that spiral open to large blossoms with high centers. Typically, hybrid teas carry one blossom at the end of each flowering stem. They bloom profusely in spring, then continue

Hybrid tea rose
'Mister Lincoln'

to produce blossoms—either in flushes or continuously—until frosty weather. Their strong, long stems make them ideal for cutting and bringing indoors.

Hybrid tea bushes tend to have an upright, narrow, almost stiff look. They grow 2–6 ft. tall, depending on variety and climate. Group three or more together to create a generous, bushy look. Consider planting low-growing perennials beneath them or a low hedge in front of them to hide their bare ankles (bases of canes are usually sparsely foliaged). Hybrid teas need good growing conditions and more care than some other types, but for many gardeners, their spectacular blooms are worth the extra effort.

Grandiflora rose
'Queen Elizabeth'

Grandiflora, floribunda, and polyantha roses. These are the workhorses of rose gardens, noted for producing large quantities of flowers all summer long. Many have hybrid tea ancestry, evident in the long stems and/or elegant shape of the flowers. Unlike hybrid teas, however, they produce clusters of blossoms rather than a single flower at the end of each stem; this makes them excellent for providing masses of color.

Grandifloras are taller than hybrid teas, sometimes reaching 8–10 ft. tall, so place them at the back of a flower bed; they also make useful barrier plants. Floribundas are smaller than hybrid

Grandiflora rose 'Gold Medal'

Polyantha rose
'Margo Koster'

teas—both in flower size and in height; use them for informal hedges, for low flower borders, or as container plants. 'Iceberg', one of the best-selling roses ever, is a floribunda.

Polyanthas produce small blossoms in large sprays; they are compact bushes, generally not much more than 2 ft. tall. The first polyanthas appeared in the late 19th century. Two of the early polyanthas are now classics: 'Cécile Brünner' (often called Sweetheart Rose) has light pink flowers of perfect hybrid tea form; and 'Perle d'Or' (sometimes called 'Yellow Cécile Brünner') is similar but has pinkish apricot flowers.

Miniature roses. These are perfect replicas of hybrid teas and floribundas, but plant size is 1–1½ ft. tall, with flowers and foliage in proportion. Grow outdoors in containers, window boxes, rock gardens, and flower gardens; a few also make sweet climbers. Or grow them indoors: pot in rich soil in containers at least 6 in. wide and place in a cool, bright window. Miniatures are shallow rooted and need regular water and fertilizer.

Miniature rose 'Starina'

OLD ROSES

Strictly speaking, old roses are varieties belonging to the rose classes that existed before 1867—the year that the first hybrid tea was introduced. However, in cata-

logs that specialize in old roses, you'll find some related varieties introduced in the 20th century, even roses such as 'Sutter's Gold' from the 1950s.

Old roses are a diverse group. They are popular because of their history and the beautiful fragrance many offer. Some are climbers; others are large mounding shrubs. Some are quite disease resistant, while others are prone to mildew or black spot in damp climates. Cold hardiness varies considerably: some are more cold hardy than hybrid teas; others are not.

The old European roses that existed before 1867 are the albas, centifolias, damasks, gallicas, and moss roses; they originated from wild roses native to Europe and western Asia. Most flower only in spring. Most are hardy in Zone 2b with no protection; some albas and gallicas bloom reliably only with some winter chill.

China and tea roses originated from eastern Asia; they were taken to Europe and crossed with European roses to produce the other classes of old garden roses: Bourbons, Portlands, hybrid perpetuals, and Noisettes. Repeat flowering is a characteristic of this group; hardiness varies, but even the hardiest—the hybrid perpetuals, Portlands, and Bourbons—are not quite as hardy as the old European roses.

Alba roses. Zones 2a–24. These were developed from *R. alba,* the white rose that symbolized the House of York in England's Wars of the Roses in the 15th century. The flowers come only in spring but generally are very fragrant. They are single to very double, white to delicate pink.

The plants themselves are upright, vigorous, and long lived, with green stems and handsome, disease-resistant gray-green leaves. Varieties include white 'Alba

Alba rose 'Alba Semi-plena'

R

Rosa centifolia

Semi-plena', and pink 'Celestial', 'Félicité Parmentier', 'Great Maiden's Blush', and 'Königin von Dänemark'.

Centifolia roses. Zones 2b–24. Centifolias were developed from *R. centifolia*, the cabbage rose; these are the gorgeous roses often portrayed by Dutch painters. Plants are open growing, with prickly stems that can reach 6 ft. long, arching under the weight of the blossoms. Intensely fragrant spring flowers typically are packed with petals, often with large outer petals that cradle a multitude of smaller petals within.

Colors include white and pink shades. 'Rose des Peintres' is a typical rich pink; 'Paul Ricault' produces deep pink silken flowers on an upright plant; 'Tour de Malakoff' is a tall, rangy plant with peony-like blossoms of pink fading to grayish mauve. Dwarf varieties (to 3 ft. or less) include 'Petite de Hollande', 'Pompon de Bourgogne', and 'Rose de Meaux'.

Damask roses. Zones 2b–24. These descendants of *R. damascena* reach 6 ft. or more, typically with long, arching, thorny canes and light or grayish green, downy leaves. Their flowers are intensely fragrant.

The summer damasks flower only in spring; forms of these are cultivated to make attar of roses (the rose oil used in the perfume industry). Varieties include 'Celsiana', blush pink; 'Léda', white with crimson markings; 'Mme Hardy', white; and 'York and Lancaster' (*R. d. versicolor*), with petals that may be pink, white, or a blend of pink and white.

'Autumn Damask' (*R. d. semperflorens, R. d. bifera*) flowers more than once a year; slender buds open to loosely double, pure pink blossoms. This is the Rose of Castile of the Spanish missions.

Gallica roses. Zones 2a–24. These are cultivated forms of *R. gallica*, the French Rose. Fragrant spring flowers run the gamut from pink through red to maroon and purple shades. Plants reach 3–4 ft. tall, with upright to arching canes bearing prickles but few thorns; leaves are dark green and often rough textured. Grown on their own roots, these plants will spread into clumps from creeping rootstocks.

Historic *R. g. officinalis*, known as the Apothecary's Rose, is presumed to be the red rose emblematic of the House of Lancaster in England's Wars of the Roses; its semidouble, cherry red flowers are held on a dense, medium-height plant. *R. g. versicolor*—generally known as 'Rosa Mundi'—has pink petals boldly striped and stippled red. Other gallicas include 'Belle de Crécy', pink aging to violet; 'Cardinal de Richelieu', slate purple; 'Charles de Mills', crimson to purple; and 'Tuscany', dark crimson with gold stamens.

Gallica rose 'Rosa Mundi'

Moss roses. Zones 2b–24. Naturally occurring sports of centifolia and damask roses, these plants have mosslike, balsam-scented glands, like little hairs, on their buds and flower stems and sometimes even on their leaflets. The "moss" of centifolias is soft; that of damasks is more prickly. Flowers are white, pink, or red, and are often intensely fragrant. 'Communis' ('Centifolia Muscosa') is a typical pink centifolia with the added moss characteristic; 'White Bath' ('Shailer's White Moss') is the same, in white. Other varieties are 'Comtesse de Murinais', pale pink to white; 'Gloire des Mousseux', deep pink; 'Mme Louis Lévêque', salmon pink; 'Nuits de Young', dark red; and 'William Lobb', dark red to purple. Repeat bloomers include 'Alfred de Dalmas', creamy pink; 'Gabriel Noyelle', apricot; 'Henri Martin', red; and 'Salet', bright pink.

China roses. Best in Zones 4–9, 12–24; H1, H2. The first two China roses to reach Europe (around 1800) were garden forms of *R. chinensis* that had been grown by the Chinese for centuries. Flowers were pink or red, under 3 in. across, and borne in small clusters on 2–4-ft. plants. 'Old Blush' ('Parsons' Pink China'), one of the original two, is still sold; others include red 'Cramoisi Supérieur' ('Agrippina'), white 'Ducher', and crimson 'Louis Philippe'. 'Mutabilis' opens yellow then turns pink.

China roses were the primary source of the repeat-flowering trait in modern roses. Modern miniature roses owe their small size to *R. c. minima*.

Tea roses. These are elegant, sweetly scented, virtually ever-blooming roses that are relatively tender; they grow best in Zones 6–9, 12–24; H1, H2. Plants are long lived, building on old wood and responding poorly to heavy pruning. Flowers are white, cream, light yellow, apricot, buff, pink, or rosy red. Though variable, many resemble hybrid teas—in fact, tea roses were crossed with hybrid perpetuals to produce the first hybrid teas.

Varieties include 'Duchesse de Brabant', warm pink; 'Lady Hillingdon', saffron; 'Maman Cochet', creamy rose pink; 'Marie van Houtte', soft yellow and pink; and 'Sombreuil', creamy white. The cross of a tea and the tea ancestor *R. gigantea* produced 'Belle Portugaise' ('Belle of Portugal'), a rampant, spring-flowering climber with large pale pink blooms.

Bourbon roses. Zones 2b–24. The original Bourbon rose was a semi-climbing hybrid between 'Old Blush', a China rose, and 'Autumn Damask'. Later came shrubs, climbers, and more semiclimbers with flowers in white, pink shades, and red, most of which were fragrant. Best known today are 'Mme Ernst Calvat', 'Mme Pierre Oger', 'Reine Victoria', 'Souvenir de la Malmaison', and 'Zéphirine Drouhin' (all pink) and the supremely fragrant 'Mme Isaac Pereire' (magenta red).

A famous Bourbon-China hybrid, 'Gloire des Rosomanes', gained widespread distribution as an understock (known popularly as 'Ragged Robin') for budded modern roses. Occasionally offered as a hedge plant, it is upright to fountainlike, with coarse foliage and semidouble

Bourbon rose
'Mme Isaac Pereire'

cherry red flowers throughout the growing season.

Portland roses. Zones 2b–24. Named after the first of the group, 'Duchess of Portland', these roses appeared around 1800. They were the first hybrids between China roses (mostly 'Slater's Crimson China') and old European roses (in particular, 'Autumn Damask'); sometimes they are called damask perpetuals. All are fairly short, bushy repeat bloomers with centifolia- and gallica-like flowers that are generally fragrant. Among those sold are 'Comte de Chambord', cool pink; 'Duchess of Portland', crimson; 'Jacques Cartier', bright pink; 'Rose de Rescht', fuchsia crimson; and 'Rose du Roi', crimson purple.

Portland rose
'Rose du Roi'

Hybrid perpetual roses. Zones 2b–24. In the 19th and early 20th centuries, hybrid perpetuals were *the* garden roses: big, vigorous, and hardy to about –30°F/–34°C with minimal protection. Flowers often are large (to 6–7 in.), full, and strongly fragrant; buds usually are shorter and plumper than standard hybrid tea buds. Prune high, thin out oldest canes, and arch over remaining canes to encourage bloom in quantity. Hybrid perpetuals need more water and fertilizer than hybrid teas in order to produce their repeated bursts of bloom. Watch for rust.

Colors range from white through pink shades to red and maroon. Varieties still sold include 'Baronne Prévost', deep rose pink; 'Dupuy Jamain', reddish pink; 'Frau Karl Druschki', white; 'Général Jacqueminot', cherry red; 'La Reine', silvery pink with lilac undertones; 'Marchesa Boccella', light pink; 'Mrs. John Laing', rose pink; 'Paul Neyron', deep pink; 'Reine des Violettes', deep purple fading to violet; and 'Ulrich Brünner Fils', carmine red.

Noisette roses. The crossing of a China rose, 'Old Blush', and the musk rose (*R. moschata*) produced the first Noisette rose, 'Champneys' Pink Cluster', a fragrant, repeat-flowering shrubby climber with small pink flowers in medium-size clusters. Crossing 'Champneys' Pink Cluster' with other China roses led to similar roses in white, pink shades, and red; crossed with tea roses, it yielded large-flowered, climbing tea-Noisettes. Noisettes are generally fragrant. All are best in milder climates (Zones 6–9, 12–24; H1, H2).

Small-flowered Noisettes include 'Aimée Vibert', white; 'Blush Noisette', light pink; and 'Fellenberg', cherry red. Larger-flowered tea-Noisettes are 'Alister Stella Gray', yellow; 'Crépuscule', apricot; 'Lamarque', white; 'Maréchal Niel', yellow; 'Mme Alfred Carrière', white; and 'Rêve d'Or', buff apricot.

SPECIES ROSES AND THEIR HYBRIDS

Species roses are the very old, wild roses. They grew in the natural landscape for hundreds, perhaps thousands, of years before modern breeding programs began. Among the following species and their hybrids are excellent shrub roses, climbing roses, and roses that will help control erosion on slopes. Some are extremely vigorous and cold hardy.

R. banksiae. LADY BANKS' ROSE. Evergreen climber (decidu-

Rosa banksiae 'Lutea'

ous in cold winters). Zones 4–24; H1, H2. From China. Vigorous grower to 20 ft. or more. Aphid resistant, practically immune to disease. Stems have few if any prickles. Large clusters of small flowers in early to late spring, depending on zone. Good for covering banks, ground, fence, or arbor. The two forms sold are 'Lutea', with scentless, double yellow flowers; and *R. b. banksiae* ('Alba Plena' or 'White Banksia'), with violet-scented, double white flowers. 'Fortuniana' (*R. fortuniana*) sometimes is sold by the name "double white banksia"; it differs from true *R. b. banksiae* in having thorny canes, larger leaves, and larger flowers that are held on single stems rather than in clusters.

R. bracteata. MACARTNEY ROSE. Evergreen climber. Zones 4–9, 12–24; H1, H2; except as noted. Native to southeastern China; naturalized in southeastern U.S. Creamy white, 2–3-in. flowers appear in spring. Without support, it trails and roots as it spreads; as a climber, it can reach 10–20 ft. Its celebrated offspring 'Mermaid' is a thorny, vigorous, tough, and disease-resistant evergreen or semievergreen climber, hardy in Zones 7–9, 12–24; H1, H2. It takes partial shade and reaches 50 ft., with profuse bloom from spring into fall; creamy yellow, single flowers are 5 in. across and lightly fragrant. Plant 'Mermaid' 8 ft. apart for quick ground cover.

R. eglanteria (R. rubiginosa). SWEET BRIAR, EGLANTINE. Deciduous shrub or climber. Zones A2, A3; 1–24. From Europe, western Asia, North Africa; naturalized in parts of the West. Vigorous grower to 12 ft. tall, 8 ft. wide. Stems are prickly; leaves are dark green with fragrance of green apples, especially after a rain. Single pink flowers to 2½ in. across

Rosa eglanteria

Rosa foetida bicolor

in late spring. Red-orange hips. Good hedge, barrier, or screen (plant 3–4 ft. apart and prune annually in early spring); can be held to 3–4 ft. tall. Hybrid forms include 'Lady Penzance'.

R. foetida. AUSTRIAN BRIER. Deciduous shrub. Zones A2, A3; 1–21. From central and western Asia. To 6 ft. tall and wide. Especially susceptible to black spot. Flowers (in mid- to late spring) are single, bright yellow, 2–3 in. across, with odd scent. This species and its well-known variety *R. f. bicolor*, commonly called Austrian Copper, are the source of orange and yellow in modern roses. *R. f. bicolor* is a 4–5-ft.-tall shrub with brilliant coppery red petals backed with yellow.

R. glauca (R. rubrifolia). Deciduous shrub. Zones A1–A3; 1–24. From central and southern Europe. To 6 ft. tall, 5 ft. wide. Valued particularly for its leaves, which combine gray green and coppery purple. Small, single pink flowers in spring are followed by small, oval hips that turn red in the autumn.

R. × harisonii. HARISON'S YELLOW ROSE. Deciduous shrub. Zones A2, A3; 1–24. Hybrid between *R. foetida* and *R. spinosissima;* very old rose that was taken westward by pioneers and still persists in California's Gold Country and around old farmhouses. To 6 ft. tall and 4 ft. wide, forming thickets of thorny stems and fine-textured foliage. Flowers (in late spring) are profuse, semidouble, bright yellow, and fragrant. Occasionally reblooms in fall in warmer climates. Showy hips. Vigorous, disease free, hardy to cold, and (once established) resistant to aridity. Useful deciduous landscaping shrub.

R. moschata. MUSK ROSE. Deciduous shrub. Zones 4–9,

12–24; H1. Probably from western Asia. Vigorous, arching plant to 10 ft. high and wide. Densely covered with matte-finish, medium green foliage that turns butter yellow in late fall. Clustered, single ivory white flowers appear in late spring, continue through summer; scent is delicious, somewhat like honey. *R. m. plena* has double blossoms, though their effect is lessened because inner petals wither before outer ones do.

R. moyesii. Deciduous shrub. Zones 3–10, 14–21. From western China. Loose shrub to 10 ft. high, 8 ft. wide. Spring display of single, bright red flowers to 2½ in. across, carried singly or in groups of two. In fall, large, bottle-shaped hips ripen to brilliant scarlet. 'Nevada', from a cross between a form of *R. moyesii* and a hybrid tea, is a large, arching shrub. In spring, it is covered with 4-in., pink-tinted, single white flowers; lesser displays follow later in the year. 'Marguerite Hilling' is a pink sport of 'Nevada'.

R. multiflora. Deciduous shrub. Zones 1–24. From Japan. Dense, vigorous, arching growth to 8–10 ft. tall and wide. Susceptible to mildew and spider mites. Profuse clusters of small white flowers akin in scent to honeysuckle (*Lonicera*); blooms in mid- to late spring. In fall, there follows a heavy crop of red, ¼-in. hips that are much loved by birds (and may cause unwelcome multitudes of volunteer seedlings). Useful as hedge but only on largest properties. Set plants 2 ft. apart for fast fill-in. Can help control erosion.

Several distinctive climbing roses, known as multiflora ramblers, are hybrids of *R. multiflora*. Best known are several so-called blue ramblers, all of which are nearly thornless and have reddish purple blooms that fade to lilac or gray violet: 'Bleu Magenta', 'Rose-Marie Viaud', 'Veilchenblau', and 'Violette'.

R. nutkana. NOOTKA ROSE. Deciduous shrub. Zones A1–A3; 1–11, 14–21. Native from Alaska to

Rosa nutkana (hips)

Northern California and eastward to the Rockies. To 6 ft. tall and 4 ft. wide. Somewhat arching stems hold gray-green leaves with sharply toothed edges. Blooms in spring, bearing single, deep pink blossoms to 2½ in. wide (primarily borne singly). Showy, rosy red hips.

R. pimpinellifolia. See R. spinosissima

R. rubiginosa. See R. eglanteria

R. rubrifolia. See R. glauca

R. rugosa. RAMANAS ROSE, SEA TOMATO. Deciduous shrub. Zones A1–A3; 1–24. From northern China, Siberia, Korea, Japan. Vigorous shrub with prickly stems and wonderfully fragrant flowers. To 3–6 ft. tall and wide. Glossy bright green leaves have distinctive heavy veining that gives them a crinkled appearance. Flowers are 3–4 in. across and, in the many varieties, range from single to double and from pure white and creamy yellow through pink to deep purplish red. Blooms in spring, summer, early fall. Bright red, tomato-shaped hips, an inch or more across.

Rosa rugosa
'Frau Dagmar Hartopp'

All rugosas are extremely tough and hardy, withstanding hard freezes, wind, aridity, and salt spray. They make fine hedges. Plants grown on their own roots will make sizable colonies and help prevent erosion. Foliage remains quite free of diseases and insects, except possibly aphids. Among the most widely sold rugosas and rugosa hybrids are 'Blanc Double de Coubert', double white; 'Frau Dagmar Hartopp', single pink; 'Hansa', double purplish red; and 'Will Alderman', double pink. Two unusual choices are 'F. J. Grootendorst' and 'Grootendorst Supreme'; their double flowers have deeply fringed petals and resemble carnations (*Dianthus*) more than roses.

R. spinosissima (R. pimpinellifolia). BURNET ROSE. Deciduous shrub. Zones A1–A3; 1–24. From western Europe eastward to Korea. To 3–4 ft. tall, spreading wider by suckers with age. Bristly stems are also armed with sharp thorns; leaves are dense and ferny. White to pink, 1½–2-in.-wide spring flowers are followed by dark brown to blackish hips. Handsome bank cover in good soil; helps prevent erosion.

Noteworthy hybrids include 'Stanwell Perpetual', with double blush pink blooms from spring to fall; and 'Golden Wings', a 6-ft. bush with single, 4-in.-wide, light yellow blossoms with red stamens from spring to fall. 'Frühlingsmorgen', also 6 ft. tall, bears large, single yellow flowers with cherry pink edges and maroon stamens in spring, sometimes reblooming in late summer or fall.

R. wichuraiana. MEMORIAL ROSE. Evergreen or partially evergreen climber (deciduous in cold winters). Zones 3–9, 12–24; H1, H2. From Japan, Korea, eastern China. Trailing stems grow 10–12 ft. long in one season, root in contact with moist soil. Midsummer flowers are white, to 2 in. across, held in clusters. Good ground cover, even in relatively poor soil.

Wichuraiana ramblers, produced in the first 20 years of the 20th century, are hybrids between the species and various garden roses: 'Albéric Barbier' is creamy white; 'François Juranville', coral pink; 'Gardenia', light yellow; 'Paul Transon', coppery salmon; and 'Sander's White Rambler', white.

ROSA DE MONTANA.
See **ANTIGONON leptopus**

ROSARY VINE.
See **CEROPEGIA linearis woodii**

ROSE. See **ROSA**

ROSE CAMPION.
See **LYCHNIS coronaria**

ROSE CRESS.
See **ARABIS blepharophylla**

ROSE-MALLOW.
See **HIBISCUS moscheutos**

ROSE MOSS. See **PORTULACA**

ROSE OF SHARON.
See **HIBISCUS syriacus**

ROSEWOOD.
See **DALBERGIA sissoo**

ROSEWOOD, ARIZONA.
See **VAQUELINIA californica**

ROSMARINUS officinalis
ROSEMARY
Lamiaceae (Labiatae)
EVERGREEN SHRUB

| 🌡 ZONES 4–24; H1, H2 |
| ☀ FULL SUN |
| 🌢🌢 LITTLE TO MODERATE WATER |

Genus name means "dew of the sea," reflecting the plant's native habitat on seaside cliffs in the Mediterranean region. Tough and versatile, rosemary grows most luxuriantly just above the tide line, braving wind and salt spray—but it will thrive inland, even enduring blistering sun and poor alkaline soil, if given moderate water and infrequent light feeding.

The various forms of rosemary vary in habit from stiff, erect types through rounded shrubs and squat, dense tufts to rock-hugging creepers. Height ranges from as low as 1 ft. to as tall as 6 ft. or more. Plants are thickly clothed in narrow, typically 1–1½-in.-long, resinous, aromatic leaves that are usually glossy dark green above, grayish white beneath. Small clusters of ¼–½-in. blossoms in various shades of blue (rarely pink or white) bloom through winter and spring; bloom occasionally repeats in fall. Blossoms attract birds, butterflies, bees; produce excellent honey. Leaves are widely used as a seasoning. Flowers also are edible; add them to salads or use as a garnish.

Good drainage is essential; lighten heavy soils with plenty of organic matter. Heavy feeding and too much water result in rank growth, subsequent woodiness. Control growth by frequent tip-pinching when plants are small. Prune older plants frequently but lightly; cut to side branch or shear. If plants become woody and bare in center, cut back selected branches by half so plant will fill in with new growth (be sure to cut into leafy wood; plants will not regrow from bare wood). Or discard plant and start over with a new one. Branches root wherever they touch the ground; creeping varieties will spread indefinitely, forming extensive colonies. To get new plants, root tip cuttings or dig and replant layered branches.

Cold hardiness varies considerably, depending on selection. In general, upright varieties are hardier, while prostrate ones (originally from Majorca and Corsica) are more tender, suffering damage at 20°F/−7°C or even higher. In cold-winter areas, choose the hardiest types and shelter them from winter winds; wrap upright growers in plastic sheeting (leaving top uncovered) in late fall to prevent branches from breaking under weight of snow. Note that even the hardiest types can succumb to cold if they have wet feet. Beyond hardiness range, grow rosemary in pots and winter indoors on a sunny windowsill; or treat as annual.

Use taller types of rosemary as clipped or informal hedges or in dry borders with native and gray-leafed plants. Lower kinds are good ground or bank covers, useful in erosion control. Set container-grown plants or rooted cuttings 2 ft. apart for moderately quick cover. Foliage of most types has culinary uses, but flavor and fragrance vary; the best have a mildly pungent flavor and a complex aroma with sweet as well as resinous notes. Rosemary is also used in medicines, cosmetics, potpourri, moth repellents.

Rosemary plants sold without names are frequently seedlings, which lack the uniformity of cutting-grown, named selections. Unfortunately, variety names are often confused, and many have synonyms; but named plants are still a better bet than nameless plants.

'Albus' ('Albiflorus'). Semi-upright grower, eventually reaching 6 ft. tall and wide. White flowers veined in pale lavender. Hardy to 0°F/−18°C.

Rosmarinus officinalis
'Albus'

'Arp'. The hardiest rosemary, taking temperatures as low as −10°F/−23°C. Discovered in Arp, Texas. Open grower to 4 ft. tall and wide; best with frequent pruning. Dark green foliage has grayish tinge. Bright medium blue flowers.

'Benenden Blue' ('Balsam'; also called pine-scented rosemary). Semiupright plant to 3 ft. high, 4 ft. or more wide. Especially narrow leaves with strong pine fragrance; light blue flowers. Bitter flavor with turpentine overtones. Tender.

R

'Blue Boy'. Young plant makes a dense, symmetrical mound 8–12 in. high, 14–18 in. across, reminiscent of a dwarf spruce (*Picea*). Leaves are just ½ in. long; flowers are light blue. Plant creeps with age, but habit becomes irregular; shear to maintain domed appearance. Good in rock gardens, pots. Pleasant fragrance and flavor. Tender.

'Blue Spires'. Strong vertical grower, to 5–6 ft. tall and as wide or wider with age; can be pruned for narrower form. Deep blue flowers. Superb landscape variety; makes tight sheared hedge. Excellent for seasoning.

'Collingwood Ingram' ('Ingramii', 'Rex #4'). To 2–2½ ft. high, sprawling to 4 ft. or wider; narrower and more upright with pruning. Branches curve gracefully. Flowers in rich, bright deep blue with violet veining. Tallish bank or ground cover that provides excellent color. Not good for seasoning; flavor is too piny. Tender.

'Corsican Prostrate'. Arching, spreading, 1–1½ ft. tall, with dark blue flowers. Tender.

'Golden Rain' ('Joyce DeBaggio'). Bushy, upright growth to 2–3 ft. high and wide. Green leaves with irregular golden edges; variegation is most prominent in cool weather, fades in summer. Deep violet-blue flowers.

'Gorizia'. Vigorous, rigidly upright, to 4–5 ft. high and wide. Reddish brown stems. Leaves to 2 in. long, broader than those of most selections. Light blue flowers. Sweet, gingery fragrance.

'Hill Hardy'. Compact, bushy plant grows semiupright to 5 ft. high and wide. Stiff foliage. Light blue flowers; repeat bloom in fall. Pleasant, light fragrance. Hardy to 0°F/–18°C.

'Huntington Carpet' ('Huntington Blue'). To 1½ ft. high; spreads quickly yet maintains a dense center. Pale blue flowers. Best variety for ground or bank cover.

'Irene'. Vigorous spreader that covers 2–3 ft. or more per year, eventually mounding to 1–1½ ft. high. Deep lavender-blue flowers. Reputedly one of the cold-hardiest prostrate varieties.

'Ken Taylor'. Sport of 'Collingwood Ingram'. Has the same deep blue flower color but is a little lower growing, with a greater tendency to trail. Tender.

'Lockwood de Forest' ('Santa Barbara', 'Lockwoodii', 'Forestii'). Resembles 'Prostratus' but mounds up to 2½ ft. or more; has lighter,

brighter green foliage and bluer flowers.

'Majorca Pink'. Initially erect to 2–4 ft. tall and 1½–2 ft. wide; eventually twists into picturesque shape, flopping to 3–4 ft. wide. Lilac-pink flowers. Slightly fruity fragrance.

'Miss Jessop's Upright' ('Fastigiatus'). Erect growth to 4 ft. or taller, 1½–2 ft. wide, with thin, pointed leaves on slender stems. Pale violet-blue flowers. A little too sparse for a good hedge.

'Prostratus'. To 2 ft. tall, with 4–8-ft. spread. Will trail straight down over wall or edge of raised bed to make a green curtain. Pale lavender-blue flowers come in waves from fall into spring. With age, tends to mound up and become woody and bare in center (except at seashore, where it remains lush throughout). Effective in hanging containers. Tender.

Rosmarinus officinalis 'Prostratus'

'Severn Sea'. Trails widely; builds up to 1–1½ ft. high. Broader leaves than other trailing types. Profuse show of sky blue flowers. Said to be one of the cold-hardiest trailers.

'Tuscan Blue'. Vita Sackville-West's original, brought to England from Tuscany, had relatively broad (to ¼-in.-wide), 1–1½-in.-long leaves; deep violet-blue flowers; upright habit to 6–7 ft. tall and 1½–2 ft. wide. A plant long sold as 'Tuscan Blue' in the U.S. fits this description but has light blue flowers; with age, turns woody and bare at base. Some nurseries sell 'Blue Spires' under this name.

ROUNDLEAF FERN.
See **PELLAEA rotundifolia**

ROYAL CHARLIE. See
PLECTRANTHUS oertendahlii

ROYAL FERN.
See **OSMUNDA regalis**

ROYAL PALM. See **ROYSTONEA**

ROYAL POINCIANA.
See **DELONIX regia**

ROYSTONEA
ROYAL PALM
Arecaceae (Palmae)
PALMS

🗡 ZONES 24; H2
☀ FULL SUN
💧 REGULAR WATER

Stately, symmetrical feather palms. Tall, smooth gray trunk is marked with rings and topped by a green crownshaft formed by the overlapping bases of the feathery fronds. Grow at a moderate to fast rate. Do best in moist, well-drained soil. Good wind and salt resistance. Can be used as street or avenue trees, to frame large buildings, in groups with other palms. Look especially majestic planted in rows.

R. oleracea. CABBAGE PALM, CARIBBEE ROYAL PALM. Native to the Caribbean and South America. May reach over 100 ft. tall, 35 ft. wide. Green fronds grow as long as 20 ft.; they are usually semiupright or spreading.

Roystonea regia

R. regia. ROYAL PALM, CUBAN ROYAL PALM. Native to Cuba. To 50–75 ft. high, 30 ft. wide. Trunk is swollen at base, tapering toward top, sometimes swollen toward middle. Bright green, 10–20-ft.-long fronds arch gracefully in all directions.

RUBBER TREE.
See **FICUS elastica**

RUBUS
BRAMBLE
Rosaceae
DECIDUOUS AND EVERGREEN SHRUBS

🗡 ZONES VARY BY SPECIES
☀ ◐ FULL SUN OR LIGHT SHADE
💧 MODERATE WATER

Though best known for blackberry and raspberry (see separate entries), the brambles include

many ornamental plants, most of them thornless. The species described here differ from blackberry and raspberry not only in their lack of prickles but also in having perennial rather than biennial stems. Spring flowers are followed by small, edible berries that attract birds. Need good drainage; spread widely by rhizomes. Plant ground cover types about 2 ft. apart.

R. arcticus 'Kenai Carpet'. NAGOONBERRY. Deciduous. Zones A1–A3; 1–3. Native to Alaska and other northern climates. Creeping ground cover plant to 6 in. high. Smooth green leaves have three to five ovate, sawtoothed leaflets; foliage turns reddish in fall. Inch-wide hot pink flowers are followed by dark red berries.

Rubus deliciosus

R. deliciosus. ROCKY MOUNTAIN THIMBLEBERRY, BOULDER RASPBERRY. Deciduous. Zones 1–6, 10. Native to Rocky Mountains in New Mexico, Colorado, Wyoming. Graceful, arching plant to 3–5 ft. tall, 6 ft. wide. Bright green, lobed, nearly round leaves. White, 2–3-in.-wide flowers resemble single roses. Dark purple berries. Profuse blooming hybrid between this species and *R. trilobus* is *R.* 'Benenden', which grows 8–10 ft. tall.

R. rolfei (R. pentalobus, R. calycinoides, R. fockeanus). Evergreen. Zones 4–6, 14–17. Native to mountains of Taiwan. Thickly foliaged stems spread at a moderate rate to form a dense carpet to 1 ft. high. Rounded, 1–1½-in. leaves have three to five broad, ruffled-edged lobes; upper surfaces are lustrous dark green and rough textured, undersides are grayish white and felted. Small white flowers like those of strawberry. Salmon-colored berries. 'Emerald Carpet' is a commonly sold variety with superior foliage that turns raspberry red in fall with the onset of cool nights. The plant spreads 5 ft. in 3 years; makes a durable ground cover for sun or partial shade.

R

RUDBECKIA
Asteraceae (Compositae)
PERENNIALS AND BIENNIALS

- ZONES 1-24, EXCEPT AS NOTED
- FULL SUN
- MODERATE TO REGULAR WATER

The showy garden rudbeckias that brighten summer and fall borders are descended from wild plants native mainly to the eastern U.S. All are tough and easy to grow. Blossoms have yellow or orange rays and a raised central cone. They make good cut flowers; cutting also encourages rebloom late in season. Divide perennials when they become crowded, usually every few years.

R. fulgida. Perennial. Initially to 3 ft. tall, 2 ft. wide; after a few years, spreads by rhizomes to form a larger clump. Branching stems; broadly lance-shaped, 5-in.-long, hairy dark green leaves. Yellow, 2–2½-in.-wide flowers with black to brown central cone bloom in summer. Varieties are more often grown than the species; among the most popular is *R. f. sullivantii* 'Goldsturm', bearing 3-in., black-eyed yellow flowers on 2–2½-ft. stems. Some nurseries offer the taller, more variable seed-grown Goldsturm strain.

R. hirta. GLORIOSA DAISY, BLACK-EYED SUSAN. Biennial or short-lived perennial; often grown as annual because it blooms the first summer from seed sown in early spring. Grown as winter annual in Zones 12, 13. To 3–4 ft. tall, 1½ ft. wide, with upright, branching habit. Stems and lance-shaped leaves to 4 in. long are rough and hairy. Daisylike, 2–4-in.-wide flowers have orange-yellow rays and a prominent purplish black cone.

Rudbeckia hirta

Gloriosa Daisy strain has 5–7-in.-wide daisies in yellow, orange, russet, or mahogany, often zoned or banded. Gloriosa Double Daisy strain has somewhat smaller (to 4½-in.) double flowers, nearly

all in lighter yellow and orange shades. 'Indian Summer' produces 6–9-in., single to semidouble flowers in golden yellow. 'Irish Eyes' ('Green Eyes') has 2–3-in., golden yellow flowers with a light green central cone that ages to brown. 'Prairie Sun' produces 5-in. golden yellow blooms with pale yellow tips and a light green central cone. For front of border, try lower-growing selections 'Goldilocks' (double flowers) and 'Toto', both 8–10 in. high; Becky Mix (12–15 in.); 'Sonora' (15 in.); 'Marmalade' (2 ft.); and 'Cherokee Sunset' (2–2½ ft. high, with large double or semidouble blooms).

R. laciniata. Perennial. The species can reach 10 ft. tall, 4 ft. wide; it has light green, deeply lobed leaves to 4 in. long and blooms from summer to fall, bearing 2–3½-in.-wide flowers with drooping yellow rays and a green cone. More widely grown in gardens are the following two selections. 'Hortensia' ('Golden Glow'), to 6–7 ft. tall, bears bright yellow double flowers 2–3½ in. wide. Good summer screen or tall plant for back of borders. Does not seed, but spreads rapidly (sometimes aggressively) by underground stems. Seems to attract aphids. 'Goldquelle', with double blooms in lemon yellow, is a less aggressive form growing 3 ft. tall, 1½ ft. wide.

R. nitida. Perennial. Zones 2–9, 14–24. Similar to *R. laciniata* but shorter (to 6 ft. tall). More widely grown than the species is 'Herbstsonne' ('Autumn Sun'), which may be a hybrid between *R. laciniata* and *R. nitida*. It grows to 6 ft. tall, 2 ft. wide; bears single, 4–5-in.-wide flowers with yellow rays and a bright green cone that ages to yellow.

RUE. See **RUTA graveolens**

RUELLIA
Acanthaceae
EVERGREEN SHRUBS AND SHRUBBY PERENNIALS

- ZONES VARY BY SPECIES
- FULL SUN OR LIGHT SHADE
- WATER NEEDS VARY BY SPECIES

Ruellias have opposite leaves and flaring, bell-shaped flowers with five shallow lobes. Beyond their hardiness range, they are commonly grown in greenhouses.

R. brittoniana. Shrubby perennial. Zones 8, 9, 12–24; H1, H2. Mexican native naturalized in many areas of the southern and southwestern U.S. To 3 ft. high; initially

1–1½ ft. wide, but can be invasive and should be contained (by an edging, for example). Narrow dark green leaves to 3 in. long, ¾ in. wide; 2-in.-long, lavender-blue flowers throughout warm times of year. 'Chi Chi' has soft pink blossoms; 'Alba' has white flowers. 'Katie' is a dwarf (10–12-in.), noninvasive variety. Regular water.

R. californica. Shrub. Zones 12, 13. Native to Sonoran Desert of Mexico. To 2–4½ ft. tall and wide, with oval light green leaves to 1¼ in. long that drop in cold spells or after protracted dry periods. Deep purple, violet, or pink flowers to 2¼ in. long appear after spring and summer rains. Needs no irrigation but will bloom nearly all year if given little to moderate water.

R. macrantha. Shrub. Zones 21–24; H1, H2. Native to Brazil. To 3 ft. high and wide, with oval dark green leaves to 6 in. long. Clusters of rose pink, 3–4-in. flowers with deeper pink veining. Blooms from earliest winter to spring. Best grown as a container plant and given shelter during frosty weather. Regular water.

Ruellia peninsularis

R. peninsularis. Shrub. Zones 12, 13, 21–24. Somewhat larger flowered than *R. californica* but otherwise very similar in appearance and bloom season; has same watering needs as *R. californica* and same propensity for dropping leaves in cold or dry periods.

RUMOHRA adiantiformis
LEATHER FERN
Polypodiaceae
FERN

- ZONES 14-17, 19-24; H1, H2
- FULL SUN OR PARTIAL SHADE
- MODERATE TO REGULAR WATER

From many tropical and subtropical areas of the Southern Hemisphere. To 3 ft. high and wide, spreading wider by rhizomes. Deep glossy green, triangular, finely cut fronds are firm textured, last well in arrangements. Good choice for hanging basket. Hardy

Rumohra adiantiformis

to 24°F/–4°C. Sometimes sold as *Aspidium capense*.

RUPTURE WORT.
See **HERNIARIA glabra**

RUSCUS
BUTCHER'S BROOM
Liliaceae
EVERGREEN SHRUBS

- ZONES 4-24; H1
- BEST IN SHADE, TOLERATE SOME SUN
- LITTLE TO REGULAR WATER

Native to Mediterranean region. Unusual leafless plants with some value as small-scale ground cover, curiosity, or source of material for dried arrangements. Flattened, leaflike branches do work of leaves and bear tiny greenish white flowers in centers of upper surfaces. If male and female plants are present, or if you have a plant with male and female flowers, bright red (sometimes yellow), marble-size fruit follows flowers. Plants spread widely by rhizomes. Tolerate competition from tree roots. Subject to chlorosis in desert.

R. aculeatus. To 1–4 ft. tall, with branched stems. Spine-tipped "leaves" are 1–3 in. long, a third as wide, leathery, dull dark green.

R. hypoglossum. To 1½ ft., with unbranched stems. "Leaves" to 4 in. long, 1½ in. wide, glossy green, not spine tipped. Spreads faster than *R. aculeatus*. Superior as small-scale ground cover.

Ruscus hypoglossum

RUSH. See **JUNCUS**

RUSSELIA
equisetiformis
CORAL FOUNTAIN,
FIRECRACKER PLANT
Scrophulariaceae
SHRUBBY PERENNIAL

🌡 **ZONES 14, 19–24; H1, H2;**
OR INDOORS

☼ ◐ **SUN OR PARTIAL SHADE; BRIGHT**
INDIRECT LIGHT

💧💧 **MODERATE TO REGULAR WATER**

Native to Mexico. To 5 ft. high and
wide, with trailing, almost leafless
bright green stems that look
attractive spilling from a hanging
basket or over the top of a wall.
Stems can also be fastened to a
trellis or other vertical surface.
Can be grown in a rock garden.
Throughout spring and summer
(all year in Hawaii), many side
branches bear a profusion of
bright red, narrowly tubular flowers that look like little firecrackers.
Needs regular fertilizing. Hardy to
about 32°F/0°C, but comes back
vigorously if cut down by frost.
Easy to propagate from pencil-size
stem cuttings taken in spring.

Russelia equisetiformis

RUSSIAN OLIVE.
See **ELAEAGNUS angustifolia**

RUSSIAN SAGE.
See **PEROVSKIA**

RUTABAGA.
See **TURNIP and RUTABAGA**

RUTA graveolens
RUE, HERB-OF-GRACE
Rutaceae
PERENNIAL

🌡 **ZONES 2–24**

☼ **FULL SUN**

💧💧 **MODERATE TO REGULAR WATER**

To 2–3 ft. high and wide, with aromatic, ferny-looking blue-green
leaves. Small greenish yellow
flowers are followed by decorative

Ruta graveolens
'Jackman's Blue'

brown seed capsules. 'Jackman's
Blue' is dense and compact, with a
fine gray-blue color. 'Blue Mound'
and 'Curly Girl' are more compact
still. Sow seeds in flats; transplant
to 1 ft. apart. Rue needs good garden soil; add lime to strongly acid
soil. Cut back in early spring to
encourage bushiness. Dry seed
clusters for use in wreaths or
swags. Sap causes dermatitis in
some people.

RYEGRASS. See LOLIUM

SABAL
PALMETTO
Arecaceae (Palmae)
PALMS

🌡 **ZONES 12–17, 19–24; H1, H2**

☼ **FULL SUN**

💧 **MODERATE WATER**

Slow-growing fan palms; some
have trunks, some do not. Mature
plants bear large clusters of tiny
flowers among the leaves. Tolerate
salt spray. All withstand 20°F/−7°C.

**S. domingensis (S. blackburn-
iana, S. umbraculifera).** HIS-
PANIOLA PALMETTO. Native to
the Caribbean. Ultimately 80 ft. or
taller, 20 ft. wide, with fan-shaped,
immense gray-green leaves to 9 ft.
across.

S. mexicana (S. texana).
OAXACA PALMETTO. Native from
Texas to Guatemala. To 30–50 ft.
high, 12 ft. wide. Bright green, 3-ft.
leaves. Leaf stems persist on trunk
in young trees, later drop to show
attractive, slender trunk.

S. minor. Native to southeastern
U.S. To 3–6 ft. tall, 10 ft. wide.
Green to blue-green, 6-ft. leaves.

Tree is usually trunkless but sometimes has a short trunk. Old leaves
fold at base, hang down like a
closed umbrella.

S. palmetto. CABBAGE PALM.
From southeastern U.S. To 20 ft.
tall, 10 ft. wide; much taller in its
native habitat. Big (5–8-ft.) green
leaves form a dense, globular head.

Sabal palmetto

SAFFLOWER.
See **CARTHAMUS tinctorius**

SAGE. See SALVIA

SAGE, RUSSIAN.
See **PEROVSKIA**

**SAGEBRUSH. See ARTEMISIA
californica, A. tridentata**

SAGINA subulata
IRISH MOSS, SCOTCH MOSS
Caryophyllaceae
PERENNIAL

🌡 **ZONES 1–11, 14–24**

☼ ◐ **FULL SUN OR PARTIAL SHADE**

💧 **REGULAR WATER**

Of two different prostrate plants of
similar appearance, *Sagina subulata*
is the more common. The other is
Arenaria verna, usually called
A. v. caespitosa. Both of these European natives make dense, compact,
mosslike masses of slender leaves
on slender stems. But *A. verna* has

Sagina subulata

tiny white flowers in few-flowered
clusters, while *S. subulata* bears
flowers singly and differs in other
technical details. In common usage,
however, green forms of the two
species are called Irish moss, and
golden green forms (*A. v.* 'Aurea' and
S. s. 'Aurea') are called Scotch moss.

Both *Sagina* and *Arenaria* are
grown primarily as ground covers
for limited areas. They're useful for
filling gaps between paving blocks.
In cool-summer gardens, they can
seed themselves and become pests.

These plants won't grow well
under conditions that suit true
mosses. They need good soil, good
drainage, and occasional feeding
with controlled-release fertilizer.
They take some foot traffic and
tend to hump up in time; control
humping by occasionally cutting
out narrow strips, then pressing or
rolling lightly. Control snails, slugs,
cutworms. Cut squares from flats
and set 6 in. apart for fast cover. To
avoid lumpiness, plant so that soil
line of squares is at or slightly
below planted soil surface.

SAGO PALM.
See **CYCAS revoluta**

SAGUARO.
See **CARNEGIEA gigantea**

ST. AUGUSTINE GRASS. See
STENOTAPHRUM secundatum

ST. CATHERINE'S LACE.
See **ERIOGONUM giganteum**

ST. JOHN'S LILY.
See **CRINUM asiaticum**

ST. JOHNSWORT.
See **HYPERICUM**

SAINTPAULIA
AFRICAN VIOLET
Gesneriaceae
PERENNIALS GROWN AS
HOUSEPLANTS

◑ ● **FILTERED EARLY SUN; INDIRECT**
BRIGHT LIGHT

💧💧 **WATERING IS AN ART; SEE TEXT**

Most popular of all flowering
houseplants; given proper care,
they bloom almost continuously.
Most of the African violets grown
are hybrids; they are derived from
several species native to East
Africa. Form rosettes of velvety
green (sometimes variegated)
leaves that may be roundish or
pointed, with a smooth or quilted
surface and scalloped or smooth
margins. The original species bear
pale blue to lavender and purple
blossoms that are typically five

S

petaled—with two smaller petals at the top of the flower, three larger ones below. Hybrids also include flowers in bell, cup, and star shapes, in colors including not only blues and purples but also white, various pink shades, burgundy, and crimson. Creamy yellows exist, but they tend to revert to pink or purple. Some hybrids have bands of color, contrasting veining, or dark accents on paler petals. All have bright yellow centers. Flowers may be single, semidouble, or fully double, sometimes with fringed or ruffled petals.

African violets need a moisture-retentive yet fast-draining potting mix. You can buy packaged mixes; if you prefer to make your own, use 3 parts peat moss to 1 part perlite and 1 part compost or sterilized loam. Don't use too large a pot; plants bloom best when roots are crowded. Choose a location where temperatures average 60 to 70°F/16 to 21°C. Humidity should be high; if house air is quite dry, increase humidity around plant by setting each plant on a saucer filled with wet gravel. Water plants from above or below, but avoid watering root crown or leaves. Wick-irrigated pots work well. Use room-temperature or slightly warmer water; wet potting mix thoroughly, then wait to water again until mix is dry to the touch. Don't let water stand in saucer for more than 2 hours after watering. Feed well-established plants (only when soil is moist) with slightly acid fertilizer once every 2 to 4 weeks. Propagate from seeds, leaf cuttings, or divisions. Common pests are aphids, cyclamen mites, thrips, and mealybugs. Pick off spent leaves and flowers.

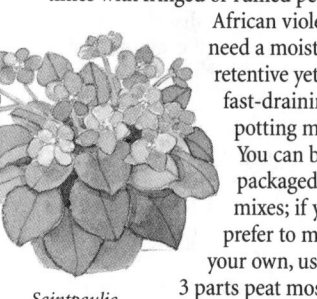

Saintpaulia

SALAL.
See **GAULTHERIA shallon**

SALIX
WILLOW
Salicaceae
DECIDUOUS TREES AND SHRUBS

✎ ZONES VARY BY SPECIES

☼ FULL SUN

◗ ◖◗ REGULAR TO AMPLE WATER

Fast-growing, weak-wooded, short-lived plants. Weeping willows are best used as single trees near a stream or lake, though they can, with training, become satisfactory shade trees for patio or terrace. They leaf out very early in spring and hold their foliage late. Shrubby willows are grown mainly for catkins (this group goes by the name "pussy willow") or colorful twigs, as screen plants, or for erosion control on stream or river banks. For this last purpose, locally offered native types are best. Pussy willow branches can be cut in bud and brought indoors to bloom. Willows take any soil; most even tolerate poor drainage. All have shallow, invasive roots and are difficult to garden under. Most are subject to pests (tent caterpillars, aphids, borers, spider mites). Twig blight may be a problem in the Northwest (spray copper fungicide on new foliage); Texas root rot may cause trouble in the desert. Species hybridize readily, resulting in much confusion of names in the nursery trade.

S. alba. WHITE WILLOW. Tree. Zones A2, A3; 1–11, 14–24. From Europe, North Africa. Upright to 75–100 ft. tall, 50–100 ft. wide. Yellowish brown bark. Narrow, 1½–4-in., bright green leaves are silvery beneath, may turn golden in fall. The following forms are valued for colorful twigs.

'Tristis' (*S. babylonica aurea*, *S.* 'Niobe'). GOLDEN WEEPING WILLOW. To 50–70 ft. tall and as wide or wider, with pendulous form. Young stems are bright yellow. Among the most attractive weeping willows.

S. a. vitellina. Upright, with brilliant yellow twigs in winter. Can grow to tree size, but cutting back gives best color display: lop to 1 ft. high yearly, just before spring growth begins. Stems may grow 8 ft. in a season. 'Britzensis' has red or orange-red winter stems; often confused with 'Chermesina'.

S. babylonica. WEEPING WILLOW. Tree. Zones 3–24; H1, H2. From China. To 30–50 ft. tall and wide (or wider). Longer (3–6-in.) leaves, more pronounced weeping habit than *S. alba tristis*. Greenish or brown branchlets. 'Crispa' ('Annularis'), ringleaf or corkscrew willow, has leaves curled into rings or circles; it is somewhat narrower than the species.

S. b. pekinensis 'Tortuosa' (*S. matsudana* 'Tortuosa'), DRAGON-CLAW WILLOW, CORKSCREW WILLOW. Zones 3–11, 14–24. Grows 30 ft. tall, 20 ft. wide, with branches that are fantastically twisted into upright, spiraling patterns. 'Snake' is similarly contorted but grows 40 ft. high, 30 ft. wide, with branches that weep at the tips; attractive cinnamon brown bark. Both are valued for winter silhouette and cut branches for arrangements.

S. caprea. FRENCH PUSSY WILLOW, PINK PUSSY WILLOW. Shrub or tree. Zones 2–11, 14–24. Native from Europe to northeastern Asia. Grows to 15–25 ft. tall, 12–15 ft. wide. Broad, 3–6-in.-long leaves are dark green above, gray and hairy beneath. Before leafout, male plants produce fat, woolly, pinkish gray catkins about 1 in. long. Can be kept to shrub size by cutting to ground every few years. 'Pendula' (a male plant known as Kilmarnock willow) and 'Weeping Sally' (its female counterpart) are two selections that will naturally sprawl on the ground; they are more effective grafted or staked to form small weeping trees 6–8 ft. tall, 6 ft. wide.

S. discolor. PUSSY WILLOW. Shrub or tree. Zones 1–11, 14–24. Native to eastern U.S. To 15–25 ft. tall, 12–15 ft. wide. Slender red-brown stems; bright green, 2–4-in. leaves with bluish undersides. Catkins of male plants are main draw—soft, silky, pearl gray, to 1½ in. long.

S. 'Flame'. Shrub or tree. Zones 2–11, 14–24. To 15–20 ft. high and wide, with compact, dense habit. Branch tips curl upward and inward. Glossy green, lance-shaped leaves to 3 in. long turn a good golden yellow rather late in autumn; twigs turn brilliant orange red in winter. May actually be a variety of *S. alba vitellina.*

Salix babylonica

S. 'Golden Curls' ('Erythroflexuosa'). Shrub or tree. Zones 3–11, 14–24. To 30 ft. tall and wide, with somewhat weeping and twisting branches. Leaves like those of *S.* 'Flame' but somewhat curled. Bark on new growth is bright yellow. After plant has established a framework, cut it back hard in winter to keep colorful new growth coming on.

S. gracilistyla. ROSE-GOLD PUSSY WILLOW. Shrub. Zones 3–11, 14–24. To 6–10 ft. tall, 12 ft. wide. Narrowly oval, 2–4-in.-long leaves are gray green above, bluish green beneath. Male plants produce plump, gray, furry, 1½-in.-long catkins with numerous stamens with rose-and-gold anthers. Cut branches for arrangements to curb plant's size. Every 3 or 4 years, cut the plant back to short stubs; you'll get very vigorous shoots with large catkins. 'Melanostachys' catkins are black with red anthers.

S. integra 'Hakuro Nishiki'. DAPPLED WILLOW. Shrub. Zones 3–9, 14–17. Native to Korea, Japan. To 4–6 ft. tall and wide; somewhat weeping. Stems and leaf buds are salmon pink; leaves are 4 in. long, ½–1¼ in. wide, light green mottled with white and pink. Best in partial shade.

S. matsudana. HANKOW WILLOW. Tree. Zones 3–11, 14–24. Upright, pyramidal growth to 40–50 ft. tall, 30–40 ft. wide. Bright green, narrow, 2–4-in.-long leaves. Can thrive on less water than most willows. This species and its varieties are popular in the high desert.

'Navajo'. GLOBE NAVAJO WILLOW. Large, spreading, round-topped tree to 70 ft. tall and wide.

'Tortuosa'. See S. babylonica pekinensis 'Tortuosa'

'Umbraculifera'. GLOBE WILLOW. To 35 ft. high and wide. Umbrella-shaped crown with upright branches, drooping branchlets.

S. nakamurana yezoalpina. CREEPING ALPINE WILLOW. Zones 2–6, 15–17. Native to Japan. To 2 ft. high and 10 ft. wide in 10 years; continues to spread but doesn't get taller. Heart-shaped, bright green leaves to 2 in. across are covered with silky white hairs when young, turn gold in fall. Male plants produce creamy white catkins. Interesting ground cover for rock gardens, where it seems to flow over and around stones. Needs well-drained soil that is not too high in nitrogen (add peat and fine gravel at planting time).

S. × pendulina. Zones 2–11, 14–24. Hybrid best known for two selections. 'Blanda', Wisconsin weeping willow, grows 40–50 ft. tall or taller, 70 ft. wide; it has a less strongly weeping habit than *S. babylonica,* with broader leaves in a bluer shade of green. The similar 'Fan-Giant', fan giant blue weeping willow, is resistant to borers and twig blight.

S. purpurea. PURPLE OSIER, ALASKA BLUE WILLOW. Shrub. Zones A2, A3; 1–11. From Europe, North Africa, central and eastern Asia. To 15 ft. high and wide, with purple branches. Narrow, 1–3-in.-long leaves are dark green above, bluish beneath. Cut shrub to ground if overgrown. 'Gracilis' ('Nana'), dwarf purple osier, has slimmer branches and narrower leaves; it is usually grown as clipped hedge and kept 1–3 ft. high and wide. 'Pendula', weeping arctic blue willow, is a prostrate grower but is usually sold as a standard, grafted onto a 6–8-ft. trunk; a nice weeping plant for small gardens.

S. udensis 'Sekka' (S. sacha-linensis 'Sekka'). JAPANESE FANTAIL. Shrub or tree. Zones 2–11, 14–24. Male selection of a Japanese species. To 10–15 ft. tall, spreading twice as wide. Narrow leaves are 2–4 in. long, green above, silvery beneath. Silvery catkins to 2 in. long. Main feature is the plant's structure: branches are flattened, often 1–2 in. wide, twisted and curled, picturesque in arrangements.

SALPIGLOSSIS
sinuata
PAINTED TONGUE
Solanaceae
ANNUAL

- ZONES 1–24
- FULL SUN
- REGULAR WATER

Native to South America. Upright, open habit to 2–3 ft. tall, 1 ft. wide. Stems and narrowly oblong, 4-in.-long leaves are sticky. Flowers are 2–2½ in. wide, resemble petunias in shape but offer more unusual colors—mahogany red, reddish orange, yellow, purple, and pink shades, marbled and penciled with contrasting colors. Plants bloom most heavily in late spring and early summer, but in cool-summer climates they'll carry on until frost

Salpiglossis sinuata

if regularly deadheaded. Good background plant for border; handsome cut flower. Bolero (to 2 ft. tall) and Royale (12–16 in.) are compact strains.

Seeds are rather difficult to start, especially when sown directly in garden. A better way to start them is to plant in potting mix in peat pots, several seeds to a pot, in late winter or early spring. Keep pots in a warm, protected location; thin seedlings to one per pot. When young plants are well established and frost danger is past, plant outdoors. Performs best in rich soil. Stake tall types. Tip-pinch growing plants to induce branching.

SALTBUSH. See **ATRIPLEX**

SALT CEDAR. See **TAMARIX chinensis**

SALVIA
SAGE
Lamiaceae (Labiatae)
EVERGREEN OR DECIDUOUS SHRUBS, PERENNIALS, BIENNIALS, AND ANNUALS

- ZONES VARY BY SPECIES
- FULL SUN, EXCEPT AS NOTED
- REGULAR WATER, EXCEPT AS NOTED

Largest genus in the mint family, including some 900 species from throughout the world. In recent years, scores of new species and selections have appeared in Western nurseries; many tender perennials and shrubs are even being offered as annuals in cold-winter climates. All sages have square stems and whorls of two-lipped flowers, either distinctly spaced along flower stalks or so tightly crowded that they look like one dense spike; some species have branched inflorescences. Flower colors range from white and yellow through salmon and pink to scarlet and pure red, from pale lavender to true blue and darkest purple. A few sages have fragrant blossoms. Many have aromatic foliage. Sages attract hummingbirds, bees, butterflies.

Plant sages in an area with good air circulation to help deter mildew and other fungal diseases. Most require good drainage, especially in winter; waterlogged plants rarely make it through hard freezes. If soil is heavy, work in plenty of organic matter and apply a thick mulch of well-rotted compost. When it comes to watering, "deep" is the operative word. Most of the plants discussed here come from areas with summer rainfall;

they need regular (or, in some cases, moderate) water during dry spells. Plants described as drought tolerant require a deep soaking at least once a month during the heat of summer to retain their foliage and prolong their bloom period.

Most sages resent severe pruning at any time other than late winter or early spring, when weather is cool and vigorous new growth is emerging from plant base. To shape during the growing season, either tip-pinch shoots or cut them back by no more than one-third (keeping most of the leaves on each stem).

Give lax varieties inconspicuous support by letting them grow through a cylinder of green-painted wire mesh. In many sages, aromatic compounds in the foliage repel pests—but this is not true for all species. Some are often damaged by slugs and snails; in warm climates, others can be demolished by Mexican giant whitefly. Aphids may be a problem for many. Sages are generally easy to propagate from cuttings or seeds; you can also propagate perennial kinds by dividing roots.

Nurseries in the West offer nearly 100 species as well as dozens of selections and hybrids. Those listed here are among the best.

S. africana-lutea. See S. aurea.
S. ambigens. See S. guaranitica
S. apiana. CALIFORNIA WHITE SAGE, BEE SAGE. Evergreen shrub. Zones 7–9, 11, 13–24. From Southern California, Baja California. Coarse plant to 3–5 ft. tall and wide. Aromatic, woolly silvery gray leaves are elliptical, 3–4 in. long. In spring, lavender-tinged white flowers appear in whorls along unbranched, sometimes pinkish stems to 2 ft. long. Attractive at night; reflects moon, garden lighting. To keep neat, shear lightly after flowering. Drought tolerant. 'Vicki Romo' (a hybrid between S. apiana and S. clevelandii) is more compact, has lavender-blue flowers.

S. argentea. SILVER SAGE. Biennial or short-lived perennial. Zones 1–24. From southern Europe, northwestern Africa. Soft, scallop-edged, silky-haired, silvery white leaves grow 6–10 in. long, form a low foliage rosette to 2 ft. wide. In summer, many-branched, 3–4-ft. flowering stems bear 1¼-in.-long, hooded white flowers (sometimes tinged pink or yellow) with silvery calyxes. Cut to ground when flowers fade. Handsome focal point for front of border. Protect from slugs and snails.

S. aurea (S. africana-lutea). GOLDEN SAGE, BEACH SAGE. Evergreen shrub. Zones 14–17, 19–24. From South Africa. Dense grower to 3–4 ft. high and wide; becomes sparse and woody with age. Young plants thickly covered with elliptical, woolly gray-green leaves to 1¼ in. long. Carried on 2–4-in. stems are whorls of interesting inch-long flowers in bright yellow aging to rusty brown; they emerge from brown, papery calyxes that persist long after blossoms fall. Main bloom in winter, early spring; sporadic through fall. When flowering decreases in late spring, shear plants back by one-third to encourage new basal growth; when plants become too woody (after 3 to 5 years), discard and replace. Prefers sandy soil. Drought tolerant. Top growth hardy to 20°F/−7°C; may resprout from roots in colder temperatures. 'Kirstenbosch' is a dwarf selection 1½–2 ft. high.

S. azurea grandiflora (S. pitcheri). PRAIRIE SAGE, PITCHER SAGE. Shrubby perennial. Zones 1–24. Native from Colorado and Texas east to Michigan and Georgia. Slender, vertical, usually unbranched stems to 5 ft. form a 2–3-ft.-wide clump. Plant is lax, needs support. Smooth or hairy, medium green to deep green, narrow leaves to 4 in. long. Pure azure blue flowers with white-blotched lower lip on spikes to 1 ft. long; blooms summer to frost. Not always permanent in wet winters.

S. 'Bee's Bliss'. Evergreen perennial ground cover. Zones 7–9, 14–24. Drought-tolerant hybrid between *S. leucophylla* and *S. sonomensis*. Grows 1–1½ ft. tall and spreads 4–6 ft. wide, with narrow, soft-looking, gray-green leaves. Whorled spikes of lavender-blue flowers are held above the foliage from spring into summer. Good on slopes, spilling over rock wall. Little to moderate water; avoid overhead irrigation, which encourages powdery mildew.

S. blepharophylla. EYELASH SAGE. Shrubby perennial. Zones 14–24. From northeastern Mexico. To 1½–2 ft. tall, spreading indefinitely by creeping rhizomes. Thin, hairy, purplish stems; oval, glossy dark green leaves to 1½ in. long, edged with fine hairs resembling eyelashes. Inch-long scarlet flowers on stems that lengthen to about 1 ft. as season goes on. Blooms from spring to frost, nearly all year in mild-winter climates. If confined, makes a good ground cover in partial shade. ▶

S. brandegeei. BRANDEGEE SAGE, BAJA SAGE, SANTA ROSA ISLAND SAGE. Evergreen shrub. Zones 15–17, 19–24. Native to Santa Rosa Island and coastal Baja California. Sprawling plant to 4–5 ft. high, 5–7 ft. wide. Linear, scalloped, 3–4-in.-long leaves are shiny, rough-textured dark green above, woolly white beneath. Tight, widely spaced whorls of ½-in., pale lavender, broad-lipped flowers on stems to 10 in. long; persistent violet-gray calyxes. Early spring bloom. Shorten branches by one-third during or right after bloom. Long-lasting cut flowers. Drought tolerant. 'Pacific Blue' has dark lavender-blue flowers.

S. buchananii. BUCHANAN SAGE. Shrubby perennial. Zones 14–24. Thought to be native to Mexico. Rounded growth to 1–2 ft. high and wide, with widely spaced, glossy dark green, oval leaves to 2 in. long. Lax, 8–12-in. stems support drooping, 2-in., brilliant magenta flowers. Blooms in summer and fall, and sporadically in other seasons in milder part of range. Sets no seed; propagate from cuttings. Handsome in containers; winter it indoors in cold climates.

S. cacaliifolia. Perennial. Zones 14–24. From southern Mexico, Guatemala, Honduras. Arching, trailing mass of interlocking stems grows to 2–3 ft. tall, 6–8 ft. or more wide. Will cascade over a bank or retaining wall, rooting where it touches ground. Evergreen, arrow-shaped kelly green leaves are 2–3 in. long. Blooms midsummer through fall (continuing all winter, in mild climates), bearing rich blue, ½-in. flowers on 6–8-in.-long stems. Tolerates full sun but blooms better in partial shade. Moderate water.

S. canariensis. CANARY ISLAND SAGE. Evergreen shrub. Zones 9, 12, 14–24. Native to Canary Islands. To 6–7 ft. tall, 8–10 ft.

wide; can reach that size in a single season. Angular, arching branches covered with stiff white hairs. Triangular, 4–6-in.-long, gray-green leaves with woolly white undersides. Big (to 8-in.-long, 6-in.-wide), branched flower clusters from spring to late fall. Pinkish purple, ¾-in. blossoms have red-violet calyxes that persist long after flowers fade. In winter, cut to 1 ft. from ground to encourage fresh basal growth. When plant becomes too woody, discard and replace it. 'Alba' has white flowers, pink calyxes.

S. chamaedryoides. GERMANDER SAGE. Perennial. Zones 8, 9, 12, 14–24. From eastern Mexico. Rounded plant to 1–2 ft. tall, spreading 2–3 ft. or more by underground runners. Silvery, ¾-in.-long leaves; brilliant true blue, 1-in. flowers on stems to 8 in. long. Heaviest bloom comes in late spring and fall, with intermittent flowering during rest of growing season. Deadhead to encourage rebloom. Elegant front-of-border plant. Drought tolerant but blooms longer and better with more water.

S. chiapensis. CHIAPAS SAGE. Perennial. Zones 17, 23, 24. From cloud forests of Chiapas, Mexico. Many 1½–2-ft. stems form a relaxed clump 3–4 ft. or more wide; growth is taller and laxer in shade. Evergreen, elliptical, glossy dark green leaves up to 3 in. long. Deep hot pink, ¾-in. flowers in widely spaced whorls on stems to 1 ft. long; blooms from early summer through winter in frost-free area or greenhouse. Reseeds freely. Succeeds with moderate water but appreciates frequent wetting of leaves. Good ground cover for dryish shade; good in containers. Needs at least partial shade in hottest climates.

S. clevelandii. CLEVELAND SAGE, CALIFORNIA BLUE SAGE. Evergreen shrub. Zones 8, 9, 12–24. Hardy to 20°F/–7°C. From South-

ern California, northern Baja California. Rounded, arching growth to 3–5 ft. high, 5–8 ft. wide. Wrinkled, toothed gray-green leaves to 2 in. long are elliptical or lance-shaped, deliciously fragrant. Foliage makes a refreshing tea and is also used as a preservative in potpourri. Fragrant, inch-long, pale lavender to violet-blue flowers in widely spaced whorls along 1½–2-ft. stems. Blooms in early summer; remove faded spikes to encourage rebloom. Drought tolerant. 'Winnifred Gilman' is more compact (3 ft. high and wide), with dark red flower stems and calyx tubes, dark violet-blue flowers. Hybrid 'Allen Chickering' grows like a typical Cleveland sage and bears abundant bright lavender-blue flowers. Hybrid 'Pozo Blue' is similar but hardier; it has endured temperatures to 10°F/–12°C. 'Aromas', also a hybrid, bears larger, darker blue flowers than the species.

S. coahuilensis. COAHUILA SAGE. Shrubby perennial. Zones 8, 9, 12–24. From mountains of Coahuila, Mexico. To 2½ ft. high and wide. Many slender, upward-sweeping woody branches, sparsely clothed with evergreen, 1-in., linear olive green leaves. Deep violet, 1-in. flowers appear on 3–5-in. stems from early summer to frost, all year in mild-winter climates; heaviest bloom in early summer and fall. Cut back to about 8 in. from ground in late winter. Moderate water.

S. coccinea. TROPICAL SAGE. Perennial in Zones 12–24, H1, H2; usually grown as annual in all zones. From Mexico; naturalized and weedy in Hawaii. Bushy, upright; to 2–3 ft. tall, 2½ ft. wide. Dark green, hairy, oval to heart-shaped leaves to 2½ in. long. In summer, slender stems to 1 ft. long carry many ¾–1-in. flowers with broad lower lip. Colors range from bright red through orange red to

pink and white, including many bicolors. Widely used as bedding plant, border filler. Stems are brittle; shelter from wind. Deadhead to encourage rebloom.

If plant lives over, cut back to 4–6 in. when new spring growth begins, then fertilize. By end of second season, plant will be woody and in decline. Reseeds copiously. Good seed-grown selections include scarlet 'Lady in Red'; salmon 'Brenthurst' ('Lady in Pink'); 'Coral Nymph' ('Cherry Blossom'), near white with coral lower lip; and white 'Lactea' ('Lady in White') and 'White Nymph'.

S. confertiflora. Perennial. Zones 16, 17, 22–24. Native to Brazil. Upright grower to 4–6 ft. high and wide (about twice that size in mildest climates). Lance-shaped, scalloped leaves to 8 in. long are dark green with yellowish tinge, densely hairy (especially on undersides); they have an unpleasant odor when bruised. Flowers offer a glowing color combination: flowering stems and calyx tubes are covered with red-brown velvet, and crowded ½-in. blossoms are dark orange. Blooms in fall, continuing through winter in mild areas. Stake plant; shelter from wind. Top growth may burn even in light frosts.

S. corrugata. Evergreen shrub. Zones 14–24. From high elevations of South America. Dense, upright habit, 5–6 ft. tall and almost as wide. Quilted, corrugated leaves are deep green on top, with prominent light veining and delicate, pale tan hairs beneath. From summer into fall, the plant is crowned with upright 4-in.-long spikes of tightly clustered, deep blue flowers held in dark purple calyxes. Pretty alongside roses or in shrub borders. Excellent in containers. Give weekly deep irrigation through the growing season.

S. 'Costa Rica Blue'. Evergreen shrub. Zones 15–17, 19–24. To 8 ft.

Salvia argentea

Salvia chamaedryoides

Salvia coccinea 'Coral Nymph'

Salvia farinacea

Salvia guaranitica

tall and wide; can be kept lower by cutting back to 1 ft. in early spring. Broadly oval to heart-shaped, hairy, shiny bright green leaves to 5 in. long. Brilliant true blue, 1–1½-in. flowers on 1–1½-ft. stems. Blooms from the end of summer until frost (through spring in mildest climates). Needs support, shelter from wind and cold. 'Omaha Gold' is a sport with leaves irregularly edged in yellowish green. A violet-flowered form also exists.

S. daghestanica. PLATINUM SAGE, DWARF SILVER-LEAF SAGE. Perennial. From western Asia. Zones 2b–24. Forms low, tight rosettes of textured, nearly white foliage 6 in. tall, to 1½ ft. wide. In spring, showy spikes of large blue flowers rise 10–12 in. tall. Bloom period lasts 3–4 weeks, but plants look good even out of flower. Attractive as edging for path or perennial border; excellent companion for other heat lovers like *Agastache* and lavender (*Lavandula*). Moderate water.

S. 'Dara's Choice'. Evergreen shrub. Zones 7, 14–24. A hybrid between *S. sonomensis* and *S. mellifera*. Bushy, spreading, to 2–3 ft. high, 3–6 ft. wide, rooting where it touches ground. Lance-shaped, 2½–3½-in.-long leaves are medium green with a grayish cast. Tight whorls of violet-blue, ½-in. spring, flowers are widely spaced along many 6–12-in. stems. Good as bank cover or draped over a wall. Sometimes subject to verticillium wilt; some branches die, but plant usually survives. Best in areas with coastal influence. Drought tolerant. Hybrid 'Mrs. Beard' has grayer foliage, lower growth (to 2 ft. high), pale lavender flowers; it is not prone to verticillium wilt.

S. darcyi (S. schaffneri, S. oresbia). DARCY SAGE. Perennial. Zones 8, 9, 12, 14–24. From northeastern Mexico. Upright growth to 3–4 ft. tall; spreads by rhizomes to 3 ft. or more. Softly hairy, triangular light green leaves to 1½ in. long have a pleasant, fruity aroma. Widely spaced whorls of 1½-in., coral red blossoms on unbranched stems from early summer to late fall. Stems are 6–12 in. tall, sometimes as high as 2 ft. They are brittle; shelter from wind. Protect from slugs, snails. Dies back to ground in winter. Tolerates partial shade.

S. dolomitica. DOLOMITE SAGE. Evergreen shrub. Zones 15, 17, 22–24. From mountains of South Africa. Handsome plant to

3–5 ft. tall and wide; may spread wider by short rhizomes. Elliptical, prominently veined gray leaves to 1½ in. long. Unassuming 1-in. summer flowers, arranged in pairs along 4-in. stems, are pale lilac with cream streak extending into throat. Bell-shaped, green or rose-colored, lemon-scented calyxes are persistent. Drought tolerant. Full sun or partial shade.

S. dorisiana. PEACH SAGE, FRUIT-SCENTED SAGE. Perennial. Zones 23, 24. From Honduras. Upright, branching habit to 5 ft. high and wide. Hairy, broadly oval, lime green, 5–7-in.-long leaves emit enticing pineapple-grapefruit scent when touched. Hot pink, 2-in. flowers with lime green calyx tubes on 6–8-in. stems. Blooms in winter and early spring, so must be grown in frost-free site or moved indoors to sunny window or greenhouse. Elegant potted plant. Morning sun or dappled shade.

S. dorrii. DESERT SAGE, GREAT BASIN BLUE SAGE. Evergreen shrub. Zones 2, 3, 10–13, 18, 19. Native to high deserts from Washington and Idaho south to California and Arizona. May have a rounded habit or form a spreading mat; grows 1–3 ft. high, 2–4 ft. wide. Branches densely clothed in gray, linear or spoon-shaped, ¼–1¼-in. leaves. Blooms in late spring; each 1–2-ft.-long stem bears three to five widely spaced whorls of light to deep blue, 1-in. flowers with deep blue bracts and calyxes. Needs sandy soil, perfect drainage. Drought tolerant. Good in dry desert garden.

S. elegans. PINEAPPLE SAGE. Perennial. Zones 5–24. Native to southern Mexico, Guatemala. In the wild, this species is variable in habit, bloom time, leaf fragrance. The most commonly grown form, 'Scarlet Pineapple' (*S. rutilans*), grows upright to 3–4 ft. high and wide, with branching, brittle stems; in part shade, growth is lush and needs support. Densely hairy, bright green leaves to 4 in. long, broadly oval with pointed tip. Foliage has a strong aroma of ripe pineapple; used in cool drinks, fruit salads. Slender, 1½-in., bright red flowers in loose clusters of 8–12 are carried on 6–8-in. stems. In mild-winter areas or indoors, blooms from late fall through spring; elsewhere, it is cut off by frost. Hybrid 'Frieda Dixon' is similar but has pinkish red flowers. 'Golden Delicious' grows just 1–3 ft. tall, with yellow-green foliage that makes for an

eye-catching contrast with the fire-engine red flowers; long bloom period. 'Honey Melon Sage' grows half as high as the species and spreads rapidly to form a dense ground cover; it has slightly smaller blooms and smaller, more rounded leaves that smell something like ripe honeydew melon. Blooms from early summer through fall (shear off faded flower stems two or three times a season to produce a new crop).

S. farinacea. MEALYCUP SAGE, TEXAS VIOLET. Perennial in Zones 7–10, 12–24, H1, H2; usually grown as annual in all zones. Native to southern New Mexico, Texas, Mexico. Upright growth to 3–4 ft. tall, half as wide. Narrowly lance-shaped leaves to 3 in. long are smooth above, woolly white below. Tall, densely packed spikes of ¾–1-in. flowers on stems 6–12 in. long, late spring to frost. Blossom color varies from deep violet blue to white; cuplike calyxes are covered with white hairs, often have a blue or violet tinge. Many strains are sold for bedding and container use; typically have heavier bloom, better branching, more compact habit. 'Cirrus', to 14 in. high, has silvery white blossoms, calyxes, stems. 'Rhea', 14–16 in. high, has intense deep blue flowers, bluish calyxes; starts blooming earlier in spring. 'Strata', 12–14 in. high, has blue flowers and large, densely woolly, silvery white calyxes. 'Victoria', to 18–20 in. high, has intense violet-blue flowers and calyxes; 'Victoria White' is white flowered.

S. gesneriiflora. Shrubby perennial. Zones 9, 14–17, 19–24. From west-central Mexico. To 4–8 ft. tall and wide. Heart-shaped, yellow-green, heavily felted, strongly aromatic leaves to 6 in. long. Stems 8–12 in. long bear brilliant orange-red, drooping, 2–2½-in. flowers with bell-shaped, usually yellow-green calyxes. Blooms from late fall into spring; to limit growth, cut back to 1–2 ft. after bloom. Best in areas with mild, sunny winters. Prone to damage from wind, rain; grow next to wall and support with stakes if needed. 'Mole Poblano', with chocolate brown calyxes, is more compact and floriferous than the species. 'Tequila' has violet calyxes.

S. greggii. AUTUMN SAGE. Evergreen or deciduous shrub. Zones 8–24. Dies to the ground in coldest winters but comes back. Native to southwest Texas, north-central Mexico. Rounded plant,

branching from base; typically grows 1–4 ft. high and wide. Slender, hairy stems are closely set with glossy green, ¾–1¼-in.-long leaves that vary in shape from rounded to linear. Blooms throughout summer and fall, bearing ¼–1-in. flowers on 3–6-in. stems, in colors ranging from deep purplish red through true red to various rose and pink shades to white. To keep plants tidy and free blooming, prune and remove dead flower stems frequently. Before new spring growth begins, shorten and shape plants, removing dead wood. Good low hedge. Replace plants every 4 or 5 years, when they become woody and unproductive. Drought tolerant but does best with moderate water. Full sun or partial shade (be sure to give some shade in hottest climates). A few of the best selections are pure white 'Alba'; hot pink 'Big Pink', with extra-large lower lip; peachy pink 'Cotton Candy'; deep raspberry 'Dark Dancer'; 'Desert Blaze', with brilliant true red flowers and gold-edged leaves; deep red 'Furman's Red', and hot pink 'Wild Thing'. (Varieties sold as *S. greggii* with flowers in shades of orange, orange red, or yellow actually belong with *S. × jamensis*.)

S. guaranitica (S. ambigens). ANISE-SCENTED SAGE. Perennial in Zones 8, 9, 14–24; annual in colder climates. From South America. Upright, branching plant to 4–5 ft. high and nearly as wide. Spreads by short underground runners; roots form tubers resembling small sausages. Narrowly heart-shaped, sparsely hairy, mint green leaves to 5 in. long. Blooms from early summer to frost. Most common form bears 2-in. cobalt blue blossoms, carried several to each foot-long stem; calyxes are bright green, turning purplish on sunny side. Needs support. Where it grows as a perennial, it gets woody by season's end—but that wood dies during winter and must be cut back to ground. Elegant container plant. Can be demolished by Mexican giant whitefly. Tolerates partial shade, especially in hottest climates.

'Argentine Skies' has light blue flowers. 'Black and Blue' bears blossoms that are deep blue with dark purplish blue calyxes. 'Blue Ensign' bears large blue flowers with bright green calyxes. 'Costa Rica Blue' can reach 6 ft. tall and wide, with broader, lighter green leaves than the species and brilliant, true blue flowers (best in Zones 15–17,

19–24). 'Omaha Gold' is similar but has leaves irregularly marked in yellowish green.

S. holwayi. HOLWAY SAGE. Perennial. Zones 9, 14–24. From mountains of southeastern Mexico, Guatemala. Spectacular where it has room to grow. Rambling plant to 4–5 ft. high, spreading to 8–10 ft. in a growing season, rooting wherever its lax stems touch the soil. Triangular, yellowish green, prominently veined leaves to 3 in. long. Bright red, 1-in. flowers in showy pyramidal spikes to 8 in. long; blooms from late fall through early spring. Partial shade under high, open tree canopy suits it well.

S. 'Indigo Spires'. Shrubby perennial. Zones 8, 9, 14–24. Can build up to a sprawling 6–7 ft. by 10 ft. but is easily kept to 3–4 ft. high, 2–3 ft. wide with support and selective pruning. Soft, silky, oval to oblong leaves (to 6 in. long near base of plant, shorter higher up) have a grayish sheen above, are white and woolly beneath. Narrow, twisted spikes of closely spaced, ½-in., violet-blue flowers can reach 3 ft. or longer. Blooms from early summer to frost (almost all year in mildest climates). Indigo calyxes are colorful long after blossoms fall. Excellent cut flowers. Top growth damaged by frost. Full sun or partial shade.

S. involucrata. ROSELEAF SAGE. Shrubby perennial. Zones 8–24; H1, H2. From eastern Mexico. To 5–6 ft. high and wide, often in one season. Oval, minutely toothed, 5–6-in.-long, rich green leaves with purple undersides and midribs. Foot-long stems hold numerous clusters of three purplish red, 2-in. flowers enclosed by a pair of bright purplish rose bracts that fall just as flowers open. Blooms from mid- or late summer to midautumn. Good cut flowers. Usually evergreen in mild-winter climates. Does best with afternoon shade. 'Bethellii' produces an almost spherical cluster of deep pink bracts at the top of its short flower spike. 'Boutin' is more compact (to 4 ft. tall, 5–6 ft. wide), with 6–10-in. flower stems. Hybrid 'Mulberry Jam' is similar to 'Boutin' but narrower (to 2–3 ft. wide).

S. × jamensis. JAMÉ SAGE. Evergreen shrub. Zones 8–24. Plants sold under this name are hybrids involving *S. greggii*, *S. microphylla*, an unknown yellow-flowered species, and possibly other sages; they are found wild in Mexico. Habit varies from upright to horizontal, but plants are usually

under 3 ft. tall, with fairly open branching; stems often root where they touch soil. Glossy green, oval to elliptical, toothed leaves ¾–1¼ in. long. Stems 3–6 in. long bear ½–¾-in. flowers in many colors: violet, wine red, orange red, hot pink, coral, salmon, yellow, white, and bicolors. Best in moderate climates without extreme temperature swings. Drought tolerant but perform best with moderate water. Good houseplants for sunny spot. Excellent varieties include 'Cienega de Oro' (creamy yellow flowers) and 'Sierra de San Antonio' (light peach blooms with pastel yellow lips); both grow 1½–2 ft. high, 2–3 ft. wide. 'San Isidro Moon' has an open, horizontal habit to 2 ft. high, 2–4 ft. wide; it bears two-tone flowers in peach shades. Varieties often sold as forms of *S. greggii* include light salmon pink 'Caviar'; soft orange-red 'Coral'; coral, yellow-throated 'Lowry's Peach'; and pale yellow 'Moonlight'.

S. leucantha. MEXICAN BUSH SAGE, VELVET SAGE. Evergreen shrub. Zones 12–24; H1, H2. From central and eastern Mexico. Vigorous, upright, velvety plant to 3–4 ft. tall, 3–6 ft. or more wide; sprawls in bloom. Lance-shaped to linear, 5–6-in.-long leaves are dark grayish green above, whitish below. Stems to 1 ft. long bear whorls of ¾–1¼-in. white flowers with purple calyxes. Bloom period runs from fall through spring in mild-winter areas, stops with frost in colder climates. To limit plant size and renew flowering stems, cut back close to ground before spring growth begins or at end of bloom cycle; where growing season is especially long, cut back again in early to midsummer. Also limit watering to every 2 or 3 weeks and remove blossoms as soon as they fade. 'Eder' has leaves with creamy white edges. 'Midnight' ('Purple Velvet'), considered by many to be the best-looking form, has purple flowers and calyxes. 'Santa Barbara' has similar flowers but is a compact grower to just 2½ ft. tall and 3–4 ft. wide.

S. leucophylla. PURPLE SAGE, GRAY SAGE. Evergreen shrub. Zones 8, 9, 14–17, 19–24, except as noted. Native to Coast Ranges of Southern California. Graceful plant to 3–5 ft. high with equal or greater width; arching branches have upturned tips, root where they touch soil. Stems and foliage thickly covered with fine white hairs. Wrinkled, oblong to lance-shaped leaves to 3 in. long are

apple green when they emerge, turn whiter as days get hotter. In spring, each 6–8-in. stem carries three to five tightly packed whorls of 1-in., pinkish purple flowers with gray calyxes. Good bank cover. Drought tolerant. 'Point Sal Spreader' (often sold as 'Point Sal') is prostrate, 1–2½ ft. high, 10–12 ft. wide; has broader, grayer leaves than species. 'Figueroa' (Zones 7–9, 14–24), to 3–4 ft. high and twice as wide, is especially silvery and exceptionally tolerant of drought, heat, cold.

S. madrensis. FORSYTHIA SAGE. Perennial. Zones 14–17, 19–24. From west-central Mexico. Strong grower, building up to 5–8 ft. tall and wide. Spreads by rhizomes to make a broad thicket (but stems are easily pulled out). Square stems are very thick—to 2 in. on a side at base. Bright green, elongated heart-shaped, rough-textured leaves reach 6 in. long at bottom of plant, become smaller toward top. Butter yellow, 1-in. flowers on 1–2-ft. stems; good for cutting. Blooms from fall until frost (through spring in mild-winter areas). Top growth damaged by frost.

S. melissodora. GRAPE-SCENTED SAGE. Evergreen or deciduous shrub. Zones 9, 14–17, 19–24. From Mexico. Graceful plant to 6 ft. tall, 4 ft. wide. Medium green, oval leaves to 1½ in. long; veins on leaf undersides are coated with yellowish tan wool. Blooms from late spring to frost; 6–8-in. stems carry ½–¾-in. lavender flowers with violet upper lip. Fragrance is like that of ripe grapes. Evergreen in mild winters. Worthy addition to a scented garden.

S. mellifera. BLACK SAGE, HONEY SAGE. Evergreen shrub. Zones 7–9, 14–24. Native to coastal California and Baja California. To 3–6 ft. tall, 3–5 ft. or more wide; upright to spreading. Oblong to lance-shaped, deeply veined, aromatic leaves 1–2¼ in. long; olive-tinged dark green above, woolly gray beneath. In late spring, bears tightly packed whorls of whitish or lavender-tinged flowers less than ½ in. long on 8–16-in.-long stems. Not spectacular looking, but butterflies and bees love it. Good cover for dry banks. Drought tolerant. Will stand some shade.

'Repens' is a creeping, cascading form to 1–2 ft. high, 4–6 ft. wide. 'Terra Seca' is an extra-tough variety to 2 ft. high, more than 6 ft. wide; makes a good cascading ground cover if you pinch or shear

upward-growing branches to keep foliage in center of plant.

S. mexicana. MEXICAN SAGE. Shrubby perennial. Zones 9, 14–17, 19–24. From central Mexico. Robust, erect growth to 10 ft. or taller, 3–5 ft. wide. Leaves to 6 in. long, typically elongated oval or heart shaped; they may be medium green and smooth above, fuzzy beneath, or gray to gray green and densely hairy on both sides. Pleasant pine fragrance. Tightly spaced whorls of 1–2½-in. flowers on 12–20-in.-long stems; blossoms are dark blue or violet with green or reddish purple calyxes. Blooms from early fall through spring in mild-winter climates; stops with hard frost elsewhere. Protect from wind. To keep compact, remove flower stems and shape plant as blooms are fading. Tolerates some shade; good under high-branching trees. Best with moderate water; more frequent watering produces excessive, brittle growth.

S. microphylla. Evergreen shrub. Zones 7–24. From southeastern Arizona through southern Mexico, with many local variant forms. Full sun or partial shade. Moderate water.

'Hot Lips' is upright, to about 1½–2 ft. tall, with striking flowers that vary from fire-engine red to white to red-and-white bicolors throughout the growing season.

S. m. microphylla (*S. grahamii*) is a tough, dense, wiry-looking plant to 3–4 ft. high, 3–6 ft. wide. Triangular to oval, tooth-edged leaves are dark green, ½–1 in. long. Rosy red, 1-in. flowers have small, hooded upper lip, three-lobed lower lip. Blooms most heavily in late spring and fall, sporadically at other times of year. 'Alba' has white blooms. 'Belize Form' (5 ft. tall, 8 ft. wide) is long-blooming but more tender, with bright green leaves and brilliant red flowers. 'Berzerkeley' (2 ft. tall, 3–4 ft. wide) bears glowing pinkish red blossoms. 'San Carlos Festival' (2–3 ft. tall, 4–6 ft. wide) has raspberry pink flowers. Hybrids with *S. greggii* include vigorous 'Maraschino', 3–4 ft. high, 6 ft. wide, with bright cherry red flowers; purplish pink 'Plum Wine', 3–4 ft. high and 2½–3½ ft. wide; and 'Raspberry Royale', 2½ ft. high, 3–4 ft. wide, with purplish red upper lip, dark red lower lip.

S. m. neurepia 'Forever Red'. To 3–4 ft. tall, 4 ft. wide. More open-branched plant than *S. m. microphylla*, with yellowish green leaves, brilliant red flowers. With deadheading, plants bloom from June until frost.

S. muelleri. ROYAL PURPLE SAGE. Evergreen shrub. Zones 8–24. From northeastern Mexico. Like *S. greggii* but lower, more spreading. Grows 2–3 ft. high, spreads 4–6 ft. by rhizomes. Oval, 1–2-in.-long, shiny green leaves. Violet, inch-long flowers, spaced along 8–12-in. stems, all year in mildest climates, spring to fall in colder ones; most profuse when days are short. Drought tolerant but needs weekly soakings in summer heat.

Salvia nemorosa 'Ostfriesland'

S. nemorosa. Perennial. Zones 2–10, 14–24. From eastern Europe, eastward to central Asia. To 1½– 3 ft. tall, spreading 2–3 ft. wide by rhizomes. Forms tight foliage rosette from which rise erect, branching flower stems. Wrinkled, dull green, finely toothed leaves are oval or lance-shaped. Lower leaves are stalked, to 4 in. long; upper ones are smaller, virtually stalk- less, clasping flower stem. Sprawls if not supported. Stems 3–6 in. long hold ¼–½-in. flowers in vio- let, purple, pink, or white, with persistent violet, purple, or green bracts. Blooms summer through fall if spent stems are removed. 'Caradonna' has violet blossoms. 'Ostfriesland' ('East Friesland') has intense violet-blue flowers. 'Plumosa' has unusual astilbe-like

plumes of mulberry purple. 'Rosen- wein' has rose-hued blossoms.

S. officinalis. GARDEN SAGE, COMMON SAGE. Shrubby peren- nial. Zones 2–24; H1, H2. From the Mediterranean region. Traditional culinary and medicinal sage. To 1–3 ft. tall, 1–2½ ft. wide; stems often root where they touch soil. Aromatic, oval to oblong, wrin- kled, 2–3-in. leaves are gray green above, white and hairy beneath. Branching, 8–12- in. stems bear loose, spikelike clusters of ½-in. flowers in late spring, summer. Usual color is lavender blue, but violet, red violet, pink, and white forms exist. Delay pruning until new leaves begin to unfurl, then cut just above fresh growth; cut- ting into bare wood usually causes dieback. Replace plants when woody or leggy (every 3 or 4 years). Subject to root rot where drainage is less than perfect. Give afternoon shade in hottest climates.

'Berggarten' ('Mountain Garden'). Compact; to 16 in. high. Denser growth, rounder leaves, fewer flowers than species; may be longer lived.

'Compacta' ('Nana', 'Minimus'). A half-size (or even smaller) ver- sion of the species, with narrower, closer-set leaves.

'Holt's Mammoth'. Leaves (4–5 in. long) used in making condiments.

'Icterina'. Gray-green leaves with golden border. Does not bloom.

'Purpurascens' ('Red Sage'). Leaves are flushed with red violet when new, slowly mature to gray green.

'Tricolor'. Gray-green leaves with irregular cream border; new foli- age is flushed with purplish pink.

S. oresbia. See *S. darcyi*
S. patens. GENTIAN SAGE. Perennial. Zones 9, 14–24; H1, H2. From central Mexico. Upright to 2–3 ft. or taller, 1–2 ft. wide. Spreads slowly by tuberous roots. Arrow-shaped, toothed, softly hairy leaves are bright green, 2–4 in. long. Pairs of brilliant blue, 2-in. blossoms on 6– 15-in.-long stems; upper lip is hooded, lower one flared and ruffled. Bloom peaks in early summer but repeats through fall if plant is fertilized and deadheaded. Best in mixed plant- ings; not showy enough for bed- ding. Established clumps can be divided. Easy from seed, though color of seedlings may vary. Partial shade in hottest climates. 'Oxford Blue' has deep blue flowers, 'Cambridge Blue' light sky blue ones. 'Guanajuato', to 3 ft. or taller, bears deep blue flowers to 3 in. long; leaves often have a brown central blotch.

Salvia officinalis 'Icterina'

S. 'Phyllis's Fancy'. Evergreen shrub. Zones 16, 17, 21–24. Vigo- rous. Habit like *S. leucantha,* which apparently is involved in its paren- tage. To 4–5 ft. tall, 6–8 ft. wide; spreads by rhizomes. Wrinkled green leaves to 6 in. long, twice as wide as those of *S. leucantha.* Bluish stems to 1½ ft. or longer bear ¾–1¼-in., lavender-tinged white flowers with blue-violet calyxes, late spring through fall (nearly all year in mildest cli- mates). 'Waverly' ('Mark's Mystery Sage') is a similar but less vigorous hybrid (3 ft. tall, 4–5 ft. wide). Its 1-ft. flower stems are flushed with red violet, as are calyxes; blooms are white tinged pinkish lilac.

S. 'Purple Majesty'. Shrubby perennial. Zones 9, 14–24. To 3 ft. tall, 4 ft. wide. Hybrid of *S. guaranit- ica,* with leaves of a yellower green; brilliant royal purple flowers with

violet-black calyxes. Blooms from summer until frost in colder cli- mates, nearly all year in mild-winter regions (where it is evergreen).

S. recognita. TURKISH SAGE. Perennial. Zones 2–24. Native to Turkey. From a 1½–2-ft.-wide basal clump, densely hairy flowering stems rise 3 ft. or more. Mildly aromatic, 5–8-in.-long leaves have wine red stalks and five to nine grayish green, scalloped, oval to lance-shaped, silky-haired leaflets. Terminal leaflet to 4–5 in. long, others less than half that size. Widely spaced whorls of four to six 1½-in. lilac-pink flowers; hairy calyxes glisten with oil glands. Blooms in early summer, sporadi- cally through fall. Short lived but reseeds freely. Partial shade.

S. regla. MOUNTAIN SAGE. Evergreen or deciduous shrub. Zones 7–10, 14–24. Native to west- ern Texas, central Mexico. Upright stems to 4–6 ft. high; these arch and branch out to form an almost equally wide mass. Scalloped, puckered, fan-shaped leaves (drawn out to sharp points in some forms) are 1 in. across. Orange-scarlet, 1-in. flowers with flaring calyxes appear in short clusters at branch ends; calyxes persist for several weeks after flowers drop. Profuse bloom from fall until frost (through early spring—though less profusely— in mild areas). Prune this plant (if ever) only when it is growing strongly in summer; winter- pruned plants recover slowly, may even die. Loses leaves at 28°F/ –2°C. Excellent nectar source for hummingbirds. 'Huntington' has larger flowers, spreading habit (3–4 ft. tall, to 6 ft. wide); 'Royal' is an upright grower to 6–7 ft.

S. reptans. COBALT SAGE, WEST TEXAS GRASS SAGE. Semievergreen perennial. Zones 5–9, 14–24. From Texas, Mexico, and Central America. Two forms of this plant are sold, one more

Salvia 'Maraschino' (*S. microphylla* hybrid)

Salvia nemorosa 'Ostfriesland'

Salvia officinalis 'Purpurascens'

Salvia splendens

Salvia uliginosa

S

upright than the other. The most commonly offered form has a graceful habit, with somewhat lax growth to about 3 ft. tall and wide. Thin stems hold needlelike, light green leaves. Wisteria blue flowers are produced in summer; these are ½ in. long, with tiny, dark calyxes. Native to dry, gravelly, mountain washes; give it well-drained soil in the garden. Use in drifts or as a soft accent among stones. Cut stems to the ground after bloom for a bushier plant the following year; new growth appears in spring from tuberous roots. Dies to the ground when temperature falls below 30°F/−1°C.

S. roemeriana. CEDAR SAGE. Perennial. Zones 7–24. Native to south-central Texas, northeastern Mexico. To 1–2 ft. high and wide. Reminiscent of coral bells (*Heuchera*), with basal clump of scalloped, rounded leaves to 1 in. long. Foliage has a cedar fragrance. Sparsely branched flowering stalks bear few-flowered whorls of scarlet, 1¼-in. blossoms on 4–8-in. stems. Deadhead to keep the brilliant show going from spring through fall. Reseeds to form colonies. Rich soil, half-day shade.

S. schaffneri. See S. darcyi

S. sclarea. CLARY SAGE. Biennial or short-lived perennial. Zones 2–24. Native to southern Europe, southwestern and central Asia. Foliage clump to 2–3 ft. wide. Oval to lance-shaped, 1–1½-ft.-long, toothed, dull grayish green leaves are wrinkled, unpleasant smelling when bruised. In late spring or early summer, produces much-branched 3–4-ft. flower stalks with 6–12-in. stems bearing whorls of two to six 1¼-in. flowers. Blossoms are typically lilac or lavender blue, with arched upper lip and cream-colored lower lip; large, aromatic, purplish or lilac-pink bracts remain showy for weeks after the flowers drop. Cutting stems before seeds form sacrifices this display, but it often produces rebloom in early fall and may prolong the plant's life. (Allow some seeds to form for replacement plants.) Leaves, flowers, bracts are used to flavor wines and liqueurs; oil is used in perfume, potpourri. Little to moderate water. 'Alba' has white flowers, bracts. 'Turkestanica' is especially vigorous, with creamy white blooms and white bracts flushed deep pink on edges.

S. semiatrata. BICOLOR SAGE. Evergreen shrub. Zones 16, 17, 21–24. Native to cool, high mountains of southern Mexico. Upright

growth to 3–6 ft. tall, 2–3 ft. wide, with brittle, woody stems. Wrinkled, velvety, yellowish green leaves to 1¼ in. long are triangular with rounded corners. Whorls of 1–2-in. flowers on 4–6-in. stems. Dusky lavender-blue blooms, with velvety, blackish violet upper lip, throat, and blotch on lower lip. Calyxes are pinkish maroon, velvety. Blooms summer through fall; some winter flowers in mildest areas. Pinch regularly and trim lightly two or three times a year; avoid hard pruning. Protect from slugs, snails. Needs perfect drainage in winter. Give afternoon shade in hottest climates. Elegant container plant.

S. sinaloensis. SINALOA SAGE. Perennial. Zones 15–17, 20–24. From foothills of western coastal Mexico. Low, mounding, dense plant with slender, 6–12-in.-long, prostrate stems. Spreads to 1–2 ft. or more by rhizomes; stems also root where they touch soil. Good ground cover. Closely spaced, lance-shaped, finely toothed leaves to 1 in. long. Foliage is purple when new, turning green in shade; to preserve purplish color, give full sun (but not in hottest climates unless well watered). Stems 4–6 in. long bear cobalt blue, ¾-in. flowers with two small white patches on lower lip and persistent, wine-colored calyxes. Main bloom in summer; sometimes repeats in fall. Shear back near ground just as new spring growth emerges from base.

S. sonomensis. SONOMA SAGE, CREEPING SAGE. Shrubby perennial. Zones 7, 9, 14–24. Native to dry foothills of California Coast Ranges and Sierra Nevada. Mat-forming creeper grows 8–12 in. high and spreads 3–4 ft. or more, rooting where branches touch soil. Evergreen, rough, irregularly notched leaves are dull green or gray green; they may be narrow and 3–4 in. long or much wider and shorter. Small (less than ½-in.) lavender-blue flowers rise above foliage on leafless, 6-in. stems in late spring or early summer. Needs perfect drainage, gritty soil. Drought tolerant. Best with some high shade in hottest climates.

S. spathacea. HUMMINGBIRD SAGE, PITCHER SAGE. Perennial. Zones 7–9, 14–24. Native to low elevations of Coast Ranges in California. Hardy to 20°F/−7°C. Foliage mass to 1–2 ft. high, 3–4 ft. or more wide, spreading by rhizomes. Evergreen, scalloped, wrinkled leaves are 6–10 in. long, lance shaped or arrow shaped; light

green above, paler and hairy beneath. Foliage has a light, fruity aroma. Flower stems rise 2–3 ft. above leaves, carrying many large, ball-shaped whorls of 2-in., magenta or rosy red flowers with maroon bracts and calyxes. Bracts and calyxes remain conspicuous for weeks after flowers fade. Blooms throughout spring, with some repeat in fall. A magnet for hummingbirds. Give rich soil, partial shade. Drought tolerant but prefers moderate water; tolerates regular garden water. 'Kawatre' has deep magenta flowers that age to orange red; it is hardier than the species (to 10°F/−12°C). 'Powerline Pink' forms a 3-ft.-high foliage mass, with flowering stems rising another 3 ft.; blossoms are rosy pink.

Salvia spathacea

S. splendens. SCARLET SAGE. Perennial in Zones 21–24, H2; usually grown as annual in all zones. Native to Brazil. The traditional bright scarlet bedding sage now comes in a range of colors, from vivid true red through salmon and pink to purple shades. White forms are also available. Plants vary in size from compact 1-ft. dwarfs to 3–4-ft. kinds. Leaves are bright green, heart shaped, 2–4 in. long. Blooms late spring or summer through fall (all year in mild-winter areas); 4–12-in. stems bear 2-in. flowers from 1-in. calyxes of same color. Can be ravaged by Mexican giant whitefly. Give afternoon shade in hottest climates. Seed-grown strains include 'Firecracker', to 1 ft. high and wide, in many single colors and bicolors; and 'Sizzler', an early bloomer offering mixed colors that grows a little taller. 'Van Houttei' is a vigorous old cutting-grown selection to 3 ft. tall, 4 ft. wide (even larger in mild-winter climates). Bears maroon flowers with an orange-scarlet tinge from early fall through spring where temperatures remain above 28°F/−2°C.

S. × superba. Perennial. Zones 2–10, 14–24. Form generally available is 'Superba', but many plants sold under this name are seedlings or selections of S. × *sylvestris* or S. *nemorosa*. The real 'Superba' forms a tight foliage clump that spreads 2–3 ft. by rhizomes and sends up erect, much-branched, 3-ft.-tall flowering stems. Smooth, scallop-edged green leaves are lance shaped; basal ones are stalked and 3–4 in. long, upper ones stalkless and smaller. At bloom time, top 6–8 in. of stems bear clusters of ½-in. violet-blue flowers with reddish purple bracts that persist long after flowers fall. (Bracts on most seedlings are green, sometimes with a purple tinge.) Blooms midsummer to fall if deadheaded. Plant will sprawl 5–6 ft. wide unless staked.

S. × sylvestris. Perennial. Zones 2–10, 14–24. Like its parent S. *nemorosa* but more compact, with stems that are less leafy. Oblong to lance-shaped, medium green, scalloped leaves are wrinkled, softly hairy, to 3 in. long. Typically unbranched or few-branched flowering stems to 6–8 in. long, set with pinkish violet, ½-in. blossoms. Blooms summer through fall if faded flowers are removed. 'Blauhügel' ('Blue Hill'), to 2 ft., has medium blue flowers. 'Mainacht' ('May Night'), 2–2½ ft., bears ¾-in. indigo flowers with green bracts (purplish at base), begins blooming in midspring. Two 1½–2-ft. forms are 'Rosakönigen' ('Rose Queen'), with purplish pink flowers and crimson bracts, and 'Schneehügel' ('Snow Hill'), bearing pure white blossoms with green bracts.

S. uliginosa. BOG SAGE, BLUE SPIKE SAGE. Perennial. Zones 6–9, 14–24. From moist lowlands in South America. Upright, dense; to 4–6 ft. tall, 3–4 ft. wide, spreading aggressively by rhizomes. Smooth green leaves are lance shaped, toothed; they reach 3½ in. long near plant's base, decrease in size toward top. Branched inflorescence with 5–6-in. stems carries whorls of ½-in., intense sky blue flowers with white throat, wide lower lip. Blooms summer through fall. To restrain spread, give only moderate water or confine roots by planting in 15-gal. nursery can sunk in ground to rim.

S. verticillata. WHORLED CLARY. Perennial. Zones 2–10, 14–24. From central Europe, western Asia. Foliage clump to 2½ ft. wide sends up branching, 2½–3-ft.-tall flower stems. Wavy-edged, medium green, softly hairy leaves to 5–6 in. long; shape varies from oval to elliptical or oblong. Basal leaves often divided into one or two pairs of smaller leaflets. Widely spaced whorls of 20–40 buds open to violet or lavender-blue flowers nearly ½ in. long, with purple-tinged, persistent calyxes. Blooms from early summer through fall if deadheaded. Protect from slugs, snails. 'Alba' has pure white flowers and calyxes. 'Purple Rain' is 1–2 ft. high, with profuse, showy deep purple blossoms and calyxes.

S. viridis comata (S. hormium). ANNUAL CLARY. Annual. All zones. Native to the Mediterranean, western Asia. Rapid, upright growth to 1½–2 ft. high, 1 ft. wide. Medium green, 2-in., oval to oblong leaves with blunt ends, notched edges. Inconspicuous cream or pinkish flowers with showy 1½-in., dark-veined bracts in violet, pink, or white. Blooms in early summer; another wave of bloom may follow if stems are cut before flowers go to seed. Bracts remain showy after flowers fade, dry well for winter bouquets. Sow indoors early; sow outdoors in midspring. Claryssa is a mix offering bushy, compact plants (to 16 in.) with bracts in intense shades of the typical colors.

SAMBUCUS

ELDERBERRY
Caprifoliaceae
DECIDUOUS SHRUBS OR TREES

- 🖊 ZONES VARY BY SPECIES
- ☼ ☽ FULL SUN OR LIGHT SHADE
- 💧 REGULAR WATER, EXCEPT AS NOTED
- ⚠ RAW FRUIT OF RED-BERRIED SPECIES CAN CAUSE NAUSEA, VOMITING, DIARRHEA IF INGESTED

In their natural state, these are rampant, fast-growing, wild-looking plants—but they can be tamed to a degree. Use as you would spirea or other large deciduous shrubs. In big gardens, they can be effective as screens or windbreaks. To keep shrubby types dense, prune hard during each dormant season: cut out older stems and head back last year's growth to a few inches. Overgrown plants can be cut to the ground. Types that grow into trees need early training to single or multiple trunks. Botanists tend to assign different names to the same plant. The various elder species have bright to dark green leaves and near-black, blue, or red berries. Birds eat fruit of all types, but the fruit of red-berried species can cause gastric

upset in humans if consumed raw in large quantities. (Red-fruited forms of black- and blue-berried species are not poisonous.)

S. callicarpa. See S. racemosa racemosa

S. nigra. BLACK ELDER, EUROPEAN ELDER. Shrub or tree. Zones 2–7, 14–17. Native to Europe, North Africa, Asia. Shrubby, upright growth to 20–30 ft. high and wide. Foliage has an almost tropical look; each leaf is up to 10 in. long and divided into many oval, pointed leaflets. Scented white flowers come in flat-topped, 5–8-in.-wide clusters in late spring or early summer. Fruits are purple-black berries less than ½ in. across; for maximum fruit production, plant two different varieties. 'Haschberg' is a heavy producer of large, black berries. A number of smaller-growing ornamental forms are available. 'Aurea', 10–20 ft. tall and broad, has yellow new growth maturing to yellow green. 'Guincho Purple', to 15 ft. tall and 10 ft. wide, has green foliage that matures to deep purple, then turns red in fall; purple flower stems bear pink buds that open to pink-tinged white blossoms. 'Black Beauty' ('Gerda') is similar but retains its black color throughout the growing season. Several varieties grow 6–8 ft. tall and wide: 'Aureomarginata', green leaves edged in yellow; 'Laciniata', very finely cut green foliage; and white-fruited 'Marginata' ('Albovariegata', 'Variegata'), green leaves bordered in creamy white. Two smaller selections (4–5 ft. high and wide) are 'Madonna', bearing green leaves that are variegated in light green to chartreuse when young, in cream, yellow, or gray-green when mature; and 'Pulverulenta', with leaves that unfold white, then mature to green splashed and striped with white.

S. n. canadensis (S. canadensis). AMERICAN ELDERBERRY. Zones A1–A3; 1–7, 14–17. Native to central and eastern North America. Seldom grown except in cold-winter climates. Spreading, suckering shrub to 12 ft. tall and wide. Each leaf has seven 2–6-in.-long leaflets. Blooms in early summer, bearing flat, creamy white flower clusters to 10 in. wide; these are followed by tasty purple-black berries. The fruit is used for pies; both flowers and fruit are used for wine. Strictly fruiting varieties include 'Adams', 'Johns', and many more; plant any two for cross-pollination. Ornamental varieties include 'Aurea', with golden green foliage

(golden in full sun) and red berries; 'Laciniata', cutleaf or fernleaf elder, with finely cut foliage and near-black berries; and 'Maxima', with leaves to 1–1½ ft. long, flower clusters 10–18 in. wide, and black fruit.

S. n. mexicana (S. mexicana, S. caerulea). BLUE ELDERBERRY. Zones 2–24; H1. Shrub or tree. Native from California north to British Columbia, east to the Rockies. To 10–30 ft. tall, 8–20 ft. wide. Leaves divided into five to nine toothed, 1–6-in.-long leaflets. White or creamy white flowers in flat-topped, 2–8-in.-wide clusters in spring, summer. Clusters of blue to nearly black berries, usually covered with whitish powder, follow the flowers. Fruit is often used in jams, jellies, pies, wine. Drought tolerant, but it looks better (and keeps its foliage in summer) if given moderate water.

Sambucus nigra mexicana

S. pubens. SCARLET ELDER. Shrub. Zones 1–6. Native to northern latitudes in North America. To 12–25 ft. tall and wide. Leaves divided into five or seven 2–4-in.-long leaflets. Blooms in late spring, bearing tall (up to 5-in.), loose flower clusters; inedible bright red berries follow flowers.

S. racemosa. RED ELDERBERRY. Zones A2, A3, 1–6, except as noted. Native to northern latitudes in North America, Europe, Asia. To 8–10 ft. tall and wide. Smooth leaves to 9 in. long are divided into five or seven sharply toothed leaflets. Small, creamy white flowers in dome-shaped clusters to 2½ in. wide, late spring into summer; inedible bright red berries. Leaves of 'Plumosa Aurea' and 'Sutherland Gold' are bright yellow when they unfurl, then turn to green late in the season. A shrub sold as S. callicarpa is probably the same as S. racemosa racemosa; it grows in Zones 4–7, 14–17, 19–23.

SAND CHERRY.
See **PRUNUS besseyi**

SANDHILL SAGE.
See **ARTEMISIA pycnocephala**

SANDPAPER VINE.
See **PETREA volubilis**

SAND PEAR.
See **PYRUS pyrifolia**

SAND STRAWBERRY.
See **FRAGARIA chiloensis**

SANDWORT. See **ARENARIA**

SANGUISORBA

BURNET
Rosaceae
PERENNIALS

- 🖊 ZONES VARY BY SPECIES
- ☼ ☽ LIGHT SHADE IN HOTTEST CLIMATES
- 💧 REGULAR WATER

These plants grow from creeping rhizomes. Leaves are divided featherwise into toothed, oval or roundish leaflets. Small flowers are carried in dense, feathery spikes resembling small bottlebrush (*Callistemon*) blossoms. Often sold as *Poterium*.

S. canadensis. GREAT BURNET, CANADIAN BURNET. Zones 1–6, 15–17. Native to eastern North America. To 3–6 ft. tall, 3 ft. wide, with bright green foliage and 8-in. spikes of white flowers in late autumn. Dies to the ground even in mild climates.

S. minor. GARDEN BURNET, SALAD BURNET. Zones 1–10, 14–21. Grown as winter annual in mild-winter desert. Native to Europe, western Asia. Can reach 1½ ft. high and wide but is usually kept clipped to a few inches to maintain a fresh supply of new foliage. Leaves have a mild cucumber flavor and are used in salads, soups, cool drinks. Can be used as an edging for border or herb garden. If not sheared too low, bears roundish, inch-long clusters of red flowers late spring to midsummer.

▶

Sanguisorba minor

S

Self-sows prolifically if allowed to go to seed. Evergreen in mild-winter regions.

S. obtusa. Zones 2–6, 15–17. Native to Japan. To 4 ft. tall, 2 ft. wide, with grayish green leaves and pink flower spikes to 4 in. tall in summer. Evergreen in mild-winter regions.

SAN JOSE HESPER PALM. See **BRAHEA brandegeei**

SANSEVIERIA trifasciata
BOWSTRING HEMP, SNAKE PLANT, MOTHER-IN-LAW'S TONGUE
Agavaceae
PERENNIAL

🌡	ZONES 13, 23, 24; H1, H2; OR INDOORS
☼ ◐	SOME SHADE IN HOTTEST CLIMATES; BRIGHT OR DIM LIGHT
💧	MODERATE WATER

From western tropical Africa. Grown outdoors in mildest-winter climates; houseplant anywhere. Often sold as *S. zeylanica.* Appreciated for thick, rigidly upright, patterned leaves that grow from thick rhizomes to form 2-ft.-wide rosettes. Leaves are dark green

Sansevieria trifasciata laurentii

banded with gray green, grow 4 ft. tall, 2 in. wide. Bears erect, narrow clusters of fragrant greenish white flowers in Hawaii but seldom on mainland. *S. t. laurentii* is identical to the species but has broad, creamy yellow stripes on leaf edges. Dwarf 'Hahnii' has rosettes of 6-in.-long, broadly triangular, dark green leaves with silvery banding; rosettes pile up to make a mass 1 ft. tall and wide. Other varieties and species are collectors' items; scores can be found in catalogs of succulent plants.

First common name comes from use of tough leaf fibers as bowstrings; second comes from leaf banding or mottling, which resembles some snakeskins; third probably comes from toughness of plants. Outdoors, plants tolerate many soil types, take salt air and drought; indoors, grow in much or little light, seldom need repotting. Withstand dry air, fluctuating temperatures, and scanty, capricious watering.

SANTA BARBARA DAISY. See **ERIGERON karvinskianus**

SANTOLINA
Asteraceae (Compositae)
EVERGREEN SHRUBS

🌡	ZONES VARY BY SPECIES
☼	FULL SUN
💧	LITTLE OR NO WATER TO MODERATE WATER

These Mediterranean natives are notable for their attractive foliage, profuse summer show of small, round, buttonlike flower heads, and stout constitutions. All are aromatic if bruised. Unpruned plants tend to become sparse and woody in the center. Cut back yearly, before spring growth begins; you can simply trim as needed around the edges (as if giving the plant a haircut) or cut the whole plant back to a few inches high. After blossoms fade, shear or clip off flowering shoots. Remove and replace plants if they become too woody. In coldest part of range, plants may die to the ground, but they should grow back from roots. Good as ground covers, bank covers, edgings for walks or borders, low informal or sheared hedges. Grow in any well-drained soil.

S. chamaecyparissus (S. incana). LAVENDER COTTON. Zones 2–24; H1, H2. To 2 ft. tall,

Santolina chamaecyparissus

3 ft. wide. Brittle, woody stems are densely clothed with rough, finely divided, whitish gray leaves. Bright yellow flower heads. Smaller versions of the species include 'Nana', to 1 ft. tall, 2–3 ft. wide; and 'Pretty Carol', to 16 in. high and wide. 'Lemon Queen', to 2 ft. tall and wide, has creamy yellow flowers.

S. pinnata (S. ericoides). Zones 3–24. To 2–2½ ft. tall, 3 ft. wide; narrow, tooth-edged dark green leaves, cream-colored flowers. *S. p. neapolitana* is 12–15 in. tall, has silvery foliage, bright yellow flowers.

S. rosmarinifolia (S. virens). Zones 3–9, 14–24. To 2 ft. tall, 3 ft. wide, with narrow green leaves like those of rosemary. Leaves may have tiny teeth or none at all. Bright yellow flowers. 'Morning Mist' is similar but more compact.

SANVITALIA procumbens
CREEPING ZINNIA
Asteraceae (Compositae)
ANNUAL

🌡	ZONES 1–24
☼	FULL SUN
💧	MODERATE TO REGULAR WATER

This Mexican native is not really a zinnia, but it looks enough like one to fool most people. Grows only 4–6 in. high but spreads or trails to 1½ ft. or wider. Leaves are like miniature (to 2-in.-long) zinnia leaves. Flowers are nearly 1 in. wide, with bright yellow or orange rays around a dark purple-brown center. Blooms from midsummer until frost. Varieties include 'Mandarin Orange' and double-flowered 'Gold Braid'.

Sanvitalia procumbens

Needs good drainage. Resents transplanting, so sow seeds where plants will grow. Plant from earliest spring (in mildest-winter climates) to late spring (where soil is slow to warm up). Heat resistant. Use as temporary filler in borders or edgings, as annual cover for slope or bank; or plant in hanging baskets or pots.

SAPIUM sebiferum
CHINESE TALLOW TREE
Euphorbiaceae
DECIDUOUS TREE

🌡	ZONES 8, 9, 12–16, 18–21; H1
☼	FULL SUN
💧💧	MODERATE TO REGULAR WATER
☣	MILKY SAP IS POISONOUS IF INGESTED

From China, Japan. To 30–40 ft. tall, 25–30 ft. wide, with a dense, round or conical crown. Tends toward shrubbiness, multiple trunks, and suckering but is easily trained to a single trunk. In colder areas, branch tips may freeze back

Sapium sebiferum

in winter, but new growth will quickly cover damage. Leafs out late in spring. Foliage is dense but flutters in the slightest breeze, giving tree an airy look. Light green leaves are roundish, tapering to a slender point; with moderate autumn chill, they can turn flaming red, plum purple, yellow orange, or mixed colors. For good color, select a tree while it is in fall leaf. Spikes of tiny yellowish flowers at branch tips are followed in fall by clusters of small fruits with a waxy grayish white coating.

Though this tree was once considered suitable for all landscapes, it is best not to plant it if you garden near wetlands, rivers, or native plant habitats. It has become a self-seeding pest in southeastern U.S. and has now naturalized along the American River near Sacramento and in Yolo County, California. Away from areas where it can do damage, it's an attractive tree for lawn, street, patio, terrace; gives light to moderate shade. Good as a screen. Resistant to oak root fungus.

SAPONARIA
Caryophyllaceae
PERENNIALS

- ZONES 1–11, 14–24, EXCEPT AS NOTED
- FULL SUN
- MODERATE TO REGULAR WATER

Generally low-growing European natives, closely related to *Lychnis* and *Silene*. Easy to grow in well-drained soil. Useful in border or rock garden.

S. ocymoides. Trailing habit to 1 ft. high, 3 ft. across. Oval dark green leaves. In spring, plants are covered with small pink flowers in loose bunches similar to those of phlox. Useful for draping over walls and as ground cover. 'Alba' is a white-flowered form; 'Rubra Compacta' has deeper pink flowers than the species.

Saponaria ocymoides

S. officinalis. SOAPWORT, BOUNCING BET. To 2 ft. high, spreading by underground runners. Elliptical to ovate, dark green leaves. Loose clusters of inch-wide summer flowers in red, pink, or white. Roots crushed in water produce a sudsy, detergent-like lather. This is a tough plant; before the days of herbicides, it could be seen growing in the cinders along railroad rights-of-way. 'Rosea Plena', with double light pink flowers, is the common garden form. 'Rubra Plena' has crimson blooms that turn paler as they age.

S. pumilio (S. pumila). Zones 2–7, 14–17. Linear, inch-long, bright green leaves form a tight cushion to 2 in. high and 1 ft. wide. Inch-wide, purplish pink flowers are borne singly at branch ends in spring, making a ring of blossoms around the plant's base.

SAPOTE, WHITE.
See **WHITE SAPOTE**

SARCOCOCCA
SWEET BOX
Buxaceae
EVERGREEN SHRUBS

- ZONES 4–9, 14–24, EXCEPT AS NOTED
- PARTIAL OR FULL SHADE
- MODERATE TO REGULAR WATER

Native to Himalayas, China. Grown for handsome, waxy dark green leaves and tiny, powerfully fragrant white blossoms that bloom in late winter or early spring, hidden in the foliage. Small berrylike fruit follows the flowers. Useful in shaded areas—under overhangs, in entryways, beneath low-branching evergreen trees. Plants maintain slow, orderly growth and polished appearance in deepest shade. Tolerate sun in cool-summer climates if soil is not allowed to become too dry. Grow best in organically enriched soil. Scale insects are the only pests.

S. confusa. Similar to *S. ruscifolia* and generally sold as such. However, *S. ruscifolia* has red fruit, while that of *S. confusa* is black.

S. hookeriana humilis (S. humilis). Zones 3–9, 14–24. Low growing, seldom more than 1½ ft. high; spreads by underground runners to 8 ft. or more. Branches are thickly set with pointed leaves 1–3 in. long, ½–¾ in. wide. Glossy blue-black fruit. Good ground cover.

Sarcococca ruscifolia

S. ruscifolia. Slow growth to 4–6 ft. high, 3–7 ft. wide. If grown against a wall, it will form a natural espalier, with branches fanning out to create patterns. Oval to elliptical leaves to 2 in. long, densely set on branches. Red fruit.

SASA. See **BAMBOO**

SASKATOON.
See **AMELANCHIER alnifolia**

SATUREJA
Lamiaceae (Labiatae)
ANNUALS AND PERENNIALS

- ZONES VARY BY SPECIES
- EXPOSURE NEEDS VARY BY SPECIES
- REGULAR WATER, EXCEPT AS NOTED

The first of these aromatic plants has long been used as a tonic, while the other two are favorite culinary herbs.

S. douglasii (Micromeria chamissonis). YERBA BUENA. Perennial. Zones 4–9, 14–24. Native from Los Angeles area to British Columbia. This is the plant for which San Francisco was given its original name of Yerba Buena. Plant grows to 6 in. high, spreading to 3 ft. wide by slender stems that root as they grow. Roundish, scallop-edged, 1-in. leaves have strong minty scent. Small white or lavender-tinted flowers in spring and summer. Grown as a ground cover. Dried leaves make a pleasant tea, which early settlers drank to treat a variety of ailments, hence the plant's common name (Spanish for "good herb"). Prefers part shade but tolerates full sun in cool-summer climates. Grows best in rich, moist soil but takes drought as well as boggy conditions.

S. hortensis. SUMMER SAVORY. Annual. All zones. From southeastern Europe. Upright to 1½ ft., with loose, open habit. Aromatic, rather narrow leaves to 1½ in. long; use fresh or dried as seasoning for meats, fish, eggs, soups, beans, vegetables. Whorls of tiny, delicate, pinkish white to rose flowers in summer. Grow in light, well-drained, organically enriched soil. Sow seeds in place; thin to 1–1½ ft. apart. Full sun. Good potted plant.

S. montana. WINTER SAVORY. Shrubby perennial. Zones 3–11, 14–24. From southern Europe. To 15 in. high, 2 ft. wide. Stiff, narrow to roundish leaves to 1 in. long; not

Satureja montana

as delicate in flavor as summer savory. Use leaves fresh or dried; clip at start of flowering season for drying. Blooms profusely in summer, bearing whorls of small white to lilac flowers that are attractive to bees. Use in rock garden, as dwarf clipped hedge in herb garden (space plants 1½ ft. apart). Grow in light, well-drained soil. Cut back as needed to keep compact. Full sun. Moderate water.

SAVORY. See **SATUREJA**

SAXIFRAGA
SAXIFRAGE
Saxifragaceae
PERENNIALS

- ZONES VARY BY SPECIES
- EXPOSURE NEEDS VARY BY SPECIES
- REGULAR WATER

Some saxifrages are native to mountainous areas of North America; most are from Europe. They do best in rock gardens of the Pacific Northwest, where specialists grow dozens of kinds. Require good drainage and light soil; rot easily in soggy soil. Most grow in full sun or light shade, but those listed here—all evergreen species—are shade plants. Although exacting in their requirements, forms offered by specialists are among the choicest of rock garden plants.

S. decipiens (S. rosacea). Zones 2–7, 14–17. Native to Europe. Plants grown under this name are generally known as "mossy saxifrages." Form low, compact or loose foliage cushions to 2–4 in. high, 1 ft. wide. Glossy green leaves less than 1 in. long are neatly divided into three to five segments. In spring, wide-open flowers are borne on 2–8-in. stems. The species typically has white flowers, but numerous named forms bear blossoms in cream, pink, or red. Widely sold 'Sternbergii' has white flowers strongly tinged pink. Afternoon shade is best in cool-summer areas; full shade is essential where summers are hot.

S. stolonifera (S. sarmentosa). STRAWBERRY GERANIUM. Zones 2–9, 14–24; or indoors. Native to China, Japan. Creeping plant forms a rosette to 6–8 in. high, 1 ft. wide, but expands fairly rapidly, sending out runners like strawberry. Nearly round green leaves to 4 in. across have white veins, pink undersides. Blooms from late summer to fall, bearing inch-wide white flowers

Saxifraga stolonifera

in loose clusters on stems to 2 ft. tall. Good ground cover where hard freezes are infrequent. Partial or full shade. To use as houseplant, grow in hanging basket; give bright indirect light.

S. umbrosa. Zones 2–7, 14–17. Native to the Pyrenees. Tongue-shaped, shiny green leaves to 1½ in. long form a foot-wide rosette only a few inches high. Blooms in spring, bearing open clusters of tiny pink flowers on wine red, 1-ft.-high stalks. Good ground cover for small areas; effective near rocks, stream beds. Best in full shade. This species is often called London pride, a common name that correctly belongs to *S. × urbium*, a hybrid between *S. umbrosa* and the similar *S. hirsuta*.

SCABIOSA
PINCUSHION FLOWER
Dipsacaceae
ANNUALS AND PERENNIALS

�	ZONES VARY BY SPECIES
☼	FULL SUN, EXCEPT AS NOTED
◖◗	MODERATE TO REGULAR WATER

Stamens protrude beyond curved surface of flower head, giving illusion of pins stuck into a cushion. Bloom begins in midsummer, continues until frost if flowers are deadheaded or cut regularly. Good in mixed or mass plantings. Excellent cut flowers.

S. atropurpurea. PINCUSHION FLOWER, MOURNING BRIDE. Annual in Zones 1–24, H1, H2; may persist as perennial where winters are mild. May also be sold as *S. grandiflora*. From southern Europe. To 2½–3 ft. tall, 1 ft. wide. Oblong, coarsely toothed leaves. Many long, wiry stems carry flowers to 2 in. or more wide, in colors from blackish purple to salmon pink, rose, white. Double Mixed strain and 'Salmon Queen' reach 3 ft. tall; Dwarf Double Mixed grows to 1½ ft. high.

S. caucasica. PINCUSHION FLOWER. Perennial. Zones 1–10, 14–24. From the Caucasus, Turkey, Iran. To 1½–2½ ft. high, 1–2 ft. wide. Leaves vary from finely cut to uncut. Flowers 2½–3 in. across, in blue to bluish lavender or white, depending on variety. Needs par-

tial shade in hottest climates. 'Alba' has white blossoms. 'Blue Perfection' bears lavender-blue flowers with fringed rays. 'Fama' has branching stalks carrying 3-in. blue flowers with broad rays. House's Hybrids (House's Novelty Mix) contains a mixture of blue shades and white. 'Ultra Violet' has deep violet-blue flowers.

S. columbaria. Perennial. Zones 2–11, 14–24. Grown as winter annual in Zones 12, 13. From Europe, Africa, Asia. To 2 ft. high and wide. Finely cut gray-green leaves. Flowers to 3 in., in lavender blue, pink, or white; almost all year in mildest climates. 'Butterfly Blue' (deep lavender blue) and 'Pink Mist' (bright pink) are superior selections.

Scabiosa columbaria

S. ochroleuca. Biennial or short-lived perennial. Zones 4–24. From Europe, western Asia. To 2 ft. high and wide, with light yellow flowers to 2½ in. across.

S. stellata. Annual. Zones 1–24. From western Mediterranean. To 1½ ft. tall, 1 ft. wide. Many heads of pale blue, 1½-in. flowers; these quickly dry to papery bronze drumsticks, useful in dried arrangements.

SCADOXUS
multiflorus katherinae
(Haemanthus katherinae)
BLOOD LILY
Amaryllidaceae
PERENNIAL FROM BULB

✿	ZONES 21–24; OR INDOORS
☼	LIGHT SHADE; BRIGHT INDIRECT LIGHT
◖	REGULAR WATER DURING GROWTH AND BLOOM

Tender South African plant closely related to amaryllis. Large (4-in.-diameter) white bulb stained red (hence common name). Lance-shaped to ovate, bright green, wavy-edged leaves are 12–15 in.

Scadoxus multiflorus katherinae

long. In late spring or summer, ball-shaped clusters (to 9 in. wide) of narrow-petaled, salmon-colored flowers are borne atop thick flower stems 1–2 ft. tall. Many threadlike, bright red stamens protrude from each bloom, giving clusters the look of spherical bottlebrushes.

In late winter or early spring, plant in rich, well-drained soil, keeping bulb tip even with soil surface. Can be grown in ground in frost-free regions (set bulbs 2 ft. apart) and the clumps left undisturbed indefinitely, but even there it is usually grown in pots. Choose a pot big enough to leave 2 in. between all sides of bulb and container edges. Place planted pot in fairly warm spot (no cooler than 55°F/13°C at night, around 70°F/21°C during the day). Water sparingly until leaves appear (in about 8 weeks); can be brought outdoors then. Water regularly and feed monthly with liquid fertilizer. After bloom, stop feeding and gradually cut back on water; let plant dry out in a cool, protected place. Do not repot next season; either add new mix on top of original soil or tip out root ball, scrape off some soil, and replace with fresh soil.

SCAEVOLA
Goodeniaceae
PERENNIALS AND EVERGREEN SHRUBS

✿	ZONES 8, 9, 14–24; H1, H2; EXCEPT AS NOTED
☼	FULL SUN
◖◗	MODERATE TO REGULAR WATER

Notable for flower form: blossoms are fan shaped, with all the segments on one side. Named for the Roman hero Mutius Scaevola, who burned off one of his hands to prove his bravery. Most are native to Australia, but some are beach plants from Asia, the Pacific Islands, and the Caribbean. The Australian species are evergreen in mild-winter climates and nearly

everblooming as well. In colder regions, where they are often grown as annuals, they bloom from late spring until frost and are useful in hanging baskets, window boxes, and pots.

S. aemula. Perennial. From Australia. Variable. Some forms are prostrate, others upright to 2½ ft.; fleshy stems of some spread to 3 ft. wide, while those of others trail or sprawl to twice that width. Bright green, 1½–2-in.-long leaves; lavender-blue, 1½-in. flowers all along the branches. Species available mainly through its named varieties, with flowers in various shades, including popular 'Blue Wonder' and 'New Wonder' (lavender-blue), 'Bombay Pink' (soft pink), 'White Charm' (pure white), and 'Zig Zag' (white petals with a central stripe of lavender blue). All these varieties grow 10–12 in. high and 2–3 ft. wide. Leaves are less than 1 in. long.

S. 'Mauve Clusters'. Perennial. From Australia. Flowers are smaller and stems less fleshy than those of *S. aemula*. Forms a mat 4–6 in. high, eventually spreading to 3–5 ft. across. Half-inch-wide flowers in lilac-tinged mauve. Often grown as ground cover (set plants 2 ft. apart).

Scaevola 'Mauve Clusters'

S. taccada (S. sericea). BEACH NAUPAKA, NAUPAKA KAHAKAI. Evergreen shrub. Zone H2. Native to Hawaii. Thick-stemmed plant to 6–10 ft. tall and broad. Fleshy light green leaves to 6 in. long and nearly as wide are clustered near branch ends. Flowers are ¾ in. wide, white with purple markings; followed by fleshy white fruits. Tolerates heat, wind, salt spray. Useful as hedge plant or windbreak, especially at the beach.

SCARBOROUGH LILY. See **CYRTANTHUS elatus**

SCARLET BUGLER. See **PENSTEMON barbatus, P. centranthifolius**

SCARLET BUSH.
See **HAMELIA** patens

SCHEFFLERA
Araliaceae
EVERGREEN SHRUBS OR TREES

🗺	ZONES VARY BY SPECIES; OR INDOORS
☀ ◐	SOME SHADE IN HOTTEST CLIMATES; BRIGHT INDIRECT LIGHT
💧	REGULAR WATER

Fast-growing, tropical-looking plants; long-stalked leaves are divided into leaflets that spread out like fingers of a hand. Summer flowers (showy in some species) are followed by tiny dark fruits. All need rich, moisture-retentive, well-drained soil. Love humidity but are quite tolerant of drier air. Useful near swimming pools. Good container plants for patio or lanai. As houseplants, they are unlikely to bloom.

S. actinophylla (Brassaia actinophylla). QUEENSLAND UMBRELLA TREE, OCTOPUS TREE, SCHEFFLERA. Zones 21–24, H1, H2; precariously hardy in Zones 16–20 with protection of overhang. Native to Australia. Fast growth to 20–40 ft. tall and wide. The "umbrella" of the common name comes from the foliage form: the long-stalked, glossy bright green leaves are divided into 7–16 large (to 1-ft.-long) leaflets that radiate outward like ribs of an umbrella. Foliage grows in tiers. "Octopus" refers to showy flower heads: narrow, raylike structures to 3 ft. long, set all along their length with little blossoms, radiate from a central point. Flowers age from greenish yellow to pink to dark red. Use for striking tropical effects, for silhouette, for contrast with ferns and other foliage plants. Cut out tips occasionally to keep plant from becoming leggy. Overgrown plants can be cut back nearly to ground level; they will branch and grow

Schefflera actinophylla

back with better form. This species has become a serious pest in some lowland areas of Hawaii.

S. arboricola (Heptapleurum arboricolum). HAWAIIAN ELF SCHEFFLERA. Zones 23, 24; H1, H2. Native to Taiwan. To 20 ft. tall with equal or greater spread, but easily kept smaller with pruning. Dark green leaves are much smaller than those of *S. actinophylla,* with 3-in. leaflets that broaden toward rounded tips. If plants are set into the ground with stems at an angle, they'll continue to grow at that angle—which can give attractive multistemmed effects. Yellowish flowers are clustered in flattened, foot-wide spheres; they turn bronze with age. Overall, produces a denser, darker, less treelike effect than *S. actinophylla.*

S. elegantissima (Dizygotheca elegantissima). Zones 16, 17, 22–24; H1, H2. Native to New Caledonia. As a juvenile, it is a houseplant; when mature, it's a garden plant to 25 ft. tall and wide. Leaves are divided like fans into leaflets with notched edges. Young plants are unbranched, with narrow (1-in.), lacy-looking leaflets to 9 in. long; foliage is shiny dark green above, reddish beneath. Plant branches as it matures, and leaflets grow slightly longer, broaden to 3 in., and become less glossy. Greenish yellow flowers in clusters to 1 ft. long.

S. pueckleri (Tupidanthus calyptratus). Zones 19–24; H1, H2. Native to southern Asia. Resembles *S. actinophylla* but is a denser plant that branches from the base. May be trained to single trunk. Leaves to nearly 2 ft. wide are divided into seven to nine stalked, glossy bright green leaflets, each to 7 in. long, 2½ in. wide. Flowers are greenish, borne on shorter, fewer "rays" than those of *S. actinophylla.*

SCHINUS
PEPPER TREE
Anacardiaceae
EVERGREEN TREES

🗺	ZONES VARY BY SPECIES
☀	FULL SUN
💧	WATER NEEDS VARY BY SPECIES
❀	FOLIAGE CAN CAUSE DERMATITIS; BERRIES OF S. TEREBINTHEFOLIUS CAN CAUSE GASTRIC DISTRESS IF INGESTED

Pepper trees are praised by some gardeners, heartily disliked by others. The two species discussed

here differ markedly, though both are tolerant of many soils, and leaves of both can cause dermatitis. Female trees bear fruit that attracts birds.

S. molle. CALIFORNIA PEPPER TREE. Zones 8, 9, 12–24; H1, H2. Thrives in Zone 11 but will die in severe freezes. Native to Peruvian Andes. Fast growth to 25–40 ft. tall and wide. Trunks of old trees are heavy and fantastically gnarled, with knots and burls that often sprout leaves or small branches. Heavy limbs; light, gracefully drooping branchlets. Bright green leaves with many narrow leaflets to 2 in. long. Drooping, 4–6-in. clusters of tiny yellowish white summer flowers; rosy berries in fall, winter. (Some trees have nearly all male flowers; these do not bear fruit.)

Schinus molle

This tree produces copious litter, is subject to scale infestation, and has greedy surface roots that make it difficult to garden beneath. Nonetheless, it's handsome when used properly. Plant away from paving, sewers, or drains; give room to spread. A fine choice for shading a play area or gravel-surfaced, outdoor living space. Among the brightest green trees in the desert. Can be planted 2 ft. apart and pruned into a graceful, billowy hedge. Can be killed by root rots, especially Texas root rot. Little or no water to moderate water. In Hawaii, best at higher elevations.

S. terebinthefolius. BRAZILIAN PEPPER TREE. Zones 13, 14 (with shelter), 15–17, 19–24; H1, H2. Native to Brazil; naturalized in Hawaii. Moderate growth to 30 ft. tall and wide; train to single or multiple trunks. Nonpendulous growth. Has darker green, coarser, glossy leaves than *S. molle,* with 5–13 oval leaflets; showy bright red berries in winter.

Individuals of this species show much variation; for best success, select a tree during fruiting season, looking for the largest, showiest berries and best foliage. Dried berries are sold as pink peppercorns; eaten in quantity, they can cause gastric distress. Wood is subject to breakage, so shorten long, lanky limbs and thin canopy to let winds pass through. Prone to verticillium wilt. Attractive shade tree for patio or garden. Self-sown seedlings can be a problem. In Hawaii, the plant has become so invasive that gardeners are advised to forgo the attractive berries and grow male plants only. Moderate to regular water (applied deeply).

SCHIZACHYRIUM
scoparium
LITTLE BLUESTEM
Poaceae (Gramineae)
PERENNIAL GRASS

🗺	ZONES 1–24
☀	FULL SUN
💧	MODERATE TO REGULAR WATER

Native to much of North America; an important grass in the native tall-grass prairie. Formerly known as *Andropogon scoparius.* Clump-forming grass 2–4 ft. tall, 1–2 ft. wide, with narrow leaves that may be erect or arching. Late summer

Schizachyrium scoparium

flowers are inconspicuous but age to an attractive silvery shade. Leaf color varies from bright green to distinctly bluish in summer, from light brown to dark red in fall and winter. Types that are bluer in summer take on the deeper cold-weather colors: blue-green leaves of 'Blaze' turn a strong red in fall, while 'The Blues' has striking light blue leaves that turn burgundy red. Needs well-drained soil. Keep mulch a few inches away from base of plant.

S

SCHIZANTHUS
pinnatus

POOR MAN'S ORCHID,
BUTTERFLY FLOWER
Solanaceae
ANNUAL

| ⚡ ZONES 1–9, 14–24; BEST IN ZONES 1–6, 15–17, 21–24 |
| ☼ FILTERED SUNLIGHT |
| 💧 REGULAR WATER |

Chilean native to 1½ ft. high, 1 ft. wide. Profuse, small orchidlike flowers in pink, rose, lilac, purple, or white, all with markings in various colors. Blossoms look quite showy against the ferny foliage, make long-lasting cut flowers. Buy potted plants or start seeds indoors 4 weeks before planting time (germination is slow). Sensitive to frost and heat. Plant in early spring where summers are moderate, in fall where summers are hot and winters are normally frostless. Give well-drained, rich soil in a wind-sheltered site. Good potted plant. Often grown in greenhouses.

Schizanthus pinnatus

SCHIZOCENTRON elegans.
See **HETEROCENTRON elegans**

SCHIZOPHRAGMA
hydrangeoides

JAPANESE HYDRANGEA VINE
Hydrangeaceae
DECIDUOUS VINE

| ⚡ ZONES 2–9, 14–17 |
| ☼ PARTIAL SHADE |
| 💧 REGULAR WATER |

Native to Korea, Japan. Resembles climbing hydrangea (*Hydrangea anomala petiolaris*). Climbs by holdfasts to 30 ft. or more. Pointed, tooth-edged dark green leaves are 3–5 in. long. Blooms in summer, producing flat, 8–10-in.-wide clusters of white flowers. Like the blossom clusters of lacecap hydrangeas, these feature tiny fertile flowers surrounded by ring of sterile ones—but the sterile blossoms of this plant have only a

Schizophragma hydrangeoides

single "petal" (those of hydrangea have four). 'Moonlight' has blue-green foliage with a silvery cast. 'Roseum' is a pink-flowered variety. Use species or varieties to climb shaded walls or trees. Plant in good, well-drained soil. Prune only to remove errant growth.

SCHIZOSTYLIS
coccinea

CRIMSON FLAG
Iridaceae
PERENNIAL FROM RHIZOME

| ⚡ ZONES 5–9, 14–24; H1, H2 |
| ☼ ☽ FULL SUN OR LIGHT SHADE |
| 💧💧 REGULAR TO AMPLE WATER |

Virtually evergreen South African native. Like gladiolus, it has upright, swordlike leaves and a spike of closely set flowers, but the blossoms themselves—star shaped, brightly colored, 2 in. wide—recall another relative, watsonia. Flowers are carried on slender, 1½–2-ft.-tall stems. The species has crimson blooms; color variants include white 'Alba', watermelon red 'Oregon Sunset', and several in pink shades ('Mrs. Hegarty', 'Sunrise', 'Viscountess Byng'). All bloom in autumn. Excellent cut flowers. Plant in spring, in organically enriched, well-drained soil. Set rhizomes ½–1 in. deep, 1 ft. apart. Water generously from planting time until flowering ends; then water

Schizostylis coccinea

more sparingly until growth resumes in spring. If clumps become crowded, divide them in early spring; each division should have at least five shoots. In cold-winter regions, grow in pots and protect in winter. Some classify this plant as *Hesperantha coccinea*.

SCHLUMBERGERA

Cactaceae
CACTI

| ⚡ ZONES 16, 17, 21–24; H1, H2; OR INDOORS |
| ☼ PARTIAL SHADE; BRIGHT INDIRECT LIGHT |
| 💧 REGULAR WATER |

In nature, these cacti live on trees, as epiphytic orchids do. Need rich, porous soil, such as a mix of equal parts coarse sand, peat moss, and leaf mold. Feed with liquid fertilizer every 7 to 10 days during growth and bloom. Plants are often confused with *Zygocactus*. The many available kinds differ principally in flower color.

S. × buckleyi. CHRISTMAS CACTUS. Sometimes sold as *S. bridgesii*. Old favorite to 2 ft. high, 3 ft. wide. Arching, drooping bright green branches of flattened, scallop-edged, smooth, spineless, 1½-in. joints. Can bear hundreds of many-petaled, long-tubed, 3-in.-long, rosy purplish red flowers at Christmastime. To ensure bud set for late December bloom, give plant cool night temperatures (50 to 55°F/10 to 13°C) and 12 to 14 hours of darkness per day during November.

S. gaertneri. See Rhipsalidopsis gaertneri

Schlumbergera truncata

S. truncata. CRAB CACTUS. Native to Brazil. To 1 ft. high and wide. Bright green, 1–2-in., toothed joints; two large teeth at tip of last joint on each branch. Short-tubed, 3-in.-long, scarlet flowers with spreading, pointed petals from late fall through winter. Many varieties are sold in white, pink, salmon, orange.

SCHOENOPLECTUS
lacustris
tabernaemontani
'Zebrinus'

ZEBRA RUSH
Cyperaceae
PERENNIAL

| ⚡ ZONES 5–24 |
| ☼ ☽ FULL SUN OR LIGHT SHADE |
| 💧💧 AMPLE WATER |

Variety of a somewhat grasslike species found in many parts of the world. Forms an upright clump to 2–4 ft. high and wide. Hollow, apparently leafless, dark green stems are banded horizontally with light yellow; striping tends to fade late in season and in strong sun. Will grow in several inches of water. Best used at edges of pools and ponds. To increase your planting, divide clumps in spring.

Schoenoplectus lacustris tabernaemontani 'Zebrinus'

SCIADOPITYS
verticillata

UMBRELLA PINE
Sciadopityaceae
EVERGREEN TREE

| ⚡ ZONES 4–9, 14–24 |
| ☼ ☽ AFTERNOON SHADE IN HOTTEST CLIMATES |
| 💧 REGULAR WATER |

In its native Japan, this tree reaches 100–120 ft. tall, but in Western gardens it is not likely to exceed 25–40 ft. tall and 25–30 ft. wide. Very slow grower. In youth, it is symmetrical, dense, and rather narrow; with age, it is more open, and limbs tend to droop. Small, scalelike leaves are scattered along branches and bunched at branch ends. Glossy dark green needles grow in whorls of 20–30 at branch and twig ends, radiating out like spokes of an umbrella; they are flattened, firm, fleshy, 3–6 in. long. Woody, 3–5-in. cones may appear on older trees.

S

Sciadopitys verticillata

Choice decorative tree for open ground or containers. Plant in rich, well-drained, neutral or slightly acid soil. Watch for mites in hot, dry weather. Leave unpruned; or thin to create Oriental effect. Good for bonsai.

SCILLA

SQUILL, BLUEBELL
Liliaceae
PERENNIALS FROM BULBS

- ZONES VARY BY SPECIES
- FULL SUN DURING BLOOM, PARTIAL SHADE AFTER
- REGULAR WATER DURING GROWTH AND BLOOM
- ALL PARTS ARE POISONOUS IF INGESTED

The three hardier species are native to cold-winter regions of Europe and Asia and need some winter chill. Gardeners in cold-winter climates know them as harbingers of spring; the earliest ones bloom with winter aconite (*Eranthis*) and snowdrop (*Galanthus*). Less hardy to cold is Peruvian scilla (*S. peruviana*); despite its name, it is native to the Mediterranean region. All squills have bell-shaped or starlike flowers that come on leafless stems that rise from clumps of strap-shaped leaves.

Cold-hardy species look best when naturalized; grow them in small patches or larger drifts. *S. peruviana* is most attractive in clumps along pathways, at edges of mixed plantings, in pots. Plant all types in fall, in well-drained, organically enriched soil. Set bulbs of cold-hardy species 2–3 in. deep, 4 in. apart; set those of *S. peruviana* 3–4 in. deep, 6 in. apart. Reduce watering when foliage yellows after bloom. Hardy kinds will tolerate less moisture during summer dormancy, but don't let soil dry out completely. *S. peruviana* will accept summer moisture but doesn't need any. Divide clumps (during dormancy) only when vigor and bloom quality decline.

S. bifolia. Zones 2–11, 14–21. Each 8-in. stem carries three to eight inch-wide, star-shaped flowers in turquoise blue. White, pale purplish pink, and violet-blue varieties are available. Each bulb produces only two leaves.

S. campanulata. See Hyacinthoides hispanica

S. hispanica. See Hyacinthoides hispanica

S. mischtschenkoana. Zones 1–11, 14–21. Each 6-in. stem bears nodding clusters of three or four starlike flowers in pale blue with darker blue stripes.

S. non-scripta. See Hyacinthoides non-scripta

S. peruviana. PERUVIAN SCILLA. Zones 14–17, 19–24. Large bulb produces numerous, rather floppy leaves; in late spring, 10–12-in. stems appear, each topped with dome-shaped cluster of 50 or more starlike flowers. Most forms have bluish purple blooms, but a white-flowered variety is sometimes sold. Bulbs are dormant only for a short time after leaves wither.

Scilla peruviana

S. siberica. SIBERIAN SQUILL. Zones A2, A3; 1–7, 10. Each 3–6-in. stem bears several flowers shaped like flaring bells. Typical color is intense medium blue, but there are varieties in white, lilac pink, and light to dark shades of violet blue, often with darker stripes. 'Spring Beauty' has brilliant violet-blue blooms that are larger than those of species.

SCIRPUS cernuus.
See **ISOLEPIS cernua**

SCOTCH BROOM.
See **CYTISUS scoparius**

SCOTCH HEATHER.
See **CALLUNA vulgaris**

SCOTCH MOSS.
See **SAGINA subulata**

SCRAMBLED EGGS.
See **SENNA surattensis**

SCREW BEAN.
See **PROSOPIS pubescens**

SCREWPINE.
See **PANDANUS tectorius**

SCROPHULARIA

Scrophulariaceae
PERENNIALS

- ZONES VARY BY SPECIES
- FULL SUN OR PARTIAL SHADE
- WATER NEEDS VARY BY SPECIES

Though it has lent its name to a large and important plant family, this genus is relatively little known in gardens. Like other members of Scrophulariaceae, it has more or less tubular, two-lipped flowers.

S. auriculata 'Variegata'. WATER BETONY, WATER FIG-WORT. Zones 3–9, 14–24. From western Europe. To 4 ft. tall, 2 ft. wide. Stems have flattened "wings." Wrinkled, toothed, lance-shaped green leaves are strongly marked with cream, grow 2–10 in. long. Green, ½-in.-long flowers with a purplish brown upper lip bloom from summer into early fall. Ample water. Showy plant for waterside plantings or damp borders.

Scrophularia macrantha

S. macrantha. REDBIRDS IN A TREE. Zones 2b–10, 12–24. From high mountains of the Southwest. To 3–4 ft. tall and 1½ ft. wide, with lance-shaped, glossy dark green, 1–3-in.-long leaves. Stems are leaning, with a tendency to recline; plant with other tall perennials for support. Bright red, puffy, ¾-in.-long flowers in 12–15-in. spires bloom from midsummer until frost. Little to regular water.

SCUTELLARIA

SKULLCAP
Lamiaceae (Labiatae)
PERENNIALS

- ZONES VARY BY SPECIES
- FULL SUN OR LIGHT SHADE
- REGULAR WATER

Clump-forming mint relatives, with the family's typical square stems and paired leaves. Long, tubular flowers flare out into two lips, the upper one narrow and hooded, the lower one broad. Blossoms are clustered in roundish or elongated inflorescences. Easy to grow if given good drainage.

S. alpina. Zones 1–9, 14–24. From southern Europe to Siberia. Sprawling, mat-forming plant to 6 in. high, 1 ft. wide, with dark green, oval, 1-in. leaves. Tight clusters of 1-in., purple or white flowers in late spring, early summer.

Scutellaria baicalensis

S. baicalensis. Zones 1–9, 14–24. Native to Siberia, China, Japan. Stems first spread, then grow upright, forming a clump 1½ ft. tall and wide. Narrowly ovate, 1½-in.-long, medium green leaves. Dense, one-sided clusters of blue-purple, inch-long flowers in summer and fall.

S. costaricana. Zones 23, 24; H2; or indoors. From Central America. Erect plant to 3 ft. or taller, half as wide, with dark green, heavily veined, ovate to elliptical leaves to 6 in. long; showy clusters of 1½-in., orange-scarlet flowers with yellow throat. Outdoors, blooms in late spring, early summer; anytime in greenhouse or indoors.

S. resinosa. Zones 3–10, 14–24. Native from Kansas and Colorado south to Texas and Arizona. Mounding plant 6–8 in. tall, 1 ft. wide, with roundish, resinous, grayish green leaves less than ½ in. long. Elongated clusters of deep purple-blue, 1-in. flowers in late spring. Deadhead for intermittent bloom through autumn.

SEA BUCKTHORN.
See **HIPPOPHAE rhamnoides**

SEAFORTHIA elegans.
See **ARCHONTOPHOENIX cunninghamiana**

SEA GRAPE.
See **COCCOLOBA uvifera**

SEA HOLLY. See **ERYNGIUM**

SEA KALE.
See **CRAMBE maritima**

SEA LAVENDER.
See **LIMONIUM**

SEA OATS.
See **CHASMANTHIUM latifolium**

SEA PINK. See **ARMERIA**

SEA POPPY. See **GLAUCIUM**

SEASIDE DAISY.
See **ERIGERON glaucus**

SEA URCHIN.
See **HAKEA laurina**

SEDGE. See **CAREX**

SEDUM
STONECROP
Crassulaceae
SUCCULENT PERENNIALS

| 🖋 ZONES VARY BY SPECIES |
| ☀ ☼ FULL SUN OR PARTIAL SHADE, EXCEPT AS NOTED |
| ○ ◑ LITTLE TO MODERATE WATER, EXCEPT AS NOTED |

Native to many parts of the world. Some are quite hardy to cold, others fairly tender; some are tiny and trailing, others much larger and upright. Fleshy leaves are evergreen (unless otherwise noted) but highly variable in size, shape, and color. Typically small, star-shaped flowers, sometimes brightly colored, are usually borne in fairly large clusters.

Smaller sedums are useful in rock gardens, as ground or bank covers, in small areas where unusual texture is needed. Some are prized by collectors of succulents, who grow them in pots, dish gardens, or miniature gardens. Larger types are good in borders or containers. Most sedums are easy to propagate by stem cuttings; even detached leaves will root and form new plants. Soft and easily crushed, they will not take foot traffic, but they are otherwise tough, low-maintenance plants.

S. acre. GOLDMOSS SEDUM. Zones A2, A3; 1–24. Native to Europe, North Africa, Turkey. To 2–5 in. high, with upright branchlets rising from trailing, rooting stems. Light green leaves to ¼ in. long; clustered yellow flowers bloom in spring. Extremely hardy but can get out of bounds and become a weed. Use as ground cover (set plants 1–1½ ft. apart), between stepping-stones, or in chinks of dry walls.

S. album. Zones 1–24. Often sold as *S. brevifolium.* From Europe, Siberia, western Asia, North Africa. Creeping plant grows to 2–6 in. high. Leaves to ½ in. long, light to medium green, sometimes red tinted. White or pinkish summer flowers. Plant 1–1½ ft. apart for ground cover. Roots from the smallest fragment; beware of planting it near choice, delicate rock garden plants. 'Coral Carpet' displays coral pink new growth and turns reddish bronze in winter.

S. altissimum. See S. rupestre, S. sediforme

S. anglicum. Zones 1–24. From western Europe. Low, spreading plant 2–4 in. high. Dark green leaves are tiny, to just ⅛ in. long. Pinkish or white spring flowers. For ground cover, set plants 9–12 in. apart.

S. 'Autumn Joy' (S. 'Herbstfreude'). Zones 1–10, 14–24. Hybrid of *S. telephium* and *S. spectabile.* To 1–2 ft. tall, 2 ft. wide, with green leaves to 2–3 in. long and about as wide. Rounded clusters of blossoms are pink when they open in late summer or autumn, later age to coppery pink and finally to rust. Dies down in winter.

Sedum 'Autumn Joy'

S. brevifolium. Zones 8, 9, 14–24. Native to the Mediterranean region. Grows just 2–3 in. high, slowly spreading to 1 ft. wide. Gray-white, red-flushed leaves are tiny (less than ⅛ in. long), tightly packed on stems. Pinkish or white summer flowers. Needs acid soil and good drainage. Best in rock garden or with larger succulents

in containers, miniature garden. Sunburns in hot, dry places.

S. cauticola. Zones 1–11, 14–24. Native to Japan. Slowly forms a mound 4–6 in. high, 1–1½ ft. wide. Blue-gray, slightly toothed, 1-in. leaves. Clusters of small rose red flowers top stems in late summer or early fall. Dies to ground in winter.

S. confusum. Zones 8, 9, 14–24. Native to Mexico. Spreading, branching plant grows 6–18 in. high and wide. Shiny dark green, ¾–1½-in.-long leaves tend to cluster in rosettes toward branch ends. Dense clusters of yellow flowers in spring. Makes a good ground cover but is sometimes plagued by dieback in wet soils, hot weather; it looks best during cooler weather. Use in borders or containers, as edging, in miniature garden. A similar, smaller plant with light green leaves is the closely related *S. kimnachii.*

S. dasyphyllum. Zones 2–24; H1, H2. Native to the Mediterranean region. Forms a low (1½–4½-in.-high) mat that spreads to 1 ft. or wider. Gray-green, ⅛–¼-in. leaves are densely packed on stems. Blooms in summer, bearing white flowers with pink streaks. Pink-blossomed 'Riffense' has silver-gray leaves that are especially plump and succulent. Partial shade.

S. dendroideum. Zones 8, 9, 12, 14–24. Native to Mexico. Branching plant to 3 ft. tall and wide. Rounded leaves to 2 in. long are yellow green, often bronze tinted. Deep yellow flowers in spring and summer. For the plant sometimes sold as *S. d. praealtum,* see S. praealtum.

S. guatemalense. See S. × rubrotinctum

S. kamtschaticum. Zones 1–11, 14–21. Native to Korea, Japan. Variable species to 4–12 in. high, 2 ft. wide, with trailing stems set with thick, somewhat triangular, 1–1½-in., medium green leaves, toothed on the upper third. Summer flowers open yellow, age to red. Useful in colder climates as a rock garden plant or small-space ground cover (set plants 1 ft. apart). 'Variegatum' has cream-edged leaves. *S. k. ellacombianum* (sometimes sold as *S. ellacombianum*) is a shorter plant (4–6 in. high) with more compact growth, unbranched stems, and brighter green leaves. *S. k. floriferum* (sometimes sold as *S. floriferum*) is a more profuse bloomer with smaller, paler flowers; its variety 'Weihenstephaner Gold' has golden blossoms that age to orange.

S. kimnachii. See S. confusum
S. lineare. Zones 1–24. Often sold as *S. sarmentosum.* Native to China, Japan. To 4 in. high. Trailing, rooting stems to 1 ft. long are closely set with narrow, inch-long light green leaves. Profuse yellow flowers in late spring, early summer. For ground cover, set plants 1–1½ ft. apart. 'Variegatum', with white-edged leaves, is often grown in containers.

S. morganianum. DONKEY TAIL, BURRO TAIL. Zones 17, 22–24; H1, H2; with protection of lath or eaves in Zones 13–16, 18–21; or indoors. From Mexico. Produces long, trailing stems that reach 3–4 ft. in 6 to 8 years. Thick, ¾-in.-long, light gray-green leaves overlap each other along stems to form braided-looking "tails" less than 1 in. thick. Pink to deep red flowers may appear from spring to summer but are only rarely seen. Because of its long stems, this

Sedum morganianum

species is best grown in a hanging basket or wall pot; in mildest climates, try it spilling from top of a wall or in rock garden. Provide rich, fast-draining soil. Protect from wind and give partial shade. Similar relatives include *S. burrito* (*S.* 'Burro'), with fatter (1-in.-thick) tails composed of densely packed, ½-in. leaves; and giant donkey tail (sometimes sold as *S. orpetii*), with somewhat shorter, thicker tails.

S. oxypetalum. Zones 16, 17, 21–24. Native to Mexico. To 3 ft. tall (usually much less), 1½ ft. wide. Even when tiny, the plant has the look of a gnarled tree. Narrow, 1–1½-in.-long, olive green leaves; dull red, aromatic summer flowers. Evergreen or semievergreen in mildest areas; deciduous elsewhere. Handsome container plant.

S

S. praealtum. Zones 8, 9, 12, 14–24. Native to Mexico. Similar to *S. dendroideum* (and sometimes sold as *S. d. praealtum*) but has a wider spread and is less treelike (to 5 ft. high and wide), with greener leaves and lighter yellow flowers. Blooms in spring and summer.

S. × rubrotinctum. PORK AND BEANS. Zones 8, 9, 12, 14–24; H1, H2. Thought to be native to Mexico. Sometimes sold as *S. guatemalense*. Sprawling, leaning, 6–8-in. stems are set with ¾-in. leaves that look like jelly beans; they are green with reddish brown tips, often entirely bronze red in sun. Detach easily and root readily. Yellow spring flowers. Grow in rock garden, in pots, as small-space ground cover (set plants 8–10 in. apart). Leaves of 'Aurora' are bright pink.

S. rupestre (S. reflexum). Zones 2–24. Native to Europe. Often sold as *S. altissimum*. Much like *S. sediforme* but more vigorous, with shorter leaves and yellow summer flowers. Spreads freely; set plants 9–12 in. apart for ground cover.

S. sarmentosum. See *S. lineare*

S. sediforme (S. altissimum). Zones 2–24. Mediterranean native. Spreading, creeping plant grows to 16 in. high, 1 ft. wide. Narrow, light blue-gray leaves to 1½ in. long, closely set on stems. Small greenish white to light yellow flowers in summer. Use in rock garden, for blue-green effect in pattern planting, as small-space ground cover (set plants 1 ft. apart).

S. sieboldii. Zones 2–9, 12, 14–24. Native to Japan. Low-growing plant just 4 in. high, 8–12 in. wide, with spreading, trailing, unbranched stems to 8–9 in. long. Blue-gray leaves with red edges are carried in threes; they are nearly round, stalkless, toothed along upper half. Plant turns coppery red in fall, dies to ground in winter. Each stem bears a broad, dense, flat cluster of dusty pink flowers in autumn. Leaves of 'Variegatum' have yellowish white markings. Species and variety are beautiful in rock gardens, hanging baskets. Light shade.

S. spathulifolium. Zones 2–9, 14–24. Native from California's Coast Ranges and Sierra Nevada north to British Columbia. Spoon-shaped, ½–1-in. blue-green leaves tinged with reddish purple are packed into rosettes on short, trailing stems. Light yellow flowers bloom in spring and summer. Use it as ground cover (set plants 1–1½ ft. apart), in rock garden.

Sedum spathulifolium 'Purpureum'

Very drought tolerant. 'Cape Blanco' is a selected form with good leaf color; 'Purpureum' has deep purple foliage.

S. spectabile. Zones 1–24. Native to China, Korea. To 1½ ft. tall and wide, with upright or slightly spreading stems thickly clothed in blue-green, roundish, 3-in. leaves. Dense, 6-in.-wide, dome-shaped flower clusters appear atop stems in late summer and fall; they open pink, mature to dark brown seed heads that put on a long-lasting show. Dies to ground in winter. Full sun. Regular to moderate water. Varieties include 'Brilliant', with deep rose red flowers; 'Carmen', soft rose; 'Indian Chief', coppery red; 'Meteor', carmine red; and 'Ruby Jewel', deep maroon.

S. spurium. Zones 1–10, 14–24. Native to Caucasus. Low-growing plant with trailing stems and dark green or bronze-tinted leaves just an inch or so long; spreads 2 ft. or wider. In summer, pink, purple, or white flowers appear in dense clusters at ends of 4–5-in. stems. For rock garden, pattern planting, ground cover. 'Bronze Carpet' has bronze leaves and pink flowers; 'Dragon's Blood' ('Schorbuser Blut') has purplish bronze leaves, dark red blooms. Red-leafed varieties include 'Red Carpet' (with red blossoms) and 'Fuldaglut' (with rosy pink flowers). Leaves of 'Tricolor' are variegated in green, creamy white, and pink; its flowers are pink.

S. telephium. Zones 1–24. To 2 ft. high, 1–2 ft. wide. Native from Europe eastward to Japan. Resembles *S. spectabile* but has gray-green, somewhat narrower leaves. Long-lasting floral display begins in late summer and fall; blossom clusters open purplish pink, age to brownish maroon. Plant dies to ground in winter. 'Matrona' has dark pink–edged gray-green leaves that age to gray-ish brown (retaining the pink edge), large heads of pink flowers borne on red stems. 'Mohrchen' has purple new growth and rosy pink

flowers. *S. t. maximum* 'Atropurpureum' has burgundy foliage all season and dusty pink flowers. Plant in full sun (stems tend to flop in shaded sites). Regular to moderate water.

S. 'Vera Jameson' (Hylotelephium 'Vera Jameson'). Zones 1–9, 14–24. Cross between *S. telephium maximum* 'Atropurpureum' and *S.* 'Ruby Glow' (a low-growing hybrid with purple-gray leaves and ruby red flowers). To 8–12 in. high and about 1½ ft. wide, with spreading purple stems clothed in pink-ish purple leaves. Rose pink flowers in late summer, fall. Dies to ground in winter.

SEGO LILY. See **CALOCHORTUS**

SELF-HEAL. See **PRUNELLA**

SEMIARUNDINARIA. See **BAMBOO**

SEMPERVIVUM

HOUSELEEK
Crassulaceae
SUCCULENT PERENNIALS

🌿 ZONES 2–24
☼ ◐ LIGHT SHADE IN HOTTEST CLIMATES
◐ ◓ LITTLE TO MODERATE WATER

Native to mountains of Europe. Form tightly packed rosettes of fleshy, evergreen leaves; spread by little offsets that cluster around parent rosette. Clustered, star-shaped summer flowers in white, yellowish, pink, red, or greenish; pretty in detail but not showy. Blooming rosettes die after setting seed, but offsets (easily detached and replanted) carry on. Many species, all good in rock gardens, pots, even in pockets in boulders or pieces of porous rock. Need excellent drainage. Water only to prevent shriveling. Protect from full sun in hot desert regions.

S. arachnoideum. COBWEB HOUSELEEK. Gray-green rosettes of many leaves are joined by fine hairs for a cobweb-covered look. Larger rosettes (to 3 in. wide) are surrounded by host of smaller

Sempervivum tectorum

rosettes. Spreads slowly to make dense mat to 1 ft. or wider. Bright red flowers on 4–6-in. stems.

S. tectorum. HEN AND CHICK-ENS. Gray-green, 2–5-in.-wide rosettes spread quickly to form clumps to 2 ft. or wider. Leaves have red-brown, bristly tips. Red or reddish blossoms are borne on stems to 2 ft. tall. Colored-leaf varieties in red, purple, chartreuse, and silvery blue are available.

SENECIO

Asteraceae (Compositae)
PERENNIALS AND EVERGREEN OR
DECIDUOUS SHRUBS AND VINES

🌿 ZONES VARY BY SPECIES
☼ ◐ ● EXPOSURE NEEDS VARY BY SPECIES
◐ ◓ ● WATER NEEDS VARY BY SPECIES

This group of daisy relatives includes the well-known dusty miller and florist's cineraria as well as less familiar garden plants and even a few weeds. Succulent species are often sold as *Kleinia*, an earlier name.

S. cineraria. DUSTY MILLER. Shrubby perennial. Zones 4–24; H1, H2. From the Mediterranean region. To 2–3 ft. high and wide, with woolly white leaves cut into many blunt-tipped lobes. Blooms at almost any season in mild-winter climates, during summer in colder regions, bearing clustered heads of yellow or creamy yellow flowers. Striking in a night garden. Gets leggy unless sheared occasionally. Full sun. Provide good drainage, little to moderate water. For the plant sometimes labeled as *S. cineraria* 'Candissimus', see *S. viravira*.

Senecio cineraria

S. confusus (Pseudogynoxys chenopodioides). MEXICAN FLAME VINE. Evergreen or decid-uous vine. Zones 13, 16–24; H1, H2; mild frost kills it to the ground, but it comes back fast from roots. Sometimes grown as a summer annual in colder climates. Native from Mexico to Honduras. Twines to 10–15 ft. in California, as much as 40 ft. in Hawaii. Light

S

green, rather fleshy leaves to 4 in. long are broadly lance shaped, coarsely toothed. Large clusters of ¾–1-in., startling orange-red blooms with golden centers appear at branch ends; blossoms of 'São Paulo' are a deeper orange, almost brick red. Blooms from midspring into fall, sometimes year-round in frostless areas. Provide light soil, moderate to regular water. Full sun or light shade. Use on trellis or column, let cascade over a bank or wall, or plant in a hanging basket.

S. cruentus. See S. × hybridus

S. greyi. Evergreen shrub. Zones 5–9, 14–24. Plant commonly sold under this name is actually *Brachyglottis* Dunedin Group 'Sunshine'. To 4–5 ft. high, 6 ft. or more wide. Stiff, slightly curving stems bear 3½-in.-long, leathery gray-green leaves outlined in silvery white. Blooms profusely in summer, producing inch-wide yellow daisies in flattish, 5-in.-wide clusters. Full sun. Moderate to regular water. Prune out oldest growth yearly. Cut branches are long lasting in arrangements.

S. × hybridus (Pericallis × hybrida, S. cruentus). FLORISTS' CINERARIA. Perennial usually grown as an annual; or indoors. Best in Zones 16, 17, 22–24, where it may overwinter or reseed. To 2 ft. high and wide. Valuable for bright colors in cool, shady places; not for hot, dry climates. Most common are large-flowered dwarf kinds generally sold as Multiflora Nana or Hybrida Grandiflora. These are compact, 12–15-in. plants with broad clusters of 3–5-in. daisies in colors ranging from white through pink and purplish red to blue and purple, often with contrasting eyes or bands. Bloom in late winter and early spring in mild-winter areas, spring and early summer elsewhere. Plants sold as *Cineraria stellata* (an invalid botanical name) are taller (to 2½–3 ft.), with clusters of smaller, star-shaped daisies. Grow in loose, rich soil. Plant in fall or

Senecio × hybridus

spring; protect plants set out in fall from frost by choosing a location under shrubs, trees, overhang, or lath. Effective in mass plantings or combined with other shade-loving plants; excellent in containers on lanai, patio. Even where perennial, usually discarded after bloom. Principal pests are leaf miners, spider mites, slugs, snails. Partial or full shade. Regular water.

S. leucostachys. See S. viravira

S. macroglossus. KENYA IVY, NATAL IVY, WAX VINE. Evergreen vine. Zones 12 and 13 (if given northern or eastern exposure), 22–24; H1, H2; or indoors. Native to southeastern Africa. Thin, succulent stems twine to 6½ ft. or more. Thick, waxy or rubbery, 2–3-in.-wide leaves are shaped like those of ivy (*Hedera*), with three, five, or seven shallow lobes. Tiny yellow daisies in summer. Leaves of 'Variegatum' are sharply splashed with creamy white. Little to moderate water. Can be grown as a houseplant in a sunny window; water only when soil is dry.

Senecio mandraliscae

S. mandraliscae (Kleinia mandraliscae). Succulent shrubby perennial. Zones 12, 13, 16, 17, 21–24; H1, H2. Native to South Africa. To 1–1½ ft. high, 2 ft. wide. Cylindrical, slightly curved, striking blue-gray leaves to 6 in. long. Use as ground cover where blue-gray effect is desired. Partial shade in the desert; full sun elsewhere. Little to moderate water. Beyond hardiness range, grow in a container and provide winter protection.

S. mikanioides (Delairea odorata). GERMAN IVY. Evergreen vine; dies to the ground in cold winters. Zones 14–24, H1, H2; or indoors. Native to South Africa. Twines to 18–20 ft. Roundish leaves resemble those of ivy (*Hedera*), have five or seven ½–3-in.-long, sharply pointed lobes. Winter flowers are small yellow "buttons"— daisies without rays. Good screening vine or trailer for window

boxes. Full sun or part shade. Little to moderate water. A noxious weed in coastal California and in Hawaii.

S. petasitis. VELVET GROUNDSEL, CALIFORNIA GERANIUM. Shrubby perennial. Zones 15–17, 21–24. From Mexico. Bulky plant to 6–8 ft. or taller, equally wide. Velvety, evergreen leaves have a tropical look: they are large (to 8 in. across), lobed, fanlike. Blooms in midwinter, bearing large clusters of small bright yellow daisies that stand well above the foliage mass. Prune hard after bloom to limit height and sprawl. Can be kept to 2–4 ft. in tubs. Good filler in tropical gardens. Full sun or light shade. Regular water.

S. serpens (Kleinia repens). Succulent perennial. Zones 16, 17, 21–24. From South Africa. This species resembles S. mandraliscae, but it is a smaller plant (to 6 in. high and 1 ft. wide) with smaller (1¼-in.) leaves.

S. viravira (S. leucostachys, S. cineraria 'Candissimus'). DUSTY MILLER. Shrubby perennial. Zones 4–24. Native to Argentina. Sprawling plant to 4 ft. tall and wide. Leaves resemble those of S. cineraria, but they are more strikingly white and are cut into much narrower, pointed segments. Creamy white summer flowers are not showy. Grown in full sun, plant is brilliantly white and densely leafy; in part shade, it is looser and more sparsely foliaged, with larger, greener leaves. Tip-pinch young plants to keep them compact. Little to moderate water.

SENNA
Fabaceae (Leguminosae)
EVERGREEN AND DECIDUOUS SHRUBS OR TREES

⚡ ZONES VARY BY SPECIES
☼ ◗ **FULL SUN OR LIGHT SHADE, EXCEPT AS NOTED**
◊ ◖ **LITTLE TO MODERATE WATER, EXCEPT AS NOTED**

Previously included in *Cassia* and still often sold as such, these species have been reclassified as *Senna*—a move not accepted by all botanists. Grown for their lavish show of bright yellow, five-petaled flowers that look something like those of potentilla. Blossoms are followed by seedpods that may create litter; to reduce pod production, prune lightly after flowering. Rangy, rank growers should also be cut back periodically to encourage more compact growth. Good for screens, massing, background plantings. Prefer well-drained soil.

Senna artemisioides

S. artemisioides (Cassia artemisioides). FEATHERY CASSIA. Evergreen shrub. Zones 8, 9, 12–16, 18–23. Native to Australia. To 3–5 ft. tall and wide, with attractive, light, airy structure. Gray leaves divided into six to eight needlelike, 1-in.-long leaflets. Bears ¾-in. flowers in clusters of five to eight in winter and spring, with bloom often continuing into summer. In the desert, plants may rest in summer, then resume flowering in fall. Heavy seed production. Very drought tolerant but looks better with moderate to regular water.

S. corymbosa (Cassia corymbosa). FLOWERY SENNA. Evergreen shrub. Zones 12, 13, 21–24; H1, H2. Native to South America. Rangy growth to 10 ft. tall, 10–12 ft. wide. Dark green leaves with six narrow, oblong, 1–2-in. leaflets. Rounded clusters of 1½-in. flowers, spring to fall. Self-seeding can be a problem.

S. didymobotrya (Cassia didymobotrya, C. nairobensis). Evergreen shrub. Zones 13, 22–24; H2. Native to eastern Africa. Rangy growth to 8 ft. tall, 8–10 wide. Blooms from winter into spring, bearing 1½-in.-wide flowers in dense, upright clusters to 1 ft. long. Olive green to dark green leaves made up of 16 to 32 leaflets, each about 2 in. long. Foliage is smelly when cut or bruised, but plant is nonetheless attractive in large wild gardens. Full sun. Moderate to regular water.

S. multiglandulosa (Cassia tomentosa). WOOLLY SENNA. Evergreen shrub. Zones 13, 17, 22–24. Native to many parts of the tropics. Vigorous, rank growth to 12–15 ft. tall and wide. Upright clusters of 1½-in. flowers at branch ends in winter, early spring. Leaves are green above, white and hairy beneath, divided into 12–16 leaflets, each about 2½ in. long. Regular water.

S

S. nemophila (S. artemisiodes filifolia, Cassia eremophila). DESERT CASSIA. Evergreen shrub. Zones 12–24. Australian native similar to *C. artemisioides* but with green rather than gray foliage and somewhat greater cold tolerance.

S. phyllodinea (S. artemisioides petiolaris, Cassia phyllodinea). SILVER LEAF CASSIA. Evergreen shrub. Zones 12–24. Native to Australia. Rapid growth to 4–6 ft. tall and wide. Silvery gray leaves are narrow, curved, 1–2 in. long. Flowers are ¾ in. wide, blooming over a long season—from winter (sometimes as early as fall) into spring. Full sun.

S. splendida (Cassia splendida). GOLDEN WONDER SENNA. Evergreen shrub. Zones 12, 13, 21–24; H1, H2. Native to Brazil. Open growth to at least 9–12 ft. tall, 6–10 ft. wide; habit varies from fairly upright to horizontal. Bright green leaves with four elliptical to oblong leaflets to 3 in. long. Loose clusters of 1½-in. flowers appear at branch ends from autumn into winter. Heavy seed production.

S. sturtii (S. artemisioides sturtii, Cassia sturtii). Evergreen shrub. Zones 12–14. Native to Australia. Bushy growth to 3–6 ft. tall, 3–4 ft. wide. Gray-green leaves with four to ten narrow, 1-in. leaflets. Tidier looking than *S. artemisioides.*

S. surattensis (Cassia surattensis). SCRAMBLED EGGS, KOLOMANA. Evergreen shrub or tree. Zones 19–24; H1, H2. Native to tropical Asia, Polynesia, and Australia. In Hawaii, it reaches 25 ft. tall and nearly as wide and is used as a flowering shade or street tree. In California, grows 6–8 ft. high and wide, makes a handsome flowering shrub for a small garden. Blooms nearly year-round, producing small clusters of ¾-in. flowers at branch ends. Each green leaf has 12–20 roundish, 1½-in. leaflets.

S. wislizenii (Cassia wislizenii). Deciduous shrub. Zones 10–13. From southern Arizona into Texas, Mexico. Rounded habit to 5–8 ft. tall, 5–10 ft. wide, with rigid, upright branches. Bright green leaves have four to six leaflets, each to 1¼ in. long. Clusters of 1-in. flowers appear at branch ends from early summer into fall.

SENTRY PALM.
See **HOWEA belmoreana**

SEQUOIA
sempervirens
REDWOOD, COAST REDWOOD
Taxodiaceae
EVERGREEN TREE

🌿 ZONES 4–9, 14–24
☀️ ◑ FULL SUN OR LIGHT SHADE
💧💧 MODERATE TO REGULAR WATER

Native to Coast Ranges from southern Oregon to central coastal California. One of the West's most famous native trees (equally renowned is its close relative *Sequoiadendron,* called giant sequoia or big tree). Coast redwood is the tallest of the world's trees: some individuals in the wild are over 350 ft. high. Fine landscaping tree—almost entirely pest free and almost always fresh looking and woodsy smelling. In its native range, a redwood tree grows rapidly (3–5 ft. a year in its early years) but will reach only about 70–90 ft. tall, 15–30 ft. wide in 25 years. In less favorable areas, grows more slowly and tops out at perhaps 50 ft. Typically forms a symmetrical pyramid of soft-looking foliage. Flat, pointed, narrow, inch-long leaves are typically medium green on top, grayish beneath; they grow in one plane on both sides of stem, giving stem a featherlike look. Small (½–1½-in.), roundish brown cones. Red-brown, fibrous-barked trunk goes straight up. A trunk with nearly parallel sides indicates a healthy redwood; one with a noticeable taper means the tree is struggling. Habit is somewhat variable, but most redwoods have main branches that grow straight out from trunk and curve up at tips; slightly drooping branchlets grow from these.

The tree's natural variability has led to selection of distinct variants. 'Aptos Blue' has dense blue-green foliage on nearly horizontal branches with drooping branchlets. 'Los Altos' features a thick canopy of dark green leaves on horizontal, arching branches. 'Majestic Beauty' has dense blue-green foliage, horizontal branches with pendulous branchlets. 'Santa Cruz' has soft, light green leaves and slightly downward-angled branches. Fine-textured 'Soquel' bears blue-tinged green foliage on horizontal branches that turn up at tips. 'Filoli' and 'Woodside' are similar if not identical to each other; both are

Sequoia sempervirens

nearly as blue as Colorado blue spruce (*Picea pungens glauca*). They have an irregular habit, with branches that tend to droop, and need careful training when young to establish good form. 'Simpson's Silver' is somewhat slower growing than other redwood varieties; it has stiffly horizontal branches and silvery blue leaves that fade to blue green with maturity. 'Adpressa' ('Albo-Spica'), to 3 ft. high and 6 ft. wide, is a dwarf variety for rock gardens; it has white-tipped new growth that turns solid green as summer advances.

Grow redwood trees singly or in groves (spaced 7 ft. apart); can also be used for a hedge (plant 3–4 ft. apart and top at least once yearly). One of the best planting locations is in or directly next to a lawn, since the tree thrives on regular moisture (in 10–20 years, however, it may defeat a lawn). Away from lawns, it needs occasional feeding and regular summer watering (at least for first 5 years). Where it is best adapted, an established tree gets all the moisture it needs from fog drip. Resistant to oak root fungus.

Troubles the tree encounters are mostly physiological. Inadequate moisture or a hot, dry site will make it sulk and grow slowly; too much competition from bigger trees and structures makes it lanky, thin, and open. Lack of available iron makes needles turn yellow in summer, especially on new growth; solve the problem by applying iron sulfate or chelates. Keep in mind, however, that it is normal for oldest leaves to turn from green to yellow to brown, then drop in late summer and early fall; short twigs also turn brown and drop.

SEQUOIADENDRON
giganteum
(Sequoia gigantea)
GIANT SEQUOIA, BIG TREE
Taxodiaceae
EVERGREEN TREE

🌿 ZONES 1–9, 14–23
☀️ FULL SUN
💧 MODERATE WATER

Native to western slope of central and southern Sierra Nevada. Old specimens reach a towering 325 ft.

Sequoiadendron giganteum

and have the most massive trunk in the world (to 30 ft. in diameter), yet young trees ("young" in terms of a 3,000-year life span) are neat, handsome trees for larger gardens, reaching 60–100 ft. tall, 30–50 ft. wide. This tree has always shared fame and comparisons with its close relative, coast redwood (*Sequoia*), but horticulturally the similarities are few.

Giant sequoia is hardier to cold than coast redwood; it grows somewhat more slowly (2–3 ft. a year) and needs less water. Outside its natural habitat, this tree is subject to fungal diseases that can disfigure or kill it; seems more successful in colder interior climates than near the coast.

Giant sequoia's dense foliage is bushier than that of coast redwood. It is a somewhat prickly tree to reach into. Branchlets are clothed with short gray-green leaves; each leaf is a pointed scale overlapping the next, like prickly cypress (*Cupressus*) foliage. Dark reddish brown, oval, 2–3-in.-long cones. Lower branches hang on for many years, so that tree form is a dense pyramid; lowest branches sometimes root where they touch the ground, forming secondary "trees" that blend into the original. Removing lower branches reveals a fissured, craggy-looking trunk covered in dark red-brown bark. In gardens, giant sequoia is primarily used as a featured tree in a large lawn (roots may surface there) or other open space. Grow in good, deep, well-drained soil. 'Glaucum' has blue-green leaves. 'Pendulum' has an irregular form and strongly weeping branches; it can be trained into tall pillar to about 25 ft. high and 4 ft. wide or a little wider.

SERIPHIDIUM canum,
S. tridentatum. See **ARTEMISIA cana, A. tridentata**

S

SERVICEBERRY.
See **AMELANCHIER**

SESLERIA
MOOR GRASS
Poaceae (Gramineae)
PERENNIAL GRASSES

🌿	ZONES VARY BY SPECIES
☀️ 🌤️	FULL SUN TO PARTIAL SHADE
💧 💧	MODERATE TO REGULAR WATER

Tufted evergreen to semievergreen perennial grasses from the hills and mountains of southeastern Europe. Tough, long-lived, low-maintenance plants that can take considerable drought once established. Use as fillers among other ornamentals or mass as ground covers among trees and shrubs, in meadow plantings.

Sesleria caerulea

S. autumnalis. AUTUMN MOOR GRASS. Zones 3b–10, 14–24. Spiky clumps of narrow, lime green leaves grow 8–18 in. high and wide. Attractive light tan flowers are held in elongated spikes 6–8 in. above the foliage in late summer and fall.

S. caerulea. BLUE MOOR GRASS. Zones 2b–10, 14–24. To 6–8 in. high and wide. Narrow leaves are powder blue on top, dark green beneath; their slightly twisted shape makes both colors visible. Short spikelike flowers held above the leaves in late spring emerge purplish black and lighten as they age; pretty but not showy. Best near the coast. Plant in partial shade inland.

SETCREASEA pallida 'Purple Heart'. See **TRADESCANTIA pallida 'Purpurea'**

SEVEN SONS FLOWER. See **HEPTACODIUM miconioides**

SHADBLOW. See **AMELANCHIER**

SHADSCALE. See **ATRIPLEX confertifolia**

SHALLOT
Liliaceae
PERENNIAL OFTEN GROWN AS ANNUAL

🌿	ALL ZONES
☀️	FULL SUN
💧	REGULAR WATER

Closely related to onion and, like it, a member of the genus *Allium*. Thought to have originated in western or central Asia. The bulb is divided into sections that grow on a common base; it is prized in cooking for its distinctive flavor, a combination of mild onion and pungent garlic. Young green shoots are also edible. Dutch shallots have golden brown skin and white cloves; red shallots have coppery skin, purple cloves.

In mild climates, you can plant shallots in fall to harvest green tops through winter and early spring, bulbs in late spring and summer. In cold-winter regions, plant in early spring for green shoots in summer, bulbs in autumn.

Shallot

Shallots are usually grown from cloves (sections of bulbs). You can purchase these from a seed company or simply buy shallots in the grocery store and separate them into cloves. Plant cloves with their pointed end up, 4–8 in. apart; cover them with ½ in. of soil. You'll have green shoots in about 60 days, new bulbs in 90 to 120 days. Some seed companies sell shallot seeds; plant 12 seeds per foot. Bulbs will be ready to harvest in about 100 days. Nurseries with stocks of herbs may sell growing plants.

When bulbs are mature, shoots yellow and die. To harvest, pull up clumps and separate the bulbs; before using them, let dry for about a month in a cool, dry place. If stored properly, shallots will keep for up to 8 months.

Around St. Patrick's Day, nurseries and florists sell "shamrocks." These are small potted plants of *Medicago lupulina* (hop clover, yellow trefoil, black medick), an annual plant; *Oxalis acetosella* (wood sorrel), a perennial; or *Trifolium repens* (white clover), also a perennial. The last is the most commonly sold. All of these have leaves divided into three leaflets, symbolic of the Trinity. They can be kept on a sunny windowsill or planted out, but they have little ornamental value and are likely to become weeds.

SHASTA DAISY. See **CHRYSANTHEMUM maximum**

SHELL FLOWER. See **ALPINIA zerumbet, MOLUCCELLA laevis**

SHELL GINGER. See **ALPINIA zerumbet**

SHE-OAK. See **CASUARINA**

SHEPHERDIA
BUFFALOBERRY
Elaeagnaceae
DECIDUOUS SHRUBS

🌿	ZONES VARY BY SPECIES
☀️	FULL SUN
💧💧💧	LITTLE TO REGULAR WATER

These are tough plants for harsh growing conditions—withstand cold and wind, take most soils, tolerate drought. Related to Russian olive (*Elaeagnus*), another plant that readily endures difficult situations. If a male plant is nearby, females will bear small, sour bright red or orange berries that can be used for jams and jellies. Birds like the fruit.

S. argentea. SILVER BUFFALO-BERRY, SILVERBERRY. Zones 1–3, 7, 10. Native from Canada into intermountain areas of the West. Spreading, suckering plant to 6–12 ft. high and wide, with spine-tipped branchlets. Elongated oval leaves to 1 in. long, silvery on

Shepherdia argentea

both sides. Looks grayer than *S. canadensis*.

S. canadensis. BUFFALOBERRY, SOAPBERRY. Zones A1–A3; 1–3, 7, 10. Native from Newfoundland west to Alaska and south to Oregon. Rounded habit to 6–8 ft. high and wide, with thornless branches. Leaves reach 2 in. long, half as wide; upper surfaces are green, undersides silvery with brown scales. Two-tone foliage gives the plant an overall grayish green appearance.

SHIELD FERN. See **DRYOPTERIS carthusiana**

SHIMPAKU. See **JUNIPERUS sargentii**

SHISO. See **PERILLA frutescens**

SHOOTING STAR. See **DODECATHEON**

SHRIMP PLANT. See **JUSTICIA brandegeeana**

SHUNGIKU. See **CHRYSANTHEMUM coronarium**

SIAM TULIP. See **CURCUMA alismatifolia**

SIBERIAN CARPET CYPRESS. See **MICROBIOTA decussata**

SIDA fallax
'ILIMA
Malvaceae
EVERGREEN SHRUB

🌿	ZONES 23, 24; H1, H2
☀️	FULL SUN
💧	LITTLE WATER

Native to Hawaii; widespread in the Pacific Islands and China. There are many forms of this plant, from ground covers to medium-size shrubs to shrubs 10 ft. high and nearly as wide. Roundish, bright green to silvery green leaves to ½ in. long. Blooms all year, producing hibiscuslike, ½–1-in. flowers in colors ranging from yellow and orange to dull red. Blossoms are used in leis. Good wind tolerance.

Sida fallax

S

Does best in well-drained, rocky or sandy soil. 'Ilima papa is a very low-growing form, to just 3 in. high and 2 ft. wide; it is useful as a ground cover. 'Kaneohe Gold', to 3 ft. high and wide, has double blooms in bright golden orange.

SIDALCEA
CHECKERBLOOM, MINIATURE HOLLYHOCK
Malvaceae
PERENNIALS

🌿	ZONES 2–10, 14–24, EXCEPT AS NOTED
☀	FULL SUN
💧	REGULAR WATER, EXCEPT AS NOTED

All are grown for clusters of five-petaled flowers like little hollyhocks (*Alcea*). The plants described here range from erect to sprawling; leaves are typically dark green, roundish to kidney-shaped, about 3 in. across. Basal leaves are shallowly lobed, stem leaves more deeply cut.

S. candida. Native to High Plains. To 2–3 ft. high, spreading by rhizomes to 1½ ft. Unbranched stems bear bluish green leaves to 8 in. across. Crowded spikes of white, 1-in. flowers in mid- or late summer.

S. hybrids. Most sidalceas grown in gardens are hybrids between *S. candida* and *S. malviflora*. They form clumps to about 2 ft. wide and bear 1½–2-in. flowers; bloom all summer if deadheaded. Choices include 3-ft. 'Elsie Heugh', with fringed pale pink flowers; 2½-ft. 'Loveliness' (shell pink); and 2–3-ft. 'Party Girl' (deep pink).

Sidalcea malviflora

S. malviflora. CHECKER-BLOOM. Zones 2–9, 14–24. Native to Oregon, California, and Baja California. May grow erect to 2 ft. high and wide; or may sprawl and spread more widely by rooting at the nodes. Pink or purplish pink,

2-in. flowers in early spring. Moderate water (without moisture, they go dormant in summer and reappear with fall rains).

S. neomexicana. Zones 2, 3, 10–13, 18–24. Native from eastern Oregon to Wyoming, south to Mexico. To 3 ft. tall, 1–1½ ft. wide; branched or unbranched spikes of white or pinkish, ¾-in., summer flowers.

SILENE
Caryophyllaceae
PERENNIALS AND ANNUALS

🌿	ZONES VARY BY SPECIES
☀ ◐	FULL SUN OR PARTIAL SHADE
💧	WATER NEEDS VARY BY SPECIES

Many species; some are erect, others cushionlike. Good choices for front of border, rock garden. Flowers are typically single. Need well-drained soil.

S. acaulis. CUSHION PINK, MOSS CAMPION. Perennial. Zones A1–A3; 1–11, 14–16, 18–21. From the Arctic, mountains of North America, Eurasia. Small (¼–½-in.), narrow bright green leaves form a mosslike mat to 2 in. high, 8 in. wide. Reddish purple, ½-in. flowers are borne singly in spring. Good for gravelly, moist but well-drained spot. Regular water.

S. alpestris (S. quadrifolia). Perennial. Zones 2–9, 14–24. From eastern Alps. Creeping plant to 8 in. high and wide. Medium green, very narrow leaves to 1¼ in. Fine spring show of ½-in., double white flowers in loose sprays; scattered bloom later. Moderate water.

S. californica. CALIFORNIA INDIAN PINK. Perennial. Zones 3, 6–9, 14–24. Native to foothills of California and southern Oregon. Loosely branching plant to 1 ft. high and wide. Blooms in spring, producing flaming red, 1½-in. flowers with cleft and fringed petals in clusters of few to many. Gray-green, hairy, lance-shaped to ovate leaves to 3 in. long are some-

Silene californica

what sticky. Occasionally sold in seed packets. In its native range, it receives no moisture during the summer months, but it can take water then if given excellent drainage.

S. coeli-rosa (Lychnis coeli-rosa, Agrostemma coeli-rosa). VISCARIA. Annual. All zones. Mediterranean native to 1 ft. tall, half as wide, with gray-green, lance-shaped to oblong leaves to 2 in. long. Loose clusters of saucer-shaped, 1-in. flowers in blue, lavender, pink, or white, often with a contrasting eye. Long bloom period. Sow seed in rich soil in early spring for summer bloom; in mild-winter climates, sow in fall for winter and spring bloom. Good cut flower. Regular water.

S. schafta. MOSS CAMPION. Perennial. Zones 2–9, 14–16, 18–21. From western Asia. Upright, wiry stems form a tuft 6–12 in. high, 1 ft. wide. Small (½–¾-in.), tongue-shaped, bright green leaves. Profuse rosy purple, ¾-in. flowers, one or two per stalk, late summer into fall. Moderate water.

S. uniflora (S. vulgaris maritima). Perennial. Zones 1–9, 14–24. From coastal regions of western and northern Europe. Forms a low (6-in.-high, 8-in.-wide) cushion of ¾-in., lance-shaped gray-green leaves. Abundant white, 1-in. summer flowers, each nearly enclosed by a balloonlike calyx; borne one to four per stem. Moderate water.

SILK FLOWER. See **ABELMOSCHUS moschatus**

SILK OAK. See **GREVILLEA robusta**

SILKTASSEL. See **GARRYA**

SILK TREE. See **ALBIZIA julibrissin**

SILVER BELL. See **HALESIA carolina**

SILVERBERRY. See **ELAEAGNUS commutata, E. pungens, SHEPHERDIA argentea**

SILVER DOLLAR. See **CRASSULA arborescens**

SILVER DOLLAR GUM. See **EUCALYPTUS polyanthemos**

SILVER DOLLAR TREE. See **EUCALYPTUS cinerea**

SILVER FERN. See **PTERIS quadriaurita 'Argyraea'**

SILVER GRASS. See **MISCANTHUS**

SILVER JADE PLANT. See **CRASSULA arborescens**

SILVER LACE VINE. See **FALLOPIA baldschuanica**

SILVERLEAF. See **LEUCOPHYLLUM**

SILVER SPEAR. See **ASTELIA chathamica**

SILVER SPREADER. See **ARTEMISIA caucasica**

SILVER TREE. See **LEUCADENDRON argenteum**

SILVERVEIN CREEPER. See **PARTHENOCISSUS henryana**

SIMMONDSIA chinensis
JOJOBA, GOATNUT
Simmondsiaceae
EVERGREEN SHRUB

🌿	ZONES 7–24
☀	FULL SUN
💧	LITTLE WATER

Native to deserts of Southern California, Arizona, Mexico. Dense plant with rigid branches; typically to 3–6 ft. high and wide, occasionally larger. Dull gray-green leaves are leathery, narrowly egg shaped, 1–2 in. long. Inconspicuous flowers. If a male plant is present,

Simmondsia chinensis

females bear edible, nutlike fruit ¾ in. long; flavor is like that of filbert but slightly bitter until fruit is dried or roasted. Fruit's high oil content gives plant commercial value as crop for marginal land, though such plantings are chancy in soil infested with verticillium wilt or Texas root rot. Useful as informal or clipped hedge, foundation planting in desert garden. Young plants are rather tender; established ones will take 15°F/–9°C.

SINARUNDINARIA. See **BAMBOO, Fargesia**

S

SINNINGIA speciosa (Gloxinia speciosa)

GLOXINIA
Gesneriaceae
PERENNIAL FROM TUBER;
GROWN AS HOUSEPLANT

- ☼ BRIGHT INDIRECT LIGHT
- ◐ SEE INSTRUCTIONS BELOW

Native to Brazil. Squat, full-foliaged plant to 1 ft. high and wide. Broad, oval leaves reach 6 in. or longer, look like quilted green velvet. Blooms in summer, producing showy, velvety-sheened, ruffled bells to 4 in. wide in cluster near top of plant. Colors include white, red, pink, blue, and light to dark shades of purple. Some flowers have dark dots or blotches, others contrasting bands at edges.

Sinningia speciosa

Gloxinias need constant warmth and are most often grown in a greenhouse or as houseplants; can be taken outdoors in warm weather. Tubers usually available in winter, spring. For each tuber, choose a container big enough to leave 2 in. between all sides of tuber and container edges. Fill with soil mix of equal parts peat moss, perlite, and leaf mold or compost; set tuber ½ in. deep. Place in warm spot (about 72°F/22°C during day, no cooler than 65°F/18°C at night) with plenty of bright light but no direct sun. Water sparingly until first leaves appear, then increase watering as roots and leaves grow. Apply water to soil only, or pour it into drip saucer to be absorbed through pot's drainage holes (pour off any water left unabsorbed after an hour). Apply half-strength liquid fertilizer every 2 weeks, starting when leaves emerge and continuing until flowers fade. After bloom has finished, gradually dry off plants. When leaves have died down completely, move container to dark place where temperatures remain around 60°F/16°C. Mist soil just enough to keep tubers from shriveling. When tubers show signs of resuming growth in midwinter, repot in fresh soil mix. If roots have filled container, move tuber to a larger pot.

SISYRINCHIUM

Iridaceae
PERENNIALS

- ✁ ZONES 4–9, 14–24, EXCEPT AS NOTED
- ☼ ◐ FULL SUN OR LIGHT SHADE
- ◐◐◐ WATER NEEDS VARY BY SPECIES

Iris relatives with narrow, leaves and small, six-segmented flowers that open in sunshine. Pretty but not showy; best suited for informal gardens or naturalizing.

S. californicum. YELLOW-EYED GRASS. From coastal areas, California to British Columbia. To 6 in.–2 ft. high, 8–10 in. wide. Dull green leaves are broader than those of *S. idahoense bellum*. Yellow flowers in late spring or early summer. Succeeds in wet or low spots. Ample water.

S. idahoense bellum (S. bellum). BLUE-EYED GRASS. Zones 2–9, 14–24. Native to coast of California and Oregon. To 4 in.–2 ft. high, 6 in.–2 ft. wide. Green or bluish green leaves. Purple to bluish purple, ½-in. flowers in spring. Several named forms, many of them dwarf, are available. Plants sold as *S. macounii* (purple blooms) or *S. m.* 'Album' (white flowers) are probably forms of *S. idahoense bellum*. Moderate to regular water.

S. striatum. Native to Chile, Argentina. To 3 ft. tall, 1 ft. wide, with attractive gray-green leaves. In spring, produces spikelike clusters of many ½-in. flowers in pale yellow streaked with brown; blooms well into summer if old flower clusters are removed (if you don't remove them, you may have hordes of unwanted seedlings the next year). Leaves of 'Aunt May' ('Variegatum') are striped with creamy yellow. Moderate water.

Sisyrinchium idahoense bellum

SKIMMIA japonica

Rutaceae
EVERGREEN SHRUB

- ✁ ZONES 4–9, 14–22
- ◐ PARTIAL SHADE
- ◐ REGULAR WATER

Native to Japan, China. Compact, slow grower to 5 ft. tall, 6 ft. wide. Glossy rich green leaves to 3–4 in. long are oval, blunt ended, mostly clustered near twig ends. Blooms in spring, when pinkish to reddish buds held well above the foliage open to tiny, lightly scented white flowers (typically larger and more fragrant on males than on females). In fall and winter, female plants will bear hollylike red berries if a male plant is nearby. Plants tend to be sold simply as "male" or "female" rather than by variety name. A white-berried form is sold. *S. j. reevesiana* (often sold as *S. reevesiana*), a dwarf form to 1½–2 ft. high, 2–3 ft. wide, is self-fruitful and bears dull crimson berries.

Skimmia japonica

Handsome beside shaded walks, under windows, flanking entryways, in containers. Prefers moist, highly organic, acid soil. Grows best in Zones 4–6, 17. Thrips and red spider mites are potential pests throughout its range. In the Northwest, it is prone to attack by several kinds of mites that give leaves a stippled, silvery look. Water mold is a problem in hot regions.

SKULLCAP. See **SCUTELLARIA**

SKUNKBUSH. See **RHUS trilobata**

SKY FLOWER. See **DURANTA, THUNBERGIA grandiflora**

SMILACINA racemosa. See **MAIANTHEMUM racemosum**

SMOKE TREE. See **COTINUS, PSOROTHAMNUS spinosus**

SNAIL VINE. See **VIGNA caracalla**

SNAKE PLANT. See **SANSEVIERIA trifasciata**

SNAKESHEAD. See **FRITILLARIA meleagris**

SNAPDRAGON. See **ANTIRRHINUM majus**

SNEEZEWEED. See **HELENIUM**

SNOWBALL, FRAGRANT. See **VIBURNUM × carlcephalum**

SNOWBELL. See **STYRAX**

SNOWBERRY. See **SYMPHORICARPOS**

SNOW BUSH. See **BREYNIA nivosa**

SNOWDROP. See **GALANTHUS**

SNOWDROP TREE. See **HALESIA carolina**

SNOWFLAKE. See **LEUCOJUM**

SNOW-IN-SUMMER. See **CERASTIUM tomentosum**

SNOW MYRTLE. See **CALYTRIX alpestris**

SNOW-ON-THE-MOUNTAIN. See **EUPHORBIA marginata**

SOAPBARK TREE. See **QUILLAJA saponaria**

SOAPWEED. See **YUCCA glauca**

SOAPWORT. See **SAPONARIA officinalis**

SOCIETY GARLIC. See **TULBAGHIA violacea**

SOFT SHIELD FERN. See **POLYSTICHUM setiferum**

SOLANDRA maxima

CUP-OF-GOLD VINE
Solanaceae
EVERGREEN VINE

- ✁ ZONES 15–24; H2
- ☼ FULL SUN
- ◐ REGULAR WATER

Native from Mexico to Venezuela and Colombia. Fast-growing, sprawling, rampant vine to 40 ft.; must be tied to its support. Heavy stems bear highly polished, broadly oval, rich green leaves to 6 in. long. Inflated-looking buds open to big (6–8-in.), leathery, bowl-shaped, five-lobed blossoms that are fragrant at night; flowers are golden yellow, with a red-brown stripe running down each lobe to flower center. Main bloom

S

Solandra maxima

period runs from winter into early spring, but scattered flowering can occur at any time.

Give good, well-drained soil for best growth. Use on big walls and pergolas, along eaves, as bank cover. Spectacular along fence near swimming pool. Cut back long, vigorous shoots to induce branching and more flowers. To make it easy to see inside the big flowers, encourage growth low on plant by tip-pinching. Can be trimmed back to make rough hedge. Takes seacoast conditions, wind, fog. Provide shade for roots in hottest climates; give overhead cold protection in Zones 15, 16, 18–20. Light frost blackens the leaves, but plants usually recover to produce new growth. Often sold as *S. guttata.*

SOLANUM

Solanaceae
EVERGREEN, SEMIEVERGREEN, AND DECIDUOUS SHRUBS, VINES, PERENNIALS

✎	ZONES VARY BY SPECIES
☼ ◐	FULL SUN OR PARTIAL SHADE
◐ ●	MODERATE TO REGULAR WATER, EXCEPT AS NOTED
◆	MANY SPECIES ARE POISONOUS IF INGESTED; MOST ARE SUSPECT

In addition to eggplant and potato (described under those names), *Solanum* includes a number of ornamental plants. All have small, star-shaped, five-petaled blue or white flowers with reproductive parts that form a pointed yellow structure in the blossom's center. A few of the species described here produce decorative fruit—edible in the case of *S. muricatum,* but usually poisonous (if fruit is not described as edible, you are better off not sampling it).

S. av180iculare. Evergreen shrub. Zones 15–17, 21–24. From Australia, New Zealand. Fast growth to 6–10 ft. tall, 5–8 ft. wide. Lance-shaped deep green leaves are smooth and deeply cut, reach 1 ft. long. Purple, 1-in.-wide flowers in spring and summer are followed

by inedible scarlet fruit about 1 in. across.

S. crispum. Evergreen vine. Zones 8, 9, 12–24. From Chile, Peru. Modest (even shrubby) climber to 12 ft., with ovate to lance-shaped, soft green, often wavy-edged leaves to 5 in. long. In summer, bears 4-in. clusters of fragrant lilac-blue flowers with yellow centers. Small, inedible yellowish fruit. Must be fastened to its support; well suited to trellises, walls, posts. May lose leaves in hard frost. 'Glasnevin' has deeper blue flowers in larger clusters.

S. jasminoides. See S. laxum
S. laxum (S. jasminoides). POTATO VINE. Evergreen or semievergreen vine. Zones 8, 9, 12–24; H1, H2. From Brazil. Twines rapidly to 30 ft. Purplish-tinged, arrow-shaped, 1½–3-in.-long leaves. White, 1-in. flowers are carried on threadlike stalks in clusters of up to 12; bloom is almost continuous all year, heaviest in spring. Grown for flowers or for light overhead shade. Cut back severely at any time to prevent tangling, promote vigorous new growth. Control rampant runners that grow along ground.

S. muricatum. PEPINO. Perennial. Zones 17, 23, 24; H2. Thought to have originated in Colombia, Peru, Chile. Grows 2–3 ft. high, sprawling to about 4 ft. wide. Ovate to lance-shaped, bright green leaves to 3 in. long. Clear blue flowers in spring and early summer are not especially showy; they are followed later in summer by football-shaped greenish yellow fruit with purple stripes. Fruit weighs ¼–1 lb. and tastes like a cross between melon and cucumber. Same culture as tomato. Plant is grown as much for ornament as for edible crop. Makes a handsome choice for a hanging basket.

S. pseudocapsicum. JERUSALEM CHERRY. Evergreen shrub. Zones 23, 24; H2; annual or indoor/outdoor plant anywhere. Native to

Solanum pseudocapsicum

Madeira; widely naturalized in tropics and subtropics. To 3–4 ft. high and wide (about half that size if grown as an annual). Shiny deep green, smooth, elliptical leaves to 4 in. long. White, ½-in. summer flowers are followed in autumn by a fine show of scarlet (rarely yellow), ½-in. fruits that look like cherry tomatoes but are poisonous. In mildest-winter areas, plant bears flowers and fruit (and self-sows) year-round. More popular than taller kinds are the many dwarf strains, which grow to 1 ft. high and bear larger fruit (to 1 in. across).

S. rantonnetii (Lycianthes rantonnetii). Evergreen shrub. Zones 12, 13, 15–24; H1, H2. From Paraguay, Argentina. As freestanding plant, it makes a shrub 8–12 ft. tall and 6–10 ft. wide, but it can be staked into tree form or, with support, grown as a vine to 12–15 ft. or more. Can also be allowed to sprawl and used as a ground cover. Bright green, oval leaves to 4 in. long; violet-blue, ½–1½-in. flowers throughout warm weather, often nearly year-round. Informal, fast growing, not easy to use in tailored landscape; prune hard to keep it neat. In severe cold, leaf drop is heavy and branch tips may die back. The species is seldom seen; common plant in the nursery trade is 'Grandiflorum'. 'Royal Robe' is more compact (to 6–8 ft. high and wide), bears darker purple flowers over a longer season. A variety with white-variegated leaves is sometimes offered.

S. seaforthianum. BRAZILIAN NIGHTSHADE. Evergreen or semievergreen vine. Zones 16, 21–24; H1, H2. Slender-stemmed plant to 15 ft.; must be fastened to its support. Oval, 4–8-in.-long, medium green leaves are either undivided or quite deeply cleft into three or more lobes. Clusters of violet-blue, 1-in.-wide flowers bloom in summer. Pea-size red fruits are enjoyed by birds but shouldn't be eaten by people.

S. wendlandii. COSTA RICAN NIGHTSHADE. Deciduous vine. Zones 16, 21–24; H1, H2. To 15–20 ft., climbing by twining stems and hooked spines. Glossy green, ovate or (sometimes) lobed leaves 4–10 in. long are corrugated in texture. Foliage forms a lush backdrop for dense, domed clusters of lavender-blue, 2½-in. summer flowers. Somewhat reminiscent of bougainvillea. Let it clamber into tall trees, cover a pergola, decorate eaves of large house. Loses leaves

in low temperatures, even without frost; slow to leaf out in spring.

S. xantii. Evergreen shrub. Zones 7–9, 11, 14–24. From California. Erect or sprawling to 2–3 ft. high, 3 ft. wide. Ovate green leaves to 1¾ in. long. Purple, 1-in. flowers in late winter, spring. Superior forms are seen in California native plant gardens. Little or no water.

SOLEIROLIA
soleirolii
(Helxine soleirolii)

BABY'S TEARS, ANGEL'S TEARS
Urticaceae
PERENNIAL

✎	ZONES 4–24; H1, H2
☼ ◐	FULL SUN OR PARTIAL SHADE
● ◐	REGULAR TO AMPLE WATER

From western Mediterranean. To 2–4 in. high, spreading indefinitely by creeping stems to form a lush, medium green mat. Inconspicuous flowers. Stems and tiny leaves are tender, juicy, easily injured, but aggressive growth repairs damage

Soleirolia soleirolii

quickly. Roots easily from pieces of stem and can become an invasive pest. Freezes to black mush in hard frosts but comes back. Cool-looking, neat underplanting for ferns or other shade-loving plants. Can be used to carpet terrariums or space under greenhouse benches. Plant 10 in. apart for small-space ground cover. With enough water, tolerates full sun in cooler climates. There is a golden green variety and one with white variegation.

SOLENOSTEMON
scutellarioides
(Coleus × hybridus)

COLEUS
Lamiaceae (Labiatae)
PERENNIALS USUALLY GROWN AS ANNUALS

✎	ZONES 24; H1, H2; ANYWHERE AS ANNUAL; OR INDOORS
☼ ◐	SOME TYPES ARE SUN TOLERANT
●	REGULAR WATER

Group of tropical plants (sometimes sold as *Coleus blumei*) grown for brilliantly colored

S

leaves. Blue flower spikes are attractive, but they spoil the plant's shape and are best pinched out in bud (pinching also encourages more vigorous leafy growth).

Seed-grown, large-leaf strains, such as Giant Exhibition and Oriental Splendor, grow 1½–2 ft. high and wide, with leaves 3–6 in. long. Plants in the Kong series have leaves up to 8 in. long. Dwarf strains, such as Carefree, Fairway, and Wizard, grow 8–12 in. tall and wide, with leaves 1–1½ in. long. Colors include green, chartreuse, yellow, buff, salmon, orange, red, purple, and brown; a single leaf often shows many colors. The more red pigment the foliage has, the more sun tolerant the plant tends to be. Most coleus perform best in strong indirect light or light shade, but the relatively new, cutting-grown "sun coleus" also thrive in sun; they come in a variety of leaf colors, shapes, and plant habits.

Solenostemon scutellarioides

All types of coleus are useful for summer borders, indoor and out-door containers, and hanging baskets. They are perennial in frost-free regions, but you'll typically get the best performance by starting new plants annually from seed or cuttings—which is easy to do. Plant in spring. Sow seeds indoors or, with frost protection, outdoors when weather is warm. Cuttings will root in water as well as other media. Started plants need warm temperatures and rich, loose, well-drained soil. Feed plants regularly with high-nitrogen fertilizer. Be sure to pinch stems often to encourage branching and compact habit.

SOLIDAGO

GOLDENROD
Asteraceae (Compositae)
PERENNIALS

| ✎ ZONES 1–11, 14–23 |
| ☼ ◑ FULL SUN OR LIGHT SHADE |
| ◐ MODERATE WATER |

From mid- or late summer into fall, these eastern U.S. natives enliven the garden with large, branching clusters of small bright yellow flowers. Blossoms are carried on leafy stems that rise from tough, woody, spreading

rootstocks. Leaves are narrow, generally linear to lance shaped. Goldenrods are not as widely grown as they deserve to be, largely due to the mistaken belief that their pollen causes hay fever (in fact, other plants are responsible). All are tough plants that thrive in not-too-rich soil. Use in informal borders or naturalize in meadows.

S. hybrids. The following are among the best garden varieties.

'Crown of Rays'. To 2–3 ft. tall, 1–2 ft. wide, with flattish flower clusters.

'Golden Baby'. To 2 ft. high, 1½ ft. wide; flower clusters are plumelike.

'Goldenmosa'. To 2½ ft. tall, 1½ ft. wide. Very large clusters of blossoms are reminiscent of florists' mimosa (*Acacia baileyana*).

Solidago 'Goldenmosa'

S. rugosa 'Fireworks'. To 3 ft. tall, 2 ft. wide. Narrow streamers of flowers arch outward and downward like the vapor trails of a skyrocket.

S. sphacelata 'Golden Fleece'. To 1½ ft. tall, 2 ft. wide, with many sprays of flowers. Makes a tough, fast-growing ground cover; set plants 15 in. apart for a solid mat in a year.

SOLLYA heterophylla (S. fusiformis)

AUSTRALIAN BLUEBELL CREEPER
Pittosporaceae
EVERGREEN SHRUB OR VINE

| ✎ ZONES 8, 9, 14–24; H1, H2 |
| ☼ ◑ PARTIAL SHADE IN HOTTEST CLIMATES |
| ◐◐ MODERATE TO REGULAR WATER |

Native to Australia. Loose, spreading shrub to 2–3 ft. high, 4–5 ft. wide. Given support and training, climbs to 6–8 ft. Glossy green foliage has a light, delicate look—leaves are narrow, 1–2 in. long.

Sollya heterophylla

Clusters of small, bell-shaped, brilliant blue flowers bloom almost all summer. 'Alba' has white blooms; 'Rosea' bears pink flowers. *S. h. parviflora* (*S. parviflora*) is more vining in habit and has somewhat smaller flowers in a darker blue.

Drought tolerant but prefers some moisture. Good drainage is crucial, however; plant will die in poorly drained soil. Prune frequently to encourage dense habit. Use as ground or bank cover, in borders, along steps, draped over low walls, in containers. Will grow under eucalyptus trees.

SOLOMON'S SEAL.
See **POLYGONATUM**

SOPHORA

Fabaceae (Leguminosae)
EVERGREEN AND DECIDUOUS TREES AND SHRUBS

| ✎ ZONES VARY BY SPECIES |
| ☼ ◑ FULL SUN OR PARTIAL SHADE |
| ◐◐ WATER NEEDS VARY BY SPECIES |
| ✿ SEEDS OF S. SECUNDIFLORA ARE POISONOUS IF INGESTED |

Handsome flowering trees with showy, drooping clusters of sweet pea–shaped blossoms. Seedpods are constricted between the seeds, giving them a bead-necklace look. Leaves divided into many leaflets. Provide good drainage.

S. arizonica. Evergreen shrub. Zones 10–13. Native to Arizona. Grows slowly to 3–10 ft. high and wide. Dark gray-green leaves have five to nine ½–1-in.-long leaflets. Clusters of 1–1¼-in., purple to lavender flowers in spring; these are followed by 4–7-in.-long seedpods. Use as an informal hedge, in borders. Takes heat. Tolerates drought but does better with moderate to regular water applied deeply during hot months.

S. japonica. JAPANESE PAGODA TREE, CHINESE SCHOLAR TREE. Deciduous tree. Zones 2–24; bloom is unreliable where summers are cold and damp. Native to China, Korea. Grows at a moderate rate to 50–70 ft. high and wide. Young wood is smooth, dark gray green; old branches and trunk gradually take on rugged look, with rough, deeply furrowed bark. Dark green, 6–10-in. leaves divided into 7–17 leaflets, each 1–2 in. long. Undistinguished yellow fall color. Long (to 1-ft.), open clusters of ½-in., yellowish white flowers in summer; 2–3½-in. pods. 'Regent' is an exceptionally vigorous and uniform grower. This species is one of best trees for shading a lawn or patio, though stains from flowers and pods may be a problem on paved surfaces. Good for Rocky Mountain area, though it is subject to damage from ice storms there. Resistant to oak root fungus. Moderate water.

Sophora japonica

S. secundiflora. MESCAL BEAN, TEXAS MOUNTAIN LAUREL. Evergreen shrub or tree. Zones 8–16, 18–24. Native to Texas, New Mexico, northern Mexico. To 15–25 ft. tall, 10–15 ft. wide; very slow growing, especially in cool-summer regions. Naturally shrubby but can be trained into tree with short, slender trunk or multiple trunks, narrow crown, upright branches. Leaves 4–6 in. long, divided into seven to nine glossy dark green, 1–2-in.-long leaflets. Blooms from midwinter to early spring, bearing sweet-scented violet-blue flowers in drooping, 4–8-in. clusters reminiscent of wisteria. A white-flowered form is occasionally available. 'Silver Peso' has silvery foliage. Silvery gray or

S

brown, woody, 1–8-in.-long seedpods open when ripe to show poisonous, bright red, ½-in. seeds. If possible, remove pods from plant before they mature. Choice small tree for street, lawn, patio. If left untrained, makes a good large screen or background hedge. Thrives in heat and alkaline soil. Moderate water.

S. tetraptera. KOWHAI, YELLOW KOWHAI. Evergreen or deciduous shrub or tree. Zones 15–17. Native to New Zealand. Slow to 15–20 ft. tall and wide. Slender, open habit. Leaves 3–6 in. long, with 20–40 tiny leaflets; they are silky gray above, reddish beneath. In summer, golden yellow, 2-in.-long flowers appear in hanging clusters of four to eight. Seedpods are 2–8 in. long. Does not take low humidity. Regular water.

SORBARIA

FALSE SPIREA
Rosaceae
DECIDUOUS SHRUBS

🌿	ZONES VARY BY SPECIES
☀️ ◐	FULL SUN OR LIGHT SHADE
💧	REGULAR WATER

Green, ferny-looking leaves are finely divided into many narrow, toothed leaflets. Bloom from mid- to late summer, producing big, plumelike clusters of tiny white or creamy flowers at branch ends. Flowers mature into brown seed clusters; cut off faded blossoms unless you like the look of brown plumes. Use in large shrub borders or at edge of woodland, near water; effect is almost tropical. These shrubs spread by suckering and will cover large areas if not curbed.

S. sorbifolia. Zones A1–A3; 1–10, 14–21. Native to eastern Asia. Grows 3–8 ft. tall and 10 ft. wide. Leaves 6–12 in. long; flower plumes to 1 ft. long.

S. tomentosa angustifolia (S. aitchisonii). Zones 3–10, 14–21. Native to Afghanistan, Pakistan. To 10 ft. tall and wide. Leaves to 1½ ft. long; flower plumes to 16 in. long.

Sorbaria sorbifolia

SORBUS

MOUNTAIN ASH
Rosaceae
DECIDUOUS TREES AND SHRUBS

🌿	ZONES VARY BY SPECIES
☀️ ◐	FULL SUN OR LIGHT SHADE
💧 💧	MODERATE TO REGULAR WATER

These natives of mountainous areas are valued for showy flowers and showier fruit. Blossoms are grouped in broad, flat clusters that are scattered over the foliage canopy in spring; they develop into hanging clusters of small, berrylike fruit that colors up in late summer or early autumn. Most species have red or orange-red fruit, but white, pink, and golden forms are occasionally available. Birds feed on the fruit, but usually not until after leaves have fallen. Foliage is typically finely cut and somewhat fernlike, though some less widely planted species have undivided leaves. Some mountain ashes have good fall color; these are noted below. Plants need good, well-drained soil and some winter chill. Cankers are a problem for trees under stress. Watch for fireblight. Good small garden or street trees, though the fruit can make a mess on paved surfaces.

Sorbus aria

S. alnifolia. KOREAN MOUNTAIN ASH. Tree. Zones 1–10, 14–17. From China, Korea, Japan. Dense growth to 40–50 ft. tall, 20–30 ft. wide. The specific name *alnifolia* refers to the leaves, which are undivided (like those of alder, *Alnus*); they are 2–4 in. long, toothed, dark green, turning yellow to orange in fall. Reddish pink to orange-red fruit.

S. americana. Tree or shrub. Zones 1–6. From eastern North America. To 10–30 ft. tall and wide. Dark green leaves with paler undersides reach 10 in. long, consist of 11–17 leaflets; turn yellow

in fall. Orange-red fruit. This species is very hardy and tolerates damp soil, but it is not the choicest of mountain ashes. 'Red Cascade' is an attractive variety with an oval crown and compact growth to 16 ft. high and 8 ft. wide.

S. aria. WHITEBEAM. Tree. Zones 3–10, 14–17. From Europe. Dense-crowned tree to 30–45 ft. tall, 20–30 ft. wide (probably larger in age). Undivided, 2–4-in.-long leaves are dull green above, whitish beneath. Variable fall color; the best trees turn yellow. Red or orange-red fruit.

Sorbus aucuparia

S. aucuparia. EUROPEAN MOUNTAIN ASH. Tree. Zones A1–A3; 1–10, 14–17. Native from Europe to western Asia and Siberia; naturalized in North America. To 20–40 ft. tall (or taller), 15–25 ft. wide. Sharply rising branches form a dense, oval to round crown. Leaves are 5–9 in. long, with 9–15 leaflets; they are dull green above, gray green below, turning tawny yellow to reddish in autumn. Orange-red fruit. 'Cardinal Royal' has especially large bright red berries. 'Black Hawk' and 'Fastigiata' are slightly narrower, upright forms.

S. hupehensis. Tree. Zones 2–10, 14–17. From China. To 25 ft. tall and wide, eventually much larger. Bluish green leaves to 7 in. long, with 13–17 leaflets; turn orange red in fall. Pure white or pink-tinged white fruit. The form in cultivation is fireblight-resistant 'Coral Cascade', with red fruit and red fall foliage.

S. × hybrida. Tree. Zones 2–10, 14–17. Erect habit to 20–30 ft. tall and wide. Foliage is blue green above, whitish beneath. Leaves are a little over 5½ in. long, with a large upper portion that is merely lobed (not divided) and one or two pairs of small leaflets at base. Red fruit.

S. reducta. Shrub. Zones 3–6, 14–17. From China. To 1–2 ft. high, 3 ft. wide, spreading by underground runners. Dark green, 4-in.-

long leaves with 9–15 leaflets; bronze-red fall color. Pink fruit. For rock garden or bonsai.

S. scopulina. WESTERN MOUNTAIN ASH. Shrub or tree. Zones A1–A3; 1–7. Native to western North America. To 3–15 ft. tall and wide, often with reddish bark. Leaves to 2½ in. long, with up to 15 deeply toothed leaflets; shiny dark green above, paler beneath. Orange-red fall color. Orange to bright red fruit.

S. × thuringiaca. Tree. Zones 3–6, 14–17. Similar to *S. × hybrida* but with longer leaves (to 8 in.) and smaller fruit.

SORREL, GARDEN

Polygonaceae
PERENNIAL OFTEN GROWN AS ANNUAL

🌿	ZONES VARY BY TYPE; ANYWHERE AS ANNUAL
☀️	FULL SUN
💧	REGULAR WATER

Two similar species are grown for their edible leaves, which can be used raw in salads or cooked in soups, sauces, egg dishes. Flavor is like that of a sharp, sprightly spinach, but sorrel is more heat tolerant and produces throughout the growing season. Common sorrel is the larger plant (to 3 ft. tall), with leaves to 6 in. long, many shaped like elongated arrowheads. It is native to northern climates and perennial in Zones A1–A3, 1–9, 14–17. French sorrel is a somewhat sprawling plant to 1½ ft. high, with shorter, broader leaves and a milder, more lemony flavor than common sorrel. Native to Europe, western Asia, and North Africa, it is perennial in Zones 3–10, 14–24.

Grow sorrel in reasonably good soil. Sow seeds in early spring; thin seedlings to 8 in. apart. Or set out transplants at any time, spacing them 8 in. apart. Pick tender leaves when they are big enough to use; cut out flowering stems to encourage leaf production. Replace (or dig and divide) plants after 3 or 4 years.

Garden sorrel

S

SORREL, WOOD or REDWOOD.
See **OXALIS**

SORREL TREE.
See **OXYDENDRUM arboreum**

SOTOL.
See **DASYLIRION wheeleri**

SOUR GUM.
See **NYSSA sylvatica**

SOURWOOD.
See **OXYDENDRUM arboreum**

SOUTHERNWOOD.
See **ARTEMISIA abrotanum**

SPANISH BAYONET.
See **YUCCA aloifolia**

SPANISH BROOM.
See **GENISTA hispanica**

SPANISH DAGGER.
See **YUCCA gloriosa**

SPANISH SHAWL.
See **HETEROCENTRON elegans**

SPANISH THYME. See
PLECTRANTHUS amboinicus

SPARAXIS tricolor
HARLEQUIN FLOWER
Iridaceae
PERENNIAL FROM CORM

🌿	ZONES 9, 12–24; OR DIG AND STORE
☀️	FULL SUN
💧	REGULAR WATER DURING GROWTH AND BLOOM

Native to South Africa. Makes a clump of sword-shaped leaves to 1 ft. high and wide. Blooms over a long period in late spring; 1–1½-ft.-tall flowering stems bear loose, spikelike clusters of small, funnel-shaped blossoms to 2 in. across. Each flower has a yellow center, a dark color surrounding this, and another color—red, pink, orange, or purple—on the rest of the petals. Looks best when naturalized or grouped as accent in

Sparaxis tricolor

border, along pathway. For planting and culture, see *Ixia* (to which *Sparaxis* is closely related).

SPARTINA pectinata
PRAIRIE CORD GRASS
Poaceae (Gramineae)
PERENNIAL GRASS

🌿	ZONES 1–9, 14–24
☀️	FULL SUN
💧💧💧	MODERATE TO AMPLE WATER

Native to wet soils and bogs—even brackish bogs—in northern U.S. Forms a foliage clump to 5 ft. tall, spreading by rhizomes to 3 ft. wide. Arching, nodding bright green leaves ('Aureomarginata' bears yellow-bordered foliage). Plant can reach 7 ft. tall in bloom; the narrow, 8–10-in., one-sided brown flower spikes are handsome in fresh or dried arrangements.

Spartina pectinata

Highly attractive plant grown as aquatic perennial in shallow pond: keep plant in pot to prevent it from spreading, and submerge in water to 6 in. deep. In the winter, move plant to garden and bury pot up to rim in soil. When grown directly in the ground in moist locations, it can be invasive, particularly in mild-winter areas. Tolerates drier soil, where rhizomes spread more slowly.

SPATHE FLOWER.
See **ANTHURIUM**

SPATHIPHYLLUM
Araceae
PERENNIALS

🌿	ZONES 24; H2; OR INDOORS
◐⬤	SOME SHADE; LOW TO BRIGHT INDIRECT LIGHT
💧💧	REGULAR TO AMPLE WATER

From the tropics, mainly in the Americas. The various types range from dwarf forms a few inches high to 8-footers; foliage color ranges from light to dark green. Leaves are carried on slender stalks that rise directly from the

Spathiphyllum
'Mauna Loa'

soil; they are generally large for the plant size, oval or elliptical, narrowed to a point. Flowers—fragrant in some species and varieties—resemble those of calla (*Zantedeschia*) or anthurium, consisting of a leaflike white or greenish white bract surrounding a central club-shaped structure of closely setting tiny flowers. Outdoors, use as border plants or accents, for ground cover, in containers on shaded lanai or patio. Provide rich soil, wind protection. Among the few flowering plants that grow and bloom readily indoors; grow in loose, fibrous potting mix and feed weekly with dilute liquid fertilizer. Good choices include *S. wallisii* 'Clevelandii', to 2 ft. high, 20 in. wide; *S.* 'Mauna Loa', 3½ ft. high, 2 ft. wide; and *S.* 'Sensation', 4–6 ft. tall, 3 ft. wide.

SPATHODEA campanulata
AFRICAN TULIP TREE
Bignoniaceae
EVERGREEN TREE

🌿	ZONES 21–24; H1, H2
☀️	FULL SUN
💧	MODERATE WATER

From tropical Africa. Very showy, fast-growing tree to 40–75 ft. tall, 20–50 ft. wide. Glossy deep green leaves to 1½ ft. long, divided featherwise into 9–19 oblong to

Spathodea campanulata

ovate leaflets. Clusters of spectacular, tulip-shaped, 4-in. flowers in scarlet to blood red appear at branch ends. In Hawaii, blossoms come throughout the year; in California, bloom is most profuse in spring, but flowers may appear at any time. Give good drainage and a warm site. This tree grows rapidly and blooms young, but it can be devastated by frosts. Likely to attain size stated above only in truly frost-free locations.

SPEARMINT.
See **MENTHA spicata**

SPEEDWELL. See VERONICA

SPHAERALCEA
GLOBE MALLOW
Malvaceae
PERENNIALS

🌿	ZONES VARY BY SPECIES
☀️	FULL SUN
💧	LITTLE WATER

Grown for attractive downy leaves and bright flowers shaped like miniature hollyhocks (*Alcea*), these upright to trailing plants have a persistent woody base with softer stems above. Need well-drained soil. Any more than a little water causes weedy growth and rust. Cut old stems almost to ground before spring growth begins. Colorful accent plants for hot, dry locations.

Sphaeralcea ambigua

S. ambigua. APRICOT MALLOW. Zones 3, 7–24. Native to Utah, Arizona, Nevada, California, and Mexico. Grows to 3–4 ft. tall, 2–3 ft. wide, with many stems covered in white or yellowish down. Broad, rounded gray-green leaves to 2½ in. long are crinkled and slightly lobed. Each stem bears many inch-wide flowers; usual color is glowing pink or orange, but white-flowered forms are occasionally available.

Blooms in summer and fall; in hot deserts, main bloom season is spring, with a sparse showing of flowers in summer and fall. May become partly deciduous where summers are very hot and dry. Best adapted to desert climates; cannot withstand wet winters. 'Louis Hamilton' has deep orange-red flowers.

S. coccinea. PRAIRIE MALLOW. Zones 1–3, 10–13. Native from Manitoba south to Texas, Arizona. Spreading plant with branching stems and rounded olive green leaves that are deeply lobed, to 1½ in long. Usually grows 2–3 ft. tall and wide but can spread wider if given summer moisture. Produces short wands of cup-shaped, orange to red flowers to 1½ in. across throughout summer.

Sphaeralcea coccinea

S. incana. ORANGE MALLOW. Zones 2, 3, 7–13, 18. Native to Arizona, New Mexico, and Texas. Forms slowly spreading clump to 2–4 ft. high, 2 ft. wide, with many upright stems clothed in rounded, 2-in. long, yellowish green leaves. In summer (spring, in desert regions), bears a succession of clustered 1-in., light to deep orange blossoms. More tolerant of wet winters than *S. ambigua*.

S. munroana. Zones 1–3, 7–10, 14–24. Native to intermountain West and Rocky Mountain foothills. Grows to 3 ft. tall and 1½–2 ft. wide, with upright stems and rounded, slightly lobed gray-green leaves to 2 in. long. Bears many wands of inch-wide salmon to reddish orange flowers from midsummer to early fall. Plants sold in California under this name may be the Argentine native *S. philippiana,* which grows to 1½ ft. high and 4–5 ft. wide and has leaves that are more deeply cut than those of *S. munroana*.

SPHAEROPTERIS cooperi. See CYATHEA cooperi

SPICE BUSH. See CALYCANTHUS occidentalis

SPICEBUSH. See LINDERA

SPIDER FLOWER. See CLEOME hasslerana

SPIDER LILY. See CRINUM asiaticum, LYCORIS

SPIDER PLANT. See CHLOROPHYTUM comosum

SPIDERWORT. See TRADESCANTIA virginiana

SPINACH
Chenopodiaceae, Aizoaceae, Basellaceae
ANNUALS AND PERENNIALS

> 🖊 ZONES VARY BY TYPE
>
> ☀ FULL SUN
>
> 💧 REGULAR WATER

One of the three plants described here is true spinach; the other two are warm-season vegetables used as substitutes for the real thing, which needs cool weather to succeed. All are grown for their edible leaves, used raw or cooked. All do best in rich, well-drained soil.

True spinach. This cool-season annual is thought to have originated in southwestern Asia. Grows in all zones. Matures slowly during fall, winter, and spring; long days of late spring and heat of summer make it go to seed quickly. To get successive harvests, make small

True spinach

sowings at weekly intervals in fall or early spring. Thin established seedlings to 3–4 in. apart. When plants have reached full size (6–12 in. high; takes about 7 weeks), harvest by cutting entire clump at ground level. Leaf miner is often a pest.

New Zealand spinach. Native to Australia and New Zealand. This succulent evergreen is a perennial in mild-winter areas (most likely to live over in Zones 15–17, 21–24; H1, H2) but goes dormant in heavy frosts. In colder climates, it can be

New Zealand spinach

grown as a summer annual. Sow seed in early spring after danger of frost is past; thin established seedlings to 1–1½ ft. apart. Mature plants are spreading, 1–2 ft. high. Harvest greens by plucking off top few inches of tender stems and attached leaves; a month later, new shoots will have grown up for another harvest. New Zealand spinach tolerates heat and drought but also thrives in cool, damp conditions.

Malabar spinach. This native of India is a perennial vine in H1 and H2; grown as annual in Zones 3–24. It needs night temperatures above 58°F/14°C; it will not survive frost. There is an especially attractive red-stemmed form. Sow seeds in early summer; thin established seedlings to 1 ft. apart. When young plants are about 1 ft. high, train them on wires or a trellis. At 2 ft. high, pinch out a few inches of stem tip (harvesting any young, tender leaves) to encourage the plants to branch and form more stems. Vine grows about 4 ft. tall. As leaves reach full, succulent size, pick them individually. They are bigger and thicker than leaves of true spinach, so you'll need fewer per serving.

SPINDLE TREE. See EUONYMUS europaeus

SPIRAEA
SPIREA
Rosaceae
DECIDUOUS SHRUBS

> 🖊 ZONES VARY BY SPECIES
>
> ☀ 🌓 FULL SUN OR LIGHT SHADE
>
> 💧💧💧 REGULAR TO MODERATE WATER, EXCEPT AS NOTED

There are two distinct kinds of spireas: the bridal wreath type, with clusters of white flowers cascading down arching branches in spring or early summer; and the shrubby type, with pink, red, or

white flowers clustered at branch ends in summer to fall. Blossoms on both types are usually single.

These are tough, easy-to-grow plants; with few exceptions, they are not fussy about soil. Prune bridal wreath spireas after flowers have finished; cut to the ground wood that has produced flowers. Prune shrubby spireas in winter or earliest spring, before new growth begins; they generally need less severe pruning than bridal wreaths. If you remove spent flower clusters, plants will produce a second (but less lavish) bloom.

S. × bumalda. See S. japonica 'Bumalda'

S. cantoniensis 'Flore-Pleno'. DOUBLE BRIDAL WREATH. Zones 3–11, 14–23. From China, Japan. To 5–6 ft. tall, 10 ft. wide, with arching branches. Double white flowers wreathe the leafy branches in late spring to early summer. Lance-shaped blue-green leaves to 2½ in. long; they drop late, show no fall color. Plant is nearly evergreen in mildest climates.

S. densiflora. MOUNTAIN SPIREA. Zones 1–9, 14–21. Native from central Sierra Nevada to British Columbia. To 1–3 ft. high and wide. Ovate to elliptical, dark green leaves to 2 in. long are woolly white beneath, turn yellow in fall. In summer, branch ends bear rosy pink flowers in dense, flat-topped clusters to 2 in. wide. 'Summer Song', to 2½ ft. high and wide, has bronzy new growth, bronzy fall, leaf color.

S. douglasii. WESTERN SPIREA. Zones 1–9, 14–24. Native to Coastal Ranges from Northern California to British Columbia, eastward to Rocky Mountains. Forms a clump 3–6 ft. high and wide; suckers freely and can be invasive. Narrowly oblong, 1–3½-in.-long leaves are dark green above and velvety white beneath; turn yellowish in fall. Pale to deep purplish pink flowers in long (to 8-in.), narrow clusters at branch ends in summer. Needs acid soil, regular to ample water. Useful for wild plantings near streams.

S. japonica. Zones A2, A3; 2–10, 14–21. Native to Japan, China. Upright, shrubby spirea to 4–6 ft. tall and wide, with flat, 8-in.-wide clusters of pink flowers carried above oval, sharply toothed green leaves. Best known through its selections, which are typically lower than the species and bloom between summer and fall. They include plants formerly classified

S

Spiraea japonica
'Anthony Waterer'

as hybrids of *S. × bumalda,* itself now considered merely a variety.

'Anthony Waterer'. To 3–5 ft. tall and wide. Carmine pink blossoms. Leaves are reddish purple when new, maturing to bright green.

'Bumalda'. To 3 ft. high and wide. Dark pink flowers; bronze-tinted new growth.

'Coccinea'. To 2–3 ft. tall and wide. Maroon-tinged foliage; red flowers.

'Dolchica'. To 3 ft. high, 4 ft. wide. Purplish pink flowers.

'Fortunei'. To 5 ft. tall and wide. Pink flowers.

'Froebelii'. Resembles 'Anthony Waterer' but is somewhat taller.

'Goldflame'. To 2½ ft. high and wide. Bronze new growth matures to yellowish green, turns dark reddish orange in fall. Pink flowers.

'Goldmound'. To 3 ft. tall, 4 ft. wide. Leaves emerge golden, mature to pronounced yellow green; hold color well in sun. Pink flowers.

'Limemound'. To 3 ft. tall, 6 ft. wide. Lemon yellow new leaves mature to lime green, then turn orange red in fall. Light pink flowers.

'Little Princess'. To 3 ft. tall, 6 ft. wide. Rose pink blossoms.

'Magic Carpet'. To 1½–2½ ft. tall, slightly wider. Reddish bronze new leaves turn chartreuse to yellow as they mature. Pink flowers.

'Nana' ('Alpina'). ALPINE SPIREA. To 2 ft. tall, 5 ft. wide. Pink flowers. Good red fall foliage in some years.

'Neon Flash'. To 3–4 ft. tall, 4–5 ft. wide. Purple-tinted foliage; bright rosy pink flowers.

'Shirobana'. To 2–3 ft. high and wide. Red buds open to bicolored blossoms in white and deep pink.

S. nipponica 'Snowmound'. Zones 1–11, 14–21. From Japan. Compact, spreading bridal wreath spirea to 2–3 ft. tall, 3–5 ft. wide. Profusion of white flowers in late spring or early summer. Ovate to roundish, dark green leaves to 1¼ in. long; little autumn color.

S. prunifolia 'Plena'. BRIDAL WREATH SPIREA, SHOE BUTTON SPIREA. Zones A2, A3; 2–11, 14–21. From China, Taiwan. Graceful, arching branches on a suckering, clump-forming plant to 6–7 ft. tall and wide. In early to midspring, bare branches are lined with small, double white flowers resembling tiny roses. Small dark green leaves turn bright shades of red, orange, and yellow in autumn.

S. thunbergii. Zones 1–11, 14–21. From China, Japan. Showy, billowy, graceful bridal wreath species 3–6 ft. or taller, 6 ft. wide, with many slender, arching branches. Round clusters of small white flowers appear all along bare branches in early spring. Bluegreen, extremely narrow leaves to 1½ in. long turn soft reddish brown in fall.

S. trilobata 'Swan Lake'. Zones 1–11, 14–17. Native from Siberia to northern China. Like a small version of *S. prunifolia* 'Plena'. Grows 3–4 ft. tall and wide, with a massive show of tiny white flowers in mid- to late spring. Leaves reach 1 in. long, are often three lobed. 'Fairy Queen' is similar but more compact, seldom exceeding 3 ft.

S. × vanhouttei. Zones A1–A3; 1–11, 14–21. Widely planted hybrid between *S. cantoniensis* and *S. trilobata.* The classic bridal wreath spirea. Arching branches form a fountain to about 6 ft. high by 8 ft. or wider. Leafy branches are covered with circular, flattened clusters of white blossoms in mid- to late spring, continuing into early summer in colder regions. Dark green, diamond-shaped leaves to 1½ in. long may turn purplish in fall.

SPLIT-LEAF PHILODENDRON. See **MONSTERA deliciosa**

SPOROBOLUS

DROPSEED
Poaceae (Gramineae)
PERENNIAL GRASSES

🗡 ZONES VARY BY SPECIES
☼ FULL SUN
◐ ◖ LITTLE TO MODERATE WATER

Graceful, fine-textured, clumping grasses that are as tough as they are good-looking. Deep-rooted and drought tolerant; excellent for massing in hot, dry areas and effective in meadow gardens, mixed borders, naturalized areas, rock gardens, even by swimming

Sporobolus airoides

pools. Plumelike flower heads appear in summer and fall. After they fade, tiny seeds drop to the ground; hence the common name. These plants tolerate a wide range of soil conditions.

S. airoides. ALKALI SACATON. Zones 1–24. Native from South Dakota and Missouri, west to eastern Washington, south to Southern California. Foliage clump grows 3 ft. high and wide; leaves are grayish green during growing season, yellow in fall, beige in winter. At bloom time in summer or fall, showy, erect or arching flower plumes increase plant height to 5 ft.; plumes are pinkish, eventually fading to pale straw color. Extremely tough, deep-rooted plant. Good grass for alkaline conditions.

S. heterolepis. PRAIRIE DROPSEED. Zones 1–10, 14–17. Native to the Midwest, High Plains, and much of the eastern U.S. Emerald green, hairlike leaves form a billowing mass to 15 in. tall and 1½ ft. wide. Foliage turns golden to orange in fall, then fades to light bronze in winter. Slender-stemmed, airy panicles of flowers rise to 3 ft. tall, soaring above the foliage in late summer. Blossoms are pink to light brown and smell faintly of buttered popcorn. The seeds are highly nutritious and were ground into flour by the Plains Indians. Self-sows mildly; volunteer seedlings are seldom a problem. Plants tolerate any soil but like it on the dry side.

S. wrightii. GIANT SACATON. Zones 3b, 7–16, 18–24. Native to sandy open areas and hillsides in southwestern Canada and southwestern U.S. Narrow, arching, blue-green leaves form a clump 3–4 ft. high and wide. Feathery, golden yellow seed heads nearly double the plant's height in late summer to early fall; good in dried arrangements. Evergreen in all but the coldest climates. Quite drought tolerant but looks best with occasional deep watering.

SPREKELIA
formosissima

JACOBEAN LILY, ST. JAMES LILY, AZTEC LILY
Amaryllidaceae
PERENNIAL FROM BULB

🗡 ZONES 9, 12–24; OR DIG AND STORE
☼ FULL SUN
● REGULAR WATER DURING GROWTH AND BLOOM

Mexican native often sold as *Amaryllis formosissima.* Foliage looks like that of daffodil *(Narcissus),* but each 1-ft.-tall stem is topped with a dark red, 6-in.-wide bloom resembling an orchid, with three erect upper segments and three drooping lower ones that are united at their bases (near the flower's center) to form a tube. Bloom comes primarily in early summer. In mild climates, foliage may be evergreen and plant may blossom several times a year if you can give it a dry period after flowering, then resume regular watering to trigger a new growth cycle.

Sprekelia formosissima

Where bulbs are hardy, plant them in fall, setting them 3–4 in. deep and 8 in. apart in good, well-drained soil. Look most effective in groups. Display increases if plants are left undisturbed for several years. Where winters are cold, set out bulbs in spring; lift plants in fall when foliage yellows and store in a cool, dark, dry place over winter (leave dry tops on). Or grow in pots like amaryllis *(Hippeastrum);* repot every 3 to 4 years.

SPRING STAR FLOWER. See **IPHEION uniflorum**

SPRUCE. See **PICEA**

SPURGE. See **PACHYSANDRA**

SPURGE OLIVE. See **CNEORUM tricoccon**

S

SQUASH

Cucurbitaceae
ANNUAL

- ✓ ALL ZONES
- ☼ FULL SUN
- ● REGULAR WATER

There are two forms of squash. Types planted for a warm-weather harvest and eaten when immature are called summer squash; this group includes scalloped white squash (pattypan squash), yellow crookneck and straightneck varieties, and cylindrical, green or gray zucchini or Italian squash. The other form is winter squash, grown for harvest in late summer or fall; it stores well and is used for baking and for pies. Varieties come in many shapes (turban, acorn, and banana are a few), sizes, and colors; all have hard rinds and firm, close-grained, good-tasting flesh. In both forms of squash, blossoms and tiny, developing fruit at base of female flowers can be eaten as delicacies.

Summer squash yields prodigious crops from just a few plants within 50 to 65 days after sowing, and it continues to bear for weeks. Vines are large (2½–4 ft. across at maturity) and need plenty of room; if space is limited, look for bush varieties. There are many vine and bush varieties to choose from.

Summer squash

Winter squash is planted and grown on vines like pumpkins; it typically needs even more space than summer squash. There are a few bush varieties, such as 'Cream of the Crop', a yellow acorn type, and 'All Seasons Hybrid', a buttercup type. Most kinds of winter squash are ready to harvest 60 to 110 days after sowing. Types for storing include small kinds such as 'Table Ace' and other acorn types, butternuts, and buttercups; and the large blue Hubbard varieties and banana squash. Spaghetti squash stores as well as any other winter squash, but when you cut it open after cooking, you find that the nutty-tasting flesh is made up

of long, spaghettilike strands. Winter squash doesn't grow well in high heat and humidity.

Bush varieties of summer squash can be planted 2–4 ft. apart in rows. If planted in circles ("hills"), they need more room; allow a 4-ft. diameter for each. Vining summer or winter squash needs 5-ft. spacing in rows, 8-ft.-diameter hills. The few bush varieties of winter squash can be spaced as for bush varieties of summer squash.

Give all kinds of squash rich soil, periodic fertilizer. Roots need regular moisture, but leaves and stems should be kept as dry as possible to prevent leaf and fruit diseases. Pick summer squash when it is small and tender. Winter squash should stay on vines until thoroughly hardened; harvest with an inch of stem and store in cool place (about 55°F/13°C).

Squash bugs cause leaves to wilt and may damage fruit. To control, destroy yellowish to brown egg clusters on undersides of leaves; trap adults with boards or burlap set in the garden at night, then collect and destroy your catch each morning. Various insecticides are also labeled for control of squash bugs.

SQUAWBUSH.
See **RHUS trilobata**

SQUILL. See **SCILLA**

SQUIRREL'S FOOT FERN.
See **DAVALLIA trichomanoides**

STACHYS

Lamiaceae (Labiatae)
PERENNIALS

- ✓ ZONES VARY BY SPECIES
- ☼ ◑ FULL SUN OR LIGHT SHADE
- ● MODERATE WATER

These mint-family members have the typical square stems and leaves in opposite pairs; foliage ranges from rough textured to furry. Except for *S. macrantha*, the species described here have short-stalked or stalkless leaves. Spike-like clusters of small, usually two-lipped flowers bloom in late spring and summer; blossoms are attractive to bees. All are fairly unfussy about soil type, needing only good drainage. Green-leafed species need some shade where summers are hot. Clumps often die out in center; divide and replant outer sections.

S. albotomentosa. HIDALGO. Zones 7–10, 12–24. Native to Mexico. To 2½ ft. tall, sprawling to

5–6 ft. wide. Green, heavily veined leaves have a felty texture, elongated heart shape. Stems and leaf undersides are covered with woolly hairs. Flowers open peach to salmon pink, age to brick red. Sometimes listed as *S. coccinea* 'Hidalgo'.

S. byzantina (S. lanata, S. olympica). LAMB'S EARS. Zones 1–24. Native to Caucasus, Iran. To 1½ ft. high, spreading freely by surface runners. Dense, ground-hugging rosettes of soft, thick, rather tongue-shaped, woolly white leaves to 4–6 in. long. Blossom stalks 1–1½ ft. high bear small purplish flowers; many gardeners feel that these detract from the foliage and so cut off or pull out flowering stems. Continued rains can mash plants down and make them mushy, and frost can damage foliage, but recovery is strong.

Stachys byzantina

'Silver Carpet' does not produce flower spikes and is somewhat less vigorous than the species. 'Big Ears' ('Countess Helen von Stein') has larger leaves. Flowers of 'Cotton Boll' are like little balls of fluff spaced along the stem. 'Primrose Heron' has furry yellow leaves that mature to chartreuse, then turn gray green.

Use all forms for contrast with dark green foliage and with different leaf shapes, such as those of strawberry or some sedums. Good edging for paths, flower beds. Excellent ground cover in high, open shade, such as under tall oaks; space plants 2 ft. apart.

S. coccinea. SCARLET HEDGE NETTLE. Zones 7–10, 12–24. Native to southern Texas, New Mexico, Arizona. Forms a clump to 1½ ft. high and wide, with wrinkled, heavily veined, elongated oval leaves to 3 in. long. Bears short spikes of scarlet flowers. For the form sometimes sold as 'Hidalgo', see *S. albotomentosa*.

S. macrantha (S. grandiflora). BIG BETONY. Zones 1–24. Native to Caucasus, Turkey, Iran. Dense foliage clump to 1 ft. high and wide, with long-stalked, heart-shaped, scallop-edged dark green

leaves to 3 in. across; they are wrinkled and roughly hairy. Showy purplish pink blossoms on 1½–2-ft.-tall stems. 'Robusta' and 'Superba' offer larger flowers; 'Alba' has white blooms.

STACHYURUS
praecox

Stachyuraceae
DECIDUOUS SHRUB

- ✓ BEST IN ZONES 4–6; ALSO GROWS IN ZONES 14–17
- ☼ ◑ FULL SUN OR LIGHT SHADE
- ● REGULAR WATER

Native to Japan. Slow grower to 10 ft. tall and nearly as wide, with slender, polished-looking, chestnut brown branches. Pendulous, 3–4-in.-long flower stalks, each carrying 12–20 buds, hang from branches in fall and winter. In late winter, buds open into bell-shaped, pale yellow or greenish yellow flowers ⅓ in. wide. Greenish yellow, berrylike fruit follows in late summer. Bright green, toothed leaves are 3–7 in. long, tapering to sharp tip; foliage is often somewhat sparse. Rosy red and yellowish fall color is pleasant but not vivid. Grow this plant under a deciduous tree to shelter its winter buds from heavy freezes.

Stachyurus praecox

S

STAGHORN FERN.
See **PLATYCERIUM**

STAR CLUSTERS.
See **PENTAS lanceolata**

STAR JASMINE.
See **TRACHELOSPERMUM**

STAR OF BETHLEHEM.
See **CAMPANULA isophylla,**
ORNITHOGALUM arabicum,
O. umbellatum

STAR OF PERSIA.
See **ALLIUM cristophii**

STAR TULIP.
See **CALOCHORTUS**

STATICE. See **LIMONIUM**

STENOCARPUS
sinuatus
FIREWHEEL TREE
Proteaceae
EVERGREEN TREE

🌿	ZONES 16, 17, 20–24
☼	FULL SUN
◐ ●	MODERATE TO REGULAR WATER

Native to Australia. Slow-growing, densely foliaged plant to 30 ft. tall, 15 ft. wide. Shiny deep green leaves; to 1 ft. long and lobed on young plants, smaller and usually unlobed on older ones. Tubular, 2–3-in., scarlet-and-yellow flowers arranged in clusters like spokes of a wheel. Flowering usually is at its peak in early fall, but plant may bloom at any time. Blooms sometimes emerge from the bark of the trunk—an unusual sight. Plants do not bloom until established for several years.

Stenocarpus sinuatus

Rather tender, especially when young. Does best in deep, rich, well-drained, acid soil. Prune to shape in early years. Showy flowering tree near patio or terrace. Also good in lawn or near swimming pool (has little leaf drop). Beautiful juvenile leaves make it an interesting indoor potted plant.

STENOCEREUS
thurberi
(Lemaireocereus
thurberi)
ORGANPIPE CACTUS
Cactaceae
CACTUS

🌿	ZONES 12–24
☼	FULL SUN
◌	LITTLE WATER

Native to southern Arizona, northern Mexico. Columnar cactus branching from base (also from top, if injured) to form a clump to 12 ft. wide. Dark green or gray-green stems grow quite slowly to

Stenocereus thurberi

15–20 ft. tall; each stem reaches 6 in. thick, has 12–19 ribs, and is covered with black spines ½–1 in. long. In old plants, clump may contain 30 or more stems of varying heights; the arrangement is said to resemble a pipe organ. Blooms from mid- to late spring; funnel-shaped, 3-in. flowers in white with a touch of pink to reddish purple open at night. Rounded, 1½-in.-long fruits are olive green, becoming red tinged when ripe. They split open to reveal edible, sweet, bright red pulp with black seeds. Needs excellent drainage.

STENOLOBIUM stans.
See **TECOMA stans**

STENOTAPHRUM
secundatum
ST. AUGUSTINE GRASS
Poaceae (Gramineae)
PERENNIAL GRASS

🌿	ZONES 12, 13, 18–24; H1, H2
☼ ◐	BEST IN SUN, TOLERATES SOME SHADE
●	REGULAR WATER

Coarse-textured grass from tropical and subtropical regions. Spreads fast by surface runners that root at joints. Dark green leaves to ⅜ in. wide on coarse, wiry, flattened stems. Turns brown during short winter dormancy, can creep into planting beds, produces thick thatch, must be cut with a power mower. On the plus side, it takes much traffic, has few pest problems, is fairly tolerant of salt and shade, and is easily removed from plantings (roots are shallow).

*Stenotaphrum
secundatum*

Plant from sod, plugs, or stolons. Mow to 1½–3 in. Needs somewhat less water than bluegrass (*Poa*). A variegated form is sometimes used in hanging baskets.

STEPHANOTIS
floribunda
MADAGASCAR JASMINE
Asclepiadaceae
EVERGREEN VINE

🌿	ZONES 23, 24; H2; OR INDOORS
◐	ROOTS COOL, TOPS IN FILTERED SUN; BRIGHT LIGHT
●	REGULAR WATER

Native to Madagascar. Twines to 15–30 ft. Waxy, glossy green, oval leaves to 4 in. long. Valued for intense fragrance of its funnel-shaped, 1–2-in.-long, waxy white blossoms. Borne in open clusters, the flowers are a favorite for bridal bouquets and are also used in leis. Blooms in late winter and spring in Hawaii, from late spring through summer in Southern California. Needs warmth. Provide support; train on trellis or fence, along eaves. Give good drainage.

Stephanotis floribunda

As houseplant, will bloom if given ample light; better suited to greenhouse. Feed liberally; watch for scale, mealybugs. Give indoor plants a rest period by letting them dry out in winter. Can be brought outdoors during warm times of year. May be sold as *Marsdenia floribunda*.

STERCULIA.
See **BRACHYCHITON**

STERNBERGIA lutea
Amaryllidaceae
PERENNIAL FROM BULB

🌿	ZONES 3–10, 14–24
☼	FULL SUN
●	REGULAR WATER DURING GROWTH AND BLOOM

Native from western Mediterranean to central Asia. Golden yellow, 1½-in. flowers, one on each

6–9-in. stem, appear in early fall; they are chalice shaped at first, then open out to a star. Narrow leaves emerge with or just after flowers, reach about 1 ft. long; they remain green through winter, die back in spring. Good alongside paths, in rock gardens or pockets in paved patios.

Sternbergia lutea

Plant bulbs in mid- to late summer, as soon as they are available. Set them 4 in. deep, 6 in. apart in well-drained soil. Where winter temperatures drop to 20°F/–7°C or lower, protect planting area with thick layer of mulch. Divide clumps (at normal planting time) only when vigor and flower quality decline. If planting cannot be kept dry during summer dormancy, grow in pots and move to a dry spot in summer. Don't be in a hurry to repot; plant blooms better when pot-bound.

STEWARTIA
Theaceae
DECIDUOUS TREES OR SHRUBS

🌿	ZONES 4–6, 14–17, 20, 21
☼ ◐	FULL SUN OR PARTIAL SHADE
●	REGULAR WATER

Mountain stewartia (*S. ovata*) is from southeastern U.S.; the others are native to Japan, Korea. All are slow-growing, all-season performers that show off fresh green leaves in spring, white flowers resembling single camellias in summer, and colorful foliage in fall. In winter, distinctive pattern of bare branches is on show, as is smooth bark that flakes off in varying degrees, depending on species. All grow best in acid, organically enriched soil. Good in woodland garden and as foreground specimens against backdrop of larger, darker-leafed trees.

S. koreana. See S. pseudocamellia Koreana group

S. monadelpha. TALL STEWARTIA. Tree. To 25 ft. tall, 20 ft. wide, with slender, upward-angled branches. Leaves are 1½–3 in.

Stewartia pseudocamellia
Koreana Group

long, turn brilliant red in fall. Small (to 1½-in.) flowers. Rich brown, scaly bark when young; smooth cinnamon-colored bark when older.

S. ovata. MOUNTAIN STEWARTIA. Shrub or tree. To 10–15 ft. tall and wide. Leaves grow 2–5 in. long, turn orange to scarlet in fall. Flowers reach 3 in. wide, have frilled petals. Bark not as handsome as that of other species. *S. o. grandiflora* has 4-in. flowers with lavender anthers; it blooms even as a young plant.

S. pseudocamellia. JAPANESE STEWARTIA. Tree. Pyramidal form; may reach 30–40 ft. tall, 20–25 ft. wide after many years. Leaves 2½–3 in. long; turn orange-red to purple in autumn. Cup-shaped, 2½-in.-wide flowers have orange anthers. Very showy bark: it flakes off to show a patchwork of green, gray, brown, rust, terra-cotta, and cream. Members of Koreana group (*S. koreana, S. pseudocamellia koreana*) have orange or orange-red fall color and 3-in.-wide flowers that open out flatter than the usual.

STIPA
FEATHER GRASS
Poaceae (Gramineae)
PERENNIAL GRASSES

🌿 ZONES VARY BY SPECIES

☀ FULL SUN

💧 REGULAR WATER, EXCEPT AS NOTED

These clump-forming grasses produce large, open, airy inflorescences that can add lightness and motion to the garden. The genus has undergone much revision by botanists, and some of its former members are now known by other names; see *Nassella* for descriptions of California native needle grasses and the highly ornamental Mexican feather grass.

S. arundinacea (Anemanthele lessoniana). PHEASANT'S-TAIL GRASS. Zones 14–24. From New Zealand. Arching, semievergreen foliage in clump to 2 ft. tall and wide. Medium green leaves have a coppery tinge (strongest in fall, winter). Feathery green flowers

with purple tints appear in early summer, rising barely higher than leaves. Tolerates light shade.

S. gigantea. GIANT FEATHER GRASS. Zones 4–9, 14–24. From Spain, Portugal, Morocco. Narrow, arching, evergreen leaves in clump growing 2–3 ft. tall and slightly wider. Open, airy sheaves of yellowish flowers bloom in summer, forming a broad, shimmering cloud that rises 6 ft. tall and as wide or slightly wider. Little to moderate water.

Stipa gigantea

S. ramosissima (Austrostipa ramosissima). PILLAR OF SMOKE. Zones 14–24. From Australia. To 6–7 ft. tall, 3 ft. wide. The erect column of evergreen foliage and blossoms does somewhat resemble a pillar of smoke. Flowering is almost continuous; the airy, light tan inflorescences make up half (or a little more) of the plant's total height.

STOCK. See MATTHIOLA

STOKESIA laevis
STOKES' ASTER
Asteraceae (Compositae)
PERENNIAL

🌿 ZONES 2–10, 12–24

☀ FULL SUN

💧 REGULAR WATER

Native to southeastern U.S. Rugged, adaptable plant. Evergreen in warmer part of range; semievergreen in cold climates. To 2 ft. tall, 1½ ft. wide, with stiff, erect, much-

Stokesia laevis
'Bluestone'

branched stems. Smooth, firm-textured, medium green leaves, 2–8 in. long, sometimes toothed at base. Leafy, curved, finely toothed bracts surround tight flower buds; in summer or early fall, these open to 3–4-in., asterlike blooms in blue, purplish blue, or white. Long-lasting cut flowers. Performs best in well-drained soil. Provide winter cover of evergreen boughs in coldest regions. Good in pots. Selections include lavender 'Blue Danube' (blooms into winter in the mildest climates); white 'Silver Moon'; deep purple 'Wyoming'; and 10-in.-high, medium blue 'Bluestone'.

**STONECRESS.
See AETHIONEMA**

STONECROP. See SEDUM

STONEFACE. See LITHOPS

STRAWBERRY
Rosaceae
PERENNIALS

🌿 ZONES A1–A3; 1–9, 14–24; H1, H2; DIFFICULT IN ZONES 10–13

☀ FULL SUN, EXCEPT AS NOTED

💧 REGULAR WATER

Standard market strawberries are hybrids (*Fragaria × ananassa*). Plants have toothed, roundish, medium green leaves and white flowers. They grow 6–8 in. tall, spreading by long runners to about 1 ft. across. June-bearing types produce one crop per year in late spring or early summer; in general, they are the highest-quality strawberries you can grow. Ever-bearing and day-neutral kinds (which are nearly identical in garden performance) have the potential to flower and set fruit over a longer season. Their harvest tends to peak in early summer, then it continues (often unevenly) through fall. The exact fruiting pattern depends on variety and temperature: plants stop flowering when the thermometer rises above 85°F/29°C, so in practice you can expect everbearing performance along the coast and two crops a year—spring and fall—in hot-summer interior climates. Ever-bearers put out fewer runners than June bearers.

Strawberries of one variety or another can be grown in every part of the West, though it is hard to succeed with them where soil and water salinity are very high. Plant on flat ground if soil drains well or is high in salts, on a 5–6-in. mound if soil is heavy or drains

poorly. (If soil is high in salts and drains poorly, plant in containers.) For a small harvest, grow a dozen plants in a sunny flower or vegetable garden; or put them in boxes, tubs, or hanging baskets on the patio. For a big crop of berries, set plants 14–18 in. apart, in rows 2–2½ ft. apart.

Planting season usually depends on when local nurseries offer plants. In mild-winter areas, set out June bearers in late summer or fall for a crop the next spring; in colder climates, plant in early spring for harvest the following year. Set out everbearing plants in spring for summer and fall berries (in mild-winter areas, they may be available for fall planting). Plant carefully (see "What Strawberries Need" on the next page). Mulch to deter weeds, conserve moisture, and keep berries clean. Hasten

What Strawberries Need

SOIL Be sure it is well-drained and acidic (most varieties do not tolerate alkalinity).

PROPER PLANTING The crown should be above soil level (a buried crown will rot); topmost roots should be ¼ in. beneath soil (exposed roots will dry out).

WATERING Plants need consistent moisture during bearing season.

FERTILIZING Feed June bearers twice a year—very lightly when growth begins and again, more heavily, after fruiting. Everbearing types prefer consistent light feedings. Heavy feeding of either type in spring leads to excessive plant growth, soft fruit, and fruit rot.

THINNING AND RENEWING Crowding leads to diseases and lower yields of poorer-quality fruit. To keep a planting from becoming too dense, remove runners as needed. Get rid of older plants every few years and replace with offsets.

Everbearing strawberry

spring growth by planting through clear or black plastic mulch, and by covering plants with floating row covers (remove covers as soon as flowers appear). Pinch off the earliest blossoms produced in the first year to increase plants' vigor. Don't let plants dry out. Drip irrigation is ideal to help reduce disease problems, but overhead irrigation is satisfactory.

The majority of varieties reproduce by runners, though some make few or no offsets. Pinch off all runners to get large plants with smaller yields of big berries; let offsets grow 7–10 in. apart for heavy yields of smaller berries. When your plants have made enough offsets, pinch off additional runners.

Most June bearers benefit greatly from renovation. After harvest, remove foliage with a lawn mower set high so it won't injure the crowns. If diseases were a problem, send leaves out with the trash. Water and fertilize to encourage new growth. This is also a good time to reduce a dense planting by removing the old "mother" plants

and leaving younger, more productive "daughter" plants.

Some home gardeners follow the example of commercial growers, who treat strawberries as annuals. Plant in summer or early fall, usually with a plastic mulch; remove runners as they develop; after harvest, tear out plants; set out new plants in another location the following year (don't replant in the same location until at least 2 years have passed). Benefits are healthier plants, fewer weeds, and bigger fruit. June-bearing 'Chandler' is especially well adapted to this system, but almost any variety can be grown this way if planted at just the right time (you may have to experiment). In Alaska, home gardeners are treating some everbearing varieties, particularly 'Quinault', as spring-planted annuals.

Strawberries need winter mulch in cold climates. Cover with a 4–6-in. layer of straw or other light, weed-free, organic material in late fall. When temperatures warm in spring, rake mulch between plants.

Plants are subject to many diseases: fruit rots (botrytis, anthracnose, leather rot), leaf diseases (leaf spot, leaf scorch, leaf blight), crown diseases (anthracnose), root diseases (verticillium wilt, red stele, black root rot), and—especially in the Pacific Northwest—viruses. Root weevils, aphids, mites, slugs, and snails are among potential pests. To reduce problems, use certified disease-free plants; also remove diseased foliage and ripe or rotten fruit. Replace plants with new ones as they begin to decline, usually after 3 years; or, better yet, start a new bed with new plants.

Varieties tend to be regionally adapted. Also consider musk strawberries: these shade-tolerant, June-bearing varieties from Italy are renowned for their intense aroma and flavor with hints of raspberry and pineapple. 'Profumata di Tortona' and 'Capron' are popular. For information on alpine strawberry, or fraise du bois, which produces tiny, delectable berries often used to edge flower and herb beds, see *Fragaria vesca*. The *Fragaria* entry also contains descriptions of ornamental strawberries.

JUNE-BEARING VARIETIES

'Benton'. Good crop of flavorful, somewhat soft berries. Virus

tolerant, mildew resistant. Outstanding in Northwest, especially in mountain and intermountain areas.

'Camarosa'. Huge, conical berries over a long season. Susceptible to mildew. Adapted to California, especially southern areas.

'Cavendish'. Attractive large fruit. Can produce well the first year it's planted, and resists red stele. Bred for winter hardiness. Performs well east of the Cascades.

'Chandler'. Large, juicy berries over long period. Excellent flavor, good texture. Some resistance to leaf spot. Grows well in California, particularly Santa Barbara area and southward. Good as an annual elsewhere.

'Guardian'. Large, all-purpose fruit with good flavor. Disease resistant. Recommended for cold-winter regions.

'Honeoye'. Large, symmetrical, bright red fruit with sweet-tart flavor. Recommended for cold-winter regions.

'Hood'. Large, conical to wedge-shaped berries for fresh eating and processing. Excellent flavor and early ripening. Resists mildew. Good in Pacific Northwest.

'Mesabi'. Heavy-yielding variety with large, smooth berries, excellent flavor. Resists red stele and leaf diseases. Particularly strong performance east of the Cascades.

'Pajaro'. Large, conical berries with good flavor. Long fruiting period. Best in California.

'Puget Reliance'. Large crop of big, tasty berries; excellent flavor when processed. Vigorous plant. Tolerant of viruses. Adapted to Pacific Northwest.

'Puget Summer'. A heavy-yielding, late-season variety. Holds its fruit up off the ground, avoiding fruit rot. Susceptible to powdery mildew; disease resistant otherwise. Excellent, sweet flavor. Best in the Pacific Northwest.

'Rainier'. Good-size berries that hold size throughout long season. Fine flavor. Vigorous plant. Fair tolerance to root rot. Best in Pacific Northwest, west of Cascades.

'Sequoia'. One of the tastiest strawberries. Bears for many months. Resistant to alkalinity, yellows, and most leaf diseases.

Strawberry

Developed for coastal California, but widely adapted, even to cold winters.

'Shuksan'. Soft, mealy berries. Excellent frozen; good fresh. Tolerant of alkalinity. Resistant to botrytis, viruses, red stele. Good in Pacific Northwest, east of Cascades.

'Tillamook'. Large, sweet, attractive berries with red flesh and skin. Open habit makes picking easy; high yielding. Virus tolerant. Good in Pacific Northwest.

'Toklat'. Large, sweet berries. Susceptible to botrytis. Well suited to Alaska.

EVERBEARING VARIETIES

'Albion'. Long, conical fruit with excellent flavor. Resists verticillium wilt and crown rot. For California.

'Fort Laramie'. Good yield of berries over long season. Excellent flavor. Tolerates −30°F/ −34°C without mulch. Hardy in mountain states, High Plains, milder parts of Alaska. Also good in Southern California.

'Quinault'. Large, attractive berries are tasty, rather soft. Good producer of runners. Resists viruses and red stele. Susceptible to botrytis. Developed for the Pacific Northwest but is widely adapted. This variety is grown as an annual in Alaska.

'Seascape'. Good producer of large berries. Very good for eating fresh, for jam, and for freezing. Excellent virus resistance. For California, the Pacific Northwest, Hawaii. Good choice for annual production in colder climates.

'Selva'. First flush of fruit comes as late as July, but produces heavily through fall. Mild flavor develops best in warm areas; huge for everbearing variety. Gets red spider mite, leaf spotting in mild parts of Pacific Northwest, but has good resistance to red stele. Does best in California.

'Tribute.' Medium to large berries with excellent flavor. Resists red stele and verticillium wilt. Prone to viruses in Pacific Northwest. Widely adapted.

'Tristar'. Large berries with excellent flavor. Bears well the first year. Resists red stele and mildew but is moderately susceptible to viruses. Widely adapted.

S

STRAWBERRY, ORNAMENTAL.
See **FRAGARIA**

STRAWBERRY BUSH.
See **EUONYMUS americanus**

STRAWBERRY GERANIUM.
See **SAXIFRAGA stolonifera**

STRAWBERRY SNOWBALL
TREE. See **DOMBEYA cacuminum**

STRAWBERRY TREE.
See **ARBUTUS unedo**

STRAWFLOWER.
See **HELICHRYSUM bracteatum**

STRELITZIA
BIRD OF PARADISE
Strelitziaceae
PERENNIALS

- ☼ ZONES VARY BY SPECIES
- ☼ ◑ LIGHT SHADE IN HOTTEST CLIMATES
- ● REGULAR WATER

From South Africa. Evergreen plants with long-stalked, leathery leaves and highly individual flowers. Blossoms are produced intermittently throughout year; they are long lasting on plant and as cut flowers. Both species are good for poolside plantings; they produce no litter and withstand some splashing. Hardy to about 28°F/−2°C.

S. nicolai. GIANT BIRD OF PARADISE. Zones 22–24; H1, H2; with protection in Zones 12, 13. Clumping, treelike plant to 30 ft. tall and wide. Grown mainly for its dramatic foliage (similar to that of banana plants): gray-green, 5–10-ft.-long leaves arranged fanwise on erect or curving trunks. Flowers are larger than those of *S. reginae* but not as colorful. Floral envelope is purplish gray; flower is white with dark blue "tongue." Feed young plants frequently until they reach full dramatic size; then give little or no fertilizer.

Strelitzia reginae

S. reginae. BIRD OF PARADISE. Zones 22–24, H1, H2; under overhangs where heat can be trapped in Zones 9, 12–21. Grown for spectacular flowers, which bear a startling resemblance to the heads of crested tropical birds. Flowers combine orange, blue, and white, are borne on long, stiff stems. Flowering is best in cooler seasons (though blooms appear year-round). Trunkless plant grows 5–6 ft. high and about as wide; blue-green leaves are 1½ ft. long. This species benefits greatly from frequent, heavy feeding.

Divide infrequently, since large, crowded clumps bloom best. Good in containers. Recovers slowly from frost damage.

STREPTOCARPUS
CAPE PRIMROSE
Gesneriaceae
PERENNIALS

- ☼ ZONES 17, 22–24; H2; OR INDOORS
- ◑ ● SOME SHADE; BRIGHT INDIRECT LIGHT
- ●● REGULAR TO AMPLE WATER

Related to African violet *(Saintpaulia)* and gloxinia *(Sinningia)* and look something like a cross between the two. Fleshy, sometimes velvety leaves; trumpet-shaped flowers with long tube and spreading mouth. Long bloom season; some kinds flower intermittently all year. Many species and hybrids of interest to fanciers; most widely available kinds are hybrids. All types are typically grown in containers. When grown indoors, take same care as African violet.

Streptocarpus 'Constant Nymph'

Large-flowered hybrids. Form 2-ft.-wide clump of long, narrow leaves. Foot-tall stems carry 1½–2-in. flowers in white, blue, pink, rose, red, purple, often with blotches in a contrasting color. Medium blue 'Constant Nymph' is best known of the cutting-grown Nymph series.

S. saxorum. From eastern Africa. Unlike others, this species forms a shrubby, much-branched, spreading mound to 6 in. high, 2 ft. wide. Furry, fleshy gray-green leaves to 1½ in. long. Bloom comes in waves over much of the year; the two-tone flowers are pale blue and white, 1½ in. wide, carried on long, slender stems. Splendid in hanging baskets. Hybrids developed from *S. saxorum* include 'Concord Blue', a nonstop bloomer with medium blue flowers.

STREPTOSOLEN
jamesonii
MARMALADE BUSH
Solanaceae
EVERGREEN VINING SHRUB

- ☼ ZONES 13, 16, 17, 23, 24; H2
- ☼ ◑ PARTIAL SHADE IN HOTTEST CLIMATES
- ● REGULAR WATER

From South America. To 4–6 ft. tall and as wide; to 10–15 ft. trained against a wall, on a bank or trellis. Ribbed, oval bright green leaves to

Streptosolen jamesonii

1½ in. long. Large, loose clusters of 1-in., orange (sometimes yellow) flowers are carried at branch ends from spring to early fall (nearly all year in frost-free areas). Grow in warm spot; give fast-draining soil. Provide protection from frosts; cut back dead wood after last frost. Effective spilling over a wall, lining garden stairs, in hanging basket.

STROBILANTHUS
dyeranus
PERSIAN SHIELD
Acanthaceae
TENDER SHRUB

- ☼ ZONES 23, 24; H1, H2; ALSO 16, 17, 19–22 WITH PROTECTION
- ◑ PARTIAL SHADE
- ● REGULAR WATER

Native to Burma. Beautiful foliage plant for areas that are mostly frost free. Grows to 4 ft. tall and 3 ft. wide; soft stems more like a perennial than a shrub. Broadly oval,

Strobilanthus dyeranus

pointed leaves are 6–8 in. long, somewhat puckered, dark green but richly variegated with purple and silvery blue tints. Leaf undersides are bright purple. Pale violet, tubular flowers come in summer in 1–1½-in. spikes less showy than the foliage. Needs rich soil. Becomes straggly with age; pinch regularly, replace, or start over from cuttings. May survive temperatures slightly below freezing if heavily mulched in late fall; or grow in containers and move to shelter in winter. Can be overwintered indoors in a sunny window.

STYRAX
Styracaceae
DECIDUOUS TREES AND SHRUBS

- ☼ ZONES 4–9, 14–21
- ☼ ◑ FULL SUN OR PARTIAL SHADE
- ● REGULAR WATER

These plants deserve to be better known for their subtly attractive springtime show of white, bell-shaped flowers in hanging clusters. Blossoms are fragrant (only faintly so in *S. japonicus*). Nonaggressive roots. Provide reasonably good, well-drained, nonalkaline soil. Prune to control shape; tend to be shrubby unless lower side branches are suppressed.

S. japonicus. JAPANESE SNOW-DROP TREE, JAPANESE SNOW-BELL. Tree. Native to eastern Asia. Grows to 30 ft. tall; often narrower

Styrax japonicus

S

than high in youth, but spreads as wide or wider than tall in maturity. Slender, graceful trunk. The branches are often strongly horizontal, giving the tree a broad, flat top. Oval, scallop-edged dark green leaves to 3 in. long; may turn a good red or yellow in fall. Small clusters of ¾-in.-wide flowers hang on short side branches; leaves angle upward from branches while flowers hang down, giving effect of parallel green and white tiers. Splendid tree to look up into; plant it in raised beds near outdoor entertaining area or on high bank above path. 'Carillon' ('Pendula') is a shrubby variety with weeping branches. 'Pink Chimes', also shrubby, is a more upright form with pink flowers. 'Snow Charm' has larger leaves and a dependably rounded form, to 20 ft. high and wide. 'Snowcone' forms a dense, broad pyramid 25 ft. high and 20 ft. wide.

S. obassia. FRAGRANT SNOW-BELL. Tree. From eastern Asia. To 20–30 ft. tall, about two-thirds as wide. Oval to round, deep green, 3–8-in.-long leaves. Where frosts come very late, leaves may color yellow in autumn. Flowers to 1 in. long are carried in drooping, 6–8-in. clusters at branch ends. Good against background of evergreens, or for height and contrast above border of rhododendrons and azaleas. Same culture as for *S. japonicus.*

S. officinalis redivivus. CALIFORNIA SNOWDROP. Zones 6–10, 14–24; best in 14–16, 18–24. Native to dry, rocky areas of California below 3,000-ft. elevation. Upright deciduous shrub to 6–10 ft. high and about 6 ft. wide. Rounded to oval, gray-green leaves are 1–2 in. wide, with fuzzy undersides; turn yellow in fall. Small, waxy, fragrant white flowers with prominent yellow-tipped stamens are held in clusters at branch tips in spring. Useful in native or drought-tolerant gardens.

SUCCULENTS

Plants in this diverse group have in common fleshy leaves, stems, or roots that store water in order to withstand periods of drought. Cacti technically are succulents, but their needlelike spines and desert growing conditions put them in a category of their own (see Cactus). Plants commonly referred to as succulents—which encompass more than 50 genera—do not necessarily have spines, nor do they require desert conditions.

In fact, many will not thrive in the summer heat of interior valleys or deserts even if given some shade. Succulent fanciers tend not to include fleshy, tropical orchids in their collections, but may include dry-climate plants such as *Dasylirion, Puya,* and *Yucca.*

Most succulents come from warm, dry, frost-free regions of the world, notably Mexico, South Africa, and Madagascar. The majority are frost tender and will not tolerate prolonged wet conditions, but a few thrive in colder, rainier climates; among these are species of *Lewisia* native to the Pacific Northwest, *Sempervivum* (from Europe), and many sedums.

In mild-climate areas of the Southwest, massed plantings of succulents serve as low-water alternatives to lawns and flower beds; they combine well with drought-tolerant perennials. Shrubby types include *Bulbine, Crassula, Portulacaria,* and *Sansevieria.* Quite a few succulents make good ground covers, though none withstand foot traffic. Creeping, spreading succulents such as *Sedum* and *Senecio* are useful between stepping-stones, for filling niches in rock gardens, and for creating patterns in geometric gardens. Such plants, along with *Ceropegia* and *Graptopetalum,* are also attractive tumbling over terraces or cascading from hanging baskets. For succulents that produce vivid sheets of bloom and rapidly cover large banks, see Ice Plants.

Their wide range of sizes, shapes, and leaf colors make succulents useful foliage plants. Larger types that form sculptural rosettes lend interest to landscapes and serve as garden focal points. *Agave, Aloe,* and *Furcraea* in particular have dramatic silhouettes. Succulents with colorful leaves are eye-catching when grown in masses and contrasted with each other; see *Aeonium arboreum* 'Zwartkop', *Cotyledon orbiculata, Crassula ovata, Euphorbia tirucalli* 'Sticks on Fire', *Kalanchoe luciae, Senecio mandraliscae,* and *S. serpens.* Leaf color may intensify when plants are stressed by drought, nipped by frost, or grown in intense sun. Some succulents with daisylike overlapping leaves, notably aeoniums, suggest giant flowers. Numerous varieties also are striped or spotted. Tree succulents tend to have bulbous trunks, fat branches, and/or stiff, fleshy leaves; see *Adenium obesum, Aloe*

barberae, Dracaena draco, Euphorbia tirucalli, Nolina, and *Pachypodium lamerei.*

Blooms tend to be long lasting and brightly colored. The flowers of aloes are especially noteworthy, ranging from reddish orange to yellow, and held in spires a foot or more in height. Most larger aloes bloom in midwinter, enlivening otherwise dormant gardens.

New succulent varieties are continually being introduced, and many that once were rare now are readily available. Look for *Beschorneria yuccoides,* with lancelike leaves and vivid pink flower spikes; *Calandrinia grandiflora,* with airy purple flowers; and cabbagelike *Echeveria* varieties with ruffled, pastel leaves. Curiosities that deserve prominent display include *Dudleya, Haworthia, Hoya, Lithops,* and *Schlumbergera.*

Succulents require fast-draining soil; liberally amend ordinary garden soil with pumice, coarse sand, or decomposed granite. Although they are among the most drought tolerant of plants, prolonged periods without water may cause leaves of succulents to lose color, shrivel, or drop. The amount of irrigation needed depends on heat, humidity, and rainfall. Give plants just enough water to keep them plump and attractive. When siting them near plants that need more water, position succulents atop a small mound of amended soil so that water drains away from the roots.

Most succulents grow well in containers, and many make excellent, no-fuss houseplants. Plant in fast-draining cactus mix (available from nurseries and garden centers); let soil of potted succulents go dry or nearly so between waterings. Provide good air circulation.

Succulents require little maintenance, but they will look shabby if neglected. Their thick leaves last season to season, sometimes year to year. Many need little tending other than removal of spent flower stalks. When well grown and well tended, they are attractive year-round. One light feeding at the start of the growing season should be enough for most garden succulents; larger and later-blooming kinds, as well as container-grown plants, may benefit from additional fertilizing. Introduce nursery-grown succulents to sunny locations gradually or their leaves may sunburn.

Propagation of many succulents is quite easy. When taking cuttings from stem-forming types, let the

cut ends callus before planting. To propagate *Agave, Aloe, Sempervivum,* and other rosette-forming succulents, remove and replant offsets that form around the parent plant.

SUGAR BUSH. See **RHUS ovata**

SUGAR-SCOOP. See **TIARELLA**

SULFUR FLOWER. See **ERIOGONUM umbellatum**

SUMAC. See **RHUS**

SUMMER CYPRESS. See **KOCHIA scoparia**

SUMMER FORGET-ME-NOT. See **ANCHUSA capensis**

SUMMER HOLLY. See **COMAROSTAPHYLIS diversifolia**

SUMMER HYACINTH. See **GALTONIA candicans**

SUMMER LILAC. See **BUDDLEJA davidii**

SUMMERSWEET. See **CLETHRA alnifolia**

SUNDROPS. See **CALYLOPHUS, OENOTHERA**

SUNFLOWER. See **HELIANTHUS**

SUNRAY. See **HELIPTERUM**

SUNROSE. See **HALIMIUM, HELIANTHEMUM nummularium**

SURINAM CHERRY. See **EUGENIA uniflora**

SUTERA cordata
BACOPA
Scrophulariaceae
PERENNIAL

☀ ZONES 15–17, 21–24, H2; ANYWHERE AS ANNUAL

◐ AFTERNOON SHADE IN HOTTEST CLIMATES

● REGULAR WATER

From moist regions of South Africa. Wiry-stemmed creeper with green, roughly heart-shaped, toothed leaves. Usually sold as "bacopa"—the botanical name of water hyssop, a member of the same family. Blooms from late spring to frost, producing small, five-petaled, golden-throated flowers. Use in hanging basket or as small-scale ground cover. Needs good drainage, good air circulation; likes rich soil, regular fertilizer. Pinch branches often to keep plant shapely, but avoid severe

Sutera cordata

pruning. If a thick layer of dead stems builds up under foliage mass, remove dead material and cut plant back to leave 5–6-in.-long branches with leafy growth.

Original variety (sold as 'Snowflake') has ¼-in. white flowers and grows 1–2 in. high, spreading 1–2 ft. in a growing season; eventually covers 3–4 ft. or more in mild climates. 'Giant Snowflake' is more vigorous, reaching 6–8 in. high, 3–4 ft. wide in a season; its white flowers are ½ in. wide. 'Snowstorm' resembles 'Giant Snowflake' but blooms more profusely and has greater heat tolerance. 'Olympic Gold' has leaves irregularly splotched with golden yellow but is otherwise identical to 'Snowstorm' (to which it sometimes reverts). 'Lavender Showers', with ¼-in. lavender-blue flowers, is a small grower like 'Snowflake'; flower color notwithstanding, it is sometimes sold as 'Mauve Mist' or 'Pink Diamond'.

SWAMP MAHOGANY.
See **EUCALYPTUS robusta**

SWAN PLANT.
See **ASCLEPIAS fruticosa**

SWAN RIVER DAISY.
See **BRACHYSCOME**

SWEDISH IVY.
See **PLECTRANTHUS oertendahlii, P. verticillatus**

SWEET ALYSSUM.
See **LOBULARIA maritima**

SWEET BALM.
See **MELISSA officinalis**

SWEET BAY. See **LAURUS nobilis, MAGNOLIA virginiana**

SWEET BOX.
See **SARCOCOCCA**

SWEET BRIAR.
See **ROSA eglanteria**

SWEET FLAG. See **ACORUS**

SWEET GUM.
See **LIQUIDAMBAR**

SWEET OLIVE.
See **OSMANTHUS fragrans**

SWEET PEA. See **LATHYRUS**

SWEET-PEA SHRUB.
See **POLYGALA × dalmaisiana**

SWEET POTATO
Convolvulaceae
PERENNIAL GROWN AS ANNUAL

✿	ZONES 8–10, 12–15, 18–24; H1, H2
☀	FULL SUN
💧	REGULAR WATER

Not a potato, but the thickened root of a trailing tropical vine closely related to morning glory *(Convovulus, Ipomoea);* scientific name is *Ipomoea batatas* (see that entry for ornamental varieties of sweet potato). Bush and short vine varieties are also available. Needs long, hot, frost-free growing season; easiest to grow in Hawaii. Also requires well-drained soil (preferably sandy loam) and plenty of room. Start with certified disease-free slips (rooted cuttings) from a garden center or mail-order nursery. Look for disease-resistant varieties. To avoid buildup of disease organisms in the soil, don't grow sweet potatoes in the same location 2 years in a row.

Sweet potato

There are two classes of sweet potatoes. One has soft, sugary, yellow-orange flesh (examples are 'Centennial', 'Jewel', 'Kona-B', 'Vineless Puerto Rico'); the other has firm, dry, whitish flesh (examples are 'Onokeo', 'Waimanalo Red', 'Yellow Jersey'). The sweet yellow-orange type is incorrectly sold under the name "yam" in grocery stores. Most varieties of both classes are ready to harvest 110 to 120 days after planting.

Plant in late spring, when soil temperature has warmed to 70°F/ 21°C. (You can plant year-round in Hawaii, but spring-planted crops mature faster.) Work in a low-nitrogen fertilizer before planting;

too much nitrogen produces leafy growth at expense of roots. Set slips so only stem tips and leaves are exposed; space 1 ft. apart, in rows 3 ft. apart. To ensure good drainage, mark off rows and ditch between them to form planting ridges. Row covers provide added heat and keep out many pests.

Harvest before first frost; if tops are killed by sudden frost, harvest immediately. Dig carefully to avoid cutting or bruising roots. Flavor improves in storage (starch is converted to sugar). Let roots dry in the sun until soil can be brushed off; then cure by storing 10 to 14 days in warm (about 85°F/ 29°C), humid place. Store in a cool, dry environment (not below 55°F/13°C).

SWEETSHADE.
See **HYMENOSPORUM flavum**

SWEETSPIRE. See **ITEA**

SWEET SULTAN.
See **CENTAUREA moschata**

SWEET WILD GARLIC.
See **TULBAGHIA natalensis**

SWEET WILLIAM.
See **DIANTHUS barbatus**

SWEET WOODRUFF.
See **GALIUM odoratum**

SWISS CHARD
Chenopodiaceae
BIENNIAL GROWN AS ANNUAL

✿	ALL ZONES
☀	FULL SUN
💧	REGULAR WATER

A form of beet grown for leaves and stalks instead of roots; probably originated in the Mediterranean area. One of the easiest-to-grow vegetables for home gardens. Sow big, crinkly, tan seeds in spaded soil, any time from spring to early summer. Thin seedlings to 1 ft. apart. About 2 months after sowing (plants will generally have reached 1–1½ ft. tall), you can

Swiss chard

begin to cut outer leaves as needed for the table. New leaves grow up in center of plants. Plants yield all summer and seldom bolt to seed (if one does, pull it up and throw it away or add it to the compost pile). Where winters are mild, can be grown as fall-into-spring crop.

Regular green-and-white chard looks presentable in flower garden, but 'Bright Lights' is more decorative; it has leaves ranging from green to burgundy, stalks in various shades of yellow, orange, pink, purple, red, green (and in white). Red stems and reddish green leaves of 'Rhubarb' are very decorative in the garden and in floral arrangements. Cook leaves and leafstalks of all types separately, since stalks take longer.

SWISS CHEESE PLANT.
See **MONSTERA friedrichsthalii**

SWITCH GRASS.
See **PANICUM virgatum**

SWORD FERN.
See **NEPHROLEPIS, POLYSTICHUM munitum**

SYAGRUS
romanzoffianum
(Arecastrum romanzoffianum)
QUEEN PALM
Arecaceae (Palmae)
PALM

✿	ZONES 12, 13, 15–17, 19–24; H1, H2
☀	FULL SUN
💧	REGULAR WATER

Brazilian native to 50 ft. tall, 20–25 ft. wide, with exceptionally straight trunk. Arching, glossy bright green, 10–15-ft.-long leaves (they break in high winds). May produce decorative orange dates. Give well-drained soil. In alkaline soils, plants yellow and slowly die. Grows quickly with fertilizer. ▶

Syagrus romanzoffianum

S

Subject to mites; wash young plants frequently. Damaged at 25°F/–4°C but has recovered from 16°F/–9°C freezes.

SYCAMORE. See PLATANUS

SYMPHORICARPOS
SNOWBERRY, CORALBERRY
Caprifoliaceae
DECIDUOUS SHRUBS

🌿	ZONES VARY BY SPECIES
☼ ◐ ●	EXPOSURE NEEDS VARY BY SPECIES
◊ ◊	LITTLE TO MODERATE WATER

North American natives. The various plants described here are upright or arching, typically 2–6 ft. high and wide, often spreading by root suckers. Most are best used as wild thicket for erosion control on steep banks. Clusters of small pink or white flowers in spring or early summer. Attractive round, berry-like fruit remains on stems after leaves drop in autumn; attracts birds. Cut stems look good in winter arrangements.

Symphoricarpos albus

S. albus (S. racemosus). COMMON SNOWBERRY. Zones A3; 1–11, 14–21. Native from California to Alaska, east to Montana. Roundish, dull green, ¾–2-in.-long leaves (to 4 in. and often lobed on sucker shoots). Pink flowers are followed by white fruit from late summer to winter. Produces most fruit in full sun but takes shade. Not a first-rate shrub but useful for its tolerance of poor soil, lower light, general neglect.

S. × chenaultii. Zones 1–11, 14–21. Hybrid of *S. orbiculatus.* Has larger leaves than its parent, greenish white flowers, and red fruit lightly spotted with white. Can take full sun in cooler climates; needs partial or full shade in hot areas. 'Hancock' is foot-high dwarf valued as woodland ground or bank cover.

S. mollis. CREEPING SNOWBERRY, SPREADING SNOWBERRY.

Zones 2–10, 14–24. Native to western North America. Like *S. albus* but usually less than 1½ ft. high, with earlier, sparser bloom, smaller fruit. Spreads like a ground cover, its trailing branches rooting where they touch soil. Partial shade.

S. orbiculatus (S. vulgaris). CORALBERRY, INDIAN CURRANT. Zones 1–11, 14–21. From eastern U.S. Resembles *S. albus* but bears white or sometimes pink-tinged flowers that are followed by small purplish red fruit. Fruit is bright and plentiful enough to provide a good fall-into-winter show. Full sun.

SYMPHYTUM officinale
COMFREY
Boraginaceae
PERENNIAL

🌿	ZONES 1–24
☼ ◐	PARTIAL SHADE IN HOTTEST CLIMATES
●	REGULAR WATER
◊	LEAVES CAN BE HARMFUL IF INGESTED

From Eurasia. Deep-rooted plant forms a clump to 3–4 ft. high, 2 ft. wide. Furry leaves set with stiff hairs; basal leaves 8 in. or longer, upper leaves smaller. Small (½-in.-long), unshowy flowers are usually dull rose in color but sometimes white, cream, or purple. In virtually frost-free climates, plant remains leafy through winter; elsewhere, it dies to the ground in fall.

Symphytum officinale

Comfrey has a long history as a folk remedy. Leaves can be dried and brewed to make a medicinal tea, though this use is no longer recommended (leaves have been found to contain potentially carcinogenic substances). Herb enthusiasts claim that the plant adds minerals to compost, but think hard before establishing it in your garden: it spreads freely from roots and is difficult to eradicate.

SYRINGA
LILAC
Oleaceae
DECIDUOUS SHRUBS, RARELY TREES

🌿	ZONES VARY BY SPECIES
☼ ◐	LIGHT SHADE IN HOTTEST CLIMATES
●	REGULAR WATER

A garden staple in cold-winter regions, cherished for big, flamboyant, fragrant flower clusters at branch tips. Best known are common lilac *(S. vulgaris)* and its many named varieties, but there are other species of great usefulness. All are medium-size to large shrubs with medium to deep green foliage and no special appeal when out of bloom. Floral show comes from number of small flowers packed into dense pyramidal to conical clusters; individual flowers are tubular, flaring into four petal-like lobes (in single types) or into a clutch of "petals" (in double kinds). Depending on climate, bloom comes from early spring (in the earliest kinds) to early summer, always after leaves have formed.

Leaf miner, scale, and stem borer are the only important pests;

> ## What Lilacs Need
>
> **WINTER CHILL** Most lilacs bloom best in regions with decidedly chilly winters, but some do well with only light winter chill.
>
> **SOIL** Give well-drained, neutral to slightly alkaline soil. If soil is strongly acid, dig lime into it before planting.
>
> **PRUNING** Until plants are established, just pinch back any overlong stems. Once they begin blooming, prune yearly for best flower production. Most lilacs bloom on wood formed the previous year, so prune just after flowering ends. Remove spent blossom clusters, cutting back to a pair of leaves. For the few types that bloom on new growth, prune in late dormant season, cutting previous year's growth to varying lengths. To encourage young shoots, cut out a few of the oldest stems yearly.
>
> *Syringa pubescens patula* 'Miss Kim'

bacterial blight, leaf spot, downy mildew may be problems.

Syringa × laciniata

S. × chinensis. CHINESE LILAC. Zones A2, A3; 1–11, 14–16, 18–21. Hybrid between *S. vulgaris* and *S. × persica.* To 15 ft. high and wide, usually much less. More graceful than *S. vulgaris,* with finer-textured foliage. Profuse, open clusters of fragrant, rosy purple flowers. Does well in mild-winter, hot-summer climates. 'Alba' has white blossoms. 'Lilac Sunday' has single, light purple blooms.

S. × hyacinthiflora. Zones A2, A3; 1–12, 14–16, 18–22. Group of hybrids between *S. vulgaris* and *S. oblata,* a Chinese species. Resemble *S. vulgaris* but generally bloom 7 to 10 days earlier. 'Assessippi' (lavender) and 'Mount Baker' (white) are earliest. Other varieties include 'Alice Eastwood' (double magenta), 'Blue Hyacinth' (lavender), 'Clarke's Giant' (lavender; larger flowers than others), 'Esther Staley' (pink), 'Excel' (light lavender), 'Gertrude Leslie' (double white), 'Pocahontas' (purple), 'Purple Heart' (purple), and 'White Hyacinth' (white).

S. josikaea. HUNGARIAN LILAC. Zones 1–11, 14–16, 18–21. From Hungary. Dense, upright growth to 12 ft. tall and wide. Leaves 2–5 in. long. Lilac purple, slightly fragrant flowers in narrow, 4–7-in.-long clusters.

S. × laciniata (S. × persica laciniata). Zones 3–12, 14–16, 18–22. Open-structured plant to 5–8 ft. tall and wide. Leaves to 2½ in. long, divided nearly to midrib into three to nine segments; good rich green color. Many small clusters of fragrant, lilac-colored blooms.

S. meyeri 'Palibin'. Zones A2, A3; 1–9, 14–16. Dense, twiggy growth to a possible 5 ft. tall and wide; often stays at about 3 ft. Sometimes grafted high to make a standard tree with 3–4-ft. trunk. Produces 5-in. clusters of faintly fragrant flowers in purple fading to pink. Leaves to 1¾ in. long.

S. × persica. PERSIAN LILAC. Zones A2, A3; 2–12, 14–16, 18–22. Graceful, loose form to 6 ft. high and wide; leaves 2½ in. long. Fragrant, pale violet flowers appear all along arching branches.

S. × prestoniae. Zones A1–A3; 1–11, 14–16. Group of extra-hardy hybrids developed in Canada. To 12 ft. tall and wide. Flowers come on new growth at the end of the lilac season, after S. vulgaris has bloomed. Bulky, dense plants resemble S. vulgaris, but individual flowers are smaller and are not as fragrant. Good selections include 'Donald Wyman' (dark rosy purple), 'Isabella' (lilac), 'Jessica' (violet), 'Minuet' (pale lilac), 'Miss Canada' (bright pink), 'Nocturne' (bluish lilac), and 'Royalty' (purple to violet). See S. × swegiflexa for 'James MacFarlane'.

S. pubescens patula 'Miss Kim'. Zones A2, A3; 1–9, 14–16. Dense, twiggy, rounded; to 8–9 ft. tall and wide. Sometimes grafted high to make a standard tree. Purple buds open to very fragrant ice blue flowers. Leaves to 2–4½ in. long.

S. reticulata. JAPANESE TREE LILAC. Zones A2, A3; 1–12, 14–16. From Japan. To 30 ft. tall, 20 ft. wide; grow as large shrub or train as single-stemmed tree. Smooth, glossy red-brown bark. Leaves to 5 in. long. Blooms on new growth in late spring, bearing white, musky-scented flowers in clusters to 1 ft. long. Useful small shade or street tree in cold climates. 'Ivory Silk' is a compact tree to 20 ft. tall, with cream-colored flowers borne in profusion even at a young age.

S. r. pekinensis (S. pekinensis). PEKING LILAC. From Mongolia and northern China. Grows quickly in youth, then slows, reaching 20–30 ft. tall and not quite as wide, with arching branches, fragrant flowers, and dark green leaves. 'Beijing Gold' sports primrose yellow flowers and glossy, cinnamon-colored bark. 'China Snow' has pure white flowers and amber-colored peeling bark. 'Summer Charm' has a finer overall texture, with blossoms of creamy white. All are known for their abundant bloom.

S. × swegiflexa. Zones 3–9, 14–16. Hybrid of S. reflexa and S. sweginzowii; sometimes called pink pear lilac. To 12 ft. tall, 8 ft. wide. Deep reddish buds; pink flowers in clusters to 8 in. on new growth, about 3 weeks after S. vulgaris. 'James MacFarlane' is best-known variety.

S. villosa. LATE LILAC. Zones A1–A3; 1–11, 14–16. From northern China. Stiff, erect bush 6–10 ft. tall and wide. Pinkish lilac to white flowers have a somewhat musky scent, appear on new growth late in the lilac season. Important chiefly as one parent of the S. × prestoniae hybrids.

S. vulgaris. COMMON LILAC. Zones A1–A3; 1–11, 14. In Zones 12–16, 18–22, the standard varieties bloom irregularly after mild winters; gradually discontinue watering near end of summer to force dormancy. From eastern Europe. Can eventually reach 20 ft. tall, with nearly equal spread. Suckers strongly; prune out suckers on grafted plants (no need to do so on own-root plants.) Leaves to 5 in. long, roundish oval with

Syringa vulgaris

pointed tips. Needs 2 to 5 years to bear flowers of full size and true color. Pinkish or bluish lavender flowers in clusters to 10 in. or longer ('Alba' has pure white flowers) in midspring. Fragrance is legendary; lilac fanciers say species and its older varieties are more fragrant than newer types. Superb cut flowers.

Varieties, often called French hybrids, number in the hundreds. They generally flower a little later than the species and have larger clusters of single or double flowers in wide range of colors. Singles are often as showy as doubles, sometimes more so. Choices include: 'Charles Joly' (double dark purplish red), 'Miss Ellen Willmott' (double pure white), 'Ludwig Spaeth' (reddish purple to dark purple), 'President Lincoln' (Wedgwood blue), 'President Poincaré' (double two-tone purple), 'Sensation' (wine red with white picotee edge), 'William Robinson' (double pink). Newer varieties include 'Adelaide Dunbar', double purple; early-blooming 'Burgundy Queen', single burgundy red; 'Krasavitsa Moskvy' ('Beauty of Moscow'), double white from pink buds; 'Nadezhda' ('Hope'), double deep lilac blue from purple buds; 'Primrose', unusual creamy yellow.

Descanso Hybrids, developed for mild winters, excel in Zones 18–22. Try 'Lavender Lady' (best known), 'Blue Skies' and 'Blue Boy' (both blue), 'Chiffon' (lavender), 'Forrest K. Smith' (light lavender), 'Sylvan Beauty' (rose lavender), and 'White Angel' ('Angel White').

SYZYGIUM
paniculatum
BRUSH CHERRY, AUSTRALIAN BRUSH CHERRY
Myrtaceae
EVERGREEN SHRUB OR TREE

| ZONES 16, 17, 20–24; H1, H2 |
| BEST IN SUN; TOLERATES SOME SHADE |
| MODERATE TO REGULAR WATER |

Australian native often sold as *Eugenia myrtifolia* or *E. paniculata*. If unclipped, makes a single- or multitrunked tree to 30–60 ft. tall, 10–20 ft. wide, with dense foliage crown. Often sheared into formal shapes and hedges; common background or screen plant. Oblong, 1½–3-in.-long leaves in rich glossy green, often bronze tinged; reddish bronze new growth. Small, creamy white summer flowers have conspicuous tufts of stamens that look like little brushes. Blossoms are followed by showy, edible, ¾-in., rosy purple fruit that is insipid raw but good in jellies. Several named varieties selected for good leaf color or dwarf form are sold.

Will not stand heavy frost; foliage burns at 25°F/–4°C, and even old plants may die if temperature drops much lower. Thrives in well-drained soil. Heavy root system makes it difficult to grow other plants nearby. Hedges need frequent clipping to stay neat. Eugenia psyllid can cause defoliation; control is a predatory wasp.

Syzygium paniculatum

S

Syringa × chinensis

Syringa × hyacinthiflora 'Excel'

Syringa meyeri 'Palibin'

Syringa × persica

Syringa reticulata

Syringa vulgaris 'Primrose'

T

TABEBUIA

TRUMPET TREE
Bignoniaceae
DECIDUOUS, EVERGREEN, AND
SEMIEVERGREEN TREES

	ZONES 15, 16, 20–24, H1, H2, EXCEPT AS NOTED
☼	FULL SUN
💧	REGULAR WATER

Native to tropical America. Showy, trumpet-shaped flowers are borne in rounded clusters that become larger and more profuse as trees mature. Leaves are typically green; may be simple (undivided) or divided into as many as seven leaflets arranged like fingers of hand. Number of leaflets is often variable within a species.

Tend to be gangly or irregular when young; benefit from training in early years. Need well-drained soil; respond well to regular fertilizing. All are useful as color accents, stand-alone flowering trees for display. Larger types are excellent as street or park plantings; smaller species make beautiful patio trees or container plants.

T. chrysotricha. GOLDEN TRUMPET TREE. Briefly deciduous. Zones 13, 15, 16, 20–24; H1, H2. To 25–50 ft. high and wide. Young twigs, leaf undersides covered with tawny fuzz. Golden yellow flowers are 3–4 in. long, often with maroon stripes in throat. Blooms most heavily in spring, when tree loses leaves for brief period. May also bloom lightly at other times, when in leaf. Sometimes sold as *T. pulcherrima.*

T. donnell-smithii (Cybistax donnell-smithii). GOLD TREE, PRIMAVERA. Deciduous. Zones H1, H2. Upright grower to 75–100 ft. high, 30–50 ft. wide. Bloom season is variable: spectacular clusters of yellow blossoms to 1½ in. long are commonly produced in winter or spring before leafout, but occasionally they appear later in the year.

T. heterophylla. PINK TECOMA, PINK TRUMPET TREE. Evergreen to semievergreen. Slender habit to 40 ft. tall, 20 ft. wide; sometimes grown as a large shrub. Flowers 2–3 in. long, in

Tabebuia heterophylla

colors ranging from pinkish purple through pink shades to white. Blossoms appear abundantly in spring but may also be seen occasionally throughout the rest of the year.

T. impetiginosa (T. ipe). PURPLE or PINK TRUMPET TREE. Semievergreen. Slow to 25–50 ft. high and wide. In late winter or spring, bears 2–3-in. flowers in white to light pink and purple. Sometimes reblooms in late summer or fall. Does not bloom as a young tree.

TAGETES

MARIGOLD
Asteraceae (Compositae)
ANNUALS AND PERENNIALS

	ZONES VARY BY SPECIES
☼	FULL SUN
💧	REGULAR WATER, EXCEPT AS NOTED

Native to Mexico, Central America. Robust, free-branching, nearly trouble-free plants ranging from 6 in. to 6 ft. tall, with flowers from pale yellow through gold to orange and brownish maroon. Finely divided, ferny, usually strongly scented leaves. Annuals will bloom early summer to frost if old flowers are picked off; in the desert, they bloom best from fall until frost. Handsome, long-lasting cut flowers; strong aroma from leaves, stems, and flowers permeates a room (some odorless varieties are available). Easy to grow from seed, which sprouts in a few days in warm soil; to get earlier bloom, start seeds in containers indoors or buy nursery plants. Smog will damage tender young plants, but they soon toughen up.

T. erecta. AMERICAN MARIGOLD, AFRICAN MARIGOLD. Annual. All zones. Original strains were single-flowered plants 3–4 ft.

tall, 2 ft. wide. Modern strains are more varied; most have fully double flowers. Choices include Antigua (10–12 in.); Guys and Dolls, Inca, and Inca II series (12–14) in.; Galore, Lady, and Perfection (16–20 in.); and Climax (2½–3 ft.). Novelty tall strains include Odorless (2½ ft.). Sweet Cream has creamy white flowers on 16-in. stems. Triploid hybrids, crosses between *T. erecta* and *T. patula,* have exceptional vigor, bear profuse 2-in. flowers over a long bloom season; they are generally shorter than other *T. erecta* strains. Examples are Trinity Mix and Nugget, both 10–12 in. high.

Avoid overhead sprinkling on taller kinds; stems will sag and even break under weight of water. To make tall types stand as firmly as possible (perhaps stoutly enough to do without staking), dig planting hole extra deep, strip any leaves off lower 1–3 in. of stem, and plant with stripped portion below soil line.

T. filifolia. IRISH LACE. Annual. All zones. Forms a mound of bright green, finely divided foliage to 6 in. high and wide; resembles an unusually fluffy, rounded fern. Used primarily as edging plant for its foliage effect, but tiny white flowers are attractive.

T. lemmonii (T. palmeri). COPPER CANYON DAISY. Shrubby perennial. Zones 8–10, 12–24; H1. To 3–6 ft. tall and wide. Finely divided, 2–4-in.-long leaves are strongly fragrant when brushed against or rubbed—they smell like a blend of marigold, mint, and lemon. Golden orange flowers are carried at branch ends sporadically all year, peaking in winter and spring. Damaged by frost in open situations; cut back to remove damaged growth or to correct shape. Tends to be short lived. Moderate to regular water.

T. lucida. MEXICAN MARIGOLD, MEXICAN TARRAGON. Perennial in Zones 8–10, 12–24; often grown as an annual in all zones. To 3 ft. high and wide, typically with unbranched stems. Narrow, uncut, smooth dark green leaves have strong scent and flavor

Tagetes erecta

of tarragon or licorice (stems and roots are similarly fragrant). Unimpressive yellow flowers, produced in fall and spring, are less than ½ in. wide. Moderate to regular water.

T. patula. FRENCH MARIGOLD. Annual. All zones. Varieties from 6 in. to 1½ ft. high and wide, in flower colors from yellow to rich maroon brown. Blossoms may be fully double or single; many are strongly bicolored. Excellent for edging are dwarf, very double strains such as Janie (8 in.), Bonanza (10 in.), and Hero (10–12 in.), with 2-in. flowers in a range of colors from yellow through orange to red and brownish red. Aurora and Sophia strains have flowers that are larger (2½ in. wide) but not as double.

T. tenuifolia (T. signata). SIGNET MARIGOLD. Annual. All zones. Infrequently grown species. Flowers are small (just 1 in. wide) and single, but bloom is incredibly profuse. Finely cut foliage. Gem strain offers golden yellow, lemon yellow, and tangerine orange blossoms on 10–12-in.-tall plants.

TAHOKA DAISY. See **MACHAERANTHERA tanacetifolia**

TAM. See **JUNIPERUS sabina 'Tamariscifolia'**

TAMARACK. See **LARIX occidentalis, PINUS contorta murrayana**

TAMARILLO. See **TREE TOMATO**

TAMARIX

TAMARISK
Tamaricaceae
DECIDUOUS SHRUBS OR TREES

	ZONES VARY BY SPECIES
☼	FULL SUN
💧	LITTLE OR NO WATER TO MODERATE WATER

In desert regions, tamarisks have no equal in resistance to wind and aridity, and they will grow in saline soils that are toxic to other plants. Also useful in other areas where wind, salt, and poor soil pose challenges, such as seacoast gardens. They demand only a full-sun location with good drainage. On the minus side, this same tenacious adaptability makes several of these species seriously invasive pests in Western natural areas, especially along watercourses. Millions of dollars a year are spent removing them. Because of deep taproots, nurseries can't hold them in containers. But they are easy to grow from ½–1-in.-thick cuttings set in the soil where the plant is to grow and kept watered until roots are established.

Tamarisks are difficult to classify, which has led to much confusion in labeling among botanists and in nurseries. Leaves are tiny, as are flowers (a hand lens is necessary to see flower details). However, you don't have to know a tamarisk's identity for pruning purposes. If it blooms only in the earlier part of spring, prune after bloom. If it starts bloom later in spring or in summer, prune just before new spring growth begins. The first two species described here can be kept shrubby by cutting back to ground yearly. If you are growing them as trees, prune only to remove dead or broken branches.

Tamarix aphylla

T. aphylla (T. articulata). ATHEL TREE. Zones 7–24. Native to eastern Mediterranean. Cuttings grow fast after planting, to 10 ft. or more in 3 years; with deep soil and some water, reach 30–50 ft. tall, 25–50 ft. wide in 15 years. True leaves are minute; the plant's evergreen appearance is due to greenish, jointed branchlets. Where soils are saline, takes on grayish look in late summer due to secretions of salt. White to pinkish, very small flowers grow in clusters at ends of branches in late summer. Tree is not as spectacular in bloom as other tamarisks. Heavily damaged at 0°F/−18°C but recovers rapidly. Can be sheared into a hedge.

Excellent windbreak. Has invasive roots; not a good choice for highly cultivated gardens.

T. chinensis. SALT CEDAR. Zones 4–24. Native to eastern Asia; naturalized in southwestern U.S. To 6–20 ft. tall, 4–10 ft. wide. Blue-green foliage. Flowers ranging from white to pink and deep purple appear mainly at branch ends. Blooms from late spring through summer. Resists heat and cold. Widely seen in desert regions but disliked there: its aggressive spreading and deep, thirsty roots displace native vegetation. Efforts are being made to remove it from many desert areas. *T. ramosissima* may be the same plant.

T. parviflora. Zones 2–24. Native to southeastern Europe. Variable habit; typically a graceful, arching large shrub to 6–15 ft. tall and wide. Profuse spring-only display of pink flowers that turn to tan, then brown. Prune to emphasize arching habit; or remove lower branches to achieve a treelike plant. An invasive pest plant in deserts, wetlands, and riparian habitats. Often sold as *T. tetrandra;* sold as *T. africana* in California.

TAMPALA. See **AMARANTHUS tricolor**

TANACETUM
Asteraceae (Compositae)
PERENNIALS

- 🌿 **ZONES VARY BY SPECIES**
- ☼ **FULL SUN**
- 🌢🌢 **MODERATE TO REGULAR WATER**

Most species have finely divided leaves (often aromatic) and clusters of daisylike flower heads. Some have gray to nearly white foliage.

T. balsamita. See Chrysanthemum balsamita

T. coccineum. See Chrysanthemum coccineum

T. densum amani. Zones 3–24. Native to Turkey. Sometimes sold as *Chrysanthemum haradjanii.* Low-growing (6–8-in.-high) plant, spreading slowly to make mat about 1½ ft. wide. Leaves are finely cut, silvery white, featherlike in appearance. Small yellow flower heads appear a few inches above foliage in late spring. Use in rock garden, as small-scale ground cover in bright, sunny area with good drainage. Can withstand some dry spells when established. One of the whitest-looking plants.

T. parthenium. See Chrysanthemum parthenium

T. ptarmiciflorum. See Chrysanthemum ptarmiciflorum

T. vulgare. TANSY. Zones 1–24. Native to Europe. Coarse, rather weedy garden plant to 3 ft. tall, 2 ft. wide, with finely divided, bright green, aromatic (some say smelly) leaves. Small, buttonlike yellow flowers appear in late summer. Thin clumps yearly to keep in bounds. This plant is no longer used medicinally, though it is still grown in herb gardens. *T. v. crispum,* fern-leaf tansy, grows 2½ ft. tall; it has finely cut foliage and is more decorative than the species.

Tanacetum vulgare

TANBARK OAK. See **LITHOCARPUS densiflorus**

TANGELO. See **CITRUS**

TANGERINE. See **CITRUS: Mandarin**

TANGOR. See **CITRUS**

TANSY. See **TANACETUM vulgare**

TARO. See **COLOCASIA esculenta**

TARRAGON, FRENCH or TRUE. See **ARTEMISIA dracunculus**

TARRAGON, MEXICAN. See **TAGETES lucida**

TASMANIAN TREE FERN. See **DICKSONIA antarctica**

TASSEL FERN. See **POLYSTICHUM polyblepharum**

TASSEL FLOWER. See **AMARANTHUS caudatus**

TAXODIUM
Taxodiaceae
DECIDUOUS AND EVERGREEN TREES

- 🌿 **ZONES VARY BY SPECIES**
- ☼ **FULL SUN**
- 🌢🌢🌢🌢 **ANY AMOUNT OF WATER**

Very tough, tolerant conifers of great size, with shaggy, cinnamon-colored bark and graceful sprays of short, narrow, flat, needlelike leaves. Small, roundish cones.

T. distichum. BALD CYPRESS. Deciduous. Zones 2–10, 12–24. From southeastern U.S. Can grow into 100-ft.-tall, broad-topped tree in the wild, but young and middle-aged garden trees are pyramidal to 50–70 ft. high, 20–30 ft. wide. Feathery, delicate foliage sprays with narrow, ½-in.-long leaves in a pale, delicate, yellow-tinged green. Foliage turns orange-toned brown before dropping. Interesting winter silhouette. Takes any except strongly alkaline soils. Tolerates extremely wet conditions (even grows in swamps) but also takes rather dry soil. Trunk is buttressed near base. When growing in water-logged soil, develops knobby growths called knees. No particular pests or diseases. Requires only corrective pruning to remove dead wood and unwanted branches. Outstanding tree for stream bank or edge of lake or pond. 'Cascade Falls' is a weeping form; grows quickly to 20 ft. tall and wide. 'Shawnee Brave' grows into a narrow pyramid just 15–20 ft. wide.

Taxodium distichum

T. mucronatum. MONTEZUMA CYPRESS. Evergreen in mild climates; partially or wholly deciduous in cold regions. Zones 5–9, 12–24. From Mexico. Given regular moisture, it quickly attains 40 ft. in 14 years, then grows at a more moderate rate to an eventual 75 ft. tall, 50 ft. wide. Under dry conditions, growth is uniformly slow. Extremely graceful tree with strongly weeping branches. Foliage is finer in texture, lighter in color than that of *T. distichum;* in colder part of range, it turns dull gold in autumn (color change and leaf drop both come very late). Beautiful tree for large lawns.

TAXUS
YEW
Taxaceae
EVERGREEN SHRUBS OR TREES

🌿	ZONES VARY BY SPECIES
☼ ◐ ●	SUN OR SHADE
◐ ●	MODERATE TO REGULAR WATER
💧	FRUIT (SEEDS) AND FOLIAGE ARE POISONOUS IF INGESTED

Yews are conifers, but they do not bear cones. Instead, they produce fleshy, scarlet (rarely yellow), cup-shaped, single-seeded, berrylike fruit. In general, yews are darker green, more formal looking, and more tolerant of shade and moisture than most cultivated conifers. Long lived; take much shearing and pruning, since they sprout from bare wood. Excellent for hedges, screens.

Yews can be moved without harm even when large, but since they grow at a slow to moderate rate, big plants are luxury items. They take many soils but do not thrive in strongly alkaline or strongly acid conditions. Do not take extreme heat, and reflected heat from a hot south or west wall will burn foliage. Even cold-hardy kinds show needle damage when exposed to dry winds, very low temperatures. Only female plants produce berries, and many do so without male plants nearby. Subject to vine weevils, scale insects, spider mites. During prolonged spells of hot, dry weather, hose off plants every 2 weeks.

T. baccata. ENGLISH YEW. Tree or shrub. Zones A3; 3–9, 14–24. From Europe, North Africa, western Asia. To 25–40 ft. or taller, 15–25 ft. wide, with broad, low crown. Needles ½–1½ in. long, dark green and glossy above, pale beneath; spirally arranged. Far more common than the species

Taxus baccata 'Fastigiata'

are garden varieties, including the following.

'Adpressa'. Usually sold as *T. brevifolia,* a name correctly belonging to the native Western yew. Wide-spreading, dense shrub to 4–5 ft. high, 6–8 ft. wide.

'Aurea'. Broad pyramid to 25 ft. tall, 12 ft. wide after many years. New foliage is golden yellow from spring to fall, then turns green.

'Fastigiata' ('Stricta'). IRISH YEW. Dark green column to 15–30 ft. tall, 3–10 ft. wide. Has larger needles and more crowded, upright branches than the species. Branches tend to spread near top, especially in snowy regions or where moisture is plentiful. Branches can be tied together with wire. Plants that outgrow their space can be reduced by heading back and thinning; old wood sprouts freely. There is a form with yellowish white variegation.

'Repandens'. SPREADING ENGLISH YEW. Long, horizontal, spreading branches make 2–4-ft.-high ground cover; extend to 8–10 ft. after many years. Useful low foundation plant. Will arch over wall.

T. brevifolia. WESTERN YEW, OREGON YEW. Zones A3; 3–7, 14–17. Native to moist places, California northward to Alaska, inland to Montana. Tree. Loose, open growth to 50–60 ft. tall, 30–40 ft. wide, with peeling red bark and dark yellowish green needles. Not common in nature and difficult to grow; not a garden tree. Most plants sold under this name are actually *T. cuspidata* 'Nana'.

T. cuspidata. JAPANESE YEW. Tree or shrub. Zones A2, A3; 2–6, 14–17. In its native Japan, a tree to 50 ft. tall; in North America, usually seen as a compact, pyramidal tree to 10–25 ft. (possibly taller), half as wide. Can be kept lower by pinching new growth. Fruits heavily. Most useful yew in cold-winter areas east of Cascades. Will succeed in shaded areas of Rocky Mountain gardens. Needles ½–1 in. long, dark green above, tinged yellowish beneath; usually arranged in two rows along twigs to make a flat or V-shaped spray. The following two varieties are commonly available.

'Capitata'. Plants sold under this name are probably ordinary *T. cuspidata.*

'Nana'. Often sold as *T. brevifolia.* Grows 1–4 in. a year; can reach 3 ft. tall, 6 ft. wide in 20 years. Serves as a good low barrier or foundation plant for many years.

T. × media. Shrubs. Zones 2–6, 14–17. Group of hybrids between *T. baccata* and *T. cuspidata;* intermediate between the two in color and texture. Of the dozens of selections available, these (all with dark green foliage) are among the most widely offered.

'Brownii'. Compact, rounded plant to 6–8 ft. tall, 8–10 ft. wide. Good dense hedge.

'Hatfieldii'. Broad column or pyramid. Reaches 12 ft. tall, 10 ft. wide after 20 years.

'Hicksii'. Upright-growing variety to 10–12 ft. tall, 3–4 ft. wide; grows larger with age.

TEA. See **CAMELLIA sinensis**

TEABERRY.
See **GAULTHERIA procumbens**

TEA TREE.
See **LEPTOSPERMUM**

TECOMA
Bignoniaceae
EVERGREEN SHRUBS, TREES, AND VINES

🌿	ZONES VARY BY SPECIES
☼ ◐	FULL SUN OR LIGHT SHADE
💧	MODERATE WATER, EXCEPT AS NOTED

Various trumpet vines once lumped together as *Tecoma* now have different names. Remaining in this genus are several showy shrubs, one of which can be grown as a vine, another as a tree. All have 2-in.-long, trumpet-shaped flowers in the yellow-orange-red range and leaves divided featherwise into many leaflets. Heat tolerant. Take drought but look best with periodic soakings. Tip-pinch young growth to induce branching, reduce tendency toward legginess. Cut faded flowers to prolong bloom and lessen production of seedpods. Prune to remove unwanted seedpods and wood damaged by freezes.

T. × alata (T. × smithii). ORANGE BELLS. Shrub. Zones 12, 13, 21–24. To 8 ft. tall, 4–5 ft. wide, with bright green foliage and orange flowers throughout warm weather. Tolerates light frost; may die to ground in a hard freeze but recovers quickly in warm weather. Some consider 'Orange Jubilee' to be a selection of this plant; others identify it as a hybrid between *T. capensis* and *T. stans.*

T. australis. See Pandorea pandorana

T. capensis (Tecomaria capensis). CAPE HONEYSUCKLE. Vine or shrub. Zones 12, 13, 20–24, H1,

H2; with protection in 14, 15, 18, 19. From South Africa. If tied to a support, can scramble to 15–30 ft.; with hard pruning, makes an upright shrub 6–8 ft. tall, 4–5 ft. wide. Shiny dark green leaflets give it a fine-textured look. Brilliant orange-red flowers in compact clusters appear from fall into spring (almost all year in Hawaii). Takes wind, salt air. Use as espalier, bank cover (especially good on hot, steep slopes), coarse barrier hedge. Little water. 'Aurea' has lighter green foliage and yellow flowers; it is somewhat less vigorous than the species. 'Buff Gold' has golden orange blossoms.

T. garrocha. ARGENTINE TECOMA. Shrub. Zones 12, 13, 21–24. From Argentina. To 5 ft. (possibly 10 ft.) tall and wide. Clusters of salmon to orange blossoms throughout warm weather. Reacts to freezes like *T. × alata.*

T. jasminoides. See Pandorea jasminoides.

T. stans (Stenolobium stans). YELLOW BELLS, YELLOW TRUMPET FLOWER, YELLOW ELDER. Zones 12, 13, 21–24, H1, H2, except as noted. Native from southern U.S. to Guatemala. In mildest climates, can be trained as a tree. Where frosts are common, it is usually a large shrub. Wood may die back in hard freezes, but new growth comes on quickly. Can reach 25 ft. tall, 10–20 ft. wide. Large clusters of bright yellow flowers from late spring to early winter. Good for boundary planting, big shrub border, screening. Needs heat, deep soil, fairly heavy feeding.

Tecoma stans

T. s. angustata. Zones 12, 13. Native from Arizona to Texas and adjoining Mexico. To 4–10 ft. tall, 3–8 ft. wide. Narrow leaflets. Blooms from midspring to late fall. Needs less water and fertilizer than the species.

TEDDYBEAR CACTUS.
See **OPUNTIA bigelovii**

TELLIMA grandiflora
FRINGE CUPS
Saxifragaceae
PERENNIAL

🌿	ZONES 2–9, 14–17
◐ ●	PARTIAL OR FULL SHADE
💧	REGULAR WATER

Native from central California to southern Alaska. To 2½ ft. tall, 1½ ft. wide. Often confused with *Tiarella*. Creeping rootstock sends up leafstalks to 8 in. long set with rounded to triangular, lobed, light green, softly hairy leaves to 4 in. across. Foliage is evergreen where

Tellima grandiflora

winters are mild. Small, urn-shaped spring flowers with tiny fringed petals open green, age to deep red; though not showy, they are attractively arranged along tall, slender stems. Provide rich, moist soil. Choice plant to combine with ferns in a woodland garden.

TERNSTROEMIA gymnanthera
(T. japonica)
Theaceae
EVERGREEN SHRUB

🌿	ZONES 4–9, 12–24
◐ ●	PARTIAL OR FULL SHADE
💧💧	REGULAR TO AMPLE WATER

Camellia relative from China, Japan. May eventually reach 6–8 ft. but is usually seen as a rounded plant 3–4 ft. tall, 4–6 ft. wide. This plant's appeal lies in its glossy, leathery foliage. Red-stalked leaves are rounded oval to narrowly oval, 1½–3 in. long, bronzy red when new; color at maturity varies. In deep shade, mature foliage tends to be dark green; with some sun, it may be bronzy green to purplish red. Red tints are deeper in cold weather. Creamy yellow, ½-in. summer flowers are fragrant but not

Ternstroemia gymnanthera

showy. Fruits (uncommon on small plants) resemble small yellow to red-orange holly berries or cherries; they split to reveal black seeds.

Grow in well-drained soil. Leaves turn yellow if soil isn't acid enough; fertilize with acid plant food if necessary. Tip-pinch to encourage compact growth. Use as basic landscaping shrub, informal hedge, tub or poolside plant. Cut foliage keeps well. Good companion for shade-loving plants. Tolerates full sun in cool-summer climates.

TETRANEURIS
(Hymenoxys)
Asteraceae (Compositae)
PERENNIALS

🌿	ZONES VARY BY SPECIES
☼	FULL SUN
💧💧	LITTLE TO MODERATE WATER

Taprooted plants with narrow, grassy, aromatic leaves that form small, evergreen foliage tufts about 8 in. high, 1 ft. wide. Somewhat reminiscent of thrift (*Armeria*). Blooms during warm months (nearly all year in mild-winter climates). Yellow daisies to 1½ in. wide have rays with notched edges; blossoms are usually carried singly on stems. Give well-drained soil. Cut off faded flower spikes to neaten plants and prolong bloom. Tolerant of heat, cold, drought. With some moisture, will reseed. Attractive in containers.

T. acaulis. ANGELITA DAISY. Zones 1–3, 7–14, 18–24. Native to

Tetraneuris acaulis

plains from Canada to Texas. Golden yellow flowers on stems to 1 ft. high.

T. scaposa. CLUSTERED GOLDFLOWER. Zones 2, 3, 10–14, 18–24. Native from Colorado to Kansas, south to New Mexico, Texas. Leaves are sometimes lobed. Bright yellow flowers on stems to 16 in. high; rays may have red-brown veins on undersides.

TETRAPANAX papyrifer
(Aralia papyrifera)
RICE PAPER PLANT
Araliaceae
EVERGREEN SHRUB

🌿	ZONES 15–24; H1, H2
☼ ◐	AFTERNOON SHADE IN HOTTEST CLIMATES
💧	REGULAR WATER

From China. Fast growing to 10–15 ft. tall and wide; often multi-trunked. Big, bold, long-stalked leaves are 1–2 ft. wide, deeply lobed, gray green above, white and felted beneath, carried in clusters at ends of stems. Fuzz on new growth can irritate eyes or skin. Tan trunks often curve or lean. Big, branched clusters of creamy white flowers on furry tan stems appear in winter.

Tetrapanax papyrifer

Young plants sunburn easily; older ones adapt. Seems to suffer only from high winds, which break or tatter leaves, and from frost—foliage is severely damaged at 22°F/−6°C (however, it recovers fast and often puts up suckers to form thickets). Digging around roots stimulates sucker formation; suckers may arise 20 ft. from parent plant. Use for silhouette against walls, on patios; combine with other sturdy, bold-leafed plants for tropical effect. Name comes from the thick pith of the stems, which is used to make Chinese rice paper.

TETRASTIGMA voinieranum
(Cissus voinierana)
Vitaceae
EVERGREEN VINE

🌿	ZONES 13, 17, 20–24; H1, H2
☼	ROOTS COOL, TOPS IN SUN, EXCEPT AS NOTED
💧	REGULAR WATER

Native to Laos. Climbs quickly by tendrils to 50–60 ft. Thick, fleshy stems carry glossy, leathery dark green leaves to 1 ft. across, divided fanwise into three to five oval leaflets with toothed edges. New growth is covered with silvery fuzz. Flowers and fruit rarely seen. Good growing along eaves, near swimming pools. Makes a large-scale bank or ground cover in milder part of range. Feed until well established. Needs shade in Zone 13.

Tetrastigma voinieranum

TEUCRIUM
GERMANDER
Lamiaceae (Labiatae)
SHRUBBY PERENNIALS

🌿	ZONES VARY BY SPECIES
☼	FULL SUN
💧	MODERATE WATER

Mediterranean natives with aromatic foliage and whorls of little flowers. These are tough plants that endure poor, rocky soils; they can't stand wet or poorly drained soils but will tolerate regular watering where drainage is good.

T. cossonii majoricum (**T. majoricum**). Zones 7–9, 14–24. Narrow, silvery gray leaves to 1 in. long form a mound to 8 in. high, 1½ ft. wide. Virtually continuous show of small, rosy purple, honey-scented flowers in dense heads (most profuse in late spring, early summer). Good rock garden plant or small-scale ground cover. ▶

T

Also sold as *T. majoricum* and *T. cussonii;* a very similar plant is *T. polium pii-fontanii.*

T. fruticans. BUSH GERMANDER. Zones 4–24. Loose, silvery-stemmed plant to 4–8 ft. tall and wide (or wider). Gray-green, 1¼-in.-long leaves have silvery white undersides, giving plant an overall silvery gray appearance. Blooms almost year-round, bearing lavender-blue flower spikes at branch ends. Thin and cut back before spring growth begins. 'Azureum' has deeper blue flowers than the species; 'Compactum', also with dark blue blooms, grows just 3 ft. high and wide.

Teucrium × lucidrys

T. × lucidrys (T. chamaedrys). Zones 2–24. To 1 ft. tall and 2 ft. wide, with many upright, woody-based stems densely clothed in toothed, dark green, ¾-in.-long leaves. Red-purple or white summer flowers in loose spikes (white-flowered form is looser). Attracts bees. Use as edging, foreground, low clipped hedge, or small-scale ground cover. Shear back once or twice a year to keep neat and force side branching. 'Prostratum' is 4–6 in. high, spreading to 3 ft. or more.

T. marum. CAT THYME. Zones 3–9, 14–24. To 1½ ft. high and wide. Upright, densely clustered stems are closely set with tiny gray-green leaves. Blooms profusely in summer, when stems are covered with many deep pink or purplish flowers in 2-in. spikes. Attracts cats.

TEXAS MOUNTAIN LAUREL.
See **SOPHORA secundiflora**

TEXAS OLIVE.
See **CORDIA boissieri**

TEXAS RANGER, TEXAS SAGE.
See **LEUCOPHYLLUM**

TEXAS TUBEROSE.
See **MANFREDA maculosa**

THALICTRUM
MEADOW RUE
Ranunculaceae
PERENNIALS

- 🌿 **ZONES 2–10, 14–17**
- ◐ **LIGHT SHADE**
- 💧 **REGULAR WATER**

Foliage clumps resemble those of columbine (*Aquilegia*). Plants typically bloom in late spring or summer, sending up sparsely leafed stems topped by puffs of small flowers, each consisting of four sepals and a prominent cluster of stamens. Superb for airy effect; delicate tracery of leaves and flowers is particularly effective against dark green background. Offers a pleasing contrast to sturdier perennials. Foliage good in arrangements. Most meadow rues need some winter chill; all thrive in dappled sunlight at woodland edges, tolerate full sun in cooler climates. Protect from wind. Divide clumps every 4 or 5 years.

T. aquilegiifolium. From Europe, northern Asia. To 2–3 ft. tall, 1 ft. wide, with bluish green foliage. Earliest of the meadow rues to bloom: clouds of fluffy stamens (the white or greenish sepals drop off) appear for a couple of weeks in mid- to late spring. Rosy lilac is the usual color, but white and purple selections are available. If left in place, spent flowers are followed by attractive, long-lasting seed heads. Heat tolerant.

Thalictrum aquilegiifolium

T. delavayi (T. dipterocarpum). CHINESE MEADOW RUE. From western China. To 3–4 ft. (even 6 ft.) tall, 1½–2 ft. wide, with thin, dark purple stems that need support. Green foliage. Lavender to violet sepals, yellow stamens. 'Hewitt's Double' has double lilac-colored flowers (one row of sepals, another of modified stamens that resemble petals); bloom continues for 2 months or longer.

T. flavum glaucum (T. speciosissimum). DUSTY MEADOW RUE. From Spain, Portugal, northwest Africa. Upright growth to 3–5 ft. tall, 2 ft. wide; stems are mauve tinged in youth. Powdery blue-green leaves are divided into many leaflets. In summer, plant is topped with clouds of small, fragrant yellow flowers. Plants may need staking.

T. rochebrunianum. From Japan. To 4–6 ft. tall, 1½–2 ft. wide, with sturdy stems that don't need staking. Flowers consist of white or lavender sepals and pale yellow stamens. 'Lavender Mist', with violet sepals, is a superior selection.

THEA sinensis.
See **CAMELLIA sinensis**

THEVETIA
Apocynaceae
EVERGREEN SHRUBS OR TREES

- 🌿 **ZONES VARY BY SPECIES**
- ☀ **FULL SUN**
- 💧 **REGULAR WATER**
- ⬥ **ALL PARTS ARE POISONOUS IF INGESTED**

Fast-growing plants with narrow, glossy deep green leaves and clusters of showy, funnel-shaped flowers at branch ends. Thrive in heat; can take very little frost.

T. peruviana (T. neriifolia). YELLOW OLEANDER, LUCKY NUT. Zones 13, 21–24; H1, H2. From tropical America. In frostless areas, it can be trained as a tree to 20–30 ft. tall and wide. Where frosts are light or rare, an 8-ft. (or larger) shrub; makes a good hedge, screen, or background plant. Leaves 3–6 in. long, with edges rolled under. Fragrant, 2–3-in., yellow to apricot flowers bloom from early summer into fall (all year where winters are warm). Small (1-in.), squat, four-angled fruits are red at first, aging to black. Provide good drainage, wind protection. In colder part of range, mound sand 6–12 in. deep around base of stem. Dies back in

Thevetia peruviana

freezes but recovers quickly; new growth will bloom same year.

T. thevetioides. GIANT THEVETIA. Zones 22–24, H2; with protection in 12, 13. From Mexico. Open growth to 12 ft. or more tall and wide. Leaves are darker green than those of *T. peruviana;* they resemble oleander (*Nerium*) leaves but are corrugated, heavily veined beneath. Large clusters of brilliant yellow, 4-in. flowers bloom from late spring through fall. Desert heat wilts flowers in summer. Makes an attractive patio tree, but fruit (2½ in. wide, green ripening to black) can be a litter problem.

THIMBLEBERRY.
See **RUBUS deliciosus**

THRIFT. See **ARMERIA**

THUJA
ARBORVITAE
Cupressaceae
EVERGREEN TREES OR SHRUBS

- 🌿 **ZONES VARY BY SPECIES**
- ☀◐ **PARTIAL SHADE IN HOTTEST CLIMATES**
- 💧 **MODERATE TO REGULAR WATER**

Neat, symmetrical plants often trimmed into geometrical forms—globes, cones, cylinders. Juvenile foliage is feathery, with small, needlelike leaves; mature foliage is scalelike, carried in flat sprays. Foliage in better-known varieties is often yellow green or bright golden yellow. Small (½–¾-in.-long) cones are green or bluish green, turning to brownish. Although arborvitaes will take both damp and fairly dry soils, they grow best in well-drained soil. Generic name is sometimes spelled *Thuya.*

T. occidentalis. AMERICAN ARBORVITAE. Zones A2, A3; 1–9, 15–17, 21–24; H1, H2. Native to eastern U.S. Upright, open growth to 30–60 ft. tall, 10–15 ft. wide, with branches that tend to turn up at ends. Bright green to yellowish green leaf sprays. Foliage turns brown in severe cold, will scorch badly in winter in coldest, windiest Rocky Mountain gardens unless plants are shaded, watered. Needs moist air to look its best. Spider mites may cause trouble. Basic species is seldom seen, but smaller garden varieties are common. Among these, the taller ones make good informal or clipped screens, while lower kinds are often used around foundations, along walks or walls, as hedges. The following are some good varieties.

'Brandon'. Fast growth to 12–15 ft. tall, 6–8 ft wide. Useful as screen.

'Douglasii Pyramidalis'. Vigorous-growing pyramid to 15 ft. tall (or taller), 10 ft. wide.

'Emerald' ('Emerald Green', 'Smaragd'). Neat, dense-growing, narrow cone to 10–15 ft. tall, 3–4 ft. wide. Holds its color throughout winter.

'Fastigiata' ('Pyramidalis', 'Columnaris'). Dense, columnar growth to 25 ft. tall, 5 ft. wide. Tends to get a bit unruly as it puts on size, with branches spreading out; they can be tied together to keep plant looking neat. Set 4 ft. apart for screen. Especially valuable in damp soils and cold regions, where few other columnar choices are available.

'Globosa' ('Little Gem', 'Little Giant', and 'Nana' are similar varieties). GLOBE ARBORVITAE, TOM THUMB ARBORVITAE. Dense and rounded, with bright green foliage. To about 4 ft. high and wide in 10 years; eventually larger.

'Golden Globe'. Dense, rounded growth to 3–5 ft. tall and wide. Bright golden foliage contrasts beautifully with deep green or blue-green evergreens.

'Hetz Midget'. Globe shaped, with rich green foliage. Not likely to exceed 3–4 ft. tall and wide.

'Lutea' ('George Peabody'). Narrow, conical tree to 30–35 ft. tall and 10–15 ft. wide. Soft yellow new growth ages to gold; holds color through most of the season.

'Nigra'. Dense dark green cone to 20–30 ft. tall, 4–5 ft. wide.

'Rheingold' ('Improved Ellwangeriana Aurea'). Cone-shaped, slow-growing, bright golden plant with a mixture of scale and needle foliage. Even very old plants seldom exceed 6 ft. tall and wide.

'Spiralis'. Fast-growing tree 30–45 ft. high, 10–15 ft. wide, with dark green foliage on branchlets that spiral around the branches for a full, ferny look.

'Sunkist'. Grows slowly to form a cone 4–6 ft. tall and 2–3 ft. wide, with bright golden foliage. Popular in landscapes and for bonsai.

'Teddy'. Slow grower to just 1–2 ft. tall and wide, with dense blue-green foliage. Perfect for small gardens, containers, narrow borders.

'Woodwardii'. Widely grown dense, globe-shaped shrub with rich green color. May attain considerable size with age but stays small over a reasonably long period; to 4 ft. high and wide in 10 years.

'Yellow Ribbon'. To 8–10 ft. tall, 2–3 ft. wide, with bright yellow foliage throughout the year.

T. orientalis. See Platycladus orientalis

T. plicata. WESTERN RED CEDAR. Zones A3; 1–9, 14–24. Native from coastal Northern California northward to Alaska and inland to Montana. Plants grown from inland seed are hardy anywhere in the West; those from coastal seed are less hardy to cold. Can reach over 200 ft. high in coastal belt of Washington, but more typical garden size is 50–100 ft. tall, 25–60 ft. wide. Slender, drooping branchlets are closely set with dark green leaf sprays. Single trees are magnificent in large lawns, but bear in mind that their lower branches spread quite broadly—and that the trees lose their characteristic beauty if these are cut off.

Thuja plicata

Varieties include the following.

'Collyer's Gold'. Slow-growing, upright shrub to 4–6 ft. tall, half as wide, with dense foliage that emerges yellow and turns bright green with age.

'Fastigiata'. HOGAN CEDAR. Very dense, narrow, erect to 80–90 ft. tall, 20–25 ft. wide. Fine for tall screen.

'Green Giant'. Hybrid between *T. plicata* and *T. standishii*, a Japanese species. Can grow 3–5 ft. a year, ultimately reaching 30–50 ft. tall, 10–20 ft. wide. Shear as a tall hedge or use as a tall screen.

'Hillieri'. Irregularly shaped, dense plant to 6–10 ft. high and wide, eventually larger.

'Spring Grove'. To 8–10 ft. high in 5 years; ultimately reaches 40–60 ft. tall, 10–15 ft. wide. Can be sheared as a hedge.

'Stoneham Gold'. Dense, slow-growing dwarf to 6 ft. tall, 2 ft. wide. Orange-yellow new growth.

'Sunshine'. Bright golden foliage on a fast-growing, upright plant to

15–30 ft. tall, 10–15 ft. wide. Color develops best in full sun.

'Zebrina'. Slow grower; same size as species. Foliage is banded in green and golden yellow. Often sold as 'Aurea', a less commonly seen variety with green foliage tinted golden.

THUJOPSIS
dolabrata

FALSE ARBORVITAE, DEERHORN CEDAR, HIBA CEDAR
Cupressaceae
EVERGREEN TREE

🌿 ZONES 3B–7, 14–17
☼ ◑ PARTIAL SHADE IN HOTTEST CLIMATES
💧💧 MODERATE TO REGULAR WATER

Native to Japan. Pyramidal, coniferous, often shrubby; very slow growing to 30–50 ft. tall, 10–20 ft. wide. Foliage resembles that of *Thuja*, but sprays are coarser, glossy, branching in staghorn effect. Best where summers are cool and humid. Plant as single tree where foliage details can be appreciated. Slow growth makes it a good container plant. 'Nana' is a dwarf variety to 3 ft. high and wide; 'Variegata' has white branch tips that tend to revert to green.

Thujopsis dolabrata

THUNBERGIA

Acanthaceae
PERENNIAL VINE IN ZONES 23, 24; H1, H2

🌿 ZONES VARY BY SPECIES
☼ ◑ PARTIAL SHADE IN HOTTEST CLIMATES
💧 REGULAR WATER

Tropical, typically twining plants noted for showy flowers. Some of the perennial sorts grow fast enough to bloom the first season and can be treated as annuals. Those grown as perennials are evergreen in mildest climates. In cooler part of range, tops may be killed by light frost, but roots usually stay

alive to send up new stems. Provide rich, well-drained soil. Good greenhouse plants.

T. alata. BLACK-EYED SUSAN VINE. Perennial vine grown as annual. May live over in Zones 23, 24; H2. To 10 ft., with triangular, 3-in., medium green leaves. Blooms all summer long; tubular flowers flare out to 1 in. wide, come in white and a variety of colors, all with purple-black throat. Start seed indoors; set plants out in good soil in a sunny spot as soon as weather warms. Display in hanging basket or window box,

Thunbergia alata

use as ground cover, or train on strings or low trellis. 'African Sunset' has blooms in shades of red-blushed yellow, salmon, rose, copper, and terra-cotta; flowers open in pastel shades and deepen as they age, so each plant shows many colors at once. 'Raspberry Smoothie' has creamy pink blossoms. 'Lemon Star' ('Sunny Lemon Star') has soft yellow flowers that bloom over a long period.

T. erecta. KING'S MANTLE. Vining shrub. Zones 16, 21–24; H1, H2. To 6 ft. tall and wide. Erect, sometimes twining, with dark green, ovate to oblong leaves to 3 in. long. Velvety dark blue flowers with orange or cream throats resemble those of gloxinia (*Sinningia*); they appear in joints of upper leaves throughout the summer and fall (for much of the year in Hawaii). 'Alba' is a white-flowered form.

T. grandiflora. SKY FLOWER. Perennial vine. Zones 16, 21–24; H1, H2. Vigorous growth to 20 ft. or more (as much as 80 ft. in Hawaii), with 8-in., heart-shaped, medium to dark green leaves. Slightly drooping clusters of tubular, flaring, sky blue flowers to 3 in. across appear through summer and into fall (throughout much of the year in Hawaii). Use on arbor, large tellis, or wire fence;

T

casts dense shade. There is a white variety.

T. gregorii (T. gibsonii). ORANGE CLOCK VINE. Perennial vine. Zones 21–24, H1, H2; with protection in Zones 13, 16, 17; anywhere as annual. Twines to 6 ft. high or sprawls over ground to cover a 12-ft. circle. Gray-green, triangular, tooth-edged leaves to 3 in. long. Tubular, flaring, bright orange flowers are borne singly on 4-in. stems. Blooms nearly all year long in mildest climates, in summer where winters are cool. Set plants 3–4 ft. apart to cover a wire fence, about 6 ft. apart as ground cover. Plant it above a wall and let it cascade down; or grow in hanging basket. Showy and easy to grow.

T. mysorensis. Perennial vine. Zones 16, 21–24; H1, H2. Tall climber (15–35 ft.), with narrow, elliptical dark green leaves to 6 in. long. Spectacular, pendent, 1–1½-ft.-long clusters of gaping flowers that are red on the outside, yellow within. Blooms much of the year, most heavily in spring. Train on pergola, arbor, or other overhead structure to permit flowers to dangle. Protect from frost.

THYME. See **THYMUS**

THYMOPHYLLA
(Dyssodia)
Asteraceae (Compositae)
PERENNIALS, SOME GROWN AS ANNUALS

🌱 ZONES 8–14, 18–23
☀️ FULL SUN
💧 MODERATE WATER

These low-growing plants with little yellow daisies start easily and quickly from seed planted in flats or sown in place. Not particular about soil type but must have good drainage.

T. acerosa. PRICKLY-LEAF DOGWEED. Shrubby perennial. Native from Nevada and Utah to Texas and Mexico. Much-branched, mounding plant to 6–8 in. high, 1 ft. wide. Covers itself with daisies from late spring to fall. Sharp-pointed, needle-thin, medium green leaves to ½ in. long. Good in beds, in cactus gardens, as edging, as informal ground cover. Especially useful for erosion control on slopes.

T. pentachaeta. GOLDEN DYSSODIA, FIVE-NEEDLE DOGWEED. Perennial. Native from California and Nevada to southern Texas, Mexico. To 4–6 in. high and

wide, with open, sparse appearance. Needlelike dark green leaves are ½–1 in. long; stems are covered with fine silky hairs. Blooms most profusely in late spring, sporadically later in the year. Short lived. Use like *T. acerosa*.

Thymophylla tenuiloba

T. tenuiloba. DAHLBERG DAISY, GOLDEN FLEECE. Short-lived perennial usually grown as annual. Heat-loving plant native from Texas to Florida and Mexico. Mounding growth to 1 ft. high, 1½ ft. wide. Divided, threadlike leaves make dark green background for flowers that look like miniature golden marguerites (*Anthemis*). Blooms from early summer to fall. Use for mass display or pockets of color. When plants become ragged with age, pull them out. In warm-winter areas, can be planted in fall for winter-to-spring bloom.

THYMUS
THYME
Lamiaceae (Labiatae)
SHRUBBY PERENNIALS

🌱 ZONES 1–24, EXCEPT AS NOTED
☀️ ◐ LIGHT SHADE IN HOTTEST CLIMATES
💧 💧 LITTLE TO MODERATE WATER

Diminutive Mediterranean members of the mint family with tiny, usually heavily scented leaves and masses of little flowers in whorls. Well suited to herb garden, rock garden; prostrate, mat-forming types make good small-space ground covers. Attractive to bees. Provide light, well-drained soil. Shear or cut back established plants to keep them compact. Easy to propagate from cuttings taken in early summer. Botanical names are constantly undergoing revision.

T. camphoratus. CAMPHOR THYME. Zones 7–9, 14–24. To 1½ ft. high and wide, with narrow gray-green leaves that smell like camphor. Blooms in late spring, early summer; flower clusters con-

sist of woolly, rosy purplish bracts and tiny white flowers.

T. × citriodorus. LEMON THYME. Variable hybrid with erect or spreading growth to 1 ft. high, 2 ft. wide. Ovate to lance-shaped, medium green leaves with lemon fragrance. Pale lilac flowers in summer. Leaves of 'Argenteus' are splashed with silver, those of 'Aureus' with gold. 'Lime' has lime green foliage. 'Doone Valley', with yellow-spotted leaves, reaches only 5 in. high.

T. herba-barona. CARAWAY-SCENTED THYME. Fast growing to 2–4 in. high, 2 ft. or more wide; stems root as they spread. Forms a dense mat of wiry stems set with widely spaced ovate to lance-shaped, dark green leaves with caraway fragrance. Clusters of rose pink flowers in midsummer.

T. lanuginosus. See T. pseudolanuginosus

T. praecox arcticus (T. drucei). MOTHER-OF-THYME, CREEPING THYME. Zones A2, A3; 1–24. Variable species to 3 in. high, 3 ft. wide, with roundish dark green leaves and purplish summer flowers. Good for small areas or as filler between stepping-stones where foot traffic is light. Soft and fragrant underfoot. Leaves can be used in seasoning and in potpourri. Often incorrectly sold as *T. serpyllum*.

The many varieties include the following. 'Album' ('Albus') has light green leaves and white flowers; 'Coccineum' produces purplish red flowers. 'Creeping Pink' grows 2 in. high, 1 ft. wide, with pink flowers and thick, dark green leaves. Nonblooming 'Elfin' grows 2 in. high and 5 in. wide. 'Minus' is extremely fine textured, forming a carpet to ½ in. high, 1 ft. wide. 'Pink Chintz' (may actually be a variety of *T. polytrichus*) grows 1 in. high and 1½ ft. wide, bears salmon pink flowers; 'Pink Ripple' has lemon-scented leaves and pink flowers. 'Reiter's', with lavender blooms, is a tough, vigorous ground cover for sun or shade; it grows 3 in. high and 2½ ft. wide. 'Reiter's Red', to 1 in. high and 1½ ft. wide, has red flowers; its leaves are smaller than those of 'Reiter's'.

T. pseudolanuginosus (T. lanuginosus). WOOLLY THYME. Zones A2, A3; 1–24. Sometimes sold as *T. praecox arcticus* 'Pseudolanuginosus'. Forms a flat to undulating mat 2–3 in. high, 3 ft. wide. Stems are densely clothed with elliptical, woolly gray

leaves. Blooms seldom and sparsely; when it does, produces pinkish flowers in leaf joints in midsummer. Becomes slightly rangy in winter. Use in rock crevices, between stepping-stones, spilling over bank or raised bed, covering small patches of ground. 'Hall's Woolly' is a profuse bloomer.

T. pulegioides. PENNSYLVANIA DUTCH TEA THYME. Fast-growing plant to 3 in. high, 1 ft. wide, with shiny green, oval, lemon-scented leaves. Dark purple to white flowers in summer. 'Goldstream' has dark green leaves with bright yellow variegation; they are lemon scented but not lemon flavored. 'Kermesinus' bears abundant star-shaped, deep pink flowers. 'Lemon Frost' has white blooms.

Thymus vulgaris

T. vulgaris. COMMON THYME. Variable plant to 1 ft. high, 2 ft. wide, with gray-green, narrow to oval leaves. White to lilac flowers in late spring, early summer. Low edging for flower, vegetable, or herb garden. Good container plant. Use leaves fresh or dried for seasoning fish, shellfish, poultry stuffing, soups, vegetables. 'Argenteus', called silver thyme, has leaves variegated with silver. 'Hi-Ho' has even more pronounced silver variegation and is more compact. 'Italian Oregano Thyme' has a strong oregano flavor. 'Orange Balsam' has narrow, orange-scented leaves.

TIARELLA
FOAMFLOWER, SUGAR-SCOOP
Saxifragaceae
PERENNIALS

🌱 ZONES VARY BY SPECIES
◐ ● PARTIAL OR FULL SHADE
💧 REGULAR WATER

Clump-forming plants to about 1½ ft. tall (in bloom) and 1½–2 ft. wide; spread by rhizomes (and by aboveground runners, in the case of *T. cordifolia*). Leaves arise directly from rhizomes; they are evergreen but may change color in autumn. Selections with year-round colorful foliage are becoming popular; look for new introductions in addition to those described below. Narrow, erect flower stems carry many small white or pink flowers. Useful in shady rock gardens; make pretty ground covers but will not bear foot traffic.

T. cordifolia. FOAMFLOWER. Zones A3; 1–9, 14–24. Rapid spreader from eastern North America. Light green, lobed, 4-in. leaves show red-and-yellow fall color. Creamy white flowers on foot-tall stalks. Leaves of 'Eco Red Heart' have dark red centers and veins; those of 'Oak Leaf' are deeply lobed. Both selections have pink blossoms.

T. selections and hybrids. Zones 1–9, 14–21. Many of the choicest foamflowers are of uncertain origin. 'Cygnet' has star-shaped leaves with purple markings along the veins; its white flowers open from pink buds. In 'Mint Chocolate', deeply lobed leaves have a central zone of deep brownish purple; flowers are pinkish white. 'Ninja', also with pinkish white blooms, has leaves that are marbled with blackish purple and turn almost entirely purple in winter. 'Skeleton Key' has very deeply cut leaves with deep purple midrib; blooms are white.

T. trifoliata unifoliata (T. unifoliata). SUGAR-SCOOP, WESTERN FOAMFLOWER. Zones A3; 1–7, 14–17. Native from Alaska to Northern California, east to Rocky Mountains. Dark green leaves divided into three tooth-edged leaflets. Tiny white flowers on 1½-ft. stalks are followed by little fruits that look like sugar scoops.

Tiarella wherryi

T. wherryi (T. cordifolia collina). Zones 2–9, 14–21. From southeastern U.S. Like *T. cordifolia* but lacks aboveground runners, is slower to spread. Flower clusters are somewhat more slender, often tinged pink.

TIARE TAHITI. See **GARDENIA taitensis**

TIBOUCHINA
Melastomataceae
EVERGREEN SHRUBS

> 🗡 ZONES VARY BY SPECIES
>
> ☼ ◑ PARTIAL SHADE IN HOTTEST CLIMATES
>
> 💧 REGULAR WATER

Brazilian natives with showy flowers at branch ends and broadly oval, prominently veined, velvety leaves. Prefer slightly acid, fast-draining soil. Protect from strong winds, hard frosts. Pinch young growth to induce branching; prune out damaged or badly placed branches before new growth begins. If flower buds fail to open, check for geranium (tobacco) budworm.

T. heteromalla. Zones 16, 17, 21–24; H1, H2. Shrub. To 4–6 ft. tall and wide. Silvery green leaves with silver undersides to 6 in. or longer. Dark purple, 1–1½-in. flowers in 1½-ft.-long clusters from early fall into winter.

Tibouchina urvilleana

T. urvilleana (T. semidecandra). PRINCESS FLOWER. Zones 16, 17, 21–24, H1, H2; with protection in 14, 15. The only species widely available. Fast, rather open growth to 5–18 ft. tall, 3–10 ft. wide. Branch tips, buds, new growth shaded with satiny hairs in orange and bronzy red. Green, 3–6-in.-long leaves, often edged red. Older leaves add spots of orange, red, or yellow, especially in winter. Brilliant royal purple, 3-in. flowers appear intermittently from late spring into winter. Prune lightly and feed after each bloom cycle.

Has naturalized in Hawaii, forming thickets in wet areas. Can be used as indoor/outdoor plant in colder climates.

TIDYTIPS. See **LAYIA platyglossa**

TIGRIDIA pavonia
TIGER FLOWER, MEXICAN SHELL FLOWER
Iridaceae
PERENNIAL FROM BULB

> 🗡 ZONES 4–24; H1; OR DIG AND STORE
>
> ☼ ◑ PARTIAL SHADE IN HOTTEST CLIMATES
>
> 💧 REGULAR WATER DURING GROWTH AND BLOOM

Mexican native with flashy summertime flowers. Fans of narrow, swordlike, ribbed leaves to 1½ ft. long send up erect, 2½-ft. flower stems bearing triangular blossoms

Tigridia pavonia

to 6 in. across. Flowers have three large outer segments in orange, red, pink, yellow, or white; cuplike center and three small inner segments are usually boldly blotched with contrasting color. (Immaculata strain is unspotted.) Each flower lasts only one day, but the bloom period usually lasts for several weeks.

Plant in spring, after weather warms up (night temperatures should not fall below 60°F/16°C). Plant in well-drained soil, setting bulbs 2–4 in. deep, 4–8 in. apart. Stop watering after flowering is finished and when leaves turn yellow. Can be left in ground where hardy; divide every 3 or 4 years, digging in fall and waiting until spring planting time to separate bulbs and replant. Spider mites are main pest (they cause yellowish or whitish streaks on foliage); begin control when leaves are several inches long. Gophers are fond of the bulbs. Beyond hardiness range, dig bulbs after leaves yellow and store as for gladiolus; or grow in pots and protect in winter.

TILIA
LINDEN
Tiliaceae
DECIDUOUS TREES

> 🗡 ZONES 1–17, EXCEPT AS NOTED
>
> ☼ FULL SUN
>
> 💧 REGULAR WATER

Dense trees. Stately good looks, moderate growth rate. All have irregularly heart-shaped leaves and small, fragrant, yellowish white flowers in drooping clusters in late spring, early summer. Flowers develop into nutlets, each with an attached papery bract. Best in deep, rich, moist soil. In cold-winter areas, fall color varies from negligible to good yellow. Young trees need shaping, older ones only corrective pruning. Aphids can cause honeydew, which drips disagreeably and encourages sooty mold.

T. americana. AMERICAN LINDEN, BASSWOOD. Native to eastern North America. To 40–60 ft. tall, 20–25 ft. wide. Straight-trunked tree with a narrow crown. Dull dark green leaves to 4–6 in. long, nearly as wide. 'Redmond' is a pyramidal form with glossy foliage.

T. cordata. LITTLE-LEAF LINDEN. Native to Europe. Dense pyramid to 30–50 ft. tall and 15–30 ft. wide. Leaves 1½–3 in. long and as wide (or wider), dark green above, silvery beneath. Excellent lawn or street tree. Given room to develop its crown, it can be a fine patio shade tree (but expect bees in flowering season). Can be sheared into hedges. Very tolerant of city conditions. Selected forms include 'Chancellor', with a tight pyramidal form; 'Glenleven' (*T. × flavescens* 'Glenleven'), a fast grower to 65 ft. tall, 40 ft. wide, with a loosely pyramidal or oval canopy; 'Greenspire', with an oval to pyramidal canopy; 'June Bride', an especially heavy bloomer; 'Olympic', which forms a broad, symmetrical pyramid; and 'Summer Sprite', a slow-growing dwarf to just 20 ft. tall, 10 ft. wide. ▸

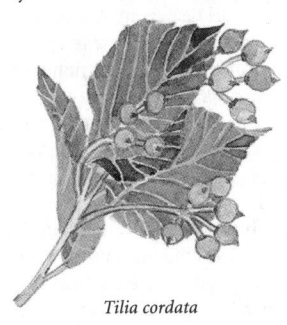

Tilia cordata

T

T. × euchlora. CRIMEAN LINDEN. Hybrid derived from *T. cordata*. To 25–35 ft. (perhaps eventually to 50 ft.) tall, almost as wide. Slightly pendulous branches. Rich glossy green leaves have paler undersides, reach 2–4 in. long and wide. Casts more open shade than *T. cordata*.

T. tomentosa. SILVER LINDEN. Zones 2–21. Native to Europe, western Asia. To 40–50 ft. tall, 20–30 ft. wide. Leaves are 3–5 in. long and about as wide, light green above, silvery beneath; they turn and ripple in the slightest breeze. More tolerant of heat, drought than other species. 'Sterling' has silvery young leaves and an especially handsome winter silhouette.

TILLANDSIA
AIR PLANT
Bromeliaceae
PERENNIALS

🌡	ZONES 22–24; OR INDOORS
☀ ☼	EXPOSURE NEEDS VARY BY SPECIES
💧 💧	WATER NEEDS VARY BY TYPE (SEE TEXT)

Large genus of bromeliads native to Texas, Mexico, and South America. Most are epiphytes (tree dwellers) that depend on rain, fog, and dew for moisture. Plants vary greatly in size and appearance; leaves may be wide or narrow (even hairlike), twisted or curled. Flowers are often shockingly bright, sometimes fragrant, and usually quite long lasting (weeks to months). Plants of many species die after blooming but first produce offsets; over time, a single plant becomes a cluster of plants at different stages of maturity and bloom.

Usually seen mounted on plaques of wood hung on walls, indoors or out. Site where air circulation is good. Types with green leaves generally need regular water and filtered light; types with gray-green to bluish foliage need less water and tolerate more sun. Drench plants every few days; if leaves curl or dry up, submerge the plant in water for several hours at a time. Once a month or so from spring to midautumn, spray with an acidic liquid fertilizer diluted to quarter-strength. Air plants need somewhat drier conditions in winter.

T. bulbosa. Thick, undulating green leaves to 4 in. long emerge from a swollen base. As plants prepare to bloom, their central leaves

Tillandsia cyanea

redden. Red flower spike appears in late winter or early spring.

T. cyanea. Narrow, arching, bright green leaves up to 1 ft. long produce a showy flower cluster in spring or autumn: a flattened plume of deep red or pink bracts, from which violet-blue flowers emerge one or two at a time over a long season.

T. ionantha. Minute gray scales cover narrow, arching green leaves (just 1½ in. long), giving them a powdery look. Leaves turn red or coral red in spring as plant prepares to produce its central bract of bright purple, tubular flowers.

T. juncea. Fine, arching, grasslike leaves are gray green, 10–12 in. long, and held in a rosette. In summer, erect red or pink flower stalks emerge from the center, each topped with a small purple flower.

TI PLANT.
See **CORDYLINE fruticosa**

TIPUANA tipu
TIPU TREE
Fabaceae (Leguminosae)
SEMIEVERGREEN OR DECIDUOUS TREE

🌡	ZONES 12 (WARMEST AREAS), 13–16, 18–24; H1, H2
☀	FULL SUN
💧	REGULAR WATER

From South America. Grows to 25–40 ft. tall, 30–60 ft. wide (or larger). Has broad, flattened crown that is wider than high, but can be pruned to make a denser, narrower, umbrella-shaped crown. Light green leaves divided into 11–21 oblong, 1½-in.-long leaflets. Blooms from late spring to early summer, bearing clusters of apricot to yellow, sweet pea–shaped flowers; 2½-in. seedpods follow the flowers. Will not take strongly alkaline conditions but is otherwise not particular about soil. Flowers best in warm-summer areas out of

immediate ocean influence. Good street tree or lawn tree. Useful as a shade tree for patio or terrace, though litter from flowers can be a slight nuisance. Hardy to 25°F/ –4°C; well-ripened wood will take 18°F/–8°C with minor damage.

Tipuana tipu

TITHONIA rotundifolia (T. speciosa)
MEXICAN SUNFLOWER
Asteraceae (Compositae)
PERENNIAL GROWN AS ANNUAL

🌡	ALL ZONES
☀	FULL SUN
💧	REGULAR WATER

Native from Mexico to Central America. Husky, rather coarse plant with velvety green leaves, spectacular gaudy flowers. Grows rapidly to 6 ft. tall, 4 ft. wide. Blooms from summer to frost, bearing 3–4-in.-wide blossoms with orange-scarlet rays and tufted yellow centers. Use as a temporary screen. Arcadian Blend grows 2–2½ ft. tall and produces gold, orange, and yellow flowers. 'Aztec Sun', to 4 ft. tall, has apricot gold flowers. 'Fiesta del Sol', to 2½ ft. high, bears 2–3-in. orange flowers, starts blooming earlier than the others. 'Goldfinger', a bushy 4-footer with deep orange flowers,

Tithonia rotundifolia

makes a good temporary summer hedge. All have hollow stems; cut carefully for bouquets to avoid bending stalks. Sow seed in place in spring, in well-drained, not-too-rich soil. Tolerates intense heat, some drought. Attractive to butterflies, hummingbirds.

TOADFLAX. See **LINARIA**

TOAD LILY. See **TRICYRTIS**

TOBIRA.
See **PITTOSPORUM tobira**

TOLMIEA menziesii
PIGGYBACK PLANT
Saxifragaceae
PERENNIAL

🌡	ZONES A3; 4–9, 14–17, 20–24; OR INDOORS
☼ ●	SOME SHADE; INDIRECT LIGHT
💧 💧	REGULAR TO AMPLE WATER

Native to Coast Ranges from Northern California northward to Alaska. Chief asset is abundant production of attractive, medium green, triangular to heart-shaped, shallowly lobed leaves of variable size (up to 5 in. long), carried at ends of leafstalks that also vary in length. Leaves are covered in ⅛-in.-long hairs. Tiny, rather inconspicuous reddish brown flowers top 1–2-ft.-high stems. 'Taff's Gold' has foliage irregularly mottled with chartreuse and yellow; great for brightening shady corners.

Tolmiea menziesii

Good ground cover for shade. Spreads indefinitely by producing new plantlets at junction of leafstalk and leaf blade; plantlets root in the soil. Handsome in hanging basket. Start new plants any time of year; take leaf with plantlet and insert in moist potting mix so base of plantlet contacts soil. As houseplant, needs cool temperatures, filtered light (bright light is fine if it's indirect). Mealybugs, spider mites are occasional pests.

TOMATILLO

Solanaceae
ANNUAL

- ✎ ALL ZONES
- ☼ FULL SUN
- ◗ REGULAR WATER

From Mexico. Easy-to-grow, summer-fruiting tomato relative known botanically as *Physalis ixocarpa*. Bushy, sprawling growth to 4 ft. high and at least as wide. Fruit swells to fill—and eventually split—the loose, papery husk (calyx) that surrounds it. When fully ripe, fruit is yellow to purple, about 2 in. wide, and very sweet, but it is usually picked when green and tart and used in sauces and other dishes.

Tomatillo

Sow seeds directly in fertile soil 4 to 6 weeks after last frost, when the soil has warmed; in moist, warm soil, seeds will germinate in 5 days. Thin seedlings to 10 in. apart. Or start plants indoors and set out in the garden; plant deep, as for tomatoes. Use floating row covers in short-summer areas. Tomatillos can be trained to a trellis like tomatoes but are usually left to sprawl. Once fruiting begins, cut back on water but don't let plants become stressed. Harvest fruit when walnut size (or smaller, if it seems fully developed) and deep green. Don't remove the papery husk until you are ready to use the fruit.

TOMATO

Solanaceae
PERENNIAL GROWN AS ANNUAL

- ✎ ALL ZONES
- ☼ FULL SUN
- ◗ REGULAR WATER

Andean native. Easy to grow and prolific, tomatoes are just about the most widely grown of all garden plants, edible or otherwise. Amateur and commercial growers have varying ideas about how best to raise tomatoes. If you've developed a successful method, continue to follow it—but if you're a novice or are dissatisfied with previous attempts, you may find the following information useful.

Choose varieties suited to your climate that will yield the kind of tomatoes you like on plants you can handle. Some varieties are determinate, others indeterminate. Determinate types are bushier, need little or no staking or trellising. Indeterminate ones are more vinelike, need more training, and generally bear over a longer period. (Though the tomato plant is really a sprawling plant incapable of climbing, you'll often see it referred to as a vine.) Plant a few each of early, midseason, and late varieties for longest possible production. (Or plant in spring and again in summer where growing season is long.) Typically, six plants can supply a family of four with enough fruit to enjoy fresh and to use for canning or sauce.

Set out tomato plants after frost danger is past and the soil has warmed. Plant in February or early March in Zones 12, 13; in April, May, or early June in Zones 7–9, 14–24; in May or early June in Zones A1–A3, 1–6, 10, 11. In Hawaii, tomatoes can be planted year-round in most locations. To grow tomatoes from seed, sow seeds in pots of light soil mix 5 to 7 weeks before you intend to set out plants. Cover seeds with ½ in. of fine soil; firm soil over seeds and keep surface damp. Place seed container in cold frame or sunny window—a temperature of 65 to 70°F/18 to 21°C is ideal, although a range of 50°F/ 10°C at night to as warm as 85°F/ 29°C in the day will give acceptable results. When seedlings are 2 in. tall, transplant each into a 3- or 4-in. pot; keep seedlings in sunny area until they reach planting size. When buying tomato plants, look for compact ones with sturdy stems; avoid those that are tall for the pot or have flowers or fruit.

Plant in a sunny site in well-drained soil. Tomato plants prefer neutral to slightly acid soil; add lime to very acid soil or sulfur to alkaline soil the autumn before setting out plants. Space plants 1½–3 ft. apart (staked or trained) to 3–4 ft. apart (untrained). Make planting holes extra deep and set in seedlings so lowest leaves are just above soil level. Additional roots will form on buried stem and provide a stronger root system.

If you live in an area where summers are cool or short (such as the Pacific Northwest, Alaska, or high-elevation regions), or if you want to get an early start, take steps to speed growth and protect tomatoes from frost. A combination of plastic mulch and floating row covers is probably most effective. Individual plants can be protected with paper or plastic caps known as hotcaps (some have water-filled cylinders that trap heat effectively to provide maximum protection).

Tomato management and harvest will be most satisfying if you train plants to keep them off the ground as much as possible. Untrained plants will sprawl, and some fruit will lie on soil, where it often suffers from rot, pest damage, and discoloration. For training indeterminate varieties, the usual practice is to drive a 6-ft.-long stake (at least 1 by 1 in.) into ground a foot from each plant. Use soft ties to hold the plant to the stake as it grows.

Slightly easier in the long run—but more work at planting time—is to grow each plant in a wire cylinder made of concrete reinforcing screen (6-in. mesh). The screen is 7 ft. wide, which is just right for cylinder height. Put stakes at opposite sides of cylinder and tie cylinder firmly to them. As the vine grows, poke protruding branches back inside the cylinder.

Tomato

Tomato plants need regular moisture at root level; they are deep rooted, so water heavily each time you water. If soil is fairly rich, you won't need to fertilize at all. In ordinary soils, feed lightly every 2 weeks from the time first blossoms set until the end of harvest; or give a single application of controlled-release fertilizer when planting.

Whiteflies are common pests of tomato plants. Large green cater-

pillars with diagonal white stripes that feed upside down on leaf undersides are hornworms; handpick them. In Hawaii, wrap developing fruit clusters in paper or cloth bags to protect from melon flies. Tomatoes are subject to a long list of diseases, some common only in certain regions. Your Cooperative Extension Office is the best source of control measures for most tomato diseases. If plants

T

are growing strongly, then suddenly wilt and die, they may have been sabotaged by gophers. If you can find no evidence of these rodents, plants probably are suffering from verticillium wilt, fusarium wilt, or both; pull them out and discard them. Diseases live over in soil, so plant in a different location every year and try varieties resistant to wilt or certain other diseases (see introduction to "Tomato varieties," below).

In Pacific Northwest, lessen chance of late blight (which spots leaves and stems, rots fruit) by avoiding overhead sprinkling. Blight declines as weather warms; destroy plant debris after harvest.

Some tomato problems—leaf roll, blossom-end rot, cracked fruit—are physiological and can usually be corrected (or prevented) by maintaining uniform soil moisture. Mulching will help conserve moisture in very hot or dry climates.

If you have done everything right and your tomatoes fail to set fruit in the spring, use hormone spray on blossoms. Tomatoes often fail to set fruit when night temperatures drop below 55°F/13°C. In chilly-night areas, select cold-tolerant varieties (especially small-fruited strains). Fruit-setting hormone often speeds up bearing in the earlier part of the season. Tomatoes can also fail to set fruit when temperatures rise above 100°F/38°C, but hormones are not effective under those conditions.

Harvest fruit when it is fully red and juicy; keep ripe fruit picked to extend season. When frost is predicted, harvest all fruit, both green and partly ripe. Store in a dry place away from direct sunlight at 60 to 70°F/16 to 21°C; check often for ripening.

TOMATO VARIETIES

Following are types of tomatoes you can buy as seeds or started plants. The number of varieties is enormous and increases every year; there are choices for every taste and every region. It's wise to consult a knowledgeable nursery, your Cooperative Extension Office, and other gardeners to find out which varieties flourish in your local climate and soil.

If certain diseases or nematodes cause trouble locally, you may be able to grow varieties that resist one or more problems. Keys to resistance you may see on plant labels or in catalog descriptions include V (verticillium wilt),

F (fusarium wilt), FF (Race 1 and Race 2 fusarium), T (tobacco mosaic virus), N (nematodes), A (alternaria leaf spot), and L (septoria leaf spot). For example, a variety labeled VFFNT means that it resists verticillium wilt, two races of fusarium wilt, nematodes, and tobacco mosaic virus.

Cool-summer tomatoes. These will ripen fruit where accumulated heat is too low for most tomatoes. Nurseries in cool-summer areas usually offer locally adapted varieties, such as 'San Francisco Fog', 'Oregon Pride', and 'Seattle Best of All'. Many early varieties, especially 'Early Girl' and 'Stupice', also do well where summers are cool.

Early tomatoes. These tomatoes set fruit at lower night temperatures than other tomatoes do; 'Early Girl', 'Burpee's Early Pick', and 'Quick Pick' are standards. Very short-season regions, such as Alaska and high-elevation areas, have their own very early varieties, which set fruit at surprisingly low temperatures; 'Early Tanana' and 'Subarctic Maxi' are examples.

Hawaiian tomatoes. Varieties developed especially for Hawaii resist nematodes and common diseases found there. They include 'N-5', 'N-52', 'N-65', 'N-69', 'Anahu', 'Healani', 'Kalohi', and 'Puunui'.

Heirloom tomato 'Cherokee Purple'

Heirloom tomatoes. Varying in size, appearance, and plant habit, these represent old varieties that have been maintained by enthusiasts in different parts of the country. Most are grown for excellent flavor. 'Brandywine' and 'Cherokee Purple' are among the many popular heirloom varieties.

Hybrid tomatoes. Some suppliers tout certain tomatoes as hybrids. They are usually referring to first-

generation offspring of controlled parent lines, sometimes indicated by F1 after the name. These varieties are more predictable and uniform in growth and fruit quality. Some are giants like 'Beefmaster' and 'Big Beef', but hybrid paste tomatoes are also available.

Large-fruited tomatoes. These grow to full size in areas where both days and nights are warm. Fruits can weigh a pound or even more. 'Beefsteak', 'Beefmaster', and 'Big Beef' are typical. 'Burpee's Supersteak Hybrid' can produce 2-lb. fruits; 'Delicious' has borne a 7¾-lb. tomato.

Main crop or standard tomatoes. 'Celebrity', 'Big Boy', and 'Better Boy' are widely grown. 'Heatwave' is popular in extremely hot climates. 'Ace' and 'Pearson' are local favorites in California.

Novelty tomatoes. Among these are yellow and orange varieties such as 'Orange Queen', 'Mountain Gold', 'Husky Gold', and 'Lemon Boy'. 'Caro Rich' is very high in vitamin A and beta carotene. There are also tomatoes that are deep reddish brown ('Black Prince'), white ('New Snowball', 'White Beauty'), tomatoes with striped fruit ('Green Zebra', 'Tigerella'), and even one with fruit that is green when fully ripe ('Evergreen'). 'Long Keeper' will stay fresh in storage for 3 months. 'Stuffer' and 'Yellow Stuffer' yield large, nearly hollow fruits that resemble bell peppers.

Paste tomatoes. Bears huge crops of small, oval, thick-meated fruits with small seed cavities. Sometimes called plum tomatoes. Favorites for canning, sauces, and tomato paste; also good for drying. 'Roma', 'San Marzano', 'Viva Italia', and yellow 'Italian Gold' are examples.

Cherry tomato 'Sun Gold'

Small-fruited tomatoes. Bear fruits ranging from very tiny (currant size) to the size of large marbles. Shapes and colors are indicated by names: 'Red Cherry', 'Red Pear', 'Yellow Cherry', 'Yellow Pear'. Those with very small fruits include 'Gardener's Delight', 'Sun Gold', 'Supersweet 100', 'Sweet 100', and 'Sweet Million'. Grape tomatoes, such as 'Juliet', produce large grapelike clusters of smallish fruit. Small-fruiting types that grow on small plants suitable for pots or hanging baskets include 'Tiny Tim', 'Small Fry', and 'Patio'.

TONGUE FERN.
See **PYRROSIA lingua**

TOONA sinensis (Cedrela sinensis)

Meliaceae
DECIDUOUS TREE

🌿 ZONES 2B–9, 14–24
☼ FULL SUN
💧 REGULAR WATER

Native to China. Slow to medium growth to 50 ft. tall, 30 ft. wide. Leaves have many leaflets (up to 26) and somewhat resemble those of Tree-of-heaven (*Ailanthus*).

Toona sinensis

Prized for beauty of new growth, which is tinted in shades of cream, soft pink, and rose. Long, pendulous clusters of white flowers appear in spring. These are followed by woody, star-shaped seed capsules that contain winged seeds and are attractive in dried arrangements. Suckers freely.

TORCH GINGER.
See **ETLINGERA elatior**

TORCH LILY. See **KNIPHOFIA**

TORENIA fournieri
WISHBONE FLOWER
Scrophulariaceae
ANNUAL

| 🌱 ZONES 1-24; H1, H2 |
| ☀️ 🌤️ PARTIAL SHADE IN HOTTEST CLIMATES |
| 💧 REGULAR WATER |

From tropical Asia. Compact, bushy, to 1 ft. high and wide. Blooms from summer into fall; flowers look like miniature gloxinias (*Sinningia*), have stamens arranged in wishbone shape. Species has pale lavender blossoms with deeper purple markings and bright yellow throats; a white-flowered form is also sold. Sow seeds in pots and transplant to

Torenia fournieri

garden after frost danger is past; or buy nursery plants. Use as edging or in pots and window boxes. If grown in sun, keep roots cool with a mulch. Summer Wave hybrids thrive in heat; their spreading habit makes them a good choice for hanging baskets. Duchess strain is more compact (6–8 in. tall and wide), offers blooms in four color combinations: light blue with blue throat, blue with white throat, deep blue with blue throat, and pink with white throat.

TORREYA californica
CALIFORNIA NUTMEG
Cephalotaxaceae
EVERGREEN TREE

| 🌱 ZONES 4-9, 14-24 |
| ☀️ 🌤️ FULL SUN OR PARTIAL SHADE |
| 💧 MODERATE WATER |

Native to cool, shaded canyons in California mountain regions below 4,500 ft. Slow-growing conifer to 15–20 ft. tall, 12–15 ft. wide, with trunk 1–3 ft. in diameter. Wide, open pyramidal crown, domelike with age. Branches are horizontal,

Torreya californica

slender, somewhat drooping at tips. Flat sprays of rigid, sharp-pointed, flat, dark green leaves with two whitish bands underneath; 1¼–2½ in. long, ⅛ in. wide. Plumlike fruit is pale green with purplish markings.

TOTARA. See PODOCARPUS nivalis, P. totara

TOUCH-ME-NOT. See IMPATIENS

TOVARA virginiana. See PERSICARIA virginiana

TOWER OF JEWELS. See ECHIUM wildpretii

TOYON. See HETEROMELES arbutifolia

TRACHELIUM caeruleum
Campanulaceae (Lobeliaceae)
PERENNIAL

| 🌱 ZONES 7-9, 14-24; ELSEWHERE AS ANNUAL |
| ☀️ FULL SUN |
| 💧 REGULAR WATER |

Tough, undemanding Mediterranean native to 2½ ft. tall and wide. Forms a clump of stems clothed with narrow, sharply toothed, dark green leaves. Blooms over a long summer season, when sparsely foliaged flowering stems are topped by broad, dome-shaped

Trachelium caeruleum

clusters of tiny blossoms in blue, mauve, pink, or white. Good cut flowers. If sown early, will bloom first year (and so can be treated as a summer annual in colder climates or as a winter annual in mild-winter desert).

TRACHELO-SPERMUM
STAR JASMINE
Apocynaceae
EVERGREEN SHRUBS OR VINES

| 🌱 ZONES VARY BY SPECIES |
| ☀️ 🌤️ LIGHT SHADE IN HOTTEST CLIMATES |
| 💧 REGULAR WATER |

Ground covers, trailers, or climbers bearing delightfully fragrant, pinwheel-shaped blossoms in spring or early summer. Among the most versatile and useful of plants. Prefer well-drained soil. For lush plants, fertilize once before spring growth begins, again after flowering. Prune back as needed to shape. Cut stems exude a milky sap. Formerly sold as *Rhynchospermum*.

T. asiaticum. Zones 6–24. From Japan, Korea. Like *T. jasminoides* but has smaller leaves in darker, duller green and smaller flowers in creamy yellow or yellowish white. Dense, low growth habit makes it an excellent ground cover. 'Red Top' has red new growth.

Trachelospermum jasminoides

T. jasminoides. STAR JASMINE, CONFEDERATE JASMINE, MAILE HAOLE. Zones 8–24; H1, H2. From China. Given support, a twining vine to 20–30 ft.; without support and with some tip-pinching, a spreading shrub or ground cover to 2 ft. tall, 10 ft. wide. Oval leaves to 3 in. long are glossy light green when new, mature to lustrous dark green. Profusion of white, inch-wide flowers in small clusters on short side branches. Attractive to bees. If grown as shrubby plant, it is

good in raised beds or entry gardens, for edging walk or drive, as extension of lawn, spilling over walls, as ground cover under trees and shrubs. Set plants 5 ft. apart for ground cover. 'Variegatum' has leaves bordered and blotched with white.

TRACHYCARPUS fortunei
WINDMILL PALM
Arecaceae (Palmae)
PALM

| 🌱 ZONES 4-24 |
| ☀️ 🌤️ FULL SUN OR LIGHT SHADE |
| 💧 REGULAR WATER |

From China. Medium-size, very hardy fan palm (to 10°F/–12°C or lower). Moderate to fast growth to 30 ft. high, 10 ft. wide. Trunk is usually thicker at top than at bottom and is covered with dense, blackish fiber; as trunk elongates,

Trachycarpus fortunei

fiber falls off its lower portion. Toothed, 1½-ft. stalks carry 3-ft.-wide leaves. May look untidy in high winds. May be sold as *Chamaerops excelsa*. Young plants can be grown indoors in bright indirect light; plant them outdoors when they become too big.

TRACHYMENE coerulea
BLUE LACE FLOWER
Apiaceae (Umbelliferae)
ANNUAL

| 🌱 ZONES 1-24 |
| ☀️ FULL SUN |
| 💧 REGULAR WATER |

From Australia. Upright growth to 2 ft. tall and 10 in. wide. Finely divided leaves. Numerous small lavender-blue flowers are borne in 2–3-in.-wide, flat-topped clusters that are quite lacy in appearance. ▶

T

Trachymene coerulea

Good cut flowers. Grow in light, rich, well-drained soil. Sow seeds in place; taproot makes transplanting difficult. Does not perform well in heat. Where summers are mild, sow in early spring for summer bloom; in hot-summer, mild-winter regions, sow in fall for bloom in winter and spring. Once sold as *Didiscus coeruleus*.

TRADESCANTIA
Commelinaceae
PERENNIALS

☀	ZONES 12–24; H1, H2; EXCEPT AS NOTED; OR INDOORS
☀ ◐ ●	EXPOSURE NEEDS VARY BY SPECIES; BRIGHT INDIRECT LIGHT
◓ ◑ ◒	WATER NEEDS VARY BY SPECIES

Most are virtually indestructible plants with long, trailing stems. Usually seen in pots or hanging baskets, but can be used as ground covers—though the most vigorous, rambling types are likely to be invasive. On variegated forms, pinch out any growth that reverts to solid green.

T. × andersoniana. See T. virginiana

T. fluminensis. WANDERING JEW. From South America. Rapid grower to 2 in. high, with indefinite spread. Succulent stems have swollen joints where dark green, oval or oblong, 2½-in.-long leaves are attached. Tiny, unshowy white flowers. Easy to grow. Excellent for window boxes and dish gardens. If plants are overgrown, renovate by cutting back severely; or discard them and start new plants with fresh tip growth. Partial or full shade. Regular to ample water. Stems will live a long time in water, rooting quickly and easily. Variegated forms include 'Albovittata', leaves finely and evenly streaked with white; 'Aurea' ('Gold Leaf'), bright yellow-green foliage; 'Laekenensis' ('Rainbow'), leaves

banded in white and pale lavender; and 'Variegata', yellow- or white-striped foliage.

T. pallida 'Purpurea' (Setcreasea pallida 'Purple Heart'). PURPLE HEART, PURPLE QUEEN. From Mexico. Creeping plant to 1–1½ ft. high, 1 ft. wide; stems tend to flop. Pointed, rather narrowly oval leaves are strongly shaded with purple, particularly on undersides. Pale or deep purple flowers (not showy). Pinch back after bloom. Generally unattractive in winter. Frost may kill tops, but recovery is fast in warm weather. Use as ground cover, for bedding, in pots. Full sun or light shade. Moderate water.

Tradescantia pallida 'Purpurea'

T. spathacea (Rhoeo spathacea). MOSES-IN-THE-CRADLE, MOSES-IN-THE-BOAT. From Mexico, Central America. To 2 ft. tall, 1 ft. wide. Each plant has a dozen or so broad, sword-shaped, rather erect leaves that are dark green above, deep purple beneath. Small, white, three-petaled blooms are interesting rather than beautiful, crowded into boat-shaped bracts borne down among leaves. There is also a dwarf form. 'Variegata' has leaves striped in red and yellowish green. Most often used as a pot plant or in hanging baskets; grown as a ground cover and edging in Hawaii. Tough plant; takes heat, low humidity, sun or shade. Best with regular moisture but withstands inconsistent watering. Try to keep water out of leaf joints when irrigating.

T. virginiana. SPIDERWORT. Zones 1–24; H1. From eastern U.S. Clump-forming border plant to 1½ ft. high and wide. Long, grassy-looking, deep green, erect or arching leaves. Three-petaled flowers last for only a day, but buds come in large clusters and plants are seldom out of bloom in summer. May self-sow and become somewhat invasive.

Divide clumps when crowded. Sun or shade. Regular to ample water. Named garden varieties come in white, blue shades, lavender, purple, shades of pink from pale to near-red; these plants are often sold as Andersoniana Group.

T. zebrina (Zebrina pendula). WANDERING JEW. Zones 24; H1, H2. From southern Mexico. Similar to *T. fluminensis* but not as hardy; bears pinkish or bluish flowers. Most widely grown are forms with colorful leaves, including 'Quadricolor', purplish green leaves with longitudinal bands of silver, pink, and red; and 'Purpusii', dark red or greenish red foliage. Attractive ground covers for shady, frost-free sites. Partial or full shade. Provide regular water.

TRANSVAAL DAISY. See GERBERA jamesonii

TRAVELER'S TREE or **PALM.** See RAVENALA madagascariensis

TREE ARALIA. See KALOPANAX septemlobus

TREE FERN. See BLECHNUM, CIBOTIUM glaucum, CYATHEA cooperi, DICKSONIA

TREE MALLOW. See LAVATERA

TREE-OF-HEAVEN. See AILANTHUS altissima

TREE TOMATO, TAMARILLO
Solanaceae
EVERGREEN OR SEMIEVERGREEN SHRUB

☀	ZONES 14–24; H1, H2
☀ ◐	FULL SUN OR PARTIAL SHADE
●	REGULAR WATER

Treelike Andean native known botanically as *Cyphomandra betacea*. Fast growth to 10–18 ft. tall, about two-thirds as wide.

Tree tomato

Pointed oval, 4–10-in.-long leaves; small pinkish flowers in summer and fall. In winter, bears egg-shaped, 2–3-in.-long red fruit (there are also yellow varieties). Grow from seed like tomato. Harvest fruit when it is fully colored; pluck from tree by snapping off, leaving stem attached. Fruit has acid flavor somewhat like that of tomato—if you find it too tart, try stewing it with a little sugar. Bears on new growth. In late winter, prune back branches that have fruited by one-fourth to one-third (this will prevent fruit from developing ever farther out from center of plant). Control sucking insects. Frost sensitive; give overhead protection in Zones 14, 15, 18–21. Fruiting is more reliable in warmer part of range.

TRICHOSTEMA lanatum
WOOLLY BLUE CURLS
Lamiaceae (Labiatae)
EVERGREEN SHRUB

☀	ZONES 14–24
☀	FULL SUN
◯	NO IRRIGATION NEEDED

Native to dry, sunny slopes of California Coast Ranges. Much-branched, neat plant to 3–5 ft. high, 4–8 ft. wide. Narrow, 1¼–2-in.-long leaves, pungently aromatic when bruised, are shiny dark green

Trichostema lanatum

on upper surface, white and woolly beneath; leaf edges are rolled under. Flowers, in separated clusters on a long stalk, are blue with conspicuous, arching stamens. Stalks and flowers are covered with blue, pink, or whitish wool. Blooms in spring; continues throughout summer and early fall if old flower stems are cut back. Temperamental plant; needs perfect drainage.

T

TRICUSPIDARIA dependens.
See **CRINODENDRON patagua**

TRICYRTIS
TOAD LILY
Liliaceae
PERENNIALS

- ZONES VARY BY SPECIES
- PARTIAL SHADE
- AMPLE WATER

Woodland plants that resemble false Solomon's seal (*Maianthemum racemosum*) in foliage. Interesting, heavily spotted, inch-long flowers appear at leaf joints and in terminal clusters in late summer and fall. They are complex in structure, somewhat orchidlike: each blossom has three petals and three sepals, with a column of decorative stamens and styles rising from the center. Need soil enriched with plenty of organic matter. Excellent companion to ferns and hostas; lovely with *Gunnera*.

T. formosana (T. stolonifera). Zones 3–9, 14–17. From Taiwan. To 2½ ft. tall. Spreads by aboveground runners to form a clump 1½ ft. or wider (but is not invasive). More erect than *T. hirta*, with flowers mostly in terminal clusters. Leaves are green, mottled with deeper green; brown or maroon buds open to white to pale lilac flowers spotted with purple. 'Amethystina' blooms several weeks earlier than species, bearing lavender-blue blossoms with a red-spotted white throat.

Tricyrtis hirta

T. hirta. Zones 2–9, 14–17. From Japan. To 3 ft. tall, 2 ft. wide; it lacks runners. Arching stems bear pale green, softly hairy foliage. White to pale lilac blossoms peppered with purple; appear in leaf joints all along the stems. 'Miyazaki' bears pink to white flowers with crimson spots; 'Miyazaki Gold' is similar but has gold-edged leaves.

TRIFOLIUM repens
WHITE CLOVER, WHITE DUTCH CLOVER
Fabaceae (Leguminosae)
PERENNIAL

- ZONES 2–24
- FULL SUN OR PARTIAL SHADE
- REGULAR WATER

Sometimes mixed with lawn grass or dichondra seed. Prostrate stems root freely, send up lush cover of leaves with three ¾-in. leaflets. Can stain clothing; white flowers attract bees. These colored-leaf varieties grow 4 in. high, spread indefinitely, and are used as ground covers or at front of borders: 'Atropurpureum', blackish purple leaves edged

Trifolium repens

in green; 'Green Ice', lime green with dark green margin; 'Purpurascens', maroon outlined in green. *T. r. minus* is one of the shamrocks. All take nitrogen from air and fix it in soil through action of bacteria on their roots.

TRILLIUM
WAKE ROBIN
Liliaceae
PERENNIALS

- ZONES VARY BY SPECIES
- PARTIAL OR FULL SHADE
- REGULAR WATER

Bloom in early spring; need some winter chill. Each stem is topped with a whorl of three leaves; a single three-petaled flower appears in the center of the whorl (sometimes on a stalk, sometimes virtually stalkless). Plant in shady, woodsy site. Left undisturbed, plants will gradually increase by rhizomes. Die to ground in mid- to late summer. In addition to species listed below, many others are offered by specialists in native plants.

T. chloropetalum (T. sessile californicum). Zones 4–9, 14–17. Native to California. To 1–1½ ft. high, 1 ft. wide, with 6-in.-long

Trillium grandiflorum

leaves mottled in maroon. Stalkless flowers have greenish white to yellowish petals about 2½ in. long. *T. c. giganteum* has deep maroon petals.

T. erectum. PURPLE TRILLIUM. Zones 1–6. From eastern North America. To 2 ft. tall, 1 ft. wide, with 7-in.-long leaves. Erect, 2–3-in. flowers are dark reddish purple, carried on stalks; they have an odd odor.

T. grandiflorum. Zones 1–6. From eastern North America. To 1½ ft. tall, 1 ft. wide, with stout stems and 2½–6-in.-long leaves. Nearly stalkless flowers are nodding, to 3 in. across, white aging to rose. There are several choice double-flowered forms.

T. luteum. YELLOW TRILLIUM. Zones 2b–6. Native primarily to the southeastern and midsouthern U.S. Grows about 1 ft. high and wide, with 6-in.-long, medium green leaves mottled with pale green. Canary yellow flowers, with petals up to 3½ in. long, are held upright; their fragrance is lemony and sweet.

T. ovatum (T. californicum). Zones 2–7, 14–17. Western native. Resembles *T. grandiflorum* but has narrower petals; flowers are usually upright and are borne on stalks.

TRISTANIA conferta.
See **LOPHOSTEMON confertus**

TRISTANIOPSIS laurina (Tristania laurina)
WATER GUM
Myrtaceae
EVERGREEN TREE OR SHRUB

- ZONES 15–24
- FULL SUN
- REGULAR WATER

From eastern Australia. Slow-growing, rather formal-looking plant with conical, dense crown. To 10 ft. tall, 5 ft. wide at 8 years

old; may eventually reach 45 ft. or taller, 30 ft. wide. Mahogany-colored bark peels off, revealing satiny white new bark beneath. Glossy green, narrow leaves to 4 in. long. Clusters of small, faintly fragrant yellow flowers appear in late spring or early summer, borne profusely enough to put on a good show. Seedpods like those of eucalyptus but much smaller (to ¼ in. wide); they don't create a litter problem. 'Elegant' has broad leaves that are red when they emerge, turn green only when shaded by later growth.

Tristaniopsis laurina

Water gum is densely shrubby when young and can be kept that way with a little pinching. Can be trained as a single- or multi-stemmed tree; once established, trees need only light shaping. Excellent tall screen, boundary, background planting. Good in large containers.

TRITELEIA
Liliaceae
PERENNIALS FROM CORMS

- ZONES 3–9, 14–24, EXCEPT AS NOTED
- FULL SUN
- NO IRRIGATION NEEDED

Plants of this name were formerly known as *Brodiaea*. General descriptions and culture are same as for *Brodiaea*, which differs only in technical details. Spring and early summer bloom.

T. grandiflora (Brodiaea grandiflora). Flowering stalk to 2 ft. tall; many 1¼-in.-long, blue to white trumpets.

T. hyacinthina (B. hyacinthina, B. lactea). WHITE BRODIAEA. Zones 2–9, 14–24. Clusters of 10–40 papery-textured white,

T

Triteleia laxa

purple-tinged flowers with greenish veins. Flowering stalk is 9–20 in. high.

T. ixioides (B. ixioides, B. lutea). PRETTY FACE, GOLDEN BRODIAEA. Flower stalk to 2 ft.; flowers 1 in. long, golden yellow with purple-black midrib and veins.

T. laxa (B. laxa). GRASS NUT, ITHURIEL'S SPEAR. Zones 5–9, 14–24. Flower stalk to 2½ ft.; purple-blue, 1½-in. trumpets.

T. 'Queen Fabiola'. Flower stalk to 2½ ft. tall; deep violet flowers.

T. × tubergenii. Flower stalk to 2½ ft. tall; light blue flowers.

T. uniflora. See Ipheion uniflorum

TRITONIA crocata
Iridaceae
PERENNIALS FROM CORMS

- **ZONES 9, 13–24; OR DIG AND STORE**
- **FULL SUN**
- **REGULAR WATER DURING GROWTH AND BLOOM**

South African native related to freesia, harlequin flower (*Sparaxis*), ixia, montbretia (*Crocosmia*). Often called flame freesia. Fans of swordlike leaves to 1 ft. long grow in early spring, followed in late spring by flower spikes holding bright orange-red flowers above the foliage. Blooms are funnel

Tritonia crocata

shaped, up to 2 in. across, and long lasting in a vase. Foliage dies down after bloom, re-emerges the next spring.

Plant corms in well-drained soil, setting them 2–3 in. deep, 3 in. apart. Plant in fall where winter temperatures remain above 20°F/−7°C; wait until spring in colder areas. Corms can remain in the ground where hardy, but they are likely to rot unless planting area is kept fairly dry during summer dormancy. Divide overcrowded plantings during dormant period. Where corms cannot be protected and in colder regions, dig and store over winter or grow in pots. Good in rock gardens, borders.

T. c. miniata has bright red blooms. 'Princess Beatrix' has deep orange flowers. Others may be offered in white, yellow, and pink shades. For the plant sometimes called *T. crocosmiiflora*, see *Crocosmia × crocosmiiflora*.

TROCHODENDRON aralioides
WHEEL TREE
Trochodendraceae
EVERGREEN TREE OR SHRUB

- **ZONES 4–9, 14–24**
- **FULL SUN OR LIGHT SHADE**
- **REGULAR WATER**

From Japan, Korea. Handsome foliage plant to 30 ft. tall, 25 ft. wide, with horizontal branching pattern. Oval, 5-in.-long, glossy dark green leaves cluster near

Trochodendron aralioides

branch tips. In late spring, elongated (to 5-in.) clusters of 10–20 bright green flowers appear at branch ends. Each ¾-in. blossom is made up of a flat disk surrounded by stamens. Blossoms are followed by fruits consisting of small pods clustered around the disk. Prefers organically enriched soil.

TROLLIUS
GLOBEFLOWER
Ranunculaceae
PERENNIALS

- **ZONES A2, A3; 1–6**
- **FULL SUN IN COOLER CLIMATES ONLY**
- **REGULAR TO AMPLE WATER**

Clumps of finely cut, shiny dark green leaves put up 2–3-ft.-tall stems terminating in yellow to orange flowers typically shaped like globes or rounded cups. Deadhead to prolong bloom. Excellent cut flowers. Cannot take drought, heat; constantly damp area near a pond or stream is an ideal planting site. If growing globeflowers in a regular garden bed, liberally amend soil with organic matter and keep well watered. Divide clumps only when they thin out in center.

Trollius chinensis

T. chinensis (T. ledebourii). From China, Siberia. To 3 ft. tall, 1½ ft. wide. Light orange-yellow, 2-in. flowers with open bowl shape; summer bloom. 'Golden Queen' has pure orange flowers.

T. × cultorum. Group of hybrids includes 'Earliest of All' (pale orange yellow; midspring) and 'Lemon Queen' (light yellow; late spring, early summer). Both bear 3-in. blooms, reach 2 ft. tall and 1½ ft. wide.

TROPAEOLUM
NASTURTIUM
Tropaeolaceae
ANNUALS AND PERENNIALS

- **ZONES VARY BY SPECIES**
- **EXPOSURE NEEDS VARY BY SPECIES**
- **REGULAR WATER**

Old-fashioned favorites from South America. Distinctive appearance, rapid growth, and easy culture are three of their many strong points.

Tropaeolum majus

T. majus. GARDEN NASTURTIUM. Annual. All zones. Two main kinds: climbing types, which trail over ground or climb to 6 ft. by coiling leafstalks; and compact, bushy, dwarf kinds to 1½ ft. high and wide (dwarf types are more widely sold). Both have round bright green leaves on long stalks. Long-spurred flowers to 2½ in. across have a refreshing fragrance, come in colors including maroon, red brown, orange, yellow, red, creamy white. You can get seeds of mixed colors in several strains; some single colors are also sold. Both single- and double-flowered forms are available. All varieties make good cut flowers. Young leaves, flowers, and unripe seedpods have a peppery flavor and are frequently used in salads.

Easy to grow in most well-drained soils, but does best in sandy soil. Sow in early spring; plant grows and blooms quickly, reseeds (it has naturalized in parts of Zone 17). In mild-winter, hot-summer areas, sow in fall for winter and spring bloom. Use climbing types to cover fences, banks, stumps, rocks; use dwarf kinds for bedding, to hide fading bulb foliage, for quick color. Somewhat drought tolerant. Full sun or light shade.

T. peregrinum. CANARY BIRD FLOWER. Perennial in Zones 15–24; H1, H2; annual elsewhere. Climbs to 10–15 ft. Deeply five-lobed leaves. Frilled, fringed, ¾–1-in.-wide, canary yellow flowers with curved green spur. Sow in spring for bloom from summer until frost. Provide support such as stakes or netting; or let plant climb into a shrub. Light shade.

TRUMPET CREEPER, TRUMPET VINE. See **CAMPSIS, DISTICTIS**

TRUMPET TREE. See **TABEBUIA**

TSUGA
HEMLOCK
Pinaceae
EVERGREEN TREES

ZONES VARY BY SPECIES

FULL SUN OR PARTIAL SHADE, EXCEPT AS NOTED

REGULAR WATER

These are mostly big, shallow-rooted trees with unusually graceful appearance. Horizontal to drooping branches bear needlelike leaves that are banded with white beneath, flattened and narrowed at the base to form distinct, short stalks. Small, oval brown cones hang down from branches. Deeply furrowed bark. Need some winter chill. Do best with acid soil, summer humidity, protection from hot sun and wind. Take well to heavy pruning; make excellent clipped hedges, screens. Easily damaged by salt and drought. In the Northwest, the hemlock woolly aphid can weaken these plants, especially those grown as hedges; it affects mainly *T. heterophylla*.

T. canadensis. CANADA HEMLOCK. Zones A3; 2–7, 17. From eastern North America. Dense, pyramidal tree to 40–70 ft. or taller, half as wide. Tends to produce two or more trunks. Outer branchlets droop gracefully. Dark green, ½-in.-long needles, mostly arranged in opposite rows. Fine lawn tree, good background plant, outstanding clipped hedge. 'Pendula', Sargent weeping hemlock, grows slowly to 5 ft. tall and 10 ft. wide, has pendulous branches. 'Cole's Prostrate' is 1 ft. tall (usually less) and spreads to 3 ft. or more. 'Gentsch White', to 2 ft. high and 1½ ft. wide, has white-tipped new growth. Many other dwarf, weeping, and variegated selections are sold.

Tsuga canadensis

T. diversifolia. NORTHERN JAPANESE HEMLOCK. Zones A2, A3; 2–7, 17. From northern Japan. Grows slowly into a pyramid 35–60 ft. tall, 25 ft. wide. Often multitrunked, with graceful, sweeping branches densely clothed in short, glossy, dark green needles ¼–½ in. long. Bark is reddish brown. Grows near the timberline in its native habitat; more tolerant of wind and frost than other hemlocks. More pest resistant than *T. canadensis*.

T. heterophylla. WESTERN HEMLOCK. Zones A2, A3; 2–7, 14–17. Native along coast from Alaska to Northern California, inland to northern Idaho and Montana. Handsome tree with narrow, pyramidal crown. Grows fairly fast to 70–130 ft. tall, 20–30 ft. wide. Somewhat drooping branchlets; fine-textured, dark green to yellowish green foliage with a fernlike quality. Needles are ¼–¾ in. long, grow in two rows. Picturesque large conifer for background, screens, hedges. 'Thorsen's Weeping' is a prostrate form that can be grown as a ground cover or staked in youth as a weeping specimen; best growth in part shade.

T. mertensiana. MOUNTAIN HEMLOCK. Zones A1–A3; 1–7, 14–17. Native to high mountains, from Alaska south through higher Sierra Nevada in California and to northern Idaho, Montana. To 50–90 ft. in the wild but is slow growing, smaller (20–30 ft. tall, half as wide) in gardens. Needles are ½–1 in. long, blue green with a silvery cast; grow all around stems to give branchlets a plump, tufty appearance. Trees at timberline frequently grow in horizontal or twisted fashion. Thrives on cool slopes with highly organic soil. Least adapted to lowland, hot-summer areas. Needs partial shade in Zone 14. Somewhat resistant to hemlock woolly aphid. Good for large rock gardens, containers, bonsai.

TUBEROSE.
See **POLIANTHES tuberosa**

TULBAGHIA
Amaryllidaceae
PERENNIALS FROM RHIZOMES

ZONES 13–24; H1, H2

FULL SUN

REGULAR WATER

From South Africa. Dense clumps of straight, narrow, evergreen leaves send up slim, 1–2-ft. stems topped by clusters of small, trumpet-shaped, pinkish lavender flowers. Suffer frost damage at 20 to 25°F/–7 to –4°C but recover quickly. Start plants from containers or divisions at any time (though early spring or early fall is best in hot-summer areas). Give well-drained, organically enriched soil. Divide clumps to increase plantings.

T. natalensis. SWEET WILD GARLIC. Narrow, shiny green leaves on a plant rarely more than 1 ft. tall. Open clusters of clove-scented flowers come in white and shades of pink to violet, with a greenish or yellow center.

T. simmleri (T. fragrans). Gray-green, 1-in.-wide leaves. Lightly fragrant flowers in clusters of 20–30 in winter or early spring. Good cut flower. 'Alba' has white blossoms.

Tulbaghia violacea

T. violacea. SOCIETY GARLIC. Bluish green, very narrow leaves. Clusters of 8–20 flowers; bloom is heaviest in spring and summer. Leaves and flower stems have onion or garlic odor if cut or crushed; leaves can be used in cooking. 'Variegata' has a creamy stripe down the middle of each leaf; in 'Silver Lace', each leaf is edged in white. Leaves of 'Tricolor' have white edges with a pinkish cast that intensifies in cool weather.

TULIPA
TULIP
Liliaceae
PERENNIALS FROM BULBS

ZONES 1–24, EXCEPT AS NOTED

FULL SUN DURING BLOOM, PART SHADE AFTER IN HOT CLIMATES

REGULAR WATER DURING GROWTH AND BLOOM

Tulips vary considerably. Some are stately and formal, others dainty and whimsical; a few look decidedly bizarre. Bloom comes at some time from March to May, depending on type.

Use larger tulips in colonies or masses, in company with low, spring-blooming plants. Use smaller, shorter types for close-up viewing—in rock gardens, near paths, in raised beds, in patio insets. Tulips are superb container plants; unusual kinds such as Rembrandt and Parrot are especially suited to this use.

Nearly all hybrid tulips and most species (wild) tulips need an extended period of winter cold for best performance. In mild climates, provide the necessary chill by refrigerating bulbs for 6 weeks (not near ripening fruit) before planting; then treat the plants as annuals.

Even in cold-winter regions, there's no guarantee of consistent performance after the first year. Tulip bulbs form offsets that take a few years to reach blooming size, but as offsets mature, they draw energy from the mother bulb. The result is a decline in flowering. For this reason, most tulips are often treated as short-lived perennials in cold climates, though you can encourage repeat flowering by fertilizing with nitrogen before bloom and by letting foliage wither before removing it after bloom.

Some species tulips are exceptions to the above; they give good repeat bloom even where winters are mild.

Plant as described in "What Tulips Need" (next page). To protect tulips from gophers and other burrowing animals, plant in baskets of ¼-in. wire mesh. Thwart ground squirrels and other animals who like to dig up bulbs by securing chicken wire over new plantings. Aphids are another pest.

If tulips do persist from year to year, they will eventually need separating. Dig and divide clumps in late summer; replant at best time for your climate. Species tulips can be left undisturbed for many years.

Tulips have been classified into many divisions, defined mainly by flower type. For the convenience of gardeners, we have arranged the divisions into additional groupings; the first three groupings are by bloom season, while the fourth contains species and their hybrids.

EARLY TULIPS
Single early tulips. Single flowers on 10–16-in. stems. Colors include white, yellow, salmon, pink, red, dark purple. Popular for forcing

T

What Tulips Need

CLIMATE Most tulips do best in areas with a distinct winter chill, but even there they may be short lived. Species tulips are more likely to persist year after year; some will even succeed where winters are mild.

EXPOSURE Tulips need sunshine at least while in bloom; they will lean toward the source of light if planting area is partly shaded. It's fine to plant under deciduous trees if the trees won't leaf out until after bloom is finished (this is a good practice in hot-summer areas).

SOIL Rich, sandy soil is ideal, though tulips will grow in any good, fast-draining soil. They perform poorly if planted in soil where other tulips were recently growing; choose a new site or dig out soil to the requisite planting depth and replace it with fresh soil from elsewhere in the garden.

PROPER PLANTING Set bulbs three times as deep as they are wide (a little shallower in heavy soils). Space 4–8 in. apart, depending on eventual size of plant. Where temperatures regularly dip below 32°F/0°C, plant in October or November, after soil has cooled. In warmer regions, plant in December or January.

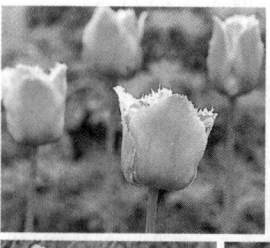

Double late tulip 'Fringed Beauty'

and growing indoors in pots. Not adapted to mild-winter areas.

Double early tulips. Peonylike double flowers, often measuring 4 in. across, on 6–12-in. stems. Same color range as Single Early tulips. Effective massed in borders. In rainy areas, mulch around plants or surround with ground cover to keep mud from splashing the short-stemmed flowers.

MIDSEASON TULIPS

Triumph tulips. Single flowers on sturdy stems to 20 in. tall. Wide range of solid colors, including red, white, and yellow, and bicolors.

Darwin hybrid tulips. Spectacular group with brightly colored flowers on 24–28-in. stems. Most are in scarlet-orange to red range; some have contrasting eyes or penciling. Some reach 7 in. across. Pink, yellow, and white varieties exist.

LATE TULIPS

Single late tulips. Graceful plants with large, oval or egg-shaped blooms on 1½–3-ft. stems. Clear, beautiful colors: white, yellow, orange, pink, red, mauve, lilac, purple, maroon. May have contrasting margins. Includes old Darwin and Cottage groups.

Lily-flowered tulips. Graceful, lilylike flowers with recurved, pointed segments; come in white and shades of yellow, pink, red, and magenta, often with contrasting markings. Stems 20–26 in. high.

Fringed tulips. Flower edges are finely fringed. Colors include white, yellow, pink, red, and violet; fringing is often in a different color than rest of flower. Stems 16–24 in. high.

Viridiflora tulips. Flowers edged in green or colored in blends of green with other hues—white, yellow, rose, red, buff. Stems 10–20 in. high. Good cut flowers.

Rembrandt tulips. Streaks and variegation on the original Rembrandts were caused by a transmittable virus; these infected bulbs can no longer be imported and should not be planted. Tulips now sold as Rembrandts have patterning of genetic, not viral, origin. The division now includes other variegated types and the old Bizarre and Bybloem groups.

Darwin hybrid tulip

Parrot tulips. Large, long, deeply fringed and ruffled flowers atop 16–20-in. stems are striped, feathered, and flamed in various colors, including green. They once had weak, floppy stems, but modern types are stouter.

Double late tulips. Often called peony-flowered tulips, these have very large (to 5-in.-wide), heavy-textured double blossoms on 14–20-in. stems. Colors include orange, rose, yellow, and white.

SPECIES TULIPS

Kaufmanniana tulips. Often called waterlily tulip, *T. kaufmanniana* is a very early bloomer with 3-in., creamy yellow flowers (marked red on petal backs) with dark yellow centers; the flowers open flat in sun. Stems 6–8 in. high. Hybrids come in various colors, usually with flower centers in a contrasting color; many have mottled leaves like Greigii tulips.

Fosteriana tulips. Early-blooming *T. fosteriana* has the largest flowers—to 8 in. wide—of any tulip. The huge red blossoms appear atop 8–10-in. stems. Hybrids include varieties with flowers in red, orange, yellow, pink, and white. The 16-in.-high 'Red Emperor' ('Mme Lefeber') has fiery red flowers.

Greigii tulips. Midseason-blooming *T. greigii* has big (6-in.) flowers borne on 10-in. stems; leaves are heavily spotted and streaked with brown. Hybrids have flowers in white, pink, orange, red; many feature several colors in a single blossom.

Other species. Sold mainly by bulb specialists. Most are native to western and central Asia. They tend to be simpler looking than large hybrid tulips, with a wildflower charm. Generally best in rock gardens or wild gardens, where plant-

: Fringed tulip 'Blue Heron'
: Triumph tulip 'Annie Schilder'

: Lily-flowered tulip 'Queen of Sheba'
: Greigii tulip 'Red Riding Hood'

: Fosteriana tulip
: Darwin hybrid tulip 'Pink Impression'

: *Tulipa clusiana* 'Lady Jane'
: Double late tulip 'Angelique'

: *Tulipa tarda*
: Parrot tulip 'Texas Flame'

ings can remain undisturbed for many years; plant 4 in. apart. Also good in pots. Species that will persist from year to year in mild-winter areas are noted.

T. acuminata. Flowers have long, twisted, spidery segments of red and yellow on 1½-ft.-tall stems. Late.

T. bakeri. Zones 2–24. Similar to and often listed as *T. saxatilis.* Lilac to purple flowers with a yellow base open to a wide, flat star; they are borne in clusters of three or four on stems to 1 ft. high. 'Lilac Wonder', to 6–7 in. high, has rosy purple flowers with a large, circular lemon yellow base. Midseason. Good in mild-winter areas.

T. batalinii. Soft yellow flowers on 6–10-in. stems. Very narrow leaves. 'Yellow Jewel' has lemon yellow blossoms tinged with rose. Midseason.

T. clusiana. LADY or CANDY TULIP. Slender flowers on 9-in. stems are rosy red outside, white inside. Blossoms of 6-in.-high *T. c. chrysantha (T. stellata chrysantha)* are star shaped when fully open; they have rose carmine outer segments (shading to buff at base), bright yellow inner segments. *T. clusiana* and *T. c. chrysantha* both bloom in midseason, make good permanent tulips in mild-winter areas.

T. humilis (T. pulchella). One to three pale pink or purplish pink flowers with a yellow center atop each 4–6-in. stem. Early. 'Violacea' has deep violet flowers, usually with a yellow base.

T. praestans. Up to six orange-red flowers on each 2-ft. stem. Midseason. 'Fusilier' is an improved selection growing 10–14 in. high.

T. pulchella. See T. humilis

T. saxatilis. Zones 2–24. Fragrant, yellow-based pale lilac flowers open nearly flat, are carried one to three to each 1-ft. stem. Early bloom. Good choice in mild-winter areas.

T. stellata chrysantha. See T. clusiana chrysantha

T. sylvestris. Yellow, 2-in. flowers, one or two to each 1-ft. stem. Late. Good choice in mild-winter areas.

T. tarda. Zones A1–A3; 1–24. Each 3–5-in. stem has three to six upward-facing, starlike flowers with golden centers, white-tipped segments. Early. Often sold as *T. dasystemon,* a different species.

T. undulatifolia (T. eichleri). Foot-tall stems bear shining scarlet flowers with jet black centers outlined in yellow. Early.

TULIP TREE.
See **LIRIODENDRON**, **MAGNOLIA×** soulangeana

TULIP TREE, AFRICAN.
See **SPATHODEA** campanulata

TUPELO. See **NYSSA** sylvatica

TUPIDANTHUS calyptratus.
See **SCHEFFLERA** pueckleri

TURKEYFOOT.
See **ANDROPOGON** gerardii

TURKISH HAZEL.
See **CORYLUS** colurna

TURNIP and RUTABAGA
Brassicaceae (Cruciferae)
BIENNIALS GROWN AS ANNUALS

🗓 ALL ZONES
☀ FULL SUN
💧 REGULAR WATER

These Mediterranean natives are cabbage relatives and, like cabbage, belong to the genus *Brassica.* Turnips are best known for roots, though foliage is also edible (some varieties are grown for leaves only). Roots come in various colors (white, white with purple on upper part, creamy yellow) and shapes (globe, flattened globe). Rutabaga is a tasty turnip relative with large yellowish roots; its leaves are palatable only when very young. Turnip

Turnip

roots grow fast and should be harvested and used as soon as they are big enough to eat. Rutabaga is a late-maturing crop that stores well in the ground; its flavor improves with light frost.

Grow turnip and rutabaga in rich, loose, well-drained soil. Plant in early spring (for early summer harvest) where winters are cold or in summer (for fall harvest). Where winters are mild, plant in fall for a winter crop. Sow seeds

1 in. apart. Thin turnips to 2–6 in. apart for roots, 1–4 in. apart for greens. Thin rutabaga plants to 5–8 in. apart; each one needs ample space for root to reach full weight of 3–5 lbs. Roots of turnip and rutabaga are milder if soil is kept moist, become more pungent under drier conditions. Turnip roots are ready to harvest about 75 days after sowing, rutabaga in 90 to 120 days. Root maggot is a pest of turnip (less likely to infest rutabaga); see Cabbage for control.

TURTLEHEAD.
See **CHELONE** lyonii

TWINBERRY.
See **MITCHELLA** repens

TWINFLOWER.
See **LINNAEA** borealis

TWINSPUR. See **DIASCIA**

U

UGNI molinae (Myrtus ugni)
CHILEAN GUAVA
Myrtaceae
EVERGREEN SHRUB

🗓 ZONES 14–24
☀◐ PARTIAL SHADE IN HOTTEST CLIMATES
💧 REGULAR WATER

South American native grown for foliage, flowers, and fruit. Slow to moderate growth to 3–6 ft. high and wide. Scraggly and open in youth but has a compact, rounded form when mature. Small, oval, leathery leaves are dark green with bronze tints above, whitish beneath; edges are slightly rolled under. Rose-tinted white flowers resembling little bottlebrushes appear in late

Ugni molinae

spring, early summer. These are followed by purplish or reddish, ½-in., pleasant-tasting fruit that smells like apples and can be eaten fresh or used in jams and jellies. Tidy, restrained plant for patios, terraces, near walks and paths. Give neutral to acid soil. For related plants that are grown primarily for fruit, see Feijoa and Guava.

ULMUS
ELM
Ulmaceae
DECIDUOUS OR SEMIEVERGREEN TREES

🗓 ZONES VARY BY SPECIES
☀ FULL SUN
💧 REGULAR WATER

Once highly prized shade trees, elms have fallen on hard times. Dutch elm disease (spread by a bark beetle) has killed millions of American elms in North America and can attack most other elm species. Many of the larger elms are appealing fare for various types of beetles, leafhoppers, aphids, and scale, making them time consuming to care for, messy, or both. Elms have other problems not related to pests. They have aggressive, shallow root systems, so you'll have trouble growing other plants beneath them. Many types produce suckers; branch crotches are often narrow, splitting easily in storms. Still, elms are widely planted and researchers continue to devote much effort to finding disease-resistant varieties. All elms are fairly soil tolerant, have handsome oval leaves. Poor yellow fall color, except as noted.

U. americana. AMERICAN ELM. Deciduous. Zones 1–11, 14–21. Native to eastern North America. This majestic, arching tree once graced lawns and streets throughout its range, but it has been decimated by Dutch elm disease. Fast growth to 100 ft. or taller with nearly equal—sometimes greater—spread. Main branches upright, outer ones pendulous. Rough surfaced, 3–6-in.-long, toothed dark green leaves; great variation in shade of yellow fall color. Leafs out very late where winters are mild. Pale green, papery seeds make a mess in spring. Two of the most disease resistant are 'Princeton' (upright, to 65 ft. tall) and 'Valley Forge' (vase shaped, to 70 ft. tall). Most trees show resistance only when young.

U. glabra. SCOTCH ELM. Deciduous. Zones 2–11, 14–21. ▶

U

Native to Europe. Fairly upright habit to 120 ft. tall, 80 ft. wide. Sharply toothed, rough-surfaced, 3–6-in.-long leaves on very short stalks. Rarely planted now, but old trees are sometimes seen. 'Camperdownii', Camperdown elm, generally 10–20 ft. tall and wide, has weeping branches that reach to ground, making a tent of shade.

U. hybrids. Zones 2–9, 14–21. Many institutions have been carrying on breeding experiments involving various elms to produce trees resistant to Dutch elm disease. Among them 'Accolade' has the best track record so far; it grows 70 ft. tall and 60 ft. wide, with arching limbs and a vase shape much like that of American elm. 'Danada Charm' has a similar size and shape but is more gangly in youth. 'Frontier', just 40 ft. tall and 30 ft. wide, features reddish purple leaves in fall. 'Homestead', to 55 ft. tall and 35 ft. wide, has a symmetrical oval to pyramidal form. 'Patriot' forms a narrow vase shape to 50 ft. tall and half as wide. 'Triumph' grows 55 ft. tall, 50 ft. wide; it forms an upright oval with a strong central leader.

U. parvifolia. CHINESE ELM, CHINESE EVERGREEN ELM. Semievergreen or deciduous, according to winter temperatures and individual tree's heredity. Zones 3–24. From China, Korea, Japan. Fast growth to 40–60 ft. tall, 50–70 ft. wide; often reaches 30 ft. in 5 years. Form is extremely variable, but trees are generally spreading, with long, arching, eventually weeping branchlets. On older trees, bark of trunk sheds in patches (somewhat like bark of sycamore, *Platanus*), often creating beautiful mottling. Leathery dark green, ¾–2½-in.-long, evenly toothed leaves. Round fruit produced in fall. Patio tree, sun screen, or (with careful pruning) street tree. Rub or cut out small branches along trunk for first few years; shorten overlong branches or strongly weeping ones to strengthen scaffolding. Older trees may need thinning to lessen chance of storm damage. Subject to Texas root rot in desert but otherwise little bothered by pests or diseases.

Forms that hold their leaves are often sold as 'Sempervirens', but that is not a true variety. Two commonly offered, more or less evergreen varieties are 'Brea', with larger leaves and more upright habit than the species; and 'Drake', with smaller leaves, weeping habit. A more reliably evergreen variety is round-headed 'True Green', with small, deep green leaves. Newer selections include 'Allee' ('Emer II'), vase-shaped tree to 70 ft. tall, 60 ft. wide; 'Athena Classic' ('Emer I'), moderately fast grower to 35 ft. tall, 50 ft. wide; and 'Dynasty', to 40 ft. by 40 ft., vaselike when young, later rounded. Novelty selections include 'Corticosa', with thick, corky bark; it can reach tree size but usually doesn't get the chance—it's a favorite for bonsai. Dwarf varieties suitable for bonsai include 'Frosty', 3-ft. shrub with leaves edged in tiny white teeth; 'Hokkaido', tiny-leafed, very slow-growing but shapely miniature tree (just 1 ft. tall in 20 years); and 'Seiju', a sport of 'Hokkaido' with larger leaves and corky bark.

A note of caution: A less desirable species, *U. pumila* (Siberian elm) is sometimes sold as Chinese elm.

U. pumila. SIBERIAN ELM. Deciduous. Zones A1–A3; 1–11, 14–21; used chiefly in Zones A1–A3, 1, 2, 10, 11, where climate limits tree choices. From Russia, northern China. To 50 ft. tall, 40 ft. wide. Smooth dark green leaves are ¾–2 in. long. Resists Dutch elm disease and endures cold, heat, aridity, and poor soil—but has brittle wood and weak crotches and is not a desirable tree. Possibly useful in holding soil against erosion; fast growth also makes it suitable for windbreak or shelterbelt. Papery, winged seeds disperse seedlings over wide area.

U. wilsoniana 'Prospector'. Zones 3–9, 14–21. Fairly new variety from western China; similar in shape to *U. americana*. Likely ultimate size is 40 ft. tall, 30 ft. wide. Leaves are orange red when new, mature to deep shiny green, turn yellow in fall. Resistant to Dutch elm disease and elm leaf beetles.

Ulmus parvifolia

UMBELLULARIA californica
CALIFORNIA LAUREL, CALIFORNIA BAY, OREGON MYRTLE, PEPPERWOOD
Lauraceae
EVERGREEN TREE

🌡 ZONES 4–9, 14–24
☀ ◐ ● SUN OR SHADE
○ ◑ ● LITTLE TO REGULAR WATER

Native to southwestern Oregon, California Coast Ranges, lower elevations of Sierra Nevada. In the wild, form varies. On windy hillsides near coast, it is a huge, gum-drop-shaped shrub; in forests, it's a tree to 75 ft. tall, over 100 ft. wide. In gardens, it tends to grow slowly (about 1 ft. a year) to 20–25 ft. high and wide. Lance-shaped, 2–5-in.-long leaves are medium to deep yellow green and glossy above, dull light green beneath.

Umbellularia californica

Leaves can be substituted for sweet bay (*Laurus nobilis*) in cooking, but they have a more pungent flavor. Clusters of tiny yellowish flowers give plant a yellowish cast in spring. Blossoms are followed by olivelike, purplish, inedible fruit.

Grows best and fastest in deep soil with regular water but tolerates many other conditions, including aridity. Will grow in deep shade and ultimately get big enough to become shade maker itself (casts very dense shade unless thinned). Though often afflicted with sooty mold resulting from aphid or scale infestation, it is nonetheless useful for screen, background planting, tall hedge. Heavy drop of yellow to tan leaves in autumn.

California laurel is the main host of *Phytophthora ramorum*, the fungus that causes sudden oak death (see page 688); it can transmit the fungus but is not usually killed by it. In the Coast Ranges

from California's Big Sur through Curry County in southern Oregon, growing California laurel within 35 ft. of any of the following plants is likely to result in their infection and death: California black oak (*Quercus kelloggii*), coast live oak (*Q. agrifolia*), and tanbark oak (*Lithocarpus densiflorus*).

UMBRELLA PINE.
See **SCIADOPITYS verticillata**

UMBRELLA PLANT.
See **CYPERUS alternifolius, DARMERA peltata**

UMBRELLA TREE, QUEENSLAND.
See **SCHEFFLERA actinophylla**

UNCINIA rubra
RED HOOK SEDGE
Cyperaceae
PERENNIAL

🌡 ZONES 4–6, 15–17
☀ ◐ FULL SUN OR PARTIAL SHADE
● REGULAR WATER

From the mountains of New Zealand. Stiff, narrow, slightly arching leaves form a tuft 8–15 in. tall and wide. Foliage is rich, dark mahogany to bronze green; lovely when backlit. Black, sharply

Uncinia rubra

pointed seed heads are produced in summer. Good choice for container, pond, or stream edge. Reseeds a bit, but not enough to be a problem. Dislikes intense heat; mulch to keep roots cool.

URSINIA anethoides
Asteraceae
PERENNIAL USUALLY GROWN AS ANNUAL

🌡 ALL ZONES
☀ FULL SUN
◑ ● MODERATE TO REGULAR WATER

Native to the Cape region of South Africa. Fast growing, bushy plant to 15 in. tall and wide, with very finely divided, bright green leaves reminiscent of dill. Golden orange flowers 2 in. across have a maroon

U

Ursinia anethoides 'Solar Fire'

circle around a central golden eye. Flowers open during the day, close in the evening and on cloudy days. Bloom period lasts for several months, peaking in summer. Tolerant of heat and drought once established. 'Solar Fire' is an excellent variety with larger flowers.

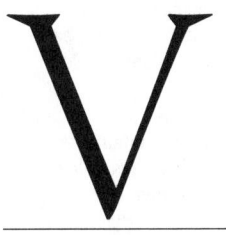

VACCINIUM
Ericaceae
EVERGREEN OR DECIDUOUS SHRUBS

- ⬚ ZONES VARY BY SPECIES
- ☼ ◑ ● EXPOSURE NEEDS VARY BY SPECIES
- ◐ ◑ ◑◑ WATER NEEDS VARY BY SPECIES

Excellent ornamental shrubs. Clusters of bell-shaped flowers in spring; colorful, edible berries that attract birds. Provide organically enriched, acid soil. Good for woodland gardens. For species grown largely for fruit, see Blueberry.

V. macrocarpon. CRANBERRY. Evergreen. Zones 1–6, 17. Native to northeastern U.S., eastern Canada. To 2–6 in. high, spreading and rooting from stems to indefinite width. Narrow, dark green, ½–¾-in. leaves turn coppery or purplish in winter. Tiny pinkish flowers; tart red berries in autumn. Commercial growers raise this plant in bogs— beds that can be flooded to control weeds and pests and make harvesting easier. Gardeners can use cranberry as an attractive small-scale ground cover in full sun (space plants 2 ft. apart). Provide ample water.

V. ovatum. EVERGREEN HUCKLEBERRY. Zones 4–7, 14–17, 22–24. Native to Pacific coastal region, from Santa Barbara area of Southern California north to British Columbia. Erect growth to 2–3 ft. high and wide in sun, 8–10 ft. tall and broad in shade. Leathery, lustrous dark green leaves to 1¼ in. long; bronzy or reddish when new. White or pinkish flowers are followed by black berries good in pies, jams, jellies, syrups. Can be trimmed as a hedge or grown in containers. Cut branches are popular for arrangements. Sun or shade. Moderate to regular water.

Vaccinium ovatum

V. parvifolium. RED HUCKLEBERRY. Deciduous. Zones A3; 2–7, 14–17. Native to Sierra Nevada, Coast Ranges from Northern California to Alaska. Slow-growing plant, eventually reaching 4–12 ft. (rarely 18 ft.) tall, 6 ft. wide. Thin green branches with spreading or cascading habit provide an intricate winter silhouette. Oval, thin-textured light green leaves ½–¾ in. long. Greenish or whitish flowers are good in arrangements. Showy bright red berries can be used in jams, jellies, pies. Partial or full shade. Regular water.

V. vitis-idaea. COWBERRY, FOXBERRY. Evergreen. Zones 2–7, 14–17, except as noted. Native to Europe. Slow growth to 1 ft. high; spreads widely by rhizomes if grown in highly organic or thickly mulched soil. Glossy dark green leaves to 1 in. long; new growth often tinged bright red or orange. White or pinkish flowers followed by sour red berries something like tiny cranberries; these are valued for preserves, syrups. Handsome little plant for informal edging around larger plantings; good small-scale ground cover (space plants 2–3 ft. apart). Best without potassium fertilizer. Regular to ample water. Prefers partial or full shade, but if given ample water will take full sun in cool-summer areas. European varieties grown for fruit production are sometimes seen. 'Erntdank' produces one crop in spring, another in summer. 'Koralle' also bears two crops; its berries are darker red and somewhat larger than those of the species, and the later crop (if not harvested) can remain on the plant all winter.

V. v. minus. LINGONBERRY. Zones A1–A3; 1–7, 14–17. Cold-hardier form from arctic North America. Has smaller leaves (to ½ in.), is attractive in rock gardens, containers.

VALERIANA
officinalis
VALERIAN, GARDEN HELIOTROPE
Valerianaceae
PERENNIAL

- ⬚ ZONES 1–24
- ☼ ◑ FULL SUN OR PARTIAL SHADE
- ◐ REGULAR WATER

From Europe and western Asia. To 5 ft. tall in bloom, spreading to 4 ft. wide. Most of the foliage remains fairly close to ground. Light green leaves, each with eight to ten pairs of narrow, jagged-edged leaflets. Tall, straight flowering stems carry tiny, fragrant pink blossoms in rounded clusters at stem ends in summer; useful for cut flowers.

Valeriana officinalis

White- and red-flowered forms exist. Strong-smelling roots are widely used in herbal preparations said to have sedative qualities. Roots also attract cats. Start new plants from seed or divisions. Grow in mixed herb or flower borders, but be aware that it can become invasive; don't let it crowd other plants.

VALERIANA rubra.
See **CENTRANTHUS ruber**

VALLOTA speciosa.
See **CYRTANTHUS elatus**

VANCOUVERIA
Berberidaceae
PERENNIALS

- ⬚ ZONES VARY BY SPECIES
- ◑ PARTIAL SHADE
- ◐ ◐ MODERATE TO REGULAR WATER

Closely related to *Epimedium* and likewise used as ground covers in shady spots. Wiry leafstalks grow directly from creeping underground stems; leaves have numerous broad leaflets that resemble small ivy (*Hedera*) leaves. Threadlike flower stalks rise above foliage in late spring or early summer, bearing drooping clusters of small blossoms. Petals and sepals are sharply reflexed, giving flowers a windswept look. Plants spread slowly from ever-enlarging mat of roots, forming sizable patches in time. Set plants about 1½ ft. apart. Need cool, moist, acid conditions.

V. chrysantha. Zones 5, 6, 14–17. Native to mountains of southwestern Oregon and extreme northwestern California. To 16 in. high, with bronzy gray-green, 1½-in.-long, evergreen leaflets and yellow, ½-in. flowers.

V. hexandra. Zones 4–7, 14–17, 19–24. Native to coastal forests from Northern California to Washington. To 1 ft. high, with light green, 2½-in. leaflets and white, ½-in. flowers. Dies back in winter.

Vancouveria planipetala

V. planipetala (V. parviflora). INSIDE-OUT FLOWER. Zones 4–7, 14–17. Native to coastal areas of California and southwestern Oregon. To 2 ft. tall, with light to medium green, 1½-in., shallowly lobed leaflets. White flowers are tiny—only about ⅛ in. wide—but are carried in clusters of 25–50. May die back in winter in colder part of range.

VANDA
Orchidaceae
EPIPHYTIC ORCHIDS

- ZONE H2; OR INDOORS
- FILTERED SUNLIGHT; BRIGHT INDIRECT LIGHT
- REGULAR WATER

About 60 species of warm-growing orchids native from India to New Guinea. In the wild, they grow on trees or rock outcroppings. They produce stout stems without pseudobulbs. Stems may be short or tall; tall stems are either self-supporting or climbing. Leaves are arranged in two rows, enveloping stem at base; showy flowers are produced in clusters at leaf joints. Hybrid 'Miss Joaquim' (*V. teres* × *V. hookeriana*) is widely grown for its attractive lavender blooms, which are popular in Hawaii for orchid leis. It has self-supporting stems, may reach 3–4 ft. or taller.

Vanda

Vandas are generally too demanding to make good house-plants; they do better in a green-house. Best grown on a coarse medium that provides complete drainage (tree fern fiber, for example). See also Orchids.

VAUQUELINIA
Rosaceae
EVERGREEN SHRUBS OR TREES

- ZONES 10–13
- FULL SUN OR PARTIAL SHADE
- LITTLE TO MODERATE WATER

Rather open-growing plants to 20 ft. tall, 15 ft. wide, with upright, sometimes twisted branches. Somewhat reminiscent of oleander (*Nerium*) in habit. Narrow, leathery, typically tooth-edged leaves are dark green above, grayish beneath. Small white flowers in 2–3-in. clusters decorate branch tips in spring. Blossoms are followed by woody seed capsules that last through fall and winter. Grow

Vauquelinia californica

as large shrubs or train as single- or multitrunked trees. Very drought tolerant but look best with some water during hot months.

V. californica. ARIZONA ROSEWOOD. Native to southern Arizona, Baja California, Mexico. Leaves to 4 in. long.

V. corymbosa angustifolia. SLIMLEAF VAUQUELINIA. Native to western Texas, northern Mexico. Has longer (6-in.), usually narrower leaves and showier flower clusters than *V. californica*. Often sold as *V. corymbosa*.

VELTHEIMIA
bracteata
Liliaceae
PERENNIAL FROM BULB

- ZONES 13, 16–24; OR INDOORS
- PARTIAL SHADE; BRIGHT INDIRECT LIGHT
- REGULAR WATER DURING GROWTH AND BLOOM

Handsome foliage is reason enough to grow this South African native. Each bulb produces a fountainlike rosette of wavy-edged, glossy green leaves to 1 ft. long, 3 in. wide. In winter or early spring, brown-mottled flower stems to about 1 ft. tall are topped by elongated clusters of tubular, drooping, pinkish purple flowers tipped in green. Leaves turn yellow and die back in late spring; new

Veltheimia bracteata

growth resumes in fall. Most plants sold as *V. capensis* are actually *V. bracteata*; the true *V. capensis* has nonglossy blue-green leaves and green-tipped, pale pink flowers.

In virtually frostless areas, veltheimia can be grown in the ground, but even there it is usually grown in pots. For each bulb, use a pot large enough to allow about 3 in. between all sides of bulb and container edges. Plant in fall, in fast-draining soil, set top of bulb neck just above soil surface. Fertilize every 2 weeks throughout growing season. Keep soil dry during summer dormancy. Can remain outdoors where temperatures stay above 25°F/–4°C; where light frosts are possible, give overhead protection.

VELVET GROUNDSEL.
See **SENECIO petasitis**

VENIDIUM fastuosum.
See **ARCTOTIS fastuosa alba**

VERBASCUM
MULLEIN
Scrophulariaceae
BIENNIALS AND PERENNIALS

- ZONES VARY BY SPECIES
- FULL SUN
- MODERATE WATER

Large group of rosette-forming, summer-blooming plants that send up spikes closely set with nearly flat, five-petaled, circular flowers about an inch across. Both foliage and stems are often covered in woolly hairs. Taller mulleins make striking vertical accents. Grow all in well-drained soil. Cut off spent flowers to encourage a second round of blooming. Mulleins self-sow freely—and some are downright weedy, such as the attractive roadside weed *V. thapsus*.

V. blattaria. MOTH MULLEIN. Biennial. Zones 1–11, 14–24. Native from Europe to central Asia. To 6 ft. tall, 2 ft. wide, with smooth-textured, dark green, cut or toothed leaves to 10 in. long. Yellow or creamy white flowers. 'Rose Form' has rose pink blooms opening from red buds.

V. bombyciferum 'Arctic Summer'. Biennial. Zones 2–11, 14–24. Selection of a species native to Turkey. To 6 ft. tall, 2 ft. wide, with furry gray-green leaves to 1½ ft. long. Yellow flowers on powdery white stems.

V. chaixii. Perennial. Zones 2–11, 14–24. From Europe. To 3 ft.

Verbascum bombyciferum
'Arctic Summer'

tall and 2 ft. wide, with hairy green leaves to 6 in. long. Red-eyed, pale yellow flowers in narrow, often branching spikes. 'Album' has white flowers with purple centers.

V. dumulosum. Perennial. Zones 7–9, 14–24. Dwarf to 1 ft. high, 1½ ft. wide, with velvety white leaves. Short, branching spikes of lemon yellow blossoms with purple centers. Hybrid 'Letitia' has a longer summer bloom season than the species.

V. hybrids. Zones 3–10, 14–24. Many hybrids are obtainable, either as blends or in single colors. Most must be grown from seed.

'Banana Custard'. Biennial. To 5–6 ft. tall, 2 ft. wide. Bright yellow flowers.

Benary Hybrids, Cotswold Hybrids. Perennials. These resemble *V. phoeniceum* but come in white, cream, pink, and purple. Named varieties are sometimes seen; these include 'Helen Johnson' (peach pink) and 'Pink Domino' (bright pink).

'Copper Rose'. Perennial. To 4–6 ft. high, 2 ft. wide, with flowers in buff, apricot, rose, or tan. Bloom first year from seed sown in late winter, earliest spring.

'Sierra Sunset'. Perennial. Rosettes 8 in. tall and 14–18 in. wide produce flower stalks 1½ ft. tall that hold large blossoms in shades of melon and salmon, with rose accents.

V. olympicum. Perennial. Zones 3–10, 14–24. From Greece. To 5 ft. high, 3 ft. wide, with soft, downy white leaves to over 2 ft. long. Bright yellow flowers; many flowering stems.

V. phoeniceum. PURPLE MULLEIN. Perennial. Zones 1–10, 14–24. To 2–4 ft. high, 1½ ft. wide. Dark green leaves to 6 in. long are smooth on top, hairy beneath. Slender spikes of purple flowers. 'Violetta' grows 2–3 ft. tall, with deep purple flowers.

VERBENA

Verbenaceae
PERENNIALS, SOME GROWN
AS ANNUALS

- ☑ ZONES VARY BY SPECIES
- ☼ FULL SUN
- ◐◑● WATER NEEDS VARY BY SPECIES

Bear clusters of small, tubular, five-petaled flowers, usually in summer. Most are fast-growing ground covers, good in parking strips, along driveways, on dry banks; also attractive in wall crevices, hanging baskets. Best in hot weather. Need good air circulation (to avoid mildew) and well-drained soil, especially in winter.

V. bipinnatifida. Perennial. Zones 1–24. Native from western Great Plains to Mexico. To 8–16 in. high, 1½ ft. or wider. Finely divided leaves and blue flowers. Self-sows. 'Valley Lavender' is low growing, just 3–6 in. tall, with bright lavender flowers over a long period. Little water.

V. bonariensis. Perennial in Zones 8–24; annual in colder climates. Native to South America; naturalized in California. Border plant to 3–6 ft. tall, 1½–3 ft. wide, with airy, branching stems carrying purple flowers. Leaves are mostly basal. Plant's see-through quality makes it suited for foreground as well as back of border. Self-sows freely. Little water.

V. gooddingii. Short-lived perennial. Zones 7–24. Native to Southwest deserts. To 1½–2 ft. tall, 3–4 ft. wide, with small, deeply cut leaves. Pinkish lavender flowers at ends of short spikes. Blooms first summer from seed sown in spring. Can reseed where moisture is present. Little to moderate water.

V. 'Homestead Purple'. Perennial in Zones 2–24; often treated as annual. To 1–2 ft. high, 2–3 ft. wide, with dark green leaves and deep purple flowers. Resistant to mildew. Regular water.

V. × hybrida (V. × hortensis). GARDEN VERBENA. Short-lived perennial in Zones 8–24, H1, H2; often treated as annual in all zones. Many-branched plant 6–12 in. high, 1½–3 ft. wide. Oblong, 2–4-in., bright green or gray-green leaves with toothed margins. Flowers in flat, compact clusters to 3 in. wide. Colors include white, pink, red, purple, blue, and combinations. Superior strains include Romance (6 in.) and Showtime (10 in.). Deep rose pink 'Showtime Trinidad' can withstand light frosts. 'Coral Red' grows only a few inches high, bears coral to rosy red flowers. 'Peaches 'N Cream' has blooms in a combination of pastel pink and cream. If growing these plants as perennials, prune severely before spring growth begins. Good ground covers in Zones 12, 13. Moderate water.

V. lilacina. CEDROS ISLAND VERBENA. Perennial. Zones 12–24. Native to Baja California. To 1 ft. high, 3 ft. or wider. Light green, deeply cut leaves. Lilac-colored flowers bloom from spring to fall (nearly all year, in mildest areas). Useful ground cover for hot, dry sites. 'De La Mina' forms a 3-ft. mound, has darker purple flowers. Little to moderate water.

Verbena peruviana
hybrid

V. peruviana (V. chamaedrifolia). Perennial in Zones 8–24; usually treated as annual in all zones. Native to South America. Forms a flat mat that spreads rapidly by aboveground runners. Set out plants 2 ft. apart for a solid cover in one season. Neat, small, closely set dark green leaves. Flat-topped clusters of scarlet-and-white flowers on slender stems cover foliage. Hybrids aren't as flat, spread more slowly, have slightly larger leaves and stouter stems, are available in several colors. They include many purplish varieties, a fine pure white, 'Starfire' (red), and these in pink and rose tones: 'Appleblossom', 'Cherry Pink', 'Little Pinkie', 'Princess Gloria', 'Raspberry Rose', 'St. Paul'. Especially popular in Southern California and the desert. Moderate water.

V. pulchella gracilior (V. tenuisecta). MOSS VERBENA. Perennial in Zones 7–9, 14–24; annual in colder climates. From South America. To 6–12 in. high and 2–5 ft. wide, with finely cut dark green leaves. Blue, purple, or violet flowers. 'Alba' is a white-flowered form. Moderate water.

V. rigida. (V. venosa). Perennial in Zones 3–24; can be grown as annual (blooms in 4 months from seed). Native to South America. To 1–2 ft. high, 3–4 ft. wide. Rough, strongly toothed dark green leaves to 2–4 in. long. Lilac to purple-blue flowers in cylindrical clusters on tall, upright stems in summer and fall. Useful in low-maintenance gardens. Moderate to regular water. 'Flame', to just 4 in. high, is a cutting-grown selection with bright scarlet flowers.

V. 'Sissinghurst'. Perennial. Zones 3–24. To a few inches high, 4 ft. wide. Dark green, finely cut leaves. Bright red flowers. Give regular water.

V. stricta. Perennial. Zones 2–24. Native from Massachusetts to Montana, south to Mexico. Upright growth to 3 ft. tall, 1½ ft. or wider. Hairy stems bear narrow to rounded, tooth-edged leaves to 4 in. long; medium green above, whitish beneath. Flower stems are also densely hairy, bear deep lavender or purple flowers. Regular water.

V. Tapien hybrids. Perennials in Zones 4–9, 12–24, H1, H2; annuals anywhere. Prostrate plants to 4 in. high, 1–1½ ft. wide, with finely cut dark green leaves. Wide range of colors, including pink, lavender, pale blue, deep purple, red. Resistant to mildew. Provide regular water.

V. Temari hybrids. Perennials in Zones 4–9, 12–24, H1, H2; annuals anywhere. Low, spreading plants to 3 in. high, 2½ ft. wide. Broad dark green leaves. Bright pink, burgundy, or violet flowers. Regular water.

VERBENA, LEMON. See **ALOYSIA triphylla**

VERONICA

SPEEDWELL
Scrophulariaceae
PERENNIALS

- ☑ ZONES VARY BY SPECIES
- ☼ FULL SUN, EXCEPT AS NOTED
- ◐◑● WATER NEEDS VARY BY SPECIES

Handsome plants ranging from less than an inch tall to 2 ft. in height. Masses of small (¼–½-in.-wide) flowers in white, rose, pink, or pale to deep blue make an effective display. Use in borders and rock gardens. Prostrate kinds are good between stepping-stones, as bulb covers. Named varieties are not easily assigned to a species; authorities differ. For shrubby plants sometimes sold as *Veronica*, see *Hebe*.

V. alpina. Zones 1–7, 14–17. From Europe, Eurasia, North America. Creeping rootstock forms low foliage rosette 4–8 in. high, 1 ft. wide; oval to elliptical leaves to 1 in. long, ½ in. wide. Spikelike clusters of blue flowers in spring or early summer; in warmer parts of range, often reblooms in fall. White-flowered 'Alba' grows 10 in. high. Regular water.

V. austriaca teucrium 'Crater Lake Blue'. Zones 1–9, 14–21. Selection of a species native to Europe. To 12–15 in. high and wide, with tooth-edged, 1½-in.-long leaves. Short spikes of intensely blue flowers in mid-summer. Regular water.

V. gentianoides. GENTIAN SPEEDWELL. Zones 1–9, 14–21. From the Caucasus. Creeping rootstock forms a dense mat to 1–2 ft. high and wide. Oblong, glossy dark green, 2–3-in.-long leaves. In spring, foliage is topped by leafy stems carrying 10-in. spikes of ice blue flowers with darker veining. 'Variegata' has leaves marked with white. Regular water.

V. hybrids. The following are among the best varieties. Regular water, except as noted.

'Blue Reflection'. Zones 2–9, 14–21. Forms a gray-green foliage mat to 3 in. high and 1½ ft. wide, covered with blue flowers in mid-spring. Little to moderate water.

'Goodness Grows'. Zones 1–7, 14–17. To 1 ft. tall and wide. Violet-blue blossoms over long bloom period—from late spring to frost, if old flowers are removed.

Veronica
'Sunny Border Blue'

'Sunny Border Blue'. Zones A2, A3; 1–9, 14–21. Compact, clump-forming plant to 1½–2 ft. tall, 1 ft. wide, with crinkled dark green leaves. Spires of dark violet-blue flowers appear in late spring or early summer; deadheading prolongs the show until frost.

'Waterperry Blue' ('Waterperry'). Zones 2–9, 14–21. Low,

trailing plant to 4–6 in. high and 1½ ft. or more wide; roots as it spreads. Small, rounded, bronze-tinted leaves. Loose clusters of pale blue flowers veined in deeper blue; main bloom in spring, with sporadic flowering throughout summer and fall.

V. liwanensis. Zones 3–9, 14–24. From Turkey. Creeping ground cover to 1–2 in. tall, 1½ ft. wide. In spring, the tiny, waxy deep green leaves are concealed by bright blue flowers. Foliage takes on purplish tints in hot sun. Little to regular water.

V. pectinata. Zones 1–9, 14–24. Western Mediterranean native. Forms prostrate mat of foliage to 3 in. high and 1 ft. wide; spreads by creeping stems that root at joints. Small grayish leaves have scalloped or deeply cut edges. Profuse spring or early summer show of deep blue flowers with white centers; blossoms are borne on 5–6-in. spikes among the leaves. Little to moderate water.

Veronica prostrata

V. prostrata (V. rupestris). Zones 1–9, 14–24. Stems are hairy and tufted. Some are prostrate and form 1–1½-ft.-wide foliage mat; other stems grow erect to 8 in. high and are topped by short clusters of pale blue flowers in late spring or early summer. 'Heavenly Blue' is almost entirely prostrate, with flower stems reaching 6 in. high. 'Mrs. Holt' has pale pink flowers. 'Trehane' has golden yellow leaves, bright blue flowers. Little to moderate water.

V. repens. Zones 3–9, 14–24. Mediterranean native. Flat mat to ½ in. high, 1 ft. or wider. Small, shiny green leaves clothe the prostrate stems, give plant a mossy look. Clusters of tiny lavender to white flowers appear in spring. Tolerates some shade. Needs little to moderate water.

V. spicata. Zones A2, A3, 1–9, 14–21, except as noted. From

Europe, Asia. Rounded, 1½–2-ft.-wide clump sends up 2-ft.-tall stems clothed in pointed oval, glossy green leaves and topped in summer with spikes of bright blue flowers. Long bloom season if faded flowers are removed. 'Icicle', to 15–18 in. high, has white flower spikes. 'Nana' grows only 6 in. high, bears violet-blue blossoms. 'Red Fox' ('Rotfuchs'), to 15 in. tall and wide, has deep rosy red blooms. Regular water.

V. s. incana (V. incana). SILVER SPEEDWELL. Zones A1–A3; 1–7, 14–17. Furry, silvery white foliage forms a 1–1½-ft.-wide mat. Blooms in summer, producing deep violet-blue blossoms on stems to about 1 ft. high. Little to moderate water.

V. umbrosa 'Georgia Blue'. Zones 2–9, 14–24. From country of Georgia. Forms a 6–8-in.-high mat that spreads to several feet wide; small dark green leaves turn bronze in cool weather. Profuse, white-eyed cobalt blue flowers in spring, with a few blossoms appearing throughout summer and fall. Regular water.

VERTICORDIA plumosa
FEATHERFLOWER
Myrtaceae
EVERGREEN SHRUB

> 🗡 ZONES 16, 17, 22–24
>
> ☼ ◑ SUN OR PARTIAL SHADE
>
> ◔ LITTLE WATER

From southwestern Australia. To 3 ft. tall and wide, with wavy branches covered in soft, needle-like foliage. From late winter into spring, produces a profusion of tiny lavender flowers at branch tips. Excellent cut flower. Requires well-drained soil; feed occasionally with low-phosphorus fertilizer. 'Pink Lace' is a compact grower to

Verticordia plumosa 'Pink Lace'

just 1½–2 ft. tall and wide, with lightly fragrant, lavender pink flowers.

VETIVERIA zizanioides
VETIVER
Poaceae (Gramineae)
PERENNIAL GRASS

> 🗡 ZONES 20–24; H1, H2
>
> ☼ ◑ FULL SUN OR PARTIAL SHADE
>
> ◑ ◑ ◑ MODERATE TO AMPLE WATER

A large, coarse grass native to tropical India. Erect growth to 8 ft. tall, 2–4 ft. wide, forming a dense cluster of stiff, narrow leaves, often bent at a point 1–2 ft. below the tips. Seldom flowers. Foliage is light green and takes on attractive bronze tints in cold weather.

Vetiveria zizanioides

Historically grown for its massive, fibrous, very fragrant roots, which were woven into mats or distilled for an oil used in perfume. Will grow in just about any type of soil, taking considerable drought or wet conditions—even seasonal flooding. Use in the middle or rear of a perennial border, grow in a large container, or use as a screening plant. Good for erosion control.

VIBURNUM
Caprifoliaceae
DECIDUOUS AND EVERGREEN SHRUBS OR TREES

> 🗡 ZONES VARY BY SPECIES
>
> ☼ ◑ FULL SUN OR PARTIAL SHADE, EXCEPT AS NOTED
>
> ◑ REGULAR WATER, EXCEPT AS NOTED

Large, diverse group of plants with generally oval, often handsome leaves and clusters of typically white, sometimes fragrant flowers. Blossoms are usually followed by single-seeded, often brilliantly colored fruit much appreciated by birds. Many viburnums are grown for their flower display, a few for their showy fruit. Many evergreen types are valuable as foliage plants. Several species (noted below) can be grown as small trees.

V. davidii needs acid soil, but the other viburnums are very soil tolerant. Prune to prevent legginess; some evergreen species can be sheared. Aphids, thrips, spider mites, scale, and root weevils are potential pests. Keep sulfur sprays off foliage.

V. awabuki. SWEET VIBURNUM. Evergreen. Zones 15–24; at some risk of frost damage in Zones 8, 9, 14. From Asia. Often sold as *V. odoratissimum.* Shrub or small tree to 12 ft. tall, 8 ft. wide. Glossy dark green leaves to 8 in. long. Conical, 3–6-in. clusters of fragrant flowers in spring. Pendulous clusters of red fruit that ripens to black. 'Chindo' has smaller leaves, denser habit; makes a good tall hedge or screen.

V. × bodnantense. Deciduous. Zones 4–9, 14–24. To 10 ft. (or more) tall, 6 ft. wide. Dark green, 1½–4-in.-long leaves are deeply veined, turn dark scarlet in fall. Blooms from fall to spring, bearing loose clusters of very fragrant deep pink flowers that age to paler pink. Red fruit is not showy. Best known is 'Dawn' ('Pink Dawn'). Flower buds freeze in coldest Northwest winters.

V. × burkwoodii. Deciduous in coldest areas, nearly evergreen elsewhere. Zones 2–12, 14–24, except as noted. To 6–12 ft. tall, 4–8 ft. wide. Glossy dark green leaves reach 3½ in. long, have white, hairy undersides; turn purplish red in cold weather. Dense, 4-in. clusters of pink buds open to very fragrant flowers in late winter or early spring. Blue-black fruit is not showy. Early growth is straggly, but mature plants are dense. Can be espaliered.

'Chenault' (*V. chenaultii*). Denser, more compact, slightly later blooming, more deciduous in mild climates than the species.

'Mohawk'. Zones 1–12, 14–24. To 7 ft. tall, 5 ft. wide. Red buds are showy long before they open into white flowers. Showy orange-red fall color.

V. × carlcephalum. FRAGRANT SNOWBALL. Deciduous. Zones 3–11, 14–24. To 6–10 ft. tall and wide. Dull grayish green, 2–3½-in.-long leaves are downy beneath; turn reddish purple in autumn. Long-lasting, waxy, sweetly perfumed spring flowers in dense, 4–5-in. clusters. No fruit. As showy as *V. opulus* 'Roseum' but has the bonus of fragrance.

V. carlesii. KOREAN SPICE VIBURNUM. Deciduous. Zones A3; 2–11, 14–24. From Korea, Japan.

Loose, open habit to 4–8 ft. tall and wide. Leaves like those of *V. × carlcephalum;* inconsistent reddish fall color. Pink buds in 2–3-in. clusters open to sweetly fragrant white flowers in spring. Blue-black fruit is not showy. Does best with part shade during hottest months.

V. davidii. Evergreen. Zones 4–9, 14–24. From western China. Compact mound to 3–4 ft. high and wide. Handsome, glossy dark green, deeply veined leaves to 6 in. long. White flowers in 3-in. clusters open from dull pinkish red buds in spring; they are not showy but are followed by an arresting show of metallic turquoise blue fruit. Grow with acid-loving plants. Partial shade. Especially good viburnum for Zones 4–6, 17.

V. dentatum. ARROWWOOD. Deciduous. Zones 1–11, 14–21. From eastern and central North America. To 6–10 ft. or taller, equally wide. Cream-colored flowers in late spring are followed by blue-black fruit. Dark green, oval to rounded, 4-in. leaves turn yellow, orange, or deep red in fall.

V. edule. HIGHBUSH CRANBERRY. Deciduous. Zones A1–A3; 1–11. Native to northern Asia and America, including Alaska. Coarselooking plant to 4–8 ft. tall, 2–4 ft. wide. Roundish dark green leaves are three lobed toward the tip, turn reddish maroon in fall. Inch-wide clusters of flowers in late spring or early summer are followed by small, musty-smelling red fruits that are tart but edible.

V. farreri (V. fragrans). Deciduous. Zones 3–9, 14–24. From northern China. Loose habit to 10 ft. tall, 8 ft. wide. Smooth, heavily veined, 1½–3-in.-long green leaves turn soft russet red to reddish purple in fall. Fragrant white to pink flowers in 2-in. clusters on bare stems at some point between late fall and spring. Blooms survive to 20 to 22°F/−7 to −6°C but freeze at lower temperatures. Bright red fruit. Prune to prevent leggy growth. 'Candidissimum' ('Album') has pure white flowers, pale yellow fruit. 'Nanum' is pink flowered, grows 2½ ft. high, 3 ft. wide.

V. hybrids. These springblooming viburnums all have complex ancestry.

'Cayuga'. Deciduous. Zones 2–11, 14–24. To 5 ft. tall and wide. Dark green, 1–3-in.-long leaves. White flowers open from pink buds.

'Chesapeake'. Semievergreen. Zones 3–11, 14–24. To 8 ft. tall,

10 ft. wide, with wavy-edged, glossy dark green leaves. Two-inch clusters of fragrant white flowers open from pink buds; dull red fruit ages to black.

'Conoy'. Evergreen. Zones 3–12, 14–24. Dense growth to 5 ft. high and wide. Lustrous dark green, 2–2½-in. leaves are whitish beneath; take on maroon tinge in cold winters. Slightly fragrant flowers are followed by long-lasting red berries. Tolerates shearing.

'Eskimo'. Semievergreen. Zones 3–12, 14–24. Dense, compact habit to 5 ft. tall and wide. Shiny dark green leaves to 4 in. long; unscented flowers in 3–4-in., snowball-like clusters.

V. japonicum. Evergreen. Zones 5–10, 12, 14–24. From Japan. To 10–15 ft. tall, 8–12 ft. wide; can be trained as a small tree. Leathery, glossy dark green leaves to 6 in. long. Sparse spring show of fragrant flowers in 4-in. clusters. Red fruit is likewise sparse—but very attractive. Best with some shade in hottest climates.

V. × juddii. Deciduous. Zones 2–9, 14–24. To 4–8 ft. tall, 6–10 ft. wide. More spreading and bushy than *V. carlesii* but similar to it in other respects, including fragrance.

V. lantana. WAYFARING TREE. Deciduous. Zones A3; 2–9, 14–17. From Europe, Asia Minor. Rounded habit to 10–20 ft. tall and wide; can be trained as a small tree. Dark green, 2–5-in.-long leaves turn an inconsistent purplish red in fall. Flat, 3–5-in. clusters of midspring flowers develop into yellow fruits that gradually age to red, then black; all colors are sometimes present at once. 'Mohican' is more compact (to 9 ft. high and wide), with fruit that holds its red color longer.

V. macrocephalum (V. m. 'Sterile'). CHINESE SNOWBALL. Deciduous in coldest areas, nearly evergreen elsewhere. Zones 3–9, 14–24. This species originated in cultivation (not in the wild). Rounded habit to 12–20 ft. tall and wide. Dull green, oval to oblong, 2–4-in.-long leaves. Spectacular big, rounded, 6–8 in. flower clusters bloom in spring (or any time during warm weather); they are

composed of sterile flowers that start out lime green, change to white. No fruit. Can be espaliered. *V. m. keteleeri,* wild form from China, has sterile and fertile flowers in lacecap effect; sometimes produces fruit.

V. odoratissimum. See V. awabuki

V. opulus. EUROPEAN CRANBERRY BUSH. Deciduous. Zones A2, A3; 1–9, 14–24. From Europe, North Africa, central Asia. To 8–15 ft. tall and wide, with arching branches. Lobed, maplelike dark green leaves to 2–4 in. long and as wide or wider. Fall foliage color may be yellow, bright red, or reddish purple. Blooms in spring; flower heads have a lacecap look, with a 2–4-in. cluster of small fertile blossoms ringed with larger sterile blossoms. Large, showy red fruit persists from fall into winter. Takes moist to boggy soils. Control aphids.

'Aureum'. Golden yellow foliage. Give some shade to prevent sunburn.

'Compactum'. Like the species but smaller—to 4–5 ft. high and wide.

'Nanum'. To 2 ft. high and wide. Needs no trimming as low, informal hedge. Cannot take poorly drained, wet soils. No flowers or fruit.

'Roseum' ('Sterile'). COMMON SNOWBALL. Resembles the species but has snowball-like flower clusters 2–2½ in. across, composed entirely of sterile flowers (so bears no fruit). Aphids are especially troublesome.

V. plicatum (V. tomentosum 'Sterile'). JAPANESE SNOWBALL. Deciduous. Zones 3–9, 14–24. From China, Japan. To 8–15 ft. tall and wide; horizontal branching pattern gives plant a tiered look. Strongly veined, 3–6-in.-long, dull dark green leaves turn purplish red in autumn. Showy, 3-in., snowball-like clusters of sterile flowers look like those of *V. opulus* 'Roseum', but this plant is less bothered by aphids. Midspring bloom. No fruit.

V. p. tomentosum. DOUBLEFILE VIBURNUM. Deciduous. From China, Japan. A truly beautiful viburnum. Resembles the species but has lacecap flower heads: flat, 2–4-in. clusters of small fertile

Viburnum opulus 'Roseum'

flowers edged with 1–1½-in. sterile ones. Fruit is red aging to black; showy but not always profuse. 'Mariesii' grows 6–8 ft. tall, 8–10 ft. wide, has larger sterile flowers. 'Shasta' has a very wide-spreading habit (6 ft. tall, 12 ft. wide). Varieties blooming from spring to the end of the growing season include 'Nanum Semperflorens' ('Watanabe'), 'Summer Snowflake', and 'Summer Stars'; all grow 4–6 ft. tall and wide.

V. × pragense. PRAGUE VIBURNUM. Evergreen. Zones 3–11, 14–24. Fast-growing, rounded plant to 10 ft. tall and broad. Shiny dark green, 2–4-in.-long leaves. Faintly fragrant white flowers in 3–6-in. clusters open from pink buds in early spring.

V. × rhytidophylloides. Zones 3–9, 14–24. These are hybrids between *V. rhytidophyllum* and *V. lantana*. Among the best is 'Allegheny', a dense, rounded plant 6–8 ft. tall and broad; it is evergreen in most winters. Leaves resemble those of *V. rhytidophyllum* but are broader and less wrinkled. Flowers and fruit are also similar.

V. rhytidophyllum. LEATHERLEAF VIBURNUM. Evergreen. Zones 3–9, 14–24. Upright to 8–15 ft. tall, 6–12 ft. wide. Narrowish, 4–10-in.-long leaves are deep green and wrinkled above, fuzzy beneath. Yellowish white spring flowers in 4–8-in. clusters; scarlet fruit that ages to black. Leaves droop in cold weather, and plant looks tattered where cold winds blow. Tolerates deep shade. Some find this plant striking; others consider it coarse.

Viburnum rhytidophyllum

V. sargentii. Deciduous. Zones 1–9, 14–21. From northeastern Asia. Erect, rounded growth to 12–15 ft. tall and wide. Lobed, somewhat maplelike, 2–5-in.-long leaves. Foliage is bronze purple when new, matures to dark green by summer, may turn yellow or red in fall. Lacecap flower heads in late spring: 2–4-in. clusters of small fertile flowers edged with 1-in. sterile flowers. Bright red fruit colors up in late summer and fall, hangs on into winter. 'Onondaga', to 6 ft. tall and broad (or larger), has foliage that emerges deep maroon and maintains its purple tinge throughout summer; its flowers are pink-tinged white.

V. setigerum. TEA VIBURNUM. Deciduous. Zones 3–9, 14–21. From China. To 8–12 ft. tall, 6–8 ft. wide. Multistemmed, rather erect; often bare at base (plant lower-growing shrubs around it for concealment). Leaves were once used for making tea; they are 3–6 in. long, dark green or blue green turning to purplish in fall. Spring flowers in 1–2 in. clusters are not striking, but heavy production of scarlet fruit makes this the showiest of fruiting viburnums.

V. suspensum. SANDANKWA VIBURNUM. Evergreen. Zones 12–24; possible in Zones 8–10 but risky in cold winters there. From Japan. To 8–10 ft. tall and broad. Leathery, 2–4-in.-long leaves are glossy deep green above, paler beneath. Blooms in early spring; loose, 2–4-in. clusters of flowers have a scent that some people find objectionable. Red fruit ages to black, is not long lasting. Serviceable screen or hedge. Watch for thrips, spider mites, aphids. Little to moderate water.

V. tinus. LAURUSTINUS. Evergreen. Zones 4–10, 12–24, except as noted. Mediterranean native. To 6–12 ft. tall, half as wide. Leathery dark green, 2–3-in.-long leaves with edges slightly rolled under. Wine red new stems. Blooms from fall to spring; tight clusters of pink buds open to lightly fragrant white flowers. Bright metallic blue fruits last through summer. Dense foliage right to ground makes it good for screens, hedges, clipped topiary shapes. Can be trained as a small tree. Susceptible to mites; prone to mildew near ocean. Varieties include the following.

'Dwarf'. To 3–5 ft. tall and wide. Good for low screens, hedges, foundation plantings.

'Lucidum'. SHINING LAURUSTINUS. Zones 8, 9, 12–24. Less hardy than the species, with larger leaves. Less prone to mildew.

'Robustum'. ROUNDLEAF LAURUSTINUS. Leaves are coarser, rougher than those of species; flower buds are almost white. Less prone to mildew. Excellent small, narrow tree.

'Spring Bouquet' ('Compactum'). Upright to 4–6 ft. high and wide; good for hedges. Leaves are deeper green, slightly smaller than those of the species.

'Variegatum'. Zones 4–9, 14–24. Leaves are marbled with white and pale yellow.

V. trilobum. CRANBERRY BUSH. Deciduous. Zones A1–A3; 1–11, 14–20. Native to Canada, northern U.S. To 15 ft. tall, 12 ft. wide. Leaves look much like those of *V. opulus;* they emerge reddish tinged, mature to dark green, turn yellow to red-purple in fall. Lacecap flowers appear in midspring. Fruit is similar to that of *V. opulus* but is used for preserves and jellies. Less susceptible to aphid damage than *V. opulus.* 'Wentworth' has larger berries and bright red fall foliage. 'Compactum' is a smaller form, reaching only 6 ft. high and wide.

VICK'S PLANT. See **PLECTRANTHUS cylindraceus**

VICTORIAN BOX. See **PITTOSPORUM undulatum**

VIGNA caracalla (Phaseolus caracalla)
SNAIL VINE
Fabaceae (Leguminosae)
PERENNIAL VINE SOMETIMES GROWN AS ANNUAL

🌿 ZONES 12–24; H1, H2; ELSEWHERE AS ANNUAL
☀️ FULL SUN
💧 REGULAR WATER

Tropical American native that generally resembles pole bean in form and foliage. The flowers are different, though: fragrant, cream to pale purple spring and summer blossoms have lilac or purple markings, twisted keel petals that are coiled like a snail shell—odd and pretty. Twines rapidly to 10–20 ft.; good summer screen or bank cover. Evergreen in frostless areas; in colder regions, cut plant to the ground if frost kills top. Sometimes sold as *Phaseolus gigantea.*

Vigna caracalla

VIGUIERA
GOLDENEYE
Asteraceae (Compositae)
SHRUBBY PERENNIALS

🌿 ZONES VARY BY SPECIES
☀️ FULL SUN
💧 LITTLE WATER

Desert plants with yellow daisies that are borne singly or in loose clusters at stem ends. Cut plants back after bloom or before new growth begins to encourage bushiness and good looks. Useful in restoring native vegetation and in stabilizing soil.

V. deltoidea (V. parishii). Zones 10–24. Native to California, Arizona, Nevada, Mexico. Freely branching, sprawling plant to 3 ft. high and wide (possibly larger), with triangular, toothed, densely hairy, green to gray-green leaves ½–2 in. long. Spring flowers are 1–1½ in. wide.

Viguiera multiflora

V. multiflora. Zones 2, 3, 10–13. Native from Montana to California, Arizona. To 1–3 ft. tall, 1½ ft. wide, with hairy, lance-shaped green leaves 1–2 in. long. Spring or summer flowers to 2 in. wide; blooms first year from seed.

VINCA
PERIWINKLE
Apocynaceae
PERENNIALS

🌿 ZONES VARY BY SPECIES
☀️ 🌤️ ● FULL SUN IN COOLER CLIMATES ONLY
💧 🌢 LITTLE TO MODERATE WATER

Trailing, arching stems that root where they touch soil make these plants useful as ground and bank covers. Shiny dark green, oval to oblong leaves. Lavender-blue, five-petaled, pinwheel-shaped flowers appear in leaf joints in early spring. Plant the larger species and its

Vinca minor

varieties 2–2½ ft. apart, dwarf kinds 1½ ft. apart. When plantings mound up or are layered with old stems, shear or mow before new spring growth begins. Will grow in almost any soil. Compete successfully with surface tree roots.

V. major. Zones 5–24. The larger, more aggressive species. Leaves to 3 in. long, flowers to 2 in. across; mounds to 1–2 ft. high. Spreads rapidly; can be extremely invasive in sheltered, forested areas. 'Variegata', probably as common as the green form, has leaves strongly edged in white.

V. minor. DWARF PERIWINKLE. Zones 1–24. Miniature version of *V. major,* with ¾–1¾-in.-long leaves, flowers to 1 in. wide, and a height of just 4–6 in. More restrained, less likely to invade adjacent plantings. Varieties include 'Alba', with white flowers; 'Atropurpurea', deep purple flowers, small leaves; 'Bowles' Variety' ('La Grave'), deeper blue flowers, larger leaves; 'Green Carpet', with dense foliage and few flowers; 'Gertrude Jekyll' ('Miss Jekyll'), smaller grower with white flowers; 'Ralph Shugert', white-edged leaves, blue flowers, repeat autumn bloom; and 'Sterling Silver', blue flowers, white-edged leaves speckled with pale green.

V. rosea. See Catharanthus roseus

VINE MAPLE. See **ACER circinatum**

VIOLA
VIOLA, VIOLET, PANSY
Violaceae
ANNUALS AND PERENNIALS, SOME TREATED AS ANNUALS

🌿 ZONES VARY BY SPECIES
☀️ 🌤️ ● EXPOSURE NEEDS VARY BY SPECIES
💧 REGULAR WATER

Botanically speaking, violas, pansies, and almost all violets are perennials belonging to the genus *Viola.* However, violas and pansies are usually treated as annuals, invaluable for winter and spring bloom in mild-winter areas, for spring-through-summer color in colder climates. Typically used for mass color in borders and edgings, as covers for spring-flowering bulbs, in containers. Violets are more often used as woodland or rock garden plants. Violas and pansies take sun or partial shade; violets grow in part or full shade (except as noted), but most are natives of deciduous forests and bloom best with at least some sun during the flowering season.

Almost all violets have two kinds of flowers: normal, conspicuous ones that rise above the foliage and may be pollinated and set seed, and short-stemmed, inconspicuous cleistogamous (Greek for "closed spouse") flowers that set copious seed without pollination and produce offspring identical to the parent. Many violets also spread by aboveground runners. Some reproduce so freely they can crowd out other small plants.

In cold-winter climates, set out nursery plants of pansies and violas in spring for summer bloom; in mild climates, plant in autumn for winter-to-spring (or longer) bloom. Or start from seed: in cold climates, sow in mid- to late summer and overwinter seedlings in cold frame until spring; or sow indoors in winter, plant in spring. In mild-winter areas, sow in mid- to late summer, plant out in fall. To prolong bloom, pick flowers (with some foliage) regularly and remove faded blooms before they set seed. In hot areas, plants get ragged by midsummer and should be removed.

Violas and pansies have such complex ancestries that many botanists are unwilling to assign them to species, preferring to list them by variety name. However, we believe it will avoid confusion if we retain these plants under their former names, invalid though they now may be.

V. adunca. CALIFORNIA SWEET VIOLET, WESTERN DOG VIOLET. Zones 1–9, 14–24. Native to coastal bluffs and Sierra foothills in central California, Pacific Northwest east to New England. To 3–6 in. high, spreading indefinitely by stolons and seeds. Dark green, heart-shaped leaves to 3 in. long. Half-inch or larger flowers in lavender blue with white petal bases and conspicuous bright orange stigmas. Extremely fragrant. Blooms in spring in cold climates, fall to spring in mild-winter areas. Best with at least half-day winter sun, summer shade. Takes various soils and exposures, tolerates some drought. Can be invasive. Often sold as *V. odorata.*

V. blanda. SWEET WHITE VIOLET. Zones 1–10, 14–24. From eastern North America. To 2–3 in. high, spreading indefinitely by runners. Fragrant white flowers with purple veining have sharply reflexed petals. Likes moist soil with lots of organic material.

V. cornuta. VIOLA, TUFTED PANSY. All zones as annuals; Zones 1–10, 14–24 for kinds grown as perennials. To 6–8 in. high and 8 in. wide, with smooth, wavy-edged leaves. Purple, pansy-like, slender-spurred flowers about 1½ in. across. Modern strains and varieties are complex hybrids with larger, shorter-spurred flowers; they come in solid colors (purple, blue, yellow, apricot, ruby red, white) or with elaborate markings ("faces"). Plants in the frost-tolerant Penny series grow 4–6 in. tall and wide, with spring and fall flowers in bold colors. Sorbet strain comes in pastel bicolors; tolerates heat and cold.

Some nurseries offer English violas—named varieties propagated by cuttings or division. These form 2-ft.-wide clumps and are reliably perennial. Varieties include 'Better Times', 2-in. yellow flowers; 'Columbine', creamy white liberally splashed with purple; 'Etain', pale yellow with purple border;

'Mt. Spokane', white with a shading of palest blue; and 'Whiskers', cream marked with thin purple lines.

V. corsica. CORSICAN VIOLET. Zones 2b–10, 14–24. From Corsica and Sardinia. Mounding perennial to 6–10 in. tall and wide, with trailing foliage and many flat, violet-blue flowers marked in deep purple and white. Blooms spring into fall; tolerates extreme temperatures. Plant in well-drained (or gravelly) soil amended with plenty of organic matter. Nice addition to the rock garden. Reseeds a bit. Full sun to partial shade.

V. cucullata (V. obliqua). MARSH BLUE VIOLET. Zones 1–9, 14–24. From eastern and central North America. To 6 in. high, 10 in. wide. Toothed, heart-shaped leaves to 4 in. across. Blue, ¾-in.-wide flowers are held well above the leaves in early spring. Good ground cover; no runners, but self-sows liberally and can become a pest. The violet often sold as 'White Czar'—white, with yellow throat veined in black— is a selection of this species; the name, however, correctly belongs to an old variety of *V. odorata.*

V. grypoceras exilis (V. koreana). Zones 1–10, 14–24. From Japan. Unlike most other violets, an annual, but will maintain itself by self-sowing once established. To 2 in. high, 6–8 in. wide. Deep green, 1–1½-in.-long leaves have heavy silver gray veining, maroon red undersides. Small light purple flowers in spring, with a scattering of summer bloom. Attractive small-scale ground cover for shady, moist places. Sometimes sold as *V. koreana* 'Syletta'.

V. hederacea. AUSTRALIAN VIOLET. Zones 7–9, 14–24. From Australia. To 1–4 in. high; eventually covers several feet, spreading by runners at slow to moderate rate. Kidney-shaped leaves to 1½ in. long. Nearly spurless, ¼–¾-in. flowers—broader than high and rather flat—in summer. They come in violet, blue, or white; commonly seen form is white with heavy blue-violet veining in throat. 'Baby Blue' has pure sky blue flowers. Plants go dormant at about 30°F/–1°C. Use as ground cover in light shade or (with abundant water) in sun.

V. koreana. See *V. grypoceras exilis*

V. labradorica. Zones A3; 1–6. From northeastern U.S., Canada, Greenland. An infrequently cultivated deciduous species with tiny

Viola odorata

(¾-in.-long), purple-tinged leaves and pale purple flowers in summer. Most plants sold under this name are *V. riviniana* 'Purpurea'.

V. obliqua. See *V. cucullata*

V. odorata. SWEET VIOLET. Zones 1–24. The violet of song and story. To 8 in. high, 1½ ft. wide. In cool, mild climates, can spread widely by seeds and runners, possibly becoming a pest. Dark green, heart-shaped, 2½-in.-long leaves with toothed margins. Fragrant, short-spurred flowers ¾ in. or wider in deep violet, bluish rose, or white. Selections include 'Rosina' (pink), 'Royal Elk' (violet), and 'Royal Robe' (deep violet). Clump-forming 'Charm' has small white flowers. Tolerates full sun in cool-summer areas. For better spring display, remove runners and shear rank growth in late fall, then apply complete fertilizer in earliest spring.

V. Parma violets. Zones 4–9, 14–24. Hybrids of uncertain parentage with small, usually double, intensely fragrant flowers. They resemble *V. odorata* in form and growth habit, but are far less vigorous and less inclined to spread; they advance slowly by runners. Give them rich soil, cool location. 'Duchesse de Parme' (lavender), 'Marie Louise' (deep violet), and 'Swanley White' are sometimes available. Beyond hardiness range, grow in pots and winter in a cool greenhouse or indoor room.

V. pedata. BIRD'S-FOOT VIOLET. Zones 1–7. From eastern North America. So named because its finely divided leaves resemble a bird's foot. Forms a clump to 2 in. high, 4 in. wide; does not spread by runners. Blooms from early spring to early summer; 4-in. stems bear inch-wide, typically two-tone violet-blue flowers with darker veining. Not as easy to grow as other violets; likes excellent drainage, filtered sun or high shade, and acidic soil.

V. riviniana. Zones 1–24. From southern Europe, North Africa.

Viola × wittrockiana

V

Tiny violet to 3 in. high or less, spreading (sometimes aggressively) by runners and seed. Heart- or kidney-shaped, 1-in. leaves; tiny lavender-blue flowers in spring (fall through late spring in mild-winter areas). Useful for small-scale ground cover in partial shade or morning sun (away from choice small perennials) or as filler between stepping-stones or paving blocks. Most often seen is 'Purpurea', with leaves that emerge deep maroon and eventually mature to dusky green. Succeeds with moderate water if shaded from summer heat.

V. sororia. DOORYARD VIOLET. Zones 1–11, 14–24. From eastern and central North America. To 4–6 in. high, 8 in. wide; does not spread by runners but self-sows freely. Leaves are somewhat heart shaped, to 5 in. wide, vary from densely hairy to almost smooth. Good ground cover under woodland shrubs. Nearly scentless, ½–¾-in. flowers in spring to early summer are held close to leaves; colors range from red-violet to blue-violet to white. Most commonly seen are the following smooth-leafed varieties (all come true from seed): 'Albiflora', pure white with yellow in throat; 'Freckles', white liberally spotted with blue; 'Priceana' (popularly known as Confederate violet), white with blue-violet veining in throat.

V. tricolor. JOHNNY-JUMP-UP. All zones. From Europe, Asia. Spring bloomer to 6–12 tall and broad; spreads widely by profuse self-sowing. Oval, deeply lobed leaves to 1¼ in. long. Pert, ½–¾-in., velvety purple-and-yellow or blue-and-yellow flowers are the original wild pansies. Same planting and care as pansy. Crosses with closely related small-flowered species have produced forms with flowers in violet, blue, white, yellow, lavender, mauve, apricot, orange, red—with or without markings ("faces"). Flowers of 'Molly Sanderson' are very dark purple—almost black.

V. × wittrockiana. PANSY. All zones. Erect and bushy to 6–10 in. high and 9–12 in. wide. Many strains with 2–4-in. flowers in white, blue, mahogany red, rose, yellow, apricot, purple; also bicolors and multicolor blends. Most have dark blotches on the lower three petals; such flowers are often said to resemble faces. Shiny green leaves are oval to nearly heart shaped, slightly lobed, 1½ in. or longer.

Strains are almost too numerous to mention; here are just a few. Clear Sky, Crystal Bowl (Clear Crystal), and Delta strains bear flowers without blotches or other markings. Contessa has ruffled, 2-in. blooms. Flowers of Ghost Mix are 2½ in. wide, carried on long stems good for cutting. Imperial Hybrids and Majestic Giants offer extra-large (to 4-in.-wide) flowers. Unlike the others, Sprite Mix is a ground cover pansy—4–5 in. high, 1½ ft. wide, with 2-in. blossoms.

A few named selections deserve mention. Flowers of 'Jolly Joker' show striking contrast between bright orange lower petals and deep purple upper petals; 'Padparadja' has flowers of pure reddish orange; 'Springtime Black' has 2-in., velvety black blooms. Unusual colors are featured in the Ultima series, which includes 'Ultima Baron Red' (deep scarlet and golden), 'Ultima Beacon Bronze', (orange fading to bronze), and 'Ultima Morpho' (pastel blue and yellow, the same color combination found on the rare and beautiful Morpho butterfly from Costa Rica).

VIOLET.
See **VIOLA**

VIOLET TRUMPET VINE.
See **CLYTOSTOMA callistegioides**

VIRGINIA BLUEBELLS.
See **MERTENSIA pulmonarioides**

VIRGINIA CREEPER.
See **PARTHENOCISSUS inserta, P. quinquefolia**

VIRGINIAN STOCK.
See **MALCOLMIA maritima**

VISCARIA.
See **SILENE coeli-rosa**

VITEX
CHASTE TREE
Verbeneaceae
DECIDUOUS AND EVERGREEN SHRUBS OR TREES

🌿	ZONES VARY BY SPECIES
☀	FULL SUN
💧💧	MODERATE TO REGULAR WATER

One is a shrub or tree and the other a shrubby ground cover, but both have handsome foliage and clustered flowers. Prefer well-drained soil.

V. agnus-castus. CHASTE TREE. Deciduous shrub or small

Vitex agnus-castus

tree. Zones 4–24; H1, H2. Native from Mediterranean region to central Asia. In warmest part of range, grows fast to make a tree to 25 ft. tall and wide, typically with multiple trunks; train high to make a good small shade tree. In colder areas, growth is slower and ultimate size is smaller—to 8–10 ft. high and wide. Where it usually freezes to the ground in winter, it is a shrubby perennial about 3–5 ft. high and wide.

Aromatic leaves are divided fanwise into five to seven narrow, 2–6-in.-long leaflets, grayish green above, gray beneath. No real fall color. Blooms summer to fall; small, fragrant lavender-blue flowers held in 6–12-in. spikes at branch ends and in leaf joints. Varieties include 'Alba' and 'Silver Spire', with white flowers; 'Latifolia' (sometimes sold as *V. macrophylla*), a sturdy plant with large leaflets; and 'Rosea', with pink flowers.

Thrives in heat, resists oak root fungus. Good in shrub border. Cut plants treated as perennials to 1 ft. high in spring; they will bloom on new growth.

V. rotundifolia. BEACH VITEX, POHINAHINA. Evergreen shrub. Zones 13–24; H1, H2. Native to coastal areas of Hawaii, Australia, Asia. Sprawls to 1½–4 ft. high, 6–8 ft. wide; roots as it spreads to make a dense ground cover. Aromatic, medium green, broadly oblong to roundish leaves to 2½ in. long. Short spikes of bluish purple, ½-in. flowers (popular in leis) appear all year in warmest areas, in summer in colder part of range. Tiny bluish black fruits. Thrives at seacoast or inland.

VITIS
GRAPE
Vitaceae
DECIDUOUS VINES

🌿	ZONES VARY BY SPECIES
☀ ◐	FULL SUN OR PARTIAL SHADE
◌💧💧	WATER NEEDS VARY BY SPECIES

For grapes grown for edible fruit, see Grape. Those plants are handsome in leaf and fruit, but the following species produce relatively tiny fruit and are grown instead for good looks. All climb by tendrils and have large, roundish, slightly lobed leaves that turn attractive colors in autumn. Prune as needed before spring growth begins.

Vitis coignetiae

V. californica. CALIFORNIA WILD GRAPE. Zones 4–24. From California, Oregon. To 30 ft., with 2–4-in. leaves that emerge grayish, mature to green, and turn red or yellow in autumn. 'Roger's Red' holds its gray-green leaf color all summer, turns brilliant red in fall. 'Walker Ridge', to 6–10 ft., has brilliant red and orange fall color. *V. girdiana* is a nearly identical species native to Southern California.

Plants grow naturally along rivers and streams, but are well adapted to periods of drought. A variety of wild animals use this plant for food and cover; bees favor the flowers.

V. coignetiae. CRIMSON GLORY VINE. Zones 3–10, 14–21. From Japan, Korea. Vigorous vine to 50 ft. tall, with foot-wide deep green leaves that turn brilliant red in fall. Provide moderate to regular water.

V. vinifera 'Purpurea'. Zones 4–9, 14–23. To 20 ft. or more. Leaves to 6 in. across emerge downy green, mature to deep purple, turn deeper purple in fall. Moderate to regular water.

W

WAKE ROBIN. See **TRILLIUM**

WALKING IRIS.
See **NEOMARICA gracilis**

WALLFLOWER. See **ERYSIMUM**

WALNUT
Juglandaceae
DECIDUOUS TREE

🌿	ZONES 4–9, 14–23; SOME VARIETIES IN ZONES 1–3
☼	FULL SUN
💧	REGULAR WATER

For walnut species grown mainly as landscape trees producing bonus crops of nuts, see *Juglans.* The species described here, English walnut (*J. regia*), is a widely grown orchard plant native to southeast Europe, southwest Asia; its nuts are the familiar ones sold commercially.

Species is hardy to –5°F/–21°C, but certain varieties are injured by late and early frosts. Reaches 60 ft. high and wide; grows fast, especially when young. Trunk and heavy, horizontal or upward-angled branches have smooth gray bark; leaves have five to seven (rarely more) 3–6-in.-long leaflets. Walnut husks open in fall, dropping nuts to ground; to hasten drop, knock nuts from tree. Gather fallen nuts immediately, remove any adhering husks, and dry in single layer in airy shade until kernels are brittle (crack a nut open to test); then store.

Plant English walnut as a landscape tree only on large lots. It's

Walnut

out of leaf a long time, messy in leaf (honeydew drip and sooty mold due to aphid infestations), and messy in fruit (husks can stain). Many people are allergic to the wind-borne pollen. Grow in deep soil. Established plants survive with no supplemental moisture but need deep watering for top-quality nuts. Keep other plants beyond drip line, where feeder roots grow. Train young trees to a central leader; mature ones need pruning only to remove dead wood or correct shape. In addition to aphids, pests include scale, codling moths, spider mites. Walnut husk fly attacks husks, causing them to turn black and adhere to shell. Husks are difficult to remove and shell is stained, but nutmeats are not damaged.

In Zones 1–3, grow walnuts described as Carpathian or Hardy Persian. Varieties include 'Ambassador', 'Cascade', 'Chopaka', 'Hansen', 'Russian', and 'Somers'; these range in hardiness from –25°F/–32°C to –35°F/ –37°C. Here are best choices for other zones. In Zones 4–7, 'Chambers', 'Cooke's Giant Sweet', 'Franquette', and 'Spurgeon' bloom late enough to escape spring frosts, yield high-quality nuts. In Zones 8, 9, grow 'Carmelo', 'Chandler', 'Cooke's Giant Sweet', 'Hartley', 'Idaho', 'Payne', 'Pedro', or 'Serr'. In Zones 14–16 and warm parts of 17, try 'Carmelo', 'Chandler', 'Cooke's Giant Sweet', 'Franquette', 'Hartley', 'Payne', 'Pedro', and 'Serr'. In Zones 18–20, grow 'Payne', 'Pedro', or 'Placentia'. In Zones 21–23, best choices are 'Pedro' and 'Placentia'.

WANDERING JEW.
See **TRADESCANTIA**

WASHINGTONIA
Arecaceae (Palmae)
PALMS

🌿	ZONES 8, 9, 10 (WARMER PARTS), 11–24; H1, H2
☼	FULL SUN
💧	LITTLE TO REGULAR WATER

These fast-growing fan palms are too tall for most suburban gardens; they are best suited to large properties, avenues, parkways. The two species often hybridize if growing near each other.

W. filifera. CALIFORNIA FAN PALM. From California, Arizona. Hardy to 18°F/–8°C. To 60 ft. tall, 20 ft. wide, with thicker trunk than *W. robusta.* Long-stalked, 3–6-ft., light green leaves stand well apart

Washingtonia filifera

in open crown. As leaves mature, they bend down to form a "skirt" of thatch. In native stands in desert, this species always grows near springs or other moist spots.

W. robusta. MEXICAN FAN PALM. From Mexico. Hardy to 20°F/–7°C. To 100 ft. tall, 10 ft. wide; trunk is slightly curved or bent, slimmer than that of *W. filifera.* Head of bright green foliage is more compact; leafstalks are shorter, with a red streak on the undersides.

WASHINGTON THORN.
See **CRATAEGUS phaenopyrum**

WATCH CHAIN.
See **CRASSULA lycopodioides**

WATER BETONY or **FIGWORT.**
See **SCROPHULARIA auriculata** **'Variegata'**

WATER GUM.
See **TRISTANIOPSIS laurina**

WATER HAWTHORN.
See **APONOGETON distachyus**

WATER HYACINTH.
See **EICHHORNIA crassipes**

WATER HYSSOP.
See **BACOPA monnieri**

WATER LETTUCE.
See **PISTIA stratiotes**

WATER LILY. See **NYMPHAEA**

WATERMELON
Cucurbitaceae
ANNUAL

🌿	ZONES 1–24; H1, H2
☼	FULL SUN
💧	REGULAR WATER

From southern Africa. Needs a long growing season, more heat than most other melons, and more

space than other vine crops— about 8 ft. by 8 ft. for each hill (circle of seed). Other than that, culture is as described under Melon. If you garden where watermelons are grown commercially (Zones 8, 9, 12–14, 18–21), choose any variety you like. If your summers are short or cool (Zones 1–7, 10, 11, 15–17, 22–24), choose a fast-maturing ("early") variety (described in catalogs and on seed

Watermelon

packets as taking 70 to 75 days from seed to harvest). Also plant through clear plastic mulch and cover with floating row covers. In Hawaii, grow proven varieties such as 'Sugar Baby', 'Summer Festival', and 'Top Yield'. Watermelon does not become sweeter after harvest—it must be picked ripe. To check for ripeness, thump the melon (it should produce a hollow "thunk"); check to see that underside has turned from white to pale yellow; and make sure tendrils where melon attaches to stem have darkened and withered. Cut (do not pull) melon from vine.

Look for 'Sweet Beauty', a sweet, crisp 5–7-lb. melon with red flesh (80 days to maturity). 'Golden Crown' bears oval 6½-lb. fruits with yellow flesh (60 days). 'New Queen' produces 5–6-lb. fruits with bright orange-yellow flesh and few seeds (63 days).

WATSONIA
Iridaceae
PERENNIALS FROM CORMS

🌿	ZONES 4–9, 12–24; OR DIG AND STORE DECIDUOUS TYPE
☼	FULL SUN
💧	REGULAR WATER DURING GROWTH AND BLOOM

Native to South Africa. Somewhat similar to gladiolus, but there are differences. Watsonia's sword-shaped, 2½-ft.-long leaves are less rigid, and it has taller, slimmer flower spikes set with smaller, more trumpetlike, fragrant blossoms. Tolerates many soils but prefers good drainage. Plant in early fall, setting corms 4 in. deep, 6 in. apart. Where hardy, corms can be left undisturbed for many years. In colder areas, you can grow *W. borbonica* as you would gladiolus: plant in spring for late spring and early summer bloom, then dig and store after foliage dies down. Because *W. pillansii* is evergreen, it cannot be dug and stored.

Watsonia borbonica

W. borbonica (W. pyramidata). Deciduous. Blooms in late spring, bearing 2½-in. flowers in pink, rosy red, or white on 4–6-ft. stems. Hybrid forms have pink, red, or lavender blooms. Foliage dies back after bloom, reappearing in fall. Does not need regular moisture during summer dormancy but accepts it if soil is well drained.

W. pillansii (W. beatricis). Evergreen. Blooms in midsummer, with slightly branched, 3½-ft. stems bearing 3-in., bright reddish apricot flowers. Hybrids come in colors ranging from peach to nearly red. This species can take less moisture in summer after bloom is over.

WATTLE. See ACACIA

WAUKE.
See BROUSSONETIA papyrifera

WAX FIG.
See FICUS microcarpa crassifolia

WAX FLOWER, WAX PLANT.
See HOYA

WAXFLOWER, GERALDTON. See CHAMELAUCIUM uncinatum

WAX VINE.
See SENECIO macroglossus

WAYFARING TREE.
See VIBURNUM lantana

WEDELIA trilobata
Asteraceae (Compositae)
PERENNIAL

- ✏️ ZONES 12, 13, 21–24; H1, H2
- ☀️ ◑ FULL SUN OR LIGHT SHADE
- 💧 REGULAR WATER

From Central and South America. Trailing evergreen plant to 1½–2 ft. high, spreading to 6 ft. or more by stems that root where they touch damp earth. Fleshy, dark glossy green leaves to 4 in. long, half as wide, with a few coarse teeth or shallow lobes toward tips. Inchwide flowers resembling tiny yellow zinnias or marigolds (*Tagetes*) bloom almost year-round. Spreads fast; easily propagated by lifting rooted pieces or placing tip cuttings in moist soil. Best in sandy, fast-draining soils but takes heavier soils if drainage is good. If killed to ground by frost, it makes a fast comeback. Tolerates desert heat, seaside conditions. Can take lower light but blooms more sparsely in shady conditions. Good for erosion control on slopes: plant 1½ ft. apart, feed lightly. Shear close to ground if planting mounds up or becomes stemmy.

Wedelia trilobata

WEEPING MYALL.
See ACACIA pendula

WEIGELA
Caprifoliaceae
DECIDUOUS SHRUBS

- ✏️ ZONES 1–11, 14–21
- ☀️ ◑ FULL SUN OR LIGHT SHADE
- 💧 REGULAR WATER

From China, Korea, Japan. Weigelas are valued for lavish springtime display of funnel-shaped, 1-in.-long flowers. They aren't attractive out of bloom, have no real fall color. Most are rather coarse leafed and stiff, becoming rangy unless pruned. After flowering, cut back stems that have bloomed to side

shoots that have not flowered; leave only one or two of these to each stem. Cut some of the oldest stems to ground. Thin new suckers to a few of the most vigorous. Another method is to cut back entire plant about halfway just after blooms fade; do this every other year. Resulting dense new growth will provide plenty of flowers the next spring. Use as background plants for flower borders, as summer screens, in mixed borders.

W. coraeensis. WHITE WEIGELA. To 12–15 ft. tall and wide, with leaves to 6 in. long. Flowers are 1½ in. long, white or light pink aging to red.

Weigela florida

W. florida (W. rosea). Fast growth to 6–10 ft. tall, 9–12 ft. wide, with branches often arching to the ground. Leaves 2–4½ in. long. Pink to rose red flowers. The following selections grow about 6 ft. high and wide: 'Bristol Snowflake', white flowers opening from pinkish buds; 'Java Red', red-tinted foliage, red buds opening to deep pink flowers; 'Pink Princess', lilac-pink flowers. 'Wine and Roses' ('Alexandra') reaches 5 ft. tall and wide, with deep purple new leaves that contrast nicely with its bright pink flowers; foliage matures to purplish green, turns blackish purple in autumn. 'Pink Poppet' grows slowly to 2 ft. tall and wide, with bright green leaves; its light pink flowers appear in spring and again in late summer. 'Midnight Wine' ('Elvera') reaches just 1½–2 ft. tall and wide, with metallic burgundy foliage and deep pink flowers.

W. hybrids. These are hybrids between *W. florida*, *W. praecox*, and other species.

'Briant Rubidor' ('Rubidor', 'Olympiade'). A sport of 'Bristol Ruby' with yellow foliage. To 6 ft. high and wide.

'Bristol Ruby'. To 6–7 ft. tall and nearly as wide, with ruby red

flowers. Some repeat bloom in midsummer and fall.

'Candida' ('Alba'). To 5 ft. tall and wide, with white flowers that are tinged with green.

'Carnaval'. To 4–5 ft. tall and wide, with 1½-in.-wide, blush pink to vivid pink flowers that appear a little later in spring than others listed here; reblooms in early fall. A hummingbird favorite.

'Dark Horse'. Compact growth to 3 ft. tall and wide. Bronzy purple leaves with lime-colored veins and bright magenta pink flowers make for a striking contrast. Good for low hedge or midborder shrub.

'Minuet'. Dwarf variety to 3 ft. tall, 5 ft. wide. Purplish leaves. Flowers blend red, purple, and yellow.

'Newport Red' ('Cardinal', 'Rhode Island Red', 'Vanicek'). To 6 ft. tall and wide, with bright red flowers. Young stems are bright green in winter.

'Red Prince'. To 5–6 ft. tall and wide, with red flowers, some summer rebloom.

'Variegata'. Compact growth to 4–6 ft. tall and wide, with deep rosy red flowers and creamy yellow to white leaf edges. 'Variegata Nana' is 3 ft. tall and wide.

WELSH POPPY.
See MECONOPSIS cambrica

WESTERN HOUND'S TONGUE.
See CYNOGLOSSUM grande

WESTERN RED CEDAR.
See THUJA plicata

WESTERN SAND CHERRY.
See PRUNUS besseyi

WESTRINGIA fruticosa
COAST ROSEMARY
Lamiaceae (Labiatae)
EVERGREEN SHRUB

- ✏️ ZONES 8, 9, 14–24
- ☀️ FULL SUN
- 💧◐ LITTLE TO MODERATE WATER

From Australia. Spreading, rather loose growth to 3–6 ft. tall, 5–10 ft. wide. Medium green to gray-green leaves have white undersides, are slightly finer and filmier in texture than rosemary leaves. Small white flowers bloom from midwinter through spring in colder areas, all year in milder climates. Needs light, well-drained soil. Good near coast; wind tolerant. Often sold as *W. rosmariniformis*. 'Wynyabbie Gem' has light lavender flowers.

Westringia fruticosa

'Morning Light' grows 3 ft. tall and wide, has white flowers and white-edged leaves.

WHEATGRASS.
See **AGROPYRON**

WHEEL TREE. See **TROCHODENDRON aralioides**

WHITEBEAM. See **SORBUS aria**

WHITE CEDAR.
See **CHAMAECYPARIS thyoides**

WHITE SAPOTE
Rutaceae
EVERGREEN OR DECIDUOUS TREE

🌿 ZONES 8, 9, 14–16, 18–24; H1, H2
☀ FULL SUN
💧 REGULAR WATER

Beautiful tropical tree, botanically known as *Casimiroa edulis*. Native to Mexico; withstands more cold than most avocados, does well wherever lemons are grown. To 25–50 ft. tall, 25–30 ft. wide, with luxuriant glossy green leaves divided fanwise into three to seven oval, 3–5-in.-long leaflets. To keep tree lower and create a wide, umbrellalike crown, pinch out terminal bud. Roots are invasive; choose planting location carefully.

Heavy crop of round, 3–4-in. fruit with pale green to yellow skin and white or creamy yellow flesh with custardlike consistency and tropical flavor. Fruit tastes best when allowed to ripen on tree, but

White sapote

it usually drops before reaching ripeness. Pick it when firm-ripe, at which point the flavor is mellow and sweet. (Some varieties become sweeter if left to stand at room temperature; others turn bitter.) To harvest, cut from tree, leaving a small piece of stem attached; pick carefully to avoid bruising. Eat with a spoon. California varieties include 'Bravo!', 'Lemon Gold', 'Louise', 'McDill', 'Suebelle', and 'Vernon'. 'Denzler' is grown in Hawaii.

Needs consistent feeding. Mature tree may produce several hundred pounds of fruit, far more than any one family can use. Cleanup becomes a chore, so plant where dropping fruit can be raked up or disappear into a ground cover. May become partially deciduous in frosty or very hot weather.

WHITE SNAKEROOT.
See **EUPATORIUM rugosum**

WHITE THORN.
See **ACACIA constricta**

WILD FOXGLOVE.
See **PENSTEMON cobaea**

WILD GINGER. See **ASARUM**

WILD INDIGO. See **BAPTISIA**

WILD LILAC. See **CEANOTHUS**

WILD RYE. See **LEYMUS**

WILD SNAPDRAGON.
See **PENSTEMON cobaea,
P. grandiflorus**

WILGA.
See **GEIJERA parviflora**

WILIWILI. See **ERYTHRINA sandwicensis**

WILLOW. See **SALIX**

WILLOW-LEAFED PEPPERMINT.
See **EUCALYPTUS nicholii**

WINDFLOWER. See **ANEMONE**

WINDMILL PALM.
See **TRACHYCARPUS fortunei**

WINE CUPS.
See **CALLIRHOE involucrata**

WINTER ACONITE.
See **ERANTHIS hyemalis**

WINTERBERRY.
See **ILEX verticillata**

WINTER CREEPER.
See **EUONYMUS fortunei**

WINTER FAT.
See **CERATOIDES lanata**

WINTERGREEN.
See **GAULTHERIA procumbens**

WINTER HAZEL.
See **CORYLOPSIS**

WINTER'S BARK.
See **DRIMYS winteri**

WINTERSWEET.
See **CHIMONANTHUS praecox**

WIRE VINE.
See **MUEHLENBECKIA**

WISHBONE FLOWER.
See **TORENIA fournieri**

WISTERIA
Fabaceae (Leguminosae)
DECIDUOUS VINES

🌿 ZONES VARY BY SPECIES
☀ FULL SUN, EXCEPT AS NOTED
💧 LITTLE TO MODERATE WATER

Twining, woody vines of great size, long life, and exceptional beauty in flower. Very adaptable; can be grown as trees, shrubs, or vines. All have large, fresh green leaves divided into many leaflets, spectacular clusters of blue, white, or pinkish springtime blossoms, and velvety, pealike pods to 6 in. long. Subdued fall color in shades of yellow. To get off to a good start, buy a cutting-grown or grafted wisteria; seedlings may not bloom for many years. If you start with grafted plants, keep suckers removed or they may take over. Wisteria is not fussy about soil, but it does need good drainage. In alkaline soil, watch for chlorosis.

Pruning and training are important to control size and shape and encourage bloom production. Let newly planted wisteria grow to establish the framework you want, with either single or multiple trunks. Remove stems that interfere with framework; pinch back side stems and long streamers. For single-trunked specimens, rub off buds that develop on trunk; for multiple trunks, select as many vigorous stems as you wish and let them develop. If the plant has only one stem, pinch it back to encourage others to develop. Remember that main stem will become good-size trunk, and that weight of mature vine is considerable.

Tree wisterias can be bought already trained; or you can train your own. Remove all but one main stem and stake this one securely. Tie stem to stake at frequent intervals, using plastic tape to prevent girdling. When plant has reached height at which you

wish head to form, pinch or prune out tip to force branching. Shorten branches to beef them up. Pinch back long streamers and rub off all buds that form below head. Replace stakes and ties as needed. Wisterias can be trained as big shrubs or multistemmed, small, semiweeping trees; permit well-spaced branches to form the framework, shorten side branches, and nip long streamers. Unsupported plants make a vigorous bank cover.

In general, wisterias do not need fertilizer. Prune blooming plants every winter; cut back or thin out side shoots from main or structural stems and shorten back to two or three buds the flower-producing spurs that grow from these shoots. You'll have no trouble recognizing fat flower buds on these spurs.

In summer, cut back long streamers before they tangle up in main body of vine; save those you want to use to extend height or length of vine and tie them to support—eaves, wall, trellis, arbor. If old plants grow rampantly but fail to bloom (and you have been fertilizing), withhold all nitrogen fertilizers for an entire growing season (buds for the next season's bloom are started in early summer). If that fails to produce bloom the next year, you can try pruning roots in spring—after you're sure no flowers will be produced—by cutting vertically with spade into plant's root zone.

W. brachybotrys (W. venusta). SILKY WISTERIA. Zones 3–24. Native to Japan. Silky-haired leaves, 8–14 in. long, are divided into 9–13 leaflets. Very large white, long-stalked, highly fragrant flowers in 4–6-in. clusters open all at once during leafout. Older plants, especially in tree form, have remarkably profuse bloom. 'Shiro Kapitan' ('Alba') is the most commonly sold; it bears white (sometimes double) flowers with yellow markings. 'Murasaki Kapitan' ('Violacea') bears blue-violet blossoms with white markings.

W. floribunda. JAPANESE WISTERIA. Zones 2–24. From Japan. Leaves are 12–16 in. long, divided into 15–19 leaflets. Fragrant, 1½-ft. clusters of violet or violet-blue flowers during leafout. Clusters open gradually, starting from the base; this prolongs bloom season but makes for a less spectacular display of color than that provided by *W. sinensis*. Many varieties in white, pink, and shades of blue, purple, and lavender, usually marked with yellow and white. 'Alba' ('Longissima Alba') bears white flowers in 2-ft.-long clusters; 'Issai Perfect' and 'Ivory Tower' are similar. 'Multijuga' ('Longissima', 'Macrobotrys') has long (1½–3 ft.) clusters of violet flowers. 'Rosea' is a good lavender-pink variety. 'Plena' has very full clusters of double, deep blue-violet flowers. 'Texas Purple' blooms at an early age.

Wisteria sinensis

W. sinensis. CHINESE WISTERIA. Zones 3–24. Native to China; the most common wisteria in the West. Leaves are 10–12 in. long, divided into 7–13 leaflets. Blooms before leafout. Clusters of violet-blue, slightly fragrant flowers are shorter (to 1 ft.) than those of *W. floribunda*—but they make quite a show, since flowers open all at once nearly all along the cluster. 'Alba' has white flowers. 'Caroline' and 'Cooke's Special' are grafted forms. 'Prolific' flowers at an early age. Plants will bloom in sun or considerable shade.

WITCH HAZEL.
See **HAMAMELIS**

WOADWAXEN.
See **GENISTA tinctoria**

WONGA-WONGA VINE.
See **PANDOREA pandorana**

WOODBINE.
See **LONICERA periclymenum, PARTHENOCISSUS inserta**

WOOD FERN. See **DRYOPTERIS**

WOOD HYACINTH.
See **HYACINTHOIDES**

WOOD ROSE. See **MERREMIA**

WOODRUFF, SWEET.
See **GALIUM odoratum**

WOODWARDIA
CHAIN FERN
Polypodiaceae
FERNS

🌿	ZONES VARY BY SPECIES
◐	PARTIAL TO FULL SHADE
💧💧	REGULAR TO AMPLE WATER

These are medium to large, mostly evergreen ferns with arching fronds and bold texture. Common name refers to the chainlike pattern of spores beneath frond segments. Excellent as focal points or grouped on banks or near water. All grow best in moist, organically enriched soil with a thick layer of mulch.

W. fimbriata. GIANT CHAIN FERN. Zones 2b–9, 14–24. Native from British Columbia to Mexico. This species is among the largest native Western ferns, topping out at 9 ft. in mild, wet coastal regions; in gardens, it typically reaches 4–5 ft. tall and 3 ft. wide. Thick, leathery, medium green fronds are upright but spreading toward the top. Foliage is twice cut but still somewhat coarse.

Use alongside a stream or brook, against a shaded wall, or in a woodland garden. Sometimes seen in desert areas where shady seeps exist. Slow to get going if dug from existing clumps; nursery plants are fast growing and vigorous, but not invasive. Withstands neglect once well established.

Woodwardia fimbriata

W. orientalis. ORIENTAL CHAIN FERN. Zones 5–9, 14–24. From Himalayas, China, Japan. Elegant and easy to grow. Lustrous green fronds are 3–5 ft. long and more drooping than those of *W. fimbriata*. New growth is an intense reddish orange. Tiny wedge-shaped plantlets appear on mature fronds, giving them a somewhat ruffled look. These can

root where they touch soil; to make more plants, remove plantlets and root in damp potting mix. Likes a bit more sun than other chain ferns listed here.

W. radicans. EUROPEAN CHAIN FERN. Zones 14–24; 5–9 with protection. Native to southern Europe. Resembles a larger version of *W. fimbriata*, reaching 6 ft. tall, 10 ft. wide; give it plenty of room. Cascading fronds produce inch-long bulbils at their tips that root when they touch the ground. Outstanding choice for a woodland bank, where a colony will slowly spread downhill.

WOOLFLOWER, CHINESE.
See **CELOSIA**

WOOLLY BLUE CURLS.
See **TRICHOSTEMA lanatum**

WOOLLYBUSH.
See **ADENANTHOS**

WORMWOOD. See **ARTEMISIA**

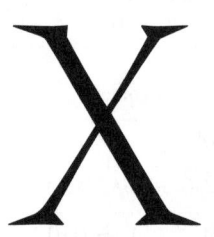

XANTHOCYPARIS nootkatensis.
See **CHAMAECYPARIS nootkatensis**

XANTHORRHOEA
GRASS TREE
Liliaceae
PERENNIALS

🌿	ZONES 12-24
☀	FULL SUN
○	LITTLE OR NO WATER

Native to Australia. Dense tufts of narrow, grasslike, 2–4-ft.-long leaves radiate from the top of a

Xanthorrhoea preissii

thick, woody, nearly black, slow-growing stem. Foliage mass stays at about 3–5 ft. tall, 3 ft. wide for many years, but as stem gradually lengthens, plant height eventually increases to 12–15 ft. Sometimes blooms; white flowers are borne in a dense, narrow spike on a tall stem that increases the plant's height further. *X. preissii* and *X. quadrangulata* are similar species. Best used with yuccas or with agaves or other succulents in dry, loose, sandy soil.

XANTHOSOMA
Araceae
PERENNIALS

🌿	ZONES 12, 13, 16, 17, 21–24; H1, H2; OR INDOORS
◑	FILTERED SUNLIGHT; BRIGHT INDIRECT LIGHT
💧	AMPLE WATER

Tropical plants related to *Alocasia*. Both species are stemless, grow to 6 ft. tall and wide, produce big, arrow-shaped leaves on long stalks. Flowers more curious than attractive; resemble those of calla (*Zantedeschia*), with a central spike surrounded by a usually greenish or yellowish bract. These plants need moist, rich soil for best performance. They can grow in standing water or in pots submerged in a pond or pool. Protect from hard frosts.

Xanthosoma sagittifolium

X. sagittifolium. Dark green, 3-ft.-long leaves on 3-ft. stalks. Greenish white, 7–9-in.-long bracts.

X. violaceum (**X. nigrum**). Grows from edible tubers. Dark green leaves to 2 ft. long have paler undersides, purplish veins and margins, powdery appearance. Purple, 2½-ft. leafstalks have a heavy, waxy, bluish or grayish coating. Yellowish white bracts to 1 ft. long.

XERANTHEMUM annuum

COMMON IMMORTELLE
Asteraceae (Compositae)
ANNUAL

- ALL ZONES
- FULL SUN
- REGULAR WATER

Mediterranean native to 2½ ft. high, 1½ ft. wide. Bears so-called everlasting flowers, with daisylike heads of papery bracts to 1½ in. across in pink, lavender, white, shades of purple. Scanty foliage is silvery green.

Xeranthemum annuum

Sow seeds directly in garden beds where plants are to grow; sow in spring for summer and fall bloom. Accepts almost any soil. Cut flowers are often dried for use in winter bouquets.

XEROCHRYSUM bracteatum.
See **BRACTEANTHA bracteata**

XEROPHYLLUM tenax

BEAR GRASS, INDIAN BASKET GRASS
Liliaceae
EVERGREEN PERENNIAL

- ZONES 1–7, 14–17
- FULL SUN OR LIGHT SHADE
- LITTLE TO MODERATE WATER

Native to open forests and meadows in the cool subalpine elevations of the western U.S. Tough, wiry, grasslike leaves grow from deep, fibrous roots to form clumps 2–3 ft. tall and wide; foliage is olive green. In early summer, a tall stalk rises from the center of each clump to produce a poker-shaped inflorescence packed with small, creamy white, star-shaped blooms. Remove entire stalks when flowers turn brown. Fibrous roots and leaves were used for traditional weaving in the Pacific Northwest.

Xerophyllum tenax

Needs well-drained soil that is not too rich; give occasional deep soakings in summer. Bear grass takes a few years to reach flowering stage and may not bloom reliably in the garden, but its attractive evergreen foliage is reason enough to grow it.

XYLOSMA congestum

Flacourtiaceae
EVERGREEN OR DECIDUOUS SHRUB OR TREE

- ZONES 8–24
- FULL SUN OR PARTIAL SHADE
- MODERATE WATER

From China. Basic landscape foliage plant. Loose, spreading growth to 8–10 ft. tall and as wide or wider. Shiny yellowish green leaves are ovate with pointed tips, 1½–3 in. long; new growth is bronzy. Flowers are insignificant and rarely seen. Some plants are spiny. Left alone, xylosma develops an angular main stem that takes its time zigzagging upward. Meanwhile, long, graceful side branches develop; these are arching or drooping, sometimes lying on the ground. Can be trained as single or multitrunked small tree, espaliered

Xylosma congestum

on wall or fence, used as clipped or unclipped hedge. 'Compacta' grows slowly to half the size of species.

Hardy to 10°F/–12°C but may lose many (or all) leaves in hard frosts. Normally sheds many old leaves when new spring growth begins; frost at that time will kill new growth. This is a useful and versatile plant, though its unattractive appearance in nursery cans (especially in winter, when stems may be nearly bare) and slow start in ground may discourage gardeners. Tolerates heat, most soils. Scale, spider mites are occasional pests. Chlorosis may be a problem.

Y

YARROW. See **ACHILLEA**

YAUPON. See **ILEX vomitoria**

YELLOW ARCHANGEL.
See **LAMIUM galeobdolon**

YELLOW BELLS, YELLOW ELDER. See **TECOMA stans**

YELLOW-EYED GRASS. See **SISYRINCHIUM californicum**

YELLOW FLAX. See **LINUM flavum, REINWARDTIA indica**

YELLOW FOXTAIL GRASS. See **ALOPECURUS pratensis 'Aureus'**

YELLOW MORNING GLORY.
See **MERREMIA**

YELLOW OLEANDER.
See **THEVETIA peruviana**

YELLOW SHOWER.
See **CASSIA fistula**

YELLOW TRUMPET FLOWER.
See **TECOMA stans**

YELLOW TRUMPET VINE.
See **MACFADYENA unguis-cati**

YELLOW WAXBELLS.
See **KIRENGESHOMA palmata**

YELLOW WOOD.
See **CLADRASTIS kentukea**

YELLOWWOOD.
See **PODOCARPUS henkelii, P. latifolius**

YERBA BUENA.
See **SATUREJA douglasii**

YESTERDAY-TODAY-AND-TOMORROW. See **BRUNFELSIA pauciflora 'Floribunda'**

YEW. See **TAXUS**

YEW PINE.
See **PODOCARPUS macrophyllus**

YUCCA

Agavaceae
EVERGREEN TREES, SHRUBS, AND PERENNIALS

- ZONES VARY BY SPECIES
- FULL SUN, EXCEPT AS NOTED
- LITTLE TO MODERATE WATER, EXCEPT AS NOTED

Yuccas grow over much of North America. All have tough, sword-shaped leaves and large clusters of typically white or whitish, rounded to bell-shaped flowers. Some are stemless clumps; others have trunks and reach tree size. Best in well-drained soil. Most need only occasional deep soakings. Group yuccas with cacti or with agaves or other succulents; or grow them with softer-leafed tropical foliage plants. Taller kinds have striking silhouettes, and even stemless species provide important vertical accents when in bloom. Keep those with stiff, sharp-pointed leaves away from walks, terraces, and other well-traveled areas. (Some people clip off the sharp tips with nail clippers.)

Young plants of some species can be used as indoor plants; they tolerate dry air and grow well in hot, sunny windows. For this use, buy plants at gallon-can size or smaller; transplant them outside when they become too large for the house. The following are successful indoors: *Y. aloifolia* (but beware of its sharp-pointed leaves), *Y. elephantipes, Y. filamentosa, Y. gloriosa, Y. recurvifolia.*

Y. aloifolia. SPANISH BAYONET. Zones 7–24; H1, H2. From southern

Yucca aloifolia

Y

U.S., Mexico. Slow to 10 ft. by 5 ft. or larger. Single or branching trunk; sometimes sprawls for picturesque effect. Stems densely clothed in sharp-pointed dark green leaves to 2½ ft. long, 2 in. wide. Foliage of 'Variegata' is marked with yellowish white. White (sometimes purple-tinged) flowers to 4 in. across are carried in dense, erect clusters to 2 ft. tall in late spring or summer.

Y. baccata. BANANA YUCCA, DATIL. Zones 1–3, 7, 9–14, 18–24. From southwestern U.S., Mexico. Slow to 3 ft. high, 5 ft. wide. Foliage clump may have no stem or several short, prostrate ones. Sharp-tipped, light bluish green or yellowish green leaves to 2 ft. long, 2 in. wide, with fibers along the edges. Large (2–6-in.), fleshy flowers from spring into summer are red brown outside, white inside, carried in dense, 2-ft.-long clusters. Fleshy, edible, bananalike fruits to 6 in. long.

Y. brevifolia. JOSHUA TREE. Zones 7, 9–16, 18–23. From deserts of Southern California, Nevada, Utah, Arizona. Few-branched, slow-growing plant to 15–30 ft. by 30 ft.; both trunk and branches are heavy. Gray-green, spiny-tipped leaves to 16 in. long, 1 in. wide, clustered near branch ends. Old, dead leaves hang on. Dense, foot-long clusters of greenish white, about 3-in. flowers in late winter and spring. Collected plants are sometimes sold; nursery plants are very slow to form trunks. Best in dry, well-drained soil in desert gardens. Difficult under ordinary garden conditions.

Y. elata. SOAPTREE YUCCA. Zones 7–24. From southwestern U.S., northern Mexico. Slow to 6–20 ft. tall, 8–10 ft. wide; single or branched trunk. Pale green, sharp-pointed leaves to 4 ft. long, ½ in. wide. Dead leaves hang on to form a straw-colored, shaggy "skirt" on trunk. Tall stems are topped by white, 2¼-in. flowers in spikes to 3 ft. long; blooms late spring into summer. May not bloom every year.

Y. elephantipes (Y. gigantea). GIANT YUCCA. Zones 12, 13 (protected from afternoon sun, hard frosts), 16, 17, 19–24; H1, H2. From Mexico, Central America. Fast growing (to 2 ft. per year) to an eventual 15–30 ft. by 8 ft. Usually has several trunks. Rich deep green, soft-tipped leaves to 4 ft. long, 3 in. wide. Striking silhouette alone or combined with other big foliage plants; looks out of proportion in smaller gardens. Tall

(3–6-ft.) spikes of creamy white, 1½-in. flowers in spring. Does best in good, well-drained soil with moderate to regular water.

Y. filamentosa. ADAM'S NEEDLE. Zones 1–24. From southeastern U.S. To 2½ ft. tall, 5 ft. wide; stemless. Stiff dark green leaves to 1½ ft. long, 1 in. wide, with long, loose fibers at edges. In late spring and summer, bears yellowish white, 2–3-in. flowers (lightly fragrant in evening) in narrow clusters to 4–7 ft. or taller. One of the hardiest, most widely planted yuccas in colder regions. Varieties include 'Bright Edge', with yellow-striped leaves; 'Color Guard', with leaves striped white and cream. Regular water.

Y. flaccida. Zones 1–9, 14–24. From southeastern U.S. Resembles *Y. filamentosa,* but flower clusters are somewhat shorter and leaves are less rigid, with straight fibers on edges. 'Golden Sword' has yellow-variegated foliage; 'Ivory Tower' bears outward-facing rather than drooping flowers. Give regular water.

Y. glauca. SOAPWEED. Zones 1–13. Native from New Mexico and Texas to South Dakota. To 3–4 ft. high and wide or larger, with short or prostrate trunk. May remain in a single rosette or form clumps. Stiff leaves, 2 ft. long, 2 in. wide, grayish green edged with a hairline of white and a few thin threads. White, 2½-in. flowers on 3-ft. stalks in spring or early summer.

Y. gloriosa. SPANISH DAGGER, SOFT-TIP YUCCA. Zones 7–9, 12–24; H1, H2. True species is native to southeastern U.S. Plants sold under this name in the West are most likely a form of *Y. elephantipes* or a hybrid between that form and *Y. gloriosa.* Much like *Y. aloifolia* in appearance. To 10 ft. tall, 8 ft. wide, generally with multiple trunks—except in colder part of range, where it is usually a smaller, stemless plant. Soft-tipped leaves with good green color that blends well with lush, tropical-looking plants. Summer bloom. Moderate to regular water; too much moisture may produce black areas on leaf margins.

Y. recurvifolia (Y. pendula). Zones 7–10, 12–24. From southeastern U.S. To 6–10 ft. tall, 6–8 ft. wide, with single, unbranched trunk (may be lightly branched in age). Can be cut back to keep single trunked. Spreads by offsets to make large groups. Beautiful blue-gray leaves are 2–3 ft. long, 2 in. wide, sharply bent downward. Leaf

tips are spined but bend to the touch; they won't cause injury. Not stiff and metallic looking like many yuccas. White, about 3-in. flowers in late spring or early summer are borne in loose, open, 3–5-ft.-tall clusters. Easy to grow under all garden conditions. Moderate to regular water.

Y. rigida. BLUE YUCCA. Zones 10 (with protection), 11–13. From Chihuahuan Desert of Mexico. To 12 ft. by 5 ft.; trunk may branch with age. Each stem is topped with rosette of stiff, spiny-tipped, blue-green leaves to 2 ft. long, 1½ in. wide. Old leaves form tan thatch on trunk. Dense spikes of white, 2¼-in. flowers appear in spring or early summer.

Y. rostrata (Y. thompsoniana). Zones 7–24. Native from extreme southwestern Texas into Chihuahuan Desert of Mexico. Treelike yucca to 12 ft. by 9 ft. or larger. Notable feature is the trunk, which is covered with soft gray fuzz (fibers remaining from old leaf bases). Needle-pointed leaves to 2 ft. long, ½ in. wide. Blooms in late spring, bearing 2-ft. clusters of white, 2½-in. flowers on a 2-ft. stalk.

Y. schidigera (Y. mohavensis). Zones 7–16, 18–24. From deserts of California, Nevada, Arizona, Baja California. Short-stemmed plant to 3–12 ft. tall, 3 ft. wide (or wider if stem branches). Tough, sharp-tipped, medium green leaves 2–3 ft. long, 1–2½ in. wide. Purple-tinted white flowers about 1¾ in. wide, in 2-ft. clusters. Spring bloom.

Y. schottii. MOUNTAIN YUCCA. Zones 10–13. Native from Arizona and New Mexico to northern Mexico. To 6–15 ft. tall, 3–4 ft. wide, with single (rarely branching) trunk. Gray-green, sharp-tipped leaves 1½–3 ft. long, 2 in. wide. Dead leaves hang on for a long time. Clusters of white, 1½-in. flowers from spring to midsummer. Full sun or light shade.

Yucca whipplei

Y. whipplei. OUR LORD'S CANDLE. Zones 2–24. From California coast, Southern California mountains, Baja California. Dense, trunkless rosette to 3 ft. tall, 6 ft. wide. Gray-green leaves are 1–2 ft. long, ¾ in. wide, with sharply toothed edges, needlelike tips; don't locate this plant where people can walk into it. Blooms in summer; 6–14-ft.-long stems carry drooping, 1–2-in., creamy white blossoms in large, branched, 3–6-ft.-long spikes. Plant dies after flowering; new plants come from seeds or offsets.

YUSHANIA.
See BAMBOO: Otatea

ZABEL LAUREL. See PRUNUS laurocerasus 'Zabeliana'

ZAMIA

Zamiaceae (Cycadaceae)
CYCADS

⚡ ZONES 21–24; H1, H2; OR INDOORS
☀ ◐ ● EXPOSURE NEEDS VARY BY SPECIES
💧 REGULAR WATER

Of 100 or so species, only the following two are generally seen. Slow-growing plants. Short trunks (may be completely or partially beneath soil level) are usually marked with scars from old leaf bases. Circular crowns of leaves resembling stiff fern fronds or small palm fronds. Need organically enriched, fast-draining soil.

Zamia pumila

Z. furfuracea. CARDBOARD PALM. From southeastern coastal Mexico. To 3 ft. high, 6 ft. wide. Stem short, sometimes subterranean. Fronds to 3 ft. long, usually much less; have as many as 12 pairs (usually fewer) of extremely stiff, leathery, dark green leaflets to 4½ in. long, 1½ in. wide. Leaflets may have a few teeth toward the tip. Best in full sun, tolerates partial or full shade.

Z. pumila (Z. integrifolia). COONTIE. From Florida, Cuba, West Indies. To 4 ft. high, 6 ft. wide. Short trunk is largely below soil level. Fronds to 3 ft. long, with as many as 30 pairs of dark green leaflets to 5 in. long, 1¼ in. wide. Partial shade.

ZAMIOCULCAS zamiifolia
AROID PALM
Araceae
PERENNIAL

🌡	ZONES 24; H1, H2; OR INDOORS
◐ ●	PARTIAL TO FULL SHADE; BRIGHT FILTERED LIGHT
◑ 💧	MODERATE TO REGULAR WATER

This tropical African perennial looks like a cycad or a palm but is actually in the same family as calla (*Zantedeschia*) and *Philodendron*. It grows to about 4–5 ft. tall, 3–4 ft. wide. Leafstalks emerge like fingers from base of plant and unfurl to reveal oval, pointed, dark green leaves that are waxy and so shiny they look as if they'd been polished. As stalks mature, they become swollen at base. Rarely produces yellowish flowers on a short spike.

Zamioculcas zamiifolia

Slow growing and tolerant of low light, aroid palm makes an excellent houseplant. Place container on tray of moistened pebbles or mist occasionally. During active growth, feed monthly with half-strength, balanced liquid fertilizer and keep soil evenly moist; in cooler months, stop feeding and water only when top inch of soil is dry (plant is often killed by overwatering during winter dormancy). In summer, plants benefit from being moved to a partially shaded location outdoors. Rarely bothered by pests.

ZANTEDESCHIA
CALLA
Araceae
PERENNIALS FROM RHIZOMES

🌡	ZONES 5, 6, 8, 9, 12–24; H1, H2; OR DIG AND STORE ALL BUT Z. AETHIOPICA
☼ ◑	EXPOSURE NEEDS VARY BY SPECIES
● 💧	WATER NEEDS VARY BY SPECIES

From South Africa. Clumps of long-stalked, shiny rich green, usually arrow-shaped leaves, sometimes spotted in white. Flower bract (spathe) surrounds a central spike (spadix) tightly covered with tiny true flowers.

Common calla (*Z. aethiopica*) has different cultural needs than other callas. It is soil tolerant and thrives in moist, even boggy, soil all year. Where summers are hot, grow in light shade; in milder climates, give full sun or light shade. Plant fall through early spring; set rhizomes 4 in. deep, 1 ft. apart. Needs year-round moisture. Dig and divide only when performance declines. Plants are evergreen to semievergreen and cannot be dug and stored over winter in cold climates. Beyond hardiness range, grow in pots and protect in winter.

The other callas described here die to the ground in fall, reappear in spring. Need regular water during growth and bloom, less during dormancy. In fall, set rhizomes 2 in. deep, 8–12 in. apart, in organically enriched, well-drained, and (ideally) slightly acid soil. Grow in full sun; in hot-summer areas, give light shade. As for *Z. aethiopica*, dig and divide when overcrowded. Beyond hardiness limits, plant in spring for summer bloom; then dig when leaves die back, store over winter in cool, dark place, replant in spring.

Z. aethiopica. COMMON CALLA. To 2–4 ft. tall, with unspotted leaves to 1½ ft. long, 10 in. wide. In spring (sometimes continuing into summer), pure or

Zantedeschia aethiopica

creamy white spathes to 8 in. long appear on stems slightly taller than foliage.

Varieties include robust 'Green Goddess', with large spathes that are white at base, green toward tip; and 'Hercules', larger than species, with big spathes that open flat, curve backward. Dwarf types include 'Childsiana' (to 1 ft.) and 'Minor' (to 1½ ft.).

Z. albomaculata. SPOTTED CALLA. To 2 ft. tall, with bright green, white-spotted leaves 1–1½ ft. long, 10 in. wide. Creamy yellow or white spathes to 5 in. long, with red-purple blotch at base. Blooms from spring into summer.

Z. elliottiana. GOLDEN CALLA. To 2 ft. tall, with bright green, white-spotted leaves to 10 in. long, 6 in. wide. Spathes to 6 in. long, greenish yellow aging to rich golden yellow. Summer bloom. Tolerates full sun, even in hot climates.

Z. hybrids. Plants are usually about the size of *Z. rehmanii* and bloom in late spring and summer. Leaves are typically unspotted, though some selections have spots on foliage. Spathe colors include cream, buff, orange, pink shades, lavender, purple.

Z. pentlandii. Resembles *Z. albomaculata*, but leaves are unspotted and spathes are deep golden yellow with purple throat. Summer bloom.

Z. rehmanii. RED or PINK CALLA. To 1½–2 ft., with narrow, lance-shaped, unspotted green leaves to 1 ft. long, 2½ in. wide. Pink or rosy pink spathes to 5 in. long in midspring. 'Superba' has dark pink spathes.

ZANTHOXYLUM piperitum
JAPAN PEPPER, SANSHO
Rutaceae
DECIDUOUS SHRUB OR TREE

🌡	ZONES 6–9, 14–17
☼	FULL SUN
💧	MODERATE WATER

Native to China, Japan, Korea. Dense growth to 8–20 ft. tall and wide. Handsome dark green, 3–6-in.-long leaves with 11–23 oval, 2-in.-long leaflets; may turn yellow in autumn. Flat, ½-in.-long spines in pairs along stems. Inconspicuous green flowers. Small, aromatic red fruits ripen in fall; they have black seeds that are pulverized and used as seasoning in Japan. Peppery-tasting leaves are

Zanthoxylum piperitum

slightly numbing to the tongue; they too are used in Japanese cuisine.

ZAUSCHNERIA (Epilobium)
CALIFORNIA FUCHSIA, HUMMINGBIRD FLOWER
Onagraceae
SHRUBBY PERENNIALS

🌡	ZONES 2–11, 14–24, EXCEPT AS NOTED
☼	FULL SUN, EXCEPT AS NOTED
◐ ◑	LITTLE TO MODERATE WATER, EXCEPT AS NOTED

Typically low, spreading plants with narrow, ½–1½-in.-long leaves in green, gray-green, or gray. In late summer or fall, they put on a profuse show of bright orange or scarlet (sometimes white or pink), narrowly trumpet-shaped flowers that attract hummingbirds. Drought tolerant, but look best with an occasional soaking in summer; prefer excellent drainage but adapt to heavier soils. These fast-growing plants can get a bit rangy. After their first year of growth, cut back to 1–2 in. tall in late fall or winter when flowering has finished. To keep taller types bushy, lightly shear or pinch back new growth in late spring. Some species spread by invasive roots or reseeding. Good in informal gardens, among stones, or to help stabilize banks or hillsides. Botanists assign California fuchsias to *Epilobium*, while horticulturists prefer to call them *Zauschneria*, as do wildflower enthusiasts and home gardeners.

Z. californica (Epilobium canum). HUMMINGBIRD TRUMPET, CALIFORNIA FUSCHIA. Native to much of the western U.S. and northern Mexico. Upright or arching growth from 6 in. to 4 ft. tall (depending on variety), spreading as wide as 3–4 ft. As there is no real consensus when it comes to sorting these plants into various subspecies—and since

Z

Zauschneria californica

several hybrids are of uncertain parentage—the following list is organized by variety names alone for convenience. All are improvements over the basic species. Flowers are orange to red unless otherwise noted.

'Bowman' ('Bowman's Hybrid'). Upright growth to 2 ft. tall, 2–3 ft. wide, with narrow, gray-green leaves.

'Calistoga'. Especially large, gray-green leaves and somewhat trailing growth to about 1½ ft. tall and 3–4 ft. wide.

'Catalina'. Fast, vigorous growth to 2–4 ft. tall and wide, with broad, light gray leaves and profuse blooms.

'Cloverdale'. Prostrate grower with broad, olive green leaves.

'Dublin'. Upright grower to 1 ft. tall, 1–2 ft. wide, with narrow, medium green leaves and scarlet flowers.

'Everett's Choice'. Low grower, just 2–4 in. tall and 3–5 ft. wide, with flared flowers. Reseeds to form colonies.

'Orange Carpet' (*Z. garretti* 'Orange Carpet'). Compact growth to 4–6 in. high and 1½ ft. wide. Profuse bloomer with bright orange flowers. Prefers afternoon shade and regular water.

'Route 66'. Grows 2–3 ft. tall and 3–4 ft. wide. Bright green leaves. Very heavy bloom, with flowers appearing a bit later than others listed here.

'Solidarity Pink'. Open, billowing growth to 1–3 ft. high and wide, with flared, pale coral pink blossoms and narrow, pale green leaves. Tolerates a bit more water than most.

'Summer Snow'. Grows 3–12 in. tall and up to 3 ft. wide, with pale, gray-green leaves and flared white flowers.

Z. septentrionalis (Epilobium septentrionale). HUMBOLDT COUNTY FUCHSIA. Zones 5–7, 14–17, 19–24. From Northern

California Coast Ranges. Mat-forming species to 6–12 in. high, 1–1½ ft. wide, with gray-green to silvery leaves. Needs afternoon shade in hottest climates. 'Etteri', a probable hybrid with *Z. californica*, grows just 7 in. high and wide, with large (1½-in.) flowers; prefers regular water. 'Select Mattole' grows 8 in. tall and is wide spreading (to 3 ft.) but not invasive. 'Wayne's Silver' is a cutting-grown selection with a uniform, dense habit and large, metallic silvery leaves.

ZEBRA GRASS. See **MISCANTHUS sinensis** 'Zebrinus'

ZEBRA PLANT. See **APHELANDRA squarrosa, CALATHEA zebrina, HAWORTHIA attenuata**

ZEBRA RUSH. See **SCHOENOPLECTUS lacustris tabernaemontani** 'Zebrinus'

ZEBRINA pendula. See **TRADESCANTIA zebrina**

ZELKOVA serrata
SAWLEAF ZELKOVA
Ulmaceae
DECIDUOUS TREE

| 🌿 ZONES 3–21 |
| ☀ FULL SUN |
| 💧💧 MODERATE TO REGULAR WATER |

Eastern Asian relative of elm (*Ulmus*). Good shade tree; sometimes used as a substitute for American elm (*U. americana*),

Zelkova serrata

which is highly prone to Dutch elm disease (zelkova is also susceptible but rarely succumbs). Grows at moderate to fast rate to 60 ft. or higher, equally wide. Silhouette ranges from vase shaped to quite spreading. Has smooth gray bark. Narrowly oval, sawtoothed, 2–

3½-in.-long leaves are similar to those of elm but rougher in texture. Fall color varies from yellow to dark red to dull reddish brown. Among vase-shaped varieties, 'Halka' is the fastest growing and the best American elm mimic; 'Green Vase' has a narrower vase shape than vigorous 'Village Green'. 'Wireless' ('Schmidtlow') is compact, just 25 ft. tall and 35 ft. wide, and has excellent red fall color.

Takes wide range of soils. Fairly tolerant of drought, wind. You may need to train and prune young trees to establish a good framework; thin out crowded ascending branches.

ZEPHYRANTHES
ZEPHYR FLOWER, FAIRY LILY
Amaryllidaceae
PERENNIALS FROM BULBS

| 🌿 ZONES VARY BY SPECIES |
| ☀ ◐ FULL SUN OR PARTIAL SHADE |
| 💧 REGULAR WATER DURING GROWTH AND BLOOM |

Clumps of foot-long, bright green, grassy leaves give rise to slender, hollow stems, each bearing a single funnel-shaped blossom with six segments. In their native Central and South America, often bloom after rains (hence another common name, rain lily). Species described here bloom in late summer and early fall.

Plant bulbs in well-drained soil at any time (though fall planting is ideal), setting them 1–2 in. deep, 3 in. apart. In mild-winter areas with a long growing season, plants may bloom several times a year if you provide a short dry period after bloom, then resume watering to initiate another growth cycle. In other regions, give little or no water after foliage dies back. Can remain undisturbed for many years. Pretty in rock garden or foreground of border. Excellent pot plant for patio or greenhouse.

Zephyranthes candida

Z. candida. Zones 4–9, 12–24; H1, H2. White, 2-in. flowers, sometimes stained pink in throat. Evergreen in warmer part of range. Usually sold as potted plants; can be planted out at any time.

Z. citrina. Zones 7–9, 12–24; H1, H2. Similar to *Z. candida* but has bright yellow flowers.

Z. grandiflora. Zones 7–9, 12–24; H1, H2. Extra-large flowers (to 4 in. across). Rose pink blossoms have a lily shape in the morning, open out flat by midday, close in late afternoon.

ZEXMENIA hispida
Asteraceae (Compositae)
SHRUBBY PERENNIAL

| 🌿 ZONES 10–13 |
| ☀ ◐ FULL SUN OR LIGHT SHADE |
| 💧 💧 LITTLE TO MODERATE WATER |

Native to Texas, Mexico. Compact, rounded plant to 2–3 ft. tall and wide; puts on a good show of bright orange-yellow daisies from late spring into autumn. Rough-textured, somewhat sticky dark

Zexmenia hispida

green leaves, 1–2 in. long, are oval to lance shaped. In cold winters, plant can lose leaves or even die to the ground, but it recovers quickly in spring. In light shade, it blooms less and sprawls more, making an attractive ground cover. Give well-drained soil.

ZINGIBER officinale
TRUE GINGER
Zingiberaceae
PERENNIAL FROM RHIZOME

| 🌿 ZONES 9, 14–24; H1, H2 |
| ◐ PARTIAL SHADE |
| 💧💧 REGULAR TO AMPLE WATER |

This tropical Asian plant's rhizomes are the source of the ginger root used in cooking. To 2–4 ft. tall, with indefinite spread. Narrow, glossy bright green leaves to 1 ft.

Z

Zingiber officinale

long. Summer flowers are yellowish green, with purple lip marked yellow; they are only rarely seen and not especially showy. Needs heat and humidity. Buy roots (fresh, not dried) at grocery store in early spring; cut into 1–2-in.-long sections, each with well-developed growth buds. Let cut ends of sections dry, then plant just below surface of rich, moist soil (pot culture is common). Water cautiously until top and root growth are active. Feed once a month. Plants are dormant in winter; rhizomes may rot in cold, wet soil. Harvest roots at any time—but allow several months after planting for them to reach some size. Grown commercially in Hawaii.

ZINNIA
Asteraceae (Compositae)
ANNUALS AND PERENNIALS

🌱	ZONES 1–24; H1, H2; EXCEPT AS NOTED
☀	FULL SUN
💧	REGULAR WATER, EXCEPT AS NOTED

Longtime favorites for colorful, round flowers, typically in summer and early fall. These are hot-weather plants that do not gain from being planted early; they merely stand still until weather warms up. Subject to mildew in foggy places, if given overhead water, and when autumn brings longer nights, more dew and shade. Sow seeds where plants are to grow (or set out nursery plants) from late spring to early summer. Give good garden soil, feed generously. Most garden zinnias belong to *Z. elegans*.

Z. acerosa. Perennial. Zones 10–24. From southern Arizona, Texas, Mexico. To 6–10 in. high, 2 ft. wide, with hairy, needlelike, ¾-in.-long leaves. Flowers are 1½ in. wide, with relatively large, creamy white rays veined in green on underside. Blooms sporadically from spring through fall, whenever moisture is present; goes dormant during extended periods of drought.

Z. angustifolia. Annual. Compact growth to 16 in. high and wide, with very narrow leaves to 2½ in. long. Orange, inch-wide flowers; each ray has a paler stripe. Blooms in 6 weeks from seed, continues late into fall. 'Classic' grows to 1 ft. high and 2 ft. wide, has 1½-in. flowers. The Star series, also to 1 by 2 ft., has 2-in. blooms in orange, yellow, and white. 'Golden Eye' is much like 'Star White': both have white rays, yellow centers.

Zinnia elegans

Z. elegans. Annual. From Mexico. The common garden zinnia, sold in strains ranging from less than a foot high and wide to 4 ft. tall, half as wide. Oval to lance-shaped leaves to 5 in. long; summer flowers from less than 1 in. to as much as 5–7 in. across. Forms include full double, cactus flowered (with quilled rays), and crested (cushionlike center surrounded by rows of broad rays); the many colors available include white, pink, salmon, rose, red, yellow, orange, lavender, and purple. 'Envy' is a novelty type with lime green flowers.

Among extra-small dwarf bedding types (under 1 ft.), look for Short Stuff, Thumbelina, and Zinnita. For bicolors, try the Swizzle series.

Dwarf bedding types (about 1 ft. tall) include the Dreamland series, Magellan, and Pulcino Mix.

Intermediate types include the following. 'Candy Stripe', to 2 ft., has white flowers striped pink, rose, or red. Ruffles Mix hybrids, 2½ ft. tall, have blossoms with ruffled rays. Sun hybrids, 2–2½ ft. tall, have blooms in a range of colors. Flowers in the Peppermint Stick series grow 2–3 ft. tall and have petals striped in pink, white, yellow, purple, or scarlet. 'Whirligig', about the same height, sports bicolored combinations of white, pink, yellow, and orange. Award-winning 'Zowie!' grows 2½–3 ft. tall, with blooms in a combination of flame colors that change hues as they age.

Tall plants for cutting and back-of-border planting include the following 3-footers: 'Big Red Hybrid', with bright red, fully double blooms to 6 in. across; Dahlia-flowered Mix, with 4–5-in. double blooms; Giant Cactus-flowered Mix, with 4–5-in. semidouble blooms; and 'Uproar Rose', with 5–6-in. blooms in deep rose red. Oklahoma Mix grows 3–3½ ft. tall, with 1½–2-in. flowers on a mildew-resistant plant. State Fair Mix reaches 3–4 ft. tall, with blooms to 5 in. across. Benary Giants can grow 4 ft. tall, with fully double flowers up to 6 in. across in a wide range of colors, including the recent addition of lime.

Z. grandiflora. Perennial in Zones 2–24; annual elsewhere. Native to Rocky Mountains, south into Mexico. To 4–6 inches tall. Bright green leaves to 1 in. long, ⅛ in. wide. Spring-into-fall flowers are 1½ in. wide, bright yellow with orange eye. Survives with no supplemental moisture but needs regular water to bloom satisfactorily.

Z. haageana. Annual. From southeastern U.S., Mexico. To 2 ft. tall, 1 ft. wide. Narrow, 3-in. leaves. Persian Carpet (1 ft. tall) and Old Mexico (16 in. tall) have double blossoms in mahogany red, yellow, and orange, with all three colors usually mixed in the same flower. Long summer bloom season.

Z. hybrida. Annual. These mildew-tolerant varieties originated with a cross between *Z. angustifolia* and *Z. elegans*. They include the Profusion series in cherry, orange, and white—all national award winners—as well as apricot and fire (orangish red). Plants grow 1–1½ ft. high and wide, with 2½-in. flower heads containing more than one row of rays.

Z. peruviana. Annual. Native from southern U.S. to Argentina. Grows to 3 ft. tall and as wide; leaves to 3 in. long, 1¼ in. wide. In summer, bears profuse, 1½-in. flowers in brick red or soft gold.

Blossoms dry well for arrangements, either in a vase or on the plant. Also called Bonita zinnia or *Z. pauciflora*.

ZIZIPHUS jujuba. See **JUJUBE**

ZOYSIA
Poaceae (Gramineae)
PERENNIAL GRASSES

🌱	ZONES VARY BY SPECIES
☀ ◑	BEST IN SUN; TOLERATE SOME SHADE
💧💧	MODERATE TO REGULAR WATER

These Asian natives tend to spread slowly, are fairly deep rooted. Dormant and straw colored during the winter; turn green in spring. Use for lawns, ground covers. Plant using sod, sprigs, stolons, or plugs. Mow lawns 1–2 in. high.

Z. 'Emerald'. EMERALD ZOYSIA. Zones 8, 9, 12–14, 18–24; H1, H2. Hybrid between *Z. japonica* and *Z. tenuifolia*. Makes wiry, dark green, prickly-looking turf. Dense blades are hard to cut. More frost tolerant than other zoysias.

Z. japonica 'Meyer'. MEYER ZOYSIA. Zones 12, 13. Resembles bluegrass (*Poa*). Turns brown earliest in winter, turns green latest in spring.

Z. matrella. MANILA GRASS. Zones 8, 9, 12–14, 18–24; H1, H2. Also similar to bluegrass in appearance. Holds color a little better than *Z. japonica* 'Meyer'.

Zoysia tenuifolia

Z. tenuifolia. KOREAN GRASS. Hardy in Zones 8, 9, 12–24; H1, H2. Creeping, fine textured, bumpy. Makes a beautiful grassy meadow or gives mossy Oriental effect in areas impossible to mow or water often. The farther inland, the longer the dormant season.

ZUCCHINI. See **SQUASH**

ZYGOCACTUS.
See **SCHLUMBERGERA**

Z

A Practical Guide to Gardening

A good understanding of certain basic gardening principles and procedures will make you a better gardener. In these pages, you'll also find help in dealing with garden problems—plant diseases, insects, animal pests, and weeds—based on the principles of Integrated Pest Management (IPM). This approach emphasizes the least-toxic means for preventing and controlling many gardening challenges.

An array of seed-starting equipment includes pots, flats, labels, seeds, and potting mix.

ANNUALS

Annuals germinate, grow, flower, set seed, and die in less than a year. Some tender perennials (see page 702), such as geranium *(Pelargonium)*, are grown as annuals where winters are cold. And a few hardier perennials, such as snapdragon *(Antirrhinum majus)*, are grown as annuals because older plants don't perform as well as young ones. Favorite annuals are listed in the Plant Selection Guide on pages 70–71.

Cool-season (or hardy) annuals, such as calendula, sweet pea *(Lathyrus odoratus)*, and some primroses *(Primula)*, develop their roots and foliage in the mild temperatures of fall and early spring, and they can withstand fairly heavy frosts. Gardeners in cold-winter areas should plant cool-season annuals in very early spring, as soon as the soil can be worked. Where winters are mild, plant in fall for winter and early-spring bloom. To ensure winter flowers, plant while the days are still warm enough to encourage growth but when day length is decreasing. In mild-winter regions, cool-season annuals can also be planted in late winter or very early spring for spring bloom.

Warm-season annuals make up a large group of plants that includes familiar summer flowers such as cosmos, sunflower *(Helianthus annuus)*, and zinnia. They grow best during the warm months and cannot withstand low temperatures. In cold-winter climates, set them out after all danger of frost has passed; in mild-winter climates, plant in midspring. In desert regions, you can plant some warm-season annuals in early fall for winter bloom.

Start annuals from seed sown in containers or, in many cases, directly in the garden (for more on starting seeds, see page 717). Or choose nursery-grown annuals that are relatively small, with healthy foliage and few or no flowers. Avoid plants with yellowing leaves and those that are leggy, root-bound, too big for their pots, or already in full bloom.

Plant annuals in the early morning or late afternoon when the weather is cool. Prepare the planting bed (see page 712), then push the plants out of their cell-packs and loosen matted roots with your fingers. Mix a complete fertilizer into the soil before planting. Plant so the top of the root ball is even with surrounding soil. Firm the soil around the roots. Apply a 1- to 2-inch-thick layer of mulch.

Annual California poppies (Eschscholzia californica).

Caring for Annuals

Water annuals thoroughly after planting. Thereafter, water enough to keep soil moist but not soggy. Younger plants may need more water in warm weather.

In cold-winter areas, give an additional feeding after bloom begins. Where winters are warmer and the growing season is longer, feed both after flowering starts and again in late summer.

To deadhead annuals, pinch or cut off individual spent flowers or shear the flower heads, removing no more than one-third of the plant. Deadheading encourages more flowers and keeps the plant tidy.

BIENNIALS

Biennials typically complete their life cycle in two years. During their first year, they grow from seed into leafy but nonblooming plants. They live through the winter, and most actually require this period of low temperatures for bloom. Then, in the following year, they flower, set seed, and die. Biennials sold in nurseries, however, usually bloom the year you buy them, because they have gone through their first year of growth.

Familiar biennials include common foxglove *(Digitalis purpurea)*, hollyhock *(Alcea rosea)*, and Canterbury bells *(Campanula medium)*, as well as vegetables like carrots and onions.

To grow biennials, sow seeds in containers or directly in the garden at the time indicated on the seed packet, typically mid- to late spring or summer. (For more on starting seeds, see page 717.) Transplant young plants into the garden in early fall, setting them in well-prepared soil; water as needed. Where the ground freezes, place a protective mulch of straw or chopped leaves around the plants. In spring, feed plants with a complete fertilizer as soon as new growth begins.

Biennial foxgloves (Digitalis purpurea) *may re-grow as short-lived perennials in mild climates.*

BULBS

What we call bulbs are several kinds of plants with specialized roots or stem bases that store nutrients and energy for the plants' growth. Five basic bulbous plants are described here. For a selection of favorite bulbs, see the Plant Selection Guide on pages 68–69.

Selecting and Planting Bulbs

Choose plump, firm bulbs that feel heavy; avoid any that are soft, squashy, or shriveled. Bulbs graded as "large" generally yield more flowers, but they are also the priciest. For mass planting, buy midsize specimens (they will soon build up).

See page 712 for information on preparing a planting bed. If your soil drains very poorly, plant on a slope or in raised beds. Work a complete fertilizer into the soil in the entire bed or mix a tablespoon of fertilizer into the bottom of individual holes, add 2 inches of compost or soil over that, and place the bulb in the hole.

In most soils, true bulbs and most corms should be planted about three times as deep as the bulb is wide. In hot climates or sandy soils, plant slightly deeper; in heavy soils, plant a bit shallower. For depth and spacing for specific bulbs, check the entries in the Western Plant Encyclopedia.

Caring for Bulbs

Bulbs need water while they're growing actively. For most, this period begins after planting and continues until the foliage dies back, until flowering is finished, or—for some types—until autumn. If you must supplement rainfall, water deeply enough to penetrate the root zone; the roots grow beneath the bulb. When growth begins, apply a high-nitrogen fertilizer to enhance the quality of the current season's flowers. After bloom ends, much or all of a bulb's stored nutrients are depleted. To ensure a good show next year, those nutrients must be replenished. As long as the leaves are green and growing, they will continue to manufacture food for

the coming year, so leave them on the plant —bedraggled and weary though they may appear—until they yellow and pull away easily. If you want to hide this dying foliage, try over-planting with annuals or a ground cover. After flowering is finished, apply a complete fertilizer such as a 10-10-10 formula or a "bulb food" high in phosphorus and potassium. For these last two nutrients to be effective, they must

To improve drainage, encase bulbs in a sand "sandwich": Add a 2-inch layer of construction-grade sand atop the soil, place the bulbs on top, then cover them with another inch of sand. If you're planting in containers, use a fast-draining mix, such as 40 percent fir bark, 40 percent sand, and 20 percent pumice.

reach the root zone. Scratch the fertilizer into the soil or apply it in narrow trenches dug near the bulbs, then water thoroughly.

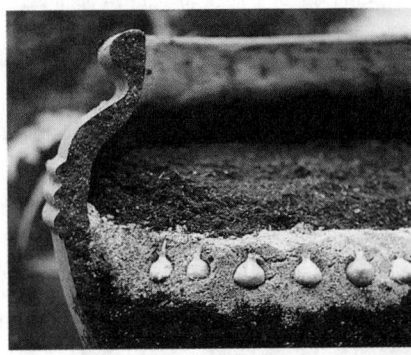

The Five Bulb Types and Ways to Divide Them

For information on the best time to divide and replant specific bulbs, consult the Western Plant Encyclopedia. The illustrations here show bulbs oriented the way they should be planted.

A true bulb is an underground stem base containing an embryonic plant surrounded by scales—modified leaves that overlap each other. A basal plate at the bottom of the bulb holds the scales together and produces roots. Most true bulbs have a protective papery outer skin called a tunic. Lilies, however, lack a tunic, making them more susceptible to drying and damage than other true bulbs; handle them with care. Most true bulbs produce offsets (also called increases). To divide, simply separate these from the mother bulb.

Allium (onion)
Tunic
Fleshy leaves (scales)
Embryonic plant
Roots   Basal plate

Narcissus (daffodil)
Bulblet (offset)

Lilium (lily)
Bulbil
Leaf

A corm is a swollen underground stem base, but unlike a true bulb, it's composed of solid tissue rather than scales. Roots grow from a basal plate at the corm's bottom, and the growth point is at the top. Many corms have a tunic formed from the dried bases of the previous season's leaves. Each corm lasts a single year. As it shrinks away, a new corm and, in many species, small increases (cormels) form on top of it. To divide, separate healthy new corms and any cormels from the old corms (cormels may take as long as 2 to 3 years to reach flowering size).

Gladiolus
Dead leaf bases
Roots
New corms
Cormels   Old corms

A rhizome is a thickened stem growing partially or entirely below ground. Its roots grow directly from the underside. The primary growing point is at one end of the rhizome, and additional growing points form along the sides. To divide, cut into sections that have visible growing points.

Tubers, like corms, are swollen underground stem bases, but they lack the corm's distinct organization. There is no basal plate, so roots can grow from all sides. Instead of just one or a few growing points, a tuber has multiple growth points scattered over its surface. Each is a scalelike leaf with a growth bud (eye) in its axil. Some tubers, such as cyclamen and begonia, are perennials that increase in size each year. Others (the potato is the best-known example) are annual. As new tubers grow, the old ones disintegrate. To divide either kind of tuber, cut it into sections, making sure each has one or more growing points.

Zantedeschia (calla)
Growth bud (eye)
Leaves
Growth bud (eye)

Tuberous begonia
Growth bud (eye)
Roots

Tuberous roots, unlike the other four bulb types, are true roots, thickened to store nutrients. Fibrous roots for the uptake of water and nutrients develop from its sides and tip. Tuberous roots grow in a cluster, with the swollen portions radiating out from a central point. The growth buds are at the bases of old stems rather than on the roots themselves. To divide, cut the root cluster apart so each division contains both roots and part of a stem base with one or more growth buds.

Dahlia
Growth bud (eye)
Old stalk
Roots

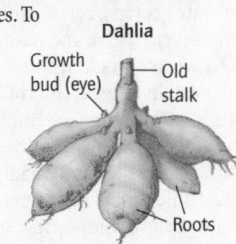

B

Naturalizing Bulbs

A number of bulbous plants can be planted in meadows, fields, or light woodlands, where they'll form a carpet of wildflower-like blooms year after year. Consult the Western Plant Encyclopedia to see whether the bulbs you want to naturalize are good candidates for this treatment and to check their climate, exposure, and moisture needs. If they aren't likely to receive enough water naturally, be prepared to supply it through irrigation.

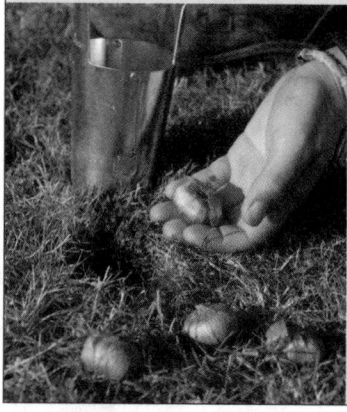

The traditional naturalizing method is to broadcast a handful of bulbs over the desired planting area, then plant them where they fall. To achieve the most realistic effect, you may need to adjust the pattern slightly. The drift should be denser at one end or toward the center, as if the bulbs began to grow in one spot, then gradually spread to colonize outlying territory. Once you have the pattern you want, use a trowel or bulb planter (shown at left) to set the bulbs at their preferred depths.

After bloom, fertilize the bulbs and allow the foliage to remain until it withers. After a number of years, overcrowding may cause a decrease in the number of flowers. When this happens, it's time to dig, divide, and replant.

COMPOSTING

Composting is a natural process that converts raw organic materials into a valuable soil conditioner. In addition to being good for your garden, composting lightens the load at the landfill, as you recycle garden and kitchen debris at home rather than consign it to the dump.

A pile of leaves, branches, and other garden trimmings will eventually decompose in a process called slow or cold composting. If you create optimum conditions for the organisms responsible for decay (by giving them the mixture of air, water, and the carbon- and nitrogen-rich nutrients they need), the compost pile will heat up quickly and decompose in a few months. This hot composting method also destroys many weeds and disease pathogens.

You can make compost in a freestanding pile or use some sort of enclosure. Regardless of the method, the fundamentals of composting are the same.

Basic Composting

Gather approximately twice as much (by volume) brown matter as green matter. Brown matter is high in carbon and includes dry leaves, hay, sawdust, straw, wood chips, and woody prunings. Green matter is high in nitrogen and includes grass clippings, fruit and vegetable scraps, coffee grounds, tea bags, crushed eggshells, and manure from cows, horses, goats, poultry, and rabbits. The compost will heat up faster if you collect all the ingredients in advance and assemble the pile all at once. Don't use bones, dairy products, cat or dog waste, meat scraps, badly diseased or insect-infested plants, or pernicious weeds that might survive composting, such as bindweed, quackgrass, and oxalis.

Raked leaves add brown matter to the compost bin.

Shredding or chopping large, rough materials into smaller pieces (the smaller, the better— but no larger than 1 to 2 inches) speeds up the composting process. Shredder-chippers and lawn mowers are good tools for this purpose. To shred dry leaves, collect them in an open area and run a lawn mower over them.

Building the pile like a layer cake makes it easier to judge the ratio of brown to green materials. Start by spreading a 4- to 8-inch layer of brown material, then add a layer of green material about 2 to 4 inches deep. Layers of grass clippings should be only 2 inches thick; less-dense green materials can be layered more thickly. Add another layer of brown material and sprinkle the pile with water. Mix these first three layers with a spading fork. If you're short on green matter, sprinkle the brown matter with a high-nitrogen product such as lawn fertilizer. To speed up decomposition in a new pile, add a few shovelfuls of old compost, which already contains bacteria and fungi. Continue adding layers, watering, and mixing.

Turn the pile weekly. In just a few days, the pile should have heated up dramatically. In time, it will decompose on its own, but you can hurry things along by turning the contents to introduce more oxygen. Using a spading fork or pitchfork, restack the pile, redistributing it so that the materials originally on the outside are moved to the pile's center, where they'll be exposed to higher heat. If necessary, add more water. The pile should be as moist as a wrung-out sponge.

Mix the compost into your planting beds or use it as a mulch. If some of the material from the compost pile is still coarser than you prefer, simply incorporate it into your next compost pile. To obtain a finer-textured compost for potting soil or for starting seeds, sift the finished compost through a screen with ¼-inch to ½-inch mesh.

Composting Systems

A freestanding compost pile should be at least 3 feet high and wide. At this size, its mass is great enough to generate the microbial activity needed for heating the materials. The upper size limit is about 5 feet high and wide; a pile larger than that may not receive enough air at its center. When siting the pile, allow space alongside for turning.

Wire cylinders or cages consist of hardware cloth, chicken wire, or snow fencing. Secure the wire to a framework or support it with stakes. A cylinder or hoop should be about 4 feet in diameter and 3 to 4 feet tall (some gardeners also use cylinders of flexible plastic with many small holes). To turn the pile, lift the cylinder or cage and move it to one side, then fork the materials back into it.

Three-bin systems are more complex than freestanding piles, but they also offer a more flexible way to make compost.

The left bin holds new green and brown material, the center one contains partly decomposed material, and the right bin holds finished or nearly finished compost. Turn the material in each bin weekly, moving decomposed material to the right. (The middle and right bins will take a few weeks to fill.)

2 × 6

4 × 4   1 × 1   2 × 2 spacer

Manufactured composters include various tumblers that make it easier to turn materials and produce finished compost quickly. Most are turned with a crank, but some roll on the ground. Such devices provide a tidy way to make compost, especially in small gardens.

Another manufactured composter is the static compost bin, in which the contents sit without turning (though occasional aerating with a spading fork is helpful). You add new materials at the top, and the finished compost is removed through a door at the base. Though tidy, these units produce fairly small amounts of compost, and they do so rather slowly.

Door

CONTAINER GARDENING

Growing plants in containers lets you have a garden even when the space for one is limited or nonexistent. For instance, you can install a planter box below a window or use containers to turn a tiny balcony or patio into a leafy haven. Gardeners with plenty of room appreciate containers too, valuing the versatility they offer. Blooming pot plants bring seasonal color to garden beds, a porch, or the front steps, and they are easily replaced with new ones when their flowers fade. In addition, containers give you the chance to experiment with new plant combinations and with kinds not suited to native conditions. For instance, if your soil is alkaline or clay-like, but you are longing to raise acid-loving plants or those that demand fast drainage, just fill their pots with the sort of soil they need. Plants too tender for your winters can be moved to shelter when cold weather hits.

PREPARING CONTAINERS Choose containers with at least one drainage hole so that water won't accumulate around plant roots. Submerge terra-cotta pots in clean water and let them soak thoroughly. If the pots are too dry, they can initially draw water away from the potting mix. Scrub used containers with a solution of 1 part household bleach to 9 parts hot water. Cover the drainage hole or holes with a small piece of fine wire screen to keep soil from washing out.

Ingredients of a lightweight potting mix, from top: compost, perlite, sphagnum moss, and controlled-release fertilizer.

Composting with Worms

For gardeners with no room for a traditional composting system, worm composting, or vermicomposting, is an efficient way to recycle fruit and vegetable scraps from the kitchen in a small amount of space. Red wiggler worms and bins for housing them are sold in many nurseries. You can also use a covered homemade wooden bin about 2 feet square and 8 to 16 inches deep. Fill the bin with bedding made from shredded newspaper, then place it in a shaded, rain-protected location where it won't freeze or overheat from sun exposure. Feed the worms kitchen scraps; 2 pounds of worms will process about 7 pounds of fruit and vegetable scraps each week. After three to six months, you can begin harvesting the compost, which will look like dark, rich soil.

CHOOSING A POTTING MIX A good potting soil allows roots to grow easily. It should be fast draining yet moisture retentive. Quick drainage means roots won't suffocate in soggy soil, while good water retention saves you from having to water too often. Regular garden soil, even good loam, is too dense for container use. For best success, most gardeners turn to packaged potting mixes, which don't contain soil. Instead they contain organic materials such as ground bark, sphagnum peat moss, and/or compost, plus mineral matter like perlite, pumice, or sand. Limestone may be added to balance the acidity of peat moss, and fertilizers and wetting agents may also be included. Before planting, flush the mix with water once or twice to eliminate excess salts.

Container Options

In recent years, container gardening has soared in popularity, so manufacturers have responded by introducing a mind-boggling variety of container styles and materials. Retailers and catalogs still stock traditional pots, planters, and urns made of terra-cotta, wood, and cast iron. But you can also pot up your plants in recycled polypropylene, high-tech thermoplastics, resin, fiberglass, or metals ranging from venerable-looking bronze to gleaming stainless steel. Some of these new models mimic classic designs while others feature sleek contemporary lines. As diverse as they are, most of the new materials have several things in common. They're unbreakable, they can stand up to any kind of weather, and even the biggest sizes are light enough to use on rooftops and balconies.

Ceramic

Zinc

Polyethylene

Polyethylene

How Much Mix?

A 2-cubic-foot bag of potting mix holds enough to transplant 8 to 10 plants from 1-gallon nursery cans into individual 10- to 12-inch pots.

An 18-inch-wide planting bowl calls for 1 cubic foot of potting mix.

A typical planter box measuring 3 feet long and 6 inches deep holds approximately 1 1/2 cubic feet of potting mix.

To fill a large container such as a half-barrel, you'll need two 2-cubic-foot bags of potting mix.

WATERING Because container plants have only a limited area from which to draw moisture, they must be watered more often than those grown in the ground. In hot or windy weather, some—especially those in hanging baskets—may need watering several times a day. In cool weather, it may be sufficient to water weekly or even less often. Test with your finger: If the soil is dry beneath the surface, it's time to water.

Apply water over the entire soil surface until it flows from the pot's drainage holes. This moistens the entire soil mass and prevents any potentially harmful salts from accumulating in the mix. If the water drains out too fast—virtually the instant you pour it in—there's

Container plants *benefit from periodic repotting.*

probably air space between the soil and the container walls. In this case, completely submerge the container in a tub of water for about half an hour. For large pots, set a hose on the soil surface near the plant's base and let the water trickle slowly into the mix.

A drip irrigation system (see page 744) can make watering container plants almost effortless. Kits for this purpose are widely available.

FERTILIZING Container plants need regular feeding, as the necessary frequent watering leaches nutrients from the potting mix. Apply a liquid fertilizer every two weeks during the growing season, following the directions on the label. Or mix a controlled-release type (see page 689) into the potting mix before planting.

Soil Mix

For a basic no-soil mix, combine 2/3 cubic yard nitrogen-stabilized ground bark, coir dust, or sphagnum peat moss; 1/3 cubic yard washed 20-grit sand; 6 pounds 0-10-10 granular fertilizer; and 10 pounds dolomite or dolomite limestone. Mix all ingredients in a wheelbarrow.

REPOTTING If roots are crowded and protruding from the drainage holes, the plant has outgrown its container and needs a roomier home. Because you want to keep the soil mass fairly well filled with roots, it's best to shift the plant to a slightly larger container rather than a much bigger one. If the pot is too large, the ratio of soil to roots will be too great for the roots to absorb all the moisture after watering—a situation that often leads to root rot. Select a new container that allows just an inch or two of fresh mix on all sides of the root mass. If the root ball is compacted (with tightly twined roots), make four shallow vertical cuts down its sides with a sharp knife to encourage the roots to move out into the new soil.

If you want to keep an older plant in the same large pot indefinitely, you can root-prune the plant periodically. Gently turn it out of its container and use a sharp knife to shave off an inch or two from all four sides and the bottom of the root ball. Place fresh potting mix in the bottom of the container, put the plant back in, and add fresh mix around the sides.

Colorful Themes

One way to design your container planting is to choose the pot first in a color you like, and one plant you've fallen in love with that matches or contrasts well with the pot. Then pick everything else to flatter rather than compete with them. Following are some popular pot colors and plants we like in them:

BLACK Tropicals such as bromeliads, caladiums, and orchids, with a fringe of Spanish moss trailing over pot edges; tuberous begonias (bright colors), blue and bronze grasses.

BRONZE-CARAMEL *Diascia* (coral), *Carex buchananii,* dwarf gaillardia (yellow and rust), *Heuchera* 'Dolce Peach Melba' (peach tones with purplish undersides) or 'Amber Waves' (amber and green), *Pelargonium* 'Golden Ears' or 'Vancouver Centennial' (both have bronzy-red leaves with wide chartreuse edges), *Sedum* 'Angelina' (chartreuse), violas (apricot).

Planting Big Pots

1 Using a drill with a ½-inch glass-and-tile bit, drill three or four additional holes around the existing center drain in the pot. Pour a small but steady amount of water on the hole to keep the drill bit cool.

2 Fill the pot with potting mix to about 6 inches below the rim. Add water, blending it in well to completely moisten the mix. Tamp down the soil with your hands.

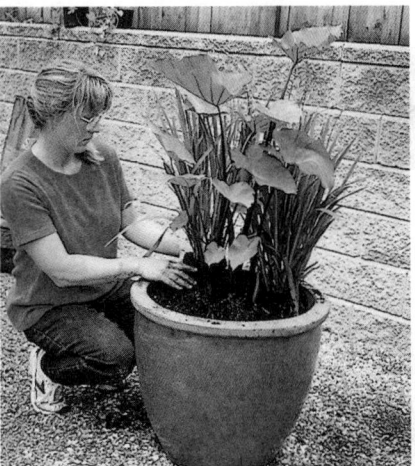

3 Arrange plants in their nursery containers, adjusting the design until you are pleased with the arrangement. Remove the tallest plant from its nursery container, rough up its root ball, and plant.

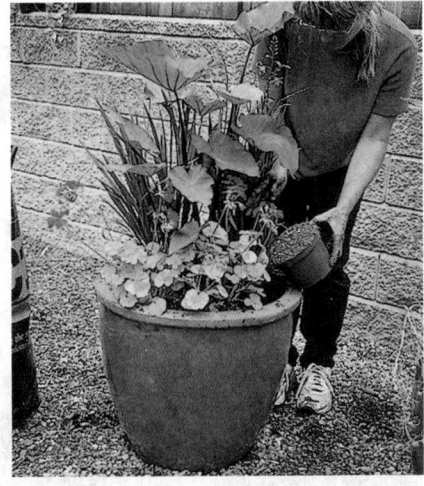

4 Repeat the process with lower-growing plants, placing trailers around the edge. Add soil to raise the level to 1 to 2 inches below the rim. Scatter controlled-release fertilizer over the soil. Water.

5 The finished pot displays elephant's ear (*Alocasia macrorrhiza*), *Crocosmia* 'Norwich Canary', *Pelargonium*, *Lantana* 'Professor Raoux', *Anagallis monelli*. Design: Tina Dixon.

Slender veldt grass (Pennisetum spathiolatum) *fans out above a plump rosette of echeveria and mounding* Plectranthus *'Blue Yonder' in a glazed celadon-colored pot. Design: John Greenlee.*

CELADON *Caladium bicolor* 'White Queen', cyclamen (pink to coral shades), *Nemesia* 'Bluebird', forget-me-nots (sky blue), Iceland poppies (apricot, coral, and pale yellow), stock (rose-pink or lavender), succulents, grasses.

CHOCOLATE BROWN *Bougainvillea* (hot-pink bush types), chocolate cosmos, *Calibrachoa* (bright rose-pink), *Carex* 'Toffee Twist', *Dahlia* 'Japanese Bishop' (bright red flowers, bronze-brown foliage), tuberous begonias (bright orange or pink).

COBALT BLUE *Angelonia* (purple), calendula (bright yellow or orange), *Calibrachoa* (rose-pink or bright cherry pink), cosmos (white), delphiniums (mixed blues), nasturtiums or nemesia (brilliant orange), heliotrope (deep purple), violas (lavender to purple).

GRASS GREEN Fairy or English primroses (rose-pink), maidenhair fern, snapdragons (bright lemon yellow), Iceland poppies (yellow, orange, apricot mix).

LEMON YELLOW Cheerful and sunny with white cosmos, freesias, *Salvia farinacea*, *Coreopsis verticillata* 'Moonbeam', *Phormium* 'Yellow Wave', violas (yellow and blue).

LIME GREEN Refreshing with *Sedum* 'Angelina' (chartreuse), basils (green and 'Dark Opal'), coleus (especially Kong series), leaf lettuce (mix), Scotch moss.

RED Crisp and striking with white flowers—cosmos, dahlias, nicotiana, zinnias—perhaps with a hint of red (Candystripe or red zinnias).

C

Seasonal Strategies

Like a canvas waiting for paint, an empty pot can become anything you desire: a meditation in violet, a carnival of oranges and limes, or a quiet study of leaf shapes and textures. You have more control with containers than anywhere else in the garden. To create a successful container planting every time, see the tips below.

One plant, one pot, one season
The easiest way to ensure a steady stream of container displays during each season is to pot up a single perennial, grow it in a side yard that gets the right light, then move it out to center stage when it's in bloom. Or plant several pots, each with the same plant, to cluster on a patio or porch. Some reliable plant choices for pots: **Spring:** delphinium (low-growing types such as Blue Fountains), *Diascia*, primrose. **Summer:** canna, dwarf Oriental lilies, *Geum chiloense* 'Lady Stratheden' or 'Mrs. Bradshaw', heliotrope, *Pelargonium*, Shasta daisy. **Fall:** asters, chrysanthemums. **Winter:** cyclamen, *Euryops pectinatus*.

One to three plants for all seasons
For containers that look good in any season, pair two or three foliage plants for color and texture in a single pot. Choose ones that can live for a few years in the pot before they'll need planting out in the garden, and make sure they have the same requirements for water and exposure (sun or shade). Some combinations are:
• Leatherleaf sedge *(Carex buchananii)* or New Zealand hair sedge (*C. comans* 'Frosty Curls') with creeping thyme. • Dwarf hinoki false cypress (*Chamaecyparis obtusa* 'Aurea') with tassel fern *(Polystichum setosum)* and Scotch moss. • Australian silver rush *(Juncus polyanthemos)* with *Plectranthus* 'Heigh-Ho Silver'. • Golden rocket rush (*Baumea rubiginosa* 'Variegata') with Scotch moss. Or make it really simple by choosing a single dramatic foliage plant, such as *Phormium* 'Yellow Wave', as a focal point.

One pot, a changing bloom show
A single large pot can provide splashes of color in each season if you plan it well. Just build your design around permanent small shrubs, grasses, and trailing plants. Then fill in with annuals or bulbs that you'll replace during the year. **Fall:** In a large (18 to 22 inches in diameter) pot, plant a mahonia, dwarf nandina, or New Zealand flax such as *Phormium* 'Tom Thumb'. In the front of the pot, tuck in seasonal bloomers such as apricot-colored violas, bulbs of orange to red tulips, and peach-colored *Primula obconica*. The blooms will carry the show into spring, when the tulips appear. **Late spring:** After spring bloom is through, replace the fillers with French marigolds and *Gaillardia*.

Plant closely; feed and water regularly. The planting can last two years or more before the shrubs need to be replaced.

Bulbs in Pots

October is the perfect time to prepare giant pots of bulbs for the following year. Such containers flower four to seven months after planting, cost no more than a florist's bouquet (about $60, including pot, potting soil, and bulbs), and give three weeks of portable spring color. If you live in a mild-winter climate, refrigerate the bulbs in paper bags (away from ripening fruit) for six weeks before planting. Most nurseries sell a variety of bulbs.

Start by filling 16- to 24-inch terra-cotta containers with a fast-draining potting mix, to within 5 inches of the rim. (The containers have drainage holes drilled into the bottom.) Plant a solid layer of bulbs shoulder to shoulder (as shown at right) in each—the 24-inch container pictured below holds up to 70 large tulip bulbs. A 16-inch-diameter pot holds 40 to 50 bulbs. Cover the bulbs with 4 inches of potting mix, and water well. Set the container in shade until stems first emerge, then move it to full sun and water regularly. This display features extra-tall white 'Maureen' tulips.

Containers for All Seasons

When you grow plants in pots, you're really creating a garden in miniature. And because you're planting for a season instead of a lifetime, you have more freedom to experiment. To celebrate the seasons, plant a single pretty combo for each—like the spring, summer, and fall ones pictured here—to dress up a patio or porch. Pick a predominant plant first, then build the composition around it.

SUMMER: Cool Whites

A. White campanula **B.** *Cosmos* 'Sonata White' **C.** Licorice plant (*Helichrysum petiolare* 'Variegatum') **D.** *Plectranthus forsteri* 'Marginatus'

SPRING: Easter Egg Pastels

A. *Primula obconica* (lavender) **B.** Lady fern **C.** English primrose (yellow) **D.** Blue star creeper **E.** White flag (grass) **F.** Viola (lavender) **G.** Fairy primrose (lavender-pink)

FALL: Autumn Fire

A. *Phormium* 'Platt's Black' **B.** *Loropetalum* 'Plum Delight' **C.** Gloriosa daisy (*Rudbeckia hirta*) **D.** *Zinnia* 'Profusion Orange' **E.** Creeping fig (*Ficus pumila*)

Taste Treats

A. 'Sunburst Squash'. Other compact squash varieties for pots: 'Gold Rush' yellow zucchini, 'Spacemiser' green zucchini. **B.** 'Early Girl' tomato (use sturdy 5-foot wire cages to support this and other tall-growing types like 'Sun Gold' and 'Supersweet 100'). Or grow bush types such as 'Bush Celebrity'.

C

COVER CROPS

Also known as green manure, cover crops are legumes or grasses planted solely to improve garden soil, prevent erosion, and loosen compacted soil. Most cover crops are planted in fall (after the rains begin in mild-winter climates; six to eight weeks before the first hard frost in cold regions) and dug into the soil in spring. As they decay, they form humus, which improves the soil's structure and increases its ability to hold moisture.

Legumes such as fava beans, bell beans, Austrian peas, clovers, and vetch also add extra nitrogen to the soil, thanks to their association with nitrogen-fixing bacteria (*Rhizobium*). These bacteria draw nitrogen from air in the soil and "fix" it in nodules on a legume's roots. When the plants eventually decompose, the nitrogen is released back into the soil.

Grass or cereal cover crops such as rye, barley, buckwheat, and mustard don't contribute extra nitrogen to the soil, but they do produce plenty of organic matter. Gardeners often combine legumes and grasses as cover crops to enjoy the benefits of both.

Before planting, till or dig the area and rake it smooth. Treat legume seeds with an inoculant powder (available from seed companies selling cover-crop seeds) to be certain that bacteria are present. Sow seeds of cover crops directly over the plot in rows 1 foot apart and about 3 inches deep. Use 2 to 3 pounds per 1,000 square feet.

After the cover crop starts to flower, but before it sets seed (above), cut or mow it down and till it into the soil (above right). You can also cut the stems and leaves and add them to your compost pile, then dig just the lower stems and roots into the soil. Don't use a rotary tiller for mixes that include vetch, as the plants will tangle in the blades. After a couple of days, till again. Allow soil to sit another two days before planting. Rake the soil smooth (right), then plant.

DISEASES

The Integrated Pest Management (IPM) approach discussed on page 704 applies to diseases as well as pests. IPM aims to maintain an attractive, productive garden with minimal, if any, use of synthetic controls. The goal is to reduce diseases and pest populations to tolerable levels, not to eradicate them entirely—which is rarely possible in any case.

Plant Pathogens

Virtually all plant diseases are caused by three kinds of organisms: fungi, bacteria, and viruses. Any of the three may be responsible for leaf, stem, and flower diseases, but the vast majority of soilborne diseases are caused by fungi. Note that often what appears to be a disease is actually a result of cultural problems, such as nutrient deficiency (or excess), sunscald, or soil compaction (see page 727).

Fungi are microscopic, typically multicellular organisms. Some obtain their food parasitically from green plants, causing diseases in the process. Most produce spores that spread from one plant to another by wind, insects, splashing water, garden equipment, or handling. Given the right conditions, each spore will produce a new infection.

Bacteria are single-celled organisms. They feed on organic matter, including plants, and they must remain inside the host plant or in plant debris to survive, where they multiply rapidly by cell division. Because they require moisture and warmth for reproduction, bacterial diseases are generally more prevalent in rainy or humid regions. Garden watering can also provide the moisture they need to flourish. Bacteria are spread by insects, splashing water, garden equipment, and handling.

Viruses are ultramicroscopic particles capable of invading plant tissue and reproducing in it, usually at the expense of the host plant. They produce a variety of symptoms, including stunting and other abnormalities in growth, spots or discoloration on leaves, and damaged fruit. (Some attractive plants, such as variegated-leaf abutilon and certain tulips with flamboyantly striped flowers, owe their variegation to a harmless virus.) Most garden plants are susceptible to at least one viral disease. Especially prone are a number of vegetables, including beans, cucumbers, squash, tomatoes, and peppers.

Viral diseases are most commonly spread by plant-eating insects such as aphids, leafhoppers, and whiteflies. However, depending on the virus, spread can also occur via infected seeds and pollen; through pruning, grafting, budding, and other forms of vegetative propagation; and, in some cases, by contaminated hands, clothing, and tools.

To prevent viral diseases, plant resistant varieties (if available) and buy certified virus-free stock. Control virus-spreading insects and remove weeds, which are hosts for some viruses. If you find a virus-infected plant, the best course of action is to destroy it.

Dealing with Diseases

Because many diseases cannot be eradicated once their symptoms are apparent, prevention is of prime importance. Choose certified and disease-free plants and, whenever possible, plant resistant varieties. Many are noted in the entries in the Western Plant Encyclopedia, or consult your Cooperative Extension Office. Bear in mind, though, that "resistant" does not mean immune; rather, it means a plant is less likely to succumb.

Give each plant the climate, exposure, and amount of moisture and fertilizer it prefers— and no more. Allow plenty of space between plants to ensure good air circulation.

Control weeds, which may harbor pathogens and insects that spread diseases. Clean up the garden each fall so disease organisms can't overwinter in plant debris. Soil solarization (see page 747) can help destroy soil-dwelling pathogens, but it also kills many beneficial organisms, so use it only as a last-ditch effort before resorting to chemical measures.

If diseases do appear in your garden, immediately remove infected annuals and vegetables to keep the problem from spreading. On larger plants, including perennials, remove diseased flowers, leaves, and, if possible, branches. Between pruning cuts, dip tools in a solution of 1 part household bleach to 9 parts water to help keep the disease from spreading to other plants. Discard all infected material in the trash, not the compost bin.

Plant Diseases

Many diseases exhibit similar symptoms. If you are unsure of a diagnosis, contact your local Cooperative Extension Office for help. For lawn diseases, see page 693.

DISEASE & TARGETS	SYMPTOMS	PREVENTION & CONTROL
Anthracnose Fungal disease. Affects many different plants, both edible and ornamental, but seldom kills them.	Symptoms depend on plant type, but include sunken, gray, or tan to dark brown spots on leaves, stems, fruit, or twigs. Leaves wither and drop. Spores that cause it are spread by rain and garden sprinkling.	Plant resistant varieties. Clip off affected plant parts and destroy them. Avoid overhead watering, mulch the soil, and provide good air circulation around plants. Apply fungicides containing lime sulfur (during the dormant season), copper compounds, or chlorothalonil.
Damping Off Fungal disease. Affects all types of seedlings.	Seedlings collapse at or near the soil surface. In some cases, seeds rot before they can sprout.	Treat seeds, potting soil, or seedlings with a biological fungicide or buy pretreated seeds. Use sterilized medium and containers. Provide good air circulation. Avoid crowding seedlings; thin if necessary. Water seedlings from bottom trays. Discard infected seedlings and starting medium.
Fireblight Bacterial disease. Affects pome-producing members of the rose family, including apple, cotoneaster, crabapple, hawthorn, pear, pyracantha, quince, and toyon.	Shoots (and sometimes entire plants) blacken, appear scorched, and die suddenly. Appears in moist weather, especially early spring. Spread by insects, splashing water.	Plant resistant varieties. Using disinfected pruners, remove and discard diseased branches, cutting 6 to 8 inches below blighted tissue. Spray at 3- to 5-day intervals during the bloom season with Serenade or copper compounds.
Oak Root Fungus Caused by the fungus *Armillaria mellea*; destroys woody plants, especially native oaks and other dry-soil lovers.	Symptoms may not appear until the disease is well established, then plants suddenly wilt and die. Early indicators are patches of dull or yellowed leaves and/or sparse foliage. Look for whitish fungal tissue or dark shoestring-like structures under the bark of stems and trunks (at or below the soil line), or on large roots. Tan mushrooms may appear around the bases of diseased plants.	Plant resistant species. Excavate soil from the base of the plant so it can dry out. Remove turf grass or other plants that are growing within 6 to 10 feet of the trunk. Water only as much as necessary. Replace infected plants, removing stumps and as many roots as possible. Let the soil dry out thoroughly before replanting. There are no effective chemical controls.
Peach Leaf Curl Caused by the fungus *Taphrina deformans*. Affects leaves, shoots, twigs, blossoms, and fruit of peaches and nectarines.	In spring, thick, puckered reddish areas appear on leaves, which turn velvety and yellowish gray in color. Leaves eventually turn yellow or brown and drop. Tree growth and fruit production may decrease. Affected shoots become thickened and distorted and often die.	Minimize stress by irrigating deeply, applying a high-nitrogen fertilizer, and harvesting fruit promptly. Prune and spray trees each autumn after the leaves have fallen, or just before bud-break in spring. Use a copper-based fungicide that contains at least 50 percent copper.
Powdery Mildew Fungal disease. Infects leaves, buds, flowers, and/or stems, depending on the host plant and the particular fungus.	Small white or gray circular patches appear, then spread rapidly. New growth and blossoms may be stunted. Most powdery mildews thrive in humid air, but the spores—unlike those of other fungi—need dry surfaces.	Plant resistant varieties. Pick off and destroy infected plant parts. Give plants sufficient light and air circulation. Spray thoroughly with a garlic-based fungicide or the biofungicide *Ampelomyces quisqualis* (see page 688). During the growing season, spray with baking soda mixtures or a fungicide containing garlic or jojoba oil. Apply an antitranspirant such as Cloud Cover or Wilt-Pruf. Spray infected plants with jets of water early in the day.
Root Rots & Water Molds Fungal diseases (notably caused by *Pythium* and *Phytophthora*). Active in warm soils (55 to 80°F/13 to 27°C), but can lie dormant in cool conditions.	Plants wilt, and their leaves discolor, become stunted, and drop prematurely. Branches or even the entire plant may die.	Plant resistant varieties. Remove and destroy dead plants or branches. Improve drainage or plant in raised beds. Do not overwater. In the early stages, drench the soil with a garlic-based fungicide (commercial or homemade).
Rust Fungal disease, many specific to particular plants.	Powdery pustules form on undersides of leaves. Upper surfaces may be spotted with yellow; eventually, the whole leaf may discolor, then drop.	Plant resistant varieties. Remove and destroy infected leaves, or dig up and destroy badly infected plants. Provide good air circulation. In winter, clean up all fallen leaves and other debris. Avoid overhead watering and water early in the day. Spray with a garlic-based fungicide. Other sprays that may be effective (depending on the kind of rust and the infected plant) include copper soap fungicide, sulfur, triadimefon, triforine, or tebuconizole.

D

DISEASE & TARGETS	SYMPTOMS	PREVENTION & CONTROL
Sooty Mold Fungal disease. Grows on honeydew produced by sap-sucking insects.	The fungus itself does not injure plants but can block sun from the leaves, which may then turn yellow and drop prematurely.	Wash or wipe the fungus from leaves. Control honeydew-excreting insects (see pages 704–710).
Texas Root Rot Fungal disease found in the arid Southwest at elevations below 3,500 feet.	Leaves become slightly yellow or bronze and soon wilt but remain firmly attached to the plant. Small plants may die within a few days, while trees and shrubs may survive for several years.	Plant resistant species. Remove badly infected plants. Improve the soil by incorporating organic matter and lowering the pH (see page 728). There are no effective chemical controls.
Verticillium Wilt Fungal disease that plugs the water-conducting tissues in crops such as tomatoes and strawberries, and in woody plants.	One side of the plant may wilt and die. Leaves, then branches, turn yellow or brown, then die. Small plants may be destroyed in one season; mature trees may survive longer.	Plant resistant varieties. Dig up and destroy infected crops, and prune out dead branches with sterile tools. Give deep but infrequent irrigation. Fertilize neglected plants (but do not fertilize infected plants that show lush growth). Grow crops in containers or raised beds filled with sterile soil. Soil solarization may destroy the fungus (see page 747).

Products for Disease Control

Controls described below are the most useful and commonly available ones. Other products, generally less widely sold, are mentioned in the descriptions of specific plant diseases above and on the previous page.

Synthetic fungicides are manufactured. Natural fungicides and bactericides are products whose active ingredients originate in a plant, animal, or mineral, or whose action results from a biological process (as in the biofungicides discussed later). "Natural" does not mean "harmless"; some of these substances can harm people, pets, or plants if not used properly. New natural disease-control formulas are continually arriving on the market, so by necessity the list below is a partial one. To locate these, and biological pest controls, see page 704.

Caution: When applying any disease-control preparation, read label directions carefully and follow them exactly. The package will clearly state the plants and diseases for which the product should be used if the substance is not subject to registration. (This is the case with a number of new products made from food-grade ingredients such as vinegar, garlic, and citrus oils.) Always follow the safety directions on the label and dispose of any chemicals in a safe manner.

The following products are listed by the accepted common name of the active ingredient—the actual chemical that prevents or controls the disease or diseases listed on the package label. Before you buy, check the label to make sure you're getting the active ingredient you need.

NATURAL FUNGICIDES AND BACTERICIDES

- **Baking soda, sodium bicarbonate.** Helps to control powdery mildew on roses. You can make your own solution by mixing 2 teaspoons each of baking soda and fine-grade horticultural oil with 1 gallon of water. Commercial versions contain a "sticker" ingredient to help keep the spray on the plant.

- **Biofungicides.** These preventive products use naturally occurring fungi and bacteria to protect plants from harmful fungi without upsetting the soil's natural microbial balance. Used as a foliar spray, *Ampelomyces quisqualis* (sold as AQ-10) prevents powdery mildew on both edibles and ornamentals, and it will also parasitize newly established spores. A strain of *Bacillus subtilis*, sold as Serenade Garden Disease Control, is a broad-spectrum product that controls numerous bacterial and fungal diseases. Other biofungicides, used as soil drenches at planting time, prevent a number of seed, stem, and root rots, including rhizoctonia, phytophthora, pythium, and fusarium wilt. Other products available in the West include Mycostop (*Streptomyces griseo-viridis*), Rootshield (*Trichoderma harzianum*), and SoilGard (*Gliocladium virens*).

- **Copper compounds.** General-purpose fungicides and bactericides used to prevent brown rot, fireblight, peach leaf curl, shot hole, and other foliar diseases.

- **Copper soap fungicide.** Broad-spectrum fungicide used to control many plant diseases, including rust, powdery mildews, and black spot.

- **Garlic.** Controls many fungal diseases, including rust, black spot, mildews, and dollar spot and brown patch on lawns. You can buy commercial sprays and soil drenches, or make your own using this recipe: Blend

---

Sudden Oak Death (SOD)

In 1995, the previously unknown *Phytophthora ramorum* fungus started killing tanbark oaks and coast live oaks in California's Santa Cruz and Marin counties. Still centered there, the outbreak has spread as far north as Curry County on the southern Oregon coast and south to California's Big Sur coast. This pathogen thrives in the cool, moist evergreen forests of coastal canyons. There are scores of potential host plants, from bigleaf maple, camellias, and rhododendrons to coast redwoods and toyon. But none is so virulent as California bay laurel (*Umbellularia californica*), which suffers leaf damage but usually survives to become a contagious host. Susceptible oaks (see *Quercus* entry to learn which species are susceptible and which are immune) and tanbark oaks in turn become fatally infected. The tanbark oaks (*Lithocarpus densiflorus*) usually die within a few weeks of first visible symptoms, while true oaks (*Quercus*) often survive for a couple of years.

Spores commonly spread from a host plant during wet weather. They travel in wind-driven rain splash, in mud on shoes and tires, and perhaps even on animals. But for susceptible plants to be infected, they apparently need to receive a heavy dose of spores. Therefore, rural gardens adjacent to areas populated by host plants are at much higher risk for infection than are urban gardens, which are at less risk of being contaminated by the relatively small number of spores found on boots, tires, and (rarely) infected nursery plants.

If you live in the San Francisco Bay Area or in the coastal hills between the Big Sur coast and the southern Oregon coast and have a susceptible oak in your garden, there are two good strategies for protecting your tree:

- Remove any California bay laurel on your property that is growing within 35 feet of your susceptible oak or tanbark oak.

- If your neighbors have lost a tree to sudden oak death, or if they are growing a California bay laurel within 35 feet of your susceptible tree, you or an arborist can treat your tree with phosphonate (sold as Agri-Fos) to boost its immune system. The treatment must be repeated about every 18 months to provide protection.

3 ounces of minced garlic with 1 ounce of mineral oil, and let it soak for at least 24 hours. Strain, stir in 1 tablespoon of liquid castile soap, and store the mixture in a sealed glass container. It will keep at room temperature for several months. To use it, mix 2 tablespoons of the garlic oil with 1 pint of water.

- **Lime sulfur, calcium polysulfide.** Used as a dormant spray in winter to prevent various leaf spots and peach leaf curl later in the season.

- **Neem oil.** Used to prevent and control black spot, powdery mildews, and some other foliar diseases. Also used as an insecticide and miticide. Toxic to fish.

- **Potassium bicarbonate.** Used to control powdery mildews. May not be registered in all states.

- **Sulfur.** Controls powdery mildews, rust, and other diseases. Do not use in conjunction with horticultural oil sprays or when the outdoor temperature is above 85°F/29°C.

SYNTHETIC FUNGICIDES

- **Chlorothalonil.** Broad-spectrum liquid fungicide used to prevent powdery mildews, leaf spots, gray mold, scab, and a variety of lawn and other diseases. Toxic to fish.

- **Tebuconazole.** Liquid systemic fungicide used to treat and prevent black spot, leaf spot, petal blight, powdery mildew, rust, and scab on landscape plants.

- **Triadimefon.** Wettable powder; systemic used for the prevention or eradication of powdery mildews, rust, and some lawn diseases.

- **Triforine.** Liquid systemic for prevention and eradication of powdery mildews, rust, black spot, and a variety of other diseases.

- **Note:** Be sure to read all manufacturer's instructions before applying any synthetic fungicide to your garden, particularly if you grow edible plants.

FERTILIZERS

When plants are actively growing, they need a steady supply of nutrients. Though many of these are present in soil, water, and air, gardeners need to supply others. Most likely to require supplemental feeding are fast-growing annuals (such as vegetables and flowers), lawns, perennials, fruit trees, and immature plants of numerous kinds. Mature trees and shrubs, on the other hand, may need little or no fertilizing.

Knowing exactly what to supply, in what quantities, and at what times begins with understanding the nutrients plants need, when—and why. The entries in the Western Plant Encyclopedia cover fertilizing needs for many plants.

Keep in mind that plants' needs often change during the season. And at any given time, a plant may need more of one nutrient—phosphorus, for example—than others. The trick is to give it just the right amount, in order to maintain a nutrient balance in the the soil. Give it too much phosphorus, for example, and something else (perhaps nitrogen) will be in short supply.

For more information on plant nutrients and nutritional disorders of plants, see pages 711–712.

Getting Specific

SIMPLE VS. COMPLETE Complete fertilizers contain the three macronutrients nitrogen (N), phosphorus (P), and potassium (K). Some may also include secondary and/or micronutrients, which will be listed on the label. Simple fertilizers supply just one macronutrient. Most familiar are the nitrogen-only types, such as ammonium sulfate (21-0-0), and phosphorus-only superphosphate (0-20-0). Falling between complete and simple types are incomplete fertilizers. An example is 0-10-10, providing phosphorus and potassium but no nitrogen.

GENERAL- AND SPECIAL-PURPOSE The various fertilizers labeled "general-purpose" or "all-purpose" contain equal or nearly equal amounts of the macronutrients N, P, and K (a 10-10-10 formula, for example). They are intended to meet most plants' requirements throughout the growing season. Other formulas are designed to meet specific needs. For instance, high-nitrogen blends (such as 29-3-4) help keep lawns green and growing quickly, while higher-phosphorus mixes (6-10-4, for example) are intended to promote flowering and fruiting. Some packaged fertilizers are formulated for particular types of plants. Those designed for acid lovers such as camellias, rhododendrons, and azaleas are especially useful, as are fertilizers for citrus.

Types of Fertilizer

Inorganic (chemical) fertilizers are made from synthetic substances with concentrated amounts of specific nutrients, primarily nitrogen, phosphorus, and potassium. When you apply an inorganic fertilizer, you see almost instant results because the nutrients are immediately available to your plants.

Organic (natural) fertilizers are made from the remains or by-products of living or once living organisms. Manure, fish emulsion, bonemeal, and kelp meal are all examples of organic fertilizers that can be used alone or in various combinations. They release their nutrients more slowly than inorganic fertilizers. Many manufacturers combine several natural fertilizers to produce a complete fertilizer.

Dry fertilizers come as powders, granules, or pellets that can be spread on the ground or scratched or dug into the soil. Controlled-release types may be beadlike granules, spikes, or tablets. Dig granules into soil at planting time or scratch them into the soil surface (they're especially useful for containers). Use a mallet to pound spikes into the ground, and dig holes for tablets.

Liquid fertilizers are sold as crystals, granules, or liquid concentrates that you mix with water and apply with a hose, watering can, or spray bottle. The spray types, known as "foliar feeds," are generally used to deliver instant supplies of specific nutrients. Liquid fertilizers must be reapplied frequently, as their nutrients leach through the root zone rapidly.

To avoid burning leaves, water plants thoroughly before spraying them, follow label directions, and don't apply if outdoor temperatures rise above 85°F/29°C.

Reading a Fertilizer Label

Every fertilizer label states the percentage by weight of the three macronutrients used in mineral form, in this order: nitrogen (**N**), phosphorus (**P**), and potassium (**K**). So a fertilizer labeled 10-8-6 contains 10 percent nitrogen, 8 percent phosphorus, and 6 percent potassium. The label also tells you the source of each nutrient.

- **Nitrogen** may be included in a fertilizer in nitrate form. If so, it will be water soluble and fast acting, especially in cool soils, but is easily leached (requiring frequent replenishment) and can pollute surface and ground water if used to excess. Nitrogen in the form of ammonium is from organic sources (such as blood meal) and IBDU (isobutylidene diurea, a synthetic organic fertilizer). These are released more slowly and last longer in the soil.

- **Phosphorus** is expressed on product labels as phosphate, P_2O_5, and listed as "available phosphoric acid."

- **Potassium** is expressed as potash, K_2O, and may be described in various ways, including "available phosphate" and "water-soluble potash." Phosphorus and potassium do not move readily through the soil in solution and must be applied near plant roots to do the most good.

Before planting a new bed, *work in a fertilizer containing phosphorus and potassium (see page 712). For growing plants, apply liquid fertilizer into a watering basin with a watering can (right) or with a hose-end sprayer or an injector device through an irrigation system. Apply dry fertilizer as a side dressing by digging a shallow trench a few inches away from the plants. Scatter fertilizer in the trench (below), cover it with soil, then water. For plants with roots growing close to the soil, use a cultivator to gently scratch the soil beneath the plant, sprinkle fertilizer, and water thoroughly. Be sure to spread fertilizer to the full extent of the plants' root zones.*

Wildfires can be sparked in suburban areas when conditions are dry.

F

FIRE, LANDSCAPING TO PREVENT

In wilderness plant communities such as chaparral, oak woodland, and forest, wildfires are part of the natural cycle, clearing out dead and diseased plants and helping some seeds germinate. However, as more homes are built in these ecosystems, resulting in fires being routinely suppressed, the fuel load of living and dead plants builds up. When fires do occur, they are larger and more damaging.

Researchers have noted an increase in fire-season duration, with large forest fires starting both earlier and later in the year than in the past. With global temperatures projected to rise, officials anticipate a pattern of even fiercer fires over a longer burn season in the coming years. To reduce the chances of fire destroying your home, make sure that roofing, siding, and fencing materials are fire resistant.

A Fire-resistant Landscape

Consult the following sources for current information on landscaping to prevent fires: Firewise Communities (www.firewise.org) and the National Interagency Fire Center (www.nifc.gov).

Maintain a greenbelt zone around your home at least 30 feet wide (wider on steep slopes) of well-irrigated, low-growing plants. Remove any trees growing close to the house. Thin crowns of others and trim limbs so the lowest ones are 10 to 20 feet above ground. Cut back branches of large specimens to 15 to 20 feet from the house.

Reduce fuel load by pruning trees and shrubs. Cut grasses back to 4 inches when they turn brown, remove brush, and cut back ground covers and native chaparral annually. Clear leaf litter from the ground, rooftops, and gutters.

Eliminate fire ladders—plants of different heights that grow adjacent to each other—by removing midsize plants.

Clear flame pathways—horizontal bands of foliage that provide pathways for fire.

Choose low-fuel-volume herbaceous perennials such as common yarrow (*Achillea millefolium*), gazania, and poppy (*Papaver*), or low-growing ground covers. Keep them well watered. If you must let them dry out because of drought, be sure to cut them back. Avoid highly flammable woody shrubs such as California sagebrush (*Artemisia californica*), junipers (*Juniperus*), and California buckwheat (*Eriogonum fasciculatum*). Check with

your Cooperative Extension Office for more information on locally adapted fire-resistant plants.

Create a transition zone about 70 feet wide, spacing clumps of shrubs at least 18 to 20 feet from each other and from structures. Leave enough plants to stabilize slopes and prevent erosion, and leave only a few widely spaced trees.

Ease fire truck access to your property. Clear out overhanging tree branches and prune shrubs along driveways and access roads. Also make sure that driveways are at least 12 feet wide to allow fire trucks to maneuver easily. Gates should open inward and easily, and the lock shouldn't be so strong that firefighters cannot break it in an emergency.

FROST AND COLD PROTECTION

The best defense against cold damage is to choose permanent plants that are hardy in your zone. Use tender plants for summer displays, or plant them in containers and move them indoors in winter.

Also learn your garden's microclimates—areas that are warmer or colder. The riskiest spots are stretches of open ground exposed to air, particularly from the north. Other high-risk locations include hollows and low, enclosed areas that catch cold air. The warmest part of any garden is beside a south-facing wall with an overhang. Lath structures and the branches of evergreen trees also protect from frost.

To some extent, you can condition plants and soil for cold weather. Water and fertilize in late spring and early summer, while plants are growing the fastest. In late summer, taper off nitrogen feeding; don't stimulate new growth that won't have time to mature (harden off) before cold weather arrives. Keep soil moist through the onset of the frost season, as damp soil holds more heat than dry soil.

An early-fall or late-spring frost is more damaging than one striking when plants are semidormant or dormant. Be alert for still air, clear skies, low humidity, and, of course, low

temperatures. Check weather bulletins as well. To protect from such unseasonal frosts, move container plants indoors and give in-ground plants temporary shelter (see box at right). For ways to protect vegetables from frost, see page 739.

Cutting back frost-damaged plants too soon can stimulate tender new growth that will be nipped by later frosts. Wait until new growth begins in spring to remove wood that you can see is clearly dead.

In climates where the ground freezes hard and temperatures drop below 0°F/–18°C, both roses and broad-leafed evergreens such as boxwood (*Buxus*), euonymus, holly (*Ilex*), pieris,

To protect broad-leafed evergreens, water thoroughly before the ground freezes, then apply a thick mulch to protect the plants' roots. Spray exposed plants with an antitranspirant near the time of the first hard freeze; it forms a thin film that seals in moisture and prevents desiccation. Drive stakes into the ground around the plants, then nail or staple burlap to the stakes. (Don't use plastic film, as it hinders air circulation.)

and rhododendron need help to survive harsh winters. See the Western Plant Encyclopedia for more information on winter protection for roses (page 596).

Protection from Occasional Frost

Make a frame of four strong stakes around the plant. Lay plastic or burlap over the tops of the stakes, making sure it does not touch the leaves—as this would cause them to freeze. If you need more heat, place one or two trouble lights or a string of holiday lights in the shelter. Plug the lights into an extension cord or outlet intended for outdoor use. Do not let them contact the plastic or burlap.

For a quick cover for smaller plants, use a large cardboard box. Cut the bottom on three sides to make a lid you can open and close as needed.

Gardeners in cold climates can start seeds in a greenhouse before the last frost.

GREENHOUSES

For avid gardeners in many climates, a greenhouse is essential for a variety of purposes:

- Providing winter shelter for tender plants, such as potted citrus trees.
- Starting seeds (see pages 718–719) of annuals and vegetables in early spring.
- Rooting cuttings (see page 720) that need a protected, moist location.
- Raising vegetables and flowers to maturity where the growing season is short.
- Growing specialty crops such as orchids and tropical plants that require controlled temperatures and humidity.

Greenhouses vary widely in size and complexity, from small bay windows attached to the house to simple lean-tos to more elaborate freestanding structures. Greenhouse frame materials include wood, aluminum, and PVC pipe. The glazing used for the building's walls and roof may be single- or double-walled glass, fiberglass, double-walled polycarbonate plastic, double-walled polyethylene, or acrylic. Double-walled glazing holds heat most efficiently. If you garden where heavy snowfalls are common, be sure the greenhouse can stand up to the snow load.

GROUND COVERS

The term "ground cover" typically refers to nongrassy plants, among them shrubs, vines, and many perennials. Ground-cover plants blanket the soil, adding variety to the garden and suppressing weeds. If chosen carefully, they require considerably less maintenance and water than lawns do.

Choosing Ground Covers

Start by considering your site. Is it level or sloping, sunny or shady? How much water will be available for the plants? Also decide whether you want a ground cover you can walk across or one that will serve as a traffic barrier. Choose between a deciduous cover or an evergreen one and decide whether you want flowers or prefer just foliage. Ask yourself how the ground cover will fit in with the garden's other plants and hardscape. For ideas, see the Plant Selection Guide on pages 94–97.

Planting and Caring for Ground Covers

In most of the West, fall planting gives plants time to establish their roots over winter. In the coldest areas, wait until spring to plant. Prepare the planting area as directed on page 712. Some ground covers, however, can be planted directly in native soil with little or no amendment. This group includes various tough, shrubby types, many of them Western natives.

Before planting, install landscape fabric (see page 747) to help control weeds, if desired.

On a steep slope where erosion may occur, arrange plants in staggered rows. Make an individual terrace for each plant and create a basin or low spot behind each one to catch water. Set the crowns of the plants high, so they won't become saturated and rot after watering.

When planting ground covers purchased in small pots or flats, set them in holes the same depth as and slightly wider than the root ball. For directions on setting out plants from gallon-size containers, see page 715. Water thoroughly after planting, then keep the soil moist (but not soggy) as the plants settle in. Apply a mulch to help conserve moisture and to prevent weed seeds from growing.

Once ground covers are established, their water needs vary depending on the particular plant and its soil. Fertilizer requirements differ, too. As a rule of thumb, though, most woody, shrubby ground covers, especially drought-tolerant sorts, have fairly low nutrient needs; many get along with little or no fertilizing. Perennial ground covers with softer, lusher growth generally have higher nutrient requirements and should receive an annual feeding in spring.

For fastest coverage, set ground-cover plants in offset rows. Form diamond patterns with groups of four plants. Spacing varies with the plant; check entries in the Western Plant Encyclopedia for details. For even distances, measure with a piece of wood cut to the desired spacing.

Rows of seedlings and potted plants in a greenhouse.

HERBS

The word "herb" applies to any plant that, at some time in history, has been valued for seasoning, medicine, fragrance, or general household use. This includes tall, willowy plants like dill as well as low, fragrant, fine-textured creepers like thyme. Many herbs are annuals and biennials grown for their leaves and seeds. Others, such as French tarragon and oregano, are perennials. Still others are tough landscape shrubs such as rosemary.

Planting and Caring for Herbs

Choose a planting spot that receives six to eight hours of full sun each day. Well-drained soil is essential. If drainage is poor, dig in plenty of organic matter, or plant in raised beds. Work in a complete fertilizer before planting (herbs aren't heavy feeders).

Most perennial and shrubby herbs are easier to start from transplants than from seed. Nurseries offer many kinds, typically in 2- or 4-inch pots. Some are also sold in gallon containers. Annual and biennial herbs such as basil, dill, and parsley, on the other hand, can easily be started from seed.

After planting herbs from containers, water regularly until the plants are growing steadily. Thereafter, most will need only occasional irrigation. Exceptions are basil, chives, mint, and parsley, which prefer evenly moist soil.

When perennial herbs resume growth in early spring, feed them lightly with a complete fertilizer or spread compost around the base of each plant, taking care not to cover the crown.

You can mix herbs with flowers or plant them in beds and borders. They can, of course, be grouped in an all-herb garden, be it a sunny corner of the vegetable plot, a special raised bed, or a traditional circular planting centered with a birdbath or sundial. The plan below shows one way to combine herbs in a 5- by 5-foot plot. Plant taller herbs such as rosemary in the center, lower-growing plants around the edges. Clockwise from top: parsley, sage, thyme, oregano, majoram, oregano, thyme, sage. Chives fringe the bed.

Drying Herbs

Harvest herbs for drying just as the first flower buds begin to open, when the oils in the leaves are most concentrated. Cut sprigs or branches in the morning, after dew has evaporated. Tie them together at the cut ends and hang them upside down in a warm, dry, well-ventilated place out of direct sunlight. When the leaves are crisp and crumble readily, strip them from the stems and store them whole in airtight jars.

Another way to dry herbs is to remove the leaves from the stems and spread them on screens placed in a warm, dry, airy place out of direct sun. Stir them every few days as they dry. Once they feel crisp, they're ready to store in airtight containers.

With herbs grown for their seeds, harvest seed heads or pods when they turn brown. Dry them in paper bags until you can shake the seeds loose; then store seeds in airtight containers.

Herbs make excellent container plants.
Pot culture is a good way to grow them near the kitchen door, handy for snipping. Plant soft-stemmed herbs that you will harvest frequently, or choose small plants of larger herbs such as sage. You can plant these out in beds at the end of the season. Clockwise from top: oregano, golden sage, 'Tricolor' sage, chives, lemon thyme.

LAWNS

The classic lush, crisply mowed lawn was a landscaping staple in the arid West early in the 20th century, when dams, pipelines, and electric pumps made water easily available. Today, however, water shortages have made obvious the fact that traditional turf grasses require more water per square foot than almost any other garden plant. As a result, some homeowners have eliminated the lawn entirely, while others have sharply reduced its size. Other useful steps include planting lawns in simple geometric shapes, which allows irrigation without overspray, keeping them fairly level to minimize runoff. Perhaps most important, choose the right grass for your climate, and prepare and plant the site carefully.

WATERING AND FERTILIZING LAWNS

To encourage deep rooting and conserve water, irrigate lawns as deeply and infrequently as possible. In mild climates, once or twice a week should be adequate during warm weather; in hotter regions, you'll probably have to water

---

To keep a lawn healthy, mow it regularly. Leave the clippings on the lawn to decompose and add nutrients to the soil.

more often. Check with local water agencies or your Cooperative Extension Office for guidelines, which are often based on evapotranspiration (ET)—a localized, weather-based measurement of how much water a plant uses and how much evaporates from the soil. To determine how thirsty the lawn really is, you can also perform a few informal tests. First, just step on the grass. If the blades don't spring back from your footprint, it's time to water. Or push a screwdriver into the soil; if it doesn't penetrate easily, the lawn probably needs water. A soil sampling tube (see page 716) gives a more accurate measurement.

Many sprinklers apply water faster than the soil can absorb it. To prevent runoff, water in cycles. Sprinkle until just before runoff or puddling occurs (typically 10 to 15 minutes), then repeat the cycle in an hour. Adjust sprinklers so they don't overshoot onto paving. To improve water penetration and reduce runoff, aerate and dethatch your lawn once a year. Local nurseries offer information and equipment to help you with these tasks.

Most lawns are heavy feeders, requiring regular applications of high-nitrogen fertilizer. In the desert, iron may also be beneficial. Give cool-season lawns two applications of fertilizer in spring and two in fall. Fertilize warm-season lawns monthly in late spring and summer (Bermuda grass only lightly in summer, to restrain its growth). Numerous bagged lawn fertilizers, both synthetic and natural, are sold. Check the packages for recommended application rates. If you cut back on watering because of drought, hold back on fertilizer as well.

Grass is weakened if allowed to grow too long between mowings. Recommended mowing heights are given in the grass descriptions on the following page.

The Right Lawn Grass for Your Region

For more information on specific grasses, consult the individual listings in the Western Plant Encyclopedia.

Cool-season grasses withstand winter cold but typically languish in hot, dry summers. Most grow best in the Northwest, in parts of the Rocky Mountains with (usually) abundant summer rainfall, and in areas with cooling marine influences. These grasses are often sold as mixes of several kinds. Even if one of them is not adapted to the soil or sun and shade conditions in your garden, chances are that others in the package will do well.

BENT GRASSES (*Agrostis*, p. 177) Fine-textured. Requires ample water and more care than other lawn grasses. Grow it in acid soil, in sun or light shade. Mow at ½ to ¾ inch. Sold as seed, sod.

CRESTED WHEATGRASS (*Agropyron cristatum*, p. 176) Light bluish green color. Tough, drought-tolerant lawn. Grow it in sunny areas. Adapted to Rocky Mountains and High Plains. Goes dormant and turns brown in hot weather. Mow at 2 inches. Sold as seed.

FINE FESCUE (*Festuca rubra* and others, p. 352) Fine-bladed grasses that succeed in well-drained soil in shaded sites. Fairly drought tolerant. Sometimes blended with Kentucky bluegrass or perennial ryegrass; used to overseed warm-season grasses. Mow at 1½ to 2 inches. Sold as seed.

TALL FESCUE (*Festuca arundinacea*; also called coarse fescue, p. 351) Tough grass that tolerates heat and some drought and flourishes in sun or shade. It freezes out in the coldest climates. Newer selections (dwarf tall fescue) are finer bladed, deeper green. Mow at 2 to 3 inches. Sold as seed, sod.

KENTUCKY BLUEGRASS (*Poa pratensis*, p. 553) Classic grass for cooler regions. Needs regular water. Takes sun, light shade. Mow at 2 to 2½ inches. Sold as seed, sod.

PERENNIAL RYEGRASS (*Lolium perenne*, p. 451) Deep green grass that does best in sun. Needs frequent watering. Used as year-round lawn in cooler regions or to overseed winter-dormant grasses. Mow at 2 inches. Sold as seed, sod.

Warm-season grasses thrive in hot weather and turn dormant and brown in cold winter weather. Most are choice grasses for California and the Southwest. For a year-round green lawn, overseed warm-season grasses with cool-season grasses for the colder months.

BERMUDA GRASS (*Cynodon dactylon*, p. 305) Good, drought-tolerant lawn for large, sunny areas. Mow at 1 inch. Sold as seed. Finer-textured hybrids do not self-sow. Mow at ½ to ¾ inch. Sold as sod, sprigs, plugs.

BLUE GRAMA (*Bouteloua gracilis*, p. 229) Tolerates drought, extremes of temperature, and a wide range of soils. Does best in sun. Makes a better-quality turf when blended with buffalo grass. Mow at 2 to 3 inches. Sold as seed.

BUFFALO GRASS (*Buchloe dactyloides*, p. 233) Very drought-tolerant lawn for sun; slow growing. Mow at 3 inches. Sold as seed, sod, plugs. Best in mountain regions. Can be invasive.

ST. AUGUSTINE GRASS (*Stenotaphrum secundatum*, p. 634) Adapted to wide range of soils but does best along coast. Grows best in sun but tolerates shade. Needs regular water. Stolons can invade other parts of the garden. Mow at 1½ to 3 inches. Sold as sod, sprigs, plugs.

ZOYSIA (*Zoysia*, p. 677) Tolerates drought and heat, sun or shade. Mow at 1 to 2 inches. Sold as sod, sprigs, plugs.

Lawns can suffer *from many problems, including sod webworms, fairy ring, mushrooms, rust, red thread, and thatch.*

keep the lawn wet for three to five days. Aerate the lawn. There are no effective chemical controls.

Mushrooms can be a sign of fairy ring or oak root fungus (see page 687). To control, apply a nitrogen fertilizer and aerate the lawn.

Rust fungi can afflict Kentucky bluegrass, perennial ryegrass, tall fescue, and zoysia lawns. Infected lawns have an overall yellowish to reddish color. Small, reddish pustules form in round or elongated patches on older leaf blades and stems. Blades eventually shrivel and die.

To control, apply adequate but not excessive nitrogen fertilizer. For rust spores to germinate, leaf surfaces must be wet for four hours. Water in the morning so that grass will dry out during the day. The fungicides triadimefon and chlorothalonil may be effective.

Sod webworms are larvae of several kinds of moths. These pests attack all turf grasses. Small dead patches appear in spring and gradually enlarge during summer. Pale moths fly close to the lawn in a zigzag pattern at dusk. To confirm the presence of sod webworms, drench an affected patch of lawn with a solution of 1 tablespoon dishwashing soap and 1 gallon water. Larvae will float to the surface; if you find 15 or more per square yard, treat the lawn. To control these pests, try parasitic nematodes (see page 705). For chemical control, use a product containing permethrin (a pyrethroid, see page 709).

White grubs are the larvae of several species of beetles; they are 1 to 1½ inches long with three pairs of legs. When exposed they curl into a C shape. White grubs feed on the roots of all turf grasses. Distinct, irregularly shaped brown patches appear in afflicted lawns; symptoms are most severe in late summer. Sections of dead turf pull up easily.

To control, apply parasitic nematodes (see page 705), first checking that the species you buy is recommended for use against white grubs. Chemical controls include carbaryl and imidacloprid. They work best if you first dethatch the lawn.

L

PLANTING A NEW LAWN Whether you start a lawn from seed, sod, sprigs, or plugs, proper site preparation is essential. Remove any existing sod with a sod cutter (available from rental yards); for easier removal, you can kill the grass with an herbicide (see page 750). Have the soil's pH tested (see page 728) to determine whether any specific amendments are needed. Till the site to a depth of about 8 inches and spread it with a 3- to 4-inch layer of an organic amendment. Also apply a complete fertilizer and any materials recommended to adjust the pH. Till again, then rake the area smooth and water it thoroughly. Let the soil settle for a few days; then sow seed, lay sod, or set out plugs or sprigs as shown on the next page. All except sod require diligent weed control after planting.

LAWN PROBLEMS To avoid lawn problems, plant grass that's well adapted to your area and care for it properly. If you do encounter problems, the following information will help you identify and correct them. (For lawn weeds, see pages 748–749.)

Chinch bugs—when exposed, the grubs curl into a C shape. Adults are black with white wings folded over their backs; nymphs may be reddish or orange and pink with white bands. The pests suck plant juices, mid-summer to fall, and are especially troublesome on St. Augustine grass.

To control, eliminate thatch. Keep lawn moist to promote beneficial fungi that attack chinch bugs. For chemical control, use a product containing cyfluthrin and bifenthrin (pyrethroids, see page 709).

Dog urine causes yellowing patches on grass. To restore affected areas, sprinkle with horticultural lime and water deeply.

Fairy ring, a fungal disease, is common in lawns growing in soil that is high in organic matter or that contains wood debris such as boards or old roots. Symptoms include small circular patches of dark green grass surrounding areas of dead or light-colored grass. Mushrooms may or may not be present.

To control, apply a nitrogen fertilizer, then

Seed, Sod, Sprigs, or Plugs?

SEED is the least expensive way to start a lawn. Package labels should list the named varieties of the grasses included and indicate a high rate of germination for those grasses. It should also show a low percentage of crop or weed seeds in relation to the percentage of lawn grass seeds.

Fall seeding is recommended for most grasses. In the coldest climates, seed in early fall so the lawn can grow before winter.

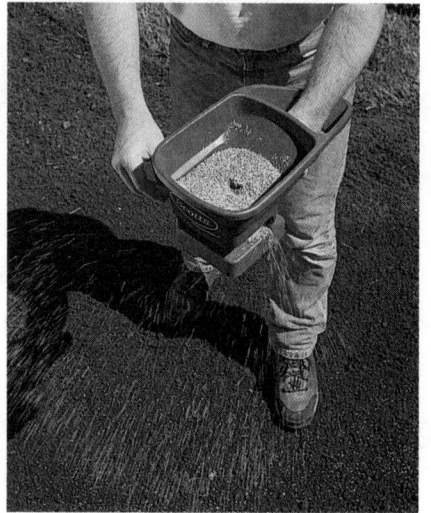

1 After preparing the area, scatter seed. A mechanical spreader helps sow seed evenly.

2 Lightly rake seed into the soil.

3 Spread a ½-inch layer of mulch, such as aged or nitrogen-fortified sawdust, over the area. Roll with an empty roller to press seed into soil. Water thoroughly. Keep the seedbed moist with frequent, light watering until the seed sprouts.

SOD is the most expensive way to start a lawn, but it does give instant coverage with almost no weed problems. Local suppliers offer varieties adapted to your area. The lawn will establish itself most quickly in the cooler weather of spring or fall.

1 After preparing the site, moisten the soil. Unroll the strips and lay them out with their ends staggered, pressing the edges together firmly.

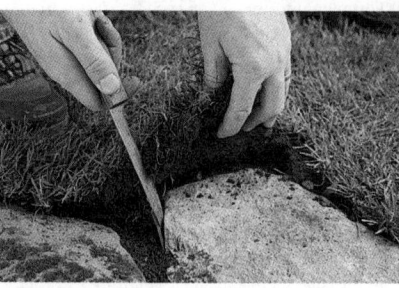

2 Use a knife to trim sod so it fits snugly around paving and other obstacles.

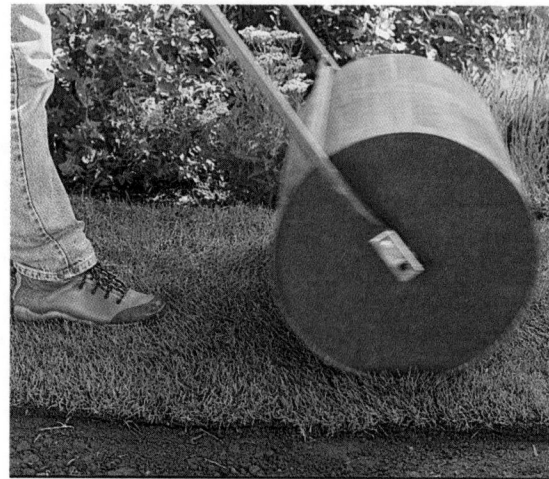

3 To press roots firmly into the soil, roll the lawn with a roller half-filled with water. Water the new lawn once daily (more often in hot weather) for six weeks.

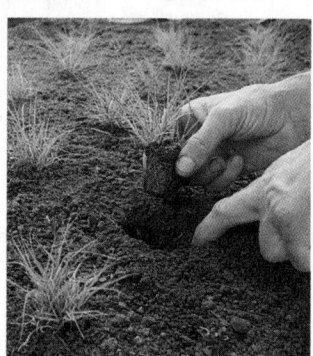

SPRIGS are pieces of grass stem and root. They're used to plant spreading warm-season grasses. Plant in spring, following the supplier's directions; water often until roots take hold.

Sprigs of hybrid Bermuda grass root and spread quickly in well-prepared soil.

Two-inch plugs of buffalo grass and some other spreading warm-season grasses are sold in trays. Planted at 8-inch intervals, they'll grow together in a year.

PLUGS are small rooted plants. They're used for warm-season spreading grasses, such as buffalo, hybrid Bermuda, St. Augustine, and zoysia. Plant them in spring, following the supplier's directions. Water often until roots take hold.

Bermuda grass sprig

Buffalo grass plug

L

MULCHING

Mulch is any material that covers soil surfaces and allows air and water through. It helps hold moisture in the soil, and it provides insulation from extreme or rapid changes in temperature. Mulch prevents most weed seedlings from becoming established (and makes it easier to remove any that do grow); keeps mud from splashing up onto foliage, flowers, fruit, and surfaces such as house walls; helps prevent erosion; and makes your garden beds look tidy. Before applying any mulch, clear away existing weeds. When applying mulch, take care not to cover plants' crowns, as too much moisture can cause rot.

ORGANIC MULCHES   Derived from once living matter, organic mulches break down slowly, improving the soil and adding nutrients as they decompose. Choices include chopped leaves, compost, grass clippings (be sure to apply clippings in thin layers, letting each layer dry before applying another), pine needles, shredded bark, ground bark, wood chips, sawdust, straw, and coir dust. Other good organic mulches are agricultural by-products such as crushed nut hulls or shells, and pomace, the pulpy remains of grapes or apples that have been pressed to make wine or juice. (Let pomace dry before using it.)

INORGANIC MULCHES Options include gravel and other kinds of rock, plastic sheeting, and landscape fabrics. Stones make permanent mulches that can discourage weeds effectively. Check with the supplier for the amount you need. Plastic warms the soil, and black plastic suppresses weeds.

Landscape fabrics, unlike plastic, are porous, allowing air, water, and dissolved nutrients to reach the soil. Sold in nurseries and garden supply centers, these fabrics are best used in permanent plantings around trees and shrubs. They aren't really suited for beds of vegetables or annuals, where you change plants often. Install around existing plants or cut slits in them to accommodate new ones. After installation, cover the fabric with a 2- to 3-inch layer of a weed-free organic mulch.

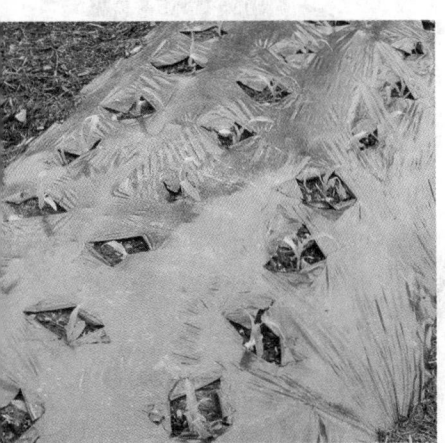

Black plastic mulch *suppresses weeds and warms the soil. Install plastic first, then cut X-shaped holes for young plants.*

How Much Mulch?

Bulk quantities of organic mulch are sold by the cubic yard. Determine how many square feet you want to cover (multiply the area's length by its width), then consult the chart below.

To cover this area	2 inches deep	3 inches deep	4 inches deep
100 square feet	$2/3$ cubic yard	1 cubic yard	$1\,1/3$ cubic yards
250 square feet	$1\,2/3$ cubic yards	$2\,1/2$ cubic yards	$3\,1/3$ cubic yards
500 square feet	$3\,1/3$ cubic yards	5 cubic yards	$6\,1/3$ cubic yards
1,000 square feet	$6\,2/3$ cubic yards	10 cubic yards	$13\,1/3$ cubic yards

Types of Mulches

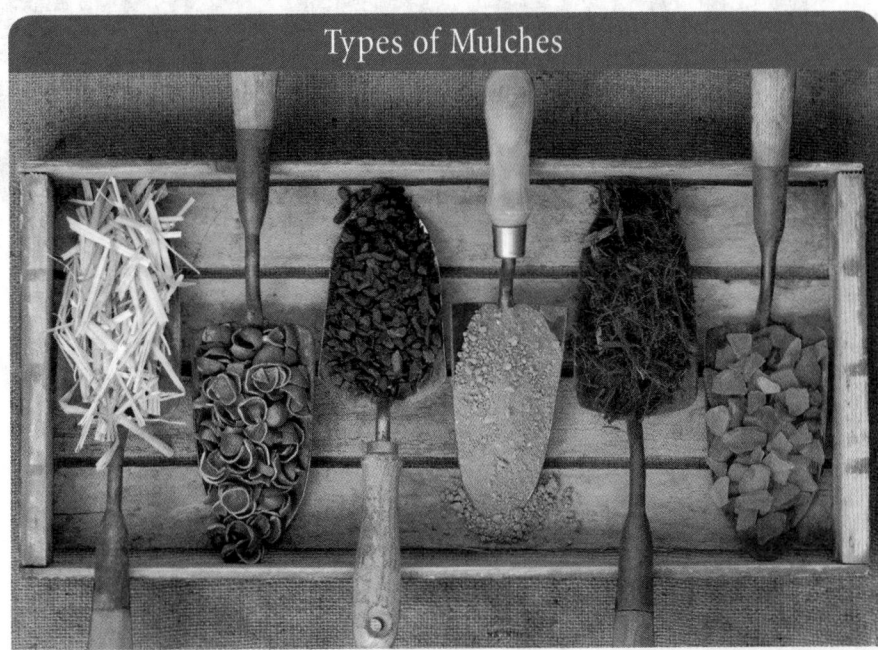

Straw is a light, loose option that lets water pass through easily. It is good around vegetable and strawberry beds. Buy at livestock-feed stores (avoid hay, which has seed heads). Apply 4 to 5 inches.

Hazelnut hulls are good for general use and ideal for paths. Most readily available around Oregon's Willamette Valley. Apply 2 to 3 inches.

Cut bark is made from various woods, depending on your location. This is a good, all-purpose mulch. Mini size gives landscapes a polished look. Apply 1 to 2 inches.

Decomposed granite (DG) compacts quickly and doesn't tend to blow away. Attractive in Southwestern and desert landscapes. Can be prone to weeds. Apply 1 to 2 inches.

Shredded bark is slow to decompose, and it knits together so that it stays in place. Useful on slopes and in windy areas. Has a woodsy, natural look. Apply 2 inches.

Tumbled glass is pricey, so use it mainly to add color and punch to small areas. Apply 1 to 2 inches.

NATIVE PLANTS

Native plants give your garden a sense of place, harmonizing it with your region's landscape. They attract wildlife, including birds, butterflies, lizards, and insects, to the garden. And because they're naturally suited to the climate in your region, natives are generally self-sufficient, needing little care once established.

The West is home to desert, chaparral, oak woodland, coniferous forest, and various wetlands. Local native plant societies, demonstration gardens, parks, and field guides can all teach you more about groups of plants indigenous to your area. For a list of plants native to several Western regions, see the Plant Selection Guide on pages 105–113.

Your garden may offer enough diversity to accommodate natives from different communities. A hot, dry, well-drained slope is an excellent site for chaparral plants. A damp, low-light spot will suit shade-loving natives adapted to moist locales, while a little-watered area beneath trees is right for those that prefer dry shade. A permanently wet, even boggy area is ideal for moisture-loving species.

N

A dark backdrop of native Douglas firs (Pseudotsuga menziesii) *is bordered by a drift of heaths that echoes the rolling hills leading to Mount Rainier.*

Designing with Natives

Growing natives doesn't have to be an all-or-nothing proposition. You can have sagebrush and a patch of lawn too, just not side by side. Here are ways to incorporate natives into your landscape.

- **Perimeter plants.** Plant natives with low irrigation needs, like brittlebush or ceanothus, on the edges of your property, saving your irrigation water for a more oasis-like planting closer to the house. Or, if you have a wilderness view, use some of the same plants that grow naturally on your property's borders.

- **Problem-solvers.** To help stabilize slopes, try mahonia, manzanita, *Ribes,* or sumac. For dry shade, consider bush anemone, Pacific Coast iris, or Western sword fern. Where you need plants resistant to oak root fungus (see page 687), try bush anemone, Catalina cherry, or spice bush. Near windy coasts, where salt spray is a problem, use coyote brush or lemonade berry.

- **Water-tolerant natives.** Some natives cannot tolerate any summer water (flannel bush, for example). But others happily adapt to regular garden irrigation: coral bells, monkey flowers, Western columbine, wild ginger, and wild strawberry are examples. As always, match the plant's water needs to the conditions in each part of your garden.

- **Mediterranean mates.** Western natives and Mediterranean plants thrive in similar growing conditions, but many Mediterraneans tend to bloom later than natives, in late spring and summer. Combining the two gives you a longer season of interest.

Planting and Caring for Natives

In mild-winter climates you can plant natives any time of the year, but the best time is fall through early spring, when cool and rainy weather allows plants to establish themselves more easily.

In cold-winter climates, plant in early fall, stopping six weeks before the ground freezes, or in spring after the ground thaws.

Many natives need well-drained soil, so before planting, test the soil's drainage (see page 728). In most areas, there's no need to add amendments such as compost to the soil at planting time. Set plants in planting holes and backfill with native soil. However, if the native topsoil has been scraped off or the soil is compacted, replace a third of the native soil with well-composted organic matter.

When setting out container-grown plants, start with young ones that are not root-bound. They may not be much to look at when first planted, but they'll adapt more successfully than larger plants.

Water immediately after planting, being sure to saturate the soil. Then water carefully and steadily for the first summer or two. Don't inundate the plants, but don't let them dry out, either. Once you've taken care to establish your natives through their first two years, and assuming you have planted them where the natural conditions suit them, they should do well with little or no supplemental watering. In general, Western natives don't require fertilizing and some are actually weakened by it. A light mulch is beneficial, but to avoid rot, keep it away from the plants' crowns.

Southwest gardens *often imitate the natural desert landscape, where cactus can emerge between boulders.*

Dave Fross on Natives for Beginners

When Dave Fross started his business, Native Sons Wholesale Nursery in Arroyo Grande, California, native plants were a tough sell. People reacted to *Muhlenbergia rigens,* for instance, as if it were a weed. Now, the same ornamental grass flies out of the nursery. "I sell thousands of plants a year," he says.

A big reason for this change of heart, says Fross, is the latest generation of gardeners. "They've been taught ecological principles since kindergarten, they embrace nature rather than try to conquer it, and they want gardens that reflect the Western landscape."

No natives in your garden yet? Try one of the following garden-friendly species, suggests Fross. "They're all great for beginners."

- *Ceanothus.* Shrubs and ground covers with flowers in a stunning range of blues; all are perfect for coastal gardens. Two showy cultivars: 'Ray Hartmann' (dark blue flowers), 'Concha' (cobalt blue flowers).
- Desert willow *(Chilopsis linearis).* "Simply the best summer-blooming large shrub or small tree for the Southwest." 'Burgundy Lace' is an especially choice cultivar.
- *Woodwardia fimbriata.* Native from British Columbia to Mexico, this bold fern adds drama to woodland gardens.

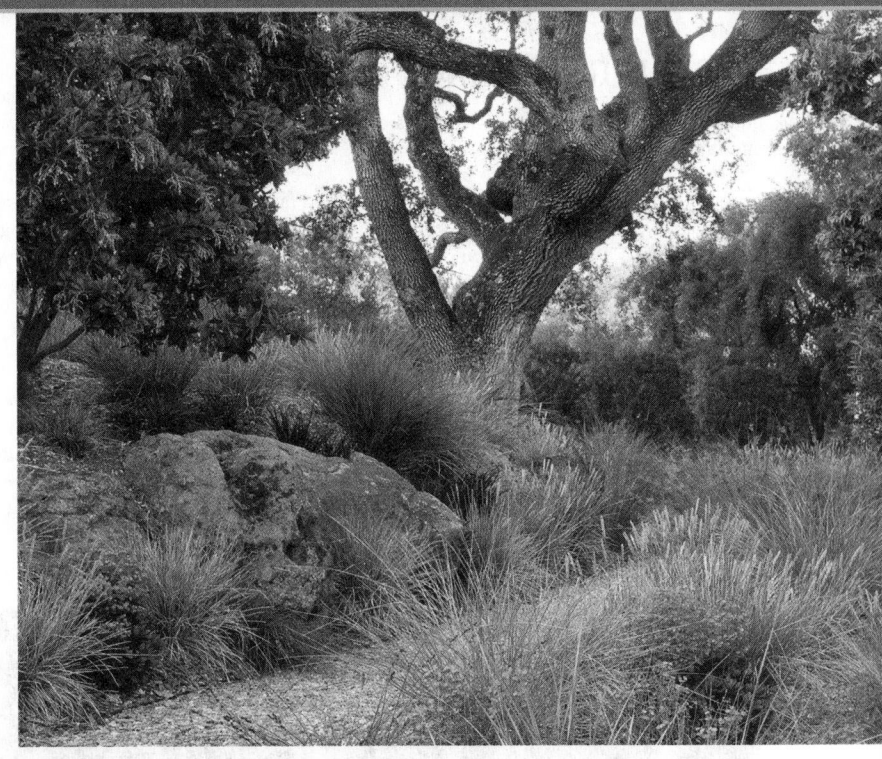

California oaks need dry summers, *so grasses and rocks make natural companions.*

N

Clockwise from left, *a riot of wildflowers cloaks the rear garden of this home in Breckenridge, Colorado. Favorite natives pictured close-up are* Ceanothus, Western columbine (Aquilegia formosa), Mahonia, *and* Lewisia cotyledon.

ORGANIC GARDENING

Also known as chemical-free or natural gardening, organic gardening is often associated with edible gardens, but its principles apply to any sort of garden, not just the vegetable plot and the fruit orchard. Organic gardeners and farmers strive to produce the healthiest plants possible with minimal impact on the environment and minimal risk to all creatures—human and otherwise—who enjoy the garden. They avoid using chemical fertilizers and pesticides, focusing instead on creating healthy soil, which in turn promotes strong plants that are less susceptible to disease and insects. Organic gardeners aim for biological diversity in their gardens, choosing plants that will attract a wide variety of organisms, including the beneficial creatures that help keep damaging pests under control.

As noted below, many aspects of organic gardening are covered elsewhere in this guide to gardening.

Building Healthy Soil

Healthy garden soil is home to earthworms and numerous other beneficial creatures. Its structure is hospitable to plant roots—neither too dense nor too loose, fast draining yet moisture retentive. To achieve this kind of soil, treat your planting beds with organic amendments such as compost and manure (see pages 680 and 729 for more on composting and soil amendments). Cover crops (page 686) offer an easy way to add large amounts of organic material to the soil. Organic gardeners prefer natural fertilizers (page 689), which, though slower acting than chemical ones, provide a more sustained release of nutrients and encourage beneficial soil-dwelling organisms.

Problem Solving

Be diligent about monitoring the garden so you know which problems are present and what natural controls (beneficial insects, for example) may already be at work. Physical controls such as barriers, handpicking, and spraying water jets can curtail insect damage. Choosing

O

plant varieties that are resistant to specific diseases and pests is important; you will find many such varieties listed in the Western Plant Encyclopedia. Crop rotation prevents diseases and insects that are specific to certain plants from building up in any one part of the garden. Mulching keeps weeds down. Physical management techniques such as pulling and hoeing weeds (page 746) are also effective.

Tea Time for Plants

One of the best liquid fertilizers is a simple brew that you can easily make yourself: compost tea. Not only does it provide balanced nutrition for plants, but evidence suggests that it can also help prevent plant diseases. All you need are a bucket and some compost. If you don't have access to a fresh supply, a high-

quality bagged compost from a nursery will work. To make the tea:

Fill the bucket about one-third of the way with compost. Add water to fill the bucket, then let the mixture steep for three to four days. Strain the mixture through cheesecloth. Return the remaining solids to your compost bin or add them to the potting mix in one of your containers.

Before using the brew, dilute it until it reaches the color of weak tea and apply it as you would any liquid fertilizer. To use compost tea as a foliar feed, add ⅛ teaspoon of vegetable oil or mild dishwashing liquid to each gallon of tea. This will help the solution adhere to plants' foliage. One caution: Strong sunlight can damage the wet leaves, so do your spraying in the morning or on an overcast day.

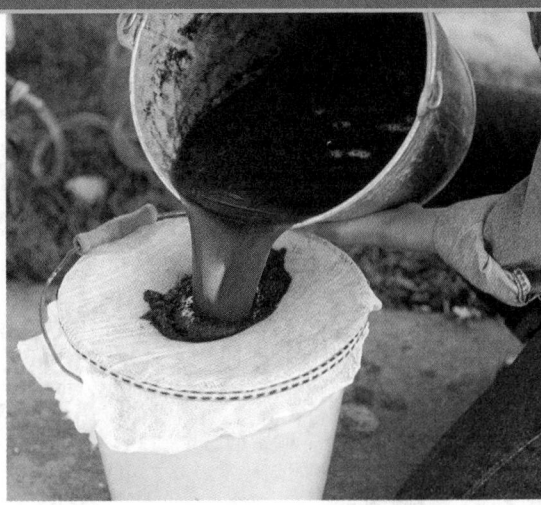

Strain compost-tea mixture through cheesecloth.

An Organic Test Garden

The 400-square-foot garden at Sunset's Menlo Park, California, headquarters (left) is designed around a zigzag split-rail fence that runs east to west. Tall plants like corn and sunflowers grow on the north side of the fence so they won't shade shorter plants, while tomatoes grow against the fence for support. On the south side of the fence, triangular planting beds hold low-growing crops, such as melons, peppers, and squash; herbs; and flowers, such as bee balm and scabiosa, that attract beneficial insects. Across the pathway, zinnias and shorter varieties of sunflowers grow in an informal row. Pole beans climb a trellis at the west end of the row.

Preparing the Garden *The top 8 inches of soil were turned with a rotary tiller (available at tool-rental yards). A 3-inch layer of compost was spread over the soil, then tilled in. The varieties chosen are well adapted to the California climate. (Local nurseries and regional seed suppliers can help you choose the best plants for your area.) Plants are spaced closely together to minimize weeds. Vegetables and flowers are intermingled to keep pollinating insects and birds circulating.*

Caring for the Garden *In spring and summer, compost tea (see above) adds nutrients to the soil and increases the amount of microbial life in the soil. That in turn reduces the load of soil pathogens, keeping plants healthier. In fall, a cover crop is sown to add nitrogen to the soil and improve soil texture and water penetration.*

O

Biodynamics

In northern California, biodynamic farming of wine grapes is catching on with growers. But its earth-friendly principles are finding their way into vineyards elsewhere, and into home gardens as well. What is biodynamics?

"It's the highest form of organic farming," says Michael Benziger, whose Benziger Sonoma Mountain vineyards in Glen Ellen, California, have earned his Benziger Family Winery numerous environmental awards. Like organic farming, biodynamics relies on crop rotation, tilling, and composting to maintain soil health, and on natural rather than chemical methods to control pests, weeds, and diseases. Like permaculture and sustainable farming, it emphasizes the creation of a self-sustaining ecosystem. But biodynamics goes a few steps further. It incorporates the environment in and around the farm or growing area, and works with natural forces (such as the life cycles of beneficial creatures) to create the balanced ecosystem.

At Benziger Vineyards, a large Insectary Garden hums at the heart of the vineyard; every plant is carefully chosen to bloom at a certain time in order to attract a pollinator needed just then. Bees zip through lavenders, Russian sage, and *Verbascum bombyciferum*, hummingbirds dart among *Kniphofia* and *Salvia*. The place is alive with a high-pitched buzz as nature's pollinators give the farmers a hand.

- Be observant. Check how plants are responding to sun or shade, wet or dry conditions, different soils. Learn all things that affect plant growth, and move the plant if it isn't happy where it is.

- Keep the soil vital. A healthy soil is alive with microorganisms and earthworms. Use compost and cover crops to replenish the soil.

- Time the cycles of soil preparation, cultivating, and harvesting to the seasons in your area.

Creeping wild rye *mingles with mixed sedges, including* Carex praegracilis, *in this Santa Cruz, California, meadow.*

ORNAMENTAL GRASSES

Grown for their graceful form and varying textures, ornamental grasses provide a handsome foil to shrubs and perennials. Many are excellent container plants too. Warm-season grasses are mainly deciduous; they grow from spring through summer, bloom in fall, and then go dormant. They bring beauty to the fall and winter garden with their dried leaves and flower plumes. Warm-season grasses include most species of *Miscanthus, Molinia, Panicum,* and *Pennisetum.*

Cool-season grasses are typically evergreen, though some may die back in cold climates. They begin new growth in fall, then flower in spring and summer. This group includes *Calamagrostis, Deschampsia, Festuca, Helictotrichon sempervirens,* and *Sesleria,* as well as the sedges *(Carex).*

Grasses also have two different growth habits. Running grasses (also called spreading grasses) multiply by spreading stolons or rhizomes. A few can be invasive. Most ornamental grasses, however, have a clumping growth habit, and there is no danger of their invading lawns or flower beds.

A few species of ornamental grasses are tender perennials often grown as annuals in cool climates—fountain grass *(Pennisetum setaceum)* is an example. For help in choosing these plants, see the Plant Selection Guide on pages 102–103.

John Greenlee on Meadow Making

The term "meadow" means different things to different people. It describes various natural and cultivated plantings, from expansive grasslands to woodland clearings to natural sedge *(Carex)* lawns. Grass grower and designer John Greenlee calls a designed meadow "a blend of sedges and grasses with small bulbs and wispy perennials." The result is a natural-looking area of grassy planting, with flowering plants providing spots of color through the grasses.

A meadow can be as large or as small as you like, Greenlee says. "They're ideal replacements for small patches of lawn that serve no purpose." Choose your accent plants well and the meadow should provide a constantly changing display through the seasons. As a bonus, a meadow needs very little care—just a few mowings per year. Set the lawn mower blade high—about 4 inches—so that you can mow over other plants without damaging their foliage.

To create a meadow in a small backyard, keep it simple. Start with an evergreen ground-cover sedge such as *Carex pansa* to create the framework, then mix in low-growing flowering perennials in clusters here and there, along with small spring-blooming bulbs. Add taller grasses in back for variation. Or tuck in a licorice-scented sweet flag for subtle fragrance underfoot.

Listed below are some of Greenlee's favorite meadow inhabitants.

Low-growing Grasses and Sedges
Bouteloua gracilis Blue grama
Buchloe dactyloides Buffalo grass
Carex pansa California meadow sedge
C. texensis Catlin sedge
Festuca idahoensis

Taller Accent Grasses
Eragrostis Love grass
Muhlenbergia capillaris Pink muhly
Nassella tenuissima Mexican feather grass

Meadow "Sweeteners"
Bulbs
Chionodoxa Glory-of-the-Snow

Crocus speciosus
Ipheion uniflorum Spring star flower
Iris (smaller types)
Scilla Squill

Perennials and Annuals
Antennaria Pussy toes
Chamaemelum nobile Chamomile
Coreopsis
Gaillardia Blanket flower
Geranium Cranesbill
Pratia pedunculata Blue star creeper
Sisyrinchium
Viola

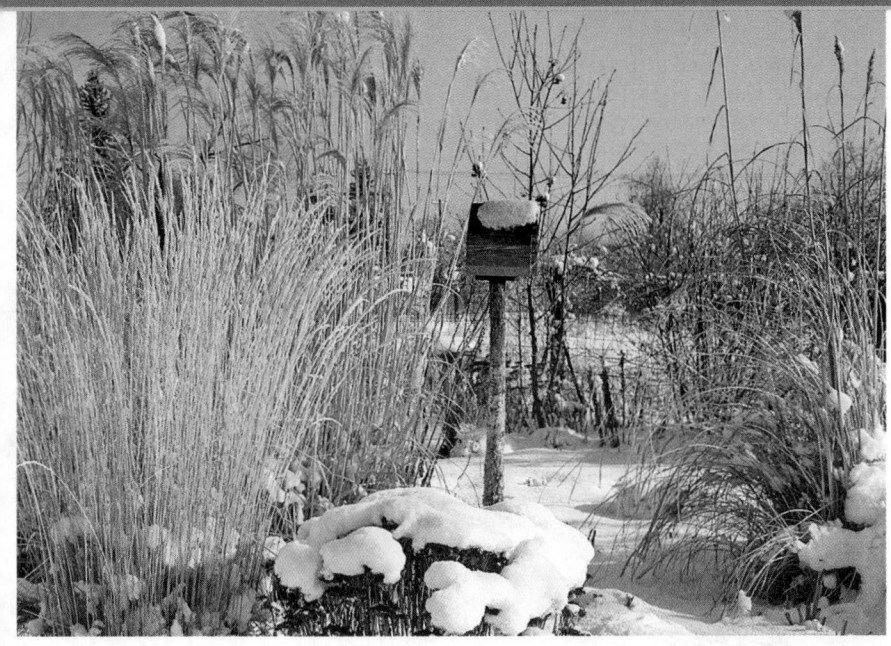

In cold-weather areas, you can choose to leave faded stalks and flower heads through the winter. The subtle buff tones of grasses bring warmth, structure, and interest to a snowy landscape.

Grooming Grasses

Most grasses benefit from an annual cleanup in late winter.

Warm-season grasses' foliage turns brown in fall before the plants go dormant. Wait to cut them back until later winter or early spring, when new growth appears from the base. Plants will regrow quickly. If necessary, divide large clumps of grasses. Dig out the plant, then use a saw or shovel to cut the root ball into sections. Replant the divisions immediately.

Cut back cool-season grasses just as you see new growth emerging in spring, using pruning shears to trim dead foliage and flowering stems to within a few inches of the ground. If you have a number of large clumps, electric hedge shears or a mechanical weed trimmer will make quick work of this project. Evergreen grasses needn't be cut back every year. Instead, "comb" out old growth by running your fingers through the clumps (wear gloves for grasses with sharp blades). After a few years, however, the grasses may develop a great deal of unattractive or dead leaves. At that point, cut them back by two-thirds in fall or early spring to encourage fresh new growth. Divide old clumps in fall, winter, or spring.

Planting and Caring for Ornamental Grasses

Garden care for ornamental grasses is much like that for perennials. Most should be planted in spring, though cool-season sorts can also be set out in autumn. Before planting, work organic matter, such as compost, and a complete fertilizer into the soil.

Don't bury the plants' crowns when you set them in, as this can lead to rot. A mulch will help keep down weeds and conserve soil mois-ture, but again, be careful not to let it pile up around the grasses' crowns.

Ornamental grasses vary greatly in their moisture requirements. Some need water regularly, others only rarely. Check the listings in the Western Plant Encyclopedia for details. If planted in well-prepared beds and mulched, most ornamental grasses can do without feeding, but if they're growing poorly, give them an application of general-purpose fertilizer in early spring.

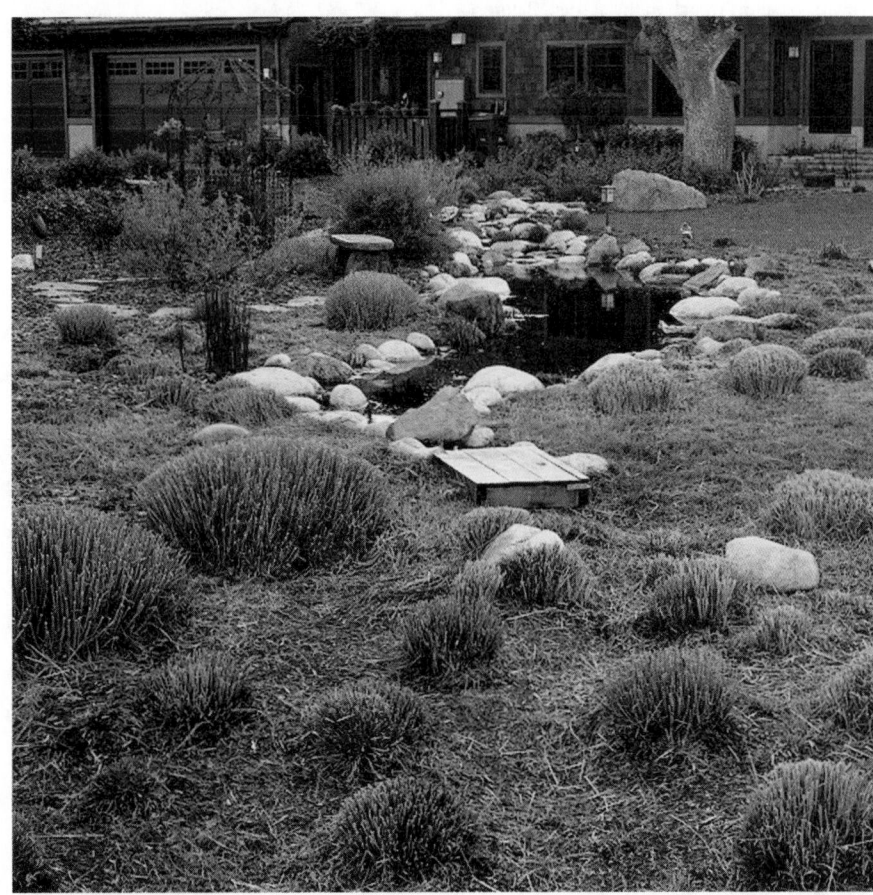

In early spring, use sharp hedge shears or pruners to cut off one section of foliage at a time (above). Work through the plant, leaving a small, neat mound (right). Small grasses (shorter than 3 feet) can be cut down to 3 inches or less. Larger grasses can be cut to 4 to 6 inches.

PERENNIALS

Perennial plants have widely varying growth habits, but all live for more than 2 years, in contrast to annuals and biennials (page 678). Some perennials—including hosta and peony (*Paeonia*)—die down to the ground at the end of each growing season, then reappear at the start of the next. These are often called "herbaceous" perennials. Others, such as Shasta daisy (*Chrysanthemum maximum*) and coral bells (*Heuchera*), go through winter as low tufts of leaves, ready to grow when spring arrives. A third type of perennial is truly evergreen, persisting almost unchanged throughout the winter months. Thrift (*Armeria maritima*) and yucca are two examples.

Planting Perennials

Nurseries and garden centers offer perennials in containers that range from cell-packs to 1-gallon pots; for information on planting these, see page 715.

Nurseries and mail-order catalogs also sell some perennials bare-root during their dormant period. As the name implies, bare-root plants have had most or all of the soil removed from around their roots, which are then surrounded with organic packing material and enclosed in plastic bags. If you'll be planting bare-root perennials within a day or two after purchase or receipt, open the bags slightly, add a little water, and hold them in a cool place. If planting must be delayed by more than a few days, however, pot up the plants in small containers or heel them in—plant them temporarily in a shallow trench in the garden. Before setting out bare-root perennials in their permanent location, prepare the soil as described on page 712. Then plant as shown on page 714.

Caring for Perennials

Although routine watering during growth and bloom will satisfy most perennials, some plants prefer drier soil, while others demand lots of moisture. These are noted in the Western Plant Encyclopedia. Young plants require more frequent watering; mulch them to help retain water in the soil. Feed established perennials once annually in late winter or early spring, using a complete fertilizer.

Throughout the bloom season, deadhead your perennials (that is, remove the spent flowers), both to keep the plants tidy and to prevent them from setting seeds. Certain perennials have attractive seedheads that many gardeners prefer to leave in place until winter or early spring, both for decoration and to provide food for seed-eating birds.

Later in the year (in fall or winter) clean up most perennials by removing old, dead, and fallen foliage, flowers, and stems. This neatens the garden and deprives pests (especially snails and slugs) of hiding places.

Staking Perennials

Some perennials are naturally inclined to sprawl or flop over, so you need to prop them up. Here are three useful staking techniques.

Metal hoop support

Stakes and string

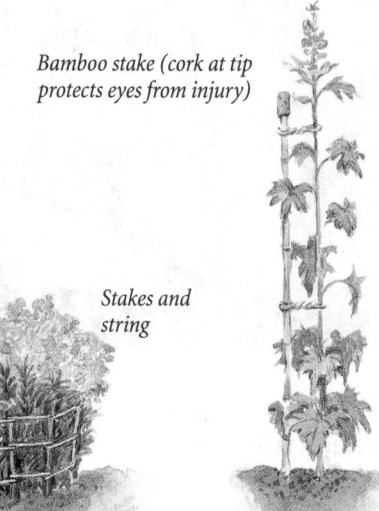
Bamboo stake (cork at tip protects eyes from injury)

Many gardeners in cold-winter climates mulch perennials over the winter to protect them from alternate freezing and thawing. As soon as the ground freezes, apply a lightweight mulch that won't pack down into an airtight mass; evergreen boughs, salt hay, marsh hay, and pine needles are all good choices.

Dividing Perennials

Over time, many perennials form such thick clumps that the plants are too crowded to turn in a good performance. When this happens, dig and divide them.

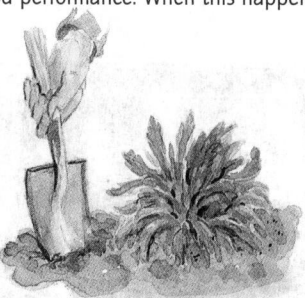

1 Loosen the soil in a circle around the clump, cutting 6 to 12 inches beyond the plant's perimeter with a shovel or spading fork, then dig under the roots to free them from the soil. Lift the whole clump out of the ground; or, if it's too heavy to lift, cut it into sections.

2 Gently tease some soil from the root ball. For larger, fibrous-rooted perennials such as daylilies (*Hemerocallis*), hose off as much soil as possible. Note the natural dividing points between stems and root sections.

3 Some perennials can be easily pulled apart by hand. Others will have to be cut with a knife, small pruning saw, or trowel. Types with thick, tough roots may require a sharp-bladed shovel or an ax. Divide clumps into good-sized sections.

4 Trim any damaged roots, stems, or leaves. Replant the divisions as soon as possible, then keep them well watered while they get established. You can also put divisions into containers to set out later or to share with other gardeners.

P

Secrets of an Effective Perennial Border

Curving borders are more interesting—and more complementary with casual landscapes —than straight-edged ones. Before planting, put down a rope or hose and adjust it until you form a pleasing design. If your border space follows a straight line along a driveway or curb strip, for instance, soften its edges by clustering low plants there to billow and ramble.

Lacy, small-flowered plants such as asters, coral bells, nemesia, and yarrow are great fillers. Place them in drifts between larger-flowered plants. To edge your border, use low, mounding plants such as creeping zinnia, curly sedge, lamb's ears, 'Lime' thyme, Santa Barbara daisy, sweet alyssum, or—in shade— *Lamium maculatum* or Semperflorens begonias.

Use accents to give the border visual punch, clustering a few plants whose flowers are bigger or of a deeper color than those that surround them. Also, plants that have unusual foliage, such as burgundy-leafed rhododendron, make dramatic accents, as do clusters of candle delphiniums and ornamental grasses such as maiden grass. Or tuck a hefty terra-cotta urn or a birdbath among plants.

Layer plants by height, from the lowest ones in the front to the tallest ones in back. Space plants close together so their "shoulders" will touch when they are grown. Make sure to include backbone plants to give the border some structure in winter— small evergreen shrubs, perennials, grasses, or dwarf conifers, for instance. If space allows, add plants for seasonal interest, such as bulbs and deciduous Japanese maples.

Create color echoes. A cohesive border has a primary color theme— pastels, perhaps, or sunny yellows and blues. These colors repeat throughout the design. Plant in clusters or drifts, by plant type, or by flower and foliage color. When choosing your plants, keep in mind the colors of the house, as well as hardscaping such as paving, fences, and walls.

P

PESTS AND PEST MANAGEMENT

A healthy garden hosts an abundance of life, including insects and wildlife. Most of these share the yard and garden without causing any problems. Many are welcome visitors, performing vital functions such as pollinating plants, feeding on undesirable insects, and helping to break down plant matter, building soils and recycling nutrients. However, some garden visitors may injure plants and unacceptably damage the garden. These we call pests.

Approach pests with Integrated Pest Management (IPM), a philosophy whose primary aim is prevention. If insects, diseases, or other problems become serious, IPM offers a number of techniques to reduce their effects to tolerable levels.

IPM begins with good cultural practices. Choose plants that are adapted to your climate and garden conditions. Look for varieties that are resistant to diseases, unpalatable to browsing deer, or otherwise unlikely to suffer from problems that may occur in your garden. Prepare planting beds well, and periodically amend the soil with organic matter, such as compost, to improve conditions for root growth. Water, fertilize, and prune to promote healthy growth. A vigorously growing plant often can outgrow the injuries caused by garden pests.

Check your plants frequently to spot problems before they get out of hand. Being able to diagnose problems and recognize pests—and beneficial species—is fundamental to the IPM approach. Learning a bit about specific pests will allow you to judge the seriousness of the problem, and whether any actions should be taken. To help with identification, read the descriptions given in this section or contact your local Cooperative Extension office.

Physical Controls

There are many things you can do to limit pest problems. Good cultural practices can keep pests at bay and allow plants to tolerate some injury. Physical controls include actions that can directly kill or capture pests. Chemical controls, involving use of pesticides, need be employed only as a last resort.

Handpick to destroy snails, caterpillars, insect egg masses, and other pests that can easily be found among the plants. Take care to leave the lady beetle larvae and other beneficial insects that are sometimes mistaken as pests (see facing page).

Prune and destroy branches, canes, and other plant tissues that show evidence of actively developing pests such as borers, scales, fire blight, and any plant diseases.

Spray plants with a strong jet of water to dislodge or kill small insects such as aphids, thrips, and spider mites. Regular spraying may also help manage powdery mildew.

Erect barriers to deter pests. These may range from a high, continuous fence around an entire garden to row covers protecting a bed of plants and caps or protective collars around individual plants. Diatomaceous earth can deter some crawling insects. Wood ashes and copper strips can deter slugs and snails.

Rotate the location of plants in your garden from season to season. This is particularly helpful for reducing plant diseases that survive in soils.

Use traps to capture and monitor pests. Yellow sticky cards are used to capture flying insects such as whiteflies and aphids. Damp newspaper or other cover can concentrate slugs, millipedes, and earwigs that seek daytime shelter (see below). Adults of some moths can be captured with pheromone traps that include as a lure the chemicals used by the female moth to attract a mate. Such traps are particularly useful in helping you know when to spray for fruit insects, such as codling moth in apples and pears.

Biological Controls

Every garden has a built-in array of pest-control measures. Among the most obvious of these are biological controls—predators and parasites that feed on garden pests and help control diseases.

Birds, toads, and garter snakes all prey on insects. Plants that provide food and shelter for birds can increase their beneficial activities around a garden (see page 752).

Many insects prey on pest insects and mites. Lady beetles and mantids are perhaps the best known, but a number of other predators, such as lacewings, ground beetles, syrphid flies, and hunting wasps, occur in gardens. Spiders all feed on insects and can provide tremendous benefits in plant protection. Other insects, such as parasitic wasps and tachinid flies, lay eggs inside pests; as the larvae develop, they kill the pest. Many of these beneficial insects can be encouraged by planting flowers that they use as sources of nectar and pollen (see pages 114–117).

Mosaic virus (transmitted by insects) · *Snails and slugs* · *Thrips* · *Mealybugs* · *Aphids* · *Scale insects* · *Weevils* · *Beetles* · *Caterpillars* · *Spider mites*

Insects, mites, and even many plant diseases are themselves subject to diseases caused by viruses, fungi, and bacteria. Perhaps the most common attackers are fungi such as *Beauveria bassiana* that kill many garden insects, particularly in moist conditions. One bacterial disease of insects, *Bacillus thuringiensis (Bt)*, is used in many plant protection products.

Sources for Beneficial Insects

Many of these "good bugs" may be in your garden already, or can be encouraged to appear. Several mail-order companies sell biological pest and disease control products, as well as natural pesticides and organic fertilizers. These include:

Golden Harvest Organics, Fort Collins, Colorado **www.ghorganics.com**

Harmony Farm Supply, Sebastopol, California **www.harmonyfarm.com**

M & R Durango Inc., Bayfield, Colorado **www.goodbug.com**

Peaceful Valley Farm Supply, Grass Valley, California **www.groworganic.com**

Rincon-Vitova Insectaries, Inc., Ventura, California **www.rinconvitova.com**

The Bio-Integral Resource Center in Berkeley, California, publishes a Directory of Least-Toxic Pest-control Products. See **www.birc.org** or call (510) 524-2567

For more on IPM, visit the University of California's website **www.ipm.ucdavis.edu**

Trapping Slugs, Snails, and Earwigs

Overturned clay pots and damp newspapers set in the garden can attract slugs and earwigs. Fermenting liquids, such as beer or sugar, are attractive to slugs and snails and can be placed in traps to lure the pests. Earwigs are attracted to vegetable oils, wheat bran, and wheat germ. Dispose of trapped pests in sealed plastic bags.

Beneficial Insects

Assassin bugs are slim insects with long legs and even longer, angled antennae. Most are green or gray, but some are brightly colored. They feed on caterpillars, beetle larvae, and various flying insects that rest on plants. One type, known as the ambush bugs, commonly hide among flowers and capture visiting insects late in the season.

Damsel bugs are small gray or brownish insects that are difficult to spot. These also are general predators that feed on small caterpillars, aphids, and many other pests.

Ground beetles are black or metallic colored beetles up to an inch long. They are most active at night but may be spotted under rocks or boards during the day. They will feed on almost any insect—and some slugs—that live on or around the soil surface.

Hunting wasps come in many sizes and shapes. Many capture whole insects that they paralyze, then place in a small cavity to provide food for their young. Others, such as the paper wasps, produce colonies and feed their young with caterpillars, sawfly larvae, and other insects. The paper wasps can sting humans, but when their nests are located in an area where they are not disturbed they can be very useful for controlling garden insects.

Lacewing adults are delicate insects with fine lacy wings. Although they usually feed on nectar and pollen, their young are voracious predators. Often called "aphid lions," they somewhat resemble miniature alligators with long, curved jaws that they use to capture aphids—and almost any insect that is smaller than they are. Lacewing eggs are available through many mail-order suppliers.

Lady beetles, also known as ladybugs, are familiar to gardeners and over 100 species are found in the West. Adults of most lady beetles are brightly colored and patterned, although some are black. The larvae are ¾ inch long, and dark with some bright patterns. They are useful for controlling aphids, spider mites, scale insects, and many other garden pests. Attract them by planting flowers that provide nectar and pollen for the adults, and by allowing some aphids to remain on a few plants or plant parts.

Mantids are one of the best known and most spectacular of the insect predators, but they are relatively rare in most gardens and so their effect on managing pests is probably minimal. Some native species of mantids occur in the West, and eggs of the Chinese mantid are available from some nurseries and mail-order suppliers.

Minute pirate bugs are tiny black and white insects most commonly found in flowers. These prey on smaller pests like spider mites, aphids, and thrips.

Parasitic nematodes are nearly microscopic roundworms that kill insects through introducing a bacterium into their body. Nematodes can help control pests that spend part of their lives in the soil, such as white grubs, root weevils, and cutworms. Beneficial nematodes are available from many mail-order suppliers. They must be applied to moist soil to be effective.

Parasitic wasps include thousands of species, each of which attacks specific kinds of pests. Typically, females lay their eggs in or on the pest insect and the young wasps then kill it, usually in a week or so. Gardeners may see the cocoons produced by the pupal stage of the wasps after they emerge from caterpillars (see below).

Predatory stink bugs are large, broad insects that feed on caterpillars and beetle larvae, as well as some plants. You can often see their egg masses, which resemble small colored barrels.

Plants that Attract Beneficial Insects

Integrate these plants into a border or place them in swaths around the garden. Mix many kinds, as the wider the range of food and shelter you provide, the more varieties of insects you'll attract and the more likely they'll be to stay. Plan your garden so that some plants are in flower throughout the year.

Buckwheat (*Eriogonum*)
Clovers (*Trifolium* and other species)
Coriander (*Coriandrum sativum*)
Coreopsis
Corn cockle (*Agrostemma githago*)
Cosmos (*Cosmos bipinnatus*)
Dill (*Anethum graveolens*)
Evening primrose (*Oenothera*)
Fennel (*Foeniculum vulgare*)
Feverfew (*Chrysanthemum parthenium*)
Fleabane (*Erigeron*)
Mustard (*Brassica*)
Parsley (*Petroselinum crispum*)
Sweet alyssum (*Lobularia maritima*)
Tansy (*Tanacetum vulgare*)
Tidytips (*Layia platyglossa*)
Wild lilac (*Ceanothus*)
Yarrow (*Achillea*)

Soldier beetles are narrow-bodied red or orange insects with black markings. Adults eat aphids and other soft-bodied insects while the larvae feed on soil-dwelling insects. You can often spot common soldier beetles in late summer feeding on pollen and mating among the flowers.

Spiders are arachnids, not insects, but their prodigious appetite for garden pests puts these eight-legged creatures high on the beneficial list. Most useful to gardeners are not those that make webs—as they capture flying insects that often are not harmful to plants—but spiders that hunt on the ground, such as crab spiders, jumping spiders, and wolf spiders, which feed on many insects.

Syrphid flies, also known as flower or hover flies, often superficially resemble bees or wasps. Most are marked with orange, yellow, or black bands. They are harmless to humans and feed on nectar and pollen. Their larvae are among the most important natural enemies of aphids, but these tapered inconspicuous maggots are hard to spot.

Tachinid flies are generally hairy flies that are easily mistaken for house flies. However, their habits are very different, because they develop as parasites of insects. Adults lay their eggs on various caterpillars and beetles, which are then killed by the developing larvae.

Assassin bug

Ground beetle

Lady beetle larvae

Parasitic wasp cocoons

Praying mantis

Syrphid fly

Plant Pests

These are some of the pests you're most likely to find on any number of plants in Western gardens. Other pests target only one or two kinds of plants; those are covered in the Western Plant Encyclopedia.

PEST	DAMAGE	CONTROLS	PESTICIDES
Ants Most ants don't damage plants, but some species protect sap-sucking insects—such as aphids, mealybugs, soft scales, and whiteflies—for the honeydew they produce.	Many susceptible plants. Sooty mold may develop from honeydew (see page 688).	Place sticky barriers around tree and shrub trunks; prune off branches that touch the ground. Wrap the lower trunk with cloth, cover it with plastic wrap, and smear with a sticky pest barrier such as Tanglefoot.	Baits and traps may eliminate colonies. Ditomaceous earth (DE) Pyrethroids (check product label for targeted pest) Acephate (nonedibles only)
Aphids Soft-bodied, sap-sucking insects, from pinhead to matchhead sized. May be black, white, pink, or pale green.	Aphids remove sap, causing wilted, discolored, and/or stunted leaves. Sooty mold may develop from honeydew (see page 688).	Blast aphids from leaves with strong jets of water. Encourage lady beetles, lacewing larvae, soldier beetles, and syrphid flies.	Insecticidal soap Horticultural oil (overwintering eggs) Pyrethroids (check product label for targeted pest) Acephate (nonedibles only) Imidacloprid
Borers Larvae of beetles or moths; tunnel into branches, trunk, or roots of woody plants.	Attracted to weakened, injured or stressed plants, restricting water and nutrient flow, killing, deforming or weakening branches or limbs.	Encourage healthy plant growth. Prune out heavily infested limbs before beetles emerge.	Parasitic nematodes (on roots) Pyrethroids (check product label for targeted pest) Imidacloprid (for flatheaded borers only; check product label)
Caterpillars (including tobacco budworm, hornworms, cabbage-worms) Soft-bodied crawling insects, often striped or spotted.	Chew leaves or tunnel through buds and blossoms.	Handpick, especially at dusk or in early morning. Release *Trichogramma* wasps and green lacewings.	*Bacillus thuringiensis (Bt)* Pyrethrins Pyrethroids (check product label for targeted pest) Spinosod Carbaryl
Cucumber beetles Spotted beetle resembles a lady beetle with 12 black spots on its back. Striped cucumber beetle is yellowish orange with three black stripes.	Adults chew holes in leaves and flowers and damage stems of cucumbers, melons, squash, and other vegetables. Spotted beetles also feed on roses. Underground larvae may damage roots.	Handpick and destroy. Vacuum beetles from plants; dispose of bag. Use pheromone traps. Encourage birds, soldier beetles, and tachinid flies.	Parasitic nematodes Diatomaceous earth (DE) Pyrethrins Pyrethroids (check product label for targeted pest)
Cutworms Hairless larvae of many species of night-flying moths. During the day, they curl up in a C shape underground.	Worms cut off seedlings at or just above ground level. Some cut-worms crawl up into plants and eat buds, leaves, and fruit.	Surround seedlings with a protective collar such as a cut-down milk carton. Sprinkle cornmeal or bran on the soil around plants.	Parasitic nematodes *Bacillus thurengiensis (Bt)* Diatomaceous earth (DE) Pyrethroids (check product label for targeted pest)
Earwigs These familiar pests aren't all bad—they also prey on aphids and other insects.	Feed on tender new growth.	Keep the garden clean, removing hiding places such as weedy areas and dead foliage. Set traps and dispose of earwigs in sealed bags (see page 704).	Pyrethroids (check product label for targeted pest) Diatomaceous earth (DE) Carbaryl (especially as bait)
Flea beetles These tiny ($1/10$ inch long), oval, shiny beetles may be blue, black, brown, or bronze. They jump like fleas.	Adult beetles riddle leaves with small holes. They feed on many vegetable crops and seedlings, especially cabbage and potato-family plants.	In fall, remove weeds and garden debris, where adult beetles overwinter. Protect seedlings with row covers. Keep plants healthy (see page 739).	Diatomacecus earth (DE) Azadirachtin (neem extract) Pyrethroids (check product label for targeted pest) Carbaryl Imidacloprid
Gall-forming insects and mites Larvae of several hundred different species of wasps, midges, mites, aphids, and other insects.	Distorted swellings may appear on leaves, stems, or flowers of many plants, including oaks. Despite their unsightliness, most galls are harmless.	Prune off those on smaller branches or simply remove the whole branch. Large galls (and large branches) are usually better left in place, as pruning them out may harm the plant.	There are no effective chemical controls.

P

PEST	DAMAGE	CONTROLS	PESTICIDES
Grasshoppers Eggs hatch from spring to early summer, depending on temperature and climate. Newly hatched nymphs resemble adults, but are wingless and smaller and feed voraciously.	When their populations soar, grasshoppers devour any plant in sight, but corn and ornamental grasses are favorite targets, as are seedlings of every kind.	Adults are very difficult to control so grasshoppers are best treated in dry, undisturbed bed soil where eggs are laid. Encourage predators, including blister beetles, ground beetles, toads, birds, spiders, and praying mantis. Row covers (see page 739) can be effective, though in severe outbreaks grasshoppers may chew through them.	*Nosema locustae,* a disease of young grasshoppers, can be sprayed in breeding areas. Pyrethroids (check product label for targeted pest) Acephate (nonedibles only)
Leaf miners The larvae of certain moths, beetles, and flies. Adults are rarely seen.	Developing leaf miners tunnel within foliage, leaving twisting trails on the surface. Damage is mostly cosmetic, although yield of some crops may be reduced.	Use row covers (see page 739) on vegetables to deter egg-laying adults. At the end of the growing season, remove debris, where pupae overwinter, and till the soil. Pick off and destroy infested leaves; use yellow sticky traps to catch adults.	Imidacloprid Acephate (nonedibles only)
Mealybugs Have an oval body with overlapping soft plates and a white, cottony covering. They move around slowly.	They suck plant juices, causing stunting. Sooty mold may develop from honeydew (see page 688). In warm climates, they target a wide range of plants, but azaleas, hibiscus, and citrus trees of all kinds are prime targets.	Control ants (see page 706), which nurture mealybugs. Encourage or purchase lady beetles, lacewings, and predatory wasps. Dab pests with a cotton swab dipped in rubbing alcohol.	Horticultural oils Insecticidal soap Pyrethrins Azadirachtin (neem extract) Acephate (nonedibles only) Imidacloprid
Mites Tiny spider relatives look like flecks of red, yellow, or green. To check plants for mites, hold a piece of white paper under the affected foliage and briskly tap it. The pepper-like pests will drop onto the paper.	Some mites are host-specific but others—notably spider mites—attack a variety of plants. Drought-stressed plants are prime targets. Symptoms include yellow-stippled leaves, fine webbing across leaves, and a tan or bronze cast to the foliage. Heavily infested plants may eventually die.	Keep plants well watered to avoid drought stress. Hose off foliage frequently to remove dust (which encourages mites) and raise humidity. Encourage beneficial insects and birds. Purchase and release predatory mites. Spray with strong blast of water.	Insecticidal soap Horticultural oil Sulfur Chemical miticides are available, but most insecticides are ineffective, and actually can make mites reproduce faster.
Pill bugs and sowbugs Soil-dwelling crustaceans. When disturbed, pillbugs roll up into balls about the size of a large pea; sowbugs are usually gray and don't roll up.	Both pests eat decaying vegetation (which they help break down into humus), very young seedlings, the skins of melons and cucumbers, and berries.	Trap pests with small saucers, wooden boards, or ripening fruit.	Pyrethroids (check product label for targeted pest)
Root weevils Many species of long-snouted, hard-shelled insects. Among the most troublesome in Western gardens are black vine weevils and (in lawns) billbugs.	Adult black vine weevils feed on leaves, flowers, and bark of rhododendron, yew, grape, and other plants, while the larvae consume roots. Billbugs target mainly lawns planted in poorly drained soil. Larvae eat grass roots, leaving small, distinct circles of yellowish turf. If you pull it up, you'll see the roots covered with a light brown powder.	Keep planting beds free of debris, especially around plants' crowns, where adults overwinter. To help prevent billbug infestation, improve soil drainage or replace grass with plants that thrive in damp soil. If you can grow fescue or perennial ryegrass, choose endophytic varieties, which kill billbugs and other lawn pests. Trap adult weevils in late May with sticky traps or by shaking plants in the evening and gathering fallen insects.	Control larvae with parasitic nematodes. Azadirachtin (neem extract) Pyrethroids (on adults) (check product label for targeted pest) Acephate (adults; nonedibles only) Imidacloprid (larvae)
Scales Classified as "armored" (hard) or soft. In spring or summer, young scales ("crawlers") emerge. Adult scale insects have a waxy, scale-like covering.	As scales suck out plant juices, yellow spots appear on foliage, and leaves may drop off. If the infestation is left unchecked, the whole plant turns sickly and stunted.	Difficult to control. Lady beetles and parasitic wasps target scales. Control ants (see page 706), which tend and protect soft scales.	Horticultural oil (crawlers) Insecticidal soap (crawlers) Imidacloprid (soft scales only)
Slugs and snails These mollusks are similar creatures—a slug is simply a snail without a shell. They hide by day and feed at night, though they may be active on gray or rainy days.	The pests' tooth-like jaws make large, ragged holes in leaves and flowers. Seedlings and new transplants may be eaten entirely.	Trap and dispose of pests (see page 704). Wrap copper strips around containers and tree trunks. Keep the copper clean. Sprinkle wood ashes, diatomaceous earth (DE), or pine needles on the soil around plants. Release decollate snails, which prey on brown snails.	Sprinkle slugs with salt. Baits containing iron phosphate Baits containing metaldehyde

P

PEST	DAMAGE	CONTROLS	PESTICIDES
Thrips Almost microscopic, the light or dark brown adults measure less than $^1/_{20}$ inch long, with narrow, feathery wings. The wingless, light green or pale yellow nymphs are even smaller.	Feed on almost every kind of plant. In heavy infestations, both flowers and leaves are discolored and fail to open normally. Leaves may take on a silvery or tan cast.	Encourage predators, which include nearly all beneficial insects. Clip off and destroy infected plant parts. Spray with strong jets of water. Hang light blue or yellow sticky traps.	Insecticidal soap Spinosad Pyrethroids (check product label for targeted pest) Acephate (nonedibles only) Imidacloprid
Whiteflies Tiny (about $^1/_8$ inch long) winged insects fly up in clouds when you touch an infested plant. Nymphs are nearly transparent.	Affected foliage may first show yellow stippling, then curl and turn brown. They can't survive low temperatures, but they can move into the garden in warm months.	In the greenhouse, release the parasitic wasps *Encarsia formosa* or *Eretmocerus californicus*. Use floating row covers (see page 739). Hang white or yellow sticky traps. Spray plants with strong jets of water.	Imidacloprid

Disposing of Pesticides

You may need to dispose of pesticides, including fungicides and herbicides, if you have mixed more solution than you need or if you have a product that is no longer considered safe because of changes in its registration status. Until you can dispose of such pesticides properly, keep them—and all others—under lock and key, well away from children and pets.

Never pour any chemical down any type of drain, including a storm drain, as it could pollute the water supply. Instead, contact your city or county public works department, garbage company, or Cooperative Extension Office to find out where you can discard such products. Many communities sponsor hazardous waste disposal sites, which typically accept used motor oil and leftover paint as well as undiluted pesticides in their original containers and diluted solutions that you have mixed. Federal law requires that products containing hazardous ingredients be labeled, so carefully pour leftover solutions into a glass or plastic container with a tight-fitting lid and attach a label stating the product's trade name, the active ingredient(s), and the dilution ratio. Empty any powdered or granular pesticide (such as a lawn-care product applied with a spreader) into a heavy-duty garbage bag, then seal and label the bag.

Animal Pests

Most gardeners welcome some wildlife into their yards. (See page 752 for ways to attract wildlife.) Certain birds and animals, however, can cause significant damage to plants. Here are some of the West's worst troublemakers, along with suggestions for controlling them.

BIRDS. Most birds rank as pest-control superstars, consuming aphids, grasshoppers, scales, and all kinds of caterpillars. At certain times of the year, though, some birds can make mischief, eating newly planted seeds, tender seedlings, and tiny transplants, as well as fruits, nuts, and berries.

Distract them from your fruits, nuts, and berries by planting things birds usually prefer over favorite human foods. For plants that attract birds, see pages 118–122.

Wrap fruit trees and bushes with ¾-inch nylon or plastic netting. Put it on two to three weeks before the fruit ripens, tying it around the trunk beneath the lowest branches or securing it to the ground.

Use row covers (see page 739) to protect sprouting seedlings and maturing vegetables, or make freestanding frames from wood or plastic pipe and attach screen, aviary wire, or netting to cover the top and all sides. Remove the shelter once flowers form, so insects can get in to pollinate them.

Note: Such classic deterrents as fluttering objects, reflectors, and scarecrows may reduce damage briefly, but birds soon become accustomed to them.

DEER As wild vegetation becomes less available during droughts or winter snows—or simply as land development depletes their food supply—deer move into gardens to forage. They develop feeding patterns, visiting tasty gardens regularly, most often in the evening. Fond of many flowering plants, especially roses, they'll also eat the foliage or fruit of nearly anything you grow for the table. For a list of plants that deer usually ignore, see pages 143–148.

Build a fence. On level ground, a 7- to 8-foot board or woven wire fence will usually do the trick. On slopes, you may need to erect a 10- to 11-foot barrier to guard against animals jumping from higher ground. A horizontal "outrigger" extension on a fence makes it harder for deer to clear. Or build two parallel fences, 4 to 5 feet high and 4 to 5 feet apart. Although deer can jump high and they jump far, they can't do both at the same time.

Build chicken-wire cages around young plants and cylinders of wire

Browsing deer

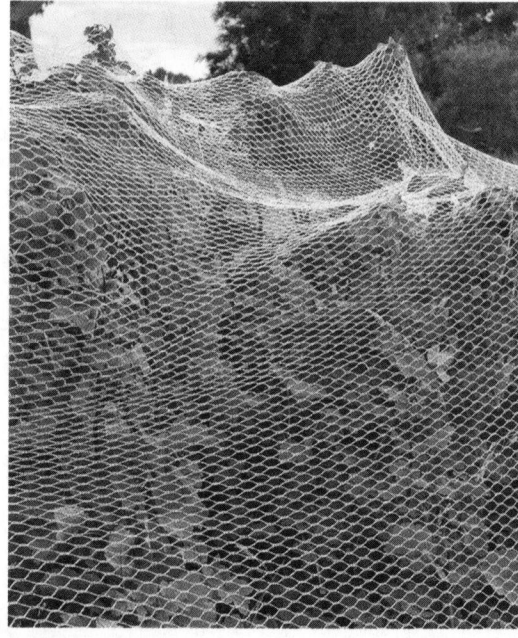

Bird netting

Products for Pest Control

In recent years there has been considerable change in the pesticides available to control insects, mites, slugs, and other garden pests. Many of the older synthetic insecticides have been removed from the market due to concerns about their effects on animals and human health. They have been replaced with pesticides of natural origin and with new classes of synthetic pesticides.

Synthetic pesticides are manufactured compounds that do not normally occur in nature. Natural pesticides, on the other hand, are products whose active ingredients originate in a plant, animal, or mineral, or whose action results from a biological process (as in the case of *Bacillus thuringiensis*). Be aware that "natural" does not mean "harmless." Some natural products can still harm people, pets, or plants if they are used incorrectly, and most of them will kill beneficial insects along with the pests. For some sources of natural pesticides, as well as beneficial insects, see page 704.

Pesticides come in many forms. Some are sprayed or dusted onto plants. Some can be applied to the soil and are systemically absorbed through plant roots. Pesticides formulated as baits can be particularly selective in their effects.

When using any pesticide, read the label carefully and follow the manufacturer's directions exactly. The label will clearly state the plants and pests for which the control is registered.

The following products are listed by the common name of the active ingredient—the chemical that controls the pest or pests listed on the package label.

NATURAL PESTICIDES

Azadirachtin, neem oil is derived from a tropical tree (*Azadirachta indica*). It repels pests and, once ingested, interrupts their growth cycle. Effective against aphids, beetles, caterpillars, grasshoppers, leaf miners, mealybugs, root weevils and whiteflies. Products that contain only neem oil (with no azadirachtin) act much like other horticultural oils.

Bacillus thuringiensis, Bt is a naturally occurring bacterium. Several strains exist; each targets different kinds of insects. The most common, *Bt kurstaki,* controls leaf-feeding caterpillars. *Bt tenebrionis* is effective against leaf beetles. All *Bt* products must be ingested by the target insect.

Diatomaceous earth (DE) is a powdery substance made from the skeletons of microscopic marine organisms. Works by damaging the protective coats of pests such as ants, aphids, cutworms, slugs, snails, and cucumber beetles. Be sure to use the horticultural product, not the one intended for swimming pool filters. Wear a breathing mask during application to avoid inhaling the dust. Sometimes combined with pyrethrins.

Food-grade oils and extracts are commercial versions of homemade repellents and pesticides that gardeners have relied on for centuries. Active ingredients include such kitchen standbys as citrus peels, sesame oil, garlic, hot pepper, mint, and rosemary. Effectiveness varies. To find many of them, see page 704.

Horticultural oils are mainly highly refined petroleum oils, but some are also derived from seeds (such as cottonseed, neem, or soybean) or fish. The oil must be mixed with water and acts primarily by smothering the insect; they are widely effective against such pests as scale insects, mites, and whiteflies. Do not apply oils when plants are under drought stress and temperatures are high.

Insecticidal soap is made not from dish detergent, but from potassium salts of fatty acids found in plants and animals. Soaps work on contact against pests such as aphids, mealybugs, mites, scales, thrips, and whiteflies. Hard water inactivates the soap, so mix the concentrate with soft water, distilled water, or rainwater.

Pyrethrins are derived from compounds found in the dried flowers of the marigold *Tanacetum cinerariifolium.* Work as both a contact and a stomach poison, and are lethal to many pests. Break down quickly in sunlight; to give them more time to act, apply after sundown. Some products combine pyrethrins with other pesticides. The dried flowers, known as pyrethrum, are also sold as an insecticide.

Spinosad is a newer insecticide made from the extracts of a soil microbe, *Saccharopolysproa spinosa.* It is primarily used to control caterpillars and thrips, but can also help control some beetles and sawflies. Although it is quite selective, some beneficial species can be killed if directly sprayed.

Sulfur is dusted or sprayed over plants to control mites and psyllids as well as some plant diseases. Do not use sulfur in conjunction with horticultural oils or when the air temperature is above 85°F/29°C. Can irritate the eyes.

SYNTHETIC PESTICIDES

Acephate is a systemic poison (one absorbed by the plant and incorporated into its tissues); it is a broad-spectrum product used against many pests. Hazardous to beneficials. Use on non-edibles only.

Carbaryl is a broad-spectrum contact insecticide. Controls most chewing insects but is not effective against many sucking types—in fact, it often increases problems with the latter by destroying natural predators. Registered for use on edible crops.

Imidacloprid is a systemic that controls a variety of pests. Registered for use on some tree crops primarily as a soil drench, but not for use otherwise on edibles.

Pyrethroids, synthetic versions of plant-based pyrethrins, are increasingly being used in pesticides and are effective against many garden and household pests. Active ingredients include bifenthrin, permethrin, cyfluthrin, and esfenvalerate.

Mole

fencing around larger specimens. Cover raised beds with mesh or row covers (see page 739).

Use repellents, either commercial or homemade. Although this method can be quite effective, it is labor-intensive: you need to spray often enough to keep new growth covered with repellent and to replace what rain and irrigation wash away. To achieve lasting results, you also have to change deterrents frequently. Do not apply commercial repellents to edible plants unless the label indicates you can do so.

MOLES Contrary to popular belief, moles are not rodents, and they do not eat plants. They belong to the biological order *Insectivora,* which means they eat insects, including grubs, beetles, and even an occasional snail. In tunneling through the soil, they sever roots, heave plants from the ground, generally make a mess of lawns. Moles are especially attracted to good, loamy soil that receives frequent moisture from either rain or irrigation. They dig an extensive network of tunnels; the main runways, usually 6 to 10 inches underground, are heavily used. Tunnel entrances are surrounded by simple, round piles of loose dirt that resemble volcanoes.

Control grubs (beetle larvae; see page 706).

Use a commercial repellant that contains castor oil; they are widely available in garden centers and catalogs.

Trap them. The spear- or harpoon-type trap is the easiest to set, since you simply position it above the soil. A scissor-jaw trap must be carefully positioned in a main runway (probe with a sharp stick to find it), and if it's improperly set, a wily mole can spring it, heave it out, or walk around it.

Use toxic gas "mole bombs," available commercially. To be successful, though, you need to set the bombs directly in the main runways, block all holes, and be persistent with follow-up treatments.

POCKET GOPHERS, named for the external, fur-lined cheek pouches they use to carry food to storage areas, are serious pests in much of the West. They use their strong, long-clawed forefeet to dig a network of tunnels, usually 6 to 18 inches below the surface. You'll know gophers are at work when you find that roots, bulbs, and sometimes entire plants have been pulled underground (and into their burrows). They can also chew irrigation pipes. The mounds they make at tunnel entrances are crescent- or horseshoe-shaped; a plug of earth is used to close the hole, which is off to one side.

Protect plants by lining the sides and bottom of planting holes, or the bottom of raised beds, with hardware cloth or chicken wire.

Use a commercial repellant that contains castor oil; they are widely available in garden centers and catalogs (see page 704).

Set commercial traps. Dig down to the main horizontal runway connecting with the surface hole and place two traps in it, one on either side of your excavation. Use chain or wire to attach each trap to a stake on the surface (this prevents a trapped gopher from dragging the trap farther into a burrow). The Macabee trap is the most effective. Box-type traps also work and are easier to set, but they require a larger hole for insertion.

When the traps are in place, plug the hole with a ball of carrot tops, fresh grass, or other tender greens. Next, place a board or soil over the greens to block all light. Check the traps frequently; clear the tunnels if the gopher has pushed soil into the traps. Be persistent: a clever gopher may avoid your first traps.

GROUND SQUIRRELS Most troublesome in areas that border fields or wild lands, ground squirrels live in underground burrows, where they store food, raise their young, and hide from predators such as foxes and hawks. They are most active in midmorning or the late afternoon (except in very hot weather); most hibernate in winter. When they're up and about, they feed on fruits, nuts, and vegetables as well as eating roots and bark.

Install metal rodent guards around trunks to keep ground squirrels out of trees.

Spray vulnerable plants with a commercial hot-pepper repellent.

Destroy burrows by tilling as deeply as possible. Or flood the burrows with water.

Before resorting to traps or poison baits, check with your local Cooperative Extension Office; some squirrels are protected by law.

TREE SQUIRRELS Familiar pests in much of the West, tree squirrels include several native and introduced species. They behave differently from ground squirrels when alarmed, heading for the safety of a tree rather than retreating to a burrow. Tree squirrels eat fruits, nuts, vegetables, and some kinds of bulbs; they also raid bird feeders and birds' nests.

Reduce food sources by cleaning up fallen fruits and nuts and using squirrel-proof bird feeders and houses.

To protect vulnerable trees, use metal rodent guards; prune low branches (if practical) and try to place the guards a minimum of 6 feet up from the ground, as the squirrels can leap at least that high. (Bear in mind, however, that if there are structures or other trees nearby, the agile pests will still be able to jump into trees you wish to protect.)

Cover bulb beds with fine-mesh chicken wire. Protect container plants with river-rock mulch or circles of shade cloth.

Before resorting to traps or poison baits, check with your local Cooperative Extension Office; some squirrels are protected by law.

VOLES Also known as meadow mice, voles are small rodents (5 to 8 inches long at maturity) with short ears and tails. They feed on a wide variety of vegetables, grasses, bulbs, and tubers, and gnaw on the bark of trees, just above or below ground. Voles travel in aboveground runways, usually hidden beneath tall grasses or ground covers.

Cut back ground covers and mow weeds —especially at the edges of fields near your garden. Use light mulches, keeping mulch several inches away from the trunks of trees and shrubs. And when snow falls, clear it away from those plant bases, too.

Protect the lower trunks of shrubs and young trees with hardware-cloth cylinders, being sure to bury the bottom edges so voles can't dig beneath them.

Dig a trench around an area you wish to protect. The trench should be a foot deep and 6 to 8 inches wide. Fill it to the top with small pebbles or crushed gravel.

Trap voles using simple wooden mouse traps, baited with peanut butter or apple slices. Set traps along the runways, and be sure to put them inside milk cartons or coffee cans, or cover them with "bridges" made of boards on bricks—thus keeping them away from birds, pets, and small human fingers.

Gophers: What Works, What Doesn't

If gophers have you fighting mad after you've tried trapping and baiting them without success, you're probably willing to try anything to save your prized plants. What about those other available gopher-getters? How well do they work?

Plants. Some gardeners say they've discovered plants that gophers don't seem to like, including breath-of-heaven, borage, calla, catmint, *Ceanothus,* coral bells, clivia, ferns, fuchias, fortnight lily, holly, hydrangeas, lantana, lavender, *Nandina,* Natal plum, penstemon (mature plants), rosemary, salvias, and toyon. They're worth a try, but intrepid gophers can dig around them. Stems of the gopher plant *(Euphorbia lathyrus)* have a poisonous, caustic, milky juice thought to bother a gopher enough to make it beat a hasty retreat. But the sap can also burn human hands and eyes.

Noisemakers emit sound that gophers are not supposed to like. But considering that gophers sometimes burrow along train tracks and airport runways, noise alone won't drive them away. For the same reason, electronic vibrating or ultrasound stakes are probably useless; their sound penetrates at most a few feet through the soil.

Realize that there's no surefire way to rid your garden of gophers completely, and protect roots of vulnerable plants with chicken wire. Before planting a small number of bulbs, sink wire baskets into planting holes. Then place bulbs in the baskets and cover them with soil.

Pocket gopher

Ground squirrel

Tree squirrel

PLANT ANATOMY AND NUTRITION

Understanding a plant's basic structure and the role each part plays in growth and reproduction is one fundamental to successful gardening. And a good knowledge of the relationship between a plant's growth and its environment—water, light, soil, air, and nutrients—helps gardeners provide the best possible conditions for each plant in its location in the garden.

Leaves carry out photosynthesis, *taking sunlight and combining it with carbon dioxide and water to make carbohydrates and oxygen. Small openings on the leaves called* stomata *transfer gases and water vapor.*

Oxygen is released through stomata.

Carbon dioxide is absorbed through stomata.

Water is released through stomata.

After **flowers** bloom and are pollinated, they produce **seeds** and **fruits,** which are dispersed by animals or wind.

Xylem in stems transports water and dissolved minerals from roots, while **phloem** carries carbohydrates (food) from the leaves. **Cambium** is a growth layer that forms each year and eventually becomes wood.

Water, air, and nutrients are absorbed by **roots.** Larger roots contain **xylem** and **phloem.** **Root hairs** increase the absorptive surface air. Roots also anchor the plant in the soil.

Xylem
Cambium
Phloem
Wood
Bark

P

What Plants Need

MACRONUTRIENTS These are substances that all plants need in fairly large quantities. Three—carbon, oxygen, and hydrogen—are found in air and water. Plants use the others in mineral form.

Nitrogen (N) is used in the synthesis of proteins, chlorophyll, and enzymes—all of which plant cells require. Nitrogen is the nutrient most likely to be inadequate in garden soils. Too much nitrogen can make plants overly lush and leafy and prone to attack by aphids and other sap-sucking insects.

Phosphorus (P) promotes flowering and fruiting, strong root growth, and the transfer of energy from one point in the plant to another. An overdose can interfere with a plant's absorption of other essential elements and cause all manner of symptoms.

Potassium (K) is important for regulating the synthesis of proteins and starches that make sturdy plants. It also helps increase resistance to diseases, heat, and cold. Too much potassium interferes with the absorption of calcium and magnesium, making plants grow poorly.

SECONDARY NUTRIENTS Plants need these in about the same amounts as they do the macronutrients. However, because they're less likely to be deficient in most soils, they are called secondary nutrients.

Calcium (Ca) plays a fundamental role in cell formation and growth, and most roots require some calcium right at the growing tips.

Magnesium (Mg) forms the core of the chlorophyll molecules in the cells of green leaves.

Sulfur (S) acts with nitrogen in the manufacture of protoplasm for plant cells.

MICRONUTRIENTS Also known as trace elements, micronutrients are required in very small quantities. In fact, excess amounts can be toxic. Among them are zinc (Zn) and manganese (Mn)—both thought to function as catalysts in the utilization of other nutrients—and iron (Fe), essential for chlorophyll formation. Some plants, particularly vegetables such as cabbage and Swiss chard, need boron (B), an element often lacking in the alkaline soils of the West.

Chlorosis. This disorder affects citrus, some other fruit trees, rhododendrons and azaleas, and some vegetables and annuals. Leaves lose their green color from the edges inward though their veins usually remain green. The newest leaves are the most noticeably affected as they may be unusually small and either white or bright yellow in color. Chlorosis is usually caused by a deficiency of iron, though it occasionally results from lack of another mineral, such as zinc or manganese. When plants are chlorotic, the soil itself is not necessarily iron poor. It may simply be alkaline, a con-

Nutrient Deficiencies

Often, the first signs of a nutrient deficiency—major or minor—appear in a plant's leaves. Here are some symptoms to watch for. In each case, your local nursery can recommend a foliar spray to solve the immediate problem and a fertilizer supplement for long-term care.

LEAF SYMPTOMS	DEFICIENCY
Yellow and smaller than normal. On some plants they may turn red or purple. Overall growth is stunted or dwarfed.	Nitrogen
Small, with edges scorched, purplish, or blue-green in color. May fall early. Overall growth is reduced and weakened. Flower and fruit production diminished.	Phosphorus
Tips and edges become yellow and scorched-looking, with brownish-purple spotting underneath.	Potassium
Turn dark from the base outward and die.	Calcium
Yellow between the veins, which remain green or slightly yellow.	Iron
Leaf centers turn reddish or yellow. Dead spots appear between veins.	Magnesium
Upper leaves yellow in center, between veins, with no sign of red.	Manganese
Veins grow lighter in color than the tissue in between.	Sulfur

dition under which iron becomes unavailable to roots. Soggy, poorly aerated soils also delay or hinder the release of iron to plant roots.

Adjusting soil pH by adding organic matter or, if necessary, sulfur, is the best long-term solution to chlorosis. Improving drainage also helps. Chelated iron, applied according to the directions on the label, can temporarily correct the problem.

PLANTING BEDS

Before sowing seeds or setting out annuals, perennials, or vegetables, you should prepare a planting bed. In most gardens, a simple one will suffice. In some cases, however—notably when soil or drainage is poor—constructing raised beds may be a better choice.

Making a Planting Bed

Good soil preparation is the first step toward success with new plantings. Begin by eliminating weeds (see page 746). Then loosen

the soil with a spading fork or tiller. Soil should be slightly damp when you work it, not wet or bone-dry. Dig down 10 to 12 inches if you can, breaking up clods and removing stones as you go. Over the area, spread a 3- to 4-inch-layer of organic matter such as compost or nitrogen-fortified ground bark or sawdust. Because both phosphorus and potassium benefit plants most when placed near the roots, work a fertilizer high in these nutrients such as a 5-10-10 or similar formula into the soil before planting, rather than applying it to the surface afterward. Also add any amendments needed to alter soil pH at this time.

Incorporate all the amendments evenly with a spading fork or tiller, then level out the planting bed with a rake.

P

PLANTING

Planting techniques depend on the plant and how it is sold. Many plants—vegetables, annuals, and some perennials and ground covers—are sold as seedlings in small containers or flats during the growing season. Many of these, as well as vegetables and some ground covers, are sold in plastic cell-packs, individual plastic pots, peat pots, and flats. (Some perennials, perennial vegetables, and strawberries may also be sold bare-root during their dormant season; for planting instructions, see page 714.)

Peat pots go into the ground, pot and all. The roots then grow through the pot into the soil, while the pot eventually decomposes. Moisten pots before planting by letting them soak in a tray of water for several minutes. When planting, cover the tops of the pots with soil, as exposed peat draws water from the soil.

Removing Plants from Containers

*Turn **small pots** upside-down, holding the plant in place with your fingers. The plant should slip out.*

*Separate plants in a **flat** by slicing between them with a knife or spatula.*

*Turn over **cell-packs** and push down on the bottom of each cell with your thumb.*

Root-bound Plants

1 Loosen coiled roots before planting so they will grow into the soil. Tease the roots apart with your fingers, then clip off any extra-long roots.

2 Another method is to spray the root ball with strong jets of water from a hose, then use your fingers to loosen and uncoil the roots.

3 For severely root-bound plants, make several vertical slits in the root ball with a knife.

Planting Annuals and Perennials

1 Dig a hole for each plant, the same depth as the containers and an inch or two wider.

2 Lightly separate matted roots. If roots are more tightly matted, use the techniques shown above.

3 Place each plant in its hole so that the top of the root ball is even with the soil surface. Firm the soil, then water each plant with a gentle flow of water.

P

Planting Bare-root Shrubs and Trees

Larger plants, such as shrubs, trees, and certain vines and more mature perennials, may be offered in several ways: In containers of various sizes during the growing season; as bare-root plants; or with the root ball enclosed in burlap, typically from late fall to early spring. At the nursery, choose stocky young plants with good leaf color and a root ball that holds together but is not tangled or matted.

Bare-root plants are sold in late winter and early spring by retail nurseries and mail-order companies. Though venturing out in the cold and wet of winter to set out bare-root plants takes a certain amount of determination, the effort is worthwhile. Such plants typically cost only 40 to 70 percent as much as the same varieties purchased in containers later in the year. In addition, they usually establish more quickly and grow better initially than containerized plants. This faster growth is in part due to the fact that when you set out a bare-root plant, you refill the planting hole with soil dug from that hole. Thus the plant's roots grow in just one kind of soil.

When buying from a local nursery, select bare-root plants with strong stems and fresh-looking, well-formed roots. Avoid any with slimy roots or dry, withered ones. Also reject any that have already leafed out. It's always best to plant bare-root plants as soon as possible after purchase. If you cannot plant right away, heel in the plants by laying them temporarily in a trench dug in a shady spot in the garden and covering the roots with moist soil or potting mix.

Most shrubs and trees grow best if planted in the soil native to your garden rather than in amended soil, but B-and-B plants are sometimes an exception. They are generally grown in clay or heavy soil that holds together well when the plants are dug up and wrapped. If you have medium- to heavy-textured garden soil (such as fairly heavy loam or clay), there's no need to amend the soil you return to the

Dig a planting hole with sides that taper outward into the soil. Make the hole at least twice as wide as the plant's roots. Roughen the sides with a spading fork. To keep the plant from settling too much after planting, make the hole a bit shallower than the root ball, then dig deeper around the edges of the hole's bottom. In heavy clay or hardpan, make the hole somewhat wider. This lets the plant establish faster by providing a larger area of loosened soil that's easier for roots to penetrate.

Planting Bare-root Plants

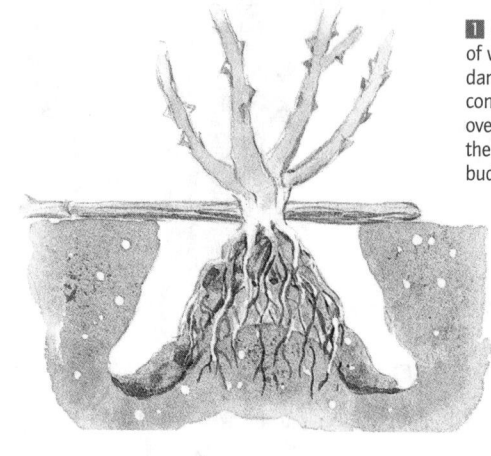

1 Soak the plant (in this case, a rose) in a bucket of water for at least four hours. Cut any broken or damaged roots back to healthy tissue. Make a firm cone of soil in the planting hole. Spread the roots over the cone so the plant is at the same depth as the soil line (usually visible on the plant's crown or bud union). Use a stick to check the depth.

2 Hold the plant upright as you firm soil around the roots. When backfilling is almost complete, add water to settle the soil around the roots. If the plant settles below the level of the surrounding soil, raise it to the proper level.

3 Finish filling the hole with soil; then water again. Do not overwater while the plant is still dormant. When the growing season begins, make a ridge of soil around the planting site to form a watering basin (see 716).

Planting from a Container

1 Dig a hole as shown on the facing page. Spread roots out over the central plateau of firm soil. The top of the root ball should be 1 to 2 inches above the surrounding soil.

2 Backfill, with the unamended soil you dug from the hole. Add the soil in stages, firming it around the roots with your hands as you work.

3 Make a berm of soil to form a watering basin. Irrigate gently. Spread a layer of mulch around the plant, keeping it several inches away from the stem or trunk.

planting hole. If the B-and-B soil is denser than your garden's soil, however, the plant may have a hard time getting established. The heavy soil around its roots will absorb water more slowly than the surrounding garden soil—so the B-and-B's soil can be dry even if the garden soil is kept moist. To prevent this problem, mix an organic amendment such as compost or nitrogen-fortified ground bark or sawdust into the soil removed from the planting hole, mixing about one shovelful of amendment for every three shovelfuls of soil. Use this blend to fill in around the roots.

Setting Out Plants from Containers

Most of the broad-leafed evergreen shrubs and trees that are the West's landscaping staples are offered only in containers. But that's not the main reason containerized plants are popular. You can buy them throughout the growing season, choosing from a variety of sizes and prices; they're relatively easy to transport; and they do not need to be planted immediately. Further, because you can buy these plants with flowers, fruit, or autumn leaf color on display, you're able to see exactly what you are getting.

When selecting container-grown plants, look for healthy foliage and strong shoots. Check that no insects are present. Do your best to avoid root-bound plants. Two common signs of this condition are roots protruding above the container's soil level and husky roots growing through the drainage holes. Additional indicators are plants that are large for the size of the container, leggy plants, and dead twigs or branches.

To remove plants from 1-gallon or larger plastic containers, tap sharply on the bottom and sides to loosen the root ball. The plant should slide out easily. With fiber or pulp pots, tear the pot away from the root ball, taking care not to damage the roots.

Planting in the Southwest

Soil with Caliche

Ideally, the workable soil should be 18 to 24 inches; if it isn't, you can bring in more topsoil or build a raised bed or mound. Dig a hole that's three to five times the width of the root ball and no deeper than the root ball. Drill or dig through the caliche layer with a soil auger or jackhammer to create two drainage chimneys at opposite ends of the hole. Set the plant in the center of the hole, staking it if necessary. Add backfill and topsoil as needed to make the soil level with the root ball. Build a small berm of soil around the root ball and water thoroughly. Spread a layer of mulch around the plant, keeping it several inches from the stem or trunk.

Drainage chimney

Drainage chimney

Stakes

Mulch

Planting hole

Soil without Caliche

Dig a hole three to five times the width of the root ball and no deeper than the root ball. Set the plant on undisturbed soil in the center of hole, with the top of the root ball at or slightly above soil level. For trees that need staking (see page 736), sink two wooden stakes into the soil. Partially backfill the hole, firm the soil, water thoroughly and finish backfilling. Build a small berm of soil around the root ball and water thoroughly. Spread a layer of mulch around the plant, keeping it several inches from the stem or trunk.

P

Planting a Balled-and-Burlapped Plant

1 Measure the root ball from top to bottom. Dig the planting hole a bit shallower than this distance, so that the top of the root ball will be about 2 inches above the surrounding soil. Adjust the hole to the proper depth, then set in the plant.

2 Untie the covering. If it's burlap, it will eventually rot, so just spread it out to uncover about half the root ball. If it's a synthetic material, remove it entirely. If the plant requires staking (see page 736), do it now. Fill the hole with soil to within 4 inches of the top and water gently.

3 Continue to fill the hole, firming the soil as you go. Form a watering basin, then water the plant. As the plant becomes established, keep the soil moist but not soggy.

Planting Balled-and-Burlapped Shrubs and Trees

Some kinds of woody plants have root systems that won't survive bare-root transplanting, while others are evergreen and cannot be bare-rooted. Instead, such plants are dug from the field with a ball of soil around their roots, and the soil ball is then wrapped in burlap or a synthetic material and tied with twine or wire. These are called balled-and-burlapped (B-and-B) plants. Some deciduous trees and shrubs, especially large specimens, evergreen shrubs such as rhododendrons and azaleas, and various conifers, are sold this way from late fall to early spring.

When buying B-and-B plants, look for healthy foliage and an even branching structure. The covering should be intact (so that the roots are not exposed), and the root ball should feel firm and moist.

B-and-B plants can be damaged if handled roughly. Always support the bottom of the root ball when moving the plant. Don't pick the plant up by the trunk or drop it, which might shatter the root ball. Because a B-and-B plant is usually quite heavy, it's a good idea to have the nursery deliver it or have a friend help you move it to and from your vehicle in a sling of stout canvas. Once home, you can move the plant by sliding it onto a piece of plywood and pulling it to the planting spot.

Below left: *Newly planted shrubs and trees benefit from a watering basin that concentrates water on the root zone. Form the main berm just outside the tree's drip line. Make a second berm 4 to 6 inches from the trunk to keep water off the plant's crown.*

Below right: *To determine how dry or moist the soil is, invest in a soil-sampling tube to "read" your soil. Push the tube into the ground and twist it back out, extracting a 12-inch or longer core showing in cross section how wet or dry the soil is.*

P

PLANT PROPAGATION

New plants can be started in several ways, either sexually or asexually. *Sexual propagation* involves the union of male and female parts of a flower to produce seed. These plants reflect the characteristics of both their parents. In *asexual (vegetative) propagation,* the new plant is produced from a vegetative part (root, stem, bud, or leaf) of just one plant. This new plant is a clone, genetically identical to its single parent. Asexual propagation maintains uniformity —assuring, for example, that each plant of the rose 'Queen Elizabeth' is like every other. Methods of asexual propagation include taking cuttings, dividing plants, layering, budding, and grafting.

How Seeds Germinate

To sprout, all seeds require adequate moisture, a preferred temperature, and a loose-textured soil that provides oxygen to the sprouting seed. Beyond these needs, the seeds of some plants have specialized requirements. For example, seeds of plants native to areas with cold winters normally need a period of low temperatures before they will sprout. In the wild, this occurs naturally. The seeds mature in late summer or autumn, are moistened by rain in fall and chilled throughout the winter, then sprout in spring. Gardeners can mimic this cold period by *stratifying* the seeds—either sowing them in containers that are set outdoors for the winter, or placing them between layers of moist paper towels enclosed in a plastic bag, then refrigerating them for a month or two.

Some seeds—including those of acacia, false indigo *(Baptisia),* lupine *(Lupinus),* and locust *(Robinia)*—have a hard seed coat that does not allow water to penetrate. Before they can germinate, they must be *scarified.* In nature, soil fungi and bacteria partially decompose the seed coat, or birds or animals excrete the seeds. Gardeners can scarify seeds by nicking the seed coat with a file or scratching it with sandpaper.

Other species require light, meaning that no newspaper or other covering should be placed over the planted seed.

Once these conditions are met, the *radicle*— the embryonic root—emerges and begins growing downward as shown below, with root hairs and lateral roots developing from it. The lower part of the stem (the *hypocotyl*) pulls the seed leaves or *cotyledons* upward. Food stored here nourishes the seedling until the first true leaves begin photosynthesis.

The plant pictured is a *dicot,* a plant with two cotyledons. Other plants—grasses, corn, onions, lilies—have only one cotyledon and are called *monocots.*

Sowing Seeds Outdoors

Whether you are planting rows of vegetables, broadcasting a wildflower mixture, or sowing several kinds of annuals for a showy border, start by preparing a planting bed (see page 712).

PLANTING SEEDS IN ROWS

Make furrows, following the seed packet instructions for their depth and spacing. If possible, lay out the rows in a north-south direction so that both sides will receive an equal amount of sunlight. Form the furrows with a hoe, rake, or stick, using a board or taut string as a guide.

Sow seeds evenly, spacing them as the packet directs. You can tear off a small corner of the packet and tap the seeds out as you move along, or pour a small quantity into your palm and scatter pinches of seed as evenly as possible, as shown above. Place larger seeds, such as beans, individually.

Water the furrows with a fine spray, then keep the soil surface moist but not dripping wet until seeds sprout. After the seedlings are up and growing, gradually cut back on watering, being sure to keep the root zone moist. Thin seedlings once they've developed two sets of true leaves. Thinned plants can be transplanted into any empty spaces in the rows.

Leaves

Cotyledon

Hypocotyl

Radicle

For straight rows, *stretch a string between two stakes and plant beneath it. Or lay a board on the surface of the soil, then plant along its edge.*

Broadcasting Seeds

1 For a patterned planting, outline the areas for each kind of seed to be sown with gypsum, flour, or stakes and string.

2 To achieve an even distribution, shake each kind of seed or seed mixture in a covered can with several times its bulk of sand.

3 Scatter the seed/sand mixture as evenly as possible over the bed or individual planting areas. Then rake lightly, barely covering the seeds with soil.

4 Spread a very thin layer of fine mulch over the bed to help retain moisture, keep the surface from crusting, and hide the seeds from birds.

5 Water with a fine spray. Keep the soil surface barely damp until the seeds sprout. Once seedlings are up, gradually decrease watering.

6 When seedlings have two sets of true leaves, thin those that are too closely spaced. Transplant the thinning seedlings to fill empty spaces in the bed.

P

BROADCASTING SEEDS This technique is the best way to plant wildflowers. It also makes natural-looking plantings of other easy-to-grow annuals, such as sweet alyssum (*Lobularia maritima*) and nasturtium (*Tropaeolum majus*).

Sowing Seeds in Containers

Many plants get off to a better start when sown in containers and transplanted to garden beds later in the season. It's easier to provide plants in containers with the temperatures and bright light they need and to protect them from birds and insects. The information given on the seed packet will help you decide when to plant. Most annual flowers and vegetables should be sown four to eight weeks before it's time to transplant them outdoors.

Container Choices

Plastic flats with or without dividers are an old favorite. They are readily available from garden supply stores and mail-order catalogs, and free when you buy seedlings at nurseries.

Plastic cell-packs and 2- to 4-inch plastic pots are easy to obtain and use.

Buy a seed-starting mix or planting mix at the nursery, or make your own by combining 1 part peat moss or finely shredded bark with 1 part perlite. Before using purchased mixes, flush them with water to eliminate excess salts. The mix should be moist but not soggy when you plant seeds.

Sowing Seeds in a Container

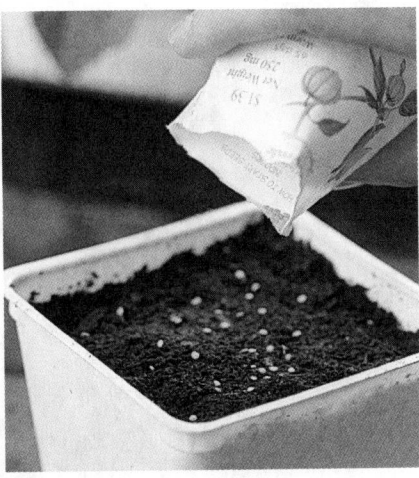

1 Scatter seeds thinly over the surface of the planting mix and cover with mix (a general rule is to cover seeds to a depth equal to twice their diameter; or consult the seed package). Label with the date and variety. Moisten the soil lightly. Place containers in a warm spot or on a heating mat.

2 When seedlings germinate, move them to a spot with plenty of light—either a sunny window, a greenhouse, or under 12 to 14 hours of fluorescent light each day. Keep moist. When they develop a second set of true leaves, it's time to transplant. Fill new containers with planting mix. Remove dampened seedlings from their original container, lifting carefully by the leaves.

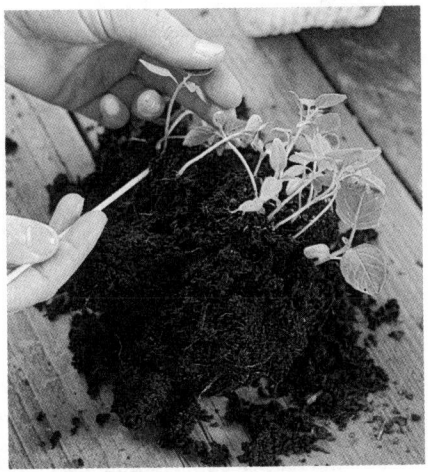

3 Separate fragile root balls with your fingers or a toothpick, gently teasing apart their separate root sections with a bamboo skewer as shown.

4 Poke a hole in the new container's planting mix and place each seedling in its new hole. Firm the mix and water. Fertilize weekly with a liquid fertilizer designated for starting seeds. When the seedlings are ready to be planted outside, stop fertilizing and set them outside for several hours each day in a sheltered spot. Over the next week or so, gradually increase exposure until the plants are in full sun. Then plant the seedlings out in the garden.

Peat pots (above) are inexpensive but not reusable. However, because you plant seedlings pot and all, such pots minimize disturbance to roots.

Peat plugs (below) are compressed peat held in netting. When water is added, the plug expands to hold two or three seeds.

Plastic foam flats with tapered individual cells are sold by nurseries and through mail-order catalogs. They come in several cell sizes and some have capillary matting that draws water from a reservoir, making seedling care easier.

You can also use recycled household items—plastic cups, cut-down milk cartons, foil baking pans. Be sure to punch drainage holes in any container that lacks them, as seedlings will die if water collects around their roots. If you're reusing old containers, scrub them out and soak them for 30 minutes in a solution of 1 part household bleach to 9 parts hot water to prevent infection by damping-off fungi (page 687).

P

Protect tender seedlings from frost by covering them with a cardboard box or an empty milk carton, or by propping up a wooden board. Remove the shelter during the day to avoid burning the plant.

Cuttings

Plants can be propagated from cuttings in several ways, depending on the plant part used for propagation. Any plant that produces sprouts from its roots will grow from *root cuttings*. Some kinds of plants will root successfully from a *leaf* or a portion of a leaf. *Stem cuttings* —in which roots are induced to grow from stem sections—are described as softwood, semihardwood, or hardwood, depending on the maturity of the stems.

ROOT CUTTINGS

Numerous perennials and other plants can be propagated by root cuttings, including Japanese anemone, globe thistle (*Echinops*), trumpet vine *(Campsis),* Oriental poppy *(Papaver orientale),* blackberry, and raspberry.

Make root cuttings when the plant is dormant—in late fall or early winter for most species. Dig up an entire plant or just a section of its roots. With a sharp knife, remove vigorous, healthy pieces of root 2 to 4 inches long; those growing close to the crown will form new plants most quickly. If you have only a few cuttings, place them upright in a container filled with damp rooting medium, with the top cut ends (those that were closest to the crown on the parent plant) at soil level (**A**). For larger numbers of cuttings, fill a flat to within an inch of the top with potting mix; lay the cuttings flat on top of the mix (**B**), then cover them with ½ inch more mix. Water, and place in a greenhouse or cold frame away from direct sunlight. Once stems and leaves have formed, move the containers into full light and water as needed.

When the young shoots are several inches tall and new roots have formed (check by gently digging up a cutting), transplant them to individual pots and feed with liquid fertilizer.

Root Cuttings

LEAF CUTTINGS

Some plants can form roots from a leaf or a portion of one. For rooting medium, use a mix of 1 part peat moss and 1 part perlite or coarse builder's sand.

To propagate rex begonias, make cuts across the large veins on the underside of a mature leaf (**A**). Lay the leaf flat, cut side down, on the rooting medium, then enclose the container in a plastic bag. New roots will form at each cut (**B**).

African violets can also be propagated by

Leaf Cuttings

cuttings; simply insert a young leaf with an inch or two of stem into the rooting medium (**C**). New plants form at the base of the stem. To root leaf cuttings of mother-in-law's tongue (*Sanseveria*), cut a leaf into 3- to 4-inch-long sections. Insert these into the rooting medium, covering as much as three-fourths of their length (**D**). Enclose with a plastic bag to retain humidity.

SOFTWOOD AND SEMIHARDWOOD CUTTINGS

Easy to take and fast to grow, softwood cuttings are taken during the growing season from relatively soft, flexible new growth. Take semihardwood cuttings somewhat later in the growing season, usually in summer or early autumn (a semihardwood stem is firm enough if it snaps when bent sharply; if it just bends, it's too mature for satisfactory rooting). Use a half-and-half mixture of perlite and peat moss, or perlite alone.

Gather cuttings early in the day and cut off an 8- to 12-inch length of stem. Discard flower buds, flowers, and side shoots. Then slice the stem into 3- to 4-inch pieces, each with at least two nodes (**A**). Dip the lower end of the cuttings in a rooting hormone (**B**). Poke holes in the rooting medium and insert the cuttings. Water with a fine spray and set the container in a warm spot that's shaded but not dark.

Enclose each container in a plastic bag to maintain humidity; open the bag for a few minutes each day for ventilation. Once cuttings have taken root and are sending out new leaves, open the bags. When the new plants are acclimated to open air, transplant each to its own pot of lightweight potting soil.

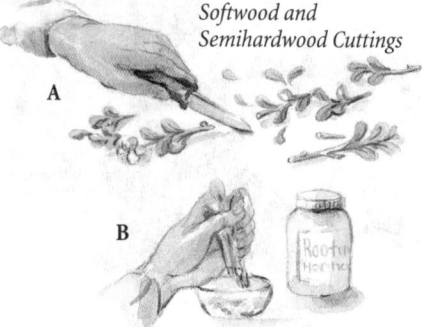

Softwood and Semihardwood Cuttings

HARDWOOD CUTTINGS

Most deciduous shrubs and trees can be propagated by this method. Some fruit species, such as fig, grape, mulberry, and some plums, are also propagated this way.

Take hardwood cuttings during the dormant season. Take pencil-thick cuttings from the previous season's growth, which is often lighter in color than older wood. Slice off the top inch or two of each stem, then cut the stems into 6- to 9-inch lengths, each with two or three nodes. Make the top cuts at a slant. Dip the bottom ends in rooting hormone (**A**). In climates where the ground is frozen in winter, store the cuttings in a box filled with slightly moist sawdust or sand (**B**). In warmer areas, bury the cuttings in an outdoor trench filled with regular soil (**C**). In early spring, plant the cuttings in a narrow trench in a sheltered spot (**D**). Fill in the trench with compost or perlite, leaving

Hardwood Cuttings

the top bud of each cutting exposed. Water as needed to keep soil moist. Protect cuttings from direct sun until they are ready for planting in the garden (usually in fall or in the following spring).

Layering

Layering is a technique that encourages new roots to form on branches still attached to the parent plant. The parent plant supplies the layer—the new plant—with water and nutrients during the rooting process.

GROUND LAYERING

Also called simple layering, ground layering is an easy way to produce a few new plants, though it may take as long as a year. This technique can be used to propagate many shrubs and perennials that have low-growing or trailing branches.

In spring, select a young, pliable shoot from low on the plant. Loosen the soil where the shoot will be buried and work in a shovelful of compost. Dig a shallow hole in the prepared area. With a sharp knife, cut about halfway through the underside of the shoot where it will touch the soil. Dust the cut with rooting

Ground Layering

hormone powder and insert a pebble or wooden matchstick to hold it open. Lay the shoot (the layer) in the hole and secure it with a piece of wire (**A**). Some gardeners tie the layer's tip to a stake to help it grow upward.

Fill in the hole, firming the soil around the layer. Place a rock on top to help hold the layer in place (**B**). During the growing season, mulch around the plant and keep the soil moist. When you are sure roots have formed (anywhere from a few months to more than a year; gently dig into the soil to check), cut the new plant free from the parent. Dig it up, keeping plenty of soil around the roots, and plant in the garden.

AIR LAYERING This process involves the same principle as ground layering but is used for branches higher on a plant. Use it to propagate large house plants—overgrown rubber plants (*Ficus elastica*), for example—but it's also successful in some outdoor trees and shrubs, including citrus, witch hazel (*Hamamelis*), magnolia, and rhododendron.

To encourage growth in houseplants, fertilize the plant to be layered, then place it in a sunny window. When new leaves appear, proceed with layering. Make a slanting cut (**A**) and insert a wooden shim to keep it open (**B**) or remove a ring of bark (**C**). Dust cut with rooting hormone, encase in damp sphagnum moss, and then cover with plastic wrap to keep the moss moist (**D**). If layering succeeds, roots will appear in the moss after a few months and you can then sever the rooted stem from the parent and pot it. Remove about half the new plant's leaves to prevent excessive moisture loss through transpiration while it gets established.

Air Layering

| A | B | C | D |

Budding and Grafting

These methods involve joining parts of two different but closely related plants, such as roses, grapes, and fruit and ornamental trees, or to add a new variety to an existing fruit or nut tree. The part that will become the upper or aboveground portion of the plant is known as the *scion;* it may be a piece of a branch or a single bud. The scion gives the new plant the desired qualities of flowering, fruiting, or form. The part that provides the roots is called the *stock, rootstock,* or *understock.* In some cases, the stock is a young plant chosen because it causes the new plant to be hardier, more disease resistant, or smaller in size (as in dwarf fruit trees). In other cases, the stock may be a mature tree that you want to graft over to a new variety.

Successful budding and grafting depend upon uniting the cambium layers of scion and stock; only then can new growth emerge. Use a very sharp knife, as the cleaner the cut, the better the chance for a successful union.

T-Budding

BUDDING Also called bud-grafting, this operation is carried out in summer or early fall when plants are actively growing. Roses and some other flowering shrubs, as well as grapes and fruit trees, are propagated by this method. Budding involves inserting a growth bud (the scion) from one plant beneath the bark of a related plant (the stock). The stock is either a pencil-thick rooted cutting of a sort known to produce a strong root system or a seedling plant of such a species.

Choose a stock stem ¼ to ½ inch in diameter. Make a T-shaped cut in the bark (**A**); gently pry up the corners of the T (**B**). Choose a vegetative bud (usually small and pointed rather than a plumper flower bud) from the budwood plant. Remove the leaf but retain its stalk. Cut a shield-shaped patch containing the bud (**C**), leaving a bit of wood attached to the back (**D**).

Push the bud patch down between the bark flaps of the T-cut (**E**). All of the patch should fit between the flaps. Bind the budding site with plastic grafting tape (**F**), covering the top of the T while leaving the bud exposed. It will stay plump but dormant through fall and winter, then begin to grow in spring, when all the plant's buds burst into growth. At this point, cut the stock stem back to just above the new, growing bud. The flowers, fruit, and leaves arising from the bud will have the characteristics of the plant from which it was taken.

GRAFTING This technique unites a short length of stem—the scion—with a stock. It is most often done to convert fruit and nut trees to new varieties. The stock plant may be a slim seedling to be grafted near ground level or an old fruit tree to be grafted on its major limbs. Make cleft grafts in early spring, when the growth buds of the stock are beginning to swell. However, the scion wood should be dormant so gather it in late fall or winter. Cut ¼- to ½-inch-thick tip growth, making sure each piece has three or four buds. Bundle the cut stems together, label them, and place in a sealed plastic bag in the refrigerator. (Some mail-order companies also sell scion wood in winter.)

Prepare the stock by splitting it several inches down into a smooth, straight-grained section (**A**). Shape the bottom end of the scions into long, gradually tapering wedges (**B**). Hold open the split stock with a block of wood (**C**) and insert the scions into the stock so that the cambium layers of stock and scion match (**D**). Remove the block and cover the entire union with grafting wax (**E**). If the graft is successful, buds will emerge during spring.

Cleft Grafting

PRUNING

Pruning tasks vary from pinching out new growth on perennials to removing large tree branches. Here are a few reasons why you may need or want to prune.

To maintain plant health. Trees and shrubs benefit when you remove branches that are badly diseased, dead, densely branched, or rubbing together.

To direct growth. Pruning stops growth in one direction and encourages it in another, because growth continues in the buds and branches that are left behind.

To remove undesirable growth. Prune out wayward branches and remove suckers (stems growing up from the roots) and water sprouts (upright shoots growing from the trunk and branches). If you have to cut back a plant continually to keep it in bounds, it is probably too large for its location.

To increase flowers or fruit. Regular pruning of fruit trees and flowering trees and shrubs produces good annual crops of fruit or blossoms.

To maintain safety. Split or broken branches can fall, injuring people or causing damage.

To create hedges or topiary. Suitable plants can be shaped through regular shearing.

Pruning and Plant Growth

Some kinds of pruning cuts are made near a growth bud. The location of that bud determines how the plant will grow after pruning.

The *terminal bud* grows at the tip of a shoot, gradually elongating the shoot. Actively growing terminal buds produce hormones that inhibit growth of other buds on that stem.

Lateral buds grow along the sides of the shoot at leaf attachment points (nodes); they produce the sideways growth that makes a plant bushy. These buds stay dormant until the shoot has grown long enough to diminish the influence of the hormones produced by the terminal bud, or until the terminal bud is pruned off.

Latent buds lie dormant beneath the bark. If a branch breaks or is cut off near a latent bud, that bud may develop into a new shoot.

What sets apart the four basic pruning techniques is where you cut in relation to growth buds and side branches. *Thinning* eliminates the entire shoot back to a main branch or trunk. *Heading* removes part of the shoot; *shearing* is a drastic form of heading. *Pinching* removes only the terminal growth.

Types of Pruning

Pinching is the most basic pruning cut, used primarily on annuals and perennials. Use your thumb and forefinger or a pair of shears to nip off the tips of new growth. Pinching side shoots (above left) causes stems to lengthen; removing terminal growth causes side shoots to grow (above right).

Heading removes a stem or branch back to a bud or to a twig or branch too small to take over the terminal role. Heading stimulates the growth of lateral buds just below the cut, producing clusters of shoots.

For maintenance pruning of most woody plants, heading is less desirable than thinning. Though it may initially make a plant more compact, the plant will soon produce vigorous growth from lateral buds, eventually ruining the natural shape of the plant. However, it's useful on young fruit trees to force branching at a particular point on a branch or stem, on a tree to fill a hole in the crown, on flowering shrubs to increase blooms, or to rejuvenate old or neglected shrubs.

Thinning is the most common pruning cut. It opens up a plant and stimulates minimal regrowth. Remove an entire stem or branch, taking it back to its point of origin, or to its junction with another branch. In the case of plants that send up stems directly from the roots, cut it all the way to the ground. When removing one branch at a junction, be sure the remaining branch is at least one-third the diameter of the one being removed.

Shearing is an indiscriminate form of heading that involves clipping a plant's outer foliage to create an even surface. The plants best suited to shearing have main and lateral branches bearing closely spaced buds, so almost every cut ends up near a growing point.

What's Wrong with Topping?

Topping—reducing the height of a mature tree by sawing off its top limbs—is the fastest way to ruin a tree's appearance. It doesn't reduce height for long either. Unlike a bushy hedge that soon sprouts new growth even after severe shearing, an older tree does not grow back in a natural-looking way when its upper limbs are pruned to stubs. Instead, it sends out scores of weak shoots from buds near the cutoff points, and these shoots are often taller, coarser, denser, and less strongly attached than the natural top was. Topping may also shorten a tree's life, both because the resultant large wounds are exposed to decay and insect attack and because the process removes much of the leafy growth needed to manufacture food for the plant.

Though some topped trees can eventually recover their form, it may take decades. A good professional arborist will not top a tree that has grown too large for its space. Instead, he or she will gradually scale it back by making thinning cuts to groups of branches in the upper part of the canopy.

To avoid ripping the bark, shorten the branch to a stub before cutting it off just outside the branch collar. First, about a foot from the branch base, make a cut from the underside approximately a third of the way through. Then, about an inch farther out on the branch, cut through the top until the branch splits cleanly between the two cuts. Make the final cut just outside the branch bark ridge. Cut downward to just outside the branch collar. If the crotch is very narrow, cut up from the bottom to avoid cutting the branch collar.

Making Pruning Cuts

Always cut back to a part that will continue to grow—to the trunk, another branch, a bud, or even to the plant's base, if it sends up stems from the roots. At these points of active growth, callus tissue will start to grow and, in time, the wound will seal off. Clean cuts callus over faster than ragged ones, so use an appropriate, well-sharpened blade (for more on tools, see pages 730–731).

If you cut too close to a bud it may die; too far from a bud and you'll leave a stub that will wither and drop off, leaving an open invitation to disease or insect infestation. Look for healthy buds pointing in the direction you want the new shoot to grow.

When removing a branch, position your shears, loppers, or saw just outside the branch collar, the wrinkled area (or bulge) at the branch's base where it meets another branch or the trunk. Refrain from cutting into the branch bark ridge (raised bark in the branch crotch).

When to Prune

In general, pruning is done in late winter or during mid- to late summer. Specific pruning times for many plants are given in the Western Plant Encyclopedia. Dead or badly diseased wood should be removed as soon as you notice it. If you see frost-damaged wood, be sure that it is truly dead before you remove it.

Deciduous trees and shrubs are typically pruned in late winter or early spring before or as they resume growth but after the danger of frost has passed. When the plants are leafless, it's easier to see their overall shape and to spot broken and awkwardly placed branches.

Before pruning flowering trees and shrubs, find out whether they bloom on old or new wood. Plants that flower in spring on old wood (which grew the preceding year) should be pruned after they have flowered; if you prune before then, you'll eliminate the flower buds. Woody plants that flower on the current season's growth, however, can be pruned in late winter without sacrificing blossoms. Check to see to which category your plants belong. Older

branches are usually darker, less pliable, and woodier looking than new growth.

Many deciduous plants can also be pruned in midsummer. This is a good time to thin out excess growth, suckers, and water sprouts. Be sure to complete such summer pruning a month before the usual first-frost date, as pruning may stimulate tender new growth.

Broad-leafed evergreen trees and shrubs slow in their growth to a level approaching dormancy during late winter or early spring. Most can be pruned during this period or in summer. For flowering broad-leafed evergreens, however, timing is more precise. For those flowering on last season's growth, prune after bloom. For those that bloom on new wood, prune before spring growth begins.

The angle of your cut is determined by the bud pattern of the plant. When a plant's buds occur alternately along the shoot, cut on the diagonal just above an outward-facing bud (above left). For a plant with buds opposite each other, make a straight cut directly above both buds (above right).

Tools for shearing shrubs include clippers (top) and hedge shears (bottom).

Conifers often require no pruning. For those that do, timing depends on the growth habit. Fir (*Abies*), spruce (*Picea*), and most pines (*Pinus*) are whorl-type conifers. They produce new growth in spring, with buds appearing all along new shoots. (On pines, the new shoots are called candles.) In early spring, cut new shoots back about halfway to induce more branching, making sure to cut above growth buds. Or cut them out entirely to force branching from buds at their bases.

Random-branching conifers include cedar (*Cedrus*), cypress (*Cupressus*), juniper (*Juniperus*), arborvitae (*Thuja*), yew (*Taxus*), and hemlock (*Tsuga*). Prune them much like other evergreens. Cut branches so that the remaining portion bears some foliage, as new growth will sprout from the branches below your cuts. (Hemlock and yew are exceptions; they can sprout from bare branches.) The best time for the job is usually right before spring growth begins.

Espalier Forms

Double U-shaped

Candelabra

Belgian fence

Belgian arch

Belgian doublet

Fan

Training an Espalier

The art of training a tree or shrub to grow more or less flat against a wall or fence, espalier is a classic space saver. Dwarf, potted fruit trees make good candidates, as do berry-bearing shrubs such as firethorn (*Pyracantha*) and cotoneaster.

1 Choose two strong branches to form the first tie; remove all other shoots and cut back the leader to just above the bottom wire. Bend the branches at a 45-degree angle and secure them with soft cloth or plastic ties.

2 During the first growing season, gradually tighten the ties so that the branches are drawn horizontal against the first wire. When the newly sprouted leader is long enough, hold it erect and tie it to the second wire.

3 During the dormant season, cut back the leader to the second wire. Choose two branches for the second tier and remove competing shoots. Cut lateral growth on the lower branches back to three buds.

4 The next growing season, gradually bring the second-tier branches to a horizontal position, as you did for the first tier in step 2. Keep the leader upright and tie it to the third wire.

5 Repeat the process for more wires, if desired. When the leader reaches the top wire, cut it back to just above the top branch. Prune back horizontal branches to downward-facing side branches in late spring and summer.

P

RAISED BEDS

In addition to solving problems that involve poor soil and limited drainage, raised beds have other advantages. Their soil warms earlier in spring, and because it is typically not walked upon, it remains loose and easier for roots to penetrate. You can also fill these beds with particular types of soil to suit specific plants—acid soil for blueberries, for example.

The simplest raised beds are made with amended soil piled on the area you wish to plant. You can buy the soil or dig it from elsewhere in the garden. It's a good idea to first loosen the soil that will be under the bed as much as possible to ease penetration by water and roots.

Many gardeners enclose their raised beds with a low border. Two-inch-thick wood is most common, but rocks or cinder blocks also work well. Plan to make enclosed beds at least 8 inches high, though a height of 12 inches gives roots even more growing space. The bed can be any length that fits the space and available building materials, but it's usually best to limit its width to about 4 feet, so that you can reach the center from either side. If pocket gophers are a problem, line the bottom of the bed with hardware cloth, fastening it to the sides. Fill the raised beds with good topsoil amended with plenty of organic matter, such as compost or nitrogen-fortified ground bark or sawdust.

Building a Raised Bed

You can build a basic raised bed in a few hours, then add versatility by mounting PVC pipes inside to hold hoops that elevate bird netting or row covers over your crops. Orient your bed north-south to give it maximum sun exposure. The best lumber choices are redwood or cedar—both are beautiful and rot-resistant. You'll need a power saw to cut the wood or you can have it cut at the lumberyard. Paint the wood on all sides with an oil-based sealer. An electric drill is helpful, though not essential.

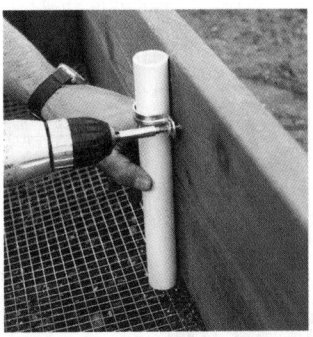

1 Build the bed upside down. Set a 4-foot 2 by 6 on its thin edge, and place a 16-inch post at one end. Secure the post with two 3-inch screws. Repeat at other end of board and with other short board. Join short sides with an 8-foot board, then add the other long side. Add a second layer of 2 by 6s.

2 Flip the bed right side up. Move it into position, marking with a trowel each corner post's location. Move the bed aside; dig a 5- to 6-inch-deep hole for each post. Put the bed back into place, with posts in holes; fill around posts with soil.

3 Rake the existing soil at the bottom of the bed to level it, then tamp it smooth. Line the bed with hardware cloth to keep out gophers or other burrowing pests.

4 To hold hoops for bird netting or row covers, attach four 12-inch pieces of 1-inch PVC pipe inside the bed. On the long sides, space pipes 4 feet apart, 2 feet from each end; screw on two tube straps to secure each pipe. Fill the bed with planting mix, and moisten it with a gentle spray from the hose.

5 To cover newly planted seedlings with bird netting or season-extending row covers, simply bend two 6-foot pieces of 1/2-inch PVC pipe to form semi-circles, and slip their ends into the 1-inch pipes inside the bed. Then drape the bird netting or row covers over them.

R

SHRUBS

Shrubs are woody plants that live for many years, providing a long-lasting framework that helps unite a garden's various elements. Some shrubs establish a permanent woody structure, then increase in size by sending out new branches from older ones. Others send out woody stems (canes) each year from the base as the older stems decline.

Shrubs may be rounded, vase shaped, columnar or conical. In size, they range from ankle-high to the height of small trees. Unlike trees, however, most shrubs sport foliage all the way to the ground.

Planting and Caring for Shrubs

Choose shrubs that will thrive in your region's conditions. Review the Plant Selection Guide on pages 85–89 for choices, both evergreen and deciduous.

Remember that a little tuft of greenery in a gallon pot can ultimately reach 12 feet in all directions. Consider maintenance; many of the most attractive shrubs grow according to their natural inclinations, without excessive shaping. (Shrubs grown as hedges are an exception. For a list, see pages 90–91.) Finally, look for ornamental features such as foliage texture, colored leaves, attractive flowers, and colorful fruits.

Shrubs may be sold bare-root, in containers, or balled-and-burlapped (B-and-B). Bare-root plants must be set out soon after you purchase them. This is also true of B-and-B shrubs, available from late fall to early spring. You can plant container-grown shrubs at any time during the growing season, but it's best to plant in spring or fall rather than in the heat of summer. See pages 713–716 for planting instructions.

Water and mulch newly planted shrubs immediately, then keep the soil moist but not soggy as the plants settle in. Once established after a year or two in the garden, many native shrubs and others that are well adapted to Western climates may survive on rainfall alone, while others will need supplemental water, especially in the dry season.

Some shrubs (notably roses) do best with regular fertilizing, and other flowering sorts may also benefit from at least an annual application of fertilizer. But many shrubs grow well with no supplemental nutrients. If the shrub puts out strong new growth with good color each year, it's doing well without any feeding. Prune shrubs as shown on pages 722–724.

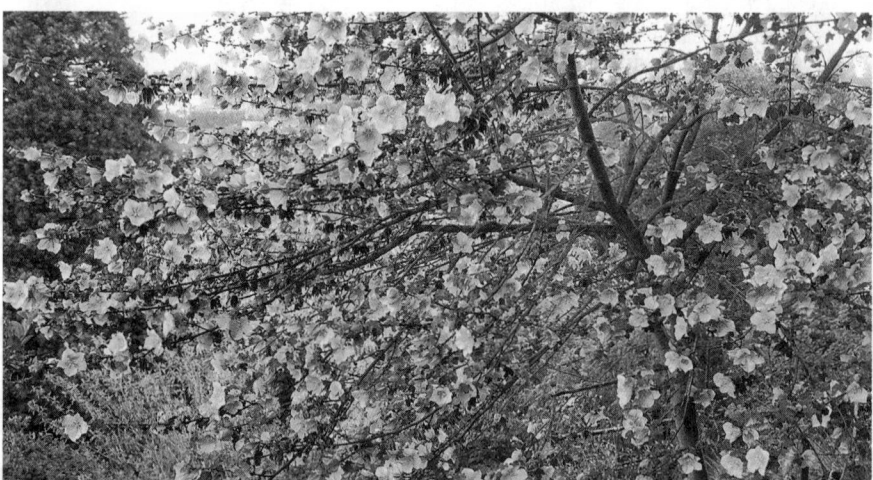

Favorite shrubs for Western gardens include, clockwise from top left, fragrant lilac (Syringa), Callicarpa, which sports striking purple berries in fall; and California native Fremontodendron.

Rejuvenating Shrubs from the Base

Shrubs that have become overgrown with long, straggling, tangled branches may require rejuvenation. This method works best on shrubs that send up canes from the roots.

On most cane-producing shrubs, it's safest to remove about a third of the oldest growth annually for three years (below left). In any case, once you have snipped off the old stems, keep the shrub under control by continuing to remove just a few of the oldest stems each spring.

Shrubs that can withstand severe pruning include glossy abelia (*Abelia grandiflora*), barberry (*Berberis*), common butterfly bush (*Buddleja davidii*), forsythia, mock orange (*Philadelphus*), shrubby willows (*Salix*), and spiraea. For these, cut back the entire plant before new spring growth begins (below right).

SOIL

Soil supports plant roots and gives them access to nutrients, water, and air. Most roots grow in the uppermost soil layer, called *topsoil,* which is biologically active and most directly affected by weather. Below the topsoil is the subsoil. Although it contains plant nutrients, it is not as hospitable to roots as topsoil. Improving your topsoil has the most beneficial effect on plant health. Good garden soil contains approximately 50 percent pore spaces filled with water and air, 45 percent minerals (rock particles), and at least 5 percent organic matter, including roots, decaying leaves and stems, materials added by gardeners, and soil-dwelling organisms.

The network of pore spaces includes large pores *(macropores)* and small ones *(micropores).* Macropores permit water and air to enter the soil easily and allow excess water to drain away. Micropores determine a soil's water-holding capacity. They hold water against the force of gravity, making it available when needed. Soils that contain a preponderance of large pores are loose in texture. They are well aerated but cannot retain water for long and need more frequent irrigation. Soils with many small pores, on the other hand, are dense and can hold a lot of water but not much air.

Soil Texture

Texture describes the size of a soil's mineral particles. These include large, coarse sand particles; smaller silt particles; and tiny particles of clay. Soil texture affects watering and fertilizing schedules, and in some cases it determines the kinds of plants you'll be able to grow.

Sandy soils contain particles that are comparatively large and irregularly rounded. Their size and shape allow for larger pore spaces between particles than in clay soils. Consequently, sandy soils contain lots of air and drain well. In a given volume of sandy soil, the surface area of the particles is less than in a similar volume of clay, so the amount of soluble nutrients in sandy soil is correspondingly lower. That's why plants in sand need watering and feeding more often. Sandy soils also warm more quickly in spring than clay soils.

Loam is considered the ideal garden soil. It contains a balance of all three particle types—clay, silt, and sand. With a combination of large and small pore spaces, it drains well (but does not dry out too fast), loses nutrients at a moderate rate, and contains enough air for healthy root growth.

Clay soils, also called adobe, gumbo, or simply "heavy" soils, are composed of flattened microscopic particles that pack closely together, leaving little pore space. But because these particles offer the largest surface area per volume of all

Soil Particles Determine Texture

Soil Particles

Clay
Less than $1/12{,}500$ inch

Silt
Up to $1/500$ inch

Fine sand
Up to $1/250$ inch

Medium sand
Up to $1/50$ inch

Coarsest sand
$1/12$ inch

soil particles, clay soils can hold the greatest volume of nutrients in soluble form. Drainage is slow in clay soils, so they retain water longer and the loss of soluble nutrients through leaching is also slow. Because of their high density, clay soils are the slowest to warm in spring.

To determine soil texture, thoroughly wet a patch of soil and then let it dry out for a day.

Now pick up a handful of soil and squeeze it firmly in your fist. If it forms a tight ball and has a slippery feel, it's predominantly clay. If it feels gritty, doesn't hold its shape, and crumbles when you open your hand, it's sandy. If it is slightly crumbly but still holds a loose ball, it is closer to loam.

Soil Structure

Structure is determined by the way a soil's particles bind to form small clumps, which are called aggregates. In soil with a good structure, the pores between and within the aggregates are large enough to contain air and allow water to drain through easily, yet they are small enough to retain some water for roots.

Though you can't change a soil's basic texture, you can improve its structure by adding organic matter to bind particles into larger aggregates. In sandy soils, organic matter lodges in the pore spaces and acts like a sponge, holding water and nutrients. In clay soils, improvement is especially important, as it increases porosity. Gypsum and lime, both inorganic amendments, are sometimes used to improve structure in clay soils. For advice on using them, consult soil professionals or your Cooperative Extension Office.

Soil structure can be damaged, especially in clay soils. Running heavy machinery over the soil or even walking on planting areas compresses the pore spaces, as does tilling soil when it's too wet.

Hardpan is an impervious layer of soil that is found naturally in some regions—in the Southwest, for example, where the most common natural hardpan is called *caliche.* Hardpan can also be created, as when builders spread excavated subsoil over the soil surface and then drive heavy equipment over it. Though a thin layer of topsoil may conceal hardpan, roots cannot penetrate it nor water drain through it.

If the hardpan layer is thin and close to the surface, you may break it up by plowing the

The three basic soil types, *from left to right: Sandy soil, loam, and clay soil.*

S

Areas of poor drainage are evident after heavy rainfall.

Porous soil

Hardpan

Porous soil

Soil pH

Soil pH is a measure of how soil ranges from acid through neutral to alkaline. This characteristic is stated as a pH number. Soil with a pH of 7 is neutral—neither acid nor alkaline. A pH below 7 indicates acidity, while one above 7 indicates alkalinity. If the pH is extreme in either direction, key nutrients are chemically "tied up" in the soil and not available to plant roots. The best way to determine your soil's pH is to have the soil tested.

A soil analysis will determine your soil's pH (acidity or alkalinity) and can reveal nutrient deficiencies. A simple test kit gives you a general indication of your soil's condition. For a more precise reading, you can have the test done at a laboratory. In some Western states, a Cooperative Extension Office will test your soil or can direct you to commercial soil laboratories. You can also search on the Internet or look in the phone book under "Laboratories—

pH range for most garden soil

Acid

3

4 — Extremely* acid soil

5 — pH range in high-rainfall regions

6

Neutral 7

8 — pH range in arid regions

9

10 — Extremely* alkaline soil

11

Alkaline

pH range preferred by acid-loving plants

pH range preferred by most garden plants

*Soils nearing extremes require professional intervention to modify pH.

soil to a depth of 1 foot or more. If plowing is impractical, you may be able to create drainage chimneys as shown on page 715. Thick hardpan may require the installation of a subsurface drainage system, a project that usually requires hiring a contractor. Or you can grow plants in raised beds filled with good soil (see page 725).

Soil Drainage

Poor drainage causes water to remain in the pore spaces, and air, necessary both to roots and beneficial soil-dwelling organisms, is unable to enter the soil. Soil texture, a low-lying location, and hardpan can all contribute to poor drainage.

As noted earlier, clay soils frequently drain poorly. To improve the situation, work in plenty of organic matter. Planting in raised beds filled with good well-drained soil is another option (see page 725). In the garden's low spots, you can install drainage pipes to carry away excess water. If this is impractical, consider adapting your garden to the site and growing plants suited to moist areas.

To check drainage, dig a 2-foot-deep hole and fill it with water. After it drains, fill it again. If this second amount of water drains away in an hour or less, the drainage is good. If it remains for several hours or longer, the soil drains poorly.

Analytical." The lab will tell you where and how to collect a soil sample.

Acid soil is most common in regions that have heavy rainfall and is often associated with sandy soils and those high in organic matter. In the West, overly acid soil typically occurs in Alaska, British Columbia, western Washington, Oregon, along the northern coast of California, and in parts of Hawaii. Though most plants grow well in mildly acid soil, highly acid soils are inhospitable. Adding calcium carbonate (lime) is one way to raise pH.

Alkaline soil, found in many regions where rainfall is light, is high in calcium carbonate. Many plants grow well in moderately alkaline soil. Others, notably camellias, rhododendrons, and azaleas, do not.

Sulfur can be used to lower soil pH. You can also lower pH over time with regular (at least annual) applications of organic amendments such as compost. Another option for growing plants that need acid soil is to plant them in containers or raised beds filled with an appropriate soil mix. Note that if your water is also alkaline, these remedies may not work.

Salty soils are found near the seashore and in arid regions, or they can result from the overuse of fertilizers and fresh manures. Salty soil pulls water from plant roots, making it difficult for plants to take up enough moisture or

S

nutrients. Symptoms include scorched and yellowed leaves or browned and withered leaf margins. Seed germination is also inhibited. Salty soils include saline and sodic types.

Saline soils contain large quantities of soluble salts, such as compounds of calcium, sulfate, chloride, or sodium. To correct these, you can improve drainage by adding organic matter and leach the soil periodically with water to wash the salts below the plants' root zones.

Sodic soils are high in insoluble sodium, which bonds to soil particles. Such soils, also known as black alkali, are alkaline and poorly drained. In many areas, it's effective to incorporate calcium sulfate (gypsum), then leach the soil to wash away the sodium. However, if the calcium level of your soil is already high (a soil test can tell you this), a better course is to lower the alkalinity by incorporating organic amendments or through the use of sulfur. Check with a soil-testing laboratory or with your Cooperative Extension Office for advice specific to your area.

Organic Soil Amendments

The decaying remains of plants and animals, organic matter is vital to the fertility and structure of all soils, especially those high in clay and sand. The final product of the breakdown of organic matter is humus, a soft, sticky material that decomposes slowly and improves soil structure.

However, the nitrogen released by decaying organic matter must first be converted by

Animal manure—from vegetarian animals only, including cows, sheep, and horses—is an excellent soil booster. However, it should be well aged or added to the compost pile to kill any weed seeds or harmful organisms.

A Substitute for Peat

For soil amendments, many gardeners prefer sphagnum peat moss to ground bark. Peat breaks down more slowly, and, unlike bark, it won't compact in the container and limit aeration. But there are concerns over the ecological damage that may result from the overmining of some peat bogs. A good alternative to peat is coir fiber. A by-product of the coconut fiber industry, it's sold in compressed bales, bricks, and discs that expand when soaked in water to make anywhere from 5 to 10 quarts of fluffy material. Used in potting mixes, it breaks down slowly and retains moisture and air well. It's also useful as a soil additive or mulch in the garden. Keep in mind, though, that coir fiber won't help acidify the soil the way peat does, as its pH is closer to neutral.

various microorganisms—such as bacteria, fungi, and actinomycetes—into ammonia, then into nitrites, which can be absorbed by plant roots.

Soils high in organic matter contain high populations of the microorganisms that ultimately produce humus. They also have plenty of earthworms. As the animals tunnel, they improve drainage and aeration, while their castings add nutrients.

Many types of organic amendments are available. One choice is well-aged manure, which contains more nutrients than most other amendments. Homemade compost is another excellent amendment (see page 680). Some municipalities gather and compost grass clippings, leaves, and tree prunings. Mushroom compost tends to be high in salts, so use it in smaller quantities than other composts.

New Soil Amendments

Two new soil amendments are appearing in nurseries alongside more familiar products, though both have been in the natural world for a very long time.

Mycorrhizal fungi are naturally occurring soil organisms that colonize the roots of plants, helping them use water and nutrients more efficiently and suppressing diseases.

Researchers have found that the extensive use of synthetic fertilizers and pesticides seems to inhibit these fungi—and that adding them to garden soil or potting mixes can improve plant growth and production. You can find mycorrhizae in tablet form or as additives in organic fertilizers.

Rock powders function much like any other organic amendment, improving soil structure

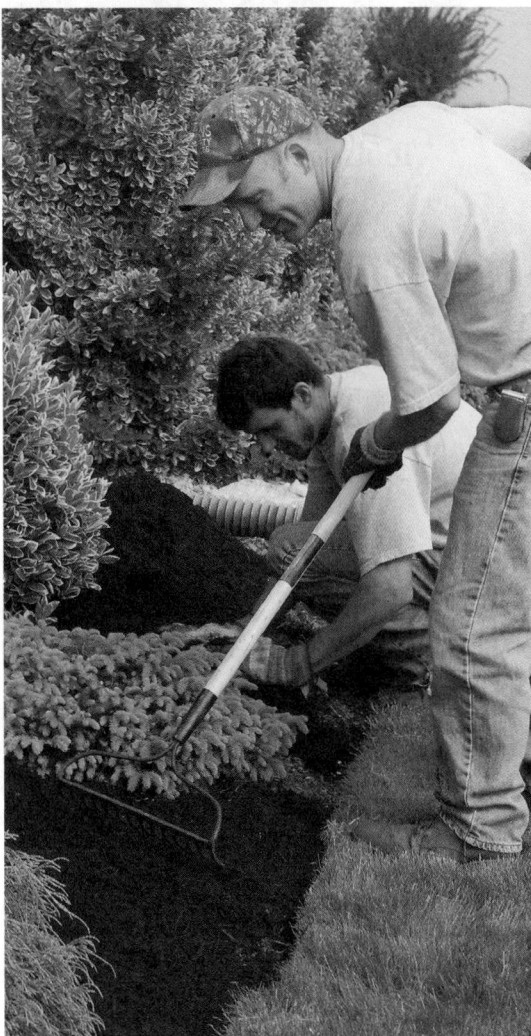

Applying organic amendments. Around established plantings, spread organic material over the soil surface as a mulch. Earthworms, microorganisms, and water will help mix it into the top layer of soil. If the established plants are deep rooted—as are most mature trees and shrubs, for example—gently work the amendment into the top inch or so of soil. To use peat as an amendment, always mix it into the top few inches of soil.

S

and adding minerals that are released slowly over time. Proponents claim that rock powders—or dusts, as they're also called—make plants more resistant to pests and diseases, improve the flavor of edible crops, and even brighten flower colors.

Before using any rock powder, order a soil test and then choose a formula that supplies any deficient minerals. Bear in mind that no rock powder contains nitrogen. Widely available products include rock phosphate, which supplies phosphorus and trace minerals; rock dust, a mixture of potassium and trace minerals; greensand, an iron-potassium silicate; and lime rock powder, a source of calcium and magnesium. Don't confuse lime rock powder with the dolomitic limestone sold in most garden centers, which is high in magnesium but low in calcium.

TOOLS

Stores, nurseries, and specialized mail-order catalogs offer gardening tools in bewildering array. This section describes a number of useful tools—many of them quite versatile—and offers tips for selecting them and using them comfortably and efficiently.

Tools

TOOL	USES	LOOK FOR	NOTES
Round-point Shovel	Loosens soil, transfers soil to a pile or wheelbarrow, digs planting holes.	For general digging, use a larger shovel (one with a 9-inch-long, 12-inch-wide head). In a confined space, use a smaller model, called a floral shovel, which has a 6-by-8-inch head and a shorter handle.	Round-point shovels vary in lift—the angle formed between the ground and the shovel handle when the shovel head is laid flat on the ground. To make digging easier by minimizing the amount of bending you'll have to do, choose a tool with generous lift.
Square-nose Shovel	Scoops up loose compost or gravel from a flat surface.	The correct size picks up the greatest amount of material you can lift repeatedly without tiring.	Not meant for general digging.
Border Spade	Digs in confined spaces such as flower beds and borders.	Blade is about 6 inches wide and 8 inches long.	In contrast to shovels, spades have longer, narrower, relatively flat heads.
English Garden Spade	Prepares soil for planting and digs narrow, straight-sided trenches.	Has an almost flat blade (about 7 inches wide by 11 inches long) and forward-turned steps (the ledges at the top of the blade where you place your foot when you dig). The handle, often a short D type, extends almost straight up from the blade with little or no lift.	Can also be used on occasion to prune roots of trees and shrubs.
Transplanting Spade	Digs holes for deep-rooted plants. Also good for replanting.	Features slightly dished blades about 5 inches wide and 14 or 16 inches long.	
Spading Fork	Breaks large clods of soil into smaller clumps.	May have shorter D handle or longer straight handle. Look for four tines that are square or rectangular in cross-section and about 1/2 inch wide.	Substitutes for spades in clay or rocky soils.
Manure Fork	Moves manure or piles of prunings. Also turns compost.	Forged tines are stronger than welded ones.	T-shaped handle makes turning compost easier.
American-style Hoe	Flat front edges cut weeds off at ground level. Sharp corners work like small picks to dig furrows.	Most common kind has a 6-inch-wide blade. Narrower blades (2 1/2 inches wide) are useful for tight spots, while a wider blade (8 inches) is ideal for paths and driveways.	
V-hoe	Point makes small furrows, and well-sharpened sides slice weeds.		Especially useful in vegetable gardens.
Eye and Grape Hoes	Break ground, chop tough weeds, scrape away dense growth, and move soil.	Heavy-duty hoes with wide, deep blades set perpendicular to the handle.	
Weeding Hoes	Cut off weeds below soil surface.	Draw hoe versions come in a variety of shapes, such as circles and diamonds. Others are push hoes, such as the Dutch hoe shown opposite, or oscillating hoes, which cut on both the push and draw strokes.	When using any of these hoes, run the blade just under the soil surface to cut off weeds at ground level. Disturb the soil as little as possible to avoid bringing more weed seeds to the surface, where they will be able to germinate.
Garden or Soil Rake	Breaks up clods of dirt, levels soil, tamps seedbeds to make them firm, and works amendments into the top few inches of a planting bed.	Thick steel tines may be straight or curved. Tines may be attached to the handle directly by a tang or socket, or indirectly by a curving bow. The bow type has more spring or resilience. Soil rakes are available with 6, 8, 14, or 16 tines.	Select a rake with some weight in its head. If it's too light, you'll have to work harder to provide the downward force needed to break clods or move soil.
Leaf Rake	Rakes leaves and gathers grass clippings and other lightweight materials into piles.	Tines are closely spaced and curve downward and slightly inward at the tip, arranged in a curving fan with a stabilizing brace about 8 inches up from the tip of the tines. Widths may be as great as 4 feet.	Smaller versions (8 or 10 inches wide) are useful for raking between shrubs and perennials. A leaf rake should be light but sturdy, allowing you to apply firm pressure to the ground with minimal effort.

T

TOOL	USES	LOOK FOR	NOTES
Thatching Rake	Clears thatch out of lawn grasses.	Semicircular metal tines are attached with rounded edge facing forward.	Keep the head on the ground. Pull through dense grass to rip out thatch. A push or forward stroke clears material from the tines.
Cultivator	Breaks up compacted soil and works amendments into the upper few inches of soil. Also effective for weeding.	Comes in a single-tine type (known as a finger hoe) or with two to five tines spaced 1½ to 2 inches apart. Tines may be long or short, curved or straight. Ends are pointed in some models, flattened to form a lozenge-shaped tooth in others.	Select a narrow cultivator if you plan to cultivate between closely spaced plants or if your soil is heavy. The fewer the tines, the more concentrated your pulling force will be. A cultivator with tines arranged in a V shape rather than lined up in a row is also easier to pull through heavy soils. If plants are widely spaced, a four- or five-tine cultivator is more practical. It also works best in sandy or well-amended soils.
Half-moon Edger	Maintains a neat edge between lawn and adjacent beds of flowers or ground covers, or between lawn and paving.		

Garden Tools

Round-point shovel

Oscillating hoe

Square-nose shovel

Spading fork

Dutch hoe

Garden spade

Garden rake

Hand Tools

TOOL	USES	LOOK FOR	NOTES
Trowel	Plants, cultivates soil, weeds, scoops fertilizers and amendments from bags.	A trowel should be both strong and sharp. The best ones are made of forged steel and have a wooden handle driven and pinned into a socket at the base of the blade.	For general use, select one with a shallowly dished blade about 4 inches wide and 6 inches long. Transplanting trowels are narrower (about 3 inches wide), tapered, and deeply dished. They may have marks on the blade to help you gauge planting depth. Potting trowels are even narrower and only shallowly dished. Crevice or rockery trowels are just 1 1/4 inch wide.
Knife	Divides roots of plants, opens bags of soil or soil amendments, carves points on the ends of stakes.		The Japanese farmer's knife (Hori Hori) features a slightly dished blade that can be used as a trowel; one side of the blade is saw-toothed, while the other has a sharp edge that can cut roots and burlap.
Dibble	Pokes holes in prepared soil to plant bulbs, bedding plants, and vegetables.	Usually carrot shaped, with an iron point and a rounded or T-shaped handle.	
Weeder	Digs or slices off weeds.	Look for a hand weeder that has a bent shaft or with a ball attached to the shaft to serve as a fulcrum. The tool's head should be small and forked.	Other models include circle or half-moon shaped blades to slice weed stems just below soil level.
Bypass Pruners	Remove branches no thicker than a little finger, snip stems, deadhead.	Have a curved hook and a curved blade.	The branch to be cut rests against the hook; the blade cuts it, passing the hook as it slices through the branch. In some models, the cutting blade bends away from the handle at an angle up to 45 degrees; this gives you more cutting power and minimizes strain on your wrists.
Anvil Pruners	Remove branches no thicker than a little finger, snip stems.	Anvil pruners have a flat anvil (instead of a hook) and a straight blade.	The blade cuts through the branch until it hits the anvil.
Loppers	Remove thicker and thornier branches.	Range from 1 to 3 feet in length and may have either bypass or anvil construction. The largest loppers will cut 3-inch-thick branches.	Long handles give you much more leverage than the short handles of hand pruners. Smaller loppers are good for cutting among thorny branches without scratching your hands and arms. Select loppers with strong handles, preferably bolted on. A shock absorber, located below the pivot point, saves wear on your arms.
Pruning Saws	Remove branches.	May have straight or curved blades; a curved one fits more easily into tight spots. May also have fixed or folding blades. Some models come with gullets—deep slots about every fourth tooth that accumulate and release sticky sawdust.	Most modern pruning saws cut on the pull rather than the push stroke.
Japanese-style Saws	Remove branches 1 to 5 inches in diameter.	Each tooth is ground on three edges, giving a smoother, faster cut. A 13-inch Japanese-style saw with a fixed blade is a good choice for most gardens.	Japanese saws can snap if you apply too much force or try to cut on the push stroke, and they cannot be resharpened, but most gardeners feel that their ease of use and cutting speed more than make up for these drawbacks.
Pole Pruners	Remove high branches 3/4 to 1 inch thick.	Typically come with both shears and a saw, which you attach to a pole. To make the shears work, pull a cord or press a lever to draw the blade through the branch.	Poles are available in various lengths; some are telescoping, while others fit together in sections. In either case, the pruners will be easiest to use if the pole is fairly stiff.
Hedge Shears	Trim hedges, shear flowering shrubs, cut back perennials.	For heavy-duty pruning of hedges with dense, woody growth, select shears with a short (7-inch) blade. One blade will often be serrated and notched; the notch helps to hold bigger twigs in place while you cut.	Hedge shears with longer blades (up to 11 inches) are meant for light-duty shearing of leafy tip growth; the longer blades shear a larger area with each stroke. Be sure any hedge shears you buy are equipped with shock absorbers.
Garden Sprayer	Applies fungicides, pesticides, herbicides, and foliar fertilizers.	A 1-quart, hand-pumped compression sprayer allows you to mix small amounts of chemicals, avoiding waste. Select one with a brass spray nozzle.	For more extensive spraying, choose a 2-gallon-capacity hand pump model. It should have a polyethylene tank, a brass valve wand, and an adjustable brass nozzle. An extra-long hose allows you to move around as you spray.

T

Hand Tools

Cape Cod
weeder

Dandelion
weeder

Anvil pruners

Bypass pruners

Trowel

Sprayer heads

Snips

Tool Handles

When choosing tools for your garden, select high-quality models that fit your body type. For example, shovels, spades, and spading forks are available with either shorter D-type handles or long handles. D handles are best for shorter gardeners (though they're also useful in confined spaces), while tall people are usually more comfortable using long-handled tools. If possible, buy hoes, cultivators, and rakes that are at least as tall as you are (preferably an inch taller). This allows you to use them in a standing rather than a stooping position.

Handles made of straight-grained, knot-free wood are generally the best choice for most garden tools. Make sure the handle and head are attached with a rivet that passes all the way through the handle. Tubular aluminum handles are easily bent, while tubular fiberglass ones can be shattered, especially on heavily used digging tools. What's more, these handles are usually narrower than wooden ones and thus more tiring to grasp for long periods.

Forging—heating metal until it is almost molten, then pounding it into the desired shape—produces a denser tool head that is less likely to bend or break and takes an edge better than less expensive stamped steel. Highly polished, forged stainless-steel tools are preferred by some gardeners because they don't rust and they slide easily into the soil. However, they're somewhat more brittle than tools made of conventional carbon steel, which makes them more difficult to sharpen and more likely to fracture if used improperly.

Ergonomic Tools

Designed primarily to make digging, pruning, and general puttering possible for people with physical limitations, these handy helpers also appeal to young, able-bodied gardeners for one reason: they make even the most strenuous chores a lot more comfortable. Innovations range from handles made of a gel-like material that cushions the user's hand to ratcheting pruners that cut with a fraction of the effort required by tradi-

tional models. Some lines of hand tools feature upright "fist grips" that maximize the user's power and lessen the chance of injury to hands and wrists. And trowels, pruners, and hand rakes with extra-long handles make life easier for people in wheelchairs, or those who simply have limited mobility.

Ergonomic tools are sold in in garden centers, but catalogs and specialty shops offer the most extensive selection. Online sources include Life with Ease (www.lifewithease.com), Wellhaven Gifts for Seniors (www.wellhaven. com), and Clean Air Gardening (www.cleanair gardening.com).

T

Hand-tool Tips

- Store hand tools where you use them most often—in the garden. One easy way is to buy a mail box and mount it on top of a redwood post. Tucked in a perennial bed within easy reach of a path, it keeps trowel, clippers, and gloves handy for quick jobs such as clipping spent blooms.

- Use a rockery or crevice trowel, just 1 1/4 inches wide, to shoehorn plants into tight spaces, such as between pavers.

- For weeding between plants in flower beds, try a circle hoe; it has an O-shaped blade that slices off weeds below the soil line.

Hanging your tools off the ground in a sheltered spot will ensure years of use.

Tool Maintenance

Fall is a good time to care for your gardening tools so they'll be ready in spring. To clean and oil the metal parts of digging tools, fill a bucket about three-fourths full with coarse sand. Mix in 1 quart or more of general-purpose oil. Jab your tools into the mixture until the sand has abraded away the dirt and the blades are coated with oil. Brush off the sand and store the tools. Oiled sand can be used indefinitely. If you need to discard it, take it to a hazardous-waste disposal station.

Caring for Garden Tools

Well-made tools not only make gardening easier but, given proper care, will last for years. All tools need cleaning after use, and any tool with an edge—be it a shovel, spade, hoe, or pruning tool—should be kept sharp. When blades eventually become dull, you will find it's easiest to have a professional restore them; many garden supply and hardware stores can recommend a reliable sharpening service.

Cleaning tools. To remove accumulated sap and rust from pruning shears, use a little oil and steel wool. You can also buy special oil/solvent mixtures to clean sap and dirt from pruning tools and to lubricate them. To maintain the smoothest operation, occasionally disassemble the tool and work a dab of synthetic white lithium grease onto the pivot bolt and into the area around the bolt hole.

Clean the sawdust from pruning saws after each use and remove any sap and rust with steel wool and oil. Apply a thin coat of paraffin to the blade before using.

A barbecue brush with a scraper is handy for cleaning digging tools. Use the scraper to remove layers of dirt and mud as you work in the garden. The bristles give a final cleanup before you store the tool.

Give tool heads a thorough cleaning annually. Remove rust with medium steel wool and a little oil; then use paint thinner to clean off the oily residue. Finally, apply a rust-proofing paint.

Maintaining wooden handles. Wooden handles on all types of garden tools last for many years if kept clean and oiled. Wipe them off after every use. Once a year or so, sand them lightly and apply a coat of boiled linseed oil with a cloth; if the oil soaks in completely, apply another coat. Then buff the handles.

A specialized sharpener can hone any tool that has one beveled edge. These include hoes, lawn mower blades, and pruning shears.

The Right Way to Dig and Hoe

Learning to dig and hoe properly can literally save your back. When digging with a shovel, don't drive the tool into the ground at a low angle, bend over to lever the soil loose, and then lift with your back bent. Instead, drive the shovel blade straight down, as close to your body as you can manage comfortably. The shovel handle will angle away from you. When you have driven the blade in as far as possible, step back with the foot that is not on the shovel's step or tread and pull the handle toward the center of your chest. Then, grasping the handle at the top with one hand and sliding the other hand toward the bottom, bend your knees and lower your body, keeping your back straight. Lift the shovelful of soil, using the strength of your legs, not your back.

Using a spade involves the same techniques, except that you'll usually be turning the soil over in a bed instead of lifting and moving it.

When using a hoe, rake, or cultivator, stand sideways to the work, as if you were using a kitchen broom. Grasp the handle with your thumbs wrapped around it near the top. As you work, flex your knees slightly and pull the tool across the front of your body. This position keeps your back straight, and if you hit a buried rock or large root, you'll naturally pull with the strong muscles in your upper legs instead of straining your lower back.

Pink blossoms *of flowering dogwood* (Cornus florida).

TREES

Trees are the backbone of the garden, providing shade and shelter and bringing year-round beauty through their foliage, flowers, fruits, leaves, bark, and branch structure. The distinction between a tree and a large shrub is sometimes blurred, but trees typically are tall plants with one dominant trunk (though some kinds may have several trunks) topped by a crown of foliage. In contrast, most shrubs (see page 726) are smaller and have foliage all the way to the ground.

The Value of Trees

Trees are your garden's most valuable assets. Their size alone can make or break the mood. Deciduous types mark the passing seasons in their own stunning way: bare branches in winter breaking forth with fresh, tender leaves or pastel blossoms in early spring, followed by lush foliage in summer, then the breathtaking autumn leaves of red, yellow, orange or burgundy. Trees lend a sense of permanence and age to the garden, while a home without any trees can have an unfinished appearance.

Trees have a practical side too. Deciduous ones, strategically placed to shade walls and windows, can reduce home cooling costs by up to 50 percent. Then they conveniently shed their leaves in fall so that sunlight can stream through house windows all winter long. Trees can also reduce noise, curb soil erosion, and provide food and shelter for birds and other wildlife, which in turn feast on

destructive and disease-spreading insects. What's more, attractive landscaping with established, well-placed trees increases both the sales appeal and the monetary value of a home.

Selecting Trees

Because trees are so important to the landscape and are generally slow growing, you'll want to choose them carefully. Consult local nursery personnel and look at the trees in your neighborhood to see which ones perform particularly well. Also review the Plant Selection Guide on pages 79–84.

DECIDUOUS TREES These varieties start their growth with a burst of new leaves (and often flowers) in early spring, then remain in leaf through summer. In autumn, the foliage drops to reveal bare limbs, often changing color before it falls. The tree then goes dormant for winter.

EVERGREEN TREES Evergreens include both broad-leafed types and conifers (though there are a few deciduous conifers). Both kinds serve well as screens and windbreaks. Broad-leafed evergreens may drop some leaves, but there's always enough foliage on the branches to give the tree a well-clothed look. Most conifers have leaves that are narrow and needle-like or tiny and scale-like. They may drop some of their leaves year-round.

LANDSCAPE FUNCTION If you need shade, choose a tree with a wide canopy. Deciduous trees provide shade in summer, then admit sun to warm the house after their leaves drop in fall. If you want to block views into your home or garden, choose relatively tall, dense trees. For a specimen tree to serve as a garden focal point, search for interesting

foliage or a striking display of blossoms or berries. Fruit trees have special appeal, providing delicious fruit as well as lovely form and flowers (see page 737).

ADAPTABILITY AND GROWTH RATE Be sure that any tree you consider planting is well adapted to your climate zone and to the conditions in your garden. Select those that will grow well in the soil you have, with the amount of water they'll receive naturally or that you can easily provide.

If you need a tree to shade a south-facing window or to provide privacy, select a fast-growing kind, though not one that will outgrow its site. In fact, it's important to visualize the ultimate height and spread of a tree you consider for any role. Not only is an overly large one out of scale in most gardens, but it will eventually crowd structures and other plants and may ultimately have to be removed.

A tree with a network of surface roots is a poor candidate for planting in a lawn or garden, but it may be just right at the garden's fringes or along a country drive. Some trees have surface roots that can lift and crack nearby pavement, making them less than ideal choices for a patio, entryway, or driveway.

If you want to plant trees beneath utility lines, choose ones that naturally top out at least 10 feet below the lines. Cutting back a tall tree that has grown too close to the line is hazardous.

MAINTENANCE Trees that produce a fair amount of litter from falling leaves, flowers, or fruits shouldn't be planted beside a patio, in a lawn, or near a pond or pool. Such trees are better candidates for background areas, where the litter can remain where it falls. In regions with regular high winds or heavy annual snow-

Trees offer year-round interest *with (clockwise from top left) winter berries of mountain ash* (Sorbus), *delicately pink spring blooms of a hybrid magnolia, drooping cones of a pine tree, and the yellow autumn leaves of* Ginkgo biloba.

fall, avoid trees with weak or brittle wood. They can be hazardous, and removing broken limbs may both ruin the tree's beauty and cost you a tidy sum.

Make sure the trees you're considering aren't overly susceptible to pests or diseases. Keep in mind that a particular tree may be trouble free in one climate but plagued with problems in another.

LONGEVITY Some trees can be planted for future generations to enjoy, while others grow and decline quickly. Trees that are planted for screening or shade should be long lived, but for specimen planting, shorter-lived kinds may be an excellent choice. Plant the latter only where removal will be relatively easy and won't compromise your overall landscape. For example, many attractive flowering trees run their course in about 20 years, but when they die,

you can fill the resulting gap with another tree of the same sort.

Planting and Caring for Trees

Many deciduous trees are sold bare-root during the dormant season, from late fall through early spring. Deciduous trees as well as conifers and broad-leafed evergreens may also be sold balled-and-burlapped from early fall into the following spring, or in containers throughout the year. For instructions on planting all types, see pages 714–716.

The exposed trunk of a newly planted tree needs protection from drying winds, hot sun, freezing temperatures, gnawing animals (such as rabbits, deer, and rodents), and damage from lawn mowers or string trimmers. To keep a trunk free from harm, wrap it loosely in burlap or a manufactured trunk-wrapping material. Remove the wrapping after a year, when the bark has become thicker and tougher. Don't leave wrapping in place longer than this, as it can eventually girdle the tree.

All trees, even drought-tolerant kinds, need regular watering during the first several years after planting, until their roots have grown deep enough to carry them through dry periods. Once established, many kinds require only infrequent irrigation.

Regular fertilizing is also needed for a few years after planting. By ensuring a good supply of nitrogen for the springtime growth surge, you'll encourage young trees to establish quickly.

Once a tree is well settled in, though, it may grow satisfactorily with no further feeding. In fact, fertilizing a tree that continues to put out healthy, vigorous new growth is a waste of both time and fertilizer. However, feeding may be in order if a tree's new growth is weak, sparse, or unusually pale, or if it has a fair amount of dieback that cannot be ascribed to overwatering or underwatering.

Training and Pruning

Most young trees benefit from some early training or pruning. The idea is to encourage the development of a sturdy trunk from which will radiate strong, well-placed main limbs (scaffold branches). Conifers are an exception. They seldom need training unless they develop more than one leader (central upward-growing stem). If that occurs, remove the weaker of the two stems. Deciduous and broad-leafed evergreen trees, on the other hand, are more likely to require training, but don't rush to do the job. Prune newly planted trees as little as possible, removing only any dead, broken, or rubbing branches and the weaker limb of a double leader. Wait a full year, until the tree's roots are growing well, before doing any more than this. Prune the tree gradually over the next three to five years, but don't remove too much wood in any one year.

Though you may be tempted to begin training a tree by removing lower limbs, it's best to leave these in place for the first few years. Don't remove the lower limbs of conifers such as spruces, firs, and others with a strongly pyramidal shape at all. They look most natural when allowed to branch all the way to the ground.

As the tree grows, encourage well-placed scaffold branches by selecting shoots at fairly evenly spaced intervals, both up the trunk and spiraling around it. Whenever possible, favor wide-angled branches forming more or less U-shaped crotches over narrow-angled ones that have V-shaped crotches. If the angle is very narrow, branches tend to be weakly attached to the trunk and split off easily. Remove badly placed and superfluous branches before they become too large, keeping the ultimate shape of the tree in mind. Also remove suckers, water sprouts, and lateral branches growing toward the center of the tree.

When They Have to Go

Sometimes, when a tree grows bigger than you thought it would, or when you've inherited someone else's inappropriate choice, you can solve the size problem with a little creative thinning. Under other circumstances, such as the ones listed below, your only choice may be to remove it.

- The tree has been planted too close to a building, under power lines, or where its roots will damage paved areas.

- A dead or dying tree could spread a pest or disease to other trees or shrubs.

- Young trees were planted too close together, resulting in overcrowding.

- Your view is blocked. In this case, the view-versus-tree decision may be yours to make, or it may be in the hands of others. Many towns and homeowners' associations have laws that mandate view preservation, while others come down in favor of the trees. The bottom line: Check before you chop.

T

Staking a Weak Trunk

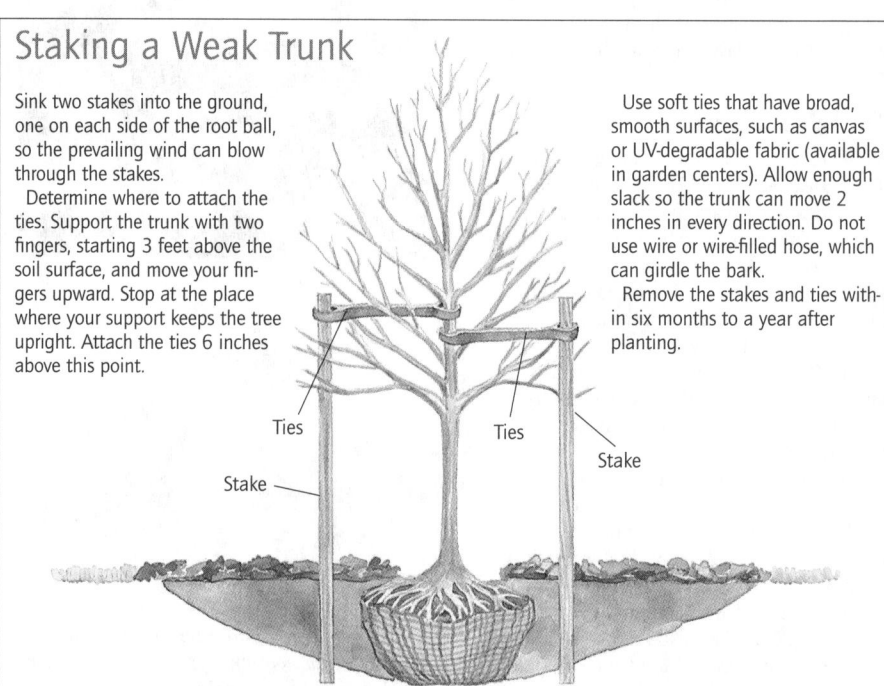

Sink two stakes into the ground, one on each side of the root ball, so the prevailing wind can blow through the stakes.

Determine where to attach the ties. Support the trunk with two fingers, starting 3 feet above the soil surface, and move your fingers upward. Stop at the place where your support keeps the tree upright. Attach the ties 6 inches above this point.

Use soft ties that have broad, smooth surfaces, such as canvas or UV-degradable fabric (available in garden centers). Allow enough slack so the trunk can move 2 inches in every direction. Do not use wire or wire-filled hose, which can girdle the bark.

Remove the stakes and ties within six months to a year after planting.

Ties

Ties

Stake

Stake

Inheriting a Tree

If you've just bought your first house, or one that you simply plan to renovate, take an inventory of the mature trees on the property and decide if there are any you wish to keep. Before you start pruning, landscaping around them, or remodeling too close to them, follow the steps below to preserve their value and beauty. All too often, a mature tree is mutilated or killed by the actions of well-meaning gardeners. For instance, a native oak—which may have taken more than a century to attain a majestic beauty—can be seriously damaged in months if a water-guzzling lawn is planted above its roots.

Even if a tree's value seems insignificant to you, keep in mind the ambience it adds to the neighborhood. In some communities, cutting down a "heritage" tree whose girth or size exceeds certain measurements is against the law. Before you remove trees on your property, check your local ordinances.

- **Find out what kind of trees you have.** If the property's previous owner doesn't know, call an arborist. Better yet, hire an arborist certified by the International Society of Arboriculture (ISA) to survey all the trees on your property. The arborist can evaluate the trees' health, age, present and future size, and any hazards they may pose, and tell you whether they're structurally sound or in need of pruning.

- **Learn about your trees' needs.** Do they need regular water during dry times? Fertilizing occasionally? Pruning every year? Do they need room to grow unencumbered? Trees such as ginkgo thrive in lawns, while the roots of magnolias tend to grow close to the soil surface, which can make a lawn difficult to grow. Native oaks cannot tolerate summer water and will do better when surrounded with a carpet of decomposed granite, perhaps accented with boulders, or a wide tapestry of native plants that thrive in dry shade. Check the cultural information provided for each species in the Western Plant Encyclopedia.

- **Protect the tree during a remodel.** If low branches must be removed to make way for heavy equipment, hire an arborist to do it. Use a rope to tie thinner, flexible branches up and out of the way. To protect a tree's trunk from gouges and its roots from compaction by heavy equipment, erect a barrier around the tree, ideally out to its dripline. If heavy equipment must be moved over the tree's root zone, cover the area from the trunk out to the dripline with a 12-inch layer of wood chips.

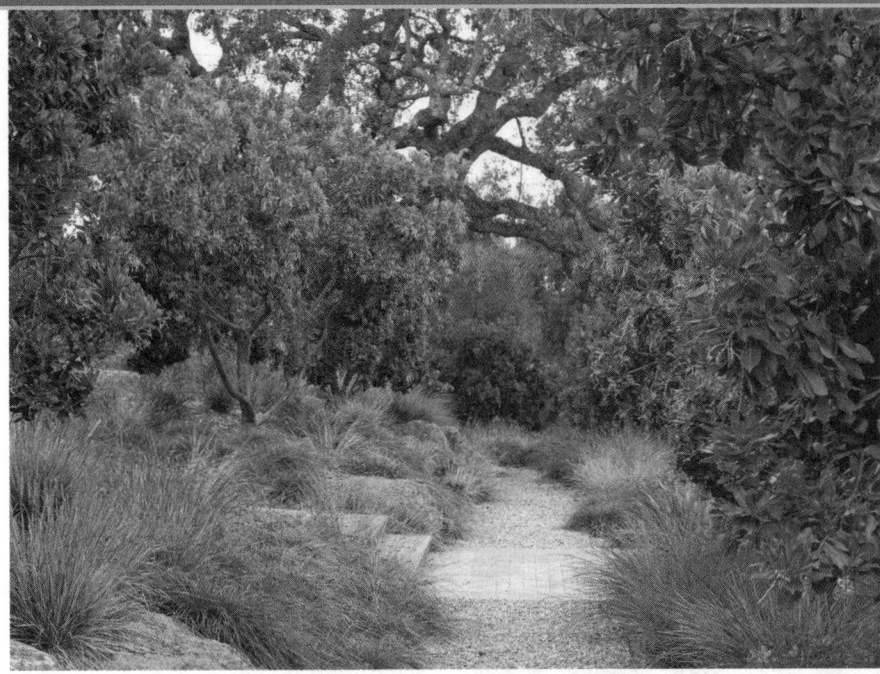

Many native trees, such as oaks and Arbutus, *cannot tolerate excessive summer water and should be surrounded with plants that thrive in dry shade.*

For more information on pruning methods, including instructions for removing large limbs, see page 723.

Staking Young Trees

A young tree develops a sturdier trunk if it grows unsupported and can sway with the wind. (The technical reason is that as the stem of a plant moves in the breeze, it releases chemicals called cytokinins, which cause cells in the stem to enlarge and thicken, thereby strengthening plant tissues.) But there are times when staking is necessary: when a tree is planted in a very windy location, when the main trunk is too weak to stand upright on its own, or when the crown is very large in proportion to the trunk. To stake a tree properly, see facing page.

Selecting Fruit Trees

Which fruit trees are best for you? To answer that question, you'll need to take several factors into account. First decide how much room you have available. A standard full-size apple or cherry tree can reach 40 feet high and 30 to 40 feet wide—too large for many gardens. But a number of choices are available to fit a more limited space. *Semidwarf* trees typically reach one-half to three-fourths normal height. *Dwarfs* grow only 5 to 10 feet tall, depending on the species. Some fruit trees are also available as genetic dwarfs—plants bred to be naturally small (just 4 to 10 feet high). These are well adapted to container culture.

Multiple-variety trees offer another way to grow fruit trees in a limited area. Such trees have three to five varieties of the same or a closely related species grafted onto a single trunk and rootstock.

When choosing fruit trees, also think about your climate. To grow and bloom well, many kinds need a certain amount of cold weather each year. Known as the chill requirement, this is measured in hours needed at temperatures below 45° F/7° C. If you live in a mild-winter region, it's important to choose varieties with a low chill requirement.

Cold tolerance is a third factor to consider. Though varieties differ in hardiness, many kinds of apples, sour cherries, and hardy hybrid plums can withstand temperatures as low as –30° F/–34° C, while pears, sweet cherries, and Japanese and European plums tolerate temperatures down to –20° F/–29° C. Peaches and apricots may be injured at –15° F/–26° C, and most citrus trees are damaged if the temperature falls below 32° F/0° C for any length of time. By taking advantage of your garden's microclimates, however, you may be able to grow fruit trees beyond their normal hardiness range. Siting trees away from frost pockets can also minimize damage inflicted on blossoms by spring frosts.

Many kinds of fruit trees require cross-pollination for good fruit set. If you live in an area where there are few other fruit trees, check the pollination requirements of those you want to grow. If cross-pollination is needed, you don't necessarily have to plant another tree. You may be able to graft a pollenizer branch onto the chosen tree or even place a bouquet of flowers from another variety in a bucket of water at its base.

VEGETABLE GARDENING

Growing your own vegetables is rewarding and enjoyable. In return for your efforts, you'll harvest food that's fresh and bursting with flavor. To make your vegetable patch a success, plan before you plant. If you're new to vegetable gardening, start small. An area of just 100 to 130 square feet can provide a substantial harvest.

To decide which vegetables to plant, first list the kinds your family really enjoys. Then consider how much room each type requires. If space is limited, raise vegetables that give a good yield for the area they occupy. Beans, tomatoes, and some summer squash, for example, can overwhelm you with produce from a very small plot. At the other extreme are melon and squash varieties that grow on long vines. Like corn, these require a great deal of space relative to their yield.

Vegetables grow best with at least six hours of full sun each day. To avoid both shade and root competition, locate the garden away from trees and large shrubs. It's also important to choose a spot protected from cold winds in spring and hot, dry winds in summer. Steer clear of frost pockets—low-lying areas that may experience frosts later in spring and earlier in fall than other parts of the garden. To make watering and other routine tasks easier, aim for a level site. If only sloping land is available, try to find a south- or southeast-facing slope to take full advantage of the sun. Lay out rows along the slope's contours to minimize water runoff and erosion. On very steep sites, terraces will make gardening much easier.

Planting Tomatoes

Unlike most other plants, tomatoes prefer deep planting. Bury one half to three-quarters of the stem after removing the leaflets along that portion of the stem. Roots will form along the buried stem to anchor the plant.

Planting Vegetables

The first step toward a satisfying vegetable garden is careful soil preparation, which will promote faster growth and a substantially larger harvest. Follow the steps on page 712 for preparing your planting bed.

You may choose to plant vegetables in rows separated by paths that give you access to the plants and let you easily till or hoe the soil. This layout works well for tall-growing plants like corn and for those that need support, such as tomatoes and pole beans. Other plants grow best in hills—grouped in a cluster but not necessarily on a mound. This method is useful for sprawling plants such as most varieties of melons and winter squash. Smaller vegetables, such as beets, carrots, spinach, and lettuce, can be grown efficiently in wide beds. In this arrangement, you prepare a bed about 3 feet wide, then broadcast the seeds over it rather than sow them in rows. Paths on both sides allow access to the plants.

If your soil is very poor or does not drain well, you may elect to grow your vegetables in raised beds (see page 725) filled with a mixture of compost and good topsoil.

You can start vegetables by planting seeds outdoors in the garden or by setting out transplants that you have either started yourself or purchased from a nursery. Vegetables requiring a long growing season such as peppers and tomatoes need many weeks of warm weather before they produce fruit, so they are best set out as transplants. But other types, including beans, carrots, corn, and peas, do not transplant well and grow best if started from seed sown directly in the garden. For more on sowing seeds and on starting and setting out transplants, see pages 717–719.

Caring for Vegetables

For the best harvest, keep your vegetables growing steadily throughout the season, trying to avoid any checks in their development. Those started from seed sown in the ground usually require thinning, so that each plant will have enough space to develop properly. Thin the plants when they're a few inches tall, making sure to space them as indicated in descriptions provided in the Western Plant Encyclopedia or on the seed packet.

Provide a steady supply of moisture from planting until harvest. Until transplants are well established, they will need frequent watering—enough to keep the soil moist but not soggy. Rows or beds of seeds and young seedlings likewise need steady moisture, sometimes requiring a sprinkling as often as two or three times a day in hot weather. As transplants and seedlings grow and their roots reach deeper, you can water less often—but when you do, be sure to moisten the entire root zone thoroughly. To water the garden, use sprinklers, furrows, or a drip system (see page 742).

Mulching the garden is important, as it conserves moisture and suppresses weed growth. An organic mulch such as straw or compost also improves soil structure as it decomposes, making the top few inches looser and more crumbly. However, because organic mulches also keep the soil cool, it's best not to apply them until warm weather arrives; avoid putting them down too early in spring. A mulch of plastic sheeting, on the other hand, helps warm the soil quickly—making it especially useful for growing heat-loving crops such as melons and eggplant in regions with cool or short summers. After preparing the soil, cover it with black plastic and then cut small holes where you want to sow seeds or set out plants (see page 695).

For many vegetables, the fertilizer you apply when you prepare the bed at planting time will be sufficient for the entire season. However, heavy feeders, such as corn, and those requiring a long growing season, including tomatoes and some varieties of cabbage and broccoli, may need one or two follow-up feedings. Lightly scratch dry granular fertilizer into the soil, keeping it off plant foliage. Then water it in thoroughly. You can also use a water-soluble fertilizer.

Preventing Problems

As is true for the garden as a whole, caring for a vegetable plot involves preventing pest and disease damage. You'll find information on many diseases and pests and advice for controlling them on pages 686–688 and 704–710 and in the entries for specific vegetables in the Western Plant Encyclopedia. The following measures will also help keep your garden productive and healthy.

Keep the garden clean. Composting or discarding spent plants and tilling the soil (especially in fall) can help you avoid trouble, as some insects and diseases overwinter or spend certain developmental stages on plant debris.

Plant resistant varieties if they are available. Seed packets and plant tags may bear code letters noting inbred resistance to certain serious problems. Tomatoes, for example, may be designated V, F, N, and/or T, indicating resistance to verticillium wilt, fusarium wilt, harmful nematodes (which cause root knots), and tobacco mosaic virus.

Mix different kinds of plants. Expanses of just one sort can result in large populations of pests fond of that particular plant. Mixed plantings encourage more kinds of insects, including beneficial species that prey on the troublemakers.

Encourage natural controls. Toads, lizards, many birds, and beneficial insects (see page 705) all prey on pests. Avoid chemical sprays if possible, and be aware that even sprays made from natural ingredients can harm helpful creatures as well as pests, leaving the garden vulnerable to new attack.

Rotate crops from season to season. This prevents the buildup of diseases and insects specific to certain kinds of vegetables in any one part of the garden.

Warm- and Cool-season Vegetables

Depending on the weather they need for best growth, vegetables are classed as warm-season or cool-season. Cool-season crops grow best at temperatures that average from 10 to 15°F/6 to 8°C below those needed by warm-season types. Most will endure short spells of frost. Many familiar cool-season vegetables have edible leaves or roots (lettuce, spinach, carrots, and radishes), while others (broccoli, cauliflower, and artichokes) are grown for their immature flowers. A few—such as peas and broad beans—produce edible seeds. Success depends on bringing plants to maturity in cool weather; in hot conditions, many become bitter tasting and may bolt to seed rather than producing edible parts. Plant them in very early spring—so the crop will mature before summer heat settles in. Or plant in the late part of summer, for a fall or winter crop. In the West's warmer regions, cool-season vegetables can be planted from late summer to early fall to provide harvests in late fall, winter, and early spring.

Warm-season vegetables require both warm soil and high temperatures with little cooling at night to grow steadily and produce a harvest. They include traditional summer crops such as snap beans, corn, cucumbers, melons, peppers, tomatoes, and squash. So-called winter squashes such as acorn, hubbard, and banana are warm-season crops. The name refers not to when they are planted, but to the fact that the fruits can be stored for winter consumption. For almost all of these vegetables, the fruit rather than the leaves or roots is the edible part. Warm-season vegetables are killed by frost, so don't plant them until after the last frost in spring without cold protection.

Row Covers and Season Extenders

Warm-season vegetables may need protection from frost when they are first planted in spring, then again as temperatures begin to dip in fall.

Floating row covers (shown above right) made of polyethylene, polyester, or polypropylene are one of the most useful tools for protecting plants from low temperatures (as well as from certain insect pests and birds). Sold in rolls, these fabric-type covers can be laid directly over seeded beds or plants or propped on stakes. They serve as miniature greenhouses,

are extremely lightweight, transmit 80 to 95 percent of the sunlight that strikes them, and allow both water and air to pass through. Burying the cover's edges in the soil will seal out insect pests, though any pests already on the plants may proliferate. To admit pollinating insects, remove covers when plants begin to bloom.

A warming device sold variously as Wall O' Water and Wall-O-Water can help cold-climate gardeners get a head start on planting tomatoes, peppers, basil, and other warmth-loving summer crops. Essentially, the device is a collar composed of vinyl tubes that you fill with 3 gallons of water to form a self-standing, teepee-style cloche 18 inches tall. The tubes absorb solar heat by day and then release it at night, keeping the temperature inside the cloche above freezing.

A week before planting, place the empty collar around a 5-gallon bucket on the soil. Then, using a hose, fill each tube three-quarters full with water. Remove the bucket, allowing the collar to close in upon itself. Let the soil inside warm for one week, then plant the seedling in the center of the cloche. Once plants begin to grow through the top, fill the tubes completely with water to expand the top of the cloche. After all danger of frost is past, remove the collar. Gently squeeze the water out of each tube, then dry and store the collar for next year.

Cold Frames

Used to protect tender plants and root cuttings, or to start vegetables during the colder months,

a cold frame is simply a box with a transparent lid or cover. It acts as a passive solar energy collector and reservoir. The sun's rays warm the air and soil in the frame; at night, the heat absorbed by the soil radiates out, keeping the plants warm.

A cold frame is useful at other times of year as well. In spring, it provides an ideal environment for hardening off annual vegetable and flower seedlings started indoors. Seeds of many plants can be sown directly in the frame and grown there until it's time to transplant them to the garden. In summer, you can replace the cover with shade cloth or lath, creating a nursery for cuttings.

Set up your cold frame in a site protected from harsh winds by trees, shrubs, a fence, or a wall. To ensure that the frame will receive as much sunlight as possible, orient it to face south or southwest. Sinking the frame 8 to 10 inches into the ground increases heat retention significantly. Make sure the location has good drainage, as you don't want water to collect around the frame after every rain.

Building a Cold Frame

1 Start by selecting a cover. Good choices include an old window sash or storm window. You can also make a cover out of clear acrylic or fiberglass sheets sandwiched between narrow strips of wood. Make sure the cover isn't too heavy to lift easily. Don't make it too wide either. A width of 2½ to 3 feet is ideal. A length of at least 4 feet will allow you to grow a variety of plants.

Build the frame from lumber, such as rot-resistant redwood or cedar or less expensive plywood or scrap lumber. The frame should slope from about 1½ feet high at the back to a foot high at the front. For strength, reinforce the corners of the box with vertical posts. Attach the cover with galvanized steel hinges and apply weather stripping around the top edges of the box.

2 Ventilation is vital to prevent overheating. A minimum-maximum thermometer is useful for keeping track of temperature fluctuations. Plan to prop open the cover when the temperature inside reaches 70 to 75°F/21 to 24°C. Close the cover in late afternoon to trap heat. On very cold nights, drape the frame with an old blanket to provide extra insulation.

VINES

Vertically growing plants can be used to frame entryways, decorate bare walls and fences, and cover arbors with foliage and flowers. Defined in the most basic terms, a vine is simply a flexible shrub that doesn't stop extending its growth. It just keeps getting taller or longer, depending on whether you train it vertically or horizontally. If unsupported, it won't climb at all but will sprawl across the ground (some vines are grown in this manner for use as ground covers).

Selecting Vines

Vines may be deciduous, semievergreen, or evergreen. Some provide greenery alone, while others bear decorative fruits or blossoms. Some vines are lightweight enough to adorn a flimsy trellis without damaging it, but others eventually become weighty enough to pull down the side of a building. As noted below, the vine's method of attachment will also determine the kind of support needed.

Once you have a good idea of what you're looking for—an evergreen flowering vine for a delicate trellis, say—narrow the list to just those plants appropriate to your climate zone. For ideas, see the Plant Selection Guide on pages 92–93.

METHODS OF ATTACHMENT. Some vines twine around their supports with stems, others with tendrils. Some cling with special growths such as suction disks, while others need to be tied to their support to climb along it.

Twining vines. New growth twists or spirals as it elongates, coiling around a support or even around growth on the same or nearby plants. Nearly all twiners make too tight a spiral to encircle a post, so support them with cord or wire.

Vines with tendrils. Growths along stems or at leaf tips reach out and wrap around anything within reach—a wire, another stem of the same vine, or an adjoining plant. The tendrils grow out straight until they make contact, then contract into a spiral. Supply narrow supports that they can easily grasp.

Wisteria

Lonicera (Honeysuckle)

Ipomoea tricolor
(Morning glory)

Grape

Parthenocissus quinquefolia
(Virginia creeper)

Bougainvillea

Clinging vines. Growths along the stems of these vines attach to flat surfaces. Some clingers have tendrils equipped at their tips with suction disks that grip the support; others have "claws" that hook into small irregularities or crevices of a flat surface. Another type of clinger has aerial rootlets along its stems that tenaciously grip all but absolutely smooth, slick surfaces. Bear in mind that all of these clinging devices—known collectively as holdfasts—can damage brick, wood, concrete, and other building materials.

Vines that require tying. Some vines have no means of attachment. They simply thread their way through and over other plants, depending on this living support to hold their stems in place. A few—climbing roses, for example—have thorns on their stems, which help secure the stems in place as they scramble but offer no permanent support. In the garden, these vines must be tied to their supports.

Planting and Caring for Vines

Most vines are sold in containers; a few deciduous kinds such as roses and grapes are available bare-root. See pages 714 and 715 for container and bare-root planting guidelines.

Many vines grow well in ordinary soil with an annual feeding in spring and require only average amounts of water. To look their best, almost all require yearly pruning. Check the Western Plant Encyclopedia for information on the specific needs of each vine.

Vine Attachments

Twining stems   Tendrils   Suction (holdfast) disks   Aerial rootlets   Scrambles
(no means of attachment)

WATER CONSERVATION

Most of the West's climates are characterized by low rainfall, a long dry season, or both. Thus, Western gardeners typically spend a good part of the year watering plants. Only those living in parts of Alaska, the higher-rainfall regions of Hawaii, California's northern coastal fog belt, and the area north of the Siskiyous and west of the Cascades are spared this task. And although each region's overall water supply remains virtually fixed, the demand for water continues to rise. In the years to come, water management will present an ever greater challenge. Here are some ways to meet that challenge.

Choose and locate plants wisely. If you mix plants that require little or no irrigation with those that require regular moisture, you'll be wasting water on the undemanding plants and may even harm them. To avoid this, try to organize your garden into hydrozones—groups of plants with similar water needs. Doing so will simplify irrigation while giving each plant the right amount of moisture. The concept of hydrozoning was developed for arid and semi-arid climates, but it can be applied anywhere that gardeners need to supplement rainfall. High-water-use plants are typically located nearest the house, while those needing less

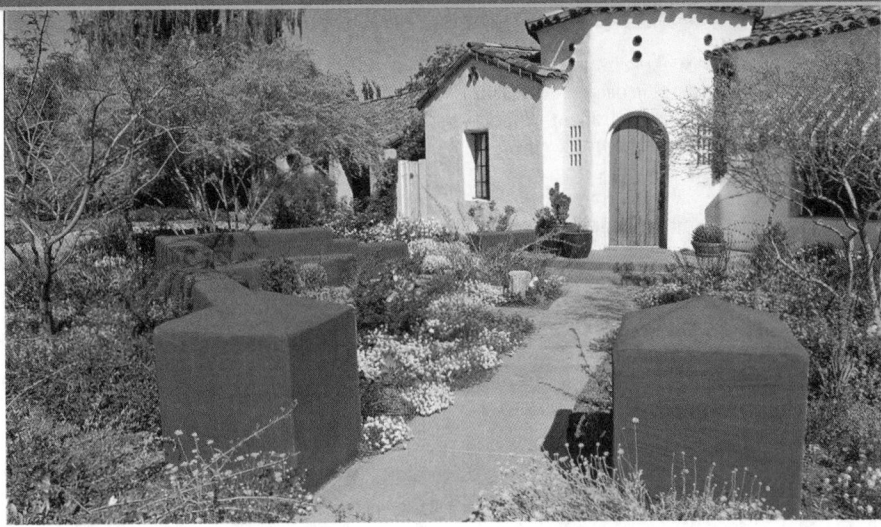

water are planted progressively farther away. (For a list of drought-tolerant plants, see the Plant Selection Guide on pages 127–132.) This scheme frees you from dragging hoses to the far reaches of the garden or extending an irrigation system farther than necessary.

Identify root zones. The roots of various plants grow to different depths. The trick is to apply just enough water to moisten a plant's entire root zone. Most tree roots are located in the top 2 feet of soil. The drip line of a tree or shrub, which runs the perimeter of the canopy, outlines much of the root zone. Focus water there.

Try a root irrigator. This hose-end device has a needle-like shaft that injects water into the ground, irrigating roots directly so that no water is lost to evaporation. Insert the shaft 6 to 12 inches or deeper into the soil around trees and shrubs. After watering in one spot along the drip line, move the irrigator to another spot until you complete one round trip.

Reconsider your lawn. Most conventional lawn grasses use water at a rate disproportionate to that of other plants, largely because they have a shallow root system that dries out quickly, especially in sandy soil. Consider reducing the size of your lawn or choosing a lawn alternative such as an unthirsty ground cover, a meadow, gravel, or a hard surface such as brick, other paving, or a wooden deck. If you

feel that a lawn is a necessary component of your garden, select a grass requiring less water than the more familiar types. See page 693 for grasses adapted to your climate.

Mulch your plantings. An organic mulch spread several inches thick over planting beds acts as an insulating blanket, slowing evaporation from the soil and keeping it cooler than it would be if unprotected. Rocks and gravel also do the job. Black plastic sheeting, sold in rolls, conserves moisture and suppresses weeds. You can also buy rolls of various plastic materials, known collectively as landscape fabrics. For more information on all these mulches, see page 695.

Eliminate runoff. Don't waste water by irrigating paved surfaces. If your sprinkler system showers water over a sidewalk, patio, or driveway, replace the heads with models that deliver water only where it is needed. If necessary, redesign the system. Sloping land and heavy clay soils invite runoff—because of gravity in the first case and slow water penetration in the second. To avoid runoff in such situations, adjust the rate at which water is applied. If you use sprinklers, you can improve penetration by watering in successive short intervals, giving the water time to soak in between sprinklings. On slopes, use terraces and basins to help prevent runoff (see below).

Runoff and Water Quality

In some areas along the Pacific Coast, runoff has caused serious pollution in coastal waters. Inland, the water quality of lakes and streams also suffers when garden runoff contains residue from chemical fertilizers and pesticides. Here are some things you can do to curb such runoff:

GARDEN SMART Don't apply any chemicals to your garden when rain is likely. You can easily miss your intended target and instead the chemicals will wash off into storm drains. In addition, avoid overwatering plants before and after you apply chemicals. Never dispose of lawn or garden chemicals in the storm drain or trash (see page 708), and bag or compost yard waste so it won't clog drains.

USE PERMEABLE PAVING Gravel and permeable concrete allow rainwater through into the soil, which acts as a filter. Impermeable surfaces simply move along rainwater or excess irrigation water to storm drains.

INSTALL AN INFILTRATIONS SYSTEM In some coastal communities, such as Santa Monica, CA, local ordinances require new building sites to include an infiltration pit or other sub-surface runoff retention system. These may be underground tanks or chambers that are connected to downspouts. They can be installed about 5 feet beneath a driveway or lawn. Before putting in new landscaping near the coast, check local ordinances, or consult a structural engineer or geologist about installing such a system.

Conserving Water on Slopes

Individual basins should extend as far as possible across the plant's drip line. Build up on the low side to increase water-holding capacity.

Terracing helps to control runoff. Because the surface reservoir is small, you need to apply water slowly.

Irrigate slowly. Slow soaking limits runoff and encourages plants to develop deep root systems that are better able to tolerate drought. The heavier your soil, the more important slow soaking is in preventing runoff. Using an oscillating sprinkler to water large areas helps reduce runoff. But if you see puddling, turn the water off for an hour, then start again. To minimize evaporation, irrigate in the early morning or evening. Soaker hoses are effective and easy to install. Drip irrigation (see page 744) is an excellent way to reduce water use. You can also upgrade an existing underground sprinkler system by installing low-volume heads or by converting the system to a drip setup, using parts and kits available at hardware stores.

Use timers. With the simplest timers, you set the dial for how long you want the water to run, then you turn on the water. The timer turns the faucet off for you. More sophisticated timers operate on batteries or household current. You set them to a schedule, and they turn the water on and off as programmed. Such timers ensure that your garden will be watered whether you're at home or away. What's more, you can select a schedule that will give your plants the precise amount of water they need to thrive.

The flaw of automatic controllers is that they follow your schedule regardless of the weather. They'll turn on the water during a deluge or apply amounts appropriate for hot summer weather on a cool fall day. To solve this problem, reset the controller, taking seasonal rainfall and weather conditions into account. Or use electronic attachments that function as weather sensors. By linking a soil moisture sensor to the controller, for example, you can trigger the sprinklers to switch on only when the sensor indicates that soil moisture has dropped to the point where water is needed. Another useful attachment is a rain shutoff device. It accumulates rainwater in a collector pan, turning off the controller when the pan is filled to a prescribed depth and triggering it to resume watering when the collected water has evaporated. Before installing either of these sensors, be sure that they are compatible with your automatic controller.

Harvest rainwater. Even in summer months, some rain usually falls, and roofs catch a lot of it. Channel runoff into a rain barrel, then use it to water plants.

WATERING

Most plants cannot survive long without water. A seed must absorb water before it can germinate. Roots can take up nutrients only when water is present in the soil, and water transports nutrients throughout plants. Water is also essential for photosynthesis.

Watering Guidelines

A number of factors—including soil texture, the particular plants, their ages and root depths, and the weather—determine how much water your plants need and how often they need it.

A soil's ability to absorb and retain water is closely related to its composition. Clay soils absorb water slowly and drain slowly too, retaining water longer than other soils. Sandy soils, in contrast, absorb water quickly and drain just as rapidly. Loam soils absorb water fairly quickly and drain well, but not too fast. Absorption patterns vary too. Water moves primarily downward, but it also moves laterally to some extent. Lateral movement is greatest in clay soils; in sandy ones, most water seeps straight down with little horizontal movement. To improve absorption and drainage in clay and to make sandy soils more moisture retentive, work in organic amendments. (For more on soil texture and organic amendments, see page 729.)

Once their roots are established, different plants have widely differing water needs. Those native to semiarid and arid climates, called xerophytes, have evolved features that allow them to survive with little water and low relative humidity. For example, they may have deep root systems or water-retaining leaves that are small, hairy, or waxy.

Many familiar garden plants, however, are adapted to moist soil and high relative humidity. Called mesophytes, they usually have broad, thin leaves that lose moisture readily.

Keep in mind that all young plants, even drought-tolerant species, need more frequent watering than mature ones until their root systems become well established. And many annuals and vegetables require regular moisture throughout the growing season if they are to bloom well or produce a good crop.

The depth of a plant's root system also influences watering practices. Irrigate enough to moisten the entire zone, encouraging roots to grow throughout that area. Shallow watering keeps roots near the soil surface. Deeper roots have access to more moisture, thus letting the plant go longer between waterings. They are also less subject to stress from heat and drying winds than shallow roots are.

Root hairs of underwatered plants will dry out and expire, causing the plant to slow its growth, wilt, and eventually die. But you don't want to overdo it either. It's important to learn

Applied to sand (left), 1 inch of water penetrates about 12 inches. Applied to loam (center), 1 inch of water reaches about 7 inches. Applied to clay (right), 1 inch of water soaks only 4 to 5 inches.

how often you must water to keep the root zone moist. Watering below the root zone is wasteful, as the water is not used. Beyond that, keeping the soil too moist can cause as many problems as letting it get too dry. Roots need air as well as water, and they absorb both from the pore spaces between soil particles. If water is applied too often, the pore spaces never have a chance to drain. They remain filled with water, cutting off the roots' air supply and making roots susceptible to various water-mold fungi, which in turn can lead to rot.

To check how far water penetrates your soil, water for a set amount of time—say, 30 minutes. Wait for 24 hours, then use a soil sampling tube (see page 716) or dig a hole to check for moisture. Sampling tubes, especially useful in lawns or around established trees and shrubs, let you test moisture at deeper levels without digging a hole that might disturb roots. A long screwdriver can also serve as a probe. Push it into the ground. It will move easily through moist soil but slow down or stop when it reaches dry soil. You'll soon learn to judge how long to water each plant or group of plants to soak the root zone thoroughly.

Weather affects water needs as well. When it's hot, dry, and windy, plants use water quickly, and young or shallow-rooted ones sometimes cannot absorb it fast enough to keep foliage from wilting. Such plants need frequent watering to keep moisture around their roots. During cool, damp weather, plants require much less water.

Because the factors just discussed—soil texture, plant characteristics and age, and weather—are variable, following a fixed watering schedule year-round or even all summer isn't the most efficient way to meet your plants' needs. Before you water, always test the soil for moisture content and look at plants for signs of wilting.

Watering Methods

Tools for applying water range from simple handheld sprayers to hose-end sprinklers to more complex underground rigid-pipe and drip

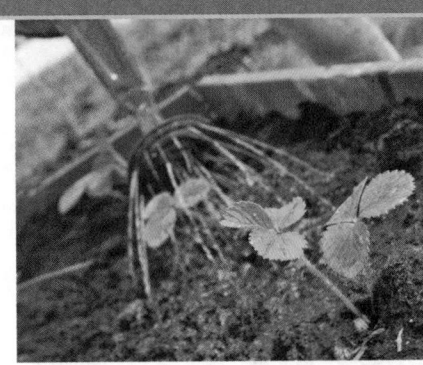

*A **gentle sprinkle** of water from a can or a sprayer is best for young seedlings.*

systems. The equipment appropriate for your garden depends on how often you need to water, the size of your garden, and how much gear you want to buy.

Hand watering. Irrigating with a handheld nozzle or a can may be a relaxing pastime, but it's usually inadequate for plants, as it takes too long to truly soak the soil. Hand watering is useful for new transplants, seedlings, and container plants, because you can apply the water gently and put it exactly where it's needed.

Hoses. While a good hose makes watering easier, a bad one can lead to plenty of frustration, so choose the highest-quality hose that meets your needs. Hoses come in lengths up to 100 feet and with standard diameters from ⅜ to 1 inch. A ⅝-inch size is best for all around use. Keep in mind that as hose length increases, water pressure decreases, so the longer the hose, the larger diameter you should consider. To avoid kinking, look for a rubber-reinforced polyvinyl chloride type with multiple layers. Some hoses are reinforced with additional layers of strengthening mesh. The best couplings are brass, and rubberized kink guards help to protect the hose ends.

Self-coiling hoses. These won't tangle or kink, and they store neatly. Look for ones made of UV-resistant polyurethane with brass couplings and rubberized kink guards on both ends. These hoses typically have a smaller interior diameter than the standard ⅝ inch. Because less water flows through, it takes longer to water, and some spray patterns on a multipattern, hose-end sprayer may only gurgle. So look for ⅜ inch, the diameter most practical for everyday needs (¼ inch hoses are suitable only for misting and watering small pots).

Sprinklers can be attached to the end of a hose or installed in underground sprinkler systems. In either case, the sprinklers apply a high volume of water over a large surface. Many plants, particularly those that like a cool, humid atmosphere, thrive with overhead sprinkling. This method also rinses dust from foliage and discourages certain pests (especially spider mites). But sprinkling has some negative aspects as well. It can be wasteful, as wind may carry off some water before it even reaches the ground, and water that falls on or runs off onto pavement is lost too. In humid climates, sprinkling encourages some foliage diseases such as black spot and rust. You can minimize this risk

by sprinkling early in the morning so that leaves dry as the day warms. Another potential drawback is that plants with weak stems and/or heavy flowers may collapse under a heavy load of water.

The wide assortment of portable, hose-end sprinklers includes stationary models that resemble salt shakers or rings; oscillating, rotating, and impulse sprinklers; and "walking" types that slowly roll through the area to be irrigated. When selecting a sprinkler, look for one with a coverage pattern that most closely matches the area to be irrigated. The shape and size of the space the sprinkler covers should be listed on the package.

Permanent underground sprinkler systems—the traditional watering method in low-rainfall areas—offer some advantages over hose-end options. They free you from moving hoses and sprinklers and can be automated to operate even if you're away from home. And recent refinements in the design of the sprinklers have improved the systems' efficiency. The newer sprinklers produce less runoff and overspray onto buildings, walkways, and fences and distribute water more evenly. For such a system to work properly, though, it must be well designed. Consult a licensed landscape contractor or a company specializing in irrigation systems.

To sprinkle effectively with a portable or an underground system, you need to know how fast water penetrates your soil and the delivery rate of your sprinklers. As the illustration on page 742 shows, 1 inch of water (from sprinkling or rainfall) moistens about 12 inches in sandy soil, 7 inches in loam, and 4 to 5 inches in clay. Thus, if you want to water to a depth of 12 inches, you'll need to apply about an inch of water to sandy soil, 2½ to 3 inches to clay soil.

***High-power lawn sprinkler** heads can be mounted on stakes.*

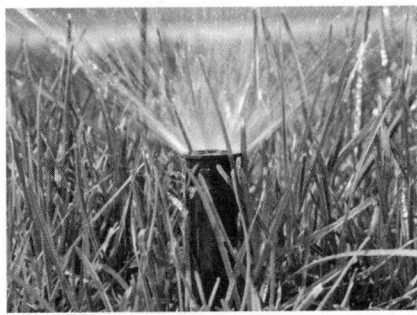

***Pop-up sprinkler heads** are part of an in-ground irrigation system.*

Watering in Furrows and Basins

Furrows 3 to 6 inches deep help irrigate straight rows on level ground. A bubbler on the hose end softens the flow of water. Note that furrows don't work well in very sandy soils, as in sand—even more so than in other soils—water moves primarily downward and has little horizontal movement.

Basins with sides 3 inches high contain water around large plants such as tomatoes and peppers and help channel it directly to the roots. On level ground, link basins to make watering easier.

W

To determine delivery rate, place a rain gauge at regular intervals outward from the sprinkler and see how long it takes to fill the gauge with 1 inch of water.

Root irrigators, which resemble giant hypodermic needles, are useful for getting water to root zones of trees growing near sidewalks, patios, or other areas with a minimum of open soil. They also help water reach deep into the soil on sloping land, where deep penetration without runoff can be a problem. Attach the tool to the end of a garden hose, then insert it into the ground as you turn the water on. Water travels down a hollow probe and shoots out of holes at the tip. Some models also supply fertilizer as they water.

Flooding or soaking is an effective way to supply sufficient water to the deep, extensive root systems of large shrubs and trees. Form two concentric rings of soil and flood the basin between them as shown on page 716. For freshly planted trees and shrubs, make the outer ring just outside the outer edge of the root ball, moving it farther out as the plant grows.

If you grow vegetables or flowers in rows, you can build adjoining basins for large plants like squash or make furrows between rows (shown on the previous page). To minimize damage to roots, construct the furrows when the plants are young, before their root systems have spread. Broad, shallow furrows are generally better than deep, narrow ones. The wider the furrow, the wider the root area you can soak, because water moves primarily downward rather than laterally. And a shallow furrow is safer for plants, as nearby roots are less likely to be disturbed when you scoop out the furrow.

Soil soaker hoses, the forerunners of drip irrigation systems, are still useful for the slow, steady delivery of water. They are long tubes made of perforated or porous plastic or rubber, with hose fittings at one or both ends. When you attach a soaker to a regular hose and turn on the water supply, water seeps or sprinkles from the soaker along its entire length. You can also water wide beds by snaking soakers back and forth around the plants. Trees and shrubs can be watered with a soaker coiled over the outermost edges of the root zone. You'll probably need to leave soakers on longer than you would sprinklers. To determine timing, check water penetration with a trowel or soil sampling tube.

Drip Irrigation

The term "drip irrigation" describes the application of water by drip emitters and microsprays. Both devices operate at low pressure, and both deliver a low volume of water compared with standard sprinklers. Because water is applied slowly on or near the ground, there should be no waste from runoff and little or no loss to evaporation. You position emitters to deliver water just where plants need it and you control penetration by varying the time the system runs and/or the emitters' delivery capacity, rated in gallons per hour (gph). You can also regulate the volume of water delivered to each plant by varying the type and number of emitters you set up for each.

In addition to water conservation, drip systems offer flexibility. You can tailor them to water individual plants by providing each with one or more emitters, or distribute water over larger areas with microsprays. A standard layout might include hookups to two or more valves and several kinds of parts. Because the lines are aboveground, they are easily concealed with mulch. And because they are made of limber plastic, changing the system is simple. Just add or subtract lines or emitters as needed.

A drip system can be attached to a hose end or provided with fittings to allow it to be screwed into a hose bibb. Or you can connect it permanently to your main water source. Like underground irrigation systems, drip systems

A Sample Drip-irrigation System

Emitters for trees

Emitters on microtubing for pots and planters

Emitter lines for flower beds

Conventional sprinkler system for lawn

Microsprays for ground covers

Emitter lines for shrubs

Emitter lines for vegetables

W

Drip-irrigation Components

Timer

Backflow preventer

Filter

Pressure regulator

Compression fitting

Emitter line

Emitter line (cutaway view)

Stakes (to hold lines in place)

Microspray

Punch
(to make holes for emitters in tubing)

Drip emitters

Goof plugs
(to close off emitter holes)

Compression fittings
(to connect lines and other components)

Tubing

should be outfitted with a backflow preventer. In addition, a filter is necessary (even when you're using municipal supplies of clean water) to keep the small openings on drip emitters and microsprays from becoming clogged. A pressure regulator is also needed, as drip systems are designed to run best at a much lower pressure than is found in most household water supplies. The regulator protects the fittings from blowing apart under excess force and allows the watering devices to work properly.

Emitters for drip systems. Emitters vary in shape, size, and internal mechanism, but all operate on the principle of dispensing water slowly. The flow rates of most range from ½ to 2 gph. Insert the emitters directly into drip irrigation tubing or thinner microtubing positioned to run from the larger tubing to each plant. Non-pressure-compensating emitters work well on flat or relatively level ground and with lines that are less than 200 feet long. But when water pressure will be lowered by gravity or friction, such as on hillsides or with long lines, opt for pressure-compensating emitters. These deliver the same amount of water throughout the system.

You can also purchase emitters factory-installed in polyethylene tubing. These may be referred to as "in-line" emitters or emitter lines. Spaced 1, 2, or 3 feet apart along the tubing, they deliver ½, 1, or 2 gph and are available in non-pressure-compensating and pressure-compensating versions. Some emitter lines are infused with a small amount of herbicide to prevent root intrusion, and can be buried to water lawns.

While the standard emitters simply drip, types that deliver water in other ways are available as well. Misters produce a fine spray—a good way to increase humidity for plants like fuchsia, tuberous begonia, and ferns. Microsprays are low-volume equivalents of standard sprinklers, particularly useful for irrigating closely spaced or dense plantings such as ground covers and flower beds.

Drip System for Containers

1 A pot up to 10 inches in diameter needs only one emitter. Here, an elbow fitting snakes the tubing over the edge of the pot. A U stake holds the tubing in place.

2 For pots 10 to 15 inches across, you'll need two emitters. A stake holds the tubing in place; emitters are attached to a T fitting.

3 Large pots can be fitted with different combinations of tubing. Here, tubing with in-line emitters encircles a plant. U stakes hold the line in place.

4 A second option for big pots is a multi-outlet emitter, sometimes called a bubbler. You can rotate the head to adjust the spray.

W

Removing weeds, *such as crabgrass, from lawns is easier when you use a weeder.*

WEEDS

Weeds are plants growing where gardeners don't want them to grow. They rob desirable plants of water, nutrients, and sunlight; they may harbor insects and diseases; and they're frequently unattractive.

Whether a plant is labeled a weed depends on several factors. Some plants, like bindweed and yellow *Oxalis,* are regarded as weeds wherever they grow. Other ones may be considered weeds in some situations, and garden plants in others. For example, common yarrow *(Achillea millefolium)* is an annoying weed when it invades a lawn, but is a very useful ornamental ground cover in a hot, dry part of the garden. Certain plants spread so aggressively that they are often thought of as weeds. Examples include some asters, bamboo, mint *(Mentha),* Mexican evening primrose *(Oenothera speciosa* 'Rosea', often sold as *O. berlandieri),* sweet woodruff *(Galium odoratum),* and Jerusalem artichoke *(Helianthus tuberosus).* And some ornamentals have gone beyond invading the garden alone, jumping the fence to overwhelm native plants in wild lands (see page 750).

Despite their frankly undesirable qualities from the gardener's point of view, weedy plants do have their positive side. An assemblage of weeds can hold the soil on a steep bank, preventing erosion. Some weeds provide nectar and shelter for beneficial insects and butterflies. When they die and decompose, weeds add humus to the soil. And even the dreaded poison oak and poison ivy are important to the deer, birds, and rabbits that eat their berries.

Identifying Weeds

Weeds are often classified by the length of their life cycle. Annual weeds, like annual garden plants, grow shoots and leaves, flower, set seed, and die within a year. Most members of this group are summer annuals, germinating in spring or summer and dying by fall. Winter annual weeds begin growth in fall or early winter, then set seed in early spring while the weather is still cool. Biennial weeds produce a cluster or rosette of leaves in their first year of growth, and in the following year, they flower, set seed, and die.

Both annuals and biennials reproduce by seed. Almost all perennial weeds, which live for several years, also reproduce by seed. Once they mature, however, most produce spreading roots, stolons, rhizomes, bulbs, or tubers as well, making control more difficult.

You'll find descriptions of some of the most common Western weeds in each of these groups on pages 748–750, along with suggestions for controlling them. You may also wish to consult your Cooperative Extension Office or a local nursery expert for advice on identifying and controlling troublesome weeds in your area.

Non-chemical Controls

As is true for other kinds of pests, it is rarely possible to eradicate weeds entirely, but you can substantially reduce infestations.

Hand pulling or hoeing is your first line of defense against most weeds. For perennial weeds that have passed the seedling stage, it's usually necessary to dig out their roots. If you just pull up or cut off the tops, the pests can resprout from fragments left behind. Even with assiduous digging, you'll probably need to repeat the process several times to manage perennial weeds. Some useful tools for weeding are discussed on pages 730–733.

Don't leave pulled or hoed-out weeds on bare ground, as they may take root again. Leafy annual or biennial types that do not yet have flowers or seeds can safely be relegated to the compost pile, as can the top growth of perennial weeds (before seeding). But roots of perennials, such as dandelions and quack grass, should be tossed into the trash rather than composted, as should any weeds that have set seed.

Rototilling or disking will do the job on annual and biennial weeds in larger areas, such as orchards, vacant lots, roadsides, and plots intended for future gardens. These methods not only knock down weeds but also incorporate them into the soil, where they eventually decay to form humus. However, perennial weeds usually sprout again from the roots or crowns, and some kinds even grow more abundantly after tilling.

Using rotary mowers or string trimmers is another good choice for seasonal weed control in larger areas. Both tools cut the weeds. String trimmers leave the severed tops behind, while mowers grind them up as they cut them. These methods are also effective for reducing weeds in fire-prone areas.

Smothering effectively kills weeds in areas earmarked for future planting. After mowing or cutting off the top growth, put down a layer of heavy cardboard, newspapers (at least three dozen sheets thick), or black plastic. Overlap the material so weeds can't grow through the cracks. Anchor the covering with a layer of bark chips or other organic mulch. Leave these smothering materials in place for at least a full growing season. Allow a year or more for tough or perennial weeds.

Flaming is another way to knock down weeds. Powered by propane or a mixture of propane and butane, flamers are not meant to burn weeds. Instead, they heat them to the point at which their cell walls burst. Though this damage is drastic enough to kill many young weeds, types with deep perennial roots usually regrow. Destroying them requires several treatments. Take care when using flamers around mulches, wooden fences, or wood-bordered raised beds, and never use them in dry, fire-prone areas.

Presprouting is a useful technique for preparing planting areas for vegetables, perennial beds, or new lawns in parts of the garden plagued by weeds. Add needed amendments, till the soil, water it, and then wait a week or two for weed seeds to germinate. When they're only a few inches high, scrape them away. Then sow or transplant your vegetables, flowers, or lawn, disturbing the soil as little as possible to avoid bringing more weed seeds to the surface.

Soil solarization (see above right) controls many kinds of weed seeds as well as harmful fungi, bacteria, and some nematodes.

Homemade sprays are yet another option. Organic gardeners have myriad herbicide recipes that use ingredients straight from the kitchen or medicine chest. One effective formula consists of 1 tablespoon of dishwashing

Soil Solarization

Soil solarization takes advantage of the sun's heat, trapped under clear plastic sheeting, to control many kinds of weed seeds as well as harmful fungi, bacteria, and some nematodes. The process is carried out in summer and works best in regions that have hot, sunny weather for four to eight weeks straight. Daytime temperatures above 80°F/27°C are ideal. Solarization isn't very effective in coastal climates with summer fog, nor does it work well in very windy areas.

Cultivate the soil, clearing it of weeds, debris, and large clods of earth. Make a bed at least 2 feet wide, as narrower beds make it difficult to build up enough heat to have much effect. Carve a small ditch along the perimeter; rake the bed level. Soak the soil to a depth of 1 foot. Cover it with 1- to 4-mil clear plastic. Use UV-resistant plastic if it's available, as it won't break down during solarization. Stretch the plastic tightly so that it is in contact with the soil. Bury the edges in the perimeter ditch. An optional second layer of plastic increases heat and makes solarization more effective. Use soda cans as spacers between the two sheets (see inset below). Leave the plastic in place for four to six weeks (eight weeks for really persistent weeds), then remove it. Don't leave it down longer than eight weeks or soil structure may suffer. You can now plant. After planting, avoid cultivating more than the upper 2 inches of soil, as weed seeds at deeper levels may still be viable.

Soda can

Black landscape fabric will help to prevent weeds from surrounding this young tomato plant.

liquid and ¼ cup of salt mixed with 1 quart of vinegar. You can also spray unwanted plants with isopropyl (rubbing) alcohol. A solution of 2 tablespoons per quart of water works for most weeds. For tougher ones, you may need to increase the amount of alcohol.

In both greenhouse and field tests, USDA scientists found that plain acetic acid eliminates many weeds, including some of the toughest perennials. For plants up to two weeks old, a 5 percent solution—the same concentration found in supermarket vinegar—will do the trick. For older plants, use pickling vinegar, which is a 9 percent concentration.

Regardless of the ingredients, apply the potion with a spray bottle and coat the plants thoroughly. Try to do the job on a hot, sunny, wind-free day, as both homemade and commercial herbicides are most effective then.

Once you've destroyed weeds in a garden area, take steps to prevent their reappearance. Mulching bare soil is an effective deterrent to weed growth. See page 695 for information on choosing and using mulches, including landscape fabrics. Ground covers, sometimes called living mulches, are also effective. Like organic and inorganic mulches, they keep sunlight from reaching weeds and their seeds. You'll usually have to do some hand weeding or apply a mulch for the first few seasons after you plant a ground cover, but as it grows and spreads to form a tight carpet, weed growth is much reduced. For more on ground covers, see page 691.

Chemical Controls

Synthetic herbicides are not recommended for food gardens. In home ornamental gardens, use them only when all other methods have failed. Beyond the risks they may pose to health and the environment, many of these chemicals can damage desirable plants if they drift through the air or run off in irrigation or rainwater. Some persist in the soil for long periods, injuring later plantings. And often the entire process of herbicide use—selecting a product, mixing and applying it, cleaning up—takes more effort than pulling or digging out the weeds.

If you use herbicides, always make sure the product is safe for the desirable plants growing in and near the areas to be treated. Also keep in mind that you can be held responsible for any damage to neighboring properties resulting from herbicides you use. Do not apply them on windy days, and warn your neighbors well in advance so they can cover their plants before you spray. See pages 748 and 750 for lists of natural and synthetic herbicides as well as explanations of terms used in describing herbicides, such as "pre-emergence" and "post-emergence."

Annual Weeds

Most annual and biennial weeds, such as mallows, can be controlled by diligent hand pulling and hoeing. Try to do the job before the plants go to seed, as most annual weeds produce prodigious amounts of seed. Discourage weed growth in lawns by maintaining a thick turf and keeping it mowed at the maximum recommended for the grass type. Taller blades cast more shade on the soil, thereby discouraging seed germination. (For more on lawns, see pages 692–694.) In garden areas, apply a thick mulch to hinder sprouting. For more thorough control in both lawns and planting beds, use corn gluten meal, a safe, pre-emergence herbicide made from corn protein. Soil solarization (see left) also destroys most annual weeds.

If you opt for a chemical herbicide, make sure it's labeled for the weed in question. Apply it in fall for winter annual weeds, in early spring for summer annuals. Spot-treat existing weeds with herbicidal soaps or one of the homemade sprays on page 750. And don't get any post-emergence herbicide—natural or synthetic—on desirable plants.

W

Consult herbicide labels to see whether the chemicals work on narrow-leafed or grasslike weeds such as crabgrass *(top)*, or on broad-leafed ones like mallow *(bottom)*.

Products for Weed Control

Herbicides are classified according to what stage of weed growth they affect, as well as by how they damage weeds.

Pre-emergence herbicides work by inhibiting the growth of germinating weed seeds and very young seedlings. They do not affect established plants. To be effective, they must be applied before the seeds sprout. Before applying these chemicals in ornamental gardens, remove any existing weeds. Some pre-emergence products are formulated to kill germinating weeds in lawns. These may be sold in combination with fertilizers, which increase the lawn's vigor and improve its ability to compete against weeds. (Such dual-purpose products should not be treated solely as fertilizers and reapplied whenever the lawn needs feeding. For that purpose, use a regular lawn fertilizer.) Some pre-emergence products must be watered into the soil, while others are incorporated into it. Some may also harm seeds you sow later in the season. Check the label to learn how long the product remains active in the soil.

Postemergence herbicides act on growing weeds rather than on seeds. Chemicals that are *translocated* must be absorbed by the plant through its leaves or stems; this kills the plant by interfering with its metabolism. *Contact herbicides* kill only the plant parts on which they are sprayed—regrowth can still occur from roots or unsprayed buds.

Synthetic herbicides are manufactured compounds that do not normally occur in nature, while natural herbicides are products whose active ingredients originate in a plant or mineral. The products listed here are widely available to Western gardeners as of this printing. Bear in mind, though, that things are in flux, with new natural brands hitting the market more frequently and synthetic formulas being pulled from the shelves. For the most up-to-date information on the regulatory status of synthetic products, contact the Pesticide Action Network at www.pesticideinfo.org.

When using any herbicide, read the label directions carefully and follow them exactly. The package will clearly state the weeds the product controls, as well as any other plants around which it can safely be used. It is illegal to apply an herbicide to any plant not designated as a target. Always dispose of pesticides in a safe manner (see page 708).

The following products are listed alphabetically by the name of the active ingredient— the actual substance that controls the weed or weeds listed on the package label. Before you buy, read the label to make sure you're getting the active ingredient you need. (For more on reading and understanding pesticide labels, see page 709.)

Synthetic Herbicides

Glufosinate-ammonium. Postemergence. Contact herbicide that damages or kills many kinds of weeds. Take care not to apply to desirable plants.

Glyphosate. Postemergence. Translocated herbicide that kills or damages any plant it touches. Effective on a broad range of troublesome weeds but must be used with caution to avoid contacting desirable plants.

Oryzalin. Pre-emergence. Used to control annual grasses and many broad-leafed weeds in warm-season turf grasses and in gardens.

Pendimethalin. Pre-emergence. Used to control many grasses and broad-leafed weeds in turf and in ornamental plantings. Toxic to fish.

Sethoxydim. Postemergence. Translocated herbicide that controls many grasses growing in ornamental plantings.

Triclopyr. Postemergence. Translocated herbicide. Depending on formulation, used on cool-season turf to control broad-leafed weeds and Bermuda grass, or to control hard-to-kill woody plants. Use with care to avoid damaging desirable plants.

Trifluralin. Pre-emergence. Controls many grasses and broad-leafed weeds in turf and ornamental plantings. Toxic to fish.

Annual Weeds

WEED	DESCRIPTION AND CONTROLS
Annual bluegrass (*Poa annua*)	Winter annual, though there are also perennial varieties. Forms a bright light green tuft of softly textured grass. Troublesome in lawns, flower borders, and winter vegetable crops. **Control:** Pull or dig when the plants are young.
Burclover (*Medicago polymorpha*)	Winter annual in most areas. Low, spreading, broad-leafed weed with yellow flowers and spiny burs. Common in lawns and garden beds with nitrogen deficiency or excess phosphorus. Also troublesome in gravel paths and driveways. **Control:** Increase nitrogen fertilizing.
Crabgrass (*Digitaria* species)	Summer annual with shallow roots. Thrives in hot, moist areas. Seeds germinate in early spring in warmer climates, later in colder areas. As the plant grows, it branches out at the base. Stems can root where they touch the soil. Typically found in lawns and flower beds that receive frequent surface watering. **Control:** Water infrequently and deeply to dry out crabgrass roots. Use corn gluten meal as a pre-emergence treatment. If chemical treatment is necessary (in ornamental beds only), use a postemergence herbicide that kills grasses.
Mallows (*Malva* species)	Winter or summer annual or biennial, depending on climate. Also known as cheeseweed (because its fruits resemble a round of cheese). Fast-growing, broad-leafed weeds with rounded, lobed leaves and pinkish white flowers. Height ranges from a few inches to 4 feet. Found in lawns, in gardens, and on roadsides. **Control:** Plants are easiest to pull when they're young because older ones develop a deep taproot.
Nettleleaf goosefoot (*Chenopodium murale*)	Summer annual. Coarse, leafy weed grows 1 to 2 feet high. Its dark green, fleshy leaves have a mealy texture. Common in gardens and orchards and on roadsides.
Purslane (*Portulaca oleracea*)	Summer annual. Prostrate broad-leafed weed with small yellow flowers and fleshy stems and leaves that are edible, with a tart, lemony flavor. Thrives in moist conditions but can withstand considerable drought. **Control:** Purslane is easy to pull or hoe, but pieces of its stem reroot readily. Remove them from the garden immediately, and don't compost any part of the plant.
Scarlet pimpernel (*Anagallis arvensis*)	Summer annual in cold climates. In milder regions, it can germinate and grow at any time of year. Low-growing plant with many branching, four-angled stems. Sometimes called "poor man's weather glass" because the pretty salmon-colored flowers open only on sunny days and close at the approach of bad weather.
Sowthistles (*Sonchus* species)	Summer annual. Upright 1- to 4-foot-tall plants with stout taproots, hollow stems, and milky sap that oozes out when a leaf or stem is broken. Yellow flowers look like those of dandelions. Common in gardens, but also grows in lawns.
Spotted spurge (*Chamaesyce maculata*; also listed as *Euphorbia maculata*)	Summer annual, though seeds can germinate in February in warm regions. Extremely aggressive. Not only does it produce large quantities of seed, but it also sets seed just a few weeks after germination—and those seeds may germinate immediately. Grows from a shallow taproot and forms a low mat of branching stems that exude a milky juice when cut or broken.

W

Perennial Weeds

This chart lists some of the West's most troublesome perennial weeds, with management options described from least to most toxic. In general, growth of perennial weeds can be controlled with landscape fabrics installed so that no light reaches the soil. Note that these must be applied after the area is cleared of weeds; see page 746. Organic mulches are not as effective, as seeds or plants sprouting from roots left in the ground often grow through them.

WEED	DESCRIPTION AND CONTROLS
Bermuda grass (*Cynodon dactylon*)	If you have a common Bermuda lawn, use 8-inch-deep barriers or edging to keep it from advancing into other parts of the garden. **Control:** Dig up stray clumps before they form sod, and remove all underground stems. Any roots that are left behind can start new shoots. Soil solarization destroys seeds and shallow-growing rhizomes, but deeply buried stems will survive. Use a pre-emergence herbicide to prevent seeds from growing. Effective postemergence herbicides kill most grasses, but can be sprayed over some broad-leafed ornamentals without harming them.
Bindweed, also called wild morning glory or field bindweed (*Convolvulus arvensis*)	Grows in open spaces throughout the West, usually in loam to heavy clay soil. One- to 4-foot-long stems crawl over the ground and twine over and around other plants. Trumpet-shaped flowers are white to pink. A single plant may produce up to 500 seeds, which can sprout even after lying dormant in the soil for 50 years. **Control:** Pull or hoe seedlings up to about a month old. Remove all flowers before they can set seed. To gradually kill established plants, cut the stems back to ground level before they set seed. Wait until the stems have grown about 6 inches long, then cut again. Each time you repeat the process, the plant must draw on stored energy in the roots to produce new growth. Eventually, it will die. Be careful not to cut through roots, as pieces form new plants quickly. Soil solarization kills seeds but not roots. In midsummer, when bindweed is growing vigorously but has not yet set seed, spot-treat isolated patches with an herbicide containing glyphosate.
Blackberry (*Rubus* species)	Several species of blackberries or brambles are pests in various parts of the West. Himalaya blackberry (*Rubus discolor*) is the most vigorous of these, thriving in the mild, moist climates of Northern California and western Oregon and Washington. Plants spread by underground stems that send up new shoots. Birds enjoy the berries and scatter the seed. **Control:** Pull young plants in spring before they develop a perennial root system. To kill established clumps, repeatedly prune back the stems as they sprout; this eventually exhausts the roots. Or mow the tops and dig out the roots.
Dandelion (*Taraxacum officinale*)	Familiar lawn weeds throughout the West, but especially troublesome in the Northwest and mountain states. Most often plague lawns that are thin and undernourished. As plants mature, they form a deep, fleshy taproot. They spread by windborne seeds that appear in fluffy heads after the yellow blossoms fade. **Control:** A healthy lawn can outcompete this weed, so thicken the turf with overseeding and proper fertilizing, watering, and mowing. Pull dandelions from lawns and gardens while they're small, before they produce a deep taproot and set seed. Once the taproot has formed, it's necessary to remove all of it to get rid of the plant, as new plants can sprout from even a small piece. A dandelion weeder with a forked blade is helpful. A hand weeder with a bent shaft (or a ball attached to the shaft) to serve as a fulcrum increases leverage, helping to pop the plants out of the ground. Use a postemergence chemical product labeled for dandelions in turf.
Kikuyu grass (*Pennisetum clandestinum*)	A native of tropical Africa, used as a lawn grass in some coastal areas, but it has escaped cultivation to become a serious pest in lawns and ornamental beds. Spreads rapidly by rhizomes and stolons, eventually forming an impenetrable mat of wiry stems. Both stems and medium-green leaves are covered with fine hairs. In Southern California, kikuyu grass also spreads by seed. **Control:** Contain turf with a strong barrier that extends 6 to 8 inches into the soil. Dig any invading kikuyu grass out of garden beds, removing as much of the root system as possible. Plan to repeat this process, as the grass will resprout from any rhizomes left in the soil. Spray with a postemergence herbicide that controls grassy weeds.
Nutsedge, yellow (*Cyperus esculentus*)	Resembles a grass, but its stems are solid and triangular in cross-section, and its leaves grow from the base in groups of three. (True grasses have hollow stems that are oval or flat in cross-section, and their leaves grow in sets of two.) Spreads by seed and by small, roundish tubers (nutlets) formed at tips of roots. **Control:** Remove plants when they are young and still small. Older, taller plants are mature enough to produce tubers. When you dig or pull the plant, the tubers remain in the soil to sprout. Repeatedly removing top growth eventually weakens tubers. Soil solarization provides only partial control.
Oxalis, yellow, also called yellow wood sorrel (*Oxalis corniculata*)	Thrives in sun or shade throughout the West, spreading quickly by seed. Seedlings start from a single, shallow taproot, which soon develops into a shallow, spreading, knitted root system. Tiny, five-petaled yellow flowers are followed by elongated seed capsules that can propel seed as far as 6 feet. **Control:** Dig out small plants before they have a chance to set seed. Keep lawns vigorous to provide tough competition. Water deeply but infrequently, since frequent shallow watering nourishes the shallow roots. Use a pre-emergence chemical herbicide on the turf grasses and around the ornamental plants listed on the label. Spot-treat with glyphosate.
Quack grass, also known as couch grass or devil's grass (*Elytrigia repens*)	Aggressively invades both lawns and gardens. Can reach 3 feet tall but stays much lower in mowed areas. Produces an extensive network of long, slender, branching, yellowish white rhizomes that can spread laterally 3 to 5 feet. The rhizomes are able to penetrate hard soil and grow into tubers and rhizomes of other plants such as potatoes and iris. **Control:** Before planting, thoroughly dig the area and remove all visible pieces of rhizome; this will slow the weed's growth for a few years. For chemical control, spray with a postemergence herbicide that controls grassy weeds. Or spot-treat with an herbicide containing glyphosate.

W

Natural Herbicides

Corn gluten meal. Pre-emergence. Prevents sprouting seeds from developing normal roots, thereby making them susceptible to dehydration in dry soil. The roots of established plants are not affected. It is most often used to control weeds, especially crabgrass, in lawns, but is also effective in garden beds. This product is also a fertilizer, serving to thicken lawns and thus suppress weed growth. It poses no risk to animals—in fact, it's a common ingredient in food for dogs, cats, fish, poultry, and cows—but some people have allergic reactions to corn and corn by-products.

Herbicidal soaps. Postemergence. Contact herbicides that degrade quickly. Made from selected fatty acids (as are insecticidal soaps), they kill top growth of young, actively growing weeds and are most effective on annual weeds.

Vinegar. Postemergence. A number of organic-gardening catalogs sell vinegar-based herbicides, usually with soap and/or lemon juice added for extra sticking and penetrating power. You can also make your own version (you'll find one recipe on page 747), but plain supermarket vinegar, either distilled or cider, kills many troublesome weeds.

Garden Runaways

While most plants brought from other parts of the world to ornament gardens (or provide timber or food) are welcome and well behaved, some have escaped from cultivation and invaded wild lands throughout the West. Unchecked by natural forces—such as diseases, insects, or animals—that helped control them in their homelands, they thrive, displacing local native plants. They change the structure of the ecosystems they enter, threatening diversity and destroying wildlife habitats. Gardeners can help stem the spread of invasive plants by not using them near natural areas, as in gardens of rural or vacation homes. Native-plant societies as well as other organizations, such as garden clubs and volunteer groups at state and national parks, sponsor weed-eradication programs and plant-restoration projects in many areas.

Fountain grass spreads unrelentingly in the Southwest and Hawaii.

Weeds of Wild Lands

Native-plant societies as well as state and federal governments maintain lists of problem plants in each state. They change frequently; for the most current news on invasive species, visit the USDA's Natural Resource Conservation Service at www.plants.usda.gov. The following are some of the West's worst offenders.

PLANT	WHERE IT IS A PROBLEM
Australian tree fern *(Cyathea cooperi)*	Hawaii
Blackberry *(Rubus* species*)*	Wild areas and gardens throughout the West; especially invasive in Northern California and western Oregon and Washington
English ivy *(Hedera helix* and *H. hibernica)*	Woodlands, suburbs, and cities throughout western Washington and Oregon
European beach grass *(Ammophila arenaria)*	Coastal dunes in California
Fountain grass *(Pennisetum setaceum)*	Arizona (especially the Sonoran Desert) and Hawaii
Giant reed *(Arundo donax)*	Riparian areas in California and Hawaii
Pampas grass *(Cortaderia selloana)* and jubata grass *(C. jubata)*	Coastal and interior habitats throughout California and Hawaii
Purple loosestrife *(Lythrum salicaria, L. virgatum,* and related hybrids*)*	Wetlands throughout the West
Scotch broom *(Cytisus scoparius)*	Coastal scrub and oak woodlands in California, Hawaii, Idaho, Oregon, and Washington
Spurge *(Euphorbia* species*)*	Forests and woodlands throughout the West
Tamarisk or salt cedar *(Tamarix)*	Large areas of the arid Southwest

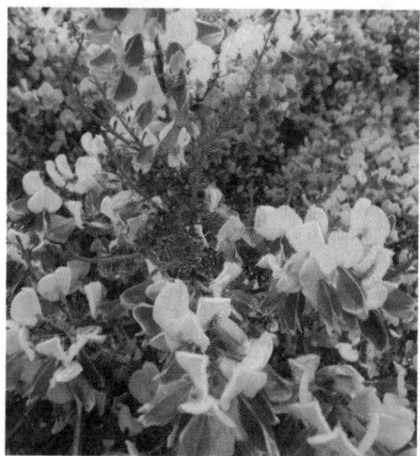

Though beautiful in bloom, Scotch broom *quickly becomes a noxious weed in California and the Northwest.*

W

WILDFLOWERS

Wildflowers provide a carefree style of gardening that's colorful and also gives great bang for a dollar. You can sow a strip to create a cheery transition between your yard and the surrounding landscape. A large space might be divided into a neatly cultivated garden close to the house and farther out a more natural area that doesn't need so much maintenance. Or you can sprinkle wildflowers in gaps between ground covers, or establish a flowering meadow instead of a lawn or flower beds.

Growing wildflowers is a purely regional affair, with different parts of the West offering locally adapted favorites. Specialty seed companies offer regional mixes that work well in many areas. Local native plant societies can also provide information on wildflowers suitable for your area.

California poppies (Eschscholzia)

Planting and Caring for Wildflowers

Plant wildflowers from seed in fall in mild winter areas.

Prepare wildflower beds as you'd prepare soil for a vegetable garden (see page 712); dig or till in a 3-inch layer of rotted manure or compost, then level the soil and water. After about three weeks, hoe or pull the weeds that come up. Then you're ready to plant.

Before sowing, check guidelines on the seed packet. But in general, scatter seed at the rate of one ounce per 300 square feet (that's 50 to 100 seeds per square foot). Rake lightly; water well. During the growing season, water regularly, and remove any weed seedlings as soon as they start to emerge.

After plants have finished blooming, they may take on a ragged appearance. Leave all the desirable plants to set seeds for the following year. Gather some seeds by hand too and save them for later plantings or to fill out any bare spots.

In early winter, mow or cut dry stems down to 6 to 8 inches. At the same time, pull out any weeds, such as oxalis or dandelion. This once-a-year trim will give perennial wildflowers room and light to spread before the next crop of annuals has emerged. In regions that typically have a lot of rain in winter, irrigate a wildflower patch only when rains are light.

In California, miner's lettuce, mild maids, sugar scoops, baby blue eyes, California pop-pies, farewell-to-spring, lupines, and shooting stars are among the many colorfully named wild plants that will thrive with minimal garden care.

In the Northwest, even delicate-looking flowers like western columbine (*Aquilegia formosa*) can fit into formal border schemes. And don't forget woodland plants such as ferns for shady gardens.

In the Southwest, reseeding annuals such as calliopsis, desert marigolds, Indian paintbrush, and bluebonnets can be grown in great sweeps in sunny areas. The drier and leaner the soil, the better these flowers seem to grow.

Camas (Camassia)

Indian paintbrush (Castilleja)

Trillium

Black-eyed Susan (Rudbeckia)

Design Tips

Here are some strategies for incorporating wildflowers into the garden.

Intersperse native species with their modern offspring. In the Northwest, this might include hybrids such as Pacific Coast irises (derived from *Iris douglasiana*).

Plant in drifts. In the wild, plant communities are often quite minimalist, with one or two plants spreading into beautiful carpets of bloom.

Mimic a native landscape. Use native shrubs to form the "bones" of the garden—coffeeberry and toyon in the Northwest and Northern California, for instance. Then fill in around them with flowering natives such as monkey flower and leopard lily.

Plant a cutting garden. Create an island of wildflowers in the backyard that doubles as a source of cut flowers. Choose varieties that hold up in bouquets, such as calliopsis, godetia, and Indian blanket.

Fill small spaces. Sow seeds in confined spaces such as around mail boxes, in raised beds, or even in containers. Or broadcast them in a new planting bed as a temporary filler until you have time to tackle a more permanent planting there.

W

Rose-red alstroemeria, orange butterfly weed, golden columbine, and, at rear, cape honeysuckle brighten the wildlife garden at Buena Creek Gardens in San Marcos, California. Pink Penstemon 'Apple Blossom' and Salvia 'Blue Hills' are further draws for hummingbirds.

WILDLIFE IN THE GARDEN

Making your garden attractive to wildlife—including songbirds, hummingbirds, butterflies, toads, lizards, frogs, and other creatures—is primarily a matter of providing shelter, water, and food. It's also important to avoid using chemical pesticides. Try to emphasize native plants, as they're familiar to the local wildlife and adapted to your climate. Also remember that a garden teeming with wildlife is not overly tidy; parts of it are left to grow naturally, providing havens for creatures of all sorts. See the Plant Selection Guides on pages 114 and 118 for lists of plants attractive to butterflies and birds, including kinds that provide food for butterfly larvae (caterpillars).

A garden's wildlife looks for all the same things that people seek for survival: good food and drink, a bath, and a cozy place to bed down for the night. They can find these at the half-acre demonstration garden for butterflies and hummingbirds at Buena Creek Gardens shown above. Created by Steve and Donna Brigham, the garden features nectar-rich flowering plants, birdbaths, and shrubs to provide cover.

Attracting Wildlife

TALL TREES These provide shelter, food (seeds or fruits), and nesting places. They also protect the garden from strong winds.

HUMMINGBIRD FEEDER To prepare feeder solution, combine 1 part granulated sugar and 4 parts water. Bring to a boil and then let it cool. Keep the feeder clean, as hummers can develop a deadly infection from dirty feeders.

BIRDBATH To provide some protection from cats and other predators, place in an open area. A location 10 to 20 feet from shrubs offers a safety zone. In freezing weather, thaw ice with boiling water or use a birdbath heater.

A garden filled with wildlife attracts a range of beneficial creatures—including ladybugs, bees, toads, and spiders—that help keep harmful pests at bay.

W

POND This is a way to provide water for birds and a habitat for frogs and turtles. Birds are especially attracted to the splashing water of a small fountain. Make a "beach" at one side to provide shallow water. An "island" (a large rock) in the center offers refuge for turtles and frogs. Water plants add shelter.

VINES Flowering vines provide shelter, nesting sites, and nectar. Many also bear berries and foliage that are sources of food for both birds and butterfly larvae.

SHELTERS Arrange rocks, or place upturned flower pots where frogs and toads can hide from predators.

BIRD FEEDERS Locate feeders near trees or shrubs so birds can fly to cover. Keep them off the ground to protect the clientele from cats. Set up feeders in fall and maintain them through winter when natural foods are scarce. Keep feeders clean. Besides seeds (sunflower, millet, safflower, thistle, and so on), birds enjoy suet, offered in mesh bags or special feeders.

HEDGEROWS These provide food, shelter, and nesting sites for birds. Plant a selection of small trees and low to medium-tall shrubs. Include fruit-bearing types as well as kinds that feed butterfly larvae.

BRUSH PILE Instead of hauling away or shredding tree prunings and other brush, make piles to shelter birds and other wildlife.

FLOWER BORDERS Include a wide selection of plants that provide nectar for butterflies, beneficial insects, and hummingbirds. Also plant species whose foliage feeds butterfly larvae. Let plants go to seed to furnish food for songbirds.

NESTING BOXES Install them away from the activity around feeders and face them away from prevailing weather. Mount boxes on metal poles to keep cats and raccoons at bay.

MEADOW Plant native grasses, wildflowers, and low shrubs for food, shelter, and nest-building materials.

Pet-friendly Gardens

Dozens of common garden plants are toxic to cats, dogs, and other animals. Some plants are more potent than others and the severity of the response can vary depending on the amount of material consumed, as well as the size and general health of the animal. But the results are never pretty. They range from irritation of the mouth, lips, and tongue to severe vomiting, diarrhea, convulsions, and death. The plants listed below are some of the most likely to cause distress. For a comprehensive list of poisonous plants, along with clinical signs that a nibbling pet might display, check the ASPCA's Poison Control Center at www.ASPCA.org.

Azaleas and rhododendrons
(Rhododendron)

Cycads (Cycas and Zamia)

Cyclamen (Cyclamen)

Daylily (Hemerocallis) *

Foxglove (Digitalis purpurea)

Heavenly bamboo (Nandina domestica)

Lily (Lilium) *

Lily-of-the-Valley (Convallaria majalis)

Lily-of-the-Valley shrub (Pieris japonica)

Oleander (Nerium oleander)

Yew (Taxus)

*Affects only cats

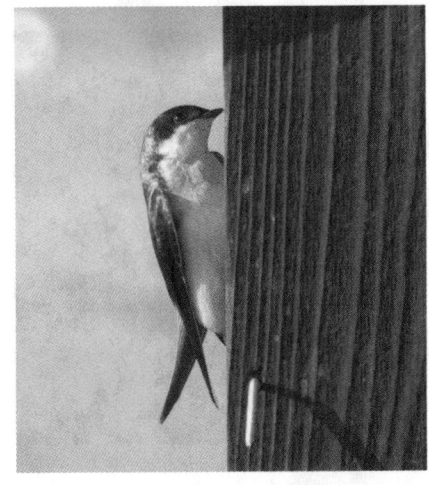

W

Demystifying Scientific Plant Names

Scientific plant names can be intimidating to gardeners. So why have they been used around the world for hundreds of years? Why do we use them in this book? And why do the plants sold at nurseries so often have scientific names printed somewhere on their labels? There's good reason: Common names for plants are often confusing and misleading. A single common name can apply to different plants in different parts of the country or the world. It can be used for two or more plants that not only look different but vary tremendously in growth habit, needs, and bloom season.

Acer palmatum

Echinacea purpurea

A COMMON LANGUAGE

Scientific names are more precise than common ones. If you tell a nursery you want to buy a dusty miller, for example, you might be asked: "Which one?" A number of plants are commonly known by that name. All are perennials with silvery foliage, but *Centaurea cineraria* has big, yellow thistlelike flowers; *Senecio cineraria* has small yellow flowers; *Senecio vira-vira* has creamy white flowers; and *Lychnis coronaria* has magenta to crimson flowers. Likewise, "Black-eyed Susan" applies to a golden-flowered perennial *(Rudbeckia hirta)* and to a vine most often planted as a summer annual *(Thunbergia alata)*.

Similar-sounding common names may also cause confusion. "Hummingbird bush" is the Australian shrub *Grevillea thelemanniana.* "Hummingbird flower" on the other hand is the California native perennial *Zauschneria,* and "Hummingbird mint" is another perennial, *Agastache.*

Finally, ornamentals and weeds may bear the same common name. "Spanish broom" is either a tidy, 2-foot shrub with yellow flowers *(Genista hispanica)* or a rangy, 6- to 10-foot shrub *(Spartium junceum)* that runs wild across many parts of the West.

Centaurea cineraria

Betula pendula

WHAT'S IN A NAME?

Scientific names, if you break them down, can tell you something about the plants. The first part of a scientific name is the **genus** name. The second part is the **species** name, which is usually a descriptive word.

Many plants are named for the person who first described them. Others hold clues to a plant's growth habit, provenance, fragrance, or other characteristics.

Sollya heterophylla, for example, combines *hetero* (heterogeneous or various) with *phylla* (leaves) to mean "various-size leaves." Indeed, some of the leaves of this evergreen shrub are lanceolate and others are oblong.

Some of the scientific names are so much like English words that there is no question as to their meaning. *Prostratum, compacta, deliciosa, fragrans,* and *pendula* all give clear clues as to a plant's qualities.

COMMONLY USED BOTANICAL NAMES

Color of Flowers or Foliage

albus—white
argenteus—silvery
aureus—golden
azureus—azure, sky blue
caeruleus—dark blue
caesius—blue-gray
candidus—pure white, shiny
canus—ashy gray, hoary
cereus—waxy
citrinus—yellow
coccineus—scarlet
concolor—one color
croceus—yellow
cruentus—bloody
discolor—two colors, separate colors
glaucus—covered with gray bloom
incanus—gray, hoary
luteus—yellow
pallidus—pale
purpureus—purple
rubens, ruber—red, ruddy
rufus—ruddy

Form of Leaf (*folius*—leaves or foliage)

acerifolius—maplelike
angustifolius—narrow
aquifolius—spiny
buxifolius—boxwood-like
ilicifolius—hollylike
laurifolius—laurel-like
parvifolius—small
populifolius—poplarlike
quercifolius—oak-like
salicifolius—willowlike

Hydrangea quercifolia

Shape of Plant

adpressus—pressing against, hugging
altus—tall
arboreus—treelike
capitatus—headlike
compactus—compact, dense
confertus—crowded, pressed together
contortus—twisted
decumbens—trailing, with tips upright
depressus—pressed down
elegans—elegant, slender, willowy

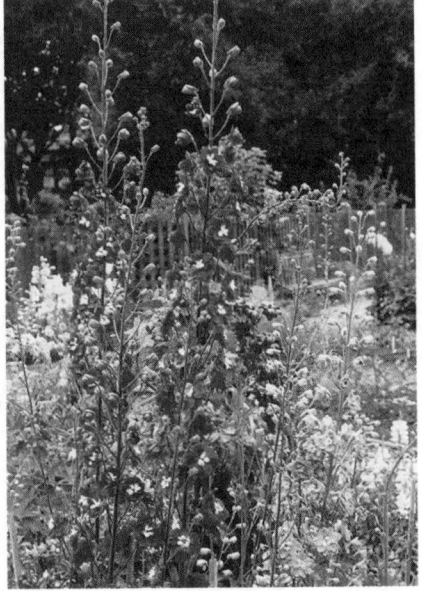

Delphinium elatum

fastigiatus—branches erect and close together
humifusus—sprawling on the ground
humilis—low, small, humble
impressus—sunken
nanus—dwarf
procumbens—trailing
prostratus—prostrate
pumilus—dwarf, small
pusillus—puny, insignificant

Coprosma repens

repens—creeping
reptans—creeping
scandens—climbing

Where It Came From

The suffix *-ensis* (of a place) is added to place names to specify the habitat where the plant was first discovered.
africanus—of Africa
alpinus—of the Alps
australis—southern

borealis—northern
campestris—of the field or plains
canadensis—of Canada
canariensis—of the Canary Islands
capensis—of the Cape of Good Hope area
chilensis—of Chile
chinensis—of China
hispanicus—of Spain
hortensis—of gardens
indicus—of India
insularis—of the island
japonicus—of Japan
littoralis—of the seashore
montanus—of the mountains
riparius—of riverbanks
rivalis, rivularis—of brooks
saxatilis—inhabiting rocks

Plant Parts

dendron—tree
flora, florum, flori, florus—flowers
phyllus, phylla—leaf or leaves

Plant Peculiarities

armatus—armed
augusta—majestic, notable
baccatus—berried, berrylike
barbatus—barbed or bearded

Campanula

campanulatus—bell or cup shaped
ciliaris—fringed
cordatus—heart shaped
cornutus—horned
crassus—thick, fleshy
decurrens—running down the stem
diversi—varying
edulis—edible
floridus—free flowering
fruticosus—shrubby
fulgens—shiny
gracilis—slender, thin, graceful
grandi—large, showy
-ifer, -iferus—bearing or having;
    e.g., *stoloniferus*, having stolons
imperialis—showy

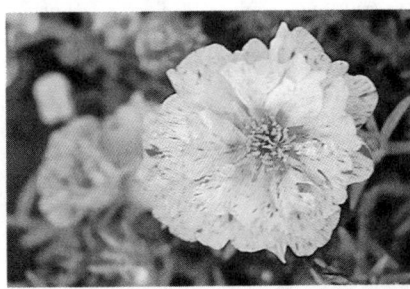

Portulaca grandiflora

laciniatus—fringed or with torn edges
laevigatus—smooth
lobatus—lobed
longus—long
macro—large
maculatus—spotted
micro—small
mollis—soft, soft-haired
mucronatus—pointed
nutans—nodding, swaying
obtusus—blunt or flattened
officinalis—medicinal
-oides—like or resembling; e.g., *jasminoides*,
    like a jasmine
patens—open, spreading growth

Cosmos bipinnatus

pinnatus—constructed like a feather
platy—broad
plenus—double, full
plumosus—feathery
praecox—early
pungens—piercing
radicans—rooting, especially along the stem

Campsis radicans

reticulatus—net-veined
retusus—notched at blunt apex
rugosus—wrinkled, rough
saccharatus—sweet, sugary
sagittalis—arrowlike
scabrus—rough feeling
scoparius—broomlike

Pronunciation Guide

Scientific names are the universal language for plants, but they are pronounced differently in various parts of the world, even among English-speaking countries. Because these names come from Latin and Greek, there is no obligatory pronunciation for them—but what follows is a list of the most familiar ways to say many scientific plant names.

Our Spelling	Pronounced as In
a	h<u>a</u>t, h<u>a</u>nd
ay	b<u>a</u>by
ah	h<u>a</u>ll
ai	<u>ai</u>r
e	m<u>e</u>t, b<u>e</u>d
ee	w<u>e</u>
i	t<u>i</u>n
ye	w<u>i</u>ne
o	h<u>o</u>t
oe	r<u>o</u>mance
u	m<u>u</u>st, b<u>u</u>rr
oo	r<u>u</u>mor
ew	h<u>u</u>man
uh	comm<u>a</u>, vap<u>o</u>r

A

Abelia—uh-BEE-lee-uh
Abutilon—uh-BEW-tuh-lon
Acacia—uh-KAY-shuh
Acer—AY-sir
Achillea—ak-il-LEE-uh
Achimenes—uh-KIM-muh-neez
Aconitum—ak-oe-NYE-tuhm
Actinidia—AK-ti-NID-ee-uh
Adiantum—ad-ee-AN-tuhm
Aesculus—ES-keew-luhs
Agapanthus—ag-uh-PAN-thuhs

Acer

Agave—ah-GAH-vay
Ageratum—ah-JER-ah-tum (usually pronounced ad-juh-RAY-tuhm)
Ailanthus—uh-LAN-thuhs
Ajuga—uh-JEW-guh
Alstroemeria—al-struh-MEE-ree-uh
Amaryllis—am-uh-RIL-is
Anemone—uh-NEM-uh-nee

Agave

Anthurium—an-THU-ree-uhm
Aquilegia—ak-wuh-LEE-jee-uh
Arabis—AIR-uh-bis
Aralia—uh-RAY-lee-uh
Arctostaphylos—ark-toe-STAF-i-luhs
Arctotheca—ark-toe-THEE-kuh
Artemisia—AHR-tuh-MEE-zee-uh
Aspidistra—as-puh-DIS-truh
Astilbe—as-STIL-bee
Atriplex—AT-rip-lex

Anemone

B

Babiana—bab-ee-AN-uh
Baccharis—BAK-uh-ris
Bauhinia—boe-HIN-ee-uh
Berberis—BUR-buh-ris
Bergenia—bur-GEN-ee-uh
Betula—BET-ew-luh
Bougainvillea—boo-guhn-VIL-ee-uh
Buddleja—BUD-lee-uh

C

Caladium—kuh-LAY-dee-uhm
Calceolaria—kal-see-oe-LAIR-ee-uh

Calendula—kuh-LEN-dew-luh
Callistemon—ka-lis-STEE-muhn
Callistephus—ka-LIS-tee-fuhs
Calochortus—kal-oh-COR-tuhs
Campanula—kam-PAN-ew-luh
Carpenteria—CAHR-pen-TEER-ee-a
Cattleya—KAT-lee-uh
Ceanothus—see-uh-NO-thuhs
Celosia—see-LOW-she-uh
Centaurea—sen-tah-REE-uh
Ceratonia—sair-uh-TONE-ee-uh
Ceratostigma—sair-uh-toe-STIG-muh
Cercidium—sir-CID-ee-uhm
Cercis—SIR-suhs
Chamaecyparis—kam-uh-SIP-uh-ris
Cheiranthus—kye-RAN-thuhs
Chionanthus—kye-oe-NAN-thuhs
Chlorophytum—klor-oe-FYE-tum
Choisya—SHOY-zee-uh

Clematis—KLEM-uh-tis
Cleome—KLEE-oe-mee
Clivia—KLYE-vee-uh
Cocculus—COC-ew-lus
Colchicum—KAHL-chik-uhm

Clematis

Convallaria—con-va-LAIR-ee-uh
Convolvulus—kon-VOL-vew-luhs
Coreopsis—kor-ee-OP-suhs
Cotinus—koe-TYE-nuhs
Cotoneaster—koe-toe-nee-AS-tuhr
Crataegus—kruh-TEE-guhs
Crocosmia—kroe-KOZ-mee-uh
Cuphea—KEW-fee-uh
Cymbidium—sim-BID-ee-uhm
Cynoglossum—sin-oh-GLOS-uhm

D

Daboecia—dab-EE-shee-uh
Daphne—DAFF-nee
Deutzia—DOOT-zee-uh or DOYT-zee-uh
Dieffenbachia—deef-uhn-BAK-ee-uh
Dizygotheca—diz-uh-GOTH-ik-uh or diz-uh-goe-THEE-kah
Dracaena—druh-SEE-nuh
Dryopteris—drye-OP-ter-uhs
Duchesnea—dew-KEZ-nee-uh

E

Echeveria—ek-uh-VAIR-ee-uh
Echinacea—ek-uh-NAY-see-uh
Echinops—EK-uh-nops
Echium—EK-ee-uhm
Elaeagnus—el-ee-AG-nuhs

Epidendrum—ep-uh-DEN-druhm
Epiphyllum—ep-uh-FIL-uhm
Equisetum—ek-wuh-SEE-tuhm
Eremurus—er-uh-MEWR-uhs
Erica—ee-RYE-kuh (correct, but universally pronounced AIR-ik-uh)
Erigeron—ee-RIJ-uh-ron
Erythrina—air-i-THRYE-nuh
Eschscholzia—eh-SCHOELT-see-uh
Eucalyptus—ew-kuh-LIP-tuhs
Euonymus—ew-ON-uh-mus
Exacum—EK-suh-kuhm
Exochorda—ek-so-KOR-duh

F

Fragaria (strawberry)

Fatshedera—fats-HED-uh-ruh
Feijoa—fay-HOE-uh
Ficus—FYE-kuhs
Forsythia—for-SITH-ee-uh
Fragaria—fra-GAIR-ee-uh
Fraxinus—FRAK-suh-nuhs
Fuchsia—FEW-shee-uh

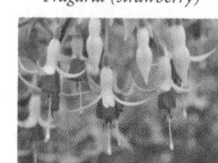
Fuchsia

G

Gaillardia—gay-LAHR-dee-uh
Gazania—guh-ZAY-nee-uh
Genista—jen-NIS-tuh
Gentiana—jen-shee-AY-nah
Gerbera—GUR-bur-uh
Geum—JEE-uhm
Gleditsia—gluh-DIT-see-uh
Gomphrena—gom-FREE-nuh
Grevillea—gruh-VIL-ee-uh
Gypsophila—jip-SOF-uh-luh

H

Hamamelis—ham-uh-MEE-luhs
Hebe—HEE-bee
Hedera—HED-uh-ruh
Helianthemum—hee-lee-AN-thuh-muhm

Helianthus—
    hee-lee-AN-thuhs
Heliopsis—hee-lee-
    OP-suhs
Heliotropium—
    hee-lee-oe-TROE-
    pee-uhm

Helianthus

Hemerocallis—hem-uh-roe-KAL-uhs
Heteromeles—het-uh-roe-MEE-leez
Heuchera—HEW-kuh-ruh
Hibiscus—hye-BIS-kuhs
Hippeastrum—hip-ee-AS-truhm
Hosta—HAHST-uh
Hydrangea—hye-
    DRAIN-jee-uh
Hymenocallis—hye-
    muh-noe-KAL-uhs
Hypericum—hye-
    PEER-ik-uhm

Hypericum

I

Iberis—eye-BEE-ruhs
Ilex—EYE-lex
Impatiens—im-PAY-shuns
Ipomoea—ip-oe-MEE-uh
Iresine—ir-uh-SYE-nee

J

Jacaranda—jak-uh-RAN-duh
Jasminum—JAZ-muh-nuhm
Juniperus—joo-NIP-uh-ruhs

K

Kalanchoe—kal-an-
    KO-ee
Kniphofia—nip-HOE-
    fee-uh
Kochia—KO-kee-uh
Koelreuteria—kell-
    rew-TEE-ree-uh
Kolkwitzia—koel-
    KWIT-zee-uh

Kniphofia

L

Lagerstroemia—lay-gur-STREE-mee-uh
Lathyrus—LATH-uh-ruhs
Leptospermum—lep-toe-SPUR-muhm
Liatris—lie-AT-ruhs
Liriodendron—lear-ee-oe-DEN-druhn
Liriope—leer-EYE-oh-pee
Lobelia—loe-BEE-lee-uh
Lonicera—lo-NIS-uh-ruh
Lychnis—LIK-nis
Lysimachia—lye-suh-MAY-kee-uh

M

Malus—MAY-lus
Mandevilla—
    man-duh-VIL-uh
Matthiola—
    ma-thee-OE-luh
Maytenus—
    MAY-te-nuhs
Melaleuca—
    mel-uh-LOO-kuh
Metrosideros—
    MET-roe-SID-uh-ruhs

Mandevilla

Mimulus—MIM-ew-luhs
Musa—MEW-zuh
Myosotis—mye-oh-SO-tuhs
Myrica—mi-RYE-kuh

N

Nandina—nan-
    DEE-nuh
Narcissus—nahr-
    SIS-uhs
Nerine—nuh-RYE-nee
Nerium—NEE-
    ree-uhm

Narcissus

Nicotiana—ni-koe-shee-AY-nuh
Nierembergia—nee-rem-BURG-ee-uh
Nyssa—NIS-uh

O

Olea—O-lee-uh
Osmanthus—oz-MAN-thuhs
Osteospermum—os-tee-oe-SPUR-muhm
Oxalis—OK-sal-uhs
Oxydendrum—OK-see-DEN-druhm

P

Pachysandra—pak-ee-SAN-druh
Papaver—puh-PAY-vur
Parthenocissus—PAHR-thuh-noe-SIS-uhs
Pelargonium—pel-ahr-GOE-nee-uhm
Pennisetum—pen-uh-SEE-tuhm
Penstemon—PEN-stuh-muhn
Philadelphus—fil-uh-DEL-fuhs
Photinia—foe-TIN-ee-uh
Phyla—FYE-luh
Phyllostachys—FIL-oe-STACK-ees

Physalis

Physalis—FYE-suh-luhs
Picea—pye-SEE-uh
Pieris—pee-AIR-uhs
Pinus—PYE-nuhs
Pittosporum—pit-TOS-poe-ruhm,
    pit-toe-SPOER-uhm
Platanus—PLAT-uh-nuhs
Platycladus—plat-i-CLAD-uhs
Podocarpus—poe-doe-KAR-puhs
Polianthes—pol-ee-AN-thez
Polygonatum—pol-ee-GON-uh-tuhm
Portulaca—por-tew-LAK-a
Potentilla—poe-ten-TIL-uh
Primula—PRIM-ew-luh
Protea—PROE-tee-uh
    or proe-TEE-uh
Pseudotsuga—soo-
    doe-TSOO-guh
Pyrostegia—
    pye-roe-STEE-
    jee-uh
Pyrus—PYE-ruhs

Protea

Q

Quercus—KWER-kuhs

R

Ranunculus—ra-NUN-kew-
    luhs
Rhaphiolepis—raf-ee-OL-uh-
    pis or
    raf-ee-o-LEP-uhs
Rhoeo—REE-oe
Romneya—ROM-nee-uh
Rosmarinus—ros-muh-RYE-nuhs
Rudbeckia—rud-BECK-ee-uh

Ranunculus

S

Salpiglossis—sal-pi-GLOS-sis
Sanvitalia—san-vi-TALE-ee-uh
Scabiosa—skay-bee-OH-suh
Schefflera—SHEF-luh-ruh
Schizanthus—ski-ZAN-thuhs
Scilla—SIL-luh
Sempervivum—sem-per-VYE-vuhm
Senecio—suh-NEE-
    shee-oe
Sequoia—suh-QUOY-uh
Sinningia—si-NIN-
    jee-uh
Solandra—soe-LAN-
    druh
Soleirolia—soe-lee-uh-
    ROE-lee-uh
Spiraea—spye-REE-uh
Strelitzia—stre-LIT-see-uh
Syngonium—sin-GOE-nee-uhm

Senecio

T

Tagetes—tuh-JEE-teez
Taxodium—taks-OE-dee-uhm
Thuja—THOO-yuh
Thymus—TYE-muhs
Tibouchina—tib-oo-KYE-nuh
Tigridia—tye-GRID-ee-uh
Tolmiea—tol-MEE-uh
Trachelospermum—tra-kee-lo-SPER-muhm
Tradescantia—trad-es-KAN-shee-uh
Trichostema—trik-oe-STEE-mah
Tropaeolum—tro-PEE-oh-luhm
Tsuga—TSOO-guh

V

Vaccinium—
    vak-SIN-ee-uhm
Vancouveria—van-koo-
    VEE-ree-uh
Verbascum—vur-BAS-
    kuhm
Verbena—ver-BEE-nuh
Vinca—VING-kuh
Vitex—VEE-teks

Verbena

W–Z

Weigela—wye-JEE-luh
Xylosma—zye-LOZ-muh
Zantedeschia—zan-tuh-DES-kee-uh
Zephyranthes—zef-i-RAN-theez
Zizyphus—ZIZ-uh-fuhs
Zoysia—ZOY-see-uh

Glossary of Gardening Terms

Acid soil. A soil with a pH below 7. See page 728.

Alkaline soil. A soil with a pH above 7. See page 728.

Alternate leaves. See Opposite leaves.

Annual. A plant that completes its life cycle in 1 year or less. For information on planting and caring for annuals, see page 678.

Anther. See Flower.

Axil. The inner angle between a leaf (or other organ of a plant) and the stem from which it springs. Organs in the axil, such as flowers and buds, are called axillary.

Balled-and-burlapped (B-and-B). Specimen shrubs and trees sold for planting with a ball of soil around the roots, wrapped in burlap or a synthetic. Usually available from late fall to early spring. For planting instructions, see page 716.

Balled-and-burlapped

Bare-root. Refers to deciduous shrubs and trees and some perennials sold for planting with the soil removed from their roots. Usually sold in winter and early spring. See page 714.

Bedding plant. Any plant suitable for massing in beds for its colorful flowers or foliage. Most bedding plants are annuals or perennials that are grown as annuals.

Biennial. A plant that germinates and produces foliage and roots during its first growing season, then blooms, produces seed, and dies during its second growing season. See page 678.

Blanching. The process of blocking light from parts of certain vegetables to keep them paler in color or milder in flavor (or both). With cauliflower and the central leaves of endive or cardoon (an artichoke relative), the outer leaves are tied over the inner head or leaves. Asparagus

Blanched asparagus

is blanched by mounding soil over the emerging spears.

Bolt. To produce seeds or flowers prematurely; the term usually refers to annual flowers and vegetables. Bolting most frequently occurs when cool-season plants (lettuce, for example) are set out in hot weather that rushes growth.

Bonsai. The word *bonsai* is Japanese for "tray planting": growing and training dwarf plants in containers selected to harmonize with them. The objective is to create a tree or landscape in miniature.

Bonsai

Bracts. Modified leaves growing on some plants below a flower or flower cluster. Bracts are usually green, but may be colorful enough to resemble flowers or petals. Bougainvillea, dogwood *(Cornus),* and poinsettia *(Euphorbia pulcherrima)* all have showy bracts.

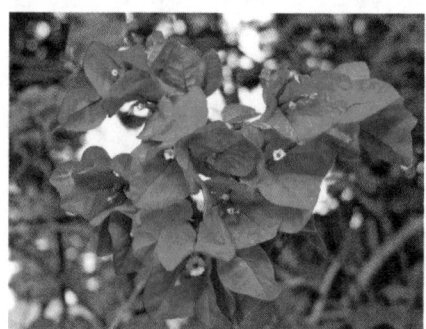

Bracts on Bougainvillea

Broad-leafed. Refers to evergreen trees and shrubs that have foliage year-round—camellia, for example—but are not conifers (such as juniper). Also refers to any weed that is not a grass.

Bud. A rudimentary organ or shoot of a plant. A flower bud develops into a blossom; a growth bud produces shoots of leafy growth. Terminal (apical) buds are produced at the end of a shoot. Lateral (axillary) buds are produced in the axil of a plant. Latent buds lie dormant until the branch is cut or breaks near it; then the bud will develop into a new shoot.

Budding. A method of propagation in which a bud (scion) from one plant is inserted beneath the bark of another related plant. See page 721.

Bud union. The point at which a shoot or bud (scion) unites with the rootstock.

Bulb. A plant that grows from a thickened underground structure. A true bulb consists of an underground stem base that contains an embryonic plant surrounded by scales—modified leaves that overlap one another. Bulblike structures include corms, rhizomes, tubers, and tuberous roots. See page 679.

Calyx. Collectively, the sepals of a flower.

Cambium. The layer of growing cells between the xylem and phloem. See page 711.

Cane. An elongated flowering or fruiting stem, usually arising directly from the roots. Examples of cane-producing plants include barberry *(Berberis),* forsythia, rose, raspberry, and grape.

Cane pruning. A method of pruning grapevines.

Catkin. A slender, spikelike, often drooping flower cluster. Alder *(Alnus),* birch *(Betula),* and willow *(Salix)* are familiar trees that produce catkins.

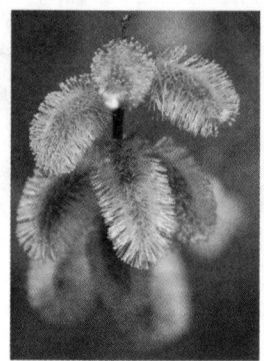

Catkin

Chill requirement. Many bulbs, perennials, and deciduous shrubs and trees (fruit trees in particular) need cold weather (as measured in hours required at temperatures below 45°F/7°C) to produce well. Many varieties of such plants—apples and lilacs *(Syringa),* for example—have been developed that require less winter chill. Bulbs can be refrigerated in warm-winter areas.

Composite head. See Inflorescence.

Compound leaf. See Leaf.

Conifer. A precise term for certain evergreens—such as cedar *(Cedrus),* juniper *(Juniperus),* and pine *(Pinus).* Conifers have leaves that are narrow and needlelike or tiny and scalelike. A few conifers, including larch *(Larix)* and dawn redwood *(Metasequoia),* are deciduous. All conifers bear seeds in cones or in modified conelike structures (juniper berries, for example). Yew *(Taxus)* and *Podocarpus* bear single seeds on fleshy bases, but because of their needlelike foliage, they are sometimes considered conifers.

Corm. A bulblike, swollen underground stem base composed of solid tissue. See page 679.

Corolla. Collectively, the petals of a flower.

Crown. A tree's crown is its entire branch structure, including foliage. Crown also refers to the point at which a plant's roots and top structure join, usually at or near the soil line.

Cultivar. Shorthand for "cultivated variety." These are genetically distinct plants, maintained in cultivation by human effort; they may be of hybrid origin or selected varieties of plants that occur in the wild. Cultivars are propagated by divisions, cuttings, or (in some cases) seed. Cultivar names are enclosed in single quotation marks and are not italicized, as in *Lobelia erinus* 'Crystal Palace'. In general usage and throughout this book, the term "variety" (see also Variety) refers both to cultivars and to varieties found in nature.

Deadhead. To remove spent flowers, neatening a plant, preventing it from setting seed, and prolonging its bloom.

Deciduous. Any plant that naturally sheds all of its foliage at any one time (usually in fall).

Defoliation. The unnatural loss of foliage, which may result from high winds, intense heat, drought, unusually early or late frosts, or severe damage caused by chemicals, insects, or diseases.

Dieback. When a plant's stems die for part of their length, beginning at the tips. Causes include inadequate moisture, nutrient deficiency, poor climate adaptation, or severe injury from pests or diseases.

Dormancy. The annual period when a plant's growth slows down. For many plants, dormancy commences as days grow shorter and temperatures colder.

Drainage. The downward movement of water through the soil. See page 728.

Drip line. The circular area of soil around a tree directly under its outermost branch tips; rainwater tends to drip from the tree at this point. Roots of established trees usually extend beyond the drip line.

Epiphyte. Epiphytes grow on another plant for support but take no nourishment from the host plant. Examples include cattleya orchids and staghorn ferns *(Platycerium)*. Epiphytes are sometimes mistakenly considered parasites, but true parasites draw nourishment from the host, while epiphytes live on nutrients drawn from the air, rainwater, and organic debris on the supporting plant.

Espalier

Espalier. A plant trained so that its branches grow in a flat pattern against a vertical surface. See page 724.

Evergreen. Plants that never lose all their leaves at one time. See also Broad-leafed; Conifer.

Family. Every plant is classified in a family whose members share certain broad characteristics that set them apart from plants in other families. Family names are in Latin and typically end in "-aceae"; examples include *Rosaceae* (the rose family) and *Iridaceae* (the iris family). Botanists often reclassify family names, so reference works may differ in their classifications.

Fertilization. The fusion of male and female gametes (fertile reproductive cells) following pollination.

Fertilize. To apply nutrients in the form of fertilizer to a plant; see page 689.

Flower. The part of a seed-bearing plant that contains the reproductive organs.

Complete Flower

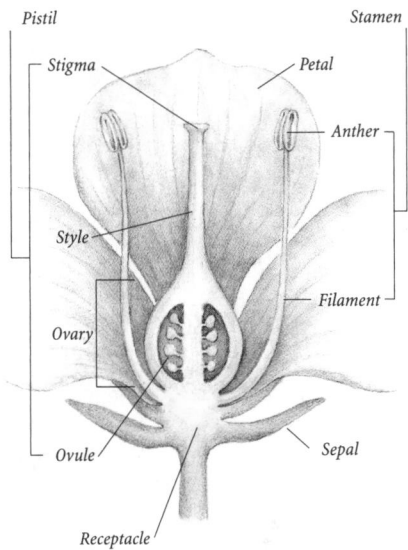

Pistil — Stigma — Style — Ovary — Ovule — Receptacle

Stamen — Petal — Anther — Filament — Sepal

Forcing. Hastening an out-of-season plant to maturity or to a flowering or fruiting stage. Usually occurs in a greenhouse, where temperature, light, and humidity can be controlled.

Foundation plant. Originally, a plant used to hide the foundation of a house. Since many of today's homes lack high or even visible foundations, the term has come to refer to any shrub planted near house walls.

Frond. In the strictest sense, fronds are the foliage of ferns. Often, however, the word is used to describe the leaves of palms or any foliage that looks fernlike.

Frond

Fruit. The mature ovary of a plant, containing one to many seeds. Fruits may be soft and fleshy, as in the case of peaches or apples, or dry, like an acorn or dried pea pod.

Genus (plural: genera). Plant families are subdivided into groups of more closely related plants called genera; the first word in a plant's botanical name is the genus. Some families contain only a single genus; for example, the family *Ginkgoaceae* includes only the genus *Ginkgo*. Others contain hundreds of genera; *Asteraceae* (the daisy family), for instance, comprises over 900 genera. The second word in a botanical name is the species (see also Species). Both genus and species are written in italics, with just the name of the genus capitalized—as in *Rosa moschata* (musk rose) and *Hemerocallis lilioasphodelus* (lemon daylily).

Girdling. The removal of bark all around a stem or branch, cutting off water and nutrients and possibly killing the plant. Girdling can occur when a woody plant has been tied tightly to a support and the growing plant becomes constricted. Gnawing rodents can also cause girdling. In some cases, a gardener may girdle a plant deliberately, removing a narrow ring of bark to reduce overly vigorous growth or to kill an unwanted plant.

Growing season. The number of days between the average dates of the last killing frost in spring and the first killing frost in fall. Also used to describe the period of time a plant is actively growing and not dormant. For information on the Western growing seasons, see pages 28–63.

Harden off. Exposing a plant that has been growing indoors to increasing periods of time outside, so that when it is planted in the garden it can make the transition with a minimum of shock.

Hardy. A plant's hardiness is its resistance to, or tolerance of, frosts or freezing temperatures. A plant hardy to –20°F/–29°C will survive undamaged by a temperature that low, for example. The word does not mean tough, pest-resistant, or disease-resistant.

Basic Flower Forms

Single

Semidouble

Double

The basic flower form is single (above left), with one row of petals (usually four, five, or six). Semidouble flowers (above center) have two or three times the minimum number of petals, usually in several rows. Double flowers (above right) have many densely packed petals that often produce a rounded blossom shape.

Herbaceous. A plant with soft or fleshy (non-woody) tissue—which might be an annual, perennial, or bulb. In the strictest sense, the term refers to plants that die to the ground each year and regrow stems the following growing season.

Humus. The soft dark substance formed when animal or vegetable matter decomposes. The term is also commonly used to describe organic materials that will eventually decompose into humus—such as sawdust, ground bark, leaf mold, and animal manure.

Hybrid. A plant that results from a cross between two species, subspecies, varieties, cultivars, strains, or any combination of the above; or, less commonly, between two plants from different genera. Hybrids may occur naturally, but more often they are deliberately bred. Hybrids are indicated with the symbol ×, as in *Buddleja* × *weyeriana,* a cross between the two butterfly bush species *B. davidii* and *B. globosa.*

Hydroponically grown watercress

Hydroponics. A method of gardening with a water-based solution rather than soil. In some systems, an inert medium such as rockwool is used to anchor plant roots.

Inflorescence. A group of individual flowers on a single stem, which can take many forms. A **spike** has flowers attached to the main stem without stalks, as in bottlebrush (*Callistemon*) or montbretia (*Crocosmia*). In an **umbel,** individual flowers spring from approximately the same point, as in the blossoms of dill (*Anethum graveolens*). In a **raceme,** flowers form on stalks arising from the main stem, as in foxglove (*Digitalis*). The flowers of lilac (*Syringa*) and privet (*Ligustrum*) are **panicles;** they have groups of flowers borne on stalks (**racemes**) arising from the main stem. A **composite head** refers to small, closely packed, stalkless flowers; these may include central disk flowers and outer ray flowers, as in sunflower (*Helianthus*).

Internode. See Node.

Lath. Any overhead structure (originally a roof of spaced laths) that reduces the amount of sunlight reaching plants beneath its cover or protects them from frost.

Leader. The central upward-growing stem of a single-trunked tree or shrub.

Leaf. The main photosynthetic organ of most plants. A **simple** leaf is a single unit, whereas

Inflorescences

Spike

Umbel

Raceme

Panicle

Composite head

Leaf Types

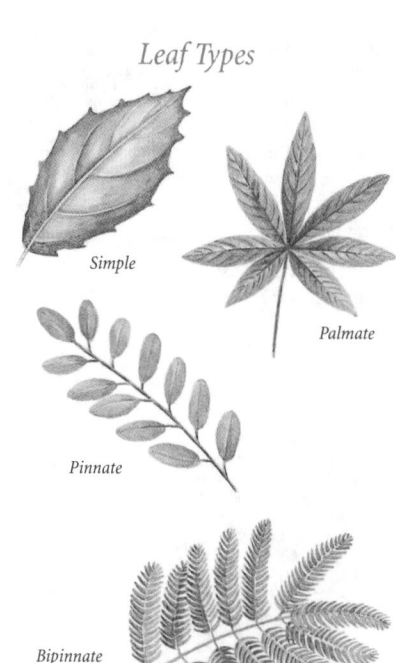

Simple

Palmate

Pinnate

Bipinnate

a **compound** leaf is divided into separate segments called leaflets. In a **palmately compound** leaf, the leaflets grow from one point at the end of a stem. In a **pinnately compound** (once-divided) leaf, the leaflets are arranged along a central axis; a **bipinnately compound** leaf is twice-divided, or twice pinnate.

Leafburn. Damage of a leaf's tissues from sunlight, chemicals, strong wind, or lack of water. Leafburn usually starts as brownish, dried-out tissue around the edge of the leaf; sometimes the whole leaf dries out. Plants sensitive to leafburn include Japanese maples (*Acer palmatum*) and azaleas (*Rhododendron*).

Leafburn

Leaflet. A division or segment of a compound leaf. See also Leaf.

Leaf mold. Partially decomposed leaves used as an organic amendment.

Leaf scar. A rounded or crescent-shaped mark on a branch where a leafstalk once was attached.

Lip. Irregular flowers (those with unequal segments) often have an upper and a lower division (each known as a lip), each bearing one or more segments. Honeysuckle (*Lonicera*) is an example.

Lip

Microclimate. A small area (such as a backyard or even a portion of it) with a slightly different climate than that of its larger surroundings. Microclimates are determined by factors such as hills, hollows, and the location of structures. Plants that might not survive in a specific climate zone may grow well in the right microclimate.

Naturalize. To set out plants (especially bulbs) randomly, without a precise pattern, and allow them to spread at will (see page 678). Also refers to plants that become established in an area where they are not native, such as foxglove (*Digitalis purpurea*), for example, which has naturalized in parts of the Pacific Northwest.

Node. The joint in a stem where a bud, branch, or leaf starts to grow. The area of stem between nodes is the **internode**.

Stem Nodes

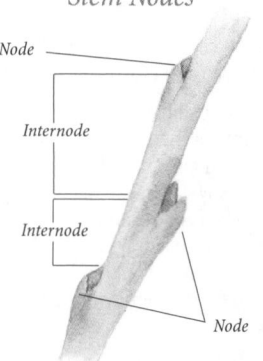

Node

Internode

Internode

Node

Offset. A young plant that develops at or near the base of the parent plant. Hen and chicks *(Echeveria)* and strawberry readily produce offsets. The word also refers to the increases of bulbs and corms.

Open-pollinated plants. Varieties or cultivars of plants produced from natural, random pollination. In contrast with hybrids, the result of deliberate crosses (controlled pollination).

Opposite leaves; alternate leaves. Leaves are opposite when they spring from the same node on a stem, but on **opposite** sides. **Alternate** leaves arise from different nodes on opposite sides of the stem.

Opposite/Alternate Leaves

Opposite

Alternate

Organic matter. Any material originating from a living organism—peat moss, ground bark, compost, or manure, for example—used as a soil amendment (see page 729).

Ovary. See Flower; Fruit.

Panicle. See Inflorescence.

Peat moss. A water-retentive organic soil amendment, peat moss is the partially decomposed remains of mosses. It increases soil acidity. Sphagnum peat moss is generally considered the highest in quality. See page 729.

Perennial. A nonwoody plant that lives for more than 2 years (often for many years). See page 703.

Petal. See Flower.

Pistil. See Flower.

Pleaching. A training method in which branches are interwoven to form a hedge or arbor. Subsequent pruning keeps a neat, rather formal pattern.

Lychnis viscaria *'Splendens' (perennial)*

Dormant pollarded tree

Pollarding. A training method in which the main limbs of a young tree are drastically cut back. In each subsequent dormant season, the growth from these branch stubs is cut back to one or two buds. In time, the branch ends become large and knobby. The result is a compact, leafy dome during the growing season and a somewhat grotesque branch structure during the dormant months. London plane tree *(Platanus × acerifolia)* is the tree most often subjected to this treatment.

Pollenizer. A plant that provides pollen for another plant, such as an apple variety planted to provide pollen for a nearby second variety that does not produce fertile pollen.

Pollination. The transfer of pollen from the male reproductive organs to the female ones, which leads to fertilization and seed production.

Pollinator. An insect or animal that transfers pollen from one part of a flower to another or from flowers on one plant to flowers on another.

Worker bee

Pseudobulb. A modified aboveground stem that serves as a storage organ. Some orchids have pseudobulbs.

Raceme. See Inflorescence.

Rhizome. A modified, horizontally growing stem. It may be long and slender, as in some perennials (and in perennial weeds like blackberry), or thick and fleshy, as in many irises (see page 679).

Rootbound. Plants grown in the same container for too long develop tangled, matted roots (see page 713).

Rootstock. The part of a budded or grafted plant that furnishes the root system and sometimes part of the branch structure (also known as an understock). See page 721.

Rosette. Leaves closely set around a crown or center, usually at or close to ground level. Hen and chicks *(Echeveria)* and partridge-breast aloe *(Aloe variegata)* both grow in rosettes.

Runner. See Stolon.

Rosette

Scion. A shoot or bud cut from one plant to graft or bud onto the rootstock of another (see page 721).

Self-seed, self-sow. When a plant sheds fertile seeds that produce seedlings.

Semidouble flower. See Basic flower forms.

Sepal. See Flower.

Simple leaf. See Leaf.

Single flower. See Basic flower forms.

Species. Each **genus** is subdivided into groups of individual **species**—generally distinct entities (though they may closely resemble other species in the genus) that reproduce from seed with only a small amount of variation. The second word in a plant's botanical name designates the species; the first word designates the genus. Both genus and species are italicized; the name of the genus is capitalized. For example, French marigold is, in botanical terms, *Tagetes patula*—genus *Tagetes,* species *patula*. See also Genus.

Specimen. A tree or shrub that makes a significant impact in a planting or in a conspicuous location in the garden.

Sphagnum. Various mosses native to bogs. Much of the peat moss sold in the West contains decomposed sphagnum. These mosses also are collected live and packaged in whole pieces, fresh or dried. In this form, they are used for lining hanging baskets and for air layering (page 721).

Spike. See Inflorescence.

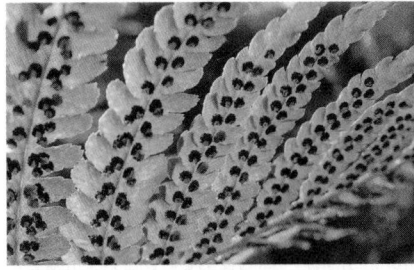

Fern spore

Spore. A simple reproductive cell. Algae, fungi, mosses, and ferns reproduce by spores.

Sport. A spontaneous mutation (variation) from the normal pattern, often a branch that differs from the rest of the plant. Examples include spurred apple varieties that occur as limb sports on standard apple varieties, and camellias propagated from branches that have shown changes in flower color or form.

Columbine (Aquilegia) *with dark pink spurs*

Spur. In grapevines and fruit trees (particularly apples and cherries), a specialized short twig that bears the plant's fruit. Also refers to short and saclike or long and tubular projections from a blossom's petals or sepals. Most species of columbine *(Aquilegia),* for example, have flowers with pronounced spurs.

Spur pruning. In winter, grapevine canes that grew and fruited in the past season are pruned from a framework of permanent arms, leaving a series of spurs (short twigs, each with two buds). These buds will produce fruit in the following summer or fall.

Stamen. See Flower.

Standard bay (Laurus nobilis) *tree*

Standard. A plant trained to a single, upright trunk topped by a rounded crown of foliage. In some standards, the trunk and top are joined by grafting.

Stolon. A stem that creeps and roots along the soil surface, forming new plants where it roots. Bermuda and St. Augustine grasses spread by stolons.

Strain. Many popular annuals and some perennials are strains (sometimes referred to as series). Examples include State Fair zinnias and Pacific delphiniums. Plants in a strain are similar but vary in some respect—usually in flower color.

Stress. Stress may result from inadequate or excess water, wind, or excessively high or low temperatures. It causes wilting, dulling or loss of foliage color, and browning of leaf edges.

Subshrub. A low-growing plant with woody stems—a small shrub. Also describes a perennial with a woody base but soft, herbaceous stems in its upper part.

Subspecies. A simple botanical name consists of two words in italics, denoting **genus** and **species.** When a third name in italics appears, it denotes a **subspecies**—a major division within a species. An example is *Eucalyptus mannifera maculosa,* red-spotted gum. (The name of the subspecies may be preceded by the abbreviation "ssp."; for example, *Eucalyptus mannifera* ssp. *maculosa.*) A third italicized name may also denote a variety (see also Variety).

Sucker. In a grafted or budded plant, suckers grow from the rootstock rather than from the grafted or budded part of the plant. See also Water sprout.

Taproot. A thick central root that may penetrate deeply into the ground. In some plants, such as carrots and parsnips, taproots are storage organs.

Tender. The opposite of hardy; tender plants have a low tolerance for frost or freezing temperatures.

Tendrils. Specialized growths along the stems or at the ends of leaves on some vines. Tendrils wrap around supports, enabling the vine to climb. See page 740.

Thin. To prune out entire branches, large or small, cutting back to the main trunk, a side branch, or the ground; see page 722. Seedlings or developing fruits are thinned by removing excess plants or fruits so that the remaining ones have enough room to grow well.

Topiary. The technique of pruning and training shrubs and trees into shapes—either geometric forms (cones, spheres, pyramids) or fanciful animals or objects.

Truss. A typically compact cluster of flowers at the end of a stem, branch, or stalk. Many rhododendrons bear their flowers in trusses.

Sucker and Water Sprouts

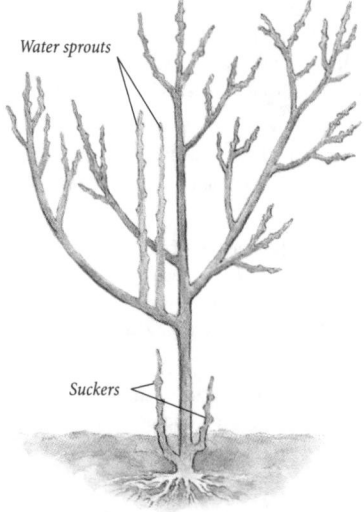

Water sprouts

Suckers

Tuber. A swollen underground stem with multiple growth points, such as the potato. See page 679.

Tuberous root. A true root, thickened to store nutrients. See page 679.

Umbel. See Inflorescence.

Underplanting. Planting one plant beneath another, such as setting out a ground cover under a tree.

Understock. See Rootstock.

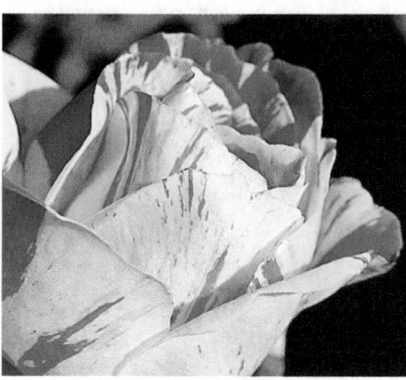

Variegated rose

Variegation. Striping, edging, or other markings in a color different from the primary color of a leaf or petal.

Variety. A variant of a basic species as it occurs in nature. Like a subspecies name, a botanical variety name is written in italics as the third word in a plant's botanical name; it may be preceded by the abbreviation "var." (such as *Ilex pernyi veitchii* or *Ilex pernyi* var. *veitchii*). The word "variety" is also used to include cultivated varieties (see also Cultivar).

Water sprout. In trees, any strong vertical shoot growing from the main framework of trunk and branches; also referred to as sucker.

Whorl. Three or more leaves, branches, or flowers growing in a circle from a node on a stem or trunk.

Woody. A plant with hardened (woody) stems or trunks. An herbaceous plant, in contrast, has soft stems.

Whorl

 Whorls

Index

NOTE: Locators in **boldface** denote maps.

Acknowledgments

SPECIAL CONSULTANTS

Randy Baldwin

Sam Benowitz

Dick Bocci

Dr. Whitney Cranshaw

Phil Edmunds

Judith Jones

Ed Laivo

Vincent Lazaneo

Tonya Lehner

Ron Ludekens

Dr. Robert Raabe

George Taylor

Ron Vanderhoff

Keith Warren

John Weeks

A special thanks to those consultants who contributed to the development of previous editions of the *Sunset Western Garden Book*, especially Pam Cornelison, Sue Eyre, Becky LaBrum, Susan Lang, Christine Miklas, Alice Rogers, and Janet Sanchez. Much of their work lives on in this edition. Our thanks also to the many experts around the West who go unnamed but nonetheless contributed to this edition, and to Eligio Hernández, Esther Kim, Audrey Mak, Susan Paris, and Sally W. Smith.

CONSULTANTS

Patrick Anderson

Mary Lu Arpaia

Lee Badger

Joan Bateman

Norm Bezona

Joe Biringer

Paul Bonine

Michael Buckner

Nancy Callister Buley

Linda Burns

Tim Cass

Betsy Clebsch

Joe Clements

John Clements

Ian Connor

Richard Criley

Alice Doyle

Dusty Eiker

Phil Favell

Sally Ferguson

Deidre Finley

Chad Finn

Robert Fowler

Frank Fujioka

Nancy Garrison

Jim Gerritsen

Roger Gossler

Harold Greer

Kelly Griffin

Mitch Hanes

Jeff Harris

Richard Heerema

Marylyn Henderson

Maurice Horn

Mary Irish

Carol Jacklin

Anni G. Jensen

Doug Johnson

Douglas Justice

Brian Kemble

Bob Kent

Pamela Koide

Kirk Larson

Karla Lortz

Edith Malek

Dick Mombell

Mel Monsen

Jeff Moore

Gary Moulton

Jim Nuccio

Tom Nuccio

Bart O'Brien

Jo O'Connell

Timothy Paine

Todd Perkins

Rick Rogers

Ellie Sather

Don Smetana

Sally Snipes

Ed Snodgrass

Mark Srull

Nicolas Staddon

Ray Stephenson

Steven Swain

Molly Thongthiraj

Lynne Tjomsland

Don & Betty Wagoner

Joe Walker

Sherry Wright

PHOTOGRAPHY CREDITS

Photographs are listed sequentially either in horizontal or vertical order. For additional clarification, the following position indicators may be used: Left (L), Center (C), Right (R); Top (T), Middle (M), Bottom (B), Upper (U).

© iStockphoto.com/DaddyBit: 705 L3. © iStockphoto.com/Ron Davey: 750 T. © iStockphoto.com/Melanie Dayus: 756 LL. © iStockphoto.com/Andrew Dean: 148 RC4. © iStockphoto.com/Geoff Delderfield: 118 RC1. © iStockphoto.com/Dainis Derics: 82 RC4; 152 LC3. William B. Dewey: 92 RC1; 118 L2; 611 RC1. © iStockphoto.com/Annette Diekmann: 160 L1. © iStockphoto.com/digger1948: 733 L2, RC2. © iStockphoto.com/Grant Dougall: 69 RC1. Andrew Drake: 697 LC2. © iStockphoto.com/Shelagh Duffett: 74 R1. Laura Dunkin-Hubby: 65 L3, LC3, L4, R2, R4; 66 L4, LC1, RC1, RC2, R2; 67 L1, L2, LC1, RC2, R2, R4; 68 LC2, RC1, R2; 69 L1, LC1, LC3, RC4, R1; 70 RC1, RC3A, RC3B, RC3C, RC4B, RC4C, R3; 71 L1, LC1, RC1, R1, L2, LC2, R2, L4, LC4, R4; 72 L2, R2, L4, LC4; 73 RC4; 74 RC1, L4, RC4, R4; 75 L1, R1, RC4; 79 R2; 80 L1; 84 LC3; 85 RC1; 86 LC2; 87 LC1, RC1B, RC2A, R4; 88 L1, RC4; 91 L1, LC1, RC1, RC4, R4; 92 LC3, LC4, RC4; 93 L1, LC1, RC1, R1, L4; 93 LC4; 94 RC2, R2; 95 L1, RC4, R4; 96 L4; 99 L4, R4; 101 LC5; 102 RC1; 104 LC2, L4, RC4; 106 RC4; 114 RC2; 116 L2, L4; 117 L1; 118 R2; 122 R3; 123 L4, RC4; 124 L1, LC2, R2, L4; 125 R2, L4; 126 LC1, RC1, L4, LC4; 127 LC2, R2, R4; 128 RC2A, R2; 129 R2, RC4; 130 LC2; 131 RC2; 132 L1, LC1, L4, R3; 134 LC1, L2, LC2; 135 RC1, L4, LC4, RC4, R4; 136 L1, LC1, L2, RC2, R3, LC4, RC4; 137 RC1, RC2, LC4; 138 RC2A, RC2B, R4; 144 LC1B, LC2B; 145 LC4; 146 RC1, RC4; 147 L1, RC3B; 148 R1, R4; 151 L1; 154 R2, R4; 155 RC4; 156 L4A, LC4, L5B, RC5; 158 RC1; 159 L2; 160 RC1A; 193 LC2; 207 ML; 385; 391; 542 M; 754 BR; 755 all; 761 BL. Anthony Dunn: 41 R. Jack Dykinga: 696 B. © iStockphoto.com/Peggy Easterly: 753 LC3. © iStockphoto.com/Pilar Echeverria: 123 LC4. © iStockphoto.com/Norman Eder: 40 BR; 155 LC1. Phil Edinger: 410 R1. © iStockphoto.com/Ståle Edstrom: 105 RC3B; 130 R4. © iStockphoto.com/Elena Elisseeva: 157 RC2. Thomas E. Eltzroth: 374. © iStockphoto.com/Enfys: 115 L1; 150 R2. © iStockphoto.com/Fred van Englelen: 117 LC1. © iStockphoto.com/Don Enright: 106 RC1; 757 BR. © iStockphoto.com/EuToch: 149 R3. © iStockphoto.com/Eva-Lisa: 744. © iStockphoto.com/Merlin Farwell: 725 L1. Derek Fell: 215 LML; 278 R1; 549 R1; 601 TR; 658 C1. © iStockphoto.com/Gary Ferguson: 153 R1. © iStockphoto.com/Ronald Flipsen: 75 L4. © iStockphoto.com/Eric Foltz: 152 RC1. © iStockphoto.com/Jake Foster: 82 L1. © iStockphoto.com/fotosav: 124 RC1. Dennis Frates: 23. © iStockphoto.com/Armando Frazao: 705 LC3. © iStockphoto.com/Douglas Freer: 150 LC4. © iStockphoto.com/David Freund: 757 BM. © iStockphoto.com/Jill Fromer: 113 L1. © iStockphoto.com/Furchin: 147 R4. © iStockphoto.com/gaffera: 759. Fiona Gilsenan: 67 L4; 73 LC4; 74 L1; 75 R4; 83 RC1; 86 R1; 91 L4; 98 LC2, RC2; 104 RC1; 128 RC2B; 133 RC4; 134 L3, RC4; 136 R1; 137 LC2, RC4; 138 RC1A, RC1B; 148 L4; 152 LC2; 520 LC1. © iStockphoto.com/Andrea Gingerich: 129 LC2. Nicholas Gitts/Swan Island Dahlias: 308 RC1, L2. © iStockphoto.com/Deb Gleason: 709. John Glover/The Garden Picture Library: 549 LC1. © iStockphoto.com/Steve Goodwin: 120 LC4. © iStockphoto.com/Joe Gough: 38 BL; 123 R3. Thayer Allyson Gowdy: 685 TR. © iStockphoto.com/grapegeek: 724. Art Gray: 7. Jeffrey Green: 59 B, 765. Harold E. Greer: 244 C1B; 332 LC1; 333 RC1; 465 LC1; 520 C1; 583; 584; 585 all; 586 R; 587 BM, BR; 589. © iStockphoto.com/Karen Grotzinger: 153 RC2. Steven Gunther: 6 L1; 14 all; 26; 49 T; 56 B; 763. Jamie Hadley: 734 TR. Joe K. Hale: 55 MR. © iStockphoto.com/Juliana Halvorson: 111 RC4, 113 RC1. © iStockphoto.com/Ulrike Hammerich: 156 L5A; 754 TM. © iStockphoto.com/han3617: 145 L4. Pamela Harper: 577 R. Marcus Harpur: 685 TL. © iStockphoto.com/Shawn Harris: 101 LC4. Lynne Harrison: 38 ML; 142 L2, LC2, L4; 159 LC2; 413 LC1; 600 C; 601 B; 696 T. © iStockphoto.com/Justin Hawthorne: 682 BL. Tom Hertz/AG Stock USA, Inc.: 377 R1. Fred Hirschmann: 29 T; 31 L, TR, BR. © iStockphoto.com/Timothy Hite: 691 T. © iStockphoto.com/Pamela Hodson: 141 R3. Neil Holmes/The Garden Picture Library: 552 L. Gary Holscher/AG Stock USA, Inc.: 375 RC1. Saxon Holt: 2 TR; 3 R; 4; 12 all; 13; 42 R; 45 B; 53 TL; 76 LC2, RC2, RC4; 77 LC4; 78 LC1, L2, RC3; 81 LC4, RC4; 82 R1; 83 L1, L4; 84 LC1, L4; 85 RC4; 86 LC1, RC4, R4; 87 L2, RC2B; 89 L2, RC2, L4, RC4; 90 L4; 91 R1; 94 RC1; 95 LC1, R1,

RC2, LC3, L4; 97 LC1, R2; 98 L4; 101 LC3, RC3; 102 RC2, RC4; 103 LC1, RC1, R1, R2, LC4, RC4, R4; 106 LC2, R2; 109 LC1, R1, L2; 111 RC1, RC3; 112 LC4; 113 LC2; 115 LC1, R3A, L4; 116 RC4; 119 R1; 120 LC1, L2; 121 RC1, R1; 122 LC1, RC1, LC3A, L4, RC4, R4; 124 R1; 126 L1; 127 RC1, LC4; 128 R4; 129 R1, L2; 130 RC2; 131 R3; 132 R2; 138 RC4; 139 L2, LC2, L4; 141 L1; 144 L1, RC1, RC2, R2; 145 L1; 147 LC4; 148 LC1, L3; 150 RC1, L4; 153 LC1, RC1; 154 RC1, RC4; 155 L3; 156 R4, R5; 157 L4, LC4; 158 R2; 160 LC3, LC4, R4; 215 L; 228 RC2; 272 LC1, RC1, LC2, C2; 278 R2; 308 LC1, R2; 332 L1; 333 C1; 377 C1; 410 L1; 412 LC1, C1; 420 RC1; 421 LC1; 445 R2; 465 RC1, R1; 491 C1, RC1, R1, L2; 522 L1, C1B; 524 C, RC1; 541 B; 542 TR; 552 LR; 575; 576 BR; 586 L; 588; 600 TL, TR; 611 LC1; 658 L1, LC1, RC1, L2, RC2, R1; 726 R1, LC2. © iStockphoto.com/Achim Holzem: 117 RC1. © iStockphoto.com/hong tong bee: 101 L2. © iStockphoto.com/Mark Hooghwerff: 690. D.A. Horchner/Design Workshop: 27; 60 BR. © iStockphoto.com/Loretta Hostettler: 79 LC4; 756 ML. © iStockphoto.com/David Hughes: 73 R1; 74 LC4; 127 L2; 143 L2; 151 R1, R2; 153 LC2; 159 R1; 735 R2; 756 LR; 761 BR. © iStockphoto.com/Juha Huiskonen: 130 LC4. © iStockphoto.com/Charles Humphries: 149 R4. © iStockphoto.com/Melissa Ide: 105 RC1. © iStockphoto.com/iwka: 35 TL; 757 C. © iStockphoto.com/jalphoto: 41 L, 109 LC4. © iStockphoto.com/jamesbenet: 705 LC4; 758 C. © iStockphoto.com/Kristen Johansen: 377 LC1. © iStockphoto.com/Ted Johns: 96 LC2. © iStockphoto.com/Alan Joyce: 150 L1. Dency Kane: 272 R2; 273; 413 L1; 491 RC1. David Karp: 519 LC1. © iStockphoto.com/Tomasz Kawka: 110 LC2. © iStockphoto.com/kevdog818: 131 RC4. Ted King/King's Mums: 272 RC2. © iStockphoto.com/Frank Kirkegaard: 761 TM. © iStockphoto.com/Satu Knape: 753 R3. © iStockphoto.com/Sebastian Knight: 678 BL. © iStockphoto.com/Ben Kopilow: 149 RC4. © iStockphoto.com/Michal Koziarski: 761 C. © iStockphoto.com/Bryce Kroll: 726 L2. © iStockphoto.com/Perry Kroll: 743 L1. Ernst Kucklich: 6 L3. © iStockphoto.com/Cay-Uwe Kulzer: 100 RC1; 105 R4. © iStockphoto.com/Emilia Kun: 140 RC1; 754 TR. © iStockphoto.com/Mary Lane: 762 R. © iStockphoto.com/Svetlana Larina: 710 R. Andrew Lawson: 142 RC4. © iStockphoto.com/Phek Thong Lee: 53 BL. © iStockphoto.com/Leeman: 140 LC3A. © iStockphoto.com/Jonathan Lenz: 111 L4; 143 RC1. © iStockphoto.com/Chee-Onn Leong: 726 LC1. George Lepp/AG Stock USA, Inc.: 550 C1B. © iStockphoto.com/Frank Leung: 118 R4. © iStockphoto.com/Adeline Lim: 144 LC1A. © iStockphoto.com/Olof M. Lindh: 743 R1. © iStockphoto.com/Henryk Lippert: 84 R4. © iStockphoto.com/Linda Loock: 733 LC2. Courtesy of the Los Angeles County Arboretum and Botanic Gardens: 52 T. Janet Loughrey: 228 R2. © iStockphoto.com/lubilub: 680 TM. © iStockphoto.com/Bruce MacQueen: 753 R4. © iStockphoto.com/Dianne Maire: 113 LC1; 124 RC4. © iStockphoto.com/Willie Manalo: 116 LC2. Allan Mandell: 40 T. Charles Mann: 2 BL; 3 TL, BL; 21 T; 32 R; 35 BL; 37 T; 59 T; 70 LC2; 79 L2; 128 LC4; 134 R1; 542 BR; 608 L1; 697 L2; 741. © iStockphoto.com/Bill Manning: 747. © iStockphoto.com/marmion: 753 L1. © iStockphoto.com/Theresa Martinez: 756 C. Ells Marugg: 244 LC1; 594. Stephanie Massey: 244 C1A. J.R. Mau/Photo Resource Hawaii: 553 LL. Mayer/Le Scanff/The Garden Picture Library: 577 L. © iStockphoto.com/Kimberly McBride: 116 R2. Jim McCausland: 683 L1, M1, R1, L2, M2. © iStockphoto.com/Chris McCooey: 76 RC1. David McDonald/Photo Garden, Inc.: 69 L4; 79 LC2; 107 L1; 160 RC1B; 215 UML; 464 LC1. © iStockphoto.com/medwhak: 743 R3. © iStockphoto.com/Matej Michelizza: 683 R3. © iStockphoto.com/Roger Milego: 157 R4. Scott Millard: 55 B. © iStockphoto.com/Mlenny: 158 L1. © iStockphoto.com/Susana Morales: 140 RC3. © iStockphoto.com/Ivy Moriber-Neal: 705 R2. © iStockphoto.com/Elizabeth Morrison: 702. © iStockphoto.com/Isabelle Mory: 94 LC4. © iStockphoto.com/Kerry Muzzey: 740 LC1. © iStockphoto.com/Eyal Nahmias: 157 RC1. © iStockphoto.com/Nalukai: 63B. © iStockphoto.com/NaturesDisplay: 118 RC2. © iStockphoto.com/Nancy Nehring: 87 R1; 101 LC2; 111 LC1; 128 R3; 130 RC1; 155 R3. © iStockphoto.com/neoloonatic:

758 TR. **Courtesy Netherlands Flower Bulb Information Center:** 490. © iStockphoto.com/Sherri Newill: 719 R1. © iStockphoto.com/Greg Nicholas: 729 L; 758 ML. © iStockphoto.com/Alexei Novikov: 692 TR. © iStockphoto.com/Dennis Oblander: 746. **Arthur N. Orans/Horticultural Photography:** 550 R1. © iStockphoto.com/PDL Design: 708 B. **Douglas Peebles:** 113 R1, RC2, RC4. © iStockphoto.com/Michael Palis: 140 L4. © iStockphoto.com/Jim Parkin: 115 RC1. © iStockphoto.com/Anita Patterson: 740 RC1. © iStockphoto.com/Rebecca Paul: 756 TM. © iStockphoto.com/Rob Pavey: 119 L1. **Jerry Pavia:** 35 TR; 53 BR; 64 RC1, R3; 66 L1, LC4; 72 RC4; 76 L4; 77 R1; 78 L1, RC1, RC2, R2, RC4; 79 RC2, RC4; 80 LC1, R1, L2, RC3, L4; 81 L1, R2; 82 RC1, RC3; 83 LC1, R1; 84 L1, RC1, R1, RC4; 85 LC4; 86 L1, RC1, L4, LC4; 87 L1, RC1A, LC4; 88 RC1, R1, RC2, LC4; 89 LC1, RC1, LC2, LC4; 91 LC4; 95 LC2; 96 R1, L2, R2, RC4; 97 L1, RC1A, RC2A, RC2B, L4, R4; 98 RC1, LC4; 99 RC1, L2, R2, RC3, RC4; 100 L1, LC1, L3, LC3, R3, RC4, R4; 101 R2, L5; 102 LC2, R3; 103 L2; 104 RC3, LC4; 105 L2, RC3A, RC4B; 106 LC4; 107 LC1, RC1, L2, LC2, RC2, RC3, LC4; 108 RC1, R1, R3, RC4, R4; 109 L1, L3, R4; 110 RC1, L2, RC4; 111 L1, L2; 112 L1, LC1, RC1, R1, RC4, R4; 113 R2; 114 RC4; 117 RC4; 119 RC1, L2; 120 L1, L4, RC4; 121 L1, RC2; 122 LC3B, LC4A, LC4B; 123 L2; 126 R2; 128 RC1A; 129 L1, LC1, RC1, RC2, LC4; 130 L1, R1, L2; 131 R4; 132 RC1; 133 RC1, L4; 134 L1; 136 RC1, LC2; 137 R2; 138 R1;140 LC1, LC3B, LC4B; 141 RC2A, LC4; 142 RC3; 143 L4, R4; 144 L2, L4, RC4; 145 LC2, RC3, RC4, R4; 146 L3, LC3, L4; 147 L2, LC2, R3, RC4A; 148 RC1; 149 L2, LC4; 151 RC4; 153 L1B; 154 LC2; 155 R1, LC3; 156 L4B, LC5; 158 RC2; 159 LC1, R3, RC4, R4; 160 L4; 207 BL; 215 R; 228 L2; 278 C2, RC2; 308 C2A; 332 C1A, C1B, RC1, R1; 333 L1, LC1; 410 LC1; 411 LC1, R1; 412 L1; 413 RC1, R1; 420 L1, LC1, R1; 421 L1, C1, RC1, R1; 423; 435; 445 L1, LC1, C2; 463 L1, RC1; 464 RC1, R1; 465 L1; 467; 491 LC2, C2; 519 L1; 524 R1; 541 T; 543 M; 549 C1A; 560; 577 M; 587 T; 597; 599 L; 608 RC1; 611 L1; 641 LC1, C1A; 658 T, C2; 701 TL. © iStockphoto.com/Marek Pawluczuk: 154 L4. © iStockphoto.com/Valda Petreikiene: 96 RC1. © iStockphoto.com/Karen Phillips: 154 RC3. © iStockphoto.com/Carl Piesch: 751 L3. **Norm Plate:** 1; 8; 9; 10; 11; 16 all; 17 all; 18 all; 37 B; 38 TR; 48 TR; 60 TL; 701 BL, BR; 703; 725 L2, LC2, RC2, R2, L3, LC3. **Norman A. Plate:** 22; 25 all; 68 RC4; 90 RC1; 193 L1; 272 C1, R1; 308 L1, C1, R1, LC2, C2B, RC2; 463 LC1; 521; 522 RC1; 608 R1; 694 all; 712 B; 717 BR; 719 L1, LC1, L2, LC2; 734 BL; 745 LC1, LC2A, RC2A. © iStockphoto.com/Tim Pohl: 114 LC2. © iStockphoto.com/Don Pool: 121 L2. © iStockphoto.com/Henry Price: 77 L1. © iStockphoto.com/Achim Prill: 731 L1. © iStockphoto.com/Hazel Proudlove: 74 LC1. © iStockphoto.com/Kathy Puckett: 699 B. © iStockphoto.com/Michelle Radin: 708 T. © iStockphoto.com/Radu Razvan: 139 RC4. © iStockphoto.com/rdsherwood: 29B. © iStockphoto.com/Jodi Red Wolf: 99 LC2. **Ian Reeves:** 745 L1, LC2B, RC1A, R1, R2. © iStockphoto.com/Tina Rencelj: 682 BR. **Howard Rice/The Garden Picture Library:** 244 RC1. © iStockphoto.com/Christina Richards: 714. © iStockphoto.com/Narelle Robson-Petch: 152 L4. © iStockphoto.com/Stan Rohrer: 158 R3. © iStockphoto.com/Rey Rojo: 762 TL. © iStockphoto.com/Malcolm Romain: 48 BR; 60 BL; 717 BL. **Susan A. Roth:** 114 L2; 207 BM; 272 L2; 412 R1; 464 C1; 491 L1, LC1; 542 BL; 543 R; 549 C1B; 599 R; 640; 695 BL. © iStockphoto.com/Anneclaire Le Royer: 64 RC4; 141 L2; 160 R2. © iStockphoto.com/Diane Rutt: 692 TM. © iStockphoto.com/Francois Sachs: 91 R2. © iStockphoto.com/Tim Sanford: 117 L4. © iStockphoto.com/Lawrence Sawyer: 116 RC2. © iStockphoto.com/Jerry Schiller: 45 ML. © iStockphoto.com/Paul Senyszyn: 149 R1. © iStockphoto.com/Olga Shelego: 158 R4; 692 TL; 740 LC2. **Richard Shiell:** 215 MR; 228 L1, LC1, RC1, R1, LC2; 244 L1; 278 L1, C1; 524 L1, LC1; 542 TM. © iStockphoto.com/sierrarat: 35 BR. © iStockphoto.com/Suzannah Skelton: 758 BL; 760. © iStockphoto.com/Craig Smith: 121 R4. © iStockphoto.com/Jeffrey Smith: 723 R4. © iStockphoto.com/William Smith: 758 TM. **Joe Solem/Photo Resource Hawaii.:** 553 BL. © iStockphoto.com/Tomislav Stajduhar: 717 TR. © iStockphoto.com/Emilia Stasiak: 141 RC4. © iStockphoto.com/step2626: 751 L4. © iStock

photo.com/Michael Stevenson: 753 L4. **Thomas J. Story:** 65 RC1; 68 L4; 69 R4; 82 L4; 105 RC2;122 R1;123 RC1;125 RC1; 142 RC1; 277; 278 L2; 678 TR; 679 TR; 684 all; 685 BR; 686 TM, TR, MR; 698 B; 712 MR; 716 L, R; 728 B; 738 M, R; 745 RC3, R3, RC4, R4. © iStockphoto.com/Geoffrey Stradling: 757 UL. **Friedrich Strauss/The Garden Picture Library:** 641 L1. **Tim Street-Porter:** 6 L4. © iStockphoto.com/Oksana Struk: 141 LC1. © iStockphoto.com/sx70: 97 R1. **Eric Tankesley-Clarke:** 411 RC1; 412 RC1. © iStockphoto.com/Robert Taylor: 121 LC4. © iStockphoto.com/Andrei Tchernov: 78 LC4; 735 LC3. © iStockphoto.com/Irene Teesalu: 97 RC1B. © iStockphoto.com/Kate Tero: 159 L4; 762 ML. **Terra Nova Nurseries, Inc.:** 136 RC3. © iStockphoto.com/Leah-Anne Thompson: 153 L2B. **Michael S. Thompson:** 21 B; 193 RC1; 194; 243; 375 L1, LC1, R1; 376 L1, LC1, R1; 444; 445 RC2; 464 L1; 519 RC1; 520 L1, RC1, R1; 522 LC1, R1; 549 L1; 550 C1A; 608 LC1, C1; 611 R1. © iStockphoto.com/Adam Tinney: 757 TM. © iStockphoto.com/Niilo Tippler: 753 LC1. © iStockphoto.com/Andrzej Tokarski: 733 LC4. **E. Spencer Toy:** 685 C; 734 BR; 742 L, M. © iStockphoto.com/trigga: 87 R2; 127 RC2; 757 LL. © iStockphoto.com/Joseph Tringali: 110 L1. © iStockphoto.com/Marian Trotter: 728 TL. © iStockphoto.com/Raymond Truelove: 122 L3. © iStockphoto.com/Tracy Tucker: 727 BR. **Mark Turner:** 5 BR; 20 L; 697 R2, R3. © iStockphoto.com/Craig Tuttle: 106 L1. © iStockphoto.com/Jaap Uilhoorn: 155 RC3. **Union Tools, Inc:** 731 L2, L3, C, R1, R2, R3; 733 L1, LC1. © iStockphoto.com/Petr Vaclavek: 40 BL. © iStockphoto.com/Astrida Valigorsky: 143 LC2. © iStockphoto.com/Liz Van: 157 RC4. © iStockphoto.com/Paul Vasarhelyi: 152 L2. **Randy Vaughn-Dotta/AG Stock USA, Inc.:** 377 RC1. © iStockphoto.com/Graça Victoria: 682 M. **Juliette Wade/The Garden Picture Library:** 52 B. **Scott Waite:** 113 L4, 153 R4. **Lance Walheim:** 278 LC1. © iStockphoto.com/William Walsh: 77 RC3. © iStockphoto.com/Richard Walters: 155 L4. © iStockphoto.com/Rewat Wannasuk: 114 RC1. **Andy Wasowski:** 5 TL. © iStockphoto.com/Robert Weber: 158 L4. © iStockphoto.com/Mark Weiss: 750 B. **Randy Wells:** 32 L. © iStockphoto.com/Michael Westhoff: 743 R2. **Stephen Whalen/Zephyr Pictures:** 55 ML. **Peter O. Whiteley:** 93 RC4. © iStockphoto.com/Roger Whiteway: 84 LC4, 723 LC1. © iStockphoto.com/Brad Wieland: 735 L1. **Bob Wigand:** 752. © iStockphoto.com/Mike Wiggins: 75 R3. **Doug Wilson:** 65 LC4; 138 L4; 146 R2; 154 L2. © iStockphoto.com/Carrie Winegarden: 761 TR. **David Winger:** 79 RC1; 81 R4; 697 LC3. **Courtesy Dave Wilson Nursery:** 519 R1. © iStockphoto.com/Joanna Wnuk: 139 LC4. © iStockphoto.com/John Wollwerth: 64 LC2; 119 R4. © iStockphoto.com/Timothy Wood: 119 R2. **Tom Woodward:** 53 MR; 65 RC2; 72 RC1; 73 L4; 75 RC1; 81 RC1; 87 LC2; 90 LC2, RC4; 105 RC4A; 110 R4; 115 RC4; 119 RC2; 123 LC2; 125 LC4; 127 L4; 133 L2; 134 R4; 146 RC2; 156 L3. **Ed Young/AG Stock USA, Inc.:** 278 RC1; 377 L1; 550 L1, LC1. © iStockphoto.com/Lisa F. Young: 736. © iStockphoto.com/Peter Zaharov: 129 R4. © iStockphoto.com/Zastavkin: 147 RC1; 735 LC2. © iStockphoto.com/Zygmund Zee: 710 L. © iStockphoto.com/Igor Zhorov: 159 L1.

DESIGN CREDITS

35 bottom left: Eileen & Pat Mangan; **37 top:** Julia Berman; **37 bottom:** Tom Berger, the Berger Partnership; **38 middle left:** Caroline Temple, structure: Little & Lewis; **40 top:** Tony Prunty, All-Oregon Landscaping; **42 right:** Freeland Tanner; **45 top right:** Bernard Trainor; **48 top right:** Urban Garden Design; **49 top:** Wayne Andrew, Andrew Landscape & Consulting; **53 top left:** Frankie Willinger; **56 top:** Joseph Marek; **56 bottom:** Nick Williams & Associates; **59 bottom:** Brian Patterson, Landscape architect for WLB Group; **683 L3:** John Greenlee; **685 top left:** Steve Lorton; **697 R1:** Bernard Trainor; **700:** John Greenlee; **725 LC2, RC2, R2, L3, LC3:** David C. Becker; **737 top:** Bernard Trainor; **741:** Carrie Nimmer Design; **763:** Nick Williams & Associates; **765:** Brian Patterson, Landscape architect for WLB Group.